# HONG KONG CIVIL COURT PRACTICE

---

## Desk Edition 2011

The Original Practitioner's Reference
on the Rules of the High Court

Incorporating relevant commentary on the Civil Procedure Rules (UK)
from The Civil Court Practice

## Lord Neuberger of Abbotsbury

Master of the Rolls
Non-permanent judge of the Hong Kong Court of Final Appeal
Editor-in-Chief

*Edited by*

## WS Clarke

BA, LLB (Brit Col), LLM (Lond)
Solicitor, Hong Kong
General Editor, Hong Kong Cases
Honorary Lecturer, Department of Professional Legal Education
University of Hong Kong

## LexisNexis

Hong Kong • Singapore • Malaysia • India

# Members of the LexisNexis Group worldwide

| | |
|---|---|
| Hong Kong | LexisNexis Hong Kong |
| | 3901, 39/F Hopewell Centre |
| | 183 Queen's Road East, HONG KONG |
| Australia | LexisNexis Australia, SYDNEY, New South Wales |
| Austria | LexisNexis Osterreich, VIENNA |
| Benelux | LexisNexis Benelux, AMSTERDAM |
| Canada | LexisNexis Canada Inc, MARKHAM, Ontario |
| Czech Republic | Novatrix sro, PRAGUE |
| France | LexisNexis SA, PARIS |
| Germany | LexisNexis Deutschland GmbH, MUNSTER |
| India | LexisNexis India, HARYANA |
| Israel | Arad-Ophir, RAMAT-HASHARON |
| Italy | Giuffrè Editore SpA, MILAN |
| Japan | LexisNexis Japan, TOKYO |
| Korea | LexisNexis Korea, SEOUL |
| Malaysia | LexisNexis Malaysia, PETALING JAYA |
| New Zealand | LexisNexis New Zealand, WELLINGTON |
| Poland | LexisNexis Polska sp z oo, WARSAW |
| PRC | LexisNexis China, BEIJING |
| Singapore | LexisNexis Asia, SINGAPORE |
| South Africa | LexisNexis SA, DURBAN |
| United Kingdom | LexisNexis, LONDON |
| USA | LexisNexis North America, DAYTON, Ohio |

ISBN : 978-988-8111-40-4

Printed in China

# LIST OF CONTRIBUTORS

### Lee JW Aitken
BA, LLB (Hons) (ANU), BCL (Oxon), Barrister of the Supreme Court of
New South Wales, Department of Law,
University of Hong Kong

### Janice Brabyn
LLB (Hons), LLM (Vict Well), Barrister and Solicitor of the High Court of New Zealand,
Department of Law, University of Hong Kong

### David Clark
BA (Hons), LLB (Otago), D Phil (Oxon), Barrister and Solicitor of the High Court of
New Zealand, Professor of Law, Flinders University of South
Australia; formerly Senior Lecturer in Public Administration,
University of Hong Kong

### WS Clarke
BA, LLB (Brit Col), LLM (Lond), Barrister and Solicitor of the Supreme Court of
British Columbia, Solicitor of the Supreme Court of Judicature in Northern Ireland,
Solicitor of the High Court of the Hong Kong Special Administrative Region,
Honorary Lecturer, Department of Professional Legal Education,
University of Hong Kong

### R Glofcheski
BA, LLB, LLM (Cantab)
Department of Law, University of Hong Kong

### Karen Kaur
LLB (Malaya), LLM (Harvard), Advocate and Solicitor of the High Court of Malaya,
formerly Associate Professor of Law, Department of Business Studies,
Hong Kong Polytechnic University

### Grace WY Lee
LLB, PCLL (HK), Solicitor of the High Court of the Hong Kong Special
Administrative Region

### Robert Margolis
BA, LLB (Brit Col), MA (W Ont), BCL (Oxon), LLM (Lond), Barrister and Solicitor
of the Supreme Court of British Columbia, Solicitor of the Supreme Court of
Judicature of England and Wales, formerly Lecturer, Department of Law,
University of Hong Kong

### Helen McCook
LLB, LLM (Hons) (Canterbury), Barrister and Solicitor of the High Court of
New Zealand, Solicitor of the Supreme Court of Judicature of England and Wales,
Solicitor of the High Court of the Hong Kong Special Administrative Region, formerly
Lecturer, Department of Professional Legal Education,
University of Hong Kong

### Gerard McCoy SBS, QC, SC
BA, LLB (Vict Well), MSc (Cantab), Senior Counsel of the bar of Hong Kong
Special Administrative Region, Barrister of the High Court of New Zealand,
Barrister of the Supreme Court of Victoria, Barrister of the Supreme Court of
New South Wales, Barrister of the Middle Temple, Professor of Law,
City University of Hong Kong

### Arthur McInnis
BA, LLB (Sask), LLM (McGill), PhD (London), Barrister and Solicitor of the
Supreme Court of British Columbia, Solicitor of the High Court of Hong Kong
Special Administrative Region, Professional Consultant, Faculty of Law,
Chinese University of Hong Kong

### Malcolm Merry
BA (Oxon), LLM (Dal), Barrister of Gray's Inn, Barrister of the High Court of the
Hong Kong Special Administrative Region, Associate Professor,
Department of Professional Legal Education,
University of Hong Kong

### Sean KF Mok
LLB (HK)

### Shane Nossal
BA (Hons) (Carleton), LLB (Ottawa), BCL (Oxon), Barrister and Solicitor of the
Supreme Court of British Columbia, formerly Lecturer, Department of Law,
University of Hong Kong

### Judith Sihombing
LLB (Melb), LLM (Malaya), Barrister and Solicitor of the Supreme Court of Victoria
and of the High Court of Australia, Faculty of Law,
Chinese University of Hong Kong

### Michael Wilkinson
BA, LLB (Cantab), Barrister of the Inner Temple,
Professor, Department of Professional Legal Education, Faculty of Law,
University of Hong Kong

# LIST OF CONTRIBUTORS TO THE CIVIL COURT PRACTICE 2011

**Editor-In-Chief**
The Right Honourable Lord Neuberger of Abbotsbury

**Consulting Editor**
The Right Honourable Lord Justice Hooper

**General Editors**
**P K J Thompson**
MA, LLB (HONS)
of Lincoln's Inn, One of Her Majesty's Counsel

**Louise Di Mambro**
LLB, (HONS) (LOND)
of the Middle Temple, Barrister, Deputy Master of Civil Appeals

**Senior Contributing Editor**
**David Di Mambro**
LLB (HONS) (LOND), FCI ARB,
of the Middle Temple, Barrister,
Fellow of the Society for Advanced Legal Studies
and a member of the Civil Procedure Rule Committee

**Editorial Board**
**Master Bowles**
A Master of the Supreme Court, Chancery Division

**Master Leslie**
A Master of the Supreme Court, Queen's Bench Division, a Barrister of the
Middle Temple, former member of the Civil Procedure Rule Committee (1997-2002)
and a former member of the working party on Practice Directions (1997-2000)

Her Honour **Judge Margaret De Haas**
Circuit Judge

His Honour **Judge David Pugsley**
Circuit Judge and formerly Chairman of Employment Tribunals

**District Judge Stephen Morley**
BA (HONS)

**Nicholas Bacon**
LLB (HONS)

**Charles Bourne**
MA (CANTAB), Maitrise (SORBONNE)
of the Middle Temple, Barrister

**Christopher Buckley**
BA (CANTAB)
of Lincoln's Inn, Barrister

**Iain Goldrein**
MA (CANTAB), FRSA
One of Her Majesty's Counsel

**David Greene**
MSC (LOND), FCI, ARB
Solicitor of the Supreme Court,
a former Member of the Civil Procedure Rule Committee and a former member of the
Working Party on Practice Directions (1997-2000)

**Robert Hendy**
LLB (HONS) (LOND), BCL (OXON)
of the Inner Temple, Barrister, Deputy Master of Civil Appeals

**Elizabeth Jeary**
of the Court Funds Office

**Stephen Jones**
MA (OXON)
of the Inner Temple, Barrister

**Lynne Knapman**
Deputy Master of the Crown Office

**Shantanu Majumdar**
BA (OXON)
of Middle Temple, Barrister

**Dov Ohrenstein**
MA (CANTAB)
of Gray's Inn, Barrister

**Alison Padfield**
BA, BCL (OXON), Lit Sp Dr Eur (Brussels)
of Lincoln's Inn, Barrister

**Robert Pearce**
MA, BCL (OXON)
of Middle Temple and Lincoln's Inn, One of Her Majesty's Counsel

**Julian C Pike**
LLB (SOTON), Solicitor

**Jamie Riley**
MA (CANTAB)
of Lincoln's Inn, Barrister

**Ashley Roughton**
BSC (LOND), PHD (CANTAB)
of the Inner Temple, Barrister

**Lydia Seymour**
BA (OXON)
of the Inner Temple, Barrister

**Alan Simons**
LLB (HONS) (LOND)
Former District Judge

**Adrian Zuckerman**
Professor of Civil Procedure, University of Oxford,
Fellow of University College, Oxford

# Preface to Desk Edition 2011

The Desk Edition 2011 is a handy and portable version of the 3 volume looseleaf edition of Hong Kong Civil Court Practice 1, up to and including Issue 54, which was published in March 2011.

The commentary in this work reflects the first two years of Hong Kong's experience with the civil justice reforms which were implemented in April 2009. The focus is and will continue to be on decisions of the Hong Kong courts. In addition, we have included extracts from our sister publication in the UK, The Civil Court Practice, reflecting the additional ten years of experience of the courts there with the Woolf reforms which were implemented in 1999. Extracts from The Civil Court Practice have been carefully chosen to ensure they are relevant in Hong Kong. Any material differences between Hong Kong's rules and those in England and Wales are highlighted to help readers to assess the persuasiveness of the extracted commentary.

We would once again like to thank Lord Neuberger of Abbotsbury, Master of the Rolls and Non-Permanent Judge of the Hong Kong Court of Final Appeal, as well as his team who produce The Civil Court Practice, for collaborating with us.

On occasion, commentary in this work goes further afield, referring to relevant authorities from Australia, Canada, Malaysia, New Zealand, Singapore and other places with common law traditions and civil procedure systems similar to Hong Kong's.

Hong Kong Civil Court Practice is the original reference work on the rules of the High Court, having first been published in 1994. It is intended for use by all members of the legal community.

The new Order 117A, regulating applications under the United Nations (Anti-Terrorism Measures) Ordinance (Cap 575), and amendments to Order 73 consequential upon the new Arbitration Ordinance (17 of 2010) came into force too late for inclusion in this Desk Edition. They are available to readers of the looseleaf edition, which is updated 4 times per year, and is now available on-line.

**WS Clarke**
June 2011

# CONTENTS

# TABLE OF CASES

*References are to paragraph numbers*

# TABLE OF LEGISLATION

## Hong Kong

## Australia

## United Kingdom

## General

## ORDER 1

### CITATION, APPLICATION, INTERPRETATION AND FORMS

PRELIMINARY

---

## NOTES

### [1.0.1]    Preliminary note on the origin of the Rules of the High Court

The Rules of the High Court date from 1988 when their predecessor was completely repealed and replaced. Since then there have been many amendments, most notably the very substantial amendments which came into force in 2009. Those substantial amendments implemented the recommendations set out in the final report of the Chief Justice's working party on civil justice reform (2004), which were made after lengthy and detailed consideration, and wide consultation. The 2009 amendments were published in the HKSAR gazette on 06.06.2008 under LN 152 of 2008 and brought into force in 2009 along with substantial amendments to relevant provisions of the High Court Ordinance (Cap 4).

The rules as enacted in 1988 were a slightly modified version of the Rules of the Supreme Court as they then were in England and Wales. Even the numbering system used in the English RSC was copied, facilitating reference to the English comparators and the authorities thereon.

In England, the RSC were largely replaced by the Civil Procedure Rules ('CPR') in 1999, implementing the 'Woolf reforms. The English CPR are considered to be an entirely new code of civil procedure. In Hong Kong, the Chief Justice's working party recommended selective amendment of the rules rather than wholesale adoption of a new code. See the discussion in Section 2 of the working party's final report.

As a result, although the 2009 Hong Kong amendments are heavily influenced by the English CPR, only selected aspects of the CPR have been adopted, and in some cases in modified format.

### [1.0.2]    Preliminary note on authority of decisions from other jurisdictions

Insofar as these rules are based on the former English Rules of the Supreme Court, and their replacement the Civil Procedure Rules, English decisions will clearly be of assistance in their interpretation. They are not binding (save pre-1997 Privy Council decisions on appeal from Hong Kong which may only be departed from by the Court of Final Appeal): *A Solicitor (24/07) v Law Society of Hong Kong* [2008] 2 HKC 1. However, they tend to be followed where they concern interpretation of an English rule which has been adopted in Hong Kong. See *Shun Kai Finance Co Ltd & Ors v Japan Leasing (HK) Ltd (in liq)* [2000] 3 HKC 705; [2001] 1 HKC 636 where the majority in the Court of Appeal declined an invitation to depart from

English authority on rules which were in the same terms in England and Hong Kong. At [2000] 3 HKC 705, 713F-I Rogers VP said:

> Whatever the correct analysis as to whether other decisions are binding or not the clarity of reasoning and sound basis of the judgments to which I have referred, in my view, makes it impossible for this court to come to any other view. Neither logic nor reasoning would lead to that conclusion and the invitation to this court to administer the rules of court oblivious to their genesis and rationale must be declined.

The English rules (both RSC and CPR) have influenced the procedural codes in many common law jurisdictions. Key provisions of the Hong Kong rules are worded substan tially if not exactly the same way as their equivalents in neighbouring jurisdic tions such as Singapore and Malaysia, and in some common law jurisdictions further afield. Decisions from such jurisdictions can be of assistance in interpreting these rules, and we make an effort to cite them, in addition to Hong Kong and English authorities.

1.    **Citation** (O. 1 r. 1)
      **These rules may be cited as the Rules of the High Court.**

2.    **Application** (O. 1 r. 2)
      **(1)   Subject to the following provisions of this rule, these rules shall have effect in relation to all proceedings in the High Court.**
      **(2)   These rules shall not have effect in relation to proceedings of the kinds specified in the first column of the following Table (being proceedings in respect of which rules may be made under the enactments specified in the second column of that Table)—**

TABLE

| Proceedings | Enactments |
| --- | --- |
| 1. Bankruptcy proceedings | Bankruptcy Ordinance (Cap. 6), section 113 |
| 2. Proceeding relating to the winding-up of companies. | Companies Ordinance (Cap. 32), section 296 |
| 3. Non-contentious or common form probate proceedings. | Probate and Administration Ordinance (Cap 10), section 72. |
| 4. Proceedings in the Court when acting as a Prize Court. | Prize Courts Act 1894, section 3 |
| 5. (Repealed 81 of 1997 s.59) | |
| 6. Matrimonial proceedings | Matrimonial Causes Ordinance (Cap. 179), sections 10 and 54; Matrimonial Proceedings and Property Ordinance (Cap. 192), section 32(20 of 2010) |
| (HK)7. Adoption proceedings. | Adoption Ordinance (Cap. 290), section 12 |
| (HK)8. Proceedings under the Domestic and Cohabitation Relationships Violence Ordinance (Cap. 189). | Domestic and Cohabitation Relationships Violence Ordinance (Cap. 189), section 8. (18 of 2009 s. 18) |

      **(3) These rules shall not have effect in relation to any criminal proceedings other than any criminal proceedings to which Order 53, Order 59,**

**Order 62, Order 70, Order 115, Order 115A, Order 116, Order 117, Order 118 or Order 119 applies.**

**(L.N. 282 of 1989; L.N. 403 of 1992; L.N. 156 of 1995; L.N. 242 of 1996; L.N. 222 of 1997; L.N. 152 of 2008)**

**(4) In the case of the proceedings mentioned in paragraphs (2) and (3), nothing in those paragraphs shall be taken as affecting any provision of any rules (whether made under the Ordinance or any other Ordinance) by virtue of which the Rules of the High Court or any provisions thereof are applied in relation to any of those proceedings.**

**(5) These rules do not have effect in relation to an election petition lodged under an enactment specified in the first column of the following Table, except to the extent that the practice and procedure of the High Court are applied to that election petition by virtue of an enactment specified in the second column of the Table —**

TABLE

| | |
|---|---|
| 1. Legislative Council Ordinance (Cap. 542), Part VII. | Legislative Council (Election Petition) Rules (Cap. 542 sub. leg. F), rule 2. |
| 2. District Councils Ordinance (Cap. 547), Part V. | District Councils (Election Petition) Rules (Cap. 547 sub. leg. C), rule 2. |
| 3. Chief Executive Election Ordinance (Cap. 569), Part 6. | Chief Executive Election (Election Petition) Rules (Cap. 569 sub. leg. E), section 3. |
| 4. Village Representative Election Ordinance (Cap. 576), Part 5 | Village Representative (Election Petition) Rules (Cap. 576 sub. leg. B), section 2. |

(L.N 152 OF 2008)

---

## NOTES

### [1.2.1]  Application to criminal proceedings

Order 1 rule 2(3) provides that these rules do not apply to criminal proceedings, save those listed by way of exception. One of the exceptions is for criminal proceedings to which Order 53 (judicial review) applies. The effect is that where appropriate, other provisions of these rules may apply to applications for judicial review arising in a criminal context. See *Chan Mei Yiu Paddy & Ors v SJ* [2008] 2 HKC 596 (CA) where it was held that Order 39 (evidence by deposition) applied in a judicial review of search warrants issued pursuant to a request from a foreign government under the Mutual Legal Assistance in Criminal Matters Ordinance (Cap 595).

In addition to the criminal proceedings listed by way of exception, there are certain criminal-like or criminal-related proceedings to which these rules apply. For example, Orders 45 and 52 lay down the procedures applicable on an application for committal for contempt of court. In this context see *Savings & Investment Bank Ltd v Gasco Investments (Netherlands) BV & Ors* [1988] Ch 422.

The Costs in Criminal Cases Ordinance (Cap 492) and the rules thereunder provide that Order 62 of these rules will apply in certain circumstances to the assessment of costs in criminal cases.

### [1.2.2]    Election petitions

Order 1 rule 2(5) was added as part of the civil justice reforms in 2009. This was done as a consequence of the fact petitions were generally abolished as an originating process for proceedings governed by these rules. As petitions continue to be prescribed by other legislation for challenges to the validity of elections, and these rules are applied to such proceedings by that legislation, it was considered appropriate for the rule 'to acknowledge the preservation of such petitions and the manner in which they adopt RHC procedures by analogy' (final report of the Chief Justice's working party on civil justice reform, para 159).

**3.      Application of Interpretation and General Clauses Ordinance** (O. 1 r. 3)
    **The Interpretation and General Clauses Ordinance (Cap. 1) shall apply for the interpretation of these rules as it applies to subsidiary legislation made after the commencement of that Ordinance.**

---

### NOTES

### [1.3.1]    Effect of Rule 3

This rule is of no practical effect. In so far as it purports to apply Cap 1 of the Laws of Hong Kong to the interpretation of the rules it is redundant, as Cap 1 applies to the rules by its own force (see section 2(1) and the definition of 'Ordinance' in section 3 of Cap 1). Moreover, the 1988 amendment to this rule, purporting to apply Cap 1 to the rules 'as it applies to subsidiary legislation made after the commencement of that Ordinance', is meaningless. Cap 1, by its own terms, applies to legislation, whether coming into force before or after it (section 2(1)). The 1988 amendment is taken from a similar amendment introduced in England in 1982. In adopting the English amendment, the Hong Kong Rules Committee appears to have overlooked the fact that the amendment was tailored to fit in with section 23 of the UK's Interpretation Act 1978, which is substantially different from its Hong Kong counterpart (Cap 1, section 2). This rule should be ignored, and reference made, where necessary, to section 2 of Cap 1.

**4.      Definitions** (O. 1 r. 4)
    **(1)   In these rules, unless the context otherwise requires, the following expressions have the meanings hereby respectively assigned to them, namely—**
**"aided person" means an aided person within the meaning of the Legal Aid Ordinance (Cap. 91); (L.N. 152 of 2008)**
**"Amendment Rules 2008" means the Rules of the High Court (Amendment) Rules 2008 (L.N. 152 of 2008)**
**"an action for personal injuries" means an action in which there is a claim for damages in respect of personal injuries to the plaintiff or any other person or in respect of a person's death, and "personal injuries" includes any disease and any impairment of a person's physical or mental condition;**
**(HK) "bailiff" means a bailiff of the Court and any person lawfully authorized to execute the process of the Court;**

"cause book" means the book or other record kept in the Registry in which the letter and number of, and other details relating to, a cause or matter are entered; (L.N. 275 of 1998)

(HK) "Full Bench" means a Bench consisting of 2 or more Judges of the Court of First Instance;

"judgment rate" means the rate of interest determined by the Chief Justice under section 49(1)(b) of the Ordinance; (Ordinance No 18 of 2003)

"master" means a master of the High Court, and includes the Registrar of the High Court and a Senior Deputy Registrar, Deputy Registrar or Assistant Registrar of the High Court; (L.N. 99 of 1993) (Ordinance No 10 of 2005)

(HK) "money lender's action" has the meaning assigned to it by Order 83A;

"notice of intention to defend" means an acknowledgment of service containing a statement to the effect that the person by whom or on whose behalf it is signed intends to contest the proceedings to which the acknowledgment relates;

"officer" means an officer of the High Court;

"originating summons" means every summons other than a summons in a pending cause or matter;

"pleading" does not include a petition, summons or preliminary act; "practice direction" means

(a) a direction issued by the Chief Justice as to the practice and procedure of the Court; or

(b) a direction issued by a specialist judge for his specialist list; (L.N. 152 of 2008)

"probate action" has the meaning assigned to it by Order 76; "receiver" includes a manager or consignee;

(HK) "Registrar" means the Registrar of the High Court; and includes a Senior Deputy Registrar, Deputy Registrar or Assistant Registrar of the High Court; (Ordinance No 10 of 2005)

(HK) "Registry" means the Registry of the High Court; (HK) "the Ordinance" means the High Court Ordinance (Cap. 4);

"vacation" means the interval between sittings of the High Court as prescribed by Order 64;

"writ" means a writ of summons;

(HK) "written law" includes "Ordinance" and "enactment" as defined in section 3 of the Interpretation and General Clauses Ordinance (Cap. 1). (L.N. 152 of 2008)

(2)    In these rules, unless the context otherwise requires, "the Court" means the Court of First Instance or any one or more of the judges thereof whether sitting in court or in chambers or the Registrar or any master but the foregoing provision shall not be taken as affecting any provision of these rules and, in particular, Order 32, rule 11 by virtue of which the authority and jurisdiction of the Registrar is defined and regulated.

(3)    In these rules unless the context otherwise requires, any reference to acknowledging service of a document or giving notice of intention to defend any proceedings is a reference to lodging in the Registry an acknowledgment of

**service of that document or, as the case may be, a notice of intention to defend those proceedings.**

---

**NOTES**

**[1.4.1]     Definition of 'the Court'**
The effect of rule 4(2) is to create for these rules a different definition for the term 'the Court' than that which usually applies. For the purpose of these rules, the term includes the Registrar or any master as well as any judge. In primary legislation, on the other hand, 'the Court' means a judge or judges sitting in open court: see *American Express International Inc v Ng Pak Sang* [1987] 1 HKC 522, 524G-525E, quoting with approval from *Firman v Ellis* [1978] QB 886 per Lord Denning MR.

**5.       Construction of references to Orders, rules, etc.** (O. 1 r. 5)
     **(1)     Unless the context otherwise requires, any reference in these rules to a specified Order, rule or Appendix is a reference to that Order or rule of, or that Appendix to, these rules and any reference to a specified rule, paragraph or sub-paragraph is a reference to that rule of the Order, that paragraph of the rule, or that sub-paragraph of the paragraph, in which the reference occurs.**
     **(2)     Any reference in these rules to anything done under a rule of these rules includes a reference to the same thing done before the commencement of that rule under any corresponding rule of court ceasing to have effect on the commencement of that rule.**
     **(3)     Except where the context otherwise requires, any reference in these rules to any written law shall be construed as a reference to that written law as amended, extended or applied by or under any other written law.**

**6.       Construction of references to action, etc. for possession of land** (O. 1 r. 6)
     **Except where the context otherwise requires, references in these rules to an action or claim for the possession of land shall be construed as including references to proceedings against the Government for an order declaring that the plaintiff is entitled as against the Government to the land or to the possession thereof. (29 of 1998 s.105)**

**(HK) 7A. Construction of references to Registrar** (O. 1 r. 7A)
     **(HK) Wherever the word "Registrar" appears in these rules and forms there may be substituted the word "Master" when and where appropriate.**

**9.       Forms** (O. 1 r. 9)
     **(1) The forms in the Appendices shall be used where applicable with such variations as the circumstances of the particular case require.**

---

**NOTES**

**[1.9.1]     Variation of prescribed forms**
Order 1 rule 9 provides that the forms in the Appendices shall be followed where

appropriate but may be modified to suit the circumstances of a particular case. See also section 37 of the Interpretation and General Clauses Ordinance (Cap 1) which provides that deviation from a prescribed form, not affecting the substance, does not result in invalidity. Citing both provisions, it was held in Secretary for *Justice v Choy Bing Wing* [2005] 4 HKC 416, 443DI that a warrant of committal in form 85A which had been modified by the court so as to give the contemnor an opportunity to be heard, was valid. The mandatory language used in these rules with respect to some forms (eg Order 6 rule 1, Order 42 rule 1) should be read accordingly.

In *Hongkong & Shanghai Banking Corp v Star Trans International Ltd* [1988] 2 HKLR 549, 553EF (CA) it was doubted that the slip rule (Order 20 rule 11) could be used to amend an order which mistakenly omitted parts of the prescribed form. It was also doubted that the terms of the prescribed form could be implied into the order as drawn up.

In *The Djatisari* [1997] 4 HKC 548 the court granted leave to a party in Admiralty proceedings to file a form substantially different from that prescribed.

**[1.9.2]    Standardised headings on court documents**
The judiciary has adopted a system of standardising the headings for use on court forms and other documents to be filed in court, including abbreviations for the various case types. The relevant information (current as at mid2010) is that set out in the following appendices (which were circulated to solicitors under Law Society circular 09675):

Appendix "A": standardised headings for all court documents

Appendix "B": official names of all levels of court and tribunal in the HKSAR together with the case types to be used on documents filed therein

**Appendix A**

**Sample 1**

(Chinese)

FACV12345/1997

香港特別行政區<br>終審法院<br>終院民事上訴 1997 年第 12345 號<br>（原本案件編號：高院民事上訴 1996 年第 6789 號）

(English)

FACV12345/1997

IN THE COURT OF FINAL APPEAL OF THE<br>HONG KONG SPECIAL ADMINISTRATIVE REGION  FINAL APPEAL (CIVIL) NO.<br>12345 OF 1997  (ON APPEAL FROM CACV 6789 OF 1996)

**Sample 2**

(Chinese)

CACV 12345/97

香港特別行政區
高等法院
上訴法院
高院民事上訴 1997 年第 12345 號
（原本案件編號：高院民事訴訟 1996 年第 6789 號）

(English)

CACV 12345/97

IN THE HIGH COURT OF THE
HONG KONG SPECIAL ADMINISTRATIVE REGION  COURT OF APPEAL
CIVIL APPEAL NO. 12345 OF 1997
(ON APPEAL FROM HCA 6789 OF 1996)

**Sample 3**

(Chinese)

HCA 12345/97

香港特別行政區
高等法院
原訟法院
高院民事訴訟 1997 年第 12345 號

(English)

HCA 12345/97

IN THE HIGH COURT OF THE
HONG KONG SPECIAL ADMINISTRATIVE REGION  COURT OF FIRST INSTANCE
ACTION NO. 12345 OF 1997

**Sample 4**

(Chinese)

DCCJ 12345/97

香港特別行政區
區域法院
民事訴訟 1997 年第 12345 號

(English)

DCCJ 12345/97

IN THE DISTRICT COURT OF THE
HONG KONG SPECIAL ADMINISTRATIVE REGION
CIVIL ACTION NO. 12345 OF 1997

**Sample 5**

(Chinese)

FCMC 12345/97

香港特別行政區
區域法院
婚姻訴訟 1997 年第 12345 號

(English)

FCMC12345/97

IN THE DISTRICT COURT OF THE
HONG KONG SPECIAL ADMINISTRATIVE REGION
MATRIMONIAL CAUSES NO. 12345 OF 1997

**Sample 6**
(Chinese)

LDPA12345/97

香港特別行政區
土地審裁處
LDPA 申請 1997 年第 12345 號

(English)

LDPA12345/97

IN THE LANDS TRIBUNAL OF THE
HONG KONG SPECIAL ADMINISTRATIVE REGION
Application No. LDPA 12345 of 1997

**Appendix B**

香港特別行政區
司法機構
法庭 / 案件類別

COURTS AND CASES TYPES
JUDICIARY, HONG KONG SPECIAL ADMINISTRATIVE REGION

THE COURT OF FINAL APPEAL OF THE HKSAR
[ 香港特別行政區終審法院 ]

| Case Type<br>類別 | Type (Chinese)<br>中文名稱 | Prefix<br>簡稱 |
|---|---|---|
| Final Appeal (Civil) | 終院民事上訴 | FACV |
| Final Appeal (Criminal) | 終院刑事上訴 | FACC |
| Miscellaneous Proceedings (Civil) | 終院民事雜項案件 | FAMV |
| Miscellaneous Proceedings (Criminal) | 終院刑事雜項案件 | FAMC |
| Miscellaneous Proceedings | 終院雜項程序 | FAMP |

THE COURT OF APPEAL OF THE HIGH COURT OF THE HKSAR
[ 香港特別行政區高等法院上訴法庭 ]

| Case Type<br>類別 | Type (Chinese)<br>中文名稱 | Existing Prefix<br>現時簡稱 | Revised Prefix<br>新簡稱 |
|---|---|---|---|
| Civil Appeal | 民事上訴 | Civ. App. | CACV |
| Criminal Appeal | 刑事上訴 | Cri. App. | CACC |
| Application for Review | 覆核申請 | AR | CAAR |
| Secretary for Justice's reference | 由律政司司長轉交的<br>法律問題 | - | CASJ |

| Case Type 類別 | Type (Chinese) 中文名稱 | Existing Prefix 現時簡稱 | Revised Prefix 新簡稱 |
|---|---|---|---|
| Reservation of Question of Law | 法律問題考慮 | - | CAQL |
| Attorney General's Reference | 由律政司轉交的法律問題 | A.G.'s Reference | CAAG |

## THE COURT OF FIRST INSTANCE OF THE HIGH COURT OF THE HKSAR
（ 香港特別行政區高等法院原訟法庭 ）

### CIVIL MATTERS
民事案件

| Case Type 類別 | Type (Chinese) 中文名稱 | Existing Prefix 現時簡稱 | Revised Prefix 新簡稱 |
|---|---|---|---|
| Civil Action | 高院民事訴訟 | HCA | HCA |
| Constitutional and Administrative Law Proceedings | 高院憲法及行政訴訟 | HCAL | HCAL |
| Admiralty Action | 高院海事訴訟 | HCAJ | HCAJ |
| Adoption Application | 高院收養申請 | HC Adoption | HCAD |
| Bankruptcy Proceedings | 高院破產案件 | HCB | HCB |
| Commercial Action | 高院商業訴訟 | HCCL | HCCL |
| Companies Winding-up Proceedings | 高院公司清盤案件 | HCCWU | HCCW |
| Application to set aside a Statutory Demand (*under Bankruptcy Ordinance*) | 申請將法定要求償債書作廢 ( 依據破產條例 ) | *New* | HCSD |
| High Court Bankruptcy Interim Order | 高院破產案臨時命令 | *New* | HCBI |
| Construction and Arbitration Proceedings | 高院建築及仲裁訴訟 | HCCON | HCCT |
| Matrimonial Causes | 高院婚姻訴訟 | HCDJ | HCMC |
| Miscellaneous Proceedings | 高院雜項案件 | HCMP | HCMP |
| Confidential Miscellaneous Proceedings | 機密雜項案件 | HCCMP | HCCM |
| Personal Injuries Action | 高院傷亡訴訟 | HCPI | HCPI |
| Bookdebt Registration | 高院帳面債項登記 | - | HCBD |
| Bill of sale Registration | 高院賣據登記 | - | HCBS |
| Stop Notice | 停止通知書 | - | HCSN |
| Application for Discharge | 高院釋放申請 | - | HCCD |
| Intended Action | 高院擬進行的訴訟 | - | HCZZ |
| Application under the Mental Health Ordinance | 根據 《精神健康條例 》提出的申請 | HCMP | HCMH |

## CRIMINAL & APPEAL CASES
刑事及上訴案件

| Case Type 類別 | Type (Chinese) 中文名稱 | Existing Prefix 現時簡稱 | Revised Prefix 新簡稱 |
|---|---|---|---|
| Criminal Case | 高院刑事案件 | HCCC | HCCC |
| Magistracy Appeal | 高院裁判法院上訴 | HCMA | HCMA |
| Labour Tribunal Appeal | 高院勞資審裁處上訴 | HCLTA | HCLA |
| Inland Revenue Appeal | 高院稅務上訴 | IRA | HCIA |
| Small Claims Tribunal Appeal | 高院小額錢債審裁處上訴 | SCTA | HCSA |
| Minor Employment Claims Appeal | 高院小額薪酬上訴 | MECA | HCME |
| Obscene Articles Tribunal Appeal | 高院淫褻物品審裁處上訴 | OATA | HCOA |
| Trade Unions Appeal | 高院工會上訴 | *New* | HCUA |
| Estate Duty Appeal | 高院遺產稅上訴 | *New* | HCED |

## PROBATE MATTERS
遺產承辦處案件

| Case Type 類別 | Type (Chinese) 中文名稱 | Existing Prefix 現時簡稱 | Revised Prefix 新簡稱 |
|---|---|---|---|
| Probate Action | 遺囑認證訴訟 | HCAP | HCAP |
| Application for Grant | 申請授予書 | HCAG | HCAG |
| Caveat Application | 知會備忘 | HCCA | HCCA |
| Ex-parte Application | 單方面申請書 | HCEA | HCEA |
| Referral Case | 呈交案件 | HCRC | HCRC |
| Citation Application | 傳喚書申請 | HCCI | HCCI |
| (Pre-system) Application for Grant | 申請授予書（系統電腦化之前） | - | HCCV |

## THE DISTRICT COURT OF THE HKSAR
[ 香港特別行政區區域法院 ]

| Case Type 類別 | Type (Chinese) 中文名稱 | Existing Prefix 現時簡稱 | Revised Prefix 新簡稱 |
|---|---|---|---|
| Civil Action | 區院民事訴訟 | DCCJ | DCCJ |
| Criminal Case | 區院刑事案件 | DCCC | DCCC |
| Distraint Case | 區院財物扣押案件 | DCDT | DCDT |
| District Court Tax Claim | 區院稅款申索 | | DCTC |
| Employee's Compensation Case | 區院僱員補償案件 | DCEC | DCEC |

| Case Type<br>類別 | Type (Chinese)<br>中文名稱 | Existing Prefix<br>現時簡稱 | Revised Prefix<br>新簡稱 |
|---|---|---|---|
| Equal Opportunities Action | 平等機會訴訟 | E.O. No.<br>(Equal<br>Opportuni-<br>ties Commis-<br>sion) | DCEO |
| Miscellaneous Appeals | 區院雜項上訴 | | DCMA |
| Miscellaneous Proceedings | 區院雜項案件 | DCMP | DCMP |
| Occupational Deafness (Compensation) Appeal | 職業性失聰（補償）上訴 | Occupational<br>Deafness<br>(Compensa-<br>tion) Appeal<br>No. | DCOA |
| Personal Injuries Action | 區院傷亡訴訟 | | DCPI |
| Pneumoconiosis (Compensation) Appeal | 肺塵埃沉著病（補償）上訴 | P.C.A No. | DCPA |
| Stamp Duty Appeal | 印花稅評稅上訴 | Stamp Appeal No. | DCSA |

## FAMILY COURT
[ 家事法庭 ]

| Case Type<br>類別 | Type (Chinese)<br>中文名稱 | Existing Prefix<br>現時簡稱 | Revised Prefix<br>新簡稱 |
|---|---|---|---|
| Matrimonial Causes | 婚姻訴訟 | FCDJ | FCMC |
| Joint Application | 離婚共同申請 | FCJA | FCJA |
| Miscellaneous Proceedings | 家事雜項案件 | FCMP | FCMP |
| Adoption Application | 收養申請 | FCAD | FCAD |

## LANDS TRIBUNAL
[ 土地審裁處 ]

(A) Applications under Landlord and Tenant (Consolidation) Ordinance
引用業主與租客（綜合）條例的申請

| Case Type<br>類別 | Type (Chinese)<br>中文名稱 | Existing Prefix<br>現時簡稱 | Revised Prefix<br>新簡稱 |
|---|---|---|---|
| Part I Possession Application *(Application for Possession/Exclusion Order for premises under Part I)* | 條例第 I 部收回管有申請 | H<br>K<br>HE<br>KE | LDPA (merging) |
| Part II Possession Application *(Application for Possession for premises under Part II)* | 條例第 II 部收回管有申請 | | LDPB |
| Part IV Possession Application *(Application for Possession for premises under Part IV)* | 條例第 IV 部收回管有申請 | LTP (splitting) | LDPD |
| Part V Possession Application *(Application for Possession for premises under Part V)* | 條例第 V 部收回管有申請 | | LDPE |
| New Tenancy Application *(Application for New Tenancy)* | 新租賃申請 | NT | LDNT |

| Case Type 類別 | Type (Chinese) 中文名稱 | Existing Prefix 現時簡稱 | Revised Prefix 新簡稱 |
|---|---|---|---|
| Landlord & Tenant Appeal *(For appeal vs the decision of the Commissioner of Rating and Evaluation)* | 租務上訴 | L&TA | LDLA |

## (B) Applications under various Ordinances
引用其他條例的申請

| Case Type 類別 | Type (Chinese) 中文名稱 | Existing Prefix 現時簡稱 | Revised Prefix 新簡稱 |
|---|---|---|---|
| Rating Appeal | 差餉上訴 | RA | LDRA |
| Buildings Ordinance Application *(Application under Buildings Ordinance)* | 建築物條例申請 | HB/KB | LDBG |
| Government Rent Appeal | 地租上訴 | *New* | LDGA |
| Land Resumption Application *(Application under Crown Land Resumption Ordinance)* | 收回土地申請 | CLR | LDLR |
| Housing Ordinance Appeal | 房屋條例上訴 | HA | LDHA |
| Building Management Application *(Application under the Building Management Ordinance)* | 建築物管理申請 | BM | LDBM |
| Demolished Buildings Application *(Application under Demolished Buildings (Re-development of sites) Ordinance-for compensation to the occupier/tenant)* | 已拆卸建築物申請 | DB | LDDB |
| Demolished Buildings Appeal *(Application under Demolished Buildings (Re-development of sites) Ordinance-for appeal against decisions of Director of Lands)* | 已拆卸建築物上訴 | DBA | LDDA |
| MTR Ordinance Application *(Application under the MTR (Land Resumption and Related Provisions) Ordinance)* | 地下 . 路條例申請 | MTR | LDMT |
| Land Compulsory Sale Application *(Application under the Land (Compulsory Sale for Redevelopment) Ordinance)* | 土地強制售賣申請 | - | LDCS |
| Railway Ordinance Application | 鐵路條例申請 | *New* | LDRW |

(C) Others
其他

| Case Type<br>類別 | Type (Chinese)<br>中文名稱 | Existing Prefix<br>現時簡稱 | Revised Prefix<br>新簡稱 |
|---|---|---|---|
| Miscellaneous References Application:<br><br>Applications under:<br>a. Foreshore and Seabed (Reclamations) Ordinance<br>b. Land Acquisition (Possessory Title) Ordinance<br>c. Country Park Ordinanced.<br>d. Hong Kong Airport (Control of Obstructions) Ordinancee.<br>e. Electricity Networks (Statutory Easements) Ordinancef.<br>f. Air Pollution Control Ordinance<br>g. Water Pollution Control Ordinance<br>h. Roads (Works, Use and Compensation) Ordinance<br>i. Sewage Tunnels (Statutory Easements) Ordinance | 雜項申請 | MR | LDMR |
| Miscellaneous Proceedings Application | 雜類申請 | - | LDMP |

## MENTAL HEALTH REVIEW TRIBUNAL
[ 精神健康覆查審裁處 ]

| Case Type<br>類別 | Type (Chinese)<br>中文名稱 | Existing Prefix<br>現時簡稱 | Revised Prefix<br>新簡稱 |
|---|---|---|---|
| Mental health Review Application | 精神健康覆核申請 | MHRT | MHRA |
| Mental health Review Referral | 精神健康覆核轉介申請 | MHRT | MHRR |

## SMALL CLAIMS TRIBUNAL
[ 小額錢債審裁處 ]

| Case Type<br>類別 | Type (Chinese)<br>中文名稱 | Existing Prefix<br>現時簡稱 | Revised Prefix<br>新簡稱 |
|---|---|---|---|
| Small Claims Tribunal Claim | 小額錢債申索 | SCTC | SCTC |

## CORONER'S COURT
[ 死因裁判法庭 ]

| Case Type<br>類別 | Type (Chinese)<br>中文名稱 | Existing Prefix<br>現時簡稱 | Revised Prefix<br>新簡稱 |
|---|---|---|---|
| Miscellaneous Applications | 雜項申請 | B01/97 HK | CCMA<br>(merging) |
| | | B01/97K | |
| | | B01/97/NT | |
| | | C01/97 HK | |
| | | C01/97K | |
| | | C01/97/NT | |
| Reportable Deaths | 須予報告的死亡個案 | *New* | CCRD |
| Death Investigation / Inquests | 死亡個案的調查 / 研訊 | DR1/97 HK | CCDI<br>(merging) |
| | | DR1/97 K | |
| | | DR1/97 NT | |
| | | DI1/97 HK | |
| | | DI1/97 K | |
| | | DI1/97 NT | |

## LABOUR TRIBUNAL
[ 勞資審裁處 ]

| Case Type<br>類別 | Type (Chinese)<br>中文名稱 | Existing Prefix<br>現時簡稱 | Revised Prefix<br>新簡稱 |
|---|---|---|---|
| Labour Tribunal Claim | 勞資申索 | LT | LBTC |

## OBSCENE ARTICLES TRIBUNAL
[ 淫褻物品審裁處 ]

| Case Type<br>類別 | Type (Chinese)<br>中文名稱 | Existing Prefix<br>現時簡稱 | Revised Prefix<br>新簡稱 |
|---|---|---|---|
| Obscene Article Tribunal Determination | 淫褻物品裁定申請 | OAT | OATD |
| Obscene Article Tribunal Classification (Comics Book) | 淫褻物品評定類別申請<br>（漫畫） | OAT/CB | OACC |
| Obscene Article Tribunal Classification (Compact Disk, CD Rom VCD) | 淫褻物品評定類別申請<br>（光碟） | OAT/CD | OACD |
| Obscene Article Tribunal Classification (Laser Disk) | 淫褻物品評定類別申請<br>（雷射光碟） | OAT/LD | OACL |
| Obscene Article Tribunal Classification (Magazine) | 淫褻物品評定類別申請<br>（雜誌） | OAT/MA | OACM |
| Obscene Article Tribunal Classification (Others) | 淫褻物品評定類別申請<br>（其他） | OAT/OT | OACO |
| Obscene Article Tribunal Classification (Video Tape) | 淫褻物品評定類別申請<br>（錄像帶） | OAT/VT | OACV |
| Obscene Article Tribunal Classification (Government Comics Book) | 淫褻物品評定類別申請<br>（政府漫畫） | OAT/GCB | OAGC |

| Case Type<br>類別 | Type (Chinese)<br>中文名稱 | Existing Prefix<br>現時簡稱 | Revised Prefix<br>新簡稱 |
|---|---|---|---|
| Obscene Article Tribunal Classification (Government Compact Disk, CD Rom & VCD) | 淫褻物品評定類別申請<br>（政府光碟） | OAT/GCD | OAGD |
| Obscene Article Tribunal Classification (Government Laser Disk) | 淫褻物品評定類別申請<br>（政府雷射光碟） | OAT/GLD | OAGL |
| Obscene Article Tribunal Classification (Government Magazine) | 淫褻物品評定類別申請<br>（政府雜誌） | OAT/GMA | OAGM |
| Obscene Article Tribunal Classification (Government Others) | 淫褻物品評定類別申請<br>（政府其他出版物） | OAT/GOT | OAGO |
| Obscene Article Tribunal Classification (Government Video Tape) | 淫褻物品評定類別申請<br>（政府錄像帶） | OAT/GVT | OAGV |

## MAGISTRATES' COURTS
### ［裁判法院］

Court Types (Magistrates' Courts)（裁判法院）

| Court Types<br>裁判 | Type (Chinese)<br>中文名稱 | Revised Prefix<br>新簡稱 |
|---|---|---|
| Eastern Magistrates' Court | 東區裁判法院 | ES |
| Fanling Magistrates' Court | 粉嶺裁判法院 | FL |
| Kowloon City Magistrates' Court | 九龍城裁判法院 | KC |
| Kwun Tong Magistrates' Court | 觀塘裁判法院 | KT |
| North Kowloon Magistrates' Court | 北九龍裁判法院 | NK |
| Shatin Magistrates' Court | 沙田裁判法院 | ST |
| Tuen Mun Magistrates' Court | 屯門裁判法院 | TM |
| Tsuen Wan Magistrates' Court | 荃灣裁判法院 | TW |
| Western Magistrates' Court | 西區裁判法院 | WS |

Case Types (Magistrates' Courts)（裁判法院案件分類）

| Court Types<br>裁判 | Type (Chinese)<br>中文名稱 | Revised Prefix<br>新簡稱 |
|---|---|---|
| Fixed Penalty Distress Warrant | 定額罰款扣押令 | A |
| Distress Warrant (Company) | 扣押令（公司） | B |
| Charges Case | 刑事案件 | CC |
| Driving Offence Points | 交通違例扣分傳票 | D |
| Fixed Penalty Notice of Order | 定額罰款令 | FN |
| Fixed Penalty Summons | 定額罰款傳票 | FS |
| Fixed Penalty Summons (Parking) | 定額罰款（違例泊車）傳票 | K |
| Fixed Penalty Notice (Public Cleanliness Offences) | 定額罰款令（公．地方潔淨罪行） | L |
| Fixed Penalty Notice (Moving) | 定額罰款令（交通違例） | M |
| Miscellaneous Proceeding | 雜項案件 | MP |

| Court Types *裁判* | Type (Chinese) *中文名稱* | Revised Prefix *新簡稱* |
|---|---|---|
| Juvenile Miscellaneous Proceeding | 未成年兒童雜項案件 | JP |
| Departmental Notice | 聆訊通知書 | N |
| Fixed Penalty Notice (Parking) | 定額罰款令 （違例泊車） | P |
| Fixed Penalty Summons (Public Cleanliness Offences) | 定額罰款 （公．地方潔淨罪行）傳票 | R |
| Departmental Summons | 傳票 | S |
| Fixed Penalty Summons (Moving) | 定額罰款 （交通違例）傳票 | V |
| Non-Payment Warrant | 未有繳交罰款手令 | X |
| Non-Appearance Warrant | 未有出庭應訊手令 | Y |
| Hawker Case | 小販案件 | HW |
| Distress Warrant (Charge Case) | 付款令發出後所發出的財物扣押令 | AW |

## [1.9.3]     Chinese language endorsements

All of the forms in the appendices to these rules have official Chinese and English versions. Where a court document prepared in English is proposed to be served on a Chinese-speaking person who may not be proficient in English, it is required to include Chinese language endorsements so as to ensure that the party to be served understands its effect. See practice direction 24.2, which is set out below. Note that the schedules to PD 24.2 are out of date and should be read in light of the fact the Rules of the Supreme Court are now the Rules of the High Court, and the forms applicable in the district court are now found in the Rules of the District Court.

PRACTICE DIRECTION 24.2

ENDORSEMENTS IN THE CHINESE LANGUAGE TO BE MADE ON COURT DOCUMENTS

1.      This Practice Direction shall apply to the court forms set out in Appendix A to the Rules of the Supreme Court (Cap 4) and in the Second Schedule to the District Court Civil Procedure (Forms) Rules (Cap 336).

2.      This Practice Direction shall apply to a party or intending party to an action proposing to serve a court form on a party or intended party who is likely to be Chinese-speaking and who may not be proficient in English.

3.      The party or intending party proposing to serve in the circumstances set out in paragraph 2 hereof shall:

  (a)   ensure that the court form is accompanied by the appropriate Chinese language version as set out in the respective rules of court referred to in paragraph 1 hereof;

  (b)   ensure that the Chinese language version is completed as to formal particulars identifying the cause and giving the names and addresses of parties and relevant dates;

  (c)   where there is no prescribed Chinese language version of a particular court form, ensure that a brief explanation in Chinese of the purpose of the form is prominently endorsed upon it;

(d) where the form requires the completion of other than formal particulars, as set out in the First and Second Schedules hereto, include a summary in Chinese of the relief claimed or other particulars required; and

(e) ensure in any event that the dates and effects of any time limit sought to be imposed are briefly explained in Chinese.

4.    Every court form intended to be served in the circumstances set out in paragraph 2 hereof shall in addition be prominently endorsed in Chinese with the following:

因這是法律文件，忽視它可帶來嚴重的後果。如有疑問，請儘早向發出文件的法庭登記處（地址）查詢。你亦應考慮聽取律師的意見或是申請法律援助。

(This is a legal document. The consequences of ignoring it may be serious. If in doubt, you should enquire as soon as possible at the Registry of the Court issuing the document, namely (insert address) . . . You should also consider taking the advice of a solicitor or applying for legal aid.)

5.    This Practice Direction shall have effect from 1 October 1991.

SCHEDULE 1
RULES OF THE SUPREME COURT

Appendix A: Forms

| Form No. | Title of Form | The special particulars required to be filled in |
|---|---|---|
| Form 1 | Writ of summons | (1) statement of claim |
| Form 8 | Originating summons - general form | (1) plaintiff's claim or questions sought to be determined |
| Form 10 | Originating summons - expedited form | (1) plaintiff's application |
| Form 13 | Notice of originating motion | (1) order or relief applied for <br> (2) grounds of application or appeal |
| Form 20 | Third party notice claiming contribution or indemnity or other relief or remedy | (1) respective claims of plaintiff and defendant <br> (2) relief or remedy sought |
| Form 21 | Third party notice where question or issue to be determined | (1) question or issue sought to be determined <br> (2) relief or remedy sought |
| Form 23 | Notice of payment into court | (1) cause of action |
| Form 38 | Notice of motion | (1) the motion |
| Form 46 | Judgement after trial before judge with jury | (1) finding of jury <br> (2) judgement of the court |
| Form 48 | Judgment after decision of preliminary issue | (1) finding of the court <br> (2) order of the court |
| Form 49 | Judgement for liquidated sum against personal representative | (1) order of the court |
| Form 50 | Judgment for defendant's costs on discontinuance | (1) plaintiff's claim |
| Form 51 | Judgment for costs after acceptance of money paid into court | (1) plaintiff's cause of action |
| Form 52 | Notice of judgment or order | (1) judgment or order of the court |
| Form 85 | Order of committal | (1) particulars of the contempt <br> (2) terms requiring defendant to comply with for not executing the order of the court |

| Form No. | Title of Form | The special particulars required to be filled in |
|---|---|---|
| Form 86A | Notice of application for leave to apply for judicial review | (1) judgment, order, decision or other pro- ceeding in respect of which relief is sought<br>(2) relief sought<br>(3) grounds on which relief is sought |
| Form 102 | Order of issue of warrant of arrest for examination | (1) conditions other than specified in the Form upon which the bailiff is authorised to release the judgment debtor |
| Form 103 | Order of imprisonment pending further examination | (1) conditions other than those specified in the Form upon which the bailiff is authorised to release the judgment debtor |
| Form 106 | Order prohibiting departure from Hong Kong | (1) conditions other than those specified in the Form upon which the order shall have no effect |

## SCHEDULE II
## DISTRICT COURT CIVIL PROCEDURE (FORMS) RULES

| Form No. | Title of Form | The special particulars required to be filled in |
|---|---|---|
| Form 4 | Writ - Debt or liquidated dam- ages | (1) particulars of the debt or liquidated damages |
| Form 5 | Writ - Debt or liquidated dam- ages | (1) particulars of claim |
| Form 5A | Notice to be served with writ | (1) reasons for defendant's disputing plaintiff's claim<br>(2) defendant's counter-claim |
| Form 6 | Writ - Recovery of immovable property | (1) particulars of claim |
| Form 7 | Writ - Recovery of immovable property | (1) particulars of claim |
| Form 8 | Writ - General | (1) particulars of claim |

Certain queries were raised by the Law Society as a result of the above practice direction. In Law Society Circular 253/91 it was sought to clarify the points which had arisen. Although that circular has been deleted from the archives on the Law Soci ety's website, it contains useful guidance. It reads as follows:

**CIRCULAR 253/91**                                        **4th November, 1991**

## ENDORSEMENT IN THE CHINESE LANGUAGE TO BE MADE ON COURT DOCUMENTS

Reference is made to the Practice Direction issued by the Chief Justice relating to Chinese endorsements on Court documents (See Circulars 194/91 and 202/91).

The Civil Litigation Committee has since been in correspondence with the Reg istrar of the Supreme Court seeking his clarification on various matters arising out of the Practice Direction. In order to assist members the Committee has prepared the following questions and answers which are based upon information provided by the Registrar in response to the Committee's enquiries. The Committee would like to hear from members who have or may have encountered any practical difficulties in complying with the Practice Direction.

| *Questions* | *Answers* |
|---|---|
| 1. Will the Registry refuse to issue a court document for lack of a Chinese language endorsement be available? | As the Practice Direction is aimed at what is served rather than what is filed, the Registry will not be refusing to file documents which, on the face of them, do not comply with the Direction. |
| 2. On whom is the burden to establish proficiency (or lack of it) in English? Is it the Plaintiff or the Defendant? | On neither. The Registrar says that paragraph 2 of the Practice Direction is quite clear and that it must be accepted that the decision by the party serving the documents may not always be correct. It is a matter of judgment. The same applies to firms and companies as to individuals. |
| 3. Will (a) firms, and (b) companies be presumed to be proficient in English? | The same applies to firms and companies as to individuals. |
| 4. Is the Practice Direction designed for information only? | No. |
| 5. What will be the consequence of a wrong translation? | It will be a matter for the Court to whose attention any breach of the Direction is brought. |
| 6. In cases of discrepancies, would the English version prevail? | The intention of the Direction is that the Chinese version should be informative and it is not intended that it should form any formal part of the document. |
| 7. In paragraph 3(ii) of the Practice Direction, what is the meaning of 'identifying the cause'? | The Registrar says that there should be no difficulty in understanding this. This paragraph deals with formal matters but the further particulars would come under paragraph 3(iv) of the Direction. |
| 8. In paragraph 3(iv), what is the meaning of 'or other particulars required'? Does it mean a summary in the form of an endorsement of claims? | The aim is to inform the recipient of the document what it is all about and that could well include a summary of the claim. |
| 9. Would the examples of summary in Chinese set out below be in accordance with paragraph 3(iv) of the Practice Direction?<br>(a) The Plaintiff's claim is for the sum of HK$ ____ together with interest and costs being repayment of banking facilities made available to you.<br>(b) The Plaintiff's claim is for the sum of HK$ ____ together with interest and costs being monies due under a guarantee dated ____ of the obligations of ____.<br>(c) The Plaintiff's claim is for the sum of HK$ ____ together with interest and costs and possession of the property known as ____ pursuant to the terms of a mortgage dated ____ made between the Plaintiff and you.<br>(d) The Plaintiff's claim is for possession of the property known as ____ together with mesne profits until the date of possession under the terms of a tenancy agreement made between the Plaintiff and you.<br>(e) The Plaintiff's claim is for damages for breach of a contract dated ____ whereby you have failed to deliver goods as contracted.<br>(f) The Plaintiff's claim is for HK$ ____ being the price of goods sold and delivered to you pursuant to invoices numbers____. | The Registrar says that he would think that the summaries suggested are, very likely, suitable and he would doubt whether any criticism would be made were they to be used. He cautions that that is simply his opinion and cannot bind any Court that may be called upon to decide the matter. |

**[1.9.4]     Marking of form number**

Whenever the statutory forms in the appendices to these rules are used, as prescribed by Order 1 rule 9, the form number should be marked at the top of the first page of the document. See practice direction 24.1, para 5.

**10.     Rules not to exclude conduct of business by post** (O. 1 r. 10)

**Nothing in these rules shall prejudice any power to regulate the practice of the Court by giving directions enabling any business or class of business to be conducted by post.**

## ORDER 1A

### OBJECTIVES

1.     **Underlying objectives** (O.1A r.1)
       **The underlying objectives of these rules are -**
     **(a)**     **to increase the cost-effectiveness of any practice and procedure to be followed in relation to proceedings before the Court;**
     **(b)**     **to ensure that a case is dealt with as expeditiously as is reasonably practicable;**
     **(c)**     **to promote a sense of reasonable proportion and procedural economy in the conduct of proceedings;**
     **(d)**     **to ensure fairness between the parties;**
     **(e)**     **to facilitate settlement of disputes; and**
     **(f)**     **to ensure that the resources of the Court are distributed fairly.**
                                                              **(L.N. 152 of 2008)**

---

## NOTES

### [1A.1.1]  Introduction of the 'underlying' objectives
Order 1A rule 1 sets out the 'underlying' objectives of the Rules of the High Court. It took effect in 2009 when the recommendations of the Chief Justice's working party on civil justice reform were implemented.

### [1A.1.2]  Origin and scope of the underlying objectives in Order 1A
The underlying objectives set out in Order 1A rule 1 are a modified version of the 'overriding' objective set out in CPR 1.1 in England. In Hong Kong the working party's final report (paras 95-100) recommended the word 'underlying' instead of 'overriding'. This was done in light of experience in England where, in the words of the final report (para 97(d)), 'over-reliance on the overriding objective has sometimes led to absurd results'. The final report continues (at para 98):

> The trap into which the misguided are likely to be led would involve regarding the overriding objective as providing all the answers and, because of its "overriding" character, as permitting specific procedural provisions to be ignored or given insufficient weight. This would be a fundamental error since such rules will in many cases have been refined over the years to deal fairly with the specific procedural issues to hand.

As a consequence, the final report recommended (at para 100) against the new rule having an 'overriding' character, 'to avoid encouraging over-elaborate and misguided reliance placed on it'. Instead, the final report recommended that:

> It should be made clear that such a rule merely makes explicit what are implicit objectives which 'underlie' specific rules of the RHC, supporting the internal logic of such rules. Such specific rules should accordingly continue to demand intelligent application informed, but not overridden, by the underlying principles.

The English rule lays down the single objective of 'enabling the court to deal with cases justly'. That phrase does not appear in the Hong Kong rule, but Order 1A rule 2(2) is arguably to a similar effect. The English rule then elaborates the single objective with a list of factors included in 'dealing with a case justly'. Hong Kong's rule lists 'objectives' in the plural, which are similar to the factors by which the English single objective is elaborated. Despite the differences in wording, the overall thrust of the two is similar.

### [1A.1.3]   The individual objectives
The wording and arrangement of the underlying objectives set out in rule 1 are different from the overriding objectives in CPR 1.1. Although the overall thrust appears to be broadly similar, the Hong Kong rules are couched in more moderate terms.

We now turn to look at Hong Kong's underlying objectives one by one.

### [1A.1.4]   Objective (a) - cost-effectiveness
Order 1A rule 1(a) states the objective of increasing the 'cost-effectiveness' of any practice and procedure to be followed in the court. This must mean that the court, when exercising its powers with regard to procedural matters, should bear in mind cost implications. It is obviously desirable that the just resolution of civil disputes should be obtainable as cheaply as possible.

This objective closely resembles CPR 1.1(2)(b), which is simply 'saving expense'. The Civil Court Practice, our sister publication in the UK, has the following commentary on that provision of the CPR (at para CPR 1.1 [4]):

> **Saving expense** In *Little v George Little Sebire & Co* [1999] The Times, 17 November, it was held that the power to award indemnity costs and enhanced interest under the former CPR 36.21 (now CPR 36.14(3)) (where a reasonable offer had been rejected) [in Hong Kong see O 22 r 23 & 24] should be exercised so as to concentrate the minds of the parties on offers to settle and thereby to save expense. Active case management, including the power to dispose of claims or issues summarily is to be implemented with a view to saving expense: see *Swain v Hillman* [2001] 1 All ER 91 (CA) [and see Order 1A rule 4 in Hong Kong]. However, the provisions of CPR 1 cannot be invoked so as to require a claimant to include claims he does not wish to raise, or to increase the quantum of his claim: *Khaiban v Beard* [2002] EWCA Civ 358 [2003] 3 All ER 362. It is incumbent on practitioners appearing in any court to take all steps they can in accordance with CPR 1.1 and CPR 1.3 [in Hong Kong Order 1A rules 1 & 3] to reduce the costs of proceedings and such steps include the use of video conferencing: *Pastouna v Black* [2005] EWCA Civ 1389, [2005] NLJR 1847.

As to when evidence may be taken by video-link in Hong Kong, see the commentary under Order 39 rule 1.

In *Ip Tsz Lam Ada v Pearl Wisdom Ltd* HCA 2482/2007 (Sakhrani J; 30.04.2009) the court referred to this objective, and objective (c) (reasonable proportion and procedural economy) on a summary assessment of the costs of an amendment application. It found the claim for more $600,000 was 'both unreasonable and disproportionate', and allowed less than $100,000.

### [1A.1.5]   Objective (b) - expeditiousness
Order 1A rule 1(b) states the objective 'to ensure that a case is dealt with as expeditiously as is reasonably practicable'. This must mean that the court should, in exercising its powers, strive to avoid unnecessary delay in the resolution of civil disputes.

This objective closely resembles CPR 1.1(2)(d), which is 'ensuring that [a case] is dealt with expeditiously and fairly'. The following commentary on the English objective is taken from our sister publication in the UK, The Civil Court Practice (para CPR 1.1 [6]):

**Expedition and fairness** Applications for permission [in Hong Kong the term 'leave' is retained instead of 'permission' used in the CPR] to amend often raise particular difficulties. In *Cobbold v Greenwich LBC* (09.08.1999, unreported) [accessible on the BAILII website as [1999] EWCA Civ 207] Peter Gibson LJ said that an amendment should generally be allowed to 'permit the real dispute between the parties to be adjudicated', provided that 'the public interest in the effective administration of justice is not significantly harmed'. However, it may well normally be right to refuse permission to amend when the application is made during trial and would result in the adjournment of the trial and a re-hearing, even where the party seeking the amendment is prepared to bear all the costs thrown away: see *Worldwide Corp Ltd v GPT Ltd* [1998] All ER (D) 667 (CA). When granting permission [leave] to amend, it may be right to impose conditions which would reduce or limit the cost or delay implications of the amendment: see *Southern & Eastern District Finance pic v Turner* [2003] EWCA Civ 1574, [2003] All ER (D) 112 (Nov), at para 34.

Although the above commentary focuses on the court's power to grant leave to amend, it is clear that the expeditiousness objective should apply broadly. Its essence is the resolution of disputes without avoidable delay. Thus in *Interasia Bag Manufacturers Ltd v Commissioner of Inland Revenue* [2009] 5 HKLRD 818 the court took this objective into account in striking out an appeal for want of prosecution.

The expeditiousness objective is furthered by the court's power to fix case management timetables which are generally expected to be complied with. See Order 25 rule IB and the commentary thereunder.

**[1A.1.6]    Objective (c) - reasonable proportion and procedural economy**
Objective (c) seeks to 'promote a sense of reasonable proportion and procedural economy in the conduct of proceedings'. It is a modified version of CPR 1.1 (2)(c) which mandates the English court to deal with cases in ways which are proportionate to (i) the amount of money involved, (ii) the importance of the case, (iii) the complexity of the issues, and (iv) the financial position of each party. The specificity of the English provision was deliberately avoided in Hong Kong. The Chief Justice's working party recommended (para 106 of its final report) that the Hong Kong provision 'should try to avoid spawning minute analysis and argument', and 'should instead be a reminder that commonsense notions of reasonableness and a sense of proportion should inform the exercise of a judicial discretion in the procedural context'.

The Chief Justice's working party said (final report, para 103, referring to the UK publication Civil Procedure 2003) that proportionality requires:

(a) litigation costs to bear a reasonably proportionate relationship with the amount at stake in the dispute;

(b) procedures to be appropriately matched to the case, that is, ensuring that elaborate procedures (which may be appropriate for big and complex cases) are not used unnecessarily in ordinary cases;

(c) applications for drastic forms of relief, such as *Anton Piller* orders or orders for committal for contempt, to be avoided where such relief would be disproportionate in the circumstances;

(d) procedural sanctions and orders to be issued in a manner proportionate to the requirements of procedural and substantive justice, for instance, not striking out the entire claim when a lesser sanction would suffice, and not ordering extensive particulars or further discovery where the benefits are likely to be slight and would not justify the expense and effort involved;

(e) cases to be instituted in the correct tribunal, avoiding the High Court where the simpler procedures of a lower court or tribunal would suffice; and

(f) procedural orders to be made which are proportionate to the financial position of each party . . .

As to what the concept entails, in *Szeto v Dwyer* [2010] NLCA 36 (CanLII), the Newfoundland Court of Appeal said (para 54) that proportionality:

> means dealing with a proceeding in ways such that the time and the types of processes involved as well as the expense and convenience of the parties are proportionate to factors such as: the nature of the issues engaged; the amount of money involved; the time reasonably necessary to resolve the issue; the complexity of the issues and the overall cost of the litigation that can be reasonably expected.

The Chief Justice's working party noted (at para 105) that some elements of the proportionality concept were already found in the rules prior to the civil justice reforms. Specific mention is made of the requirement in relation to discovery (Order 24 rule 8) and interrogatories (Order 26 rule 1) that an order not be made unless necessary for disposing fairly of the case, or for saving costs; and the stipulation in Order 38 rule 2A(1) that the court's power to order exchange of witness statements shall be exercised for the purpose of fair and expeditious disposal of the case, and saving costs, having regard to all the circumstances. Order 1A rule 1(c) now makes it clear that proportionality underlies the rules as a whole.

Proportionality will be of particular relevance when the court exercises a discretion. Our sister publication in the UK, the Civil Court Practice gives the following examples (at para CPR 1.1 [5]):

- Amendment: *McPhilemy v Times Newspapers Ltd* [1999] 3 All ER 775
- Assessment of costs: *Lownds v Home Office* [2002] EWCA Civ 365
- Leave to appeal: *Piglowska v Piglowska* [1999] 3 All ER 632 644-5 (HL).

Examples from Hong Kong include:

- *Ma Hoi Ki v Li Chi Chuen & Anor* [2009] 2 HKC 488 (para 18): proportionality would militate against allowing counsel's fee for advising on settlement in straightforward low quantum proceedings.
- *Ip Tsz Lam Ada v Pearl Wisdom Ltd* HCA 2482/2007 (Sakhrani J; 30.04.2009): a claim for more than $600,000 for an amendment application was said to be 'both unreasonable and disproportionate', and was reduced to less than $100,000.

Examples from other jurisdictions include:

- *London Enterprises Ltd v Smith* [2010] BCSC 1666 (CanLII): an application for disclosure of the identity of the 11,000 'Names' who were personally liable under a Lloyd's insurance syndicate was refused as disproportionate, considering the time, effort, complexity and possible cost.

### [1A.1.7] Objective (d) - fairness between the parties

The objective in Hong Kong is to ensure 'fairness' between the parties, whereas in England's CPR 1.1(2)(a) the court is enjoined to ensure that the parties are on an 'equal footing'. The Chief Justice's working party on civil justice reform recommended the objective of 'greater equality between parties' (final report, para 99) but the wording was changed to 'fairness' when Order 1A was made by the rules committee. In England the 'fairness' objective is coupled with that of 'expeditiousness', as to which see above. 'Fairness' appears to be broader than 'equality', though clearly equality is a part of fairness.

The Civil Court Practice, our sister publication in the UK, says of the English 'equal footing' provision (at para CPR 1.1 [3]):

> **Equal footing** The right of a litigant to be represented by the solicitors or advocates of his or her choice is fundamental and well-established, and that right is not removed by the "level playing field" or the requirement of proportionality in CPR 1.1(2) [in Hong Kong Order 1A rule 1(c)]: *Maltez v Lewis* [1999] 21 LS Gaz R 39 ChD. However, CPR 1.1(2) (a) [in Hong Kong Order 1A rule 1(d)] may be invoked on the issue of costs, both at the assessment [taxation] stage - see R on the application of *Wolfsohn v Legal Services Commission* [2002] EWCA Civ 250, [2002] All ER (D) 120 (Feb) - and in relation to an application for a costs order - *R (CPRE) v Hammersmith and Fulham London Borough Council* [1999] Times, 26 Oct. The equal footing provision may also be invoked in relation to an application for permission [leave] to amend: see *Woods v Chaleff* [2002] NJLR 1276.

> The denial of legal assistance to a person who needs to be represented in proceedings may in some circumstances involve a breach of human rights under Article 6 [of the European Convention on Human Rights]. *But the mere fact that one party has legal representation which the other cannot afford does not by itself entitle the lay litigant to legal aid in order to achieve equality of arms. A judge should not cease hearing a case, or application, where a party appearing in person has asserted that judges in general, including those listed to hear his case, were likely to favour submissions by members of the legal profession over those of a lay litigant. Nor should such an assertion by itself justify the court in urging the Legal Services Commission [Legal Aid Department in Hong Kong] to grant legal aid. Both points were made by the Court of Appeal in *Trio dos Bank NV v Dobbs* [2005] EWCA Civ 630; [2005] Times, 11 May.

* The Civil Court Practice here refers readers to the following commentary elsewhere in the work (III HUM [28.2A]), on the European Convention, which may be relevant in Hong Kong under the Basic Law and the Bill of Rights:

> **Legal assistance in the determination of civil rights and obligations** The provision of free legal assistance may sometimes be required because of the complexity of the procedure or the case: *Airey v Ireland* (Application 6289/73) [1979] 2 EHRR 305, followed in *P C & S v United Kingdom* (Application 56547/00) [2002] 3 FCR 1, [2002] Times 16 Aug ECHR, a freeing for adoption case. A denial of free legal assistance in the defence of libel proceedings is not necessarily a breach of Articles 6 or 10: *McVicar v United Kingdom* (Application 46311/99 [2002] NLJR 759, ECHR. A litigant who wishes to establish that without legal aid his right to effective justice would be violated has a relatively high threshold to cross: *Perrotti v Collyer-Bristow (a firm)* [2003] EWCA Civ 1521, [2004] 2 All ER 189.

> The denial of legal aid to the defendants in a substantial libel case has been held to contravene the requirements of fairness in Article 6.1: *Steel v United Kingdom* (Application No 64816/01 [2005] Times, 16 Feb, ECHR.

In England, a party who wishes to rely on 'equal footing' as a ground for the court to restrain another party in the conduct of the litigation, should demonstrate that it is conducting the proceedings in a manner conducive to limiting expense as far as practicable: *McPhilemy v Times Newspapers* [1999] 3 All ER 775 (CA). The same should be true with regard to the objective of 'fairness' in Hong Kong.

In *Ma Hoi Ki v Li Chi Chuen & Anor* [2009] 2 HKC 488 (para 18) this objective was cited in obiter dicta to the effect that the court might refuse to allow counsel's fee for advising on settlement in straightforward low quantum proceedings in the District Court involving a party under disability and thus requiring approval of the court under Order 80. The court said (at para 14) that on implementation of the civil justice reforms, it must be vigilant to ensure that costs incurred by parties are reasonable and proportionate 'not only from the perspective of the person under disability but also from an inter partes perspective'.

### [1A.1.8]   Objective (e) - facilitate settlement

Objective (e), to facilitate settlement of disputes, does not have a direct equivalent in CPR 1.1. However, there is something similar in CPR 1.4 which deals with the court's duty of active case management. That has been replicated in Hong Kong's Order 1A, rule 4(2)(f). See the commentary thereunder.

The rules have always had the objective of encouraging settlement. The costs sanction normally imposed on the losing party is a good example, being a strong incentive to settle. This objective requires more - settlement should not only be encouraged, but facilitated. Thus on an application for discovery or interrogatories (or any other type of interlocutory order) the court should now take into account whether the order sought might facilitate settlement, by clarifying issues or otherwise.

### [1A.1.9]   Objective (f) - fair distribution of court resources

Objective (f), that the resources of the court shall be distributed fairly, closely resembles CPR 1.1(2)(e) which gives the English court the task of 'allotting to [a case] an appropriate share of the court's resources, while taking into account the need to allot resources to other cases'. By this objective the court should take into account not only the needs of the particular case, but those of others which are waiting to be heard. The civil courts are a public dispute resolution service available to everyone and this objective makes clear that litigants with large budgets cannot necessarily expect to be allowed whatever court time they can afford. However, there will continue to be 'big' cases calling out for a greater share of court resources than most, and the proportionality objective in rule 1(c) should be taken into account along with fair distribution in rule 1(f) when considering whether they should be allotted such a share.

The Civil Court Practice, our sister publication in the UK, says (at para CPR 1.1[7]) of the equivalent English provision:

> **Allotting an appropriate share of the court's resources** In *SBJ Stephenson Ltd v Mandy* [1999] The Times, 21 July, the Court of Appeal said that it would not be a good use of the court's resources to explore the merits of an appeal against an interlocutory injunction when the trial date was less than a month away, and the claimant had given a cross-undertaking in damages. In *Arbuthnot Lathan Bank Ltd v Trafalgar Holdings Ltd* [1997] The Times, 29 December; [1998] 1 WLR 1426 (CA) Lord Woolf MR explained that delay or disruption resulting from a proposed course would be assessed not solely by reference to the effect on the parties, but also by reference to other litigants.

## 2.   Application by the Court of underlying objectives (O. 1A r. 2)

**(1)   The Court shall seek to give effect to the underlying objectives of these rules when it -**

(a)    exercises any of its powers (whether under its inherent jurisdiction or given to it by these rules or otherwise); or

(b)    interprets any of these rules or a practice direction.

(2)   In giving effect to the underlying objectives of these rules, the Court shall always recognize that the primary aim in exercising the powers of the Court is to secure the just resolution of disputes in accordance with the substantive rights of the parties.

(L.N. 152 of 2008)

---

## NOTES

### [1A.2.1]    When does the court apply the underlying objectives?

Order 1A rule 2(1) derives from CPR 1.2 which likewise provides that the court must give effect to the underlying [in England 'overriding'] objectives when it exercises its powers or interprets the rules. Unlike the Hong Kong rule, the English equivalent is expressly subject to CPR 76.2 which provides for modification of the overriding objective in proceedings under the Prevention of Terrorism Act 2005.

It has been held that the underlying objectives are applicable to actions commenced before the civil justice reforms came into force on 2 April 2009:

*Nanjing Iron & Steel Group Int'l Trade Co Ltd & Ors v STX Pan Ocean Co Ltd & Anor* HCAJ 177/2006 (Reyes J; 07.09.2009) (para 14). The Court of Appeal agreed in *Interasia Bag Manufacturers Ltd v Commissioner of Inland Revenue* [2009] 5 HKLRD 818. However, in *Re Wing Fai Construction Co Ltd* [2010] 3 HKC 593 (CA) (para 12) it was held that on an application to dismiss for want of prosecution, the correct approach is to consider delay which occurred prior to implementation of the civil justice reforms in the context in which it occurred, not with regard to the underlying objective of expeditiousness (O 1A, r 1(b)).

### [1A.2.2]    Rule 2(2) - primacy of just resolution and rights of the parties

Order 1A rule 2(2) states that the underlying objectives should be given effect by the court bearing in mind that the 'primary aim' is just resolution of disputes in accordance with the rights of the parties. Inclusion of this provision was recommended by the Chief Justice's working party on civil justice reform (final report, recommendation 3) in response to concerns that 'the new methodology might divert the court from deciding cases in accordance with their substantive merits' (final report, para 89(a)).

It is arguable that this provision has a similar effect to the English overriding objective of enabling the court to deal with cases justly. See the commentary under Order 1A rule 1.

3.    **Duty of the parties and their legal representatives.** (O. 1A r. 3)

The parties to any proceedings and their legal representatives shall assist the Court to further the underlying objectives of these rules.

(L.N. 152 of 2008)

## NOTES

### [1A.3.1]    Duty to assist the court

Order 1A rule 3 imposes a duty on the parties to assist the court in furthering the underlying objectives. It derives from CPR 1.3, but is broader in that it expressly extends to the parties' legal representatives. The following points are taken from the commentary on the duty to assist the court as set out in our sister publication in the UK, The Civil Court Practice (at paras CPR 1.3[1] & [2]):

> **The duty of the parties** The duty plainly extends to the legal advisors and legal representatives of the parties: see *Geveran Trading Co Ltd v Skjevesland* [2002] EWCA Civ 1567, [2003] 1 All ER (para 37). The duty of the parties extends to cooperating with each other and with the court in relation to fixing the trial date. Further, where the dates upon which an expert witness will be available are given to the court, a party should indicate which dates are merely inconvenient, and which dates are effectively impossible eg because the expert is committed to give evidence in another matter: *Matthews v Tarmac Bricks & Tiles Ltd* [1999] All ER (D) 692 (CA). CPR 1.3 also requires a publicly funded litigant to honour his obligations to the Legal Services Commission [Legal Aid Department in Hong Kong] so far as they relate to the continuation of his certificate: *R (Murray) v Hampshire CC* (No 2) [2003] EWCA Civ 760.
>
> Similarly, parties must cooperate in explaining any procedural points which they intend to take: where one party warned the other that it would oppose an application (by reason of a failure to comply with the rules) but refused to identify the basis on which there had been noncompliance (the contention being a failure to comply with the requirements of CPR 36 in respect of a Part 36 offer [in HK see O 22]), the court rejected the undisclosed and technical objection on the ground that the objecting party should not be allowed to reap any benefit from noncooperation in breach of CPR 1.3 and CPR 1.4 [Order 1A rules 3 & 4]: *Hertsmere Primary Care Trust v Estate of BabindraAnandh* [2005] EWHC 320 (Ch), [2005] 3 All ER 274.
>
> In complex cases 'the advocates who are expected to be instructed to appear at the trial should attend case management conferences or pretrial reviews before the judge so that they can discuss with him in a collaborative manner ways in which the conduct of the trial might be made less burdensome if the issues are handled in a particular way': *Morris v Bank of America National Trust & Savings Ass'n* [2000] 1 All ER 954 (CA) (para 52).
>
> It is incumbent on practitioners appearing in any court to take all steps they can in accordance with CPR 1.1 and CPR 1.3 [in Hong Kong Order 1A rule 1 and 3] to reduce the costs of proceedings and such steps include the use of video conferencing: *Pastouna v Black* [2005] EWCA Civ 1389, [2005] NLJR 1847.

As to when evidence may be taken by videolink in Hong Kong, see the commentary under Order 39 rule 1. The above passage continues:

> **Duty to keep the court informed of likely settlement or adjournment** The parties must inform the court immediately when a case or application has been settled, or is unlikely to proceed. Otherwise there is a risk of serious waste of resources, including waste of judicial time, and the possible harm to other parties of getting their application or case heard: see *Tasyurdu v Immigration Appeal Tribunal* [2003] EWCA Civ 447. Similarly, where judgment has been reserved by the court, the parties must inform the court as soon as they become aware of any development which might make it

unnecessary for judgment to be delivered: *HFC Bank plc v HSBC Bank plc* [2000] 144 Sol Jo LB 182 (CA).

    If a case of any complexity, due for hearing on a Monday, settles, or is about to settle, late on Friday, the parties should not wait until Monday to inform the court, but should try and pass the information on by whatever means may be available. In particular they should take advantage of the 24 hour telephone service: *Yell Ltd v Garton* [2004] EWCA Civ 87, 80 (Feb).

The duty to inform the court if hearing dates will need revision was recognised in Hong Kong even before this rule came into force. See *Mandecly Ltd & Anor v Hao Wei & Ors* [2005] 2 HKLRD 592, and see the commentary under Order 34 rule 2. In Hong Kong the clerk to the duty judge can be reached outside court hours on mobile telephone number 9137 9005 (High Court) and 9137 9004 (District Court).

### [1A.3.2]    Duty to assist court does not require disclosure of unfavourable evidence

The duty of legal representatives to assist the court does not require them to disclose evidence favourable to the other side. The legal representative's duty to the client remains paramount in this regard. See *Khudados v Hayden & Ors* [2007] EWCA Civ 1316 (13.12.2007) where it was argued that the defendant's counsel, appearing to oppose an adjournment application, ought to have disclosed a medical report obtained by their side, which would have substantiated the health grounds relied upon by the unrepresented applicant, who was absent from the hearing. Dismissing this argument, Ward LJ said (at paras 38-9):

> The question is to what extent if at all a barrister who must promote and protect fearlessly and by all proper and lawful means his lay client's best interests is bound to disclose evidence favourable to the other side. I draw the distinction between evidence favourable to the other side and law in the form of all relevant decisions and legislative provisions which may be unfavourable towards the contention which he argues. It seems to me that the better view is that a barrister would fail in his duty to his own client were he to supplement the deficiencies in his opponent's evidence. The fact that the other side is a litigant in person cannot make any difference as to the manner in which he fulfils his duties to the client, to the other side and above all to the court. In my judgment, counsel cannot be criticised for failing to disclose the further report.

The learned judge went on specifically to consider whether the duty to assist the court under CPR 1.3 (Order 1A rule 3 in Hong Kong) affected the position stated above. He said:

> ...it is at most a duty to the court, not to the other side. The duty is to help the court further the overriding objective ['underlying objectives' in Hong Kong]. The primary duty to further the overriding objective is imposed on the court itself. It is the court which must dispose of cases justly . . . In my judgment fairness does not require counsel to place his own client at a substantial disadvantage by acting contrary to his interests. Whatever may be the requirement to help the court, it cannot in my judgment, extend so far as to impose upon counsel a duty in conflict with his proper duty to his client.

Counsel's duty to lay client is found inter alia in paragraphs 110 and 135 of the Code of Conduct of the Hong Kong Bar Association. The duty to the court to make known relevant law is found in para 136. With regard to solicitor advocates, see chapter 10 of the Hong Kong Solicitors' Guide to Professional Conduct vol 1 (2nd ed).

**[1A.3.3]    Duty to assist the court reinforces duty not to put forward unarguable case**

Even in the absence of express provision in the conduct guide, solicitors are under a professional duty '(i) not to include in court documents that they drafted any contention which they did not consider to be properly arguable and (ii) not to instruct counsel to advance contentions which they did not consider to be properly arguable': *Richard Buxton (Solicitors) v Mills-Owens* [2010] EWCA Civ 122 (23.02.2010) (para 43). There it was held that this duty is 'reinforced' by the English equivalent of Order 1A rule 3. As a result, a firm of solicitors was entitled to terminate the retainer of a client who persisted in instructions that they take unarguable points on an appeal.

**4.      Court's duty to manage cases** (O. 1A r. 4)

     **(1)    The Court shall further the underlying objectives of these rules by actively managing cases.**

     **(2)    Active case management includes -**

         **(a)    encouraging the parties to co-operate with each other in the conduct of the proceedings;**

         **(b)    identifying the issues at an early stage;**

         **(c)    deciding promptly which issues need full investigation and trial and accordingly disposing summarily of the others;**

         **(d)    deciding the order in which issues are to be resolved;**

         **(e)    encouraging the parties to use an alternative dispute resolution procedure if the Court considers that appropriate, and facilitating the use of such a procedure;**

         **(f)    helping the parties to settle the whole or part of the case;**

         **(g)    fixing timetables or otherwise controlling the progress of the case;**

         **(h)    considering whether the likely benefits of taking a particular step justify the cost of taking it;**

         **(i)    dealing with as many aspects of the case as practicable on the same occasion;**

         **(j)    dealing with the case without the parties needing to attend at court;**

         **(k)    making use of technology; and**

         **(l)    giving directions to ensure that the trial of a case proceeds quickly and efficiently.**

                                                **(L.N. 152 of 2008)**

---

**NOTES**

**[1A.4.1]    Origin and scope of Order 1A r 4**

Order 1A rule 4 imposes on the court a duty to further the underlying objectives by actively managing cases, and goes on to set out a non-exhaustive list of some spe cific things the court should do in that regard.

     The Chief Justice's working party on civil justice reform considered (final report, para 108) that the court ought to engage in 'active case management' in the sense of having power to reject the proposals of both parties as to directions, and make orders which it considers appropriate even if neither party has sought them. The working party continued (at para 109) by sounding a note of caution against 'unwarranted proactivity' by the court:

> It should, however, be made clear that the Working Party is not in favour of unwarranted proactivity by the court. The case management powers are there to curb the excesses of the adversarial system, not to displace that system. What the Working Party favours, reflected in proposal 3, is to make more systematic the approach to case management presently accepted as a matter of common law, as discussed in the Interim Report (paras 234-9).

Order 1A rule 4 derives from CPR 1.4 which is in the same terms, save that it uses the English 'overriding' objective.

Our sister publication in the UK, The Civil Court Practice, includes (at paras CPR 1.4 [1]&[2]) the following commentary on the equivalent English provision:

> **General** For the preliminary stage at which the court routinely commences its management of a case, see CPR Pt 26 [which deals with allocation of cases between different 'tracks', and was not adopted in Hong Kong; in this jurisdiction see Order 25 which deals with the case management summons and conference]. The duty of the court to manage a case is fundamental. It normally starts with the allocation questionnaire and the consequent allocation of a case to the appropriate track.

The above passage must be read in Hong Kong in light of the fact that although Order 25 rule 1 provides for a questionnaire, leading to the giving of pre-trial directions by the court, cases in this jurisdiction are not allocated to separate tracks. The above passage continues:

> The various factors listed in [Order 1A rule 4] may sometimes conflict, and the court must reconcile them appropriately giving such weight as it thinks appropriate to each factor: see *Re Rotodata Ltd* [2000] 1 BCLC 122 (ChD). In many instances, case management may involve the imposition of a sanction falling short of dismissing a claim or disallowing a defence: see *Biguzzi v Rank Leisure plc* [1999] 4 All ER 934, [1999] 1 WLR 1926 (CA).
>
> **Duty of the parties and legal representatives to assist the court**
>
> The duty of the court to manage cases actively requires the active assistance and cooperation of the parties (and hence of their legal representatives): see [Order 1A rule 3]. This means that all the parties in a particular case are under a duty to assist the court, and cooperate, in relation to active case management of their dispute, and in particular of the various components identified in [Order 1A rule 4(2)]. Thus, the parties should be ready to assist the court on any matter which may be raised at an allocation hearing [not applicable in Hong Kong], a case management conference, or any other hearing. The parties should also consider what directions the court should be asked to give, and, when a party considers that it is necessary or appropriate to make an application, he should do so with dispatch: see CPR PD 29, para 3.8 [English practice direction on the multi-track, which has not been adopted in Hong Kong]. Further a party is obliged to raise all matters which can conveniently be disposed of in the same claim, and failure to do so may amount to an abuse of the court's process: CPR 7.3 and CPR 3.4(2)(b).

In Hong Kong the court has ample power under Order 18 rule 19(1)(d) to strike out proceedings which raise matters that could and should have been litigated in an earlier action. See the commentary under that rule. The above passage from the Civil Court

Practice continues:

> The parties' legal representatives have a duty to keep up to date with reported decisions of the Court of Appeal and to bring them to the attention of the court whenever they are in point: *Copeland v Smith* [2000] 1 All ER 457 [2000] 1 WLR 1371 (CA).

### [1A.4.2] The individual items of case management
The individual items of case management in Order 1A rule 4(2) are worded identically to the English equivalents (in CPR 1.4). We now turn to look at them one by one.

### [1A.4.3] Order IA rule 4(2)(a) — duty to encourage co-operation
Order 1A rule 4(2)(a) lays down a duty to further the underlying objectives by encouraging co-operation between the parties in the conduct of the proceedings. Its wording is identical to CPR 1.4 (2) (a). The Civil Court Practice, our sister publication in the UK says (at para CPR 1.4[3]) of this item:

> **Encouraging cooperation: [rule 4(2)(a)]** One of the most important aspects in this connection is the pre-action protocol [in Hong Kong the personal injuries practice direction is an example — see the commentary under Order 72 rule 2]. Many other provisions of the CPR are based on the obligation to cooperate, and require cooperation between the parties to be fully effective. An example is the appointment of a single joint expert under CPR 35.7 [in Hong Kong O 38 r 4A].
>
> The court's duty to encourage cooperation gives rise, in an appropriate case, to a duty on a party to draw promptly to the court's attention any failure on the part of the other party not to cooperate [sic]. However, whether and if so when, it is appropriate for such a matter to be drawn to the attention of the court is inevitably fact-sensitive. Any failure to cooperate can, and indeed often should, be appropriately penalised in costs: see CPR 44.5 (3) (a) [in Hong Kong O 62 r 5(1)(e) and r 32C(1)(b)].

### [1A.4.4] Order 1A rule 4(2)(b) — duty to identify issues early
Rule 4(2) (b) includes identifying issues at an early stage among the non-exhaustive list of case management powers. Its wording is identical to CPR 1.4(2)(b). Of that provision our sister publication in the UK, The Civil Court Practice says (at para CPR 1.4[4]):

> Identifying issues early: [rule 4(2)(b)] It is important for the court to be told of all the real issues between the parties at an early stage, and to be kept informed of this throughout the progress of the case. Otherwise its case management powers cannot be utilised properly, and often will be misdirected. If costs are increased due to a party's failure to assist the court in identifying all the real issues, adverse costs consequences should follow.

### [1A.4.5] Order 1A rule 4(2)(c) — prompt disposal of issues
Rule 4(2)(c) specifies as part of case management, the need for prompt decisions as to which issues need to go to trial, and which can be disposed of summarily. Its wording is the same as CPR 1.4(2)(c), of which our sister publication in the UK, The Civil Court Practice, says (at para CPR 1.4[5]):

> Disposing of issues appropriately under [rule 4(2)(c)] While a hopeless head of claim or defence should be dismissed promptly, any point raised in a statement of case [statement of claim] which may be arguable should be permitted to go to trial. Further, where a number of connected issues are raised, it may well be inappropriate to dispose

of only some of them at a summary stage: see *Tawil v Harrods Ltd* [2001] EWCA Civ 1695 [2001] All ER (D) 41 (Nov).

The test under CPR Part 24 [summary judgment — in Hong Kong see Order 14, which is not identical] is whether there is a real prospect of success in the sense that the prospect of success is realistic rather than fanciful. When considering that matter, the court should consider not only the evidence currently available, but also the evidence which could reasonably be expected to be available at trial. However, it is not appropriate for the court to undertake an examination of the evidence without a trial, and to adopt the standard of proof applicable to a trial, namely the balance of probabilities: see *Royal Brompton Hospital NHS Trust v Hammond* [2001] EWCA Civ 550 [2001] BLR 297.

See also Order 18 rule 12(3A) by which the court may seek to clarify issues by ordering, of its own motion, a party to provide particulars of a pleading.

### [1A.4.6]    Order 1A rule 4(2)(d) — order of dealing with issues

Order 1A rule 4(2)(d) includes 'deciding the order in which issues are to be resolved' in the list of case management powers. Its wording is the same as CPR 1.4(2)(d), of which our sister publication in the UK, The Civil Court Practice, says (at para CPR 1.4[6]):

Deciding the order of issues to be resolved under [rule 4(2) (d)] It may be inappropriate to determine some issues preliminarily, especially if there is an overlap between the evidence and/or arguments on those issues and the other issues left to be determined later: see *Worsley v Tambrands Ltd* [2000] The Times, 11 Feb (CA).

### [1A.4.7]    Order 1A rule 4(2)(e) — encouraging use of ADR

Order 1A rule 4(2)(e) mandates the court, in exercise of its case management powers, to encourage and facilitate the use of alternative dispute resolution ('ADR') procedures. It is worded identically to CPR 1.4(2)(e).

The Chief Justice's working party had mediation principally in mind. It considered that mediation of commercial cases had proved successful and cost-effective in the UK (final report, paras 788-9), and that there had been similar success in the pilot scheme for family mediation in Hong Kong (para 792). It noted the following advantages of mediation:

(a) the possibility of 'very substantial savings in costs' in suitable cases (para 798) (though the working party also acknowledged the risk that if mediation fails 'this would add to the costs and might possibly delay resolution of the dispute': para 821)

(b) the fact that 'mediation can produce flexible and constructive outcomes as between the parties which traditional legal remedies cannot offer'(para 799)

(c) 'Mediation also provides the chance of a swifter resolution of the dispute in conditions of confidentiality and in an atmosphere where the parties are channeled towards seeking settlement rather than towards inflicting maximum adversarial damage on each other' (para 800).

The working party rejected arguments that Hong Kong lacks the infrastructure to support ADR or mediation, noting the existence of the Hong Kong Mediation Council (part of the Hong Kong International Arbitration Centre) with mediation rules which can be viewed on www.hkiac.org, and the Hong Kong Mediation Centre (www.mediation-centre.com.hk) (paras 907-813).

Subsequently the judiciary has published a pamphlet on mediation (which may be viewed on the judiciary's website www.judiciary.gov.hk) which gives additional referrals. See also the judiciary's dedicated webpage mediation.judiciary.gov.hk,and for venues available for mediation free-of-charge, see Law Society circular 10-15.

The working party also doubted the validity of concerns about the right of access to the courts (Basic Law, art 35) (paras 801-4), though it limited its recommendation to encouragement of purely voluntary mediation (recommendation 138), rejecting mandatory mediation (recommendation 139).

The Civil Court Practice, our sister publication in the UK, says (at para CPR 1.4[7]) of the equivalent provision in England, CPR 1.4(2)(e):

> **Encouraging ADR: [rule 4(2)(e)]** Since the coming into effect of the CPR in April 1999 the courts have adopted a variety of stances towards ADR, ranging from more or less gentle persuasion, through the standard Admiralty and Commercial Court order [which does not appear to have a direct equivalent in Hong Kong], to the making of direct orders to the parties to submit to mediation.
>
> The encouragement to use alternative dispute resolution procedures is reinforced by procedures [practice direction, protocols and court guides, which have no direct equivalents in Hong Kong].
>
> In the CPR 'alternative dispute resolution' (ADR) means any 'method of resolving disputes otherwise than through the normal trial process' [definition in the glossary appended to the CPR. There is no such glossary in Hong Kong, nor is the term defined elsewhere in the rules, but it must have same meaning in the two jurisdictions]. In practice this is most likely to be mediation.
>
> Mediation is a flexible procedure. As stated by Colman J in *Cable & Wireless pic v IBM UK Ltd* [2003] EWHC 316 (Comm), [2003] All ER (D) 391 (Feb):
>
> > "[M]ediation as a tool for dispute resolution is not designed to achieve solutions which reflect the precise legal rights and obligations of the parties, but rather solutions which are mutually commercially acceptable at the time of the mediation"
>
> It is a procedure which is suitable not only for commercial disputes but for disputes between individuals and the government and between individuals and statutory authorities. In 2001 the Lord Chancellor directed that government departments have recourse to ADR whenever the other party agrees. . . In *Royal Bank of Canada v Secretary of State for Defence* [2003] EWHC 1841 (Ch) (Lewison J), the substantially successful defendant - a government department - was refused an order for costs in its favour where it had declined to accept the claimant's proposal for mediation. In *Halsey v Milton Keynes General NHS Trust* [2004] EWCA Civ 576, [2004] 4 All ER 920, [2004] 1 WLR 3002 (para 35) the Court of Appeal disagreeing with the approach taken by Lewison J in that case, commented that the [Lord Chancellor's] 'pledge'was no more than an undertaking, 'that ADR would be considered and used in all suitable cases' (court's emphasis). Halsey is addressed in some detail below.
>
> Subsequently, in *Cowl v Plymouth City Council* [2001] EWCA Civ 1935, [2002] 1 WLR 803 Lord Woolf CJ stressed the value of ADR, 'even in disputes between public authorities and the members of the public for whom they are responsible'.

The above passage from The Civil Court Practice continues by quoting from the decision of the English Court of Appeal in *Halsey v Milton Keynes General NHS Trust* [2004] EWCA Civ 576 (11.05.2004); [2004] 4 All ER 920 where it was said that the court should not seek to compel parties to participate in ADR, but encourage them to do so in appropriate cases, making clear the possible costs and other consequences of failure to do so. In Halsey Dyson LJ said:

> 9. We heard argument on the question whether the court has power to order parties to submit their disputes to mediation against their will. It is one thing to encourage the parties to agree to mediation, even to encourage them in the strongest terms. It is another to order them to do so. It seems to us that to oblige truly unwilling parties to refer their disputes to mediation would be to impose an unacceptable obstruction on their right of access to the court. The court in Strasbourg has said in relation to article 6 of the European Convention on Human Rights [in Hong Kong see art 35 of the Basic Law] that the right of access to a court may be waived, for example by means of an arbitration agreement, but such waiver should be subjected to 'particularly careful review'to ensure that the claimant is not subject to 'constraint': see *Deweer v Belgium* (1980) 2 EHRR 439 (para 49). If that is the approach of the EctHR to an agreement to arbitrate, it seems to us likely that *compulsion* of ADR would be regarded as an unacceptable constraint on the right of access to the court and, therefore, a violation of article 6. Even if (contrary to our view) the court does have jurisdiction to order unwilling parties to refer their disputes to mediation, we find it difficult to conceive of circumstances in which it would be appropriate to exercise it. We would adopt what the editors of Volume 1 of [the UK Civil Procedure 2003] say at para 1.4.11:
>
> > 'The hallmark of ADR procedures, and perhaps the key to their effectiveness in individual cases, is that they are processes voluntarily entered into by the parties in dispute with outcomes, if the parties so wish, which are non-binding. Consequently the court cannot direct that such methods be used but may merely encourage and facilitate.'
>
> 10. If the court were to compel parties to enter into a mediation to which they objected, that would achieve nothing except to add to the costs to be borne by the parties, possibly postpone the time when the court determines the dispute and damage the perceived effectiveness of the ADR process. If a judge takes the view that the case is suitable for ADR, then he or she is not, of course, obliged to take at face value the expressed opposi tion of the parties. In such a case, the judge should explore the reasons for any resistance to ADR. But if the parties (or at least one of them) remain intransigently opposed to ADR, then it would be wrong for the court to compel them to embrace it.
>
> 11. Parties sometimes need to be encouraged by the court to embark on an ADR. The need for such encouragement should diminish in time if the virtue of ADR in suitable cases is demonstrated even more convincingly than it has been thus far. The value and importance of ADR have been established within a remarkably short time. All members of the legal profession who conduct litigation should now routinely consider with their clients whether their disputes are suitable for ADR. But we reiterate that the court's role is to encourage, not to compel. The form of encouragement may be robust: see para 30 below . . .
>
> 29. So far we have been considering the question whether a successful party's refusal of ADR was unreasonable without regard to the impact of any encouragement that the court may have given in the particular case. Where a successful party refuses to agree to ADR despite the court's encouragement, that is a factor which the court will take into account when deciding whether his refusal was unreasonable. The court's encouragement may take different forms. The stronger the encouragement, the easier it will be for the unsuc cessful party to discharge the burden of showing that the successful party's refusal was unreasonable.
>
> 30. An ADR order made in the Admiralty and Commercial Court ['Draft ADR Order' in Appendix 7 to the 'Admiralty & Commercial Courts Guide', reproduced in our sister publication in the UK, The Civil Court Practice, following CPR Part 61] is the strongest

form of encouragement. It requires the parties to exchange lists of neutral individuals who are available to conduct 'ADR procedures', to endeavour in good faith to agree a neutral individual or panel and to take 'such serious steps as they may be advised to resolve their disputes by ADR procedures before the neutral individual or panel so chosen'. The order also provides that if the case is not settled, 'the parties shall inform the court what steps towards ADR have been taken and (without prejudice to matters of privilege) why such steps have failed'. It is to be noted, however, that this form of order stops short of actually compelling the parties to undertake an ADR. [There is no equivalent draft order in Hong Kong, but see the mediation practice direction.]

31. Nevertheless, a party who, despite such an order, simply refuses to embark on the ADR process at all would run the risk that *for that reason alone* his refusal to agree to ADR would be held to have been unreasonable, and that he should therefore be penalised in costs. It is to be assumed that the court would not make such an order unless it was of the opinion that the dispute was suitable for ADR.

32. A less strong form of encouragement is mentioned in the other court guides . . . A particularly valuable example is the standard form of order now widely used in clinical negligence cases, and which was devised by Master Ungley. The material parts of this order provide:

> 'The parties shall by ___ consider whether the case is capable of resolution by ADR. If any party considers that the case is unsuitable for resolution by ADR, that party shall be prepared to justify that decision at the conclusion of the trial, should the judge consider that such means of resolution were appropriate, when he is considering the appropriate costs order to make. The party considering the case unsuitable for ADR shall, not less than 28 days before the commencement of the trial, file with the court a witness statement without prejudice save as to costs, giving reasons upon which they rely for saying that the case was unsuitable.'

33. This form of order has the merit that (a) it recognises the importance of encouraging the parties to consider whether the case is suitable for ADR, and (b) it is calculated to bring home to them that, if they refuse even to consider that question, they may be at risk on costs even if they are ultimately held by the court to be the successful party. We can see no reason why such an order should not also routinely be made at least in general personal injury litigation, and perhaps in other litigation too. A pary who refuses even to *consider* whether a case is suitable for ADR is always at risk of an adverse finding at the costs stage of litigation, and particularly so where the court has made an order requiring the parties to consider ADR.

### [1A.4.8]    Costs penalty for refusal to mediate

Although the court can only encourage, not compel, the use of alternative dispute resolution procedures, it can take into account a refusal to undertake mediation or another ADR procedure in deciding on costs. In Hong Kong the court is required to take into account the conduct of the parties when exercising its discretion as to costs: Order 62 rule 5(1)(e) and (2). In this regard, The Civil Court Practice, continuing the above quoted passage, says:

> It was held in *Halsey* [above], that a party who refuses mediation and wins in court should not be deprived of costs unless the unsuccessful party shows that the winner acted unreasonably in refusing to take part in ADR. Relevant considerations include:
>
> • the nature of the dispute
>
> • the merits of the case

- the extent to which other settlement methods have been attempted
- whether the costs of ADR would have been disproportionately high
- whether any delay in setting up and attending ADR would have been prejudicial
- whether the ADR should result in a costs penalty.

The rule and the case law have been reinforced and supplemented by [English practice direction] CPR PD 29, para 4.10(9).

*Halsey* was cited with approval in this regard in *Supply Chain & Logistics Technology Ltd v NEC Hong Kong Ltd* HCA 1939/2006 (Lam J; 29.01.2009).

Even where a party agrees to mediate, but not until a late stage when the vast majority of costs have already been incurred, it may face an adverse costs order: see *Nigel Witham Ltd v Smith & Isaacs* [2008] EWHC 12 (TCC) and see the discussion of that case and other in Sorabji, 'Costs - Further Developments from Halsey' (2008) 27 CJQ 427.

See generally the commentary under Order 62 rule 5(1)(e) concerning conduct being taking into account in exercising the court's discretion as to costs.

With regard to cases in the construction and arbitration list, reference should also be made to practice direction 6.3 which established a pilot scheme for voluntary mediation for two years from 1 September 2006.

### [1A.4.9]    Mediation practice direction

A practice direction on mediation, PD 31, took effect on 01.01.2010. It applies to proceedings in the Court of First Instance commenced by writ, except those on the construction and arbitration list or the personal injuries list, which have their own practice directions containing provisions relating to mediation. It also applies to proceedings commenced by writ in the District Court, save personal injuries, equal opportunities and tax cases. See Appendix A to the practice direction, which sets out the exceptions. By its own terms, the practice direction also applies to proceedings commenced by originating summons which are subsequently ordered to be continued as if begun by writ (under O 28 r 8).

The mediation practice direction provides for a certificate to be filed by parties stating whether they are willing to participate in mediation. The certificate is required to be filed along with the timetabling questionnaire under Order 25 rule 1, in proceedings where all the parties are legally represented. It also provides for a mediation notice whereby a party who wishes to attempt mediation may propose terms such as scope of the mediation, governing rules, name of mediator and venue. The form of notice is set out in Appendix C to the practice direction. The other parties are required to respond to the notice in the form set out in Appendix D to the PD. The text of the practice direction can be downloaded from the judiciary website or that of HKLII, both of which are accessible free of charge.

### [1A.4.10]    Information available to the court to assist it in encouraging use  of ADR

The court's duty to encourage use of ADR procedures is facilitated by the provision of information by the parties pursuant to the mediation practice direction (PD 31) (in force from 01.01.2010). It is there provided that a mediation certificate, setting out information about the parties' attempts and attitude to mediation, must be filed together with the case management questionnaire filed under Order 25 rule 1. See the commentary under that rule. The practice direction also provides that a party which wishes to pursue mediation may serve notice setting out its proposals with regard to ADR, to which the opposing party must respond, usually within 14 days. The notice and response are filed in court and thus may be considered pursuant to the duty to encourage use of ADR. With regard to personal injury actions, see also part D of the personal injury list practice direction (PD 18. 1) which deals with mediation in such actions.

**[1A.4.11]   Solicitor's duty to encourage use of ADR at early stage**
The court's duty under Order 1A rule 4(2)(e) to encourage the use of ADR in any particular action can, obviously, only be exercised after proceedings have been com menced. This does not mean that parties should wait until costs have been incurred in getting an action underway before considering ADR such as mediation. As expressed in *Egan v Motor Services (Bath) Ltd* [2007] EWCA Civ 1002, in appropriate cases solicitors should encourage clients to consider mediation at the earliest possible stage. In that case Ward LJ said (at para 52):

> ... this is a paradigm case which, if it could not have been settled by the parties themselves, customer and dealer, then it behoved both solicitors to take the firmest grip on the case from the first moment of instruction. That, I appreciate, may not always be easy, but perhaps a copy of this judgment can, at the first meeting, be handed to the client, bristling with righteous indignation, in this case the customer who has paid a small fortune for a motor car which does not meet his satisfaction, and the dealer anxious to preserve the reputation of his prestige product. "This case cries out for mediation", should be the advice given to both the claimant and the defendant. Why? Because it is perfectly obvious what can happen. Feelings are running high, early positions are taken, positions become entrenched, the litigation bandwagon will roll on, experts are inevitably involved, and, before one knows it, there will be two/ three day trial and even, heaven help them, an appeal. It is on the cards a wholly dis-proportionate sum, £100,000, will be to fight over a tiny claim, £6,000. And what benefit can mediation bring? It brings an air of reality to negotiations . . . Mediation can do more for the parties than negotiation. In this case the sheer commercial folly could have been amply demonstrated to both parties sitting at the same table but hearing it come from somebody who is independent . . .The commercial possibilities are endless for finding an acceptable solution which would enable the parties to emerge, one with some satisfaction, perhaps a replacement vehicle and the other with its and Audi's good name intact and probably enhanced, but perhaps with each of them just a little less wealthy. The cost of such mediation would be paltry by compar ison with the costs that would mount from the moment of the issue of the claim. In so many cases, and this is just another example of one, the best time to mediate is before the litigation begins. It is not a sign of weakness to suggest it. It is the hallmark of commonsense. Mediation is a perfectly proper adjunct to litigation. The skills are now well developed. The results are astonishingly good. Try it more often.

In *iRiver HK Ltd v Thakral Corp (HK) Ltd* [2008] 6 HKC 391 (CA) (para 102) Yeung JA, giving the judgment of the Court of Appeal, referred to the above judgment as containing 'useful suggestions as regards how a solicitor could proffer advice on mediation to a client effectively'.

The solicitor's duty with regard to ADR is now a matter of professional conduct.

The Hong Kong Solicitors' Guide to Professional Conduct, vol 1, principle 10.17, commentary 3 provides that a solicitor should consider and if appropriate advise on ADR procedures. See also para 4 of the mediation practice direction (PD 31) where it is provided that legal representatives should advise clients of the possibility of an adverse costs order where a party unreasonably fails to engage in mediation, and see the commentary under Order 62 rule 5(1)(e) concerning such costs orders.

While the emphasis appears to be on encouraging mediation at an early stage, the fact that proceedings have reached an advanced stage should not be regarded as a barrier. In *Leung Catherine v Tary Ltd* HCPI 805/2007 (Fung J; 12. 10.2009) (para 22) the court said 'better late than never, especially when time, expenses and uncertainty of the trial can be avoided'.

### [1A.4.12]   Application to the court for directions on mediation
Where parties are unable to agree between themselves on the manner in which mediation is to proceed, they may apply to the court for directions. Such application is provided for by para 13 of PD 31. The court may give directions to resolve disagreements in the mediation notice and response. This may include choice of rules to govern the mediation, of mediator and venue. Guidance as to the approach the court will adopt in deciding the choice of mediator was set out in *Upplan Co Ltd v Li Ho Ming & Anor* [2010] 6 HKC 457. At paras 13-15 Registrar KW Lung said:

13. First the court will consider all the relevant objective data, in the following priority:

    (a)   the nature of the matter and the issues for mediation;

    (b)   the amount involved and the importance of the matter to the parties;

    (c)   the mediators' knowledge and experience in respect of the issues in order to determine whether the mediators are the appropriate persons to deal with the issues concerned;

    (d)   the experience of the mediators in mediation;

    (e)   the other relevant experiences such as that of legal practice, arbitration or social experience;

    (f)   the fees and expenses for the mediation;

    (g)   the availability of the mediators, bearing in mind that mediation will be taking place near the trial;

    (h)   other relevant factors.

14. Second the court will, on the materials and information before it, make an assessment of the nominated mediators to determine, on the balance of probabilities, who will most likely be able to conduct the mediation smoothly, successfully and economically.

15. Third the court will make its rational and dispassionate decision accordingly.

### [1A.4.13]   Stay of proceedings to facilitate mediation
Where the parties do not embark upon mediation until after proceedings have been commenced, the court is prepared to stay the proceedings for the time being. This is done pursuant to the court's duty under these rules to encourage the use of ADR and to help parties reach settlement. The power to grant a stay is found in Order 1B rule 1(2)(e). See also para 16 of the mediation practice direction (PD 31), where it is provided that such a stay may be granted on application of one or more of the

parties, or on the court's own motion. The power to make orders on the court's own motion is found in Order 1B rule 2. A stay pending mediation allows the parties to focus on the mediation and prevents costs which may prove to be unnecessary from being incurred.

The mediation practice direction provides that the stay may be for such period and on such terms as the court thinks fit, bearing in mind the importance of avoiding disruption to timetabled dates, especially milestone dates. Thus in *Hui Ling Ling v Sky Field Dev't Ltd* HCA 35/2007 (Registrar AuYeung; 22.07.2009) the court directed that a case management conference proceed despite an agreement to mediate having been reached, the CMC being a milestone date. It seems likely that the court will generally favour relatively short stays, perhaps requiring the parties to report back to the court at the end of the stay period.

**[1A.4.14]   Recovery of cost of mediation**
The cost of mediation, a private service, can be a disincentive. However, it has been held in Hong Kong that such costs may, in principle, be recoverable where they are incidental to legal proceedings. See the commentary under Order 62 rule 28 referring to *Chun Wo Construction & Eng'g Co Ltd v China Wing Eng'g Ltd* HCCT 37/2006 (Lam J; 12.06.2008).

**[1A.4.15]   Mediation in legally aided cases**
The Legal Aid Department has indicated a willingness to approve the appointment of a feecharging mediator in legally aided cases, though assigned solicitors are advised to consider the availability of pro bono mediation services. The cost of mediation is subject to the first charge provided for under the Legal Aid Ordinance. Solicitors were informed of the position in Law Society circulars 09378 and 09521, which can be viewed on the members' zone of the Law Society's website.

**[1A.4.16]   Confidentiality of mediation**
An agreement to mediate typically provides for confidentiality. This confidentiality will be respected by the court and evidence of what took place in a mediation will not be received in court proceedings. See *S v T* [2010] 4HKC 501 where it was said that otherwise, 'the whole system of mediation will come to naught and people will use mediation as a tactical advantage and then seek to introduce evidence which has come from an unsuccessful mediation and somehow bring that into court proceedings'. See also para 6 of the mediation practice direction (PD 31) which provides:

> What happens during the mediation process, being without prejudice communications, is protected by privilege. It must be emphasized that there is no question of the Court undermining the protection afforded by privilege.

And see Koo, 'Mediation Confidentiality', in Hong Kong Lawyer July 2010 (which can be viewed on www.hklawyer.com) for an interesting discussion of some possible exceptions which could lead to loss of confidentiality in mediation.

**[1A.4.17]   Order 1A rule 4(2)(f) - helping parties reach settlement**
Order 1A rule 4(2)(f) mandates the court, in exercise of its case management powers, to help the parties to settle all or part of their dispute. The Civil Court Practice, our sister publication in the UK, (at para CPR 1.4[8]) says of the equivalent provision in England,

CPR 1.4(2)(f), which is identical to the Hong Kong provision:

> **Encouraging settlement: [rule 4(2)(f)]** While the court should encourage parties to settle their differences, it should be careful of putting unfair pressure on a party. Further, when encouraging settlement, the court cannot look at privileged material unless all the parties who have the benefit of the privilege agree - cf *Al Fayed v Metropolitan Police Commr* [2002] EWCA Civ 780, [2002] All ER (D) 450 (May).

See also Order 1A rule 1(e) by which facilitating settlement of disputes is included in the underlying objectives of these rules.

Also relevant is Order 62 rule 5(1)(e) whereby the court may take into account a refusal to negotiate as conduct relevant to exercise of its discretion in ordering costs. See the commentary under that provision.

### [1A.4.18]   Order 1A rule 4(2)(g) - timetables and control of case

Order 1A rule 4(2)(g) mandates the court, in exercise of its case management powers, to control progress of a case by fixing timetables or otherwise. Its wording is identical to CPR1.4(2)(g). The fixing of timetables is dealt with in detail in Order 25.

As a result of this case management duty of the court, late interlocutory applications which may have significant impact on trial, are unlikely to be viewed sympathetically by the court. Late applications 'should be rare occurrences after the CJR': *Liu Chen v Chan Poon Wing & Anor* HCPI 779/2006 (Master Marlene Ng; 07.10.2009) (para 589). With regard to late interlocutory applications generally, see the commentary under Order 32 rule 11A.

### [1A.4.19]   Order 1A rule 4(2)(h) - cost/benefit considerations

Order 1A rule 4(2)(h) provides that the court's active case management duty includes considering whether a particular step in proceedings is justified by the cost. The provision is identical to CPR 1.4(2)(h), of which our sister publication in the UK, The Civil Court Practice says (at para CPR 1.4 [9]):

> Benefits of taking a particular step [rule 4(2)(h)] - The court can, where appropriate, dismiss summarily an application made before trial simply on the ground that it is likely to increase the costs without producing any real benefit to the conduct of the case: *Norwich Union Linked Life Assurance Ltd v Mercantile Credit Co Ltd* [2003] EWHC 3064 (Ch),[2003] All ER (D) 376 (Dec).

### [1A.4.20]   Order 1A rule 4(2)(i) - Court should deal with outstanding matters at one stage

Order 1A rule 4(2)(i) stipulates that the court should, as part of case management, deal with as many aspects of a case as it can on the same occasion. Its wording is identical to CPR 1.4(2)(i). See also Order 25 rule 7 by which all relevant matters are to be considered under the case management summons (formerly summons for directions).

### [1A.4.21]   Order 1A rule 4(2)(j) - Court may deal with cases in absence of parties

Order 1A rule 4(2)(j), like CPR 1.4(2)(j), which is worded identically, allows the court to deal with cases without requiring the parties to attend before it, as part of case management. This provision should be read together with Order 1B rule 2 (court's power to make an order of its own motion) and Order 1B rule 3 (court's power to give directions by way of order nisi). Together these provisions enable the court to take a proactive approach in managing cases by reviewing progress from what appears in the court file, without any input or application from the parties, and to give directions in their absence on a nisi basis, enabling them to seek to set aside or vary such directions if they are of the view they are inappropriate.

See also:

(a) Order 32 rule 11A which expressly empowers masters to deal with interlocutory applications without an oral hearing;

(b) Order 59 rule 2A(5) which provides for applications for leave to appeal interlocutory decisions to the Court of Appeal to be dealt with on paper; and

(c) Order 62 rule 21B(1)(a) by which the taxing master may tax a bill of costs without an oral hearing.

### [1A.4.22]   Order 1A rule 4(2)(k) - use of technology

Order 1A rule 4(2)(k) provides that making use of technology is part of the court's duty of active case management. It is in the same terms as CPR 1.4(2) (k), of which our sister publication in the UK, The Civil Court Practice says (at para CPR 1.4[10]):

> **The use of technology - [rule 4(2)(k)]** - . . . The use of IT systems in complex cases is to be encouraged - see the observations in *Morris v Bank of America National Trust & Savings Ass'n* [2000] 1 All ER 954 (CA) (paras 5460).

Court No 7 on the 5th Floor of the High Court building is equipped with technological equipment including a videoconferencing system and electronic documentation and exhibits handling system (DEHS) allowing documents to be retrieved and displayed electronically during a hearing. See practice direction 29 as to the facilities available and the use of this court. See also the commentary under Order 39 rule 1 as to when it is appropriate to direct that the technology court's videoconferencing facility be used in taking evidence.

### [1A.4.23]   Order 1A rule 4(2)(l) - directions for quick and efficient trial

Order 1A rule 4(2)(1) includes the giving of directions to ensure quick and efficient trials as part of case management. It is in the same terms as CPR 1.4(2) (1). In this regard, reference should also be made to Order 1B rule 1(2) (j) which gives the court an express power to exclude an issue from consideration, and Order 35 rule 3A which expressly empowers the court to impose time limits including restrictions on the time to be allowed for examination of witnesses and making submissions.

## ORDER 1B

### CASE MANAGEMENT POWERS

1. **Court's general powers of management** (O. 1B r. 1)

(1) The list of powers in this rule is in addition to and not in substitution for any powers given to the Court by any other rule or practice direction or by any other enactment or any powers it may otherwise have.

(2) Except where these rules provide otherwise, the Court may by order -

(a) extend or shorten the time for compliance with any rule, court order or practice direction (even if an application for extension is made after the time for compliance has expired);

(b) adjourn or bring forward a hearing;

(c) require a party or a party's legal representative to attend the Court;

(d) direct that part of any proceedings (such as a counterclaim) be dealt with as separate proceedings;

(e) stay the whole or part of any proceedings or judgment either generally or until a specified date or event;

(f) consolidate proceedings;

(g) try two or more claims on the same occasion;

(h) direct a separate trial of any issue;

(i) decide the order in which issues are to be tried;

(j) exclude an issue from consideration;

(k) dismiss or give judgment on a claim after a decision on a preliminary issue;

(l) take any other step or make any other order for the purpose of managing the case and furthering the underlying objectives set out in Order 1A.

(3) When the Court makes an order, it may —

(a) make it subject to conditions, including a condition to pay a sum of money into court; and

(b) specify the consequences of failure to comply with the order or a condition.

(4) Where a party pays money into court following an order under paragraph (3), the money is security for any sum payable by that party to any other party in the proceedings.

(L.N. 152 of 2008)

---

**NOTES**

**[1B.1.1] Order 1B rule 1(1) & (2) — Origin and scope of the express case management powers**

Order 1B rule 1(1) and (2) confer express case management powers on the court.

The sub-rules are taken from CPR 3.1(1) and (2), the language of which is virtually identical. However there are some differences:

(a) CPR 3.1 (2)(d), which expressly empowers the English court to 'hold a hearing and receive evidence by telephone or by using any other method of direct oral communication', is omitted in Hong Kong. The Chief Justice's working party concluded in its final report (at para 528) that in a geographically small jurisdiction like Hong Kong the savings which would be achieved by conducting hearings by telephone or video conference would be slight, if any. Nevertheless the Hong Kong court does have a video-conferencing facility: see the commentary under Order 39 rule 1.

(b) CPR 3.1(2)(II) (inserted by amendment to the CPR) which expressly empowers the English court to order any party to file and serve an estimate of costs, is not included in the list of express case management powers in Hong Kong's Order 1B. However such a power is given to masters in respect of interlocutory applications by Order 32 rule 11 A(3)(c). In addition, it is established practice in Hong Kong for estimates of costs to be placed before the court on applications for security for costs under Order 23, or on summary assessment of costs under Order 62 rules 9 and 9A (previously known as gross sum assessment).

(c) CPR 3.1(4), empowering the English court to take into account compliance with pre-action protocols, has not been included in Hong Kong. At the consultation stage such a power was included in the draft Order 2 rule 3(1), but it was omitted when the rules implementing the civil justice reforms were made by the rules committee.

(d) The power in CPR 3.1(7) to vary or revoke an order, rather than requiring the aggrieved party to appeal, has not been adopted in Hong Kong, but there is a new broad power given to the Hong Kong court by Order 1B rule 3 to make orders *nisi* which may be set aside on application of a party. See the commentary under that rule.

**[1B.1.2]  Express case management powers supplemental to pre-existing powers**
The case management powers listed in rule 1(2) are intended to be supplementary to the court's other powers from whatever source (whether elsewhere in the rules, practice direction or other legislation). This is a result of rule 1(1) which provides that the powers in the rule are 'in addition to *and not in substitution for*' other powers. The highlighted words, which do not appear in CPR 3.1(1), make this point expressly in Hong Kong.

The Chief Justice's working party on civil justice reform recognised that most of these powers already exist, 'scattered in various provisions of the RHC or to be found in the court's inherent jurisdiction' (final report, para 109). It said that the purpose of CPR 1.4 (Order 1A rule 4), 3.1 and 3.3 (Order 1B rules 1 and 2) is to 'draw these powers together and place them on a clear and transparent legal footing' (para 110).

**[1B.1.3]  Case management powers do not override provisions elsewhere in the rules**
Where a case management power in Order 1B rule 1 exists in another form elsewhere, the former does not override the latter. This follows from the opening words of rule 1(2) 'except where these rules provide otherwise'. Thus in England it has been held that the power in rule 1(2)(a) to 'extend or shorten time' does not apply to extension of time for service of a writ, since that is covered by specific provision elsewhere (Order 6 rule 8 in Hong Kong): see *Vinos v Marks & Spencer plc* [2001[3 All ER 784 (CA).

**[1B.1.4]   Order 1B rule 1(2)(a) — power to extend or shorten time**
Order 1B rule 1(2)(a) is an express power to extend or shorten the time for compliance with any rule, order or practice direction. In England the equivalent provision (CPR 3.1(2)(a)) is now the court's general power to extend or abridge time, replacing Order 3 rule 5 of the former RSC. In Hong Kong Order 3 rule 5 is retained along with this new power. Since the new power is expressly in addition to and not in substitution for other powers, its real significance lies in situations where Order 3 rule 5 may not apply.

Our sister publication in the UK, The Civil Court Practice, says (at para 3.1[1]) of the English equivalent:

> **Extend or shorten time for compliance** "**Extension of time for service of claim form [writ]** The court does not, under this rule, have the power to extend the time for the service of a claim form [writ or originating summons]; by [Order 1B rule 1(2)] the court's general powers of management under [rule 1] apply "Except where these rules provide otherwise…"; [Order 6 rule 8] does provide otherwise and such power is given by and regulated by that rule: *Vinos v Marks & Spencer plc* [2001] 3 All ER 784, May LJ and see also: *Kaur v CTP Coil Ltd* (2000) 10 July CA (where the court made a similar decision in relation to CPR 3.10 (general power of the court to rectify error of procedure) [in Hong Kong see Order 2 rule 1]). The court has a general discretion to extend time for serving the particulars of claim [statement of claim in Hong Kong] and the very narrow restrictions in relation to permitting extra time for service of the claim form [writ or originating summons] [Order 6 rule 8] do not apply: *Totty v Snowden* [2001] EWCA Civ 1415 [2001] 4 All ER 577…
>
> **Application for extension of time: regard to [Order 2 rule 5]** Where a court is considering an application for an extension of time to comply with any rule, it should have regard to the list of factors set out in [Order 2 rule 5] (relief from sanctions): *Sayers v Clarke Walker* [2002] EWCA Civ 645 [2002] 3 All ER 490 [2002] All ER (D) 189 (May) (a case concerning an extension of time to appeal [see the commentary under Order 59 rule 4]].
>
> Where, however, the application is in relation to an extension of time for service and the application is made before the time for service has expired there is no requirement to go through the [Order 2 rule 5] checklist; in such a case the focus of attention should be on the prejudice caused by the extension of time not pre-existing prejudice: *Robert v Momentum Services Ltd* [2003] EWCA Civ 299 [2003] 2 All ER 74.
>
> **Extension of time to comply with court order** Where a party applies for an extension of time within which to comply with a court order and makes it clear that he seeks relief from sanctions imposed for failure to comply with the order if the extension is refused, then the overriding objective to deal with the case justly [no direct equivalent in Hong Kong, but see Order 1A rule 2(2)] requires the court to consider [the factors listed in Order 2 rule 5] before deciding what order to make notwithstanding that the applicant has not specifically made an application under [Order 2 rule 5]: *Keith v CPM Field Marketing Ltd* [2000] Times 29 Aug, CA …

In Hong Kong the court has given guidance as to the exercise of the power under rule 1(2)(a) to extend time to comply with an order for filing evidence in opposition to an interlocutory application. See *Fortune Asset Dev't Ltd v De Monsa Investments Ltd* [2009] 2 HKC 420 where such an application was made in the context of an Order 14 summary judgment application after the time ordered by the court had expired. The court said (para 14) that on such an application all the circumstances would be taken into account including, but not limited to the following:

(i)   What was the original time allowed and when had it expired? The more   the original time allowed, the more difficult to justify an extension.

(ii)  Was the original time laid down by consent or at the suggestion of the  applicant? Under the civil justice reform a party is held more to his own  bargain.

(iii) Why was the original time not adhered to?

(iv)  When was the application for extension of time taken out? The greater  the delay, the more difficult it would be to obtain an extension.

(v)   Had the applicant used its best endeavours to secure the attendance of a  witness to take instructions and impressed upon that witness the  importance of attending on a certain date to affirm?

(vi)  Was a witness's availability within the 'control' of the applicant? For  example, if a witness is an unwilling ex-employee, the court may have  more sympathy with the applicant.

(vii) That a client or witness had to travel frequently out of the jurisdiction  was not a good reason in itself given the advanced means of   communication. It was incumbent upon the applicant to obtain  instructions for drafting the affirmation in good time and to impress upon  the witness the need to turn up on a designated date to affirm.

(viii) If the witness was an expert, had the expert been informed of the time  laid down by legislation, PD or the court, and committed himself to  provide a report by that time? If he had not so committed himself, why  was that particular expert still engaged?

(ix)  What realistically was the further time needed to complete and file the  affirmation? An applicant should not just casually pick a multiple of 7  days without regard to its adequacy for completing the affirmation.

(x)   Was there any de facto extension of time already enjoyed by the applicant,  whether by way of consent, or in waiting for his time summons  to be heard?

(xi)  Would the extension of time sought have impact on any hearing date or  milestone date?

The court added that a last minute change of legal team was not in itself a good reason for an extension.

The Civil Court Practice continues:

> **Extension of time in an "unless" order where timetable agreed by the parties** The court has power under [Order 1B rule 1(2)(a) and Order 3 rule 5] to allow extra time beyond that agreed by the parties as the basis of an "unless" order but the court should place very great weight on what the parties had agreed and be slow to intervene: *Repac Ltd v Inntrepreneur Pub Co* [2000] 26 LS Gaz R 38, Neuberger J.
>
> The making and entering of an "unless" order does not preclude the exercise of the power conferred by [Order 1B rule 1(2)(a)] to extend the time for compliance (eg to allow time for an application for permission [leave] to appeal): *Omega Engineering Inc v Omega SA* [2003] EWHC 1482 [2003] All ER (D) 267 (May), Pumfrey J.

With regard to extension of time for compliance with peremptory or 'unless' orders in Hong Kong, see also the commentary under Order 42 rule 2.

The Civil Court Practice continues:

> **Extension of time for service of witness statements** Where a party fails to serve witness statements on time, the court will usually extend time for service and will only in very extreme circumstances use its power to exclude that party from adducing evidence at trial; such circumstances may include the deliberate flouting of court orders or inexcusable delay such that the only way that the court could fairly entertain the evidence would be by

adjourning the trial: see *Mealey Horgan plc v Horgan* [1999] Times, 6 July, Buckley J. In *Cowland & Kendrick v District Judges of the West London County Court* (20 July 1999, unreported), CA [available on the BAILII website as [1999] EWCA Civ 1894] (a case involving an issue of whether the court had been notified of a dispute as to ownership in respect of goods to be taken in execution), the Court of Appeal overturned the decision of the trial judge to refuse permission [leave] for a witness to give evidence at the hearing concerning the sending of the relevant fax; neither party had had the foresight to obtain a witness statement from him and ought to have done so; the witness was "not the claimant's witness"; the defendants could not protest at the calling of a witness whom they could have "proofed" and called themselves. On the other hand, in *Rose Stroh v London Borough of Haringey* (13 July 1999, unreported), CA, [available on the BAILII website as [1999] EWCA Civ 1825]the Court of Appeal decided that the judge was correct to refuse the defendant's application to adduce the evidence of four witnesses; the reason for the delay had been the defendants' failure to investigate the matter with diligence; the court concluded that the prejudice to the claimant of being faced with the evidence outweighed the prejudice to the defendant of being unable to adduce the evidence, even though the effect of refusing the application was that the judge went on to order that judgment be entered for the claimant.

On the topic of extension of time for exchange of witness statements in Hong Kong, see also the commentary under Order 38 rule 2A.

### [1B.1.5]   Order IB rule1(2)(b) - power to adjourn or bring forward

Order IB rule 1(2)(b) gives the court an express power to adjourn or bring forward a hearing. So far as adjournments are concerned, this power is not new, already being found in Order 32 rule 4(1) (for summonses), Order 35 rule 3 (adjournment of trial), and inherent jurisdiction (*St Edmundsbury & Ipswich Diocesan Board of Finance v Clark* [1973] Ch 323, 327D). This may be the first time the court has been given an express power to bring forward a hearing, but that too has probably existed in inherent jurisdiction all along. The court has long had power under Order 3 rule 5 to abridge time - see the commentary under that rule.

Rule 1(2)(b) is in the same terms as CPR 3.1(2)(b). Our sister publication in the UK, The Civil Court Practice, says (at CPR 3.1[1A]) of that provision:

> **Application for an adjournment by a litigant in person who does not attend** Where a litigant in person was seeking an adjournment for the first time the court should be very careful indeed before concluding that it would be appropriate to proceed with the application or appeal in his absence; the court should only take such a course where it was satisfied either that it was right to grant the litigant the relief he sought or it was satisfied that the application or appeal brought by the litigant in person was plainly hopeless: *Fox v Graham Group Ltd* [2001] The Times, Aug, Neuberger J.

The court should not bring forward a hearing without the consent of the parties or other compelling reasons. See *Lu Quo Xiang v Hong Kong Ming Wall Shipping Co Ltd* HCMP 52/2010 (Tang VP & Cheung JA; 22.01.2010) where the Court of Appeal set aside a bringing forward order. Tang VP said (para 23):

> just as litigants are expected to obey the orders of the Court, I believe it is important for the Court not to take litigants by surprise. Certainty and predictability are important for the fair administration of justice.

In that case the court, of its own motion (see Order 1B rule 2), brought forward an assessment of damages by 10 months, leaving the parties with only 6 more days to prepare. The defendant opposed bringing forward because of unavailability of its principal witness.

**[1B.1.6]   Order IB rule 1(2)(c) - power to require attendance at court**
Order 1B rule 1(2)(c), which is in the same terms as CPR 3.1(2)(c), gives the court a new power to require a party, or legal representative, to attend before the court. Our sister publication in the UK, The Civil Court Practice, says (at para CPR 3.1 [1B]) of the English equivalent:

> **3.1(2) (c) require a party or a party's legal representative to attend the court** It may well be appropriate to require a party's attendance in order to facilitate a settlement or to encourage alternative dispute resolution, but it is inappropriate to order the attendance of a board of directors of an overseas company in order to put pressure on the company to discontinue the company's claim: *Tarajan Overseas Ltd v Kaye* [2001] EWCA Civ 1859, [2001] All ER (D) 385 (Nov), [2002] The Times 22 January.

**[1B.1.7]   Order IB rule 1(2)(d) - severance of proceedings**
Order 1B rule 1(2)(d) empowers the court to direct that part of any proceedings be dealt with separately. Counterclaims are given as an example. The provision is the same terms as CPR 3.1(2)(e) in England. This provision on its face is broader than the similar (and pre-existing) Order 15 rule 5 which is expressly subject to certain criteria which must be met before it may be exercised. See the opening commentary under Order 1B rule 1 as to which should take precedence.

**[1B.1.8]   Order 1B rule 1(2)(e) - stay of proceedings or judgment**
Order 1B rule 1(2)(e), which is in the same terms as CPR 3.1(2)(f), expressly empowers the court to stay any proceedings or judgment generally or until a future event. It supplements pre-existing powers which continue to exist. The express power to stay proceedings such as where there is a jurisdictional dispute is an example (see Order 12 rule 8 and the commentary thereunder). Likewise the power to stay execution of a judgment (under Order 14 rule 3 where summary judgment is granted but a counterclaim will go to trial, under Order 59 rule 13 where an appeal is pending and under Order 45 rule 11 and Order 47 rule 1 as well as inherent jurisdiction: *Credit Lyonnais v SK Global HK Ltd* [2003] 4 HKC 104).

Our sister publication in the UK, The Civil Court Practice, says (at para CPR 3.1[2]) of the equivalent provision in the CPR:

> **CPR 3.1(2)(f): stay of proceedings** - It is not appropriate to stay a second claim pending the payment of costs for the unsuccessful first claim unless the bringing of a second claim involved an element of needless procedural duplication: *Society of Lloyd's v Jaffray* [1999] 1 All ER (Comm) 354. In a case where a firm of solicitors acting for the claimant has previously acted for the defendant it may be appropriate to direct a stay of the proceedings until a different firm has been appointed but the court has no power to order a party to appoint different solicitors: *SMC Eng'g (Bristol) Ltd v Fraser* [2001] The Times 26 Jan (CA).

With regard to the final sentence of the above passage, concerning the situation of solicitors acting against their own previous client, see also *Time Success Profits Ltd v Andrew Lam & Co* [2004] 1 HKC 214 where the court granted an injunction to restrain solicitors from accepting instructions, discussed in the commentary under Order 29 rule 1.

**[1B.1.9]    Order 1B rule 1(2)(f) - power to consolidate proceedings**
Order 1B rule 1(2) (f) gives the court an express power to consolidate proceedings, in the same terms as CPR 3.1(2)(g). In Hong Kong this power does not seem to add anything to the pre-existing consolidation power under Order 4 rule 9, which is subject to specific criteria as to when a consolidation order may be made. See the commentary under that rule. And see the opening commentary under Order 1B rule 1 as to which power should take precedence.

**[1B.1.10]    Order 1B rule 1(2)(g) - trial of claims together**
Rule 1(2)(g) gives the court an express power to order that two or more claims be tried on the same occasion, in the same terms as CPR 3.1(2)(h). In Hong Kong this power does not seem to add anything to the pre-existing power under Order 4 rule 9 to order that claims be tried together, which is subject to specific criteria. See the commentary under that rule. And see the opening commentary under Order 1B rule 1 as to which should take precedence.

**[1B.1.11]    Order 1B rule 1(2)(h) - separate trial of issue**
Order 1B rule 1(2)(h) gives the court power to direct the separate trial of any issue. It is in the same terms as CPR 3.1(2)(i). In Hong Kong this provision does not appear to add anything to the pre-existing powers under Order 33 rules 3 and 4. See the commentary under those rules. And see the opening commentary under Order 1B rule 1 as to which should take precedence.

**[1B.1.12]    Order 1B rule 1(2)(i) - power to decide order of trial of issues**
With the regard to the power under rule 1(2)(i) to decide the order in which issues are to be tried, it has been held in England that the saving of time and expense are relevant criteria to exercise of the equivalent power under CPR 3.1(2) (j). See *GKR Karate (UK) Ltd v Yorkshire Post Newspapers Ltd* [2000] 2 All ER 931 (CA) where the defence of qualified privilege in a defamation action was ordered to be tried prior to the other issues. In *Steele v Steele* [2001] The Times 5 June the English court, considering this power, noted the pre-CPR observation of *Lord Scarman in Tilling v Whiteman* [1980] 1 AC 1, 25, that separate trials of preliminary issues can be 'treacherous shortcuts which could lead to delay, anxiety and expense'.

In Hong Kong reference should also be made to Order 33 rules 3 and 4, which continue to provide for separate trials of distinct issues, and split trials of liability and quantum particularly in personal injury cases. See the commentary under those rules. And see the opening commentary under Order 1B rule 1 as to whether those rules should take precedence over the provision being commented on here.

**[1B.1.13]    Order 1B rule 1(2)(j) - exclusion of issue from consideration**
Order 1B rule 1(2)(j), which is in the same terms as CPR 3.1(2)(k), gives the court an express power to exclude an issue from consideration. The commentary in our sister publication in the UK, The Civil Court Practice, suggests that this power is not much different from the pre-existing powers to enter summary judgment and to strike out. However, unlike the pre-existing powers it is not restricted to application by interlocutory summons. Hence it should be exercisable by the court of its own motion under Order 1B rule 2, and at any stage including trial. The Civil Court Practice says of the English provision:

> **CPR 3.1(2)04) [Order 1B rule 1(2)(j)]: excluding issues at the trial** - At the trial it is open to the court to strike out a claim or for the court to give summary judgment on the claim or part of the claim ...

The commentary goes on to discuss the criteria laid down in CPR 24 (dealing, inter alia, with summary judgment). To that extent it is not relevant in Hong Kong, which retains Order 14 summary judgment.

### [1B.1.14]  Order 1B rule 1(2)(k) — disposition of claim after trial of preliminary issue

Order 1B rule 1(2)(k), which is in the same terms as CPR 3.1(2)(1), gives the court an express power to dismiss a claim, or give judgment, after decision on a preliminary issue. In Hong Kong this provision does not appear to add much, if anything, to the pre-existing Order 33 rule 7.

### [1B.1.15]  Order 1B rule 1(2)(l) — power to make other order for case management

Order 1B rule 1(2)(1) empowers the court to take any other step or make any other order for the purpose of managing a case and furthering the underlying objectives. It is in the same terms as CPR 3.1(2)(m), save that Hong Kong's objectives are 'underlying' rather than 'overriding'. The English equivalent was described as a 'sweeping-up' provision in *Forcelux Ltd v Binnie* [2009] EWCA Civ 854 (para 41).

In *Asia-Pac Infrastructure Dev't Ltd v Ing & Ors* HCA 16778/1999(Stone J; 03.12.2010) (para 33-5) it was held that rule 1(2)(l) permits the court to reconsider and vary case management decisions without an appeal. The rule was relied upon by the trial judge at a pre-trial case management conference to set aside another judge's earlier case management order permitting a witness's evidence to be taken by video conference. The court was of the view that it is in principle always open to a trial-designated judge to consider afresh signally important case management directions.

Commentary in The Civil Court Practice 2008, our sister publication in the UK (at para CPR 3.1[4]), referring to *Sleeman v Highway Care Ltd* [1999] The Times 3 Nov (CA), suggests that this provision empowers the court to direct that final submissions be put in writing without each side necessarily having the opportunity to see or comment on the other's. In this regard see also Order 35 rule 3A, which empowers the court to impose time limits for various stages of a trial, which can easily be facilitated by directing that submissions be reduced to writing.

### [1B.1.16]  'Cost Capping' orders

The Civil Court Practice 2008 goes on to discuss cases in which the English equivalent of this rule has been referred to as empowering the court to make 'cost-capping' orders, that is orders which fix in advance an upward limit on the amount of costs that a party may recover from the opposing party, or be liable to pay, or even the amount of money that a party may spend on the litigation. It says (at para CPR3.1[4A]):

> **Capping the claimant's costs under [rule 1(2)(1)]** The court has power under s 51 of the Supreme Court Act 1981 and this rule to cap the claimant's [plaintiffs] costs on the application of the defendant and did so in *AB v Leeds Teaching Hospitals NHS Trust* [2003] EWHC 1034 [QB (09.05.2003)], and *King v Telegraph Group Ltd* [2004] EWCA Civ 613, [at para 78 et seq], [2004] The Times 21 May. . .

The costs-capping order was endorsed by the House of Lords in *Campbell v MGN Ltd* [2005] UKHL 61 (20.10.2005). However that case, and the cases cited in the above passage, concerned costs arising in legal proceedings of types which do not exist in Hong Kong, and therefore must be examined carefully before being applied in this jurisdiction. *AB v Leeds* concerned 'group litigation', the English equivalent of the class action, for which there is no provision in Hong Kong. Both *King* and *Campbell* concerned recovery of success or up-lift fees under conditional fee arrangements, which do not exist in Hong Kong. That said, insofar as the rule gives a legislative basis to the court's power to make protective costs orders in public interest cases, the English authorities are likely to be relevant in Hong Kong. In relation to such orders, see the commentary under Order 62 rule 3.

**[1B.1.17]   Order 1B rule 1(3)(a)&(4) — conditions such as payment of money as security**

Order 1B rules 1(3)(a) and (4) are a simplified version of CPR 3.1(3)-(6A). In both, provision is made for the court to impose conditions when making an order, including payment of money into court as security for any sum which might be payable to another party. The following points are taken from the commentary on the CPR provisions set out in our sister publication in the UK, The Civil Court Practice (paras CPR 3.1[5A]-[7]):

> **Conditions** Conditions should not be imposed unless the party concerned has some prospect of compliance: *Chappie v Williams* [1999] CPLR 731 (CA). On the other hand, the fact that a defendant company has ceased trading does not necessarily preclude the court from making a conditional order for money to be paid into court: *Foot & Bowden v AngloEuropeCorp Ltd The Times* 17.02.2000 (CA).
>
> **Order that party pay money into court: evidence of means** A court should not impose a condition requiring a party to make a payment into court under [this rule] in the absence of evidence about the defendant's means, unless the defendant had been given prior warning that such an order would be sought: *Anglo-Eastern Trust Ltd v Kermanshahchi* [2002] EWCA Civ 198 [2002] All ER (D) 321 (Feb) …
>
> **The court 'may' order a party to pay a sum of money into court** As a sanction, the court will only make such an order where that party had repeatedly breached the rules and/or was not acting in good faith and the other party needed to be protected; where both sides had failed to comply with the procedural timetable such an order was not likely to be appropriate: see *Mealey Horgan plc v Horgan The Times* 06.07.1999, a case concerning the late service of witness statements.

The above commentary continues with reference to *Olatawura v Abiloye* [2002] EWCA Civ 998; [2002] 4 All ER 903; [2002] The Times, 24 July, in which the equivalent English provisions (which are more detailed than the Hong Kong rules) were interpreted as empowering the court to order security for costs in circumstances outside the main provision in that regard (Order 23 in Hong Kong).

In Hong Kong reference should also be made to Order 2 rule 3, dealing with orders for payment into court for failure to comply with a procedural requirement.

**[1B.1.18]   Order 1B rule 1(3)(b) — power to specify consequences of failure to comply**

Order 1B rule 1(3)(b) provides that as part of the court's case management powers it may, when making an order, specify the consequences of failure to comply with the order or any condition imposed in it. This provision is in the same terms as CPR 3.1(3)(b).

In its final report, the Chief Justice's working party on civil justice reform referred to such orders as 'self-executing'. The purpose of such orders is to implement 'a shift from requiring the innocent party to enforce compliance to placing the burden on the errant party to seek relief' (final report, para 509). Thus under Order 2 rule 4 the sanction specified in such an order takes effect unless the party in default applies under Order 2 rule 5 and is granted relief from the sanction. See the commentary under those rules.

Insofar as orders made on interlocutory applications are concerned, this provision should be read together with Order 32 rule 1 IB which sets out detailed provisions in relation to self-executing interlocutory orders. See the commentary under that rule.

**2. Court's power to make order of its own motion** (O.1B r. 2)

    **(1)** Except where a rule or some other enactment provides otherwise, the Court may exercise its powers on an application or of its own motion.

    **(2)** Where the Court proposes to make an order of its own motion—

        **(a)** it may give any person likely to be affected by the order an opportunity to make representations; and

        **(b)** where it does so, it shall specify the time by and the manner in which the representations must be made.

    **(3)** Where the Court proposes —

        **(a)** to make an order of its own motion; and

        **(b)** to hold a hearing to decide whether to make the order, it shall give each party likely to be affected by the order at least 3 days' notice of the hearing.

    **(4)** The Court may make an order of its own motion, without hearing the parties or giving them an opportunity to make representations.

    **(5)** Where the Court has made an order under paragraph (4) —

        **(a)** a party affected by the order may apply to have it set aside, varied or stayed; and

        **(b)** the order must contain a statement of the right to make such an application.

    **(6)** An application under paragraph (5)(a) must be made —

        **(a)** within such period as may be specified by the Court; or

        **(b)** if the Court does not specify a period, not more than 14 days after the date on which notice of the order was sent to the party making the application.

                          **(L.N. 152 of 2008)**

---

**NOTES**

**[1B.2.1]**      **Origin and scope of Order 1B rule 2**

Order 1B rule 2 derives from CPR 3.3. The wording is not identical, but to the same effect. The English rule refers to the court making orders 'of its own initiative', where as the Hong Kong rule says 'of its own motion'. CPR 3.3(7), concerning the

English court's power to strike out of its own motion, is omitted in Hong Kong, but Hong Kong's Order 1B rule 1(2)(j) probably fills the gap.

Rule 2(4) allows the court to make an order of its own motion without hearing the parties or giving them an opportunity to be heard. However, any such order may be set aside, varied or stayed by application under rule 2(5), and the order must contain a statement of the right to make an application for such relief.

The rule should be read together with Order 1A rule 4(2)(j) which includes dealing with a case without the parties' presence as part of the court's duty of case management.

The following extract from our sister publication in the UK, The Civil Court Practice (para CPR 3.3[2]) is relevant in Hong Kong:

> **Application to vary or set aside order made of court's own initiative** When an application is made under [Order 1B rule 2(5)] to set aside or vary an order made of the court's own initiative, it is good practice to require the application to be made at a hearing rather than on paper: *Leeson v Marsden, Glass v Surrendran* [2006] EWCA Civ 20 (paras 20-40) [2006] The Times 3 Feb.

**3.    Court's power to give procedural directions by way of order nisi** (O. 1B r. 3)

**(1)    Where the Court considers that it is necessary or desirable to give a direction on the procedure of the Court and that the direction is unlikely to be objected to by the parties, it may of its own motion and without hearing the parties, give the direction by way of an order nisi.**

**(2)    The order nisi becomes absolute 14 days after the order is made unless a party has applied to the Court for varying the order.**

**(L.N. 152 2008)**

---

**NOTES**

**[1B.3.1]    Procedural directions by order nisi**

Order 1B rule 3 makes it clear that the court may, of its own motion and without hearing the parties, give directions on matters of procedure. The power may be exercised when the court considers that the direction is necessary or desirable, and that the parties are unlikely to object. Such a direction is given by way of order nisi, meaning that the order is provisional and may be varied or set aside on application within 14 days (rule 3(2)).

The rule largely overlaps with rule 2(5) which also provides for setting aside, variation or stay of an order made by the court without a hearing, whether or not the order is expressed to be made 'nisi'. Both rules operate as a salutary adjunct to the express duty of the court under Order 1A rule 4(2)(j) to deal with cases without the parties needing to attend court where appropriate as a matter of case management, and Order 32 rule 11A which empowers a master to determine an interlocutory application without an oral hearing.

## ORDER 2

### EFFECT OF NON-COMPLIANCE

1. **Non-compliance with Rules** (O. 2 r. 1)

    **(1)   Where, in beginning or purporting to begin any proceedings or at any stage in the course of or in connection with any proceedings, there has, by reason of any thing done or left undone, been a failure to comply with the requirements of these rules, whether in respect of time, place, manner, form or content or in any other respect, the failure shall be treated as an irregularity and shall not nullify the proceedings, any step taken in the proceedings, or any document, judgment or order therein.**

    **(2)   Subject to paragraph (3), the Court may, on the ground that there has been such failure as is mentioned in paragraph (1), and on such terms as to costs or otherwise as it thinks just, set aside either wholly or in part the proceedings in which the failure occurred, any step taken in those proceedings or any document, judgment or order therein or exercise its powers under these rules to allow such amendments (if any) to be made and to make such order (if any) dealing with the proceedings generally as it thinks fit.**

    **(3)   The Court shall not wholly set aside any proceedings or the writ or other originating process by which they were begun on the ground that the proceedings ought to have begun by an originating process other than the one employed, but shall instead give directions for the continuation of the proceedings in an appropriate manner. (L.N. 152 of 2008)**

---

## NOTES

### [2.1.1]   Court's power to overlook procedural irregularity

Order 2 rule 1 gives effect to the modern approach that the court should avoid treating procedural errors as fatal, and should, so far as possible without injustice to the other parties, allow them to be remedied by amendment (under Order 20), or otherwise. As Litton PJ concisely observed in *Roe Investment Ltd v Prince Good Ltd* [2000] 1 HKC 548, (CFA) 560A, referring to this rule, 'Long gone are the days when justice can be denied because of some procedural irregularity'.

    The rule was introduced in England in 1964. In *Harkness v Bell's Asbestos & Eng'g Ltd* [1967] 2 QB 729, 735-6 Lord Denning MR said of its purpose:

> The new rule does away with the old distinction between nullities and irregularities. Every omission or mistake in practice or procedure is henceforward to be regarded as an irregularity which the court can and should rectify so long as it can do so without injustice.

Those words were quoted with approval in the Hong Kong case of *Fabrique Ebel Société Anonyme v MBO Far East (UK) Ltd* [1985] 1 HKC 166, where the court retrospectively rectified a failure to obtain leave to apply for committal for contempt.

    In England, the equivalent of Order 2 rule 1 is now CPR 3.10.

    Another example of a case where the rule has been used in Hong Kong is *Hong-Kong and Shanghai Banking Corp Ltd v Ong Tong Sing Lawrence & Ors* [2008] 3

HKC 421. There the court relied on the rule to overlook irregular service of a writ on the partners of a firm where the writ had actually been received and no prejudice was caused.

Despite the statements of eminent judges, the courts are not prepared to use this rule to cure every kind of procedural error. The court retains power under Order 2 rule 2 to set aside on grounds of procedural irregularity. Fundamental errors may be regarded as being beyond the court's curative powers, or at least not appropriate for the exercise of those powers. In *Lee Tain Tshung v Hong Leong Finance Bhd* [2000] 3 MLJ 364 the Malaysian Court of Appeal said:

> The power given to the court by O 2 r 1 is a power to cure irregularities consisting of failure to comply with the rules. There is no power to remedy failures of a more fundamental kind.

Thus in *C v C & A* [2003] 4 HKC 141, 152D-G (CA) the Hong Kong court was not prepared to use this rule to overlook the fact that proceedings below had taken place in chambers rather than in open court, which was an irregularity 'of a fundamental nature' (at the time all chambers hearings were closed to the public). Ma JA (as he then was) made this point in terms of the court being slow to exercise its discretion in such cases, rather than the court lacking power.

See also *Leal v Dunlop Bio-processes Int'l Ltd* [1984] 1 WLR 874.

### [2.1.2]   Defects of form
See the commentary under Order 1 rule 9.

### [2.1.3]   Incorrect originating process not fatal
Order 2 rule 1(3) provides that the court shall not set aside proceedings on the ground the wrong originating process has been used, requiring the court instead to give directions for continuation of the proceedings in an appropriate manner. See also Order 28 rule 8 which specifically empowers the court to order proceedings inappropriately commenced by originating summons to be continued as if they had been begun by writ. And see Order 18 rule 21 by which an action commenced by writ can proceed to trial without pleadings, rather as if it had been commenced by originating summons. The provisions of Order 5 as to choice of originating process should be read in light of these powers.

In *Ye Hong Ying v Chan Lup Ying* [1996] 3 HKC 426, 431F-G it was said that as a result of this rule it is not appropriate for proceedings to be 'struck out' on the ground the wrong originating process has been used.

Rule 1(3) was previously limited to failure to comply with the requirements of these rules as to originating process. Thus it might not have been applicable where the correct originating process was stipulated in other rules or legislation. That should no longer be the case as a result of the amendment of the wording of the rule with effect from 2009.

### [2.1.4]   Failure to give notice of intention to proceed
In *Kung Wong Sau Hin v Sze To Chun Keung* [1996] 2 HKC 616, LePichon J expressed the view (obiter) that she could invoke this rule to 'waive' the irregularity caused by failure to give notice of intention to proceed under Order 3 rule 6. On appeal to the Court of Appeal, it was held (again, obiter) that the learned judge had

discretion to do so ([1996] 3 HKC 292, 297E).

### [2.1.5]  Practice directions

Practice directions are issued under the inherent power of the court to regulate its own process and not under these rules or other statutory power: see *Re Boon Voon King & Ors* [1998] 3 HKC 537 (CA), and see the definition of 'practice direction' in Order 1 rule 4. The situation is different in England, where the power to make practice directions is now regulated by statute: see the historical discussion in *Secretary of State v Bovale Ltd & Anor* [2009] EWCA Civ 171. It was there held (at para 69) that a practice direction cannot disapply or vary the rules of court, because the rules have the force of subsidiary legislation. This is also the case in Hong Kong: *I v L* [2005] 4 HKLRD 301. The purpose of practice directions was described by Kaplan J in *Tong Yi Sang & Anor v Fung Law & Ng & Ors* [1993] 2 HKC 665 (at 669E-F) in the following terms:

> Practice directions are intended to be complied with. They are designed, in consultation with the profession, to ensure the efficient, expeditious and economical dispatch of the court's business.

The above passage was quoted with approval in *Re Boon Voon King & Ors* (above) at 540B, per LePichon J.

Failure to comply with practice directions has been the subject of adverse comment by members of the judiciary. See for example *Sanyo Electric Trading Co Ltd v Leung Kwok Hing* [1992] 2 HKC 509; [1993] 1 HKLR 253, 261 cited with approval in *Tong Yi Sang & Anor v Fung Law & Ng & Ors* [1993] 2 HKC 665. In the latter case Kaplan J warned of the costs consequences of failure to comply with practice directions in the following terms (at 670B-E):

> If in future, these Practice Directions are ignored, save in the most exceptional circumstances, I propose to refuse to hear the case and adjourn it to a date to be fixed by which time I will expect the Practice Directions to be fully complied with. I will expect an undertaking from solicitors who have ignored the Practice Directions to the effect that they will not seek to charge their clients for the costs thrown away. If not given, then I will consider inviting the solicitors to show cause why they should not pay the costs personally.

**2.  Application to set aside for irregularity** (O. 2 r. 2)

**(1) An application to set aside for irregularity any proceedings, any step taken in any proceedings or any document, judgment or order therein shall not be allowed unless it is made within a reasonable time and before the party applying has taken any fresh step after becoming aware of the irregularity.**

**(2) An application under this rule may be made by summons and the grounds of objection must be stated in the summons. (Enacted 1988) (LN 152 of 2008)**

---

### NOTES

### [2.2.1]  Fresh step a bar to setting aside irregularity

Under Order 2 rule 2(1) a party who wishes to rely upon a procedural irregularity as a ground to avoid proceedings against it must apply to set aside the proceedings before taking any fresh step. For example, if a party wishes to contend that a writ has not properly been served, this point must be raised before serving a defence. In *Morigood Development Ltd v Sunny Trading Co (a firm)* [1999] 2 HKC 710 at 716G-I a defendant sought to set aside judgment on the ground of improper service. The plaintiff objected that the application was barred under this rule by virtue of the defendant having previously resisted execution of the judgment. It was not necessary for the court to decide the point as the judgment was found to be regular, hence this rule did not apply. Nevertheless the court set aside the judgment on other grounds.

**3.     Non-compliance with rules and court orders** (O. 2 r. 3)
        **(1) The Court may order a party to pay a sum of money into court if that party has, without good reason, failed to comply with a rule or court order.**
        **(2) When exercising its power under paragraph (1), the Court shall have regard to -**
                **(a)the amount in dispute; and**
                **(b)the costs which the parties have incurred or which they may incur.**
        **(3) Where a party pays money into court following an order under paragraph (1), the money is security for any sum payable by that party to any other party in the proceedings.**

**(LN 152 of 2008)**

---

**NOTES**

**[2.3.1]     Origin and scope of Order 2 rule 3**
Order 2 rule 3 derives from CPR 3.1(4)-(6A). Both provide that the court may order a party who is in procedural default to pay money into court as security for any sum payable to another party. The rule is a sanction against parties who fail, without good reason, to comply with the rules or a court order. An order would be appropriate under this rule against a party who deliberately tries to delay an action. In *Leung Wai Kee v Tan Yuet Sheung* DCCJ 5716/2007 (Judge Mimmie Chan; 11.05.2009) the court warned that such an order would be made in the event of further failure to comply with court directions. The court said (para 22) that it was doing so 'to make sure that no one is using this as an attempt to delay the trial'.

An order may be made under this rule to secure payment of past costs. Such an order should only be made if it is just to do so: *CIBC Mellon Trust Co v Mora Hotel Corp NV* [2002] EWCA Civ 1688, [2003] 1 All ER 564, [2002] The Times, 28 Nov. 28 Nov. See the full discussion of that case and other English authorities in *Lee Wai Man v Chan Che Ming & Anor* DCPI 1719/2008 (Judge Marlene Ng; 19. 08.2009) (para 55 et seq). In *Lee Wai Man* (para 126) it was held that an order for payment into court under this rule should not be in an amount that would stifle the party's right of access to the court, being an amount beyond the party's means. The court ordered a party to pay $5,000 into court for failure to meet its discovery obligations under an order.

Reference should also be made to Order 1B rule 1(3) & (4) and the commentary thereunder as to when it is appropriate to require a party to pay money into court as a condition of an order.

**4.      Sanctions have effect unless defaulting party obtains relief** (O. 2 r. 4)

**Where a party has failed to comply with a rule or court order, any sanction for failure to comply imposed by the rule or court order has effect unless the party in default applies to the Court for and obtains relief from the sanction within 14 days of the failure.**

**(L.N. 152 of 2008)**

---

**NOTES**

**[2.4.1]      Origin and scope of Order 2 rule 4**

Order 2 rule 4 provides that sanctions for failure to comply with the rules or a court order take effect unless the party in default applies for and obtains relief therefrom. See Order 32 rule 11B on 'self executing' orders, and see Order 1B rule 1(3)(b) on the power to specify consequences of failure to comply. Applications for relief from sanctions are governed by rule 5.

Although an order specifying sanctions which will take effect in default may itself be appealable, no appeal lies against the sanctions themselves once they take effect. This is because they take effect automatically, and there is no judicial decision to appeal. See *Piper Jaffray Asia Securities Ltd v Lam Ying Yu* HCA 38/2009 (Deputy Judge L Chan; 15.09.2010) (para 7) where an appeal against judgment entered in default of compliance with an unless order was astruck out, though the party was permitted to proceed with an application for relief under rule 5.

Rule 4 is a shortened version of CPR 3.8. The English rule goes on, in para (3) to provide expressly that time may not be extended by agreement between the parties. Hong Kong has not adopted that restriction, and retains Order 3 rule 5(3) which expressly provides that the parties may agree on extensions in relation to service of pleadings, etc, without intervention of the court. The Civil Court Practice 2008, our sister publication in the UK, says of the English provision (at para CPR 3.8[3]):

> **Court may extend time in the absence of an application for an extension** The power to extend time does not depend on the making of an application for relief: the court has inherent jurisdiction to extend time whether applied for or not: *Keen Phillips (a firm) v Field* [2006] EWCA Civ 1524; (2006) The Times, 7 Dec; [2007] 1 WLR 686 (CA).

Quite apart from any such inherent jurisdiction the court has an express power to make orders of its own motion under Order 1B rule 2. That should extend to making orders to extend time for compliance so as to relieve a defaulting party from sanctions.

**5.      Relief from sanctions** (O. 2 r. 5)

**(1)      On an application for relief from any sanction imposed for a failure to comply with any rule or court order, the Court shall consider all the circumstances including -**

**(a)      the interests of the administration of justice;**

**(b)      whether the application for relief has been made promptly;**

**(c)      whether the failure to comply was intentional;**

**(d)      whether there is a good explanation for the failure to comply;**

**(e)      the extent to which the party in default has complied with**

other rules and court orders;

(f)     **whether the failure to comply was caused by the party in default or his legal representative;**

(g)     **in the case where the party in default is not legally represented, whether he was unaware of the rule or court order, or if he was aware of it, whether he was able to comply with it without legal assistance;**

(h)     **whether the trial date or the likely trial date can still be met if relief is granted;**

(i)     **the effect which the failure to comply had on each party; and**

(j)     **the effect which the granting of relief would have on each party.**

(2)    **An application for relief must be supported by evidence.**

**(L.N. 152 of 2008)**

---

## NOTES

### [2.5.1]    Origin and scope of Order 2 rule 5

Order 2 rule 5 derives from CPR 3.9. The broad purpose of both provisions is to set out the factors to be considered by the court on an application by a party in default of its obligations under the rules or a court order for relief from a sanction taking effect pursuant to the preceding rule. The wording of the two provisions is similar, but not identical. One important difference relates to unrepresented parties. Rule 5(1)(g), which sets out special considerations to be taken into account where the party in default is not legally represented, does not appear in the CPR.

### [2.5.2]    Relief from sanctions imposed in 'self executing' orders

Order 32 rule 11B empowers the court to specify, in interlocutory orders, the consequences of failure to comply. The provision was recommended by the Chief Justice's working party on civil justice reform, which called this type of order the 'self-executing' order. See generally the commentary under Order 32 rule 11B.

Order 2 rule  5 enables a party who has failed to comply with a selfexecuting order to seek relief from the specified consequences. The working party envisaged that applications for relief would be scrutinised carefully and that terms would be imposed. It said (final report, para 515):

> Relief should not automatically be granted upon a defaulting party's application. A reasonable explanation for noncompliance should be required and consideration given to the extent of prejudice to the innocent party if relief is granted. Any relief should generally be ordered on suitable terms as to costs, putting up security, and so forth, with a view to deterring non-compliance.

See also the working party's recommendation 84.

In *Piper Jaffray Asia Securities Ltd v Lam Ying Yu* HCA 38/2009 (Deputy Judge L Chan; 15.09.2010) (para 50-52) an application under this rule was refused where the applicant had intentionally failed to comply with an unless order well knowing the consequences.

In Australia the courts take the view that relief from sanctions which flow from non-compliance with a self-executing order should not be granted in cases of 'inattention or laxity'. In *MTQ Holdings Pty Ltd v Lynch* [2007] WASC 49, approved in *Jorgensen v Slater & Gordon Pty Ltd* [2008] VSCA 110 (18.06.2008) it was said:

> The authority of the court will equally be undermined, and the quality of justice for the innocent party eroded, if the ultimate sanction effected by the operation of a [self-executing] order can be avoided by showing that non-compliance with [that] order came about by the same sort of inattention or laxity that caused the order to be made in the first place.

As to the power to impose conditions on making an order such as one granting relief from sanctions, see Order 1B rule 1(3).

## [2.5.3]    Factors to be considered on application for relief from sanctions

Order 2 rule 5 requires the court to consider all the circumstances including those listed. In addition the right of access to the courts may be relevant, as discussed in a subsequent paragraph. Relevant commentary in our sister publication in the UK, The Civil Court Practice, says (at CPR 3.9[1]-[2A]) of the equivalent English provision:

> **'The court will consider all the circumstances'** [note that the word 'shall, is used instead of 'will' in Hong Kong's Order 2 rule 5(1)] -As well as these circumstances the court must take into account the overriding objective ['underlying objectives' in Hong Kong — see Order 1A rule 1]. It is essential for courts to consider the matters listed in [Order 2 rule 5] systematically (as in a s 33 Limitation Act 1980 exercise) [in Hong Kong see section 30 of the Limitation Ordinance (Cap 347) — court's power to override time limits for personal injury and fatal accident claims] and to consider whether the order proposed was just: *Bansal v Cheema* [2000] All ER (D) 2565, CA (where an appeal against an order striking out was allowed; the Court of Appeal held that an unless order in relation to the serving of evidence should have been made) (and see also *Woodhouse v Consignia plc, Stelliou v Compton* [2002] EWCA Civ 275 [2002] 2 All ER 737 [2002] All ER (D) 79 (Mar); *RC Residuals Ltd v Linton Fuel Oils Ltd* [2002] EWCA Civ 911 [2002] 1 WLR 2782 [2002] The Times, 22 May).
>
>> Where a party applies for an extension of time within which to comply with a court order and makes it clear that he seeks relief from sanctions imposed for fail ure to comply with the order if the extension is refused, then the overriding objective to deal with the case justly [CPR 1.1(1), which has not been included in the 'underlying objectives' set out in Order 1A rule 1 in Hong Kong, but may be said to find expression in Order 1A rule 2(2) — see the commentary thereunder] requires the court to consider [the factors set out in rule 5] before deciding what order to make notwithstanding that the applicant has not specifically made an application under [rule 5]: *Keith v CPM Field Marketing Ltd* [2000] The Times 29 Aug (CA).
>>
>> Where a party who has been struck out for non-attendance applies promptly for relief, with evidence of a reasonable excuse and reasonable prospects of success in the main proceedings, the court should restore the claim unless there are exceptional grounds for not so doing: *Thakerar v Northwick Park Hospital NHS Trust* [2002] EWCA Civ 617 [2002] All ER (D) 216 (Apr).

With regard to striking out for non-attendance as mentioned in the above passage, see Order 25 rule 1C which provides that if a plaintiff fails to appear at a case management conference or PTR, the court shall provisionally strike out the claim.

The above commentary from The Civil Court Practice continues:

**'An application for relief must be supported by evidence' [rule 5(2)]** The application itself, if it is verified by a statement of truth may constitute evidence in support for this purpose otherwise a witness statement has to be used: for applications generally see CPR Pt 23 [in Hong Kong an affidavit or affirmation would normally be used under Order 32 — Order 41A does not require statements of truth for interlocutory applications].

> Where a party contends that a condition in the nature of a payment into court would be impossible to meet, then that party must put before the court the evidence relied upon in support of that contention; it is not incumbent upon the court to request such evidence: *Redcliffe Close (Old Brompton Road) Management Ltd v Kamal* [2005] EWHC 858 (Ch) [2005] All ER (D) 166 (Jan).

> In the case of an 'unless' order the evidence should not be directed solely at the difficulty of complying with the order on the last day: *RC Residuals Ltd v Linton Fuel Oils Ltd* [2002] EWCA Civ 911 [2002] 1 WLR 2782 [2002] The Times 22 May (although a refusal by the other side to accept service by email on the final day might tell in favour of granting relief) [in Hong Kong there is no provision for service by fax or e-mail -see the commentary under O 65 r 5].

**Extension of time in respect of an 'unless' order where timetable agreed by the parties** The court has power under [Order 1B rule 1(2)(a) and this rule] to allow extra time beyond that agreed by the parties as the basis of an 'unless' order but the court should place very great weight on what the parties agreed and be slow to intervene: *Ropac Ltd v Inntrepreneur Pub Co* [2000] 26 LS Gaz R 38, Neuberger J.

For additional commentary on extensions of time for compliance with unless orders, see the discussion on peremptory orders following Order 42 rule 2.

**[2.5.4]    Hearing required**
Applications under Order 2 rule 4 (and 5) for relief from sanctions are expressly excepted from the general power of masters to deal with interlocutory applications without a hearing. See Order 32 rule 11A(5)(a).

**[2.5.5]    Human rights considerations on application for relief from sanction**
In England it is accepted that on an application for relief against a sanction it is relevant for the court to consider the right to a fair trial under art 6 of the European Convention on Human Rights and Fundamental Freedoms. Any restriction on that right must be proportionate and for a legitimate purpose. See *Momson v Azeez* [2009] EWCA Civ 202 (18.03.2009) (para 36), a case where the defendant had been barred from defending because of failure to comply with orders for discovery. The same should be true in Hong Kong bearing in mind the right to a fair hearing in art 14(1) of the ICCPR (and art 10 of the HK Bill of Rights), and the right of access to the court under art 35 of the Basic Law.

**ORDER 3**

**TIME**

**1.**     **"Month" means calendar month** (O. 3 r. 1)

**Without prejudice to section 3 of the Interpretation and General Clauses Ordinance (Cap. 1) in its application to these rules, the word "month", where it occurs in any judgment, order, direction or other document forming part of any proceedings in the High Court, means a calendar month unless the context otherwise requires.**

**2.**     **Reckoning periods of time** (O. 3 r. 2)

**(1)    Any period of time fixed by these rules or by any judgment, order or direction for doing any act shall be reckoned in accordance with the following provisions of this rule.**

**(2)    Where the act is required to be done within a specified period after or from a specified date, the period begins immediately after that date.**

**(3)    Where the act is required to be done within or not less than a specified period before a specified date, the period ends immediately before that date.**

**(4)    Where the act is required to be done a specified number of clear days before or after a specified date, at least that number of days must intervene between the day on which the act is done and that date.**

**(5)    Where, apart from this paragraph, the period in question, being a period of 7 days or less, would include a Sunday or a general holiday, that day shall be excluded.**

**In this paragraph "general holiday" means a day which is, or is to be observed as, a general holiday under the General Holidays Ordinance (Cap. 149). (35 of 1998 s. 5)**

---

**NOTES**

**[3.2.1]    Interpretation and General Clauses Ordinance**

See also section 71 of the Interpretation and General Clauses Ordinance (Cap 1) which deals with the same matter. As section 71 is contained in an Ordinance it takes precedence over this and any other provision in the rules to the extent of any inconsistency (see section 28(1)(b) of Cap 1 and *Mohan v McElney* [1983] HKLR 308). Moreover, whereas rule 2, being general, must give way to specific provision to the contrary elsewhere in the rules, this is not the case with respect to section 71, due to the latter's superior status as a provision of an Ordinance.

Section 71 of Cap 1, as amended in 1995 (see Ordinance No 68 of 1995), provides in essence as follows:

     (a)   Subsection (1)(a) provides that the day from which time is to run is excluded in calculating the time within which the act must be done. This is essentially the same as rule 2(2) of this Order.

(b) Subsections (1)(b) and (c) provide that where the day for doing any act or taking any step falls on a public holiday or a day on which either a gale warning or black rainstorm warning is issued, time is extended to the next normal business day. However, this does not apply to acts or steps the time limited for which is six days or less (subsection (1)(d)). For the purpose of section 71, 'black rainstorm warning' is defined as such issued by the Royal Observatory and 'gale warning' is given the meaning assigned by the Judicial Proceedings (Adjournment During Gale Warnings) Ordinance (Cap 62).

The question of when the act, in respect of which the time limitation exists, has been done arose before the Hong Kong Court of Appeal in *Wo Fung Paper Making Factory Ltd v Sappi Kraft (Pty) Ltd* [1988] 2 HKLR 346. In that case, a solicitor's clerk had presented a summons at the registry on the last day of the time limited for making the particular application. The registry queried the summons with the result that it was taken back to the solicitor and not accepted by the registry until the next day. It was later argued that the application had been made within the prescribed time, ie when the summons was first presented to the registry. Their Lordships were divided in their opinion on this issue. Fuad VP held that the application had not been made in time because the registry had made a perfectly sensible and proper query about the summons; Hunter JA felt it was unnecessary to decide the point, and Penlington JA held that application had been made to the court in time.

### [3.2.2]    Legal Aid Ordinance

Section 15 of the Legal Aid Ordinance (Cap 91) and regulations thereunder provide that there shall be a stay of proceedings where notice of an application for legal aid is filed (42 days) or where legal aid is discharged (14 days). The effect of such a legal aid stay is that the time prescribed by these rules for the taking of any step in proceedings ceases to run so long as the stay lasts. This includes the time within which a party may appeal from an adverse decision: see *Brook v Law Society of Hong Kong (No 1)* [1998] 1 HKC 595.

Under the terms of the Legal Aid Ordinance a legal aid stay may be lifted by the court.

In *Lee Shiu Ming v Yeo Hiap Seng (Hong Kong) Ltd* [1994] 1 HKC 18 the Court of Appeal considered the circumstances in which such a stay of proceedings might be lifted.

In *Chan Chun Shing v Chang Chen Chin t/a Tong Tak Co* HCPI 395/2008 (Fung J; 04.05.2009) the court lifted a legal aid stay to prevent trial dates from being lost, referring to the need to preserve 'milestone' dates. See Order 25 rule 1B as to variation of such dates.

### 3.    Summer Vacation excluded from time for service, etc., of pleadings
(O. 3 r. 3)

**Unless the Court otherwise directs, the period of the Summer Vacation shall be excluded in reckoning any period prescribed by these rules or by any order or direction for serving, filing or amending any pleading.**

---

**NOTES**

#### [3.3.1]    Comparison with English rule

The equivalent English rule was repealed in 1990.

#### [3.3.2]    Time does not run during summer vacation

Order 3 rule 3 provides that the time for serving, filing or amending pleadings does not run during the court's summer vacation, unless the court otherwise directs. The summer vacation is the month of August — see Order 64 rule 1 and the definition of 'vacation' in Order 1 rule 4. The court also has brief vacations at Christmas and Easter and, prior to 1988, the running of time was suspended during those vacations as well.

The suspension of the running of time under this rule applies only with respect to any 'pleading'. Order 1 rule 4 provides that 'pleading' does not include a petition, summons or preliminary act. The ordinary meaning of the word suggests that it applies only to documents which 'plead' a party's case. The Concise Oxford dictionary defines 'pleading' as 'formal statement of cause of action or defence'. Thus a notice of appeal is not a pleading for this purpose: *Chung Fai Engineering Co v Maxwell Engineering Co Ltd* [2001] 3 HKC 24. However, reading the rule together with section 31(1) of the High Court Ordinance, the suspension of time applies more broadly.

Section 31(1) of the High Court Ordinance provides as follows:

> Where by any law regulating civil procedure, or by any special order of the High Court, any period not exceeding one month is appointed or allowed for the doing of any act or the taking of any proceeding, no days included in the Summer vacation shall be reckoned in the computation of such time, unless the Court otherwise directs:
>
> Provided that nothing in this section shall be deemed to extend the time for entering appearance to any writ endorsed with a statement of claim.

It will be noted that unlike Order 3 rule 3, section 31(1) is not restricted to pleadings. Hence the time for serving notice of appeal is suspended by the latter, though not by the former: Chung Fai Engineering Co (above), at 31D-E. Likewise the time for issuing a summons under Order 12 rule 8 (to challenge jurisdiction) is suspended by section 31(1) though not by Order 3 rule 3: The Artemis CACV 81/1982 (Leonard VP, Cons & Fuad JJA; 04.11.1982).

#### [3.3.3]    Power of court to direct time to run during summer vacation

Both Order 3 rule 3 and section 31(1) of the High Court Ordinance leave with the court a discretion to direct that the suspension of time shall not operate in a particular case. Thus when the court gives directions which are likely to span the August vacation, consideration will be given to the question whether time should run during that period.

It is obviously desirable that a direction that time shall run during the August vacation be stated expressly in the court's order. However, such a direction may be implied, as in *Guang Xin Enterprises Ltd (in liq) v Kwan Wong Tang & Fong (a firm)* HCA 2788/2001 (Chung J; 09.08.2001) where a master's order extending time to a date within the summer vacation was construed as a direction that time shall run.

**4.    Time expires on Sunday, etc. (O. 3 r. 4)**

**Where the time prescribed by these rules, or by any judgment, order or direction, for doing any act at an office of the Court expires on a Sunday or other day on which that office is closed, and by reason thereof that act cannot be done on that day, the act shall be in time if done on the next day on which that office is open.**

5.       **Extensions, etc., of time** (O. 3 r. 5)

        **(1)    The Court may, on such terms as it thinks just, by order extend or abridge the period within which a person is required or authorized by these rules, or by any judgment, order or direction, to do any act in any proceedings.**

        **(2)    The Court may extend any such period as is referred to in paragraph (1) although the application for extension is not made until after the expiration of that period.**

        **(3)    The period within which a person is required by these rules, or by any order or direction, to serve, file or amend any pleading or other document may be extended by consent (given in writing) without an order of the Court being made for that purpose.**

        **(4)    In this rule references to the Court shall be construed as including references to the Court of Appeal and a single judge of that Court.**

---

## NOTES

### [3.5.1]    Cross-references
With regard to the court's general power to extend and abridge time, see also Order 1B rule 1(2)(a). Concerning the time within which an act is required to be done pursuant to a judgment or order, see Order 45 rule 6. And with regard to peremptory or 'unless' orders, see the commentary under Order 42 rule 2.

### [3.5.2]    Court's power to extend or abridge time
Order 3 rule 5 gives the court a broad discretion to extend or abridge the time within which any step in legal proceedings is required to be taken under these rules or otherwise, such as under an order.

    However, Order 3 rule 5 does not apply so as to permit an extension of time stipulated under any other enactment: see Re Merck Sharp & Dohme Ltd [2002] 2 HKC 475 where the Court of Appeal upheld a decision of Kwan J to the effect that this rule does not apply so as to permit an extension of the time limited by rule 39 of the Patents (General) Rules (Cap 514) to file notice of amendment of a patent.

### [3.5.3]    Abridgement of time
Abridgement (or shortening) of time is necessary where a party wishes a hearing before a stipulated notice period has expired. For example Order 32 rule 3 provides that a summons must normally be served not less than two clear days before the hearing (or on the day prior to the hearing in the case of a time summons). The court may abridge the notice period in case of urgency or where there is other good reason, for example where a more proximate date has already been fixed for hearing related matters.

    Where an application for abridgement of time relates to something more substantial than an interlocutory summons the court may be more strict. In *Talent Hope Ltd v Magnificent Estates Ltd* [1995] 3 HKC 593, 597E-F, an application for abridgment of the time for hearing an originating summons was refused. Waung J noted (at 597C-F) that such an order would cut into the other party's rights and said 'very special or urgent reasons must be shown'. In *Lo Siu Lan & Anor v Hong Kong Housing Authority* CACV 378/2004 (Ma CJHC, Stock & Le Pichon JJA; 17.12.2004) the Court of

Appeal, citing Talent Hope, allowed an abridgement of time for lodging an appeal which was acceptable to the other party. However, Ma CJHC opined that in the absence of consent 'exceptional reasons' would have to be shown, 'urgency is not necessarily enough by itself'.

### [3.5.4]   Principles upon which extension to be granted
The principles on which the court will exercise its discretion under Order 3 rule 5 to extend time have been expressed in different ways over time. There may be a trend to focus on the merits. Let us look first at the law as it was stated in Hong Kong in the early 1990s. In *Chiu Sin-chung v Yu Yan-yan Angela & Anor* [1993] 1 HKLR 225, at 227-228, the principles which should guide the court on an application for extension of time under Order 3 rule 5(1) were given by Keith J as follows:

   (i)   'The rules of court must prima facie be obeyed, and in order to justify a court in extending the time during which some step in procedure requires to be taken there must be some material upon which the court can exercise its discretion. If the law were otherwise, a party in breach would have an unqualified right to an extension of time which would defeat the purpose of the rules, which is to provide a time table for the conduct of litigation': *Thamboo Ratnam v Thamboo Cumarasamy & Cumarasamy Ariamany* [1965] 1 WLR 8 at p 12A-B, applied in *Revici v Prentice Hall Inc* [1969] 1 WLR 157 and in Re Adhiguna Meranti [1988] 1 HKLR 410.

   (ii)   Accordingly, the prerequisite of an application to extend time is a clear statement as to the reasons for the time limits not having been observed and for any delay in then applying for an extension.

   (iii)   'Once the time for appealing has elapsed, the respondent who was successful in the court below is entitled to regard the judgment in his favour as being final. If he is to be deprived of this entitlement, it can only be on the basis of a discretionary balancing exercise, however blameless may be the delay on the part of the would be appellant': *Norwich & Peterborough Building Society v Steed* [1991] 1 WLR 449 at p 454G.

   (iv)   The factors which are normally to be taken into account in that balancing exercise are (a) the length of the delay, (b) the reasons for the delay, (c) the chances of the appeal succeeding if an extension of time for appealing is granted, and (d) the degree of prejudice to the would-be respondent if the application for an extension is granted: Steed, p 454H.

   (v)   As for the reasons for the delay, 'the fact that the omission to appeal in due time was due to a mistake on the part of the legal adviser, may be a sufficient cause to justify the court in exercising its discretion': *Gatti v Shoosmith* [1939] 3 All ER 916 at p 919G. Indeed, in that case, the Court of Appeal extended the time without consideration of the merits at all: the period involved was only a matter of a few days, the appellant's solicitors had informed the respondent's solicitors within time of the appellant's intention to appeal, and the mistake was one 'which, to anyone who was reading the rule without having the authorities in mind, might very well have arisen'.

   (vi)   Although the existence of prejudice to a would-be respondent is a ground for refusing an extension of time, the absence of prejudice to a would-be respondent is not a ground for extending time: *Re Adhiguna Meranti*, p 411H.

   (vii)   As for the merits, they will play little part in the balancing exercise if the delay is short and is wholly excusable, but where the delay is substantial and is not wholly excusable, much  more merit is required to overcome it: *Steed*, p 455G-H, distinguishing *Palata Investments  Ltd v Burt & Sinfield Ltd* [1985] 1 WLR 942 from *Rawasdeh v Lane* (Court of Appeal (Civil Division) Transcript No 327 of 1988).

In 2001 Deputy Judge McCoy considered afresh the power to extend time under Order 3 rule 5. See *Zida Technologies Ltd v Tiga Technologies Ltd & Ors* [2001] 4 HKC 163. The learned Deputy Judge expressly held (at 173D-E) that the Privy Council's decision in *Ratnam v Cumarasamy* [1965] 1 WLR 8 no longer represents the law in Hong Kong on extension of time and likewise the subsequent English cases of *Revici v Prentice Hall Inc* [1969] 1 WLR 157 (CA) and *Savill v Southend Health Authority* [1995] 1 WLR 1254 (CA) were no longer to be followed. Those decisions had been 'overtaken by a new jurisprudential approach to time limits in civil law, as exemplified by *Finnegan v Parkside Health Authority* [1998] 1 WLR 411 (CA)' (Deputy Judge McCoy's judgment at 172C-D). The learned Deputy Judge preferred the approach adopted by Hartmann J in *Mobil Petroleum Co Inc v Registrar of Trade Marks* [2000] 4 HKC 670 concerning extension of time under rule 91 of the Trade Marks Rules and found that the 'critical' criterion is the prospect of injustice, meaning the merit or the prospect of success. The merits were the 'dominant consideration' (1731), and, quoting from *Mortgage Corp Ltd v Sandoes* [1997] PNLR 263 (CA) 'the overriding principle was that justice must be done' (at 173I-174A). In addition, Deputy Judge McCoy held, the following other criteria are also relevant, in descending order of importance: length of delay, reason for delay and degree of prejudice to the opposing party (at 173 C-G). So far as prejudice is concerned, Deputy Judge McCoy cited the judgment of Le Pichon J in *Birkenhead Properties and Investments Ltd v Leung Yiu* [1998] 1 HKLRD 527, 539C and stated that lack of prejudice per se is not a reason to refuse an extension -'an additional period of uncertainty is prejudice in itself' (at 173 H-I).

In *Nantong Angang Garments Co Ltd v Hellmann Int'l Fowarders & Ors* [2005] 4 HKC 86, 96B-E the Court of Appeal also endorsed the approach adopted by Hartmann J in the Mobil Petroleum case, whereby instead of focusing on whether there is an acceptable explanation for the delay, the court weighs all matters including the reason for the delay.

**[3.5.5]    Extension of time at interlocutory stage**

The court will be more ready to grant an extension of time at the interlocutory stage as compared to a later stage when the parties' rights have been determined. Time for taking an interlocutory step will normally be extended where the delay is not excessive, the party in default pays costs and no injustice would be done to the opposing party. On the other hand a different view may be taken in cases of repeated or persistent delay, procedural abuse or questionable tactics. See *Po Kwong Marble Factory Ltd v Wah Yee Decoration Co Ltd (No 2)* [1997] 3 HKC 509 (CA) quoting with approval from *Costellow v Somerset County Council* [1993] 1 All ER 952.

**[3.5.6]    Power to extend time after expiration**

Order 3 rule 5(2) provides that the court may exercise its power to extend time even though application is not made until that time has already expired. In *CSI Investment Management Ltd v Ke Jun Xiang* CACV 17/2006 (Tang JA; 16.05.2006) the court readily granted such an extension, on terms as to costs, where the delay was only one day.

See also section 72 of the Interpretation and General Clauses Ordinance (Cap 1) which likewise provides that extensions of time may be granted after expiration. Section 72 is broader than this rule in that it applies to time limits prescribed by any Ordinance (which includes subsidiary legislation such as these rules -see Cap 1, s 3) whereas this rule is confined to the time limits laid down in these rules. On the other hand section 72 is narrower in that it applies only to time limits laid down in legislation, whereas this rule extends to time limits prescribed in any judgment, order or direction.

### [3.5.7]    Peremptory orders

Peremptory or 'unless' orders, stipulating that a particular consequence will follow if a party fails to take a specified step in the proceedings within a given time, are governed by practice directions in Hong Kong (see the commentary under Order 42 rule 2).

### [3.5.8]    Extension of time to comply with consent order

The court's power under Order 3 rule 5 extends to permitting an extension of time to comply with a consent order unless the consent order embodies a contract between the parties by which the court's jurisdiction is ousted, such as where the time for compliance is 'of the essence'. See *Lee Hung Yam v Lee Sou Fai* HCA 4390/1983 (Deputy Judge Nazareth QC; 23.05.1985) [1985] HKLY 788 and *Leung Yee & Anor v Ng Yiu Ming & Anor* [2001] 1 HKC 342 (CA). In the Leung Yee case the Court of Appeal held (at 354D) that the consent order in that case embodied an agreement between the parties which was construed as superadding the court's powers including that under Order 3 rule 5. The Court of Appeal was reinforced in this conclusion by the inclusion of a 'liberty to apply' clause (at 354G). In its decision the Court of Appeal applied the English decisions in *Purcell v FC Trigell Ltd* [1971] 1 QB 358, *Siebe Gorman & Co Ltd v Pneupac Ltd* [1982] 1 All ER 377, *Wentworth v Bullen* (1829) 9 B&C 840, and *Tigner-Roche & Co Ltd v Spiro* [1982] 126 SJ 525.

It is noteworthy that in the Leung Yee case the Court of Appeal ordered the party in default to pay costs on an indemnity basis, in view of the lengthy delay.

### [3.5.9]    Extension of time without order

Order 3 rule 5(3) permits extensions of time by written consent of the parties. Extensions of time to serve, file or amend any pleading or document are within its scope. No order of the court is required. The usual practice is that consent is simply indorsed on the back of the document concerned: *Lai Cheung Textiles Ltd v China Profit Enterprises Ltd* HCA 2346/2003 (Registrar Chan; 08.09.2003).

**6.    Notice of intention to proceed after year's delay** (O. 3 r. 6)
    **Where a year or more has elapsed since the last proceeding in a cause or matter, the party who desires to proceed must give to every other party not less than one month's notice of his intention to proceed.**
    **A summons on which no order was made is not a proceeding for the purposes of this rule.**

## NOTES

### [3.6.1]    Where notice required

In *Kung Wong Sau Hin v Sze To Chun Keung* [1996] 2 HKC 616 the question arose as to whether notice of intention to proceed was required where there had been a step taken against some but not all defendants within the previous year. Le Pichon J held that no notice was required. To hold otherwise would be to read into the rule words which were not there: (see at 623B-624D). The learned judge's decision on this point was upheld on appeal to the Court of Appeal: see [1996] 3 HKC 292, 296E-297E.

### [3.6.2]    Failure to give notice

In *Kung Wong Sau Hin v Sze To Chun Keung* [1996] 3 HKC 292, the Court of Appeal expressed the view (obiter) that it was appropriate for a judge, as a matter of discretion, to consider applying Order 2 rule 1 so as to waive any irregularity caused by failure to give notice of intention to proceed.

## ORDER 4

### ASSIGNMENT, TRANSFER AND CONSOLIDATION OF PROCEEDINGS COMMENCEMENT AND PROGRESS OF PROCEEDINGS

---

## NOTES

### [4.01]   Comparison with English rule

It will be noted that Order 4 in the Hong Kong rules contains only two rules whereas the equivalent in England contains nine. It would appear that the balance of the English rules have been omitted in Hong Kong because they deal with administrative and other matters which are inapplicable in this jurisdiction.

**2.   Companies** (O. 4 r. 2)

**Where an order has been made by the Court for the winding up of a company, all proceedings in chambers in any action against that company at the instance or on behalf of debenture holders shall be dealt with by an officer of the Court of First Instance who is a registrar within the meaning of any rules for the time being in force relating to the winding up of companies.**

**9.   Consolidation, etc., of causes or matters** (O. 4 r. 9)

**(1)   Where two or more causes or matters are pending, then, if it appears to the Court—**

**(a)   that some common question of law or fact arises in both or all of them, or**

**(b)   that the rights to relief claimed therein are in respect of or arise out of the same transaction or series of transactions, or**

**(c)   that for some other reason it is desirable to make an order under this rule,**

**the Court may order those causes or matters to be consolidated on such terms as it thinks just or may order them to be tried at the same time, or one immediately after another, or may order any of them to be stayed until after the determination of any other of them.**

**(2)   Where the Court makes an order under paragraph (1) that two or more causes or matters are to be tried at the same time but no order is made for those causes or matters to be consolidated, then, a party to one of those causes or matters may be treated as if it were a party to any of those other causes or matters for the purpose of making an order for costs against him or in his favour.**

---

## NOTES

### [4.9.1]   Consolidation and joint trial of proceedings

Order 4 rule 9(1) empowers the court to order that proceedings be consolidated, tried together or one after another. The power may be exercised where separate sets of proceedings are closely connected by law, fact or otherwise. In *Sincere View Int'l Ltd v Kenco Investments Ltd* HCA 301/2005 (Kwan J; 03.02.2006) it was said:

> In deciding whether to order consolidation of actions the court has an unfettered discretion. The power is to be exercised in a flexible way with regard to the particular circumstances of the situation. The objective of such an order is to save time and costs. There is no hard and fast rule that just because the parties are identical and some common question of fact or law is involved in both actions, it would be expedient and proper to order consolidation.

In addition to saving time and costs, the court will be concerned with avoidance of delay, undue complexity and overloading of issues: *Re The Prudential Enterprises Ltd* HCCW 594/1999 (Chu J; 19.08.2003).

An application for consolidation should be made 'at the earliest convenient moment' in order to avoid waste of expense and effort: *Re Shui On Construction Co Ltd & Schindler Lifts (HK) Ltd* [1986] HKLR 1177, 1185I-J. In *Comtech Engineering & Consultant Co Ltd v Thorn Security (HK) Ltd* HCCT 53/1999 (Ma J; 20.06.2002) the court refused to consolidate two actions which were at different stages, where to do so would result in having to vacate trial dates which had already been fixed for one.

Consolidation results in a single action in which there should be a single set of pleadings. By contrast an order for joint trial leaves the actions and their pleadings distinct. Thus consolidation may be appropriate where two actions can proceed as claim and counterclaim. On the other hand joint trial, or trial one after the other may be preferable where the parties are not identical in the separate actions: *Kader Industrial Co Ltd v Ngai Hing Hong Plastics Materials Ltd* HCA 1534/2003 (Deputy Judge Saunders; 23.02.2004).

See also Order 1B rule 1(2)(g).

**[4.9.2]  Costs of actions tried at same time**
Order 4 rule 9(2) provides that where actions are tried at the same time, but not consolidated, the court may order a party to one of the actions to pay costs of the other action. There was previously some doubt in Hong Kong as to the vires of this provision as it conflicted with section 52A(2) of the High Court Ordinance which prohibited costs orders against non-parties in the absence of specific primary legislation. Thus it was arguable that *Aiden Shipping Co Ltd v Interbulk Ltd* [1986] 1 AC 965, 982 (HL), so far as it dismissed the suggestion that the English equivalent of this rule was ultra vires, was not applicable in Hong Kong. However, section 52A(2) was replaced with effect from 2009 with an express power to order costs against a non-party. Thus there should no longer be any doubt about the validity of the power expressed in this rule. See the commentary on costs against non-parties under Order 62 rule 6A.

**[4.9.3]  Consolidation of arbitration proceedings**
Consolidation of arbitrations is governed by section 6B of the Arbitration Ordinance (Cap 341). That section is based on Order 4 rule 9 and similar, though not identical, factors apply: *Shui On Constructions Ltd v Moon Yik Co & Ors* HCMP 1275/1987 (Deputy Judge Cruden; 31.07.1987); *Linfield Ltd v Brooke Hillier Parker (a firm)* HCA 7693/2000 (Ma J; 19.08.2002).

**ORDER 5**

**MODE OF BEGINNING CIVIL PROCEEDINGS IN THE COURT OF FIRST INSTANCE**

**1.      Mode of beginning civil proceedings** (O. 5 r. 1)
      **Subject to the provisions of any written law and of these rules, civil proceedings in the Court of First Instance may be begun by writ or originating summons.**
      **(25 of 1998 s. 2) (L.N. 152 of 2008)**

——————————————

**NOTES**

**[5.1.1]     Court of First Instance or District Court?**
Certain types of claim may be pursued in either the Court of First Instance or the District Court. For example, money claims above the Small Claims Tribunal's exclusive jurisdiction and up to the District Court's upward limit of HK$1 million may be brought in either court. However, actions which are within the jurisdiction of the District Court should not be commenced in the CFI without good reason. Section 43 of the District Court Ordinance (Cp 336) provides that in the absence of good reason such as importance or complexity of any issue in the action, the CFI is required to transfer such an action to the District Court. It may do so either on application or of its own motion: section 43(1). See the commentary under Order 25 rule 3.
      There were once procedural differences between the two courts which might lead plaintiffs to choose the CFI over the District Court. See, for example, *Diners Club International (HK) Ltd v Wilson Cheung Wing-yim* (1981) 11 HKLJ 247; *Kwangtung Provincial Bank v Tang Chik Leung* [1985] 1 HKC 93. However the District Court rules were amended in 2000 so as to largely bring them into line with the High Court rules.

**[5.1.2]     Types of originating process**
Order 5 rule 1 provides that civil proceedings may be begun by writ or originating summons. The rule previously listed the originating motion and petition as additional modes of commencing proceedings. The Chief Justice's working party on civil justice reform concluded that the previous system was unnecessarily complex (final report, para 151 et seq) and recommended that originating motions and petitions should be abolished save where prescribed for excluded proceedings (recommendation 14). They are preserved by Order 5 rule 5 for proceedings where their use is required or authorised by written law. Thus winding-up and matrimonial proceedings, which are governed by their own rules, continue to be initiated by petitions. However Orders 53 and 54 have been amended so that applications for judicial review and habeas corpus are no longer brought by motion, but by special types of originating summons.
      Petitions and motions also continue to exist for some proceedings governed by these rules. Order 102 rule 5 continues to prescribe the petition for certain applications under the Companies Ordinance (Cap 32), and Order 59 rule 3(1) continues to provide that appeals to the Court of Appeal must be brought by a type of motion known as notice of appeal.

See Order 5 rule 7 for transitional provisions concerning petitions and originating motions pending at the time the rules were amended.

In choosing between writ and originating summons reference should be made to rule 4 of this Order. Note also Order 2 rule 1(3) which provides that the court shall not set aside proceedings commenced with the wrong originating process, but give directions for continuation of the proceedings in an appropriate manner.

### [5.1.3]    Originating process to be indorsed as to nature of claim
By practice direction 24.1 a writ or originating summons must be indorsed, at the top of the front page, as to (a) whether the claim is monetary only, non-monetary only, or mixed; and (b) as to the nature of the claim eg commercial land, tort, etc. A list of categories of 'nature' of claim is annexed to the practice direction.

### [5.1.4]    Date of issue of originating process
The date on which originating process is issued can be important, especially where a limitation point may be taken. See the commentary under Order 63 rule 3.

**2.      (Repealed – L.N. 152 of 2008)**

----

**NOTES**

### [5.2.1]    Repeal of Order 5 rule 2
Order 5 rule 2 previously provided that certain types of civil proceedings were required to be commenced by writ of summons. These included claims in tort (other than trespass to land), claims based on fraud and personal injury actions. Now see rule 4 of this Order. The Chief Justice's working party on civil justice reform considered that there was no need to require certain actions to be commenced in a particular way and that Order 5 rule 4(2) was sufficient guidance for choosing between writ of summons and originating summons as the means of commencing an action (final report, para 154). As a result Order 5 rule 2 was repealed and Order 5 rule 4(2) retained in the civil justice reform amendments implemented in 2009.

**3.      (Repealed – L.N. 152 of 2008)**

----

**NOTES**

### [5.3.1]    Repeal of Order 5 rule 3
Order 5 rule 3 previously provided that an originating 'application' to the court under written law was to be made by originating summons. An example is the vendor purchaser application under section 12 of the Conveyancing and Property Ordinance (Cap 219). The rule was repealed as part of the civil justice reforms which took effect in 2009, for the same reasons as the former Order 5 rule 2, as to which see the commentary above.

**4.      Proceedings which may be begun by writ or originating summons** (O. 5 r. 4)
     **(1)    Except in the case of proceedings which under any written law are required or authorized to be begun by a specific form of originating process,**

proceedings may be begun either by writ or by originating summons as the plaintiff considers appropriate. (L.N. 152 of 2008)

 (2) Proceedings—

   (a) in which the sole or principal question at issue is, or is likely to be, one of the construction of any written law or of any instrument made under any written law or of any deed, will, contract or other document, or some other question of law, or

   (b) in which there is unlikely to be any substantial dispute of fact,

are appropriate to be begun by originating summons unless the plaintiff intends in those proceedings to apply for judgment under Order 14 or Order 86 or for any other reason considers the proceedings more appropriate to be begun by writ.

---

## NOTES

### [5.4.1]    Writ or originating summons

Order 5 rule 4 allows the plaintiff to choose to commence civil proceedings by writ of summons or originating summons in cases where there is no specific requirement as to the type of originating process to be used. As guidance in making the choice, rule 4(2) points to cases concerned with points of law or construction, or which otherwise are unlikely to involve factual disputes, as being suitable for the originating summons procedure.

The consequence of choosing a writ over an originating summons is that there will be more elaborate interlocutory procedures such as discovery of documents and case management summons, and full trial with oral evidence. Procedure by way of originating summons is usually simpler and often quicker.

Although the rule appears to leave the choice solely to the plaintiff, reference should be made to the provisions of these rules whereby the court may give directions as to the manner in which proceedings shall continue where it is of the view that an inappropriate originating process has been used. See the commentary under Order 2 rule 1(3).

### [5.4.2]    Actions based on fraud or undue influence

Under the former Order 5 rule 2(b) actions based on an allegation of fraud were required to be commenced by writ of summons. 'Fraud' was considered for that purpose to include undue influence: *In re Deadman, deceased* [1971] 1 WLR 426. Although there may now be greater flexibility as to choice of originating process, such an action should still normally be commenced by writ. This is because there will almost always be factual disputes in such an action, requiring full trial with oral evidence which follows from adopting the writ procedure.

### [5.4.3]    Costs considerations

In *Secretary for Justice v HK Cable Television Ltd* HCA 1398/2005 (Saunders J; 22.03.2007) it was argued that costs should be ordered on the common fund basis rather than party and party basis because the paying party had proceeded by way of writ, rather than originating summons, which would have been more appropriate in the circumstances. The court declined to make such an order on the ground that the extra costs incurred by the receiving party as a consequence of the writ procedure being adopted were covered by a party and party costs order, and it was not appropriate to punish the paying party.

In *So Mariko v Tse Chun Chung John & Anor* HCA 579/2010 (Deputy Judge Carlson; 06.10.2010) (para 6-8) it was said that there could be costs implications where a conveyancing dispute was brought before the court by writ of summons rather than originating summons. Although it was open to the plaintiff to issue a writ, the vendor and purchaser summons procedure (Conveyancing and Property Ordinance (Cap 219), s 12) was 'more appropriate and convenient'.

**5.      Proceedings to be begun by motion or petition** (O. 5 r. 5)

**Proceedings may be begun by originating motion or petition if, but only if, under any written law the proceedings in question are required or authorized to be so begun.**

**(L.N. 152 of 2008)**

**[5.5.1]     Originating motions and petitions**

Originating motions and petitions are forms of originating process which continue to be prescribed by legislation for commencing limited types of specialist proceedings. Examples of proceedings where the petition is prescribed are matrimonial, bankruptcy and winding-up proceedings which are governed by their own rules, and certain other applications under the Companies Ordinance (Cap 32) (see Order 102 rule 5). Appeals to the Court of Appeal are brought by way of motion: Order 59 rule 3(1).

See the commentary under Order 5 rule 1 as to the reduced use of petitions and motions following amendment of these rules implementing civil justice reform in 2009.

**6.      Right to sue in person** (O. 5 r. 6)

**(1)     Subject to paragraph (2) and to Order 80, rule 2, any person (whether or not he sues as a trustee or personal representative, or in any other representative capacity) may begin and carry on proceedings in the High Court by a solicitor or in person.**

**(2)     A body corporate may not begin or carry on any such proceedings in the Court otherwise than by a solicitor except—**

> **(a)     as expressly provided by or under any enactment; or**
>
> **(b)     where leave is given under paragraph (3) for it to be represented by one of its directors.**

**(3)     (a)     An application by a body corporate for leave to be represented by one of its directors shall be made ex parte to a Registrar and supported by an affidavit, made by the director and filed with the application, stating and verifying the reasons why leave should be given for the body corporate to be represented by the director.**

**(L.N. 99 of 1993) (L.N. 108 of 2002)**

> **(b)     The relevant resolution of the board of the body corporate authorizing the director to appear on its behalf if leave is granted shall be exhibited to the affidavit.**

**(4)    No appeal shall lie from an order of the Registrar under paragraph (3) giving or refusing leave.**

**(5)    Leave given by a Registrar under paragraph (3) may be revoked by the Court at any time.**

**(6)    No appeal shall lie from an order of the Court revoking leave given by a Registrar.**

-----------

## NOTES

**[5.6.1]    Cross-reference**
See also Order 9 rule 6 and Order 12 rule 1(2A) dealing with proceedings by way of Petition and Originating Summons respectively.

**[5.6.2]    Litigants in person**
Order 5 rule 6(1) preserves the right of an individual to sue in person. The equivalent for bodies corporate is rule 6(2) – see the commentary below. Individuals and bodies corporate may also defend in person – see Order 12 rule 1 and the commentary thereunder.

As to when a litigant in person may be assisted at a court hearing by a '*McKenzie* friend', see the commentary on rights of audience under Order 35 rule 7.

**[5.6.3]    Restriction on vexatious legal proceedings**
The court has both statutory and inherent power to prevent litigants from abusing the process of the court by commencing or continuing vexatious legal proceedings. The statutory power is found in sections 27 and 27A of the High Court Ordinance, and the procedure under it is regulated by Order 32A of these rules. See the commentary under that rule for discussion of the statutory and inherent powers.

As observed by Li CJ in *Ng Yat Chi v Max Share Ltd & Anor* [2005] 1 HKLRD 473 (CFA) abusive litigants who commence vexatious proceedings are invariably unrepresented. As a result, the court's power to restrain them effectively operates so as to qualify the right to act in person as set out in Order 5 rule 6.

**[5.6.4]    Companies**
The right to sue in person does not extend to bodies corporate, such as companies. Under Order 5 rule 6(2) such a body is required to act through a solicitor except as provided. The rule goes on to provide that a company may, with leave, be represented by one of its directors. There are cases in which a director appears to have been appointed with a view to obtaining leave to represent the company. Only a director may be granted leave under the rule: *China Top Consultants Ltd v Prosperity Construction & Decoration Ltd* HCA 6903/2000 (Chu J; 29.08.2003); *Bank of China (HK) Ltd v Expert Promise Ltd* HCMP 1136/2003 (Lam J; 17.09.2003). In *Wing Hang Bank Ltd v Kit Choy Dev't Ltd & Anor* HCMP 5172/2002 (Barma J; 04.08.2006) it was said that where no leave has been sought or obtained under this rule a company 'must be treated as being absent' at trial, even though a person purports to appear for it. However, *M Bergmann AG v Tsinlien Metals & Minerals Co Ltd* HCCL 198/1997 (Stone J; 22.11.2000), where the court heard a non-director on behalf of a company applying for an adjournment, suggests (at para 11) that the court has an 'overriding discretion' apart

from the provisions of this rule.

In *Hondon Dev't Ltd & Anor v Powerise Investments Ltd* CACV 296/2003 (Yuen JA; 11.12.2003) (para 15) the court expressed the view, without deciding, that Order 5 rule 6 does not apply to appeals, with the result that a master has no jurisdiction to grant leave for a company to be represented by a director in the Court of Appeal.

Application for leave is made ex parte on affidavit to the registrar. The jurisdiction to grant leave lies solely with the Registrar, and the Court of Appeal may neither entertain such an application nor an appeal from the Registrar: *Kone Elevator (HK) Ltd v Senfield Ltd* CACV 216/2002 (Leong CJHC, Woo & Cheung JJA; 24.02.2003). Prior to an amendment in 2002 the affidavit was required to demonstrate 'lack of resources or…other good reasons'. Now the rule merely stipulates that the affidavit should state 'why leave should be given'. The result of the amendment is that 'a company's lack of resources is no longer *per se* a "good reason" for the grant of leave': *Hondon Dev't* (above, para 18). In that decision the court, referring to *Radford v Freeway Classics Ltd* [1994] 1 BCLC 445 said that 'the normal principle' is that a company must pursue litigation through lawyers and, although there are exceptions, it is 'not enough' for a company to show it lacks resources or to plead that it has a good cause of action.

As to companies *defending* otherwise than through a solicitor, see Order 12 rule 1(2).

Companies acting 'in person' under this rule, through a director, may be entitled to recover costs as a litigant in person under Order 62 rule 28A. See the commentary under that rule.

### [5.6.5]    Solicitor litigants

A firm of solicitors may sue in person and directly instruct counsel to appear on its behalf 'unless there are clear grounds for considering that the interests of justice will be prejudiced': *George Y C Mok & Co v Trade Advisers Co Ltd & Anor* [2003] 4 HKC 96.

## 7.    Transitional provision relating to rule 16 of Amendment Rules 2008
(O. 5 r. 7)

**Any civil proceedings begun by originating motion or petition before the commencement of the Amendment Rules 2008 and pending immediately before the commencement may be continued and disposed of as if rule 16 of the Amendment Rules 2008 had not been made.**

**(L.N. 152 of 2008)**

---

## NOTES

### [5.7.1]    Transitional provision for originating motions and petitions issued before 2009 reforms

Order 5 rule 7 is a transitional provision preserving Order 5 as it existed prior to implementation of the civil justice reforms in 2009 for proceedings commenced by originating summons or petition before implementation of the reforms.

See also Order 8 rule 6 with regard to motions and originating motions of other types, eg those making an application rather than commencing proceedings.

## ORDER 6

## WRITS OF SUMMONS: GENERAL PROVISIONS

**1.    Form of Writ, etc.** (O. 6 r. 1)
**Every writ must be in Form No. 1 in Appendix A.**

---

## NOTES

### [6.1.1]    Form of writ from 2009
It is important to note that the prescribed form of writ (Form No 1 in Appendix A) was amended as part of the civil justice reforms which came into force in 2009.

### [6.1.2]    Defective form of writ
In principle failure to complete a writ or any other prescribed form in accordance with the rules does not render the proceedings void: see Order 2 rule 1. Non-compliance can be cured by amendment under Order 20. However, there are cases in which the form of originating process used has been held so defective as to constitute a nullity. See, for example, *MacFoy v United Africa Co* [1962] AC 152, *Re Pritchard* [1963] Ch 502 and *Bleile v Coventry Estates Ltd* (1979) 10 BCLR P-53. See also the commentary under Order 1 rule 9.

**2.    Indorsement of claim** (O. 6 r. 2)
    **(1)    Before a writ is issued it must be indorsed—**
        **(a)    with a statement of claim or, if the statement of claim is not indorsed on the writ, with a concise statement of the nature of the claim made or the relief or remedy required in the action begun thereby;**
        **(b)    where the claim made by the plaintiff is for a debt or liquidated demand only, with a statement of the amount claimed in respect of the debt or demand and for costs and also with a statement that further proceedings will be stayed if, within the time limited for acknowledging service, the defendant pays the amount so claimed to the plaintiff, his solicitor or agent; and**
        **(c)    where the only remedy that the plaintiff is seeking is the payment of money, with a statement that the defendant may make an admission in accordance with Order 13A within the period fixed for service of his defence. (L.N. 152 of 2008)**

---

## NOTES

### [6.2.1]    Order 6 rule 2(1)(a) – statement of claim or general indorsement
Order 6 rule 2(1)(a) gives the plaintiff a choice whether to indorse the writ with a full formal statement of claim (which should comply with Order 18), or a 'concise statement' of the

claim and the relief or remedy required. The latter is known as a 'general indorsement'. If the writ is generally indorsed, and the action proceeds, a full statement of claim must later be served: Order 18 rule 1. Costs will be a consideration in making the choice, particularly where it is anticipated the dispute may be undefended or settled.

### [6.2.2]    The general indorsement – degree of particularity required

A general indorsement should state both the nature of the plaintiff's claim (ie the cause of action such as 'breach of contract' or 'negligence') and the relief or remedy sought: the word 'or' the second time it appears in rule 2(1)(a) should be read as 'and': *Sterman v Moore* [1970] 1 QB 596, 603D-E (CA).

An insufficiently particular general indorsement is not a nullity, but an irregularity which may be cured by amendment: *Hill v Luton Corp* [1951] 2 KB 387. See also *Kanada Tejapaibulnational v Thai Mercantile Development Finance Ltd* (in liq) [1988] HKC 295 (CA) where the majority were of the view that a general indorsement stating only the relief sought was technically sufficient.

It was once thought that an insufficiently particular general indorsement was cured by the subsequent service of a proper statement of claim: *Pontin v Wood* [1962] 1 QB 594. In *Beacon College Ltd v Yiu Man Hau Alfred* HCA 2529/2001 (Chu J; 26.06.2001) this proposition was repeated. However it should no longer apply because Order 18 rule 15(2) now provides that a statement of claim may not include allegations in relation to a cause of action not mentioned or arising from the general indorsement: *Sterman v Moore* (above). Now amendment should be required to cure an insufficiently particular general indorsement.

### [6.2.3]    Order 6 rule 2(1)(b) – the '14 days costs indorsement'

Order 6 rule 2(1)(b) requires that where the plaintiff's claim is for a debt or liquidated sum, the writ should be indorsed with a statement that the action will be stayed if the amount claimed, plus fixed costs, is paid within the time for acknowledgment of service (usually 14 days from service). The form of the required indorsement is included in the form of writ of summons (form No 1 in Appendix A to these rules). The amount of fixed costs required to be paid should be calculated in accordance with the second schedule to Order 62. Order 6 rule 2(1)(b) does not apply to litigants in person: see Order 62 rule 28A(5).

*Meaning of 'liquidated' sum* – The indorsement is required on all writs claiming a debt or liquidated amount. A 'liquidated' amount is one which 'can be ascertained by calculation' or which is 'fixed by any scale of charges or other positive data': *GL Baker Ltd v Barclays Bank Ltd* [1956] 1 WLR 1409; [1956] 3 All ER 519. A claim in quantum meruit may be a liquidated claim where the amount claimed for services rendered is stated in the writ: *Lagos v Grunwaldt* [1910] 1 KB 41. By contrast, a money claim is 'unliquidated' if its quantification 'depends upon the circumstances of the case and is fixed by opinion or by assessment or by what might be judged reasonable': *GL Baker* (above). Hence a claim for unspecified damages is unliquidated and the 14 days costs indorsement need not be included in the writ. Both the *GL Baker* case and *Lagos v Grundwalt* were cited with approval in *Indian Overseas Bank Ltd v Asi Tai & Co* [1965] HKLR 128.

**[6.2.4]　　Order 6 rule 2(1)(c) – indorsement as to admission procedure**
Order 6 rule 2(1)(c) requires that a writ be indorsed with a statement alerting the defendant to the procedure under Order 13A whereby liability to pay a sum of money may be admitted and, if wished, a request for payment on terms may be submitted at the same time. See the commentary under that Order.

Rule 2(1)(c) was added to Order 6 with effect from 2009 as part of the civil justice reforms. At the same time, the prescribed form of writ (Form No 1 in Appendix A) was amended so as to add the indorsement required by this provision.

In addition to the indorsement required by rule 2(1)(c), the form for making admission is required to be served together with the originating process: Order 13A rule 13.

3.　　**Indorsement as to capacity** (O. 6 r. 3)
　　**Before a writ is issued it must be indorsed—**
　　　　**(a)　　where the plaintiff sues in a representative capacity, with a statement of the capacity in which he sues;**
　　　　**(b)　　where a defendant is sued in a representative capacity, with a statement of the capacity in which he is sued.**

**NOTES**

**[6.3.1]　　Application of Order 6 rule 3**
Order 6 rule 3 is expressed to apply to persons suing or being sued in representative capacities, which usually means trustees and personal representatives. It should, however, be read as also applying to representative proceedings in which one or some of a numerous group are named as representatives for the group pursuant to Order 15 rule 12.

In *Shing Hai-doing v Genuius Knitting Factory Ltd* [1978] HKLR 305, it was suggested that it is not sufficient simply to describe the person as a trustee (or other type of representative) in the heading of the writ, and that the rule requires a full statement of representative capacity to be indorsed on the back of the writ.

In proceedings against deceased persons, the estate may be named as defendant under Order 15 rule 6A pending the appointment of a personal representative.

Non-compliance with this rule should be curable by amendment, notwithstanding the judgment in *Shing Hai-doing v Genuius Knitting Factory Ltd* [1978] HKLR 305. There it was suggested that proceedings might be struck out for failure to comply with this rule, though in the circumstances of that case no such order was made. However, that reasoning was based on English authority pre-dating the present liberal rules on non-compliance and amendment (see Order 2 rule 1 and Order 20 rule 5(4)) which today could be invoked to prevent non-compliance with this rule from being fatal. Neither the *Shing Hai-doing* case nor the English authority it applied (*Bowler v John Mowlem & Co Ltd* [1954] 3 All ER 556) should be followed any longer insofar as they deal with the consequences of non-compliance with this rule.

5.      **Indorsement as to solicitor and address** (O. 6 r. 5)

    (1)     Before a writ is issued it must be indorsed—

        (a)     where the plaintiff sues by a solicitor, with the plaintiff's address and the solicitor's name or firm and a business address of his within the jurisdiction and also (if the solicitor is the agent of another) the name or firm and business address of his principal;

        (b)     where the plaintiff sues in person, with the address of his place of residence and, if his place of residence is not within the jurisdiction or if he has no place of residence, the address of a place within the jurisdiction at or to which documents for him may be delivered or sent.

    (2)     The address for service of a plaintiff shall be—

        (a)     where he sues by a solicitor, the business address to which may be added a numbered box at a document exchange of the solicitor indorsed on the writ;

        (b)     where he sues in person, the address within the jurisdiction indorsed on the writ.

    (3)     Where a solicitor's name is indorsed on a writ, he must, if any defendant who has been served with or who has acknowledged service of the writ requests him in writing so to do, declare in writing whether the writ was issued by him or with his authority or privity.

    (4)     If a solicitor whose name is indorsed on a writ declares in writing that the writ was not issued by him or with his authority or privity, the Court may on the application of any defendant who has been served with or who has acknowledged service of the writ, stay all proceedings in the action begun by the writ.

6.      **Concurrent writ** (O. 6 r. 6)

    (1)     One or more concurrent writs may, at the request of the plaintiff, be issued at the time when the original writ is issued or at any time thereafter before the original writ ceases to be valid.

    (2)     Without prejudice to the generality of paragraph (1), a writ for service within the jurisdiction may be issued as a concurrent writ with one which is to be served out of the jurisdiction and a writ which is to be served out of the jurisdiction may be issued as a concurrent writ with one for service within the jurisdiction.

    (3)     A concurrent writ is a true copy of the original writ with such differences only (if any) as are necessary having regard to the purpose for which the writ is issued.

---

## NOTES

### [6.6.1]    Power to issue concurrent writs

Order 6 rule 6 gives the court power to issue concurrent writs at the request of the plaintiff. The power is stated to be exercisable any time before the original writ ceases to be valid: r 6(1). However, in *Yau Ngai & Ors v Yau Tak & Ors* HCA 1309/ 2007 (Deputy Judge L Chan; 09.01.2009) the court dismissed an argument that a concurrent writ had been issued invalidly because the original writ had already expired, saying that if necessary it would have no hesitation in renewing the original writ.

Concurrent writs are sometimes issued under rule 6(2) after leave has been obtained to issue out of the jurisdiction. See the commentary under Order 6 rule 7.

**7.     Issue of writ** (O. 6 r. 7)

**(1)     No writ which is to be served out of the jurisdiction shall be issued without the leave of the Court:**

**Provided that if every claim made by a writ is one which by virtue of any written law the Court of First Instance has power to hear and determine notwithstanding that the person against whom the claim is made is not within the jurisdiction of the Court or that the wrongful act, neglect or default giving rise to the claim did not take place within its jurisdiction, the foregoing provision shall not apply to the writ.**

**(3)     Issue of a writ takes place upon its being sealed by an officer of the Registry.**

**(4)     The officer by whom a concurrent writ is sealed must mark it as a concurrent writ with an official stamp.**

**(5)     No writ shall be sealed unless at the time of the tender thereof for sealing the person tendering it leaves at the office at which it is tendered a copy thereof signed, where the plaintiff sues in person, by him or, where he does not so sue, by or on behalf of his solicitor.**

---

**NOTES**

**[6.7.1]     Comparison with English rule**
The English equivalent of Order 6 rule 7(1) (prior to the Woolf reforms) contained the additional words 'for such service' after the word 'issued'.

**[6.7.2]     Concurrent writ for service out of the jurisdiction**
On its face Order 6 rule 7(1) prohibits the issue of a writ to be served out of the jurisdiction without leave. In practice the registry will, when the address stated on the writ for a defendant is outside Hong Kong, allow the writ to be issued and endorse it with a statement that it is not for service out of the jurisdiction. It is then up to the plaintiff to apply under Order 11 rule 1 for leave to serve the writ on that defendant out of the jurisdiction. If such leave is granted the registry will issue a 'concurrent writ' which may be served on the defendant outside Hong Kong. This practice was upheld in *Hui Suet Ying v Sharp Corp* HCPI 1269/1997 (Suffiad J; 15.02.2000), rejecting an argument that leave must be obtained under this rule before issue of the original writ, as opposed to the concurrent writ.

A concurrent writ must be marked as such by official stamp: rule 7(4). See also rule 6, which deals with concurrent writs generally.

**8.      Duration and renewal of writ** (O. 6 r. 8)

**(1)      For the purpose of service, a writ (other than a concurrent writ) is valid in the first instance for twelve months beginning with the date of its issue and a concurrent writ is valid in the first instance for the period of validity of the original writ which is unexpired at the date of issue of the concurrent writ.**

**(2)      Where a writ has not been served on a defendant, the Court may by order extend the validity of the writ from time to time for such period, not exceeding twelve months at any one time, beginning with the day next following that on which it would otherwise expire, as may be specified in the order, if an application for extension is made to the Court before that day or such later day (if any) as the Court may allow.**

**(3)      Before a writ, the validity of which has been extended under this rule, is served, it must be marked with an official stamp showing the period for which the validity of the writ has been so extended.**

**(4)      Where the validity of a writ is extended by order made under this rule, the order shall operate in relation to any other writ (whether original or concurrent) issued in the same action which has not been served so as to extend the validity of that other writ until the expiration of the period specified in the order.**

---

**[6.8.1]      Writ valid for service for 12 months**

Order 6 rule 8(1) provides that a writ is valid for service for 12 months from issue. In the case of a concurrent writ the 12-month period runs from issue of the original writ. If not served within time, there is the possibility of extension of validity, as to which see below.

A plaintiff is entitled to withhold service of a writ, and it is not an abuse of process to do so. A defendant who is unhappy with such a situation may give notice under Order 12 rule 8A requiring the plaintiff to serve the writ or discontinue the action. See *Lau William John v Wan Yuk Lin Alison & Ors* HCA 1255/2006 (Recorder P Fung SC; 22.06.2007).

*Dixon v Grand Hyatt HK Co Ltd* [1994] 2 HKC 489 (citing *Leal v Dunlop Bio Processes Int'l Ltd* [1984] 1 WLR 874 (CA)) suggests that the court has power to validate purported service of an expired writ by extension of time under Order 3 rule 5 and use of the court's power under Order 2 rule 1 to overlook irregularity. See also *Bank of China (HK) Ltd v Chen Jianren* HCA 2844/2001 (Deputy Judge Carlson; 18.12.2007). Insofar as *Bernstein v Jackson* [1982] 2 All ER 806 (CA) may suggest otherwise, it is clear from *Leal* (above) that it should not be followed.

**[6.8.2]      Comparison with English rule**

Whereas in Hong Kong the validity of a writ for service remains at 12 months, the period was shortened in England in 1990 to four months for most cases. Under CPR 7.5 the period remains four months in most cases in England.

**[6.8.3]      Extension of validity of writ**

Order 6 rule 8(2) gives the court power to extend the validity of a writ for the purpose of service. In exercising the power the court adopts a two-stage process. First it considers whether there is 'good reason' for extension. If so, a discretion arises and the court may go on to consider factors such as the balance of hardship. See *Netherby v Personal Representative of Hinings* HCA 2418/1993 (Findlay J; 14.11.1995), *Chow Ching Man v Sun Wah Ornament Manufactory Ltd* [1996] 2 HKC 460, 463F-H (CA) and *Grand Pacific Equity Ltd v RSH Sports (HK) Ltd* [2006] 4 HKLRD 617 (CA), all referring to *Kleinwort Benson Ltd v Barbrak Ltd* [1987] AC 597 and *Waddon v White Scovell Ltd* [1988] 1 WLR 309 (HL).

'Good reason' may be found where the defendant is evading service or cannot be traced (*Can-Asia Capital Co Ltd v Kwok Yee William* [1989] 2 HKC 355), or where the plaintiff has been unsuccessful in effecting service 'despite reasonable efforts': Grand Pacific (above). The desire to withhold service with a view to saving costs may be good reason for extension: *Miruvor Ltd v Panama-Globe Steamer Lines SA* [2006] 2 HKC 617 (para 27) (appeal allowed on other grounds – [2007] 1 HKLRD 804), for example where the defendant requests or agrees that service be withheld while investigations or negotiations are underway: *Re Chittenden* [1970] 1 WLR 1618, 1625–1626; *Kun Kay Hong v Tan Teo Huat* [1985] 1 MLJ 404. In such cases the court may require a clear agreement between the parties to withhold service, as in *Kwok Chung Fai Andy v Citybus Ltd* HCPI 739/1999 (Deputy Judge Woolley; 18.10.2001). Good reason in this context does not arise where there has been a deliberate decision not to serve: *Chow Ching Man* (above); or where solicitors are at fault: *Lee Fai v Chan Kui* [1997] 3 HKC 228 (CA).

*Application to be made ex parte by affidavit* – An application to extend the validity of a writ must be made ex parte since at that stage there is no defendant before the court *Lee Fa*i (above). The application may be made by affidavit which will usually be considered by a master without attendance of the parties: see the commentary under Order 32 rule 1. The affidavit should set out the evidence in support of the application. In *Netherby* (above) an application made by letter without supporting evidence was rejected.

*Further extensions* – The rule provides that no single extension may be for longer than 12 months, but further extensions are clearly contemplated.

*Extension after expiration* – The power to extend validity of a writ may be exercised even after the writ has expired, though the court may require 'exceptional circumstances' in such cases: *Heaven v Road & Rail Wagons Ltd* [1965] 2 QB 355, 365. In *Hong Kong Housing Authority v Hsin Yieh Architects & Associates Ltd* HCCT 39/2001 (*Reyes J*; 04.04.2006) a retrospective extension of time was granted to validate service which had been effected after expiry. The court held that the defendant suffered no prejudice, and observed that 'pedantic' points were being taken. In *Chappell v Cooper* [1980] 1 WLR 958, 966C-D (CA) it was held that once a writ has been expired for 12 months the court has no power under the rules to grant an extension. This results from the fact rule 8(2) provides for a maximum 12 months extension to begin from the date of expiry. However in *Bank of China (HK) Ltd v Chen Jianren* HCA 2844/2001 (Deputy Judge Carlson; 18.12.2007) the court used Order 2 rule 1 and Order 3 rule 5 to extend validity of a writ which had expired five years earlier and to deem good service to have been effected.

*Order dispensing with service where extension no longer possible* – In *Bank of China (HK) Ltd v All World Int'l Ltd & Ors* [2008] 6 HKC 348 the court made an order dispensing with service where no extension of validity was possible because the writ had expired more than 12 months previously. On appeal [2009] 3 HKC 411 that order was set aside on the ground the defendant was not in Hong Kong at the relevant time and there had been no order for *ex juris* service. However the Court of Appeal did not doubt the existence of the inherent jurisdiction to dispense with service in a proper case even when the validity of the writ can no longer be extended.

*Extension where limitation period has expired* – Where the limitation period has expired the applicant for renewal faces an added difficulty as the court will be very reluctant to deprive the defendant of a limitation defence. See *Siy Ramon v BPI International Finance Ltd* [1987] 3 HKC 317, 323H–I & 326C–F. In *Kleinwort Benson* (above) it was said (at 615) that only where both the validity of the writ and the limitation period have expired can it be said that the defendant has an accrued right of limitation.

*Setting aside extension of validity of writ* – An order extending the validity of a writ may be set aside under Order 12 rule 8(1)(d). Such an application does not constitute submission to the jurisdiction of the court whereas if the defendant takes any other step in the proceedings any jurisdictional defect may be taken to have been waived: *Lee Fai v Chan Kui* [1997] 3 HKC 228 (CA).

*Appeal* – Extension of validity of a writ being a matter of discretion, the Court of Appeal will not interfere unless the judge below erred in law or in fact: *Waan Chuen Ming v Lo Kin Nam* CACV 101/2005 (Rogers VP & Le Pichon JA; 18.01.2006). Different considerations apply on an appeal from a master to a single judge of the Court of First Instance, where the discretion may be exercised afresh – see the commentary under Order 58. On such an appeal the single judge may take into account matters which occur after the order on the application for an extension: see the determination of the Court of Final Appeal (FAMV 22/2007; 08.06.2007) refusing leave to appeal *Grand Pacific* (above).

**[6.8.4]    Service of extended writ**

A writ which has been extended must be marked with an official stamp showing the period of the extension: Order 6 rule 8(3). Service without such a stamp will be irregular and may be set aside: *Hongkong & Shanghai Banking Corporation v Bittker & Ors* HCCL 83/1985 (Sears J; 24.03.1988). However, in *Hui Suet Ying v Sharp Corp & Ors* HCPI 1269/1997 (Suffiad J; 15.02.2000) the court was prepared to overlook such an irregularity. In that case a writ was stamped showing that it had been extended, but the period of the extension was not stated. As this was an omission of the registry, the court was of the view that it would be 'quite wrong to penalise the plaintiffs' and declined to find that valid service had not been extended, but the period of the extension was not stated. As this was an omission of the registry, the court was of the view that it would be 'quite wrong to penalise the plaintiffs' and declined to find that valid service had not been effected.

## ORDER 7

### ORIGINATING SUMMONS: GENERAL PROVISIONS

**1.    Application** (O. 7 r. 1)
**The provisions of this Order apply to all originating summonses subject, in the case of originating summonses of any particular class, to any special provisions relating to originating summonses of that class made by these rules or by or under any written law.**

---

**NOTES**

**[7.1.1]    Originating summons procedure – cross references**
Order 7 makes provision for the commencement of proceedings by way of originating summons. As to when it is appropriate to proceed by way of originating summons rather than writ, see Order 5 rules 3 and 4.

See Order 28 for originating summons procedure following commencement of proceedings.

**2.    Form of summons, etc.** (O. 7 r. 2)
**(1)    Every originating summons (other than an ex parte summons) shall be in Form No. 8 or, if so authorized or required, in Form No. 10 in Appendix A, and every ex parte originating summons shall be in Form No. 11 in Appendix A.**
**(1A) Form No. 8 in Appendix A is to be used in all cases except where another form is prescribed under a written law or there is no party on whom the summons is to be served. (L.N. 152 of 2008)**
**(1B) Form No. 10 in Appendix A is to be used if it is prescribed under a written law. (L.N. 152 of 2008)**
**(1C) Form No. 11 in Appendix A is to be used if there is no party on whom the summons is to be served. (L.N. 152 of 2008)**
**(2)    The party taking out an originating summons (other than an ex parte summons) shall be described as a plaintiff, and the other parties shall be described as defendants.**
**(3)    This rule is subject to Order 53, rule 5(1) and Order 54, rule 2(3). (L.N. 152 of 2008)**

---

**NOTES**

**[7.2.1]    Types of originating summons**
Order 7 rule 2 provides for three different types of originating summons, the prescribed forms for which are set out in appendix A to these rules. The forms are:

- Form No 8 – the 'general' or 'long' form of originating summons;
- Form No 10 – the 'expedited' or 'short' form; and
- Form No 11 – the form of *ex parte* originating summons.

Note that there is also the originating summons 'for possession' in form No 11A, which is required to be used in summary proceedings for possession of land under Order 113 rule 2. Note also that applications for judicial review and habeas corpus have their own specific types of originating summons: this rule is specifically subject to Order 53, rule 5(1) and Order 54, rule 2(3) which prescribe the use of forms 86 and 87 for those types of application respectively.

The general form of originating summons must be used save where use of one of the other forms is mandated. Prior to the civil justice reforms implemented in 2009 the question of which type of originating summons to use was governed by practice direction 5.8. The effect of rule 2(1A), (1B) and (1C) is to give a legislative basis to the information set out in that practice direction. As to when one of the forms other than the general form should be used, see the discussion in the ensuing paragraphs.

We now turn to look at when it is appropriate to use the expedited and *ex parte* forms of originating summons.

### [7.2.2]   Use of the expedited form of originating summons

As its name suggests, the expedited form of originating summons will normally result in a speedier hearing. In this regard see Order 28 rule 2.

Order 7 rule 2(1) provides that the expedited form of originating summons may only be used where 'authorized or required'. This means authorised or required by these rules, not by the circumstances of the particular case: *Hong Kong Ping Jeng Lau Co Ltd v Incorporated Owners of United Centre* HCMP 2971/1989 (Godfrey J; 04.12.1989). It was there held that it was improper to use the expedited form in an ordinary case. To do so would defeat the provisions of these rules setting out a timetable. As a consequence the defendant would be 'deprived of the time provided by the rule for the filing of evidence'. The position is made crystal clear with rule 2(1B), added in 2009, stating that the expedited form is only to be used where 'prescribed' by written law.

Examples of provisions prescribing use of the expedited form of originating summons include the following:

*   Order 24 rule 7A – application for discovery before action under section 41 of the High Court Ordinance.
*   Order 73 rule 3(3) – application for leave to appeal against arbitration award.
*   Order 102 rule 3(2) – application for rectification of register of members of a company.
*   Order 118 rule 3 – application under section 84(3) of Cap 1 in relation to search and seizure of journalistic material.

In *A Co v B Co* [2002] 2 HKC 497, 500E, it was suggested that the expedited form should have been used on an application for *Norwich Pharmacal* discovery; however it is not clear from the judgment why this should be so.

It is not appropriate to use the expedited form in issuing a vendor and purchaser summons under section 12 of the Conveyancing and Property Ordinance (Cap 219): *Talent Hope Ltd v Magnificent Estates Ltd* [1995] 3 HKC 593. If the application is urgent, for example where a completion date is forthcoming, the applicant should use the general form and seek an expedited hearing: *Hingold Investments Ltd v Kadesy Development Ltd* HCMP 1311/1995 (Rogers J; 07.06.1995).

Improper use of the expedited form will not necessarily be fatal to the proceedings.

In *Hong Kong Ping Jeng Lau Co Ltd* (above) the court, citing Order 2 rule 2(1), held it had 'power to do what is just to cure the matter'. See also *Hiew Fook Loi v Yau Wai Yin & Anor* HCMP 272/2002 (Deputy Judge A Cheung; 22.11.2002) where the court took the same view, citing Order 2 rule 1. In *Talent Hope Ltd v Magnificent Estates Ltd* [1995] 3 HKC 593 the court allowed a party who had wrongly commenced proceedings by way of the expedited form to amend it into the general form.

**[7.2.3]    Use of ex parte originating summons**

It is only rarely appropriate to make an ex parte originating application to the court. Paragraph 1 of Practice Direction 5.8 (which may be viewed on the judiciary website) provides that the *ex parte* originating summons should only be used where authorised or required by the Rules or other statutory provision. Examples of such provisions include the following:

- Applications under the Evidence Ordinance for the taking of evidence in aid of a foreign court (Order 70 rule 2) or for letters of request to a foreign court (*AG v L* [1990] 1 HKLR 195, 197H–I) (notwithstanding the Bill of Rights: *AG v Osman* HCMP 2793/1985 (Jones J; 28.10.91)).
- Order 90 rule 3(2) under which the court may grant leave to issue an ex parte originating summons in wardship cases where there is no person other than the child who is a suitable defendant.
- Order 115A rule 4 – application for registration of an external confiscation order under the Mutual Legal Assistance in Criminal Matters Ordinance (Cap 525).
- Order 117 rule 4 – application for restraint order or charging order under the Organized and Serious Crimes Ordinance (Cap 455).
- Order 118 rule 4 – application for a warrant for search and seizure of journalistic material under the Interpretation and General Clauses Ordinance (Cap 1).

It has been held that use of the *ex parte* procedure may also be authorised or required by implication. See *Re Cheung Chi Wang & Anor* [2002] 1 HKC 326, 334I–335F where it was held that the procedure may be used in seeking relief under section 12A of the Conveyancing and Property Ordinance (Cap 219) (in relation to stale mortgages). See also *Director of Social Welfare v Official Solicitor* HCMP 44/2004 (Lam J; 05.03.2004) where the same judge came to the same conclusion in relation to an application for appointment of a committee under the Mental Health Ordinance (Cap 136). There are examples of applications for vesting orders under section 45(e) of the Trustee Ordinance (Cap 29) (deceased trustee with no personal representative) being made by *ex parte* summons. See *Re Trustee Ordinance* HCMP 2133/1987 (Godfrey J; 02.11.1987) and *Re Trustee Ordinance section 45(e)* HCMP 4522/2000 (Kwan J; 16.11.2000).

It has been held that it is not appropriate to proceed by way of *ex parte* originating summons in the following cases:

- Application for declaration as to title to property: *Re Kwong Sin Tong* HCMP 2797/1993 (Godfrey J; 03.08.1993)
- Application for exemption from jury service: *Re Jury Ordinance* HCMP 3270/1994 (Yam J; 25.11.1994).
- Application for order that dissolution of a company be declared void: *Axa*

*China Region Insurance Co Ltd v Maratz (HK) Ltd & Ors* HCMP 2166/2001 (Yuen J; 04.05.2001).

**[7.2.4]      Parties and headings**

Order 7 rule 2(2) provides that the parties to an inter partes originating summons shall be described as plaintiff and defendant, just as in a writ. The parties will be named accordingly in the heading to the originating summons.

It is common practice also to state in the heading that the application is brought 'in the matter of' a particular statute, parcel of land, contract or deed. This practice is catered for by the forms of originating summons in Appendix A. Lengthy descriptions of the matter in which an originating summons is brought were criticised in *Wong Shui Yun Bernadette v Lau Wai Pui* [1987] 3 HKC 513, 514H–I as a waste of time and money. In *Re Trustee Ordinance* HCMP 2133/1987 (Godfrey J; 02.11.1987) it was said:

> It is quite unnecessary to follow the archaic practice of referring to the subject matter of the proceedings by the use of unnecessary verbiage. A short description of the property affected is quite sufficient.

Where the application is *ex parte*, a short description of the matter or property affected is sufficient: *Re Trustee Ordinance* HCMP 2133/1987 (Godfrey J; 02.11.1987). Parties should not be named because there are no parties to ex parte proceedings: *AG v L* [1990] 1 HKLR 195, 197H–I; *Sham Wan Keung, deceased & Anor v Leung Suet Fan, deceased* CACV 56/1994 (Nazareth & Bokhary JJA; Barnett J; 29.06.1994).

**[7.2.5]      Originating summons procedure**

See Order 28 and the commentary thereunder.

**3.      Contents of summons** (O. 7 r. 3)

**(1)   Every originating summons must include a statement of the questions on which the plaintiff seeks the determination or direction of the Court of First Instance or, as the case may be, a concise statement of the relief or remedy claimed in the proceedings begun by the originating summons with sufficient particulars to identify the cause or causes of action in respect of which the plaintiff claims that relief or remedy.**

**(2)    Order 6, rules 3 and 5, shall apply in relation to an originating summons as they apply in relation to a writ.**

**4.      Concurrent summons** (O. 7 r. 4)

**Order 6, rule 6, shall apply in relation to an originating summons as it applies in relation to a writ.**

**5.      Issue of summons** (O. 7 r. 5)

**(1)    An originating summons shall be issued out of the Registry.**

**(3)    Order 6, rule 7 (except paragraph (2)), shall apply in relation to an originating summons as it applies in relation to a writ.**

**6.      Duration and renewal of summons** (O. 7 r. 6)

**Order 6, rule 8, shall apply in relation to an originating summons as it**

applies in relation to a writ.

**7.     Ex parte originating summonses** (O. 7 r. 7)

(1)     Rules 2(1) and (1C), 3(1), and 5(1) shall, so far as applicable, apply to ex parte originating summonses; but, save as aforesaid, the foregoing rules of this Order shall not apply to ex parte originating summonses. (L.N. 152 of 2008)

(2)     Order 6, rule 7(3) and (5), shall, with the necessary modifications, apply in relation to an ex parte originating summons as they apply in relation to a writ.

**(Enacted 1988)**

## ORDER 8

### ORIGINATING AND OTHER MOTIONS: GENERAL PROVISIONS

1.      **Application** (O. 8 r. 1)
**The provisions of this Order apply to all motions required or authorized under a written law, subject to any provisions relating to any class of motion made by that written law or any other written law. (L.N. 152 of 2008)**

---

### NOTES

#### [8.1.1]    Limited use of motions
Order 8 rule 1 applies the provisions of the Order to motions required or authorised under a written law. The rule was amended with effect from 2009 along with the amendment to Order 5 rule 1 making it clear that proceedings under these rules are normally to be commenced by writ or originating summons. Appeals to the Court of Appeal continue to be brought by motion: Order 59 rule 3(1).

See the commentary under Order 5 rule 1.

2.      **Notice of motion** (O. 8 r. 2)
**(1)    Except where an application by motion may properly be made ex parte, no motion shall be made without previous notice to the parties affected thereby, but the Court, if satisfied that the delay caused by proceeding in the ordinary way would or might entail irreparable or serious mischief, may make an order ex parte on such terms as to costs or otherwise, and subject to such undertaking, if any, as it thinks just; and any party affected by such order may apply to the Court to set it aside.**

**(2)    Unless the Court gives leave to the contrary, there must be at least 2 clear days between the service of notice of a motion and the day named in the notice for hearing the motion.**

---

### NOTES

#### [8.2.1]    Ex parte motion
Order 8 rule 2 provides that an application by motion shall not normally be made ex parte. The court has inherent jurisdiction to set aside an order made on a motion without prior notice to affected parties: *Commissioner of Inland Revenue v Registrar of Companies* [1998] 1 HKLRD 875, 877D.

3.      **Form and issue of notice of motion** (O. 8 r. 3)
**(1)    The notice of an originating motion must be in Form No. 13 in Appendix A and the notice of any other motion in Form No. 38 in that Appendix.**

**Where leave has been given under rule 2(2) to serve short notice of motion, that fact must be stated in the notice.**

(2)    The notice of a motion must include a concise statement of the nature of the claim made or the relief or remedy required.

(3)    Order 6, rule 5, shall, with the necessary modifications, apply in relation to notice of an originating motion as it applies in relation to a writ.

(4)    The notice of an originating motion by which proceedings are begun must be issued out of the Registry.

(6)    Issue of the notice of an originating motion takes place upon its being sealed by an officer of the Registry.

4.    **Service of notice of motion with writ, etc.** (O. 8 r. 4)
Notice of a motion to be made in an action may be served by the plaintiff on the defendant with the writ of summons or originating summons or at any time after service of such writ or summons, whether or not the defendant has acknowledged service in the action.

5.    **Adjournment of hearing** (O. 8, r. 5)
The hearing of any motion may be adjourned from time to time on such terms, if any, as the Court thinks fit.
(**Enacted 1988**)

6.    **Transitional provision relating to originating and other motions** (O. 8 r. 6)
Where, immediately before the commencement of the Amendment Rules 2008, an application, request or appeal by motion or originating motion made under a provision amended by Part 5 of the Amendment Rules 2008 is pending, then the application, request or appeal is to be determined as if that provision had not been so amended.
(**L.N. 152 of 2008**)

---

**NOTES**

**[8.6.1]    Additional transitional provision for motions pending at time of 2009 reforms**
Order 8 rule 6 is a transitional provision for motions and originating motions pending when the civil justice reforms were implemented in 2009. It preserves the pre-existing rules for such motions. This transitional provision is in addition to that in Order 5 rule 7 which applies to proceedings which were commenced by originating motion prior to the implementation of the civil justice reforms in 2009.

# ORDER 9

## PETITIONS: GENERAL PROVISIONS

1.      **Application** (O. 9 r.1)
        **The provisions of this Order apply to all petitions required or authorized under a written law, subject to any provisions relating to any class of petition made by that written law or any other written law. (L.N. 152 of 2008)**

---

NOTES

**[9.1.1]     Restricted use of petitions**
Order 9 rule 1 applies the provisions of the Order to petitions required or authorised under a written law. The rule was amended to that effect in 2009 along with the amendment to Order 5 rule 1 limiting the use of forms of originating process other than the writ or originating summons to proceedings governed by special rules. See the commentary under Order 5 rule 1.

2.      **Contents of petition** (O. 9 r. 2)
        **(1)    Every petition must include a concise statement of the nature of the claim made or the relief or remedy required in the proceedings begun thereby.**
        **(2)    Every petition must include at the end thereof a statement of the names of the persons, if any, required to be served therewith or, if no person is required to be served, a statement to that effect.**
        **(3)    Order 6, rule 5, shall, with the necessary modifications, apply in relation to a petition as it applies in relation to a writ.**

3.      **Presentation of petition** (O. 9 r. 3)
        **A petition may be presented by leaving it at the Registry.**

4.      **Fixing time for hearing petition** (O. 9 r. 4)
        **(1)    A day and time for the hearing of a petition which is required to be heard shall be fixed by the Registrar.**
        **(2)    Unless the Court otherwise directs, a petition which is required to be served on any person must be served on him not less than seven days before the day fixed for the hearing of the petition.**

5.      **Certain applications not to be made by petition** (O. 9 r. 5)
        **No application in any cause or matter may be made by petition.**

6.      **Right to defend in person** (O. 9 r. 6)
        **(1)    Subject to paragraph (2) and to Order 80, rule 2, a respondent to proceedings begun by petition may (whether or not he is sued as a trustee or personal representative or in any other representative capacity) defend the proceedings by a solicitor or in person.**

  (2) Where the respondent to such proceedings is a body corporate, except as expressly provided by or under any enactment or where leave is given under paragraph (3) for such respondent to be represented by one of its directors, such respondent may not take any step in the proceedings otherwise than by a solicitor.

  (3) (a) An application by a body corporate for leave to be represented by one of its directors shall be made ex parte to a Registrar and supported by an affidavit, made by the director and filed with the application, stating and verifying the reasons why leave should be given for the body corporate to be represented by the director.

    (b) The relevant resolution of the board of the body corporate authorizing the director to appear on its behalf if leave is granted shall be exhibited to the affidavit.

  (4) No appeal shall lie from an order of the Registrar under paragraph (3) giving or refusing leave.

  (5) The Court may at any time revoke the leave given by a Registrar under paragraph (3).

  (6) No appeal shall lie from an order of the Court revoking leave given by a Registrar.

  **(Enacted 1988) (L.N. 108 of 2002)**

## ORDER 10

### SERVICE OF ORIGINATING PROCESS: GENERAL PROVISIONS

1.      General provisions (O. 10 r. 1)

(1)    A writ must be served personally on each defendant by the plaintiff or his agent.

(2)    A writ for service on a defendant within the jurisdiction may, instead of being served personally on him, be served—

(a)    by sending a copy of the writ by registered post to the defendant at his usual or last known address, or

(b)    if there is a letter box for that address, by inserting through the letter box a copy of the writ enclosed in a sealed envelope addressed to the defendant.

(L.N. 404 of 1991)

(3)    Where a writ is served in accordance with paragraph (2)—

(a)    the date of service shall, unless the contrary is shown, be deemed to be the seventh day (ignoring Order 3, rule 2(5)) after the date on which the copy was sent to, or as the case may be, inserted through the letter box for, the address in question;

(b)    any affidavit proving due service of the writ must contain a statement to the effect that—

(i)    in the opinion of the deponent (or, if the deponent is the plaintiff's solicitor or an employee of that solicitor, in the opinion of the plaintiff) the copy of the writ, if sent to, or as the case may be, inserted through the letter box for, the address in question, will have come to the knowledge of the defendant within 7 days thereafter; and

(ii)    in the case of service by post, the copy of the writ has not been returned to the plaintiff through the post undelivered to the addressee.

(4)    Where a defendant's solicitor indorses on the writ a statement that he accepts service of the writ on behalf of that defendant, the writ shall be deemed to have been duly served on that defendant and to have been so served on the date on which the indorsement was made.

(5)    Subject to Order 12, rule 7, where a writ is not duly served on a defendant but he acknowledges service of it, the writ shall be deemed, unless the contrary is shown, to have been duly served on him and to have been so served on the date on which he acknowledges service.

(6)    Every copy of a writ for service on a defendant shall be sealed with the seal of the High Court and shall be accompanied by a form of acknowledgment of service in Form No. 14 in Appendix A in which the title of the action and its number have been entered.

(7)    This rule shall have effect subject to the provisions of any Ordinance and these rules and in particular to any enactment which provides for the manner in which documents may be served on bodies corporate.

## NOTES

### [10.1.1]   Comparison with English rules
Order 10 rule 1 is based on the equivalent of the same number in the former English RSC. An important difference in Hong Kong is that the rule stipulates that service by post is to be effected by registered post. According to commentary in the English Supreme Court Practice 1999, registered post was deliberately eschewed because the defendant would have an opportunity to refuse to accept the letter. In England the equivalent provision is now CPR 6.2.

### [10.1.2]   Application of Rule 1
Application to other types of originating process – Note that although this rule speaks only of the 'writ', its provisions also apply, subject to any necessary modifications, to most originating summonses and to notices of originating motion and petitions (see Order 10 rule 5).

### [10.1.3]   Application to companies
Service of limited companies is provided for elsewhere. The better view seems to be that Order 10 rule 1 also applies. See the commentary under Order 65 rule 3.

### [10.1.4]   Rule 1(1) - Personal service requirement
Although the wording of this sub-rule is mandatory, there are in fact alternatives to personal service. The following sub-rule, introduced in 1979, permits service by post or delivery (see below).

As to the manner in which personal service should effected, see Order 65 rule 2 and the commentary thereunder.

### [10.1.5]   Rule 1(2) - Defendant must be within the jurisdiction
Rule 1(2) permits service by post or insertion in a letter box of a 'writ for service on a defendant within the jurisdiction'. These words have been interpreted as meaning that service will not be valid unless the defendant is within the jurisdiction on the date of service: see *Desirable International Fashions Ltd (in liq) v Chiang Shi Chau* [1997] 3 HKC 170, 174B–C per Waung J citing *Barclays Bank of Swaziland Ltd v Hahn* [1989] 2 All ER 398, [1989] 1 WLR 506. See also *Honest Billion Investment Ltd v Wang Xian Chou* [1997] 3 HKC 161, *Wing Lung Bank Ltd v Ho Man Iam* [1999] 3 HKC 368, *Chu Kam Lun v Yap Lisa Susanto* [1999] 3 HKC 378 (CA); *Victor Chandler (Int'l) Ltd v Zhou Chu Jian He* [2006] 3 HKC 90 and *Cosec Nominees Ltd & Anor v Lau Hon Ming Alan* [2001] 3 HKC 290, 296A-–B. Default judgment will be set aside as of right if it is obtained following service which is irregular in that the defendant is not within the jurisdiction at the time: *Shanghai Land Holdings Ltd (in receivership) v Chau Ching Ngai & Anor* [2004] 3 HKC 573, 577–79. This is the case even if the defendant had actual notice of the writ despite absence from Hong Kong: *Deng Minghui v Chau Shuk Ling Elaine* [2007] 2 HKC 414 (CA), holding that *Penrose Industries Ltd v Tam Yan Lung* HCA 5783/2000 (Yeung J; 10.05.2001) is incorrect in this regard.

In *Yongheng Nevada Int'l Co Ltd v Chan Mau Tak* [2000] 2 HKC 584 and again in *Haifa Int'l Finance Co Ltd v Concord Strategic Investments Ltd & Ors* HCA 2308/

2006 (Deputy Judge Carlson; 16.07.2009) the defendant was not in Hong Kong on the actual date of service, but was present on the deemed date of service (as to which see the commentary a few paragraphs hence). In both cases it was argued that service was good. In *Yongheng* the court decided the matter before it on other grounds, and in *Haifa* the court rejected the argument, saying (para 9) that the position is well-settled, and that there was 'no warrant' to interpret the rule in any way other than that once it is shown that the defendant was not in Hong Kong on the date when the writ was inserted into the letter-box of his address, service will be held to have been invalid.

As a result, proof of the actual date of service can be important, especially in a place like Hong Kong where travel outside the jurisdiction is so frequent. See the commentary below on rule 1(3) and the provision therein as to deemed date of service. Likewise proof of when a defendant was or was not present in Hong Kong can be crucial. This can be established definitively by obtaining a statement of travel records from the Immigration Department.

**[10.1.6] Rule 1(2)(a) and (b) – service by post or insertion in letter box**
Service by post under Order 10 rule 1(2)(a) is 'a permissible variant to personal service. It is not a second class variant, but an effective variant, given proper compliance with the rules': *Honour Finance Co Ltd v Chui Mei-mei* [1989] 2 HKLR 146, 150G–H (CA). The same comment should apply to service by insertion into the defendant's letter box under rule 1(2)(b).

*Service by post* – Postal service of a document is deemed to be effected by 'properly addressing, pre-paying the postage thereon and dispatching it': see section 8 of the Interpretation and General Clauses Ordinance (Cap 1).

*The 'registered post' requirement* – In 1991 Order 10 rule 1(2)(a) was amended so as to require postal service to be effected by means of registered post. This differs from the equivalent rule in the former English RSC, and the current CPR 6.2, which provide for service by 'first class post'. Service by ordinary, as opposed to registered, post, in Hong Kong is defective and any judgment obtained is liable to be set aside as irregular: *Electronic Spider Technology Ltd & Anor v Au Cheong Tat & Ors* DCCJ 17323/2000 (Judge A Cheung; 20.07.2001).

*'Usual or last known address'* – Order 10 rule 1(2) provides that a document for service by post or insertion in a letter box should be directed to the defendant's 'usual or last known address'. The following points can be stated as to the meaning of those words:

- 'Usual' address means a place where a person may usually be reached, and although there is a habitual or frequent connotation, a person may have a number of usual addresses: *Hong Kong Mortgage Corp Ltd v Chung Kit Yu & Anor* HCMP 2226/2002 (Deputy Judge To; 15.04.2003) (para 13). In *Varsani v Relfo Ltd* [2010] EWCA Civ 560 (27.05.2010) it was held that service at an address in England occupied by a defendant's family members was valid as service at the defendant's 'usual' residence even though he was working abroad for most of each year.
- The word 'or' must be read disjunctively: *Hong Kong Mortgage Corp* (above) (para 10).
- 'Last known' address is intended to be an alternative to 'usual' address in case the plaintiff is unaware of a recent change of address: *Guangdong Int'l*

Trust & Investment Corp HK (Holdings) Ltd v Yuet Wah (HK) Wah Fat Ltd [1997] 2 HKC 696, 701F.

• 'Last known' address refers to the address last known to the plaintiff: *Guangdong Int'l Trust* (above) (citing *Austin Rover Group Ltd v Crouch Butler Savage Associates* [1986] 3 All ER 50); *Hong Kong Mortgage Corp Ltd* (above) (para 12). It does not matter that with further inquiry a different address might have been discovered by the plaintiff: *Law Kwok Hung v Tse Ping Man* [1999] 4 HKC 397, 403H–I, citing *National Westminster Bank v Betchworth Investments Ltd* (1975) 234 EG 675. The last known address may be known to the plaintiff from a source other than the defendant: *Phillip Securities (HK) Ltd v Lam Chi Bin Stanley* [2002] 1 HKC 432, 436G–H.

• 'Address' is not confined to a person's residence but extends to place of work and other places where the person can be found such as student hostel and work quarters: *Hong Kong Mortgage Corp Ltd* (above) (para 11).

*Consequence of non-receipt* – The wording of Order 10 rule 1(2) and of section 8 of the Interpretation and General Clauses Ordinance (Cap 1) suggests that service is effective upon dispatch of the postal packet, or insertion into the letter box in compliance with the rules. As a result the Court of Appeal held in *Honour Finance Co Ltd v Chui Mei-mei* [1989] 2 HKLR 146, 150D–G that such service is effective even if the document does not come to the notice of the defendant. The Court of Appeal expressly doubted the earlier decision in *AG v Geoffrey Watson* [1989] 1 HKLR 386. The decision in the *Honour Finance* case has since effectively been over-ruled insofar as it concerns the circumstances in which default judgments will be set aside (see the commentary under Order 13 rule 9). It has also been doubted on the question of what constitutes effective service by post or insertion: see *Cosec Nominees Ltd v Lau Hon Ming Alan* [2001] 3 HKC 290, 296C–F. There Deputy Judge Jeremy Poon, citing a number of other decisions, stated that on a true construction of Order 10 rule 1(2) service is effected when the proceedings are brought to the notice of the defendant and not merely by delivery of the writ to his last known address. See also *Phillip Securities (HK) Ltd v Lam Chi Bin Stanley* [2002] 1 HKC 432, citing the robust judgment of *Sir Thomas Bingham MR in Forward v West Sussex County Council* [1995] 1 WLR 1469. There the English Court of Appeal found that the requirement in rule 1(3)(b) for an affidavit of service stating the deponent's opinion that the particular mode of service will bring the writ to the attention of the defendant supports the view that service takes place when notice is actually received. With great respect the Editor of this work is of the view that the English Court of Appeal's decision is not applicable in this jurisdiction. In Hong Kong section 8 of the Interpretation and General Clauses Ordinance (Cap 1) expressly deems service to be effected upon dispatch by post. Being enacted in Ordinance, that section takes precedence over anything in these rules (see s 28(1)(b) of Cap 1). The practical difference between the two approaches arises on an application to set aside default judgment, as to which see the commentary under Order 13 rule 9.

*Acceptance of postal packet by agent* – It has been held that service by post is effective when the postal packet is received by an agent for the defendant: see *Hecny Transportation (Thailand) Ltd v Tam Suet Fong Amedeo* [1999] 1 HKC 833.

## [10.1.7]   Rule 1(3)(a) – deemed date of service

In order to facilitate the calculation of the time within which the defendant must acknowledge service, Order 10 rule 1(3)(a) deems service to have been effected on the seventh day after posting or insertion into the defendant's letter box, unless the contrary is shown. See also section 8 of the Interpretation and General Clauses Ordinance (Cap 1) which provides that service is deemed to be effected on the day the postal packet would reach the defendant 'in the ordinary course of post'.

To the extent that the two deeming provisions are in conflict, the provisions of the Ordinance should be treated as prevailing: under general principles and indeed section 28(1)(b) of Cap 1 an Ordinance prevails over subsidiary legislation such as these rules.

It is a question of fact when a postal packet will be delivered 'in the ordinary course of post': see *Treasure Land Property Consultants (a firm) v United Smart Development Ltd* [1995] 3 HKC 30; [1995] 2 HKLR 176 (CA). There it was held that the judge below had been wrong to take judicial notice of what he believed to be the 'ordinary course of post'. With effect from 2nd October 2003 Practice Direction 19.2 seeks to inject some certainty into the question of when a postal packet is delivered 'in the ordinary course of post', but it does not apply to service of originating process. See the commentary under Order 65 rule 5.

*'Unless the contrary is shown'* – Both provisions deeming date of service are subject to the proviso 'unless the contrary is shown'. It is thus open to a party to seek to prove that the actual date of service was different from the deemed date. Subject to proof, the actual date of service is the date on which the defendant receives notice of the proceedings, not the date of insertion or postal delivery: see *Phillip Securities (HK) Ltd v Lam Chi Bin Stanley* [2002] 1 HKC 432, 437F–438I applying *Forward v West Sussex County Council* [1995] 1 WLR 1469. In *Honest Billion Investment Ltd v Wang Xian Chou* [1997] 3 HKC 161 immigration records were used to prove the presence of the defendant in Hong Kong and the court held that service had been effected on the actual date of insertion into his letter box.

## [10.1.8]   Service on defendant both personally and by post

Where a defendant is served personally, and also by post, the time within which he may give notice of intention to defend runs from the earlier date: see *Tindixs Services Ltd v Cheng Wing Chun* [1998] 4 HKC 194.

## [10.1.9]   Rule 1(3)(b)– Affidavit of service

*By whom affidavit of service to be made* – Where service is by registered post, the appropriate person to make the affidavit of service is the person who caused the writ to be dispatched by post, not the postman who delivers it. This is because the service is effected by dispatching the document by post.

Where, however, service is under rule 1(2)(b), by delivery by a messenger or courier, then, it is submitted, the affidavit should be made by the person actually inserting the envelope containing the writ into the letter box. This is because it is the act of insertion rather than the act of sending the messenger on his way which constitutes service.

*Content of affidavit of service* – Rule 1(3)(b)(i) requires that the affidavit of service must state that in the opinion of the deponent service at the particular address will result in the writ coming to the knowledge of the defendant within seven days. In *Law Kwok Hung v Tse Ping Man & Anor* [1999] 4 HKC 397 Yuen J considered this requirement. She held that the opinion must be 'reasonably held'. If the opinion of the deponent is impeached, or if there were no reasonable grounds for the belief, service may be set aside. In that case service had been effected at the address which the defendant had provided to his professional body. The learned judge held that there were reasonable grounds to believe service at that address would be effective and service was not irregular (at 404E–G). See also practice direction 24.1, para 8, which stipulates that an affidavit of service in support of an application for judgment in default of notice of intention to defend a monetary claim should depose to the fact that the relevant form under Order 13A for making an admission has been served with the writ.

*Cross-examination of process server* – In *Kwan Kam Wah v Chan Wai Ming* [2000] 2 HKC 378 the defendant, on an application to set aside default judgment, sought leave to cross-examine the process server on his affirmation of service. The court has power to order any person making an affidavit or affirmation to be cross-examined thereon: see Order 38 rule 2. In the particular case the application was resolved in favour of the defendant without the need to cross-examine the process server. Deputy Judge Carlye Chu went on to observe, at 382F–H:–

> I accept that in appropriate cases, a defendant is entitled to impeach the good faith of the opinion stated by a plaintiff in an affirmation of service. I also accept that if a defendant does take this course, the court has to find whether the plaintiff has reasonable ground for holding the opinion so asserted in the affirmation of service and, if not, the service will be irregular. However, that does not confer upon the defendant a right to cross-examine ... [i]t is still incumbent upon the defendant to provide a proper foundation for the exercise of the court's discretion.

Deputy Judge Chu held that there was no proper basis to cross-examine the process server because he had no actual knowledge as to the whereabouts of the defendant, and instead relied solely on what he had been informed by the plaintiff. See also:

- *Bank of Credit & Commerce HK Ltd v Mirchandani* HCA 3150/1997 (Master Jones; 04.05.1998) where a process server was cross-examined by way of trial of a preliminary issue.
- *Leung Chi Kwan v Chan Chi Ko* HCMP 4150/1997 (Yuen J; 29.12.1998) where a process server was cross-examined in a mortgage action.
- *Wei Bingqing v Xie Diangrong* HCA 2654/2003 (Chung J; 01.04.2006) where the court declined to order cross-examination on the plaintiff's affidavit of service, but nevertheless found that it lacked credibility.
- *Nelson Telecommunications Group (Asia) Ltd v United Land Network Technologies Ltd* DCCJ 5962/2005 (Judge Lok; 24.11.2008) where a default judgment was set aside on the basis of evidence that it would have been impossible for the process server to have served the writ in the manner set out in the affidavit of service. It appears the process server was not cross-examined in this case.

*Cross-examination of defendant who disputes service* – See the commentary under Order 13 rule 9.

### [10.1.10]  Rule 1(4) – acceptance of service by solicitor
It is common practice for service to be accepted' by solicitors on behalf of a defendant. This can save time and costs. The practice is based on Order 10 rule 1(4).

It has been held that where solicitors accept service under this provision on behalf of a defendant who is outside Hong Kong, the validity of the service per se may not later be challenged, though it is open to the defendant to dispute the court's jurisdiction under Order 12 rule 8. See *New Link Consultants Ltd v Air China* [2005] 2 HKC 260, 274B.

### [10.1.11] Rule 1(5) – deemed service

A defendant who has not been served but wishes to defend may give notice under Order 12 rule 8A or may simply acknowledge service. In the latter case due service is deemed by Order 10 rule 1(5) on the date of acknowledgement of service unless the contrary is shown. In *Wong Kim Fung & Anor v Wong Kwing Tung* HCPI 454/1997 (Godfrey JA; 06.08.1999) the defendant, despite having acknowledged service, succeeded in having the action dismissed on the ground the writ had not in fact been served, but merely sent to insurers for information.

### [10.1.12] Failure to comply with requirements as to service

Where it is contended that service has not been validly effected, a defendant may acknowledge service and apply under Order 12 rule 8(1)(b) for a declaration to that effect. The acknowledgement of service is deemed, by Order 12 rule 7, not to be a waiver of any irregularity in service.

Applications for a declaration that service has not been validly effected are not looked at favourably by the court where the alleged defect in service is purely technical. If the writ has actually come to the attention of the defendant, and no prejudice has been caused, the court may consider treating the defect as a mere irregularity under Order 2 rule 1. See the following cases as examples:

- *Transamerica Occidental Life Insurance Co v King Sound Industry Co Ltd & Anor* [2005] 1 HKLRD 125, 133D-G.
- *Bank of China (HK) Ltd v Chen Jianren* HCA 2844/2001 (Deputy Judge Carlson; 18.12.2007) (para 23)
- *Hongkong & Shanghai Banking Corp Ltd v Ong Tong Sing Lawrence & Ors* [2008] 3 HKC 421.

2. **Service of writ on agent of overseas principal** (O. 10 r. 2)
    (1) **Where the Court is satisfied on an ex parte application that—**
        (a) **a contract has been entered into within the jurisdiction with or through an agent who is either an individual residing or carrying on business within the jurisdiction or a body corporate having a registered office or a place of business within the jurisdiction, and**
        (b) **the principal for whom the agent was acting was at the time the contract was entered into and is at the time of the application neither such an individual nor such a body corporate, and**
        (c) **at the time of the application either the agent's authority has not been determined or he is still in business relations with his principal,**
**the Court may authorize service of a writ beginning an action relating to the**

contract to be effected on the agent instead of the principal.

(2)   An order under this rule authorizing service of a writ on a defendant's agent must limit a time within which the defendant must acknowledge service.

(3)   Where an order is made under this rule authorizing service of a writ on a defendant's agent, a copy of the order and of the writ must be sent by post to the defendant at his address out of the jurisdiction.

## NOTES

**[10.2.1]   Service on agent**
See the commentary under Order 65 rule 3.

3.   **Service of writ in pursuance of contract** (O. 10 r. 3)
   **(1)   Where—**
       **(a)**   a contract contains a term to the effect that the Court of First Instance shall have jurisdiction to hear and determine any action in respect of a contract or, apart from any such term, the Court of First Instance has jurisdiction to hear and determine any such action, and
       **(b)**   the contract provides that, in the event of any action in respect of the contract being begun, the process by which it is begun may be served on the defendant, or on such other person on his behalf as may be specified in the contract, in such manner, or at such place (whether within or out of the jurisdiction), as may be so specified, then, if an action in respect of the contract is begun in the Court and the writ by which it is begun is served in accordance with the contract, the writ shall, subject to paragraph (2), be deemed to have been duly served on the defendant.

(2)   A writ which is served out of the jurisdiction in accordance with a contract shall not be deemed to have been duly served on the defendant by virtue of paragraph (1) unless leave to serve the writ out of the jurisdiction has been granted under Order 11, rule 1(1) or service of the writ is permitted without leave under Order 11, rule 1(2).

## NOTES

**[10.3.1]   Contractual provisions as to place and mode of service**
It is common practice for commercial contracts to specify the place and manner in which service of court process may be effected in the event of a dispute arising. The legal basis for such clauses is Order 10 rule 3, by which a writ is deemed to have been duly served on the defendant if such an agreed term is followed. In *Hong Kong Mortgage Corp Ltd v Ching Kit Yu & Anor* HCMP 2226/2002 (Deputy Judge To; 15.04.2003) it was argued that such a term may not prevail over the provisions of Order 10 rule 1 as to service. The argument was rejected because 'Order 10 rule 3

specifically permits such service' (para 19).

It is necessary that the action be one over which the court has jurisdiction, whether by agreement or otherwise: rule 3(1)(a). Such a clause may provide for service at a place outside Hong Kong, but in that event it is necessary to obtain leave under Order 11 rule 1 if it is a case where such leave is required: rule 3(2).

For service to be effective under Order 10 rule 3, the term of the agreement must be strictly complied with. In the HK Mortgage Corp case (above) it was held that valid service had not been effected because although the originating summons was sent to the agreed address, the agreed mode of service had not been followed. The originating summons had been inserted into the letter box at that address, rather than by being left or sent by prepaid post as provided in the agreement.

**4. Service of writ in certain actions for possession of premises or land**
(O. 10 r. 4)
**(1) Where a writ is indorsed with a claim for the recovery, or delivery of possession, of premises or land, the Court may—**

(a) if satisfied on an ex parte application that no person appears to be in possession of the premises or land and that service cannot be otherwise effected on any defendant, authorize service on that defendant to be effected by affixing a copy of the writ to some conspicuous part of the premises or land;

(b) if satisfied on such an application that no person appears to be in possession of the premises or land and that service could not otherwise have been effected on any defendant, order that service already effected by affixing a copy of the writ to some conspicuous part of the premises or land shall be treated as good service on that defendant.

**(HK)(2) Where a writ is indorsed with a claim for the recovery, or delivery of possession, of premises or land, in addition to, and not in substitution for any other mode of service, a copy of the writ shall be posted in a conspicuous place on or at the entrance to the premises or land recovery or possession of which is claimed.**

---

## NOTES

**[10.4.1] Service of originating summons for possession of land**
Separate provision is made in Order 113 rule 4 for service of originating summonses seeking possession of land.

**5. Service of originating summons, notice of motion, or petition** (O. 10 r. 5)
**(1) The foregoing rules of this Order shall apply, with any necessary modifications, in relation to an originating summons (other than ex parte originating summons or an originating summons under Order 113) as they apply in relation to a writ, except that an acknowledgement of service of an originating summons shall be in Form No. 15 or 15A in Appendix A, whichever is appropriate. (L.N. 152 of 2008)**

**(2) Rule 1(1), (2), (3) and (4) shall apply, with any necessary modifications, in relation to a notice of an originating motion and a petition as they apply in relation to a writ.**

**(Enacted 1988)**

---

## NOTES

### [10.5.1]   Application of Order 10 to originating summonses, motions and petitions

Order 10 rule 5 has the effect of applying some of the provisions of the Order regarding service of writs to other types of originating process. Originating summonses which are *ex parte*, or invoke Order 113 (summary proceedings for possession of land) are outside the scope of the rule.

### [10.5.2]   Form of acknowledgement of service to be served with originating summons

The general form of acknowledgement of service is form No 14 in Appendix A, which must, according to Order 10 rule 1(6), accompany every writ. Order 10 rule 5(1) prescribes form No 15 as the appropriate form of acknowledgement of service in proceedings commenced by originating summons. The rule was amended with effect from 2009 as part of the civil justice reforms to prescribe, in addition, form 15A in Appendix A for use in 'costs only proceedings' under section 52B of the High Court Ordinance (as to which see Order 62 rule 11A and the commentary thereunder).

## ORDER 11

### SERVICE OF PROCESS, ETC., OUT OF THE JURISDICTION

1.     **Principal cases in which service of writ out of jurisdiction is permissible**
(O. 11 r. 1)

(1)     Provided that the writ is not a writ to which paragraph (2) of this rule applies, service of a writ out of the jurisdiction is permissible with the leave of the Court if in the action begun by the writ—
(L.N. 363 of 1990)

- (a)     relief is sought against a person domiciled or ordinarily resident within the jurisdiction;

- (b)     an injunction is sought ordering the defendant to do or refrain from doing anything within the jurisdiction (whether or not damages are also claimed in respect of a failure to do or the doing of that thing);

- (c     the claim is brought against a person duly served within or out of the jurisdiction and a person out of the jurisdiction is a necessary or proper party thereto;

- (d)     the claim is brought to enforce, rescind, dissolve, annul or otherwise affect a contract, or to recover damages or obtain other relief in respect of the breach of a contract, being (in either case) a contract which—
  - (i)     was made within the jurisdiction, or
  - (ii)     was made by or through an agent trading or residing within the jurisdiction on behalf of a principal trading or residing out of the jurisdiction, or
  - (iii)     is by its terms, or by implication, governed by Hong Kong law, or
  - (iv)     contains a term to the effect that the Court of First Instance shall have jurisdiction to hear and determine any action in respect of the contract;

- (e)     the claim is brought in respect of a breach committed within the jurisdiction of a contract made within or out of the jurisdiction, and irrespective of the fact, if such be the case, that the breach was preceded or accompanied by a breach committed out of the jurisdiction that rendered impossible the performance of so much of the contract as ought to have been performed within the jurisdiction;

- (f)     the claim is founded on a tort and the damage was sustained, or resulted from an act committed, within the jurisdiction;

- (g)     the whole subject matter of the action is land situate within the jurisdiction (with or without rents or profits) or the perpetuation of testimony relating to land so situate;

- (h)     the claim is brought to construe, rectify, set aside or enforce an act, deed, will, contract, obligation or liability affecting land situate within the jurisdiction;

- (i)     the claim is made for a debt secured on immovable property or is made to assert, declare or determine proprietary or possessory rights, or rights of security, in or over movable property, or to obtain authority to dispose of movable property, situate within the jurisdiction;

(j)　　the claim is brought to execute the trusts of a written instrument being trusts that ought to be executed according to Hong Kong law and of which the person to be served with the writ is a trustee, or for any relief or remedy which might be obtained in any such action;

(k)　　the claim is made for the administration of the estate of a person who died domiciled within the jurisdiction or for any relief or remedy which might be obtained in any such action;

(l)　　the claim is brought in a probate action within the meaning of Order 76;

(m)　　the claim is brought to enforce any judgment or arbitral award;

(n)　　the claim is brought under the Carriage by Air Ordinance (Cap. 500); (13 of 1997 s. 20)

(o)　　(Repealed by L.N. 296 of 1996)

(oa)　　the claim is made under the Mutual Legal Assistance in Criminal Matters Ordinance (Cap. 525); (87 of 1997 ss. 1(2) & 36)

(ob)　　the claim is for an order for the costs of and incidental to a dispute under section 52B(2) of the Ordinance; (L.N. 152 of 2008)

(oc)　　the claim is for interim relief or appointment of a receiver under section 21M(1) of the Ordinance; (L.N. 152 of 2008)

(od)　　the claim is for a costs order under section 52A(2) of the Ordinance against a person who is not a party to the relevant proceedings; (L.N. 152 of 2008)

(p)　　the claim is brought for money had and received or for an account or other relief against the defendant as constructive trustee, and the defendant's alleged liability arises out of acts committed, whether by him or otherwise, within the jurisdiction.

(L.N. 404 of 1991)

(2)　Service of a writ out of the jurisdiction is permissible without the leave of the Court provided that each claim made by the writ is—

(b)　　a claim which by virtue of any written law the Court of First Instance has power to hear and determine notwithstanding that the person against whom the claim is made is not within the jurisdiction of the Court or that the wrongful act, neglect or default giving rise to the claim did not take place within its jurisdiction.

(3)　Where a writ is to be served out of the jurisdiction under paragraph (2), the time to be inserted in the writ within which the defendant served therewith must acknowledge service shall—

    (c)    **be limited in accordance with the practice adopted under rule 4(4).**

**(HK) (4)  This rule shall not apply to a writ—**

    (a)    **to enforce a claim for damage, loss of life or personal injury arising out of—**

        (i)    **a collision between ships;**

        (ii)    **the carrying out of or omission to carry out a manoeuvre in the case of one or more of 2 or more ships; or**

        (iii)    **non-compliance, on the part of one or more of 2 or more ships, with the regulations made under section 93, 100 or 107 of the Merchant Shipping (Safety) Ordinance (Cap. 369);**

    (b)    **for the limitation of liability in a limitation action as defined in Order 75, rule 1(2); or**

    (c)    **to enforce a claim under section 1 of the Merchant Shipping (Oil Pollution) Act 1971 (1971 c. 59 U.K.) or section 4 of the Merchant Shipping Act 1974 (1974 c. 43 U.K.). (L.N. 363 of 1990)**

---

## NOTES

### [11.1.1]  Territorial basis of court's jurisdiction

The jurisdiction of the High Court of the Hong Kong Special Administrative Region has a territorial basis in that it is usually confined to claims against defendants who are properly served with process within the territorial boundaries of Hong Kong. This is a principle of common law, which finds expression in decisions such as *Ex p Blain; Re Sawers* (1879) 12 Ch D 522 and *Colt Industries Inc v Sarlie* [1966] 1 All ER 673; [1966] 1 WLR 440.

### [11.1.2]  Extra-territoriality

Order 11 rule 1 provides for service of process on persons outside Hong Kong. Although the rule refers only to service of writs, it extends to originating summonses and other forms of process by virtue of Order 11 rule 9.

    By permitting service outside Hong Kong this rule has an extra-territorial effect. In the common law system the legislature and the courts are reluctant to interfere in matters which are primarily the concern of other jurisdictions. Thus the scheme of Order 11 is to limit the circumstances in which Hong Kong process may be served in other jurisdictions to cases where the claim has a substantial connection with the SAR. Likewise the courts view the jurisdiction conferred by this rule as exceptional (*The Siskina* [1979] AC 210, 254) and have described it as an 'exorbitant' jurisdiction not to be lightly exercised: *Tay Choo Wah v Singapore-Johore Express (Pte) Ltd* [1991] 2 HKC 180, 196 (CA).

    During the colonial era there were theoretical limitations on the legislature's competence to make laws having extra-territorial effect. See Wesley-Smith 'Extraterritoriality and Hong Kong' [1980] Public Law 150. Analogy with other jurisdictions having limited constitutional power suggests that the vires of Order 11 could be challenged on this basis. See *Cotter v Workman* (1972) 20 FLR 318 in relation to the Australian Capital Territory. On the other hand *Ashbury v Ellis* [1893] AC 339 (PC from NZ) suggests

Order 11 is supportable. In the unlikely event a court could be persuaded that Order 11 was beyond the power of Hong Kong's colonial legislature (and hence its delegate, the rules committee, which enacted these rules in 1988) it should follow that the Order did not become part of the law of the HKSAR on reunification: *Solicitor v Law Society of HK & Secretary for Justice* (2003) 6 HKCFAR 570.

### [11.1.3]   Leave requirement

Except as provided in rule 1(2) (see below), a plaintiff who wishes to serve a writ on a defendant outside Hong Kong must first obtain leave of the court under rule 1(1). As to the procedure for such application, see below.

To secure a grant of leave, the plaintiff must demonstrate on his application for leave, that his claim comes within one of the heads listed in rule 1(1). In addition, it must be made 'sufficiently to appear' to the court that the case is a 'proper one' for service out of the jurisdiction (Order 11 rule 4(2)). As stated by Barnes J in *Deak Perera Far East Ltd (in liquidation) v R Leslie Deak et al* [1988] 2 HKLR 95, at 100C:

> Under O 11 the Court is faced with two issues: a 'jurisdictional issue' as to whether the applicant's claim falls within any of the 'permissible' categories mentioned in r 1(1), and the 'discretion issue' raised by r 4(2).

The second issue as set out by Barnes J will necessarily include an examination of the merits of the plaintiff's claim.

Furthermore, it must be noted that the terms of Order 11 do not spell out the entirety of the court's jurisdiction to refuse leave (*Johnson v Taylor Brothers & Co Ltd* [1920] AC 144, at 154, per Lord Dunedin). Even where the case falls within the terms of Order 11 rule 1, leave may be refused on the ground of lis alibi pendens or forum non conveniens, and other factors which may be relevant to a grant or refusal of the order to stay or set aside the leave to serve out (*Kuwait Asia Bank EC v National Mutual Life Nominees Ltd* [1991] 1 AC 187, at 212, per Lord Lowry). These considerations do not affect the existence of jurisdiction, but entitle the court to decline to exercise that jurisdiction. They are considered under rule 4(2) or, more often, will be raised after ex parte leave has been granted, and the defendant applies pursuant to Order 12 rule 8 to have that leave set aside.

### [11.1.4]   The principles on which leave to serve out of the jurisdiction may be granted

The principles which guide the court on an application under Order 11 for leave, or under Order 12 rule 8 to set aside such leave, were set out as follows by Hunter JA in *Wo Fung Paper Making Factory Ltd v Sappi Kraft (Pty) Ltd* [1988] HKC 10, 22-3; [1988] 2 HKLR 346, 356B-357H:

> I think it convenient at the outset to attempt to summarise what I see as the main relevant principles governing applications of this nature under Orders 11 and 12. I have drawn them principally, but not exclusively, from three decisions in the House of Lords; *The Brabo* [1949] AC 326; *Vitkovice Horni v Korner* [1951] AC 869, and *Spiliada Maritime Corp v Cansulex Ltd* [1987] AC 460. They can be summarised in this way:
>
> (1)   This is what has been called an exorbitant jurisdiction. The Court's basic jurisdiction is territorial. It is therefore a strong thing for the Court to go outside its territory and to compel the foreigner to come here to defend himself. It must therefore be exercised

with great caution: see *Spiliada* [1987] AC 460 at p 481.

(2)    There are two safeguards for the foreigner. First the applicant has to bring himself within one of the subparagraphs in Order 11 rule 1. Secondly the applicant has to satisfy Order 11 rule 4(2) and 'make [it] sufficiently to appear to the court that the case is a proper one for service out'. That as Lord Radcliffe pointed out in *Vitkovice* [1951] AC 869 is really the heart of the rule.

(3)    In contract, the question whether a case is a proper one for service out falls to be answered by the tests in *Spiliada* [1987] AC 460. There are two ways, it seems to me, of expressing substantially the same concept. The first is Lord Keith's formulation of 'natural forum' in the *The Abidin Daver* [1984] AC 398 at p 415 where he defines the natural forum as being 'that with which the action has the most real and substantial connection'. The second is what Lord Goff called the basic principle and in his paraphrase of Lord Kinnear's test in *Sim v Robinow* (1892) 19 R 665. It is expressed by Lord Goff in these words at p 476: 'the appropriate forum for the trial of the action ie in which the case may be tried more suitably for the interests of all the parties and the ends of justice.' The onus of establishing that falls upon the plaintiff applicant.

(4)    The phrase 'sufficiently to appear' in Order 11 rule 4(2) is a guarded one, and is carefully chosen, I think, to cover the two very different positions of the court, on an application like this, in relation to the law and the facts. As far as the law is concerned, if the facts are clear the court can readily decide that for itself. That conclusion may be decisive, directly or indirectly: see *The Brabo* [1949] AC 326. Equally, and this is one of the court's primary functions under this rule, it can decide whether the facts alleged are sufficient in law to support the cause of the action alleged. But on pure fact, and particularly upon disputed fact, it is in a very different position. It cannot make any finding for the simple reason that it cannot conduct a mini pre-trial in order to decide whether a proper trial is to take place. It therefore has basically to act upon asserted fact.

(5)    There are two stages to the enquiry. The first is the *ex parte* stage under Order 11. I emphasise that it is *ex parte* on documents. The practice does not envisage oral submissions ever being made except at specific request. Order 11 rule 4(1) specifies what the supporting affidavit has to show. At that stage it seems to me that the court has to come to a provisional view (it being an *ex parte* application) on three matters. The first is whether the applicant shows a *prima facie* case. I read the speeches in *Vitkovice* [1951] AC 869 as accepting that that is the burden of that stage, it may be for the simple reason that when the court has only got one party's version before it, it can do very little more. That is how I read the speeches of Lord Simonds at p 876, Lord Radcliffe at p 884, Lord Tucker at p 891. Secondly it has to consider the sufficiency in law of the facts alleged: for example whether the applicant brings himself within any of the sub-rules and whether the facts alleged are sufficient *prima facie* to establish the cause of action alleged. Thirdly the court has to consider the facts within the limited scope available. This really comes down to considering whether the facts are sufficiently asserted in an apparently credible manner. The manner was put in this way in a case in contract by Lord Buckmaster giving the opinion of the *Privy Council in Hemelryck v William Lyall Shipbuilding* [1921] 1 AC 698 at p 701. He said:

> 'For the purpose of exercising the discretion which is conferred by the rules to be exercised (that is Order 11) it is sufficient if there appears reasonable

evidence that a contract has been made.'

(6)     The second stage which may or may not be reached, follows a proper application under Order 12 rule 8. Then the court has to consider all the evidence before it, and to determine in the light of that whether the plaintiff shows a good arguable case. That is the test laid down in *Vitkovice* [1951] AC 869 at that stage. But the court's position on fact and law is the same as it was at the *ex parte* stage. It cannot make any findings of fact. It can certainly consider the legal sufficiency of the facts, and whether there are legal holes or obvious failings in the plaintiff's case. It can in the words of Lord Goddard CJ in *Malik v National Bank of Czechoslovakia* 176 LT 136 cited in *Vitkovice* [1951] AC 869 at p 888, 'if it can see by what appears on the affidavits that the case put up is a perfectly groundless one and one in which there is no substance at all, the court can refuse to give leave'. Similarly if the case is demurrable or nearly so. But that is about the limit of the court's power and function on disputed facts under this jurisdiction. It follows that the existence of disputed facts is normally quite irrelevant to the question as to whether or not a good arguable case has to be shown. Putting it in another way, the showing of a good arguable case does not postulate an Order 14 case, and is not negatived by the fact that good arguable defences may exist. The relevance of the dispute goes really to little more than the question of the suitability of the forum evidentially and it may be a factor to be brought in there. Otherwise normally speaking factual disputes are quite irrelevant.

Distilling the above comments down to their essence, and reading them together with the approach adopted by the court in other cases such as *Deak & Anor v Deak Perera FE Ltd* (in liq) [1991] 1 HKLR 551, 554C-I (CA) and *National Union Fire Insurance Co of Pittsburgh v Grand Union Insurance Co Ltd* CACV 105/1992 (*Kempster, Penlington & Litton JJA*; 24.03.1993) (para 10), it might be said that the following three elements are relevant:

(1)     whether there is a *prima facie* or good arguable case on the merits;
(2)     whether the facts come within one of the lettered heads of rule 1(1);
(3)     whether the case is a proper one under rule 4(2) for service out of the jurisdiction, that is the question of *forum conveniens*.

## [11.1.5]   The merits - standard of proof

A line of cases emanating from *The Brabo* (1949) 82 Lloyd LR 251; [1949] AC 326 and *Vitkovice Horni A Hutni Tezirstvo v Korner* [1951] AC 869 suggests that the plaintiff must show a 'good arguable case on the merits'. For a Hong Kong case, see *Komala Deccof & Co SA & Ors v Perusahaan Pertambangan Minyik Dan Gas Bumi Negara (Pertamina)* [1981] HKLR 116, especially at 118. In considering whether there is a 'good arguable case' the court does not exercise a discretion but makes a 'judgment of fact': *Continental Mark Ltd v Verkehrs-Club De Schweiz* [2001] 4 HKC 469, 481B (affirmed on appeal: see [2002] 2 HKC 513).

The English cases in this line of authority include *Metall und Rohstoff v Donaldson Lufkin & Jenrette Inc & Anor* [1990] 1 QB 391; *Attock Cement Co v Romanian Bank for Foreign Trade* [1989] 1 Lloyd's Rep 572; [1989] 1 WLR 1147; *Hutton (EF) (London) Ltd & Co v Mofarrij* [1989] 2 Lloyd's Rep 348; [1989] 1 WLR 488; *Société Commerciale de Reassurance v Eras International Ltd* [1992] 1 Lloyd's Rep 570; *Overseas Union Insurance Ltd v Incorporated General Insurance Ltd* [1992] 1 Lloyd's Rep 439; *Banque*

*Paribas v Cargill International SA* [1992] 2 Lloyd's Rep 19; and *Seaconsar Far East Ltd v Bank Markazi Jomhouri Islami Iran* [1993] 1 Lloyd's Rep 236; [1994] 1 AC 438 (HL).

In the lengthy extract from the judgment of Hunter JA in *Wo Fung Paper Making Factory Ltd v Sappi Kraft (Pty) Ltd* [1988] 2 HKLR 346, set out above, his Lordship interpreted the leading English cases as stipulating that on the *ex parte* application for leave the court need be satisfied that the plaintiff has shown a *prima facie* case, whereas in the event of a subsequent *inter partes* application under Order 12 rule 8 to set aside leave, the appropriate test was 'good arguable case'.

In *Tay Choo Wah v Singapore-Johore Express (Pte) Ltd* [1991] 2 HKC 180, at 196, Clough JA expressed the required standard of proof as follows:

> It is well settled that the exercise of the exorbitant jurisdiction of the Court under Order 11, rule 1 is not lightly to be exercised. However, the plaintiff is not required to discharge the standard of proof which must be attained at the trial or to prove the matter beyond all reasonable doubt, but he must show a good arguable case, something better than a prima facie case assessed by looking primarily at the plaintiff's case and not attempting to try the disputed facts on affidavit.

From time to time the requisite test is expressed differently. There is no particular magic in any particular formulation. In *National Union Fire Insurance Co of Pittsburgh v Grand Union Insurance Co Ltd* [1993] HKLD C78 the Court of Appeal expressed the test as a 'good chance of succeeding on the merits'. In *Seaconsar Far East Ltd v Bank Markazi Jomhouri Islami Iran* [1994] 1 AC 438 'serious question to be tried' was used. Referring to *Seaconsar, the Privy Council, in Hague & Anor v Nam Tai Electronics Inc* [2008] UKPC 13, [2008] 2 HKC 315 set aside leave in proceedings which it considered to be 'misconceived', disclosing 'no cause of action' against the defendants. In *Continental Mark Ltd v Verkehrs-Club de Schweiz* [2001] 4 HKC 469 (affirmed on appeal: see [2002] 2 HKC 513), 481G–H Deputy Judge McCoy said 'In essence the court must reach a provisional conclusion that the plaintiff is probably right', citing *Yee Sang Metal and Building Supplies Co Ltd v Taiyo Maritime SA* [1991] 2 HKC 291(CA).

It is not necessary for the plaintiff to show that he would succeed on an application for Order 14 summary judgment but the evidence he puts forward must be consistent and complete. See *Continental Mark Ltd v Verkehrs-Club de Schweiz* [2001] 4 HKC 469, 482A–B (affirmed on appeal: see [2002] 2 HKC 513), citing *Chetan v Jhaveri Shailain Hirachand* [1990] 2 HKC 170 (CA). In both those cases it was held that the plaintiff had failed to show a good arguable case when its evidence was inconsistent. In *Continental Mark Deputy Judge McCoy* said that while the court should not 'attempt to try disputes of fact on the affidavits' it is open to a defendant to try to demonstrate that the plaintiff's evidence is 'incomplete or plainly wrong or attendant with some sustained doubt.'

The merits of the potential defence are also relevant in assessing whether the jurisdictional ground has been made out and in exercising the court's discretion to grant leave: *Deak & Anor v Deak Perera Far East Ltd* (in liq) [1991] 1 HKLR 551, 555 (CA) ; *Overseas Union Insurance Ltd v Incorporated General Insurance Ltd* [1992] 1 Lloyd's Rep 439, 445–448. Failure to disclose a potential defence at the *ex parte* stage may result in leave being set aside: see the commentary under Order 11 rule 4 below.

**[11.1.6]** **The court's approach on an application for leave to serve out of Hong Kong**

In order to obtain leave to serve out of the jurisdiction, the plaintiff must demonstrate that the case comes within one or more of the lettered paragraphs under Order 11 rule 1(1). This often requires the court to make provisional findings of fact, a task it will approach strictly: *Société Commerciale de Reassurance v Eras Int'l Ltd* [1992] 1 Lloyd's Rep 570, 587 (CA).

If the court is satisfied that the case comes within one of the heads under Order 11 rule 1(1), it must then consider whether it is appropriate to exercise its discretion: see Order 11 rule 4(2) and the commentary thereunder.

**[11.1.7]** **Rule 1(1)(a) – relief is sought against a person domiciled or ordinarily resident within the jurisdiction**

Order 11 rule 1(1)(a) empowers the court to grant leave to serve a writ out of the jurisdiction where relief is sought against a person domiciled or ordinarily resident within Hong Kong. The alternative 'or ordinarily resident' was inserted into the Hong Kong rule when it was adapted from the English equivalent of the same number. Now see CPR 6.20(1) under which, in England, domicile remains the sole criterion.

As to when a natural person is 'ordinarily resident' in Hong Kong, see the authorities cited in the commentary under Order 23 rule 1. A body corporate is resident in the place where its central management and control is exercised, whether or not that be its place of incorporation: *Tait Marketing & Distribution Co Ltd v Tait Int'l Ltd* HCA 10308/2000 (Deputy Judge Longley; 11.05.2001). A body corporate may be resident in more than one jurisdiction if its management and control is divided: *Tait* (above); *Osman v Elders Finance Asia Ltd* [1992] 1 SLR 369, 374H–I (Sing CA).

**[11.1.8]** **Rule 1(1)(b) – injunction cases**

The court may grant leave to serve out where the writ claims an injunction to do or refrain from doing something in Hong Kong. This power exists only where the claim is for a final injunction: see *Mercedes Benz AG v Leiduck* [1995] 3 HKC 1, 15C–I (PC) where it was held that an application for a *Mareva* injunction, which is purely interlocutory in nature, was not within this paragraph. The effect of *Leiduck* has been reversed by the enactment of section 21M of the High Court Ordinance (in force in 2009) and there is now specific provision in Order 11 rule 1(1)(oc) permitting the court to grant leave for service out of the jurisdiction in such cases. See the commentary below concerning that provision, as well as Order 29 rule 8A and the commentary thereunder with regard to applications in Hong Kong for a *Mareva* injunction in aid of proceedings in another jurisdiction.

In *Securities and Futures Commission v C & Ors* [2009] 4 HKC 167 (CA) it was held that one of the defendants could not be served out of the jurisdiction under this provision because it had no assets or other connection with Hong Kong and was not involved in any act within the jurisdiction constituting the alleged wrongdoing. However, that defendant was a necessary and proper party to proceedings which had been duly served against other defendants, and thus leave to serve it out of Hong Kong could be granted under rule 1(1)(c).

**[11.1.9]  Rule 1(1)(c) - claim against a person out of the jurisdiction who is a necessary or proper party**

Where a writ has already been duly served on a defendant, the court may grant leave for service on a 'necessary or proper' party outside Hong Kong. The 'or' between 'necessary' and 'proper' is disjunctive, with the result that a party may be 'proper' without being 'necessary' to the proceedings: *Inchcape JDH Ltd v Baltrans Exhibition & Removal Ltd & Anor* [1997] 3 HKC 314, 322G.

A proper party for the purpose of this sub-paragraph is one 'who could have been properly joined in the action had that party been within the jurisdiction': *Deak Perera (FE) Ltd (in liq) v Deak & Ors* [1988] 2 HKLR 95, 98C–D; *Inchcape* (above), 321B–G. A defendant out of the jurisdiction may be a necessary or proper party even though the defendant who has been served within the jurisdiction has made a formal admission that it is the party who would be liable. See *Mahajan v HCL Technologies (HK) Ltd & Ors* HCA 954/2005 (Burrell J; 24.01.2008) where, despite such an admission, the court permitted service *ex juris* of two defendants who were said to be liable in the alternative to the locally served defendant (appeal to the Court of Appeal dismissed: CACV 46/2008).

The court may refuse leave if it appears that a defendant has been named and served solely with a view to establishing jurisdiction against another defendant: *Bhojwani v Bhojwani* [1997] 2 SLR 682, 687B. The court will not permit an existing defendant, against which there is no live issue, to become a 'jurisdictional Trojan horse': *Dallah Albaraka (Ireland) Ltd v Symphony Gems NV* [2005] 2 HKC 404, 411C–E.

The writ must already have been duly served on a defendant. If not, the application for leave to serve another defendant out of the jurisdiction is unsustainable: *Heliopolis Co Ltd v Euroscan Express (HK) Ltd* [1998] 1 HKC 323, 327E, *et seq*. The defendant who has already been served may have been served in or out of Hong Kong.

The affidavit in support of an application under this paragraph must state 'the ground for the deponent's belief that there is between the plaintiff and the person on whom a writ has been served a real issue which the plaintiff may reasonably ask the court to try': see rule 4(1)(d). This is an 'important jurisdictional requirement', but compliance does not require that the precise terms of rule 4(1)(d) be followed: *Tay Choo Wah v Singapore-Johore Express (Pte) Ltd* [1991] 2 HKC 180, 194A-D (CA). Rule 4(1)(d) does not require that there be a cause of action against the overseas party:  *HK Housing Authority v Hsin Yieh Architects & Associates Ltd* [2005] 2 HKC 201; [2006] 1 HKC 116 (CA).

Default judgment entered against the defendant within the jurisdiction may render the claim against the overseas party nugatory resulting in leave to serve out being set aside, if the claims are alternative: *Bonus Garment Co v Karl Rieker GMBH* [1997] 2 HKC 460 (PC), considering *Morel Bros & Co Ltd v Earl of Westmoreland* [1904] AC 11.

**[11.1.10]Rule 1(1)(d) - contracts closely connected with Hong Kong**

Leave may be granted for service out of the jurisdiction in cases seeking relief under contracts closely connected with Hong Kong. A contract will come within this paragraph if it was made in Hong Kong, made through an agent in Hong Kong; if it is governed by Hong Kong law or if the parties expressly agreed that the Hong Kong court shall have jurisdiction. The English equivalent is now CPR 6.20(5), which is in very similar terms.

The paragraph presupposes the existence of a contract; hence it does not apply where the plaintiff claims a declaration that there is no contractual relationship: *Finnish Marine Insurance Co Ltd v Protective National Insurance Co* [1990] 1 QB 1078. The situation is now different in England, as a result of CPR 6.20(7).

A claim brought on a bill of exchange accepted outside Hong Kong may nevertheless be the subject of leave under paragraph (d) if the underlying contract in respect of which payment was to be made was made in Hong Kong: *United Links Int'l Ltd v The Price Co* [1994] 2 HKC 617, 619F–H.

A contract made through an agent in Hong Kong must be a contract made by a foreign *defendant* through an agent in Hong Kong for the purpose of rule 1(1)(d)(ii), notwithstanding the literal wording of the rule. See *Transamerica Occidental Life Insurance Co v King Sound Industry Co Ltd & Anor* [2005] 1 HKLRD 125, referring to *Union Int'l Insurance Co Ltd v Jubilee Insurance Co Ltd* [1991] 1 All ER 740.

Where the only head of jurisdiction relied on is that the contract is governed by local law, there is a 'heavy burden' in the plaintiff to show that Hong Kong is the appropriate forum: *Novus Aviation Ltd v Onur Air Tasimacilik AS* [2009] EWCA Civ 122 (para 32). That consideration is relevant in deciding whether the case is a 'proper one' for service out of the jurisdiction in accordance with rule 4(2). One relevant factor will be the language of the contractual document. The court may come to the conclusion that it is in the interests of the parties and the ends of justice that the contract be interpreted in a forum whose native language is that of the contractual document: *The Magnum* [1989] 1 Lloyd's Rep 47, 51. However, the court should be wary of placing too much emphasis on this factor: Novus (above, loc cit).

As to when a contract may come within paragraph (d) by virtue of impliedly being governed by Hong Kong law, it has been held that the test is what the parties would have agreed if they had directed their minds to the question: *Century Yachts Ltd v Xiamen Celestial Yacht Ltd* [1994] 1 HKC 331, 339F-G (CA). See also *Continental Mark Ltd v Verkehrs-Club de Schweiz* [2001] 4 HKC 469, 482F (affirmed on appeal: [2002] 2 HKC 513) where the court looked for the system of law with which the transaction had the 'closest and most real connection'.

**[11.1.11]    Rule 1(1)(e) – contracts breached in Hong Kong**
The court may grant leave to serve a writ out of the jurisdiction where the claim is for breach, in Hong Kong, of a contract.

Failure to pay the price of goods or services is a breach in the place where the creditor is to be found, unless the contract stipulates another place for payment: *Robey & Co v The Snaefell Mining Co, Ltd* (1887) 20 QBD 152.

In *Century Yachts Ltd v Xiamen Celestial Yacht Ltd* [1994] 1 HKC 331, 340D–G (CA) it was held that a repudiatory breach, in the form of a letter faxed from the Mainland severing all business ties, took place on the Mainland.

**[11.1.12]    Rule 1(1)(f) - claims in tort**
Leave to serve out of the jurisdiction may be granted under this paragraph for claims in tort where the damage was sustained in Hong Kong, or resulted from an act committed in Hong Kong. The two limbs are independent; thus where damage has been sustained in Hong Kong it is not necessary to show any act committed in Hong Kong: *Hui Suet*

*Ying v Sharp Corp* HCPI 1269/1997 (Suffiad J; 15.02.2000). The rule was amended in 1984 (LN 148) to cater for cases of damage sustained in Hong Kong. Earlier authorities such as *English Sewing (HK) Ltd v Eastern Shipping Lines Inc* [1984] HKLR 5, 11J, to the effect that it is necessary to show a tort committed within the jurisdiction, should no longer be followed.

In considering whether damage has been sustained in Hong Kong 'it is sufficient if some significant damage had been sustained here': *Dynasty Line Ltd (provisional liquidators appointed) v Sukamto Sia & Anor* [2009] 4 HKC 184 (CA) (para 33), referring to *Metall und Rohstoff AG v Donaldson Lufkin & Jenrette Inc & Anor* [1990] 1 QB 391.

A plaintiff with a reputation in Hong Kong suffers damage in Hong Kong when libellous remarks are published here. As a result proceedings in Hong Kong are appropriate under this paragraph and it would not be right to require the plaintiff to seek vindication elsewhere: *Investasia Ltd v Kodansha Co Ltd* [1999] 3 HKC 515. Slander takes place at the location the words are uttered: *Buttes Gas & Oil Co v Hammer* [1971] 3 All ER 1025.

#### [11.1.13]   Rule 1(1)(g) - claims to land within the jurisdiction

Leave to serve out of the jurisdiction may be granted under rule 1(1)(g) where the 'whole subject-matter' of the action is land situate within the jurisdiction. In *Banca Carige SpA v Banco Nacional de Cuba* [2001] 3 All ER 923 (para 32) it was said that the authorities on the equivalent English provision established that 'an action only fell within the rule if the claim was confined to a claim to a proprietary or possessory interest in the land and that the rule did not extend to a claim for any other relief *eg* damages arising from a breach of contract or tort relating to the land'.

In England under the CPR the situation is now different. CPR 6.20(10) is not limited to land, but extends to all kinds of property, and the claim need not be confined to a proprietary or possessory interest. See *Banca Carige* (above) (paras 31–33). Hong Kong not having followed that amendment, the older authorities should be preferred.

Rule 1(1)(g) also applies to actions for perpetuation of testimony relating to land, as to which see Order 39 rule 15.

#### [11.1.14]   Rule 1(1)(h) - instrument or liability affecting land within the jurisdiction

Rule 1(1)(h) provides for service out of the jurisdiction in relation to claims under instruments or for obligations or liabilities 'affecting land' in Hong Kong.

In *Clare County Council v Wilson* [1913] 2 IR 89, 110-11 (CA) a similarly-worded rule was construed in Ireland. It was held that the instrument, obligation or liability must affect the land in the sense that there must be 'an obligation to do something physically to the land, as in the case of a covenant to repair, or an obligation which may be enforced against the land as in the case of a mortgage . . .' Thus the provision did not apply to a money claim for damages arising from injury to land – the liability was to pay money, and although it may have been connected with land it did not 'affect' land. A similar, strict, approach is evident in the Australian case of *BHP Petroleum Pty Ltd v Oil Basins Ltd* [1985] VR 725, 735-6, where it was held that litigation in relation to royalties for petroleum extracted within the jurisdiction was not within the provision.

In England such a strict approach is not always applied. See, for example, *Official*

*Solicitor v Stype Investment Ltd* [1983] 1 WLR 214. There it was held that a declaration of trust was clearly a deed or contract affecting land situate within the jurisdiction, even though the land had been sold and the dispute was over the cash proceeds.

### [11.1.15]   Rule 1(1)(i)
Broadly speaking Order 11 rule 1(1)(i) provides for service out of the jurisdiction in cases concerning security interests over movable or immovable property. It is clear that the movable property must be situate within the jurisdiction. It does not seem so clear whether the same is true with regard to immovable property. However, that should be the case because as a general rule disputes over land should be decided only in the jurisdiction where the land is located.

### [11.1.16]   Rule 1(1)(j) – trusts
Paragraph (j) deals inter alia with claims to enforce trusts governed by Hong Kong law.  See the Recognition of Trusts Ordinance (Cap 76) implementing the Hague Convention on Trusts and their Recognition 1986. The predecessor to this provision applied only to trusts located in Hong Kong. Now the requirement is simply that the trust ought to be 'executed' according to Hong Kong law. *Winter v Winter* [1894] 1 Ch 421 should no longer be followed.

### [11.1.17]   Rule 1(1)(k) – administration of estates
Actions concerning the administration of estates are governed by Order 85. Order 11 rule 1(1)(k) permits the court to grant leave to serve out of Hong Kong provided that the deceased died domiciled in the jurisdiction.

### [11.1.18]   Rule 1(1)(l)– probate action
Leave is required to commence a probate action: see Order 76 rule 2. Order 11 rule 1(1)(*l*) empowers the court to grant leave to serve out of the jurisdiction where such an action is brought against a defendant out of Hong Kong.

### [11.1.19]   Rule 1(1)(m) – action to enforce judgment or arbitral award
Rule 1(1)(m) empowers the court to grant leave to serve out of the jurisdiction where the claim is to enforce 'any' judgment or arbitral award. The use of the word 'any' clearly extends application of the paragraph to claims for enforcement of judgments of other jurisdictions.  See the commentary under Order 71.

In *Mercedes Benz AG v Leiduck* [1995] 3 HKC 1 (PC) it was held that an application for a *Mareva* injunction does not come within this paragraph since such an injunction does not enforce a judgment, but simply preserves the position until a judgment is given. The effect of that decision has been reversed by the enactment of section 21M of the High Court Ordinance (in force in 2009) which empowers the court to grant such an injunction in aid of proceedings in other jurisdictions, and Order 11 rule 1(1)(oc) which makes specific provision for the court to grant leave for service out of the jurisdiction in such cases. See Order 29 rule 8A and the commentary thereunder with regard to proceedings in Hong Kong for a *Mareva* injunction in aid of proceedings in another jurisdiction.

### [11.1.20]   Rule 1(1)(n) - Carriage by Air Ordinance
Order 11 rule 1(1)(n) empowers the court to grant leave to serve out of the jurisdiction

where a claim is made under the Carriage by Air Ordinance (Cap 500).

The Ordinance gives the force of law to several international agreements regulating liability of international air carriers. Among them is the Warsaw Convention, as amended, which is set out in Schedule 1 of the Ordinance. Article 28 of that convention provides that proceedings may be brought against an air carrier, at the option of the plaintiff, in (i) its place of ordinary residence (ii) its principal place of business (iii) the place at which it has 'an establishment by which the contract has been made', or (iv) at the place of destination.

The Warsaw convention, as amended, also provides for an optional waiver of sovereign immunity for carriage performed by a state or public body. Thus, service on a foreign state may be necessary, and in that event the procedure set out in Order 11 rule 7A should be followed. See the commentary under that rule.

### [11.1.21]　Rule 1(1)(oa) - claims under the Mutual Legal Assistance in Criminal Matters Ordinance

Claims under the Mutual Legal Assistance in Criminal Matters Ordinance (Cap 525) come within this paragraph. See generally Order 115A.

### [11.1.22]　Rule 1(1)(ob) - costs only proceedings

Rule 1(1)(ob) concerns claims under section 52B of the High Court Ordinance for costs only. That section, which was enacted by the Civil Justice (Miscellaneous Amendments) Ordinance 2008 (in force 2009), provides for proceedings in the Court of First Instance claiming an order for costs (and taxation thereof) where a dispute is settled without an action having been commenced, but the issue of costs remains unresolved. Rule 1(1)(ob) empowers the court to grant leave to serve out of the jurisdiction, originating process claiming such a costs order. With regard to costs only proceedings generally, see the commentary under Order 62 rule 11A.

### [11.1.23]　Rule 1(1)(oc) - claim for interim relief or appointment of receiver

Rule 1(1)(oc) provides for service out of the jurisdiction in respect of claims under s 21M of the High Court Ordinance. That section was added by the Civil Justice (Miscellaneous Amendments) Ordinance 2008 (in force 2009) as part of the civil justice reforms. The explanatory memorandum to the bill (clause 6) said of the section:

> The new section 21M empowers the Court of First Instance to grant interim relief or appoint a receiver in aid of foreign proceedings which are capable of giving rise to a judgment that is capable of being enforced in Hong Kong. Under the new section, the interim relief or the appointment of a receiver may be sought as an independent, free-standing form of relief without being ancillary or incidental to substantive proceedings in Hong Kong.

It is clear from the final report of the Chief Justice's working party (para 327 et seq) that insofar as section 21M relates to 'interim relief', it is intended to enable the court to grant Mareva injunctions and Anton Piller orders ancillary to proceedings in other jurisdictions. With regard to such interim relief generally, see Order 29 rule 8A and the commentary thereunder. The section also provides for appointment of a receiver in such circumstances, as to which see Order 30 rule 9.

**[11.1.24]    Rule 1(1)(od) - claim for costs against non-party**

Order 11 rule 1(1)(od) empowers the court to grant leave to serve proceedings out of Hong Kong where they relate to claims under section 52A(2) of the High Court Ordinance for costs against non-parties. Section 52A(2) was amended by the Civil Justice (Miscellaneous Amendments) Ordinance 2008 (in force 2009) as part of the civil justice reforms in order to give the court an express power to make costs orders against non-parties. At the same time, rule 1(1)(od) was added to Order 11 to permit service of such non-parties who are outside Hong Kong. Even before the insertion of rule 1(1)(od) the court had granted leave for service out of the jurisdiction of a summons seeking a pre-emptive costs order against an insurer: *HK Housing Authority v Hsin Yieh Architects & Associates Ltd & Ors* [2005] 2 HKC 201, 207A-B (upheld on appeal – CACV 85/2005).

With regard to costs orders against non-parties generally, see Order 62 rule 6A and the commentary thereunder.

**[11.1.25]    Rule 1(1)(p) - claims against constructive trustee**

Rule 1(1)(p) provides for service out of the jurisdiction of a constructive trustee, where the alleged liability arises out of acts committed within the jurisdiction. In *ISC Technologies Ltd v Guerin* [1992] 2 Lloyd's Rep 430, 433 it was said that the provision was primarily designed for cases in which foreign entities have been used as receptacles for the proceeds of wrongful acts committed within the jurisdiction. The provision specifically refers to claims for money had and received or for an account. However, it is not limited to such claims - it expressly extends to claims for 'other relief' as well. Thus it extends to personal claims against a constructive trustee as well as proprietary claims: *Ghana Commercial Bank v C* [1997] TLR 111. It is provided that the acts committed within the jurisdiction may have been committed by the defendant or another person. It is sufficient to show that liability arises from 'substantial and efficacious' acts committed within the jurisdiction, irrespective of whether other substantial and efficacious acts were committed elsewhere: *Dynasty Line Ltd (provisional liquidators appointed) v Sukamto Sia & Anor* [2009] 4 HKC 184 (CA) (para 37).

**[11.1.26]    Application for leave to be made ex parte by affidavit**

An application for leave to serve out of the jurisdiction is normally made before the writ is issued. It should be made *ex parte* on paper: *Wo Fung Paper Making Fty Ltd v Sappi Kraft (Pty) Ltd* [1988] HKC 10, 22H-I (CA). In practice this means the application is made by submitting to the registry an affidavit headed 'in the matter of an intended action between ...', which will then be considered by a master. As to what the affidavit must contain, see Order 11 rule 4.

Where there is more than one defendant, at least one of which is in Hong Kong, the registry will permit the writ to be issued before leave to serve out has been granted, and will at that stage mark the writ as being 'not for service out of the jurisdiction'.

Where *ex parte* leave to serve out of the jurisdiction has been granted, the affected party may apply inter partes for that order to be set aside: see Order 12 rule 8(1)(c) and the commentary thereunder.

**[11.1.27]    Where service cannot be effected ex juris**

Where a defendant cannot be served ex juris because, for example, it is a body corporate which has no domicile anywhere, the court may order substituted service in Hong Kong but only if the requirements of Order 11 rule 1 are met: see *Tillemont Shipping Corp SA & Anor v Taitexma Enterprise Corp & Ors* [1993] 2 HKC 129 (CA).

### [11.1.28]   Service out without leave – Order 11 rule 1(2)

Leave to serve out of the jurisdiction is not required in the somewhat unusual circumstances where extra-territorial jurisdiction is expressly conferred by statute. Examples may be found in the fields of aviation and shipping law.

This paragraph was discussed with respect to a claim under section 26 of the High Court Ordinance and the relevant provision of the Guardianship of Minors Ordinance in *Re S (a minor)* [1992] 2 HKLR 39, where the judge held that the relevant statutory provisions did not permit service without leave.

### [11.1.29]   Numbering

There is no rule 2 or rule 3 in Order 11. Rule 3 previously prescribed the procedure whereby notice of a writ rather than the writ itself was served out of the jurisdiction, and was repealed in 1988.

**4.      Application for, and grant of, leave to serve writ out of jurisdiction**
        (O. 11 r. 4)

**(1)   An application for the grant of leave under rule 1(1) must be supported by an affidavit stating—**

> **(a)     the grounds on which the application is made;**
> **(b)     hat in the deponent's belief the plaintiff has a good cause of action;**
> **(c)     in what place the defendant is, or probably may be found; and**
> **(d)     where the application is made under rule 1(1)(c), the grounds for the deponent's belief that there is between the plaintiff and the person on whom a writ has been served a real issue which the plaintiff may reasonably ask the Court to try.**

**(2)   No such leave shall be granted unless it shall be made sufficiently to appear to the Court that the case is a proper one for service out of the jurisdiction under this Order.**

**(4)   An order granting under rule 1 leave to serve a writ out of the jurisdiction must limit a time within which the defendant to be served must acknowledge service.**

---

## NOTES

### [11.4.1]   The affidavit in support of application for leave

Order 11 rule 4(1) states that the affidavit in support of an application for leave to serve out of the jurisdiction must include the following:

•     *Rule 4(1)(a)* – the grounds upon which the application is made. It should be sufficient to adapt the wording of the particular head under rule 1 which is relied upon.

•     *Rule 4(1)(b)* – the deponent's belief the plaintiff has a good cause of action. It is not necessary to have a cause of action against the party to be served out of Hong Kong so long as there is a good cause of action against another defendant. See *HK Housing Authority v Hsin Yieh Architects & Associates Ltd* [2006] 1 HKC 116, 122C (CA) where leave to serve an insurer out of Hong Kong was granted where there was no cause of action against the insurer itself, but against its insured in Hong Kong.

•   *Rule 4(1)(c)* – the location of the defendant. In other words the country or territory in which it is sought to serve the defendant should be stated.

•   *Rule 4(1)(d)* – where the application is based on rule 1(1)(c) (application to serve a 'necessary or proper party' out of the jurisdiction, where another defendant has already been duly served), the affidavit must state the deponent's belief there is a real issue to be tried as against the party already duly served. The purpose is to prevent the use of a 'jurisdictional Trojan horse' solely to create a ground for serving a party out of Hong Kong. See the commentary under rule 1(1)(c).

The requirements in rule 4(1)(b) and (d) that the affidavit state the deponent's belief as to certain matters is complied with where the deponent confirms the facts relied on – a 'ritual incantation' of the words set out in those paragraphs is not necessary: *Tay Choo Wah v Singapore-Johore Express (Pte) Ltd* [1991] 2 HKC 180, 194A-D; (CA); *Century Yachts Ltd v Xiamen Celestial Yacht Ltd* [1994] 1 HKC 331, 335I-336E (CA). In the latter of those two cases the court expressed the view that failure to comply with these requirements could be regarded as cured by a subsequent affidavit even though filed for another purpose – summary judgment.

### [11.4.2]   Full disclosure

In order to obtain an order for service out the plaintiff must make full disclosure by affidavit (*Mattel Inc v Tonka Corp* [1991] 2 HKC 411; *George Monro, Ltd v American Cyanamid and Chemical Corp* [1944] KB 432, at 441–442, per Du Parcq LJ). The duty of full disclosure is that which applies on all *ex parte* applications. (See the fuller discussion of the duty to make full disclosure in the commentary to Order 32 rule 1.)

Failure to make full and frank disclosure may result in the application being refused or leave being set aside. See for example *A J Lucas (HK) Ltd v Drilltec Gut Gmbh* HCCT 36/2005 (Burrell J; 14.02.2006) where failure to disclose the existence of an exclusive jurisdiction clause was considered sufficient for leave to be set aside. And see *China Chance Corp Ltd v Rockefeller Group Int'l Inc* [2010] 6 HKC 337 (paras 85-93) where leave was set aside for failure to disclose, at the ex parte stage, a defence under the foreign law which governed the contract between the parties. However, non-disclosure of a defence available to the opposing party will not necessarily be fatal.

'It is not for a plaintiff preparing evidence in support of an application under O 11 r 1 to anticipate all the arguments or all the points which might be against his case. The duty is one of degree': *Continental Mark Ltd v Verkehrs-Club de Schweiz* [2001] 4 HKC 469, 480H–I, per Deputy Judge McCoy citing *McCauley (Tweeds) Ltd v Independent Harris Tweed Producers Ltd* [1961] RPC 184, 194. In *United Links International Ltd v The Price Co* [1994] 2 HKC 617 Godfrey J stated at 619H–J that he was:

> not prepared to hold that the failure of the plaintiff to disclose, in its evidence in support of its application for leave to serve the writ out of the jurisdiction, the fact that an allegation of fraud had been made against it in connection with the underlying contract, is an omission of so serious a character as to disentitle the plaintiff to rely on the leave which it obtained.

Where leave to serve out is refused or set aside for non-disclosure, a renewed application based on a proper affidavit may be possible. See *Pacific Electric Wire & Cable Co Ltd v Texan Management Ltd & Ors* [2007] 4 HKC 372 (CA) where Rogers VP said (at para 16) 'there is certainly no absolute bar' to such an application.

### [11.4.3]    Discretion - must be a 'proper' case for service out
Order 11 rule 4(2) provides that the court shall not grant leave unless the case is a 'proper' one for service out of the jurisdiction. The effect is to leave the court with a discretion to refuse an application even though the case comes within one of the heads of rule 1(1). This is the basis on which the court may refuse leave on grounds such as lis alibi pendens and *forum non conveniens*: *Deak Perera (FE) Ltd v Deak* [1988] 2 HKLR 95, 98. For discussion of these grounds, see the commentary under Order 12 rule 8. At the initial *ex parte* stage the burden on the plaintiff is to demonstrate that Hong Kong is 'clearly and distinctly' the appropriate forum for trial of the action: *Hargreaves v Taian Insurance Co Ltd* [2006] 3 HKLRD 70 (para 50). This is the opposite of the situation where a stay is sought of proceedings started in Hong Kong as of right, on grounds such as forum non conveniens: *Dynasty Line Ltd (provisional liquidators appointed) v Sukamto Sia & Anor* [2009] 4 HKC 184 (CA) (para 56, 75).

The requirement of Order 11 rule 4(2) that the court be satisfied the case is a proper one for a grant of leave to serve out of the jurisdiction also involves consideration of the merits of the claim. This topic is discussed in the commentary under Order 11 rule 1.

### [11.4.4]    Procedure on application for leave to serve out
An application under Order 11 for leave to serve a writ out of the jurisdiction should be made *ex parte* by affidavit in accordance with the procedure discussed in the commentary under Order 32 rule 1. The application will normally be dealt with by a master, without a hearing. The application may be made before the writ is issued, seeking leave to issue a writ for service out of the jurisdiction. Alternatively, if a writ has already been issued naming a defendant out of the jurisdiction, it will have been marked 'not for service out of the jurisdiction', and the application will be for issue of a concurrent writ under Order 6 rule 6 and leave to serve *ex juris*.

### [11.4.5]    Setting aside leave to serve out
A party who is the subject of an *ex parte* order granting leave to serve out of the jurisdiction may apply to discharge that order. Such an application is specifically provided for in Order 12 rule 8(1)(c). Leave may be set aside on the ground the requirements discussed above are not met. Those were succinctly set out in *Hargreaves v Taian Insurance Co Ltd* [2006] 3 HKLRD 70 (para 24) as a burden on the plaintiff to show:

(i)     that there is a good arguable case that the facts fall within one of the relevant heads of Order 11 rule 1(1);
(ii)    that in terms of the dispute itself there is a serious issue to be tried; and
(iii)   that the case is one which falls within the rubric of Order 11 rule 4(2), namely that 'No such leave shall be granted unless it shall be made sufficiently to appear to the Court that the case is a proper one for service out of the jurisdiction'.

In addition, non-disclosure at the *ex parte* stage may be a ground for setting aside leave to serve out of the jurisdiction: see the discussion of the full disclosure requirement above. In *Friis & Anor v Colburn* [2009] EWHC 903 (Ch) (01.05.2009) the English court took cost into account in setting aside leave to serve out of the jurisdiction. The court noted that more than £500,000 in costs had already been incurred, that there were already proceedings underway in two other jurisdictions and concluded (at para 54) that the plaintiffs were 'running up costs oppressively'. In Hong Kong, the court's discretion under Order 11 rule 4, coupled with the underlying objective of reasonable proportion and procedural economy (Order 1A rule 1(c)) should make a similar result possible in a suitable case.

**5.     Service of writ out of jurisdiction: general** (O. 11 r. 5)

**(1)     Subject to the following provisions of this rule, Order 10, rule 1(l), (4) and (5) and (6) and Order 65, rule 4, shall apply in relation to the service of a writ notwithstanding that the writ is to be served out of the jurisdiction, save that the accompanying form of acknowledgment of service shall be modified in such manner as may be appropriate.**

**(2)     Nothing in this rule, rule 5A or in any order or direction of the Court made by virtue of it shall authorize or require the doing of anything in a country or place in which service is to be effected which is contrary to the law of that country or place. (L.N. 39 of 1999)**

**(3)     A writ which is to be served out of the jurisdiction—**

**(a)     need not be served personally on the person required to be served so long as it is served on him in accordance with the law of the country or place in which service is effected; and**

**(b)     need not be served by the plaintiff or his agent if it is served by a method provided for by rule 5A, rule 6 or rule 7. (L.N. 39 of 1999)**

**(5)     An official certificate stating that a writ as regards which rule 5A or rule 6 has been complied with, has been served on a person personally, or in accordance with the law of the country or place in which service was effected, on a specified date, being a certificate—**

**(a)     by a British consular authority in that country or place, or**

**(b)     by the government or judicial authorities of that country or place, or**

**(c)     by any other authority designated in respect of that country or place under the Hague Convention,**

**shall be evidence of the facts so stated. (L.N. 39 of 1999)**

**(6)     An official certificate by the Chief Secretary for Administration stating that a writ has been duly served on a specified date in accordance with a request made under rule 7 shall be evidence of that fact. (L.N. 362 of 1997)**

**(7)     A document purporting to be such a certificate as is mentioned in paragraph (5) or (6) shall, until the contrary is proved, be deemed to be such a certificate.**

**(8)     In this rule and rule 6 "the Hague Convention" means the Convention on the service abroad of judicial or extra judicial documents in civil or commercial matters signed at The Hague on 15 November 1965.**

---

**NOTES**

### [11.5.1]   Interpretation of Order 11 rule 5 after 1 July 1997

Order 11 rule 5, dealing with service outside Hong Kong, continues to contain provisions which have ceased to be relevant since the resumption of Chinese sovereignty on 1 July 1997. The rule should now be interpreted in accordance with the provisions of the Reunification Ordinance and in particular, Schedule 8 of the Interpretation and General Clauses Ordinance (Cap 1) enacted thereby. See the 'blue pages' published with Issue 8 of this work in August 1997.

### [11.5.2]   Address at which service abroad may be effected

An order granting leave for service out of the jurisdiction commonly states the place at which leave to serve is granted. See, for example High Court practice form PF 6 (in volume 2 of the looseleaf edition of this work). Usually the order will continue with words such as 'or elsewhere in . . .'. Whether or not those additional words appear, the inclusion of an address in the order does not have the effect of limiting the court's leave to serve at that place. The order grants leave to serve out generally and the reference to an address is 'a reference to where the defendant may be served, not where he must be served': *Mattel Inc v Tonka Corp* [1991] 2 HKC 411, 419H-I (Deputy Judge Andrew Li QC, as he then was). In that case and again in *Precieux Garment Fty Ltd v Ralph Lauren Womenswear Co LP* HCA 11705/1996 (Suffiad J; 07.05.1998) service in a state of the United States other than the one specified in the order was not considered a ground for setting aside.

### [11.5.3]   Mode of service outside the jurisdiction

Order 11 rule 5(3) provides that service of a writ out of the jurisdiction must be effected in accordance with the law of the place of service. Failure to comply may result in service being set aside, as in *ITC Global Holdings Pte Ltd v ITC Ltd* [2007] SGHC 127 (13.08.2007) (Sing HCt). In *Hartando Hady v Radnaabazar Bazar* HCA 89/2008 (Deputy Judge L Chan; 12.08.2010) a default judgment was set aside on the ground that the mode of service of the writ in Mongolia was not in accordance with the law of that jurisdiction.

     For mode of service in the mainland of China see rule 5A, and for other jurisdictions see rule 6.

### [11.5.4]   Rule 5(5) - official certificate of compliance

Order 11 rule 5(5) provides that an official certificate of compliance with the provisions of rule 5A and 6 for service outside Hong Kong shall be evidence of the facts stated. In *Hong Kong Housing Authority v Hsin Yieh Architects & Associates Ltd* HCCT 39/2001 (Reyes J; 04.04.2006) it was held that in the absence of compelling evidence to the contrary the court was entitled to assume, on the basis of such a certificate, that proper service had been effected.

**5A.    Service of writ in the Mainland of China through judicial authorities**
     (O. 11 r. 5A)

     **(1)    Where in accordance with these rules, a writ is to be served on a person to be served in the Mainland of China, the writ shall be served through the judicial authorities of the Mainland of China.**

     **(2)    A person who wishes to serve a writ under paragraph (1) must**

lodge in the Registry a request for such service, together with 2 copies of the writ and 2 additional copies thereof for the person to be served.

(3)    The request lodged under paragraph (2) must contain—

    (a)    the full name and address of the person to be served;

    (b)    a description of the nature of proceedings; and

    (c)    if a particular method of service by the judicial authorities of the Mainland of China is desired by the person making the request, an indication of that particular method.

(4)    Every copy of a writ lodged under paragraph (2) must be in Chinese or accompanied by a Chinese translation.

(5)    Every translation lodged under paragraph (4) must be certified by the person making it to be a correct translation; and the certificate must contain a statement of that person's full name, of his address and of his qualifications for making the translation.

(6)    Documents duly lodged under paragraph (2) shall be sent by the Registrar to the judicial authorities of the Mainland of China with a request that they arrange for the writ to be served or, where a particular method of service is indicated under paragraph (3)(c), to be served by that method. (L.N. 39 of 1999)

---

**NOTES**

**[11.5A.1]    Service of Hong Kong process in the Mainland**

Order 11 rule 5A provides for the service of Hong Kong writs in the Mainland of China. By virtue of rule 9(7) it applies to the service of other Hong Kong court documents as well. It does not apply to documents which are not issued by the court, such as a statutory demand: *Re Fung Kwok On William* HCB 9590/2008 (Recorder Patrick Fung SC; 06.08.2010) (para 36). Documents to be served in the Mainland should be submitted to the registry under this rule, together with an undertaking as to expenses as required by rule 8A.

Rule 5A dates from 1999. Its purpose was to implement in Hong Kong the terms of an arrangement for mutual service of judicial documents between the Mainland and the Hong Kong SAR. Although the terms of the arrangement themselves do not have the force of law in Hong Kong, they may be useful in understanding the underlying framework of the system put in place by the rules for service in the Mainland. They will also be useful in understanding the means by which Mainland court process may be served in Hong Kong. The terms of the arrangement can be viewed on the website of the Department of Justice (www.doj.gov.hk), under Treaties and International Agreements – Arrangements with the Mainland and the Macao SAR.

**6.    Service of writ abroad through foreign governments, judicial authorities and British consuls** (O. 11 r. 6)

(1)    Save where a writ is to be served pursuant to paragraph (2A) this rule does not apply to service in—

    (HK)(a)    The United Kingdom of Great Britain, Northern Ireland, the Channel Islands and the Isle of Man;

    (b)    any independent Commonwealth country;

    (HK)(c)    any British protectorate;

(HK)(d)    any British colony;

     (e)    the Republic of Ireland.

(2)    Where in accordance with these rules a writ is to be served on a defendant in any country with respect to which there subsists a Civil Procedure Convention (other than the Hague Convention) providing for service in that country of process of the Court, the writ may be served—

     (a)       through the judicial authorities of that country; or

     (b)       through a British consular authority in that country (subject to any provision of the convention as to the nationality of persons who may be so served).

(2A) Where in accordance with these rules, a writ is to be served on a defendant in any country which is a party to the Hague Convention, the writ may be served—

     (a)       through the authority designated under the Convention in respect of that country; or

     (b)       if the law of that country permits—

          (i)       through the judicial authorities of that country, or

          (ii)       through a British consular authority in that country.

(3)    Where in accordance with these rules a writ is to be served on a defendant in any country with respect to which there does not subsist a Civil Procedure Convention providing for service in that country of process of the Court of First Instance, the writ may be served—

     (a)       through the government of that country, where that government is willing to effect service; or

     (b)       through a British consular authority in that country, except where service through such an authority is contrary to the law of that country.

(4)    A person who wishes to serve a writ by a method specified in paragraph (2), (2A) or (3) must lodge in the Registry a request for service of the writ by that method, together with a copy of the writ and an additional copy thereof for each person to be served.

(5)    Every copy of a writ lodged under paragraph (4) must be accompanied by a translation of the writ in the official language of the country in which service is to be effected or, if there is more than one official language of that country, in any one of those languages which is appropriate to the place in that country where service is to be effected:

Provided that this paragraph shall not apply in relation to a copy of a writ which is to be served in a country the official language of which is, or the official languages of which include, English, or is to be served in any country by a British consular authority on a British subject, unless the service is to be effected under paragraph (2) and the Civil Procedure Convention with respect to that country expressly requires the copy to be accompanied by a translation.

(6)    Every translation lodged under paragraph (5) must be certified by the person making it to be a correct translation; and the certificate must contain a statement of that person's full name, of his address and of his qualification for making the translation.

(7)    Documents duly lodged under paragraph (4) shall be sent by the

**Registrar to the Chief Secretary for Administration with a request that he arrange for the writ to be served by the method indicated in the request lodged under paragraph (4) or, where alternative methods are so indicated, by such one of those methods as is most convenient.**

---

## NOTES

### [11.6.1]  Construction of Order 11 rule 6 after 1 July 1997

Following Hong Kong's reunification with the Mainland of China this rule must be read subject to the legislative amendments brought about by the Hong Kong Reunification Ordinance (No 110 of 1997).

As a result, references in this rule to the British government and officials thereof should now be construed as references to the Central People's Government of the People's Republic of China (schedule 8 of the Interpretation and General Clauses Ordinance (Cap 1) as amended by Ordinance No 110 of 1997).

Further, insofar as this rule might be construed as conferring privileges on the United Kingdom or other parts of the Commonwealth, it shall have no further effect (section 2A(2)(b) of Ordinance No 110 of 1997) save where reciprocal arrangements exist.

### [11.6.2]  Scope of Order 11 rule 6

Order 11 rule 6 makes provision for the manner of service of Hong Kong process in other jurisdictions. It should be read together with rules 5 and 5A. Service in jurisdictions which are parties to the Hague Convention, and jurisdictions which are not, is covered.

The 'Hague Convention' referred to in rule 6 is the 1965 Hague Convention on Service Abroad: see Order 11 rule 5(8). As noted in the commentary under that rule, the text of the convention can be viewed on the internet.

Note that at the time of reunification the central government took the necessary steps to ensure that the Hague Convention continues to apply in relation to the Hong Kong SAR. Formal announcement was made by the Department of Justice. See Law Society circular 97-287 dated 15.09.1997.

### [11.6.3]  Manner of service outside Hong Kong

See also rule 5 and the commentary thereunder. For service in the Mainland of China see rule 5A.

The manner of service in other jurisdictions which are parties to the Hague Convention is governed by the convention itself, and the instrument by which it became applicable in respect of the particular jurisdiction. As pointed out in *Continental Mark Ltd v Verkehrs-Club de Schweiz* [2001] 4 HKC 469, 476G the relevant information is available on the convention web-site www.hcch.net. In that case it was conceded that purported service of a writ in Switzerland by airmail was not valid. The terms of the Swiss accession to the Hague Convention did not allow for service by post. However, where a state party has not objected to article 10(a) of the convention, service by post is valid: *Hui Suet Ying v Sharp Corp* HCPI 1269/1997 (Suffiad J; 15.02.2000).

Rule 6(2), (2A) and (3) provide for service abroad through judicial or governmental authorities of the jurisdiction in which service is to be effected, or through consular authorities. To effect such service it is necessary to comply with rule 6(4) and submit the required documents to the registry. Form JUD (HC 220) (1/98) (which is available in the High Court registry) should be completed.

### [11.6.4]    Service in Japan under the Hague Convention
Information circulated to solicitors by the Law Society states that Hong Kong process may be served in Japan through a Chinese consular official or by the Japanese judicial authorities. See Law Society circular 96-253. It is there noted that Japan had not formally objected to article 10(a) of the Hague Convention such that service by post (preferably registered post) might be possible in that jurisdiction. In *Hui Suet Ying* (above) the court upheld service by post on a defendant in Japan.

### [11.6.5]    Service in the USA under the Hague Convention
In 2003 the United States adopted new procedures for service of process under the Hague Convention. These are set out fully in Law Society circular 03-189 dated 09.06.2003. Service is now handled through a private business. Hong Kong parties wishing to serve process in the United States and its territories should complete the required form (see above) naming Process Forwarding International of 910, 5th Avenue, Seattle, Wa, USA 98104 as the receiving authority. A fee of US$95.00, payable by bank draft to that business, is prescribed for 2006 and 2007.

### [11.6.6]    Service in Switzerland under the Hague Convention
As mentioned above, in *Continental Mark Ltd* (above) it was held that the terms of Switzerland's accession to the Hague Convention do not permit service by post.

### [11.6.7]    Service in India
In *ITC Global Holdings Pte LTd v ITC LTd* [2007] SGHC 127 (13.08.2007) the Singapore High Court considered expert evidence as to what forms of service of a foreign writ were permitted in India. The evidence was to the effect that Indian law does not recognise service by the Indian government or through consular authorities, but service is possible through certain Indian courts provided that certain local procedural requirements are complied with. However, the Singapore court's judgment appears to have been superseded – the Hague Convention's website says that the convention took effect in India in the month that judgment was delivered.

**7.**      **Service of process on a foreign State** (O. 11 r. 7)
     **(1)**    **Subject to paragraph (4) where a person to whom leave has been granted under rule 1 to serve a writ on a State, as defined in section 14 of the State Immunity Act 1978 (1978 c. 33 U.K.), wishes to have the writ served on that State, he must lodge in the Registry—**
         **(a)**      **a request for service to be arranged by the Chief Secretary for Administration; and**
         **(b)**      **a copy of the writ; and**
         **(c)**      **except where the official language of the State is, or the official languages of that party include, English, a translation of the writ in the official language or one of the official languages of the State.**
     **(2)**    **Rule 6(6) shall apply in relation to a translation lodged under paragraph (1) of this rule as it applies in relation to a translation lodged under**

paragraph (5) of that rule.

(3)   Documents duly lodged under this rule shall be sent by the Registrar to the Chief Secretary for Administration with a request that the Chief Secretary for Administration arrange for the writ to be served on the State or the government in question, as the case may be.

(4)   Where section 12(6) of the State Immunity Act 1978 (1978 c. 33 U.K.) applies and the State has agreed to a method of service other than that provided by the preceding paragraphs, the writ may be served either by the method agreed or in accordance with the preceding paragraphs of this rule.

---

**NOTES**

**[11.7.1]   Interpretation of Order 11 rule 7 after 1 July 1997**
Like a number of other provisions of these rules, Order 11 rule 7 contains provisions which were enacted during the colonial era and have not yet been amended as part of the on-going Adaptation of Laws exercise. Pending such amendment the rule should be read in conjunction with the Reunification Ordinance and specifically Schedule 8 to the Interpretation and General Clauses Ordinance (Cap 1) introduced thereby.

**7A .   Service of writ in certain actions under Carriage by Air Ordinance**
     (O. 11 r. 7A)
(HK)(1) Where a person to whom leave has been granted under rule 1 to serve a writ on a High Contracting Party or State Party, as may be appropriate, within the meaning of section 2(1) of the Carriage by Air Ordinance (Cap 500), being a writ beginning an action to enforce a claim in respect of carriage undertaken by that Party, wishes to have the writ served on that Party, he must lodge in the Registry (13 of 1997 s 20; 22 of 2005 s 26)—

(a)   a request for service to be arranged by the Chief Secretary for Administration; and

(b)   a copy of the writ; and

(c)   except where the official language of the High Contracting Party or State Party, as may be appropriate, is, or the official languages of that Party include, English, a translation of the writ in the official language or one of the official languages of that Party. (22 of 2005 s 26)

(2)   Rule 6(6) shall apply in relation to a translation lodged under paragraph (1) of this rule as it applies in relation to a translation lodged under paragraph (5) of that rule.

(3)   Documents duly lodged under this rule shall be sent by the Registrar to the Chief Secretary for Administration with a request that the Chief Secretary for Administration arrange for the writ to be served on the High Contracting Party or State Party, as may be appropriate. (22 of 2005 s 26)

---

**NOTES**

**[11.7A.1]  Wording of Order 11 rule 7A**

The wording of Order 11 rule 7A as printed above is accurate. Some works, in print and on–line, reproduce the wording of the rule incorrectly by failing to include amendments which were made in 1997 and 2005, or by including them inaccurately.

**[11.7A.2]  Service of air transport claims against governments and public bodies**

Order 11 rule 7A provides for service on states (and other high contracting parties) of writs making claims under the Carriage by Air Ordinance (Cap 500). Leave to serve out of the jurisdiction must first have been obtained under Order 11 rule 1(1)(n). Service will be arranged by the office of the Chief Secretary for Administration, who should be approached through the court registry in the manner set out in rules 7A and 8.

   The Ordinance gives the force of law to several international agreements regulating liability of international air carriers. Among them is the Warsaw Convention, as amended, which is set out in Schedule 1 of the Ordinance. Article 2 of that convention provides that it applies to carriage performed by states and public bodies, but an option is given in the additional protocol set out at the end of the amended convention for states and high contracting parties to opt out of this waiver of sovereign immunity at the time of ratification or accession. Governments which have not opted out are deemed by section 9(1) of the Ordinance to have submitted to the jurisdiction of the Hong Kong court, provided that the proceedings are properly brought in accordance with article 28 of the amended convention. Article 28 provides that proceedings may be brought at the option of the plaintiff, in (i) its place of ordinary residence (ii) its principal place of business (iii) the place at which it has 'an establishment by which the contract has been made', or (iv) at the place of destination.

**8.     Undertaking to pay expenses of service by the Chief Secretary for Administration** (O. 11 r. 8)

   **Every request lodged under rule 6(4), rule 7 or rule 7A must contain an undertaking by the person making the request to be responsible personally for all expenses incurred by the Chief Secretary for Administration in respect of the service requested and, on receiving due notification of the amount of those expenses, to pay that amount to the Treasury and to produce a receipt for the payment to the Registrar. (L.N. 362 of 1997)**

**8A.    Undertaking to pay expenses of service by the Registrar** (O. 11 r. 8A)

   **Every request lodged under rule 5A must contain an undertaking by the person making the request to be responsible personally for all expenses incurred by the Registrar in respect of the service requested and, on receiving due notification of the amount of those expenses, to pay that amount to the Treasury and to produce a receipt for the payment to the Registrar. (L.N. 39 of 1999)**

**9.     Service of originating summons, petition, notice of motion, etc.** (O. 11 r. 9)

   **(1)    Subject to Order 73, rule 7, rule 1 of this Order shall apply to the service out of the jurisdiction of an originating summons, notice of motion or petition as it applies to service of a writ.**

   **(4)    Subject to Order 73, rule 7, service out of the jurisdiction of any**

summons, notice or order issued, given or made in any proceedings is permissible with the leave of the Court, but leave shall not be required for such service in any proceedings in which the writ, originating summons, motion or petition may by these rules or under any written law be served out of the jurisdiction without leave.

(5)   Rule 4(1), (2) and (3) shall, so far as applicable, apply in relation to an application for the grant of leave under this rule as they apply in relation to an application for the grant of leave under rule 1.

(6)   An order granting under this rule leave to serve out of the jurisdiction an originating summons must limit a time within which the defendant to be served with the summons must acknowledge service.

(7)   Rules 5, 5A, 6, 8 and 8A shall apply in relation to any document for the service of which out of the jurisdiction leave has been granted under this rule as they apply in relation to a writ. (L.N. 39 of 1999)

(Enacted 1988)

---

## NOTES

**[11.9.1]   Service of other originating process, summonses and orders out of the jurisdiction**

Order 11 rule 9 provides that leave to serve out of the jurisdiction is normally required for other forms of originating process, as well as summonses, notices and orders. Leave is not required for documents not issued by the court, such as a statutory demand: *Re Fung Kwok On William* HCB 9590/2008 (Recorder Patrick Fung SC; 06.08.2010) (para 36).

Rule 9(1) extends the provisions of rule 1 to originating summonses, notices of motion and petitions, with the result that the leave will only be granted where the case comes within one of the grounds set out in that rule.

Rule 9(4), providing that leave is normally required for *ex juris* service of summonses, notices and orders, does not expressly apply rule 1. It follows that it is not necessary to bring the application within one of the lettered paragraphs in that rule. See *A & B v C* HCMP 2261/2006 (A Cheung J; 06.07.2007) (para 5) where, in relation to an *inter partes* summons, it was said that the relevant provisions of rule 9 'form a code of their own', so there is 'no need to bring the application within a limb of rule 1(1)'.

The leave requirements of rule 9 expressly do not apply to *ex juris* service of originating or interlocutory process in arbitration proceedings, which is catered for by Order 73 rule 7.

Failure to obtain leave, where required, may result in service being set aside. In both *Li Fook Chu v Chung Shau Ching* [2001] 4 HKC 681 (CA) and *Gainford Int'l Ltd v Kingbo Holdings Ltd* DCCJ 5079/2004 (Deputy Judge ST Poon; 08.02.2006) default judgments were set aside where leave had not been obtained for service of an order (in the first of those cases) and an *inter partes* summons (in the second case).

## ORDER 12

### ACKNOWLEDGMENT OF SERVICE OF WRIT OR ORIGINATING SUMMONS

1. **Mode of acknowledging service** (O. 12 r. 1)

   (1)   Subject to paragraph (2) and to Order 80, rule 2, a defendant to an action begun by writ may (whether or not he is sued as a trustee or personal representative or in any other representative capacity) acknowledge service of the writ and defend the action by a solicitor or in person.

   (2)   The defendant to such an action who is a body corporate may acknowledge service of the writ and give notice of intention to defend the action either by a solicitor or by a person duly authorized to act on the defendant's behalf but, except as expressly provided by or under any enactment or where leave is given under paragraph (2A) for such defendant to be represented by one of its directors, such defendant may not take any further step in the action otherwise than by a solicitor.

   (2A) (a)   An application by a body corporate for leave to be represented by one of its directors shall be made ex parte to a Registrar and supported by an affidavit, made by the director and filed with the application, stating and verifying the reasons why leave should be given for the body corporate to be represented by the director. (L.N. 103 of 1994) (L.N. 108 of 2002)

   (b)   The relevant resolution of the board of the body corporate authorizing the director to appear on its behalf if leave is granted shall be exhibited to the affidavit.

   (2B) No appeal shall lie from an order of the Registrar under paragraph (2A) giving or refusing leave.

   (2C) Leave given by a Registrar under paragraph (2A) may be revoked by the Court at any time.

   (2D) No appeal shall lie from an order of the Court revoking leave given by a Registrar.

   (3)   Service of a writ may be acknowledged by properly completing an acknowledgment of service as defined by rule 3 and handing it in at, or sending it by post to, the Registry.

   (4)   If two or more defendants to an action acknowledge service by the same solicitor and at the same time, only one acknowledgment of service need be completed and delivered for those defendants.

   (5)   The date on which service is acknowledged is the date on which the acknowledgment of service is received at the Registry.

---

## NOTES

**[12.1.1]   Manner of acknowledging service**

Service of a writ is acknowledged by properly completing the appropriate form of acknowledgement of service (as to which see rule 3 and the commentary thereunder) and handing it in or sending it by post to the court registry. See Order 12 rule 1(3).

Upon receipt of the acknowledgment of service, the court registry is required to take the steps set out in Order 12 rule 4, which includes sending it by post to the plaintiff. The defendant acknowledging service is not required to effect service on the plaintiff.

#### [12.1.2]   Body corporate defending in person

Order 12 rule 1(2) allows a body corporate to acknowledge service and give notice of intention to defend by person authorised to do so. Thereafter a body corporate may not take any step to defend the action save by solicitor unless the body corporate applies for and obtains leave to be represented by one of its directors. In 2002 the previous requirement in Order 12 rule 1(2A)(a) that the affidavit in support of such an application demonstrate 'lack of resources or … other good reasons' was repealed.

As to companies commencing proceedings otherwise than through a solicitor, see Order 5 rule 6. And see Order 9 rule 6 in relation to Petitions.

A company which obtains leave to be represented by one of its directors may be entitled to claim costs as a litigant in person under Order 62 rule 28A. See the commentary under that rule.

In *Wing Hang Bank Ltd v Kit Choy Development Ltd & Anor* [2005] 3 HKC 312, 315B-H (CA), the court rejected a submission that where both a company and a director thereof are named as defendants in an action, the director may represent the company without leave.

#### [12.1.3]   Acknowledgment of service by partnership

Particular provisions as to acknowledgment of service of partners sued in the name of the partnership or firm are set out at Order 81 rule 4.

#### [12.1.4]   Numbering

There is no rule 2 in Order 12.

3.    **Acknowledgment of service** (O. 12 r. 3)

(1)    **An acknowledgment of service must be in Form No. 14, 15 or 15A in Appendix A, whichever is appropriate, and except as provided in rule 1(2), must be signed by the solicitor acting for the defendant specified in the acknowledgment or, if the defendant is acting in person, by that defendant. (L.N. 152 of 2008)**

(2)    **An acknowledgment of service must specify—**

(a)    **in the case of a defendant acknowledging service in person, the address of his place of residence and, if his place of residence is not within the jurisdiction or if he has no place of residence, the address of a place within the jurisdiction at or to which documents for him may be delivered or sent, and**

(b)    **in the case of a defendant acknowledging service by a solicitor, a business address to which may be added a numbered box at a document exchange of his solicitor within the jurisdiction;**

**and where the defendant acknowledges service in person the address within the jurisdiction specified under sub-paragraph (a) shall be his address for service, but otherwise his solicitor's business address shall be his address for service.**

In relation to a body corporate the references in sub-paragraph (a) to the defendant's place of residence shall be construed as references to the defendant's registered or principal office.

(3)  Where the defendant acknowledges service by a solicitor who is acting as agent for another solicitor having a place of business within the jurisdiction, the acknowledgment of service must state that the first-named solicitor so acts and must also state the name and address of that other solicitor.

(4)  If an acknowledgment of service does not specify the defendant's address for service or the Court is satisfied that any address specified in the acknowledgment for service is not genuine, the Court may on application by the plaintiff set aside the acknowledgment or order the defendant to give an address or, as the case may be, a genuine address for service and may in any case direct that the acknowledgment shall nevertheless have effect for the purpose of Order 10, rule 1(5), and Order 65, rule 9.

---

## NOTES

### [12.3.1]  Acknowledgment of service by solicitor
Only a Hong Kong qualified solicitor may acknowledge service of proceedings issued out of the Hong Kong court: see *Li Fook Chu v Chung Shau Ching* [2001] 4 HKC 681 (CA).

### [12.3.2]  Address for service
Order 12 rule 3(2) requires that the defendant give an address within the jurisdiction for service of documents. In *Li Fook Chu v Chung Shau Ching* [2001] 4 HKC 681 the Court of Appeal held that an acknowledgment of service by an English solicitor, giving an address in England for service was defective. Service at that address of pleadings and summonses was set aside.

### [12.3.3]  Service of documents after acknowledgment of service of originating process
After the filing of an acknowledgement of service, documents relating to the proceedings should be served at the address for service stated on the acknowledgement. At this stage service is known as 'ordinary service' and the provisions of Order 65 rule 5 apply.

### [12.3.4]  Acknowledgement of service of amended writ
It is clear from form No 14 in Appendix A that an acknowledgement of service giving notice of intention to defend relates to 'the proceedings', which should mean the legal action identified by the unique proceedings number. It should follow that the acknowledgement is good for the entire proceedings no matter how they may subsequently be modified by amendment or otherwise, and a fresh acknowledgement of service should not be required when an amended writ is served. This was the position under the pre-1981 procedure whereby a defendant was required to enter an 'appearance' rather than an acknowledgement of service. See *Paxton v Baird* [1893] 1 QB 139 (CA) where Lord Coleridge CJ said (at 141) that it is 'not necessary that there should be a fresh appearance where a writ is amended'. In *Thian Sui Ching v Au Yeung Kwai Chuen & Ors* HCPI 1245/1998 (Suffiad J; 22.10.1999) the court left no room for doubt as to whether a

fresh acknowledgement of service would be required by including in an order granting leave to amend the writ, a direction that the previous acknowledgement of service do stand.

**[12.3.5]   Form of acknowledgement of service**
Rule 3(1) prescribes 3 different forms of acknowledgement of service, for use in different types of proceedings. Note that Forms 14 and 15 (for acknowledgement of service of a writ and originating summons respectively) were amended as part of the civil justice reforms taking effect in 2009, notably to reflect the admission procedure under the new Order 13A.

**4.     Procedure on receipt of acknowledgment of service** (O. 12 r. 4)
**On receiving an acknowledgment of service an officer of the Registry must —**

    **(a)     affix to the acknowledgment an official stamp showing the date on which he received it;**

    **(b)     enter the acknowledgment in the cause book with a note showing, if it be the case, that the defendant has indicated in the acknowledgment an intention to contest the proceedings or to apply for a stay of execution in respect of any judgment obtained against him in the proceedings;**

    **(c)     make a copy of the acknowledgment, having affixed to it an official stamp showing the date on which he received the acknowledgment, and send by post to the plaintiff or, as the case may be, his solicitor at the plaintiff's address for service.**

---

**NOTES**

**[12.4.1]   Tasks for registry on receipt of acknowledgement of service**
Order 12 rule 4 prescribes what the court registry is required to do when it receives an acknowledgement of service. This includes sending a copy to the plaintiff or the plaintiff's solicitor by post. It is thus the duty of the court, not the defendant, to bring the acknowledgement of service to the plaintiff's attention.

Rule 4(b) requires that the registry note in the cause book if the defendant has indicated in the acknowledgement an intention to apply for a stay of execution. This requirement is obsolete. It refers to the previous form of acknowledgement of service in which the defendant could indicate an intention to apply for a stay of execution of judgment when giving notice that it did not intend to defend the proceedings. The purpose was to enable the defendant to apply for terms of payment so as to discourage frivolous defences designed to procure delay and postpone an inevitable judgment. The forms of acknowledgement of service were amended as part of the civil justice reforms which took effect in 2009: see the commentary under rule 3. Rather than allowing the defendant to indicate an intention to apply for a stay of execution they now allow the defendant to indicate an intention to make an admission under the new Order 13A procedure whereby payment terms can be requested and fixed by the court if not agreed.

**5.      Time limited for acknowledging service** (O. 12 r. 5)

**References in these rules to the time limited for acknowledging service are references—**

<table>
<tr><td>(a)</td><td>in the case of a writ served within the jurisdiction, to fourteen days after service of the writ (including the day of service) or, where that time has been extended by or by virtue of these rules, to that time as so extended; and</td></tr>
<tr><td>(b)</td><td>in the case of a writ served out of the jurisdiction, to the time limited under Order 10, rule 2(2), Order 11, rule 1(3), or Order 11, rule 4(4), or, where that time has been extended as aforesaid, to that time as so extended.</td></tr>
</table>

---

**NOTES**

**[12.5.1]   Service must be acknowledged within 14 days**

Order 12 rule 5(a) provides that where a writ is served within Hong Kong, the time limited for acknowledging service is normally 14 days. In the case of a writ served outside Hong Kong, the time limited for acknowledging service will have been fixed by the court granting leave to serve out under one of the provisions referred to in rule 5(b).

Failure to acknowledge service and give notice of intention to defend within the prescribed time may result in default judgment being entered under Order 13. However, if judgment has not been entered, late acknowledgement of service may be given under rule 6.

**6.      Late acknowledgment of service** (O. 12 r. 6)

**(1)   Except with the leave of the Court, a defendant may not give notice of intention to defend in an action after judgment has been obtained therein.**

**(2)   Except as provided by paragraph (1) nothing in these rules or any writ or order thereunder shall be construed as precluding a defendant from acknowledging service in an action after the time limited for so doing, but if a defendant acknowledges service after that time, he shall not, unless the Court otherwise orders, be entitled to serve a defence or do any other act later than if he had acknowledged service within that time.**

**[12.6.1]   Late notice of intention to defend**

Order 12 rule 6 provides that a defendant may acknowledge service after the time limited for doing so, and may give notice of intention to defend provided that judgment has not been entered. Such late notice of intention to defend is valid, and any default judgment entered thereafter will be irregular, even if an application for such judgment was submitted before notice of intention to defend was given: *Kwan Tat Chung v Ho Cheuk Kwun (t/a Fat Fai Eng'g Co)* HCPI 381/2002 (Suffiad J; 05.12.2002); *Kerry Freight (HK) Ltd v Del Prado Asia Ltd* [2005] 3 HKLRD 804.

**7.      Acknowledgment not to constitute waiver** (O. 12 r. 7)

**The acknowledgment by a defendant of service of a writ shall not be treated as a waiver by him of any irregularity in the writ or service thereof or in**

any order giving leave to serve the writ or extending the validity of the writ for the purpose of service.

**8.     Dispute as to jurisdiction** (O. 12 r. 8)

(1)     A defendant who wishes to dispute the jurisdiction of the court in the proceedings by reason of any such irregularity as is mentioned in rule 7 or on any other ground shall give notice of intention to defend the proceedings and shall, within the time limited for service of a defence, apply to the Court for—

- (a)     an order setting aside the writ or service of the writ on him, or
- (b)     an order declaring that the writ has not been duly served on him, or
- (c)     the discharge of any order giving leave to serve the writ on him out of the jurisdiction, or
- (d)     the discharge of any order extending the validity of the writ for the purpose of service, or
- (e)     the protection or release of any property of the defendant seized or threatened with seizure in the proceedings, or
- (f)     the discharge of any order made to prevent any dealing with any property of the defendant, or
- (g)     a declaration that in the circumstances of the case the court has no jurisdiction over the defendant in respect of the subject-matter of the claim or the relief or remedy sought in the action, or
- (ga)     an order staying the proceedings, or (L.N. 152 of 2008)
- (h)     such other relief as may be appropriate.

(2)     A defendant who wishes to argue that the Court should not exercise its jurisdiction in the proceedings on one or more of the grounds specified in paragraph (2A) or on any other ground shall also give notice of intention to defend the proceedings and shall, within the time limited for service of a defence, apply to the Court for –

- (a)     a declaration that in the circumstances of the case the Court should not exercise any jurisdiction it may have, or
- (b)     an order staying the proceedings, or
- (c)     such other relief as may be appropriate, including the relief specified in paragraph (1)(e) or (f). (L.N. 152 of 2008)

(2A)     The grounds specified for the purposes of paragraph (2) are that –

- (a)     considering the best interests and convenience of the parties to the proceedings and the witnesses in the proceedings, the proceedings should be conducted in another court,
- (b)     the defendant is entitled to rely on an agreement to which the plaintiff is a party, excluding the jurisdiction of the Court, and
- (c)     in respect of the same cause of action to which the proceedings relate, there are other proceedings pending between the defendant and the plaintiff in another court. (L.N. 152 of 2008)

(3)     An application under paragraph (1) or (2) must be made by summons and the summons must state the grounds of the application. (L.N. 152 of 2008)

(4)    An application under paragraph (1) or (2) must be supported by an affidavit verifying the facts on which the application is based and a copy of the affidavit must be served with the summons by which the application is made. (L.N. 152 of 2008)

(5)    Upon hearing an application under paragraph (1) or (2), the Court, if it does not dispose of the matter in dispute, may give such directions for its disposal as may be appropriate, including directions for the trial thereof as a preliminary issue. (L.N. 152 of 2008)

(6)    A defendant who makes an application under paragraph (1) or (2) shall not be treated as having submitted to the jurisdiction of the court by reason of his having given notice of intention to defend the action; but if the Court makes no order on the application or dismisses it, the notice shall stand unless otherwise directed by the Court and the defendant shall be treated as having given notice of intention to defend the action. (L.N. 152 of 2008)

(6A)   If the Court makes no order on an application under paragraph (1) or (2) or dismisses it, it may give such directions as may be appropriate for service of a defence and the further conduct of the proceedings. (L.N. 152 of 2008)

(7)    Except where the defendant makes an application in accordance with paragraph (1) or (2), the acknowledgment by a defendant of service of a writ shall, unless the acknowledgment is withdrawn by leave of the Court under Order 21, rule 1, be treated as a submission by the defendant to the jurisdiction of the Court in the proceedings. (L.N. 152 of 2008)

---

## NOTES

### [12.8.1]    Vires of Order 12 rule 8 – admiralty jurisdiction
See *The Tian Sheng No 8* [2000] 3 HKC 285 (CFA) dismissing an argument that Order 12 rule 8 is *ultra vires*. See in particular the judgment of Sir Anthony Mason NPJ at 308I *et seq.*

### [12.8.2]    Order 12 rules 7 and 8 – disputes as to jurisdiction
Order 12 rules 7 and 8 provide for the resolution of disputes as to the jurisdiction of the court over an action or party. At one time a party could not raise such issues before the court without the risk of being taken to have submitted to the jurisdiction: *Henry v Geoprosco Int'l Ltd* [1976] 1 QB 726 (CA). The effect of that decision was reversed by the introduction of rules 7 and 8 in Hong Kong in 1981. They provide expressly that acknowledging service does not constitute waiver of irregularity (rule 7), and that a defendant may appear before the court to raise a jurisdictional point without being taken to have submitted to the jurisdiction (rule 8(6)&(7)), provided that an appropriate application is made within the time limited for service of a defence.

### [12.8.3]    Consequences of unsuccessful jurisdictional challenge
Order 12 rule 8(6) previously provided that if the court dismissed a jurisdictional challenge, or made no order, the defendant's notice of intention to defend would cease to have effect. It was then up to the defendant to decide whether to give a fresh notice

of intention to defend. That remains the position in England under CPR 11(7)(b). In Hong Kong, however, the rule was amended as part of the civil justice reforms which took effect on 2 April 2009 so as to provide that the notice of intention to defend stands unless the court orders otherwise. In *Iu Po Shing Patrick v Empresa Hoteleira de Macau Lda & Anor* HCMP 1495/2009 (Rogers VP & Le Pichon JA; 01.09.2009) (para 6) it was said that this gives the court a discretion, and that 'the rule is directed to facilitate the administration of justice by treating the defendant as having given notice to defend and thus avoiding any unnecessary further delays, unless the court saw good reason otherwise'.

The 2009 amendment to rule 8(6) was made at the suggestion of the Law Society, which considered a fresh notice of intention to defend to be an unnecessary additional step. See the Law Society's comments on the draft rules published by the steering committee on civil justice reform.

If the defendant's notice of intention to defend stands, but it takes no further steps, it will be open to the plaintiff to seek judgment in default of defence under

### [12.8.4]   Types of order

Order 12 rule 8(1) lists various heads of relief which may be sought by a party who seeks to avoid having to defend proceedings against it in Hong Kong on jurisdictional grounds. The party may seek a declaration that the writ has not been validly served on him (rule 8(1)(b)) or the discharge of an *ex parte* order under Order 11 rule 1 granting leave to serve the writ out of the jurisdiction (rule 8(1)(c)). The provision also extends to discharge of an order under Order 6 rule 8 extending the validity of a writ for service (rule 8(1)(d)) and a declaration that the court has no jurisdiction over the party in respect of the particular claim (rule 8(1)(g)). Applications for orders by which the court will decline to exercise its jurisdiction by granting a stay of proceedings in favour of another forum are now (with effect from 2009) also covered by the rule. See the commentary below.

### [12.8.5]   Application of Order 12 rule 8 to stay applications

Rule 8(1)(ga), inserted as part of the civil justice reform package with effect from 2009, brings applications for a discretionary stay of proceedings within the scope of the rule. Thus applications to bring proceedings to an end on the ground the dispute should be resolved by litigation in another forum, are now within the rule. Such applications seek a stay on the ground that although the court has jurisdiction, it should decline to exercise it. They are additionally dealt with in rule 8(2A), also inserted as part of the 2009 package.

Previous authorities such as *Royal Skandia Life Assurance Ltd v Sparkle Consultants (HK) Ltd & Ors* HCMP 1453/2006 (Cheung & Yeung JJA; 25.09.2006) in which it was said that it was 'misconceived' to rely on Order 12 rule 8 in a *forum non conveniens* application, should no longer be followed (save when the transitional provisions of Order 12 rule 11 apply). Likewise cases such as *Hwoo Huang Linda v Fu Being San & Ors* HCA 4888/2001 (Deputy Judge Reyes SC; 10.04.2002) which say that inherent jurisdiction is the proper basis of such a stay application.

The Chief Justice's working party on civil justice reform recommended that discretionary stay applications be brought within rule 8 to add to 'procedural certainty' (final report, para 166).

The court's inherent jurisdiction to grant a stay is not displaced by rule 8, but continues to exist. An application for a stay should be brought under rule 8 if there are circumstances which would justify a stay at the time the proceedings are first served; but may be brought under inherent jurisdiction if those circumstances arise after the time prescribed by rule 8(1) has expired. See *Texan Management Ltd & Ors v Pacific Electric Wire & Cable Co Ltd* [2009] UKPC 46 (paras 73, 77), a decision of the Privy Council construing similar provisions in the rules applicable in the British Virgin Islands.

Although discretionary stay applications are now within Order 12 rule 8, certain practical differences remain between them and other jurisdictional applications under the rule. For example, a stay granted by the court can always be lifted 'for example to enforce a security or to facilitate execution', whereas 'a successful challenge to the jurisdiction often results in practical terms in the termination of the action': *Rambas Marketing Co LLC v Chow Kam Fai David* [2001] 3 HKC 250, 253F (per Recorder G Ma SC, as he then was) (appeal to the Court of Appeal dismissed – see CACV 1055/2001).

We now turn to look at stay applications of various types one by one.

**[12.8.6] Stay of Hong Kong proceedings in favour of another jurisdiction**
The court may decline to exercise jurisdiction which it undoubtedly has in a particular case. This will be done where some other forum is considered more appropriate, whether that be the courts of another jurisdiction (by agreement or otherwise), or arbitration (where there is an arbitration agreement). The discretion is exercised in suitable cases by grant of a stay of the Hong Kong proceedings.

The power to grant such a stay exists at common law and is expressed in section 16(3) of the High Court Ordinance (Cap 4) which has the effect of 'statutorily recognising or preserving such a power': *The Nedlloyd Colombo* [1995] 2 HKC 655, 662F-I (CA). In *Linfield Ltd v Taoho Design Architects Ltd* [2002] 2 HKC 204 (para 10) section 16(3) was said to be a 'statutory codification of an inherent jurisdiction'. On the other hand it has been said that the power to stay proceedings in favour of arbitration derives from the Arbitration Ordinance alone: see section 6 thereof and article 8 of the UNCITRAL Model Law, and see the commentary below on the circumstances in which such a stay will be granted.

**[12.8.7] Who may apply for stay of proceedings**
Section 16(3) of the High Court Ordinance provides that such a stay of proceedings may be granted by the court on its own motion or on the application of any person, whether or not a party. In practice it is usually the defendant who will apply, objecting to being sued in the Hong Kong court.

In the rather unusual case of *The Al Dhabiyyah* [1999] 4 HKC 414 it was the plaintiff who applied for and obtained a stay of proceedings in Hong Kong. The plaintiff had commenced proceedings in Singapore, but jurisdiction there was being disputed. With the limitation period about to expire the plaintiff issued a protective writ in Hong Kong. When the defendant sought to compel the plaintiff to proceed with the Hong Kong action the plaintiff sought and obtained a temporary stay of its own proceedings pending resolution of the jurisdictional dispute in Singapore.

**[12.8.8] Foreign jurisdiction clause**

It is common for commercial agreements to specify that disputes shall be resolved in a particular jurisdiction. Where proceedings are commenced in Hong Kong in breach of such an agreement the court may give effect to the agreement by granting a stay. Application for such a stay is now made under Order 12 rule 8(2A)(b). On an application for such a stay the Hong Kong court has followed decisions of courts in other common law jurisdictions.

See, for example *Sport-Billy Productions v DHL International Ltd* [1987] HKLR 729 applying *The Eleftheria* [1969] 1 Lloyd's Rep 237; [1970] P 94. In *Konsumex Foreign Trade Co & Ors v Sun Luen Transportation Co* [1990] 1 HKC 247 and *The Frinton* [1990] 2 HKLR 700 (CA) the principles laid down in the following passage from the judgment of Brandon J in *The Eleftheria* were quoted with approval. Brandon J said, at [1970] P 94, 99:

> The principles established by the authorities can, I think, be summarised as follows:
>
> (1)   Where a plaintiff sues in England in breach of an agreement to refer disputes to a foreign court and the defendants apply for a stay, the English court, assuming the claim to be otherwise within its jurisdiction, is not bound to grant a stay but has a discretion whether to do so or not;
>
> (2)   The discretion should be exercised by granting a stay unless some strong cause for not doing so is shown;
>
> (3)   The burden of proving such strong cause lies on the plaintiffs;
>
> (4)   In exercising its discretion, the court should take into account all the circumstances of the particular case;
>
> (5)   In particular, but without prejudice to (4), the following matters, where they arise, may properly be regarded:
>
>> (a)   in what country the evidence on the issues of fact is situated or more rapidly available and the effect of that on the relative convenience and expense of trial as between the English and foreign courts;
>>
>> (b)   whether the law of the foreign court applies and if so, whether it differs from English law in any material respects;
>>
>> (c)   with what country either party is connected and how closely;
>>
>> (d)   whether the defendants genuinely desire a trial in the foreign country or are only seeking procedural advantages;
>>
>> (e)   whether the plaintiffs will be prejudiced by having to sue in the foreign court because they would:
>>
>>> (i)    be deprived of security for their claim;
>>>
>>> (ii)   be unable to enforce any judgment obtained;
>>>
>>> (iii)  be faced with a time bar not applicable in England; or
>>>
>>> (iv)   for political, racial, religious or other reasons be unlikely to get a fair trial.

In *The K H Enterprise* [1994] 2 HKLR 134 (PC, from Hong Kong) it was held that the general principles applicable on an application for a stay are those set down in the judgment of Brandon LJ in *The El Amria* [1981] 2 Lloyd's Rep 119. In the words of Lord Goff (at [1994] 2 HKLR 134, 150):

> According to those principles, the court has a discretion whether to grant a stay of

proceedings brought in breach of an agreement to refer disputes to a foreign court; but the discretion should be exercised by granting a stay, unless strong cause for not doing so is shown.

See also *Chan Chi Keung & Anor v Delmas HK Ltd* [2004] 4 HKC 28, 39B–C. In The *K H Enterprise* the Privy Council held that one of the matters to be taken into account on a stay application is whether the plaintiff would be prejudiced by having to sue in the foreign court. In that case the plaintiff alleged it would be prejudiced since it faced a time bar in the foreign court but not in Hong Kong. However, the Privy Council upheld the grant of a stay because the plaintiff had deliberately and advisedly allowed the foreign limitation period to expire.

A distinction must be drawn between cases where the agreement confers exclusive jurisdiction on the chosen forum, and cases where the agreed jurisdiction is non-exclusive. Where the agreement provides for exclusive jurisdiction elsewhere, the court will stay proceedings brought in Hong Kong unless 'strong cause' is shown: *Prime Deal (HK) Enterprises Ltd v HSBC* [2006] 3 HKC 74 (para 24). In *Yu Lap Man v Good First Investment Ltd* [1999] 1 HKC 622 (CA) a stay was refused in an action where the parties had agreed that disputes would be subject to the jurisdiction of the courts of the Mainland of China, but there was no agreement to exclude other jurisdictions. The Court of Appeal cited *Sohio Supply Co v Gatoil (USA) Inc* [1989] 1 Lloyd's Rep 588 and *Contractors Ltd v MTE Control Gear Ltd* [1964] SASR 47. See also *Noble Power Investments Ltd v Nissei Stomach Tokyo Co Ltd* [2008] 1 HKLRD 134 where (at para 45 *et seq*) the court reviewed a number of authorities on enforcement of non-exclusive jurisdiction clauses in the context of a *forum non conveniens* application.

An agreement that the law of another jurisdiction shall apply exclusively does not mean that a choice of jurisdiction clause which goes with it is necessarily exclusive: *Wynn Las Vegas LLC v Lam Kwok Hung* HCA 2161/2007 (Sakhrani J; 26.05.2008). In that case it was held that a choice of Nevada law may have been exclusive, but the choice of Nevada jurisdiction was permissive only.

Many of the cases dealing with choice of forum clauses arise in Admiralty proceedings – see also the commentary preceding Order 75 rule 1.

## [12.8.9]   Forum non conveniens

A defendant who takes the view that a jurisdiction other than Hong Kong is more appropriate for a particular dispute may apply to the court to stay the Hong Kong proceedings on the grounds of *forum non conveniens*. Such an application is now made pursuant to Order 12 rule 8(2A)(a). The summons or motion by which such an application is made should identify the jurisdiction said to be more appropriate: *Rambas Marketing Co LLC v Chow Kam Fai David* [2001] 3 HKC 250.

The principles to be applied on an application of this nature were laid down by Lord Goff in *Spiliada Maritime Corp v Cansulex Ltd* [1987] AC 460, see in particular pages 480–481. A useful *précis* of those principles can be found in the judgment of Bingham LJ in *DuPont v Agnew* [1987] 2 Lloyd's Rep 585, 588. Both of those judgments and the principles enunciated in them have been applied in many Hong Kong cases. See, for example, *The Adhiguna Meranti* [1987] 2 HKC 126; [1987] HKLR 904 (CA); *The Andhika Samyra* [1989] 1 HKLR 198; *Tay Choo Wah v Singapore-Johore Express (Pte) Ltd* [1991] 2 HKC 180, 191 (CA); *Rambas Marketing Co LLC v Chow Kam Fai David* [2001] 3 HKC 250 and *LG Electronics Hong Kong Ltd v Bank of Taiwan* [2001]

4 HKC 421.

More recent English cases should be considered in light of the fact that in the European Union it is not open to a national court to decline jurisdiction on grounds of forum *non conveniens* in cases involving a person domiciled in the jurisdiction. See *Owusu v Jackson & Ors* [2005] QB 801 (Eur Ct Grand Chamber). There is no such restriction in Hong Kong.

An application for a stay of proceedings on the ground of *forum nonconveniens* is a matter within the discretion of the court. The court asks itself a single question to be answered in three stages. The single question derives from *Spiliada Maritime Corp v Cansulex Ltd* [1987] AC 460, per Lord Goff, quoted with approval by Hunter JA in *The Adhiguna Meranti* [1987] 2 HKC 126, 129H –130E; [1987] HKLR 904, 907F-908B in the following terms.

> The court has now to answer a single question, namely:
>
>> 'Is there some other available forum, having competent jurisdiction, which is the appropriate forum for the trial of the action, *ie* in which the case may be tried more suitably for the interests of all the parties and the ends of justice'.

According to Hunter JA in *Louvet v Louvet & Anor* [1990] 1 HKLR 670 (CA) this question was first formulated in *Sim v Robinow* (1892) 19 R (Ct of Sess) 665. The three stages by which the question is to be answered were laid down by Hunter JA in *The Adhiguna Meranti* (above) in the following terms:

> (I)    Is it shown that Hong Kong is not only not the natural or appropriate forum for the trial, but that there is another available forum which is clearly or distinctly more appropriate than Hong Kong? The evidential burden is here upon the applicant. The emphasis is upon 'appropriate' rather than 'convenient' because this is not simply a matter of practical convenience. The purpose is to identify the forum 'with which the action has the most real and substantial connection', per Lord Keith in the *Abidin Daver* [1984] AC 398. Failure by the applicant at this stage is normally fatal.

> (II)    If the answer to (I) is yes, will a trial at this other forum deprive the plaintiff of any 'legitimate personal or juridical advantages'? The evidential burden here lies upon the plaintiff.

> (III)    If the answer to (II) is yes, a court has to balance the advantages of (I) against the disadvantages of (II), *Abidin Daver* per Lord Brandon at 419. Deprivation of one or more personal or juridical advantages will not necessarily be fatal to the applicant provided that the court is satisfied that notwithstanding such loss 'substantial justice will be done in the available appropriate forum'. The court must try to be objective. Proof of this, which can fairly be called the ultimate burden of persuasion, rests upon the applicant for the stay. By these means he establishes that on balance the other forum is more suitable 'for the interests of all the parties and the ends of justice'. This may be another way of saying that the plaintiff's choice of forum has been shown to be so inappropriate as to deserve the pejorative description of 'forum shopping' and to be restrained accordingly, (cp Lord Reid in *The Atlantic Star* [1974] AC 436).

This test continues to be used. See for example *Ho Siu Pui & Ors v Yue Sheng Finance Ltd & Anor* [2003] 1 HKC 621 (CA); *DGC v SLC* [2005] 3 HKC 293 (CA); *Esquel Enterprises Ltd v Tal Apparel Ltd* [2006] 2 HKC 384 (CA).

It will be noted that in para (I) of the above passage from *The Adhiguna Meranti* it is said that the burden is on the applicant, that is the defendant applying for a stay on grounds of *forum non conveniens*. This is the opposite of the situation where the defendant is not present within the jurisdiction and leave is needed for service of the writ *ex juris*. See *Dynasty Line Ltd (provisional liquidators appointed) v Sukamto Sia & Anor* [2009] 4 HKC 184 (CA) (para 56, 75).

One ground on which it is frequently argued that Hong Kong is not the appropriate forum for resolution of a dispute is that the law of another jurisdiction is applicable. In such a case it is up to the party so asserting to establish what the foreign law is and how it is different from the Hong Kong law: see, for example, *LG Electronics Hong Kong Ltd v Bank of Taiwan* [2001] 4 HKC 421. In the absence of evidence as to the state of the foreign law, the Hong Kong court will proceed on the assumption that it is the same as Hong Kong law.

Another ground frequently raised on *forum non conveniens* applications is the availability of witnesses. It is obviously cheaper and more appropriate to have a trial in the place where witnesses are to be found and are compellable. However, in *Greenwood Ltd v Pearl River Container Transportation Ltd & Anor* [1994] 1 HKC 585, the court took the view that given the proximity of Hong Kong to Guangzhou and the facilities for travel, Hong Kong was not an inappropriate forum for a trial involving witnesses from that part of China. The decision of Deputy Judge Yam in *Greenwood* was upheld on appeal to the Court of Appeal (CACV 27/1994; Power VP, Nazareth & Litton JJ A; 25.05.1994, unreported). In *Continental Mark v Verkehrs-Club de Schweiz* [2001] 4 HKC 469, 483I–484B (affirmed on appeal: see [2002] 2 HKC 513) it was held that Switzerland rather than Hong Kong was the appropriate forum in a case where the alleged contract had been negotiated in German, the witnesses were in Europe and if their evidence were to be given in Hong Kong interpretation would be required. The fact that a witness is resident out of the jurisdiction will only be of significance if his or her attendance will mostly likely be required at trial: *Rambas Marketing* (above, at 261G-262A).

*Forum non conveniens* applications may be opposed on the ground the plaintiff would be deprived of a personal or juridical advantage if compelled to litigate elsewhere. An example is where the proceedings would be time-barred in the other jurisdiction: *Peregrine Fixed Income Ltd v JP Morgan Chase Bank* [2005] 2 HKC 374, 386; *Mayar (HK) Ltd v Sayal* [2005] 2 HKC 389, 402. In *Xinjiang Xingmei Oil-Pipeline Co Ltd v China Petroleum & Chemical Corp* [2005] 2 HKC 292 it was argued that proceedings should be allowed to continue in Hong Kong because of perceived risks that justice would not be done in the natural forum, Mainland China. The argument was rejected. Such an argument was taken very seriously, but ultimately rejected in *Pacific Int'l Sports Clubs Ltd v Surkis* [2010] EWCA Civ 753 (02.07.2010) where there was evidence of grave deficiencies in the judicial system of the natural forum, Ukraine. In *Ho Yuen Ki Winnie v Ho Hung Sun Stanley & Anor* [2007] 4 HKC 416 (CFI); [2008] 4 HKC 544 (CA); leave to appeal to the CFA refused (FAMV 52/2008) the court declined to stay Hong Kong proceedings where the plaintiff had a rational fear she would be the victim of physical violence if she had to go to Macau, the natural forum, to give evidence.

The place where a tort is committed is *prima facie* the natural forum for determination of the dispute: see *Chow Tak Sung v Tse Ching* [2002] 4 HKC 664, 669H–I citing *Distillers Co (Bio-Chemicals) Ltd v Thompson* [1971] AC 458 and *Berezovsky v Michaels*

[2000] 1 WLR 1004 (HL). In *Chow Tak Sung* Judge Wong granted a stay of proceedings in the District Court claiming damages for malicious prosecution and false imprisonment which had allegedly occurred in Shenzhen. The plaintiff had submitted that he would not be able to have a fair hearing in Shenzhen and that he was concerned for his personal safety should he have to travel there for trial. The judge found that there was no evidence to substantiate these claims and stated (at 670B) 'The courts of Hong Kong have always shown their respect to the People's Republic of China Courts and have always regarded People's Republic of China Courts as courts of competent jurisdiction'. See also *Emperor (China Concept) Investments Ltd v SBI E-2 Capital Securities Ltd* [2006] 1 HKC 266 where an action in defamation was stayed on the ground that Singapore, the place of publication, was the appropriate forum.

In *The Kapitan Shvetsov* [1997] 1 HKC 485 (CA) proceedings were commenced in both Hong Kong and Singapore in respect of a collision between a Singaporean vessel and a Russian vessel in Thailand. Both parties had rejected the natural forum, Thailand. In the circumstances it was held that Hong Kong's jurisdiction should not be ousted on the ground of *forum non conveniens*.

*Appeal* – The court has a discretion on an application for a stay of proceedings on the ground of *forum non conveniens* and the Court of Appeal will be slow to interfere unless the judge's decision is demonstrably wrong: see *Nan Tung Bank Ltd, Zhu Hai v Wangfoong Transportation Ltd* [1999] 2 HKC 606 (CA); *Lungerhausen & Anor v Dillon* CACV 226/2003 (Rogers VP & Le Pichon JA; 05.02.2004); and *Louvet v Louvet & Anor* [1990] 1 HKLR 670 (CA).

In *Greenwood Ltd v Pearl River Container Transportation Ltd & Anor* CACV 27/1994 (Power VP, Nazareth & Litton JJ A; 25.05.1994, unreported), the Court of Appeal set down three 'very limited circumstances' in which it will interfere with the exercise of discretion on a *forum non conveniens* application. These derive from the *Abidin Daver* [1984] 1 AC 398, 420A–C and are:

(i)     where the judge had misdirected himself with regard to the principles in accordance with which his discretion had to be exercised;

(ii)    whether the judge, in exercising his discretion, had taken into account matters which he ought not to have done or failed to take into account matters which he ought to have done; or

(iii)   where his decision is plainly wrong.

The above passage was quoted with approval in *Ho Siu Pui & Anor v Yue Sheng Finance Ltd & Ors* [2003] 1 HKC 621, 628F–G (CA).

Considerations of *forum non conveniens* may also be relevant where a party seeks not to stay proceedings in Hong Kong, but to restrain another party from proceeding elsewhere. See the commentary under Order 29 rule 1 concerning the court's power to grant an injunction to restrain a party from proceeding in another jurisdiction by means of 'anti-suit' injunction.

### [12.8.10]   Litigating in different jurisdictions simultaneously

A defendant who is being sued in Hong Kong and another jurisdiction simultaneously in respect of the same cause of action may apply for a stay of the Hong Kong proceedings on the basis of *lis alibi pendens*. Application for such a stay is now made under Order 12 rule 8(2A)(c).

While it is highly undesirable to have the same cause of action being litigated concurrently in different jurisdictions, this does not automatically justify an order to prevent the actions from continuing at the same time: *Hing Fat Plastic Manufacturing Co Ltd v Advanced Technology Products (HK) Ltd* [1992] 2 HKLR 350. There is no presumption that a multiplicity of proceedings is vexatious: *Choi Sai Yiu & Ors v Widepower Ltd & Ors* [1994] 3 HKC 274. A plaintiff will be permitted to continue with simultaneous proceedings if it demonstrates that it derives some personal or juridical advantage so that to prevent the actions continuing would amount to a positive injustice. If, after considering the facts, no such advantage appears, then the plaintiff will be restrained from proceeding and may be ordered to pay the defendant's costs on an indemnity basis: *The Abidin Daver* [1984] AC 398; *Australian Commercial Research and Development Ltd v ANZ McCaughan Merchant Bank Ltd* [1989] 3 All ER 65.

The plaintiff itself may also apply for a stay of its own proceedings. In *Allson Classic Hotel (HK) Ltd v Abundance Assets Ltd* [1994] 2 HKC 154 the Court of Appeal granted a stay of proceedings sought by a plaintiff who had earlier commenced parallel proceedings in Hawaii and had issued a writ in Hong Kong only to preserve its rights under the Transfer of Businesses (Protection of Creditors) Ordinance (Cap 49).

The matter is one of discretion and the decision of the trial judge will not be lightly interfered with on appeal (*National Union Fire Insurance Co of Pittsburgh v Grand Union Insurance Co Ltd* [1993] HKLD C78).

In *The Kapitan Shvetsov* [1997] 1 HKC 485 (CA) the Court of Appeal reversed the decision below to order a stay of Hong Kong proceedings when parallel proceedings were already well advanced in Singapore. Citing *The Atlantic Star* [1974] AC 436 as interpreted in *The Tillie Lykes* [1977] 1 Lloyd's Rep 124, Litton JA stated (at 494E–F) that 'the mere existence of a multiplicity of proceedings was not to be taken into account as a disadvantage to the defendant; a clear case of oppression or vexation had to be made out to justify a stay'.

In *Intel Corp v Via Technologies Inc & Anor* [2002] 3 HKC 650 an application to stay Hong Kong proceedings in favour of on-going proceedings in England, which had progressed further, was refused. It was held that although there would be duplication of work if the Hong Kong proceedings were allowed to continue, there were important differences between the two actions. In particular, the proceedings in England involved an additional defendant, and the Hong Kong proceedings fell to be determined by local legislation which had different wording. See the judgment of Sakhrani J at 657G–658B.

The court also has power to grant an injunction to restrain a party from continuing proceedings in another jurisdiction – see the commentary under Order 29 rule 1.

**[12.8.11] Stay of proceedings in favour of arbitration**

The court may grant a stay of proceedings in order to compel parties to abide by an agreement to submit a dispute to arbitration. The agreement must be in writing: Arbitration Ordinance (Cap 341), s 6. As to what constitutes sufficient writing for this purpose see *Ocean Park Corp v Proud Sky Co Ltd & Ors* HCCL 10/2006 (Stone J; 28.11.2007).

The power to order such a stay is found in section 6 of the Arbitration Ordinance and art 8 of the UNCITRAL model law (sched 5 to the Ordinance). Those provisions expressly limit the court's power to applications by a party who has not yet taken a substantive step in the proceedings. In *Chok Yick Interior Design & Eng'g Co Ltd v Fortune World Enterprises Ltd* [2010] 2 HKC 360 it was held that the plaintiff, who had already served a statement of claim, could get round this restriction by relying on inherent jurisdiction and Order 1B rule 1(2)(e) rather than the Ordinance and the model law. However, see *Tommy CP Sze & Co v Li & Fung (Trading) Ltd & Ors* [2003] 1 HKC 418, 423G-H where it was said, apparently *obiter*, that there is no inherent jurisdiction and the power is entirely statutory.

The power in section 6 of the Ordinance is worded in discretionary terms ('the court . . . may'), whereas art 8 of the model law uses mandatory language ('the court shall'). In *Paquito Lima Buton v Rainbow Joy Shipping Ltd* [2007] 2 HKC 503 (CA) it was held that the grant of a stay is mandatory under the legislation. However, on further appeal ([2008] 4 HKC 14) the Court of Final Appeal held that the mandatory stay provisions are inoperative where their application is precluded by a law granting exclusive jurisdiction to a court, such as the Employees' Compensation Ordinance which grants exclusive jurisdiction to the District Court.

Applications for a stay in favour of arbitration are now brought under Order 8 rule 12(2A)(b). In *Tommy CP Sze* (above) Ma J set out four questions the court should ask itself when dealing with such a stay application:

1.    Is the clause in question an arbitration agreement?
2.    Is the arbitration agreement null and void, inoperative or incapable of being performed?
3.    Is there in reality a dispute or difference between the parties?
4.    Is the dispute or difference between the parties within the ambit of the arbitration agreement?

With regard to the first two questions, the burden on the party applying for a stay is merely to show there is a *prima facie* or plainly arguable case that the parties are bound by an arbitration clause: *Pacific Crown Eng'g Ltd v Hyundai Eng'g & Construction Co Ltd* [2003] 3 HKC 659; *PCCW Global Ltd v Interactive Communications Service Ltd* [2007] 1 HKC 327 (CA) (leave to appeal to the CFA refused – FAMV 12/2007; 19.04.2007). Otherwise the court would be 'usurping the function of the arbitrator': *Private Co 'Triple V' Inc v Star Universal Co Ltd & Anor* [1995] 3 HKC 129 (CA). This is because an arbitral tribunal is, under art 16 of the UNCITRAL Model Law, competent to rule on its own jurisdiction: *Cathay Pacific Airways Ltd v Hong Kong Air Cargo Terminals Ltd* [2002] 2 HKC 193, 202E. The situation may be different where the UNCITRAL Model Law does not apply.

It has been held that where it is sought to argue that an arbitration clause is overridden by consumer protection legislation (in Hong Kong see the Control of Exemption Clauses (Cap 71), s 15 and the Arbitration Ordinance, s 6(3)) the court should not interfere with the arbitrator's jurisdiction to decide the issue in the first instance: *Rogers Wireless Inc v Muroff* [2007] SCC 35 (SCC).

An 'option' to arbitrate may constitute a binding arbitration agreement entitling the defendant to a stay: *Grandeur Electrical Co Ltd v Cheung Kee Fung Cheung Construction Co Ltd* [2006] 4 HKC 423 (CA), explaining *Thorn Security (HK) Ltd v Cheung Kee Fung Cheung Construction Co Ltd* [2005] 1 HKC 252 (CA).

With regard to question 3 set out in *Tommy C P Sze & Co* (above), an unequivocal admission of liability and quantum means there is no dispute to refer to arbitration and in principle the plaintiff should be free to proceed with court action to recover the debt. See *Louis Dreyfus Trading Ltd v Bonarich Int'l (Group) Ltd* [1997] 3 HKC 597 and *Leung Kwok Tim v Builders Federal (HK) Ltd* [2001] 3 HKC 527.

Even in the absence of any suggestion of an arbitration agreement the court may stay proceedings pending the outcome of a related arbitration involving other parties: *Linfield Ltd v Taoho Design Architects Ltd* [2002] 2 HKC 204, 208H–I per Ma J, refusing a stay on the facts.

### [12.8.12]   Procedure on application

Order 12 rule 8(3) provides that a jurisdictional application under the rule must be made by summons. It must be emphasised that the sub-rule specifically requires that the summons must state the grounds of the application. It is probably sufficient simply to refer to one or more of the heads set out in rule 8(1) and (2A) without elaboration, so long as the applicant's position is made clear.

The application must be supported by an affidavit verifying the facts relied upon, and the affidavit must be served with the summons: rule 8(4). In *Texan Management Ltd & Ors v Pacific Electric Wire & Cable Co Ltd* [2009] UKPC 46 (paras 87) the Privy Council, construing a similar provision in the rules applicable in the British Virgin Islands, held that a failure to serve the evidence with the application was 'a minor procedural defect', and that the judge at first instance had properly exercised discretion to excuse it. Such a discretion may be found in Hong Kong's Order 2 rule 1.

### [12.8.13]   Time for making application

Order 12 rule 8(1) provides that an application under the rule must be made within the time for service of a defence (as to which see Order 18 rule 2). Prior to amendment in 1988 the rule stipulated 14 days from the giving of notice of intention to defend.

Where the time for service of the defence is extended, the time for applying under rule 8 is likewise extended. See *Texan Management Ltd & Ors v Pacific Electric Wire & Cable Co Ltd* [2009] UKPC 46 (paras 82-85), where the Privy Council preferred *Lawson v Midland Travellers Ltd* [1993] 1 WLR 735 (CA) over other authorities.

The time limit does not apply to applications for a stay made under the inherent jurisdiction of the court, and it is appropriate to rely on inherent jurisdiction where the circumstances said to justify a stay arise only after that time has expired. See *Texan Management Ltd* (above) (paras 73, 77), a decision of the Privy Council construing similar provisions in the rules applicable in the British Virgin Islands.

### [12.8.14]   Extension of time for making application

The time within which an application must be made under Order 12 rule 8 may be extended under Order 3 rule 5 even after it has expired. See, for example, *The Tian Sheng No 8* [2000] 3 HKC 285 (CFA), in particular the judgment of Bokhary PJ at 299F *et seq.* Earlier authorities such as *Wo Fung Paper Making Fty Ltd v Sappi Kraft (Pty) Ltd* [1988] 2 HKLR 346 (CA), based on the former rule 8(2) (which purported to exclude such extension power) should no longer be followed.

On an application for extension of time the court will expect a satisfactory explanation for the delay: *Yeung Fu Lin & Anor v Wong Kam Hung & Anor* [1997] 3 HKC 809, 811D-F. Where the grounds for a stay emerge only after the time to make an application has expired, there is 'no reason to suppose that the court should be reluctant to extend time to allow the application to be made': *Chan Chin Cheung v Chan Fatt Cheung & Ors* [2010] 1 SLR 1192 (CA) (para 24), quoting Dicey & Morris.

### [12.8.15]     Abandonment of jurisdictional point by taking a step in the proceedings

Notwithstanding the scheme laid down in Order 12 rules 7 and 8 a party may be taken to waive a jurisdictional point by taking a step in the proceedings. The party will be taken to have waived the jurisdictional point if the step it takes demonstrates an election to abandon the right to contest the court's jurisdiction: *Deak Perera Far East Ltd (in liq) v R Leslie Deak* [1988] 2 HKLR 95, 101I–J citing *Eagle Star Insurance Co v Yuval Insurance Co* [1978] 1 Lloyd's Rep 357 and *Ives and Barker v Willans* [1894] 2 Ch 478. The principle and its operation are illustrated by the following points set out in *Hwoo Huang Linda v Fu Being San & Ors* HCA 4888/2001 (Deputy Judge Reyes SC; 10.04.2002):

(1)     A party may be treated as having submitted to the jurisdiction if he files a pleading setting out his case on the substantive merits of an action.

(2)     A party may be treated as having submitted to the jurisdiction if he invokes the court's jurisdiction to obtain an interlocutory or final order requiring the opposite party to perform some act (for example, disclose documents, provide further and better particulars, or answer interrogatories).

(3)     A party does not submit to the jurisdiction if he merely acts to preserve the *status quo* pending the mounting and resolution of an application to challenge forum.

(4)     A party does not submit to jurisdiction if he merely takes defensive action in interlocutory injunction proceedings brought by the other side.

(5)     A party may be able to preserve an option to challenge forum, despite having engaged in conduct which might be regarded as submission to the jurisdiction if before or at the time of such conduct he makes it clear that his action is without prejudice to the bringing of a challenge to forum.

(6)     The court should adopt a common sense approach. It must not be overly subtle or astute to find that a party has submitted to the jurisdiction. Otherwise, the question of submission could easily become a technicality trap for the unwary. The real question is whether a party's conduct is so inconsistent with maintaining an option to challenge forum that the party should be assumed to have waived such option. In the case of any doubt, the party proposing to challenge forum should probably be given the benefit of that doubt.

The same considerations apply where a defendant seeks a stay of proceedings in favour of arbitration or litigation in another jurisdiction even though Order 12 rule 8 does not apply: see *Hwoo Huang Linda* (above, para 23).

Additional guidance on submission to jurisdiction can be obtained from the following cases:

•     *Lee Fai v Chan Kui* [1997] 3 HKC 228 (CA) where the defendant was taken to have submitted to the jurisdiction by applying to set aside a default judgment and appearing at an assessment of damages, albeit under protest, without making an application under Order 12 rule 8.

•     In *ABN Ambro Bank NV v Fortgang* HCA 537/2007 (Sakhrani J; 11.01.2008) the defendant was taken to have submitted to the jurisdiction by, after issuing a summons under Order 12 rule 8, serving a bare denial defence (later said to have been done 'purely as a precaution') without any indication that this was done without prejudice to the pending application.

* *Winnitex Investment Co Ltd v Oxford Products (Int'l) Ltd* [2004] 4 HKC 660 (DCt) where the defendant applied (in the alternative) to strike out the plaintiff's claims under Order 18 rule 19 in the same summons as it sought a stay of proceedings on jurisdictional grounds.

### [12.8.16]    Time for service of defence
The time for service of a defence does not run against a defendant pending determination of a jurisdictional issue under Order 12 rule 8: see Order 18 rule 2(3). The plaintiff should not be entitled to enter judgment in default of defence and any such judgment would be liable to be set aside. However, in the unusual case of *Dongguan Dongxiang Decoration Co Ltd v Universal Right Ltd* [1999] 1 HKC 790 Barnett J refused to set aside judgment in default of defence where the defendant had brought its application under Order 12 rule 8 only after the court had made an unless order for service of a defence.

### [12.8.17]    Merits irrelevant
It has been observed in the Hong Kong Court of Appeal that the merits of a case are irrelevant on an application under this rule to challenge the jurisdiction of the court: see *Mercedes-Benz AG v Leiduck & Anor* [1995] 1 HKC 448. The judge below had held that it would be 'absurd to require the usual affidavit of merits' on an application of this nature and Litton JA (at 455E–F) agreed. The Court of Appeal's judgment was affirmed in the Privy Council: see [1995] 3 HKC 1. But note that *Leiduck* has in other respects been reversed by legislation: see Order 11 rule 1(1)(oc) and the commentary thereunder.

See, however, *Bayer Polymers Co Ltd v Industrial and Commercial Bank of China, Hong Kong Branch* [2000] 1 HKC 805 where Stone J dismissed an application for a stay on the grounds of *forum non conveniens* where he was satisfied that there was no arguable defence such that there would be no real issues between the parties whether the trial took place in Hong Kong or elsewhere. The learned judge went on to hold that the plaintiff had satisfied him that there was a risk that the plaintiff would not receive substantial justice in the jurisdiction which the defendant contended for (the Mainland of China) and that this further justified dismissal of the application.

### [12.8.18]    Rule exclusive
Order 12 rule 8 is the exclusive source of the court's power to dispute jurisdictional issues and all applications must be made under it. See *Wo Fung Paper Making Factory Ltd v Sappi Kraft (Pty) Ltd* [1988] 2 HKLR (especially at 352) where the Court of Appeal dismissed an application to challenge jurisdiction brought under Order 32 rule 6 and inherent jurisdiction. There the Court of Appeal described Order 12 rule 8 as a 'code'. See also the judgment of Sir Anthony Mason NPJ in *The Tian Sheng No 8* [2000] 3 HKC 285, at 308D *et seq* where the learned judge held that this rule is intended to be 'a comprehensive and exclusive code for the taking of jurisdictional objections'.

*Miruvor v Panama-Globe Steamer Lines SA & Ors* [2007] 1 HKLRD 804 (CA) (para 8) suggests that Order 12 rule 8 is *not* a complete code and may be considered to be *per incuriam* in this regard.

**8A.**  **Application by defendant where writ not served** (O. 12 r. 8A)

(1)  Any person named as a defendant in a writ which has not been served on him may serve on the plaintiff a notice requiring him within a specified period not less than 14 days after service of the notice either to serve the writ on the defendant or to discontinue the action as against him.

(2)  Where the plaintiff fails to comply with a notice under paragraph (1) within the time specified the Court may, on the application of the defendant by summons, order the action to be dismissed or make such other order as it thinks fit.

(3)  A summons under paragraph (2) shall be supported by an affidavit verifying the facts on which the application is based and stating that the defendant intends to contest the proceedings and a copy of the affidavit must be served with the summons.

(4)  Where the plaintiff serves the writ in compliance with a notice under paragraph (1) or with an order under paragraph (2) the defendant must acknowledge service within the time limited for so doing.

**9.**  **Acknowledgment of service of originating summons** (O. 12 r. 9)

(1)  Each defendant named in and served with an originating summons (other than an ex parte originating summons or an originating summons under Order 113 or an application under Order 121) must acknowledge service of the summons as if it were a writ.

(3)  The foregoing rules of this Order shall apply in relation to an originating summons (other than an ex parte originating summons or an originating summons under Order 113 or an application under Order 121) as they apply to a writ except that after the word "extended" wherever it occurs in rule 5(a), there shall be inserted the words "or abridged" and for the reference in rule 5(b) to Order 11, rules 1 (3) and 4(4), there shall be substituted a reference to Order 11, rule 9(6). (L.N. 119 of 1998)

---

NOTES

**[12.9.1]**  **When acknowledgement of service of originating summons required**
Order 12 rule 9 extends to most originating summonses the requirement that service be acknowledged. The exceptions, where acknowledgement of service is not required, are:
* *Ex parte* originating summons (since it is not served).
* Originating summons claiming summary possession of land under Order 113.
* Originating summons under Order 121 claiming relief under the Child Abduction and Custody Ordinance (Cap 512).

**10.**  **Acknowledgment of service to be treated as entry of appearance**
(O. 12 r. 10)
For the purpose of any enactment referring expressly or impliedly to the entry of appearance as a procedure provided by rules of court for responding to a writ or other process issuing out of the Court of First Instance, or of any

**rule of law, the acknowledgment of service of the writ or other process in accordance with these rules shall be treated as the entry of an appearance to it, and related expressions shall be construed accordingly.**

---

NOTES

**[12.10.1]   Entry of 'appearance'**
The acknowledgement of service procedure was introduced in 1981 replacing a procedure whereby a defendant, once served, was required to make a notional 'appearance' before the court on paper. Order 12 rule 10 is transitional, providing that an acknowledgement of service shall be treated as entry of an appearance where any legislation continues to refer to the former procedure.

**11.    Transitional provision relating to rule 86 of Amendment Rules 2008**
     (O.12, r. 11)
     **Where an application under rule 8(1) is pending immediately before the commencement of the Amendment Rules 2008, then the application is to be determined as if rule 86 of the Amendment Rules 2008 had not been made. (L.N. 152 of 2008]**

---

NOTES

**[12.11.1] Prior applications not affected by CJR amendments**
Order 12 rule 11 makes transitional provision for applications under rule 8(1) which were pending when the civil justice reforms came into force in 2009. Such applications will not be affected by the amendments. One result with regard to pending discretionary stay applications is that they will continue to be based on inherent jurisdiction rather than these rules. However that is largely a conceptual matter without much practical significance.

## ORDER 13

### FAILURE TO GIVE NOTICE OF INTENTION TO DEFEND

**1.     Claim for liquidated demand** (O. 13 r. 1)

**(1)   Where a writ is indorsed with a claim against a defendant for a liquidated demand only, then, if that defendant fails to give notice of intention to defend, the plaintiff may, after the prescribed time, enter final judgment against that defendant for a sum not exceeding that claimed by the writ in respect of the demand and for costs, and proceed with the action against the other defendants, if any. (See App. A, Form 39)**

**(2)   A claim shall not be prevented from being treated for the purposes of this rule as a claim for a liquidated demand by reason only that part of the claim is for interest under section 48 of the Ordinance at a rate which is not higher than that payable on judgment debts at the date of the writ.**

---

**NOTES**

**[13.1.1]   Types of claim where default judgment may be entered**
Judgment in default of notice of intention to defend may be taken as of right, but subject to being set aside (see rule 9), in respect of claims for most, but not all, types of relief. The types of claim which come within the scope of the Order are the following:

(1)     Rules 1 and 2 – claims for liquidated and unliquidated sums of money respectively. As to the distinction between those two types of claims for money, see *GL Baker Ltd v Barclays Bank Ltd* [1956] 1 WLR 1409; [1956] 3 All ER 519 and *Lagos v Grundwalt* [1910] 1 KB 41, both of which were cited with approval in *Indian Overseas Bank Ltd v Asi Tai & Co* [1965] HKLR 128.
(2)     Rule 3 – claims in detinue.
(3)     Rule 4 – claims for possession of land.
(4)     Rule 5 – mixed claims, being claims for more than one of the above types of relief.

In each case, the plaintiff's entitlement to enter judgment in default of notice of intention to defend arises 'after the prescribed time', as to which, see rule 6A and the commentary thereunder.

Note that leave is required to enter judgment in default of notice of intention to defend in certain types of case. See, for example, Order 83A in respect of money lenders' actions and Order 84A dealing with actions to enforce hire-purchase and conditional sale agreements.

Other claims, in respect of which there is no provision for default judgment, are dealt with by Order 13 rule 6. See the commentary under that rule.

**[13.1.2]   Effect of default judgment**
A default judgment is binding on the parties and takes effect like any other judgment. Such a judgment is capable of giving rise to estoppel *per rem judicatam* even though there has been no adjudication on the merits. See *Kok Hoong v Leong Cheong Kweng*

*Mines Ltd* [1964] AC 993, 1010 (PC). However, such estoppel will arise only in respect of what must necessarily be taken to have been decided: *New Brunswick Railway Co v British and French Trust Corp Ltd* [1939] AC 1.

In *Lam Chi Fat v Liberty International Insurance* [2003] 2 HKC 260, 265I the Court of Appeal, citing *Cribb v Freyberger* [1919] WN 22 held that on failing to give notice of intention to defend, a defendant had admitted all of the allegations in the statement of claim.

### [13.1.3]   Enforcement of default judgment abroad

Because a default judgment is not a judgment on the merits, enforcement in international cases is 'notoriously difficult': *Habib Bank Ltd v Central Bank of Sudan* [2007] 1 WLR 470; [2006] EWHC 1767 (Comm) (para 8). Although the common law permits enforcement of such judgments (see the commentary under Order 71 rule 2), different legal systems may take a different view. Thus in *Berliner Bank AG v Karageorgis & Anor* [1996] 1 Lloyd's Rep 426, and again in *Habib* (above) the English court permitted the plaintiffs to proceed to trial rather than enter default judgment, in order that they could obtain judgment on the merits which would more likely be enforceable abroad.

### [13.1.4]   Effect of default judgment against one defendant

Where relief is sought against more than one defendant, default judgment entered against one of them may, but does not necessarily, render the claim against the other nugatory. In *Bonus Garment Co (a firm) v Karl Rieker GMBH & Anor* [1997] 2 HKC 460 the Privy Council considered *Morel Bros & Co Ltd v Earl of Westmoreland* [1904] AC 11 where it was held that where a plaintiff has pleaded in the alternative against more than one defendant the taking of default judgment against one of them precluded it from proceeding against the others. The board was of the opinion that the claim against the remaining defendant was not alternative to that against the party against whom judgment in default had been entered and reversed the decision of the Court of Appeal setting aside leave to serve out of the jurisdiction.

With regard to assessment of damages where default judgment is entered against one defendant, see Order 37 rule 3.

### [13.1.5]   Costs

As to the quantum of costs which may be claimed by a plaintiff in favour of whom judgment is entered under this rule, see Order 62, Second Schedule, Part I.

**2.      Claim for unliquidated damages** (O. 13 r. 2)

**Where a writ is indorsed with a claim against a defendant for unliquidated damages only, then, if that defendant fails to give notice of intention to defend, the plaintiff may, after the prescribed time, enter interlocutory judgment against that defendant for damages to be assessed and costs, and proceed with the action against the other defendants, if any. (See App. A, Form 40)**

------

## NOTES

### [13.2.1]   Form of default judgment on claim for unliquidated amount

Default judgment for a liquidated amount cannot be entered on a claim for unliquidated damages even though those damages are particularised: *UDL Contracting Ltd v Apple Daily Printing Ltd & Anor* [2008] 2 HKC 534. In that case the court set aside such a judgment as irregular.

The prescribed forms of default judgment are set out in appendix A to the rules, as forms 39, 40, 41 and 42.

**3.     Claim for detention of goods** (O. 13 r. 3)

**(1)     Where a writ is indorsed with a claim against a defendant relating to the detention of goods only, then, if that defendant fails to give notice of intention to defend the plaintiff may, after the prescribed time and subject to Order 42, rule 1A—**

>    **(a)     at his option enter either—**
>
>>        **(i)     interlocutory judgment against that defendant for delivery of the goods or their value to be assessed and costs; or**
>>
>>        **(ii)     interlocutory judgment for the value of the goods to be assessed and costs; or**
>
>    **(b)     apply by summons for judgment against that defendant for delivery of the goods without giving him the alternative of paying their assessed value,**

**and in any case proceed with the action against the other defendants, if any. (See App. A, Form 41)**

**(2)     A summons under paragraph (1)(b) must be supported by affidavit and notwithstanding Order 65, rule 9, the summons and a copy of the affidavit must be served on the defendant against whom judgment is sought.**

**4.     Claim for possession of land** (O. 13 r. 4)

**(1)     Where a writ is indorsed with a claim against a defendant for possession of land only, then, if that defendant fails to give notice of intention to defend the plaintiff may, after the prescribed time, and on producing a certificate by his solicitor, or (if he sues in person) an affidavit, stating that he is not claiming any relief in the action of the nature specified in Order 88, rule 1, enter judgment for possession of the land as against that defendant and costs, and proceed with the action against the other defendants, if any. (See App. A, Form 42)**

**(5)     Where there is more than one defendant, judgment entered under this rule shall not be enforced against any defendant unless and until judgment for possession of the land has been entered against all the defendants.**

**5.     Mixed claims** (O. 13 r. 5)

**Where a writ issued against any defendant is indorsed with two or more of the claims mentioned in the foregoing rules, and no other claim, then, if that defendant fails to give notice of intention to defend, the plaintiff may, after the prescribed time, enter against that defendant such judgment in respect of any such claim as he would be entitled to enter under those rules if that were the only claim indorsed on the writ and proceed with the action against the other defendants, if any.**

**6.** **Other claims** (O. 13 r. 6)

(1) **Where a writ is indorsed with a claim of a description not mentioned in rules 1 to 4, then, if any defendant fails to give notice of intention to defend, the plaintiff may, after the prescribed time and, if that defendant has not acknowledged service, upon filing an affidavit proving due service of the writ on him and, where the statement of claim was not indorsed on or served with the writ, upon serving a statement of claim on him, proceed with the action as if that defendant had given notice of intention to defend.**

(2) **Where a writ issued against a defendant is indorsed as aforesaid, but by reason of the defendant's satisfying the claim or complying with the demands thereof or any other like reason it has become unnecessary for the plaintiff to proceed with the action, then, if the defendant fails to give notice of intention to defend, the plaintiff may, after the prescribed time, enter judgment against that defendant for costs.**

(3) **(Repealed L.N. 99 of 1993)**

---

**NOTES**

**[13.6.1] Claims where default judgment cannot be entered**
Order 13 rule 6 deals with the situation where a defendant fails to give notice of intention to defend, but the claim is not one in respect of which there is provision for entering default judgment. The rule provides that the plaintiff can proceed as if notice of intention to defend had been given by filing an affidavit of service and serving a statement of claim. If no defence is served, the plaintiff may then consider proceeding under Order 19 rule 7. It has been held that it is not open to the plaintiff to apply for summary judgment under Order 14 instead: *Incorporated Owners of 3-3E Wang Fung Terrace v Law Chi Wing* DCCJ 230/2006 (Judge Ng; 28.03.2006). If there is no need to proceed because, for example, the defendant has satisfied the claim, Order 13 rule 6(2) allows the plaintiff to enter judgment for costs.

Claims which require the court to exercise a discretion come within this rule. They include claims for relief such as a declaration (see, for example, *Yau Yuk Tai v Ip Shuck Po* HCA 14760/1996 (Chung J; 18.11.1999)), specific performance or injunction and other equitable remedies.

**6A.** **Prescribed time** (O. 13 r. 6A)
**In the foregoing rules of this Order "the prescribed time" in relation to a writ issued against a defendant means the time limited for the defendant to acknowledge service of the writ or, if within that time the defendant has returned to the Registry an acknowledgment of service containing a statement to the effect that he does not intend to contest the proceedings, the date on which the acknowledgment was received at the Registry.**

---

**NOTES**

**[13.6A.1] 'Prescribed time' after which default judgment may be entered**
Order 13 rule 6A defines the term 'prescribed time', used in rules 1, 2, 3, 4, 5 and 6,

after which a plaintiff may apply for default judgment if the defendant has not given notice of intention to defend. In most cases the prescribed time is the time within which the defendant may acknowledge service (as to which see Order 12 rule 5). However, if the defendant acknowledges service stating that the proceedings will not be contested, default judgment may be entered immediately.

A defendant may acknowledge service after the prescribed time, and may give notice of intention to defend provided that judgment has not been entered. Such late notice of intention to defend is valid, and any default judgment entered thereafter will be irregular, even if an application for such judgment was submitted before notice of intention to defend was given: *Kwan Tat Chung v Ho Cheuk Kwun (t/a Fat Fai Eng'g Co)* HCPI 381/2002 (Suffiad J; 05.12.2002); *Kerry Freight (HK) Ltd v Del Prado Asia Ltd* [2005] 3 HKLRD 804.

**7.    Proof of service of writ** (O. 13 r. 7)

**(1)    Judgment shall not be entered against a defendant under this Order unless—**

    **(a)    the defendant has acknowledged service on him of the writ; or**

    **(b)    an affidavit is filed by or on behalf of the plaintiff proving due service of the writ on the defendant; or**

    **(c)    the plaintiff produces the writ indorsed by the defendant's solicitor with a statement that he accepts service of the writ on the defendant's behalf.**

**(2)    Where, in an action begun by writ, an application is made to the Court for an order affecting a party who has failed to give notice of intention to defend, the Court hearing the application may require to be satisfied in such manner as it thinks fit that the party failed to give such notice.**

**(3)    Where, after judgment has been entered under this Order against a defendant purporting to have been served by post under Order 10, rule 1(2)(a), the copy of the writ sent to the defendant is returned to the plaintiff through the post undelivered to the addressee, the plaintiff shall, before taking any step or further step in the action or the enforcement of the judgment, either—**

    **(a)    make a request for the judgment to be set aside on the ground that the writ has not been duly served, or**

    **(b)    apply to the Court for directions.**

**(4)    A request under paragraph (3)(a) shall be made by producing to an officer of the Registry and leaving with him for filing, an affidavit stating the relevant facts, and thereupon the judgment shall be set aside and the entry of the judgment and of any proceedings for its enforcement made in the book kept in the Registry for that purpose shall be marked accordingly.**

**(5)    An application under paragraph (3)(b) shall be made ex parte by affidavit stating the facts on which the application is founded and any order or direction sought, and on the application the Court may—**

    **(a)    set aside the judgment; or**

    **(b)    direct that, notwithstanding the return of the copy of the writ, it shall be treated as having been duly served: or**

    **(c)    make such other order and give such other direction as the circumstances may require.**

## NOTES

### [13.7.1]    Affidavit of service

An application for judgment in default of notice of intention to defend under this Order must be supported by an affidavit of service unless either paragraph (a) or (c) of this rule applies.

For affidavits of service generally, see the commentary under Order 10 rule 1(3)(b), and with regard to formal requirements, see Order 65 rule 8.

The affidavit of service in support of an application for default judgment in a monetary claim 'should additionally depose to the fact that the relevant statutory forms under Order 13A for making admissions have been served together with the writ and acknowledgement of service on the defendant': practice direction 24.1, para 8. The relevant forms are forms 16 and 16C in appendix A, depending on whether the amount of money claimed is liquidated or unliquidated. The appropriate form is required by Order 13A rule 13 to be served together with the writ or originating summons where the only remedy sought is payment of money.

**7A.    Judgment against a State** (O. 13 r. 7A)

  (1)   **Where the defendant is a State, as defined in section 14 of the State Immunity Act 1978 ("the Act") (1978 c. 33 U.K.), the plaintiff shall not be entitled to enter judgment under this Order except with the leave of the Court.**

  (2)   **An application for leave to enter judgment shall be supported by an affidavit—**

  **(a)    stating the grounds of the application,**

  **(b)    verifying the facts relied on as excepting the State from the immunity conferred by section 1 of the Act, and**

  **(c)    verifying that the writ has been served by being transmitted to the Chief Secretary for Adminstration and by him to the Foreign and Commonwealth Office for onward transmission to the State concerned, or in such other manner as may have been agreed to by the State, and that the time for acknowledging service, as extended by section 12(2) of the Act (by two months) where applicable, has expired.**

  (3)   **The application may be made ex parte but the Court hearing the application may direct a summons to be issued and served on that State, for which purpose such a direction shall include leave to serve the summons and a copy of the affidavit out of the jurisdiction.**

  (4)   **Unless the Court otherwise directs, an affidavit for the purposes of this rule may contain statements of information or belief with the sources and grounds thereof, and the grant of leave to enter judgment under this Order shall include leave to serve out of the jurisdiction—**

  **(a)    a copy of the judgment, and**

  **(b)    a copy of the affidavit, where not already served.**

  (5)   **The procedure for effecting service out of the jurisdiction pursuant to leave granted in accordance with the rule shall be the same as for the service of the writ under Order 11, rule 7(1), except where section 12(6) of the Act**

**applies and an alternative method of service has been agreed.**

---

**NOTES**

**[13.7A.1]   Interpretation of Order 13 rule 7A after 1 July 1997**
Following the resumption of Chinese sovereignty and pending amendment of the High Court rules under the on-going Adaptation of Laws exercise, Order 13 rule 7A must be read in conjunction with the Reunification Ordinance and in particular Schedule 8 of the Interpretation and General Clauses Ordinance (Cap 1) enacted thereby.

The State Immunity Act 1978 (UK) referred to in rule 7A(1) no longer applies in Hong Kong. In *FG Hemisphere Associates LLC v Democratic Republic of Congo* [2009] 1 HKC 111 the court, without deciding, favoured the view that the common law on state immunity as it had developed before the 1978 Act was extended to Hong Kong, revived upon the 1978 Act ceasing to have effect in this jurisdiction. That judgment was reversed on appeal on another point: [2010] 2 HKC 487, and it is understood the matter will be taken to the Court of Final Appeal.

The Foreign and Commonwealth Office, referred to in rule 7A(2)(c) is a UK government office which no longer has any function in regard to Hong Kong's relations with other countries. The reference to that office in the rule should now be read as a reference to the Foreign Ministry of the PRC, which has an office in Hong Kong.

**8.     Stay of execution on default judgment** (O. 13 r. 8)
**Where judgment for a debt or liquidated demand is entered under this Order against a defendant who has returned to the Registry an acknowledgment of service containing a statement to the effect that, although he does not intend to contest the proceedings, he intends to apply for a stay of execution of the judgment by writ of fieri facias, execution of the judgment by such a writ shall be stayed for a period of 14 days from the acknowledgment of service and, if within that time the defendant issues and serves on the plaintiff a summons for such a stay supported by an affidavit in accordance with Order 47, rule 1, the stay imposed by this rule shall continue until the summons is heard or otherwise disposed of, unless the Court after giving the parties an opportunity of being heard otherwise directs.**

**9.     Setting aside judgment** (O. 13 r. 9)
**Without prejudice to rule 7(3) and (4), the Court may, on such terms as it thinks just, set aside or vary any judgment entered in pursuance of this Order.**

---

**NOTES**

**[13.9.1]   Power to set aside default judgment – Distinction between regular**
            **and irregular default judgments**
Order 13 rule 9 gives the court a general discretion to set aside judgments entered in

default of notice of intention to defend. The court also has a power under Order 19 rule 9 to set aside judgment in default of pleading. The commentary set out below is largely applicable to applications under that rule as well.

It is generally accepted that applications to set aside judgment in default of notice of intention to defend fall into two groups. The first group are cases where the default judgment is irregular in some way, such as where the writ was not properly served, or where the plaintiff jumped the gun by taking default judgment before the prescribed period had elapsed. The second group are cases where the judgment has been entered regularly, but the defendant seeks to have it set aside on the basis of an excuse for having failed to act in time, such as inability to give notice of intention to defend in time on account of illness or absence.

Default judgments falling into the first category have traditionally been thought to be liable to be set aside *ex debito justitiae*, or as of right (see *Analby & Ors v Praetorius* (1888) 20 QBD 764), whereas default judgments falling into the second category required an exercise of discretion turning in part on the defendant satisfying the court that it had a plausible defence. It remains the case that where a default judgment is irregular, it will normally be set aside on proof of the irregularity alone. Where, however, the default judgment was regularly taken, the invariable practice is to require an affidavit of merits demonstrating that the defendant has a prospect of succeeding if the judgment is set aside and the matter be permitted to proceed to trial. See *Park Kit Investment Ltd v Cheung Wan Ping* [1999] 3 HKC 841 (CA).

**[13.9.2] Setting aside irregular default judgments**
With respect to irregular default judgments there was a state of flux following the judgment of the Court of Appeal in *Honour Finance Co Ltd v Chui Mei-mei* [1989] 2 HKLR 146. There, Hunter JA said, at 148:

> It is we think desirable to enter a caveat about the use of these two phrases 'as of right' or 'ex debito justitiae'. They may be convenient ways of summarising the position of a party against whom an irregular judgment has been entered, and they are frequently used. But they are not precisely accurate. In *Evans v Bartlam* [1937] AC 473, the House of Lords authoritatively held that a court under the predecessor to O 13 r 9 exercised a discretion which was not and could not be fettered; and the court's practice in relation to regular and irregular judgments only constituted 'rules to guide ... the normal exercise of ... discretion' : per Lord Atkin p 480. Lord Wright was quite specific when he said: 'A discretion necessarily involves a latitude of individual choice according to the particular circumstances, and differs from a case where the decision follows ex debito justitiae once the facts are ascertained' (p 489). The victim of an irregular judgment therefore enjoys a confident expectation rather than a right.

The decision in *Honour Finance* was doubted in *Fok Chun Hung v Lo Yuk Shi* [1995] 2 HKC 648 (CA). The conflict between the two Court of Appeal decisions was noted by Yam J in *Honest Billion Investment Ltd v Wang Xian Chou* [1997] 3 HKC 161 at 164G.

The Court of Appeal subsequently affirmed the traditional rule that an irregular judgment in default will be set aside *ex debito justitiae*, that is without consideration of the merits of the proposed defence. See *Wing Lung Bank Ltd v Ho Man Iam* [1999] 3 HKC 368 and see *Chu Kam Lun v Yap Lisa Susanto* [1999] 3 HKC 378 (CA). In *Chu Kam Lun* the Court of Appeal reviewed the Hong Kong decisions.

Leong JA observed (at 384H) that the 'weight of the Hong Kong authorities is where the judgment is irregular, it should be set aside without going into the merits of the defence'. The court went on to consider the effect of an unreported 1998 judgment of the English Court of Appeal (*Faircharm Investments Ltd v Citibank International plc* [1998] The Times 20 February 1998). That judgment supported the view that where the proposed defence is hopeless the court would decline to set aside default judgment notwithstanding irregular service. In *obiter* (the defence in the Hong Kong case was found not to be hopeless) the Hong Kong Court of Appeal doubted the English decision and Leong JA expressly noted that it was not binding in Hong Kong (at 384I).

In *Kwan Kam Wah v Chan Wai Ming* [2000] 2 HKC 378 Deputy Judge Carlye Chu followed the Court of Appeal's reaffirmation of the traditional rule and set aside two default judgments where notice of the proceedings had not actually been received by the defendant. The learned deputy judge said (at 385 B–D):

> It would appear that as a result of the latest Court of Appeal judgment in *Chu Kam Lun* in 1999, the Hong Kong position is the same as the English position, namely, the emphasis is not on the delivery but on the receipt or notice of the writs. Applying the test in *Chu Kam Lun*, the service of the writs herein, albeit in accordance with the Rules, would be ineffective in bringing notice of the proceedings to the defendant. Although the plaintiff had no reason to believe that service of the writs was unsuccessful, the reality is that the defendant had not been afforded an opportunity to be heard.

The learned deputy judge went on to hold (at 386C–D) that as service was irregular the default judgments should be set aside without consideration of the merits of the proposed defence. She referred to the judgment of Yuen J in *Law Kwok Hung v Tse Ping Man & Anor* [1999] 4 HKC 397, 406 and concluded that she was bound by the decision of the Court of Appeal in *Po Kwong Marble Factory Ltd v Wah Yee Decoration Co Ltd* [1996] 4 HKC 157; therefore 'where a judgment has been obtained irregularly, a defendant would *not* need to show merits, although the court may consider all the other circumstances of the case in deciding whether to impose conditions'. See also *Liu Chong Hing Bank Ltd v Union World (HK) Ltd & Ors* [2005] 1 HKC 20 (CA).

**[13.9.3]   Discretion to set aside regularly entered default judgment**
The court has a discretion under Order 13 rule 9 to set aside a default judgment which has been regularly entered, that is a default judgment properly entered after a defendant duly served fails to give notice of intention to defend within the prescribed time. The principles on which the court's discretion will be exercised were succinctly stated by Ribeiro JA in *L & M Specialist Construction Ltd v Wo Hing Construction Co Ltd* [2000] 3 HKC 335, at 339B *et seq*. His Lordship stated first that the discretion exists to avoid injustice and continued:

> Where … the judgment was regularly entered, the court will consider the nature of and reasons for the default but it will focus primarily on whether the defence has sufficient merits.

Hence the burden on the defendant in seeking to set aside a regular default judgment is twofold: he must provide an explanation for having failed to act within the prescribed time and, more important, he must satisfy the court that he has a potential defence on the merits. These requirements, which are not expressed in the rule, 'must necessarily enter into the judge's consideration' but it cannot be said that their proof is a 'condition precedent to the existence or exercise of the discretionary power': *Evans v Bartlam* [1937] AC 473, 482.

*Explanation for the failure to comply on time* – The court will clearly be satisfied with an explanation of illness, accident or other impediment making it impracticable for the defendant to act within the prescribed time. Where, however, the delay results from procrastination, incompetence or contumelious disregard for the court's process, the application will be looked on less favourably: see *Wong Pak v Ng Po Chui* [1982] HKC 243 where Rhind J held that failure to act within time was attributable to 'inexcusable incompetence' on the part of an insurance company and, citing *Gail Stevenson & Anor v Chartered Bank* [1977] HKLR 165, concluded that the court did not wish to see its way to lend assistance in such circumstances.

*Meritorious defence* – To prevail on an application to set aside a regular default judgment the defendant must go on to satisfy the court that he has a meritorious defence. This will normally entail an affidavit of merit setting out the points of defence the defendant proposes to raise. The affidavit should be sworn by the defendant himself (or a person with personal knowledge) and should preferably be in narrative form 'explaining precisely what the proposed defence will be' – see *Tong Yi Sang & Anor v Fung Law & Ng & Ors* [1993] 2 HKC 665, 667. In that case Kaplan J held, citing *The Saudi Eagle* [1986] 2 Lloyd's Rep 221, that the applicant bears a 'substantial onus' and that an affidavit merely exhibiting a draft defence was insufficient.

The affidavit of merit must disclose a defence which has a 'real prospect of success': *Yeu Shing Construction Co Ltd v Pioneer Concrete (HK) Ltd* [1987] 2 HKC 187 (CA); *Treasure Land Property Consultants (a firm) v United Smart Development Ltd* [1995] 1 HKC 686; [1995] 3 HKC 30, 38C–D (CA). Where a provisional view of the probable outcome of the action cannot sensibly be formed without an assessment of the witnesses the court may ask itself whether the defence 'could well be established at trial': see *Guangdong International Trust and Investment Corp HK (Holdings) Ltd v Yuet Wah (HK) Wah Fat Ltd* [1997] 2 HKC 696, per Keith J.

The party seeking to uphold the default judgment is, of course, entitled to dispute the merit of the proposed defence but it is wrong to require him to provide 'incontrovertible evidence' against it: *Premier Fashion Wears Ltd v Li Hing Chung* [1994] 1 HKC 213, 219C (CA).

*Delay in application* – The length of delay in applying to set aside the default judgment may also be taken into account: see *Wong Pak v Ng Po Chui* [1982] HKC 243 where an application to set aside default judgment was dismissed after a lapse of six months. It was held that irreparable mischief would be caused by setting aside the judgment as the memories of eye witnesses would have faded. See also *Hung Ling Chun Felicia v Chow Yung Fong & Anor* [2001] 3 HKC 209 where the court declined to set aside a default judgment even though it was satisfied the defendant had a real prospect of success, on the grounds of delay of five years and of prejudice to the plaintiff.

### [13.9.4] Irregular service by post

Where default judgment has been entered but the writ though properly served was not actually received by the defendant on time or at all, is the default judgment regular, and thus liable to be set aside by exercise of discretion, or is it irregular and liable to be set aside *ex debito justitiae*? There are authorities going both ways. It seems fair to say that the prevailing view is in favour of irregularity. However the Editor of this work favours the regularity view because of section 8 of the Interpretation and General Clauses Ordinance (Cap 1). See the commentary under Order 10 rule 1 next to the sub-heading *'Consequence of non-receipt'*. This is not an arid question, for it is clear that only if such a default judgment is regular will the merits of the proposed defence be relevant on an application to set it aside.

The situation is different where after default judgment has been entered the writ is returned by the post office undelivered. In such a case the plaintiff has a duty under Order 13 rule 7(3) to apply to set aside the judgment or for directions. In *Fok Chun Hung v Lo Yuk Shi* [1995] 2 HKC 648 the Court of Appeal set aside such a judgment unconditionally where the plaintiff had failed to apply as required.

### [13.9.5]   Irregular service by insertion in letter box
In *Phillip Securities (HK) Ltd v Lam Chi Bin Stanley* [2002] 1 HKC 432, 437B–F Deputy Judge Lam accepted uncontradicted affidavit evidence to the effect that a writ could not have been served by insertion in the letter box at 'Room 203', because there was no longer a separate Room 203 and there was no letter box.

### [13.9.6]   Affidavit of service - dispute as to truth
Where the truth of an affidavit of service is in dispute, such as where, on an application to set aside default judgment, a defendant alleges that service has not in fact been effected, it can 'scarcely ever be apropriate' to seek cross-examination of the defendant: *Ambridge Investments Ltd v Lexcon Investment Lt & Anor* HCA 9743/2000 (Recorder G Li SC; 04.10.2001). However the court is not obliged to accept a defendant's assertion 'no matter how improbable': *Bank of China (HK) Ltd v Cheung King Fung* [2007] 1 HKLRD 462, 469I-J (CA). In that case the Hong Kong court referred to *Forward v West Sussex County Council* [1995] 1 WLR 1469, 1473G – 1474H (CA), where it was said that the defendant is required to show 'convincing' or 'compelling' evidence of non-receipt.

As for cross-examination of a process server, see the commentary under Order 10 rule 1.

### [13.9.7]   Setting aside default judgment for too large a sum
A default judgment entered for too large a sum is considered to be irregular, and liable to be set aside unless it is amended: *Pollard Construction Co Ltd v Yung Yat Fan (t/a Golden Year & Co)* [1999] 3 HKC 109. The defendant is entitled to have the judgment set aside *ex debito justitiae* unless the plaintiff obtains an amendment so as to reduce it to the proper sum: *Muir v Jenks* [1913] 2 KB 412, 417; *Au Chow Electrical Co Ltd v Cherison Eng'g Ltd & Anor* HCA 2736/2008 (Suffiad J; 30.06.2009) (para 50). Thus in *Connaught Real Estate Ltd & Anor v Primocargo Agency Ltd* DCCJ 935/2008 (Judge Mimmie Chan; 14.08.2008), where it was conceded that amendment was not possible because of a dispute over one of the claims, a judgment entered without giving credit for $71,440 paid after issue of the writ was set aside without consideration of the merits.

### [13.9.8]   Court's power to impose terms on setting aside default judgment
The court's power under Order 13 rule 9 to set aside judgment in default of notice of intention to defend expressly provides for the imposition of such terms as the court may think just. The obvious term is one requiring payment into court of all or part of sum claimed as a condition of setting aside the judgment. However, in *Wong Kam*

*Wing v Cheng Pui Lun* CACV 21/2003 (Rogers VP & Le Pichon JA; 11.07.2003), where quantum was very much in dispute, it was held that payment into court was not appropriate. Different considerations apply depending on whether the default judgment being set aside was regular or irregular.

*Regular default judgments –* In *L & M Specialist Construction Ltd v Wo Hing Construction Co Ltd* [2000] 3 HKC 335 (CA) the court accepted that there is power to require payment into court as a condition of setting aside a regular default judgment. However, Ribeiro JA (at 342G-H) took the view that it would be exceedingly rare for such an order to be made because 'there is a certain logical tension between a court deciding that the defendant has real prospects of succeeding in his defence and the court considering at the same time that the defence is in shadowy realms'. Reference was made to *City Construction Contracts (London) Ltd v Adam* [1988] The Times 4 Jan (CA) where it was said that the purpose of the power to impose such a condition even where there is a good arguable defence is 'not to punish the defendant, but to encourage the proper future conduct of the litigation and to provide a measure of security for the plaintiff'. The *L & M* case concerned an application under Order 19 rule 9 to set aside judgment in default of pleading, but in principle its reasoning should be applicable under Order 13 rule 9 as well. In *Wang Ruiyan v Gem Global Yield Fund Ltd* HCCL 16/2006 (Stone J; 27.10.2010) the court, troubled by the fact that the defendant had apparently made a conscious decision not to comply with a court order, resulting in interlocutory judgment being entered, ordered the defendant to pay 70% of the plaintiff's net claim into court (or provide bank guarantee) as a condition of having the judgment set aside. The court also made a 'stringent' costs order against the defendant, on the common fund basis.

*Irregular default judgments -* In the case of an irregular default judgment, which is set aside as of right, without consideration of the merits, the court has a residual discretion to have regard to the conduct of the parties and impose terms 'which accord with justice having regard to the facts of the particular case'. See *Po Kwong Marble Factory Ltd v Wah Yee Decoration Co Ltd* [1996] 4 HKC 157, 161C-E (CA) where a defendant was required to pay the amount claimed into court when it succeeded in having default judgment set aside on the ground that as a result of 'virtually disguising' its registered office, the writ had in fact been served at the wrong place. Conduct of the defendant has also been considered in the following cases:

- *Guangdong Int'l Trust and Investment Corp HK (Holdings) Ltd v Yuet Wah (HK) Wah Fat Ltd* [1997] 2 HKC 696 where the court declined to impose a condition, not agreeing with an argument that there had been an attempt to evade service.
- *Chu Kam Lun v Yap Lisa Susanto* [1999] 3 HKC 378, 385D-F (CA) where no substance was found in an argument based on conduct in countermanding payment at the last minute before leaving Hong Kong, and default judgment was set aside unconditionally.

In *Bank Austria AG v Sukamto* [2002] 1 HKC 232 this was described as the 'limited right' approach, in that the right to have an irregular default judgment set aside is limited in the sense that the court may take conduct into account in deciding what, if any, terms to impose.

**[13.9.9]   Costs of setting aside default judgment**
The costs of an unsuccessful application to set aside a default judgment will normally follow the event and be paid by the defendant. Where the application is successful, the court's order as to costs will depend on the reason for setting aside the judgment. See *Ko Sin Yun v Chan Chuen* CACV 147/2006 (Le Pichon & Cheung JJA and A Cheung J; 14.12.2006) where it was said (at para 21):

> Generally speaking if an irregular judgment is set aside then the plaintiff should be ordered to bear the costs of the setting aside of the default judgment because the judg ment was not properly obtained in the first place. However, where a judgment was set aside not because of it being irregular but because of a meritorious defence, the general rule is that the defendant should bear the costs of the application to set aside the default judgment. As an alternative the costs of the application can be in the cause of the action.

## ORDER 13A

### ADMISSIONS IN CLAIMS FOR PAYMENT OF MONEY

**1.     Interpretation** (O. 13A r.1)

**(1) In this Order –**

**"claim" means –**

    **(a)     where in an action the plaintiff makes only one claim, that claim; and**

    **(b)     where in an action the plaintiff makes more than one claim, all the claims in the action.**

**(2) For the purposes of rules 6(1)(b) and 7(1)(b), the amount of a claim is treated as unliquidated if the claim consists of a claim for a liquidated amount of money and a claim for an unliquidated amount of money.**

    **(L.N. 152 of 2008)**

---

NOTES

**[13A.1.1]   Origin and scope of Order 13A**

Order 13A is derived from CPR part 14. Its addition to these rules with effect from 2009 resulted from recommendation 18 of the final report of the Chief Justice's working party on civil justice reform. It provides a mechanism whereby a defendant can admit liability to pay a sum of money and obtain an order for payment on terms such as deferred payment or payment by instalments. It was introduced with a view to reducing the number of cases in which debtors defend simply in the hope of postponing judgment. The working party's final report described the problem which Order 13A seeks to address, at para 171:

> Where the defendant has no defence against debt-collection type cases, he will, in most cases, face up to this and not resist the claim, allowing judgment to be entered under the present rules. However, in a significant number of cases, although the defendant (usually unrepresented) realises that he has no defence to the whole or most of the claim, he may be unwilling, for various reasons, to allow judgment unconditionally to be entered against him. This leads to more or less desperate attempts to stave off judgment, requiring the plaintiff to incur the effort, delay and expense of applying to the court for summary judgment or even having to take the matter towards trial.

Thus Order 13A now enables such a defendant to admit liability, and to obtain terms as to payment by order of the court, even if the plaintiff is not agreeable to such terms.

    The Order is also useful in cases where the only real defence is a set-off or counterclaim, by which the net amount of money changing hands would be reduced. Such a defendant can take advantage of Order 13A by offering to pay an amount less than that claimed, indicating that it will waive the set-off or counterclaim if the lesser sum is accepted. Thirdly, the Order caters for early settlement of unliquidated claims by allowing the defendant to propose a quantum.

    Specific provision is made in rule 2(3) for the court to grant leave to amend or withdraw an admission.

In order to encourage use of the Order 13A admission procedure, Order 6 rule 2(1)(c) requires that every writ be indorsed with a statement informing the defendant that an admission may be made in accordance with Order 13A (included in the amended form of writ, Form No 1 in Appendix A), and Order 13A rule 13 requires that the appropriate form for admission be served with every originating process commencing a money claim.

### [13A.1.2]   Order 13A rule 1(2) – mixed claims

Rule 1(2) makes it clear that a mixed claim (consisting of a claim for a liquidated amount and an unliquidated amount) is to be treated as unliquidated so that admission of liability to pay is governed by rules 6 and 7 rather than rules 4 and 5. As to the distinction between liquidated and unliquidated amounts, see the commentary under Order 13 rule 1.

**2.     Making an admission** (O. 13A r. 2)

**(1)   Where the only remedy that a plaintiff is seeking is the payment of money, the defendant may make an admission in accordance with —**

   **(a)   rule 4 (admission of whole of claim for liquidated amount of money);**

   **(b)   rule 5 (admission of part of claim for liquidated amount of money);**

   **(c)   rule 6 (admission of liability to pay whole of claim for unliquidated amount of money); or**

   **(d)   rule 7 (admission of liability to pay claim for unliquidated amount of money where defendant offers a sum in satisfaction of the claim).**

**(2)   Where the defendant makes an admission as mentioned in paragraph (1), the plaintiff may enter judgment except where –**

   **(a)   the defendant is a person under disability; or**

   **(b)   the plaintiff is a person under disability and the admission is made under rule 5 or 7.**

**(3)   The Court may allow a party to amend or withdraw an admission if the Court considers it just to do so having regard to all the circumstances of the case.**

**(4)   In this rule, "person under disability" has the meaning assigned to it in Order 80, rule 1.**

   **(L.N. 152 of 2008)**

---

## NOTES

### [13A.2.1]   Order 13A rule 2 - admission of liability to pay money

Order 13A rule 2(1) provides that a defendant may admit liability to pay all or part of a claim for money. It enhances the admission procedure provided for in Order 27 rule 1, which continues to exist.

Claims for a liquidated amount of money may be admitted in whole or in part under rule 2(1)(a) and (b). This is elaborated in rules 4 and 5. Claims for an unliquidated amount of money may be admitted in whole under rule 2(1)(c) and where a settlement offer is made, under rule 2(1)(d) (elaborated in rules 6 and 7). There is no specific procedure in the Order for admission of partial liability to pay an unliquidated claim for money, but see Order 16 rule 10 which may partially fill the gap.

Upon any such admission, the plaintiff may enter judgment: rule 2(2).

### [13A.2.2] Should notice of intention to defend be given by party who intends to make an admission?

The forms for acknowledgement of service of a writ and originating summons (forms 14 and 15 respectively) were amended as part of the civil justice reforms, giving the defendant an opportunity to indicate whether it is intended to make an admission under Order 13A. The question whether an admission will be made is not expressed as an alternative to the question whether the defendant intends to contest the proceedings: it appears that both questions should be answered. A defendant who does wish to make an admission, and to invoke the jurisdiction under Order 13A to request payment terms, should probably give a positive answer to the question whether he intends to contest the proceedings, or at least make sure that there is little or no time gap from filing and service of the acknowledgement of service, and the making of the admission and application for payment terms. This is because if he ticks the 'no' box in answer to this question, the plaintiff might try to pre-empt an application for payment terms by entering default judgment under Order 13 rule 1. Once default judgment is entered it may still be possible to invoke the Order 13A jurisdiction, but only within the time for service of a defence: see rule 3 and the commentary thereunder.

### [13A.2.3] Judgment on admission

Order 13A rule 2(2) provides that judgment may be entered on admission of liability to pay money under the Order. Such a judgment is obtained simply by filing a request in the appropriate form as prescribed in the subsequent rules of this Order. It is not necessary to issue a summons for judgment on admissions as under Order 27 rule 3.

The more significant difference between judgment on admission under this Order, and the equivalent procedure under Order 27 rule 3, is that under this Order the defendant, when making admission of liability to pay, may make a proposal as to the amount to be paid, or for payment on terms. See the commentary under Order 13A rules 5, 7 and 9. Furthermore Order 13A does not apply to admissions made pre-action, whereas Order 27 rule 3 is capable of doing so: *Sowerby v Charlton* [2005] EWCA Civ 1610, [2006] 1 WLR 568.

### [13A.2.4] Restrictions on judgment on admissions where party under disability

The right to enter judgment on admission under Order 13A is restricted in most cases where a party is under disability. In such cases the procedure for approval of a compromise under Order 80 rules 10 and 11 should be followed.

### [13A.2.5] Amendment and withdrawal of admissions

Order 13A rule 2(3) provides that the court may allow a party to amend or withdraw an admission. This is not a new power but a legislative expression of a power which was previously recognised by the courts. See the commentary under Order 27 rule 1 which remains in force in the same terms as prior to Order 13A being inserted into the rules with effect from 2009. This new express power may be regarded as limited to admissions made under Order 13A.

Rule 2(3) simply states that the court may exercise its power to grant leave to amend or withdraw an admission where it considers it 'just to do so having regard to all the circumstances'. The factors the court will take into account, as discussed in the commentary under Order 27 rule 1, should be relevant here as well. In its final report, the Chief Justice's working party on civil justice reform noted the approach the Hong Kong courts have taken and recommended against regulating it by introduction of new rules (paras 175–183).

However in England, where Order 27 has been repealed, the Court of Appeal has said that authorities concerning withdrawal of admissions under Order 27 should be 'approached with caution' in relation to the equivalent of Order 13A, because there were features of the pre-CPR practice which would no longer be acceptable: *Sowerby v Charlton* [2005] EWCA Civ 1610; [2006] 1 WLR 568 (para 34-35). The English court appeared to prefer the 'valuable guidance' laid down in *Braybrook v Basildon & Thurrock University NHS Trust* (unreported, 07.10.2004) (para 45):

1.   In exercising its discretion the court will consider all the circumstances of the case and seek to give effect to the overriding objective [in Hong Kong, underlying objectives].

2.   Amongst the matters to be considered will be:

   (a)   the reasons and justification for the application which must be made in good faith;

   (b)   the balance of prejudice to the parties;

   (c)   whether any party has been the author of any prejudice they may suffer;

   (d)   the prospects of success of any issue arising from the withdrawal of an admission.

3.   The nearer any application is to a final hearing the less chance of success it will have even if the party making the application can establish clear prejudice. This may be decisive if the application is shortly before the hearing.

**3.   Period for making admission** (O. 13A, r. 3)

   **(1)   The period for filing and serving an admission under rule 4, 5, 6 or 7 is –**

   **(a)   where the defendant is served with a writ, the period fixed by or under these rules for service of his defence;**

   **(b)   where the defendant is served with an originating summons, the period fixed by or under these rules for filing of his affidavit evidence; and**

   **(c)   in any other case, 14 days after service of the originating process.**

   **(2)   A defendant may file an admission under rule 4, 5, 6, or 7 –**

   **(a)   after the expiry of the period for filing it specified in paragraph (1)(a) if the plaintiff has not obtained a default judgment under Order 13 or 19; and**

   **(b)   after the expiry of the period for filing it specified in paragraph (1)(b) if the admission is filed and served before the date or the period fixed under Order 28, rule 2 for the hearing of the originating summons.**

**(3)** **If the defendant files an admission under paragraph (2), this Order applies as if he had made the admission specified in paragraph (1)(a) or (b), as the case may be.**

**(L.N. 152 of 2008)**

---

## NOTES

**[13A.3.1]** **Time considerations**

Order 13A rule 3 sets out the times within which defendants may admit liability to pay under the Order. They are clearly encouraged to do so at an early stage. Order 6 rule 2(1)(c) requires that a writ be indorsed with a statement notifying the defendant of the Order 13A procedure (see the amended from of writ, Form no 1 in Appendix A), and 13A rule 13 requires that the form of admission (which contains explanatory notes) be served with the originating process. Rule 3 lays down a relatively short period within which the defendant may make admissions, which in the case of proceedings commenced by writ, is the time for service of a defence. However rule 3(2) expressly allows late admissions by defendants, without the need to apply for an extension of time, provided the plaintiff has not already obtained default judgment or, in the case of actions commenced by originating summons, provided the summons has not been fixed for hearing.

**4.** **Admission of whole of claim for liquidated amount of money** (O. 13A r 4)
    **(1)** **This rule applies where –**
        **(a)** **the only remedy that the plaintiff is seeking is the payment of a liquidated amount of money; and**
        **(b)** **the defendant admits the whole of the claim.**
    **(2)** **The defendant may admit the claim by –**
        **(a)** **filing in the Registry an admission in Form No. 16 in Appendix A; and**
        **(b)** **serving a copy of the admission on the plaintiff.**
    **(3)** **The plaintiff may obtain judgment by filing in the Registry a request in Form No. 16A in Appendix A and, if he does so –**
        **(a)** **where the defendant has not requested time to pay, paragraphs (5), (6) and (7) apply;**
        **(b)** **where the defendant has requested time to pay, rule 9 applies.**
    **(4)** **If the plaintiff does not file a request for judgment within 14 days after the copy of the admission is served on him, the claim is stayed until he files the request.**
    **(5)** **The plaintiff may specify in his request for judgment –**
        **(a)** **the date by which the whole of the judgment debt is to be paid; or**
        **(b)** **the times and rate at which it is to be paid by instalments.**
    **(6)** **Upon receipt of the request for judgment, the Court shall enter judgment.**
    **(7)** **Judgment shall be for the amount of the claim (less any payments made) and costs to be paid –**
        **(a)** **by the date or at the times and rate specified in the request for**

> **judgment; or**
>   **(b)  if none is specified, immediately.**
> **(L.N. 152 of 2008)**

---

**NOTES**

**[13A.4.1]  Origin and scope of Order 13A rule 4**

Order 13A rule 4 derives from CPR 14.4. It sets out the procedure whereby a defendant may admit liability to pay the whole of a claim for a liquidated amount of money, and the plaintiff may obtain judgment thereon. The wording of the English rule is different in some respects. For example, in England the word 'specified' is used instead of 'liquidated' to describe an ascertained amount of money.

In admitting liability to pay the defendant may request time for payment pursuant to rule 9.

Rule 4(3) provides that the plaintiff 'may' obtain judgment on an admission under this rule, by filing a request in the appropriate form. In reality the plaintiff does not have any other option: rule 4(4) provides that if the plaintiff does not do so within 14 days, the proceedings are stayed.

The judgment will be for the amount claimed and admitted, coupled, where appropriate, with time to pay if the plaintiff in applying for judgment accepts the terms proposed by the defendant. Alternatively if the plaintiff does not accept the payment terms proposed by the defendant, judgment will be for payment on terms to be decided by the court under rule 10.

Rule 4(5) provides that the plaintiff, in requesting judgment on admission of liability to pay, may specify terms as to payment. This will be appropriate where the defendant has not applied under rule 9 for terms as to payment, or where the parties have reached an agreement thereon, or by way of counterproposal to terms requested by the defendant.

In Hong Kong, unlike England, Order 13A rule 9(8) provides that where judgment is entered on terms allowing the defendant time to pay, and the defendant defaults, the plaintiff may immediately take enforcement action for the whole outstanding balance.

Admission of liability to pay the whole of a liquidated claim under rule 4 effectively brings the proceedings to an end. The plaintiff must file a request for judgment within 14 days, failing which the claim is stayed. The only matters which may be outstanding would be determination by the court (under rule 10) of the date or the times and rate of payment where this has not been agreed, and taxation or assessment of costs.

**5.  Admission of part of claim for liquidated amount of money** (O. 13A r. 5)
  **(1)  This rule applies where –**
    **(a)  the only remedy that the plaintiff is seeking is the payment of a liquidated amount of money; and**
    **(b)  the defendant admits part of the claim in satisfaction of the whole claim.**
  **(2)  The defendant may admit part of the claim by –**
    **(a)  filing in the Registry an admission in Form No. 16 in Appendix A; and**
    **(b)  serving a copy of the admission on the plaintiff.**

(3)   Within 14 days after the copy of the admission is served on him, the plaintiff shall –

    (a)   file in the Registry a notice in Form No. 16B in Appendix A, stating that –

        (i)   he accepts the amount admitted in satisfaction of the whole claim;

        (ii)   he does not accept the amount admitted by the defendant and wishes the proceedings to continue; or

        (iii)   if the defendant has requested time to pay, he accepts the amount admitted in satisfaction of the claim, but not the defendant's proposals as to payment; and

    (b)   serve a copy of the notice on the defendant.

(4)   If the plaintiff does not file the notice in accordance with paragraph (3), the whole claim is stayed until he files the notice.

(5)   If the plaintiff accepts the amount admitted in satisfaction of the whole claim, he may obtain judgment by filing in the Registry a request in Form No. 16B in Appendix A and, if he does so –

    (a)   where the defendant has not requested time to pay, paragraphs (6), (7) and (8) apply;

    (b)   where the defendant has requested time to pay, rule 9 applies.

(6)   The plaintiff may specify in his request for judgment –

    (a)   the date by which the whole of the judgment debt is to be paid; or

    (b)   the times and rate at which it is to be paid by instalments.

(7)   Upon receipt of the request for judgment, the Court shall enter judgment.

(8)   Judgment shall be for the amount admitted (less any payments made) and costs to be paid –

    (a)   by the date or at the times and rate specified in the request for judgment; or

    (b)   if none is specified, immediately.

(L.N. 152 of 2008)

---

## NOTES

### [13A.5.1]   Origin and scope of Order 13A rule 5

Order 13A rule 5 derives from CPR 14.5. It provides that a defendant to a claim for a liquidated amount of money may admit liability to pay part of it in satisfaction of the whole claim. Such an admission is made by completing the appropriate part of form No 16 in appendix A, which requires that the defendant state the amount of money for which liability is admitted. The plaintiff is required to respond by filing the appropriate form stating whether the amount admitted by the defendant is accepted, not accepted or whether any requested terms as to payment are unacceptable. If the plaintiff does not do so, the proceedings are stayed under rule 5(4).

### [13A.5.2]   Consequences of rejection of defendant's admission of part of claim

Rule 5(3)(a)(ii) expressly provides that the plaintiff may in the notice in response to a defendant's admission of liability to pay part of a liquidated claim state that he does not accept the amount admitted by the defendant and wishes the proceedings to continue. In reality the defendant's admission is just an offer which the plaintiff is free to reject. If rejected, the action will proceed to trial. In that event, there does not appear to be an express prohibition on the earlier admission (or offer) being brought to the attention of the court on the question of liability. In this respect such an admission differs from a without prejudice offer, which is protected by rules as to admissibility (see the commentary under Order 24 rule 2); or a sanctioned proposal under Order 22, disclosure of which is restricted by Order 22 rule 25.

**6.     Admission of liability to pay whole of claim for unliquidated amount of money** (O. 13A, r. 6)

**(1)     This rule applies where –**

    **(a)     the only remedy that the plaintiff is seeking is the payment of money;**

    **(b)     the amount of the claim is unliquidated; and**

    **(c)     the defendant admits liability but does not offer to pay a liquidated amount of money in satisfaction of the claim.**

**(2)     The defendant may admit the claim by –**

    **(a)     filing in the Registry an admission in Form No. 16C in Appendix A; and**

    **(b)     serving a copy of the admission on the plaintiff.**

**(3)     The plaintiff may obtain judgment by filing in the Registry a request in Form No. 16D in Appendix A.**

**(4)     If the plaintiff does not file a request for judgment within 14 days after the copy of the admission is served on him, the claim is stayed until he files the request.**

**(5)     Upon receipt of the request for judgment, the Court shall enter judgment.**

**(6)     Judgment shall be for an amount to be decided by the Court and costs.**

**(L.N. 152 of 2008)**

---

## NOTES

### [13A.6.1]     Origin and scope of Order 13A rule 6

Order 13A rule 6 derives from CPR 14.6. It provides for admission by a defendant of liability to pay the whole of a claim for an unliquidated amount of money by filing and serving the appropriate form. In England the word 'unspecified' is now used in place of 'unliquidated'. As to the distinction between liquidated and unliquidated claims, see the commentary under Order 13 rule 1.

When such an admission is made, the plaintiff 'may' obtain judgment thereon by filing the appropriate form: rule 6(3). In reality the plaintiff does not have a choice, as the proceedings will be stayed by rule 6(4) if no such request is filed within 14 days.

Judgment under this rule is for an amount to be decided by the court and costs: rule 6(6). Directions may be given under rule 8 with a view to assessment of quantum.

7.      **Admission of liability to pay claim for unliquidated amount of money where defendant offers a sum in satisfaction of the claim** (O. 13A r. 7)

     **(1)**    This rule applies where –

         **(a)**   the only remedy that the plaintiff is seeking is the payment of money;

         **(b)**   the amount of the claim is unliquidated; and

         **(c)**   the defendant –

             **(i)**    admits liability; and

             **(ii)**   offers to pay a liquidated amount of money in satisfaction of the claim.

     **(2)**    The defendant may admit the claim by –

         **(a)**   filing in the Registry an admission in Form No. 16C in Appendix A; and

         **(b)**   serving a copy of the admission on the plaintiff.

     **(3)**    Within 14 days after the copy of the admission is served on him, the plaintiff shall –

         **(a)**   file in the Registry a notice in Form No. 16E in Appendix A, stating whether or not he accepts the amount in satisfaction of the claim; and

         **(b)**   serve a copy of the notice on the defendant.

     **(4)**    If the plaintiff does not file the notice in accordance with paragraph (3), the claim is stayed until he files the notice.

     **(5)**    If the plaintiff accepts the offer he may obtain judgment by filing in the Registry a request in Form No. 16E in Appendix A and if he does so –

         **(a)**   where the defendant has not requested time to pay, paragraphs (6), (7) and (8) apply;

         **(b)**   where the defendant has requested time to pay, rule 9 applies.

     **(6)**    The plaintiff may specify in his request for judgment –

         **(a)**   the date by which the whole of the judgment debt is to be paid; or

         **(b)**   the times and rate at which it is to be paid by instalments.

     **(7)**    Upon receipt of the request for judgment, the Court shall enter judgment.

     **(8)**    Judgment shall be for the amount offered by the defendant (less any payments made) and costs to be paid –

         **(a)**   by the date or at the times and rate specified in the request for judgment; or

         **(b)**   if none is specified, immediately.

     **(9)**    If the plaintiff does not accept the amount offered by the defendant, he may obtain judgment by filing in the Registry a request in Form No. 16E in Appendix A.

     **(10)** Judgment under paragraph (9) shall be for an amount to be decided by the Court and costs.

     (L.N. 152 of 2008)

## NOTES

### [13A.7.1]  Origin and scope of Order 13A rule 7
Order 13A rule 7 derives from CPR 14.7. It enables a defendant to admit liability to pay a claim for an unliquidated amount, and at the same time make a formal proposal as to the amount to be paid in satisfaction of the claim, and the time of payment. The plaintiff is required to respond stating whether or not the proposed amount is accepted in satisfaction of the claim. If the plaintiff does not respond, the proceedings are stayed.

### [13A.7.2]  Rule 7(9) - judgment for an amount to be assessed
Order 13A rule 7(9) introduces an innovative new procedure whereby instead of merely rejecting a proposal to settle a claim for an unliquidated amount of money which it considers to be too low, the plaintiff may enter judgment for an amount to be assessed by the court under rule 7(10). This will ensure that costs and court time are not wasted on a trial on liability in such cases. Defendants making settlement proposals must consider this new procedure when making proposals. Defendants are not able to reserve the right to contest liability if their settlement proposals under this rule are rejected.

**8.     Power of Court to give directions** (O. 13A r. 8)
**Where the Court enters judgment under rule 6 or 7 for an amount to be decided by the Court, it may give such directions as it considers appropriate.**
        **(L.N. 152 of 2008)**

## NOTES

### [13A.8.1]  Directions for assessment of damages
Order 13A rule 8 derives from CPR 14.8. It empowers the court to give directions when judgment is entered under the preceding rules on a claim for an unliquidated amount. Directions will be required if the judgment is for an amount to be determined by the court. See part I of Order 37 concerning assessment of damages.

**9.     Request for time to pay** (O. 13A r. 9)
        **(1)     A defendant who makes an admission under rule 4, 5 or 7 may make a request for time to pay.**
        **(2)     A request for time to pay is a proposal about the date of payment or a proposal to pay by instalments at the times and rate specified in the request.**
        **(3)     The defendant's request for time to pay must be filed with his admission.**
        **(4)     If the plaintiff accepts the defendant's request for time to pay, he may obtain judgment by filing in the Registry a request for judgment in Form No. 16A, 16B or 16E (as the case may be) in Appendix A.**
        **(5)     Upon receipt of the request for judgment, the Court shall enter judgment.**

(6)    **Judgment shall be –**

    (a)    **where rule 4 applies, for the amount of the claim (less any payments made) and costs;**

    (b)    **where rule 5 applies, for the amount admitted (less any payments made) and costs; or**

    (c)    **where rule 7 applies, for the amount offered by the defendant (less any payments made) and costs,**

**and (in all cases) shall be for payment by the date or at the times and rate specified in the defendant's request for time to pay.**

(7)    **Where judgment is for payment by instalments at the times and rate specified in the defendant's request for time to pay, then unless the Court otherwise orders and subject to paragraph (8), execution of the judgment is stayed pending payment.**

(8)    **If the defendant fails to pay an instalment or part of an instalment in accordance with the judgment, the stay of execution pursuant to paragraph (7) immediately ceases and the plaintiff may enforce the payment of the whole amount adjudged to be paid or the whole of any unpaid balance.**

    **(L.N. 152 of 2008)**

---

## NOTES

### [13A.9.1]    Origin and scope of Order 13A rule 9

Order 13A rule 9 derives from CPR 14.9. It provides that a defendant may, when admitting liability to pay a specified sum of money claimed in legal proceedings, request terms as to time for payment or payment by instalment. If the plaintiff agrees those terms, judgment may be entered accordingly. It has always been possible for this result to be achieved by agreement between the parties, and consent or *Tomlin* order. However the formal procedure laid down in rule 9 is a key innovation in the civil justice reforms, in effect from 2009.

The Hong Kong rule differs from its English counterpart in that it goes on to provide for the consequences if a defendant defaults in making payment in accordance with the agreed terms.

### [13A.9.2]    Defendant may request payment on terms

A request for payment on terms is made by completing the appropriate part of form No 16 in appendix A, the form of admission. The defendant must give information as to ability to pay and state the terms requested.

### [13A.9.3]    Entry of judgment on acceptance of request for payment on terms

If the plaintiff accepts the defendant's proposal for payment on terms, the plaintiff may enter judgment on the terms proposed by the defendant, pursuant to rule 9(4), (5) and (6). If the plaintiff does not accept the defendant's proposal to pay on terms, the timing and rate of payment will be determined by the court under rule 10. See the commentary under that rule.

### [13A.9.4]    Stay of execution on acceptance of request for payment on terms

Rule 9(7) provides for an automatic stay of execution pending payment under a judgment for payment by instalments, unless the court orders otherwise.

### [13A.9.5]   Enforcement in case of breach terms of payment

Rule 9(8) provides for an automatic lifting of the stay of execution under rule 9(7), if the defendant fails to make payment in accordance with the terms of the judgment. The paragraph does not make any provision for overlooking even trifling breaches, but in principle it should be possible for a defendant to apply under Order 1B rule 1(2)(a) or Order 3 rule 5 for an extension of time to pay.

The court may be reluctant to grant an extension of time where the plaintiff has accepted the defendant's proposals as to payment terms because such acceptance may be construed as giving rise to a contract. See the commentary under Order 3 rule 5 concerning extension of time to comply with consent orders, and see also the commentary under Order 42 rule 5A concerning setting aside such orders. However, there should be no such impediment to an extension of time where the terms of payment have been determined by the court under rule 10. In England practice direction 14 expressly provides that either party may, on account of change in circumstances since the date of the court's determination of terms of payment, apply for a variation thereof.

### [13A.9.6]   Comparison with Tomlin order

The procedure for judgment on terms as to payment under rule 9 is rather like a formalised and streamlined version of the *Tomlin* order which was developed by the courts. See the commentary on the *Tomlin* order under Order 42 rule 5A.

**10.**     **Determination of rate of payment by Court** (O. 13A r. 10)

    **(1)**   **This rule applies where the defendant makes a request for time to pay under rule 9.**

    **(2)**   **If the plaintiff does not accept the defendant's proposal for payment, he shall file in the Registry a notice in Form No. 16A, 16B or 16E (as the case may be) in Appendix A.**

    **(3)**   **When the Court receives the plaintiff's notice, it shall enter judgment for the amount admitted (less any payments made) to be paid by the date or at the times and rate of payment determined by the Court.**

    **(4)**   **Where the Court is to determine the date or the times and rate of payment, it –**

       **(a)**   **may do so without a hearing; but**

       **(b)**   **shall consider –**

          **(i)**   **the information set out in the defendant's admission filed in the Registry;**

          **(ii)**   **the reasons why the plaintiff does not accept the defendant's proposal for payment; and**

          **(iii)**   **all other relevant matters.**

    **(5)**   **If there is to be a hearing to determine the date or the times and rate of payment, the Court shall give each party at least 7 days' notice of the hearing.**

    **(L.N. 152 of 2008)**

**NOTES**

**[13A.10.1]  Origin and scope of Order 13A rule 10**
Order 13A rule 10 derives from CPR 14.10. It provides for determination by the court of the times and rate of payment where a defendant has admitted liability to pay and has requested time to pay, but the plaintiff has rejected the proposal as to payment terms. The Hong Kong rule differs from its English counterpart in that it specifically empowers the court to make the determination without a hearing.

**[13A.10.2]  Court's power to determine times and rate of payment**
Order 13A rule 10 gives the court power to override a plaintiff's objection to the defendant's request for time to pay. The rule provides that where the plaintiff rejects the defendant's admission and request for time to pay, the court 'shall' enter judgment for payment at times and a rate to be determined by the court. That determination may be made without a hearing, but in that event the court is required to consider the matters set out in rule 10(4)(b). The guidance set out there as to how the court is to determine the times and rate of payment appears to be based on para 5.1 of English practice direction CPR PD 14.

In the event of the court proceeding without a hearing, its decision is subject to the right of either party to apply under rule 11 for a re-determination.

**11.     Right of re-determination** (O. 13A, r. 11)
      **(1)     Where the Court has determined the date or the times and rate of payment under rule 10(4) without a hearing, either party may apply for the decision to be re-determined by the Court.**
      **(2)     An application for re-determination must be made within 14 days after the applicant is served with notice of the determination.**
      **(L.N. 152 of 2008)**

**NOTES**

**[13A.11.1]  Origin and scope of Order 13A rule 11**
Order 13A rule 11 derives from CPR 14.13. It is consequential to the express power of the court under rule 10(4) to determine the times and rate of payment without a hearing. It enables a party dissatisfied with the times and rate determined by the court in such circumstances to apply within 14 days for a re-determination.

Rule 11 does not expressly require an oral hearing for a re-determination. It is thus conceivable that it could be dealt with by way of written submissions to a master under Order 32 rule 11A.

**12.     Interest** (O. 13A r. 12)
      **(1)     Judgment under rule 4, 5 or 7 must include the amount of interest claimed to the date of judgment if –**
                  **(a)     the plaintiff is seeking interest and he has stated in the endorsement of the writ or the statement of claim or the originating summons that he is doing so –**

                **(i)**      **under the terms of a contract;**
                **(ii)**      **under a specified enactment; or**
                **(iii)**     **on some other specified basis;**

     **(b)**      **where interest is claimed under section 48 of the Ordinance, the rate is no higher than the rate of interest payable on judgment debts at the date when the writ or the originating summons was issued; and**

     **(c)**      **the plaintiff's request for judgment includes a calculation of the interest claimed for the period from the date up to which interest was stated to be calculated in the statement of claim or the originating summons to the date of the request for judgment.**

    **(2)**    **In any case where judgment is entered under rule 4, 5 or 7 and the conditions specified in paragraph (1) are not satisfied, judgment shall be for an amount of interest to be decided by the Court.**

    **(L.N. 152 of 2008)**

---

## NOTES

### [13A.12.1]  Origin and scope of Order 13A rule 12

Order 13A rule 12 derives from CPR 14.14. The Hong Kong rule is broader and more specific. It provides for interest to be included in a judgment for a specified amount entered on admission of liability to pay under this Order.

### [13A.12.2]  Pre-judgment interest on admission of liability to pay

Order 13A rule 12(1) requires that judgment on admission of liability to pay under this Order must include interest if interest is claimed, the basis of that claim has been pleaded, and a calculation of the amount of accrued interest is included in the request for judgment. Where those conditions are not met, the amount of interest will be decided by the court under rule 12(2). That will be the case where instead of specifically stating the basis on which interest is claimed, the plaintiff's indorsement or statement of claim merely contains a general statement such as 'and the plaintiff claims interest'.

    See also the commentary under Order 18 rule 8 as to pleading interest, and that under Order 42 rule 1 concerning the award of interest on judgment for a sum of money.

**13.**     **Form for admission to be served with writ or originating summons**
     (O. 13A r. 13)

    **(1)**    **This rule applies where the only remedy that the plaintiff is seeking is the payment of money, whether or not the amount is liquidated.**

    **(2)**    **Where a writ of summons, an originating summons or any other originating process is served on a defendant, it must be accompanied by —**

     **(a)**      **if the amount of money which the plaintiff is seeking is liquidated, a copy of Form No. 16 in Appendix A for admitting the claim; and**

     **(b)**      **if the amount of money which the plaintiff is seeking is unliquidated, a copy of Form No. 16C in Appendix A for**

**admitting the claim.**
**(L.N. 152 of 2008)**

---

## NOTES

**[13A.13.1] Form for admission must be served with originating process**
Order 13A rule 13 obliges the plaintiff, in any money claim, to serve along with the writ or other originating process, the appropriate form whereby the defendant may admit the claim and ask for time to pay, or in the case of an unliquidated claim, offer a specified amount to satisfy the claim. This requirement is in addition to Order 6 rule 2(1)(c) by which a writ must be indorsed with a statement informing the defendant of the procedure under Order 13A for admission of liability to pay.

It is implicit in rule 13 that where proceedings are commenced by a generally endorsed writ, the admission form must be served with it, and cannot be deferred to the later stage when a statement of claim is prepared.

**14.    Application (O. 13A r. 14)**

   **(1)   This Order (other than rule 13) applies in relation to a writ of summons, an originating summons or any other originating process served before the commencement of this Order if –**

      **(a)   in the case of a writ of summons, the plaintiff has not obtained a default judgment under Order 13 or 19;**

      **(b)   in the case of an originating summons, the admission is filed and served before the date or the period fixed under Order 28, rule 2; and**

      **(c)   in the case of any other originating process, the period specified in rule 3(1)(c) for filing and serving an admission under rule 4, 5, 6 or 7 has not expired.**

   **(2)   This Order applies in relation to a counterclaim with the necessary modifications as if –**

      **(a)   a reference to a claim or statement of claim were a reference to a counterclaim;**

      **(b)   a reference to a plaintiff were a reference to the party making the counterclaim; and**

      **(c)   a reference to a defendant were a reference to the defendant to the counterclaim.**

   **(3)   Where a defendant has made a claim against a person not already a party to the action under Order 16, rule 1 or 8, this Order applies in relation to that claim and any other claim made under Order 16, rule 9 with the necessary modifications as if –**

      **(a)   a reference to a plaintiff were a reference to the person who makes the claim; and**

      **(b)   a reference to a defendant were a reference to the person against whom the claim is made.**

   **(L.N. 152 of 2008)**

**NOTES**

**[13A.14.1]  Limited application of Order 13A to pre-2009 actions**
Order 13A rule 14(1) provides that the admission procedures under the Order apply to actions commenced prior to the Order coming into force in 2009 save in the limited circumstances set out in paragraphs (a), (b) and (c) of rule 14(1).

**[13A.14.2]  Application of Order 13A to counterclaims and 3$^{rd}$ party proceedings**
Order 13A rule 14(2) and (3) extend the admission of liability to pay procedure under the Order, to counterclaims and third party proceedings.

**ORDER 14**

SUMMARY JUDGMENT

**1. Application by plaintiff for summary judgment** (O. 14 r. 1)
    **(1)   Where in an action to which this rule applies a statement of claim has been served on a defendant and that defendant has given notice of intention to defend the action, the plaintiff may, on the ground that that defendant has no defence to a claim included in the writ, or to a particular part of such a claim, or has no defence to such a claim or part except as to the amount of any damages claimed, apply to the Court for judgment against that defendant.**
    **(2)   Subject to paragraph (3) this rule applies to every action begun by writ other than—**
        **(a)   an action which includes a claim by the plaintiff for libel, slander, malicious prosecution, false imprisonment or seduction,**
        **(b)   an action which includes a claim by the plaintiff based on an allegation of fraud, or**
        **(c)   an Admiralty action in rem.**
    **(3)   This Order shall not apply to an action to which Order 86 or Order 88 applies.**

---

**NOTES**

**[14.1.1]   Scope of Order 14 – comparison with English rule**
Order 14 provides a mechanism for 'summary' judgment in cases where although the defendant has given notice of intention to defend it is demonstrable on written evidence that there is no genuine defence justifying the time and expense involved in a full trial with oral evidence.

Summary judgment under Order 14 is not available in those types of action listed in sub-rule 1(2). In addition, actions for specific performance or rescission, and mortgage actions are catered for by specific provision elsewhere: see Orders 86 and 88 respectively. See also Order 77 rule 7 which precludes summary judgment in actions against the government.

In England the exception for cases involving an allegation of fraud (Order 14 rule 1(2)(b)) was repealed some time before the Woolf reforms. The distinction between the Hong Kong rule and its pre-Woolf English counterpart was noted by the Court of Appeal in *Skink Ltd (in liq) v Comtowell Ltd & Anor* [1994] 2 HKC 286.

**[14.1.2]   No summary judgment in an action based on fraud**
Order 14 rule 1(2)(b) provides that summary judgment is not available in cases 'based on an allegation of fraud'. This is a matter of jurisdiction: see *Pacific Electric Wire & Cable Co Ltd v Harmutty Ltd & Ors* [2009] 2 HKC 330 (CA), referring to *Kays Impex Corp (HK) Ltd v Arbuthnot Export Services Ltd* [1973-76] HKC 109, 111H where Briggs CJ said that 'O 14 is inapplicable' to such cases.

The reason for the fraud exception was explained by Kaplan J in *Skink Ltd (in liq) v Comtowell Ltd & Anor* [1994] 1 HKC 646E-G:

I can only think that the fraud exception to O 14 was inserted in England and maintained in Hong Kong because the O 14 jurisdiction was wholly inappropriate for cases where the court had to consider whether a person was guilty of fraud or at the material time had an intention of fraud.

In *Skink* it was held that an application under section 60 of the Conveyancing and Property Ordinance (Cap 219) to set aside an assignment of landed property on the ground it was intended to defraud creditors would necessarily involve a finding of fraud, and was thus not susceptible to a summary judgment application.

There is a line of authorities to the effect that the fraud exception is confined to claims founded on fraud as strictly defined in *Derry v Peek* (1889) 14 App Cas 337. See, for example, *Tan Eng Guan & Anor v Southland Co Ltd* [1996] 2 HKC 100, 106G (CA) where Godfrey JA expressed the view that the fraud exception applies only to cases of 'false representation made knowingly without belief in its truth' and that it did not catch a derivative action claiming fraud on the minority. Liu JA agreed with Godfrey JA, but Nazareth VP preferred not to express any view on the issue, which he considered not to have been sufficiently addressed in the particular case. More recently a differently constituted Court of Appeal took a different view. See *Pacific Electric Wire & Cable* (above) where (at para 29) Rogers VP expressed the view that the exception extends to other types of fraud claims such as 'conspiracy, bribery or a claim for money had and received or under constructive trusts', with the result that there is no jurisdiction to grant summary judgment in such cases. The learned judge (with whom Le Pichon JA agreed) suggested that what Godfrey JA said in *Tan Eng Guan* might be confined to fraud on the minority. On an application for leave to appeal (FAMV 28/2009; 14.09.2009), the appeal committee of the CFA considered the point to be 'reasonably arguable and of importance', but considered that the particular case was not an appropriate one for leave to be granted.

Even where an allegation of fraud is outside the confines of the exception, such that Order 14 applies, the court may decline to grant summary judgment on the ground of the seriousness of the allegation. In *Wavefront Trading Ltd v Po Sang Bank Ltd* [1999] 2 HKC 130, 134B-D Keith J said that 'save in the clearest possible case, it is inappropriate for the court to decide in summary proceedings whether a defendant has been dishonest'. That view was endorsed by the Court of Appeal in *Comsec Travel Ltd v Fok Hing Tours Co Ltd* [2002] 4 HKC 679, 684C-D where Sakhrani J said:

> Where, as here, the plaintiff alleges that the defendant entered into a conspiracy to defraud the plaintiff it cannot be right for a court to conclude that the defendant was guilty of it in summary proceedings save in the clearest possible case and where the evidence is overwhelming.

### [14.1.3] Where summary judgment appropriate

Summary judgment is not appropriate in cases where there are 'real disputes of fact, or where the factual matrix is unclear': *Sin Hua Bank Ltd v Sung Foo Kee Ltd* [1993] 1 HKC 65 (CA), per Litton JA 76 I.

Summary judgment should only be sought in cases where it is clear that the defendant has no good defence. In *Man Earn Ltd v Wing Ting Fong* [1996] 1 HKC 225 (CA), Godfrey JA stated:

> Since the policy which underlies the summary procedure is to prevent the defendant

from delaying the plaintiff from obtaining judgment in a case in which the defendant has clearly no defence to the plaintiff's claim, the procedure should be invoked only where this condition is satisfied (at 227I–228A).

His Lordship continued:

> Unless it is obvious that the defence put forward by the defendant is 'frivolous and practically moonshine, Order 14 ought not to be applied: see *Codd v Delap* (1905) 92 LT 510, per Lord Lindley at 511' (at 228E).

Godfrey JA discouraged practitioners from applying for summary judgment in all but clear cases, stating that the result of failed applications would be further delay (at 228H–I). In the particular case the court dismissed an appeal against a High Court judge's decision to set aside summary judgment under Order 86 rule 1. The principles stated are equally applicable under this Order. See also *Kan Chi Chuen v New Happy Ltd & Ors* CACV 1531/2001 (Woo & Cheung JJA; 22.01.2002).

Summary judgment is not appropriate where there are doubts or suspicions as to the plaintiff's case. In that event the proper course is to grant leave to defend. See *Billion Silver Development Ltd v All Wide Investments Ltd* [2000] 2 HKC 262 (CA), citing *Extraktion Gesellschaft Fur Anlagenbau MbH v Oskar* (1984) 128 SJ 417.

Summary judgment is also inappropriate where the application would require extensive argument. See *Pacific Electric Wire & Cable Co Ltd v Harmutty Ltd & Ors* [2009] 2 HKC 330 where the Court of Appeal was highly critical of a summary judgment application which required a 12-day hearing with 10,000 pages of documents.

### [14.1.4] Time for making application for summary judgment

An application for summary judgment may not be made until a statement of claim has been served and notice of intention to defend given: Order 14 rule 1(1). There is no time limit for making the application, though the rules 'clearly contemplate' that ordinarily the application will be made before a defence has been filed: *Morison, Son & Jones (HK) Ltd v Yiu Wing Construction Co Ltd* [1989] 1 HKC 11, 17I–18A (CA).

### [14.1.5] Delay

In a suitable case, 'delay of itself would entitle the court to refuse to entertain an application for summary judgment': *Resona Bank Ltd v Lam Sie & Ors* [2004] 4 HKC 601, 612F. In that case the court decided against dismissing the application because a trial in the absence of a *bona fide* defence would be a waste of court time. Where a late application for summary judgment is made, it is good practice to submit an explanatory affidavit: *Kaufman v Maker Industrial Co Ltd* [1982] HKLR 20, 21I–22C.

**2. Manner in which application under rule 1 must be made** (O. 14 r. 2)

**(1) An application under rule 1 must be made by summons supported by an affidavit verifying the facts on which the claim, or the part of a claim, to which the application relates is based and stating that in the deponent's belief there is no defence to that claim or part, as the case may be, or no defence except as to the amount of any damages claimed.**

**(2) Unless the Court otherwise directs, an affidavit for the purposes of this rule may contain statements of information or belief with the sources and grounds thereof.**

**(3)    The summons, a copy of the affidavit in support and of any exhibits referred to therein must be served on the defendant not less than 10 clear days before the return day.**

---

## NOTES

### [14.2.1]    Application by summons and affidavit

Order 14 rule 2 provides that an application for summary judgment shall be made by summons supported by affidavit evidence. The summons and affidavit must be served at least 10 clear days before the return day. The affidavit in support must verify the claim, and state the deponent's belief that there is no defence or no full defence. Statements of 'information and belief' may be included in the affidavit, as to which see below. It has been held that the requirements as to the affidavit in support are strict, and failure to comply will deprive the court of jurisdiction to make the order sought: *Lagos v Grunwaldt* [1910] 1 KB 41 (per Cozens-Hardy MR at 45).

The affidavit in support 'cannot supplement the statement of claim and make assertions of fact which are not pleaded': *Lai Yuen Wah v Hoi Kwong Printing Co Ltd & Ors* [2003] 1 HKC 447, 452B-C, citing *Gold Ores Reduction Co Ltd v Parr* [1892] 2 QB 14. In *Lai Yuen Wah*, Deputy Judge Saunders set aside summary judgment which had been entered for a sum not readily ascertainable from the statement of claim and was instead based on affidavit evidence.

### [14.2.2]    Appropriate person to make the affidavit in support

It is not required that the affidavit or affirmation in support of a summary judgment application be made by the party in whose name the application is brought. However, in Hong Kong as in England, it has been held that where someone other than the plaintiff swears the affidavit he should give his means of knowledge (*Pan American World Airways v Great China Trading Co* (1950) 34 HKLR 80, citing *Chirqwin v Russell* 27 TLR 21 with approval).

In practice the Hong Kong courts may not permit Order 14 affidavits to be sworn by persons other than the parties quite as readily as do their English counterparts. It has been said:

> In Hong Kong we require the parties themselves to swear or affirm to matters of fact unless there is some very good reason such as absence from Hong Kong. The idea behind this is very simple. Both plaintiffs and defendants have been known, more often than ought to be the case to put forward stories that are eventually shown to be demonstrably false. When they swear or affirm to those stories they can and will be prosecuted for perjury. Where such stories are put forward through a solicitor or clerk who swears he is 'informed of and verily believes' the same, the client escapes the sanction of the criminal law and the solicitor acquires (with the court) the reputation of being a fool or a villain or both. (Betts, 'Practice and Procedure: A Master's View', in *Law Lectures for Practitioners 1987* (Hong Kong: Hong Kong Law Journal Ltd, 1987) pp 227, 234–235.)

### [14.2.3]    Requirement that affidavit state there is no defence

Order 14 rule 2(1) stipulates that the affidavit or affirmation in support of an application for summary judgment must state the deponent's belief that there is no defence to the claim. In *Hongkong Chinese Bank Ltd v Delon Photo & Hi-fi Centre Ltd* [2000] 3 HKC 71 the court had before it a case where the applicant for summary judgment had failed to comply with this requirement. Recorder Kenneth Kwok SC held that the omission was a fundamental slip, but capable of being cured (at 75C). The solicitors for the plaintiff gave an undertaking to produce an affidavit meeting the requirement before the conclusion of the hearing and on that being done, the issues before the court were resolved otherwise than on the basis of the procedural defect.

## [14.2.4]   Statements of 'information or belief'

Order 14 rule 2(2) expressly provides that an affidavit in support of a summary judgment application may contain statements based on 'information or belief' (unless the court otherwise directs). The rule is similar to Order 41 rule 5(2), dealing with affidavits in support of interlocutory applications generally. See the commentary under that rule.

Order 14 rule 2(2) overrules *Lagos v Grunwaldt* [1910] 1 KB 41, 46–47 insofar as it was there held that evidence on information or belief was not acceptable on an application for summary judgment. (That decision was based on the former requirement that the plaintiff's affidavit in support of a summary judgment application be made by the plaintiff personally or by someone who could swear positively to the facts.)

Evidence based on information or belief is hearsay. Although admissible for the purpose of a summary judgment application it is inherently less credible than evidence based on first hand knowledge. On a summary judgment application the court does not resolve issues of credibility (see the commentary under Order 14 rule 1) but there may be cases where first hand evidence will be viewed more favourably than hearsay.

**3.      Judgment for plaintiff** (O. 14 r. 3)

**(1)    Unless on the hearing of an application under rule 1 either the Court dismisses the application or the defendant satisfies the Court with respect to the claim, or the part of a claim, to which the application relates that there is an issue or question in dispute which ought to be tried or that there ought for some other reason to be a trial of that claim or part, the Court may give such judgment for the plaintiff against that defendant on that claim or part as may be just having regard to the nature of the remedy or relief claimed. (See App. A, Form 44)**

**(2)    The Court may by order, and subject to such conditions, if any, as may be just, stay execution of any judgment given against a defendant under this rule until after the trial of any counterclaim made or raised by the defendant in the action.**

---

## NOTES

### [14.3.1]   Procedure for hearing application – the call-over

The court has adopted a two-stage procedure for the hearing of Order 14 summonses. The initial hearing will be fixed for 15 minutes only. If at that hearing it is evident to the master that the application cannot be resolved without argument, it will be adjourned to a date to be fixed, and directions may be given as to the filing of further affidavits etc. The call-over hearing is also an appropriate occasion for the court to consider whether the substantive application should be heard by a master or transferred to a judge pursuant to Order 32 rule 12. See the commentary under that rule.

It has been held that the first call-over hearing of an Order 14 summons is not an appropriate occasion for 'muscular case management', even after the advent of the civil justice reforms. See *Win Profit Corp Ltd v World Orient Investment Ltd* HCA 1487/2009 (Deputy Judge Carlson; 29.12.2009) (para 9) where strict terms imposed by a master at a first call-over hearing in respect of an extension of time to file evidence, were set aside.

In *Win Profit* it was also held (para 17) that it is inappropriate to grant a certificate for counsel appearing at an Order 14 call-over hearing. Although a party is entitled to instruct counsel to appear at a call-over if it so wishes, this is not something which the opposing party 'should ever be expected to pay for'. The sort of issue which arises on such a call-over is 'well within the range of advocacy that a solicitor would be expected to undertake'.

### [14.3.2]   Type of order to be made on Order 14 summons

By virtue of Order 14 rules 3, 4 and 7, read together, there are three types of order which the court may make on an Order 14 summons. These are an order dismissing the application, an order granting the defendant leave to defend, and an order that judgment be entered for the plaintiff.

An order granting judgment to the plaintiff is made under Order 14 rule 3. See the commentary below.

It is appropriate for the court to dismiss an application which is irregular in some respect (such as where the affidavit in support does not comply with Order 14 rule 2), or where the plaintiff knew that the defendant relied on a contention which would entitle it to unconditional leave to defend. See Order 14 rule 7.

On the other hand, the grant of leave to defend implies that the defendant has satisfied the court that the matter should proceed to trial. See Order 14 rule 4 and the commentary thereunder.

Dismissal and leave to defend are alternatives, and should not be ordered at the same time: *Wordcap Investment Ltd v Bosswell Estates Ltd* [1988] HKC 328, 333D-F (CA). This is at least partly because the different orders have different costs consequences: *Ho Kuen Fai (t/a Sun Hing Electrical Eng'g) v Chun Wo Construction & Eng'g Co Ltd* HCA 1790/2007 (Deputy Judge Lisa Wong SC; 07.08.2008).

With regard to the costs consequences of a grant of leave to defend, see the commentary under Order 14 rule 4, and for costs consequences of dismissal of an application for summary judgment, see Order 14 rule 7.

### [14.3.3]   Burden on defendant

Upon the plaintiff filing and serving an affidavit which complies with Order 14 rule 2 the burden in effect shifts to the defendant to show that a trial is justified: *Manciple Ltd v Char On Man* [1995] 3 HKC 459, 466E–F. In the words of Order 14 rule 3, the burden on the defendant is to show that there is an issue or question which ought to be tried or that for some other reason there ought to be a trial. In short the defendant's burden is to show a triable issue: *Fung Kau t/a Fung Kau Kee Contractors, Salvage & Eng Co v Lam Yau Cheong* [1967] HKLR 156, 158; *Murjani v Bank of India* [1990] 1 HKLR 586, 589H (CA). The defendant need not show a complete defence, merely an issue to be tried: *Ray v Barker* (1879) 4 Ex D 279, 283.

*Triable issue of fact* – Although the court should not embark on a 'mini-trial' on affidavit evidence (see below), it is not obliged to find a triable issue of fact where the defendant puts forward a factual defence which is simply not believable, or is 'practically moonshine': see the commentary under Order 14 rule 1 as to when summary judgment is appropriate. If what the defendant says is believable, the court will then consider whether it amounts to an arguable defence in law: *Schindler Lifts (HK) Ltd v Ocean Joy Investments Ltd* [2003] 1 HKC 438 (para 10).

*Triable issue of law* – In deciding whether a point of law gives rise to a triable issue the court will ask whether the issue is 'misconceived or can be shown by relatively short argument to be unsustainable': *Ryoden Eng'g Ltd Co Ltd v Paul Y Construction Co Ltd* [1994] 2 HKC 578, 584G-H. If so the court may decide the point under the Order 14 summons, but otherwise leave to defend will be granted as it is not appropriate for the Order 14 procedure to be used to decide points of law which may require lengthy argument and the citation of many authorities: *Home & Overseas Insurance Co Ltd v Mentor Insurance Co (UK) Ltd (in liq)* [1990] 1 WLR 153, 158D-F; [1989] 3 All ER 74 (CA). Instead of granting leave to defend, the court may direct that the point be decided under Order 14A. See the commentary under that Order.

*Other reason for trial* – Order 14 rule 3 provides that the court may refuse summary judgment where there is 'some other reason' why there ought to be a trial. Such other reasons include:

- Where there are circumstances which call for further investigation: *Talent Wise Ltd v Cheung Shui Ching* [1998] 2 HKLRD 744, 748H *et seq*, citing *Miles v Bull* [1969] 1 QB 258.
- Where the defendant is searching for a witness who might be able to provide material for a defence; where the claim is of a highly complicated or technical nature which could only be properly understood with oral evidence; or where it is desirable that if a plaintiff who may have acted harshly and unconscionably is to be given judgment it should be in the full light of publicity: *Bank für Gemeinwirtschaft AG v City of London Garages Ltd* [1971] 1 WLR 149, 158 (CA).
- Where there are cross-claims and it would be 'just and reasonable' for all matters in dispute between the parties to be determined together: *Trafalgar House Construction (Regions) Ltd v General Surety & Guarantee Co Ltd* [1996] 1 AC 199, 210C-H.
- Where the case is complicated: *United Malayan Banking Corp Bhd v Lim Meng Hua & Ors* [1990] 1 MLJ 54; but not where the defendant 'is embarking upon a fishing expedition in the hope of finding some ground for delaying a judgment against him: *Cheng Ah Hung Bernard v Chintung Commodities Ltd* [1985] 1 HKC 318, 328B-C (CA).
- Where the case requires mature consideration such as in an evolving area of law: *Wavefront Trading Ltd v Po Sang Bank Ltd* [1999] 2 HKC 130, 134D-G.

It may be sufficient for the defendant to show that he has an arguable defence based on set-off, whereby the plaintiff's claim might be extinguished. See, for example, *Charmway Development Ltd v Long China Engineering Ltd* [2001] 3 HKC 515, 520 where it was stated (*obiter*) that where the defendant has a cross-claim so closely connected with the plaintiff's claim 'that it would be manifestly unjust to enforce one without regard to the other' there may be a right to equitable set-off justifying a refusal of summary judgment. *Esso Petroleum Co Ltd v Milton* [1997] 1 WLR 938, 950D and *Dole Dried Fruit & Nut Co v Trustin Kerwood Ltd* [1990] 2 Lloyd's Rep 309, 311 were referred to. As to the defence of set-off see the commentary under Order 18 rule 17.

'Some other reason' for trial in Order 14 rule 3(1) 'has to be a reason that goes, or is relevant, to a defence to the summary judgment application': *Tianjin Jinfu Expressway Co Ltd v Lucky Money Ltd & Ors* CACV 266/2007 (Le Pichon JA & Sakhrani J; 09.04.2008) (para 38).

### [14.3.4]  Defendant's affidavit

Order 14 rule 4(1) provides that the defendant may resist a summary judgment application 'by affidavit or otherwise'. Although an affidavit is not strictly required, in most cases, where the plaintiff's application is in order and demonstrates a *prima facie* case, the defendant has little prospect of being granted leave to defend unless its defence is set out in an affidavit: *Koninklijke Philips Electronics NV v Wealth Full Technology Ltd* [2002] 3 HKC 87.

Some exceptional circumstances in which a defendant's affidavit may not be necessary are mentioned in *Chinakong Manufactory Ltd v Uniden HK* [1992] 1 HKC 481, 485, *et seq*:

*   Statement of claim fails to set out the necessary ingredients of the cause of action, for example failure to plead that notice has been given in respect of an agreement terminable by notice
*   Plaintiff's cause of action unknown to law
*   Defendant enjoys immunity from suit
*   It is plain from the statement of claim that the limitation period has expired and the defendant has filed a defence taking the point
*   Cause of action not within the scope of Order 14, for example libel [see Order 14 rule 1(2)]
*   Action against the government [see Order 77 rule 7].

The three common forms of defendant's affidavit in Order 14 proceedings were described as follows in *Chinakong* (above, at 485E-F):

> The most common method is for the defendant to file an affidavit(s) deposing to the fact that there is a defence on the merits and setting out the matters which give rise to the defence.
>
> A variation of the first method is, in addition to this narrative, to exhibit to the affidavit a draft defence which it is proposed to file.
>
> The third method is simply to exhibit a defence and verify its truth and content by affidavit.

The defendant's affidavit may contain 'information or belief' evidence: rule 4(2).

The defendant's affidavit should 'state clearly and concisely what the defence is, and what facts are relied on to support it', and if fraud is relied on, particulars should be given: *Wesco China Ltd v Liu Fu Tien* [2007] 1 HKC 576, 597A (DCt), quoting from *Wallingford v Mutual Society* (1880) 5 App Cas 685. In *Wesco* leave to defend was refused where the proposed defence of fraud was put forward in oral submissions only.

**[14.3.5]  No 'mini-trial' of issues of fact**

On a summary judgment application the court is not in a position to resolve issues of fact on the affidavit evidence. It follows that where there is a genuine factual dispute the court should not embark on a 'mini-trial', but should grant leave to defend so that the factual issues can be resolved at a full trial. In *Ng Shou Chun v Hung Chun San* [1994] 1 HKC 155, 158G-H (CA) it was said the court should ask itself:

> 'Is what the defendant says credible?' If so, he must have leave to defend. If not, the plaintiff is entitled to summary judgment. The issue is not whether the defendant's assertions are to be believed; it is whether those assertions are believable.

The question whether the defendant's assertions are believable 'is a question to be answered not by taking those assertions in isolation but rather by taking them in the context of so much of the background as is either undisputed or beyond reasonable dispute': *Re Safe Rich Industries Ltd* CACV 81/1994 (Nazareth VP, Litton & Bokhary JJA; 03.11.1994) (para 13); [1994] HKLY p 115 (Case No 183).

See also *Mass Int'l Ltd v Hillis Industries Ltd* [1996] 1 HKC 434, 439E (CA) and *Kan Chi Chuen v New Happy Ltd & Ors* CACV 1531/2001 (Woo & Cheung JJA; 22.01.2002).

It is not appropriate for the court to make 'findings' on the affidavit evidence – reasons for refusing summary judgment need only consist of a few words why the plaintiff has not satisfied the court there is no defence: *Man Earn Ltd v Wing Ting Fong* [1996] 1 HKC 225, 230B–D (CA).

**[14.3.6]  Oral evidence on summary judgment application**

Order 14 rule 4(4)(b) provides for oral examination of the defendant in 'special circumstances'. This power is rarely if ever used because the court will normally grant leave to defend if there is a genuine factual issue, leaving it to the trial judge to decide whether the defence is to be believed. The court should not use this provision so as to treat the Order 14 application as trial of the action: *Phonographic Performance (SEA) Ltd v California Entertainments Ltd* [1988] 2 HKLR 237, 243G (CA).

**[14.3.7]  Types of relief which may be the subject of Order 14 summary judgment**

Order 14 rule 3 empowers the court to give 'such judgment… as may be just having regard to the nature of the remedy or relief claimed'. The court will not give judgment for relief which is not specifically claimed in the statement of claim, and the usual prayer for 'further or other relief' does not assist in this regard: *Chang Man v Ma Shou Yung* [2002] 2 HKC 213.

**[14.3.8]  Form of judgment**

Where the court grants summary judgment under this rule, judgment should be drawn up in accordance with Form No 44 in Appendix A to these rules.

**[14.3.9]  Summary judgment on part of a claim**

Order 14 rule 3(1) provides that the court may grant summary judgment on part of a claim. In *Wing Siu Co Ltd v Goldquest International Ltd* [2002] 4 HKC 420 the court granted summary judgment on liability and ordered that damages be assessed. At the same time the court made an order for an interim payment of damages (as to which see Order 29 rules 11 and 12 and the commentary thereunder).

#### [14.3.10]  Summary judgment where set-off or counterclaim

Where an application for summary judgment is made out, but at the same time there is an arguable defence of set-off or a counterclaim, the court will normally make an order accommodating both sides. In *Shenzhen Baoming Ceramics Co Ltd v Companion-China Ltd* [2000] 2 HKC 790, 796F *et seq* (CA) the court quoted with approval the summary of the law in the English *Supreme Court Practice 1999*. Shortly stated, the following points are made there:

(a)    leave to defend should be granted to the extent of an arguable set-off;

(b)    where there is a counterclaim:

    (i)    unconditional leave to defend should be granted where the counterclaim arises out of the same subject matter as the action;

    (ii)   judgment should be granted to the plaintiff coupled with a stay of execution under rule 3(2) (see below) where there is a plausible counterclaim which could extinguish the plaintiff's claim;

    (iii)  judgment should be granted to the plaintiff without a stay of execution where there is a counterclaim wholly unconnected with the claim.

See also *Pacific Century Insurance Co Ltd v Top Glory Insurance Co (Bermuda) Ltd & Anor* CACV 293/2002 (Woo & Ma JJA; 27.12.2002).

With regard to summary judgment *on* a counterclaim, see rule 5.

#### [14.3.11]  Stay of execution pending trial of counterclaim

Order 14 rule 3(2) empowers the court to order a stay of execution of a summary judgment pending trial of a counterclaim.

The power is discretionary, and in exercising the discretion the court may consider the merits of the counterclaim: *Fu Tai Industrial Ltd v Decapio Int'l Industrial Ltd* [2000] 3 HKC 259, 263H-I (distinguishing *TC Trustees Ltd v JS Darwen (Successors) Ltd* [1969] 2 QB 295 which suggests that in other circumstances, *eg* Order 47 rule 1, the court will not consider the merits on an application for such a stay).

In *Parkie Trading Ltd & Anor v Wong Tsun Tsun Thai Kitchen Ltd & Ors* HCA 1462/1996 (Stone J; 18.07.1997 the court declined to grant a stay where the counterclaim was not brought in the same action but by way of separate action in mainland China.

#### [14.3.12]  Costs on grant of summary judgment

Where the court grants summary judgment, it will usually make an order that costs follow the event, that is that the defendant pay the plaintiff's costs of the action including the Order 14 application. The quantum of costs is normally limited by the scale set out in Part II of the 2$^{nd}$ Schedule to Order 62. However the court retains a discretion to order that costs be taxed in the usual way. See *Cobalt Industrial Co Ltd v Kin Sun Electronics Ltd* HCA 7320/1995 (Patrick Chan J; 08.11.1996); [1997] 2 HKC 402 (CA). Where the court so orders quantum is not restricted to the amounts in the scale: Order 62 rule 32(4). Only in exceptional circumstances is it appropriate for the court to order taxed costs instead of scale costs: see the Court of Appeal's judgment in *Cobalt* (above, per Godfrey JA at 404D).

See also rule 7 which makes specific provision for costs of summary judgment applications which should never have been brought.

**[14.3.13] Appeal against grant of summary judgment**

A grant of summary judgment is exempt from the general requirement under section 14AA of the High Court Ordinance that leave be obtained for an appeal to the Court of Appeal from an interlocutory order. See Order 59 rule 21 and the commentary thereunder. There is no leave requirement for appeals from a master to a single judge of the High Court under Order 58.

**4.      Leave to defend** (O. 14 r. 4)

**(1)    A defendant may show cause against an application under rule 1 by affidavit or otherwise to the satisfaction of the Court.**

**(2)    Rule 2(2) applies for the purposes of this rule as it applies for the purposes of that rule.**

**(3)    The Court may give a defendant against whom such an application is made leave to defend the action with respect to the claim, or the part of a claim, to which the application relates either unconditionally or on such terms as to giving security or time or mode of trial or otherwise as it thinks fit.**

**(4)    On the hearing of such an application the Court may order a defendant showing cause or, where that defendant is a body corporate, any director, manager, secretary or other similar officer thereof, or any person purporting to act in any such capacity—**

**(a)      to produce any document;**

**(b)      if it appears to the Court that there are special circumstances which make it desirable that he should do so, to attend and be examined on oath.**

---

**NOTES**

**[14.4.1]   Leave to defend**

A defendant who is able on the hearing of an Order 14 application to demonstrate that there is a triable issue will normally be granted leave to defend. Such an order puts the defendant in a better position than an order simply dismissing the Order 14 application. Leave to defend is a determination that the defendant shall be permitted to defend the action. Such leave can only be over-turned on appeal. On the other hand an order simply dismissing an Order 14 application merely suggests that the application may not have been put together properly. Theoretically a fresh application, properly constituted, could be brought.

Where the court has doubts or suspicions about a plaintiff's case, it should grant the defendant unconditional leave to defend so as to allow those matters to be ventilated at trial: *Billion Silver Development Ltd v All Wide Investments Ltd* [2000] 2 HKC 262, 266D–E (CA).

Leave to defend must be granted where there is a 'question as to what on the true state of the account is payable': *Lai Yuen Wah v Hoi Kwong Printing Co Ltd* [2003] 1 HKC 447, 452F–G, citing *Lynde v Waithman* [1895] 2 QB 180 and *Wallingford v Mutual Society and Official Receiver* (1880) 5 App Cas 685.

## [14.4.2]   Conditional leave to defend

Where the court grants leave to defend, it may do so unconditionally or on terms. Order 14 rule 4(3) mentions terms as to security, time and mode of trial, but it is clear that other terms are not excluded.

Terms as to posting security for the amount claimed are appropriate where the defence put forward by the defendant, although possible, is 'shadowy' (*Wu Cho Mei t/ a Mui Far Chung Restaurant v Wang Siau Yu* [1994] 1 HKC 188, 190; *Tong Nai Kan v Cheung King Fung Francis* [2005] 2 HKC 249, 254B-) or 'far-fetched' (*Pitamberas Chatomal Kalwani t/a Kalwani Corp v Jacobson Van Den Berg (HK) Ltd* [1964] HKLR 842, 862). In the *Kalwani* case Blair-Kerr J said, at 862:

> In Hong Kong it not infrequently happens that when a defendant is asked to show cause why judgment should not be given against him, he puts forward by way of defence an allegation which, on the face of it, may strike a court as being rather far-fetched, although the court may hesitate to shut him from the seat of judgment. For my part, I think that the court should not hesitate to grant conditional leave in such cases; and payment into court of the sum in dispute should ordinarily be considered.

Faced with implausible, inconsistent or seemingly incredible evidence which nevertheless could be believed at trial, the court cannot enter judgment against the defendant – there can be no trial on the affidavit evidence – but it is proper in such cases to require the posting of security. Requiring the defendant to pay the amount in dispute into court will prevent him from putting forward an unmeritorious defence simply for the purpose of delaying the inevitable judgment against him.

It has been suggested that the Hong Kong courts may be more ready to impose such a term than their English counterparts: see *Fung Tin Keung v Hong Kong Wah Yuen Investment Co & Anor* [1967] HKLR 650, 657–658.

*Quantum of security* – The court may order the defendant to give security for all or part of the claim. In *Pitamberdas Chatomal Kalwani t/a Kalwani Corp v Jacobson Van Den Berg (HK) Ltd* [1964] HKLR 842, 862, Blair-Kerr J held that the court should at least consider requiring the defendant to pay the full amount into court. However, it has been held in a trio of decisions of the Hong Kong Court of Appeal that it is not appropri ate to impose a condition which the defendant is unable to fulfil: see *Hwang Yiou Kwa Victor & Anor v Morgan Guaranty Trust Co of New York* [1985] 1 HKC 294 (CA), *Muhammad Ibrahim v Khan* [1986] HKLR 580 (CA) and *Wu Cho Mei t/a Mui Far Chung Restaurant v Wang Siau Yu* [1994] 1 HKC 188. In the third of those cases the defendant had been granted leave to defend on condition he pay $750,000 into court. On appeal he filed an affidavit of means suggesting he could not pay more than $200,000. Citing *MV Yorke Motors (a firm) v Edwards* [1982] 1 WLR 444 (HL) the court allowed the appeal. Godfrey JA said (at 189D–E):

> It is clear that the court will not impose upon a defendant a condition with which it is satisfied he is unable to comply before giving him leave to defend, for that would be tantamount to refusing him leave to defend altogether.

The court may of its own motion raise the issue of the defendant's ability to comply with a proposed condition and may postpone imposing the condition until the defendant's means have been investigated: *Paclantic Financing Co Inc v Moscow Narodny Bank Ltd* [1983] 1 WLR 1063 (affirmed on appeal – [1984] The Times, 22 February). However, in *Wu Cho Mei t/a Mui Far Chung Restaurant v Wang Siau Yu* [1994] 1 HKC 188 the court accepted the defendant's 'jejune' evidence as to means where the plaintiff neither put in any evidence to the contrary nor sought an adjournment to do so.

The court's approach where a defendant alleges inability to pay security as a condition of leave to defend was summarised in *Kwong Key Construction & Eng'g Ltd v Sunlink Ltd* [2003] 4 HKC 300, 305H–306B (CA) as follows:

(1) Where a defendant seeks to argue his impecuniosity in order to avoid a financial condition being imposed, the onus is on him to put sufficient and proper evidence before the court as to his means. He must make full and frank disclosure. The reason for this evidential burden (on top of the legal burden) is that usually it is the defendant rather than the plaintiff who will have any knowledge of his own financial position.

(2) A defendant must show not that it is difficult for him to fulfil the condition sought to be imposed, but that it is impossible for him to fulfil it. Here, the possibility of a defendant obtaining financial assistance from, say, friends, relatives, financial institutions or (in the case of a company) related or associated companies, must be satisfactorily dealt with by him.

As to the full and frank disclosure requirement referred to at point (1) above, see also *Lam Kam Hung v Yick Kwok Man* CACV 216/1996 (Bokhary JA, P Chan & Rogers JJ; 30.01.1997).

A defendant who would not be able to pay security as a condition of leave to defend need not necessarily prepare evidence as to its means in advance of a summary judgment application. It is appropriate to wait for the court to give an indication that conditional leave is likely. See *Wang Yiou Kwa Victor v Morgan Guaranty Trust Co of New York* [1985] 1 HKC 294, 296 (CA). In *Kwong Key Construction & Engineering Ltd v Sunlink Ltd* [2003] 4 HKC 300, 305D (CA) this practice was approved as 'correct … even though some delay may be involved'. However in *Wing Lung Finance Ltd v Cheng Ho Yin & Ors* HCA 1494/2008 (Chu J; 19.08.2009) the court took a different view. Costs of the resumed hearing to consider evidence of means were ordered to be 'plaintiff's costs in the cause in any event' (meaning they could not be recovered by the defendant regardless of the outcome – see the commentary on costs orders on interlocutory applications under Order 62 rule 3). The court considered the hearing would not have been necessary if the defendant had prepared its evidence on this issue in advance. When produced, evidence of impecuniosity should be given on affidavit. In *Tadano South China Co Ltd v Brightford Ltd* CACV 152/2006 (Le Pichon & Yuen JJA; 17.08.2006) (application for leave to appeal to the CFA dismissed 15.01.2007) the court described as 'wholly inadequate' evidence of impecuniosity put forward from the bar table without a supporting affidavit.

*Other terms* – In *O Mark Polyethylene Products Fty Ltd v Reap Star Ltd* [2000] 2 HKC 330 a master had ordered a defendant to pay $45,000 wasted costs into court as a condition of leave to defend. The Court of Appeal overturned that order in the particular circumstances of the case.

**[14.4.3] 'Appropriation' of money paid as condition of leave to defend**
Order 22 rule 23(2) provides that a defendant who pays money into court under Order 14 as a condition of being granted leave to defend, may 'appropriate' that sum in whole or in part, and even together with another payment, in satisfaction of the plaintiff's claim. This is done by notice, for which no form is prescribed. Such an appropriation is deemed, by Order 22 rule 23(3), to be a sanctioned payment or payment with a plea of

tender. As to sanctioned payments generally, see Order 22. As to the defence of tender, see Order 18 rule 16 and the commentary thereunder.

**[14.4.4]   Appeal against unconditional leave to defend**
Section 14(3)(b) of the High Court Ordinance previously provided that no appeal lay from an order of the Court of First Instance giving unconditional leave to defend an action. The provision applied only to appeals to the Court of Appeal, and not to appeals from a master to a single judge under Order 58: *Thiam Joc (HK) Ltd & Ors v Sanday Investment Ltd* [1985] 1 HKC 298 (CA). It was repealed in 1987, so that appeals are possible whether from a master to a single judge, or from a judge to the Court of Appeal. However, under section 14AA of the High Court Ordinance, which came into force on 02.04.2009 along with the civil justice reforms, such an appeal, if to the Court of Appeal, now requires leave, which should be sought in accordance with Order 59 rule 2B. Although a grant of summary judgment is exempt from the leave requirement (see Order 59 rule 21 and the commentary thereunder), a grant of leave to defend is not.

Even before the leave requirement was introduced it was clear that the Court of Appeal would be slow to interfere with a grant of unconditional leave to defend, particularly where made on the basis of a triable issue of fact. See *Strong Base Services Ltd v Geroma Electronic Ltd & Anor* [1996] 2 HKC 94, 96A–E (CA) *citing Lloyds Bank Ltd v Ellis-Fewster* [1983] 1 WLR 559 and *European Asian Bank AG v Punjab & Sind Bank* (No 2) [1983] 1 WLR 642. See also *The General of the Salvation Army v Hong Kong Cat Salvation Army Ltd* [2004] 3 HKC 144 (CA).

The approach is different where questions of law are involved 'since the views of the court below are either correct or not correct'. See *Trewell Development Ltd v Tsang Chun Wah* [2003] 4 HKC 401, 405C–F, per Ma JA.

The above factors will now undoubtedly be taken into account on an application for leave to appeal against a grant of unconditional leave to defend.

The approach may also be different where the appeal is from a master to a single judge. On such an appeal the application is heard over again. See the commentary under Order 58 rule 1.

**[14.4.5]   Appeal against conditional leave to defend**
Under section 14AA of the High Court Ordinance, which came into force as part of the civil justice reforms on 02.04.2009, an appeal against a grant of conditional leave to defend will only lie with leave of the court. The leave requirement applies only to appeals to the Court of Appeal, and not appeals from a master to a single judge under Order 58. Such leave should be obtained under Order 59 rule 2B. Although a grant of summary judgment is exempt from the leave requirement (see Order 59 rule 21 and the commentary thereunder), a grant of leave to defend is not. On such an application for leave, the court will no doubt take into account the previous cases concerning the general reluctance of the Court of Appeal to interfere with discretionary decisions. In *Banque Nationale de Paris v Chan U Tong* [1968] HKLR 151 (CA) the court doubted that an order imposing a condition on leave to defend is a matter of discretion. It set aside the condition imposed below on the ground that it could cause injustice. In *Cheung Hong v Lau Kwok Mong* CACV 320/2006 (Cheung JA & A Cheung J; 06.02.2007) (para 13), without referring to the earlier authority, the court proceeded on the basis that the

imposition of conditions is an exercise of discretion such that the Court of Appeal will not interfere unless there has been an error of principle.

Different considerations may apply on an appeal from a master to a judge under Order 58, as the application is heard afresh. Note that *Wong Hung Yu Richard v Wu Ming Fat Simon* [2002] 2 HKC 687 firmly establishes that an appeal lies under Order 58 against the imposition of terms on a grant of leave to defend.

### [14.4.6]  Costs on grant of leave to defend

When leave to defend is granted by a master, the usual order as to costs is costs in the cause. However the matter remains one of discretion and the master may make another order in the circumstances of an individual case. Where a master does so, an appellate court will be slow to interfere. See *Li Kwong Wong v Ever Property Management Ltd* CACV 62/1995 (Litton VP, Godfrey JA & Ryan J; 13.12.1995).

The situation is different where leave to defend is refused in the first instance and it is necessary for the defendant to appeal to a single judge, or to the Court of Appeal. In that event the costs of the hearing before the master will be in the cause, and the costs of the appeal will follow the event, that is, they will be to the defendant who obtains leave to defend only by bringing such appeal. See *Teh Yee Lee William v Nikko Securities Co (Asia) Ltd* CACV 78/1983 (Huggins VP, Cons & Fuad JJA; 13.10.1983); *Shahdan Ltd v Siu Wing Keung* HCA 4861/1994 (Findlay J; 01.08.1995).

In the case of conditional leave to defend, it is appropriate for the costs order to be one which is contingent on the condition being complied with. Such an order may provide that if the condition is complied with, costs will be in the cause; but if the condition is not complied with, the plaintiff will be at liberty to enter judgment with costs. See *Wu Yi Dev't Co Ltd v Big Island Construction (HK) Ltd* HCA 714/2007 (Chu J; 19.07.2007) as an example. Where it is necessary for the defendant to appeal to obtain conditional leave to defend, the costs of the appeal will normally follow the event, as in *Dragages et Travaux Publics (HK) Ltd v Citystate Insurance Ltd* [2001] 1 HKC 196 (CA).

**5.  Application for summary judgment on counterclaim** (O. 14 r. 5)

**(1)  Where a defendant to an action begun by writ has served a counterclaim on the plaintiff, then, subject to paragraph (3), the defendant may, on the ground that the plaintiff has no defence to a claim made in the counterclaim, or to a particular part of such a claim, apply to the Court for judgment against the plaintiff on that claim or part.**

**(2)  Rules 2, 3 and 4 shall apply in relation to an application under this rule as they apply in relation to an application under rule 1 but with the following modifications, that is to say—**

> **(a)  references to the plaintiff and defendant shall be construed as references to the defendant and plaintiff respectively;**
>
> **(b)  the words in rule 3 (2) "any counterclaim made or raised by the defendant in" shall be omitted; and**
>
> **(c)  the reference in rule 4(3) to the action shall be construed as a reference to the counterclaim to which the application under this rule relates.**

(3)    **This rule shall not apply to a counterclaim which includes any such claim as is referred to in rule 1(2).**

6.    **Directions** (O. 14 r. 6)

    (1)    **Where the Court—**

        (a)    **orders that a defendant or a plaintiff have leave (whether conditional or unconditional) to defend an action or counterclaim, as the case may be, with respect to a claim or a part of a claim, or**

        (b)    **gives judgment for a plaintiff or a defendant on a claim or part of a claim but also orders that execution of the judgment be stayed pending the trial of a counterclaim or of the action, as the case may be,**

**the Court shall give directions as to the further conduct of the action, and Order 25, rules 2 to 7, shall, with the omission of so much of rule 7(1) as requires parties to serve a notice specifying the orders and directions which they require and with any other necessary modifications, apply as if the application under rule 1 of this Order or rule 5 thereof, as the case may be, on which the order was made were a case management summons. (L.N. 152 of 2008)**

    (2)    **In particular, and if the parties consent, the Court may direct that the claim in question and any other claim in the action be tried by a master under the provisions of these rules relating to the trial of causes or matters or questions or issues by masters.**

---

**NOTES**

**[14.6.1]    Directions on grant of leave to defend**

Where an application for summary judgment is wholly or partly unsuccessful, with the result that some or all of the issues in dispute between the parties will proceed to trial, the court may, under Order 14 rule 6, give directions as to the further conduct of the action. Such directions may include any which could be granted on a case management summons under Order 25. In addition, it is specifically provided in rule 6(2) that if the parties consent the court may order trial by a master. See Order 36 for general provisions concerning trial by master.

7.    **Costs** (O. 14 r. 7)

    (1)    **If the plaintiff makes an application under rule 1 where the case is not within this Order or if it appears to the Court that the plaintiff knew that the defendant relied on a contention which would entitle him to unconditional leave to defend, then, without prejudice to Order 62 and in particular to rule 4(1) thereof, the Court may dismiss the application with costs and may require the costs to be paid by him forthwith.**

    (2)    **The Court shall have the same power to dismiss an application under rule 5 as it has under paragraph (1) to dismiss an application under rule 1, and that paragraph shall apply accordingly with the necessary modifications.**

**NOTES**

**[14.7.1]   Power to dismiss inappropriate summary judgment application**
Order 14 rule 7(1) gives the court power to dismiss with costs a summary judgment application which is 'not within this Order', or where the plaintiff knew that the defendant relied on a contention which would result in the grant of unconditional leave to defend.

Cases where the court has dismissed summary judgment applications as not being appropriate for the procedure, or 'not within this Order', include:

• *Hui Ting Hang v Grand Union Motor Insurance Co Ltd* [1988] HKC 142, 144C (CA) where Fuad VP said that the judge below had been entitled under this rule to dismiss an application for summary judgment, instead of granting leave to defend, where the underlying claim had no prospect of success as a matter of law.

• *Wordcap Investment Ltd v Bosswell Estates Ltd* [1988] HKC 328, 332D-F (CA), a case that was 'hopeless' as far as Order 14 was concerned; where it 'stood out on the face of the documents from the outset' that 'full elucidation of the facts' was required before the court could decide on the meaning of those documents.

• *Simba-Toys (HK) Ltd v Fullmore Corp Ltd* HCA 1599/2008 (Deputy Judge A Chow SC; 05.03.2009) (para 5) where, although the court was of the view that this rule did not apply, it dismissed with costs an Order 14 application on the ground that it was 'plain' that the plaintiff had no *locus* to sue, and had no cause of action against the defendant.

There are at least two categories of cases where summary judgment applications have been dismissed under the second limb of rule 7, that is where the plaintiff knew that the defendant relied on a contention which would result in the grant of unconditional leave to defend. First there are cases where the substance of a defence giving rise to a triable issue had been set out in correspondence before proceedings were commenced, such as *Lam Wai Na v Lam Wai Yu* HCA 280/2004 (Tang J; 24.12.2004) and *National Bank of Can ada v Yeebo (Int'l Holdings) Ltd* HCCL 201/ 1995 (Le Pichon J; 26.02.1996). Secondly, there are cases where a formal defence pleading a triable issue had been served before the Order 14 summons was issued. These include *Sterling Services Ltd v Tan Kee Cheang & Anor* [2003] 3 HKLRD 894 where, 'in embarking upon this application the plaintiff knew the substance of the principal defence raised, given that the pleaded defence antedated the institution of the summary judgment application by almost four months' (per Stone J; para 15). See also *Bang & Olufsen a/s v To Hok Chung t/a Mirage Electronics Industrial Co* HCA 2596/2005 (Deputy Judge Muttrie; 08.05.2006 (appeal allowed on other grounds – [2007] 1 HKLRD 85).

**8.   Right to proceed with residue of action or counterclaim** (O. 14 r. 8)
   **(1)   Where on an application under rule 1 the plaintiff obtains judgment on a claim or a part of a claim against any defendant, he may proceed with the action as respects any other claim or as respects the remainder of the**

claim or against any other defendant.

(2) Where on an application under rule 5 a defendant obtains judgment on a claim or part of a claim made in a counterclaim against the plaintiff, he may proceed with the counterclaim as respects any other claim or as respects the remainder of the claim or against any other defendant to the counterclaim.

**9.    Judgment for delivery up of chattel** (O. 14 r. 9)

Where the claim to which an application under rule 1 or rule 5 relates is for the delivery up of a specific chattel and the Court gives judgment under this Order for the applicant, it shall have the same power to order the party against whom judgment is given to deliver up the chattel without giving him an option to retain it on paying the assessed value thereof as if the judgment had been given after trial.

**10.   Relief against forfeiture** (O. 14 r. 10)

A tenant shall have the same right to apply for relief after judgment for possession of land on the ground of forfeiture for non-payment of rent has been given under this Order as if the judgment had been given after trial.

**11.   Setting aside judgment** (O. 14 r. 11)

Any judgment given against a party who does not appear at the hearing of an application under rule 1 or rule 5 may be set aside or varied by the Court on such terms as it thinks just.

(Enacted 1988)

---

## NOTES

**[14.11.1]   Setting aside judgment on ground of failure to appear**

Under Order 14 rule 11 the court has power to set aside summary judgment where the defendant has failed to appear. Keith J considered this rule in *Morigood Development Ltd v Sunny Trading Co (a firm)* [1999] 2 HKC 710. The learned judge stated that this rule removed an anomaly whereby summary judgment could not be set aside, unlike other judgments (at 713E–F). His Lordship expressly declined to decide whether the test for an application under this rule is that applicable on an application for summary judgment or that applicable on setting aside a judgment in default. In the event, the summary judgment was set aside on the ground that the defendant had not received notice of the Order 14 hearing and that she had a real prospect of succeeding in her proposed defence. The question of the test applicable on an application under Order 14 rule 11 was considered by the Court of Appeal in *O Mark Polyethylene Products Fty Ltd v Reap Star Ltd* [2000] 2 HKC 330. Godfrey JA stated, at 337H–I (obiter) that 'there is or should be no difference in the test to be applied in Hong Kong on an application to set aside judgment made under Order 14 rule 11 from that to be applied on such an application made under Order 13 rule 9'. See also *Secretary for Justice v Lam Chi Bin Stanley* HCA 148/2001 (Deputy Judge Poon; 04.09.2001).

### [14.11.2]    Setting aside fraudulent judgment

In *Lau Kak v Cheung Mo Kit* [1996] 1 HKC 79, Le Pichon J reviewed the authorities and principles on which the court has jurisdiction to set aside a completed judgment on the ground of fraud. See the commentary under Order 42 rule 3.

**ORDER 14A**

**DISPOSAL OF CASE ON POINT OF LAW**

**1.     Determination of questions of law or construction** (O. 14A r. 1)

**(1)     The Court may upon the application of a party or of its own motion determine any question of law or construction of any document arising in any cause or matter at any stage of the proceedings where it appears to the Court that—**

> **(a)     such question is suitable for determination without a full trial of the action; and**
>
> **(b)     such determination will finally determine (subject only to any possible appeal) the entire cause or matter or any claim or issue therein.**

**(2)     Upon such determination the Court may dismiss the cause or matter or make such order or judgment as it thinks just.**

**(3)     The Court shall not determine any question under this Order unless the parties have either—**

> **(a)     had an opportunity of being heard on the question; or**
>
> **(b)     consented to an order or judgment on such determination.**

**(4)     The jurisdiction of the Court under this Order may be exercised by a master.**

**(5)     Nothing in this Order shall limit the powers of the Court under Order 18, rule 19 or any other provision of these rules.**

---

**NOTES**

**[14A.1.1]     Purpose and scope of Order 14A**

Order 14A provides for the determination by the court of points of law or construction where it appears this can be done without a full trial, and that the result may be resolution of all or part of the dispute. In *Shell HK Ltd v Yeung Wai Man Kiu Yip Co Ltd* (2003) 6 HKCFAR 222 (paras 23–25) guidance, which may be summarised as follows, was given as to when this procedure is appropriate:

(1)     The procedure can be invoked for the purpose of finally determining not only the entire cause or matter but also 'any claim or issue' in the cause or matter. It is not necessary that the whole action would be finally determined. However, it is not contemplated that the parties would submit a trivial matter for determination under O 14A. That would be contrary to the spirit and purpose of the procedure and should be refused by the court in exercise of its discretion.

(2)     It is inappropriate to use this procedure if the issues of fact are interwoven with the legal issues to be determined.

(3)     Even if the conditions are satisfied, the court still has a discretion under r 1 to decide whether to entertain an application under the Order.

**[14A.1.2] Approach of the court on application under Order 14A**

The approach which the court will adopt on an application under Order 14A was set out succinctly by Recorder Geoffrey Ma SC in *Rockwin Enterprises Ltd v Shui Yee Ltd & Ors* [2003] 3 HKC 174, 183. He said:

> Once seized of an application under Order 14A, the court's approach is essentially a three-step approach:
>
> > (1) Is the relevant question one of law or of the construction of a document?
> > (2) If so, is that question one that should be determined under the O 14A procedure?
> > (3) If the answer to (2) is 'yes', what is the determination of that question and what orders should the court make as a consequence of determining that question?
>
> Usually, step (1) will cause little difficulty for the court to ascertain. Step (2) requires the court to be satisfied of the following:
>
> > (a) That the question of law or construction is one that is suitable for determination without a trial. In other words, the court has all the necessary facts and matters before it in order to determine the question of law or construction.
> > (b) That if so suitable and should it be determined by the court, that it will finally determine (subject to a possible appeal) the entire cause or matter or any issue or claim therein.
> > (c) Even if the above two conditions are fulfilled, that the court in its discretion is satisfied that the question is one that ought to be determined under O 14A.

As to point (a) above, see also *PCCW-HKT International Ltd v New World Telephone Ltd* [2001] 2 HKC 416. There the Court of Appeal upheld a judge's decision not to proceed with an Order 14A application on the ground it was not possible safely to conclude that there were no issues of fact interwoven with the issues of law. See also *Netwell Properties Ltd v JCG Finance Co Ltd* [2003] 4 HKC 566 (CA) where Rogers VP said (at 569 A-B) 'Where a claimant seeks judgment under O 14A the facts would have to be based on either established facts or agreed facts'. In the same case Stone J said (at 570 C-D) 'I venture to suggest that, in practice, there are few cases which are sufficiently 'fact insensitive' to jus tify the invocation of O 14A . . .'

In *Rockwin Enterprises* Recorder Geoffrey Ma SC went on to elaborate point (c) above. He held (at 183I) that even where the conditions set out as (a) and (b) above are met, the court has a residual discretion whether to proceed to make a determination under Order 14 A. This followed from the use of the word 'may' in Order 14A r 1(1). At 184G – 185E, Recorder Ma gave examples of factors which might be relevant in this exercise of discretion, including:

- whether the question of construction was a 'dominant' feature of the case;
- whether determination of the question might facilitate settlement;
- whether determination would result in a saving of time or costs.

**[14A.1.3] Court may proceed of its own motion**

It is expressly provided in Order 14A rule 1(1) that the court may determine any question of law or construction under this Order either on application of a party or of its own motion. In *Ho Yee Ming Theresa v Chung Loi Tai & Anor* [1994] 1 HKC 618 the court of its own motion (and after hearing counsel) ordered that applications which had been brought under Order 14 (for summary judgment) and under Order 18 rule 19 (to strike out) proceed as an application under Order 14A for determination of a point of law.

**[14A.1.4]    Timing of Order 14A application**
Order 14A rule 1(1) expressly provides that the rule may be invoked at any stage of the proceedings.  In *Man Wing Fun Stephen & Anor v Ho Ching Yee Susanna* HCA 3724/ 1997 (Recorder Edward Chan SC; 25.02.1999) (paras 15, 16) the court was of the view that it had no discretion to decline to entertain a late application under Order 14A, even though delay and cost could have been avoided by proceeding to trial instead. In *Hong Kong Kam Lan Koon Ltd v Realray Investments Ltd (No 2)* [2005] 1 HKC 565, 575C *et seq* the court relied on the rule to dismiss a claim during the course of a trial because of an intervening binding appellate decision by which the claim must fail.  The court did so not withstanding the fact the intervening appellate decision was subject to further appeal. However, an Order 14A application may be inappropriate before the close of pleadings: *Dream Property Sdn Bhd v Atlas Housing Sdn Bhd* [2008] MYFC 19 (CommonLII). In that case, the Federal Court of Malaysia was considering a provision in the same terms as Hong Kong's. Reference was made to *Watson & Anor v Dutton Forshaw Motor Group Ltd & Ors* [1998] EWCA Civ 1270 which suggests that a question of law or construction must be apparent on the pleadings.

**[14A.1.5]    Formulation of the question of law or construction**
An application under Order 14A should state the question of law or construction to be answered by the court 'in clear, careful and precise terms, so that there should be no difficulty or obscurity, still less any ambiguity, about what is the question that has to be determined': *Dragages et Travaux Public (HK) Ltd v American Home Assurance Co* CACV 295/1999 (Godfrey & Rogers JJA; 10.12.1999) (para 14).

**2.     Manner in which application under rule 1 may be made** (O. 14A r. 2)
     **An  application  under  rule  1  may  be  made  by  summons  or (notwithstanding Order 32, rule 1) may be made orally in the course of any interlocutory application to the Court.**
     **(L.N. 165 of 1992) (L.N. 152 of 2008)**

---

**NOTES**

**[14A.2.1]    Application by summons and affidavit**
An application under Order 14A will normally be made by interlocutory summons leading to an *inter partes* hearing before a master in chambers. Rule 1(4) expressly provides that masters have jurisdiction. If the matter is complicated or requires mature consideration the master may transfer the application to a judge under Order 32 rule 12. Note that the rule also permits application to be made orally in the course of any interlocutory application. This would be exceptional, unless the opposing party has had a full opportunity to prepare and the court has sufficient time to proceed. In *Rockwin Enterprises* (above) (para 14) the court allowed such an application to proceed where there was no objection. Rule 2 was amended with effect from 2009 to delete the reference to making an application under Order 14A by motion.
     There is no express requirement for an affidavit in support of an application under Order 14A. However, the court does not operate in a factual vacuum and it will usually be useful to place the salient facts before the court in an affidavit or

affirmation. Where the application relates to construction of a document, that document should be exhibited. Information and belief evidence is not admissible since an application under Order 14A is not considered to be interlocutory: see the commentary under Order 41 rule 5. The opposing party may submit an affidavit in response if it wishes, but it should be remembered that if material factual disputes are apparent on the affidavits the court will not proceed under Order 14A since factual disputes can only be resolved by trial: see the commentary under rule 1.

## ORDER 15

## CAUSES OF ACTION, COUNTERCLAIMS AND PARTIES

**1.     Joinder of causes of action** (O. 15 r. 1)
       **(1)     Subject to rule 5(1), a plaintiff may in one action claim relief against the same defendant in respect of more than one cause of action—**

> **(a)     if the plaintiff claims, and the defendant is alleged to be liable, in the same capacity in respect of all the causes of action, or**

> **(b)     if the plaintiff claims or the defendant is alleged to be liable in the capacity of executor or administrator of an estate in respect of one or more of the causes of action and in his personal capacity but with reference to the same estate in respect of all the others, or**

> **(c)     with the leave of the Court.**

       **(2)     An application for leave under this rule must be made ex parte by affidavit before the issue of the writ or originating summons, as the case may be, and the affidavit must state the grounds of the application.**

---

## NOTES

**[15.1.1]   Order 15 rule 1 – joinder of causes of action**
Order 15 rule 1 provides that a defendant may be sued for different, even unrelated, causes of action in a single action. Leave is not required where it is alleged that the defendant is liable for more than one cause of action in the same capacity (Order 15 rule 1(a)).

       In the case of an executor or administrator who is alleged to be liable in that capacity as well as his personal capacity, more than one cause of action may be pleaded provided that liability arises with reference to the same estate (Order 15 rule 1(b)).

       In any other case causes of action may be joined with leave of the court (Order 15 rule 1(c)).

       Joinder of causes of action under Order 15 rule 1 is subject to the court's power under Order 15 rule 5 to order separate trials.

       Where plaintiffs join in an action in respect of which they are entitled to joint relief they may also claim individually in the same action separate relief against defendants: *Harris & Anor v Ashworth & Anor* [1962] 1 All ER 438. In effect, one should first look at Order 15 rule 4 and choose the appropriate parties, then, having done so, look at Order 15 rule 1 as to which causes of action may be alleged against them.

**2.     Counterclaim against plaintiff** (O. 15 r. 2)
       **(1)     Subject to rule 5(2), a defendant in any action who alleges that he has any claim or is entitled to any relief or remedy against a plaintiff in the action in respect of any matter (whenever and however arising) may, instead of bringing a separate action, make a counterclaim in respect of that matter; and**

**where he does so he must add the counterclaim to his defence.**

**(2)   Rule 1 shall apply in relation to a counterclaim as if the counterclaim were a separate action and as if the person making the counterclaim were the plaintiff and the person against whom it is made a defendant.**

**(3)   A counterclaim may be proceeded with notwithstanding that judgment is given for the plaintiff in the action or that the action is stayed, discontinued or dismissed.**

**(4)   Where a defendant establishes a counterclaim against the claim of the plaintiff and there is a balance in favour of one of the parties, the Court may give judgment for the balance, so, however, that this provision shall not be taken as affecting the Court's discretion with respect to costs.**

---

NOTES

**[15.2.1]   Counterclaims**
Order 15 rule 2 permits a defendant to make a counterclaim back against the plaintiff under the rubric of the same proceedings. This is a remedial provision – at common law a defendant who had a claim back against the plaintiff could not have that dispute adjudicated in the plaintiff's proceedings but had to commence a separate action: see *Stooke v Taylor* (1880) 5 QBD 569, 573–4.

See also section 16(2) of the High Court Ordinance (Cap 4), by which the court is required to exercise its jurisdiction so that 'as far as possible, all matters in dispute between the parties are completely and finally determined, and all multiplicity of legal proceedings with respect to any of those matters is avoided'.

A counterclaim may only be brought by a defendant against a plaintiff. It is not possible for a defendant to counterclaim against another defendant: *Yan How Yee v Yu Kin Sang Paul & Ors* HCA 1069/2008 (Recorder Yuen SC; 04.11.2009). Instead the procedure under Order 16 rule 8 should be considered.

*Counterclaim distinguished from set-off* – The counterclaim procedure must be distinguished from the defence of set-off (as to which see the commentary under Order 18 rule 17). A set-off is a shield operating as a defence to the plaintiff's claims in the strict sense. A counterclaim on the other hand can be used as a sword, alleging a completely unrelated claim which may exceed the plaintiff's claim in value: *Stooke v Taylor* (1880) 5 QBD 569, 575.

*Manner of bringing counterclaim* – A counterclaim is brought by adding it to the defence: Order 15 rule 2(1). The result is a pleading known as a 'defence and counterclaim'. This pleading is commonly divided into two parts, the first being the defence setting out the points on which the defendant joins issue on the plaintiff's claim, and the second being the counterclaim which is, in effect, the defendant's statement of claim against the plaintiff. When served with a counterclaim the plaintiff is required to respond with a defence to counterclaim if he intends to defend it: see Order 18 rule 3(2).

*Judgment on claim and counterclaim* – The counterclaim procedure allows the court at the end of the day to give judgment for the net balance owing by one to the other: see Order 15 rule 2(4). However, in *Chell Engineering Ltd v Unit Tool and Engineering Co Ltd* [1950] 1 All ER 378 it was held that where both the plaintiff's claim and the defendant's counterclaim succeed it is 'usually better' for the court to pronounce separate judgments and separate orders for costs (per Singleton LJ at 382A). It is a matter of discretion whether to pronounce a single net judgment or separate judgments. In *Lundi (a firm) v The Prudential Enterprise Ltd* CACV 82/1987 (Cons VP, Fuad & Clough JJA; 09.10.1987) a single net judgment was considered appropriate where the claim and counterclaim in reality related to the same issue.

*Separate existence of counterclaim* – In some respects a counterclaim retains the characteristics of a separate action. Limitation periods are applicable in the same way as if a separate action were commenced: *Lowe v Bentley* (1928) 44 TLR 388; *Bankes v Jarvis* [1903] 1 KB 549. Discontinuation or compromise of the plaintiff's claims does not necessarily bring the counterclaim to an end: see Order 15 rule 2(3) and see *McGowan v Middleston* (1883) 11 QBD 464. Further, under Order 15 rule 3 the defendant may bring his counterclaim against another person (whether or not already a party) in addition to the plaintiff.

*Counterclaim must be against plaintiff in same capacity* – A counterclaim may only be made against a plaintiff in respect of his liability in the same capacity in which he sues: *Nelson v Roberts* (1893) 69 LT 352.

*Costs of counterclaim* – See the commentary under Order 62 rule 3.

*Interest on judgment for counterclaim* – See the commentary under Order 42 rule 2.

*Dismissal of counterclaim for want of prosecution* – See the commentary under Order 34 rule 2.

**3. Counterclaim against additional parties** (O. 15 r. 3)

**(1)     Where a defendant to an action who makes a counterclaim against the plaintiff alleges that any other person (whether or not a party to the action) is liable to him along with the plaintiff in respect of the subject-matter of the counterclaim, or claims against such other person any relief relating to or connected with the original subject-matter of the action, then, subject to rule 5(2), he may join that other person as a party against whom the counterclaim is made.**

**(2)     Where a defendant joins a person as a party against whom he makes a counterclaim, he must add that person's name to the title of the action and serve on him a copy of the counterclaim and, in the case of a person who is not already a party to the action, the defendant must issue the counterclaim out of the Registry and serve on the person concerned a sealed copy of the counterclaim together with a form of acknowledgment of service in Form No. 14 in Appendix A (with such modifications as the circumstances may require) and a copy of the writ or originating summons by which the action was begun and of all other pleadings served in the action; and a person on whom a copy of a counterclaim is served under this paragraph shall, if he is not already a party to the action, become a party to it as from the time of service with the same rights in respect of his defence to the counterclaim and otherwise as if he had been duly sued in the ordinary way by the party making the counterclaim. (L.N. 404 of 1991)**

**(3)     A defendant who is required by paragraph (2) to serve a copy of the counterclaim made by him on any person who before service is already a party to the action must do so within the period within which, by virtue of Order 18,**

rule 2, he must serve on the plaintiff the defence to which the counterclaim is added.

(4)    The appropriate office for issuing and acknowledging service of a counterclaim against a person who is not already a party to the action is the Registry. (L.N. 404 of 1991)

(5)    Where by virtue of paragraph (2) a copy of a counterclaim is required to be served on a person who is not already a party to the action, the following provisions of these rules, namely, Order 6, rule 7(3) and (5), Order 10, Order 11, Orders 12 and 13 and Order 75, rule 4, shall, subject to the last foregoing paragraph, apply in relation to the counterclaim and the proceedings arising from it as if—

       (a)      the counterclaim were a writ and the proceedings arising from it in an action; and

       (b)      the party making the counterclaim were a plaintiff and the party against whom it is made a defendant in that action.

(L.N. 404 of 1991)

(5A) Where by virtue of paragraph (2) a copy of a counterclaim is required to be served on any person other than the plaintiff, who before service is already a party to the action, the provisions of Order 14, rule 5 shall apply in relation to the counterclaim and the proceedings arising therefrom, as if the party against whom the counterclaim is made were the plaintiff in the action. (L.N. 363 of 1990)

(6)    A copy of a counterclaim required to be served on a person who is not already a party to the action must be indorsed with a notice, in Form No. 17 in Appendix A, addressed to that person.

**4.**      **Joinder of parties** (O. 15 r. 4)

(1)    Subject to rule 5(1), two or more persons may be joined together in one action as plaintiffs or as defendants with the leave of the Court or where—

       (a)      if separate actions were brought by or against each of them, as the case may be, some common question of law or fact would arise in all the actions, and

       (b)      all rights to relief claimed in the action (whether they are joint, several or alternative) are in respect of or arise out of the same transaction or series of transactions.

(2)    Where the plaintiff in any action claims any relief to which any other person is entitled jointly with him, all persons so entitled must, subject to the provisions of any written law and unless the Court gives leave to the contrary, be parties to the action and any of them who does not consent to being joined as a plaintiff must, subject to any order made by the Court on an application for leave under this paragraph, be made a defendant.

This paragraph shall not apply to a probate action.

(HK)(3) Where relief is claimed in an action against a defendant who is jointly liable with some other person and also severally liable, that other person need not be made a defendant to the action; but where persons are jointly, but not severally, liable under a contract and relief is claimed against some but not all of those persons in an action in respect of that contract, the Court may, on the

**application of any defendant to the action, by order stay proceedings in the action until the other persons so liable are added as defendants.**

---

## NOTES

### [15.4.1]   Scope of Order 15 rule 4

Order 15 rule 4 deals with the circumstances in which two or more persons *may* be joined together in one action as plaintiffs or defendants, and also with circumstances where such joinder is *required*.

This is a convenient place to deal with other issues as to parties as well.

### [15.4.2]   Order 15 rule 4(1) – plaintiffs may join in certain circumstances

Order 15 rule 4(1) provides that a plaintiff may join together with others claiming relief where there is a common question of law or fact, or where the claim arises from the same transaction or series of transactions. Otherwise plaintiffs may be joined with leave of the court. This permissive rule must be read subject to Order 15 rule 4(2) which requires joinder of other parties in certain circumstances.

### [15.4.3]   Order 15 rule 4(2) – plaintiff must join parties jointly entitled to the relief claimed

Order 15 rule 4(2) stipulates that a plaintiff must join into the proceedings any other person who is jointly entitled to the relief claimed, unless the court grants leave otherwise. Examples will be joint bank account holders where relief is sought in respect of the account, and joint property-owners seeking to enforce rights in respect of the property.

Where a person jointly entitled to the relief sought does not consent to be a plaintiff, this rule provides that he should be joined as a defendant. Such a person 'becomes a defendant simply to be bound by the result of the litigation and to ensure that the plaintiff's claim is not thwarted by a lack of proper parties before the court': *Kao, Lee & Yip (a firm) v Koo Hoi Yan Donald & Ors* [2002] 3 HKC 323, 332H–I, per Ma J. The position is different with respect to partners. A partner may be compelled to be a co-plaintiff without his consent, but the unwilling partner will be entitled to seek an indemnity from the other partners as to costs. See *Kao, Lee & Yip* at 332D, citing *Whitehead v Hughes* (1834) 2 C&M 318, 319, and see the commentary under Order 81 rule 1.

The proviso to this sub-rule provides that it shall not apply to probate proceedings.

Proceedings to enforce a deed of mutual covenant in respect of a multi-storey building might be thought to come within this rule, since all parties bound by the DMC are arguably entitled to the relief. However, it has been held that individual owners are entitled to enforce their interests in the land without joining the others: *Incorporated Owners of Chungking Mansions v Shamdasani* [1991] 2 HKC 342, 353A-B. There are many cases in which one flat owner sues another without joining other parties having an interest in the building. So far as common areas are concerned, the owners' incorporation has the exclusive right to enforce the DMC: Building Management Ordinance (Cap 344), s 16; *Snowland Ltd v Topland Holdings Ltd* [2006] 4 HKC 188, hence it is not appropriate for any other interested party to be named as a plaintiff.

**[15.4.4]  Joinder of defendants**

The provisions of Order 15 rule 4 as to joinder of defendants depend on the nature of the alleged liability. Where it is alleged that more than one defendant is liable in respect of the same cause of action, jointly or severally, the provisions of rule 4(3) apply. Otherwise it is rule 4(1) which applies.

*Rule 4(3) – joint or several liability of defendants* – Where more than one potential defendant is alleged to be liable on a joint and several basis, the plaintiff is entitled under Order 15 rule 4(3) to issue proceedings naming only one or some among them. The cause of action may be said to be complete without the absent party: *Kao, Lee & Yip (a firm) v Koo Hoi Yan Donald & Ors* [2002] 3 HKC 323, 333B (obiter). However, where the claim is in contract, and more than one person is liable jointly but not severally, the defendant(s) named may apply to the court for a stay of proceedings pending joinder of the other person(s) jointly liable. The power under rule 4(3) to stay proceedings pending joinder of other parties jointly liable under a contract is discretionary. In *Great Success Development (HK) Ltd v Towa Concrete Ltd* [2002] 1 HKC 116 the District Court declined to exercise the discretion where it was alleged the defendant was only one of two partners who were jointly and not severally liable. Judge Lok, after citing *Robinson v Geisel* [1894] 2 QB 685 said, at 119G–120B:

> Based on the aforesaid authorities, the law can be summarised as follows. If two or more partners are jointly liable to a third party for breach of contract, all the partners ought normally to be sued jointly. However, it is not mandatory and the court does have a wide discretion to allow the action to be proceeded against some and not all the partners of the firm.

The learned judge then went on to list instances where it is appropriate to allow such an action to proceed, including cases where additional partners cannot be found and cases where the objection is raised too late. In this connection see the *Transfer of Businesses (Protection of Creditors) Ordinance (Cap 49)* which deems the transferee of a business to be liable for the debts of the transferor unless proper notice has been given. See also *DDK Trading & Development Co Ltd v Multi Best Manufacturers Ltd* [1986] HKLR 155.

*Effect of judgment against one defendant* – Where judgment is obtained against a defendant who is jointly liable with another, the plaintiff may proceed against the other for the balance of the amount claimed. Section 5 of the Civil Liability (Contribution) Ordinance (Cap 377) removes the bar which existed at common law and section 7 provides likewise where there is a settlement agreement (but subject to the terms of the agreement). See *Chien Ngan Sang v Lai Kam Hing & Anor* [2002] 2 HKC 448, 454I-455A, and see *Asia Television Ltd v Mak Chi Kin* [2006] 4 HKC 347 (CA) where the development of the law is outlined.

*Rule 4(1) – other cases* – Where there is no question of joint or several liability of defendants Order 15 rule 4(1) applies and defendants may only be joined where there are common questions of law or fact or the relief sought arises out of the same, or a series of transactions, or with leave of the court.

**[15.4.5]  Representation of joined parties**

Where there is more than one plaintiff in an action they must be represented by the same solicitors: see *Lewis v Daily Telegraph Ltd* [1964] 2 QB 601; [1964] 1 All ER 705 (per Pearson LJ at 620 QB) and see *Attorney General v Canadian Pacific Ltd* (1981) 30 BCLR 230. The same rule may apply to counsel, save in exceptional circumstances:

*Black King Shipping Corp v Massie* [1984] The Times, 9 July. Defendants are entitled to separate representation, but there may be costs implications if there is no conflict of interest such that separate representation is not strictly necessary. See *Milillo v Kon necke* [2009] NSWCA 109 where one of the two successful defendants was denied costs.

**[15.4.6]   Companies**
It is essential that bodies corporate be properly named when they are joined in legal proceedings. A body corporate exists only by virtue of the legal instrument by which it is created. In the case of limited companies this will be the certificate of incorporation under the Companies Ordinance, which states precisely what its name is. In other cases the founding legal instrument may be a statute (as is the case with many religious and charitable organisations) or executive charter (for example, Standard Chartered Bank, though not the Hong Kong branch thereof which is now operated by a limited company – see Cap 1174).

In *WA Somerville & Co Ltd v Golden Carriage Restaurant (a firm)* [1966] HKLR 273 judgment was obtained against a company which had wrongly been named in the writ as a firm. The judgment was set aside, but leave to amend and re-serve was granted.

In *Re Nos 55 and 57 Holmes Road, Kentish Town* [1959] Ch 298; [1958] 2 All ER 711 it was held that it was not a mere misnomer to name the wrong company in legal proceedings.

A company must duly authorise proceedings brought in its name. This normally means a directors' resolution is required. However, proceedings started without authority are not a nullity and the defect may be cured by ratification: *Danish Mercantile Co Ltd v Beaumont* [1951] 1 Ch 680; *Swire Timber Products Ltd v So Kwok Kuen* CACV 55/1982 (Cons & Zimmern JJA, Hooper J; 17.06.1982).

**[15.4.7]   Action by struck off company**
Legal proceedings commenced by a company which has been struck off may retrospectively be validated upon restoration of the company to the register. See *El Vince Ltd v Wu Wen Sheng* [2001] 4 HKC 107, 113G–115D where a writ issued by a company which was at the time struck off under s 290A of the Companies Ordinance (for failure to file an annual return) was found to be valid because of the subsequent restoration of the company.

**[15.4.8]   Action against wound-up company**
The court has power to make a '*Lazarus*' order granting leave to commence proceedings against a company which has been wound up: see the Companies Ordinance (Cap 32) s 290; and see *Wong Pui Sau & Anor v Cheung Kwong Min* [2000] 2 HKC 810 where such an order was made.

*Lazarus* orders can be useful where, although the defendant has been wound up, a judgment would be satisfied by an insurer or by a compensation fund such as TAVAS.

**[15.4.9]   Right of foreign corporation to commence proceedings**
Under the Foreign Corporations Ordinance (Cap 437) a body corporate incorporated in a territory which is not recognised as a state may nevertheless commence proceedings in

Hong Kong: see *Taiwan Via Versand Ltd v Commodore Electronics Ltd* [1993] 2 HKC 650. Note, however, that an order of a court in such a jurisdiction may not be recognised in Hong Kong: see *Ting Lei Miao v Chen Li Hung & Anor* [1997] 2 HKC 779.

**[15.4.10]    Action by receiver**
Receivers have no title to sue in their own name on a cause of action accruing to the party for whose benefit they have been appointed. Only in limited circumstances where they have an independent cause of action may they sue. See *Liu Yiu Keung Stephen v Keen Lloyd Resources Ltd (in liq)* [2007] 1 HKC 605.

**[15.4.11]    Enemy aliens**
An enemy alien may not invoke the jurisdiction of the court, nor can he continue proceedings commenced prior to the outbreak of war. He may, however, be sued and may defend the proceedings brought against him. See *Porter v Freudenberg* [1915] 1 KB 857. The question whether any foreign jurisdiction is an 'enemy' for this purpose is a matter for the sovereign and a certificate issued by the competent authority will be conclusive: see *R v Bottrill ex p Kuechenmeister* [1946] 1 All ER 635.

This rule should not apply to persons and entities from Taiwan. Although they may be considered enemies of the state, Taiwan is considered to be a part of China and its people Chinese nationals, hence they are not aliens.

**[15.4.12]    Vexatious and abusive litigants**
See the discussion of this topic in the commentary under Order 5 rule 6 and Order 32A.

**[15.4.13]    Sovereign and diplomatic immunity**
Foreign governments and their representatives are entitled to claim immunity from the jurisdiction of the Hong Kong courts. See the Consular Relations Ordinance (Cap 557) which provides that key provisions of the Vienna Convention on Consular Relations 1963 have the force of law in Hong Kong. Those provisions are set out in the schedule to that Ordinance. See also *FG Hemisphere Associates LLC v Democratic Republic of Congo* [2010] 2 HKC 487 (CA) in regard to the common law position in post-1997 Hong Kong.

Likewise international organisations and their representatives are entitled to immunity. See the International Organizations and Diplomatic Privileges Ordinance (Cap 190) and the International Organizations (Privileges and Immunities) Ordinance (Cap 558).

Immunity must be claimed, and may be waived. Proceedings may be issued, leaving it to the party entitled to immunity to assert it by applying to strike out the proceedings or for a stay, as in *Ilan v Belmonte-Jover & Ors* [2006] 1 HKC 546. However a plaintiff would be unwise to risk an adverse order as to costs by commencing proceedings without first enquiring whether immunity will be asserted.

*Trading entities owned by a foreign sovereign* – the right to claim sovereign immunity from the process of the court does not extend to trading entities owned by a foreign sovereign. See *Trendtex Trading v Central Bank of Nigeria* [1977] 1 All ER 881; *FG Hemisphere Associates* (above).

It has been held that sovereign immunity is a matter of substantive, not procedural law. Thus where a dispute is governed by the law of another jurisdiction, it is the laws of the other jurisdiction with regard to sovereign immunity, not the laws of the forum, which apply: *Garsec Pty Ltd v Sultan of Brunei* [2008] NSWCA 211.

### [15.4.14]   Immunity of Mainland government and instrumentalities
The government of Mainland China, and its instrumentalities, are entitled to claim immunity from the jurisdiction from the Hong Kong courts on grounds arising from the common law concept of 'crown' immunity. See *The Hua Tian Long (No 3)* [2010] 3 HKC 557. In that case a Mainland government department was found entitled to claim immunity in respect of its vessel which had been arrested in Hong Kong, but was found to have waived immunity on the facts of the case.

### [15.4.15]   Judicial immunity
Members of the judiciary are entitled to immunity from legal action in the performance of their judicial functions: Basic Law, art 85. In *Choy Bing Wing v CE & Ors* [2006] 1 HKC 225 the court, of its own motion, struck out a contemnor's claim against the two judges who had found him guilty of contempt. In *Park Young Sook v Melloy* [2010] 5 HKC 329 the Secretary for Justice successfully applied to strike out an action against a District Court judge brought by a litigant who was unhappy with the judge's decision in a family dispute.

See also section 39 of the High Court Ordinance concerning protection of the registrar.

### [15.4.16]   Unknown persons
Problems arise where the identity of a potential defendant is not known. In *Tang Chi Wai v Person Unknown* [2001] 2 HKC 299 the plaintiff was unable to identify the paper owner of a piece of land in respect of which title by adverse possession was claimed and as a result commenced proceedings against 'Person Unknown'. Recorder Geoffrey Ma SC adjourned the proceedings expressing the view (at 300D) that in the absence of a named defendant the proceedings *prima facie* offended 'the basic requirement that parties need to be named in the writ of summons'. The learned Recorder cited *Friern Barnet UDC v Adams* [1927] 2 Ch 25 and 37 Hals (4th) 215 n 4.

On occasion it will be necessary to issue proceedings before it is possible to identify the proper defendant. For example the limitation period may be about to expire in the case of a running down action where the culprit has not been identified. In such cases the fictional defendants 'John Doe' and 'Richard Roe' have sometimes been named. See *Barnett v French* [1981] 1 WLR 848, 853B–854B citing *Levy v Levy* (English CA, 09.11.1979, unreported). Later on, if and when the wrongdoer is identified, the court has power to substitute him for the fictional defendant even after expiration of the limitation period: see Order 15 rule 6(5). In *Barnett v French* the English court cited the use of the fictional characters as long ago as 1656 in England and thereafter in the USA and held that there was 'no legal, constitutional or ethical objection' to their use in proceedings, which in that case were of a criminal nature.

### [15.4.17]   Married women
In this day and age we take it for granted that a married woman may sue or be sued like any other person. This was not always so. The relevant provision in Hong Kong law is the Married Persons Status Ordinance (Cap 182), which dates back to 1936.

From time to time one sees proceedings where a married woman is specifically described as such in a writ. As a result of the Ordinance this is unnecessary, superfluous and possibly offensive. Similarly, the description of a female litigant as 'femme sole' (previously used to describe a divorced woman) is no longer necessary or appropriate.

### [15.4.18] Unincorporated associations

Organisations which do not enjoy the status of a body corporate (whether under the Companies Ordinance (Cap 32) or other statute or prerogative instrument of Hong Kong or other jurisdiction) may not normally be joined as parties to legal proceedings in their own name. This is because at common law such an organisation does not exist as a juridical entity: *Trustees of the Roman Catholic Church v Ellis & Anor* [2007] NSWCA 117 (para 47). See *Tang Man Kit & Anor v Hip Hing Timber Co Ltd* [2001] 4 HKC 11. The members of such organisations should be joined in accordance with Order 15 rule 12, which deals with representative proceedings.

Express exceptions are made in these rules for partnerships (see Order 81 rule 1) and sole proprietorships (see Order 81 rule 9) which may in certain circumstances be named as parties notwithstanding the lack of corporate personality.

### [15.4.19] Trade unions

By virtue of section 13 of the Trade Unions Ordinance (Cap 332) a trade union enjoys the status of body corporate and may institute and defend legal proceedings in its own name.

### [15.4.20] Claims for costs against non-parties and costs-only proceedings

Order 62 rule 6A makes provisions as to parties where the court is considering exercise of its power under sections 52A or 52B of the Ordinance to make costs orders in favour of or against non-parties. The non-party must be joined into the proceedings and given an opportunity to be heard.

Section 52A(2) of the Ordinance provides for costs orders against non-parties, and section 52B provides for costs-only proceedings where terms of settlement are reached before action is commenced. See the commentary under Order 62 rules 6A and 11A.

### [15.4.21] Solicitor's warranty on commencing proceedings on behalf of a party

When solicitors commence proceedings on behalf of a party they warrant that the plaintiff exists and that they have proper instructions to act. Any breach of such warranty renders the solicitors liable to costs. The governing principles, deriving from *Nelson v Nelson* [1997] 1 WLR 233, were stated by Yuen J in *Tang Man Kit & Anor v Hip Hing Timber Co Ltd (No 2)* [2002] 1 HKC 630, 633F–634B, in the following words:

(1) A solicitor who commenced proceedings warranted that

    (i) he had a client

    (ii) the client bore the name of the party to the proceedings, and

    (iii) that the client had authorized the proceedings (*Nelson* 235).

    Where these are satisfied, the other party to the proceedings would have to look to the client to pay the costs of the action (*Nelson* 237).

    (2)    Where the person for whom the solicitor purports to act does *not exist* (eg a defunct corporation), then by analogy with breach of warranty of authority, the solicitor would ordinarily be held liable to pay the other party's costs (*Nelson* 239–240).

    (3)    Where the person does exist but is at law *incapable* of instructing a solicitor (eg a minor, or a person of unsound mind), then the solicitor would, on the same analogy, similarly be ordinarily held liable to pay the other party's costs, because he had no principal who had authorized him to commence the proceedings (*Nelson* 239–240).

    (4)    In the situations in (2) and (3) above, there is no effective retainer and the proceedings are a nullity (*Nelson* 236).

    (5)    In those cases, although the solicitor is not under a strict liability to pay the costs as the court always has a discretion when dealing with matters in its inherent jurisdiction, ordinarily one would expect the solicitor to be held liable to pay the costs, because otherwise the other party would be left without any person or entity against whom an order for costs could be obtained (*Nelson* 241).

    (6)    In any case, a solicitor does not warrant that his client has a good cause of action, or that his client is solvent (*Nelson* 237).

Where a solicitor's authority to act for a party is in issue, the burden of proof rests on the solicitor asserting this authority to prove that he is duly authorised: *Shanghai Land Holdings Ltd (in receivership) v Chau Ching Ngai & Anor* [2004] 3 HKC 573, 580F–G, not following *AG v Foley & Anor* [2000] 2 All ER 609, 615 (CA).

See also the commentary under Order 15 rule 6 concerning challenge to a plaintiff's standing, which may occur where it is alleged that the plaintiff does not have the mental capacity to instruct a solicitor.

A solicitor who acts without proper authority may be personally liable for the opposing party's costs: see *Grand Field Group Holdings Ltd v Tsang Wai Lun Wayland & Ors* [2010] 5 HKC 441.

### [15.4.22]   Anonymity order in respect of parties

The court has an inherent jurisdiction to make an 'anonymity order', that is an order to prohibit the public disclosure of the identity of a party to proceedings. See *L v Equal Opportunities Commission & Ors* [2002] 3 HKC 571, 573D where the Court of Appeal cited *Scott v Scott* [1913] AC 417 and held that an anonymity order operates by way of exception to the general principle that a trial should be open to the public.

In *Chao Pak Ki Raymond & Anor v Hong Kong Society of Accountants* [2004] 2 HKC 469, 472G-I, an anonymity order was refused where it was sought to protect the applicants from public attention and not to protect the integrity of the administration of justice.

The making of an anonymity order involves the balancing of the right to privacy and family life against the freedom of the press to report judicial proceedings (in Hong Kong, arts 14 and 16 of the Bill of Rights). Two examples of this balancing exercise being undertaken at the highest level in the UK are *Re BBC* [2009] UKHL 34, [2009] 3 WLR 142; and *Guardian News & Media Ltd & Ors v HM Treasury* [2010] UKSC 1. In both cases anonymity orders were set aside on the ground that the public interest in identifying the party outweighed the privacy and family life right.

See also the discussion under Order 29 rule 1 of the 'gagging' order whereby the court may order that the fact proceedings have been commenced be concealed from a wrongdoer or party.

### [15.4.23]    'Norwich Pharmacal' action to disclose identity of potential defendant

An action may be brought for discovery alone against a defendant to obtain information as to the identity of a wrongdoer (*Norwich Pharmacal Co v Commissioners of Customs and Excise* [1974] AC 133; [1973] 2 All ER 943).

In *Norwich Pharmacal*, the House of Lords held that where a person 'has got mixed up in the tortious acts of others so as to facilitate their wrong-doing he may incur no personal liability but he comes under a duty to assist the person who had been wronged by giving him full information and disclosing the identity of the wrongdoers' (per Lord Reid).

### [15.4.24]    Characteristics of Norwich Pharmacal order

The characteristics of a *Norwich Pharmacal* order were set out concisely by Ma J in *A Co v B Co* [2002] 2 HKC 497, 503C–G as follows:

(1)    It is made against an innocent party whose only involvement is to become mixed up in the tortious or wrongful activities of others. There is at that stage no evidence of any wrongdoing on the part of the innocent party.

(2)    Instead, whatever wrongdoing there is, exists only on the part of a person or persons against whom no relief may be sought at that stage and indeed against whom there is probably insufficient evidence to found an action. In other words, this person or these persons will most probably not be before the court and would not be able to answer what are often very serious allegations made against them.

(3)    Usually, there will, moreover, exist a legal relationship between the innocent per son against whom a discovery order is sought and the alleged wrongdoer and this relationship may involve strict duties to be observed on the innocent party's part. The present case offers what is a common scenario: the innocent defendant is a bank and the alleged wrongdoers its customers. In this situation, any discovery to be made by the innocent party may well, apart from a court order, expose that innocent party to liability, both civil and possibly even crimi nal. At the very least, a breach of confidentiality is involved.

(4)    The court, accordingly, in applications for *Norwich Pharmacal* relief must, in its discretion, balance the competing interests of the victim of the alleged wrongdoing and an innocent party caught up in the wrongdoing.

### [15.4.25]    Criteria for Norwich Pharmacal order

The criteria for obtaining a *Norwich Pharmacal* order were summarised succinctly in *BMG Canada Inc & Ors v John Doe & Ors* (Federal Court of Canada 2004 FC 488; Finckenstein J 31.03.2004). The learned judge said he read the decision of the House of Lords in the *Norwich Pharmacal* case and that in *Glaxo Wellcome PLC v Canada (Minister of National Revenue)* (1998) 81 CPR (3rd) 372 as laying down the following criteria:

(a)    the applicant must establish a *prima facie* case against the unknown alleged wrongdoer;

   (b)    the person from whom discovery is sought must be in some way involved in the matter under dispute, he must be more than an innocent bystander;

   (c)    the person from whom discovery is sought must be the only practical source of information available to the applicants;

   (d)    the person against whom discovery is sought must be reasonably compensated for his expenses arising out of compliance with the discovery order in addition to his legal costs

   (e)    the public interests in favour of disclosure must outweigh the legitimate privacy concerns.

It is clear that the party against whom discovery is ordered need not be guilty of any wrongdoing; further that an order may be made even where the applicant does not intend to commence legal proceedings, but merely seeks information. See *Ashworth Hospital Authority v MGN Ltd* [2002] 1 WLR 2033 (HL).

### [15.4.26]   The Norwich Pharmacal case – as extended

See the commentary under Order 24 rule 1 for a discussion of the manner in which *Norwich Pharmacal* has been extended to disclosure of documents and information.

### [15.4.27]   Juridical basis of the Norwich Pharmacal order

The juridical basis of *Norwich Pharmacal* discovery, as it has come to be known, is judicial necessity: see *Lonrho plc v Fayed (No 2)* [1992] 1 WLR 1; *Yew Seng Computer (HK) Ltd v Computerland Corp* [1986] HKLR 283, 285G (CA); *Re Greater Beijing Region Expressways Ltd (No 2)* [2000] 2 HKC 118, 129G *et seq* and *Manufacturer's Life Ins Co of Canada v Harvest Hero Int'l Ltd* [2001] 1 HKC 435, 442H (CFI) (reversed on appeal on other grounds: see [2002] 1 HKLRD 828 (CA)). In the *Lonrho* case Millett J said at 13–14:

> The jurisdiction is founded on judicial necessity: its justification lies in the fact that the information will not otherwise become available, so that to withhold relief would amount to a denial of justice.

### [15.4.28]   Exception to 'mere witness' rule

*Norwich Pharmacal* discovery operates as an exception to the 'mere witness' rule whereby discovery will not be ordered against a third party who could be called as a witness. *Norwich Pharmacal* discovery is not intended as an alternative to calling a witness or obtaining a *subpoena duces tecum:* see *Ho Tsui-chun v Attorney General* [1980] HKLR 854 where it was said:

> Had the recipient in the Education Department filed the letters and taken no further action, it would have fallen into the category of a 'mere witness' . . . and the plaintiff would have been debarred from relief ... In the present case the Education Department was involved in the performance of its duty to investigate complaints against school staff. The libels were published to at least four members of the department. This is a sufficient involvement in the tort to enable the plaintiff to succeed in these proceedings.

See also *Seacliff Ltd v Decca Ltd & Ors (No 2)* [2001] 1 HKC 588 where the 'mere witness' rule and its exceptions were set out by Deputy Judge Gill at 593H *et seq.*

### [15.4.29]   Discretion

A *Norwich Pharmacal* order is equitable in nature and hence discretionary: see *A Co v B*

*Co* [2002] 2 HKC 497, 502H *et seq.* The jurisdiction 'is to be exercised only if it is just and necessary to do so': *Sham v Eastweek Publisher Ltd* [1994] 1 HKC 687, 693B–C (reversed on other grounds – [1995] 1 HKC 264). In exercising its discretion the court must 'balance the competing interests of the victim of the alleged wrongdoing and an innocent party caught up in the wrongdoing': see *A Co v B Co* [2002] 2 HKC 497, 503G where Ma J held it was necessary to take into account the potential civil and criminal liability which may result from an order requiring breach of confidentiality.

The factors to be borne in mind by the court on a *Norwich Pharmacal* application were set down concisely by Ma J in *A Co v B Co* [2002] 2 HKC 497, 503I–504E in the following terms:

(1)    There must be cogent and compelling evidence to demonstrate that serious tortious or wrongful activities have taken place. And where fraud or similar allegations are made, the degree of proof must correspondingly be high: see *Re H (Minors)* [1996] AC 563 at 586C–H. All the more so when the alleged wrongdoer is not and will not likely be before the court.

(2)    It must also be clearly demonstrated that the order will or will very likely reap substantial and worthwhile benefits for the plaintiff. Where, as in the present case, the plaintiff is likely to make a tracing claim, there must be a serious possibility that the discovery sought must either allow the plaintiff to preserve what may well be his assets or realistically lead to the discovery of such assets: see *Arab Monetary Fund v Hashim (No 5)* [1992] 2 All ER 911 at 916D–E, 918J–919A.

(3)    The discovery sought must not be unduly wide. There is no entitlement to general discovery (by general discovery is meant discovery in the *Peruvian Guano* sense): see *Arab Monetary Fund* at 918D–E, 919H. It follows therefore that not only must any order be specific, it must also be restricted to those or those classes of documents that are necessary to enable the plaintiff to preserve or discover assets. This is not to say that discovery orders cannot be wide; what is important is that the discovery, whether wide or narrow, is necessary.

**[15.4.30]    Standard of proof on Norwich Pharmacal application**
The standard of proof required on a *Norwich Pharmacal* application was not specifically raised in that case, but it has been touched on in subsequent cases. In *Lonrho plc v Fayed (No 2)* [1992] 1 WLR 1, Millett J described the standard of proof applicable on an application for *Norwich Pharmacal* discovery in the following words (at 13–14):

It is, however, a prerequisite for the exercise of the jurisdiction that the applicant can demonstrate a prima facie cause of action against a party or parties whose identity cannot be ascertained without the information sought.

In *Wellcome Foundation Ltd v A-G* [1992] 1 HKC 171 Kaplan J was of the view (at 188B) that the suggestion a 'strong case' had to be made out was putting the matter too high (note that that decision was overturned on appeal on other points: see [1992] HKC 158). In *A Co v B Co* [2002] 2 HKC 497, 503C, Ma J said that a *Norwich Pharmacal* order is 'not one that a court would lightly grant in the absence of powerful factors'.

Averments of fact giving rise to the duty to assist on the part of the defendant must be clearly pleaded: *Allied Arab Bank Ltd v Taj El Arefin Hajjar & Ors* HCCL 9/1987 (Deputy Judge Litton QC, 12. 06. 1987) at page 37.

**[15.4.31]   Hong Kong examples**
Hong Kong courts have ordered *Norwich Pharmacal* disclosure in a range of situations. These include:

- *Untraceable business* – in *Easey Garment Factory Ltd v AG* [1980] HKLR 18 the Postmaster General was ordered to disclose the names and addresses of persons who operated a post office box which had been used by an untraceable business allegedly involved in passing off.

- *Anonymous complainant* – in *Ho Tsui Chun v AG* [1980] HKC 720 a *Norwich Pharmacal* order was made against the Education Department requiring disclosure of documents to enable the plaintiff, a school principal, to ascertain the identity of a person who had allegedly made libelous complaints against him.

- *Breach of confidentiality* – an employer obtained a *Norwich Pharmacal* order requiring a party suing it in the Labour Tribunal to disclose the identity of an employee who allegedly disclosed confidential documents, even though this information would later be available on discovery. See *Nam Tai Management Services Ltd & Anor v Ng Yiu-ming* [1990] 1 HKLR 445.

- *Nominee company* – the court has made *Norwich Pharmacal* orders against company secretarial services providing nominee directors and shareholders, requiring disclosure of the identity of the persons behind such companies. See *State Bank of India v Fleet National Bank & Ors* HCMP 1919/2004 (Deputy Judge Gill; 18.08.2006) and *Kensington Int'l Ltd v ICS Secretaries Ltd (No 1)* [2007] 3 HKC 644.

- *Internet piracy* – in *Cineopoly Records Co Ltd & Ors v HK Broadband Network Ltd & Ors* [2006] 1 HKC 433 the court ordered internet service providers to disclose the names, postal addresses and identity card numbers of persons using the internet to download music files in breach of copyright. In *Dish Network LLC & Ors v Zentek Int'l Co Ltd & Anor* [2009] 3 HKC 52 satellite broadcasters obtained *Norwich Pharmacal* relief against the owners of servers hosting websites selling pirate hardware and software to enable illegal descrambling of their signals.

- *Unknown source of defamatory statement* – a person who claimed to have been wrongly named in court proceedings as having provided a document used in cross-examination obtained a *Norwich Pharmacal* order requiring disclosure of the true source of the document, in order to bring a defamation action. See *Chang Wa Shan v Chan Chun Chuen* [2009] 6 HKC 201.

**[15.4.32]   Proper parties to an action for discovery alone**
In ancillary proceedings seeking discovery only against a stranger to the main action (proceedings in the nature of the *Norwich Pharmacal* case), the opposing party in the main action may be refused leave to be joined where he would subsequently have a full opportunity to be heard in the main action: see *Kwan Chi On v Hong Kong Baptist University & Anor* [1998] 1 HKC 88.

**[15.4.33]   Norwich Pharmacal order to require disclosure of journalistic sources**
The 'newspaper rule' whereby the court will not at the discovery stage compel disclosure of the source of information published in news media is recognised in Hong Kong: *Sham v*

*Eastweek Publisher Ltd* [1995] 1 HKC 264. In that case the Court of Appeal set aside a *Norwich Pharmacal* order, holding that the public interest in the free flow of information as expressed in the 'newspaper rule' took precedence in the absence of special circumstances. In *Ashworth Hospital Authority v MGN Ltd* [2002] 1 WLR 2033 the House of Lords upheld a *Norwich Pharmacal* order requiring disclosure of a newspaper's sources, saying that such an order could be made where it was a necessary and proportionate response in the circumstances of the case.

**[15.4.34]** **Norwich Pharmacal order in aid of proceedings outside HK**
The court may make a *Norwich Pharmacal* order in aid of potential proceedings in a place outside Hong Kong: *Manufacturer's Life Ins Co of Canada v Harvest Int'l Ltd* [2002] 1 HKLRD 828 (CA) (reversing the judgment reported at [2001] 1 HKC 435). The Court of Appeal held that the *Norwich Pharmacal* jurisdiction is not limited by the statutory powers under the Evidence Ordinance (Cap 8) and Order 70 to order discovery in aid of foreign proceedings.

**[15.4.35]** **Norwich Pharmacal order in aid of criminal proceedings**
In *Sony Corp v Anand* [1981] FSR 398 it was suggested that a *Norwich Pharmacal* order may be made in aid of criminal proceedings. In *Secretary for Justice v Cheung Kwok Kuen & Anor* HCMP 55/2000 (Lugar-Mawson J; 26.04.2000) the court held it had an inherent power to make a *Norwich Pharmacal*-like order requiring disclosure of information relating to property the government sought to freeze under the Organized and Serious Crimes Ordinance (Cap 455) in circumstances where the statutory power under that Ordinance did not apply.

**[15.4.36]** **Privacy considerations**
The court's power to make a *Norwich Pharmacal* order for disclosure of the identity and particulars of a wrongdoer is not restricted by the Personal Data (Privacy) Ordinance (Cap 486): *Cinepoly Records Co Ltd & Ors v HK Broadband Network Ltd & Ors* [2006] 1 HKC 433, 447I. In that case the court granted a *Norwich Pharmacal* order to compel internet service providers to disclose the names, postal addresses and identity card numbers of persons who were using the internet to download music files in breach of copyright. It was also held that disclosure would not infringe the providers' duty of confidentiality under their telecommunications licences.

**[15.4.37]** **Is use of information obtained by Norwich Pharmacal order subject to restriction?**
There are conflicting authorities on the question whether the use of information obtained under a *Norwich Pharmacal* order is subject to any restriction such as the implied undertaking which applies to documents obtained by means of discovery (as to which see the commentary under Order 24 rule 14A). In *Ashworth Hospital Authority v MGN Ltd* [2002] UKHL 29; [2002] 1 WLR 2003 (HL) (para 60) Lord Woolf suggested that information obtained under a *Norwich Pharmacal* order may only be used for purposes disclosed to the court on the application for the order, unless and until the court permits it to be used for other purposes. That remark was doubted in *Kensington Int'l Ltd v ICS Secretaries Ltd & Ors (No 3)* [2008] 4 HKC 137 (CA) where Rogers VP said:

. . . it is my view that the suggestion that there should be an implied undertaking results from confusion between the discovery orders which are granted because a defendant has come under a duty as described in the *Norwich Pharmacal* case in distinction from the very different form of discovery namely that in the course of an action which is governed by Order 24 RHC.

The comments in both cases are *obiter dicta*. In the Hong Kong case, one member of the 3-judge bench considered it best to leave the point open as it had not been fully argued.

What is clear is that if there are any restrictions on use of information obtained under a *Norwich Pharmacal* order, they cease to have effect once that information is referred to in open court. That is the real ratio of *Kensington Int'l Ltd* (above), referring with approval to *Long Beach Ltd v Global Witness Ltd* [2007] EWHC 1980 (15.08.2007) (paras 29, 52).

**[15.4.38]    Costs of Norwich Pharmacal application**
The defendant in proceedings for *Norwich Pharmacal* discovery, being an innocent party, will normally be entitled to indemnity costs of the application and of compliance with the order made: *A Co v B Co* [2002] 2 HKC 508B. In *Cinepoly Records Co Ltd & Ors v HK Broadband Network Ltd & Ors* [2006] 1 HKC 433, 450 a defendant was granted indemnity costs despite unsuccessfully resisting the *Norwich Pharmacal* application. It was held that the defendant had acted understandably in ventilating its concerns before the court. See also *State Bank of India v Fleet National Bank & Ors* HCMP 1919/2004 (Deputy Judge Gill; 18.08.2006) (indemnity costs of application and compliance awarded to defendants) and *Kensington Int'l Ltd v ICS Secretaries Ltd (No 1)* [2007] 3 HKC 644 (party and party costs of application and indemnity costs of compliance).

It is submitted that costs paid by the applicant in a *Norwich Phamacal* application should ultimately be recoverable against the wrongdoer if liability is established.

**5.    Court may order separate trials, etc. (O. 15 r. 5)**
**(1)    If claims in respect of two or more causes of action are included by a plaintiff in the same action or by a defendant in a counterclaim, or if two or more plaintiffs or defendants are parties to the same action, and it appears to the Court that the joinder of causes of action or of parties, as the case may be, may embarrass or delay the trial or is otherwise inconvenient, the Court may order separate trials or make such other order as may be expedient.**
**(2)    If it appears on the application of any party against whom a counterclaim is made that the subject-matter of the counterclaim ought for any reason to be disposed of by a separate action, the Court may order the counterclaim to be struck out or may order it to be tried separately or make such other order as may be expedient.**

---

**NOTES**

**[15.5.1]    Power of court to sever proceedings**
Order 15 rule 5(1) empowers the court to order separate trials of issues arising in an action, and Order 15 rule 5(2) provides for striking out a counterclaim where the

court is of the view it should be disposed of by separate action.

See also Order 1B rule 1(2)(d) which empowers the court to make similar orders as part of case management.

**6.     Misjoinder and nonjoinder of parties** (O. 15 r. 6)

(1)    No cause or matter shall be defeated by reason of the misjoinder or nonjoinder of any party; and the Court may in any cause or matter determine the issues or questions in dispute so far as they affect the rights and interests of the persons who are parties to the cause or matter. (L.N. 167 of 1994)

(2)    Subject to the provision of this rule, at any stage of the proceedings in any cause or matter the Court may on such terms as it thinks just and either of its own motion or on application—

(a)    order any person who has been improperly or unnecessarily made a party or who has for any reason ceased to be a proper or necessary party, to cease to be a party;

(b)    order any of the following persons to be added as a party, namely—

(i)    any person who ought to have been joined as a party or whose presence before the Court is necessary to ensure that all matters in dispute in the cause or matter may be effectually and completely determined and adjudicated upon, or

(ii)    any person between whom and any party to the cause or matter there may exist a question or issue arising out of or relating to or connected with any relief or remedy claimed in the cause or matter which in the opinion of the Court it would be just and convenient to determine as between him and that party as well as between the parties to the cause or matter.

(3)    An application by any person for an order under paragraph (2) adding him as a party must, except with the leave of the Court, be supported by an affidavit showing his interest in the matters in dispute in the cause or matter or, as the case may be, the question or issue to be determined as between him and any party to the cause or matter.

(4)    No person shall be added as a plaintiff without his consent signified in writing or in such other manner as may be authorized.

(5)    No person shall be added or substituted as a party after the expiry of any relevant period of limitation unless either—

(a)    the relevant period was current at the date when proceedings were commenced and it is necessary for the determination of the action that the new party should be added, or substituted; or

(b)    the relevant period arises under the provisions of section 27 or 28 of the Limitation Ordinance (Cap. 347) and the Court directs that those provisions should not apply to the action by or against the new party.

In this paragraph "any relevant period of limitation" means a time limit under the Limitation Ordinance (Cap. 347).

(6)    The addition or substitution of a new party shall be treated as

necessary for the purposes of paragraph (5)(a) if, and only if, the Court is satisfied that—

(a)    the new party is a necessary party to the action in that property is vested in him at law or in equity and the plaintiff's claim in respect of an equitable interest in that property is liable to be defeated unless the new party is joined, or

(b)    the relevant cause of action is vested in the new party and the plaintiff jointly but not severally, or

(c)    the new party is the Secretary for Justice and the proceedings should have been brought by relator proceedings in his name, or

(d)    the new party is a company in which the plaintiff is a shareholder and on whose behalf the plaintiff is suing to enforce a right vested in the company, or

(e)    the new party is sued jointly with the defendant and is not also liable severally with him and failure to join the new party might render the claim unenforceable.

## NOTES

### [15.6.1]   Curing misjoinder and nonjoinder of parties

At one time the failure to name the correct parties could be fatal to the proceedings. This is remedied by Order 15 rule 6 which in sub-rule (1) specifically provides that no cause or matter shall be defeated by such a mistake. Sub-rule (2) empowers the court to delete or add parties so as to correct any such error.

The court's power to cure misjoinder and nonjoinder of parties is discretionary. The discretion is exercisable in the circumstances set down in rule 6(2)(a) where it is sought to remove a party, and rule 6(2)(b) where it is sought to add a party. For the history and scope of these provisions see *Wong Chun Loong Tony v Ada Ltd* [1991] 1 HKC 86, 93D *et seq* (CA). The rule is designed 'to secure the determination of all disputes relating to the same subject matter without the delay and expense of separate actions, and to ensure that the proper parties necessary for determining the point at issue are before the court': *Kwan Chi On v Hong Kong Baptist University & Anor* [1998] 1 HKC 88, 96G-H.

The power to cure misjoinder and nonjoinder is expressed in terms of ordering that a person 'cease to be a party', or 'added as a party'. In some cases both types of order are made at the same time and the court speaks of 'substituting' parties. See, for example, *East Touch Publisher Ltd v TELA* [1996] 3 HKC 195, 198F.

### [15.6.2]   Stage of proceedings at which application should be made

Order 15 rule 6(2) provides that an order to remove or add a party may be made 'at any stage of the proceedings'. However, in *Nguyen Tuan Cuong & Ors v Secretary for Justice* [1999] 1 HKC 242 (CA) the court declined to do so at the assessment of damages stage in judicial review proceedings. The power may be exercised on appeal, so as to add a party who was not involved at first instance: *Ming An Insurance Co (HK) Ltd v Chan Man Dun & Anor* CACV 96/2005 (Yuen JA; 15.03.2006).

### [15.6.3]   Affidavit in support

The requirement in Order 15 rule 6(3) for an affidavit applies only where a party applies to add himself as a party. There is no such requirement in other circumstances, such as where an existing party applies for substitution of a different plaintiff: see *Wong Kam Hong v Triangle Motors Ltd* [1998] 2 HKC 219.

**[15.6.4]**    **Addition and substitution of plaintiffs**

In *Wong Kam Hong v Triangle Motors Ltd* [1998] 2 HKC 219 the court allowed a substitution of a plaintiff where an agent which had commenced proceedings sought to have its principal substituted for itself.

It may not be improper for the administrator of the estate of a deceased person to be made a plaintiff in proceedings by the estate against a company of which the administrator is a director: see *Chan King Wan & Ors v Honest Scaffold General Contractor Co Ltd & Anor* [1998] 2 HKC 358.

A new plaintiff's consent in writing (or other authorised form) is required for joinder: rule 6(4). A proposed new plaintiff who does not consent may instead be named as a defendant to ensure a judgment binding on all persons concerned: *Kao, Lee & Yip (a firm) v Koo Hoi Yan Donald & Ors* [2002] 3 HKC 323, 332H-I.

**[15.6.5]**    **Challenge to plaintiff's standing**

Where a defendant challenges the authority of the plaintiff to sue, the issue as to standing should be determined before trial: see *Tang Man Kit (suing as sole manager of Wah Yan Mo Fan Heung) v Hip Hing Timber Co Ltd* [1999] 3 HKC 104, 107H, per Yuen J, citing *Banco de Bilbao v Rey* [1938] 2 All ER 253 and *Russian Commercial & Industrial Bank v Comptoir d'Escompte de Mulhouse* [1925] AC 112. The reason is that time and costs would be wasted in dealing with the merits if the plaintiff has no standing: *Foshan Hongda Development Co Liquidation Ctee v East Legend Investment Ltd* HCA 581/ 2002 (Deputy Judge To; 07.06.2007) (para 9). Although the court may consider such a challenge whenever raised, a late challenge may have costs consequences. See *HSBC Private Trust (HK) Ltd v Au Yeung Chung* HCA 1662/2001 (Deputy Judge Carlson; 04.01.2008) (para 31).

An application to challenge the plaintiff's standing to sue should be made by way of application to strike out the plaintiff's name rather than by way of pleading the point in the defence: *Tang Kam Sheung v Tang Kit Yee* HCA 677/2007 (Chu J; 25.09.2009) (para 13), referring to *Kammy Town Ltd v Super Glory Corp Ltd* HCA 3524/2003 (A Cheung J; 14.01.2005) (para 12).

See also the related topic of the solicitor's warranty on commencing proceedings on behalf of a party, in the commentary under Order 15 rule 4.

**[15.6.6]**    **Addition, substitution and deletion of defendants**

The court has power under Order 15 rule 6(2) to order the removal or addition of defendants on application or of its own motion during the course of proceedings.

The power to order a person to cease to be a party is expressed in Order 15 rule 6(2)(a) in terms of parties who have been improperly or unnecessarily joined. Thus a defendant which enjoys immunity from the action may be removed under this power: *Cheng Wai Leung v Martin Construction Co Ltd & Ors* [1991] 1 HKC 466, citing English authority.

A defendant will only be removed from the proceedings on its own application if its joinder is an abuse of process: *Murray-Jones v Hongkong & Shanghai Banking Corp*

[1982] HKC 127; [1982] HKLR 191 (CA). In *Incorporated Owners of Repulse Bay Tower v Ling & Chan* HCCT 100/1999 (Burrell J; 25.01.2000) the court dismissed an application by the defendants that they be replaced by a limited company which they said was the true contracting party, holding that there was an issue for the trial judge as to the identity of the contracting parties.

### [15.6.7]   Limitation considerations on addition or substitution of defendants

Subject to limited exceptions, it is not generally possible to add or substitute defendants into an on-going action after the limitation period has expired as against them. See *Refco Inc v Troika Bullion Ltd & Ors* [1989] 2 HKC 548. Three main exceptions are as follows:

First, Order 20 rule 5(3) allows the court to *correct* the name of a party after expiration of the limitation period notwithstanding an allegation that this amounts to joinder of a new defendant, provided there was a genuine mistake and no one was misled.

Secondly, Order 15 rule 6(5)(a) permits joinder of a new defendant after expiry of the limitation period if that period was current at the time the proceedings were commenced, provided that the joinder is 'necessary' in the narrow circumstances defined by rule 6(6). Those circumstances include the case where the proposed new defendant holds property which is the subject of the action. Some guidance on when joinder is 'necessary' in this context may be found in the decisions of the English Court of Appeal which are usefully summarised in *Parkinson Eng'g Services plc v Swan & Anor* [2009] EWCA Civ 1366 (21.12.2009) (para 17 *et seq*). See also the judgment of the UK Supreme Court in *Roberts v Gill & Co* [2010] UKSC 22 (19.05.2010). The relevant legislative provisions in England are similar, but not identical, to those in Hong Kong.

Thirdly, Order 15 rule 6(5)(b) caters for joinder of a new defendant when the court has exercised its power to disapply the limitation period in a personal injury case (see the commentary under Order 32 rule 9A).

The question whether the limitation period has expired is examined with reference to the date on which the application to join the new defendant was filed in court, not the later date on which the court may hear the application. See *Lim Ban Thoon v Chintung Securities Ltd* [1991] 2 HKC 204, 209F-I (CA).That decision remains good law in Hong Kong despite subsequent developments in England: see *Bowardley Enterprises Ltd v Millennium Group Ltd* [2006] 4 HKC 329 (CA).

Where there is an issue as to whether the limitation period has expired, it may be appropriate for the court to allow the new defendant to be joined, leaving it to that defendant to plead the time bar as a defence. See *Wong Kam Lee v Shimizu Corp & Ors* [1997] 1 HKC 61 where the court held it was not possible to resolve the question of when the limitation period had expired before hearing the evidence. The court allowed joinder of the new defendant to stand, leaving it to that defendant to raise a limitation defence if it wished.

There is no power to order joinder of a defendant after expiration of a contractual limitation period: *Win's Marine Trading Co v Wan Hai Lines (HK) Ltd & Anor* [1999] 3 HKC 701.

A new defendant who is joined after expiration of the usual limitation period against it is deprived of a limitation defence by section 35(1) and (2) of the Limitation

Ordinance (Cap 347) which deems the claim against that defendant to have been made on the same date as the original action.

### [15.6.8]   Costs on change of parties

A plaintiff who finds it necessary to change the parties originally named in its originating process will normally be required to pay the costs of and occasioned by such amendment, just as is the case with amendment under Order 20 rule 5 (see the commentary thereunder). Where an additional plaintiff is joined the court may make a conditional order that the original plaintiff pay all the costs of the action up to that point if at trial it turns out that the original plaintiff was not entitled to maintain the action. See *Chan Chi Ngon v Hung Ling Chun Felicia* [2001] 3 HKLRD 20 where such an order was made, referring to *Ayscough v Bullar* (1889) 41 Ch D 341.

### [15.6.9]   Intervention of new party on own application

Occasionally a stranger to the action may apply to be joined as a defendant. This will only be done against the will of the plaintiff where the proposed new party 'would be affected in his legal right or his pocket by the determination of the dispute': *Idmiston Ltd v Asian Master Enterprises Ltd* [1988] HKC 588, 592H-I, quoting from *Gurtner v Circuit* [1968] 2 QB 587. A mere commercial interest in the outcome 'divorced from the subject matter of the action' is not enough: *Wong Chun Loong Tony v Ada Ltd* [1991] 1 HKC 86 (CA), quoting from *Sanders Lead Co Ltd v Entores Metal Brokers Ltd* [1984] 1 WLR 452 (CA). See also *United States Garment Fty Ltd & Anor v Sealand Service Inc & Ors* [1995] 1 HKC 515. A party seeking to be joined as an additional defendant does not need to show a real prospect of success: *Wing Hang Bank, Ltd v Tsang Sze Yin & Ors* HCMP 1689/1998 (Ribeiro J; 30.12.1999) (para 13); *Flying Mortgage Ltd v Chan Kuen Kwong & Ors* DCCJ 5004/2006 (Judge Lok; 13.02.2008).

Cases in which the court has considered exercise of this power include the following:

(a)    *Chan Shum Sum v Chan Kwan Chin & Anor* [1989] 2 HKC 609 where the Attorney General was granted leave to intervene in wardship proceedings. It was contended that the wardship proceedings were instituted to thwart exercise of the powers of the Director of Immigration to remove a child.

(b)    *Plastimoda SpA v Fung Siu Man & Anor* [1990] 1 HKC 445 where a non-party affected by an *Anton Piller* order was allowed to join as a defendant on its own application.

(c)    *Tai Ping Insurance Co Ltd v Hong Leong Investment Co Ltd* [1991] 2 HKC 8 (CA) where a trustee-in-bankruptcy was joined as a defendant in proceedings concerning a bond under which the bankrupt was jointly and severally liable with the defendant.

(d)    *Yu Cho Wah v Ho Chi Kwong Michael & Ors* [1999] 3 HKC 68 where Pang J granted leave to the daughters of a deceased property owner to be joined as defendants in a dispute over the rights to the property. The daughters claimed an interest in the property under Chinese customary law: and

(e)    *Man Whi Chung v Man Ping Man & Anor* [2003] 1 HKC 549 where a member of a traditional Chinese *Wui* was allowed to intervene as a defendant, on his own application, in proceedings concerning property owned by the *Wui*.

(f)    *Gallium Electronics Ltd v Bridisco (HK) Ltd* DCCJ 6485/2005 (Judge HC

Wong; 07.12.2006) where the court allowed application by a principal to join in proceedings against its agent.

### [15.6.10]  Application by insurer to be joined as defendant

An insurer normally has a contractual right to 'stand in the shoes' of the insured and to defend in his name. Where this right is exercised the insurer need not be named as a defendant. Indeed it may be inappropriate for the insurer to be named. See *Lee Kwan-hung v Hung Kwok Cheung & Anor* HCA 1606/1973 where Cons J said:

> Where an insurance company has a contractual right to take over the conduct of proceedings, it does not seem to me to be necessary for that company to be joined in its own right under Order 15 rule 6(2). This view is confirmed by Diplock LJ in *Gurtner v Circuit* [1968] 2 QB 587 at 603.

See also *Cheung For Kuen v Tang Wai Kwong* [1973–76] HKC 485 where the above passage was cited with approval and see *Sheppard v Richstone Industries Co Ltd* DCEC 113/1984 (Judge Roy; 30.04.1985). The same applies to the Motor Insurance Bureau: *Mak Kin Cheung v Chan Man Lok* [1996] 1 HKC 394.

The contractual right may normally be exercised without prejudice to the insurer's right to deny liability as between itself and the insured for breach of the terms of the policy.

However, where the proceedings give rise to an issue as to which the insurer and the insured have adverse interests it will be appropriate for the insurer to be joined as a defendant in its own right. See *Sami'an Sutinah v Leung Wai Kuen Katrina* [2002] 2 HKC 706, citing *Chu Yuen Wah v Lee Kwok Kee* [1995] 3 HKC 629, *Woo Kin Wah v Somec (Hong Kong) Ltd* [1993] 1 HKLR 300 and *Gurtner v Circuit* [1968] 2 QB 587 (CA). See also *Chan Man v Lam Chan Shing* (1979) 9 HKLJ 82 and *Shahid v Fame Rich Co Ltd* [2009] 1 HKLRD 302. In *Sami'an Sutinah* an insurer was joined in order that it might be heard on the issue whether the alleged wrongful acts were within the scope of employment and thus covered by an employee's compensation policy.

Delay is a relevant factor to be taken into account on an application by an insurer to be joined: *Lau Pui Kei (administrator) v Leung Chi Wai & Ors* HCPI 532/2006 (Deputy Judge Gill; 14.07.2008). In that case a late application was allowed where the court was assured trial dates would not be disturbed.

### [15.6.11]  Joinder of public interest groups in private litigation

In *Tsang Helen v Cathay Pacific Airways Ltd* [2001] 4 HKC 182 (CA) the Equal Opportunities Commission applied to be added as a party in an appeal against a finding that an employer's retirement policy was discriminatory on the basis of sex. The court dismissed the application, which had been brought under Order 15 rule 6(2)(b), on the ground that the Commission did not come within either limb of that subrule. Keith JA held (at 186A–F) that it would be more appropriate for the Commission to seek leave to provide the court with the services of counsel as *amicus curiae* as had been done in *Secretary for Justice v Chan Wah & Ors* [2000] 3 HKC 565. See also *Leung TC William Roy v Secretary for Justice* CACV 317/2005 (Tang JA; 24.03.2006) where the EOC was given leave to provide the court with services of counsel as an *amicus* in a case which was said might have implications on the work of that body.

**[15.6.12]　Service of newly joined defendant**

Where a defendant is substituted or added to an action under Order 15 rule 6(2) the time for service of the new party is not calculated from the date of issue of the writ but from the date of the amendment: see *Seabridge v H Cox & Sons (Plant Hire) Ltd & Anor* [1968] 2 QB 46, cited with approval in *Lee Yuk Yung & Anor v Yeung Kwok Keung & Ors* [1985] HKLR 468.

**6A.　Proceedings by and against estates** (O. 15 r. 6A)

　　(1)　**Where any person against whom an action would have lain has died but the cause of action survives, the action may, if no grant of probate or administration has been made, be brought against the estate of the deceased.**

　　(2)　**Without prejudice to the generality of paragraph (1), an action brought against "the personal representatives of A.B. deceased" shall be treated, for the purposes of that paragraph, as having been brought against his estate.**

　　(3)　**An action purporting to have been commenced by or against a person shall be treated, if he was dead at its commencement and the cause of action survives, as having been commenced by his estate or against it in accordance with paragraph (1) as the case may be, whether or not a grant of probate or administration was made before its commencement. (L.N. 363 of 1990)**

　　(4)　**In any such action as is referred to in paragraph (1) or (3)—**

　　　　(a)　**the plaintiff shall, and the defendant, the personal representatives of the deceased or any person interested in the deceased's estate may, during the period of validity for service of the writ or originating summons, apply to the Court for an order appointing a person to represent the deceased's estate for the purpose of the proceedings or, if a grant of probate or administration has been made, for an order that the personal representative of the deceased be made a party to the proceedings, and in either case for an order that the proceedings be carried on by or against the person so appointed or, as the case may be, by or against the personal representative, as if he had been substituted for the estate; (L.N. 363 of 1990)**

　　　　(b)　**the Court may, at any stage of the proceedings and on such terms as it thinks just and either of its own motion or on application, make any such order as is mentioned in sub-paragraph (a) and allow such amendments (if any) to be made and make such other order as the Court thinks necessary in order to ensure that all matters in dispute in the proceedings may be effectually and completely determined and adjudicated upon.**

　　(5)　**Before making an order under paragraph (4) the Court may require notice to be given to any insurer of the deceased who has an interest in the proceedings and to such (if any) of the persons having an interest in the estate as it thinks fit.**

**(5A)** Where an order is made under paragraph (4) at the instance of a plaintiff appointing the Official Solicitor to represent the deceased's estate, the appointment shall be limited to his accepting service of the writ or originating summons by which the action was begun unless, either on making such an order or on a subsequent application, the Court, with the consent of the Official Solicitor, directs that the appointment shall extend to taking further steps in the proceedings. (L.N. 363 of 1990; L.N. 375 of 1991)

**(6)** Where an order is made under paragraph (4), rules 7(4) and 8(3) and (4) shall apply as if the order had been made under rule 7 on the application of the plaintiff.

**(7)** Where no grant of probate or administration has been made, any judgment or order given or made in the proceedings shall bind the estate to the same extent as it would have been bound if a grant had been made and a personal representative of the deceased had been a party to the proceedings. **(L.N. 363 of 1990)**

---

## NOTES

### [15.6A.1]   Comparison with English rule
The rule of the same number in the former English RSC was confined to proceedings against estates, whereas the Hong Kong rule applies to proceedings by estates as well. In England the relevant rule is now CPR 19.8.

### [15.6A.2]   Scope of rule
Where there has been a grant of representation in respect of the estate of a deceased, the proper procedure is to commence proceedings in the name of or against the executor or administrator, with an indorsement as to capacity in accordance with Order 6 rule 3. Order 15 rule 6A does not apply in such cases. Rather it deals with actions by or against the estate of a deceased person where there has not been a grant of representation.

Rule 6A permits proceedings to be commenced by or against the deceased's estate itself. It applies to both testate and intestate estates where there has not yet been any grant of representation.

In relation to testate estates where there is a valid will appointing an executor who is willing to act it may not be necessary to use rule 6A, at least not where the estate would stand as plaintiff. An executor can commence proceedings on behalf of the estate before probate is granted: *Yeung Yuk Yin v Chu Tat Si* [2006] 2 HKC 142; *Tang Ka Hung Robert v Tang Tim Chue* [2006] 2 HKC 582. The situation is different for intestate estates. Whereas an executor derives title and authority from the will, an administrator has no authority until there is a grant of representation: *Chetty v Chetty* [1916] 1 AC 603, 608 (PC from Singapore); *Chan Pak-man v Chan Pang-fee & Anor* [1981] HKLR 483, 503; *European Asia (HK) Investment Ltd v Wong Shun On Anthony* CACV 120/2010 (Rogers VP, Le Pichon JA & Stone J; 16.11.2010) (para 11).

In relation to intestate estates, there are other procedures which may be considered. The intestate estate of a deceased person vests in the Official Administrator ('OA') (who is the Registrar of the High Court): Probate and Administration Ordinance (Cap

10), s 9, 10. If no surviving relative comes forward to apply for administration in the order of priority set out in rule 21 of the Non-contentious Probate Rules, Cap 10A, administration can be granted to the OA under s 16 of the Ordinance. In that event the OA is entitled to commission in accordance with s 19.

The advantage of the Order 15 rule 6A procedure is twofold. First it avoids delay. Whereas any application for probate or administration takes time, rule 6A allows proceedings to be commenced straight away. This can be particularly important if there is a limitation period about to expire. Secondly, rule 6A provides for the proceedings to be carried on after they have been commenced. The OA, if appointed under the procedure mentioned above, may not be able to carry on the proceedings for lack of instructions.

Rule 6A(1) expressly confines application of the rule, in cases of actions against the estate of a deceased person, to causes of action which arose against the deceased person during the lifetime of the deceased, and survive his death. So far as actions *by* a deceased person are concerned, they must likewise be causes of action which survive death; otherwise there would be nothing to claim. By virtue of section 20(1) of the Law Amendment and Reform (Consolidation) Ordinance (Cap 23) ('LARCO'), causes of action 'subsisting against or vesting in' a person who dies after 26 October 1951 survive against or for the benefit of the person's estate. By proviso to section 20(1), the section does not apply to causes of action in defamation, seduction, inducing a spouse to leave or remain apart or for damages for adultery.

The statutory underpinning of rule 6A is section 55A of the High Court Ordinance by which the power to make rules of court includes the power to make provision for proceedings by or against the estate of a deceased person where there has been no grant of probate or administration.

## [15.6A.3]  Proceedings against estate

This rule authorises action being commenced against the estate of a deceased person before a grant of probate or administration has been made. It will be useful in cases where there is a delay in obtaining a grant of probate or administration which may stretch beyond the limitation period. Without this rule it might be possible for an estate to avoid liability for the deceased's civil obligations simply by never seeking a grant of probate or administration.

The plaintiff in a case to which this rule applies may commence proceedings against the estate, naming 'the personal representatives of AB deceased' as defendant, in accordance with sub-rule (2) and serve it on the person appointed in accordance with sub-rules (4), (5) and (5A). By virtue of sub-rule (7) any judgment will be binding just as if there had been a grant of probate or administration. However, sub-rule (7) would not appear to apply in a case where there is a grant of probate or administration during the course of the proceedings and, accordingly, where there is such a grant subsequent to the commencement of proceedings, the style of cause should be amended (under rule 6 (above)) to reflect the grant.

## [15.6A.4]  Proceedings by estate

There is nothing in this rule expressly authorising an action to be commenced in the name of a deceased person. However, paragraph 6A(3) deems an action purporting to have been commenced by a person who was in fact dead at the date of commencement to have been commenced by his estate. Thus such an action would appear to be unobjectionable, so long as the additional criterion is met: the cause of action must survive the death of the putative plaintiff (as to which see LARCO (Cap 23), section 20, summarised above).

Originally this rule applied only to proceedings *against* estates and that remains the case in England (even after implementation of the Woolf reforms). The Hong Kong rule was amended in 1990 (LN 363/90) to facilitate actions *by* estates as well. However some printings of the rule overlooked that amendment. And the initial Chinese language version of the rules was a translation of such a printing.

An action in the name of a person holding a power of attorney on behalf of the relatives of a deceased entitled to relief under *LARCO* is not valid under rule 6A(3). By its own terms rule 6A(3) is confined to actions commenced in the name of the deceased person. See *Chung Yi Yuen v Lau Koon Shing & Anor* [1999] 3 HKC 43.

### [15.6A.5]  Proceedings under Fatal Accidents Ordinance

With regard to claims under the Fatal Accidents Ordinance (Cap 22), see section 5 thereof which provides that where there has been no grant of representation, an action under the Ordinance may be brought in the names of all or any of the persons on whose behalf a personal representative could have brought it.

Where, in addition to a claim under the FAO, there is a common law cause of action, that can be claimed in the name of the deceased under Order 15 rule 6A if there has been no grant of representation. Alternatively, as one helpful reader has suggested, the common law claims can be added later by amendment, once a grant has been obtained.

### [15.6A.6]  Appointment of representative

Although proceedings may be commenced by or against the estate of a deceased person, they cannot be continued unless and until someone is appointed to represent the estate. Absent a representative, any default judgment obtained against the estate would be a nullity: *Chan Chu Hang & Ors v Man Yun Sau* [1997] 2 HKC 144, 151D-F, citing *Re Amirteymour (deceased)* [1978] 3 All ER 637.

Order 15 rule 6A(4) provides that where a grant of representation (probate or administration) is made after the action is commenced, the personal representative should be joined as a party and the proceedings carried on as if the personal representative has been substituted for the estate. Where there is more than one personal representative all should be joined, and if one refuses to be joined as a plaintiff he or she should be named as a defendant: *Chan King Wan v Honest Scaffold General Contractor Co Ltd* [1998] 2 HKC 358, 361C-F.  If there has not been a grant of representation the rule provides that a person must nevertheless be appointed to represent the estate for the purpose of the action. This may be the Official Solicitor if there is no other suitable person. Where the Official Solicitor is appointed to represent a defendant estate, the appointment is limited to accepting service unless otherwise ordered: rule 6A(5A). See Law Society circular 05-647 as to the information the Official Solicitor requests in the event of a request to extend such appointment.

With regard to issues which arise when the person it is sought to appoint to represent the estate is unwilling, see the commentary under Order 15 rule 15, which should be equally applicable here.

In *Trustee of the Property of Law Ip Po (a bankrupt) v Yuen Yip Kan & Anor*

[1994] 3 HKC 493, 500 it was held that although it is possible to appoint a bankrupt as representative for the purposes of Order 15 rule 6A, this is generally undesirable.

### [15.6A.7]  Limited grant

Reference should also be made to the related procedure for appointment of a personal representative solely for the purpose of litigation.

It is possible to procure a limited grant for the purposes of litigation; see *Overseas Trust Bank Ltd v Ho Pui-wah & Anor* [1987] 2 HKC 459. In that case Barnes J approved as 'an accurate statement of the practice' the following passage from *Tristram & Coote's Probate Practice*, 24th ed, p 392:

> Grant limited to an action. Where it is necessary for the personal representative of a deceased person to be made a party to legal proceedings, for example, an action by or against the estate of the deceased, but the executors or other persons entitled to obtain a grant will not constitute themselves as personal representatives, application may be made for a grant of administration to a nominee limited to bringing, defending or being a party to the action or proceedings in question. The grant will in no case be a general grant.

**7.      Change of parties by reason of death, etc.** (O. 15 r. 7)

**(1)     Where a party to an action dies or becomes bankrupt but the cause of action survives, the action shall not abate by reason of the death or bankruptcy.**

**(2)     Where at any stage of the proceedings in any cause or matter the interest or liability of any party is assigned or transmitted to or devolves upon some other person, the Court may, if it thinks it necessary in order to ensure that all matters in dispute in the cause or matter may be effectually and completely determined and adjudicated upon, order that other person to be made a party to the cause or matter and the proceedings to be carried on as if he had been substituted for the first mentioned party.**

**An application for an order under this paragraph may be made ex parte.**

**(3)     An order may be made under this rule for a person to be made a party to a cause or matter notwithstanding that he is already a party to it on the other side of the record, or on the same side but in a different capacity; but—**

> **(a)     if he is already a party on the other side, the order shall be treated as containing a direction that he shall cease to be a party on that other side, and**
>
> **(b)     if he is already a party on the same side but in another capacity, the order may contain a direction that he shall cease to be a party in that other capacity.**

**(4)     The person on whose application an order is made under this rule must procure the order to be noted in the cause book, and after the order has been so noted that person must, unless the Court otherwise directs, serve the order on every other person who is a party to the cause or matter or who becomes or ceases to be a party by virtue of the order and serve with the order on any person who becomes a defendant a copy of the writ or originating summons by which the cause or matter was begun and of all other pleadings served in the proceedings and a form of acknowledgment of service in Form No.**

**14 or 15 in Appendix A, whichever is appropriate. (L.N. 404 of 1991)**

(5)    Any application to the Court by a person served with an order made ex parte under this rule for the discharge or variation of the order must be made within 14 days after the service of the order on that person.

---

## NOTES

### [15.7.1]   Death or bankruptcy of party

By virtue of section 20 of the Law Amendment and Reform (Consolidation) Ordinance (Cap 23), when a person dies, most causes of action survive against or for the benefit of the estate of the deceased. See the commentary under Order 15 rule 6A above. As a consequence, Order 15 rule 7(1) provides that on-going proceedings in respect of such a cause of action do not 'abate', or come to an end, by reason of death.

Rule 7(1) also applies when a party to proceedings becomes bankrupt. The proceedings do not abate, despite section 12 of the Bankruptcy Ordinance (Cap 6), by which the Official Receiver becomes trustee of the bankrupt's property and claims against a bankrupt are restricted. Thus in *HRA Investments Ltd v Lee Yik Kwong* DCCJ 1291/2005 (Judge Mar lene Ng; 12.07.2007) it was held that a defendant's application for leave to appeal had not abated on his bankruptcy, though it could be pursued only by the Official Receiver.

In the case of death or bankruptcy of a party, the action continues to exist, and provision is made in rule 7(2) for joinder of a new party in his place, and for the proceedings to be carried on as if that person had been substituted for the deceased or bankrupt.

### [15.7.2]   Substitution of parties on death, bankruptcy, assignment, etc

Order 15 rule 7(2) empowers the court to order joinder of a substitute party where the interest or liability of a party in on-going proceedings is assigned, transmitted or devolves upon some other person. The power clearly applies upon death or bankruptcy of a party, as well as other situations.

It is clear from the use of the permissive 'may' that the power is discretionary.

### [15.7.3]   Substitution order not a bar to argument on locus standi

It has been held that a substitution order under rule 7(2) may be made without prejudice to the opposing party's right to challenge the *locus standi* of the new party. See *Crédit Agricole Indosuez Shanghai Branch v China Textile Machinery Co Ltd & Anor* HCA 651/2003 (Chung J; 19.03.2010).

### [15.7.4]   Who may be appointed as substitute party?

A literal reading of rule 7(2) suggests that only the person to whom the interest or liability of a party is assigned, transmitted or devolves can be appointed in substitution. However, the identically worded provisions in Malaysia and Singapore have been interpreted otherwise. In *Government of Malaysia v Taib bin Abdul Rahman* [1991] 2 MLJ 174 it was held that 'to give effect to the principal object of the rule, which is to avoid delay in the disposal of cases', the provision should not be so read. The court upheld appointment of the deceased's son pending a grant of letters of administration despite the fact that in the interim the estate was vested in the Official Administrator. In *Chern Chiow Yong v Cheng Chew Chin* [1998] 2 SLR 615 the Singapore court appointed the executors of a deceased defendant's will, despite the fact that probate (which had been granted) had not yet been extracted. The court dismissed an objection that the action ought to be stayed until probate formalities were completed. In the subsequent Singapore case of *Tan Keaw Chong v Chua Tiong Guan & Anor* [2009] SGHC 127 (26.05.2009) the court appointed the 2nd defendant, who intended to apply for a grant of representation, but had not yet done so. Enquiries were still being made as to whether the deceased had made a will or died intestate. In *Tan* it was said (para 10) that although it would 'normally be appropriate' for the personal representative to be appointed, this did not mean that another person could not be appointed. However, (*Tan* 17, *obiter*) it would 'be going one step too far' to appoint a person who has 'no interest whatsoever in the deceased's estate'.

### [15.7.5]   The test
Rule 7(2) provides that the court must think joinder of the substitute party to be 'necessary' to ensure effective and complete determination of the dispute. In *Tan* (above) the Singapore court was of the view (para 16) that it may not be strictly necessary to appoint a substitute shortly after death of a party, when family members are still taking steps with a view to obtaining a grant of representation. However, the joinder order was allowed to stand in order to avoid delay.

### [15.7.6]   Procedure on application
Order 15 rule 7(2) expressly provides that an application under the provision may be made *ex parte*. Any person served with such an *ex parte* order may apply within 14 days of service for its discharge or variation: rule 7(5).

   An order appointing someone who is already a party as substitute for another may result in a person appearing as both plaintiff and defendant, or in inconsistent capacities. Rule 7(3) make provision for avoidance of such consequences.

   An order made under rule 7 must be served on every other party, including anyone who becomes or ceases to be a party under the order. In the case of a person becoming a defendant, the originating process, all pleadings and a form of acknowledgement of service must also be served: rule 7(4).

### [15.7.7]   Where there is a counterclaim
An order under rule 7 can make provision for a counterclaim to continue against the original plaintiff despite the fact that the plaintiff has assigned the cause of action in respect of which it commenced the proceedings. See *Sun Hung Kai Bank Ltd v Chan Park Chi* CACV 165/1986 (Silke VP, Clough & Power JJA; 05.06.1987) where the plaintiff assigned its cause of action after it had commenced proceedings, and an order was made to substitute the assignee to carry on the proceedings. The Court of Appeal made an order restoring the assignor to its capacity as defendant to counterclaim despite the substitution of the assignee as plaintiff in the main claim. Such an order is necessary in such cases because the assignee of a cause of action does not normally assume the burden under the counterclaim. See *Sun Legend Investments Ltd v Ho Yuk Wah David* [2010] 2 HKC 139. The situation may be different where the counterclaim would have been available as an equitable set-off, as the assignee may take subject to the equities which existed as between the assignor and the debtor: *Sun Legend* (paras 17, 30), referring to *Bank of Boston Connecticut v European Grain & Shipping Ltd* [1989] 1 AC 1056 (HL).

**[15.7.8]    Failure to apply for substitution of party**
As to the consequences of failure to apply under rule 7(2) for substitution of a party who has died, see Order 15 rule 9.

**8.    Provisions consequential on making of order under rule 6 or 7** (O. 15 r. 8)
(1)    Where an order is made under rule 6 the writ by which the action in question was begun must be amended accordingly and must be indorsed with—

(a)    a reference to the order in pursuance of which the amendment is made, and

(b)    the date on which the amendment is made;

and the amendment must be made within such period as may be specified in the order or, if no period is so specified, within 14 days after the making of the order.

(2)    Where by an order under rule 6 a person is to be made a defendant, the rules as to service of a writ of summons shall apply accordingly to service of the amended writ on him, but before serving the writ on him the person on whose application the order was made must procure the order to be noted in the cause book.

(2A) Together with the writ of summons served under paragraph (2) shall be served a copy of all other pleadings served in the action. (L.N. 404 of 1991)

(3)    Where by an order under rule 6 or 7 a person is to be made a defendant, the rules as to acknowledgment of service shall apply accordingly to acknowledgment of service by him subject, in the case of a person to be made a defendant by an order under rule 7, to the modification that the time limited for acknowledging service shall begin with the date on which the order is served on him under rule 7(4) or, if the order is not required to be served on him, with the date on which the order is noted in the cause book.

(4)    Where by an order under rule 6 or 7 a person is to be added as a party or is to be made a party in substitution for some other party, that person shall not become a party until—

(a)    where the order is made under rule 6, the writ has been amended in relation to him under this rule and (if he is a defendant) has been served on him, or

(b)    where the order is made under rule 7, the order has been served on him under rule 7(4) or, if the order is not required to be served on him, the order has been noted in the cause book;

and where by virtue of the foregoing provision a person becomes a party in substitution for some other party, all things done in the course of the proceedings before the making of the order shall have effect in relation to the new party as they had in relation to the old except that acknowledgment of service by the old party shall not dispense with acknowledgment of service by the new.

(5)    The foregoing provisions of this rule shall apply in relation to an action begun by originating summons as they apply in relation to an action begun by writ.

NOTES

**[15.8.1]   Amendment consequent upon change of parties**
Order 15 rule 8(1) requires that where an order has been made to cure misjoinder or nonjoinder of parties under Order 15 rule 6, the writ must be amended accordingly.

In *Li Ming Cheong v Li Wai Ki & Ors* HCA 10334/2000 (Deputy Judge Longley; 01.02.2002) it was argued that this implies a two-stage process involving first an order as to parties and subsequent amendment. The learned Deputy Judge rejected this argument and held that a wholly new defendant could be added into existing proceedings by amendment without leave under Order 20 rule 1 without exercise of the court's discretion under Order 15 rule 6.

**[15.8.2]   When joinder of new party takes effect**
An order of the court is not of itself sufficient for the joinder of a new party to take effect: *Kalimantan Timbers v Mighty Dragon Shipping Co SA* [1980] HKC 228, 235F-G (CA). Joinder takes effect at the time stipulated by Order 15 rule 8(4). In most cases that is when the writ has been amended in accordance with Order 20 rule 9 and, if the new party is a defendant, served.

In *Plastimoda SpA v Fung Siu Man & Anor* [1990] 1 HKC 445 it was argued that prior to joinder taking effect the new party has no *locus standi* to be heard in the action. However, the court entertained the submissions of the new party, citing the interests of justice.

**[15.8.3]   Service of newly joined defendant**
Order 15 rule 8(2) and (2A) provide that a defendant newly joined under Order 15 rule 6 must be served with the writ of summons together with copies of the pleadings. By rule 8(3), the rules as to acknowledgement of service apply to defendants joined into an action under rule 6 or rule 7.

**[15.8.4]   Effect of change of parties**
In *Chorlton v Dickie* (1879) 13 ChD 160 it was said that the new defendant by order of 'revivor' on bankruptcy of the original defendant was placed in the 'exact position' of the original defendant. Thus it was not necessary to file fresh pleadings as against the new defendant. Order 15 rule 8(2) requires that the new defendant be provided with copies of the pleadings already served (see above) but makes no mention of refiling. Thus *Chorlton v Dickie* should apply in that regard. However, the remark about the substitute party being placed in the 'exact position' of the original party should be taken as limited to procedural matters, leaving substantive rights unaffected. See *Sun Legend Investments Ltd v Ho Yuk Wah David* [2010] 2 HKC 139 (paras 23–25) where an order under rule 7 changing plaintiffs following assignment of a cause of action did not render the new plaintiff liable under a counterclaim. The defendant could have applied to retain the original plaintiff as defendants to the counterclaim, but having not done so, could not succeed on the counterclaim.

**9.    Failure to proceed after death of party** (O. 15 r. 9)
   **(1)   If after the death of a plaintiff or defendant in any action the cause**

of action survives, but no order under rule 7 is made substituting as plaintiff any person in whom the cause of action vests or, as the case may be, the personal representatives of the deceased defendant, the defendant or, as the case may be, those representatives may apply to the Court for an order that unless the action is proceeded with within such time as may be specified in the order the action shall be struck out as against the plaintiff or defendant, as the case may be, who has died; but where it is the plaintiff who has died, the Court shall not make an order under this rule unless satisfied that due notice of the application has been given to the personal representatives (if any) of the deceased plaintiff and to any other interested persons who, in the opinion of the Court, should be notified.

(2) Where in any action a counterclaim is made by a defendant, this rule shall apply in relation to the counterclaim as if the counterclaim were a separate action and as if the defendant making the counterclaim were the plaintiff and the person against whom it is made a defendant.

**10.   Actions for possession of land** (O. 15 r. 10)

(1) Without prejudice to rule 6, the Court may at any stage of the proceedings in an action for possession of land order any person not a party to the action who is in possession of the land (whether in actual possession or by a tenant) to be added as a defendant.

(2) An application by any person for an order under this rule may be made ex parte, supported by an affidavit showing that he is in possession of the land in question and if by a tenant, naming him.

The affidavit shall specify the applicant's address for service and Order 12, rule 3(2), (3) and (4), shall apply as if the affidavit were an acknowledgment of service.

(3) A person added as a defendant by an order under this rule must serve on the plaintiff a copy of the order giving the added defendant's address for service specified in accordance with paragraph (2).

---

## NOTES

### [15.10.1]   Cross-references
See also:
* Order 10 rule 4 which empowers the court to authorise service of originating process claiming possession of land to be effected by affixing a copy at a conspicuous part of the premises or land;
* Order 45 rule 3(3) which requires that occupiers of land be given notice of proceedings before leave to issue a writ of possession may be granted; and
* Order 113 rule 5 with regard to applications for joinder into summary proceedings for possession of land against persons who entered into occupation as trespassers.

### [15.10.2]   Application to be joined in action for possession of land
Order 15 rule 10 provides that a person in possession of land may apply to be joined as a defendant in an action for possession of that land.  The applicant may be in

actual possession or have let to a tenant.

The rule is 'designed to safeguard the rights of any person who is not made a party but who is in possession of part or all of the premises sought to be recovered': *Wong Chi Shing v Cheung Choi Lee* [1982] HKC 560, 572C (CA). Such persons must be given notice of the proceedings before leave may be granted to issue a writ of possession for enforcement of an order for possession: see Order 45 rule 3.

### [15.10.3]    Stage at which order may be made

The rule provides that an order for joinder may be made 'at any stage of the proceedings', which means 'application can be made even after judgment': *Wong Chi Shing* (above) (at 572C). However, the power is discretionary and the court will be slow to order joinder at a very late stage such as after judgment has been given and execution carried out: *Yuen Ka-kwok v Ho Nai-sun & Anor* [1980] HKLR 646, 647 (CA). As interpreted by *Liu Chong Hing Bank Ltd v Homex Rattan HK Ltd & Ors* HCMP 1043/1984 (Mantell J; 12.10.1984), *Yuen Ka-kwok* stands for the proposition that where a late application is made, it must be demonstrated that the delay is 'not due to wilful default'.

### [15.10.4]    Grounds on which joinder will be ordered

In *Yu Wing Kan v Lau Shuk Lan* CACV 68/1989 (Fuad VP, Kempster & Clough JJA; 28.06.1990) it was said (at para 29) that the 'leading case' on joinder under Order 15 rule 10 is *Minet v Johnson* (1890) 6 TLR 417 (CA). The Hong Kong Court of Appeal was of the view that the effect of that English case is as follows (from the judgment of Clough JA in *Yu Wing Kan*, at para 31):

> *Minet v Johnson* is authority for the proposition that any person in actual possession of land who is not made a party to an action for possession of that land by a plaintiff against a defendant is entitled to be added under Order 15 rule 10 as a defendant before or after judgment, provided he has a *bona fide* independent claim to be in possession. However, as Lord Esher pointed out [in that case], if the applicant has no independent claim because his rights are wholly dependent upon those of the defendant in the action, out he must go. If the application is made after judgment, *Minet v Johnson* confirms that if there are grounds for the application the judgment must be set aside so far as it affects the application but not as against the original defendant.

See also *AIG Finance (HK) Ltd v Wu Sing Cheung* [2003] 3 HKC 553 (CA) where an application for joinder under this rule was allowed after considering the merits of the applicant's claim to an interest in the property by way of proprietary estoppel.

### [15.10.5]    No necessity for amendment following joinder

Where an order for joinder of a new party is made under Order 15 rule 6 the writ must be amended accordingly: see rule 8(1). However, there is no such requirement when joinder is ordered under Order 15 rule 10. In *Yue Wan Loy Ltd v Chow Hok Lam & Anor* HCA 2336/1979 (Commr Hooper; 27.02.1980) it was held that an application for summary judgment could proceed against a defendant joined under Order 15 rule 10 even though the pleadings had not been amended to claim relief specifically against it. The court was of the view that the original prayer for relief was sufficient. However, it would be good practice for the plaintiff to amend the pleadings following joinder of a defendant under rule 10.

**10A.    (Repealed L.N. 127 of 1995)**

**11.    Relator actions** (O. 15 r. 11)
**Before the name of any person is used in any action as relator, that person must give a written authorization so to use his name to his solicitor and the authorization must be filed in the Registry.**

---

**NOTES**

**[15.11.1]    'Relator' actions**
A 'relator' action is an action to enforce a public right brought by a private individual rather than the competent public authority, who is the Attorney General or, in Hong Kong, the Secretary for Justice.

A public right is one which is enjoyed by every member of the public equally, as opposed to a private right, which is one to which individual members of society have personal claims. For example, the right to travel along a public highway is a public right, to which every member of society is equally entitled. It should be enforced by proceedings in the name of the Secretary of Justice for the benefit of the public at large against any person or persons who are alleged to impede the same. On the other hand, the right to occupy property to the exclusion of others is a private right enforceable by means of ordinary civil proceedings in the claimant's name against those sought to be excluded.

As a general rule it is the Secretary for Justice, as guardian of the public interest, who enforces public rights. However, where the Secretary for Justice declines to take proceedings, a member of the public may seek his or her permission to bring proceedings in the name of the Secretary to enforce the public right. Such proceedings are known as 'relator' proceedings with the individual citizen borrowing or using the name of the Secretary being the 'relator'. The style of cause will reflect the fact that the Secretary's name is being borrowed by the relator, for example, the plaintiff may be described as 'Secretary for Justice *ex rel AB v CD*'.

The Secretary's consent to relator proceedings is required. See *Gouriet v Union of Post Office Workers* [1978] AC 435 where the House of Lords overturned a decision of Lord Denning which would have allowed a private individual to challenge an interruption of public postal and telecommunications services with South Africa. As a result, if the Secretary declines to enforce a public right, and further declines permission for relator proceedings, the public right will go unenforced.

Order 15 rule 11 requires that the relator's consent to act be filed in court in the form of a written authorisation.

It is generally thought that a relator should act through a solicitor, and not in person.

**12.    Representative proceedings** (O. 15 r. 12)
**(1)    Where numerous persons have the same interest in any proceedings, not being such proceedings as are mentioned in rule 13, the proceedings may be begun, and, unless the Court otherwise orders, continued, by or against any one or more of them as representing all or as representing all except one or more of them.**

(2)   At any stage of proceedings under this rule the Court may, on the application of the plaintiff, and on such terms, if any, as it thinks fit, appoint any one or more of the defendants or other persons as representing whom the defendants are sued to represent all, or all except one or more, of those persons in the proceedings; and where, in exercise of the power conferred by this paragraph, the Court appoints a person not named as a defendant, it shall make an order under rule 6 adding that person as a defendant.

(3)   A judgment or order given in proceedings under this rule shall be binding on all the persons as representing whom the plaintiffs sue or, as the case may be, the defendants are sued, but shall not be enforced against any person not a party to the proceedings except with the leave of the Court.

(4)   An application for the grant of leave under paragraph (3) must be made by summons which must be served personally on the person against whom it is sought to enforce the judgment or order.

(5)   Notwithstanding that a judgment or order to which any such application relates is binding on the person against whom the application is made, that person may dispute liability to have the judgment or order enforced against him on the ground that by reason of facts and matters particular to his case he is entitled to be exempted from such liability.

(6)   The Court hearing an application for the grant of leave under paragraph (3) may order the question whether the judgment or order is enforceable against the person against whom the application is made to be tried and determined in any manner in which any issue or question in an action may be tried and determined.

---

## NOTES

### [15.12.1]   Representative proceedings

Where numerous persons have the same interest in litigation they may sue or defend by one or more representatives under Order 15 rule 12. For example, an unincorporated club, which does not have legal capacity to sue in its own name, may seek to enforce the interests of its members by action in the name of its president or other representative, for and on behalf of the members. No court order is necessary for such proceedings save under Order 15 rule 12(2) after proceedings have been commenced against a body of persons.

By virtue of Order 15 rule 12(3) judgment in the proceedings will be binding against all persons represented.

Without the procedure laid down in Order 15 rule 12, proceedings involving groups with large numbers of members would be extremely unwieldy – each and every member of an unincorporated organisation would have to be named in the action in order for relief to be binding on them all. The rule exists for convenience, to ensure that all persons affected are before the court and will be bound by its judgment: *Hong Kong Kam Lan Koon Ltd v Realray Investments Ltd* [2004] 2 HKC 673, *citing John v Rees* [1970] Ch 345.

The members of the group represented in the proceedings must have the same interest in the litigation: rule 12(1). The 'same interest' test should be applied permissively and not rigidly: *TND Group Ltd v Lau Chiang Chu Vivien* [2010] 5 HKLRD 330 (para 18). The fact that individual members of the group may have different rights against the opposing party does not prevent them from being represented in respect of those issues which are common to all: *Duke of Bedford v Ellis* [1901] AC 1. It is sufficient that there is some matter of commonality and that the represented persons have a community of interest in the determination of any substantial question of law or fact in the proceedings: *TND* (above) (para 20). The court may review the assessment of the commonality of interest of the represented parties as the case develops, and vary the form of the proceedings if necessary: *Hong Kong Kam Lan Koon Ltd v Realray Investments Ltd (No 2)* [2005] 1 HKC 565, 572F–H.

Where there is a dispute amongst the members of an organisation, such that they do not have the same interest in the litigation, the representative proceedings must make this fact clear. For example, proceedings may be issued by AB, Chairman of the CD Club, for and on behalf of the members of the CD Club, except E, F, G & H, in which case E, F, G & H should be named as defendants. See *Re the Pentecostal Mission, Hong Kong and Kowloon* [1962] HKLR 171 and *Sung Sheung-hong & Ors v Leung Wong Soo-ching & Ors* [1965] HKLR 602.

**[15.12.2]    The represented parties must be properly before the court**
Representative proceedings brought under this rule should expressly state in the style of cause and in the statement of claim that the plaintiff brings the proceedings as representative of a group of persons – for example, 'ABC, Chairman of the XYZ Club, for and on behalf of the members of the XYZ Club'.

In *Re the Pentecostal Mission, Hong Kong and Kowloon* [1962] HKLR 171, there was a dispute between two factions within an unincorporated religious association. The applicants, who described themselves as the Chairman and Secretary of the association, commenced proceedings seeking relief against the Treasurer of the association or a branch of it. The court held that the proceedings were improperly constituted and should be amended so as to bring all members of the two rival factions before the court in representative proceedings.

The group or class of persons represented must be clearly defined because there are practical implications such as who will be bound by the judgment, and who might be liable for costs: *Right to Inherent Dignity Movement Ass'n v HKSAR* HCAL 74/2008 (Lam J; 21.08.2008). Thus in *Chinachem Charitable Foundation Ltd v Chan Chun Chuen & Anor* HCAP 8/2007 (Lam J; 19.03.2009) the court refused leave for an unincorporated body to join in a probate action, where the putative representative refused to disclose the names of the members of the association.

**[15.12.3]    Choice of representatives**
The persons named as representatives of the group may be self–elected; the consent of the members of the group is not necessary: *Sung Sheung-hong & Ors v Leung Wong Soo-ching & Ors* [1965] HKLR 602, 612. This will sometimes be the case when the group are plaintiffs. Members who do not wish to be plaintiffs should be joined as defendants pursuant to Order 15 rule 4(2) in order to ensure that all members of the group are before the court.

The court may compel a person to represent other members even against his wishes: *TND Group Ltd v Lau Chiang Chu Vivien* [2010] 5 HKLRD 330 (para 12), referring to *Wood v McCarthy* [1893] 1 QB 775.

### [15.12.4]   New Territories associations
See the interesting case of *Tang Man Kit & Anor v Hip Hing Timber Co Ltd* [2001] 4 HKC 11; [2003] 4 HKC 278 (CA) as to the circumstances in which a New Territories association such as a 'heung' or 't'ong' may have the legal capacity to bring proceedings in its own name like a body corporate. In the absence of such capacity it may be appropriate to use the representative proceedings procedure under this Order.

### [15.12.5]   Agents
An agent may not normally bring representative proceedings under this rule: an agent is required to sue in the name of his principal: see *Chinavest II-A, LP v Chan Keung Un Roy* [1998] 4 HKC 453 (CA), per Godfrey JA at 459A citing *Jones v Gurney* [1913] WN 72. In the *Chinavest* case the Court of Appeal held that an action by agent on behalf of a group of sellers was properly constituted by virtue of this rule, but went on to decide that the situation was not satisfactory and that all the sellers should be added as plaintiffs.

### [15.12.6]   Enforcement of judgment against unincorporated association
Though a judgment or order made in representative proceedings is binding on all represented persons, it may not be enforced against individual members without leave. See *Hong Kong Kam Lan Koon Ltd v Realray Investments Ltd* [2004] 2 HKC 673, citing *City of London Sewers Commissioners v Gellatly* (1876) 3 Ch D 610.

### [15.12.7]   Shareholder's derivative action
The derivative action, in which a shareholder brings proceedings for the benefit of the company as a whole, may be regarded as a form of representative proceeding. See *Tang Kwok Ham & Ors v Pengurusan Danaharta Nasional Bhd* [2006] 5 MLJ 60 (CA) (para 26). In England the Rules of the Supreme Court contained Order 15 rule 12A regulating the procedure to be followed (now see CPR 19.9). In Hong Kong the Chief Justice's working party on civil justice reform initially proposed that Order 15 rule 12A of the English RSC be adopted, but this was dropped in the final report (2004) as a result of amendments to the Companies Ordinance.

Derivative actions developed as a common law exception to the rule in *Foss v Harbottle* (1843) 67 ER 189. Part IVAA of the Companies Ordinance (Cap 32), which came into force in mid-2005 and traces back to recommendations of the Standing Committee on Company Law Reform on corporate governance, now provides for a statutory derivative action. The common law derivative action is preserved by section 168BC(4) of the Companies Ordinance so it appears that a shareholder has a choice.

There are key differences between the statutory and common law derivative actions. First, leave is required to bring a derivative action under the Ordinance. An application for leave is made by originating summons under Order 102 rule 2 (see the commentary thereunder). In order to obtain leave the applicant must satisfy the court of the matters set out in section 168BC(3) of the Ordinance. See *Re F&S Express Ltd* [2005] 4 HKLRD 743 and *Re Grand Field Group Holdings Ltd* [2009] 3 HKC 81 (para 19 *et seq*) for discussion of those matters. There is no leave requirement for a common law derivative action, though the plaintiff might seek the court's sanction in order to be indemnified as to costs as in *Chung Sau Ling v Asia Women's League Ltd*

[2001] 3 HKC 410, and the court might exercise its striking out power, as in *Cheung Tse-ming v Cheung Yuk May Ida & Ors* HCA 9995/1995 (Rogers J; 21.12.1995). Secondly, in a statutory derivative action the company must be named as plaintiff: section 168BC(2). By contrast in a common law derivative action the shareholder bringing the action will be named as plaintiff (perhaps with a statement to the effect that he brings the action for the benefit of himself and other shareholders, though this is not strictly necessary: *Lau William John v Wan Yuk Lin Alison & Ors* HCA 1255/2006 (Deputy Judge Au; 28.07.2008) (para 23). In the common law action the company should be named as a defendant: *Kwong Ian (HK) Construction & Real Estate Dev't Co Ltd v Glorious Sun Highway Dev't Ltd & Ors* HCA 260/2006 (Deputy Judge L Chan; 09.08.2006). Thirdly a statutory derivative action may not be discontinued or settled without leave of the court: section 168BJ.

The court's statutory power in relation to derivative actions extends to granting leave to intervene 'for the purpose of continuing, discontinuing or defending' proceedings: Companies Ordinance, s 168BC(1)(b). It also extends to granting leave to bring an appeal: *Re Lucky Money Ltd* HCMP 505/2006 (Kwan J; 17.08.2007).

It has been held that a 'double' or 'multiple' derivative action is maintainable in Hong Kong. In such an action a shareholder seeks, on behalf of the company, redress for a wrong not to the company itself, but to a subsidiary. See *Waddington Ltd v Chan Chun Hoo & Ors* [2006] 2 HKLRD 896 (CA), (2008) 11 HKCFAR 370.

Judgment for the plaintiff in a derivative action must be entered in favour of the company, not the shareholder who brings it. This follows from the fact that a derivative action is brought for the benefit of the company as a whole. See *Ng Yee Wah v Lam Chun Wah & Anor* CACV 309/2008 (Rogers VP, Le Pichon JA & Stone J; 25.02.2009).

As to the costs of a derivative action brought by a minority shareholder, see the commentary under Order 62 rule 3.

**[15.12.8]   Derivative action by beneficiary of a trust**
As a general rule it is for the trustee, not the beneficiary, to bring proceedings on behalf of the trust against third parties. See Order 15 rule 14. However the beneficiary may act in exceptional circumstances where the trustee is in breach of duty: *Hayim v Citibank NA & Anor* [1987] 2 HKC 1 (PC). In *Roberts v Gill & Co* [2010] UKSC 22 (19.05.2010) such an action by a beneficiary was described as a derivative action. The allegedly errant trustee should be joined as a defendant to such an action.

**13.    Representation of interested persons who cannot be ascertained, etc.**
     (O. 15 r. 13)
   **(1)  In any proceedings concerning—**
       **(a)    the estate of a deceased person, or**
       **(b)    property subject to a trust, or**
       **(c)    the construction of a written instrument, including an Ordinance or any other written law,**
**the Court, if satisfied that it is expedient so to do, and that one or more of the conditions specified in paragraph (2) are satisfied, may appoint one or more persons to represent any person (including an unborn person) or class who is or may be interested (whether presently or for any future, contingent or**

unascertained interest) in or affected by the proceedings.

(2) The conditions for the exercise of the power conferred by paragraph (1) are as follows—

(a) that the person, the class or some member of the class, cannot be ascertained or cannot readily be ascertained;

(b) that the person, class or some member of the class, though ascertained, cannot be found;

(c) that, though the person or the class and the members thereof can be ascertained and found, it appears to the Court expedient (regard being had to all the circumstances, including the amount at stake and the degree of difficulty of the point to be determined) to exercise the power for the purpose of saving expense.

(3) Where in any proceedings to which paragraph (1) applies, the Court exercises the power conferred by that paragraph, a judgment or order of the Court given or made when the person or persons appointed in exercise of that power are before the Court shall be binding on the person or class represented by the person or persons so appointed.

(4) Where, in any such proceedings, a compromise is proposed and some of the persons who are interested in, or who may be affected by, the compromise are not parties to the proceedings (including unborn or unascertained persons) but—

(a) there is some other person in the same interest before the Court who assents to the compromise or on whose behalf the Court sanctions the compromise, or

(b) the absent persons are represented by a person appointed under paragraph (1) who so assents,

the Court, if satisfied that the compromise will be for the benefit of the absent persons and that it is expedient to exercise this power, may approve the compromise and order that it shall be binding on the absent persons, and they shall be bound accordingly except where the order has been obtained by fraud or non-disclosure of material facts.

---

## NOTES

### [15.13.1] Representation of unascertained persons

Order 15 rule 13 provides the court with a discretion to appoint representatives for unascertained persons who may be interested in the outcome of litigation involving an estate, a trust or the construction of a written instrument (whether an enactment or private instrument such as a contract).

### [15.13.2] 'Class' and 'group' actions

Apart from rules 12 and 13, there is no specific provision in Hong Kong for 'class' or 'group' actions. Class actions are used in some other common law jurisdictions (particularly in North America) as a means of seeking redress for large numbers of plaintiffs with similar claims. In England CPR Part 19 was introduced in 2000 to provide for 'group' actions which likewise may involve large numbers of claimants.

In Hong Kong the Consumer Council, incorporated under the Consumer Council Ordinance (Cap 216) provides an avenue for redress in some such cases. The Chief Justice's Working Party on Civil Justice Reform recommended in its final report (2004) that in principle Hong Kong should adopt a scheme for multi-party litigation and that such schemes in other jurisdictions should be studied.

For a comparison between class actions and representative proceedings see Debelle, 'Class Actions for Australia? Do They already exist?' [1980] ALJ 508. See also Glenn, 'Class Actions in Ontario and Quebec' (1984) 62 Can Bar Rev 248, which highlights the reluctance of common law courts to allow actions to proceed where not all parties have been identified.

**13A.   Notice of action to non-parties** (O. 15 r. 13A)

**(1)   At any stage in an action to which this rule applies, the Court may, on the application of any party or of its own motion, direct that notice of the action be served on any person who is not a party thereto but who will or may be affected by any judgment given therein.**

**(2)   An application under this rule may be made ex parte and shall be supported by an affidavit stating the grounds of the application.**

**(3)   Every notice of an action under this rule shall be in Form No. 52 in Appendix A and the copy to be served shall be a sealed copy and accompanied by a copy of the originating summons or writ and of all other pleadings served in the action, and by a form of acknowledgment of service in Form No. 14 or 15 in Appendix A with such modifications as may be appropriate.**

**(4)   A person may, within 14 days of service on him of a notice under this rule, acknowledge service of the writ or originating summons and shall thereupon become a party to the action, but in default of such acknowledgment and subject to paragraph (5) he shall be bound by any judgment given in the action as if he was a party thereto.**

**(5)   If at any time after service of such notice on any person the writ or originating summons is amended so as substantially to alter the relief claimed, the Court may direct that the judgment shall not bind such person unless a further notice together with a copy of the amended writ or originating summons is issued and served upon him under this rule.**

**(6)   This rule applies to any action relating to—**

**(a)     the estate of a deceased person; or**

**(b)     property subject to a trust.**

**(7)   Order 6, rule 7(3) and (5) shall apply in relation to a notice of an action under this rule as if the notice were a writ and the person by whom the notice is issued were the plaintiff.**

**(L.N. 404 of 1991)**

---

**NOTES**

**[15.13A.1]   Scope of Order 15 rule 13A**

Order 15 rule 13A provides for non–parties to be given an opportunity to join as parties to on–going litigation by service of notice on them by order of the court.

An important aspect of the rule is that the non–party who has been served with notice under the rule will be bound by the court's judgment in that case whether or not it chooses to join in the litigation: rule 13A(4).

### [15.13A.2] Costs of non–parties served with notice

In *Chiu Tak Kwong v Tan Yufang* HCAP 9/2006 (Deputy Judge L Chan; 11.06.2010); [2010] 5 HKLRD 718 a probate action by one of the deceased's children against the deceased's second wife was unsuccessful, and costs were ordered in favour of the second wife. Notice of the action had been given to the plaintiff's siblings under Order 15 rule 13A, and although they did not choose to join as defendants, they did actively assist the plaintiff hoping to receive part of the benefit by virtue of rule 13A(4). The court took the view that the siblings should be jointly and severally liable for the costs ordered against the plaintiff and made an order to that effect pursuant to Order 62 rule 6A.

**14.     Representation of beneficiaries by trustees, etc.** (O. 15 r. 14)

**(1)     Any proceedings, including proceedings to enforce a security by foreclosure or otherwise, may be brought by or against trustees, executors or administrators in their capacity as such without joining any of the persons having a beneficial interest in the trust or estate, as the case may be; and any judgment or order given or made in those proceedings shall be binding on those persons unless the Court in the same or other proceedings otherwise orders on the ground that the trustees, executors or administrators, as the case may be, could not or did not in fact represent the interests of those persons in the first-mentioned proceedings.**

**(2)     Paragraph (1) is without prejudice to the power of the Court to order any person having such an interest as aforesaid to be made a party to the proceedings or to make an order under rule 13.**

---

### NOTES

### [15.14.1]     Cross reference

See also Order 85 concerning administration and similar actions.

### [15.14.2]     Parties in action concerning trust property

Order 15 rule 14 provides that action can be brought by or against a trustee (or executor or administrator) in relation to trust property without joining the beneficiaries. Any judgment or order in the proceedings will normally be binding on the beneficiaries. Thus in *Nu Life Int'l Ltd v Healthy Living Products Int'l Ltd & Anor* HCA 1157/2006 (Deputy Judge Gill; 12.09.2007) proceedings brought by the beneficiary of an alleged trust were struck out on the ground the matter had already been litigated as against the trustee. In that case (para 63-65) the court rejected an argument that this rule applies only to express trusts as opposed to trusts arising out of the operation of law such as resulting or constructive trusts.

Rule 14 is permissive: proceedings 'may' be brought by or against the trustee without naming the beneficiary. In most cases there is not a genuine choice and the proper party is the trustee: *Choi Sze Fai v Pretty Full Development Ltd* [1999] 3

HKC 261. However, in certain circumstances it will be appropriate for trustee and beneficiary to be named separately, for example where their interests are adverse or there is a dispute between them.

As for the exceptional circumstances in which a beneficiary may on his own initiative commence proceedings for the benefit of the trust, see the commentary under Order 15 rule 12 concerning 'derivative' actions by beneficiaries.

#### [15.14.3]   Action may proceed against untraceable trustee
Section 58 of the Trustee Ordinance (Cap 29) expressly provides that an action may proceed, and judgment may be given, in the absence of a trustee defendant who, despite diligent search, could not be found and served.

#### [15.14.4]   Action concerning property of a bankrupt
Under section 58 of the Bankruptcy Ordinance (Cap 6) the property of a bankrupt passes to the trustee in bankruptcy. It follows that actions in relation to a bankrupt's property should be brought by or against the trustee in bankruptcy rather than the bankrupt personally. An exception is personal claims, meaning 'claims which relate to the bankrupt's body, mind or character without immediate reference to his rights of property': *Chung Kau v HK Housing Authority* [2004] 2 HKLRD 650 (CA) (para 8). In *Cheong Shing Investment Loan & Exchange Co Ltd v Ho Wan Cheung & Anor* CACV 395/2006 (Tang VP, Cheung JA & Lam J; 06.11.2007) an appeal was struck out partly on the ground it was brought by a bankrupt personally, in respect of a property matter. In *Choi Sze Fai* (above) at 262I–263C a bankrupt was permitted to proceed with a claim in his own name where it was alleged that the suit property had not beneficially belonged to him and thus had not passed to the trustee in bankruptcy.

#### 15.   Representation of deceased person interested in proceedings (O. 15 r. 15)
**(1)   Where in any proceedings it appears to the Court that a deceased person was interested in the matter in question in the proceedings and that he has no personal representative, the Court may, on the application of any party to the proceedings, proceed in the absence of a person representing the estate of the deceased person or may by order appoint a person to represent that estate for the purposes of the proceedings; and any such order, and any judgment or order subsequently given or made in the proceedings, shall bind the estate of the deceased person to the same extent as it would have been bound had a personal representative of that person been a party to the proceedings.**

**(2)   Before making an order under this rule, the Court may require notice of the application for the order to be given to such (if any) of the persons having an interest in the estate as it thinks fit.**

---

### NOTES

#### [15.15.1]   Order 15 rule 15 – Procedure where interested estate lacks representation
Order 15 rule 15 empowers the court to proceed in the absence of representation of an estate which has an interest in on-going legal proceedings, or to appoint a representative for the estate.

The court is unlikely to proceed without appointing a representative where the estate has any substantial interest in the litigation. This is because unless the estate is represented the court's judgment may not be binding on it, giving rise to the risk of a multiplicity of proceedings and inconsistent decisions when there is a grant of representation. See *Ip Cheung-kwok v Sin Hua Bank Trustee Ltd* [1990] 1 HKLR 497, 511G (CA).

The preferable course is for the court to exercise its power under this rule to appoint a representative for the estate. As noted in *Wong Moy (administratrix) v Soo Ah Choy* [1996] 1 SLR 586, 595F (appeal allowed on other grounds at [1996] 3 SLR 398) there are four requirements for such an order to be made:

(a)      presence of existing proceedings;
(b)      the deceased must have been interested in the matter in question in the proceedings;
(c)      the deceased must not have a personal representative; and
(d)      the applicant must be a party to the existing proceedings.

It follows from (a) that the power can only be exercised in on-going proceedings with the consequence that it cannot be used to appoint a person to *commence* proceedings on behalf of a deceased's estate: *Re Estate of Yam Wong Tak* HCAP 406/1975 (Yang J; 29.09.1975). However proceedings wrongly commenced on behalf of an estate without a grant of representation are not a nullity and may be cured by an order under this rule: *Ip Cheung-kwok* (above). As an example see *Cheung Lily v Official Solicitor & Anor* HCMP 635/2006 (Poon J; 27.10.2008). For the proper procedure to be followed in commencing proceedings on behalf of an unrepresented estate see Order 15 rule 6A and the commentary thereunder.

There is longstanding authority to the effect that a person cannot be appointed to represent an estate against his or her wishes: *Re Curtis & Betts* [1887] WN 126; *Pratt v London Passenger Transport Board* [1937] 1 All ER 473 (CA); *Firth Finance & General Ltd v McNarry* [1987] NI 125. However, it has been held that those authorities should no longer be followed in light of the entrenched rights to a fair trial and access to the court: *Turner v Kearney* [2010] NIMaster 10 (BaILII) (17.12.2010). Such rights are found in art 10 of the Hong Kong Bill of Rights and in 14 of the ICCPR. In *Turner* a Northern Ireland Queen's Bench master appointed a deceased's widow to represent the estate against her wishes, but limited the appointment to acceptance of service. In addition, it should be noted that there is authority in Hong Kong to the effect that the Official Solicitor is duty bound to act if requested by the court: see the commentary on the role of the Official Solicitor under Order 80 rule 3.

A representative appointed under this rule should be made a party to the proceedings: *Ip Cheung-kwok* (above, at 517F-G).

**16.      Declaratory judgment** (O. 15 r. 16)
**No action or other proceeding shall be open to objection on the ground that a merely declaratory judgment or order is sought thereby, and the Court may make binding declarations of right whether or not any consequential relief is or could be claimed.**

**NOTES**

**[15.16.1]     Cross reference**
Order 15 rule 16 deals with the court's power to make declarations of right. It should be read subject to Order 53, which deals with the court's power to grant declarations by way of judicial review in the public law context. Reading the two together, Order 15 rule 16 is, in effect, confined to declarations involving private rights.

**[15.16.2]     Circumstances in which declaration may be granted**
The court's power to grant a declaration traces back to the Court of Chancery and is discretionary. See *Wu Chiu Ting v Ng Sun Wah & Anor* HCA 7927/1988 (Liu J; 21.02.1990).

   Important principles as to the manner in which the court will exercise this discretion include the following:

(a)     The power to grant declarations is wide, but will not be exercised lightly: *Oriental Peer Co Ltd v Terrian Ltd & Ors* [1987] 2 HKC 61 (CA), citing *Ibeneweka v Egbuna* [1964] 1 WLR 219 (PC). In the latter case the Privy Council referred to the 'counsels of moderation' to the effect that the power should be exercised 'sparingly', with 'great care and jealousy', with 'extreme caution'.

(b)     The discretion must be exercised judicially, *Oriental Peer* (above) citing *Hanson v Radcliffe Urban City Council* [1922] 2 Ch 490, 507.

(c)     It is not necessary for the applicant to have a cause of action, but there must be a justiciable issue. Thus a statement of claim seeking declaratory relief only will not be struck out as disclosing no reasonable cause of action, but the court will not grant the relief unless the case raises 'justiciable matters, that is, legal or equitable rights but not moral, social or political matters' *Dicks v Easy Finder Ltd* [1996] 3 HKC 65, 67I.

(d)     Declarations of a purely advisory or hypothetical nature will not normally be granted. Thus in *Jackson v AG* [1980] HKC 182 (CA) the court refused to grant a declaration as to the manner in which a public servant's pension should be calculated because there was no right to a pension, merely an expectation. In *Charter View Development Ltd v Golden Rich Enterprises Ltd & Anor* [2000] 2 HKC 77 (CA) Ribeiro JA reiterated the court's reluctance to grant declarations on hypothetical questions or of an advisory nature. However, there are cases in which the court has been prepared to depart from that general principle. With regard to public law cases, see the discussion on advisory or hypothetical applications for judicial review in the commentary under Order 53 rule 1. In relation to private law cases, see the interesting discussion in *Rolls-Royce plc v Unite the Union* [2009] EWCA Civ 387 (14.05.2009) (para 38 *et seq*), where it is said that different considerations may arise in 'friendly actions' and test cases.

The court will not normally exercise its discretion to grant a declaration of right in default of defence or on admissions. See the commentary under Order 19 rule 7.

**[15.16.3]    Arbitration clause**

The court will not make a declaration of the rights of the parties where the subject matter comes within the scope of an arbitration agreement, except where there is agreement that a preliminary point of law should be determined under section 23A of the Arbitration Ordinance (Cap 341): see *AG v Shimizu Corp* [1994] 1 HKC 664.

An application for a declaration that an arbitral award is not binding for want of jurisdiction should normally be made by motion under Order 73 rule 2(3). See the commentary under that rule.

**17.    Conduct of proceedings** (O. 15 r. 17)

**The Court may give the conduct of any action, inquiry or other proceedings to such person as it thinks fit.**

## ORDER 16

### THIRD PARTY AND SIMILAR PROCEEDINGS

**1.    Third party notice** (O. 16 r. 1)

**(1)    Where in any action a defendant who has given notice of intention to defend—**

**(a)    claims against a person not already a party to the action any contribution or indemnity; or**

**(b)    claims against such a person any relief or remedy relating to or connected with the original subject-matter of the action and substantially the same as some relief or remedy claimed by the plaintiff; or**

**(c)    requires that any question or issue relating to or connected with the original subject-matter of the action should be determined not only as between the plaintiff and the defendant but also as between either or both of them and a person not already a party to the action;**

**then, subject to paragraph (2), the defendant may issue a notice in Form No. 20 or 21 in Appendix A, whichever is appropriate (in this Order referred to as a third party notice), containing a statement of the nature of the claim made against him and, as the case may be, either of the nature and grounds of the claim made by him or of the question or issue required to be determined.**

**(2)    A defendant to an action may not issue a third party notice without the leave of the Court unless the action was begun by writ and he issues the notice before serving his defence on the plaintiff.**

**(3)    Where a third party notice is served on the person against whom it is issued, he shall as from the time of service be a party to the action (in this Order referred to as a third party) with the same rights in respect of his defence against any claim made against him in the notice and otherwise as if he had been duly sued in the ordinary way by the defendant by whom the notice is issued.**

---

## NOTES

### [16.1.1]    Purpose and scope of Order 16

Order 16 provides that a defendant may join a third party against which it claims relief for any liability which may be found against it in respect of the plaintiff's claims. The relief which the defendant seeks to claim against the proposed third party must come within one of heads (a), (b) and (c) of rule 1(1).

Head (a) applies where the defendant claims contribution or indemnity against the proposed third party. With regard to contribution, see the Civil Liability (Contribution) Ordinance (Cap 377). Indemnity might be claimed by joining an insurer as third party where the insurer has denied liability under the policy.

Heads (b) and (c) were explained in *Wong Wai Lan v Tam Fung Lan Sandra* [2003] 1 HKLRD 674. In that case, the purchaser in a collapsed property transaction commenced proceedings against the vendor. The vendor issued a third party notice against her former solicitors seeking to shift the ultimate loss to them. This was permissible under head (b) as 'substantially the same' relief or remedy was proposed to be claimed against the solicitors as the purchaser had claimed against the vendor. At the same time the vendor sought to claim damages from the solicitors for another property transaction which could not complete, because of shortage of funds consequent upon collapse of the first transaction. It was held that this was not permissible under head (b) because the relief or remedy was not substantially the same. However, it was permissible under head (c) because of the common question or issue, namely whether the solicitors had been negligent.

By issuing a third party notice the defendant does not relieve itself of liability to the plaintiff, but is able to obtain from the court, in the same proceedings, an adjudication of its rights as against the third party.

**[16.1.2]   Third party claims in tort – Civil Liability (Contribution) Ordinance (Cap 377)**

An independent tortfeasor may be named as a third party under this Order. In *Kwan Man Ling v Chan Pui Shan Patsy & Anor* [1998] 4 HKC 695 it was held that where each of several persons, not acting in concert, commits a tort against another person substantially contemporaneously and causing the same or indivisible damage, each several tortfeasor is liable for the whole damage. Hence the defendant who alleges that another, possibly independent, tortfeasor, is wholly or partly responsible for the damage, may issue third party proceedings against that other claiming contribution under the Civil Liability (Contribution) Ordinance (Cap 377).

**[16.1.3]   Third party proceedings not appropriate against co-defendant**

This rule, by its own terms, does not apply to the situation where a defendant wishes to claim relief against one of his co-defendants in the action. There are cases in which leave has been granted to one defendant to issue a third party notice against another defendant, with the result that the other defendant is both a defendant and third party in the proceedings. In principle, no such leave should be granted. Instead the defendant who wishes to shift liability onto a co-defendant should issue a notice under rule 8 of this Order.

**[16.1.4]   Effect of settlement of main action**

Third party proceedings are not affected by settlement as between the plaintiff and defendant of the main claim. The third party proceedings may continue without the need to commence a fresh action: see *Lam Chun Lin v Lee Wai Chao & Ors* [1998] 2 HKC 68.

**2.      Application for leave to issue third party notice** (O. 16 r. 2)

**(1)   Application for leave to issue a third party notice may be made ex parte but the Court may direct a summons for leave to be issued.**

**(2)   An application for leave to issue a third party notice must be supported by an affidavit stating—**

      **(a)   the nature of the claim made by the plaintiff in the action;**

      **(b)   the stage which proceedings in the action have reached;**

(c)     **the nature of the claim made by the applicant or particulars of the question or issue required to be determined, as the case may be, and the facts on which the proposed third  party notice is based; and**

(d)     **the name and address of the person against whom the third party notice is to be issued.**

---

## NOTES

### [16.2.1]   Leave to issue third party notice
A defendant who wishes to serve a third party notice requires leave of the court unless the action was begun by writ and the notice is issued before service of the defence: Order 16 rule 1(2).

The grant of leave to issue a third party notice is within the discretion of the court: *FIL Leveraged US Government Bond Fund Ltd & Ors v TCW Funds Management Inc* HCCL 231/1998 (Stone J; 28.11.2000) (para 10); *So Kai Hau v YSK2 Eng'g Co Ltd* [2010] 5 HKLRD 278 (para 35).

Order 16 rule 2 governs the procedure to be followed on an application for leave to issue a third party notice. The rule provides that the application may be made *ex parte*. That will usually be done by affidavit exhibiting the proposed third party notice as in *Ever–Long Capital Ltd v Rich Delta Dev't Ltd & Anor* HCA 509/2006 (Deputy Judge L Chan; 27.11.2008) (para 16). The affidavit must give the information required by rule 2(2). See *Safdar v Chesco Eng'g Ltd* [2008] 5 HKLRD 725 in which rule 2(2) was treated as mandatory.

Where application is made *ex parte*, the court may direct that a summons be issued in order that the plaintiff or even the proposed third party may be heard: rule 2(1). Such a hearing is appropriate where there are concerns such as delay, as in *Ever–Long* (above).

### [16.2.3]   Late application for leave to issue third party notice
The possibility of causing delay in prosecution of the main action and prejudice to the plaintiff are factors which the court should take into account in exercising its discretion to grant leave to issue a third party notice: *Henshaw v Sovereign Marine & General Insurance Co Ltd* [1988] HKC 115, 125B (CA). In *Chea Kam Wing Victor v Kwan Kin Travel Services Ltd* HCPI 970/2005 (Sakhrani J; 18.12.2006) an application made only after the action had been set down for trial was refused on the ground that it would delay the trial by a year, causing prejudice to the plaintiff in his claim for damages. On the other hand, the court was prepared to adjourn hearing of a vendor purchaser summons to accommodate the late joinder of the defendant's former solicitors as third party in *Lee Sau Ling v Chan Man Sang* HCMP 1731/1998 (Yuen J; 30.06.1999). The court was of the view the issue of solicitor's negligence in a conveyancing transaction should be tried with the main action.

**3.      Issue, service and acknowledgment of service, of third party notice**
(O. 16 r. 3)
**(1)     The order granting leave to issue a third party notice may contain**

directions as to the period within which the notice is to be issued.

(2) There must be served with every third party notice a copy of the writ or originating summons by which the action was begun and of the pleadings (if any) served in the action and a form of acknowledgment of service in Form No. 14 in Appendix A with such modifications as may be appropriate.

(3) The appropriate office for acknowledging service of a third party notice is the Registry.

(4) Subject to the foregoing provisions of this rule, the following provisions of these rules, namely, Order 6, rule 7(3) and (5), Order 10, Order 11, Order 12 and Order 75, rule 4, shall apply in relation to a third party notice and to the proceedings begun thereby as if—

    (a) the third party notice were a writ and the proceedings begun thereby an action; and

    (b) the defendant issuing the third party notice were a plaintiff and the person against whom it is issued a defendant in that action:

Provided that in the application of Order 11, rule 1(1)(c) leave may be granted to serve a third party notice outside the jurisdiction on any necessary or proper party to the proceedings brought against the defendant.

---

## NOTES

### [16.3.1] Issue of third party notice

When leave is granted to issue a third party notice the court may give directions as to the period within which the notice is to be issued: rule 3(1). Whether or not leave was required for the issue of the third party notice, it must be in form 20 or 21 in appendix A of these rules: rule 1(1). A third party notice is issued on the date it is sealed by the court, and issues as to whether a limitation period has been complied with must be judged with reference to that date. See *Parshad v Chit Hing Construction Eng'g* [2011] 1 HKLRD 217 (para 93-120).

### [16.3.2] Third party notice must be sealed

A third party notice is issued by the court. Being effectively the originating process against the third party, requiring him to acknowledge service and give notice of intention to defend or face default judgment under rule 5, a third party notice should be sealed with the seal of the court just like a writ or originating summons. Order 6 rule 7(3), which provides that a writ is issued upon being sealed, applies to a third party notice by virtue of Order 16 rule 3(4). In *Keen Lloyd Ltd v Sam Lee Lightering & Transport Co Ltd* [1995] 2 HKC 350, 351B it was said that by virtue of those provisions there is 'no doubt at all' that third party notices 'must be sealed'. In *Parshad* (see case above, para 103 et seq) a third party notice which had not been sealed was treated as ineffective and the court held that the procedural defect could not be cured under Order 2 rule 1.

### [16.3.3] Service of third party notice

A third party notice must be served on the third party in the same manner as a writ or originating summons: Order 16 r 3(4) expressly provides that various other provisions of these rules relating to service shall apply.

Rule 3(2) provides that together with the third party notice there must be served a copy of the originating process by which the main action was commenced, together with any pleadings, and a form of acknowledgement of service. The third party must acknowledge service in the same way as must a defendant, and failure to do so may result in default judgment under rule 5.

**4.      Third party directions** (O. 16 r. 4)

**(1)    If the third party gives notice of intention to defend, the defendant who issued the third party notice must, by summons to be served on all the other parties to the action, apply to the Court for directions.**

**(2)    If no summons is served on the third party under paragraph (1), the third party may, not earlier than 7 days after giving notice of intention to defend, by summons to be served on all the other parties to the action, apply to the Court for directions or for an order to set aside the third party notice.**

**(3)    On an application for directions under this rule the Court may—**

**(a)      if the liability of the third party to the defendant who issued the third party notice is established on the hearing, order such judgment as the nature of the case may require to be entered against the third party in favour of the defendant; or**

**(b)      order any claim, question or issue stated in the third party notice to be tried in such manner as the Court may direct; or**

**(c)      dismiss the application and terminate the proceedings on the third party notice;**

**and may do so either before or after any judgment in the action has been signed by the plaintiff against the defendant.**

**(4)    On an application for directions under this rule the Court may give the third party leave to defend the action, either alone or jointly with any defendant, upon such terms as may be just, or to appear at the trial and to take such part therein as may be just, and generally may make such orders and give such directions as appear to the Court proper for having the rights and liabilities of the parties most conveniently determined and enforced and as to the extent to which the third party is to be bound by any judgment or decision in the action.**

**(5)    Any order made or direction given under this rule may be varied or rescinded by the Court at any time.**

---

## NOTES

### [16.4.1]   Directions for trial of third party dispute

A defendant who issues a third party notice is required to apply to the court for directions: Order 16 rule 4(1). The summons for directions should be served within 7 days of the third party giving notice of intention to defend; otherwise the third party can apply under rule 4(2) to have the third party notice set aside.

Third party directions will normally provide for service of a statement of claim by the defendant on the third party, with consequential directions for service of a defence, for discovery and so forth. Useful references include the form of summons for third party directions in Chitty & Jacob's Queen Bench forms, and the directions given in *Paul Y Management Ltd v Eternal Unity Dev't Ltd & Ors* HCA 571/2007 (A Cheung J; 01.06.2009) (para 32).

Rule 4(3)(b) empowers the court to direct that a third party claim be tried in a particular way. It is within the court's power to direct that there be a separate and subsequent trial of the third party claim. This can save costs in the event that the main claim fails and the third party trial becomes unnecessary. Where such a direction is given, the court may additionally grant leave to the third party to appear at the trial of the main action and oppose to the plaintiff's claim, as in *Wing Mou Construction Co Ltd v Cosmic Insurance Corp Ltd & Anor* HCCT 40/2001 (Ma J; 20.06.2002).

Rule 4(3)(c) empowers the court, at the directions stage, to bring the proceedings under a third party notice to an end. In *Deks Air (HK) Ltd v Freight Management International* HCA 4261/1980 (Commr Litton QC; 19.12.1980) this provision was relied upon in an (unsuccessful) application to strike out a third party notice for failure to disclose any ground of complaint against the third party.

In *Sabstex Trading Corp v Law Sau Kin & Anor* HCA 3215/1986 (Liu J; 25.06.1987) the court held that it was not appropriate to order two separate hearings if the result would be the same evidence having to be taken twice. Instead the appropriate direction is for the evidence given in the action between the plaintiff and the defendant to be taken as evidence in the third party proceedings, with counsel for the third party to have equal right in cross-examination.

### [16.4.2]   Where third party wishes to defend main claim
A third party who wishes to take an active part in defending the main claim against the defendant should seek a direction under rule 4(4) rather than applying to be joined as a defendant: *Wing Mou Construction Co Ltd v Cosmic Insurance Corp Ltd* HCCT 40/2001 (Ma J; 20.06.2002).

**5.     Default of third party, etc.** (O. 16 r. 5)

**(1)   If a third party does not give notice of intention to defend or, having been ordered to serve a defence, fails to do so—**

   **(a)   he shall be deemed to admit any claim stated in the third party notice and shall be bound by any judgment (including judgment by consent) or decision in the action in so far as it is relevant to any claim, question or issue stated in that notice; and**

   **(b)   the defendant by whom the third party notice was issued may, if judgment in default is given against him in the action, at any time after satisfaction of that judgment and, with the leave of the Court, before satisfaction thereof, enter judgment against the third party in respect of any contribution, and, with the leave of the Court, in respect of any other relief or remedy claimed therein.**

**(2)   If a third party or the defendant by whom a third party notice was issued makes default in serving any pleading which he is ordered to serve, the Court may, on the application by summons of that defendant or the third party, as the case may be, order such judgment to be entered for the applicant as he is**

entitled to on the pleadings or may make such other order as may appear to the Court necessary to do justice between the parties.

(3)   The Court may at any time set aside or vary a judgment entered under paragraph (1)(b) or paragraph (2) on such terms (if any) as it thinks just.

---

## NOTES

### [16.5.1]   Default in 3rd party proceedings
Order 16 rule 5 lays out the consequences of default in 3rd party proceedings.

Rule 5(1)(b) provides that where default judgment has been entered against a defendant the court may grant leave for that defendant to enter judgment against a 3rd party. That power applies only where judgment in default has been entered against the defendant – where judgment by some other means, such as summary judgment, has been entered, the court's power to enter judgment against the 3rd party is in rule 7.  See *Premier Fashion Wears Ltd v Li Hing Chung* [1994] 1 HKC 213 (CA).

Rule 5(3) expressly empowers the court to set aside any default judgment entered under the rule.

## 6.     Setting aside third party proceedings (O. 16 r. 6)
Proceedings on a third party notice may, at any stage of the proceedings, be set aside by the Court.

---

## NOTES

### [16.6.1]   Test on application to set aside third party notice
In the Singapore case of *Lee Kuan Yew v Devan Nair* [1993] 1 SLR 723 it was held that the principles applicable on an application to set aside a third party notice are the same as on a strike out application under Order 18 rule 19.  The Singapore rule considered in that case is identical to Order 16 rule 6.

## 7.     Judgment between defendant and third party (O. 16 r. 7)
(1)   Where in any action a defendant has served a third party notice, the Court may at or after the trial of the action or, if the action is decided otherwise than by trial, on an application by summons, order such judgment as the nature of the case may require to be entered for the defendant against the third party or for the third party against the defendant. (L.N. 152 of 2008)

(2)   Where judgment is given for the payment of any contribution or indemnity to a person who is under a liability to make a payment in respect of the same debt or damage, execution shall not issue on the judgment without the leave of the Court until that liability has been discharged.

(3)   For the purpose of paragraph (2)—
"liability" includes liability under a judgment in the same or other proceedings and liability under an agreement to which section 3(4) of the Civil Liability (Contribution) Ordinance (Cap. 377) applies.

---

## NOTES

### [16.7.1]   Power to enter default judgment against 3$^{rd}$ party
The provisions of Order 16 rule 7 are wide enough to permit the entry of default judgment against a third party where summary judgment has already been entered against the defendant: *Premier Fashion Wears Ltd v Li Hing Chung* [1994] 1 HKC 213 (CA).

### [16.7.2]   Locus standi of plaintiff
A plaintiff who has obtained judgment against a defendant has standing on an application concerning a claim by that defendant for indemnity against a third party. See the concurring judgment of Litton JA in *Premier Fashion Wears Ltd v Li Hing Chung* [1994] 1 HKC 213 (CA).

### [16.7.3]   Appeal by third party
A third party may appeal any judgment in favour of the defendant on the third party claim. However leave is required for an appeal by a third party against a judgment awarded in favour of the plaintiff except in the circumstances laid down in *Asphalt & Public Works Ltd v Indemnity Guarantee Trust Ltd* [1969] 1 QB 465, 472F-473B. Those are:
(i)     where the 3$^{rd}$ party is bound by the judgment between the plaintiff and the defendant - see *On Park Parking Ltd v SJ* [2006] 3 HKC 132, 140B-E (CA) where it was held a third party had a right to appeal judgment given in favour of the plaintiff where there had been an order that it be bound by that judgment;
(ii)    Where the 3rd party has been substituted as a defendant; and
(iii)   Where there has been an order enabling the 3$^{rd}$ party to defend.

### [16.7.4]   Costs of third party proceedings
Costs as between a defendant and a third party will normally be awarded in favour of the party who prevails in the third party proceedings. Where the defendant succeeds as against the plaintiff, with the result that the third party succeeds against the defendant, the court will normally order the plaintiff to reimburse the defendant for costs the defendant has to pay the third party. See *Liu Ma Cheung & Ors v Liau Yin Fu & Ors* HCA 181/2004 (Recorder Kwok SC; 21.12.2007), referring to *Johnson v Ribbins* [1977] 1 WLR 1459.

**8.      Claims and issues between a defendant and some other party** (O. 16 r. 8)
     **(1)   Where in any action a defendant who has given notice of intention to defend—**
               **(a)    claims against a person who is already a party to the action any contribution or indemnity; or**
               **(b)    claims against such a person any relief or remedy relating to or connected with the original subject-matter of the action and substantially the same as some relief or remedy claimed by the plaintiff; or**
               **(c)    requires that any question or issue relating to or connected**

with the original subject-matter of the action should be determined not only as between the plaintiff and himself but also as between either or both of them and some other person who is already a party to the action;

then, subject to paragraph (2), the defendant may, without leave, issue and serve on that person a notice containing a statement of the nature and grounds of his claim or, as the case may be, of the question or issue required to be determined.

(2)    Where a defendant makes such a claim as is mentioned in paragraph (1) and that claim could be made by him by counterclaim in the action, paragraph (1) shall not apply in relation to the claim.

(3)    No acknowledgment of service of such a notice shall be necessary if the person on whom it is served has acknowledged service of the writ or originating summons in the action or is a plaintiff therein, and the same procedure shall be adopted for the determination between the defendant by whom, and the person on whom, such a notice is served of the claim, question or issue stated in the notice as would be appropriate under this Order if the person served with the notice were a third party and (where he has given notice of intention to defend the action or is a plaintiff) had given notice of intention to defend the claim, question or issue.

(4)    Rule 4(2) shall have effect in relation to proceedings on a notice issued under this rule as if for the words "7 days after giving notice of intention to defend" there were substituted the words "14 days after service of the notice on him".

---

## NOTES

### [16.8.1]   Contribution notice to be sealed by court

A contribution notice served under this rule must be issued by the registry and must be sealed by the court (see *Keen Lloyd Ltd v Sam Lee Lightering and Transport Co Ltd* [1995] 2 HKC 350).

### [16.8.2]   Effect of settlement of main action

Contribution proceedings under this rule are not affected by settlement as between the plaintiff and defendant of the main claim. The claim for contribution or indemnity may continue without the need to commence a fresh action: see *Lam Chun Lin v Lee Wai Chao & Ors* [1998] 2 HKC 68.

**9.**    **Claims by third and subsequent parties** (O. 16 r. 9)

(1)    Where a defendant has served a third party notice and the third party makes such a claim or requirement as is mentioned in rule 1 or rule 8, this Order shall, with the modification mentioned in paragraph (2) and any other necessary modifications, apply as if the third party were a defendant; and similarly where any further person to whom by virtue of this rule this Order applies as if he were a third party makes such a claim or requirement.

(2)    The modification referred to in paragraph (1) is that paragraph (3)

shall have effect in relation to the issue of a notice under rule 1 by a third party in substitution for rule 1 (2).

(3)  A third party may not issue a notice under rule 1 without the leave of the Court unless the action in question was begun by writ and he issues the notice before the expiration of 14 days after the time limited for acknowledging service of the notice issued against him.

---

## NOTES

### [16.9.1]  Fourth party notice

Order 16 rule 9 provides that a third party may itself issue a third party notice against someone it alleges is ultimately liable. Such a notice is sometimes called a 'fourth party notice' as in *Man Sun Finance Holdings Ltd v Foo Sau Chun Richard & Ors* HCA 1297/2002 (Deputy Judge Saunders; 24.03.2004). A fourth party is itself entitled to the benefit of rule 9, with the result that there is the possibility of a fifth party notice and so on.

**10.    Offer of contribution** (O. 16 r. 10)

(1)  If, at any time after he has acknowledged service, a party to an action who stands to be held liable in the action to another party to contribute towards any debt or damages which may be recovered against that other party in the action, makes (without prejudice to his defence) a written offer to that other party to contribute to a specified extent to the debt or damages, then subject to paragraph (2) and, notwithstanding that he reserves the right to bring the offer to the action of the judge at the trial, the offer shall not be brought to the attention of the judge until after all questions of liability and amount of debt or damages have been decided.

(2)  Where the question of the costs of the issue of liability falls to be decided, that issue having been tried and an issue or question concerning the amount of the debt or damages remaining to be tried separately, any party may bring to the attention of the judge the fact that a written offer under paragraph (1) has or has not been made and the date (but not the amount) of such offer or of the first such offer if more than one.

---

## NOTES

### [16.10.1]  *'Calderbank'* offers as to contribution

Order 16 rule 10 provides that a party who stands to be held liable to contribute to any debt or damages which may be ordered against another party in an action may make a written offer to contribute to a specified extent. The offer is expressly without prejudice to the offeror's defence, meaning that if it is not accepted the offeror is entitled to oppose liability to make any contribution at trial, without the court being informed that it was once prepared to agree to contribute. By virtue of Order 62 rule 5(1)(a) such an offer shall be taken into account by the court when exercising its discretion as to costs. As a result such an offer functions like a *'Calderbank'* offer, as to which see the commentary under Order 62 rule 5(1)(d). If such an offer is not accepted, but the offeree fails to do better by proceeding to trial, the court may award costs from the time the offer ought to have been accepted to the offeror.

**11.    Counterclaim by defendant** (O. 16 r. 11)

**Where in any action a counterclaim is made by a defendant, the foregoing provisions of this Order shall apply in relation to the counterclaim as if the subject-matter of the counterclaim were the original subject-matter of the action, and as if the person making the counterclaim were the plaintiff and the person against whom it is made a defendant.**

## ORDER 17

### INTERPLEADER

1.  **Entitlement to relief by way of interpleader** (O. 17 r. 1)
    **(1)  Where—**
    - **(a)    a person is under a liability in respect of a debt or in respect of any money, goods or chattels and he is, or expects to be, sued for or in respect of that debt or money or those goods or chattels by two or more persons making adverse claims thereto, or**
    - **(b)    claim is made to any money, goods or chattels taken or intended to be taken by a bailiff in execution under any process, or to the proceeds or value of any such goods or chattels, by a person other than the person against whom the process is issued,**

**the person under liability as mentioned in sub-paragraph (a), or (subject to rule 2) the bailiff, may apply to the Court for relief by way of interpleader.**

**(2)    References in this Order to a bailiff shall be construed as including references to any other officer charged with the execution of process by or under the authority of the Court of First Instance.**

---

## NOTES

### [17.1.1]    Relief by way of interpleader

Relief by way of interpleader enables the holder of property claimed by others to stay out of the dispute between the others. The basic principles were set out concisely in *China Dragon Int'l Ltd v Pang Hong & Anor* [2007] 2 HKC 514 (para 29):

(1)    Where 2 or more persons claim the same thing or fund, the holder of the thing or fund does not claim any interest in the property, and not knowing to which of the claimants he ought to deliver the property, and he is sued or fears that he may be sued by some of them, he may apply for interpleader relief against the claimants.

(2)    The relief is discretionary and it will not be granted unless there appears to be some real foundation that the applicant may be sued.

(3)    The applicant does not in any manner collude with any claimant, or has not voluntarily put himself into the situation from which he calls on the court to extricate him.

(4)    He is ready to bring into court, or to pay or dispose of the subject matter of the action in such manner as the court may direct.

See also *Unionix Dev't Ltd v Roe Investment Ltd & Anor* [1999] 1 HKC 593, 601I (CA) (appealed to the CFA – see *Roe Investment Ltd & Anor v Prince Good Ltd & Anor* [2000] 1 HKC 548).

### [17.1.2]   Meaning of 'chattels'

In *Roe Investment Ltd v Prince Goods Ltd & Ors* [1998] 4 HKC 338 it was held at first instance that shares in a company are 'chattels' within the meaning of Order 17 rule 1(1)(a). As a result relief by way of interpleader could be granted. When that decision came under scrutiny of the Court of Final Appeal (see [2000] 1 HKC 548) it was held that interpleader was not appropriate in the circumstances of the case because there had not been adverse claims by two or more parties to the company shares (per Litton PJ at 555E). In coming to that conclusion the CFA did not interfere with the first instance decision as to the meaning of the word 'chattels' in this rule.

### [17.1.3]   Meaning of 'expects to be sued'

In order to seek relief by way of interpleader a person must have been sued or expect to be sued by two or more persons making adverse claims: Order 17 rule 1(1)(a). In this context 'expects to be sued' is not to be construed subjectively – there must be a 'real foundation' for the expectation: *Bank of America v Oxford Properties & Finance Ltd & Ors* HCA 8540/1984 & 1817/1985 (Mortimer J; 26.09.1985); *NYK (HK) Ltd v Wilford Ltd* [1997] 3 HKC 127 (CA). There can be no real foundation for any expectation to be sued 'unless a prima facie case exists': *Chan King Sheen v KC Tsang & Co & Ors* [2002] 3 HKC 209 (CA), per Le Pichon JA at 221I. However, the competing claims need not co-exist in the sense of being actively pursued at the same time: *Bank of America* (above).

### [17.1.4]   Costs

The court has a general discretion as to the costs of an application for relief by way of interpleader: see Order 17 rule 8 and the commentary thereunder.

**2.     Claim to goods, etc., taken in execution** (O. 17 r. 2)

**(1)   Any person making a claim to or in respect of any money, goods or chattels taken or intended to be taken in execution under process of the Court, or to the proceeds or value of any such goods or chattels, must give notice of his claim to the bailiff charged with the execution of the process and must include in his notice a statement of his address, and that address shall be his address for service.**

**(2)   On receipt of a claim made under this rule the bailiff must forthwith give notice thereof to the execution creditor and the execution creditor must, within 7 days after receiving the notice, give notice to the bailiff informing him whether he admits or disputes the claim.**

**An execution creditor who gives notice in accordance with this paragraph admitting a claim shall only be liable to the bailiff for any fees and expenses incurred by the bailiff before receipt of that notice.**

**(3)   Where—**

    **(a)   the bailiff receives a notice from an execution creditor under paragraph (2) disputing a claim, or the execution creditor fails, within the period mentioned in that paragraph, to give the required notice, and**

    **(b)   the claim made under this rule is not withdrawn, the bailiff may apply to the Court for relief under this Order.**

(4)   A bailiff who receives a notice from an execution creditor under paragraph (2) admitting a claim made under this rule shall withdraw from possession of the money, goods or chattels claimed and may apply to the Court for relief under this Order of the following kind, that is to say, an order restraining the bringing of an action against him for or in respect of his having taken possession of that money or those goods or chattels.

3.    Mode of application (O. 17 r. 3)

(1)   An application for relief under this Order may be made by originating summons unless made in a pending action, in which case it must be made by summons in the action. (L.N. 152 of 2008)

(2)   Where the applicant is a bailiff who has withdrawn from possession of money, goods or chattels taken in execution and who is applying for relief under rule 2(4), the summons must be served on any person who made a claim under that rule to or in respect of that money or those goods or chattels, and that person may attend the hearing of the application.

(3)   An originating summons under this rule shall be in Form No. 10 in Appendix A.

(4)   Subject to paragraph (5), a summons under this rule must be supported by evidence that the applicant—

    (a)   claims no interest in the subject-matter in dispute other than for charges or costs,

    (b)   does not collude with any of the claimants to that subject-matter, and

    (c)   is willing to pay or transfer that subject-matter into court or to dispose of it as the Court may direct.

(5)   Where the applicant is a bailiff, he shall not provide such evidence as is referred to in paragraph (4) unless directed by the Court to do so.

(6)   Any person who makes a claim under rule 2 and who is served with a summons under this rule shall within 14 days serve on the execution creditor and the bailiff an affidavit specifying any money and describing any goods and chattels claimed and setting out the grounds upon which such claim is based.

(7)   Where the applicant is a bailiff a summons under this rule must give notice of the requirement in paragraph (6).

---

## NOTES

### [17.3.1]   Mode of application for relief by way of interpleader

Order 17 rule 3(1) provides that an application for relief by way of interpleader should be made by originating summons or by *inter partes* summons in pending proceedings.

In *Bank of America v Oxford Properties & Finance Ltd & Ors* HCA 8540/1984 and HCA 1817/1985 (Mortimer J; 26.09.1985) it was held that an interpleader application had wrongly been brought by summons in pending proceedings. The issue giving rise to the interpleader application was who was entitled to payment of rent, but that issue would not necessarily be resolved in the pending proceedings.

**[17.3.2] Hearing of application**

An interpleader summons will not normally be listed on the three-minute list. However, this will be possible where there is likely to be agreement as to the form of Order.

**[17.3.3] Order 17 rule 3(4)(b) – meaning of 'collusion'**

A party seeking relief by way of interpleader is required to demonstrate in its evidence that it does not 'collude' with any of the claimants to the property in dispute: see Order 17 rule 3(4)(b). It is intended that the party seeking relief be 'in a real position of impartiality' between the claimants to the property: *Chan King Sheen v KC Tsang & Co & Ors* [2002] 3 HKC 209 (CA), per Le Pichon JA at 220H–I, citing *Murietta v South American etc Co Ltd* (1893) 62 LJQB 396, 397. Collusion in this context is an equivalent for 'playing the game' and does not necessarily involve anything morally wrong (*Chan King Sheen*) or 'connote anything sinister' (*Famous Zone Electronics Ltd v Hongkong and Shanghai Banking Corporation Ltd & Anor* [1998] 3 HKC 723, 727F–G).

In *Chan King Sheen* the Court of Appeal found there was abundant evidence of collusion when the conduct of the party (a firm of solicitors) was viewed against the backdrop of family connections which made it obvious there was a lack of impartiality.

In the *Famous Zone* case the court was not satisfied that the bank claiming relief had not colluded with one of the parties when it had transferred money from one party's account to another's. It was suggested that the bank was asking the court to help it by getting the other parties to litigate a different question to that which applied to it and the application for interpleader was dismissed.

**5.      Powers of Court hearing summons** (O. 17 r. 5)

    **(1)    Where on the hearing of a summons under this Order all the persons by whom adverse claims to the subject-matter in dispute (hereafter in this Order referred to as "the claimants") appear, the Court may order—**

        **(a)    that any claimant be made a defendant in any action pending with respect to the subject-matter in dispute in substitution for or in addition to the applicant for relief under this Order, or**

        **(b)    that an issue between the claimants be stated and tried and may direct which of the claimants is to be plaintiff and which defendant.**

    **(2)    Where—**

        **(a)    the applicant on a summons under this Order is a bailiff, or**

        **(b)    all the claimants consent or any of them so requests, or**

        **(c)    the question at issue between the claimants is a question of law and the facts are not in dispute,**

**the Court may summarily determine the question at issue between the claimants and make an order accordingly on such terms as may be just.**

    **(3)    Where a claimant, having been duly served with a summons for relief under this Order, does not appear on the hearing of the summons or, having appeared, fails or refuses to comply with an order made in the proceedings, the Court may make an order declaring the claimant, and all persons claiming under him, forever barred from prosecuting his claim against the applicant for such relief and all persons claiming under him, but such an**

**order shall not affect the rights of the claimants as between themselves.**

---

NOTES

**[17.5.1]  Mode of resolution of interpleader dispute**
Order 17 rule 5 provides, *inter alia*, for the court to determine the mode by which any issue between claimants in interpleader proceedings will be resolved. The court may order that an issue be stated and tried (Order 17 rule 5(1)(b)); alternatively summary determination is possible (Order 17 rule 5(2)). In *Bank of America v Oxford Properties & Finance Ltd*, HCA 8540/1984 and 1817/1985 (Mortimer J; 26.09.1985) the court indicated a reluctance to order summary determination where it was possible evidence would have to be adduced.

**[17.5.2]  Leave to appeal against summary determination**
Where a question arising in interpleader proceedings is summarily determined by a judge under rule 5(2)(b) or (c), the judge's decision is deemed to be final unless leave to appeal to the Court of Appeal is granted. See Order 58 rule 7. The rule does not apply to decisions by masters.

**6.      Power to order sale of goods taken in execution** (O. 17 r. 6)
**Where an application for relief under this Order is made by a bailiff who has taken possession of any goods or chattels in execution under any process, and a claimant alleges that he is entitled, under a bill of sale or otherwise, to the goods or chattels by way of security for debt, the Court may order those goods or chattels or any part thereof to be sold and may direct that the proceeds of sale be applied in such manner and on such terms as may be just and as may be specified in the order.**

**7.      Power to stay proceedings** (O. 17 r. 7)
**Where a defendant to an action applies for relief under this Order in the action, the Court may by order stay all further proceedings in the action.**

**8.      Other powers** (O. 17 r. 8)
**Subject to the foregoing rules of this Order, the Court may in or for the purposes of any interpleader proceedings make such order as to costs or any other matter as it thinks just.**

---

NOTES

**[17.8.1]  Power of the court**
The powers of the court under Order 17 rule 8 'are wide and may be exercised notwithstanding that the order may interfere with property rights': *Leung Ho Yiu t/a Kent Long Trading Co v Winner Godown Ltd* [1994] 1 HKC 503, 505B–C.

**[17.8.2]  Costs**
The party interpleading ('the custodian') will normally be protected as to costs

where it has not acted wrongly or improperly in any way. Payment of those costs may be ordered to be a first charge on the property interpleaded: see *Leung Ho Yiu t/a Kent Long Trading Co v Winner Godown Ltd* [1994] 1 HKC 503D–G. In *Roe Investment Ltd v Prince Good Ltd* [2000] 1 HKC 548 the Court of Final Appeal held that the party which had commenced the interpleader proceedings should be denied its costs. The CFA found that the proceedings were not properly constituted under Order 17 rule 1 because the subject property (shares in a company) was not in fact subject to competing claims from other parties.

In *DLA Piper Hong Kong (a firm) v China Ppty Dev't (Holdings) Ltd* [2010] 1 HKLRD 903 (CA), where the custodian was denied interpleader relief on the ground that one of the claimants had no *prima facie* case, the court ordered the custodian to pay the successful party's costs, those costs to be indemnified by the unsuccessful claimant. In a subsequent decision in the *DLA* litigation (CACV 142/2009; 25.01.2010) the custodian was also allowed its own costs against the unsuccessful claimant.

### [17.8.3] Security for costs of interpleader proceedings
The court has power to order security for costs of interpleader proceedings against the party who is the "attacker" or true plaintiff: *Buxbaum LLP v Samuel-Rozenbaum Diamond Ltd & Ors* [2003] 1 HKLRD 600, 606.

**9.**      **One order in several causes or matters** (O. 17 r. 9)
     **Where the Court considers it necessary or expedient to make an order in any interpleader proceedings in several causes or matters pending before the Court, the Court may make such an order; and the order shall be entitled in all those causes or matters and shall be binding on all the parties to them.**

**10.**      **Discovery** (O. 17 r. 10)
     **Orders 24 and 26 shall, with the necessary modifications, apply in relation to an interpleader issue as they apply in relation to any other cause or matter.**

**11.**      **Trial of interpleader issue** (O. 17 r. 11)
     **(1)    Order 35 shall, with the necessary modifications, apply to the trial of an interpleader issue as it applies to the trial of an action.**
     **(2)    The Court by whom an interpleader issue is tried may give such judgment or make such order as finally to dispose of all questions arising in the interpleader proceedings. (Enacted 1988)**

---

## NOTES

### [17.11.1]    Application for directions after final disposition of interpleader summons
After an interpleader summons has been determined the court is *functus* so far as the disposal of the subject matter of the summons is concerned. There is no power to give directions other than as to the implementation or manner of carrying out the order. See *George YC Mok & Co v Tang Kwong Ming & Anor* [2000] 3 HKC 445

where Deputy Judge Carlye Chu refused an application by a firm of solicitors which had obtained an order for distribution of funds held by it and later sought a direction that it be permitted to apply part of the funds to costs owing to it.

**[17.11.2]  Appeal**

See Order 58 rule 7 for the provisions governing appeals from decisions of a judge in interpleader proceedings.

## ORDER 18

### PLEADINGS

1.    **Service of statement of claim** (O. 18 r. 1)
      **Unless the Court gives leave to the contrary or a statement of claim is indorsed on the writ, the plaintiff must serve a statement of claim on the defendant or, if there are two or more defendants, on each defendant, and must do so either when the writ is served on that defendant or at any time after service of the writ but before the expiration of 14 days after that defendant gives notice of intention
to defend.**

---

## NOTES

### [18.1.1]    When statement of claim required
Order 18 rule 1 provides for service of a statement of claim in cases where the writ of summons has been generally indorsed under Order 6 rule 2, and notice of intention to defend is subsequently given. If notice of intention to defend is not given, the plaintiff may enter default judgment under Order 13 without incurring the cost of setting out its claim with the precision required in a formal statement of claim.

The court may, under Order 18 rule 1, give leave to dispense with service of a statement of claim. Such leave will be appropriate in cases which may be tried without pleadings and an order to that effect is made under Order 18 rule 21.

### [18.1.2]    Time for service of statement of claim
The plaintiff is required by Order 18 rule 1 to serve a full statement of claim within 14 days of the defendant giving notice of intention to defend. Time may be extended under Order 3 rule 5 by agreement or by order of the court. Extension of time may be granted under Order 3 rule 5 even where application is not made until after expiration of the 14 day time limit, and even after the limitation period has expired: *Walker v Howard* [1997] TLR (13.11.1997) (CA).

### [18.1.3]    Manner of service of statement of claim
When a defendant gives notice of intention to defend, it is required to give an address for service. See form 14 in appendix A to these rules. Subsequent documents, including the statement of claim, may be served by 'ordinary service' (by hand, post or DX) pursuant to Order 65 rule 5. Personal service is not required.

### [18.1.4]    Failure to serve statement of claim
If a plaintiff fails to serve a statement of claim, the defendant may apply under Order 19 rule 1 for an order dismissing the action. In some cases it may be appropriate to rely on the power under Order 18 rule 19(1)(d) to strike out for abuse of process on the ground that the plaintiff has no intention to proceed to trial. Alternatively, after lapse of time, the plaintiff may apply to dismiss for want of prosecution, as to which see the commentary under Order 34 rule 2.

**[18.1.5]   Filing of statement of claim**

A statement of claim served under Order 18 rule 1 must be filed in court within the same time limit: Order 18 rule 5A.

**2.      Service of defence (O. 18 r. 2)**

**(1)   Subject to paragraphs (2) and (3), a defendant who gives notice of intention to defend an action must, unless the Court gives leave to the contrary, serve a defence on every other party to the action who may be affected thereby before the expiration of 28 days after the time limited for acknowledging service of the writ or after the statement of claim is served on him, whichever is the later. (L.N. 383 of 1996) (L.N. 152 of 2008)**

**(2)   If a summons under Order 14, rule 1, or under Order 86, rule 1, is served on a defendant before he serves his defence, paragraph (1) shall not have effect in relation to him unless by the order made on the summons he is given leave to defend the action and, in that case, shall have effect as if it required him to serve his defence within 28 days after the making of the order or within such other period as may be specified therein. (L.N. 152 of 2008)**

**(3)   Where an application is made by a defendant under Order 12, rule 8(1) or (2), paragraph (1) shall not have effect in relation to him unless the application is dismissed or no order is made on the application and, in that case, shall have effect as if it required him to serve his defence within 28 days after the final determination of the application or within such other period as may be specified by the Court. (L.N. 383 of 1996) (L.N. 152 of 2008)**

---

**NOTES**

**[18.2.1]   Time for service of defence**

Order 18 rule 2 requires a defendant to serve a defence within 28 days of the time limited for giving notice of intention to defend (see Order 12) or within 28 days of service of the statement of claim, whichever is later. In practical terms this means:

(a)      a defendant may give notice of intention to defend immediately, without thereby shortening the time within which he must serve his defence; and

(b)      where the writ is generally indorsed under Order 6 rule (2)(1)(a) with a concise statement short of a full statement of claim the 28-day period for service of a defence does not begin to run until the full statement of claim has been served.

Where the plaintiff issues a summons for summary judgment under Order 14 or Order 86 before the defence has been served, the time for service of the defence is suspended until further order: Order 18 rule 2(2). Similarly, rule 2(3) provides that where a defendant applies under Order 12 rule 8 disputing the jurisdiction of the court, time for service of the defence is suspended.

Prior to the amendment of rule 2 with effect from 2009, the period for service of a defence was only 14 days. The increase to 28 days was recommended in the final report of the Chief Justice's working party on civil justice reform (para 244) because more time would be required on implementation of the reforms for defendants to deal substantively with the plaintiff's allegations and verify the case with a statement of truth. It was suggested that without the increase there would be more applications for extension of time, adding to costs.

The lengthened period does not apply to certain proceedings which were underway when the amendment came into force: see the transitional provision in Order 18 rule 24.

### [18.2.2] Filing of defence
Although Order 18 rule 2 refers only to service of a defence, the practice in Hong Kong is to file the defence in court as well. See Order 18 rule 5A which provides that pleadings shall be filed in court within the time limited for service of the same.

### [18.2.3] Multiple defendants – severance of defences
Where more than one defendant is named in a writ and their interests are identical they may file and serve a common defence. However, separate or 'severed' defences will be required in other cases, in particular where one defendant seeks to shift liability to another.

### [18.2.4] Extension of time for filing and service of defence
The court's general discretion to order an extension of time under Order 3 rule 5 extends to the filing and service of a defence. The power may be exercised even where the application is not brought until after expiration of time. See the commentary under Order 3 rule 5.

The issue of a summons seeking an extension of time to file and serve a defence does not stop the time from running. If the time has already expired, and notice has been given pursuant to Order 19 rule 8A, it is open to the plaintiff to enter default judgment pending the hearing of the summons. See *Schindler Lifts (HK) Ltd v Ocean Joy Investments Ltd* [2002] 1 HKLRD 279 (para 10); *Stevenson, Wong & Co (a firm) v Goldsense Technology Ltd* [2007] 1 HKLRD 217 (para 16). Such a default judgment is not irregular and is not liable to be set aside save on the usual principles: see the commentary under Order 19 rule 9. Likewise time continues to run pending an application for transfer to the District Court, meaning that the defendant is not relieved of its obligation to serve a defence unless an express stay is ordered: *Tai Chao Cheng v Cheung Chun* HCA 770/2003 (Recorder Jat SC; 19.04.2004) (para 23).

**3.    Service of reply and defence to counterclaim** (O. 18 r. 3)

   **(1)   A plaintiff on whom a defendant serves a defence must serve a reply on that defendant if it is needed for compliance with rule 8; and if no reply is served, rule 14(1) will apply.**

   **(2)   A plaintiff on whom a defendant serves a counterclaim must, if he intends to defend it, serve on that defendant a defence to counterclaim.**

   **(3)   Where a plaintiff serves both a reply and a defence to counterclaim on any defendant, he must include them in the same document.**

   **(4)   A reply to any defence must be served by the plaintiff before the expiration of 28 days after the service on him of that defence, and a defence to counterclaim must be served by the plaintiff before the expiration of 28 days after the service on him of the counterclaim to which it relates. (L.N. 152 of 2008)**

**NOTES**

**[18.3.1]  Where reply or defence to counterclaim must be served**
Order 18 rule 3 deals with the circumstances in which the plaintiff may respond to
the defendant's pleading.

It is not necessary for the plaintiff to respond to the defendant's defence in most
cases because Order 18 rule 14 deems there to be joinder of issue in the absence of a
response. Non-admission of the defence is deemed by that rule. However, if the
plaintiff intends at trial to challenge any part of the defence with an allegation which
is of the type which must be pleaded under Order 18 rule 8, then he must respond
with a 'reply': Order 18 rule 3(1). Furthermore, if the defendant has counterclaimed,
the plaintiff must serve a defence to counterclaim if he intends to defend the same:
Order 18 rule 3(2).

A reply is the plaintiff's response to the defence. It should not be used to plead a
new cause of action. Amendment of the statement of claim is the appropriate way to
introduce a new cause of action. See *First Laser Ltd v Fujian Enterprises Holdings
Co Ltd & Anor* CACV 126/2008 (Cheung, Yeung & Yuen JJA; 08.07.2010) (para
8.1-8.3). That enables the defendant to seek leave to amend its defence so as to
defend the new claim.

**[18.3.2]  Time for serving reply or defence to counterclaim**
Order 18 rule 3 was amended with effect from 2009 as part of the civil justice
reforms to extend the time for serving a reply or defence to counterclaim from 14
days to 28 days. This is in line with the increase of the time under rule 2 for service
of a defence, implemented at the same time. See the commentary under that rule. As
is the case with rule 2, the lengthened period under rule 3 does not apply to some
proceedings which were underway at the time the amendment came into force: see
the transitional provision in Order 18 rule 24.

**4.      Pleadings subsequent to reply** (O. 18 r. 4)
**No pleading subsequent to a reply or a defence to counterclaim shall be
served except with the leave of the Court.**

**NOTES**

**[18.4.1]  Leave to serve subsequent pleadings**
At one time pleadings commonly continued for round after round. Nowadays
Order 18 rule 20 deems them to close no later than 14 days after service of the
Reply and/or Defence to Counterclaim, if any. Order 18 rule 4 requires leave for
any subsequent pleading. Leave will not be granted unless there is a real need for
the subsequent pleading. In *First Laser Ltd v Fujian Enterprises Holdings Co Ltd
& Anor* CACV 126/2008 (Cheung, Yeung & Yuen JJA; 08.07.2010) (para 8.7) the
court considered that it would be appropriate to grant leave to a defendant to serve
a rejoinder pleading a point of foreign law in response to the plaintiff's reply. This
was appropriate because foreign law is a matter which must be specifically

pleaded under Order 18 rule 8.Where there is a split trial, rule 4 may be used to enable the parties to refine issues on quantum following trial on liability, but any such subsequent pleading may not make claims outside the scope of the indorsement of claim and statement of claim: *Magic Score Ltd v Hongkong & Shanghai Banking Corporation Ltd* HCA 11077/1994 (Lam J; 23.06.2006).

**5.      Service of pleadings in Summer Vacation** (O. 18 r. 5)
**Pleadings or amended pleadings shall not be served during the Summer Vacation, except with the leave of the Court or with the consent of all the parties to the action.**

---

**NOTES**

**[18.5.1]   Effect of Order 18 rule 5**
By virtue of Order 18 rule 5 pleadings are not to be served during the court's summer vacation, which is the month of August. The rule should be read together with Order 3 rule 3 and section 31 of the High Court Ordinance by which the running of time during the month of August is suspended.

The English equivalent of Order 18 rule 5 was repealed in 1990 along with companion legal provisions there suspending the running of time during the court vacation in that jurisdiction.

**(HK)5A.  Filing of pleadings and originating process** (O. 18 r. 5A)
**(1)      Subject to Order 3, rule 5(3) and subject to the provisions of this rule, every pleading and originating process shall be filed in the Registry within the time during which that pleading or originating process may be served by him on any other party.**
**(2)      A party may apply to the court for further time to file a pleading or originating process on a summons stating the further time required.**
**(3)      If a party fails to file a pleading or originating process within the time allowed under paragraph (1) or further time allowed under paragraph (2), he shall not be at liberty to file that pleading or originating process without the leave of the Court.**

---

**NOTES**

**[18.5A.1]   Comparison with English rules**
Order 18 rule 5A had no counterpart in the previous English Supreme Court Rules. Unlike Hong Kong, it was not necessary to file pleadings in England. The Civil Procedure Rules 1998 introduced the filing requirement in England. See for example CPR 7.4 and 15.2.

**6.      Pleadings: formal requirements** (O. 18 r. 6)
**(1)      Every pleading in an action must bear on its face—**
**(a)      the year in which the writ in the action was issued and the number of the action,**
**(b)      the title of the action,**

(d)    the description of the pleading, and

(e)    the date on which it was served.

(2)    Every pleading must, if necessary, be divided into paragraphs numbered consecutively, each allegation being so far as convenient contained in a separate paragraph.

(3)    Dates, sums and other numbers must be expressed in a pleading in figures and not in words.

(4)    Every pleading must be indorsed—

(a)    where the party sues or defends in person, with his name and address;

(b)    in any other case, with the name or firm and business address of the solicitor by whom it was served, and also (if the solicitor is the agent of another) the name or firm and business address of his principal.

(5)    Every pleading must be signed by counsel, if settled by him, and, if not, by the party's solicitor or by the party, if he sues or defends in person.

---

## NOTES

### [18.6.1]    Practice direction 19.1 – formal requirements of pleadings

Part I of practice direction 19.1, in effect since 01.02.1999 stipulates, pursuant to Order 18 rule 6, that pleadings which are required to be served must, when presented for filing in the High Court Registry, bear the date or dates on which served. The full text of the practice direction can be viewed on the judiciary's website, www.judiciary.gov.hk, or that of the Hong Kong Legal Information Institute www.hklii.org, both of which are accessible by the general public free-of-charge.

### [18.6.2]    Rule 6(5) – pleadings must be signed

The requirement of Order 18 rule 6(5) that every pleading be signed by counsel or solicitor, or by the party if in person, is not to be read literally. In *Max Share Ltd & Anor v Ng Yat Chi (No 1)* [1998] 1 HKC 123 the Court of Final Appeal dismissed an application to set aside a party's Case which appeared not to have been signed in accordance with the equivalent rule in the CFA Rules, referring to the following authorities:

- *London County Council v Agricultural Food Products Ltd* [1955] 2 QB 218 where it was said 'at common law a person sufficiently signs a document if it is signed in his name with his authority by somebody else'.
- *R v Kent Justices* (1873) LR 8 QB 305 – where a statute requires that a document be signed it is a question of construction whether the statute displaces the common law rule and 'makes a personal signature indispensable'.
- *Goodman v J Eban Ltd* [1954] 1 QB 550 – where a rubber stamp facsimile signature was considered sufficient.

The CFA considered the common practice of printing counsel's name at the end of a pleading to be acceptable.

### [18.6.3]   Language of pleadings

Pleadings may be in either Chinese or English: Basic Law, art 9; High Court Civil Procedure (Use of Language) Rules (Cap 5), r 4. However, a pleading should not be written in a mixture of the two languages: if in an English pleading it is necessary to include Chinese words, such as allegedly defamatory words spoken in Chinese, an English translation should be provided. See *Cheung Kong (Holdings) Ltd v Chan Wai Yip Albert* [2000] 4 HKC 591, approved by the Court of Appeal in *Chan Kong v Chan Li Chai Medical Factory (HK) Ltd* [2009] 2 HKLRD 455 (para 21).

**7.     Facts, not evidence, to be pleaded** (O. 18 r. 7)

**(1)   Subject to the provisions of this rule and rules 7A, 10, 11 and 12, every pleading must contain, and contain only, a statement in a summary form of the material facts on which the party pleading relies for his claim or defence, as the case may be, but not the evidence by which those facts are to be proved, and the statement must be as brief as the nature of the case admits.**

**(2)   Without prejudice to paragraph (1), the effect of any document or the purport of any conversation referred to in the pleading must, if material, be briefly stated, and the precise words of the document or conversation must not be stated, except in so far as those words are themselves material.**

**(3)   A party need not plead any fact if it is presumed by law to be true or the burden of disproving it lies on the other party, unless the other party has specifically denied it in his pleading.**

**(4)   A statement that a thing has been done or that an event has occurred, being a thing or event the doing or occurrence of which, as the case may be, constitutes a condition precedent necessary for the case of a party is to be implied in his pleading.**

---

## NOTES

### [18.7.1]   The general rules of pleading

The general rules of pleading are found in Order 18 rule 7 and elsewhere in Order 18. They may be stated as follows:

(1)   *Plead facts, not conclusions of law* – Order 18 rule 7 requires a pleader to confine himself to allegations of fact. It is not appropriate to plead the conclusion of law which it is hoped the court will draw therefrom. See *Philipps v Philipps* (1878) 4 QBD 127; and see *Yeung Wah James v Alfa Sea Ltd* [1993] 1 HKC 440, citing *Drane v Evangelous* [1978] 1 WLR 455 where Lord Denning MR said, at 458:

> It is sufficient for the pleader to state the material facts. He need not state the legal result. If, for convenience, he does so, he is not bound by, or limited to, what he has stated. He can present, in argument, any legal consequence of which the facts permit.

In *Re Vandervell's Trusts No 2* [1974] 3 WLR 257 it was held that in a trust case it was sufficient to plead that one person gave property to another to hold for the former's benefit; it was not necessary to plead a 'trust'. In *NW Salt Co Ltd v Electrolytic Alkali Co Ltd* [1913] 3 KB 422 it was held unnecessary for a pleading to allege that a contract was 'illegal' – illegality was merely the consequence of the pleaded restraint of trade. In *Middlesex County Council v Nathan* [1937] 2 KB 272 it was held that an allegation to the effect that X was 'legally liable' to support Y was a pleading of a conclusion of law and not one of fact.

Note, however, that under Order 18 rule 11 a pleader may raise a point of law. This permits a pleader to raise, for example, a defence under the Limitation Ordinance. See the commentary under that rule.

(2) *Plead facts, not evidence* – Order 18 rule 7 expressly provides that a pleading should not set out the evidence by which the alleged facts are to be proved. In this connection see *Davy v Garrett* (1878) 7 Ch D 473 and see *Lumb v Beaumont* (1884) 49 LT 772 where it was held that it is incorrect to plead the opposing party's admissions. See also *GE v Simplex-GE Ltd* [1971] FSR 106; [1971] RPC 351. In *Total Lubricants HK Ltd & Ors v de Chanterac & Ors* HCA 1694/2008 (Poon J; 15.12.2009) the court struck out pleas of inferences which were admitted to be evidence, which 'littered' a statement of claim.

(3) *All the material facts must be pleaded* - 'Material' facts for the purpose of rule 7(1) means the facts 'necessary for the purpose of formulating a complete cause of action': *Bruce v Odhams Press Ltd* [1936] 1 All ER 287, 294 (CA). There it was held that if any one material allegation is omitted, the statement of claim is bad. This is because evidence will not be admitted at trial to prove an allegation which has not been pleaded; therefore, if there is no allegation of an essential element of the cause of action, the claim cannot succeed: *Waghorn v George Wimpey & Co Ltd* [1969] 1 WLR 1764. Likewise a defendant who wishes to put forward a positive defence (as opposed to simply putting the plaintiff to proof) should plead all the facts relied on. Failure to do so, resulting in the plaintiff being taken by surprise at trial, may result in the need for a last minute amendment with costs consequences. See *Davie v New Merton Board Mills Ltd* [1956] 1 WLR 233.

**[18.7.2]   What pleadings should do**
A useful *précis* of the law and practice relating to pleadings can be found in the judgment of Bokhary JA in *Aktieselskabet Dansk Skibsfinansiering v Wheelock Marden* [1994] 2 HKC 264 (CA) at 269E–270E. The learned judge said:

> Our procedure aims to ensure that litigation, particularly the trial itself, is conducted fairly, openly, free from surprise, and without unnecessary delay or expense. In the attainment of that objective, pleadings have a fundamental role to play. Accordingly, there are a number of things which pleadings should do. Ideally, they would do them from the outset. In any event, they must do them by the time they have been properly particularized – whether particularized on the pleader's own initiative, upon the other side's request, or pursuant to the court's order.
>
> What those things are is to be gathered from the decided cases. That exercise has been performed by the learned editors of the 1993 *Supreme Court Practice*. And, as one sees from the note 18/12/2 at pp 307–308 of Vol 1 thereof, the things which properly particularized pleadings must do are to:
>
> (1)   inform the other side of the nature of the case they have to meet as distinguished from the mode in which that case is to be proved;
>
> (2)   prevent the other side from being taken by surprise at the trial;

(3)     enable the other side to know what evidence they ought to be prepared with and to prepare for trial;

(4)     limit the generality of the pleadings, the claim and the evidence;

(5)     limit and define the issues to be tried, and as to which discovery is required; and the hands of the party so that he cannot without leave go into any matters not included (although if the opponent omits to ask for particulars, evidence may be given which supports any material allegation in the pleadings).

*... and especially where fraud is alleged*
To the generality of the foregoing must be added the special rule that allegations of fraud must be pleaded distinctly and with the utmost particularity. The word 'distinctly' is the one used by Thesiger LJ in his well-known statement in *Davy v Garrett* (1878) 7 Ch D 473 at p 489 as to how fraud is to be pleaded. And the expression 'utmost particularity', as one sees from note 18/8/8 at p 297 of Vol 1 of the *1993 Supreme Court Practice*, is the one chosen by its learned editors and has the authority of their combined experience. That special rule arises in this case.

*Never before as much as now*
None of the basic rules of pleading have anything to do with technicality. All of them have everything to do with practical justice. They have always been of importance. Never before as much as now. For these days, there are more and more cases so vast and so complex that they push practically to its limit our system's capacity effectively to cope with them. Any laxity in their proper management, whether in regard to pleadings or anything else, can all too easily result in such cases spinning into confusion if not chaos — even before trial but especially at trial. The present case, for the trial of which half a year has been reserved, is such a case.

## [18.7.3]   Pleading in the alternative
See Order 18 rule 12A.

## [18.7.4]   A party is bound by his pleadings
Subject to the court's broad power to allow amendment of pleadings (as to which, see Order 20) a party is bound by what he has pleaded. Evidence outside the scope of what has been pleaded will not be relevant and hence not admissible at trial. Nor can the court find liability on a basis other than that pleaded, unless the opposing party has had a full opportunity to deal with it: *Poon Hau Kei v Hsin Cheong Construction Co Ltd* [2003] 2 HKC 408 (CA). In the same case, on further appeal to the Court of Final Appeal (see [2004] 2 HKC 235), these points were not doubted. However, the Court of Final Appeal allowed the appeal since, although the plaintiff had not pleaded the scenario which was found as fact by the trial judge, the defendant had done so. There had been cross-examination on the scenario as found by the trial judge. The court held that in result there was no unfairness in allowing the plaintiff to succeed on the scenario not pleaded by him.

## [18.7.5]   Pleading content of document or conversation – Order 18 rule 7(2)
Order 18 rule 7(2) provides, in effect, that it is not usually necessary to plead the complete words of a document or conversation relied upon. The 'effect' of a document or the 'purport' of a conversation must be stated, but the precise words need not be, unless material. Where there is a dispute as to the meaning of words in a document those words are material and should be set out: *Darbyshire & Ors v Leigh & Anor*

[1896] 1 QB 554. Likewise, in a defamation action the actual language used should be pleaded: see Order 82 rule 3 and the commentary thereunder.

### [18.7.6]   Occurrence of condition precedent implied in pleading – Order 18 rule 7(4)

Order 18 rule 7(4) provides that a condition precedent 'necessary for the case of a party', is implied in the party's pleading. Thus notice of termination of a lease may be implied in a pleading claiming relief for failure to deliver vacant possession upon expiration of the lease: *Treasure Rock Dev't Ltd v Splendid Duesseldorf Production Ltd* [1996] 1 HKC 86. The party's 'case' which may be assisted by this rule is the pleaded case, not the case which emerges from evidence or submissions: *Chan Wai Sheung v SHNET Audio Visual Technology Ltd* DCCJ 610/2007 (Deputy Judge R Cheung; 21.05.2007).

**7A.    Conviction, etc. to be adduced in evidence: matter to be pleaded**
(O. 18 r. 7A)

**(1)    If in any action which is to be tried with pleadings any party intends, in reliance on section 62 of the Evidence Ordinance (Cap. 8) (convictions as evidence in civil proceedings) to adduce evidence that a person was convicted of an offence by or before a court in Hong Kong, he must include in his pleading a statement of his intention with particulars of—**

    **(a)    the conviction and the date thereof,**

    **(b)    the court which made the conviction, and**

    **(c)    the issue in the proceedings to which the conviction is relevant.**

**(2)    If in any action which is to be tried with pleadings any party intends, in reliance on section 63 of the Evidence Ordinance (findings of adultery as evidence in civil proceedings) to adduce evidence that a person was found guilty of adultery in matrimonial proceedings, he must include in his pleading a statement of his intention with particulars of—**

    **(a)    the finding and the date thereof,**

    **(b)    the court which made the finding and the proceedings in which it was made, and**

    **(c)    the issue in the proceedings to which the finding is relevant.**

**(3)    Where a party's pleading includes such a statement as is mentioned in paragraph (1) or (2), then if the opposite party—**

    **(a)    denies the conviction or finding of adultery to which the statement relates, or**

    **(b)    alleges that the conviction or finding was erroneous, or**

    **(c)    denies that the conviction or finding is relevant to any issue in the proceedings,**

**he must make the denial or allegation in his pleading.**

---

## NOTES

### [18.7A.1]   Conviction, etc must be pleaded where relied upon

Order 18 rule 7A provides that where it is sought to rely on the fact of a criminal conviction (or a finding of adultery), notice of the party's intention to do so must be pleaded, with particulars including the issue to which the conviction is said to be relevant. Such facts are admissible by virtue of sections 62 and 63 of the Evidence Ordinance (Cap 8).

In certain circumstances the fact of a criminal conviction is sufficient of its own to prove the case, meaning that the burden of proof shifts to the defendant to prove on the balance of probabilities that he was not guilty of the offence. See *Kwai Fun Luk Vanessa v Kwai Kun Choi* HCA 4261/2003 (Chu J; 18.12.2006), referring to *Stupple v Royal Insurance Co Ltd* [1971] 1 QB 50.

A defendant denying liability despite a conviction is likewise required to plead the denial expressly: rule 7A(3). Where the defendant denies the relevance of the conviction it is up to the plaintiff to prove that the conviction supports the cause of action, and the defendant will not be ordered to particularise the denial of relevance: *The Kang Oh v Wong Yik Fai* HCPI 791/1995 (Woo J; 10.07.1996).

An interesting question arises where the offence of which the defendant was convicted was one of strict liability. Can such a conviction constitute evidence of negligence? This question was raised in *Wong Yiu Wing v To Chark Wah* DCCJ 30743/1992 (Judge Downey; 28.06.1993) but not resolved as the court found that strict liability was not involved.

**8.**      **Matters which must be specifically pleaded** (O. 18 r. 8)

(1)    **A party must in any pleading subsequent to a statement of claim plead specifically any matter, for example, performance, release, any relevant statute of limitation, fraud or any fact showing illegality—**

         (a)     **which he alleges makes any claim or defence of the opposite party not maintainable; or**

         (b)     **which, if not specifically pleaded, might take the opposite party by surprise; or**

         (c)     **which raises issues of fact not arising out of the preceding pleading.**

(2)    **Without prejudice to paragraph (1), a defendant to an action for recovery of land must plead specifically every ground of defence on which he relies, and a plea that he is in possession of the land by himself or his tenant is not sufficient.**

(3)    **A claim for exemplary damages or for provisional damages must be specifically pleaded together with the facts on which the party pleading relies.**

(4)    **A party must plead specifically any claim for interest under section 48 of the Ordinance or otherwise.**

---

**NOTES**

**[18.8.1]**    **Scope and effect of Order 18 rule 8**

Order 18 rule 8 provides that certain matters must be specifically pleaded. Rule 8(1) applies only to pleadings subsequent to the statement of claim, and rule 8(2) applies only to defendants in actions for recovery of land. However rules 8(3) and (4) apply to any pleading.

Each of the paragraphs of rule 8 uses the mandatory 'must' as to matters which must be specifically pleaded. It has been held that the requirements of the rule are, accordingly, mandatory: *Shell Chemicals UK Ltd & Anor v Vinamul Ltd* [1991] TLR 122 (The Times 07.03.1991) (CA). In *Clico Holdings (B'dos) Ltd v Royal Bank of Canada* [2001] BBSC 14 (CommonLII) the Barbados Court of Appeal, construing a provision in the same terms as Hong Kong's rule 8(1), held that a defence based on release from a contract of guarantee could not succeed because it had not been specifically pleaded.

### [18.8.2]   Pleading fraud

Order 18 rule 8(1) provides that an allegation of fraud must be pleaded specifically. However, it has been held that it is not necessary to use the word 'fraud' or 'dishonesty' if the facts which make the conduct complained of fraudulent are pleaded, 'but, if the facts pleaded are consistent with innocence, then it is not open to the court to find fraud': *Armitage v Nurse & Ors* [1998] Ch 241, 256-7 (CA), quoted with approval in *Haifa Int'l Finance Co Ltd v Concord Strategic Investments Ltd & Ors* CACV 168/2008 (Cheung JA & Sakhrani J; 23.03.2009).

Although rule 8(1) by its own terms applies only to pleadings subsequent to the statement of claim, see also Order 18 rule 12(1)(a) by which particulars of any alleged fraud must be given in any pleading, and see *Scales v Wong* [1983] 2 HKC 199; [1983] HKLR 110 (CA).

It is 'well-established that fraud cannot and should not be pleaded unless the pleader has clear instructions to plead fraud and he has before him reasonably credible material which, as it stands, establishes a *prima facie* case of fraud': *Hui Yin Sang & Anor v Tsoi Ping Kwan* [2010] 1 HKC 585, referring to para 113 of the bar Code of Conduct. In *Medcalf v Mardell & Ors* [2003] 1 AC 120 (HL) (paras 22, 79) it was held that at the preparatory stage this duty does not require that there be admissible evidence of fraud. What is necessary is that there be material 'of such a character as to lead responsible counsel to conclude that serious allegations could properly be based upon it'. However, at a hearing, counsel cannot persist in an allegation of fraud which is unsupported by admissible evidence. The duty is owed to the court, and 'must take precedence over pressure from lay clients to which counsel must not succumb': *Tam Chi Kok Garbriel v Fok Eugenia* HCA 1859/1992 (Deputy Judge A Cheung; 12.06.2003) (para 84). Litigation solicitors have comparable professional duties: Guide to Professional Conduct, vol 1 (2nd ed) 10.01.

As to the degree of particularity required when pleading fraud, see the commentary under Order 18 rule 12.

### [18.8.3]   Defence of set-off

A defence of set-off must be specifically pleaded: see, for example, *SC Chow & Associates Ltd v Chow Kit Ming (t/a Modern World Printing Design Co)* [1997] 2 HKC 96. In that case Master Cannon was assessing damages in an action brought by a landlord against a tenant for early termination of two leases. The tenant (who was in person) sought to set-off the rental deposit of $130,000 against the damages awarded. The Master refused to allow the set-off because it had not been pleaded.

As to set-off generally, see the commentary under Order 18 rule 17.

### [18.8.4]   Illegality

Order 18 rule 8(1) requires that allegations of illegality must be specifically set out in any pleading subsequent to the statement of claim. The requirement is mandatory and a party will not be permitted to rely on illegality at trial unless it has complied: *Shell Chemicals UK Ltd & Anor v Vinamul Ltd* [1991] TLR 122 (07.03.1991) (CA). In *Treasure Spot Finance Co Ltd v Li Chik Ming* HCA 5387/2001 (Recorder P Fung SC; 10.07.2007) an allegation of failure to comply with section 18 of the Money Lenders Ordinance (Cap 163) (which requires a memorandum setting out the terms of a loan) was treated as an allegation of illegality which should, under this rule, be pleaded. With regard to money lenders actions, see also Order 83A.

### [18.8.5]    Contributory negligence
An allegation of contributory negligence 'is a positive allegation which ought to be clearly pleaded': *Liu Jianhui v Graham* [1996] 3 HKC 383, 388B-C (CA).  See also *Fookes v Slaytor* [1978] 1 WLR 1293 and *Chow Wai Hung v King Rise Engineering Ltd & Anor* CACV 213/2005 (Rogers VP, Le Pichon & Cheung JJA; 14.10.2005).

If the pleading is not clear, the proper course is for the opposing party to seek further and better particulars as to whether the defence of contributory negligence is relied upon: *Liu Jianhui*, at 388.

### [18.8.6]    Volenti non fit injuria
The defence of *volenti non fit injuria* should be pleaded where it is sought to be relied upon: see *Lau Kam Tai v United Soundfair Engineering Co Ltd & Ors* [1999] 2 HKC 299 per Suffiad J, citing *James v Wellington City* [1971] NZLR 978.

### [18.8.7]    Res ipsa loquitur
A party who wishes to rely on '*res ipsa loquitur*' to prove negligence must plead the allegations of fact which it is contended demonstrate that the accident was of the type which would not normally happen in the absence of negligence. However, since *res ipsa loquitur* 'adds nothing to the cause of action' (*Kwan Shiu Cheong Charles v Ferrari SpA & Anor* [1994] 2 HKC 179, 188B-C (CA), citing *Bennett v Chemical Construction (GB) Ltd* [1971] 1 WLR 1571) and is really 'a mode of inferential reasoning' (*Sanfield Building Contractors Ltd v Li Kai Cheong* (2003) 6 HKCFAR 207; [2003] 3 HKLRD 48) it need not be specifically pleaded as if it were itself an allegation of fact.

### [18.8.8]    Defence to action for recovery of land
Order 18 rule 8(2) provides that the defence to an action for recovery of land must plead specifically every ground of defence relied upon. In *Luen Wo Land Investment Co Ltd v Yau Wai Nam* DCCJ 556/2005 (Deputy Judge H Au-Yeung; 08.09.2010) the defendant was not permitted to rely on an argument that he was a statutorily protected tenant, because this was not pleaded.

### [18.8.9]    Pleading foreign law
The state of foreign law is a question of fact and must be pleaded where it arises in proceedings in Hong Kong. See *Man Siu Hin v Man Yuen Yam* HCAP 13/2003 (Deputy Judge Muttrie; 07.02.2006), referring to Dicey & Morris on the Conflicts of Laws and *Ascherberg Hopwood & Crew Ltd v Casa Musicale Sonzogno di Piero* [1971] 1 All ER 477.

For this purpose 'foreign' law means the law of any jurisdiction outside Hong

Kong, including other parts of China.

In the absence of properly pleaded and proved evidence of foreign law, the court will proceed on the assumption that the foreign law is the same as that of Hong Kong. With regard to the manner in which the state of foreign law may be proved, see Order 38 rule 7 and the commentary thereunder.

### [18.8.10]    Pleading limitation period

Order 18 rule 8(1) expressly provides that a limitation defence must be pleaded. Otherwise the defendant, being bound by its pleadings, may not rely on the same. Failure to plead a limitation defence may be cured by amendment, but the court may refuse leave to amend if the application is made too late. In *Tengku Ismail v Sia Cheng Soon* [2006] 5 MLJ 228 (CA) a defendant who sought to raise a limitation defence for the first time in written submissions at the conclusion of trial was not permitted to do so.

### [18.8.11]    Acknowledgement of debt

An acknowledgement of debt, having the effect of causing the limitation period to begin running all over again (Limitation Ordinance (Cap 347), section 25), must be specifically pleaded in a statement of claim: *Busch v Stevens* [1962] 1 All ER 412.

### [18.8.12]    Infringement of copyright

Copyright and infringement thereof cannot be implied, and must be specifically pleaded: *Samsonite Corp v Make Rich Ltd* [2002] 1 HKC 692.

### [18.8.13]    Pleading liability to tax

A defendant in an action for lost earnings who wishes to argue that the quantum of damages should be reduced by the amount of tax which would have been payable on the earnings should plead the point: see *Wong Chi Shing v Argos Engineering & Heavy Industries Co Ltd & Ors* [1993] 1 HKC 598, 601G–602E, following *Kowloon Motor Bus Co v Ng Kung* CACV 7/1983 (Roberts CJ; Huggins VP & Barker JA; 09.05.1983), unreported.

### [18.8.14]    Estoppel

There is nothing in these rules which requires a plea of estoppel to be pleaded in any specific manner; hence the plea may be raised provided that it is specifically referred to and all the relevant facts in support have been set out: *La Chemise Lacoste SA v Crocodile Garments Ltd* [1999] 4 HKC 212, 221D–E.

A party seeking to rely on estoppel by silence is required to show detriment and it follows that the party 'must (a) plead and identify what steps it would have taken and (b) prove that it would have had a real chance of protecting or improving its situation and that it would have taken that chance': *Pertamina Energy Trading Ltd v Credit Suisse* [2006] 4 SLR 273 (para 85).

### [18.8.15]    Lack of writing

A defence of lack of writing to a claim based on a contract of a type which is not enforceable unless reduced to writing (such as a contract for the sale of land – see the Conveyancing and Property Ordinance, s 3) must be specifically pleaded: see *James v Smith* (1891) Ch D 384 and *Holland v Yates Building Co Ltd* [1989] The

Times, 5 December. However, it is not necessary to plead a specific section of the statute requiring writing. In *Lam Tin Hing & Anor v Lam Kwai Choi* [2009] 3 HKC 1 para 14 *et seq*) a defence to a claim for enforcement of an oral agreement for sale and purchase of land failed because the lack of writing point had not been pleaded.

### [18.8.16]   Pleading Interest

Order 18 rule 8(4) provides that claims to interest must be specifically pleaded. So far as it applies to pre-judgment interest under statute, the enactment of the sub-rule in 1988 ended a period of uncertainty in Hong Kong (as to which see Carver, (1986) 16 HKLJ 121). Prior to the enactment of the sub-rule the better view was that a claim to interest under statute did not need to be pleaded because it was not part of a cause of action: *Riches v Westminster Bank Ltd* [1943] 2 All ER 725. On the other hand, it has always been necessary to plead claims for interest under agreement since they are part of the cause of action.

Pre-judgment interest is provided for in section 48 of the High Court Ordinance, section 57 of the Bills of Exchange Ordinance and other specific legislation. As a result of rule 8(4) it is necessary to plead a claim to such interest just as it has always been necessary to claim contractual interest. The court will not make an award of such interest if it is not pleaded: *Ward v Chief Constable of Avon & Somerset* [1985] The Times, 17 July (CA); *Bank of China (HK) Ltd v Sze Wang* HCMP 2825/2001 (Master T So; 31.01.2004).

Rule 8(4) does not apply to post-judgment interest under section 49 of the High Court Ordinance, which need not be pleaded: *Grandyield Knitters Ltd v MBE Engineering Ltd* [2002] 2 HKLRD 88 (CA). The situation may be different where there is a contractual claim for post-judgment interest, in which case the contractual term should be pleaded if relied upon.

When interest is claimed under statute it is sufficient to plead the claim in the prayer for relief – no specific averment in the body of the statement of claim is required. However, this is not the case with a claim to interest under contract, which must be included in the body of the statement of claim. See *Prague Enterprises Ltd v Chan Miu Cheung* [1994] 3 HKC 175 (CA) where Litton JA said (at 182H *et seq*):

> A statement of claim is an entire document which includes the prayer for relief. If, from the statement of facts in the body of the statement of claim, liability for the payment of interest could arise, the pleader needs to do no more than include a claim for interest in the prayer for relief. Obviously, if the plaintiff is alleging that a liability for interest arises from contractual arrangements, then this must be pleaded in the body of the statement of claim.

In pleading a claim to pre-judgment interest under statute it is not necessary to refer to a specific statute or section number, though this may be advisable if it is not clear in the circumstances which provision is relied upon. See *Grandyield Knitters* (above).

For a discussion of the court's powers to order pre- and post-judgment interest, and interest rates, see the commentary under Order 42 rule 1.

See also Order 13A rule 12 as to the specificity with which interest must be pleaded in order for it be included in a judgment on admission of liability to pay without the need for a determination by the court.

**9.    Matter may be pleaded whenever arising** (O. 18 r. 9)

**Subject to rules 7(1), 10 and 15(2), a party may in any pleading plead any matter which has arisen at any time, whether before or since the issue of the writ.**

---

NOTES

**[18.9.1]    Pleading causes of action arising after issue of the writ**
Order 18 rule 9 provides that any matter may be pleaded, even matters arising after issue of the writ. Insofar as causes of action arising after issue of the writ are concerned this rule must be read in conjunction with the cases concerning the doctrine of 'relation back'. In this connection see the commentary under Order 20 rule 5.

**10.    Departure** (O. 18 r. 10)

**(1)    A party shall not in any pleading make any allegation of fact, or raise any new ground of claim, inconsistent with a previous pleading of his.**

**(2)    Paragraph (1) shall not be taken as prejudicing the right of a party to amend, or apply for leave to amend, his previous pleading so as to plead the allegations or claims in the alternative.**

---

NOTES

**[18.10.1]    Inconsistent pleading may be struck out**
An allegation in a pleading which is inconsistent with an allegation in an earlier pleading of the same party is said to be a 'departure'. Such a pleading is liable to be struck out to the extent of the inconsistency: see *Herbert & Anor v Vaughan & Ors* [1972] 1 WLR 1128. However, Order 18 rule 10(2) specifically preserves the right of the offending party to seek to amend.

**11.    Points of law may be pleaded** (O. 18 r. 11)

**A party may by his pleading raise any point of law.**

---

NOTES

**[18.11.1]    Circumstances in which it is appropriate to plead law**
Order 18 rule 11, expressly providing that a party may plead a point of law, should be read together with Order 18 rule 7(1) which states that a party should plead only material facts. Together they mean that although a party can plead a point of law, such as a limitation period, it is not permissible to plead law in the sense of including legal argument. As to when it is appropriate to plead a point of law, the Chief Justice's working party on civil justice reform said (at para 205):

> In some cases, the pleading of a point of law usefully makes a party's case clearer to the other side. *Barclays Bank plc v Boulter* [1999] 1 WLR 1919, 1923, is an example of such a case. The defendant wished to contend that a bank had constructive notice of alleged undue influence and misrepresentation but, while having pleaded the material

facts, had not expressly alleged such.

The working party continued by quoting the judgment of Lord Hoffman in the *Boulter* case where it was said that although the pleading may technically have been sufficient since the facts necessary for the court to be able to find constructive notice had been pleaded, failure to plead the point of law might result in the other side being taken by surprise. The working party concluded (at para 206) that in such circumstances 'a reference to the legal point helpfully conveys the nature of the party's case'.

### [18.11.2]    Statement of truth does not extend to pleaded law

A party verifying a pleading by statement of truth is not required to verify the truth of a legal point contained in the pleading. This is because of the form of statement of truth to be used in a pleading (or other document apart from a witness statement or expert report), as prescribed by Order 41A rule 5(1). The prescribed wording is limited to verification of the truth of *the facts* stated in the document. Thus in *Korea National Insurance Corp v Allianz Global Corporate & Speciality AG* [2007] EWCA Civ 1066 (30.10.20007) (para 34), referring to the equivalent English rule, CPR 22.1(4), it was said that 'the scope of a statement of truth does not extend to propositions of law set out in the document in question'.

### 12.    Particulars of pleading (O. 18 r. 12)

(1)    Subject to paragraph (2), every pleading must contain the necessary particulars of any claim, defence or other matter pleaded including, without prejudice to the generality of the foregoing—

- (a)    particulars of any misrepresentation, fraud, breach of trust, wilful default or undue influence on which the party pleading relies;
- (b)    where a party pleading alleges any condition of the mind of any person, whether any disorder or disability of mind or any malice, fraudulent intention or other condition of mind except knowledge, particulars of the facts on which the party relies; and (L.N. 404 of 1991)
- (c)    where a claim for damages is made against a party pleading, particulars of any facts on which the party relies in mitigation of, or otherwise in relation to, the amount of damages. (L.N. 404 of 1991)

(1A) Subject to paragraph (1B), a plaintiff in an action for personal injuries shall serve with his statement of claim—

- (a)    a medical report; and
- (b)    a statement of the special damages claimed. (L.N. 404 of 1991)

(1B) Where the documents to which paragraph (1A) applies are not served with the statement of claim, the Court may—

- (a)    specify the period of time within which they are to be provided; or
- (b)    make such other order as it thinks fit (including an order dispensing with the requirements of paragraph (1A) or staying the proceedings.) (L.N. 404 of 1991)

(1C) For the purposes of this rule—

"medical report" means a report substantiating all the personal injuries alleged in the statement of claim which the plaintiff proposes to adduce in evidence as part of his case at the trial;

"a statement of the special damages claimed" means a statement giving full particulars of the special damages claimed for expenses and losses already incurred and an estimate of any future expenses and losses (including loss of earnings and of pension rights).

(L.N. 404 of 1991)

(2)   Where it is necessary to give particulars of debt, expenses or damages and those particulars exceed 3 folios, they must be set out in a separate document referred to in the pleading and the pleading must state whether the document has already been served, and, if so, when, or is to be served with the pleading.

(3)   The Court may order a party to serve on any other party particulars of any claim, defence or other matter stated in his pleading, or in any affidavit of his ordered to stand as a pleading, or a statement of the nature of the case on which he relies, and the order may be made on such terms as the Court thinks just.

(3A) The Court may make an order under paragraph (3) upon the application of a party or of its own motion. (L.N. 152 of 2008)

(3B) No order shall be made under paragraph (3) unless the Court is of the opinion that the order is necessary either for disposing fairly of the cause or matter or for saving costs. (L.N. 152 of 2008)

(4)   Where a party alleges as a fact that a person had knowledge or notice of some fact, matter or thing, then, without prejudice to the generality of paragraph (3), the Court may, on such terms as it thinks just, order that party to serve on any other party—

      (a)    where he alleges knowledge, particulars of the facts on which he relies, and

      (b)    where he alleges notice, particulars of the notice.

(5)   An order under this rule shall not be made before service of the defence unless, in the opinion of the Court, the order is necessary or desirable to enable the defendant to plead or for some other special reason.

(6)   Where the applicant for an order under this rule did not apply by letter for the particulars he requires, the Court may refuse to make the order unless of opinion that there were sufficient reasons for an application by letter not having been made.

(7)   Where particulars are given pursuant to a request, or order of the Court, the request or order shall be incorporated with the particulars, each item of the particulars following immediately after the corresponding item of the request or order.

---

NOTES

[18.12.1]   Particulars of fraud

In *Aktieselskabet Dansk Skibsfinansiering v Wheelock Marden* [1994] 2 HKC 264 the Court of Appeal considered the requirements for pleading fraud in the context of an application to strike out an allegation of conspiracy in a statement of claim. Bokhary JA stated (at 270 B–C):

> ... allegations of fraud must be pleaded distinctly and with the utmost particularity. The word 'distinctly' is the one used by Thesiger LJ in his well-known statement in *Davy v Garrett* (1878) 7 Ch D 473 at p 489 as to how fraud is to be pleaded. And the expression 'utmost particularity', as one sees from note 18/8/8 at p 297 of Vol 1 of the 1993 *Supreme Court Practice*, is the one chosen by its learned editors and has the authority of their combined experience.

In *Haifa Int'l Finance Co Ltd v Concord Strategic Investments Ltd & Ors* CACV 168/2008 (Cheung JA & Sakhrani J; 23.03.2009) (paras 17-19) the court struck out a claim based on fraud which was admittedly inadequate, despite a submission that the plaintiff should be allowed to conduct discovery and administer interrogatories so that the particulars of fraud could be supplied later. The court appears to have distinguished *Deak Perera Far East Ltd v Deak & Ors* [1995] 2 HKC 28, 36C (CA) where a claim based on fraud was allowed to stand on the basis that full particulars could be given after discovery.

See also Order 18 rule 8 and the commentary thereunder.

### [18.12.2]   Dishonesty

An allegation of dishonesty, like fraud, must be distinctly pleaded, particularised and proved: *Three Rivers District Council & Ors v Bank of England (No 3)* [2003] 2 AC 1, cited with approval in the dissenting judgment of Yuen JA in *Great Source Enterprise Ltd v Sino Estates Management Ltd* [2004] 4 HKC 49, 62E-G (CA), and in the concurring judgment of Cheung JA in *Peconic Industrial Development Ltd v Yu Ka Hong Paul & Anor* [2006] 4 HKC 406 (CA) (para 33).

The word 'dishonesty' (or 'fraud') need not necessarily be used: *Davy v Garrett* (1878) 7 Ch D 473, 489; *Armitage v Nurse & Ors* [1998] Ch 241, 256-7 (CA), quoted with approval in *Haifa Int'l Finance* (above). However, if the language used is unclear or equivocal this may be fatal: *Belmont Finance Corp Ltd v Williams Furniture Ltd & Ors* [1979] Ch 250; [1978] 1 All ER 118 (CA).

### [18.12.3]   Restraint of trade

An allegation that a contractual non–competition clause or restrictive covenant is an unenforceable restraint of trade must be fully particularised. See *Hummingbird Music Ltd v Acconci* CACV 40/2009 (Rogers VP, Le Pichon JA & Stone J; 05.01.2010); [2010] 1 HKLRD 587 (CA) (para 38), where in a concurring judgment Stone J said:

> ...restraint of trade is one of those areas in which it is essential to set out in the relevant pleading the very particular matters which are asserted to invoke operation of the doctrine, and thus to apprise the opposing party of the specific reason why it now should be said that the existing contractual obligation is unenforceable as a restraint of trade.

### [18.12.4]   Pleading tort of conspiracy

In a claim in the tort of conspiracy the pleader must allege at least one overt act. In *Aktieselskabet Dansk Skibsfinansiering v Wheelock Marden* [1994] 2 HKC 264 Bokhary JA stated (at 272 B–C):

When it comes to a claim in the tort of conspiracy, what the pleader has to do in regard to pleading an overt act or overt acts is this. He has to plead at least one overt act which is the act of all the alleged conspirators or, failing that, a number of overt acts which include at least one act on the part of each conspirator. And the overt act or overt acts pleaded must be such as to show: (i) that the conspiratorial agreement alleged against the defendants had been entered into by each and every one of them; (ii) that the agreement, and not merely the intention of one person alone, was implemented; and (iii) that such implementation caused the damage complained of.

> If the pleader fails to do that, then, depending on whether the failure is in respect of all the defendants or only some or one of them, then either the plea is liable to be struck out altogether or it is liable to be struck out as against some or one of the defendants.

### [18.12.5]   Pleading particulars of damages

Order 18 rule 12, in requiring that every pleading include particulars of the claim, is taken as requiring that amounts claimed by way of 'special' damages be pleaded specifically. Special damages are those which are readily quantifiable at the time the claim is made, such as out-of-pocket expenses which have been incurred. The distinction between special and general damages was set out in *British Transport Commission v Gourley* [1956] AC 185, 206 where Lord Goddard said:

> First there is what is referred to as special damage, which has to be specially pleaded and proved. This consists of out-of-pocket expenses and loss of earnings incurred down to the date of trial, and is generally capable of substantially exact calculation. Secondly there is general damage which the law implies and is not specially pleaded. This includes damages for pain and suffering and the like, and if the injuries suffered are such as to lead to continuing or permanent disability, compensation for loss of earning power in the future.

See also *Pang Yau v Cheung Kwok Hing* [1977] HKLR 412 where it was pointed out that although loss of earnings up to trial are special damages, such loss after trial is not capable of precise calculation and is an item of general damages.

The purpose of requiring special damages to be pleaded is to facilitate settlement, whether by payment into court or otherwise: *Perestrello e Companhia Ltda v United Paint Co Ltd* [1969] 1 WLR 570.

A party is limited to the amount of special damages claimed: *Ilkiw v Samuels & Ors* [1963] 1 WLR 991 (CA).

It is now well established that claims to general damages which might otherwise take the opposing party by surprise at trial, should also be pleaded: *Perestrello* (above). Thus special circumstances which may cause future losses should be pleaded: *Domsalla v Barr* [1969] 1 WLR 630, 634. Likewise a claim to loss of future earning capacity should be pleaded: *Chan Wai Tong & Anor v Li Ping Sum* [1985] HKLR 176, [1985] 2 WLR 396 (PC) (doubting *British Transport Commission v Gourley* (above) in this regard). It is the facts giving rise to such claims which should pleaded – it remains unnecessary to plead a specific amount as that is a matter for judicial determination, rather than a question of fact.

In personal injury cases rule 12(1A) requires the plaintiff to serve a statement of special damages with the statement of claim, and sub-rule (1C) includes loss of future earnings and pension rights as special damages for this purpose. See the commentary on the statement of damages below.

The special damages rule applies to a contractual claim for legal costs as damages:

see *Hang Seng Credit Card Ltd & Ors v Tsang Nga Lee & Ors* [2000] 3 HKC 269, and see the commentary on pleading costs under Order 18 rule 15.

In *Hayward v Pullinger & Partners Ltd* [1950] 1 All ER 581 it was held that a statement of claim which failed to plead special damages was 'defective' with the result the plaintiff was not entitled to recover the same. However, in *Industrial & Commercial Bank of China (Asia) Ltd v BC Chow & Co* [2004] 1 HKC 371, 394F–398F an objection that a claim to damages was insufficiently pleaded was rejected on the ground it could be found in the 'tenor' of the pleading, and the opposing party had not been taken by surprise.

### [18.12.6]    Statement of special damages and medical report in personal injury cases

Order 18 rule 12(1A) requires that the plaintiff in a personal injury claim serve a medical report and a statement of special damages with the statement of claim. Rule 12(1B) provides that the court may stay the proceedings in cases of non-compliance. Such an order was made in *Yau Lee Construction Co Ltd v Chan Yau Ho* [1994] 3 HKC 560.

*Medical report* – according to rule 12(1C), the medical report should substantiate the alleged personal injuries. See also paragraph 65(1) of the personal injuries list practice direction (PD 18.1) which stipulates in addition that there should be at least one medical report describing the plaintiff's condition no more than 4 months prior to service and that a post mortem report should be included in fatal accident cases, if one exists. Service of a medical report in compliance with this provision does not make the medical evidence admissible as expert evidence at trial. It is still necessary to seek leave to adduce expert evidence under Order 38 rule 36. See *Chu Sin Yung v Lee Hon Kwong & Ors* HCPI 191/2008 (Master Yu; 18.11.2009) (para 12). However, if the report is confined to evidence of treatment of the patient, it is not of an expert character and leave is not required. See the commentary under Order 38 rule 36.

*Statement of special damages* – The purpose of the statement of special damages is to require the plaintiff to quantify the claim as early as possible 'so that all the parties will know exactly where they stand', thus facilitating settlement or payment into court: *Yau Lee Construction* (above, 562G-H). The rule is expanded upon in para 65(2) of practice direction 18.1 which stipulates that the statement should also set out amounts claimed in respect of items such as pain, suffering and loss of amenities which were traditionally regarded as 'general' rather than 'special' damages. The practice direction lays down additional requirements for fatal accident cases and extends to medical negligence cases. The statement should be in the form of a schedule as set out in *Yau Lee Construction* (above, at 562D-F). Part G provides for contemporaneous service of additional documents in particular types of cases. Note that a statement of damages, and an answer to a statement of damages, are considered to be pleadings for the purpose of the verification by statement of truth requirement: see Order 41A and the commentary thereunder, and see practice direction 19.3.

### [18.12.7]    Claim on dishonoured cheque

When a cheque is dishonoured, the payee is required to give notice thereof to the drawer: Bills of Exchange Ordinance (Cap 19), section 48. Such notice must be given in accordance with the rules laid down in section 49. By way of exception section 50(2) of the Ordinance provides that notice of dishonour is dispensed with in certain circumstances.

Where a payee sues on a dishonoured cheque 'the statement of claim must contain either an allegation that due notice of dishonour was given to the defendant, stating the date when, the manner in which and the person by whom such notice was given, or else it must contain a statement of the facts relied on dispensing with such notice under s 50(2)': *Thong Ko Sine v Wilkinson & Anor* [1988] HKC 56, 57H (CA). Failure to plead the ground on which notice of dishonour is dispensed with may be overlooked by the court, or readily cured by amendment, where the drawer obviously knows precisely why the cheque was dishonoured (such as where the drawer has countermanded payment): *Yuen Chak Construction Co Ltd v Tak Son Contractors Ltd* [1997] 3 HKC 294, 299G et seq; *Tong Nai Kan v Cheung King Fung Francis* [2005] 2 HKC 249.

Where notice of dishonour is required, it must be given within a reasonable time: section 49(1). It has been suggested that the date of presentation of the cheque should be pleaded in order that the court can judge whether the notice of dishonour was given within such reasonable time. See *Wong's Kong King HK Ltd v Polyware Co (a firm)* HCA 1339/1990 (Kaplan J; 29.08.1990).

### [18.12.8]    Misrepresentation or undue influence

Allegations of misrepresentation or undue influence, or other matters rendering a contract unenforceable, must be made 'abundantly clear' in the pleading: *Wing Hang Bank Ltd v Crystal Jet International Ltd* [2005] 2 HKC 638, 642D–F (CA), citing Order 18 rule 12(1)(a). See also Order 18 rule 8(1)(a).

### [18.12.9]    Rule 12(3), (3A) and (3B) – power to order further and better particulars

The court has power under rule 12(3) to order that a party provide particulars of a pleading. Where particulars exist, but are inadequate, the order is commonly referred to as one for 'further and better particulars'. Rule 12(3A), inserted as part of the civil justice reforms which took effect in 2009, makes it clear that this power may be exercised on application of a party or by the court of its own motion. That ties in with the court's duty by way of active case management (Order 1A rule 4(2)(b)) to identify issues early. Where it is a party who takes the initiative, the particulars should first be requested by letter: rule 12(6).

A party is not justified in opposing a request for particulars on the ground that it too is seeking particulars: *East Seas Shipping Corp v Liu Chong Hing Bank Ltd* [1982] HKLR 102. However, objection that the particulars sought are unnecessary or peripheral is a valid ground to resist. See rule 12(3B) which makes it clear that particulars will not be ordered unless necessary for fair disposal of the action or for saving costs. Rule 12(3B) implements recommendation 34 of the final report of the Chief Justice's working party on civil justice reform. The working party said (at paras 268-9):

> 268. As between themselves, the parties ought to have leeway to request, by correspondence, such further and better particulars of each other's pleadings as they consider desirable. However, where voluntary particulars are refused, applications to the court for particulars to be ordered should only be launched where there is a genuine need for clarification of the nature of the other side's case in order to ensure fairness or to avoid wasting costs.

> Attempts should also be made to schedule any such applications to be heard at general directions hearings rather than as specific pieces of satellite litigation.
>
> 269. As emphasised in *McPhilemy v Times Newspapers Ltd* [1999] 3 All ER 775, given the modern practice of requiring witness statements, expert reports and so forth to be exchanged, satellite litigation merely to clarify the pleadings is seldom necessary. A pleading which conveys the nature of a party's case, stating the material facts, should not attract an application for particulars even if certain details (which are peripheral or likely to emerge in the usual course) are not disclosed ... unnecessary applications should attract appropriate costs sanctions.

The necessity requirement in rule 12(3B) is similar to that which has long existed in respect of applications for discovery and interrogatories: see Order 24 rule 8 and Order 26 rule 1 and the commentary thereunder. Even before the necessity requirement was introduced as part of the civil justice reforms it was held that further and better particulars would not be ordered on matters of evidence or where each party already knows the case to be met: see *Midland Realty Int'l Ltd v Wise Surplus Ltd* [2002] 3 HKC 318, 322B-F. This continues to be the case: *Libertarian Investments Ltd v Hall* HCA 2533/2006 (Deputy Judge A Chan SC; 14.05.2009), quoting from *British Airways Pension Trustees Ltd v Sir Robert McAlpine & Sons Ltd & Ors* (1994) 72 BLR 26.

Vague allegations in a pleading will result in an order for further and better particulars. See *Discreet Ltd v Cubiertas y Mzov SA & Ors* [1998] 1 HKC 108 where the plaintiff had made 'vague' allegations of unlawful interference with a right of way along a road without specifying where the road was, and of damages arising therefrom, without giving any particulars of special damage. The court ordered that the pleading be particularised, failing which the plaintiff would not be permitted to adduce evidence thereon at trial.

Previously the court would not order further and better particulars of a simple traverse or denial in a defence; only where a traverse was 'pregnant' with or suggested a positive allegation would an order be made: *East Seas Shipping Corp v Liu Chong Hing Bank Ltd* [1982] HKLR 102. However, with the amendment of Order 18 rule 13 as part of the civil justice reforms, a party who traverses an allegation by denial is now required to state reasons for doing so. A failure to do so might arguably now result in an order for further and better particulars. See the commentary concerning Order 18 rule 13(6).

Where further and better particulars provided by a party are inadequate, they may be the subject of an application for 'further and better particulars of the further and better particulars': see *La Chemise Lacoste SA v Crocodile Garments Ltd* [1999] 4 HKC 212, at 224A-G.

An application for further and better particulars cannot be resisted on the ground the party is unable to formulate the claim. See *Wharf Properties Ltd & Anor v Eric Cumine Associates* [1991] 2 HKLR 154, 166 (PC) where Lord Oliver said:

> It is for the plaintiff in an action to formulate his claim in an intelligible form and it does not lie in his mouth to assert that it is impossible for him to formulate it and that it should, therefore, be allowed to continue unspecified in the hope that, when it comes to trial he may be able to reconstitute his case and make good what he then feels able to plead and substantiate.

In appropriate circumstances the court will be prepared to allow a party to delay providing full particulars until discovery has been completed. See *Deak Perera Far East Ltd v Deak & Ors* [1995] 2 HKC 28, 36C (CA). However, in *Haifa Int'l Finance Co Ltd v Concord*

*Strategic Investments Ltd & Ors* CACV 168/2008 (Cheung JA & Sakhrani J; 23.03.2009) (paras 17–19) the court struck out a claim based on fraud which was admittedly inadequate, despite a submission that the plaintiff should be allowed to conduct discovery and administer interrogatories so that the particulars of fraud could be supplied later.

### [18.12.10]  Failure to comply with order to provide particulars
A party's pleadings may be struck out for failure to comply with an order that it provide particulars. Where there is formal compliance in that particulars are provided, but those particulars are inadequate, a striking out order may be made only if the original required full disclosure: *Fong Yin Cheung v Ho Kwan Chu & Ors* HCA 436/2005 (Suffiad J; 07.08.2009).

### [18.12.11]  Verification of particulars by statement of truth
Particulars of a pleading, whether given voluntarily, pursuant to request or by order of the court, are subject to the requirement that they be verified by statement of truth just like any pleading. See the definition of 'pleading' in Order 41A rule 1.

### [18.12.12]  Particulars of 'statement of case' in proceedings commenced by originating summons
In proceedings commenced by way of originating summons, where there are no formal pleadings, the court may order a party to serve a statement of the nature of its case: Order 18 rule 12(3). Although such a document is not the same thing as a pleading, it may be the subject of an application for further and better particulars: *Cheung Man Yu v Lau Yuen Ching & Ors* HCMP 2421/2000 (Deputy Judge Saunders; 22.04.2005).

### [18.12.13]  Defamation actions
See Order 82.

**12A.  Pleading with inconsistent alternatives** (O. 18, r. 12A)
   **A party may in any pleading make an allegation of fact which is inconsistent with another allegation of fact in the same pleading if –**
   **(a)    the party has reasonable grounds for so doing; and**
   **(b)    the allegations are made in the alternative.**
   **(L.N. 152 of 2008)**

---

## NOTES

### [18.12A.1]  Pleading in the alternative
Inconsistent pleadings are generally prohibited. Inconsistency within a single pleading would probably be considered embarrassing and be liable to be struck out under Order 18 rule 19(1)(c). Where the inconsistency is in a subsequent pleading, it is considered to be a 'departure', and is expressly prohibited by Order 18 rule 10.

   However it has long been the case that a party may plead in the alternative, even though the alternatives cannot each be true. An example would be an allegation along these lines:

> The plaintiff says that the accident was caused by the 1st defendant, alternatively that it was caused by the 2nd defendant, and in the further alternative that it was caused by

both the 1$^{st}$ and 2$^{nd}$ defendants.

Order 18 rule 12A gives a legislative basis to this form of alternative pleading. This was recommended by the Chief Justice's working party on civil justice reform (recommendation 32). The recommendation was that this form of pleading should be permissible if a party has 'reasonable grounds', and that wording is repeated in the new rule. It is clear from the final report that by including the reasonable grounds requirement the working party had in mind cases where a party 'has no personal knowledge of the facts, but has evidence pointing to alternative possibilities' (para 263). What the working party said in this regard is now reflected in *Hui Yin Sang & Anor v Tsoi Ping Kwan* [2010] 1 HKC 585, where it was said, at para 25(10) that one of the objectives of Order 18 rule 12A 'is to prevent a party from pleading inconsistent cases in relation to a matter which is plainly within his knowledge...' In that case the court considered that proposed amendments to a statement of claim fell foul of rule 12A, and refused leave to amend. The working party said that each alternative should be justified by some evidence (referring to the Bar's Code of Conduct), and that it was 'not intended to exclude honest claims reasonably advanced on the basis of incomplete information which points to alternative sets of fact, each of which would be legally viable as part of the party's case', referring to *Clarke v Marlborough Fine Art (London) Ltd* [2002] 1 WLR 1731, 1742-3 & 1745.

The working party also recommended that the requirement for verification by state ment of truth be applied to alternative pleadings, despite some conceptual difficulty. The result is Order 41A rule 2(2). See the commentary concerning that provision.

Special considerations arise where a plaintiff pleads in the alternative two entirely different sets of facts in relation to a single incident where it is not possible for both sets of facts to be true. In such a case the party may be required to make an election as to which version he is going to advance. See *Poon Hau Kei v Hsin Cheong Construction Co Ltd & Ors* [2003] 2 HKC 408, 417 D–F where Ma JA discussed this scenario in *obiter*. That decision was appealed to the Court of Final Appeal (see [2004] 2 HKC 235) where, without doubting Ma JA's *obiter* comments, it was held that in the particular circumstances of the case no election was called for.

A party pleading inconsistent alternatives should decide which is primary and which secondary and expend effort and costs in preparation accordingly. Costs unreasonably incurred on inconsistent claims may be disallowed under Order 62 rule 5(2) (by which, when taking into account a party's conduct in exercising its discretion as to costs, the court will consider whether it was reasonable for the party to raise, pursue or contest a particular allegation or issue). See *Lam So Chai v Cheung Sai Lui t/ a Hoi Fung Stevedore & Transportation Co* HCPI 360/2007 (Fung J; 03.07.2009) (para 18) (*obiter*).

### 13.    **Admissions and denials** (O. 18 r. 13)

**(1)   Subject to paragraph (6), an allegation of fact made by a party in his pleading is deemed to be admitted by the opposite party unless it is traversed by that party in his pleading or a joinder of issue under rule 14 operates as a non-admission of it. (L.N. 403 of 1992) (L.N. 152 of 2008)**

**(2)   Subject to paragraph (5), a traverse may be made either by a denial or by a statement of non-admission and either expressly or by necessary implication. (L.N. 152 of 2008)**

**(3)   Every allegation of fact made in a statement of claim or counterclaim**

which the party on whom it is served does not intend to admit must be specifically traversed by him in his defence or defence to counterclaim, as the case may be; and a general denial of such allegations, or a general statement of non-admission of them, is not a sufficient traverse of them. (L.N. 403 of 1992)

(4)    (Repealed L.N. 403 of 1992)

(5)    Where an allegation made in a statement of claim or counterclaim is traversed by a denial, the party who denies the allegation shall in his defence or defence to counterclaim –

    (a)    state his reasons for doing so; and

    (b)    if he intends to put forward a different version of events from that given by the claimant, state his own version.

(L.N. 152 of 2008)

(6)    A party who –

    (a)    fails to deal with an allegation; but

    (b)    has set out in his defence or defence to counterclaim the nature of his case in relation to the issue to which that allegation is relevant,

is to be taken to require that allegation to be proved.

(L.N. 152 of 2008)

---

## NOTES

### [18.13.1]    Rule 13(5) – bare denial no longer permitted

By Order 18 rule 13(5) a defendant is no longer entitled to plead bare denials of the plaintiff's allegations. The Chief Justice's working party recommended this change, saying (at para 207 of its final report) 'A defence consisting of bare denials and non-admissions does nothing to advance the proper functions of pleadings'. Now a defendant must state his reasons for a denial, and state his own version of events if he intends to put one forward at trial. Such elaboration is not expressly required in the case of a non-admission, though that appears to have been within the working party's contemplation. This is possibly explained by the fact that non-admission is only appropriate where a party is unable to admit or deny for lack of knowledge, so the reason is implied. For example, if a plaintiff has pleaded that he is a teacher, and the defendant responds with a non-admission, it means that the defendant does not know the plaintiff's occupation. Similarly, it should not be necessary to elaborate a non-admission with a different version of events because non-admission necessarily implies the defendant does not have a different version of events to put forward.

Order 18 rule 13(5) derives from CPR 16.5(2). The Civil Court Practice, our sister publication in the UK, says of the English provision (at CPR 16.5[1]):

> **Contents of defence** The defendant may not meet the claimant's particulars of claim with a bare denial; he must state which allegations he admits, which he denies (with his reasons for so doing) and which allegations he is unable either to admit or to deny but nevertheless requires the claimant to prove. If he wishes to put forward a different version of events from that given by the claimant then he must state that version. See the CPR Pt 16 Practice Direction, paras 10-13 [which describes generally what is required in a defence, and may serve as a useful guide in Hong Kong].

Where, for example, in a claim for damages for personal injuries the defendant's case is that the claim is fabricated he does not need to put forward a substantive case of fraud in order to succeed; it is sufficient to set out fully the facts from which the defendant would be inviting the judge to draw the inference that the claimant had not in fact suffered the injuries which he asserted; if the defendant's medical examiner has examined the claimant and has concluded on the basis of thorough interview and clinical examination that there are substantive reasons for disbelieving the claimant's account then those reasons ought to be positively asserted in the defence: *Kearsley v Klarfeld* [2005] EWCA Civ 1510 paras 45 and 48, [2005] All ER (D) 98 (Dec).

In *Kearsley*, referred to in the above passage, the English Court of Appeal was of the view that a defence pleading that the plaintiff was 'fabricating his symptoms and that no injuries were truly sustained' was sufficient, and that it was not necessary in the defence to plead a substantive case of fraud. What seems to be clear is that supporting a denial with a reason such as 'because it is not true' is unlikely to be sufficient; that something more specific must be stated, such as 'because no such accident happened', or 'because there was no such agreement'.

## [18.13.2]    Rule 13(6) – defendant may require allegation to be proved

Order 18 rule 13(6) provides that a party is taken to require an allegation against it to be proved where although the allegation is not specifically dealt with, the nature of that party's case in relation to the issue is set out in its defence or defence to counterclaim. Its adoption was recommended by the Chief Justice's working party in order to prevent defences from becoming overly lengthy as a result of the introduction of rule 13(5) whereby a bare denial is no longer permitted. In para 209 of their final report, the working party said:

> There is, however a danger that such a rule [Order 18 rule 13(5)], aimed at countering insufficient pleading, may result in the opposite defect of prolixity or inordinate detail. It should accordingly be made clear that in pleading a defence substantively, the defendant should not deal obsessively with each and every allegation in the statement of claim but that he should aim to strike the balance mentioned above.

The balance referred to in the above passage is the balance between 'excessive sparsity and excessive detail' in pleadings, referred to at para 195 of the final report.

Order 18 rule 13(6) derives from CPR 16.5(3). The Civil Court Practice, our sister publication in the UK, says of the English equivalent of this rule (at CPR 16.5[2]):

> **'fails to deal with an allegation'** If a defendant fails to deal with an allegation specifically but has nevertheless set out in the defence the nature of his case on that issue, he will be taken to have required that issue to be proved (CPR 16.5(3)) [in Hong Kong Order 18 rule13(6)]. If, on the other hand, the defendant fails to deal with an allegation at all, then he will be taken to admit that allegation (CPR 16.5(5)) [in Hong Kong Order 18 rule 13(1)]. In either event it is open to the claimant to request further information under CPR Pt 18 [in Hong Kong, an application for particulars under Order 18 rule 12(3)]. If the defence does not make the nature of the defendant's case sufficiently clear in the sense that the claimant does not really know what is admitted or denied or what he is required to prove, then the defence or any offending part of it may be struck out as an abuse of the process or because it will obstruct the just disposal of the proceedings: CPR 3.4 [in Hong Kong Order 1B rule 1(2)(j) and Order 18 rule 19(1)]. The court may take such a step of its own initiative or upon application: CPR 3.3 [in Hong Kong Order 1B rule 2 and Order 18 rule 19(1)].

See also the discussion of *Kearsley v Klarfeld* in the preceding paragraph.

## [18.13.3]   What a defence must do

In the words of Jessel MR 'the whole object of pleadings is to bring the parties to an issue': see *Thorp v Holdsworth* (1876) 3 Ch D 637, 639. This is facilitated by Order 18 rule 13(1) which provides that a defendant is deemed to admit any particular allegation against him unless it is 'traversed'. The effect of this rule is that a defendant must admit, deny or refuse to admit each allegation against him in the statement of claim or be deemed to admit the same. This deemed admission rule does not apply to parties under disability: see Order 80 rule 8.

An allegation in a statement of claim may be traversed in several ways. Order 18 rule 13(2) provides that a traverse may take the form of (i) express denial, (ii) non-admission or (iii) denial by necessary implication. In *Warner v Sampson* [1959] 1 QB 297, 319 it was said that 'there is no effective line to be drawn between non-admission, on the one hand, and denial on the other'. That is probably no longer strictly true, given that rule 13(2) is now expressly subject to rule 13(5) & (6), by which reasons for a denial must be given, and any positive case contrary to that of the plaintiff must be pleaded in the case of denial or non-admission.

Denial implies that it is within the defendant's own knowledge that the allegation is false, whereas refusal to admit indicates the defendant has no knowledge as to the truth of the allegation and wishes to put the plaintiff to proof. Denial by necessary implication is where the defence contains a specific allegation which is inconsistent with what is pleaded in the statement of claim.

## [18.13.4]   Traverse must be specific

Order 18 rule 3(3) provides that every allegation which a defendant does not intend to admit must be *specifically* traversed. This means that the allegations in the statement of claim should be traversed paragraph by paragraph. Failure to comply may result in the defendant being deemed by virtue of Order 18 rule 13(1) to admit the allegations against him. In *Harris v Gamble* (1878) 7 Ch D 877 a defence stating 'the defendant puts the plaintiffs to proof of the several allegations in their statement of claim' was held not to be sufficient. The same result occurred in *Rutter v Tregent* (1879) 12 Ch D 758 with a defence stating 'defendant does not admit the correctness of the allegations in the statement of claim and requires proof thereof'. It is sufficient, however, to deny generally an entire paragraph in the statement of claim: see *John Lancaster Radiators Ltd v General Motor Radiators Co Ltd* [1946] 2 All ER 685. It is not considered necessary to traverse particulars adumbrated under a particular paragraph of a statement of claim where the paragraph as a whole is denied.

*Sweeping up clause* – It was long the practice to conclude a defence with a 'sweeping up' clause purporting to oust the application of the deemed admission rule in Order 18 rule 13(1) by stating that the defendant denied anything not expressly admitted. Such a clause would state that each and every allegation in the statement of claim not expressly admitted was not admitted as if set out and denied seriatim, or one by one. The efficacy of such a clause was accepted by Lord Denning in *Warner v Sampson* [1959] 1 QB 297, 310–11, but in *Jim Mai-gi v Choy Kwun-ping* [1981] HKLR 674 (CA) it was held that such a clause can only be effective in denying inconsequential matters, not substantial allegations. Now, as a result of rule 13(5) & (6) by which bare denials are no longer per mitted, and any positive case which is the basis for a denial or non-admission must be expressly pleaded, it is arguable that such a clause is, of itself, of no effect at all.

*Negative pregnant* – A denial which is worded in such a way as to suggest that the generality of the allegation in the statement of claim may be correct, and only a detail incorrect, is considered improper and evasive. The term 'negative pregnant' is sometimes used. Such a denial will not prevent operation of the deemed admission rule in Order 18 rule 13(1). For example a defence to the effect that 'the defendant never offered a bribe of $500' suggests there may have been a bribe of another amount and the allegation of paying a bribe will be deemed admitted for failure specifically to traverse: see *Tildesley v Harper* (1878) 7 Ch D 403. To avoid this result the pleader ought to add 'or any other amount'. In *Thorp v Holdsworth* (1876) 3 Ch D 637 a defence to the effect that 'the defendant denies that the terms of the arrangement between himself and the plaintiffs were definitely agreed upon as alleged' was held insufficient to deny the existence of an agreement. The pleader ought to have concluded the passage 'whether as alleged or at all'.

### [18.13.5]   Defence as to quantum of damages – effect of repeal of former Order 18 rule 13(4)

Order 18 rule 13(4) (which was repealed in 1992) provided that allegations that damage was suffered and as to the quantum thereof were deemed to be traversed. Damages are always in issue, it used to be said. This is no longer the case as demonstrated by the decision in *Kuan Heng Choi v Ma Pui Tung* [2002] 1 HKC 111. In that case Deputy Judge Lam ruled that a defendant who had not pleaded the point could not pursue a defence that the damages alleged by the plaintiff had not actually been incurred. The Deputy Judge noted that under Order 18 rule 12(1)(c) a defendant is now required to plead facts in relation to a claim for damages and said (at 114B):

> The rules of pleadings as to damages have undergone changes. There has been a trend to apply the same rules on liability as well as quantum. In the old days O 18 r 13(4) provided that allegation about damage being suffered and amount thereof was deemed to be traversed. Even so, in the case of *Speidel v Plato Films Ltd* [1961] AC 1090 at 1104 and 1105, the English Court of Appeal held that new issues of facts pertaining to question of damages should not be raised without pleadings … I cannot see any distinction between issues of facts touching upon quantum and issues of facts touching upon questions like mitigation or remoteness. Pleading serves to inform the other side what case he has to meet. There is no reason why the rule should be different with regard to quantum.

### [18.13.6]   Effect of admission in a defence

Where an allegation is admitted by a defendant, whether expressly or by failure to traverse the same, he is not entitled to adduce any evidence at trial to rebut that allegation: *Pioneer Plastic Containers Ltd v Commrs of Customs & Excise* [1967] Ch 597.

**14.    Non-admission by joinder of issue** (O. 18 r. 14)

   **(1)   If there is no reply to a defence, there is an implied joinder of issue on that defence.**

      **(2)   Subject to paragraph (3)—**

         **(a)   there is at the close of pleadings an implied joinder of issue on the pleading last served, and**

         **(b)   a party may in his pleading expressly join issue on the next**

preceding pleading.

(3)   There can be no joinder of issue, implied or expressed, on a statement of claim or counterclaim.

(4)   A joinder of issue operates as a non-admission of every material allegation of fact made in the pleading on which there is an implied or expressed joinder of issue unless, in the case of an expressed joinder of issue, any such allegation is excepted from the joinder and is stated to be admitted, in which case the expressed joinder of issue operates as a non-admission of every other such allegation. (L.N. 152 of 2008)

**15.   Statement of claim** (O. 18 r. 15)

(1)   A statement of claim must state specifically the relief or remedy which the plaintiff claims; but costs need not be specifically claimed.

(2)   A statement of claim must not contain any allegation or claim in respect of a cause of action unless that cause of action is mentioned in the writ or arises from facts which are the same as, or include or form part of, facts giving rise to a cause of action so mentioned; but subject to that, a plaintiff may in his statement of claim alter, modify or extend any claim made by him in the endorsement of the writ without amending the endorsement.

(3)   Every statement of claim must bear on its face a statement of the date on which the writ in the action was issued.

---

**NOTES**

**[18.15.1]   Relief or remedy must be stated in statement of claim**
Order 18 rule 15(1) provides that a statement of claim must state specifically the relief or remedy required. This is usually done in the form of a 'prayer for relief' set out at the end of the statement of claim.

In granting relief the court may depart from what is claimed in the statement of claim. For example the court may grant judgment for a smaller amount than that claimed, without the need for amendment. However it cannot grant relief which has not been claimed at all: *Belmont Finance* (above, [1979] Ch 250, 269F-G, 275 A-B) (CA).

In *Lau Wing Hong v Wong Wor Hung* [2006] 4 HKC 221 (para 140-148) the court held it could grant a declaration of possessory title to a lesser amount of land than claimed in the prayer for relief, without requiring an amendment. The test was whether 'genuine prejudice' would be caused.

**[18.15.2]   Claim to costs need not be stated in statement of claim**
Order 18 rule 15(1) expressly provides that a claim to costs need not be pleaded. This is the consequence of the fact that a claim to costs is not usually a cause of action, but a compensatory award by the court pursuant to statutory power (section 52A, High Court Ordinance). It is sometimes said that 'costs are always in issue'. The situation should be different where a claim to costs, or to costs at a particular level, arises from a contractual term. In such cases the claim is, or is part of, the cause of action and in principle the relevant contractual terms should be pleaded. See

*Hang Seng Credit Card Ltd & Ors v Tsang Nga Lee & Ors* [2000] 3 HKC 269, and see the commentary under Order 62 rule 3 as to contractual claims to costs.

### [18.15.3]   Claim to interest must be pleaded
Relief in the form of interest, whether under statute or otherwise, must be specifically claimed. See Order 18 rule 8(4) and the commentary thereunder.

### [18.15.4]   Order 18 rule 15(2) – statement of claim must conform to general indorsement
Where a writ is generally indorsed under Order 6 rule 2(1)(a) the general indorsement lays down the boundaries of the claim and by virtue of Order 18 rule 15(2) the subsequent state ment of claim may not plead any matter outside those boundaries. See also *Sterman v Moore* [1970] 1 QB 596. In the converse situation where a claim is made in the general indorsement and then not included in the subsequent statement of claim, it is taken to have been abandoned: *Harries v Ashford* [1950] 1 All ER 425.

**16.   Defence of tender** (O. 18 r. 16)
    **Where in any action a defence of tender before action is pleaded, the defendant must pay into court in accordance with Order 22 the amount alleged to have been tendered, and the tender shall not be available as a defence unless and until payment into court has been made.**

---

## NOTES

### [18.16.1]   Defence of tender
Order 18 rule 16 provides that payment into court by way of sanctioned payment under Order 22 is required before a defendant may rely on a pleaded defence of tender. The wording of the rule is such that the requirement for payment in arises only when the defence is pleaded. In *Maysun Eng'g Co Ltd v Wormald Eng'g Services Ltd* CACV 199/2006 (Tang VP, Yuen JA & Waung J; 11.01.2007) (paras 33-39) it was argued that a defence of tender need not necessarily be pleaded, but the court did not find it necessary to decide this point.

    The defence of tender is, in effect, that the defendant had already tendered payment of the sum due before the plaintiff commenced the action. In contract cases, the defence is in essence that the defendant has always been ready to perform the contract: see *Citadines Ashley TST (HK) Ltd v Quenchers Ltd* HCA 2704/2006 (Burrell J; 23.07.2007) (at para 13, quoting Chitty on Contract).

    At common law, the defence of tender was only available in respect of liquidated claims: *Davys v Richardson* (1888) 21 QBD 202, 204–5. By section 30 of the Law Amendment and Reform (Consolidation) Ordinance (Cap 23), inserted by section 8 of the Civil Justice (Miscellaneous Amendments) Ordinance 2008, in force from 2009, the defence is extended to apply to all monetary claims, whether liquidated or unliquidated.

    Since a defence of tender goes to the question of liability, the prohibition on disclosure to the court of payments into court before issues of liability have been decided does not apply where the defence is pleaded (Order 22 rule 25(3)(a); Order 59 rule 12A(1)).

    Order 22 rule 23(2) provides that a party who has paid money into court under

Order 14 (see Order 14 rule 4(3) which empowers the court to order payment into court as security for the amount claimed on grant of leave to defend), may appropriate the payment as a tender. This may be done in the party's pleading. Order 22 rule 23(3) deems the money so appropriated to be a sanctioned payment in accordance with that Order, with the enhanced costs and interest consequences set out therein.

## 17. Defence of set-off (O. 18 r. 17)

**Where a claim by a defendant to a sum of money (whether of an ascertained amount or not) is relied on as a defence to the whole or part of a claim made by the plaintiff, it may be included in the defence and set-off against the plaintiff's claim, whether or not it is also added as a counterclaim.**

---

## NOTES

### [18.17.1] Set-off

Order 18 rule 17 provides that a cross-claim by a defendant against the plaintiff, for money, may be pleaded in the defence. The rule provides that such a cross-claim may instead, or in addition, be pleaded as a counterclaim. As to counterclaims, see the commentary under Order 15 rule 2.

The purpose of set-off and counterclaim is to avoid multiplicity of proceedings in cases where both sides have claims against each other.

### [18.17.2] Distinction between set-off and counterclaim

Both set-off and counterclaim are types of cross-claim which may be used to advance a claim which a defendant has back against the plaintiff. The primary difference is that set-off operates as a defence whereas counterclaim has some of the characteristics of an independent action. Hence a claim to set-off is only good to the amount of the plaintiff's claim: *Stooke v Taylor* (1880) 5 QBD 569, 575. Where a defendant's cross-claim exceeds the amount of the plaintiff's claim, the whole amount can only be recovered if put forward as a counterclaim.

There are also costs consequences to the choice of proceeding by way of set-off or counterclaim. See below.

### [18.17.3] Historical origin of legal and equitable set-off

Order 18 rule 17 does not distinguish between legal and equitable set-off, but there are important differences in the substantive law, arising from their different historical origins.

By the Statutes of Set-Off 1728 and 1734, legal set off was introduced as a defence. The court of Chancery developed equitable set-off for circumstances which the law did not provide. Relief by way of equitable set-off would be provided by way of injunction 'to restrain the claimant at law from enforcing his claim at law': *BICC plc v Burndy Corp & Anor* [1985] 1 All ER 417, 426g (CA). Thus, equitable set-off is and has always been available as a defence against claims for common law damages, and is not restricted to claims for equitable remedies.

For discussion of the historical distinction between the two types of set-off see *The Brede* [1973] 3 All ER 589, quoted with approval in *Golden Jet Forwarders Ltd & Anor v Transmeridian Air Cargo Ltd & Anor* [1982] HKLR 228.

**[18.17.4]    Juridical basis for legal set-off in Hong Kong**

There does not appear to be any direct equivalent to the English Statutes of Set-Off in Hong Kong, nor were they applied in Hong Kong under the pre-1997 Application of English Law Ordinance. In *Re Finbo Engineering Co Ltd* [1998] 2 HKC 480; [1998] 2 HKLRD 695 Le Pichon J took the view that the English statutes had been incorporated in Hong Kong law prior to the 1966 enactment of that Ordinance, and the issue was whether that Ordinance had repealed them. If so, they were not part of post-1997 Hong Kong law. Unfortunately, it was not necessary for the court to decide the issue in the particular proceedings.

It was argued in *Re Finbo* that set-off, being a matter of pure procedure, did not require express inclusion in the list of statutes under the Application of English Law Ordinance.

It has also been argued that section 12(2)(a) of the High Court Ordinance is sufficient to incorporate legal set-off in Hong Kong law. See Morrow, 'Progress in Practice and Proce dure' [1986] *Law Lectures for Practitioners* (HKLJ) 51, 58. Section 12(2)(a) provides that the Court of First Instance shall have jurisdiction and authority of like nature as the High Court of Justice in England. Another possible statutory basis is section 16(2) of the High Court Ordinance, which provides that the court's jurisdiction should be exercised in such a way as to ensure that 'all matters in dispute between the parties are completely and finally determined, and all multiplicity of legal proceedings with respect to any of those matters is avoided'.

**[18.17.5]    Circumstances in which legal and equitable set-off available**

The requirements for legal and equitable set-off are different. The situation was summarised succinctly by Yuen JA in *Wong Wai Kuen t/a Mei Tak Decoration & Engineering Co v Polygon Contracting Ltd* [2002] 2 HKLRD 569:

> The distinction between the two are that at law, so long as debts are liquidated and there is mutuality, set-off can apply even though the debts are not connected; in equity, even unliquidated debts may be set-off so long, however, as the debts are connected.

We now turn to deal with the major differences between legal and equitable set-off in greater detail.

*(1) The close connection requirement for equitable set-off*

There must be a close connection between the two claims for equitable set-off to be available: *BICC plc v Burndy Corp* [1985] 1 All ER 417; *Lee Wing Fung v Lee Wing Chiu* DCCJ 3357/1985 (Judge E Li; 09.08.1985). It is not sufficient that the parties' claims arise under the same agreement or the same trading relationship – the connection must be so close that the cross-claim impeaches the main claim such that it would be unjust to allow it: *British Anzani (Felixstowe) Ltd v International Marine Management (UK) Ltd* [1979] 3 All ER 451; [1980] QB 137; *Selwood Ltd v ICE Far East (HK) Ltd* HCA 4403/2001 (Deputy Judge Lam; 21.11.2001) citing *Esso Petroleum Co Ltd v Milton* [1997] 1WLR 938, 950. In *Ridge Ltd v Golden Castle Ltd* [2005] 3 HKC 592 it was held that there could be no equitable set-off of damages for breach of the covenant of quiet possession against rent since payment of rent was not dependent upon the landlord's compliance. For a fuller discussion of equitable set-off see *Geldof Metaalconstructie NV v Simon Carves Ltd* [2010] EWCA Civ 667 (11.06.2010).

(2) *Legal set-off requires only mutuality*

Legal set-off is available where there is mutuality in the cross-claims. The equitable requirement of showing that the cross-claim impeaches the main claim need not be met. In this context mutuality means that the claims must be between the same parties in the same capacities: *Wong Wai Kuen t/a Mei Tak Decoration & Engineering Co v Polygon Contracting Ltd* [2002] 2 HKLRD 569; *Nelson v Roberts* (1893) 69 LT 352. An obvious example is where a depositor has a credit balance but also owes money to the financial institution (though in most such cases set-off would be provided for by contract).

It is not always easy to discern when there is sufficient mutuality for legal set-off to be available. In *Wong Wai Kuen* (above) it was held that legal set-off was available in respect of a statutory claim (under the Employment Ordinance) against a contractual claim for work done. However in *Karpex (HK) Ltd v Yasmine Printing (China) Ltd* CACV 124/2006 (Cheung JA & Chu J; 10.07.2006) it was held that a cross-claim arising under a separate contract was properly the subject of a counterclaim rather than set-off.

(3) *The issue as to liquidated and unliquidated claims*

It is clear that equitable set-off is available regardless of whether the main claim and the cross-claim are liquidated or unliquidated, whereas historically this has not been the case with legal set-off. This state of the law has repeatedly been described as unsatisfactory: see, for example, *Mass International Ltd v Hillis Industries Ltd & Anor* [1996] 1 HKC 434, 441 (CA) referring to *Axel Johnson Petroleum AB v MG Mineral Group AG* [1992] 1 WLR 270, 275.

The Hong Kong court continues to proceed on the basis that legal set-off is not available in respect of unliquidated claims. See, for example *Alco International Ltd v Akai Electronic Co Ltd* [2000] 3 HKC 724; *Heng Hing Metal Factory Ltd v Unionwest Ltd* HCA 9328/2000 (Sakhrani J; 20.04.2001) and *Lau Kwok Yin v Cheong Tit Ping* HCA 4559/2002 (Deputy Judge Muttrie; 03.06.2003). The significance is that an unliquidated claim may only be set off where the more stringent close connection test applicable in equity can be met.

However there may be room for argument that legal set-off should, in fact, be available in respect of unliquidated claims. Order 18 rule 17 expressly extends the right to plead set-off to any money claim 'whether of an ascertained amount or not'. Further, no such restriction can be found in section 16(2) of the High Court Ordinance, if that be the juridical basis of legal set-off in Hong Kong.

**[18.17.6]  Set-off and non-monetary claims**

It is now accepted that both legal and equitable set-off can be available against claims for relief other than money, at least where the non-monetary claim is consequent upon failure to pay a sum of money. *See BICC plc v Burndy Corp* [1985] 1 All ER 417, 426b (CA). In that case, the court allowed set-off of a claim for money against a claim for assignment of patent rights under a penalty clause.

**[18.17.7]  Contractual exclusion of right to set-off**

The right to plead a defence of set-off may be excluded by contract: *Young's Engineering Co Ltd v Hang Sing Construction Co Ltd* HCA 469/1984 (Penlington J; 12.10.1984), citing *Gilbert-Ash (Northern) Ltd v Modern Engineering (Bristol) Ltd* [1974] AC 689

(HL). However, 'clear words are required to rebut the presumption that a party does not intend to abandon rights of set-off': *Euroasia Dockyard Enterprise & Development Ltd v Foredragon Shipping Ltd* HCA 7554/1998 (Yuen J; 30.03.1999).

It has been held in England that a contractual term excluding the right to set-off may not survive the equivalent of the Control of Exemption Clauses Ordinance (Cap 71): *Stewart Gill Ltd v Horatio Myer & Co Ltd* [1992] QB 600, 604 (CA). The point was raised in *Natamon Protpakorn v Citibank NA* HCA 190/2005 (Deputy Judge Muttrie; 23.11.2005) but it was not necessary for the court to reach a decision on it. Note that the Ordinance only applies to standard form consumer contracts and does not affect commercial contracts negotiated at arm's length.

### [18.17.8]    Claims by and against government
There are restrictions on the right to raise a defence of set-off in proceedings by and against the government. See Order 77 rule 6 and the commentary thereunder.

### [18.17.9]    Abatement
A claim of abatement (reduction in price in defence to an action for the price of goods sold and delivered on the ground of breach of warranty) is a form of set-off developed at common law. See *Mondel v Steel* (1841) 151 ER 1288 and *Hanak v Green* [1958] 2 QB 9.

Abatement is now codified in section 55 of the Sale of Goods Ordinance (Cap 26).

### [18.17.10]  Costs
Since set-off operates as a defence, where it succeeds in ousting the plaintiff's claim entirely, the defendant will normally be entitled to costs. See *Incorporated Owners of King Yip Factory Building v Kwun Wah Flower & Plant Mfy Ltd* CACV 128/2003 (Yuen JA & Yam J; 13.11.2003) (para 33). The situation is different with counterclaims: see the commentary under Order 15 rule 2.

**18.    Counterclaim and defence to counterclaim** (O. 18 r. 18)

**Without prejudice to the general application of this Order to a counterclaim and a defence to counterclaim, or to any provision thereof which applies to either of those pleadings specifically—**

      **(a)    rules 12(1A), (1B) and (1C) and 15(1) shall apply to a counterclaim as if the counterclaim were a statement of claim and the defendant making it a plaintiff; (L.N. 404 of 1991)**

      **(b)    rules 8(2), 16 and 17 shall, with the necessary modifications, apply to a defence to counterclaim as they apply to a defence.**

**19.    Striking out pleadings and indorsements** (O. 18 r. 19)

    **(1)    The Court may, either of its own motion or on application, at any stage of the proceedings order to be struck out or amended any pleading or the indorsement of any writ in the action, or anything in any pleading or in the indorsement, on the ground that—**

      **(a)    it discloses no reasonable cause of action or defence, as the case may be; or**

      **(b)    it is scandalous, frivolous or vexatious; or**

      **(c)    it may prejudice, embarrass or delay the fair trial of the**

**action; or**

**(d)     it is otherwise an abuse of the process of the court;**

**and may order the action to be stayed or dismissed or judgment to be entered accordingly, as the case may be. (L.N. 152 of 2008)**

**(2)     No evidence shall be admissible on an application under paragraph (1)(a).**

**(3)     This rule shall, so far as applicable, apply to an originating summons and a petition as if the summons or petition, as the case may be, were a pleading.**

---

## NOTES

### [18.19.1]     Scope of Order 18 rule 19

Order 18 rule 19 gives the court an express power to strike out a pleading or indorsement on 4 specified grounds, which are discussed below. This striking out power exists in parallel with an inherent jurisdiction to strike out, as to which see *Reichel v Magrath* (1889) 14 App Cas 665.

Order 18 rule 19 also empowers the court to order a pleading to be amended on the same 4 specified grounds.

In practice, where the court strikes out a pleading because the whole claim is bad, it will also dismiss the action; however if the defect appears capable of being cured the court may strike out and make an order for amendment. *Sun Focus Investment Ltd v Tang Shing Bor & Anor* HCA 538/2007 (Recorder Shieh SC; 22.10.2009) is an example of the latter course being taken.

### [18.19.2]     Application to strike out pleading – principles

The principles applicable on an application to strike out a pleading or indorsement under this rule or under the court's parallel inherent jurisdiction are well established in English cases which are regularly applied in the Hong Kong courts. The burden on a defendant seeking to strike out a statement of claim is 'high', and to succeed it 'must show to the court that [the] issues are unarguable and that on a trial of the action the plaintiff is bound to fail': see *BSC Building Materials Co Ltd v Cheung Chi Hung Michael* [1998] 2 HKC 425, 433D–E, per Waung J. In *Drummond-Jackson v BMA* [1970] 1 WLR 688 the power to strike out was described as 'drastic' and it was held that it should be exercised 'sparingly', only in 'plain and obvious' cases (see per Sir Gordon Willmer at 699H).

### [18.19.3]     Evidence on application to strike out

No evidence is admissible on an application under rule 19(1)(a) to strike out on the ground a pleading or indorsement discloses no reasonable cause of action or defence. This is expressly provided in rule 19(2). On such an application the court 'simply looks at the Statement of Claim and determines whether, on the assumption that the facts pleaded in it are true, the plaintiff has a cause of action in law': *Hong Kong Polytechnic University & Ors v Next Magazine Publishing Ltd & Anor* [1997] 2 HKLRD 260. However, the bar is not absolute. In *Hong Kong Polytechnic University* (above) (para 9) the court was prepared to consider agreed facts not pleaded in the statement of claim. In *Hotung v Hillhead Ltd & Ors* [2008] 3 HKC 301 (paras 49-50) it was held that although the bar applies in deciding whether there is a viable cause of action on the pleadings, it did not prevent the court from looking at correspondence in determining whether, despite inadequate pleadings, there was a good reason why the action ought to be allowed to proceed.

With regard to strike out applications brought under rule 19(1)(b), (c) or (d) there is no restriction on admissibility of evidence. Thus affidavits may and often are relied upon on applications to strike out on grounds that the pleading or indorsement is (b) scandalous, frivolous or vexatious, (c) may prejudice, embarrass or delay a fair trial, or (d) is otherwise an abuse of process. The affidavit evidence may be used 'to show, for example that a plaintiff simply has no factual basis to support the cause of action pleaded': *Oh Jae-hoon Eugene v Richdale* [2004] 4 HKC 315 (CA) (para 15).

Where affidavit evidence is relied upon, the court is not in a position to resolve issues of fact. Thus 'it is wrong to expect the court to have to conduct a protracted analysis of affidavit evidence in a strike out application'; that can only be done in 'the rarest of cases' where 'the ultimate issue is quite simple': *Chuang Yue Chien Eugene v Ho Yau Kwong Kevin* [2002] 4 HKC 245 (para 14(2)). Care must be taken 'to ensure that a plaintiff is not prevented from going to trial unless the material facts before the court at the strike out stage are either uncontroversial or cannot seriously be in dispute': *Oh v Richdale* (above) (para 15). In *Overseas Trust Bank Ltd v Coopers & Lybrand (a firm) & Ors* [1990] 1 HKLR 568, 583H-I (CA), a case in which 'unusual and possibly extravagant' claims were made, it was held that a third party was entitled to rely on affidavit evidence to seek to show the court that the statement of claim against it should be struck out:

> ...not on the ground that the facts disclosed were improbable or that it was difficult to believe that they could be proved, (see per Lord Herschell in *Lawrence v Lord Norreys* (1888) 39 Ch D 213, 217) but on the ground that 'the case has not a solid basis capable of proof ... the story told in the pleadings is a myth ... and has no solid foundation' (per Lord Herschell at 220) and one where 'the statement of claim presents . . . a tissue of improbabilities, which ought not to be sent to proof' (per Lord Watson, at 222).

Such cases will be rare. Strike out applications are more suitable for determination of issues of law based on uncontested certain facts. See *Chuang* (above) (para 14(3)).

## [18.19.4]　Advance disclosure of grounds for application to strike out

Part III of practice direction 19.1 provides that the grounds of an application to strike out a pleading must be disclosed to the opposing party in advance. The requirement applies to 'applications to strike out pleadings as disclosing no reasonable cause of action or where no letter has been written by counsel for the applicant to counsel for the respondent signifying his intention to make the application and the broad grounds upon which he will rely'. In such cases the practice direction stipulates that 'the applicant shall inform the respondent of the said grounds in writing at least 5 clear working days before the day fixed for the hearing.'

The full text of the practice direction can be viewed on the judiciary's website www.judiciary.gov.hk or that of the Hong Kong Legal Information Institute www.hklii.org, both of which are accessible by the general public free-of-charge.

## [18.19.5]    Delay in making application to strike out

Order 18 rule 19(1) provides that a striking out order may be made 'at any stage of the proceedings'.

In *Tang Woung Shiu v Tang Kun Yeung & Anor* [2003] 1 HKC 195 such an application was objected to on the ground that it was not made until trial. Commentary in *Hong Kong Civil Procedure 2002* was cited in support of the objection. Recorder Kenneth Kwok SC held (at 204D–E) that the interpretation contended for was contrary to the wording of the rule and ordered that the claim be struck out. He cited *Goodwill v British Pregnancy Advisory Service* [1996] 2 All ER 161 where it was held that although litigants should be encouraged to bring a strike out application at an early stage this was not an absolute requirement. Further he declined to follow the decision in *Halliday v Shoesmith* [1993] 1 WLR 1 (CA) where it was held that the court should not hear such an application 'at the eleventh hour' save in exceptional circumstances. See, however, *Poon Lai Bing v Gold Dragon Ltd* CACV 136/2007 (Cheung JA & Stone J; 13.12.2007) where Cheung JA said (at para 30) that a striking out application brought as late as the beginning of trial should only be allowed to proceed 'in the clearest circumstances where, for example, the particulars were totally lacking and the allegations were clearly unsustainable'.

## [18.19.6]    Court may exercise power to strike out of its own motion

With effect from 2009, as part of the civil justice reforms, Order 18 rule 19(1) was amended so as to state expressly that the power to strike out may be exercised by the court either on application or of its own motion. The amendment gave a legislative basis to what had previously been recognised in the cases. See *Ng Yat Chi & Anor v China Resources Holdings Ltd & Ors* [2005] 3 HKC 506, 523–526, citing various examples.

## [18.19.7]    Order 18 rule 19(1)(a) – No reasonable cause of action or defence

No evidence is admissible on an application under rule 19(1)(a) to strike out a pleading or indorsement on the ground that it discloses no reasonable cause of action or defence (see Order 18 rule 19(2) and see *Republic of Peru v Peruvian Guano Co* (1887) 36 Ch D 489). The viability of the cause of action or defence must be judged by reference to the pleadings alone. Hence it has been said that such an application 'raises a pure pleading point': *Yue Xiu Finance Co Ltd v Agnew & Ors (formerly t/a Deloitte Haskins & Sells (a firm)) & Anor* [1996] 2 HKC 122 (CA) per Litton VP at 123I.

In the *Yue Xiu* case, Litton VP stated that rule 19(1)(a) provides 'a drastic remedy', further 'it follows that no court should give effect to it unless it is satisfied that the legal basis of the claim is unarguable or almost incontestably bad ...' (at 127B). Citing *E (a minor) v Dorset County Council* [1994] 3 WLR 853, 865, Litton VP cautioned that 'where the legal viability of the cause of action is sensitive to the facts, an order to strike out should not be made'. His Lordship's observations should, in principle, be equally applicable to an application to strike out a defence. The *Yue Xiu* case was cited with approval by Nazareth JA in *Beijing Television v Brightec Ltd & Ors* [1999] 2 HKC 665 (CA).

See also *Karex (HK) Ltd v Fortune Talent Development Ltd & Ors* [1999] 4 HKC 203 (CA) where it was held that a claim which is 'arguable' should not be struck out (per Mayo JA at 209C–D) and Rogers JA held '[i]t is not for the court to strike out a pleading simply on the basis that there is a slim chance of success' (at 210F).

In *BSC Building Materials Supply Co Ltd v Cheung* [1998] 2 HKC 425, 433E Waung J stated that a defendant seeking to strike out a statement of claim assumes a 'high burden', and that to succeed it must show that the plaintiff is 'bound to fail' at trial.

In the circumstances an application to strike out under Order 18 rule 19(1)(a) will only be appropriate where it is arguable that a claim or defence cannot succeed as a matter of law. For example, it might be argued that the law does not recognise a particular cause of action: see *Hubbuck & Sons Ltd v Wilkinson, Heywood & Clark Ltd* [1989] 1 QB 86,91 and see *Tang Chai On v AG* [1970] HKLR 209. Or it may be argued that no cause of action had arisen by the date of issue of the writ: see *Grandregal Enterprises Ltd v Sitwell Estates Ltd* [2003] 2 HKC 306 (DC). In *Lam Fung Ying v Ho Tung Sing* [1993] 2 HKC 28 (CA), an action to enforce a compromise of proceedings was struck out where the plaintiff had elected to proceed with the original action. In *Sun Zhongguo v BOC Group Ltd* [2003] 2 HKC 239, a claim based on an alleged implied term arising from 'business efficacy' was struck out where it was contrary to the terms of the Employment Ordinance (Cap 57).

Striking out defence – in *Hutchvision Asia Ltd v Asia Television Ltd* [1993] 2 HKC 510, citing *Reichel v Magrath* (1889) 14 App Cas 665, 669 it was held that 'the court will be particularly careful in exercising this exceptional jurisdiction when the pleading sought to be struck out is a defence, though it will do so if it is satisfied that the defendant "has not a shadow of a defence"?'. Example – see *Kar Ho Development Co Ltd v Axis Investment Ltd* [2001] 1 HKC 86 (CA) where a two-member bench of the Court of Appeal struck out part of a purchaser's defence in an action under a contract relating to property. The purchaser had not given express notice that the contract was at an end and relied solely on its failure to complete. Mayo VP held (at 94G) 'while the defendant's silence may have indicated that the contract was at an end it could not in any sensible way be interpreted as being the exercise of a right to rescind.' Keith JA (at 97H–I) stated that the purchaser's argument was 'plainly and obviously unsustainable' in the absence of express notice giving the reason for non-completion.

**[18.19.8]    Order 18 rule 19(1)(b) – scandalous, frivolous or vexatious**

The test for striking out an action as frivolous or vexatious was considered by the Court of Appeal in *Numatic Engineering Ltd v Peter Ying Hiu-tan t/a Onward Trading Co* [1981] HKLR 4. Huggins JA held (at 6A) that the case for striking out must be 'very clear', citing *Gleeson v J Wippell & Co Ltd* [1977] 1 WLR 510, 518C.

An action may be struck out as scandalous, frivolous or vexatious where it discloses no cause of action known to law: see *Chaffers v Goldsmid* [1894] 1 QB 186. To this extent there is an overlap with rule 19(1)(a). The difference between the two provisions is that evidence is admissible on an application under rule 19(1)(b) but not rule 19(1)(a) – see Order 18 rule 19(2).

A pleading will not be struck out as 'scandalous' in Order 18 rule 19(1)(b) unless it is irrelevant. It is permissible to plead an immoral relationship where that relationship is relevant: see *Anonymous* (1835) 1 My & Cr 78 where it was held that it was permissible to plead an immoral relationship between a man and a woman where the cause of action was based on undue influence of the one on the other. However, a pleading which seeks to cast irrelevant aspersions on the opposing party's character is 'scandalous' and liable to be struck out: see *Edmunds v Lord Brougham* (1866) 13 LT 790, 791 where it was held that an irrelevant pleading of spite and anger could be struck out.

**[18.19.9]     Order 18 rule 19(1)(c) – prejudice, embarrass or delay**

A pleading which may prejudice, embarrass or delay the fair trial of an action may be struck out, wholly or in part (to the extent of the defect) under Order 18 rule 19(1)(c). The rule applies to pleadings which unnecessarily impede or complicate an action or put the opposing party in difficulty as to how to respond. For example:

- *ambiguous pleading* – an ambiguous pleading may be struck out if it creates doubt as to what the party's case is: *Fleming v Dollar* (1889) 23 QBD 388; *Lo Ka Chun v Lo To & Anor* HCA 2015/1980 (Clough J; 11.06.1984).

- *irrelevant pleading* – allegations which are 'so irrelevant that to allow them to stand would involve useless expense, and would also prejudice the fair trial of the action by involving the parties in a dispute that is wholly apart from the issues' are liable to be struck out: *Mayor & Councillors of City of London v Horner* (1914) 111 LT 512, 514 (followed in *So Pak Hung v Cheung Chow* [1997] 3 HKC 694, 699).

- *prolix pleading* – a pleading which is prolix in that it is too lengthy a statement of necessary facts, or a statement of facts unnecessary to be stated, may be struck out: *Davy v Garrett* (1877) 7 Ch D 473, 486. In *Leung Wing Tak v IT Catering & Services Ltd* DCPI 1267/2006 (Deputy Judge W C Li; 03.10.2006) such a pleading was struck out on the ground it would involve the opposing party in useless expense and would unnecessarily prolong matters.

- *unnecessary pleading* – a pleading which is unnecessary to the extent it may prejudice, embarrass or delay trial will be struck out: *Knowles v Roberts* (1888) 38 Ch D263 (CA) quoted with approval in *Saunders v JSM & Ors* HCA 2981/1972 (Registrar Jones; 12.01.1973).

- *unintelligible pleading* – a pleading which is unintelligible, such that the opposing party cannot plead properly in response, is embarrassing and may be struck out: *Saunders v JSM & Ors* (above) citing *Davy v Garrett* (above).

- *contrary to rules of pleading* – a pleading which infringes the rules of pleading may be struck out: *Knowles v Roberts* (above). For example a pleading which improperly pleads law or evidence, making it difficult for the opposing party to respond properly.

- *Unparticularised or incomplete pleading* – the court may strike out a pleading which the party cannot or will not properly particularise: *Wharf Properties Ltd & Anor v Eric Cumine Associates* [1991] 2 HKLR 154 (PC). However, where an incomplete pleading is capable of 'curative amendment' the court will generally accommodate an application to do so, though not where no useful purpose would be served: *Akai Holdings Ltd v Ko & Ors* HCCL 20/2005 (Stone J; 09.06.2006) (para 29).

The word 'embarrass' in rule 19(1)(c) is not used in the sense of making a person feel awkward or ashamed. There is no barrier to pleading in a proper fashion relevant facts which may embarrass the opposing party in that sense: *Millington v Loring* (1880) 6 QB 190 (CA); *Lumb v Beaumont* (1884) 49 LT 772.

The court will only strike out a pleading under rule 19(1)(c) in clear cases. If the problem can be cured in some other way the court will be unlikely to strike out. For example in *Mak Yiu v Chinachem Realty Ltd* HCA 10335/1998 (Ribeiro J; 17.11.1999) the court declined to strike out an embarrassing pleading where the opposing party's difficulty could be overcome by a request for particulars or interrogatories.

**[18.19.10]  Order 18 rule 19(1)(d) – abuse of process**

The court has power under Order 18 rule 19(1)(d) and under its inherent jurisdiction to strike out proceedings on the ground of abuse of process. The power 'must be exercised with extreme caution' because it is 'a very serious matter to prevent a party from commencing litigation or pursuing it': *Tsang Chin Keung v Employees Compensation Assistance Fund Board (No 2)* [2003] 1 HKC 499, 510G-H (CA). The categories of 'abuse of process' are by no means closed, but it has been held that there is no discretion to strike out a genuine claim where the party bringing it has participated in an abuse of process by a co-litigant. See *Shah v Ul-Haq & Ors* [2009] EWCA Civ 542. In that case it was held that the genuine claims of two accident victims could not be struck out despite the fact they had participated in an abuse of process by fraudulently maintaining that a third plaintiff had also been injured.

There are well-recognised circumstances in which the power to strike out will be exercised. These are discussed below.

(1)    *Relitigation of matters previously decided*

It is an abuse of process for a litigant to seek to re-litigate a dispute which has already been decided in prior proceedings. The dispute is said to be *res judicata* and the subsequent proceedings may be struck out: *Stephenson v Garnett* [1898] 1 QB 677. Similarly an issue which has been decided may not be re-opened in subsequent proceedings even though the cause of action is not exactly the same – issue estoppel applies: *Arnold v National Westminster Bank plc* [1991] 2 AC 93; *Keen Lloyd Energy Ltd v Bank of China (HK) Ltd* HCA 1299/2004 (Poon J; 11.01.2008) (appeal dismissed – CACV 34/2008).

In *Wong Wang Sum v Lee Kam Engineering Co (a firm)* [1996] 3 HKC 627, 630 Cheung J held that the ingredients which must be established to make out a claim of *res judicata* or issue estoppel are those laid down in *Carl Zeiss Stiftung v Rayner & Keeler Ltd (No 3)* [1970] Ch 506:

1.    a prior judicial decision by a competent court or tribunal;
2.    of a final character;
3.    of the same question;
4.    between the same parties.

The prior decision must be 'final and conclusive on the merits' and 'the cause of action must be extinguished by the decision which is said to create the estoppel': *Kung Wong Sau Hing v Sze To Chun Keung* [1996] 2 HKC 616, 625 (affirmed on appeal at [1996] 3 HKC 292) citing *Carl Zeiss Stiftung v Rayner & Keeler Ltd (No 2)* [1967] 1 AC 853, 935C–D. See also *Hung Fan Keung Henry v Yeung Man Fung* [1996] 2 HKC 329 (CA).

In *Union (V-Tex) Shirt Factory Ltd v Union V-Tex Realty Ltd & Ors* [1985] HKLR 152 it was held that a decision based on a concession made by counsel gave rise to issue estoppel.

Where the previous proceedings came to a conclusion at an interlocutory stage, without adjudication on the merits, it may not be appropriate to strike out the subsequent proceedings as an abuse of process: *AG v Lo Chak Man Joseph & Ors* [1993] 1 HKC 548, 551B–D; *Tsang Yu v Tai Sang Container Cold Storage and Wharf Ltd* [2000] 1 HKLRD 780.

It appears that *res judicata* and issue estoppel technically do not arise from procedural interlocutory decisions. Nevertheless where it would be 'unjust and unreasonable' to permit the same issue to be relitigated between the same parties the court may in its discretion refuse to entertain the subsequent application. See *Pocklington Foods Inc v R in right of Alberta* (1995) 123 DLR (4th) 141 (Alta CA), quoted extensively in *Chu Hung Ching v Chan Kam Ming* [2001] 1 HKC 396, 401–402 (CA). It may not be considered 'unjust and unreasonable' for a party to make a fresh application for an interlocutory order where there has been a change of circumstances or new evidence (fresh applications for security for costs are an example), but where the fresh application amounts to unnecessary harassment it will not be allowed to proceed: *Pei Zheng Middle School & Anor v China Pui Ching Educational Foundation Ltd* CACV 2/2007 (Rogers VP & Le Pichon JA; 06.08.2007) (para 11-12).

There may be special circumstances in which *res judicata* does not apply but these do not include the nature of the proceedings such as personal injury litigation: *Sze Lai Man v Wing On Department Stores (HK) Ltd* [2001] 1 HKC 297, 300G.

*Res judicata* may arise from a foreign judgment: *Wee Koon Sim Anthony v UBS* [2006] 2 HKC 1 (appeal dismissed – CACV 96/2006). Likewise issue estoppel: *Traffic Stream (BVI Infrastructure Ltd v JP Morgan Chase Bank & Ors* [2005] 2 HKC 1, 8C, citing *The Sennar (No 2)* [1985] 1 WLR 490. Similarly court proceedings which seek to re-open issues already decided in an arbitration may be struck out under this rule: *Parakou Shipping Pte Ltd v Jinhui Shipping & Transportation Ltd & Ors* HCAJ 184/ 2009 (Reyes J; 30.09.2010) (subject to appeal – CACV 225/2010).

Similarly it is an abuse of process to launch a 'collateral attack' on an earlier decision by bringing new proceedings in a different form or against a different party. Such proceedings are liable to be struck out even though *res judicata* or issue estoppel may not technically arise. See *Hunter v Chief Constable* [1982] AC 529 (HL); *Cosby v USA* [2000] 3 HKC 688, 695I-696G; *Wong Shui Kee Roger v Thomas & Anor* HCA 2207/2003 (Reyes J; 17.09.2003).

(2)    *Multiplicity of proceedings*

The doctrine of *res judicata* has a wider sense under which it is 'an abuse of process to raise in subsequent proceedings matters which could and therefore should have been litigated in earlier proceedings': *Yat Tung Investment Co Ltd v Dao Heng Bank Ltd & Anor* [1975] AC 581; [1973]–[1976] HKC 194 (PC) per Lord Kilbrandon at 201A. See also *Yeo Teo Bok v Yeung Kai Pun* [1984] HKC 47; *Berthier Godown Ltd v E Wah Realty Ltd & Anor* [1986] HKC 8 and *Re Law Kin-man* [1993] 1 HKLR 83. In *Tso Joe-tak v AG* [1980] HKLR 120 a statement of claim was struck out where criminal proceedings were afoot touching on the same issue. A medical negligence claim was struck out in *Chan Chung Sau v Hospital Authority* DCPI 189/2004 (Deputy Judge S T Poon; 08.05.2006) where the plaintiff's whole loss had already been the subject of a prior personal injury action. In *Harvest Good Dev't Ltd v SJ & Ors* HCAL 32/2006 (Hartmann J; 19.12.2006) (affirmed on appeal: [2007] 4 HKC 424 (CA)), where squatters had succeeded in establishing adverse possession in litigation which went all the way to the CFA, the court struck out claims against them in a subsequent judicial review application asserting that the law of adverse possession violated the Basic Law. The court was satisfied the Basic Law issue could have been raised in the earlier proceedings.

The above-quoted passage from the speech of Lord Kilbrandon in *Yat Tung* has been criticised as being 'too dogmatic' insofar as it suggests that it is an abuse of process to raise matters which *could and therefore should* have been litigated in earlier proceedings. See *Chen Ray v Wan Ching Lam Anita & Anor* [2006] 1 HKC 454, (paras 25-6) citing *Johnson v Gore Wood & Co* [2002] 2 AC 1. In *Chen Ray* the court considered itself bound by *Yat Tung*, but in other cases, both in Hong Kong and elsewhere, courts have proceeded on the basis that there are circumstances in which a party may justifiably refrain from litigating an issue in one proceeding yet wish to raise it in another. In *Port of Melbourne Authority v Anshun Pty Ltd* (1981) 147 CLR 589 the High Court of Australia held that estoppel does not arise unless the matter relied upon in the second action was so relevant to the subject matter of the first action that it would have been unreasonable not to raise it earlier. That decision, and *Bradford & Bingley Building Society v Seddon Hancock* [1999] 1 WLR 1482 (CA), were referred to in *Tang Kin Wah v Cheng Choy Kam Chee Connie & Anor* [2002] 1 HKC 552 where it was held that to justify striking out in this context there must be some additional element such as a 'collateral attack on a previous decision, some dishonesty or successive actions amounting to unjust harassment'. In *Ngai Few Fung v Cheung Kwai Heung* [2008] 2 HKC 111 (CA) it was held that *Yat Tung* had been explained in *Brisbane City Council v AG* [1979] AC 411 (PC) and that subsequent proceedings should only be struck out if they are an abuse of process. In the *Ngai Few Fung* case, the Court of Appeal allowed the subsequent proceedings to continue, referring to the requirements of justice in the circumstances of the case.

In 'special circumstances' the court may permit subsequent proceedings to continue notwithstanding *res judicata* in its wider sense. This traces back to *Henderson v Henderson* (1843) 67 ER 313, 320, quoted with approval in *Yat Tung* (at 201 HKC). *Obiter dicta* in *Chun Yip Construction Co Ltd v E Bon Building Materials Co Ltd* HCCT 77/2002 (Burrell J; 16.01.2003) and in *Ngai Few Fung* (above) suggest that in addition to being special, the circumstances should explain why the matter was not raised in the earlier proceedings, and must be such as to lead to injustice if the subsequent proceedings are not allowed to continue.

See also the commentary under Order 34 rule 2 as to when a subsequent action may be struck out as an abuse of process where the prior action was dismissed for want of prosecution.

## (3)    *Public policy*

In *Derbyshire County Council v Times Newspapers Ltd* [1993] AC 534 it was held that for reasons of public policy a local authority could not maintain an action for defamation. Any such action would be liable to be struck out as an abuse of process. The *Derbyshire* case was applied in *Hong Kong Polytechnic University v Next Magazine Ltd* (No 2) (1996) 7 HKPLR 41, [1997] 1 HKLRD 102 (CFI) where a libel action by a university was struck out on the ground that as a public body which ought to be open to scrutiny it was contrary to public policy for a university to maintain such a claim. The decision was reversed on appeal: [1997] 1 HKLRD 514 on the ground the *Derbyshire* case does not apply to a university.

## (4) *Lack of intention to proceed to trial*

'Maintaining an action when there is no intention of carrying it to trial is an abuse of process rendering the action liable to be struck out': *New China Hong Kong Group Ltd (in liq) & Anor v AIG Asian Infrastructure Fund LP & Ors* [2005] 1 HKC 281,

288I per Woo VP summarising in his own words the *ratio* of *Grovit v Doctor* [1997] 1 WLR 640 (HL).

Abuse of process of this type can be established with evidence of inactivity on the part of the plaintiff. However delay alone is not sufficient. There must in addition be contumelious conduct such as disregard of a court order. See *New China Hong Kong Group* (above) at 289E-F, citing *Barclays Bank plc v Maling* [1997] EWCA Civ 1480 (23.04.1997) and *Teale v McKay* [1994] PIQR 508. In addition it is necessary for the court to consider whether it would be 'fair' to strike out: *Hoi Sing Construction Co Ltd v ITC Corp Ltd* HCA 11433/1998 (Deputy Judge Carlson; 22.04.2005), citing the *New China* case. In *Chevalier (E&M Contracting) Ltd v Rotegear Development Ltd* HCA 1717/1990 (Deputy Judge Fung; 09.06.2005) the court used this power to dismiss an action on the ground the plaintiff, which had delayed more than 10 years, 'never intended to comply with the scheme of the rules'.

Abuse of process of this type is confined to cases of an 'exceptional nature': *Hoi Sing Construction* (above).

The power to strike out on the ground of abuse of process of this type closely resembles the power to dismiss for want of prosecution (as to which see the commentary under Order 34 rule 2). However, there is no need to demonstrate prejudice: *New China Hong Kong Group* (above); *Hoi Sing Construction* (above).

On a *Grovit v Doctor* strike out application it is not appropriate to infer that the plaintiff has no intention to bring the matter to trial where, even after long delay, the plaintiff puts forward uncontradicted evidence that it does now intend to do so: *Super Worth Contracting Co Ltd v Top Glory Holdings Co Ltd & Anor* HCA 3754/2000 (Suffiad J; 22.04.2009).

### (5) *Vexatious litigants*
See the commentary under Order 5 rule 6 as to the court's powers to prevent vexatious litigants (who usually act in person) from commencing or continuing hopeless or misconceived proceedings.

### (6) *Injunction to restrain proceedings in another jurisdiction*
See the commentary under Order 29 rule 1 as to the circumstances in which the court will grant an injunction to restrain the commencement or continuation of proceedings in another jurisdiction.

### [18.19.11]  Dismissal for want of prosecution
The court has ample power to dismiss an action for want of prosecution, that is for failure to proceed with due alacrity. The juridical basis of such power is inherent jurisdiction and in addition the express powers under Order 25 rule 1(4) and Order 34 rule 2(2). For a fuller discussion of this topic see the commentary under Order 34 rule 2. The court's power to strike out for abuse of process under Order 18 rule 19(1)(d) is sometimes cited on such applications.

### [18.19.12]  Inconsistent claims against various defendants
A statement of claim is not liable to be struck out solely on the ground that it raises allegations which are not consistent as between defendants. See *Charter View Development Ltd v Golden Rich Enterprises Ltd & Anor* [2000] 2 HKC 77 (CA). There Ribeiro JA, delivering the judgment of the court, held (at 82B–C):

The viability of the claim must be judged separately in respect of each defendant. In any particular case, the averments contained in the statement of claim and the relief sought may disclose a perfectly good case against some defendants but not against others.

### [18.19.13] Striking out reply to request for further and better particulars

A reply to a request for further and better particulars forms part of the party's pleadings and are liable to be struck out under this rule: see *So Pak Hung v Cheung Chow & Anor* [1997] 3 HKC 694. In that case it was held that it sat ill with the party seeking the particulars to seek to strike them out once given.

### [18.19.14] Striking out superfluous pleadings

A superfluous pleading may be struck out under the court's inherent jurisdiction. See *Welwin Knitting Garment Factory Ltd v Welmade Fabric Mfg Ltd* [1983] 2 HKC 378 (Rhind J; 02.05.1983) where a counterclaim to a counterclaim was struck out.

### [18.19.15] Striking out statute-barred action

An action which is commenced after expiration of the limitation period may be struck out on the frivolous or vexatious ground: see *New China Hong Kong Group Ltd (in liq) & Ors v Ernst & Young (a firm)* HCCL 41/2004 (Recorder A Ho SC; 29.08.2008) (para 49), where the court adopted the approach set out in the following passage from the judgment of Stephenson LJ in *Ronex Properties Ltd v John Laing Construction Ltd* [1983] 1 QB 398, 408 (CA):

> There are many cases in which the expiry of the limitation period makes it a waste of time and money to let a plaintiff go on with his action. But in those cases it may be impossible to say that he has no reasonable cause of action. The right course is therefore for a defendant to apply to strike out the plaintiffs' claim as frivolous and vexatious and an abuse of the process of the court, on the ground that it is statute-barred . . .

However, it must be 'plain and obvious' that the limitation point is bound to succeed - where there is 'room for serious argument whether or not the limitation point is a good one' the court will not exercise its striking out power: *Lam Kee On v Lam Hing* [1992] 2 HKC 317, 320C.

### [18.19.16] Originating summons treated as writ

In *Kung Wong Sau Hin v Sze To Chun Keung* [1996] 2 HKC 616, it was argued that where it had been ordered that proceedings commenced by originating summons be continued as if begun by writ, issue estoppel arose and an application under this rule could no longer be brought. Le Pichon J rejected the submission stating (at 625C–D):

> If the contention ... is sound, then whenever an originating summons is treated as a writ, it would have the effect of precluding an application under O 18 r 19. That cannot be right as a matter of principle.

### [18.19.17] District Court

This rule did not apply in the District Court prior to 1 September 2000. Rule 38A of the District Court Civil Procedure (General) Rules covered similar ground and its existence negatived the application of RSC Order 18 rule 19. See *Kwangtung Provincial Bank v Tang Chik Leung* [1985] 1 HKC 93, 101.

As from 1 September 2000, the District Court rules contain Order 18 rule 19 in terms virtually identical to the High Court rules.

20. **Close of pleadings** (O. 18 r. 20)
    **(1)    The pleadings in an action are deemed to be closed—**
    **(a)    at the expiration of 14 days after service of the reply or, if there is no reply but only a defence to counterclaim, after service of the defence to counterclaim, or**
    **(b)    if neither a reply nor a defence to counterclaim is served, at the expiration of 28 days after service of the defence. (L.N. 152 of 2008)**
    **(2)    The pleadings in an action are deemed to be closed at the time provided by paragraph (1) notwithstanding that any request or order for particulars has been made but has not been complied with at that time.**

20A.  **Pleading, etc. to be verified by statement of truth** (O. 18, r 20A)
    **(1)    A pleading and the particulars of a pleading specified in paragraph (2) must be verified by a statement of truth in accordance with Order 41A.**
    **(2)    The particulars of a pleading referred to in paragraph (1) are particulars given by a party to any other party, whether voluntarily or pursuant to –**
    **(a)    a request made by that other party; or**
    **(b)    an order of the Court made under rule 12(3) or (4).**
    **(L.N. 152 of 2008)**

---

**NOTES**

**[18.20A.1]  Origin and scope of Order 18 rule 20A**
Order 18 rule 20A extends to pleadings and particulars the requirement in Order 41A that documents filed in court be verified by statement of truth. The rule derives from CPR 22.1(2). Insofar as it relates to pleadings, it covers the same ground as Order 41A rule 2(1)(a). See also the commentary concerning that rule.

**[18.20A.2]  Verification of pleadings and particulars by statement of truth**
The Chief Justice's working party on civil justice reform recommended adoption of the English requirement that pleadings and particulars be verified by statement of truth. The purpose was to address one of the 'main defects often found in pleadings … namely, the fact that such pleadings do not accurately reflect the true case of the party in question' (final report, para 217). The working party quoted (final report, para 222) the following passage from *Clarke v Marlborough Fine Art (London) Ltd* [2002] 1 WLR 1731, 1742:

> The purpose of Part 22 [in Hong Kong Order 18 rule 20A] is simply to exclude factual allegations which to the knowledge of the claimant or other party are untrue or which the party putting forward the pleading to the court is unable to say are true.
>
> In the most simple case the requirements of CPR 22.1 [Order 18 rule 20A(1) in Hong Kong] will, if observed, exclude untruthful or fanciful claims but the notes to Part 22 also indicate that the purpose of the new rule was to discourage the pleading of

cases which when settled were unsupported by evidence and which were put forward in the hope that something might turn up on disclosure or at trial.

The working party also noted (para 221) that verification of the facts alleged is appropriate given that in certain circumstances a Statement of Claim may be relied on as evidence.

For further discussion of the statement of truth procedure, see the commentary under Order 41A.

**[18.20A.3]  Consequences of failure to verify pleading by statement of truth**
Order 41A rule 6 provides that the court may strike out a pleading that is not verified by a statement of truth, and that any party may apply for such an order.

**[18.20A.4]  Extension of statement of truth requirement to statement of damages**
The practice direction on statements of truth (PD 19.3) provides, in para 1, that a statement of damages and answer to statement of damages, and any revision thereof are regarded as pleadings for the purpose of the statement of truth requirement, and must be verified accordingly.

**[18.20A.5]  Verification of amended pleadings by statement of truth**
Amendments to a pleading or particulars of a pleading must be verified by statement of truth: Order 20 rule 13. When this is done, the original statement of truth should not be deleted, and a new statement of truth underlined in the appropriate colour should be added: see para 2 of the practice direction on statements of truth (PD 19.3).

In the unusual case of *Binks v Securicor Omega Express Ltd* [2003] EWCA Civ 993 (16.07.2003) a party felt constrained not to amend his pleadings because the amendment would advance a case wholly inconsistent with evidence he had already given. The English court suggested (para 8) that in the circumstances it might be appropriate to exercise the power to dispense with a statement of truth. That power is found in Order 41A rule 2(3) in Hong Kong.

With regard to the appropriate colour for amendments, re-amendments and so forth, see practice direction 19.1, and see the commentary under Order 20 rule 10.

**[18.20A.6]  Verification of alternative pleading by statement of truth**
A pleading which alleges inconsistent alternatives in accordance with Order 18 rule 12A must be verified by statement of truth even though the alternatives cannot both be true. See Order 41A rule 2(2) and the commentary thereunder.

**21.   Trial without pleadings** (O. 18 r. 21)
    **(1)   Where in an action to which this rule applies any defendant has given notice of intention to defend in the action, the plaintiff or that defendant may apply to the Court by summons for an order that the action shall be tried without pleadings or further pleadings, as the case may be.**
    **(2)   If, on the hearing of an application under this rule, the Court is satisfied that the issues in dispute between the parties can be defined without pleadings or further pleadings, or that for any other reason the action can properly be tried without pleadings or further pleadings, as the case may be,**

the Court shall order the action to be so tried, and may direct the parties to prepare a statement of the issues in dispute or, if the parties are unable to agree such a statement, may settle the statement itself.

(3) Where the Court makes an order under paragraph (2), it shall, and where it dismisses an application for such an order, it may, give such directions as to the further conduct of the action as may be appropriate, and Order 25, rules 2 to 7 shall, with the omission of so much of rule 7(1) as requires parties to serve a notice specifying the orders and directions which they desire and with any other necessary modifications, apply as if the application under this rule were a case management summons. (L.N. 152 of 2008)

(4) This rule applies to every action begun by writ other than one which includes–

(a) a claim by the plaintiff for libel, slander, malicious prosecution or false imprisonment; or (L.N. 363 of 1990)

(b) a claim by the plaintiff based on an allegation of fraud.

**22. Saving for defence under Merchant Shipping Acts etc.** (O. 18 r. 22)

Nothing in Order 75, rules 37 to 40, shall be taken as limiting the right of any shipowner or other person to rely by way of defence on any provision of the Merchant Shipping Acts 1894 to 1979 in their application to Hong Kong or the Merchant Shipping (Local Vessels) Ordinance (Cap 548), the Merchant Shipping (Seafarers) Ordinance (Cap. 478) or the Merchant Shipping (Safety) Ordinance (Cap. 369), which limits the amount of his liability in connection with a ship or other property. (L.N. 356 of 1988; 44 of 1995 s. 143; 24 of 2005 s. 55)

---

**NOTES**

**[18.22.1] Wording of Order 18 rule 22**

Order 18 rule 22 continues to refer to United Kingdom legislation which ceased to apply in Hong Kong on the resumption of Chinese sovereignty. See the commentary under Order 75 rule 1. Note that this rule was amended with effect from 02.01.2007 when the Merchant Shipping (Local Vessels) Ordinance (Cap 548) was brought into force (LN 282/2006).

As a transitional measure some United Kingdom legislation may continue to apply in Hong Kong if adopted by the legislature: see section 2A(2)(e) of Cap 1, and with regard to shipping legislation see the commentary under Order 75 rule 1.

**23. Transitional provision relating to rule 93 of Amendment Rules 2008**
(Order 18 r. 23)

Where a statement of claim has been served on a defendant before the commencement of the Amendment Rules 2008, then rule 93 of the Amendment Rules 2008 does not apply to the defence to the claim and if a counterclaim has been served on the plaintiff, to the defence to the counterclaim, and rule 13 as in force immediately before the commencement continues to apply as if rule 93 of the Amendment Rules had not been made. (L.N. 152 of 2008)

**NOTES**

**[18.23.1]    Defence not affected by 2009 amendments if claim served prior to commencement**

The practical effect of Order 18 rule 23 is that the provisions of rule 13, by which a bare denial or non-admission is no longer permitted, do not apply to a defence to an action in which a statement of claim had already been served when that rule was amended as part of the civil justice reforms with effect from 2009. In such cases a bare denial will still be possible. The same is true with respect to a defence to counterclaim in such an action.

**24.    Transitional provision relating to rules 96 and 97 of Amendment Rules 2008** (O. 18, r. 24)

**Where a statement of claim has been served on a defendant before the commencement of the Amendment Rules 2008, then rules 96 and 97 of the Amendment Rules 2008 do not apply –**

    **(a)    in relation to the service of the defence and the reply to that defence; and**

    **(b)    if a counterclaim has been served on the plaintiff, in relation to the service of the defence to the counterclaim,**

**and rules 2 and 3 as in force immediately before the commencement continue to apply as if rules 96 and 97 of the Amendment Rules 2008 had not been made.**

    **(L.N. 152 of 2008)**

**NOTES**

**[18.24.1]    Times for service not affected by 2009 amendments if claim served prior to commencement**

The practical effect of rule 24 is that the provisions of rules 2 and 3 enlarging the time for service of a defence, reply or defence to counterclaim do not apply to an action in which a statement of claim had already been served when the amendments to those rules came into force as part of the civil justice reforms in 2009. The previous period of 14 days will apply instead of the enlarged time of 28 days.

**ORDER 19**

**DEFAULT OF PLEADINGS**

1.     **Default in service of statement of claim** (O. 19 r. 1)
      **Where the plaintiff is required by these rules to serve a statement of claim on a defendant and he fails to serve it on him, the defendant may, after the expiration of the period fixed by or under these rules for service of the statement of claim, apply to the Court for an order to dismiss the action, and the Court may by order dismiss the action or make such other order on such terms as it thinks just.**

_____

NOTES

**[19.1.1]   Power to dismiss for failure to serve statement of claim**
Where proceedings are commenced by generally indorsed writ, the plaintiff will normally be required to serve a statement of claim within 14 days of the defendant giving notice of intention to defend. See Order 18 rule 1. Failure to do so may result in an application under Order 19 rule 1 to dismiss the action. The power to dismiss under this rule is discretionary as a result of the use of the permissive 'may' in the rule's grant of power to the court. In this regard the power differs from that in Order 19 rule 2 to enter judgment in default of defence.

      Where the delay is short, and the defendant seeks an extension of time, the court will normally exercise its discretion in favour of the defendant, as in *Higginbottom v Aynsley* (1876) 3 Ch D 288 (delay of only 2 days as a result of clerical error). However each case depends on its own merits: *Canadian Oil Works Corp v Sir J Hay* (1878) 38 LT 549.

      An application under this rule is sometimes referred to as an application to dismiss for want of prosecution, especially where there has been long delay, as in *Chan Yiu Cheong Raymond v AG* HCPI 1159/1995 (Suffiad J; 05.10.1998) (para 2). Prejudice must sometimes be shown on an application to dismiss for want of prosecution. See the commentary on want of prosecution under Order 34 rule 2. However this does not appear to be required on an application under Order 19 rule 1.

2.     **Default of defence: claim for liquidated demand** (O. 19 r. 2)
      **(1)   Where the plaintiff's claim against a defendant is for a liquidated demand only, then, if that defendant fails to serve a defence on the plaintiff, the plaintiff may, after the expiration of the period fixed by or under these rules for service of the defence, enter final judgment against that defendant for a sum not exceeding that claimed by the writ in respect of the demand and for costs, and proceed with the action against the other defendants, if any. (See App. A, Form 39)**
      **(2)   Order 13, rule 1(2) shall apply for the purpose of this rule as it applies for the purposes of that rule.**

## NOTES

**[19.2.1]   Judgment in default of defence**
Order 19 rule 2 provides for entry of judgment in default of defence as of right in cases of claims for a liquidated sum. In cases involving claims for unliquidated damages, Order 19 rule 3 applies.

The right to enter judgment in default of defence is of general application but subject to exceptions elsewhere in these rules. See, for example, Orders 83A and 84A under which leave of court is required to enter judgment in default of defence in the actions to which those Orders apply. Although Order 19 rule 2 makes reference to the claims in the writ, it is not limited to actions commenced by writ. See *Smolar v Prosport Management Ltd & Anor* HCA 7744/2000 (Recorder Tang SC; 17.08.2001) where it was held that the rule applied to an action which had been commenced in the Labour Tribunal and directions for service of pleadings were given under Order 79 following transfer to the Court of First Instance.

Two clear days notice of intention to enter default judgment under rule 2 or rule 3 is required by Order 19 rule 8A.

**3.      Default of defence: claim for unliquidated damages** (O. 19 r. 3)
**Where the plaintiff's claim against a defendant is for unliquidated damages only, then, if that defendant fails to serve a defence on the plaintiff, the plaintiff may, after the expiration of the period fixed by or under these rules for service of the defence, enter interlocutory judgment against that defendant for damages to be assessed and costs, and proceed with the action against the other defendants, if any. (See App. A, Form 40)**

## NOTES

**[19.3.1]   Judgment in default of defence – unliquidated claim**
Whereas Order 19 rule 2 provides for judgment in default of defence to a liquidated claim, rule 3 provides for such judgment in respect of claims for an unliquidated amount of damages. Unliquidated claims are those the amount of which is not precisely ascertainable in advance, and require assessment by the court. See the discussion of this topic under Order 6 rule 2(1)(b). The distinction is perhaps best illustrated by example. Claims for special damages such as reimbursement for medical bills are liquidated, whereas claims for monetary compensation for a non-monetary loss such as pain and suffering are unliquidated.

Because unliquidated claims require assessment by the court, judgment in default under rule 3 is a judgment on liability only, with the quantum to be assessed. Assessment of damages will normally be conducted before a master in open court pursuant to Order 37 rule 1.

**4.      Default of defence: claim in detinue** (O. 19 r. 4)
**(1)   Where the plaintiff's claim against a defendant relates to the detention of goods only, then, if that defendant fails to serve a defence on the**

plaintiff, the plaintiff may, after the expiration of the period fixed by or under these rules for the service of the defence and subject to Order 42, rule 1A—

    (a)    at his option enter either—

        (i)    interlocutory judgment against that defendant for delivery of the goods or their value to be assessed and costs, or

        (ii)    interlocutory judgment for the value of the goods to be assessed and costs, or

    (b)    apply by summons for judgment against that defendant for delivery of the goods without giving him the alternative of paying their assessed value,

and in any case proceed with the action against the other defendants, if any. (See App. A, Form 41)

(2)    A summons under paragraph (1)(b) must be supported by affidavit and, notwithstanding Order 65, rule 9, the summons and a copy of the affidavit must be served on the defendant against whom judgment is sought.

**5.    Default of defence: claim for possession of land** (O. 19 r. 5)

(1)    Where the plaintiff's claim against a defendant is for possession of land only, then, if that defendant fails to serve a defence on the plaintiff, the plaintiff may, after the expiration of the period fixed by or under these rules for service of the defence, and on producing a certificate by his solicitor, or (if he sues in person) an affidavit, stating that he is not claiming any relief in the action of the nature specified in Order 88, rule 1, enter judgment for possession of the land as against that defendant and for costs, and proceed with the action against the other defendants, if any. (See App. A, Form 42)

(5)    Where there is more than one defendant, judgment entered under this rule shall not be enforced against any defendant unless and until judgment for possession of the land has been entered against all the defendants.

**6.    Default of defence: mixed claims** (O. 19 r. 6)

Where the plaintiff makes against a defendant two or more of the claims mentioned in rules 2 to 5, and no other claim, then, if that defendant fails to serve a defence on the plaintiff, the plaintiff may, after the expiration of the period fixed by or under these rules for service of the defence, enter against that defendant such judgment in respect of any such claim as he would be entitled to enter under those rules if that were the only claim made, and proceed with the action against the other defendants, if any.

**7.    Default of defence: other claims** (O. 19 r. 7)

(1)    Where the plaintiff makes against a defendant or defendants a claim of a description not mentioned in rules 2 to 5, then, if the defendant or all the defendants (where there is more than one) fails or fail to serve a defence on the plaintiff, the plaintiff may, after the expiration of the period fixed by or under these rules for service of the defence, apply to the Court for judgment, and on the hearing of the application the Court shall give such judgment as the plaintiff appears entitled to on his statement of claim.

(2)    Where the plaintiff makes such a claim as is mentioned in

paragraph (1) against more than one defendant, then, if one of the defendants makes default as mentioned in that paragraph, the plaintiff may—

      **(a)**       if his claim against the defendant in default is severable from his claim against the other defendants, apply under that paragraph for judgment against that defendant, and proceed with the action against the other defendants; or

      **(b)**       set down the action for judgment against the defendant at the time when the action is set down for trial, or is set down for judgment, against the other defendants. (L.N. 152 of 2008)

    **(3)**   An application under paragraph (1) must be by summons. (L.N. 152 of 2008)

---

**NOTES**

**[19.7.1]    Judgment in default of defence – other claims, such as declaration**

Order 19 rule 7 provides that a plaintiff may apply to the court for judgment in default of defence where the relief sought is of a type not dealt with in the preceding rules.

Application under this rule may be made by summons before a master or by motion before a judge: *Lau Siu Kwong David & Ors v The personal representative of Lee On Yuen, deceased* HCA 10001/2000 (Mr Recorder Edward Chan SC; 09.04.2001). In that case it was held that applications appropriate to be heard in open court should be made by motion to a judge.

Rule 7(1) uses mandatory language providing that the court 'shall' give judgment where the defendant is in default of defence. However the courts proceed on the basis that the power is discretionary. See *Lam Shing Shou v Lam Hon Man & Ors* HCA 361/ 2001 (Chu J; 15.01.2002); *California Insurance Co Ltd & Ors v Choung Suk Wah & Ors* HCA 172/2002 (Deputy Judge A Cheung; 19.09.2002).

On the hearing of an application under this rule the court confines itself to the plaintiff's pleadings and does not receive evidence going to the merits: *Lam Shing Shou* (above); *California Insurance* (above). The court's task on such an application is 'to examine the statement of claim to see if it appears that the plaintiff is entitled to judgment': *China Construction Realty Ltd v Sino Business Services Pty Ltd & Ors* HCA 1294/2005 (Recorder Edward Chan SC; 24.03.2006). The court will also have regard to any proposed defence if the defendant resists the application and seeks an extension of time: *California Insurance* (above).

This rule extends to actions in which the relief claimed is a declaration, but it is not the normal practice for the court to grant a declaration without a trial: *Wong Kwok-chiang & Ors v Longo Construction Ltd & Anor* [1987] HKLR 345, 353B-D citing *Wallersteiner v Moir* [1974] 1 WLR 991; [1974] 3 All ER 217 (CA); *Lam Shing Shou v Lam Hon Man & Ors* HCA 361/2001 (Mr Recorder R Tang SC; 31.07.2001). However, where a proper trial is not possible because the defendant cannot be traced, and justice will not be done unless a declaration is granted, the court will do so. See *Lam Shing Shou v Lam Hon Man & Ors* HCA 361/2001 (Chu J; 15.01.2002); *Lai Wai Kuen v Wong Shau Kwong* [2004] 4 HKC 528. In *Kin Ming Holdings Int'l Ltd v Lam Moon Yuen* HCA 2350/2005 (Deputy Judge L Chan; 27.01.2006) the court granted declarations by default where the defendant had chosen not to take part in the proceedings despite being served.

**8.      Default of defence to counterclaim** (O. 19 r. 8)
      **A defendant who counterclaims against a plaintiff shall be treated for the purposes of rules 2 to 7 as if he were a plaintiff who had made against a defendant the claim made in the counterclaim and, accordingly, where the plaintiff or any other party against whom the counterclaim is made fails to serve a defence to counterclaim, those rules shall apply as if the counterclaim were a statement of claim, the defence to counterclaim a defence and the parties making the counterclaim and against whom it is made were plaintiffs and defendants respectively, and as if references to the period fixed by or under these rules for service of the defence were references to the period so fixed for service of the defence to counterclaim.**

      **(HK)8A. Notice of intention to enter judgment** (O. 19 r. 8A)
      **(1)   No party shall enter judgment under the provisions of this Order against a party who has filed an acknowledgment of service giving notice of intention to defend, or on a counterclaim, unless—**
      **(a)   after such acknowledgment of service or counterclaim has been filed, and not less than 2 clear days before entering judgment, the party intending to enter judgment has served notice in writing of his intention to do so on the party against whom judgment is sought or, if that party is legally represented, on his solicitor;**
      **(b)   evidence of such service by way of affidavit has been filed in the Court.**
      **(2)   This rule shall not apply where—**
            **(a)   the Court has made an order prescribing or extending the time for service of defence or defence to counterclaim; or**
            **(b)   the party against whom it is sought to enter judgment does not have a solicitor of record in the proceedings and has failed to state an address within the jurisdiction in the proceedings at which he can be served.**
      **(L.N. 223 of 1995)**

---

**NOTES**

**[19.8A.1]   Origin and scope of Order 19 rule 8A**
Order 19 rule 8A provides that in most cases two clear days notice must be given to the defendant before judgment in default of defence may be entered. The rule was added in 1995, replacing a voluntary system previously operated by the Law Society, under which many (but not all) firms of solicitors gave undertakings not to take judgment in default of defence without such prior notice.
      Rule 8A is unique to Hong Kong in the sense that it was not adopted from the former English RSC. Default judgment is now dealt with in CPR Part 12 in England, which likewise contains no notice provision.

**[19.8A.2]   When notice may be given**
Under the terms of rule 8A, notice of intention to enter judgment in default of defence may be given at any time after the defendant has acknowledged service giving notice of intention to defend. There is no express requirement in the rule that the plaintiff must wait until default has occurred before giving notice, nor can any such requirement be implied from the language of the rule: *Ho Yuen Tsan v Hop Wing Transportation Co Ltd* [1997] 4 HKC 259. It follows that notice 'may be served at any time, whether or not the defendant is already in default': *Schindler Lifts (HK) Ltd v Ocean Joy Investments Ltd* [2002] 1 HKLRD 279 (para 9).

**[19.8A.3]   Manner of service of notice**
Notice of intention to enter judgment in default of defence under Order 19 may be served by post, and if the defendant is legally represented the notice should be addressed to his solicitors. See *Ng Ngon Kwan Stephen v Hideaki Minami & Anor* DCCJ 7989/2001 (Judge A Cheung; 15.11.2001).

**9.      Setting aside judgment** (O. 19 r. 9)
**The Court may, on such terms as it thinks just, set aside or vary any judgment entered in pursuance of this Order.**
**(Enacted 1988)**

---

**NOTES**

**[19.9.1]    When judgment in default of pleading may be set aside**
See also the commentary under Order 13 rule 9, dealing with setting aside judgment in default of notice of intention to defend. The principles set out there are largely applicable to applications under Order 19 rule 9 for judgment in default of pleading.

Judgment in default of pleading which is irregularly entered is liable to be set aside *ex debito justitiae*, just as is the case with an irregular judgment in default of notice of intention to defend.

Judgment in default of defence which is entered after the defendant has set down an application to extend the time for serving a defence is not irregular as the application to extend the time does not operate as a stay of proceedings: *GP Vickers & Co Ltd v Humanbo Enterprises Ltd* HCA 12076/1983 (Power J; 16.01.1984); *Ng Ngon Kwan Stephen v Hideaki Minami & Anor* DCCJ 7989/2001 (Judge A Cheung; 15.11.2001). The application for an extension of time does not prevent time from running nor does it render a default judgment obtained before the application is heard liable to be set aside: *Schindler Lifts (HK) Ltd v Ocean Joy Investments Ltd* [2002] 1 HKLRD 279 (para 10).

Where judgment in default of pleading has been entered regularly it may be set aside in the discretion of the court. In the case of judgment in default of defence there is an almost inflexible rule that an affidavit of merits will be required: *GP Vickers & Co Ltd v Humanbo Enterprises Ltd* HCA 12076/1983 (Power J; 16.01.1984). In that case the defendant relied on the affirmation of a solicitor's clerk to which was exhibited the proposed defence and counterclaim. It was held that this was not an affidavit of merits as there was nothing in it showing a defence on the merits.

**[19.9.2]      Conditions on setting aside judgment in default of pleading**

The court has power under Order 19 rule 9 to impose terms when it sets aside judgment in default of pleading. The Court of Appeal has held that only in rare circumstances will a defendant be ordered to make a payment into court on account of the amount claimed as a condition of judgment being set aside: see *L & M Specialist Construction Ltd v Wo Hing Construction Co Ltd* [2000] 3 HKC 335, per Ribeiro JA at 342G. See the discussion of that case and others in the commentary concerning terms under Order 13 rule 9.

## ORDER 20

### AMENDMENT

---

## NOTES

### [20.0.1] Comparison with English Order

Note that there is no rule 6 in Order 20 of the Hong Kong rules.

**1.**     **Amendment of writ without leave** (O. 20 r. 1)

**(1)**    **Subject to paragraph (3), the plaintiff may, without the leave of the Court, amend the writ once at any time before the pleadings in the action begun by the writ are deemed to be closed.**

**(2)**    **Where a writ is amended under this rule after service thereof, then, unless the Court otherwise directs on an application made ex parte, the amended writ must be served on each defendant to the action.**

**(3)**    **This rule shall not apply in relation to an amendment which consists of—**

       **(a)**     **the addition, omission or substitution of a party to the action or an alteration of the capacity in which a party to the action sues or is sued, or**

       **(b)**     **the addition or substitution of a new cause of action, or**

       **(c)**     **(without prejudice to rule 3(1)) an amendment of the statement of claim (if any) indorsed on the writ,**

**unless the amendment is made before service of the writ on any party to the action.**

---

## NOTES

### [20.1.1] Amendment of writ without leave

Order 20 rule 1 provides that a plaintiff may amend the writ once, without leave of the court, at the early stages of the proceedings. Substantial amendments, of the type enumerated in rule 1(3) may be made without leave at any time before any party has been served with the writ. Other amendments may be made without leave at any time before pleadings are deemed to have closed (as to which see Order 18 rule 20). An amendment without leave under Order 20 rule 1 may be set aside under Order 20 rule 4. It is there provided that the court 'shall' set aside any such amendment if leave would have been refused under Order 20 rule 5.

Is joinder of a wholly new party into existing proceedings an 'amendment' which may be made under this rule? In *Li Ming Cheong v Li Wai Ki & Ors* (2002) HCA 10334/2000 (Deputy Judge Longley; 01.02.2002) it was argued that it is not. Order 15 rule 6 was said to be the appropriate provision to cure 'non-joinder'. The distinction is that leave of the court is required under Order 15 rule 6. Deputy Judge Longley rejected this argument and allowed an appeal from a master who had invoked Order 20 rule 4 to set aside an amendment made without leave under this rule to join a wholly new defendant into existing proceedings. The Deputy Judge further held that the amendment was not required to be struck out under Order 20 rule 4 because it was within the scope of Order 20 rule 5 despite the fact that rule 5 is expressly 'subject to' Order 15 rule 6. The 'subject to' provision of Order 20 rule 5 did not oust such an amendment in favour of Order 15 rule 6, rather it merely required the court to have regard to that rule. The Deputy Judge doubted commentary in the post-Woolf English *White Book* which suggests that only after the 1999 Woolf reforms could joinder of a wholly new defendant be achieved by amendment without leave.

**[20.1.2]  Service of amended writ**
There is no requirement in the rules for an *amended* writ to be served personally, nor does Order 10 rule 1 (service by post) expressly apply. As a result, it should be permissible to serve an amended writ by 'ordinary' service under Order 65 rule 5. However common sense dictates that this should only be done where the original writ was properly served and service has been acknowledged. If not, the amended writ should be served as if it were the original writ. Otherwise there may later be argument that the proceedings were never properly served. It should make no difference whether the amendment is made with or without leave.

To save time and cost, where the proposed amended writ has already been seen by the defendant (such as where it is attached in draft to a summons seeking leave to amend) the plaintiff sometimes seeks an order that service of the amended writ be dispensed with.

**2.      Amendment of acknowledgment of service** (O. 20 r. 2)
**(1)  Subject to paragraph (2), a party may not amend his acknowledgment of service without leave of the Court.**

**(2)  A party whose acknowledgment of service contains a statement to the effect that—**
- **(a)  he does, or**
- **(b)  he does not**

**intend to contest the proceedings to which the acknowledgment relates may, without the leave of the Court, amend the acknowledgment by substituting for that statement a statement to the opposite effect, provided that in a case falling under sub-paragraph (b) the amendment is made before judgment has been obtained in the proceedings.**

**(3)  Where an acknowledgment of service is authorized to be amended under this rule, a fresh acknowledgment, amended as so authorized, must be handed in at or sent by post to the Registry, and Order 12, rule 4, shall apply.**

**3.  Amendment of pleadings without leave** (O. 20 r. 3)
**(1)  A party may, without the leave of the Court, amend any pleading of his once at any time before the pleadings are deemed to be closed and, where he does so, he must serve the amended pleading on the opposite party.**

**(2)  Where an amended statement of claim is served on a defendant—**
- **(a)  the defendant, if he has already served a defence on the plaintiff, may amend his defence, and**
- **(b)  the period for service of his defence or amended defence, as the**

case may be, shall be either the period fixed by or under these rules for service of his defence or a period of 14 days after the amended statement of claim is served on him, whichever expires later.

(3) Where an amended defence is served on the plaintiff by a defendant—

(a) the plaintiff, if he has already served a reply on that defendant, may amend his reply, and

(b) the period for service of his reply or amended reply, as the case may be, shall be 14 days after the amended defence is served on him.

(4) In paragraphs (2) and (3) references to a defence and a reply include references to a counterclaim and a defence to counterclaim respectively.

(5) Where an amended counterclaim is served by a defendant on a party (other than the plaintiff) against whom the counterclaim is made, paragraph (2) shall apply as if the counterclaim were a statement of claim and as if the party by whom the counterclaim is made were the plaintiff and the party against whom it is made a defendant.

(6) Where a party has pleaded to a pleading which is subsequently amended and served on him under paragraph (1), then, if that party does not amend his pleading under the foregoing provisions of this rule, he shall be taken to reply on it in answer to the amended pleading, and Order 18, rule 14(2), shall have effect in such a case as if the amended pleading had been served at the time when that pleading, before its amendment under paragraph (1), was served.

---

## NOTES

**[20.3.1] Costs of amendment without leave**
The costs of and occasioned by an amendment without leave shall normally be borne by the party making the amendment: see Order 62 rule 3(3).

**4. Application for disallowance of amendment made without leave** (O. 20 r. 4)

(1) Within 14 days after the service on a party of a writ amended under rule 1 (1) or of a pleading amended under rule 3(1), that party may apply to the Court to disallow the amendment.

(2) Where the Court hearing an application under this rule is satisfied that if an application for leave to make the amendment in question had been made under rule 5 at the date when the amendment was made under rule 1(1) or rule 3(1) leave to make the amendment or part of the amendment would have been refused, it shall order the amendment or that part to be struck out.

(3) Any order made on an application under this rule may be made on such terms as to costs or otherwise as the Court thinks just.

---

## NOTES

**[20.4.1]   Disallowance of amendment without leave**
Order 20 rule 4 provides for a measure of control over amendments made without leave under rules 1 and 3 of this Order. It empowers the court to set aside any such amendment and indeed requires the court to do so if leave to amend would not have been granted under rule 5.

**5.     Amendment of writ or pleading with leave** (O. 20 r. 5)
**(1)   Subject to Order 15, rules 6, 7 and 8 and the following provisions of this rule, the Court may at any stage of the proceedings allow the plaintiff to amend his writ, or any party to amend his pleadings, on such terms as to costs or otherwise as may be just and in such manner (if any) as it may direct.**

**(2)   Where an application to the Court for leave to make the amendment mentioned in paragraph (3), (4) or (5) is made after any relevant period of limitation current at the date of issue of the writ has expired, the Court may nevertheless grant such leave in the circumstances mentioned in that paragraph if it thinks it just to do so.**

**(3)   An amendment to correct the name of a party may be allowed under paragraph (2) notwithstanding that it is alleged that the effect of the amendment will be to substitute a new party if the Court is satisfied that the mistake sought to be corrected was a genuine mistake and was not misleading or such as to cause any reasonable doubt as to the identity of the person intending to sue or, as the case may be, intended to be sued.**

**(4)   An amendment to alter the capacity in which a party sues may be allowed under paragraph (2) if the new capacity is one which that party had at the date of the commencement of the proceedings or has since acquired.**

**(5)   An amendment may be allowed under paragraph (2) notwithstanding that the effect of the amendment will be to add or substitute a new cause of action if the new cause of action arises out of the same facts or substantially the same facts as a cause of action in respect of which relief has already been claimed in the action by the party applying for leave to make the amendment.**

---

**NOTES**

**[20.5.1]   Principles to be applied on application for leave to amend**
The court's power under Order 20 rule 5 to grant leave to amend is discretionary. The principles on which that discretion will be exercised are well established. See, for example, *Kwan Shiu Cheong Charles v Ferrari SpA & Anor* [1994] 2 HKC 179 (CA), 184E–I where Nazareth JA explained the scope of Order 20 rule 5 in the following terms:

> Sub-rule (1) of O 20 r 5 is the general provision empowering leave to be granted to amend pleadings. The well-established and well-known principles that apply to the exercise of this power may conveniently be taken from the summary given by Lord Brandon in *Ketteman v Hansel Properties Ltd* [1987] AC 189, 212F ... Lord Brandon summarized them in the following four propositions:
>
> > First, all such amendments should be made as are necessary to enable the real

questions in controversy between the parties to be decided. Secondly, amendments should not be refused solely because they have been made necessary by the honest fault or mistake of the party applying for leave to make them: it is not the function of the court to punish parties for mistakes which they have made in the conduct of their cases by deciding otherwise than in accordance with their rights. Thirdly, however blameworthy (short of bad faith) may have been a party's failure to plead the subject matter of a proposed amendment earlier, and however late the application for leave to make such amendment may have been, the application should, in general, be allowed, providing that allowing it will not prejudice the other party. Fourthly, there is no injustice to the other party if he can be compensated by appropriate orders as to costs.

Hence a party who opposes an application for leave to amend must demonstrate that he will suffer some injustice which cannot be compensated by an award of costs: see *Kwan Shiu Cheong Charles v Ferrari SpA & Anor* [1994] 2 HKC 179 (CA) per Nazareth JA at 185D–H quoting with approval from *The Casper Trader; Hancock Shipping Co v Kawasaki Heavy Industries Ltd* [1992] 3 All ER 132. In that case Staughton LJ described the burden which must be discharged on an application for leave to amend as one of 'persuasion', rather than of 'proof'.

Since the advent of the civil justice reforms in 2009, the court should take into account the underlying objectives in Order 1A when considering an application for leave to amend. These include cost-effectiveness, expeditiousness and the fair distribution of court resources. In *Aon Risk Services Australia Ltd v Australian National University* [2009] HCA 27 (05.08.2009) the High Court of Australia took into account similar factors in setting aside leave to amend which had been granted at trial. In a joint judgment of five justices it was said (at para 111):

An application for leave to amend a pleading should not be approached on the basis that a party is entitled to raise an arguable claim, subject to payment of costs by way of compensation. There is no such entitlement. All matters relevant to the exercise of the power to permit amendment should be weighed. The fact of substantial delay and wasted costs, the concerns of case management, will assume importance on an application for leave to amend.

In a concurring judgment, French CJ said (at para 5):

In the proper exercise of the primary judge's discretion, the applications for adjournment and amendment were not to be considered solely by reference to whether any prejudice to Aon could be compensated by costs. Both the primary judge and the Court of Appeal should have taken into account that, whatever costs are ordered, there is an irreparable element of unfair prejudice in unnecessarily delaying proceedings. Moreover, the time of the court is a publicly funded resource. Inefficiencies in the use of that resource, arising from the vacation or adjournment of trials, are to be taken into account.

The court may also take into account the fact that a pleading which it is sought to amend was verified by a statement of truth in its original form. Order 18 rule 20A and Order 41A rule 2(1)(a) both require verification of pleadings by statement of truth. See the commentary under those provisions. In *Tong Kin Hing v Autron Mauritius Corp & Ors* [2010] 1 HKLRD 77 (CA) the court declined to permit amendment of a statement of claim where the party who had verified it by statement of truth must have known facts had been suppressed rendering a key allegation false. The court said (para 20) that 'when faced with a situation where a pleading has been verified in circumstances where it has been demonstrated that the verification should never have been made, the Court should be very slow to permit any amendment to that pleading'.

The court and the other parties are entitled to scrutinise proposed amendments. As a result it is usual for the party seeking leave to amend to put forward draft amendments for consideration of the other parties and the court. This can conveniently be done by attaching the draft amended pleading to the summons seeking leave to amend. If the proposed amendments violate the rules of pleading, leave to amend may be refused. For example, proposed amendments which are insufficiently particularised may be rejected: *Perak Pioneer Ltd v Carrian Holdings Ltd* CACV 59/1985 (Cons, Fuad & Kempster JJA; 13.06.1985). This is particularly so where the amendments are sought close to trial: *Wellfit Investments Ltd v Poly Commence Ltd* [1995] 3 HKC 56, 61 (CA). Likewise, leave to amend so as to introduce a cause of action which is unsustainable may be refused. See *Sam Woo Bore Pile Foundation Ltd v China Overseas Foundation Engineering Ltd* HCCT 76/1996 (Reyes J; 21.02.2006) where leave to amend so as to introduce a claim which was time-barred and 'bad' on a true construction of a contract was refused. Likewise an amendment to introduce a new cause of action which is unsustainable and liable to be struck out: *Ip Tsz Lam Ada v Pearl Wisdom Ltd* HCA 2482/2007 (Sakhrani J; 17.04.2009) (para 48). The court should not undertake a 'deep and detailed analysis' of the validity of the proposed new claim – it should refuse leave only if on superficial consideration the new claim is 'hopeless', or 'bound to fail': *Greater Beijing Region Expressways Ltd v Cosco (HK) Group Ltd* HCA 474/2005 (Burrell J; 11.08.2006), referring to *Hancock Shipping Co Ltd v Kawasaki Heavy Industries Ltd* [1992] 1 WLR 1025, 1031C-D (CA) where it was said that leave should be granted if the new claim is 'fairly arguable'. See also *Natamon Protpakorn v Citibank NA* HCA 190/2005 (Deputy Judge Carlson; 11.03.2008).

## [20.5.2]   Construction of Order 20 rule 5

Order 20 rule 5(1) sets out the court's broad power to amend, and the subsequent paragraphs of the rule deal with the circumstances in which leave to amend may be granted after expiration of the limitation period.

In *Sterman v Moore* [1970] 1QB 596 it was held that the broad power in rule 5(1) should not be taken to be cut down by the subsequent subrules even where the application is made after expiry of the limitation period. In that case it was argued that a writ may only be amended after expiration of the limitation period if it comes within Order 20 rule 5(2), (3), (4) or (5). Lord Denning MR held that 'full effect' should be given to the 'wide words' of Order 20 rule 5(1) – they should not be 'cut down' by reference to the subsequent sub-rules: see 391B–C. In result the court allowed an amendment to plead a cause of action after the expiration of the limitation period even though the original writ pleaded no cause of action at all and on the face of it, rule 5(5) was not engaged. See, however, *Grewal v National Hospital for Nervous Diseases & Anor* [1982] The Times, 15 October; [1982] CLY para 2588, where Dunn LJ preferred the view that addition of a new cause of action after expiration of the limitation period is only possible if it comes squarely within the wording of rule 5(5).

*Parties* – Order 20 rule 5 is expressly subject to Order 15 rules 6, 7 and 8, which deal with curing misjoinder and nonjoinder of parties as well as change of parties on death. In *Li Ming Cheong v Li Wai Ki & Ors* HCA 10334/2000 (Deputy Judge Longley; 01.02.2002) it was argued that the result is to require a party to proceed under Order 15 when any such issue as to parties arises. The learned Deputy Judge rejected this argument and held that the phrase 'subject to' merely requires the court, when exercising its discretion under Order 20 rule 5, to have regard to the relevant provisions of Order 15. The significance is that amendments of the type envisioned by Order 20 rule 5 may at early stages of proceedings be achieved without leave under Order 20 rule 1, whereas Order 15 rule 6 requires a grant of leave. Thus where the application for leave to amend is brought during the currency of the limitation period one need only have regard to rule 5(1) and the test is whether it is 'just' to allow the amendment: *Wong Kam Hong v Triangle Motors Ltd* [1998] 2 HKC 219, 226B–H.

### [20.5.3]  Timing of application for leave to amend

The court's power to grant leave to amend applies 'at any stage of the proceedings': rule 5(1). It may even be exercised after judgment has been delivered, at any time before the order is perfected: *Rich Circle Co Ltd v Lucky Time Finance Co Ltd* [1993] 2 HKC 429; *Wu Han Sin v Leung Fat* HCA 2430/2005 (Recorder B Yu SC; 31.08.2009). Some authorities suggest that pleadings can be amended even after formal judgment has been entered: see *Wing Han Trading Co Ltd v Tang Yan Kit & Anor* [1990] 2 HKC 445; *Lui Lai Tuen v Leung Kwai Hing Omango* HCA 1193/2008 (Master Levy; 01.11.2010).

However, the timing of the application is clearly relevant to the exercise of the court's discretion. The application may be refused if it is made too late in the proceedings. In *Fairview Park Property Management Ltd v Sun Wai Chun* [1999]4 HKC 42 (CA) leave to amend at trial, (after all factual witnesses had given their evidence) so as to plead for the first time an entirely new point, was refused. See also *Elliot v Healthy Living Products Int'l Ltd* CACV 40/2006 (Rogers VP & Le Pichon JA; 24.02.2006) where a late application to raise a dubious defence was refused. In *C&A Consultants Ltd & Anor v Hong Kong Airlines Ltd* HCA 279/2007 (Deputy Judge Carlson; 17.08.2010) (para 29) an application for leave to amend was refused where the result would have been loss of the trial dates. Trial dates are 'milestone' dates under Order 25 rule 1B and will not be disturbed save in exceptional cir cumstances.

Undue delay may not on its own be sufficient to justify refusal of leave to amend. See the judgment of Godfrey JA in *Tang Shun Hay v Jetline Co Ltd & Ors* [2000] 1 HKC 417, 423H–I. There the learned judge, referring to English authority, said, at 423 I, that '[t]here must also be prejudice to the opponent of the party seeking leave to amend'. In that case the Court of Appeal dismissed an appeal against refusal of leave to amend on the basis of delay and prejudice. The applicant had sought to raise a limitation defence at a late stage. See also *Good Year Import & Export (a firm) v Yiu Fung Cold Storage & Warehousing Ltd & Anor* HCA 4957/1980 (Penlington J; 12.03.1986) where leave to re-amend a statement of claim was refused where the proceedings had been commenced five and a half years earlier and it was felt there was a risk witnesses would have difficulty remembering events. See also *Tang Kam Wah & Ors v Tang Ming Yat & Anor* [2003] 1 HKC 532 where the Court of Appeal allowed an appeal against an order refusing a defendant's application to amend the defence first made only when the plaintiff closed its case.

An application for leave to amend so as to withdraw an admission will be carefully weighed, especially after expiration of the limitation period: see *Li Fat Mui v Able Engineering Co Ltd & Ors* [1998] 1 HKC 469. There the defendant sought to amend so as to withdraw an admission that it was the employer of the plaintiff in a personal injuries action. Leave was refused on the ground that prejudice would be caused to the plaintiff in that the limitation period had expired and it would no longer be possible for the plaintiff to commence proceedings against the person which the applicant maintained was the true employer.

### [20.5.4]  No power to reverse order granting leave to amend
Once the court has given leave to amend, the court is *functus officio* so far as that amendment is concerned and has no jurisdiction to reverse the order: *Chau Mei Lee Fragrance & Anor v Ng Yee Tim* [1996] 4 HKC 46 (CA) per Ching JA at 52H.

### [20.5.5]  Costs of amendment with leave
Where an application for leave to amend has been resisted but is allowed, the usual order is that there be two sets of costs: *Lessy SARL v Pacific Star Development Ltd & Anor* [1996] 2 HKC 326, per Yam J at 327B–C, namely:

(a)  costs of and occasioned by the amendment shall be to the other side … in any event; but

(b)  costs of the hearing before the tribunal shall be to the party who is successful in the argument [as to whether leave to amend ought to be granted] …

However, the court retains a discretion to order otherwise. See *Wong Wai Lung & Anor v Bondfield Development Ltd* CACV 214/2006 (Le Pichon JA & Stone J; 31.08.2006) where a party which not unreasonably resisted an application for leave to amend was awarded costs of the hearing despite being unsuccessful.

### [20.5.6]  Costs of action where result affected by late amendment
Under Order 62 rule 9(4)(a) the court may make different costs orders as to different stages of an action. Where the result of a case is affected by a late amendment the court will generally make such an order. See *Dah Seng Decoration Property Agency Ltd v Sze Kie Set & Anor* CACV 1074/2000 (Rogers VP, Keith & Le Pichon JJA; 22.06.2001) (para 5), referring to *Beoco Ltd v Alfa Laval Co Ltd* [1995] QB 137; [1994] 4 All ER 464 (CA) where Stuart-Smith LJ said (at 154A–B):

> As a general rule, where a plaintiff makes a late amendment as here, which substantially alters the case the defendant has to meet and without which the action will fail, the defendant is entitled to the costs of the action down to the date of the amendment.

The above passage continues with an acknowledgement that there may be 'special reasons' why the general rule should not be applied. *Kaines (UK) Ltd v Osterreichische Warrenhandelsgesellschaft* [1993] 2 Lloyd's Rep 1 is cited as an example. There, in the words of Stuart-Smith LJ, 'the judge was satisfied that, even if the amendment had been made earlier, the action would have been vigorously resisted'. In *Re Jinro (HK) Int'l Ltd* [2004] 2 HKLRD 221 Kwan J referred (at para 12-13) to the same example and ordered that a petitioner be entitled to the costs of winding-up proceedings despite the fact it succeeded only as a result of a late amendment. This was because the amendment made no difference to the company's approach which was 'to generate as much delay as possible by raising as many issues as it could to buy time'. However, the costs of and occasioned by the amendment itself were ordered in favour of the company.

### [20.5.7]   Amendment after expiration of limitation period

Under Order 20 rule 5(2) the court may grant leave for certain types of amendment even after expiration of a relevant limitation period. Those types of amendment are: sub-rule (3) – correction of the name of a party; sub-rule (4) – alteration of capacity in which a party sues; and sub-rule (5) – addition or substitution of causes of action.

The power in subrule (3) to correct the name of a party after expiry of the limitation period is confined to cases of genuine mistake where no one has been misled. It does not extend to joinder of a new defendant against whom the limitation period has expired: *Refco Inc v Troika Bullion Ltd & Ors* [1989] 2 HKC 548. In *Davies v Elsby Bros, Ltd* [1960] 3 All ER 672, 676D–F it was said that the test is:

> How would a reasonable person receiving the document take it? If, in all the circumstances of the case and looking at the document as a whole, he would say to himself: 'Of course, it must mean me, but they have got my name wrong', then there is a case of mere misnomer. If, on the other hand, he would say: 'I cannot tell from the document itself whether they mean me or not and I shall have to make inquiries' then it seems to me that one is getting beyond the realm of misnomer.

Order 20 rule 5(5) provides that amendment so as to plead a new cause of action that is statute-barred is only permissible where it arises out of the same or substantially the same facts as already relied upon. As to what constitutes a 'new' cause of action for this purpose, see the discussion in *Bank of China (HK) Ltd v Leong Mei Yong & Anor* HCA 4588/2002 (Sakhrani J; 19.03.2008). In deciding whether the new cause of action arises from the same facts it is necessary for the court to consider the evidence which will likely be led to prove the new cause of action and to ask itself whether that is substantially the same evidence as is already required: see *Ng Kam Chuen v AG* [1991] 2 HKC 560 per Patrick Chan J quoting with approval from *Grewal v National Hospital for Nervous Diseases & Anor* [1982] The Times, 15 October. In *Leung Kin Fook & Ors v Eastern Worldwide Co Ltd (No 2)* [1997] 1 HKC 524 the Court of Appeal held that the words of Order 20 rule 5(5) 'are not to be narrowly construed: they should be given a broad and liberal interpretation in order to attain the objective of the rules' (per Litton JA at 528C–D). Litton JA held that the fact there was not a 'complete overlap of facts' did not take the case out of the rule. Liu JA, concurring, held that leave to amend ought to be granted as there was a 'significant overlap' of factual matrix (at 529I). In *Keen Lloyd Energy Ltd v Bank of China (HK) Ltd* HCA 1299/2004 (Deputy Judge L Chan; 12.04.2006) (para 17) an amendment was set aside on the ground the misrepresentation it would plead was not part and parcel of the transaction already pleaded, but distinct.

An amendment after expiration of the limitation period is deemed to have been made on the date of the original action or third party proceeding: Limitation Ordinance (Cap 347), s 35.

The court's power to grant leave to amend after expiration of a relevant limitation period does not extend to amendments which would deprive a party of a substantive defence under a contract stipulating that a claim must be brought within a specified period. The power may only be exercised in relation to limitation periods prescribed by law, such as those under the Limitation Ordinance. See *Win's Marine Trading Co v Wan Hai Lines (HK) Ltd & Anor* [1999] 3 HKC 701, per Stone J at 707I citing *The 'Jay Bola'* [1992] 1 QB 907. This is because a contractual time-bar extinguishes the claim whereas a statutory limitation period merely renders the claim unenforceable.

## [20.5.8]    Vires of Order 20 rule 5

In *Mohan v McElney* [1983] HKLR 308 (CA) it was held that Order 20 rule 5(5) was *ultra vires* on the ground it went beyond the rules committee's power to make rules on matters of practice and procedure, and affected the substantive right to plead a time bar. Shortly thereafter the same conclusion was reached with regard to rule 5(4): *Kwok Cheung & Ors v Kowloon Motor Bus (1933) Ltd & Anor* HCA 2057/ 1980 (Mayo J; 15.02.1984). The legislature retrospectively reversed the effect of those decisions and broadened the powers of the rules committee with the enactment of section 35 of the Limitation Ordinance (Cap 347). See in particular section 35(12).

## [20.5.9]    Court's power to order amendment of its own motion

In addition to the power to grant leave to amend under Order 20 rule 5, the court has an express power under Order 20 rule 8 to order a party to amend its pleadings or documents. See the commentary under that rule.

## [20.5.10]    Amendment to introduce causes of action arising after issue of writ

An amendment to a Statement of Claim is said to 'relate back' to the date of issue of the writ (see *Sneade v Wotherton* [1904] 1 KB 295). As a consequence, a Statement of Claim may not be amended so as to introduce a cause of action which arose after the issue of the writ: see *Lark International Finance Ltd v Lam Kim Marisa & Anor* [2000] 4 HKC 688 (CA) at 699I, citing *Eshelby v Federated European Bank Ltd* [1932] 1 KB 254 and other English authority. See also *Moscow Narodny Bank Ltd v Wong Wing Cheung Edward* [1981] HKC 416. In *Wing Siu Co Ltd v Goldquest International Ltd* [2003] 2 HKC 64, 70I, the Court of Appeal affirmed the application of the *Eshelby* decision in Hong Kong. The Court of Appeal distinguished amendments to plead events arising after issue of the writ which relate to a cause of action already pleaded (which is possible - see Order 18 rule 9) from amendments to plead an entirely new cause of action which did not exist when the writ was issued (not permissible). See also *Smith v Tam* HCA 2638/2004 (Deputy Judge Gill; 20.03.2007) where the same distinction was made.

In *Chan Chook Tim v Wong Kwok Hung* [2004] 1 HKC 18 a defamation action failed because the allegedly defamatory statement (pleaded by amendment) had been made after the issue of the writ.

In *Lead Mile Ltd v Sino Peak Finance Ltd & Ors* [2004] 4 HKC 646 the court held that an action could not be cured by amendment where it was sought to introduce a plea as to a condition precedent which had not occurred at the date of issue of the writ (claim against guarantor which was conditional upon prior default of the principal debtor).

In some cases it has been suggested that the prohibition on amendment to include a new cause of action does not apply where there is consent of the parties. See *Wing Siu Co Ltd v Goldquest International Ltd* [2003] 2 HKC 64, 68C–D(CA), citing *Lark International*, and see *Geoglobal Partners LLC v Peaktop Technologies (USA) HK Ltd* HCCW 87/2007 (Kwan J; 12.12.2007) (para 8), referring in addition to *Eshelby*.

In cases where a debtor is sued for failing to make instalment payments the creditor may not later add into the Statement of Claim by way of amendment a claim for subsequent instalments unpaid. As observed by the Court of Appeal in the *Lark International* case, this result is not unusual since loan agreements frequently provide that in the event of default all subsequent instalments become immediately payable (at 700B–C).

See also *Luk Por v Chau Kim Hung* [2001] 1 HKC 674 where Sakhrani J allowed an appeal against a master's decision to allow an amendment to plead a settlement agreement which had allegedly been made after the proceedings were commenced.

But see *Zea Star Shipping Co SA v Parley Augustsson (Invest) A/S* [1984] 2 Lloyd's Rep 605 where the operation of the doctrine of relation back in the context of instalment payments was criticised, not followed in *The 'C' and the 'J'* [1984] 2 Lloyd's Rep 601. See also *DDK Trading and Development Co Ltd v Multi Best Manufacturers Ltd* [1986] HKLR 155 where it was held that relation back did not apply to joinder of a new defendant into an existing action, and see *Woo Suk King v Lam Lee Yuet Ha Lilian* [1995] 3 HKC 701 where it was held that the court's wide powers of amendment could not be fettered by the doctrine of relation back. In *Chan Yuen Yee v Chan Chuck Kwong & Anor* [2005] 2 HKLRD 416 the court was strongly critical of the authorities by which it could not permit an amendment which would in the particular case save time and costs, but considered itself bound.

A counterclaim does not relate back to the date of issue of the writ. This is because a counterclaim has the characteristics of a separate action – see the commentary under Order 15 rule 2. It follows that an 'amendment' to a defence so as to plead a counterclaim in respect of a cause of action arising after the issue of the writ is unobjectionable. See *Hong Kong Jie Hing Trading Co Ltd v Pacific Commercial Co Ltd* HCA 2167/2005 (Deputy Judge Gill; 18.10.2006).

The relation back rule does not apply to recovery of damages under a continuing cause of action. Order 37 rule 6 provides for recovery of such damages occurring after the issue of the writ, down to the date of assessment. Nor does it apply to evidence of matters arising after the issue of the writ, which may be relied upon to prove the facts alleged: *Pearldelta Group Ltd v Huge Winners Int'l Ltd & Ors* HCA 595/2008 (Saunders J; 11.02.2009).

### [20.5.11]    Effect of amendment

Once a pleading has been amended, what stood before is no longer material and cannot be relied upon: *Warner v Sampson* [1959] 1 QB 297 (CA). In that case it was held that a landlord could not invoke a denial of the lease in the unamended defence as constituting a forfeiture thereof.

### [20.5.12]    Wholesale amendments

Where a party seeks to completely redraft a pleading, the court may permit it to 'put a line right through' the whole of it and set out an entirely new pleading: *Chow Wing Yuet Elton v Carry Express Investment Ltd* HCCT 18/2007 (Saunders J; 04.11.2009) (para 15). There the court said (para 16) that in doing so 'great care' must be taken to ensure that admissions made in the original pleading are maintained unless leave to withdraw them is granted under Order 13A rule 2(3).

In *FEB Finance Ltd & Anor v Tse Yim* CACV 92/1989 (Cons VP, Clough & Pen lington JJA; 15.02.1990) the court struck out a statement of claim with leave to file a new one where it was of the view that a completely new pleading was appropriate where amendments which would substantially change the nature of the case were sought.

See also rule 10(1) which provides for the preparation of a fresh document where amendments are numerous or lengthy, and requires that in the case of a writ or originating summons, the originating process be re-issued.

### [20.5.13]    Amendment in other official language
It has been held that a party may in amending a document, cross it out entirely and replace it with a document in the other official language: *Hebei Enterprises Ltd v Livasiri & Co* HCA 20094/1998 (Yuen J; 26.11.1999). Where this is done to a writ or originating summons the procedure under rule 10(1) for reissuance should be followed.

### [20.5.14]    Amendment during August vacation
The previous Order 20 rule 6 imposed restrictions on the making of amendments during the court's summer vacation, that is the month of August. It was repealed in England in 1982 and omitted from the Hong Kong rules when they were repealed and re-enacted in 1988. Order 3 rule 3 continues to provide that the month of August will not be included in the reckoning of time for amendment of pleadings (unless the court otherwise directs): see the commentary under that rule.

### [20.5.15]    Numbering
There is no rule 6 in Order 20. It was repealed in 1988. See the commentary above.

**7.    Amendment of other originating process** (O. 20 r. 7)
    **Rule 5 shall have effect in relation to an originating summons, a petition and an originating notice or motion as it has effect in relation to a writ.**

**8.    Amendment of pleading and certain other documents** (O. 20 r. 8)
    (L.N. 152 of 2008)
    **(1)    For the purpose of determining the real question in controversy between the parties to any proceedings, or of correcting any defect or error in any proceedings, the Court may at any stage of the proceedings and either of its own motion or on the application of any party to the proceedings order a pleading or any other document in the proceedings to be amended on such terms as to costs or otherwise as may be just and in such manner (if any) as it may direct. (L.N. 152 of 2008)**
    **(1A) The Court shall not under paragraph (1) order a pleading to be amended unless it is of the opinion that the order is necessary either for disposing fairly of the cause or matter or for saving costs. (L.N. 152 of 2008)**
    **(2)    This rule shall not have effect in relation to a judgment or order. (L.N. 152 of 2008)**

---

## NOTES

### [20.8.1]    Power to order amendment
Order 20 rule 8 empowers the court to order parties to amend their documents in the proceedings. The rule was broadened with effect from 2 April 2009, so as to apply to pleadings. Thus the court now has an express power to order parties to amend their pleadings whereas previously it was solely up to the parties to take the initiative. At the same time rule 8(1A) was inserted to make it clear that the court should not order a pleading to be amended under the rule unless necessary for fair disposal of the

action or for saving costs. This requirement is similar to that which has long existed in respect of applications for discovery and interrogatories: see Order 24 rule 8 and Order 26 rule 1 and the commentary thereunder.

By its own terms, this power is exercisable by the court of its own motion. See generally Order 1B rule 2 and the commentary thereunder as to orders made by the court of its own motion. In *Chau Mei Lee Fragrance & Anor v Ng Yee Tim* [1996] 4 HKC 46, 51H-52G (CA) it was held that the court below was wrong to make an amendment order without hearing the parties. Although that decision pre-dates the power under Order 20 rule 8 to order amendment of the court's own motion, the same principle should apply under this rule.

The rule does not apply to judgments and orders: rule 8(2).

The 2009 amendments to rule 8 implement recommendation 33 in the final report of the Chief Justice's working party on civil justice reform. The working party's intention was to introduce into Hong Kong procedure something similar to CPR 18.1 by which the English court may order a party to clarify matters in dispute or give additional information. As to the circumstances in which the working party envisaged this power being exercised, the final report says (at para 267):

(a)     The power should only be exercised when the pleading is seriously inadequate and fails to convey the nature of the party's case or is such as to pose a serious risk of requiring significant expenditure of unnecessary costs. The power should, in other words only be used when its exercise is necessary for disposing fairly of the matter or for saving costs. It should not be exercised in respect of peripheral imperfections.

(b)     The power should only be exercised when the defective pleading comes to the court's notice in the ordinary course. It is not suggested that the court should proactively schedule a case management hearing simply to deal with defective pleadings.

See also Order 20 rule 13 which requires that an amendment of a pleading, whether under this rule or otherwise, must be verified by statement of truth.

**9.      Failure to amend after order** (O. 20 r. 9)

**(1)   Where the Court makes an order under this Order giving any party leave to amend a writ, pleading or other document, then, if that party does not amend the document in accordance with the order before the expiration of the period specified for that purpose in the order or, if no period is so specified, of a period of 14 days after the order was made, the order shall cease to have effect, without prejudice, however, to the power of the Court to extend the period.**

**(2)   Paragraph (1) is subject to any directions given by the Court. (L.N. 152 of 2008)**

_____

**NOTES**

**[20.9.1]   Time for formal amendment after order**
After an order granting leave to amend has been obtained, it is necessary to go through the formal process of making the amendments within the time stipulated in

Order 20 rule 9. That is 14 days from the date of the order granting leave, or such other period stipulated in the order. Failure to do so results in the order ceasing to have effect. It is sufficient to file the amended document in the registry within time: delay thereafter on the part of the registry does not result in a failure to comply: *Cheng Hang Guan & Ors v Perumaham Farlim (Penang) Sdn Bhd & Ors* [1993] 3 MLJ 352, 376G-I.

See Order 20 rule 10 as to the manner of making the formal amendments.

**[20.9.2]   Extension of time to make formal amendment**
Order 20 rule 9 expressly preserves the power of the court to extend the time for making formal amendment. That power is found in Order 3 rule 5. In *Malaysia Building Society Bhd v Ghazi* [1994] 2 MLJ 1, 8-9 extension of time was opposed for lack of an affidavit explaining the delay. The court regarded the objection as of no real substance. In *Kalimantan Timbers v Mighty Dragon Shipping Co SA* [1980] HKC 228, 235H *et seq* (CA) it was suggested extension of time to amend can be granted even after expiration of a limitation period.

**10.     Mode of amendment of writ, etc. (O. 20 r. 10)**
**(1)   Where the amendments authorized under any rule of this Order to be made in a writ, pleading or other document are so numerous or of such nature or length that to make written alterations of the document so as to give effect to them would make it difficult or inconvenient to read, a fresh document, amended as so authorized, must be prepared and, in the case of a writ or originating summons, re-issued, but, except as aforesaid and subject to any direction given under rule 5, or 8, the amendments so authorized may be effected by making in writing the necessary alterations of the document and in the case of a writ or originating summons, causing it to be resealed and filing a copy.**

**(2)   A writ, pleading or other document which has been amended under this Order must be indorsed with a statement that it has been amended, specifying the date on which it was amended, the name of the Judge, master or Registrar by whom the order (if any) authorizing the amendment was made and the date thereof, or, if no such order was made, the number of the rule of this Order in pursuance of which the amendment was made.**

**NOTES**

**[20.10.1]   Manner of making amendment**
Order 20 rule 10 prescribes the procedures to be followed when making formal amendment to a writ, pleading or other document. See also practice direction 19.1 by which amendments are to be made in coloured ink – red, green, violet and yellow for the 1st, 2nd, 3rd and 4th amendments respectively. The text of the practice direction can be viewed on the judiciary's website, www.judiciary.gov.hk, or that of the Hong Kong Legal Information Institute www.hklii.org, both of which are accessible by the general public free-of-charge.

**11.     Amendment of judgment and orders** (O. 20 r. 11)
     Clerical mistakes in judgments or orders, or errors arising therein from any accidental slip or omission, may at any time be corrected by the Court on summons without an appeal. (L.N. 152 of 2008)

---

## NOTES

### [20.11.1]    'Slip rule' for amendment of judgments and orders
Order 20 rule 11 empowers the court at any time to correct any clerical mistake or error in a judgment or order arising from accidental slip or omission. The rule is colloquially referred to as the 'slip rule'.

### [20.11.2]    Purpose of the 'slip rule'
The purpose of the slip rule is to allow the court, without the need for an appeal, to correct an error or omission in a judgment or order so as to express its manifest intention: *Bank of China v Xinyuan Trading Co Ltd & Anor* CACV 276/1998 (Godfrey VP, Rogers & Ribeiro JJA; 21.06.2000).

### [20.11.3]    Manner of making application under slip rule
Order 20 rule 11 provides that an application under the slip rule should be made by summons. The rule was amended in 2009 removing the possibility of making such an application by motion. In principle the application should be returnable before the judge or judicial officer whose judgment or order it is sought to correct.

### [20.11.4]    Time considerations
The rule provides that the slip rule may be invoked 'at any time'. It is clear that the rule applies after the court's formal order or judgment has been drawn up and entered: *Combi (Singapore) Pte Ltd v Winston Camera & Radio Co Ltd* CACV 160/1987 (Yang VP, Kempster & Power JJA; 17.03.1988). Delay may be a relevant consideration: *Bank of China (HK) Ltd v Sze Wang & Anor* HCMP 2825/2001 (Chu J; 16.02.2005).

### [20.11.5]    'Slip rule' may not be used to vary substance of judgment or order
The slip rule may only be used for 'rectification of an accidental slip or omission' and does not 'entitle a court to reconsider a final and proper order once it had been perfected or to make variations of a significant nature to it': *Lo Ka Chun v Lo To & Anor* CACV 44/1985 (Roberts CJ, Cons VP & Fuad JA; 02.01.1987), citing *R v Cripps, ex p Muldoon & Ors* [1984] 1 QB 686. See also *Lee Wai Man v Tso Yan* HCA 11301/1997 (Sakhrani J; 23.09.2000) and *Ng Yee Wah v Lam Chun Wah* HCMP 4616/2001 (Kwan J; 10.02.2006).
     It follows that the slip rule can only be used to provide relief which was actually claimed in the proceedings. In *Bank of China v Xinyuan Trading Co Ltd & Anor* CACV 276/1998 (Godfrey VP, Rogers & Ribeiro JJA; 21.06.2000) the court refused to use the slip rule to add into its order a certificate for two counsel. The application was 'misconceived and improper' because no such certificate had been sought in the proceedings leading up to the order. See also *Credit Agricole v Crossland Industries Corp & Anor* [1988] HKC 676 where the court declined to use the slip rule to give effect to a contractual provision providing for costs on the solicitor and own client

basis, which had not been pleaded.

In *Hong Kong & Shanghai Banking Corp v Star Trans International Ltd* [1988] 2 HKLR 549, 553E–F (CA) it was doubted that the slip rule could be used to amend an order which mistakenly omitted important parts of the prescribed form.

In *Olding v Singapore Airlines Ltd* DCPI 1145/2001 (Judge Carlson; 02.07.2002) the court cited the slip rule as the basis to set aside its own judgment and order a retrial on the basis of a mistake in the evidence. The mistake had become apparent after judgment had been delivered but before it had been perfected. Since in that case the court went beyond amendment of an accidental slip or omission, the source of power should not be the slip rule, but the court's inherent jurisdiction to reopen a judgment or order which has not been perfected – see the discussion on that topic below.

### [20.11.6]   Examples

Interest which is claimed but mistakenly omitted from a judgment or order may be provided for by amendment under the slip rule: *Yee Sang Metal Supplies Co v Defag Construction Co & Anor* HCA 2212/1966 (Pickering J; 07.07.1970) (appeal to Privy Council reported at [1973] 1 WLR 300); *Newtech Rich Ltd v Chan Shuk Yin Ada & Anor* HCA 8726/1997 (Suffiad J; 04.10.1999).

In *Aqua-Leisure Industries Inc & Anor v Aqua Splash Ltd* [2003] 2 HKLRD 422 the Court of Appeal used the slip rule to amend an order which mistakenly set aside a judgment below against all parties, whereas the court's intention had been to set it aside only as against those parties which had appealed.

In *Chow Tai Fook Jewellery Co Ltd v Shun Kai Bullion Co Ltd* HCMP 6992/1998 (Suffiad J; 12.10.2000) the court used the slip rule to reverse its decision to dismiss an appeal from a master in a mortgage action when it became apparent that the decision was based on the wrong documentation having been provided to the judge.

### [20.11.7]   Costs of amendment under 'slip rule'

Where amendment of an order is necessitated by an error on the part of the party drawing it up, the costs thereof should be borne by that party. It is that party who has the primary responsibility for the correctness of the order. See *Chung Shan Investment & Dev't Co Ltd v Pioneer Metals Holdings Co Ltd* HCMP 2104/2007 (Barma J; 31.10.2008) where such an order was made even though the mistaken order was approved by the court and sealed.

### [20.11.8]   Inherent jurisdiction to reconsider and vary before order sealed

The court has an inherent jurisdiction to reconsider and vary its judgments and orders before they are sealed. The jurisdiction is 'implicit in the court's power to determine the matter in controversy', and extends to both civil and criminal cases: *HKSAR v Tin's Label Factory Ltd* [2009] 1 HKC 254 (CFA) (para 16). This jurisdiction is discretionary, and although broad, it is exercised with restraint. In *Wong Kam Hung v Triangle Motors Ltd* [1998] 2 HKC 219, 223I; [1998] 2 HKLRD 330, 336, citing *Re Harrison* [1955] Ch 260, Cheung J said (*obiter*) that the court 'has jurisdiction to reconsider and rehear' a matter before the order is perfected. See also *Lau Tang Su Ping May v Lau Chu* [1988] HKC 128 (CA). In *Chan Wai Yin v Wong Sau Ping Ada* DCEC 97/2004 (Judge Ng; 24.11.2006) it was said (at para 15):

> I have no doubt that until the order has been perfected, this court retains control over

the order and reasons, and can permit argument to be re-opened which may result in modification or reversal of the decision which has already been made. Rather, the issue is how the discretion should be exercised.

The discretion to re-open the merits of a decision should be exercised 'sparingly', or only in 'exceptional circumstances': *Stewart v Engel* [2000] 1 WLR 2268 (CA); *Chan Wai Yin* (above, para 36). It should not be used to subvert the appeal process: *Cie Noga v Abacha* [2001] 3 All ER 513. Examples of circumstances where the court might exercise its discretion in favour of reconsidering a decision were mentioned in *Re Blenheim Leisure (Restaurants Ltd (No 3)* [1999] TLR 755 (09.11.1999), quoted with approval in *Stewart v Engel* (above) and *Chao Keh Lung v Don Xia* HCA 9289/2000 (Deputy Judge Carlson; 03.10.2002) and adopted by the Hong Kong Court of Appeal in *Sun Jianqiang v Trans-Island Limousine Service Ltd* [2004] 1 HKC 533 (para 28):

> ... a plain mistake on the part of the court; a failure of the parties to draw to the court's attention a fact or point of law that was plainly relevant; or discovery of new facts subsequent to the judgment being given. Another good reason was if the applicant could argue that he was taken by surprise by a particular application from which the court ruled adversely to him and that he did not have a fair opportunity to consider.

In *Chan Wai Yin* (above) an application for reconsideration of an earlier order was refused on the ground that the new points sought to be relied upon could have been made at the original hearing. In *Re Kennedy* [2007] 5 HKC 75 (CA) the court used this power to reverse its decision where it became apparent that the original decision was based on a misapprehension of the facts. In *The Goodeast* [1997] 3 HKC 250 the court reversed an interlocutory order (not yet sealed) with the benefit of new material. In *Tseung Tsan Fai v Tang Shui Ching* HCPI 172/2006 (Chu J; 17.01.2008) the court varied the quantum of a judgment before it was sealed, on the basis of information which had not previously been before it.

See, however, the anomalous case of *Skink Ltd & Anor v Comtowell Ltd & Anor* [1998] 1 HKLRD 542(CA) where it was held that like the slip rule, the court's inherent jurisdiction only extends 'to the correction of errors in expressing the court's intention' and that the court has 'no power to correct mistakes of its own; even where it is satisfied that it has indeed made such a mistake'.

This inherent jurisdiction of the court may only be exercised prior to the judgment or order being perfected. Thereafter, apart from the restricted power under the slip rule to correct clerical mistakes, *etc*, the court is *functus officio* and the only remedy is appeal. See *Andayani v Chan Oi Ling* [2000] 4 HKC 233, 237D; *Ampittia Inc v B-Tech (Holdings) Ltd & Ors* [2001] 2 HKC 574, 579C-H; *Kwan Chui Kwok Ying & Anor v Tao Wai Chun & Ors* CACV 194/2002 (Woo & Cheung JJA; 13.12.2002). However in *Dragon House Investment Ltd v Secretary for Transport* FACV 13/2004 (Bokhary, Chan & Ribeiro PJJ; Nazareth & Lord Millett NPJJ; 12.01.2006) the Court of Final Appeal held that it was not *functus* in relation to costs where although the judgment of the court had been perfected, the parties had not been heard on that issue.

An order is 'perfected' when it has been drawn up and entered in accordance with Order 42 rule 5. See *China Resources Electric Appliance (Zhuhai) Co Ltd & Anor v Decosonic HK Ltd* HCCL 39/2001 (Chung J; 25.08.2001) where it was held that an order signed by a judge had not yet been perfected. Where the court varies its own order under this inherent power, the result is one order, not two, and only a single order should be drawn up and entered. See *Super Century Investments Ltd v Advance Ltd &*

*Anor* [2005] 1 HKC 480, 485I-486A.

The power to review a judgment or order before it is sealed includes a discretion to permit amendment of pleadings so as to enable a new argument to be put forward, or new evidence to be adduced: *Charlesworth v Relay Roads Ltd (in liq) & Ors* [1999] 4 All ER 397; [2000] 1 WLR 230.

See also the closely related topic of the power to permit a case to be re-opened after evidence has been heard, discussed in the commentary under Order 35 rule 7.

**[20.11.9]   Inherent jurisdiction to clarify judgment or order**
The court has inherent power to clarify its judgments and orders. Unlike the power to reconsider and vary an order, this power may be exercised at any stage, even after the order has been sealed. This is because the court is merely clarifying what it has already decided, so it does not involve the court acting when *functus officio*. See *Man Ping Nam & Anor v Man Fong Hang* [2007] 1 HKLRD 763 (CFA) (para 10-11), referring to *Lawrie v Lees* (1881) 7 App Cas 19. In *Man Ping Nam* it was said that this discretionary power is available to courts 'at all levels'.

An example of a case where the court appears to have used this inherent jurisdiction to clarify an order after it had been sealed is *AG v Paterson-Todd* [1987] 3 HKC 266, citing *R v Michael* [1976] 1 All ER 629. In *Paterson-Todd* the court altered the wording used in a sealed order after it became apparent that it had conveyed an unintended meaning to the magistrate to whom it was directed.

**[20.11.10]   Cross references**
See also Order 35 rule 2 which gives the court a discretion to set aside any judgment, order or verdict obtained in the absence of a party, and see the commentary under Order 42 rule 3 as to when a judgment obtained by fraud may be set aside.

**12.    Amendment of pleadings by agreement** (O. 20 r. 12)
    **(1)    Notwithstanding the foregoing provisions of this Order any pleading in any cause or matter may, by written agreement between the parties, be amended at any stage of the proceedings.**
    **(2)    This rule shall not have effect in relation to an amendment which consists of the addition, omission or substitution of a party.**
    **(Enacted 1988)**

**13.    Amendment of pleadings or particulars of pleadings to be verified by statement of truth** (O. 20 r. 13)
    **(1)    An amendment to a pleading or to the particulars of a pleading specified in paragraph (2) must be verified by a statement of truth in accordance with Order 41A.**
    **(2)    The particulars of a pleading referred to in paragraph (1) are particulars given by a party to any other party, whether voluntarily or pursuant to –**
        **(a)    a request made by that other party; or**
        **(b)    an order of the Court made under Order 18, rule 12(3) or (4).**
    **(Enacted 1988) (L.N. 152 of 2008)**

## NOTES

### [20.13.1]    Amendment must be verified by statement of truth

Order 20 rule 13 extends to amendments of pleadings and particulars the requirement in Order 18 rule 20A that pleadings and particulars be verified by statement of truth. It derives from CPR 22.1(2). See the commentary under Order 18 rule 20A. As to statements of truth generally, see Order 41A.

In *Binks v Securicor Omega Express Ltd* [2003] EWCA Civ 993 (16.07.2003) a party sought, in closing submissions, to advance a case wholly inconsistent with the evidence he had already given. It was felt he could not do this by amending his pleadings because in the circumstances he was not in a position to give a statement of truth. However the appellate court was of the view (para 8) that such an amendment could be made, along with a direction dispensing with the statement of truth requirement. In Hong Kong the dispensation power is found in Order 41A rule 2(3).

## ORDER 21

### WITHDRAWAL AND DISCONTINUANCE

1.    **Withdrawal of acknowledgment of service** (O. 21 r. 1)

A party who has acknowledged service in an action may withdraw the acknowledgment at any time with the leave of the Court.

2.    **Discontinuance of action, etc., without leave** (O. 21 r. 2)

(1)    Subject to paragraph (2A) the plaintiff in an action begun by writ may, without the leave of the Court, discontinue the action, or withdraw any particular claim made by him therein, as against any or all of the defendants at any time not later than 14 days after service of the defence on him or, if there are two or more defendants, of the defence last served, by serving a notice to that effect on the defendant concerned.

(2)    Subject to paragraph (2A) a defendant to an action begun by writ may, without the leave of the Court—

    (a)    withdraw his defence or any part of it at any time,

    (b)    discontinue a counterclaim, or withdraw any particular claim made by him therein, as against any or all of the parties against whom it is made, at any time not later than 14 days after service on him of a defence to counterclaim or, if the counterclaim is made against two or more parties, of the defence to counterclaim last served,

by serving a notice to that effect on the plaintiff or other party concerned.

(2A) A party in whose favour an interim payment has been ordered, in accordance with Order 29, may not discontinue any action or counterclaim, or withdraw any particular claim therein, except with the leave of the Court or the consent of all the other parties.

(3)    Where there are two or more defendants to an action begun by writ not all of whom serve a defence on the plaintiff and the period fixed by or under these rules for service by any of those defendants of his defence expires after the latest date on which any other defendant serves his defence, paragraph (1) shall have effect as if the reference therein to the service of the defence last served were a reference to the expiration of that period.

This paragraph shall apply in relation to a counterclaim as it applies in relation to an action begun by writ with the substitution for references to a defence, to the plaintiff and to paragraph (1), of references to a defence to counterclaim, to the defendant and to paragraph (2) respectively.

(3A) The plaintiff in an action begun by originating summons may, without the leave of the Court, discontinue the action or withdraw any particular question or claim in the originating summons, as against any or all of the defendants at any time not later than 14 days after service on him of the defendant's affidavit evidence filed pursuant to Order 28, rule 1A(2) or, if there are two or more defendants, of such evidence last served, by serving a notice to that effect on the defendant concerned.

(3B) When there are two or more defendants to an action begun by originating summons not all of whom serve affidavit evidence on the plaintiff, and the period fixed by or under these rules for service by any of those defendants of his affidavit evidence expires after the latest date on which any other defendant serves his affidavit evidence, paragraph (3A) shall have effect as if the reference therein to the service of the affidavit evidence last served were a reference to the expiration of that period.

(4)    If all the parties to an action consent, the action may be withdrawn without the leave of the Court at any time before trial by producing to the Registrar a written consent to the action being withdrawn signed by all the parties.

---

**NOTES**

**[21.2.1]    Bringing proceedings to an end by withdrawal or discontinuance**
Under Order 21 a party may abandon all or part of his claim or defence by 'discontinuance' of the action, statement of claim or counterclaim, or 'withdrawal' of the acknowledgment of service, defence or of a particular claim pleaded.

Where an action is discontinued it comes to an end, but a counterclaim made in the action may continue: see Order 15 rule 2(3).

Where a particular claim in an action or counterclaim is discontinued the claim will continue in its reduced form. Where an acknowledgment of service or defence is withdrawn, the opposing party will be at liberty to enter judgment in default provided that the terms of Order 13 or 19 are complied with.

**[21.2.2]    Discontinuation without leave**
Leave of the court is not required to discontinue an action, claim or counterclaim at the early stages of the proceedings, generally up to 14 days after the opposing party's pleading in response has been served. In other circumstances an action may be withdrawn with consent of all the parties (Order 21 rule 2(4)) or with leave of the court under Order 21 rule 3. An acknowledgment of service may not be withdrawn without leave (Order 21 rule 1). Where there has been order for an interim payment under Order 29, proceedings may not be discontinued or withdrawn save by consent of all the parties or with leave of the court (Order 21 rule 2(2A)).

**[21.2.3]    Order 21 rule 2 – comparison with English rule**
Order 21 rule 2 is similar but not identical to the rule of the same number in the previous English RSC. The equivalent provision in England is now in CPR Part 38.

Order 21 rule 2(2A) (which provides that a party in whose favour an interim payment has been ordered must obtain leave to discontinue or withdraw) was, under the English RSC, confined to interim payments under Order 29 rule 11, whereas the Hong Kong rule simply refers to Order 29. Hence the Hong Kong rule is wide enough to cover interim payments under Order 29 rule 12 as well.

**[21.2.4]    Wording of Order 21 rule 2**
Order 21 rule 2(3A) (which provides for discontinuance or withdrawal of claims in proceedings commenced by originating summons) mistakenly refers to sub-rule 1A(2) of Order 28, which deals with plaintiffs' rather than defendants' evidence. It

should refer to sub-rule 1A(4), as did its counterpart under the English RSC.

**[21.2.5]   Costs on withdrawal or discontinuance without leave**
A plaintiff who withdraws or discontinues without leave under Order 21 rule 1 or 2 is liable for costs up to that point and the defendant may proceed to taxation under Order 62 rule 10(1). The situation is different where leave is sought under Order 21 rule 3, in which case the court has a discretion as to costs. See the commentary under that rule.

It is open to a party who might withdraw or discontinue without leave instead to apply for leave under rule 3 simply in order to have an opportunity to seek a more favourable order as to costs: *Trend Publishing (HK) Ltd v Vivien Chan & Co* [1996] 3 HKC 433, 436D-G.

In *Supply Chain Logistics Technology Ltd v NEC Hong Kong Ltd* HCA 1939/2006 (Lam J; 24.11.2008) notice of discontinuance was served without leave after the expiration of the period within which that is permitted. The court treated the notice as an application for leave to discontinue and held that it retained jurisdiction to decide what costs order to make.

**3.      Discontinuance of action, etc., with leave** (O. 21 r. 3)
   **(1)   Except as provided by rule 2, a party may not discontinue an action (whether begun by writ or otherwise) or counterclaim, or withdraw any particular claim made by him therein, without the leave of the Court, and the Court hearing an application for the grant of such leave may order the action or counterclaim to be discontinued, or any particular claim made therein to be struck out, as against any or all of the parties against whom it is brought or made on such terms as to costs, the bringing of a subsequent action or otherwise as it thinks just.**
   **(2)   An application for the grant of leave under this rule may be made by summons or by notice under Order 25, rule 7. (L.N. 152 of 2008)**

---

**NOTES**

**[21.3.1]   Discretion to grant leave to discontinue or withdraw**
The court has a broad discretion under Order 21 rule 3 to grant leave to discontinue or withdraw. It is necessary to make an *inter partes* application for leave in any case outside Order 21 rule 2 (relating to discontinuance and withdrawal without leave or by consent).

In *Hang Seng Bank Ltd v Yeung Sau-min* [1986] HKLR 273 it was held that the court's power under Order 21 rule 3 extends to granting leave to discontinue foreclosure proceedings even after an order *nisi* has been granted. *Stevens v Theatres Ltd* [1903] 1 Ch 860 was not followed.

**[21.3.2]   Power to impose terms on leave to discontinue or withdraw**
Under Order 21 rule 3(1) the court has power to impose terms when it grants leave to discontinue or withdraw. The rule specifically mentions terms as to costs and as to the bringing of a subsequent action. Terms prohibiting the bringing of subsequent proceedings have the effect of ousting application of Order 21 rule 4 which provides

that in the absence of such terms discontinuance or withdrawal is not a bar to fresh proceedings for the same cause of action. See the commentary under Order 21 rule 4.

The court's power to impose terms on leave to discontinue or withdraw is discretionary. The circumstances in which the court will exercise the discretion were considered in *Inchroy Credit Corp Ltd v Cheung Man Cheung* [1992] 1 HKLR 120. There Kaplan J cited with approval the test laid down in *Chappie Ltd v Warrington Canners Ltd* (1955) 72 RPC 343, where Wynn-Parry J said, at 344:

> It is quite clear from the authorities that I ought only to impose conditions if, upon a fair view of the whole of the relevant circumstances, the imposition thereof is necessary, either for the protection of the defendants or in the public interest.

In the *Inchroy Credit* case the plaintiff sought leave to discontinue an action claiming outstanding instalment payments under a hire-purchase agreement. The debt had been paid by a third party. Kaplan J upheld a master's order granting leave to discontinue subject to the condition that no fresh proceedings be commenced against the defendant under the hire-purchase agreement. In *Trend Publishing (HK) Ltd v Vivien Chan & Co (a firm)* [1996] 3 HKC 433 it was held that an order prohibiting fresh proceedings is appropriate where leave to discontinue is granted in circumstances where the dispute is at an end.

**[21.3.3]    Costs on withdrawal or discontinuance with leave**

The court's power under Order 21 rule 3(1) to impose terms on granting leave to discontinue or withdraw expressly extends to terms as to costs. In considering what order to make the court has a 'complete discretion to do justice between the parties': *Trend Publishing (HK) Ltd v Vivien Chan & Co* [1996] 3 HKC 433, 437A.

In exercising the discretion the court will normally order costs against the party given leave to withdraw or discontinue, particularly where the application for leave can be equated with an acknowledgement of likely defeat: *Trend Publishing* (above); *Inchroy Credit Corp Ltd v Cheung Man Cheung* [1991] 2 HKC 619; [1992] 1 HKLR 120. However even in such cases the court retains a discretion: see *Trend Publishing* (above at 437A) and *Inchroy* (above). In 'exceptional' cases the court may depart from the usual rule: *Leung Yuet Ching v Leung Yuet Kuen* [2001] 4 HKC 562, 569G, citing *Drown v Gaumont-British Picture Corp Ltd* [1937] 2 All ER 609. In *Lai Kwok Wah Kenneth & Ors v Leung Kwok Hung Jonathan & Ors* LDBM 292/2004 (Judge Wong; 25.05.2010), adopting the approach in *Brawley v Marczynski & Anor* [2004] 4 All ER 1060, no order as to costs was made where it was not possible to say what the likely outcome would have been. In *Robbins & Anor v Peaktop Technologies (USA) HK Ltd* HCMP 2456/2006 (Barma J; 16.05.2007) the court went so far as to make an order for costs in favour of the applicants on granting them leave to withdraw an application. Examples of circumstances where the court might exercise its discretion differently include:

- The matter has become academic: *Standard Chartered Bank (HK) Trustee Ltd v Brogan* [1990] 2 HKC 560, 564G-H, particularly where this results from something done by the defendant: *Hachette Filipacchi Presse v Kador Ltd* [1995] 1 HKC 352, 356D.
- An additional defendant has been reasonably joined but need no longer be pursued: *General Accident Insurance Asia Ltd v Hampton Winter & Glynn* [1998] 4 HKC 398, 415H *et seq.*

- The parties have jointly decided not to contest the matter: *Leung Yuet Ching* (above, at 569H-570B).

The discretion under rule 3 to order costs cannot be exercised independently of an order for withdrawal or discontinuance bringing the particular claim or action to an end: *Ta Tung China & Arts Ltd v Fontana Restaurant Ltd* [1999] 1 HKC 404 (CA).

### [21.3.4] Withdrawal by agreement

An agreement between the parties whereby the plaintiff will abandon some of its claims is binding and will be given effect by the court: *Macedonia Maritime Co & Ors v Austin & Pickersgill Ltd* [1989] 2 Lloyd's Rep 73.

**4. Effect of discontinuance** (O. 21 r. 4)

**Subject to any terms imposed by the Court in granting leave under rule 3, the fact that a party has discontinued an action or counterclaim or withdrawn a particular claim made by him therein shall not be a defence to a subsequent action for the same, or substantially the same, cause of action.**

---

### NOTES

### [21.4.1] Subsequent proceedings for same cause of action

Under Order 21 rule 4 discontinuance or withdrawal of a claim is not of itself a barrier to commencement of fresh proceedings on the same, or substantially the same, cause of action. A party who takes advantage of the provisions of this Order by which he may discontinue or withdraw without leave will be at liberty to start over again. Hence a party who early on realises that there is a serious defect in his proceedings as framed, may choose to discontinue and start afresh rather than amend.

Such fresh proceedings may be stayed under Order 21 rule 5 until the party commencing them pays costs owing in respect of the prior proceedings.

Similarly, discontinuance with leave of the court does not 'by itself preclude a plaintiff from starting an identical proceeding': *Suen Wah Ling v China Harbour Engineering Co* HCMP 1952/2005 (Tang JA; 18.10.2005). The plaintiff will only be barred from commencing fresh proceedings if the court, on granting leave to discontinue, imposes such a term under Order 21 rule 3(1). Such a term should be imposed where the dispute between the parties is at an end: *Trend Publishing (HK) Ltd v Vivien Chan & Co (a firm)* [1996] 3 HKC 433, 438H-439C.

**5. Stay of subsequent action until costs paid** (O. 21 r. 5)

**(1) Where a party has discontinued an action or counterclaim or withdrawn any particular claim made by him therein and he is liable to pay any other party's costs of the action or counterclaim or the costs occasioned to any other party by the claim withdrawn, then, if, before payment of those costs, he subsequently brings an action for the same, or substantially the same, cause of action, the Court may order the proceedings in that action to be stayed until those costs are paid.**

**(2) An application for an order under this rule may be made by summons or by notice under Order 25, rule 7. (L.N. 152 of 2008)**

**NOTES**

**[21.5.1]   Stay of fresh proceedings pending payment of costs**
Order 21 rule 5 empowers the court to order a stay of fresh proceedings pending payment of outstanding costs of proceedings which have been discontinued or withdrawn. This rule operates to qualify Order 21 rule 4 under which a party who has discontinued or withdrawn may generally commence fresh proceedings in respect of the same or substantially the same cause of action.

**6.      Withdrawal of summons** (O. 21 r. 6)
      **A party who has taken out a summons in a cause or matter may not withdraw it without the leave of the Court.**
      **(Enacted 1988)**

## ORDER 22

### OFFERS TO SETTLE AND PAYMENTS INTO COURT

### I. PRELIMINARY

**1.  Interpretation** (O. 22 r. 1)

     **(1)  In this Order –**

"claim" includes, where the context so permits or requires, a counterclaim.

"counterclaim" includes, where the context so permits or requires, a claim;

"defendant" includes, where the context so permits or requires, a defendant to a counterclaim;

"offeree" means the party to whom an offer is made;

"offeror" means the party who makes an offer;

"plaintiff" includes, where the context so permits or requires, a counterclaiming defendant;

"sanctioned offer" means an offer made (otherwise than by way of a payment into court) in accordance with this Order;

"sanctioned payment" means an offer made by way of a payment into court in accordance with this Order;

"sanctioned payment notice" means the notice relating to a sanctioned payment required to be filed under rule 8(2).

     **(2)  Where in an action the plaintiff makes more than one claim, a reference in this Order to –**

       **(a)**    the whole claim is to be construed as a reference to all the claims in their entirety;

       **(b)**    a part of a claim is to be construed as a reference to any one or more of the claims or a part of any one or more of the claims; and

       **(c)**    an issue arising from a claim is to be construed as a reference to an issue arising from one or more of the claims.

     **(L.N. 152 of 2008)**

---

## NOTES

### [22.1.1]  Origin and scope of Order 22

Order 22 was completely replaced on implementation of the civil justice reforms in 2009. The new Order 22 is based on Part 36 of the English CPR. It provides for sanctioned offers and sanctioned payments whereby parties may seek to settle civil disputes short of full trial. To encourage settlement the Order provides for sanctions against a party who rejects a sanctioned settlement proposal but fails to achieve a better result by continuing with the proceedings. Those sanctions include costs and interest penalties.

The sanctioned offer provided for in Order 22 is similar to the *Calderbank* offer which was developed by the courts, and latterly expressed in the former Order 22 rule 14. The sanctioned payment is similar to the former procedure whereby a defendant could make a payment into court as an offer of settlement. What distinguishes the new procedures is the enhanced costs and interest sanctions for a party who refuses to settle but does not achieve a better result by continuing the proceedings. See Order 22 rules 23 and 24.

There are some significant differences between Hong Kong's new Order 22 and CPR Part 36. (Note that CPR part 36 was amended in 2007, and Hong Kong's Order 22 appears to have been based on the earlier version.) First, the Hong Kong procedure differentiates between money claims and non-money claims to some extent with the 'sanctioned payment' and 'sanctioned offer' procedures, the latter being applicable to both (see rule 2), whereas in the English rules there is just the 'Part 36 offer' procedure applying to all types of claim. Secondly, a sanctioned payment under the Hong Kong rules requires actual payment into court, rather than a mere offer to pay as in England: see the definition of 'sanctioned payment' in rule 1. The Chief Justice's working party deliberately chose to retain, in Hong Kong, the requirement that a defendant must make an actual payment to qualify for costs protection: see para 303 of the working party's final report. Thirdly, the English procedure applies even before commencement of proceedings (CPR 36.3(2)(a)), whereas the Hong Kong rules expressly preclude this possibility (Order 22 rules 3(3) and 5(6)). At the consultation stage it was proposed that the new Order 22 procedure be applicable at the pre-action stage if so provided by pre-action protocol, but no such provision is found in Order 22.

### [22.1.2]   Order 22 rule 1(2) – meaning of 'claim'

Order 22 rule 1(2) qualifies the definition of 'claim' in rule 1(1) where more than one claim is made. It was added as a result of comments from the Bar Association on an earlier draft of the new Order 22. The steering committee said that the paragraph should be added to make it clear that in this Order 'the word "claim" can mean a claim in a cause of action or that "claims" can mean the claims made in more than one cause of action' (Judiciary Administration paper CJRS 3/2008, para 26).

### [22.1.3]   Objective of Order 22

The objective of the payment into court procedure under the former Order 22 was to encourage the parties to settle and avoid further litigation. This is equally true of the refined sanctioned payment and sanctioned offer procedures under the current Order 22. The intention that this be so is clear from the final report of the Chief Justice's working party which says (at para 292) of the proposal to adopt a modified version of CPR Part 36 in Hong Kong:

> The proposed sanctioned offers and payments aim to encourage the parties to take possible settlement seriously and to avoid unproductive prolongation of the litigation. A plaintiff who rejects a sanctioned offer or payment and then fails to achieve a better result at the trial may, despite winning the case, be ordered to pay all of the defendant's costs incurred after the time when the plaintiff could have accepted the offer. This substantially mirrors the rules [on payment into court in the former] Order 22 of the RHC. The major change brought about by CPR 36 involves rules providing that a defendant who rejects a plaintiff's sanctioned offer and then finds that the plaintiff does better at the trial, may be ordered to pay indemnity costs and additional interest up to base rate plus 10% on the sum awarded.

So far as costs are concerned, of the previous procedure it was said, in *Findlay v*

*Railway Executive* [1950] 2 All ER 969 (CA):

> The main purpose of the rules for payment into court is the hope that further litigation
> will be avoided, the plaintiff being encouraged to take out the sum paid in, if it be a
> reasonable sum, whereas, if he goes on and gets a smaller sum, he will be penalised
> wholly or to some extent in costs. Once, therefore, the money has been paid in, the *lis*
> between the parties simply is: Is that sum sufficient to cover the damage which has
> been suffered.

In addition, some or all of the interest payable on the judgment sum may be disallowed:
rules 23(2) and 24(2).

The commentary on the objective of CPR Part 36 in our sister publication in the
UK, The Civil Court Practice, is relevant to understanding Hong Kong's new Order
22. It says (at CPR 36[4.2]):

> **The Rule** The fundamental objective of CPR 36 is to provide a clear and simple structure
> within which parties may make offers to settle and, if those offers are accepted, to provide
> for various consequences which will generally ensue. It is of the essence of the revised CPR
> Part 36 [Part 36 was extensively revised with effect from 06.04.2007] that there should be
> certainty as to whether or not an offer qualifies or does not qualify as a Part 36 Offer as
> defined in the rule. Parties retain the freedom to negotiate or to compromise as they wish but
> in order to obtain the benefits of CPR 36 the requirements of CPR part 36 must be fulfilled.
>
> Thus, CPR 36.1(2) [in Hong Kong see Order 22 rule 2(4), which is worded slightly
> differently] provides that:
>
> Nothing in this Part prevents a party making an offer to settle in whatever way he
> chooses, but if the offer is not made in accordance with rule 36.2, it will not have the
> consequences specified in rules 36.10, 36.11 and 36.14 [in Hong Kong Order 22 pt
> IV].
>
> By implication, an offeree may accept an offer in any way he chooses but, if his
> acceptance is not in accordance with CPR 36, then it will not have the consequences
> specified in those rules [unless the court so orders, a proviso to Hong Kong's rule 2(4)
> which does not appear in the English rule]. The acceptance which is envisaged by Part
> 36 is simple and unconditional. This is entirely consistent with the language of CPR
> 36.11 generally where, in CPR 36.11(2) [in Hong Kong Order 22 rule 22(2)(a)] the
> rule refers to the stay being on the terms of the "offer" (and not of the acceptance) and
> where, in CPR 36.11(8) [in Hong Kong Order 22 rule 22(5)(a)], the rule refers to the
> enforcement of the "offer".
>
> If the offeree states that he accepts, or wishes to accept, the offer but adds conditions
> for which the rules do not provide (for instance, more onerous costs or interest than
> provided for in the rules), then such purported acceptance is not acceptance at all but,
> in fact, constitutes a counter-offer.

**[22.1.4]   Contract of settlement**
As is apparent from the above passage, the learned authors of The Civil Court Practice
see settlement under Order 22 as a matter of contract. That observation is equally
applicable in Hong Kong. See, for example Order 22 rule 22(6)(b)(ii) which refers to
breach of contract as the remedy where a party fails to comply with a sanctioned offer
which has been accepted.

However, Order 22 being part of a legislative enactment, it will take precedence over
common law rules of contract in case of any inconsistency. Thus, in *Gibbon v Manchester*

*City Council* [2010] EWCA Civ 726 (25.06.2010) it was held that the common law with regard to an offer lapsing upon being rejected did not apply to a sanctioned offer under Part 36 of the CPR, because the express wording of the English rule allowed acceptance 'at any time'. The wording of the Hong Kong rules is different (see Order 22 rules 15 and 16 and the commentary thereunder); however it has been held that under the Hong Kong rules a sanctioned offer is not withdrawn by the making of a subsequent without prejudice offer outside the scope of Order 22: *Wealthy Century Investment Ltd v DBS Bank (HK) Ltd (No 2)* [2010] 6 HKC 130.

On the topic of contract in this context, our sister publication in the UK, The Civil Court Practice says (at CPR 36 [4.1]):

> **Accord and satisfaction** The principle of accord and satisfaction is the purchase of a release from an obligation, whether arising under contract or tort (or, presumably, arising on any other basis – *eg* in equity), by means of any valuable consideration, not being the performance of the obligation itself (see *Arrale v Costain Civil Engineering Ltd* [1976] 1 Lloyd's Rep 98, (1975) 119 Sol Jo 527 (CA); and *BCCI SA v Ali* [2001] UKHL 8, [2001] 1 All ER 961). The accord is the agreement by which the obligation is to be discharged. The satisfaction is the consideration which makes the agreement operative.
>
> A claimant may agree to accept as satisfaction (1) the promise of the substituted obligation or (2) only the actual performance of the substituted obligation.
>
> In the former case, the original obligation will be discharged from the moment of the new agreement; in the later case, it will not be discharged until the substituted obligation has been performed (*British Russian Gazette and Trade Outlook Ltd v Associated Newspapers Ltd* [1933] 2 KB 616, 644, 654, CA). (See Halsbury's Laws [of England] vol 9 paras 1043 to 1051 inclusive and Chitty on Contracts 29th ed, vol 1, paras 22-12 to 22-23 inclusive).
>
> Whether or not it is a term of the compromise that the original obligation will only be discharged upon performance of the substituted obligation will normally be a matter of construction of the compromise into which the parties have entered, to which the normal rules of interpretation of contracts will apply.
>
> Subject to any question of illegality, parties are free to negotiate and to compromise their disputes as they wish. The question arises as to how that freedom may be exercised and yet the parties obtain and retain the benefits of Part 36.

A completed settlement agreement which forms a valid and enforceable contract must be given effect by the court: *Robertson v Walwyn Stodgell Cochrane Murray Ltd* [1988] CanLII 188; [1988] 4 WWR 283 (BCCA). The agreement may be varied or set aside on general principles of the law of contract: see the commentary on variation of contractual orders under Order 42 rule 5A.

## [22.1.5]  Performance of the substituted obligation

The fact that settlement under Order 22 is rooted in contract has certain consequences with regard to performance of the substituted obligation which arises under a contract of settlement. This is true with any settlement agreement, whether under Order 22 or otherwise. So far as settlement by acceptance of a sanctioned payment under Order 22 is concerned, these consequences are unlikely to be of much practical significance since there is no possibility of a sanctioned payment not being performed, as the money must be paid into court when the offer is made. See the commentary under

Order 22 rule 8. However they will be of significance on acceptance of a sanctioned offer.

Our sister publication in the UK, The Civil Court Practice says (at CPR 36 [4.3]) of this topic:

> **Performance of the substituted obligation** Two particular points arise.
>
> **(1) If a Part 36 offer is the promise of a substituted obligation which is accepted and the offeror fails to fulfil his obligation, can the offeree continue his claim or may he only enforce the terms of the offer which he has accepted?**
>
> In accordance with the normal rules of interpretation, the contract created by the making of the Part 36 offer and its acceptance must be construed within the context in which the parties have created their contract. The contract is made in the context of the procedure provided by CPR Part 36. CPR Part 36 provides that if a Part 36 offer is accepted, the claim is stayed (CPR 36.11(1)) [in Hong Kong Order 22 rule 22]. "Stayed" in this context does not mean that the proceedings temporarily go to sleep: it means that the case is effectively over, bar the assessment [taxation] of costs and any subsequent enforcement proceedings. The notion of continuation of the claim by the offeree in the event of default by the offeror is manifestly inconsistent with CPR 36. In other words, once the offeree has accepted such a Part 36 offer, he may only enforce the terms of that offer, and in the event of default by the offeror, he may not resume his claim. **(See also sub para (2) "may the offeree ..." below).**

The above passage continues with discussion of the similar result which follows in relation to acceptance of pre-action proposals in the United Kingdom. That commentary is not relevant in Hong Kong, where the rules expressly require that a sanctioned offer or sanctioned payment may only be made after proceedings have been commenced. The Civil Court Practice continues:

> **(2) May the offeree, when accepting the offer which is the promise of a substituted obligation, specify that the offeror's liability will not be discharged unless the compromise is performed?**
>
> Save that the acceptance must be in writing (CPR 36.9 [in Hong Kong Order 22 rule 16(1)] the rules are silent in relation to the form and content of the acceptance [in Hong Kong this is true only in the case of acceptance of sanctioned offers – Form No 24 in Appendix A is prescribed for the acceptance of sanctioned payments – see Order 22 rule 15(4)]. CPR Part 36, however, provides that if a Part 36 offer is accepted, the claim is stayed (CPR 36.11) [in Hong Kong Order 22 rule 22] and various costs consequences follow (CPR 36.10 and CPR 36.12) [in Hong Kong Order 22 rules 20 and 21]. The rules also provide for the enforcement of the offer (CPR 36.11(6), (7) and (8)) [in Hong Kong Order 22 rule 22(5) and (6)]. If, however, the offeree specifies that his acceptance of the offer is on the basis that the offeror's liability is not discharged, an initial problem is that this would not qualify as an acceptance because the offeree is in effect seeking to add a fresh term to the offer. Assuming, however, that the offeror accepts this additional term, there would still be a difficulty in treating such an arrangement (valid contract though it may be) as being within Part 36.
>
> As already mentioned, "stayed" in this context does not mean that the proceedings go to sleep: acceptance of a Part 36 offer means that the case is effectively over, bar the assessment [taxation] of costs and any subsequent enforcement.
>
> The continuation of the claim by the offeree whilst retaining the benefit of the costs consequences of CPR 36 would seem to be manifestly inconsistent with the rules.

It would appear, therefore, that the offeree has an election.

(1) If the offeree wishes that the costs consequences of Part 36 should ensue then he simply accepts the offer. If the compromise is not satisfied then he enters judgment as provided under CPR 36.11(7) [which relates to money claims and has no equivalent in Hong Kong where the rules provide that the money must actually be paid into court when the proposal is made] or seeks to enforce the compromise under CPR 36.11(8), as appropriate [in Hong Kong Order 22 rule 22(5) and (6)].

(2) Alternatively, if he is willing to forgo the automatic costs and other consequences of CPR 36 then he is free so to do; he may specify that he is prepared to "accept" the offer outside the ambit of CPR 36 and that the offeror's liability will only be discharged if the offeror satisfies the terms of the compromise. If the offeror accepts this counter-offer and then fails to perform his obligations under the compromise, the offeree retains the opportunity to bring his claim for the full amount and/or for the full relief.

### [22.1.6] Application of Order 22 to arbitration proceedings
In response to comments received at the consultation stage, it was said that arbitration proceedings are 'clearly covered' by Order 22, 'although it will be rare for sanctioned offers or payments to be made in O 73 proceedings'. (Judiciary Administration paper CJRS 3/2008, para 27).

### [22.1.7] Offers and payments in relation to costs
With regard to proposals to settle a liability for unquantified costs, see Order 62A.

**2.    Offer to settle with specified consequences** (O. 22 r. 2)

    **(1)    A party to an action containing a money claim or a non-money claim or both arising from any cause or causes of action may make an offer to settle the whole claim, a part of it or any issue arising from it in accordance with this Order.**

    **(2)    An offer made under paragraph (1) may take into account any counterclaim or set-off in the action.**

    **(3)    An offer made under paragraph (1) has the consequences specified in rules 20, 21, 22, 23 and 24 (as may be applicable).**

    **(4)    Nothing in this Order prevents a party from making an offer to settle in whatever way he chooses, but if that offer is not made in accordance with this Order, it does not have the consequences specified in this Order, unless the Court so orders.**

    **(L.N. 152 of 2008)**

---

**NOTES**

### [22.2.1] Types of offer to settle under Order 22
Order 22 rule 2 provides that any party may make an offer to settle in accordance with this Order. The Order provides for two types of offer to settle, the sanctioned offer and the sanctioned payment. The procedures for making such proposals are set out in rules 5 and 8 respectively.

### [22.2.2]    Other types of offer to settle – 'Calderbank' offers

Order 22 rule 2(4) expressly preserves the right of a party to make an offer to settle of any type, whether of the type contemplated by this Order or not. However a proposal not of the Order 22 type will only have Order 22 consequences if the court so orders. The equivalent provision in England is CPR 36.1(2).

The court retains a discretion to take into account a proposal not of the Order 22 type in making an order for costs. See Order 62 rule 5(1)(g). The Chief Justice's working party specifically recommended that this be stated expressly in the rules (final report, recommendation 42). With regard to '*Calderbank*' offers (offers 'without prejudice save as to costs') that discretion is restricted by Order 62 rule 5(1)(d) by which the court may not take such an offer into account if the party making it could have protected its position as to costs by making a sanctioned offer or sanctioned payment under Order 22. Thus, there is no impediment to making a '*Calderbank*' offer despite the repeal of the former Order 22 rule 14 which gave such offers recognition within these rules. However, such an offer will only afford costs protection in the unusual event that the sanctioned proposals under Order 22 were not available or appropriate. For discussion of the costs consequences of such offers, see the commentary under Order 62 rule 5.

With regard to awards of enhanced interest, the Chief Justice's working party chose to confine the possibility of such an order to settlement proposals within Order 22 (final report, recommendation 43). As a result only the normal provisions as to interest apply to non-Order 22 settlement proposals (as to which see the commentary under Order 42 rule 1, and as to interest on costs see the commentary under Order 62 rule 3) .

### [22.2.3]    Application to money and non-money claims

It is clear from Order 22 rule 2(1) that the sanctioned payment and sanctioned offer procedures under the Order are both intended to be available in respect of both money and non-money claims. However, it is difficult to see how a payment of money alone can satisfy a non-monetary claim such as a claim for an injunction or a declaration. Under the previous Order 22 it was held that a payment into court could not satisfy a claim for a declaration: *Associated Engineers Ltd v Lo Chee Pui* [2003] 2 HKC 316 (CA).

### [22.2.4]    Application to Admiralty proceedings

Order 22 applies to Admiralty proceedings, subject to certain modifications. See Order 75 rule 24.

### [22.2.5]    Stage at which sanctioned settlement proposal may be made

Sanctioned offers and sanctioned payments may only be made after proceedings have been commenced: rules 3(3) and 5(6). See the commentary under those rules. This is different from the situation in England under CPR Part 36. The Chief Justice's working party noted resistance in Hong Kong to adopting the English position, and decided against it (final report, para 301). This does not mean that the parties are not encouraged to settle their disputes before action is commenced. It simply means that the costs and other consequences laid down in Order 22 will not apply to a pre-action proposal. The Chief Justice's working party made it clear that 'parties should be encouraged to settle their disputes by negotiation' even where Order 22 is not extended to apply to pre-action proposals (recommendation 40).

The Chief Justice's working party did envisage the possibility that sanctioned offers (though not sanctioned payments) could be made before proceedings have been commenced in specialist proceedings if provision is made accordingly by pre-action protocol (final report, para 301). At the consultation stage, the draft Order 22 contained provision to that effect, but it was omitted when the Amendment Rules 2008 were made. The requirement that proceedings have been commenced is discussed further under rule 3.

Once proceedings have been commenced there is no time limitation for making a settlement proposal under either procedure. It is even possible to make a proposal after trial has begun. However, late proposals (made less than 28 days before commencement of trial) may only be accepted if the parties agree on liability for costs or with leave: rules 15(2) and 16(2). Late proposals which are not accepted may not be fully effective in protecting the offeror as to costs. See *Standard Metal Mfy (HK) (a firm) v Ace Accessories Ltd* [1990] HKDCLR 1 where the court considered whether a plaintiff had sufficient time to consider a payment into court made only 4 days before trial. And see rule 23(6)(b) and rule 24(5)(b) which require the court to take into account the 'stage in the proceedings' at which a sanctioned proposal was made, in deciding whether it might be unjust to impose the enhanced costs and interest sanctions.

### [22.2.6]   Offer to settle not an admission of liability

Under the former Order 22 payment into court procedure it was held that a payment into court was not an admission as to liability or the merits: *Sun Jianqiang v Trans-Island Limousine Service Ltd* [2004] 1 HKC 533 (CA). See also *Ng Ming Chor v Pui Hing Construction Co Ltd & Ors* DCCJ 496/1996 (Judge To; 26.05.1998) citing *French v Kingswood Hill Ltd* [1961] QB 96. The same should be true of a sanctioned payment or sanctioned offer under the current Order 22.

II. Manner of Making Sanctioned Offer or Sanctioned Payment

**3.      Defendant's offer to settle** (O. 22 r. 3)

**(1)      An offer by a defendant to settle the whole or part of a claim or an issue arising from the claim does not have the consequences specified in this Order unless it is made by way of a sanctioned offer or a sanctioned payment or both.**

**(2)      Where an offer by a defendant involves a payment of money to the plaintiff, the offer must be made by way of a sanctioned payment.**

**(3)      A sanctioned payment may only be made after the proceedings have commenced.**

**(L.N. 152 of 2008)**

---

**NOTES**

### [22.3.1]    Consequences of Order 22 flow only from sanctioned offer or payment

Order 22 rule 3(1) provides that the costs and interest consequences of the Order flow only from a sanctioned offer or payment made under its terms, and rule 3(2) provides that an offer involving payment of money must be made by way of sanctioned payment. These provisions should be read together with rule 2(4), which makes it clear that parties are free to make settlement proposals in any way they choose, and Order 62 under which the court has a discretion as to costs. Thus even where a settlement proposal does not come within Order 22, the court has powers which may be exercised to give an Order 22-like effect, at least to some extent. So far as costs are concerned, this point is made in the final report of the Chief Justice's working party on civil justice reform where it is said (at para 319):

> In Hong Kong, s 52A of the HCO provides that, subject to the provisions of rules of court, the costs of and incidental to all civil proceedings in the High Court are in the court's discretion. The introduction of sanctioned offers would not affect this residual discretion which would enable the court to make an adverse costs order reflecting an unreasonable rejection of an 'unsanctioned' offer.

The working party makes a similar point with regard to interest at para 323 *et seq* of its final report.

See also generally the commentary on contract of settlement under Order 22 rule 1.

### [22.3.2]    Payment required for offer to settle money claim

Order 22 rule 3(2) provides that a defendant's offer to settle a money claim must be made by way of a sanctioned payment. It does not mean that other forms of offer outside the scope of Order 22 are not possible. In fact the right of a party to propose settlement of any type is preserved by rule 2(4). What rule 3(2) means is that if a defendant wishes to make a settlement proposal carrying the sanctions provided for by Order 22, it must, if it involves payment of money, be made by way of sanctioned payment. Thus in the case of mixed claims, seeking both monetary and non-monetary relief, it is necessary to make a sanctioned payment in respect of the monetary claim rather than including it in a sanctioned offer in respect of the non-monetary claim.

### [22.3.3]    Rule 3(3) – no sanctioned payment before action

Order 22 rule 3(3) expressly provides that a sanctioned payment may only be made after proceedings have been commenced. Order 22 rule 5(6) makes the same provision for sanctioned offers – see the commentary under that rule.

In Hong Kong at the pre-action stage a potential defendant may consider making a *Calderbank* offer or tendering the amount of the potential plaintiff's claim. A *Calderbank* offer may be made before action: *Oriental Press Group v Apple Daily* [1996] 3 HKC 615 (CA) and may be taken into account by the court on the question of costs pursuant to Order 62 rule 5(1)(d). A tender before action will give rise to a defence if proceedings are commenced (provided it is then paid into court: see Order 18 rule 16 and the commentary thereunder) and could be taken into account by the court on the question of costs under Order 62 rule 5(1)(e) as a matter of conduct of the parties, which expressly includes preaction conduct: rule 5(2)(d).

### [22.3.4]    Sanctioned payment not a bar to jurisdictional challenge

In *Towers v Morley* [1992] 1 WLR 511 (CA) it was held that a defendant who made a payment into court under the former Order 22 could still challenge the validity of service of the writ. The same should be equally true of a sanctioned payment.

**4.      Plaintiff's offer to settle** (O. 22 r. 4)
**An offer by a plaintiff to settle the whole or part of a claim or an issue arising from the claim does not have the consequences specified in this Order unless it is made by way of sanctioned offer.**
**(L.N. 152 of 2008)**

---

**NOTES**

**[22.4.1]   Origin and scope of Order 22 rule 4**
Order 22 rule 4 provides that the enhanced costs and interest consequences set out in the Order apply only to offers of settlement which are made by way of sanctioned offer. Thus, although a party remains free to put forward a *Calderbank* offer (see the commentary under rule 2 above), and such an offer may in some circumstances affect the incidence of costs, it is likely to attract only the usual level of costs and interest. The equivalent provisions in England are found in CPR 36.1.

This rule may be read as conflicting with the closing words of Order 22 rule 2(4) which appear to reserve to the court a power to order that the enhanced costs and interest consequences shall apply to an offer to settle not made in accordance with this Order. The two provisions might be reconciled by reading rule 2(4) as merely preserving the court's broad discretionary powers as to costs and interest which exist outside Order 22.

**5.      Form and content of sanctioned offer** (O. 22 r. 5)
     **(1)    A sanctioned offer must be in writing.**
     **(2)    A sanctioned offer may relate to the whole claim or to part of it or to any issue arising from it.**
     **(3)    A sanctioned offer must –**
          **(a)    state whether it relates to the whole claim or to part of it or to an issue arising from it and if so to which part or issue;**
          **(b)    state whether it takes into account any counterclaim or set-off; and**
          **(c)    if it is expressed not to be inclusive of interest, give the details relating to interest set out in rule 26(2).**
     **(4)    A defendant may make a sanctioned offer limited to accepting liability up to a specified proportion.**
     **(5)    A sanctioned offer may be made by reference to an interim payment.**
     **(6)    A sanctioned offer may be made at any time after the commencement of proceedings but may not be made before such commencement.**
     **(7)    A sanctioned offer made not less than 28 days before the commencement of the trial must provide that after the expiry of 28 days from the date the sanctioned offer is made, the offeree may only accept it if –**

          (a)     **the parties agree on the liability for costs; or**

          (b)     **the Court grants leave to accept it.**

    **(8)  A  sanctioned  offer  made  less  than  28  days  before  the commencement of the trial must provide that the offeree may only accept it if –**

          (a)     **the parties agree on the liability for costs; or**

          (b)     **the Court grants leave to accept it.**

    **(L.N. 152 of 2008)**

---

## NOTES

### [22.5.1]   Origin and scope of Order 22 rule 5

Order 22 rule 5 derives, in part, from CPR 36.2 which likewise deals with the form and content of offers which will have the consequences provided for in the rules. However, the two provisions are by no means identical. The English rule is shorter.

### [22.5.2]   Form and content of sanctioned offer

Order 22 rule 5(1) stipulates that a sanctioned offer must be in writing, however there is no prescribed form. It should be sufficient to set out the offer in a letter. Care should be taken to include all of the information required by rule 5(3).

In addition a sanctioned offer must provide that acceptance will in certain circumstances require leave. Rule 5(7) applies where the offer is made 28 or more days before trial, and requires the offer to provide that if not accepted within 28 days, leave to accept it will be required unless the parties agree on the liability for costs. Rule 5(8) applies where the offer is made less than 28 days before trial, and requires that the offer provide that any acceptance is only possible with agreement as to liability for costs, or with leave. Those two provisions reflect the requirements set out in rules 15 and 16 as to when leave to accept a sanctioned proposal is required.

### [22.5.3]   The need for precision in formulating terms of sanctioned offer

The terms of a sanctioned offer should be clear. This is especially important in cases where there are cross claims or multiple causes of action. The recipient of the offer needs to know precisely which parts of the case it is being asked to settle and on what terms. In *Prudential Mall Ltd v PH Shek Ltd & Anor* [1992] 1 HKC 7 a dispute over an insufficiently clear notice of payment into court under the former Order 22 went all the way to the Privy Council. The notice failed to indicate whether interim payments which had already been made were taken into account, but was treated as an irregularity rather than a nullity, pursuant to Order 2 rule 1.

Not only do the terms of a sanctioned offer need to be clear, but the offeror's case needs to be clear from correspondence, pleadings, affidavits and so on. The Chief Justice's working party noted this need at para 307 of its final report. Clarity of the offeror's case is necessary in order for the offer to be properly assessed by the offeree. The working party said (at para 308) that lack of clarity may be one of the grounds on which the court would in its discretion order that the consequences of a sanctioned offer not follow in a particular case, or only follow after the case has been made clear by amendment (referring to *Factortame Ltd v Secty of State* [2002] 1 WLR 2438).

The following commentary from CPR 36.2[2] of The Civil Court Practice, our sister publication in the UK, on the terms of a Part 36 offer is relevant in Hong Kong:

> **Terms of the offer** The requirements in respect of the content and terms of a Part 36 offer are strict. The court does not have an express discretion within the rule itself to apply the normal consequences of Part 36 if the offer does not fully comply with the terms of CPR 36 [but see the closing words of rule 2(4) in Hong Kong]. It is anticipated that the court will not readily exercise its power to rectify errors of procedure (under CPR 3.10 [Order 2 rule 1(3) in Hong Kong]) where there has been a failure to comply with the clear requirements of CPR 36.2, 36.3 and 36.4 [in Hong Kong see in particular Order 22 rules 5 and 8].

The above passage continues by pointing out that in England the court is obliged to take into account any offer when deciding what order as to costs to make (CPR 44.3). In Hong Kong see Order 62 rule 5 (which is not so broad in scope as to what the court is obliged to take into account) and section 52A of the High Court Ordinance by which the court's discretion with regard to costs is broad enough that it may take into account any relevant factor.

See also Order 22 rule 14 as to an offeree's right to request clarification of a sanctioned proposal.

### [22.5.4]   Consequences of non-compliance with formal requirements
In England, a sanctioned proposal which does not comply with the formal requirements as to form and content set out in the equivalent of Order 22 rule 5 may nevertheless be treated as having the consequences of a sanctioned proposal. This may be done by exercise of the power under rule 2(4) to order that an offer which is not technically a sanctioned proposal, have those consequences. See *Mitchell v James* [2002] EWCA Civ 997; [2003] 2 All ER 1064, and *Neave v Neave* [2003] EWCA Civ 325. In both those cases sanctioned proposals failed to comply with the requirement in the English equivalent of rule 5(7) that a sanctioned offer must provide that after the expiry of 28 days from the date of the offer (21 days in England), the offeree may only accept if (a) the parties agree on costs, or (b) the court grants leave to accept it. In *Mitchell* Peter Gibson J said (at para 25):

> In my judgment whilst in other circumstances the court might not be prepared to waive the defect of the omission from the offer of words to comply with r 36.5(6)(b) [r 5(7) in Hong Kong], in the present case, with the Defendants having legal advisers and there being no evidence that the Defendants were misled, I cannot accept that this defect in the offer is other than technical. Accordingly, if this had been the only objection, I would have been prepared to use the power in r. 36.1(2) [r 2(4) in Hong Kong] to order that in relation to the non-compliance with r 36.5(6)(b) the offer has the consequences specified in Part 36 [Order 22 in Hong Kong].

In *Neave* the English Court of Appeal applied *Mitchell* in a case where the non-compliance 'was of no material significance, led to no prejudice of any kind' (per Potter LJ at para 49).

### [22.5.5]   Sanctioned offer between defendants
Order 22 rule 5(4) expressly provides that a defendant may make a sanctioned offer to accept liability up to a specified proportion. In *Tang Hung On v Crown Rich Transportation Ltd & Ors* HCPI 304/2006 (Saunders J; 12.03.2010) such an offer was made not to the plaintiff, but by one defendant to another in respect a claim for contribution and indemnity. The sanctioned offer was not accepted and when the

offeror defendant did substantially better at trial, it successfully applied for enhanced costs and interest sanctions against the offeree defendant.

**[22.5.6]    Rule 5(3)(c) – interest**
A sanctioned offer need not include interest, but if it is silent on this question it will be taken to include interest: Order 22 rule 26(1). Rule 5(3)(c) together with rule 26(2) provides that where a sanctioned offer does not include interest, the notice must state whether interest is offered and if so the terms.

**[22.5.7]    Rule 5(6) – no sanctioned offer before action**
Rule 5(6) provides that a sanctioned offer may not be made before commencement of proceedings. The situation is different in England: see *Huck v Robson* [2002] 3 All ER 263 (CA), and see CPR 36.3(2)(a) as amended in 2007. The Chief Justice's working party decided not to adopt the English position for Hong Kong, in light of opposition to 'the general adoption of pre-action protocols', and 'the court assuming powers to penalise the parties' pre-commencement conduct'. The opposition was said to be based on the ground that the result would be 'unnecessary front-loaded costs' (final report, para 301). The working party continued (para 302):

> In consequence, although parties would be encouraged to settle their disputes before starting proceedings, their rejection of any pre-commencement offers which would otherwise qualify as sanctioned offers would not subsequently be taken into account by the court (subject to the aforementioned exception concerning pre-action protocols) [which appears to have been omitted from Order 22 as made]. The court would only attach any adverse consequences to the non-acceptance of sanctioned offers made with or after service of the Writ (such consequences to take effect from the end of the period allowed for acceptance).

In Hong Kong at the pre-action stage consideration may be given to making a *Calderbank* offer, which may have costs consequences even where made before commencement of proceedings: *Oriental Press Group v Apple Daily* [1997] 3 HKC 615 (CA). See also para 24 of the personal injury practice direction (PD 18.1), which reminds parties that under Order 62 rule 5 such offers may be taken into account on costs.

**[22.5.8]    No filing requirement for sanctioned offer**
A sanctioned offer itself need not be filed in court. This point was made in response to comments received on a draft of the new Order 22. In a summary of responses to the earlier draft, it was said 'it is not anticipated that the offer will be filed in court' (Judiciary Administration paper CJRS 3/2008, para 28). However acceptance of a sanctioned offer is required to be filed in court: see rules 15(1) and 16(1).

The situation is different with regard to sanctioned payments, in respect of which both notice of making the payment (see Order 22 rule 8(2)) and of acceptance (Order 22 rule 15(1)) must be filed in court.

**[22.5.9]    Rule 5(7) – late acceptance**
Rule 5(7) provides that a sanctioned offer made 28 or more days before trial must provide that late acceptance, that is acceptance more than 28 days after the offer is made, is only possible if the parties agree on liability for costs, or with leave of the court.

**[22.5.10]  Rule 5(8) – late offers**

Order 22 rule 5(8) imposes additional requirements on sanctioned offers made less than 28 days before trial. The offer must stipulate that it may only be accepted if (a) there is agreement on liability for costs, or (b) the court grants leave. These additional requirements were thought to reflect the view of the Chief Justice's working party that late sanctioned offers could cause unfairness. At para 311 of its final report the working party said:

> It would be undesirable to enable a plaintiff to place a defendant under the significant threat of additional interest at potentially punitive rates at the very door of the court (having already incurred the bulk of the defence costs) as a means of forcing what may be an unfair settlement.

However, in *Tsoi Hak Kong Herbert (administrator) v Kok Wai Chun & Ors* [2009] 3 HKC 344 it was held that the enhanced costs and interest sanctions may apply to a plaintiff's sanctioned offer made less than 28 days before trial, if it is not accepted. See the commentary under rule 24.

**6.      Service of sanctioned offer** (O. 22 r. 6)

**An offeror shall serve the sanctioned offer –**

  **(a)      on the offeree; and**

  **(b)      where the offeree is an aided person, on the Director of Legal Aid.**

**(L.N. 152 of 2008)**

---

**NOTES**

**[22.6.1]   Service of sanctioned offer**

Order 22 rule 6 requires that a sanctioned offer be served on the plaintiff and, where appropriate, the Director of Legal Aid. The Director has power to withdraw legal aid from an aided person who unreasonably refuses to settle.

In England practice direction CPR PD 36 para 1.2 provides that where an offeree is legally represented, service must be on the legal representative. This is consistent with Hong Kong's Order 65 rule 5, which provides for ordinary service of documents after the commencement of proceedings. See the commentary thereunder.

It has been held that defective service may be overlooked: *Charles v NTL Group Ltd* [2002] EWCA Civ 2004. In that case an offer which was sent by fax was treated as being a sanctioned offer despite the fact it was not formally served.

**7.      Withdrawal or diminution of sanctioned offer** (O. 22 r. 7)

  **(1)   A sanctioned offer made not less than 28 days before the commencement of the trial may not be withdrawn or diminished before the expiry of 28 days from the date the sanctioned offer is made unless the Court grants leave to withdraw or diminish it.**

  **(2)   A sanctioned offer made less than 28 days before the commencement of the trial may be withdrawn or diminished if the Court grants leave to withdraw or diminish it.**

  **(3)   If there is subsisting an application to withdraw or diminish a**

sanctioned offer, the sanctioned offer may not be accepted unless the Court grants leave to accept it.

(4)   If the Court dismisses an application to withdraw or diminish a sanctioned offer or grants leave to diminish the sanctioned offer, it may by order specify the period within which the sanctioned offer or diminished sanctioned offer may be accepted.

(5)   If a sanctioned offer is withdrawn, it does not have the consequences specified in this Order.(L.N. 152 of 2008)

---

## NOTES

### [22.7.1]   Duration of sanctioned offer
Order 22 rule 7 should be read together with Order 22 rule 15. They provide, in effect, that a sanctioned offer remains open for acceptance for 28 days, unless the court gives leave to withdraw or diminish it. After expiration of the 28-day period the offer may be accepted, but only if the parties agree on liability for costs or the court grants leave.

### [22.7.2]   Withdrawal or diminution of sanctioned offer
Order 22 rule 7 deals with the question of when a sanctioned offer may be withdrawn or diminished. Leave is generally required. See the commentary under Order 22 rule 10, concerning withdrawal and diminution of sanctioned payments, which is largely relevant here as well.

### [22.7.3]   Is automatic withdrawal of sanctioned offer possible?
The learned authors of our sister publication in the UK, The Civil Court Practice 2008 (at 36.3[2]) submit that although it is not free from doubt, it should be possible to stipulate in a sanctioned offer that the same will be treated as withdrawn (if not accepted) at the end of the relevant period.

### [22.7.4]   Does sanctioned offer lapse upon being rejected?
It has been held in England that a sanctioned offer remains open for acceptance even after it has been rejected. See *Gibbon v Manchester City Council* [2010] EWCA Civ 726 (25.06.2010). It was there held that the common law rule that an offer lapses upon rejection was ousted by CPR 36.9(2), which provides that a sanctioned offer may be accepted 'at any time', unless formally withdrawn. The Hong Kong rules are worded differently. In particular Order 22 rules 15 and 16 provide that a sanctioned offer or sanctioned payment may only be accepted after 28 days if liability to costs is agreed, or with leave of the court. However it has been held that under the Hong Kong rules a sanctioned offer is not withdrawn by the making of a subsequent without prejudice offer outside the scope of Order 22: *Wealthy Century Investment Ltd v DBS Bank (HK) Ltd (No 2)* [2010] 6 HKC 130.

**8.     Notice of sanctioned payment** (O. 22 r. 8)
**(1)   A sanctioned payment may relate to the whole claim or to part of it or to an issue arising from it.**
**(2)   A defendant who makes a sanctioned payment shall file with the**

Court a notice in Form No. 23 in Appendix A, that –

- **(a)** states the amount of the payment;
- **(b)** states whether the payment relates to the whole claim or to part of it or to an issue arising from it and if so to which part or issue it relates;
- **(c)** states whether it takes into account any counterclaim or set-off;
- **(d)** if an interim payment has been made, states that the interim payment has been taken into account;
- **(e)** if it is expressed not to be inclusive of interest, gives the details relating to interest set out in rule 26(2); and
- **(f)** if a sum of money has been paid into court (other than as security for costs), states whether the sanctioned payment has taken into account that sum of money.

(L.N. 152 of 2008)

---

## NOTES

### [22.8.1]   Settlement proposal by way of sanctioned payment

The sanctioned payment procedure is a revised version of the payment into court procedure under the former Order 22. Like the former payment into court procedure, it enables a defendant to make a proposal to compromise a money claim by paying a sum into court, with costs consequences for a plaintiff who chooses not to accept it but fails to do any better at trial. The main difference with the new procedure is the court's express power to impose enhanced costs and interest sanctions on the plaintiff under Order 22 rule 23.

Order 22 rule 8 sets out the basic procedures to be followed when making a compromise proposal by way of sanctioned payment. Although the rule does not itself say so, it is clear from the definition of 'sanctioned payment' in rule 1, and from form No 23 in Appendix A to these rules, that the money offered must be paid into court at the time the offer is made.

### [22.8.2]   The sanctioned payment notice

Order 22 rule 8 provides that a party who wishes to make a settlement proposal following the sanctioned payment procedure must file and serve notice in form 23 in Appendix A to these rules. The form must be completed providing the information stipulated by rule 8(2)(a)-(f).

*Rule 8(2)(d) – interim payments* — The notice must state that any interim payment has been taken into account. The effect is that the offeror need only pay into court the balance required to top up the interim payment to the amount of the full offer. This applies whether the interim payment was made voluntarily or pursuant to order: see Order 29 rule 16.

*Rule 8(2)(e) – interest* – A sanctioned payment need not include interest, but if it is silent on this question it will be taken to include interest: Order 22 rule 26(1). Rule 8(2)(e) together with rule 26(2) provide that where a sanctioned payment does not include interest, the notice must state whether interest is offered and if so the terms.

*Rule 8(2)(f) – money in court –* The notice must state whether the sanctioned payment takes into account money which has previously been paid into court other than as security for costs. See *inter alia* Order 1B rule 1(3)(a) and (4) as to the court's power to order payment of money into court by a party in procedural default, and Order 14 rule 4 as to the power to require payment into court as a condition of leave to defend.

In *Prudential Mall Ltd v PH Shek Ltd & Anor* [1992] 1 HKC 7; [1993] 1 HKLR 195 (PC) it was held that defects in a notice of payment into court under the former Order 22 should have been treated as mere irregularity pursuant to Order 2 rule 1.

**[22.8.3]    Sanctioned payment in foreign currency**
Practice direction 16.2 has long made provision for claims for amounts of foreign currency, including payment into court thereof by adapting the form of notice of payment in. The same should apply with sanctioned payments.

**[22.8.4]    Sanctioned payment where more than one plaintiff**
Special considerations will arise when a defendant makes a sanctioned payment in respect of the claims of more than one plaintiff. The plaintiffs' interests in the claim may not be equal. Under the former payment into court procedure the defendant was entitled to make one unapportioned payment in respect of all the plaintiffs' claims. However the court could require the defendant to apportion the payment if some but not all plaintiffs wished to accept it. See *Walker & Anor v Turpin & Anor* [1994] 1 WLR 196. Now see also  the power under Order 22 rule 14 to order clarification of a sanctioned proposal.

**[22.8.5]    Sanctioned payment by more than one defendant**
Under the former payment into court procedure, the court had no power to require defendants making a single payment into court to apportion it so as to indicate how much had been contributed by each, or as between heads of damages claimed. See *Driscoll v Nye Saunders & Partners (a firm)* [1988] The Times, 27 June (CA). Now the court might, in an appropriate case, use its power under Order 22 rule 14 to order clarification.

**[22.8.6]    Sanctioned payment where more than one cause of action**
Neither rule 8 nor the form of notice of sanctioned payment (form No 23 in appendix A) appears to require a party making a sanctioned payment to apportion it between various causes of action (though it may be limited to part of a claim or an issue arising). Order 73 rule 11(5) provides that the court may require a defendant to apportion such a payment between 'more than one matter in dispute' in arbitration proceedings, but there does not appear to be any express equivalent for sanctioned payments under Order 22, though the clarification power under rule 14 might be used.

**9.    Service of sanctioned payment** (O. 22 r. 9)
**A defendant who makes a sanctioned payment shall —**
    **(a)    serve the sanctioned payment notice —**
        **(i)    on the plaintiff; and**
        **(ii)    where the plaintiff is an aided person, on the Director of Legal Aid; and**

**(b)      file with the Court a certificate of service of the notice.**
**(L.N. 152 of 2008)**

---

## NOTES

**[22.9.1]   Service of sanctioned payment notice**
Order 22 rule 9 requires that a sanctioned payment notice be served on the plaintiff and, where appropriate, the Director of Legal Aid. The Director has power to withdraw legal aid if an aided person unreasonably refuses a settlement. A certificate of service must be filed in court. The certificate need only be signed – the formality of an affirmation of service is not expressly required.

In England practice direction CPR PD 36 para 1.2 provides that where an offeree is legally represented, service must be on the legal representative. This is consistent with Hong Kong's Order 65 rule 5, which provides for ordinary service of documents after the commencement of proceedings. See the commentary thereunder.

It has also been held in England that defective service may be overlooked so that the proposal is not deprived of the sanctions provided for in this Order: *Charles v NTL Group Ltd* [2002] EWCA Civ 2004.

**10.      Withdrawal or diminution of sanctioned payment** (O. 22 r. 10)
**(1)    A sanctioned payment may not be withdrawn or diminished before the expiry of 28 days from the date the sanctioned payment is made unless the Court grants leave to withdraw or diminish it.**

**(2)    If there is subsisting an application to withdraw or diminish a sanctioned payment, the sanctioned payment may not be accepted unless the Court grants leave to accept it.**

**(3)    If the Court dismisses an application to withdraw or diminish a sanctioned payment or grants leave to diminish the sanctioned payment, it may by order specify the period within which the sanctioned payment or diminished sanctioned payment may be accepted.**

**(4)    If a sanctioned payment is withdrawn, it does not have the consequences specified in this Order.**
**(L.N. 152 of 2008)**

---

## NOTES

**[22.10.1]   Withdrawal or reduction of sanctioned offer or payment**
Order 22 rule 7 contemplates that a sanctioned offer may be withdrawn or reduced. Rule 10 does the same for sanctioned payments. Leave is required if it is sought to withdraw or reduce the proposal within the 28 day period during which it is normally open for acceptance or, in the case of sanctioned offers, if made less than 28 days before the commencement of the trial. This differs from the situation in England where it has been held that offers (as opposed to payments) may be withdrawn at any time before acceptance: *Scammell v Dicker* [2001] 1 WLR 631. The Chief Justice's working party decided not to adopt the English position for Hong Kong (final report, para 312).

The equivalent provision in England expressly gives the offeror a right to withdraw or amend a proposal without the need for leave after the expiry of the 28 day period: CPR 36.3(6). Although that express provision does not appear in Hong Kong's Order 22, there is nothing inconsistent with it, so the same result should obtain.

Where leave is required, the court is likely to be guided by the authorities concerning withdrawal or amendment of a payment into court under the previous Order 22. In *Tsang Kam Ming v Artchamp Investment Ltd* [2002] 2 HKC 693, 696B-E, referring to *Cumper v Pothecary* [1941] 2 KB 58 (CA) it was held that the power to grant leave to withdraw is discretionary and the defendant must satisfy the court there are good reasons. Good reasons include a change of circumstances increasing the prospects of the defence, or decreasing the likely quantum of damages. This may arise from a discovery of further evidence, putting 'a wholly different complexion on the case' as in *Cumper* (above, at 70) or finding a key witness only after payment in has been made, as in *Tsang Kam Ming* (above). In *Wong Pan v Eastern Pacific Circuits (HK) Ltd* DCPI 1283/2004 (Judge CB Chan; 16.11.2005) a defendant was granted leave to withdraw a payment into court where subsequently discovered documents gave rise to a new defence.

Under the former payment into court procedure it was thought that a defendant who wished to reduce the amount of the offer should withdraw the existing notice with liberty to substitute a new one: *Unistress Building Construction Co Ltd v Humphreys Estate (Forrestdale) Ltd* HCMP 3268/1991 (Kaplan J; 16.03.1992), referring to *Cumper* (above).

**[22.10.2]    Return of funds where sanctioned payment withdrawn**
Under the former payment into court procedure it was held that the court has an implied or inherent power to order the release of funds to a defendant who is granted leave to withdraw a payment in: *Tsang Kam Ming* (above, 698), citing *Garner v Cleggs* [1983] 1 WLR 862 (CA). Such payment out is now contemplated by Order 22A rule 1(2)(b).

**[22.10.3]    Costs consequences of withdrawal of sanctioned payment**
Under the former Order 22 a payment into court might still be relevant to the question of costs even after it had been withdrawn. In *Garner v Cleggs* (above, at 872H) it was said:

> … where notice of the payment into court is withdrawn by the defendant with leave after expiry of the [period during which it may be accepted], the costs previously incurred by the defendant during the period which has elapsed since the payment in, during which the money was in reality available to the plaintiff to be taken out, should ordinarily be borne by the plaintiff.

The same has been held with regard to Part 36 offers under the English CPR: *Trustees of Stokes Pension Fund v Western Power Distribution (SW) plc* [2005] EWCA Civ 854, though it is another question whether the enhanced costs and interest sanctions under Order 22 would apply: see rule 10(4).

**[22.10.4]    Increase of sanctioned payment**
The rules do not expressly deal with the possibility of making a further sanctioned payment on top of an earlier one. However, it is clear from the wording of the form of notice of sanctioned payment (form No 23 in appendix A) that this can be done simply by making an additional payment into court and serving a fresh notice,

expressly indicating that the payment is "a further amount".

**11.      Offer to settle claim for provisional damages** (O. 22 r. 11)

(1)      **A defendant may make a sanctioned payment in respect of a claim that includes a claim for provisional damages.**

(2)      **Where the defendant makes a sanctioned payment under paragraph (1), the sanctioned payment notice must specify whether or not the defendant is offering to agree to the making of an award of provisional damages.**

(3)      **Where the defendant is offering to agree to the making of an award of provisional damages, the sanctioned payment notice must also state —**

(a)      **that the sum paid into court is in satisfaction of the claim for damages on the assumption that the injured person will not develop the disease or suffer the type of deterioration specified in the notice;**

(b)      **that the offer is subject to the condition that the plaintiff shall make any claim for further damages within a limited period; and**

(c)      **what that period is.**

(4)      **Where a sanctioned payment is —**

(a)      **made in accordance with paragraph (3); and**

(b)      **accepted within the relevant period specified in rule 15,**

**the sanctioned payment has the consequences specified in rule 20, unless the Court orders otherwise.**

(5)      **If the plaintiff accepts the sanctioned payment he must, within 7 days of doing so, apply to the Court for an order for an award of provisional damages under Order 37, rule 8.**

(6)      **The money in court may not be paid out unless the Court has disposed of the application made under paragraph (5).**

(7)      **In this rule, "provisional damages" means damages for personal injuries that are to be assessed on the assumption that the injured person will not develop the disease or suffer the deterioration referred to in section 56A of the Ordinance.**

(**L.N. 152 of 2008**)

---

**NOTES**

**[22.11.1]      Origin and scope of Order 22 rule 11**
Order 22 rule 11 is based on CPR 36.6, though the latter is much shorter.

**[22.11.2]      Sanctioned payments in respect of claims for provisional damages**
Order 22 rule 11 extends the sanctioned payment procedure to claims for provisional damages. Where such a payment is made the notice must give the information prescribed by rule 11(3).

Provisional damages relate to claims for personal injuries where there is allegedly a possibility of a future disease or deterioration. The claim may be settled on the assumption that the future disease or deterioration will not happen, leaving it open to the plaintiff to claim additional damages in the event it does. With regard to provisional damages generally, see section 56A of the High Court Ordinance (Cap 4) and see Order 37 rules 7-10 and the commentary thereunder.

It is clear from rule 11(7) that the rule is intended to deal only with the initial lot of damages, which may be agreed or awarded on the assumption that the future condition will not eventuate. This point was noted in the Judiciary Administration's paper CJRS 3/2008 at the consultation stage where it was said (at para 33):

> O 22 r [11] is not intended to deal with the further damages an injured person might be awarded.

This does not mean that there is no possibility of a sanctioned payment in respect of further damages claimed at a later stage if and when the future condition materialises. Such a claim should come within rule 8(1) as a part of a claim or an issue arising from it.

**12.    Time when sanctioned offer or sanctioned payment is made and accepted** (O. 22 r. 12)

**(1)    A sanctioned offer is made when it is served on the offeree.**

**(2)    A sanctioned payment is made when a sanctioned payment notice is served on the offeree.**

**(3)    An amendment to a sanctioned offer is effective when its details are served on the offeree.**

**(4)    An amendment to a sanctioned payment is effective when notice of the amendment is served on the offeree.**

**(5)    A sanctioned offer or a sanctioned payment is accepted when notice of its acceptance is served on the offeror.**

**(L.N. 152 of 2008)**

---

**NOTES**

**[22.12.1]    Time when sanctioned offer or payment is made**
Order 22 rule 12(1) and (2) provide that a sanctioned offer or sanctioned payment is made when served on the offeree, and rule 12(3) and (4) provide the same for amendments thereto. These provisions derive from CPR 36.7.

**[22.12.2]    Time when sanctioned offer or payment is accepted**
A sanctioned offer or payment is accepted when notice of acceptance is served on the offeror: rule 12(5).

**13.    Service of notice of acceptance of plaintiff's sanctioned offer** (O. 22 r. 13)

**(1)    Where there is more than one defendant, a defendant who serves on the plaintiff a notice of acceptance of the plaintiff's sanctioned offer shall at the same time serve a copy of the notice on the other defendant or defendants.**

**(2)    A defendant on whom a copy of the notice has been served may within 14 days after the service apply to the Court for –**

**(a)    a direction as to any question of costs between him and the defendant who has accepted the plaintiff's sanctioned offer;**

**and**

(b) **any other direction relating to the acceptance of the plaintiff's sanctioned offer.**

(3) **No application may be made under paragraph (2) after the expiry of the 14-day period referred to in that paragraph.**

(L.N. 152 of 2008)

---

## NOTES

### [22.13.1] Acceptance of sanctioned offer must be served on co-defendants
Order 22 rule 13(1) provides that a defendant who accepts a plaintiff's sanctioned offer must serve the notice of acceptance not only on the plaintiff, but on any co-defendants.

### [22.13.2] Application by co-defendant for directions
Where a defendant has accepted a plaintiff's sanctioned offer, any co-defendant may apply under Order 22 rule 13(2) for directions as to costs or otherwise, within 14 days. The purpose of the rule is to provide an opportunity for a co-defendant to claim its costs. That may be by way of '*Bullock*' or '*Sanderson*' order or otherwise. See the commentary under Order 62 rule 3 concerning such orders.

**14. Clarification of sanctioned offer or sanctioned payment notice** (O. 22 r. 14)

(1) **The offeree may, within 7 days of a sanctioned offer or sanctioned payment being made, request the offeror to clarify the offer or payment notice.**

(2) **If the offeror does not give the clarification requested under paragraph (1) within 7 days of service of the request, the offeree may, unless the trial has commenced, apply for an order that he does so.**

(3) **If the Court makes an order pursuant to an application made under paragraph (2), it shall specify the date when the sanctioned offer or sanctioned payment is to be treated as having been made.**

(4) **Where a cause of action under the Fatal Accidents Ordinance (Cap. 22) and a cause of action under Part IV or IVA of the Law Amendment and Reform (Consolidation) Ordinance (Cap. 23) are joined in an action, with or without any other cause of action, the plaintiff is not entitled under paragraph (1) to request the defendant to make an apportionment of the sanctioned payment between the causes of action under those Ordinances.**

(L.N. 152 of 2008)

---

## NOTES

### [22.14.1] Origin and scope of Order 22 rule 14
Order 22 rule 14 derives from CPR 36.8. That rule, apart from inconsequential differences in terminology, is the same terms as Order 22 rule 14(1), (2) and (3). Rule 14(4) is unique to Hong Kong, reflecting local statutory provisions concerning claims on death.

## [22.14.2]    Right to seek clarification of sanctioned offer or payment

Rule 14(1), (2) and (3) concern the right of an offeree to seek clarification of a sanctioned offer or sanctioned payment notice, and give the court power to compel the offeror to provide clarification unless the trial has started. The Civil Court Practice, our sister publication in the UK, in commenting on the equivalent English provision, refers readers (at 36.8[1]) to the duty of the parties to co-operate:

> **Duty to co-operate** In addition to this requirement in CPR 36.8 [in Hong Kong Order 22 rule 14(1), (2) and (3)], parties are obliged by CPR 1.3 and 1.4 [in Hong Kong see Order 1A rules 3 and 4(2)(a)] to co-operate; this obligation extends to explaining any procedural points which they intend to take: *Hertsmere Primary Care Trust v Estate of Balasubramanium Rabindra-Anandh* [2005] EWHC 320 (Ch), [2005] 3 All ER 274, [2005] The Times, 24 Apr.

## [22.14.3]    Rule 14(4) - claims on death

The apportionment of money accepted on settlement of claims made under the Fatal Accidents Ordinance (Cap 22) and LARCO (Cap 23) is a matter for the court under Order 80 rule 15. See the commentary under that rule. As a result, Order 22 rule 14(4) provides that a plaintiff in such an action may not require a defendant to clarify a sanctioned payment by apportioning it between those entitled to share in the damages.

III. Acceptance of Sanctioned Offer or Sanctioned Payment

**15.    Time for acceptance of defendant's sanctioned offer or sanctioned payment** (O. 22 r. 15)

**(1)    Subject to rules 7(3) and 10(2), a plaintiff may accept a sanctioned offer or a sanctioned payment made not less than 28 days before the commencement of the trial without requiring the leave of the Court if he files with the Court and serves on the defendant a written notice of acceptance not later than 28 days after the offer or payment was made.**

**(2)    If –**

> **(a)    a defendant's sanctioned offer or sanctioned payment is made less than 28 days before the commencement of the trial; or**
>
> **(b)    the plaintiff does not accept it within the period specified in paragraph (1),**

**then the plaintiff may –**

> > **(i)    if the parties agree on the liability for costs, accept the offer or payment without the leave of the Court; and**
> >
> > **(ii)    if the parties do not agree on the liability for costs, only accept the offer or payment with the leave of the Court.**

**(3)    Where the leave of the Court is required under paragraph (2), the Court shall, if it grants leave, make an order as to costs.**

**(4)    A notice of acceptance of a sanctioned payment must be in Form No. 24 in Appendix A.**

(L.N. 152 of 2008)

---

**NOTES**

**[22.15.1]  Time considerations with regard to acceptance of sanctioned proposal**
A settlement proposal under Order 22 is generally open for acceptance for 28 days: see rules 15(1) and 16(1). In England CPR 36.9 provides for acceptance 'at any time' unless the proposal has been withdrawn.

Where a proposal is made at a late stage, *ie* less than 28 days before the commencement of trial, it may only be accepted if the parties agree on liability for costs, or with leave.

**[22.15.2]  Solicitor's duty in advising on sanctioned offer or sanctioned payment**
Under the former Order 22 payment into court procedure it was considered that a prudent solicitor should advise the client of the possible consequences of failure to accept, and should record that advice in writing: *Poon Yat Lam Ilum v Chan Chi Wai* HCPI 462/2003 (Deputy Judge Saunders; 15.09.2006). There it was said:

> If that advice is not given, and the client is left to believe that they have the security of a payment in which may be accepted at any time, only to find upon late acceptance that there are adverse costs consequences, then the client would have every right to look to the solicitors . . . it would be difficult for the solicitors to resist a demand that they themselves should meet the costs.

The above remarks should apply all the more strongly to the sanctioned offer and sanctioned payment procedures under the current Order 22, given the enhanced interest and costs consequences which may follow from failure to accept.

See also the revised practice direction on personal injury actions (PD 18.1) which expressly stipulates that a solicitor should bring the costs consequences of sanctioned offers and sanctioned payments to the attention of the party concerned.

**[22.15.3]  Late acceptance of sanctioned proposal**
Acceptance of a sanctioned offer or sanctioned payment out of time is possible if the parties agree on the liability for costs, or with leave of the court: rules 15(2) and 16(2). In deciding whether to grant leave, the court's main concern will likely be costs. Rules 15(3) and 16(3) require that the court make an order as to costs when granting leave. An offeree who wishes to accept out of time might be denied costs incurred after the expiry of the usual 28 day period during which the proposal could have been accepted without leave.

In *Modern Fashion Ltd v Hong Kong Prudential Knitting Factory Ltd* [1996] 3 HKC 267 the court allowed a plaintiff to accept a payment into court under the former Order 22, out of time, and against the wishes of the defendant. However the court will not normally do so if there has been a material change in risk: *Gaskins v British Aluminium Co Ltd* [1976] 1 QB 530 (CA); *X v Y* [1990] TLR 726 (CA). In *Lee Yiu Pui v Wong Tat Man Simon* DCPI 1331/2008 (Deputy Judge Frederick Chan; 29.09.2008) the court found that it had discretion under Order 3 rule 5 to extend the time for acceptance of a payment into court under the former Order 22. However it declined to extend time in the particular case, partly on the ground that it was not clear whether the plaintiff would actually accept the payment in. It was suggested the plaintiff should have applied for payment out rather than merely for an extension of time.

**[22.15.4]  Sanctioned proposal less than 28 days before trial**
The requirements of rule 15(2) and 16(2) as to obtaining leave of the court for late

acceptance of a sanctioned payment or sanctioned offer unless the parties agree on liability for costs, also apply to proposals made less than 28 days before commencement of trial. The commentary above should be of guidance.

### [22.15.5]    Duty to inform listing officer of acceptance

Order 34 rule 8(3) provides that a party who accepts a sanctioned payment or sanctioned offer in an action which has been set down for trial has a duty to inform the officer who keeps the list.

**16.      Time for acceptance of plaintiff's sanctioned offer** (O. 22 r. 16)

     **(1)    Subject to rule 7(3), a defendant may accept a sanctioned offer made not less than 28 days before the commencement of the trial without requiring the leave of the Court if he files with the Court and serves on the plaintiff a written notice of acceptance not later than 28 days after the offer was made.**

     **(2)    If –**

         **(a)     a plaintiff's sanctioned offer is made less than 28 days before the commencement of the trial; or**

         **(b)     the defendant does not accept it within the period specified in paragraph (1),**

**then the defendant may –**

             **(i)     if the parties agree on the liability for costs, accept the offer without the leave of the Court; and**

             **(ii)     if the parties do not agree on the liability for costs, only accept the offer with the leave of the Court.**

     **(3) Where the leave of the Court is required under paragraph (2), the Court shall, if it grants leave, make an order as to costs.**

     **(L.N. 152 of 2008)**

---

### NOTES

### [22.16.1]    Time considerations and solicitor's duty

See the commentary under Order 22 rule 15 in relation to defendants' proposals, which is equally relevant to plaintiffs' proposals as dealt with in rule 16.

### [22.16.2]    Sanctions applicable to late plaintiff's offer

The court's power under Order 22 rule 24 to impose enhanced costs and interest sanctions on a defendant who has failed to accept a plaintiff's sanctioned offer, but is ultimately found liable for more, applies even to a plaintiff's sanctioned offer made less than 28 days before trial. This is despite rule 16 which provides that such an offer may only be accepted if the parties agree on liability for costs, or with leave of the court, and rule 24, which provides that those sanctions apply only from the last date on which the offer could have been accepted without leave. See *Tsoi Hak Kong Herbert (administrator) v Kok Wai Chun & Ors* [2009] 3 HKC 344.

**17.  Payment out of a sum in court on acceptance of sanctioned payment**
(O. 22 r. 17)

Subject to rules 18(4) and 19 and Order 22A, rule 2, where a sanctioned payment is accepted, the plaintiff may obtain payment out of the sum in court by making a request for payment in Form No. 25 in Appendix A.
**(L.N. 152 of 2008)**

---

NOTES

**[22.17.1]  Order not required for payment out**
The effect of Order 22 rule 17 is that an order is not normally required for payment out of court of money accepted under a sanctioned payment. However, this is subject to exceptions. See the commentary under the rules to which rule 17 is expressly subject.

On the form for making application for payment out (Form 25) the party applying for payment out is required to declare that none of the exceptions whereby leave is required (which are set out in tick-boxes) applies. The form also stipulates that a copy should be 'sent' to the opposing party.

In legally aided cases, payment out may only be made in favour of the Director of Legal Aid: see Order 22A rule 2(1).

**18.  Acceptance of sanctioned offer or sanctioned payment made by one or more, but not all, defendants** (O. 22 r. 18)

(1)  This rule applies where the plaintiff wishes to accept a sanctioned offer or a sanctioned payment made by one or more, but not all, of a number of defendants.

(2)  If the defendants are sued jointly or in the alternative, the plaintiff may accept the offer or payment without requiring the leave of the Court in accordance with rule 15(1) if –

(a)  he discontinues his claim against those defendants who have not made the offer or payment; and

(b)  those defendants give written consent to the acceptance of the offer or payment.

(3)  If the plaintiff alleges that the defendants have a several liability to him, the plaintiff may –

(a)  accept the offer or payment in accordance with rule 15(1); and

(b)  continue with his claims against the other defendants.

(4)  In all other cases the plaintiff shall apply to the Court for –

(a)  an order permitting a payment out to him of any sum in court; and

(b)  such order as to costs as the Court considers appropriate.
**(L.N. 152 of 2008)**

---

NOTES

**[22.18.1]  Origin and scope of Order 22 rule 18**
Order 22 rule 18 derives from CPR 36.12. The English provision is shorter, but

largely to the same effect.

The purpose of the rule is to enable a plaintiff to accept a sanctioned offer or sanctioned payment which is not made by all the defendants to the action. Where the defendants are sued jointly or in the alternative, the plaintiff is required to discontinue the action against the defendants who are not participating in the settlement proposal, and their consent is required. On the other hand where the action is based on several liability of the defendants, the plaintiff may accept the settlement and continue the action against the other defendants. In other cases the plaintiff is required by rule 18(4) to apply to the court.

**19.    Other cases where court order is required to enable acceptance of sanctioned offer or sanctioned payment (O. 22 r. 19)**

**(1)    Where a sanctioned offer or a sanctioned payment is made in proceedings to which Order 80, rule 10 (Compromise, etc., by person under disability) applies —**

**(a)    the offer or payment may be accepted only with the leave of the Court; and**

**(b)    the money in court may not be paid out except in pursuance of an order of the Court.**

**(2)    Where the Court grants leave to a plaintiff to accept a sanctioned offer or sanctioned payment after the trial has commenced –**

**(a)    the money in court may not be paid out except in pursuance of an order of the Court; and**

**(b)    the Court shall, in the order, deal with the whole costs of the proceedings.**

**(3)    Where a plaintiff accepts a sanctioned payment after a defence of tender before action has been put forward by the defendant, the money in court may not be paid out except in pursuance of an order of the Court.**

**(4)    Where a plaintiff accepts a sanctioned payment made in satisfaction of —**

**(a)    a cause of action under the Fatal Accidents Ordinance (Cap. 22) and a cause of action under Part IV or IVA of the Law Amendment and Reform (Consolidation) Ordinance (Cap. 23); or**

**(b)    a cause of action under the Fatal Accidents Ordinance (Cap. 22) where more than one person is entitled to the money,**

**the money in court may not be paid out except in pursuance of an order of the Court.**

**(L.N. 152 of 2008)**

---

**NOTES**

**[22.19.1]    Leave required for acceptance of sanctioned proposal by party under disability**

Order 22 rule 19(1) provides that leave is required for acceptance of a sanctioned offer or sanctioned payment on behalf of a party under disability. The purpose is to facilitate operation of Order 80 rule 10 whereby the court's approval is required for any compromise of a claim on behalf of any such person. See the commentary under Order 80 rules 10 and 11.

Furthermore the rule provides that an order of the court is required for payment out of court of money which has been paid in by way of sanctioned proposal to settle the claims of a party under disability. This operates by way of exception to rule 17, by which leave is not normally required for payment out of money accepted by way of sanctioned payment.

It has been held that where a sanctioned offer made by a party under disability is not accepted, the enhanced costs and interest sanctions do not apply. This is because Order 22 rule 24 provides that those sanctions may be imposed only from the latest date on which the offer could have been accepted without leave. There can be no such date in proceedings involving a party under disability, because leave is always required. See *Law Ping Leung by Siu Siu Wa (next friend) v Ng Sze Pong* HCPI 601/2008 (Deputy Judge Benjamin Yu SC; 24.11.2009).

### [22.19.2]   Leave required for payment out of court after commencement of trial
Rule 19(2) sets up a second exception to the provision of rule 17 whereby leave is not normally required for payment out of money accepted by way of sanctioned payment. It applies where leave is granted to accept a sanctioned proposal after commencement of trial, and provides that in such cases an order of the court is required for payment out of the money.

See Order 22 rules 15 and 16 as to the circumstances in which leave is required for late acceptance of a sanctioned proposal, or for acceptance of a sanctioned proposal made late in the proceedings.

### [22.19.3]   Leave required for payment out of court where defence of tender
Rule 19(3) sets up a third exception to the provision of rule 17 whereby leave is not normally required for payment out of money accepted by way of sanctioned payment. It applies where a defence of tender has been 'put forward'. That presumably means where the defence has been pleaded and, in accordance with Order 18 rule 16, the money has been paid into court as a sanctioned payment.

The purpose of this provision would appear to be to give the court an opportunity to consider what order as to costs would be appropriate, since if the defence has, in effect, been successful, the plaintiff might be deprived of costs.

With regard to the defence of tender before action generally, see the commentary under Order 18 rule 16.

### [22.19.4]   Leave required for payment out in FAO and LARCO cases
Rule 19(4) is the fourth exception to the general provision in rule 17 that leave is not normally required for payment out of a sanctioned payment which has been accepted. It applies to cases raising a cause of action under the Fatal Accidents Ordinance (Cap 22) or LARCO (Cap 23). The purpose of the leave requirement is to facilitate Order 80 rule 15, by which the court is required to apportion settlement money in such cases. See the commentary under that rule.

IV. Consequences of Sanctioned Offer or Sanctioned Payment

**20.     Costs consequences of acceptance of defendant's sanctioned offer or sanctioned payment** (O. 22 r. 20)

**(1)     Where a defendant's sanctioned offer or sanctioned payment to settle the whole claim is accepted without requiring the leave of the Court, the plaintiff is entitled to his costs of the proceedings up to the date of serving notice of acceptance, unless the Court otherwise orders.**

**(2)     Where –**

**(a)     a sanctioned offer or a sanctioned payment relating to a part of the claim or an issue arising from the claim is accepted; and**

**(b)     at the time of serving notice of acceptance the plaintiff abandons the other parts of the claim or other issues arising from the claim,**

**the plaintiff is entitled to his cost of the proceedings up to the date of serving notice of acceptance, unless the Court otherwise orders.**

**(3) The plaintiff's costs include any costs attributable to the defendant's counterclaim or set-off if the sanctioned offer or the sanctioned payment notice states that it takes into account the counterclaim or set-off.**

**(L.N. 152 of 2008)**

---

## NOTES

**[22.20.1]     Costs on acceptance of defendant's sanctioned offer or payment**
Order 22 rule 20 provides that a plaintiff who accepts a sanctioned offer or payment will normally be entitled to the costs of the action up to the date of the acceptance. See also Order 62 rule 10(5) which deems an order for costs to have been made.

Rule 20 is similar, but by no means identical, to CPR 36.10. The Civil Court Practice, our sister publication in the UK, says of the English rule:

> **Costs will be assessed on the standard [party and party] basis if the amount of costs is not agreed** Costs will therefore be assessed [taxed] in accordance with CPR 44.4 and 44.5 [in Hong Kong Order 62 rule 28(2)] if agreement cannot be reached on the amount of those costs beforehand . . .

> The court has no discretion to award indemnity costs to a claimant [plaintiff] who had accepted a payment into court in settlement of its claim where the sum paid in was better than an offer which the claimant had made under Part 36 [Order 22 in Hong Kong] and which the defendant had rejected; in the absence of a hearing to assess the quantum of damages, the court could not properly rule on the reasonableness of the defendant's rejection of the claimant's Part 36 [Order 22 in Hong Kong] offer: *Dyson Appliances Ltd v Hoover Ltd (No 3)* [2002] The Times, 06 Nov.

**[22.20.2]     Scale of costs where settlement amount below court's jurisdictional threshold**
The above commentary from The Civil Court Practice goes on to say that in England, where the sum offered and accepted is within the small claims limit the court may, as a matter of discretion order the payment of costs appropriate to small claims, citing *E Ivor Hughes Educational Foundation v Leach* [2005] EWHC 1317 (Ch), [2005] All

ER (D) 127 (Jun).

In Hong Kong there are conflicting authorities on the similar question of the scale of costs to be applied on taxation following acceptance of a payment of an amount below the court's jurisdictional threshold. The cases were decided in relation to the payment into court procedure under the former Order 22. In *Cho Ho Kuen v Yu Kwok Wah* [2001] 3 HKC 566 (CA) (over-ruling *Ho Kin Chung v Tsang Hiu Sang* [2001] 1 HKC 110) it was held that a plaintiff who, in a District Court action, accepted payment in of an amount within the Small Claims Tribunal's jurisdiction, was entitled to taxed costs on the District Court scale. Similarly, in *Wellegant Dev't Ltd v Fine Telecom Ltd* [2007] 2 HKC 427 it was held that the statutory scheme entitles the plaintiff in an action in the Court of First Instance to costs on the High Court scale on acceptance of an amount within the District Court's jurisdiction. However in *Wong Lan v Hong Chang Construction Transportation Eng'g Co Ltd* [2007] 3 HKC 499 (para 41) the court expressly disagreed with *Wellegant*. Instead the procedure set out in *Lai Ki v B+B Construction Co Ltd* [2003] 3 HKC 322 (para 22) was approved. There it had been held that there is a discretion in such cases and the plaintiff should apply to a master for determination of the scale of costs. In *Park Avenue Toys Ltd v Candy Novelty Works Ltd* HCA 11135/1997 (Master de Souza; 29.06.2007) the court preferred *Wong Lan* over *Wellegant*. Likewise in *Hung Yuet Wan v Lau Yan Shing & Anor* HCPI 1011/2005 (Master Levy; 25.01.2008) *Wong Lan* was preferred.

If *Lai Ki* is followed, the court will decide which scale of costs to apply on the basis of whether, when the action was commenced, there was a reasonable prospect of obtaining an amount in excess of the District Court's jurisdiction. See the discussion of the related topic of the costs of High Court proceedings which result in judgment for an amount within the District Court's jurisdiction, in the commentary under Order 62 rule 28.

**21.    Costs consequences of acceptance of plaintiff's sanctioned offer**
        (O. 22 r. 21)
        **(1)    Where a plaintiff's sanctioned offer to settle the whole claim is accepted without requiring the leave of the Court, the plaintiff is entitled to his costs of the proceedings up to the date upon which the defendant serves notice of acceptance, unless the Court otherwise orders.**
        **(2)    The plaintiff's costs include any costs attributable to the defendant's counterclaim or set-off if the sanctioned offer states that it takes into account the counterclaim or set-off.**
        **(L.N. 152 of 2008)**

---

**NOTES**

**[22.21.1]    Costs on acceptance of plaintiff's sanctioned offer**
Order 22 rule 21 provides that a plaintiff whose sanctioned offer is accepted will normally be entitled to costs up to that point. Like rule 20 it derives from CPR 36.10. The commentary under rule 20 above is largely relevant.

**22.** **Other consequences of acceptance of sanctioned offer or sanctioned payment** (O. 22 r. 22)

(1)    If a sanctioned offer or sanctioned payment relates to the whole claim and is accepted, the claim is stayed.

(2)    In the case of acceptance of a sanctioned offer which relates to the whole claim —

    (a)    the stay is upon the terms of the offer; and

    (b)    either party may apply to enforce those terms without the need to commence new proceedings.

(3)    If a sanctioned offer or a sanctioned payment which relates only to a part of the claim or an issue arising from the claim is accepted —

    (a)    the claim is stayed as to that part or issue, and in the case of the sanctioned offer, the stay is upon the terms of the offer;

    (b)    either party may apply to enforce those terms without the need to commence new proceedings; and

    (c)    unless the parties have agreed on costs, the liability for costs shall be decided by the Court.

(4)    If the approval of the Court is required before a settlement can be binding, any stay which would otherwise arise on the acceptance of a sanctioned offer or a sanctioned payment takes effect only when that approval has been given.

(5)    Any stay arising under this rule does not affect the power of the Court —

    (a)    to enforce the terms of a sanctioned offer;

    (b)    to deal with any question of costs (including interest on costs) relating to the proceedings; or

    (c)    to order payment out of court of any sum paid into court.

(6)    Where —

    (a)    a sanctioned offer has been accepted; and

    (b)    a party alleges that —

        (i)    the other party has not honoured the terms of the offer; and

        (ii)    he is therefore entitled to a remedy for breach of contract,

the party may claim the remedy by applying to the Court without the need to commence new proceedings unless the Court otherwise orders.

    **(L.N. 152 of 2008)**

---

**NOTES**

**[22.22.1]    Origin and scope of Order 22 rule 22**
Order 22 rule 22 derives from CPR 36.11. It provides for a stay of proceedings on acceptance of a sanctioned offer or sanctioned payment, and for enforcement of such sanctioned offers.

**[22.22.2]    Stay of proceedings on acceptance**
Order 22 rule 22(1) provides that proceedings are stayed upon acceptance of a sanctioned

payment or offer, on the terms thereof. Where the settlement relates to part of a claim, only that part is stayed. The Civil Court Practice, our sister publication in the UK, has the following to say (at 36.11[2], so far as relevant) about the stay provided for in the equivalent English rule:

> **Consequences of acceptance** Upon acceptance of the offer, the proceedings are stayed (CPR 36.11 [in Hong Kong Order 22 rule 22(1), which applies to both sanctioned offers and sanctioned payments]; "stayed" in this context does not mean that the proceedings temporarily go to sleep: it means that the case is effectively over, bar the assessment [taxation] of costs and any subsequent enforcement proceedings...

## [22.22.3]    Effect of acceptance of sanctioned payment which is part of the terms of a sanctioned offer

According to Form No 23 in Appendix A, the form for acceptance of a sanctioned payment, acceptance of a sanctioned payment which is part of a sanctioned offer, constitutes acceptance of the sanctioned offer as well.

## [22.22.4]    Resiling from acceptance of sanctioned offer or sanctioned payment

Under the former Order 22 there was a stay of proceedings on acceptance of a payment into court just as there is under the current Order 22 on acceptance of a sanctioned payment or sanctioned offer. It was considered that a plaintiff who wished to resile from acceptance of a payment into court should apply for the stay to be lifted rather than commence fresh proceedings. Any such proceedings were liable to be struck out as an abuse of process: *Buckland v Palmer* [1984] 1 WLR 1109. It was further considered that the court had a discretion to lift the stay of proceedings in rare circumstances: *Cooper v Williams* [1963] 2 QB 567, 580 (CA).

It seems possible that a similar discretion will be found to exist in relation to the sanctioned payment and sanctioned offer procedures under the current Order 22. Certainly The Civil Court Practice, our sister publication in the UK, suggests (at 36.11[2]) that there may be circumstances in which the court will be prepared to lift the stay under the equivalent English provision, and that in doing so it would have regard to what in Hong Kong are the underlying objectives (Order 1A rule 1) and the principles applied in deciding whether to set aside a consent order (as to which see the commentary under Order 42 rule 5A). However there does not appear to be any express power in the rules in England or in Hong Kong to lift the stay. Any such power must derive from inherent jurisdiction.

In *Tsui Wai Kam v Wang Fung Machinery & Eng'g Ltd* DCEC 530/2009 (Deputy Judge Clement Lee; 27.10.2010) it was held that there was no jurisdiction to permit a plaintiff to 'cancel' or 'withdraw' acceptance of a sanctioned payment. The court took the view (para 7) that on acceptance an agreement binding in contract was made (as to which see the commentary on contract of settlement under Order 22 rule 1). No authorities are cited in the judgment, and it would appear that the court did not have the benefit of full legal argument as the applicant was acting in person.

Under the former Order 22 the discretion to lift the stay was exercised 'with very great care', only in 'rare' cases, because litigation ought not lightly be allowed to be reopened: *Lambert v Mainland Market Deliveries Ltd* [1977] 1 WLR 825. In principle, circumstances should be shown which undermine the contract of settlement which underlies the acceptance of the payment. Examples would be where the payment was accepted under mistake or fraud. In *Derrick v Williams* [1939] 2 All ER 559 (CA) the court would not allow the plaintiff to resile from acceptance of a payment into court where it sought to rely on a subsequent decision of the House of Lords which might have allowed it to recover more.

**[22.22.5]    Cases where court approval required for settlement**
In cases where the court's approval is required for a settlement (for example, where the plaintiff is under disability – see Order 80 rules 10 and 11 and the commentary thereunder), rule 22(4) provides that the stay only comes into effect upon that approval being given. In England it is provided by practice direction (CPR PD 36 para 3.2) that an application for the court's approval of a settlement of this type must be heard by a judge other than the trial judge or likely trial judge, unless the parties agree otherwise. This is because of the restrictions on disclosure, as to which see Order 22 rule 25. In Hong Kong these applications are often heard by masters.

**[22.22.6]    Enforcement**
Order 22 rule 22 provides that a sanctioned offer which has been accepted, but not honoured, may be enforced by application to the court within the same action. See in particular rule 22(6). The use of the permissive 'may' might be read as suggesting that the non-defaulting party may choose between enforcement within the same action, or proceeding to trial. Our sister publication in the UK, The Civil Court Practice, suggests that this is not the case. It says (at CPR 36.11[2]) of the English equivalent, CPR 36.11(8), which also uses 'may':

> If the offer is accepted then the offeree must enforce that compromise. He may not resume the proceedings …

See also the passage from the Civil Court Practice on contract of settlement reproduced in the commentary under Order 22 rule 1.

At the consultation stage the Law Society queried the need for an application to the court for enforcement, suggesting that the non-defaulting party might instead be permitted simply to enter judgment on the terms of the offer. In response it was noted that the position is the same in England under CPR 36.11(8), and said that an application to the court 'ought to be required as opposed simply to enforcing the accepted offer without more'. See the Judiciary Administration's paper CJRS 3/2008 para 35.

Enforcement of a sanctioned offer by application to the court within the same action is similar to the procedure under a 'Tomlin' order. See the commentary under Order 42 rule 5A.

With regard to sanctioned payments which have been accepted, in Hong Kong problems as to enforcement cannot arise as the money is required to have been paid into court. On acceptance the plaintiff need only apply for payment out under Order 22 rule 17.

**23.    Costs consequences where plaintiff fails to do better than sanctioned offer or sanctioned payment** (O. 22 r. 23)
    **(1)    This rule applies where a plaintiff —**
        **(a)    fails to obtain a judgment better than the sanctioned payment; or**

    (b)    **fails to obtain a judgment that is more advantageous than a defendant's sanctioned offer.**

  (2)    The Court may by order disallow all or part of any interest otherwise payable under section 48 of the Ordinance on the whole or part of any sum of money awarded to the plaintiff for some or all of the period after the latest date on which the payment or offer could have been accepted without requiring the leave of the Court.

  (3)    The Court may order the plaintiff to pay any costs incurred by the defendant after the latest date on which the payment or offer could have been accepted without requiring the leave of the Court.

  (4)    The Court may also order that the defendant is entitled to —

    (a)    his costs on the indemnity basis after the latest date on which the plaintiff could have accepted the payment or offer without requiring the leave of the Court; and

    (b)    interest on the costs referred to in paragraph (3) or sub-paragraph (a) at a rate not exceeding 10% above judgment rate.

  (5)    Where this rule applies, the Court shall make the orders referred to in paragraphs (2), (3) and (4) unless it considers it unjust to do so.

  (6)    In considering whether it would be unjust to make the orders referred to in paragraphs (2), (3) and (4), the Court shall take into account all the circumstances of the case including —

    (a)    the terms of any sanctioned payment or sanctioned offer;

    (b)    the stage in the proceedings at which any sanctioned payment or sanctioned offer was made;

    (c)    the information available to the parties at the time when the sanctioned payment or sanctioned offer was made; and

    (d)    the conduct of the parties with regard to the giving or refusing to give information for the purposes of enabling the payment or offer to be made or evaluated.

  (7)    The power of the Court under this rule is in addition to any other power it may have to award or disallow interest.

                                     **(L.N. 152 of 2008)**

## NOTES

### [22.23.1]   Power to impose costs and interest sanctions on plaintiff for failure to accept sanctioned offer or payment

Order 22 rule 23 provides for costs and interest sanctions to encourage plaintiffs not to refuse reasonable sanctioned offers and payments. Those sanctions may be applied if a plaintiff refuses such an offer or payment, and instead continues with the action, but does no better than the settlement proposal which could have been accepted. This is similar to the approach the court has long taken with regard to plaintiffs who fail to better a payment into court or a *Calderbank* offer (see the commentary under Order 62 rule 5), but goes further. So far as sanctioned offers are concerned, the rule goes further, first by providing what the Chief Justice's working party intended to be a *'prima facie* entitlement' to costs, whereas under the *Calderbank* procedure the court was merely required to take the offer into account in deciding on the incidence of costs (see para 297 of the final report). Secondly, the rule provides for new sanctions in the event of failure to accept a payment or offer which at the end of the day, is not bettered.

The sanctions provided for by rule 23 are:

(a)    the court may disallow all or part of the interest which would otherwise be payable under section 48 of the High Court Ordinance – rule 23(2);

(b)    the plaintiff may be ordered to pay the defendant's costs after the time by which the settlement proposal could have been accepted – rule 23(3);

(c)    those costs may be ordered on the indemnity basis – rule 23(4)(a); and

(d)    costs may be subject to enhanced interest, up to 10% above the judgment rate – rule 23(4)(b).

For discussion of these sanctions, see the commentary under Order 22 rule 24, which deals with the situation where similar sanctions may be imposed on a defendant.

Rule 23 derives from CPR 36.14. The Civil Court Practice 2008, our sister publication in the UK, says (at CPR 36.14[1]-[2]) of the English rule:

> **Usual practice: if claimant fails to achieve better result** This Rule follows the long-standing practice that if a claimant [plaintiff] fails, at trial, to achieve a judgment which is more advantageous than the compromise offered by the defendant, the claimant will have to pay the costs of the defendant incurred after the period for which the offer was open for acceptance. The court retains its discretion in accordance with CPR 44.3 [in Hong Kong see Order 62 rules 3 and 5] and there may be other factors which it will take into account under that Rule in deciding what costs order to make. The claimant must, however, overcome the hurdle of the usual order being "unjust" in order to secure an order to the contrary...
>
> **"claimant fails to obtain a judgment more advantageous than a defendant's Part 36 offer . . ." case law** Where a defendant made a payment into court which, had it been accepted, amounted to more than the claimant [plaintiff] would have received at trial, the court was entitled to assess damages as at the date of payment in and not as at the date of trial: *Johnson v Gore Wood & Co (No 2)* [2004] EWCA Civ 14, [2004] All ER (D) 248 (Jan)...
>
> Where the claimant beats an initial offer into court but not a second offer, the costs consequences should ignore the first offer. The normal rule should be for the claimant to be awarded his costs up to the date for acceptance of the second offer but that he should be liable for the defendant's costs after that date: *Johnsey Estates (1990) Ltd v Secretary of State* [2001] EWCA Civ 535, [2001] All ER (D) 135 (Apr), [2001] 2 EGLR 128...

### [22.23.2]    Enhanced interest and costs sanctions to be ordered 'unless unjust to do so'

The court is directed by rule 23(5) to apply the enhanced interest and costs sanctions against a plaintiff who has failed to accept a sanctioned offer or sanctioned payment, but ultimately fails to do better, unless it is unjust to do so. See also rule 24(4) and the commentary thereunder, concerning the similar situation of a plaintiff who betters his own offer which was not accepted.

As to when it would be unjust to do so, our sister publication in the UK, The

Civil Court Practice 2008 says (at CPR 36.14[3]):

> **Unjust to do so** In deciding whether it would be unjust to make an order for costs against a claimant [plaintiff] who has failed to do better than a payment into court, the court may take account of the defendant's non-disclosure of material matters: *Ford v GKR Construction Ltd* [2000] 1 All ER 802 (CA). Conversely, the court should not allow the claimant [plaintiff] costs for the period after Part 36 payment (under the new regime, Part 36 offer) [in Hong Kong it may be a sanctioned payment or sanctioned offer under Order 22] where the claimant [plaintiff] decides to take the risk of recovering less at trial when further medical evidence is made available: *Jones v Jones* [1999] The Times 11 Nov (CA).
>
> The disclosure by the defendant in a personal injuries action of an expert medical report which suggested that the claimant was malingering did not justify a departure from the general rule that a claimant [plaintiff] who failed to beat an offer should not be entitled to his costs thereafter notwithstanding that the claimant [plaintiff] had felt obliged to pursue the claim to trial in order to rebut the allegation of dishonesty: *Burgess v British Steel* [2000] 05 LS Gaz R 33 (CA).
>
> Two examples of situations where it would be unjust to award indemnity costs and interest are: (1) where the rejection of the offer appeared reasonable in the light of the law as it then stood or (2) where inadequate disclosure meant that the offeree could not assess the validity of the offer: *Mamidoil-Jetfoil Greek Petroleum Co SA v Okta Crude Oil Refinery AD* [2002] EWHC 2462 (Comm), [2003] 1 Lloyd's Rep 42, [2002] The Times, 27 Dec.

In *Sulaman v AXA Insurance plc & Anor* [2009] EWCA Civ 1331 (11.12.2009) the court denied full costs to a defendant who had lied in her evidence, despite the fact she had made a sanctioned payment which was not bettered at trial. In Hong Kong such an exercise of discretion could be justified by Order 62 rule 5(1)(e), by which the court is directed to take into account the conduct of parties. See the commentary under that provision. However, in *P4 Ltd v United Integrated Solutions plc* [2006] EWHC 2924 (TCC) (17.11.2006) it was held that a defendant's refusal to mediate, conduct which may be relevant under Order 62 rule 5(1)(e), did not render it unjust to impose costs sanctions on the plaintiff for having failed to better the defendant's sanctioned proposal.

In *Factortame Ltd & Ors v Secretary of State* [2002] EWCA Civ 22 (28.01.2002) (paras 24-27); [2002] 1 WLR 2438 it was accepted that in a suitable case the court might not apply the usual consequences for the full period after a sanctioned proposal is not accepted, if only upon a later amendment did it become clear that the proposal ought to have been accepted.

It is clear that the Chief Justice's working party intended these rules to adopt the English position with regard to circumstances where it would be unjust to impose the sanctions. See paras 305-309 of the final report, referring, *inter alia*, to *Ford v GKR Construction Ltd* (above).

### [22.23.3]    Meaning of 'better' or 'more advantageous' judgment in rules 23 and 24

Order 22 rules 23 and 24 both provide for costs consequences when a sanctioned payment or sanctioned offer has not been accepted and the case proceeds in the usual way. The costs consequences depend on whether the judgment is 'better' than the sanctioned payment or 'more advantageous' than the sanctioned offer. So far as the former payment into court procedure was concerned, this topic was previously dealt with in Order 62 rule 5. That rule is still relevant to *Calderbank* offers 'without prejudice save as to costs'.

It is relatively easy to determine whether a plaintiff who has failed to accept a sanctioned payment, or whose sanctioned offer is not accepted by the defendant, does better at trial in a money claim – 'better' is obviously a higher amount. If the judgment amount is higher than the sanctioned offer, the defendant will normally be ordered to pay the plaintiff's costs, with the penalties set out in rule 24(3). If, however, the judgment amount is lower than the sanctioned payment not accepted by a plaintiff, it is the plaintiff who will suffer those consequences under rule 23(4). In each case those consequences follow only from the last date on which the sanctioned payment could have been accepted. This was the position under the former payment into court procedure (with the difference that the enhanced costs provision did not then exist). See *Hulquist v Universal Pattern & Precision Eng'g Co Ltd* [1960] 2 QB 467; *Yuen Yiu Kwong v Chan Kwok Chuen & Ors* [2003] 2 HKC 617. In *Dmetrichuk v Tung Wah Group of Hospitals* [2006] 4 HKC 616 the court rejected an argument that such a plaintiff be entitled to costs in relation to the issue of liability incurred after a payment into court which was not bettered at trial.

In the unusual case of *Wagman v Vare Motors Ltd* [1959] 1 WLR 853 (CA) judgment was given in exactly the same sum as had previously been paid into court. It was held that the plaintiff, having proceeded with the litigation after the payment in, hoping for a judgment in a higher sum, was unsuccessful in that regard and was therefore liable in costs.

In England the court does not confine itself to the amount of money in deciding whether a sanctioned payment has been bettered. It takes into account factors such as the conduct of the parties and asks itself 'who was the real winner in this litigation?' See, for example, *Painting v University of Oxford* [2005] EWCA Civ 161 (03.02.2005) (para 21). The same should apply in Hong Kong where Order 62 rule 5 requires the court, in the exercise of its discretion as to costs, to take into account factors such as the conduct of the parties. In *Painting*, the court took into account the plaintiff's refusal to negotiate and deprived her of a portion of her costs. Where a refusal to negotiate is raised, the court should avoid a detailed investigation of how the negotiations would have gone: *Straker v Tudor Rose (a firm)* [2007] EWCA Civ 368 (25.04.2007). In *Jones v Associated Newspapers Ltd* [2007] EWHC 1489 (QB); [2008] 1 All ER 240 the plaintiff contended that he was entitled to indemnity costs because he was awarded £5,000 in a defamation action, whereas he had earlier on made a sanctioned offer to accept £4,999 and an apology. It was held that the plaintiff had not in fact bettered his sanctioned offer because the ultimate vindication came only after an additional 11 months distress and because the worth of the apology which had been part of the sanctioned offer had to be taken into account.

It has been held that a term in a sanctioned offer relating to costs should not be taken into account in deciding whether it was more advantageous than a subsequent judgment. See *Sunbeam Investments Ltd v IO Villa Veneto* [2011] 1 HKC 86 (para 25), referring to *Mitchell v James* [2002] EWCA Civ 997; [2003] 2 All ER 1064 (CA). In *Mitchell* Peter Gibson LJ said (para 35):

> I therefore conclude that a term as to costs is not within the scope of a Part 36 offer. That does not of course mean that a claimant cannot make an offer which includes a term as to costs; the court will have regard to that in exercising its usual discretion in

relation to inter partes costs at the end of the case. As r 36.1(2) states, nothing in Part 36 prevents a party making an offer to settle in whatever way he chooses. However, nothing in r 36(1)(2) permits a party to include a term as to costs as part of a Part 36 offer for the purpose of obtaining an order for costs on an indemnity basis.

The references to Part 36 in the above passage are, of course, to the equivalent of Hong Kong's Order 22 in the English CPR.

### [22.23.4]  Cases of obtaining judgment only marginally 'better' or 'more advantageous'

The English courts have on several occasions considered whether a result only marginally better than the party could have got under a sanctioned proposal is in fact more advantageous. In *Carver v BAA plc* [2008] 3 All ER 91; [2008] EWCA Civ 412 (CA) Ward LJ said (para 31) that no 'reasonable litigant would have embarked upon this campaign for £51' and that factors such as emotional stress and having incurred unrecoverable costs could be taken into account. However in *Morgan v UPS* [2008] EWCA Civ 1476 (11.11.2008), where the plaintiff had beaten a sanctioned payment 'only by a whisker', *Carver* (above) and *Painting v University of Oxford* [2005] EWCA Civ 161 (03.02.2005) were not followed and the sanctioned payment was considered to have been bettered. It was emphasised that the judge had a broad discretion which the appellate court would be slow to interfere with.

*Carver* was cited in *Lau Chi Keung v Wong Wai Kei & Anor* [2010] 5 HKC 582 where a deputy judge of the District Court ordered that each party bear its own costs after the date of a sanctioned payment which was beaten by the plaintiff only marginally.

Subsequently in *Gibbon v Manchester City Council* [2010] EWCA Civ 726 (25.06.2010) the English court sought to downplay *Carver* as an exercise of discretion on the particular facts of an individual case. Moore-Bick LJ noted (at para 40) that *Carver* had been criticised by many and expressed the view that 'In most cases obtaining a judgment for an amount greater than the offer is likely to outweigh all other factors'. Carnwath LJ (at para 51) agreed, and said that *Carver* 'should not be interpreted as opening the way to a wide ranging investigation of emotional and other factors in every case'.

The similar situation of a defendant offering a token amount of damages, where liability is contested and ultimately not established, has been considered in British Columbia. In *Skinner v Fu* [2010] BCSC 30 and *Oh v Usher* [2010] BCSC 122 (CanLII website) the court declined to impose enhanced sanctions against plaintiffs who had failed to accept offers of $1 damages, and ultimately achieved nothing. In *Skinner* it was said (para 17) that otherwise 'all defendants in similar positions would follow suit' and enhance their entitlement to costs without promoting the underlying objective of the relevant rule. In British Columbia the court may order double costs against a party who does not accept an offer, but ultimately does no better.

### [22.23.5]  Application of enhanced costs and interest consequences to judgment obtained short of trial

The enhanced costs and interest consequences of a sanctioned offer or sanctioned payment (under rules 23 and 24) which is not accepted are not limited to cases which proceed all the way to trial. The consequences flow from a 'judgment' which is no more favourable than could have been obtained under the sanctioned proposal. This point was noted in response to comments on a draft of the new Order 22 (Judiciary Administration paper CJRS 3/2008, para 30.) where it was said:

> It may be possible for there to be costs consequences where a Plaintiff fails to better a sanctioned offer or sanctioned payment after obtaining judgment other than after trial.

**[22.23.6]  Appeals, indemnity costs, interest on costs, and amendment**
The commentary following Order 22 rule 24 concerning appeals, indemnity costs, interest on costs, clarification and amendment should be equally applicable under rule 23.

24.  **Costs and other consequences where plaintiff does better than he proposed in his sanctioned offer** (O. 22 r. 24)
 (1)  This rule applies where —
  (a)  a defendant is held liable for more than the proposals contained in a plaintiff's sanctioned offer; or
  (b)  the judgment against a defendant is more advantageous to the plaintiff than the proposals contained in a plaintiff's sanctioned offer.
 (2)  The Court may order interest on the whole or part of any sum of money (excluding interest) awarded to the plaintiff at a rate not exceeding 10% above judgment rate for some or all of the period after the latest date on which the defendant could have accepted the offer without requiring the leave of the Court.
 (3)  The Court may also order that the plaintiff is entitled to—
  (a)  his costs on the indemnity basis after the latest date on which the defendant could have accepted the offer without requiring the leave of the Court; and
  (b)  interest on those costs at a rate not exceeding 10% above judgment rate.
 (4)  Where this rule applies, the Court shall make the orders referred to in paragraphs (2) and (3) unless it considers it unjust to do so.
 (5)  In considering whether it would be unjust to make the orders referred to in paragraphs (2) and (3), the Court shall take into account all the circumstances of the case including —
  (a)  the terms of any sanctioned offer;
  (b)  the stage in the proceedings at which any sanctioned offer was made;
  (c)  the information available to the parties at the time when the sanctioned offer was made; and
  (d)  the conduct of the parties with regard to the giving or refusing to give information for the purposes of enabling the offer to be made or evaluated.
 (6)  The power of the Court under this rule is in addition to any other power it may have to award interest.
 (L.N. 152 of 2008)

## NOTES

**[22.24.1]**    **Power to order defendant to pay enhanced costs and interest for failure to accept plaintiff's sanctioned offer**

Order 22 rule 24 is similar to rule 23, save that it applies to the different situation where it is a defendant who failed to accept a sanctioned offer. If the ultimate result is more advantageous to the plaintiff than the sanctioned offer, the court will impose costs and interest sanctions on the defendant unless it would be unjust to do so: rule 24(2), (3) and (4).

**[22.24.2]**    **Application of sanctions to late offers**

A plaintiff's sanctioned offer made less than 28 days before trial may only be accepted if the parties agree on liability for costs, or with leave of the court: Order 22 rule 16. However, if such an offer is not accepted, and the plaintiff achieves a better result after trial, the enhanced costs and interest sanctions under rule 24(2) and (3) are available just as with an offer made more than 28 days before trial. This is so despite the fact that rule 24(2) and (3) apply those sanctions only from the last day on which the offer could have been accepted without leave. See *Tsoi Hak Kong Herbert (administrator) v Kok Wai Chun & Ors* [2009] 3 HKC 344.

The same is true with a late sanctioned payment made by a defendant: *Cheng Kai Kit v Kwong Kam Tim Marble Co Ltd & Anor* DCPI 2627/2008 (Judge Leung; 01.02.2010) (para 15)

**[22.24.3]**    **Rule 24(2) – enhanced interest on judgment sum**

Order 22 rule 24(2) provides that where a plaintiff's sanctioned offer is not accepted, and the matter proceeds with the plaintiff achieving a better result ultimately, the court may order the defendant to pay enhanced interest on any sum of money awarded to the plaintiff. The enhancement may be up to 10% above the judgment rate. The intention appears to be to empower the court to order interest at up to 10 percentage points above the judgment rate, meaning that when the judgment rate is 8%, the court could order interest at up to 18%. However, the rule does not refer to percentage *points*; thus it might be argued that the power is limited to enhancing a judgment rate of 8% by an additional 0.8%, resulting in interest at 8.8%.

The Civil Court Practice 2008, our sister publication in the UK, says (at CPR 36.14[4]) of the equivalent English rule, so far as relevant to rule 24:

> **Where claimant [plaintiff] does better than proposed in his offer** In order for the defendant to be liable for indemnity costs and enhanced interest, the Part 36 offer [sanctioned offer under Order 22] has to be a genuine offer to settle for less than the full amount claimed, not merely a tactical ploy: *East West Corpn v DKBS 1912 (No 2)* [2002] EWHC 253 (Comm), [2002] 2 Lloyd's Rep 222, [2002] All ER (D) 361 (Feb). A claimant's offer to accept liability on 95/5 split was held to be a genuine offer in *Huck v Robson* [2002] EWCA Civ 398, [2002] 3 All ER 263, [2002] All ER (D) 316 (May) although a reduction of a mere 1% would have been regarded as purely tactical.

> The rule does not apply where there has been no judgment but only an acceptance of an offer; the court has no discretion to award indemnity costs to a claimant who had

accepted settlement of its claim where the sum offered was better than an offer which the claimant had made under Part 36 and which the defendant had rejected; in the absence of a hearing to assess the quantum of damages, the court could not properly rule on the reasonableness of the defendant's rejection of the claimant's Part 36 offer: *Dyson Appliances Ltd v Hoover Ltd (No 3) (Costs)* EWHC 2229 (Ch), [2002] The Times 6 Nov…

## [22.24.4] No enhanced interest for damages which do not normally attract interest

Enhanced interest should not be awarded to a plaintiff who beats a sanctioned offer in respect of a type of damages which does not normally attract interest. These include damages for defamation: *McPhilemy v Times Newspapers* [2001] EWCA Civ 933; *Power Color Scanning & Lithographics Co Ltd v Kam Kong Food Factory* DCCJ 3902/2007 (Judge Mimmie Chan; 09.11.2010) (para 16) and damages for future loss in personal injury actions (*Pankhurst v White* [2010] EWCA Civ 1445).

## [22.24.5] Appeals

The sanctions provided for by Order 22 rules 23 and 24 may become relevant when an appeal is successful. The Civil Court Practice 2008, our sister publication in the UK says (at para CPR 36.14[4]):

> Where . . . enhanced interest is awarded following a decision of the Court of Appeal, the period for which the enhanced interest is awarded should not extend beyond the date of the original judgment, unless a further Part 36 offer has been made in the appeal proceedings: *KR v Bryn Alyn Community (Holdings) Ltd* [2003] EWCA Civ 85, [2003] 1 FCR 385.

Note that in England CPR 36.3(2)(b) expressly provides for a Part 36 offer to be made in appeal proceedings. There appears to be no express equivalent in Hong Kong.

## [22.24.6] Costs on indemnity basis

The Civil Court Practice 2008, our sister publication in the UK, contains the following commentary (at CPR 36.14[5]) concerning the circumstances in which the court will use the indemnity costs sanction. It is relevant to both rules 23 and 24 of Hong Kong's Order 22 in relation to sanctioned offers and sanctioned payments which are not bettered.

> **Costs on indemnity basis** An award of costs on the indemnity basis is not to be regarded as penal; such an award should not be refused on the ground that it would be interpreted as an indication of the court's disapproval of a party's conduct: *McPhilemy v Times Newspapers* [2001] EWCA Civ 933, [2001] All ER (D) 200. If the claimant's [plaintiff's] offer had been on the terms that each side bear their own costs and the claimant subsequently obtains an order for costs, an application for costs on the indemnity basis should be refused on the ground that offers and orders as to costs are not to be taken into account in deciding whether the judgment was "more advantageous": *Mitchell v James* [2002] EWCA Civ 997, [2003] 2 All ER 1064 (applied in *Ali Reza-Delta Transport Co Ltd v United Arab Shipping Co SAG (No 2)* [2003] EWCA Civ 811, [2003] 3 All ER 1297, in which it was held that concessions as to interest uplift over the ordinary rate were not intended to be any part of an offer to settle made under CPR Part 36 nor were such concessions to be taken into account in determining the entitlement to indemnity costs).

The above commentary goes on to suggest that where a plaintiff fails on some issues but nevertheless succeeds in beating a sanctioned payment or offer, the court 'may confine the award of indemnity costs to the costs in relation to those issues on which the claimant succeeded'. *Kastor Navigation Co Ltd v AGF MAT (No 2)* [2003] EWHC 472 (Comm), [2003] 1 All ER (Comm) 277 is cited as authority. Although that case was decided under a provision of Part 36 which is no longer in force, the learned authors of The Civil Court Practice 2008 express the opinion that 'it is likely that the court will retain this approach'.

### [22.24.7]   Enhanced interest on costs

Order 22 rule 23(4)(b) and 24(3)(b) both empower the court to order enhanced interest on costs where a sanctioned offer or payment has not been bettered. Each rule mandates the court to impose this sanction unless it would be unjust to do so (see the discussion on that topic above).

The enhancement of interest is up to a maximum of 10% above the judgment rate. At the consultation stage the Bar Association questioned the use of the judgment rate instead of the prime rate as the base (the judgment rate is usually higher), noting that an award of the enhanced interest is intended to be compensatory rather than punitive. The Law Society observed that the court's discretion as to the rate of enhancement would mean that use of the judgment rate as the base would not necessarily result in higher enhanced interest than use of the prime rate, and this view found favour. See the Judiciary Administration's paper CJRS 3/2008, paras 31 and 26. The Law Society's view is in line with the prevailing view that orders for costs carry interest at the judgment rate: see the commentary under Order 62 rule 3.

In England it is the Bank of England's 'base rate' on top of which an additional 10% interest may be awarded.

It is important to bear in mind that 10% is not the norm, or even a guide, but the maximum permitted enhancement. In *KR v Bryn Alyn Community (Holdings) Ltd* [2003] EWCA Civ 85, [2003] 1 FCR 385, interest on indemnity costs was awarded at 4% above the base rate. The same 4% rate was ordered in Hong Kong in *Cheng Kai Kit v Kwong Kam Tim Marble Co Ltd & Anor* DCPI 2627/2008 (Judge Leung; 01.02.2010).

In principle, enhanced interest on costs should run from the date each item of costs was incurred, or the party put up the funds to cover them. However, that could cause difficulty in calculating the amount, with each item of work carrying interest from a different date. Thus in *Golden Eagle Int'l (Group) Ltd v GR Investment Holdings Ltd* [2010] 5 HKC 317 the court simply ordered half rate of interest on all the relevant costs incurred within a defined period, regardless of the stage within that period they were incurred.

### [22.24.8]   Enhanced interest and costs sanctions to be ordered 'unless unjust to do so'

Order 22 rule 24(4) provides that the enhanced interest and costs sanctions 'shall' be ordered unless the court considers it unjust to do so. The wording of the provision is the same as Order 22 rule 23(5), which deals with the different situation of a plaintiff who fails to do better than a sanctioned proposal made to it. Hence the commentary on the 'unjust to do so' point under rule 23 will be relevant here.

Can the public interest in resolving an issue render it unjust to order enhanced interest and costs sanctions? This issue was considered in the Australian case of *Air Link Pty Ltd v Paterson (No 2)* [2009] NSWCA 342 (20.10.2009). There a passenger was injured when disembarking from an aeroplane. The airline, which was found liable at trial, appealed. Not long before the appeal was heard, the passenger offered to accept $50,000 less than had been awarded him at first instance. The offer was not accepted, and at the end of the day the appeal was dismissed. Under the Uniform Civil Procedure Rules the passenger was entitled to indemnity costs unless the court ordered otherwise. The airline argued that indemnity costs should not be ordered because the hearing was of public importance to the airline industry and the general public. The NSW Court of Appeal ordered indemnity costs nonetheless saying:

> It is true that the matter raised considerations of some importance for the industry. However these were not matters which concerned Mr Paterson [the passenger]. He had been injured and was entitled to a judgment. His interest was in the prompt and certain resolution of the case. He was prepared to make a not insignificant deduction for the safety of a settlement of a case which was otherwise well-founded.

Somewhat similarly, it has been held in England that it is not unjust to order enhanced costs and interest against a public authority bringing legal proceedings in the public interest: *Commissioners for HM Revenue and Customs v Blue Sphere Global Ltd* [2010] EWCA Civ 1448 (para 11).

Hong Kong cases in which the court has considered whether it would be unjust to award enhanced costs and interests to a plaintiff who has bettered an unaccepted sanctioned offer include the following:

- *The Garden Co Ltd v Smart Year Ltd* [2009] 5 HKLRD 542 (para 43) – The fact that the defence was not totally devoid of merit was not a 'good reason' to consider it unjust to impose the sanctions.
- *Fung Wing Yee v Chen Jung Chien* HCPI 657/2007 (Suffiad J; 30.04.2010) (para 39) – An argument that it was not in the public interest to impose enhanced sanctions on the Motor Insurers Bureau (MIB) was rejected.
- *Ho Ming Kong & Ors v Chow Wong Hing & Ors* HCA 2829/2004 (Rogers VP; 03.08.2010 (paras 28-30) – A defendant's counter-offer did not justify 'holding out' on acceptance of the plaintiff's sanctioned offer.
- *Power Color Scanning & Lithographics Co Ltd v Kam Kong Food Fty* DCCJ 3902/2007 (Judge Mimmie Chan; 09.11.2010) (para 8) – A defendant which chose to put the plaintiff to proof of its damages at trial took a risk as to costs and was not spared from enhanced sanctions.

## [22.24.9] Effect of amendment of pleadings

The Chief Justice's working party envisioned the sanctions provided for in rules 23 and 24 being applied only in a limited fashion where it is only after a sanctioned offer or payment has been rejected that the offeror's pleadings are clarified by amendment. At para 309 of the final report it is said:

> If a case is initially insufficiently pleaded and if it is only by a later amendment that a party's true case is revealed, it is likely that any costs or interest consequences to flow from the other side's rejection of a sanctioned offer would be confined to the post-amendment period, depriving the offer of any prior effect.

The final report continues by quoting from *Factortame Ltd v Secty of State for the*

*Environment* [2002] 1 WLR 2438 where Waller LJ explained the court's discretionary approach as follows: –

> It seems to me that so far as possible the judge should be trying to assess who in reality is the successful party and who has been responsible for the fact that costs have been incurred which should not have been. It is plainly right that a full scale trial examining privileged material, and listening to *ex post facto* justification should be avoided…

> The starting point is that a claimant who fails to beat a payment in will *prima facie* be liable for the costs. An amendment may be of such a character that a judge will feel that the onus should be firmly placed on the defendant to persuade him that the *prima facie* rule should continue to apply; on the other hand the judge may be quite clear by reference to his feel of the case that the amendment is being used as an excuse to take money out of court that should have been accepted when originally made. Some cases will lie between the two extremes, and the judge will have to adjust his assessment to give effect to possibilities which it would be inappropriate to try out and thus by reference to his overall view of the case.

The situation envisaged by the working party is similar to that which prevailed under the previous Order 22 payment into court procedure. Under that procedure a plaintiff who obtained judgment for an amount higher than a sanctioned payment only because of an amendment to pleadings at a late stage, such as at trial, adding new heads of damages, might not be considered to have bettered the payment. See *Li Lai Fun v Chan Yan* [1989] 1 HKLR 211 (CA), considering *Cheeseman v Bowaters Ltd* [1971] 1 WLR 1173 (CA).

### V. Miscellaneous

**25.** **Restriction on disclosure of sanctioned offer or sanctioned payment**
(O. 22 r. 25)
**(1)** **A sanctioned offer is treated as "without prejudice save as to costs".**
**(2)** **The fact that a sanctioned payment has been made must not be communicated to the trial judge or the master hearing or determining the action or counterclaim or any question or issue as to the debt or damages until all questions of liability and the amount of money to be awarded have been decided.**
**(3)** **Paragraph (2) does not apply —**
　**(a)** **where the defence of tender before action has been raised;**
　**(b)** **where the proceedings have been stayed under rule 22 following acceptance of a sanctioned offer or a sanctioned payment; or**
　**(c)** **where —**
　　**(i)** **the issue of liability has been determined before any assessment of the money claimed; and**
　　**(ii)** **the fact that there has or has not been a sanctioned payment may be relevant to the question of the costs of the issue of liability.**
**(L.N. 152 of 2008)**

## NOTES

### [22.25.1]    Origin and scope of Order 22 rule 25
Order 22 rule 25 derives from CPR 36.13. It provides for the confidentiality of sanctioned offers and sanctioned payments which are not accepted in order to prevent them from influencing the court.

### [22.25.2]    Rule 25(1) – sanctioned offer 'without prejudice save as to costs'
Order 22 rule 25(1), in providing that a sanctioned offer is treated as 'without prejudice save as to costs' has the effect of prohibiting disclosure of the offer to the court save with consent of all relevant parties or in other exceptional circumstances. Only after substantive issues have been decided, and the court is considering what costs order to make, may the fact that an offer was made be disclosed. See generally the commentary on without prejudice communications in the commentary under Order 24 rule 2. Rule 25(1) is in roughly the same terms as CPR 36.13(1) and is similar to the former Order 22 rule 14(1) (which previously made provision for *Calderbank* offers).

### [22.25.3]    Rule 25(2) & (3) – duty not to disclose sanctioned payment
Rule 25(2) prohibits the disclosure to the court of the fact that a sanctioned payment has been made until substantive issues have been decided. That may be before quantum is decided if it is relevant to an issue of costs of the liability issue: rule 25(3)(c).

The provision is to the same effect as the former Order 22 rule 7 (which applied in relation to the former payment into court procedure).

The reason for the rule is that knowledge of the payment 'may, or may appear to, influence unjustly the decision of the court on the issue of liability, the amount to be awarded by way of damages, or the incidence of costs': Downey at (1980) 10 HKLJ 84 (note of *Shek Kam Tin v Chan Fuk Sang* [1977]-[1979] HKC 178; [1979] HKLR 532 (CA)). That decision concerned disclosure on appeal, which is the subject of Order 59 rule 12A but should apply at first instance as well. This is clear from *Millensted v Grosvenor House (Park Lane) Ltd* [1937] 1 KB 717, 727 (CA) where it was said:

> The purpose of the Order is obvious, it was made to prevent the premature disclosure of a fact which was not relevant to the issues to be tried, but the disclosure of which might prejudice one or more of the parties to the proceedings.

The closing phrase of the quoted passage from the article by Downey (a former judge of the District Court) should not be read as suggesting the fact of a payment may not be drawn to the court's attention after judgment on liability or quantum when considering what costs order to make.

### [22.25.4]    Consequences of wrongful disclosure of sanctioned payment
In *Garratt v Saxby* [2004] EWCA Civ 341, [2004] 1 WLR 2152 (para 17-18) the English Court of Appeal considered what a judge should do in the event of breach of the stipulation in rule 25 that the fact a sanctioned payment has been made should not be disclosed. It was held that the guidance laid down under the former Order 22 payment into court procedure in the case of *Millensted* (above) should still be followed under the CPR. In that case Farwell J said (at 727):

It is to be noticed, that the Order makes no express provision for the event of an infringement of the rule. It is, of course, the duty of both judge and counsel to observe the rule, but what is to be done if the rule by inadvertence or otherwise is broken? In my judgment, this is in every case a matter for the trial judge to determine, having due regard to the object for which the rule was made. If he thinks it proper or necessary for the due administration of justice, he may refuse to hear the action any further and direct it to be tried before another tribunal. On the other hand, if he is satisfied that no injustice will be done, he may allow the matter to proceed and if he adopts the latter course, that in itself affords no ground for an appeal from the order which is ultimately made.

In *Garratt v Saxby* (above) the court went on to say (at para 20) that judges should not be 'too ready' to conclude that justice demands they stand down, noting that 'the delay and extra cost occasioned by a recusal may be very considerable.'

**[22.25.5]     Exceptions to stipulation that sanctioned payment not to be disclosed**
Order 22 rule 25(3) provides that the prohibition on disclosure of the fact a sanctioned payment has been made does not apply where there is a defence of tender before action (as to which see Order 18 rule 16), where the proceedings are stayed as a consequence of a sanctioned proposal having been accepted or where the costs of the issue of liability fall to be determined before assessment of quantum.

**26.     Interest** (O. 22 r. 26)
    **(1)     Unless —**
        **(a)     a plaintiff's sanctioned offer which offers to accept a sum of money; or**
        **(b)     a sanctioned payment notice,**
**indicates to the contrary, any such offer or payment is to be treated as inclusive of all interest until the last date on which it could be accepted without requiring the leave of the Court.**
    **(2)     Where a plaintiff's sanctioned offer or a sanctioned payment notice is expressed not to be inclusive of interest, the offer or notice must state —**
        **(a)     whether interest is offered; and**
        **(b)     if so, the amount offered, the rate or rates offered and the period or periods for which it is offered.**
    **(L.N. 152 of 2008)**

---

**NOTES**

**[22.26.1]     Quantum of sanctioned proposal should reflect interest**
Order 22 rule 26 provides that unless otherwise indicated, both a sanctioned offer to accept a sum of money, and a sanctioned payment, are to be treated as including interest. If the offer or payment is expressed not to include interest, the offeror must state in the offer or payment notice whether interest is offered and on what terms. When such a sanctioned offer or payment is not accepted, and the dispute proceeds to trial, the court will have to take account of such an offer on interest in deciding whether the proposal is bettered by the judgment.

    This rule is similar to the former Order 22 rule 1(8), under the previous payment into court procedure. That rule specifically applied to interest 'whether under section 48 of the [High Court] Ordinance or otherwise'. Although those words are omitted from the current rule 22, the intention appears to be the same – note in particular the reference in the current rule to 'all' interest.

The former Order 22 rule 1(8) was introduced to reverse the effect of *Jefford v Gee* [1970] 2 QB 130, 149-50 (CA). There it had been held that since a claim for interest under statute is not itself a cause of action and forms no part of the debt or damages claimed, a defendant making a payment into court did not need to include an additional sum to cover interest that might be awarded. As noted in *Vianini Lavori SPA v AG* HCMP 3333/1991 (Kaplan J; 10.01.1991) the rule was introduced on the recommendation of the English Law Commission in its report on Interest. It was adopted in Hong Kong in 1988.

Under the former Order 22 rule 1(8) it was unclear whether the offeror could expressly exclude interest from the proposal, though in *Vianini Lavori* (above) it was suggested this could be done. The current Order 22 rule 26 expressly provides that the offeror may make a proposal exclusive of interest, provided that the particulars required by rule 26(2) are given. See also Order 22 rule 8(2)(e) which provides that this information must be included in a sanctioned payment notice.

**27.     Money paid into court under order** (O. 22 r. 27)

**(1)   On making any payment into court under an order of the Court or a certificate of a master, the party making the payment shall give notice of the payment in Form No. 25A in Appendix A to every other party to the proceedings.**

**(2)   Unless the Court otherwise orders, a defendant who has paid money into court in pursuance of an order made under Order 14 may —**

**(a)     by notice served on the plaintiff, appropriate the whole or any part of the money and any additional payment, if necessary, in satisfaction of any particular claim made by the plaintiff and specified in the notice; or**

**(b)     if he pleads a tender, by his pleading served on the plaintiff, appropriate the whole or any part of the money as payment into court of the money alleged to have been tendered.**

**(3)   Any money appropriated in accordance with paragraph (2) is deemed to be —**

**(a)     in the case of paragraph (2)(a), a sanctioned payment when the notice is served on the plaintiff; and**

**(b)     in the case of paragraph (2)(b), money paid into court with a plea of tender when the pleading is served on the plaintiff,**

**and this Order applies accordingly.**

**(4)   A notice served on the plaintiff in accordance with paragraph (2)(a) is deemed to be a sanctioned payment notice.**

**(L.N. 152 of 2008)**

---

**NOTES**

**[22.27.1]     Origin and scope of Order 22 rule 27**

Order 22 rule 27 is a modified version of the previous Order 22 rule 8. It deals with money paid into court pursuant to court order. There are many different circumstances in which the court has power to order payment of money into court. They include:

(a)     *Conditional order* – Order 1B rule 1(3)(a) empowers the court, by way of case management, to impose conditions including payment into court when making an order.

(b)     *Procedural default* – Order 2 rule 3 provides that the court may order a party who has failed to comply with a rule or court order to pay money into court.

(c)     *Conditional leave to defend* – leave to defend may be granted on a summary judgment application subject to terms, including payment of money into court. See the commentary under Order 14 rule 4.

(d)     *Security for costs* – orders for security for costs sometimes provide that the money be paid into court. See the commentary under Order 23 rule 2.

(e)     *Party under disability* – money awarded to a party under disability will normally be paid into court under Order 80 rule 12.

**[22.27.2]     Rule 27(1) - Form of notice of payment into court under order**

Order 22 rule 27(1) provides that form 25A in appendix A to these rules should be used for giving notice of payment into court under order or certificate of the court. It replaces the form previously made available by the registry for use in such circumstances (as set out in appendix 11 to the consolidated notes of High Court Registry practice circulated to solicitors under Law Society circular 06-79).

In the rather unusual case of *Modern Fashion Ltd v Hong Kong Prudential Knitting Fty Ltd* [1996] 3 HKC 267 a party making payment into court under an order mistakenly used the form appropriate for a payment into court made as a settlement proposal, the equivalent of today's sanctioned payment. The court refused leave to amend the notice and ordered the money to be paid out to the plaintiff in satisfaction of its claims.

Money paid into the court under an order, notice of which is given in the correct form making it clear that the payment is pursuant to order, cannot be accepted as if it were a sanctioned payment: *Fenn Kar Bik Lily v Goh Kim Lay* [1994] 2 HKLR 228, 241–2.

**[22.27.3]     Date of payment into court by cheque**

The effective date of a payment into court by cheque is the date the cheque is received in the court office, not the later date when the funds have cleared. See *Petroleo Brasilieiro SA v ENE Kos 1 Ltd* [2009] EWCA Civ 1127 (30.10.2009) where it was held that an order for payment into court was sufficiently complied with by delivering a cheque on the final day for compliance, even though, being a foreign currency cheque, it took a week to clear.

**[22.27.4]     Rule 27(2) & (3) – 'Appropriation' of money paid into court under Order 14**

Under Order 14 rule 4(3) the court may order a defendant to make a payment into court as security for the amount claimed as a condition of granting leave to defend. See the commentary under that rule. Order 22 rule 27(2)&(3) provides that where such security is paid into court, the defendant may 'appropriate' it (in whole or in part, and together with any additional payment) so as to make it a sanctioned payment. The rule states that this is to be done by 'notice', but no form is prescribed. It is also provided that the defendant may by pleading render the money a tender, which shall similarly be deemed to be a sanctioned payment. As to the defence of tender, see Order 18 rule 16 and the commentary thereunder.

28.   **Transitional provision relating to Part 9 of Amendment Rules 2008**
      (O. 22 r. 28)
      **Where —**
      **(a)    a payment into court has been made in accordance with Order 22 ("the repealed Order") repealed by rule 111 ("the repealing rule") of the Amendment Rules 2008; and**
      **(b)    the disposal of the payment is pending immediately before the commencement of the repealing rule,**
**then nothing in Division I of Part 9 of the Amendment Rules 2008 applies in relation to that payment, and the repealed Order and all the other provisions amended or repealed by that Division, as in force immediately before the commencement, continue to apply in relation to that payment as if that Division had not been made.**
**(L.N. 152 of 2008)**

---

**NOTES**

**[22.28.1]    Order 22 not applicable to payments into court under former procedure**
Order 22 rule 28 is a transitional provision whereby payments into court under the former Order 22 (which did not provide for enhanced costs and interest consequences) will still be governed by the previous Order if disposal of the payment was pending when the new Order 22 came into force in 2009.

See also the commentary under Order 62 rule 10 concerning the repeal of the provisions in that rule for taxation of costs on acceptance of payment into court under the previous procedure, which are likewise preserved.

## ORDER 22A

### MISCELLANEOUS PROVISIONS ABOUT PAYMENTS INTO COURT

**1.     Money remaining in court** (O. 22A r. 1)
     **(1)     Subject to Order 22, rule 17, any money paid into court in an action (whether or not in accordance with Order 22) may not be paid out except in pursuance of an order of the Court which may be made at any time before, at or after the trial or hearing of the action.**
     **(2)     Where an order under paragraph (1) is made before the trial or hearing and the money in court is a sanctioned payment made in accordance with Order 22, the money may not be paid out except –**

> **(a)     in satisfaction of the cause or causes of action in respect of which it was paid in; or**
>
> **(b)     to the extent to which the sanctioned payment may be withdrawn or diminished pursuant to Order 22.**

     **(L.N. 152 of 2008)**

---

## NOTES

### [22A.1.1]     Origin and scope of Order 22A rule 1
Order 22A rule 1 was made as part of the civil justice reforms in effect from 2009. It provides that a court order is required for payment out of money in court in all circumstances, but subject to Order 22 rule 17 whereby on acceptance of a sanc tioned payment, payment out may be obtained simply by filing a request in form No 25. The rule replaced the previous Order 22 rules 5 and rule 8(2).
     See also Order 92 rule 5 in relation to trustees.

### [22A.1.2]     Order for payment out of court
In *Harrington v CAP Gemini Ernst & Young HK Ltd* HCCL 10/2002 (Stone J; 10.09.2004) it was held that payment out should not be ordered unless to do so is 'just in all the circumstances'. In that case the court refused an application by a plaintiff for payment out to satisfy a judgment in her favour where it was argued that the funds might be needed to satisfy a costs order against the plaintiff. Any previous practice whereby funds held in court as security for costs will invariably be paid out following judgment 'must now be laid to rest'; the question 'is one of discretion' and a pending appeal may be taken into account: *First Laser Ltd v Fujian Enterprises (Holdings) Ltd & Anor* HCA 4414/2001 (Deputy Judge To; 28.04.2008) (para 21).
     Where money has been paid into court under an order for security for costs, a subsequent order that there be no order as to the costs of the proceedings may in effect be an order for payment out of those funds: see *Tsang Yuk Kiu v Lobley Co Ltd & Anor* [1997] 3 HKC 717 (CA). In that case it was argued that where money had been paid into court under an order of the Court of Appeal, only the Court of Appeal could order its payment out. The court did not find it necessary to decide that issue.

**2.     Person to whom payment to be made** (O. 22A r. 2)

    **(1)   Where the party entitled to money in court is a person in respect of whom a certificate is or has been in force entitling him to legal aid under the Legal Aid Ordinance (Cap. 91), payment shall be made only to the Director of Legal Aid without the need for any authority from the party.**

    **(2)   Subject to paragraph (1), payment shall be made to the party entitled or to his solicitor.**

    **(3)   This rule applies whether the money in court has been paid into court under Order 22 or under an order of the Court or a certificate of the Registrar.**

    **(L.N. 152 of 2008)**

---

**NOTES**

**[22A.2.1]   Origin and scope of Order 22A rule 2**
Order 22A rule 2 is in the same terms as the former Order 22 rule 10, which was repealed on implementation of the civil justice reforms in 2009.

    The rule makes provision for payment out of funds in court to the party entitled thereto, the party's solicitor or the Director of Legal Aid, in various circumstances. The rule applies to all funds in court, whether paid in as a sanctioned payment under Order 22 or otherwise.

**[22A.2.2]   Payment out of court in legally aided cases**
 Order 22A rule 2(1) provides that where a legally aided party is entitled to money in court, the money shall be paid to the Director of Legal Aid. The purpose is to protect the Director's first charge on any money or property recovered or preserved in legally aided proceedings (Legal Aid Ordinance (Cap 91), s 18A). The rule expressly provides that the authority of the legally aided person is not required for payment to the Director.

    In *Leung Kam Tai v Wong Chuen* [1998] 4 HKC 214 the court was critical of the terms of a consent order whereby a sum of money would be paid in settlement of an aided person's civil claim and in the meantime funds in court would be returned to the defendant's solicitors. It was said that such a term should never have been agreed because it put the plaintiff at risk in case the defendant became insolvent and jeopardised the legal aid first charge.

**[22A.2.3]   Other cases**
Where the party entitled to money in court is not legally aided, money in court should be paid out to that party or its solicitor: Order 22A rule 2(2).

**3.     Payment out: small intestate estates** (O. 22A r. 3)
    **Where —**
        **(a)   a person entitled to a fund in court, or a share of such fund, dies intestate;**
        **(b)   the Court is satisfied that no grant of administration of his estate has been made; and**
        **(c)   the assets of his estate, including the fund or share, do not**

**exceed \$150,000 in value,**

**it may order that the fund or share shall be paid, transferred or delivered to the person who, being a widower, widow, child, father, mother, brother or sister of the deceased, would have the prior right to a grant of administration of the estate of the deceased.**

**(L.N. 152 of 2008)**

-------------------------

## NOTES

### [22A.3.1]   Origin of Order 22A rule 3

Order 22A rule 3 is in almost the same terms as the previous Order 22 rule 11, which was repealed on implementation of the civil justice reforms in 2009. Under the new provision, the maximum value of an estate for the purpose of the rule has been raised from \$20,000 to \$150,000. The rule enables the court to order payment out of funds belonging to a person who dies intestate to the person who would have prior right to apply for letters of administration of the estate of the person who dies intestate, without the need for such letters to be granted. Priority amongst surviving family members in applying for letters of administration is governed by rule 21 of the Non-Contentious Probate Rules (Cap 10A).

**4.     Investment of money in court** (O. 22A r. 4)

**Cash under the control of or subject to the order of the Court may be invested in any manner specified in the High Court Suitors' Funds Rules (Cap. 4 sub. leg. B) and the Trustee Ordinance (Cap. 29).**

**(L.N. 152 of 2008)**

-------------------------

## NOTES

### [22A.4.1]   Origin and scope of Order 22A rule 4

Order 22A rule 4, introduced on implementation of the civil justice reforms in 2009, is in the same terms as the previous Order 22 rule 13. The rule provides for investment of money which has been paid into court. Any such investment must be in accordance with the High Court Suitors' Funds Rules (subsidiary legislation under the High Court Ordinance) and the Trustee Ordinance.

### [22A.4.2]   Dividends and interest on funds in court

Dividends or interest are credited to money in court in accordance with rule 16 of the High Court Suitors' Funds Rules. Those rules date from 1979 and were substantially amended in 1998. Earlier authorities such as *Lee Ying v Hamlett* [1977] HKLR 274 and Re Hongkew Holdings Ltd HCMP 2523/1993 (Rogers J; 17.07.1996) should no longer be followed insofar as they held that an order was required for interest to be payable on funds paid into court as security for costs, proceeds of sale, in satisfaction of a judgment debt, etc. Rule 16(3A) of the Suitors' Funds Rules now provides for interest to accrue once such funds have been held in court for 14 days.

## ORDER 23

### SECURITY FOR COSTS

1.    **Security for costs of action, etc.** (O. 23 r. 1)
    **(1)   Where, on the application of a defendant to an action or other proceeding in the Court of First Instance, it appears to the Court —**
        **(a)    that the plaintiff is ordinarily resident out of the jurisdiction, or**
        **(b)    that the plaintiff (not being a plaintiff who is suing in a representative capacity) is a nominal plaintiff who is suing for the benefit of some other person and that there is reason to believe that he will be unable to pay the costs of the defendant if ordered to do so, or**
        **(c)    subject to paragraph (2), that the plaintiff's address is not stated in the writ or other originating process or is incorrectly stated therein, or**
        **(d)    that the plaintiff has changed his address during the course of the proceedings with a view to evading the consequences of the litigation,**
    **then if, having regard to all the circumstances of the case, the Court thinks it just to do so, it may order the plaintiff to give such security for the defendant's costs of the action or other proceeding as it thinks just.**
    **(2)   The Court shall not require a plaintiff to give security by reason only of paragraph (1)(c) if he satisfies the Court that the failure to state his address or the mis-statement thereof was made innocently and without intention to deceive.**
    **(3)   The references in the foregoing paragraphs to a plaintiff and a defendant shall be construed as references to the person (howsoever described on the record) who is in the position of plaintiff or defendant, as the case may be, in the proceeding in question, including a proceeding on a counterclaim.**

---

## NOTES

### [23.1.1]    The court's power to order security for costs
The court's power to order security for costs arises from inherent jurisdiction: *GFN SA & Anor v Liquidators of Bancredit Cayman Ltd* [2009] UKPC 39 (04.11.2009) (para 9-11) and now finds expression in various legislative provisions including Order 23 rule 1, section 357 of the Companies Ordinance (Cap 32) in relation to companies and Order 59 rule 10(5) in relation to appeals.

### [23.1.2]    Principles on which security will be ordered
The principles upon which security for costs will be ordered are well established. The Hong Kong court tends to follow English decisions.
    An order for security for costs is within the discretion of the court. The closing

words of Order 23 rule 1(1) enjoin the court to have regard to all the circumstances and to order security if it thinks it just to do so. It is not appropriate for the court to make an order for payment into court which has the effect of providing security for costs without considering the factors which would be relevant on an application under this rule: *Siu King Cheung Hing Yip Co Ltd v Malaysia Borneo Finance Corp (M) Bhd* [1980] HKLR 625, 628 (CA).

Set out below is a discussion of some of the circumstances in which a party may be ordered to give security for costs and some of the factors which frequently influence the court's exercise of discretion. But first we deal with some procedural and jurisdictional issues.

**[23.1.3]    Mode of application for security for costs**

Security for costs should first be requested by letter, followed by consent summons if agreement is reached that security be paid into court. If no agreement is reached, it is then appropriate to apply to the court by summons to a master. Delay in issuing a summons after such a letter may militate against the court ordering security for costs: *Ronia Ltd v Clarke* [2003] 2 HKLRD 643.

**[23.1.4]    Time for making application for security for costs**

An order for security for costs may be made at any stage of the proceedings: *BBMB Finance (HK) Ltd v China Underwriters Life & General Insurance Co Ltd* [1991] 1 HKLR 617, 624E-F (CA). However timing is relevant to the court's exercise of discretion. In *Midland Realty Int'l Ltd v Wise Surplus Ltd* HCA 3065/2001 (Deputy Judge Muttrie; 21.06.2005) the court quoted with approval the following passage from *Croft Leisure Ltd v Gravestock & Owen* [1993] BCLC 1273, 1279:

> If one makes it too early one is reproached because one cannot forecast accurately how long the trial will take and how much it will cost. If one makes it too late, one is said to have led the plaintiffs up the garden path.

An application for security for costs will be considered late if there is delay after the applicant is aware of the grounds relied on, as in *BBMB Finance* (above), or if made too close to the trial, as in *Peconic Industrial Development Ltd & Anor v Chio Ho Cheong & Ors* HCA 16255/1999 (A Cheung J; 26.10.2005). The application may be refused in the absence of a credible explanation for the delay, as in *Senior Honor Ltd v Lee Ki Luk & Ors* HCA 4043/2001 (A Cheung J; 14.11.2003). Even where there is a credible explanation for the delay, the court will consider whether there is prejudice to the opposing party: *Peconic Industrial* (above).

Delay is relevant to the court's exercise of discretion, but not a bar — late applications for security for costs are sometimes successful. See, for example, *Andersen & Anor v Huang Kuang Yuan & Ors* [1997] HKLRD 1360 (CA) upholding a judge's decision to order security for costs on the 14th day of a lengthy trial, but reducing the amount.

**[23.1.5]    Form of order for security for costs**

It is not appropriate for an order for security for costs to be worded in such a way as to *require* the payment to be made: *Lam Fei Hong v Wong Kam Fong* [1999] 2 HKC 781. There at 783H–I Keith J disapproved the form of order found in *Atkin's Court Forms* (1992) on the ground it suggested that it would be a breach to fail to make payment. Keith J preferred a form of order whereby the proceedings would be stayed if security is not provided. The appeal committee of the CFA has since said that it is appropriate for the order to provide for the action to be dismissed without further order if security is not given within the time stipulated: *Sunchase Int'l Group (China) Ltd v Vincor Group of Companies (Investment) Ltd* FAMV 21/2004 (Bokhary, Chan & Ribeiro PJJ; 22.02.2005). In *Wong Kam San v Yeung Wing Keung & Ors* CACV 131/2007 (Rogers VP; 03.07.2007) the learned judge made an order in the following terms, which he described as 'the standard form':

> The [appellant] do on or before [date] give security to answer costs in case any shall be awarded to be paid by the [appellant] by making lodgement in court of the sum of [$XX] by cash or banker's draft, or by the provision of a bank guarantee of the like amount, which guarantee shall have been approved by the Registrar; and until such lodgement be made and notice thereof given to the Registrar and to the solicitors for the [respondent] such notice to be given on the same day as the lodgement is made, all proceedings in the said appeal are to be stayed. In default of the [appellant] making such lodgement as aforesaid within the time specified above or within such further time as the court may for special reasons allow, the said appeal do, upon the solicitors for the [respondent] certifying such default to the Registrar, stand dismissed out of this court without further order. In the event that the appeal is dismissed in the circumstances provided for above, the [appellant] do pay the [respondent's] costs occasioned by the said appeal, such costs to be taxed and the costs of this application ....

### [23.1.6] Time for compliance

An order that security for costs be provided will normally stipulate the time for compliance. See Order 23 rule 2. The court's general power to extend time under Order 3 rule 5 enables this time to be enlarged. In *Multi Sky v Hongkong Chinese Insurance Co Ltd* [1994] 1 HKC 108 the Court of Appeal granted an extension of time in the interests of justice where considerable costs had already been incurred and there was a possibility of a fresh action which would cause further delay.

### [23.1.7] Failure to comply with order for security for costs

The court has an inherent power to dismiss an action for failure to comply with an order for security for costs: *Multi Sky Ltd v Hongkong Chinese Insurance Co Ltd & Anor* [1994] 1 HKC 108, 111H–I (CA). In exercising this power the court will consider factors such as 'whether the action is being pursued with due diligence, whether there is no reasonable prospect that the security will be paid, and whether the time limit prescribed by the court has been disregarded': *Ingo Int'l Ltd v Canadian Eastern Life Assurance Ltd* HCA 19675/1999 (Deputy Judge Saunders; 04.05.2005). As discussed above, provision may be made in the order for security whereby the action will automatically be dismissed if security is not given. In the absence of such a provision application must be made to the court to dismiss the proceedings after default has occurred.

### [23.1.8] Security for costs of appeal

The provisions of Order 23 do not apply to appeals. Elsewhere in these rules there is provision for orders for security for costs of certain types of appeals.

Appeal under Order 55 – Security for costs of an appeal under Order 55 (from a tribunal to a judge of the High Court) may be ordered under Order 55 rule 7(6) in 'special circumstances'.

Appeal from master to a single judge – It has been held that there is no jurisdiction to order security for costs of an appeal under Order 58 from a master to a judge in chambers: see *Perennial Cable (HK) Ltd v Popbridge Industrial Ltd* [2000] 1 HKC 564.

Appeal to Court of Appeal – the power to order security for costs of an appeal to the Court of Appeal is found in Order 59 rule 10(5). See also the commentary under that rule.

**[23.1.9]    Non-resident plaintiff**
Order 23 rule 1(1)(a) empowers the court to make an order for security for costs against a plaintiff on the ground of ordinary residence out of the jurisdiction. The purpose is to facilitate enforcement in the event of an order for costs against the non-resident plaintiff: *Walt Disney Co v Disney Property Agency* HCA 7289/1992 (Godfrey J; 15.03.1993) quoting with approval from *The Alpha* [1991] 2 Lloyd's Rep 52, 54. It is considered *prima facie* unjust that a non-resident plaintiff, 'more or less immune' from enforcement of an adverse costs order, should be allowed to proceed in Hong Kong without putting up security for costs: *Tagliani v Lee Wai Ying Elvis* [2006] 2 HKC 194, 197E-F, citing *ElecVision Inc v Achiever Industries Ltd* [2003] 1 HKLRD 60. The possibility of enforcement of an adverse costs order in the jurisdiction where the non-resident plaintiff lives is a relevant factor: *Tagliani* (above, 200B-C); *Jollymex NV v Jollybaby Int'l Ltd* [2007] 4 HKC 66; but not of itself decisive: *Thune v London Properties Ltd* [1990] 1 WLR 562 (CA).

In most cases it will be clear where the plaintiff is resident, as the form of writ of summons requires that the plaintiff's address be stated. Where on an application for security for costs there is a dispute as to the plaintiff's place of ordinary residence, the burden of proof rests with the defendant applying for security. See *Mahajan v HCL Technologies (HK) Ltd & Ors* HCA 1510/2004 (Deputy Judge L Chan; 15.10.2010) (para 4).

Ordinary residence is a concept which has been considered in many cases and in different contexts. Essentially a person is ordinarily resident in the place where he habitually goes about his daily life apart from temporary or occasional absences: *R v Barnet LBC ex p Shah* [1983] 2 AC 309 (HL). See also the note by Pyott at (1982) 12 HKLJ 216 and the cases cited therein. Ordinary residence is a matter of fact, and differs from a legal right of residence. Thus the holder of a Hong Kong identity card is not *ipso facto* ordinarily resident here: *Chian Ker Chi Paul v Super Zone Investment Ltd* [1994] 2 HKC 679, 681G. However, a person illegally present in the jurisdiction will not be considered ordinarily resident: *Sun Jie v Registration of Persons Tribunal* CACV 320/2004 (Rogers VP, Le Pichon JA & Sakhrani J; 13.12.2005.

A non-resident plaintiff may resist an order for security for costs by showing fixed assets in Hong Kong. See *Tsang Yee Mui v Personal Representatives of Mak Chik Wing* HCA 2606/2006 (Chu J; 21.07.2008) where it was said (at para 31):

> . . . the fact that the plaintiff is known to have fixed assets in the jurisdiction is highly relevant. This is because the rationale or objective underlying Order 23 rule 1(1)(a) is to alleviate the difficulty that may be faced by a successful defendant in seeking to recover costs against a foreign plaintiff. If it is known that there are assets within the jurisdiction available for costs, then the concern that the rule sets out to address will be met.

In *Tsang* (above) the court went on to hold (at para 32) that a plaintiff who resists an application for security for costs on the basis of assets within the jurisdiction 'is obliged to make good that proposition' and 'should adduce supporting information to substantiate his assertion' and that the value of the assets is relevant. Cash deposits in bank accounts in Hong Kong are unlikely to assist a non-resident plaintiff in resisting an order for security for costs: see *Hoogland v Lin & Anor* HCA 657/2007 (Chung J; 29.05.2008) where, refusing an appeal against an order for security for costs, it was said (at para 25):

> Hong Kong is a major financial centre. Financial movements can take place swiftly. Cash deposits in bank accounts can be disposed of literally within minutes. They cannot ordinarily be regarded as assets of a fixed and permanent nature.

### [23.1.10]   Human rights considerations

It is now clear that human rights considerations are relevant on an application for security for costs. In *Nasser v United Bank of Kuwait* [2002] 1 All ER 401 (CA) it was held that it would be discriminatory if the mere fact of residence abroad could justify an order for security for costs. Reference was made to the right under the European Convention on Human Rights to access to the court without discrimination on the basis of 'national ... origin'. The ICCPR and the Hong Kong Bill of Rights both contain similar provisions. The English court held there could be no inflexible assumption that a person from abroad should provide security. The court should consider the difficulty in enforcing a costs order in the place of residence. It inferred that enforcement of an English costs order in the United States carried with it a significantly greater burden by way of cost and delay as compared to enforcement in England and upheld an order for security against an American-resident plaintiff. In *Tagliani v Lee Wai Ying Elvis* [2006] 2 HKC 194, 199F-I it was argued that an order for security for costs against a non-resident of relatively limited means would infringe the right of access to the courts under art 35 of the Basic Law. The court, without citing *Nasser* (above), held that an order for security would not infringe art 35, though it was sensitive to the possibility of stifling a genuine claim, and in result ordered security of only 1/9 of the amount claimed. *Nasser* was cited in *Izumo Mokko Co Ltd & Anor v TS Lines Ltd* [2007] 3 HKC 296 (DCt) (para 15), where the court said it reflected the 'modern approach', and that in order to avoid infringing the provisions of the Bill of Rights Ordinance, 'the Hong Kong courts, in deciding whether to order a foreign plaintiff to provide security for costs, should now focus on the difficulties faced by the defendant in enforcing the judgment rather than on the status of a particular plaintiff'. The absence of arrangements for reciprocal enforcement of judgments was considered sufficient to demonstrate difficulty in enforcing a Hong Kong costs order in the United States in both *Condumex Inc v Starasia Components Ltd* DCCJ 6287/2005 (Judge Marlene Ng; 09.08.2007) (para 80) and *Yang Wei Jenni fer & Anor v HSBC Private Trustee (HK) Ltd & Ors* HCA 5073/2001 (Chu J; 24.12.2008) (para 18). For discussion of reciprocal enforcement of judgments, see Orders 71, 71A and 71B.

In *Cano-Shearer Anne & Ors v Cathay Pacific Airways Ltd* [2003] 2 HKC 448, it was held that security for costs should be approached differently in cases seeking to enforce civil rights, as compared to commercial cases. The action concerned claims for relief under the Sex Discrimination Ordinance (Cap 480). The district judge refused an application for security for costs against non-resident plaintiffs, citing section 73B(3) of the District Court Ordinance which restricts the circumstances in which costs may be ordered against a plaintiff in such a case.

## [23.1.11] Nominal plaintiff

Under Order 23 rule 1(1)(b) security for costs may be ordered against a 'nominal' plaintiff.

A 'nominal' plaintiff in this context is one 'who is plaintiff in name but who in truth sues for the benefit of another': *Semler v Murphy* [1967] 2 All ER 185, per Lord Denning MR at 191. In that case the plaintiff was 'nominal' since he had granted a charge on the fruits of the action to another person. See also *Belgrove v Marine and General Insurance Service Pty Ltd* (1996) 5 Tas R 409 where a plaintiff who had conveyed and assigned the net benefit of a legal action was held to be a nominal plaintiff. And see *UDL Holdings Ltd & Anor v Leung Yuet Keung & Anor* [2004] 1 HKC 548 (CA) where a company was found to be a nominal plaintiff because it had entered into a scheme of arrangement under which the benefit of the legal proceedings would pass to its creditors.

In order to obtain an order that a nominal plaintiff provide security for costs, it must be shown there is 'reason to believe that he will be unable to pay the costs of the defendant if ordered to do so': rule 1(1)(b). It appears that the authorities preserving the right of an impecunious plaintiff to pursue legal proceedings without giving security for costs where to do so would prevent him from litigating a meritorious claim (see below) do not apply in this context. See the Tasmanian case of *Belgrove* cited above.

The nominal plaintiff rule expressly does not apply to plaintiffs who sue in a representative capacity. According to the Tasmanian case of *Belgrove* (above) these include an administrator (*Rainbow v Kittoe* (1916) 1 Ch D 313), a next friend (*Fellows v Barnett* (1836) 1 Keen 119; 48 ER 252) and a trustee who is required by law to pursue the matter (*Ramsey v Hartley* [1977] 2 All ER 673).

## [23.1.12] Companies

As to security for costs as against companies, see also section 357 of the Companies Ordinance (Cap 32) which provides as follows:

> Where a limited company is plaintiff in any action or other legal proceeding, any judge having jurisdiction in the matter may, if it appears by credible testimony that there is reason to believe that the company will be unable to pay the costs of the defendant if successful in his defence, require sufficient security to be given for those costs, and may stay all proceedings until the security is given.

The legal principles on which security for costs may be ordered against a company under section 357 of the Companies Ordinance (Cap 32) are in most respects the same as those which apply under this Order.

On an application under section 357 of the Companies Ordinance the defendant must satisfy the court by credible evidence that there is reason to believe the plaintiff would be unable to satisfy an order for costs. There is no jurisdiction to order security unless this threshold is crossed: *Success Wise Ltd v Dynamic (BVI) Ltd* [2006] 1 HKC 149 (para 10). It is not sufficient to show that the company 'may well' be unable to meet an adverse costs order – the Ordinance requires that it be shown the company 'will be unable to pay': *KJM Industries Ltd v JPM Resources (HK) Ltd* [2005] 4 HKC 100 (CA).

It is suggested in *San Heines Investments Ltd v THL (Holdings) Co Ltd & Anor* [2001] 1 HKC 39, 42H that once the threshold requirement is crossed the 'onus' shifts to the company against which security is sought. However in *Livingspring Pty Ltd v Kliger Partners* [2008] VSCA 93 (04.06.2008) (para 21) the Victorian Court of Appeal, dealing with similarly worded legislation, was of the view that while it would be up to the company to establish the facts to make good an assertion such as that an order for security would stultify the litigation, the burden rests on the party applying for security 'from first to last, to persuade the court that the order for security should be made'.

### [23.1.13]    Companies acting 'in person'

There is authority to the effect that a company which is granted leave (under Order 5 rule 6(2)(b)) to act by one of its directors is not entitled to recover costs and thus may not be entitled to an order for security for costs. See *Australian Telephone Distributors Pty Ltd v Golden Always Ltd & Anor* [1996] 3 HKC 401 (CA). However, the primary point, that such a company is not entitled to recover costs, was subsequently doubted by a differently constituted Court of Appeal. See *Typhoon 8 Research Ltd v Seapower Resources International Ltd & Anor* [2002] 2 HKLRD 660, and see the commentary under Order 62 rule 28A.

### [23.1.14]    Companies incorporated outside Hong Kong

Section 357 of the Companies Ordinance does not apply to companies incorporated in jurisdictions outside Hong Kong. This is because of the definition of the word 'company' in section 2 of the Ordinance, which is confined to Hong Kong companies: *Insurance Co of the State of Pennsylvania v Grand Union Insurance Co Ltd* [1988] HKC 200 (CA). Companies incorporated outside Hong Kong are subject to Order 23, but not if they have established residence in the jurisdiction (see below). As a result, Hong Kong businesses which use offshore corporate vehicles may be immune from the power to order security for costs. This unsatisfactory situation has been the subject of adverse comment in many cases. In *Akai Holdings Ltd (in liq) v Ernst & Young (a firm)* [2009] 2 HKC 439 the Court of Appeal saw this as a growing problem and decided not to follow *Insurance Co of the State of Pennsylvania* (above). The Court of Appeal held that security could be ordered against an overseas company which was registered in Hong Kong under Part XI of the Companies Ordinance. However, that decision was reversed by the Court of Final Appeal ([2009] 5 HKC 218). The Court of Final Appeal agreed that the situation is unsatisfactory, but held that a change could only be brought about by legislation. It suggested that Order 23 be amended along the lines of CPR 25.13(2)(c) which empowers the English court to order security for costs against impecunious companies incorporated anywhere, and whether or not resident within the jurisdiction.

### [23.1.15]    Company 'ordinarily resident out of jurisdiction'

The power under Order 23 rule 1(1)(a) to order security for costs against a non-resident plaintiff applies to bodies corporate just as it applies to natural persons. A company's place of residence is not necessarily in the jurisdiction where it is incorporated. The test is 'where its central management and control abides': *Insurance Co of the State of Pennsylvania v Grand Union Insurance Co Ltd & Anor* [1988] HKC 200, 204B (CA). Thus in *Re Greater Beijing Region Expressways Ltd (No 3)* [2000] 3 HKC 608 the court was prepared to find that a BVI company was ordinarily resident in Hong Kong, and in *Akai Holdings Ltd (in liq) v Ernst & Young* HCCL 29/2004 (Stone J; 15.07.2008) a Bermuda company was found to be resident in Hong Kong. The consequence of a foreign company being resident in Hong Kong is that there is no jurisdiction to order security for costs against it. Order 23 is inapplicable because it is not a non-resident, and section 357 of the Companies Ordinance does not apply because it is not incorporated in Hong Kong. See the discussion in the preceding paragraph referring to the decision of the Court of Final Appeal in *Akai Holdings*.

In *Charter View Holdings (BVI) Ltd v Corona Investments Ltd & Anor* [1998] 1 HKLRD 469, 471F-J Keith J expressed the view that application of the 'central management and control' test is not straightforward. He set out in his own words three propositions which he derived from *Re Little Olympian Each Ways Ltd* [1995] 1 WLR 560:

(i)    The mere assertion of where the company's central management and control is unsatisfactory. What is needed are the primary facts on which that assertion is based.

(ii)   All the circumstances in which the company carries on its business should be taken into account, though the weight to be applied to each factor will obviously differ from case to case. Those factors include the provisions of the company's objects clause, the place of incorporation, the place where the company's real trade and business is carried on, the place where the company's books are kept, the place where the company's administration is carried out, the place where the directors with power . . . meet or are resident, the place where its chief office is or where the company secretary is to be found, and the place where its most significant assets are.

(iii) In applying the test to a non-trading company, it may be more important than would otherwise be the case to have regard to the nature of the company's corporate activities.

In the *Insurance Co of the State of Pennsylvania* case (above) the Court of Appeal considered the ordinary residence of a multinational company which was incorporated in the United States but carried on business in many other places including Hong Kong. It was held that the company was ordinarily resident in the United States where 'the seat of its central management and control' was located. The fact that the company carried on business in Hong Kong (it was registered as an oversea company under the Companies Ordinance and under the Business Registration Ordinance and was authorised under the Insurance Companies Ordinance) might have made it amenable to service in Hong Kong, but did not render it ordinarily resident in Hong Kong for the purposes of rule 1(1)(a).

See also *Jade Harbour Ltd v Eltones Profits Ltd & Anor* [2005] 3 HKLRD 148 where a BVI company used as a corporate vehicle in Hong Kong was held to be ordinarily resident in Hong Kong.

### [23.1.16]    Co-plaintiffs

It was suggested in successive editions of the English *Supreme Court Practice* that there is a rule of practice whereby the court will not normally order security for costs if there is a co-plaintiff resident in the jurisdiction. Authorities of considerable antiquity were cited. As explained in *City Top Eng'g Ltd v Lee Shing Yue Construction Co Ltd* HCCT 75/1998 (Burrell J; 28.02.2000) the reason is simply that any costs order could be executed against the local plaintiff. Clearly where the co-plaintiff would likely be jointly liable for costs, and has exigible assets, it would be arguable that there is no need for security for costs. However, in the Hong Kong decisions where this 'rule of practice' has been cited, rarely, if ever, has it been applied. In *Skyriver (BVI) Ltd & Anor v Shougang Holding (HK) Ltd* HCA 17196/1999 (Deputy Judge Poon; 19.09.2002) it was said (at para 19):

> There is no inflexible rule that security for costs against a foreign plaintiff would not be ordered where there is a Hong Kong co-plaintiff in the action. It is after all a matter of discretion.

In *Ai Zhong v Metroford Ltd* HCA 2627/2008; [2010] 1 HKLRD 213 (para 16) Yam J said he had 'grave doubts about the relevance of this rule in Hong Kong today'. In *Ng Yat Chi & Anor v Max Share Ltd* [1996] 4 HKC 284, 286D-G the court ordered security for costs against a nominal plaintiff where its cause of action differed from that of its co-plaintiff and it was thought the court might not order the co-plaintiff to be responsible for the nominal plaintiff's costs. In *Polar Furs Ltd & Anor v Int'l Fur Co Ltd & Ors* HCA 2042/2005 (Master Wong; 14.05.2007) (para 9) the court said that the mere addition of a local co-plaintiff was insufficient to persuade the court to release the 1st plaintiff from security for costs, noting that the plaintiffs sued on an 'and/or' basis. In *Spectrum Plus Ltd & Anor v Konica Minolta Business Solutions (HK) Ltd* HCA 10364/2000 (Deputy Judge Carlson; 12.06.2007) (para 4) security was ordered where the co-plaintiff had already been ordered to post security.

## [23.1.17]   Defendants, counterclaims and interlocutory applications

The court's power to order security for costs under rule 1(1) is limited to applications by defendants for security to be provided by plaintiffs. Thus security for costs will not generally be ordered against a defendant: *Naamlooz v Bank of England* [1948] 1 All ER 465.

However, rule 1(3) provides that 'plaintiff' and 'defendant' shall be construed with reference to the parties' actual positions. Thus a defendant taking a stance which is more than merely defensive may be regarded as being in the 'position of plaintiff' within rule 1(3) and susceptible to an order for security for costs. Rule 1(3) specifically contemplates an order for security for costs against a defendant who counterclaims. The position is the same under section 357 of the Companies Ordinance - the power in that section to order a plaintiff to give security for costs extends to a party which is plaintiff in substance as opposed to form: *Brand Farrar Buxbaum LLP v Samuel-Rozenbaum Diamond Ltd & Ors* [2003] 1 HKLRD 60, 606A-B. Cases in which the court has considered whether a defendant is in reality in the position of plaintiff include the following:

- *Dragages et Travaux Public v Hong Kong Chinese Insurance Co Ltd & Ors* [1993] 1 HKC 617;
- *Smarking Int'l Ltd v Lau Chi Keung George & Ors* [1999] 4 HKC 669;
- *Midland Realty Int'l Ltd v Wise Surplus Ltd* HCA 3065/2001 (Deputy Judge Muttrie; 21.06.2005); and
- *Ai Zhong & Anor v Metrofond Ltd* [2010] 1 HKLRD 213.

A defendant making an interlocutory application will not normally be ordered to provide security for the costs thereof, despite the fact that as applicant it is in a plaintiff-like position. This is because an interlocutory application is not regarded as an 'action or other proceeding' within rule 1(1). See *TK Bulkhandling Gmbh v Meridian Success Int'l Ltd* HCMP 4765/1998 (Findlay J; 30.11.1998). In that case the court dismissed an application for security for the costs of an application to set aside leave to enforce an arbitral award. See also *GFN SA & Anor v Liquidators of Bancredit Cayman Ltd* [2009] UKPC 39 (04.11.2009) (para 31) where Lord Neuberger said 'a discreet order for security will not be made in relation to what is in substance an interlocutory application'. See, however, *Brand Farrar Buxbaum LLP v Samuel-Rozenbaum Diamond Limited* HCA 5191/1998 (Master K Wong; 11.11.2003) where security for costs of enforcement proceedings was granted.

Just as a counterclaiming defendant may be regarded as a plaintiff in substance, the plaintiff against whom a counterclaim is made may be regarded as in substance a defendant, and not susceptible to an order for security for costs. See *Anwide Co Ltd v AG* [1994] 2 HKC 114, 116A-F (CA), citing *CT Bowring & Co (Insurance) Ltd v Corsi & Partners Ltd* [1994] 2 Lloyd's Rep 567; and see *Policyd S A de CV v Kwan Kim Hung* HCA 11225/1997 (Suffiad J; 09.12.1998) where the court refused to order security for costs against a plaintiff who was defending a counterclaim.

Where a claim and a counterclaim raise the same issues, so that the dispute will proceed to trial whether or not the plaintiff is ordered to give security for costs, the court may in the exercise of its discretion refuse an application for security: see *Wison (Shanghai) Chemical Eng'g Co Ltd v Simmons & Simmons* [2008] 2 HKC 399 referring to *BJ Crabtree (Insulation) Ltd v GPT Communication Systems Ltd* (1990) 59 BLR 43 (CA). See also *Hung Fung Enterprises Holdings Ltd & Anor v Agricultural Bank of China* HCA 16459/1998 (Fung J; 10.07.2009).

### [23.1.18]    Where order for security would 'stifle a genuine claim'

As a general rule, an impecunious party will not be ordered to pay security for costs to such an extent as would prevent him from litigating the proceedings: see *Chian Ker Chi Paul v Super Zone Investment Ltd & Anor* [1994] 2 HKC 679. This is a matter of settled practice but has been varied by statute in the case of impecunious corporate plaintiffs which may now, as a matter of discretion, be ordered to post security for costs despite impecuniosity, under s 357 of the Companies Ordinance (Cap 32). See the discussion on companies above, and see *GFN SA & Anor v Liquidators of Bancredit Cayman Ltd* [2009] UKPC 39 (04.11.2009) (para 9), concerning an almost identical provision of Cayman Islands law.

In *Chian Ker Chi Paul* (above), the Hong Kong court overturned an order for security for costs against a non-resident plaintiff where, on account of the plaintiff's lack of funds, the effect of the order might be to 'stifle a genuine claim' (at 682B) and to prevent the plaintiff 'from getting anywhere near to the door of the court in order to present his case' (at 682D). The learned judge made his decision without consideration of the details of the claim, holding that it would be inappropriate to do so. In his judgment Kaplan J gave considerable emphasis to the fact that the plaintiff had originally commenced his claim in the Labour Tribunal where legal representation is not permitted and security for costs may not be ordered. It was only because of an order to transfer the proceedings to the Court of First Instance that the application for security could be made. In relation to companies, see *Wing Hing Provision, Wine & Spirits Trading Co Ltd v Hanjin Shipping Co Ltd* [1998] 4 HKC 461 where the Court of Appeal upheld a judge's exercise of discretion in refusing to order security for costs against an impecunious company. The evidence showed that the plaintiff company was extremely unlikely to be able to raise money with the risk that an order for security for costs would stifle its claim. In that case the relevant principles were set out in the form of a checklist, borrowed from the judgment of Peter Gibson LJ in *Keary Developments Ltd v Tarmac Construction Ltd & Anor* [1995] 3 All ER 534: This very useful checklist reads as follows: (at [1998] 4 HKC 461, 464B–F):

1.      The court has a complete discretion whether to order security, and accordingly it will act in the light of all the relevant circumstances.

2.      The possibility or probability that the plaintiff company will be deterred from pursuing- its claim by an order for security is not without more a sufficient reason for not ordering security.

3.      The court must carry out a balancing exercise. On the one hand it must weigh the injustice to the plaintiff if prevented from pursuing a proper claim by an order for security. Against that, it must weigh the injustice to the defendant if no security is ordered and the defendant finds himself unable to recover costs from the plaintiff in due course.

4.      In considering all the circumstances, the court will have regard to the plaintiff company's prospects of success. But it should not go into the merits in detail unless it can clearly be demonstrated that there is a high degree of probability of success or failure.

5.      The court may order any amount up to the full amount claimed by way of security, provided that it is more than a simply nominal sum; it is not bound to order a substantial amount.

6.      Before refusing to order security on the ground that it would unfairly stifle a valid claim, the court must be satisfied that, in all the circumstances, it is probable that the claim would be stifled. There may be cases where this can properly be inferred without direct evidence. The court should consider not only whether the plaintiff company can provide security out of its own resources to continue the litigation, but also whether it can raise the amount needed from its directors, shareholders or other backers or interested parties. It is for the plaintiff to satisfy the court that it would be prevented by an order for security from continuing the litigation.

As suggested by the final paragraph in the above quotation, where an impecunious company submits that a genuine claim would be stifled by an order for security for costs, the court may have regard to the company's ability to raise funds from its backers. This point was made in *Dragages et Travaux Public v Hong Kong Chinese Insurance Co Ltd & Ors* [1993] 1 HKC 617 where Kaplan J asked, rhetorically (at 621H-I):

> If in the past [those behind the company] have made funds available to the company, why should it be assumed that they will not find funds for security if failure to do so would prevent the claim from proceeding?

Thus in *Million Top Int'l Development Ltd v Persil Development Ltd* [1997] 4 HKC 392 security was ordered where the company's own evidence was that its holding companies would back it financially. And in *Smarking Int'l Ltd v Lau Chi Keung George & Ors* [1999] 4 HKC 669, 673H-I, security was ordered where there was no evidence that the company could not continue to raise money from outside sources such as shareholders or directors.

It is clear from the cases mentioned above that the onus is on the impecunious company to demonstrate that it would not be able to raise funds from its backers. This point was made directly in *Dae Boong Int'l Co Pty Ltd v Gray* [2009] NSWCA 11 where it was said that 'where a company resists an order for security on the ground that the order would stultify litigation, that company does have the onus to show that persons who stand behind it, and who would benefit from the litigation if it is successful, are without means.'

#### [23.1.19] Security for costs against legally aided party

It is theoretically possible for the court to order security for costs against a legally aided party. Section 18B of the Legal Aid Ordinance (Cap 91), which provides that the Director may provide security ordered against an aided person 'clearly contemplates that an order for security for costs may be made against an aided person': *Lauria v Le Salon Orient (HK) Ltd & Anor* [1996] 3 HKC 157, 164B. However, in most instances where an order for security for costs might be appropriate, such as where the aided person is plaintiff or appellant, the Director is, under section 16C of the Legal Aid Ordinance liable to pay any costs ordered against the aided person. It follows that an order for security should not be necessary since the aided person 'is in the same position as any other appellant who is backed by financial resources': *Li Hing Wan v Fung Chi Wah* [1986] HKC 333, 335 (CA). Thus it would 'rarely be just in all the circumstances for an order for security for costs to be made if the only costs are those covered by the certificate since if the plaintiff were unsuccessful, those costs would be met out of the fund': *Lauria* (above, at 164D–E).

#### [23.1.20] Consideration of the merits on application for security for costs

The merits of the case may be relevant on an application for security for costs. For example, where a party seeks to resist an application for security for costs on the grounds that it would be unable to pay and the effect of the order would be to stifle a genuine claim, the court will normally wish to look into the genuineness of the claim. In considering the merits, the court should confine itself to the party's case as pleaded and not what it might be if amended: *Mak Shiu Tong v Yue Kwok Ying & Anor* (2004) 7 HKCFAR 228; [2005] 1 HKLRD 33.

Detailed examination of the merits is not normally desirable on an application for security for costs, especially where there are disputed issues of fact which the court cannot be expected to resolve on affidavit evidence. See *DEX Asia Ltd v DBS Bank (HK) Ltd & Anor* CACV 245/2007 (Cheung JA & Chung J; 06.12.2007) (para 27) and *Ironwood Capital Ltd v KTH Capital Management Ltd* HCA 2836/2004 (Suffiad J; 16.05.2008) (para 36), both referring to *Porzelack KG v Porzelack (UK) Ltd* [1987] 1 WLR 420, 423.

In *Chian Ker Chi Paul v Super Zone Investment Ltd & Anor* [1994] 2 HKC 679, Kaplan J declined to consider the merits and set aside an order for security where the proceedings had originally been commenced in the Labour Tribunal, where legal representation is not permitted and security for costs may not be ordered.

There are cases in which the court has refused to order a non-resident plaintiff to post security for costs, even where such an order would not be stifling, on the grounds of the strength of the claim. See, for example, *Chen Kang Huang Michael v Peter Lit Ma* HCA 218/2005 (Deputy Judge Carlson; 20.07.2006) and *Liao Fu Pin v*

*Ad-Magnetics Co Ltd* HCA 1778/2006 (Fung J; 26.04.2007). In *Shantou Xinyuan Trading Co Ltd v China Medical & Bio Science Ltd* HCCW 198/2008 (Kwan J; 24.10.2008) an application for security for costs was successfully opposed solely on the ground of high probability of success.

**[23.1.21]   Quantum of security for costs**
The quantum of security for costs is a matter within the discretion of the court. The court cannot exercise its discretion in a vacuum, and the party applying for security is expected to put forward a figure and to justify it. In *Dr Pete Fashions Co Ltd v C&C Textiles Corp* HCA 6733/1995 (Jerome Chan J; 29.08.1996) (upheld on appeal: see CACV 188/1996) it was said (para 13):

> It is for the applicant in an application for security for costs to place materials before the court to enable the court to come to a view on the quantum to be ordered as security. If the applicant fails to discharge this obligation, no amount can be ordered notwithstanding that a right for security has been established.

It is common practice for the party applying for security to put forward a skeleton bill of costs with itemised estimates of solicitors' time and disbursements such as counsel's fees. A full bill of costs in taxable form is inappropriate since it is 'not the function of the court on an application for security for costs to assume the role of a taxing master and to embark upon detailed analysis and examination of the costs': *Big Island Construction (HK) Ltd v Wu Yi Dev't Co Ltd & Anor* HCA 1957/2005 (Chu J; 26.10.2007) (para 46).

The quantum of security should normally be calculated on the party and party basis: *Herman Iskandar v Bonardy Leo* CACV 117/1987 (Silke VP; 28.09.1987). The hourly rates for solicitors' time advised by the Law Society (see the commentary under Order 62 rule 21) will normally be adopted as a guideline: *Cal-Trade Pte Ltd v Mindo Commodity Trading Co Ltd* [1989] 2 HKC 112, 117I-8D (CA). The wording of rule 1 does not restrict quantum to future costs, and there are many cases in which the quantum of security ordered takes into account costs already incurred. See *Procon (GB) Ltd v Provincial Building Co Ltd* [1984] 1 WLR 557 (CA) as an example. Where security is claimed in respect of both past and future costs the skeleton bill particularising the amount claimed should clearly differentiate between the two: *Bestway Inflatables & Material Corp v Greyland Trading Ltd* HCA 3709/2002 (Deputy Judge Poon; 02.08.2004).

The substantive issues between the parties are relevant to the question of quantum of security to the extent that they are an indication of the complexity or difficulty of the case: *Cal-Trade* (above, 115H).

Some authorities suggest there is a practice whereby the court will, after deciding on a likely quantum, apply a discount of about one-third. However in *Sujanani v Middle East Finance Int'l Ltd* [1985] 2 HKC 226 (CA) it was held that there should be no automatic discount as a matter of practice. Instead the court may 'make allowance for the normal processes of taxation' by which the receiving party's claim is rarely allowed in full. Quantum may be reduced to avoid oppression: *Dragages et Travaux Public v Hong Kong Chinese Insurance Co Ltd* [1993] 1 HKC 617, 623G-624B). There the court quoted from *Innovare Displays plc v Corporate Broking Services Ltd* [1991] BCC 174 where it was said that 'sufficient' security within the English equivalent of s 357 of the Companies Ordinance is not necessarily 'complete' security, but an amount which in all the circumstances of the case is just. Quantum may also be reduced to reflect the prospect of early settlement: *Procon* (above, at 567B-D).

As with most exercises of discretion, the Court of Appeal will be slow to interfere with a decision on quantum of security for costs. However it will do so where the amount ordered is far too high. In *Procon* (above, at 559E) it was said the question to be asked is:

> . . . whether on the facts the security ordered by the judge was too much, on the ground that he did not take a sufficiently cautious view in order to protect the party against whom security was ordered, from the oppression of meeting security likely or liable to exceed the costs which the party seeking security had incurred or was likely to incur, when taxed on a party and party basis.

The above passage was quoted in *Cal-Trade* (above) where the Hong Kong Court of Appeal was of the view that the quantum of security ordered by the judge was 'much too high', and reduced it by more than 50%.

As a matter of principle, pre-action costs, such as the costs of pre-action mediation, may be the subject of an application for security: *Lobster Group Ltd v Heidelberg Graphic Equipment Ltd* [2008] EWHC (TCC); [2008] 2 All ER 1173. This follows from the fact that such costs may in certain circumstances be recoverable as costs 'incidental' to legal proceedings: see the commentary under Order 62 rule 28. In the *Lobster Group* case the English court cautioned (para 12) that it should be slow to exercise its discretion in favour of such an application. Further, the greater the distance in time between the costs being incurred and the commencement of proceedings, the greater the likelihood the paying party would have grounds to resist liability, and hence the stronger the argument that the court should not order security.

## [23.1.22]   Further security

An order for security for costs will normally be in respect of the costs up to a specified stage of the action, such as the completion of discovery, with leave to apply for further security thereafter.

In *Lessy SARL v Pacific Star Development Ltd* [1997] 3 HKC 306 (CA) an order for security for costs provided that any application for further security must be made within a specified time. The Court of Appeal doubted the jurisdiction to impose a time limit but granted an extension of time.

In *Re Max Share Ltd* HCCW 321/1996 (Yuen J; 09.09.1999) an application for further security made on the 6th day of a 12 day hearing was dismissed on the ground it was made 'far too late' – the 'due administration of justice' required the court to proceed with the substantive hearing. However in *Natuzzi SPA v Decoro Ltd* HCA 1702/2001 (Lam J; 24.07.2006) the court granted further security during a break in a trial which had been adjourned part-heard, noting that earlier orders contemplated applications for further security and that there had been changes of circumstances.

## [23.1.23]   Fresh application or appeal

Any party dissatisfied with an order made by a master on an application for security for costs may appeal to a single judge under Order 58. On such an appeal the single judge has full power to exercise the master's discretion on all questions including the quantum of security: *Million Top Int'l Development Ltd v Persil Development Ltd* [1997] 4 HKC 392.

Where an application for security for costs has been refused, the applicant may later bring a fresh application on the basis of change of circumstances: *Skytruck Int'l Holdings Ltd v Lau Nai Keung* [2005] 2 HKC 620.

The fact that an action is stayed for failure of a party to provide security for costs within the time prescribed is not a bar to an appeal against the order: see *Lam Fei Hong v Wong Kam Fong & Ors* [1999] 2 HKC 781. Otherwise 'there could never be an appeal from an order for a stay unless the order expressly permitted it' (per Keith J at 783G–H).

### [23.1.24]   Payment out of court following judgment
See the commentary under Order 22A rule 1 as to the circumstances in which the court will order payment out of security for costs following judgment.

**2.     Manner of giving security** (O. 23 r. 2)
**Where an order is made requiring any party to give security for costs, the security shall be given in such manner, at such time, and on such terms (if any) as the Court may direct.**

---

## NOTES

### [23.2.1]   Form of security
Order 23 rule 2 provides the court with a discretion as to the form of security for costs. The usual order is for payment into court. However the parties may request or agree some other form of security such as a bank guarantee. The court may direct that such a guarantee be subject to approval of the registrar as in *Oldham, Li & Nie v Wong Lin Chooi* CACV 319/2005 (Tang JA; 08.11.2005). There is no practical difference between security in the form of payment into court and security by way of bank guarantee. Thus the court will readily allow variation of the mode by which security is given: *Wing Fai Construction Co Ltd v Fitzroya Finance Co Ltd* [2006] 1 HKC 272.

Security may also take the form of a solicitor's undertaking. This will be appropriate where the parties reach agreement without formal application for an order for security.

**3.     Saving for enactments** (O. 23 r. 3)
**This Order is without prejudice to the provisions of any written law which empowers the Court to require security to be given for the costs of any proceedings.**
**(Enacted 1988)**

## ORDER 24

### DISCOVERY AND INSPECTION OF DOCUMENTS

**1.      Mutual discovery of documents** (O. 24 r. 1)

**(1)    After the close of pleadings in an action begun by writ there shall, subject to and in accordance with the provisions of this Order, be discovery by the parties to the action of the documents which are or have been in their possession, custody or power relating to matters in question in the action.**

**(2)    Nothing in this Order shall be taken as preventing the parties to an action agreeing to dispense with or limit the discovery of documents which they would otherwise be required to make to each other.**

-------------------

### NOTES

**[24.1.1]    Comparison with English rules**
Order 24 is taken from the Order of the same number in the former English Rules of the Supreme Court. The Order was replaced in England with CPR Part 31, together with a practice direction, in 1999. Under the CPR, discovery of documents is referred to as 'disclosure' of documents.

**[24.1.2]    Discovery of documents**
Discovery of documents by means of mutual service of lists of documents, followed by inspection or provision of copies, follows the close of pleadings in most actions commenced by writ of summons. See Order 24 rule 2 and the commentary thereunder. In other types of proceedings, the court may have a discretion to order discovery of documents in suitable cases.

**[24.1.3]    Limitation on scope of discovery – Deferment of discovery as to damages in intellectual property and other split trial cases**
Order 24 rule 1(2) permits the parties by agreement to limit the scope of discovery. See also rule 2(5) and (6) and rule 15A, which permit the court so to order. Discovery relating to damages may be deferred until issues of liability have been decided: *Auto-Treasure v Noble Diamond Ltd* [1992] 1 HKC 117 (CA), citing *Fennessy v Clark* (1888) 37 Ch D 184. This will be appropriate in cases like *Auto-Treasure* concerning breach of copyright where the court determines issues of liability before considering quantum. In *Nintendo Co Ltd & Anor v Supreme Factory Ltd & Ors* [2008] 2 HKC 129 (para 4) it was said of discovery in intellectual property cases:

> Only necessary discovery should be given before trial. That is discovery necessary for determination of the issues in the trial on liability. What is necessary in an intellectual property case is that each type of alleged infringement should have one example particularised in the pleadings. Discovery needs to be given in relation to that. The court can then decide whether the instance particularised is an infringement or not. The court has to decide whether the plaintiff has the rights its claims, and it has to decide whether or not each instance particularised is an infringement.

> It is only when that has been decided at the trial on liability that it is necessary to go

into reams and reams of documents which go to how many other similar things a
defendant has done which have constituted infringements. So the vast amount of
discovery which is often thought to be necessary is totally unnecessary and should
never be ordered until after trial. It is relevant for the inquiry as to damages. It is
not relevant for the trial on liability.

In other cases it will similarly be appropriate to defer discovery in relation to damages
if a split trial has been ordered: *Sinocard Technology Ltd v Lee Chi Keung* HCA 2022/
2005 (Master J Wong; 04.01.2008).

### [24.1.4]    Agreement to dispense with or limit discovery

Order 24 rule 1(2) expressly provides that the parties may by agreement dispense with
or limit the scope of discovery of documents. Such an agreement will be appropriate if
the result would be a saving of costs. See *Wong Tsu Yew Charles v Bermuda Trust
(HK) Ltd* [2002] 4 HKC 196, 200H-I, quoting *Sveriges Angfartygs Assurans Forening
v The 1976 Eagle Insurance Co SA* (English QBD; 28.03.1990) where it was said that
although in general a disciplined approach to the procedures prescribed by the rules is
more efficient, expeditious and economical, 'there may be cases where costs can be
saved by adopting a flexible and fairly informal approach to discovery'.

With regard to limiting the scope of discovery by order of the court, see rule
2(5)&(6), and rule 15A, and the commentary concerning them.

### [24.1.5]    Electronic and other non-paper 'documents'

It is clear that for the purpose of discovery of documents in civil proceedings,
'document', as used in Order 24 includes not just paper documents but other means of
storing information. In *Grant v Southwestern & County Properties Ltd* [1975] 1 Ch 185
it was held that a tape recording was a document, and in *Senior v Holdsworth* [1976] 1
QB 23 (CA), television film. Computer files and e-mails were treated as documents in
*CSAV Group (HK) Ltd v Safdar* CACV 55/2007 (Le Pichon JA & Sakhrani J;
31.05.2007) (leave to appeal to the CFA refused: FAMV 52/2007).

In England CPR 31.4 now defines 'document' to mean 'anything in which
information of any description is recorded'. CPR PD 2A.1 elaborates as follows:

> Rule 31.4 contains a broad definition of a document. This extends to electronic documents,
> including e-mail and other electronic communications, word processed documents and
> databases. In addition to documents that are readily accessible from computer systems and
> other electronic devices and media, the definition covers those documents that are stored on
> servers and back-up systems and electronic documents that have been 'deleted'. It also
> extends to additional information stored and associated with electronic documents known
> as metadata.

Insofar as that definition is a legislative expression of what had been decided in pre-
CPR cases it will be of assistance in Hong Kong, though the definition itself has not
been adopted in this jurisdiction.

### [24.1.6]    Other remedies for inspection of documents Anton Piller order

See the commentary under Order 29 for discussion of the *Anton Piller* order as a
means of obtaining discovery without prior notice where there is a risk evidence will
be destroyed.

**[24.1.7]    Inspection of bank records**

Section 21 of the Evidence Ordinance (Cap 8) gives the court a discretion to order that a party be at liberty to inspect and take copies of any entries in a banker's record for the purpose of legal proceedings. Such records are admissible under section 20 of the Ordinance.

An order for disclosure may include a provision restraining the bank from informing its customer: *Banco Ambrosiano Andino SA v BNP* [1985] HKLR 72.

Section 2 of the Evidence Ordinance defines 'banker's record' so as to include any document or record used in the ordinary course of a bank's business. It has been observed that this definition is much wider than that of 'banker's books' in the equivalent UK legislation (Bankers' Books Evidence Act 1879). See *R v Keung Cam-yuen* [1986] HKLR 916, 919. It was there held (at 920) that the Hong Kong definition is not confined to 'ledger sheets' but extends to any letter, telex, commercial invoice or bill of lading which a bank has retained in the course of business.

In *ITP Systems NV v Reichenback & Anor* [1985] 2 HKC 148, 156 it was held that the discretion should be exercised in accordance with four principles which may be summarised as follows:

(1)    The section is to be applied in accordance with the normal rules for discovery.
(2)    There have to be strong grounds for suspicion almost amounting to certainty that there are items in the account material on matters in issue.
(3)    Sufficiently strong grounds may arise from proven criminality or the need to trace money arising from fault, misappropriation or breach of trust.
(4)    It is too wide and sweeping a contention to assert that when granting the application it is open to the court to make any order necessary to ensure justice.

**[24.1.8]    Criteria applicable on application for inspection of bank records**

On an application under section 21 of Cap 8 for inspection of bank records 'it must be shown that there is a probability that the account will contain materials germane to an issue to be tried . . . In short the issue is one of relevance': *Chan Wai Sun & Anor v Law Shiu Kai Andrew* [2004] 1 HKC 180, 183C-E. The court will not allow the provision to be used for a fishing expedition going beyond normal discovery: *Assets Investments PT Ltd v The United Islamic Investments Foundation & Ors* HCA 4392/1993 (Barnett J; 21.01.1994) citing *Williams v Summerfield* [1972] 2 QB 512. The power should be exercised 'with great caution' and only where it is established that the account is that of a party to the proceedings 'or that the party is so closely connected with it that it would be evidence against him': *Chan Wai Sun* (above) at 183B, citing *South Staffordshire Tramways Co v Ebbsmith* [1895] 2 QB 669.

It has been held that as with an application under Order 24 rule 13, a party seeking an order under section 21 of Cap 8 must show that the order is necessary either for disposing fairly of the cause or matter or for saving costs. See *Re Wong The Huei (deceased)* [2002] 3 HKC 312 citing *Macmillan Inc v Bishopsgate Investment Trust plc* [1993] 1 WLR 1372 (CA).

**[24.1.9]    Procedure on application for inspection of bank records**

An application under section 21 of Cap 8 for inspection of bank records may be made *ex parte* if necessary on account of time constraints or the need for secrecy. See *Assets Investment PT Ltd v The United Islamic Investments Foundation & Ors*

HCA 4392/1993 (Barnett J; 21.01.1994). In *Chan Wai Sun* [2004] 1 HKC 180 the application was made *inter partes* and the bank was served but not the account holder. The court made the order, noting that information about the account holder such as its place of incorporation and the identity of those behind it would not be available unless and until the order was made.

Section 20(2) of the Evidence Ordinance provides that the application must be brought before a judge.

The bank being an innocent party would normally expect to have its costs (including the costs of complying with the order) paid. In *Chan Wai Sun* [2004] 1 HKC 180 the party applying for the order was required to pay the bank's costs in the first instance. It was understood such costs might be recoverable as a disbursement if there were eventually an *inter partes* costs order in favour of the applicant.

**[24.1.10]    Company records**
There are common law and statutory rights enabling shareholders, directors and in some instances members of the public to inspect the records of a company. With regard to the common law right of a director to inspect the company's documents, see the concise statement of the relevant legal principles in *Ng Yu Wah v Lam Chun Wah* HCMP 4616/2001 (Kwan J; 28.06.2005) (para 29).

The right of a director to inspect company documents is not lost by appointment of provisional liquidators: *Re Gold Pleasure Industrial Co Ltd* [2006] 4 HKC 398. For discussion of the manner in which the court will grant assistance to a director seeking to exercise the  right to inspect the company's books, see *Ling Yun Sang v Chan Hak Kong* HCA 3347/1985 (Deputy Judge Barnett; 12.06.1985), *Re Armour Insurance Co Ltd* [1990] 2 HKC 227 (CA) and *Ho Pui Tin Terence v Wah Nam Group Ltd* [2006] 3 HKC 40.

Relevant provisions of the Companies Ordinance (Cap 32) concerning inspection of company records include section 90 (mortgages and charges), 98 (register of members), 120 (minute books), 121 and 124 (accounts) and 221 (power to order production of books and papers of a company). With regard to section 121, see *Cornforth v Alvarez & Marsal Asia Ltd* [2009] 3 HKC 41 (CA), and for section 221 see *Re New China HK Group Ltd (in liq)* [2003] 3 HKC 252, *Joint & Several Liquidators of Kong Wah Holdings Ltd v Grande Holdings Ltd* [2007] 1 HKLRD 116 (CFA) and *Re Nardu Co Ltd (in liq)* [2008] 3 HKC 381.

As a general rule, a company may not assert privilege to resist disclosure to its own shareholders: *Re NDT (BVI) Trading Ltd* [2009] 2 HKLRD 409 (para 14). However legal professional privilege may be asserted when the company is in hostile litigation with its own shareholders: *NDT (loc cit)*. In *Akai Holdings Ltd (in liq) v Ernst & Young* [2009] 2 HKC 245 (CFA) it was held that transcripts and notes of private examinations and interviews conducted pursuant to (or under threat of) section 221 were susceptible to a claim of privilege.

**[24.1.11]    The Norwich Pharmacal case – disclosure of identity of tortfeasor**
In the landmark case of *Norwich Pharmacal v Customs & Excise Commissioners* [1974] AC 133 the House of Lords held that a party seeking relief in tort, who is unable to identify the potential defendant, may bring action against a stranger who has knowledge of the identity of the tortfeasor, for disclosure thereof. For discussion of the

manner in which the court should exercise its discretion to make a *Norwich Pharmacal* order and the characteristics thereof, including the manner in which the Hong Kong courts have approached this jurisdiction, see additionally the commentary under Order 15 rule 4.

**[24.1.12]     The Norwich Pharmacal case – as extended**

It is now clear that the principles laid down by the House of Lords in *Norwich Pharmacal* have been extended beyond disclosure of identity of a tortfeasor who is a potential defendant. See *Radio Corporation of America v Reddington's Rare Records* [1975] RPC 95; *Bankers Trust Co v Shapira* [1980] 1 WLR 1274; *Yew Seng Computer (HK) Ltd v Computerland Corp* [1986] HKLR 283 (CA); and *Philip Lawrence Choy v Nissei Sangyo America Ltd* [1992] 2 HKLR 177.

In particular, *Norwich Pharmacal* discovery now extends to disclosure of information. As stated by Le Pichon J in *Re Greater Beijing Region Expressways Ltd (No 2)* [2000] 2 HKC 118, 129G:

> *Norwich Pharmacal* is not limited to pure identity: information may be obtained and used in appropriate cases. See per Cons JA in *Yew Seng Computer (HK) Ltd v Computerland Corp* [1986] HKLR 283 at 286D–E. So the fact that the identity of the wrongdoer is known is not necessarily a bar to the application of the principle.

In the *Greater Beijing* case Le Pichon J ordered disclosure of information which could not be obtained from any other source in order to assist the applicant in making an informed decision in the context of winding-up proceedings.

It is not necessary that the information sought to be obtained from the innocent party is relevant to an issue in *existing* proceedings: see the *Greater Beijing* case at 129H–I, citing *P v T Ltd* [1997] 1 WLR 1309 and *British Steel Corp v Granada Television Ltd* [1981] AC 1096.

See also *Sabah Shipyard Sendirian Bhd v SP P'ng & Co Certified Public Accountants & Macfarlance Ltd* HCMP 415/2009 (Deputy Judge Carlson; 04.11.2009 where a *Norwich Pharmacal* order was made for disclosure of information to assist in enforcement of a BVI court judgment. And see *Secretary for Justice v Cheung Kwok Kuen & Anor* HCMP 55/2000 (Lugar-Mawson J; 26.04.2000) where it was held that the court had jurisdiction to order disclosure of information regarding the proceeds of crime which the government sought to seize.

For discussion on the question whether the use of information obtained under a *Norwich Pharmacal* order is subject to restriction, see the commentary under Order 15 rule 4.

**[24.1.13]     Other forms of discovery against strangers**

In addition to the *Norwich Pharmacal* principles there are some other circumstances in which discovery may be ordered against a stranger. In the context of personal injuries claims, discovery may be ordered under section 42 of the High Court Ordinance and Order 24 rule 7A. See the commentary under that rule. It may also be possible to obtain discovery against someone who, although in form not a party, is in substance taking part in the proceedings. See *The SS Claus Rickmers* (1937) 29 HKLR 2, referring to *James Nelson & Sons Ltd v Nelson Line (Liverpool) Ltd* [1906] 2 KB 217. The definition of 'party' in section 2 of the High Court Ordinance is relevant in this context.

**[24.1.14]    Discovery in aid of foreign proceedings**
Part VIII of the Evidence Ordinance (Cap 8) and Order 70 of these rules empower the court to order discovery in aid of proceedings in another jurisdiction. See the commentary under Order 70 rule 1.

**[24.1.15]    Discovery in representative proceedings**
The represented parties in representative proceedings under Order 15 rule 12 are not themselves parties, and there is no general power to order them, or the person representing them, to make discovery of their documents: *Ventouris v Mountain* [1990] 1 WLR 1370.

**[24.1.16]    Trade unions**
As to the inspection of the account books and registers of registered trade unions by members, see sections 36 and 37(1) of the Trade Unions Ordinance (Cap 332).

**[24.1.17]    Trusts**
Beneficiaries of a trust are entitled to disclosure by the trustee, and privilege may not be asserted save where the parties are in hostile litigation: *Re NDT (BVI) Trading Ltd* [2009] 2 HKLRD 409 (para 14). See also *McKay v Rysaffe Ltd & Ors* [1983] 2 HKC 436 referring to the right of a beneficiary to disclosure of documents in which a proprietary interest, as defined in *Re Londonderry's Settlement* [1965] Ch 918, is claimed.

**2.      Discovery by parties without order** (O. 24 r. 2)
      **(1)    Subject to the provisions of this rule and of rule 4, the parties to an action between whom pleadings are closed must make discovery by exchanging lists of documents and, accordingly, each party must, within 14 days after the pleadings in the action are deemed to be closed as between him and any other party, make and serve on that other party a list of the documents which are or have been in his possession, custody or power relating to any matter in question between them in the action.**
      **Without prejudice to any directions given by the Court under Order 16, rule 4, this paragraph shall not apply in third party proceedings, including proceedings under that Order involving fourth or subsequent parties.**
      **(2)    Unless the Court otherwise orders, a defendant to an action arising out of an accident on land due to a collision or apprehended collision involving a vehicle shall not make discovery of any documents to the plaintiff under paragraph (1).**
      **(3)    Paragraph (1) shall not be taken as requiring a defendant to an action for the recovery of any penalty recoverable by virtue of any written law to make discovery of any documents.**
      **(4)    Paragraphs (2) and (3) shall apply in relation to a counterclaim as they apply in relation to an action but with the substitution, for the reference in paragraph (2) to the plaintiff, of a reference to the party making the counterclaim.**
      **(5)    On the application of any party required by this rule to make discovery of documents, the Court may—**

    **(a)**    **order that the parties to the action or any of them shall make discovery under paragraph (1) of such documents or classes of documents only, or as to such only of the matters in question, as may be specified in the order, or**

    **(b)**    **if satisfied that discovery by all or any of the parties is not necessary, or not necessary at that stage of the action, order that there shall be no discovery of documents by any or all of the parties either at all or at that stage;**

**and the Court shall make such an order if and so far as it is of opinion that discovery is not necessary either for disposing fairly of the action or for saving costs.**

    **(6)**  **An application for an order under paragraph (5) must be by summons, and the summons must be taken out before the expiration of the period within which by virtue of this rule discovery of documents in the action is required to be made.**

    **(7)**  **Any party to whom discovery of documents is required to be made under this rule may, at any time before the case management summons in the action is taken out, serve on the party required to make such discovery a notice requiring him to make an affidavit verifying the list he is required to make under paragraph (1), and the party on whom such a notice is served must, within 14 days after service of the notice, make and file an affidavit in compliance with the notice and serve a copy of the affidavit on the party by whom the notice was served. (L.N. 152 of 2008)**

---

## NOTES

### [24.2.1]    Automatic discovery of documents

Order 24 rule 2 provides for automatic discovery of documents by means of service, by each party on the other, of lists of documents. Discovery under the rule is automatic in the sense that no order is required. The practice direction on case management, which took effect when the civil justice reforms came into force in 2009, expressly provides that the parties should proceed with discovery without the need to wait for an order of the court.

The rule applies only to the parties to an 'action', which is defined in section 2 of the High Court Ordinance to mean civil proceedings commenced by writ of summons 'or in such other manner as may be prescribed by any law'. Although the quoted words suggest that there may be such a thing as an action commenced by an originating process other than a writ of summons, this is not taken as meaning that rule 2 extends to proceedings commenced by originating summons, petition or originating motion. In such proceedings discovery is considered to be available only on application to the court for an appropriate order.

The obligation is on the 'parties' to make discovery. The definition of the word 'party' in section 2 of the High Court Ordinance is broad, extending beyond named plaintiffs and defendants. In practice, however, the obligation to make automatic discovery is confined to the named parties as it is only as between them there is likely to be any 'matter in question' as required by rule 2(1). Discovery against others is available in some circumstances, discussed elsewhere in this commentary, on application to the court for an order.

## [24.2.2]    Lists of documents

As to the form of lists of documents and the manner in which documents are to be listed therein, see Order 24 rule 5 and the commentary thereunder.

## [24.2.3]    Time for filing and service of lists of documents

Order 24 rule 2 provides that lists of documents are to be served within 14 days after the close of pleadings. As to calculation of the time at which pleadings close see Order 18 rule 20.

Prior to the implementation of the civil justice reforms in April 2009, it was common for parties to wait until a later stage to make discovery, and to seek directions in that regard in the summons for directions. Now it is specifically provided in the case management practice direction (PD 5.2) para 5 that the parties should proceed to discovery without waiting for an order of the court.

Order 24 rule 2 does not require that lists of documents be filed in court. Practice direction 24.1, para 9 makes it clear that unless the court has directed that the lists be filed, it is not necessary to do so, and it is sufficient only to serve them.

## [24.2.4]    Supplemental lists of documents

Frequently parties find that their lists of documents need to be supplemented. Additional documents may come to light, or may become relevant as issues are refined. The rules do not make any provision to cover these circumstances but clearly discovery is required if a party wishes to rely on additional documents at trial and it is in practice accepted that this may be done by means of supplemental list of documents. This was recognised in *Hong Lok School Ltd v Chow Sai Yiu* [2003] 2 HKLRD 782 (para 4) where it was said that discovery 'is a continuing obligation and supplemental lists of documents have to be filed from time to time to fulfil such obligation'.

## [24.2.5]    Affidavit required to explain last minute supplemental list

It has been held that where a party wishes to rely on documents which are disclosed only shortly before trial, an explanatory affidavit should be made. See *Hong Lok School Ltd* (above, para 6) where it was said:

> . . . it behoves a litigant giving discovery at the eleventh hour . . . to provide the court and the other side with full and accurate information at least as to the following to enable the court to exercise its discretion properly in dealing with possible objections from his opponents:
>
> (a)    the reasons why these documents were not disclosed earlier;
>
> (b)    the provenance and the makers of these documents;
>
> (c)    the relevance of these documents to the issues before the court;
>
> (d)    the availability or non-availability of the makers to attend trial for cross-examination in case his opponents make an application under section 48 [of the Evidence Ordinance (Cap 8) – power to make an order for cross-examination of the maker of a hearsay statement – see also Order 38 rule 21].

The judgment in *Hong Lok School* has been adopted in a number of other judgments, including four of Judge Ng in the district court: *Yeung Chung Wai v St Paul's Hospital* DCEO 7/2003 (24.102005), *Kai Hon Electroplate (Shenzhen) Co Ltd v Marble Watch Manufacturing Ltd* DCCJ 2192/1999 (12.06.2006), *Leung Suet Ha v Lo Ki Ling* DCCJ 309/2005 (12.02.2007) and *Headwin Eng'g Ltd v United Soundfair Eng'g Co Ltd* [2008] 1 HKC 369.

With regard to late interlocutory applications generally, see the commentary under Order 32 rule 11A.

### [24.2.6]    Duty to disclose subsequent developments

Because the obligation to make discovery of documents is ongoing, a party has a duty to disclose developments, adverse to his own case, which occur after the normal discovery process. In *Vernon v Bosley* [1997] 1 All ER 614 (CA) failure to disclose documents showing that a party's expert witnesses had given different evidence on the party's condition in other legal proceedings resulted in an action being re-opened after trial.

### [24.2.7]    Inspection of documents

The service of lists of documents leads to a right to inspect. See Order 24 rule 9 and the notice to inspect included in the form of list of documents. Since the advent of the photocopy machine, parties often dispense with inspection of originals, and simply request copies under rule 11A.

### [24.2.8]    'Documents which are or have been in his possession, custody or power'

Discovery of documents under Order 24 rule 2 is limited to documents which are in the 'possession, custody or power' of a party. The meaning of that phrase was explained concisely in *B v B* [1978] Fam 181, 186D-E; [1979] 1 All ER 801, 805h-j as follows:

> For this purpose 'possession' means, the right to the possession of a document. 'Custody' means the actual, physical or corporeal holding of a document regardless of the right to its possession, for example, a holding of a document by a party as servant or agent of the true owner. 'Power' means an enforceable right to inspect the document or to obtain possession or control of the document from the person who ordinarily has it in fact. The requirements of the rules are disjunctive in their operation, so far as possession, custody and power are concerned.

A party has 'possession or power' of documents which have been entrusted to his solicitor by a witness for the purpose of the case: *Ng Yuen Hing v Lap Kee* (1908) 3 HKLR 9.

The concept of documents being in the 'power' of a party was considered in *Lonrho Ltd & Ors v Shell Petroleum Co Ltd & Ors* [1980] 1 WLR 627, 635 (HL). There Lord Diplock used language slightly different from that in the above passage from *B v B*. He said that 'power' in this context:

> ... must, in my view, mean a presently enforceable legal right to obtain from whoever actually holds the document inspection of it without the need to obtain the consent of anyone else.

*Documents accessible by data access request* - Applying the test as set out in *Lonrho* (above), it has been held that a document is not within a party's 'power' merely because a copy might be obtained under the Personal Data (Privacy) Ordinance (Cap 486): *Gotland Enterprises Ltd v Kwok Chi Yau & Ors* HCMP 4550/2003 (Deputy Judge Muttrie; 01.12.2006). The situation is the same in the Australian state of Victoria (*Theodore v Australian Postal Commission* [1988] VR 272) but different in New Zealand (*Johansen v American Int'l Underwriters (NZ) Ltd* [1997] 3 NZLR 765), both of which were considered in *Gotland.*

*Company and partnership documents* – Questions have arisen as to whether company or partnership documents must be disclosed on discovery by a party who is a director, shareholder or one of the partners. A director who is sued in a private capacity is not necessarily considered to have 'power' over company documents: see *B v B* (above, at 807) (approved without discussion in *E v E* HCMC 1057/1988 (Bokhary J; 23.06.1989)). See also Phillips, 'Family Companies' (1986) 16 HKLJ 196, 199-202. A director will not be compelled to disclose company documents against the wishes of the board of directors unless the refusal to consent is contrived: *B v B* (above, 806). In regard to application of this principle to a partnership see *Yuen v Yuen* CACV 46/1985 (Cons, Fuad & Kempster JJA; 24.05.1985). A shareholder or director who has unfettered control, or possibly, is in a position of dominance, or is the alter-ego of a company, may be required to disclose company documents: *Innovisions Ltd v Chan Sing Chuk Charles & Ors* [1992] 1 HKC 348 (CFI); CACV 55/1992 (Cons VP, Power JA & Sears J; 04.08.1992). However mere dominance is not enough. The fact that documents are owned by a party's 'sister' or 'associated' company does not of itself mean they are in the possession, custody or power of that party: *Suen Yuet Tai Ltd v BAT (HK) Ltd* CACV 95/1999 (Godfrey & Rogers JJA; 04.06.1999); *Morinda Int'l HK Ltd v Next Magazine Publishing Ltd* [2003] 1 HKC 492.

**[24.2.9]    'Relating to any matter in question between them'**
Order 24 rule 2 naturally confines the scope of discovery to documents which are relevant to the issues between the parties. The relevance test is found in the phrase 'relating to any matter in question between them'. Those words were given a broad interpretation in the classic case of *Compagnie Financiere du Pacifique v Peruvian Guano Co* (1883) 11 QBD 55 where Brett LJ held (at 63) that the court should judge relevance by reference not only to the statement of claim, but to the defence as well. Documents 'which may – not which must – either directly or indirectly enable a party . . . either to advance his own case or to damage the case of his adversary' were within the test.

The *Peruvian Guano* case has long been acknowledged as applicable in Hong Kong: see, for example, *Iqbal Hussain Khan v AG* [1974] HKLR 63, 93; *Overseas Trust Bank Ltd v Cooper & Lybrand (a firm) & Ors* HCA 5764/1986 (Godfrey J; 27.03.1990); *Man Won Co Ltd & Anor v Tay Vi Bing & Ors* HCA 2553/1989 (Bokhary J; 06.12.1991). In *Guess? Inc & Ors v Lee Seck-mon & Ors* [1989] 1 HKLR 399 the Court of Appeal quoted the following summary of the relevance test as laid down by Lord Edmund-Davies in *Air Canada v Secretary of State* [1983] 2 AC 394, 441:

> ...discovery of documents between parties to an action with pleadings ...is restricted to documents 'relating to matters in question in the action' ...any document which, it is reasonable to suppose, contains information which may enable the party applying

for discovery either to advance his own case or to damage that of his adversary, if it is a document which may fairly lead him to a train of inquiry which may have either of those two consequences, must be disclosed.

There is some subsequent authority in support of a narrower scope to discovery obligations. In *O Company v M Company* [1996] 2 Lloyd's Rep 347, 350-51 it was said that Brett LJ's formulation in *Peruvian Guano* 'was never intended to justify demands for disclosure of documents at the far end of the spectrum of materiality'. Parties should not be required 'to turn out the contents of their filing systems as if under criminal investigation merely on the off chance that something might show up'. On the contrary, it was said, the party seeking discovery must show 'a real possibility of evidential materiality in the sense that it must be a document or class of documents which in the ordinary way can be expected to yield information of substantial evidential materiality to the pleaded claim and the defence to it'. In *Robert Hitchins Ltd v International Computers Ltd* [1996] EWCA Civ 1163 (10.12.1996) *O Company* was described as a 'gloss put upon the *Peruvian Guano* approach', and in *Portman Building Society v Royal Insurance plc & Anor* [1998] EWCA Civ 150 (04.02.1998) Simon Brown LJ commented that it was 'a valuable antidote to the potentially poisonous effect' of an over-literal application of *Peruvian Guano*. However *O Company* has not gained wide currency in England, because it was shortly superseded by the Civil Procedure Rules which replaced the *Peruvian Guano* test (see below).

In Hong Kong *O Company* has found favour in a number of first instance decisions including *Tridant Eng'g Co Ltd v Paul Y-ITC (E&M) Contractors Ltd* HCCT 40/1996 (Findlay J; 19.05.1998); *Wing Fai Construction Co Ltd (in liq) v Benefit Holdings Int'l Ltd & Ors* HCA 810/2003 (Deputy Judge Saunders; 04.07.2005); *Chau Ka Chik Tso v Lam Chi Fai & Ors* HCA 10670/2000 (Deputy Judge Muttrie; 21.11.2005); *Yung Yuen Ling Alice v Wong Ming Kan Michael* HCA 231/2004 (Deputy Judge Wright; 01.12.2006) and *Chan Kwok Hong v AXA China Region Insurance Co (Bermuda) Ltd & Anor* HCA 2563/2007 (Fung J; 19.05.2009). However, in *Mariner Int'l Hotels Ltd & Ors v Atlas Ltd & Ors* HCA 10714/1998 (Burrell J; 18.01.2002) the court, while praising the sentiments in *O Company* as 'laudable', declined to apply them in 'an overly restrictive way' (para 7). And in *Chan Hung v Yung Kwong Chung* HCA 216/2004 (Deputy Judge H Wong SC; 15.01.2009) (para 29) the court doubted that it was open to the Court of First Instance to adopt the *O Company* approach given that the Hong Kong Court of Appeal had accepted *Peruvian Guano* as the appropriate test in *Deak & Co (FE) Ltd v NM Rothschild & Sons Ltd* [1981] HKC 78. Notably, there is no mention of the *O Company* line of authority in the reports which led to the 2009 civil justice reforms in Hong Kong. In fact the interim report of the Chief Justice's working party (para 406) quoted the above passages from *Peruvian Guano* as stating the test '[a]t present in Hong Kong'. In *Moulin Global Eyecare Holdings Ltd & Ors v KPMG* HCA 118/2007 (Barma J; 08.06.2010) (para 15) the parties accepted that the *O Company* approach was the correct one to adopt, and the court proceeded on that basis.

In England the *Peruvian Guano* test was replaced when the CPR came into force in 1999. There, Part 31 of the CPR provides that unless the court otherwise directs, discovery is limited to 'standard disclosure', which includes only the documents on which a party relies, and documents which adversely affect his own case, another party's case or support another party's case (CPR 31.5 and 31.6). The Chief Justice's working party on civil justice reform initially proposed replacing the *Peruvian Guano* test with the narrower discovery obligations found in the CPR Part 31. However this proposal was not adopted in the final report. At para 478 of the final report the working party expressed the view that encouragement should instead be given to use of case management powers to 'fashion a discovery regime suitable to the needs of the particular case – preferably by agreement, but otherwise by order'. In this regard note the new Order 24 rule 15A which gives the court a new express power to limit discovery. See the commentary under that rule.

Where relevance is in dispute the court is not bound to accept at face value an affirmation stating that a document is not relevant: see *Pacific Link Communications Ltd v Wong Man Him Melvyn & Anor* [1996] 1 HKC 474 (CA), citing *Jones v Monte Video Gas Co* (1880) 5 QBD 556 and *Thornett v Barclays Bank (France) Ltd* [1939] 1 KB 675.

There is no issue susceptible to discovery where, by prior agreement between the parties, facts are deemed to be final and conclusive: *HKFE Clearing Corp Ltd v Yicko Futures Ltd* [2006] 2 HKC 233 (CA).

## [24.2.10]  Interpleader proceedings
The provisions of Order 24 apply in interpleader actions: see Order 17 rule 10.

## [24.2.11]  Action for recovery of a penalty
Order 24 rule 2(3) provides that there will not be automatic discovery of documents in an action for recovery of a penalty under statute. Rule 2(4) extends this to counterclaims for such relief, with necessary modifications. See also the commentary below on the privilege against self-incrimination.

## [24.2.12]  Automatic discovery not available against the government
Order 24 rules 1 and 2 do not apply in civil proceedings to which the government is a party: Order 77 rule 12(1). This reflects the common law position under which discovery could not be ordered against the government: *Cowie v AG* [1948] HKLR 42. Discovery may now be ordered against the government under the Crown Proceedings Ordinance (Cap 300) s 24(1)(a). See the commentary under Order 77 rule 12.

## [24.2.13]  Actions for infringement of a patent
Order 24 rules 1 and 2 do not apply to actions for infringement of patent rights: Order 103 rule 26(3).

## [24.2.14]  Collision cases
Order 24 Rule 2(2) provides that the automatic discovery of documents procedure does not apply in cases arising from collision or apprehended collision of vehicles, unless the court otherwise orders. An automatic direction by which the parties are so ordered in personal injury cases (which will be the bulk of collision cases) is provided for by Order 25 rule 8. Practice direction 18.1 (concerning the personal injuries list) is also relevant in this regard – see the commentary under Order 72 rule 2.

## [24.2.15]  Defamation actions
There are limitations on the discovery process in defamation actions. See the commentary under Order 82 rule 3.

## [24.2.16]   Third party proceedings

There is no automatic discovery of documents in third party proceedings: see the qualifying paragraph at the end of Order 24 rule 2(1). In such cases, if there is to be discovery, an appropriate direction should be sought under Order 16 rule 4.

## [24.2.17]   Order limiting scope of discovery

Order 24 rule 2(5) & (6) empower the court to make an order limiting the scope of discovery of documents, or dispensing with it altogether, if necessary in the circumstances of the particular case for disposing of the case fairly or for saving costs. In *Deacons v White & Case* HCA 2433/2002 (Deputy Judge Poon; 13.03.2003) (paras 19–31) the court used this power to excuse a party from making discovery of documents in relation to irrelevant allegations in the opposing party's pleading. In addition see the express power to limit the scope of discovery in Order 24 rule 15A.

See also rule 1(2) under which the parties may by agreement dispense with or limit discovery.

## [24.2.18]   Affidavit of documents

Any party may require another party to make an affidavit verifying its list of documents at any time before the summons for directions is taken out: Order 24 rule 2(7). See also rule 3(2) which empowers the court (without restriction as to the stage of proceedings) to order a party to verify its list of documents by affidavit. And see rule 5(3) as to the form of affidavit of documents.

The purpose of an affidavit of documents is to add the sanction of perjury so as to ensure full disclosure.

Failure to make an affidavit of documents when required to do may result in an adverse order under Order 24 rule 16.

## [24.2.19]   Privilege

The common law recognises a number of heads of privilege which may be claimed by a party to legal proceedings so as to justify refusal to allow the opposing party to inspect a relevant document. Privilege is not automatic but must be asserted. A claim to privilege is made by listing the relevant document in part 2 of schedule I of the party's list of documents. Privilege may be lost or waived if not asserted or if voluntary disclosure is made – see below.

Of the various heads of privilege it is legal professional privilege which is most often asserted in civil proceedings.

## [24.2.20]   Legal professional privilege

Legal professional privilege (sometimes called 'solicitor client privilege') protects communications the dominant purpose of which is to seek legal advice or which are made in contemplation of litigation. An outline of the history of the development of this privilege at common law, and its interaction with modern statute and human rights law can be found in the judgment of Lord Phillips in *Re McE & Ors* [2009] UKHL 15 (para 3 *et seq*). See also the interesting exposition of cases from around the common law world in the Singapore Court of Appeal's decision in *Skandinaviska Enskilda Banken AB v Asia Pacific Breweries (Singapore) Pte Ltd & Ors* [2007] SGCA 9; [2007] 2 SLR 367 (paras 23-26). The common law principle was stated in the often-cited English case of *Anderson v Bank of British Columbia* (1876) 2 Ch D 644 which has been applied in

Hong Kong all along. See for example *The Chun Loong v G Martini* (1919) 14 HKLR 29.

A concise up-to-date statement of the common law rule can be found in *Lui Yiu Nga v Hospital Authority* [2002] 4 HKC 204, 207D–H, per Suffiad J, quoting Phipson on Evidence (15th ed). The learned judge said as follows:

> The statement of the law which I rely upon can be found in *Phipson on Evidence* (15th ed). There, the author of *Phipson* categorizes privilege into two categories: Legal Advice privilege and Litigation privilege. Under the first category, at para 20-04, *Phipson* states:
>
>> 'Confidential communication between a lawyer and client which come into existence for the purpose of giving or getting legal advice are privileged at all times. The privilege may be asserted by successors in title. It covers direct communications and communications through agents. It covers all documents generated for the purpose of giving or getting legal advice, not merely letters to and from solicitors and instructions to and opinions from counsel, but also all working papers and drafts. The privilege exists whether or not litigation is contemplated or pending.'
>
> As for Litigation privilege, *Phipson* says this at para 20-05:
>
>> 'The second category of legal professional privilege is wider than the first but arises only when litigation is in prospect or pending. From that moment on, any communications between the client and his solicitor or agent or between one of them and a third party will be privileged if they come into existence for the sole or dominant purpose of either giving or getting advice in regard to the litigation or collecting evidence for use in the litigation. This is the basis for claiming privilege for correspondence with witnesses of fact or experts and proofs, reports or documents generated by them.'

In multi-party litigation communications between parties who have a common interest may be privileged from production by any of them: *AXA China Region Insurance Co Ltd v Pacific Century Insurance Co Ltd (No 2)* [2005] 3 HKC 359. However where parties have jointly retained solicitors and subsequently fall out and sue one another, neither can claim privilege against the other in respect of documents generated under the joint retainer: *Chan King Sheen v KC Tsang & Co* [2002] 3 HKC 209, 219D–E, quoting *Phipson on Evidence* (15th ed).

The policy underlying legal professional privilege is to enable clients to obtain legal advice in confidence. In *Pang Yiu Hung Robert v Commissioner of Police & Anor* [2002] 4 HKC 579 Hartmann J quoted with approval the following passage from the speech of Lord Taylor CJ in *R v Derby Magistrates Court ex p B* [1996] 1 AC 487, 507:

> The principle which runs through all these cases . . . is that a man must be able to consult his lawyer in confidence, since otherwise he might hold back half the truth. The client must be sure that what he tells his lawyer in confidence will never be revealed without his consent. Legal professional privilege is thus much more than an ordinary rule of evidence, limited in its application to the facts of a particular case. It is a fundamental condition on which the administration of justice as a whole rests.

Where a document has come into existence for more than one purpose, it will only be protected if the dominant purpose was one to which legal professional privilege attaches. See the formulation of the rule in *Waugh v British Railways Board* [1980] AC 521, 532G–533D, quoted with approval in *AXA* (above, 368C), and see the thorough discussion of this point in *Esso Australia Resources Ltd v Commissioner of Taxation* (1999) 201 CLR 49 (HC Aust). See also the commentary some paragraphs below on accident reports, where the 'dominant purpose' question often arises.

### [24.2.21]    Constitutional status of legal professional privilege

In *Pang Yiu Hung Robert v Commissioner of Police & Anor* [2002] 4 HKC 579 Hartmann J held that legal professional privilege now has constitutional status, being protected by article 35 of the Basic Law. It is there provided that Hong Kong residents shall have the right to confidential legal advice. Further he cited *R (Morgan Grenfell & Co Ltd) v Special Commissioners of Income Tax* [2002] 2 WLR 1299 where Lord Hoffmann said that legal professional privilege 'is today recognised as a fundamental human right' protected by the ICCPR.

Subject to constitutional restraints, legal professional privilege may be limited by legislation. See *Pang Yiu Hung Robert* at 589I. However no such limitation will be found without express statutory language or by necessary implication. Applying that principle of statutory construction in *Pang Yiu Hung Robert* Hartmann J found (at 595D–596F and 606E–G) that section 25A of the Organized and Serious Crimes Ordinance (Cap 455) does not abrogate legal professional privilege, even prior to amendment by Ordinance No 26 of 2002 expressly to protect the privilege.

In *Pang Yiu Hung* it was not necessary to decide whether the impugned legislation infringed the constitutional guarantee. However the Court of Final Appeal was faced squarely with the issue, with regard to other legislation, in *A Solicitor 23/05) v Law Society of HK* [2006] 2 HKC 429 (CFA). It was held that section 8B(2) of the Legal Practitioners Ordinance (which provides that a solicitor must produce documents to Law Society inspectors notwithstanding any claim of solicitor client privilege) does not infringe the Basic Law.

For an analysis of the constitutional guarantee readers may also wish to refer to *Lavallee & Ors v AG of Canada* [2002] 3 SCR 209.

### [24.2.22]    Common law exceptions to legal professional privilege

By way of exception at common law legal professional privilege does not attach to 'communications made in order to obtain legal advice for a criminal purpose' (*Pang Yiu Hung Robert v Commissioner of Police & Anor* [2002] 4 HKC 579 per Hartmann J at 590A–591C citing *R v Cox and Railton* (1884) 14 QBD 153, 168; *Banque Keyser Ullmann SA v Skandia (UK) Insurance Co Ltd* [1986] 1 Lloyd's Rep 336; *Bullivant v AG for Victoria* [1901] AC 196, 201 and *O'Rourke v Darbishire* [1920] AC 581, 632). In *Re McE & Ors* [2009] UKHL 15 Lord Phillips said (at para 11) that it is questionable whether this is a true exception to the common law privilege, seemingly preferring the view that the privilege simply does not extend to protect 'consultations or communications between a lawyer and his client that are in furtherance of crime or fraud'.

Other common law exceptions where communication between a client and legal adviser are not protected by legal professional privilege are referred to in the judgment of Hartmann J in *Pang Yiu Hung Robert v Commissioner of Police & Anor* [2002] 4 HKC 579, 591D–593E:

(a)    The record of time on an attendance note, and the record of an appointment which in themselves have nothing to do with obtaining legal advice (citing *R*

(b)    Records of a conveyancing transaction (citing *R v Crown Court at Inner London Sessions, ex p Baines & Baines (a firm)* [1987] 3 All ER 1025).

(c)    Information as to dealings with clients' money which 'stand in isolation unconnected to advice given or sought' (citing *Re Furney* [1964] ALR 814; *Packer v Deputy Commissioner of Taxation* (1984) 1 Qd R 275; *Re Ontario Securities Commission and Greymac Credit Corp* (1983) 146 DLR (3d) 73).

See also *Rmbsa Corporate Services Ltd v SJ* [2008] 2 HKC 81 (CA) (para 43–44) citing *Kilbreath & Ors v AG* [2004] SKQB 489; [2005] 4 WWR 462 (Sask QB) as to documents which are not privileged although held by lawyers on behalf of their clients.

In addition see *Maranda v Richer* [2003] 3 SCR 193; (2003) 232 DLR (4th) 14 where Deschamps J adumbrated the following additional common law exceptions to legal professional privilege:

(a)    pressing social needs such as safety and the public interest (*R v McClure* [2001] 1 SCR 445), and

(b)    where an accused's innocence depends on privileged information being admitted in evidence.

In contentious probate actions, communications between a solicitor and an attesting witness of a will are not subject to legal professional privilege to the extent that they concern evidence on attestation and execution: *Chinachem Charitable Foundation Ltd v Chan Chun Chuen & Ors* [2009] 2 HKC 365 (para 15).

### [24.2.23]   Information as to lawyers' fees

In *Chong Hin Pong & Anor v District Judge Gould & Anor* [1995] 2 HKC 221 it was held that information as to lawyers' fees is confidential and the court has no power to compel disclosure. In *Maranda v Richer* [2003] SCR 193; (2003) 232 DLR (4th) 14 the Supreme Court of Canada held that the amount of a lawyer's fees is information protected by solicitor-client privilege.

### [24.2.24]   Search warrant over solicitor's office

Care must be taken by law enforcement authorities when seeking a warrant to search a solicitor's office or other premises where material covered by legal professional privilege is likely to be found. See *Philip KH Wong & Kennedy YH Wong (a firm) v ICAC* [2009] 5 HKC 335 (CA) (para 94) where it was held that although such a warrant need not necessarily include conditions to protect privilege, the following points needed to be emphasised:

(1)    There is a duty on an officer applying for a search warrant to disclose any circumstances giving rise to reasonable cause to believe that the premises to be searched are likely to contain material covered by legal professional privilege or in respect of which a claim to privilege may be made.

(2)    A search warrant may not be issued to search for (or seize) material known to be subject to legal professional privilege.

(3)    Any magistrate to whom an application is made for a warrant which will authorise search of solicitor's premises must examine the application with particular vigilance to satisfy himself that sufficient safeguards will be in place to protect privileged material until such time as claims are determined.

Conditions may be imposed.

## [24.2.25]   Expert reports – privilege

Expert reports obtained for the purpose of legal advice or in contemplation of litigation are clearly susceptible to a claim of legal professional privilege: *Chung Fung Chu v SJ* [2007] 5 HKC 446 (CA). It is not improper for a party to put forward favourable expert reports and claim privilege in respect of others which may be less favourable. The result is not entirely unfair to the opposing party since it is at liberty to obtain its own reports. Furthermore, the opposing party may subpoena the expert who gave the unfavourable report and adduce his opinion before the court, though not privileged communications. See *Harmony Shipping Co SA v Davis & Ors* [1979] 1 WLR 1380 discussed in Plunkett, 'Solicitor-Third Party Communications' (1991) 21 HKLJ 100, 102.

A party who wishes to change experts may be required to waive privilege in the report it no longer wishes to rely upon: see the commentary on change of experts under Order 38 rule 36, referring to *Vasilou v Hajigeorgiou* [2005] EWCA Civ 236; [2005] 3 All ER 17.

Two points concerning expert reports are made in *Lui Yiu Nga v Hospital Authority* [2002] 4 HKC 204. First the privilege may apply even where no legal professional is involved. In that case a claim to privilege was upheld where the plaintiff obtained a report on her own with a view to seeking legal advice. Secondly, the privilege extends to the expert's notes and other papers generated in the process of preparing the report.

## [24.2.26]   Accident reports – privilege

In *Mutual Underwriters Ltd & Ors v Yu Kam Chung* [1978] HKLR 447, the question arose as to whether a notice of accident was privileged. The Court of Appeal held:

> [A] notice of accident is not *ipso facto* a document prepared for the purpose of submission to a solicitor. There may well be situations where one of the substantial purposes of such a notice is to pass it on to a solicitor for his legal advice but we are unable to accept that proposition as having general application. Nor are we able to accept the contention that at the time a notice of accident is made, litigation is anticipated as a matter of course … The correspondence between the plaintiff and the insurers which came into existence for the purpose of ascertaining the details of the motor accident is prima facie relevant … [W]e think counsel should examine it and that any correspondence which came into existence for the purpose of finding out the details of the accident as opposed to obtaining legal advice should be disclosed. (At 451–452, per Yang J.)

*A Crompton Ltd v Customs and Excise* [1974] AC 405 and *Jones v Great Central Railway* [1910] AC 4 were preferred over *Westminster Airways Ltd v Kuwait Oil Co Ltd* [1951] 1 KB 134.

In *Tam Yuk Kwan v Chu Cheuk Tao & Ors* [1989] 1 HKC 231, *Waugh v British Railways Board* [1980] AC 521 was applied on the question of whether privilege attaches to accident reports. It was held that a report as to the cause of an accident is only privileged from discovery if the dominant purpose for its preparation, or at least the ordering of its preparation, was that of submitting it to a legal advisor for advice in connection with, or use in, reasonably anticipated litigation arising out of the accident. Discovery was refused in this case because the court was satisfied, on the sworn evidence of a manager of the relevant defendant's insurance company, that preparation for contemplated litigation was the dominant purpose for which the report was requested.

An accident or incident report, which would have been prepared irrespective of any intention to obtain legal advice, is unlikely to be susceptible to a claim of privilege: *Carter Holt Harvey Wood Products Australia Pty Ltd v Auspine Ltd* [2008] VSCA 59 (Vic CA).

On the 'dominant purpose' requirement generally, see the introductory commentary some paragraphs above on legal professional privilege.

**[24.2.27]   Copies, lists and extracts of documents**
No privilege attaches to a copy, extract, list or verbatim note of unprivileged documents, even where created by a solicitor in connection with giving legal advice or as an *aide-mémoire*: *LMH v KLH* [2007] 1 HKC 320 (CA).

**[24.2.28]   Unintentional disclosure of privileged documents**
Where privileged documents unintentionally come into the possession of the opposing party the extent to which the opposing party may make use of the same is circumscribed. The party in whom the privilege vests may be able to obtain an injunction requiring return of the documents: *AG v Tin Shui Wai Development Ltd & Ors* [1989] 1 HKC 360; *English and American Insurance Co Ltd v Herbert Smith* [1987] NLJ 148; [1988] FSR 232. Further, the rules of professional conduct impose special duties on legal professionals which supersede their duties to their clients (as to which, see below).

*Calcroft v Guest* [1898] 1 QB 759 is authority for the proposition that, as a matter of the law of evidence, a party may use evidence in his/her hands as secondary evidence of a document for which privilege is claimed by the other party. This is so even if the secondary evidence, for example, a copy, was improperly obtained, a consequence of the Privy Council decision in *Kuruma v R* [1955] AC 197. However, provided the party holding the secondary evidence has not yet used it as such, equity may intervene. The party in whom the privilege in the original vests may be able to obtain an injunction demanding delivery up of any documents comprising the secondary evidence and restraining his/her opponent from disclosing or making use of any information contained in them (May LJ in *Goddard v Nationwide Building Society* [1986] 3 WLR 734, at 743). This is so even where it was through a party's negligence that his/her opponent was able to inspect and take copies of a privileged document provided the negligent party's mistake was one which was or should have been obvious to the opponent (*Guinness Peat Properties v Fitzroy Robinson Partnership* [1987] 2 All ER 716, at 731, per Slade LJ).

In *Zheng Lie Lie & Ors v Prosperfield Ventures Ltd & Anor (No 2)* [2003] 2 HKC 47, an injunction was granted to restrain use at trial of a privileged document which had inadvertently found its way into the hands of the opposing party. In addition the opposing party was ordered to return the document and all copies of it.

**[24.2.29]   Lawyer's duty in respect of unintentionally disclosed privileged documents**
Barristers and solicitors are both subject to rules of professional conduct which restrict the use of privileged documents belonging to the opposing party which unintentionally come into their hands.

The Code of Conduct of the Hong Kong Bar Association provides that counsel intending to use a document belonging to the other side should inform the opposing advocate in sufficient time to enable an objection to be made: see para 139A of the code, the full text of which can be viewed on the Bar Association's website. English barristers appear to be subject to more stringent standards. The English bar's 'Written Standards for the Conduct of Professional Work' (which are not part of the Code of Conduct, but a guide) provides that a barrister who comes into possession of a document belonging to another party otherwise than through proper channels, should at once return the document unread. If the document has been read, the barrister may have to withdraw. See part 7 of the written standards, the full text of which can be viewed on the website of the Bar Council of England and Wales.

Hong Kong solicitors have a duty to pass on to their clients and to make use of all material information regardless of the source: see principle 8.03 of the Hong Kong Solicitors' Guide to Professional Conduct vol 1 (2nd ed). However the duty is subject to exceptions which are discussed in the commentary to that principle. For example para 6 of the commentary states that where it is obvious that privileged documents have mistakenly been disclosed on discovery, a solicitor must immediately cease to read them, inform the other side and advise the client that the court could grant an injunction to prevent use of the information gleaned. The full text of the guide and commentary can be viewed on the Law Society's website.

### [24.2.30]    Privilege against self-incrimination

The common law privilege against self-incrimination entitles a person to refuse to answer any question which would, in the opinion of the court, tend to expose the deponent to any criminal charge, penalty or forfeiture which the court regards as reasonably likely to be preferred or sued for: *Blunt v Park Lane Hotel Ltd* [1942] 2 KB 253, 257 (CA). The privilege is now refined in statute and constitutionally entrenched. Section 65 of the Evidence Ordinance (Cap 8) expressly extends the privilege to production of documents and incrimination of one's spouse. Article 11(2)(g) of the Hong Kong Bill of Rights guarantees the right, but only where a person faces a criminal charge and only to the extent that the person cannot be compelled to testify against himself or to confess guilt. See *HKSAR v Lee Ming Tee & Anor* (2001) 4 HKCFAR 133 (paras 97-105). There it was said that the constitutional protection is 'of much narrower scope' than the common law privilege. It follows that statutory encroachment on the common law privilege will not necessarily infringe the constitutional guarantee.

The privilege extends to any piece of information which might be used in establishing guilt or deciding whether to prosecute: *Pheby v Paier & Ors* [2003] 2 HKC 328, 336A-B, citing *Den Norske Bank ASA v Antonatos* [1999] QB 271.

The court is entitled to consider the validity of a claim to the privilege and in so doing will consider whether there is 'reasonable ground to apprehend danger to the witness': *R v Boyes* (1861) 1 B&S 311, 330; 121 ER 730 (quoted with approval in *Pheby* (above, at 336D)).

There are conflicting authorities in different common law jurisdictions on the question whether a body corporate may claim the privilege. See the discussion in *Salt & Light Development Inc & Anor v SJTU Sunway Software Industry Ltd* [2006] 2 HKC 440, 454-5 where the Hong Kong court came down in favour of the privilege being available. It was held that the privilege is personal to the body corporate and not descendible to its directors. Thus directors may not invoke the privilege when asked questions which might incriminate the company.

The privilege may be claimed only as regards offences under Hong Kong law: Evidence Ordinance s 65(1)(a). However the court has a discretion to excuse a witness from answering where there is a risk of self-incrimination under the law of another jurisdiction, including other parts of China: *Salt & Light Development* (above, at 459).

**[24.2.31]   Statutory encroachments on the privilege against self-incrimination**
Subject to the constitutional guarantee (which applies only in criminal proceedings – see above), the privilege against self-incrimination may be reduced in scope or taken away by statute: *Fu Kin Chi Willy v Secretary for Justice* [1998] 1 HKC 411, 423 (CFA). This has been done in Hong Kong in respect of some specific types of proceedings, including:

- *Anton Piller orders* – the privilege is no longer normally available to resist compliance with such an order: High Court Ordinance (Cap 4), s 44A. See the commentary under Order 29 rule 3.
- *Proceedings for recovery or administration of property, execution of a trust or for an account of property* – the privilege is abolished by section 66 of the Crimes Ordinance (Cap 200) and section 33 of the Theft Ordinance (Cap 210).
- *Companies inspector* – the privilege is abolished in respect of an investigation of a company by an inspector appointed by the Financial Secretary: Companies Ordinance (Cap 32), s 145(3A). The information obtained may be used in a subsequent criminal prosecution as such 'derivative' use is not prohibited by the statute nor does it infringe the constitutional guarantee or the right to a fair trial: *HKSAR v Lee Ming Tee & Anor* (2001) 4 HKCFAR 133 (paras 117–125).
- *SFC investigations* – the privilege does not excuse a person from providing information to SFC investigators, but information provided may only be used in the prosecution of a limited group of offences: Securities and Futures Ordinance (Cap 571), s 183 & 187. This encroachment on the privilege does not infringe the constitutional guarantee in the Bill of Rights: *Koon Wing Yee v SFC* [2008] 1 HKC 240 (appeal dismissed – CACV 369/2007).
- *Proceedings for recovery of drug trafficking proceeds* – the privilege is abolished by section 5(6) of the Drug Trafficking (Recovery of Proceeds) Ordinance (Cap 405).
- *Forfeiture* – Section 66 of the Evidence Ordinance (Cap 8) abolishes, for civil proceedings, the rule whereby a person could not be compelled to answer questions or produce any document if the result could be exposure to forfeiture.

**[24.2.32]   Public interest immunity**
The government is entitled to resist disclosure of information on grounds of public interest. In *Chu Woan Chyi & Ors v Director of Immigration* HCAL 32/2003 (Hartmann J; 08.05.2006) this public interest immunity or privilege was described in the following terms:

> The administration of justice requires that all facts relevant to a dispute should be before the court. The principle, however, is subject to qualifications. One of those qualifications recognises that there may be occasions when the public interest in the administration of justice must give way to a greater public interest; namely, the protection of society in order to ensure what was once described as the peace of the realm.

The above passage continues with a reference to *Conway v Rimmer* [1968] AC 910, 980 where it was said that the court will not order the production of documents 'where this would imperil the state or harm the public interest as a whole'.

**[24.2.33]  Assertion of public interest privilege by means of certificate**
Public interest immunity is usually asserted by means of executive certificate. The certificate is sometimes put forward in the form of an affidavit. The official giving the certificate should be one discharging functions equivalent to those of a Minister of State in the United Kingdom: *Edwards v Almao (No 4)* [1957] HKLR 365, 382 (FC). In practice in Hong Kong the task usually falls to the Chief Secretary for Administration. However, since the matter is one of public interest, the claim for immunity may be raised by any person interested or by the court itself: *Rogers v Home Secretary* [1973] AC 388, 400E-G; *Sankey v Whitlam* (1978) 142 CLR 1, 59 (HCA). In such a case there may then be an adjournment to enable the government to consider whether a certificate should be issued.

The effect of a deliberate decision by the executive not to assert public interest immunity is unclear: *Sankey* (above, at 54).

Natural justice will normally require that the certificate be made available to the other parties. However in *Chu Woan Chyi & Ors* (above, para 92) the government was permitted to submit a 'special' certificate, to be seen by the court only, on the ground that any open discussion would undermine the public interest.

**[24.2.34]  Judicial scrutiny of claim to public interest immunity**
It was once thought that an executive certificate asserting public interest immunity was conclusive and that a court was bound to accept it: *Duncan v Cammell Laird & Co* [1942] AC 587; *Edwards v Almao (No 4)* (above), at 397-8); *Cheung Yan Lung v Yeung Yim Ming* [1957] HKLR 233, 236-7. Now it is recognised that the court may look behind such a certificate and determine the legitimacy of the claim to public interest immunity: *Conway v Rimmer* [1968] AC 910; *Burmah Oil Co Ltd v Bank of England* [1980] AC 1090; *Air Canada v Secretary of State for Trade (No 2)* [1983] 2 AC 394. That line of authority has been followed in Hong Kong since *Kwok Kwan v Wai Keung Iron Works Co* [1968] DCLR 68.

It is now clear that a party may contest a claim to public interest immunity and apply for an order to compel disclosure. Where this arises in the context of discovery of documents, such an application may be made under Order 24 rule 11. In *R (Mohammed) v Secretary of State* [2010] EWCA Civ 65 the English court upheld a challenge to public interest immunity certificates in the context of a *Norwich Pharmacal* application.

**[24.2.35]  Procedure on challenge to claim of public interest immunity**
On an application for disclosure of documents in respect of which public interest immunity has been claimed, the court must first consider the *prima facie* validity of the claim. The claim will be *prima facie* valid if on the face of the certificate it appears that:

(1)     the subject matter or the class of documents has been recognised as worthy of protection before;

(2)     there is no reason to suppose the document sought does not deal with such subject matter or fall within such class of documents; and

(3)     the official signing the certificate has given specific attention to the matter and the reasons or basis for the claim are adequately stated.

In *Wan Chung Yiu v Amerasia Garment Manufacturers Ltd* [1963] HKDCLR 53 the claim was unsuccessful where made by a civil servant acting on a general direction from the Colonial Secretary. If the certificate does not adequately state the reasons or basis of the claim the court may seek clarification or even inspect the document concerned: *Conway v Rimmer* (above, at 953); *Kwok Kwan v Wai Keung Iron Works* (above).

If the claim is *prima facie* valid, the next step is to consider whether the party seeking disclosure can make out a case that disclosure of the evidence would advance the public interest in the administration of justice. The court will consider the nature of the claim for immunity, the issues and the evidence already available in the case. If no sufficient counter-balancing public interest in disclosure is found, the claim to immunity will be upheld. However, if the court is undecided or tending toward disclosure, it may proceed to inspect the documents concerned. The court may do so if it is of the view that the document is likely to support or further the case of the party seeking disclosure: *Air Canada* (above).

If the party seeking disclosure is able to establish the requisite public interest in production, the two competing public interests must be balanced by the court: *R v Lau Alexander* [1982] HKC 174, 178; [1982] HKDCLR 53, 56; *Cheung Yan Lung v Yeung Yim Ming (No 2)* [1957] HKLR 310. Only if the public interest in the administration of justice is dominant will disclosure be ordered. Actual production may be delayed or the order stayed pending any possible appeal.

See Generally Cross & Tapper on Evidence (10th ed, 2004) 510-513, and see also CPR 31.19 which in England provides for an application for permission to withhold disclosure.

**[24.2.36]   Claim in respect of a class of documents**
It has been held that when public interest immunity has been asserted in respect of a class of documents the court has no residual discretion to engage in 'surgery' so as to make available those parts where disclosure would not be prejudicial. See *Chu Woan Chyi & Ors* (above, para 79 *et seq*) referring to *Apple Daily Ltd v Commissioner of the ICAC* [2000] 1 HKC 295 (CA).

**[24.2.37]   Hong Kong cases on public interest immunity Pre-Conway v Rimmer cases which might be decided the same way today**
(1)     In *Chang Lan-Sheng v Attorney-General* [1968] HKLR 487 (CA), immunity was upheld for a file containing minutes of meetings of the Hong Kong Executive Council, the nearest equivalent in Hong Kong to minutes of meetings of the British Cabinet, sought for the purpose of revealing decisions affecting the land policy of the government and the reasons therefor. No reasons other than the class of the documents concerned is recorded in the report.

(2)     In *Yeung Chik Fook & Anor v Lim Ho U* (1924) 19 HKLR 58 and *Cheung Yan Lung v Yeung Yim Ming* [1957] HKLR 233, at 310, immunity upheld in respect of testimony and memoranda by an official of the Secretariat of Chinese Affairs as to what took place in the official's office during a meeting in which he attempted to mediate between the Chinese parties in a tenancy dispute was

claimed on the ground that disclosure would destroy the trust of the Chinese community in the confidentiality of such meetings thereby destroying an important part of the Secretariat's usefulness. The claim was successful notwithstanding that testimony as to what took place could be given by either of the parties present. These cases may have been more appropriately considered by analogy with 'without prejudice' privilege, discussed below. Compare the English case of *Broome v Broome* [1955] 1 All ER 201, followed in *Cheung Yan Lung* (above), in which oral evidence as to what took place during a marriage counselling session for a soldier and his wife was also protected, and the Hong Kong case of *Wan Chung Yiu v Amerasia Garment Manufacturers Ltd* [1963] HKDCLR 53, in which *Cheung Yan Lung* (above) was distinguished. It has been doubted whether *Broome v Broome* would be followed in England today *as a matter of public interest immunity* (and see *Gain v Gain* [1961] 1 WLR 1469, as to the admissibility of oral evidence of the proceedings or contents of the documents, but note the existence of a distinct privilege for any communications made in the course of an attempt at matrimonial reconciliation quite unconnected with any question of national security or the public service (*Cross on Evidence*, 7th ed, pp 454–455). This may also be the most appropriate rationalisation of *Young Hay v Wong Kit Mui* [1967] HKLR 708).

### [24.2.38]     Post Conway v Rimmer

(1)     In *Kwok Kwan v Wai Keung Iron Works Co* [1968] DCLR 68, immunity was upheld in respect of the testimony of an officer of the Labour Department and the production of documents concerning labour conciliation proceedings between the plaintiff and the defendant; a class claim case heard soon after a period of violent labour unrest about which the judge made comment.

(2)     In *R v Lau Alexander* [1982] HKC 174; [1982] HKDCLR 53, oral and written communications between a magistrate, on the one hand, and the Chief Justice and Registrar of the Supreme Court, on the other, concerning the magistrate's future prospects as a member of the judiciary sought to be adduced by the prosecution in the trial of the magistrate for attempting to pervert the course of justice and misconduct in a public office, were said to fall within a class of documents the disclosure of which would be prejudicial to the proper administration of the judicial service in Hong Kong. Disclosure was refused on two grounds: the prosecution was unable to say that nothing in the proposed evidence would be in any way prejudicial to the proper administration of the judicial service in Hong Kong; and there was insufficient relevance to issues in the trial given other evidence available.

(3)     In *Y Khan v PG O'Dea & Anor* [1987] HKLR 150, public interest immunity was upheld with respect to a file of the ICAC Complaints Committee concerning a complaint against the ICAC made by the plaintiff to that committee and files created by the ICAC in consequence of two complaints made to the ICAC again by the plaintiff; in each case on the ground that both the ICAC and the Committee could only start to perform their proper functions and give effect to the relevant statutory purposes '...if they can act in complete confidence. The suggestion that their files are on risk of discovery in civil proceedings must in my judgment be put aside completely.' (per Hunter J, at 155). Authorities

relied upon included *Neilson v Laugharne* [1981] QB 736 and *Hehir v Commissioner of Metropolitan Police* [1982] 2 All ER 335. Hunter J's very strong statements must be read first subject to the qualification that disclosure may, nevertheless, be ordered when to do so is necessary for the proper presentation of a defence to a criminal charge (*R v Brown and Daley* (1987) 87 Cr App R 52).

(4)     As to the public interest in keeping secret the identity of police informers see *Lau Biu v AG & Anor* HCA 392/1981 (Mr Commissioner Gittins QC; 15.07.1981) and *R v Lam Kwok-hung* CACC 477/1988 (Yang CJ, Silke VP & Power JA; 23.03.1989).

(5)     In *PV v Director of Immigration* [2004] 3 HKC 637, 647H–I, judicial review proceedings concerning the detention and removal of a person, the judge, having reviewed the documents in respect of which public interest immunity was claimed, upheld the claim on the ground that 'disclosure would not only reveal the identity of sources whose anonymity was fundamental to the order and safety of Hong Kong but would constitute a gross breach of solemn confidential arrangements necessary to the good governance of this Territory'

## [24.2.39]   Appointment of 'special advocate' in cases where public interest immunity upheld

Circumstances may arise where the government wishes to rely on privileged material in support of its case, but at the same time keep it confidential from the opposing litigant and the public for public interest reasons such as national security. In *PV v Director of Immigration* [2004] 3 HKC 637, 648-50, applying *R v H & Ors* [2004] 2 WLR 335 (HL) the court allowed this to be done by appointing a 'special advocate' to represent the opposing litigant in respect of the privileged material. The special advocate was appointed on terms which restricted the usual right to communicate with the client, and required that submissions on the privileged material be made at an *in camera* hearing in the absence of the client. The special advocate's role was limited to the privileged material with the balance of the case being conducted in the usual way by the litigant's own legal team. The special advocate procedure will only be adopted in exceptional cases such as where liberty is at stake, or a person faces deportation to a place where there is a risk of persecution: *Chu Woan Chyi & Ors v Director of Immigration* HCAL 32/2003 (Hartmann J; 08.05.2006). In that case the court declined to adopt the special advocate procedure and decided to consider the confidential documents itself.

The special advocate procedure is Canadian in origin: *Chahal v UK* (1996) 23 EHRR 413. It has been adopted in the UK in the Special Immigration Appeals Commission Act 1997. Although the procedure deprives a person of the right to know the whole of the case against him, it is a justifiable infringement of that right where there are compelling national security considerations: see *Charkhaoui v Canada* [2007] 1 SCR 350 where it was suggested that the procedure would not infringe constitutionally entrenched rights. See, however, the trenchant condemnation of the special advocate procedure in *Epoch Group Ltd v Director of Immigration* HCMP 2475/2010 (Rogers VP; 05.01.2011) where (para 7, *obiter*) the procedure was described as 'abhorrent', 'a denial of the fundamental principles of the common law and natural justice' and 'the tool of the oppressor'.

In *V v Director of Immigration* HCAL 60/2005 (Chu J; 17.10.2005) an application by the government to use the special advocate procedure was dismissed on the ground the evidence the government wished to rely on without disclosure to the opposing party was irrelevant. It is now recognised that the special advocate procedure is not limited to national security situations: *Murungaru v Secretary of State* [2008] EWCA Civ 1015 (12.09.2008) (para 18).

For a succinct statement of the principles to be borne in mind when considering appointment of a special advocate, see *Secretary of State for the Home Department v AHK & Ors* [2009] EWCA Civ 287 (para 37).

The special advocate or 'closed material' procedure was developed in the context of cases involving issues of public law, and appears to be limited to such cases. In *Al Rawi & Ors v Security Service & Ors* [2010] EWCA Civ 482 (04.05.2010) it was held the procedure may not, in the absence of statutory power or (arguably) agreement of the parties, be adopted in an ordinary civil claim such as a claim for damages for tort or breach of statutory duty.

### [24.2.40]  Privilege as between spouses

Section 7 of the Evidence Ordinance (Cap 8) provides that spouses cannot be compelled to disclose communications between them during the course of their marriage. The section was amended by Ordinance 25/1969 to restrict its application to criminal proceedings.

Other provisions in the Evidence Ordinance extend the privilege against self-incrimination to incrimination of one's spouse. See sections 65 and 65A thereof.

### [24.2.41]  Legal aid

Information obtained from applicants for legal aid, apart from that relating to the applicant's financial means, is privileged from disclosure (Legal Aid Ordinance (Cap 91), section 24).

### [24.2.42]  'Without prejudice' communications

Communications between parties with a view to settle their dispute, such as 'without prejudice' letters, are normally inadmissible without consent of both sides. This rule is based on the public policy of encouraging litigants to settle their disputes: *Rush & Tompkins Ltd v GLC & Ors* [1989] AC 1280, 1299 (HL). It enables parties to have candid negotiations with a view to settlement knowing that if agreement is not reached, whatever has been said cannot be used against them at trial. The privilege may attach to both oral and written communications.

The law concerning without prejudice communications was set out concisely in *Standard Chartered Bank (HK) Ltd v Ma Lit Kin Cary* HCA 62/2006 (Reyes J; 22.01.2007) in the following terms:

    (1)    For a claim of 'without prejudice' privilege to succeed, the party claiming it must show that the communication was made:-

        (a)    in a *bona fide* attempt to settle a dispute between the parties; and

        (b)    with the intention that, if negotiations failed, the communication could not be disclosed without the consent of the party making the communication.

    (2)    In establishing that there was a *bona fide* attempt to settle a dispute, the party seeking to assert privilege must show that, at the time of his communication:-

        (a)    a dispute existed between the parties in respect of which legal proceedings had commenced or were contemplated; and,

(b) the communication was made in an attempt to further negotiations to settle that dispute.

(3) The mere fact that a communication concerns a dispute between the parties is
not sufficient to confer privilege.

(4) The communication need not be expressed to be 'without prejudice' if it is clear
from the surrounding circumstances that the parties were generally seeking to
compromise their dispute.

(5) But there is an exception to the 'without prejudice' privilege. This exception
applies where the exclusion of the evidence would act as a cloak for perjury or
other 'unambiguous impropriety'. This exception should only apply in the
clearest of cases, since otherwise it could undermine the 'without prejudice'
privilege altogether.

In 1985 the Law Society circulated guidance on without prejudice communications
based on advice of leading counsel. Although the Society's website says the circular
(No 85-115) has been deleted from the archives, it remains useful, and we reproduce
it here:

1.   The rule is that statements made in the course of bona fide negotiations for the
settlement of a dispute may not afterwards be given in evidence without the consent
of both parties. For the purposes of the rule it is neither necessary nor sufficient that the
letter containing the statement should be marked "without prejudice." If the contents of
the letter show that it was written with a view to the settlement of dispute, it will be
treated as having been without prejudice even though not so marked. On the other hand,
letters not concerned with the resolution of a dispute or not written in good faith will
not be privileged even though they purport to be written without prejudice. The use of
the label "without prejudice" is however a strong indication that the writer regards the
letter as part of a negotiation with a view to a settlement.

2.   The circumstances in which letters marked "without prejudice" may be given in
evidence are not so much exceptions to the rule as cases which, when the rule is correctly
formulated, can be seen to fall outside its scope. So for example –

(a) Without prejudice correspondence which is alleged to have resulted in a
binding agreement will be admissible to establish the existence and terms of
such agreement in the same way as any other contractual correspondence.
As Lindley LJ said in *Walker v Wilshire*:

"What is the meaning of the words 'without prejudice'? I think they
mean without prejudice to the position of the writer of the letter if the
terms he proposes are not accepted."

(b) On the other hand, if the terms are accepted (or it is alleged that they were),
the original dispute is no longer in issue and the letters are admissible to
establish the existence of the compromise agreement.

If a letter marked "without prejudice" contains a statement which is
"wholly unconnected" with the dispute, that statement will be admissible.
This is because such a statement cannot be said to have been made in the
course negotiation for the settlement of the dispute. But the policy of the
without prejudice rule is to encourage litigants to settle their disputes and
the courts therefore give a liberal interpretation to the question of whether
statements in a letter without prejudice is connected with the dispute. It
would not be in the public interest if parties were discouraged from put-

ting forward settlement proposals by the thought that some statement in the letter might be dissected as insufficiently connected with the dispute and proved in evidence against them.

    (c)    The fact that negotiations without prejudice have been taking place is admissible to rebut a plea of laches or a suggestion that there has been delay in taking proceedings. Thus, in *Jones v Foxall* Sir John Romilly MR said:

> "In my opinion, ... letters and offers (without prejudice) are admissible for one purpose only, namely, to show that an attempt has been made to com promise the suit, which may sometimes be necessary; as, for instance, in order to account for the lapse of time, but never for the purpose of fixing the person making them with any admissions contained in such letters."

    (d)    In cases in which payment into court is not possible under the Rules of the Supreme Court, a party may qualify the "without prejudice" nature of an offer by saying that he reserves the right to draw the offer to the attention of the court after judgment in connection with an application for costs. In such a case, the correspondence will be admissible for this purpose only.

3.   If there is a dispute about whether a particular statement is covered by the privilege or not, the judge is entitled (if he thinks it necessary) to examine the letter in order to determine the question. Although the judge in a civil action now combines the former functions of judge and jury, the rules of evidence were evolved on the assumption that they would be separate. When the judge is called upon to rule upon a question of admissibility of a letter, he may therefore read the letter in his capacity as judge in order to decide whether to allow himself to read it in his capacity as jury. However, since most judges acknowledge that they are human and might have some difficulty in dismissing from their minds in one capacity what they have just read in another (or at any rate accept that litigants might not credit them with such strength of mind) they will try to avoid reading a letter of questionable admissibility unless this is plainly necessary to decide the issue. In Leading Counsel's view it is the duty of Counsel in propounding such a letter to tell the judge that its admissibility may be in issue so as to give his opponent time to object before the contents of the letter are actually disclosed. It is desirable that Counsel should, where appropriate, be reminded of this.

4.   In the case of an application *ex parte*, the duty of the utmost good faith cast upon the applicant also requires him to tell the judge that the admissibility of any evidence he proposes to adduce on the application may be disputed and to do so before actually disclosing its contents. If he does this and makes full disclosure of the reasons why the evidence may be inadmissible, he will in Leading Counsel's view have fully discharged his duty and cannot be blamed if the judge allows the evidence to be read but afterwards appears to have made a mistake in doing so.

## [24.2.43]   Discovery of 'without prejudice' communications

The position appears to be that a party should include in its list of documents without prejudice communications which are already known to the opposing party, leaving it to the opposing party to object to admissibility at trial, but such communications are protected from disclosure to other parties to whom they were not addressed. These propositions derive from *Gross Fortune Int'l Ltd v Set Win Int'l Ltd* [2000] 1 HKC 269 (CA) and *Rush & Tompkins Ltd v GLC* [1989] 1 AC 1280 (HL), discussed below.

    In *Gross Fortune* the court declined to order a defendant to delete from its list of documents items which the plaintiff alleged were subject to the without prejudice rule. It was held that the documents should be listed, leaving the issue of admissibility for trial. This followed from the fact that the without prejudice rule is really one of admissibility rather than one of privilege.

However in *Rush & Tompkins* the House of Lords declined to order disclosure to the 2nd defendant of without prejudice communications which had passed between the plaintiff and the 1st defendant and had resulted in a settlement with the 1st defendant.

The different results in the two cases was explained by Ribeiro J (as he then was) in *Gross Fortune* (at 273I-274C). He noted that whereas *Gross Fortune* concerned com munications between the parties themselves, the contents of which were well-known to both sides, *Rush & Tompkins* concerned an attempt by a 2nd defendant to obtain without prejudice communications which had passed between the plaintiff and another defendant. In *Rush & Tompkins* Lord Griffiths (at 1304E-F) quoted with approval from *Waxman & Sons Ltd v Texaco Canada Ltd* [1968] 1 OR 642; [1968] 2 OR 452 (Ontario CA) where it was held that without prejudice communications are protected from disclosure 'on discovery or at trial in proceedings by or *against the third party*' (emphasis added).

It is submitted that the refusal to disclose in *Rush & Tompkins* was justified on the basis that the communications did not relate to a 'matter in question' in relation to the party seeking disclosure. Or to put it another way, the communications were irrelevant because they were inadmissible.

**[24.2.44]    Improper disclosure of without prejudice communications**
Where without prejudice communications have improperly been disclosed to the court, the question may arise whether the matter should be transferred to another judge. In *Berg v IML London Ltd* [2002] 1 WLR 3271 it was said (at para 20) that the court should not too easily come to the conclusion that a case should be transferred as this would hamper the procedure of the court and increase costs. The court then set out (at paras 21–22) two circumstances in which it is appropriate for the matter to be transferred. They are first, where 'subjectively the judge considers that he is disabled from fairly continuing with the case', in which event the matter must be transferred; and secondly, where whatever the subjective feeling of the judge, there is a 'real possibility or a real danger of there being seen to be, by a fair-minded and informed observer, an unfair trial'.

**[24.2.45]    Exceptions to the 'without prejudice' rule**
There must be a live dispute between the parties for the without prejudice rule to apply. Thus it has been held that a conversation in which one party admits a debt and asks for time to pay is not covered by the rule since there is no dispute as to quantum or liability: *Standard Chartered Bank (HK) Ltd v Ma Lit Kin Cary* HCA 62/2006 (Reyes J; 22.01.2007).

A party can bring without prejudice correspondence to an end by giving a clear indication that subsequent correspondence is intended to be open. See *Chun Lee Engineering Co Ltd v Hopewell Construction Co Ltd* [1989] 2 HKC 592, 594H *et seq* referring to *India Rubber v Chapman* (1926) 20 BWCC 184 and *Scott Paper Co v Drayton Paper Works Ltd* (1927) 44 RPC 151.

Without prejudice communications may be admitted to show that they resulted in a binding agreement: *Re Y (Infants)* [1946]-[1972] HKC 378. As stated in the above Law Society guidance they may also be admitted to rebut a plea of laches or an allegation of delay. For example, such communications may be admitted to explain delay to counter an application to strike out for want of prosecution: *Unilever plc v The Procter & Gamble Co* [2001] 1 All ER 783 (CA) (NB at 792e-f); [2000] 1 WLR 2436; *Barton v Potash Corp of Saskatchewan* [2009] SKCA 7 (para 15). This exception is said in *Unilever* to trace back to *Walker v Wilsher* (1889) 23 QBD 335. Further a statement wholly unconnected with the dispute contained in what is otherwise a 'without prejudice' communication, may be admitted.

It is now well established that 'without prejudice' communications will be admissible where 'exclusion of the evidence would act as a cloak for perjury ... or other "unambiguous impropriety" '. See *Re Jinro (HK) International Ltd* [2002] 4 HKC 90, 96E–I, citing *Unilever* (above, at 2444 WLR) and *Forster v Friedland* (English CA, 10.11.1992). However, this exception will only be applied in the 'clearest cases of abuse of a privileged occasion', otherwise 'the value of the without prejudice rule would be seriously impaired if its protection could be removed by anything less than unambiguous impropriety': *Re Jinro (HK)* citing in addition *Fazil-Alizadeh v Nikbin* ((English CA, 25.02.1993). As to the meaning of 'unambiguous impropriety' in this context see *Golden King Holdings Ltd v Kinwell Group Ltd* DCCJ 6209/2002 (Judge CB Chan; 20.05.2003) and the authorities cited therein. See also *Dynamic Creations Ltd v Mint Gem & Jewelry Manufacturing Co Ltd* HCA 378/2006 (Chu J; 12.04.2006) where the court refused to expunge without prejudice communications from an affidavit where they cast doubt on the truth of what was put forward in another affidavit.

In *Lo Chi Wai Arthur v Liu Wing Cheung Wilfred* [1983] 1 HKC 416 the court was of the view that 'without prejudice' correspondence could be admitted to counter an allegation of a failure to mitigate. Mantell J held (at 424D) that it would be 'quite unfair to prevent the other party from answering the allegation by pointing not only to the fact of without prejudice correspondence but also to its content'. In *Chen v Hardoon* (1953) 37 HKLR 31 an admission of liability was held admissible where it had been offered as part of a compromise and the offer had been accepted and acted upon.

In *Ofulue & Anor v Bossert* [2009] UKHL 16 the House of Lords held (by a majority) that a without prejudice acknowledgement of title to property was not admissible to defeat a claim for adverse possession.

### [24.2.46]   Copies of non-privileged originals

Generally, if an original document is not privileged, whether in the hands of one of the parties or of a third person, then any copy of that document is not privileged notwithstanding it may have come into existence for the purpose of litigation (*Bank of Dubai v Galadari* [1989] 3 All ER 769). This is subject to an exception in the case of a collection of documents where the documents '... are procured by the advisers themselves for the purposes of the litigation, since where such a collection of documents has been so prepared its principles of selection, editing, organisation and classification might themselves indicate the substance of the party's case.' (*Cross on Evidence*, 7th ed, p 434, citing *Lyell v Kennedy (No 3)* (1884) 27 Ch D 1). It is doubtful whether *R v Board of Inland Revenue, ex p Goldberg* [1988] 3 All ER 248 remains good law, but see *Hodgkinson v Simms* (1988) 55 DLR (4th) 577.

## [24.2.47]    Waiver or loss of privilege

Privilege may be waived, either expressly or by implication. Actual disclosure bringing a document into the public domain is an example of the latter, but not limited disclosure to parties having a common interest: *Redfern Ltd v O'Mahony & Ors* [2009] IESC 18 (SC Ireland). Likewise privilege is impliedly waived by a client bringing proceedings in negligence against its former solicitors: *Paragon Finance plc v Freshfields* [1999] 1 WLR 1183 (CA); *Nam Tai Electronics Inc v PWC* [2008] 1 HKC 427 (CFA) (para 46); or where a client makes a wasted costs application against its own legal representative: *Ma So So Josephine v Chin Yuk Lun Francis & Anor* [2004] 3 HKLRD 294 (CFA) (para 11) (as to which see the commentary under Order 62 rule 8).

The right to claim privilege reposes with the client and may be waived only by the client or on the client's instructions: *Anderson v Bank of British Columbia* (1876) 2 ChD 644, 649.

Waiver of privilege in a document will normally apply to the whole of its contents but waiver in respect of one of a series of documents does not necessarily extend to the others: *Great Atlantic Insurance Co v Home Insurance Co* [1981] 2 All ER 485 (CA); *Lyell v Kennedy* (1884) 27 ChD 1. A party waiving privilege on a particular issue is not entitled to do so selectively. The court may order all relevant material to be disclosed in order to ensure there is no 'cherry picking'. See *Goldion Properties Ltd & Ors v Regent National Enterprises Ltd* [2005] 4 HKC 500, 521D (CA). There the court preferred the English test of fairness to the Australasian 'putting in issue' approach.

Reference to a privileged communication in a witness statement or expert report may result in waiver of the privilege: *Fleming v Houlder Marine Services (HK) Ltd* HCA 5623/1986 (Deputy Judge Findlay QC; 01.02.1990); *Chan Mun Kui v Lau Yuk Lai* HCPI 301/1998 (Seagroatt J; 23.09.1999). Likewise a reference to a privileged communication in a pleading or affidavit: *Roberts v Oppenheim* (1884) 26 ChD 724 (CA); *Goldion Properties* (above); *AXA China Region Insurance Co Ltd & Anor v Pacific Century Insurance Co Ltd & Ors (No 2)* [2005] 3 HKC 359 (para 12). Underlying these authorities seems to be a principle based on fairness, that it is unfair to allow a party to rely on a document but refuse to disclose it on the ground of privilege. Merely citing the existence of the privileged communication will not result in waiver – there must be reference to its contents and reliance thereon: *Ma Man Wan Helen v Hong Kong Land Group Ltd* HCPI 381/2005 (Deputy Judge Muttrie; 10.01.2006); *Treasure Spot Finance Co Ltd v Li Chik Ming & Anor* HCA 5387/2001 (Deputy Judge Poon; 20.07.2006), both referring to *Bourns Inc v Raychem Corp & Anor* [1999] 3 All ER 154, 166j–177a (CA).

A passing reference in an open letter to a previous without prejudice communication was held not to constitute waiver of the privilege in *Tonkin & Anor v UK Insurance (No 2)* [2006] EWHC 1185 (TCC) (18.05.2006) (para 9).

In *Rockefeller & Co Inc v Secretary for Justice & Anor* [2000] 3 HKC 48 (CA) the court refused to restrain disclosure by the prosecution of documents which had been provided to the SFC on a confidential basis, to be used for limited purposes only. The majority appear to have been of the view that privilege had not been waived, but that it was outweighed by the prosecution's duty to disclose unused material to a criminal defendant.

**[24.2.48]    Public policy may over-ride privilege**
There exist at common law certain circumstances in which the privilege against disclosure of documents may be over-ridden by considerations of public policy.

In *Rockefeller & Co Inc v Secretary for Justice & Anor* [2000] 3 HKC 48, 50B–C Godfrey VP held that the public interest in protecting confidential documents (which had been found to be subject to legal professional privilege) was outweighed by the public interest in allowing a defendant in criminal proceedings to use them in his defence. Disclosure was allowed. In support Godfrey VP cited *Taylor v Director of the Serious Frauds Office* [1999] 2 AC 177, 217–8.

**[24.2.49]    Discovery of confidential documents**
The fact that a document is confidential does not mean it is privileged or subject to public interest immunity. Nevertheless, where obtained in confidential circumstances and pursuant to compulsion such as in an enquiry into the affairs of a listed company, there is a 'powerful argument' that the court should not order disclosure even where the provisions of Order 24 have been satisfied: *British and Commonwealth Holdings plc (in administration) v Barclays de Zoete Wedd L*td [1999] 1 BCLC 86, quoted in *Cheeroll Ltd v Tose & Ors* [2003] 2 HKC 422, 431 F-H.

In the *Cheeroll* case the party opposing disclosure referred to *Wallace Smith Trust Co Ltd (in liq) v Deloitte Haskins & Sells* (a firm) [1996] 4 All ER 403 as setting out the circumstances in which disclosure will be ordered. See the judgment of Deputy Judge Fung in *Cheeroll* at 431H – 432 A, quoting the following passage from the judgment of Simon Brown LJ:

> Disclosure will be necessary if:
>
> (a)    it will give 'litigious advantage' to the party seeking inspection;
>
> (b)    the information sought is not otherwise available to the party by, for example, admissions, or some other form of proceeding (e.g. interrogatories) or from some other source; and
>
> (c)    such order for disclosure would not be oppressive, perhaps because of the sheer volume of the documents.

In *Cheeroll*, Deputy Judge Fung went on to order disclosure of confidential information which had been obtained in the course of preparing a report under the Companies Ordinance into the affairs of a Hong Kong listed company. The documents were highly relevant to the litigation, it was admitted they were of litigious advantage and the court could not say they were only of little probative value (per Deputy Judge Fung at 432 G-H).

In England 'exceptional measures of a kind now well established' may be put in place to protect sensitive information which is disclosed on discovery. See *Virgin Media Ltd v BSkyB plc* [2008] 1 WLR 2854; [2008] EWCA Civ 612 (para 3) where the parties agreed that commercially sensitive information be restricted to identified external legal advisers subject to express undertakings not to disclose them or their contents to anyone, including their own clients.

In *Yuen Wendy v Yuen Philip* [1984] HKLR 431 (CA), a solicitor objected to disclosure of the financial records of his firm in matrimonial proceedings. The solicitor's partners objected to disclosure of their confidential information. The Court of Appeal did not decide on the question of confidentiality, but ordered that the solicitor be cross-examined on his affidavit of means.

3.      **Order for discovery** (O. 24 r. 3)

        **(1)   Subject to the provisions of this rule and of rules 4 and 8, the Court may order any party to a cause or matter (whether begun by writ, originating summons or otherwise) to make and serve on any other party a list of the documents which are or have been in his possession, custody or power relating to any matter in question in the cause or matter, and may at the same time or subsequently also order him to make and file an affidavit verifying such a list and to serve a copy thereof on the other party.**

        **(2)   Where a party who is required by rule 2 to make discovery of documents fails to comply with any provision of that rule, the Court, on the application of any party to whom the discovery was required to be made, may make an order against the first-mentioned party under paragraph (1) of this rule or, as the case may be, may order him to make and file an affidavit verifying the list of documents he is required to make under rule 2 and to serve a copy thereof on the applicant.**

        **(3)   An order under this rule may be limited to such documents or classes of document only, or to such only of the matters in question in the cause or matter, as may be specified in the order.**

---

**NOTES**

**[24.3.1]   Stage at which discovery may be ordered**
In *Dragages et Travaux Publics v Lau Ching Kit t/a Man Shun Construction & Decoration Co & Ors* HCA 6414/1980 (Liu J; 26.06.1981), discovery was ordered in advance of the defence being served. The registrar had ordered discovery of two classes of documents by the plaintiffs and granted the fourth defendants leave to file a defence out of time within seven days after inspection of the documents ordered to be disclosed. On appeal Liu J found:

> These defendants have set a course for their defence in this action, and they do not seem to be on any fishing expedition. The documents ordered in the discovery are limited in nature, and no difficulty should be expected by the plaintiff. A peripheral indication, if acceptable as a pleading, would inevitably necessitate extensive amendments and incur unwarranted litigation costs. The information sought from the documents desired, so counsel concluded, were necessary for disposing fairly of the controversy between the parties ... These contentions are formidable. In the circumstances, the exercise of discretion of the learned Registrar cannot in any way be faulted.

**[24.3.2]   Verification**
The various provisions in Order 24 rules 2, 3(1) and (2) suggest a somewhat narrow discretion in the courts to refuse an invitation to impose a term of verification when ordering discovery after default. Terms should readily be imposed if an applicant has not been shown to have made a real effort in his preparation of a list of documents, with usual care and sincerity. However, there is such a discretion and the court may exercise it in favour of not ordering verification in other types of cases (*Tanfory Ltd t/a Volvo Nightclub v China City Night Club Ltd & Ors* HCA 2482/1987 (Liu J; 15.03.1989)).

**[24.3.3] Application for a further and better list of documents**

The court has power under this rule to order that a further and better list of documents be served. See *Shailain Hirachand Jhaveri t/a Kiran Diamonds v Jayantilal Chunilal Jhaveri & Ors* HCA 1237/88 (Liu J; 26.06.1989) where the principles applicable in England were applied on such an application.

**[24.3.4] Court will not allow 'fishing expedition'**

It is well settled that the court will not order discovery to assist a 'fishing expedition', that is an attempt to find something as yet unknown to 'turn a non-issue into an issue': *HKFE Clearing Corp Ltd v Yicko Futures Ltd* [2006] 2 HKC 233 (CA), para 17. In *Vo Thi Do v Director of Immigration* [1998] 1 HKLRD 729 (CA) Litton VP memorably condemned as a departure from the 'discipline of law' an application for a large number of documents in the hope that 'by a microscopic examination of those papers... some procedural defect or blunder on the part of the authorities might be discovered'. See also *Chau Ka Chik Tso v Secretary for Justice* [2006] 2 HKC 95, para 35, quoting *Re State of Norway's Application* [1987] 1 QB 433, 482 where it was said that impermissible fishing is:

> ...where what is sought is not evidence as such, but information which may lead to a line of inquiry ... It is the search for material in the hope of being able to raise allegations of fact, as opposed to elicitation of evidence to support allegations of fact which have been raised *bona fide* with adequate particularisation'.

**[24.3.5] Right of client to be heard on application for discovery of privileged documents**

The right to claim privilege reposes with the client, not the solicitor: *Anderson v Bank of BC* (1876) 2 Ch D 644, 649. As a result, it has been suggested that the client is entitled to be heard on an application for discovery of documents which may be privileged. See *McMullen v Kennedy* [2008] IESC 69 (16.12.2008) (para 25) (Supreme Court of Ireland). In that case, a plaintiff was seeking discovery against a firm of solicitors in respect of documents relating to a matter in which it acted on behalf of another client.

**4. Order for determination of issue, etc., before discovery** (O. 24 r. 4)

**(1) Where on an application for an order under rule 2 or 3 it appears to the Court that any issue or question in the cause or matter should be determined before any discovery of documents is made by the parties, the Court may order that that issue or question be determined first.**

**(2) Where in an action begun by writ an order is made under this rule for the determination of an issue or question, Order 25, rules 2 to 7, shall, with the omission of so much of rule 7(1) as requires parties to serve a notice specifying the orders and directions which they desire and with any other necessary modifications, apply as if the application on which the order was made were a case management summons. (L.N. 152 of 2008)**

**5. Form of list and affidavit** (O. 24 r. 5)

**(1) A list of documents made in compliance with rule 2 or with an order under rule 3 must be in Form No. 26 in Appendix A, and must enumerate**

the documents in a convenient order and as shortly as possible but describing each of them or, in the case of bundles of documents of the same nature, each bundle, sufficiently to enable it to be identified.

(2)   If it is desired to claim that any documents are privileged from production, the claim must be made in the list of documents with a sufficient statement of the grounds of the privilege.

(3)   An affidavit made as aforesaid verifying a list of documents must be in Form No. 27 in Appendix A.

---

**NOTES**

**[24.5.1]     Manner in which documents should be listed**
A list of documents under Order 24 must be in form 26, Appendix A to these rules. The form of list prescribes that documents be divided into categories depending whether they are, or are no longer, in the party's possession, and prescribes a separate part for documents in respect of which privilege is claimed.

It is not always necessary to list each document individually. It is permissible to list a bundle of documents of a similar nature as a single item: see Order 24 rule 5(1). In *Wong Tsu Yew Charles & Ors v Bermuda Trust (Hong Kong) Ltd* [2002] 4 HKC 196, 202A–C, Chung J held that in deciding whether documents listed as a bundle are of the same nature and can be listed accordingly, regard should be had to the character of the documents, the nature of the action and the issues. The learned judge quoted extensively from the judgment of Hobhouse J in *Sveriges Angfartygs Assurans Forening v The 1976 Eagle Insurance Co SA* (QBD, 28 March 1990, unreported).

Documents in respect of which privilege is claimed need not be identified individually. See *Re Kong Wah Holdings Ltd* HCCW 49/2000 (Kwan J; 13.09.2007) where the court referred to a line of English cases including *Ventouris v Mountain* [1990] 3 All ER 157 and *Derby & Co Ltd & Ors v Weldon & Ors (No 7)* [1990] 3 All ER 161, [1990] 1 WLR 1156, and said (para 57):

> Thus, in respect of documents for which privilege is claimed, it would not be required to list them individually and it would be permissible to give a compendious description by type or category, so long as it is possible to identify them, and provided that the ground of privilege and the facts giving rise to the claim for privilege are clearly stated. See, for example, the formulas usually adopted and as approved in *Ventouris* [above, at 160g] and *Derby v Weldon* [above, at 178i All ER]. The rationale behind this is that a more detailed description of the documents might be capable of undermining the privilege by revealing information . . .

In *Re Kong Wah Holdings* (above, at para 61) the court went on to consider the '*Kadlunga* order' whereby the court may order a party 'to give a supplementary list of documents identifying individually the documents over which privilege was claimed, by reference to the date, author, addressee and a brief description of the nature of the document without disclosing its contents'. That type of order derives from a line of Australian cases emanating from *Kadlunga Proprietors v Electricity Trust of SA* (1985) 39 SASR 410. The court made an order along those lines in *Re Kong Wah Holdings*, albeit in respect of discovery under section 221 of the Companies Ordinance (Cap 32) rather than this Order.

**6.      Defendant entitled to copy of co-defendant's list** (O. 24 r. 6)

(1)    A defendant who has pleaded in an action shall be entitled to have a copy of any list of documents served under any of the foregoing rules of this Order on the plaintiff by any other defendant to the action; and a plaintiff against whom a counterclaim is made in an action begun by writ shall be entitled to have a copy of any list of documents served under any of those rules on the party making the counterclaim by any other defendant to the counterclaim.

(2)    A party required by virtue of paragraph (1) to supply a copy of a list of documents must supply it free of charge on a request made by the party entitled to it.

(3)    Where in an action begun by originating summons the Court makes an order under rule 3 requiring a defendant to the action to serve a list of documents on the plaintiff, it may also order him to supply any other defendant to the action with a copy of that list.

(4)    In this rule "list of documents" includes an affidavit verifying a list of documents.

**7.      Order for discovery of particular documents** (O. 24 r. 7)

(1)    Subject to rule 8, the Court may at any time, on the application of any party to a cause or matter, make an order requiring any other party to make an affidavit stating whether any document specified or described in the application or any class of document so specified or described is, or has at any time been, in his possession, custody or power, and if not then in his possession, custody or power when he parted with it and what has become of it.

(2)    An order may be made against a party under this rule notwithstanding that he may already have made or been required to make a list of documents or affidavit under rule 2 or rule 3.

(3)    An application for an order under this rule must be supported by an affidavit stating the belief of the deponent that the party from whom discovery is sought under this rule has, or at some time had, in his possession, custody or power the document, or class of document, specified or described in the application and that it relates to one or more of the matters in question in the cause or matter.

---

## NOTES

**[24.7.1]      Grounds for making order for specific discovery**

The relevant principles on an application for specific discovery under Order 24 rule 7 were summarised as follows in *Paul's Model Art GMBH & Co KG v UT Ltd* [2006] 1 HKC 238, 247D-H (CA):

(1)    There is no jurisdiction to make an order under Order 24 rule 7 for the production of documents unless:

    (a)    there is sufficient evidence that the documents exist which the other party has not disclosed;

    (b)    the document or documents relate to matters in issue in the action;

(c) there is sufficient evidence that the document is in the possession, custody or power of the other party.

(2) When it is established that those three prerequisites for jurisdiction do exist, the court has a discretion whether or not to order disclosure.

(3) The order must identify with precision the document or documents or categories of document which are required to be disclosed, for otherwise the person making the list may find himself in serious trouble for swearing to a false affidavit, even though doing his best to give an honest disclosure. (See *Berkeley Administration Inc v McClelland* [1990] FSR 381).

In *Deak & Co (Far East) Ltd v N M Rothschild & Sons Ltd & Ors* [1981] HKC 78, 80H–I (CA) and in *Full Range Electronics Co Ltd v General-Tech Industrial Ltd & Anor* [1997] 1 HKC 541, 544C (appeal dismissed – see CACV 59/1997 (Nazareth VP, Godfrey JA & Rogers J; 11.06.1997)) it was said that the burden is on the party seeking specific discovery to satisfy the court on a *prima facie* basis.

In addition the court must be satisfied that discovery is necessary for disposing fairly of the cause or matter or for saving costs: see Order 24 rule 8.

**[24.7.2]    Affidavit in support**

An application for a specific discovery order must be supported by an affidavit setting out the matters required by rule 7(3).

**[24.7.3]    Order for discovery of 'class' of document**

Order 24 rule 7 encompasses an order for discovery of a 'class' of document. It has been held that to constitute a 'class', the relevant documents must be of the same nature. See *Deak & Co (Far East) Ltd v NM Rothschild & Sons Ltd* [1981] HKC 78. Thus 'correspondence ... relating to the accident' is a class of document: *Seabrook v British Transport Commission* [1959] 1 WLR 509. However 'any other documentation held in any medium showing details ... of visits ... to the electronic version of the Magazine' does not describe a class of document: see *Morinda International Hong Kong Ltd v Next Magazine Publishing Ltd* [2003] 1 HKC 492.

**[24.7.4]    Privilege as a ground for opposing specific discovery**

An application for an order for specific discovery may be opposed on the ground that the relevant documents are privileged from production. In such a case it is appropriate for the court to be allowed to inspect the relevant documents in order to decide whether the claim to privilege is well founded. See for example *Lui Yiu Nga v Hospital Authority* [2002] 4 HKC 204. Production of privileged documents to a judge for such a purpose does not constitute waiver of the privilege: *Goldstone v Williams* [1899] 1 Ch 47. It has been held that a simple assertion by counsel without further information is insufficient to establish privilege on a contested application for specific discovery: *Shooting Star Amusements Ltd v Prince George Agricultural & Historical Ass'n* [2009] BCCA 452 (22.10.2009).

In *The Bank of Tokyo, Ltd & Ors v Regentcourt Ltd & Ors* CACV 86/1987 (Silke VP, Kempster & Hunter JJA; 22.10.1987) it was argued that an order for specific discovery should be made first, leaving it to the discovering party to claim privilege in complying with the order. The Court of Appeal rejected this argument.

**[24.7.5]     Early discovery under Order 24 rule 7**

Order 24 rule 7(1) provides that the court may make an order for discovery 'at any time'. Thus there is no requirement that a party must wait for service of the opposing party's list of documents before making an application: *Allaha Ditta v Rodney Engineering Co Ltd* HCPI 981/2005 (Suffiad J; 29.12.2006). However it has been held that the rule may not be invoked pre-action: *Chan Ka Kit v AS Watson & Co Ltd* HCPI 554/2007 (Master B Kwan; 04.12.2007).

At the early stages of an action discovery will only be ordered in exceptional circumstances: see *McKay v Rysaffe Ltd & Ors* [1983] 2 HKC 436, 438I *et seq* where it was said:

> There is no doubt that in a proper case, a party can seek and obtain disclosure of documents at a very early stage in the proceedings . . . But it will only be ordered in exceptional circumstances (see *RHM Foods Ltd v Bovril Ltd* [1982] 1 All ER 673) and not where the sole object is to seek discovery before a full and proper pleading in the statement of claim and merely to substantiate suspicions and thereby assist in obtaining interlocutory relief.

The exceptional circumstances requirement for early discovery finds justification in the scheme of Order 24. First, discovery relates only to 'matters in question in the action' (see rules 1(1) and 7(3)). Until there is a statement of claim 'the court can seldom know what are the matters in question in the action': *RHM Foods* (above, at 677); and the same may be said with regard to a defence: *Bank of India v Sadhwani* HCA 4939/1983 (Kempster J; 05.12.1983). Secondly rule 8 enjoins the court to refuse an application for discovery unless it is necessary for fair disposition of the action or for saving costs. In many cases this will be an insurmountable hurdle given that discovery would, in the usual course of events, be available at a later stage.

The 'exceptional circumstances' test was satisfied and early discovery ordered in *Lim Siew Peng v Glaxo Wellcome HK Ltd* [1997] 3 HKC 802 where the court ordered discovery, before service of the statement of claim, of a former employer's reference letter in an action for damages for negligent mis-statement, breach of duty or libel contained in that letter.

**[24.7.6]     Scope of discovery which may be ordered**

An application for specific discovery should be confined within reasonable limits. If it is too wide, or would place an undue burden on the opposing party, it may be refused on grounds such as lack of relevance, oppression or waste of costs. In *Daiwa Bank Ltd v Hing Yip Hing Fat Co Ltd* [1990] 2 HKC 82 the Court of Appeal set aside an order for discovery the scope of which was 'impossibly wide', going beyond matters at issue in the action. In *Wharf Properties Ltd v Eric Cumine Associates* HCA 13431/1983 (Mortimer J; 25.04.1987) a discovery application was dismissed on grounds of irrelevance, oppression due to the huge number of documents which would require sifting and failure to meet the criteria laid down by rule 8.

Likewise in *Lee Annabell v Lee Wing Kim* HCAP 5/2003 (Chu J; 05.03.2003) (para 27) an application for specific discovery was refused where it sought 'an unduly wide scope of documents' and lacked precision such that it would be 'both oppressive and difficult to comply in full'.

It appears that applications for specific discovery in cases on the commercial list (as to which see Order 72) may be subject to particular scrutiny in this regard. See

*Anbest Electronic Ltd v CGU Int'l Insurance plc* CACV 17/2007 (Rogers ACJHC & Burrell J; 25.04.2007) (para 8) where it was said:

> It is a feature of the commercial court that an effort is made to restrict discovery to that which is essential. Discovery has become more and more extensive. It is often extremely onerous. Sometimes, it would appear that it is used as a means of frustrating the progress of a case by deliberate excessive demands for discovery. It is for this reason that in specialist lists an effort is made to contain discovery.

## [24.7.7]    Repeat application for specific discovery

Where an application for specific discovery has been dismissed, a fresh application for the same specific discovery on the same grounds is liable to be dismissed as an attempt to relitigate an issue already decided. See *Re Prudential Enterprises Ltd (No 2)* [2004] 2 HKC 205, 209B-D. However, there are exceptions to this rule. In the *Prudential case* (at 210D-E), Chu J said:

> In my view, if there is fresh evidence that shows the existence or relevance of documents previously sought but refused, then there can be no doubt that a renewed application for discovery is permissible. But where, as the petitioners contend here, fresh evidence arises casting doubt on the assertion on oath by the party from whom discovery is sought that he does not have the documents asked for, then the applying party cannot make a renewed discovery application on the basis that the responding party has not been truthful in his assertion on oath.

In the *Prudential case*, Chu J dismissed a fresh application for specific discovery which was based on inadmissible hearsay from a newspaper and judicial decisions overseas.

**7A.    Application under section 41 or 42(1) of the Ordinance** (O. 24 r. 7A)

**(1)    An application for an order under section 41 of the Ordinance for the disclosure of documents before the commencement of proceedings shall be made by originating summons (in Form No. 10 in Appendix A) and the person against whom the order is sought shall be made defendant to the summons. (L.N. 404 of 1991)**

**(2)    An application after the commencement of proceedings for an order under section 42(1) of the Ordinance for the disclosure of documents by a person who is not a party to the proceedings shall be made by summons, which must be served on that person personally and on every party to the proceedings other than the applicant.**

**(3)    A summons under paragraph (1) or (2) shall be supported by an affidavit which must—**

    **(a)    in the case of a summons under paragraph (1), state the grounds on which it is alleged that the applicant and the person against whom the order is sought are likely to be parties to subsequent proceedings in the Court of First Instance; (L.N. 152 of 2008)**

    **(b)    in any case, specify or describe the documents in respect of which the order is sought and show, if practicable by reference to any pleading served or intended to be served in the proceedings, that the documents are relevant to an issue**

arising or likely to arise in the proceedings and that the person against whom the order is sought is likely to have or have had them in his possession, custody or power. (L.N. 152 of 2008)

(3A) In the case of a summons under paragraph (1), paragraph 3(b) shall be construed as if for the word "relevant", there were substituted the words "directly relevant (within the meaning of section 41 of the Ordinance)". (L.N. 152 of 2008)

(4) A copy of the supporting affidavit shall be served with the summons on every person on whom the summons is required to be served.

(5) An order under section 41 or 42(1) for the disclosure of documents may be made conditional on the applicant's giving security for the costs of the person against whom it is made or on such other terms, if any, as the Court thinks just, and shall require the person against whom the order is made to make an affidavit stating whether any documents specified or described in the order are, or at any time have been, in his possession, custody or power and, if not then in his possession, custody or power, when he parted with them and what has become of them.

(6) No person shall be compelled by virtue of such an order to produce any documents which he could not be compelled to produce—

(a) in the case of a summons under paragraph (1), if the subsequent proceedings had already been begun; or

(b) in the case of a summons under paragraph (2), if he had been served with a writ of subpoena duces tecum to produce the documents at the trial.

(7) (Repealed L.N. 152 of 2008)

(8) For the purposes of rules 10 and 11 an application for an order under section 41 or 42(1) shall be treated as a cause or matter between the applicant and the person against whom the order is sought.

## NOTES

### [24.7A.1] Applications for disclosure before action and against non-parties – now available in all proceedings

Order 24 rule 7A applies to applications for disclosure of documents under sections 41 and 42 of the High Court Ordinance, and should be read in conjunction therewith. Section 43 is also relevant. It specifically authorises the rules committee to make provision in the rules of court for disclosure orders under those sections.

Section 41 provides for discovery before action in certain circumstances, and section 42 provides for discovery against non-parties. Previously both sections applied only to claims concerning personal injuries or death. The Chief Justice's working party on civil justice reform recommended in its final report (recommendations 75 and 78) that both sections be amended so as to apply to all types of cases. That was done with effect from 2009. As a consequence, references to claims for personal injuries or in respect of a person's death were removed from rule 7A as part of the CJR, also with effect from 2009.

The amendments recommended by the Chief Justice's working party follow those which were made in the United Kingdom some years earlier. The relevant provisions in England and Wales are now CPR 31.16 (disclosure before action) and 31.17 (non-party pre-trial disclosure). Although the broad thrust of the provisions in Hong Kong is similar to those in England, the provisions in the two jurisdictions are by no means identical.

**[24.7A.2]   Exercise of court's power to order disclosure before action**
The requirements for exercise of the court's power to order disclosure of documents before action under section 41 of the High Court Ordinance may be summarised as follows:

(a)    application must be made by a person who appears to be likely to be a party to subsequent proceedings; and

(b)    application must be against a person who appears to be likely to be a party to the contemplated proceedings, and is likely to have or have had documents directly relevant to an issue arising or likely to arise out of that claim.

The above matters must be demonstrated to the court by evidence in accordance with rule 7A(3). For the purposes of point (b) above, a document is only to be regarded as 'directly relevant' if it would be 'likely to be relied upon by any party in evidence in the proceedings', or it 'supports or adversely affects any party's case'. See section 41(2). The latter requirement ('supports or adversely affects …') is similar to one of the criteria in CPR 31.6 for 'standard disclosure', which in England replaces *Peruvian Guano* as to the scope of discovery between parties in the ordinary course of an action. Reading rule 7A(3)(b) and 7A(3A) together, it can be seen that the affidavit in support of a section 41 application must demonstrate that the documents are directly relevant in that sense.

The power extends only to requiring the respondent to disclose whether the documents sought are in its possession custody or power, and to produce those documents to the applicant or, subject to conditions which may be specified, to the applicant's legal adviser (if any) or medical or other professional advisers. See section 41(1)(a) and (b). It is thus clear that the court may, on granting an order for pre-action disclosure, restrict the applicant's access to the documents disclosed.

See also Order 24 rule 8(2) by which the court is enjoined not to make an order for pre-action disclosure unless it is of the opinion that the order is necessary either for fair disposal of the case or for saving costs.

In England it is recognised that the power is discretionary (*Black v Sumitomo Corp* [2001] EWCA Civ 1819, [2002] 1 WLR 1562) and that the jurisdictional threshold for making an order is not a high one. That should be the case in Hong Kong as well.

The Chief Justice's working party (final report, para 488) advised that it was not necessary to specify in the rule as a discretionary factor the desirability of pre-action disclosure in aid of early settlement because pre-action protocols were not being generally adopted in Hong Kong.

The English rule differs from its Hong Kong equivalent in that the former expressly requires the court to be satisfied that if proceedings had already been commenced, the usual obligations as to discovery would extend to the documents sought.

Because of the differences between the legislation in the two jurisdictions, English cases should be considered with care with regard to applications for pre-action disclosure in Hong Kong. The following extract from the commentary at CPR 31.16[1A] in our sister publication in the UK, The Civil Court Practice does appear to have some relevance in Hong Kong:

> Before making an order under this rule the court needs to be satisfied as to the likely issues in the litigation and that the documents sought, being those which would be disclosed on standard disclosure [the latter requirement not adopted in Hong Kong], would either support or adversely affect the case of one side or the other [a requirement expressly included in s 41(2)(b) in Hong Kong]; it was then for the court to determine, as a balancing exercise, whether an order was desirable: *Bermuda Int'l Securities Ltd v KPGM (a firm)* [2001] EWCA Civ 269, (2001) 145 Sol Jo LB 70.

> > One of the factors against making an order might be the likelihood of the proposed claim being struck out: *K v Secretary of State for the Home Office* [2001] CP Rep 39.

> > There are practical dangers which arise when deciding any substantive issue as a preliminary issue on any application for pre-action disclosure; a court should be hesitant, in the context of such an application, about embarking upon any determination of substantive issues in the case; it would normally be sufficient to found an application under [the rule] for the substantive claim pursued in the proceedings to be properly arguable and to have a real prospect of success, and it would normally be appropriate to approach the conditions [as to exercise of the power] on that basis: *Rose v Lynx Express Ltd* [2004] EWCA Civ 447, [2004] 1 BCLC 455.

> > In *Black v Sumitomo* [above], it was held that the word 'likely' in CPR 31.16(3) [in Hong Kong s 41(1) and rule 7A(3)(a)] meant, in effect 'may well', and that it applied to the issue of whether the applicant and respondent would be parties to proceedings, if they were issued, and it did not apply to the issue of such proceedings themselves. So the position appears to be that the applicant has to show that he and the respondent may well be parties to proceedings, if such proceedings take place.

> > An application for pre-action disclosure may be refused if the party seeking the disclosure could have sought the same under a pre-action protocol but has failed so to do and the lack of pre-action disclosure had not prevented their writing a letter of claim [letter before action]: *Steamship Mutual Underwriting Ass'n Trustees (Bermuda) Ltd v Baring Asset Management Ltd* [2004] EWHC 202 (Comm) [2004] All ER (D) 272 (Feb), Aikens J (a case where, additionally, there had been sufficient disclosure already and the issues were clear; consequently, the pre-action disclosure was not necessary).

See also *Moresfield Ltd & Ors v Banners (a firm) & Anor* [2003] EWHC 1602 (Ch) (03.07.2003) (para 32) where the English court summarised the principles established by the authorities, especially *Black v Sumitomo Corp* (above) and *Bermuda Int'l Securities Ltd v KPMG* (above) in the following terms:

(a)  [the equivalent English legislation] does not require that the proceedings are likely, but rather that the respondent is likely to be a party if proceedings are issued, where 'likely' means 'may well';

(b)  because disclosure will only be ordered in relation to documents which would be the subject of standard disclosure the court must be clear what the issues in the litigation are likely to be [note that Hong Kong retains the *Peruvian Guano* test as to the scope of discovery, and has not adopted England's 'standard discovery' – see the commentary under Order 24 rule 2];

(c)   the court is only permitted to consider a grant of pre-action disclosure where there is a real prospect in principle of such an order being fair to the parties if litigation is commenced, or of assisting the parties to avoid litigation, or of saving costs in any event;

(d)   if there is such a real prospect the court should go on to consider the question of discretion which has to be considered on all the facts and not merely in principle but also in detail;

(e)   pre-action disclosure should not be ordered as a matter of course, at any rate where the parties at the pre-action stage have been acting reasonably;

(f)   the discretionary elements include the clarity and identification of the issues raised by the complaint, the nature of the documents requested, and the opportunity which the complainant has to make its case without pre-action disclosure;

(g)   the more focused the complaint and the more limited the disclosure sought, the easier it is for the court to exercise its discretion in favour of an order on the basis that transparency was what the interests of justice and proportionality most required.

## [24.7A.3]   Procedure on application under HCO s 41

An application for disclosure of documents before action under section 41 of the High Court Ordinance should be made by originating summons in form No 10 in appendix A, which is the expedited form. See rule 7A(1).

The rule does not expressly provide that the originating summons must be served on the prospective defendant, but this must necessarily follow from the fact that it is the expedited form of originating summons which is required to be used, rather than the *ex parte* form of originating summons.

The application must be supported by evidence on affidavit or affirmation setting out the matters required by rule 7A(3).

## [24.7A.4]   Order against non-party for disclosure under HCO s 42

Section 42(1) of the High Court Ordinance empowers the court to order disclosure, in existing proceedings, against non-parties. The section was amended in 2009 so that it now applies to all types of cases, whereas previously it was restricted to personal injuries and fatal accident cases. In recommending this amendment, the Chief Justice's working party on civil justice reform noted (final report, para 492) *O'Sullivan v Herdmans Ltd* [1987] 1 WLR 1047, 1056 (HL) where Lord Mackay said the previous procedure whereby in non-personal injuries actions it was necessary to issue a subpoena *duces tecum* returnable at trial in order to compel disclosure by a non-party was not in the interests of justice. It was also noted that this form of disclosure in non-personal injuries actions was already possible under the procedure improvised by Lord Donaldson MR in *Williams v Williams* [1988] QB 161, 169 whereby a trial would be split so that after disclosure is obtained under a subpoena *duces tecum* at the initial stage, there would be a break during which the parties could consider the material disclosed, before the trial resumes.

See also Order 24 rule 8(2) by which the court is enjoined not to make an order for disclosure against a non-party unless it is of the opinion that the order is necessary either for fair disposal of the case or for saving costs.

Application may be made by a 'party'. See the broad definition of that word in section 2 of the Ordinance, which extends beyond persons named on the record. A third party may apply under the section: *Cheung Kai Wing v Mok Sheung Shun (Tigu Insurance Co Ltd, 3ʳᵈ party)* [1993] 2 HKC 113, 119D *et seq* (CA).

Disclosure under section 42(1) is in respect of 'documents which are relevant to an issue arising out of [the] claim'. In *Chan Tam-sze v Hip Hing Construction Co Ltd* [1990] 1 HKLR 473 it was held that those words have the same meaning as 'relating to matters in question in the action' in Order 24 rule 1(1), and that the *Peruvian Guano* test as to the ambit of discovery under that rule applies. See also rule 7A(3)(b) (by which the affidavit in support of the application must show that the documents are relevant to an issue arising or likely to arise), and see *Chan Ho Yeung Jason v Dr Chang Wai Julian* HCPI 248/2003 (Suffiad J; 09.11.2005).

The court's power under section 42(1) extends to making an order against the first clerk of a magistrate's court to disclose the minutes of proceedings in such court, and is not limited by section 35A of the Magistrates Ordinance: *Wong Siu Hing & Anor v Lo Che Keung* [1991] 1 HKC 412.

In *Chan Tam-sze* (above) the court made an order under section 42(1) requiring the Commissioner for Labour to disclose documents relating to an accident investigation. It was held that at the same time it was necessary to make an order under section 5(4) of the Factories and Industrial Undertakings Ordinance (Cap 59), but that should no longer be necessary as section 5 was repealed in 1997.

The equivalent procedure in England is governed by CPR 31.17. The Civil Court Practice, our sister publication in the UK, says of that provision:

> **Disclosure by non-party** The two requirements of CPR 31.17(3) [in Hong Kong, Order 24 rules 7A and 8, so far as relevant to applications under section 42 of the High Court Ordinance] must both be satisfied in relation to a document before the court can make an order under this rule in respect of it. However, where a number of documents are the subject of an application under this rule, the court may conclude that an order should be made for disclosure of all of the documents in a specified class, even though the first requirement ["the documents of which disclosure is sought are likely to support the case of the applicant or adversely affect the case of one of the other parties"] may not be satisfied in respect of every one of them. This was justified on the ground of practicality, but also on the basis that any document has to be read in its context – *Three Rivers (No 4)* [*Three Rivers District Council v Bank of England (No 4)* [2002] EWCA Civ 1182, [2002] 4 All ER 881, [2003] 1 WLR 210]. Even where the two conditions are satisfied, the court still has a discretion which will normally involve carrying out a balancing exercise. On an application under this rule, the Court must first decide whether disclosure was necessary for the purpose of fairly disposing of the claim which is said to justify disclosure (or to save costs) [see rule 8 in Hong Kong]. If the Court is also satisfied that, absent an order under this rule, the applicant could not get the document (or the information it contains), then it must balance the competing interests, as in *Frankson v Home Office* [2003] EWCA Civ 655, [2003] All ER (D) 80, [2003] 1 WLR 1952.

> As this rule overrides any rights to privacy [see below], the court will exercise its discretion particularly carefully. In the event that the court orders the production of a list, the list will state which documents are in the person's control and those documents which he has had but which are no longer in his control and what has happened to them. The court may consider that the requirement to provide a list of documents is too onerous and order inspection only of identified documents.

In *Tajik Aluminium Plant v Hydro Aluminium AS* [2005] EWCA Civ 1218, [2005] 4 All ER 1232, the Court of Appeal emphasised the distinction between a disclosure order against a non-party under [this rule] and a witness summons under CPR 34.2 [which makes provision for something like the procedure improvised in *Williams v Williams* [1988] QB 161, 169, above]. When deciding whether to make an order under this Rule or under CPR 34.2(4) … the court will take into account, amongst other factors, the likely evidential value of the documents and the burden upon the witness of complying with the order.

If an order for disclosure is made under [this rule] then the person in respect of whom it is made will be obliged to produce a disclosure list and specify not only those documents which he has but those documents which he has had and where they are now. If an order is made under CPR 34.2(4) [the procedure improvised in *Williams v Williams* [1988] QB 161, 169 involving use of a subpoena *duces tecum*] then, strictly speaking, he will be obliged to attend court and produce the document. In practice, once an order under CPR 34.2 has been made, copies of the documents are often delivered to the party who obtained the order without an attendance at court. If a party requires, prior to any hearing, not only documents but oral evidence from a person who has refused to co-operate in producing a witness statement or affidavit then consideration should be given to making an application under CPR 34.8 (evidence by deposition) [in Hong Kong see Order 39].

Where it is contended that, on the grounds of privilege (for example), it is inappropriate to produce some or all of the documents under CPR 34.2(4) [the *Williams v Williams*-like procedure] then the course that should be adopted is to apply for disclosure under this rule.

The above commentary goes on to note that this rule may be used against banks to require the production of relevant documents which are outside the scope of the Banker's Books Evidence Act 1879, but this may not be necessary in Hong Kong where the equivalent legislation is broader than its English counterpart – see the commentary under Order 24 rule 1 above.

### [24.7A.5] Privacy considerations in relation to HCO s 42

In *Tse Lai Yin Lily v IO of Albert House & Ors* [1999] 1 HKC 386 it was held that the court's power under section 42(1) is not restricted by the Personal Data (Privacy) Ordinance (Cap 486). The police had objected to disclosure of unedited statements taken from witnesses of an accident on the ground they contained personal data protected by that Ordinance. It was held that Cap 486 was not intended to impede the administration of justice by restricting the court's power under section 42, and that the documents concerned were exempt from protection under Cap 486 by virtue of section 58 and principle 3 in schedule 1 thereof.

However there may be constitutional issues related to privacy. The Civil Court Practice, our sister publication in the UK, says of the privacy issue in relation to CPR 31.17, the equivalent English provision:

An order under this rule may risk infringing the respondent's rights under art 8 or art 10 of the ECHR [right to respect for private life and right to freedom of expression respectively]. So far as art 8 is concerned, it may be invoked in many cases to justify a claim for confidentiality, but it may be overridden if the interests of justice require – *MS v Sweden* (1997) 28 EHRR 313; *R v Local Authority in the Midlands, ex p LM* [2000] 1 FCR 736. In *South Tyneside Metropolitan Borough Council v Wickes Building Supplies Ltd* [2004] EWHC 2428 (Comm), [2004] All ER (D) 69 (Nov), Gross J refused to order disclosure on the ground of commercial confidentiality, as disclosure would have had the effect of "opening up [the respondent's] commercially sensitive information to its rival", a course which could only have been even arguably justified if a "very clear case of necessity" had been made out.

As for art 10, it ensures that freedom of the press is given great weight (as indeed it is at common law, and under statute – see section 10 of the Contempt of Court Act 1981). The importance of protecting the press's sources was emphasised by the European Court in *Goodwin v UK* (1996) 22 EHRR 123 – see especially at para [39]. See also the decision of the House of Lords in *Ashworth Hospital Authority v MGN Ltd* [2002] UKHL 29, [2002] 4 All ER 193. As the latter case shows, there will be circumstances where even the freedom of the press must yield to other interests. However, before ordering disclosure in such a case, the court must be satisfied that a pressing social need for disclosure existed and disclosure was proportionate to a legitimate aim. However, in the subsequent, closely related, case of *Mersey Care NHS Trust v Ackroyd (No 2)* [2006] EWHC 107 (QB), 88 BMLR 1, it was held (Tugendhat J) that, largely due to the effect of the passage of time, but also for other reasons not available to the court in *Ashworth*, there was not a pressing social need for further disclosure. Where the national interest is at stake, freedom of the press is unlikely to stand in the way of a disclosure order under this rule – see *Secretary of State for Defence v Guardian Newspapers Ltd* [1985] AC 339, [1984] 3 All ER 601; *Re Company Securities (Insider Dealing) Act 1985* [1988] AC 660, [1988] 1 All ER 203. [With regard to freedom of the press and the 'newspaper rule' see the commentary under Order 82 rule 3].

In determining applications under this rule, the court may often have to balance the public interest in keeping the document sought confidential and the public interest in ensuring that any trial is conducted by reference to all the relevant material: see *Frankson* [above].

**[24.7A.6]   Procedure on application under HCO s 42 for disclosure before action**

Rule 7A(2) provides that an application for disclosure under section 42 of the High Court Ordinance should be made by summons in the action, which should be served on all other parties. In addition, it is provided by that rule that the summons must be served personally on the non-party against whom disclosure is sought. This follows from the fact that such person will not have been served with the writ, not being a party to the proceedings.

The application must be supported by an affidavit or affirmation which sets out the matters prescribed by rule 7A(3)(b).

**[24.7A.7]   Form of order under rule 7A**

An order under section 41 for disclosure before action, or under section 42 for disclosure against a non-party, should specify or describe the documents to be disclosed. In addition, the order 'shall' require the person against whom it is made to state on affidavit whether those documents are or have been in that person's possession, custody or power, and if no longer, since when, and what has become of them. See Order 24 rule 7A(5).

**[24.7A.8]   Costs of application under rule 7A**

The person against whom an order for disclosure is made under section 41 or 42 of the Ordinance may be an innocent bystander. Any such innocent bystander is normally entitled to the costs of the application and of compliance with the order. See Order 62 rule 3(12).

The equivalent provision in England is CPR 48.1(2), of which Moore-Bick LJ said in *SES Contracting Ltd v UK Coal plc* [2007] EWCA Civ 791 (26.07.2007) (para 17):

> By laying down a general rule that the respondent will be awarded his costs, therefore, I think that the Rules implicitly recognise that it will not usually be unreasonable for him to require the applicant to satisfy the court that he ought to be granted the relief which he seeks. The reason for that (if it be necessary to find one) lies, I think, in a recognition that a private person who is not a party to existing litigation which brings with it an obligation of disclosure is entitled to maintain the privacy of his papers unless sufficient grounds can be shown for overriding it and that it is for the person seeking to invade that privacy to justify doing so. At all events, the rule is clear in its terms and provides the point of departure for a judge dealing with the costs of an application of this kind.

The situation may be different if the person against whom the order is granted had unreasonably refused a prior request by letter. The situation may also be different where the person against whom the order is granted is in control of the litigation, as in *Wong Chong Yip v Chan Yin Fong* HCPI 755/2006 (Deputy Judge L Chan; 21.02.2007). In that case an insurer and its investigation agent were ordered to pay part of the costs of an application against them under this rule.

In England express provision is made for such situations by CPR 48.1(3), by which the court, in considering whether to make a different order, is required to have regard to 'the extent to which it was reasonable for the person against whom the order was sought to oppose the application'. Thus in *Samuel R (a child) v W Primary Care Trust* [2004] EWHC 2085 (Fam) (03.09.2004) the court held that it was not appropriate to grant costs to a respondent which objected to disclosure on the reasonable ground of protecting the confidence of the child concerned, but failed itself to indicate what arrangements could be made to meet that objection. Each party was ordered to pay its own costs. In *Bermuda Int'l Securities Ltd v KPMG* [2001] EWCA Civ 269 (27.02.2001); [2001] Lloyd's Rep PN 392 the court made no order as to costs where the party from which disclosure was sought 'dug their heels in', and 'resisted the production of documents root and branch'. However that party was nevertheless entitled to its costs of the actual disclosure exercise. Waller LJ said (para 32):

> . . . it is important that it is recognised that in relation to pre-action disclosure, the cost of the actual exercise will be paid by the applicant for that disclosure. But so far as the application is concerned if it has been unreasonably resisted, those are the very circumstances contemplated where the order for costs may be different.

It is submitted that in principle, the party required to pay the innocent bystander's costs should be entitled to recover those costs against the wrongdoer in the main action if liability is eventually established and an order for costs is made against the wrongdoer. Such costs may be regarded as coming within the 'necessary or proper' test under Order 62 rule 28(2) and should potentially be recoverable by including them in the bill of party and party costs claimed against the wrongdoer.

### [24.7A.9] Security for costs of order under rule 7A

Order 24 rule 7A(5) gives the court a specific power to order security for costs when making an order under section 41 or 42.

**8. Discovery to be ordered only if necessary** (O. 24 r. 8)

(1)    On the hearing of an application for an order under rule 3 or 7 the Court, if satisfied that discovery is not necessary, or not necessary at that stage of the cause or matter, may dismiss or, as the case may be, adjourn the application and shall in any case refuse to make such an order if and so far as it is of opinion that discovery is not necessary either for disposing fairly of the cause of matter or for saving costs.

(2)    No order for the disclosure of documents shall be made under section 41 or 42 of the Ordinance, unless the Court is of opinion that the order is necessary either for disposing fairly of the cause or matter or for saving costs.

(L.N. 152 of 2008)

---

**NOTES**

**[24.8.1]    The necessity requirement**

Order 24 rule 8 provides that an order for discovery shall be refused if not necessary for disposing fairly of the cause or matter or for saving costs. This is the same test as found in Order 26 rule 1 in respect of interrogatories.

In *Morinda International HK Ltd v Next Magazine Publishing Ltd* [2003] 1 HKC 492, 494E it was held that the burden of proving that discovery is not necessary lies with the party opposing the application.

The rule applies not only to discovery of documents in the usual course of an action, but to applications under rule 7A for disclosure before action and against non-parties pursuant to sections 41 and 42 of the Ordinance. The rule was amended in 2009 as part of the civil justice reforms so as to deal with rule 7A applications separately (in rule 8(2)) whereas previously they were subject to the same provision as regular discovery.

**9. Inspection of documents referred to in list** (O. 24 r. 9)

A party who has served a list of documents on any other party, whether in compliance with rule 2 or with an order under rule 3, must allow the other party to inspect the documents referred to in the list (other than any which he objects to produce) and to take copies thereof and, accordingly, he must when he serves the list on the other party also serve on him a notice stating a time within 7 days after the service thereof at which the said documents may be inspected at a place specified in the notice.

---

**NOTES**

**[24.9.1]    Party making discovery must give notice of inspection**

Order 24 rule 9 provides that a party making discovery of documents must permit other parties to inspect those documents and must together with the list of documents give notice of a time and place where the documents may be inspected within 7 days. The form of notice to inspect is set out at the conclusion of the form of list of documents prescribed by Order 24 rule 5, that is form 26 in appendix A to these rules.

Compliance with rule 9 may be ordered under rule 11. That rule also empowers the court to direct the time, place and manner in which inspection is to take place.

**10.    Inspection of documents referred to in pleadings and affidavits** (O. 24 r. 10)
    **(1)    Any party to a cause or matter shall be entitled at any time to serve a notice on any other party in whose pleadings, affidavits or witness statements served under Order 38, rule 2A, or experts' reports reference is made to any document requiring him to produce that document for the inspection of the party giving the notice and to permit him to take copies thereof.**
    **(L.N. 223 of 1995; L.N. 383 of 1996)**
    **(2)    The party on whom a notice is served under paragraph (1) must, within 4 days after service of the notice, serve on the party giving the notice a notice stating a time within 7 days after the service thereof at which the documents, or such of them as he does not object to produce, may be inspected at a place specified in the notice, and stating which (if any) of the documents he objects to produce and on what grounds.**

---

**NOTES**

**[24.10.1]    Inspection of documents referred to in documents filed in court**
Order 24 rule 10(1) provides that any party may require the production, inspection and copying of any document to which 'reference is made' in another party's pleadings, affidavits, witness statements or expert reports. If the requested party objects he must give notice within four days stating the grounds of objection (rule 10(2)). Application may then be made by the requesting party under rule 11 for an order to compel production.
    In *Quilter v Heatley* (1883) 23 Ch D 42 (CA) it was said (at 45) that the 'main object' of this rule is to prevent fictitious documents from being invented and pleaded. In modern times the purpose is arguably much broader, to enhance openness in the conduct of civil litigation and to prevent surprise at trial. However, verification of copies which have been produced is still within the scope of rule 10: see *Re Ming John Fook* [1998] 3 HKC 712, 722E–F (CA).
    *Meaning of document 'to which reference is made'* – By its own terms Order 24 rule 10 applies only to documents 'to which reference is made' in a party's pleadings, affidavits, witness statements or expert reports. In *Zida Technologies Ltd v Tiga Technologies Ltd & Ors* [2001] 4 HKC 163 the meaning of this phrase was considered. Deputy Judge McCoy SC held that 'documents need not be identified or individually described – a general reference will suffice . . . [b]ut a direct allusion to the document is required'. See also *Easewin Properties Ltd & Anor v Registrar of Companies & Ors* [2004] 4 HKC 41, 44F–I.
    *'Pleadings' includes particulars* – For the purpose of Order 24 rule 10 'pleadings' includes particulars: see *Milbank v Milbank* [1900] 1 Ch 376 (CA), cited with approval in *Zida Technologies Ltd v Tiga Technologies Ltd* [2001] 4 HKC 163, 176C.
    *'Affidavits' includes exhibits* – In *Zida Technologies Ltd v Tiga Technologies Ltd & Ors* [2001] 4 HKC 163 Deputy Judge McCoy SC considered whether a document referred to in an exhibit to an affirmation could be said to be one to which 'reference is made' in the affirmation itself. He answered that question in the affirmative, citing

*Dynamic Way International Ltd v Ho Kui Chee* [2000] 4 HKC 138 (CA). The learned Deputy Judge agreed that the Court of Appeal had adopted too narrow an approach in *Bank of India v BK Murjani* CACV 84/1989 (Cons VP, Clough & Hunter JJA; 11.07.1989) (unreported). The decision in *Zida Technologies* was applied in *AXA China Region Insurance Co Ltd v Pacific Century Insurance Co Ltd (No 2)* [2005] 3 HKC 359, 367.

*Supporting affidavits and witness statements* – The literal wording of Rule 10(1) suggests that only a party's own affidavits and witness statements are covered. However, the rule has been interpreted liberally and has been held to extend to supporting affidavits and witness statements made by other persons in support of a party's position: see *Dubai Bank v Galadari* [1990] 2 All ER 738 (CA).

*Request may be made 'at any time'* – Rule 10(1) expressly stipulates that a request for production of documents may be made 'at any time'. Those words 'mean what they say, so that for example, even before a defence is filed, a document referred to in a statement of claim may be sought': *Zida Technologies Ltd v Tiga Technologies Ltd & Ors* [2001] 4 HKC 173, 177. Similarly delay in making the request is immaterial: *Dun and Bradstreet Ltd v Typesetting Facilities Ltd* [1992] FSR 320, 328–329.

*Parallel inherent jurisdiction* – In *Re Ming John Fook* [1998] 3 HKC 712 (CA) it was suggested that in addition to its power under Order 24 rule 10 the court has an inherent jurisdiction to order inspection.

*Privilege* – an application for inspection under Order 24 rule 10 may be resisted on the ground of privilege. Privilege is not waived by mere reference to a document in a pleading or affidavit, though reproduction of substantial parts of the document may, and full reproduction certainly will, constitute waiver: *Buttes Gas & Oil Co v Hammer (No 3)* [1981] 1 QB 223, 252E–F (CA). In the *AXA* case (above, para 31) the Hong Kong court was of the view a document must be deployed, that is its effect or contents must have been referred to or relied upon, for there to be any waiver of privilege. See also *Expandable Ltd & Anor v Rubin* [2008] EWCA Civ 59 (11.02.2008) where it was held that the position remains unchanged in England following the implementation of the CPR.

**[24.10.2]   Implied undertaking as to use of documents not applicable**
The implied undertaking restricting the use of documents obtained on discovery (see the commentary under Order 24 rule 14A) does not arise on disclosure of documents under this rule. See *Shun Kai Finance Co Ltd & Ors v Japan Leasing (HK) Ltd (in liq) (No 2)* [2001] 1 HKC 636 (CA), applying *Eagle Star Insurance Ltd v Arab Bank plc* (English High Court, 25 February 1992, unreported). The law may not rest there, as Keith JA gave a spirited dissent in the Hong Kong decision, based on a principled view of what ought to be.

**11.   Order for production for inspection** (O. 24 r. 11)
**(1)   If a party who is required by rule 9 to serve such a notice as is therein mentioned or who is served with a notice under rule 10(1)—**

     **(a)   fails to serve a notice under rule 9 or, as the case may be, rule 10(2), or**
     **(b)   objects to produce any document for inspection, or**
     **(c)   offers inspection at a time or place such that, in the opinion of**

the Court, it is unreasonable to offer inspection then or, as the case may be, there,

then, subject to rule 13(1), the Court may, on the application of the party entitled to inspection, make an order for production of the documents in question for inspection at such time and place, and in such manner, as it thinks fit.

(2) Without prejudice to paragraph (1), but subject to rule 13(1), the Court may, on the application of any party to a cause or matter, order any other party to permit the party applying to inspect any documents in the possession, custody or power of that other party relating to any matter in question in the cause or matter.

(3) An application for an order under paragraph (2) must be supported by an affidavit specifying or describing the documents of which inspection is sought and stating the belief of the deponent that they are in the possession, custody or power of the other party and that they relate to a matter in question in the cause or matter.

---

## NOTES

### [24.11.1] Order to compel production of documents for inspection

Order 24 rule 11 gives the court a power to order production of documents for inspection where the requested party fails to comply or objects to production or imposes unreasonable conditions. It applies both to the obligation under rule 9 to include in a list of documents notice of the place and time at which inspection may take place, and to a party's right under rule 10 to inspect documents referred to in another party's pleadings, affidavits or witness statements. No such order will be made unless the court 'is of the opinion that the order is necessary either for disposing fairly of the cause or matter or for saving costs': see Order 24 rule 13 and the commentary thereunder.

It has been held that the requirements of Order 24 rule 11(3) are the same as those applicable on an application for an order for discovery of documents under Order 24 rule 7(3): see *Asia Television Ltd v Golden Star Video Bhd* [1983] 2 HKC 239.

### [24.11.2] Order to require documents to be brought to Hong Kong for inspection

Rule 11(1) empowers the court, when making an order to compel production of documents for inspection, to specify the time, place and manner of the inspection. In *Re NDT (BVI) Trading Ltd* [2009] 2 HKLRD 409 inspection was ordered to be given in Hong Kong where a party had offered inspection only in Beijing.

### [24.11.3] Affidavit in support of application under rule 11

Order 24 rule 11(3) provides that an application for an order requiring documents to be produced must be supported by an affidavit which must cover the following three points:

(1) *description of the documents* – The documents sought must be described with sufficient clarity for the requested party to be able to identify them;

(2) *belief of the deponent that the documents are in the possession, custody or power of the requested party* – The party seeking production is required to state that he is

of the belief that the documents sought are in the possession, custody or power of the requested party. It has been held, however, that the fact of possession, custody or power is not a pre-requisite to exercise of the court's power: see *Rafidain Bank v Agom Universal Sugar Trading Co Ltd & Anor* [1987] 3 All ER 859 (CA) where it was held that the absence of possession may amount to good cause, but not invariably. As stated by Deputy Judge McCoy SC in *Zida Technologies Ltd v Tiga Technologies Ltd & Ors* [2001] 4 HKC 163, 178E–G, the jurisdiction exists even without possession;

(3)    *that the documents relate to a matter in question* – The party seeking production must state the manner in which it is contended the documents sought relate to the issues as defined by the pleadings. As to the meaning of the phrase 'relate to a matter in question' see the commentary under Order 24 rule 2.

On an application under this rule the onus is on the requested party: *Quilter v Heatley* (1883) 23 Ch D 42, 48 (CA). The applicant is *prima facie* entitled to production of the documents requested: *Dynamic Way International Ltd v Ho Kui Chee* [2000] 4 HKC 138 (CA).

Where a document is only partly relevant the party producing it may seal off the irrelevant parts: *Asia Television Ltd v Golden Star Video Bhd* [1983] 2 HKC 239. However, if the court is satisfied that relevant material has been improperly sealed up or that relevant material has not been disclosed, the appropriate order is to require the offending party to make a further affidavit. After that the court may go further by exercising its powers under Order 24 rule 16. See *Guess? Inc & Ors v Lee Seck-mon & Ors* [1989] 1 HKLR 399.

**[24.11.4]    Cross-references**
As to the court's power to compel production of documents in marine insurance claims, see Order 72 rule 10.

For the inspection, preservation and testing of property, see Order 29 rules 2, 3 and 7A; High Court Ordinance, sections 42(2), 44(1) and 45.

**11A.    Provision of copies of documents** (O. 24 r. 11A)
    **(1)    Any party who is entitled to inspect any documents under any provision of this Order or any order made thereunder may at or before the time when inspection takes place serve on the party who is required to produce such documents for inspection a notice (which shall contain an undertaking to pay the reasonable charges) requiring him to supply a true copy of any such document as is capable of being copied by photographic or similar process.**
    **(2)    The party on whom such a notice is served must within 7 days after receipt thereof supply the copy requested together with an account of the reasonable charges.**
    **(3)    Where a party fails to supply to another party a copy of any document under paragraph (2), the Court may, on the application of either party, make such order as to the supply of that document as it thinks fit.**

**12.    Order for production to Court** (O. 24 r. 12)
    **At any stage of the proceedings in any cause or matter the Court may, subject to rule 13(1), order any party to produce to the Court any document in**

his possession, custody or power relating to any matter in question in the cause or matter and the Court may deal with the document when produced in such manner as it thinks fit.

---

## NOTES

### [24.12.1]    Power to order production of documents to court

Order 24 rule 12 empowers the court to order the production of relevant documents. It is a form of order for specific discovery (as to which see Order 24 rule 7 and the commentary thereunder). The rule expressly provides that the order may be made at any stage of the proceedings. In *Silver Stone Development Ltd v Lau Kwong Ching James* [2006] 4 HKC 100 such an order was made at the outset of trial, even though an earlier application for specific discovery had been dismissed and there was no appeal.

**13.    Production to be ordered only if necessary, etc.** (O. 24 r. 13)

**(1)    No order for the production of any documents for inspection or to the Court or for the supply of a copy of any document shall be made under any of the foregoing rules unless the Court is of opinion that the order is necessary either for disposing fairly of the cause or matter or for saving costs.**

**(2)    Where on an application under this Order for production of any document for inspection or to the Court or for the supply of a copy of any document privilege from such production or supply is claimed or objection is made to such production or supply on any other ground, the Court may inspect the document for the purpose of deciding whether the claim or objection is valid.**

---

## NOTES

### [24.13.1]    Discretion to order production of documents

The court's power to order production of documents under Order 24 rule 13 is discretionary. See *Easewin Properties Ltd & Anor v Registrar of Companies & Ors* [2004] 4 HKC 41, 43H.

### [24.13.2]    Court may only order production of documents where necessary

Order 24 rule 13 provides that an order for production of documents (see rules 11 and 12) will only be made where the court is satisfied that disclosure is necessary either for disposing fairly of the cause or matter or for saving costs. The burden is on the party seeking production to satisfy the court that production is necessary in this sense: see *Dolling-Baker v Merrett* [1990] 1 WLR 1205, 1209, quoted with approval in *Au Shui-yuen, Alick v Sir David Ford & Ors* [1991] 1 HKLR 525.

Where the requested party itself wishes to rely on a document, it will be difficult to persuade a court that disclosure is not necessary. See *Dynamic Way International Ltd & Anor v Ho Kui Chee & Ors* [2000] 4 HKC 138 (CA). There Godfrey VP stated (at 142D) that by referring to a document in an affirmation a deponent had given a 'clear indication' that he considered it necessary to bring the document to the attention of the court. Rogers JA said (at 141E–F) that except in 'very unusual circumstances' a party should not have to deal with evidence which he is not permitted to see. See also *Interlego AG v Tyco Industries Inc & Ors* [1985] HKLR 115, citing *WEA Records Ltd & Ors v Visions Channel 4 Ltd & Ors* [1984] FSR 404. However, in *Realink Industries Ltd & Anor v Yeung Wai Wing & Ors* [2002] 3 HKC 584 the court refused to make an order for production of a computer programme which had been exhibited to an affirmation. It was held that an order was unnecessary since the purpose for which production was sought was to enable authorship of the programme to be determined, but that could be done by the party's own expert anyhow.

Relevance alone is not sufficient to show necessity. Thus where the issue to which the document is said to be relevant can be determined on the basis of other available evidence disclosure may be refused. See *Au Shui-yuen, Alick v Sir David Ford & Ors* [1991] 1 HKLR 525, 531A–C (citing *Air Canada v Secretary of State* [1983] 2 AC 394, 441) and at 533G.

The 'necessary' test applies at all stages of the proceedings. The question 'is not properly examined by a view of only the (distant) horizon' and it follows that production of a document may be ordered where necessary for the disposal of an interlocutory application: see *Zida Technologies Ltd v Tiga Technologies Ltd & Ors* [2001] 4 HKC 163, 177C–H, per Deputy Judge McCoy SC citing *Dubai Bank Ltd v Galadari (No 2)* [1990] 1 WLR 731, 737D–E. See, however, *Auto-Treasure Ltd v Noble Diamond Ltd* [1992] 1 HKC 117 (CA) where it was held in a copyright case that documents relevant solely to quantum might not be subject to an order for discovery prior to liability being established (citing *Fennessy v Clark* (1888) 37 Ch D 184).

Under rule 13(2) the court may inspect the document which is the subject of the application to assist it in deciding whether to make an order. In *Dynamic Way International Ltd & Anor v Ho Kui Chee & Ors* [2000] 4 HKC 138 (CA) such an inspection was conducted. In *Asia Television Ltd v Golden Star Video Bhd* [1983] 2 HKC 239 the Court of Appeal held that a judge had not wrongly exercised his discretion by failing to inspect.

## 14.    Production of business books (O. 24 r. 14)

**(1)    Where production of any business books for inspection is applied for under any of the foregoing rules, the Court may, instead of ordering production of the original books for inspection, order a copy or any entries therein to be supplied and verified by an affidavit of some person who has examined the copy with the original books.**

**(2)    Any such affidavit shall state whether or not there are in the original book any and what erasures, interlineations or alterations.**

**(3)    Notwithstanding that a copy of any entries in any book has been supplied under this rule, the Court may order production of the book from which the copy was made.**

## 14A.    Use of documents (O. 24 r. 14A)

**Any undertaking, whether express or implied, not to use a document for any purposes other than those of the proceedings in which it is disclosed shall cease to apply to such document after it has been read to or by the Court, or referred to, in open court, unless the Court for special reasons has otherwise**

**ordered on the application of a party or of the person to whom the document belongs.**

---

NOTES

**[24.14A.1] Undertaking not to use discovered documents for collateral purpose**
Documents which are obtained on discovery are subject to an implied obligation not to make use of them for any purpose other than 'the proper conduct of the litigation': *Harman v Secretary of State for the Home Department* [1983] 1 AC 280; *Bentley & Anor v Parry & Anor* [1993] 1 HKC 298 (CA). The obligation takes the form of an implied undertaking by the solicitor or litigant who receives documents but 'is in reality an obligation imposed by operation of law': *Taylor v Serious Fraud Office* [1999] 2 AC 177, 207 quoted with approval by Le Pichon JA in *Shun Kai Finance Co Ltd v Japan Leasing (HK) Ltd (in liq)* [2001] 1 HKC 636 (CA). A party who breaches the obligation is liable to be punished by way of contempt. A party who has disclosed documents on discovery is entitled to the court's protection by way of injunction against misuse of those documents: *Distillers Co (Biochemicals) Ltd v Times Newspapers Ltd* [1975] 1 QB 613.

Documents obtained on discovery may not be used for the purpose of other litigation, not even an unrelated counterclaim within the same action: *Bentley & Anor v Parry & Anor* [1993] 1 HKC 298. Nor, according to the Supreme Court of Canada, is there an exception permitting disclosure to the police of discovered material tending to show criminal misconduct: *Juman v Doucette* [2008] 1 SCR 157, except possibly where there is an 'immediate and serious danger': *Smith v Jones* [1999] 1 SCR 455.

The rationale for the implied undertaking is that a litigant is compelled to disclose the documents: *Shun Kai Finance Co Ltd v Japan Leasing (HK) Ltd (in liq)* [2001] 1 HKC 636 (CA). There it was held that the implied undertaking does not arise in respect of documents obtained under Order 24 rule 10 or 11 as these are considered to have been voluntarily disclosed. See the judgment of Le Pichon JA at 642A–B citing *Derby v Weldon (No 2)* [1988] The Times, 20 October and at 643G–H quoting from the judgment of Hobhouse J in *Prudential Assurance Co Ltd v Fountain Page Ltd* [1991] 1 WLR 756. Note that in *Shun Kai Finance* Keith JA disapproved of the English authorities and gave a spirited dissenting judgment.

The purpose of Order 24 rule 14A is to discharge the implied (or express) undertaking where the document disclosed has been read out in open court. The effect of this rule is to reverse previous English decisions whereby a person could be found guilty of contempt of court for disclosing discovered documents which had been dealt with in open court.

A party may be released from the implied undertaking by the court. It will do so only 'in special circumstances and where the release or modification will not occasion injustice to the person giving discovery': *Crest Homes plc v Marks* [1987] 2 All ER 1074, 1083; [1987] 1 AC 829 (HL). The court's power to release a party from the undertaking is discretionary, and the factors to be taken into account will vary from case to case; it is not possible to give an exhaustive list: *Re NDT (BVI) Trading Ltd* [2009] 5 HKLRD 615, referring to *Mead Corp v Carbonless Papers (Australia) Pty Ltd & Ors* [2002] WASC 237. In *Mead* (para 45) the Australian court said that on an application to release the undertaking in order to use the documents in other legal proceedings, relevant factors would include:

> the nature of the document, the circumstances under which it came into existence, the attitude of the author of the document and any prejudice the author may sustain, whether the document pre-existed litigation or was created for that purpose and therefore expected to enter the public domain, the nature of the information in the document (in particular whether it contains personal data or commercially sensitive information), the circumstances in which the document came into the hands of the applicant for leave and, perhaps most important of all, the likely contribution of the document to achieving justice in the second proceeding.

In *NDT* (above) the court permitted documents disclosed in winding-up proceedings to be used for making a criminal complaint and a complaint against solicitors to the Law Society. The documents appeared to contradict parts of witness statements and affirmations. In *Re Murjani ex parte Bank of India* [1991] 2 HKC 432 the court permitted documents obtained in an earlier Order 49B application to be used in subsequent bankruptcy proceedings. In *Bentley* (above) a defendant was refused leave to be released from the implied undertaking where he sought to do so to found a counterclaim which had little connection with the main claim in which the documents had been discovered.

See also *Allied Group Ltd & Anor v Secretary for Justice & Anor* [2003] 4 HKC 359 (CA) concerning use in civil proceedings of documents disclosed as 'unused material' in a prior criminal case.

**15.    Document disclosure of which would be injurious to public interest: saving** (O. 24 r. 15)
**The foregoing provisions of this Order shall be without prejudice to any rule of law which authorizes or requires the withholding of any document on the ground that the disclosure of it would be injurious to the public interest.**

---

**NOTES**

**[24.15.1]    Cross-reference**
See also the commentary on public interest immunity under Order 24 rule 2, and see Order 77 rule 12 which expressly preserves the government's right not to disclose documents on discovery where to do so would be injurious to the public interest.

**15A.    Order for limiting discovery** (O. 24 r. 15A)
**For the purpose of managing the case in question and furthering any of the objectives specified in Order 1A, the Court may make any one or more of the following orders –**

> **(a)    an order limiting the discovery of documents which the parties to the case would otherwise be required to make to each other under rule 1(1);**
>
> **(b)    an order directing that the discovery of documents required to be made under this Order to any party to the case shall, notwithstanding anything in this Order, be made in the manner specified in the order; and**

     **(c)    an order directing that documents which may be inspected under this Order shall, notwithstanding anything in rule 9 or rule 10, be inspected at a time or times specified in the order.**

**(L.N. 152 of 2008)**

---

**NOTES**

**[24.15A.1] Court's power to limit scope of discovery**

Order 24 rule 15A stipulates that the court may limit the scope of discovery as an exercise in case management and for the purpose of furthering the underlying objectives set out in Order 1A. The rule implements recommendation 80 in the final report of the Chief Justice's working party on Civil Justice Reform.

The working party's intention in recommending introduction of this rule was to enable the court to tackle the 'excesses of discovery' by appropriate case management. This was consequent upon the decision to retain full *Peruvian Guano* discovery (see the commentary under Order 24 rule 2), the scope of which may in some circumstances need to be 'narrowed by appropriate case management'. See para 500 of the final report.

The power to limit the scope of discovery is not new – Order 24 rule 2(5) & (6) have long provided for limitation on the discovery obligations of parties by court order. However unlike those provisions, rule 15A is not expressed to be available only on application of a party. This suggests the power under rule 15A may be exercised by the court of its own motion. See Order 1B rule 2 generally with regard to the court making orders of its own motion.

In exercising this power, the court should take into account the underlying objectives in Order 1A. Thus, an order limiting discovery might be made where full discovery would cause delay, be out of proportion, overly expensive or unfair. In recommending this new rule, the working party appears to have indorsed the comments made in the interim report which suggest the court should not hesitate to use this power. In the interim report (proposal 29) it was said:

> The court should be expected to exercise its case management powers with a view to tailoring an appropriate discovery regime for the case at hand. It should have a residual discretion both to direct what discovery is required – to narrow or widen the scope of discovery required, to include, if necessary and proportionate, full *Peruvian Guano* style discovery – and in what way discovery is to be given.

It is at least possible, and probably likely, that exercise of the power under the new rule will result in full *Peruvian Guano* style discovery becoming somewhat of a rarity.

**16.    Failure to comply with requirement for discovery, etc. (O. 24 r. 16)**

    **(1)    If any party who is required by any of the foregoing rules, or by any order made thereunder, to make discovery of documents or to produce any documents for the purpose of inspection or any other purpose or to supply copies thereof fails to comply with any provision of that rule or with that order, as the case may be, then, without prejudice, in the case of a failure to comply with any such provision, to rules 3(2) and 11(1), the Court may make such order as it thinks just including, in particular, an order that the action be**

dismissed or, as the case may be, an order that the defence be struck out and judgment be entered accordingly.

(2)   If any party against whom an order for discovery or production of documents is made fails to comply with it, then, without prejudice to paragraph (1), he shall be liable to committal.

(3)   Service on a party's solicitor of an order for discovery or production of documents made against that party shall be sufficient service to found an application for committal of the party disobeying the order, but the party may show in answer to the application that he had no notice or knowledge of the order.

(4)   A solicitor on whom such an order made against his client is served and who fails without reasonable excuse to give notice thereof to his client shall be liable to committal.

------

## NOTES

### [24.16.1]   Order to strike out, etc, for failure to comply with obligations on discovery

When a party fails to meet its obligations on discovery, the court may, under Order 24 rule 16, make such order as may be just, and may go so far as to dismiss the action, strike out the defence or even make an order of committal for contempt. The power is clearly discretionary: *Arnhold & Co Ltd v China Marine Investment & Anor* HCA 2174/1971 (Registrar Jones; 08.01.1973).

The Court will only exercise its discretion to make a drastic order such as striking out in 'rare and exceptional circumstances': *Pang Po King Connie v Celestial Securities Ltd* HCA 3319/2002 (Deputy Judge Poon; 29.08.2005); *Tai Fook Futures Ltd v Cheung Moon Hoi Jeff* [2006] 4 HKC 81 (para 14). Such circumstances include breach of a peremptory or 'unless' order, risk that a fair trial is no longer possible and contumelious conduct: *LDB Sales Co Ltd v Germain Electronic Ltd & Ors* [2006] 4 HKC 602; [2006] 2 HKLRD 865 (CA). We now set out some examples:

(1)   *Breach of unless order* – See the commentary under Order 42 rule 2.

(2)   *Fair trial no longer possible* – In *Jademan (Holdings) Ltd & Ors v Tony Wong Chun Loong* HCCL 15/1990 (Jones J; 17.06.1992); [1992] HKLY 736 the court found there had been contumelious delay of more than 2 years in complying with an order for discovery, rendering a fair trial impossible, and as a result ordered the defence struck out.

(3)   *Contumelious conduct* – In *Ka Wah Bank Ltd v Low Chung-song & Anor* [1989] 1 HKLR 451 (CA) the court struck out a defence on the basis the defendants' purported compliance with an order for discovery was deliberately evasive and illusory. In *Image Technology (HK) Ltd & Ors v Ho Ying Cheong & Ors* HCA 6861/1993 (Yam J; 13.02.1995) the court was satisfied that one of the plaintiffs had deliberately suppressed documents and failed to give a full explanation for the default, and in result dismissed that plaintiff's claims saying a fair trial may no longer be possible.

In *Tsoi Kay v Wu John Baptist* [1992] 1 HKC 475 leave to cross-examine on a discovery affidavit was sought in the hope of demonstrating lies which would justify striking out under Order 24 rule 16. Leave to cross-examine was set aside on appeal, the court disapproving of such an 'interlocutory diversion' in the particular case.

Where instead of immediately making a drastic order such as striking out the court is prepared to give the party in default another chance, an extension of time on an 'unless' basis may be appropriate: *Sadhwanis (Japan) Ltd v Sadhwanis (HK) Ltd* HCA 6088/1982 (Jones J; 24.06.1986). Failure to comply with such an order would clearly justify a drastic order at a later stage.

Even after an action has been dismissed or defence struck out for failure to comply with discovery obligations, the court has power to grant an extension of time to enable the action to continue: *John Walker & Sons Ltd v Henry Ost & Co Ltd* [1970] RPC 151 (CA); *Samuels v Linzi Dresses Ltd* [1981] QB 115 (CA).

**17.    Revocation and variation of orders** (O. 24 r. 17)

**Any order made under this Order (including an order made on appeal) may, on sufficient cause being shown, be revoked or varied by a subsequent order or direction of the Court made or given at or before the trial of the cause or matter in connection with which the original order was made.**

**(Enacted 1988)**

## ORDER 25

### CASE MANAGEMENT SUMMONS AND CONFERENCE

1.    Case management summons and conference (O. 25 r. 1)

(1)   For the purpose of facilitating the giving of directions for the management of a case, each party shall, within 28 days after the pleadings in an action to which this rule applies are deemed to be closed —

    (a)    complete a questionnaire prescribed in a practice direction issued for that purpose by providing the information requested in the manner specified in the questionnaire; and

    (b)    serve it on all other parties and file it with the Court in the manner specified in the practice direction.

(L.N. 152 of 2008)

(1A) Where, upon completion of the questionnaire, the parties are able to reach an agreement on —

    (a)    the directions relating to the management of the case that they wish the Court to make; or

    (b)    a timetable for the steps to be taken between the date of the giving of those directions and the date of the trial,

they shall procure an order to that effect by way of a consent summons.

(L.N. 152 of 2008)

(1B) Where there is no agreement on any of the matters specified in paragraph (1A)(a) and (b) —

    (a)    each party shall in the questionnaire make a proposal on the matter; and

    (b)    the plaintiff shall, within the time specified in the practice direction, take out a summons (in these rules referred to as a case management summons) returnable in not less than 14 days, so that the Court may give directions relating to the management of the case.

(L.N. 152 of 2008)

(2)   This rule applies to all actions begun by writ except—

    (a)    actions in which the plaintiff or defendant has applied for judgment under Order 14, or in which the plaintiff has applied for judgment under Order 86, and directions have been given under the relevant Order;

    (b)    actions in which the plaintiff or defendant has applied under Order 18, rule 21, for trial without pleadings or further pleadings and directions have been given under that rule;

    (c)    actions in which an order has been made under Order 24, rule 4, for the trial of an issue or question before discovery;

    (d)    actions in which directions have been given under Order 29, rule 7;

    (e)    actions in which an order for the taking of an account has been made under Order 43, rule 1;

(f)     **actions in which an application for transfer to the commercial list is pending;**

(h)     **actions for the infringement of a patent; and**

(j)     **actions for personal injuries for which automatic directions are provided by rule 8.**

(k)     **(Repealed L.N. 152 of 2008)**

(3)     **(Repealed L.N. 152 of 2008)**

(4)     **If the plaintiff does not file the questionnaire in accordance with paragraph (1)(b) or take out a case management summons in accordance with paragraph (1B)(b), the defendant or any defendant may —**

(a)     **take out a case management summons; or**

(b)     **apply for an order to dismiss the action.**

**(L.N. 152 of 2008)**

(5)     **On an application by a defendant to dismiss the action under paragraph (4) the Court may either dismiss the action on such terms as may be just or deal with the application as if it were a case management summons. (L.N. 152 of 2008).**

(6)     **In the case of an action which is proceeding only as respects a counterclaim, references in this rule and rule 1A(1)(c) to the plaintiff and defendant shall be construed respectively as references to the party making the counterclaim and the defendant to the counterclaim. (L.N. 152 of 2008)**

(7)     **Notwithstanding anything in paragraph (1B), any party to an action to which this rule applies may take out a case management summons at any time after the defendant has given notice of intention to defend, or, if there are two or more defendants, at least one of them has given such notice. (L.N. 152 of 2008)**

---

## NOTES

### [25.1.1]     Application of Order 25 rule 1

Subject to some exceptions, the case management summons procedure laid down in Order 25 must be followed in all actions begun by writ. The exceptions are listed in rule 1(2) and include, notably, patent infringement actions and personal injuries claims. However, practice direction 18.1 concerning personal injury actions applies Order 25 to actions in the personal injury list, though not the practice direction on case management. Instead practice direction 18.1 contains its own provisions for case management of personal injury cases. There are also exceptions for general claims when circumstances arise which make it unnecessary to follow the Order 25 procedure, such as where a summary judgment application is pending, or where directions have been given under Order 29 rule 7 on hearing an application for an interlocutory injunction or similar relief.

### [25.1.2]     Amendments to Order 25 in 2009

In 2009 substantial amendments to Order 25 came into force. The Order previously provided for the summons for directions procedure whereby the parties would appear before a master at an early stage for directions as to the pre-trial conduct of an action.

The summons for directions procedure has been replaced by the 'case management summons', and the hearing before the master is now known as the 'case management conference'. The changes go beyond terminology. The substantive innovations implemented by the amendments may be summarised as follows:

(a)     A questionnaire has been introduced for completion by the parties at an early stage, with a view to enabling the court to tailor its directions to the particular case (rule 1(1)).

(b)     Procedures whereby attendance at court may be dispensed with by the parties agreeing the directions to be given (rule 1(1A)), or the court dealing with the matter without a hearing, have been formalised (rule 1A(4)).

(c)     In addition to giving directions the court is now required to set a timetable for the pre-trial progress of an action, including 'milestone dates' (rules 1A and 1B).

(d)     Where a party fails to attend the case management conference or pre-trial review, the court is required to strike out the action on a provisional basis (rule 1C).

## [25.1.3]     The questionnaire procedure

Order 25 rule 1(1) provides that each party must serve and file a questionnaire within 28 days of the close of pleadings. The close of pleadings is calculated by reference to Order 18 rule 20. The form of questionnaire is set out in appendix A to practice direction 5.2 on case management. In the practice direction the questionnaire is referred to as the 'timetabling questionnaire'. The practice direction and the form of timetabling questionnaire can be downloaded from the judiciary's website www.judiciary.gov.hk or that of the Hong Kong Legal Information Institute www.hklii.org, both of which are accessible by the general public free-of-charge. The prescribed form includes a declaration by the party or solicitor signing it that the answers set out in it are true and accurate to the best of the person's information and belief.

Parties are expected to consider their cases properly before completing the questionnaire. The court requires compliance in substance, not only in form. See *Yip Kee Wai v So Kim Wah* HCA 1504/2009 (Registrar Lung; 20.10.2010); [2010] 5 HKLRD 440.

The purpose of the questionnaire is to enable the court to tailor a timetable for pre-trial matters suitable for the individual case. The Chief Justice's working party was of the view that timetabling under the previous summons for directions procedure was 'hardly ever effective' (final report, para 361). The working party continued:

> Parties often ask for 'standard' time-limits to be imposed, without sufficient thought given to the exigencies of the particular case. The court is often not equipped to form an independent judgment as to the realism or otherwise of the directions proposed.

The questionnaire was recommended by the working party to remedy the situation it described in those words. It said (at para 370):

> For there to be a better-tailored court-determined timetable, the court must be given accurate information about the case. To achieve this, it is proposed that each party be required:-
>
> (a)     to fill in a questionnaire giving the court and the other parties information and his best estimates regarding the nature, size, complexity and case management

needs of the case, and

(b)    to propose directions and time limits for compliance linked to his view of the needs of the case up to and including a proposed trial date or proposed trial period, that is, a period during which the trial is to commence.

The working party said the questionnaire it had in mind was similar to the information sheet required in construction and arbitration proceedings (see appendix A to practice direction 6.1, and see the commentary on the Construction and Arbitration List under Order 72).

The form of timetabling questionnaire is based on the recommendations of the Chief Justice's working party which envisaged it as touching on the following topics (final report, para 372):

(a)    whether the parties are presently or anticipate that later they will be legally represented;

(b)    whether the parties have attempted ADR (giving details) and if not, whether any of the parties has offered to or is willing to engage in ADR (giving details) [see Order 1A rule (4)(2)(3)];

(c)    whether any persons are intended to be joined as parties [Order 15 rule 6(2)(b)] or brought in as Third Parties [Order 16];

(d)    whether any interlocutory applications are intended or outstanding;

(e)    whether any amendments to the pleadings are intended [Order 20];

(f)    whether requests for further and better particulars of the pleadings are intended or outstanding [Order 18 rule 12(3), (3A) & (3B)];

(g)    whether interrogatories are likely to be served or outstanding [Order 26];

(h)    whether any directions for modifying discovery obligations or the manner of their implementation are proposed with a view to achieving economies in respect of discovery [Order 24 rules 2(5)&(6) and 15A];

(i)    the approximate volume of the documents considered relevant to the case and how much time it would take to assemble and list them;

(j)    the number of factual witnesses likely to be called;

(k)    how long it is likely to take to prepare witness statements for such witnesses [Order 38 rule 2A];

(l)    whether expert evidence may be needed, in what fields and broadly in relation to what matters [Order 38 rules 35-44];

(m)    if expert evidence is needed, whether appointment of a single joint expert is considered appropriate and if not, why not [Order 38 rule 4A];

(n)    if party-appointed experts are to be appointed, how much time it is likely to take to have their expert reports ready for exchange [Order 38 rule 37];

(o)    whether a case management conference should be held [Order 25 rule 1A(1)(b)];

(p)    the extent to which the proceedings may be conducted in Chinese [High Court Civil Procedure (Use of Language) Rules (Cap 5C)];

(q)    whether the Technology Court may beneficially be used for all or any part of the proceedings [practice direction 29; and see the commentary under Order 39 rule 1]; and,

(r)    the estimated length of trial.

**[25.1.4]     Mediation certificate to be filed with timetabling questionnaire**

The mediation practice direction (PD 31, in force from 01.01.2010) provides that together with the timetabling questionnaire which must be filed under Order 25 rule 1(1), there must be filed a mediation certificate. A specimen form of certificate, to be signed by a solicitor, and counter-signed by the client, is annexed to the practice direction. It is necessary to certify that the availability of mediation, and the practice direction itself, have been explained by the solicitor and are understood by the client.

With regard to the court's duty to encourage use of alternative dispute resolution procedures such as mediation, and related topics, see the commentary concerning Order 1A rule 4(2)(e). For possible costs consequences of unreasonable refusal to mediate, see the commentary under Order 62 rule 5(1)(e).

**[25.1.5]     Questionnaire obligations of unrepresented parties**

The Chief Justice's working party suggested that parties acting without the benefit of legal representation might not always be required to complete the questionnaire. At para 375 of the final report it is said:

> Unrepresented litigants ought to be given suitable latitude. While they should be encouraged, if possible, to complete the questionnaire, it may be appropriate in some cases to require such a litigant only to provide information about his case (as to how many documents he has and how many witnesses he is likely to call, etc), relaxing the requirement regarding the proposal of directions and a timetable, leaving such matters to be formulated by the court on all the available information. A case management conference is likely to be needed in all such cases, with the court providing procedural guidance to the unrepresented litigant.

There is nothing in Order 25 rule 1 to cater to the views expressed above. In fact the rule requires the timetabling questionnaire of all parties without making any distinction between those who are represented and those who are not. However, there is room for the court to take into account the working party's views in the event of failure of an unrepresented litigant to complete the questionnaire: see rule 1(5) which provides that the court may deal with an application to dismiss a plaintiff's claim for failure to comply with the questionnaire procedure as if it were a case management summons.

With regard to the mediation certificate, to be filed together with the questionnaire (see above), the practice direction on case management does not appear to require compliance by a litigant in person.

**[25.1.6]     Parties encouraged to agree directions and timetable**

It is clear that the parties are encouraged to try to agree the matters covered by the timetabling questionnaire. Paragraph 8 of the practice direction on case management (PD 5.2) provides that the parties should consult each other, but not so as to delay filing of the timetabling questionnaire.  Where there is agreement the parties are required by rule 1(1A) to procure an order by way of consent summons giving directions and setting a timetable. It is not stated expressly whether this requirement applies where there is partial agreement, but there seems no reason why the parties could not by consent summons seek directions and a timetable so far as agreed, leaving other matters to be dealt with by the court.

To facilitate agreement being reached, the Chief Justice's working party envisaged the plaintiff completing the questionnaire first, and then passing it to each defendant 'who would indicate in columns alongside those filled in by the plaintiff, whether they agree with the plaintiff's estimates and proposed directions, and if not, what their own estimates and proposals are' (final report, para 374). The working party continued:

> The questionnaire would then be returned to the plaintiff who would consider whether, in the light of the defendants' responses, he ought to modify any of his own estimates or proposals before filing the questionnaire in court. Relatively short time-limits for each of these steps should be provided.

The steps envisaged by the working party, as set out above, are not entirely formalised in the rules of court, the matter being left primarily to the practice direction on case management. It is there additionally provided that if the parties are able to agree on pre-trial directions, they may seek a trial date by each filing with the consent summons a certificate setting out their time estimates for opening submissions, evidence-in-chief, cross-examination and closing submissions.

### [25.1.7] Case management summons where parties fail to agree directions and timetable

Where the parties do not agree on directions and a timetable, they are required to set out their proposals in the questionnaire, and the plaintiff must take out a case management summons (rule 1(1B)). The court will decline to hear the case management summons unless the timetabling questionnaire is also filed: *Faith Bright Dev't Ltd v Ng Kwok Kuen* HCA 9058/1999 (Registrar Lung; 20.10.2010); [2010] 5 HKLRD 425. However, the listing questionnaire (discussed below) should not be filed at this stage as it is intended for use at the case management conference which will only be fixed at the case management summons hearing: *Yip Kee Wai v So Kim Wah* HCA 1504/2009 (Registrar Lung; 20.10.2010); [2010] 5 HKLRD 440. A sample form of case management sum mons is set out in appendix B to the practice direction on case management (PD 5.2). The court will then, in accordance with rule 1A, consider what directions to give and an appropriate timetable to fix. That may be done with or without a hearing. See the commentary under rule 1A.

Practitioners have been reminded that all proposed directions should be included in the case management summons. See *Bank of China (HK) Ltd v Sze See & Anor* HCA 2383/2008 (Registrar Au-Yeung; 15.07.2009) (para 5) where it was said that this is important because under para 31 of the case management practice direction (PD 5.2), the later in time and closer to trial date an application is made, the less likely the court will entertain it.

### [25.1.8] Rule 1(4)&(5) – failure of plaintiff to comply– dismissal for want of prosecution

Order 25 rule 1(4) provides that if the plaintiff fails to file a questionnaire or take out a case management summons, a defendant may take out the summons or apply for an order to dismiss the action. If the defendant applies to dismiss the action the court will proceed under rule 1(5).

Rule 1(4) and (5) are in similar terms to the provisions of equivalent number under the former Order 25 summons for directions procedure. Under the former procedure, the Hong Kong courts followed English cases on applications to dismiss an action for failure to proceed to the directions stage. See *Can-Asia Capital Co Ltd v Kwok Yee William & Ors* [1995] 1 HKC 521, 529F-G (CA). See also Order 34 rule 2(2) and the commentary thereunder concerning dismissal for want of prosecution.

**1A.    Case management timetable** (O. 25 r. 1A)

**(1)    Subject to paragraph (4), as soon as practicable after the completed questionnaire has been filed with the Court, the Court shall, having regard to the questionnaire and the needs of the case —**

   **(a)    give directions relating to the management of the case and fix the timetable for the steps to be taken between the date of the giving of those directions and the date of the trial;**

   **(b)    fix a case management conference if the Court is of the opinion that it is desirable to do so; or**

   **(c)    direct the plaintiff to take out a case management summons if he has not already done so under rule 1(1B)(b).**

**(2)    Where the Court has fixed a case management conference it shall —**

   **(a)    give directions relating to the management of the case and fix the timetable for the steps to be taken between the date of the giving of those directions and the date of the case management conference; and**

   **(b)    at the case management conference, fix a timetable for the steps to be taken between the date of the conference and the date of the trial, and the timetable must include —**

      **(i)    a date for a pre-trial review; or**

      **(ii)    the trial date or the period in which the trial is to take place.**

**(3)    Where the Court has not fixed a case management conference, any timetable fixed under paragraph (1)(a) must include —**

   **(a)    a date for a pre-trial review; or**

   **(b)    the trial date or the period in which the trial is to take place.**

**(4)    The Court may, without a hearing of the case management summons and having regard to the completed questionnaire, by an order nisi, give directions relating to the management of the case and fix the timetable for the steps to be taken between the date of the giving of those directions and the date of the trial.**

**(5)    The order nisi becomes absolute 14 days after the order is made unless a party has applied to the Court for varying the order.**

**(6)    The Court shall, on an application made under paragraph (5), hear the case management summons.**

   **(L.N. 152 of 2008)**

---

**NOTES**

**[25.1A.1]    Order 25 r 1A – court shall give directions and fix case timetable**
Order 25 rule 1A provides for the court to give directions on the pre-trial conduct of an action, and to fix a timetable for pre-trial steps, having regard to the questionnaire completed by the parties and the needs of the case. It implements recommendation 52 of the Chief Justice's working party on civil justice reform. The working party considered that the previous procedure for setting a timetable (under the former

summons for directions procedure) was 'hardly ever effective' (final report, para 361). One of the reasons it was not effective was the court not being equipped to form an independent judgment as to the realism or otherwise of the directions proposed by the parties. That is sought to be remedied by the questionnaire procedure (see above). The next stage (unless the parties are in agreement and follow the procedure under rule 1(1A) to obtain directions by consent summons) is consideration of the questionnaire by the court, and the setting of a court-determined timetable under rule 1A. The working party had in mind 'a court-determined timetable which realistically takes into account the reasonable wishes of the parties and the needs of the particular case' (final report, para 365). It said that the 'timetable as initially set should, so far as possible, be realistic and workable so that the parties can reasonably be held to its deadlines' (final report, para 382).

See also Order 1A rule 4(2)(g) by which the fixing of timetables or otherwise controlling the progress of cases is included in the court's duty of active case management.

### [25.1A.2]   Directions and timetable by order nisi without a hearing

Importantly, rule 1A(4) empowers the court to fix a case timetable by order *nisi* without a hearing. Previously, it was possible for the parties to dispense with a hearing of the summons for directions only if there was agreement which could be put forward to the court in the form of a consent summons. Rule 1A(4) now allows the court to fix the timetable by order *nisi* in the absence of agreement, and there will be a hearing only if a party applies within 14 days under rule 1A(5) for the order *nisi* to be varied. Such a hearing is a hearing of the case management summons: rule 1A(6).

The Chief Justice's working party envisaged such orders *nisi* being the norm rather than the exception. In recommendation 54 of the final report it said that unless it appears to the court that a hearing is desirable, 'the court ought to make orders *nisi* giving such directions and fixing such timetable for the proceedings as it thinks fit in the light of the questionnaire and without a hearing', but subject to the right of any party who objects to one or more of the directions given to call for a hearing.

As to the court's power to give directions by order *nisi* generally, see Order 1B rule 3 and the commentary thereunder.

### [25.1A.3]   Timetable may be fixed in stages

The timetable may, in appropriate cases, be fixed by the court in stages. Rule 1A(1)(b) & (2) provide that instead of fixing the whole timetable up to and including trial date in one go, the court may instead, on considering the questionnaire, fix a case management conference and the timetable for steps leading to that. Then at the case management conference the court will fix dates up to pre-trial review or trial: rule 1A(2)(b). This reflects the comments of the working party at para 384 of the final report:

> At the summons for directions stage [now the case management summons stage], equipped with the pleadings and the questionnaire, the court would have the flexibility to decide whether a case management conference is required. If so, it would give directions and set a timetable which runs in the first place only up to the case management conference as the first milestone, with further timetabling to be done at that conference. If a case management conference is not considered necessary, the court would give directions setting a timetable

with the date of the pre-trial review as the first milestone and the trial date or trial period as the second and final milestone.

Accordingly the working party recommended that where in the court's view a case management conference is desirable, 'the court should fix a timetable up to the date of the case management conference, that date constituting the first milestone, with further milestones to be fixed when the case management conference is held': final report, recommendation 55.

As to the meaning of 'milestone' and 'non-milestone' dates, see rule 1B and the commentary thereunder.

### [25.1A.4]   When case management conference appropriate

As to when it would be appropriate for the court to fix a case management conference under rule 1A(1)(b), the working party said (final report, para 385):

> A court might order a case management conference where the case is heavy and procedural complications are likely to arise, for instance, where strongly contested interlocutory applications or interlocutory appeals are intended or pending (as disclosed in the questionnaire) making it difficult to fix a realistic trial date or trial period at the summons for directions [now case management summons] stage.

> (a)   The court might in such cases fix a case management conference for a time when it is envisaged that most of the outstanding pending interlocutory disputes would have been dealt with, giving directions only up to that stage.

> (b)   The case management conference would be used to clear any still outstanding interlocutory questions and then to fix a timetable for the further progress of the case, including dates for the pre-trial review and the trial (or the trial period).

> (c)   By fixing the milestones progressively in this way, flexibility would be preserved, allowing the state of progress to be taken into account at the stage of the case management conference.

> (d)   … a case management conference might also be useful in relation to proceedings brought by or against unrepresented litigants.

The working party was of the view that in 'many if not most cases', a case management conference will not be necessary (final report, para 386). In *Au Yeung Wing Hau & Anor v Cheung Pak Chuen* HCAP 4/2009 (Master Levy; 12.11.2009) a CMC was dispensed with in a simple probate action where the plaintiffs were only required to prove the will in solemn form and the defendant was not putting forward any positive case.

### [25.1A.5]   The listing questionnaire

The practice direction on case management (PD 5.2) makes provision for a second questionnaire, known as the listing questionnaire, to be filed and served no less than 7 days before the date fixed for a case management conference or pre-trial review. The form of listing questionnaire is set out in appendix C to the practice direction, which can be downloaded from the judiciary's website www.judiciary.gov.hk or that of the Hong Kong Legal Information Institute www.hklii.org.hk, both of which are accessible by the general public free-of-charge. Care should be taken to complete the listing questionnaire accurately and fully. In *Lo Shu Man t/a Lam Sing Machinery Eng'g Co v Kin Ming Construction Co Ltd* HCA 191/2008 (Registrar Au-Yeung; 13.10.2009) (para 17), where a listing questionnaire was 'so poorly prepared by the plaintiff's solicitor that it was tantamount to no preparation', the court directed the solicitor to show cause why an order disallowing costs as between solicitor and client should not be made. By paragraph 25 of the practice direction, if a trial date is sought, each party is required to file and serve with the listing questionnaire a certificate giving that party's estimates for the time that party will require for various stages of the trial. There is no prescribed form of certificate, but the practice direction says it should preferably be prepared by counsel who will handle the trial, and should give time estimates for the following, without taking into account the other parties' estimates:

(1)     his own opening submission;
(2)     evidence-in-chief of each of his own witnesses;
(3)     cross-examination of each of the other side's witnesses; and
(4)     his own closing submission.

The purpose of the above information is to enable the court to allocate an appropriate number of days for the trial of the action. The information will also be useful if the court is minded to exercise its power under Order 35 rule 3A to limit the time to be taken by any part of the proceedings. See the commentary under that rule.

### [25.1A.6]   The CMC bundle

The plaintiff is required to lodge a 'CMC bundle' with the court no later than 3 clear days before a case management conference. See para 26 of PD 5.2. The bundle should contain copies of the pleadings, witness statements, expert reports and a draft index for the document bundle to be used at trial. (With regard to compilation of the document bundle see the commentary under Order 34 rule 8.) The bundle may be re-used at subsequent case management conferences and pre-trial reviews, if any, and if updated for such subsequent hearing, the updated parts should be highlighted.

According to a letter from the Registrar dated 20 March 2009 and circulated to solicitors from time to time (for example, Law Society circular 09-981), parties may seek a direction that the CMC bundle be treated as the setting down bundle which is required to be lodged at the time of setting down for trial (Order 34 rule 3).

### [25.1A.7]   Adjourned case management conference

The court may adjourn a case management conference pursuant to para 32(4) of PD 5.2. This may be appropriate where there are steps yet to be taken before the action is ready to be set down for trial.

At a resumed case management conference the parties may rely on their previous timetabling questionnaires, but if there are 'drastic changes' fresh questionnaires should be filed: *Faith Bright Dev't Ltd v Ng Kwok Kuen* HCA 9058/1999 (Registrar Lung; 20.10.2010) (para 30); [2010] 5 HKLRD 425.

### [25.1A.8]   Pre-trial review

The court long ago adopted a practice of ordering pre-trial reviews in complex cases so as to provide an opportunity to take stock of progress and readiness for trial. See the commentary under Order 34 rule 8. Order 25 rule 1A now expressly provides the court with a power to order pre-trial reviews as part of case management. It is clear that the power is discretionary, and that a pre-trial review will not be required in every case. The circumstances in which a pre-trial review will be considered appropriate will be similar to those militating in favour of a case management conference (see above).

As to the timing of the pre-trial review, the Chief Justice's working party said (final report, para 388):

> The pre-trial review should be fixed to occur after completion of discovery, exchange of expert reports and witness statements. It should be listed to take place two to three months before the trial date or the start of the trial period.

The practice direction on case management (PD 5.2) says (at para 33) that where the court decides to hold a PTR, it will normally be held about 8 to 10 weeks before the trial date or the start of the trial period, and that it will generally be dealt with by the trial judge.

The working party continued by setting out a list of the matters it considered should be dealt with at a pre-trial review. It said:

> At the pre-trial review, the judge or master would:–
>
> (a)   fix the starting date for the trial if a trial period has been fixed at the summons for directions or case management conference stage;
>
> (b)   confirm or vary the estimated length of the trial in the light of completed interlocutory steps;
>
> (c)   give any further directions needed (including any needed extensions of time for interlocutory tasks not yet completed, on any appropriate 'unless order' terms or terms as to costs) provided that such directions will not impinge upon the trial date.

Prior to Order 25 rule 1A coming into force, when the court exercised an inherent power to direct that there be a pre-trial review in some cases, it was held that directions given at a pre-trial review should not be interfered with lightly on appeal. See *Cheung Yee Mong Edmond (an infant) v So Kwok Man Bernard* [1996] 1 HKC 604 (CA), 606C-E where it was said that directions given on a pre-trial review are 'a matter of case management peculiarly within the province of the judge of first instance', and that the Court of Appeal 'will not review decisions of a judge of first instance on matters of case management unless it is satisfied that the judge's decision was plainly wrong'. Those remarks should be equally applicable under Order 25 rule 1A in force in 2009 giving the pre-trial review a legislative basis.

### [25.1A.9]   Attendance of counsel at case management conference and PTR

The practice direction on case management (PD 5.2) provides (in para 45), that unless otherwise directed, trial counsel should attend any case management conference or pre-trial review before a judge. It is envisaged that PTRs will generally be dealt with by the trial judge. The situation is different for actions on the personal injuries list, where the solicitor with prime responsibility for the case should attend, or counsel if there is an issue or argument fit for counsel, in which event a certificate for counsel may be granted if appropriate. See para 131 of the PI list practice direction (PD 18.1), and see *Lau Koon Loi v Wong Wai Sing & Anor* HCPI 445/2007 (Fung J; 13.07.2009) (para 3).

Case management conferences before a master may, according to the PD, be attended by a representative of the solicitors' firm instructed by the party, but it should be the person responsible for the case and in any event the person attending must be familiar with the case and be able to provide the court with the information it is likely to need to make decisions with regard to case management.

**[25.1A.10]          Fixing the trial date or period**
The timetable fixed by the court under Order 25 rule 1A culminates with the trial date or the period during which trial will take place.

The Chief Justice's working party envisaged that the 'trial period' would be 'a period of say, four to six weeks during which the trial is to commence, the precise starting date being fixed at the pre-trial review' (final report, para 387).

It seems most likely that a trial date will be fixed in cases where previously it was considered appropriate that they be set down on the fixture list, and that a trial period will be fixed for cases appropriate for the running list. However, fixing the trial period may result in less uncertainty than setting down on the running list, given that it is envisaged that a starting date for the trial will be fixed by the pre-trial review: see above. Note also that the Chief Justice's working party was alive to the problems caused by the uncertainty of a running list, and envisaged that court-directed timetabling would eventually replace that list entirely (final report, para 403).

So far as the length of the trial is concerned, it is fixed on the basis of the time estimates given by the parties in the listing questionnaire (see above), and any order of the court under Order 35 rule 3A limiting the time to be taken by the parties at trial.

**[25.1A.11]  Interlocutory orders after case management stage to be 'self-executing'**
Once a case management summons has been taken out, or court has given directions as to management of the case under Order 25 rule 1A, any subsequent orders made on interlocutory applications should be 'self-executing', meaning that they should specify the consequences of non-compliance. See Order 32 rule 11B and the commentary thereunder.

**1B.     Variation of case management timetable** (O. 25 r. 1B)
**(1)    The Court may, either of its own motion or on the application of a party, give further directions relating to the management of the case or vary any timetable fixed by it under rule 1A.**

**(2)    A party may apply to the Court if he wishes to vary a milestone date.**

**(3)    The Court shall not grant an application under paragraph (2) unless there are exceptional circumstances justifying the variation.**

**(4)    A non-milestone date may be varied by procuring an order to that effect by way of a consent summons.**

**(5)    A party may apply to the Court if he wishes to vary a non-milestone date without the agreement of the other parties.**

**(6)    The Court shall not grant an application under paragraph (5) unless sufficient grounds have been shown to it.**

**(7)    Whether or not sufficient grounds have been shown to it, the Court shall not grant an application under paragraph (5) if the variation would make it necessary to change a trial date or the period in which the trial is to take place.**

**(8)    In this rule —**
**"milestone date" means —**
          **(a)     a date which the Court has fixed for —**

      (i)      **a case management conference;**
      (ii)     **a pre-trial review; or**
      (iii)    **the trial; or**
    **(b)    a period fixed by the Court in which a trial is to take place;**
**"non-milestone date" means a date or period fixed by the Court, other than a**
       **date or period specified in the definition of "milestone date".**
    **(L.N. 152 of 2008)**

---

## NOTES

### [25.1B.1]   Variation of dates fixed by the court – general principles

The timetable fixed by the court under Order 25 rule 1A is intended to be firm. However rule 1B introduces an element of flexibility by providing for the timetable to be varied.

    The Chief Justice's working party was of the view that although an element of flexibility is appropriate, firmness in sticking to the timetable laid down by the court will generally be preferable. It said (final report, para 379):

> The benefits of having a firm timetable are obvious. It would set the pace at which the parties and their legal advisers need to work and make deliberate procrastination more difficult. Everyone would be able to assess the progress of the case and to plan and prepare for the next phase. The parties would be better able to consider settlement, knowing where they have got to, how much further there is to go and when the next major tranche of litigation costs has to be incurred. The court would be able to deploy judicial resources more efficiently.

The working party continued (at para 380) by saying that if the benefits it described above are to be enjoyed, 'the court must be resolute in holding the parties to the essentials of the timetable, anchored by the trial date or trial period, which are not to be moved save in very exceptional circumstances'.

### [25.1B.2]   Variation of timetable by the court of its own motion

Rule 1B(1) expressly contemplates the court giving further directions or varying the timetable fixed by it, of its own motion.

### [25.1B.3]   Variation of milestone dates

Milestone dates are defined by rule 1B(8) as dates fixed by the court for a case management conference, pre-trial review, trial or trial period. Variation of such dates at the instigation of a party or the parties is only possible by application to the court: rule 1B(2). 'Exceptional circumstances' must be shown: rule 1B(3).

    The Chief Justice's working party envisaged that on such an application, variation would not be ordered lightly. It said (final report, para 383) that 'milestone dates, once set, should largely be immovable'. This is reflected in the practice direction on case management which says (PD 5.2, para 42) that milestone dates will be immovable 'save in the most exceptional circumstances'. The practice direction goes on to state that for this purpose 'exceptional circumstances' does not include the following:

(a)    late instructions from client

(b)    change of lawyers

(c)    absence of prejudice to other party which cannot be compensated for by costs.

In *Chan Chun Shing v Chang Chen Chin t/a Tong Tak Co* HCPI 395/2008 (Fung J; 04.05.2009) the court lifted the stay of proceedings which took effect under section 15(4) of the Legal Aid Ordinance (Cap 91) when the plaintiff made a late application for legal aid. The action was already in the running list and the court reasoned that 'the trial period is a milestone date, and cannot be changed unless for exceptional reason'. In *Incorporated Owners of Kin Ho Ind Bldg v Tam Wing Pak* HCA 2137/2006 (Deputy Judge L Chan; 14.05.2010) the court refused an application for transfer of an action to the District Court on the ground that the trial date already fixed in the Court of First Instance would be lost. In *C&A Consultants Ltd & Anor v Hong Kong Airlines Ltd* HCA 279/2007 (Deputy Judge Carlson; 17.08.2010) (para 29) an application for leave to amend was refused where the result would have been loss of trial dates. In *Honour v Canada (AG)* [2008] BCCA 346 (paras 7, 15 & 17) the British Columbia court refused leave to appeal an interlocutory decision where such an appeal would result in the trial dates, which had already been fixed, being lost. In *Calden v Dr Nunn & Partners* [2003] EWCA Civ 200 (19.02.2003) leave to adduce additional expert evidence was refused where the 'trial window' or trial period as it is known in Hong Kong, would be lost. The appellate court referred to the English equivalent of the underlying objective of ensuring that a case is dealt with expeditiously (Order 1A rule 1(b)), and said (para 41) that it was a 'central objective' that 'cases must be managed towards the trial window or the trial date'.

A late interlocutory application which may affect milestone dates should be supported by an affidavit explaining the delay: *Chan Sang Nam v Chan Shiu Hung* DCCJ 4278/2009 (Deputy Judge C Lee; 07.07.2010).

**[25.1B.4] Variation of non-milestone dates where the parties are in agreement**
Non-milestone dates are dates fixed by the court other than milestone dates: rule 1B(8). The Chief Justice's working party was of the view that where there is agreement between the parties as to variation of a non-milestone date, which would not affect milestone dates, the parties should be allowed flexibility. At para 390 of the final report it said:

> ... parties should be allowed a great deal of flexibility to vary time-limits by agreement for events falling between milestones (without the need for applying to the court), so long as the milestone dates themselves are not affected.

Implementing this aspect of the working party's final report, rule 1B(4) provides that the parties may seek a variation of a non-milestone date by consent summons. Although the rule does not differentiate between agreed variations which may affect a milestone date and those which will not, the practice direction on case management makes it clear that variation of non-milestone dates by consent summons should only be sought where milestone dates will not be affected. A consent summons requires scrutiny by the court, and it is clear that an order will likely be refused if it would affect a milestone date. See also part J of the practice direction on case management (PD 5.2).

The Chief Justice's working party also recommended that an agreed variation of a non-milestone date could be given effect 'by recording the agreement in counter-signed correspondence to be filed as a matter of record with the court, provided that the agreed variations do not involve or necessitate changes to any milestone date' (recommendation 57). However there is no express provision in rule 1B or the case management practice direction for such a procedure.

**[25.1B.5]    Variation of non-milestone dates where the parties are not in agreement**

Where the parties are not in agreement as to variation of a non-milestone date, application may be made to the court by the party seeking the variation: rule 1B(5). The application should be taken out as soon as possible: practice direction on case management (PD 5.2), para 41(1). 'Sufficient grounds' must be shown: rule 1B(6). The working party envisaged the court taking a fairly strict approach on such an application. In recommendation 58 it said:

> Where a party cannot secure the agreement of all the other parties for a time extension relating to a non-milestone event, a court should have power to grant such extension only if sufficient grounds are shown and provided that any extension granted does not involve or necessitate changing the trial date or trial period. It should be made clear in a practice direction that where an extension is granted, it is likely to involve an immediate 'unless order' specifying a suitable sanction.

Even where such sufficient grounds are shown, the court is enjoined not to grant an application for variation of a non-milestone date if the result would be a need to change the trial date or trial period: rule 1B(7). As recommended in the above passage, the case management practice direction provides (PD 5.2, para 41) that where variation of a non-milestone date by extension of time, which is not agreed, will only be granted on 'unless order' terms prescribing a suitable sanction should there be any further non-compliance. See Order 32 rule 11B and the commentary thereunder in relation to such orders.

If the party in default does not apply for variation, any other party may apply for 'an order to enforce compliance or for a sanction to be imposed or both': practice direction on case management (PD 5.2), para 41(2).

**[25.1B.6]    Duty of parties to inform court of failure to comply with dates**

In *Ip Sau Lin v Hospital Authority* [2009] 2 HKC 383 it was said that it is incumbent on the non-compliant party and the other party alike to assist the court in discharging its active case management function by bringing to the court's notice anticipated or actual non-compliance with court-ordered case management directions or timetable. Failure to do so could result in short-scheduled self-executing sanctions (as to which see Order 32 rule 11B and the commentary thereunder) or refusal of extension of time. The court went on to warn that in clear cases where legal representatives are responsible for non-compliance, consideration could be given to the making of a wasted costs order under Order 62 rule 8. The particular case concerned delay in exchange of witness statements and filing expert reports in an employee's compensation application, but the court's remarks appear to have been intended to be of more general application.

**1C.    Failure to appear at case management conference or pre-trial review**
(O. 25 r. 1C)

**(1) Where the plaintiff does not appear at the case management conference or pre-trial review, the Court shall provisionally strike out the plaintiff's claim.**

**(2) Where the defendant has made a counterclaim in the action and he does not appear at the case management conference or pre-trial review, the Court shall provisionally strike out the defendant's counterclaim.**

**(3) Where the Court has provisionally struck out a claim or counterclaim**

under paragraph (1) or (2), the plaintiff or the defendant may, before the expiry of 3 months from the date of the case management conference or pre-trial review, as the case may be, apply to the Court for restoration of the claim or counterclaim.

(4) The Court may restore the claim or counterclaim subject to such conditions as it thinks fit or refuse to restore it.

(5) The Court shall not restore the claim or counterclaim unless good reasons have been shown to the satisfaction of the Court.

(6) If the plaintiff or the defendant does not apply under paragraph (3) or his application under that paragraph is refused, then —

    (a)    the plaintiff's claim or the defendant's counterclaim stands dismissed upon the expiry of 3 months from the date of the case management conference or pre-trial review, as the case may be; and

    (b)    (i)    in the case of the plaintiff's claim, the defendant is entitled to his costs of the claim; and

            (ii)    in the case of the defendant's counterclaim, the plaintiff is entitled to his costs of the counterclaim.

(L.N. 152 of 2008)

---

## NOTES

### [25.1C.1]   Provisional striking out as consequence of failure to appear at case management conference or pre-trial review

The court has long had a power under Order 35 rule 1 to strike out an action from the list if neither party appears at trial. Order 25 rule 1C extends that power so that the court may strike out a plaintiff's claim or a defendant's counterclaim for non-appearance by such party at a case management conference or pre-trial review. The rule was introduced to deal with cases which 'go to sleep', whether because the plaintiff gets cold feet or runs out of money, or because settlement is reached without the court being informed. See para 395 of the final report of the Chief Justice's working party on civil justice reform.

It should be noted that the power under rule 1C is mandatory rather than discretionary – the rule provides that the court 'shall' strike out the claim or counterclaim of the party who fails to appear. It should also be noted that such striking out is 'provisional', being subject to the right to apply for restoration, as to which see below.

The working party was of the view that a distinction should be drawn between cases which 'go to sleep' before a timetable is fixed, and those which do so afterward, resulting in the timetable not being adhered to. It recommended that the former could be tolerated, but not the latter. In recommendation 60 the working party said:

> Where the parties fail to obtain a timetable, the court should not compel them to continue with the proceedings. However where a pre-trial milestone date has been set, the court should, after giving prior warning, strike out the action provisionally if no one appears at that milestone hearing.

As to the 'prior warning' referred to in the above recommendation, the working party had in mind the court's computer system automatically sending the parties a reminder of an approaching milestone date, 'asking to be informed if the case has settled, and warning that the action will be struck out if the milestone is ignored' (final report, para 398).

**[25.1C.2]  Restoration of an action which has been provisionally stuck out**
An order under Order 25 rule 1C striking out a claim or counterclaim for non-appearance at a case management conference or pre-trial review is provisional only: the plaintiff or defendant may apply, within 3 months, for the claim or counterclaim to be restored: rule 1C(3).

The court will deal with such an application to restore a claim or counterclaim in three stages: *World Chinese Business Investment Foundation Ltd & Ors v Shine Rainbow Marketing Ltd & Ors* [2010] 2 HKC 294 (Registrar Au-Yeung; 12.02.2010). The three stages are:

(1)   The applicant should meet the threshold of showing 'good reasons'. An explanation for the failure to attend is required. Rule 1C(5) provides that the court shall not restore the claim or counterclaim unless good reasons are shown.

(2)   Then the court will consider whether, as a matter of discretion, it should grant the application. The applicant should normally put forward evidence of the merits of its claim.

(3)   If the court decides to restore the claim, it will consider whether to impose conditions pursuant to rule 1C(4).

In *World Chinese* it was held that a solicitor's fault in failing to attend might constitute a good reason.

The Civil Court Practice 2008, our sister publication in the UK says (at CPR 3.1[1]), in the slightly different context of applications for relief from sanctions (Order 2 rule 5):

Where a party who has been struck out for non-attendance applies promptly for relief, with evidence of a reasonable excuse and reasonable prospects of success in the main proceedings, the court should restore the claim unless there are exceptional grounds for not doing so: *Thakerar v Northwick Park Hospital NHS Trust* [2002] EWCA Civ 617, [2002] All ER (D) 216 (Apr).

On granting an application to restore a claim or counterclaim which has been provisionally struck out, the court is expressly empowered to impose 'such conditions as it thinks fit': rule 1C(4). Unless the non-appearance of the party which resulted in the provisional striking out is entirely excusable (for example, where caused by accident or illness), it is likely that the defaulting party will face an adverse (possibly enhanced) costs order, and perhaps an order for payment of money into court under Order 1B(3), as a condition of the claim or counterclaim being restored.

**[25.1C.3]  Dismissal of claim or counterclaim which is not restored**
If the party in default does not apply within 3 months for restoration of a claim or counterclaim which has been provisionally struck out (or if such application is refused), rule 1C(6)(a) provides that the claim or counterclaim 'stands dismissed' and the costs thereof will be to the other side: rule 1C(6)(b). The use of the word 'dismissed' suggests an intention that there be little if any possibility of extending the 3 month time period during which application for restoration may be made. Whereas conceptually an action which has been struck out may be restored, dismissal of an action connotes a refusal to allow any further hearing, just as if there has been an adjudication on the merits rendering the matter *res judicata*.

**[25.1C.4]    Continuation of balance of the action**

Where a claim or counterclaim is struck out on non-appearance of the plaintiff or the defendant at a case management conference or pre-trial review, the balance of the action should not be affected. Thus where the plaintiff's claim is struck out, the defendant should be able to continue with its counterclaim, and *vice versa*. This seems to follow from the fact that under the rule it is the defaulting party's claim or counterclaim, rather than the action itself, which is struck out.

**2.    Duty to consider all matters** (O. 25 r. 2)

**(1)    When the case management summons first comes to be determined, the Court shall consider whether—**

    **(a)    it is possible to deal then with all the matters which, by the rules of this Order, are required to be considered at the case management summons; or**

    **(b)    it is expedient to adjourn the consideration of all or any of those matters until a later stage.**

**(L.N. 152 of 2008)**

**(2)    If when the case management summons first comes to be determined the Court considers that it is possible to deal then with all the said matters, it shall deal with them forthwith and shall endeavour to secure that all other matters which must or can be dealt with on interlocutory applications and have not already been dealt with are also then dealt with. (L.N. 152 of 2008)**

**(3)    If, when the case management summons first comes to be determined, the Court considers that it is expedient to adjourn the consideration of all or any of the matters which, by the rules of this Order, are required to be considered at the case management summons, the Court shall deal forthwith with such of those matters as it considers can conveniently be dealt with forthwith and adjourn the consideration of the remaining matters and shall endeavour to secure that all other matters which must or can be dealt with on interlocutory applications and have not already been dealt with are dealt with either then or at such time as the Court may specify. (L.N. 152 of 2008)**

**(4)    Subject to paragraph (5), and except where the parties agree to the making of an order under Order 33 as to the place or mode of trial before all the matters which, by the rules of this Order, are required to be considered at the case management summons have been dealt with, no such order shall be made until all those matters have been dealt with. (L.N. 152 of 2008)**

**(5)    If, at the determination of the case management summons, an action is ordered to be transferred to the District Court or some other court, paragraph (4) shall not apply and nothing in this Order shall be construed as requiring the Court to make any further order at the case management summons. (L.N. 152 of 2008)**

**(7)    If the determination of the case management summons is adjourned without a day being fixed for its resumption, any party may restore the summons to the list on 2 days' notice to the other parties. (L.N. 152 of 2008)**

## NOTES

**[25.2.1]    Numbering**
There is no paragraph (6) in Order 25 rule 2. The paragraph of the same number in the former Rules of the Supreme Court in England and Wales related to actions which might be tried before an official referee. In Hong Kong there is no provision for trial by official referee (see Order 33 rule 2 and Order 36 rule 1), hence paragraph (6) was omitted in this jurisdiction.

**[25.2.2]    Case management summons may be heard in stages**
Order 25 rule 2 provides that the court may consider the matters to be dealt with under a case management summons in stages. If the court considers it possible to deal with all matters when the summons first comes to be determined, it 'shall deal with them forthwith': rule 2(2). If not the court may adjourn certain matters to be dealt with later: rule 2(3). The latter is the course likely to be taken where there are contested interlocutory applications to be dealt with. Place and mode of trial will not normally be determined until all other matters under the case management summons have been dealt with: rule 2(4).

**3.    Particular matters for consideration** (O. 25 r. 3)
     **At the determination of the case management summons, the Court shall in particular consider, if necessary of its own motion, whether any order should be made or direction given in the exercise of the powers conferred by any of the following provisions, that is to say—**
>     **(a)    any provision of Part IV and Part V of the Evidence Ordinance (Cap. 8) (hearsay evidence of fact or opinion in civil proceedings) or of Part III and Part IV of Order 38;**
>     **(b)    Order 20, rule 5 and Order 38, rules 2 to 7;**
>     **(c)    section 43 of the District Court Ordinance (Cap. 336).**
>                                                  **(L.N. 152 of 2008)**

## NOTES

**[25.3.1]    Order 25 rule 3 – other matters to be considered at case management stage**
Order 25 rule 3 requires the court at the stage of the case management summons to consider whether directions are required with regard to the court's powers under certain particular legislative provisions. They are:
(a)    hearsay evidence (Order 38, Part III)
(b)    expert evidence (Order 38 part IV);
(c)    amendment of the writ or pleadings (Order 20 rule 5);
(d)    the giving of evidence at trial by affidavit (Order 38 rule 2);
(e)    exchange of witness statements (Order 38 rule 2A);
(f)    evidence at trial on information or belief, by production of documents or books, or copies thereof, or by production of a newspaper stating a fact which

is common knowledge (Order 38 rule 3);

(g)    limiting the number of expert witnesses (Order 38 rule 4);

(h)    admission of plans, photographs or models without proof (Order 38 rule 5);

(i)    revocation of any order previously made under Order 38 rules 2-5 (see the points immediately above) (Order 38 rule 6);

(j)    fixing the period within which notice of intention to rely on a finding or decision in relation to foreign law must be given (Order 38 rule 7);

(k)    transfer of the action to the District Court (District Court Ordinance (Cap 336), section 43) – see the discussion below.

It will be noted that the rule expressly provides that the court is to consider these matters of its own motion if necessary.

### [25.3.2]    Order 25 rule 3(c) – transfer to the District Court

Order 25 rule 3(c) provides that at the determination of the case management summons the court must consider whether to exercise its power under section 43 of the District Court Ordinance (Cap 336) to transfer the action to that court.

Section 43(3) of Cap 336 provides that the Court of First Instance is required to make an order for transfer of an action to the District Court where it appears to be within the jurisdiction of that court unless for any reason such as the importance or complexity of any issue in the action it ought to remain in the CFI. See also section 44 of Cap 336 which provides for transfer from the CFI to the District Court, by consent of the parties, of actions which are beyond the monetary limits of the District Court's jurisdiction.

In some cases, such as claims for liquidated amounts of money under the monetary limit of the District Court's jurisdiction, it will be clear that the action can be transferred to that court. It has been suggested such cases should be transferred by order *nisi* of a master shortly after being commenced in the Court of First Instance: *Hang Seng Credit Card Ltd & Ors v Tsang Nga Lee & Ors* [2000] 3 HKC 269, 281I. The exercise is more complicated with claims for unliquidated amounts. In such cases the court must come to a view as to the likely quantum achievable by the plaintiff at the end of the day. In *Wong Miu Kwan v FPD Savills Property Management Ltd* [2006] 1 HKC 575, 580B-H it was said that in doing so any employee's compensation already paid to the plaintiff should be taken into consideration (s 32(2)(b), Cap 336). Likewise, contributory negligence should be taken into account if admitted (s 32(2)(c), Cap 336). The court continued, saying that the following matters should be considered:

(a)    In the absence of abuse, a plaintiff should be entitled to frame his case in the manner that he wishes.

(b)    At the interlocutory stage, it would not be proper for the court or a master to view the plaintiff's claim in the same way as it would be viewed at trial by weighing the different evidence or by believing or disbelieving some or all of the evidence …

(c)    Accordingly, the plaintiff's case on quantum as framed by him ought to be viewed at its highest when determining the proper jurisdiction where the case should be brought.

See also *Hung Chor Hung John v Li Kwok Kin & Anor* HCPI 251/2009 (Master Marlene Ng; 10.11.2009) (para 16).

Both section 43 and Order 25 rule 3 provide that a transfer order may be made by the CFI of its own motion. However the parties should first be given an opportunity to be heard: *Inchcape HK Ltd v Performa (Asia) Ltd* [1992] 2 HKC 364.

Section 43(2) of Cap 336 provides that transfer may be ordered at any stage of the proceedings. In *American Express Bank Ltd v Cheung Kam Fung Betty* [2000] 2 HKC 510 (CA) it was held that transfer may be ordered even after judgment has been entered in the CFI. That decision was based on the former section 40, but is probably still good law. However, as a matter of discretion a late transfer to the District Court may not be appropriate. See *Incorporated Owners of Kin Ho Ind Bldg v Tam Wing Pak* HCA 2137/2006 (Deputy Judge L Chan; 14.05.2010) where a transfer order was refused on the ground that the trial had already been fixed to start in just ten days in the Court of First Instance.

In *Hung Chor Hung* (above) (para 71–72) practitioners were reminded that the personal injuries list practice direction (PD 18.1, paras 96–97) provide that where it becomes clear that a case is appropriate for transfer to another court, application should be made as soon as possible. The court warned of costs consequences if there is 'unjustified failure or refusal to promptly transfer' appropriate cases from the High Court to the District Court.

With regard to the costs consequences of transfer between the CFI and the District Court, see section 44A of the District Court Ordinance and the commentary under Order 78.

**4.    Admissions and agreements to be made** (O. 25 r. 4)

**At the determination of the case management summons, the Court shall endeavour to secure that the parties make all admissions and all agreements as to the conduct of the proceedings which ought reasonably to be made by them and may cause the order on the summons to record any admissions or agreements so made, and (with a view to such special order, if any, as to costs as may be just being made at the trial) any refusal to make any admission or agreement. (L.N. 152 of 2008)**

---

**NOTES**

**[25.4.1]    Court to encourage admissions and agreements at case management stage**

Order 25 rule 4 places a duty on the court to try to get the parties to make admissions and reach agreement on the conduct of the proceedings at the case management stage. The rule contemplates the making of 'special' orders as to costs as a possible sanction against parties who refuse to admit or agree.

Rule 4 is subject to rule 5.

**5.    Limitation of right of appeal** (O. 25 r. 5)

**Nothing in rule 4 shall be construed as requiring the Court to endeavour to secure that the parties shall agree to exclude or limit any right of appeal, but the order made on the case management summons may record any such agreement. (L.N. 152 of 2008)**

**NOTES**

**[25.5.1]     Agreement to limit right of appeal – exception to rule 4**
Order 25 rule 5 excludes agreement to limit the right of appeal from the scope of rule
4. The result is that the court has no obligation to try to secure such agreement from
the parties at the case management stage. However the rule contemplates the order
made on the case management summons recording any such agreement. Where that
is done the agreement goes onto the court record, perhaps lessening the chance of
disputes arising as to its existence or terms.

**6.     Duty to give all information at determination of case management
       summons** (O. 25 r. 6)
       **(1)    Subject to paragraph (2), no affidavit shall be used at the
determination of the case management summons except by the leave or
directions of the Court, but, subject to paragraph (4), it shall be the duty of the
parties to the action and their advisers to give all such information and produce
all such documents as the Court may reasonably require for the purposes of
enabling it properly to deal with the summons. (L.N. 152 of 2008)**
       **The Court may, if it appears proper so to do in the circumstances,
authorize any such information or documents to be given or produced to the
Court without being disclosed to the other parties but, in the absence of such
authority, any information or document given or produced under this
paragraph shall be given or produced to all the parties as well as to the Court.**
       **(2)    No leave shall be required by virtue of paragraph (1) for the use of
an affidavit by any party at the determination of the case management
summons in connection with any application thereat for any order if, under any
of these rules, an application for such an order is required to be supported by
an affidavit. (L.N. 152 of 2008)**
       **(3)    If the Court at the determination of the case management summons
requires a party to the action or his solicitor or counsel to give any information
or produce any document and that information or document is not given or
produced, then, subject to paragraph (4), the Court may– (L.N. 152 of 2008)**
              **(a)    cause the facts to be recorded in the order with a view to such
                     special order, if any, as to costs as may be just being made at
                     the trial, or**
              **(b)    if it appears to the Court to be just so to do, order the whole or
                     any part of the pleadings of the party concerned to be struck
                     out, or if the party is plaintiff or the claimant under a
                     counterclaim, order the action or counterclaim to be dismissed
                     on such terms as may be just.**
       **(4)    Notwithstanding anything in the foregoing provisions of this rule,
no information or documents which are privileged from disclosure shall be
required to be given or produced under this rule by or by the advisers of any
party otherwise than with the consent of that party.**

**NOTES**

**[25.6.1]    Provision of information and documents at case management stage**
Order 25 rule 6 provides that at the case management stage, affidavits are not normally required, but the parties have a duty to provide the court and the other parties with information and documents needed by the court to give appropriate directions. Confidentiality may be protected by disclosure to the court only, and not the other parties, under the proviso to rule 6(1). Privileged information and documents are protected by rule 6(4) which provides the court may not compel their disclosure without consent.

It is clear that the court has power to direct a party to provide specific information in pursuance of this duty. This can be seen in the following cases:

(a)    *Luigi Benetton SRL v Face Time Int'l Ltd* HCA 4135/1993 (J Chan J; 24.11.1995) where the court ordered a party to indicate on affidavit whether it intended to call any witness at trial. The defendant had failed to comply with an earlier direction to exchange witness statements.

(b)    *Fila Marketing (HK) Ltd v Faithful Properties Ltd & Anor* HCCL 66/1997 (Findlay J; 23.08.1999) where the defendants were ordered to supply information on their assets in order to assist the plaintiff to decide whether it was worthwhile continuing with the proceedings. There was reason to believe the defendants had already divested themselves of their assets and the plaintiff was concerned that it may be a waste of costs and court time to proceed to assessment of damages.

**[25.6.2]    Sanctions for failure to comply with duty to provide information and documents at case management stage**
Order 25 rule 6(3) provides for sanctions against a party, or legal representative, who fails to give information or provide documents required by the court at the case management stage. The rule envisages the making of a 'special' order as to costs, and goes so far as to empower the court to strike out the defaulting party's pleadings. Cases in which the striking out power has been exercised include the following:

(a)    *Luigi Benetton SRL v Face Time Int'l Ltd* HCA 4135/1993 (J Chan J; 24.11.1995) where the court made an unless order requiring the defendant to file and serve witness statements within 21 days, in default of which judgment would be entered against it. The defendant had indicated it intended to call witnesses at trial, but had failed to comply with an earlier direction to exchange witness statements.

(b)    *Aqua-Leisure Industries Inc & Anor v Aqua Splash Ltd (No 2)* [1999] 3 HKC 343, 347I-348C where the defendant's defence was struck out after it failed to attend a hearing and failed to respond to written questions put to it by the plaintiff's solicitors on direction of the court. The court said that it was 'reluctant to make an order which has the effect of debarring the defendant from defending the action', but decided it must 'take a robust view' by assuming the defendant did not intend to defend the action, and struck out the defence thereby enabling the plaintiff to enter default judgment rather than having to go to the trouble and expense of proving an undefended case.

(c)    *Top One Int'l (China) Property Group Co Ltd* HCA 1244/2009 (Fok J; 09.12.2010) where defendants' failure to comply with an unless order requiring them to answer the plaintiff's questions as to whether they intended to continue to defend resulted in their defence being automatically struck out.

With regard to striking out for non-appearance at a case management hearing or pre-trial review see also Order 25 rule 1C.

**7.    Duty to make all interlocutory applications at case management summons** (O. 25 r. 7)

**(1)    Any party to whom the case management summons is addressed must so far as practicable apply at the time fixed for determination of the summons for any order or directions which he may desire as to any matter capable of being dealt with on an interlocutory application in the action and must, not less than 7 days before the time fixed for determination of the summons, serve on the other parties a notice specifying those orders and directions in so far as they differ from the orders and directions asked for by the summons. (L.N. 152 of 2008)**

**(2)    If the determination of the case management summons is adjourned and any party to the proceedings desires to apply for any order or directions not asked for by the summons or in any notice given under paragraph (1), he must, not less than 7 days before the resumption of the determination of the summons, serve on the other parties a notice specifying those orders and directions in so far as they differ from the orders and directions asked for by the summons or in any such notice as aforesaid. (L.N. 152 of 2008)**

**(3)    Any application subsequent to the case management summons and before judgment as to any matter capable of being dealt with on an interlocutory application in the action must be made under the summons by 2 clear days' notice to the other party stating the grounds of the application. (L.N. 152 of 2008)**

---

**NOTES**

**[25.7.1]    Matters to be dealt with under case management summons**
Order 25 rule 7(1) places a duty on all parties to apply on 7 days notice for all interlocutory orders and directions required at the determination of the case management summons. Subsequent interlocutory applications may be made on two clear days' notice: rule 7(3). The rule is the same as that which applied under the former summons for directions procedure, adapted only to reflect the change to case management summons.

The questionnaire or case management summons in an action will comprehensively raise matters which it is necessary for the court to consider in giving directions for pre-trial conduct of an action and fixing a timetable. With regard to the former summons for directions procedure, it was said, in *Li Fook Chu v Chung Shau Ching* [2001] 4 HKC 681, 688F (CA):

When a summons for directions is heard, that must never be treated as a formality. It is the master's duty to consider all matters which will lead to a speedy and effective hearing of the trial of the action.

Those comments should apply *a fortiori* to the case management summons procedure, given the questionnaire, which is designed to allow the court to give directions tailor-made to the individual case. See the commentary under Order 25 rule 1 concerning the questionnaire.

### [25.7.2]　Long cases

In regard to cases which are likely to require lengthy trials, practice direction 5.7 requires additional matters to be considered at the case management stage. The parties are required to alert the listing judge by letter if they are in agreement that the trial is likely to last 15 days or longer, or apply by summons if they are not in agreement on this point.

As amended when the civil justice reforms came into force, the practice direction provides that long cases are assigned to a trial judge at an early stage, who will take charge of case management of the action and preside at any subsequent hearing of the case management summons or pre-trial review. The text of the practice direction can be viewed on the judiciary's website www.judiciary.gov.hk or that of the Hong Kong Legal Information Institute www.hklii.org, both of which are accessible by the general public free-of-charge. The Chief Justice's working party on civil justice reform regarded it as providing for what is essentially a 'docket' system, whereby cases are assigned to a particular judge's list, and supported its continuation (final report, recommendation 63).

### [25.7.3]　Reconsideration of case management decisions

A master's order *nisi* on a case management summons may be varied on application to the master. See Order 25 rule 1A(4) and the commentary thereunder. A case management order absolute may be appealed to a single judge of the Court of First Instance under Order 58 at which the court is entitled to exercise discretion afresh. In the case of appeals from a judge to the Court of Appeal, the court is generally reluctant to interfere with discretionary decisions and leave to appeal is unlikely to be granted. See the commentary under Order 59 rule 2B.

It is open to a trial–designated judge to reconsider and vary case management decisions made earlier on by a judge of the same court. See *Asia–Pac Infrastructure Dev't Ltd v Ing & Ors* HCA 16778/1999 (Stone J; 03.12.2010) (para 33–5) where jurisdiction to do so was found in PD 5.2, para 39, and in Order 1B rule 1(2)(l). The practice direction contemplates variation of earlier case management decisions only when there has been a change of circumstances, but in *Asia–Pac* the court was of the view that it should in principle always be open to the trial–designated judge to do so.

**8.　　Automatic directions in personal injury actions** (O. 25 r. 8)

　　**(1)　When the pleadings in any action to which this rule applies are deemed to be closed the following directions shall take effect automatically —**

　　　　　　**(a)　there shall be discovery of documents within 14 days in accordance with Order 24, rule 2, and inspection within 7 days thereafter, save that where liability is admitted, or where the action arises out of a road accident, discovery shall be limited**

to disclosure by the plaintiff of any documents relating to special damages;

(b)  **(Repealed L.N. 152 of 2008)**

(c)  **(Repealed L.N. 152 of 2008)**

(d)  photographs, a sketch plan and the contents of any police accident report shall be receivable in evidence at the trial and shall be agreed if possible;

(HK)(dd  the record of any proceedings in any court or tribunal shall be receivable in evidence upon production of a copy thereof certified as a true copy by the clerk or other appropriate officer of the court or tribunal;

(f)–(g)  **(Repealed L.N. 99 of 1993)**

(2)  **(Repealed L.N. 152 of 2008)**

(3)  Nothing in paragraph (1) shall prevent any party to an action to which this rule applies from applying to the Court for such further or different directions or orders as may, in the circumstances, be appropriate or prevent the making of an order for the transfer of the proceedings to the District Court. **(L.N. 152 of 2008)**

(4)  For the purpose of this rule —

"a road accident" means an accident on land due to a collision or apprehended collision involving a vehicle; and

"documents relating to special damages" include —

(a)  documents relating to any industrial injury, industrial disablement or sickness benefit rights, and

(b)  where the claim is made under the Fatal Accidents Ordinance (Cap. 22), documents relating to any claim for dependency on the deceased.

(5)  This rule applies to any action for personal injuries except–

(a)  any Admiralty action; and

(b)  any action where the pleadings contain an allegation of a negligent act or omission in the course of medical treatment.

---

## NOTES

**[25.8.1]  Directions in personal injuries actions**

Order 25 rule 1 exempts personal injury actions from the questionnaire procedure. The questionnaire is not necessary in such actions because standard directions automatically take effect under Order 25 rule 8. However practice direction 18.1, concerning the personal injuries list, applies Order 25 to personal injury actions generally, and additionally sets out specific and detailed directives for the conduct of such actions and the time within various steps are to be taken. See the commentary under Order 72 rule 2 concerning the personal injuries list practice direction. The practice direction can be viewed on the judiciary's website www.judiciary.gov.hk or that of the Hong Kong Legal Information Institute www.hklii.org, both of which are accessible by the general public free-of-charge.

Note that Order 25 rule 8 does not apply to Admiralty actions or medical negligence claims: rule 8(5). The personal injuries practice direction does apply to Admiralty actions if they are transferred to the personal injury list, and it applies to medical negligence claims (PD 18.1, paras 10 & 12).

Order 25 rule 8 previously contained automatic directions with regard to expert evi dence in personal injury actions. These were deleted with implementation of the civil justice reforms in 2009. Now reference should be made to Order 38 rule 4A, which applies not just to personal injuries claims, but to all actions, and makes provision for the appointment of a single joint expert in any case where expert evidence is required. See also Order 38 rule 4 (power to limit the number of expert witnesses), rule 35 (expert's overriding duty to the court) and rule 37A (expert report to be verified by statement of truth).

In cases where there is a split trial, see also Order 37 rule 1(1A) which sets out automatic directions which take effect upon the court giving judgment for damages to be assessed.

### [25.8.2]    Stay of proceedings where plaintiff refuses medical examination

The court has power to stay a personal injuries action until the plaintiff submits to medical examination by the defendant's expert: *Edmeades v Thames Board Mills Ltd* [1969] 2 QB 67 (CA); *Ho Ki Hung v Chan Ngai Ho Ki Hung v Chan Ngai Ho & Anor* DCCJ 8177/1984 (Judge Li; 29.05.1985); *Ma Oi Lin Irene v Ma Hing Ming & Anor* [2008] 5 HKC 289. This power is not found in the rules, but in inherent jurisdiction: *Edmeades* (above, at 71).

The criteria for making such an order were set out in *Lane v Willis* [1972] 1 All ER 430, 435j-436b (CA) in the following terms:

> An order for a medical examination of any party to an action has been well said to be an 'invasion of personal liberty'. Accordingly, it should only be granted when it is reasonable in the interests of justice so to order. When the refusal of a medical examination is alleged to be unreasonable, the onus lies on the party who says that it is unreasonable and who applies for the order to show, on the particular facts of the case, that he is unable properly to prepare his claim (or defence) without that examination.

In *Wong See Ming v Alfulso Ltd* [1998] 4 HKC 300, 304I-305B the above criteria were regarded as applicable in Hong Kong.

The question of reasonableness is to be judged by reference to both the request and the refusal to undergo examination: *Aspinall v Sterling Mansell Ltd* [1981] 3 All ER 866. There the court refused a stay where a party objected to undergo 'patch' testing to determine the cause of dermatitis. It was held that the right of personal liberty had to prevail where the proposed examination carried a risk of injury. In *Prescott v Bulldog Tools Ltd* [1981] 3 All ER 869 it was held reasonable for a party to refuse to undergo a fifth round of testing which would last 3-5 days and would involve radiation and a risk of infection.

### 9.    (Repealed L.N. 152 of 2008)

---

## NOTES

### [25.9.1]    Repeal of Order 25 rule 9

Prior to the implementation of the civil justice reforms in 2009, Order 25 rule 9(3) empowered the court to give further directions on application of a party or of its own motion. (Rule 9(1) had been repealed in 1993 and rule 9(2) was omitted at the time of the 1988 revision). The repeal of rule 9(3) with effect from 2009 was probably on account of the fact it was no longer necessary in view of the express powers included elsewhere to make orders by way of case management. See in particular Order 1B.

**10.     Application to action in specialist list** (O. 25, r.10)
         **Notwithstanding anything in this Order, a specialist judge may, by a practice direction, determine the extent to which this Order is to apply to an action in a specialist list.**
         **(L.N. 152 of 2008)**

---

**NOTES**

**[25.10.1]     Application of Order 25 to specialist proceedings**
Specialist proceedings such as commercial cases, construction and arbitration proceedings, personal injury actions and applications for judicial review are governed by practice directions in Hong Kong. See generally Order 72 and the commentary thereunder. The purpose of Order 25 rule 10 is to enable such practice directions to set out the extent to which the case management summons and case management conference procedures provided for by Order 25 will apply to such proceedings.

**11.     Transitional provisions relating to Part 11 of Amendment Rules 2008**
         (O. 25 r. 11)
         **(1)     A summons for directions taken out before the commencement of the Amendment Rules 2008 and pending immediately before the commencement is deemed to be-**
                   **(a)     if the summons for directions was taken out by the plaintiff, a case management summons taken out under rule 1(1B)(b); or**
                   **(b)     if the summons for directions was taken out by a defendant, a case management summons taken out under rule 1(4)(a).**
         **(2)     Where the pleadings in an action to which rule 1 applies are deemed to be closed but no summons for directions has been taken out before the commencement of the Amendment Rules 2008, rule 1(1) has effect as if for the words "the pleadings in an action to which this rule applies are deemed to be closed", there were substituted the words "the commencement of the Amendment Rules 2008".**
         **(L.N. 152 of 2008) (Enacted 1988)**

---

**NOTES**

**[25.11.1]     Transitional provision – summons for directions deemed to be case management summons**
A summons for directions taken out before that procedure was replaced by the case management summons with effect from 2009 is deemed, by rule 11 to be a case management summons. It follows that the new procedures will apply despite the fact

that the action, and the summons, pre-date the amendments coming into force. There is no express requirement for the questionnaire under Order 25 rule 1 to be completed in such cases, but it would certainly be helpful to the court for that to be done.

Where no summons for directions had been taken out in an action pending at the time of the civil justice reforms coming into force in 2009, a case management summons must be taken out within 28 days of the commencement of the new rules: rule 11(2).

## ORDER 26

### INTERROGATORIES

**1. Discovery by interrogatories** (O. 26 r. 1)

(1)   A party to any cause or matter may in accordance with the following provisions of this Order serve on any other party interrogatories relating to any matter in question between the applicant and that other party in the cause or matter which are necessary either—

(a)   for disposing fairly of the cause or matter; or

(b)   for saving costs.

(2)   Without prejudice to the provisions of paragraph (1), a party may apply to the Court for an order giving him leave to serve on any other party interrogatories relating to any matter in question between the applicant and that other party in the cause or matter.

(3)   A proposed interrogatory which does not relate to such a matter as is mentioned in paragraph (1) may not be administered notwithstanding that it might be admissible in oral cross-examination of a witness.

(4)   In this Order—

"interrogatories without order" means interrogatories served under paragraph (1);

"ordered interrogatories" means interrogatories served under paragraph (2) or interrogatories which are required to be answered pursuant to an order made on an application under rule 3(2) and, where such an order is made, the interrogatories shall not, unless the Court orders otherwise, be treated as interrogatories without order for the purposes of rule 3(1).

(5)   Unless the context otherwise requires, the provisions of this Order apply to both interrogatories without order and ordered interrogatories.

(L.N. 404 of 1991)

---

## NOTES

### [26.1.1]   Nature of interrogatories

Interrogatories are written questions which one party may require another party to answer concerning matters at issue in an action. They should be in the form as prescribed by Order 26 rule 2. A court order is not generally required for service of interrogatories (see Order 26 rule 3), but if the party on whom they are served does not respond, an application to the court may be made under Order 26 rule 4.

The basic principles with regard to interrogatories were set out succinctly in *Sit Ka Yin Priscilla v EOC & Ors* DCEO 11/1999 (Judge Lok; 17.09.2008) (para 8), summarising the judgment in *Lee Nui Foon v Ocean Park (No 2)* [1995] 2 HKC 395 as follows:

(a)   the interrogatories must relate to 'a matter in question' between the parties and must be 'necessary' either for disposing fairly of the cause or matter or for saving costs (at 396G);

(b) the interrogatories must not be fishing, oppressive, prolix or imprecise, and interrogatory will be oppressive if the answer cannot be given without an examination of the respondent's record, with the expenditure of much time and trouble (at 396H-398E);

(c) the interrogatories must not be questions which go to the evidence the opposing party intends to adduce (at 398E-I);

(d) the interrogatories must not be questions which require an answer which is a matter of opinion or for an expert (at 399A);

(e) the interrogatories must not be questions which go to the facts which would assist in establishing the opposing party's case as opposed to the case of the party seeking to interrogate (at 399A-B)

(f) the interrogatories must not be effectively asking for documents or discovery (at 399B-D); and

(g) even if the interrogatories comply with all the requirements of the rules under O 26, the court nevertheless retains an overriding discretion as to whether or not to allow them to be administered (at 399E).

The above points are discussed in greater detail below.

**[26.1.2]    Interrogatories must relate to a matter in question**

Interrogatories must relate to a matter in question in the proceedings: Order 26 rule 1(1). In other words they must be relevant to the factual issues. The relevance may be direct or indirect: see *Lau Tak Wah Andy v Hang Seng Bank Ltd (No 2)* [2001] 2 HKC 548 where Cheung J, at 552C–D quoted with approval from *Marriott v Chamberlain* (1886) 17 QBD 154 where Lord Esher MR stated:

> The right to interrogate is not confined to the facts directly in issue, but extends to any facts the existence or non-existence of which is relevant to the existence or non-existence of the facts directly in issue.

See also *Cocoa Merchants Ltd v Ferryview Holdings Inc &Ors*[1987] HKLR 577 citing *Nash v Layton* [1911] 2 Ch 71 where a defendant pleading that the plaintiff was an unlicensed money lender was permitted to interrogate on the details of other loans made. However in *Prudential Assurance Co Ltd v Ho* HCA 1231/2004 (Suffiad J; 09.10.2007) the court disallowed interrogatories seeking 'general information' relating not to the particular party but to non-parties who might be in a similar position. The court said (at para 19) that the interrogatories were 'quite irrelevant to the issues in the case'.

The relevance of interrogatories is to be judged by reference not only to the case of the party putting forward the question, but also with reference to his opponent's case. See *Plymouth Mutual Society Ltd v Traders' Publishing Association Ltd* [1906] 1 KB 403.

It is not permissible to go on a 'fishing expedition' by administering interrogatories in the hope of finding a case of which nothing is yet known: *Hennessy v Wright (No 2)* (1890) 24 QBD 445, 448. In other words, interrogatories based on 'mere speculation or suspicions', without pleaded allegations or *prima facie* evidence in support, will not be allowed: *Rai Ramesh v Nesco-China State-Hip Hing Joint Venture* HCPI 436/2007 (Master Kwan; 10.06.2008) (paras 12-17).

**[26.1.3]    Interrogatories must be 'necessary'**
Under Order 26 rule 1 interrogatories may only be administered where 'necessary' for fairly disposing of the action, or for saving costs. The necessity requirement is stringent: see *Lau Tak Wah Andy v Hang Seng Bank Ltd (No 2)* [2001] 2 HKC 548 quoting with approval from *Hall v Sevalco Ltd* [1996] PIQR 344 where it was said:

> Necessity is a stringent test… The interrogator must be able to show that his interrogatories, if answered when served, will serve a clear litigious purpose by saving costs or promoting the fair and efficient conduct of the action.

**[26.1.4]    Necessary ... for fair disposition of matter**
In *Lovell v Lovell* [1970] 1 WLR 1451 it was held that an interrogatory was not fair in that if compelled to answer it the defendant might acknowledge the debt in respect of which he pleaded the statute of limitations. Such an acknowledgment would deprive him of that defence.

**[26.1.5]    'Necessary ... for saving costs'**
Interrogatories may be considered necessary 'for saving costs' within the meaning of rule 1(1)(b) even though the possibility of saving costs depends on what answer is given. The phrase should be interpreted as necessary 'if costs are to be saved', or 'if any saving of costs is to be achieved'. See *Baroness Dunn v Li Kwok Po David* [1994] 2 HKC 597, 600F-G.

Interrogatories are not normally considered necessary for saving costs when directed to a person who will inevitably give evidence at trial: *Griebart v Morris* [1920] 1 KB 659. However they will be permitted if the interrogator could be irremediably prejudiced, or the trial could be interrupted, by late emergence of the information: *Det Danske Hedeselskabet v KDM Int'l plc* [1994] 2 Lloyd's L R 534, 537, quoted with approval in *Ma Tak Kin John v Dr Yu Chung Ping* HCPI 614/2002 (Suffiad J; 07.06.2006).

It is not proper to interrogate on matters which will require the witness to consult an expert: *Rofe v Kevorkian* [1936] 2 All ER 1334 (CA).

**[26.1.6]    Timing of interrogatories**
In *Ngai Hung Chau v Kwok Keung & Ors* HCA 3731/1994 (Jerome Chan J; 26.10.1995); [1995] HKLY 1007) it was held that interrogatories were not appropriate before the exchange of witness statements. The information sought by way of interrogatories might be revealed in the witness statements; hence it could not be said that the interrogatories were necessary for saving costs at that stage of the proceedings. The learned judge declined to follow *Lee Nui Foon v Ocean Park Corp (No 2)* [1995] 2 HKC 395. In *Lau Tak Wah Andy v Hang Seng Bank Ltd (No 2)* [2001] 2 HKC 548 it was held that interrogatories relating to damages should not served before issues of liability in a passing off case was established. The rationale was to preserve confidentiality in the information.

**2.    Form and nature of interrogatories** (O. 26 r. 2)

(1)    **Where interrogatories are served, a note at the end of the interrogatories shall specify—**

(a)    **a period of time (not being less than 28 days from the date of service) within which the interrogatories are to be answered;**

    **(b)**     **where the party to be interrogated is a body corporate or unincorporate which is empowered by law to sue or be sued whether in its own name or in the name of an officer or other person, the officer or member on whom the interrogatories are to be served; and**

    **(c)**     **where the interrogatories are to be served on two or more parties or are required to be answered by an agent or servant of a party, which of the interrogatories each party or, as the case may be, an agent or servant is required to answer, and which agent or servant.**

    **(2)   Subject to rule 5(1), a party on whom interrogatories are served shall, unless the Court orders otherwise on an application under rule 3(2), be required to give within the period specified under paragraph (1)(a) answers, which shall (unless the Court directs otherwise) be on affidavit.**

    **(L.N. 404 of 1991)**

---

## NOTES

### [26.2.1]     Answer to interrogatories to be on affidavit

Order 26 rule 1(2) provides that the answers to interrogatories shall be given on affidavit unless the court directs otherwise. The affidavit should normally be made by the party to whom the interrogatories are addressed, or someone with personal knowledge. In *Chan Kin Lam v Sunray Cave Ltd* HCA 1997/2006 (Recorder Yuen SC; 21.09.2009) (para 10) the court found the affirmation of the party's solicitor acceptable, where the solicitor was explaining a typographical error for which he was responsible.

**3.     Interrogatories without order** (O. 26 r. 3)

    **(1)   Interrogatories without order may be served on a party not more than twice.**

    **(2)   A party on whom interrogatories without order are served may, within 14 days of the service of the interrogatories, apply to the Court for the interrogatories to be varied or withdrawn and, on any such application, the Court may make such order as it thinks fit (including an order that the party who served the interrogatories shall not serve further interrogatories without order).**

    **(3)   Interrogatories without order shall not be served on the Crown.**

    **(L.N. 404 of 1991)**

---

## NOTES

### [26.3.1]     Order required for interrogatories against government

Order 26 rule 3(3) provides that interrogatories without order may not be served on the government. However interrogatories may be ordered against the government under the Crown Proceedings Ordinance (Cap 300) s 24(1)(b). See the commentary under Order 77 rule 12.

**[26.3.2]**      **Order required for interrogatories in District Court**

Order 26 rule 3 is omitted from the Rules of the District Court (Cap 336) with the result that an order is always required for service of interrogatories in that court: *Regent Land Asia Ltd v Lee Chau Hung Eva & Ors* DCCJ 4460/2007 (Deputy Judge Kent Yee; 26.03.2010) (para 22). Note that there are other differences between Order 26 in the RHC and the RDC as well.

**4.**      **Ordered interrogatories** (O. 26 r. 4)

     **(1)**      Where an application is made for leave to serve interrogatories, a copy of the proposed interrogatories shall be served with the summons or the notice under Order 25, rule 7, by which the application is made.

     **(2)**      In deciding whether to give leave to serve interrogatories, the Court shall take into account any offer made by the party to be interrogated to give particulars, make admissions or produce documents relating to any matter in question and whether or not interrogatories without order have been administered.

     **(L.N. 404 of 1991)**

**5.**      **Objections and insufficient answers** (O. 26 r. 5)

     **(1)**      Without prejudice to rule 3(2), where a person objects to answering any interrogatory on the ground of privilege he may take the objection in his answer.

     **(2)**      Where any person on whom ordered interrogatories have been served answers any of them insufficiently, the Court may make an order requiring him to make a further answer, either by affidavit or on oral examination as the Court may direct.

     **(3)**      Where any person on whom interrogatories without order have been served answers any of them insufficiently, the party serving the interrogatories may ask for further and better particulars of the answer given and any such request shall not be treated as service of further interrogatories for the purposes of rule 3(1).

     **(L.N. 404 of 1991)**

**6.**      **Failure to comply with order** (O. 26 r. 6)

     **(1)**      If a party fails to answer interrogatories or to comply with an order made under rule 5(2) or a request made under rule 5(3), the Court may make such order as it thinks just including, in particular, an order that the action be dismissed or, as the case may be, an order that the defence be struck out and judgment be entered accordingly.

     **(2)**      Without prejudice to paragraph (1), where a party fails to answer ordered interrogatories or to comply with an order made under rule 5(2), he shall be liable to committal.

     **(3)**      Service on a party's solicitor of an order to answer interrogatories made against the party shall be sufficient service to found an application for committal of the party disobeying the order, but the party may show in answer to the application that he had no notice or knowledge of the order.

     **(4)**      A solicitor on whom an order to answer interrogatories made

against his client is served and who fails without reasonable excuse to give
notice thereof to his client shall be liable to committal.
    **(L.N. 404 of 1991)**

**7.      Use of answers to interrogatories at trial** (O. 26 r. 7)
    A party may put in evidence at the trial of a cause or matter, or of any
issue therein, some only of the answers to interrogatories, or part only of such
an answer, without putting in evidence the other answers or, as the case may be,
the whole of that answer, but the Court may look at the whole of the answers
and if of opinion that any other answer or other part of an answer is so
connected with an answer or part thereof used in evidence that the one ought
not to be so used without the other, the Court may direct that that other answer
or part shall be put in evidence.

**8.      Revocation and variation of orders** (O. 26 r. 8)
    Any order made under this Order (including an order made on appeal)
may, on sufficient cause being shown, be revoked or varied by a subsequent
order or direction of the Court made or given at or before the trial of the cause
or matter in connection with which the original order was made.
    **(Enacted 1988)**

## ORDER 27

### ADMISSIONS

**1. Admission of case of other party** (O. 27 r. 1)
      **Without prejudice to Order 18, rule 13, a party to a cause or matter may give notice, by his pleading or otherwise in writing, that he admits the truth of the whole or any part of the case of any other party.**

---

## NOTES

### [27.1.1]    Admissions of allegations of fact

Order 27 rule 1 provides for the making of formal, binding admissions of the whole or part of the case against a party. Where the whole of the case against a party is admitted judgment may be entered on the admissions under Order 27 rule 3. The rule should be read together with Order 13A, which provides a separate formal procedure for admission of liability to pay the whole or part of a claim for money, with or without a request for payment on terms.

      Formal binding admissions may be made in pleadings (Order 18 rule 13), in response to a Notice to Admit under Order 27 rule 2, or even in a solicitors' letter (see, for example, *Rankine v Garton Sons & Co Ltd* [1979] 2 All ER 1185 and see *Bird & Ors v Birds Eye Walls Ltd* [1987] The Times, 24 July, where it was held that a letter admitting liability was equivalent to an admission on the pleadings).

      An admitted fact is taken to have been proved and evidence is not required at trial. By contrast, there is a view that admissions made in evidence, such as in an affirmation or in answer to interrogatories, are only part of the evidence to be weighed by the trier of fact; hence a party should be free to contradict himself at trial: see *Lyell v Kennedy (No 3)* (1884) 27 Ch D 1, 15 and 29, and see *Endeavour Wines Ltd v Martin* [1948] WN 338. It is another matter whether a party who contradicts his own previous evidence will be believed.

### [27.1.2]    Withdrawal of admissions

Withdrawal of a formal binding admission will normally require leave of the court, whether by way of leave to amend the pleading in which it is made, or under Order 27 rule 2(2) to withdraw an admission made in response to a Notice to Admit. Likewise leave is required to withdraw an admission made in a letter: *Singh Balwinder v Sino Phil Engineering Services Ltd* [2007] 1 HKLRD 560 (DCt). Leave to withdraw 'should normally be granted if the application is made in good faith, raises a triable issue with a reasonable prospect of success, and will not prejudice the plaintiff in a manner which cannot be adequately compensated': *Gale v Superdrug Stores plc* [1996] 1 WLR 1089 (CA), quoted with approval in *Burlington Air Express Ltd v Nuovo Collection Ltd* DCCJ 8865/2001 (Deputy Judge K Lin; 15.08.2002) and in *Singh Balwinder* (above). On such an application the court will 'balance the prejudice suffered by the admitting party if deprived of his right to resile against any prejudice which the relying party has specifically established he will suffer if the admission is withdrawn': *Re Chung Wong Kit* [1999] 1 HKC 684, 688E-F. As Barnett J attractively put it in *The Amigo* [1991] 2 HKC 491, 497G, 'the guiding principle is whether or not it would be just to allow the withdrawal'.

A party seeking to withdraw an admission made by mistake will normally be expected to give a 'credible explanation of the circumstances' in which the admission was made: *Tse Yuk-tin (administrator) v Chee Cheung Hing & Co Ltd & Anor* [1984] HKLR 391. Nevertheless in *Taisei Kogyo Kaisha Ltd v Billiongold Co Ltd* [1992] 2 HKC 153 the Court of Appeal allowed withdrawal of an admission in a defence which, by comparison to what was contained in the rest of the defence, was obviously made in error.

Admissions which have deliberately been made may also be withdrawn if 'good reason' is shown: *Tse Yuk-tin* (above, at 395E).

The Chief Justice's working party on civil justice reform, referring to *Gale* (above) and some of the Hong Kong cases referred to above, expressed the view that the approach in Hong Kong 'has tended to be somewhat stricter' than that in England, saying (final report para 179):

> The courts in this jurisdiction have generally required the party seeking to resile from an admission to provide a proper explanation for its withdrawal and at the same time required the party resisting to provide evidence of any prejudice it might suffer should the admission be withdrawn.

The working party concluded (at para 183) that the courts are 'well-equipped to perform such balancing exercises in the exercise of discretion' and that amendment of the rules was not necessary.

**2.     Notice to admit** (O. 27 r. 2)
**(1)   A party to a cause or matter may not later than 21 days after the cause or matter is set down for trial serve on any other party a notice requiring him to admit, for the purpose of that cause or matter only, such facts or such part of his case as may be specified in the notice.**

**(2)   An admission made in compliance with a notice under this rule shall not be used against the party by whom it was made in any cause or matter other than the cause or matter for the purpose of which it was made or in favour of any person other than the person by whom the notice was given, and the Court may at any time allow a party to amend or withdraw an admission so made by him on such terms as may be just.**

---

**NOTES**

**[27.2.1]     Comparison with English rules**
Order 27 rule 2 derives from the rule of the same number in the former English RSC. The equivalent rule in England under the CPR is 32.18.

**[27.2.2]     The notice to admit procedure**
Order 27 rule 2 enables a party to serve notice on another party requiring the other to make admissions of fact. If made, such an admission is binding on the party making it, for the purpose of the proceedings in which it is made. A party who is not prepared to make a full admission of a point under a notice to admit may make a qualified admission.

The rule provides that a party may amend or withdraw such an admission with leave. As to withdrawal of admissions, see the commentary under rule 1 above.

The rule provides that notice to admit may be served any time up to 21 days after an action is set down for trial. No express time is stated for the party served with the notice to respond. However Order 62 rule 3(5) provides for costs consequences (see below) if the party fails to respond within 7 days. That period compares with 14 days under the equivalent provision in the former English RSC.

### [27.2.3]    Form of notice to admit

Practice forms 60 and 61 (reproduced in volume 2 of the loose-leaf edition of this work) are respectively the form of Notice to Admit Facts and the form of Admission in response thereto. The form followed in England under the CPR (form N266) is substantially different.

### [27.2.4]    Costs consequences of failure to admit

A party who fails to make an admission sought under a notice to admit will normally be ordered to pay the costs of proving the particular fact in any event: see Order 62 rule 3(5). However the court retains a discretion and may make a different order: *Large Land Investments Ltd v Cheung Siu Kwai Pansy* HCA 434/1998 (Deputy Judge Gill; 28.01.2002); *Man Ping Nam v Man Mei Kwai* HCA 9852/1998 (A Cheung J; 21.05.2002) (paras 9-15). In the latter of those two cases the court departed from Order 62 rule 3(5) where the costs consequences of a party having refused to make the required admissions were 'minimal'.

Refusal to make any admission at all where a qualified admission would be appropriate may have costs consequences, as in *Wong Sai Chung t/a Concord Int'l Trading Co v Kwan Min* HCA 7023/1984 (Penlington J; 14.05.1986).

**3.    Judgment on admissions** (O. 27 r. 3)

**Where admissions of fact or of part of a case are made by a party to a cause or matter either by his pleadings or otherwise, any other party to the cause or matter may apply to the Court for such judgment or order as upon those admissions he may be entitled to, without waiting for the determination of any other question between the parties, and the Court may give such judgment, or make such order, on the application as it thinks just.**

**An application for an order under this rule may be made by summons. (L.N. 152 of 2008)**

---

### NOTES

### [27.3.1]    Application for judgment on admissions

Under Order 27 rule 3 the court may grant judgment on admissions of fact. Those admissions may be made in the party's pleadings or otherwise, such as under a Notice to Admit.

The admissions 'may be express or implied, but they must be clear and unambiguous': *Re Chung Wong Kit* [1999] 1 HKC 684, 686G, per Rogers JA. Allegations of fact in a pleading may also be deemed to be admitted if not traversed by the party against whom they are made: Order 18 rule 13(1).

Admissions of fact can only be used against the party making them. In *Re Chung Wong Kit* [1999] 1 HKC 684 Rogers JA held (at 688I) that admissions made by persons in their personal capacities could not be used against a company of which they were directors and shareholders.

It is a curious feature of the tort of negligence that negligence alone is not sufficient to found liability – there must also be loss or damage occasioned thereby. As a result, an admission of 'negligence' alone is not sufficient for judgment under Order 27 rule 3: *Rankine v Garton Sons & Co Ltd* [1979] 2 All ER 1185 (CA).

### [27.3.2]    Comparison with judgment on Order 13A admissions

Entry of judgment on admissions under Order 27 rule 3 is entry of judgment to the extent of the admissions only. Other questions between the parties may be left for determination.

The court may enter such judgment as the beneficiary of the admissions is entitled to. Thus judgment for any type of relief is theoretically possible. However the court will not normally grant discretionary remedies (such as a declaration or injunction) without a hearing on the merits: see the commentary under Order 19 rule 7.

With regard to money claims, judgment under Order 27 rule 3 may be for an ascertained amount or on liability alone, with quantum to be assessed later. The procedure differs from Order 13A in that it does not carry with it a right on the part of the party making the admissions to request time to pay. Clearly in that regard the Order 13A procedure will be more attractive to many defendants.

Judgment under Order 27 rule 3 is by application to the court, which means *inter partes* application by summons, or possibly by consent summons. Under Order 13A on the other hand application is made by filing the appropriate form and no hearing is required.

### [27.3.3]    Comparison with summary judgment

It has been held that it would be 'unusual' for a court to grant judgment on admissions under Order 27 rule 3 where it refused summary judgment under Order 14: see *Louis Drefus Trading Ltd v Bonarich International (Group) Ltd* [1997] 3 HKC 597, 604I–605A. The two types of judgment are notionally different. On an Order 14 application the court must consider not what has been admitted but whether there is a triable issue of fact or law. As noted by Rogers JA in *Re Chung Wong Kit* [1999] 1 HKC 684 at 686I–687A, on an Order 14 application it is open to the court to draw inferences from primary facts whereas under Order 27 rule 3 the court is confined to the actual admissions.

### [27.3.4]    Exercise of discretion where there is a claim to set-off or counterclaim

Order 27 rule 3 expressly provides that judgment on admissions may be granted 'without waiting for the determination of any other question between the parties'. This gives the court discretion to grant judgment on admissions, leaving a set-off or counterclaim to proceed to trial. In *Townearn Industrial Ltd v Golden Globe Holdings Ltd* [2003] 1 HKC 186, 191I it was held that in the exercise of this discretion the court should consider whether the set-off or counterclaim 'relates to the same or closely connected subject matter as the claim which is being made by the plaintiff'.

**4.     Admission and production of documents specified in list of documents**
     (O. 27 r. 4)

     (1)   Subject to paragraph (2) and without prejudice to the right of a party to object to the admission in evidence of any document, a party on whom a list of documents is served in pursuance of any provision of Order 24 shall, unless the Court otherwise orders, be deemed to admit—

          (a)     that any document described in the list as an original document is such a document and was printed, written, signed or executed as it purports respectively to have been, and

          (b)     that any document described therein as a copy is a true copy.

     This paragraph does not apply to a document the authenticity of which the party has denied in his pleading.

     (2)   If before the expiration of 21 days after inspection of the documents specified in a list of documents or after the time limited for inspection of those documents expires, whichever is the later, the party on whom the list is served serves on the party whose list it is a notice stating, in relation to any document specified therein, that he does not admit the authenticity of that document and requires it to be proved at the trial, he shall not be deemed to make any admission in relation to that document under paragraph (1).

     (3)   A party to a cause or matter by whom a list of documents is served on any other party in pursuance of any provision of Order 24 shall be deemed to have been served by that other party with a notice requiring him to produce at the trial of the cause or matter such of the documents specified in the list as are in his possession, custody or power.

     (4)   The foregoing provisions of this rule apply in relation to an affidavit made in compliance with an order under Order 24, rule 7, as they apply in relation to a list of documents served in pursuance of any provision of that Order.

------

NOTES

**[27.4.1]     Authenticity of listed documents admitted unless notice to the contrary given**

Order 27 rule 4 provides that a party on whom a list of documents is served is deemed to admit the authenticity of the documents listed unless this is denied in the party's pleading, or notice of non-admission of authenticity is given. Likewise documents listed as copies are deemed to be true copies.

     Rule 4(2) provides that notice of non-admission of authenticity should be given within 21 days of the time for inspection of documents. That time may be extended. See *Silver Stone Dev't Ltd v Lau Kwong Ching James* [2006] 4 HKC 100 where an extension was granted at the outset of trial notwithstanding the time had expired nearly 5 years earlier.

     Where deemed admission applies, it is not open to a party to question the authenticity of the document at trial, in cross-examination or otherwise, unless the court grants leave: *World Food Fair Ltd v HK Island Dev't Ltd* HCA 4602/2000 (Deputy Judge Carlson; 08.08.2003) (para 7). The admission is restricted to authenticity – it remains open to a party to dispute the truth of the contents of the document, and it is a matter for the court what weight it should be given: *Leung Tsang Hung & Ors v Tse Yiu Pui & Ors* HCPI 595/ 2002 (Deputy Judge To; 12.05.2004) (para 49); *Guangzhou Green-Enhan Bio-Eng'g Co Ltd v Green Power Health Products Int'l Co Ltd* HCA 4651/2002 (Lam J; 08.04.2005) (paras 228-229). Similarly, deemed authenticity is expressly without prejudice to a party's right to object to admissibility: rule 4(1).

Bundles of documents prepared for use at trial should make clear which documents are deemed or agreed to be authentic: see para 3 of practice direction 5.6, which can be viewed on the judiciary website.

### [27.4.2]     Costs sanction for non-admission of authenticity of document

Order 62 rule 3(6) provides that a party who gives notice of non-admission under Order 27 rule 4 or rule 5 may be ordered to pay the costs of proving authenticity in any event.

**5.**       **Notices to admit or produce documents** (O. 27 r. 5)

    **(1)**   **Except where rule 4(1) applies, a party to a cause or matter may within 21 days after the cause or matter is set down for trial serve on any other party a notice requiring him to admit the authenticity of the documents specified in the notice.**

    **(2)**   **If a party on whom a notice under paragraph (1) is served desires to challenge the authenticity of any document therein specified he must, within 21 days after service of the notice, serve on the party by whom it was given a notice stating that he does not admit the authenticity of the document and requires it to be proved at the trial.**

    **(3)**   **A party who fails to give a notice of non-admission in accordance with paragraph (2) in relation to any document shall be deemed to have admitted the authenticity of that document unless the Court otherwise orders.**

    **(4)**   **Except where rule 4(3) applies, a party to a cause or matter may serve on any other party a notice requiring him to produce the documents specified in the notice at the trial of the cause or matter.**

    **(Enacted 1988)**

---

**NOTES**

### [27.5.1]     Notice to admit authenticity of documents

Order 27 rule 5 enables a party to serve notice requiring an opposing party to admit the authenticity of documents in circumstances where the deemed admission of authenticity under rule 4 does not apply. Failure to admit authenticity under such a notice may lead to costs consequences (see above).

## ORDER 28

### ORIGINATING SUMMONS PROCEDURE

**1.  Application** (O. 28 r. 1)
The provisions of this Order apply to all originating summonses subject, in the case of originating summonses of any particular class, to any special provisions relating to originating summonses of that class made by these rules or by or under any written law; and subject as aforesaid, Order 32, rule 5, shall apply in relation to originating summonses as they apply in relation to other summonses.

---

## NOTES

**[28.1.1]  Forms of originating summons**
There are various prescribed forms of originating summons in appendix A to these rules. See the discussion under Order 7 rule 2 as to when it is appropriate for each to be used.

**1A.  Affidavit evidence** (O. 28 r. 1A)
(1)  In any cause or matter begun by originating summons (not being an ex parte summons) the plaintiff must, before the expiration of 14 days after the defendant has acknowledged service, or, if there are two or more defendants, at least one of them has acknowledged service, file with the Court the affidavit evidence on which he intends to rely.

(2)  In the case of an ex parte summons the applicant must file his affidavit evidence not less than 4 clear days before the day fixed for the hearing.

(3)  Copies of the affidavit evidence filed in the Court under paragraph (1) must be served by the plaintiff on the defendant, or, if there are two or more defendants, on each defendant, before the expiration of 14 days after service has been acknowledged by that defendant.

(4)  Where a defendant who has acknowledged service wishes to adduce affidavit evidence he must within 28 days after service on him of copies of the plaintiff's affidavit evidence under paragraph (3) file his own affidavit evidence in the Court and serve copies thereof on the plaintiff and on any other defendant who is affected thereby.

(5)  A plaintiff on whom a copy of a defendant's affidavit evidence has been served under paragraph (4) may within 14 days of such service file in the Court further affidavit evidence in reply and shall in that event serve copies thereof on that defendant.

(6)  No other affidavit shall be received in evidence without the leave of the Court.

(7)  Where an affidavit is required to be served by one party on another party it shall be served without prior charge.

(8)  The provisions of this rule apply subject to any direction by the Court to the contrary.

**(9)    In this rule references to affidavits and copies of affidavits include references to exhibits to affidavits and copies of such exhibits.**

**2.        Fixing time for attendance of parties before Court** (O. 28 r. 2)

**(1)    In the case of an originating summons which is in Form No. 8 in Appendix A the plaintiff must, within one month of the expiry of the time within which copies of affidavit evidence may be served under rule 1A, obtain an appointment for the attendance of the parties before the Court for the hearing of the summons, and a day and time for their attendance shall be fixed by a notice (in Form No. 12 in Appendix A) sealed with the seal of the Court.**

**(2)    A day and time for the attendance of the parties before the Court for the hearing of an originating summons which is in Form No. 10 in Appendix A, or for the hearing of an ex parte originating summons, may be fixed on the application of the plaintiff or applicant, as the case may be and in the case of a summons which is required to be served, the time limited for acknowledging service shall, where appropriate, be abridged so as to expire on the next day but one before the day so fixed, and the time limits for lodging affidavits under rule 1A(2) and (3) shall, where appropriate, be abridged so as to expire, respectively, on the fifth day before, and the next day but one before, the day so fixed.**

**(3)    Where a plaintiff fails to apply for an appointment under paragraph (1), any defendant may, with the leave of the Court, obtain an appointment in accordance with that paragraph provided that he has acknowledged service of the originating summons.**

---

## NOTES

### [28.2.1]    Call-over hearing

The court has adopted a call-over procedure whereby an originating summons will initially come on for a short directions hearing before a judge in chambers. The initial hearing is commonly called a 'call-over'. It is governed by paragraph 2 of practice direction 5.8, in force from 1 March 1998, and applies only to originating summonses set down for hearing by a judge. That paragraph reads as follows:

   2. Hearing

   (a)    The hearing of an originating summons on the date fixed under O 28 r 2 shall be a first hearing before a judge sitting in chambers at which directions as to the further conduct of the proceedings will be given, but nothing herein shall affect the court's power to dispose of an originating summons at such hearing under O 28 r 4 should the nature of the case so require.

   (b)    In future, the first hearing of all originating summonses will be listed for hearing on Tuesday mornings (or any other morning as circumstances may require) at 9.30 am before the judge assigned to hear such summonses.

   (c)    The first or any subsequent hearing at which directions are to be given may be vacated, *inter alia*, if on a written application by the parties by consent for leave to fix a date for the substantive hearing made at least two working days prior hereto [sic], the judge is satisfied that no further directions are required and the estimated length of the hearing is stated in the application.

**3.**      **Notice of hearing** (O. 28 r. 3)

(1)    **Not less than 14 days before the day fixed under rule 2 for the attendance of the parties before the Court for the hearing of an originating summons which is in Form No. 8 in Appendix A, the party on whose application the day was fixed must serve a copy of the notice fixing it on every other party. (L.N. 404 of 1991)**

(2)    **Not less than 4 clear days before the day fixed under rule 2 for the hearing of an originating summons which is in Form No. 10 in Appendix A, the plaintiff must serve the summons on every defendant or, if any defendant has already been served with the summons, must serve on that defendant notice of the day fixed for the hearing.**

(3)    **Where notice in Form No. 12 in Appendix A is served in accordance with paragraph (1), such notice shall specify what orders or directions the party serving the notice intends to seek at the hearing; and any party served with such notice who wishes to seek different orders or directions must, not less than 7 days before the hearing, serve on every other party a notice specifying the other orders and directions he intends to seek. (L.N. 404 of 1991)**

(4)    **If the hearing of an originating summons which is in Form No. 8 or 10 in Appendix A is adjourned and any party to the proceedings desires to apply at the resumed hearing for any order or direction not previously asked for, he must, not less than 7 days before the resumed hearing of the summons, serve on every other party a notice specifying those orders and directions. (L.N. 404 of 1991)**

(5)    **Where a party is required by any provision of this rule or rule 5(2) to serve a notice or a copy of a notice on "every other party" he must—**

> (a)    **where he is the plaintiff, serve it on every defendant who has acknowledged service of the originating summons; and**

> (b)    **where he is a defendant, serve it on the plaintiff and on every other defendant affected thereby. (L.N. 404 of 1991)**

---

**NOTES**

**[28.3.1]**      **Wording of Order 28 rule 3**

Some printings of these rules refer to 'orders of directions' rather than 'orders or directions', in Order 28 rule 3(3). An examination of LN 404 of 1991 by which rule 3(3) was enacted indicates that 'orders or directions' (as above) is correct.

**3A.**      **Originating summons to be heard in open court** (O. 28 r. 3A)

**An originating summons must be heard in open court unless the Court otherwise directs.**

**(L.N. 152 of 2008)**

## NOTES

### [28.3A.1]   Originating summons normally heard in open court

Order 28 rule 3A stipulates that originating summonses are to be heard in open court unless the court otherwise directs. The rule was inserted to implement recommendation 15 in the final report of the Chief Justice's working party on civil justice reform. The rule does not represent a change in the previous practice, but simply states in legislative form the practice established by cases dating back to the 1980s.

Until the late 1980s, originating summonses were often heard in chambers in Hong Kong. At the time all chambers hearings were closed to the public. That practice was condemned by the court as 'improper' in *Wong Shui Yun Bernadette v Lau Wai Pui* [1987] 3 HKC 513, and as 'wrong' in *Pak Lan Ching v Crown Great Co Ltd* [1988] HKC 784, 786C. In *Yau Fook Hong Co Ltd v CIR* [1989] 2 HKC 514, 516B-D it was said:

> ... an action commenced by originating summons is an action just like any other, although commenced by a different originating process ... unless there are some special reasons, the substantive hearing has to be in open court.

Vendor and purchaser summonses under section 12 of the Conveyancing and Property Ordinance (Cap 219) should be heard in open court: *Cheung Kai Wei Sandra v Fuk Ka Pak & Anor (No 2)* [1990] 2 HKC 401, 407B-D.

### [28.3A.2]   Exceptional circumstances where originating summons may be heard in chambers

Exceptional circumstances in which it may be appropriate for the court to direct that an originating summons be heard in chambers, or 'special reasons' as they were described in the above passage from *Yau Fook Hong* were said, in that case, to include the following:

> ... security of the state or the protection of the interests of infants or disabled persons, or the protection of trade secrets. Generally speaking, apart from such cases, actions commenced by originating summons, like, as I say, any other action, ought to be heard in open court: *Scott v Scott* [1913] AC 417.

In addition to the special reasons mentioned in the above passage for hearing an originating summons in chambers, such a hearing may be appropriate where the case raises matters of 'private concern ... such as the execution of trusts or the administration of estates', as opposed to hostile litigation like a construction summons: *Pak Lan Ching* (above, at 785D-E). See also *Yu Hong Ping v Yuen* HCMP 1104/2009 (Lam J; 24.08.2009) where an uncontested application under s 33(3) of the Probate and Administration Ordinance (Cap 10) for removal of an executor was adjourned to chambers to be dealt with by a master. In making that direction under this rule, the court said there was no reason the application could not be dealt with on the papers (as to which see Order 32 rule 11A).

In *Mayluck Investment Ltd v Lee Yih Ping & Ors* [1996] 3 HKC 245 the court heard an originating summons seeking relief under the Partition Ordinance (Cap 352) in chambers, but only because the parties appeared by solicitors and it was thus not practicable to proceed in open court. At the time all chambers hearings in Hong Kong were closed to the public. Judgment was delivered in open court.

**[28.3A.3] Originating summonses heard before a master in chambers**

Before Order 28 rule 3A came into force the practice was for certain types of originating summonses to be set down for hearing before a master in chambers. At the time rule 3A came into force practice direction 14.2 was amended to state expressly that the following applications by originating summons should in the first instance be returnable before a master in chambers (open to the public):

(a)  application for summary determination of interpleader under Order 17 rule 5;

(b)  application for default judgment under Order 83A (money lenders' actions);

(c)  application for default judgment under Order 84A (hire purchase and conditional sales actions);

(d)  application for default judgment under Order 88 (mortgage actions);

(e)  costs only proceedings under Order 62 rule 11A;

(f)  application for solicitor and own client taxation of a bill of costs under section 67 of the Legal Practitioners Ordinance (Cap 159) and Order 106 rule 2;

(g)  application for summary possession of land under Order 113 rule 1.

In addition mortgage actions under Order 88 are by long-established practice normally heard by a master in chambers, unless they are not suitable for summary determination and are referred by the master to a judge to be dealt with in open court. See the commentary under Order 88 rule 1.

**4.  Directions, etc., by Court** (O. 28 r. 4)

**(1) The Court by whom an originating summons is heard may, if the liability of the defendant to the plaintiff in respect of any claim made by the plaintiff is established, make such order in favour of the plaintiff as the nature of the case may require, but where the Court makes an order under this paragraph against a defendant who does not appear at the hearing, the order may be varied or revoked by a subsequent order of the Court on such terms as it thinks just.**

**(2) In any case where the Court does not dispose of any originating summons altogether at a hearing or order the cause or matter begun by it to be transferred to a District Court or some other court or makes an order under rule 8, the Court shall give such directions as to the further conduct of the proceedings as it thinks best adapted to secure the just, expeditious and economical disposal thereof.**

**(3) Without prejudice to the generality of paragraph (2), the Court shall, at as early a stage of the proceedings on the summons as appears to it to be practicable, consider whether there is or may be a dispute as to fact and whether the just, expeditious and economical disposal of the proceedings can accordingly best be secured by hearing the summons on oral evidence or mainly on oral evidence and, if it thinks fit, may order that no further evidence shall be filed and that the summons shall be heard on oral evidence or partly on oral evidence and partly on affidavit evidence, with or without cross-examination of any of the deponents, as it may direct.**

**(4) Without prejudice to the generality of paragraph (2), and subject to paragraph (3), the Court may give directions as to the filing of evidence and as to the attendance of deponents for cross-examination and any directions which it could give under Order 25 if the cause or matter had been begun by writ and**

the summons were a case management summons under that Order. (L.N. 152 of 2008)

(5)    The Court may at any stage of the proceedings order that any affidavit, or any particulars of any claim, defence or other matters stated in any affidavit, shall stand as pleadings or that points of claim, defence or reply be delivered and stand as pleadings. (L.N. 404 of 1991)

---

## NOTES

### [28.4.1]    Summary disposal of originating summons

Order 28 rule 4(1) empowers the court to give an appropriate judgment to the plaintiff where at the hearing of an originating summons it is satisfied that the plaintiff's claim is established. The power is interpreted as a power of summary disposal akin to summary judgment under Order 14: *Bank of China (HK) Ltd v Twin Profit Ltd & Ors* HCMP 874/2009 (Fok J; 30.03.2010) (para 6-8). The difference is that there is no burden on the defendant: *Wing Hang Bank Ltd v Liu Kam Ying* [2002] 2 HKC 57 (para 7). The court may be satisfied that there is no triable issue where the defendant has filed no evidence, or where its evidence is 'not credible', or 'defies belief': *Bank of China (HK) Ltd v Keen Lloyd Resources Ltd* CACV 1787/2001 (Mayo VP & Yeung J; 26.02.2002) (para 29).

### [28.4.2]    Application to vary order made in absence of defendant

Order 28 rule 4(1) provides, *inter alia*, that where the court makes an order against a defendant who does not appear at the hearing, that order may subsequently be varied or revoked. In *Liu Chong Hing Bank Ltd v Union World (HK) Ltd & Ors* [2005] 1 HKC 20 (CA) such an application was made on the ground of irregular service of the defendant. It was held that in the circumstances the principles applicable on an application under Order 13 rule 9 to set aside default judgment were appropriate.

See also Order 35 rule 2.

**5.    Adjournment of summons** (O. 28 r. 5)

(1)    The hearing of the summons by the Court may (if necessary) be adjourned from time to time, either generally or to a particular date, as may be appropriate, and the powers of the Court under rule 4 may be exercised at any resumed hearing.

(2)    If the hearing of the summons is adjourned generally, any party may restore it to the list on 14 days' notice to every other party and rule 3(4) shall apply in relation to any such adjourned hearing. (L.N. 404 of 1991)

**6.    Applications affecting party who has failed to acknowledge service** (O. 28 r. 6)

Where in a cause or matter begun by originating summons an application is made to the Court for an order affecting a party who has failed to acknowledge service of the summons, the Court hearing the application may require to be satisfied in such manner as it thinks fit that the party has so failed.

**7.      Counterclaim by defendant** (O. 28 r. 7)

(1)   A defendant to an action begun by originating summons who has acknowledged service of the summons and who alleges that he has any claim or is entitled to any relief or remedy against the plaintiff in respect of any matter (whenever and however arising) may make a counterclaim in the action in respect of that matter instead of bringing a separate action.

(2)   A defendant who wishes to make a counterclaim under this rule must at the first or any resumed hearing of the originating summons by the Court but, in any case, at as early a stage in the proceedings as is practicable, inform the Court of the nature of his claim and, without prejudice to the powers of the Court under paragraph (3), the claim shall be made in such manner as the Court may direct under rule 4 or rule 8.

(3)   If it appears on the application of a plaintiff against whom a counterclaim is made under this rule that the subject-matter of the counterclaim ought for any reason to be disposed of by a separate action, the Court may order the counterclaim to be struck out or may order it to be tried separately or make such other order as may be expedient.

---

**NOTES**

**[28.7.1]     Court direction required for counterclaim**
Under Order 28 rule 7 the court's direction is required as to the manner of bringing a counterclaim to an originating summons. 'There should be an express direction as to how a counterclaim to an originating summons should be presented in every case': *Yeung Kwok Fan v Standard Chartered Bank* [2001] 4 HKC 486, 494I, per Deputy Judge McCoy, citing *Ng Wing See v Chang Chi Ching* [1973] HKLR 170 (FC). The court may direct that the counterclaim be formulated by affidavit, but in no case may the counterclaim proceed without direction from the court: *Yeung Kwok Fan v Standard Chartered Bank* [2001] 4 HKC 486, 494G.

**8.      Continuation of proceedings as if cause or matter begun by writ** (O. 28 r. 8)

(1)   Where, in the case of a cause or matter begun by originating summons, it appears to the Court at any stage of the proceedings that the proceedings should for any reason be continued as if the cause or matter had been begun by writ, it may order the proceedings to continue as if the cause or matter had been so begun and may, in particular, order that any affidavits shall stand as pleadings, with or without liberty to any of the parties to add thereto or to apply for particulars thereof.

(2)   Where the Court decides to make such an order, Order 25, rules 2 to 7, shall, with the omission of so much of rule 7(1) as requires parties to serve a notice specifying the orders and directions which they require and with any other necessary modifications, apply as if there had been a case mangement summons in the proceedings and that order were one of the orders to be made thereon. **(L.N. 152 of 2008)**

(3)   This rule applies notwithstanding that the cause or matter in question could not have been begun by writ.

**(4)**     **Any reference in these rules to an action begun by writ shall, unless the context otherwise requires, be construed as including a reference to a cause or matter proceedings in which are ordered under this rule to continue as if the cause or matter had been so begun.**

---

## NOTES

### [28.8.1]     Order that proceedings commenced by originating summons continue as if commenced by writ

Order 28 rule 8 gives the court power to order that proceedings commenced by way of originating summons be continued as if commenced by writ. When making such an order the court may give consequential directions, including an order that any affidavits already filed shall stand as pleadings. See also Order 18 rule 12(3) which provides that the court may order a party to proceedings commenced by originating summons to serve a statement of the nature of its case. Such a statement is not a pleading but may be the subject of an application for further and better particulars. See *Cheung Man Yu v Lau Yuen Ching & Ors* HCMP 2421/2000 (Deputy Judge Saunders; 22.04.2005) as an example.

In *Cheney Communications Pte Ltd v Cheney* HCMP 2942/1992 (Godfrey J; 02.08.1993) an order was made under this rule in a case involving construction of a written contract. The defendant had raised an issue outside the contract itself, being waiver or estoppel by conduct from relying on the terms of the agreement. Godfrey J said:

> That is not an issue which can possibly be tried on originating summons. It raises a dispute of fact which can only properly be tried in an action commenced by writ. I cannot possibly decide such a matter without pleadings defining the issues and evidence tested by cross-examination so that I can come to a proper conclusion on the issues.

His Lordship went on to hold that the effect of sub-rule (2) of this rule was that he could 'treat this application as if it were the summons for directions in the action' and he proposed to lay out an attenuated timetable to enable the action to come on for trial quickly.

In *Ye Hong Ying v Chan Lup Ying* [1996] 3 HKC 426, Keith J took a different view. The learned judge held (at 430H–I) that the existence of issues of fact between the parties did not render the originating summons procedure inappropriate. Under Order 28 rule 4(3) and (4) the court had power to direct the taking of oral evidence and the attendance of deponents to be cross-examined on their affidavits. In the case before the learned judge there would be no particular advantage to pleadings and it was not appropriate to make an order under this rule that the proceedings continue as if begun by writ.

### [28.8.2]     Consequences of order that proceedings commenced by originating summons be continued as if commenced by writ

The scope of proceedings may be enlarged following an order that proceedings commenced by originating summons be continued as if commenced by writ, even so as to include claims for relief that would not be within the scope of an originating summons. See *Board of Trustees of Chung Chi College & Anor v Chanway Investment*

*Co Ltd* [1993] 1 HKLR 203, 206 (CA). In that case Kempster JA said 'one of the purposes of the rule is to extend the range of remedies open to a plaintiff without requiring discontinuance and the issue of a fresh originating process'. However see *Hanton Development Ltd v Secretary for Justice* HCMP 5973/2000 (Recorder Fok SC; 15.12.2005) where the court proceeded on the basis that new claims, going beyond the scope of the originating summons, are liable to be struck out for infringement of Order 6 rule 2 unless introduced by amendment.

An order under Order 28 rule 8 'relates back to the date when proceedings were begun': *Chung Chi College* (above, at 206). This has an important effect in relation to limitation periods. See the commentary on the doctrine of relation back under Order 20 rule 5.

Once it is ordered that proceedings begun by originating summons continue as if begun by writ, the interlocutory procedures applicable to action by writ, such as discovery, will ensue.

## [28.8.3] Costs of application for originating summons proceedings to continue as if commenced by writ

The costs of an application for an order that proceedings commenced by originating summons be continued as if commenced by writ will normally be costs in the cause. However, a plaintiff who ought to have known that there would be substantial issues of fact, such that the originating summons procedure would be inappropriate, may be ordered to pay the costs. See *Lam Pak Cheung v Lin Zhen Lue* [2009] 1 HKLRD 35 (para 49), referring to *Lai Kwong-ma & Anor v Tang Hop-wan & AG* [1976] HKLR 51, 56.

## 9. Order for hearing or trial (O. 28 r. 9)

**(1) Except where the Court disposes of a cause or matter begun by originating summons in chambers or orders it to be transferred to a District Court or some other court or makes an order in relation to it under rule 8 or some other provision of these rules, the Court shall, on being satisfied that the cause or matter is ready for determination, make such order as to the hearing of the cause or matter as may be appropriate.**

**(3) The Court shall by order determine the place and mode of the trial, but any such order may be varied by a subsequent order of the Court made at or before the trial.**

**(4) Order 33, rule 4(2) and Order 34, rules 1 to 8, shall apply in relation to a cause or matter begun by originating summons and to an order made therein under this rule as they apply in relation to an action begun by writ and to an order made therein under the said rule 4 and shall have effect accordingly with any necessary modifications and with the further modification that for references therein to the case management summons there shall be substituted references to the first or any resumed hearing of the originating summons by the Court. (L.N. 152 of 2008)**

---

**NOTES**

**[28.9.1]     Hearing of originating summons in chambers**

Order 28 rule 9(1) clearly contemplates the hearing of an originating summons in chambers. However, it must be read together with rule 3A and the commentary thereunder as to the limited circumstances in which such a hearing will be appropriate.

**10.     Failure to prosecute proceedings with despatch** (O. 28 r. 10)

**(1)     If the plaintiff in a cause or matter begun by originating summons makes default in complying with any order or direction of the Court as to the conduct of the proceedings, or if the Court is satisfied that the plaintiff in a cause or matter so begun is not prosecuting the proceedings with due despatch, the Court may order the cause or matter to be dismissed or may make such other order as may be just.**

**(2)     Paragraph (1) shall, with any necessary modifications, apply in relation to a defendant by whom a counterclaim is made under rule 7 as it applies in relation to a plaintiff.**

**(3)     Where, by virtue of an order made under rule 8, proceedings in a cause or matter begun by originating summons are to continue as if the cause or matter had been begun by writ, the foregoing provisions of this rule shall not apply in relation to the cause or matter after the making of the order.**

---

**NOTES**

**[28.10.1]     Defendant's remedy for delay on part of plaintiff**

Order 28 rule 10 'provides a salutary remedy for a defendant to an originating summons who finds that the case against him is not being prosecuted "with dispatch"': *Yau Fook Hong Co Ltd & Ors v CIR* [1989] 2 HKC 514, 516F. It empowers the court to make such order as may be just, including dismissal of the action, where the plaintiff does not proceed expeditiously. The rule applies equally to a counterclaim to an originating summons, but not to an originating summons where there has been an order that the proceedings continue as if commenced by writ.

In *Au Yeung On v Che Shing Cheong Wilfred & Ors* HCMP 4745/1999 (Deputy Judge To; 20.06.2006) the court proceeded on the basis that the principles relating to an application to strike out for want of prosecution should be followed on an application under Order 28 rule 10. This accords with the decision in *Halls & Anor v O'Dell & Ors* [1992] QB 393, 404C-F (CA) where it was held that those principles should be followed on such an application (disapproving *United Bank Ltd v Maniar & Ors* [1988] 1 Ch 109 in this regard). See the discussion of striking out for want of prosecution under Order 34 rule 2.

**11.     Abatement, etc., of action** (O. 28 r. 11)

**Order 34, rule 9, shall apply in relation to an action begun by originating summons as it applies in relation to an action begun by writ.**

**(Enacted 1988)**

## ORDER 29

### INTERLOCUTORY INJUNCTIONS, INTERIM PRESERVATION OF PROPERTY INTERIM PAYMENTS, ETC.

I. Interlocutory Injunctions, Interim Preservation of
Property, etc.

**1.      Application for injunction** (O. 29 r. 1)

(1)   An application for the grant of an injunction may be made by any party to a cause or matter before or after the trial of the cause or matter, whether or not a claim for the injunction was included in that party's writ, originating summons, counterclaim or third party notice, as the case may be.

(2)   Where the applicant is the plaintiff and the case is one of urgency such application may be made ex parte on affidavit but, except as aforesaid, such application must be made by summons. (L.N. 152 of 2008)

(3)   The plaintiff may not make such an application before the issue of the writ or originating summons by which the cause or matter is to be begun except where the case is one of urgency, and in that case the injunction applied for may be granted on terms providing for the issue of the writ or summons and such other terms, if any, as the Court thinks fit.

---

## NOTES

### [29.1.1]     Power of the court to grant injunctions
The power of the court to grant injunctions, including interlocutory injunctions, is governed by section 21L of the High Court Ordinance, which reads as follows:

> 21L.(1)The Court of First Instance may by order (whether interlocutory or final) grant an injunction or appoint a receiver in all cases in which it appears to the Court of First Instance to be just or convenient to do so.

> (2) Any such order may be made either unconditionally or on such terms and conditions as the Court thinks just.

Section 21L(1) and (2) derive from section 37 of the Supreme Court Act 1981 (UK).

### [29.1.2]     Comparison with English rules
In England the rules governing grant of interlocutory injunctions are now included in CPR Part 25, which deals with interim remedies of various types and security for costs. The Chief Justice's working party on civil justice reform noted (final report, para 326) that CPR 25 is a consolidation which effected only minor changes to the pre-existing law. It decided against making any recommendation to change the framework in Hong Kong. However, it did recommend adoption from England of some specific procedures such as the *Mareva* injunction in aid of foreign proceedings, as to which see Order 29 rule 8A.

### [29.1.3]     Procedure for making application for interlocutory injunction
An application for an interlocutory injunction may be made *ex parte* by affidavit or

affirmation, or *inter partes* by summons in an action. See Order 29 rule 1(2). Prior to amendment as part of the civil justice reforms with effect from 2009, the rule also contemplated application by motion.

### [29.1.4]   Interlocutory injunctions – jurisdiction
Order 32 rule 11(1)(d) excludes injunctions under part I of Order 29 from the jurisdiction of the registrar and masters, except where in terms agreed by the parties. Applications for injunctions should, accordingly, be made to a judge.

### [29.1.5]   No need to claim injunction in originating process
Order 29 rule 1(1) provides that a party may apply for an injunction even though no such a claim is included in that party's originating process. An example of a case where such an injunction was granted on an interlocutory basis is *Chanway Shatin New Town Dev't Ltd v Sun Mate Holdings (HK) C1070 Ltd* HCA 2018/2006 (Deputy Judge Carlson; 10.04.2007).

### [29.1.6]   Interlocutory injunction will only be granted where cause of action against defendant
An interlocutory injunction will only be granted in aid of a claim for relief in respect of a recognised cause of action. In *The Siskina* [1979] AC 210, 256C-E Lord Diplock said:

> A right to obtain an interlocutory injunction is not a cause of action. It cannot stand on its own. It is dependent upon there being a pre-existing cause of action against the defendant arising out of an invasion, actual or threatened by him, of a legal or equitable right of the plaintiff for the enforcement of which the defendant is amenable to the jurisdiction of the court. The right to obtain an interlocutory injunction is merely ancillary and incidental to the pre-existing cause of action.

The above passage was referred to with approval and applied in *Tsai Shui Sheng & Ors v Ho Hong Chu* HCA 662/2007 (Recorder Kwok SC; 19.09.2007).

It follows that an interlocutory injunction can only be granted against a party to the proceedings, since a pleaded cause of action can only relate to other parties: see *Xinyuan Trading Co Ltd & Anor v Bank of China* [1999] 4 HKC 686 (CA).

Notwithstanding what was said in *The Siskina* (above) it has been held that a defendant, who claims no relief by way of counterclaim, may be granted an interlocutory injunction against the plaintiff. See *Raingate Ltd v CHCP Investment Co Ltd* HCA 734/2007 (Deputy Judge Gill; 31.07.2008) (paras 37-51) (believed to be under appeal).

There are authorities to the effect that the court will not grant an interlocutory injunction of the *Mareva* type ancillary to an anticipated claim (see the commentary below on *Mareva* injunctions). However an interlocutory injunction should be available ancillary to a claim for a *quia timet* injunction, since a claim for such an injunction is itself a cause of action.

### [29.1.7]   Interlocutory injunction after judgment
The court's power to grant interlocutory injunctions continues after final judgment has been given. The *Mareva* injunction in aid of execution is a common example. However the jurisdiction is not limited to that type of post-judgment interlocutory injunction. Rather the court may grant any post-judgment interlocutory injunction

'reasonably necessary and ancillary to the administration of justice': *Tang Che Tai & Ors v Tang On Kwai & Ors* HCA 331/2002 (Deputy Judge To; 13.12.2007) (paras 17-22), referring to *Smith v Peters* (1875) LR 20 Eq 511.

### [29.1.8]     Interlocutory injunctions – principles governing grant

The House of Lords' landmark decision in *American Cyanamid Co v Ethicon* [1975] AC 396; [1975] 1 All ER 504 was quickly adopted by the Hong Kong courts as laying down the principles applicable on an application for an interlocutory injunction: see *JC Penney Co Inc v Penneys Ltd* [1975] HKLR 598. Decades later *American Cyanamid* (as explained in a host of subsequent cases) remains authoritative. See for example *Wah Nam Holdings Co Ltd & Ors v Excel Noble Development Ltd & Ors* [2000] 3 HKC 118 (CA) where Ribeiro J stated (at 125D) 'A judge … considering whether to uphold or set aside an *ex parte* injunction at the *inter partes* stage, applies the principles established by *American Cyanamid*'.

The impact of *American Cyanamid* was to relax the burden on the applicant for an interlocutory injunction insofar as it is incumbent on him to demonstrate that he has a meritorious claim. Previously the applicant had been required to show a good *prima facie* case. In *American Cyanamid* the House of Lords held that the applicant need only show 'a serious question to be tried', that is a 'real prospect of succeeding'. As Ribeiro J stated in *Wah Nam Holdings Co Ltd & Ors v Excel Noble Development Ltd & Ors* [2000] 3 HKC 118, 125D–E (CA):

> The important change effected by that decision is that the court is no longer concerned even to ask whether the plaintiff has demonstrated a prima facie case (except in *extremis* where the balance of convenience cannot be resolved in favour of either party). The approach now, so far as the merits of the plaintiff's claim are concerned, is to ascertain merely whether there is a serious question to be tried.

Since an interlocutory injunction is not a cause of action in itself (see above), there can only be a serious question to be tried if a case of actual or threatened infringement of a legal or equitable right is put forward: *Hiew Fook Siong & Ors v Fung Tak Keung & Ors* [2006] 4 HKC 384 (paras 10-11). A finding that there is no serious question to be tried is interlocutory, not final; thus it is not necessarily an abuse of process to continue with the claim: *Mascioli v Unilux Boiler Corp* [2008] ONCA 344 (Ont CA).

*Whether damages an adequate remedy and the balance of convenience* — If the court is satisfied there is a serious question to be tried, it will go on to evaluate the degree of harm either party might suffer if the interlocutory injunction is, or is not, granted, and the extent to which such harm could be compensated in damages. If the plaintiff can demonstrate a possibility of irreparable harm (that is, harm which would not be redressed by an award of damages), this must be balanced against the adequacy of the defendant's remedy in damages if an interlocutory injunction is wrongly granted against it. In *Wah Nam Holdings Co Ltd & Ors v Excel Noble Development Ltd & Ors* [2000] 3 HKC 118, 125F–G (CA) Ribeiro J summarised this exercise as follows:

> [T]he court proceeds to consider whether, if the plaintiff were to succeed in obtaining a permanent injunction at the trial, it could adequately be compensated by an award of damages in respect of any loss which it might suffer by reason of the defendant continuing to act unrestrained pending the trial. If damages would not be an adequate remedy, the court then considers whether the defendant would be adequately protected

> by the plaintiff's … undertaking in damages, should it later be found that the plaintiff should not have been granted an interlocutory injunction.

> If the court is in doubt as to the respective remedies of damages, then the court considers where the balance of convenience lies, this involving a discretionary assessment of the effects of granting or withholding interlocutory relief, the court seeking to preserve the status quo.

It is clear that the court will not grant an interlocutory injunction where damages would be an adequate remedy to the plaintiff; nor will it refuse an interlocutory injunction on the ground of possible harm to the defendant where that could be compensated in damages. However adequacy of damages is not to be measured solely by common law principles for the assessment of damages or compensation: the fact that damages would be quantifiable and reducible to a monetary sum does not necessarily mean that they would be an adequate remedy: *Wong Chun Ming Dev't Fund Co Ltd v Profit Surplus Ltd* [2009] 3 HKC 19 (CA) (para 21–23).

*Examination of the merits where the balance is even* — Where at this stage the balance appears even, the court may seek to resolve the issue by comparing the relative strengths of each party's case:

> It is only where 'the uncompensatable disadvantage to each party would not differ widely' that 'it may not be improper to take into account in tipping the balance the relative strength of each party's case as revealed by the affidavit evidence adduced on the hearing of the application'. However, even then, this exercise can only be undertaken 'where it is apparent upon the facts disclosed by the evidence as to which there is no credible dispute that the strength of one party's case is disproportionate to that of the other party'. (*Wah Nam Holdings Co Ltd & Ors v Excel Noble Development Ltd* [2000] 3 HKC 118, 125H–126A per Ribeiro J in the Court of Appeal, quoting from *American Cyanamid* at [1975] AC 396, 409).

*Special factors* — The court does not proceed as if bound by a straight-jacket but will consider all relevant factors when exercising its discretion on an application for an interlocutory injunction. Special considerations may lead the court to come to a result different from that which would pertain if *American Cyanamid* were followed to the letter. See *JC Penney Co Inc v Penneys Ltd* [1975] HKLR 598 per Huggins J. For example, where there is no arguable defence, the 'balance of convenience' need not be considered by the court: see *Yeko Trading Ltd v Chow Sai Cheong Tony & Ors* [2000] 2 HKC 612, 618B–I, per Chung J. Further, considerations of public policy may also be taken into account: *Her Majesty's Attorney General In and For the United Kingdom v South China Morning Post Ltd & Ors* [1988] 1 HKLR 143.

In *JC Penney Co Inc v Penneys Ltd* [1975] HKLR 598, Huggins J expressed a preference for *American Cyanamid* as 'explained' by Sir John Pennycuick in *Fellowes & Anor v Fisher* [1975] 2 All ER 829. There emphasis was given to the House of Lords' dictum in *American Cyanamid* that 'special factors' may be taken into account in 'individual cases', and an interlocutory injunction, in a case in which it might have been granted under the relatively liberal rule laid down by the House of Lords, was refused.

Other relevant Hong Kong decisions include *Gucci Co Ltd v Ng Kwok Pun t/a Kwok Hang Co* [1984] HKC 335 and *Watanmal (Liberia) Inc v Chase Manhattan Bank NA* [1987] 2 HKC 427.

**[29.1.9]     Delay in applying for interlocutory injunction**

An interlocutory injunction may be refused if there is delay after the grounds for making the application come to light. This is because such delay makes it difficult for a plaintiff to satisfy the court the injunction is needed to prevent irreparable loss, that is loss which could not be compensated by damages. See *King Fung Vacuum Ltd & Anor v Toto Toys Ltd & Anor* [2006] 2 HKLRD 785 (CA) where it was said (at para 20) that 'if a party is prepared to allow matters to proceed and takes no action with respect to matters which have been extant for lengthy periods, it lies ill in their mouth to say that there is likely to be irreparable damage'. See also *International Connex Holdings Pte Ltd v Wealth Resources Enterprises Ltd* [2006] 3 HKC 601. In the *King Fung* case it was said that promptness in applying for an interlocutory injunction is 'commonly understood to be a period of six weeks or so of unexplained delay and three months with an explanation . . .'

Other Hong Kong cases in which interlocutory injunctions have been refused on grounds of delay include:

*   *Chan Cheung Hing v Chan Tang Lan & Ors* HCA 4568/1987 (Mayo J; 10.11.1987) – delay of one year in applying for a *Mareva* injunction to restrain dealings in disputed properties.

*   *Husky Injection Molding Systems China Ltd v Lau Kwong Fat & Anor* [2002] 3 HKC 223, 228B-E – delay of 15 months in seeking an interlocutory injunction against former employees, for at least 4 of which the plaintiff was aware of the grounds.

Once an interlocutory injunction has been granted, preserving the *status quo* pending trial, the plaintiff has an obligation to bring the action on for trial as soon as possible. Undue delay may result in the injunction being set aside. This topic is discussed in the commentary on *Mareva* injunctions, some paragraphs hence.

**[29.1.10]     Interlocutory injunction which will determine outcome of the action**

Special considerations arise where the grant or refusal of an interlocutory injunction is likely to determine the final outcome of the dispute. This situation may arise where, for example, there is insufficient time for a full trial before a forthcoming event which is the subject of the injunction application, or where the grant of an injunction would put the defendant out of business. In such cases the balance of convenience test laid down in *American Cyanamid* does not apply. The court should approach the application with a view to avoid injustice and bear in mind that the result may be to deprive the defendant of the right to trial. See *Zheng Lie Lie v Prosperfield Ventures Ltd & Anor (No 1)* [2003] 2 HKC 33, 43D-44A, citing *Cayne v Global Natural Resources plc* [1984] 1 All ER 225 and *Entec (Pollution Control) Ltd v Abacus Mouldings* [1992] FSR 332 (CA). In such cases the court should have regard to the prospects of success if the matter were to go to a full trial: *Fortune Realty Co Ltd v Chan Hiu Yeung Dick* HCA 1582/2001 (Chu J; 24.05.2001); *Time Success Profits Ltd & Anor v Andrew Lam & Co* [2004] 1 HKC 214 (para 9); *Midland Business Management Ltd v Ng Pe Lok & Ors* [2006] 3 HKC 249 (DCt) (paras 13-15). The burden on the plaintiff with regard to the prospects of success is to show that 'it has at least good prospects of success': *Abbott GmbH & Co KG & Anor v Pharmareg Consulting Co Ltd & Anor* HCA 166/2005 (Sakhrani J; 17.04.2009) (para 27). In that case the court doubted commentary in another work suggesting that the plaintiff must satisfy the court that it has a 'high likelihood of success at trial', and (at para 22-24), quoting with approval from *Lansing Linde Ltd v Kerr* [1991] 1 WLR 251, said that all that is required is 'some consideration' as to whether the plaintiff would be likely to succeed at trial.

**[29.1.11]    Application for interlocutory injunction – may be treated as trial of the action**

In a case where there is no dispute as to the material facts, the court may, with agreement of the parties, treat an application for an interlocutory injunction as the trial of the action and make a final order (*The Incorporated Owners of Viking Garden v Golden Brains Ltd & Anor* [1991] 1 HKC 353).

**[29.1.12]    Service on non-parties**

There is a duty to inform the court where it is intended to serve an interlocutory injunction on a third party, that is someone who is not a party to the proceedings in which the injunction is sought: *Loerie Investments Ltd v Liu Hong Shu* HCA 1908/ 2007 (Chu J; 04.12.2008) (para 37). The court will normally require an undertaking to indemnify such a third party for any costs, expenses or fees reasonably incurred in complying with the order: *Re Liu Lee Yuk-ching* [1982] HKLR 399. See also the commentary some paragraphs below on *Mareva* injunctions which are served on third parties.

**[29.1.13]    Ex parte applications**

An application for an interlocutory injunction should normally be made *inter partes* after the issue of the writ or originating summons, by motion or summons. In case of urgency, however, the plaintiff may make the application *ex parte* on affidavit (Order 29 rule 1(2)), and this may be done even before issue of originating process (Order 29 rule 1(3)). An *ex parte* injunction, like any *ex parte* order, should be made on a provisional basis with a subsequent return date at which the matter can be re-heard *inter partes*: *Goldie v Grandtag Financial Consultancy & Insurance Brokers Ltd* [2006] 3 HKC 302, paras 30-36. The party against whom an *ex parte* injunction has been granted may apply under Order 32 rule 6 for it to be set aside at any time. See the commentary under that rule.

In *Tyece Ltd v Max Concept Technology Ltd* [2003] 3 HKC 116, an *ex parte* injunction was set aside on the ground the applicant had failed to disclose material which showed there was in fact no urgency. In that case at 118D-F Sakhrani J quoted *Seapower Resources International Limited & Ors v Lau Pak Shing & Ors* HCA 10715/1993 (Rogers J; 15.12.1993) as to what constitutes 'urgency' in this context:

> 'For an *ex parte* application for an injunction to be urgent on the grounds of urgency, it must be so urgent but you cannot give even five minutes warning to the other side.'

See also *Ho Tak Eng v Fame Brilliant Ltd* DCCJ 2138/2005 (Rogers VP & Le Pichon JA; 20.12.2005) where the Court of Appeal emphasised that *ex parte* applications are exceptional and should only be made in cases of real urgency.

Where an application for urgent interlocutory relief is made prior to the filing of originating process, the applicant will be required to undertake to file the appropriate originating process as soon as reasonably practicable. This applies even if no order is made on the application and even if it is decided not to continue with the proceedings: *Dragon Capital Partners LP v Merrill Lynch Capital Services Inc* [1996] 4 HKC 198.

No action number or miscellaneous proceedings number will be assigned to any such proceedings until the proceedings have been commenced by some form of originating process.

Although rule 1 mentions the making of the application *ex parte* only in cases were there is urgency, which suggests limited time, it is accepted that such an application can be justified where there are other strong grounds. For example, the typical *Anton Piller* or *Mareva* injunction application is based on the apprehension that the alleged wrongdoer will behave in a less than scrupulous manner by transferring his assets out of the jurisdiction or concealing evidence; accordingly the application is brought *ex parte* to ensure that the alleged wrongdoer is not given an opportunity to render the order nugatory by acting prior to the order being made.

In *Seapower Resources International Ltd & Ors v Lau Pak Shing & Ors* HCA 10715/1993 (Rogers J; 15.12.1993) this additional ground for seeking an *ex parte* interlocutory injunction was described as the need for 'secrecy'. Rogers J went on to summarise the position as follows:

> '*Ex parte* applications should only be made where either the delay would cause to the applicant injustice or the defendant would take action which would nullify the effect of the injunction. An *ex parte* injunction goes against the normal way litigation is conducted. It is an infringement of the rights of natural justice of each party to be heard. Those making such applications have a duty to bear that in mind and they can not pass their responsibility to the court when they do so.'

In support of the above summary Rogers J cited, *inter alia, Jademan (Holdings) Ltd v Francis Leung Pak To & Ors* [1989] 2 HKLR 151.

**[29.1.14]   Duty of full and frank disclosure on application for ex parte interlocutory injunction**

On an *ex parte* application for an interlocutory injunction, as with any *ex parte* application, the applicant is required to make full and frank disclosure to the court. This means that in addition to putting forward its own case, the applicant should disclose the opposing (absent) party's likely case and any evidence which supports it. See *Third Chandris Shipping Corp v Unimarine SA* [1979] 2 All ER 972; [1979] 3 WLR 122 which deals with these requirements in the context of an *ex parte* application for a *Mareva* injunction. For a fuller discussion of the duty to make full and frank disclosure, and the consequences of breach, see the commentary under Order 32 rule 6.

It has been held that the duty of full and frank disclosure continues into the *inter partes* stage of an application for an interim injunction: see *Chu Hung Ching v Chan Kam Ming & Ors* [2001] 1 HKC 396, 402H-I (CA); *Hong Jing Co Ltd v Zhuhai Kwok Yuen Co Ltd* HCA 146/2006 (Deputy Judge Saunders; 14.09.2006) (para 9).

**[29.1.15]   Ex parte application 'on notice'**

In some cases it is appropriate for the party applying for an *ex parte* injunction to give notice to the opposing party prior to the hearing. This will not be the case where there is a risk that notice will defeat the applicant's rights (such as with many *Anton Piller* applications). However in urgent cases where there is no such risk, it may be appropriate for such notice to be given. In this context see *Rever (AMA) Salon Ltd v Kung Wai For Danny & Ors* [2001] 1 HKC 241, 250G. The effect of such notice is to give the opposing party the opportunity to be heard on an *inter partes* basis.

**[29.1.16]   Consideration of encouraging peaceful resolution of disputes**
In an interesting *dictum* Godfrey JA has observed that the public policy of encouraging parties to resolve their disputes by peaceful means was 'the court's primary consideration' on an application for an *ex parte* injunction: see *New Asia Energy Ltd v Concord Oil (HK) Ltd* [2000] 2 HKC 681, 692A–B. His Lordship opined that *ex parte* relief enabled the sta tus quo to be preserved until both sides had the opportunity to be heard. In that case Godfrey JA dissented in result; nevertheless it is submitted that his comment on public policy is of considerable merit.

**[29.1.17]   Practice direction 11.1 – urgent and ex parte applications for injunctive relief**
Practice direction 11.1 gives guidance as to the procedure to be followed in making applications which are urgent or *ex parte*. It applies to applications for interlocutory injunctions. The practice direction dates from October 1989, shortly after Hunter JA condemned the 'Pearl Harbour tactics' adopted by plaintiffs in seeking such relief (*Pappadis & Anor v Chan Shing Sheung Barry & Ors* [1989] 2 HKLR 511, 515C-F). Since then the practice direction has been revised, and its current wording can be viewed on the judiciary's website www.judiciary.gov.hk or that of the Hong Kong Legal Information Institute www.hklii.org, both of which are accessible by the general public free-of-charge.

**[29.1.18]   Terms of interlocutory injunction must be clear**
The terms of an order granting an interlocutory injunction (whether made *inter partes* or *ex parte*) must be sufficiently clear that the party restrained may know precisely what 'he may do and what he may not do'. See *Seapower Resources International Ltd & Ors v Lau Pak Shing & Ors* HCA 10715/1993 (Rogers J; 15.12.1993), citing *Potters v Ballotoni* [1977] RPC 202, 206 and *Locke v Beswick* [1989] 3 All ER 373, 389. In the *Seapower* case, Rogers J criticised as too wide the terms of an *ex parte* interlocutory injunction to restrain disclosure of confidential information.

The requirement that the terms of an injunction be clear is particularly important in the case of a mandatory injunction. See *Tech Focus Ltd v Austria Property Management Ltd & Anor* [2004] 1 HKC 343 where Rogers VP said (at 345B-C):

> It is very important when mandatory injunctions are framed that they are framed in precise terms so that everybody, including in particular the defendant, must know exactly what he must do and what steps he must take.

**[29.1.19]   Undertaking as to damages**
An undertaking as to damages will normally be required when any interlocutory injunction is granted, *ex parte* or *inter partes*, and the undertaking will be continued until final determination of the rights of the parties at trial.

The purpose of the undertaking is to protect the party against whom the injunction is made (and, in some cases, third parties as well). In *American Cyanamid Co v Ethicon Ltd* [1975] AC 396; [1975] 1 All ER 504 (HL), this point was made in the following terms:

> ...since the middle of the 19th century [the granting of interlocutory injunctions] has been made subject to [the plaintiff's] undertaking to pay damages to the defendant for any loss sustained by reason of the injunction if it should be held at the trial that the plaintiff had not

been entitled to restrain the defendant from doing what he was threatening to do (per Lord Diplock, at 509 B–C All ER).

The requirement of an undertaking in damages has been described as 'a necessary part of the mechanism for granting injunctions': (*Wah Nam Holdings Co Ltd & Ors v Excel Noble Development Ltd* [2000] 3 HKC 188, 126B (CA), per Ribeiro J. His Lordship continued that the undertaking 'is a safeguard for the defendant which enables the court to grant the plaintiff an order for interim restraint without the merits having been canvassed' and went on to quote from Lord Diplock's speech in *American Cyanamid*.

The undertaking is given to the court, not the other party, and is thus enforceable by contempt proceedings: *King Fung Vacuum Ltd & Anor v Toto Toys Ltd & Anor* [2006] 2 HKLRD 785.

Where by oversight an interlocutory injunction is granted without recording an undertaking in damages, this will readily be corrected on application to the court: see *Refco Inc v Troika Investment Ltd* [1988] 2 HKLR 623, per Sears J at 632A.

It is good practice in all cases for the applicant to give information to the court as to his financial ability to meet the undertaking and, where the applicant is low on or devoid of means, to give information as to such circumstances as would, in the interests of justice, require that the injunction should nevertheless be granted: *Hang Cheong Mould Fty (a firm) v Rodopi Ltd & Ors* HCA 912/1992 (Deputy Judge Neoh QC; 10.03.1992) (para 28).

A plaintiff who would be unable to give an undertaking as to damages because of impecuniosity is entitled to apply for a permanent injunction without seeking an interlocutory injunction to preserve the status quo. In *Oxy Electric Ltd v Zainuddin* [1990] 2 All ER 902, the plaintiff had applied for a permanent injunction to restrain the defendant from breaching a restrictive covenant. The defendant argued that the claim for a permanent injunction should be struck out unless the plaintiff was willing to apply for an interlocutory injunction supported by an undertaking as to damages with adequate security. Hoffman J rejected this argument saying that the defendant was not entitled to stifle an action in this way.

### [29.1.20]  Ability to honour undertaking in damages – fortification

The financial capacity of a party to honour its undertaking in damages is relevant in an application for an interlocutory injunction. This is to ensure that the protection given to the defendant by the undertaking is 'real and not illusory': *Wah Nam Holdings Co Ltd & Ors v Excel Noble Dev't Ltd* [2000] 3 HKC 118, 128E (CA).

Where the undertaking is given, with nothing further said, it will be assumed that the party giving it is of sufficient substance to meet it: *Wah Nam Holdings Co Ltd & Ors v Excel Noble Dev't Ltd & Ors* [2000] 3 HKC 118, 128I–129B (CA), quoting *Manor Electronics Ltd v Dickson* [1988] RPC 618, 623.

Where doubt arises about the party's ability to honour the undertaking, it is incumbent on the party applying for the injunction to give full and frank disclosure of its financial position: *Wah Nam Holdings* (above) (129 C–I); *Cheung Kam Wah v Cheung Hon Wah & Ors* [2005] 1 HKC 136 (CA) (para 28). Although both those judgments speak of 'full' disclosure, it would presumably be sufficient to give partial disclosure of sufficient assets to meet the undertaking in cases where the party's total assets substantially exceed the amount of damages which could reasonably be caused by the injunction. Absence of adequate disclosure might justify the drawing of an adverse inference as to ability to meet the undertaking: *Hui Chi Ming v Koon Wing Yee & Ors* HCA 1479/2009 (Deputy Judge Coleman SC; 25.11.2010) (para 45). In *CTO (HK) Ltd v Li Man Chiu & Ors* HCA 5165/ 2001 (Chu J; 15.01.2002) disclosure of means given at the *ex parte* stage was ambiguous and omitted important adverse information. The injunction was set aside for material non–disclosure, though it was re–granted on fortification.

If doubts about the party's ability to honour the undertaking are not dispelled, the court may refuse the injunction or require fortification: *Wah Nam Holdings* (above) (129C–F). Fortification may take the form of payment into court, provision of bank guarantee or such other form as may be agreed or ordered. Failure to put up fortification when required will result in the injunction being refused, or if already granted, in not taking effect: *Hui Chi Ming* (above) (para 17).

Any question as to a party's ability to honour its undertaking should be raised at the time the interlocutory injunction is sought, or if granted *ex parte*, when it first comes on for *inter partes* hearing: *Hui Chi Ming* (above) (para 18). The court has power to revisit the question of a party's capacity to honour an undertaking in damages, at a later stage, if there are compelling circumstances, or if there has been some significant change of circumstances: *Elegant Jump Ltd v Tribune Bridge Ltd & Ors* [2000] 3 HKC 133, 138H–I. The test for ordering fortification on such a later application is the same on an application at the time the injunction is granted: *Hui Chi Ming* (above) (para 35–38).

**[29.1.21]     Exceptions to requirement for undertaking in damages**
The court will dispense with the requirement for an undertaking as to damages where there is good reason. For example, an undertaking will not normally be required in matrimonial and children's matters: *Will v Will* [1993] 2 HKLR 398 (CA). Similarly the court may refrain from requiring an undertaking from a public authority or regulatory body acting under a duty to enforce the law: *Securities and Futures Commission v A* [2008] 1 HKC 89 (paras 54-59), referring to the House of Lords decisions in *Hoffmann-La Roche & Co AG v Secty of State* [1975] AC 295 and *Kirklees Metropolitan Borough Council v Wickes Building Supplies Ltd* [1993] AC 227. In the *SFC* case the court distinguished *Customs & Excise Commissioners v Anchor Foods Ltd* [1999] 3 All ER 268 (where an undertaking was required on grant of an injunction on a claim for customs duty) on the basis the injunction there was for protection of proprietary right rather than one resembling a prosecution function.

**[29.1.22]     Quantum of damages**
In *Ho Wing Cheong (t/a Hong Leong Securities) v Graham Margot* [1990] 1 HKC 235, Godfrey J held that where a plaintiff obtains an interlocutory injunction and gives the usual undertaking as to damages, but fails at the trial, the damages awarded to the defendant, if any, must be assessed in accordance with the rules governing an award of damages for breach of contract. In reaching this conclusion the learned judge followed *Hoffman-LaRoche v Secretary of State for Trade* [1975] AC 295, at 361, and *Air Express v Ansett Transport Industries Pty Ltd* (1981) 146 CLR 149 (H Ct of Australia). As to the approach in dealing with issues of foreseeability and remoteness of damages allegedly caused by an interlocutory injunction, see *European Bank Ltd v Robb Evans* [2010] HCA 6 (10.03.2010) (H Ct of Australia).

Although the court has power to require an undertaking that covers legal costs, the form of undertaking set out in practice direction 11.2 does not extend to costs: *Re New China HK Highway Ltd* [2010] 3 HKC 361.

### [29.1.23]  Costs

The usual practice is to order that the costs of a successful application for an interlocutory injunction be costs in the cause. The reason is that the merits of the case have not yet been investigated and determined. See *King Fung Vacuum Ltd & Anor v Toto Toys Ltd & Anor* [2006] 2 HKLRD 785; *Golite Int'l Ltd v Golden Power Industries Ltd* HCA 2262/2004 (Chu J; 18.03.2005); *Beacon College Ltd v Yiu Man Hau Alfred & Ors* [2001] 4 HKC 433, 444F-G. In *TKI Ltd & Anor v New Happy Ltd & Anor* [1995] 1 HKC 551, 555B-C (CA) a costs order in favour of the successful applicant in any event was described as 'unusual' and 'plainly wrong'.

The traditional order was that the successful party's costs be in the cause, but now the court more frequently orders that the costs of both parties be in the cause: *King Fung* (above).

This is not an inflexible rule. The court retains a discretion to make a final order for costs. An unjustifiable application or wholly unmeritorious opposition may result in a party being penalised with such an order. See *Golite* (above) referring to *Fortuna Investments Ltd v Hoo Tony* HCA 1384/2004 (Chu J; 09.03.2005) and see *Ho Shuk Ching Portia v Wong Mei Chu & Ors* HCA 1213/2003 (Chu J; 22.08.2005). In *Wah Cheong Construction Co Ltd v Super Bright Engineering Ltd* HCCT 10/2003 (Deputy Judge To; 06.06.2003) the court made a final order as to the costs of an interlocutory injunction where there was doubt whether the matter would proceed to full trial. In *AXA China Region Insurance Co Ltd v Pacific Century Insurance Co Ltd* HCA 9093/ 2000 (Deputy Judge To; 22.11.2001) the court made an order against defendants 'for unnecessary costs which should never have been incurred' and for 'wasting time and money' in contesting an application for an interlocutory injunction. In *Cheung Sai Lun v Lau Tai Chin Francis & Anor* HCCW 677/2004 (Barma J; 19.09.2007) (the 2nd of two decisions of that date) it was argued that it was unnecessary for the plaintiff to apply for an *ex parte Mareva* injunction and there should be no order as to costs. The defendant said he did not intend to dissipate the assets concerned and he did not object to continuation of the injunction at the return date. The court held (at para 17) that the key question for consideration was whether it was 'reasonable' for the plaintiff to have made the *ex parte* application in the circumstances.

### [29.1.24]  Costs against solicitor

A solicitor may be ordered to pay the costs of an application for an interlocutory injunction where he fails in his duty to the court. In *KB Chau & Co (a firm) v China Finance Trust and Investment Corp Ltd* [1996] 1 HKC 420 (CA), a solicitor was ordered to pay costs to the opposing party against whom his client had obtained an *ex parte Mareva* injunction. The client had made an affirmation in support of the *ex parte* application which was false in important respects. The solicitor, to whom the client had not previously been known, had not made enquiries to check the client's financial status. The Court of Appeal held that the solicitor's duty was not only to his client, especially in an *ex parte* application, and *a fortiori* where the order sought was of an extreme nature such as a *Mareva* injunction. See also the commentary under Order 62 rule 8.

## [29.1.25]     Appeals

The Court of Appeal will be slow to interfere with a decision of a judge whether to exercise his discretion in favour of granting an interlocutory injunction. See *Advance Finance Ltd v Pang Sze-mui, Loretta & Ors* [1986] HKLR 523 (CA) and *Cheung Kam Wah v Cheung Hon Wah & Ors* [2005] 1 HKC 136, 142F–H (CA). In *Centalic Technology Development Ltd v Worldwide Industrial Ltd* [1996] 3 HKC 498, Godfrey JA said (at 510D–G):

> If the judge can be shown to have misapprehended the evidence, and that in consequence his assessment of the applicant's chances of obtaining a permanent injunction was plainly wrong, this court is bound to reconsider the matter; and decide whether, on that evidence, the judge should have granted, or refused, the interlocutory relief sought. Otherwise this court is not entitled to interfere with the judge's exercise of his discretion.

## [29.1.26]     Undertaking in lieu of injunction

A defendant who might otherwise be compelled by interlocutory injunction can give an undertaking in the same terms instead. Such an undertaking might be given to the other party in correspondence without intervention of the court, or it may be recorded in a consent order instead of or in substitution for an interlocutory injunction. It is common for an undertaking to replace an *ex parte* injunction when the matter comes on for *inter partes* hearing a few days hence.

A consent order recording such an undertaking is in practice just as effective as an interlocutory injunction. An undertaking, like an injunction, is binding on the conscience, and does not create any interest in the affected property. In each case the remedy for breach lies in contempt. An undertaking in lieu of injunction at the interlocutory stage is not an admission of any right on the part of the plaintiff. Rather it is a voluntary act of restraint on the part of the person giving it, pending trial, in the full knowledge that he could be compelled by interlocutory injunction.

A party who wishes to be released from an undertaking in lieu of injunction may apply by summons, just as if he were applying to set aside an interlocutory injunction.

As discussed above, a plaintiff who obtains an interlocutory injunction is required to give an undertaking in damages. In the case of an undertaking in lieu of injunction, there is an implied cross-undertaking from the plaintiff in damages. As to the circumstances in which such an undertaking in damages may be implied, and when it may be excluded by express statement or agreement, see *Oberrheinische Metallwerke GmbH v Cocks* [1906] WN 127 and see Aitken, 'Undertakings and Judicial Vigilance' *New Gazette* (HK), August 1990, p 25 citing the Supreme Court of Victoria in *Bond Brewing Holdings v National Australia Bank Ltd* (unreported; 03.04.1990).

## [29.1.27]     Inherent jurisdiction to discharge interlocutory injunction

A decision to grant an interlocutory injunction does not give rise to *res judicata* or issue estoppel, hence it is 'always open to the court to entertain an application to discharge an interlocutory injunction': *Chu Hung Ching v Chan Kam Ming & Ors* [2001] 1 HKC 396, 401D-402F (CA) referring to *Pocklington Foods Inc v R* (1994) 123 DLR (4th) 141. This is an 'inherent jurisdiction': *Chou Yi Feng v Chou Yi Chen & Ors* HCA 4393/ 2001 (Chung J; 23.11.2002) (para 56).

The court will discharge an interlocutory injunction when it is 'just and convenient' to do so: *Chou Yi Feng* (above, para 56), referring to *RD Harbottle (Mercantile) Ltd v*

*National Westminster Bank Ltd* [1977] 3 WLR 752, 763H. 'Just and convenient' is an apparent reference to the court's power to *grant* injunctions as set out in section 21L of the High Court Ordinance. Note, however, that the statute actually says 'just *or* convenient'.

Examples of circumstances in which the court will discharge an interlocutory injunction include the following:

(1)     *New evidence comes to light* – see *Chu Hung Ching* (above, at 403 B-C) citing *Brink's Mat Ltd v Elcombe* [1988] 1 WLR 1350.

(2)     *Material change of circumstances* – see *Chou Yi Feng* (above, para 56), referring to *London Underground Ltd v NUR (No 2)* [1989] IRLR 343 and *Chu Hung Ching* (above).

(3)     *Delay* - where after the interlocutory injunction is granted, the plaintiff is guilty of inordinate and inexcusable delay in prosecuting the action: *Magnitogorsk Integrated Iron & Steel Works & Anor v Varex & Co GmbH & Ors* HCA 17492/1999 (Deputy Judge Gill; 27.11.2007), referring to *Newsgroup Newspapers Ltd v Mirror Group Newspapers (1986) Ltd* [1991] FSR 487. However, where the defendant has also delayed in prosecuting a counterclaim the court may refuse to discharge the injunction: the application may be dismissed on that ground: *China Merchants Bank v I-China Holdings Ltd & Ors* [2003] 1 HKLRD 271 (paras 25, 27).

(4)     *Error of law* – the court may discharge an interlocutory injunction when it becomes apparent that it was granted on an erroneous view of the law: *Cartiman Int'l Ltd v Polymer Resources Int'l (USA) Inc & Anor* HCCL 132/1995 (Keith J; 13.11.1996) (para 24).

Absent such factors, the court will be inclined to leave it to the aggrieved party to appeal, if there is still time to do so, rather than apply for discharge of the interlocutory injunction. Examples of cases in which the court appears to have adopted such an inclination include *EPRC Ltd & Anor v Century City Developments Ltd* HCA 6692/2000 (Chung J; 21.12.2001), where the aggrieved party had made a conscious decision not to attend the hearing at which the interlocutory order was made, and *Department of Justice v Yeung Chun Pong & Ors* HCMP 5021/2003 (Deputy Judge M Poon; 15.03.2004), concerning a restraint order under the Organized and Serious Crimes Ordinance (Cap 455) (as to which see Order 117).

**[29.1.28]     Particular instances – Banking**
There are many instances in which the court has been asked to grant interlocutory injunctions in relation to banking matters. The following are some examples:

•     *Duty of confidentiality* – In *Chase Manhattan Bank NA v FDC Co Ltd* [1985] 2 HKC 470 (CA) an interlocutory injunction was granted to restrain breach of the implied duty of confidentiality in the banker-customer relationship.

•     *Guarantee* – An interim injunction to restrain a bank from making payment under a guarantee was refused in *Guangdong Transport Ltd v Ancora Transport NV* [1987] HKLR 923 (CA). The court noted (at 931) the 'undesirability of issuing injunctions to restrain those engaged in international commerce, the life-blood of Hong Kong, from carrying out obligations freely entered into by them'. Similarly in *Watanmal (Liberia) Inc v Chase Manhattan Bank NA* [1987] 2 HKC 427 the court described bank guarantees as having 'special status', and quoted *Harbottle (Mercantile) Ltd v National Westminster Bank* [1978] QB 146, 155 where it was said that only in 'exceptional circumstances' will the courts interfere with irrevocable obligations assumed by banks. In this regard see also *United Trading Corp SA v Allied Arab Bank Ltd* [1985] 2 Lloyd's Rep 554 (CA) and *Bolvinter Oil SA v Chase Manhattan Bank* [1984] 1 Lloyd's Rep 251, both referred to by the Hong Kong court in *Watanmal*.

•   *Letter of credit* – As is the case with bank guarantees, the court will be very slow to restrain a bank from honouring a letter of credit. See *Ever Eagle Co Ltd v Kincheng Banking Corp* [1993] 2 HKC 157 (CA), referring to *Tukan Timber Ltd v Barclays Bank plc* [1987] 1 Lloyd's Rep 171, 174-5 where it was said that only in 'the most extremely exceptional circumstances' should the court interfere. An example of such circumstances may be where the bank has notice of a fraud committed by the beneficiary: *Edward Owen Eng'g Ltd v Barclays Bank Int'l Ltd* [1978] QB 159. See also *Sinom Shanghai Import & Export Co Ltd v Exfin (India) Mineral Ore Co Pvt Ltd* HCCT 45/2006 (Recorder Kwok SC; 19.06.2006).

Because of the commercial considerations which militate against the court interfering with operation of the banking system, the applicant's duty of disclosure is more 'acute' on an *ex parte* application to restrain a bank from making payment on a letter of credit: *Prime Deal (HK) Enterprises Ltd v HSBC* [2006] 3 HKC 74 (para 20).

**[29.1.29]     Injunction to prevent mortgagee from exercising power of sale**
The court may restrain a mortgagee from exercising its power of sale, in order to preserve the *status quo* pending resolution of a dispute. It is usual to require payment of the mortgage debt into court as a condition of such an injunction: *Inglis v Commonwealth Trading Bank of Australia* [1972] ALR 591. However the condition may be dispensed with wholly or in part: *Wong Chun Loong Tony v Lam Kin Ming* [1990] 1 HKC 188, 192 (CA).

**[29.1.30]     Breach of deed of mutual covenant**
There are many cases in which interlocutory injunctions have been granted to restrain threatened breach of a deed of mutual covenant ('DMC') governing the rights of owners of units in multi-storey buildings in Hong Kong. Examples include the following:

•   *Incorporated Owners of Mai On Industrial Bldg* HCA 6529/1987 (Godfrey J; 18.12.1987), where an injunction was granted to restrain the defendant from erecting a chimney on the building of which its unit formed part, pending trial of the action.

•   *Hon Hing Enterprises Ltd v Skai Import Export Ltd* [1994] 1 HKLR 248 (CA) where an interlocutory injunction was granted to restrain the defendant from opening up a wall to provide easier access to a lift lobby. Godfrey JA said that an urgent *ex parte* order was appropriate, otherwise the allegedly wrongful building works would be completed by the time a full *inter partes* hearing could be brought on.

•   *Incorporated Owners of South Seas Centre v Great Treasure Dev't Ltd* [1994] 1 HKC 197 (CA) where an interlocutory injunction was granted to prevent one owner from erecting a signboard on the external wall of the building in breach of the DMC.

The provisions of a typical DMC which may be the subject of an application for injunctive relief, will often be 'negative covenants'. Special considerations apply on an application for an injunction in respect of such a covenant. See the commentary on that topic a few paragraphs hence.

**[29.1.31] Breach of lease**
An interlocutory injunction to restrain a breach of a lease of commercial premises was granted in *Chanway Shatin New Town Dev't Ltd v Sun Mate Holdings (HK) Co Ltd* HCA 2018/2006 (Deputy Judge Carlson; 10.04.2007), pending trial of an action for forfeiture of the lease and damages.

**[29.1.32] Contracts for the sale of land**
The Court of Appeal held in *Chinapro Ltd v Century Fame Ltd* [1993] 1 HKLR 234 (per Kempster JA) that, where there was a contract for the sale of land which clearly would entitle a purchaser to a decree of specific performance, the court would grant an injunction restraining the vendor from selling elsewhere. Further, the grant of an injunction would substantially increase the chances of performance of the agreement (per Yang CJ).

**[29.1.33] Injunction to secure obedience to the law**
The court may grant an injunction to prevent a breach, or threatened breach, of the law. See *Re Lee Suk-ping* [1988] 1 HKLR 566 where the court suggested that injunctive relief could be sought to stop unlicensed premises from illegally selling alcohol, and illegal hawkers causing potential danger. The court referred to *Stafford BC v Elkenford Ltd* [1977] 1 WLR 324 and quoted *Hamersmith LBC v Magnum Ltd* [1978] 1 WLR 5054 where Lord Denning MR said:

> The High Court has inherent power to secure by injunction obedience to the law by everyone in the land, whenever a person with a sufficient interest brings the case before the court.

The court noted that the above principle was approved by the House of Lords in *Stoke-on-Trent City Council v B&Q (Retail) Ltd* [1984] AC 754 where Lord Templeman (at 776A-B) referred to the 'right to invoke the assistance of the civil court in aid of the criminal law' as a 'comparatively modern development'.

The court exercises this jurisdiction with caution: *Secretary for Justice v Ocean Technology Ltd & Ors* HCA 70/2008 (Hartmann J; 21.01.2008), referring to *Gouriet v Union of Post office Workers* [1978] AC 435, 481 and *Portsmouth County Council v Richards* [1989] 1 CMLR 673, 710. In *Ocean Technology,* the court refused to extend an injunction which had been granted to secure obedience to a statute prohibiting unlicensed radio broadcasts. There was an outstanding issue as to the constitutionality of the relevant provisions. In reaching its decision the court distinguished (at para 32) *AG v Bastow* [1957] 1 QB 514, 521 where it was suggested that the court would readily grant an injunction to enforce a clear provision of the law.

At common law an application for such an injunction must be brought by the Secretary for Justice (equivalent in Hong Kong of the Attorney General) or, with the Secretary's permission, by a 'relator' (as to which see Order 15 rule 11). In England local authorities may, by statute, now bring such applications in their own right. See *Birmingham City Council v Shafi & Anor* [2008] EWCA Civ 1186 (30.10.2008) (para 23).

**[29.1.34]     Interlocutory mandatory injunctions**

The 'serious question to be tried' test laid down in *American Cyanamid* does not apply on an application for an interlocutory mandatory injunction. A 'higher standard of proof' is required as compared to prohibitory injunctions: *TKI Ltd v New Happy Ltd* [1995] 1 HKC 551, 554B (CA). The court's concern in this regard is which course is likely to involve 'the least risk of injustice if it turns out to be wrong': *Trade Advisers Co Ltd v Silkart Ltd* [1999] 2 HKC 806 (quoting *Nikitenko v Leboeuf Lamb Greene & Macrae* [1999] TLR 61). The court should feel 'a high degree of assurance' that at trial it will appear that the injunction was rightly granted: *Shepherd Homes Ltd v Sandham* [1971] 1 Ch 340, 351; *Lau Wing Mou (a firm) v Lo Kong* [1992] 1 HKLR 60 (CA). But even if the court does not feel such a 'high degree of assurance', it may be appropriate to grant an interlocutory mandatory injunction if withholding it would carry a greater risk of injustice: *Music Advance Ltd v IO of Argyle Centre* HCA 2574/2002 (Ma J; 30.08.2002); [2010] 2 HKLRD 1041 (para 12(g)).

**[29.1.35]     Threatened breach of negative covenant**

In *Doherty v Allman* (1878) 3 App Cas 709, 720 it was held that the court has no option but to grant an injunction to restrain the breach of a negative covenant, regardless of the balance of convenience. This principle was applied at the interlocutory stage in *Incorporated Owners of Mai On Industrial Bldg v Hedit Ltd* HCA 6529/1987 (Godfrey J; 18.12.1987). The court preferred *Hampstead & Suburban Properties Ltd v Diomedous* [1969] 1 Ch 248 over *Texaco Ltd v Mulberry Filling Station* [1972] 1 WLR 814 on the question whether *Doherty v Allman* applies at the interlocutory stage. An interlocutory injunction was granted to restrain the owner of part of an industrial building from erecting a chimney in breach of the DMC pending trial of the action, notwithstanding the concession that the balance of convenience lay against the granting of the interim injunction. *Incorporated Owners of South Seas Centre v Great Treasure Dev't Ltd* [1994] 1 HKC 197 (CA) is another case where an interlocutory injunction was granted to restrain breach of a negative covenant in a DMC. There the principle was reformulated in the following terms (at 202B-D):

> where a defendant is proposing to act in breach of an express negative stipulation binding upon him, he will normally be enjoined from doing so, and, save in exceptional cases, damages will not be regarded as an adequate remedy. However, the defendant may, nonetheless, be able to establish special circumstances of such a nature that the hardship that the making of the order would cause him would so far outweigh the inconvenience to the plaintiff through denying the plaintiff specific relief that the court considers that its intervention would be unjust. In addition, general discretionary considerations, such as unfairness, acquiescence or delay, may make the grant of an interlocutory injunction inappropriate.

With regard to the balance of convenience it was observed (at 203E-F) that 'where a defendant is proposing to act in breach of an express negative stipulation, the balance of convenience would have to come down very much more heavily on his side to justify the court in withholding interlocutory relief from the plaintiffs'.

Different considerations may apply where an interlocutory mandatory injunction is sought to enforce a negative covenant. See *Dollfus Mieg & Cie v CDW Int'l Ltd* HCA 3517/2002 (Deputy Judge Barma SC; 30.01.2003) (para 65) where the court adopted the approach in *Nottingham Building Society v Eurodynamics Systems plc*

[1993] FSR 468, 474, being the 'least risk of injustice' approach used in applications for interlocutory mandatory injunctions (see above).

**[29.1.36]    Contract for personal services**

The court does not grant specific performance of contracts for personal services. Damages are considered a sufficient remedy. As a result, the court will be reluctant to grant an injunction to prevent breach of a contract for personal services where the effect could be the same as a decree of specific performance. See *Worth Achieve Associates v Huang Sheng Yi* [2007] 3 HKC 7 and *Hummingbird Music Ltd v Acconci* HCA 836/2007 (A Cheung J; 18.06.2007).

**[29.1.37]    Defamation cases**

On an application for an interlocutory injunction to restrain repetition of alleged defamatory remarks pending trial, the *American Cyanamid* 'balance of convenience' test does not apply: *Target Newspapers Ltd & Ors v Narain* [1989] 2 HKC 16 (CA), and see *Chan Shui Shing Andrew v Ironwing Holdings Ltd* [2001] 2 HKC 376, 378E-F citing *Khashoggi v IPC Magazines Ltd* [1986] 1 WLR 1412 (CA). The burden on the applicant in such a case 'is a much heavier one': *Wang Lin Jia v Ng Kai Cheung* HCA 113/2008 (Deputy Judge Carlson; 18.02.2008). This is because of the importance of leaving free speech unfettered: *Ki Ming Po v Yeung Wai Hong & Ors* [1993] 1 HKC 595, referring to *Bonnard v Perryman* [1891] 2 Ch 269, 284 (CA). In *Chan Shui Shing* (above, at 378H–I) the court said that such an interim injunction will only be granted where:

(a)     the statement is unarguably defamatory;
(b)     there are no grounds for concluding the statement may be true;
(c)     there is no other defence which might succeed;
(d)     there is evidence of an intention to repeat or publish the defamatory statement.

In *Chan Shui Shing,* the court went on to say that where the defendant swears the words complained of are true, an injunction will not be granted unless the plaintiff satisfies the court that such defence cannot succeed.

In *Amuse Hong Kong Ltd v Chan Kin Tim Leslie & Anor* [1994] 1 HKC 175 (CA) the court went so far as to grant an interlocutory injunction not only restraining repetition of defamatory statements contained in a letter, but requiring it to send all recipients of the letter an unconditional retraction.

**[29.1.38]    Confidential information**

The court may grant an interlocutory injunction to restrain the use of confidential information. Such injunctions have been sought against former employees joining competing enterprises (*Seapower Resources Int'l Ltd v Lau Pak Shing* HCA 10715/1993 (Rogers J; 15.12.1993); *ICAP (HK) Ltd v BGC Securities (HK) LLC* [2005] 3 HKC 137); a financial advisor acting against the interests of a former client (*Jademan (Holdings) Ltd v Francis Leung Pak To & Ors* [1989] 2 HKLR 151) and a firm of solicitors accepting instructions to act against a former client (*Time Success Profits Ltd v Andrew Lam & Co* [2004] 1 HKC 214). In *AXA China Region Insurance Co Ltd v Pacific Century Insurance Co Ltd* [2003] 3 HKC 1 insurance agents who switched companies were prevented by such an injunction from using the former principal's clients' confidential information.

In *Commissioner of Police v Bermuda Broadcasting Co Ltd* [2008] UKPC 5 (23.01.2008) the Privy Council upheld a decision not to grant an interlocutory injunction to protect the confidentiality of police documents on the ground that the competing public interest in freedom of the press took precedence.

**[29.1.39]    Non-competition covenants**
The court will carefully scrutinise an application for an interlocutory injunction to enforce a non-competition covenant pending trial. This is because the decision at the interlocutory decision is often, in effect, final – such covenants will often have expired by the time it takes to bring an action on for trial. Furthermore the court will not enforce a covenant if the effect is to deprive a party of the means of making a living or to force him to continue to work for the same employer. In this regard see *Beacon College Ltd v Yiu Man Hau Alfred & Ors* [2001] 4 HKC 433 citing *Lumley v Wagner* (1852) 1 DeGM & G 604 and *Whitwood Chemical Co v Harman* [1891] 2 Ch 416.

In *Ho Wing Cheong (t/a Hong Leong Securities) v Graham Margot* [1990] 1 HKC 235, the Court granted an interlocutory injunction restraining the defendant from taking up employment with another firm. The court subsequently, however, ruled that the restraint clause was unenforceable as being of unreasonable duration and the plaintiff was held liable on its undertaking for damages. In *Sea Wave Hair Design (WTS) Ltd v Choy Kwong Yiu* HCA 2743/1992 (Deputy Judge Tong QC; 02.06.1992), the court granted an interlocutory injunction in favour of the operator of hair salons to restrain ex-employees from working as hair stylists within Tsim Sha Tsui district or one mile from the owner's branch, subsidiary company, agency or joint venture.

**[29.1.40]    Infringement of intellectual property rights**
Cases in which the court has considered applications for interlocutory injunctions to restrain breach of intellectual property rights include the following:

- *Takmay Industrial Co Ltd v Wah Sang Industrial Co* [1977–1979] HKC 115 (CA) where an interlocutory injunction was granted restraining the defendant from infringing the plaintiff's rights in respect of dolls manufactured and sold by it. It was said that the grant of the interim injunction was a matter of discretion and the Court of Appeal would hesitate to interfere.
- *RJP Electronics Ltd v Far East United Electronics Ltd* [1983] HKLR 428 where the court granted an interlocutory injunction to restrain the defendant from continuing to manufacture or sell a ruler containing a clock and a calculator, which was said to constitute passing off and to infringe the plaintiff's copyright and registered design. Although the court was satisfied that the defendants were good for any foreseeable amount of damages, it considered that the plaintiff might suffer disruption to its marketing over a period of months which could cause loss 'very difficult to be assessed in terms of dollars and cents'.
- *Caesars World Inc v Delman Co Ltd* [1988] HKC 421 where an interlocutory injunction was granted to restrain the defendant from operating its nightclub under the name used by the plaintiff for its casino complex in Las Vegas.
- *Improver Corp & Ors v Raymond Industrial Ltd & Anor* [1989] 1 HKC 397 where the court, not being satisfied that the defendant would be in a position

to meet an award of damages, granted an interlocutory injunction to restrain it from allegedly infringing the plaintiff's patent rights.

- *Reebok Int'l Ltd & Ors v Laws Fashion Knitters Ltd* HCA 1056/1989 (Mayo J; 23.05.1989) where the court refused to restrain the defendants from dealing in allegedly infringing sports shoes on the ground that damages would be an adequate remedy.

- *Ten-Ichi Co Ltd v Jancar Ltd & Ors* [1989] 2 HKC 330 where the court granted an interlocutory injunction restraining the defendant from using the plaintiff's name for a Japanese restaurant.

- *Lau Wing Mou (a firm) v Lo Kong* [1991] 2 HKC 569 where an interlocutory mandatory injunction was granted requiring the defendant to alter the appearance of its shop, which was said to mimic the plaintiff's to facilitate the defendant passing off the plaintiff's goods.

- *Samsonite Corp v Make Rich Ltd* [2002] 1 HKC 692 where the court refused an interim injunction to restrain the defendant from manufacturing and marketing luggage which allegedly infringed the plaintiff's intellectual property rights on the ground that infringement of copyright had not been specifically pleaded, and the mere possibility of copying was insufficient to give rise to a serious question to be tried on passing off.

- *Harbour Fit Industrial Ltd v Tan Kwai Garden Seafood Restaurant Ltd* [2002] 2 HKC 487, a 'name' passing off case, where, although the court was satisfied damages would not be an adequate remedy for the plaintiff, it refused an interlocutory injunction to restrain the defendant from using a particular name for its restaurant, and instead ordered that the matter proceed to trial on an urgent basis.

- *Gold Source Jewellery Ltd v Jewel Arts Ltd* HCA 2708/2006 (Deputy Judge L Chan; 18.02.2008) where an interim injunction was granted restraining the defendant from offering for sale jewellery which was allegedly copied from the plaintiff's designs.

- *Aqua Concepts Ltd & Ors v Hong Kong Resort Co Ltd* HCA 1658/2007 (Deputy Judge L Chan; 31.03.2008) where an interlocutory injunction was granted restraining the defendants from using a restaurant name similar to the plaintiffs'.

## [29.1.41]   Sale of goods
In *Tung Wing Steel Co Ltd v Brasimet Comercio e Industria SA & Ors* CACV 38/1990 (Cons VP, Kempster JA & Sears J; 25.09.1990) it was held that an interlocutory injunction to restrain a defendant from receiving a shipment of goods, which the plaintiff contended it had bought, was not appropriate since it was open to the plaintiff to procure replacement goods on the open market and claim damages if it succeeded at trial. See also *Alpha (Asia) Ltd v Dyno Nobel HK Ltd* HCA 1501/2007 (Recorder Shieh SC; 07.11.2007).

## [29.1.42]   Injunction to restrain commencement or continuation of legal proceedings
The court has jurisdiction to grant an injunction to restrain a person from instituting proceedings in Hong Kong: *Lenka Investments Ltd v Cheung Kong (Holdings) Ltd* [1983] HKLR 258, 265E-G (CA), referring to *Doleman & Sons v Ossett Corp* [1912] 3 KB 257

and *Bryanston Finance v De Vries (No 2)* [1976] 2 WLR 41. In *Lenka Investments* (where the injunction was refused) it was alleged that the threatened proceedings would be in breach of an arbitration agreement, and vexatious. The grant of such an injunction will be rare as the court has ample power to stay such proceedings if instituted – see the commentary under Order 12 rule 8.

The court may also grant an injunction restraining a party from continuing proceedings in another jurisdiction. Such an injunction operates *in personam* only as the court will 'recoil' from making an order which might infringe on the jurisdiction of courts elsewhere: *China Light & Power Co Ltd v Wong To Sau Heung* [1993] 2 HKC 238 (CA). In that case such an injunction was granted *ex parte* on an interim basis. This type of injunction is sometimes called an 'anti-suit' injunction.

The applicable principles for grant of an anti-suit injunction were discussed (*obiter*) in *First Laser Ltd v Fujian Enterprises (Holdings) Ltd* HCA 4414/2001 (Deputy Judge Lam; 12.12.2002) (para 60 *et seq*), referring to the following authorities from other jurisdictions:

- *Société Aérospatiale v Lee Kui Jak* [1987] 1 AC 871 (PC from Brunei) – the discretion to grant an anti-suit injunction must be exercised with caution (at 892E–F). The injunction will be appropriate where the ends of justice so require such as where the foreign proceedings are vexatious or oppressive.
- *Amchem Products Inc v Workers' Compensation Board* (1993) 102 DLR (4th) 96, 120-1 (SCC) – the party invoking the foreign jurisdiction may be restrained where the exercise of that jurisdiction is inconsistent with our rules of private international law.
- *Airbus Industrie v Patel* [1999] 1 AC 119, 138G-H – an anti-suit injunction should not be granted unless the forum has sufficient interest in or connection with the matter in question to justify the indirect interference with a foreign court.

Subsequently, the key principles in relation to anti-suit injunctions emerging from the above cases and others were set out in *Highland Crusader Offshore Partners LP & Ors v Deutsche Bank AG & Anor* [2009] EWCA Civ 725 (13.07.2009). Toulson LJ said (para 50):

1. Under English law the court may restrain a defendant over whom it has personal jurisdiction from instituting or continuing proceedings in a foreign court when it is necessary in the interests of justice to do so.

2. It is too narrow to say that such an injunction may be granted only on grounds of vexation or oppression, but, where a matter is justiciable in an English and a foreign court, the party seeking an anti-suit injunction must generally show that proceeding before the foreign court is or would be vexatious or oppressive.

3. The courts have refrained from attempting a comprehensive definition of vexation or oppression, but in order to establish that proceeding in a foreign court is or would be vexatious or oppressive on grounds of forum non conveniens, it is generally necessary to show that

    (a) England is clearly the more appropriate forum ('the natural forum'), and

    (b) Justice requires that the claimant in the foreign court should be restrained from proceeding there.

4. If the English court considers England to be the natural forum and can see no legitimate personal or juridical advantage in the clamant in the foreign proceedings being allowed to pursue them, it does not automatically follow that an anti-suit injunction should be granted. For that would be to overlook the important restraining influence of considerations of comity.

5. An anti-suit injunction always requires caution because by definition it involves interference with the process or potential process of a foreign court. An injunction to enforce an exclusive jurisdiction clause governed by English law is not regarded as a breach of comity, because it merely requires a party to honour his contract. In other cases the principle of comity requires the court to recognise that, in deciding questions of weight to be attached to different factors, different judges operating under different legal systems with different legal policies may legitimately arrive at different answers, without occasioning a breach of customary international law or manifest injustice, and that in such circumstances it is not for an English court to arrogate to itself the decision how a foreign court should determine the matter. The stronger the connection of the foreign court with the parties and the subject matter of the dispute, the stronger the argument against intervention.

6. The prosecution of parallel proceedings in different jurisdictions is undesirable but not necessarily vexatious or oppressive.

7. A non-exclusive jurisdiction agreement precludes either party from later arguing that the forum identified is not an appropriate forum on grounds foreseeable at the time of the agreement, for the parties must be taken to have been aware of such matters at the time of the agreement . . .

8. The decision whether or not to grant an anti-suit injunction involves an exercise of discretion and the principles governing it contain an element of flexibility.

It has been suggested that the Hong Kong court should not entertain an application for an anti-suit injunction until the foreign court has ruled on jurisdiction and any issues of *forum non conveniens*: *Kara Mara Shipping Co Ltd v World Tanker Carriers Corp* [1996] 2 HKLR 8, 17A-B. In *Sumitomo Bank Ltd v Xin Hua Estate Ltd* HCCL 256/ 1998 (Stone J; 05.02.1999) an anti-suit injunction application was adjourned pending a decision of the Guangdong court on jurisdiction.

It may even be possible to seek an 'anti-anti-suit' injunction to restrain a party from proceeding with an anti-suit injunction in another jurisdiction. See *Lloyd's Underwriters v Cominco Ltd* [2007] BCCA 249 (para 22) where it appears that such an injunction was granted.

### [29.1.43] Restraint on publication
The court is frequently asked to grant injunctive relief to prevent publication of defamatory material. Such relief may also be granted in respect of publications which would be illegal in the sense that they would breach official secrecy and threaten national security (*Her Majesty's AG in and for the UK v South China Morning Post Ltd* [1988] 1 HKLR 143 (CA), or infringe proprietary rights under contract (*Laidler v Lui Patrick* [1987] 3 HKC 411).

### [29.1.44] Passing off
In *Television Broadcasts Ltd v Home Guide Publication Co* [1982] HKLR 313, an interlocutory injunction was granted to prevent a magazine proprietor from changing

the name of a magazine with a minimal circulation published by him to that of a highly successful television programme televised by the plaintiff. The court held that there was a serious question to be tried; that there was no evidence that the defendant would be able to meet an award for damages, whereas the plaintiff could well afford to compensate the defendant for any damages the latter might suffer as a result of the injunction. In any case the injunction would be granted to preserve the status quo.

#### [29.1.45]   Gagging order – the superinjunction
The court's jurisdiction under section 21L of the High Court Ordinance (Cap 4) to grant injunctions extends to the making of a 'gagging' order whereby a party is restrained from disclosing information relating to court proceedings. See *A Co v B Co* [2002] 2 HKC 497, 508H–509D, citing *Banco Ambrosiano Andino SA v BNP* [1985] HKLR 72. In *A Co v B Co* Ma J stated (at 509F–H) that a gagging order is exceptional, to be granted only where a 'strong case' is made out. The learned judge upheld such an order in the context of *Norwich Pharmacal* proceedings for disclosure of the identity of a wrongdoer (as to which, see the commentary under Order 15 rule 4).

In *Re X Ltd* HCCW 382/2006 (Harris J; 04.05.2010) a gagging order was made permitting a writ to be entered in the court registry in the names 'A' and 'B' to conceal from interested parties the fact that proceedings had been commenced. The purpose was to permit confidential investigations to continue before the action was proceeded with.

In England the court has been known to grant the 'superinjunction', whereby the names of the parties, the terms of the order and even the fact that the injunction has been sought and obtained are suppressed. See the discussion in *Ntuli v Donald* [2010] EWCA Civ 1276 where such an order was made *ex parte* at first instance to protect the privacy of a musician from intimate details being sold to the press by a woman with whom he had been in a relationship. The anonymity aspects of the judgment were set aside on appeal.

#### [29.1.46]   Interim injunction to restrain compliance with court order
It has been held that the court has power to grant an interim injunction to stay or restrain compliance with another court order. See *J&C New Poly Catering Sdn Bhd v TTMP Bakum Consortium Sdn Bhd* [2006] 1 MLJ 587 where the Malaysian court held that an injunction could issue to restrain a garnishee from complying with a garnishee order absolute pending an application to set aside the underlying judgment (though in that case the injunction was set aside for lack of standing).

#### [29.1.47]   The *Mareva* injunction –Interlocutory freezing of assets
In 1975 the English Court of Appeal departed from long-standing authority and held that an interlocutory order restraining a defendant from disposing of his own assets could be issued. This type of order has since come to be known as the '*Mareva* injunction', after one of the seminal cases in which it was developed (*Mareva Compania Naviera SA v International Bulk Carriers SA* [1980] 1 All ER 213). In England *Mareva* injunctions are now known as 'freezing' injunctions. See CPR 25.1.

In the *Mareva* case, the English Court of Appeal held that, where a debt is owing to a plaintiff and it is reasonably feared that a defendant resident outside the jurisdiction may send its assets offshore to avoid enforcement of the judgment, the court may grant an interlocutory injunction to restrain the defendant from doing so.

Subsequent developments have broadened the scope of the *Mareva* injunction so that it is now available against residents and non-residents alike and to prevent assets from being removed from the jurisdiction or dissipated within the jurisdiction.-

The 'basic rationale' of the *Mareva* injunction 'is to ensure that the plaintiff is given adequate protection from the possibility of being left with a barren judgment in circumstances where a real risk exists of the defendant dissipating its assets before judgment': *Yau Chiu Wah v Gold Chief Investment Ltd & Anor* [2002] 1 HKC 383, 391G-H, per Ma J. This form of ancillary relief had previously been thought to be unavailable. See *Lister & Co v Stubbs* (1890) 45 Ch D 1 (CA) where it was held that a plaintiff claiming a money judgment has no interest in the property of the defendant, so the court will not grant interlocutory relief to restrain the defendant from dealing with that property in any way.

**[29.1.48]**   *Mareva* **injunction requires independent cause of action**
As with all other interlocutory injunctions, a *Mareva* injunction will only be granted ancillary to a claim for a recognised cause of action against the defendant. See the discussion of *The Siskina* [1979] AC 210 above, at the outset of the commentary under Order 29 rule 1.

The court will, therefore, be unwilling to grant a *Mareva* injunction in respect of an anticipated claim, no matter how strong the evidence that the defendant was likely to dissipate his assets (*Veracruz Transportation Inc v VC Shipping Co Inc* [1992] 1 Lloyd's Rep 353; *The P* [1992] 1 Lloyd's Rep 470; *Zucker v Tyndall Holdings plc* [1992] 1 WLR 1127 (CA)). An illustration of the application of this principle in Hong Kong is *Gainluxe Investments Ltd v Superstand Developments Ltd & Anor* [1994] 3 HKC 641.

At one time the decision in *The Siskina* was taken to mean that it was not possible to seek a *Mareva* injunction in Hong Kong in aid of proceedings in another jurisdiction. That position has been reversed by section 21M of the High Court and Order 29 rule 8A. See the commentary under that rule.

**[29.1.49]**   **No Mareva injunction against non-party**
A *Mareva* injunction will only be issued against a party to proceedings. See *Louvet v Louvet* [1990] 2 HKLR 596, 602A–B (CA). However non-parties who have notice of a *Mareva* injunction must not do anything which would facilitate breach. Thus where a *Mareva* injunction is issued against a bank account holder, the bank should be served and it may be responsible for the consequences if it allows the account holder to breach the injunction.

**[29.1.50]**   *Mareva* **injunction before action**
The court has power to grant a *Mareva* injunction before proceedings have been commenced in respect of the substantive claim. However this power should only be exercised on the undertaking of the applicant to commence proceedings, particularly where the application is made *ex parte*. See *Fourie v Le Roux & Ors* [2007] UKHL 1 (HL). There it was said that this restriction is imposed by the court to protect defendants, and that on granting a *Mareva* injunction before action the court should give directions for the institution of proceedings.

For an example of a case where a *Mareva* injunction was granted before action in Hong Kong, see *Sunchase Int'l Group (China) Ltd v Chik Wai Wan Stephen* [1999] 1 HKC 671 (CA).

**[29.1.51]   *Mareva* injunction after judgment**
The *Mareva* injunction was originally conceived as a remedy to provide a plaintiff a degree of protection prior to judgment. However it is now clear that such an injunction can be granted even after judgment. In *Wu Choi Yau v Beelee Industries Ltd* HCA 5811/1990 (Godfrey J; 28.01.1991), (referring to *Orwell Steel (Erection & Fabrication) Ltd v Asphalt & Tarmac (UK) Ltd* [1984] 1 WLR 1097) the court said: 'There is no doubt about the jurisdiction of this court to grant such an order in aid of execution'.

**[29.1.52]   *Mareva* injunction does not affect property rights**
A *Mareva* injunction, being an injunction, and therefore equitable in nature, operates *in personam* only, and does not give the plaintiff any right in or lien over the defendant's assets (*Cretanor Maritime Co Ltd v Irish Marine Management Ltd* [1978] 3 All ER 164 (CA)). A *Mareva* injunction is thus distinguishable from a proprietary injunction: *MSR Capital Ltd v KTH Recovery Fund II Ltd & Ors* [2005] 1 HKC 371, 375C-E (CA). The *Mareva* injunction does, however, carry with it the sanction of committal for contempt of court in the event that a defendant disposes of his assets in violation of the order. This sanction enables it to act as an effective form of pre-trial security for judgment in cases where an unscrupulous defendant would otherwise attempt to deprive the plaintiff of the fruits of his action by placing his assets beyond the reach of the procedures for the execution of a judgment of the court.

Compare the similar remedy of interim attachment under Order 44A rule 7, which does appear to operate against the debtor's property.

**[29.1.53]   *Mareva* injunction does not affect priority of creditors**
A *Mareva* injunction does not create any interest in or charge over the property affected. This flows from the fact that like all injunctions, the *Mareva* injunction is a creature of equity, operating *in personam* only. Thus the party in whose favour a *Mareva* has been granted remains a general unsecured creditor over whom any secured creditor has priority even if the security is granted subsequent to the injunction.

It follows that a judgment creditor may levy execution against property subject to a *Mareva* injunction in favour of another creditor, without regard to that other creditor's interests: *Kanematsu-Gosho (HK) Ltd v Lee Boon Chean* [1986] HKLR 59. Further, a mortgagee may take possession and exercise its power of sale of property subject to a *Mareva* injunction in favour of another creditor: *SA Development Ltd v Wing Hang Bank Ltd* [1997] 1 HKC 82 (CA).

**[29.1.54]   Remedy for breach of a *Mareva* injunction**
The remedy for breach of a *Mareva* injunction, like any injunction, lies in contempt of court. See the interesting discussion of the circumstances in which a party (or a third party) will be found in contempt for breach of a *Mareva* injunction in the judgment of the Singapore Court of Appeal in *Pertamina Energy Trading Ltd v Karaha Bodas Co LLC & Ors* [2007] SGCA 10 (01.03.2007). With regard to contempt of court generally see Order 52 and the commentary thereunder, and for sentencing considerations see the commentary under Order 52 rule 9.

## [29.1.55]    Joint property

A *Mareva* injunction may extend to cover property jointly owned by the restrained party and another. Indeed the wording of the forms of *Mareva* injunction prescribed by PD 11.2 expressly extends to property 'whether solely or jointly owned'.

## [29.1.56]    Trust and similar property

A *Mareva* injunction may extend to property in which the restrained party has a beneficial interest under a trust. Indeed the wording of the forms of *Mareva* injunction prescribed by PD 11.2 extends to property held in trust for the restrained party ('whether in his own name or not'). The order can also extend to the assets of a third party which the restrained party 'does not own but against which he has some legal right of recourse which, if exercised, would make those assets available to his own judgment creditors': *JSC BTA Bank v Kythreotis & Ors* [2010] EWCA Civ 1436 (para 32), referring to *C Inc plc v L* [2001] EWHC 550 (Comm). The wording used in the standard forms in PD 11.2 does not extend to property which the restrained party holds as trustee for the benefit of another. 'His assets' in those forms 'refers to assets belonging to that person, not to assets belonging to another person': *Federal Bank of the Middle East Ltd v Hadkinson & Ors* [2000] 1 WLR 1695, 1709E–1711B (CA); *Hui Chi Ming v Koon Wing Yee & Ors* HCA 1479/2009 (Fok J; 01.04.2010) (para 25). In England, differently worded forms are now prescribed in the Commercial Court Guide. It is provided that a freezing injunction applies to assets 'whether the Respondent is interested in them legally, beneficially or otherwise'. In *JSC BTA Bank* (above) it was held that a *Mareva* injunction in that form does extend to property held by the restrained party as trustee and that judges granting such an injunction should ensure that the undertaking in damages protects the beneficial owner as well as the trustee.

See also the commentary on the forms prescribed by PD 11.2, which appears at the end of the commentary on Order 29 rule 1.

## [29.1.57]    The *Mareva* injunction in Hong Kong

The efficacy of the *Mareva* injunction was quickly recognised in Hong Kong and has been applied in numerous cases. The statutory basis of the *Mareva* injunction in Hong Kong is now section 21L(1) of the High Court Ordinance which provides in the broadest possible terms that the Court of First Instance may grant an injunction in all cases where it appears to be just or convenient to do so.

The writ of foreign attachment, which was previously available in Hong Kong under Order 49A, was abolished as a result of the success enjoyed by the *Mareva* injunction.

## [29.1.58]    Property outside Hong Kong – the 'worldwide' *Mareva* injunction

The court may grant a *Mareva* injunction covering assets inside as well as outside Hong Kong. This was recognised by the English Court of Appeal in *Republic of Haiti v Duvalier* [1989] 1 All ER 456 and *Derby & Co Ltd v Weldon (Nos 3 & 4)* [1990] Ch 65, and by the Hong Kong Court of Appeal in *Bank of India v BK Murjani* [1989] 2 HKLR 318. Such an injunction is often referred to as a 'worldwide' *Mareva*. In the *Bank of India* case (above) the Hong Kong Court of Appeal set out the criteria for the grant of a worldwide *Mareva* injunction in the following terms (at 319H–J):

> In our opinion a *Mareva* injunction affecting assets outside the jurisdiction may be granted when there is a good arguable case that the plaintiff will recover judgment, reason to think that the defendant, properly before the court, has such assets available to satisfy it but insufficient assets within the jurisdiction for the purpose and the Court is satisfied that there is a real risk that the defendant may take steps designed so to dispose of or conceal such foreign assets as to render the judgment nugatory by the time that it is given.

Those criteria continue to be applied, as in *Yin Chin v Weng Tzu Ting* HCA 1435/ 2010 (Deputy Judge Carlson; 08.12.2010).

The recognition by the courts of the power to order a worldwide *Mareva* injunction occurred in stages. The pre-1989 authorities should, generally, no longer be followed. See the commentary some paragraphs hence on the process by which the courts came to the present position.

In order to avoid unwarranted interference with matters in other jurisdictions, the form of worldwide *Mareva* injunction set out in practice direction 11.2 (see below) contains special terms in relation to assets outside Hong Kong. Some of these are discussed in the ensuing paragraphs.

**[29.1.59]    Defendant need not be in Hong Kong**

Initially the *Mareva* injunction was available only against persons not resident in the jurisdiction. Now section 21L(3) of the High Court Ordinance provides:

> The power of the Court of First Instance under subsection (1) to grant an interlocutory injunction restraining a party to any proceedings from removing from the jurisdiction of the Court of First Instance, or otherwise dealing with, assets located within that jurisdiction shall be exercisable in cases where that party is, as well as in cases where he is not, domiciled or resident or present within that jurisdiction.

**[29.1.60]    Use and misuse of the Mareva injunction**

Because of its drastic nature, the *Mareva* injunction has been described (along with the *Anton Piller* order) as one of the law's nuclear weapons. That description traces back at least to *Bank Mellat v Nikpour* [1982] FSR 87, 92, and has been adopted in many Hong Kong cases including *Grand Trade Dev't Ltd v Bonance Int'l Ltd* CACV 776/2000 (Rogers VP, Stock & Le Pichon JJA; 03.11.2000) (para 17).

As a result the court is cautious both in deciding whether to grant a *Mareva* injunction, and as to its scope. The purpose of the *Mareva* injunction must be borne in mind. That purpose is to prevent the plaintiff from being defrauded, as colourfully described in *Kanematsu-Gosho (HK) Ltd & Anor v Lee Boon Chean* [1986] HKLR 59, 64E-G, 'by some quick-witted or light-footed defendant who, whilst keeping the proceedings alive and holding off an apparently good claim by a plaintiff, is busily getting his assets out of the jurisdiction'.

Thus the court is vigilant to ensure that *Mareva* injunctions are not granted for improper purposes such as an attempt to obtain security in the defendant's assets or priority over other creditors: *Pappadis v Chan Shing Sheung Barry* [1989] 2 HKLR 511, 516A-B (CA). Where the risk to the plaintiff arises from possible insolvency of the defendant, the plaintiff should issue a bankruptcy or winding-up petition rather than apply for a *Mareva* injunction: *Wu Choi Yau v Beelee Industries Ltd* HCA 5811/1990 (Godfrey J; 28.01.1991).

The plaintiff clearly shoulders a burden in ensuring that the *Mareva* injunction is not misused. In *Pappadis* (above, at 517G-H) the court quoted with approval *Z v A-Z Ltd* [1982] QB 558, 588 where Kerr LJ said:

> It is the duty of the plaintiff and his legal advisers to do the following:
>
> (i)   To consider carefully whether an application for a *Mareva* injunction is justified ...
>
> (ii)  If so, to consider very carefully what should be the extent of the injunction in order to safeguard the plaintiff's *prima facie* justified claim ...

## [29.1.61]   Smaller claims

It will not normally be appropriate to apply for a *Mareva* injunction where the amount of the claim is relatively small: see *American Express Bank Ltd v Cheung Kam Fung Betty* [2000] 2 HKC 510. There the Court of Appeal held that a *Mareva* injunction was not appropriate where the amount claimed was $54,000 and the costs of obtaining the injunction could be 'out of all proportion' (per Godfrey JA at 515A–B).

## [29.1.62]   Application ex parte

Applications for *Mareva* injunctions are normally made *ex parte* at the initial stage in order not to give the defendant an opportunity to dissipate assets before the court has considered the matter. If the injunction is granted *ex parte* a return date will be fixed to give the defendant an opportunity to be heard. In *1638 Ltd v Power Cycles Ltd* [2007] 3 HKC 306 the court considered it inappropriate to hear a *Mareva* application *ex parte* and adjourned the matter to the following day to give the defendant an opportunity to be heard at the initial stage.

## [29.1.63]   Setting aside ex parte Mareva injunction

*Ex parte Mareva* injunctions, like all *ex parte* orders are liable to be set aside at a subsequent *inter partes* hearing: an appeal is not necessary. As to setting aside *ex parte* orders generally, see Order 32 rule 6 and the commentary thereunder. A ground frequently relied upon for setting aside *ex parte Mareva* injunctions is failure of the applicant to meet its duty of full and frank disclosure at the *ex parte* stage. In *Leviathan Shipping Co Ltd v Sky Sailing Overseas Co Ltd* [1998] 4 HKC 347 an *ex parte Mareva* injunction was set aside on the ground that the applicant had failed to disclose, at the *ex parte* stage, the fact that a similar order had been refused in an overseas court, and the fact that that overseas court had ordered that the dispute be referred to arbitration.

An application to set aside an *ex parte Mareva* injunction is not an appeal: see the commentary under Order 32 rule 6. The application will be made to the judge who made the order complained of and not to the Court of Appeal. However, in *AIG (Asia) Direct Investment Fund Ltd & Ors v Ngai Wai Lun William* [1999] 1 HKC 415, the Court of Appeal permitted an appeal against a *Mareva* injunction to proceed where the opposing party had been given notice and had appeared at the *ex parte* stage.

## [29.1.64]   Duty of full and frank disclosure

Any party making an *ex parte* application has a duty to make full and frank disclosure, particularly of matters which the absent party would want the court to know. This duty is of particular importance on application for a *Mareva* injunction because of the drastic nature of this pre-emptive remedy.

The consequences of non-disclosure will depend upon the nature and extent of the non-disclosure. For a more detailed discussion of this topic, see the annotation under Order 32 rules 1–6. The fact of previous non-disclosure will not, however, prevent a fresh injunction being granted subsequent to the former being set aside (*Shenzhen Universal Enterprises Industry and Trade Company Supplies v Wei Bun Co Ltd* [1989] 1 HKLR 470 (CA)).

**[29.1.65]    What the applicant must show to obtain a *Mareva* injunction**

To succeed on an application for a *Mareva* injunction the applicant must establish at least the following:

*(a) Good arguable case on the merits*

The applicant must establish that there is a 'good arguable case' on the merits: *Liu Hong Fai v Wong Man Fai* CACV 56/1986 (Fuad JA, Power & Clough JJ; 20.06.1986); *Anglo-Eastern (1985) Ltd v Knutz* [1987] 3 HKC 80 (CA), both referring to *Ninemia Maritime Corp v Trave* [1983] 1 WLR 1412 (CA). A good arguable case in this context is the same thing as 'a serious question to be tried', the test established in *American Cyanamid* for other types of interlocutory injunctions: see *Kanada Tejapaibulnational v Thai Mercantile Development Finance Ltd* [1988] HKC 295, 298B (CA) where Kempster JA treated the two tests as interchangeable in the *Mareva* context.

The 'good arguable case' test carries with it the need for the applicant to show it has a pre-existing cause of action: *Kanada* (above) per Fuad VP at 303 (dissenting in result). See the commentary above on the need for a pre-existing cause of action.

When there is a dispute on the merits of the applicant's underlying claim the court will not attempt to resolve conflicts of evidence as a *Mareva* application is interlocutory: *Mandarin Resources Corp Ltd v Cheng* [1988] 1 HKLR 108.

*(b) A real risk of dissipation*

The applicant must establish that there is a real risk the defendant will dissipate assets, that is render them unavailable to satisfy a judgment: *Anglo-Eastern* (above, at 89G *et seq*); *Lai Sau-lin v World Speed Co Ltd* [1990] 2 HKLR 317 (CA). It was once thought the applicant had to show a risk the defendant would remove assets from the jurisdiction, and that dissipation within Hong Kong was not sufficient for grant of a *Mareva* injunction: *Chen v Chen Lee Hong-man* [1981] HKLR 628 (CA). Now it is well–established that dealing with assets inside Hong Kong in a manner which makes them unavailable to satisfy a judgment is sufficient: *Z Ltd v A-Z* [1982] QB 558, 571D–H (CA); *Assets Investments Pte Ltd v United Islamic Investments Foundation* [1995] 1 HKC 560, 563C–D (CA).

The burden on the plaintiff is to show 'a clear basis on which the court can conclude that there is a risk of dissipation of assets': *Grand Trade Dev't Ltd v Bonance Int'l Ltd* CACV 776/2000 (Rogers VP, Stock & Le Pichon JJA; 03.11.2000) (para 17) 'Solid evidence' is required: *Advance Finance Ltd v Pang Sze Mui Loretta* HCCL 5/1985 (Jones J; 09.07.1985) (reversed on appeal on other grounds – see [1986] HKLR 523); *Ha Sheung Ping v Lo Siu Yin* [1996] 3 HKC 144, both referring to *Ninemia* (above). In *Advance Finance* the court quoted from the first instance judgment in *Ninemia* (unreported) where 'solid evidence' was described in the following terms:

> This evidence may take a number of different forms. It may consist of direct evidence that the defendant has previously acted in a way which shows that its probity is not to be relied upon. Or the plaintiff may show what type of company the defendant is (where it is incorporated, what are its corporate structure and assets, and so on) so as to raise an inference that the company is not to be relied upon. Or, again, the plaintiff may be able to found his case on the fact that inquiries about the characteristics of the defendant have led to a blank wall. Precisely what form the evidence may take will depend upon the particular circumstances of the case.

See also *Chow Chor-leung v Rafaella Sportswear Inc* [1990] 1 HKLR 449, 451, quoting extensively from *Third Chandris Shipping Corp v Unimarine SA* [1979] 1 QB 645.

It has been suggested that in Hong Kong it may be easier for the court to infer a risk that assets may be removed from the jurisdiction: see *Intercontinental Housing Development Ltd v Queck* HCCL 1/1986 (Mortimer J; 15.01.1986) (reversed on appeal on other grounds – see [1986] HKLR 1153) where it was said:

> In Hong Kong with the cosmopolitan nature of its community, the international nature of its financial institutions, its international connections, its ease of travel and the ease with which liquid assets can be moved both in and out of the jurisdiction are matters which necessarily have to be considered. In Hong Kong it may be easier to infer from the evidence that there is a risk that assets may be removed from the jurisdiction than in places lacking some of these facilities which in every other respect are admirable.

The fact that the defendant is a foreign company is probably not enough on its own to infer a risk of dissipation: *Anglo-Eastern* (above, at 89G-H). However it is clearly a relevant factor. In *Honsaico Trading Ltd v Hong Yiah Seng Co Ltd* [1990] 1 HKLR 235 (affirmed on appeal – CACV 171/1989) the court took into account the fact the defendant was a foreign company from a jurisdiction with no provision for reciprocal enforcement of Hong Kong judgments. The appellate court noted it could take 6-9 years to enforce a Hong Kong judgment there.

Dubious behaviour will be taken into account and may be a sufficient basis to infer a real risk: *Honsaico* (above) where (at 240H HKLR) it was said:

> . . . the defendant has exhibited an unacceptably low standard of commercial morality in its dealings with the plaintiff; and this drives me to conclude that there is a danger that if the defendant thought it was in its best interests to do so, it would not shrink from attempting to defeat the interests of the plaintiff under any judgment . . .

*Honsaico* was followed in this regard in *Standard Chartered Securities Ltd v Lai Arthur & Ors* [1993] 1 HKC 375, 394A, and again in *Top One Int'l (China) Property Group Co Ltd & Anor v Top One Property Group Ltd & Ors* HCA 1244/2009 (Poon J; 16.10.2009) (para 63). See also *Nienaber v Bravery Co Ltd* HCA 2942/1989 (Liu J; 05.09.1989) (para 11) where 'steps and measures taken in haste by the defendant in closing down without the slightest warning' were held to be 'indicative' of a risk of dissipation of assets.

Conversely, evidence 'which might tend to support a claim by the defendants that they honestly believed they were entitled to do what they had done would reduce the likelihood of fraud and, consequently, tend to destroy the basis for an inference that there was a real risk of disposal of property...': *Scales & Anor v Wong William & Anor* [1983] 2 HKC 119, 204H-I (CA).

*(c) Just or convenient*

The court must be satisfied that it is 'just or convenient' to grant the injunction. This requirement is found in s 21L(1) of the High Court Ordinance and applies to all injunctions. The requirement is misstated as 'just *and* convenient' in *Advance Finance* (above) and *Liu Hong Fai* (above).

In *Macy's Candies Ltd v Chan Man Hong* [1996] 2 HKC 602 a *Mareva* injunction was discharged on this ground. The court said (at 613F-G) that the injunction was neither just nor convenient *inter alia* because it would deprive the defendant of the opportunity to earn a living and the plaintiff already had substantial security for its claim.

*(d) Defendant has assets*

The applicant must satisfy the court that the defendant has assets. Those assets may be in or outside of Hong Kong. See the discussion elsewhere in this commentary on extraterritorial or 'worldwide' *Mareva* injunctions.

The court will not grant a *Mareva* injunction to cover assets in which the defendant has no equity or beneficial interest. In *Wong King Lun v Hong Kiao Go* DCCJ 67/2005 (Judge CB Chan; 17.08.2005) a *Mareva* injunction was set aside on the ground the defendant's only known asset was landed property in negative equity so that the injunction would serve no purpose. In *Prekookeanska Plovidba v LNT Lines SrL* [1988] 3 All ER 897 it was held that a *Mareva* should not be granted against funds in a solicitor's client account where the solicitor had a lien over the funds for unpaid costs.

Where the defendant is plainly insolvent, the appropriate remedy is winding-up rather than a *Mareva* injunction: *Wu Choi Yau v Beelee Industries Ltd* HCA 5811/1990 (Godfrey J; 28.01.1991).

**[29.1.66]     Time at which injunction takes effect**

A *Mareva* injunction, like all judgments and orders of the court, takes effect from the moment it is pronounced: see Order 42 rule 3 and the commentary thereunder. In practice, however, *Mareva* injunctions are granted *ex parte* in private, which means no one can be expected to comply until notice of the order is given or it is served. The means of enforcement is contempt proceedings, but a person can hardly be guilty of contempt of an order of which he is ignorant.

**[29.1.67]     *Mareva* injunction in dispute subject to arbitration**

Section 2GC(1)(c) of the Arbitration Ordinance (Cap 341) empowers the court to grant interim injunctions in relation to arbitration proceedings. Such an injunction may be of the *Mareva* type and *Mareva* principles will apply: *Hsin Chong Construction (Asia) Ltd v Henable Ltd* [2005] 3 HKC 27. In *Interbulk (HK) Ltd v Safe Rich Industries Ltd* [1992] 2 HKLR 185 the court was of the view (under the previous legislation) that such an injunction may not be granted in Hong Kong in relation to an arbitration to be conducted in another jurisdiction.

**[29.1.68]     *Mareva* injunctions affecting banks**

Injunctions which interfere with the usual obligations of a bank to repay depositors and to honour instruments such as guarantees and letters of credit will not be granted lightly. Commercial confidence in the banking system will be taken into account. See *Prime Deal (HK) Enterprises Ltd v HSBC* [2006] 3 HKC 74 (para 14) and the authorities cited therein, and see *Polly Peck Int'l plc v Nadir* [1992] 4 All ER 769;

[1992] 2 Lloyd's Rep 238 (CA).

The receipt by a bank of notice of a *Mareva* injunction affecting a customer's account may override the customer's instructions regarding that account and make it unlawful for the bank to honour the customer's cheques.

**[29.1.69]    Mareva injunction to restrain disbursement of sale price– 'poisoned pill' completion**

In *Gainluxe Investment Ltd v Superstand Dev't Ltd* [1994] 3 HKC 641 a *Mareva* injunction in aid of a 'poisoned pill' completion was set aside. On such a completion the purchaser of property tenders the purchase price to the vendor's solicitors in accordance with the sale and purchase agreement, and at the same time serves a *Mareva* injunction preventing the solicitors from disbursing the funds to the vendor. In *Gainluxe* the court noted the different opinions expressed in the English Court of Appeal in *Ninemia Maritime Corp v Trave* [1983] 1 WLR 1412 and *Zucker v Tyndal Holdings plc* [1992] 1 WLR 1127, and whilst not prepared to lay down a general rule that such injunctions are not allowed, set aside the injunction in the circumstances of the particular case.

**[29.1.70]    Effect of Mareva injunction on third parties**

A *Mareva* injunction is effective not just against the party whose assets are frozen, but against anyone with knowledge of the order. In *Z Ltd v A-Z* [1982] QB 558, 572 Lord Denning MR said:

> Every person who has knowledge of [the order] must do what he reasonably can to preserve the asset. He must not assist in any way in the disposal of it. Otherwise he is guilty of a contempt of court.

However, it is usual to limit a world-wide *Mareva* injunction so as to apply to third parties outside Hong Kong only in restricted circumstances. See the form of world-wide *Mareva* injunction set out in practice direction 11.2 (below). Briefly, it is there provided that the order does not affect any person outside Hong Kong until it is declared enforceable or is enforced by a court in another jurisdiction, unless the person is:

(a)    a person to whom the order is addressed (or an agent, officer or attorney of such person) or

(b)    a person subject to the jurisdiction of the Hong Kong court who has been served at a place of residence or business in Hong Kong and is in a position to prevent breach of the order outside Hong Kong.

**[29.1.71]    Notification of third parties**

Where assets owned by a party against whom a *Mareva* injunction is granted are held by a third party, the third party should be notified of the terms of the injunction. For example, where the injuncted party has money on deposit in a bank, the bank should be informed. The standard undertakings set out in the schedule to form of order in practice direction 11.2 provide that anyone notified of the order should be provided with a copy. This is the most effective way of ensuring the bank has knowledge of the order and is thus bound to comply with it. It also ensures that the bank or other third party is answerable to the court in case of breach – see below. In the absence of an express direction of the court, formal service on third parties is not required: *Guinness Peat Aviation (Belgium) NV v Hispania Lineas Aereas SA* [1992] 1 Lloyd's Rep 190, 196.

On an application for a *Mareva* injunction the court should be informed of the third parties who may be affected. This is part and parcel of the duty of full and frank disclosure.

### [29.1.72]   Terms of Mareva injunction in relation to third party

A bank or other third party notified or served with a *Mareva* injunction is entitled to know with precision exactly what it is prohibited from doing, and should be given as much information as possible to enable it to comply. For example the amount to which the injunction is effective, and the injuncted party's account details such as account number and branch of account should be expressly set out so far as possible.

The standard form of *Mareva* injunction set out in practice direction 11.2 (see below) contains information directed to third parties such as banks concerning their obligations, the consequences of disobedience and the right to apply to vary the order.

In England it is recognised that a *Mareva* injunction in respect of assets outside the jurisdiction may be modified so as to provide that a third party is not prevented from complying with its obligations under the law of the jurisdiction where the assets are held: *Bank of China v NBM LLC* [2001] 4 All ER 954 (CA). Such a provision is sometimes referred to as a '*Baltic* proviso', after *Baltic Shipping Co v Translink Shipping Ltd & Anor* [1995] 1 Lloyds Rep 673. The jurisdiction to insert a *Baltic* proviso into a *Mareva* injunction was recognised in Hong Kong (*obiter*) in *Illustrious Assets Ltd v Lu Chung Chun & Ors* HCA 2426/2007 (Deputy Judge Carlson; 27.03.2008).

### [29.1.73]   Undertaking to indemnify third party served with *Mareva* injunction

A third party such as a bank notified of a *Mareva* injunction is regarded as an 'innocent' party in that the alleged wrongdoer in the litigation is not itself but its customer. As a result it is well established that the court may require the plaintiff to provide an indemnity to the third party for the costs and expenses of compliance with a *Mareva* injunction, and to compensate for lost income. See *Clipper Maritime Co Ltd ('The Marie Leonhardt')* [1981] 1 WLR 1262; [1981] 3 All ER 664. The standard form undertakings which are annexed to the form of order prescribed by practice direction 11.2 include an undertaking to compensate a third party and to fortify this obligation by bank guarantee.

### [29.1.74]   Consequence of breach by third party served with *Mareva* injunction

A third party notified of a *Mareva* injunction which breaches its obligations thereunder, acts in disobedience thereof or assists its customer to do so, is answerable to the court in the law of contempt. Specific warning to that effect is included in the standard form of order set out in practice direction 11.2. However, a third party will only be liable for contempt if it is proved beyond reasonable doubt that 'there was an intention on his part to interfere with or impede the administration of justice': *AG v Punch Ltd* [2003] 1 AC 1046, cited with approval in relation to a *Mareva* injunction served on a bank in *Customs & Excise Commissioners v Barclays Bank plc* [2006] 3 WLR 1 (HL).

In the interesting case of *Pertamina Energy Trading Ltd v Karaha Bodas Co LLC & Ors* [2007] SGCA 10 (01.03.2007) the Singapore Court of Appeal found a Hong Kong solicitor (but not the solicitor's firm) guilty of contempt of court for using information obtained under a Singapore *Mareva* injunction to obtain a garnishee order in the Hong Kong court.

Service of the *Mareva* injunction or knowledge by some other means does not of itself give rise to a duty of care rendering a third party liable in damages for breach. See the *Barclays Bank* case (above) where a bank was found not liable for failing to take reasonable care to ensure that money was not paid out of an account frozen by a *Mareva* injunction.

### [29.1.75]   Amount to be covered by Mareva injunction

The court has power to grant a *Mareva* injunction in an unlimited amount but should only do so in 'wholly exceptional circumstances': *Ng Chun Fai Stephen v Tamco Electrical & Electronics (HK) Ltd* [1994] 1 HKLR 289, 293 (CA). The rationale 'is to avoid unnecessary interference with the defendant's freedom to use his own assets, there being no justification for freezing assets over and above the ceiling established by the amount of the plaintiff's claim': *Macy's Candies Ltd v Chan Man Hong & Ors* [1997] 2 HKC 602, 608C-D. The appropriate amount may be lower where the defendant has a need for living, business or legal expenses. In *Chow Chor Leung t/a Rayontex Trading Co v Rafaella Sportswear Inc & Anor* [1990] 1 HKLR 449 an 'all-assets' injunction was set aside and replaced with one with a monetary limit so as not to prevent the defendant from conducting business in the ordinary way. The court cited *Avant Petroleum v Gatoil Overseas* [1986] 2 Lloyd's Rep 236, 243 where it was held that *Mareva* injunctions should be tailored to the facts of the case.

The applicant should put forward evidence to demonstrate the loss or damage it claims in the proceedings and make good its claim for a *Mareva* injunction to a particular amount. In *Bright Rims Manufacturing Sdn Bhd v Victor Taichung Machinery Works Co Ltd* [2008] 4 MLJ 380 the Malaysian Court of Appeal upheld the refusal of a *Mareva* injunction partly on the ground there was no evidence to support the claim for substantial special damages. However, the fact that the applicant is unable to quantify its claim may not preclude the grant of a *Mareva* injunction. See *Sunchase Int'l Group (China) Ltd v Chik Wai Wan Stephen* [1999] 1 HKC 671, 676H-I (CA) where the applicant had 'established a very high probability at least of substantial loss or damage', notwithstanding being unable to 'quantify the precise amount'.

There is a duty upon the plaintiff and his legal advisers to consider very carefully what should be the extent of the injunction (*Z Ltd v A-Z* [1982] QB 558, applied in *Pappadis v Chan Shing Sheung Barry* [1989] 2 HKLR 511 (CA)).

### [29.1.76]   Variation of amount covered by Mareva injunction – release of funds to meet expenses

Anyone affected by a *Mareva* injunction may apply at any time for variation (or discharge) of the injunction. Notice of the right to do so is expressly given in the forms of *Mareva* injunction prescribed by practice direction 11.2 (see below).

Applications to vary *Mareva* injunctions are commonly made by defendants so as to permit the release of funds to meet living expenses, legal costs, and debts. Variation to meet such expenses is possible where the funds available are not enough to cover the amount of the claim against the defendant, since a *Mareva* injunction does not give the plaintiff an interest in or a charge over the defendant's assets. See *Cheung Sai Lun v Lau Tai Chin Francis & Anor* HCCW 677/2004 (Barma J; 19.09.2007) (the 1st of two decisions of that date) (paras 7-9) where it was said that where it is sought to release funds to meet 'proper' or 'normal' expenses, there is:

> no dissipation of assets or injustice to the plaintiff or intending plaintiff as the assets are being used in the ordinary course for the normal expenses of the defendant concerned. They are not being used or transferred or expended with the objective of defeating the potential claim or actual judgment of the plaintiff.

The court went on to say that release of funds to meet living expenses and reasonable legal costs is 'not in any way contradictory of the purpose' of a *Mareva* injunction.

The onus is on the defendant to satisfy the court that the release of funds would not conflict with the policy underlying the *Mareva* injunction: *Kanematsu-Gosho v Lee Boon Chean* [1986] HKLR 59, quoting with approval *A v C (No 2)* [1981] 1 QB 961. The defendant must put forward evidence to show that there are no other assets which could be used to meet the particular expense: *M Corp v B Inc & Anor* [1986] HKLR 657. Release of funds should not be permitted where there are other assets which could be used to meet the expenditure: *Assets Investments Pte Ltd v United Islamic Investments Foundation & Ors* [1995] 1 HKC 560, 563C-G. In this connection 'other assets' is not limited to funds over which the defendant has a legal right – release may be refused if the defendant could obtain money some other way: *Atlas Maritime Co SA v Avalon Maritime Ltd (No 3)* [1991] TLR 305 (CA). In *Liu Xian Feng Sam & Anor v Liu Bo & Ors* [2006] 4 HKLRD 33 (CA) release to meet legal expenses was refused where the defendant had entered into a credit arrangement with solicitors.

Funds may be released from a *Mareva* injunction to meet trade debts when they fall due: *M Corp v B Inc* (above, at 658H-I), referring to *The Angel Bell* [1981] 1 QB 65. In *Atlas Maritime Co SA v Avalon Maritime Ltd (The Coral Rose) (No 1)* [1991] 4 All ER 769 (CA) release was refused on the ground the debt had not been incurred in the ordinary course of business where it was discovered that the 'creditor' was in fact the parent company of the party subject to the injunction.

Where a *Mareva* injunction has been granted in aid of a proprietary claim to assets in the defendant's name the court will take a stricter approach to release of funds: see *Liu Xian Feng Sam* (above) applying *Ostrich Farming Corp Ltd v Ketchell* [1997] EWCA Civ 2953 (10.12.1997). See also *Sime Winner Holdings Ltd & Anor v Tan Wan Hong & Anor* HCA 793/2005 (Saunders J; 12.02.2009). In *Northwest Airlines Inc v Chen & Ors* [1989] 1 HKLR 382 release of funds was refused where the plaintiffs had established an arguable case that they were trust moneys that belonged to them.

**[29.1.77]     Exception for payments in ordinary course of business**

The standard form of *Mareva* injunction prescribed by practice direction 11.2 (below) contains an optional provision that the party injuncted shall not be prevented from dealing with its assets in the ordinary and proper course of business. This term traces back to decisions of the UK courts in the early years after the *Mareva* jurisdiction was recognised such as *Iraqi Ministry of Defence v Arcepey Shipping Co SA* [1981] QB 65, 71. In *Polly Peck Int'l plc v Nadir (No 2)* [1992] 4 All ER 769, 785h-j Lord Donaldson MR said:

> … no defendant, whether a natural or juridical person, can be enjoined in terms which will prevent him from carrying on his business in the ordinary way or from meeting his debts or other obligations as they come due prior to judgment being given in the action.

In *Kanematsu-Gosho (HK) Ltd & Anor v Lee Boon Chean* [1986] HKLR 59, 64F-G it was said that in granting a *Mareva* injunction 'the court is not in the least bit concerned with and should not stop the payment of *bona fide* debts or the conduct of a *bona fide* business'.

In practice the general provision in the standard form may not be sufficient, as a bank which has notice of the injunction will not always be in a position to be sure whether a payment is in the ordinary course of the defendant's business. In *Indian Corridor Sdn Bhd & Anor v China Idea Dev't Ltd & Ors* HCA 1/2008 (Deputy Judge Carlson; 25.01.2008) the court assisted by fixing an amount which could be paid, and directing that the plaintiff be provided with details of payments made on a fortnightly basis.

**[29.1.78]    Duration of ex parte injunction**

An *ex parte Mareva* injunction should be granted for a few days until the defendant can be served and the bank or other third party can be given notice. Thereafter an *inter partes* hearing will be held as to whether the *Mareva* injunction ought to be continued pending final resolution of the litigation: see the form of order prescribed by practice direction reproduced below, specifically that part of the prescribed order under the heading '*Duration of this order*'.

**[29.1.79]    Setting aside Mareva injunction on ground of delay**

A *Mareva* injunction may be set aside if there is subsequent delay in proceeding to trial. See the commentary some paragraphs above concerning the court's inherent jurisdiction to discharge any interlocutory injunction.Where a *Mareva* is in place the duty on the plaintiff to proceed diligently is stricter, since such an injunction is particularly onerous, infringing the defendant's liberty pending trial. See *Sanwa Dev't Ltd v Chan Kar Keung* [1999] 1 HKC 847 and *Yung Yuen Ling Alice v Wong Ming Kan Michael* HCA 231/2004 (Wright J; 11.04.2007) both referring to *Newsgroup Newspapers Ltd v Mirror Group Newspapers (1986) Ltd* [1991] FSR 487.

**[29.1.80]    Uusuccessful ex parte application - whether other party to be notified**

When an *ex parte* application for a *Mareva* injunction is dismissed, it is not the practice to require the applicant to inform the party against which it had sought the injunction. See *Deiulemar Shipping SpA & Anor v Transfield ER Futures Ltd* [2011] 1 HKLRD 75 (CA) (para 82).

**[29.1.81]    Order for disclosure or protection of assets ancillary to Mareva injunction**

It is well established that to make a *Mareva* injunction effective, 'the court has a discretion to order the defendant to make a statement of his assets and to give discovery of documents for the purpose of ascertaining the existence, nature and location of assets and in the case of a proprietary claim, the whereabouts of the missing trust funds': *CTO (HK) Ltd v Li Man Chiu & Ors* [2002] 2 HKLRD 875 (Poon J; 09.07.2002) referring to *A v C* [1981] 1 QB 956. The primary purpose of such an order is 'to preserve the assets or property which might otherwise be dissipated notwithstanding the injunction': *CTO* (above). Other Hong Kong cases considering this jurisdiction include *American Express Int'l Banking Corp v Yu* [1983] HKLR 148 and *Advance Finance Ltd v Pang Sze Mui Loretta* HCCL 55/1985 (Jones J; 09.07.1985) (appeal allowed at [1986] HKLR 523).

It has been suggested that discovery should not normally be ordered at the *ex parte* stage. Rather, if a *Mareva* injunction is granted *ex parte*, the question of discovery should be considered at the subsequent *inter partes* hearing. See *Nicolas Pappadis & Anor v Chan Ching Sheung, Barry* [1989] 2 HKLR 511, 517C-D (CA) where it was said:

> If a court is minded to order discovery, the simple and proper remedy is to grant the restrictive *Mareva* for a short return date, then the application for discovery can be considered. The great advantage of the short return date is that the matter is dealt with *inter partes...*

Disclosure of assets under a *Mareva* injunction will normally be by affidavit, as in *Pheby v Paier & Ors* [2003] 2 HKC 328.

In addition to its power to order discovery, the court has jurisdiction to make the following other types of order to assist in gathering information in relation to a *Mareva* injunction:

(1)    *Inspection of bank records* – The court may order inspection of bank records under section 21 of the Evidence Ordinance (Cap 8) (as to which see the commentary under Order 24 rule 1) ancillary to a *Mareva* injunction. See *Wharf Ltd & Ors v Lau Yuen How & Ors (No 2)* [2009] 1 HKC 479 and the authorities cited therein. In such cases the plaintiff may be required to give an undertaking to use the information obtained only for the purpose of the proceedings: *Bankers Trust Co v Shapira* [1980] 1 WLR 1274.

(2)    *Anton Piller order* - In *Refco Inc v Troika Investment Ltd* [1988] HKLR 623 it was held that the court may grant an *Anton Piller* order to preserve documentary evidence as to assets covered by a *Mareva* injunction. At 627B-C Sears J said:

> In my judgment an *Anton Piller* can be utilized to ensure that the *Mareva* injunction is effective over the assets it ought to cover, that is assets which are or should be the subject of the *Mareva* injunction.

(3)    *Tracing order* – In *Chow Wai Lan v Cheung Siu Fong & Ors* HCA 5218/1989 (Liu J; 07.10.1989) and again in *Hang Seng Bank Ltd v Lau Ching Che & Ors* [2008] 1 HKC 385 the court granted tracing orders in aid of *Mareva* injunctions. In the first of those cases, the court held that the burden on the applicant for such an order is the same as for a *Mareva* injunction, rejecting an argument that the heavier burden applicable to an *Anton Piller* application was required.

(4)    *Interrogatories* – The court has power to order interrogatories in support of a *Mareva* injunction: *AJ Bekhor & Co Ltd v Bilton* [1981] QB 923. In *Kanematsu-Gosho (HK) Ltd & Anor v Lee Boon Chean & Ors* [1986] HKLR 59, 66B the court ordered interrogatories where cross-examination of a party would be inconvenient because of his absence from the jurisdiction. In *United Technology Products Co Ltd v Atari Int'l (HK) Ltd* [1985] 1 HKC 33, 38C-D an application for leave to administer interrogatories in support of a *Mareva* injunction was refused where the questions sought to be put did not relate to removal or dissipation of assets.

The court will not order disclosure of assets or information beyond the scope of what is claimed in the proceedings: *RACP Pharmaceutical Holdings Ltd v Li Xiaobo* CACV 139/2007 (Rogers VP & Le Pichon JA; 19.09.2007).

Failure to comply with an asset discovery order ancillary to a *Mareva* injunction is punishable as a contempt of court. In addition the court may use its power under Order 24 rule 16 to dismiss an action or strike out the defence of a defaulting party. See *Jademan (Holdings) Ltd & Ors v Tony Wong Chun Loong* HCCL 15/1990 (Jones J; 17.06.1992); [1992] HKLY 736 where the defaulting party's defence was struck out, referring to *Re Jokai Tea Holdings Ltd* [1992] 1 WLR 1196 and *Grand Metropolitan Nominee (No 2) Co Ltd v Evans* [1992] 1 WLR 1191.

### [29.1.82]    Cross-examination on assets disclosure affidavit

The court may order the cross-examination of a party on an assets disclosure affidavit made pursuant to a *Mareva* injunction. The power so to order is found in Order 38 rule 2(3). In the former English Rules of the Supreme Court, Order 29 rule 1A, which was not adopted in Hong Kong, provided for such cross-examination to be conducted before a master or examiner.

In *Yau Chiu Wah v Gold Chief Investment Ltd & Anor* [2002] 1 HKC 383 Ma J held (at 389C–D) that there is 'undoubtedly jurisdiction in the court to order cross-examination of a deponent on any affidavit or affirmation made by him in compliance for an order for discovery under a *Mareva* injunction'. The learned judge cited *AJ Bekhor & Co Ltd v Bilton* [1981] QB 923, 944 and *House of Spring Gardens Ltd v Waite* [1985] FSR 173, 176 and went on to state that it was a matter of discretion. The learned judge usefully set down the principles on which the discretion will be exercised as follows (at 389E–390H):

(1)   The object of an order for cross-examination is to enable a *Mareva* injunction to be made more effective: cf *Bekhor v Bilton*. This after all is the justification for an order for discovery as an ancillary order to a *Mareva* injunction in the first place. It has to be remembered that the purpose of such cross-examination is to obtain more information as to a defendant's assets and as to the whereabouts of such assets in circumstances where the court has already formed the view that there exists a risk of dissipation. The purpose is not to enable information to be gathered so as to impugn the defendant's credit or to investigate whether there has been a breach of the *Mareva* injunction and thereby obtaining material for possible contempt proceedings: see *Bayer v Winter (No 2)* [1986] 1 WLR 540.

(2)   An order for cross-examination is far from being automatic. On the contrary, such orders, if made pre-judgment, are rare. The court is most likely to make such an order post-judgment than pre-judgment. This is because, pre-judgment, there is no certainty that at the end of the day the plaintiff will win and if the claim fails, then the time (and expense) involved in a cross-examination exercise would have been wasted, not to mention the injustice to a defendant of being subject to what is often likely to be hostile cross-examination. I would also observe here that the cross-examination of a deponent is not simply an examination on an appointed date. It is possible if not probable that further discovery in preparation for the hearing may be required. The production of accounts in the case of a company is perhaps an example of this. Pre-judgment, therefore, the making of such an order runs the risk of producing a trial within a trial resulting in the court and the parties being distracted at least to a certain degree from what is the real purpose of an action, namely, the proper adjudication of the dispute between the parties. It has been commented that the granting of an order for cross-examination pre-judgment is exceptional and a strong step often difficult to justify: see *Mareva Injunctions and Anton Piller Relief* by Steven Gee QC (4th Ed) at p 354. See also in this context: *Wendy Wenta Seng Yuen v Philip Pak-Yiu Yuen* [1984] HKLR 431 at

436E–H per Fuad JA.

(3)     I would also add here that it is not permissible for a cross-examination to be conducted for the purpose of eliciting material to be used at trial: see *CBS United Kingdom Ltd v Perry* [1985] FSR 421 at 425–426. Where the cross-examination will deal with the same issues as those at trial, exceptional circumstances will have to be shown. In *Grand Empire Holdings Ltd v Marco International (HK) Ltd* (HCA 14891/1999, 7 December 1999, Burrell J, unreported), it was said at p 4:

> In my judgment, if the cross-examination is to be on the same issues as those which form the basis of the dispute between the parties, an order under O 38 r 2, should rarely, if ever, be made. In this case, there are no exceptional circumstances which would merit such an order.

(4)     True that the court therefore has to undertake a balancing exercise, but ultimately the key to whether an order should be made lies in my view on the justice of the situation facing the court. I gratefully adopt the simple and practical formulation of the discretion by Burrell J in *Grand Empire Holdings Ltd v Marco International (HK) Ltd,* where at p 2, the learned judge said:

> The court has an unfettered discretion to order cross-examination and that discretion should be exercised in favour of the parties seeking it when the court is satisfied that it is necessary in the interests of justice. In other words, if there is a real risk that justice would not be done if cross-examination is not allowed, then leave should be granted.

(5)     Put simply, the question for the court is this: Would the making of an order result in justice being achieved; conversely if an order were not made, would there be injustice?

It may be appropriate in some cases, before ordering cross-examination on an affidavit in the *Mareva* context, first to give the deponent an opportunity to file a further affidavit to explain the situation. In *Yau Chiu Wah v Gold Chief Investment Ltd & Anor* [2002] 1 HKC 383, 393G–H Ma J considered this possibility, but refused it, citing *House of Spring Gardens Ltd v Waite* [1985] FSR 173 where Cumming-Bruce LJ said:

> It may be said that there are situations in which the circumstances demonstrate that it is more sensible, if only for reasons of speed and urgency, not to order further affidavits in order to fill the vacuum alleged to exist in the affidavits filed pursuant to the original order, but to proceed at once to order that the defendants attend for cross-examination upon their affidavits. The purpose of the cross-examination would be to elicit with greater particularity the extent and the whereabouts of the defendants' assets.

## [29.1.83]     Privilege and disclosure of assets

An order for disclosure of assets is subject to the common law rules as to privilege. A party may refuse to disclose assets by making a valid claim to privilege. For cases concerning use of the privilege against self-incrimination to justify refusal to make full disclosure under a *Mareva* injunction, see *Petroliam Nasional Bhd v George Tan Soon Gin* [1989] 2 HKLR 109 (CA); *AT&T Istel Ltd & Anor v Tully & Ors* [1992] 2 All ER 28 (CA); and *Pheby v Paier & Ors* [2003] 2 HKC 328.

The court may order a party to make disclosure despite a claim to privilege against self-incrimination, provided that adequate safeguards are put in place to ensure that the party is not in fact prosecuted: *Manufacturer's Life Insurance Co of Canada v Harvest Hero Int'l Ltd & Ors* [2002] 1 HKLRD 828 (para 34). In *Hui Chi*

*Ming v Koon Wing Yee & Ors* HCA 1479/2009 (Poon J; 25.09.2009) the court directed that the Department of Justice be informed of the application in order that its view could be made known.

**[29.1.84]    Restriction on use of information disclosed pursuant to Mareva injunction**

As with the case with regard to information obtained by normal means of discovery (see the commentary under Order 24 rule 14A), there is an implied undertaking to the court on grant of a *Mareva* injunction that information obtained will not be used for a collateral purpose. Breach is a contempt of court. See the judgment of the Singapore Court of Appeal in *Pertamina Energy Trading Ltd v Karaha Bodas Co LLC & Ors* [2007] SGCA 10 (01.03.2007), referring to several UK authorities, in particular *Prudential Assurance Co Ltd v Fountain Page Ltd* [1991] 1 WLR 756, 764-5.

**[29.1.85]    Solicitor's duty in relation to discovery under Mareva injunction**

A solicitor has important duties to the court in respect of disclosure by the client under a *Mareva* injunction. In *Yau Chiu Wah v Gold Chief Investment Ltd & Anor (No 2)* [2003] 3 HKC 91, Ma JA considered these duties at 102G-I. The learned judge said:

> A solicitor's duty in relation to discovery is to ensure that his client properly complies with his obligations . . . The duty is not limited merely to preventing the client filing an affidavit which, to his knowledge, is false. The solicitor must actually explain to his client the extent of his obligations in relation to discovery and take reasonable steps to ensure that this obligation is fulfilled.

In this regard Ma JA cited *Myers v Elman* [1940] AC 282, 304 and *Rockwell Machine Tool Co Ltd v EP Barrus (Concessionaires) Ltd* [1968] 1 WLR 693, 694.

**[29.1.86]    Dispute as to ownership**

Where there is a question as to the ownership of assets, such as where they appear on their face to belong to a third party, the court will not include them within the scope of a *Mareva* injunction without evidence that in truth they belong to the defendant. In such cases the court may direct the issue of ownership to be tried as a separate issue. See *Lee Boon Chean v Alfred Kao & Ors* HCA 8146/1984 (Hunter J; 22.05.1985) and *Standard Chartered Securities Ltd v Lai Arthur & Ors* [1993] 1 HKC 375, 390D-I, both applying *SCF Finance Co Ltd v Masri* [1985] 1 WLR 876.

**[29.1.87]    The evolution of the 'worldwide' Mareva injunction**

As mentioned above, the court may grant a *Mareva* injunction against assets inside as well as outside Hong Kong. Such an injunction is often referred to as a 'worldwide' *Mareva*.

The decisions in which the worldwide *Mareva* injunction evolved show concern that the court should not arrogate to itself an extraterritorial power to interfere in matters which on grounds of comity should be left to the courts of other jurisdictions. That concern remains relevant and finds expression in aspects of the form of worldwide *Mareva* injunction set out in practice direction 11.2 (see below). Hence a brief consideration of the development of the worldwide *Mareva* may be instructive.

In *Ka Wah Int'l Merchant Finance Ltd v Asean Resources Ltd* HCA 386/1987

(Sears J; 05.03.1987) the court recognised a power to grant a worldwide *Mareva* injunction against a person within Hong Kong in restricted circumstances. Referring to the decision in *Ashtiani v Kashi* [1986] 3 WLR 647 (CA) the Hong Kong court held that the power to grant a *Mareva* covering assets in other jurisdictions should be restricted to cases where:

(1)    the assets have been deliberately removed from Hong Kong to frustrate control by the court;

(2)    assets have been disguised as 'foreign' when in reality they are 'national';

(3)    the document of title to extraterritorial assets is in Hong Kong;

(4)    the extraterritorial assets are held by a Hong Kong company and can be specifically identified.

In *Cheung Lily v Standard Chartered Bank HK Trustee Ltd* [1988] 1 HKLR 613 (CA) *Ashtiani* was again referred to and the court limited a *Mareva* injunction to assets in Hong Kong saying (at 618F-G) that such an injunction 'should not purport to inhibit dealings with assets outside the jurisdiction'.

In 1989 the position changed radically with a quartet of decisions of the English Court of Appeal:

(1)    In *Babanaft Int'l Co SA v Bassatne* [1989] 1 All ER 433 (CA) it was held that although the court should not claim an exorbitant extraterritorial jurisdiction of an *in rem* nature, a *Mareva* injunction could cover assets elsewhere if qualified by a proviso making it clear that the injunction was directed to the defendant *in personam* and did not affect the rights of third parties or seek to control their activities.

(2)    *Republic of Haiti v Duvalier* [1989] 1 All ER 456 (CA) – the proviso to a worldwide *Mareva* should protect third parties outside the jurisdiction only to the extent that the order is not enforced by the courts of the place where the assets are located.

(3)    In *Derby & Co Ltd v Weldon* [1989] 1 All ER 469 (CA) the court held it had jurisdiction to grant a worldwide *Mareva* in exceptional circumstances such as where the assets within the jurisdiction were wholly inadequate in view of the sum involved in the action, and there was a high risk of dissipation of the extra-territorial assets. Such a *Mareva* should, held the court, by undertaking or proviso protect the position of third parties.

(4)    In *Derby & Co Ltd v Weldon (Nos 3 & 4)* [1990] Ch 65 (reported at [1989] 1 All ER 1002 as *Derby & Co Ltd v Weldon (No 2)*) it was held that a worldwide *Mareva* could be granted even where the defendant had no assets within the jurisdiction. A sufficient sanction existed against the defendant in the event of disobedience in that the court could bar the defendant's right to defend. The court should protect the position of third parties outside the jurisdiction by including a proviso that, insofar as the order purported to have extraterritorial effect, no person should be affected by it or concerned with its terms until it was declared enforceable or recognised or enforced by the court of the extraterritorial jurisdiction. Even then, it should only affect such third persons to the extent they are:

(a)    persons to whom the order is addressed or an officer or agent of such persons, or

(b)    persons who are subject to the jurisdiction of the court and (i) have been given written notice of the order within the jurisdiction, and (ii) are able to prevent acts or omissions outside the jurisdiction of the court which would assist in breach.

Those qualifications are now set out in the form of worldwide *Mareva* injunction prescribed by practice direction 11.2 (see below).

In *Bank of India v BK Murjani* [1989] 2 HKLR 318 (CA) the English authorities, in particular *Derby & Co Ltd v Weldon (Nos 3 & 4)* (above) were applied in Hong Kong, with the court holding (at 320A-B) that the same principles are applicable whether the *Mareva* injunction covers assets within or without the jurisdiction. *Cheung Lily* (above) was effectively overruled.

## [29.1.88]    Restriction on proceedings and enforcement elsewhere

The forms of *Mareva* injunction stipulated by practice direction 11.2 (see below) suggest that an undertaking should be required that the plaintiff will not, without leave of the court, commence proceedings or seek to enforce the injunction in any other jurisdiction. The circumstances in which such leave will be granted were considered in Hong Kong for the first time in *RACP Pharmaceutical Holdings Ltd v Li Xiaobo* [2007] 3 HKC 1 (CFI). There the court, satisfied the defendant's assets in Hong Kong were well below the amount covered by the injunction, granted leave to enforce a worldwide *Mareva* in Canada. In doing so the Hong Kong court adopted the '*Dadourian* guidelines' as the English Court of Appeal has dubbed them. Those guidelines are set out in *Dadourian Group Int'l Inc v Simms* [2006] 3 All ER 48 (CA) (para 25) in the following terms:

> Guideline 1: The principle applying to the grant of permission to enforce a WFO ['world freezing order', as a worldwide *Mareva* is now known in England] abroad is that the grant of that permission should be just and convenient for the purpose of ensuring the effectiveness of the WFO and . . . not oppressive to the parties to the English proceedings or to third parties who may be joined to the foreign proceedings.
>
> Guideline 2: All the relevant circumstances and options need to be considered. In particular consideration should be given to granting relief on terms, for example, terms as to the extension to third parties of the undertaking to compensate for costs incurred as a result of the WFO and as to the type of proceedings that may be commenced abroad. Consideration should also be given to the proportionality of the steps proposed to be taken abroad, and in addition to the form of any order.
>
> Guideline 3: The interests of the applicant should be balanced against the interests of other parties to the proceedings and any new party likely to be joined to the foreign proceedings.
>
> Guideline 4: Permission should not normally be given in terms that would enable the applicant to obtain relief in the foreign proceedings which is superior to the relief given by the WFO.
>
> Guideline 5: The evidence in support of the application for permission should contain all the information (so far as it can reasonably be obtained in the time available) necessary to enable the judge to reach an informed decision, including evidence as to the applicable law and practice in the foreign court, evidence as to the nature of the proposed proceedings to be commenced and evidence as to the assets believed to be located in the jurisdiction of the foreign court and the names of the parties by whom such assets are held.
>
> Guideline 6: The standard of proof as to the existence of assets that are both within the

WFO and within the jurisdiction of the foreign court is a real prospect, that is the applicant must show that there is a real prospect that such assets are located within the jurisdiction of the foreign court in question.

Guideline 7: There must be evidence of a risk of dissipation of the assets in question.

Guideline 8: Normally the application should be made on notice to the respondent, but in cases of urgency, where it is just to do so, the permission may be given without notice to the party against whom relief will be sought in the foreign proceedings but that party should have the earliest practicable opportunity of having the matter reconsidered by the court at a hearing of which he is given notice.

**[29.1.89]   Mareva injunction to secure costs**
A *Mareva* injunction may be granted to secure a plaintiff's claim for costs: *Fenn Kar Bak Lily v Goh Kim Lay* [1994] 2 HKLR 228 (Woo J); [1995] 3 HKC 313, 315C-D (CA). This may be done simply by taking into account the amount of likely costs when fixing the amount to be covered by the *Mareva* injunction. Care should be exercised so as not to eradicate the protection given to defendants by Order 23 rule 1 whereby security for costs may not be ordered against them (per Woo J at 233). See also *Faith Panton Ppty Plan Ltd v Hodgetts* [1981] 2 All ER 877 (CA), cited in the *Fenn* decision at first instance.

**[29.1.90]   Draft order to be submitted when applying for Mareva**
The provisions of practice direction 11.1 concerning interlocutory injunctions generally (see above) apply to *Mareva* injunctions. This includes the obligation to submit a draft of the order sought to the court at the time of making the application.

**[29.1.91]   Form of Mareva injunction**
Practice direction 11.2 sets out the standard forms of *Mareva* injunctions (in both official languages) which the court will normally follow. It contains a form of injunction prohibiting disposal of assets in Hong Kong, as well as a form for an injunction prohibiting disposal of assets worldwide, in both official languages. The practice direction, which also deals with *Anton Piller* orders (see below), stipulates that where an order in English is likely to be served on a Chinese-speaking person who may not be proficient in English, a brief explanation in Chinese of its contents must be added.

The text of the practice direction may be viewed on the judiciary's website www.judiciary.gov.hk, or that of the Hong Kong Legal Information Institute www.hklii.org, both of which are accessible by the general public free-of-charge.

**2.     Detention, preservation etc., of subject-matter of cause or matter** (O. 29 r. 2)
   **(1)   On the application of any party to a cause or matter the Court may make an order for the detention, custody or preservation of any property which is the subject-matter of the cause or matter, or as to which any question may arise therein, or for the inspection of any such property in the possession of a party to the cause or matter.**
   **(2)   For the purpose of enabling any order under paragraph (1) to be carried out the Court may by the order authorize any person to enter upon any land or building in the possession of any party to the cause or matter.**
   **(3)   Where the right of any party to a specific fund is in dispute in a**

cause or matter, the Court may, on the application of a party to the cause or matter, order the fund to be paid into court or otherwise secured.

(4)   An order under this rule may be made on such terms, if any, as the Court thinks just.

(5)   An application for an order under this rule must be made by summons or by notice under Order 25, rule 7.

(6)   Unless the Court otherwise directs, an application by a defendant for such an order may not be made before he acknowledges service of the writ or originating summons by which the cause or matter was begun.

---

## NOTES

### [29.2.1]    Power to order preservation
Order 29 rule 2 allows a party to any legal proceedings to apply to the court for an order to preserve any property concerned in the proceedings. It appears that the power is intended for situations where property is perishable or has some intrinsic value that justifies its preservation *in specie*. In *Feng Loy-chuen v Lim Yiong-lin* [1977] HKLR 471 the court refused an application for a preservation order to restrain sale of gemstones, on the ground payment would be sufficient compensation if the plaintiff's claim were to succeed.

### [29.2.2]    Power to order inspection
Order 29 rule 2(1) empowers the court to order inspection of property. It has been suggested that there may also be a parallel, perhaps broader, inherent power to order inspection: *Re Ming John Fook* [1998] 3 HKC 712, 719C (CA).

The power under this rule applies in respect of property which is the subject-matter of the proceedings, or as to which any question may arise. The property must be in possession of a party. Possession in this context means physical or legal possession – the rule does not apply in respect of property over which a party merely has the power to obtain possession from someone else: *Simba-Toys (HK) Ltd v Fullmore Corp Ltd* HCA 1599/2008 (Deputy Judge A Chow SC; 20.02.2009) (para 19).

An inspection order under this rule is discretionary: *Laguna Properties Ltd v New Trend Investment Ltd* HCA 19128/1998 (Tang J; 13.05.2004) (para 9). In that case the court dismissed an inspection application on the ground that it was a fishing expedition, and because it was made too late in the proceedings.

*Examples* – In *The Mare del Nord* [1990] 1 Lloyd's Rep 40 the power under this rule was used to order inspection of the plans of a ship to assist in determining whether oil had leaked into non-cargo space of the vessel. In *Wong Man Tat v Chan Yuen Man & Ors* CACV 347/2007 (Cheung, Yeung & Yuen JJA; 24.04.2008) (para 34) it was suggested that the power under this rule could be used to require a flat owner to allow inspection by a neighbour seeking to ascertain the source of leaking water.

With regard to Admiralty proceedings, see also Order 75 rule 28 which empowers the court to order inspection of any ship or other property.

### [29.2.3]    Land – lis pendens
Where a party wishes to preserve a claimed interest in land pending litigation there is no

need to make an application under Order 29 rule 2. The party need only register the writ or originating summons making the claim in the land registry. The effect of such registration is that the pending claim ('*lis pendens*') will have priority over subsequently created interests in the land, meaning that such interests take subject to the *lis pendens*.

In *Wong Kum Chi v Lee Tit Ying* [2002] 2 HKC 230 an application was made to the District Court to vacate registration of a *lis pendens*. It was held that the application was within the exclusive jurisdiction of the Court of First Instance and it was transferred accordingly.

**[29.2.4]     Power to authorise entry on land or building**
Order 29 rule 2(2) empowers the court to authorise any person to enter upon any land or building in possession of a party for the purpose of carrying out an order under the rule for detention, custody or preservation of property. In *First Majestic Silver Corp v Davila* [2010] BCSC 279 (CanLII) (04.03.2010) the British Columbia court dismissed an application for such an order which it considered to be too broad. The order sought was objectionable in that it 'amounts to allowing the plaintiffs to freely rove over the defendants' property as virtual owners' (para 17) and would permit employees of the plaintiff to attend along with an independent expert (para 18).

**[29.2.5]     Rule 2(3) – payment into court of specified fund in dispute**
The court has power to order a 'specific fund' in dispute in a case to be paid into court or otherwise secured: rule 2(3). The power is discretionary: *Questnet Ltd v Rinck* HCA 1475/2006 (Deputy Judge Saunders; 16.08.2006) (para 9).

The 'specific fund' must be one to which a proprietary right is claimed. See *Wenden Eng'g Service Co Ltd v Technic Construction Co Ltd & Anor* HCCT 120/1997 (Burrell J; 14.06.2001) (para 13) where an order was refused in respect of money held in an active bank account, to which the plaintiff conceded it did not have a proprietary claim.

The rule stipulates that the fund must be in dispute in the proceedings. In *City Famous Ltd v Profile Ppty Ltd* HCA 7926/1998 (Cheung J 28.01.1999) (para 22) the court held that an application under the provision was misconceived where there was not in fact a dispute over ownership of a sum of money and the applicant was merely trying to obtain security for a judgment which had not yet been obtained. In *Lai Wai Pang v Kwok Li Shuk Han* HCAP13/2000 (Deputy Judge A Cheung; 16.05.2003) (para 6) the court (without coming to a firm conclusion) expressed the view that an order could not be made where the parties were agreed on ownership the fund, or where the dispute as to the fund was not a matter raised in the particular proceedings.

In *Lai Wai Pang* (above) (para 9) it was held the applicant should show good reason to make an order under rule 2(3), such as a risk of dissipation of assets.

An example of a case in which this power was exercised is *To Hoi Yip & Ors v Lai Siu Wai Louis & Ors* HCA 1607/2004 (Deputy Judge L Chan; 11.08.2005) where the court ordered payment into court of past and future income from letting a plot of land in dispute.

**3.     Power to order samples to be taken, etc.** (O. 29 r. 3)
**(1)     Where it considers it necessary or expedient for the purpose of obtaining full information or evidence in any cause or matter, the Court may, on the application of a party to the cause or matter, and on such terms, if any,**

as it thinks just, by order authorize or require any sample to be taken of any property which is the subject-matter of the cause or matter or as to which any question may arise therein, any observation to be made on such property or any experiment to be tried on or with such property.

(2)    For the purpose of enabling any order under paragraph (1) to be carried out the Court may by the order authorize any person to enter upon any land or building in the possession of any party to the cause or matter.

(3)    Rule 2(5) and (6) shall apply in relation to an application for an order under this rule as they apply in relation to an application for an order under that rule.

---

## NOTES

### [29.3.1]    Jurisdiction of master
The registrar and masters have jurisdiction to make orders under Order 29 rules 2, 3 and 4. This is clear from the grant, by the rules, of power to 'the Court', which term is defined in Order 1 to include the registrar and masters. See also *The Mare del Nord* [1990] 1 Lloyd's Rep 40 rejecting an argument that because an order under these rules is an injunction, only a judge should have jurisdiction.

### [29.3.2]    Cross-reference
See also Order 75 rule 28 which preserves the court's powers under Order 29 rules 2 and 3 in connection with inspection orders in the Admiralty jurisdiction.

### [29.3.3]    Rule 3 – order for samples to be taken
Order 29 rule 3 gives the court power to order that a sample be taken of any property which is the subject of litigation or in relation to which any question may arise; further to order that any observation or experiment be tried thereon.

The power was interpreted widely in *Ho Wai Yin v Cheng Suet Yee* HCAP 18/ 2003 (A Cheung J; 17.12.2004). There the court rejected an argument that 'property' as used in the rule was confined to a tangible thing to which a proprietary right or interest may be claimed as a matter of law. Authorisation was given for samples to be taken from the remains of two deceased persons for the purpose of DNA testing, despite the fact that human remains are not recognised as 'property' in that sense. Although the remains were not the subject matter of the action, a question arose in respect of them, in that they might provide evidence pertinent to a crucial issue in dispute, being the parentage of a party.

On the other hand, 'property' in rule 3 may be confined to tangible things. See *UMCI Ltd v Tokio Marine & Fire Insurance Co (Singapore) Pte Ltd* [2006] 4 SLR 95 where the Singapore court held that the power does not extend to requiring samples of handwriting to be given (though it was suggested there might be an inherent jurisdiction to order a party to provide handwriting samples in exceptional circumstances).

In *The Inchon Glory* HCAJ 117/1992 (Barnett J; 17.06.1992) (para 5) the court set out a list of 'the principal matters which a court should take into account when exercising its discretion whether or not to order that samples be taken'. The list derives from *The Mare del Nord* [1990] 1 Lloyd's Rep 40 and is non-exhaustive. Although its wording reflects the fact it was formulated in the context of Admiralty proceedings, it would appear to be generally applicable in other cases, with necessary modifications. It reads as follows:

1.    The plaintiffs' evidence on affidavit must show a good arguable case on the merits. Particularly, the evidence must show that there was damage which should not be treated as *de minimis*.

2.    The taking of a sample (or such other relief as may be granted) must be shown to be such that it may assist the judge at trial. The longer the lapse of time between the moment when damage occurred and the moment when a sample is to be taken, the more difficult it will be to show that the order is likely to be of assistance at trial. If there is any doubt, it is in the interest of justice to preserve evidence rather than let pass an opportunity of obtaining such evidence.

3.    Shipowners must be protected from unnecessary interference with the running of their ships. Provided, however, a shipowner is fully protected against any damage which he may suffer, the type of relief being afforded to a plaintiff may be no more burdensome than discovery which can put a shipowner to a great deal of trouble and inconvenience . . .

4.    A plaintiff should be required to give an undertaking in damages.

5.    If satisfied that the plaintiff has a good arguable case and that the evidence obtained may assist at trial, the court should take account of undertakings given by the plaintiff and balance the inconvenience that might be caused to the shipowner and others against the possible benefit to the plaintiff.

**[29.3.4]    Conduct of experiment**
The court has power under Order 29 rule 3(1) to order any observation to be made, or experiment to be tried on any property connected with litigation.

In *Teck Cominico Metals Ltd v Foster Wheeler Pyropower Inc* [2010] BCCA 51 (CanLII) (04.02.2010) the plaintiff was permitted a consultation and monitoring role in the testing of its industrial equipment by the defendants. This was permitted in the interests of fairness, and in spite of objection based on privilege.

**[29.3.5]    Anton Piller order to preserve evidence**
In addition to the powers of the court under Order 29 to order detention or preservation of property, the court has inherent power to prevent destruction of evidence by making an *Anton Piller* order. Such an order is a type of mandatory injunction requiring a person alleged to be in possession of evidence that is at risk of destruction or concealment to permit a plaintiff's representatives to enter premises and take it away. The order takes its name from *Anton Piller KG v Manufacturing Processes Ltd* [1976] Ch 55 (CA), though the first reported case was *EMI v Pandit* [1975] 1 All ER 418; [1975] 1 WLR 302. In the *Anton Piller* case Lord Denning MR stated (at 61) that this type of order derives not from these rules, but from the inherent jurisdiction of the court. The jurisdiction has long been recognised in Hong Kong. For a discussion of the development of the *Anton Piller* order in England and Hong Kong, see Wilkinson 'Recent Developments Affecting Anton Piller Orders' (1993) 23 HKLJ 79.

**[29.3.6]    Types of cases in which Anton Piller order will be made**
The *Anton Piller* case concerned infringement of copyright, and the order named after it has since been closely associated with intellectual property litigation. In Hong Kong, such orders have often been used to require persons in possession of fake goods to permit

rep resentatives of the owner of the copyright, patent or trademark being infringed to enter premises and take the infringing goods away to preserve them as evidence. The order is particularly useful in such cases because people who deal in fake goods are notorious for destroying or concealing them to avoid civil and criminal liability. However, *Anton Piller* orders are by no means limited to intellectual property cases. They have been granted in a wide range of cases as can be seen from the following examples:

- *Family litigation* – In *Emmanuel v Emmanuel* [1982] 2 All ER 342; [1982] 1 WLR 669 an *Anton Piller* order was made in relation to matrimonial litigation to enable the wife's solicitor to enter the husband's premises and remove documents concerning the latter's financial status. The husband had previously breached an undertaking not to dispose of assets pending financial settlement with the wife. However, it has been observed that 'in family proceedings, *Anton Piller* orders remain a rare weapon for use only in extreme or exceptional cases': *Overholt v Overholt* [1999] 2 HKLRD 445, referring to *Burgess v Burgess* [1996] 2 FLR 34.
- *Money claims* - An *Anton Piller* order was made in a case claiming for an accounting of the amount due under a commercial contract in *Yousif v Salama* [1980] 1 WLR 1540.
- *Admiralty jurisdiction* - In *The Inchon Glory* HCAJ 117/1992 (Barnett J; 17.06.1992) the court granted an order to permit the plaintiff's surveyors and solicitors to inspect and photograph a vessel's hold and machinery and to take copies of navigational records, log books and plans. The order was made under Order 75 rule 28, but was granted *ex parte* in the *Anton Piller* fashion. The order was set aside in part at the *inter partes* stage on the ground of lack of urgency.
- *Execution* – In *United Reliance Corp Ltd v Metalimex* (HK) Ltd HCCL 73/1983 (Deputy Judge H Wong; 07.03.1986) the court granted a *Mareva* injunction coupled with an *Anton Piller* order in aid of execution of a judgment where there was reason to believe the judgment debtor was concealing or disposing of its assets. The court referred to *Orwell Steel (Erection and Fabrication) Ltd v Asphalt & Tarmac (UK) Ltd* [1985] QB 747 and *Distributori Automatici Italia SpA v Holdford General Trading Co* [1985] 3 All ER 750.
- *Companies court* – In *Re Central Pacific Enterprises Ltd* HCMP 799/2005 (Kwan J; 09.05.2005) the court was satisfied it had jurisdiction to make an *Anton Piller* order in aid of an application for inspection of the documents of a company in liquidation.

**[29.3.7]**    **Procedure on application for Anton Piller order**

An *Anton Piller* order may be made *ex parte* in proceedings closed to the public (see schedule 2 to practice direction 25.1, which provides that *ex parte* applications for injunctions will usually not be open to the public by reason of their nature). This enables such orders to be granted without forewarning to the defendant. Often such orders are sought before or immediately after issue but before service of the writ, based on information obtained through confidential enquiries, so the defendant does not even know of the legal proceedings until served with the order. As with other types of *ex parte* order there will be a subsequent *inter partes* hearing at which the defendant may apply for the order to be set aside. The standard form of *Anton Piller* order (see practice direction 11.2 above) expressly provides that the *ex parte* order continues only until the *inter partes* return date which should be the first summons day after the expiry of two clear days after the order is made and served. 'Summons day' is dealt with in practice direction 5.3, as to which see above. The standard form also provides that the defendant may apply to set the order aside 'at once': see the commentary below on setting aside *Anton Piller* orders.

## [29.3.8]    Anton Piller order not a search warrant

An *Anton Piller* order is not a search warrant: *Refco Inc v Troika Investment Ltd & Anor* [1988] 2 HKLR 623, 626J. Rather it may be described as a form of mandatory injunction requiring the party to whom it is directed to allow persons to enter premises to search for and take material away. If the defendant refuses entry, the plaintiff's representative is not entitled to use force. Failure to comply may constitute contempt of court. See the discus sion below on failure to comply with the order.

## [29.3.9]    Requirements for grant of Anton Piller order

The requirements for grant of an *Anton Piller* order were set out in *Giant Electronics Ltd v In-Tech Electronics Ltd* HCA 15823/1999 (Deputy Judge Woolley; 22.12.1999) (para 16) in the following words:

(i)    there must be an extremely strong *prima facie* case;

(ii)    the damage to the plaintiff, potential or actual, must be very serious;

(iii)    there must be clear evidence that the defendants have in their possession incriminating documents [editorial note: or other evidence such as goods]; and

(iv)    there must be a real possibility that they may destroy such material.

These requirements derive from the *Anton Piller* case itself, see in particular the judgment of Ormrod LJ at [1976] Ch 55, 62. The requirements are discussed one by one below.

## [29.3.10]    The 'strong prima facie case' requirement

The party applying for an *Anton Piller* order must satisfy the court that it has a strong *prima facie* case of a cause of action: *Lock Int'l plc v Beswick & Ors* [1989] 3 All ER 373, 385j. This is done by placing evidence before the court, by affidavit or affirmation. Evidence which shows mere suspicion that the defendant is infringing the plaintiff's intellectual property (or other) rights is insufficient: *Giant Electronics* (above, para 18-19).

## [29.3.11]The 'serious damage' requirement

The plaintiff is required to satisfy the court that it has actually or will potentially suffer serious damage as a result of the defendant's alleged infringement of its rights. In *Giant Electronics* (above) evidence that a customer of the plaintiff had switched its business to the defendant, who was allegedly producing goods in breach of the plaintiff's copyright, was considered evidence of damage.

## [29.3.12]    The possession requirement

The purpose of an *Anton Piller* order is to enable the plaintiff to obtain evidence of breach of its rights from the defendant. Because of its intrusive nature, the court will only grant such an order where it is satisfied that the defendant is in possession of such evidence. In *Giant Electronics* (above, para 21) the court took evidence that the defendant used the plaintiff's designs as evidence that the defendant was in possession of the same.

### [29.3.13]    The real possibility of destruction requirement

The purpose of an *Anton Piller* order being to preserve evidence which might otherwise be destroyed, it is incumbent on the plaintiff to satisfy the court that there is a real possibility of such destruction. The requirement is 'real possibility' not 'mere possibility'. This means there must be a 'likelihood': see *Technica Electronics Ltd & Anor v Shin-Shirasuna Denki Kabushiki Kaisha* [1981] HKLR 425 (CA), 426F *et seq* where Huggins VP said:

> One can become embroiled in semantics, but it seems to me that clearly 'a real possibility' is intended to convey something more than a mere possibility. There has, I think, to be some evidence which suggests that there is some likelihood and not just circumstances, which would arise in every case, that the defendant might destroy evidence: there could not be a case where that mere possibility did not exist. Obviously something more is intended, and I think there has to be some likelihood shown.

In *Ng Chun Fai Stephen & Anor v Tamco Electrical & Electronics (HK) Ltd* [1993] 1 HKC 160 (CA) the court said (at 173I et seq) that an *Anton Piller* order should not be granted 'unless there is real reason to believe that without such an order the respondent would disobey an injunction for the preservation of the evidence the destruction of which would defeat the ends of justice'.

In *Giant Electronics* (above) the court was prepared to infer the possibility of destruction from the strength of the evidence of culpability. Deputy Judge Woolley said (at para 22):

> Once a strong likelihood of culpability is established, it is a short step to imagine what someone in the defendants' place would do if given advance warning that their premises will be searched, or that an injunction will be applied for requiring delivery up of incriminating material.

In *Four Seasons Industrial Co Ltd v Sheen Long Industries Ltd* [1993] 2 HKC 706, 709A an *Anton Piller* order was discharged partly on the ground that the alleged risk that evidence would be destroyed was 'wholly unsupported by any basis'.

### [29.3.14]    Duty of full and frank disclosure

As is the case on any *ex parte* application, a party applying for an *Anton Piller* order has a duty to make full and frank disclosure to the court: *Reily Leisure plc v Dokyo Co Ltd & Anor* CACV 80/1986 (Fuad JA & Clough J; 05.08.1986) (para 13), citing *Thermax v Schott Industrial Glass Ltd* [1981] FSR 289, 298. See generally the commentary under Order 32 rule 6 on this duty.

It has been suggested that because of their intrusive nature, the duty of full and frank disclosure 'is almost more important in *Anton Piller* cases than in other *ex parte* applications': *Thermax* (above, at 298), quoted with approval in *Pioneer Int'l Buying Agencies (HK) Ltd v Tung Chien Kwok* HCA 346/1985 (Penlington J; 25.01.1985).

It appears that the duty of full and frank disclosure is owed to the opposing party as well. In *Four Seas Industrial Co Ltd v Sheen Long Industries Ltd* [1993] 2 HKC 706, 711I *et seq* it was held that the plaintiff who obtains an *Anton Piller* order cannot keep from the defendant information relied upon in support of the application. In so holding the court relied on *Re K (Infants)* [1963] Ch 381, *WEA Records Ltd v Vision Channel 4 Ltd* [1983] 1 WLR 721 and *VNU Business Publications BV v Ziff Davis (UK) Ltd* [1992] RPC 269.

## [29.3.15]    Consideration of harm to defendant

In deciding whether to grant an *Anton Piller* order the court must take the defendant's interests into consideration. As pointed out in *Giant Electronics* (above, para 23) there is 'inevitably a degree of disruption to any business premises in the execution of such an order'. Further there is likely to be intrusion into the defendant's property and privacy rights in and over its premises, goods and possessions. In *Lock Int'l plc v Beswick & Ors* [1989] 3 All ER 373, 384e; [1989] 1 WLR 1268, 1281F Hoffman J spoke of a need for 'careful balancing':

> The more intrusive orders allowing searches of premises or vehicles require a careful balancing of, on the one hand, the plaintiff's right to recover its property or to preserve important evidence against, on the other hand, violation of the privacy of a defendant who has no opportunity to put his side of the case.

In *Ng Shun Fai Stephen* (above, at 174G-H) the Hong Kong Court of Appeal, referring to *Columbia Picture Industries Inc v Robinson* [1987] Ch 38, put it this way:

> . . . a decision whether or not an *Anton Piller* order should be granted required a balance to be struck between the plaintiff's need that the remedies allowed by the law for the breach of his rights should be attainable and the requirement of justice that the defendant should not be deprived of his property without being heard.

When the order is sought *ex parte*, as is usually the case, the applicant's duty of full and frank disclosure encompasses putting forward material concerning the defendant's interests.

The court requires that an *Anton Piller* order contain provisions to safeguard the defendant's rights. See the discussion below on execution of an *Anton Piller* order.

## [29.3.16]    Judicial restraint in granting Anton Piller order

The court exercises restraint in considering whether to grant an *Anton Piller* order, because of the order's drastic nature. The order has, along with the *Mareva* injunction, been described as one of the law's nuclear weapons: *Bank Mellat v Nikpour* [1982] FSR 87, 92. This is not least because, as pointed out in *Columbia Picture Industries Inc v Robinson* [1986] 3 All ER 38 and *Lock Int'l plc v Beswick* [1989] 3 All ER 373, 382, the *Anton Piller* order may involve serious inroads into recognised freedoms such as the presumption of innocence, the right not to be condemned unheard, protection against arbitrary search and seizure and the sanctity of the home. In *Ng Chun Fai Stephen & Anor v Tamco Electrical & Electronics (HK) Ltd* [1993] 1 HKC 160 (CA) the court (at 173I et seq) cited the above authorities, and said, referring to both *Anton Piller* orders and *Mareva* injunctions:

> They are powerful and valuable weapons against fraud or dishonesty. But the more powerful the weapon, the more important it is that the user should take care about its handling. And these remedies are extremely powerful . . . Plainly, no such order should ever be made unless necessary in the interests of justice; nor in terms wider than necessary to achieve the legitimate object of the order; nor unless there is real reason to believe that without such an order the respondent would disobey an injunction for the preservation of the evidence the destruction of which would

defeat the ends of justice.

*Ng Chun Fai Stephen* was followed in *Four Seas Industrial Co Ltd v Sheen Long Industries Ltd* [1993] 2 HKC 706.

The 'nuclear weapons' description has been adopted in many Hong Kong cases including *Grand Trade Dev't Ltd v Bonance Int'l Ltd* CACV 776/2000 (Rogers VP, Stock & Le Pichon JJA; 03.11.2000) (para 17).

### [29.3.17]    Anton Piller order must be clear and unambiguous

An *Anton Piller* order must be clear and unambiguous so that the defendant will know precisely what is required. In *Ng Chun Fai Stephen v Tamco Electrical & Electronics (HK) Ltd* [1993] 1 HKC 160, 179B-C the Court of Appeal was highly critical of the terms of an *Anton Piller* order permitting the plaintiff's representatives to enter the defendant's premises for the purpose of 'removing therefrom into the custody or control of the plaintiff's solicitors all documents and articles relating to or connected with the claim set out in the statement of claim endorsed on the writ herein . . .' The statement of claim was not in fact indorsed on the writ and did not come into existence until some time later. The learned judges considered some of the terms of the order to be 'oppressive, unreasonable, and unjustified' (at 180B).

### [29.3.18]    Form of Anton Piller order

Practice direction 11.2 prescribes a standard form of *Anton Piller* which should normally be followed. The form is available in both official languages. The practice direction, which also deals with *Mareva* injunctions, stipulates that where an order in English is likely to be served on a Chinese-speaking person who may not be proficient in English, a brief explanation in Chinese of its contents must be added.

The text of the practice direction may be viewed on the judiciary's website www.judiciary.gov.hk, or that of the Hong Kong Legal Information Institute www.hklii.org, both of which are accessible by the general public free-of-charge.

### [29.3.19]    Anton Piller in support of Mareva injunction

The court has power and will grant an *Anton Piller* order where necessary to ensure that a *Mareva* injunction is effective over the assets it ought to cover. See *Refco Inc v Troika Investment Ltd & Anor* [1988] 2 HKLR 623.

### [29.3.20]    Privilege against self-incrimination

Prior to the enactment of section 44A of the High Court Ordinance, the privilege against self-incrimination inhibited the effectiveness of the *Anton Piller* order. This is because in many cases infringement of intellectual property rights is both a civil and criminal wrong. Thus a defendant could refuse to hand over infringing goods under an *Anton Piller* order by invoking the privilege. See *Rank Film Distributors Ltd v Video Information Centre* [1981] 2 AC 380; *Lincoln International Ltd v Eagleton Direct Exports Ltd* [1981] HKC 380.

Section 44A, which came into force in 1982 and is taken from section 72 of the English Supreme Court Act 1981, abolishes the privilege against self-incrimination in this context and goes on to provide that information obtained under an *Anton Piller* or similar order may not subsequently be used in a criminal case against its source.

The abolition of the privilege applies only in respect of 'related offences' which are defined as offences committed 'by or in the course of the infringement or passing off', or involving fraud or dishonesty. It may still be invoked when there is a reasonable apprehension of prosecution for conspiracy: *Sociedade Nacional de Combustiveis de Angola UEE v Lundqvist* [1991] 2 QB 310; *Tate Access Floors Inc v Boswell* [1991] Ch 512. In *International Management Group (Overseas) Inc v Lun* [2006] 2 HKC 463 it was held the privilege was available to defeat an *Anton Piller* order granted in a civil action to recover money which had allegedly been misappropriated by an employee. Further, that where a claim to the privilege will be available, the order should not be made at all – it is insufficient to draw attention to the right to assert the privilege and leave it to the defendant to decide whether to do so.

As to the privilege against self-incrimination generally, and the constitutional protection thereof, see the commentary under Order 24 rule 2.

### [29.3.21]     Execution of Anton Piller order

Because of the intrusive nature of an *Anton Piller* order, and in order to safeguard the defendant's interests, such an order is required to include stringent terms as to its execution. These terms were developed by the courts in decisions such as *Columbia Picture Industries Inc v Robinson* (above), *Lock Int'l plc v Beswick* (above) and *Universal Thermosensors Ltd v Hibben* [1992] 1 WLR 840. The Hong Kong Court of Appeal endorsed those decisions in *Ng Chun Fai Stephen* (above, at 177G *et seq*). Many of the requirements laid down by the courts are now included in the standard form of *Anton Piller* order prescribed by practice direction 11.2 (see above). These requirements, which may be varied to suit the circumstances of the individual case, include the following:

(1)     *Execution by a solicitor* – Since at least *Universal City Studios Inc v Mukhtar* [1976] 1 WLR 568 it has been held that an *Anton Piller* order should be executed by a solicitor, preferably one with experience in the field. The purpose is to protect the interests of the defendant. Now see paragraph 1(1) of the standard form order, which provides that the solicitor must be identified by name, and that the number of accompanying persons be stated.

(2)     *Supervision by independent solicitor* – It has been suggested that the service and execution of an *Anton Piller* order should be supervised by an independent solicitor experienced in the field: *Universal Thermosensors* (above). However, para 2(3) of Hong Kong's standard form stipulates that it is the plaintiff's solicitor serving the order who should supervise its execution.

(3)     *Place of execution* - In schedule 1 of the standard form order the address of the premises to which access is required to be given must be set out. This requirement dates back at least to *Protector Alarms Ltd v Maxim Alarms Ltd* [1978] FSR 442. Para 1(1) of the standard form requires that access be given to the stated premises, vehicles under the defendant's control on or around the premises, and any other premises disclosed pursuant to an ancillary order for disclosure of information.

(4)     *Presence of a woman* – Where an *Anton Piller* order is likely to be served on an unaccompanied woman, by a male solicitor, the plaintiff's team serving it should also include a woman. This is expressly provided for in para 2(3) of the standard form, and derives from *Universal Thermosensors* (above).

(5)     *Office hours* – Para 1(1) of the standard form order limits commencement of execution of an *Anton Piller* order to the hours of 9.30 a.m. to 5.30 pm Monday to Friday, and 9.30 am to 1.00 pm on Saturdays (excluding public holidays). Execution may continue until 8.00 pm on weekdays and 3.00 pm on Saturdays, and on the next following working day if necessary. These requirements trace back to *Universal Thermosensors* (above) and are included to ensure that the defendant's representative would be able to contact a solicitor during office hours to seek legal advice.

(6)     *Presence of defendant's representative* – An *Anton Piller* order directed to a body corporate should be served on a representative of that body: *Universal Thermosensors* (above). Paragraph 1(2) of the Hong Kong standard form requires that it be complied with by any employee of the defendant or other person appearing to be in control of the premises and having authority to permit entry.

(7)     *Explanation in everyday language* – The standard form of order exists in both official languages, and begins with 11 paragraphs explaining in short form its effect. Para 3 of this summary informs the person on whom it is served that he or she is entitled to have the solicitor serving it explain what it means in everyday language. An incomplete or inaccurate explanation may be a contempt of court even where the error arises from negligence or error of judgment rather than malice: *VDU Installations Ltd v Integrated Computer Systems & Cybernetics Ltd* [1988] The Times, 13 Aug.

(8)     *Documents to be served* – Along with the *Anton Piller* order itself, there should be served (a) the writ of summons (or a draft); (b) the *inter partes* summons for continuation of the *ex parte* order; (c) copies of the affidavits and exhibits (so far as practicable) relied upon by the plaintiff (see *Booker McConnell v Plascow* [1985] RPC 425 (CA)); (d) a note of any additional allegation of fact made orally to the judge at the *ex parte* hearing, and (e) a copy of the plaintiff's skele ton argument. Schedule 3 to the standard form order records (in para (4)) an undertaking by the plaintiff that these documents will be served with the order.

(9)     *Legal advice and application to the court* – Before permitting entry and execution of the order, the defendant is entitled to seek legal advice and to apply to the court for variation or discharge of the order. This is expressly provided for in para 3 of the standard form order. The defendant is not in contempt by refusing to allow execution of the order pending such an application: *Bhimji & Ors v Chatwani & Ors* [1991] 1 All ER 705, 713b-f.

(10)    *Exclusion of privileged material* – Para 3 of the standard form order permits the defendant to gather and deliver to its own solicitor anything which it considers to be, or likely to be, subject to privilege or to be incriminating, before complying with the order.

(11)    *Restriction on what may be taken away* – The standard form order is restricted to documents and articles listed in schedule 2 thereof. By para 2(6) of the standard order, nothing may be removed until a list of the items the plaintiff proposes to remove has been prepared and served. The defendant is entitled to an opportunity to check the list and to object to anything on it, in which event the objected item must be sealed in a container to be retained by

the plaintiff's solicitors until the *inter partes* return day. Improper removal may constitute contempt: *Columbia Pictures Industries Inc v Robinson* [1987] Ch 38.

(12)    *Report on execution* – The plaintiff's solicitor is required to prepare a report on the execution of the order, and para (5) of schedule 3 to the standard form records an undertaking that this will be served on the defendant as soon as practicable after it is prepared.

(13)    *Post execution* – Schedule 4 of the standard form records an undertaking by the plaintiff to return the defendant's original documents no later than two working days after removal, and to deliver to the defendant's solicitors any item of disputed ownership, on their undertaking to retain it in safe keeping and to produce it to the court.

## [29.3.22]    Ancillary orders

Paragraph 5 of the standard form of *Anton Piller* order prescribed by practice direction 11.2 (above) sets out ancillary relief which the court may grant requiring disclosure of information. If included in an *Anton Piller* order, the paragraph requires the defendant to disclose on affidavit the location of goods and the names and addresses of suppliers and customers with details of dates and quantities. Paragraph 6 prohibits the defendant from informing others of the order (except for the purpose of obtaining legal advice), and from destroying, tampering with, (*etc*) the material which is the subject of the order.

## [29.3.23]    Restriction on use of material

There is an implied undertaking on the part of solicitors and client obtaining material under an *Anton Piller* order 'not to permit the use of any of the documents or information obtained . . . for any collateral or ulterior purposes': *Computerland Corp v Yew Seng Computer (HK) Ltd* [1986] HKC 494, 500C-F, referring to *Customs & Excise Commrs v AE Hamlin & Co* [1984] 1 WLR 509, 517. An express undertaking to this effect is now recorded in para (6) of schedule 3 to the standard form order. The effect of the undertaking is that the material may only be used for the purposes of the proceedings in which the order is granted: *Stack Electronics Asia Ltd v Lu Da Lin & Ors* HCA 1850/2007 (Reyes J; 16.11.2007) (para 82). The express undertaking in the standard form contemplates an application for leave to use the material for another purpose.

Breach of the undertaking is a contempt of court in the same way as breach of the undertaking which applies under other forms of discovery: *Computerland* (above, at 498I *et seq* and 500F-I), referring to *Sybron Corp & Anor v Barclays Bank plc* [1984] 3 WLR 1055 and *Harman v Secty of State* [1983] 1 AC 280. See the discussion of the implied undertaking on discovery in the commentary under Order 24 rule 14A.

## [29.3.24]    Undertaking in damages

The standard form of *Anton Piller* order includes in para (1) of schedule 3 an undertaking by the plaintiff to comply with any order the court may make as to damages or otherwise if the order or carrying it out causes loss to the defendant. When an *Anton Piller* order is set aside, this undertaking may be enforced by an order that there be an inquiry as to damages, as in *Nobs & Anor v Kantec Electronics Co Ltd* [1998] 1 HKLRD 935. In *Giant Electronics Ltd v In-Tech Electronics Ltd & Ors* HCA 15823/1999 (Deputy Judge

Woolley; 22.12.1999) (para 66) the court considered that immediate enforcement of the undertaking on discharge was not appropriate, and adjourned the matter to be dealt with by the judge at trial. The court may direct that the inquiry be conducted by a master, as in *Overholt v Overholt* [1999] 2 HKLRD 445 (para 89). Inquiries before masters are governed by Orders 36 and 43.

### [29.3.25]    Failure to comply with Anton Piller order

As discussed above, an *Anton Piller* order is not a search warrant. If the defendant fails to comply the plaintiff's representatives are not permitted to use force to enter. The remedy against the defendant for failure to comply is an application for committal for contempt of court.

### [29.3.26]    Breach of Anton Piller order constitutes contempt

A defendant who breaches an *Anton Piller* order is guilty of contempt of court and is liable to be imprisoned or fined upon proof beyond reasonable doubt. See generally the commentary on contempt under Order 52.

Examples of Hong Kong cases in which the court has punished a person for contempt of an *Anton Piller* order include the following:

(1)     *Chopard et cie SA v Ace King Watch Ltd & Anor* HCA 7413/1983 (Mantell J; 06.04.1984) – a director of the defendant was fined $20,000 and ordered to pay indemnity costs for breach of an *Anton Piller* order by making an affirmation minimising the number of copy watches which had been dealt with.

(2)     *Le Clip SA & Ors v Wai Tat Metal Enterprise Co (a firm) & Ors* [1987] 3 HKC 354 – a defendant who through his sole proprietorship and limited company breached an *Anton Piller* order requiring him to cease manufacturing copy watches was sentenced to one month in prison and ordered to pay costs on the common fund basis.

(3)     *Guccio Gucci SpA Severin Montres AG v Ng Ping Tin* CACV 71/1993 (Macdougall VP, Bokhary JA & Sears J; 10.06.1994) – the defendant was fined $3,000 and ordered to pay indemnity costs for making a false affirmation pursuant to an *Anton Piller* order requiring him to give full disclosure relating to copy watches he had dealt in. The Court of Appeal set aside the finding of contempt (by a majority) on the ground there had been insufficient proof.

(4)     *Ebewe Arznemittel GmbH & Anor v Lai Shu Lam* HCA 16387/1998 (Yeung J; 05.07.1999) – the defendant was fined $30,000 and ordered to pay costs on the full indemnity basis for understating the number of counterfeit instruction leaflets he had produced.

Where the defendant succeeds in having an *Anton Piller* order set aside, there may no longer be any basis on which he can be punished for contempt. An order made without jurisdiction is void *ab initio* and cannot have been breached: *Wardle Fabrics Ltd v G Myristis Ltd* [1984] FSR 263, 271 *et seq*. Further, the court appears to have power to set aside an *Anton Piller* order *ab initio* where it has been made on the wrong basis: *Cheng Cheung Wang v Lo Noi Yung & Ors* [1984] HKC 575, 578H-I referring to *Fields & Anor v Watts & Ors* [1984] The Times 22 Nov. However, for policy reasons, failure to comply with an *Anton Piller* order may be a contempt even though it is later set aside, provided the order was valid at the time of the breach: *Wardle Fabrics* (above).

**[29.3.27]    Setting aside Anton Piller order**

Like any interlocutory injunction, and any order made *ex parte*, an *Anton Piller* order may be set aside at any time. The *inter partes* hearing which follows *ex parte* grant of an *Anton Piller* order provides an early opportunity for such an application to be made. However, the application may be made even earlier, and in advance of execution of the order: para 9 of the notice to defendant in the standard form of *Anton Piller* order expressly states that the defendant may ask the court to vary or discharge the order 'at once', permitting the plaintiff's solicitors to enter in the meantime, but not to commence the search. An application to set aside will normally be appropriate before appealing to the Court of Appeal: *Guess? Inc & Ors v Jordache Int'l (HK) Ltd* [1987] 1 HKC 99 (CA).

Affected persons other than the defendant may apply to set aside an *Anton Piller* order. See *Plastimoda SpA v Fung Siu Man & Anor* [1990] 1 HKC 445 where an importer and wholesaler which had no proprietary interest in the goods seized on execution of an *Anton Piller* order, but whose trading activities were disrupted, was permitted to join in the proceedings for the purpose of applying to set aside the order.

As mentioned above, the court may set aside an *Anton Piller* order *ab initio*, with the effect that in law it never existed.

There are procedural and substantive grounds on which an *Anton Piller* order may be set aside. These include:

(1)    *Material non-disclosure* – As discussed some paragraphs above, there is a duty of full and frank disclosure when applying for an *Anton Piller* order. Failure to discharge this duty may result in the order being set aside: see *Overholt v Over holt* [1999] 2 HKLRD 445 (para 69) as an example, and see generally the commentary on setting aside *ex parte* orders under Order 32 rule 6. Where solicitors are at fault they may be responsible in costs, as in *J v C&E* [1995] 1 HKLR 19. Although the matter is not free from doubt, it appears that the court will not, on an application to set aside for non-disclosure, take into account the 'yield' (that is the evidence obtained on *ex parte* execution of an *Anton Piller* order): *Guess? Inc v Lee Seck Mon & Ors* CACV 63/1986 (Cons VP & Fuad JA; 15.10.1986) (para 21); *Giant Electronics* (above, at para 43). However, there is clear authority that the 'yield' may be taken into account in considering whether to re-grant an *Anton Piller* order which has been discharged for non-disclosure: *Nobs v Kantec Electronics Co Ltd* [1998] 1 HKLRD 935; *Sportless Plastic Pty Ltd & Anor v Keen Resource Industrial Ltd & Ors* HCA 17865/1998 (Cheung J; 10.11.1998), both referring to *Naf Naf SA & Anor v Dickens (London) Ltd* [1993] FSR 424.

(2)    *Fishing exercise* – An *Anton Piller* order which amounts to a fishing exercise, such as a search for a cause of action where there is not yet a firm basis for a case, is liable to be set aside. See *Hytrac Conveyors Ltd v Conveyors Int'l Ltd* [1983] 1 WLR 44 (CA) cited in *Yeung On Nan v Weizen Industry Co Ltd* [1988] HKC 305.

(3)    *Abuse of process* – In *Lam Yung-tak Philip v Old Hand Ltd & Ors* HCA 1084/1990 (Sears J; 05.03.1990) a number of *Anton Piller* orders were set aside on the ground of gross abuse of process. The plaintiff had surreptitiously induced the defendants to breach his patent rights with a view to obtaining cash payments in

settlement of his claims.

(4) *Other relief more appropriate* – In *Overholt v Overholt* [1999] 2 HKLRD 445 (para 80) an *Anton Piller* order was set aside partly on the ground that it was unnecessary, as a preservation order under Order 29 rule 2 would have sufficed. *Ng Chun Fai Stephen v Tamco Electrical & Electronics (HK) Ltd* [1993] 1 HKC 160 suggests (at 174B-C) that an *Anton Piller* order should not be granted 'unless there is real reason to believe that without such an order the respondent would disobey an injunction for the preservation of the evidence the destruction of which would defeat the ends of justice'.

**[29.3.28] Costs**
The principles applicable to interlocutory injunctions will normally be followed in regard to the costs of an *Anton Piller* order. See the discussion in *Centaline Property Agency Ltd v Hong Kong Property Service (IC&I) Ltd* DCCJ 4937/2005 (Deputy Judge K W Wong; 12.12.2005).

**4. Sale of perishable property, etc.** (O. 29 r. 4)
**(1) The Court may, on the application of any party to a cause or matter, make an order for the sale by such person, in such manner and on such terms (if any) as may be specified in the order of any property (other than land) which is the subject-matter of the cause or matter or as to which any question arises therein and which is of a perishable nature or likely to deteriorate if kept or which for any other good reason it is desirable to sell forthwith.**

**In this paragraph "land" includes any interest in, or right over, land.**

**(2) Rule 2(5) and (6) shall apply in relation to an application for an order under this rule as they apply in relation to an application for an order under that rule.**

---

**NOTES**

**[29.4.1] Power to order sale of perishable property**
Order 29 rule 4 empowers the court to order the sale of property which is perishable or likely to deteriorate, or where there is other good reason.

The purpose of this power is to allow the court 'to prevent injustice which would arise if the goods, which are liable to deteriorate or perish, are allowed to do so, with the consequence that they will become of no value while the dispute between the parties is pending': *Taxfield Shipping Ltd v Asiana Marine Inc & Ors* HCCT 15/ 2006 (Deputy Judge L Chan; 07.03.2006).

The power to order sale is discretionary. It extends to property (other than interests in land) which is the subject of the action or as to which any question arises. The power extends to enable the court to order sale of a ship which has been arrested as security for an admiralty claim, even where the validity of the arrest is questioned. See *The Athenian Zoe (No 2)* [1985] 1 HKC 367.

**5. Order for early trial** (O. 29 r. 5)
**Where on the hearing of an application, made before the trial of a cause or matter, for an injunction or the appointment of a receiver or an order under**

rule **2, 3** or **4** it appears to the Court that the matter in dispute can be better dealt with by an early trial than by considering the whole merits thereof for the purposes of the application, the Court may make an order accordingly and may also make such order as respects the period before trial as the justice of the case requires.

Where the Court makes an order for early trial it shall by the order determine the mode of the trial.

**6.    Recovery of personal property subject to lien, etc.** (O. 29 r. 6)

Where the plaintiff, or the defendant by way of counterclaim, claims the recovery of specific property (other than land) and the party from whom recovery is sought does not dispute the title of the party making the claim but claims to be entitled to retain the property by virtue of a lien or otherwise as security for any sum of money, the Court, at any time after the claim to be so entitled appears from the pleadings (if any) or by affidavit or otherwise to its satisfaction, may order that the party seeking to recover the property be at liberty to pay into court, to abide the event of the action, the amount of money in respect of which the security is claimed and such further sum (if any) for interest and costs as the Court may direct and that, upon such payment being made, the property claimed be given up to the party claiming it.

---

## NOTES

### [29.6.1]    Scope of Order 29 rule 6

Order 29 rule 6 empowers the court to order the release of property (other than land) being held under a lien or as security, in return for payment of the amount in dispute into court. Although the rule mentions only payment by the party claiming return of the property, in *Dynamic Creations Ltd v Mint Gem & Jewelry Manufacturing Co Ltd* HCA 378/2006 (Chu J; 12.04.2006) the court granted relief under the rule on payment in by a parent company.

**7.    Directions** (O. 29 r. 7)

**(1)**    Where an application is made under any of the foregoing provisions of this Order, the Court may give directions as to the further proceedings in the cause or matter.

**(2)**    If, in an action begun by writ, not being any such action as is mentioned in sub-paragraphs (a) to (c) and (e) to (h) of Order 25, rule 1 (2), the Court thinks fit to give directions under this rule before the case management summons, rules 2 to 7 of that Order shall, with the omission of so much of rule 7(1) as requires parties to serve a notice specifying the orders and directions which they desire and with any other necessary modifications, apply as if the application were a case management summons. (**L.N. 152 of 2008**)

---

## NOTES

**[29.7.1]    Court's power to give directions on application for interlocutory injunction, etc**

Order 29 rule 7 provides that the court may, on an application for interim relief, such as an interlocutory injunction, give directions for the conduct of the action. Where that is done, the requirement to issue a case management summons is dispensed with: see Order 25 rule 1(2)(d) and Order 29 rule 7(2). These provisions reflect the fact that an interim remedy such as an interlocutory injunction is usually determined shortly after proceedings are commenced, and will usually require a substantial degree of preparedness, with the result that the court hearing the application will be in a position to give appropriate directions without the need for the questionnaire under the case management summons procedure in Order 25 rule 1.

**7A.    Inspection, etc. of property under sections 42 and 44(1) of the Ordinance**
       (O. 29 r. 7A)

**(1)    An application for an order under section 44(1) of the Ordinance in respect of property which may become the subject-matter of subsequent proceedings in the Court or as to which any question may arise in any such proceedings shall be made by originating summons and the person against whom the order is sought shall be made defendant to the summons.**

**(2)    An application after the commencement of proceedings for an order under section 42(2) of the Ordinance in respect of property which is not the property of or in the possession of any party to the proceedings shall be made by summons, which must be served on the person against whom the order is sought personally and on every party to the proceedings other than the applicant.**

**(3)    A summons under paragraph (1) or (2) shall be supported by affidavit which must specify or describe the property in respect of which the order is sought and show, if practicable by reference to any pleading served or intended to be served in the proceedings or subsequent proceedings, that it is property which is or may become the subject-matter of the proceedings or as to which any question arises or may arise in the proceedings.**

**(4)    A copy of the supporting affidavit shall be served with the summons on every person on whom the summons is required to be served.**

**(5)    An order made under section 42(2) or 44(1) may be made conditional on the applicant's giving security for the costs of the person against whom it is made or on such other terms, if any, as the Court thinks just.**

**(6)    No such order shall be made if it appears to the Court—**
    **(a)    that compliance with the order, if made, would result in the disclosure of information relating to a secret process, discovery or invention not in issue in the proceedings; and**
    **(b)    that the application would have been refused on that ground if—**
        **(i)    in the case of a summons under paragraph (1), the subsequent proceedings had already been begun; or**
        **(ii)    in the case of a summons under paragraph (2), the person against whom the order is sought were a party to the proceedings.**

**NOTES**

**[29.7A.1]  Order for inspection, etc, against non-party or before action**
Sections 42(2) and 44 of the High Court Ordinance empower the court to order inspection, photographing, preservation, custody and detention of property, or the taking of samples and carrying out of experiments against a non-party or before action. Order 29 rule 7A regulates the procedure for such applications. Such an order should normally grant costs of the application and of compliance to the party against which the order is made: Order 62 rule 3(12).

**8.     Allowance of income of property pendente lite** (O. 29 r. 8)
**Where any real or personal property forms the subject-matter of any proceedings, and the Court is satisfied that it will be more than sufficient to answer all the claims thereon for which provision ought to be made in the proceedings, the Court may at any time allow the whole or part of the income of the property to be paid, during such period as it may direct, to any or all of the parties who have an interest therein or may direct that any part of the personal property be transferred or delivered to any or all of such parties.**

**8A.    Application for interim relief under section 21M(1) of the Ordinance**
**(O. 29 r. 8A)**
**(1)     An application for interim relief under section 21M(1) of the Ordinance must be made by originating summons in Form No. 10 in Appendix A.**
**(2)     Rules 1, 2, 3, 4, 7(1), 7A and 8 of this Order apply with any necessary modifications to the application as they apply to an application for interlocutory relief in an action or proceeding in the High Court.**
**(3)     Upon hearing of the originating summons, the Court may direct that all or any part of the hearing be conducted in open court.**
**(L.N. 152 of 2008)**

**NOTES**

**[29.8A.1]  Origin and scope of Order 29 rule 8A**
Order 29 rule 8A derives from the rule of the same number in the former Rules of the Supreme Court in England and Wales (which came into force in April 1997). The rule regulates the procedure for applications under section 21M of the Ordinance for interim relief in aid of proceedings outside Hong Kong. That section empowers the court to appoint a receiver or grant other interim relief in relation to proceedings which have been commenced or are contemplated in another jurisdiction, provided that those proceedings are capable of giving rise to a judgment enforceable in Hong Kong. The section derives from section 25(1) of the Civil Jurisdiction and Judgments Act 1982.

Section 21N of the High Court Ordinance is also relevant to such applications. It sets out certain factors which the court is to bear in mind in exercising its power under section 21M. These are referred to below.

With regard to appointment of a receiver under section 21M, see also Order 30 rule 9.

With regard to *Mareva* injunctions in support of arbitration proceedings outside Hong Kong, see the commentary under Order 73 rule 4.

**[29.8A.2]   Application for Mareva injunction in aid of proceedings outside Hong Kong**

This rule, and HCO section 21M, implement recommendations 45, 46 and 47 in the final report of the Chief Justice's working party on civil justice reform. The working party had in mind the possibility of the Hong Kong court granting a *Mareva* injunction in aid of proceedings in another jurisdiction. The intention evident in the final report was to reverse the effect of *The Siskina* [1979] AC 210 and *Mercedes Benz AG v Leiduck* [1995] 3 HKC 1; [1996] 1 AC 284 (PC from HK) insofar as those decisions stood for the propo sition that the Hong Kong court had no power to grant a free-standing *Mareva* injunction in support of proceedings which had no other connection with Hong Kong. In the *Mercedes Benz* case a *Mareva* injunction granted by the Hong Kong court to preserve assets in Hong Kong pending resolution of litigation in Monaco was set aside for lack of jurisdiction. See the discussion at para 328 *et seq* of the working party's final report. As a result of section 21M and rule 8A the position in Hong Kong would now appear to be as the House of Lords expressed it to be in England in *Channel Tunnel Group Ltd v Balfour Beatty Construction Ltd* [1993] AC 334. The Chief Justice's working party summarised the effect of that judgment in the following words (at para 335):

> The approach of the House of Lords in the *Channel Tunnel* case is particularly strik-ing. While maintaining that an interim injunction had to be incidental to an attempt to enforce a substantive right and could not exist in isolation, and that the defendant had to be amenable to the court's jurisdiction, it was held not to be necessary that it should be ancillary to a claim for relief to be granted by an English court, but could be ordered in aid of proceedings in a foreign court or before a foreign arbitral tribunal . . .

With regard to foreign arbitral tribunals, see Order 73 rule 4 and the commentary thereunder.

As to when it is appropriate for the court to exercise its discretion to grant a *Mareva* injunction in aid of proceedings outside Hong Kong, the Chief Justice's working party anticipated that guidance would be derived from English cases. At para 358 of its final report the working party said:

> It is probably unnecessary for the legislation or the rules to go much further in providing guidance for the exercise of the court's discretion. Our courts would no doubt have regard to the relevant English case-law and decide on the extent to which it should be applied in Hong Kong. Thus, for instance, the English courts have held that:–
>
> (a)   The proper approach is to consider first whether the facts would warrant the relief sought if the substantive proceedings were brought in England, and if so, to ask whether, in the terms of s 25(2) [of the Civil Jurisdiction and Judgments Act 1982; in Hong Kong see section 21M(4) of the High Court Ordinance], the fact that the Court has no jurisdiction apart from that given to it by the Act makes it inexpedient [in Hong Kong's s 21M(4) 'unjust or inconvenient'] to grant the interim relief sought (*Refco Inc v Eastern Trading Co* [1999] 1 Lloyd's Rep 159, 170-1).
>
> (b)   The interim relief which an English court can grant is not limited to that which

would be available in the court trying the substantive dispute. It should be willing to assist the other court by providing such interim relief as would be available if English courts were seized of the substantive proceedings (*Alltrans Inc v Interdom Holdings Ltd* [1991] 4 All ER 458, 468; *Crédit Suisse Fides Trust SA v Cuoghi* [1998] QB 818, 827).

(c)  In exercising the discretion, the English court would pay great heed to whether the grant of relief would obstruct or hamper the management of the case by the court seized of the substantive proceedings or give rise to a risk of conflicting, inconsistent or overlapping orders. It would consider whether the primary court has itself declined to grant such relief and generally would avoid treading on the toes of the primary court or any other court involved in the case (*Crédit Suisse* (above) at 831-2).

(d)  Since such orders are often made effective by serving notice of the order on a third party (such as a bank at which the defendant has an account) within the local court's jurisdiction, such third parties should be given all reasonable protection, for instance, by ensuring that the court's order does not require them to breach their contractual or other legal obligations abroad (*Bank of China v NBM LLC* [2002] 1 WLR 844) [see the discussion concerning third parties affected by *Mareva* injunctions under Order 29 rule 1].

The working party then indicated that reference could also be made to *Ryan v Friction Dynamics Ltd & Ors* [2000] TLR 459 (14.06.2000). There Neuberger J (as he then was) set out the following 9 general principles to be applied by the court when asked to exercise its jurisdiction under section 25 of the 1982 Act to grant a *Mareva* injunction (or 'freezing order' as it is now called in England) in aid of proceedings in another jurisdiction:

1.  The court should always exercise caution before granting any freezing order.

2.  As Lord Justice Millett emphasised in *Crédit Suisse Fides Trust SA v Cuoghi* [1998] QB 818 particular caution was required when a freezing order was sought under section 25. The fact that the primary forum for the litigation was abroad meant that the court was likely to be even less fully appraised of the facts than in a case where it was exercising primary jurisdiction: see *Refco Inc v Eastern Trading Co* [1999] 1 Lloyd's Rep 159, 164.

3.  However, factors such as comity and the need to stop international fraud meant that the High Court should not be too worried about granting an injunction under section 25 where it was satisfied that good grounds existed. As was pointed out in *Cuoghi*, section 25(2) indicated that an order should be made unless it was inexpedient to do so.

4.  Just as when exercising its primary jurisdiction to grant a freezing order, the court should not make an order under section 25 unless the basic requirements were satisfied, namely that the claimant had a good arguable case and that there was a real risk of dissipation: see *Refco* (at pp 164 and 171).

5.  Although it should be slow to do so, it might be appropriate for the High Court to grant a freezing order even where the foreign court had refused to grant an order.

6.  The fact that there was a world-wide freezing order granted by the principal foreign court did not prevent the High Court from granting a freezing order at least in relation to British assets and/or against defendants resident or domiciled within the

jurisdiction. To hold otherwise would be inconsistent with the practice of the High Court. World-wide freezing orders were frequently granted by the High Court as the primary court on terms that specifically envisaged that the claimant would apply for freezing orders in the courts of the Channel Islands; the Isle of Man or Gibraltar in respect of assets within those jurisdictions. Further, to hold otherwise would involve implying an absolute fetter on a statutory jurisdiction which, on its face, appeared to be intended to give a wide and flexible jurisdiction.

7.      However, before such an overlapping freezing order was made under section 25 the court should expect to be given cogent reasons to justify it. Overlapping orders meant overlapping applications which in turn resulted in substantially increased costs and court time. Furthermore, overlapping injunctions in different jurisdictions could lead to a risk of double jeopardy for defendants and the opportunity for forum shopping by the claimants: see *In re Bank of Credit and Commerce Int'l SA* [1994] 1 WLR 708, 713.

8.      Where it was appropriate to grant a freezing order under section 25 in respect of British assets and the order overlapped with a world-wide or similar freezing order from a foreign court with primary jurisdiction, it would be sensible to include some provision which indicated which court was to have the primary role for enforcing the overlapping injunction. That would substantially reduce the risk of double jeopardy and forum shopping. Save in the case of good reason to the contrary, it would generally be the foreign court to which such application should be made.

9.      Where an overlapping order was made under section 25, it was in general desirable that it should track precisely the terms of the order made by the foreign court. Any inconsistency could lead to uncertainty and extra complications for the defendant. Worse, it could lead to a position where a defendant found itself bound to breach one order or the other: see the dictum of Mr Justice Jacob in *State of Brunei Darussalam v Prince Jefri Bolkiah* (unreported, March 20, 2000). However, in particular cases there may be good reason why an order made under section 25 should be in different terms from the order made by the primary court.

It has been held in England that a *Mareva* injunction in aid of proceedings elsewhere should not be granted unless it is shown that the respondent has some sufficient connection with the jurisdiction: *Mobil Cerro Negro Ltd v Petroleos de Venezuela SA* [2008] EWHC 532. In that case a freezing order was set aside because the respondent had neither a presence nor assets in England. This was done for reasons of comity. See the interesting discussion of this case and others in Johnson, 'Interim Injunctions and International Jurisdiction' (2008) 27 CJQ 433.

In recommendation 50 the working party expressed the view that while the grant of a *Mareva* injunction in aid of proceedings outside Hong Kong was a matter entirely in the court's discretion, 'the court is to bear it in mind that its jurisdiction is only ancillary and intended to assist the processes of the court or arbitral tribunal which has primary jurisdiction'. This is implemented by section 21N(1) of the High Court Ordinance. The working party envisaged the legislation empowering the court to make incidental orders, such as for disclosure of relevant assets, to ensure the effectiveness of the *Mareva* injunction granted: final report para 359 and recommendation 51. This is implemented by section 21N(2) of the High Court Ordinance.

In *Hornor Resources (Int'l) Co Ltd v Savvy Resources Ltd* [2010] 4 HKC 50 a *Mareva* injunction which had been granted in Hong Kong proceedings was continued after those proceedings were stayed because of an arbitration clause and an exclusive jurisdiction clause. In considering continuation of the injunction the court took into account the usual factors on which a *Mareva* injunction will be granted.

### [29.8A.3]   Application for other interim relief in aid of proceedings outside Hong Kong

In addition to interlocutory injunctions, rule 8A expressly provides that the court's powers under other rules in Order 29 will apply on an application for interim relief in aid of a proceedings outside Hong Kong. Those rules include rule 2 (detention or preservation of property), rule 3 (taking of samples) and rule 4 (sale of perishable property).

The wording of the rule suggests that those other powers are available in relation to the application in Hong Kong, rather than directly in aid of the proceedings in another jurisdiction.

See also Order 30 rule 9 with regard to appointment of interim receivers.

### [29.8A.4]   Procedure on application for interim relief in aid of proceedings outside Hong Kong

Rule 8A provides that an application under section 21M of the High Court Ordinance is to be commenced by originating summons in form No 10, which is the expedited form. Any affidavit evidence relied upon must be filed and served in accordance with Order 28 rule 1A.

### [29.8A.5]   Service out of originating summons out of Hong Kong

An application under section 21M of the High Court Ordinance will often involve parties who must be served outside Hong Kong. Order 11 rule 1(1)(oc) makes specific provision for the court to grant leave to serve out of the jurisdiction in such cases.

II.   Interim Payments

**9.     Interpretation of Part II** (O. 29 r. 9)

**"Interim payment", in relation to a defendant, means a payment on account of any damages, debt or other sum (excluding costs) which he may be held liable to pay to or for the benefit of the plaintiff; and any reference to the plaintiff or defendant includes a reference to any person who, for the purpose of the proceedings, acts as next friend of the plaintiff or guardian of the defendant. (L.N. 99 of 1993)**

**10.     Application for interim payment** (O. 29 r. 10)

**(1)     The plaintiff may, at any time after the writ has been served on a defendant and the time limited for him to acknowledge service has expired, apply to the Court for an order requiring that defendant to make an interim payment.**

**(2)     An application under this rule shall be made by summons but may be included in a summons for summary judgment under Order 14 or Order 86.**

    **(3)**    **An application under this rule shall be supported by an affidavit which shall—**

        **(a)**      **verify the amount of the damages, debt or other sum to which the application relates and the grounds of the application;**

        **(b)**      **exhibit any documentary evidence relied on by the plaintiff in support of the application; and**

        **(c)**      **if the plaintiff's claim is made under the Fatal Accidents Ordinance (Cap. 22), contain the particulars mentioned in section 5(4) of that Ordinance.**

    **(4)**    **The summons and a copy of the affidavit in support and any documents exhibited thereto shall be served on the defendant against whom the order is sought not less than 10 clear days before the return day.**

    **(5)**    **Notwithstanding the making or refusal of an order for an interim payment, a second or subsequent application may be made upon cause shown.**

---

## NOTES

### [29.10.1]    Cross-reference to High Court Ordinance

The underpinning statutory power to make rules governing the making of an order for interim payment is section 56 of the High Court Ordinance.

### [29.10.2]    Application by summons before master or judge

An application for an interim payment should be made by interlocutory summons in the action in which it is sought. Order 29 rule 10(2) expressly provides that such an application may be included in a summons for summary judgment. Where so included, the application for interim payment would normally be in the alternative to the application for summary judgment as in *Morison, Son & Jones (HK) Ltd v Yiu Wing Construction Co Ltd* [1989] 1 HKC 11 (CA) and *Ocean Air-Condition Engineering Co v Chevalier (HK) Ltd* HCCT 85/2002 (Burrell J; 24.01.2003). See the commentary under Order 29 rule 12 as to the circumstances in which an interim payment may be ordered where an application for summary judgment is unsuccessful.

    The application will normally be heard by a master in accordance with Order 32 rule 11, but may also be heard by a judge: *Smith & Ors v Glennon* [1990] TLR 494. It is submitted that the application should only be listed before a judge where a point of law is involved.

### [29.10.3]    Time

Order 29 rule 10 expressly provides that an application for interim payment may be made at any time after the time for acknowledgement of service has expired. On this basis the court rejected an argument that an interim payment application should wait until damages have been assessed: see *Sony Computer Entertainment Inc v Lik Sang Int'l Ltd* HCA 3583/2002 (Recorder J Leong SC; 11.04.2003).

### [29.10.4]    The affidavit in support

An application for interim payment must be supported by an affidavit which complies with Order 29 rule 10(3). In *Yeung Sek Sung v Cheung For Ming* [1991] 1 HKLR 1, 5C it was held that although the affidavit may be made by the applicant's solicitor, this is undesirable unless there are good reasons such as physical incapacity of the plaintiff or absence abroad.

**11.    Order for interim payment in respect of damages** (O. 29 r. 11)

**(1)    If, on the hearing of an application under rule 10 in an action for damages, the Court is satisfied—**

    **(a)    that the defendant against whom the order is sought (in this paragraph referred to as "the respondent") has admitted liability for the plaintiff's damages; or**

    **(b)    that the plaintiff has obtained judgment against the respondent for damages to be assessed; or**

    **(c)    that, if the action proceeded to trial, the plaintiff would obtain judgment for substantial damages against the respondent or, where there are two or more defendants, against any of them,**

**the Court may, if it thinks fit and subject to paragraph (2), order the respondent to make an interim payment of such amount as it thinks just, not exceeding a reasonable proportion of the damages which in the opinion of the Court are likely to be recovered by the plaintiff after taking into account any relevant contributory negligence and any set-off, cross-claim or counterclaim on which the respondent may be entitled to rely.**

**(2)    No order shall be made under paragraph (1) in an action for personal injuries if it appears to the Court that the defendant is not a person falling within one of the following categories, namely—**

    **(a)    a person who is insured in respect of the plaintiff's claim or whose liability in respect of the plaintiff's claim will be met by the following person—**

        **(i)    an insurer under section 10 of the Motor Vehicles Insurance (Third Party Risks) Ordinance (Cap. 272); or**

        **(ii)    an insurer who is a party to an agreement with the Motor Insurers' Bureau of Hong Kong; or**

        **(iii)    the Motor Insurers' Bureau of Hong Kong;**
        **(L.N. 108 of 2002)**

    **(b)    a public authority; or**

    **(c)    a person whose means and resources are such as to enable him to make the interim payment.**

**(3)    In paragraph (2)(a)(ii), "agreement"** (*Chinese text omitted*) **means the domestic agreement between the Motor Insurers' Bureau of Hong Kong and the insurance companies and Lloyd's underwriters authorized to carry on motor vehicle insurance business in Hong Kong, made on 1 February 1981, as amended from time to time.**

**(L.N. 108 of 2002)**

**12.    Order for interim payment in respect of sums other than damages** (O. 29 r. 12)

**If, on the hearing of an application under rule 10, the Court is satisfied—**

    **(a)    that the plaintiff has obtained an order for an account to be taken as between himself and the defendant and for any amount certified due on taking the account to be paid; or**

**(b)**    **that the plaintiff's action includes a claim for possession of land and, if the action proceeded to trial, the defendant would be held liable to pay to the plaintiff a sum of money in respect of the defendant's use and occupation of the land during the pendency of the action, even if a final judgment or order were given or made in favour of the defendant; or**

**(c)**    **that, if the action proceeded to trial, the plaintiff would obtain judgment against the defendant for a substantial sum of money apart from any damages or costs,**

**the Court may, if it thinks fit, and without prejudice to any contentions of the parties as to the nature or character of the sum to be paid by the defendant, order the defendant to make an interim payment of such amount as it thinks just, after taking into account any set-off, cross-claim or counterclaim on which the defendant may be entitled to rely.**

---

## NOTES

**[29.12.1]    Order for interim payment under rules 11 and 12**

According to Order 29 rule 11 the court may order the defendant to make an interim payment in respect of damages; under Order 29 rule 12 the court may order an interim payment in respect of sums other than damages, *eg* a sum due on an account. It has been held, in *Shearson Lehman Bros Inc & Anor v Maclaine, Watson & Co Ltd* [1987] 1 WLR 480 (CA), that rules 11 and 12 could be read together to permit the court to make an order for interim payment where it is satisfied that, if the action proceeded to trial, the plaintiff would obtain judgment either for substantial damages within rule 11(1)(c), or for a substantial sum of money apart from damages, within rule 12(c), even though it might not be certain which. Lord Justice Lloyd said that, although this conclusion does some violence to the language of the rules, it was justified in order to make sense of the rules as a whole.

Both rule 11 and rule 12 contain provisions whereby the court must be satisfied either that the plaintiff has already established liability or would be able to do so if the action proceeded to trial. The test is whether the plaintiff will, not 'will be likely to', obtain judgment: *Shenzhen Envirotex Electronics Co Ltd v Cellplus (HK) Ltd* [2005] 4 HKLRD 217 (para 19). This test is a 'high' one: *Guo Jing Jing v Art Master Investment Ltd & Ors* HCA 1008/2009 (Au J; 11.12.2009) (para 88), and will normally involve an examination of the merits, as in *Lin Chiu Lung v ILE Co Ltd* HCPI 1056/2002 (Master B Kwan; 08.12.2005).

**[29.12.2]    Limitation on power in personal injury cases**

The court's power to order an interim payment in personal injury cases is limited by Order 29 rule 11(2) so as to protect impecunious defendants. An order will only be made against a defendant whose liability will be met by insurance, is a public authority or has sufficient resources of its own. So far as insurance is concerned, this rule previously allowed an interim payment order only against a defendant who was himself an insured. By amendment in 2002 this was expanded so as to allow an order to be made against any defendant whose liability will be met under an insurance policy (whether he is the insured himself or not) or under the uninsured motorists' scheme run by the Motor Insurers' Bureau.

## [29.12.3]     Factors to be taken into account in exercise of discretion

The court's power to order an interim payment under Order 29 rules 11 and 12 is clearly discretionary.

There are many cases touching upon the manner in which the court should exercise its discretion. The cases have canvassed the questions whether any particular need must be demonstrated by the applicant, the extent to which delay in the proceedings is relevant and the question whether any distinction should be drawn between personal injury cases and other cases. Suffiad J conducted a review of the relevant cases in *Sun Jianqiang v Chan Tai Kau & Anor* [2001] 2 HKC 702 and held as follows (at 708I–709G):

> Viewing all these cases, and the somewhat confused state of the law, the time has come when there should be a standard practice adopted in respect of applications for interim payment irrespective whether the case is a personal injury case or not. This is the effect of the decision by the Court of Appeal in *Stringman v McArdle* [1994] 1 WLR 1653 (CA). Of particular note are the following passages of the judgment of Stuart-Smith LJ in *Stringman v McArdle* at 1657 where he said:
>
> > 'Once the threshold conditions in RSC Ord 29 r 11(1), sub-paragraphs (a), (b) or (c) are satisfied, what the court has to do, if it thinks fit, is to make an interim payment of such amount as it thinks just not exceeding a reasonable proportion of the damages which in the opinion of the court are likely to be recovered by the plaintiff after taking into account contributory negligence and any set-off or counterclaim. It should be noted that the plaintiff does not have to demonstrate any particular need over and above the general need that a plaintiff has to be paid his or her damages as soon as reasonably may be done. It will generally be appropriate and just to make an order where there will be some delay until the final disposal of the case. Therefore what the court is concerned with in fixing the quantum is that it does not exceed a reasonable proportion of the damages which in the opinion of the court are likely to be recovered ...'

Suffiad J continued in the *Sun Jiangqiang* case by saying he was in full agreement with the above words of Stuart-Smith LJ and that those words should henceforth be taken to apply equally to personal injury cases as to other cases (at 709E).

On the question whether the applicant is required to show any particular hardship or need for an interim payment, Suffiad J held that these factors could be taken into account by the court but 'not in a restrictive way in the exercise of the court's discretion' (at 709F–G). In this respect Suffiad J was of the view that the following cases should no longer be followed: *Yeung Sek Sung v Cheung For Ming* [1991] 1 HKLR 1; *Paul Y Construction Co Ltd v AG* [1992] 2 HKLR 120; and *Pham Van Ngo v AG* HCA 4895/1990 (Jones J; 12.06.1992).

## [29.12.4]     Quantum of interim payment

When the court decides that it is appropriate to order an interim payment the question of the quantum of that payment is also a matter of discretion. Under both rule 11 and rule 12 the court shall fix the quantum at the amount it thinks just, after taking into account any claim to set-off, cross-claim or counterclaim. Under rule 11, but not rule 12, the court must also take into account contributory negligence, and should fix the quantum at an amount not exceeding a reasonable proportion of the damages likely to be recovered.

In personal injury cases no distinction is to be made between the various heads of damages which may be awarded: see *Sun Jianqiang v Chan Tai Kau* [2001] 2 HKC 702, 710H where Suffiad J rejected a submission that in fixing the quantum of an interim payment he should not have regard to damages for pain and suffering and future loss.

In exercising its discretion as to quantum the court will also take into account the fact that liability and/or quantum remain in issue so that at the end of the day the plaintiff may be required to re-pay all or part of the interim award (see Order 29 rule 17). Thus the question of solvency will be relevant, though the court will not be concerned with the manner in which the plaintiff proposes to spend the interim award (unless he is a party under disability): see *Stringman v McArdle* [1994] 1 WLR 1653 (CA), approved by Suf fiad J in *Sun Jianqiang v Chan Tai Kau & Anor* [2001] 2 HKC 702.

In *BIS Consultants Ltd v Dao Heng Bank Ltd* [1989] 1 HKLR 446 the quantum of an interim payment was fixed with reference to the amount of funds held by the defendant mortgagee surplus to its claim.

## [29.12.5]    No power to order interim periodic payment
The power under Order 29 rules 11 and 12 is to order 'an' interim payment, meaning there is no jurisdiction to order interim *periodic* payments. See *Ho Shuk Man v Sunflower Travel Service Ltd* DCEC 618/2009 (Judge Chow; 12.02.2010) in which an application for interim monthly payments was dismissed.

## [29.12.6]    Interim payment where two defendants
It has been held, in *Ricci Burns Ltd v Toole* [1989] 1 WLR 993 (CA), that in an application for an interim payment on account of damages under Order 29 rule 11, in a case where the plaintiff is suing two defendants, it is not sufficient for the plaintiff to show that he is bound to succeed against one or the other of the defendants; proof of success to the necessary standard (see below) against a particular defendant is required before an order can be made against him.

## [29.12.7]    Leave to defend under Order 14 not a barrier to order for interim payment
It may be conceptually possible for the court to make an order for interim payment even though the defendant has been granted leave to defend. The difficulty is that failure of an Order 14 application suggests the plaintiff cannot demonstrate that he 'would' obtain judgment at trial in accordance with Order 29 rule 11(1)(c) or rule 12(c).

In *Ricci Burns Ltd v Toole* [1989] 1 WLR 993 the English Court of Appeal held that doubt about the plaintiff's prospects of success sufficient to preclude Order 14 summary judgment did not prevent the court from concluding on the same evidence that the plaintiff would succeed at trial and thus should have an interim payment. However, in *British and Commonwealth Holdings plc v Quadrex Holdings Inc* [1989] 3 All ER 492 the same court was of the view that an interim payment order is inconsistent with unconditional leave to defend, though it might be possible to justify an interim payment order where on the Order 14 summons the court had sufficient doubt about the prospects of a defence to grant leave to defend on terms.

In *Chun Lee Engineering Co Ltd v Aoki Construction* HCCT 19/1989 (Kaplan J; 03.05.1991); [1991] HKLY 87 Kaplan J preferred the decision in the *British and Commonwealth Holdings* case over that in *Ricci Burns*.

**[29.12.8]    Order 29 rule 12(b) – interim payment for use and occupation of land**

For an interim payment to be ordered under Order 29 rule 12(b) in respect of use or occupation of land pending judgment, there are two 'pre-conditions'. They are, as set out in *Wong Wai Ming v Sai Kung Flea Market & BBQ Paradise Co Ltd* HCA 2289/2008 (Chu J; 20.03.2009) (para 18):

    (1)    The plaintiff's action has included a claim for possession of land; and

    (2)    If the action proceeds to trial, the defendant will be held liable to pay to the plaintiff a sum of money in respect of the defendant's use and occupation of the land during the pendency of the action, even if a final judgment or order were given or made in favour of the defendant: *Winsworld Properties Ltd v Chance Full Int'l Dev't Ltd & Anor* HCA 4161/2002 (Deputy Judge Lam; 14.02.2003) (para 9) and *Maxon Investment Ltd v Million Nice Dev't Ltd & Anor* HCA 2332/2003 (Chu J; 06.07.2004) (para 7).

Thus, interim payment will not be ordered where a purchaser claiming specific per formance has gone into possession of the land: *Lee Shu Man v Chu Wing Hung* [1996] 3 HKC 88 (CA). This is because if the purchaser succeeds, it would not be liable for mesne profits. However, a tenant resisting a claim for possession is liable for rent or mesne profits whether or not it succeeds, so an interim payment may be ordered: *New Jet Harbour Ltd v Yueh Hsi HK Transportation Co Ltd* [2005] 1 HKC 190 (CA). In that case it was suggested (at 196H-197B) that the claim for rent or *mesne* profits must be pleaded, or the pleading amended to include such a claim.

**[29.12.9]    Order 29 rule 12(c) – Set-off or counterclaim relevant in making order**

According to *Shanning International Ltd v George Wimpey International Ltd* [1988] 3 All ER 475 (CA), on an application under Order 29 rule 12(c), the court has first to satisfy itself that the plaintiff would succeed at trial in obtaining judgment for a substantial sum and only then decide, as a matter of discretion, whether an interim payment should be ordered. At each of these two stages the court must take into account any set-off or counter claim claimed by the defendant. The same principle would presumably apply to applications under Order 29 rule 11(1)(c).

**[29.12.10]    The burden on the applicant for an interim payment**

Both Order 29 rule 11 and rule 12 state that to grant an order for an interim payment the court must be 'satisfied' of one of the relevant criteria. In *Yeung Sek Sung v Cheung For Ming* [1991] 1 HKLR 1, 4H Jones J cited with approval the following passage in the judgment of Croom-Johnson LJ in *Brian Breeze v R McKennon & Son Ltd* [1985] 32 BLR 41, 49–50:

    The onus of proof to 'satisfy' the court on liability under rule 11(1)(c) is high. It is equivalent to being sure that the plaintiff will recover. A mere *prima facie* case is not enough … The court cannot be satisfied under rule 11(1)(c) without evidence. This should be provided by the affidavit under rule 10(3)(a) setting out the grounds of the application.

In *Gibbons & Anor v Wall* [1988] The Times, 24 February (CA) it was held that the civil standard of proof is flexible and that on an application for an interim payment the standard to be applied is at the high end of the range.

In *Tang Cheuk Him v Hospital Authority* HCPI 1123/2006 (Reyes J; 07.09.2007) an application for an interim payment was refused on the ground that liability was 'far from a foregone conclusion' (para 99).

## [29.12.11]  Remedy for breach of order for interim payment
The remedy for failure to make an interim payment under order of the court is to levy execution under Order 45 *et seq* of these rules. It is not appropriate to seek an 'unless' order with a view to striking out the defaulting party's pleading: see *Law Shek Po v Team Ease Ltd* [1998] 1 HKC 81 (CA).

## 13.    Manner of payment (O. 29 r. 13)
**(1)    Subject to Order 80, rule 12, the amount of any interim payment ordered to be made shall be paid to the plaintiff unless the order provides for it to be paid into court, and where the amount is paid into court, the Court may, on the application of the plaintiff, order the whole or any part of it to be paid out to him at such time or times as the Court thinks fit.**

**(2)    An application under paragraph (1) for money in court to be paid out may be made ex parte, but the Court hearing the application may direct a summons to be issued.**

**(3)    An interim payment may be ordered to be made in one sum or by such instalments as the Court thinks fit.**

**(4)    Where a payment is ordered in respect of the defendant's use and occupation of land the order may provide for periodical payments to be made during the pendency of the action.**

---

## NOTES

### [29.13.1]    Interim payment to be made to the plaintiff
Order 29 rule 13 provides that an interim payment shall be made to the plaintiff, save in cases where the plaintiff is under disability, in which event the funds should be dealt with in accordance with Order 80 rule 12.

In a note dated 5 May 2003 the judge then in charge of the personal injury list reminded practitioners that an interim payment is intended for the plaintiff, not the lawyers, and that it should be directly and without deduction remitted to the plaintiff. The full text of the note can be found in Law Society circular 03-286, dated 25 August 2003. See also the commentary under Order 72 rule 2 on the personal injury practice direction.

## 14.    Directions on application under rule 10 (O. 29 r. 14)
**Where an application is made under rule 10, the Court may give directions as to the further conduct of the action, and, so far as may be**

applicable, Order 25, rules 2 to 7, shall, with the omission of so much of rule 7(1) as requires the parties to serve a notice specifying the orders and directions which they require and with any other necessary modifications, apply as if the application were a case management summons, and, in particular, the Court may order an early trial of the action. (L.N. 152 of 2008)

**15.    Non-disclosure of interim payment** (O. 29 r. 15)
The fact that an order has been made under rule 11 or 12 shall not be pleaded and, unless the defendant consents or the Court so directs, no communication of that fact or of the fact that an interim payment has been made, whether voluntarily or pursuant to an order, shall be made to the Court at the trial, or hearing, of any question or issue as to liability or damages until all questions of liability and amount have been determined.

---

## NOTES

### [29.15.1]    Disclosure and non-disclosure of interim payment
Order 29 rule 15 provides that the fact an interim payment has been made shall not be made known to the court at the trial or hearing of any question relating to liability or damages, until such question has been determined.

However in guidance to the profession issued in the form of a note from the judge in charge of the personal injury list (dated 5 May 2003) the contrary is stipulated for such cases. It is expressly stated that the solicitors for the plaintiff in such cases 'must notify the court of any interim payment received'. The full text of this note can be found in Law Society circular 03-286(PA) which is available on the society's website. See also the commentary on the personal injury list under Order 72 rule 2. It may be that the guidance was intended only for cases where the plaintiff is under a disability, as in the case which gave rise to the judge's comments. In such cases money recovered is required to be dealt with in accordance with directions of the court pursuant to Order 80 rule 12.

**16.    Payment into court in satisfaction** (O. 29 r. 16)
Where, after making an interim payment, whether voluntarily or pursuant to an order, a defendant pays a sum of money into court under Order 22, the notice of payment must state that the defendant has taken into account the interim payment. (L.N. 152 of 2008)

---

## NOTES

### [29.16.1]    Interim payments and payment in
According to Order 29 rule 16 where, after making an interim payment, whether voluntarily or pursuant to an order of the court, a defendant pays a sum of money into court under Order 22 rule 1, the notice of payment must state that the defendant has taken into account the interim payment.

The effect of failure to comply with Order 29 rule 16 was considered in *Prudential Mall Ltd v PH Shek Ltd* [1992] 1 HKC 7 (PC). The defendants had been ordered before trial to make interim payments on account of their liability in respect of the use and occupation of premises. They then paid money into court but failed to state in the notice of payment in whether the payment in took into account the interim payments already made. Judgment was given for the plaintiffs and the court had to decide, for the purpose of assessing costs, whether the sum paid in by the defendants had taken into account the sums already paid by way of interim payments. At first instance, the trial judge held that failure to state in the notice of payment in that the interim payments had been taken into account must lead to those sums being excluded from the payment in. Costs would, therefore, be awarded to the plaintiffs. The defendants appealed and the Court of Appeal reversed the holding at first instance on the grounds that the plaintiffs must have realised that the payment in had taken the interim payments into account and related only to the balance remaining. This decision was upheld by the Privy Council. In the view of the Privy Council, failure to comply with Order 29 rule 16 was a mere irregularity. Further, the court still retained a discretion as to the award of costs even if there were defects in the notice of payment in.

**17.    Adjustment on final judgment or order or on discontinuance** (O. 29 r. 17)
    **Where a defendant has been ordered to make an interim payment or has in fact made an interim payment, whether voluntarily or pursuant to an order, the Court may, in giving or making a final judgment or order, or granting the plaintiff leave to discontinue his action or to withdraw the claim in respect of which the interim payment has been made, or at any other stage of the proceedings on the application of any party, make such order with respect to the interim payment as may be just, and in particular—**

    (a)    **an order for the repayment by the plaintiff of all or part of the interim payment; or**

    (b)    **an order for the payment to be varied or discharged; or**

    (c)    **an order for the payment by any other defendant of any part of the interim payment which the defendant who made it is entitled to recover from him by way of contribution or indemnity or in respect of any remedy or relief relating to or connected with the plaintiff's claim.**

**18.    Counterclaims and other proceedings** (O. 29 r. 18)
    **The preceding rules in this Part of this Order shall apply, with the necessary modifications, to any counterclaim or proceeding commenced otherwise than by writ, where one party seeks an order for an interim payment to be made by another.**
    **(Enacted 1988)**

## ORDER 30

### RECEIVERS

**1.    Application for receiver and injunction** (O. 30 r. 1)

**(1)    An application for the appointment of a receiver may be made by summons. (L.N. 152 of 2008)**

**(2)    An application for an injunction ancillary or incidental to an order appointing a receiver may be joined with the application for such order.**

**(3)    Where the applicant wishes to apply for the immediate grant of such an injunction, he may do so ex parte on affidavit.**

**(4)    The Court hearing an application under paragraph (3) may grant an injunction restraining the party beneficially entitled to any interest in the property of which a receiver is sought from assigning, charging or otherwise dealing with that property until after the hearing of a summons for the appointment of the receiver and may require such a summons, returnable on such date as the Court may direct, to be issued.**

---

## NOTES

### [30.1.1]    Power to appoint receiver

The court's power to appoint receivers is found in section 21L of the High Court Ordinance. The power may be exercised where it appears 'just or convenient' to do so. There are well recognised circumstances in which a receiver will be appointed. The two main classes of cases in which the appointment will be made are described as follows in Kerr & Hunter on Receivers and Administrators (18th ed) 2005:

(1)    to enable persons who possess rights over property to obtain the benefit of those rights and to preserve the property pending realization, where ordinary legal remedies are defective; and

(2)    to preserve property from some danger which threatens it.

Thus in *Chan Cheung Hing v Tang Lan & Ors* HCA 4568/1987 (Deputy Judge Litton QC; 13.01.1989) a receiver was appointed in respect of trust property where the court felt it did not have power to order sale. And in *Chau Hung Kau v Texgar Ltd & Ors* HCMP 1372/2000 (Kwan J; 23.01.2001) a receiver was appointed to protect property pending trial where there was *prima facie* evidence of a scheme of 'fraudulent ingenuity' which, if unchecked, could be repeated.

### [30.1.2]    Cross-reference

See also Order 51, which deals with appointment of receivers by way of equitable execution, and Orders 116 and 117 which deal with the Organized and Serious Crimes Ordinance (Cap 455), under which a receiver may be appointed in respect of the proceeds of crime.

### [30.1.3]    Effect of appointment of a receiver

The appointment of a receiver does not affect underlying property rights, contracts

599

or legal status, but transfers their exercise to the receiver under supervision of the court. *See Parsons v Sovereign Bank of Canada* [1913] AC 160, 167 (PC).

In *Jinlin Sun & Anor v Kenneth Chi Shing Cheung & Ors* HCA 3544/2003 (Reyes J; 13.10.2003) it was argued that an appointment of a receiver could be confined to such powers as circumstances might warrant, but the court did not find it necessary to decide the point.

**[30.1.4]     Receiver an officer of the court**
A receiver is an officer of the court and subject to the court's supervision: *Shanghai Land Holdings Ltd v Chau Ching Ngai & Anor* [2005] 3 HKC 302, 308A-D, citing *Deloitte & Touche AG v Johnson & Anor* [1999] 1 WLR 1605. Receivers are obliged 'not only to act lawfully but fairly and honourably'; the court 'requires of them strict standards': *Bank of China (HK) Ltd v New Nongkai Global Investments Ltd* HCA 2062/2003 (Deputy Judge Poon; 31.07.2003).

**[30.1.5]     Interlocutory appointment of receiver**
Section 21L of the High Court Ordinance expressly permits appointment of a receiver either on an interlocutory or a final basis.

The test for appointment of an interim receiver, that is appointment on an interlocutory basis, is the same as that for an interlocutory injunction: *Re Niceline Co Ltd* [2003] 2 HKLRD 725. The power is discretionary and is to be exercised flexibly: *Guo Jing Jing v Art Master Investment Ltd & Ors* HCA 1008/2009 (Au J; 11.12.2009) (para 36). The principles for granting interlocutory injunctions in *American Cyanamid Co v Ethicon Ltd* [1975] AC 396 apply by analogy, and the court needs to consider (1) whether there is a serious case to be tried, (2) whether there is a proper basis for appointing a receiver such as a jeopardy to assets, and (3) the balance of convenience: *Cenky Ltd v Zealot & Co Ltd & Anor* [2008] 1 HKLRD 386. In *Re Full Billion Shipping Ltd* [2003] 2 HKLRD 674 (para 18) the court expressed consideration (2) as 'whether financial compensation is an adequate remedy'.

It is appropriate for the court's discretion to be exercised in favour of appointment of an interim receiver where there is reason to fear dissipation of the assets pending a full trial, as in *Chau Hung Kau* (above). Dispute over ownership of the assets may be a relevant consideration, but is not of itself a bar to appointment of an interim receiver: *Re HK Sindy Footwears Ltd* [2007] 1 HKC 64 (para 22).

In *Stewart v E Excel Ltd* HCA 2493/2001 (Stone J; 30.08.2001) the court proceeded on the basis that it has power to appoint a receiver on an interlocutory basis to preserve property pending resolution of a dispute in another jurisdiction.

**[30.1.6]     Undertaking in damages**
An undertaking in damages is an 'essential condition' to appointment of an interim receiver: *Re HK Sindy Footwears Ltd* [2007] 1 HKC 64 (para 40).

**2.     Giving of security by receiver** (O. 30 r. 2)
     **(1)   A judgment or order directing the appointment of a receiver may include such directions as the Court thinks fit for the giving of security by the person appointed.**
     **(2)   Where by virtue of any judgment or order appointing a person**

named therein to be a receiver, a person is required to give security in accordance with this rule he must give security approved by the Court duly to account for what he receives as receiver and to deal with it as the Court directs.

(3)    Unless the Court otherwise directs, the security shall be by guarantee.

(4)    The guarantee must be filed in the Registry, and it shall be kept as of record until duly vacated.

---

## NOTES

### [30.2.1]    Order requiring receiver to post security

Order 30 rule 2 provides that the court may require a receiver to post security. Such an order is usual.

Appointment of a receiver takes effect from the date of the order, but the receiver is not able to act until security has been posted: *Ridout v Fowler* [1904] 1 Ch 658; [1904] 2 Ch 92 (CA).

**3.    Remuneration of receiver** (O. 30 r. 3)

A person appointed receiver shall be allowed such proper remuneration, if any, as may be authorized by the Court and the Court may direct that such remuneration shall be fixed by reference to such scales or rates of professional charges as it thinks fit.

**4.    Service of order and notice** (O. 30 r. 4)

A copy of the judgment or order appointing a receiver shall be served by the party having conduct of the proceedings on the receiver and all other parties to the cause or matter in which the receiver has been appointed.

**5.    Receiver's accounts** (O. 30 r. 5)

(1)    A receiver shall submit such accounts to such parties at such intervals or on such dates as the Court may direct.

(2)    Any party to whom a receiver is required to submit accounts may, on giving reasonable notice to the receiver, inspect, either personally or by an agent, the books and other papers relating to the accounts.

(3)    Any party who is dissatisfied with the accounts of the receiver may give notice specifying the item or items to which objection is taken and requiring the receiver within not less than 14 days to lodge his accounts with the Court and a copy of such notice shall be lodged in the Registry.

(4)    Following an examination by or on behalf of the Court of an item or items in an account to which objection is taken the result of such examination must be certified by the Registrar and an order may thereupon be made as to the incidence of any costs or expenses incurred.

---

## NOTES

### [30.5.1]    Passing of receiver's accounts

Order 30 rule 5 provides the procedures whereby a receiver is obliged to submit accounts to the court for approval. Note that prior to 1988 the rule was number 4.

A party who objects to an item in the receiver's accounts should raise the issue in the context of the action in which the receiver was appointed. It is not appropriate to commence fresh proceedings against the receiver. See *Kwok Hang-tat & Anor v Chan Kwok-man* [1985] HKLR 471 (CA) where a fresh action was struck out and the parties were left to go back to the master since the certificate required by rule 5(4) had not yet been signed, meaning the master was not *functus officio*.

In *Kwok Hang-tat* it was held that the procedures in Order 43 apply on an application for approval of a receiver's accounts.

**6.     Payment into court by receiver** (O. 30 r. 6)

**The Court may fix the amounts and frequency of payments into court to be made by a receiver.**

**7.     Default by receiver** (O. 30 r. 7)

**(1)    Where a receiver fails to attend for the examination of any account of his, or fails to submit any account, provide access to any books or papers or do any other thing which he is required to submit, provide or do, he and any or all of the parties to the cause or matter in which he was appointed may be required to attend in chambers to show cause for the failure, and the Court may, either in chambers or after adjournment into court, give such directions as it thinks proper including, if necessary, directions for the discharge of the receiver and the appointment of another and the payment of costs.**

**(2)    Without prejudice to paragraph (1), where a receiver fails to attend for the examination of any account of his or fails to submit any account or fails to pay into court on the date fixed by the Court any sum required to be so paid, the Court may disallow any remuneration claimed by the receiver and may, where he has failed to pay any such sum into court, charge him with interest at the rate currently payable in respect of judgment debts in the Court of First Instance on that sum while in his possession as receiver.**

---

## NOTES

### [30.7.1]    Challenge to receiver's improper acts

A party which wishes to challenge alleged improper acts by a receiver should proceed under Order 30 rule 7, or seek leave to bring an action against the receiver, rather than applying for injunctive relief in the proceedings in which the receiver was appointed: *Achieve Goal Holdings Ltd v Zhong Xie Ore-Mineral Holding Co Ltd* HCA 1987/2005 (Chung J; 03.07.2009) (paras 18-21) (*obiter*).

**8.     Directions to receivers** (O. 30 r. 8)

**A receiver may at any time request the Court to give him directions and such a request shall state in writing the matters with regard to which directions are required. (Enacted 1988)**

## NOTES

**[30.8.1]**     **Scope of Order 30 rule 8**

Order 30 rule 8 permits a receiver to apply to the court for directions. Such directions must be confined to the parties to the particular proceedings – the rule does not give the court jurisdiction over non-parties: *Bank of China (HK) Ltd v New Nongkai Global Investments Ltd* (Deputy Judge Poon; 31.07.2003).

It has been argued that once the court has given directions, the receiver has no power to appeal, since to do so would be inconsistent with the duty to remain neutral as between competing creditors. Rather only a party adversely affected may appeal. *See Arthur Anderson Inc v Artisan Corp* (2002) 220 DLR (4th) 351 where this argument was rejected on the basis a receiver has power to appeal to ensure the 'correct' advice or directions are given by the court.

**9.     Application for appointment of receiver under section 21M(1) of the Ordinance** (O. 30 r.9)

**This Order applies to an application for appointment of a receiver under section 21M(1) of the Ordinance as it applies to an application for appointment of a receiver in an action or proceeding in the High Court subject to the following modifications —**

        **(a)     the application must be made by originating summons in Form No. 10 in Appendix A and accordingly rule 1(1) does not apply; and**

        **(b)     rule 1(3) and (4) does not apply to the application.**

                                      **(L.N. 152 of 2008) (Enacted 1988)**

## NOTES

**[30.9.1]**     **Power to appoint receiver in aid of proceedings outside Hong Kong**

Order 30 rule 9 applies most of the provisions of the Order to applications under section 21M of the Ordinance for appointment of a receiver in aid of proceedings outside Hong Kong. That section empowers the court to appoint a receiver or grant other interim relief in relation to proceedings which have been commenced or are contemplated in another jurisdiction, provided that those proceedings are capable of giving rise to a judgment enforceable in Hong Kong. Section 21M and this rule were enacted as part of the civil justice reforms which took effect in 2009. For the background see the commentary under Order 29 rule 8A.

**[30.9.2]**     **Procedure on application to appoint receiver in aid of proceedings outside Hong Kong**

As to commencement of such proceedings see also Order 29 rule 8A. It is there, and again in Order 30 rule 9, specified that an application for appointment of a receiver under section 21M should be commenced by originating summons in form No 10, which is the expedited form.

## ORDER 31

### SALES ETC OF LAND BY ORDER OF COURT

1.      **Power to order sale of land** (O. 31 r. 1)

**Where in any cause or matter relating to any land it appears necessary or expedient for the purposes of the cause or matter that the land or any part thereof should be sold, the Court may order that land or part to be sold, and any party bound by the order and in possession of that land or part, or in receipt of the rents and profits thereof, may be compelled to deliver up such possession or receipt to the purchaser or to such other person as the Court may direct.**

**In this Order "land" includes any interest in, or right over, land.**

---

**NOTES**

**[31.1.1]**      **Scope of Order 31 rule 1**

Order 31 rule 1 does not confer on the court power to order the sale of land. Rather its purpose is to provide that such power, where it exists, may be exercised 'where necessary for the purposes of the cause or matter'. See *Ip Cheung Kwok v Sin Hua Bank Trustee Ltd* HCA 7440/1984 (Godfrey J; 17.10.1988). Thus Order 31 does not empower the court to enforce a charging order by sale of land. That should be done under Order 88 instead: *Ken Kee Securities Co v Wong Ying Cheong (No 2)* [1973-76] HKC 446. Order 31 does apply in the context of an administration action or proceedings for execution of a trust under Order 85: *Ip Kwok Cheung* (above).

The court's power under Order 31 is discretionary, and like all discretions, must be exercised judicially: *Kwok Shui Fong v Wong Kam & Anor* HCMP 145/1969 (Briggs J; 12.08.1969).

2.      **Manner of carrying out sale** (O. 31 r. 2)

     **(1)    Where an order is made, whether in court or in chambers, directing any land to be sold, the Court may permit the party or person having the conduct of the sale to sell the land in such manner as he thinks fit, or may direct that the land be sold in such manner as the Court may either by the order or subsequently direct for the best price that can be obtained, and all proper parties shall join in the sale and conveyance as the Court shall direct.**

     **(2)    The Court may give such directions as it thinks fit for the purpose of effecting the sale, including, without prejudice to the generality of the foregoing words, directions**

             **(a)    appointing the party or person who is to have the conduct of the sale;**

             **(b)    fixing the manner of sale, whether by contract conditional on the approval of the Court, private treaty, public auction, tender or some other manner;**

             **(c)    fixing reserve or minimum price;**

             **(d)    requiring payment of the purchase money into court or to**

trustees or other persons;

(e)    **for settling the particulars and conditions of sale;**

(f)    **for obtaining evidence of the value of the property;**

(g)    **fixing the security (if any) to be given by the auctioneer, if the sale is to be by public auction, and the remuneration to be allowed him;**

(h)    **requiring an abstract of the title to be referred to counsel for his opinion thereon and to settle the particulars and conditions of sale.**

## NOTES

### [31.2.1]    Comparison with English rules – conveyancing counsel

In the former English Rules of the Supreme Court, Order 31 rule 2(2)(h) provided for an abstract of title to be referred to 'conveyancing counsel of the Court or some other conveyancing counsel' for an opinion. In Hong Kong the rule merely provides for an abstract of title to be referred to 'counsel'. There being no 'conveyancing counsel of the Court' in Hong Kong, part II of the former English Order 31 is omitted in this jurisdiction.

The fees of 'conveyancing counsel of the Court' were, under the former English Order 62 rule 25, fixed by a taxing officer. There is no equivalent provision in Hong Kong.

The relevant provisions in England are now found in CPR 40.18 and CPR PD 44 para 8.8.

### [31.2.2]    Scope of Order 31 rule 2

Order 31 rule 2 empowers the court to give directions as to the manner in which a court-ordered sale of land will take place. By virtue of rule 4 it also applies to the 'mortgage, exchange or partition' of land under order of the court. The equivalent provisions in England are now CPR 40.16 and CPR PD 40D, para 2.

**3.    Certifying result of sale** (O. 31 r. 3)

(1)    **If either the Court has directed payment of the purchase money into court or the Court so directs, the result of a sale by order of the Court must be certified**

(a)    **in the case of a sale by public auction, by the auctioneer who conducted the sale; and**

(b)    **in any other case, by the solicitor of the party or person having the conduct of the sale;**

**and the Court may require the certificate to be verified by the affidavit of the auctioneer or solicitor, as the case may be.**

(2)    **The solicitor of the party or person having the conduct of the sale must file the certificate and any affidavit in the Registry.**

**4.    Mortgage, exchange or partition under order of the Court** (O. 31 r. 4)

**Rules 2 and 3 shall, so far as applicable and with the necessary modifications, apply in relation to the mortgage, exchange or partition of any**

land under an order of the Court as they apply in relation to the sale of any land under such an order.

(Enacted 1988)

## ORDER 32

### APPLICATIONS AND PROCEEDINGS IN CHAMBERS

I. general

**1.     Mode of making application** (O. 32 r. 1)

**Except as provided by Order 25, rule 7, every application in chambers not made ex parte must be made by summons, and where, under the provisions of these rules, such summons must be supported by affidavit, such affidavit shall be filed at the same time as the summons. (L.N. 127 of 1995)**

---

## NOTES

### [32.1.1]     Jurisdiction in chambers

Most applications in chambers are heard by masters. See Order 32 rule 11 and the commentary thereunder as to the jurisdiction of masters. See also Order 32 rule 12 which provides for a master to refer any matter to a judge.

### [32.1.2]     Ex parte application by affidavit

Routine *ex parte* applications may be made by submitting an affidavit or affirmation, which will be considered by a master without a hearing. This includes most applications which are made *ex parte* because there is as yet no other party before the court. Examples are applications under Order 11 for leave to serve out of the jurisdiction, and under Order 65 rule 4 for a substituted service order. Applications made *ex parte* because of a need for secrecy are usually of the type which under Order 32 rule 11 should be made to a judge – *Mareva* injunction applications, for example. Such applications will require an *ex parte* hearing, from which the public will be excluded under practice direction 25.1.

### [32.1.3]     Inter partes applications in chambers

Order 32 rule 1 requires that applications in chambers other than *ex parte* applications be made by summons. See also Order 25 rule 7 whereby a party responding to a summons for directions may by notice apply for different directions.

Applications to a master in chambers will normally be listed initially for a three-minute hearing. If at such a hearing it is apparent that the application cannot be resolved within three minutes the summons will normally be adjourned to a date to be fixed for argument and a direction will be given as to the time required for hearing. This will be the case where any of the orders sought is contested. The presiding master will seek the opinions of the parties' representatives as to the time required before making the direction as to the time required for hearing. The onus will then be on the party who has issued the summons to invite the other parties concerned to attend before the Clerk of the Court to fix a hearing date in accordance with the direction made.

Where an action has been assigned to a particular list (for example, the personal injuries list), special procedures may apply to chambers applications. See the practice directions governing the particular lists reproduced in the commentary under Order 72 rule 2.

### [32.1.4]   Filing of affidavit in support of summons

Where an application in chambers is required to be supported by an affidavit, the affidavit must be filed at the same time as the summons. This is expressly required by Order 32 rule 1.

### [32.1.5]   Chambers hearings open to public

Practice direction 25.1 provides that with effect from 18 July 2005 most chambers hearings are open to the public. Exceptions include applications relating to family matters and *ex parte a*pplications for injunctions. The less formal procedure previously adopted in chambers, and solicitors' rights of audience, are unaffected by the change. See also practice direction 25.2 as to reports of proceedings held in chambers *not* open to the public. Both practice directions can be viewed on the judiciary's website.

For discussion of the circumstances where proceedings may be closed to the public see *Huang Hsin Yang v Bank of China (HK) Ltd* [2007] 4 HKC 572 (CA), concerning applications to set aside a statutory demand (closed) and for recusal of a judge (open).

### [32.1.6]   Repeated application by summons

Where an application by summons has been dismissed, a repeated application by fresh summons is liable to be dismissed on the ground that it 'traverses' the same ground: *Tong Yi Sang & Anor v Fung Law & Ng & Ors* [1993] 2 HKC 665, 667F-G. The appropriate remedy if dissatisfied with a decision on a summons is to appeal (which will be under Order 58 if the summons was heard by a master, or under Order 59 if heard by a judge).

### [32.1.7]   Co-operation of parties to save costs by avoiding need to attend chambers

The court encourages parties to save costs by dealing with routine and unopposed matters by agreement or consent summons rather than appearing in chambers. In a letter to the President of the Law Society, dated 15.04.2003 (reproduced in Law Society circular 03-141), the Registrar of the High Court said:

> Dear Sir
>
> Re: Master Chambers Hearing
>
> The Masters of both the High Court and the District Court in one of their regular meetings have generally discussed the question of how to save the litigants' costs and the Court's time. They have expressed their views in the following areas.
>
> 3-Minute Chambers Hearing
>
> Every morning the High Court Masters have to deal with approximately fifty to sixty applications. More than half of them are related to time summonses, the results of which are almost predictable; Masters usually allow the extension applied for, on some occasions grant the applications in the form of an unless order, and very rarely dismiss them. As the applicants are seeking the indulgence

of the Court, costs are usually awarded to the respondents. To avoid unnecessary taxation, costs are assessed immediately, and usually without having the benefit of hearing submission from either party, at a rate of $800.00 for attendance by solicitors, $500.00 by trainees and $400.00 by legal executives. Such practice has been criticized: it seems to encourage the respondents to withhold their consent until the last minute at the doorway of the courtroom in order to gain the costs to be awarded to them.

The gross sum assessment of the costs in those applications was originally designed to penalize the defaulters by making them pay the costs forthwith. We hope by doing so parties may be more vigilant in observing the time stipulated by the rules. It does not seem to produce the desired results.

It is trite to say that costs are a matter of discretion of the Court and the respective rates of $800.00, $500.00 and $400.00 are only suggested rates for assessment. In appropriate circumstances the rates can be varied. It should not be assumed that the costs order will be granted automatically at the aforesaid rates. The Court has to look at the circumstances of each case before a costs order is imposed. We take the view that parties should be more co-operative and communicate with each other before an application is made. They should try to come to a sensible solution by way of a consent summons or consent order without attending court. It any party acts unreasonably or deliberately withholds its consent resulting in application, such matter should be reported to the Court at the hearing and I am sure that the Court after considering it will make an appropriate order as to costs.

Summons for Directions in High Court

Summons for Directions in High Court are usually made in certain standard form. The only variables are the number of days to be given for various directions. Our experience shows that the summonses are seldom contested. Many practitioners attend court just to give their consent and to obtain the date for appearance before the Listing Clerk at Room LG108B for fixing an appointment before the Listing Master to hear the application to set down. If parties can agree to a date for the atten dance, the Court will endorse it provided that it is reasonable. Normally, the date for attending before the Listing Clerk is fixed by Masters hearing the summons with reference to the longest period for performance of certain act in the order plus four to six extra weeks, giving the allowance for contingencies. We do not see why summons for directions in most of the cases cannot be disposed of by way of con sent summons. It is not right that litigants' money be spent unnecessarily or Court's time be wasted on such hearing. I would ask practitioners to note that for cases where the parties should have the directions made by consent summons or consent order but nevertheless choose to attend the hearing unnecessarily, the Court may consider making no order as to costs or asking the solicitors to bear their own costs.

Call-over hearings and the like

Similar thoughts have been given to the call-over hearing of different types e.g. Order 14 applications, taxation etc. when the opposing party contests. Parties can easily agree their directions for Court approval. This also applies to many other applications in the 3-minute list like requests for further and better particulars, applications for security for costs and applications to set aside default judgment etc., where the respondent party contests and the first hearing is no more than a direction hearing. Solicitors are surely aware of the usual directions for filing of affidavit evidence in support, the affidavit in opposition and the affidavit in reply within certain period of time, which can easily be agreed between the parties without court attendance.

I wish to emphasize that parties should act reasonably and sensibly. Practitioners should try to co-operate with each other. Adversarial system does not mean every step should be challenged and contested for no good reason. The Court is determined to sanction by way of costs orders against any party who acts unreasonably.

We expect parties to communicate with each other before an application is made to Court. Court hearing should be avoided, if possible. If an application is inevita ble, before the hearing the parties should narrow down the issues and try to understand the case of the other side. It will facilitate the hearing. Please be reminded once again that the Court will not automatically grant costs orders against the party asking for the Court's indulgence. It will look at all circum stances of the case including ther manner and the way the proceeding is conducted. As far as possible, parties should enter into agreement by exchange of correspondence or by way of consent summons. It will help to minimize costs and reduce the workload of the Court.

We understand the difficulty or obtaining consent or agreement from a party not legally represented. Under those circumstances, an application may be necessary.

I hope that you will bring it to the attention of your members by publishing this letter in your weekly circular. This letter is an expression of the general view of the Masters. It will not affect their right or discretion in making their decisions in individual cases.

Yours Faithfully

## [32.1.8]    Paper disposal of interlocutory applications

In 2007 the court introduced a 'trial run' of a procedure whereby, with the consent of the parties, certain types of contested interlocutory applications might be dealt with on paper. That procedure has now been formalised in Order 32 rule 11A. See that rule and the commentary thereunder.

## [32.1.9]    Hearing bundles, skeleton arguments and authorities for proceedings in chambers

Practice direction 5.4 sets out the requirements for hearing bundles, *dramatis personae*, chronology of events, skeleton arguments and lists of authorities for interlocutory sum monses listed before a judge, or before a master for 30 minutes or longer, and for appeals to a judge in chambers under Order 58. The practice direction was revised along with the civil justice reforms taking effect in 2009. The practice direction can be viewed on the judiciary's website, www.judiciary.gov.hk, or that of the Hong Kong Legal Information Institute www.hklii.org, both of which are accessible by the general public free-of-charge.

Non-compliance with the predecessors to the current practice direction 5.4 was the subject of criticism from the bench. See, for example, *Leung Kwok Hing v Sanyo Electric Trading Co Ltd* [1992] 2 HKC 509, 519E *et seq*, and *Tong Yi Sang v Fung Law & Ng & Ors* [1993] 2 HKC 665, 669H-I. In the second of those cases the court warned that it would refuse to hear cases where the practice direction has not been complied with, and adjourn them to a date to be fixed on terms that the solicitors not charge their clients for the costs thrown away, with consideration to be given to the making of a wasted costs order against the solicitors at fault (as to which see Order 62 rule 8).

Para 30 of the current PD 5.4 expressly provides that parties not observing or complying with directions may, in the absence of a satisfactory explanation, be penalised in costs irrespective of whether they succeed on the application. In *Ng Pik Hak & Ors v Ho Chiu* HCA 2359/2008 (Master Kwang; 12.05.2009) the court considered making such an order where there had been delay in filing documents. It was said (para 39) that compliance with the practice direction is necessary to ensure the court is in a position to read all the papers in good time, to understand them and to digest the arguments on the issues in question.

### [32.1.10]   Urgent applications

Practice direction 11.1 gives guidance as to the procedure to be followed when making an urgent application for interlocutory relief. The text of the practice direction can be viewed on the judiciary's website www.judiciary.gov.hk, or that of the Hong Kong Legal Information Institute www.hklii.org, both of which are accessible by the general public free-of-charge. The practice direction was revised with effect from 1 November 2009.

### [32.1.11]   Duty of full and frank disclosure on ex parte application

The Hong Kong court, like its counterparts in other common law jurisdictions, is particularly anxious to ensure full disclosure on an *ex parte* application, and rightly so. The duty to make full and frank disclosure was considered by the Hong Kong Court of Appeal in *Jordache International (HK) Ltd v Guess? Inc* [1987] HKLR 314, where, at 318, Cons VP quoted with approval the following passage from *R v Kensington Income Tax Commissioners, ex p Princess Edmond de Polignac* [1917] 1 KB 486, at 509:

> It is perfectly well settled that a person who makes an *ex parte* application to the Court, that is to say in the absence of the person who will be affected by that which the Court is asked to do, is under an obligation to the Court to make the fullest possible disclosure of all material facts within his knowledge, and if he does not make that fullest possible disclosure, he can not obtain any advantage from the proceedings and he will be deprived of any advantage he may have already obtained by means of the order which has thus wrongly been obtained by him.

The Hong Kong Court of Appeal has held that facts are 'material' in this context if they 'are relevant to the weighing operation which the court has to make in deciding whether or not to grant the order' (*Citibank NA v Express Ship Management Services Ltd & Anor* [1987] HKLR 1184, at 1190C–D, per Fuad JA, quoting from *Thermax v*

*Schott Industrial Glass* [1981] FSR 289, at 298). In the *Citibank* case, the Hong Kong Court of Appeal restored injunctions which had been set aside below on the ground of non-disclosure, holding that the non-disclosure was not material.

The duty to make full and frank disclosure requires more than exhibiting documents to the affidavit in support of the *ex parte* application. This is particularly so where those exhibits are voluminous and the judge presiding on the *ex parte* application does not have his attention drawn to the documents which might militate against an *ex parte* order being granted. See *Standard Chartered Securities Ltd v Lai Arthur & Ors* [1993] 1 HKC 375; *Rever (AMA) Salon Ltd v Kung Wai For Danny & Ors* [2001] 1 HKC 241 and *Richcombe Investment Ltd v Tin Fung* [2001] 2 HKC 115, 121A–B.

See also the commentary under Order 32 rule 6 which deals with the circumstances in which an *ex parte* order may be set aside on grounds including non-disclosure.

## 2.      Issue of summons (O. 32 r. 2)

**(1)     Issue of a summons by which an application in chambers is to be made takes place on its being sealed with the Seal of the Court.**

**(2)     A summons may not be amended after issue without the leave of the Court.**

---------------------

## NOTES

### [32.2.1]     Indorsement on summons as to rule relied on

It is established practice in Hong Kong to note in the left hand margin of a summons the rule of court under which the application is made. In some cases it may be appropriate to refer to an Ordinance or to inherent jurisdiction. Although the registrar of the district court once suggested summonses might be rejected if not so indorsed (see Law Society circular 88-2, now repealed), the practice is not mandatory. It follows that an incorrect reference will not preclude the appropriate relief from being granted where no one is prejudiced. See *Premier Fashion Wears Ltd v Li Hing Chung* [1994] 1 HKC 213, 220E-F (CA).

### [32.2.2]     Summons should state whether chambers hearing in public or private

A summons or notice for hearing in chambers should specify whether the hearing will be open to the public. See para 9 of practice direction 25.1. That practice direction provides that effective 18 July 2005, subject to numerous exceptions, the general rule is that chambers hearing shall be open to the public.

### [32.2.3]     Time at which summons is issued and application to the court is made

Order 32 rule 2(1) expressly provides that a summons is issued when it is sealed with the seal of the court. In the normal course of events the application made by the summons is considered to be made at the same time even though the hearing will not take place until later. Thus a summons issued on the last day for making a particular application is within time even though the court will not hear the application until after the time expires.

In the unusual case of *Wo Fung Paper Making Factory Ltd v Sappi Kraft (Pty) Ltd* [1988] 2 HKLR 346 (CA) a solicitor presented a summons to the registry for issue on the last day of the prescribed period. The registry asked for clarification of the estimated time for the hearing, which was not forthcoming until the next day. As a result the summons was not issued until the next day, by which time the prescribed period had expired. Fuad VP (at 335D) held that the application was late, Hunter JA expressed no view on this question and Penlington JA (at 360H-I) held that the application had been made 'to the court' in time.

**3.    Services of summons** (O. 32 r. 3)

**A summons asking only for the extension or abridgement of any period of time may be served on the day before the day specified in the summons for the hearing thereof but, except as aforesaid and unless the Court otherwise orders or any of these rules otherwise provides, a summons must be served on every other party not less than 2 clear days before the day so specified.**

---

**NOTES**

**[32.3.1]    Time and manner of service of inter partes summonses**
An interlocutory *inter partes* summons must be served within the time specified in Order 32 rule 3. The rule provides that summonses other than time summonses must be served at least two 'clear' days prior to the hearing (though the court may abridge time under Order 3 rule 5). As to the meaning of 'clear' days, see Order 3 rule 2(4). Time summonses may be served on the day prior to the hearing.

Service after 4.00 pm on a weekday (or after 1.00 pm on a Saturday) is deemed to be effected on the following day (or following Monday): see Order 65 rule 7.

Late service of a summons does not deprive the court of jurisdiction, even where no extension or abridgement of time is expressly granted. The power under Order 2 rule 1(1) to treat failure to comply with the rules as mere irregularity may be invoked: *Tung Wing Steel Co Ltd v Brasimet Comercio e Industria SA & Ors* CACV 38/1990 (Cons VP, Kempster JA & Sears J; 25.09.1990) (para 6).

Service of an interlocutory summons is effected by 'ordinary' service under Order 65 rule 5.

**4.    Adjournment of hearing** (O. 32 r. 4)

**(1)    The hearing of a summons may be adjourned from time to time, either generally or to a particular date, as may be appropriate.**

**(2)    If the hearing is adjourned generally, the party by whom the summons was taken out may restore it to the list on 2 clear days' notice to all the other parties on whom the summons was served.**

---

**NOTES**

**[32.4.1]    Discretion to adjourn hearing of summons**
Order 32 rule 4 gives the court a power to adjourn the hearing of a summons from time to time, either generally (*sine die*) or to a particular date. The power is discretionary and the court may refuse to exercise it even where the adjournment is sought by con sent of all parties. See *Lee Kwok Ning Lobo & Anor v Emcom Int'l Ltd* HCA 1338/

2008 (Registrar Au-Yeung; 26.05.2009) where the court refused a consent application for an adjournment which was sought because the parties had revised their estimated hearing time to one day, compared to 3 hours which had been allocated. In that case the court approached the application by asking two questions (para 3):

(i)     What was the reason for the adjournment?

(ii)    Was the application for adjournment made promptly?

Reference was also made (para 14) to the underlying objectives of expeditiousness and fair distribution of court resources (O 1A, r 1(b) & (f) respectively). The parties were criticised for having allowed 'two valuable weeks' to elapse without informing the court of the proposed adjournment, thus failing to comply with para 17 of PD 5.4 (which provides that the court should be notified 'in good time before the hearing' where parties take the view that the original allotted time is insufficient).

### [32.4.2]     Power to impose terms on adjournment of summons

On adjourning the hearing of a summons the court may impose terms as to costs and a timetable so as to minimise delay: *TMC (Int'l) Trading Co Ltd v Shye Lian (HK) Manufac turing Co Ltd* [1995] 2 HKC 469, 472A-B. In that case the court doubted that it had jurisdiction to require payment into court as a condition of an adjournment. However, an express case management power to impose such a condition, when making an order, is now found in Order 1B rule 1(3). That provision came into force in April 2009 as part of the civil justice reforms.

### [32.4.3]     Restoration of adjourned summons for hearing

A summons which has been adjourned generally, that is to a date to be fixed, or '*sine die*', may be restored for hearing in accordance with Order 32 rule 4. The party which issued the summons is required to give 2 clear days notice of an attendance before the office of the Chief Judicial Clerk for the purpose of fixing a date for the restored hearing.

Order 32 rule 4 does not 'place a duty' on the party which issued the summons to restore it for hearing: *The Sansinena Co Ltd v Power Tankers Inc Ltd* [1983] 1 HKC 274, 290D.

See also practice direction 5.1 concerning refixing of hearings, and see the administrative directions issued by the listing judge, both reproduced under Order 34 rule 2. See Order 35 rule 3 concerning adjournment of trial.

**5.     Proceeding in absence of party failing to attend** (O. 32 r. 5)

**(1)    Where any party to a summons fails to attend on the first or any resumed hearing thereof, the Court may proceed in his absence if, having regard to the nature of the application, it thinks it expedient so to do.**

**(2)    Before proceeding in the absence of any party the Court may require to be satisfied that the summons or, as the case may be, notice of the time appointed for the resumed hearing was duly served on that party.**

**(3)    Where the Court hearing a summons proceeded in the absence of a party, then, provided that any order made on the hearing has not been perfected, the Court, if satisfied that it is just to do so, may re-hear the summons.**

**(4)    Where an application made by summons has been dismissed**

**without a hearing by reason of the failure of the party who took out the summons to attend the hearing, the Court, if satisfied that it is just to do so, may allow the summons to be restored to the list.**

## NOTES

### [32.5.1]    Examples
For examples of cases where the court has proceeded to hear interlocutory summonses pursuant to Order 32 rule 5, despite the absence of a party, see *Banca Intesa SpA v Forward Industry Ltd* HCA 1222/2004 (Deputy Judge L Chan; 09.11.2005) and *Yuen Oi Lee Lisa v Heath Co Ltd* CACV 272/2005 (Yuen JA; 01.12.2005).

### [32.5.2]    Application to originating summonses
Order 32 rule 5 applies to originating summonses as well as interlocutory summonses: see Order 28 rule 1.

### [32.5.3]    Rehearing after order made in absence of party
Order 32 rule 5(3) provides that where the court has proceeded to hear a summons in the absence of a party, it may rehear the matter any time before the order is perfected. Once the order has been perfected there is no power to rehear the summons: *Secretary for Justice v Lam Chi Bin Stanley* HCA 148/2001 (Deputy Judge Poon; 04.09.2001). See, however, *Lee San v The Estate of Lee Man Fat & Ors* HCA 5245/2001 (Sakhrani J; 06.09.2007) where an order striking out an action for want of prosecution was set aside 2 years after it was made, on the ground the summons was never received by the plaintiff and he could not have attended in any event because he was in custody in the United States.

6.    **Order made ex parte may be set aside** (O. 32 r. 6)
      **The Court may set aside an order made ex parte.**

## NOTES

### [32.6.1]    Setting aside ex parte order
The purpose of this rule is to enable the court to set aside, on *inter partes* hearing, an order made on the basis of only one side's version of events.

*Ex parte* orders 'go against the normal way litigation is conducted' and should only be granted 'where either the delay would cause the applicant injustice or the party who would be the subject of the order would take action which would nullify the effect of the order': *see L v C* [2004] 2 HKC 387, 391B, per Rogers JA. The purpose of this rule is to allow such orders to be set aside without the need of an appeal.

An application to set aside an *ex parte* order can be made at any time and a direc tion requiring a period of prior notice is not binding: *Seapower Resources Int'l Ltd & Ors v Lau Pak Shing & Ors* HCA 10715/1993 (Rogers J; 15.12.1993). In that case it was said that an undertaking should be required that the absent party will be informed of its right to apply to vary or discharge the order. It was also held that there was no basis to suggest there should be an appeal against an *ex parte* injunction rather than application to set it aside.

In *Goldie v Grandtag Financial Consultancy & Insurance Brokers Ltd* [2006] 3 HKC 302, 313F-G an order was considered to be *ex parte* for the purpose of this rule where the prior notice to the opposing party was very late and of no 'practical value'.

### [32.6.2]    Setting aside for material non-disclosure

It is a well-established principle that on an *ex parte* application there is a duty to make full and fair disclosure, and failure to do so may itself be the ground for setting aside an *ex parte* order under this rule. In *Wo Fung Paper Making Factory Ltd v Sappi Kraft (Pty) Ltd* [1988] 2 HKLR 346, 357H-J, Hunter JA explained the purpose of the court's power to set aside an *ex parte* order on the ground of non-disclosure:

> I turn now to the two principles I conceive to be relevant, in relation to non-disclosure. First the court's power to discharge any order obtained *ex parte* for material non-disclo sure is salutary and necessary. As one of the earlier cases shows, *ex parte Polignac* [1917] 1 KB 486, it is there for the court's own protection. It is necessary to prevent its processes being abused. Secondly, there is another equally significant principle in this jurisdiction. This is to make sure that the court does not get itself in a position of what might be called 'counter-abuse': where this sort of point is regarded by litigants as 'a very present help in trouble'; and where problems arise on the substance to resort to attack as the best method of defence.

And see *Continental Mark Ltd v Verkehrs-Club De Schweiz* [2001] 4 HKC 469, 480G (affirmed on appeal: see [2002] 2 HKC 513) where Deputy Judge McCoy emphasised that the duty to make full and frank disclosure applies 'particularly of anything which casts doubt on [the deponent's] case', citing *The Electric Furnace Co v Selas Corp of America* [1987] RPC 23, 28–29 (CA) and *The Hilda Maru* [1981] 2 Lloyd's Rep 510 (CA).

The courts will only exercise this power when there is *material* non-disclosure, that is, failure to disclose facts relevant to the exercise of the court's discretion on the *ex parte* application. See *Citibank NA v Express Ship Management Services Ltd & Anor* [1987] HKLR 1184, where Fuad JA said, at 1190I:

> While the courts must be vigilant and insist that full and frank disclosure be made in grounding affidavits for *ex parte* applications for injunctions, Anton Piller orders etc, it is essential to bear in mind the true principle upon which this rule is based. Unless the courts use the sanctions which the practice gives them only when the non-disclosure is of facts which are relevant to the *ex parte* judge's 'weighing operation', an impossible burden would be placed upon applicants and their advisors, and affidavits, *ex abundanti*, will tend to contain all sorts of facts and exhibits which are not really necessary for the proper exercise of the court's discretion when *ex parte* relief is sought.

In the words of Macdougall J, at 1191–92, 'Commonsense must prevail', lest encouragement be given to undeserving defendants 'to search for facts a plaintiff might innocently have failed to disclose, in the hope that a judge may consider them to be material and so discharge the injunction'.

The test enunciated in the *Citibank* case whereby non-disclosure will only be consid ered material if the undisclosed facts would have been relevant to the judge's 'weighing operation' was applied by the Court of Appeal in *New Asia Energy Ltd v Con cord Oil (HK) Ltd* [2000] 2 HKC 681, 686B–E, per Keith JA. There, in addition, the decision in *Fenn Kar Bak Lily v Goh Kim Lay & Anor* [1995] 3 HKC 313 was cited.

See also the judgment of Hunter JA in *Wo Fung Paper Making Factory Ltd v Sappi Kraft (Pty) Ltd* (above) where the same point was made in reliance on the above-quoted passage from the judgment of Fuad JA in the *Citibank* case. And see *Refco Inc v Troika Investment Ltd & Anor* [1988] 2 HKLR 623 where Sears J, at 630J, said that the test was whether there was an 'element of misinformation' arising from the non-disclosure.

The effect of failure to make full and frank disclosure was carefully analysed by Bokhary J in *AMD Pack Rack Ltd & Ors v The Barrons Group Ltd & Ors* [1992] 2 HKLR 50, at 53. The learned judge concluded that the court had a discretion to decline to intervene to discharge an injunction on the ground of inadequate disclosure where: (i) there was no dishonesty apparent; (ii) it was by no means obvious that there had been any failure to make material disclosure; (iii) it would be necessary to comb through a large body of disputed evidence to discern whether adequate disclosure had been made; and (iv) where the nature of the alleged failure was not so serious as to demand immediate investigation. See, however, *Scales v Wong* [1983] 2 HKC 199; [1983] HKLR 110 (CA) where it was held that the court may set aside for unintentional non-disclosure.

In *Richcombe Investment Ltd v Tin Fung* [2001] 2 HKC 115 Sakhrani J described the duty to make full disclosure on an *ex parte* application as 'stringent' (see at 120G) and refused an application to continue a *Mareva* injunction where the documents placed before the *ex parte* judge contained 'material and serious inaccuracies', in particular an allegation that the defendants were directors of the plaintiff when the evidence simply did not support this (see at 121E).

In *Hover Base Investments Ltd v Best Concept Management Ltd & Anor* [2004] 4 HKC 557, 562H–564E (CA) the court set aside an *ex parte* injunction on the ground the applicant had failed to disclose a letter which 'would undoubtedly have undermined' its case.

**[32.6.3]    Setting aside ex parte order granting leave to serve ex juris**
Order 32 rule 6 does not apply to an application to set aside an *ex parte* order under Order 11 granting leave to serve a writ out of the jurisdiction. The procedure under Order 12 rule 8 whereby a defendant served pursuant to such an order may apply for a stay of proceedings is a 'complete code' for the purpose of setting aside such orders. See *Wo Fung Paper Making Factory Ltd v Sappi Kraft (Pty) Ltd* [1988] HKC 10, 21D; [1988] 2 HKLR 346, 355H (CA), per Hunter JA.

**[32.6.4]    Appropriate time at which to apply to set aside ex parte order on ground of non-disclosure**
When there is no urgency, the question of whether an *ex parte* injunction should be discharged on the ground of material non-disclosure may be adjourned to be considered at trial (*Steeltex Hong Kong Ltd v Steeltex Scaffold Services Ltd* [1989] 1 HKLR 135, at 140A–C, referring to *Dormeuil Freres SA and Dormeuil Ltd v Nicolian International (Textiles) Ltd* [1988] 3 All ER 197). In the *Dormeuil* case, the court held that it was inappropriate to deal with the issue in advance of trial because the result would be protracted argument.

**[32.6.5]    Fresh relief on setting aside ex parte order**
When an *ex parte* injunction is set aside on the ground of material non-disclosure, the

court has jurisdiction to grant fresh relief; however, 'if the non-disclosure was both material and deliberate I find it difficult to envisage circumstances in which it could ever be proper to exercise the court's discretion in the applicant's favour by granting fresh relief' (*Intercontinental Housing Development Ltd v Quek Teck-huat & Ors* [1986] HKLR 1153, at 1162F–G, per Fuad JA, citing *Bank Mellat v Nikpour* [1985] FSR 87 and *Yardley & Co Ltd v Higson* [1984] FSR 304). Nevertheless, in *Shenzhen Universal Enterprises Industry & Trade Company Supplies & Anor v Wei Bun Trading Co Ltd & Anor* [1989] 1 HKLR 470, the Hong Kong Court of Appeal granted fresh *Mareva* injunctions with immediate effect upon setting aside *ex parte Mareva* injunctions in the same terms for material non-disclosure. Kempster JA found it unnecessary to make a finding as to whether the non-disclosure was deliberate, and no mention of this question was made by the other members of the presiding bench.

As to the circumstances in which the court will exercise its discretion to grant fresh relief on discharging an *ex parte* order, see *Cheung Kam Wah v Cheung Hon Wah & Ors* [2005] 1 HKC 136, 155–156 (CA).

**[32.6.6]    Application to set aside ex parte order not an appeal**
All relevant matters will be considered on an application to set aside an order granted *ex parte*. Such an application to set aside will normally be heard by the judge or master who made the order concerned, and is not in the nature of an appeal; rather it is an open reconsideration at which all relevant evidence may be adduced. In *Builders Federal (HK) Ltd v Elemeta Holdings Ltd* HCA 709/1986 (Hunter J; 04.08.1986) it was said at the hearing of such an application:

> I do not think for a moment that this put me in the bizarre position of appealing from myself. I think the correct approach is that any ex parte order which a judge makes should be regarded as provisional in the sense that when full or further facts are placed before him, he should have no hesitation in reconsidering the matter as a whole in the light of all the evidence that is put before him.

See, however, *AIG (Asia) Direct Investment Fund Ltd & Ors v Ngai Wai Lun William* [1999] 1 HKC 415 where the Court of Appeal permitted an appeal to proceed notwithstanding the fact that there had not been an application to the judge below to set it aside. In the particular case the opposing party had been given notice of the *ex parte* application and had appeared and been heard by the judge making it.

**7.    Subpoena for attendance of witness** (O. 32 r. 7)
      **(1)    A writ of subpoena ad testificandum or a writ of subpoena duces tecum to compel the attendance of a witness for the purpose of proceedings in chambers may be issued out of the Registry, if the party who desires the attendance of the witness produces a note from a judge or from the Registrar or a master, as the case may be, authorizing the issue of the writ.**
      **(2)    The Registrar or any master may give such a note or may direct the application for it be made to the judge before whom the proceedings are to be heard.**

_____

**NOTES**

### [32.7.1]     Leave to issue subpoena for proceedings in chambers

Order 32 rule 7 provides for the issue of subpoenas to compel the attendance of witnesses for proceedings in chambers. Leave of court, in the form of a note from a judge, registrar or master, is required.

The purpose of the leave requirement, in the words of Godfrey JA in *Li Man York Evelyn v Li Wai Tat Walton* [1997] 3 HKC 532, 535C-D (CA), is:

> to provide a filter, so that, where it is plain and obvious that the case is one in which it would be an abuse of the process of the court to issue the subpoena the judge or master can nip it in the bud.

In *Li Man York*, Mortimer VP (at 534 G-I) held that at the leave stage the judge or master should not go into issues such as the relevance and usefulness of the evidence; rather it is sufficient to ask:

> are the proceedings of such a nature as one would expect evidence to be called? Is this a cause or matter being heard in chambers in which oral evidence is appropriate? Is the application for a subpoena an abuse of process?

and if the answers to such questions are in favour of the applicant the judge or master should issue the note required by rule 7(1) and grant leave. See also *Waters v Malahon Credit Co Ltd* [2004] 2 HKC 94 (CA) applying the decision in *Li Man York*.

In *McKay v Rysaffe Ltd & Ors* [1983] 2 HKC 436, failure to obtain the required leave was treated as a mere irregularity under Order 2 of these rules and it was ordered that the subpoenas continue. Mantell J (at 439E-F), citing *Re Saunders* (1919) 147 LT Jo 212, held that the real question was 'whether the judge would have given his authority if asked for'.

With regard to subpoenas generally, see Order 38 rules 14-19 and the commentary thereunder.

**8.     Registrar, etc., may administer oaths, etc.** (O. 32 r. 8)

**(1)     The Registrar or any master shall have authority to administer oaths and take affidavits for the purpose of proceedings in the Court.**

**9.     Applications under the Mental Health Ordinance** (O. 32 r. 9)

**(1)     The jurisdiction of the Court to grant leave under section 69 of the Mental Health Ordinance (Cap. 136) to bring proceedings against a person may be exercised in chambers by a judge.**

**(2)     An originating summons by which an application for leave under the said section 69 is made shall be in Form No. 10 in Appendix A.**

**(3)     The application must be supported by an affidavit setting out the grounds on which such leave is sought and any facts necessary to substantiate those grounds.**

---

### NOTES

### [32.9.1]     Application for leave to bring proceedings against person acting under Mental Health Ordinance

Section 69 of the Mental Health Ordinance (Cap 136) limits the liability of persons exercising the removal and detention powers under that Ordinance to cases of bad faith or lack of reasonable care. Subsection (2) provides that leave of the court is required to bring proceedings. An application for leave should be made in accordance with Order 32 rule 9.

**9A.    Application for a direction under the Limitation Ordinance** (O. 32 r. 9A)
**The jurisdiction to direct, under section 30 of the Limitation Ordinance (Cap. 347), that section 27 or 28 of that Ordinance should not apply to an action or to any specified cause of action to which the action relates shall be exercisable by the Court.**

---

**NOTES**

**[32.9A.1]    Origin of Order 32 rule 9A**
Order 32 rule 9A derives from the rule of the same number in the former English RSC, dealing with the equivalent provisions of the Limitation Act 1980.

**[32.9A.2]    Purpose and scope of Order 32 rule 9A**
Order 32 rule 9A deals with applications under section 30 of the Limitation Ordinance (Cap 347). That section empowers the court to direct that the limitation periods prescribed in sections 27 and 28 of that Ordinance for personal injury and fatal accident cases shall not apply in a particular case.

The purpose of this rule is to enable such applications to be heard by a master: see *American Express International Inc v Ng Pak Sang* [1987] 1 HKC 522, 524I. The rule thus reverses the decision of Lord Denning MR in *Firman v Ellis* [1978] QB 886 in which it was held that such applications under the equivalent English legislation must be heard by a judge. This purpose is achieved by the use of the words 'the Court' at the end of the rule, those words being defined in Order 1 rule 4(2) to include the Registrar or any master.

**[32.9A.3]    The court's approach on application to override limitation period**
Section 30(1) of the Limitation Ordinance (Cap 347) provides that the court may over ride the limitation period in a personal injury or fatal accident case if it appears 'equitable' to allow the action to proceed. The onus is on the plaintiff to satisfy the court that it would be equitable to allow the claim to proceed out of time: *Lee Yuet-ling & Anor v Kwan Kwing-kai* [1985] HKLR 495, 501 (CA); *Tam Oi-kau v Tacksen Shui Hing Godown Co Ltd & Anor* [1986] HKLR 288, 294. The limitation period is not to be over ridden lightly, and the rights of a defendant to rely on it should not be dismissed on a whim: *Cheng Shiu Hong Herbert v AG* [1996] 3 HKC 333, 339F-G. The court is required to have regard to the factors set out in section 30(3). Those factors are discussed more fully in the commentary on that section in volume 2 of the loose-leaf edition of this work.

A key factor is the length and reasons for the delay. Both the period before expiration of the primary limitation period and the period after will be considered: *Donovan v Gwentoys Ltd* [1990] 1 WLR 472 (HL). The plaintiff's background may be relevant: see *Cheng Shiu Hong* (above) where Master Woolley said (at 338B-D):

> the court would be more willing to assist a plaintiff who perhaps has had little education

and whose socio-economic background is such as to place him at the lower level of the social scale than one whose education and intelligence would lead one to expect him to know, or at least be able to discover, what his legal rights are.

Delay in obtaining legal aid may, in appropriate circumstances, be a sufficient explanation of delay: *Yip Wing Hong v Maeda Corp* HCPI 518/2000 (Master Ho; 11.05.2001) (para 27-28). In both *Cheng Shiu Hong* (above) and *Yip Wing Hong* (above) it was recognised that preoccupation with medical treatment after an accident may also be an acceptable explanation for delay in commencing proceedings.

Prejudice is another key factor to be taken into account. Section 30(1) specifically requires that the court have regard to possible prejudice to both the plaintiff and the defendant. Further, section 30(3)(b) specifically directs the court to have regard to the extent to which the evidence for each side is likely to be less cogent than if the action had been brought in time. Prejudice to the plaintiff arising from possible loss of a remedy, in particular lack of an alternative remedy, should be taken into account: *London Strategic Health Authority v Whiston* [2010] EWCA Civ 195 (05.03.2010) (paras 71-75). Thus the fact that the plaintiff may have a remedy against his solicitors would militate against dis applying the limitation period: *Chan Keung v Patt Mansfield & Co Ltd* HCA 8385/1990 (Deputy Judge Mitchell QC; 07.04.1993). Where the defendant would suffer no prejudice, the discretion will normally be exercised in favour of the plaintiff: *Chau Chui Ping Winky v Cathay Pacific Airways Ltd* HCPI 261/2003 (Deputy Judge Saunders; 17.07.2006 citing *Horton v Sadler* [2006] UKHL 27; *Chuck Wai Man v Asian Television Ltd* [2008] 6 HKC 342 (CA).

**[32.9A.4] Examples**
There are several Hong Kong cases in which the court has not hesitated to disapply the limitation period in respect of new claims against parties already involved in the proceedings on the ground of lack of prejudice. See *Kwok Pat Mui & Anor v Fok Chi Wah & Ors* CACV 148/1996 (Litton VP, Godfrey & Liu JJA; 22.01.1997); *Lam Yau Tai v Denholm Ship Management Ltd & Ors* [1991] 2 HKC 554 and *Ng Ngan Chiu v Paramount Printing Co Ltd* [1998] 3 HKC 730.

Other Hong Kong cases where the court has considered its discretion to disapply the limitation period include the following:

- *Chan Keung v Patt Mansfield & Co Ltd* HCA 8385/1990 (Deputy Judge Mitchell QC; 07.04.1993) – the limitation period was disapplied where the defendant was responsible for part of the delay by encouraging the view that another company was the true employer of the injured worker. The court noted that the plaintiff did not have an 'iron-clad' remedy against his solicitors if the action against the employer could not proceed.
- *Tam Kwok Man v KMB* [2002] 4 HKC 492 – the court disapplied the limitation period where the only prejudice to the defendant resulted from its own failure to preserve evidence.
- *Ng Keung Lung v Lam Chik Suen (deceased)* HCPI 512/2004 (Deputy Judge To; 25.11.2005) – the limitation period was not disapplied in a case where no satisfactory explanation for the delay was given and the plaintiff had a likely alternative remedy against his solicitors.
- *Li Chi Hung, Lawrance v Secretary for Justice* HCPI 1036/2004 (Deputy Judge Carlson; 11.01.2006) – the limitation period was disapplied where the

defendant was expecting to be sued and suffered no prejudice by the delay, even though the plaintiff would have had an alternative remedy against his solicitors.

• *Lu Guo Xiang v Hong Kong Ming Wah Shipping Co Ltd* [2009] 1 HKC 466 – the court disapplied the limitation period on the ground (*inter alia*) that the defendant had all along led the plaintiff to believe that he would receive compensation, and this was a major reason for delay in commencing proceedings.

**10.     Application to make order of Court of Final Appeal order of High Court** (O. 32 r. 10)
**(HK) An application to make an order of the Court of Final Appeal an order of the Court of First Instance may be made ex parte by affidavit to a master.**
**(79 of 1995 s. 50; 25 of 1998 s. 2)**

II.  Powers of the Registrar, Judges and the Court

**11.     Jurisdiction of the Registrar and masters** (O. 32 r. 11)
**(1)     The Registrar and any master shall have power to transact all such business and exercise all such authority and jurisdiction as under any Ordinance or by these rules may be transacted and exercised by a judge in chambers except in respect of the following matters and proceedings, that is to say—**

> **(a)     matters relating to criminal proceedings, other than matters relating to the conditions of admission to bail and an application under Order 70 relating to criminal proceedings; (L.N.152 of 2008)**
> **(b)     matters relating to the liberty of the subject other than orders for arrest and imprisonment to enforce, secure or pursue civil claims for the payment of money and orders prohibiting persons from leaving Hong Kong;**
> **(d)     subject to paragraph (2), proceedings for the grant of an injunction or other order under Part I of Order 29;**
> **(da)   applications under section 27A of the Ordinance (leave to institute or continue proceedings) for leave to institute or continue legal proceedings; (L.N. 152 of 2008)**
> **(f)     any other matter or proceeding which by any of these rules is required to be heard only by a judge.**

**(2)     The Registrar and any master shall have power to grant an injunction, or to make an order for the detention, custody or preservation of any property, in the terms agreed by the parties to the proceedings in which the injunction or order is sought.**

---

**NOTES**

**[32.11.1]   Jurisdiction of the Registrar and masters - general**
Section 38 of the High Court Ordinance provides that the Registrar shall have the same jurisdiction, powers and duties as similar officers in England, and such other jurisdiction, powers and duties as may be laid down in rules of court or elsewhere. Order 32 rule 11 elaborates by providing that the Registrar (and any master) has the same jurisdiction as may be exercised by a judge in chambers, save the following exceptions:

(1) *Rule 11(1)(a) Criminal proceedings* –
The Registrar and masters have no jurisdiction in criminal matters save under Order 70 by which the court may take evidence from a witness in Hong Kong at the request of a foreign court.  Rule 11(1)(a) was amended in 2009 so as to enable masters to hear matters relating to conditions imposed on admitting a person to bail. See also Order 1 rule 2(3) by which the Rules of the High Court are in any event not generally applicable to criminal proceedings.

(2) *Rule 11(1)(b) Liberty of the subject* –
The Registrar and masters may make certain orders affecting the liberty of the subject in connection with the enforcement of civil claims.  These are prohibition orders (pro hibiting a debtor from leaving Hong Kong – see Order 44A), orders for arrest to secure the attendance of a judgment debtor to be examined under Order 49B and orders of imprisonment against recalcitrant debtors (Order 49B rule 1B(1)).  Otherwise only a judge may make an order restraining personal liberty.

(3) *Rule 11(1)(d) & (2) Injunctions and similar relief* –
Reading these two provisions together, the Registrar and masters have jurisdiction in proceedings for injunctions, or the detention, custody or preservation of property, (under Part I of Order 29) but may not grant relief save where the terms thereof are agreed by the parties.

(4) *Rule 11(1)(da) Vexatious litigants* –
Under section 27 of the High Court Ordinance, persons who habitually and persistently commence vexatious legal proceedings without reasonable grounds may be subjected to restrictions whereby they may not commence or continue legal proceedings without leave. See generally the commentary under Order 5 rule 6. Rule 11(1)(da) provides that applications for leave by such persons may not be heard by the Registrar or a master.

(5) *Rule 11(1)(f) Other* –
Any other type of matter which is required by provision elsewhere in these rules to be heard by a judge is excluded from the jurisdiction of the Registrar and masters by rule 11(1)(f).

**[32.11.2]   Jurisdiction of judge in chambers which may be exercised by Registrar**
As set out above, the general jurisdiction of the Registrar and of masters follows that of a judge in chambers.
    The ambit of the jurisdiction of a judge in chambers is governed by sections 32A and 33 of the High Court Ordinance.  Generally speaking a judge may sit in chambers

when dealing with matters which are interlocutory, private or administrative: *Mayluck Investment Ltd v Lee Yih Ping* [1996] 3 HKC 245 citing *Pak Lan Ching v Crown Great Co Ltd* [1988] HKC 784, 786.

The jurisdiction of the Registrar and masters under Order 32 rule 11 is not exclusive, but concurrent with that of judges: *Smith & Ors v Glennon* [1990] TLR 494. In *Great Perfect Investment Ltd v Leung Yat Wah & Ors* [1990] 2 HKC 219 (CA) it was held that an interlocutory application may be made either by summons to a master or by motion direct to a judge. Under practice direction 14.2 interlocutory applications should now be made by summons to a master. The application may then be transferred to a judge under rule 12 if the master considers appropriate. By way of exception, interlocutory applications in some specialist proceedings should be made direct to a judge – see the commentary under Order 72 concerning specialist lists.

**[32.11.3]    When powers granted to 'the Court' may be exercised by a master**
Powers granted to 'the Court' in an Ordinance are generally exercisable only by a judge: *American Express International Inc v Ng Pak Sang* [1987] 1 HKC 522, 524G-525F. However, where such power is one which may be exercised by a judge in chambers, it may, by virtue of this rule, come within the jurisdiction of the Registrar or a master.

For the purpose of these rules, the term 'the Court' is defined to include the Registrar and any master: Order 1 rule 4(2). Thus powers granted to 'the Court' by these rules may generally be exercised by the Registrar and masters.

**[32.11.4]    Jurisdiction of Registrar in open court**
The Registrar and masters have jurisdiction to deal with certain matters in open court. See part III of practice direction 14.2. These include certain types of trial, assessments of damages, unopposed bankruptcy and winding up petitions, and examinations of judgment debtors.

**11A.    Interlocutory applications** (O. 32 r. 11A)
    **(1)    A master may —**
        **(a)    determine an interlocutory application without an oral hearing; or**
        **(b)    adjourn the application to be heard before him or another master or a judge in chambers.**
    **(2)    The master may fix a date on which he may —**
        **(a)    in the case of paragraph (1)(a), hand down his determination of the application; and**
        **(b)    in the case of paragraph (1)(b), make an order that the application be heard before him or another master or a judge in chambers on a date specified in the order.**
    **(3)    The master may give such directions as he thinks necessary or desirable for the purpose of determining the application, including directions for —**
        **(a)    the setting of a timetable for the steps to be taken between the date of the giving of those directions and the date of the determination of the application;**
        **(b)    the filing of evidence and arguments;**

    (c)    **the filing of a statement of costs in respect of the application; and**

    (d)    **the filing of a statement of grounds in opposition to the statement of costs referred to in sub-paragraph (c).**

    **(4)   Where the determination of the application is adjourned for the hearing of the summons, no further evidence may be adduced unless it appears to the Court that there are exceptional circumstances making it desirable that further evidence should be adduced.**

    **(5)   Paragraph (4) is subject to a direction given under paragraph (3).**

    **(6)   This rule does not apply to —**

    (a)    **an application under Order 2, rule 4 for relief from any sanction imposed by a court order; and**

    (b)    **an application to extend or shorten the time for compliance with a court order.**

                                         **(L.N. 152 of 2008)**

---

## NOTES

### [32.11A.1]  Power of masters to deal with interlocutory applications with or without oral hearing

Order 32 rule 11A(1) provides that masters may deal with interlocutory applications with or without an oral hearing, or may transfer them to a judge. The rule applies to all interlocutory applications apart from applications for relief from sanctions imposed for failure to comply with an order and applications to extend or abridge time for compliance with an order: see rule 11A(5). See also Order 1A rule 4(2)(j) which provides that as part of active case management, the court my deal with cases in the absence of the parties.

Order 32 rule 11A implements recommendation 85 of the final report of the Chief Justice's working party on civil justice reform. The working party considered that empowering masters to deal with interlocutory applications on paper could result in substantial savings in time and costs (final report, para 519).

The right to appeal from a master to a single judge of the High Court applies whether the matter before the master was dealt with on paper or with an oral hearing: see Order 58 rule 1(1) as amended on implementation of the civil justice reforms.

### [32.11A.2]  Cases appropriate to be dealt with on paper

The Chief Justice's working party on civil justice reform envisaged a procedure where evidence, skeleton arguments and authorities from both sides would be available to enable the master to decide whether to dispense with oral hearing of an interlocutory application. The following examples were given (at paras 521-2) of circumstances where 'oral submissions are most unlikely to add to what is evident on the papers so that the master can safely deal with the matter there and then':

(a)    . . . it will often be clear that a respondent to an O 14 summons should be given unconditional leave to defend or that a striking out application should fail.

(b)    Conversely, it may be clear that the matters raised by the defendant provide no defence against the O 14 claim, or that the basis for resisting an O 18 r 19 striking out application is misconceived.

(c)      It may also be plain that a default judgment was obtained irregularly and has to be set aside.

(d)      The papers relevant to an application for further and better particulars or for leave to amend pleadings frequently enable the master to make up his mind without hearing oral argument.

The power of a master under this rule to deal with an interlocutory application without an oral hearing is a matter for the master's discretion. Although any representations from the parties should be considered, their consent is not required. In this regard it differs from the previous informal system which required the consent of the parties (see Law Society circular 07-747).

Practice direction 5.4 (para 24), as amended contemporaneously with the civil justice reforms coming into force in 2009, sets out the following non-exhaustive list of applications which will 'generally' be considered as appropriate for disposal on the papers:

(a)      Determination of the time and rate of payment under Order 13A (which enables a defendant to admit liability and request time to pay, to be determined by the court if not agreed)

(b)      Further and better particulars

(c)      Security for costs

(d)      Summary judgment under Orders 14 and 86

(e)      Interim payment (Order 29 rules 10-12)

(f)      Setting aside default judgment (Order 13 rule 9 and Order 19 rule 9)

(g)      Amendment (without argument on questions of limitation) (Order 20 rule 5)

(h)      Case management summons (Order 25).

The practice direction (para 25) also provides that a party may apply for an oral hearing if, after the master has directed paper disposal of an application, the party considers that proceeding without an oral hearing is inappropriate. It is provided that such an application shall be made not less than 7 days before the 'order date' (the date fixed for the master's decision to be made known), and it is envisaged that the master may direct that an oral hearing take place on that date.

### [32.11A.3] Unrepresented litigants – Paper applications may not be appropriate

The Chief Justice's working party on civil justice reform acknowledged that some unrepresented litigants would have difficulty in formulating their submissions on paper, and said that in such cases 'the master ought to exercise his discretion against dealing with the matter purely on paper' (final report, para 526).

### [32.11A.4] Listing and management of interlocutory applications where oral hearing dispensed with

The Chief Justice's working party envisaged (final report, para 523) that to facilitate use of the power under rule 11A(1) to deal with interlocutory applications without an oral hearing, such applications would proceed as follows:

(a)      The applicant would be required to issue and serve the summons seeking the relevant interlocutory order, accompanied by any evidence relied on. From this point onwards, automatic directions laid down in the rules and practice directions should apply, subject to the parties agreeing to adopt a different timetable.

(b)     The applicant would not be given a return day in the present sense since the application may not require an oral hearing. Instead, a date which we might call for present purposes 'an order date' would be given instead. This is the date when the master will either hand down the orders made, having determined the summons without a hearing, or hand down an order that the summons be adjourned for an oral hearing on a specified date before either a master or a judge in chambers.

(c)     The order date will be set to accommodate automatic directions applicable to interlocutory applications which will be laid down in rules and practice directions. The periods allowed for the filing of evidence, skeleton argu ments, costs statements, etc, will be provided for after consultation with the legal profession and interested parties. The periods eventually fixed may obviously differ, but for illustrative purposes, the automatic directions might allow say, 14 days from service of the summons for evidence to be filed by the respondent; say, another 14 days for any evidence from the applicant in reply; perhaps a further 7 days each to allow the parties to put in sequential skeleton arguments and costs statements (to permit a possible summary assessment of costs). On this example, the order date fixed on the issuing of the summons would fall shortly after 42 days from the date of issue to allow for the aforesaid steps to be taken. In some cases, the directions may require a shorter overall period, *eg*, where no evidence needs to be filed.

(d)     It should be open to the parties, up to a reasonable time (to be fixed in rules or practice directions) prior to the order date, to agree to modified dates, leading (subject to the court's discretion) to a revised order date. If no agreement is reached, the order date should be retained unless a master can be convinced on a time summons that there are compelling reasons for moving it. Such time summonses would have to be dealt with promptly (as discussed further below [final report, para 525]).

(e)     On the order date, the master would decide what order to make on the interlocutory application on the basis of the materials before him. If, for instance, the respondent has failed to put in any materials or submissions in time and no extension for filing such evidence has been given, the master would make his decision based on the applicant's evidence and submissions.

(f)     Where the matter is likely to go to the judge in any event, the master has a discretion to order that the summons be referred to the judge. Any request by the parties for such a reference would be given substantial weight, but the decision would lie in the master's discretion.

(g)     The rules ought to make it clear that, save in the most exceptional cases (such exceptions perhaps being defined along the lines laid down in *Ladd v Marshall* [1954] 1 WLR 1489), further evidence will not be admitted in the event of the summons being adjourned for argument or in the event of an appeal to the judge after determination on the papers by the master.

The working party was of the view that this system would likely lead to earlier hearings in most cases (final report, para 524).

See also revised practice direction 5.4 which gives guidance on the paper application procedure. With regard to points (d) and (e) above, it is emphasised in practice direction 5.4 that extensions of time which impinge on the order date will only be granted where there are compelling reasons.

### [32.11A.5] Restriction on further evidence

Order 32 rule 11A(3) empowers the master to give directions in relation to an interlocutory application. The setting of a timetable for steps to be taken before the date of determination of the application and the filing of evidence and arguments are specifically provided for in rule 11A(3)(a) and (b). Further evidence may not be adduced without leave, which may only be granted in 'exceptional circumstances': rule 11A(4). The Chief Justice's working party on civil justice reform suggested that exceptional circumstances in this context might be defined along the lines of the *Ladd v Marshall* test for leave to adduce fresh evidence on appeal (see para 523(g) of the working party's final report, quoted above; and for discussion of the *Ladd v Marshall* test see the commentary under Order 59 rule 10(2)). Thus in *Fourway (HK) Ltd v China Nantong Harbour Logistics Ltd* HCA 1618/2009 (Master J Wong; 13.01.2010) (para 9) the court refused leave where the *Ladd v Marshall* test was not satisfied. In that case, as well as in *Fortune Asset Dev't Ltd v De Monsa Investments Ltd* HCA 167/2009 (Saunders J; 21.08.2009) (para 11-12) the court took into account the underlying objectives of expeditiousness and fairness between parties (Order 1A r 1(b) and (d)). The application was dismissed in *Fortune Asset* on the ground that a proper review of the potential issues would have resulted in the evidence being filed within time.

### [32.11A.6] Late interlocutory applications

Interlocutory applications which are made at a late stage, such as at the outset of trial, will be scrutinised carefully by the court. In *Liu Chen v Chan Poon Wing & Anor* HCPI 779/2006 (Master Marlene Ng; 07.10.2009) (para 55) it was said:

> Whether the court should allow a late application for amendment of pleadings, for further discovery or for further witness evidence is a balancing exercise, and the court must exercise its discretion in a fair manner having regard to all the circumstances and the explanation given. Whilst each case must be determined in the context of its own factual and legal matrix, the considerations of the court are largely three-fold:
>
> (a)  the merits of the proposed application, namely, whether the application if granted will assist the court in securing "the just resolution of disputes in accordance with the substantive rights of the parties " (see Order 1A rule 2(2) of the RHC);
>
> (b)  the presence or absence of any real prejudice to the other party;
>
> (c)  any conscious flouting of the rules of court, practice directions and/or case management directions/timetables, or any over-reaching or deliberate manoeuvring on the part of the applicant.

The court went on to say (para 58) that it was 'unlikely to be sympathetic to any late application that has the effect of raising any new dimension or focus, especially when opportunity has been given to the applicant under previous case management directions/timetables to put forward the fullness of his case'.

### [32.11A.7] Summary assessment of costs of interlocutory applications

Order 32 rule 11A(3)(c) and (d) provide that a master may direct that statements of costs, and of ground of opposition thereto, be filed. The purpose is to facilitate summary assessment of the costs of the interlocutory application concerned. See Order 62 rule 9A and the commentary thereunder as to the power of masters to assess costs of interlocutory applications summarily.

**11B.   Court's power to specify consequences of failure to comply with court order on interlocutory application** (O. 32 r. 11B)

(1)   **Where the Court makes an order on an interlocutory application before —**

   **(a)     a case management summons in the action is taken out under Order 25; or**

   **(b)     it gives directions relating to the management of the case under Order 25, rule 1A(1)(a), 2(a) or (4),**

**it may, if it thinks appropriate to do so, specify the consequences of failing to comply with the order.**

(2)   **Where the Court makes an order on an interlocutory application after —**

   **(a)     a case management summons in the action taken out under Order 25 has been dealt with by the Court; or**

   **(b)     it has given directions relating to the management of the case under Order 25, rule 1A(1)(a), 2(a) or (4),**

**it shall, unless there are special circumstances which render it inexpedient to do so, specify the consequences of failing to comply with the Order.**

(3)   **The consequences specified under paragraph (1) of (2) must be appropriate and proportionate in relation to the non-compliance.**

   **(L.N. 152 of 2008)**

---

**NOTES**

**[32.11B.1]  'Self-executing' orders specifying consequence of failure to comply**
Order 32 rule 11B provides for what the Chief Justice's working party on civil justice reform called 'self-executing' interlocutory orders which specify the consequences of failure to comply. The rule implements recommendation 83 of the working party's final report. The purpose of the recommendation was to implement 'a shift from requiring the innocent party to enforce compliance to placing the burden on the errant party to seek relief' (final report, para 509).

   Reference should also be made to Order 1B rule 3(b) which empowers the court, as part of case management, to specify the consequences of failure to comply when making an order, and Order 2 rule 4 which provides that such sanctions take effect automatically unless the court grants relief. Applications for relief are made under Order 2 rule 5. See the commentary under those rules.

   As self-executing order under this rule is essentially the same thing as a peremptory or 'unless' order, as to which see the commentary under Order 42 rule 2.

**[32.11B.2]  When interlocutory order should be made 'self-executing'**
Rule 11B provides that an interlocutory order made before the case management stage

'may' be made self-executing, whereas an order made after that stage 'shall' normally be such an order. The reason for differentiating between interlocutory orders made before and after the case management stage is that the working party did not wish to create a flood of interlocutory applications for relief against the sanctions which flow from non-compliance with self-executing orders. At para 510 of the final report the working party said:

> In deciding which approach to take, it is important to bear in mind the existence of other proposed reforms aimed at reducing the incidence of interlocutory applications. If self-executing sanctions were to be prescribed on the summons for directions [now case management summons], this could well discourage agreements by the parties to vary non-milestone time-limits by agreement and without application to the court. With a self-executing order already in place, the innocent party may find it hard to see why he should, as it were, 'let the other side off the hook'. He is likely to feel that he cannot be criticised for allowing the self-executing order to run its pre-ordained course. Making self-executing orders on the summons for directions [case management summons] could therefore be counter-productive, leading to less cooperation and so to *more* interlocutory applications for relief from the self-executing sanctions.

### [32.11B.3] Type of sanction to be imposed for non-compliance

The Chief Justice's working party was of the view that the sanctions to be imposed in a self-executing order should be 'proportionate to the non-compliance in question' (final report, para 513). The 'proportionate' requirement is express in rule 11B(3). This reflects the need to respect the constitutionally protected right to a fair trial (art 14(1) of the ICCPR and art 10 of the HK Bill of Rights), which may be restricted by sanctions, but only by those which 'serve a legitimate aim, are proportionate and do not destroy the very essence of the right': *Stolzenberg & Ors v CIBC Mellon Trust Co Ltd & Ors* [2004] EWCA Civ 827.

The working party continued by saying that although the ultimate sanction of striking out the claim or defence would be appropriate where the non-compliance is 'such as to make a fair trial impossible', that should be a 'last resort'. The working party referred to *Biguzzi v Rank Leisure plc* [1999] 1 WLR 1926; [1999] EWCA Civ 1972 where the English Court of Appeal took the view that less Draconian sanctions 'often enable a case to be dealt with justly'. In that case the English court dismissed an appeal against a decision in which a judge had held that in considering whether to impose the ultimate sanction of striking out, the real issue was whether there was 'anything unfair in letting this case go to trial'.

In *Momson v Azeez* [2009] EWCA Civ 202 (18.03.2009) a defendant was debarred from defending the claim against him and from pursuing his counterclaim for non-compliance with an unless order for discovery of documents. Refusal to grant relief from the sanction was upheld by the English Court of Appeal as compli ant with the right of access to the court. Rimer LJ said (at para 37):

> Any other conclusion would mean that litigants could with impunity avoid compliance with court orders made for the purpose of the holding of a fair trial.

### [32.11B.4] Application for relief from consequences

The consequences specified in a self-executing order take effect automatically unless the court grants relief: Order 2 rule 4. In *Jorgensen v Slater & Gordon Pty Ltd* [2008] VSCA 110 (18.06.2008) (para 6) it was said that an application for a declaration that an appeal stands dismissed by reason of failure to comply with a self-executing order was 'redundant'. The party facing such consequences may apply for relief under Order 2 rule 5. See the commentary thereunder.

**12.     Reference of matter to judge** (O. 32 r. 12)
     **The Registrar and any master may refer to a judge any matter which he thinks should properly be decided by a judge, and the judge may either dispose of the matter or refer it back to the Registrar or to any master, with such directions as he thinks fit.**

---

**NOTES**

**[32.12.1]     Transfer of interlocutory matter to a judge**
Order 32 rule 12 provides that the Registrar or a master may refer any matter to a judge for decision. It is appropriate that this power be exercised so as to save costs of interlocutory matters which are likely to be appealed to a judge under Order 58 regardless of the outcome before the Registrar or master: *Hong Kong Polytechnic University & Ors v Next Magazine Publishing Ltd & Anor* [1996] 2 HKLR 260, 266. In that case an appeal was inevitable because of authority which was binding on the master, though not on a judge. It may also be appropriate for interlocutory applications which are complex or involve difficult points of law to be transferred to a judge, and the amount in issue is a relevant consideration. The power may be exercised in respect of preliminary legal points arising before the Registrar or master, including on taxation of costs: *Chun Wo Construction & Eng'g Co Ltd v China Win Eng'g Ltd* HCCT 37/2006 (Lam J; 12.06.2008) (para 108); *To Kan Chi & Ors v Miller Peart* HCMP 2111/2005 (Master Ho; 12.05.2010) (para 21).
     The appropriate time for exercise of this power is when the application or matter first comes on for hearing before the Registrar or a master, such as on the 3-minute list, or call-over hearing.

**13.     Power to direct hearing in court** (O. 32 r. 13)
     **(1)     The judge in chambers may direct that any summons, application or appeal shall be heard in court or shall be adjourned into court to be so heard if he considers that by reason of its importance or for any other reason it should be so heard.**
     **(2)     Any matter heard in court by virtue of a direction under paragraph (1) may be adjourned from court into chambers.**

---

**NOTES**

**[32.13.1]     Chambers hearings adjourned into open court**
Order 32 rule 13 provides for matters set down in chambers to be adjourned into open court, and then back to chambers, where appropriate. The rule was particularly significant when chambers hearings were all closed to the public. Since 18 July 2005 when, by practice direction 25.1 most chambers hearings have been opened up, the rule has less significance.

**16.    Obtaining assistance of experts** (O. 32 r. 16)

If the Court thinks it expedient in order to enable it better to determine any matter arising in proceedings in chambers, it may obtain the assistance of any person specially qualified to advise on that matter and may act upon his opinion.

**17.    Notice of filing, etc. of affidavit** (O. 32 r. 17)

Any party—

(a)    filing an affidavit intended to be used by him in any proceedings in chambers, or

(b)    intending to use in any such proceedings any affidavit filed by him in previous proceedings,

must give notice to every other party of the filing or, as the case may be, of his intention to do so.

**18.    Adjournment into or from court** (O. 32 r. 18)

The hearing of any summons or other application in chambers may be adjourned from chambers into court and subsequently from court into chambers.

**19.    Disposal of matters in chambers** (O. 32 r. 19)

The judge may by any judgment or order made in court in any proceedings direct that such matters (if any) in the proceedings as he may specify shall be disposed of in chambers.

**21.    Papers for use of Court, etc.** (O. 32 r. 21)

The original of any document which is to be used in evidence in proceedings in chambers must, if it is available, be brought in, and copies of any such document or of any part thereof shall not be made unless the Court directs that copies of that document or part be supplied for the use of the Court or be given to the other parties to the proceedings.

**22.    Notes of proceedings in chambers** (O. 32 r. 22)

(HK) A note shall be kept of all proceedings in the judge's, registrar's or master's chamber with the dates thereof so that all such proceedings in any cause or matter are noted in chronological order with a short statement of the matters decided at each hearing.

(Enacted 1988)

## ORDER 32A

### VEXATIOUS LITIGANTS

**1.    Application under section 27(1) of the Ordinance** (O. 32A r. 1)
**(1)    An application under section 27(1) of the Ordinance for an order specified in that section must be made by originating summons supported by affidavit and served on the person against whom the order is sought.**
**(2)    The application must be heard in open court by a single judge.**
**(L.N. 152 of 2008)**

---

**NOTES**

**[32A.1.1]    Court's power to restrict abusive litigants from commencing or continuing vexatious legal proceedings**
Order 32A regulates the procedure on applications under section 27 and 27A of the High Court Ordinance in relation to vexatious litigants.

Section 27 of the Ordinance empowers the Court of First Instance to impose restrictions on the commencement or continuation of proceedings by persons who have habitually, persistently and without reasonable ground instituted vexatious legal proceedings. The section provides that the court may order that the vexatious litigant not commence or continue legal proceedings without leave of the court. Prior to amendment by the Civil Justice (Miscellaneous Amendments) Ordinance (No 3 of 2008), in force in 2009, the section permitted only the Secretary for Justice to apply for such an order. The provision was criticised in that regard: see *Ng Yat Chi v Max Share Ltd & Anor* [2005] 1 HKLRD 473 (CFA). Now, in addition to the Secretary for Justice, application may be made by an 'affected person', which is defined by section 27(5) to mean a person who has been a party to the vexatious proceedings or has directly suffered adverse consequences as a result.

The legislation does not define vexatious proceedings. In *Ng Yat Chi* (above) (para 2) Li CJ said that it is not difficult to recognise the activities of a vexatious litigant, giving as examples hopeless claims, misconceived appeals, judgments not accepted, attempts to relitigate, filing of irrelevant, incoherent or scandalous materials and indecorum at hearings such as hurling abuse. Some guidance may also be obtained from the following somewhat fuller list set out in *Re Lang Michener & Fabian* (1987) 37 DLR (4th) 685, 691 (Ont HCt):
(a)    the bringing of one or more actions to determine an issue which has already been determined by a court of competent jurisdiction constitutes a vexatious proceeding;
(b)    where it is obvious that an action cannot succeed, or if the action would lead to no possible good, or if no reasonable person can reasonably expect to obtain relief, the action is vexatious;
(c)    vexatious actions include those brought for an improper purpose, including the harassment and oppression of other parties by multifarious proceedings brought for purposes other than the assertion of legitimate rights;
(d)    it is a general characteristic of vexatious proceedings that grounds and issues

raised tend to be rolled forward into subsequent actions and repeated and supple mented, often with actions brought against the lawyers who have acted for or against the litigant in earlier proceedings;

(e)    in determining whether proceedings are vexatious, the court must look at the whole history of the matter and not just whether there was originally a good cause of action;

(f)    the failure of the person instituting the proceedings to pay the costs of unsuccess ful proceedings is one factor to be considered in determining whether proceedings are vexatious;

(g)    the respondent's conduct in persistently taking unsuccessful appeals from judicial decisions can be considered vexatious conduct of legal proceedings.

The above indicia of vexatious proceedings continue to be applied in Canada. See, for example, *Bea v Owners, Strata Plan LMS 2138* [2009] BCSC 723.

Section 27A sets out the criteria to be applied by the court where a vexatious litigant who is subject to restrictions imposed under section 27(1) seeks leave to commence or continue proceedings.

As amended with effect from 2009, the statutory powers in relation to vexatious litigants in Hong Kong are based on section 42 of the Supreme Court Act 1981 in England and Wales. They implement recommendation 67 of the Chief Justice's working party on civil justice reform. The equivalent of Order 32A in England is practice direction PD 3A, para 7.

### [32A.1.2]   The court's parallel inherent powers

The court has parallel common law or inherent powers to make orders restraining vexatious and abusive litigants. These powers, which trace back to *Grepe v Loam* [1887] Ch 168, were discussed in detail in *Ng Yat Chi v Max Share Ltd & Anor* [2005] 1 HKLRD 473 where the Court of Final Appeal held they are not inconsistent with constitutional guarantees found in the Basic Law and Bill of Rights.

Subsequent to the decision in *Ng Yat Chi* (above) the Chief Justice issued practice direction 11.3 to govern the exercise of the court's inherent powers to restrain litigants. The practice direction provides for two types of order. First there is the *Grepe v Loam* type of order (referred to as the 'restricted application order' or 'RAO') whereby the court can prohibit a litigant from making further applications in existing proceedings without leave. Such an order may be made against a litigant who has abused and is likely to continue abusing the court's process by persistently making unwarranted applications. Secondly there is the 'restricted proceedings order' or 'RPO' whereby the court can prevent a litigant from commencing fresh proceedings without leave. This second type of order is aimed at preventing litigants from abusing the court's process by seeking to re-litigate matters which have already concluded.

The practice direction, as amended when Order 32A came into force, states that it concerns the court's inherent jurisdiction at common law to make RAOs and RPOs whereas the statutory power under HCO sections 27 and 27A is regulated by those provisions as well as Order 32A.

The practice direction can be viewed on the judiciary's website www.judiciary.gov.hk or that of the Hong Kong Legal Information Institute www.hklii.org, both of which are accessible by the general public free-of-charge.

As noted in section 14.3 of the Chief Justice's working party on civil justice reform, this inherent power is not recognised in some common law jurisdictions. See the interesting discussion there as to why the working party was of the view that enhanced statutory powers were necessary rather than relying solely on the inherent jurisdiction.

### [32A.1.3]   Master has no jurisdiction

A master has no jurisdiction to hear applications under section 27 of the High Court Ordinance in relation to vexatious litigants: Order 32 rule 11(1)(da) and Order 32A rule 1(2). This implements recommendation 69 of the final report of the Chief Justice's working party on civil justice reform, which was that all applications to have a person declared a vexatious litigant should be made directly to a single judge.

### [32A.1.4]   When hearing required

An application under section 27(1) for an order imposing restrictions on an alleged vexatious litigant must be heard in open court by a single judge: Order 32A rule 1(2).

   In *Choy Bing Wing v CE & Ors* [2006] 1 HKC 225 (para 35) the court, of its own motion, and without hearing the parties, made an interim restricted proceedings order and fixed a date for submissions as to whether the order should be continued. That decision was given under the inherent power of the court, prior to the amendment of sections 27 and 27A of the Ordinance, and of these rules, with effect from 2009.

   When a person who is subject to an order under section 27(1) seeks leave under sec tion 27A to commence or continue proceedings, that application may be determined without an oral hearing: see rule 3.

**2.      Application for leave for institution or continuance of proceedings, etc.**
   (O. 32A r. 2)
   **(1)   Where an order made under section 27(1) of the Ordinance is in force against a person, an application for leave to institute or continue any legal proceedings by that person must be made by a notice in Form No. 27A in Appendix A containing a statement of —**

   **(a)   the title and reference number of the proceedings in which that order was made;**

   **(b)   the name and address of the applicant;**

   **(c)   the order the applicant is seeking; and**

   **(d)   briefly, why the applicant is seeking the order.**

   **(2)   The notice of application for leave must be filed together with any affidavit evidence on which the applicant relies in support of the application.**

   **(3)   Any previous applications for leave which the applicant has made under section 27 of the Ordinance, and the results of those applications, must be listed in the notice of application.**
   **(L.N. 152 of 2008)**

---

### NOTES

### [32A.2.1]   Form of application by vexatious litigant for leave

Order 32A rule 2 provides that an application for leave to commence or continue proceedings by a person who is subject to restrictions under the legislation concerning vexatious litigants must be made by notice in form No 27A in Appendix A. The notice must contain the information set out in rule 2(1)(a)-(d) and must further list the details of previous applications by that person of the same type: rule 2(3).

### [32A.2.2]　Criteria on application by vexatious litigant for leave
The criteria to be applied by the court on an application for leave, by a person subject to a vexatious litigant order, to commence or continue legal proceedings, are set out in section 27A of the High Court Ordinance. The court is enjoined not to grant leave unless the court is satisfied (a) that the proceedings are not an abuse of process, and (b) there are reasonable grounds for the proceedings.

**3.　Hearing and determination of application for leave** (O. 32A r. 3)

**(1)　An application for leave made under rule 2 may be determined by a single judge without the attendance of the applicant unless the judge gives directions for the hearing of the application.**

**(2)　Where the judge gives directions for the hearing of the application, the hearing may be held in chambers.**

**(3)　Directions for the hearing of the application given under paragraph (2) may include an order that the notice of application be served by the applicant on the Secretary for Justice and on any person against whom the applicant wishes to institute or continue the proceedings for which leave is being sought.**

**(4)　The judge may give directions for further affidavit evidence to be supplied by the applicant before an order is made on the application.**

**(5)　Without limiting the power of the judge to refuse the application, if the leave sought, or the grounds advanced, substantially repeat those submitted in support of a previous application which has been refused, the judge may make an order refusing the application.**

**(6)　Where the applicant institutes the new proceedings or continues the proceedings for which leave has been granted, the applicant shall —**

**(a)　file the order granting the leave, together with the instrument by which the proceedings are instituted or continued; and**

**(b)　serve the order granting the leave on every other person who is a party to the proceedings, together with the instrument by which the proceedings are instituted or continued.**

**(L.N. 152 of 2008)**

---

## NOTES

### [32A.3.1]　Power to determine application for leave without oral hearing
Order 32A rule 3(1) provides that an application by a person who is subject to a vexatious litigant order for leave to commence or continue proceedings may be determined without attendance of that person. However the person will always have an opportunity to be 'heard' in writing. The form of application for leave (form No 27A in appendix A) requires that the grounds of the application be set

out, and Order 32A rule 2 requires that the form be filed together with any affida vit evidence relied upon.

In this respect such an application differs from the vexatious litigant order itself: Order 32A rule 1(2) requires that such an application be heard before a single judge in open court.

**[32A.3.2]   Appeal against refusal of leave to institute or continue proceedings**
Where an application for leave to institute or commence legal proceedings is refused under the Ordinance and these rules, leave to appeal is required: High Court Ordi nance s 27A(2). However that section applies only where the order restricting the person's right to commence or continue proceedings has been made under the statutory provisions. As noted in the practice direction on the common law power to make restricted application orders and restricted proceedings orders (RAO and RPO) (PD 11.3), an appeal lies as of right if the order is made under that power.

**4.      Service of order** (O. 32A r. 4)
      **(1)   An order granting or refusing the leave sought or an order made pursuant to rule 3(3) must be sent to the applicant at the address given in the notice of application.**
      **(2)   The applicant shall forthwith after being sent an order granting the leave sought serve a copy of the order on the Secretary for Justice if he has been served with the notice of application pursuant to rule 3(3).**
      **(L.N. 152 of 2008)**

## NOTES

**[32A.4.1]   Requirements as to service**
Order 32A rule 4(1) contemplates the court sending the applicant a copy of the order made on an application for leave to commence or continue proceedings. Rule 4(2) obliges the party then to serve the Secretary for Justice if the court had earlier directed service of the notice of application on the secretary pursuant to rule 3(3).

There are additional requirements as to service in rule 3(6), which apply in the event the application for leave is successful. It is there provided that the party who has been granted leave must, when consequentially commencing or continuing proceedings, file the relevant papers in court and serve the order granting leave on every other party to the proceedings in respect of which leave has been given.

**5.      Setting aside grant of leave** (O. 32A r. 5)
      **(1)   A person may apply to set aside a grant of leave if —**
            **(a)   the leave allows the applicant to institute or continue proceedings against that person; and**
            **(b)   the leave was granted other than at a hearing of which that person was given notice pursuant to a direction given under rule 3.**
      **(2)   An application under paragraph (1) must be made by an inter partes summons within 14 days after the order granting the leave was served on the person under rule 3(6)(b). (L.N. 152 of 2008)**

---

**NOTES**

**[32A.5.1] Application by affected party to set aside leave**

The person against whom a vexatious litigant is granted leave to commence or continue proceedings will not always have had an opportunity to be heard on the leave application: Order 32A rule 3(3) provides that the application 'may', not 'must', be served on such a person. In such cases the affected person who has not been heard on the leave application may, under rule 4, apply for the leave to be set aside.

6.  **Leave required for inspection of documents relating to application for leave under section 27A of the Ordinance** (O. 32A r. 6)

    **(1) A person may not without the leave of the Court inspect any document filed in the Registry relating to the application for leave under section 27A of the Ordinance.**

    **(2) Leave may not be granted under paragraph (1) unless the Court is satisfied that there is reasonable ground for the inspection.**

    **(3) Leave granted under paragraph (1) may be granted on such terms and conditions as the Court thinks just. (L.N. 152 of 2008)**

---

**NOTES**

**[32A.6.1] Confidentiality**

Order 32A rule 6 seeks to preserve confidentiality of applications by persons subject to vexatious litigant orders for leave to commence or continue proceedings. It requires that the documents filed in respect of such an application may not be inspected without leave, which may not be granted unless there is reasonable ground. The rule has the effect of removing such applications from the scope of Order 63 rule 4 which provides a general, though limited, right of members of the public to inspect certain documents filed in court.

7.  **Transitional** (O. 32A r 7)

    **Where, immediately before the commencement of this Order, an application for an order or for leave under section 27 of the Ordinance as in force immediately before the commencement is pending, then the application is to be determined as if this Order had not been made. (L.N. 152 of 2008)**

---

**NOTES**

**[32A.7.1] Applications for leave made before 2009 amendments**

Order 32A rule 7 provides that applications for leave to commence or continue proceedings by persons subject to restrictions under the legislation concerning vexatious litigants will be subject to the prior law if they were pending when the civil justice reform amendments came into force in 2009.

## ORDER 33

### PLACE AND MODE OF TRIAL

TRIAL

**1.    Place of Trial** (O.33 r.1)
**Subject to the provisions of these rules, the place of trial of a cause or matter, or of any question or issue arising therein, shall be determined by the Court and shall be either the High Court Building or such other place or places as may be authorized by the Chief Justice.**

---

## NOTES

### [33.1.1]    Venue of trial

Under Order 33 rule 1, trials in the Court of First Instance take place in the High Court building or other place authorised by the Chief Justice. See also section 28(1) of the High Court Ordinance which similarly provides for authorisation by the Chief Justice. The Wan Chai law courts are sometimes used, particularly where district court judges sit as deputy judges of the CFI. Choice of venue within Hong Kong is normally dealt with administratively, without input from the parties.

In *Singh v Matilda Hospital* HCPI 717/2003 (Suffiad J; 29.12.2006) a party applied for an order, subject to the authorisation of the Chief Justice, that the action be tried in London. The plaintiffs and a number of expert witnesses were resident in the UK, and London counsel had been instructed by some parties. The court considered that costs and convenience were important factors but was not satisfied on either count and rejected the application.

**2.    Mode of trial** (O. 33 r. 2)
**Subject to the provisions of these rules, a cause or matter, or any question or issue arising therein, may be tried before—**
    **(a)    a judge alone, or**
    **(b)    a judge with a jury, or**
    **(c)    a judge with the assistance of assessors, or**
    **(e)    a master.**

**3.    Time, etc. of trial of questions or issues** (O. 33 r. 3)
**The Court may order any question or issue arising in a cause or matter, whether of fact or law or partly of fact and partly of law, and whether raised by the pleadings or otherwise, to be tried before, at or after the trial of the cause or matter, and may give directions as to the manner in which the question or issue shall be stated.**

---

## NOTES

**[33.3.1]    Order for separate trial of distinct issue**

Order 33 rule 3 empowers the court to order that any distinct issue arising in civil proceedings be tried separately from the other issues.  This power overlaps with those under Order 14A (disposal of a case on a point of law or construction) and Order 33 rules 4(2) and 4(2A) (which are sometimes cited as the source of the court's power to order separate trials on issues of liability and quantum).  See also Order 1B rule 1(2)(h).

**[33.3.2]    Comparison with Order 14A (disposal of a case on a point of law or construction)**

Order 33 rule 3 differs from Order 14A in a number of respects.

First, unlike Order 14A the rule is not confined to questions of law or construction of documents – it expressly extends to questions of fact or mixed fact and law.

Secondly, unlike Order 14A there is no express requirement that the distinct issue be one which will finally determine the dispute.

Thirdly this rule expressly provides that the distinct issue may be tried before, at or after the trial of the other issues whereas Order 14A appears to contemplate preliminary determination of an issue.

Fourthly, there is no equivalent in this rule to Order 14A(1)(4) which expressly confers jurisdiction on a master.

**[33.3.3]    Comparison with Order 33 rule 4(2) and (2A) - (split trial)**

Order 33 rule 3 differs from rule 4(2) of the same Order in that the latter expressly contemplates different modes of trial for separate issues.

It differs from Order 33 rule 4(2A) in that the latter expressly caters for split trial of issues of liability and quantum in personal injury actions.

**[33.3.4]    Application of rule**

Order 33 rule 3 does not lay down any criteria to be applied when application is made for separate trial of a distinct issue.  However any court would certainly wish to be satisfied that costs or court time might be saved, or delay avoided.

In *Henshaw v Sovereign Marine and General Insurance Co Ltd* [1988] HKC 115 (CA) the Court of Appeal took into account possible delay in setting aside an order for a separate trial.

The court should be 'extremely cautious' before ordering separate trial of preliminary points: *Mai Gou v Mak Chik Lun* [2001] 3 HKLRD 248 (CA) (para 10), quoting *Allen v Gulf Oil Refining Ltd* [1981] AC 1001.

In *Chuang Eugene Yue Chien v Ho Yau Kwong Kevin* [2002] 4 HKC 245 Ma J said (at 255B-C) there is 'little point in dealing with any point of law … under Order 33 rule 3 if the relevant facts are either not before the court or are in dispute'. However the court might proceed with a preliminary issue on the basis that the pleaded case be taken at its highest, meaning that it will accept the facts as alleged for the purpose of the application, as in *Donald McArthy Trading Pte Ltd v Pankaj* [2007] SGCA 8 (14.02.2007) (para 2) (Sing CA).

In *Esman v ACMDC Ventures Inc* HCA 9553/94 (Deputy Judge Aiken QC; 29.07.1996) it was stated that a separate trial under this rule would generally be by consent of the parties and in terms agreed by them.

In *Wong Shui Kee Roger v Victor LL Chu & Ors* [2001] 3 HKC 589 the court ordered a defence of absolute privilege to be tried as a preliminary issue in a defamation case. The defence prevailed and the action was dismissed, thereby saving costs and court time which would have been taken up with a full trial.

**4.      Determining the place and mode of trial** (O. 33 r. 4)

**(1)    In every action begun by writ, the Court shall by order determine the place and mode of the trial. (L.N. 152 of 2008)**

**(2)    In any such action different questions or issues may be ordered to be tried at different places or by different modes of trial and one or more questions or issues may be ordered to be tried before the others.**

**(2A) In an action for personal injuries, the Court may at any stage of the proceedings and of its own motion make an order for the issue of liability to be tried before any issue or question concerning the amount of damages to be awarded and—**

> **(a)      notwithstanding the provisions of Order 42, rule 5(5), an order so made in the absence of the parties shall be drawn up by an officer of the Court who shall serve a copy of the order on every party; and**
>
> **(b)      where a party applies within 14 days after service of the order upon him, the Court may confirm or vary the order or set it aside. (L.N. 404 of 1991)**

**(4)    Nothing in this rule affects the provisions of Order 103, rule 26, as to actions for the infringement of a patent.**

---

## NOTES

### [33.4.1]   Power to order split trial

Under Order 33 rule 4(2) the court has power to order that there be a 'split' trial, that is a trial where issues of liability are decided prior to issues of quantum. There is also power to order trial of any preliminary issue.

The power to order a split trial is discretionary and once a decision has been reached there is no jurisdiction to reconsider unless there is a material and substantial change of circumstances: *CKW Co Ltd v Secretary for Justice* [2005] 1 HKC 96, 105B–F (CA).

See also Order 1B rule 1(2)(h).

### [33.4.2]   Single trial normally considered appropriate

A single trial of all the issues between the parties is considered appropriate unless it is demonstrated that it is 'just and convenient' to order otherwise. In *Telford Development Ltd v Shui On Construction Ltd* [1990] 2 HKC 110 (CA) it was stated (at 117):

> The general rule is that all the issues in a case are to be tried at one and the same time. There is power to order that different issues in a case be tried at different times. But that departure from the general rule is ordered only if it is just and convenient. And it is, of course, for the party who seeks such a departure to demonstrate that it is indeed just and convenient.

## [33.4.3]  Onus on party seeking split trial

The onus to satisfy the court a split trial is appropriate is on the party seeking such an order. See *Performance Properties Ltd & Anor v Yip Kim Po & Ors* [2004] 1 HKC 338 citing *Tin Shui Wai Development Ltd v AG* [1989] 2 HKC 492. And see *Telford Development* (above).

## [33.4.4]  Split trial will be ordered where 'just and convenient'

As mentioned above, the court will only depart from the general rule that there be a single trial of all issues where it would be 'just and convenient' to have a split trial. As to the meaning of 'just and convenient' in this context, in *Wincheer Investments Ltd & Ors v Lobley Co Ltd & Anor* HCA 8145/1992 (Findlay J; 23.02.1995) (para 6), after considering *Coenen v Payne* [1974] 1 WLR 984, 988 (CA), it was said:

> I take it, therefore, as the guiding principle that I should not order the issues to be tried separately unless it is just and convenient to do so; by 'just' I mean fair to both sides, without one side or the other gaining an undue advantage by a separation, and by 'convenient' I mean convenient to both sides and advantageous from the point of view of costs.

The above passage was adopted in *Paul Y Management Ltd v Eternal Unity Development Ltd & Ors* HCA 571/2007 (Suffiad J; 08.01.2010).

## [33.4.5]  Where split trial appropriate

In deciding whether it is 'just and convenient' to order a split trial the court will consider all of the circumstances. Some of the circumstances which have been taken into account in Hong Kong decisions are the following:

(1) *Risk of different conclusions regarding evidence of a witness* – In *Performance Properties* (above) Chu J rejected an application for a split trial where that might result in witnesses having to be called twice. The learned judge cited *Wincheer Investments Ltd* (above) where it was said embarrassment might be caused if different judges came to different conclusions regarding the evidence of the same witness.

(2) *Likelihood of preliminary trial disposing of the dispute* – In *Wincheer Investments* (above) citing *Emma Silver Mining Co v Grant* (1879) 11 Ch D 918 it was said that an order for a split trial is appropriate where 'the matter directed to be tried first will, when decided one way or the other, really be likely to dispose of the case'. See also *Re Tai Ping Yeung Motors Ltd* [2001] 2 HKC 611 (CA) where it was held that 'trials of prelim inary issues should only be ordered if, whichever way they are decided, they would be determinative of the case or at least part of the case (per Le Pichon JA at 614E-615B) (citing *Tilling v Whiteman* [1980] AC 1, 17H–18A and *Allen v Gulf Oil Refining Ltd* [1981] AC 1001, 1022A).

(3) *Clear demarcation of issues* – In *Wincheer Investments* it was said an order for a split trial should not be sought 'unless there is on the pleadings a clear line of demarcation between issues on liability and issues bearing on quantum of damages'. See also *Performance Properties* (above) on the question of clear demarcation.

## [33.4.6]  Split trial and case management

In *Chan Jak Tung (t/a Forward & Co) v Baltrans Ltd* [1997] 1 HKC 89, 95G–H Waung J considered the 'wise words of caution' in *Tilling v Whiteman* [1980] AC 1 and *Allen v Gulf Oil Refining Ltd* [1981] AC 1001 in light of what he called 'the new culture of case management'. The learned judge said that now 'it is open and very often incumbent on the Commercial Court to take drastic or sensible step of severing the important issues and push them forward for an early resolution'. However in result he declined to order a split trial.

In *Coenen v Payne & Anor* [1974] 1 WLR 984 Lord Denning MR said that the courts might in future be more ready to order separate trials than they used to (cited in *Wincheer Investments* – above).

An order for a split trial being an exercise in case management is 'pre-eminently a matter for the discretion of the judge' and therefore not to be interfered with lightly on an appeal: *Cable & Wireless HKT Telephone Ltd & Anor v City Telecom (HK) Ltd* CACV 197/1999 (Ribeiro J; 01.02.2000); *CKW Co Ltd v Secretary for Justice* [2005] 1 HKC 96, 109I (CA).

### [33.4.7]    Split trial in personal injury cases

Order 33 rule 4(2A) makes special provision for separate trials on liability and quantum in personal injury cases. It is perhaps in personal injury cases that the demarcation between issues of liability and quantum is most stark. In *Chan Yin Na v Union Medical Centre Ltd & Anor* HCPI 804/2003 (Suffiad J; 27.04.2006) possible costs savings were cited as a ground for a split trial of a medical negligence claim. It was said that if the defendants were successful in resisting liability, substantial costs in preparing expert reports on quantum would be saved. The court accepted that cost saving was a relevant factor, but considered that in the particular case it was outweighed by the possibility of up to an extra year's delay.

### [33.4.8]    No separate assessment of quantum in absence of order for split trial

In the absence of an order for a split trial, it is not open to the trial judge to order that there be a separate assessment of damages. Rather it is up to the plaintiff to adduce evidence on the quantum issue at trial, and if this is not done, only nominal damages will be awarded. See *Born Chief Co v Tsai George & Anor* [1996] 2 HKC 282 (CA) and *Wong Man Tat v Chan Yuen Man & Ors* CACV 347/2007 (Cheung, Yeung & Yuen JJA; 24.04.2008) (para 38 et seq). However in *HSBC Private Trustee (HK) Ltd v Au Yeung Chung* HCA 1662/2001 (Deputy Judge Carlson; 28.10.2008) the court took a different view with regard to assessment of mesne profits where there had been no order for a split trial.

**4A.    Split trial: offer on liability** (O. 33 r.4A)

**(1)    This rule applies where an order is made under rule 4(2) for the issue of liability to be tried before any issue or question concerning the amount of damages to be awarded if liability is established.**

**(2)    After the making of an order to which paragraph (1) applies, any party against whom a finding of liability is sought may (without prejudice to his defence) make a written offer to the other party to accept liability up to a specified proportion.**

**(3)    Any offer made under the preceding paragraph may be brought to the attention of the Judge after the issue of liability has been decided, but not before.**

**NOTES**

**[33.4A.1]  Without prejudice offer to accept proportion of liability**
Order 33 rule 4A expressly provides that where the court has ordered a split trial, a party may make a written offer to accept a proportion of liability. Such an offer is without prejudice to the offeror's defence, meaning that if it is not accepted, and the matter proceeds to trial on liability, the offeror may oppose any allegation of liability without the court being informed that it had earlier been prepared to accept a proportion thereof. By virtue of Order 62 rule 5(1)(c), such a written offer will be taken into account by the court in exercising its discretion as to costs. The effect of such an offer is therefore something like a *Calderbank* offer in that if it is not bettered at the trial on liability, the offeror will likely be granted costs. See generally the commentary under Order 62 rule 5.

Rather than using the Order 33 rule 4A procedure, it will be advisable in many cases to use the sanctioned offer procedure under Order 22 which carries with it the possibility of enhanced costs and interest sanctions in the event of non-acceptance.

**5.      Trial with jury** (O. 33 r. 5)
       **(1)   The provisions of rule 4(2) are, as respects any action and as respects any question of fact arising in such an action, subject to the provisions of section 33A of the Ordinance, but an application for trial with a jury under that section (the time for making which is, under that section, to be limited by rules of court) must be made before the place and mode of trial is fixed under rule 4. (L.N. 152 of 2008)**
       **(2)   The powers conferred by the said section 33A on a judge may be exercised by a master.**

**NOTES**

**[33.5.1]      Mode of trial**
Section 33A of the High Court Ordinance provides that civil actions for libel, slander, malicious prosecution, false imprisonment and seduction, and other cases as may be prescribed by rules of court, shall, on application of a party, be tried with a jury. However, the section goes on to provide that the Court may order otherwise where it is 'of the view that the trial requires any prolonged examination of documents or accounts or any scien tific or local investigation which cannot conveniently be made with a jury'. As to the approach the court should take when asked to order otherwise in this context, see *Fiddes v Channel Four Television Corp & Ors* [2010] EWCA Civ 730 (29.06.2010). An example of a case where a jury trial was refused on the scientific investigation limb is *Dr Esthetic Product Research & Production Centre Ltd & Anor v Next Magazine Publishing Ltd & Anor* HCA 2776/2006 (Deputy Judge Au; 21.08.2009). Other types of claims may be tried with a jury if the court, in its discretion, so orders: s 33A(3). In *AB Volvo v Tanfory Co Ltd t/a Club Volvo* [1990] 1 HKC 158, 160E-F (CA) it was said that the section is 'a clear directive by the legislature that . . . setting aside the five excepted cases, the normal mode of trial should be by judge alone'.

In regard to the discretion under section 33A(3), although there must be questions of fact for a jury to decide, that alone is not enough for the court to order a jury trial, especially in a personal injury case. See *Saatori v Raffles Medical Group* [2007] 1 HKLRD 672 where a jury trial was refused in such a case. The court referred to *Ward v James* [1965] 1 All ER 563 (CA) which makes it clear the court will be very slow to order a jury trial of a personal injury claim, especially in relation to questions of quantum of damages, and to *Williams v Beesley* [1973] 3 All ER 144 (HL).

In *Wong Tsz Yuk v Commissioner of Police & Anor* HCA 1699/2008 (Chung J; 29.04.2010) (para 12-13) it was suggested that increased time and cost might militate against the court ordering a jury trial; likewise the existence of questions of mixed fact and law making it difficult to separate the functions of judge and jury.

**6.      Trial with assistance of assessors** (O. 33 r. 6)
**A trial of a cause or matter with the assistance of assessors under section 53 of the Ordinance shall take place in such manner and on such terms as the Court may direct.**

**7.      Dismissal of action, etc., after decision of preliminary issue** (O. 33 r. 7)
**If it appears to the Court that the decision of any question or issue arising in a cause or matter and tried separately from the cause or matter substantially disposes of the cause or matter or renders the trial of the cause or matter unnecessary, it may dismiss the cause or matter or make such other order or give such judgment therein as may be just. (See App. A, Form 48)**
**(Enacted 1988)**

---

**NOTES**

**[33.7.1]      Powers on conclusion of trial of preliminary issue**
Order 33 rule 7 provides that once it has reached a decision on a trial of separate issue under the foregoing provisions of this Order, the court may dismiss an action or give judgment. As an example see *Ong v Malaysian Airline System Bhd* [2008] 3 HKC 26.

A similar power is included in the list of the court's case management powers: see Order 1B rule 1(2)(k).

## ORDER 34

### SETTING DOWN FOR TRIAL ACTION BEGUN BY WRIT

**1.    Application and interpretation** (O. 34 r. 1)

(1)    This Order applies to actions begun by writ and, accordingly, references in this Order to an action shall be construed as references to an action so begun.

---

**NOTES**

**[34.1.1]    Application to Admiralty actions**

Order 34 applies to Admiralty actions save as is expressly excepted in Order 75 rule 26(3).

**2.    Time for setting down action** (O. 34 r.2)

(1)    Unless the Court has fixed a trial date or a period in which the trial is to take place under Order 25, rule 1A(2)(b) or (3)(b), every order made in an action which provides for trial before a judge shall, whether the trial is to be with or without a jury, fix a period within which the plaintiff is to set down the action for trial. (L.N. 152 of 2008)

(2)    Where the plaintiff does not, within the period fixed under paragraph (1), set the action down for trial, the defendant may set the action down for trial or may apply to the Court to dismiss the action for want of prosecution and, on the hearing of any such application, the Court may order the action to be dismissed accordingly or may make such order as it thinks just.

(3)    Every order made in an action which provides for trial before a judge (otherwise than in the commercial list or in any list which may be specified for the purposes of this paragraph by directions under rule 4) shall contain an estimate of the length of the trial and, shall, subject to any such directions, specify the list in which the action is to be put.

---

**NOTES**

**[34.2.1]    When court must fix time for setting down**

Previously Order 34 rule 2(1) required the court to stipulate a time within which all actions commenced by writ were to be set down. This was normally done at the time leave to set down was granted. With effect from 2009 Order 25 was amended so that the fixing of the trial date or the period during which it will take place is now part of the case management procedure under that Order. Where dates have been fixed under that procedure, Order 34 rule 2(1) no longer applies. In other words, although an action must still be set down for trial, the grant of leave does not need to stipulate a time for doing so if the trial date or period has been fixed at the case management stage.

**[34.2.2]    Dismissal for want of prosecution**
See also Order 25 rule 1(4).

According to Order 34 rule 2(2), where the plaintiff fails to set the action down for trial within the period fixed by Order 34 rule 2(1), the defendant may apply to have the action dismissed for want of prosecution. Such application was made in *Shum Yuen Nim v United Venture Navigation Co Ltd* HCA 2283/1985 (Deputy Judge Findlay QC; 06.02.1990), where the court on the facts declined to grant such relief but made a peremptory order that, unless the action was set down by a specified date, the action would be dismissed. An appeal to the Court of Appeal was dismissed: see [1991] 2 HKC 73.

The court also has an inherent jurisdiction to dismiss an action for want of prosecu tion: *Allen v Sir Alfred McAlpine & Sons Ltd* [1968] 2 QB 229 (CA), approved by the House of Lords in *Birkett v James* [1978] AC 297 and applied in Hong Kong since at least *Poncher v P H Sin & Co* [1973] HKLR 319. In 2002 it was said that *Birkett v James* remains the leading authority: *South-East Asia Finance Co Ltd v Tsui Luen On* HCA 1997/2000 (Deputy Judge A Cheung; 16.12.2002). The same was said by the Privy Council in 2009: *Icebird Ltd v Winegardner* [2009] UKPC 24 (para 8). The discussion below largely relates to this inherent jurisdiction.

**[34.2.3]    Circumstances in which action will be dismissed for want of prosecution**
On an application to dismiss for want of prosecution the applicant must show either intentional and contumelious delay, or inordinate and inexcusable delay giving rise to prejudice or a risk that a fair trial is no longer possible. See (in addition to the above cases) *Computronics International (a firm) v Piff Shipping Ltd* [1997] 2 HKC 53, 57A-B (CA); *Bouygues SA & Ors v Red Sea Insurance Co Ltd* [1997] 4 HKC 149 (CA); *Prosperfield Ventures Ltd v Tripole Trading Ltd & Ors* [2002] 4 HKC 447; *New China Hong Kong Group Ltd (in liq) & Anor v AIG Asian Infrastructure Fund LP & Ors* [2005] 1 HKC 281, 287I (CA).

The court's power to dismiss for want of prosecution is discretionary. Where the general requirements for making an order are present the court *may*, not *must* dismiss the action: *Kerry Foodstuffs Co Ltd v Phulsawat Navy Co Ltd & Ors* [1999] 3 HKC 523, 527G-H (CA). There is still a discretion to exercise: *Wing Ming Garment Fty Ltd v Incorporated Owners of Wing Ming Industrial Centre* HCA 8805/1993 (A Cheung J; 22.04.2005). The process of exercising this discretion has been described as a 'balanc ing exercise' in relation to the rights of both sides with a view to decid ing whether it is more just to stop the action summarily or to allow it to go on: *Gobind Mohan & Anor v McElney & Ors* [1981] HKC 518, 538C, quoting from *The Mollyhawk* [1974] 1 Lloyd's Rep 32.

**[34.2.4]    Intentional and contumelious delay**
Intentional and contumelious delay in this context is delay in flagrant disregard of the obligation to the court and the opposing party to proceed expeditiously to trial. A clear example is failure to comply with a peremptory or 'unless' order. See the commentary under Order 42 rule 2 as to the circumstances in which the court will strike out an action for failure to comply with such an order.

Intentional and contumelious delay is of itself sufficient for the court to dismiss an action for want of prosecution. It is not necessary to demonstrate prejudice. By contrast an application based on inordinate and inexcusable delay requires, in addition, prejudice flowing from the delay.

### [34.2.5] Inordinate and inexcusable delay

Whether any period of delay is inordinate for the purpose of an application to strike out for want of prosecution will depend on the facts and circumstances of the particular case. One of the definitions of 'inordinate' in the Concise Oxford Dictionary is 'excessive', and this appears to be the meaning which is relevant on a such an application. In *Prosperfield Ventures Ltd v Tripole Trading Ltd & Ors* [2002] 4 HKC 447, 452B Stone J found 'a degree of delay which normally is not countenanced in modern litigation' to be sufficient. In *Nanjing Iron & Steel Group Int'l Trade Co Ltd & Ors v STX Pan Ocean Co Ltd & Anor* HCAJ 177/2006 (Reyes J; 07.09.2009) the court took into account the underlying objective in Order 1A, r 1(b) 'to ensure that a case is dealt with as expeditiously as is reasonably practicable'.

Delay prior to the issue of the writ will not of itself be considered inordinate, but it may be taken into account in assessing overall delay: *United Venture Navigation Co Ltd v Shum Yuen Nim* [1991] 2 HKC 73, 84 (CA), citing *Gobind Mohan & Anor v Hutchison Int'l Ltd* HCA 1047/1981 (Clough J; 21.02.1984). See also *Gallagher v MTR Corp & Ors* HCPI 986/1998 (Seagroatt J; 14.06.1999), citing *William C Parker Ltd v F J Ham & Son Ltd* [1972] 1 WLR 1583 and *Nip Kwok-wah v Wing Chong Engineering Co & Anor* DCEC 735/1998 (Judge Carlson; 03.07.2001). Likewise the court may take into account delay both before and after the limitation period expires: *James Investments (IOM) Ltd & Anor v Phillips Cutler Phillips Troy (a firm)* The Times 16.09.1987 (CA).

The delay must be inexcusable in all the circumstances of the case. It is up to the plaintiff to offer a credible excuse for the delay: *Kwan Man Ho & Anor v Ho Hip Lik & Anor* [1996] 2 HKC 401, 405C-D (CA) citing *Trill v Sacher* [1993] 1 WLR 1379.

A plaintiff may be excused for delay which is attributable to the defendant: *Allen v Sir Alfred McAlpine & Sons Ltd* [1968] 2 QB 229. However, the defendant's failure to restore an adjourned summons will not necessarily justify delay by the plaintiff: *The Sansinena Co Ltd v Power Tankers Inc Ltd* [1983] 1 HKC 274, 290D. A defendant cannot complain of delay which it has condoned or in which it has acquiesced: *Computronics Int'l (a firm) v Piff Shipping Ltd* [1997] 2 HKC 53, 62 (CA) citing *Roebuck v Mungovin* [1994] 2 AC 224; *Kerry Foodstuffs Co Ltd v Phulsawat Navy Co Ltd & Ors* [1999] 3 HKC 523 (CA). Similarly a defendant may be taken to waive its right to object to delay if it takes steps inducing the plaintiff to incur further costs in the belief the matter will go to trial: *Lee Yuet-ling & Anor v Kwan Kwing-kai* [1985] HKLR 495, 498D-E (CA). Where the defendant applying to dismiss the action has itself delayed in prosecuting a counterclaim, it cannot complain of the plaintiff's delay: *Zimmer Orthopaedic Ltd v Zimmer Manufacturing Co Ltd* [1968] 1 WLR 1349 (CA). The court may insist that it will only dismiss the action if the counterclaim is also dismissed: *Bank of India v BK Rekhatex (HK) Ltd & Ors* HCA 3017/1985 (Barnett J; 25.09.1992).

In some cases it is suggested that acquiescence or waiver gives rise to estoppel against the party seeking to dismiss for want of prosecution. See, for example, *Hongkong & Shanghai Banking Corp Ltd v Kuan Tao Sheng* [1998] 1 HKC 438. However, in *Hymer v Mass Transit Railway Corp & Ors* [2000] 2 HKLRD 589, 601H *et seq* (CA) it was held that acquiescence or waiver is merely a factor to be taken into account in exercise of the court's discretion: see the judgment of Ribeiro JA citing *Roebuck v Mungovin* (above) where Lord Browne-Wilkinson said it was 'confusing' to use concepts such as estoppel.

Some of the other factors which the court may take into consideration in deciding whether delay is excusable are the following:

(1)     *Negotiations between the parties with a view to settlement* – See, for example, *Hoi Sing Construction Co Ltd v ITC Corp Ltd* HCA 11433/1998 (Deputy Judge Carlson; 22.04.2005); *Wing Ming Garment Fty Ltd v Incorporated Owners of Wing Ming Industrial Centre* HCA 8805/1993 (A Cheung J; 22.04.2005). In *Hoi Sing Construction* the court examined without prejudice correspondence in considering whether it rendered the delay excusable. The court is entitled to have regard to such correspondence by exception to the without prejudice rule where 'settlement discussions are said to explain the delay in moving matters forward': *Barton v Potash Corp of Saskatchewan* [2009] SKCA 7 (para 15), referring to *Unilever plc v The Procter & Gamble Co* [2001] 1 All ER 783 (CA) (NB at 792e-f).

(2)     *Scarcity of funds or delay in obtaining legal aid* - See, for example, *Hoi Sing Construction* (above) and *Hymer* (above). Delay on account of impecuniosity must be balanced against prejudice to the defendant: *Ngan Ching Pai v Dr Chan Wai Lam William & Ors* HCA 10002/1991 (Findlay J; 27.07.1999)

(3)     *General extension of time by agreement* – In *Wycombe Investment Ltd v Leong Siu Hung* HCA 5665/1997 (Sakhrani J; 20.09.2004) the court took into account the fact the parties had agreed (pursuant to Order 3 rule 5) to extend generally the time for service of expert reports. In *Wing Ming Garment Fty* (above) the court took into account an agreement to extend generally the time for exchange of witness statements.

(4)     *Difficulty in obtaining access to evidence* – See, for example, *Hoi Sing Construction* (above) where it was alleged that the defendant had hampered the plaintiff's prepa ration of the case by taking away accounting records, but the court found an insufficiency of evidence on this point.

(5)     *Seeking advice of specialist London counsel* – This excuse for delay was raised in *Hoi Sing Construction* (above), but not relied upon by the court to any significant extent.

(6)     *Change of solicitors* – The court recognises that a party has the right to change its legal team, but this is not in itself an excuse for causing delay to the defendant: *China Link Construction Co Ltd v China Insurance Co Ltd* [2002] 1 HKLRD 844, 865E-F; *Hoi Sing Construction* (above).

(7)     *Incapacity of party* – Imprisonment and ill-health have been cited as factors rendering delay excusable: *Prosperfield Ventures Ltd v Tripole Trading Ltd & Ors* [2002] 4 HKC 447.

(8)     *Waiting for point of law to be determined in another case* – Delay may be excusable where it is motivated by a desire to wait for resolution of a contentious point of law, which affects the case, pending in another action: *Team Glory Dev't Ltd v So Luen Fai* [2008] 4 HKC 493 (reversed on appeal on the facts of the case – [2009] 2 HKC 297). See also *Desmond v MGN Ltd* [2008] IESC 56 (15.10.2008) where the Supreme Court of Ireland found delay in a libel action excusable in part because of a deliberate decision to 'park' the proceedings pending the outcome of a tribunal

investigation into the matter.

Where delay for good reason is anticipated in advance 'the plaintiff should put that reason to the defendant and seek the defendant's agreement': *Nissei Sangyo America, Ltd v Philip Lawrence Choy* CACV 35/1995 (Litton VP, Godfrey & Liu JJA; 29.06.1995); *Can-Asia Capital Co Ltd v Kwok Yee William* [1995] 1 HKC 521, 530A-B. Any such agreement would strongly militate against an application to dismiss for want of prosecution.

### [34.2.6]    Prejudice

On an application to dismiss a pending action for want of prosecution on the basis of inordinate and inexcusable delay it is necessary to demonstrate prejudice resulting from that delay. The situation may be different where the plaintiff has already had its day in court and the delay occurs in appeal or review proceedings. See *Secretary of State for the Environment v Euston Centre Investments Ltd* [1995] Ch 201 (CA) where it was held that prejudice did not need to be shown on an application to dismiss for want of prosecution an application for leave to appeal an arbitral award. And see *Interasia Bag Manufacturers Ltd v Commissioner of Inland Revenue* [2009] 5 HKLRD 818 (CA) where that case was referred to in a want of prosecution application regarding an appeal against a judicial review.

Traditionally the question of prejudice resulting from the delay has been assessed from the point of view of the opposing party. The question has been whether the defendant has been prejudiced by the plaintiff failing to prosecute the action with due expedition. However, on the eve of the CPR coming into force in England in 1999, it was suggested that thereafter delay would be assessed 'not only from the point of view of the prejudice caused to the particular litigants whose case it is, but also in relation to the effect it can have on other litigants who are wishing to have their cases heard and the prejudice which is caused to the due administration of civil justice': *Arbuthnot Lathan Bank Ltd v Trafalgar Holdings Ltd* [1997] The Times, 29 December; [1998] 1 WLR 1426, 1436E-F (CA), per Lord Woolf MR. The underlying objective of ensuring that the resources of the court are distributed fairly in Order 1A rule 1(f) would now be a basis for doing so in Hong Kong. In *Re Wing Fai Construction Co Ltd* HCCW 735/2002 (Kwan JA; 08.12.2009) (para 12) leave to appeal was granted, the court contemplating that this issue would be raised before the Court of Appeal.

The question whether a defendant has been prejudiced by the delay 'is a matter of fact and degree and each case depends upon its own facts': *Cheung Sau Chu Rosanna v Li Kwok Leung* [1994] 2 HKC 592, 594H. The burden of establishing prejudice lies on the defendant: *Gobind Mohan & Anor v McElney & Ors* [1981] HKC 518, 524D-E, citing *Allen v McAlpine* (above).

A causal link between the delay and the prejudice must be shown: *Gobind Mohan* (above), at 533; *Wong Yat Hung v Sun Kon Sin Transportation (a firm)* HCPI 116/1997 (Suffiad J; 30.12.1999) citing *Rath v C S Lawrence & Partners* [1991] 1 WLR 399, 410. Thus prejudice resulting from the defendant's own failure to gather necessary evidence will not support an application to dismiss the plaintiff's action: *Vaswani v General Accident Insurance Asia Ltd* [2002] 3 HKC 450, 454C; *Core Pacific-Yamaichi Finance Co Ltd v Leung Siu Wai & Ors* HCCL 224/1998 (Stone J; 30.05.2005); *ASM Assembly Automation Ltd & Anor v Chan Lo Kwan & Anor* HCA 7622/1999 (Deputy Judge Gill; 21.10.2005).

Usually, but not necessarily, the prejudice to be shown is prejudice in the sense that a fair trial is no longer possible. This often relates to difficulties with regard to evidence. For example:

(1)     *Disappearance of witnesses* – In *Kwan Man Ho & Anor v Ho Hip Lik & Anor* [1996] 2 HKC 401 (CA) after 11 years of delay in a probate case the solicitor and clerk in charge of execution of the will had both retired, a witness to a codicil could not be located and other witnesses had emigrated. The relevance of the missing witness's evidence may a factor in assessing whether there is prejudice, as in *CA Pacific Finance Ltd v Sin Mei Chun Nadia* HCA 838/1998 (Deputy Judge Muttrie; 23.02.2006). Where a party had an opportunity to take a statement from a witness and ought to have done so at an early stage, the court may take the view that any prejudice from the subsequent non-availability of that witness is the party's own fault and not attributable to the opposing party's delay. See *Lee Kin Yan t/a Kin Shing Eng'g Co v Honeywell Ltd* CACV 35/2000 (Rogers & Woo JJA; 19.05.2000), referring to *Hunter v Skingley* [1997] 1 WLR 1466.

(2)     *Fading of memory* – The fading of memory by reason of passage of time may be inferred and need not necessarily be specifically proved: *Wong Yat Hung v Sun Kon Sin Transportation (a firm)* HCPI 116/1997 (Suffiad J; 30.12.1999). In *Lee Shing Lai v Lou Tong Chiu Kee Construction Co Ltd* HCCT 46/2005 (Reyes J; 14.10.2005) the court was of the view that the dimming of memories 17 years after the writ had been issued was an 'insurmountable obstacle to the conduct of a fair trial'. However, faded memory does not necessarily mean a fair trial is not possible: *Hymer v Mass Transit Railway Corp & Ors* [2000] 2 HKLRD 589. There may still be sufficient documentary evidence. Further, in some cases recollection of events may be less important than the view the trial judge takes of the witnesses' integrity: *Gobind Mohan* (above) at 532. In *Re Wing Fai Construction Co Ltd* HCCW 735/2002 (Kwan J; 07.10.2009) (para 65) the court took the view that prejudice resulting from fading memory could have been avoided by taking 'detailed proofs of evidence from . . . the wit nesses at the beginning, when memories would be freshest'.

(3)     *Loss of documentary evidence* – Loss of documentary evidence may consti tute prejudice sufficient to justify striking out, but it will not often be easy to demonstrate a causal connection between the delay and the loss. In *United Venture Navigation Co Ltd v Shum Yuen Nim* [1991] 2 HKC 73, 88B-C (CA) and *Lui Chun Kwong v Kier HK Ltd & Ors* [1995] 1 HKC 695, 708G-I prejudice was not demonstrated since the documentary evidence was lost prior to the delay.

Prejudice not relating to evidential matters may also be taken into account. In *Nissei Sangyo America, Ltd v Philip Lawrence Choy* CACV 35/1995 (Litton VP, Godfrey & Liu JJA; 29.06.1995), the defendant did not intend to call any evidence at trial, but his application to dismiss for want of prosecution succeeded on what the majority, citing English authority, described as 'non-evidential prejudice'.

Non-evidential prejudice can arise from the delay itself. In *Biss v Lambeth etc Health Authority* [1978] 1 WLR 382 (CA) it was held that prejudice can arise simply from having an action hanging over one's head indefinitely. This '*Biss* type prejudice' is a 'well-recognised head of prejudice, particularly where professional men and organisations are involved': *Hymer v Mass Transit Railway Corp & Ors* [2000] 2 HKLRD 589, 614-15 (CA). 'A good example is a case in which fraud, or professional negligence, is alleged against a professional man. Charges of that nature may be most damaging to his practice and the court should do all it can to protect him from this': *Can-Asia Capital Co Ltd v Kwok Yee William* [1995] 1 HKC 525H (CA). However *Biss* type prejudice 'by itself is unlikely to provide a ground for striking out': *Trill v Sacher* [1993] 1 WLR 1379, 1399F-G (CA); *Bank of China (HK) Ltd v Simon Siu, Wong, Lam & Chan* HCA 1905/2002 (Deputy Judge Poon; 29.09.2006) para 63.

Other examples of non-evidential prejudice can be seen in the following authorities:

- In *Kwan Man Ho & Anor v Ho Hip Lik & Anor* [1996] 2 HKC 401 (CA) the court took into account the defendant's loss of an opportunity to sell property which was tied up by *lis pendens* until disposal of the action.

- In *Bouygues SA & Ors v Red Sea Insurance Co Ltd* [1997] 4 HKC 149 (CA) it was argued that prejudice arose from the fact the defendant's insurers had been liquidated (though on the facts of the case the court found no such prejudice arose: see at 158C-E).

- In *Eastgate Partners Ltd v Tejavibulya* CACV 289/2005 (Rogers VP & Le Pichon JA; 16.03.2006) it was held that the deteriorating health of one of the defendants could be relied on to show prejudice, though it was not suggested that the deterioration was caused by the delay. The court also took into account the fact that the plaintiff had led the defendant to believe it would not proceed with the action.

### [34.2.7] Multiple defendants

Where an application to dismiss for want of prosecution is brought by only one or some of a group of defendants the question arises whether, if the action is to be dismissed at all, it should be dismissed as against only the applicants or all defendants.

A 'strong case' is required to persuade the court to dismiss an action against one defendant and allow it to proceed against another: *Lui Chun Kwong v Kier HK Ltd* & Ors [1995] 1 HKC 695, 715E-G. In *Hymer v Mass Transit Railway Corp & Ors* [2002] 2 HKLRD 589, 606A-C (CA) it was said that a partial striking out would be 'exceptional'. In *Wing Ming Garment Fty Ltd v Incorporated Owners of Wing Ming Industrial Centre & Ors* HCA 8805/1993 (A Cheung J; 22.04.2005) the court declined to dismiss for want of prosecution against one defendant where there was a real chance it would be brought back into the proceedings by other defendants issuing a contribution or third party notice.

In *Kwan Man Ho & Anor v Ho Hip Lik & Anor* [1996] 2 HKC 401 (CA) the court dismissed the action as against all defendants on the appeal of one of them. Such a result will be rare. As noted by A Cheung J in *Wing Ming Garment Fty* (above) the decision in *Kwan Man Ho* was 'highly fact-sensitive' in a 'very special' probate action.

### [34.2.8] Dismissal for want of prosecution before expiration of limitation period

An application to dismiss for want of prosecution will not normally be granted during the currency of the limitation period. See *The Andros* [1987] 2 HKC 48 (PC from HK); *Hongkong & Shanghai Banking Corp Ltd v Kuan Tao Sheng & Ors* [1998] 1

HKC 438 (CA); and *New China Hong Kong Group Ltd (in liq) & Anor v AIG Asian Infrastructure Fund LP & Ors* [2005] 1 HKC 281, 298H *et seq* (CA), all citing *Birkett v James* [1978] AC 297 (note the speech of Lord Diplock at 332D). The reason is that the plaintiff could simply issue a fresh writ with the result that dismissal might result in more delay and expense: *Official Administrator v AG* [1981] HKLR 429, 432J, thereby aggravating any prejudice to the defendant: *South-East Asia Finance Co Ltd v Tsui Luen On* HCA 1997/2000 (Deputy Judge A Cheung; 16.12.2002) citing *Birkett v James* (above).

However, there may be circumstances in which the fresh action would be liable to be struck out. In such cases dismissal of the earlier action would not be futile. For example, a fresh action may be struck out as an abuse of process if it replicates proceedings which have already been dismissed for contumelious conduct such as failure to comply with a peremptory or 'unless' order. See *Tolley v Morris* [1979] 1 WLR 593 (HL) and *Janov v Morris* [1981] 1 WLR 1389 (CA). Other exceptional circumstances in which an action may be dismissed for want of prosecution during the currency of the limitation period were discussed in *South-East Asia Finance Co Ltd* (above) where it was held that the fact money had been locked up for 2 years could be taken into account. In *DHSS v Ereira* [1973] 3 All ER 421 (CA) (explaining *Spring Grove Services Ltd v Deane* (1972) 116 Sol Jo 844 (CA)) it was held that a subsequent action might be struck out as an abuse of pro cess where a witness is no longer available.

When considering the limitation period in this context, the court should normally confine itself to the cause of action as pleaded in the case before it. The fact that there might be another cause of action, which is not statute-barred, and could be the subject of another action, should not normally be taken into account. See *Chevalier (E&M Contracting) Ltd v Rotegear Development Ltd & Ors* HCA 1717/1990 (Deputy Judge Fung; 09.06.2005).

**[34.2.9]     Striking out where no intention to proceed to trial**
Closely related to the court's power to dismiss for want of prosecution is the power to strike out on the ground of abuse of process where the plaintiff has no intention to proceed to trial. See the commentary under Order 18 rule 19(1) (d).

**[34.2.10]     Appeal from decision on application to dismiss for want of prosecution**
It follows from the fact that the court's power to dismiss for want of prosecution involves an exercise of discretion that an appellate court will not interfere lightly. In *Hymer v Mass Transit Railway Corp & Ors* [2000] 2 HKLRD 589, 601B-C the Court of Appeal said it would only interfere if the court below 'erred in principle' or if there was a need to promote consistency. In *Kerry Foodstuffs Co Ltd v Phulsawat Navy Co Ltd & Ors* [1999] 3 HKC 523, 527F-G (CA) Godfrey JA expressed the view that a particularly strong case has to be shown to justify appellate interference with a decision to *refuse* an application for dismissal for want of prosecution. See also *Conticorp SA v Central Bank of Ecuador*[2007] UKPC 40 (JCPC) (para 24) where Lord Neuberger said these points have 'particular force' on a final appeal against refusal to strike out for want of prosecution.

**[34.2.11]     Leave to set down for trial and fixing of dates**
As noted above, from the coming into force of the civil justice reforms in 2009 the

procedures for seeking leave to set down for trial and fixing a trial date are now largely dealt with as part of case management under Order 25. The practice direction (5.2) may be viewed on the judiciary's website www.judiciary.gov.hk or that of the Hong Kong Legal Information Institute www.hklii.org, both of which are accessible by the general pubic free-of-charge.

**[34.2.12]    Estimating length of trial**

Order 34 rule 2(3) provides that (subject to certain exceptions) an order for trial before a judge shall state the estimated length of trial. In *Mandecly Ltd & Anor v Hao Wei & Ors* [2005] 2 HKLRD 592 Ma CJHC emphasised (at para 8) that the parties have a duty to provide the court with conscientiously considered estimates in order to avoid trials having to be adjourned part heard or other hearings having to be postponed. The Chief Judge said that this is a 'continuing obligation' and that the court 'should be informed at the earliest possible opportunity if the original dates need to be revised'. He concluded by saying that failure to take seriously the duty to provide proper estimates may result in 'sanctions against the relevant party or his legal representatives, whether by way of costs or otherwise'. See also Order 1A rule 3 and the commentary thereunder concerning the duty to assist the court.

**[34.2.13]    Listing of adjourned hearings**

Where a trial or other hearing is adjourned, the hearing will have to be refixed unless the adjournment is to a fixed date. According to practice direction 7.1 (para 10) this is an administrative function and not subject to appeal.

Administrative directions on listing of adjourned hearings have been given by the Listing Judge on 17 May 1995. Listing personnel will only consider the availability of the court and shall give the earliest available date. The state of counsel's diary will be taken into account only where an order to that effect has been made. The directions (which are included in guidance on registry practice circulated to solicitors from time to time — see, for example appendix 9 to Law Society circular 06-79), read as follows:

*Administrative Directions from the Listing Judge on listing of adjourned hearings*

1.   In the absence of a court order ordering the adjourned hearing to be fixed in consultation with counsel's diary or the consent of all affected parties, the *earliest* available date shall be given. No consideration shall be given to the state of counsel's diary in such circumstances. The sole consideration is the availability of a court.

2.   If a party wishes listing personnel to take into account the state of diary of his counsel, an order to that effect must first be obtained from the court when the adjournment was ordered or subsequent thereto but prior to the appointment for fixing the adjourned hearing.

3.   An order for dates to be fixed in consultation with counsel's diary shall be given effect in the manner as specified in paragraph 5(e) of practice direction 7.1 [which has been superseded and provided that counsel's wishes will be taken into account only so far as convenient to the court diaries, which shall have priority.]

4.   It is the responsibility of a party to seek an order from the court, at the time the adjournment was ordered or subsequent thereto but prior to the appointment for fixing the adjourned hearing, for the hearing not to be fixed before a named date if that party is alleging that a particular minimum time is required for preparation for hearing. In the absence of such a court order or the consent of all affected parties, listing personnel shall not take into account any representation that the earliest available

date will not give sufficient time to a party to prepare for the adjourned hearing.

See also Order 32 rule 4 concerning adjournment of summonses and Order 35 rule 3 concerning adjournment of trial.

**3.      Lodging documents when setting down** (O. 34 r. 3)
    **(1)    In order to set down for trial an action which is to be tried before a Judge, the party setting it down must deliver to the Registrar, by post or otherwise, a request that the action may be set down for trial, together with a bundle (for the use of the judge) consisting of one copy each of the following documents that is to say—**
      **(a)    the writ,**
      **(b)    the pleadings (including any affidavits ordered to stand as pleadings) any request or order for particulars and the particulars given,**
      **(c)    all orders made —**
         **(i)     pursuant to the questionnaire completed in accordance with Order 25, rule 1(1)(a);**
         **(ii)    pursuant to a case management summons; and**
         **(iii)   at a case management conference or pre-trial review, (L.N. 152 of 2008)**
      **(d)    the requisite legal aid documents, if any, and (L.N. 223 of 1995)**
      **(e)    all witness statements served under the provisions of Order 38 rule 2A. (L.N. 223 of 1995)**
    **(2)    The said bundle must be bound up in the proper chronological order, save that voluntary particulars of any pleading and particulars to which Order 18, rule 12(7) applies shall be placed immediately after the pleading to which they relate.**
    **(3)    In this rule "the requisite legal aid documents" means any documents which are required to be filed in the Registry under the Legal Aid Ordinance (Cap. 91) or the regulations made thereunder. (L.N. 165 of 1992)**

---

**NOTES**

**[34.3.1]      The setting down bundle**
Order 34 rule 3 provides that when setting down an action for trial, a bundle of pleadings, witness statements, *etc* must be delivered to the Registrar. The rule states that the bundle is for the use of the judge.

    Even though trial dates may now be given at an earlier stage such as the case management conference, this rule must still be complied with. Practice direction 5.1 10 states that unless the required bundle is lodged with the Registrar the action will not be set down for trial.

    According to a letter from the Registrar dated 20 March 2009, and circulated to solicitors from time to time (for example see Law Society circular 09-981), parties may seek a direction that the CMC bundle used for case management conferences pursuant to part G of PD 5.2 be treated as the setting down bundle.

**[34.3.2]    Formal application to set down**

When leave to set down for trial has been granted the party to whom it has been granted must, within the time specified in the order granting leave, comply with Order 34 rule 3 and make formal application to set down for trial.

**[34.3.3]    Form of application to set a case down for trial**

The form to be used when applying to set an action down for trial, after leave to do so has been granted, is set out in appendix D to the practice direction on case management (PD 5.2). It can be downloaded from the judiciary's website www.judiciary.gov.hk or that of the Hong Kong Legal Information Institute www.hklii.org.hk, both of which are accessible by the general public free-of-charge.

**4.    Directions relating to lists** (O. 34 r. 4)

**Nothing in this Order shall prejudice any powers of the Chief Justice to give directions—**

  (a)    **specifying the lists in which actions, or actions of any class or description, are to be set down for trial and providing for the keeping and publication of the lists;**

  (b)    **providing for the determination of a date for the trial of any action which has been set down or a date before which the trial thereof is not to take place; and**

  (c)    **as to the making of applications (whether to the Court or an officer of the Court) to fix, vacate or alter any such date, and, in particular, requiring any such application to be supported by an estimate of the length of the trial and any other relevant information.**

---

**NOTES**

**[34.4.1]    Running List and Fixture List**

Order 34 rule 4 preserves the court's powers to give directions specifying different lists for the trial of actions and for the fixing and amendment of trial dates. The manner in which these powers are exercised is dealt with in practice directions.

Practice direction 7.1 makes provision for the running list and the fixture list. An action set down on the running list will not be given a fixed hearing date in advance. Rather the action will wait in the queue for a judge to be available. The parties will be warned in advance of the month, then the week, in which the action is likely to come on for hearing. The fixture list, as its name suggests, provides for the fixing of trial dates in advance.

If the trial is estimated to last 3 days or less it will be assigned to the running list (para 2, practice direction 7.1). Shorter trials may also be assigned to the fixture list, if a party so requests, and is able to satisfy the court that this is appropriate, for example where witnesses will be coming from overseas. In such cases an affidavit may be required to justify the request.

The text of practice direction 7.1 can be found on the judiciary's website.

It is envisaged that the implementation of the civil justice reforms in 2009 will eventually result in the running list being abolished, with every case being given a fixed date. See the discussion at para 399 *et seq* of the final report of the Chief Justice's working party on civil justice reform.

### [34.4.2]    Vacation of dates in the Fixture List

When application is made to vacate a date which has been fixed notice should be given to the respondent (*Re Lawe William Enterprises Ltd* HCMP 1638/1989 (Jones J; 27.07.1989). According to the English 'Practice Statement: Listing Statement (No 3)', The Times Law Report, 5 April 1988, it is the duty of counsel and solicitors to apply to vacate a fixed date and return to the general list cases which no longer justify a fixture, for example, where an expert witness need no longer be called as expert evidence had been agreed. The principle involved would surely be appropriate to Hong Kong.

### [34.4.3]    Marking of counsel's diary

The marking of counsel's diary does not commit either counsel or solicitor. However delivery of a brief will bind the solicitor to pay counsel's brief fee unless otherwise agreed. Even where a brief has been delivered, counsel may withdraw if, for example, another case over-runs. See the Law Society's notes for guidance under circular 00-334 (PA) (reproduced in the commentary under Order 62 rule 32) and the Bar code of conduct.

### [34.4.4]    Numbering

Order 34 has no rule 5, 6 or 7. Rule 5 in the former English RSC concerned district matters which have no relevance in Hong Kong. Rules 6 and 7 were repealed in England in 1971 and were omitted from the 1988 revision of the Hong Kong rules.

**8.    Notification of setting down** (O. 34 r. 8)

**(1)    A party to an action who sets it down for trial must, within 24 hours after doing so, notify the other parties to the action that he has done so.**

**(2)    It shall be the duty of all parties to an action entered in any list to furnish without delay to the officer who keeps the list all available information as to the action being or being likely to be settled, or affecting the estimated length of the trial, and, if the action is settled or withdrawn, to notify that officer of the fact without delay and take such steps as may be necessary to withdraw the record.**

**(3)    In performance of the duty imposed by paragraph (2), a plaintiff who gives notice of acceptance of a sanctioned payment or a sanctioned offer in accordance with Order 22, shall at the same time lodge a copy of the notice with the officer mentioned in that paragraph. (L.N. 152 of 2008)**

---

## NOTES

### [34.8.1]    Procedure after setting down for trial

After an action has been set down for trial, Order 34 rule 8 requires that notice of that having been done must be given to the other parties. There is no prescribed form of notice under these rules, but the judiciary's website includes a form of 'Notice to Set Down' which may be used for this purpose.

## [34.8.2]    Pre-trial review

It has long been considered part of the court's inherent power of case management to direct that there be a pre-trial review in any particular action. Now see Order 25 rule 1A where the power is expressly stated. Previously a direction for a pre-trial review would typically made at the time of granting leave to set down for trial. Now, under Order 25 rule 1A, the direction will typically be made earlier, at the case management conference stage.

## [34.8.3]    Hearing bundles

In addition to the bundle of pleadings and other court documents which must be delivered to the court on setting down for trial (see Order 34 rule 3), the parties are required to seek to agree and prepare a loose-leaf bundle of documents they wish to place before the trial judge. This will primarily be documentary evidence. See practice direction 5.6 which may be viewed on the judiciary's website. The practice direction governs the preparation and status of this bundle, and provides it must be lodged with the court at least 72 hours (excluding Saturdays, Sundays and general holidays) before the date fixed for hearing. The importance of the parties agreeing a common bundle of documents for use at trial, rather than producing separate ones, was emphasised in *Panachand & Co Pte Ltd v Poon Lee Meng* CACV 12/1989 (Silke VP, Fuad & Hunter JJA; 21.06.1989) (paras 25–27), where it was suggested that there could be costs consequences.

In all cases care should be taken not to include in the hearing bundles unnecessary, peripheral or duplicate documents.  This is to avoid a waste of paper and judicial time. See *Tsang Wai Lun Wayland & Anor v Chu King Fai & Ors* HCA 300/2009 (Reyes J; 12.08.2009) (para 110–114) where it was said:

> It is part of a lawyer's professional duty, especially after CJR, to sift through available documents and only select those that are absolutely necessary and relevant to the issues for inclusion in the bundle. One does not discharge such duty by indiscriminately placing an undigested jumble of documents before the Court.
>
> ...
>
> It is possible that, as a result of a robust weeding-out process, an important document is inadvertently left out of the trial bundle. There is no great harm in that, as the document can be inserted in the course of trial.
>
> ...
>
> I suggest that in the future during (say) a pre-trial review the Court routinely ask the lawyers appearing before it for an assurance that every effort has been taken to minimise the bulk of the trial bundle. Where (despite assurance) the trial bundle turns out to be needlessly bulky, the Court may seriously have to consider whether the parties or their lawyers should bear the costs of such waste personally.

In *Watfield Technology Ltd v Kenworth Eng'g Ltd & Anor* HCCT 1/2008 (Reyes J; 22.01.2010) (para 91-92) the court returned a trial bundle consisting of 30 level-arch files, which it considered excessive, and not in keeping with the obligations set out above. The bundle was then reduced to 12 volumes, which the court thought was still excessive by 50%. The party was disallowed the costs of the 30 volume bundle, and 50% of the costs of the 12 volume bundle.

In the rare case of a civil trial before a judge and jury, care should be taken to exclude from the bundles prepared for members of the jury any documents which may not be admissible in evidence: *Tsui Koon Wah v Lam King Yuen & Ors* HCA 890/2003 (Chung J; 08.09.2006).

### [34.8.4]    Translation of documentary evidence

Trials in the Court of First Instance conducted in English may involve use of documentary evidence in Chinese. Unless there is a direction for the action to be tried by a bilingual judge, the Chinese documentation must be translated. The onus is on the party wishing to introduce the document into evidence to prepare or obtain privately a translation - it is not usual for the court language section to prepare translations of this type of document. A translation may then be submitted to the court language section for certification in accordance with the procedures set out in practice direction 10.2 (which can be viewed on the judiciary website). See also the guidance provided by the judiciary administrator (which can be viewed on the judiciary website) including the form by which application for certification of a translation should be made.

Parties frequently overlook the requirement in the practice direction to serve the translation on the other parties within 3 days of it being submitted for certification.

Certification of translations is not mandatory. Parties are encouraged to try to agree the accuracy of translations so as to avoid the need for certification, which is a time consuming process for which a fee is payable under the 1st Schedule of the *High Court Fees Rules*, subsidiary legislation under the *High Court Ordinance* (Cap 4). In this connection see the guidance from the registrar set out in a letter dated 07.09.2006 and circulated to solicitors under Law Society circular 06-527 (PA) which can be viewed on the Law Society's website. The guidance sets out the circumstances in which a document needs to be translated as well as when a translation needs to be certified.

Where there is a dispute over the accuracy of a certified translation, notice must be given to the other parties and the court translator in accordance with para 4 of the practice direction, together with the alleged correct translation. If the dispute is not resolved, the translator(s) may have to be called as witnesses at trial.

The court language section does not provide a certification service for translations into Chinese or English of documents written in a third language. In such case, unless the translation is agreed by the other parties, its accuracy should be proved by statutory declaration or oral evidence.

### [34.8.5]    List and bundle of authorities

Practice direction 5.5 sets out the requirements with regard to submission of authorities which a party intends to rely on at a hearing. It applies to hearings at all levels of the High Court. Each party is required to lodge with the Clerk of the Court (and the other party or solicitor) a list of authorities it intends to cite. This must be done not less than two clear days (excluding public holidays) before a hearing in the Court of Appeal or by a Full Bench, and no later than 12.00 noon on the day preceding a hearing before a judge of the High Court or a Master.

The practice direction provides that the parties should attach copies of unreported judgments and any other authorities when informed by the Clerk of Court that copies are not available in the court libraries. In practice the parties usually prepare complete bundles of authorities without waiting for any indication from the Clerk of Court. That practice is mandatory for interlocutory applications and appeals to a judge in chambers or listed before a master for more than 30 minutes: practice direction 5.4, para 10.

The Chief Judge of the High Court has indicated that only where a judgment is not reported in any recognised series of law reports should a computer report be relied upon. Further, official law report series should be preferred, such that in preference to the All England Reports, the report (if any) in the Appeal Cases, Queen's Bench or Chancery Reports (etc) should be used. See *Koon Wing Yee v Insider Dealing Tribunal & Anor* CACV 358/2005 (Ma CJHC, Tang VP & Stone J; 08.06.2009) (para 60-61).

Where at a hearing to be conducted in English, a party wishes to rely on an authority written in Chinese, practice direction 10.3 should be observed. It is there provided that where there is an official judiciary translation, that should be used. Otherwise, the party shall, unless otherwise directed, prepare an English translation of the judgment (or the relevant parts thereof) and serve it on all other parties not later than 7 clear days before the hearing. Any party who disputes the translation is required to apply for directions not later than 4 clear days before the hearing, with a supporting statement identifying the disputed parts of the translation and setting out what in its view is the correct translation.

**9.     Abatement, etc., of action** (O. 34 r.9)

**(1)     Where after an action has been set down for trial the action becomes abated, or the interest or liability of any party to the action is assigned or transmitted to or devolves on some other person, the solicitor for the plaintiff or other party having the conduct of the action must, as soon as practicable after becoming aware of it, certify the abatement or change of interest or liability and send the certificate to the officer who keeps the list, and that officer shall cause the appropriate entry to be made in the list of actions set down for trial.**

**(2)     Where in any such list an action stands for one year marked as abated or ordered to stand over generally, the action shall on the expiration of that year be struck out of the list unless, in the case of an action ordered to stand over generally, the order otherwise provides.**

**(Enacted 1988)**

## ORDER 35

### PROCEDURE AT TRIAL

**1.    Failure to appear by both parties or one of them** (O. 35 r. 1)
   **(1)   If, when the trial of an action is called on, neither party appears, the action may be struck out of the list, without prejudice, however, to the restoration thereof, on the direction of a judge.**
   **(2)   If, when the trial of an action is called on, one party does not appear, the judge may proceed with the trial of the action or any counterclaim in the absence of that party.**

---

### NOTES

**[35.1.1]    Absence of party from trial**
Order 35 rule 1 prescribes what the court should do where either or both parties fail to appear at trial.
   Where both parties fail to appear, rule 1(1) provides that the court 'may' strike out the action from the list, without prejudice to it being restored by direction of the court. The rule does not mention adjournment of the trial, but that is an obvious alternative and may be ordered under Order 35 rule 3.
   Where one party is absent, the court may proceed with the trial: rule 1(2). Again, adjournment is an alternative. Where it is the plaintiff who is absent, and the court decides to proceed with the trial, the action will almost certainly be dismissed, as there will be no evidence for the plaintiff, and thus no case for the defendant to answer. On the other hand, where it is the defendant who is absent, the plaintiff must call its witnesses and present its evidence to prove its case.
   In *Chiu Tin Yau Lesley v Ng* HCA 105/2004 (Poon J; 13.11.2009) (para 18) the court expressed the view that an absent party's witness statement did not stand as evidence, and no weight was given documentary evidence he had adduced. See, however, Order 38 rule 2 which gives the court a discretion to receive affidavit evidence at trial. In *Deng Minghui t/a Tianye Industrial (HK) Co v Chau Shuk Ling Elaine* HCA 749/2005 (Poon J; 30.09.2010) (para 10) the court disregarded the absent defendant's witness statement, and an expert report she had filed on Mainland law.
   Where the court proceeds with trial of an action involving a counterclaim, and in the absence of the plaintiff, the plaintiff's claims will almost certainly be dismissed for the reasons explained above, and the defendant may proceed to prove its counterclaim. As an example see *Joyful Sparkle Co Ltd v Ng Pik Chu* DCCJ 1881/2008 (Deputy Judge C Lee; 08.07.2010).

**2.    Judgment, etc., given in absence of party may be aside** (O. 35 r. 2)
   **(1)   Any judgment, order or verdict obtained where one party does not appear at the trial may be set aside by the Court, on the application of that party, on such terms as it thinks just.**
   **(2)   An application under this rule must be made within 7 days after the trial.**

**NOTES**

**[35.2.1]     Order 35 rule 2 – Power to set aside judgment given in absence of party**

Order 35 rule 1 permits the court to proceed with a trial despite the absence of one or both parties. Under rule 2, any resulting judgment (*etc*) may be set aside on application made within 7 days.

The power to set aside under rule 2 applies where the absence was inadvertent – it does not extend to cases of deliberate absence or where an application for an adjournment has been refused: *Yuen v Yuen* HCMC 2/2000 (Deputy Judge Woolley; 12.10.2001).

The court's approach to an application under rule 2 to set aside was set out in *HK Magnetronic Co Ltd v Lau Wah* CACV 53/1986 (Roberts CJ, Yang JA & Clough J; 06.06.1986) in the following terms:

> … as a general rule, if by some oversight or mistake by a party, or as a result of his solicitor's error or negligence, the party does not appear at the hearing of an action and judgment is given against him, then if justice can be done by compensating the other party for any costs and trouble caused to him, the judgment should be set aside on terms as to the costs thereby thrown away.

In that case the court declined to set aside the judgment on the ground the applicant had not provided any reasonable excuse or explanation for being absent from the trial. It was observed that if such an excuse or explanation had been provided the court would have gone on to consider questions of prejudice and merit. In the subsequent case of *Shocked v Goldschmidt* [1998] 1 All ER 372, 381 the English court held that each case depends on its own facts and, after a review of the relevant authorities, set out a comprehensive list of 'general indications' of when the power to set aside will be exercised. The list may be summarised as follows:

(1)     A party with notice of proceedings who disregards the opportunity to appear and participate will normally be bound by the decision.

(2)     The explanation for the absence is most important.

(3)     Where setting aside would entail a complete retrial on matters of fact already investigated by the court the application will not be granted unless there are very strong reasons for doing so.

(4)     The party applying to set aside judgment must have a real prospect of success.

(5)     Delay is relevant, particularly if the successful party has acted on the judgment, or third parties have acquired rights by reference to it.

(6)     The conduct of the person applying to set aside the judgment has to be considered: the court will be less ready to exercise its discretion in favour of a party who has failed to comply with orders of the court.

(7)     A material consideration is whether the successful party would be prejudiced by the judgment.

(8)     There is a public interest in there being an end to litigation and in not having the time of the court occupied by two trials, particularly if neither is short.

*Shocked v Goldschmidt* was applied in Hong Kong in *Lau Kam Chuen v Lee Ching*

[2003] 2 HKLRD 1018 (CA). In that case it was emphasised that the most important factor is the reason for the party's absence from the trial. In that regard applications under Order 35 rule 2 were to be distinguished from applications to set aside regular default judgments, where the most important consideration was the merits of the defence. See also *Sit Ka Yin Priscilla v EOC* [2009] 5 HKC 24 (para 26). In *Su Sh-Hsyu v Wee Yue Chew* [2007] SGCA 31; [2007] 3 SLR 673 (para 44) the Singapore Court of Appeal added to the factors considered in *Shocked* the 'overriding consideration of whether there is a likelihood that a real miscarriage of justice has occurred'. The Singapore court went on to set aside judgment which had been given against a party who had made a deliberate decision not to attend court for business reasons, on the ground there was a real possibility the claim against that party was fraudulent.

### [35.2.2]    Extension of time to set aside judgment

Order 35 rule 2(2) provides that an application to set aside a judgment (*etc*) made in the absence of a party must be made within 7 days after the trial. Where the application is not made within that time, the court's general power to extend time under Order 3 rule 5 applies. In the exceptional case of *Nantong Angang Garments Co Ltd v Hellmann Int'l Forwarders & Ors* [2005] 4 HKC 86 (CA) an extension was allowed, judgment set aside and a re-trial ordered where the application had been delayed for 2 years. The court cited the 'overall justice' of the case. In *Wealthy Channel Ltd v Yam Sam Leung* HCA 8680/1999 (Chung J; 18.11.2010) an extension of time was refused after a lapse of 4 years. It was found that the absence from trial was deliberate (para 36). The court also expressed the view that the civil justice reforms, especially Order 1A rr 1(a), (b) and (f), had heightened attention to the 8th factor from *Shocked v Goldschmidt* set out above.

### [35.2.3]    Inherent jurisdiction to re-open

Apart from its power under rule 2, the court has an inherent jurisdiction to re-open a case before judgment is given where a party was absent from the hearing. In *Chien Ngan Sang v Lai Kam Hing & Anor* [2002] 2 HKC 448 the court distinguished *Shocked v Goldschmidt* (above) and held that the following factors are relevant on such an application:

(a)    reason for failure of the party to attend;
(b)    strength and merits of the applicant's case
(c)    manner in which the applicant has conducted the case;
(d)    prejudice to the opposing party;
(e)    public interest in the efficient administration of justice.

In *Overseas Trust Bank Ltd v Moral Tact Co Ltd & Ors* [2003] 2 HKC 77, 80B-C (CA) the court, apparently referring to this inherent power, said that the power to re-hear a matter or to re-open continues until the order has been sealed.

With regard to the court's power to reconsider a judgment or order where neither party was absent, see the commentary under Order 20 rule 11.

### 3.    Adjournment of trial (O. 35 r. 3)

**The judge may, if he thinks it expedient in the interest of justice, adjourn a trial for such time, and to such place, and upon such terms, if any, as he thinks fit.**

**NOTES**

**[35.3.1]     Power to adjourn trial**
Order 35 rule 3 gives the court express power to adjourn a trial. There is in addition an inherent jurisdiction to adjourn: *St Edmundsbury & Ipswich Diocesan Board of Finance v Clark* [1973] Ch 323, 327D.

The power to adjourn a trial is discretionary. As to the factors the court will take into account, see *Dick v Piller* [1943] 1 All ER 627. When considering the application, the court should 'hold the scales between the parties', preserve the 'capacity to serve the general body of court users efficiently', and  avoid prejudicial delay and loss of judicial time: *Wellfit Investments Ltd v Poly Commence Ltd* [1995] 3 HKC 56, 62H-I (CA). The discretion is essentially for the judge, and the Court of Appeal will not lightly interfere: *Joyce & Anor v King* [1987] The Times 13 July (CA). However it will do so if the order below would result in injustice: *Maxwell v Keun* [1928] 1 KB 645, 653 (CA).

The court may be more ready to grant an adjournment of an action which comes on for trial on the running list, whereas the parties are expected to be ready for a trial which has been granted a fixed date: *Tai Shum Jewellery Trading Co v Christianos* [1946]-[1972] HKC 590.

Unlike the power under Order 32 rule 4(1) to adjourn a summons, the power to adjourn a trial expressly provides for the imposition of terms. Thus, although the court may not require payment into court as a condition of adjournment of a summons, this should be possible on adjournment of a trial: *TMC (Int'l) Trading Co Ltd v Shye Lian (HK) Manufacturing Co Ltd* [1995] 2 HKC 469. In *Dick v Piller* (above, at 629) it was suggested that where a defendant has admitted part of the claim, the court may order payment of that part to the plaintiff and that the balance be paid into court.

See also practice direction 5.1 concerning refixing of hearings, and see the administrative directions issued by the listing judge, both reproduced under Order 34 rule 2.

**3A.     Time, etc. limits at trial** (O. 35 r. 3A)
   **(1)     At any time before or during a trial, the Court may by direction —**
      **(a)     limit the time to be taken in examining, cross-examining, or re-examining a witness;**
      **(b)     limit the number of witnesses (including expert witnesses) that a party may call on a particular issue;**
      **(c)     limit the time to be taken in making any oral submission;**
      **(d)     limit the time to be taken by a party in presenting its case;**
      **(e)     limit the time to be taken by the trial; and**
      **(f)     vary a direction made under this rule.**
   **(2)     In deciding whether to make any such direction, the Court shall have regard to the following matters in addition to any other matters that may be relevant —**
      **(a)     the time limited for a trial must be reasonable;**
      **(b)     any such direction must not detract from the principle that each party is entitled to a fair trial;**

(c)     **any such direction must not detract from the principle that each party must be given a reasonable opportunity to lead evidence and cross-examine witnesses;**

(d)     **the complexity or simplicity of the case;**

(e)     **the number of witnesses to be called by the parties;**

(f)     **the volume and character of the evidence to be led;**

(g)     **the state of the Court lists;**

(h)     **the time expected to be taken for the trial; and**

(i)     **the importance of the issues and the case as a whole.**

**(L.N. 152 of 2008)**

---

## NOTES

### [35.3A.1]  Origin and scope of Order 35 rule 3A

Order 35 rule 3A represents a fundamental departure from the principle of party control whereby the trial judge traditionally took a passive role, merely adjudicating upon whatever evidence and submissions the parties chose to present. It empowers the court to impose limitations on the evidence and submissions to be presented, and on the length of trial. Previously the court would generally only discourage unnecessarily lengthy trials by adverse costs order after the event, as in *Hebei Enterprises Ltd & Ors v Livasiri & Co (a firm) & Ors* FACV 23/2007 (judgment on costs 05.12.2008).

The rule implements recommendation 108 of the Chief Justice's working party on civil justice reform and is based on Order 34 rule 5A of the Supreme Court Rules of Western Australia, which is virtually identical in wording. A similar provision also appears in CPR 32.1 in England.

The working party envisaged this rule as a case management power 'aimed both at curbing prolixity and increasing the accuracy of trial time estimates' (final report, para 637). In the interim report which preceded the working party's final report, it was also envisaged that this provision would improve the advocacy of counsel appearing at trial. See para 523 of the interim report quoting Ipp, 'Reforms to the Adversarial Process in Civil Litigation' (1995) 69 ALJ 790, 816 where it was said:

> Limiting the time for oral argument would compel counsel to concentrate on their best points, discourage them from arguing every issue including those that have no or little prospect of success, and, generally, would raise the standard of advocacy. Disorganised, unstructured arguments would be less frequent. There would be little incentive for counsel to ramble on in all directions, in the hope that eventually a persuasive point will be revealed. Counsel would not be able to afford time in tedious reading of authorities and passages from the transcript.

The Chief Justice's working party decided against going so far as empowering the court to exclude otherwise admissible evidence at trial (final report, para 636). Thus the rule has no equivalent of CPR 32.1(2) in England which expressly empowers the court in that regard.

### [35.3A.2]  Cross-reference

See also Order 1A rule 1(f) which states the underlying objective of ensuring that the resources of the court are distributed fairly, Order 1A rule 4(2)(l) which includes the giving of directions to ensure quick and efficient trials amongst the court's duties by way of case management, and Order 1B rule 1(2)(l), the catch all provision in relation to case management, under which it has been held the court may direct that final submissions be put in writing without each side seeing the other's.

**[35.3A.3]   Time limits on examination of witnesses**
Order 35 rule 3A(1)(a) expressly empowers the court to limit the time to be taken in examining, cross–examining or re–examining a witness. So far as examination–in–chief is concerned, this is sometimes dispensed with altogether by an order that the witness statements exchanged under Order 38 rule 2A stand as evidence–in–chief. See the commentary under that rule.

**[35.3A.4]   Limits on opening and closing submissions**
Order 35 rule 3A(1)(c) and (d), in empowering the court to limit the time for a party to present its case, and to limit the time to be taken by the trial, clearly permit the court to limit the time taken in opening and closing submissions. One obvious and easy way to do this is to direct that the parties follow the now common practice of reducing such submissions to writing.

**[35.3A.5]   Stage at which direction limiting trial should be made**
The power under Order 35 rule 3A to impose limits on a trial may be exercised before or during the trial (rule 3A(1)). The Chief Justice's working party was of the view that directions of the kind provided for by the rule 'ought routinely to be given at the pre-trial review' (final report, para 639). As a result the working party's recommendation 108 called for this rule to be accompanied by a practice direction 'providing that such powers should primarily be exercised at the pre-trial review'. The practice direction on case management requires parties to file and serve a listing questionnaire which, if a trial date is sought, must be accompanied by a certificate (preferably prepared by trial counsel) giving time estimates for opening submissions, evidence-in-chief, cross-examination and closing submissions. See the commentary under Order 25. With the benefit of this information the court will be in a position to exercise its powers under rule 3A at the case management or PTR stage.

**7.      Order of speeches** (O. 35 r.7)
**(1)    The judge before whom an action is tried (whether with or without a jury) may give directions as to the party to begin and the order of speeches at the trial, and, subject to any such directions, the party to begin and the order of speeches shall be that provided by this rule.**
**(2)    Subject to paragraph (6), the plaintiff shall begin by opening his case.**
**(3)    If the defendant elects not to adduce evidence, then, whether or not the defendant has in the course of cross-examination of a witness for the plaintiff or otherwise put in a document, the plaintiff may, after the evidence on his behalf has been given, make a second speech closing his case and the defendant shall then state his case.**
**(4)    If the defendant elects to adduce evidence, he may, after any evidence on behalf of the plaintiff has been given, open his case and, after the**

evidence on his behalf has been given, make a second speech closing his case, and at the close of the defendant's case the plaintiff may make a speech in reply.

(5)    Where there are 2 or more defendants who appear separately or are separately represented, then—

    (a)    if none of them elects to adduce evidence, each of them shall state his case in the order in which his name appears on the record;

    (b)    if each of them elects to adduce evidence, each of them may open his case and the evidence on behalf of each of them shall be given in the order aforesaid and the speech of each of them closing his case shall be made in that order after the evidence on behalf of all the defendants has been given;

    (c)    if some of them elect to adduce evidence and some do not, those who do not shall state their cases in the order aforesaid after the speech of the plaintiff in reply to the other defendants.

(6)    Where the burden of proof of all the issues in the action lies on the defendant or, where there are two or more defendants and they appear separately or are separately represented, on one of the defendants, the defendant or that defendant, as the case may be, shall be entitled to begin, and in that case paragraphs (2), (3) and (4) shall have effect in relation to, and as between, him and the plaintiff as if for references to the plaintiff and the defendant there were substituted references to the defendant and the plaintiff respectively.

(7)    Where, as between the plaintiff and any defendant, the party who would, but for this paragraph, be entitled to make the final speech raises any fresh point of law in that speech or cites in that speech any authority not previously cited, the opposite party may make a further speech in reply, but only in relation to that point of law or that authority, as the case may be.

---

## NOTES

### [35.7.1]    Order of speeches in civil trial

Order 35 rule 7 gives the court a wide discretion as to which party shall open its case first, and the order of speeches thereafter.

In practice, it is usually the plaintiff who begins, in accordance with rule 7(2). This is because the plaintiff must normally show a *prima facie* case before the defendant need respond, or to put it another way, because the plaintiff normally has the burden of proof. In some cases the burden of proof lies on the defendant, and rule 7(6) provides that in that event the defendant is entitled to begin. Examples of cases where the defendant has begun under rule 7(6) include the following:

•    *Tang Yau Yi Tong & Anor v Tang Mou Shau Tso & Ors* [1995] 2 HKC 245, 249H-I, where the plaintiffs claimed a declaration they were entitled to sell property without the consent of the defendants, and the defendants resisted on the basis that they had a 1/3 beneficial interest in the property. The court required the defendants to open because they had the burden to prove the alleged beneficial interest.

- *The Grande Properties Management Ltd v Siegont Ltd* DCCJ 21516/2001 (Judge Ng; 13.10.2003), where the basic elements of the plaintiff's claim for outstanding building management fees were admitted, but the defendant raised a positive defence based on failure to comply with provisions of the Building Management Ordinance (Cap 344).
- *Orient Technologies Ltd v A Plus Express (HK) Ltd* DCCJ 6747/2003 (Judge Ng; 10.08.2004) (para 11), where the consignee of goods claimed damages for goods lost while in the course of delivery by the defendant carrier and the only issue was the validity of exemption clauses relied upon by the defendant in light of the Control of Exemption Clauses Ordinance (Cap 71).
- *Wide Project Eng'g & Construction Co v Lantau Tea Gardens Ltd* DCCJ 3815/2005 (Judge S Chan; 24.09.2007), where the defendant admitted the plaintiff's claim, but resisted on the basis of a counterclaim for a higher amount.
- *Chan Kwan Yin Shirley & Anor v Wu Wing & Ors* HCA 7718/2000 (Lam J; 07.08.2009) where a claim for possession of property was resisted on grounds of alleged fraudulent misrepresentation and *non est factum*.

The plaintiff's opening is often reduced to writing and submitted to the court before trial.

The order of closing speeches is governed by rule 7(3) and (4). It is there provided that if the defendant does not call evidence, the plaintiff may on the close of its evidence make a closing speech, following which the defendant shall state its case. Where, however, the defendant does call evidence, its opportunity to make a closing speech comes at the conclusion of that evidence, following which the plaintiff may make a speech in reply.

## [35.7.2] Language of trial

A trial may be conducted in either Chinese or English. The choice of which language to use is left to the presiding judge under section 5 of the Official Languages Ordinance (Cap 5). There is no constitutional right to insist on a trial being conducted in a particular official language: *Re Cheng Kai Nam Gary* [2002] 1 HKC 41. In deciding which language to use, the judge is required to give 'paramount consideration to the just and expeditious disposal of the proceedings': High Court Civil Procedure (Use of Language) Rules (Cap 5C), r 3.

A party who wishes a case to be heard in Chinese should request, at the case management stage, that it be listed before a bilingual judge. That is done by completing the appropriate part of the Timetabling and Listing questionnaires (appendices A and C respectively, to the case management practice direction, PD 5.2) at the Order 25 stage. Such a request must be supported by reasons.

Regardless of which official language is chosen for trial, witnesses may give their evidence in any language: see the commentary under Order 38 rule 1.

In *Park Young Sook v Melloy* [2010] 5 HKC 329 the court declined to provide a Korean/English interpreter for a litigant in person, instead allowing her to engage her own interpreter.

With regard to the language of pleadings, see the commentary under Order 18 rule 6.

**[35.7.3]     No case to answer**

The judge may refuse to rule upon a submission of no case to answer unless defence counsel first makes it clear that he does not intend to call any defence witnesses. The judge is not, however, bound so to rule (*Nieh HC v Kiki Carvalho* [1970] DCLR 13).

In *Pappadis v Chan Shing Sheung Barry* [1989] 2 HKC 369 it was held that the subject of an application for committal for contempt of court had to elect whether to give evidence before proceeding with a submission of no case to answer. That judgment was overturned by the Court of Appeal ([1989] 2 HKLR 511) on other grounds. In *Re Kennedy (No 1)* [2004] 3 HKC 404 Kwan J, without referring to the earlier cases, was of the view that on a committal application it is not necessary to make an election as to giving evidence before making a submission of no case to answer.

As to the grounds upon which to base such submission the court in *Chu Suk-chun v Ma Fuk-sang* [1965] DCLR 1 applied the dictum of Ormerod LJ in *Storey v Storey* [1960] 3 WLR 653, at 656:

> There are, however, two sets of circumstances under which a defendant may submit that he has no case to answer. In the one case there may be a submission that, accepting the plaintiff's evidence at its face value, no case has been established at law, and in the other that the evidence led for the plaintiff is so unsatisfactory or unreliable that the Court should find that the burden of proof has not been discharged.

See also *Ever-Long Securities Co Ltd v Wong Sio Po* [2004] 1 HKC 702, 709E-I (CA) where the test laid down in *Storey v Storey* was affirmed as applicable in Hong Kong. In the *Ever-Long* case, the Court of Appeal refused to order a retrial after allowing an appeal to dismiss the plaintiff's case on the ground of no case to answer. The defendant was bound by the election not to call evidence.

**[35.7.4]     Court dress and mode of addressing judicial officers**

On reunification it was announced that there would be no change to the previous court attire. Directions were given as to the mode of court dress for judges of the Court of Final Appeal, with counsel appearing in that court to be attired in the same manner as in the High Court. See Law Society circular 97-218 dated 14.07.1997. See also practice direction 21.1 which provides that solicitors exercising their right of audience in open court shall wear gown, wing collar and bands. The modes of addressing judicial officers in Chinese and English are also set out in that Law Society circular. They are:

MODE OF ADDRESS IN COURT

| Legal Title | Address | |
|---|---|---|
| | English | Chinese |
| Chief Justice of the Court of Final Appeal 終審法院首席法官 | My Lord or Your Lordship | 法官閣下 |
| Permanent Judges of the Court of Final Appeal 終審法院常任法官 | My Lord or Your Lordship | 法官閣下 |
| Chief Judge of the High Court 高等法院首席法官 | My Lord or Your Lordship | 法官閣下 |
| Justices of Appeal of the High Court 高等法院上訴法庭法官 | My Lord or Your Lordship | 法官閣下 |

| | | |
|---|---|---|
| Judges of the Court of First Instance of the High Court 高等法院原訟法庭法官 | My Lord or Your Lordship My Lady or Your Ladyship | 法官閣下 |
| Registrar, Court of Final Appeal 終審法院司法常務官 | Sir or Madam or My Registrar | 法官閣下 |
| Registrar, High Court, Deputy Registrar, High Court, and Masters 高等法院司法常務官，高等 法院副司法常務官，聆案官 | Sir or Madam or My Registrar or Master | 法官閣下 |
| Chief Judge of the District Court 區域法院首席法官 | Your Honour | 法官閣下 |
| District Judges 域法院法官 | Your Honour | 法官閣下 |
| Presiding Officers and Adjudicators of Tribunals, 審裁官, Coroner, 裁判官 | Sir or Madam | 法官閣下 |
| Magistrates 裁判官 | Sir or Madam or Your Worship | 法官閣下 |

## [35.7.5]    Rights of audience in Hong Kong

Hong Kong's legal profession is divided between barristers and solicitors, each of whom is admitted to only one of those professions. The rights of audience of solicitors are limited. The Chief Justice's Working Party on Solicitors' Rights of Audience, October 2007, recommended that Hong Kong adopt a system similar to that in the UK whereby individual solicitors with advocacy experience may apply for and be granted the right of audience in higher courts. This has been given effect by the Legal Practitioners (Amendment) Ordinance 2010, inserting a new part IIIB into the principal Ordinance. It is expected to be brought into force in late 2010. In the meantime the position as to rights of audience is as set out below.

Barristers have the right of audience in all courts and tribunals of Hong Kong (save those such as the Small Claims Tribunal and the Labour Tribunal where legal representation is not permitted). The rights of audience of solicitors and trainee solicitors in Hong Kong are set out comprehensively in Law Society circular 09-165, which may be viewed on the Law Society's website. Briefly, solicitors may appear in the magistracies, any tribunal where legal representation is permitted, the district court (see practice directions 5.10 and 27) and in the following civil matters in the High Court:

- Hearings before a master in chambers - practice direction 14.1
- Hearings before a master in open court – practice direction 14.2 (para 5)
- Hearings before a judge of the Court of First Instance or of the Court of Appeal in chambers
- Formal or unopposed hearings in open court before a judge of the Court of First Instance where the court will not be called upon to exercise a discretion – practice direction 21.1
- Contested bankruptcy and winding-up proceedings - *Re Lai Yin Shan* [2001] 3 HKC 232. According to Law Society circular 04-184, this right extends to all bankruptcy and winding-up proceedings listed in practice direction 3.1.

In addition the court has inherent power to permit a solicitor to appear where the interests of justice so demand. For example, a solicitor may be allowed to appear where there is an emergency or where counsel has withdrawn: *Re Gunston & Smart's Application* [1956] HKLR 1034; *Brentwood Wig Manufacturing Ltd & Ors v Poncher & Anor* [1965] HKLR 1042.

Rights of audience are a matter of pure practice, governed by the court's inherent jurisdiction: *Abse & Ors v Smith & Anor* [1986] 1 QB 536 (CA), cited with approval in *Re Lai Yin Shan* (above). In *Abse* it was held that the test to be applied on any application to depart from the existing practice is the public interest. Only in 'exceptional circumstances' should the court do so. Further, any modification of existing practice required collective decision of the judges.

## [35.7.6]    Rights of audience of unqualified persons in proceedings before a master

Practice direction 14.1, as amended with effect from 1st May 2010, provides that trainee solicitors (including those on secondment from England) and certain legal executives may appear before a master in chambers on an uncontested application or an application listed for a 3-minute hearing. It also provides that costs clerks employed by a solicitor, and approved law costs draftsmen may appear on taxation of a bill of costs.

## [35.7.7]    'McKenzie friend'

A litigant in person may, with leave of the court, be assisted by a '*McKenzie* friend'. The friend may sit with the litigant, take notes and quietly offer advice, but should not normally be allowed to make submissions on the litigant's behalf: *Lobo v Kripalani* [1998] 2 HKLRD 325, 328C-J (CA); *Daiwa Bank Ltd v Shum Shek Chiu* [2005] 1 HKC 243, 246G *et seq*. The friend should not be permitted to take over the running of the case with the litigant merely repeating the friend's words: *Chau Siu Woon v Cheung Shek Kong* [2007] 3 HKC 29 (Deputy Judge Carlson; 17.04.2006) (para 31 *et seq*). The title '*McKenzie* friend' traces back to *McKenzie v McKenzie* [1971] P 33. The role was first recognised much earlier in *Collier v Hicks* (1831) 2 B & Ad 663: see *Bow County Court, ex p Pelling* [1999] 4 All ER 751 (CA).

The criteria applied by the court in deciding whether to permit a litigant in person to be assisted by a *McKenzie* friend are fairness and the interests of justice: *Ex p Pelling* (above). There the court said it will likely be undesirable to allow a *McKenzie* friend in proceedings heard in private, and that a judge should give reasons for refusing to allow the assistance of such a friend.

## [35.7.8]    Government counsel and Legal Aid counsel

It should be noted that the Legal Officers Ordinance and the Legal Aid Ordinance make special provision for the right of Government counsel and Legal Aid counsel to appear in the Hong Kong courts, in appropriate circumstances, whether or not they have been called to the Bar or admitted as solicitors in Hong Kong.

## [35.7.9]    Re-opening of case after evidence heard

The court has a discretion to allow a party to re-open his case after the evidence has been heard. Such an order was made in *Chow Siu Po v Wong Ming Fung* [2004] 1 HKC 10 where a party had failed to adduce evidence on the due execution of a will (possibly due to inadvertence on the part of his legal advisers). Reference was made to *Charlesworth v Relay Roads Ltd (in liq)* [2000] 1 WLR 230; *Stewart v Engel* [2000] 1 WLR 2268; *Re Barrell Enterprises* [1973] 1 WLR 19 and *Born Chief Co v Tsai George* [1996] 2 HKC 282. In *Mak Kit Ching Kitty v Tsang Yiu Wing* HCPI

811/1999 (Deputy Judge Carlson; 18.10.2006) (para 10) the court declined to allow a party to re-open the case after the close of evidence and speeches, on the ground that the new evidence sought to be adduced was not compelling.

Guidance as to the principles to be borne in mind on an application to re-open was set out in *Yuki Takahashi & Anor v Cheng Zhen Shu & Ors* HCA 2115/2004 (Fung J; 30.05.2008) (para 6), referring with approval to *Urban Transport Authority of NSW v Nweiser* (1992) 28 NSWLR 471 where Clarke JA said (at 478D–F):

> The principle which should guide the court in determining whether to grant an application for leave to re-open is whether the interests of justice are better served by allowing or rejecting the application... No doubt it is relevant to take account of a number of matters such as likely prejudice to the party resisting the application and the reasons why the evidence was not led in the first place, but there is not, in my opinion, any hard and fast rule which requires the court to reject an application where the decision not [to] call the witness in the party's case was a deliberate one. Of course that does not mean that that is not a very relevant consideration. It is. Where, for instance, a decision was based on tactical grounds it may be difficult to resist the conclusion that the interests of justice were better served by the rejection of the application. But even in that circumstance there may be cases in which it is felt that the client whose application it is should not have to suffer for his or her counsel's deliberate decision. Where the decision is not made for tactical reasons and is based on a mistaken apprehension of the law or the facts the case is more appropriately to be considered as one in which the application has resulted from an error by counsel.

In *Charlesworth* (above) Neuberger J said (at 238 WLR; [1999] 4 All ER 397, 405d-h) that the following principles apply where a party is seeking to call fresh evidence on a new point after judgment has been given but before the order has been drawn up:

(1)   The court has jurisdiction to grant an application to amend the pleadings to raise new points and/or to call fresh evidence and/or to hear fresh argument.

(2)   The court must clearly exercise its discretion in relation to such an application in a way best designed to achieve justice.

(3)   The general rules relating to amendments apply so that:

    (a)   while it is no doubt desirable in general that litigants should be permitted to take any reasonably arguable point, it should by no means be assumed that the court will accede to an application merely because the other party can, in financial terms, be compensated in costs;

    (b)   as with any other application for leave to amend consideration must be given to anxieties and legitimate expectations of the other party, the efficient conduct of litigation, and the inconvenience caused to other litigants.

(4)   Quite apart from, and over and above, those principles, because it is inherently contrary to the public interest and unfair on the other side that an unsuccessful party should be able to raise new points or call fresh evidence after a full and final judgment has been given against him, it would generally require an exceptional case before the court was prepared to accede to an application where the applicant could not satisfy the three requirements in *Ladd v Marshall*.

(5)   Almost inevitably, each case will have particular features which the court will think it right to take into account when deciding how to dispose of the application before it.

(6)     The court should be astute to discourage applications which involve parties seeking to put in late evidence, but cases where new evidence is found after judgment is given and before the order is drawn up will be comparatively rare.

The above passage was quoted in *Secretary of State for Trade & Industry v Paulin* [2005] 2 BCLC 667; [2005] EWHC 888 (Ch) (13.05.2005), where it was accepted (at para 50) that on an application to admit fresh evidence after a hearing but before judgment, the principle is 'no more restrictive than would be applied by the Court of Appeal', that is, in civil matters, the test in *Ladd v Marshall* (as to which see the commentary under Order 59 rule 10). In *Keen Lloyd Energy Ltd v Bank of China (HK) Ltd* CACV 34/2008 (Rogers VP & Le Pichon JA; 06.01.2009) (para 9) leave to appeal to the Court of Final Appeal was sought on the issue whether this English approach should be preferred over the Australian approach in *Nweiser* (above). Leave was refused on the ground the issue was not really engaged in the particular case. In *Chinachem Charitable Foundation Ltd v Chan Chun Chuen & Anor* HCAP 8/2007 (Lam J; 10.07.2009) it was said, referring to the same judge's earlier decision in *L v L* HCMC 1/2003 (Lam J; 20.04.2005), that *Charlesworth* concerned an application to re-open after judgment and that some considerations identified in it would not apply to an application to re-open before handing down of a judgment.

See also the closely related topic of the court's power to reconsider and vary its judgments and orders before they are sealed, discussed in the commentary under Order 20 rule 11.

**8.     Inspection by judge or jury** (O. 35 r. 8)

**(1)    The judge by whom any cause or matter is tried may inspect any place or thing with respect to which any question arises in the cause or matter.**

**(2)    Where a cause or matter is tried with a jury and the judge inspects any place or thing under paragraph (1), he may authorize the jury to inspect it also.**

**9.     Death of party before giving of judgment** (O. 35 r. 9)

**Where a party to any action dies after the verdict or finding of the issues of fact and before judgment is given, judgment may be given notwithstanding the death, but the foregoing provision shall not be taken as affecting the power of the judge to make an order under Order 15, rule 7(2), before giving judgment.**

**10.    Certificate of judicial clerk** (O. 35 r.10)

**At the conclusion of the trial of any action, the judicial clerk or other officer in attendance at the trial shall make a certificate in which he shall certify—**

     **(a)    the time actually occupied by the trial,**

     **(b)    any order made by the judge under Order 38, rule 5 or 6,**

     **(c)    every finding of fact by the jury, where the trial was with a jury,**

     **(d)    the judgment given by the judge, and**

     **(e)    any order made by the judge as to costs.**

**11.    List of exhibits** (O. 35 r. 11)

(1)    The judicial clerk or other officer in attendance at the trial shall take charge of every document or object put in as an exhibit during the trial of any action and shall mark or label every exhibit with a letter or letters indicating the party by whom the exhibit is put in or the witness by whom it is proved, and with a number, so that all the exhibits put in by a party, or proved by a witness, are numbered in one consecutive series.

In this paragraph a witness by whom an exhibit is proved includes a witness in the course of whose evidence the exhibit is put in.

(2)    The judicial clerk or other officer in attendance at the trial shall cause a list to be made of all the exhibits in the action, and any party may, on payment of the prescribed fee, have an office copy of that list.

(3)    The list of exhibits when completed shall form part of the record of the action.

(L.N. 103 of 1994)

(4)    For the purpose of this rule a bundle of documents may be treated and counted as one exhibit.

**12.    Exhibits retained by Registrar pending appeal** (O.35 r.12)

(HK)(1)    Unless the Court otherwise directs, the Registrar shall retain in his custody all exhibits duly marked and labelled until—

(a)    the expiration of the time limited by these rules for appealing to the Court of Appeal, or such extended period therefor as may be allowed; and thereafter

(b)    in the event of an appeal to the Court of Appeal, the final disposal of such appeal; and thereafter

(c)    the expiration of the time limited by Order in Council for applying to the Court of Appeal for leave to appeal to the Court of Final Appeal, or such extended period therefor as may be allowed; and thereafter

(d)    in the event of the Court of Appeal or Court of Final Appeal giving leave to appeal to Court of Final Appeal, the nonfulfilment of any condition for such leave to appeal or the final disposal of such appeal.

(2)    Unless the Court otherwise directs, upon the expiration of the time limited for retention of exhibits fixed under paragraph (1) it shall be the duty of every party to an action who has put in any exhibits, and where represented, of his solicitor on the record, to apply to the Registrar for the return of the exhibits and to collect the same.

**NOTES**

**[35.12.1]    Retention of exhibits pending appeal**

Order 35 rule 12 (which is a unique Hong Kong rule in the sense that it was not adopted from the English Rules of the Supreme Court) provides that the court registry shall retain exhibits produced at trial pending disposition of any appeal or final appeal.

The reference in rule 12(1)(c) to 'Order in Council' prescribing the time for appeal to the Court of Final Appeal dates back to the colonial era when final appeals were to the Privy Council. UK Orders in Council no longer apply in Hong Kong and the relevant time limitations are now found in the Hong Kong Court of Final Appeal Ordinance and Rules (Cap 484). The wording of the rule should be amended in light of the transfer of sovereignty and enactment of new local legislation.

The court may order the release of exhibits even though an appeal is pending. The power to do so is in the opening words of rule 12(1) 'Unless the Court otherwise directs'. Where an application is made for release of this type 'the prime consideration of the court must be whether the release of the exhibit would have an adverse effect on the course of the appeal': *Secretary for Justice v Chan Chun Chuen & Anor* [2010] 5 HKC 163. In that case the party who had produced the exhibit at trial failed in its bid to have the court impose a condition entitling his expert to participate in a police finger-print test on the exhibit. In a later ruling it was suggested that the application for release of the exhibit should have been made to the Court of Appeal rather than to the first instance judge whose decision was the subject of the appeal. See *Chinachem Charitable Foundation Ltd v Chan Chun Chuen & Anor* CACV 62/2010 (Rogers VP; 09.09.2010)

**13.    Impounded documents** (O. 35 r. 13)

**(1)    Documents impounded by order of the Court shall not be delivered out of the custody of the Court except in compliance with an order made by a judge on an application made by summons: Provided that where the Secretary for Justice makes a written request in that behalf, documents so impounded shall be delivered into his custody. (L.N. 152 of 2008)**

**(2)    Documents impounded by order of the Court, while in the custody of the Court, shall not be inspected except by a person authorized to do so by an order signed by a judge.**

**(Enacted 1988)**

## ORDER 36

### TRIALS BEFORE, AND INQUIRIES BY, MASTER

**1.    Trial before, and inquiry by, master** (O. 36 r. 1)
**(HK) In any cause or matter other than a criminal proceeding by the Crown, the Court may, with the consent of the parties, order that the cause or matter, or any question or issue of fact arising therein, be tried before a master or that the master do inquire and report thereon and, in the case of inquiry and report, giving consequential directions.**

---

NOTES

**[36.1.1]    Comparison with English rules**
Hong Kong's Order 36 deals with trials and inquiries by masters, whereas the Order of the same number in the former English RSC dealt also with court business conducted by official and special referees. There are no official or special referees in Hong Kong: compare RHC Order 33 rule 2 with the rule of the same number in the former English RSC.

In England CPR part 60 replaced referees with 'TCC judges', to deal with proceedings in the Technology and Construction Court. That court deals with technically complex mat ters and differs from the Technology Court established by practice direction 29 in Hong Kong, which is technological in the sense that it is equipped with electronic communications facilities.

**[36.1.2]    Order for matter to be dealt with by master**
Order 36 rule 1 provides that the court may order trial by a master, or that a master inquire and report on a question or issue of fact. Consent of the parties is required – see below.

This rule applies in companies winding-up proceedings: see *Re Peregrine Investments Holdings Ltd* [1998] 3 HKC 1, 23 where the court considered referring the question of pro visional liquidators' remuneration to a master.

In *JH Trachsler (HK) Ltd v Lohse* HCA 2906/1987 (Deputy Judge Findlay QC; 09.08.1989) the court referred a complicated calculation of interest to a master under this rule. In *Kwok Ying Lung v Ho Chi Kung* [2001] 3 HKC 480 (CA) it appears that a preliminary question whether the effective interest rate on a loan exceeded the maximum permitted by the Money Lenders Ordinance (Cap 163) was referred to a master under this rule.

**[36.1.3]    The consent requirement**
Order 36 rule 1 expressly provides that the consent of the parties is required for a trial or inquiry to be referred to a master. Consent is a 'condition precedent', and the fact of such consent should be recorded in the order as drawn up: *Kwok Ying Lung v Ko Chi Hung* [2001] 3 HKC 480, 486B (CA). In *Chiu Yu Fong (Administratrix) v Lau Kwong Wing* HCA 6099/1999 (Deputy Judge L Chan; 24.11.2010) a master's order was set aside on the ground that he had effectively conducted a trial without

the consent of the parties.

In *UBC (Construction) Ltd v Sung Foo Kee Ltd* [1993] 2 HKC 458, 461E–F the consent requirement was criticised as 'an unnecessary restriction'. Kaplan J said:

> If the court feels that it will be assisted in this way, and if it feels it will reduce the time spent before a High Court judge hearing technical evidence, then I see no reason why the court should not be able to require this course of action to be adopted on the application of a party.

The judge went on to say that Order 36 should be updated in line with trends in other jurisdictions for resolution of technical issues. This issue was not covered in the 2004 report of the Chief Justice's Working Party on Civil Justice Reform.

## [36.1.4]  Hearing in open court
According to Practice Direction 14.2, trials pursuant to Order 36 rule 1 shall be in open court. A solicitor has the right of audience on such matters and counsel and solicitors appearing before a master in open court must be appropriately robed.

## [36.1.5]  Appeal
Unlike most appeals from a master, an appeal from a master's decision on a matter referred under Order 36 rule 1 goes to the Court of Appeal rather than to a single judge of the CFI: see Order 58 rule 2(a). In *Kwok Ying Lung v Ko Chi Hung* [2001] 3 HKC 480, 486D-F the Court of Appeal appears to have doubted that it had jurisdiction to hear such an appeal until the order referring the matter to the master was amended to record the consent of the parties to the referral as required by Order 36 rule 1.

**4.    Power of master** (O. 36 r. 4)

    **(1)  Subject to any directions contained in the order made pursuant to rule 1—**

        **(a)  the master shall for the purposes of the trial or inquiry (including any interlocutory application therein) have the same jurisdiction, powers and duties (including the power of committal and discretion as to costs) as a judge, exercisable or, as the case may be, to be performed as nearly as circumstances admit, in the like cases, in the like manner and subject to the like limitations; and**

        **(b)  every trial and all other proceedings before a master shall, as nearly as circumstances admit, be conducted in the like manner as the like proceedings before a judge.**

    **(2)  Without prejudice to the generality of paragraph (1) but subject to any such directions as are mentioned therein the master before whom any cause or matter is tried shall have the like powers as the Court with respect to claims relating to or connected with the original subject-matter of the cause or matter by any party thereto against any other person and Order 15, rule 5(2) and Order 16 shall with any necessary modifications apply in relation to any such claim accordingly.**

**NOTES**

**[36.4.1]    Numbering**
Rules 2–3, 5–8 and 10–11, as they existed in the former English RSC, are omitted from Hong Kong's Order 36.

**9.      Report on reference** (O.36 r. 9)
      **(1)    The report made by a master in pursuance of a reference under rule 1 shall be made to the Court and notice thereof served on the parties to the reference.**
      **(2)    The master may in his report submit any question arising therein for the decision of the Court or make a special statement of facts from which the Court may draw such inferences as it thinks fit.**
      **(3)    On receipt of the master's report the Court may—**
            **(a)    adopt the report in whole or in part;**
            **(b)    vary the report;**
            **(c)    require an explanation from him;**
            **(d)    remit the whole or any part of the question or issue originally referred to him for further consideration by him or any other master; or**
            **(e)    decide the question originally referred to him on the evidence taken before him either with or without additional evidence.**
      **(4)    When the report of the master has been made, an application to vary the report or remit the whole or any part of the question or issue originally referred may be made on the hearing by the Court of further consideration of the cause or matter, after giving not less than 4 days' notice thereof, and any other application with respect to the report may be made on that hearing without notice.**
      **(Enacted 1988)**

## ORDER 37

### DAMAGES
### ASSESSMENT AFTER JUDGMENT AND ORDERS FOR PROVISIONAL DAMAGES

I. Assessment of Damages after Judgment

**1.** **Assessment of damages by a master** (O. 37 r. 1)

(1)  Where judgment is given for damages to be assessed and no provision is made by the judgment as to how they are to be assessed, the damages shall, subject to the provisions of this Order, be assessed by a master, and the party entitled to the benefit of the judgment may, after obtaining the necessary appointment from a master and, at least 7 days before the date of the appointment, serving notice of the appointment on the party against whom the judgment is given, proceed accordingly.

(HK)(1A)Upon judgment being given for damages to be assessed, the following directions shall, unless the Court directs otherwise, take effect automatically— (L.N. 383 of 1996)

(a)  there shall be discovery of documents within 14 days in accordance with Order 24, rule 2, and inspection within 7 days thereafter in accordance with Order 24, rule 9;

(ab)  each party shall serve on the other parties, within 6 weeks, written statements under Order 38, rule 2A of the oral evidence which the party intends to lead on any issues of fact to be decided at the trial. (L.N. 152 of 2008)

(b)  (Repealed L.N. 152 of 2008)

(c)  (Repealed L.N. 152 of 2008)

(d)  (Repealed L.N. 152 of 2008)

(e)  photographs, plans and the contents of any police investigation report shall be receivable in evidence at the hearing and shall be agreed if possible;

(f)  the record of any proceedings in any court or tribunal shall be receivable in evidence upon production of a copy thereof certified as a true copy by the clerk or other appropriate officer of the court or tribunal;

(g)  at the time of making of the application for an appointment the master shall be notified of the estimated length of the assessment and any other matter which may affect the setting down of the assessment. (L.N. 363 of 1990)

(2)  Notwithstanding anything in Order 65, rule 9, a notice under this rule must be served on the party against whom the judgment is given.

(3)  The attendance of witnesses and the production of documents before a master in proceedings under this Order may be compelled by writ of subpoena, and the provisions of Order 35 shall, with the necessary adaptations, apply in relation to those proceedings as they apply in relation to proceedings at a trial.

## NOTES

### [37.1.1] Assessment of damages before master in open court

Where judgment is given for damages to be assessed, the subsequent assessment of the quantum of damages will normally take place before a master. This follows from Order 37 rule 1(1) which provides that the matter shall be heard before a master unless otherwise directed at the time of giving judgment.

Practice direction 14.2 provides that an assessment of damages before a master shall be in open court, that solicitors have the right of audience and that advocates should be appropriately robed.

### [37.1.2] Time limitation for assessment of damages

There is no statutory time limitation within which a plaintiff must proceed to have damages assessed following entry of judgment. However, it has been held that undue delay may result in the plaintiff forfeiting the opportunity to proceed.

In *Ho Tze Bun v Incorporated Owners of 39-41 Tong Chong Street and 31-33 Hoi Wan Street* [1996] 1 HKC 95 (DCt) there was a delay of 11 years in the plaintiff bringing on for hearing an assessment of damages ordered on entry of judgment in default of defence. The court of its own motion struck out the claim for want of prosecution under inherent jurisdiction. Judge Sweeney held: 'I find that the court must have an inherent jurisdiction to police its own proceedings on grounds of public policy' (at 103D).The existence of such jurisdiction was doubted in the subsequent case of *Cheung Yuk Chun v Yeung Wo Fai* HCA 6191/1998 (Master Au Yeung; 07.08.2006). There the court expressed the view that as the legislature had not set a time limitation for assessment of damages there was no need for the court to do so, and that the decision in *Ho Tze Bun* should be confined to its own peculiar facts.

### [37.1.3] Rule 1(1A) – automatic directions for assessment of damages

Order 37 rule 1(1A) sets out automatic directions which take effect unless otherwise ordered when the court gives judgment for damages to be assessed. The directions are similar to those under Order 25 rule 8, which applies to personal injury actions. Note that the list of directions which take effect was amended with effect from 2009 so as to repeal those which related to expert evidence. At the same time similar amendments were made to Order 25 rule 8. See also part S of practice direction 18.1, concerning the personal injuries list.

Note that a direction for the exchange of witness statements is now included under this rule, though not in Order 25 rule 8.

### (HK) 1A. Assessment of costs as damages (O. 37 r. 1A)

**Where damages to be assessed pursuant to a judgment to which this Order applies consist solely of costs claimed on an indemnity basis, such assessment shall proceed as for a taxation of costs under Order 62 and the provisions of that Order shall apply as if an order for taxation of costs on the indemnity basis had been made.**

**(L.N. 404 of 1991)**

**2.      Certificate of amount of damages** (O. 37 r. 2)

**Where in pursuance of this Order or otherwise damages are assessed by a master, he shall certify the amount of the damages and the certificate shall, when judgment is entered, be filed in the Registry.**

**3.      Default judgment against some but not all defendants** (O. 37 r. 3)

**Where any such judgment as is mentioned in rule 1 is given on failure to give notice of intention to defend or in default of defence, and the action proceeds against other defendants, the damages under the judgment shall be assessed at the trial unless the Court otherwise orders.**

**4.      Power to order assessment at trial** (O. 37 r. 4)

**(1)      Where judgment is given for damages to be assessed, the Court may—**

> **(d)      order that the action shall proceed to trial before a judge (with or without a jury) as respects the damages.**

**(3)      Where the Court orders that the action shall proceed to trial, Order 25, rules 2 to 7, shall, with the omission of so much of rule 7(1) as requires the parties to serve a notice specifying the orders and directions which they desire and with any other necessary modifications, apply as if the application to the Court in pursuance of which the Court makes the order, were a case management summons under Order 25. (L.N. 152 of 2008)**

---

**NOTES**

**[37.4.1]      Numbering**

Order 37 rule 4 contains no sub-rule (2). The provision of the equivalent number in the former Rules of the Supreme Court in England concerned orders for assessment of damages by the Admiralty Registrar, which does not exist as a separate office in Hong Kong.

**[37.4.2]      Trial on question of quantum of damages**

Order 37 rule 4 provides for trial on the quantum of damages in cases where judgment has been given for an amount to be assessed. Such a judgment may be given under Order 13 or Order 19 in default of acknowledgement of service or defence, or may result from a split trial on liability alone. The rule provides that the court may order that a trial on quantum take place before a judge. More commonly assessments of damages are conducted by masters. See Order 37 rule 1. The rule applies, *mutatis mutandis*, the case management summons and conference procedures of Order 25 to actions which are ordered to proceed to trial before a judge on quantum.

**5.      Assessment of value** (O. 37 r. 5)

**The foregoing provisions of this Order shall apply in relation to a judgment for the value of goods to be assessed, with or without damages to be assessed, as they apply to a judgment for damages to be assessed, and references in those provisions to the assessment of damages shall be construed accordingly.**

**6.    Assessment of damages to time of assessment** (O. 37 r. 6)
    **Where damages are to be assessed (whether under this Order or otherwise) in respect of any continuing cause of action, they shall be assessed down to the time of the assessment.**

---

## NOTES

**[37.6.1]    Recovery of damages occurring after issue of writ**
Damage caused after the issue of the writ may be recovered on an assessment of damages by virtue of Order 37 rule 6, provided the cause of action is a continuing one which arose before and is pleaded in the writ. See, for example, *Uni Industries Ltd v Omega International Ltd & Ors* [2005] 1 HKC 415 (CA). That case concerned a claim for damage caused by water seeping from one flat into another, which continued after issue of the writ.

II. Orders for Provisional Damages for Personal Injuries

**7.    Application and interpretation** (O. 37 r. 7)
    **(1)    This Part of this Order applies to actions to which section 56A of the Ordinance (in this Part of this Order referred to as "section 56A") applies.**
    **(2)    In this Part of this Order "award of provisional damages" means an award of damages for personal injuries under which—**
        **(a)    damages are assessed on the assumption that the injured person will not develop the disease or suffer the deterioration referred to in section 56A; and**
        **(b)    the injured person is entitled to apply for further damages at a future date if he develops the disease or suffers the deterioration.**

---

## NOTES

**[37.7.1]    High Court Ordinance, section 56A**
Part II of Order 37 is enacted pursuant to section 56A of the High Court Ordinance. It applies to personal injuries actions where there is a chance the injured person may in future develop some serious disease or suffer some serious deterioration in condition. The court is empowered to make an award of provisional damages, leaving it open to the injured person to apply for further damages if the disease or deterioration eventuates.

    The power to make an award of provisional damages is a statutory exception to the general common law rule that 'damages are assessed on a once-and-for-all basis': *Wilson v Ministry of Defence* [1991] 1 All ER 638, 644g.

    The English equivalent of this legislation is section 32A of the Supreme Court Act 1981, and Part 41 of the CPR.

**8.    Order for provisional damages** (O. 37 r. 8)
    **(1)    The Court may on such terms as it thinks just and subject to the**

provisions of this rule make an award of provisional damages if—

    **(a)**    **the plaintiff has pleaded a claim for provisional damages, and**

    **(b)**    **the Court is satisfied that the action is one to which section 56A applies.**

    **(2)**    **An order for an award of provisional damages shall specify the disease or type of deterioration in respect of which an application may be made at a future date, and shall also, unless the Court otherwise determines, specify the period within which such application may be made.**

    **(3)**    **The Court may, on the application of the plaintiff made within the period, if any, specified in paragraph (2), by order extend that period if it thinks it just to do so, and the plaintiff may make more than one such application.**

    **(4)**    **An order for an award of provisional damages may be made in respect of more than one disease or type of deterioration and may in respect of each disease or deterioration specify a different period within which an application may be made at a future date.**

    **(5)**    **Orders 13 and 19 shall not apply in relation to an action in which the plaintiff claims provisional damages.**

---

## NOTES

**[37.8.1]**    **Where order for provisional damages may be made**

In *Wilson v Ministry of Defence* [1991] 1 All ER 638, 641j-642a the court approached an application to assess damages on a provisional basis with three questions:

(i)    *whether there is a 'chance'* – the word 'chance' is not defined in the legislation, but is to be given a wide meaning. In this connection see also *Wan Man Kit v Poon Chi Man* HCPI 393/1999 (Recorder Kwok SC; 16.06.2000) where the court declined to make a provisional damages award, apparently on the basis that a 'not probable' future condition was not one in respect of which there was a 'chance'.

(ii)    *whether there might be a 'serious' disease or deterioration* – this is a question of fact which depends on the circumstances including the effect on the injured person. 'For example, where a plaintiff suffers a hand injury and there is a deterioration it may be a matter of great gravity for a concert pianist but a matter of rather less importance for somebody else': *Wilson* (above).

(iii)    *whether the court should exercise its discretion* – if the injured person passes the first two hurdles the court needs still to consider whether it should exercise its discretion in the circumstances of the case.

It appears that the provisional damages procedure does not apply in cases of natural or gradual progression of a condition: *Wilson* (above). However it is available where, although causation could not be proved on the current state of medical science, it might be at the time the possible future condition manifests itself: *Fairchild v Glenhaven Funeral Services Ltd & Ors* [2002] 1 WLR 1052, 1096 (CA).

**9.**    **Offer to submit to an award (O. 37 r. 9)**

    **(1)**    **Where an application is made for an award of provisional damages,**

any defendant may at any time (whether or not he makes a payment into court) make a written offer to the plaintiff—

    (a)    to tender a sum of money (which may include an amount, to be specified, in respect of interest) in satisfaction of the plaintiff's claim for damages assessed on the assumption that the injured person will not develop the disease or suffer the deterioration referred to in section 56A and identifying the disease or deterioration in question; and

        **(L.N. 404 of 1991)**

    (b)    to agree to the making of an award of provisional damages.

(2)    Any offer made under paragraph (1) shall not be brought to the attention of the Court until after the Court has determined the claim for an award of provisional damages.

(3)    Where an offer is made under paragraph (1), the plaintiff may, within 28 days after the offer was made, give written notice to the defendant of his acceptance of the offer and shall on such acceptance make an application to the Court for an order in accordance with the provisions of rule 8(2).

10.    **Application for award of further damages** (O. 37 r. 10)

(1)    This rule applies where the plaintiff, pursuant to an award of provisional damages, claims further damages.

(2)    No application for further damages may be made after the expiration of the period, if any, specified under rule 8(2), or of such period as extended under rule 8(3).

(3)    The plaintiff shall give not less than three months' written notice to the defendant of his intention to apply for further damages and, if the defendant is to the plaintiff's knowledge insured in respect of the plaintiff's claim, to the insurers.

(4)    The plaintiff must take out a case management summons as to the future conduct of the action within 21 days after the expiry of the period of notice referred to in paragraph (3). (L.N. 152 of 2008)

(5)    At the determination of the case management summons the Court shall give such directions as may be appropriate for the future conduct of the action, including, but not limited to, the disclosure of medical reports and the place, mode and date of the hearing of the application for further damages. (L.N. 152 of 2008)

(6)    Only one application for further damages may be made in respect of each disease or type of deterioration specified in the order for the award of provisional damages.

(7)    The provisions of Order 29 with regard to the making of interim payments shall, with the necessary modifications, apply where an application is made under this rule.

(8)    The Court may include in an award of further damages simple interest at such rate as it thinks fit on all or any part thereof for all or any part of the period between the date of notification of the plaintiff's intention to apply for further damages and the date of the award. (Enacted 1988)

**ORDER 38**

**EVIDENCE**

I. General Rules

**NOTES**

**[38.0.1]** **Cross-reference to primary legislation**
Order 38 is enacted pursuant to section 55B of the High Court Ordinance which specifically empowers the rules committee to make rules regulating the manner by which particular facts may be proved and the mode by which evidence may be given. It should be read together with the Evidence Ordinance (Cap 8).

**[38.0.2]** **Scope of Order 38 Part I**
Part I of Order 38 sets out general rules concerning the use of evidence in court proceedings. It includes rule 2A under which the exchange of witness statements is usually ordered in civil actions.

**1.** **General rule: witnesses to be examined orally** (O. 38 r. 1)
**Subject to the provisions of these rules and of the Evidence Ordinance (Cap. 8) and any other written law relating to evidence, any fact required to be proved at the trial of any action begun by writ by the evidence of witnesses shall be proved by the examination of the witnesses orally and in open court.**

**NOTES**

**[38.1.1]** **When evidence to be taken orally or in writing**
Order 38 rule 1 states the general principle that the evidence of witnesses at trial should be given orally in open court. There are many exceptions by which evidence may be given in writing in specific circumstances. Some examples are the following:

- Rule 1 by its own terms applies only to actions begun by writ. In proceedings commenced by originating summons evidence is normally given by affidavit (see Order 28 rule 1A). Likewise evidence is normally given by affidavit in applications for judicial review, habeas corpus and other types of proceedings not initiated by writ.
- Order 38 rule 2A(7)(a) empowers the court to order that written witness statements stand as evidence-in-chief.
- Order 38 rule 9 provides for the use of deposition evidence at trial.
- In personal injury actions it is commonly directed that medical records of treating hospitals be admitted as agreed evidence. Such evidence is agreed in the sense that its authenticity is not challenged, so it is not necessary for the makers to be called, but no admission is made as to the truth of the contents: *Padamlal v Dashing (Holi) Co Ltd & Anor* HCPI 100/2008 (Fung J;

24.10.2008).

• Also in personal injury actions the court commonly orders that expert reports be admitted into evidence without calling the makers to give oral evidence: *Shrestha Kalyan v Acciona Infraestructuras SA* HCPI 710/2007 (Fung J; 22.09.2008)

### [38.1.2]    Oaths and affirmations

See the Oaths and Declarations Ordinance (Cap 11) and see also the commentary under Order 41.

### [38.1.3]    Refreshment of memory

Section 51(6) of the Evidence Ordinance preserves the common law with respect to the circumstances in which a document, used to refresh memory and subsequently made the subject of cross-examination, may be made evidence in the proceedings. Prior to amendment of the Ordinance in 1999 the provision was found in section 48(2).

### [38.1.4]    Hostile witnesses

As to hostile witnesses, see sections 12, 13 and 14 of the Evidence Ordinance. There has been some debate in the criminal courts in Hong Kong as to whether a judge ought to treat a witness as hostile once it is established that the witness has made a previous inconsistent statement (see *R v Au Lai Yung* [1973-76] HKC 417, [1976] HKLR 249; *Wu Man-choi v R* [1979] HKLR 174 and *R v Cheung Ting Wai* [1977-79] HKC 102). Three propositions are common ground:

(1)   there must be sufficient evidence upon which a judge may find a witness to be hostile;

(2)   whether there is such sufficient evidence is for the judge to decide; and

(3)   proof that the witness has made a previous inconsistent statement will often be sufficient.

But will proof that the witness has made a previous inconsistent statement always be sufficient? It is submitted that the effect of the latter two decisions cited above is to answer this question in the negative, but the circumstances in which proof of a previous inconsistent statement will not suffice are not clear. In *Wu Man-choi* (above), at 179, it was said that, 'So far as we are aware the only reason for treating Miss To as hostile was that she had made the previous inconsistent statements. That would have been a sufficient reason if the judge was satisfied that the previous statement had been voluntary, [denied by the witness in this case] but not other wise'. In *Cheung Ting Wai* (above), the court held:

> As we interpret *Fraser*, when read with earlier authorities, the main factor which will influence the judge in deciding whether or not to declare a witness hostile is the inconsistency between his earlier statement and his evidence. But we agree with the passage in *Wu* which states that it is not the only factor. The judge should, for instance, *consider* the degree of inconsistency as well as the fact of it, its importance to the trial, and the demeanour and attitude of the witness. But, having done so, he is entitled to declare a witness hostile on the ground of inconsistency alone.

The last sentence is ambiguous in context but it is submitted that acceptance that the declaration or non-declaration of a witness as hostile is a matter for the discretion of the court necessarily implies that a judge is not bound to find that a witness is hostile notwithstanding a previous inconsistent statement has been proved. However, absent any acceptable explanation of the inconsistency, a court may so declare without fear of being overruled.

### [38.1.5]  Previous convictions

See section 15 of the Evidence Ordinance, relating to indictable offences, and sections 2 and 3 of the Rehabilitation of Offenders Ordinance (Cap 297) relating to spent convictions.

Questions as to convictions for summary offences which are not misdemeanours, which convictions are not spent and, nevertheless, tend to weaken the character of the witness or question the witness's trustworthiness as a witness of truth may still be permissible at common law.

### [38.1.6]  Previous inconsistent statements

As to previous inconsistent statements of a witness or consistent statements adduced to rebut a suggestion of recent fabrication in civil cases, see sections 13, 14, and 51 (previously 48(1)) of the Evidence Ordinance.

### [38.1.7]  Language of evidence

Section 5 of the Official Languages Ordinance (Cap 5) provides that a party or witness may testify in any language. If a witness uses a language other than English or Chinese it will have to be translated into the official language chosen for use in the proceedings under r 3 of the High Court Civil Procedure (Use of Language) Rules (Cap 5C), as to which see the commentary under Order 35 rule 7. Sometimes translation between Chinese dialects is required.

### [38.1.8]  Payment of witnesses

Expert witnesses are usually paid by the parties who call them, and the fact of payment is irrelevant to admissibility of their evidence: *Tang Ping Choi v Secretary for Transport* [2004] 3 HKC 178, 185H-I (CA). Payment of other witnesses is not usual and may be undesirable. See *Kwan Yim Kwan Peggy v Namkung Promotions (Worldwide) Ltd* [2007] 3 HKC 314 (CA) (para 12) where it was held that payment to a non-expert witness must be disclosed to the court before the witness gives evidence, and that the fact of payment is relevant to assessment of credibility.

### [38.1.9]  Examination-in-chief and cross-examination of witnesses– defendant's obligation to put its case to plaintiff's witnesses

A defendant who intends to adduce evidence which contradicts that of a witness for the plaintiff is obliged to put that evidence to the plaintiff's witness in cross-examination so as to provide an opportunity to comment. Failure to do so resulted in parts of the defendant's evidence being excluded in *Secretary for Justice v Yu's Tin Sing Enterprises Co Ltd* HCA 398/2006 (Recorder Kwok SC; 09.09.2008).

**2.    Evidence by affidavit** (O. 38 r. 2)

**(1)    The Court may, at or before the trial of an action begun by writ, order that the affidavit of any witness may be read at the trial if in the circumstances of the case it thinks it reasonable so to order.**

**(2)    An order under paragraph (1) may be made on such terms as to the**

filing and giving of copies of the affidavits and as to the production of the deponents for cross-examination as the Court thinks fit but, subject to any such terms and to any subsequent order of the Court, the deponents shall not be subject to cross-examination and need not attend the trial for the purpose.

(3)   In any cause or matter begun by originating summons, originating motion or petition, and on any application made by summons or motion, evidence may be given by affidavit unless in the case of any such cause, matter or application any provision of these rules otherwise provides or the Court otherwise directs, but the Court may, on the application of any party, order the attendance for cross-examination of the person making any such affidavit, and where, after such an order has been made, the person in question does not attend, his affidavit shall not be used as evidence without the leave of the Court.

---

## NOTES

### [38.2.1]   Court's discretion to allow evidence by affidavit at trial

Order 38 rule 2(1) gives the court a discretion to allow evidence to be adduced at trial by way of affidavit, with or without cross-examination of the deponent. Each case must depend on its own facts and circumstances: *High Fashion Garments Co Ltd v Ng Siu Tong & Ors* [2003] 2 HKC 562, 567E-F. Where a party wishes to rely on an affidavit at trial without calling the witness, the proper procedure is to apply for directions accordingly before the case is set down for trial: see *Cheung Wei Man Vivien & Anor v Centaline Property Agency Ltd & Ors* [2004] 1 HKC 692, 695B-D. The application should be made at the case management stage pursuant to Order 25.

In the *High Fashion Garments* case, a plaintiff sought to rely on affidavit evidence of a witness in Singapore who did not wish to travel to Hong Kong for health reasons. Deputy Judge Lam was of the view that the witness's evidence could have a significant impact on the case and held that on balance, the defendants should not be deprived of an opportunity to cross-examine. In the circumstances, the learned deputy judge allowed the application to adduce affidavit evidence at trial, but subject to the condition that the witness attend for cross-examination by video-link from Singapore.

Where the affidavit evidence sought to be adduced at trial is seriously contested, it is not appropriate for the court to allow it to be adduced without the witness being required to attend for cross-examination, whether in person or by video-link: see *Cheung Wei Man Vivien & Anor v Centaline Property Agency Ltd & Ors* [2004] 1 HKC 692, 694D-E

In the *High Fashion Garments* case it was said (*obiter*, at 568G) that, the 1999 amendments relaxing the criteria under which hearsay evidence is admissible, did not change the prior law as to admissibility of affidavit evidence under this rule. The decisions in *Rover International Ltd v Cannon Film Sales Ltd* [1987] 1 WLR 1597 and *Re Dominion International Group plc* [1995] 1 WLR 649 were cited by the learned deputy judge in this regard.

### [38.2.2]   Cross-examination on affidavit

Order 38 rule 2(3) underpins the practice whereby evidence in proceedings commenced otherwise than by writ of summons, and on interlocutory applications, is normally given by way of affidavit.

The sub-rule goes on to provide that the court may order that a deponent attend to be cross-examined on his affidavit. The circumstances in which this discretion will be exer cised were considered by the Court of Appeal in *Yuen Wendy v Yuen Philip* [1984] HKLR 431. It was held that there is no generally applicable requirement that special cir cumstances must be shown and *Oriental Pacific Mills Ltd (No 2) v Nan Fung Woollen Mills Ltd & Ors* [1965] HKLR 703 was not to be read as supporting such a proposition. Cross-examination would be ordered where the interests of justice so dictate (citing *Smith and Fawcett* [1942] 1 Ch 304), and the burden on the applicant was 'to establish that in all the circumstances of the case there is a good and sufficient reason for the application'. The court would consider whether 'great delay and expense might be entailed'. It was incum bent on the applicant 'to show that the proposed cross-examination might be pro ductive of a useful result' at the interlocutory stage. Cross-examination would not be allowed in interlocutory proceedings on matters which should be canvassed at the hearing of the action. See the judgment of Fuad JA at 436 E-I. In result, the Court of Appeal upheld a judge's decision to order cross-examination on an affidavit seeking to resist an applica tion for disclosure of accounts in a matrimonial case. The judgment of the Court of Appeal in *Yuen Wendy* continues to be regarded as authoritative: see *Waters v Malahon Credit Co Ltd* [2004] 2 HKC 94 (CA); *Pacific Electric Wire & Cable Co Ltd v Texan Man agement Ltd & Ors* HCA 2203/2004 (Deputy Judge Muttrie; 28.02.2006).

With regard to fugitives from justice, who do not wish to come to Hong Kong to be cross-examined, see the commentary under Order 39 rule 2.

The court will be slow to grant leave to cross-examine on the affidavit of an alleged contemnor in contempt proceedings. This is because of the penal consequences of the proceedings. See *Comet Products UK Ltd v Hawkex Plastics Ltd & Anor* [1971] 2 QB 67 (per Lord Denning MR); *Kwan v Extra Excel (Malaysia) Sdn Bhd & Ors* [2007] 7 MLJ 250. If leave to cross-examine is given, the court may limit its scope as in *Lexi Holdings plc v Luqman* [2007] EWHC 1508 (Ch) (02.07.2007) (para 8).

**2A.   Exchange of witness statements** (O. 38 r.2A)

**(1)   The powers of the Court under this rule shall be exercised for the purpose of disposing fairly and expeditiously of the cause or matter before it, and saving costs, having regard to all the circumstances of the case, including (but not limited to)—**

    **(a)**    **the extent to which the facts are in dispute or have been admitted;**

    **(b)**    **the extent to which the issues of fact are defined by the pleadings;**

    **(c)**    **the extent to which information has been or is likely to be provided by further and better particulars, answers to interrogatories or otherwise.**

**(2)   At the determination of a case management summons, in an action commenced by writ the Court shall direct every party to serve on the other parties, within such period of the hearing as the Court may specify and on such terms as the Court may specify, written statements of the oral evidence which the party intends to adduce on any issues of fact to be decided at the trial. (L.N. 152 of 2008)**

The Court may give a direction to any party under this paragraph at any other stage of such an action and at any stage of any other cause or matter.

Order 3, rule 5(3) shall not apply to any period specified by the Court under this paragraph.

(3) Directions under paragraph (2) or (17) may make different provision with regard to different issues of fact or different witnesses.

(4) Statements served under this rule shall—

    (a) be dated and, except for good reason (which should be specified by letter accompanying the statement), be signed by the intended witness and must be verified by a statement of truth in accordance with Order 41A; (L.N. 152 of 2008)

    (b) sufficiently identify any documents referred to therein; and

    (c) where they are to be served by more than one party, be exchanged simultaneously.

(5) Where a party is unable to obtain a written statement from an intended witness in accordance with paragraph (4)(a), the Court may direct the party wishing to adduce that witness's evidence to provide the other party with the name of the witness and (unless the Court otherwise orders) a statement of the nature of the evidence intended to be adduced.

(6) Subject to paragraph (9), where the party serving a statement under this rule does not call the witness to whose evidence it relates, no other party may put the statement in evidence at the trial.

(7) Subject to paragraph (9), where the party serving the statement does call such a witness at the trial—

    (a) except where the trial is with a jury, the Court may, on such terms as it thinks fit, direct that the statement served, or part of it, shall stand as the evidence in chief of the witness or part of such evidence;

    (b) the witness may with the leave of the Court —

        (i) amplify his witness statement; and

        (ii) give evidence in relation to new matters which have arisen since the witness statement was served on the other party; (L.N. 152 of 2008)

    (c) whether or not the statement or any part of it is referred to during the evidence in chief of the witness, any party may put the statement or any part of it in cross-examination of that witness.

(7A) The Court may grant leave under paragraph (7)(b) only if it considers that there is good reason not to confine the evidence of the witness to the contents of his witness statement. (L.N. 152 of 2008).

(8) Nothing in this rule shall make admissible evidence which is otherwise inadmissible.

(9) Where any statement served is one to which the Evidence Ordinance (Cap. 8) applies, paragraphs (6) and (7) shall take effect subject to the provisions of that Ordinance and Parts III and IV of this Order.

The service of a witness statement under this rule shall not, unless expressly so stated by the party serving the same, be treated as a notice under that Ordinance; and where a statement or any part thereof would be admissible in evidence by virtue only of that Ordinance, the appropriate notice under Part III or IV of this Order shall be served with the statement notwithstanding any provision of those Parts as to the time for serving such a notice. (L.N. 152 of 2008)

(10)  Where a party fails to comply with a direction for the exchange of witness statements he shall not be entitled to adduce evidence to which the direction related without the leave of the Court.

(11)  Where a party serves a witness statement under this rule, no other person may make use of that statement for any purpose other than the purpose of the proceedings in which it was served—

(a)     unless and to the extent that the party serving it gives his consent in writing or the Court gives leave; or

(b)     unless and to the extent that it has been put in evidence (whether pursuant to a direction under paragraph (7)(a) or otherwise).

(12)  Subject to paragraph (13), the judge shall, if any person so requests during the course of the trial, direct the Clerk of Court to certify as open to inspection any witness statement which was ordered to stand as evidence in chief under paragraph (7)(a).

A request under this paragraph may be made orally or in writing.

(13)  The judge may refuse to give a direction under paragraph (12) in relation to a witness statement, or may exclude from such a direction any words or passages in a statement, if he considers that inspection should not be available—

(a)     in the interests of justice or national security;

(b)     because of the nature of any expert medical evidence in the statement; or

(c)     for any other sufficient reason.

(14)  Where the Clerk of Court is directed under paragraph (12) to certify a witness statement as open to inspection he shall—

(a)     prepare a certificate which shall be attached to a copy ("the certified copy") of that witness statement; and

(b)     make the certified copy available for inspection.

(15)  Subject to any conditions which the Court may by special or general direction impose, any person may inspect and (subject to payment of the prescribed fee) take a copy of the certified copy of a witness statement from the time when the certificate is given until the end of 7 days after the conclusion of the trial.

(16)  In this rule—

(a)     any reference in paragraphs (12) to (15) to a witness statement shall, in relation to a witness statement of which only part has been ordered to stand as evidence in chief under paragraph (7)(a), be construed as a reference to that part;

(b)     any reference to inspecting or copying the certified copy of a witness statement shall be construed as including a reference to inspecting or copying a copy of that certified copy.

**(17) The Court shall have power to vary or override any of the provisions of this rule (except paragraphs (1), (8) and (12) to (16)) and to give such alternative directions as it thinks fit.**

**(L.N. 223 of 1995)**

---

## NOTES

### [38.2A.1]  Exchange and filing of witness statements

Under Order 38 rule 2A(2) the court is required at the determination of the case management summons under Order 25 to direct the parties to serve written statements of the oral evidence they intend to adduce at trial. Rule 2A(4)(c) requires that opposing litigants should exchange their witness statements simultaneously. The rule does not require that witness statements be filed in court. That is only necessary where the court so directs: practice direction 24.1, para 9.

In *Cheung Kai Wing v Mok Sheung Shum & Anor* [1993] 2 HKC 113 (CA), Kaplan J commented on the impact the witness statement procedure has had on civil litigation. His Lordship said, at 126C–D:

> It is no exaggeration to say that Order 38 rule 2A has revolutionised the way in which civil litigation is conducted in England and in Hong Kong. Prior to the coming into force of this rule, it was frequently and authoritatively stated that litigation under our system was conducted on a 'cards on the table' approach.

His Lordship went on to quote from the judgment of Steyn J in *Mercer v Chief Constable of the Lancashire Constabulary* [1991] 1 WLR 367 where it was said:

> RSC Order 38 rule 2A has proved a most useful innovation which, to the great benefit of parties and the administration of justice, has been accommodated in our adversarial system. The system was borrowed from the tried and tested system for international commercial arbitration.

### [38.2A.2]  Formal requirements

Paragraph (4) of the rule sets out the following formal requirements for witness statements:

(a)  they must be dated;

(b)  they must be signed by the intended witness (except where there is good reason);

(c)  they must be verified by a statement of truth in accordance with Order 41A. See the commentary under that Order.

(d)  where documents are referred to, those documents should be sufficiently identified.

With regard to (c) above, that is the requirement that a witness statement be verified by statement of truth, see also Order 41A rule 2(b) which is to the same effect. For discussion of statements of truth generally, see the commentary under Order 41A. Note in particular that Order 41A rule 7 provides that a witness statement which is not verified by statement of truth is not admissible in evidence unless the court orders otherwise.

**[38.2A.3]  Scope of witness statements**

Witness statements should be comprehensive statements of the whole of the witnesses' evidence. In *Hanwa Kozai (HK) Ltd v Hangyiu Ltd* [1995] 1 HKC 841 Keith J, referring to an earlier judgment of his own, said as follows (at 842D–F):

> In *Ng Kam Chun Stephen v Chan Wai Hing Janet* HCA No A3036/92, I said that 'the witness statement should contain the whole of the witness' evidence in the detail in which the witness would have given it if his evidence had been elicited by oral questions at the trial' ... In my view, that practice should prevail whether or not the master has at the same time ordered that the statement should stand as the witness' evidence-in-chief. I see no room for a witness statement which represents a half-way house between the pleadings (which are limited to the assertions which the parties seek to prove, and are not intended to incorporate the evidence which the parties propose to call to prove those assertions) and the witness statements (which are intended to set out the evidence which the parties propose to call to prove the facts asserted in the pleadings).

Witness statements, like affidavits, should not go into legal argument nor should they contain 'lawyerese' designed to prove a case. See *Dah Sing Bank Ltd v Sing Hai Handbags Manuf'y Ltd & Ors* [2007] 3 HKC 515 and the other authorities cited in the commentary preceding Order 41 rule 1.

**[38.2A.4]  Translation of statements**

In *Cheung Kai Wing v Mok Sheung Shum & Anor* [1993] 2 HKC 113 (CA), Kaplan J dealt with the problem frequently encountered in this jurisdiction of non-English-speaking witnesses who give statements in English. At 127E–F his Lordship said:

> In cases where the witnesses cannot speak or understand English, it is crucial that the solicitor concerned should translate and explain the statement to their intended witness before it is signed and the solicitor should so declare on the face of the statement.

In some cases the court has gone further and directed that a Chinese-language version of a witness statement be prepared and signed by the deponent.

**[38.2A.5]  Witness statements as evidence-in-chief**

Order 38 rule 2A(7)(a) empowers the court to order that witness statements stand as evidence-in-chief, except where there will be a jury trial. The power is a matter for the judge's discretion: *So Amy & Ors v Au Leslie* [1995] 2 HKC 113, 118H (CA); though in *Cheung Kai Wing v Mok Sheung Shum t/a Mok Sum Kee & Anor* [1993] 2 HKC 113, 128A-C (CA) it was suggested that the parties could procure such an order by consent.

In *Cheung Kai Wing* (above) it was said (at 128D-E) that an order that witness statements stand as evidence-in-chief will likely be appropriate 'in most commercial cases and most personal injury cases'. In *Hanwa Kozai (HK) Co Ltd v Hangyiu Ltd & Anor* [1995] 1 HKC 841, 842 it was said that such an order is not appropriate where the witness statements 'reveal a significant conflict of evidence between two or more witnesses'. The most important factor for a judge to consider in deciding whether to make such an order 'is the extent to which the evidence of a particular witness is likely to be controversial, and his credibility put in issue': *So Amy* (above, at 118G-I). However all the circumstances should be taken into account and the judge retains a discretion even where there are conflicts on the evidence: see *Bam Ganesh v Hussain Maroof* CACV 47/2007 (Rogers VP, Le Pichon JA & Barma J;

16.07.2008) where Le Pichon JA said (para 18):

> As to the *So* case, I would observe that what is there stated does not take away the judge's discretion. Trials would be needlessly prolonged if in every case where the evidence of a witness is controversial and his credibility is put in issue (and that must arise in most cases), evidence in chief has to be given. The judge's discretion [is] to be exercised sensibly having regard to the circumstances of the particular case.

The judge should consider the witness statements one by one rather than making a blanket order for witness statements to stand as evidence-in-chief: *Richardson Greenshields of Canada (Pacific) Ltd v Tze Yim* HCA 6690/1987 (Kaplan J; 18.10.1991) (para 66), refer ring to *Mercer v Chief Constable of Lancashire* [1991] 1 WLR 367. Indeed 'it is wrong in principle to make orders applying to all witness statements without regard to the extent to which the witness' evidence is likely to be controversial and go to the heart of the dispute': *So Amy* (above, 118H-I), also referring to *Mercer* (at 371H).

At trial, where a statement has earlier been ordered to stand as evidence-in-chief, the witness will normally be asked to confirm or adopt the statement as his or her evidence. The statement may be supplemented by oral evidence: 'it is usual for the judge to permit some oral amplification, especially in the light of evidence already given at the trial': *Cheung Kai Wing* (above, 128E–F).

### [38.2A.6] Circumstances in which witness may give evidence beyond the scope of witness statement

Order 38 rule 2A(7)(b), read together with rule 2A(7A), permits the court to grant leave to a witness to amplify his or her witness statement, or give evidence on matters which arose after the witness statement was served, where there is good reason. The rule was amended to that effect on implementation of the civil justice reforms in 2009. The purpose was to implement recommendation 100 of the Chief Justice's working party on civil justice reform, which called for 'introducing greater flexibility in permitting a witness to amplify or supplement his witness statement'. Previously a witness was allowed to give evidence beyond the scope of his or her witness statement only with the consent of the other parties, or if there had been a direction of the court limiting the scope of the witness statement to specific issues, or if the new evidence concerned matters arising subsequent to service of the witness statement. The working party considered these to be 'very limited circumstances' (final report, para 589).

The problem addressed by the amendments under the civil justice reforms implemented in 2009 was identified in the interim report on civil justice reform at paras 471 *et seq*. It was there said:

> ... it is widely recognized that the practice which has developed in relation to witness statements, reflecting adversarial excesses, has seriously tarnished the benefits of the procedure, particularly in heavy cases. Witness statements have become regarded as documents to be carefully crafted by counsel, going through several drafts, covering every detail and with every nuance discussed in conference with the client ...
>
> If a witness will not be allowed to add to his witness statement, or if he will be criticised if he needs to correct any errors or ambiguities in it, conscientious legal advisers will quite properly consider it their duty to make the statement as comprehensive as possible, covering numerous possible lines of inquiry and minutely checking the statement for errors.

Underlying the above observations is clearly a desire to keep costs down.

The equivalent provisions in England are CPR 32.5(3) and (4), which are in the same terms as Hong Kong's Order 38 rule 2A(7) and (7A).

In proposing adoption of the more liberal English position, the Chief Justice's working party expressed the view that as a general rule, a witness statement should still cover all of the witness's evidence. Thus a grant of leave to depart therefrom may still be regarded as exceptional.

In most cases it will be preferable to seek leave to file a supplementary witness statement (as to which see below) instead of waiting in hope that the court will, in its discretion, allow additional evidence from a witness when called.

### [38.2A.7]   Hearsay in witness statements – Order 38 rule 2A(9)

Order 38 rule 2A(9) makes it clear that the provisions of the Evidence Ordinance (Cap 8) and parts III and IV of this Order (which deal with hearsay and expert evidence respectively) apply to witness statements. It is provided that where hearsay is included in a witness statement a hearsay notice shall be served with it, further that a counter-notice shall be deemed to have been served. The rule does not reflect the relaxation of the admission of hearsay for actions commenced since 1999 (as to which see the commentary under Order 38 rule 22).

### [38.2A.8]   Supplementary statements

A party may seek leave to file supplementary statements. In *Allington Investment Corp v First Pacific Bancshares Holdings Ltd* [1995] 2 HKC 567, 570B-D it was said:

> The witness statements ought, in the usual course, be mutually exchanged so that no unfair advantage would be conferred on any one party. In the premises, it is not unusual for parties to seek leave to supplement their witness statements by further statements from their witnesses to deal with matters arising from the other side's statements. However, there must be an end to such process and usually no more than one supplemental statement from a witness is necessary.

Supplemental witness statements should be confined to clarification and filling in gaps. Where it is sought by supplemental statement to *change* a witness's evidence, leave will be refused. Changes in evidence should be left for trial. See *Commerzbank Aktiengesellschaft (HK) v Peregrine Fixed Income Ltd (in liq)* CACV 296/2002 (Rogers VP & Le Pichon JA; 10.09.2002). However, leave will be granted where a witness seeks to correct a mistake made by legal advisors in preparing the witness statement: *Man Fung Choy v Man Shing Li* [2004] 4 HKC 487 (CA).

### [38.2A.9]   Time for exchange of witness statements

When the court gives a direction for the exchange of witness statements it will fix a time within which this step should be taken. That time will normally be after discovery and inspection of documents and well before the time for hearing the application for leave to set down.

### [38.2A.10]   Extension of time for exchange of witness statements

The court has long had power under Order 3 rule 5 to extend the time for exchange of witness statements.

The procedure whereby in most circumstances the parties may extend time by agreement under Order 3 rule 5(3) does not apply: see Order 38 rule 2A(2). As a result a court order is necessary for extension of time to exchange witness statements. The situation was different prior to amendment of Order 38 rule 2A in force on 25.05.1995. An agreement between parties to extend the time for exchange of witness statements made prior to that date will be considered valid. See *Wing Ming Garment Fty Ltd v IO of Wing Ming Industrial Centre* HCA 8805/1993 (A Cheung J; 22.04.2005).

The court's power under Order 1B rule 1(2)(a) to extend or shorten time by way of case management also extends to witness statements. See the commentary under that provision.

Where one side is able to comply with a direction to exchange witness statements in a timely fashion, but the opposing party is not, and the opposing party does not apply for an extension of time, the party ready to comply faces a dilemma. Should it unilaterally file and serve its witness statement, thereby running the risk that its opponent will later tailor its own statement in light of what it learns therefrom, or should it also refrain from complying in order to preserve the obvious advantage of mutual exchange? To preserve its right to simultaneous exchange of statements the compliant party may consider applying for an extension of time on a peremptory or 'unless' basis, based on the other party's default.

### [38.2A.11] 'Unless' order for exchange of witness statements

Where a party fails to comply with a direction to exchange witness statements, the court may grant an 'unless' order: *Chow Kwok Fai v Waysuntone Communication Ltd* [1997] 3 HKC 628; *Kai Yip Air-Condition Engineering Co v Ma Hei Sun* [2001] 3 HKC 458. Such an order may provide that judgment be entered unless there is compliance or simply that the defaulting party be barred from adducing evidence at trial, without leave of the court. The latter type of order was made in *Ying Chow Lung v Kowloon Motor Bus Co (1933) Ltd & Anor* HCPI 74/1998 (Suffiad J; 17.11.1998) where the party in default gave an indication that it would not call any witnesses.

In *Luigi Benetton SRL v Face Time Int'l Ltd* HCA 4135/1993 (J Chan J; 24.11.1995) the court made an unless order requiring the defendant to file and serve witness statements within 21 days, in default of which judgment would be entered against it. The defendant had failed to comply with an earlier direction to exchange witness statements, but had indicated it would call witnesses at trial.

In *Yee Tung Fibre Glass Manufactory Eng Co (a firm) v FRP (HK) Ltd* HCA 17840/1998 (Ribeiro J; 17.09.1999) the court set aside judgment which had been entered on failure to comply with an unless order for service of expert reports and witness statements where it was satisfied there had not been contumelious disregard of the court's order. The court directed that the defaulting party's solicitors have an opportunity to show cause why they should not bear the costs.

### [38.2A.12] Late witness statements

Applications for leave to rely on additional witness statements at a late stage will be scrutinised carefully by the court. This is because a late application my cause prejudice to the opposing party, or prolong or disrupt trial: *Guangzhou Green-Enhan Bio-Eng'g Co Ltd & Anor v Green Power Health Products Int'l Co Ltd* HCA 4651/2002 (Lam J; 21.08.2004). In that case it was suggested that the court might adopt the approach laid down in *Hong Lok School Ltd v Chow Sai Yiu* [2003] 2 HKLRD 782 whereby an explanatory affidavit is required where a party wishes to rely on documents disclosed at the 11<sup>th</sup> hour. See the discussion of that decision in relation to last minute supplemental lists of documents under Order 24 rule 2.

**[38.2A.13]  Failure to comply with direction for exchange of witness statements**
A party which fails to comply with a direction for the exchange of witness statements is not entitled to adduce evidence at trial except with leave of the court: rule 2A(10).

On an application for such leave, the court must have regard to the underlying objectives in Order 1A. See *Chinachem Charitable Foundation Ltd v Chan Chun Chuen & Anor* HCAP 8/2007 (Lam J; 11.06.2009); [2009] 4 HKLRD 157 (para 4). In that case the court referred to Order 1A rule 2(2) (underlying objectives to be given effect recognising that the primary aim is to secure just resolution of disputes in accordance with substantive rights) and said that the probative value of the proposed evidence was an important, though by no means the only, consideration (para 21). The court found that the proposed evidence was not of much probative value, and balancing that against prejudice to the trial (which was already underway), concluded that it would not be fair and proportionate to permit the evidence to be adduced (para 49). The court was of the view (para 50) that Order 2 rule 5 (relief from sanctions) applied, possibly because there had been an unless order.

**[38.2A.14]  Striking out inadmissible evidence from witness statement**
Order 38 rule 2A(8) expressly provides that nothing in the rule affects the admissibility of evidence. Inadmissible evidence is liable to be struck out from a witness statement. See *Kind Respect Ltd v Apex Logistics Ltd* DCCJ 502/2004 (Deputy Judge Au; 05.06.2006) where without prejudice material was struck out. In *Allington Investments Corp & Ors v First Pacific Bancshares Holdings Ltd & Ors* [1995] 2 HKC 567 the court ordered a party to amend a witness statement which contained material offending the hearsay rule. And see *Urban Renewal Authority v Agrila Ltd & Anor* HCA 1582/2002 (Deputy Judge L Chan; 19.02.2009) where inadmissible evidence of pre-contract negotiations was struck out from a witness statement (appeal dismissed – CACV 49/2009).

Evidence in a witness statement which is irrelevant in that it does not come within the case as pleaded may be struck out: *EAA Securities Ltd v Chan Lin Mui & Anor* DCCJ 4015/2003 (Deputy Judge K W Wong; 25.04.2006). In *Secretary for Justice v Yu's Tin Sing Enterprises Co Ltd* HCA 398/2006 (Recorder Kwok SC; 09.09.2008) the court held, at trial, that parts of the evidence set out in the defence witnesses' statements were inadmissible because they contradicted the evidence which had been adduced by the plaintiff, but there had been no cross-examination of plaintiff's witnesses thereon. Opinion evidence of witnesses of fact was also excluded.

An application to strike out or exclude material in a witness statement need not be reserved to the trial judge, and may instead be dealt with at the interlocutory stage by a master: *Allington* (above) (at 568I); *Dias v Cathay Pacific Airways Ltd* HCA 2372/2002 (Master Ko; 21.11.2008).

**[38.2A.15]  Immunity of witness giving statement**
Subject to certain exceptions, a witness is entitled to immunity from civil suit for what is stated in a witness statement, just as with evidence given orally in court. See the discussion in *Autofocus Ltd v Accident Exchange Ltd* [2010] EWCA Civ 788 (14.07.2010). However a witness statement must be verified by a statement of truth and there is no immunity from criminal sanctions for perjury. See the discussion under Order 41A rule 9.

**3.      Evidence of particular facts** (O.38 r. 3)
**(1)   Without prejudice to rule 2, the Court may, at or before the trial of any action, order that evidence of any particular fact shall be given at the trial in such manner as may be specified by the order.**
**(2)   The power conferred by paragraph (1) extends in particular to ordering that evidence of any particular fact may be given at the trial—**

|       |                                                                         |
|-------|-------------------------------------------------------------------------|
| **(a)** | **by statement on oath of information or belief, or**                 |
| **(b)** | **by the production of documents or entries in books, or**            |
| **(c)** | **by copies of documents or entries in books, or**                    |
| **(d)** | **in the case of a fact which is or was a matter of common knowledge either generally or in a particular district, by the production of a specified newspaper which contains a statement of that fact.** |

**NOTES**

**[38.3.1]     Stage at which court shall consider manner of giving evidence**
Order 38 rule 3 provides that the court may order that specified types of evidence be given in a particular manner. The power is stated to be exercisable 'at or before the trial of any action'. However, see also Order 25 rule 3 whereby the court is required to consider exercise of this power at the determination of the case management summons.

**4.      Limitation of expert evidence** (O. 38 r. 4)
**The Court may, at or before the trial of any action, order that the number of medical or other expert witnesses who may be called at the trial shall be limited as specified by the order.**

**NOTES**

**[38.4.1]  Power to limit number of expert witnesses**
The power under Order 38 rule 4 to limit the number of expert witnesses to be called at trial is frequently exercised in personal injury actions. The personal injuries list practice direction (PD 18.1) specifically provides for consideration to be given to exercise of this power at the check list review. Further, the specimen order on check list review (annex H to the practice direction), includes (at para 10) such an order. See the commentary under Order 72 rule 2.

**4A.** **Evidence by single joint expert** (O. 38 r. 4A)

(1) In any action in which any question for an expert witness arises, the Court may, at or before the trial of the action, order 2 or more parties to the action to appoint a single joint expert witness to give evidence on that question.

(2) Where the parties cannot agree on who should be the joint expert witness, the Court may —

    (a)    select the expert witness from a list prepared or identified by the parties; or

    (b)    direct that the expert witness be selected in such manner as the Court may direct.

(3) Where an order is made under paragraph (1), the Court may give such directions as it thinks fit with respect to the terms and conditions of the appointment of the joint expert witness, including but not limited to the scope of instructions to be given to the expert witness and the payment of the expert witness's fees and expenses.

(4) Notwithstanding that a party to the action disagrees with the appointment of a single joint expert witness to give evidence, the Court may, subject to paragraph (6), make an order under paragraph (1) if it is satisfied that it is in the interests of justice to do so after taking into account all the circumstances of the case.

(5) The circumstances that the Court may take into account include but are not limited to —

    (a)    whether the issues requiring expert evidence can readily be identified in advance;

    (b)    the nature of those issues and the likely degree of controversy attaching to the expert evidence in question;

    (c)    the value of the claim and the importance of the issue on which expert evidence is sought, as compared with the cost of employing separate expert witnesses to give evidence;

    (d)    whether any party has already incurred expenses for instructing an expert who may be asked to give evidence as an expert witness in the case; and

    (e)    whether any significant difficulties are likely to arise in relation to —

        (i)    the choosing of the joint expert witness;

        (ii)    the drawing up of his instructions; or

        (iii)    the provision to him of the information and other facilities needed to perform his duties.

(6) Where a party to the action disagrees with the appointment of a single joint expert witness to give evidence, the Court shall not make an order under paragraph (1) unless the party has been given a reasonable opportunity to appear before the Court and to show cause why the order should not be made.

(7) Where the Court is satisfied that an order made under paragraph (1) is inappropriate, it may set aside the order and allow the parties concerned to appoint their own expert witnesses to give evidence.

(L.N. 152 of 2008)

---

## NOTES

### [38.4A.1]   Power to order appointment of single joint expert

Order 38 rule 4A empowers the court to direct that the parties appoint a single joint expert ('SJE'), rather than each independently instructing their own experts. The rule goes on to make provision for resolving disputes between the parties in choosing the expert to be appointed, *etc.*

The rule implements recommendation 107 of the final report of the Chief Justice's working party on civil justice reform. The working party envisaged this power being used in a 'relatively small minority' of cases, being 'low value, low complexity' cases (final report, para 633). This was based on a submission by the Academy of Experts, summarising the experience in England and Wales. The working party (final report, para 629) quoted the following passage from the academy's submissions:

> The most likely appropriate case for the appointment of an SJE is a low value and/or low complexity case where it is in any event possible that the expert will not need to be called at all and his report should be accepted as written evidence without the need for cross-examination. In these cases the use of the SJE has been largely successful.

See Order 38 rule 41 with regard to expert reports being received in evidence without calling the maker.

The working party also noted the academy's view that appointment of an SJE might actually add to costs in cases where the parties had already consulted their own experts (final report, para 626(d)). In such cases it may not be appropriate to direct appointment of an SJE.

In England it is recognised that a single joint expert may be appointed to give evidence on an issue, even though there is more than one discipline relevant to that issue. This is accomplished by identifying a lead expert in the dominant discipline, who will prepare the general part of the report and annex or incorporate any reports from experts in other disciplines. See CPR PD 35 para 6.

See also the personal injuries list practice direction (PD 18.1) which specifically provides for consideration to the making of such an order at the check list review. Further, the specimen order on check list review (annex G to the practice direction), includes (at para 11) such an order. See the commentary under Order 72 rule 2. Rule 4A gives a legislative basis to this personal injury list practice.

### [38.4A.2]   SJE order may be made without consent

The court may make an order for appointment of a single joint expert ('SJE') despite the fact a party objects: Order 38 rule 4A(4). In this respect the rule appears to differ from its English counterpart, CPR 35.7, which applies only where two or more parties wish an SJE to be appointed.

A party who objects to appointment of an SJE must be given an opportunity to be heard on the question: rule 4A(6).

### [38.4A.3]   Factors to be considered by the court

Order 38 rule 4A(4) requires the court to take into account all the circumstances of the case in deciding whether to direct appointment of an SJE, and rule 4A(5) sets out some of the specific circumstances to be taken into account. Those are:

(a)  *Whether issues for expert can be identified in advance* – If the parties are able to identify on their own the issues requiring expert evidence the court will be more likely to make an SJE order, as compared to where the parties need first to consult experts before being able to identify the issues.

(b)  *Nature of issues and degree of controversy* – Expert evidence on a crucial issue, which is likely to be controversial between the parties, would perhaps less likely be the subject of an SJE order. See *Kam Hing Trading (HK) Ltd v The People's Insurance Co of China (HK) Ltd & Anor* HCA 1062/2008 (Registrar Au-Yeung; 27.07.2009) where it was said (para 37) that where 'issues are contested and arise under a negligence claim, it would usually be preferable to let the court have a range of opinion rather than from just one expert'.

(c)  *Value and importance as compared to cost of separate experts* – This paragraph requires the court to take into account proportionality, weighing the value of the claim and the importance of issue on which expert evidence is sought, against the cost of employing separate experts. This is consistent with the underlying objective of promoting reasonable proportion and procedural economy under Order 1A rule 1(c). See the commentary concerning that provision.

(d)  *Whether any party has already instructed expert* – This paragraph recognises that where a party has already incurred expense in instructing an expert, it may be unfair to require that party additionally to take part in instruction of a single joint expert. This consideration will be important in cases, such as personal injury claims, where an expert is sometimes instructed even before proceedings are commenced.

(e)  *Whether there is likely to be disagreement between the parties* – The court will take into account the possibility that the parties would disagree on aspects of appointment and instructing a single joint expert. Such disagreement can result in a waste of costs by necessitating correspondence and possibly an application to the court to resolve a deadlock, which might be avoided by allowing the parties to instruct their own experts.

### [38.4A.4]   Letter of instructions to SJE
The Law Society's personal injuries committee has made available sample letters of instructions to a single joint expert and to experts instructed to prepare a joint report. They were prepared with a view to compliance not only with these rules, but also relevant prac tice directions and the Solicitors' Practice Rules. See Law Society circular 09-1003, which may be viewed in the members' zone of the Law Society's website.

### [38.4A.5]   Rule 4A(3) – dispute over content of letter of instructions
In the event that the parties are unable to agree on the content of a letter of instructions to a single joint expert, application may be made under Order 38 rule 4A(3) for directions of the court. In *Tang Kam Sheung v Tang Kit Yee* HCA 677/2007 (Chu J; 25.09.2009) that rule was used by the court to resolve a dispute over the scope of questions to be put to a single joint psychiatric expert on the mental capacity of a party.

### [38.4A.6]   Rule 4A(7) – power to set aside SJE order
Order 38 rule 4A(7) provides that the court may set aside an order for appointment of

a single joint expert, and allow the parties to adduce evidence from their own separate experts, where it is satisfied that the SJE order is inappropriate. The Chief Justice's working party on civil justice reform saw such a power as enabling the court to avoid 'the counter-productive effects of SJE orders made inappropriately' (final report, para 633). Reference was made to *Daniels v Walker* [2000] 1 WLR 1382 (CA) as a case where such an order was made. Our sister publication in the UK, The Civil Court Practice, summarises the guidance set out by Lord Woolf MR in that case in the following words (at CPR 35.7[2]):

    (1)    It was perfectly proper, in the absence of agreement between the parties in relation to the joint instructions, for one party to give separate or supplementary instructions.

    (2)    The first step where a party was unhappy with the report was to ask questions of the expert; if those did not resolve the problem then the court may give permission for the instruction by that party of another expert.

    (3)    If it would be unjust in a substantial case – having regard to the overriding objective [underlying objectives in Hong Kong: see Order 1A] – to prevent a party calling other or further expert evidence then he will be permitted to call it; accordingly a party who had agreed jointly to instruct a single expert but who for reasons which were not fanciful, was unhappy with that expert's report should, subject to the court's discretion, be permitted to obtain and, if appropriate, rely on a report from another expert.

    (4)    The decision whether the report of the further expert was to be used at the trial should not be made until the experts had met to resolve their differences.

With regard to experts' meetings, see Order 38 rule 38.

The learned editors of The Civil Court Practice go on to set out the following 9 factors to be taken into account by the court when considering an application to permit a further expert, deriving from *Cosgrove v Pattison* [2001] 2 CPLR 177; [2001 The Times, 13 Feb, per Neuberger J (as he then was):

    (1)    the nature of the issue or issues and the number of issues between the parties

    (2)    the reason the new expert is wanted

    (3)    the amount at stake and, if it is not purely money,

    (4)    the nature of the issues at stake and their importance

    (5)    the effect of permitting one party to call further expert evidence on the conduct of the trial

    (6)    the delay, if any, in making the application

    (7)    any delay that the instructing and calling of the new expert will cause

    (8)    any other special features of the case and

    (9)    in a sense all embracing, the overall justice to the parties in the context of the litigation.

A Hong Kong example of a case in which the court permitted a party to adduce its own evidence to challenge that of a single joint expert is *L v L* HCMC 1/2003 (Lam J; 20.04.2005). In that case (which was decided before Order 38 rule 4A came into force), a party was permitted to subpoena a bank's valuation report to contradict a single joint expert's valuation of landed property.

**[38.4A.7]   Meeting of parties with SJE**

It has been held in England that an SJE should not meet or confer with any of the instructing parties in the absence of the others unless all parties consent in writing: *MP v Mid Kent Healthcare NHS Trust* [2001] EWCA Civ 1703; [2002] 3 All ER 688 (CA). In that case an infant plaintiff's parents were refused permission to meet with an SJE privately. They wished to do so in order to be able 'to express ourselves freely, without fear that any of our comments might be used or taken up by the other side', but the defendant objected. The court found favour with the protocol of the Academy of Experts, which says (at para 19.9):

> A single joint expert should not attend any meeting or conference that is not a joint one, unless all the parties have first agreed in writing.

**[38.4A.8]   Weight of evidence of SJE**

The evidence of a single joint expert, being unchallenged by other expert evidence, will often be compelling. However the court is not bound to accept it. In *Cooper Payen Ltd v Southampton Container Terminal Ltd* [2003] EWCA Civ 1223 it was said (at para 67):

> Where a single joint expert gives evidence on an issue of fact on which no direct evidence is called, for example as to valuation, then subject to the need to evaluate his evidence in the light of his answers in cross-examination his evidence is likely to prove compelling. Only in exceptional circumstances may the judge depart from it and then for a good reason which he must fully explain. But if his evidence is on an issue of fact on which direct evidence is given, for example the speed at which a vehicle was travelling at a particular time, the situation is somewhat different. If the evidence of a witness of fact on the issue is credible, the judge may be faced with what, if they stood alone, may be the compelling evidence of two witnesses in favour of two opposing and conflicting conclusions. There is no rule of law or practice in such a situation requiring the judge to favour or accept the evidence of the expert witness or the evidence of a witness of fact. The judge must consider whether he can reconcile the evidence of the expert witness with that of the witness of fact. If he cannot do so, he must consider whether there may be an explanation for the conflict of evidence or for a possible error by either witness, and in the light of all the circumstances make a considered choice which evidence to accept.

See also *Kam Hing Trading (HK) Ltd v The People's Insurance Co of China (HK) Ltd & Anor* HCA 1062/2008 (Registrar Au-Yeung; 27.07.2009) where it was said (para 42) that the court is 'not bound to accept the views of an expert if those views are not prop erly backed up by reasons or authorities'. An example of a case where the court declined to accept the evidence of a single joint expert is *Armstrong & Anor v First York Bus Co* [2005] EWCA Civ 277; [2005] 1 WLR 2751 (CA). In that case the evidence of the injured persons as to how an accident happened was accepted even though the single joint expert was of the opinion that it could not be true.

**5.      Limitation of plans, etc., in evidence** (O. 38 r. 5)

**Unless, at or before the trial, the Court for special reasons otherwise orders, no plan, photograph or model shall be receivable in evidence at the trial of an action unless at least 10 days before the commencement of the trial the parties, other than the party producing it, have been given an opportunity to inspect it and to agree to the admission thereof without further proof.**

**6.      Revocation or variation of orders under rules 2 to 5** (O. 38 r. 6)

Any order under rules 2 to 5 (including an order made on appeal) may, on sufficient cause being shown, be revoked or varied by a subsequent order of the Court made at or before the trial.

**7.      Evidence of finding on foreign law** (O. 38 r. 7)

(1)    A party to any cause or matter who intends to adduce in evidence a finding or decision on a question of foreign law by virtue of section 59 of the Evidence Ordinance (Cap. 8) shall—

    (a)    in the case of an action to which Order 25, rule 1, applies within 28 days after the pleadings in the action are deemed to be closed, and

    (b)    in the case of any other cause or matter, within 21 days after the date on which an appointment for the first hearing of the cause or matter is obtained,

or in either case, within such other period as the Court may specify, serve notice of his intention on every other party to the proceedings.
(L.N. 152 of 2008)

(2)    The notice shall specify the question on which the finding or decision was given or made and specify the document in which it is reported or recorded in citable form.

(3)    In any cause or matter in which evidence may be given by affidavit, an affidavit specifying the matters contained in paragraph (2) shall constitute notice under paragraph (1) if served within the period mentioned in that paragraph.

---

## NOTES

**[38.7.1]      Evidence of foreign law**

Under common law principles applicable in Hong Kong any question as to the state of the law of another jurisdiction is a question of fact. The onus to prove it is on the party who asserts that it is different from Hong Kong law. In the absence of such proof the court will assume that the foreign law is the same as Hong Kong law: *Warner Bros v Nelson* [1937] 1 KB 209; *The Griesheim* [1983] 1 HKC 251, [1984] HKC 416 (CA). The law of the other jurisdiction as the party contends it to be should be pleaded as an allegation of fact: see Order 18 rule 8 and the commentary thereunder. At trial it must be proved by evidence. Section 59(1) of the Evidence Ordinance (Cap 8) provides that such evidence may be given by any person competent to do so, whether or not a qualified legal practitioner. In the interesting case of *Cooper-King v Cooper-King* [1900] P 65 a former governor of Hong Kong was held competent to give evidence of the marriage law of the colony when the only available lawyer had demanded a prohibitive fee.

Where the state of foreign law has previously been determined in proceedings in Hong Kong the previous decision may be relied upon to prove the state of the foreign law: Evidence Ordinance, s 59(2). Advance notice is required in accordance with Order 38 rule 7. Although the rule uses the term 'foreign law' this should be construed as the law of any place outside Hong Kong, including other parts of China. This is clear from section 59 of the Ordinance.

Evidence of foreign law must be assessed like any other evidence. It is up to the court to decide what, if any, weight to attach to such evidence. See *Full Wisdom Holdings Ltd v Traffic Stream Infrastructure Co Ltd* [2004] 3 HKC 1 where the Court of Appeal held that no weight should be attached to an opinion as to the legal effect of a Notice of the State Council of the PRC. In that decision, Le Pichon JA said, at 11H–I:

> In studying the validity of any opinion based on foreign law, the court does not simply accept any stated conclusions as being correct, even where there may be no legal opinion contradicting it. The court is entitled to (and indeed must) look at the basis of the legal reasoning as well as the terms of the State Council Notice in determining what weight, if any, should be attached to the Opinion.

An application for leave to appeal to the Court of Final Appeal was dismissed: see [2004] 4 HKC 171.

In *Guangzhou Green-Enhan Bio-Engineering Co Ltd v Green Power Health Products International Co Ltd* [2004] 4 HKC 163 the court excluded expert evidence which strayed into questions of fact and issues which had already been decided in the mainland courts.

**[38.7.2]     Notice of intention to adduce evidence of foreign law**
Evidence of foreign law which is adduced by way of an opinion of a person with expertise in the law of the foreign jurisdiction concerned is expert evidence and is governed by part IV of this Order. In order to qualify as an expert for that purpose, it is not necessary that a person be qualified as a legal practitioner in the jurisdiction concerned: Evidence Ordinance (Cap 8), s 59(1).

Order 38 rule 7 deals with the situation where the party putting forward a proposition of foreign law wishes to prove it by means of a finding or decision on the particular question of foreign law. Section 59(2) of the Evidence Ordinance (Cap 8) provides for proof by that method. Its purpose is to obviate the need to prove the same point all over again. It provides that Hong Kong and English decisions at first instance or on appeal, and decisions of the Court of Final Appeal, may be used.

The purpose of Order 38 rule 7 is to require that advance notice be given by a party of its intention to rely on such a finding or decision. Note that the time within which such notice must be given, in cases which are subject to the questionnaire procedure under Order 25 rule 1 (that is, most actions commenced by writ – see Order 25 rule 1(2)), was extended with effect from 2009 from 14 to 28 days after the close of pleadings. In other cases (principally those commenced by originating summons) the time remains 21 days from the date on which an appointment for hearing is obtained.

**8.     Application to trials of issues, references, etc.** (O. 38 r. 8)
     The foregoing rules of this Order shall apply to trials of issues or questions of fact or law, references, inquiries and assessments of damages as they apply to the trial of actions.

**9.     Depositions: when receivable in evidence at trial** (O. 38 r. 9)
     **(1)     No deposition taken in any cause or matter shall be received in evidence at the trial of the cause or matter unless—**
          **(a)     the deposition was taken in pursuance of an order under**

**Order 39, rule 1, and**

(b)     **either the party against whom the evidence is offered   consents or it is proved to the satisfaction of the Court that the deponent is dead, or beyond the jurisdiction of the Court or unable from sickness or other infirmity to attend the trial.**

(2)     **A party intending to use any deposition in evidence at the trial of a cause or matter must, a reasonable time before the trial, give notice of his intention to do so to the other party.**

(3)     **A deposition purporting to be signed by the person before whom it was taken shall be receivable in evidence without proof of the signature being the signature of that person.**

---

## NOTES

### [38.9.1]     Use of deposition evidence at trial

Deposition evidence is evidence taken before trial from a witness who is unable to attend the trial because of illness, absence from the jurisdiction or other reason.  In *Hong Kong Kam Lan Koon Ltd v Realray Investments Ltd & Anor* [2004] 4 HKC 349 it was held that there is a two-stage process. Firstly, an order must be obtained under Order 39 rule 1 for the taking of the evidence, and secondly an order must be obtained under Order 38 rule 9 for the use at trial of the evidence thus taken.

### [38.9.2]     Deposition evidence as hearsay

Where evidence taken by deposition is not receivable against a party in the usual way it may nevertheless be admitted as hearsay. See *Hong Kong Kam Lan Koon Ltd v Realray Investments Ltd & Anor* [2004] 4 HKC 349, 360F–361F. In that case, an order had been obtained for the taking of evidence by deposition before the addition of a fresh party to the proceedings. It was held that at trial, the evidence could be admitted as hearsay as against that party, and leave was given to that party to cross-examine the witness by video-link.

**10.     High Court documents admissible or receivable in evidence** (O. 38 r. 10)

(1)     **Office copies of writs, records, pleadings and documents filed in the High Court shall be admissible in evidence in any cause or matter and between all parties to the same extent as the original would be admissible.**

(2)     **Without prejudice to the provisions of any enactment, every document purporting to be sealed with the seal of any office or department of the High Court shall be received in evidence without further proof, and any document purporting to be so sealed and to be a copy of a document filed in, or issued out of, that office or department shall be deemed to be an office copy of that document without further proof unless the contrary is shown.**

---

## NOTES

### [38.10.1]     Admissibility of court documents

Order 38 rule 10 provides that court documents, whether bearing the seal of the court or office copies, are admissible as evidence.

The same does not normally apply to judicial findings when it is sought to rely on them in subsequent proceedings not involving the same parties. The general rule is that 'as between a party to the earlier action and a party who is not, judicial findings are inadmissible as evidence of the facts so found'. See *Re Prudential Enterprises Ltd (No 2)* [2004] 2 HKC 205, 208C–I, citing *Hollington v Hewthorn & Co Ltd* [1943] 2 All ER 35 and *Secretary of State for Trade and Industry v Bairstow* [2003] 1 BCLC 696. In the *Prudential* case, Chu J, referring to *Symphony Group plc v Hodgson* [1993] 4 All ER 143, noted that there may be an exception to this principle 'if the connection of the non-party with the earlier proceedings was so close that he will not suffer any injustice'.

### [38.10.2]   Admissibility in Hong Kong of public documents from other jurisdictions

Prior to the transfer of sovereignty over Hong Kong in 1997 there were numerous provisions of law by which court and other public documents from Commonwealth jurisdictions were admissible in court proceedings in Hong Kong without formal proof. These included local statutory provisions such as sections 33 and 34 of the Evidence Ordinance and United Kingdom legislation extended to Hong Kong such as the Evidence (Foreign, Dominion and Colonial Documents) Act 1933.

Any such local legislation should now be read in light of the amendments to the Interpretation and General Clauses Ordinance (Cap 1) enacted on the transfer of sovereignty. In general, preference for Commonwealth jurisdictions no longer applies unless there is reciprocity.

Common law rules as to proof of foreign public documents should continue to apply. See, for example, *Lyell v Kennedy* (1889) 14 App Cas 437, 448–9.

**11.   Evidence of consent of new trustee to act** (O. 38 r. 11)

**A document purporting to contain the written consent of a person to act as trustee and to bear his signature verified by some other person shall be evidence of such consent.**

**12.   Evidence at trial may be used in subsequent proceedings** (O. 38 r. 12)

**Any evidence taken at the trial of any cause or matter may be used in any subsequent proceedings in that cause or matter.**

**13.    Order to produce document at proceeding other than trial** (O. 38 r. 13)

**(1)   At any stage in a cause or matter the Court may order any person to attend any proceeding in the cause or matter and produce any document, to be specified or described in the order, the production of which appears to the Court to be necessary for the purpose of that proceeding.**

**(2)   No person shall be compelled by an order under paragraph (1) to produce any document at a proceeding in a cause or matter which he could not be compelled to produce at the trial of that cause or matter.**

---

## NOTES

**[38.13.1]　Order to produce documents to the court – scope of Order 38 rule 13**
Order 38 rule 13 embodies the court's jurisdiction to make an order against any person to compel him to produce documents to the court. Exercise of the power is not restricted to parties to the proceedings and clearly an order may be made in relation to a non-party. See *Re Wong The Huei (deceased)* [2002] 3 HKC 312 and *Chan Wai Sun & Anor v Law Shiu Kai Andrew* [2004] 1 HKC 180. In the former of those cases Yam J (at 314C) expressed the rule in terms which would limit its application to persons within the jurisdiction.

**[38.13.2]　Effect of order under Order 38 rule 13**
An order under rule 13 is not an order for discovery. It requires production of a document to the court, not inspection thereof by a party. As such the order is in the nature of a subpoena *duces tecum*. See *Chan Wai Sun & Anor v Law Shiu Kai Andrew* [2004] 1 HKC 180 citing *Elder v Carter* (1890) 25 QBD 194.

**[38.13.3]　Order to produce bank records**
It is inappropriate to use Order 38 rule 13 when seeking an order to inspect bank records. Instead application should be made under section 21 of the Evidence Ordinance (Cap 8). See *Chan Wai Sun & Anor v Law Shiu Kai Andrew* [2004] 1 HKC 180. That section empowers the court to order that any party be at liberty to inspect and take copies of entries in a banker's record for the purpose of any proceedings. For a discussion of application under section 21, see the commentary under Order 24 rule 1.

II. Writs of Subpoena

**14.　Form and issue of writ of subpoena** (O. 38 r.14)
**(1)　A writ of subpoena must be in Form No. 28 or 29 in Appendix A, whichever is appropriate.**
**(2)　Issue of a writ of subpoena takes place upon its being sealed by an officer of the Court.**
**(3)　Where a writ of subpoena is to be issued in a cause or matter in the Court, the appropriate office for the issue of the writ is the Registry.**
**(HK)(5)Before a writ of subpoena is issued a praecipe for the issue of the writ must be filed in the Registry together with a note from a judge or master authorizing the issue of such writ and the sum of $500 shall be deposited in the Registry, in addition to any fee payable in respect of such issue, as a deposit in respect of the witness' reasonable expenses; and the praecipe must contain the name and address of the party issuing the writ, if he is acting in person, or the name or firm and business address of that party's solicitor and also (if the solicitor is the agent of another) the name or firm and business address of his principal.**
**(HK)(6)In any proceedings, whether in chambers or in court, the Court may order the reimbursement by one or more of the parties to a witness who has been served with a writ of subpoena in respect of any expenses reasonably and properly incurred by that witness.**
**(HK)(7)Any expenses so ordered by the Court to be paid shall be assessed by the Court making the order or, if no such assessment is made by the**

Court, shall be taxed (if not agreed) and paid by the party ordered to make such payment.

(HK)(8)A witness whose expenses have been ordered to be paid may, if the party ordered to make such payment is the party who made the deposit on issue of the writ of subpoena, recover such expenses, after assessment, agreement or taxation, from the said deposit and look to the party liable to make such payment for the balance, if any.

(HK)(9)The deposit (or such part of it as shall remain after payment to the witness under rule 14(8)) shall be refunded to the party that paid the deposit if—

    (a)    that party was not ordered to pay the costs of the witness; or

    (b)    that party was ordered to pay the costs of the witness and has effected payment of such costs after assessment, agreement or taxation.

## NOTES

### [38.14.1]   Cross-references

See also Order 32 rule 7 and Order 37 rule 1(3) which make specific provision for the issue of subpoenas for proceedings in chambers and for assessments of damages respectively.

The issue of subpoenas in aid of inferior courts and tribunals is governed by Order 38 rule 19.

Specific provision is made in several Ordinances for the issue of subpoenas. See, for example, section 221 of the Companies Ordinance (Cap 32).

### [38.14.2]   Arbitration

Under section 2GC(3) of the Arbitration Ordinance (Cap 341) the court has power to 'order a person to attend proceedings before an arbitral tribunal to give evidence or to produce documents or other material evidence'. By comparison, the power of the arbitral tribunal itself is merely to 'direct' the attendance of a witness (section 2GB(7)(c)), which does not carry with it the court's ultimate sanction of committal for contempt.

### [38.14.3]   Whether leave is required to issue subpoena

In *Li Man York Evelyn v Li Wai Tat Walton* [1997] 3 HKC 532, Mortimer VP contrasted the requirement under Order 32 rule 7 whereby leave is required to issue a subpoena for proceedings in chambers with proceedings in open court where, he said, a party is entitled to issue a writ of subpoena 'as of right'. In the same case, Godfrey JA, referring to Order 38 rule 14(5), said it appeared that in Hong Kong, unlike England, leave is required to issue a subpoena whether for proceedings in chambers or in open court.

An application for issue of a subpoena is made *ex parte* by praecipe: Order 38 rule 14(5). Appearance before a master or judge will not normally be required. Although leave may technically be required, the issue of a subpoena is in effect an 'administrative act': *Hsin Chong Construction Co Ltd v Hong Kong and Kowloon Wharf and Godown Co Ltd & Anor* [1986] HKLR 987, 988B.

### [38.14.4]    Types of subpoena

Subpoenas are generally of two types. A subpoena *ad testificandum* requires a named person to attend to give oral evidence. A subpoena *duces tecum* requires a person to attend together with identified documents to produce the same.

### [38.14.5]    Prescribed form of subpoena

See forms 28 and 29 in Appendix A to these rules. The former applies to proceedings in open court and the latter to proceedings in chambers.

### [38.14.6]    Procedure

Guidance on the procedure to be followed in relation to applications for subpoenas is set out in *Big Island Construction (HK) Ltd v Wu Yi Development Co Ltd & Anor* [2010] 2 HKC 356. The following points emerge from paras 2-6 of the judgment:

(1)    Parties should act with due diligence in approaching witnesses well in advance of trial.

(2)    If the witness is willing to assist, the party intending to call him should prepare his witness statement and exchange it with the other side in accordance with the court's directions. If he fails to do so he may not be allowed to call the witness (O 38 r 2A(10) RHC).

(3)    If the witness is unwilling, and the party has decided to subpoena him, he should so inform the court and the other side at the case management conference, and apply to issue the subpoena once the trial dates are known. Upon issue of the subpoena, he should inform the other side forthwith. The other side should then decide if he wishes to apply to set aside the subpoena.

(4)    Applications pertaining to the subpoena should be disposed of before the pre-trial review. A late application may be dismissed on the basis of delay alone under PD 5.2 34.

In *Big Island* an application during the course of trial for leave to subpoena additional witnesses was refused on the ground of delay.

### [38.14.7]    Principles applicable to subpoena duces tecum

The principles applicable to obtaining documentary evidence by means of subpoena *duces tecum* were set out in *To Kan Chi & Ors v Pui Man Yau & Ors* [1998] 3 HKC 371 (CA), with reference to English authority. See in particular the judgment of Nazareth VP at 377. An application for leave to appeal that decision was dismissed by the Court of Final Appeal (see [1998] 3 HKC 390) and the principles laid down were subsequently re-affirmed by the Court of Appeal in *Brisilver Investment Ltd v Wong Fat Tso & Ors* CACV 251/1999 (Mayo and Rogers JJA; 02.12.1999). In *Brisilver*, Mayo JA summarised in the following terms:

(1)    There shall be no discovery from a non party to an action [subject to certain exceptions ...] ...

(2)    A subpoena should not be used for making discovery only ...

(3)    A subpoena should not be used as a fishing exercise for documents nor speculative ...

(4)    A subpoena should not be oppressive to the witness when, say for example, the terms are too wide. The party issuing the subpoena ... has to show that these

witnesses are required to produce relevant and admissible evidence for trial and that those documents to be produced must be required and are necessary for the fair disposal of the case ...

See also *Ng Chiu Yuen Jacob v Lam Che Cheung* HCA 3364/1999 (Chung J; 04.08.2000).

The court may refuse to allow documentary evidence to be obtained by subpoena *duces tecum* where the evidence might be obtained another way, or where there is a privacy objection. See *Morgan v Morgan* [1977] 2 All ER 515, cited in *SMSE v KL (No 2)* [2009] 5 HKLRD 770 (CA). In *SMSE* it was held (para 43) that a third party to whom a subpoena *duces tecum* is directed should be entitled to redact parts of documents which are immaterial or irrelevant to the purpose for which they are subpoenaed.

## [38.14.8]  Territorial considerations
Although as a general rule the court will not make orders having extra-territorial effect, it may issue a subpoena against a person outside Hong Kong provided this is permissible under the governing legislation and appropriate in the circumstances of the case. See *Joint & Several Liquidators of B+B Construction Co v Weinmann & Ors* HCCW 114/2001 (Kwan J; 08.06.2004). In that case, subpoenas were issued against persons resident abroad in winding-up proceedings.

## [38.14.9]  Witness expenses
Under section 52 of the High Court Ordinance, a judge may order the reimbursement of any expenses reasonably incurred by a witness. Where a witness is subpoenaed, the party applying for the subpoena must deposit $500 with the court on account of witness expenses before the subpoena is issued: Order 38 rule 14(5).

## [38.14.10]  Subpoenas directed to government and similar officials
The Law Society has received comments on the calling of witnesses in an official capacity from governmental and quasi-governmental bodies. The comments are set out in consolidated form in Law Society circular 00-394, which remains valid as of early 2009. The circular can be viewed on the members zone of the Law Society's website. It touches on the calling as witnesses of government officers, police officers, representatives of the Hospital Authority, land registry staff and members of consular posts.

## [38.14.11]  Application to set aside subpoena
The court has power to set aside a subpoena on an *inter partes* application before a master or judge. The juridical basis of this power may be the court's inherent jurisdiction or the express power under Order 32 rule 6 to set aside any order which has been made *ex parte*.

A subpoena will be set aside if it 'is irrelevant, or fishing, or speculative or oppres sive'. See *Senior v Holdsworth* [1976] 1 QB 23, which is the only 'clear state ment of principle' as to when a subpoena will be set aside: *Hsin Chong Construction Co Ltd v Hong Kong and Kowloon Wharf and Godown Co Ltd* [1986] HKLR 987, 989C-G, per Hunter J.

## [38.14.12]  Setting aside subpoena duces tecum on ground of relevance

In order to justify a subpoena *duces tecum*, the documents must be 'relevant and admissible': *Brisilver Investment Ltd v Wong Fat Tso & Ors* CACV 251/99 ((Mayo and Rogers JJA; 02.12.1999), per Mayo JA (dismissing an appeal from the judgment of Chung J reported at [1999] 3 HKC 567). In *Overseas Trust Bank Ltd v Coopers & Lybrand (a firm) & Ors* HCA 5746/1986 (Godfrey J; 27.03.1990), it was held that '*Peruvian Guano*' relevance is insufficient to justify a subpoena *duces tecum* (following *Burshand v MacFarlane* [1891] 2 QB 241) – in other words it is insufficient that a document relates or may relate to a matter in question in the action – the document concerned must be 'evidence in the case for either of the parties'. In *Brisilver* (above), Rogers JA held that an attempt to obtain access to documents which would 'probably' be inadmissible on a discovery application was 'certainly' inadmissible for the purposes of a subpoena *duces tecum*.

## [38.14.13]  Setting aside subpoena duces tecum as 'fishing' or speculative

In *To Kan Chi & Ors v Pui Man Yau* [1998] 3 HKC 371, 383 (CA), it was held that a subpoena *duces tecum* for production of whole files, the contents of which were not actually known, was objectionable as being in the nature of fishing or speculation. In *Brisilver* (above), Rogers JA held that a subpoena amounting to an attempt to obtain discovery should be set aside as being 'no more than a speculative fishing exercise'. Although it may be permissible to identify documents to be produced under a subpoena *duces tecum* by class rather than individual description, a party who does so runs the risk that the subpoena will be objectionable on the ground of fishing: *Brisilver* per Rog ers JA, citing *Rio Tinto Zinc Corp v Westinghouse Electric Corp* [1978] AC 547.

## [38.14.14]  Setting aside subpoena as oppressive

In *Computer Personnel Ltd v Digital Equipment (HK) Ltd* [1987] 1 HKC 140 (CA), subpoenas requiring the attendance of four senior officers of a party were set aide. It would have been 'extremely disruptive to the defendant's business' if all four had to be together in Hong Kong. Further, the court was of the view that the real purpose of the subpoenas was not to obtain evidence but to cause inconvenience.

In *Chu Piu-wing v AG*, a subpoena was issued in breach of a promise made by the law enforcement authorities that the witness would not be required to give evidence. At first instance the court had held the subpoena was not oppressive (see [1985] 2 HKC 342) but on appeal it was set aside on the ground of abuse of process (see [1984] HKLR 411).

## [38.14.15]  Attendance of prisoners as witnesses

An ordinary subpoena is not appropriate to procure the attendance of a prisoner to give evidence. Obviously a prisoner is not at liberty to comply with a subpoena. It is, therefore, necessary to obtain an order directed to the authority detaining the prisoner.

Section 12 of the Prisons Ordinance (Cap 234) provides for what is commonly known as a 'body order'. See also section 81 of the Evidence Ordinance (Cap 8). And see Order 54 rule 9 and the commentary thereunder concerning the writ of habeas corpus *ad testificandum*.

**15.    More than one name may be included in one writ of subpoena**
(O. 38 r. 15)

The names of two or more persons may be included in one writ of subpoena ad testificandum.

**16.    Amendment of writ of subpoena** (O. 38 r. 16)

Where there is a mistake in any person's name or address in a writ of subpoena, then, if the writ has not been served, the party by whom the writ was issued may have the writ re-sealed in correct form by filing a second praecipe under rule 14(5) endorsed with the words "Amended and re-sealed".

**17.    Service of writ of subpoena** (O. 38 r. 17)

A writ of subpoena must be served personally and, subject to rule 19, the service shall not be valid unless effected within 12 weeks after the date of issue of the writ and not less than four days, or such other period as the court may fix, before the day on which attendance before the Court is required.

**18.    Duration of writ of subpoena** (O. 38 r. 18)

Subject to rule 19, a writ of subpoena continues to have effect until the conclusion of the trial at which the attendance of the witness is required.

**19.    Writ of subpoena in aid of interior court or tribunal** (O. 38 r. 19)

**(1)**    The office of the Court out of which a writ of subpoena ad testificandum or a writ of subpoena duces tecum in aid of an inferior court or tribunal may be issued is the Registry, and no order of the Court for the issue of such a writ is necessary.

**(2)**    A writ of subpoena in aid of an inferior court or tribunal continues to have effect until the disposal of the proceedings before that court or tribunal at which the attendance of the witness is required.

**(3)**    A writ of subpoena issued in aid of an inferior court or tribunal must be served personally.

**(4)**    Unless a writ of subpoena issued in aid of an inferior court or tribunal is duly served on the person to whom it is directed not less than 4 days, or such other period as the Court may fix, before the day on which the attendance of that person before the court or tribunal is required by the writ, that person shall not be liable to any penalty or process for failing to obey the writ.

**(5)**    An application to set aside a writ of subpoena issued in aid of an inferior court or tribunal may be heard by a master.

---

## NOTES

**[38.19.1]    Order 38 rule 19 – issue of subpoena in aid of inferior court or tribunal**

The High Court has an inherent power to issue a subpoena in aid of an inferior court or tribunal.  See *Secretary for Justice v Penta-Ocean Construction Co Ltd & Ors* [2004] 1 HKC 414, 418, citing *R v Greenaway* (1845) 7 QB 126, 134.  Order 38 rule

19(1) provides that such a subpoena may be issued by the registry without order of the court.

The question what constitutes an inferior tribunal for this purpose was considered by Deputy Judge To in *Secretary for Justice v Penta-Ocean Construction Co Ltd & Ors* [2004] 1 HKC 414. In deciding that question the learned judge applied the follow ing test derived from *Currie v Chief Constable of Surrey* [1982] 1 WLR 215 (per McNeill J):

> . . . a subpoena may issue . . . to assist inferior courts and tribunals by compelling the attendance of witnesses or the production or documents when the inferior court or tribunal
>
> (a)    is recognised by law;
> (b)    acts judicially or quasi judicially in the exercise of its functions;
> (c)    acts upon evidence, whether or not on oath; and
> (d)    has no or not sufficient power of its own to secure the attendance of witnesses or the production of documents.

In *Penta-Ocean* (above) the learned Deputy Judge went on to hold that the Review Body on Bid Challenges established under the World Trade Organisation was not an inferior tribunal for the purposes of this rule.

In *Chu Piu-wing v AG* [1984] HKLR 411, the Court of Appeal dismissed an argument that the court's power to issue subpoenas in aid of inferior tribunals applies only in respect of tribunals which have power to take evidence on oath (applying *Currie & Ors v Chief Constable of Surrey* [1982] 1 WLR 215).

**20.    Application and interpretation** (O. 38 r. 20)

**(1)    In this Part of this Order "the Ordinance" means the Evidence Ordinance (Cap. 8) and any expressions used in this Part and in Part IV of the Ordinance have the same meanings in this Part as they have in the said Part IV.**

**(2)    This Part of this Order shall apply in relation to the trial or hearing of an issue or question arising in a cause or matter, and to a reference, inquiry and assessment of damages, as it applies in relation to the trial or hearing of a cause or matter.**

**(3)    In this Part—**
**"hearsay evidence" means evidence consisting of hearsay within the meaning of section 46 of the Ordinance.**
**(Ord 2/99)**

---

**NOTES**

**[38.20.1]    History of Part III**
Part III of Order 38, dealing with hearsay evidence, traces back to the Evidence (Hearsay) Rules, subsidiary legislation under the Evidence Ordinance. Those rules were replaced by Part III in 1980. In 1999 Part III was substantially amended (with prospective effect only) to relax the criteria under which hearsay evidence may be admissible – see below.

**21.    Power to call witness for cross-examination on hearsay evidence and to call additional evidence to attack or support hearsay evidence** (O. 38 r. 21)

**(1)    Where a party tenders as hearsay evidence a statement made by a person but does not propose to call the person who made the statement to give evidence, the Court may, on application—**

> **(a)    allow another party to call and cross-examine the person who made who made the statement on its contents;**
> **(b)    allow any party to call—**
> > **(i)    additional evidence to attack or support the reliability of the statement;**
> > **(ii)    additional evidence to attack or support that first-mentioned additional evidence.**

**(2)    Where the Court allows another party to call and cross-examine the person who made the statement, it may give such directions as it thinks fit to secure the attendance of that person and as to the procedure to be followed. (Ord 2/99)**

**22.    Powers exercisable in chambers** (O.38 r. 22)

**The jurisdiction of the Court under rules 20 and 21 may be exercised in chambers. (Ord 2/99)**

---

**NOTES**

**[38.22.1]    Admissibility of hearsay evidence**

With effect from 1st June 1999, substantial changes to the Evidence Ordinance (Cap 8) swept away most of what remained of the common law restrictions on the use of hearsay evidence in civil proceedings.  The amendments were effected by the Evidence (Amendment) Ordinance (No 2 of 1999) and apply only to actions commenced after the amending Ordinance came into force.

Section 47 of the Evidence Ordinance now provides that hearsay evidence shall not be excluded in civil proceedings unless the opposing party objects and the court is satisfied that the exclusion of the evidence 'is not prejudicial to the interests of justice'.

The amending legislation gives effect to recommendations of the Law Reform Commission of Hong Kong published in 1995.  The full text of the Commission's report is available on its website (www.hkreform.gov.hk). The legislation is based on similar amendments in the Civil Evidence Act 1995 (UK).

**[38.22.2]    Weight to be given to hearsay evidence**

Section 49 of the Evidence Ordinance as amended sets out the factors to be considered by the court in assessing the weight of hearsay evidence.  In *Aqua-Leisure Industries Ltd & Anor v Aqua Splash Ltd* [2003] 1 HKC 1 (CA) judgment was set aside on the ground the trial judge had apparently failed to take account of the factors listed in the section.

**[38.22.3]    Notice of proposal to adduce hearsay evidence**

Section 47A(2) of the Evidence Ordinance provides that a party proposing to adduce hearsay shall give notice to the other parties to enable them to deal with matters arising and, on request, provide particulars of or relating to the evidence. Section 47A(1) contemplates the enactment of rules of court concerning such notice. However no such rules have been enacted applicable to actions com menced after the 1999 amendments came into force. This reflects the Law Reform Commission's view that no special notice provision is necessary because the exchange of witness statements and full discovery effectively put all parties on notice (LRC report, para 5.36-7). Thus the previous forms of hearsay notice and counter-notice need not necessarily be followed in actions commenced after the new legislation came into force. Nevertheless it is a good idea for a party wishing to adduce hearsay evidence at trial to ensure that the opposing party is specifically alerted. Otherwise, as the LRC noted, there is a risk of last minute adjournment should the opposing party genuinely be taken by surprise.

The formal procedures for hearsay notices under the previous rules continue to apply to actions commenced prior to 1st June 1999 and in the absence of compliance (or in the event of successful objection) the court will not have regard to the hearsay evidence: *Postwell Ltd v Cheng Kap Sang* HCA 2799/1999 (Master Rimsky Yuen SC; 23.09.2003).

**[38.22.4]    Filing of hearsay notice**

It is not necessary to file a hearsay notice in court, unless there is a direction to that effect. It is sufficient for the notice to be served on the other parties. See Practice Direction 24.1, para 8.

**[38.22.5]    Objection to hearsay evidence**

The only ground on which admission of hearsay may successfully be resisted under the new legislation is the interests of justice: Evidence Ordinance, section 47(1)(b). Where a party seeks to invoke the court's power to exclude hearsay evidence on this ground the court may deal with the issue at the beginning or the end of the trial: section 47(2). The legislation does not contemplate a prior interlocutory application, possibly because such an issue is best determined by the trial judge.

**[38.22.6]    Leave to cross-examine on hearsay evidence**

Order 38 rule 21 provides that the court may grant leave to a party to call and cross-examine a person who made a hearsay statement adduced by another party. 'This safeguard is intended to ensure that a witness whom it is reasonable and practicable to call is in fact called if his hearsay statement is challenged': LRC Report, para 5.39, citing the equivalent English Law Commission report.

The rule goes on to provide that the court may give directions to secure the attendance of the person to be cross-examined.

The court's power under rule 21 is discretionary and will not be exercised in every case. To do so might 'defeat the main purpose' of the 1999 amending legislation. See *High Fashion Garments Co Ltd v Ng Siu Tong & Ors* [2003] 2 HKC 562, 567E-H where the court went on to observe that the factors to be borne in mind in exercising the discretion might include the impact of the particular piece of hearsay evidence, the relationship of the maker with either party, the history of the case, the practicalities as to the procurement of the maker to give evidence and the factors set out in section 49 of the Ordinance (as to the weight to be attached to hearsay).

### [38.22.7] Hearsay in proceedings commenced before 1 June 1999

The amendments to the Evidence Ordinance discussed above do not apply to actions which had already been commenced when the amending legislation came into force on 1 June 1999. For the purpose of those actions the law as it stood prior to that date still applies. To assist readers we set out below the former Order 38 rules 20 to 34, with commentary, which continue to be relevant to such actions.

### [38.22.8] 20. Interpretation and application (The former O. 38 r. 20)

(1) In this Part of this Order "the Ordinance" means the Evidence Ordinance (Cap. 8) and any expressions used in this Part and in Parts IV and V of the Ordinance have the same meanings in this Part as they have in the said Parts IV and V.

(2) This Part of this Order shall apply in relation to the trial or hearing of an issue or question arising in a cause or matter, and to a reference, inquiry and assessment of damages, as it applies in relation to the trial or hearing of a cause or matter.

### [38.22.9] 21. Notice of intention to give certain statements in evidence (The former O. 38 r. 21)

(1) Subject to the provisions of this rule, a party to a cause or matter who desires to give in evidence at the trial or hearing of the cause or matter any statement which is admissible in evidence by virtue of section 47, 49 or 50 of the Ordinance must—

    (a) in the case of a cause or matter which is required to be set down for trial or hearing or adjourned into court, not later than 21 days before application is made to set down or to adjourn into court, or within such other period as the Court may specify; and
    (L.N. 99 of 1993)

    (b) in the case of any other cause or matter, within 21 days after the date on which an appointment for the first hearing of the cause or matter is obtained, or within such other period as the Court may specify,

serve on every other party to the cause or matter notice of his desire to do so, and the notice must comply with the provisions of rule 22, 23 or 24, as the circumstances of the case require.

(2) Paragraph (1) shall not apply in relation to any statement which is admissible as evidence of any fact stated therein by virtue not only of section 47, 49 or 50 of the Ordinance but by virtue also of any other statutory provision within the meaning of section 46 of the Ordinance.

(3) Paragraph (1) shall not apply in relation to any statement which any party to a probate action desires to give in evidence at the trial of that action and which is alleged to have been made by the deceased person whose estate is the subject of the action.

(4) Where by virtue of any provision of these rules or of any order or direction of

the Court the evidence in any proceedings is to be given by affidavit then, without prejudice to paragraph (2), paragraph (1) shall not apply in relation to any statement which any party to the proceedings desires to have included in any affidavit to be used on his behalf in the proceedings, but nothing in this paragraph shall affect the operation of rule 5 of Order 41, or the powers of the Court under rule 3 of this Order.

(5)     Rule 9 of Order 65 shall not apply to a notice under this rule but the Court may direct that the notice need not be served on any party who at the time when service is to be effected is in default as to acknowledgment of service or who has no address for service.

**[38.22.10]  22. Statement admissible by virtue of section 47 of the Ordinance: contents of notice (The former O. 38 r. 22)**

(1)     If the statement is admissible by virtue of section 47 of the Ordinance and was made otherwise than in a document, the notice must contain particulars of—

    (a)     the time, place and circumstances at or in which the statement was made;

    (b)     the person by whom, and the person to whom, the statement was made; and

    (c)     the substance of the statement or, if material, the words used.

(2)     If the statement is admissible by virtue of section 47 of the Ordinance and was made in a document, a copy or transcript of the document, or of the relevant part thereof, must be annexed to the notice and the notice must contain such (if any) of the particulars mentioned in paragraph (1)(a) and (b) as are not apparent on the face of the document or part.

(3)     If the party giving the notice alleges that any person, particulars of whom are contained in the notice, cannot or should not be called as a witness at the trial or hearing for any of the reasons specified in rule 25, the notice must contain a statement to that effect specifying the reason relied on.

**[38.22.11]  23. Statement admissible by virtue of section 49 of the Ordinance: contents of notice (The former O. 38 r. 23)**

(1)     If the statement is admissible by virtue of section 49 of the Ordinance, the notice must have annexed to it a copy or transcript of the document containing the statement, or of the relevant part thereof, and must contain—

    (a)     particulars of—

        (i)     the person by whom the record containing the statement was compiled;

        (ii)     the person who originally supplied the information from which the record was compiled; and

        (iii)     any other person through whom that information was supplied to the compiler of that record,

    and, in the case of any such person as is referred to in (i) or (iii) above, a description of the duty under which that person was acting when compiling that record or supplying information from which that record was compiled, as the case may be;

(b)  if not apparent on the face of the document annexed to the notice, a description of the nature of the record which, or part of which, contains the statement; and

(c)  particulars of the time, place and circumstances at or in which that record or part was compiled.

(2)  If the party giving the notice alleges that any person, particulars of whom are contained in the notice, cannot or should not be called as a witness at the trial or hearing for any of the reasons specified in rule 25, the notice must contain a statement to that effect specifying the reason relied on.

### [38.22.12]  24. Statement admissible by virtue of section 50 of the Ordinance: contents of notice (The former O. 38 r. 24)

(1)  If the statement is contained in a document produced by a computer and is admissible by virtue of section 50 of the Ordinance, the notice must have annexed to it a copy or transcript of the document containing the statement, or of the relevant part thereof, and must contain particulars of—

(a)  a person who occupied a responsible position in relation to the man agement of the relevant activities for the purpose of which the computer was used regularly during the material period to store or process information;

(b)  a person who at the material time occupied such a position in relation to the supply of information to the computer, being information which is reproduced in the statement or information from which the information contained in the statement is derived; and

(c)  a person who occupied such a position in relation to the operation of the computer during the material period,

and where there are two or more persons who fall within sub-paragraph (a), (b) or (c) and some only of those persons are at the date of service of the notice capable of being called as witnesses at the trial or hearing, the person particulars of whom are to be contained in the notice must be such one of those persons as is at that date so capable.

(2)  The notice must also state whether the computer was operating properly throughout the material period and, if not, whether any respect in which it was not operating properly or was out of operation during any part of that period was such as to affect the production of the document in which the statement is contained or the accuracy of its contents.

(3)  If the party giving the notice alleges that any person, particulars of whom are contained in the notice, cannot or should not be called as a witness at the trial or hearing for any of the reasons specified in rule 25, the notice must contain a statement to that effect specifying the reason relied on.

### [38.22.13]  25. Reasons for not calling a person as a witness (The former O. 38 r. 25)

The reasons referred to in rules 22(3), 23(2) and 24(3) are that the person in question is dead, or beyond the seas or unfit by reason of his bodily or mental condition to attend as a witness or that despite the exercise of reasonable diligence it has not been possible to identify or find him or that he cannot reasonably be expected to have any recollection of matters relevant to the accuracy or otherwise of the statement to which the notice relates.

### [38.22.14] Witness 'unfit' within the meaning of the former Order 38 rule 25
The provision in the former Order 38 rule 25 in respect of a person who is 'unfit ... to attend as a witness' does not mean unfit to attend the court. Other means of appearing as a witness, for example video-link and adjourning the court to the wit ness's home must also be ruled out. See *Ip Man Shan Henry & Anor v Ching Hing Construction Co Ltd & Anor* [2003] 1 HKC 39 where the court refused to allow the evidence of an infirm witness to be given by statutory declaration.

### [38.22.15] Court has no discretion under the former Order 38 rule 25
Once the court is satisfied that one of the reasons for not calling the witness stipulated by the former Order 38 rule 25 exists and that the notice procedure has been properly complied with, the court has no discretion to refuse to admit the statement in any case (*Cluett HK Ltd t/a Six Continents v Hercules Knitters Ltd* [1986] HKLR 1112, overrul ing *Attorney General v Lui Lok* [1984] HKLR 275 on this point).

### [38.22.16] 26. Counter-notice requiring person to be called as a witness (The former O. 38 r. 26)

(1)     Subject to paragraphs (2) and (3), any party to a cause or matter on whom a notice under rule 21 is served may, within 21 days after service of the notice on him, serve on the party who gave the notice a counter-notice requiring that party to call as a witness at the trial or hearing of the cause or matter any person (naming him) particulars of whom are contained in the notice.

(2)     Where any notice under rule 21 contains a statement that any person, particulars of whom are contained in the notice, cannot or should not be called as a witness for the reason specified therein, a party shall not be entitled to serve a coun ter-notice under this rule requiring that person to be called as a witness at the trial or hearing of the cause or matter unless he contends that that person can or, as the case may be, should be called, and in that case he must include in his counter-notice a statement to that effect.

(3)     Where a statement to which a notice under rule 21 relates is one to which rule 28 applies, no party on whom the notice is served shall be entitled to serve a counter-notice under this rule in relation to that statement, but this provision is without prejudice to the right of any party to apply to the Court under rule 28 for directions with respect to the admissibility of that statement.

(4)     If any party to a cause or matter by whom a notice under rule 21 is served fails to comply with a counter-notice duly served on him under this rule, then, unless any of the reasons specified in rule 25 applies in relation to the person named in the counter-notice, and without prejudice to the powers of the Court under rule 29, the statement to which the notice under rule 21 relates shall not be admissible at the trial or hearing of the cause or matter as evidence of any fact stated therein by virtue of section 47, 49 or 50 of the Ordinance, as the case may be.

**[38.22.17]  27. Determination of question whether person can or should be called as a witness (The former O. 38 r. 27)**

(1)      Where in any cause or matter a question arises whether any of the reasons specified in rule 25 applies in relation to a person, particulars of whom are contained in a notice under rule 21, the Court may, on the application of any party to the cause or matter, determine that question before the trial or hearing of the cause or matter or give directions for it to be determined before the trial or hearing and for the manner in which it is to be so determined.

(2)      Unless the Court otherwise directs, the summons by which an application under paragraph (1) is made must be served by the party making the application on every other party to the cause or matter.

(3)      Where any such question as is referred to in paragraph (1) has been determined under or by virtue of that paragraph, no application to have it determined afresh at the trial or hearing of the cause or matter may be made unless the evidence which it is sought to adduce in support of the application could not, with reasonable diligence, have been adduced at the hearing which resulted in the determination.

**[38.22.18]  28. Directions with respect to statement made in previous proceedings (The former O. 38 r. 28)**

Where a party to a cause or matter has given notice in accordance with rule 21 that he desires to give in evidence at the trial or hearing of the cause or matter—

(a)      a statement falling within section 47(1) of the Ordinance which was made by a person, whether orally or in a document, in the course of giving evidence in some other legal proceedings (whether civil or criminal); or

(b)      a statement falling within section 49(1) of the Ordinance which is contained in a record of direct oral evidence given in some other legal proceedings (whether civil or criminal),

any party to the cause or matter may apply to the Court for directions under this rule, and the Court hearing such an application may give directions as to whether, and if so on what conditions, the party desiring to give the statement in evidence will be permitted to do so and (where applicable) as to the manner in which that statement and any other evidence given in those other proceedings is to be proved.

**[38.22.19]  Proof (under the former O 38 r 28) of what transpired in previous proceedings**

Hearings in the Hong Kong courts are now electronically recorded. Transcripts may be obtained by the parties (on payment). There is thus little room for disagreement as to what transpired. In the unlikely event that such disagreement arises, older authorities might be referred to. See for example *Kwok Hang Kei v Quon Hing Concrete Co Ltd & Ors* [1990] 1 HKC 84 (CA).

**[38.22.20]  29. Power of Court to allow statement to be given in evidence (The former O. 38 r. 29)**

(1)      Without prejudice to sections 47(2)(a) and 49(2)(a) of the Ordinance and rule 28, the Court may, if it thinks it just to do so, allow a statement falling within section 47(1), 49(1) or 50(1) of the Ordinance to be given in evidence at the

trial or hearing of a cause or matter notwithstanding—

(a)    that the statement is one in relation to which rule 21(1) applies and that the party desiring to give the statement in evidence has failed to comply with that rule; or

(b)    that that party has failed to comply with any requirement of a coun ter-notice relating to that statement which was served on him in accordance with rule 26.

(2)    Without prejudice to the generality of paragraph (1), the Court may exercise its power under that paragraph to allow a statement to be given in evidence at the trial or hearing of a cause or matter if a refusal to exercise that power might oblige the party desiring to give the statement in evidence to call as a witness at the trial or hearing an opposite party or a person who is or was at the material time the servant or agent of an opposite party.

### [38.22.21]  Discretion to admit hearsay (in pre-1999 actions) notwithstanding failure to comply with the applicable rules

The former Order 38 rule 29 provides the court with a general discretion to admit hearsay evidence notwithstanding failure to comply with the other provisions of this Order. For illustrations as to the circumstances in which the discretion under rule 29 has been exercised in favour of the applicant, see *Bud-Burma Inc v Cougar Shirts Ltd* HCA 740/1977 (Mr Commissioner Liu QC; 12.10.1977), decided under rule 11 of the former Evidence (Hearsay) Rules, and *Chan Hoi Yan t/a Leader Enterprise v Arctic Trading Co Ltd* [1988] HKC 242. See also *China Everbright-IHD Pacific Ltd v Ch'ng Poh & Ors* [1999] 1 HKC 278, where a late application to adduce hearsay evidence, not previously disclosed, was allowed in the interests of justice, notwith standing the fact that an adjournment of the trial might have to be sought.

The discretion should be approached in the light of sections in the Evidence Ordinance whereby certain forms of hearsay statements are made admissible. In *Chan Hoi Yan t/a Leader Enterprise v Arctic Trading Co Ltd* (above), it was held:

> [R 29] ... is remedial in its intent and operation and is designed to enable the court to do what is just in the particular circumstances of the case. Each case will turn on its own particular facts and clearly non-compliance with the procedural requirements of the rules should not of itself result in the exclusion of material hearsay evidence which is otherwise admissible where the court considers it just that the evidence should be admitted.

See also *Technalloy Chemical Corp v International Merona Ltd* [1993] 2 HKC 94 where the Court of Appeal, applying dicta in *Cluett HK Ltd v Hercules Knitters Ltd* [1986] HKLR 1112, held that in exercising its discretion under this rule the court ought not to have regard to the weight of the evidence in the statements nor whether the statement might be inadmissible under any other rule. In *China Everbright-IHD Pacific Ltd v Ch'ng Poh & Ors* [1999] 1 HKC 278, Yuen J, citing the decision in *Technalloy*, exercised her discretion in favour of admitting previously undisclosed hearsay evidence on the basis that the interests of justice are best served where the court has before it all of the relevant evidence.

The court will always consider whether admission of the hearsay would cause prejudice or injustice to the opposing party. See *Ip Man Shan Henry & Anor v Ching*

*Hing Construction Co Ltd & Anor* [2003] 1 HKC 39 citing *Morris v Stratford-on-Avon Rural District Council* [1973] 1 WLR 1059. Leave to adduce may be coupled with an agreement to adjourn at the requesting party's expense so that the opposing party may have time to consider its position.

### [38.22.22] 30. Restriction on adducing evidence as to credibility of maker, etc. of certain statements (The former O. 38 r. 30)

Where—

(a)    a notice given under rule 21 in a cause or matter relates to a statement which is admissible by virtue of section 47 or 49 of the Ordinance; and

(b)    the person who made the statement, or, as the case may be, the person who originally supplied the information from which the record containing the statement was compiled, is not called as a witness at the trial or hearing of the cause or matter; and

(c)    none of the reasons mentioned in rule 25 applies so as to prevent the party who gave the notice from calling that person as a witness,

no other party to the cause or matter shall be entitled, except with the leave of the Court, to adduce in relation to that person any evidence which could otherwise be adduced by him by virtue of section 52 of the Ordinance unless he gave a counter-notice under rule 26 in respect of that person or applied under rule 28 for a direction that that person be called as a witness at the trial or hearing of the cause or matter.

### [38.22.23] 31. Notice required of intention to give evidence of certain inconsistent statements (The former O. 38 r. 31)

(1)    Where in a cause or matter a person, particulars of whom were contained in a notice given under rule 21, is not to be called as a witness at the trial or hearing of the cause or matter, any party to the cause or matter who is entitled and intends to adduce in relation to that person any evidence which is admissible for the purpose mentioned in section 52(1)(b) of the Ordinance must, not more than 21 days after service of that notice on him, serve on the party who gave that notice, notice of his intention to do so.

(2)    Rule 22(1) and (2) shall apply to a notice under this rule as if the notice were a notice under rule 21 and the statement to which the notice relates were a statement admissible by virtue of section 47 of the Ordinance.

(3)    The Court may, if it thinks it just to do so, allow a party to give in evidence at the trial or hearing of a cause or matter any evidence which is admissible for the purpose mentioned in section 52(1)(b) of the Ordinance notwithstanding that that party has failed to comply with the provisions of paragraph (1).

### [38.22.24] 32. Costs (The former O. 38 r. 32)

If—

(a)    a party to a cause or matter serves a counter-notice under rule 26 in respect of any person who is called as a witness at the trial of the cause or matter in compliance with a requirement of the counter-notice; and

(b)    it appears to the Court that it was unreasonable to require that person to be called as a witness, then, without prejudice to Order 62 and, in particular, to rule 10(1) thereof, the Court may direct that any costs to that party in respect of the preparation and service of the counter-notice shall not be allowed to him and that any costs occasioned by the counter-notice to any other party shall be paid by him to that other party.

**[38.22.25] 33. Certain powers exercisable in chambers (The former O. 38 r. 33)**
The jurisdiction of the Court under sections 47(2)(a), 47(3), 49(2)(a) and 51 (1) of the Ordinance may be exercised in chambers.

**[38.22.26] 34. Statements of opinion (The former O. 38 r. 34)**
Where a party to a cause or matter desires to give in evidence by virtue of Part IV of the Ordinance, as extended by section 56 of the Ordinance, a statement of opinion other than a statement to which Part IV of this Order applies, the provisions of rules 20 to 23 inclusive and 25 to 33 inclusive shall apply with such modifications as the Court may direct or the circumstances of the case may require.

IV. Expert Evidence

**35. Interpretation** (O. 38 r. 35)
(1) Expressions used in this Part of this Order which are used in the Evidence Ordinance (Cap. 8) have the same meanings in this Part of this Order as in that Ordinance. (L.N. 152 of 2008)
(2) A reference to an expert witness in this Part or Appendix D is a reference to an expert who has been instructed to give or prepare evidence for the purpose of proceedings in the Court. (L.N. 152 of 2008)

**NOTES**

**[38.35.1] Application of definitions in Evidence Ordinance**
Order 38 rule 35(1) provides that definitions of words and phrases in the Evidence Ordinance apply where the same words and phrases are used in part IV of Order 38 and in Appendix D to these rules (Code of Conduct for expert witnesses). See the definitions in section 2 of the Evidence Ordinance. More important see the definitions in various sections in part V of the Evidence Ordinance (section 58 *et seq*) which, like this part of Order 38, deals with expert evidence.

**35A. Expert witness's overriding duty to Court** (O. 38 r. 35A)
(1) It is the duty of an expert witness to help the Court on the matters within his expertise.
(2) The duty under paragraph (1) overrides any obligation to the person from whom the expert witness has received instructions or by whom he is paid.
(L.N. 152 of 2008)

**NOTES**

**[38.35A.1]** **Origin and scope of Order 38 rule 35A – Expert's overriding duty to the court**

Order 38 rule 35A derives from England's CPR 35.3 which is to the same effect though worded slightly differently. The rule states in legislative form that an expert witness has a duty to the court which overrides any obligation the expert may have to a party. The rule implements recommendation 102 of the Chief Justice's working party on civil justice reform. The working party expressed the view that the principles underlying this rule (and others concerning expert evidence which it recommended) were 'well-known and established in law', referring to *The Ikarian Reefer* [1993] 2 Lloyd's Rep 68. The effect of the rule, is stated in our sister publication in the UK, The Civil Court Practice (at CPR 35.1[1]) in the following terms:

> **Overriding duty** The expression of this duty is far more than a statement of good practice; it has, in effect, statutory force.

The Chief Justice's working party noted that the previously established principles continued to apply in England after implementation of the CPR, as demonstrated by *Stevens v Gullis* [2000] 1 All ER 527. It should follow that the prior decisions on an expert's duty of impartiality and not to act as an advocate should continue to be useful. These are discussed below.

One important difference between Hong Kong and England with regard to the relationship between expert witnesses and the court is with regard to seeking directions from the court. In England CPR 35.14 permits an expert witness to approach the court directly for directions. In Hong Kong the Chief Justice's working party decided against such a provision (final report, recommendation 106), noting many objections including the fact it was positively disliked by solicitors in England.

**[38.35A.2]** **Expert witness should be impartial**

An expert witness must be impartial as between the parties, 'uninfluenced as to the form or content of the exigencies of the litigation': *Rajeshkumar Nareshchandra Kantilal t/a KL Gems v DRA Trading Ltd* HCA 4193/2003 (Deputy Judge Saunders; 23.08.2005), quoting from *The Ikarian Reefer* (above). In *Rajeshkumar* it was held that as a consequence a party to the litigation can never be an expert witness therein.

There is no absolute bar to the admissibility of expert evidence on account of close connection (such as a consultancy or employment arrangement) with one of the parties: *Tang Ping Choi v Secty for Transport* [2004] 3 HKC 178, 184A-F (CA). That case is consistent with *Liverpool Roman Catholic Archdiocesan Trustees Inc v Goldberg* [2001] TLR 187 where Neuberger J expressed the view that a close personal and professional relationship did not preclude, as a matter of law, a QC from acting as expert witness for another QC who was being sued for negligence. However Neuberger J did not decide the issue, reserving it to the trial judge, who took another view, excluding the QC's expert evidence on grounds of public policy: *Roman Catholic Archdiocesan Trustees Inc v Goldberg (No 2)* [2001] 4 All ER 950; [2001] 1 WLR 2337. In *Tang Ping Choi* Rogers VP considered that the trial judge's ruling in that case had been disapproved in *R (Factortame) v Secty of State for Transport and the Regions (No 8)* [2002] 3 WLR 1104. That being the case, the judgment of Neuberger J should represent the law to be followed in Hong Kong. Thus in *Helm HK Ltd v Au Tat Kei Decky* HCA 1517/2006 (Deputy Judge Carlson; 04.06.2010) an accountant who had prepared a forensic report for one of the parties was permitted to be that party's expert witness. However, in the case of medical evidence, there should be a clear separation between treatment and expert evidence: see the discussion of this topic under Order 38 rule 36.

The fact that an expert is paid to give evidence is 'irrelevant' – experts are usually paid, otherwise they would not be likely to give up their valuable time to assist the court: *Tang Ping Choi* (above), at 185H-I.

It is recognised that the views of an expert instructed on behalf of one party may be 'coloured to some extent by that party's views': *Li Ip Man Lui v Thomas Li Wang Chung* HCMC 109/1966 (Rigby J; 08.06.1968). For this reason, and to save costs, the court may now direct the parties to appoint a single joint expert: see Order 38 rule 4A and the commentary thereunder.

### [38.35A.3]  Expert witness should not act as advocate

The guidelines laid down in *The Ikarian Reefer* (above) also require that an expert should not assume the role of advocate. In *Re Chan Yu Nam & Anor* [2006] 1 HKC 392, 406A-B expert evidence was rejected on this ground on an *ex parte* application for leave to apply for judicial review.

The duty of an expert not to act as advocate for one party or the other is now expressly stated in the Code of Conduct for expert witnesses, which is Appendix D to these rules. In the Canadian case of *Jayetileke v Blake* [2010] BCSC 1478 (CanLII) the court penalised a party in costs for having relied on expert evidence from a psychiatrist who 'was nothing more than an advocate thinly disguised in the cloak of an expert'.

### [38.35A.4]  Expert witness – conflict of interest

An expert witness who has been consulted by one party is not barred from giving evidence for the opposing party. This follows from the general principle that there is no property in a witness. The safeguard is privilege, which protects discussions between a party and an expert from being disclosed to the opposing party. See *Harmony Shipping Co SA v Saudi Europe Line Ltd* [1979] 1 WLR 1380 (CA), and in particular the judgment of Waller LJ at 1387A-E.

In England it has been recommended that experts should be instructed to end their reports with a statement as to any conflict of interest. See the following passage from our sister publication in the UK, The Civil Court Practice, para CPR 35.3[4]:

> **Conflict of interest**  A conflict of interest does not automatically disqualify an expert from giving evidence; but where an expert has a material or significant conflict of interest the court is likely to decline to act on the evidence and indeed may refuse permission [leave] for the evidence to be adduced. It is, therefore, important that any conflict should be disclosed as early as possible so that the court may decide for itself whether it can act in reliance upon the expert's evidence: *Toth v Jarman* [2006] EWCA Civ 1028, [2006] The Times 17 Aug (CA). The court went on to recommend that instructions to an expert should include a requirement on the part of the expert to end the report with statements to the effect that:
>
> (i)  he had no conflict of interest of any kind, other than any which he had disclosed in his report;
>
> (ii)  he did not consider that any interest which he had disclosed affected his suitability as an expert witness on any issue on which he had given evidence;
>
> (iii)  he would advise the party by whom he was instructed if between the date of his report and the trial, there was any change in circumstances which affected his

answers to (i) or (ii) above.

It would be a good practice to follow the above recommendation in Hong Kong.

In some Canadian cases, in order to protect privileged or confidential information, the courts have refused to permit a party to use an expert who had earlier been instructed by the opposing party. See *Andersen Enterprises Ltd v Kerrisdale Plaza Projects Ltd & Anor* [2009] BCSC 570 and the cases referred to therein.

### [38.35A.5] Breach of expert's duty
The Code of Conduct (appendix D to these rules) which must be provided to and read by expert witnesses (see Order 38 rules 37B and 37C) concludes with a note to the effect that proceedings for contempt of court may result from making a false declara tion verifying an expert report. This reflects Order 41A rule 9(4), concerning false statements of truth. Other consequences which may flow from breach of an expert's duty to the court are discussed in our sister publication in the UK, The Civil Court Practice, at CPR 35.3[2]-[2A], where it is said:

> **Power to order a witness to pay costs** The court had power to make a costs order against an expert who, by his evidence, caused significant expense to be incurred and did so in flagrant and reckless disregard of his duties to the court. An expert witness who gives evidence in breach of his, or her, duties under Part 35 [Order 38 part IV in Hong Kong] may be joined for the purposes of making a costs order [see Order 62 rule 6A] for the payment of the costs incurred and wasted by one or other of the parties as a result of the breach of duty. Although a warning might need to be given in the case of some wit nesses this was not necessary in the case of an expert who had made a declaration and statement of truth as required by [Order 38 rules 37A and 37C]: *Phillips v Symes* [2004] EWHC 2330 (Ch), [2005] 4 All ER 519, [2005] 1 WLR 2043 . . . It is suggested that such an order will be very unusual and that any such order for costs must be limited to those costs for which the witness's default can properly be held to have caused to be incurred.

> **Disciplinary proceedings by professional body** Although witnesses are generally immune from civil proceedings based on the evidence given to the court, an expert's professional body has jurisdiction to consider issues of professional misconduct, in a forensic context, for the protection of the public: *Meadow v General Medical Council* [2006] The Times, 31 Oct (CA).

### 36. Restrictions on adducing expert evidence (O. 38 r. 36)
**(1) Except with the leave of the Court or where all parties agree, no expert evidence may be adduced at the trial or hearing of any cause or matter unless the party seeking to adduce the evidence—**

    **(a) has applied to the Court to determine whether a direction should be given under rule 37 or 41 (whichever is appropriate) and has complied with any direction given on the application.**

    **(b) (Repealed L.N. 152 of 2008)**

    **(c) (Repealed L.N. 152 of 2008)**

**(2) Nothing in paragraph (1) shall apply to evidence which is permitted to be given by affidavit or shall affect the enforcement under any other provision of these rules (except of Order 45, rule 5) of a direction given under this Part of this Order.**

    **(L.N. 363 of 1990)**

**NOTES**

**[38.36.1] Nature of expert evidence**

Expert evidence is opinion evidence by a person with expertise on a relevant issue. It differs from evidence of fact in that it is not necessarily based on personal observation of events. See *Koninklijke Philips Electronics NV v Wealth Full Technology Ltd* [2002] 3 HKC 87 where Deputy Judge R Tong SC stated (at 91E–F): 'Opinion evidence, by definition, means any inference from observed facts' (citing Cross & Tapper *'Evidence'* (9th ed) 511). See also *Re Jinro (HK) International Ltd* [2002] 4 HKC 90, 97F–G, per Kwan J.

The fact that a person giving evidence has expertise in the subject matter does not necessarily mean the evidence is of expert character. As Deputy Judge R Tong SC stated in the *Philips Electronics* case (above, at 91F–G):

> The mere fact that factual evidence is given by someone with expertise in a particular discipline does not transform that evidence into expert or opinion evidence although sometimes the line between factual and opinion evidence may not be immediately apparent. For example, an explanation as to how a computer works may be purely descriptive and factual although it may require some expert training on the part of the person giving that explanation. On the other hand, evidence as to the quality of the work of a computer may be a matter of expert opinion.

In the *Philips Electronics* case Deputy Judge R Tong SC held that evidence by an engineer as to how a compact disc works was not expert evidence.

Explaining words or terms of science or art is 'within the function of experts': *Wong Hoi Fung v AIA Co (Bermuda) Ltd* [2002] 4 HKC 225 (para 14). There the court granted leave to adduce expert evidence concerning 'terms and usage in life insurance policies'.

**[38.36.2] Medical evidence – distinction between 'treatment' and expert evidence**

In cases where medical evidence is adduced, the distinction between factual and expert evidence comes into sharp focus. Both are often required in cases involving claims for personal injuries, medical negligence and employees compensation. They should be dealt with separately, as emphasised in *Wong Cheuk v Falcon Insurance Co (HK) Ltd* DCEC 688/2008 (Judge Marlene Ng; 20.05.2009), where it was said (paras 45-46):

> 45. A treating doctor renders his medical report an/or testify in court as a professional witness on observed facts (eg what the patient told him, what symptoms were reported, what investigation/examination was undertaken, what medical advice/ treatment was given, etc) rather than offer expert medical opinion (*eg* opinion on the causation, aetiology, diagnosis and/or prognosis etc of the injuries). Thus, information from the treating doctor is normally non-controversial, and his medical reports/records are usually admitted without calling him to testify in court.

> 46. On the other hand, an expert doctor is qualified by his experience and expertise in a medical specialty, and usually has no prior therapeutic involvement with the injured party. He is expected to give impartial opinion on particular medical issue(s) to assist the court on the basis of assumptions of fact provided to him in

written or other form and/or his own examination of the injured party. His opinion/report is for the benefit of the court and independent of such party. Permission of the court is generally required for adducing such expert opinion in evidence at trial.

The learned judge continued (at paras 49-50) by saying that practitioners who instruct medical doctors 'should take special care to make clear the purpose for which the reports are required', so as not to avoid 'mixing of fact and opinion', which 'can lead to confusion'. In *Ho Lai San Teresa v Orea Dental Centre Ltd & Anor* DCPI 2530/2009 (Master Lo; 04.06.2010) the court refused to permit a party to instruct an expert for a joint medical report where that expert had previously treated the party and would be a witness of fact at trial.

### [38.36.3]  Cross reference
See also Order 38 rule 4 under which the court may limit the number of expert witnesses to be called at trial, and see Order 40 as to court-appointed experts.

### [38.36.4]  Admissibility of expert and other opinion evidence
Expert evidence is admissible by virtue of section 58(1) of the Evidence Ordinance (Cap 8), subject to any rules. Section 58(2) provides for the admission of other opinion evidence, not of an expert character.

Issues as to the admissibility of expert evidence may arise when leave is sought (as to which see below) or later, once the expert reports have been served and considered. A comprehensive review of the issues which may arise on a challenge to the admissibility of expert evidence is set out in *Barings plc v Cooper & Lybrand & Ors* [2001] EWHC (Ch) 17 (09.02.2001). In that case, after reviewing authorities from the UK and other jurisdictions, the English court said (at para 45):

> In my judgment the authorities which I have cited above establish the following propositions: expert evidence is admissible under section 3 of the Civil Evidence Act 1972 [Evidence Ordinance s 58(1) in Hong Kong] in any case where the Court accepts that there exists a recognised expertise governed by recognised standards and rules of conduct capable of influencing the Court's decision on any of the issues which it has to decide and the witness to be called satisfies the Court that he has a sufficient familiarity with and knowledge of the expertise in question to render his opinion potentially of value in resolving any of those issues. Evidence meeting this test can still be excluded by the Court if the Court takes the view that calling it will not be helpful to the Court in resolving any issues in the case justly. Such evidence will not be helpful where the issue to be decided is one of law or is otherwise one on which the Court is able to come to a fully informed decision without hearing such evidence.

The above passage has been relied upon in at least two decisions in Hong Kong: *Lee Annabell v Lee Wing Kim* HCA 9522/1997 (Chu J; 06.12.2001) and *Re Ocean Time Dev't Ltd* HCCW 334/2004 (Barma J; 16.01.2008). It was also referred to in the final report of the Chief Justice's working party on civil justice reform (2004) (para 596-7) where the effect of the legislation was succinctly summarised as follows:

(a)    the subject matter of the opinion must fall within an area in which expert evidence may properly be given;

(b)    the witness must be qualified as an expert to give the evidence of the type in question; and,

(c)     his evidence must be relevant to the issues being litigated.

### [38.36.5]  Application for expert directions

A party who wishes to adduce expert evidence at trial must apply for directions pursuant to Order 38 rule 36. Paragraph 20 of the case management practice direction (PD 5.2) provides that the court will not give permission for a party to adduce expert evidence unless that party has:

(a)     identified the expert by name and field;

(b)     identified the issue to which the expert evidence will relate (a mere reference to adducing expert evidence 'limited to the issue of liability' or 'limited to the issue of quantum' is not sufficient); and

(c)     considered the appropriateness of appointing a single joint expert in the case.

See also para 72 of the personal injuries list practice direction (PD 18.1).

The requirements set out above were elaborated and explained in *Kam Hing Trading (HK) Ltd v The People's Insurance Co of China (HK) Ltd & Anor* HCA 1062/2008 (Registrar Au-Yeung; 27.07.2009). The following points were made:

• *Field of expertise* - it is 'necessary to state the profession or discipline of the expert (eg architect, investment advisor)' to avoid confusion between related disciplines such as building surveyor, quantity surveyor, architect and authorised person, which has sometimes caused hearings to be adjourned pending clarification.

• *Name of expert* – an expert must already have been identified to ensure that one is available, that issues of conflict of interest have been cleared and that realistic estimates of the time required to prepare an expert report can be put forward.

• *Issues* - these should preferably be framed as 'yes or no' or 'multiple choice' questions in the summons and order.

• *Single joint expert* – the court will appoint a single joint expert 'if doing so will reduce cost and delay and ensure that the parties litigate on equal footing'. [See also the commentary under Order 38 rule 4A].

With regard to identifying the issue for expert evidence, further guidance is set out in *Total Market Ltd v Crosby Wealth Management (HK) Ltd* [2009] 5 HKC 479 where it was said (para 2):

> A summons (or case management summons) applying for expert directions should contain a list of issues for the intended expert to answer. If both parties want expert directions, they should endeavour to agree the issues. If they cannot agree, the court will determine the issues to be put to an expert after considering the parties' submissions.

The Registrar continued by setting out the advantages of such a list of issues as follows:

(i)     It focuses the parties' minds on the real issues of a case.

(ii)    It helps the parties to consider whether they have pleaded all the issues and apply for amendment to the pleadings as early as possible.

(iii)   It avoids experts giving opinions on different issues.

(iv)    It helps the parties to decide how controversial the issues are and hence decide if it is appropriate to appoint a single joint expert ('SJE').

The Registrar also warned that failure to prepare or consider the list of issues will cause wastage of time and costs. In the particular case she considered that the parties had not been sufficiently prepared, and made a limited order as to the party and party costs.

The requisite information can be given by completing part E of the timetabling questionnaire (appendix A to PD 5.2) which parties are required to file and serve under Order 25 rule 1. For actions in the personal injuries list see part F of questionnaire set out in appendix F to PD 18.1. Whether the directions are sought under the timetabling questionnaire or in a special summons, they should be sought 'as early as possible, usually after the pleadings are closed, or as soon as possible after amendments to pleadings make it necessary to do so': *Kam Hing Trading* (above).

### [38.36.6]  Criteria for grant of leave to adduce expert evidence

In considering whether to grant leave the Hong Kong court applies a 3-prong test of necessity, relevance and probative value. This test is said to have been enunciated by Suffiad J in *Chan Kwok Ming v Hitachi Electric Service Co* HCPI 322/2002. It appears that no written judgment is available to the public in that case, but the 3-prong test said to have been laid down in it has been cited and applied in many subsequent authorities including *Arfan Muhammed v MPS Eng'g Ltd* HCPI 457/2003 (Deputy Judge Muttrie; 30.06.2005); *Lam Lai Ying v Choi Min & Anor* [2006] 3 HKLRD 572 (para 5); *Cheung Yuen Fan Sally v HKUST* HCPI 106/2003 (Master Kwan; 13.06.2006) (para 13); *Shum Tsz Yan v Union Medical Centre Ltd* DCEC 1135/2004 (Deputy Judge Au; 19.07.2006) (para 56); *Cheung Chi Keung v Chiu Wing Chuen* DCPI 101/2006 (Judge Ng; 29.06.2006) (para 44); *Wong Chok Wai v Sun Chung Luen Chinese Products Co Ltd* DCPI 1839/2006 (Judge Ng; 03.04.2007 (para 20); *Kwan Tat Kuen v Cheung Choi & Ors* HCPI 899/2006 (Deputy Judge Muttrie; 14.05.2007) (para 11); *Chan Wai Ying v Sin Kit Sang & Ors* HCPI 805/2006 (Master Kwan; 31.05.2007) (para 10); *Unibo Trading Ltd v Cool Tech Laundry Ltd* HCA 16/2006 (Sakhrani J; 14.05.2007); and *Li Siu Ping v Perfecta Dyeing, Printing & Weaving Works Ltd* (Judge Ng; 18.07.2007) (para 44).

*Proportionality and expense* – From implementation of the civil justice reforms in 2009, the underlying objective of reasonable proportion and procedural economy (Order 1A rule 1(c)) will be taken into account in addition to the above 3-prong test. See *Ip Sau Lin v Hospital Authority* [2009] 2 HKC 383 (para 38) referring to *Mann v Chetty & Patel* [2000] EWCA Civ 267 (26.10.2000). In para 17 of the *Mann* case Hale LJ said the court should take into account 'how much it will cost and the relationship of that cost to the sums at stake'.

*Personal injuries cases* – There is a 'modern trend' in personal injuries actions that expert evidence on liability is not normally allowed: *Tong Ho Wing v Wong Fuk* HCPI 1369/1999 (Suffiad J; 19.07.2000). The cause of a normal traffic accident can usually be determined by eye-witness testimony, so the 'necessity' limb of the 3-prong test cannot be satisfied. However, where there is no eye-witness to describe what happened, and deductions may have to be drawn from circumstantial evidence or from the position of vehicles, marks on the road, *etc*, expert evidence may be permitted: *Liddell v Middleton* [1996] PIQR 36, quoted in *Tong Ho Wing* (above). In *Tang Hung On v Crown Rich Transportation Ltd & Ors* HCPI 304/2006 (Saunders J; 21.01.2010) (para 17-18) the court regretted that leave to adduce expert evidence had been refused as to the cause of an unusual accident arising from a pressurised rubber hose becoming detached from a cement tanker.

*Professional negligence cases* – As to when expert evidence will be helpful to the court on a question whether a professional fell below the required standard of skill and care, see the interesting discussion in *Lee Chun Mui v Securicor Gurkha Services Ltd & Ors* HCPI 774/2005 (Deputy Judge Carlson; 27.02.2008).

*Admissibility and relevance* – Expert evidence which is not admissible (whether because it is not genuinely 'expert' evidence, or otherwise), clearly fails the 'relevance' and 'probative value' limbs of the 3-prong test. In *Wong Hoi Fung* (above, at 229G-I) the court said:

> Where the proposed expert evidence is plainly inadmissible or irrelevant, the court ought to exercise its discretion to refuse the admission of such evidence. But where the court cannot form a clear view on the relevance of the proposed expert evidence or where it considers that the proposed evidence is clearly relevant, then it should grant leave for the evidence to be adduced at trial.

It is not necessary for the court to go into detailed arguments on relevance. If the evidence is arguably relevant the court should grant leave, and then, at the end of the day, if it proves unhelpful, the court can give it little or no weight. See the final report of the Chief Justice's working party on civil justice reform (2004) (para 598) referring to *Re M & R (minors)* [1996] 4 All ER 239. In assessing the relevance of expert evidence, it is necessary for the court to form a view as to how helpful the evidence would be in resolving the issues before it: see the above-quoted passage from *Barings plc*. Thus in *Ip Sau Lin v Hospital Authority* (above) (para 38) leave to adduce psychiatric evidence on the plaintiff's ability to cope with pain was refused on the ground the court could derive sufficient help from existing clinical and orthopaedic reports, and from the plaintiff's own evidence; and in *Khan v Lau Kai Hong & Anor t/a Shun Sum Eng'g Co* HCPI 850/2008 (Fung J; 29.04.2009) (para 20) it was held that treatment records from government hospitals, if available, would be sufficient for the trial judge in assessing quantum, and leave to adduce expert evidence was refused.

**[38.36.7] Stage at which issue as to admissibility of expert evidence may be resolved**

A dispute over admissibility of expert evidence may, instead of being reserved to the trial judge, be resolved at the interlocutory stage, and the issue may be dealt with by a master: *Ko Chi Keung v Lee Ping Yan Andrew* [2001] 2 HKC 63 (doubting *Sullivan v West Yorkshire Passenger Transport Executive* [1985] 2 All ER 134 and *Woodford & Ackroyd v Burgess* [2000] CP Rep 79 in part). See also *Lee Annabell v Lee Wing Kim* HCA 9522/1997 (Chu J; 06.12.2001).

In *Roman Catholic Archdiocesan Trustees Inc v Goldberg* [2001] TLR 187 (The Times 09.03.2001) the issue of admissibility of expert evidence was not raised until the case was due to come on for trial. Neuberger J set out the following factors to be considered by the court:

> 1. If the expert evidence was said to be inadmissible then the point should be raised as soon as possible. The parties and the court should know where they were sooner rather than later and a determination of the point early would

save costs and assist case management generally. Moreover, the decision on admissibility might be challenged in the Court of Appeal. If the decision on admissibility was reached only very shortly before the trial then, particularly if the decision was that the evidence was inadmissible, if the decision turned out to be wrong the trial would go ahead on a false basis and the Court of Appeal might feel that there was no option but to order a retrial; or the trial date would be lost while the question of admissibility went to the Court of Appeal, or the appeal would have to be rushed on inconveniencing the Court of Appeal and causing unfair delay to other litigants.

2.   If the objection was raised early, the court should normally determine it unless the court was satisfied that the trial judge would be in a better position to decide the point.

3.   If the objection was raised later then the court should be slower to determine the application rather than leaving it to the trial judge. However, that did not mean that the court should not determine it if it thought it appropriate to do so.

4.   The court should be particularly slow to determine an application to exclude evidence when the application was made so late that the case was coming on for trial.

5.   If there was any real doubt whether expert evidence was admissible the issue should be determined in favour of admissibility.

## [38.36.8]   Admissibility of expert evidence in interlocutory proceedings

By exception to the general rule that expert evidence may only be adduced by agreement or with leave of the court, Order 38 rule 36(2) provides that such evidence may be adduced by affidavit where affidavit evidence is permitted. In general, this means that expert evidence may be adduced without restriction in interlocutory matters. In this regard see the *Philips Electronics* case [2002] 3 HKC 87, 91D.

## [38.36.9]   Change of expert

Our sister publication in the UK, The Civil Court Practice, contains [at CPR 35.4[2]) the following discussion concerning cases where the court has given leave for a party to adduce the evidence of an expert, but the party is later dissatisfied with that expert's report and wishes to switch to another:

> **Where a party wishes to instruct a second expert because dissatisfied with the report of the first expert** Where a party wishes to instruct a second expert because dissatisfied with the report of the first, then, if it is appropriate to give permission [leave], such permission should be conditional on the disclosure, to the other party, of the report of the first expert: *Beck v Ministry of Defence* [2003] EWCA Civ 1043, [2003] The Times, 21 July.
>
> A condition that the first report should be disclosed should not be imposed where the order of the court giving permission for expert evidence did not identify a particular expert and thus left it to the party to choose on which of two expert's reports to rely: *Vasiliou v Haji georgiou* [2005] EWCA Civ 236, [2005] 3 All ER 17. In *Hajigeorgiou* the Court of Appeal went on to state that the court can control the conduct of litigation in general, and the giving of expert evidence in particular. Expert shopping is undesirable and, wherever possible, the court should use its powers to prevent it. It should be emphasised that, if a party needs the permission of the court to rely on expert witness A in place of expert witness B, the court has the power to give permission on condition

that A's report is disclosed to the other party or parties, and that such a condition should usually be imposed. In imposing such a condition, the court is not abrogating or emasculating legal professional privilege; it is merely saying that, if a party seeks the court's permission to rely on a substitute expert, it will be required to waive privilege in the first expert's report as a condition of being permitted to do so. Furthermore, the condition of disclosure does not relate only to the first expert's final report, but also to a draft report containing the substance of his or her opinion.

*Vasiliou v Hajigeorgiou* was quoted with approval in *Chinachem Charitable Foundation Ltd v Chan Chun Chuen & Anor* [2009] 5 HKC 190 (para 20), the Hong Kong court saying that expert shopping is undesirable and should be discouraged. This was because, having regard to the underlying objectives in Order 1A, expert shopping, if unchecked, would 'not be conducive to cost-effectiveness of the proceedings nor the expeditious disposal of a case' (para 23). Reference was also made to potential unfairness to parties who could not afford to 'shop around for the opinions of more than one expert', and the need to avoid compromising the impartiality of expert evidence. However, leave was granted in the circumstances of the particular case. Leave to appeal to the Court of Appeal was refused on the ground that this was primarily a case management decision – see HCMP 901/2009.

An application for change of expert should be supported by an affidavit 'setting out the circumstances which prompted the application, and the grounds of the application, and exhibiting the opinion or, at least, the gist of the opinion of the new expert': *Law Chung Fai v Lam Ming Kuen* HCPI 96/2008 (Bharwaney J; 13.09.2010) (para 28).

**37. Direction that expert report be disclosed** (O. 38 r. 37)

**(1) Subject to paragraph (2), where in any cause or matter an application is made under rule 36(1) in respect of oral expert evidence, then, unless the Court considers that there are special reasons for not doing so, it shall direct that the substance of the evidence be disclosed in the form of a written report or reports to such other parties and within such period as the Court may specify. (L.N. 404 of 1991)**

**(2) Nothing in paragraph (1) shall require a party to disclose a further medical report if he proposes to rely at the trial only on the report provided pursuant to Order 18, rule 12(1A) or (1B) but, where a party claiming damages for personal injuries discloses a further report, that report shall be accompanied by a statement of the special damages claimed and, in this paragraph, "a statement of the special damages claimed" has the same meaning as in Order 18, rule 12(1C). (L.N. 404 of 1991)**

## NOTES

### [38.37.1] Disclosure of expert evidence

Order 38 rule 37 provides that the parties should normally be directed to disclose in advance 'the substance' of any expert evidence they intend to adduce at trial. The purpose is to 'narrow the issues and avoid surprises': *Re Estate of Ng Shum (No 1)* [1990] 1 HKLR 63, 65B.

What must be disclosed is 'the substance' of the expert evidence. In *Iskandar v Bonardy Leo* [1988] 1 HKLR 583, 605E-F (CA) Hunter JA said that in this context the 'substance' is:

> . . . the essential facts and reasoning

> (1)    upon which the expert intends to rely in evidence at the hearing in support of his opinion;

> (2)    to which counsel must be ready to direct their cross-examination; and

> (3)    in relation to which the court must be ready to make findings.

Hunter JA went on to recognise that after the exchange of expert reports, an expert may wish to 'refine, alter or amend his view in the light of any contrary report or in the light of new or different facts', and expressed the view that an order for exchange of expert reports should routinely give two time limits, eg:

> (1)    present reports within _____ weeks; and

> (2)    any amended or final reports (in a form sufficient to constitute the expert's evidence-in-chief) not less than _____ weeks before trial.

Note that in personal injury cases there is early disclosure of expert evidence to the extent that a medical report (or post-mortem report if applicable and available) must be served with the statement of claim. See the personal injury practice direction (PD 18.1), para 5.1(i), and see the commentary under Order 72 rule 2.

## [38.37.2]  Filing of expert reports
Order 38 rule 37 only requires disclosure of expert reports to the other relevant parties. It does not require such reports to be filed in court. Practice Direction 24.1 (para 8) provides that filing is not necessary unless there is a direction of the court to that effect, and that it is sufficient that they be served.

## [38.37.3]  Form and content of expert report
The requirements as to form and content of expert reports are set out in paragraphs 8 to 11 of appendix D to these rules. The requirements set out there are similar, but by no means identical, to what is laid down by practice direction CPR PD 35 in England.

Additionally, an expert report must be verified by a statement of truth by virtue of Order 38 rule 37A and Order 41A rule 2(1)(c), and must contain a declaration of duty to the court setting out the matters prescribed by Order 38 rule 37C.

See also the commentary under Order 38 rule 35A concerning the recommended inclusion in England of a statement as to absence of conflict of interest and see practice direction 18.1 concerning the personal injuries list, which contains some additional guidance on the form of content of expert reports in personal injury cases.

One important difference between the requirements as to content of an expert report in Hong Kong as compared to England is with regard to disclosure of the expert's instructions. In England CPR 35.10(3) provides that an expert report must state the substance of all material instructions, whether written or oral, on the basis of which the report was written. In Hong Kong the Chief Justice's working party on civil justice reform recommended against adopting such a requirement (final report, recommendation 105). Concern was expressed that such a mandatory provision would be an abrogation of legal professional privilege (in England CPR 35.10(4) provides that the expert's instructions are not privileged from disclosure) and might infringe the constitutional protection of confidential legal advice in article 35 of the Basic Law. As a result the equivalent Hong Kong provision (para 8(a) of appendix D to these rules) does not require disclosure of an expert's instructions, only the 'facts, matters and assumptions on which the opinions in the report are based', which *may* be done by annexing a letter of instructions.

With regard to joint expert reports, para 64 of practice direction 18.2 gives guidance as to what should be included. Although that practice direction deals with employees' compensation cases, in *Leung Wai Kee v Tan Yuet Sheung* DCCJ 5716/ 2007 (Judge Mimmie Chan; 11.05.2009) the court found the guidance in para 64 useful in a water leaking case, and said (para 16) that it is 'not restricted to medical reports and should be applicable to most, if not all types of expert reports'.

### [38.37.4] Challenge to party's expert report
Expert evidence may, in principle, be challenged by the opposing party in the same way as any other evidence. However expert reports prepared pursuant to contractual provisions are sometimes deemed by the contract to be binding such that they can be challenged only on limited grounds such as that the expert departed from instruc tions in a material respect. See *Dlugash v Mayers* [1997] 2 HKC 814, 819G– I and *Lau Yee Ching v Wong Tak Kwong* [2007] 2 HKC 593, both referring to *Jones & Ors v Sherwood Computer Services plc* [1992] 1 WLR 277 (CA). It was once thought that there was greater scope to challenge a 'speaking' valuation report, that is a valuation report supported by reasons and analysis (*Donnett v Cheung* [1988] 2 HKLR 454, 456G-I), but this line of reason ing has been discredited: *Re Golden Bright Ltd* [2007] 1 HKC 89 (para 20).

See also the commentary concerning court-appointed experts under Order 40.

### [38.37.5] Failure to comply
The court has a discretion to exclude expert evidence which has not been disclosed: *Iskandar v Bonardy Leo* [1988] 1 HKLR 583 (CA). Experts may be confined to the evidence which has been disclosed, and will not be permitted to supplement it or respond to an opposing party's expert evidence without first seeking leave to serve a supplementary report: *Re Estate of Ng Shum (No 1)* [1990] 1 HKLR 63.

### [38.37.6] Unless order as to expert reports
It has been held that the court has no power to make an 'unless' order where there has been a failure to serve expert reports in a timely fashion. See *Yee Tung Fibre Glass Manufactory Eng Co v FRP (HK) Ltd* HCA 17840/1998 (Ribeiro J; 17.09.1999), citing *Derby & Co Ltd v Weldon (No 9)* [1990] The Times, 9 November. However, the *Yee Tung* decision was doubted in part by Chung J in *Kai Yip Air-Condition Engineering Co v Ma Hei Sun* [2001] 3 HKC 458.

**37A.   Expert report to be verified by statement of truth** (O. 38 r. 37A)
   **An expert report disclosed under these rules must be verified by a statement of truth in accordance with Order 41A.**
   **(L.N. 152 of 2008)**

---

**NOTES**

**[38.37A.1]  Statement of truth requirement for expert reports**
Order 38 rule 37A requires that expert reports be verified by statement of truth. Order 41A rule 2(1)(c) provides likewise. See the commentary under Order 41A for discussion of statements of truth generally. Note in particular Order 41A rule 7 by which an expert report which is not verified by statement of truth is not admissible in evidence unless the court orders otherwise.

**37B.  Duty to provide expert witness with copy of code of conduct** (O. 38 r. 37B)
　　**(1)　A party who instructs an expert witness shall as soon as practicable provide the expert witness with a copy of the code of conduct set out in Appendix D.**
　　**(2)　Where the Court has under rule 4A(1) ordered that 2 or more parties shall appoint a single joint expert witness, paragraph (1) applies to each of the parties.**
　　**(3)　If the instruction is in writing, it must be accompanied by a copy of the code of conduct set out in Appendix D.**
　　**(L.N. 152 of 2008)**

---

**NOTES**

**[38.37.1]　The code of conduct for expert witnesses**
Appendix D to these rules, which was introduced as part of the civil justice reforms implemented in 2009, is a code of conduct for expert witnesses. It was added in order to facilitate the adoption of the provision of the New South Wales rules whereby expert evidence is inadmissible unless the expert acknowledges having read such a code and agrees to be bound by it. See paragraph 612 of the final report of the Chief Justice's working party on civil justice reform. It is there noted that the Academy of Experts offered to adapt its code for Hong Kong use.
　　Order 38 rule 37B places a duty on a party instructing an expert witness to provide the expert with a copy of the code of conduct and stipulates that the duty lies on both parties where a single joint expert is instructed.

**37C.  Expert witness's declaration of duty to Court** (O. 38 r. 37C)
　　**(1)　An expert report disclosed under these rules is not admissible in evidence unless the report contains a declaration by the expert witness that —**
　　　　**(a)　he has read the code of conduct set out in Appendix D and agrees to be bound by it;**
　　　　**(b)　he understands his duty to the Court; and**
　　　　**(c)　he has complied with and will continue to comply with that duty.**
　　**(2)　Oral expert evidence is not admissible unless the expert witness has declared, whether orally or in writing or otherwise, that—**
　　　　**(a)　he has read the code of conduct set out in Appendix D and agrees to be bound by it;**
　　　　**(b)　he understands his duty to the Court; and**
　　　　**(c)　he has complied with and will continue to comply with that**

**duty.**

**(3)    Paragraph (1) does not apply to a report that was disclosed under rule 37 before the commencement of this rule.**

**(L.N. 152 of 2008)**

---

## NOTES

### [38.37C.1]  Origin and scope of Order 38 rule 37C – Expert evidence inadmissible without declaration

Order 38 rule 37C provides that expert evidence is not admissible unless the expert wit ness declares that he has read the code of conduct in appendix D, understands his duty to the court (as to which see Order 38 rule 35A) and that he has and will comply with that duty. The requirement for a declaration derives from England's CPR 35.10(2), and the sanction whereby the evidence is inadmissible in case of non-compliance derives from the New South Wales rules. The rule implements recommendation 103 of the Chief Justice's working party on civil justice reform, which called for such a hybrid provision in Hong Kong.

In *Ip Kam Chung v Kwo Siu Kit & Anor* DCEC 797/2009 (Deputy Judge Clement Lee; 20.09.2010) (para 14) the court made an unless order by which expert reports would be expunged from the court file unless the statement of truth and declaration of compliance with the code of conduct were filed within 14 days.

### [38.37C.2]  Reports exchanged before implementation of CJR in 2009

Order 38 rule 37C(2) is a transitional provision, whereby expert reports disclosed under rule 37 before the implementation of the civil justice reforms in 2009 are not subject to the provisions of the rule requiring a declaration and restricting admissibility in case of non-compliance.

### [38.37C.3]  Breach of expert's duty

See the commentary under Order 38 rule 35A.

**38.    Meeting of experts** (O. 38 r. 38)

**In any cause or matter the Court may, if it thinks fit, direct that there be a meeting "without prejudice" of such experts within such periods before or after the disclosure of their reports as the Court may specify, for the purpose of identifying those parts of their evidence which are in issue. Where such a meeting takes place the experts may prepare a joint statement indicating those parts of their evidence on which they are, and those on which they are not, in agreement.**

---

## NOTES

### [38.38.1]  Power to order meeting of experts

Order 38 rule 38 empowers the court to direct that there be a 'without prejudice' meeting between experts for the purpose of identifying the parts of their disclosed reports which are in issue. The rule is in the same terms as the rule of the same number in the former

English Rules of the Supreme Court. The equivalent provision in England is now CPR 35.12.

As to the circumstances in which the court will exercise its discretion to order such a meeting, the following observations of Tuckey LJ in *Hubbard & Ors v Lambeth Southwark & Lewisham Health Authority & Ors* [2001] EWCA Civ 1455 (07.09.2001), [2002] Lloyd's Rep Med 8 are instructive:

> 17.   The rule is obviously salutary. Experience of the working of this rule and its RSC predecessor show that in almost every case experts are able to narrow the issues to be determined at trial even in very complex cases. The time and cost benefit which flows from this is obvious. There are of course cases where an experts' meeting would serve no purpose, in which case no order should be made. But, even if both parties object to a meeting, the Court is not prevented from making an order and should do so if it thinks that something will come of it. I see nothing wrong with a general approach that an order for such discussions to take place will usually be made where there has been an exchange of expert reports.
>
> 18.   The mere objection of one party will not be sufficient. Some very good reason for not having a meeting would have to be shown.

In *Hubbard* (para 19) it was held that the plaintiff's fear that at such a meeting their experts would be overawed by the reputation of a distinguished medical specialist against whom some of their allegations were made and would 'sell them down the river' was not a good reason not to order a meeting. Tape recording of the meeting was agreed to cater for this concern.

In *Leung Wai Kee v Tan Yuet Sheung* DCCJ 5716/2007 (Judge Mimmie Chan; 11.05.2009), where the opposing parties had filed expert reports, the court made an order under this rule directing the experts to prepare a joint statement indicating the parts of their evidence on which they were in agreement, and those on which they were not. The result was 10 'bullet points' of the experts' respective conclusions, which the court considered to be readily apparent from the expert reports filed earlier. The court was highly critical, and emphasised that reasons for disagreement should be given. Judge Mimmie Chan said (para 8-9):

> To simply repeat their different conclusions without stating the reasons for their dif ferent conclusions by reference at least to their reports is not only unhelpful, but also not in compliance with the Order of the Court . . . Further it is a dereliction of the experts' paramount and overriding duty to help the Court . . . If experts are not prepared to assume such a general duty to the Court, or if they regard such duty to be too onerous, then they should not accept instructions to act.

In result the court adjourned the trial, ordering each party to bear its own costs and disallowing the experts' costs in preparing the unsatisfactory joint statement.

## [38.38.2] Arrangements for meetings between experts

Useful advice on the arrangements to be made for discussions between experts has been given in England in part 18 of the Protocol for the Instruction of Experts to Give Evidence in Civil Claims. The following relevant extracts from that protocol may of some guidance in Hong Kong:

> 18.4   Arrangements for discussions between experts should be proportionate to the value of cases . . .

18.5  The parties, their lawyers and experts should co-operate to produce the agenda for any discussion between experts, although primary responsibility for preparation of the agenda should normally lie with the parties' solicitors.

18.6  The agenda should indicate what matters have been agreed and summarise concisely those which are in issue. It is often helpful for it to include questions to be answered by the experts. If agreement cannot be reached promptly or a party is unrepresented, the court may give directions for the drawing up of the agenda. The agenda should be circulated to experts and those instructing them to allow sufficient time for the experts to prepare for the discussion.

18.7  Those instructing experts must not instruct experts to avoid reaching agreement (or to defer doing so) on any matter within the experts' competence. Experts are not permitted to accept such instructions.

18.8  The parties' lawyers may only be present at discussions between experts if all the parties agree or the court so orders. If lawyers do attend, they should not normally intervene except to answer questions put to them by the experts or to advise about the law (*Hubbard v Lambeth Southwark & Lewisham HA* [2001] EWCA 1455).

18.9  The content of discussions between experts should not be referred to at trial unless the parties agree (CPR 35.12(4)) [in Hong Kong this is implicit in the wording of Order 38 rule 38 which provides for such talks to be 'without prejudice']. It is good practice for any such agreement to be in writing.

18.10  At the conclusion of any discussion between experts, a statement should be prepared setting out:

(a)  a list of issues that have been agreed, including, in each instance, the basis of agreement;

(b)  a list of issues that have not been agreed, including, in each instance, the basis of disagreement;

(c)  a list of any further issues that have arisen that were not included in the original agenda for discussion;

(d)  a record of further action, if any, to be taken or recommended, including as appropriate the holding of further discussions between experts.

18.11  The statement should be agreed and signed by all the parties to the discussion as soon as may be practicable.

18.12  Agreements between experts during discussions do not bind the parties unless the parties expressly agree to be bound by the agreement (CPR 35.12(5)). However, in view of the overriding objective [in Hong Kong, 'underlying objectives' taking effect in 2009 as part of the civil justice reforms], parties should give careful consideration before refusing to be bound by such an agreement and be able to explain their refusal should it become relevant to the issue of costs.

## [38.38.3]  Joint examination and report of expert witnesses

The court sometimes directs that the parties' experts, especially medical experts, carry out a joint examination and prepare a joint report. The power to make such a direction is arguably not express in Order 38 rule 38, but it may find support in general principles of case management. The personal injury practice direction (PD 18.1) provides (paras 81-84) that this procedure 'should' be followed where each party instructs its own expert.

In *Mok King Sun v Turn Round Co Ltd & Ors* HCPI 865/2007 (Fung J; 25.03.2009) (para 26) the court set out the following general observations on the benefits of joint examination and reporting:

(1)     avoidance of different observations on different occasions, or disputes on observations under single examination;

(2)     discussions amongst the experts to narrow down the issues;

(3)     specifying matters agreed and matters not agreed and the reasons for any non-agreement;

(4)     avoidance of numerous supplemental reports commenting on the reports of the other side;

(5)     minimising the need to call the experts to deal with matters which could have been dealt with under (1) to (4) above.

Many of the above benefits, and the added advantage of costs savings, can be achieved by reliance on a single joint expert pursuant to Order 38 rule 4A instead of each party instructing its own expert.

**39.     Disclosure of part of expert evidence** (O. 38 r. 39)

**Where the Court considers that any circumstances rendering it undesirable to give a direction under rule 37 relate to part only of the evidence sought to be adduced, the Court may, if it thinks fit, direct disclosure of the remainder.**

**41.     Expert evidence contained in statement** (O. 38 r. 41)

**Where an application is made under rule 36 in respect of expert evidence contained in a statement and the applicant alleges that the maker of the statement cannot or should not be called as a witness, the Court may direct that the provisions of rules 20 to 22 inclusive shall apply with such modifications as the Court thinks fit. (L.N. 152 of 2008)**

---

**NOTES**

**[38.41.1]  Order dispensing with calling author of expert report**
Order 38 rule 41 empowers the court to order that an expert report be received in evidence without the need to call the expert to give oral evidence. In the event of such an order the provisions of Order 38 part III concerning hearsay apply. It is understood that this power is sometimes exercised in personal injury cases.

The circumstances in which such an order is appropriate are similar to those where the court may exercise its power under Order 38 rule 4A to direct the parties to instruct a single joint expert: see the commentary under that rule.

**42.     Putting in evidence expert report disclosed by another party** (O. 38 r. 42)

**A party to any cause or matter may put in evidence any expert report disclosed to him by any other party in accordance with this Part of this Order.**

**43.**     **Time for putting expert report in evidence** (O. 38 r. 43)

Where a party to any cause or matter calls as a witness the maker of an expert report which has been disclosed under these rules, the report may be put in evidence at the commencement of the examination in chief of its maker or at such other time as the Court may direct. (L.N. 152 of 2008)

**44.**     **Revocation and variation of directions** (O. 38 r. 44)

Any direction given under this Part of this Order may on sufficient cause being shown be revoked or varied by a subsequent direction given at or before the trial of the cause or matter.

**(Enacted 1988)**

## ORDER 39

### EVIDENCE BY DEPOSITION: EXAMINERS OF THE COURT

**1.　Power to order depositions to be taken** (O. 39 r. 1)

**(1)　The Court may, in any cause or matter where it appears necessary for the purposes of justice, make an order (in Form No. 32 in Appendix A) for the examination on oath before a judge, an officer or examiner of the Court or some other person, at any place, of any person. (See also App. A, Form 31)**

**(2)　An order under paragraph (1) may be made on such terms (including, in particular, terms as to the giving of discovery before the examination takes place) as the Court thinks fit and may contain an order for the production of any document which appears to the Court to be necessary for the purposes of the examination.**

---

## NOTES

### [39.1.1]　Evidence by deposition
Order 39 rule 1 makes provision for the taking of evidence from a witness before trial in cases where there is reason to believe the witness might not be available to attend the trial. Evidence taken in this way is referred to as evidence 'by deposition', or 'on commission'. In cases where the witness is outside Hong Kong, see in addition, the subsequent rules of this Order.

### [39.1.2]　Comparison with English rules
Order 39 is taken from the Order of the same number in the former English RSC. That has been replaced by CPR 34.8 – 34.15, which are supplemented by practice direction.

### [39.1.3]　Evidence by video-link
It is now possible to take evidence from a witness by video-link. This has obvious advantages over evidence by deposition as the witness's evidence can be taken during the normal course of the trial. The High Court has a facility known as the 'technology court' which has video conferencing facilities ('VCF'). Its use is governed by practice direction 29, which provides that the court has a discretion as a part of case management to allow the facilities of the technology court to be used. In *Sun Legend Investments Ltd v Ho Yuk Wah David & Ors* [2008] 4 HKC 98, after reviewing various authorities, the court set out the following principles as to when it will allow evidence to be given in this manner:

(1)　Whether to permit the giving of evidence by means of VCF is a decision within the discretion of the court.

(2)　In general, the applicant should provide a valid reason for the use of VCF. The threshold for valid reason is not a high one, however.

(3)　The court should have regard to all the circumstances of the case. Relevant factors include the matters set out in paragraph 5 of practice direction 29*, the reason why the witness is unable or unwilling to attend the trial in person, the importance of the witness to the applicant's case and any prejudice to the other party.

(4)   The witness' unwillingness to testify in person at the trial because he is a fugitive from justice** may, depending on the circumstances of the case, be a good and sufficient reason for making a VCF order.

\* Paragraph 5 of practice direction 29 provides:

In making the decision, the court or tribunal shall take into account the views of all the parties, the availability of the technology court, the subject matter of the proceedings or the relevant part of the proceedings and all other material circumstances, including in particular, whether the proposed use of the technology court is likely:

(a)   to promote the fair and efficient disposal of the proceedings;

(b)   to save costs, and/or

(c)   materially to delay disposal of the proceedings.

\*\* See the commentary under Order 39 rule 2 concerning the circumstances in which a fugitive for justice might be permitted to give evidence by alternative means.

See also the commentary under Order 38 rule 2 as to the circumstances in which the court will order cross-examination on an affidavit, where similar considerations arise if the witness is unable or unwilling to attend court.

### [39.1.4]  Two-stage process

An application for an order that evidence be taken by deposition should be made by summons in form 31 in Appendix A to the rules. The order itself, if granted, should be in form 32: rule 1(1). That form of order provides that the evidence taken by deposition may be 'read and given in evidence' at trial without further proof of the absence of the witness other than an affidavit of the solicitor of the party intending to use the evidence. Notwithstanding the wording of the form, it has been held that an order under Order 39 rule 1 does not of itself render evidence by deposition admissible at trial. In *Hong Kong Kam Lan Koon Ltd v Realray Investments Ltd & Anor* [2004] 4 HKC 349 it was held that there is in fact a two-stage process: firstly, an order must be obtained under Order 39 rule 1 for the evidence to be taken by deposition, and secondly the party wishing to rely on the evidence at trial must make a subsequent application under Order 38 rule 9. That judgment was cited with approval on this point in *Credit Suisse v Lim Soon Fang Bryan* [2007] 3 SLR 414 (para 28).

### [39.1.5]  Circumstances in which order will be granted

The court's power under Order 39 rule 1 to order that evidence be taken by deposition is discretionary: *Kwong Hong Seng v Nippon Yusen Kaisha* (1920) 15 HKLR 31. The discretion will, in the words of rule 1(1), be exercised in favour of granting the order 'where it appears necessary for the purposes of justice'. In *Warner v Mosses* (1880) 16 ChD 100, 102–103, without confining the rule, the English Court of Appeal gave as examples cases where there is evidence a witness will not be able to attend trial on account of age or illness or other infirmity. In *Lee Samuel Tak v HK Chinese Christian Churches Union & Anor* HCAL 27/2008 (Chu J; 25.09.2009) (para 32) an order was refused partly on the ground that the evidence sought had no 'material relevance' to the issue to be decided.

#### [39.1.6]  Timing of application for deposition to be taken
Application for an order that evidence be taken by deposition should not normally be made until after the close of pleadings unless there are exceptional circumstances such as a witness about to depart Hong Kong as in *Yim Tak Wan v Tang Kai & Ors* [1961] 1 HKLR 539. Delay in making the application may result in it being refused. In *Kwong Hong Seng v Nippon Yusen Kaisha* (1920) 15 HKLR 31 an application to take deposition evidence in Norway was allowed despite delay, but on terms.

#### [39.1.7]  Deposition and discovery of documents
Order 39 rule 1(2) expressly empowers the court to order discovery before a deposition examination takes place, and to order production of documents necessary for the purposes of the examination. In *Lee Samuel Tak v HK Chinese Christian Churches Union & Anor* HCAL 27/2008 (Chu J; 25.09.2009) the applicant sought an order for taking deposition evidence from a witness in the United States solely for the purpose of requiring the witness to produce documents. The application was refused, partly on the ground that this was not a 'proper use' of the procedure (para 20).

#### [39.1.8]  Costs
The party applying for and obtaining an order for the taking of deposition evidence has to finance the commission. The costs will normally be in the cause. See *Midwood v Robinson* (1911) 6 HKLR 140. In that case, the court doubted that a defendant who obtains an order for the taking of deposition evidence can as a result seek security for the costs thereof against the plaintiff.

#### [39.1.9]  Before whom deposition may be taken
Rule 1(1) provides that a deposition under this Order may be taken before a judge, officer or examiner of the court 'or some other person'. Whoever is appointed, it should be a person who has power to administer an oath. In that regard see Order 114 and the commentary thereunder.

Though the rule contemplates that a deposition may take place before an *examiner* of the court, there does not appear to be any provision in Hong Kong for the appointment of such. In England CPR 34.15 expressly provides for appointment of barristers and solicitor-advocates of not less than 3 years experience to be examiners of the court.

In *Hong Kong Kam Lan Koon Ltd v Realray Investments Ltd* [2004] 4 HKC 349 the examination took place before a master.

#### [39.1.10]  Procedure at deposition
See Order 39 rule 8.

2.     **Where person to be examined is out of the jurisdiction** (O. 39 r. 2)
      **(1)   Where the person in relation to whom an order under rule 1 is required is out of the jurisdiction, an application may be made—**
            **(a)     for an order (in Form No. 34 in Appendix A) under that rule for the issue of a letter of request to the judicial authorities of**

the country in which that person is to take, or cause to be taken, the evidence of that person, or (See also App. A, Form 33)

    (b)    if the government of that country allows a person in that country to be examined before a person appointed by the Court, for an order (in Form No. 37 in Appendix A) under that rule appointing a special examiner to take the evidence of that person in that country. (See also App. A, Form 36)

    (2)   An application may be made for the appointment as special examiner of a British consul in the country in which the evidence is to be taken or his deputy—

    (a)    if there subsists with respect to that country a Civil Procedure Convention providing for the taking of the evidence of any person in that country for the assistance of proceedings in the Court, or

    (b)    with the consent of the Chief Secretary for Administration.

---

## NOTES

### [39.2.1] Order for examination of witness outside Hong Kong

Order 39 rule 2 makes provision for cases where a party wishes to take evidence by deposition (under Order 39 rule 1) from a witness who is outside Hong Kong. The rule provides for the issue of a letter of request to the competent judicial authorities in the place where the witness is, or the appointment of a special examiner or consular officer to take the evidence. The jurisdiction to issue letters of request is inherent, and the rules merely regulate its exercise: *Kwan Chui Kwok Ying & Anor v Tao Wai Chun & Ors* CACV 194/2002 (Woo & Cheung JJA; 13.12.2002), citing *Panayiotou v Sony Music Ltd* [1994] Ch 142. The power is clearly discretionary: *AG v Lui Lok* [1982] HKC 410, 415F (CA). With regard to criminal proceedings, see also sections 77E & 77F of the Evidence Ordinance (Cap 8).

An application may be made under Order 39 in judicial review proceedings. This is the case even with judicial review proceedings arising from a criminal context, by way of exception to the general rule that the RHC do not apply to apply to criminal proceedings. See Order 1 rule 2(3) and see *Chan Mei Yiu Paddy v SJ* [2008] 2 HKC 596 (CA).

### [39.2.2] Factors to be considered in application under Order 39 rule 2

The factors to be considered by the court in exercising its discretion under Order 39 rule 2 were summarised succinctly in *FWC v FSR* [1992] 1 HKC 490. Kaplan J said (at 495D–F):

Before making such an order, I must be satisfied that:

(1)    The evidence is directly material to an issue in the case and not merely evidence which may be incidentally useful in corroboration of other evidence (*Ehrmann v Ehrmann* [1896] 2 Ch 611 and *Langen v Tate* (1883) 24 Ch D 522).

(2)    The party seeking the order cannot bring the witness to this country to be examined at trial (*Lawson v Vacuum Brake Co* (1884) 27 Ch D 137).

(3)     The order is necessary for the purposes of justice (*Warner v Mosses* (1880) 16 Ch D 100 and O 39 r 1 . . .

The court should consider not only what the plaintiff's case requires, but the defendant's interests as well: *Berdan v Greenwood* (1880) 20 Ch D 764n (CA). In that case an order for the plaintiff's own evidence to be taken abroad was set aside on the ground that although there was evidence his health would suffer if he had to travel to England, it was 'still more important' in the particular case that the defendants should have a full opportunity to cross examine him before the tribunal which was to decide the case.

The court's jurisdiction to grant an order for the issue of a letter of request will not normally be exercised 'unless there is reason to suppose the foreign court would be receptive to the request': *Panayiotou v Sony Music Ltd* [1994] Ch 142, 150F. The court may be satisfied on this count by the fact that the foreign jurisdiction is a signatory to the Hague Convention 1970 (as to which see below) or, as in *Kwan Chui Kwok Ying & Anor v Kwan Chi On & Ors* CACV 194/2002 (Woo & Cheung JJA; 13.12.2002) (para 22) by evidence of the existence of an established practice in the foreign jurisdiction of executing letters of request received from abroad. In *Chan Mei Yiu Paddy & Ors v SJ (No 2)* [2008] 3 HKC 182 the court ordered issue of a letter of request despite the government's objection that it would not be acted upon by the authorities in Italy, causing humiliation to Hong Kong, and having a detrimental effect on the comity of nations.

### [39.2.3]  Fugitives from justice
Where a fugitive from justice seeks to use an alternative procedure for taking evidence, such as deposition or video-link, the court must grapple with opposing policy considerations. On the one hand, the court does not wish to be seen to assist a witness who wishes to avoid legal process. On the other hand, the court is required to do justice in the case before it. Cases in which the courts have dealt with this difficult question include the following:

- *Hongkong & Shanghai Banking Corp v Fung Wing King (Executor)* [1973]–[1976] HKC 164, where the court granted an application under Order 39 rule 2 in respect of a witness who did not wish to come to Hong Kong because of civil claims against him.
- *Okura & Co Ltd v Kowloon Container Warehouse Co Ltd (in liq) & Ors* [1977] HKLR 557 where the court refused an order in circumstances similar to those in the above case.
- *AG v Lui Lok* [1982] HKC 410; [1982] HKLR 413 where the Court of Appeal set aside an order for taking evidence abroad from a defendant who did not wish to come to Hong Kong where he faced criminal charges.
- *HKCT Trading Ltd v Li Luen Ping* [2001] 3 HKLRD 504 where the Court of First Instance considered itself bound by *AG v Lui Lok* (above) and refused an application by a defendant to give evidence by video-link. The defendant feared that if he returned to Hong Kong he would be detained by the ICAC for questioning.
- *Re Chow Kam Fai David* [2004] 2 HKC 645 (CA) where a witness who did not wish to come to Hong Kong because of an arrest warrant pursuant to Order 49B was refused permission to be cross-examined by video-link from Macau, on policy grounds.

- *Sun Legend Investments Ltd v Ho Yuk Wah David & Ors* [2008] 4 HKC 98 where a judge of the Court of First Instance acknowledged that the Court of Appeal's decision in *Re Chow Kam Fai David* (above) was binding, but came to a different result, referring to the subsequent decision of the House of Lords in *Polanski v Condé Nast Publications Ltd* [2005] 1 All ER 945. In *Polanski* the Lords (by a majority) held that the plaintiff was entitled to the assistance of the court, and could give evidence by video-link from France, although his reason for not wanting to travel to the United Kingdom was that he might face extradition to the United States on criminal charges. However *Sun Legend* was doubted and *Re Chow Kam Fai David* affirmed in *Mahajan v HCL Technologies (HK) Ltd & Ors* HCMP 1895/2010 (Rogers VP & Bharwaney J; 07.10.2010). The court sought to confine *Polanski* to its particular facts.

### [39.2.4]  Procedure on application for letter of request

An application for an order under Order 39 rule 2 should be made 'at the earliest opportunity': *FWC v FSR* [1992] 1 HKC 490, 495C. In *Re Letters of Request to Singapore and Arizona* [2003] 1 HKC 162 it was held that the party affected by the order must be given an opportunity to be heard. Such an application is considered to be interlocutory in nature with the result that hearsay may be included in the affidavit evidence under Order 41 rule 5(2): *FWC v FSR* (above, at 495A–B).

### [39.2.5]  The Hague Convention

Provision is made in an international convention which applies in Hong Kong for party states to assist each other in taking evidence. See the 'Convention on the Taking of Evidence Abroad in Civil Proceedings or Commercial Matters done at the Hague 18 March 1970', popularly known as the Hague Convention 1970. The text of the Convention and an up-to-date list of the states and territories in which it applies can be found on the Convention website (www.hcch.net).

The Hague Convention 1970 was extended to Hong Kong by the United Kingdom government with effect from 22 August 1978. China is not a party to the convention but shortly before the transfer of sovereignty on 1 July 1997 gave notice pursuant to article 153(2) of the Basic Law that the Convention would continue to apply to the HKSAR.

**3.      Order for issue of letter of request** (O. 39 r. 3)

**(1)   Where an order is made under rule 1 for the issue of a letter of request to the judicial authorities of a country to take, or cause to be taken, the evidence of any person in that country the following provisions of this rule shall apply.**

**(2)   The party obtaining the order must prepare the letter of request and lodge it in the Registry, and the letter must be in Form No. 35 in Appendix A, with such variations as the order may require.**

**(3)   If the evidence of the person to be examined is to be obtained by means of written questions, there must be lodged with the letter of request a copy of the interrogatories and cross-interrogatories to be put to him on examination.**

**(4)   Each document lodged under paragraph (2) or (3) must be accompanied by a translation of the document in the official language of the**

country in which the examination is to be taken or, if there is more than one official language of that country, in any one of those languages which is appropriate to the place in that country where the examination is to be taken unless—

      (a)    the Registrar has given a general direction in relation to that country that no translation need be provided, or

      (b)    the official language or one of the official languages of that country is English.

    (5)   Every translation lodged under paragraph (4) must be certified by the person making it to be a correct translation; and the certificate must contain a statement of that person's full name, of his address and of his qualifications for making the translation.

    (6)   The party obtaining the order must, when he lodges in the Registry the documents mentioned in paragraphs (2) to (5), also file in that office an undertaking signed by him or his solicitor to be responsible personally for all expenses incurred by the Chief Secretary for Administration in respect of the letter of request and, on receiving due notification of the amount of those expenses, to pay that amount to the Treasury and to produce a receipt for the payment to the Registrar. (L.N. 362 of 1997)

---

**NOTES**

**[39.3.1]  Letter of request to be lodged with registry**

Order 39 rule 3 provides that when the court has granted an order for the issue of a letter of request, the onus is on the party obtaining the order to prepare the letter and lodge it with the registry together with the other documents as set out in rule 3(3), (4) and (5). In the ordinary course of events the registry will send the letter to the Chief Secretary for Administration for onward transmission to the requested jurisdiction. The party obtaining the order must, at the time of lodging, file an undertaking to be responsible for all expenses incurred by the Chief Secretary (rule 3(6)).

    It is important that the letter of request be 'lodged' with the registry, and not filed. In *Kwan Chui Kwok Ying & Anor v Tao Wai Chun & Ors* CACV 194/2002 (Woo & Cheung JJA; 13.12.2002) solicitors mistakenly filed the letter of request. As a result, the registry took no action on it until the mistake came to light a year later.

**3A.    Examination otherwise than on oath** (O. 39 r. 3A)

    Notwithstanding the provisions of rule 1, where the person to be examined is out of the jurisdiction that person may be examined on oath or affirmation or otherwise in accordance with the procedure of the country in which the examination is to take place.

---

**NOTES**

**[39.3A.1]   Cross-reference**

'Oath' includes 'affirmation' in any case (see section 3 of the Interpretation and General Clauses Ordinance).

**4.     Enforcing attendance of witness at examination** (O.39 r. 4)
Where an order has been made under rule 1—

    (a)    for the examination of any person before an officer of the Court or some other person (in this rule and rules 5 to 14 referred to as "the examiner"), or

    (b)    for the cross-examination before the examiner of any person who has made an affidavit which is to be used in any cause or matter,

the attendance of that person before the examiner and the production by him of any document at the examination may be enforced by writ of subpoena in like manner as the attendance of a witness and the production by a witness of a document at a trial may be enforced.

**5.     Refusal of witness to attend, be sworn, etc.** (O. 39 r. 5)
    **(1)**     If any person, having been duly summoned by writ of subpoena to attend before the examiner, refuses or fails to attend or refuses to be sworn for the purpose of the examination or to answer any lawful question or produce any document therein, a certificate of his refusal or failure, signed by the examiner, must be filed in the Registry, and upon the filing of the certificate the party by whom the attendance of that person was required may apply to the Court for an order requiring that person to attend, or to be sworn, or to answer any question or produce any document, as the case may be.

    **(2)**     An application for an order under this rule may be made ex parte.

    **(3)**     If the Court makes an order under this rule it may order the person against whom the order is made to pay any costs occasioned by his refusal or failure.

    **(4)**     A person who wilfully disobeys any order made against him under paragraph (1) is guilty of contempt of court.

**6.     Appointment of time and place for examination** (O. 39 r. 6)
    **(1)**     The examiner must give the party on whose application the order for examination was made by a notice appointing the place and time at which, subject to any application by the parties, the examination shall be taken, and such time shall, having regard to the convenience of the persons to be examined and all the circumstances of the case, be as soon as practicable after the making of the order.

    **(2)**     The party to whom a notice under paragraph (1) is given must, on receiving it, forthwith give notice of the appointment to all the other parties.

**7.     Examiner to have certain documents** (O. 39 r. 7)
    The party on whose application the order for examination before the examiner was made must furnish the examiner with copies of such of the documents in the cause or matter as are necessary to inform the examiner of the questions at issue in the cause or matter.

**8.     Conduct of examination** (O. 39 r. 8)
    **(1)**     Subject to any directions contained in the order for examination—

     (a)    **any person ordered to be examined before the examiner may be cross-examined and re-examined, and**

     (b)    **the examination, cross-examination and re-examination of persons before the examiner shall be conducted in like manner as at the trial of a cause or matter.**

**(2)    The examiner may put any question to any person examined before him as to the meaning of any answer made by that person or as to any matter arising in the course of the examination.**

**(3)    The examiner may, if necessary, adjourn the examination from time to time.**

---

## NOTES

### [39.8.1]  Procedure at deposition

A witness being deposed under this Order is examined in much the same way as a witness at trial: rule 8(1)(b). The witness is examined in chief and the other parties are given 'a fair opportunity to cross-examine': *Hong Kong Kam Lan Koon Ltd v Realray Investments Ltd* [2004] 4 HKC 349, 359F–G.

**9.    Examination of additional witnesses** (O. 39 r. 9)

    **The examiner may, with the written consent of all the parties to the cause or matter, take the examination of any person in addition to those named or provided for in the order for examination, and must annex such consent to the original deposition of that person.**

**10.    Objection to questions** (O. 39 r. 10)

    **(1)    If any person being examined before the examiner objects to answer any question put to him, or if objection is taken to any such question, that question, the ground for the objection and the answer to any such question to which objection is taken must be set out in the deposition of that person or in a statement annexed thereto.**

    **(2)    The validity of the ground for objecting to answer any such question or for objecting to any such question shall be decided by the Court and not by the examiner, but the examiner must state to the parties his opinion thereon, and the statement of his opinion must be set out in the deposition or in a statement annexed thereto.**

    **(3)    If the Court decides against the person taking the objection it may order him to pay the costs occasioned by his objection.**

**11.    Taking of depositions** (O. 39 r. 11)

    **(1)    The deposition of any person examined before the examiner must be taken down by the examiner or a shorthand writer or some other person in the presence of the examiner but, subject to paragraph (2) and rule 10(1), the deposition need not set out every question and answer so long as it contains as nearly as may be the statement of the person examined.**

    **(2)    The examiner may direct the exact words of any particular**

question and the answer thereto to be set out in the deposition if that question and answer appear to him to have special importance.

(3)    The deposition of any person shall be read to him, and he shall be asked to sign it, in the presence of such of the parties as may attend, but the parties may agree in writing to dispense with the foregoing provision. If a person refuses to sign a deposition when asked under this paragraph to do so, the examiner must sign the deposition.

(4)    The original deposition of any person, authenticated by the signature of the examiner before whom it was taken, must be sent by the examiner to the Registry and shall be filed therein.

---

NOTES

### [39.11.1]  Wording of Order 39 rule 11
In some printings of these rules, Order 39 rule 11(4) refers to 'the examiner before them (*sic*) it was taken'. An examination of the original text of the rule in the 1988 revision shows that 'them' should be 'whom'. The wording set out above is correct, *ie* 'the examiner before whom it was taken'.

**12.    Time taken by examination to be indorsed on depositions** (O. 39 r. 12)
Before sending any deposition to the Registry under rule 11(4) the examiner must indorse on the deposition a statement signed by him of the time occupied in taking the examination and the fees received in respect thereof.

**13.    Special report by examiner** (O. 39 r. 13)
The examiner may make a special report to the Court with regard to any examination taken before him and with regard to the absence or conduct of any person thereat, and the Court may direct such proceedings to be taken, or make such order, on the report as it thinks fit.

**14.    Order for payment of examiner's fees** (O. 39 r. 14)
(1)    If the fees and expenses due to an examiner are not paid he may report that fact to the Court, and the Court may direct the Law Officer (Civil Law) to apply for an order against the party on whose application the order for examination was made to pay the examiner the fees and expenses due to him in respect of the examination. (L.N. 362 of 1997)

(2)    An order under this rule shall not prejudice any determination on the taxation of costs or otherwise as to the party by whom the costs of the examination are ultimately to be borne.

**15.    Perpetuation of testimony** (O. 39 r. 15)
(1)    Witnesses shall not be examined to perpetuate testimony unless an action has been begun for the purpose.

(2)    Any person who would under the circumstances alleged by him to exist become entitled, upon the happening of any future event, to any honour, title, dignity or office, or to any estate or interest in any real or personal property, the right or claim to which cannot be brought to trial by him before

the happening of such event, may begin an action to perpetuate any testimony which may be material for establishing such right or claim.

(3)    No action to perpetuate the testimony of witnesses shall be set down for trial.

(Enacted 1988)

## ORDER 40

### COURT EXPERT

1.    **Appointment of expert to report on certain questions** (O. 40 r. 1)
      **(1)    In any cause or matter which is to be tried without a jury and in which any question for an expert witness arises the Court may at any time, on the application of any party, appoint an independent expert or, if more than one such question arises, 2 or more such experts, to inquire and report upon any question of fact or opinion not involving questions of law or of construction.**

      **An expert appointed under this paragraph is referred to in this Order as a "court expert".**

      **(2)    Any court expert in a cause or matter shall, if possible, be a person agreed between the parties and, failing agreement, shall be nominated by the Court.**

      **(3)    The question to be submitted to the court expert and the instructions (if any) given to him shall, failing agreement between the parties, be settled by the Court.**

      **(4)    In this rule "expert", in relation to any question arising in a cause or matter, means any person who has such knowledge or experience of or in connection with that question that his opinion on it would be admissible in evidence.**

---

## NOTES

### [40.1.1]  Discretion to appoint court expert
Order 40 rule 1 provides for the appointment of a 'court expert' to inquire and report on questions of fact or opinion.  The question to be reported on must not involve a question of law or construction. In *Re Peregrine Investments Holdings Ltd* [1998] 3 HKC 1, 23I – 24A the court doubted that it has power to appoint an expert under this rule to advise on liquidators' remuneration in a winding-up case.

      The power to appoint a court expert is discretionary and a judge's decision will not be interfered with on appeal unless it is 'plainly wrong': *Nguyen Ho & Ors v Director of Immigration & Anor* CACV 135/1990 (Cons VP, Kempster JA & Sears J; 25.09.1990).

### [40.1.2]  Distinction between court expert and joint expert
In addition to the power under Order 40 to appoint a 'court expert', the court has power under Order 38 rule 4A to direct the parties to appoint a single joint expert. The distinction is that a court expert is appointed by the court, whereas a single joint expert is appointed by the parties. Order 40 applies only to the former, not the latter. See *Tang Kam Sheung v Tang Kit Yee* HCA 677/2007 (Chu J; 25.09.2009) (para 9). To a large extent the distinction is formal rather than substantive. This is because any expert witness has an over-riding duty to the court which supersedes any duty to the party or parties instructing him or her: Order 38 rule 35(2).

**[40.1.3] Considerations relevant to exercise of discretion**

Factors which have influenced the court's exercise of discretion to appoint a court expert under Order 40 rule 1 include the following:

- *Saving time and expense* - The rule contemplates appointment of a single expert on any one question to be inquired upon. Thus time and expense can be saved by adopting this procedure rather than leaving it to the parties to instruct their own experts. See *Nguyen Ho* (above) where the Court of Appeal recognised this as a relevant consideration in the exercise of discretion, though at the end of the day it did not interfere with the judge's decision not to appoint a court expert. See also *Fishenden v Higgs & Hill, Ltd* [1935] All ER Rep 435, 452-3 (CA).

- *Impartiality* – An expert appointed under this rule must be 'independent': rule 1(1). In *Abbey National Mortgages plc v Key Surveyors Ltd* [1996] 1 WLR 1534, 1542 (CA) the court noted that experts instructed by the parties sometimes tend to espouse the cause of those instructing them, and suggested that a court appointed expert might prove more reliable.

- *Encourage resolution of dispute* - In *Re Forecast Nominee Ltd* [1996] 4 HKC 12, 26G a court expert was appointed to advise on the value of shares of a company despite opposition of one of the parties. The court was of the view that the appointment could 'encourage a resolution of the present dispute'.

- *Timing* – Although Order 40 rule 1 expressly provides for the appointment of a court expert 'at any time', in *Ernest Cheong PTL Chartered Surveyors v KM Engineering & Development Sdn Bhd* [1996] 4 MLJ 438 an application made by a party after his case had closed was rejected as too late.

Some disadvantages of using court appointed experts are discussed in the Australian Law Reform Commission's background paper No 6 on Experts:

- In some cases costs might not be saved, but actually increased, for example if the parties wish to instruct their own experts to monitor, assess or challenge the opinions of the court expert.

- Court time may not be saved because the court may have to be involved in selecting and instructing the court expert.

- There is a possibility of bias or perceived bias of the court in favour of its own expert.

- Where there are distinct schools of thought within a particular discipline, choice of a single expert would tend to favour the chosen expert's school.

**[40.1.4] Identifying the expert to be appointed**

It is obviously preferable if the parties can agree which expert should be appointed by the court. If that is not possible the court may ask the parties to put forward their own nominees for its consideration (as in *Re Tai Lap Investment Co Ltd* [1998] 4 HKC 438, 447I-448A) or make a nomination of its own (as in *Re Forecast Nominee Ltd* [1996] 4 HKC 12, 26H). In *Mak Wo Ping v Mak Lam Pui Yuk* [1987] 1 HKC 136 (CA) it was ordered that in the absence of agreement on an expert, either party could apply for the report to be requisitioned by the Director of Legal Aid.

**2.    Report of court expert** (O. 40 r. 2)

    **(1)   The court expert must send his report to the Court, together with**

such number of copies thereof as the Court may direct, and the Registrar must send copies of the report to the parties or their solicitors.

(2) The Court may direct the court expert to make a further or supplemental report.

(3) Any part of a court expert's report which is not accepted by all the parties to the cause or matter in which it is made shall be treated as information furnished to the Court and be given such weight as the Court thinks fit.

---

NOTES

**[40.2.1] Scope of court expert's report**

A court-appointed expert is not confined to giving evidence from direct first-hand knowledge, but may state opinions based on reliable information obtained on making enquiries within the field of his or her professional expertise: *Abbey National Mortgages plc v Key Surveyors Nationwide Ltd* [1996] 1 WLR 1534 (CA).

**[40.2.2] Challenge to report of court expert**

The parties are not bound to accept the report of a court-appointed expert. The expert's report may be challenged and it is up to the court to attach such weight as it thinks fit. See rule 2(3). This situation differs from that of expert reports prepared pursuant to contractual provisions. Such reports are sometimes deemed by the contract to be binding and can be challenged only on limited grounds such as that the expert departed from instructions in a material respect. See the commentary concerning party-appointed experts under Order 38 rule 37. In *Re Golden Bright Ltd* [2007] 1 HKC 89 (para 31) it was observed that the court has 'more flexible powers to regulate the procedure where an independent expert is appointed under O 40 r 1(1)'.

Where the report of a court-appointed expert is challenged the court may review its order appointing the expert (as in *Jordan v Norfolk County Council* [1994] 1 WLR 1353) or it may direct the expert to prepare a further or supplemental report under rule 2(2) (as in *Re Golden Bright Ltd*, above).

There are numerous cases in which the court has dealt with allegations that a court-appointed expert's report should not be accepted on account of partiality or bias. The test in such cases is actual partiality or bias rather than the mere appear ance thereof: *Re Golden Bright Ltd* (above, at para 26), referring to *Macro v Thompson (No 3)* [1997] 2 BCLC 36, 65G.

**3.     Experiments and tests** (O. 40 r. 3)

If the court expert is of opinion that an experiment or test of any kind (other than one of a trifling character) is necessary to enable him to make a satisfactory report he shall inform the parties or their solicitors and shall, if possible, make an arrangement with them as to the expenses involved, the persons to attend and other relevant matters; and if the parties are unable to agree on any of those matters it shall be settled by the Court.

**4.     Cross-examination of court expert** (O. 40 r. 4)

Any party may, within 14 days after receiving a copy of the court expert's report, apply to the Court for leave to cross-examine the expert on his report, and on that application the Court shall make an order for the cross-examination of the expert by all the parties either—

    **(a)**    at the trial, or

    **(b)**    before an examiner at such time and place as may be specified in the order.

**5.**    **Remuneration of court expert** (O. 40 r. 5)

    **(1)**    The remuneration of the court expert shall be fixed by the Court and shall include a fee for his report and a proper sum for each day during which he is required to be present either in court or before an examiner.

    **(2)**    Without prejudice to any order providing for payment of the court expert's remuneration as part of the costs of the cause or matter, the parties shall be jointly and severally liable to pay the amount fixed by the Court for his remuneration, but where the appointment of a court expert is opposed the Court may, as a condition of making the appointment, require the party applying for the appointment to give such security for the remuneration of the expert as the Court thinks fit.

---

**NOTES**

**[40.5.1]**    **Payment of court expert**

Order 40 rule 5 provides that a court expert's remuneration is to be fixed by the court. Parties are jointly and severally liable to pay the court expert, but sums so paid may be recovered if the court makes an order for the costs of the proceedings.

    In *Re Forecast Nominee Ltd* [1996] 4 HKC 12, 27A-B the court ordered that the cost of the court expert's report in winding-up proceedings be in the cause of the petition, to first be disbursed out of the funds of the company.

**6.**    **Calling of expert witnesses** (O. 40 r. 6)

    Where a court expert is appointed in a cause or matter, any party may, on giving to the other parties a reasonable time before the trial notice of his intention to do so, call one expert witness to give evidence on the question reported on by the court expert but no party may call more than one such witness without the leave of the Court, and the Court shall not grant leave unless it considers the circumstances of the case to be exceptional.

    **(Enacted 1988)**

**ORDER 41**

**AFFIDAVITS**

---

## NOTES

### [41.0.1]  Application of Order 41 to affirmations

In Order 41, and throughout these rules, the word 'affidavit' is used. An affirmation is an equivalent document, of equal 'force and effect': Oaths and Declarations Ordinance (Cap 11), section 7(5). According to the definition of 'oath' and 'affidavit' in section 3 of the Interpretation and General Clauses Ordinance (Cap 1), those words are to be construed as including 'affirmation'.

### [41.0.2]  Distinction between affidavit and affirmation

In Hong Kong affirmations are generally used in preference to affidavits, unlike the situation in some other common law jurisdictions. The distinction between an affidavit and an affirmation is historical, and has little, if any, remaining legal significance.

Notionally an affidavit is made on oath, meaning that the maker invokes belief in a deity in swearing to tell the truth. See section 5 of the Oaths and Declarations Ordinance. Affirmations were introduced in the 19th century to enable persons without such belief to give evidence of equal weight. An interesting historical source on this point is Norton-Kyshe, History of the Laws and Courts of Hong Kong (HK: Veitch & Lee, 1971) vol 1 144-5.

Does it matter whether an affidavit or an affirmation is used? Certainly not from the point of view of the weight of the evidence given. See section 7(5) of the Oaths and Declarations Ordinance. Indeed it has been argued that the distinction should be abolished: see Litton, (1985) 15 HKLJ 1. However there may be room to argue that whereas an affidavit made by a non-believer is acceptable, an affirma tion made by a believer may not. This results from the wording of sections 6 and 7(2) of the Oaths and Declarations Ordinance. The former provides that an oath (affidavit) is acceptable whether or not the deponent has any religious belief; whereas the latter uses permissive language suggesting that only a non-believer may make an affirmation. Whatever the strict legal position, no court in modern Hong Kong is likely to welcome argument on this point.

### [41.0.3]  Purpose and use of affidavits

Affidavits are a means of placing evidence before the court in writing. They are suitable for circumstances where there are unlikely to be contentious issues of fact. They are usually used in interlocutory applications and may be used at some types of substantive hearing, such as proceedings by way of originating summons (Order 28 rule 1A) and judicial review (Order 53 rules 3 & 6). In unusual circumstances affidavit evidence may be used at the trial of an action begun by writ (Order 38 rule 2).

### [41.0.4]  Affidavits should be confined to evidence

Because an affidavit is a vehicle for putting evidence before the court, argument or submissions should not normally be included. In *Nelson Delivery Service Ltd v Wong Kan & Anor* CACV 136/1986 (Fuad JA & Power J; 11.12.1986) the court quoted with approval from *Alfred Dunhill Ltd & Anor v Sunoptic SA & Anor* [1979] FSR 337, 352 where Roskill LJ said:

> Affidavits are designed to place facts, whether disputed or otherwise, before the tribunal for whose help they are prepared. They are not designed as a receptacle for or as a vehicle for legal arguments. Draftsmen of affidavits should not, as a general rule, put into the mouths of the intended deponents legal arguments of which those deponents are unlikely ever to have heard. Legal arguments, especially in interlocutory proceedings, should come from the mouths of those best qualified to advance them and not be put into the mouths of deponents.

In the same case Megaw LJ said, at 373, that 'submissions of law' and 'forensic argument' are 'wholly out of place in an affidavit, as it would be in the oral evidence of a witness'.

In *Deak & Ors v Deak Perera FE Ltd* [1990] 2 HKC 198, 208 (CA) the court was highly critical of affidavit material which was 'extremely argumentative and, what is worse, argumentative in a heated sort of way'. It was suggested that the court should consider striking out such material, possibly with costs against the responsible solicitor. See also *Dah Sing Bank Ltd v Sing Hai Handbags Manuf'y Ltd & Ors* [2007] 3 HKC 515 (paras 14–19) where the court was highly critical of 'lawyerese' designed to prove a case being put into the affirmations of lay persons, and held that very little weight could be given to them. Similarly speculation, supposition and innuendo have no place in an affidavit or affirmation: *Re Wah Ying Cheong Co Ltd* HCCW 225/1996 (Kwan J; 05.10.2007).

See also Betts, 'Practice and Procedure: A Master's View', in Law Lectures for Practitioners 1987 (HK: Hong Kong Law Journal Ltd, 1987), 227, 235-6, where a former registrar advised practitioners that padding an affidavit with irrelevancies and arguments can obscure good points of fact.

**[41.0.5]     Cross-examination upon affidavit**
See the commentary under Order 38 rule 2.

**1.     Form of affidavit** (O. 41 r. 1)

**(1)     Subject to paragraphs (2) and (3), every affidavit sworn in a cause or matter must be entitled in that cause or matter.**

**(2)     Where a cause or matter is entitled in more than one matter, it shall be sufficient to state the first matter followed by the words "and other matters", and where a cause or matter is entitled in a matter or matters and between parties, that part of the title which consists of the matter or matters may be omitted.**

**(3)     Where there are more plaintiffs than one, it shall be sufficient to state the full name of the first followed by the words "and others", and similarly with respect to defendants.**

**(4)     Every affidavit must be expressed in the first person and, unless the Court otherwise directs, must state the place of residence of the deponent and his occupation or, if he has none, his description, and if he is, or is employed by, a party to the cause or matter in which the affidavit is sworn, the affidavit must**

state that fact. In the case of a deponent who is giving evidence in a professional, business or other occupational capacity the affidavit may, instead of stating the deponent's place of residence, state the address at which he works, the position he holds and the name of his firm or employer, if any.

(5) Whether or not both sides of the paper are used, the printed, written or typed sides of the paper of every affidavit must be numbered consecutively.

(6) Every affidavit must be divided into paragraphs numbered consecutively, each paragraph being as far as possible confined to a distinct portion of the subject.

(7) Dates, sums and other numbers must be expressed in an affidavit in figures and not in words.

(8) Every affidavit must be signed by the deponent and the jurat must be completed and signed by the person before whom it is sworn.

(HK)(9)Where any affidavit has been interpreted to the deponent before being sworn it shall contain a statement to that effect, state the name and address of the person who interpreted it, and be signed by him.

---

## NOTES

### [41.1.1]    Formal requirements for affidavits and affirmations
Order 41 rule 1 lays down certain formal requirements for affidavits and affirmations. In addition reference should be made to the Oaths and Declarations Ordinance (Cap 11) and to Practice Direction 10.1 (which may be viewed on the judiciary website, or that of HKLII).

### [41.1.2]    Oath or affirmation must be made orally
When swearing an affidavit in writing, the deponent should orally state his oath. The same applies to affirmations and statutory declarations. See *R v Low Robert Eli* [1996] 4 HKC 125.

### [41.1.3]    Prescribed form
There is no prescribed form of written affidavit in these rules. Reference may be made to the form which is posted on the judiciary's website. In addition reference should be made to relevant legislation. Section 7(4) of the Oaths and Declarations Ordinance (Cap 11) provides that an affirmation in writing shall commence with the words 'I,      , of    , solemnly and sincerely affirm' and end 'Affirmed at this     day of      19    , Before me      .' The wording in section 7(4) is mandatory. However, in practice one often encounters written affirmations which are embellished with extra words. As to the consequences of defects of form see Order 41 rule 4 and the commentary thereunder.

### [41.1.4]    Affidavit to be headed with style of cause
Affidavits and affirmations are normally made for use in legal proceedings. Order 41 rule 1(1) requires that they be headed with the style of cause of those proceedings.

**[41.1.5]    Shortened form of style of cause for use in affidavits**

Order 42 rule 1 (2) & (3) permit a shortened form of style of cause to be used on an affidavit. In order to save paper in cases where the style of cause is lengthy, the profession has been encouraged to make greater use of those paragraphs. See the letter from the Registrar dated 21 August 2003 included in Law Society circular 03-306 (PA), the text of which is available to members on the society's website.

**[41.1.6]    Rule 1(4) – affidavit to be expressed in the first person**

Affidavits and affirmations are required by rule 1(4) to be expressed in the first person. This is invariably the practice and it is difficult to imagine the third person being used, though older editions of the English Supreme Court Practice refer to that having been permitted in the past.

**[41.1.7]    Rule 1(4) – address of deponent**

Rule 1(4) requires that an affidavit state the address of the deponent. This must be the deponent's 'place of residence' but, if the affidavit is made in a 'professional, business or other occupational capacity', the place of work may be stated. An affidavit is not made in an occupational capacity merely because the cause of action arose during the course of or at the place of employment: *Tsui Koon Wah v Lam King Yuen & Ors* HCA 890/2003 (Tang J; 27.05.2004). However a solicitor, agent or employee of a party making an affidavit on its behalf may, and normally will state the place of work.

   Although mandatory language is used in the rule, the court is unlikely to reject an affidavit which does not comply with the requirement to set out the deponent's address. The purpose of the requirement is identification, and where there is no doubt as to the identity of the deponent the court will be reluctant to give effect to a technical objection: *Tsui Koon Wah* (above). Instead the court may proceed on the basis of a direction or undertaking that a corrective affidavit be filed, as in *Standfast Int'l Insurance Co Ltd v Lau Ming Kit & Anor* HCA 2295/1971 (Registrar Jones; 14.12.1971) and *Liu Yiu Keung Stephen v Akan Group Ltd* HCA 926/2004 (Chu J; 22.02.2005). See also the commentary under rule 4.

   An affidavit which gives only an 'illusory' address for the deponent may be rejected: *Ka Wah Bank Ltd v Low Chung Song & Ors* HCA 4191/1987 (Deputy Judge Cruden; 23.06.1988) (appeal allowed on other grounds – see [1989] 1 HKLR 451), citing *Hyde v Hyde* (1888) 59 LT 523.

   And see *Nelson Telecommunications Group (Asia) Ltd v United Land Network Technologies Ltd* DCCJ 5962/2005 (Judge Lok; 24.11.2008) where the court struck out two affidavits where there was evidence that the deponents were not actually residing at or occupying the addresses given.

**[41.1.8]    Rule 1(4) – occupation of deponent**

Order 41 rule 1(4) requires that an affidavit state the deponent's occupation or, if he has none, 'his description'. It is insufficient to state 'clerk' or 'trainee solicitor' without naming the firm or principal: *Shakespear v Willan* (1850) 19 LJ Ex 184; *R v Reeve* (1843) 114 ER 877. Similarly a company director should state the name of the company: *Re Church Press Ltd* (1917) 116 LT 247. Appropriate descriptions would include 'unemployed', 'retired' and 'of no occupation', but not 'gentleman': *Re Orde* (1883) 24 Ch D 271 (CA).

In *Estate of Yang Sen Hui (deceased) v Pao Yuen Tung Hsing Yieh Co Ltd* [1982] HKC 81, 101G-102D (CA) the court rejected an objection that an affirmation did not spell out clearly whether or not the deponent was an employee of the party on whose behalf the affirmation was made.

### [41.1.9]    Rule 1(5) – physical assembly of an affidavit

Order 41 rule 1(5) contemplates both sides of the paper being used in preparing an affidavit. Pages are to be numbered sequentially. In England (after implementation of the Woolf reforms) it is provided by practice direction 32 that only one side of the paper should normally be used. Unlike England there is no requirement in Hong Kong that A4 size paper be used. See also practice direction 10.1 (reproduced below) which sets out additional requirements for the physical assembly of affidavits.

### [41.1.10]    Rule 1(8) – signature and jurat

An affidavit must be signed by the deponent and the person before whom it is sworn. A clause known as the 'jurat' at the end of the affidavit will state when, where and before whom it was sworn. An affidavit may be sworn before a solicitor holding a current practising certificate (Legal Practitioners Ordinance (Cap 159), section 7A), commissioner for oaths appointed by the Chief Justice under Order 114, justice of the peace (Justices of the Peace Ordinance (Cap 510), section 5) or notary public (Legal Practitioners Ordinance (Cap 159) section 40B(2)(c)). Barristers are not empowered to administer oaths in Hong Kong, unlike the situation in England under the Commissioner for Oaths Acts.

### [41.1.11]    Rule 1(9) – language and interpretation of affidavits

Affidavits, like all other documents required to be filed or served, may be written in English or Chinese: see article 9 of the Basic Law of the HKSAR and see rule 4 of the High Court Civil Procedure (Use of Language) Rules (Cap 5). Where the deponent does not understand the language in which the affidavit is written it must be interpreted to him (Oaths and Declarations Ordinance (Cap 11), section 8). Order 41 rule 1(9) requires that where an affidavit has been interpreted this fact must be stated, along with the name, address and signature of the interpreter. Section 8 of the Oaths and Declarations Ordinance (Cap 11) additionally requires that the interpreter be sworn.

The common practice is to append to the affidavit or affirmation a declaration by the interpreter in a form similar to that set out in Schedule 1 Part III of the Oaths and Declarations Ordinance which prescribes the following form of declaration or oath by the interpreter:

> I, CD, of      , solemnly and sincerely declare [or swear] that I well understand the official language in which this document is written and [state the language in which the contents of this document are interpreted] language and that I have truly, distinctly, and audibly interpreted the contents of this document to the declarant [insert name], and that I will truly and faithfully interpret the declaration about to be administered to him.

> (Signed) CD

> Interpreter

Declared at        in Hong Kong this    day of     19
Before me,

[Signature and designation, ie
Justice of the Peace/Notary Public/
Commissioner for Oaths.]

## [41.1.12] Practice direction on affidavits

Additional requirements as to the form of affidavits and affirmations are set out in practice direction 10.1 which dates back to October 1989 and was revised with effect from February 1999. The practice direction (which can be viewed on the judiciary's website www.judiciary.gov.hk or that of the Hong Kong Legal Information Institute www.hklii.org, both of which are accessible by the general public free-of-charge) deals with the marking of affidavits, exhibits, numbering and other matters.

**2. Affidavit by 2 or more deponents** (O. 41 r. 2)

**Where an affidavit is made by 2 or more deponents, the names of the persons making the affidavit must be inserted in the jurat except that, if the affidavit is sworn by both or all the deponents at one time before the same person, it shall be sufficient to state that it was sworn by both (or all) of the "above named" deponents.**

**3. Affidavit by illiterate or blind person** (O. 41 r. 3)

**Where it appears to the person administering the oath that the deponent is illiterate or blind, he must certify in the jurat that—**

     **(a)**    **the affidavit was read in his presence to the deponent,**

     **(b)**    **the deponent seemed perfectly to understand it, and**

     **(c)**    **the deponent made his signature or mark in his presence;**

**and the affidavit shall not be used in evidence without such a certificate unless the Court is otherwise satisfied that it was read to and appeared to be perfectly understood by the deponent.**

---

## NOTES

### [41.3.1] Procedure where deponent unable to read

Order 41 rule 3 lays down special procedures to be followed when an affidavit is made by a person who is unable to read, whether by reason of blindness or illiteracy. As to the similar problem of lack of knowledge of the official language in which an affidavit is written see the commentary on Order 41 rule 1(9) above.

In the case of a blind or illiterate deponent it must be certified in the jurat that the affidavit was read to the deponent, who seemed to understand it, and that the deponent signed or marked the affidavit in the presence of the person so certifying. Such a jurat might take the following form:

AFFIRMED AT,)

Hong Kong this    day of)

20XX, Before me, through the)

interpretation of CD, the)

deponent subsequently making)

his mark hereon in my presence)


_____

Solicitor/Commissioner for Oaths


    I, EF, clerk to X & Y, Solicitors for the Plaintiff/Defendant, of [address], solemnly and sincerely declare that I well understand the official language in which this document is written and the Cantonese dialect and that I have truly, distinctly and audibly read over and interpreted the contents of this affirmation to the affirmant, AB, who seemed perfectly to understand the contents of this affirmation, and that I will truly and faithfully interpret the affirmation about to be administered to him.


DECLARED at             )

Hong Kong, this    day of     20XX)

Before me,


_____

Solicitor/Commissioner for Oaths

**4.**      **Use of defective affidavit** (O. 41 r. 4)
    **An affidavit may, with the leave of the Court, be filed or used in evidence notwithstanding any irregularity in the form thereof.**

_____

**NOTES**

**[41.4.1]**      **Leave to use irregular affidavit**
Under Order 41 rule 4 the court may permit an affidavit to be filed or used notwithstanding any irregularity in form. Examples of the circumstances in which this power has been used include the following:

•     *Failure to state address of deponent* – The court will normally grant leave to rely on an affidavit which fails to comply with the requirement in rule 1(4) to state the address of the deponent. See *Ka Wah Bank Ltd v Low Chung Song & Ors* HCA 4191/1987 (Deputy Judge Cruden; 23.06.1988) (appeal allowed on other grounds – [1989] 1 HKLR 451). See also the cases cited in the commentary under rule 1(4) in which the court has granted leave on terms that a corrective affidavit be filed.

•     *Failure to comply with requirements as to information or belief evidence* – In *Sharp Kabushiki Kaisha v Acker Trading Ltd* [1993] 2 HKC 490, 493B-C the court, without referring to any authority, found it had a discretion to admit an affirmation which breached the requirements of rule 5(2) as to information or belief evidence. If it exists, the source of this discretion may be Order 41 rule 4 or Order 2 rule 1. However, there are some cases in which failure to comply with rule 5 has been fatal – see the commentary under that rule. Could it be that rule 4 does not apply because a breach of rule 5(2) goes beyond 'irregularity in form'?

- *Affidavit in the form of statutory declaration* – In *Fort Crown Investments Ltd v Tam Virginia* CACV 173/2005 (Rogers VP, Cheung & Tang JJA; 05.01.2006) it was held that under rule 4 the court could treat a document in the form of a statutory declaration under the Oaths and Declarations Ordinance as if it were an affidavit.

- *Affirmation not using prescribed wording* – In *Ngai Po Lun Paul v Chan Cheryl* [1990] 2 HKC 291 (CA) the court cited rule 4 in allowing a document which had been affirmed without following the wording prescribed by section 7(4) of the Oaths and Declarations Ordinance to be used.

- *Incomplete jurat* – In *Hotung v Ho Yuen Ki & Ors* [2007] 2 HKC 246 (para 15) the court used its power under rule 4 to permit an affidavit to be used notwithstanding the fact the jurat did not state the address at which the affidavit was sworn. The missing information had been provided separately by e-mail.

- *Failure to produce exhibit* – In *Hotung* (above, para 11) the court was prepared to overlook failure to produce an exhibit where there was no doubt as to which document was being referred to in the affidavit.

As subsidiary legislation, rule 4 should not apply to breaches of the Oaths and Declarations Ordinance (Cap 11). See section 28(1)(b) of 1 see *Mohan v McElney* [1983] HKLR 308.

**5.     Contents of affidavit** (O. 41 r. 5)
**(1)     Subject to Order 14, rules 2(2) and 4(2), to Order 86, rule 2(1), to paragraph (2) of this rule and to any order made under Order 38, rule 3, an affidavit may contain only such facts as the deponent is able of his own knowledge to prove.**
**(2)     An affidavit sworn for the purpose of being used in interlocutory proceedings may contain statements of information or belief with the sources and grounds thereof.**

---

## NOTES

**[41.5.1]     Type of evidence an affidavit may contain**
Order 41 rule 5(1) provides that subject to specific exceptions, an affidavit should be confined to evidence within the knowledge of the deponent. Rule 5(2) goes on to permit the use of hearsay, or 'information or belief' evidence in certain circumstances. The use of information and belief evidence in affidavits is discussed at length below.

An affidavit should not contain argument or points of law, nor should a lay person's evidence be couched in 'lawyerese' designed to prove a case: see the commentary pre ceding Order 41 rule 1.

**[41.5.2]     Affidavits by solicitors and clerks — when appropriate**
It is appropriate for a solicitor or clerk to make an affidavit in respect of steps taken

on behalf of a party. An affidavit of service is a good example. The relevant facts will be within the personal knowledge of the solicitor or clerk. Likewise it is appropriate for a solicitor to make an affidavit exhibiting correspondence generated in the course of conduct of the client's matter.

However affidavits delving into the facts giving rise to the case 'should where possible be sworn by the person with the most direct knowledge of the matters deposed to, and this will usually be the party rather than the solicitor': *Williams v Hongkong Land Property Co Ltd & Anor* HCPI 522/2001 (Deputy Judge Muttrie; 22.10.2003).

Where a solicitor puts forward false evidence on behalf of a client on an information or belief basis, the client may escape prosecution for perjury, but the solicitor's reputation in the eyes of the court will suffer. See Betts, 'Practice and Procedure: A Master's View', in Law Lectures for Practitioners 1987 (HK: Hong Kong Law Journal Ltd) 227, 234-5, quoted with approval in *Mutual Luck Investment Ltd v Chiu Yim Man & Ors* [1999] 3 HKC 399, 404. In Law Society circular 86-118 (since deleted) the Secretary General of the society warned solicitors of the consequences:

> . . . it is generally undesirable, in any but the most exceptional case, for a solicitor to swear an affidavit on his client's behalf, however if he chooses to do so the burden is on him to verify the truth of what he deposes to. It is not sufficient for him simply to rely on instructions given earlier without confirming whether such instructions still hold good at the time when the affidavit is sworn, particularly when such instructions were given sometime ago. It goes without saying that an untrue statement contained in an affidavit may amount to perjury.

> The Council takes a serious view of untrue statements deposed to by a solicitor in an affidavit and offenders may render themselves liable not only to disciplinary action but also to criminal prosecution.

### [41.5.3] Rule 5(2) - 'information or belief' hearsay evidence in affidavits

Rule 5(2) provides that an affidavit for use in interlocutory proceedings may contain statements based on 'information or belief'. The deponent's sources and grounds must be stated.

Information or belief evidence is hearsay. In permitting the use of such evidence rule 5(2) operates as an exception to the usual rules relating to hearsay. See *FWC v FSR* [1992] 1 HKC 490, 495A-B. The formalities to be followed for the use of hearsay in a trial, and the court's residual discretion to exclude the same under the Evidence Ordinance (Cap 8) part IV, do not apply.

*Cross-reference* - See also Order 14 rules 2(2) and 4(2) and Order 86 rule 2(1) which make provision for the use of information or belief evidence in proceedings to which those Orders apply.

*To what proceedings does this hearsay exception apply?–* Rule 5(2) expressly applies only to affidavits for use in interlocutory proceedings. This is not a matter going to jurisdiction, and non-compliance may be waived: *Onway Eng'g Ltd v Shun Wing Construction Co Ltd* FAMV 18/2009 (14.09.2009) (para 6). For the purpose of rule 5(2), an application to the court will be considered to be 'interlocutory' 'unless determination of the application will finally dispose of the action or finally determine a substantial issue in the action, whichever party succeeds on the application': *Onway* (above, para 15); *Wai Hung Stationery Co Ltd & Ors v HKSAR & Ors* [1998] 2 HKC 229, 231

(CFA). In *Onway* the CFA's appeal committee said this is the same 'application' test as applies on an application for leave to appeal to the Court of Final Appeal. Thus, said the committee, a striking out application is interlocutory (because, if the application fails, the action will proceed to trial for final adjudication) (referring to *Sam Woo Bore Pile Foundation Ltd v China Overseas Foundation Eng'g Ltd* FAMV 21/2007 (08.06.2007). The following types of application have been held not to be interlocutory for the purpose of rule 5(2), so that the exception permitting the use of hearsay evidence in an affidavit is not available:

•   *Order 14A* – an application for determination of a case on a point of law under Order 14A: *Premier Bearing & Equipment Ltd v IFB Int'l Freightbridge (China) Ltd* HCCL 355/1996 (Stone J; 02.01.1998) (paras 27-28); *Secretary for Justice v Hongkong & Yaumatei Ferry Co Ltd* HCA 15329/1999 (Suffiad J; 18.09.2000) (para 27).

•   *Costs* – an application for costs after judgment: *Image Technology (HK) Ltd & Ors v Ho Ying Cheong & Ors* HCA 6861/1993 (Yam J; 22.02.1995) (paras 7–9).

•   *Enforcement of arbitral award* – an application for leave to enforce an overseas arbitral award: *Medison Co Ltd v Victor (FE) Ltd* [2000] 2 HKC 502, 506F-H.

## [41.5.4]   Sources and grounds must be stated
Rule 5(2) provides that information or belief evidence in an affidavit must be presented together with the 'sources and grounds' thereof. The deponent must state where the evidence came from, and give the grounds for believing it. We now turn to look at 'sources' and 'grounds' requirements one by one, and the consequences of failure to comply.

## [41.5.5]   Sources
The deponent should give the name of the person who is the source of the information or belief put forward in the affidavit. It is 'quite insufficient' simply to identify a body corporate: Betts, 'Practice and Procedure: A Master's View', in Law Lectures for Practitioners 1987 (HK: Hong Kong Law Journal Ltd). In *Leung Kin Fook & Ors v Eastern Worldwide Co Ltd & Anor* [1991] 1 HKC 55 (CA) it was held that a solicitor's affidavit identifying the sources no more particularly than 'information derived by me in the course of my conduct of the action', fell 'considerably short' of what is required. See, however, *The Jelau* [1980] HKC 393, 396H where it was said that where the deponent is a solicitor 'it is fairly obvious where the sources of the information came from without them being mentioned'.

Where the deponent's source is documentation, the documents need not necessarily be exhibited to the affidavit, provided that if subsequently required to do so, the depo nent produces the documents or provides an acceptable explanation for not doing so: *Korea Sonbak Shipping Co v Charter Harvest Shipping Ltd* [1994] 1 HKC 494, 500B-F, citing *Deputy Commissioner of Taxation v Ahern (No 2)* [1988] Qd R 158.

It is clear that second-hand hearsay may be introduced under rule 5(2): *FWC v FSR* [1992] 1 HKC 490, 495B. However, there are conflicting authorities as to whether the original source of the evidence must be stated. In Hong Kong one judge has preferred the view that an intermediate source may be identified. See *Peconic Industrial Development Ltd v Chio Ho-cheong* HCA 16255/1999 (Deputy Judge

Longley; 24.03.2000), preferring *Deutsche Ruckversicherung v Walbrook Insurance* [1995] 1 WLR 1017 over *Savings & Investment Bank Ltd v Gasco BV* [1984] 1 WLR 271.

### [41.5.6]    Grounds

Where the source of a deponent's information or belief is a trusted colleague, friend or relative, there will be little difficulty complying with the requirement to state the grounds for putting forward the evidence as truthful. It may be sufficient simply to state the existence of such a relationship with the source.

In other cases it may not be easy to state an honest reason why the deponent believes what has been heard from the source. Trust and belief in what other people say are often based on instinct and emotion rather than on rational analysis. Perhaps for this reason the requirement is frequently breached. To ensure compliance, the deponent may simply state (if it is true) that the source is a person there is no reason to doubt, or one who is known generally to be truthful. One formula which has been used is to state that the deponent believes what is put forward 'on account of my belief in the veracity' of the source.

### [41.5.7]    Consequences of failure to state sources and grounds

It has been observed that the courts have for more than a century lamented the failure to comply with the requirement to state the sources and grounds of information or belief evidence: *Continental Mark Ltd v Verkehrs-Club de Schweiz* [2001] 4 HKC 469,474B-C (affirmed on appeal: [2002] 2 HKC 513), citing *Bidder v Bridges* (1884) 26 ChD 1, 5.

Where an objection of substance is made to evidence which fails to comply, the court has a duty to observe the rule: *Wang King-fong v Fook-hong Chan* [1961] HKLR 448, 454. In that case, failure to comply left the court in doubt as to the defendant's sincerity in deposing that he had a good defence to the action. It is particularly important to ensure compliance on any point of substance such as evidence in support of an *ex parte* applica tion for leave to serve out of the jurisdiction: *Continental Mark* (above, at 479H, citing *Re JL Young Manufacturing Co Ltd* [1900] 2 Ch 753 (CA) and *Lumley v Osborne* [1901] 1 KB 532), or where it is known that the application will be seriously contested: *Leung Kin Fook & Ors v Eastern Worldwide Co Ltd & Anor* [1991] 1 HKC 55 (CA).

An affidavit which fails to comply may be considered inadmissible: *Continental Mark* (above, *loc cit*); *Ka Wah Bank Ltd v Low Chung Song & Ors* HCA 4191/1987 (Deputy Judge Cruden; 23.06.1988) (appeal allowed on other grounds – [1989] 1 HKLR 451); *Leung Kin Fook* (above, at 59F-G).

In both *Wang* and *Continental Mark* the court warned of costs consequences.

### [41.5.8]    Use of affidavits containing 'information or belief' evidence at trial

By its own terms, rule 5(2) only permits the use of 'information or belief' evidence in interlocutory proceedings. However in *Re Chan Heung Mui & Ors* [1993] 1 HKLR 126 and in *Shun Tak Holdings Ltd v Commissioner of Police* [1994] 2 HKC 363, 379 such evidence was permitted to be used in substantive judicial review proceedings. In *Re Chan* it was said that such evidence is frequently put forward on judicial review where factual challenges are rare. The evidence in the particular case was put forward simply to make known to the court what information the respondent had acted upon in reaching the decision subject to review. The evidence was accepted notwithstanding the fact the source was not disclosed. In *Cheung Francis & Anor v Insider Dealing Tribunal* [1999] 4 HKC 585, 599B-G (CA), the court referred to English authority to the effect that the principles as to admission of hearsay evidence are more relaxed generally in judicial review and habeas corpus applications.

**6.    Scandalous, etc., matter in affidavit** (O. 41 r. 6)
   **The Court may order to be struck out of any affidavit any matter which is scandalous, irrelevant or otherwise oppressive.**

**NOTES**

**[41.6.1]    Power to strike out all or part of an affidavit**
Under Order 41 rule 6 the court has power to strike out an affidavit which is 'scandalous, irrelevant or otherwise oppressive'. Where only part of an affidavit is objectionable, the court may sever the offending parts, leaving the remainder to stand. See *Kung Wong Sau-hin v CP Lin & Co* [1988] 2 HKLR 209, 213B-D.

   The power is discretionary: *Rich Idea Int'l Investment Co Ltd v Law Man Chak* CACV 93/1995 (Litton VP; Godfrey & Liu JJA; 07.06.1995), per Godfrey JA citing *Re J* [1960] 1 WLR 253. In exercise of its discretion, the court may decline to exercise the power, adopting another course instead, such as adjourning the proceedings with leave to file a further affidavit. This was done in *Deak & Anor v Deak Perera FE Ltd* [1990] 2 HKC 198 (CA) where the court considered making a costs order against the solicitors responsible.

**[41.6.2]    Principles applicable on application to strike out affidavit**
The principles on which the court will act when considering whether to strike out an affidavit were summarised in *Re Linea Trading Co Ltd* HCCW 350/2004 (Barma J; 11.07.2005), in the following terms:

(1)   Scandalous has the same meaning in Order 41 rule 6 as it does in Order 18 rule 19 dealing with the striking out of pleadings. Thus, degrading, indecent and offensive charges made in an affidavit will be regarded as scandalous if they are irrelevant or inadmissible in evidence to prove any material allegation . . .

(2)   Matters which are material will not generally be struck out even if they are offensive, although where unnecessary detail is given, that may be susceptible to being struck out . . .

(3)   Irrelevant matter may be struck out even if not scandalous . . .

(4)   It is wrong to include argumentative material in affidavits and such material may be struck out . . .

(5)   The court may take one of three approaches to an affidavit in which there is scandalous, irrelevant or oppressive matter:-

(a)   It may decline to strike the matter out, on the basis that it is capable of excluding such material from its mind when deciding the issues which arise for decision; or

(b)   It may think it appropriate to strike out some or all of the material complained of; or

(c)   It may, in an extreme case, order the entire affidavit to be taken off the court file.

Which of these courses is adopted will depend on the circumstances of the case, regard being had to the nature and extent of the objectionable material.

The power to strike out will not be exercised lightly. See *Kung Wong Sau-hin* (above) where Fuad JA said, at 212G-H: 'This necessary and salutary power must, it seems to me, be used with a measure of caution otherwise a litigant is entitled to feel a sense of grievance'.

**[41.6.3]   Examples**

Examples of objectionable material in affidavits which the court has held may be struck out under rule 6 include the following:

• *Irrelevant evidence* – In *Re Linea Trading Co Ltd* (above) the court struck out parts of an affidavit which were in 'vague and general terms', and 'irrelevant'. Irrelevance is not specifically mentioned in rule 6 as a ground for striking out, and it has been suggested that the magnitude of the irrelevance must be such as to render it scandalous: *Re Y & Anor (infants)* [1946-1972] HKC 378, 384F-G. However, the passage from *Re Linea Trading* (above) suggests otherwise.

• *Argument* – The court considered it had power to strike out material going beyond evidence, and into argument, in *Nelson Delivery Service Ltd v Wong Kan & Anor* CACV 136/1986 (Fuad JA & Power J; 11.12.1986) (referring to *Alfred Dunhill Ltd & Anor v Sunoptic SA & Anor* [1979] FSR 337). See also *Deak & Anor v Deak Perera FE Ltd* [1990] 2 HKC 198 where the Court of Appeal was highly critical of the practice of including argument in affidavits, and *Flickinger v Director of Immigration* [1988] HKLR 81.

• *Inadmissible hearsay* – Hearsay evidence, such as evidence on 'information or belief' which is not properly set out in accordance with rule 5(2) may be stricken from an affidavit: *Flickinger v Director of Immigration* [1988] HKLR 81, 94E-G.

• *Without prejudice proposals* – References in an affidavit to without prejudice communications, where the other party to the correspondence has not consented to disclosure, may be struck out from an affidavit: *Re Jinro (HK) Int'l Ltd* [2002] 4 HKC 90; *Re Dartina Development Ltd* HCCW 368/2005 (Kwan J; 30.01.2007).

• *Evidence protected from disclosure* – In *Re Boldwin Construction Co Ltd & Ors* [2003] 4 HKC 156 the court struck out parts of an affidavit which reproduced evidence which had been filed in matrimonial proceedings: rule 121 of the Matrimonial Causes Rules provides that such evidence may not be disclosed to third parties without leave.

• *Incredible evidence* – In *Kung Wong Sau-hin* (above) the Court of Appeal held that evidence lacking credibility should not be struck out as it may be contradicted by other evidence or be subject to cross-examination, but the possibility of striking out such evidence in an extreme case appears to have been left open.

**7.   Alterations in affidavits** (O. 41 r. 7)

**(1)   An affidavit which has in the jurat or body thereof any**

interlineation, erasure or other alteration shall not be filed or used in any proceeding without the leave of the Court unless the person before whom the affidavit was sworn has initialled the alteration and, in the case of an erasure, has re-written in the margin of the affidavit any words or figures written on the erasure and has signed or initialled them.

(2)    Where an affidavit is sworn at the Registry, the Seal of the Court may be substituted for the signature or initials required by this rule.

**8.      Affidavit not to be sworn before solicitor of party, etc.** (O. 41 r. 8)

No affidavit shall be sufficient if sworn before the solicitor of the party on whose behalf the affidavit is to be used or before any agent, partner or clerk of that solicitor.

---

## NOTES

**[41.8.1]    Affidavits and declarations should not be made before party's own solicitor**

Order 41 rule 8 provides that affidavits must always be sworn before a solicitor or other commissioner for oaths who is not connected with the solicitor acting for the party on whose behalf the evidence is to be given. This necessitates a trip to another firm of solicitors, or to the court's oaths and declarations office. In some jurisdictions, British Columbia for example, it is permissible for an affidavit dealing with matters not in dis pute (such as affidavits of service) to be sworn before the party's own solicitor.

The wording of this rule has not been amended since the advent of associated firms. However, it would appear to extend to a party's solicitor's partners whether in the same firm or in associated firms.

In Hong Kong, unlike England, it is not the practice for solicitors to charge each other's clients for taking affidavits.

This rule applies only to affidavits and affirmations – it does not apply to statu tory declarations, nor is there any equivalent legislative provision for statutory declarations. However, in *Lee Yeung-chun & Anor* [1990] 1 HKLR 468, Godfrey J suggested (*obiter*) that as a matter of policy, statutory declarations made before a party's own solicitor in conveyancing transactions should be treated as inadmissible in court proceedings. Godfrey J's *obiter dictum* was expressly not followed in *Kowara v Headwell Investments Ltd* [1995] 1 HKC 613 where Rogers J noted that there had long been a practice in Hong Kong of such statutory declarations being used. Although Rogers J expressed the view that a change in the law might be desirable, he held that it was a matter for the legislature and that in any event such a change should not affect statutory declarations made prior thereto.

Principle 13.09 of the Hong Kong Solicitors' Guide to Professional Conduct (which was first published in May 1995, six months after the judgment of Rogers J in *Kowara*) is also relevant in this context. Although it does not affect the question of admissibility, it does prohibit solicitors from taking oaths and affirmations or declarations in connection with matters in which they are acting. The paragraph reads as follows:

> A solicitor must not administer oaths and affirmations nor take declarations in
> proceedings or matters in which he or his firm is acting for any of the parties, or is

otherwise interested.

The Law Society brought disciplinary proceedings against a solicitor for breach of principle 13.09 in *Solicitor (301/02) v Law Society of HK* [2006] 2 HKC 40 (CA).

**9.     Filling of affidavits** (O. 41 r. 9)

**(4)     Every affidavit used in a cause or matter proceeding in the Court must be filed in the Registry.**

**(5)     Every affidavit must be indorsed with a note showing on whose behalf it is filed and the dates of swearing and filing, and an affidavit which is not so indorsed may not be filed or used without the leave of the Court.**

---

**NOTES**

**[41.9.1]     Affidavit to be indorsed on filing**
Order 41 rule 9(5) provides that an affidavit must be endorsed as to the party on whose behalf it is filed, as well as the dates of swearing and filing. See also para 1 of practice direction 10.1 (reproduced in the commentary under rule 1 above) which deals with these and other requirements as to what should be indorsed on an affidavit.

**10.     Use of original affidavit or office copy** (O. 41 r. 10)

**(1)     Subject to paragraph (2), an original affidavit may be used without the leave of the Court, notwithstanding that it has not been filed in accordance with rule 9.**

**(2)     Where an original affidavit is used then, unless the party whose affidavit it is undertakes to file it, he must immediately after it is used leave it with the judicial clerk in court or chambers, as the case may be, who shall send it to be filed.**

**(3)     Where an affidavit has been filed, an office copy thereof may be used in any proceedings.**

**11.     Document to be used in conjunction with affidavit to be exhibited to it**
(O. 41 r. 11)

**(1)     Any document to be used in conjunction with an affidavit must be exhibited, and not annexed, to the affidavit.**

**(2)     Any exhibit to an affidavit must be identified by a certificate of the person before whom the affidavit is sworn.**

**The certificate must be entitled in the same manner as the affidavit and rule 1(1), (2) and (3) shall apply accordingly.**

---

**NOTES**

**[41.11.1]     Exhibits to affidavits**
This rule must be read together with the practice direction on affidavit evidence reproduced in the commentary under Order 41 rule 1. The practice direction stipulates that court documents should never be exhibited to affidavits, as they prove themselves; that solicitors have a responsibility to ensure that every page of an exhibit is legible,

by attaching a typed copy if necessary; and that where a deponent wishes to refer to a document which has already been exhibited to an affidavit in the proceedings the document should not be re-exhibited.

In May 1987, the Law Society issued its Circular to Members No 86/87 reminding members of these requirements (previously laid down in practice direction dated 28 October 1986) at the request of the Acting Registrar, who had complained that the direction was not being sufficiently observed.

In *Lee Wai Kwai Ngor v Lee Yuet Ming* HCMP 511/1981 (Huggins VP, Li & Cons JJA; 10.06.1981), the Court of Appeal noted disapprovingly 'the growing tendency, since the advent of the photocopying machine, to attach more and more paper to affidavits, thus increasing, quite unnecessarily, the cost of litigation'. The court went on to admonish solicitors to try to reduce the amount of paper filed in court.

### [41.11.2]    Inspection of original exhibits

Paragraph 4 of the practice direction governing affidavit evidence (PD 10.1) provides that copies of documents may be exhibited to an affidavit rather than the originals. This is subject to the proviso that the originals must be made available for inspection by other parties or the judge. In this connection see also *Re Ming John Fook* [1998] 3 HKC 712 where at 722D–E Rogers JA stated:

> the court must have inherent jurisdiction to enable inspection of documents, copies of which have been exhibited in affidavits. If that were not enough, O 24 r 10 allows for inspection of documents mentioned in affidavits whether exhibited or not.

**12.     Affidavit taken in Commonwealth or foreign country admissible without proof of seal, etc.** (O. 41 r. 12)

**(1)     Any affidavit sworn in any part of the Commonwealth outside Hong Kong before any judge, officer or other person duly authorized, or before any commissioner authorized by the Court, to take affidavits therein, may be used in the Court in all cases where affidavits are admissible.**

**(2)     Any affidavit sworn in any foreign parts out of Her Majesty's dominions before a judge or magistrate, being authenticated by the official seal of the foreign court to which he is attached or of such magistrate, or before a notary public or a British consular officer, may be used in the Court in all cases where affidavits are admissible.**

**(3)     The fact that an affidavit purports to have been sworn in the manner prescribed by paragraph (1) or (2) of this rule shall be prima facie evidence of the seal or signature, as the case may be, of any such court, judge, magistrate, commissioner or other officer or person therein mentioned, appended or subscribed to such affidavit, and of the authority of such court, judge, magistrate, commissioner or other officer or person to administer oaths.**

**(Enacted 1988)**

---

**NOTES**

### [41.12.1] Scope of Order 41 rule 12 – use of affidavit evidence from outside Hong Kong

Order 41 rule 12 makes provision for the admissibility into evidence in legal proceedings in Hong Kong of evidence taken by affidavit in other jurisdictions.

### [41.12.2] Interpretation of rule 12 after 1 July 1997

Rule 12(1), which makes specific provision for the reception in Hong Kong of affidavit evidence from the Commonwealth, must, since reunification, be read subject to section 2A(2)(b) of the Interpretation and General Clauses Ordinance (Cap 1). It is provided there that legislative provisions conferring privileges on the United Kingdom and Commonwealth jurisdictions are of no effect from 1 July 1997, save where there is reciprocity.

Rule 12(2), in referring to 'foreign parts out of Her Majesty's dominions', should now be interpreted as not referring to any part of the People's Republic of China: see para 19, schedule 8, Cap 1. Insofar as the paragraph provides for use of affidavits sworn before British consular officers it is inconsistent with Chinese sovereignty and probably of no effect as a result of article 8 of the Basic Law of the HKSAR.

With regard to attestation of documents, including conveyancing documents, executed outside Hong Kong (including the Mainland) for use in Hong Kong and *vice versa*, see Law Society circular 97-226 as to the consequences of reunification in 1997. The circular, which remains valid in mid–2009, can be viewed in the members' zone of the Law Society's website www.hklawsoc.org.

### [41.12.3] Hong Kong solicitor may not take affidavit abroad

Hong Kong solicitors are not empowered to take affidavits or affirmations abroad, even for use in Hong Kong. See *Ka Wah Bank Ltd v Low Chung Song & Ors* HCA 4191/1987 (Deputy Judge Cruden; 23.06.1988) (appeal allowed on other grounds – see [1989] 1 HKLR 451) and see *Top Flying Investment Ltd v Open Mission Assets Ltd* HCA 566/2006 (Recorder McCoy SC; 01.09.2006) approving Law Society circular 00-127 in this regard. The proper procedure is to have such affidavits sworn before a notary public of the relevant jurisdiction pursuant to Order 41 rule 12(2) (an ordinary commissioner for oaths will not do: *Top Flying* (above)) or a Chinese consular official pursuant to section 10 of the Oaths and Declarations Ordinance. In the *Ka Wah Bank* case, it was held that an affidavit sworn before a Hong Kong solicitor who travelled to Taiwan for that pur pose was defective as 'a matter of substance' and not a mere irregularity which could be cured under Order 41 rule 4.

### [41.12.4] Statutory declarations made outside Hong Kong

It has been held that statutory declarations are not admissible in evidence in Hong Kong unless made within the jurisdiction. See *Yiu Ping Fong & Anor v Lam Lai Hing Lana* [1998] 4 HKC 476 where Yuen J held that the requirements of section 14 of the Oaths and Declarations Ordinance (Cap 11) are 'mandatory'. As a result, with reference to the form set out in the schedule to the Ordinance, the learned judge held that a declaration made in Taiwan before a notary of that jurisdiction was insufficient proof in a property dispute.

## [41.12.5]  Admissibility of affidavit evidence from foreign jurisdictions - apostille not required

An affidavit (or affirmation) sworn in a foreign jurisdiction (meaning a jurisdiction other than Hong Kong or any other part of China) is admissible in evidence in legal proceedings in Hong Kong just like an affidavit sworn locally, provided that Order 41 rule 12 is complied with. The affidavit must be sworn before a judge, magistrate, notary public or consular officer, and in the first two cases it should be duly authenticated in accordance with rule 12(2). See also section 10 of the Oaths and Declarations Ordinance (Cap 11) which provides that affidavits (and other documents) made at a Chinese diplomatic mission abroad are as effectual as if made before lawful authority in Hong Kong.

The internationally recognised procedure for legalisation of notarised documents by means of an apostille verifying the authority of the person before whom it is sworn or made is not a requirement for admissibility of a foreign affidavit in Hong Kong. Rule 12(3) provides that the seal or signature of the authorised officer or notary is *prima facie* evidence of the authority of the person to administer oaths. See *Hotung v Ho Yuen Ki & Ors* [2007] 2 HKC 246 where it was held (at para 17) that rule 12 is a 'code' and it is not necessary to follow the apostille procedure laid down by the Hague Convention Abolishing the Requirement of Legalisation for Foreign Public Documents, 1961.

## [41.12.6]  Affidavits from the Mainland of China

Prior to reunification it was held that an affidavit sworn before a notary public in the Mainland was admissible in Hong Kong under rule 12(2) and (3): *Europet Heimtierbedarf Gmbh & Ors v Yeh Chun Hui* HCMP 1208/1994 (Le Pichon J; 05.05.1995). However, rule 12(2) and (3) should no longer apply, since the Mainland cannot now be considered a foreign jurisdiction. See the commentary above on post-1997 interpretation of the rule. Law Society circular 97-226 (which remains valid at mid-2009) states (para 2(b)) that notarised documents from the Mainland will be authenticated by the PRC foreign ministry, but it is not clear by what legal mechanism they might be admissible in Hong Kong court proceedings.

## [41.12.7]  Affidavits for use in Mainland China

Order 41 rule 12 does not deal with the requirements for an affidavit sworn in Hong Kong for use in the Mainland. That is a matter which should be governed by the rules of procedure applicable in Mainland proceedings. Law Society circular 97-226 (which remains valid at mid-2009) states (para 2(a)) that documents prepared in Hong Kong for use in the Mainland should be attested by a China-Appointed Attesting Officer in Hong Kong and authenticated by China Legal Services (Hong Kong) Limited. A list of such officers can be found in the public zone of the Law Society's website.

## ORDER 41A

### STATEMENTS OF TRUTH

1.     **Interpretation** (O. 41A r. 1)
     **In this Order, unless the context otherwise requires —**
"expert report" means an expert report disclosed under these rules;
"pleading" includes —

(a)     particulars of a pleading given by a party to any other party, whether voluntarily or pursuant to —
     (i)     a request made by that other party; or
     (ii)     an order of the Court made under Order 18, rule 12(3) or (4); and

(b)     an amendment to a pleading or any of the particulars referred to in paragraph (a);

"witness statement" means a statement served under Order 38, rule 2A.
     (L.N. 152 of 2008)

2.     **Documents to be verified by statement of truth** (O. 41A r. 2)
     **(1)     The following documents must be verified by a statement of truth in accordance with this Order —**

(a)     a pleading;
(b)     a witness statement;
(c)     an expert report; and
(d)     any other document verification of which in accordance with this Order is required by any other provision of these rules or by a practice direction

     **(2)** A pleading must be verified by a statement of truth in accordance with this Order notwithstanding that the party has in the pleading made an allegation of fact in accordance with Order 18, rule 12A, which is inconsistent with another allegation of fact in the same pleading.

     **(3)** If the Court considers that it is just to do so in a particular case, it may direct that all or any of the documents specified in paragraph (1) need not be verified by a statement of truth.

     **(4)** All or any of the documents specified in paragraph (1) need not be verified by a statement of truth if it is so provided by a practice direction.

     **(5)** A practice direction may only provide that all or any of the documents specified in paragraph (1) need not be verified by a statement of truth if the documents or document relate to a matter that is to be heard in a specialist list.
     (L.N. 152 of 2008)

---

**NOTES**

**[41A.2.1]     General requirement for 'statement of truth'**
Order 41A rule 2 introduces a general requirement that pleadings, particulars, witness

statements, expert reports and some other documents be verified by 'statement of truth'. The rule derives from England's CPR 22.1.

As to signature, form and effect of a statement of truth, see rules 3, 4 and 5. As noted in the commentary there, a statement of truth does not require the formality of an affidavit or affirmation. However, the sanction of contempt is equally available: see the commentary under rule 9.

### [41A.2.2]  Practice direction on statements of truth
See practice direction 19.3, which contains additional provisions with regard to statements of truth. The text of the practice direction can be viewed on the judiciary's website, or that of the Hong Kong Legal Information Institute.

### [41A.2.3]  Requirement that pleading be verified by statement of truth
Order 41A, rule 2(1)(a) requires that pleadings be verified by statement of truth. In that regard it is to the same effect as Order 18 rule 20A, which also applies to particulars of pleadings. See the commentary under that rule. With regard to amendments to pleadings and particulars, see Order 20 rule 13.

A pleading which is not verified by a statement of truth may be struck out by the court: Order 41A rule 6.

The purpose of applying the statement of truth requirement to pleadings is evident in the response of the Chief Justice's working party on civil justice reform to concerns that the procedure would result in unjustified front-end loading of costs. The working party said (final report, paras 242–3):

> Thus, as discussed above, pleadings should not seek to lay out the evidence or recite every detail of a party's case. They should convey the nature of the case, stating the material facts in a manner which avoids both excessive sparsity and excessive detail. Properly drawn pleadings therefore do not call for front-end work on such detail or evidence and the verification requirement does not pre-suppose any greater exploration of the same. If, in good faith, a party reasonably verifies a pleading and subsequently discovers that it contains errors, that pleading may duly be amended, verifying the amendment.

> Of course, the verification requirement is intended to deter the pleading of a false or speculative case, or a case based on insufficient instructions. To the extent that expense has to be incurred to formulate a proper pleading, such expense is necessary and involves no unjustified front-loaded costs. On the other hand, ill-prepared or ill-conceived pleadings hamper early settlement and define false parameters for discovery, witness statements, and so forth, leading to wasteful interlocutory effort and additional costs …

What the working party said subsequently found expression in *Tong Kin Hing v Autron Mauritius Corp & Ors* [2010] 1 HKLRD 77 (CA) where it was said:

> The requirement of a statement of truth is important. Its purpose is to focus the mind of the relevant party and to deter sloppy or speculative pleadings and prevent dishonest cases being put forward. It is a very important part of the Court's process in applying the Rules. In this respect, as much as in any other, the requirement serves to help the Court and the parties to achieve the underlying objectives which are set out in Order 1A Rule 1 of the Rules of the High Court.

**[41A.2.4]   Requirement that witness statement be verified by statement of truth**
Order 41A, rule 2(1)(b), which requires that witness statements be verified by statement of truth, is to the same effect as Order 38 rule 2A(4)(a).

A witness statement which is not verified by statement of truth is not admissible in evidence unless the court orders otherwise: Order 41A rule 7.

**[41A.2.5]   Requirement that expert report be verified by statement of truth**
Order 41A, rule 2(1)(c), which requires that expert reports be verified by statement of truth, is to the same effect as Order 38 rule 37A.

**[41A.2.6]   Other documents which must be verified by statement of truth**
Order 41A rule 2(1)(d) provides that the statement of truth requirement extends to documents other than those listed in the rule, where provision is made elsewhere. Examples of other documents which are subject to the statement of truth requirement include:

- Particulars of pleadings – Order 18 rule 20A

- Amendments of pleadings and particulars – Order 20 rule 13

- Statement of damages and Answer to Statement of damages – practice direction on statements of truth, PD 19.3, para 1

- Amendments to any document verified by a statement of truth, in which case the original statement of truth shall not be deleted, and a fresh statement of truth verifying the amendments shall be added – practice direction on statements of truth, PD 19.3, para 2

- Petitions and other Originating process in matrimonial and family proceedings, and any answer or reply; statements as to arrangements for children; etc – practice direction on matrimonial and family pro ceedings, PD 15.12, part L

- Documents for use in proceedings in the Lands Tribunal – practice direction on application of the civil justice reforms to the Lands Tri bunal, PD LTPD: CJR No 1/2009, para 7(10)

The requirement for verification of particulars of pleadings extends to voluntary particulars. This was expressly recommended by the Chief Justice's working party, which noted (final report, para 271), that such a requirement had been omitted from the CPR in England.

**[41A.2.7]   Order 41A rule 2(2) – Verification of pleading in the alternative**
Order 41A rule 2(2) expressly extends to pleadings in the alternative the requirement for verification by statement of truth. Such a pleading is one in which a party pleads inconsistent versions of events on an 'either/or' basis. See the commentary under Order 18 rule 12A.

The express extension of the statement of truth requirement to alternative pleadings results from recommendation 32 of the Chief Justice's working party on civil justice reform. The working party noted (final report, para 263) that there was some difficulty to the question how verification would work in respect of alternative pleadings. It noted the approach set out in *Clarke v Marlborough Fine Art (London) Ltd* [2002] 1 WLR 1731, which it summarised as follows:

Cases may arise where the party has no personal knowledge of the facts, but has evidence pointing to alternative possibilities. Provided that each alternative can be justified by some evidence (a requirement reflected in the Bar's Code of Conduct), the pleading and verification of such alternative pleas is permissible. CPR 22 [Order 18 rule 20A in Hong Kong] is aimed at excluding dishonest or opportunistic and speculative claims. It is not intended to exclude honest claims reasonably advanced on the basis of incomplete information which points to alternative sets of fact, each of which would be legally viable as part of the party's case.

The working party expressed the view (at para 264) that a similar approach be adopted in Hong Kong and said:

Each case would have to be examined separately. If the matter pleaded is plainly within the party's knowledge so that there could be no justification for him putting forward inconsistent factual alternatives, the pleading is embarrassing and cannot properly be put forward or verified. The same is true of inconsistent and mutually destructive allegations advanced, not as alternatives, but as part of a unified case. Where, however, the party putting forward the pleading has a reasonable basis for putting forward alternative and mutually inconsistent versions, the pleading is permissible and ought to be verifiable on the basis that the party believes, on the evidence available, that the facts correspond to one or other of the possibilities pleaded.

### [41A.2.8]  Power to dispense with statement of truth

Order 41A rule 2(3) empowers the court to dispense with the statement of truth requirement where it considers that it is just to do so. In *Binks v Securicor Omega Express Ltd* [2003] EWCA Civ 993 (16.07.2003) it was said that it might be appropriate to exercise the equivalent power in England in relation to a late amendment to a pleading to advance a case wholly inconsistent with the evidence which the party had given.

Rule 2(4) provides that a practice direction in relation to a specialist list may provide that the statement of truth requirement shall not apply.

### [41A.2.9]  Modification of statement of truth requirement by practice direction

Order 41A rule 2(1)(d) provides the requirement for a statement of truth may be extended to other types of document by practice direction. In addition rule 2(4) provides that the need for a statement of truth may be abrogated by practice direction. It might be argued that these provisions are an unlawful sub-delegation by the rules committee of its rule making powers to the individual judges in charge of specialist lists.

### [41A.2.10]  Failure to comply with verification requirement

The court has power to order that a document be verified where there has been failure to comply with the verification requirements set out in these rules. See Order 41A rule 8. A pleading which is not verified may be struck out under Order 41A rule 6, and a witness statement of expert report is inadmissible (unless otherwise ordered) if it is not verified by statement of truth: rule 7.

**3.      Signing of statement of truth** (O. 41A r. 3)

**(1)    Subject to paragraphs (6), (7), (8) and (9), a statement of truth must be signed by —**

  (a)    in the case of a witness statement or expert report, the maker of the statement or report;
  (b) in any other case —
      (i)    the party putting forward the verified document or where appropriate, his next friend or guardian ad litem; or
      (ii)   the legal representative of the party or next friend or guardian ad litem.
  (2)    Subject to paragraphs (6), (7), (8) and (9), where a party is a body of persons, corporate or unincorporate, the statement of truth must be signed by a person holding a senior position in the body.
  (3)    Subject to paragraph (7), where the party is a public officer, the statement of truth must be signed by the public officer or a person holding a senior position in the public body or public authority to which the proceedings relate.
  (4)    Each of the following persons is a person holding a senior position —
      (a)    in respect of a corporation that is neither a public body nor a public authority, any director, manager, secretary or other similar officer of the corporation;
      (b)    in respect of an unincorporated association that is neither a public body nor a public authority, any corresponding person appropriate to that unincorporated association; and
      (c)    in respect of a public body or public authority, a person duly authorized by the public body or public authority for the purposes of this sub-paragraph.
  (5)    Where a statement of truth is signed by a person holding a senior position, that person shall state in the statement of truth the office or position he holds.
  (6)    Subject to paragraphs (7), (8) and (9), where the party is a partnership, the statement of truth must be signed by —
      (a)    one of the partners; or
      (b)    a person having the control or management of the partnership business.
  (7)    A statement of truth in or in relation to a pleading may be signed by —
      (a)    a person who is not a party; or
      (b)    two or more parties jointly,
if this is permitted by a practice direction.
  (8)    An insurer or the Motor Insurers' Bureau of Hong Kong may sign a statement of truth in or in relation to a pleading on behalf of a party where the insurer or the Motor Insurers' Bureau of Hong Kong has a financial interest in the result of the proceedings brought wholly or partially by or against that party.
  (9)    If more than one insurer is conducting proceedings on behalf of a plaintiff or defendant, a statement of truth in or in relation to a pleading may be signed by an officer of the insurer responsible for the case as the lead insurer, but —
      (a)    the person signing shall specify the capacity in which he signs;
      (b)    the statement of truth must be a statement that the lead

> insurer believes that the facts stated in the document are true;
> and
>
> (c)    the Court may order that the statement of truth also be signed
>        by one or more of the parties.

(10) Where a legal representative signs a statement of truth, he shall sign in his own name, and shall not sign only in the name of the firm to which he belongs.

(L.N. 152 of 2008)

---

## NOTES

### [41A.3.1]   Origin and scope of Order 41A rule 3

Order 41A rule 3 sets out detailed guidance as to who should be responsible to sign the statement of truth in various circumstances. It is based on para 3 of The English practice direction CPR PD 22. The various circumstances are discussed in detail below.

### [41A.3.2]   Formalities not required on signing statement of truth

Order 41A rule 3 requires that a statement of truth be signed. The formality of being sworn or affirmed as for an affidavit or affirmation is not required, although practice direction 19.3 does require that a person who is unable to read must sign in the presence of a commissioner for oaths: see the commentary on that subject some paragraphs below. Nevertheless serious consequences are provided for in the event such a statement is untrue. As the Chief Justice's working party on civil justice reform said (final report, para 220):

> A statement of truth lacks the formality of an affidavit or affirmation. It does not involve
> the person who makes it being sworn or affirmed and does not involve his attendance
> before a person qualified to administer oaths or take affidavits. Nevertheless, a person
> who verifies a pleading without an honest belief in the truth of the facts pleaded faces
> possible proceedings for contempt.

See Order 41A rule 9 as to proceedings for contempt against the maker of a false statement of truth.

### [41A.3.3]   Witness statements and expert reports

Order 41A rule 3(1)(a) uses mandatory language requiring that a statement of truth verifying a witness statement or expert report must be signed by the maker of the statement or report.

### [41A.3.4]   Parties under disability

The mandatory requirement that a statement of truth verifying a witness statement be signed by the maker of the statement applies to parties under disability (minors and mentally incapacitated persons – see Order 80 rule 1). In cases where this causes difficulty, the commentary below on persons unable to read or sign may be of some guidance.

Other documents may be verified by statement of truth signed by the next friend or guardian *ad litem* of the party under disability, or legal representative: rule 3(1)(b).

## [41A.3.5]    Statement of truth by legal representative

Order 41A rule 3(1)(b)(ii) provides that a document other than a witness statement or expert report may be verified by statement of truth signed by the relevant party's legal representative. The provision derives from England's CPR 22.1(6)(a)(ii).

Does 'legal representative' extend to in-house legal advisers and executives? In England CPR 2.3 defines 'legal representative' to mean a barrister, solicitor, solicitor's employee or other authorised litigator. CPR PD 22 para 3.11 suggests that this means an employed barrister or solicitor may sign, but not an in-house legal executive: only a legal executive employed by a solicitor in private practice might do so. The Chief Justice's working party referred to this discussion in CPR PD 22 in a footnote to para 230 of its final report, without comment. However, there is no definition of the term 'legal representative' for the purpose of Order 41A (there is a definition in Order 62 rule 1, but that applies only that Order). Thus it appears that the matter is open to question in Hong Kong.

A legal representative's statement of truth refers to the client's belief: see rule 5(1). As the Chief Justice working party said (final report, para 227), referring to the equivalent provisions in the CPR:

> ... although the rules permit the person signing the statement of truth to be either the party or the party's legal representative, the pleading remains the party's document which he puts forward as representing his case. The statement signed by the legal representative will refer to the client's belief, not his own.

Although a legal representative's signature verifies the client's belief, the representative who signs 'is taken to make certain representations of his own to the court' (final report, para 233). Those representations to the court are set out in rule 4(3). The working party said (final report, para 236):

> the legal representative should sign only if he can meet the requirements [of that rule]. If he cannot meet those requirements, he should decline to sign. If neither he nor his client signs the statement of truth, the pleading could still be filed and would take effect as a pleading, but it might be liable to be struck out upon application by the other side.

It is clear that the legal representative makes those representations personally, as rule 3(10) requires that the representative sign in his or her own name rather than a firm name.

A legal representative's statement of truth is not a proper substitute for evidence. See *Korea National Insurance Corp v Allianz Global Corporate & Speciality AG* [2007] EWCA Civ 1066 (30.10.2007). There it was said (at para 33) to be 'inherently unsatisfactory' for a party to rely on the statement of truth of its legal representative verifying its defence as evidence on a strike out application when it could have provided a witness statement (or affidavit).

## [41A.3.6]    Bodies corporate

Order 41A rule 3(2) provides that a statement of truth on behalf of a party which is a body corporate must be signed 'by a person holding a senior position in the body'. Although the mandatory 'must' is used, the sub-rule does not appear to oust the possibility of a body corporate's pleadings being verified by legal representative as provided for in rule 3(1)(b)(ii).

'Senior position' is defined by rule 3(4). So far as bodies corporate which are not public bodies or public authorities are concerned, the term refers to 'any director, man ager, secretary or other similar officer of the corporation'. The senior position held by the person signing must be stated in the statement of truth: rule 3(5). Positions such as 'manager' are not legally defined and the Chief Justice's working party advised (final report, para 230):

> Whether a signatory holding a particular position qualifies, for example, as 'manager' of a company, is to be approached pragmatically and in the light of his realistic ability to confirm the accuracy of the allegations made.

The Chief Justice's working party noted (final report, para 228) that issues can arise as to whether an officer of a company is authorised to make the statement of truth on its behalf. However it was decided not to address those issues in the rules. The working party said:

> The rules of court are not concerned with such issues and proceed on the assumption that the person signing is duly authorized to do so.

## [41A.3.7]    Public officers

Order 41A rule 3(3) provides that a statement of truth on behalf of a party who is a public officer should be signed by the public officer or a person holding a 'senior position' in the public body or authority concerned. The term 'senior position' for this purpose is defined by rule 3(4)(c) to mean a person duly authorised by the public body or authority. The provision refers to the authorisation having been given 'for the purposes of this sub-paragraph', which suggests that there must be a specific authorisation for the purpose of the statement of truth, and that it would not be sufficient to rely on a general delegation or authority. The senior position held by the person signing must be stated in the statement of truth: rule 3(5).

## [41A.3.8]    Unincorporated associations

Order 41A rule 3(2) and 4(b) makes provision for the signing of statements of truth on behalf of parties which are unincorporated associations.

These provisions will be of limited application. This is because unincorporated associations cannot normally be parties to legal proceedings. They lack the legal capacity to sue or be sued: see the commentary under Order 15 rule 4. In the case of partners, who may sue or be sued in the firm name (Order 81 rule 1), special provision for signing statements of truth is made in rule 3(6), so the provisions with regard to unincorporated associations should not be applicable. Nor do they appear to apply to sole proprietorships which may be sued in the business name as if they were a firm (Order 81 rule 9) because although a sole proprietorship is unincorporated, it is not an 'association'. However they might be applicable to representative proceedings under Order 15 rule 12 if the group rather than the representative is considered to be the party. They may also be applicable to some Chinese customary associations which may be able to be parties to legal proceedings in relation to land in the New Territories although they are formally unincorporated (see the commentary under Order 15 rule 12).

The requirement in rule 3(2) that a statement of truth on behalf of a body corporate be signed by a person 'holding a senior position in the body' applies equally to unincorporated associations. Such a person, in relation to an unincorporated association is, according to rule 3(4)(b) any person 'corresponding' to director, manager, secretary or similar officer of a body corporate.

### [41A.3.9]  Insurers

Order 41A rule 3(8) provides that an insurer or the Motor Insurers' Bureau may sign a statement of truth verifying a pleading. Special considerations arise where more than one insurer is involved on behalf of a particular party, which are addressed by rule 3(9), giving the responsibility to the lead insurer. These provisions derive from England's practice direction CPR PD 22 para 3.6A and 3.6B.

The Chief Justice's working party on civil justice reform recognised that difficulties can arise in insurance cases in re-establishing contact with a policy holder who has been indemnified, and may have 'little motivation to sign court documents' (final report, para 238). The working party suggested (at para 239) that the 'answer to this type of problem probably lies in steps to be taken by the insurer before indemnifying the insured'. The working party continued:

> Thus, agreement might be secured that the insured's incident report form is submitted on the basis that the facts there stated may be used to draw up pleadings on his behalf, that he believes those facts to be true and that he authorizes the insurer to sign a statement of truth relating to such facts, and so forth, thereby enabling the insurer or the legal representative to act on the insured's behalf to meet the requirements of [rule 4(3)].

### [41A.3.10]  Partnerships

A statement of truth on behalf of a partnership must be signed by one of the partners or a person having control or management of the partnership business: rule 3(6). The wording resembles part of Order 81 rule 3 as to who may be served where partners are sued in the name of the partnership.

### [41A.3.11]  Statement of truth by person who requires interpreter

A statement of truth may be in English or Chinese and should be in the language of the statement maker. See para 4 of the practice direction on statements of truth (PD 19.3). Thus an English-language document should be verified by a statement of truth in Chinese if the person verifying reads Chinese but not English: *Chok Yick Interior Design & Eng'g Co Ltd v Lau Chi Lun* HCA 1480/2008 (Lam J; 21.06.2010) (para 33). Furthermore, the contents of the document must have been interpreted to the person verifying it. By para 5 of PD 19.3 a certificate from the interpreter in the following terms must be provided:

> I certify that I [name and address of the person] have translated the contents of this document and the statement of truth to the person signing the statement of truth [if there are exhibits, add 'and explained the nature and effect of the exhibits referred to in it'] who appeared to understand (a) the document and approved its content as accurate and (b) the statement of truth and the consequences of making a false state ment, and made his signature in my presence.

The text of practice direction 19.3 can be viewed on the judiciary's website, or that of the Hong Kong Legal Information Institute.

### [41A.3.12]  Statement of truth by person unable to read

A statement of truth by a person who is unable to read must be signed, or the person's mark made on it, in the presence of an "authorized person", being a person who may administer oaths and take affidavits, but not necessarily a person independent of the parties or their representatives. The authorised person certifies in the document as follows:

> I certify that I [*name and address of the authorized person*] have read over the contents of this document and the statement of truth to the person signing the statement of truth [*if there are exhibits, add 'and explained the nature and effect of the exhibits referred to in it'*] who appeared to understand (a) the document and approved its content as accurate and (b) the statement of truth and the consequences of making a false statement, and made his [*signature/mark*] in my presence.

See practice direction 19.3, para 6, the full text of which may be viewed on the judiciary's website, or that of the Hong Kong Legal Information Institute. As to who may take an oath or affidavit, see Order 114 and the commentary thereunder.

### [41A.3.13] Modification of signature requirements by practice direction
Order 41A rule 3(7) provides that a practice direction may permit a statement of truth in relation to a pleading to be signed by a non-party, or two or more parties jointly. It might be argued that this is an unlawful sub-delegation by the rules committee of its rule making powers to the individual judges in charge of specialist lists who issue practice directions.

**4.  Effect of statement of truth** (O. 41A r. 4)

  **(1) Subject to paragraph (2), a statement of truth is a statement that —**

    **(a) the party putting forward the document believes that the facts stated in the document are true; or**

    **(b) in the case of a witness statement or expert report, the maker of the witness statement or expert report believes that the facts stated in the document are true and (if applicable) the opinion expressed in it is honestly held.**

  **(2) If a party is conducting proceedings with a next friend or guardian ad litem, the statement of truth in or in relation to a pleading is a statement that the next friend or guardian ad litem believes the facts stated in the document being verified are true.**

  **(3) Where a legal representative or insurer has signed a statement of truth on behalf of a party, the Court shall treat his signature as his statement that —**

    **(a) the party on whose behalf he has signed had authorized him to do so;**

    **(b) before signing he had explained to the party that in signing the statement of truth he would be confirming the party's belief that the facts stated in the document were true; and**

    **(c) before signing he had informed the party of the possible consequences to the party if it should subsequently appear that the party did not have an honest belief in the truth of those facts.**

                  **(L.N. 152 of 2008)**

## NOTES

### [41A.4.1]  Deemed representations on signing statement of truth

Order 41A rule 4(1)(a) effectively deems a statement of truth to be a representation that the party putting forward the document believes the facts stated in it to be true. In the case of expert reports, it is additionally represented that the opinion expressed is honestly held: rule 4(1)(b). A next friend or guardian *ad litem* makes a personal representation of belief in the truth of the facts stated in the document: rule 4(2).

In the case of a statement of truth signed by a legal representative or insurer, the court is additionally directed by rule 4(3) to treat that person's signature as a representation of having been authorised to sign, having explained to the party that the statement is confir mation of the party's belief in the truth of the facts stated, and that the party had been informed of the consequences of a false statement.

It would appear that the purpose of rule 4 in setting out such representations, is to facilitate imposition of the contempt sanction for false statements, as to which see rule 9.

## 5.      Form of statement of truth (O. 41A r. 5)

**(1)    The form of the statement of truth verifying a document other than a witness statement or expert report is as follows:—**

"[I believe] [the *(plaintiff or as may be)* believes] that the facts stated in this [*name document being verified*] are true.".

**(2)    The form of the statement of truth verifying a witness statement or expert report is as follows —**

"I believe that the facts stated in this [*name document being verified*] are true and (if applicable) the opinion expressed in it is honestly held.".

**(3)    Where the statement of truth is not contained in the document that it verifies —**

    **(a)    the document containing the statement of truth must be headed with the title of the proceedings and the action number; and**

    **(b)    the document being verified must be identified in the statement of truth as follows —**

        **(i)    pleading: "the [*statement of claim or as may be*] served on the [*name of party*] on [*date*]";**

        **(ii)    particulars of pleading: "the particulars of pleading issued on [*date*]";**

        **(iii)    amendment to a pleading or particulars of pleading: "the amendment to [*name document being verified*], made on [*date*]";**

        **(iv)    witness statement: "the witness statement filed on [*date*] or served on [*party*] on [*date*]";**

        **(v)    expert report: "the expert report disclosed to [*party*] on [*date*]".**

**(L.N. 152 of 2008)**

_____

**NOTES**

**[41A.5.1]   Origin and scope of Order 41A rule 5**
Order 41A rule 5 sets out certain basic requirements as to the form a statement of truth should take, which vary slightly according to the nature of the document being verified. The rule derives from England's practice direction CPR PD 22 para 2 which is in largely similar terms.

**[41A.5.2]   Statement of truth limited to facts and opinions**
The prescribed wordings of the different types of statement of truth set out in Order 41A rule 5 relate only to the matters of fact stated in the document verified, and to expressions of opinion in a witness statement or expert report. Thus where a document such as a pleading includes reference to a matter of law, such reference is not subject to the verification. In *Korea National Insurance Corp v Allianz Global Corporate & Speciality AG* [2007] EWCA Civ 1066 (30.10.2007) (para 34), referring to the equivalent English rule, CPR 22.1(4), it was said that 'the scope of a statement of truth does not extend to propositions of law set out in the document in question'.

The reason statements of truth are limited in this way is likely because the person making the statement of truth will often not be a person with legal knowledge, and even where it is a person with legal knowledge (as in *Korea National*) questions of law are a matter for the court

**[41A.5.3]   Statement of truth may be made in separate document**
It seems likely that a statement of truth will normally be made on the document being verified itself. This would certainly be appropriate with witness statements and expert reports. However Order 41A rule 5(3) contemplates the possibility of a statement of truth being made in a separate document and prescribes that the separate document is to be headed with the title to the action, and the manner in which the document being verified is to be identified. The use of such a separate document would be appropriate where the statement of truth requirement has been overlooked when the document is filed and served, or possibly where the person making the statement of truth is not available at that moment and makes the statement later to cure the defect.

**6.      Failure to verify pleading** (O. 41A r. 6)
      **(1)   The Court may by order strike out a pleading that is not verified by a statement of truth.**
      **(2)   Any party may apply for an order under paragraph (1).**
      **(L.N. 152 of 2008)**

**7.      Failure to verify witness statement or expert report** (O. 41A r. 7)
      **If the maker of a witness statement or expert report fails to verify the witness statement or expert report by a statement of truth, the witness statement or expert report is not admissible in evidence unless otherwise ordered by the Court.**
      **(L.N. 152 of 2008)**

**8. Power of Court to require document to be verified** (O. 41A r. 8)

**(1)** The Court may order a person who has failed to verify a document in accordance with this Order to verify the document.

**(2)** Any party may apply for an order under paragraph (1).

**(L.N. 152 of 2008)**

---

## NOTES

**[41A.8.1] Rules 7 & 8 – consequences of failure to make statement of truth**

Order 41A rule 7 provides that a witness statement or expert report will normally be inadmissible in evidence unless verified by statement of truth, and rule 8 empowers the court to order compliance.

In *Ip Kam Chung v Kwo Siu Kit & Anor* DCEC 797/2009 (Deputy Judge Clement Lee; 20.09.2010) (para 14) the court made an unless order by which expert reports would be expunged from the court file unless the statement of truth and declaration of compliance with the code of conduct were filed within 14 days.

**9. False statements** (O. 41A r. 9)

**(1)** Proceedings for contempt of court may be brought against a person if he makes, or causes to be made, a false statement in a document verified by a statement of truth without an honest belief in its truth.

**(2)** Proceedings under this rule may be brought only —

    **(a)** by the Secretary for Justice or a person aggrieved by the false statement; and

    **(b)** with the leave of the Court.

**(3)** The Court shall not grant the leave under paragraph (2) unless it is satisfied that the punishment for contempt of court is proportionate and appropriate in relation to the false statement.

**(4)** Proceedings under this rule are subject to the law relating to contempt of court and this rule is without prejudice to such law.

**(L.N. 152 of 2008)**

---

## NOTES

**[41A.9.1] Origin and scope of Order 41A rule 9 – the contempt sanction**

Order 41A rule 9 provides for proceedings for contempt of court against a person who makes a false statement of truth. Paragraphs (1) and (2) of the rule derive from England's CPR 32.14. Rule 9(3) and (4) were recommended by the Chief Justice's working party on civil justice reform (final report, recommendation 31) to reflect the analysis and approach set out in *Malgar Ltd v RE Leach (Eng'g) Ltd* [2000] FSR 393; [2000] The Times, 17 Feb, with which the working party expressly agreed. In *Malgar* it was said that the equivalent rule in England did not introduce a new category of contempt, which remained a matter of the general law, but merely provided for the possibility that a false statement would result in prosecution for contempt.

The contempt sanction applies notwithstanding the fact that a statement of truth is made without the formality of an oath or affirmation (see the commentary under Order 41A rule 3 on formalities). In *Tong Kin Hing v Autron Mauritius Corp & Ors* [2010] 1 HKLRD 77 (CA) the court set out the text of Order 41A rule 9 and said:

> Hence the seriousness of the statement of truth cannot be brushed aside. It may not be an affidavit or an affirmation but the Rules themselves treat the statement with similar seriousness.

### [41A.9.2]   Contempt sanction not impeded by witness immunity

In *KJM Superbikes Ltd v Hinton* [2008] EWCA Civ 1280 (20.11.2008) it was argued that the immunity from civil liability enjoyed by witnesses meant that they are not amenable to contempt proceedings (being civil in nature) at the instance of an aggrieved party other than the Attorney General. The argument was dismissed. Moore-Bick LJ (delivering the unanimous judgment of the Court of Appeal) said (at para 11):

> The immunity of a witness from proceedings in respect of things said in the course of giving evidence does not extend to immunity from punishment in respect of statements made under oath which are known to be false. A witness who knowingly makes a false statement in the course of giving evidence orally or in an affidavit does not expose himself to an action for damages at the suit of anyone injured as a result, but he does expose himself to the risk of prosecution for perjury and as such is publicly accountable for his attempt to interfere with the course of justice . . . Statements of truth are not made on oath, but the principle that a per son who knowingly makes a false statement intended for use in proceedings should be held accountable is equally applicable.

### [41A.9.3]   The leave requirement

Order 41A rule 9(2)(b) stipulates that proceedings for contempt against a person for making a false statement of truth may only be brought with leave of the court. The leave requirement applies whether the Secretary for Justice or a person aggrieved seeks to bring the contempt proceedings. In this regard the rule differs from its English counterpart (CPR 32.14(2)) which imposes a leave requirement only where someone other than the Attorney General seeks to bring the contempt proceedings.

### [41A.9.4]   The test on application for leave to bring contempt proceedings – public interest

It has been held in England that the test for granting leave to bring contempt pro ceedings in this context is the public interest. In *KJM Superbikes* (above) Moore-Bick LJ (delivering the unanimous judgment of the Court of Appeal) set out the factors to be considered by the court in the following terms (at para 16):

> Whenever the court is asked by a private litigant for permission to bring proceedings for contempt based on false statements allegedly made in a witness statement it should remind itself that the proceedings are public in nature and that ultimately the only question is whether it is in the public interest for such proceedings to be brought. However, when answering that question there are many factors that the court will need to consider. Among the foremost are the strength of the evidence tending to show not only that the statement in question was false but that it was known at the time to be false, the circumstances in which it was made, its significance having regard to the nature of the proceedings in which it was made, such evidence as there may be of the maker's state of mind, including his understanding of the likely effect of

the statement and the use to which it was actually put in the proceedings. Factors such as these are likely to indicate whether the alleged contempt, if proved, is of sufficient gravity for there to be a public interest in taking proceedings in relation to it.

It will be noted that the court's observations reproduced above are expressed as applicable only when a private litigant seeks leave. That is most likely because in England the Attorney General is not subject to the leave requirement. In Hong Kong, where the Secretary for Justice is subject to the leave requirement, the English court's observations may not be confined to applications by private individuals.

### [41A.9.5] Consideration of underlying objectives on application for leave
In the passage quoted above from *KJM Superbikes* the English Court of Appeal went on to say that on an application for leave to bring contempt proceedings against a person who has made a false statement of truth, the proportionality of the exercise should be taken into account. Moore-Bick LJ said:

> In addition, the court will also wish to have regard to whether the proceedings would be likely to justify the resources that would have to be devoted to them.

This is apparently a reference to the English equivalent of the underlying objectives in Order 1A rule 1(c) and (f), respectively the objectives of proportionality and ensuring fair distribution of the court's resources. See also rule 9(3) of this Order, and see *Malgar Ltd v R E Leach (Eng'g) Ltd* (2000) FSR 393, [2000] The Times, 17 Feb, where it was held that a committal application would be disproportionate.

### [41A.9.6] Timing of the application for leave
Although a witness should be warned early of possible contempt proceedings, an application for leave should not be entertained by the court until the witness has finished giving evidence. See *KJM Superbikes* (above) where the following *obiter* observations were set out by Moore-Bick LJ (at para 19):

> Although we did not hear argument on this point, I think that in general a party who considers that a witness may have committed a contempt of this kind should warn him of that fact at the earliest opportunity ... and that a failure to do so is a matter that the court may take into account if and when it is asked to give permission for proceedings to be brought. However, it is important not to impose any improper pressure on a witness who may later be called to give oral evidence. In particular, if the alleged contemnor is to be called as a witness, an application [under this rule] should not be made, and if made should not be entertained by the court, until he has finished giving his evidence.

### [41A.9.7] Cross-examination of witness on statement of truth
The privilege against self-incrimination does not impede cross-examination of a witness on the truth or falsehood of a statement of truth. Our sister publication in the UK, The Civil Court Practice 2008 says (at CPR 32.14[2]):

> **Self-incrimination** Where the maker of a witness statement or affidavit refuses to answer questions in cross-examination on the ground that an admission of having made false statements might lead to proceedings for contempt, the court has power to prevent such proceedings and to direct the witness to answer: *Great Future International Ltd v Sealand Housing Corp (Contempt of Court)* [2001] All ER (D) (Nov); [2001] CPLR 293.

**[41A.9.8]   Sentence for false statement of truth**
In *Daltel Europe Ltd & Ors v Makki* [2006] 1 WLR 2704 (CA) a party was sentenced to 5 months imprisonment for contempt of court in dishonestly making a false statement of truth in support of a statement of claim.

**10.     Transitional** (O. 41 r. 10)
        **This Order does not apply in relation to a document in any action if that document was filed, served or exchanged before the commencement of this Order.**
        **(L.N. 152 of 2008)**

---

**NOTES**

**[41A.10.1]   Statement of truth requirements prospective only**
Order 41A rule 10 provides that the statement of truth requirements in the Order do not apply to documents filed, served or exchanged prior to the Order coming into force in 2009. Some other Orders contain requirements for statements of truth, and reference should also be made to the transitional provisions in relation to those Orders, if any.

## ORDER 42

### JUDGMENTS AND ORDERS
### JUDGMENTS, ORDERS, ACCOUNTS AND INQUIRIES

**1.      Form of judgment and interest thereon, etc.** (O. 42 r. 1)

**(1)If, in the case of any judgment, a form thereof is prescribed by Appendix A the judgment must be in that form. (See App. A, Form 39–46, 48, 49)**

**(2)    The party entering any judgment shall be entitled to have recited therein a statement of the manner in which, and the place at which, the writ or other originating process by which the cause or matter in question was begun was served.**

**(3)    An order other than a consent order to which rule 5A applies must be marked with the name of the judge or master by whom it was made and must be sealed.**

---

## NOTES

**[42.1.1]    Forms of judgments and orders**
By virtue of Order 42 rule 1 judgments should be drawn up in accordance with the pre scribed forms in Appendix A to these rules, where such a form exists. In the absence of such a form, practitioners should refer to the Hong Kong Practice Forms reproduced in volume 2 of this work (under the tab 'High Court Ordinance') or consult one of the standard English reference works such as Chitty & Jacob's *Queen's Bench Forms.*

Orders of the court should be drawn up in consultation with the same forms.

Forms should not be followed slavishly, rather they should be modified to suit the circumstances of the individual case. See Order 1 rule 9 and the commentary thereunder.

**[42.1.2]    Order for payment of pre-judgment interest**
Section 48 of the High Court Ordinance provides for pre-judgment interest on money claims. In addition an award of pre-judgment interest may arise from a cause of action (such as where an agreement sued upon makes provision for interest) or under the rules of equity.

*Pre-judgment interest pursuant to agreement* – A claim to pre-judgment interest may be part and parcel of the plaintiff's cause of action. For example, there may be an express or implied agreement requiring interest to be paid on the amount due. An obvious example is a mortgage. In such cases the contractual term governs the award of interest and there is no need to invoke the court's discretion under section 48 of the High Court Ordinance. In such cases the plaintiff's claim to interest is part of the cause of action and must be pleaded. The rate of interest will be the agreed rate. The court may allow compound interest where the agreement so provides. In *BNP Paribas v Pang Kwai Ling* [2003] 1 HKC 20 compound interest was claimed on the basis of an alleged implied term arising from banking practice. The court refused to allow compound interest, not following *National Bank of Greece SA v Pinios Shipping Co (No 1)* [1990] 1 AC 637 on the basis that there was no evidence of such a banking practice in Hong Kong.

*Pre-judgment interest under section 48* – Section 48 of the Ordinance empowers the court to award pre-judgment interest on a judgment for debt or damages. Interest 'shall' be awarded in cases of personal injury or death where the damages exceed $30,000 (s 48(3)). In all other cases it is left to the court's discretion to decide whether to award interest, but in principle an award should be made where a party has been kept out of money: *Union Base Ltd v Tsang Shek Tong* [1998] 2 HKC 349 (CA), 352D-F. Where interest is awarded the court may order it to run from as far back as the date the cause of action accrued, and the rate is left to the discretion of the court. Guidance as to the date from which interest should run, and the rate, is contained in *Komala Deccof & Co SA v Perusahaan Pertambangan Minyak Dan Gas Bumi Negara (Pertamina)* [1984] HKLR 219 (CA). The following points emerge from that judgment:

1   An award of interest is not intended to punish the paying party, but to achieve *restitutio in integrum* (referring to *Tate & Lyle Distribution v GLC* [1982] 1 WLR 149).

2   In fixing the date from which interest will run in commercial cases the court will have regard to the time at which persons acting honestly and reasonably would pay (referring to *General Tyre Co v Firestone Tyre Co Ltd* [1975] 1 WLR 819).

3   Personal injuries cases are a different matter and interest will usually run from the date of issue of the writ (referring to *Birkett v Hayes* [1982] 1 WLR 816).

4   The court may take into account delay on the part of the plaintiff and reduce the award of interest accordingly.

5   In commercial cases, the rate of interest will be fixed having regard to the rate at which the plaintiff could have borrowed the money wrongly withheld. This may be 1% above prime for a large credit-worthy borrower, and higher for others.

The decision in *Komala Deccof* has stood the test of time. It was approved by the Court of Final Appeal in *Polyset Ltd v Panhandat Ltd* FACV 28/2000 (Bokhary, Chan & Ribeiro PJJ; Litton & Lord Millet NPJJ; 25.04.2002) (not the judgment reported in HKLRD and HKCFAR) with regard to the rate of interest in commercial cases, and in *Mariner Int'l Hotels Ltd v Atlas Ltd* HCA 10714/1998 (Burrell J; 15.01.2008). *Komala Deccof* leaves room for the court to be flexible in deciding the interest rate in commercial cases. In *Wong v Saccani* HCA 2061/2004 (Deputy Judge Muttrie; 23.11.2006) the court awarded interest at a lower rate where there had been no need to borrow money, and in *Mariner Int'l* (above) the court referred to the existence of a few cases in which the court's award of interest was based on HIBOR rather than the prime rate (though the court decided not to follow them in the instant case). In *Sun Legend Investments Ltd v Ho Yuk Wah David (No 2)* [2010] 2 HKLRD 559 there was evidence that the successful party was required to pay 3% above prime to its bankers, and the court ordered judgment interest at that rate.

Interest under section 48 being a matter of discretion, an appellate court will not interfere lightly: *Tago Ltd v Process Automation (Int'l) Ltd* HCA 1133/2006 (Deputy Judge Muttrie; 18.05.2006).

Only simple interest (*ie* interest which is not compounded at periodic rests) may be awarded under section 48.

*Pre-judgment interest in equity* – The court's power to award pre-judgment interest under section 48 of the High Court Ordinance is limited to claims for debt or damages. Money claims in the court's equitable jurisdiction are susceptible to awards of interest under the rules of equity themselves. It is well established that in equity, compound interest may be ordered. See *China Everbright-IHD Pacific Ltd v Ch'ng Poh* [2002] 45 HKCFAR 630; [2003] 2 HKLRD 594, citing *Wallersteiner v Moir (No 2)* [1975] 1 QB 373 and *President of India v La Pintada Compania Navigacion SA* [1985] AC 104. Thus, compound interest may be awarded in cases of breach of trust, fiduciary duty or other equitable obligation. The purpose is to deprive the defendant of any actual or notional profit made from the breach. In *China Everbright* the Court of Final Appeal upheld the trial judge's order that interest be paid at 1% above the prime rate, to be compounded at monthly rests.

### [42.1.3]    Post-judgment interest

Post-judgment interest is governed by section 49 of the High Court Ordinance. Section 49(1) provides that a judgment debt carries simple interest (a) at such rate as the court may order; or (b) in the absence of such an order, at the rate fixed by the Chief Justice from time to time.

It is appropriate for the court to determine the post-judgment interest rate under section 49(1)(a) rather than apply the rate fixed under section 49(1)(b) where the creditor has a cause of action for post-judgment interest which is pleaded and proved. An independent contractual covenant to pay a specified rate of post-judgment interest does not merge with the judgment and continues to have effect: *Freeway Finance Co Ltd v Tam Chuen On Ray mond* [2010] 4 HKC 448. However, in *The Mandarin Container & Ors* [2004] 4 HKC 505, 515B-F, the court allowed only the lower bank rate earned by the court on funds paid in during a short period when the debtor's funds were held in court.

Where there is no cause of action relating to post-judgment interest, the claim arises by operation of law and need not be pleaded. Unless the court for some reason orders a different rate, the rate fixed by the Chief Justice from time to time will apply. See the table of such rates set out below. Where the rate fixed by the Chief Justice applies, it is not necessary for the formal sealed judgment of the court to make any specific provision as to interest: see Practice Direction 16.3.

### [42.1.4]    Date from which post-judgment interest is payable

A judgment takes effect from the date it is pronounced and interest accrues on the date thereof, not from the subsequent date on which the judgment is drawn up and entered. See Order 42 rule 3(3).

In the case of a successful appeal the question arises whether interest is payable from the date of the appeal judgment or from the date of the judgment overturned. English authority suggests that it should be the former. See *Borthwick v Elderslie SS Co* [1905] 2 KB 516 and *Belgian Grain & Produce Co v Cos & Co (France) Ltd* [1919] WN 317. It is submitted that if those authorities are correct, the court should exercise its discretion under section 48 of the High Court Ordinance to order pre-judgment interest so as not to disadvantage the successful appellant.

## [42.1.5]     Rates of post-judgment interest

The post-judgment interest rates fixed by the Chief Justice pursuant to section 49(1)(b) of the High Court Ordinance are 'significantly higher' than commercial rates. This is 'to give the judgment debtor an incentive promptly to satisfy the judgment debt': *Man Ping Nam & Anor v Man Fong Hang* [2007] 1 HKLRD 763 (CFA) (para 23). A list of the pre scribed rates going back to 1975 can be viewed on the judiciary's website at www.judiciary.gov.hk/en/crt_services/interest_rate.htm. To save space here we repro duce only the prescribed rates applicable in more recent years:

**Post-judgment interest rates prescribed under HCO s 49(1)(b)**

| Year | Effective Date | % Rate of Interest |
|---|---|---|
| 2000 | 01-Jan | 11.5 |
|  | 01-Apr | 11.54 |
|  | 01-Jul | 11.98 |
|  | 01-Oct | 12.5 |
| 2001 | 01-Apr | 12.08 |
|  | 01-Jul | 10.86 |
|  | 01-Oct | 9.82 |
| 2002 | 01-Jan | 8.72 |
|  | 01-Apr | 8.14 |
|  | 01-July | 8.125 |
| 2003 | 01-Jan | 8.093 |
|  | 01-Apr | 8 |
| 2005 | 01-Jan | 8.069 |
|  | 01-Apr | 8 |
|  | 01-Jul | 8.245 |
|  | 01-Oct | 9.234 |
| 2006 | 01-Jan | 10.088 |
|  | 01-Apr | 10.711 |
|  | 01-Jul | 10.921 |
|  | 01-Oct | 11 |
| 2007 | 01-Jan | 10.934 |
|  | 01-Apr | 10.75 |
| 2008 | 01-Jan | 10.420 |
|  | 01-Apr | 9.398 |
|  | 01 Jul | 8.353 |
|  | 01-Oct | 8.250 |
| 2009 | 01-Jan | 8.192 |
|  | 01-Apr | 8 |

## [42.1.6]     Interest on costs

An award of costs in a judgment is part of the judgment and interest is payable under section 49 of the High Court Ordinance: see *Caltex Oil Hong Kong v Director of Buildings and Lands* [1994] HKDCLR 31. The prevalent view is that interest on an award of costs runs from the date of the order for costs rather than the subsequent date on which the amount of costs payable may be quantified by taxation or agreement. See the commentary under Order 62 rule 3.

## [42.1.7]     Interest on money repaid on appeal

The court has a common law or inherent power to order the payment of interest on money which is ordered to be repaid on appeal: *Man Ping Nam v Man Fong Hang* (CFA) (above, para 14), referring to *Rodger v Comptoir d'Escompte de Paris* (1871) 3 LR PC 465 (an appeal from HK) and *Central Electricity Board of Mauritius v Bata Shoe Co (Mauritius) Ltd* [1983] 1 AC 105. The opposite conclusion was reached in *Hang Sing Construction Co Ltd v Young's Engineering Co Ltd* [1985] 2 HKC 17 (CA), which would appear to be *per incuriam*.

### [42.1.8]    Interest where both claim and counterclaim successful
Where both claim and counterclaim succeed, the court may give separate judgments or may set off one against the other and give a single net judgment. See Order 15 rule 2 and the commentary thereunder. In *Union Base Ltd v Tsang Shek Tong* [1998] 3 HKC 349, 352D-F (CA), where a single net judgment was given in favour of the plaintiff after setting off the amount of the successful counterclaim, it was held that in principle the plaintiff was entitled to interest on the net amount.

**1A.    Judgment in favour of reversioner for detention of goods** (O. 42 r. 1A)

**(1)    Where a claim relating to the detention of goods is made by a partial owner whose right of action is not founded on a possessory title, any judgment or order given or made in respect of the claim shall be for the payment of damages only.**

**In this paragraph "partial owner" means one of two or more persons having interest in the goods, unless he has the written authority of every other such person to sue on the latter's behalf.**

**2.    Judgment, etc. requiring act to be done: time for doing it** (O. 42 r. 2)

**(1)    Subject to paragraph (2), a judgment or order which requires a person to do an act must specify the time after service of the judgment or order, or some other time, within which the act is to be done.**

**(2)    Where the act which any person is required by any judgment or order to do is to pay money to some other person, give possession of any land or deliver any goods, a time within which the act is to be done need not be specified in the judgment or order by virtue of paragraph (1), but the foregoing provision shall not affect the power of the Court to specify such a time and to adjudge or order accordingly.**

---

### NOTES

### [42.2.1]    Time for complying with order requiring act to be done
Order 42 rule 2 provides that certain types of judgments and orders requiring a person to do an act (for example, a mandatory injunction) must specify the time within which the act is to be done. Failure to comply with this requirement may result in the judgment being set aside: *Chou Yi Feng v Chou Yi Chen & Ors* HCA 4393/2001 (Chung J; 23.11.2002).

The time for doing the required act is normally stipulated as a specified time after service of the judgment or order. However the rule also permits 'some other time' to be stipulated. Thus the order will not be bad for stipulating a time for compliance counting from the date of the order rather than the date of service: *Lee Hung Yam v*

*Lee Sou Fai* HCA 4390/1983 (Deputy Judge Nazareth QC; 23.05.1985); [1985] HKLY 788. Further, it is permissible to state that the act must be done 'forthwith', in which case the act must be done as soon as it can reasonably be done: *Chou Yi Feng* (above).

**[42.2.2]    Peremptory orders**
A common example of an order requiring that an act be done is the peremptory or 'unless' order. Such an order provides that if something is not done by a specified time certain consequences will follow. Such orders are often made at the interlocutory stage against a party who has repeatedly sought extensions of time but has yet to comply. In such cases it is typically provided that the party will have one last extension of time, and 'unless' the party meets the final deadline judgment may be entered against it.

Guidance as to the form and wording of peremptory or 'unless' orders is given by practice direction 16.5, the text of which can be viewed on the judiciary website www.judiciary.gov.hk or that of the Hong Kong Legal Information Institute www.hklii.org.

**[42.2.3]    Cross-reference**
See also Order 45 rule 6 which empowers the court to vary the time within which an order must be complied with, or to impose a time for compliance where this has not already been done. And see Order 32 rule 11B as to 'self-executing' orders, which appear to be essentially the same thing as 'unless' orders. Self-executing orders require application under Order 2 rules 4 and 5 for relief against the sanction taking effect. It seems likely that the provisions of those rules will extend to applications for extension of time to comply with an unless order, and the commentary in the ensuing 5 paragraphs should be read with that in mind. Those paragraphs concern the position as it was before Order 32 rule 11B and Order 2 rules 4 and 6 came into force as part of the civil justice reforms in 2009.

**[42.2.4]    Power to extend time for compliance with peremptory order**
The court's general power under Order 3 rule 5 to extend time may be exercised to grant extensions of time for compliance with a peremptory or 'unless' order. Extension may be granted even after the time has expired. See *Samuels v Linzi Dresses Ltd* [1981] QB 115; *The Bayville* HCAJ 14/1983 (Power J; 16.02.1984) (not following the Full Court in *Sum v Li Pui Chuen* [1962] HKLR 209); and *CTB Australia Ltd v Kuo Kin Ling Betty* HCA 5435/2000 (Sakhrani J; 20.05.2004).

Any application for extension of time to comply with an unless order should now be considered in light of Order 2 rules 4 and 5, which concern applications for relief from sanctions for non-compliance with 'self-executing' orders. Subject to that caution, we set out below some discussion of the court's approach to applications for extension of time to comply with 'unless' orders before Order 2 rule 4 and 5 came into force as part of the civil justice reforms in 2009.

**[42.2.5]    Test for extension of time to comply with peremptory order**
The court's power under Order 3 rule 5 to extend time is discretionary. See the commentary under that rule. In the case of peremptory or 'unless' orders, the power will not be exercised lightly. Where the time has already expired the discretion should be exercised 'cautiously': *Samuels v Linzi Dresses Ltd* [1981] QB 115.

In recent times the test has been whether the failure was 'intentional and contumelious': *Tan Eddy Tansil v PT Bank Pembangunan Indonesia (Persero)* [1996] 1 HKC 231; [1997] HKLRD 57 (CA) applying *Re Jokai Tea Holdings Ltd* [1992] 1 WLR 1196; [1993] 1 All ER 630. If so the court would likely refuse an extension of time and allow the sanction specified in the unless order to take effect. If not, the court might grant an extension of time, usually on terms as to costs. Contumelious conduct in this context is any 'conscious and deliberate decision to ignore or disobey the court's order in the absence of any extraneous excuse': *Chan Chun Lung Allen & Anor v Ryland Ltd & Ors* HCA 4904/1996 (Ribeiro J; 26.08.1999) (affirmed on appeal: CACV 284/1999).

In *Hytec Information Systems Ltd v Coventry City Council* [1997] 1 WLR 1666, it was suggested that failure to comply attributable to negligence, incompetence or indolence might not be excused. This lower threshold for refusing an extension was considered not yet to represent the law in Hong Kong in *Chan Chun Lung* (above). However, 11 years later it was held that in light of the 2009 civil justice reforms, the time had come for Hong Kong to adopt the English approach in *Hytec*: see *Top One Int'l (China) Property Group Co Ltd & Anor v Top One Property Group Ltd* [2011] 1 HKC 425 (para 36–41).

In *Hytec*, Auld LJ said in his concurring judgment:

> In my judgment, there is no need to confine the test to that of an intentional disregard of a court's peremptory order, whether or not it is characterised as flouting, contumelious, contumacious, perverse, obstinate or otherwise. Such an intent may be the most usual circumstance giving rise to the exercise of this jurisdiction. But failure to comply with one or a number of orders through negligence, incompetence or sheer indolence could equally qualify...

In his judgment in *Hytec*, with which the other members of the court agreed, Ward LJ set out the following principles:

1. An Unless Order is an order of last resort, not made unless there is a history of failure to comply with other orders. It is the party's last chance to put its case in order;
2. Because that was his last chance, a failure to comply would ordinarily result in the sanction being imposed;
3. The sanction is a necessary forensic weapon which the broader interests of the administration of justice require to be deployed unless the most compelling reason is advanced to exempt his failure;
4. It seems axiomatic that if a party intentionally or deliberately (if the synonym is preferred) flouts the order then he can expect no mercy;
5. A sufficient exoneration would almost invariably require that he satisfy the court that something beyond his control has caused his failure to comply with the order;
6. The judge exercises his judicial discretion whether or not to excuse. A discretion judicially exercised on the facts and circumstances of each case on its own merits depends on the circumstances of that case; at the core is service to justice;
7. The interests of justice require that justice should be shown to the injured party for procedural inefficiencies causing the twin scourges of delay and wasted costs. The public interest in the administration of justice to contain those blights also weighs very heavily. Any injustice to the defaulting party,

though never to be ignored, comes a long way behind the other two.

## [42.2.6]    Examples

In *Ka Wah Bank Ltd v Low Chung-song & Anor* [1989] 1 HKLR 451 the Court of Appeal refused an extension of time and struck out a defence where it was satisfied the defendants had made no conscientious effort to comply with their obligations. The defendants, who were fugitives, had filed an affidavit giving an illusory address in order to conceal their whereabouts. Further, they had filed lists of documents which were 'glaringly evasive'.

In *CTB Australia Ltd v Kuo Kin Ling Betty* HCA 5435/2000 (Sakhrani J; 20.05.2004) failure to comply with an unless order was attributable to 'bad luck and incompetence' and the litigant was given one last chance. The court was satisfied the litigant had genuine difficulty complying with the order on time because not all the relevant documents were in the same place and they had previously been handled by her late husband.

In *Dongguan Dongxiang Decoration Co Ltd v Universal Right Ltd* [1999] 1 HKC 790 the court was not prepared to excuse failure to comply with an unless order even though the non-compliance was not contumelious. Barnett J held that if the failure were excused the opposing party would suffer prejudice which could not be compensated with an order for costs.

In *Monteiro v IO Blocks 41-44 Baguio Villas* HCA 362/2007 (Deputy Judge Mayo; 17.10.2008) the court set aside judgment which had been entered for failure to comply with an unless order where it was satisfied that the defendant had intended to comply but had been hampered from doing so in part by the fact the No 8 typhoon signal was hoisted on the final day for compliance.

## [42.2.7]    Failure to comply attributable to legal adviser

It is well established that where failure to comply with an unless order is attributable to a litigant's legal advisers, the litigant himself should not be made to suffer as a consequence: *Tan Eddy Tansil v PT Bank Pembangunan Indonesia (Persero)* [1996] 1 HKC 231 (CA).

See also *Chow Kai Sang v Toi Samuel & Ors* [1996] 4 HKC 330 and *Ming Pao Enterprise Corp Ltd v CIM Co Ltd* [1999] 1 HKC 497.

## [42.2.8]    Extension of time for compliance with unless order made by consent

The court's power to extend time for compliance with an unless order extends to orders made by consent. However, it has been suggested that where the consent order embodies a contract between the parties the terms of which preclude extension of time, the court may not over-ride the agreed term. See *Lee Hung Yam v Lee Sou Fai* HCA4390/1983 (Deputy Judge Nazareth QC; 23.05.1985); [1985] HKLY 788 citing *Siebe Gorman & Co Ltd v Pneupac Ltd* [1982] 1 All ER 377 and see the commentary under Order 3 rule 5. See also the commentary under Order 42 rule 5A concerning variation and setting aside of consent orders.

## 3.    Date from which judgment or order takes effect (O. 42 r. 3)

**(1)   A judgment or order of the Court takes effect from the day of its date.**

**(2)** Such a judgment or order shall be dated as of the day on which it is pronounced, given or made, unless the Court orders it to be dated as of some other earlier or later day, in which case it shall be dated as of that other day.

**(3)** A judgment or order shall take effect for the purposes of this rule notwithstanding that the reasons therefor may not be given until a later date.

---

NOTES

**[42.3.1]     Date from which judgment or order takes effect**
The word 'judgment' in this rule means the conclusion pronounced by the judge and not the formal document which in most cases is subsequently drawn up and entered: see *Chow Po Bor & Anor v Timothy Lee & Anor* [1993] 1 HKC 271 (CA).

The effect of this rule is that the parties to an action are bound by any order or judgment made within the action from the date of the delivery of the judgment or the making of the order, without further formality. Thus the subsequent rules in the Order which require that judgments and orders be drawn up and entered and that reasons be given are not pre-conditions to a judgment or order taking effect: *Re Chinascreen Ltd* [1994] 2 HKC 643.

It follows that a judgment for the payment of money is a debt which may be the subject of garnishee proceedings even before the judgment is entered (*Holtby v Hodgson* (1890) 24 QBD 103, at 106–107). So a judgment *in favour* of a judgment debtor may be garnisheed to the benefit of his judgment creditor even before it is entered. The position may be different for writs of execution (Order 46 rule 6(4)(a)(i) stipulates that a writ of execution shall not be issued without production of a copy of the judgment or order sought to be enforced).

It follows from this rule that actual notice of a judgment or order is not required for it to bind the parties to the action. See *Chung Shun Land Investment Co Ltd v Steadman* HCA 4215/1985 (Deputy Judge Barnett; 01.07.1986), [1986] HKLY 732 dismissing an application to set aside an interlocutory order on the ground the summons, which had been posted to the defendant's address for service, was returned by the post office undelivered. There are, however, exceptional circumstances in which service of a judgment or order is required. Under Order 44 rule 2 notice of a judgment should be served on certain non-parties in certain types of action, and under Order 45 rule 7 certain types of judgments and orders may not be enforced unless they have been served personally.

The situation is different where a judgment or order is not pronounced by a judicial officer, but given or made by administrative act in the registry; for example a default judgment. In *Shen Gan Finance Ltd v Yiu Tek* HCMP 4275/1998 (Stone J; 30.11.1998) it was held that such a judgment takes effect from sealing; and in *Ip Man Kei v Liu Wai Hong* HCPI 901/2006 (Deputy Judge Gill; 26.03.2007), from signing for or on behalf of the registrar.

**[42.3.2]     Setting aside fraudulent judgment**
In *Lau Kak v Cheung Mo Kit* [1996] 1 HKC 79, Le Pichon J considered the undisputed jurisdiction of the court to set aside a completed judgment on the ground of fraud, citing *Jonesco v Beard* [1930] AC 298. The learned judge held that the 'threshold question' was whether the matters alleged to be tainted were directly relevant to the

impugned judgment (at 83G–I). She posed the question in this way: 'In other words, would judgment have been in favour of the other party but for the matters alleged to be tainted? That the tainted matters must be directly material to the judgment to be set aside for fraud finds support in the judgment of Cozens-Hardy LJ in *Birch v Birch* [1902] P 130 at 136.'

In that case, it was a judgment of the Court of Appeal which was sought to be set aside. The court declined so to do on the ground that the threshold test was not met. The key conclusion of the Court of Appeal had been reached without any reliance on the tainted matter.

See the commentary under Order 71 rule 9 as to the court's power to set aside registration of a foreign judgment which has been obtained by fraud.

**[42.3.3]    Power to reconsider order or judgment not yet perfected**
The court has an inherent power to reconsider and rehear any matter on which it has given judgment or made an order, prior to the judgment or order being perfected. See the commentary on the court's inherent jurisdiction to amend under Order 20 rule 11.

**[42.3.4]    Power to backdate judgment or order**
Order 42 rule 3(2) provides that a judgment or order shall ordinarily bear the date on which it is 'pronounced, given or made'. However the provision goes on to stipulate that the court may order that a judgment or order be dated as of some earlier or later day. Hong Kong cases in which the court has considered the exercise of this power include the following:

• *Re King's Dyeing & Weaving Fty Ltd* [1986] HKC 382, 384H-I where the appointment of a provisional liquidator of a company was backdated to the date the application first came on for hearing.
• *Kailay Eng'g Co (HK) Ltd v Farrance* [1999] 2 HKC 765, 769G-I where it was said that this power cannot be used so as to confer jurisdiction on the court which it would not otherwise have.
• *ML v YJ* HCMC 13/2006 (Lam J; 20.03.2008) (para 31) where the court considered that it could not use this power to ante-date a decree absolute of divorce to a date before application had been made.

**4.    Orders required to be drawn up** (O. 42 r. 4)
    **(1)    Subject to paragraph (2), every order of the Court shall be drawn up unless the Court otherwise directs.**
        **(2)    An order—**
            **(a)    which—**
                **(i)    extends the period within which a person is required or authorized by these rules, or by any judgment, order or direction, to do any act, or**
                **(ii)    grants leave for the doing of any of the acts mentioned in paragraph (3), and**
            **(b)    which neither imposes any special terms nor includes any special directions other than a direction as to costs,**
**need not be drawn up unless the Court otherwise directs.**
        **(3)    The acts referred to in paragraph (2)(a)(ii) are—**

(a)     the issue of any writ, other than a writ of summons for service out of the jurisdiction;

(b)     the amendment of a writ of summons or other originating process or a pleading;

(c)     the filing of any document;

(d)     any act to be done by an officer of the Court other than a solicitor;

(HK)(e)     the extension of the validity of a writ;

(HK)(f)     the abridgement of time for service of a summons;

(HK)(g)     the adjournment of the hearing of a summons;

(HK)(h)     the adjournment of the trial of an action;

(HK)(i)     an order made by a Judge ordering that an application or summons shall be heard by a master or a similar order made by a master that an application or summons shall be heard by a Judge;

(HK)(j)     leave to inspect and take copies of documents filed in the Registry;

(HK)(k)     the transfer of an action from one list to another;

(HK)(l)     the vacation or variation of the dates upon which an action has been set down to be heard; and

(HK)(m)     the admission of a person as a solicitor or a barrister of the High Court under the Legal Practitioners Ordinance (Cap. 159), and any order made under rule 13 of the Admission and Registration Rules (Cap. 159 sub. leg.).

**5.     Drawing up and entry of judgments and orders** (O. 42 r. 5)

(1)     Where a judgment given in a cause or matter is presented for entry in accordance with this rule at the Registry, it shall be entered in the book kept for the purpose by the Registrar.

(2)     The party seeking to have such a judgment entered must draw up the judgment and present it to the Registrar for entry.

(3)     A party presenting a judgment for entry must produce any certificate, order or other document needed to satisfy the Registrar that he is entitled to have the judgment entered.

(4)     On entering any such judgment the Registrar shall file the judgment.

(5)     Every order made and required to be drawn up must be drawn up by the party initiating the application upon which the order was made and if that party fails to draw up the order within 7 days after it is made any other party affected by the order may draw it up.

(L.N. 103 of 1994)

(6)     The order referred to in paragraph (5) must, when drawn up, be produced at the Registry, together with a copy thereof, and when passed by the Registrar the order, after it has been sealed, shall be returned to the party producing it and the copy shall be lodged in the Registry.

---

**NOTES**

**[42.5.1]    Obligation to draw up judgment or order**

Order 42 rule 5(5) provides that the obligation to draw up an order of the court rests on the party who initiated the application under which it was made. It differs from the rule of the same number in the former English RSC, which applied to orders made in the Queen's Bench Division and placed the obligation on the party having 'custody' of the summons, which is said in some reference works to mean the party which succeeded on the application.

Where the court makes an order of its own motion there is no obligation on any party to draw it up: *Getfit Co Ltd v Joinex Industries Ltd* HCA 4781/2001 (Deputy Judge Longley; 21.12.2001). However, as a matter of good practice the parties should ensure that such an order is drawn up and entered.

Certain types of order, as listed in Order 42 rule 4, do not need to be drawn up unless the court directs.

**[42.5.2]    Practice direction on settling draft orders and judgment**

PD 16.1, which was substantially revised at the time of the civil justice reforms in 2009, gives guidance on the settling of draft orders and judgments. Para 1 of the practice direction provides that a draft order should be submitted for approval 'as soon as possible but in any case not later than 7 days after the pronouncement of the order'. The full text of the practice direction can be viewed on the judiciary's website.

**[42.5.3]    Order should recite summons and affidavits before the court**

It is a 'long established practice' for an order to be drawn up reciting the affidavits which were read by the judge or master making the order: *Deak & Anor v Deak Perera Far East Ltd (in liq)* [1990] 2 HKC 198, 200E-F. In that case it was said that failure to comply had 'occasioned uncertainty and the waste of time and money' in the course of hearing an appeal against the order concerned, and that it would cause difficulties for the taxing master.

In 2009 practice direction 16.1 was amended so as to specifically require that court orders recite the parties who attended and their representation, and all summonses, affidavits and affirmations relevant to the hearing or before the court when the order was made.

**[42.5.4]    Submission of draft order or judgment for approval**

Before an order or judgment of the court will be sealed and entered, a draft must be submitted for approval. Practice direction 16.1 provides that this should be done as soon as practicable and in any case not later than 7 days after the order is made. If the party who initiated the application leading to the order fails to draw up the order within 7 days, the other party may do so: Order 42 rule 5(5).

**[42.5.5]    Sealing of judgment or order**

Once a draft judgment or order has been approved, it should be engrossed as amended and presented to the registry (together with the approved draft) for sealing. Solicitors have been reminded of the importance of ensuring that engrossments submitted for sealing are exactly the same as the approved draft. See the letter from the Registrar dated 11.02.2003 circulated by the Law Society from time to time, for example in circular 06–79.

## [42.5.6]    When judgment or order is 'perfected'

An order is 'perfected' when it has been drawn up and entered in accordance with Order 42 rule 5. See *China Resources Electric Appliance (Zhuhai) Co Ltd & Anor v Decosonic HK Ltd* HCCL 39/2001 (Chung J; 25.08.2001) where it was held that an order signed by a judge had not yet been perfected. The significance is that although the judgment or order takes effect from the date of its pronouncement (Order 42 rule 3), it may be amenable to variation under the court's inherent jurisdiction up until it has been perfected. See the commentary under Order 20 rule 11.

**5A.    Consent judgment and orders** (O. 42 r. 5A)

    **(1)**    **Subject to paragraphs (2), (3), (4) and (5), where all the parties to a cause or matter are agreed upon the terms in which a judgment should be given, or an order should be made, a judgment or order in such terms may be given effect as a judgment or order of the Court by the procedure provided in rule 5.**

    **(2)**    **This rule applies to any judgment or order which consists of one or more of the following—**

        **(a)**    **any judgment or order for—**

            **(i)**    **the payment of a liquidated sum, or damages to be assessed, or the value of goods to be assessed;**

            **(ii)**    **the delivery up of goods, with or without the option of paying the value of the goods to be assessed, or the agreed value;**

            **(iii)**    **the possession of land where the claim does not relate to a dwelling-house;**

        **(b)**    **any order for—**

            **(i)**    **the dismissal, discontinuance or withdrawal of any proceedings, wholly or in part;**

            **(ii)**    **the stay of proceedings, either unconditionally or upon conditions as to the payment of money;**

            **(iii)**    **the stay of proceedings upon terms which are scheduled to the order but which are not otherwise part of it (a "Tomlin order");**

            **(iv)**    **the stay of enforcement of a judgment, either unconditionally or upon condition that the money due under judgment is paid by instalments specified in the order;**

            **(v)**    **the setting aside of a judgment in default;**

            **(vi)**    **the transfer of any proceedings to the District Court or the Lands Tribunal; (L.N. 152 of 2008)**

            **(vii)**    **the payment out of money in court;**

            **(viii)**    **the discharge from liability of any party;**

            **(ix)**    **the payment, taxation or waiver of costs, or such other provision for costs as may be agreed;**

        **(c)**    **any order, to be included in a judgment or order to which the preceding sub-paragraphs apply, for—**

            **(i)**    **the extension of the period required for the service or filing of any pleading or other document;**

            **(ii)**    **the withdrawal of the record;**

            **(iii)**    **liberty to apply, or to restore.**

    **(3)**    **Before any judgment, or order to which this rule applies may be entered, or sealed, it must be drawn up in the terms agreed and expressed as**

**"By Consent" and it must be indorsed by solicitors acting for each of the parties.**

**(4)    This rule shall not apply to any judgment or order in proceedings which are pending in the Admiralty jurisdiction or in the Commercial List.**

**(5)    This rule shall not apply to any judgment or order in proceedings in which any of the parties is a litigant in person or a person under a disability.**

---

## NOTES

### [42.5A.1]  Scope of Order 42 rule 5A

In the former English RSC, Order 42 rule 5A was confined to proceedings in the Queen's Bench Division. There are, of course, no formal divisions in Hong Kong's Court of First Instance, and there is no equivalent restriction in Order 42 rule 5A. However, rule 5A(4) provides that the rule does not apply to Admiralty or Commercial List proceedings. In addition, Order 76 rule 12 may be interpreted as providing that an agreed compromise of a probate action may not be formalised by consent judgment or order under Order 42 rule 5A, requiring instead a trial, which may be on affidavit evidence under that rule.

### [42.5A.2]  Consent orders

Order 42 rule 5A provides, subject to some important exceptions, that judgments and orders may be entered by consent, without the need for an appearance before a judge or master. The rule applies to the types of judgment and order listed in rule 5A(2), except in actions in the Admiralty jurisdiction or on the Commercial list (rule 5A(4)), or where there is a litigant in person or a party under disability (rule 5A(5)).

A consent judgment or order (whether entered under this rule, granted under a consent summons or at an unopposed hearing) is final and conclusive like any other judgment or order. See *Ho Shiu Kwong v Au Yeung Leung & Anor* [1946]–[1972] HKC 288, 293B-C and *Law Shi Ying v Law Kam Tai* [1994] 1 HKC 378, 382E-F, citing *Kinch v Walcott* [1929] AC 482, 493. However, because a consent order embodies an agreement between the parties it is liable to variation by subsequent agreement or by the court in circumstances where the court has jurisdiction to set aside a contract. See the commentary under 'Setting aside consent order' below.

Likewise a consent judgment or order may, in principle, be enforced like any other. However there is some authority to the effect that breach of a consent order does not constitute contempt: see *Lim Chau Leng v Wong Chee Chong* [2006] 2 MLJ 269 and the authorities cited therein.

A consent order may embody only part of an agreement between the parties. In such a case the additional terms of the agreement, outside the consent order, will be enforceable. See *Lam Hon Keung Keith & Ors v Jade Light Village Sea Food Restaurant Ltd* [1984] HKC 279. In principle a fresh action should be required, though that is not the case with terms in the schedule to a Tomlin order which go beyond the original dispute:  see the commentary on Tomlin orders below.

### [42.5A.3]  Procedure

The party seeking to enter the judgment or order which has been agreed upon should draw up the order in the agreed terms, expressing it to be 'by consent' and have it indorsed by solicitors acting for each of the parties (rule 5A(3)). The form of order then need only be left with the registrar to be entered in accordance with the procedure laid down in rule 5.

### [42.5A.4]   Jurisdiction

The parties cannot in a consent order provide for anything exceeding the court's jurisdiction or circumvent any restriction on the exercise of the court's power. See *Shen Ta-chang & Anor v Chen Lai-pui* DCCJ 6537/1980 (Judge Downey; 02.09.1981) where it was stated, citing *Choi Hau-ying v Teh Hu Steamship Co (HK) Ltd* [1969] DCLR 29, 32:

> As a matter of general principle, the parties cannot by their agreement confer upon the court a jurisdiction which it does not possess, or remove any fetter thereon, imposed by statute.

### [42.5A.5]   Distinction between consent order and consent summons

When seeking an order by consent otherwise than by appearing before the court, it is important to bear in mind the distinction between consent orders and consent summonses.

A consent order is a matter for the registry and will only be granted if the order sought comes within the ambit of Order 42 rule 5A. Where the order sought is outside the ambit of Order 42 rule 5A the parties should submit a consent summons, which will be placed before a judge or master for consideration. It is not appropriate to issue a consent summons where a consent order is possible under the rules: see *Wing Han Trading Co Ltd v Tang Yan Kit & Anor* [1990] 2 HKC 445 where Godfrey J stated (at 449C–F):

> I should draw attention to a point of practice which is consistently misapprehended by practitioners in Hong Kong. It concerns the consent order of 14 March 1990. This was obtained as often happens by the plaintiff taking out what is called a 'consent summons' seeking the order required, and placing that before a master ... for him to make an order in the terms of the summons. This practice is wrong and involves a quite unnecessary waste of money and of judicial time. The relevant rule is O 42 r 5A. Under the provisions of this rule, a party who wishes to obtain a consent order in a case to which the rule applies may do so simply by presenting it to the registrar for entry: see r 5A(1) and r 5A(2). It must be endorsed by the solicitors for the parties: see r 5A(3). But it is quite unnecessary to place it before any judge or master.

Since late 1994 the registry has refused to accept consent summonses seeking orders which could be made by consent order under Order 42 rule 5A.

### [42.5A.6]   Tomlin orders

A Tomlin order (so named for the judge who decided *Dashwood v Dashwood* [1927] WN 276) is a stay of proceedings for all purposes save the carrying out of an agreement which is set out in a schedule to the order.  Since the order involves agreement it will be made by consent and may be made by paper application under Order 42 rule 5A(2)(b)(iii). A Tomlin order is normally worded along the following lines (*Dashwood v Dashwood* [1927] WN 290 (practice note)):

> And the plaintiff and defendant having agreed to the terms set forth in the schedule hereto, it is ordered that all further proceedings in this action be stayed except

for the purpose of carrying such terms into effect. Liberty to apply as to carrying such terms into effect.

The schedule to a Tomlin order being a matter of agreement between the parties, its terms need not be approved by the court, but the court might later refuse to enforce it if, for example, it is too vague. See *Lucky Wealth Consultants Ltd v Horizon Technologies Int'l Ltd* [1991] 1 HKLR 563, 572C-E (CA) referring to *Noel v Becker* [1971] 1 WLR 355 and *Wilson & Whitworth Ltd v Express & Independent Newspapers Ltd* [1969] 1 WLR 197. A Tomlin order constitutes a contract of settlement between the parties and it is up to the court to determine its meaning and effect: *Wenden Engineering Services Co Ltd v Lee Shing Yue Construction Co Ltd* HCCT 90/1999 (Burrell J; 20.11.2000) (para 6).

The schedule to a Tomlin order may go outside the ambit of the original dispute between the parties: *Colliers Jardine Management Ltd v Natural Way Development Ltd & Ors* [2001] 2 HKC 580, 587B-C (CA). However it has been held that it may not contain provisions going beyond the jurisdiction of the court: *Shen Ta-chang & Anor v Chen Lai-pui* DCCJ 6537/1980 (Judge Downey; 02.09.1981).

The schedule to a Tomlin order is not part of the order: *Dashwood v Dashwood* [1927] WN 276, 277. As a result failure to comply is not a breach of the order: *Chu Kin-ying v R* CACC 232/1981 (Huggins & McMullin VPP, Li JA; 04.08.1981). Further the schedule cannot be enforced directly by the usual execution procedures – it is necessary for the party seeking to enforce it to apply for an order in terms of the agreement. That can be done by summons in the same action pursuant to the liberty to apply - a fresh action is not necessary: *Luk Por v Chau Kim Hung* HCA 10369/1997 (Reyes J; 08.10.2003). This is the case even with provisions in the schedule going beyond the ambit of the original dispute: *E F Phillips & Sons Ltd v Clarke* [1970] Ch 322, quoted with approval in *Lucky Wealth* (above, at 572A-B) and *Luk Por* (above) and superseding *Green v Rozen* [1955] 1 WLR 741, 744 in this regard. In *E F Phillips* Goff J stated (at 325F-H):

> … provided an order is in the normally appropriate form with a qualified stay and a liberty to apply, and provided the application is strictly to enforce the terms embodied in the order and the schedule, and does not depart from the agreed terms, an order giving effect to the terms may be obtained under the liberty to apply in the original action, notwithstanding the compromise itself goes beyond the ambit of the original dispute  and the provision sought to be enforced is something which could not have been enforced in the original action and which, indeed, is an obligation which did not then exist but arose for the first time under the compromise.

Where an application to enforce the schedule to a Tomlin order is opposed, the party resisting enforcement has a 'burden' analogous to that of a defendant resisting an application for summary judgment: *Chan Yiu Sing Peter v Lam Yat Wah & Anor* [1990] 2 HKLR 92, 96A; *Incorporated Owners of Hoi To Court v Chinluck Properties Ltd* HCA 6171/1997 (Chu J; 29.08.2006).

Where the court refuses an application to enforce the schedule to a Tomlin order, or where the plaintiff wishes, as a consequence of the defendant's failure to comply, to proceed with other claims which were made in the original action but not dealt with in the schedule, the court may lift the stay of proceedings to enable the plaintiff to continue with the original action where it had left off or a fresh action may be commenced for specific performance or breach of the agreement embodied in the schedule.

It has been suggested that the usual limitation periods apply to any application for enforcement of the terms set out in the schedule to a Tomlin order: see the *Hoi To Court* case (above).

In the Australian state of Victoria, it has long been recognised that an agreement to compromise proceedings may be enforced in those proceedings, even if not scheduled to an order. Provided that the proceedings have not been brought to an end, it is not necessary to commence a fresh action. See *Roberts v Grippsland Agricultural & Earth Moving Contract Co Pty Ltd* [1956] VLR 555 (F Ct); *Seachange Management Pty Ltd & Anor v Pital Business Pty Ltd* [2009] VSCA 139.

**[42.5A.7] 'Liberty to apply'**

It is common to include in orders made by consent a provision that there be 'liberty to apply'. The meaning of that phrase in a consent order was considered by the Court of Appeal in *Leung Yee & Anor v Ng Yiu Ming & Anor* [2001] 1 HKC 342. It was held (at 360B) that the provision 'confers on the judge the power to construe the terms of the consent order and decide on their true meaning and effect.' As a result, in the absence of an express ouster of the court's power under Order 3 rule 5 to extend time, the time for compliance with the consent order could be extended by order of the court.

Liberty to apply is not restricted to matters which could be dealt with under the 'slip rule' (see Order 20 rule 11 and the commentary thereunder): *Wing Fai Construction Co Ltd v Fitzroya Finance Co Ltd* [2006] 1 HKC 272, 275B–C, not following *Koh Ewe Chee v Koh Hua Leong* [2002] 3 SLR 643 in this regard.

See also the commentary under Order 44 rule 3.

**[42.5A.8] Variation of contractual consent order**

An order made by consent (whether entered under Order 42 rule 5A or not) may embody an agreement between the parties. If so, it may be susceptible to variation or discharge by further agreement between the parties. See *Ho Shiu Kwong v Au Yeung Leung & Anor* [1946–1972] HKC 288, 293A, citing *Australasian Automatic Weighing Machine Co v Walter* (1891) WN 170.

Furthermore, a contractual consent order may be varied or set aside by the court 'on any of the grounds upon which an agreement may be set aside': *Ng Shui Ling v Lai Hang* [1983] 1 HKC 158, 162B-C (CA). Those grounds include fraud, mistake and misrepresentation: *Cathay Pacific Airways Flight Attendants Union v Cheung & Choy* HCMP 1863/2007 (Deputy Judge Au; 03.02.2009) (para 28). In the absence of such 'exceptional circumstances' the court will not set aside a consent order as 'it is a matter of public policy that the court should enforce compromises which are agreed in good faith': *Postwell Ltd v Cheng Kap Sang* [2004] 2 HKLRD 355, 361. Since it is necessary to prove the grounds on which it is sought to set aside the agreement and hence the con sent order, a fresh action is necessary. See *Law Shi Ying v Law Kam Tai* [1994] 1 HKC 378, 382C–D (CA) citing *De Lasala v De Lasala* [1980] AC 546, 561. See also *Ng Shui Hing v Lai Hang* [1983] 1 HKC 158, 162C (CA), citing in addition *Ainsworth v Wilding* [1896] 1 Ch 673.

Unconscionability as a ground for setting aside a consent order was considered by Godfrey J in *Tsang Iu Hung v Tsang Tak Wah & Anor* [1993] 2 HKC 471. He refused to set aside an order consented to by a litigant in person who had had its terms explained to him by the court interpreter. He said the court would only set aside a consent order on this ground:

> ... if it would be unconscionable conduct on the part of the party seeking to enforce the compromise to insist on enforcing it; for example, if an unfair advantage has been taken of one party by the other party (in the sense of domination or victimization or unfair pressure) leading him into a manifestly disadvantageous transaction.

See also *Deputy Commissioner of Taxation (NSW) v Chamberlain* (1990) 93 ALR 729 where the Federal Court of Australia set aside a consent judgment on the grounds that the unilateral mistake of one party (unrepresented) had unconscionably been taken advantage of by the other. In that case a decimal point was misplaced resulting in judgment for only one-tenth the correct amount.

A consent order may also be set aside on the ground of failure to make full and frank disclosure of all material facts to the other party and to the court. See *Man Lan Ying v Leung Tsan Chung* CACV 150/2006 (Ma CJHC, Tang VP & Sakhrani J; 19.12.2006) where the court declined to set aside a consent order in a matrimonial case where one of the parties had allegedly concealed assets.

In the unusual case of *Leung Kam Tai v Wong Chuen* [1998] 4 HKC 214 the court set aside an order providing for payment out of court to the defendant in a personal injuries action which had been resolved by consent in favour of the plaintiff. The court was of the view that such a provision should never have been agreed as it put at risk the plaintiff's security for payment of damages and the first charge of the Director of Legal Aid. Application to the court should have been made. The order was set aside on the basis of a jurisdiction to set aside an order if it does not make sense, is contradictory, unclear or otherwise defective.

A review of various grounds on which the court may refuse to enforce a settlement agreement between parties can be found in *Malley v Red River Valley Mutual Insurance Co* [2010] MBQB 111 (CanLII).

**[42.5A.9]　Variation of consent order not based on contract**
In some cases the courts have found that particular consent orders do not embody a contract between the parties, such that the order may be varied without the need to demonstrate the exceptional grounds on which an agreement may be set aside. See *CY Tsun Investment Co Ltd v IO Hoi To Court* HCSA 16/2003 (A Cheung J; 02.07.2004) (para 30), referring to *Siebe Gorman & Co Ltd v Pneupac Ltd* [1982] 1 WLR 185. In both those cases this was said to be the case with consent orders made not by agreement, but by non-objection in order to save time and costs. The court has a discretion to vary such consent orders according to 'normal principles': *Cathay Pacific Airways Flight Attendants Union v Cheung & Choy* (above) (para 28). For example, the court may in its discretion grant an extension of time, the power to do so under Order 3 rule 5 not having been excluded by agreement.

**5B.　Reasons for judgment or order** (O. 42 r. 5B)
　　**(HK)(1)A Court shall give the reasons for any decision either at the time the judgment or order is pronounced or, where it is at that time announced that the reasons will be given at a later date, at such later date as may be fixed.**
　　　**(2)　Where the judgment or order is not pronounced on the day on**

which the hearing is concluded or where a decision is pronounced but it is announced in accordance with paragraph (1) that reasons therefor will be given at a later date, the Court may state that the judgment or order or the judgment or order and the reasons therefor, as the case may be, will be recorded in writing.

(3) Where a date has been fixed for delivery of a written decision or of written reasons notice shall be given to the parties, but it shall not be necessary for them to appear by counsel or in person.

(4) Where it has been announced that a judgment or order and reasons therefor or the reasons for a judgment or order previously pronounced will be recorded in writing, the Court may on the date fixed, instead of reading in full the judgment or order and reasons therefor or the reasons, as the case may be, supply copies thereof in accordance with paragraph (5). Thereupon any judgment or order contained in the writing shall be deemed to have been pronounced for the purposes of rule 3.

(5) Where the judgment or order and reasons therefor or the reasons are given at a later date and, being recorded in writing, are not read in full, the Court shall—

    (a)    hand down a copy thereof for each of the parties and endorse the record accordingly;

    (b)    lodge a copy thereof in the High Court Library; and

    (c)    make a copy thereof available for public inspection in the Registry.

(6) Where a written decision is given pursuant to this rule the Court may make therein an order nisi as to costs and, unless an application has been made to vary that order, that order shall become absolute 14 days after the decision is pronounced.

(7) Where a court consisting of more than one judge sits to deliver pursuant to this rule a decision and reasons for a decision previously pronounced, it shall be sufficient if at least one of the judges who conducted the hearing is present.

(8) Nothing in this rule shall affect the provisions of Order 63 rule 4.

(Enacted 1988)

---

## NOTES

**[42.5B.1]  Court's duty to give reasons**

Order 42 rule 5B(1) restates the fundamental common law principle that the court must give reasons for any decision.

The Court of Appeal had occasion to consider the elements of this principle in *Zhuo Cui Hao v Ting Fung Yee* [1999] 3 HKC 634. At 639D–E Chan CJHC stated that a professional judge's duty is to give adequate reasons. Justice could only be done by making losing litigants understand why their evidence is not accepted and why they lose in a case (at 639C–D). In that case the reasons were found to be so inadequate that the trial judge's decision was set aside and a re-trial ordered.

**[42.5B.2] Handing down of judgments**

As a general rule, justice should be administered in public and the court should publicly give its reasons for any decision. An exception is the court composed of judge and jury, as juries are not required to give reasons.

In many cases, the court requires time to consider a case, and therefore the judgment or reasons cannot be given immediately. Rule 5B(3) makes it possible for the court in such cases to give its reasons for judgment, in a manner accessible to the public, without the need for the parties (through counsel or otherwise) to attend, thus saving costs.

**[42.5B.3] Rule 5B(6) – Costs order nisi**

Order 42 rule 5B(6) provides that the court may make a costs order *nisi* when handing down a decision which has been reserved. The provision applies equally where the court hands down final judgment or an interlocutory decision, as in *Re UDL Holdings Ltd (No 2)* [1999] 3 HKC 220, 222H.

The rule provides that a costs order *nisi* will become absolute 14 days after it is made unless an application for variation is made. It has been held that an application made on the 14th day is within time even though that is the day on which the order *nisi* would otherwise become absolute: *Newmark Capital Corp Ltd v Coffee Partners Ltd* HCA 1271/2006 (Recorder Shieh SC; 10.04.2007).

In *Newmark* (above) it was held that an application for variation of a costs order *nisi* does not require a summons, and may be made by letter. However in the earlier case of *PCCW-HKT Telephone Ltd v Telecommunications Authority* CACV 274/2003 (Ma CJHC, Rogers VP & Le Pichon JA; 07.09.2004) (which was not referred to in *Newmark*) the Court of Appeal said application by letter was 'most unsatisfactory' and 'incorrect' (para 5). Ma CJHC said (at para 11):

> Lastly I would just like to make some observations on the way in which the TA has made the present application to vary the costs order *nisi* under O 42, r 5B(6). As mentioned above, this was done by way of letter. This is wrong. Applications to court should be made by way of summons or motion, and not by the informal way that was chosen in the present case. The reason for this requirement is to enable the other side and the Court to understand exactly the nature and extent of what is being asked for. Otherwise, there is a danger that it becomes unclear just what is being sought from the Court, thereby allowing parties to ask for relief in a haphazard manner.

Nevertheless in that case, and again in *Law Cheuk v Chan Fung Luen Margaret* HCPI 701/2006 (Saunders J; 17.07.2008) the court did entertain applications made by letter for variations of costs orders *nisi*.

The time for making an application for variation of a costs order *nisi* may be extended under Order 3 rule 5 even after the order has become absolute: *Ma Wan Farming Ltd v CE in Council* [1998] 2 HKLRD 314 (CA). On an application to extend the time to apply for variation of a costs order *nisi*, the court will normally expect a good explanation for the delay: *Tsang Mei Luen v Yip Wai Biu* DCPI 2272/2008 (Deputy Judge ST Poon; 12.08.2010). The usual practice would be for the explanation to be set out in an affidavit.

It is not appropriate to seek variation of a costs order *nisi* on the ground the substantive decision is wrong – that is a matter for appeal: *Kwan Siu Man Joshua v Yaacov Ozer (No 2)* [1998] 3 HKC 62 (CA).

## ORDER 43

### ACCOUNTS AND INQUIRIES

1.    **Summary order for account** (O. 43 r. 1)

(1)   **Where a writ is indorsed with a claim for an account or a claim which necessarily involves taking an account, the plaintiff may, at any time after the defendant has acknowledged service of the writ or after the time limited for acknowledging service, apply for an order under this rule.**

(1A)  **A defendant to an action begun by writ who has served a counterclaim, which includes a claim for an account or a claim which necessarily involves taking an account, on—**

    (a)    **the plaintiff, or**

    (b)    **any other party, or**

    (c)    **any person who becomes a party by virtue of such service,**

**may apply for an order under this rule.**

(2)   **An application under this rule must be made by summons and, if the Court so directs, must be supported by affidavit or other evidence.**

(3)   **On the hearing of the application, the Court may, unless satisfied that there is some preliminary question to be tried, order that an account be taken and may also order that any amount certified on taking the account to be due to either party be paid to him within a time specified in the order.**

---

## NOTES

**[43.1.1]**    **Scope of Order 43 rule 1 – Interlocutory order for taking account**

Order 43 rule 1 empowers the court to make a summary order for the taking of an account at the interlocutory stage. Such an order may be sought in an action claiming for an account, or which necessarily involves taking an account: rule 1(1). Rule 1(1A) provides likewise where the defendant is counterclaiming for such relief.

In some cases, such as where there is an admitted duty to account, and the only dispute is as to the amount owing, the taking of an account may resolve the entire dispute. In *Dongguan Harris Plastic Products Co Ltd & Anor v Chan Dai Chung* HCA 289/1999 (Recorder G Li SC; 27.09.2001), which appears to have been such a case, the court encouraged the parties to save costs by using the Order 43 summary procedure rather than 'deploying the armoury of interlocutory applications available in a full action'. In *Ironwood Capital Ltd v KTH Capital Management Ltd* HCA 2836/2004 (Suffiad J; 20.11.2007) the taking of an account at the interlocutory stage was considered appropriate to enable 'proper and smooth determination of the issues at trial' (para 44).

It is not appropriate for the procedure under this rule to be used to obtain specific discovery: *Ho Lee Man v Wong Wai Kai* [1993] 1 HKC 183, 191F (CA).

**[43.1.2]**    **No account to be taken where preliminary question to be tried**

An application for the taking of an account at the interlocutory stage is not appropriate where there are unresolved issues which are appropriate for determination at trial: *Ho*

*Lee Man* (above, at 191B); *Kids World Ltd v XL Machine Ltd & Ors* HCA 125/2002 (Reyes J; 18.09.2003). Indeed rule 1(3) is worded in such a way as to deprive the court of power to order an account in such circumstances. However the outstanding issues must be ones which go to the crucial question whether the defendant is under a duty to account. See *Hollingworth v Juson* [2006] 3 HKC 488 where it was held that the fact there were outstanding applications for further and better particulars and challenging the plaintiff's mental capacity did not prevent the court from ordering that an account be taken. Similarly in *Ironwood Capital* (above) the court ordered the taking of an account despite outstanding factual issues, since those factual issues did not 'touch on the question whether an account should be rendered' (para 34). In *Tang Fu Sun v Tang Lik Yuen* HCA 2028/2006 (Master Wong; 14.12.2007) the court rejected an argument that it was not possible to prepare a complete account pending trial, saying that the account could contain 'reservation and qualification' as is common in audited accounts.

**[43.1.3]     Orders ancillary to an order for taking an account**
Order 43 rule 1(3) provides that the court may, when ordering that an account be taken, also order payment within a specified time after the amount has been certified. In *Ironwood Capital* (above, at para 29) it was said that such an order is normally sought.

In *Avid Technology Inc v Cheung Ki Wing George* HCA 9956/1996 (Cheung J; 03.12.1998) it was held that once the account has been taken and the amount certified, the creditor may apply for an interim payment under Order 29 rule 12.

In *Wong Kam Wing v Cheng Pui Lun & Anor* DCCJ 3878/2002 (Deputy Judge Ko; 13.12.2005) proceedings in the action were stayed pending the taking of an account.

**2.     Court may direct taking of accounts, etc.** (O. 43 r. 2)
**(1)     The Court may, on an application made by summons at any stage of the proceedings in a cause or matter, direct any necessary accounts or inquiries to be taken or made.**

**(2)     Every direction for the taking of an account or the making of an inquiry shall be numbered in the judgment or order so that, as far as may be, each distinct account and inquiry may be designated by a number.**

**3.     Directions as to manner of taking account or making inquiry** (O. 43 r. 3)
**(1)     Where the Court orders an account to be taken or inquiry to be made it may by the same or a subsequent order give directions with regard to the manner in which the account is to be taken or vouched or the inquiry is to be made.**

**(2)     Without prejudice to the generality of paragraph (1), the Court may direct that in taking an account the relevant books of account shall be evidence of the matters contained therein with liberty to the parties interested to take such objections thereto as they think fit.**

---

**NOTES**

**[43.3.1]**     **Liberty to apply**

See the commentary under Order 44 rule 3 as to 'liberty to apply' in respect of directions under a judgment or order.

**4.**     **Account to be made, verified, etc.** (O. 43 r. 4)

    **(1)**    **Where an account has been ordered to be taken, the accounting party must make out his account and, unless the Court otherwise directs, verify it by an affidavit to which the account must be exhibited.**

    **(2)**    **The items on each side of the account must be numbered consecutively.**

    **(3)**    **Unless the order for the taking of the account otherwise directs, the accounting party must lodge the account with the Court and must at the same time notify the other parties that he has done so and of the filing of any affidavit verifying the account and of any supporting affidavit.**

**5.**     **Notice to be given of alleged omissions, etc. in account** (O. 43 r. 5)

    **Any party who seeks to charge an accounting party with an amount beyond that which he has by his account admitted to have received or who alleges that any item in his account is erroneous in respect of amount or in any other respect must give him notice thereof stating, so far as he is able, the amount sought to be charged with brief particulars thereof or, as the case may be, the grounds for alleging that the item is erroneous.**

---

## NOTES

**[43.5.1]**     **Rules 4 & 5 – procedure for taking an account**

Rules 4 and 5 set out the obligations of the respective parties to refine the issues in preparation for the taking of an account. Under rule 4 the 'accounting party', that is the party who has a duty to account, sets out the account item by item in numbered sequence. This will show, for example, the payments received by the accounting party, expenses incurred and payments out to the receiving party. The rule requires that the account be verified by affidavit.

In response any party objecting to an item in the account is obliged to give notice with particulars. This is done in a document which is sometimes called a 'Notice of Objections' – see, for example, *Wong Kam Wing v Cheng Pui Lun & Anor* DCCJ 3878/2002 (Judge Muttrie; 09.06.2004). Unlike the account, there is no requirement in the rules that the objections be verified by affidavit. However it would be appropriate to file affidavit evidence in support of an objection if such evidence is required to substantiate it.

The time and manner for taking the above steps may be fixed by directions given under Order 43 rule 3.

See generally Atkin's Court Forms (2002 issue, vol 1, p 5 *et seq*) and Chitty & Jacob's Queen's Bench Forms (1986, ch 98), both of which are cited with approval in *Lam Yim Kam Johnson v Lam Yim Hing David* HCA 642/2001 (Recorder Ronny Wong SC; 03.09.2002) and *Wong Kam Wing* (above). As to the degree of detail required, see *Hollingworth v Juson* HCA 249/2006 (Chu J; 16.10.2006).

#### [43.5.2]    Hearing

The taking of an account 'is a process of inquiry' whereby the court (master or judge) will vet the accounts produced by the accounting party and the oral and written evidence produced by both parties 'with a view to arriving at an outstand ing figure due from one party to another': *Kids World Ltd v XL Machine Ltd & Ors* HCA 125/2002 (Reyes J; 18.09.2003).

#### [43.5.3]    Appeal against order made on taking an account

An appeal against a master's order made on taking an account lies to a single judge in chambers pursuant to Order 44 rule 12. See the commentary under that rule, referring to *Chow Fu Hsien v K Vision Int'l Investment (HK) Ltd* HCA 2884/2004 (Recorder Yu SC; 20.07.2010).

**6.    Allowances** (O. 43 r. 6)

**In taking any account directed by any judgment or order all just allowances shall be made without any direction to that effect.**

---

**NOTES**

#### [43.6.1]    Meaning of 'just allowances'

The meaning of the term 'just allowances' in Order 43 rule 6 was explained by Barnett J in *Tang Wing Hong Alan (personal representative of the estate of Tang Man Sit, deceased) v Capacious Investment Ltd* [1993] 2 HKC 416. The learned judge stated (at 421D–E):

> Just allowances, as I have said, are essential expenses and disbursements which it is just to be allowed to the accounting party. The important word, in relation to this case, is 'just'. The cases to which I have been referred, all involved mortgagees acting lawfully and justifiably. In contrast, the defendant, ie the deceased, behaved unlawfully, in breach of trust. That, in my judgment, distinguishes this case. I do not consider it just that a party who is called to account for secret profits arising out of a breach of trust should be entitled to any allowances without explicit order of the court.

**7.    Delay in prosecution of accounts, etc.** (O. 43 r. 7)

**(1)   If it appears to the Court that there is undue delay in the prosecution of any accounts or inquiries, or in any other proceedings under any judgment or order, the Court may require the party having the conduct of the proceedings or any other party to explain the delay and may then make such order for staying the proceedings or for expediting them or for the conduct thereof and for costs as the circumstances require.**

**(2)   The Court may direct any party or the Official Solicitor to take over the conduct of the proceedings in question and to carry out any directions made by an order under this rule and may make such order as it thinks fit as to the payment of the Official Solicitor's costs. (L.N. 375 of 1991)**

**8.    Distribution of fund before all persons entitled are ascertained** (O. 43 r. 8)

**Where some of the persons entitled to share in a fund are ascertained, and difficulty or delay has occurred or is likely to occur in ascertaining the**

other persons so entitled, the Court may order or allow immediate payment of their shares to the persons ascertained without reserving any part of those shares to meet the subsequent costs of ascertaining those other persons.

9.      **Guardian's accounts** (O. 43 r. 9)

The accounts of a person appointed guardian of a minor's estate must be verified and passed in such a manner as the Court may direct.

**(Enacted 1988)**

## ORDER 44

### PROCEEDINGS UNDER JUDGMENTS AND ORDERS

**NOTES**

**[44.0.1]    Comparison with English rules**
Order 44 is based on the equivalent of the same number in the former English Rules of the Supreme Court. There are a few minor differences in wording, but these do not appear to be of any consequence.

Since advent of the Civil Procedure Rules, the equivalent provisions in England are no longer found in a single place, but are scattered. See para 9.17 of the Chancery Guide published when the CPR came into force.

**1.    Application to orders** (O. 44 r. 1)
**In this Order references to a judgment include references to an order.**

**2.    Service of notice of judgment on person not a party** (O. 44 r. 2)
**(1)    Where in an action for—**
  **(a)    the administration of the estate of a deceased person, or**
  **(b)    the execution of a trust, or**
  **(c)    the sale of any property,**
**the Court gives a judgment or makes a direction which affects persons not parties to the action, the Court may when giving the judgment or at any stage of the proceedings under the judgment direct notice of the judgment to be served on any such person and any person so served shall, subject to paragraph (4), be bound by the judgment as if he had originally been a party to the action.**
  **(2)    If it appears that it is not practicable to serve notice of a judgment on a person directed to be served the Court may dispense with service and may also order that such person be bound by the judgment.**
  **(2A) Order 6, rule 7(3) and (5) shall apply in relation to a notice of judgment under this rule as if the notice were a writ and the person by whom the notice is issued were the plaintiff. (L.N. 404 of 1991)**
  **(3)    Every notice of a judgment for service under this rule must be indorsed with a memorandum in Form No. 52 in Appendix A and accompanied by a form of acknowledgment of service in Form No. 15 in Appendix A with such modifications as may be appropriate and the copy of the notice to be served shall be a sealed copy.**
  **(4)    A person served with notice of a judgment may, within one month after service of the notice on him, and after acknowledging service, apply to the Court to discharge, vary or add to the judgment.**
  **(5)    A person served with notice of a judgment may, after acknowledging service of the notice, attend the proceedings under the judgment.**
  **(6)    Order 12, rules 1 to 4, shall apply in relation to the acknowledgment of service of a notice of judgment as if the judgment were a writ, and the person**

**by whom the notice is served were the plaintiff and the person on whom it is served a defendant. (L.N. 404 of 1991)**

---

## NOTES

### [44.2.1]    Notice to non-party affected by judgment or order

Order 44 rule 2 provides for notice to be given to non-parties affected by a judgment or direction of the court. It is provided that the person served with notice pursuant to the rule is bound by the judgment as if he had been a party. The rule does not require service of affected non-parties; rather it empowers the court to direct such service. The rule applies only in relation to the 3 types of action listed in rule 2(1). As an example see *Ip Cheung Kwok v Ip Siu Bun* CACV 79/1998 (Cons VP, Kempster & Clough JJA; 28.11.1989) where notice of an order for sale of trust property was served on a company which made a claim against the property in separate proceedings.

**3.      Directions by the Court** (O. 44 r. 3)

**(1)    Where a judgment given in a cause or matter contains directions which make it necessary to proceed in chambers under the judgment the Court may, when giving the judgment or at any time during proceedings under the judgment, give further directions for the conduct of those proceedings, including, in particular, directions with respect to—**

**(a)    the manner in which any account or inquiry is to be prosecuted,**

**(b)    the evidence to be adduced in support thereof,**

**(c)    the preparation and service on the parties to be bound thereby of the draft of any deed or other instrument which is directed by the judgment to be settled by the Court and the service of any objections to the draft,**

**(d)    without prejudice to Order 15, rule 17, the parties required to attend all or any part of the proceedings,**

**(e)    the representation by the same solicitors of parties who constitute a class and by different solicitors of parties who ought to be separately represented, and**

**(f)    the time within which each proceeding is to be taken,**

**and may fix a day or days for the further attendance of the parties.**

**(2)    The Court may revoke or vary any directions given under the rule.**

---

## NOTES

### [44.3.1]    Scope of Order 44 rule 3

Order 44 rule 3 stipulates that the court may give directions for the conduct of pro ceedings under a judgment. An example would be directions for the conduct of an assessment of damages. See also Order 43 rule 3 in relation to the taking of accounts and inquiries.

## [44.3.2]     Liberty to apply

It may be appropriate for directions in accordance with Order 44 rule 3 to include 'liberty to apply', but that is not appropriate in most interlocutory orders. In *Sun Yuet Tai Ltd v BAT Co (HK) Ltd* CACV 95/1999 (Godfrey & Rogers JJA; 04.06.1999) Godfrey JA said at paras 30-31:

> . . . the giving of 'liberty to apply' is not necessary or appropriate in interlocutory orders. When an action is proceeding, it is always possible for the parties at any time to apply for any relief they think to be necessary by notice under the summons for directions (if the action has got that far) or by an ordinary summons. And in any case, where 'liberty to apply' is given, this does not authorise the parties to come back to the court without taking the appropriate procedural steps. (It may be that the expression 'liberty to apply' is sometimes used when what is really meant is 'liberty to restore'. If it is desired for some reason that an application should come back before the judge or master for some further order, then it is appropriate that, in the original order, the plaintiff or the defendant be given 'liberty to restore', something which can then be done without the issue of another summons.)
>
> In contrast, 'liberty to apply' may need to be included in an order made in an action for administration of an estate or for an execution of a trust, or in an action for the winding-up of a partnership, or something of that sort. After the trial of the action, accounts and inquiries will probably need to be taken and made. For that purpose, it is appropriate that 'liberty to apply' be inserted in the order, usually to direct that further consideration of the action is to take place in chambers (rather than in open court).

See also the commentary under Order 42 rule 5A concerning liberty to apply under consent orders.

**4.      Application of rules 5 to 8** (O. 44 r. 4)
**Rules 5 to 8 apply—**
    **(a)**    **where in proceedings for the administration under the direction of the Court of the estate of a deceased person the judgment directs any account of debts or other liabilities of the deceased's estate to be taken or any inquiry for next of kin or other unascertained claimants to be made, and**
    **(b)**    **where in proceedings for the execution under the direction of the Court of a trust the judgment directs any such inquiry to be made,**
**and those rules shall, with the necessary modifications, apply where in any other proceedings the judgment directs any account of debts or other liabilities to be taken or any inquiry to be made.**

**5.      Advertisements for creditors and other claimants** (O. 44 r. 5)
    **The Court may, when giving a judgment or at any stage of proceedings under a judgment, give directions for the issue of advertisements for creditors or other claimants and may fix the time within which creditors and claimants may respond.**

**6.      Examination of claims** (O. 44 r. 6)
    **(1)     Where an account of debts or other liabilities of the estate of a**

deceased person has been directed, such party as the Court may direct must—

    (a)    examine the claims of persons claiming to be creditors of the estate,

    (b)    determine, so far as he is able, to which of such claims the estate is liable, and

    (c)    at least seven clear days before the time appointed for adjudicating on claims, make an affidavit stating his findings and his reasons for them and listing all the other debts of the deceased which are or may still be due.

    (2)    Where an inquiry for next of kin or other unascertained claimants has been directed, such party as the Court may direct must—

    (a)    examine the claims,

    (b)    determine, so far as he is able, which of them are valid, and

    (c)    at least seven clear days before the time appointed for adjudicating on claims, make an affidavit stating his findings and his reasons for them.

    (3)    If the personal representative or trustee concerned are not the parties directed by the Court to examine claims, they must join with the party directed to examine them in making the affidavit required by this rule.

**7.    Adjudication on claims** (O. 44 r. 7)

For the purpose of adjudicating on claims the Court may—

    (a)    direct any claim to be investigated in such manner as it thinks fit,

    (b)    require any claimant to attend and prove his claim or to furnish further particulars or evidence of it, or

    (c)    allow any claim after or without proof thereof.

---

## NOTES

**[44.7.1]    Costs of creditor**

A creditor which succeeds in proving its debt against an estate or trust under Order 44 rules 4-8 will normally be entitled to its costs. See Order 62 rule 3(9).

**8.    Notice of adjudication** (O. 44 r. 8)

The Court shall give directions that there be served on every creditor whose claim or any part thereof has been allowed or disallowed, and who did not attend when the claim was disposed of, a notice informing him of that fact.

**9.    Interest on debts** (O. 44 r. 9)

    (1)    Where an account of the debts of a deceased person is directed by any judgment, then, unless the deceased's estate is insolvent or the Court otherwise orders, interest shall be allowed—

    (a)    on any such debt as carries interest, at the rate it carries, and

    (b)    on any other debt, from the date of the judgment at the rate payable on judgment debts at that date.

(2)   A creditor who has established his debt in proceedings under the judgment and whose debt does not carry interest shall be entitled to interest on his debt in accordance with paragraph (1)(b) out of any assets which may remain after satisfying the costs of the cause or matter, the debts which have been established and the interest on such of those debts as by law carry interest.

(3)   For the purposes of this rule "debt" includes funeral, testamentary or administration expenses and, in relation to expenses incurred after the judgment, for the reference in paragraph (1)(b) to the date of the judgment there shall be substituted a reference to the date when the expenses became payable.

**10.    Interest on legacies** (O. 44 r. 10)

Where an account of legacies is directed by any judgment, then, subject to any directions contained in the will or codicil in question and to any order made by the Court, interest shall be allowed on each legacy at the rate of 8 per cent per annum beginning at the expiration of one year after the testator's death.

**11.    Master's order** (O. 44 r. 11)

(1)   Subject to Order 37, rule 2, the result of proceedings before a master under a judgment shall be stated in the form of an order. (L.N. 363 of 1990)

(2)   Subject to any direction of the master under paragraph (3) or otherwise an order under this rule shall have effect as a final order disposing of the cause or matter in which it is made.

(3)   An order under this rule shall contain such directions as the master thinks fit as to the further consideration, either in court or in chambers, of the cause or matter in which it is made.

(4)   Every order made under this rule shall have immediate binding effect on the parties to the cause or matter in which it is made and copies of the order shall be served on such of the parties as the master may direct.

**12.    Appeal against master's order** (O. 44 r. 12)

(1) Subject to paragraph (2), Order 58, rule 1 shall apply to an order made under rule 11 as it applies to any judgment, order or decision of a master, save that the hearing shall be in open court unless the Court directs otherwise. (L.N. 129 of 2000)

(1A) The following provisions shall have effect in the application of Order 58, rule 1 to an order made under rule 11—

    (a)   the notice referred to in Order 58, rule 1(2) shall state the grounds of the appeal;

    (b)   no fresh evidence (other than evidence as to matters which occurred after the date of the master's order) shall be admitted except on special grounds;

    (c)   the judge hearing the appeal shall have the same power to draw inferences of fact as has the Court of Appeal under Order 59, rule 10(3). (L.N. 129 of 2000)

**(2)    If the order is to be acted on by the Judiciary Accountant or is an order passing a receiver's account, notice of appeal must be issued not later than two clear days after the making of the order and, where the order is to be acted on by the Judiciary Accountant, a duplicate of it must be served on the Judiciary Accountant as soon as practicable after it is made.**

**(Enacted 1988)**

---

## NOTES

### [44.12.1]    Appeal to single judge

Order 44 rule 12 provides for an appeal against an order of a master made under rule 11. Rule 12(1) expressly provides that Order 58 rule 1 applies, which means that the appeal lies to a single judge in chambers. The intention appears to be to oust application of Order 58 rule 2, which provides that certain appeals from a master must go straight to the Court of Appeal.

In *Chow Fu Hsien v K Vision Int'l Investment (HK) Ltd* HCA 2884/2004 (Recorder Yu SC; 20.07.2010) (para 6) it was held that an appeal against a master's order after taking an account was within the jurisdiction of a single judge in chambers by virtue of this rule.

## ORDER 44A

### (HK) PROHIBITION ORDER BEFORE OR AFTER JUDGMENT AND ATTACHMENT OF PROPERTY BEFORE JUDGMENT

PROVISIONAL REMEDIES

### Prohibition order against debtor

**1.     Application of the Order to an intended action** (O. 44A r. 1)

**(1)   Subject to paragraph (2), on the hearing of an application by a plaintiff, the Judge may, if he thinks fit, order that the relief provided by this Order shall be available to the plaintiff notwithstanding that the plaintiff has not commenced his action.**

**(2)   An order shall not be made under paragraph (1) unless the plaintiff, at the hearing of his application for such order—**

**(a)     produces at the hearing of the application, a draft writ; and**

**(b)     undertakes to the Judge to issue the writ on the next day on which an office of the Court is open.**

**(3)   In paragraph (1), "plaintiff" means a person who intends to commence an action and elsewhere in this Order, where the Judge has made an order under paragraph (1), "plaintiff" includes a person who intends to commence an action and "defendant" or "debtor" includes a person against whom a plaintiff intends to commence an action.**

---

## NOTES

**[44A.1.1]   Prohibition order before action**

Order 44A rule 1 provides that the court's jurisdiction to make an order prohibiting a debtor from leaving Hong Kong may be exercised even before an action has been commenced.

When seeking a prohibition order before action the intending plaintiff is required to produce a draft writ (rule 1(2)(a)) and give an undertaking to issue it on the next day the court is open (rule 1(2)(b)). In *Murjani v Bank of India* [1989] 2 HKC 80 (CA) reference is made (at 84A-B) to a prohibition order before action having been discharged in circumstances where these procedural requirements were not complied with.

**[44A.1.2]   Application to proceedings not begun by writ**

The use of the word 'writ' in Order 44A rule 1(2) does not have the effect of restricting the grant of prohibition orders before action to claims which would be brought by writ of summons. See *Standard London (Asia) Ltd v Ho Wai Kin Robert* [1998] 4 HKC 595 where it was held that a prohibition order could be made in contemplation of issuing a bankruptcy petition.

**2.     Application for an order prohibiting a debtor from leaving Hong Kong**
(O. 44A r. 2)

**A plaintiff or judgment creditor may apply ex parte to the Court for an**

**order prohibiting a debtor from leaving Hong Kong.**

**3.      Making of prohibition order** (O. 44A r. 3)
        **(1)    Subject to the provisions of section 21B of the Ordinance the Court may make an order prohibiting the debtor from leaving Hong Kong.**
        **(2)    The order prohibiting a debtor from leaving Hong Kong shall be in Form No. 106 in Appendix A.**

---

**NOTES**

**[44A.3.1]    Jurisdiction to grant prohibition order**
The court's power under Order 44A rule 3 to make an order prohibiting a debtor from leaving Hong Kong is expressly subject to section 21B of the High Court Ordinance. That section confers jurisdiction on the court to make prohibition orders.
        The jurisdiction under section 21B is broad in that it extends not just to judgments and orders of the courts, but to 'civil claims'. Thus the court has power to grant a prohibition order even before proceedings are commenced: see Order 44A rule 1. Further, although there must be a good cause of action to found a prohibition order on a 'claim' (section 21B(3)(a)), that cause of action need not be directly against the party restrained.  See *Bunker Holdings Ltd v Asia Pacific Seafood Management Ltd & Ors* [2005] 2 HKC 62, 67H-63E where the court held it had jurisdiction to make a prohibition order against a person who was the subject of an application for committal for contempt in proceedings to which he was not a party.

**[44A.3.2]    Restrictions on jurisdiction to grant prohibition order**
The court's jurisdiction to grant prohibition orders is circumscribed in several respects.
        Perhaps most important, section 21B(1) of the High Court Ordinance states that the purpose of the jurisdiction is 'to facilitate the enforcement, securing or pursuance' of judgments and orders of the court and other civil claims. In *Avco Financial Services (Asia) Ltd v Topma Electronics Ltd & Ors* [1999] 4 HKC 193 this express purpose was cited by V Bokhary J (at 196A-B) in holding 'It would not be appropriate to make a prohibition order unless prohibiting the judgment debtor from leaving Hong Kong is reasonably and properly conducive to the enforcement of the judgment.'
        Section 21B(1) of the High Court Ordinance sets out three types of civil claim where the court may make a prohibition order. The ensuing sub-sections set out criteria and restrictions. Only claims concerning money or property are within the scope of section 21B(1). It should follow that the procedure cannot be used in connection with other types of relief which may be granted by the court.
        The three types of case are discussed one by one below.

**[44A.3.3 ]    (1) Section 21B(1)(a) – money judgments**
Section 21B(1)(a) of the Ordinance gives the court power to make a prohibition to facilitate enforcement of a judgment for the payment of a specified sum of money.  In *Avco Financial Services (Asia) Ltd v Topma Electronics Ltd & Ors* [1999] 4 HKC 193 V Bokhary J held (at 196C-D) that there must be some evidence 'that enforcement of

the judgment would be impeded in some significant way if no prohibition order were made'.

**[44A.3.4]   (2) Section 21B(1)(b) – judgment or order for amount to be assessed, etc**
Section 21B(1)(b) of the Ordinance provides for prohibition orders in cases of judgment or order for payment of an amount to be assessed or requiring the delivery of property or performance of any other act.

This jurisdiction is subject to section 21B(2) of the Ordinance which provides that the court shall not make an order unless there is 'probable cause for believing' that the debtor is about to leave Hong Kong and that if he should do so satisfaction of the judgment or order is likely to be obstructed or delayed.

**[44A.3.5]   (3) Section 21B(1)(c) – prohibition order pre-judgment**
Section 21B(1)(c) provides for prohibition orders in respect of civil claims which have not yet resulted in judgment.  There is no requirement that proceedings have been commenced and it is clear a prohibition order may be made prior to issue of a writ.  See Order 44A rule 1.

Section 21B(3) imposes on this type of case four criteria and restrictions.  The court shall not make a prohibition order unless 'it is satisfied that there is probable cause for believing that' -

(a)    *there is a good cause of action* (see *So Po Tong v Richard Patterson* HCA 6993/87 (Godfrey J; 09.10.1987) where a prohibition order was refused on the ground the affidavit evidence in support of the plaintiff's claim was 'thin in the extreme'); and

(b)    the debtor
   (i)    *incurred the alleged liability in Hong Kong while present in Hong Kong* (see *Murjani v Bank of India* [1989] 2 HKC 80, 87F – 88D as to the meaning of 'liability' in this context); *or*
   (ii)   *carries on business in Hong Kong*  (as to when a debtor can be said to be carrying on business in Hong Kong see *Chase Bank International v Carlos Shalon Abadi* [1986] HKLR 1104, 1108D-E.  It was there held that carrying on business in Hong Kong means carrying on business in a personal capacity and does not include the carrying on of business through a company)*; or*
   (iii)  *is ordinarily resident in Hong Kong* (as to when a person is 'ordinarily' resident, see the authorities cited in the commentary under Order 23 rule 1); and

(c)    *the debtor is about to leave Hong Kong*; and

(d)    *by reason of (c) any judgment which may be given against the debtor is likely to be obstructed or delayed.*

**[44A.3.6]   Debtor must be about to leave Hong Kong**
The jurisdiction to grant a prohibition order will not be exercised unless the alleged debtor is about to leave Hong Kong. This is an express requirement in respect of case types (2) and (3) above. With regard to case type (1), although there is no express prohibition on granting a prohibition order, the court will

con sider whether there is a real likelihood the debtor will leave Hong Kong in exercising its discretion: *Questnet Ltd v Rinck & Anor* HCA 1475/2006 (Chu J; 22.02.2008) (para 23), approving *Yue Wah Chuk Richard & Anor v McKeon* DCCJ 7088/2003 (Judge To; 24.08.2004) (para 45). In *REM Assets Ltd v MIR Investments Ltd & Anor* HCA 626/2008 (Reyes J; 12.02.2009) (para 17) the defendant rented accommodation in Hong Kong on a short-term basis and had no personal or family connection with Hong Kong, though he had lived here for some time. The court declined to accept that there was cogent evidence of an intention to leave Hong Kong in the near or foreseeable future.

It has been held that there must be evidence that the debtor intends to depart with a 'sense of permanence': *Edward Chan v Technical Waxes (NZ) Ltd* [1980] HKLR 526 (CA). That case was decided before the 1984 amendments to the prohibition order procedure but the rule appears to survive. See *Avco Financial Services (Asia) Ltd v Topma Electronics Ltd & Ors* [1999] 4 HKC 193 where a prohibition order against a person who travelled daily between Hong Kong and the mainland was set aside on this ground. See also *Sterling Services Ltd v Tan Kee Cheang* HCCL 72/2002 (Waung J; 26.10.2002) where the court declined to grant a prohibition order against a Shenzhen resident who commuted regularly to work in Hong Kong. See, however, *HBZ Finance Ltd v Glory Products Co Ltd & Ors* HCA 5893/2000 (Suffiad J; 30.08.2000) where the court was of the view (at least in the particular case) that it was not a question of whether the debtors would leave Hong Kong permanently, 'but whether their leaving Hong Kong is likely to obstruct or delay any judgment that may be given against them'.

Furthermore the debtor must be departing Hong Kong with a view to defeating his creditor. In *So Po Tong v Richard Patterson* HCA 6993/1987 (Godfrey J; 09.10.1987) it was said that the purpose of a prohibition order is:

> . . .to prevent a plaintiff from being deprived of the fruits of his judgment by those who are, on clear evidence, demonstrably going to use their escape from the jurisdiction as a means of escaping liability for their debts.

In that case an application for a prohibition order before action was dismissed on the ground the evidence of intention to depart Hong Kong so as to escape liability was too weak.

### [44A.3.7]   Jurisdiction of master
Section 21B(10) expressly provides that the jurisdiction to grant a prohibition order may be exercised by the Registrar or a master.

### [44A.3.8]   History
The current legislation governing prohibition orders (including the relevant provisions of the Ordinance and this Order) dates back to 1984. Earlier authorities such as *Lincoln International Ltd v Feldstein* [1973] HKLR 299 have been superseded. See generally Morrow, 'The Crumbling Walls of the Debtors' Prison' (1984) 14 HKLJ 195.

### [44A.3.9]   Constitutional considerations
In *Tam Hing-yee v Wu Tai-wai* DCCJ 6250/1989 (Judge Downey; 08.07.1991) it was held that the legislation providing for prohibition orders was inconsistent with article 8(2) of the Hong Kong Bill of Rights ('Everyone shall be free to leave Hong Kong')

and to that extent repealed. That decision was overturned on appeal (see at [1992] 1 HKLR 185). The Court of Appeal held that prohibition orders are a useful and necessary procedural device in the circumstances of Hong Kong and thus preserved by the saving clause in article 8(3) of the Bill. Further, since the particular dispute was between private individuals the Bill did not apply (Hong Kong Bill of Rights Ordinance (Cap 383) section 7 provides that the Bill is only binding on the government). As a result prohibition orders could continue to be made in litigation between private citizens, though provisions entitling the government to obtain such orders were invalid: *CIR v Lee Lai Ping (administratrix)* DCCJ 1541/1992 (Judge Cheung; 25.03.1993). (A modified form of prohibition order known as the 'departure prevention direction' was later enacted for revenue cases: see the discussion in *Wen Shang Kuang v CIR* [2003] 2 HKLRD 31, 37F *et seq.*)

Section 7 of the Bill of Rights Ordinance was amended to negate the effect of *Tam Hing-yee* on the day prior to the resumption of Chinese sovereignty. The amendment was suspended shortly after the handover and was subsequently repealed. It has been argued that the repeal did not revive *Tam Hing-yee* by reason of section 23(a) of the Interpretation and General Clauses Ordinance (Cap 1) (repeal of an Ordinance does not revive anything not in force) and in *Solicitor (301/02) v Law Society of Hong Kong* [2006] 2 HKC 40, (para 206–9) (CA) Cheung JA agreed. He held that the court was entitled to consider the Bill of Rights issue afresh, and on doing so he came to the con clusion that the Bill is engaged when the government exercises legislative power. The judgment of Cheung JA finds some support in the separate judgment of Woo VP in the same case, and in *The Joint & Several Liquidators of Kong Wah Holdings Ltd v James Henry Ting* HCCW 49/2000 (Kwan J; 07.09.2004) but cannot be said to be part of the binding *ratio* of the Court of Appeal's decision. However, if it is correct, the effect of Cheung JA's judgment is arguably to restore the first instance judgment of Judge Downey in *Tam Hing-yee* that prohibition orders are inconsistent with the Bill of Rights and repealed altogether.

**[44A.3.10]  Cross reference to Order 49B**
See also Order 49B which provides for prohibition orders for the purpose of securing attendance at an examination of a judgment debtor.

**[44A.3.11]  Comparison with English law**
The prohibition order procedure is unique to Hong Kong. There is no equivalent in England (and other common law jurisdictions) to the Hong Kong legislation under which prohibition orders are granted. However a similar result can be achieved by use of the ancient writ of *ne exeat regno* which has been revived in some jurisdictions (*Felton v Callis* [1969] 1 QB 200; *Parsons v Burk & Ors* [1971] NZLR 244; *Al Nahkel for Contracting and Trading Ltd v Lowe* [1986] 1 QB 235.

The writs of *ne exeat regno* and *ne exeat colonia* were abolished in Hong Kong in 1974: *Supreme Finance Ltd v Wan Hang Trading Ltd* [1983] HKLR 314, 323F-H.

**[44A.3.12]  Exercise of discretion to make prohibition order**
The grant of a prohibition order is clearly a matter of the court's discretion. In exercising the discretion the court will take into account human rights considerations. See *Avco Financial Services (Asia) Ltd v Topma Electronics Ltd & Ors* [1999] 4 HKC 193 where

(at 196B-C) V Bokhary J took into account the right to leave Hong Kong as enshrined in article 31 of the Basic Law.

### [44A.3.13]  Procedure on application

Order 44A rule 2 provides that an application for a prohibition order may be made *ex parte*. The *ex parte* procedure is not mandatory but is usually used, especially where there is a risk the defendant will abscond if prior notice is given. Unlike some other *ex parte* applications which may be made simply by submitting an affidavit to the registry, the practice of the court is to require the applicant to appear in support of the application. The application may be heard by a master in chambers.

### [44A.3.14]  Delay in application for prohibition order

An application for a prohibition order may be refused unless it is sought promptly upon the creditor having reason to believe that the debtor intends to abscond. See *So Po Tong v Richard Patterson* HCA 6993/1987 (Godfrey J; 19.10.1987) and *HBZ Finance Ltd v Glory Products Co Ltd & Ors* HCA 5893/2000 (Suffiad J; 30.08.2000). In the latter case delay of some 2 months was considered sufficient to refuse an order.

### [44A.3.15]  Service of prohibition order

Section 21B(6) of the High Court Ordinance provides that a prohibition order must be served on the Director of Immigration, the Commissioner of Police and, 'if he can be found', the person against whom the order is directed. There is no requirement for personal service on the person against whom the order is made, and if that person cannot be found it may not be necessary to serve him at all: *Bunker Holdings Ltd v Asia Pacific Seafood Management Ltd & Ors* [2005] 2 HKC 62, 69G-H.

'A plaintiff who obtains a prohibition order is … under a duty to take reasonable steps to serve it immediately': *Auto-Treasure Ltd t/a Albert Jewelry Creation v Pyramid International (a firm) & Ors* CACV 24/1992 (Cons VP, Bokhary & Kaplan JJ; 22.05.1992) (para 11). It is not appropriate for the plaintiff to keep the prohibition order 'up his sleeve' while negotiating resolution of the dispute: *Bunker Holdings* (above, at 70D).

### [44A.3.16]  Duration of prohibition order

A prohibition order lapses on the expiry of one month from issue, but may be extended twice for further periods of one month each so that the total period during which it is in force extends to three months. See section 21B(5)(a) of the High Court Ordinance. There is no express provision in the legislation as to whether it is possible to obtain a fresh order after an initial order has been extended and has been in force for the full three-month period. However, it has been held that this is indeed possible. See *Hong Kong Industrial and Commercial Bank Ltd v Wong Siu Leung Tommy & Ors* [1986] HKC 101 (CA).

### [44A.3.17]  Enforcement of prohibition orders

Prohibition orders are enforced by means of the 'watch list' operated by the immigration department. Persons trying to depart Hong Kong in breach of a prohibition order will not be permitted to pass through departure immigration control. They may be arrested by any immigration officer, police officer or bailiff and in that event must be brought before the court the next day: High Court Ordinance s 21B(7)&(8). Section 71 of Cap 1 expressly does not apply, which means the person must be brought before the court the next day even if that be a Sunday or holiday or the courts are closed because of inclement weather.

Once a prohibition order has been made it is the responsibility of the applicant's solicitors to ensure that the immigration department is informed so that the relevant name can be added to the watch list. This is done by informing:

(during office hours):        Immigration Department

Control Support Section

Room 1403, Immigration Tower

7 Gloucester Road

Wan Chai, Hong Kong


Tel: 2294 2004

(outside office hours):        Duty Senior Immigration Officer

Hong Kong International Airport

Chek Lap Kok


Tel: 2138 1318

As mentioned above, the Ordinance requires that the prohibition order be served on the Director of Immigration and the Commissioner of Police. The bailiff's office should also be informed. In cases so urgent that a sealed copy of the order cannot be obtained in time it is understood the authorities will act on an unsealed copy signed by the judicial officer making the order, coupled with a solicitor's undertaking to serve a sealed copy of the order.

For efficient and accurate operation of the watch list, the Director of Immigration has requested that the person prohibited from departing Hong Kong be fully identified with particulars such as date of birth, identity card number, all passport numbers and any known aliases: see Law Society circular 00-241.

It is also necessary for the contact particulars (including after hours telephone numbers) of the legal representatives of the plaintiff be provided to the authorities.

### [44A.3.18]  Breach of prohibition order
A person who breaches a prohibition order whether by attempting to leave Hong Kong or by actually leaving is liable to be committed for contempt: *Sino Wood Investment Ltd v Wong Kam Yin* [2006] 1 HKC 1 (CFA), allowing an appeal against the judgment of the Court of Appeal reported at [2004] 2 HKC 694.  Section 21B(7) of the High Court Ordinance provides that a person who attempts to breach a prohibition order may be arrested by any immigration officer, police officer or bailiff.

**4.    Application to discharge order** (O. 44A r. 4)
    **(1)    Where a debtor is prohibited from leaving Hong Kong, he may, on 2 days clear notice to the plaintiff or judgment creditor and upon being present**

in person in Court, apply for the order to be discharged.

(2)    In an application under paragraph (1) by a debtor under a judgment for money, the Court shall, after the assessment of the amount due to the judgment creditor if appropriate—

    (a)    discharge the order; and

    (b)    proceed as if the judgment debtor appears under arrest for examination under Order 49B.

(3)    Where, in an application under paragraph (1), a debtor for money, other than a judgment debtor—

    (a)    consents to judgment being entered against him; or

    (b)    satisfies the Court that he has a substantial defence to the plaintiff's claim; or

    (c)    consents to judgment being entered against him in respect of part of the plaintiff's claim and, as to the remainder of that claim, satisfies the Court that he has a substantial defence to the plaintiff's claim,

the Court shall—

    (i)    discharge the order; and

    (ii)    where the defendant consents to judgment being entered against him in respect of the whole or any part of the plaintiff's claim, give judgment in accordance with that consent and thereafter proceed as if the defendant appears under arrest for examination under Order 49B.

(4)    Where, in an application under paragraph (1), a debtor, other than a debtor for money or a debtor under a judgment for money, satisfies the Court that he has a substantial defence to the plaintiff's claim, the Court shall discharge the order.

(5)    In an application under paragraph (1), the Court may either for the purposes of the application or to achieve a speedy determination of any issue in dispute, give such directions as it thinks fit as to the filing of statements of claim, defences and counter-claims, the filing of affidavits, the assessment of the amount due or otherwise.

(6)    Paragraphs (2), (3) and (4) shall not prevent the Court from discharging the order, either absolutely or subject to conditions, in any circumstances in which it thinks fit to do so.

---

## NOTES

### [44A.4.1]    Power to discharge prohibition order

Section 21B(4)(a) of the High Court Ordinance expressly provides for the discharge of any prohibition order. Order 44A rule 4 lays down the procedure whereby application is to be made on two days' notice and sets out what the debtor needs to demonstrate. Rule 4(1) provides that the debtor must be present 'in person' in court on the application for discharge.

**[44A.4.2]   Discretion**
The court has a 'complete discretion' whether to discharge a prohibition order: *HBZ Finance Ltd v Shantilal Hargovind & Ors* HCA 1951/1985 (Penlington J; 07.05.1985). In that case a prohibition order was discharged where the court was satisfied the debtor had come to Hong Kong as a visitor in an 'honest effort' to assist his creditors and that it was in the interests of creditors for the debtor to be able to travel outside Hong Kong in pursuance of his business affairs.

**[44A.4.3]   Discharge of prohibition order where there is a good defence**
Order 44A rule 4(3)(b) provides for the discharge of a prohibition order where the court is satisfied there is a 'substantial defence'. The provision expressly does not apply to judgment debtors.

In *Grandwin Co Inc v Chang So Luis* [1989] 2 HKC 530 a prohibition order was discharged where the court was satisfied that the money claim against the defendant was unenforceable under the Money Lenders Ordinance.

**[44A.4.4]   Discharge of prohibition order on payment or posting security**
Section 21B(4)(b) of the High Court Ordinance expressly empowers the court to make a prohibition order subject to the condition that it shall cease to have effect upon payment of the judgment sum, or posting security in such amount as the court may fix. Similarly Order 44A rule 4(6) provides that the court may discharge a prohibition order subject to conditions. The form of order prescribed by Order 44A rule 3 (form 106 in Appendix A) expressly contemplates a prohibition order ceasing to have effect upon payment or posting of security.

**[44A.4.5]   Discharge of prohibition order on undertaking**
In *Lin Fung Trading Co v Hanade Wafu* [1979] HKLR 472 (CA) the court accepted an undertaking not to leave Hong Kong and surrender of travel documents in place of an order within the scope of Order 44A. The Court of Appeal held (at 475) that although there was nothing in Order 44A providing for such an order it was in the circumstances 'eminently sensible and practical' and deemed to have been made under the court's general power to obtain undertakings. The Court of Appeal rejected the creditor's argument that Order 44A was comprehensive and the judge could not act outside its scope.

Although the *Lin Fung Trading* case was decided before the 1984 amendments there does not appear to be any reason of principle why it should not continue to be applicable.

**[44A.4.6]   Discharge of prohibition order for material non-disclosure**
As is the case on any *ex parte* application, a party applying for a prohibition order has a duty to make full and frank disclosure. In *Auto-Treasure Ltd t/a Albert Jewelry Creation v Pyramid International (a firm) & Ors* CACV 24/1992 (Sir Derek Cons VP, Bokhary & Kaplan JJ; 22.05.1992) a prohibition order was discharged for breach of this duty, with indemnity costs.

Note that in the *Auto-Treasure* case Sir Derek Cons VP described the duty to make full and frank disclosure as a continuing one, obliging a party to inform the court of material changes of circumstances.

**[44A.4.7] Appeal against decision on application to discharge**
As with other exercises of discretion, the Court of Appeal will be slow to interfere with a judge's decision on an application to discharge a prohibition order: *Hongkong & Shanghai Banking Corp Ltd v Wing Hong Woo Co Ltd & Ors* CACV 38/1996 (Nazareth VP; Liu & Mayo JJA; 17.05.1996). There Nazareth VP was of the view that the Court of Appeal should only interfere 'if the judge exercises his discretion upon a material misapprehension of the facts or an erroneous inference drawn therefrom'. Liu JA said that the exercise of discretion may not be impugned 'unless the judge applied the wrong principles, took into account irrelevant matters or ignored relevant considerations or unless his decision is plainly wrong'.

5.    **Power to award compensation** (O. 44A r. 5)
      **(1)    Where it appears to the Court that the order prohibiting a debtor from leaving Hong Kong—**
           **(a)    was applied for on insufficient grounds; or**
           **(b)    was not caused to lapse by the plaintiff or judgment creditor as soon as reasonably possible after it was no longer required,**
**the Court may, on the application of the debtor, award against the plaintiff or judgment creditor reasonable compensation to the debtor for any injury or loss sustained by the debtor by reason of sub-paragraph (a) or (b):**
      **Provided that the Court shall not award a larger sum by way of compensation under this rule than is competent to the Court to award in an action for damages.**
      **(2)    An award of compensation under this rule shall bar any action for damages in respect of the prohibition order.**

### Interim attachment of property of defendant

7.    **Application for taking security from defendant or for attachment of his property in certain cases** (O. 44A r. 7)
      **(1)    If in any action the defendant, with intent to obstruct or delay the execution of any judgment that may be given against him in the action, is about to dispose of his property or any part thereof, or to remove any such property from the jurisdiction of the Court, the plaintiff may, either at the institution of the action or at any time thereafter until final judgment, apply to the Court to call upon the defendant to furnish sufficient security to produce and place at the disposal of the Court, when required, his property, or the value of the same, or such portion thereof as may be sufficient to answer any judgment that may be given against him in the action, and, in the event of his failing to furnish such security, to direct that any property, movable or immovable, belonging to the defendant shall be attached until the further order of the Court.**
      **(2)    The application shall contain a specification of the property required to be attached, and the estimated value thereof, so far as the plaintiff can reasonably ascertain the same.**
      **(3)    There shall be filed with the application an affidavit to the effect that the defendant is about to dispose of or remove his property or some part thereof, with such intent as aforesaid.**

## NOTES

### [44A.7.1]  Ex parte application

An application for attachment of property under Order 44A rule 7 may be made *ex parte*, although the rule does not state so expressly. See *Chung Wai Paper Products Mfy Ltd v Yun Fat Paper Products Fty* [1985] HKLR 352. In that case it was held that it would defeat the object of the rule if the application were made otherwise than *ex parte*.

### [44A.7.2]  Comparison with Mareva injunction

With the advent of the *Mareva* injunction (see the commentary under Order 29 rule 1) the procedure under Order 44A rule 7 for attachment of property is relatively seldom used. However, there may be an advantage to use of this procedure in that a *Mareva* injunction, being a creature of equity, operates only *in personam*, whereas it appears that attachment under Order 44A rule 7 may operate against the property itself.

### [44A.7.3]  Order only to be made before judgment

Order 44A rule 7 is applicable only before judgment and an application made after judgment will be dismissed: *Hebei Peak Harvest Battery Co Ltd v Polytek Engineering Co Ltd* HCMP 3501/1995 (Findlay J; 27.10.1997). After judgment the normal procedures for execution of a judgment should be followed instead.

### [44A.7.4]  Affidavit in support

An application under Order 44A rule 7 must, by subrule (3), be supported by an affidavit deposing that the defendant is about to dispose of or remove property with intent to obstruct or delay the execution of any judgment which may be given against him. The decision in *Hebei Peak Harvest Battery Co Ltd* (above) suggests that the evidence of intent may be direct, or indirect evidence from which an inference may be drawn.

### [44A.7.5]  Duration of order

An attachment order made before judgment under Order 44A rule 7 continues after judgment: *Che San & Co v Wa Shing Printers* [1927] HKLR 120, cited with approval in *K Yu Sein Trading Co Ltd & Anor v Talakchand* [1982] HKLR 171, 175D–E (CA).

**8.  Issue of warrant requiring defendant to furnish security or to appear and show cause, and attaching his property** (O. 44A r. 8)

**(1)  If the Court, after making such investigation as it may consider necessary, is of opinion that there is probable cause for believing that the defendant is about to dispose of or remove his property or some part thereof, with such intent as aforesaid, it shall be lawful for the Court to issue a warrant to the bailiff commanding him to call upon the defendant, within a time to be fixed by the Court, either to furnish security, in such sum as may be specified in the order to produce and place at the disposal of the Court, when required, the said property, or the value of the same, or such portion thereof as may be**

sufficient to answer any judgment that may be given against him in the action, or to appear before the Court and show cause why he should not furnish such security. (See App. C, Form 5)

(2) The Court may also in the warrant direct the attachment until further order of the whole or any portion of the property of the defendant within the Colony.

(3) The attachment shall be made, according to the nature of the property to be attached, in the manner prescribed for the attachment of property in execution of a judgment for money.

9. Showing cause, and procedure thereon (O. 44A r. 9)

(1) If the defendant shows such cause or furnishes the required security within the time fixed by the Court, and the property specified in the application, or any portion thereof, has been attached, the Court shall order the attachment to be withdrawn.

(2) If the defendant fails to show such cause or to furnish the required security within the time fixed by the Court, the Court may direct that the property specified in the application, if not already attached, or such portion thereof as may be sufficient to answer any judgment that may be given against the defendant in the action, shall be attached until the further order of the Court.

(3) The attachment shall be made, according to the nature of the property to be attached, in the manner prescribed for the attachment of property in execution of a judgment for money.

10. Saving of rights of other persons under attachment (O. 44A r. 10)

(1) The attachment shall not affect the rights of any persons not being parties to the action, and in the event of any claim being preferred to the property attached before judgment, such claim shall be investigated in the manner prescribed for the investigation of claims to property attached in execution of a judgment.

(2) Where the property consists of movable property to which the judgment debtor is entitled subject to a lien or right of some other person to the immediate possession thereof, the attachment shall be made by a written order prohibiting the person in possession from giving over the property to the judgment debtor or to any other person.

11. Removal of attachment on furnishing of security (O. 44A r. 11)

In any case of attachment before judgment the Court shall at any time remove the same on the defendant furnishing the required security together with security for the costs of the attachment.

12. Power to award compensation to defendant for unjustifiable attachment (O. 44A r. 12)

(1) If it appears to the Court that the attachment was applied for on insufficient grounds, or if the action is dismissed or judgment is given against the plaintiff by default or otherwise and it appears to the Court that there was

no probable ground for instituting the action, the Court may, on the application of the defendant, made either before or at the time of the pronouncing of the judgment, award against the plaintiff such amount, as it may deem a reasonable compensation to the defendant for any injury or loss which he may have sustained by reason of the attachment: Provided that the Court shall not award a larger sum by way of compensation under this rule than it is competent to the Court to award in an action for damages.

(2)    An award of compensation under this rule shall bar any action for damages in respect of the attachment.

(Enacted 1988)

## ORDER 45

### ENFORCEMENT OF JUDGMENTS AND ORDERS: GENERAL

---

## NOTES

### [45.0.1]    Scope of Order 45

Order 45 sets out the means by which the various types of judgments and orders may be enforced or 'executed'. The Court of Appeal has a co-extensive jurisdiction for the purposes of the amendment or enforcement of any judgment or order made on appeal (section 13(4) of the High Court Ordinance).

The combined effect of Order 42 rules 1–5 and Order 45 rules 1–7 is to render the terms 'judgment' and 'order' synonymous. 'Judgment' includes 'decree' (section 2 of the High Court Ordinance).

### [45.0.2]    The meaning of 'execution'

In *Silktex Trading Co (a firm) v Kong Sung Sin, t/a Darwin Fashion Garment Factory* [1986] 1 HKLR 559, Jackson-Lipkin J approved the following definition of 'execution' taken from *Halsbury's Laws of England*, 4th ed, vol 17, p 252:

> The word 'execution' in its widest sense signifies the enforcement of or giving effect to the judgments or orders of courts of justice. In a narrower sense, it means the enforcement of those judgments or orders by a public officer under the writ of fieri facias, possession, delivery, sequestration ...

### [45.0.3]    Persons against whom execution may be levied

'Execution may be levied only against a person who is liable upon the judgment and no person can be liable upon the judgment to pay money unless he was a party to the proceedings. It is not sufficient that he could have been made a party to the proceed ings because a cause of action had accrued against him' (Huggins DJ in *Nam Cheong Chan Yin Construction Co v Irene Smith* [1959] DCLR 163).

### [45.0.4]    Time limitations as to enforcement of judgments and orders

There is no general, statutory, time limitation in respect of the enforcement of judgments. However, where six years or more have elapsed since the date of the judgment, no 'writ of execution' (as defined by Order 46 rule 1) may be issued without the court's leave (Order 46 rule 2(1)(a)). No arrears of interest in respect of any judgment debt may be recovered after the expiration of six years from the date upon which such interest became due (section 4(4) of the Limitation Ordinance (Cap 347)).

### [45.0.5]    Methods of enforcement may be used concurrently

Order 45 rule 1 states that a judgment (or order) may be enforced by 'one or more' of the methods listed. In *Diners Club Int'l (HK) Ltd v Lau Lin Shan* CACV 187/1985 (Huggins & Cons VPP, Yang JA; 21.02.1986) it was said:

> The law as I understand it, and as is set out in *Hayter v Beall* (1881) 44 LT 131, is that the different remedies in execution are concurrent remedies.

## [45.0.6]     Practice and procedure in the bailiff's office

From time to time various aspects of the practice and procedure of the bailiff's office are brought to the attention of solicitors by Law Society circular. As of late 2006 the relevant information was contained in Law Society circular 09–3, available to solicitors on the Law Society's website.

**1.     Enforcement of judgment, etc., for payment of money** (O. 45 r. 1)

**(1)     Subject to the provisions of these rules, a judgment or order for the payment of money, not being a judgment or order for the payment of money into court, may be enforced by one or more of the following means, that is to say—**

> **(a)     writ of fieri facias;**
> **(b)     garnishee proceedings;**
> **(c)     a charging order;**
> **(d)     the appointment of a receiver;**
> **(e)     in a case in which rule 5 applies, an order of committal;**
> **(f)     in such a case, writ of sequestration;**
> **(HK)(g)     an order of imprisonment made under Order 49B.**

**(2)     Subject to the provisions of these rules, a judgment or order for the payment of money into court may be enforced by one or more of the following means, that is to say—**

> **(a)     the appointment of a receiver;**
> **(b)     in a case in which rule 5 applies, an order of committal;**
> **(c)     in such a case, writ of sequestration.**

**(3)     Paragraphs (1) and (2) are without prejudice to any other remedy available to enforce such a judgment or order as is therein mentioned or to any written law relating to bankruptcy or the winding up of companies.**

**(4)     In this Order references to any writ shall be construed as including references to any further writ in aid of the first mentioned writ.**

---

## NOTES

### [45.1.1]     Scope of order 45 rule

Order 45 rule 1 sets out the methods of enforcement in respect of what are commonly termed 'money judgments'. Included amongst these is 'an order for imprisonment made under Order 49B'. (Order 49B prescribes the court's punitive powers in respect of 'oral examination', conducted either under Order 48 or under Order 49B). In the context of civil proceedings, and 'civil debt', this particular method of enforcement is peculiar to Hong Kong.

See the Orders following Order 45 for details of the various enforcement procedures.

**3.     Enforcement of judgment for possession of land** (O. 45 r. 3)

**(1)     Subject to the provisions of these rules, a judgment or order for the giving of possession of land may be enforced by one or more of the following means, that is to say—**

> **(a)     writ of possession;**

    **(b)**    **in a case in which rule 5 applies, an order of committal;**

    **(c)**    **in such a case, writ of sequestration.**

    **(2)**    **A writ of possession to enforce a judgment or order for the giving of possession of any land shall not be issued without the leave of the Court except where the judgment or order was given or made in a mortgage action to which Order 88 applies.**

    **(3)**    **Such leave shall not be granted unless it is shown that every person in actual possession of the whole or any part of the land has received such notice of the proceedings as appears to the Court sufficient to enable him to apply to the Court for any relief to which he may be entitled.**

    **(4)**    **A writ of possession may include provision for enforcing the payment of any money adjudged or ordered to be paid by the judgment or order which is to be enforced by the writ.**

---

## NOTES

### [45.3.1]    Means by which judgment for possession may be enforced

Order 45 rule 3 provides that a judgment or order for possession of land may be enforced by writ of possession, or, where the order is in the form of an injunction to which rule 5 applies, by committal for contempt or writ of sequestration. With regard to committal see Order 52, and for sequestration see Order 46 rule 5.

### [45.3.2]    Leave required to issue writ of possession

Order 45 rule 3(2) provides that leave is required to issue a writ of possession unless the judgment or order to be enforced was given in a mortgage action under Order 88. There is also an exception for orders for possession granted under Order 113 (which makes provision for such orders as against persons who go into possession as trespassers): see rule 7(2) of that Order. As a result of those exceptions the leave requirement applies principally as against persons who remain in occupation after a tenancy comes to an end.

    The rationale for excluding mortgage actions from the leave requirement is that under Order 88 rule 5(4) an affidavit must be filed giving particulars of every person known to be in possession of the mortgaged property, with the result that the court will by that means have considered the matters set out in Order 45 rule 3: *DBS Bank (HK) Ltd v Ngai Yin Shing & Ors* [2005] 2 HKC 53 (para 9). The same may be said with regard to orders for possession under Order 113, rule 4 of which lays down similar requirements.

### [45.3.3]    Notice of proceedings required to obtain leave to issue writ of possession

Leave to issue a writ of possession may not be granted unless it is shown that every per son in actual possession of the suit premises has received notice of the proceedings: rule 3(3). The notice must be sufficient to enable any occupant to apply to the Court for relief: rule 3(3). Such an occupant may apply under Order 15 rule 10 to be joined as a defendant in the proceedings for the purpose of applying for relief. See the commentary under that rule.

## [45.3.4]     Manner of giving notice

On a strict interpretation of rule 3(3), personal service of each and every occupant of the premises would be necessary to satisfy the requirement that it be shown that each such person 'has received such notice'. Such an interpretation would cause considerable difficulty in many cases. A landlord will often not know the number or identity of members of the tenant's household, and yet the rule requires that notice be given to and received by each such person. Furthermore, there may be sub-tenants of which the landlord has no knowledge.

In order to alleviate such difficulties, a procedure has been adopted whereby the requirements of the rule may be satisfied by posting notice of the proceedings at the main door or entrance to the premises on 3 successive days, and allowing 4 clear days thereafter before submitting the application for leave. The procedure is set out in practice direction 16.4, as amended with effect from 01.08.2008. The text of the practice direction may be viewed on the judiciary's website, or that of HKLII. A specimen form of notice is annexed to the practice direction, in English and Chinese. The practice direction requires that notice in both languages be posted. The English version of the specimen notice is as follows:

(Plaintiff's address)

### NOTICE
(English version)

To: Defendant/s AND To all Persons in Actual Possession of ____

Action No.

Plaintiff(s)

vs

*Defendant(s)*

TAKE NOTICE that I, the undersigned, have on _____, at the _____ Court in the aforesaid action obtained a judgment against the above-named defendant(s) _____ for the recovery of possession of the premises known as _____ and YOU ARE HEREBY NOTIFIED THAT you should vacate these premises by the _____ and that in default of your vacating these premises or any application by you to the Court for relief or otherwise, I shall proceed to recover possession upon the said Judgment without further notice.

Dated the ____ day of _____

(Sd.)

*Plaintiff*

The Chinese version of the specimen notice can be viewed on either of the websites mentioned above. It is important to note that the practice direction requires that the notice be given in both official languages.

In *Alfonso v Tsang Yiu Kai* [1968] HKLR 68 it was held that it should be established by affidavit evidence that the notice remains in a conspicuous place on the 3 consecu tive days so that any occupant will have had an opportunity to read it. In that case the court was not prepared to grant leave where it was not clear on the affidavit evidence whether the same notice remained posted, or whether a new one had to be posted on successive days.

## [45.3.5]    Procedure on application for leave
Order 45 rule 3 is silent as to the procedure to be followed on an application for leave to issue a writ of possession. In practice such applications are made *ex parte* by submitting an affidavit showing the giving of notice to occupants as required by rule 3(3). See, for example, *Alfonso v Tsang Yiu Kai* [1968] HKLR 68.

## [45.3.6]    Form of writ of possession
See form No 66 in Appendix A to these rules.

## [45.3.7]    Execution of writ of possession
To avoid delay, the court bailiff is willing to execute a writ of possession on the 1st visit to the premises provided that the solicitor for the party in whose favour possession has been ordered waives service of Notice to Quit and undertakes to indemnify the bailiff. The prescribed form of undertaking is circulated with guidance on bailiff's office prac tice and procedure from time to time, for example under Law Society circular 06–599. It reads as follows:

To:  Chief Bailiff
     High Court
     HKSAR

**RE:(Premises – Address ('the Premises'))**

**(Action No.)**

**Undertaking**

I/We act for the Plaintiff(s)/Landlord(s) in the captioned action.

I/We do hereby direct the Bailiffs to waive service of Notice to Quit to the occupant(s) of the Premises or to make prior visit to the Premises to ascertain the situation thereof as we understand the Premises are deserted. In consideration of the Bailiffs accepting such direction, I/We shall indemnify and reimburse the Bailiffs for all liability, claims and costs that may arise, fall to and be incurred by the Bailiffs during the whole course of the execution, and undertake to pay forthwith any such sums as may be payable and due upon demand.

This undertaking is issued by the undersigned in his/her capacity as the sole proprietor/ a partner of (name of solicitors firm).

Signature(s) of Solicitor(s)

**4.    Enforcement of judgment for delivery of goods** (O. 45 r. 4)

(1)    Subject to the provisions of these rules, a judgment or order for the delivery of any goods which does not give a person against whom the judgment is given or order made the alternative of paying the assessed value of the goods may be enforced by one or more of the following means, that is to say—

(a)    writ of delivery to recover the goods without alternative provision for recovery of the assessed value thereof (hereafter in this rule referred to as a "writ of specific delivery");

(b)    in a case in which rule 5 applies, an order of committal;

(c)    in such a case, writ of sequestration.

(2)    Subject to the provisions of these rules, a judgment or order for the delivery of any goods or payment of their assessed value may be enforced by one or more of the following means, that is to say—

(a)    writ of delivery to recover the goods or their assessed value;

(b)    by order of the Court, writ of specific delivery;

(c)    in a case in which rule 5 applies, writ of sequestration.

An application for an order under sub-paragraph (b) shall be made by summons, which must, notwithstanding Order 65, rule 9, be served on the defendant against whom the judgment or order sought to be enforced was given or made.

(3)    A writ of specific delivery, and a writ of delivery to recover any goods or their assessed value, may include provision for enforcing the payment of any money adjudged or ordered to be paid by the judgment or order which is to be enforced by the writ.

(4)    A judgment or order for the payment of the assessed value of any goods may be enforced by the same means as any other judgment or order for the payment of money.

**5.    Enforcement of judgment to do or abstain from doing any act** (O. 45 r. 5)

(1)    Where—

(a)    a person required by a judgment or order to do an act within a time specified in the judgment or order refuses or neglects to do it within that time or, as the case may be, within that time as extended or abridged under Order 3, rule 5, or

(b)    a person disobeys a judgment or order requiring him to abstain from doing an act,

then, subject to the provisions of these rules, the judgment or order may be enforced by one or more of the following means, that is to say—

(i)    with the leave of the Court, a writ of sequestration against the property of that person;

(ii)    where that person is a body corporate, with the leave of the Court, a writ of sequestration against the property of any director or other officer of the body;

(iii)    an order of committal against that person or, where that person is a body corporate, against any such officer.

(2)    Where a judgment or order requires a person to do an act within a time therein specified and an order is subsequently made under rule 6

**requiring the act to be done within some other time, references in paragraph (1) of this rule to a judgment or order shall be construed as references to the order made under rule 6.**

**(3)    Where under any judgment or order requiring the delivery of any goods the person liable to execution has the alternative of paying the assessed value of the goods, the judgment or order shall not be enforceable by order of committal under paragraph (1), but the Court may, on the application of the person entitled to enforce the judgment or order, make an order requiring the first mentioned person to deliver the goods to the applicant within a time specified in the order, and that order may be so enforced.**

---

## NOTES

### [45.5.1]    Order 45 rule 5 – Enforcement of order to do or abstain from doing an act

Order 45 rule 5 stipulates the means of enforcement of judgments and orders requiring a person to do an act within a specified time or to abstain from doing an act. Typically, such orders take the form of either mandatory or prohibitory injunctions. The rule pro vides that where a person fails to comply with such an order, the order may be enforced by sequestration of the person's property or by committal. Where the order is directed to a body corporate, it may be enforced by such means against a director or other officer of the body: see Order 45 rule 5(1)(b)(ii) and the commentary below.

An order may not be enforced under Order 45 rule 5 unless the provisions of rule 7 as to service of the order and its endorsement with a penal notice have been complied with.

See Order 46 rule 5 for the procedures for issue of a writ of sequestration, and Order 52 for committal.

Privilege may justify failure or refusal to comply with an order to do an act such as make disclosure of information: see *Pheby v Paier & Ors* [2003] 2 HKC 328.

### [45.5.2]    Enforcement of order against body corporate

Order 45 rule 5(1)(b)(ii) provides that an order directed to a company to do or abstain from doing an act may be enforced by writ of sequestration against the property of 'any director or other officer' of the body, and rule 5(1)(b)(iii) provides for enforcement by committal of 'any such officer'.

*Meaning of 'officer'* – it is clear from the wording of Order 45 rule 5 that 'officer' of a body corporate includes any director thereof. The definition of 'officer' in section 2 of the Companies Ordinance (Cap 32) is also relevant (though it does not apply directly to interpretation of these rules). That definition provides that officer 'includes a director, manager or secretary'. In *Pappadis & Anor v Chan Shing Sheung Barry & Ors* [1989] 2 HKC 369, 376C–D (reversed by the Court of Appeal on other grounds at [1989] 2 HKLR 511) Liu J described the definition in the Companies Ordinance as 'somewhat circuitous' and of 'no real guidance'. The learned judge cited with approval the decisions in *Gibson v Barton* (1875) LR 10 QB 329 and *Re A Company* [1930] 1 Ch 138 where 'officer' and 'manager' were held to connote a person managing the affairs of the company as a whole. Liu J cautioned that in contempt proceedings, being punitive in nature, there is good reason to resist the temptation to adopt an enlarged meaning of 'officer' in terms of a manager, and went on to hold (at 378B–C) that ultimately it is a question of fact 'how the management of the company has in reality been conducted'.

*Committal of company director* – There are two routes by which a company director may be committed for contempt in respect of an order directed to the com pany: *Nicolas Pappadis & Anor v Chan Shing-sheung, Barry & Ors* [1989] 2 HKLR 511 (CA). First, under Order 45 rule 5, an order requiring a body corporate to do or refrain from doing an act may be enforced by committal proceedings against a director or officer thereof. Secondly, a director may be guilty of aiding and abetting another person, or the company itself, in committing the contempt. See *Cartier International BV & Ors v Kaybee International Ltd* [1985] HKLR 127, 130I–131A (CA), citing *Biba Ltd v Stratford Investments Ltd* [1973] Ch 281.

*Absence of moral blame on part of company director* – In a series of cases the Hong Kong courts have held that under Order 45 rule 5 a company director may be committed for contempt even in the absence of moral blame. However, personal misconduct must be proved in the case of aiding and abetting. See *Nicolas Pappadis & Anor v Chan Shing-sheung, Barry & Ors* [1989] 2 HKLR 511, 519G–H, where Hunter JA, citing *Cartier International BV & Ors v Kaybee International Ltd* [1985] HKLR 127 (CA), said:

> Under O 45 no moral blame or necessarily knowledge, need be shown in the director. It is sufficient to show that the order was made against the company and served upon him. Then it is the director's personal obligation to ensure that that order is complied with. When you are dealing with aiding and abetting the situation is quite different. What has to be shown is personal misconduct on the part of the director.

It has been suggested that the Hong Kong cases diverge from English law insofar as they do not require proof of wilfulness under Order 45 rule 5: see *Abu Dhabi National Tanker Co v Lam Ming Chi* [1998] 4 HKC 320, 327I–328I, per Stone J and *Aqua-Leisure Industries Inc & Anor v Aqua Splash Ltd (No 3)* [2002] 1 HKC 495, 500G–H, per Deputy Judge To. In the latter of those decisions reference was made to *AG for Tuvalu v Philatelic Distribution Corp Ltd* [1990] 1 WLR 926 for the proposition that in England it is necessary to show that a director willfully failed to take steps to ensure compliance with the order. However, in *Excel Noble Development Ltd & Ors v Wah Nam Group Ltd & Ors* [2001] 4 HKC 148 (CA) Rogers JA (at 156D–I) felt able to reconcile the Hong Kong and English authorities. The decision of Deputy Judge To was set aside by the Court of Appeal in this regard on the basis of the *Excel Noble* case: see [2003] 1 HKC 1, 18C–D.

**6.      Judgment, etc. requiring act to be done: order fixing time for doing it**
**(O. 45 r. 6)**
**(1)    Notwithstanding that a judgment or order requiring a person to do an act specifies a time within which the act is to be done, the Court shall, without prejudice to Order 3, rule 5, have power to make an order requiring the act to be done within another time, being such time after service of that order, or such other time, as may be specified therein.**
**(2)    Where, notwithstanding Order 42, rule 2(1), or by reason of Order 42, rule 2(2), a judgment or order requiring a person to do an act does not specify a time within which the act is to be done, the Court shall have power**

subsequently to make an order requiring the act to be done within such time after service of that order, or such other time, as may be specified therein.

(3)    An application for an order under this rule must be made by summons and the summons must, notwithstanding anything in Order 65, rule 9, be served on the person required to do the act in question.

7.        Service of copy of judgment, etc., prerequisite to enforcement under r. 5
         (O. 45 r. 7)

(1)    In this rule references to an order shall be construed as including references to a judgment.

(2)    Subject to Order 24, rule 16(3), Order 26, rule 6(3) and paragraphs (6) and (7) of this rule, an order shall not be enforced under rule 5 unless— (L.N. 103 of 1994)

    (a)    a copy of the order has been served personally on the person required to do or abstain from doing the act in question, and

    (b)    in the case of an order requiring a person to do an act, the copy has been so served before the expiration of the time within which he was required to do the act.

(3)    Subject as aforesaid, an order requiring a body corporate to do or abstain from doing an act shall not be enforced as mentioned in rule 5(1)(ii) or (iii) unless—

    (a)    a copy of the order has also been served personally on the officer against whose property leave is sought to issue a writ of sequestration or against whom an order of committal is sought, and

    (b)    in the case of an order requiring the body corporate to do an act, the copy has been so served before the expiration of the time within which the body was required to do the act.

(4)    There must be indorsed on the copy of an order served under this rule a notice informing the person on whom the copy is served—

    (a)    in the case of service under paragraph (2) that if he neglects to obey the order within the time specified therein, or, if the order is to abstain from doing an act, that if he disobeys the order, he is liable to process of execution to compel him to obey it, and

    (b)    in the case of service under paragraph (3) that if the body corporate neglects to obey the order within the time so specified or, if the order is to abstain from doing an act, that if the body corporate disobeys the order, he is liable to process of execution to compel the body to obey it.

(5)    With the copy of an order required to be served under this rule, being an order requiring a person to do an act, there must also be served a copy of any order made under Order 3, rule 5, extending or abridging the time for doing the act and, where the first-mentioned order was made under rule 5(3) or 6 of this Order, a copy of the previous order requiring the act to be done.

(6)    An order requiring a person to abstain from doing an act may be enforced under rule 5 notwithstanding that service of a copy of the order has

not been effected in accordance with this rule if the Court is satisfied that, pending such service, the person against whom or against whose property it is sought to enforce the order has had notice thereof either—

  (a)    by being present when the order was made, or

  (b)    by being notified of the terms of the order, whether by telephone, telegram or otherwise.

  (7)    Without prejudice to its powers under Order 65, rule 4, the Court may dispense with service of a copy of an order under this rule if it thinks it just to do so.

## NOTES

### [45.7.1]    Order 45 rule 7 – personal service requirement

Order 45 rule 7(2) provides that an order requiring a person to do or abstain from doing an act (for example, a mandatory or prohibitory injunction), shall not be enforced unless it has been served personally. In the case of an order requiring a person to do an act (such as a mandatory injunction) the order must be served before expiration of the time to do the act. These requirements are pre-conditions to enforcement but do not detract from the fact that under Order 42 rule 3 a judgment or order is binding from the moment of pronouncement.

  In *Chung Shun Land Investment Co Ltd v Steadman* HCA 4215 (Deputy Judge Barnett; 01.07.1986), [1986] HKLY 732 it was held that the personal service requirement is not applicable when it is sought only to enforce that part of the order relating to costs.

### [45.7.2]    Service of bodies corporate

Where an order to be enforced is directed to a body corporate (whether a limited company or statutory corporation), it may be enforced against an officer thereof. Prior personal service of that officer is required by rule 7(3). Note that 'officer' is defined in section 2 of the Companies Ordinance (Cap 32) to include director, manager and secretary. For further discussion of the meaning of 'officer' of a company see the commentary under Order 48 rule 1.

### [45.7.3]    Rule 7(6) - enforcement notwithstanding failure to comply with service requirement

Order 45 rule 7(6) empowers the court to enforce an order to abstain from doing an act notwithstanding failure to comply with the stipulated procedures as to service. This power is discretionary, and is available only in respect of prohibitory orders where conditions (a) and (b) prescribed by rule 7(6) are met: *Chou Yi Feng v Chou Yi Chen & Ors* HCA 4393/2001 (Chung J; 23.11.2002).

### [45.7.4]    Rule 7(7) - power to dispense with service

The court has power under Order 45 rule 7(7) to dispense with service of an order, thereby allowing enforcement notwithstanding lack of service. This power is broader than that under rule 7(6) in that it applies whether the order to be enforced is prohibitory or mandatory and, unlike rule 7(6) it is an unfettered discretion. It is not necessary to demonstrate evasion of service. See *Chou Yi Feng* (above).

There are three requirements for an order dispensing with service under rule 7(7), and they must be proved beyond reasonable doubt: *Lucky Sun Dev't Ltd v Gainsmate Int'l Ltd* HCCT 12/2007 (Deputy Judge L Chan; 03.05.2007) (para 28). The require ments are that 'the respondent (i) knew of the terms of the order; (ii) was well aware of the consequences of disobedience; and (iii) was aware of the grounds relied on as a breach with sufficient particularity to be able to answer the charge'.

Examples where this power has been exercised include the following:

(1) *Excel Noble Development Ltd & Ors v Wah Nam Group Ltd & Ors* [2001] 4 HKC 148 (CA) where, on an application to commit a company director for the company's breach of a mandatory order, the Court of Appeal upheld a judge's exercise of discretion to dispense with personal service of the director. The court was satisfied that the director was responsible for the day to day administration of the company. A copy of the order had been inserted in the letter box at the director's residence, and there was no evidence that he was unaware of it. In the absence of any such evidence the court could conclude that the officer knew of its terms: see per Rogers JA at 159D-H.

(2) *Axa China Region Insurance Co Ltd & Anor v Li Yu Ping Ellen* [2002] 3 HKC 339 (CA) where it was held that where it is in the interests of justice to do so and would result in no prejudice, an order dispensing with service may be made, retro spectively, on the contemnor's appeal against a committal order on the grounds of procedural irregularity occasioned by failure to effect personal service. The court held it appropriate to make such an order given that the mandatory injunction with which the defendant had failed to comply (itself a variation of an earlier order with which she *had* been personally served) was made at the initiative of her advisers, with her knowledge and consent and, further, that whilst her advisers had been aware of the irregularity at all material times, they had not thought fit to raise the point at the hearing of the motion to commit.

**[45.7.5]** **Penal notice**

Rule 7(4) provides that the copy of the order served must be endorsed with a penal notice warning of the consequences of failure to comply. In *Questnet Ltd v Rinck & Anor* HCA 1475/2006 (Deputy Judge Saunders; 17.11.2006) (para 30) it was suggested that where such an order is later varied, a penal notice should be attached to the order making the variation as well.

Penal notices must be carefully worded as they will be strictly construed by the court: *Pappadis & Anor v Chan Shing Sheung Barry* [1989] 2 HKC 369 (reversed on other grounds – see [1989] 2 HKLR 511 (CA)). See also *Funny Electronics Co Ltd v World Asia Plastics Die-Casting Mould Factory* [1985] 2 HKC 572 where an applica tion to commit a director for contempt by the company was dismissed on the ground that the penal notice failed to comply with the requirements of rule 7(3) and (4).

Failure to comply with the requirement for a penal notice will not necessarily be fatal. The court's powers under both rule 7(6) and rule 7(7) may be invoked. See *Excel Noble Development Ltd & Ors v Wah Nam Group Ltd & Ors* [2001] 4 HKC 148 (CA), *Axa China Region Insurance Co Ltd & Anor v Li Yu Ping Ellen* [2002] 3 HKC 339 (CA) together with the commentary, above.

**8.      Court may order act to be done at expense of disobedient party**
(O. 45 r. 8)

If an order of mandamus, a mandatory order, an injunction or a judgment or order for the specific performance of a contract is not complied with, then, without prejudice to its powers to punish the disobedient party for contempt, the Court may direct that the act required to be done may, so far as practicable, be done by the party by whom the order or judgment was obtained or some other person appointed by the Court, at the cost of the disobedient party, and upon the act being done the expenses incurred may be ascertained in such manner as the Court may direct and execution may issue against the disobedient party for the amount so ascertained and for costs.

---

## NOTES

### [45.8.1]      Court may empower another to do act where party ordered has failed to do so

Order 45 rule 8 empowers the court to appoint a person to do an act on behalf of a party who has failed to comply with an earlier order to do that act. Failure to comply with mandatory orders such as injunction and specific performance is covered. The court may order the disobedient party to bear the cost.

In *Pacific Electric Wire & Cable Co Ltd v Texan Management Ltd & Ors* HCA 2203/2004 (Saunders J; 04.07.2008) (paras 14-17) an argument that the power may only be exercised once there has been an act of disobedience was rejected, and it was held that such an order may be made in anticipation of disobedience.

The rule derives from the rule of the same number in the former English RSC. The English rule was expressed to be without prejudice to the court's power under section 39 of the Supreme Court Act 1981 which empowers the court to order a document to be executed by a person nominated by the court. The equivalent of that section in Hong Kong is section 25A of the High Court Ordinance. Although section 25A is not mentioned in the Hong Kong rule it clearly exists in tandem with the rule and the two provisions may be used together to effect conveyance of title under an order for specific performance where the party ordered to do so fails to comply. As an example, see *Yuen Lai Tui v Ho Kwok Ling & Ors* HCMP 280/2005 (Chung J; 20.11.2006) where such an order was contemplated.

The rule does not empower the court to make an order to facilitate the change of a company's name where the company itself has failed to comply with an order that it do so. This is because the Companies Ordinance (Cap 32) s 22(1) provides that only by a special resolution may a company change its name. See *Hitachi Ltd v Hitachi Wei Chu (HK) Ltd* HCA 2520/2006 (Suffiad J; 30.08.2007), referring to *Halifax plc v Halifax Repossessions Ltd* [2004] BCC 281.

### [45.8.2]      Enforcement of undertakings

In *Hussain v Hussain* [1986] 1 All ER 961 it was held that the procedural requirements for enforcement of an undertaking are not as strict as those for enforcement of a judgment or order. Sir John Donaldson MR said:

> Let it be stated in the clearest possible terms that an undertaking to the court is as solemn,

binding and effective as an order of the court in the like terms and the contrary has never been suggested. What has been suggested . . . is that the procedural requirements for enforcement are not as strict in the case of an undertaking as in the case of an order . . . because [the rules] have no direct application to committal for breach of an undertaking . . . I have no doubt that this submission is well founded. Undertakings may be recorded in an order of the court, as occurred in this case, but it is the undertaking and not the order which requires the giver of the undertaking to act in accordance with its terms.

In *Winner Food Products Ltd v Chung Yat-ming* [1988] HKC 473; [1989] 1 HKLR 371 Godfrey J quoted the above passage and held that a person giving an undertaking is presumed to know what he is doing and lack of a penal notice was not good ground to refuse to entertain an application for committal for breach thereof. This applied to both positive and negative undertakings.

**9.     Execution by or against person not being a party** (O. 45 r. 9)

**(1)     Any person, not being a party to a cause or matter, who obtains any order or in whose favour any order is made, shall be entitled to enforce obedience to the order by the same process as if he were a party.**

**(2)     Any person, not being a party to a cause or matter, against whom obedience to any judgment or order may be enforced, shall be liable to the same process for enforcing obedience to the judgment or order as if he were a party.**

---

**NOTES**

**[45.9.1]     Enforcement by and against non-parties**

Order 45 rule 9 provides for the enforcement of orders of the court made in favour of or against persons who are not parties to the proceedings.

In *Sam Ming City Forestry Economic Co & Anor v Lam Pun Hung & Anor* [2001] 3 HKC 573 the Court of Appeal, citing this rule, held that a mainland arbitral award which had been made in favour of a person not a party to the arbitration could be enforced in Hong Kong by that person.

**10.     Conditional judgment: waiver** (O. 45 r. 10)

**A party entitled under any judgment or order to any relief subject to the fulfilment of any condition who fails to fulfil that condition is deemed to have abandoned the benefit of the judgment or order, and, unless the Court otherwise directs, any other person interested may take any proceedings which either are warranted by the judgment or order or might have been taken if the judgment or order had not been given or made.**

**11.     Matters occurring after judgment: stay of execution, etc.** (O. 45 r. 11)

**Without prejudice to Order 47, rule 1, a party against whom a judgment has been given or an order made may apply to the Court for a stay of execution of the judgment or order or other relief on the ground of matters which have occurred since the date of the judgment or order, and the Court may by order grant such relief, and on such terms, as it thinks just.**

## NOTES

**[45.11.1]   Stay of execution**
There are several provisions in the rules whereby an application may be made for a stay of execution. For example, Order 13 rule 8 provides for an automatic stay where the defendant has acknowledged service and states that he does not intend to contest the proceedings but intends to apply for a stay of execution; Order 14 rule 3(2) provides for a stay of execution of judgment granted under Order 14 until the trial of a counterclaim; Order 47 rule 1 provides for a stay of execution, but is limited to cases where execution is sought by way of *fieri facias*; and Order 58 rule 1(4) and 59 rule 13(1)(a) provide respectively that an appeal from a master to a judge of the CFI or an appeal to the Court of Appeal shall not operate as a stay of execution except so far as may be ordered. For a discussion of the principles applicable on an application for stay of execution pending appeal, see the commentary under Order 59 rule 13.

The court has an inherent jurisdiction to grant a stay of execution where required to prevent injustice or abuse, to preserve the dignity of the court or to facilitate the administration of justice: *Credit Lyonnais v S K Global HK Ltd* [2003] 4 HKC 104.

Order 45 rule 11 provides generally for the granting of a stay of execution at the discretion of the court on the ground of matters that have occurred since the date of the judgment or order. In *Daiwa Bank Ltd v Shum Shek Chiu & Anor* [2005] 1 HKC 243 an application under this rule, relying on matters arising *before* the date of the relevant order, was dismissed as 'misconceived'. In *Tam Ho Man v Wong Kwok Tai* (1986) HCA 4736/1985 (Hunter J; 20.10.1986), judgment had been entered in the plaintiff's favour. The defendant applied for a stay of execution on the ground that a bankruptcy notice against him had been issued but not served. Hunter J held that 'matters which have occurred since the date of the judgment' referred to matters that went to the validity of the judgment and which, if established before the court, might justify the court in saying that this was not a judgment which, on the material now placed before it, it would allow to be executed. Accordingly, the application did not come within the terms of Order 45 rule 11 and the court had no jurisdiction to make such an order.

**12.    Forms of writs** (O. 45 r. 12)
      **(1)   A writ of fieri facias must be in such of the Forms Nos. 53 to 63 in Appendix A as is appropriate in the particular case.**
      **(2)   A writ of delivery must be in Form No. 64 or 65 in Appendix A, whichever is appropriate.**
      **(3)   A writ of possession must be in Form No. 66 or 66A in Appendix A.**
      **(4)   A writ of sequestration must be in Form No. 67 in Appendix A.**

**13.    Enforcement of judgments and orders for recovery of money, etc.**
      (O. 45 r. 13)
      **(1)   Rule 1(1) of this Order, with the omission of sub-paragraphs (e) and (f) thereof, and Orders 46 to 51 shall apply in relation to a judgment or order for the recovery of money as they apply in relation to a judgment or order for the payment of money.**

(2)     Rule 3 of this Order, with the omission of paragraph (1)(b) and (c) thereof, and Order 47, rule 3(2), shall apply in relation to a judgment or order for the recovery of possession of land as they apply in relation to a judgment or order for the giving or delivery of possession of land.

(3)     Rule 4 of this Order, with the omission of paragraphs (1)(b) and (c) and (2)(c) thereof, and Order 47, rule 3(2), shall apply in relation to a judgment or order that a person do have a return of any goods and to a judgment or order that a person do have a return of any goods or do recover the assessed value thereof as they apply in relation to a judgment or order for the delivery of any goods and a judgment or order for the delivery of any goods or payment of the assessed value thereof respectively.

**14.     Power of the Court to order immediate execution** (O. 45 r. 14)

(HK)(1)The Court may at the time of giving judgment, on the oral application of the party in whose favour the judgment is given, order immediate execution thereof without the issue of a writ of execution, except as to so much as relates to the costs, and that the judgment shall be executed as to the costs as soon as the amount thereof has been ascertained by taxation.

(2)     The order for immediate execution shall be in writing and shall be sufficient authority to the bailiff to proceed at once to execution of the judgment against the property of the party against whom judgment is given: Provided that the party obtaining the order shall as soon thereafter as practicable comply with the requirements of Order 46, rule 6: Provided further that, if the party against whom the order has been made satisfies the Court that he has sufficient means and intends to satisfy the judgment, the Court may discharge the order for immediate execution.

**15.     Judgment for money against representatives of deceased persons** (O. 45 r. 15)

(HK) If the judgment is against a party as the representative of a deceased person and such judgment is for money to be paid out of the property of the deceased person, it may be executed by the attachment and sale of any such property or, if no such property can be found and the defendant fails to satisfy the Court that he has duly applied such property of the deceased person as may be proved to have come into his possession, the judgment may be executed against the defendant to the extent of the property not duly applied by him, in the same manner as if the judgment had been against him personally.

**16.     Execution in case of cross judgments for money** (O. 45 r. 16)

(HK) If there are cross-judgments between the same parties for the payment of money execution shall be taken out by that party only who has obtained a judgment for the larger sum and for so much only as may remain after deducting the smaller sum, and satisfaction for the smaller sum shall be entered on the judgment for the larger sum as well as satisfaction on the judgment for the smaller sum, and if both sums are equal satisfaction shall be entered on both judgments.

## NOTES

**[45.16.1]    Set-off of one judgment sum against another**
Order 45 rule 16 provides that where there are cross-judgments in favour of opposing parties only the party with the larger judgment shall levy execution. The smaller judgment is, in effect, set off against the larger.

In *Re Lam Lam ex p Bank of China (Hong Kong) Limited* HCB 14221/2002 & CACV 396/2002 (Reyes J; 22.12.2003) it was held that set-off under this rule is 'automatic' – there is no need to apply to the court. The court went on to consider (without deciding) whether there is a discretion to set aside set-off under this rule.

**17.    Application for leave to issue execution by one of several persons entitled**
(O. 45 r. 17)

**(HK)(1)If a judgment has been given jointly in favour of more persons than one, any one or more of such persons, or his or their representatives, may apply to the Court for leave to issue execution on the whole judgment for the benefit of them all or, where any of them has died, for the benefit of the survivors and of the representative in interest of the deceased person.**

**(2)    If the Court grants such leave it shall make such order as it may think fit for protecting the interests of the persons who have not joined in the application.**

**(Enacted 1988)**

## ORDER 46

### WRITS OF EXECUTION: GENERAL

1.     **Definition** (O. 46 r. 1)
       **In this Order, unless the context otherwise requires, "writ of execution" includes a writ of fieri facias, a writ of possession, a writ of delivery, a writ of sequestration and any further writ in aid of any of the aforementioned writs. (See App. A, Form 69)**

---

## NOTES

**[46.1.1]     Cross-reference to High Court Ordinance**
According to section 46(1) of the High Court Ordinance, all writs other than the writs listed in the schedule to the Ordinance are abolished. Those listed in the schedule include the following writs of execution:

(1)     Writ of *fieri facias.*
(2)     Writ of possession.
(3)     Writ of delivery.
(4)     Writ of sequestration.
(5)     Writ of assistance.
(6)     Writ of restitution.

It is provided in section 46(2) that the writs listed in the schedule should be issued according to the common law except to the extent that the common law has been modified by any enactment.

**[46.1.2]     Charging order not a writ of execution**
A charging order is 'nominally a mode of execution' but is not in itself a 'writ of execution': see *Ip Hon Man v Chan Moon Kau* [2002] 2 HKC 220 (DCt), not following *Mercantile Credit Ltd v Ellis* [1987] The Times, 1 April (English CA). This is because the property subject to the charge remains in the possession of the judgment debtor and a separate step, namely Order 88 proceedings, is necessary for enforcement (per Judge Li at 225D–226C).

2.     **When leave to issue any writ of execution is necessary** (O. 46 r. 2)
       **(1)   A writ of execution to enforce a judgment or order may not issue without the leave of the Court in the following cases, that is to say—**

      **(a)   where 6 years or more have elapsed since the date of the judgment or order;**

      **(b)   where any change has taken place, whether by death or otherwise, in the parties entitled or liable to execution under the judgment or order;**

      **(c)   where the judgment or order is against the assets of a deceased person coming to the hands of his executors or administrators after the date of the judgment or order, and it is sought to issue**

execution against such assets;

(d)    where under the judgment or order any person is entitled to relief subject to the fulfilment of any condition which it is alleged has been fulfilled;

(e)    where any goods sought to be seized under a writ of execution are in the hands of a receiver appointed by the Court or a sequestrator.

(2)    Paragraph (1) is without prejudice to any written law or rule by virtue of which a person is required to obtain the leave of the Court for the issue of a writ of execution or to proceed to execution on or otherwise to the enforcement of a judgment or order.

(3)    Where the Court grants leave, whether under this rule or otherwise, for the issue of a writ of execution and the writ is not issued within one year after the date of the order granting such leave, the order shall cease to have effect, without prejudice, however, to the making of a fresh order.

## NOTES

### [46.2.1]    Origin and scope of Order 46 rule 2

Order 46 rule 2 derives from the rule of the same number in the former English RSC. There is a slight difference in the wording of rule 2(2) which in England referred to the Reserve and Auxiliary Forces (Protection of Civil Interests) Act 1951.

The rule provides that in certain circumstances leave of the court is required to issue a writ of execution to enforce a judgment or order. The rule does not apply to enforcement of the schedule to a Tomlin order (as to which see the commentary under Order 42 rule 5A) since the schedule is not part of the order itself: *Incorporated Owners of Hoi To Court v Chinluck Properties Ltd* HCA 6171/1997 (Chu J; 29.08.2006).

### [46.2.2]    Where leave to issue writ of execution required

The circumstances in which leave to issue a writ of execution is required under Order 46 rule 2 are the following:

- *Rule 2(1)(a) – judgment 6 or more years old –* leave is required to enforce stale judgments. The power to grant leave under this rule does not conflict with the limitation period for bringing action on a judgment (Limitation Ordinance (Cap 347) s 4(4)) since enforcement of a judgment is not the same thing as bringing action on a judgment: *WT Lamb & Sons v Rider* [1948] 2 All ER 402 (CA).

- *Rule 2(1)(b) – change of parties –* a winding up order does not result in a change of parties, and this rule does not apply: *Eternal Summit Dev't Ltd v Oriental Wealth Holdings Ltd* [2005] 2 HKC 557 (para 28).

- *Rule 2(1)(c) – estate of deceased person –* this paragraph appears to require leave only where the judgment is against the assets of a deceased person, not where the judgment is against the deceased person himself.

- *Rule 2(1)(d) – conditional relief –* see *Kai Fung Eng'g Co Ltd v Plasteel HK Ltd* [1983] 2 HKC 526 where leave to enforce a judgment was refused on the ground the plaintiff had failed to comply with an undertaking recorded in the consent order providing for entry of judgment in its favour.

- *Rule 2(1)(e) – receiver* - leave to levy execution by seizing goods in the hands of a receiver is required.

## [46.2.3]    Application procedure
An application for leave to enforce a judgment may be made *ex parte*: see Order 46 rule 4. As with other *ex parte* applications to a master, a hearing may not be necessary, and leave may be obtained by submitting an affidavit to the registry.

**3.      Leave required for issue of writ in aid of other writ** (O. 46 r. 3)
**A writ of execution in aid of any other writ of execution shall not issue without the leave of the Court.**

---

## NOTES

### [46.3.1]    Writ of execution in aid
Order 46 rule 3 provides that leave is required to issue a writ of execution in aid of another such writ.

The writ of assistance is an example of a writ of execution in aid. A writ of assistance may issue where a writ of delivery of chattels has not been effective: *Wyman v Knight* (1888) 39 Ch D 165. Another example is the writ of restitution, which is the appropriate remedy where, for example, after the bailiff has entered under a writ of possession, the party against whom judgment was given has wrongfully re-taken possession: *Alliance Bldg Society v Austen* [1951] 2 All ER 1068; *Chan Wai Wah, Lily Ann v Chan Sai Lun Henry & Ors* HCMP 2921/2001 (Kwan J; 31.07.2001 (para 7).

The writ of *capias ad satisfaciendum* for imprisonment of a debtor with insufficient assets to satisfy his adjudged liability was a common law writ of execution in aid, but has been abolished in Hong Kong: *Re an Application by the Official Solicitor (No 1)* [1983] 2 HKC 259, 263E-I (Full Bench).

**4.      Application for leave to issue writ** (O. 46 r. 4)
**(1)    An application for leave to issue a writ of execution may be made ex parte unless the Court directs it to be made by summons.**
**(2)    Such an application must be supported by an affidavit-**
- **(a)    identifying the judgment or order to which the application relates and, if the judgment or order is for the payment of money, stating the amount originally due thereunder and the amount due thereunder at the date of the application;**
- **(b)    stating, where the case falls within rule 2(l)(a), the reasons for the delay in enforcing the judgment or order;**
- **(c)    stating where the case falls within rule 2(1)(b), the change which has taken place in the parties entitled or liable to execution since the date of the judgement or order;**
- **(d)    stating, where the case falls within rule 2(1)(c) or (d), that a demand to satisfy the judgment or order was made on the person liable to satisfy it and that he has refused or failed to do**

so;

(e)     giving such other information as is necessary to satisfy the
Court that the applicant is entitled to proceed to execution on
the judgment or order in question and that the person against
whom it is sought to issue execution is liable to execution on it.

(3)    The Court hearing such application may grant leave in accordance
with the application or may order that any issue or question, a decision on
which is necessary to determine the rights of the parties, be tried in any manner
in which any question of fact or law arising in an action may be tried and, in
either case, may impose such terms as to costs or otherwise as it thinks just.

**5.      Application for leave to issue writ of sequestration** (O. 46 r. 5)

(1)    Notwithstanding anything in rules 2 and 4, an application for leave
to issue a writ of sequestration must be made to a judge by summons. (L.N. 152
of 2008)

(2)    Subject to paragraph (3), the summons, stating the grounds of the
application and accompanied by a copy of the affidavit in support of the
application, must be served personally on the person against whose property it
is sought to issue the writ. (L.N. 152 of 2008)

(3)    Without prejudice to its powers under Order 65, rule 4, the Court
may dispense with service under this rule if it thinks it just to do so. (L.N. 152 of
2008)

(4)    The judge hearing an application for leave to issue a writ of
sequestration may sit in private in any case in which, if the application were for
an order of committal, he would be entitled to do so by virtue of Order 52, rule
6, but, except in such a case, the application shall be heard in open court.

**6.      Issue of writ of execution** (O. 46 r. 6)

(1)    Issue of a writ of execution takes place on its being sealed by the
Registrar.

(2)    Before such a writ is issued a praecipe for its issue must be filed.

(3)    The praecipe must be signed by or on behalf of the solicitor of the
person entitled to execution or, if that person is acting in person, by him.

(4)    No such writ shall be sealed unless at the time of the tender thereof
for sealing—

(a)     the person tendering it produces—

(i)     the judgment or order on which the writ is to issue, or
an office copy thereof,

(ii)    where the writ may not issue without the leave of the
Court, the order granting such leave or evidence of the
granting of it; and

(b)     the Registrar is satisfied that the period, if any, specified in the
judgment or order for the payment of any money or the doing
of any other act thereunder has expired.

(5)    Every writ of execution shall bear the date of the day on which it is
issued.

## NOTES

### [46.6.1]     Origin and scope of Order 46 rule 6
Order 46 rule 6 derives from the rule of the same number in the former English RSC. There are some differences, notably rule 6(4)(a)(iii) and rule 6(6) are omitted in Hong Kong. Those provisions in the former English RSC dealt with service of a foreign state under Order 42 rule 3A (which has not been adopted in Hong Kong), and district registries, which do not exist in Hong Kong.

The rule makes provision for the manner in which application is made to the registry for issue of a writ of execution.

### [46.6.2]     Numbering
There is no rule 7 in Order 46; nor was there in the former English RSC when they were replaced by the CPR in 1999.

**8.     Duration and renewal of writ of execution** (O. 46 r. 8)

(1)   For the purpose of execution, a writ of execution is valid in the first instance for 12 months beginning with the date of its issue.

(2)   Where a writ has not been wholly executed the Court may by order extend the validity of the writ from time to time for a period of 12 months at any one time beginning with the day on which the order is made, if an application for extension is made to the Court before the day next following that on which the writ would otherwise expire or such later day, if any, as the Court may allow.

(3)   Before a writ the validity of which has been extended under paragraph (2) is executed either the writ must be sealed with the Seal of the Court showing the date on which the order extending its validity was made or the applicant for the order must serve a notice (in Form No. 71 in Appendix A), sealed as aforesaid, on the bailiff to whom the writ is directed informing him of the making of the order and the date thereof. (L.N. 363 of 1990)

(4)   The priority of a writ, the validity of which has been extended under this rule, shall be determined by reference to the date on which it was originally delivered to the bailiff.

(5)   The production of a writ of execution, or of such a notice as is mentioned in paragraph (3), purporting in either case to be sealed as mentioned in that paragraph, shall be evidence that the validity of that writ or, as the case may be, of the writ referred to in that notice, has been extended under paragraph (2). (L.N. 363 of 1990)

(6)   If, during the validity of a writ of execution, an interpleader summons is issued in relation to an execution under that writ, the validity of the writ shall be extended until the expiry of 12 months from the conclusion of the interpleader proceedings. (L.N. 404 of 1991)

**9.     Return to writ of execution** (O. 46 r. 9)

(1)   Any party at whose instance or against whom a writ of execution was issued may serve a notice on the bailiff to whom the writ was directed

requiring him, within such time as may be specified in the notice, to endorse on the writ a statement of the manner in which he has executed it and to send to that party a copy of the statement. (L.N. 363 of 1990)

(2)   If a bailiff on whom such a notice is served fails to comply with it the party by whom it was served may apply to the Court for an order directing the bailiff to comply with the notice.

(3)   (Repealed L.N. 404 of 1991)

(Enacted 1988)

## ORDER 47

### WRITS OF FIERI FACIAS

---

## NOTES

### [47.0.1] Cross-reference and history

When considering the law and procedure regulating the writ of *fieri facias* reference must be made both to the relevant provisions of the High Court Ordinance (sections 21C and D) and to this Order.

### [47.0.2] Application for writ of fieri facias

A stay of execution of a judgment imposed by Order 13 rule 8 does not prevent a judgment creditor issuing a writ of *fieri facias* within that period, provided that the writ is not passed to the bailiff and no enforcement of its terms is attempted during that 14-day period (*Silktex Trading Co (a firm) v Kong Sung Sin, t/a Darwin Fashion Garment Factory* [1986] HKLR 559.

### [47.0.3] Effect of issue of writ of fieri facias

The provision regulating the effect of the issue of the writ of *fieri facias* was previously found in section 28(1) of the Sale of Goods Ordinance. It is now found in section 21C(1) of the High Court Ordinance (repeating section 138 of the Supreme Court Act 1981) which says:

> Subject to subsection (2), a writ of fieri facias or other writ of execution against goods issued from the High Court shall bind the property in the goods of the execution debtor as from the time when the writ is delivered to the bailiff to be executed.

Section 21C(3) says:

> For the better manifestation of the time mentioned in subsection (1), it shall be the duty of the bailiff (without fee) on receipt of any such writ as is there mentioned to endorse on its back the hour, day, month and year when he received it.

Order 46 rule 9 repeats the duty of the bailiff to indorse the time of receipt on the writ in respect of all writs of execution.

In *Cheung Tung Leung t/a Tin Lung Electric-Plating Fty v Paulsan Fat Watch Products Co Ltd* [1985] 2 HKC 140, Mantell J, considering the effect of the former section 28(1) of the Sale of Goods Ordinance, said:

> The effect of section 28(1) of the Sale of Goods Ordinance, which has its genesis in section 15 of the Statute of Frauds, is, subject to the proviso, to bind the property in the goods of the judgment debtor from the time when the writ of fi fa is delivered to the Bailiff, but not to vest any title to the goods in either the Bailiff or the execution creditor.

Mantell J further considered the position of competing execution creditors and held that precedence went to the creditor who first delivered his writ to the bailiff. In a case where there were several competing execution creditors he approved the dictum of Lord Denman CJ in *Drewe v Lainson* (1840) 113 ER 516, 519

The duty of the sheriff, when he has several writs of execution, is clear. He is to execute them according to their priority; which, as to writs of fieri facias, is according to the time of their delivery to him. By 'executing' is meant that he is to apply the proceeds of goods seized in that manner. It is not material whether he seizes the goods under the first or the last writ: as soon as they are seized, they are, in point of law, in his custody under all the writs which he then has; and, when he sells them, he sells, in point of law, under all the writs. This is obviously so: for, if the proceeds are more than sufficient to satisfy the first, he must apply the surplus to the second, and so to the third and others; and, as the amount for which the goods will sell is uncertain, he cannot be said to sell under the first writ only.

Mantell J further said that, on the authorities, he did not doubt that there might be circumstances where, by reason of laches or by the countermanding of the writ, a party might lose his priority.

**[47.0.4]    Court has no power to order third persons to deliver up property to bailiff**

The court has no power to make an order requiring a non-party to deliver property to the bailiff for the purpose of execution. See *K Yu Sein Trading Co Ltd & Anor v Talakchand* [1982] HKLR 171, 175A–B (CA) citing *Brydges v Brydges & Wood* [1909] P 187 (CA). In *K Yu Sein* the court suggested that the plaintiff, having obtained an attachment order under Order 44A rule 7, should have applied for an order for sale and an order that the bailiff be permitted to enter the non-party's premises to seize the goods.

**[47.0.5]    Transfer of goods by debtor after writ delivered to bailiff**

Since the property in the goods remains in the debtor, he can, until sale, give a good title to a purchaser but any such transfer will be subject to the bailiff's right to follow the goods except in the following cases:

(1)    Section 21C(2) of the High Court Ordinance provides that a writ of *fieri facias* shall not prejudice the title to any goods of the execution debtor acquired by a person in good faith and for valuable consideration unless that person had, at the time when he acquired his title, notice that that writ or any other such writ by virtue of which the goods of the execution debtor might be seized or attached had been delivered to and remained unexecuted in the hands of the bailiff. According to section 21C(4)(d), an act shall be treated as done in good faith if it is in fact done honestly, whether it is done negligently or not.

(2)    Section 24(1) of the Sale of Goods Ordinance (Cap 26): purchase in good faith and without notice of any defect or want of title on the part of the seller from a shop or a market in the ordinary course of business. (The burden of proof in establishing the necessary criteria rests upon the purchaser – and what constitutes a 'shop' is a question of fact (see *Au Muk-shun v Choi Chuen-yau* [1988] 1 HKLR 413 (CA).)

(3)    Winding up of the debtor company, unless the execution was completed before the commencement of the winding up (section 269(1) of the Companies Ordinance (Cap 32)). According to section 269(2), execution against goods is completed by seizure and sale or by the making of a charging order under

section 20 of the High Court Ordinance; execution against land is completed by seizure, by the appointment of a receiver, or by the making of a charging order under section 20 of the High Court Ordinance. It must be remembered, however, that proviso (c) to section 269(1) provides that 'the rights conferred by this subsection on the liquidator may be set aside by the Court in favour of the creditor to such extent and subject to such terms as the Court may think fit'. In *Re Lake & Hot Springs Country Club (HK) Ltd* [1986] 2 HKLR 824, Jones J considered this proviso and held, following *Re Caribbean Products (Yam Importers) Ltd v Swains Packaging Ltd* [1966] 1 Ch 331, that, in order to justify an alteration to the statutory order for the payment of debts provided for under the Companies Ordinance to the effect that all unsecured creditors ranked *pari passu* in a winding up, very strong grounds had to be put forward.

According to section 270(1) of the Companies Ordinance (Cap 32), where any goods of a company are taken in execution, and, before the sale thereof or the completion of the execution by the receipt or recovery of the full amount of the levy, notice is served on the bailiff that a provisional liquidator has been appointed or that a winding-up order has been passed, the bailiff shall, on being so required, deliver the goods and any money seized or received in part satisfaction of the execution to the liquidator, but the costs of the liquidation shall be a first charge on the goods or money so delivered, and the liquidator may sell the goods, or a sufficient part thereof, for the purpose of satisfying that charge.

(4)     Bankruptcy of the debtor, unless the execution was complete before the bankruptcy order was made. According to section 12 of the Bankruptcy Ordinance (Cap 6), on the making of a bankruptcy order the Official Receiver shall be constituted receiver of the property of the debtor and thereafter no creditor shall have any remedy against the property or person of the debtor in respect of the debt or shall commence any proceedings. Section 45(1) of the Bankruptcy Ordinance provides that where a creditor has issued execution against the property of a debtor, he shall not be entitled to retain the benefit of the execution against the trustee in bankruptcy of the debtor, unless he had completed the execution before the date of the receiving order and before notice of the presentation of any bankruptcy petition by or against the debtor. According to section 45(2), execution against goods is completed by seizure and sale. In *C Cordon & Co (HK) Ltd v Hui Yuen* [1967] HKDCLR 17, the court, construing the former section 45(2) of the Bankruptcy Ordinance, held that, since money from the proceeds of execution still remained in court, execution had not been completed.

**[47.0.6]     Property of judgment debtor liable to attachment and sale**
Section 21D(1) of the High Court Ordinance (Cap 4) provides that virtually every type of property, movable as well as immovable is liable to attachment and sale in execution of a judgment. The proviso to the subsection excludes from execution the judgment debtor's tools of trade as well as bedding and wearing apparel of the judgment debtor and dependants living with him, up to a total value of HK$10,000.

*Shares in private Hong Kong companies* – Section 21D(1) also expressly excludes from availability for 'attachment and sale' shares in a Hong Kong 'private company'.

However, it has been held that whilst section 21D(1) precludes attachment and sale of such shares by means of *fieri facias* (under the provisions of Order 47, sale being con ducted by the bailiff) the section, upon its true construction (and when read together with sections 20, 20A, and 20B of the High Court Ordinance and Order 50 rule 9(a)), does not restrict or otherwise affect the court's powers to make a 'charging order' in respect of such shares (under section 20A of the High Court Ordinance) and subsequently to direct sale (under section 20B of the High Court Ordinance, the sale being conducted by and in a manner considered appropriate by the registrar). See *Tim mar Co Ltd & Anor v Erwin Hardy Corp Ltd* [2001] 3 HKC 55 overruling *Cheung Koon Ping v Muneyoshi Michiyoshi* [1994] 3 HKC 563 (DC). The result of the decision in the *Timmar* case is that the correct procedure for executing against shares in a private company is charging order and sale rather than writ of *fi fa*.

### [47.0.7]    Claim by third party that property seized belongs to him
Where a third party claims that property seized by the bailiff belongs to him, the bailiff should interplead. The rules regulating interpleader actions are found in Order 17. Order 17 rule 2(1) requires the third party to give notice of his claim to the bailiff charged with execution of the writ. Under Order 17 rule 2(4), a bailiff who, prior to receipt of such notice, has taken possession of the goods or chattels in question, may apply to the court for a protective order, restraining the bringing of an action against him and the court (pursuant to Order 17 rule 8) may make such order as it thinks just.

### [47.0.8]    Voidable preferences
Whilst a debtor may pass good title to a third party in respect of property sold or otherwise disposed of, prior to the issue of the writ, the disposition will be voidable and will be liable to be set aside where it is made with an intention to defraud creditors. Section 60 of the Conveyancing and Property Ordinance (Cap 219) says:

(1) Subject to subsections (2) and (3), every disposition of property made, whether before or after the commencement of this section, with intent to defraud creditors, shall be voidable, at the instance of any person thereby prejudiced.

(2) This section does not affect the law of bankruptcy for the time being in force.

(3) This section does not extend to any estate or interest in property disposed of for valuable consideration and in good faith  to any person not having, at the time of the disposition, notice of the intent to defraud creditors.

See also the definition of 'property' in section 3 of Cap 1 which is not restricted to land.

The incidence of the burden of proof under section 60(1) and (3) was considered by the Court of Appeal in *Honour Finance Co Ltd v Poon Ting-chau* [1990] 2 HKLR 629 (CA). The court held that whilst the burden of proving intent to defraud, under section 60(1), lies on the person seeking to avoid the disposition, the onus of proving the requirements set out in section 60(3) lies on the transferee who claims the benefit of the exception created by that subsection. In so holding, the Court of Appeal relied upon the English Court of Appeal's decision in *Glegg v Bromley* [1912] 3 KB 474 (CA) and that of Pennycuick J in *Lloyds Bank Ltd v Marcan* [1973] 1 WLR 339 (upheld by the English Court of Appeal, although the point was not in issue; [1973] 1 WLR 1387), in which the court considered, respectively, the former section 5 of the Statute of Elizabeth 1571 (UK) and its successor, formerly section 172 of the Law of Property Act 1925 (UK), upon which section 60 is based.

In *Yee Sang Metal Supplies Co v Zee Chi-ling t/a Tai Chong Building Contractor* [1965] HKLR 874 it was held that for the purposes of determining whether a particular disposition was made 'with intent to defraud', in terms of what is now section 60(1) of the Conveyancing and Property Ordinance, the crucial test was whether the transaction was a cloak or contrivance designed to secure a personal benefit to the grantor. If it was not then the transaction was valid 'even though the grantor knew at the time that execution [by writ of *fi fa*] was about to be levied by another creditor ... and the grantee entered into the transaction with the full knowledge and intention to defeat an expected execution by another judgment creditor' (at 878).

**1.    Power to stay execution by writ of fieri facias** (O. 47 r. 1)

**(1)   Where a judgment is given or an order made for the payment by any person of money, and the Court is satisfied, on an application made at the time of the judgment or order, or at any time thereafter, by the judgment debtor or other party liable to execution—**

      **(a)    that there are special circumstances which render it inexpedient to enforce the judgment or order, or**

      **(b)    that the applicant is unable from any cause to pay the money,**

**then, notwithstanding anything in rule 3, the Court may by order stay the execution of the judgment or order by writ of fieri facias either absolutely or for such period and subject to such conditions as the Court thinks fit.**

**(2)   An application under this rule, if not made at the time the judgment is given or order made, must be made by summons and may be so made notwithstanding that the party liable to execution did not acknowledge service of the writ or originating summons in the action or did not state in his acknowledgment of service that he intended to apply for a stay of execution under this rule pursuant to Order 13, rule 8.**

**(3)   An application made by summons must be supported by an affidavit made by or on behalf of the applicant stating the grounds of the application and the evidence necessary to substantiate them and, in particular, where such application is made on the grounds of the applicant's inability to pay, disclosing his income, the nature and value of any property of his and the amount of any other liabilities of his.**

**(4)   The summons and a copy of the supporting affidavit must, not less than 4 clear days before the return day, be served on the party entitled to enforce the judgment or order.**

**(5)   An order staying execution under this rule may be varied or revoked by a subsequent order.**

---

**NOTES**

**[47.1.1]   Stay of execution**

The court has several different express powers under these rules to stay execution of a judgment or order in different circumstances. In addition it has a parallel inherent jurisdiction to grant such a stay. See the commentary under Order 45 rule 11.

**[47.1.2]     Stay of execution by way of writ of fi fa**

Order 47 rule 1 gives the court an express power to order a stay of execution by way of writ of *fieri facias*. The rule is limited to execution by way of writ of *fi fa* and does not empower the court to restrain a judgment creditor from enforcing the judgment by other means: *Kwangtung Provincial Bank v Cheung Tin Ming* [1992] 1 HKC 344.

The grounds on which a stay of execution may be ordered under this rule are set out rule 1(1)(a) and (b), namely special circumstances which render it 'inexpedient' to enforce the judgment, and inability to pay.

Where it is alleged that it would be 'inexpedient' to enforce the judgment the court should ask itself 'whether the justice of the parties' mutual relations might demand a stay of execution': *BIS Consultants Ltd v Dao Heng Bank Ltd* [1989] 2 HKLR 172 (CA), citing with approval *Canada Enterprises Corp Ltd v MacNab Distilleries Ltd* [1981] Comm L R 167 and *Orri v Moundreas* [1981] Comm L R 168. 'Expediency' is to be equated with 'justice' in this context.

An application for a stay on the ground of inability to pay must be supported by an affidavit setting out the debtor's means: rule 1(3).

Rule 1(2) provides that an application for a stay may be made when the judgment is given (for example by oral application upon grant of Order 14 summary judgment) or subsequently (by summons and affidavit). Repeated applications are not permissible – if a stay is refused the remedy is to appeal: *Sanyo Electric Trading Co Ltd v Leung Kwok-hing* [1992] 2 HKC 509; [1993] 1 HKLR 253, 256 at lines 25–35.

On granting a stay the court should specify the period for which it will last and it may impose conditions: rule 1(1). A condition commonly imposed is payment of the judgment debt by instalment. In *Sanyo Electric Trading Co Ltd v Leung Kwok-hing* [1992] 2 HKC 509; [1993] 1 HKLR 253 it was held that the discretion to require instalment payments requires the court:

> 'to balance the legitimate interest of the judgment creditor to choose the best method of enforcing his judgment so as to ensure payment in full against the interest of the judgment debtor to avoid more draconian methods of enforcement by paying the judgment debt in realistic instalments'.

In that case the court held the balance tipped in favour of allowing the judgment creditor to choose how to enforce the judgment since there was doubt whether the judgment debtor could keep up instalment payments.

**[47.1.3]     No need for stay where cross-judgment**

There is no need to apply for a stay of execution by way of writ of *fi fa* (or otherwise) on the ground of set-off against another judgment. The set-off is 'automatic' under Order 45 rule 16. See *Re Lam Lam ex p Bank of China (Hong Kong) Limited* HCB 14221/2002 & CACV 396/2002 (Reyes J; 22.12.2003).

**[47.1.4]     Enforcement of judgment debt in foreign currency by way of fieri facias**

Enforcement of judgment debts expressed in foreign currency by means of a writ of *fieri facias* is governed by a practice direction 16.2, paragraph 7, of which reads as follows:

(a) Where the plaintiff wishes to enforce a judgment expressed in foreign currency by the issue of a writ of fieri facias, the praecipe for the issue of the writ must first be indorsed and signed by or on behalf of the solicitor of the plaintiff, or by the plaintiff if he is acting in person, with the following certificate:

'Hong Kong dollar equivalent of Judgment

I/We certify that the rate current in Hong Kong for the purpose of (state the unit of the foreign currency in which the Judgment is expressed) at the close of business on the ........ day of ........ 19.. (being the date nearest or most nearly preceding the date of the issue of the Writ of fi fa) was....... to the $Hong Kong and at this rate the sum of (state the amount of the Judgment debt in foreign currency) amounts to $......

Dated the ..... day of ...... 19...

Signed .............

Solicitor to the Plaintiff.'

(b) The amount so certified will then be entered in the writ of fi fa by adapting Appendix A, Form 53 to meet the circumstances of the case but substituting the following recital:

'Whereas in the above named action it was on the .... day of ..... 19 ... adjudged [or ordered] that the defendant C.D. to pay to the Plaintiff A.B. (state the sum of the foreign currency for which Judgment was entered) or the Hong Kong dollar equivalent at the time of payment, and whereas the Hong Kong dollar equivalent at the date of issue of the Writ is $...... as appears by the Certificate indorsed and signed by or on behalf of the Plaintiff on the Praecipe for the issue of this Writ.'

## [47.1.5] Rule 2 – Comparison with English rule

Order 47 rule 2 of the English rules, which confers on a party the right to issue two or more writs of *fieri facias* directed to the sheriffs in different counties to enforce the judgment or order, is omitted from the Hong Kong rules. Reference to Order 47 rule 2 has, therefore, been omitted from Order 47 rule 1(1) of the Hong Kong rules.

**3. Separate writs to enforce payment of costs, etc.** (O. 47 r. 3)

**(1) Where only the payment of money, together with costs to be taxed, is adjudged or ordered, then, if when the money becomes payable under the judgment or order the costs have not been taxed, the party entitled to enforce that judgment or order may issue a writ of fieri facias to enforce payment of the sum (other than for costs) adjudged or ordered and, not less than 8 days after the issue of that writ, he may issue a second writ to enforce payment of the taxed costs.**

**(2) A party entitled to enforce a judgment or order for the delivery of possession of any property (other than money) may, if he so elects, issue a separate writ of fieri facias to enforce payment of any damages or costs awarded to him by that judgment or order.**

## NOTES

### [47.3.1]    Comparison with English rule

Order 47 rule 4 of the English rules refers to the situation where the execution creditor has recovered less than £600 and is not entitled to costs in the action. He is obliged, therefore, to pay the expenses of the execution process himself. This rule has been omitted from the Hong Kong rules.

Order 47 rule 5 of the English rules concerns the writ *fieri facias de bonis ecclesiasticis*, which writ does not exist in Hong Kong. It has, therefore, been omitted from the Hong Kong rules.

**6.     Order for sale in execution of judgment** (O. 47 r. 6)

**(HK)(1)   Every sale in execution of a judgment shall be made under the direction of the Registrar and shall be conducted according to such orders, if any, as the Court may make on application of the person at whose instance the writ of execution under which the sale is to be made was issued, of the person against whom that writ was issued or of the bailiff to whom it was issued. In the absence of any such application the sale shall be made by public auction.**

**(2)   Such an application must be made by summons and the summons must contain a short statement of the grounds of the application.**

**(3)   Where the applicant for an order under this rule is not a bailiff, the bailiff must, on the demand of the applicant, send to the applicant a list containing the name and address of every person at whose instance any other writ of execution against the goods of the judgment debtor was issued and delivered to the bailiff (in this rule referred to as "the bailiff's list"); and where the bailiff is the applicant, he must prepare such a list.**

**(4)   Not less than 4 clear days before the return day the applicant must serve the summons on each of the other persons by whom the application might have been made and on every person named in the bailiff's list.**

**(HK)(5)   Where any goods of a debtor are taken in execution, and the bailiff has notice of another execution or other executions, the Court shall not consider an application for sale otherwise than by auction until service of the summons on the person or persons named in the bailiff's list has been effected.**

**(6)   The applicant must produce the bailiff's list to the Court on the hearing of the application.**

**(7)   Every person on whom the summons was served may attend and be heard on the hearing of the application.**

## NOTES

### [47.6.1]    Comparison with English rule

Order 47 rule 6 (1) is peculiar to Hong Kong. Formerly contained in Order 47 rule 7(2), the present rule provides greater detail as to the mode of sale. Although still conducted under the direction of the registrar and according to the orders of the court, the judgment creditor, judgment debtor or bailiff is entitled to apply by summons to the court as to the mode of sale. In the absence of any such application and consequent order, sale will be by public auction.

Order 47 rule 6(5) is peculiar to Hong Kong, although Order 47 rule 6(5) of the English rules is somewhat similar in its effect.

**[47.6.2]    Rule 6(3)**
According to Order 47 rule 6(3), where such application is made by the judgment creditor or debtor, the bailiff must send to the applicant a list ('the bailiff's list') containing the name and address of every person at whose instance any other writ of execution against the goods of the judgment debtor has been issued and delivered to the bailiff. Where the bailiff is the applicant, he must also prepare such list. The summons as to the mode of sale must then be served on all other potential applicants including those whose names appear on the bailiff's list and any of such persons may attend the hearing of the summons. The purpose of this provision is to ensure that as many creditors as possible gain some recompense from the sale of the debtor's goods and to provide the debtor with some safeguard as to his assets.

**[47.6.3]    Sale by the bailiff**
According to section 21D(2) of the High Court Ordinance (formerly Order 47 rule 7(3) RHC), where any goods in the possession of an execution debtor are sold by the bailiff without any claim having been made to them, the purchaser of the goods so sold shall acquire good title to them and no person shall be entitled to recover against the bailiff for any sale of such goods, unless it is proved that the person from whom recovery is sought had notice or might, by making reasonable inquiry, have ascertained that the goods were not the property of the execution debtor.

**[47.6.4]    Liability for acts of a bailiff**
The Hong Kong SAR government is immune from liability in respect of any tort committed by a bailiff (section 4(5) of the Crown Proceedings Ordinance). Nor can any liability attach to a bailiff, personally, in respect of the seizure and sale of goods belonging to someone other than the judgment debtor, unless it can be shown that the bailiff had knowledge as to the goods' ownership or could have acquired such knowledge by making reasonable inquiry (section 21D(2) of the High Court Ordinance). In *Tyrone Crystal Ltd v European Asian Bank* [1985] 2 HKC 762, the bailiff's inquiries at the go-down where the goods were stored, coupled with information contained in a letter sent to him by the judgment creditor's solicitor, were found to meet the 'reasonable inquiry' test. However, Mantell J was clearly of the view that had the plaintiff established the identity of the individual, within the bailiff's office, responsible for conducting the sale of the goods, an action in damages, for negligence, would lie. (The goods, which consisted of crystal glassware, had been sold at a considerable undervalue at a poorly advertised auction).

That an action against a bailiff, in negligence, might lie in respect of a carelessly conducted sale at which goods were sold for considerably less than their true value, was expressly recognised by Rogers JA in *Fu Lok Man James v Chief Bailiff of the High Court* [1999] 3 HKC 742 (CA), at 752C–F, in which he cited with approval the comment of Megaw LJ in *Newman v Bakeaway* [1983] 1 WLR 1016, at 1024. On a practical note, Rogers JA observed that where an order for sale by auction was made in any interpleader proceedings instituted by the bailiff, such order could fix a reserve price.

In the case of *Fu Lok Man James*, Rogers JA emphasised (as had Megaw LJ in the *Newman* case) that no liability would attach to a bailiff who had acted honestly unless the person against whom the writ of *fieri facias* had been executed had suffered a 'real grievance'. Moreover (per both Rogers JA and Godfrey JA), unless the bailiff had himself procured or authorised a wrongful act, he was not personally liable for acts of subordinate officers.

### [47.6.5]    Liability of the judgment creditor

In *Tyrone Crystal Ltd v European Asian Bank* (above), the court held that the general rule was that the execution creditor was not liable for wrongful execution upon a correctly indorsed writ. There was, however, an exception where an execution creditor intermeddled by directing the bailiff to levy the amount of judgment on another's goods, whether or not that direction took the form of an indorsement on the writ (see *Smith v Keal* (1882) 9 QBD 340). Similarly, in *Hock Finance Holdings Ltd v Tat Ming Godown Co Ltd* [1985] 2 HKC 495, Kempster JA held that the bailiff executes a valid writ of execution as an officer of the court and not as a servant or agent of the judgment creditor, unless that judgment creditor, by himself or his solicitors, has given him specific directions to seize particular goods or otherwise intermeddled with the bailiff's responsibility under the writ. In the absence of such specific direction or intermeddling, the judgment creditor could not be held vicariously liable for any unlawful seizure on the part of the bailiff. Further, where a bailiff seizes the goods of a wrong person under a valid writ without any direction or intermeddling from or by the judgment creditor, a subsequent ratification or approval by the judgment creditor does not render him liable to the owner of the goods seized (applying *Wilson v Tumman* (1843) 6 M & G 236 and *Morris v Salberg* (1889) 22 QBD 614).

### [47.6.6]    Obstruction of the bailiff

It is an offence under section 23 of the Summary Offences Ordinance (Cap 228) to resist or obstruct a public officer or other person lawfully engaged, authorised or employed in the performance of any public duty (see *Sun Yue Yen v R* [1964] HKLR 139 where the offence was held to be one of strict liability).

**(HK)7.    Special rules as to the sale of immovable property** (O. 47 r. 7)

**(1)    At any time within 10 days from the date of sale of any immovable property in execution of a judgment, application may be made to the Court to set aside the sale on the ground of any material irregularity in the conduct of the sale, but no such sale shall be set aside on the ground of such irregularity unless the applicant proves to the satisfaction of the Court that he has sustained substantial injury by reason of such irregularity.**

**(2)    (a)    If no such application is made the sale shall be deemed absolute.**

**(b)    If such application is made and the objection is disallowed, the Court shall make an order confirming the sale.**

**(c)    If such application is made and the objection is allowed, the**

Court shall make an order setting aside the sale for irregularity.

(3)    Whenever a sale of immovable property is set aside for irregularity the purchaser shall be entitled to receive back any money deposited or paid by him on account of such sale, with or without interest, to be paid by such parties and in such manner as it may appear to the Court proper to direct.

(4)    (a)    After a sale of immovable property has become absolute in manner aforesaid the Court shall grant a certificate to the person who has been declared the purchaser at such sale to the effect that he has purchased the right, title and interest of the judgment debtor in the property sold.

(b)    Such certificate shall be liable to the same stamp duty as an assignment of the same property and, when duly stamped as aforesaid, shall be taken and deemed to be a valid transfer of such right, title and interest and may be registered in the Land Registry under the Land Registration Ordinance (Cap. 128). (8 of 1993 s. 30)

(5)    (a)    Where the property sold consists of immovable property in the occupancy of the judgment debtor, or of some person on his behalf, or of some person claiming under a title created by the judgment debtor subsequently to the attachment of the property, the Court shall, on the application of the purchaser, order delivery of the property to be made by putting the party to whom the property has been sold, or any person whom he may appoint to receive delivery on his behalf, in possession thereof and, if necessary, by removing any person who may refuse to vacate the same.

(b)    Where the property sold consists of immovable property in the occupancy of any other person entitled to occupy the same the Court shall, on the application of the purchaser, order delivery thereof to be made by affixing a copy of the certificate of sale in some conspicuous place on the property or at the court house.

(6)    (a)    If the purchaser of any immovable property sold in execution of a judgment is, notwithstanding the order of the Court, resisted or obstructed in obtaining possession of the property, the provisions of this Order relating to resistance or obstruction to the execution of the judgment for immovable property shall be applicable in the case of such resistance or obstruction.

(b)    If it appears that the resistance or obstruction to the delivery of possession was occasioned by any person other than the judgment debtor claiming a right to the possession of the property sold as proprietor, mortgagee, lessee, or under any other title, or if in the delivery of possession to the purchaser any such person claiming as aforesaid is dispossessed, the Court, on the complaint of the purchaser or of such person claiming as aforesaid, if made within one month from the date of such resistance or obstruction or of such dispossession, as the case may be, shall inquire into the matter of the complaint and make such order as may be proper in the circumstances of the case.

(c)    The person against whom any such order is made shall be at liberty to bring an action to establish his right at any time within three months from the date of the order.

**(HK)8.**    **Special rules as to the sale of movable property** (O. 47 r. 8)

(1)    (a)    **Where the property sold consists of movable property in the possession of the judgment debtor, or to the immediate possession of which the judgment debtor is entitled, and of which actual seizure has been made, the property shall be delivered to the purchaser.**

(b)    **Where the property sold consists of movable property to which the judgment debtor is entitled subject to a lien or right of any person to the immediate possession thereof, the delivery to the purchaser shall as far as practicable be made by the bailiff giving notice to the person in possession prohibiting him from delivering possession of the property to any person except the purchaser.**

(2)    **Where the property sold consists of debts, not being negotiable instruments, or of shares in any public company or corporation, the Court shall, on the application of the purchaser, make an order prohibiting the judgment debtor from receiving the debts and his debtor from making payment thereof to any person except the purchaser, or prohibiting the person in whose name the shares are standing from making any transfer of the shares to any person except the purchaser, or receiving payment of any dividends thereon, and the manager, secretary or other proper officer of the company or corporation from permitting any such transfer or making any such payment to any person except the purchaser.**

(3)    **Where the property sold consists of a negotiable instrument of which actual seizure has been made the same shall be delivered to the purchaser.**

(4)    (a)    **If the execution of a transfer by any person in whose name any share in a public company or corporation is standing, or the indorsement by any person of any negotiable instrument, or the execution by any person of any deed or other instrument relating to immovable property or any interest therein, is lawfully required to give effect to any sale in execution of a judgment, the Registrar, with the sanction of the Court, may—**

(i)    **execute such transfer; or**
(ii)    **endorse such negotiable instrument; or**
(iii)    **execute such deed or other instrument.**

(b)    **The execution of such transfer, the endorsement of such negotiable instrument and the execution of such deed or other instrument by the Registrar shall have the same effect as the execution and the endorsement by the person whose execution or endorsement is so required as aforesaid.**

(c)    **Until the execution of such transfer or the endorsement of such negotiable instrument the Court may, by order, appoint some person to receive any dividend or interest due in respect of any such share or negotiable instrument.**

**(Enacted 1988)**

## NOTES

### [47.8.1]      Comparison with English rules

Order 47 rule 7 – Special rules as to the sale of immovable property, and Order 47 rule 8 – Special rules as to the sale of movable property, are peculiar to Hong Kong.

## ORDER 48

### EXAMINATION OF JUDGMENT DEBTOR, ETC.

---

## NOTES

### [48.0.1]    Comparison between Orders 48 and 49B

The Hong Kong Rules provide two, separate, procedures for oral examination which are contained in Orders 48 and 49B respectively. The Orders assumed their present form following the enactment of the Debtors' (Arrest and Imprisonment) Ordinance (No 1 of 1984). Both Orders provide a form of post-judgment discovery. They also enable the court to sanction, by imprisonment, those debtors who, it appears on examination, have had assets available to satisfy the judgment wholly or in part but have failed to do so, who have failed to make a full disclosure or who have disposed of assets with a view to avoiding satisfaction of the judgment. In addition the court has power to direct that the judgment debt be paid by instalments and to imprison for any failure to pay as directed. (As to the court's powers upon examination, generally, see Order 49B rule 1B, the provisions of which also apply to examinations conducted under Order 48).

That oral examination should be the subject of two, overlapping, procedures is commonly attributed to historical factors, specifically to the hurried enactment of the Debtors' (Arrest and Imprisonment) Ordinance in the face of public concern as to the procedure for imprisonment for civil debt under the pre-existing rules and conflicting views, within the judiciary, as to how those rules should be interpreted. (For the history of the current provisions, see Morrow, 'The Crumbling Walls of the Debtors' Prison' (1984) 14 HKLJ 195.)

Although the two procedures (contained in Order 48 and Order 49B respectively) operate in parallel, there remain significant differences between them. Firstly, it is only where the examination is conducted under Order 49B that the court may order the debtor's arrest for the purpose of securing his attendance at the examination and may, upon any adjournment of the examination, make a prohibition order (prohibiting the debtor from leaving Hong Kong) or, where the court has reason to believe that the debtor may not appear at the resumed hearing, order the debtor's imprisonment until such date. Secondly, it may be argued that the scope of examination under Order 49B is wider than that afforded by Order 48. Upon examination under either Order, the debtor may be required to produce documents and other records as may be specified. However, whereas under Order 48, the enquiry is limited to whether and, if so, what debts are owing to the debtor and whether the debtor has means, and if so, what means of satisfying the judgment debt (Order 48 rule 1(1)), upon examination under Order 49B, the debtor is required to 'make a full disclosure of all his assets, liabilities, income and expenditure and of the disposal of any assets or income' and must 'answer all questions put to him' (Order 49B rule 1A(2)). Thirdly, whilst Order 49B is concerned only with enforcement of 'money judgments', Order 48 facilitates examination of persons liable to satisfy other types of judgments and orders (see Order 48 rule 2). Finally, and significantly, it is only Order 48 which caters for a judgment debtor which is a body corporate. Under Order 48 rule 1, the court may order the examination of 'any officer' of the body corporate. The court is given no equivalent power by Order 49B.

**1.     Order for examination of judgment debtor** (O. 48 r. 1)

**(1)    Where a person has obtained a judgment or order for the payment, by some other person (hereinafter referred to as "the judgment debtor") of money, the Court may, on an application made ex parte by the person entitled to enforce the judgment or order, order the judgment debtor or, if the judgment debtor is a body corporate, an officer thereof, to attend before the Registrar or such officer as the Court may appoint and be orally examined on the questions—**

> **(a)     whether any and, if so, what debts are owing to the judgment debtor, and**
>
> **(b)     whether the judgment debtor has any and, if so, what other property or means of satisfying the judgment or order,**

**and the Court may also order the judgment debtor or officer to produce any books or documents in the possession of the judgment debtor relevant to the questions aforesaid at the time and place appointed for the examination.**

**(2)    An order under this rule must be served personally on the judgment debtor and on any officer of a body corporate ordered to attend for examination.**

**(3)    Any difficulty arising in the course of an examination under this rule before the Registrar or officer, including any dispute with respect to the obligation of the person being examined to answer any question put to him, may be referred to a judge and he may determine it or give such directions for determining it as he thinks fit.**

---

**NOTES**

**[48.1.1]     Application for examination order**
Order 48 rule 1 empowers the court to make an order for the oral examination of a judgment debtor on the questions whether there are any debts owing to him and what property or other means of satisfying the judgment he may have. Rule 1(1) specifically provides that the application be made *ex parte*. Such applications are usually made by affidavit filed in the registry and considered by a master without a hearing. This proce dure does not infringe human rights guarantees since any *ex parte* order may be set aside at an *inter partes* hearing under Order 32 rule 6. See *Poon Ting Chau v Wong Kwok Chi* HCMP 5314/2002 (Chu J; 20.10.2006). The order at this stage is only that an examination take place. If that order is not set aside, the matter proceeds on an *inter partes* basis to a call-over hearing (see below) and then the examination itself.

**[48.1.2]     Examination of 'officer' of body corporate**
Where the judgment debtor is a body corporate, Order 48 rule 1 empowers the court to order that 'an officer thereof' attend for examination. In *Toppan Printing Co Ltd v Champion Dragon Development Ltd* [1986] HKC 371 it was held, on the basis of English authority (*Société Generale du Commerce et de l'industrie en France v JM Farina & Co* [1904] 1 KB 794) that 'officer' is not restricted to its definition in the

Companies Ordinance (Cap 32), and that for the purposes of Order 48 the term encompasses anyone, however described, who is actively concerned in the direction or management of the company. Applying this test, it was held that the court could examine a former director who remained 'actively concerned' at the time judgment was entered despite having resigned.

In England it has been held that there is no power to order examination of an officer who is outside the jurisdiction, and no basis for service of any such order out of the jurisdiction: *Masri v Consolidated Contractors Int'l Co SAL & Ors* [2009] UKHL 43 (30.07.2009). The decision is based on the wording of CPR 71 (English equivalent of Order 48) and CPR 6 (equivalent of Order 11), which it was said did not expressly provide for extraterritorial jurisdiction over company officers. Although the court may have extraterritorial jurisdiction over the company, this did not extend to the company's officers, who are separate legal persons. The case concerned a foreign company, and may be read as inapplicable to companies registered in the jurisdiction.

In *Sano Screen Manufacturing Ltd v J & R Bossini Trading Ltd* [2001] 3 HKC 465 (CA), the judgment debtor company sought to appeal an order that a former director attend for examination upon the grounds, firstly, that the individual had ceased to be a director of the company at the time application for an order for examination was made (although it was acknowledged that at such time he remained president of a group of companies of which the judgment debtor formed part) and, secondly, that such an order should not be made when information could be sought from other individuals who remained directors of the debtor company. Rogers VP, in delivering the court's judgment dismissing the appeal, held that the original order had been properly made – the individual whose examination was sought remained, both at the time of the application and at the time when the facts took place which gave rise to the judgment, 'intimately involved' in the management of the company, by virtue of his involvement in the 'overall management and strategic planning' of the group of which the judgment debtor company formed part. Moreover, Rogers VP held that the fact that there might be other people who could also give relevant information was but one factor which the court might properly take into account when considering whether or not to make the order for examination sought.

## [48.1.3]      Directions as to call-over

The court has adopted a 'call-over' system whereby an initial hearing of short duration will be fixed for the purpose of giving directions to the parties to facilitate the examination, the hearing of which will be adjourned to a date to be fixed.

A form setting out standard directions which may be given at the call-over hearing has been in use since 1994 (see Law Society circular 94-301). Obviously the form must be adapted according to the circumstances and the directions actually made. As in use in 2006 the form reads:

### Directions under RHC Order 48

1.      The examination of _____ , a director of the Judgment Debtor Company is adjourned to a date to be fixed with an estimated time of [   ] hours.

2.      The director of the Judgment Debtor Company shall as far as possible, supply

copies of or make available originals for copying the following documents not later than 21 days before the adjourned hearing and shall also produce the following documents at that hearing:

a.   Passbooks and copies of bank statements for the last __ years of all bank accounts in Hong Kong and elsewhere in the company's sole name or jointly with any other person, or of any firm or business of which the company is sole proprietor or a partner.

b.   Accounts for the last __ years of any business in which the company is sole proprietor or a partner or a shareholder in the case of a private company.

c.   Tax returns and assessments of the company for the last __ years.

d.   All shares and stocks certificates held in the company's name.

e.   The deeds or Land Registry entries in respect of all property in the company's name or owned beneficially by the company.

f.   Registration details of all vehicles owned by or in the company's name.

g.   All documents showing outgoings and liabilities, including copies of any other judgments of a court entered against the company's name.

h.   All Company Books, Registers [and documents].

3.   Costs reserved.

Further Direction:

The Judgment Creditor shall provide a shorthand writer to take a verbatim note of evidence at the examination and the notes of evidence shall be filed in court within [   ] days of the completion of the examination or any adjournment thereof.

**Warning**

The director of the Judgment Debtor Company is warned of the requirement to make a full disclosure when complying with clause 2 herein, and if it is not done there may be another adjournment and the director of the Judgment Debtor Company may be liable for the costs incurred.

The director of the Judgment Debtor Company is further warned that he must attend the examination whenever required and if he fails to attend the examination without good cause being shown, he is liable to face Contempt of Court Proceedings.

**48.1.4]   Examination in open court**
By practice direction 13.2 examination of a judgment debtor under this Order and under Order 49B is conducted in open court before a master. Solicitors have the right of audience.

**[48.1.5]   Scope of examination under Order 48 rule 1**
The scope of an examination under Order 48 rule 1 is set down in sub-rule (1), that is to determine whether (a) there are any debts owing to the judgment debtor, and (b) what other property or means the judgment debtor may have of satisfying the judgment.

In *Bloomsbury International Ltd v Nouvelle Foods (HK) Ltd* [2005] 1 HKC 337 the court considered in detail the scope of examination permitted by rule 1(1)(b). It was held that the word 'property' should not be read narrowly. It includes choses in action such as claims for unliquidated damages or restitution of property. As a result the judgment creditor may ask questions about the judgment debtor's rights against third parties, including accounts receivable, with a view to the appointment of a liquidator or receiver by way of equitable execution. The decision in *Hua Chiao Commercial Bank Ltd v Alpha Plus International Development Ltd* [2001] 2 HKC 54 (where it was held that the examination is limited to assets which are 'instantly' or 'currently' available) was effectively over-ruled in this regard.

There is a line 'beyond which a creditor examining under Order 48 may not tread'. In deciding what can or cannot be examined the court 'must not be overly solicitous' in favour of the debtor, who has committed a wrong in failing to pay, and 'should refrain from drawing too refined distinctions'. The judgment creditor is not entitled to ask about negotiations or to ask questions with a view to seeking its own remedy against third parties. 'Order 48 is a process of discovery about the debtor's means and property rights against third parties ... not a means of obtaining discovery for use in personal actions by the creditor or anyone else against third parties': *Bloomsbury International* (above) citing *Watkins v Ross* (1893) 68 LT 423 and *McCormack v National Australia Bank Ltd* (1992) 106 ALR 647.

### [48.1.6]     Order for further disclosure
The court has power to order further disclosure of documents during the course of an examination under Order 48 or Order 49B: *Lafarge SA v Continental Cement Corp* [2007] 1 HKC 34.

### [48.1.7]     Dispute in the course of examination
Order 48 rule 1(3) provides that the master before whom the examination takes place may refer to a judge any difficulty or dispute with regard to the examinee's obligation to answer questions. This provision is 'permissive', it 'does not require that every dispute on the scope of the examination be referred to the judge'. It would be 'impractical and disruptive, not to say inefficient in terms of time and cost, if every dispute in the course of examination had to go to a judge'. The master 'has a wide discretion whether to allow a question' and jurisdiction to 'resolve the issues of scope raised by the parties'. See *Bloomsbury International Ltd v Nouvelle Foods (HK) Ltd* [2005] 1 HKC 337.

### [48.1.8]     Imprisonment
Where, upon an examination conducted under Order 48 rule 1, the court is satisfied that the judgment debtor is able to satisfy the judgment, has disposed of assets with a view to avoiding satisfaction of the judgment, either wholly or in part, or has wilfully failed to make full disclosure, the court may, in its discretion, order that the judgment debtor be imprisoned for a period not exceeding three months (Order 49B rule 1B(1)). In each case, the liability to imprisonment is that of the 'judgment debtor' and not of the person examined (where the identity of such person differs from that of the judgment debtor). Consequently, where the judgment debtor is a body corporate, there can be no imprisonment (under Order 49B rule 1B(1)) in respect of an 'officer' of that body corporate who is examined under Order 48 rule 1. The point was acknowledged in *Hua Chiao Commercial Bank Ltd v Alpha Plus International Development Ltd* [2001] 2 HKC 54. In refusing the judgment creditor's application

to order the imprisonment of the company judgment debtor's director (on the basis that the judgment debtor company was able to satisfy the judgment debt) Master Kwan stated (at 61B–E):

> … it is conceptually difficult to apply the provisions of O 49B r 1B to commit directors of corporate entities. A distinction has to be drawn between the judgment debtor company and [the examined director]. Since the case of *Salomon v A Saloman Ltd* [1897] AC 22 the common law has recognized that the legal identity of an incorporated company is distinct from its members and directing mind.'

However, it is submitted that the provisions of Order 49 rule 1B in no way restrict or curtail a court's common law power to commit, for 'contempt', any person – be it an officer of a corporate judgment debtor, upon his examination under Order 48 rule 1, or otherwise – for wilful refusal to comply with a court order.

**2.     Examination of party liable to satisfy other judgment** (O. 48 r. 2)

**Where any difficulty arises in or in connection with the enforcement of any judgment or order, other than such a judgment or order as is mentioned in rule 1, the Court may make an order under that rule for the attendance of the party liable to satisfy the judgment or order and for his examination on such questions as may be specified in the order, and that rule shall apply accordingly with the necessary modifications.**

**3.     Examiner to make record of debtor's statement** (O. 48 r. 3)

**The Registrar or officer conducting the examination shall cause to be recorded, by means of shorthand notes or mechanical, electronic or optical device or otherwise, the evidence given by the judgment debtor or other person at the examination.**

**(Enacted 1988) (L.N. 108 of 2002)**

## ORDER 49

### GARNISHEE PROCEEDINGS

**1.      Attachment of debt due to judgment debtor** (O. 49 r. 1)

**(1)    Where a person (in this Order referred to as "the judgment creditor") has obtained a judgment or order for the payment by some other person (in this Order referred to as "the judgment debtor") of a sum of money amounting in value to at least $1,000, not being a judgment or order for the payment of money into court, and any other person within the jurisdiction (in this Order referred to as "the garnishee") is indebted to the judgment debtor, the Court may, subject to the provisions of this Order and of any written law, order the garnishee to pay the judgment creditor the amount of any debt due or accruing due to the judgment debtor from the garnishee, or so much thereof as is sufficient to satisfy that judgment or order and the costs of the garnishee proceedings. (See App. A, Forms 72-74)**

**(2)    An order under this rule shall in the first instance be an order to show cause, specifying the time and place for further consideration of the matter, and in the meantime attaching such debt as is mentioned in paragraph (1), or so much thereof as may be specified in the order, to answer the judgment or order mentioned in that paragraph and the costs of the garnishee proceedings.**

---

## NOTES

### [49.1.1]      Comparison with English rule

Whereas in Hong Kong the minimum debt which may be the subject of a garnishee order is $1,000, in England it is £50.

Subrules 1(3) and 1(4) of the English rule are omitted in Hong Kong. The English subrule 1(3) (which states that moneys in bank deposit accounts are deemed to be sums 'due or accruing due' to the account holder, and are therefore liable to attachment, notwithstanding that certain conditions applicable in respect of the account may be unsatisfied, including any condition that a receipt for money deposited must be produced before any money is withdrawn) has its Hong Kong equivalent in section 21(1)(d) of the High Court Ordinance. England's subrule 1(4) (which provides that a garnishee order shall not reduce the amount on deposit in a building society or credit union to less than £1) has no equivalent in Hong Kong.

### [49.1.2]      Garnishee orders generally

Order 49 provides the procedure whereby a judgment creditor may enforce the judgment by attaching a debt owing by a third party to the judgment debtor. The effect is to require the third party (known as the 'garnishee') to pay the judgment creditor instead of the judgment debtor. By virtue of section 21(1)(d) of the High Court Ordinance, moneys in bank deposit accounts are deemed to be debts 'due or accruing due' notwithstanding that the agreement or mandate which governs the account's operation imposes conditions, as to withdrawals, which are not or cannot be met (see 'Comparison with English rule', above). The section has no application to moneys in bank 'current' accounts and the account holder's right to withdraw credit balances in such accounts remains conditional upon the making of a demand for payment (see the decisions of the English courts in *Libyan Arab Foreign Bank v Bankers Trust Co* [1989] 3 All ER 252, at 268 per Straughton J; *Richardson v Richardson* [1927] P 228, at 232–233 per Hill J; *Joachimson v Swiss Banking Corp* [1921] 3 KB 110 (CA), at 127 per Aitken LJ). However, service upon the bank of the garnishee order *nisi* has been held to constitute a sufficient demand for these purposes (see the *Joachimson* case, above).

By virtue of Order 49 rule 8 money paid to a judgment creditor under a garnishee order validly discharges the garnishee's debt to the judgment debtor dollar for dollar.

See generally Booth, Enforcing Judgments in Hong Kong (HK: LexisNexis, 2004) ch 6.

**[49.1.3]   Discretion**

The making of a garnishee order clearly involves an exercise of the court's discretion. Order 49 rule 1, which confers the power to make a garnishee order, uses the permissive 'may'. In *Rooke v HV Construction Services Ltd* [1998] 1 HKC 686 (CA) Godfrey JA noted (at 689) that whilst there were no general principles laid down as to the exercise of the court's discretion, the court should, in each case, have regard not only to the position of the judgment creditor, the judgment debtor and the garnishee but also to the position of the judgment debtor's other creditors. The court held, however, that unless winding-up proceedings had actually been commenced or a scheme of arrangement was imminent – and, in either case, a proper *pari passu* distribution was thereby assured – the court had no choice but to make a garnishee order absolute in favour of the applicant creditor. A similar conclusion was reached in the earlier case of *Wardley Ltd & Ors v Aik San Realty Ltd & Anor* [1985] 2 HKC 695 which was cited, with approval by Godfrey JA in the *Rooke* case. The rule is that in the absence of insolvency 'the person who gets in first gets the fruits of his diligence . . . but it is different if the estate is insolvent'. In that event the court may, in the exercise of its discretion, refuse a garnishee order if the effect would be to prefer one creditor over others. This is to preserve fairness amongst creditors of equal rank who should share in the available assets '*pari passu*': *Prichard v Westminster Bank Ltd* [1969] 1 WLR 547 (CA), quoted with approval in *CCIC Finance Ltd v Guangdong International Trust & Investment Corp* [2005] 2 HKC 589, 605D-607B.

It appears that the court may, in its discretion, refuse to make a garnishee order absolute where knowledge of the debt, which it is sought to attach, was obtained by the judgment creditor through a breach of confidence or where the judgment creditor has otherwise acted 'unconscionably'. This issue was also considered by the Court of Appeal in *Rooke v HV Construction Services Ltd* [1998] 1 HKC 686. However, the court held, on the facts before it, that there was no such breach of confidence or lack of conscionability as would justify the court in refusing the garnishee order sought. The judgment creditor thus succeeded in obtaining a garnishee order absolute in respect of funds held on the judgment debtor's behalf by its solicitors. The funds' existence had been disclosed at a creditor's meeting (which the judgment debtor did not attend) and the information later passed on to him by another creditor. Notably, neither at the time of the meeting, nor subsequently and prior to the date of the hearing itself, had there been presentation of any winding-up petition, any resolution to present a petition, any resolution for the voluntary winding up of the judgment debtor company or any approved scheme of arrangement.

## [49.1.4]     Procedure

An application for a garnishee order is made in two stages. The initial application is *ex parte* by affidavit under Order 49 rule 2. If the court is satisfied with the affidavit evidence it will make an initial order to show cause specifying the time and place for an *inter partes* hearing: see Order 49 rule 1(2). This order should be drawn up in accordance with Form 72 in Appendix A and served initially on the garnishee, and later on the judgment debtor (rule 3). The garnishee is bound as from service of the order to show cause: rule 3(2).

At the second stage the court will hear all concerned, *inter partes*, as to whether it should make the initial order absolute. The court will exercise its discretion in favour of making the garnishee order absolute unless the court is satisfied that there are reasonable grounds for not doing so. (See '*Discretion*', above).

The garnishee has a right to set off any cross-claim it may have against the judgment debtor, which would serve to reduce or extinguish the debt, provided the claim would qualify as a *set-off* in terms of Order 18 rule 7 and so long as it arose prior to service, upon the garnishee, of the order *nisi*: *Hale v Victoria Plumbing Co Ltd* [1966] 2 QB 746.

Garnishee proceedings may be instituted, concurrently, with other modes of enforcement (Order 45 rule 1 states that a judgment (or order) may be enforced by 'one or more' of the various methods listed).

Application for a garnishee order *nisi* may be made as soon as judgment is pronounced (or the 'order' made). Although it is no doubt desirable, it is strictly unnecessary that the judgment, or order, should have been first drawn up or sealed (see Order 45 rule 14).

*Costs* – Where a judgment creditor applies for a garnishee order, he does so at his own risk as to costs. Where the application is unsuccessful, the judgment creditor may be required to pay the costs of the garnishee, on a 'party to party' basis, even where the judgment creditor has acted reasonably in applying for the order: *Interpaul Trading Co Ltd v Jia Pai Co Ltd & Ors* [2001] 4 HKC 229 (D Ct).

## [49.1.5]     Who may obtain a garnishee order – 'person'

Order 49 rule 1(1) provides that a garnishee order may be made in favour of a 'person' who 'has obtained a judgment or order' for the payment of a sum of money.

Section 3 of the Interpretation and General Clauses Ordinance (Cap 1) provides that the term 'person' includes 'any public body and any body of persons, corporate or incorporate ...'. As to the additional requirement that such 'person' (the judgment creditor) should have obtained a 'judgment or order', see below.

## [49.1.6]     'Judgment or order' enforceable by garnishee proceedings

A garnishee order may be made to enforce a 'judgment or order': Order 49 rule 1(1). Throughout Order 49 the person in whose favour a garnishee order may be made is referred to as 'the judgment creditor'. However, this is solely for the sake of convenience and does not limit the scope of the Order. It is expressly provided in Order 49 rule 1(1) that a garnishee order may be made to enforce an order other than a judgment. Thus an interlocutory order for payment of costs may be the subject of a garnishee order (provided that payment is due).

In the English case of *Gandolfo v Gandolfo & Anor* [1981] 1 QB 359 (CA) a garnishee order was made to enforce an undertaking to pay money. Browne LJ held (at 366H–367A) that it was appropriate to treat the particular undertaking (which was recorded in an order) as being 'equivalent to an order' for the purposes of garnishee proceedings. The learned judge continued: 'I am not saying it would be appropriate in all cases.' The situation appears to be different with an obligation to pay money under a *Tomlin* order since the agreement annexed to such an order is not part of the order itself: see the commentary under Order 42 rule 5A.

A garnishee order may be granted in respect of a judgment or order from a court outside Hong Kong. In *Société Eram Shipping Co Ltd v Compagnie Internationale de Navigation & Ors* [2001] EWCA Civ 1317 (07.08.2001) the English Court of Appeal upheld a garnishee order based on a French judgment, which had been registered in England. That judgment was later reversed by the House of Lords on the ground the debt sought to be garnisheed was located outside England (*Société Eram Shipping Co Ltd v HSBC* [2003] UKHL 30, discussed below). However, the fact that the judgment to be enforced originated outside England was not a matter of concern. As to registration and enforcement in Hong Kong of judgments from other jurisdictions, see generally Order 71 and the commentary thereunder.

### [49.1.7] Against whom may a garnishee order be made – 'within the jurisdiction'

For an order to be made the proposed garnishee must be 'within the jurisdiction': Order 49 rule 1(1). This requirement reflects the territorial basis on which common law courts normally exercise their jurisdiction. The theory is that the Hong Kong courts should not interfere in matters which are more properly left to the courts of another place. Thus if the third party is in another jurisdiction, the creditor should seek to enforce the Hong Kong judgment or order there. Nevertheless a temporary, even fleeting, presence in Hong Kong should be sufficient for a garnishee order to be made: see *Colt Industries v Sarlie* [1966] 1 All ER 673; *SCF Finance Co Ltd v Masri & Anor (No 3)* [1987] 1 QB 1028 (CA), provided that the person is not induced to enter Hong Kong by fraud or trickery: *Watkins v North American Land and Timber Co Ltd* (1904) 20 TLR 534. In the *SCF Finance* case it was held that a party who had submitted to the jurisdiction by instructing her solicitors to accept service of a garnishee order is considered to be 'within the jurisdiction' for the purpose of Order 49 rule 1, though she left England shortly before the order *nisi* was granted.

### [49.1.8] Change of parties

The assignee of a judgment debt is considered a person who 'has obtained a judgment' within the meaning of Order 49 rule 1 and he may seek to enforce the debt by means of a garnishee order: see *Goodman v Robinson* (1887) 18 QBD 332.

Order 46 rule 2(1)(b) provides that where there is a change of parties whether by way of assignment, death or otherwise, leave is required to issue a writ of execution. It is doubtful whether this applies to a garnishee order since such an order is not a writ, and is not included in the definition of 'writ of execution' in Order 46 rule 1 nor in the Schedule to the High Court Ordinance. Nevertheless garnishee orders are within the discretion of the court and where an assignee or personal representative is involved evidence of the circumstances should be placed before the court on the application for a garnishee order.

**[49.1.9]    Debt must be 'due or accruing due'**

In the words of Order 49 rule 1 the debt owing by the garnishee to the judgment debtor must be 'due or accruing due'. 'It is for the judgment creditor, as plaintiff, to establish that the garnishees, as defendants, were indebted to the judgment debtors in any and, if so, what amount at the time the order *nisi* was served.': *Kwok Sin Hung v Hang On Tai Building Contractors* [1958] HKLR 215. As a general rule, garnishee orders do not attach future debts: see *Karaha Bodas Co LLC v Perusahaan Pertambangan Minyak Dan Gas Bumi Negara (Pertamina) (No 3)* [2004] 3 HKC 608, 617D. 'Accruing due' refers to debts payable in the future by reason of a present obligation: *Webb v Stenton & Ors, garnishees* (1883) 11 QBD 518. Hence a debt payable by instalment is considered to be 'accruing due', and may be the subject of an order that future instalments be paid to the judgment creditor over time. On the other hand an anticipated payment which depends upon a future event which may never happen is not an enforceable debt at all and cannot be the subject of a garnishee order. For example a payment which depends on the exercise of a trustee's discretion, or on the attainment of a certain age, or surviving until the next payment date (*Webb v Stenton & Ors, garnishees* (1883) 11 QBD 518) is neither due nor accruing due. Similarly a debt which becomes owing only upon fulfilment of certain conditions is neither due or accruing due in the meantime: *Yik Keung v Hong Kong & China Gas Co Ltd* [1959] DCLR 67.

**[49.1.10]    Cases where there is an attachable debt – moneys in bank accounts**

A credit balance in a bank account is a debt due to the account holder under the normal principles of banking law. By virtue of section 21 of the High Court Ordinance credit balances in deposit accounts of banks and other authorised financial institutions are deemed to be sums 'due or accruing due', and hence attachable by garnishee order, notwithstanding the existence of pre-conditions required for the deposit to be repayable. Specifically, the fact that any of the following types of conditions has not been satisfied does not prevent attachment of the deposit:

(1)    notice requirement;
(2)    personal application condition;
(3)    presentation of deposit book;
(4)    production of receipt.

The effect of section 21 is to over-ride, for the purpose of deposit accounts in financial institutions, the authorities cited in the preceding paragraph to the effect that a debt subject to a condition precedent is not due or accruing due: see *Panyu Chemicals Import & Export Corp v Sun Wai Man & Ors* HCA 1537/2001 (Suffiad J; 25.09.2007).

The section goes on to provide that rules of court may add to the above list, but no such rules have been enacted.

Section 21 of the High Court Ordinance has no application to credit balances held in current accounts. The account holder's right to such balances is conditional only upon his making a demand for payment. It has been held that service of the garnishee order *nisi*, itself, constitutes a sufficient demand (*Joachimson v Swiss Banking Corp* [1921] 3 KB 110 (CA)).

## [49.1.11] Debts located outside Hong Kong

Although a garnishee order may issue to enforce a judgment or order made by a court outside Hong Kong (see *Société Eram Shipping Co Ltd v Compagnie Internationale de Navigation & Ors* [2001] EWCA Civ 1317 (07.08.2001), discussed above), the debt to be garnisheed should be one which is payable inside Hong Kong. Thus the Hong Kong branch of a bank should not be required by garnishee order to pay over money held in an account at its branch in another jurisdiction. The debt due or accruing due in such a case is not located in Hong Kong and for reasons of comity the Hong Kong court should not make orders with respect to it. See *Société Eram Shipping Co Ltd v Hongkong and Shanghai Banking Corp Ltd & Ors* [2003] UKHL 30 (12.06.2003). There the House of Lords held that the English court had no power to make a garnishee order requiring the Hongkong Bank, at its London branch, to pay over money on deposit in Hong Kong. The earlier decision of the House of Lords in *Deutche Schachtbau-und Tiefbohrgesesellschaft mbh v Shell Int'l Petroleum Co Ltd* [1990] 1 AC 295 had been interpreted as deciding that this was a matter of discretion, leaving open the possibility of a garnishee order with extraterritorial reach. However, it is now clear from *Société Eram* that this is a matter of jurisdiction and such an order could only be made under an express statutory grant of extraterritorial jurisdiction.

## [49.1.12] Debts that have been assigned

A garnishee order may properly be made in relation to a debt, which has been assigned by way of mortgage, to take effect on reassignment. Such was held by Hunter J in *Wardley Ltd & Ors v Aik San Realty Ltd* [1985] 2 HKC 695, where his Lordship cited with approval the following words of Jervis CJ in *Hirsch v Coates* (1856) 25 LJ CP (NS) 315, at 317:

> A judgment creditor may obtain an *ex parte* order ... to attach debts owing or accruing to the judgment debtor, and that Order binds those debts and makes ultimately available to the judgment creditor so much as may remain after satisfying all equitable claims thereon. If the debts have been assigned, and the assignment swallows up the whole, then the judgment creditor gets nothing ... If the debtor has charged or parted with his interest in the debt, then, except as to any excess beyond the amount of the charge, no interest will go to the person obtaining the Order.

In *Wardley Ltd*, debts owing from a third party to the judgment debtor had been assigned by way of security to a bank, subject to a provision for reassignment. Hunter J held that the judgment creditor was not seeking to garnishee an equity of redemption but, as the assignment of the debts was not absolute, was seeking to garnishee the debt itself after reassignment from the bank, which it could properly do.

## [49.1.13] Debts subject to a Mareva injunction

Debts owing to the judgment debtor, which are subject to a Mareva injunction imposed on the application of a third party, may be garnisheed, although the onus rests upon the judgment creditor and judgment debtor to show that the transaction giving rise to the debt is genuine in a case where its genuineness is called into question by the third party: *Kanematsu-Gosho (HK) Ltd & Anor v Lee Boon Chean* [1986] HKLR 59.

## [49.1.14] Pensions payable under the Pensions Ordinance (Cap 89)

It has been held in *Attorney General v Ng Shiu-fai* [1977] DCLR 51 that, under section

12 of the Pensions Ordinance, money due can be attached in favour of the Government. It can only be attached under the provisions of the Pensions Ordinance, however, and not under this Order. As no procedure was laid down, the court adopted the procedure of Order 49 with such variations as circumstances required.

**[49.1.15]    Judgment in favour of judgment debtor**
A judgment in favour of the judgment debtor in other proceedings is a debt due to the judgment debtor from the moment such judgment is delivered, and it is not necessary to wait for it to be entered before it may be garnisheed (*Holtby v Hodgson* (1890) 24 QBD 103, at 106–107).

**[49.1.16]    No attachment of wages**
Section 66 of the Employment Ordinance (Cap 57) prohibits the attachment of wages, save in respect of civil debts owing to the government.

**[49.1.17]    Where judgment debtor's right to repayment of debt is conditional**
In *Yik Keung v Hong Kong & China Gas Co Ltd* [1959] DCLR 67, money had been deposited by the judgment debtor with a public utility company. Conditions were contained in the deposit receipt to the effect that the deposit could only be refunded on presentation of the receipt, duly indorsed by the depositor, subject to all accounts due having been paid. The court held, following *Bagley v Winsome and National Provincial Bank Ltd (Garnishee)* [1952] 2 QB 236, that such money could not be garnisheed as the judgment debtor was bound by the conditions and the judgment creditor could not stand in any better position. A debt owed to a judgment debtor will not be treated as 'due or accruing due' unless the debtor's right to payment is unconditional. A notable exception to this principle exists in respect of moneys held in bank deposit accounts (see under '*Garnishee orders generally*', above).

**[49.1.18]    Debt in respect of which cheque given but not presented**
In *Kwok Sin Hung v Hang On Tai Building Contractors* [1958] HKLR 215 (H Ct), Reece J held, applying *Elwell v Jackson* (1885) 1 TLR 454, that, where a cheque is tendered and accepted in satisfaction of a debt, the debt is thus extinguished, even though the cheque has not been presented for payment. However, he held that the debt would revive if the cheque was subsequently stopped or dishonoured.

**[49.1.19]    Interest on garnisheed debt ordered to be repaid**
See the commentary under Order 42 rule 1 concerning interest on money ordered to be repaid on appeal, referring to *Hang Sing Construction Co Ltd v Young's Engineering Co Ltd* [1985] 2 HKC 17 (which may be *per incuriam*).

**[49.1.20]    Effect of bankruptcy or winding up of judgment debtor Bankruptcy**
According to section 45(1) of the Bankruptcy Ordinance (Cap 6), where a creditor has issued execution against the property of a debtor or has attached any debt due to him, he shall not be entitled to retain the benefit of the execution or attachment against the trustee in bankruptcy of the debtor unless he had completed the execution or attachment before the date of the receiving order and before notice of the presentation of any bankruptcy petition by or against the debtor. According to section 45(2) of the Ordinance, an attachment of a debt is completed by the receipt of the debt.

**[49.1.21]  Winding up**

According to section 269(1) of the Companies Ordinance, where a creditor has issued execution against the goods or lands of a company or has attached any debt due to the company, and the company is subsequently wound up, he shall not be entitled to retain the benefit of the execution or attachment against the liquidator in the winding up of the company unless he has completed the execution or attachment before the commencement of the winding up. According to section 269(2)(b), an attachment of a debt is completed by the receipt of the debt. In *Chung Nan Industrial Supplies Co Ltd v Ritaworks Ltd* [1966] HKLR 338, judgment creditors obtained a garnishee order *nisi* to attach the surplus remaining of the judgment debtor company's assets after discharging a debenture debt to a garnishee bank two days after the commencement of the winding up of the judgment debtor company. The application by the judgment creditors for an order absolute was opposed by the garnishees. The court held, distinguishing *Lam Pak-luen v Lee Wing-yuen* [1964] HKLR 85, that the judgment creditors would have been able to retain the benefit of their attachment only if they had actually received the debt before the commencement of the winding up. The court's powers as to the making of orders absolute in garnishee proceedings (and in respect of charging orders) are discretionary in nature. In deciding whether to make an order *nisi*, absolute, and in determining whether to grant a stay of execution in respect of an order absolute, the court should consider not only the position of the judgment creditor, the judgment debtor and that of the garnishee but also the position of the judgment debtor's other creditors and the desirability of securing a *pari passu* distribution amongst creditors of the same class (*Chellic Industries Ltd v Datacom Wire & Cable Co Ltd* [2000] 1 HKC 646). However, where bankruptcy or winding up proceedings have not been commenced, or where there is no imminent finalisation of any scheme of arrangement for payment of debts, the court has no choice but to make the order absolute (*Rooke v HV Construction Services Ltd* [1998] 1 HKC 686 (CA) applying dicta of Cotton LJ in *Roberts v Death* (1881) 8 QBD 319 and in *Wilson (D) (Birmingham) Ltd v Metropolitan Property Developments Ltd* [1975] 2 All ER 814; and dicta of Hunter J in *Wardley Ltd v Aik San Realty Ltd* [1985] 2 HKC 695).

**[49.1.22]  Amendment of garnishee order**

A garnishee order which is incorrect may be amended if that may be done without injustice. In *Da Silva & Anor v Dias-Azedo* [2010] 6 HKC 262; [2010] 4 HKLRD 599 the court granted leave to amend a garnishee order absolute under Order 20 rule 11 where the amount stated to be owing by a bank to the judgment debtor was incorrect. The court distinguished cases where there had been mistakes of identity and garnishee orders were set aside to prevent injustice.

**2.     Application for order** (O. 49 r. 2)

**An application for an order under rule 1 must be made ex parte supported by an affidavit—**
- **(a)     stating the name and the last known address of the judgment debtor,**
- **(b)     identifying the judgment or order to be enforced and stating the amount remaining unpaid under it at the time of the application,**

    **(ba)**   if the amount remaining unpaid under the judgment or order is arrears of maintenance, stating—

        **(i)**   the interest payable in respect of the arrears of maintenance that the judgment creditor is entitled to under section 20A(2) of the Guardianship of Minors Ordinance (Cap. 13), section 9(B)(2) of the Separation and Maintenance Orders Ordinance (Cap. 16), section 53A(2) of the Matrimonial Causes Ordinance (Cap. 179) or section 28AA(2) of the Matrimonial Proceedings and Property Ordinance (Cap. 192), as the case may be; and

        **(ii)**   the surcharge payable in respect of the arrears of maintenance under section 20B(1) of the Guardianship of Minors Ordinance (Cap. 13), section 9C(1) of the Separation and Maintenance Orders Ordinance (Cap. 16), section 53B(1) of the Matrimonial Causes Ordinance (Cap. 179) or section 28AB(1) of the Matrimonial Proceedings and Property Ordinance (Cap. 192), as the case may be; (Ordinance No 18 of 2003)

    **(c)**   stating that to the best of the information or belief of the deponent the garnishee (naming him) is within the jurisdiction and is indebted to the judgment debtor and stating the sources of the deponent's information or the grounds for his belief, and

    **(d)**   stating, where the garnishee is a bank having more than one place of business, the name and address of the branch at which the judgment debtor's account is believed to be held or, if it be the case, that this information is not known to the deponent.

---

## NOTES

**[49.2.1]    Comparison with English rule**

There would appear to be a line omitted from Order 49 rule 2(b) if the intention was to reproduce the English rule. The words omitted are italicised:

> (b) identifying the judgment or order to be enforced and stating the amount *of such judgment or order and the amount* remaining unpaid under it at the time of the application.

There is also a difference in Order 49 rule 2(d) between the Hong Kong rules and the English rules in that the latter requires the number of the bank account to be stated. Notwithstanding the difference in the Hong Kong rules, it is suggested that the inclusion of the bank account number would clearly be desirable in an application in Hong Kong.

**[49.2.2]    Contents of affidavit**

It has been held in *Yau Lee Construction Co (a firm) v Ding Hsung Construction Co* [1965] HKLR 48 that, in a case where the judgment debtor stated in his affirmation that he 'understands' that money had been deposited with the garnishee, the affirmation was defective. At best it was equivocal. If the affirmant had personal knowledge of these matters he should have stated them as facts. If by 'understands' he meant that he had been informed and verily believed that money had been deposited as alleged, he should have said so.

## [49.2.3] Enforcement of judgment debt in foreign currency by garnishee proceedings

According to para 8 of Practice Direction 16.2 'Judgment: Foreign Currency':

(a) Where the plaintiff wishes to enforce a judgment expressed in foreign currency by garnishee proceedings, the affidavit made in support of an application for an order under Order 49 rule 1 must contain words to the following effect:

> The rate current in Hong Kong for the purchase of (state the amount of the Judgment in foreign currency) at the close of business on the.......day of.....19.... was........to the $Hong Kong, and at this rate the said sum of .......amounts to $........I have ascertained the above information (state the source of the information) and verily believe the same to be true.

> The Registrar will then make an order nisi for the dollar equivalent of the judgment debt as so verified.

(b) Where the plaintiff wishes to attach a debt due or accruing due to the defendant within the jurisdiction in the same unit of foreign currency as that in which the judgment debt itself is expressed, the affidavit made in support of an application for an order under 0.49 r.1 must state all the relevant facts relied upon. In such event the Registrar may make the order to attach such debt due or accruing due in that foreign currency.

**3.      Service and effect of order to show cause** (O. 49 r. 3)

**(1)    Unless the Court otherwise directs, an order under rule 1 to show cause must be served—**

**(a)    on the garnishee personally, at least 15 days before the day appointed thereby for the further consideration of the matter, and**

**(b)    on the judgment debtor, at least 7 days after the order has been served on the garnishee and at least 7 days before the day appointed for the further consideration of the matter.**

**(2)    Such an order shall bind in the hands of the garnishee as from the service of the order on him any debt specified in the order or so much thereof as may be so specified.**

---

## NOTES

### [49.3.1] History of Rule 3

Changes were made to this rule in 1988. Formerly, Order 49 rule 3 provided that notice to show cause had to be served on the garnishee and judgment debtor not less than seven days before the return date. There was a danger here. The debt is only bound in the hands of the garnishee as from the date of receipt of the notice (*Re Stanhope Silkstone Collieries Co* (1879) 11 Ch D (CA) 160). It was, therefore, important that the judgment debtor was not served before the garnishee or the former could assign the debt away from the reach of the judgment creditor. The new Order

49 rule 3 requires service on the garnishee at least 15 days before the return date and on the judgment debtor at least seven days before the return date and at least seven days after service on the garnishee. The risk of assignment of the debt is thereby eliminated.

**[49.3.2]    Objection to garnishee order by third party**
A third party may object to a garnishee order by intervening in the proceedings and applying for a stay: *Kanematsu-Gosho (HK) Ltd & Anor v Lee Boon-chean & Ors* [1986] HKLR 59. The power to grant a stay on application of a non-party is preserved by section 16(3) of the High Court Ordinance. In the *Kamematsu* case the court ordered discovery and interrogatories with a view to investigating the *bona fides* of the judgment sought to be enforced by garnishee order.

**[49.3.3]    Garnishee proceedings where the Government is garnishee**
As with other forms of execution, garnishee proceedings cannot be instituted against the government where the government is the judgment debtor (Order 77 rule 15). Provision is made, however, in Order 77 rule 16 for the case where the government is in the position of garnishee. This rule was amended in 1988. A judgment creditor may apply by summons for an order under section 23(1) of the Crown Proceedings Ordinance (Cap 300) restraining any person from receiving money payable to him by the government (note the provision does not restrain the government) and directing payment of the money to the applicant. This procedure does not apply unless the judgment debt is at least $5,000. In conformity with ordinary garnishee proceedings, the summons must be served on the government at least 15 days before the return date and on the person to be restrained at least seven days after service on the government and at least seven days before the return date. The former provisions (section 23(1) of the Crown Proceedings Ordinance and Order 77 rule 16(2)) were applied in *Lau Ka-cheung v Shin Pao Daily News* [1968] DCLR 16.

**4.      No appearance or dispute of liability by garnishee (O. 49 r. 4)**
**(1)    Where on the further consideration of the matter the garnishee does not attend or does not dispute the debt due or claimed to be due from him to the judgment debtor, the Court may make an order absolute under rule 1 against the garnishee. (See App. A, Forms 73, 74)**
**(2)    An order absolute under rule 1 against the garnishee may be enforced in the same manner as any other order for the payment of money.**

-----

**NOTES**

**[49.4.1]    Enforcement against garnishee**
Order 49 rule 4(2) provides that a garnishee order absolute may be enforced against the garnishee like any other order for payment of money. Notice of the order is not a condition precedent to enforcement and the judgment creditor may proceed even in the absence of service thereof: *Mok Yat v Ho Kwai Chik* (1934-35) 27 HKLR 35.

On enforcement against a garnishee, the judgment creditor is in the same position as an ordinary creditor and has no priority in the garnishee's assets: *Kwai Wai Chong v Bonny Glory Investment Ltd* [1988] HKC 559, 561G-I, following *Geisse v*

*Taylor* [1905] 2 KB 658.

**5.**      **Dispute of liability by garnishee** (O. 49 r. 5)
     **Where on the further consideration of the matter the garnishee disputes liability to pay the debt due or claimed to be due from him to the judgment debtor, the Court may summarily determine the question at issue or order that any question necessary for determining the liability of the garnishee be tried in any manner in which any question or issue in an action may be tried, without if it orders trial before a master the need for any consent by the parties.**

---

**NOTES**

**[49.5.1]**      **Procedure where debt disputed by garnishee**
It is provided in this rule that where the garnishee disputes the debt sought to be garnisheed, the matter may be summarily determined or referred for trial. The Court of Appeal considered this rule in *Ying Fat Plastic Factory Ltd v Hegner Ltd* [1998] 1 HKC 691. It was held that where there was a serious dispute as to the amount owing by the garnishee to the judgment debtor, there ought to be an accounting rather than a summary determination of the dispute.

**[49.5.2]**      **Application to proceedings under Order 77**
The provisions of this Order do not generally apply in respect of money owing by the government. In such cases there is a special procedure under Order 77. However, it is expressly provided in Order 77 rule 16(3) that the provisions of rules 5 and 6 of this Order will apply to proceedings under Order 77.

**[49.5.3]**      **Jurisdiction of master**
It is clear from the text of Order 49 rule 5 that a master has jurisdiction to try a dispute as to liability of a garnishee, whether or not the parties consent to trial before a master. See *Expectrade Ltd v Lee Ming Cotton Goods Co (Lin Fung Trading Co, garnishee)* [1990] 1 HKC 283, disapproving commentary in the English *Supreme Court Practice 1988* suggesting that consent was necessary.

**[49.5.4]**      **Trial in open court**
Trial of a disputed issue in garnishee proceedings should be held in open court: *Citic Ka Wah Bank Ltd v China's Best Ltd & Ors* [2008] 4 HKC 362.

**6.**      **Claims of third persons** (O. 49 r. 6)
     **(1)**    **If in garnishee proceedings it is brought to the notice of the Court that some other person than the judgment debtor is or claims to be entitled to the debt sought to be attached or has or claims to have a charge or lien upon it, the Court may order that person to attend before the Court and state the nature of his claim with particulars thereof.**
     **(2)**    **After hearing any person who attends before the Court in compliance with an order under paragraph (1), the Court may summarily determine the questions at issue between the claimants or make such other order as it thinks just, including an order that any question or issue necessary**

**for determining the validity of the claim of such other person as is mentioned in paragraph (1) be tried in such manner as is mentioned in rule 5.**

---

## NOTES

### [49.6.1]      Procedure where third party claims the debt owing by judgment debtor

Order 49 rule 6 deals with the case where a debt which a judgment creditor seeks to attach by garnishee order is claimed by a third party. The rule empowers the court to order the third person to attend in order that the matter may be resolved. Where there is a conflict of evidence as to who is entitled to the debt, 'that issue should be properly investigated before an order absolute is made': *Fubon Bank (HK) Ltd v First Prime Group Ltd & Ors* [2009] 4 HKLRD 283 referring to *Go Fun Properties & Investment Ltd v So Bik Har Winfield & Anor* [1980] HKC 66 (CA). Such a dispute may be determined summarily or be tried in any manner as any other issue in an action may be tried, including, whether or not the parties consent, trial before a master: rule 6(2).

In *George Lee & Sons (Builders) Ltd v Olink & Anor* [1972] 1 WLR 214 (CA) it was said that the money due from the garnishee should be paid into court to abide by the outcome of the inquiry into competing claims.

It appears that the court may resolve disputed claims to a garnisheed debt on affidavit evidence. In *Go Fun* (above) four affidavits were filed in opposition to a garnishee order being made absolute. The Court of Appeal said that at the very least the Registrar should have called for affidavits in reply. In *Goodpoint Holdings Ltd v Sea brook* [1997] 2 HKC 541 the court declined the judgment creditor's application for cross-examination of two claimants to the garnisheed debt. It was held that the court's power under section 6(1) to order the claimants to attend did not give rise to a duty to do so simply because there were questions of fact to be resolved. The matter was disposed of on the basis of the affidavit evidence alone since the claimants were resident abroad and the amount at issue was relatively small.

### [49.6.2]      Numbering

There is no rule 7 in Order 49. The rule of that number in the former English Rules of the Supreme Court dealt with judgment debtors resident outside England and Wales, and was repealed in 1979.

### 8.      Discharge of garnishee (O. 49 r. 8)

**Any payment made by a garnishee in compliance with an order absolute under this Order, and any execution levied against him in pursuance of such an order, shall be a valid discharge of his liability to the judgment debtor to the extent of the amount paid or levied notwithstanding that the garnishee proceedings are subsequently set aside or the judgment or order from which they arose reversed.**

**9.    Money in court** (O. 49 r. 9)

(1)    Where money is standing to the credit of the judgment debtor in court, the judgment creditor shall not be entitled to take garnishee proceedings in respect of that money but may apply to the Court by summons for an order that the money or so much thereof as is sufficient to satisfy the judgment or order sought to be enforced and the costs of the application be paid to the judgment creditor.

(2)    The money to which the application relates shall not be paid out of court until after the determination of the application.

(3)    Unless the Court otherwise directs, the summons must be served on the judgment debtor at least 7 days before the day named therein for the hearing of it.

(4)    Subject to Order 75, rule 24, the Court hearing an application under this rule may make such order with respect to the money in court as it thinks just.

---

## NOTES

### [49.9.1]    Comparison with English rule
Order 49 rule 9(2) differs from the corresponding English rule in that the English rule requires that the summons, when issued, be produced at the office of the Accountant General and a copy be left with him. There is no similar requirement in Hong Kong.

### [49.9.2]    Scope of Rule 9
Order 49 rule 9 provides that a garnishee order cannot be made against funds in court, but a judgment creditor may apply by summons for similar relief. It has been held that where the funds are held in the district court, application should be made to that court: *Chandru Heera Sakhrani t/a Sakhrani Trading Co v Yau Tack Shing (a firm)* [1969] HKLR 93. There is now an equivalent provision of the same Order and rule number in the district court rules.

**10.    Costs** (O. 49 r. 10)

The costs of any application for an order under rule 1 or 9, and of any proceedings arising therefrom or incidental thereto, shall, unless the Court otherwise directs, be retained by the judgment creditor out of the money recovered by him under the order and in priority to the judgment debt.

(Enacted 1988)

---

## NOTES

### [49.10.1]    Judgment creditor's costs of garnishee proceedings
Order 49 rule 10 provides that the judgment creditor is entitled to its costs of garnishee proceedings (unless the court orders otherwise). Further, those costs take priority over the judgment debt. This means that money received by the judgment creditor under a garnishee order goes first to satisfy those costs, and only then toward reduction of the

judgment debt.

**[49.10.2]    Garnishee's costs of garnishee proceedings**

The garnishee, often a bank, is considered to be an innocent party in proceedings under this Order. It will usually be entitled to costs as against the judgment creditor, who may later be able to recover them from the judgment debtor. However, in *Da Silva & Anor v Dias-Azedo* HCA 2158/2009 (Deputy Judge Carlson; 05.11.2010) a garnishee bank was ordered to bear its own costs of an application to amend a garnishee order which had been necessitated by the bank's mistake.

Normally the garnishee will be entitled only to the fixed costs prescribed by Part III of the 2nd Schedule to Order 62. Those costs are of modest amount and cater for the usual case where the garnishee need only prepare a *pro forma* affirmation.

However, the court retains a discretion under Order 62 rule 32(4) to order that the garnishee be entitled to costs to be assessed in the usual way by taxation or agreement. In *Ever Good Trading Corp v Cheng Ching Kwok* [1988] 1 HKLR 307, such an order was made. There, a bank successfully opposed a garnishee application. It was holding a deposit in the name of the judgment debtor as security for a guarantee which took priority over the judgment creditor's claim. The court held that the bank had a real interest in opposing the order and should be entitled to taxed costs. See also *Interpaul Trading Co Ltd v Jia Pai Co Ltd & Ors* [2001] 4 HKC 229 where a similar order was made and it was observed that a judgment creditor, even where acting reasonably, embarks on garnishee proceedings at its own risk as to the garnishee's costs.

**[49.10.3]    Numbering**

There is no Order 49A in these rules. Order 49B follows immediately after Order 49.

## ORDER 49B

### (HK) EXECUTION AND ENFORCEMENT OF JUDGMENT
### FOR MONEY BY IMPRISONMENT

**1.     Securing attendance at examination** (O. 49B r. 1)

**(1)**   Where a judgment for the payment of a specified sum of money is, wholly or partly, unsatisfied, the Court, on an ex parte application of the judgment creditor, may order that the judgment debtor be examined under rule 1A and shall, for the purpose of securing the attendance of the judgment debtor at an examination under rule 1A either—

(a)     order the judgment debtor, by an order which shall be served personally upon him, to appear before the Court at a time appointed by the Court, with such documents or records as the Court may specify; or

(b)     where it appears to the Court that there is reasonable cause, from all the circumstances of the case, including the conduct of the judgment debtor, to believe that an order under paragraph (a) may be ineffective to secure the attendance of the judgment debtor for examination, order that he be arrested and brought before the Court before the expiry of the day after the day of arrest.

**(2)**   On an application under paragraph (1), the Court may make an order prohibiting the judgment debtor from leaving Hong Kong.

**(3)**   Where a judgment debtor fails to appear as ordered under paragraph (1)(a), the Court may order that he be arrested and brought before the Court for examination before the expiry of the day after the day of arrest.

**(4)**   Section 71 of the Interpretation and General Clauses Ordinance (Cap. 1) shall not apply to this rule.

**(5)**   The order for arrest shall be in Form No 102 in Appendix A.

---

## NOTES

**[49B.1.1]   Comparison with English rules**
Order 49B was introduced in Hong Kong in 1984 to supplement the examination procedure under Order 48. See the commentary under Order 48. Order 49B is unique to Hong Kong.

**[49B.1.2]   Comparison with examination under Order 48**
There is considerable overlap between Order 48 and Order 49B (see the commentary under Order 48, generally). However, where the judgment debtor is an individual, Order 49B may be the more attractive procedure because of some of its features not found in Order 48. For example:

(1)     whereas under Order 48 it is necessary to seek an order of committal, for contempt, if the judgment debtor fails to attend the examination, Order 49B provides for an immediate order for the arrest of the judgment debtor for

failure to attend, or even in anticipation of his failure to attend (Order 49B rule 1(1)(b)); and

(2)        the scope of an examination under Order 49B may be broader in that Order 49B rule 1A(2) imposes an obligation on the judgment debtor to make 'full disclosure' at the examination. There is no equivalent in Order 48.

It has been suggested that Order 49B is intended for cases where there is reason to believe that the judgment debtor has hidden or disposed of his assets in an attempt to defeat the judgment creditor (see Betts, 'Practice and Procedure: A Master's View', in *Law Lectures for Practitioners 1987,* published by Hong Kong Law Journal Ltd).

### [49B.1.3]   Application for examination order
Order 49B rule 1 empowers the court to make an order that a judgment debtor be examined under rule 1A as to his assets, liabilities, income and expenditure etc. An application for such an order is made *ex parte* by the judgment creditor, normally by affirmation verifying the fact that the judgment debt remains wholly or partly out standing. The application will normally be considered by a master without a hearing. This procedure does not infringe human rights guarantees since any *ex parte* order may be set aside at an *inter partes* hearing under Order 32 rule 6. See *Poon Ting Chau v Wong Kwok Chi* HCMP 5314/2002 (Chu J; 20.10.2006). The order at this stage is only that an examination take place. If that order is not set aside, the matter proceeds on an *inter partes* basis to a call-over hearing (see below) and then the examination itself.

### [49B.1.4]   Natural persons only
Only the judgment debtor himself may be the subject of an examination order under Order 49B rule 1. Where the judgment debtor is a body corporate the appropriate procedure is under Order 48 rule 1 which provides for examination of an officer thereof.

### [49B.1.5]   Discretion to order examination
The court's power to order examination of a judgment debtor is discretionary – the permissive 'may' is used in rule 1. However an examination order cannot be refused on the ground the court disapproves of the recovery tactics of the judgment creditor. See *Diners Club Int'l (HK) Ltd v Lau Lin Shan* CACV 187/1985 (Huggins & Cons VPP, Yang JA; 21.02.1986). In that case it was also held that it was wrong to refuse an order on the ground the judgment creditor should pursue other methods of execution but noted that if the judgment creditor chooses to pursue more than one such method there could be an argument it is not entitled to all the costs.

### [49B.1.6]   Securing attendance of person to be examined
An order requiring a judgment debtor to attend to be examined before the court must be served personally: Order 49B rule 1(1)(a). Substituted service may be permitted under Order 65 rule 4 if personal service proves to be impracticable. The court may prohibit the judgment debtor from leaving Hong Kong pending the examination: see Order 49B rule 1(2) which should be read together with section 21B of the High Court Ordinance (Cap 4). Additionally, where there are reasonable grounds, the court may order that the judgment debtor be arrested and brought before the court:

Order 49B rule 1(1)(b) and 1(3). The power to order arrest for this purpose may be exercised by the registrar or any master, and conditions may be imposed: HCO s 21A. In January 2006 it was announced that the court would normally limit the validity of arrest warrants under this power to 12 months: see Law Society circular 06-23.

For the procedures for implementing an order prohibiting a debtor from leaving Hong Kong through the offices of the Immigration Department and the Chief Bailiff, see the commentary under Order 44A.

For the steps to be taken upon issue of a warrant of arrest under order 49B see Practice Direction 12.1.

**1A.  Examination of debtor** (O. 49B r. 1A)

**(1)  Upon appearance of the judgment debtor for examination, he shall give evidence and he may be examined on oath by the judgment creditor and the Court; and the Court may receive such other evidence as it thinks fit.**

**(2)  The judgment debtor shall, at his examination, make a full disclosure of all his assets, liabilities, income and expenditure and of the disposal of any assets or income and shall, subject to the directions of the Court, answer all questions put to him.**

**(3)  Where the examination is adjourned, the Court shall order that the judgment debtor appear at the resumption of the examination and may—**

**(a)  order that he be prohibited from leaving Hong Kong; or**

**(b)  where it appears to the Court that there is reasonable cause, from all the circumstances of the case, including any evidence heard by the Court and the conduct of the judgment debtor, to believe that he may not appear at the resumption of the examination, order that he be imprisoned until that resumption.**

**(4)  The order under paragraph (3)(b) shall be in Form No 103 in Appendix A.**

---

## NOTES

**[49B.1A.1] Examination in open court**
By practice direction 14.2 an examination of a judgment debtor under this Order shall be conducted in open court before a master. Likewise an examination under Order 48. The practice direction goes on to state that solicitors have the right of audience. The full text of the practice direction can be viewed on the judiciary's website.

**[49B.1A.2] Directions on call-over**
The court has adopted a 'call-over' procedure whereby the initial hearing will be of short duration, and primarily for the purpose of giving directions to the parties to facilitate the conduct of the examination, the hearing of which will be adjourned to a date to be fixed.

A form setting out standard directions which may be given at the call-over hearing has been in use since 1994 (see Law Society circular 94-301). Obviously the form must be adapted according to the circumstances and the directions actually made. As in use in 2006 the form reads:

### Directions under RHC Order 49B

1.   The examination of the Judgment Debtor is adjourned to a date to be fixed with an estimated time of [   ] hours.

2.   The Judgment Debtor shall as far as possible, supply copies of or make available originals for copying the following documents not later than 21 days before the adjourned hearing and shall also produce the following documents at that hearing:

    a.   Passbooks and copies of bank statements for the last __ years of all bank accounts in Hong Kong and elsewhere in his sole name or jointly with any other person, or of any firm or business of which he is sole proprietor or a partner.

    b.   Accounts for the last __ years of any business in which he is sole proprietor or a partner or a shareholder in the case of a private company.

    c.   Tax returns and assessments for the last __ years.

    d.   All shares and stocks certificates held in his name.

    e.   The deeds or Land Registry entries in respect of all property in his name or owned beneficially by him.

    f.   Registration details of all vehicles owned by or in his name.

    g.   All documents showing outgoings and liabilities, including copies of any other judgments of a court entered against his name.

    h.   Wage or salary slips from his employer for the last __ years.

3.   Costs reserved.


Further Direction:

The Judgment Creditor shall provide a shorthand writer to take a verbatim note of evidence at the examination and the notes of evidence shall be filed in court within [   ] days of the completion of the examination or any adjournment thereof.

### Warning

The Judgment Debtor is warned of the requirement to make a full disclosure when complying with clause 2 herein, and if it is not done there may be another adjourn ment and the director of the Judgment Debtor may be liable for the costs incurred.

The Judgment Debtor is further warned that he must attend the examination whenever required and if he fails to attend the examination without good cause being shown, the Court may order that the Judgment Debtor be arrested and brought before the Court for examination before the expiry day after the day of arrest.

It has been suggested that a direction as contemplated by para 2 above, whereby the judgment debtor is required to make disclosure prior to the adjourned hearing, may be open to challenge because the court's power under rule 1(1)(a) is to order the judgment debtor to appear before the court with the documents. See *Lam Shing Chin t/a New Cotton Trading Co v Luen Hing Fat Textile Ltd* [1989] 2 HKC 485, 488E.

## [49B.1A.3]  Prohibition order or imprisonment pending examination

When an examination is adjourned, such as at the call-over hearing, the court has power under rule 1A(3) to order that the judgment debtor be prohibited from leaving Hong Kong or even imprisoned until the resumption of the examination.

## [49B.1A.4]  Scope of examination under Order 49B

Order 49B rule 1A(2) provides that the judgment debtor shall on examination make full disclosure of his assets, liabilities, income and expenditure. The wording of the rule is different from that of Order 48 rule 1(1) which sets out the scope of an examination under that Order. Whereas here the rule requires disclosure of 'assets', in Order 48 the word 'property' is used. Assets may certainly include property, and the authorities referred to in the commentary under Order 48 rule 1 may contain useful guidance on Order 49B as well.

An examination under this Order is not necessarily limited to the judgment debtor's circumstances as they exist at the time of the examination, or the time judg ment was entered. Rule 1B(1)(b) clearly suggests there may be enquiry into prior disposal of assets. Thus the court may extend the investigation into the circumstances as they existed when the judgment creditor's claim came into existence. See *Citibank NA v Chow Tat Sang* HCA 9175/1983 (Mayo J; 01.02.1984).

At the call-over hearing the judgment debtor is usually ordered to disclose, prior to the resumption of the hearing, documentary evidence of assets, expenditure etc, going back a period of years. However, the judgment creditor is not entitled to disclosure of documents going long into the past, since only 'current or recent' documents will be relevant to the purpose of the examination, which is to facilitate execution of the judgment: *Hebei Enterprises Ltd v Livasiri & Co* HCA 20094/1998 (Deputy Judge Poon; 02.11.2006) (para 6).

## [49B.1A.5]  Order for further disclosure

The court has power to order further disclosure of documents during the course of an examination under Order 48 or Order 49B: *Lafarge SA v Continental Cement Corp* [2007] 1 HKC 34.

## [49B.1A.6]  Duty of judgment debtor on examination

The judgment debtor's duty on an examination under Order 49B is set out in rule 1A(2). The duty is to make full disclosure and answer all questions. There is no burden of proof on the judgment debtor. See *Citibank v Chow* (above).

## [49B.1A.7]  Costs of examination

Where a judgment creditor is justified in applying for an oral examination the costs of an incidental thereto will normally be ordered to be paid by the judgment debtor. It has been suggested that no order as to costs might be appropriate where an examination fails to reveal any hidden assets: Betts 'Practice and Procedure, a Master's View' Law Lectures for Practitioners 1987 (HK: HK Law Journal Ltd, 1987). In *Trading Consultants Ltd v Sloan* DCCJ 2548/2000 (Master Kwang; 07.11.2001) the court granted the judgment creditor the costs of and incidental to the application for an examination order, which it considered justified, but made no order as to the costs of the examination itself, which elicited no fruitful evidence. In *Hung Kai Finance Co Ltd v Teh Han King* CACV 118/1998 (Cons VP, Clough & Hunter JJA; 11.11.1988) a judgment debtor who had lied at the examination was ordered to pay indemnity costs thereof.

In *Furusawa v Leung Kwok Chia* HCA 3225/1989 (Master Jones; 13.09.1991) the court, having ordered the judgment debtor to make instalment payments on account of the judgment debt (see rule 1B(2) and the commentary thereunder), ordered that the costs of the examination be added to the judgment debt and be discharged in the same manner.

### 1AA.  Record of judgment debtor's evidence given at examination
(O. 49B r. 1AA)

**The Court shall cause to be recorded, by means of shorthand notes or mechanical, electronic or optical device or otherwise, the evidence given by the judgment debtor at the examination conducted under rule 1A. (L.N. 108 of 2002)**

### 1B.  Power of the Court following examination (O. 49B r. 1B)

**(1)   Where the Court is satisfied, following the examination conducted under rule 1A or following an examination conducted under Order 48, that the judgment debtor—**

**(a)     is able to satisfy the judgment, wholly or partly; or**

**(b)     has disposed of assets with a view to avoiding satisfaction of the judgment or the liability which is the subject of the judgment, wholly or partly; or**

**(c)     has wilfully failed to make a full disclosure as required under rule 1A(2) or at the examination under Order 48 or to answer any question as provided under that rule or Order,**

**it may, in its discretion, order the imprisonment of the judgment debtor for a period not exceeding 3 months.**

**(2)(a)     Where the Court is satisfied, following the examination conducted under rule 1A or following an examination conducted under Order 48, that the judgment debtor is able or will be able to satisfy the judgment, wholly or partly, by instalments or otherwise, it may order him to satisfy the judgment in such manner as it thinks fit.**

**(b)     The Court may, on application, discharge, vary or suspend an order made under sub-paragraph (a), either absolutely or subject to such conditions as it thinks fit.**

**(3)(a)     Where the judgment debtor fails to comply with an order made under paragraph (2), the judgment creditor may apply to the Court, on not less than 2 clear days notice to the judgment debtor, for an order for the imprisonment of the judgment debtor and the Court may, unless the judgment debtor shows good cause, order the imprisonment of the judgment debtor for a period not exceeding 3 months.**

**(b)     Notwithstanding rule 7, the Court may order the imprisonment of the judgment debtor on each occasion of a failure to comply with an order under paragraph (2) or more than once in respect**

of a continuing failure to comply with an order under that paragraph.

(4)    The order for imprisonment shall be in Form No 104 in Appendix A.

(5)    The application under paragraph (3)(a) shall be in Form No 105 in Appendix A.

(6)    An order under paragraph (1), (2) or (3) shall not prevent execution of the judgment by other means unless the Court so directs.

(7)    An order for imprisonment of a judgment debtor shall be made in open court.

---

## NOTES

### [49B.1B.1]  Quasi-criminal jurisdiction to imprison judgment debtor
Order 49B rule 1B gives the court power to imprison a judgment debtor for up to 3 months following an examination under this Order or under Order 48. The grounds on which imprisonment may be ordered are discussed below. This power may only be exercised at the conclusion of the examination: *Lam Shing Chin t/a New Cotton Trading Co v Luen Hing Fat Textile Ltd* [1989] 2 HKC 485. See rules 1(3) and 1A(3) as to the circumstances in which a judgment debtor may be arrested and imprisoned at an earlier stage.

Because the judgment debtor's liberty is at risk, proceedings under Order 49B are considered to be quasi-criminal in nature: *Hung Kai Finance Co Ltd v Teh Han King* CACV 118/1998 (Cons VP, Clough & Hunter JJA; 11.11.1988). The grounds on which imprisonment may be ordered under rule 1B are analogous to contempt and it follows that the criminal standard of proof applies: *Bank of India v Murjani* CACV 12/1991 (Cons VP, Kempster & Clough JJA; 01.05.1991), applying *Re Bramblevale Ltd* [1970] 1 Ch 128. See also *Hua Chiao Commercial Bank Ltd v Alpha Plus Int'l Development Ltd* [2001] 2 HKC 54, 62D-E.

The power to order imprisonment is discretionary: *Honour Finance Co Ltd v Chan Mang* CACV 63/1989 (Cons VP, Clough JA & Jones J; 05.01.1990). It is not right to exercise the discretion to imprison a judgment debtor for non-payment where he is unable to pay: *Ferryhill Int'l Ltd v Aziz* [1997] 4 HKC 383, 390G-H (CA).

An order for imprisonment under this rule should be in form no 104 in appendix A: see rule 1B(4).

### [49B.1B.2]  No order of imprisonment without application by judgment creditor
The court has no power to order imprisonment under Order 49B of its own motion, and may only make such an order on the application of the judgment creditor: *Hung Kai Finance* (above). This follows from the fact that the judgment creditor is required by rule 2 to pay for the prisoner's maintenance.

### [49B.1B.3]  Grounds on which judgment debtor may be imprisoned following examination
The grounds on which a judgment debtor may be imprisoned following examination are set out in rule 1B(1)(a), (b) and (c). The court 'must be satisfied of one or more'

of these matters, and the burden is on the judgment creditor: *Citibank NA v Chow Tat Sang* HCA 175/1983 (Mayo J; 01.02.1984). The grounds are that the judgment debtor:

(a)   *is able to satisfy the judgment wholly in part* – *s*ee the discussion under Order 48 rule 1 and *Bloomsbury Int'l Ltd v Nouvelle Foods (HK) Ltd* [2005] 1 HKC 337 in particular as to what constitutes 'property' from which a judgment debtor could satisfy the judgment. Where the judgment debtor is able to satisfy the judgment it would normally be more appropriate (at least initially) to seek an order under rule 1B(2) requiring the judgment debtor to pay the same by instalment or otherwise, rather than to seek imprisonment;

(b)   *has disposed of assets with a view to avoid payment* – it has been suggested that although the rule does not specify whose assets, 'it must follow that it should refer to the assets of the judgment debtor but not the others': *Trading Consul tants Ltd v Sloan* DCCJ 2548/2000 (Ag Reg Kwang; 07.11.2001) (para 9); *Secretary for Justice v Lee Siu Fung Siegfried* HCMP 2851/2004 (Master Kwang; 23.10.2006) (para 10). In those decisions the possibility of a judgment debtor reducing his worth by disposing of assets owned by a company in which he has shares, without disposing of the shares themselves, was not considered. It is submitted that in principle the rule should apply in such a case; and

(c)   *has willfully failed to make disclosure as required* – the failure to make full disclosure 'must be deliberate and intentional as opposed to accidental and negligent': *Trading Consultants Ltd* (above); *SJ v Lee Siu Fung Siegfried* (above).

### [49B.1B.4]  Appeal against order of imprisonment under Order 49B
A judgment debtor who wishes to challenge an order that he be imprisoned made under these rules should appeal against the order rather than applying for habeas corpus (*Re Yu Kin-chun, Philip* [1987] HKLR 123). By virtue of Order 58 rule 1 and rule 2(d), such an appeal should be made to the Court of Appeal rather than to a judge of the Court of First Instance. Where, however, an order of imprisonment has been made by a master wholly without jurisdiction, a single judge of the Court of First Instance may set it aside (*Lam Shing Chin t/a New Cotton Trading Co v Luen Hing Fat Textile Ltd* [1989] 2 HKC 485).

### [49B.1B.5]  Order that judgment debtor satisfy the debt
Rather than imprisoning a recalcitrant debtor, the court may, following examination under Order 49B, make an order under rule 1B(2) requiring him to pay the debt by instalment or otherwise. Failure to comply with such an order can lead to imprisonment under rule 1B(3). An application for imprisonment in such circumstances should be made in form no 105 in appendix A: see rule 1B(5).

Because an order requiring the judgment debtor to make payment may lead to imprisonment, the criminal standard of proof applies: *Bank of India v Murjani* (above); *Furusawa v Leung Kwok Chia* HCA 3225/1989 (Master Jones; 13.09.1991) (para 10).

In fixing the amount of instalment payments the court has to 'balance the creditor's right to payment with the debtor's ability both to pay and to live at a standard reasonable to his circumstances, including his debts': *Furusawa* (above) (para 21).

**1C. Imprisonment not to satisfy debt** (O. 49B r. 1C)

An order for imprisonment under this Order shall not satisfy or extinguish any judgment debt.

**2. Support and maintenance allowance to prisoner for debt** (O. 49B r. 2)

When a judgment debtor is committed to prison in execution of the judgment the Court shall fix whatever monthly allowance it may think sufficient for his support and maintenance, not exceeding $660 per diem, which shall be paid by the person at whose instance the judgment has been executed to the Commissioner of Correctional Services by monthly payments in advance, the second and subsequent such payments to be made not less than 7 days before the last preceding such payment is exhausted.

(L.N. 74 of 1989; L.N. 403 of 1992; L.N. 167 of 1994; L.N. 419 of 1995)

**3. Removal to hospital of prisoner for debt in case of serious illness**
(O. 49B r. 3)

(1) In case of the serious illness of any person imprisoned in execution of a judgment it shall be lawful for the Court, on the certificate of the medical officer of the prison in which he is confined or of the Director of Health of the Government, to make an order for the removal of the judgment debtor to a hospital and for his treatment there under custody until further order. (L.N. 76 of 1989)

(2) In any such case the period of the judgment debtor's stay in hospital shall be counted as part of his term of imprisonment and his support and maintenance money shall be paid as if no such order had been made.

**4. Release of prisoner for debt** (O. 49B r. 4)

Every person arrested or imprisoned in execution of a judgment shall be released at any time on the judgment being fully satisfied, or at the request of the person at whose instance the judgment has been executed, or on such person omitting to pay his support and maintenance money.

**5. Recovery of amount of support and maintenance money** (O. 49B r. 5)

All sums paid by a plaintiff for the support and maintenance of a person imprisoned in execution of a judgment shall be added to the costs of the judgment and shall be recoverable by the attachment and sale of the property of the judgment debtor; but the judgment debtor shall not be detained in custody or arrested on account of any sum so paid.

**6. Recovery of costs of execution** (O. 49B r. 6)

The costs of obtaining and executing the order and warrant of arrest or imprisonment shall be added to the costs of the judgment and shall be recoverable accordingly.

**7. Effect of discharge of prisoner for debt** (O. 49B r. 7)

Subject to rule 1B(3)(b), when any person imprisoned in execution of a judgment has been once discharged he shall not again be imprisoned on account of the same judgment, but his property shall continue liable, under the ordinary rules, to attachment and sale until the judgment is fully satisfied.

**8.        Meaning of "judgment creditor"** (O. 49B r. 8)

In this Order, "judgment creditor" includes any person entitled to enforce the judgment.

(**Enacted 1988**)

## ORDER 50

### CHARGING ORDERS, STOP ORDERS, ETC.

**1.    Order imposing a charge on a beneficial interest** (O. 50 r. 1)

(2)    An application by a judgment creditor for a charging order in respect of a judgment debtor's beneficial interest may be made ex parte, and any order made on such an application shall in the first instance be an order, made in Form No. 75 in Appendix A, to show cause, specifying the time and place for further consideration of the matter and imposing the charge in any event until that time. (See also App. A, Form 76)

(3)    The application shall be supported by an affidavit—

(a)    identifying the judgment or order to be enforced and stating the amount unpaid at the date of the application;

(b)    stating the name of the judgment debtor and of any creditor of his whom the applicant can identify;

(ba)    if the amount unpaid under the judgment or order is arrears of maintenance, stating—

(i)    the interest payable in respect of the arrears of maintenance that the judgment creditor is entitled to under section 20A(2) of the Guardianship of Minors Ordinance (Cap. 13), section 9(B)(2) of the Separation and Maintenance Orders Ordinance (Cap. 16), section 53A(2) of the Matrimonial Causes Ordinance (Cap. 179) or section 28AA(2) of the Matrimonial Proceedings and Property Ordinance (Cap. 192), as the case may be; and

(ii)    the surcharge payable in respect of the arrears of maintenance under section 20B(1) of the Guardianship of Minors Ordinance (Cap. 13), section 9C(1) of the Separation and Maintenance Orders Ordinance (Cap. 16), section 53B(1) of the Matrimonial Causes Ordinance (Cap. 179) or section 28AB(1) of the Matrimonial Proceedings and Property Ordinance (Cap. 192), as the case may be; (18 of 2003, s14)

(c)    giving full particulars of the subject-matter of the intended charge, including, in the case of securities other than securities in court, the full title of the securities, their amount and the name in which they stand and, in the case of funds in court, the number of the account; and

(d)    verifying that the interest to be charged is owned beneficially by the judgment debtor.

(4)    Unless the Court otherwise directs, an affidavit for the purposes of this rule may contain statements of information or belief with the sources and grounds thereof.

(5)    An application may be made for a single charging order in respect of more than one judgment or order against the debtor.

------------------------

**NOTES**

**[50.1.1]    History and comparison with English legislation**
Significant changes were introduced into the rules relating to charging orders by the Supreme Court (Amendment) Ordinance 1987 and the Rules of the Supreme Court (Revocation and Replacement) Rules 1988. The effect of these changes was to introduce into the law of Hong Kong the provisions of the English Charging Orders Act 1979. Relevant provisions relating to charging orders are now found in sections 20, 20A and 20B of the High Court Ordinance and Orders 50 and 88 of the High Court Rules. Relevant provisions relating to stop orders are found in section 55C of the High Court Ordinance and Order 50 of the High Court Rules.

In England charging orders are now dealt with in Part 73 of the CPR.

**[50.1.2]    Power to impose charges on property**
According to section 20(1) of the High Court Ordinance:

> Where, under a judgment or order of the Court of First Instance, a person (in this section and in sections 20A and 20B referred to as the 'debtor') is required to pay a sum of money to another person (in this section and in section 20A referred to as the 'creditor') then, for the purpose of enforcing that judgment or order, the High Court may make an order imposing on any such property of the debtor as may be specified in the order a charge for securing the payment of any money due or to become due under the judgment or order.

**[50.1.3]    Type of judgment or order which may be enforced by charging order**
Section 20(1) empowers the court to grant charging orders for the purpose of enforcement of a 'judgment or order of the Court of First Instance'. By section 20(3) the power is extended to cover any judgment, order, decree or award however called of any court or arbitrator, including any foreign court or foreign arbitrator, which is or has become enforceable, whether wholly or to a limited extent'.

The judgment or order to be enforced need not be final in the sense that it may arise from an interlocutory application, but it must be 'final in the sense that it is an order having permanent effect for a sum certain': *Ng Yat Chi & Anor v China Resources (Holdings) Co Ltd* HCA 424/2005 (Deputy Judge Gill; 15.09.2006).

In this context 'having permanent effect' should not mean the court has no jurisdiction to grant a charging order in respect of a judgment which is subject to appeal where there has been no stay of execution, but the fact of such an appeal would clearly go to the court's exercise of discretion, as to which see below.

The requirement that the judgment or order be 'for a sum certain' flows from the requirement in rule 1(3)(a) that the creditor state the amount unpaid in the supporting affidavit. Thus there is no power to grant a charging order to enforce a judgment for damages to be assessed, or an order for costs to be taxed: *Ho King Yim v Lau King Mo* HCMP 733/1978 (Zimmern J; 25.04.1979) citing *A&M Records Inc v Darakdjian* [1975] 1 WLR 1610; *Cheung Yuk Chun v Yeung Wo Fai* HCA 6191/1998 (Lam J; 20.07.2006).

**[50.1.4]    Property which may be charged**
The list of property which may be charged is set out in section 20A(1) of the High Court Ordinance.

20A(1). Subject to subsection (3), a charge may be imposed by a charging order only on –

    (a)    an interest held by the debtor beneficially –

        (i)    in any asset of the kind mentioned in subsection (2); or

        (ii)    under any trust; or

    (b)    an interest held by a person as trustee of a trust (in this paragraph referred to as 'the trust'), if the interest is in an asset of a kind mentioned in subsection (2) or is an interest under another trust and

        (i)    the judgment or order in respect of which a charge is to be imposed was made against that person as trustee of the trust;

        (ii)    the whole beneficial interest under the trust is held by the debtor unencumbered and for his own benefit; or

        (iii)    in a case where there are two or more debtors all of whom are liable to the creditor for the same debt, they together hold the whole beneficial interest under the trust unencumbered and for their own benefit.

    (2)    The assets referred to in subsection (1) are –

        (a)    land;

        (b)    securities of any of the following kinds –

            (i)    Government stock;

            (ii)    stock of any body incorporated in Hong Kong;

            (iii)    stock of any body incorporated outside Hong Kong or of any state or territory outside Hong Kong, being stock registered in a register kept at any place within Hong Kong;

            (iv)    units of any unit trust in respect of which a register of the unit holders is kept at any place within Hong Kong; or

        (c)    funds in Court.

    (3)    In any case where a charge is imposed by a charging order on any interest in an asset of a kind mentioned in subsection (2)(b) or (c), the Court of First Instance may provide for the charge to extend to any interest, dividend or other distribution payable and any bonus issue in respect of such asset.

    (4)    In this section – 'dividend' includes any distribution in respect of any unit of a unit trust; 'stock' includes shares, debentures loan stocks, funds, bonds, notes, any other securities issued by the body concerned, whether or not constituting a charge on the assets of that body and any rights or options to subscribe for or be allotted any of the foregoing; and 'unit trust' means any trust established for the purpose, or having the effect, of providing, for persons having funds available for investment, facilities for the participation by them, as beneficiaries under the trust, in any profits or income arising from the acquisition, holding, management or disposal of any property whatsoever.

The court's powers to impose charging orders and to enforce such orders by sale are unaffected by the provisions of section 21D of the High Court Ordinance: see *Timmar Co Ltd v Erwin Hardy Corp Ltd* [2001] 3 HKC 55 (overruling *Cheung Koon Ping v Muneyoshi Michiyoshi* [1994] 3 HKC 563 (D Ct)). Recorder Kenneth Kwok SC held that a contrary construction would be inconsistent with the terms of sections 20A and 20B of the High Court Ordinance. Consequently, whilst section 21D applies to writs of *fi fa* and restricts the court's powers of 'attachment and sale', under such writs, to the types of property there listed, no such limitations are imposed in respect of the making and the enforcement of charging orders. As a result the court held that there was no impediment to the imposition of a charge upon Hong Kong private shares and the making of a subsequent order for sale.

An equity of redemption is a beneficial interest within the meaning of section 20A(1)(a)(i) and may be the subject of a charging order. See *Bank of China (HK) Ltd v Kanishi (FE) Ltd & Ors* [2002] 2 HKLRD 52 where the court made a charging order absolute against shares which the judgment debtor had previously mortgaged to another creditor. It was recognised that the prior mortgagee's interest in the shares would take priority over the judgment creditor's interest under the charging order.

#### [50.1.5]    Trust property

Section 20A(1)(b) of the High Court Ordinance empowers the court to make a charging order against property held by a person as trustee. This provision is adopted from section 2 of the Charging Orders Act 1979 (UK) which was enacted to enable charging orders to be made against land held under joint tenancy. The purpose was to reverse *Irani Finance Ltd v Singh* [1971] Ch 59 (CA) where it had been held that a charging order could not be made against a joint tenant's interest because under the Law of Property Act 1925 that interest was a trust for sale. This was not necessary in Hong Kong where, because of the absence of legislation converting a joint tenancy into a trust for sale, it was already possible to obtain a charging order against a joint tenant's interest in land. See *Yu Pei-tseng v Mong Wing Ho Alexander* [1978] DCLR 15, *Kung Wong Sau Hin v Kung Kwok Sun & Ors* [1985] 2 HKC 547 and *Malahon Credit Co Ltd v Siu Chun Wah Alice & Anor* [1987] 2 HKC 79 (CA). For procedure see Order 50 rule 4.

Section 20A(1)(b) enables a judgment creditor to obtain a charging order binding not only on the debtor's beneficial interest in trust property, but also binding on the trustee. It is suggested in some works that the section makes it possible to obtain a charging order against property held by the debtor as trustee, without affecting the beneficial owner who is not responsible for the debt. That may be correct but it is difficult to envision circumstances in which the judgment debtor would want a charge which does not attach to the beneficial interest.

#### [50.1.6]    Priority as between charging order and purchaser of land

Once the judgment debtor has disposed of and interest in land by way of assignment, nothing remains for the judgment creditor to charge, even though the assignment may not have been registered. In *Ng Kam Ha v Vincent Sina Traders (HK) Ltd* [1987] 2 HKC 517, a charging order *nisi* was made and registered against the land after the judgment debtor had assigned his interest in the land, but before the assignment had been registered. Mayo J held that the charging order was of no effect on the land. Once the judgment debtor had assigned the land he no longer had an interest which could be charged by the judgment creditor. The fact that the assignment was not registered until after the charging order did not alter this situation.

Where a question of priority as between an assignment and a charging order arises it is legitimate to look behind the date appearing on the assignment and consider evidence of when the transaction was actually completed: see *Yau Siu Yeung & Ors v Wing Sum Lo (t/a Wing Sum Lo & Co)* [1988] HKC 693.

In *Ho King-yim v Lau King-mo* [1980] HKLR 42 (CA), the Court of Appeal grappled with the more difficult situation where a judgment creditor obtained a charging order after the judgment debtor had entered into an agreement to sell the property, but before that sale had been completed by assignment. It was held that upon entering into the sale and purchase agreement the substantial beneficial interest in the land passed to the purchaser. Whilst the vendor held the legal estate as trustee for the purchaser, he nevertheless retained, in addition, a limited beneficial interest in the property and one which was capable of being charged. However, upon completion, the vendor's beneficial interest in the property ceased and as the full relation of trustee was said, at that point, to relate back to the date of the sale and purchase agreement, and the basis of any charging order registered subsequent to the date of the agreement was inevitably destroyed (see Huggins JA at 44). *Ho King-yim* was applied in *Tse Fook Choy, Joey Callan v Kwong On Bank Ltd* [1999] 3 HKC 126 to facts described as identical (at 130G–H). In discharging the charging orders, Seagroatt J noted that whilst the vendor also retained, subsequent to the date of the sale and purchase agreement, an equitable lien in respect of the unpaid balance of purchase moneys, such a lien did not constitute an interest in land and was not property of a kind chargeable under Order 50.

For the purposes of section 3(2) of the Land Registration Ordinance, the interest of a judgment creditor, who has obtained a charging order absolute under the provisions of Order 50, is not to be equated with that of a '*bona fide* purchaser or mortgagee for valuable consideration' within the meaning of the subsection (*Financial & Investment Services for Asia Ltd v Baik Wha Int'l Trading Co Ltd* [1985] HKLR 103 and *Yau Siu Yeung v Wing Sum Lo (t/a Wing Sum Lo & Co)* [1988] HKC 693). These observations led Seagroatt J to conclude (*obiter*), in the case of *Tse Fook Choy, Joey Callan*, that a *bona fide* purchaser for value who had entered into a sale and purchase agreement in respect of property would not be affected, regardless of whether or not the sale and purchase agreement was registered, by any subsequent registration of a charging order.

In *Ho King-yim* the Court of Appeal stated (*obiter*) (at 48) that where prior to comple tion, the purchaser has notice of the charging order he is liable to account to the 'chargee' for the purchase money to the extent of the charge. One helpful reader has brought to the Editor's attention the use of the word 'chargee' by the court. In the context it is clear that the Court of Appeal was referring to the judgment creditor who had obtained the charging order, and thus must have meant 'chargor'. In result the Court of Appeal's decision and its *obiter dictum* means that the purchaser acquired title free of the charging order without paying off the debt secured by that order but, if he had notice of the charging order and had failed to pay it off at the time of completion, the judgment creditor may have a right of action against the purchaser, though no charge against the land. The dictum of the Court of Appeal was endorsed (again, *obiter*) by Seagroatt J, in the case of *Tse Fook Choy, Joey Callan*, who went on to note that in the ordinary course of events the balance of the proceeds of sale, in the hands of the vendor's (the judgment debtor's) solicitors, would be attachable. He therefore described as sensible and fair, the purchaser's decision to pay such balance into court, pending the resolution of any claims in respect of it (see 131G–I).

**[50.1.7]     The court's exercise of discretion**
According to section 20(3) of the High Court Ordinance:

(3)  In deciding whether to make a charging order the Court of First Instance shall consider all the circumstances of the case and, in particular, any evidence before it as to –

   (a)  the personal circumstances of the debtor; and

   (b)  whether any other creditor of the debtor would be likely to be unduly prejudiced by the making of the order.

Section 20(3) clearly gives the court a discretion when considering an application for a charging order. One of the relevant factors will be the interests of other creditors and interested parties. Thus Order 50 rule 1(3)(b) stipulates that an application for a charging order 'shall' be supported by an affidavit giving the name of any other creditor of the judgment debtor known to the applicant. The court may direct that the order *nisi* be served on that creditor or any other interested person (rule 2(2)) and may discharge or vary a charging order at any time on application of such a party (rule 7(1)). Where the applicant does not know of any other creditors it is good practice so to state in the affidavit in support, but failure to do so is not an irregularity: *Capacious Investment Ltd v Estate of Tang Man Sit* HCA 9745/1991 (Barnett J; 10.03.1991).

*Interests of judgment debtor's spouse* – in *Harman v Glencross* [1986] 1 All ER 545, the English Court of Appeal held that where a wife had commenced divorce proceedings together with ancillary proceedings in which she sought a property adjustment order along with other financial relief, the wife's interests in terms of those proceedings were matters which the court could properly take into account in determining whether to make a charging order absolute against the husband's (the judgment debtor's) beneficial interest, as co-owner, in the matrimonial home.

The English Court of Appeal's decision in *Harman* was cited with approval by Sakhrani J in *Chan Ting Wai William v Lam Sai Pak & Anor* [1999] 1 HKC 843 where the court set aside an order absolute against a husband's interest, as joint tenant, in the matrimonial home; the wife having instituted divorce proceedings which included a claim for ancillary relief, and having registered those proceedings against the property, prior to the date on which the charging order *nisi* was obtained. The court found that in the circumstances of the case it had a proper concern to ensure that the spouse's rights of occupation in the home were adequately protected. It held that where divorce proceedings had been commenced and where it was sought to charge an interest in a matrimonial home, the court should consider whether it was proper to make a charging order absolute, in respect of that interest, before any claim for ancillary relief had been heard. The court commented that the usual practice in such circumstances should be to transfer the application for a charging order to the Family Division, so that it could be heard together with the application for ancillary relief.

In *Harman*'s case and in that of *Chan Ting Wai William*, divorce proceedings, coupled with proceedings for ancillary relief, had been commenced prior to the date upon which the charging order *nisi* was made and the court, in both cases, clearly considered it inappropriate to decide whether or not the order *nisi* should be made absolute in isolation from a determination of the spouses' individual rights and entitlement with respect to the couple's matrimonial property, overall. However, in *Ip Hon Nam v Chan Moon Kau* [2002] 2 HKC 220, where the spouses were still in 'matrimonial union' and there was no suggestion of their parting, Judge Li had no hesitation in making absolute an order charging the judgment debtor's (the husband's) interest, as joint tenant, in the matrimonial home. Judge Li held that the facts in *Harman* and in *Chan Ting Wai William* were distinguishable in that the spouses in both cases (unlike the spouses in the case before him) had already embarked upon proceedings for divorce and property distribution 'so that the interest of wife *qua* spouse (in addition to whatever [her] rights as joint tenant) had arisen or crystallized' prior to the judgment creditor's application (see 226G–I). Judge Li emphasised that a charging order, in and of itself, does not immediately deprive the judgment debtor of the use and occupation of the property charged. Rather, such deprivation will only occur when the property is sold – either by the judgment creditor or another creditor – and under Order 88, the court has a wide discretion to refuse to make an order for sale (see 225F–I, 226A–B). As to the court's discretion upon an application for sale, see *Union Finance Ltd v Leung Wai Ling & Anor* [2000] 2 HKC 821.

*Interests of other creditors* – in *Wardley Ltd v Aik San Realty Ltd* [1985] 2 HKC 695, the court was asked to exercise its discretion against making a charging order absolute on the grounds that the judgment debtor had been for some two years in a position of near insolvency and had been trying to hold the scales equally between its several creditors. It would, therefore, be unfair to allow the judgment creditor to become a preferred creditor. The court held that since the company had not been put into liquidation there was no prospect of a true *pari passu* distribution and the charging order should be made absolute. In *Ip Hon Nam v Chan Moon Kau* [2002] 2 HKC 220 it was argued that a charging order should not be made absolute because there was no remaining equity in the property to be attached. The property was subject to a prior mortgage securing debt far in excess of the value of the property. Judge Li held (at 227C–F) that negative equity was not a consideration at this stage. It might be considered later if the judgment creditor sought an order for sale under Order 88, but at this stage the principal consideration was 'whether the property should be *preserved*' with a view to enforcement some time later when circumstances may have changed and, for example, the property market may have risen or the prior mortgage been discharged.

*Amount of judgment debt compared to value of property charged* – it is improper for a judgment creditor to charge more properties than necessary to provide sufficient security for the judgment debt. See *Choy Bing Wing v Chief Justice & Ors* HCA 125/2005 (Yam J; 14.01.2008) where the court set aside charging orders against 4 out of 5 properties, where the value of the 5th was more than sufficient to cover the whole judgment debt.

### [50.1.8] Registration and priority of charging orders against land

Section 20B(2) of the High Court Ordinance (Cap 4) provides that the Land Registration Ordinance (Cap 128) applies to charging orders as it applies to other instruments for enforcement of judgments. Registration is not required for a charging order to be valid, but it is necessary if the charging order is to have priority over subsequent dealings in the land: *Financial & Investment Services for Asia Ltd v Baik Wha Int'l Trading Co Ltd* [1985] HKLR 103, 112H. LRO section 5A provides that a charging order (like a *lis pendens*) takes priority from the day after its registration, unlike deeds which have priority back to the date of execution so long as registered within one month thereof.

For a discussion of priority as between a charging order and a purchaser of land, see above.

Where two charging orders are registered against the same interest in land, priority depends on the order of registration of the order *nisi*. See *Wong Kam Wing & Anor v Cyril Murkin (HK) Ltd & Ors* [1989] 2 HKC 603 (citing *Haly v Barry* (1868) LR 3 Ch 452 and *Brereton v Edwardes* (1888) 21 QBD 468) where it was held that a charging order absolute relates back to the order *nisi*. In *Wong Kam Wing* the court went on to express the view (605G-I) that where two charging orders are registered on the same day, the principle that the law takes no account of fractions of a day is inapplicable and the charge registered earlier in time will take priority.

**[50.1.9]　　Priority as between charging order and trustee in bankruptcy**
According to section 45 of the Bankruptcy Ordinance (Cap 6) a creditor who has completed execution or attachment of property of a bankrupt is entitled to retain the benefit of the execution or attachment against the trustee in bankruptcy. Execution against land is, by s 45(2)(c), completed by seizure, appointment of a receiver, or the making of a charging order. In *Dah Sing Bank Ltd v Daylight Industrial Co Ltd* [1987] 3 HKC 25 it was held that the reference to a charging order in s 45(2)(c) is to the charging order *nisi*; the order absolute, once made, relates back to the date of the order *nisi*. Thus execution is complete once the charging order *nisi* has been made and the judgment creditor is entitled to retain the benefit as against the trustee in bankruptcy. An appeal to the Court of Appeal (*Official Receiver v Daylight Industrial Co Ltd* [1987] 3 HKC 29) was dismissed on the ground that in the circumstances of the case section 45 was inapplicable. The Court of Appeal said (at 33E) that it expressed no opinion whether the trial judge was correct on the relation back point.

**[50.1.10]　　Priority as between charging order and liquidator of company**
According to section 269(1) of the Companies Ordinance:

> Where a creditor has issued execution against the goods or lands of a company ..., and the company is subsequently wound up, he shall not be entitled to retain the benefit of the execution ... against the liquidator in the winding up of the company unless he has completed the execution ... before the commencement of the winding up.

According to section 269(2)(c), execution against land is completed by seizure, appointment of a receiver, or the making of a charging order. If the first instance decision in *Dah Sing Bank* (above) applies, 'charging order' for this purpose means a charging order *nisi*.

**[50.1.11]　　Procedure on application for charging order**
An application for a charging order is a two-stage process. Order 50 rule 1(2) provides that initially the application should be made *ex parte* on affidavit and should be an application to show cause. The application will usually be considered on paper by a master without a hearing – see the commentary under Order 32 rule 1. The order (if granted) at this stage is usually referred to as a charging order *nisi*. In England under the CPR the term 'interim charging order' is now used. Where such an order is made against an interest in land, the usual practice is to register it in the Land Registry imme-

diately, without prior notice to the judgment debtor, in order to limit the possibility of intervening dealings in the land prior to the second stage. See the commentary on registration above.

The order *nisi* must be served pursuant to Order 50 rule 2, giving an opportunity to the judgment debtor to be heard at the second stage, where the court will further consider the application under rule 3, this time on an *inter partes* basis. At the second stage the charging order may be made absolute (with or without modifications) or discharged: see rule 3.

2.      **Service of notice of order to show cause** (O. 50 r. 2)

     **(1)**    **On the making of an order to show cause, notice of the order shall, unless the Court otherwise directs, be served as follows—**

         **(a)**    **a copy of the order, together with a copy of the affidavit in support, shall be served on the judgment debtor;**

         **(b)**    **where the order relates to securities other than securities in court, copies of the order shall also be served—**

             **(iii)**    **in the case of stock of any body incorporated within Hong Kong, on that body;**

             **(iv)**    **in the case of stock of any body incorporated outside Hong Kong, being stock registered in a register kept in Hong Kong, on the keeper of the register;**

             **(v)**    **in the case of units of any unit trust in respect of which a register of unit holders is kept in Hong Kong, on the keeper of the register;**

         **(c)**    **where the order relates to a fund in court, a copy of the order shall be served on the Registrar at the Registry, and**

         **(d)**    **where the order relates to an interest under a trust, copies of the order shall be served on such of the trustees as the Court may direct.**

     **(2)**    **Without prejudice to the provisions of paragraph (1) the Court may, on making the order to show cause, direct the service of copies of the order, and of the affidavit in support, on any other creditor of the judgment debtor or on any other interested person as may be appropriate in the circumstances.**

     **(3)**    **Documents to be served under this rule must be served at least seven days before the time appointed for the further consideration of the matter.**

3.      **Order made on further consideration** (O. 50 r. 3)

     **(1)**    **On the further consideration of the matter the Court shall either make the order absolute, with or without modifications, or discharge it.**

     **(2)**    **Where the order is made absolute, it shall be in Form 76 in Appendix A, and where it is discharged, the provisions of rule 7, regarding the service of copies of the order of discharge, shall apply.**

---

**NOTES**

**[50.3.1]** **Order to be made at the second stage**

Order 50 rule 3 provides for the type of order the court may make at the second stage, that is the *inter partes* hearing after the charging order *nisi* has been served.

It has been held that where there is a dispute over the beneficial ownership of the property charged (for example, where it is alleged that the debtor holds that property as trustee for the benefit of another) the court may order a trial of that issue and adjourn the charging order application. See *Rosseel NV v Oriental Commercial & Shipping (UK) Ltd* [1991] TLR 446 (CA).

**4.    Order imposing a charge on an interest held by a trustee** (O. 50 r. 4)

**(1)    Save as provided by this rule, the provisions of rules 1, 2 and 3 shall apply to an order charging an interest held by a trustee as they apply to an order charging the judgment debtor's beneficial interest.**

**(2)    Instead of verifying the judgment debtor's beneficial ownership of the interest to be charged, the affidavit required by rule 1(3) shall state the ground on which the application is based and shall verify the material facts.**

**(3)    On making the order to show cause, the Court shall give directions for copies of the order, and of the affidavit in support, to be served on such of the trustees and beneficiaries, if any, as may be appropriate.**

**(4)    Rules 5, 6 and 7 shall apply to an order charging an interest held by a trustee as they apply to an order charging the judgment debtor's beneficial interest, except that, where the order is made under subsection (ii) or (iii) of section 20A(1)(b) of the Ordinance references in those rules to "the judgment debtor" shall be references to the trustee.**

**(5)    Forms No. 75 and 76 in Appendix A shall be modified so as to indicate that the interest to be charged is held by the debtor as trustee or, as the case may be, that it is held by a trustee (to be named in the order) on trust for the debtor beneficially.**

**5.    Effect of order in relation to securities out of court** (O. 50 r. 5)

**(1)    No disposition by the judgment debtor of his interest in any securities to which an order to show cause relates made after the making of that order shall, so long as that order remains in force, be valid as against the judgment creditor.**

**(2)    Until such order is discharged or made absolute, the person or body served in accordance with rule 2(1)(b) shall not permit any transfer of any of the securities specified in the order, or pay any dividend, interest or redemption payment in relation thereto, except with the authority of the Court, and, if it does so, shall be liable to pay the judgment creditor the value of the securities transferred or, as the case may be, the amount of the payment made or, if that value or amount is more than sufficient to satisfy the judgment or order to which such order relates, so much thereof as is sufficient to satisfy it.**

**(3)    If the Court makes the order absolute, a copy of the order, including a stop notice as provided in Form No. 76 in Appendix A, shall be served on the person or body specified in rule 2(1)(b) as may be appropriate and, save as provided in rule 7(5), rules 11 to 14 shall apply to such a notice as they apply to a stop notice made and served under rule 11.**

**(4)   This rule does not apply to orders in respect of securities in court.**

**6.    Effect of order in relation to funds in court** (O. 50 r. 6)
**(1)   Where an order to show cause has been made in relation to funds in court (including securities in court) and a copy thereof has been served on the Registrar in accordance with rule 2, no disposition by the judgment debtor of any interest to which the order relates, made after the making of that order, shall, so long as the order remains in force, be valid as against the judgment creditor.**
**(2)   If the Court makes the order absolute, a copy of the order shall be served on the Registrar at the Registry.**

**7.    Discharge, etc., of charging order** (O. 50 r. 7)
**(1)   Subject to paragraph (2) on the application of the judgment debtor or any other person interested in the subject-matter of the charge, the Court may, at any time, whether before or after the order is made absolute, discharge or vary the order on such terms (if any) as to costs or otherwise as it thinks just.**
**(2)   Where an application is made for the discharge of a charging order in respect of the judgment debtor's land on the ground that the judgment debt has been satisfied, the applicant shall state in his application, and the Court shall specify in its order the lot number of the land and the memorial number of any relevant charge registered against the land.**
**(3)   Notice of an application for the discharge or variation of the order shall be served on such interested parties as the Court may direct.**
**(4)   Where an order is made for the discharge or variation of a charging order in respect of funds in court, a copy thereof shall be served on the Registrar at the Registry.**
**(5)   Where an order is made for the discharge or variation of a charging order in respect of securities other than securities in court, a copy thereof shall be served on the person or body specified in rule 2(1)(b) as may be appropriate, and the service thereof shall discharge, or, as the case may be, vary, any stop notice in respect of such securities which may be in force pursuant to the original order.**

---

## NOTES

**[50.7.1]    Comparison with English rules**
Order 50 rule 7(2) is essentially the same as the rule of the same number in the former English RSC, specifying the manner in which land shall be described in an application and order for discharge of a charging order. However, there are some minor differences in wording, reflecting the different land registry and conveyancing systems in the two jurisdictions.

**[50.7.2]    Who may apply for discharge of a charging order?**
Order 50 rule 7(1) enables the court to discharge or vary a charging order on application of the judgment debtor 'or any other person interested in the subject-matter of the charge'. The provision should not be interpreted narrowly, and application may be

made either by the judgment debtor or the judgment creditor. Thus, once the judgment debt has been paid, the judgment creditor has no particular obligation to apply for discharge of the charging order at its own expense, and may leave it to the judgment debtor to do so: *Jim Kiu t/a Sandwin Interior Contractor v Mdm Lam Lee Chu* DCCJ 8133/1992 (Judge Leung; 28.10.2010) (para 21-26).

**[50.7.3]     Application for discharge of charging order may be heard by master**
Masters have jurisdiction to hear applications under Order 50 rule 7 for discharge of a charging order. However, where oral evidence is required to resolve disputes of fact there should be a trial, and the master only has jurisdiction if the parties consent under Order 36 rule 1. See *Chiu Yu Fong (Administratrix) v Lau Kwong Wing* HCA 6099/1999 (Deputy Judge L Chen; 24.11.2010).

**9.     Jurisdiction of master to grant injunction** (O. 50 r. 9)
**A master shall have power to grant an injunction if, and only so far as, it is ancillary or incidental to an order under rule 1, 3 or 4 and an application for an injunction under this rule may be joined with the application for the order under rule 1, 3 or 4 to which it relates.**

**9A.     Enforcement of charging order by sale** (O. 50 r. 9A)
**(1)     Proceedings for the enforcement of a charging order by sale of the property charged must be begun by originating summons.**
**(2)     The provisions of Order 88 shall apply to all such proceedings.**

---

**NOTES**

**[50.9A.1]     Enforcement of the charging order**
According to section 20B(3) of the High Court Ordinance, a charge imposed by a charging order shall have the like effect and shall be enforceable in the same courts and in the same manner as an equitable charge created by the debtor by writing under his hand. The primary remedy of the judgment creditor is sale. Order 50 rule 9A provides that proceedings for the enforcement of a charging order by sale of the property charged must be begun by originating summons; the provisions of Order 88 apply to such proceedings (Order 50 rule 9A (2)). See also Order 31.

**[50.9A.2]     Enforcement of charging order against land**
'A charging order on an interest in land, unlike a mortgage, does not confer any proprietary right or title in the land': see *Sino Billion Ltd & Anor v Lam Chok Wai* [2003] 2 HKC 167,173E-F. It follows that a judgment creditor who has obtained a charging order, unlike a mortgagee, cannot enforce by means of foreclosure or taking possession: *Carreras Rothmans Ltd v Freeman Mathews Treasure Ltd* [1985] 1 Ch 207, 227D (cited in *Sino Billion* at 174A). Rather the judgment creditor's remedy is to apply under Order 88 for an order for sale. See in particular Order 88 rule 5A and the commentary thereunder.

In *Sino Billion* Deputy Judge Poon held that an order for sale to enforce a charging order over land does not of itself authorise the party given conduct of the sale to convey title to a purchaser. There must be an additional order under section 25A of the High

Court Ordinance or under section 48 or section 51 of the Trustee Ordinance (Cap 29) to vest someone with legal power to convey title to the purchaser. See *Sino Billion* at 174 B-D.

### [50.9A.3]   Enforcement of charging order against shares
Although shares in private companies are expressly excluded from the list of property liable to attachment and sale in execution of a judgment as set out in section 21D(1) of the High Court Ordinance, the Court has power under section 20A to grant a charging order against such shares, and to enforce the same by order for sale. See *Timmar Co Ltd & Anor v Erwin Hardy Corp Ltd* [2001] 3 HKC 55, overruling *Cheung Koon Ping v Muneyoshi Michiyoshi* [1994] 3 HKC 563 (DCt).

Where a judgment debtor's beneficial interest in company shares held for him in trust is subject to a charging order, the trustee should be joined in an application to enforce that order by sale: *Audrey PF Chow & Co v Ying Kai Leung* [1976] HKLR 166. Although that case concerned shares in a public company, it should be applicable to private company shares as well since the reasoning is based on the need for an order to compel the trustee to transfer legal title under the proposed sale.

### [50.9A.4]   Enforcement of charging order for foreign currency debt
The affidavit in support of an application to enforce a charging order in respect of a judgment debt expressed in a foreign currency should contain a statement as to the equivalent amount in Hong Kong dollars in the form set out in practice direction 16.2. See paras 8 and 9 of that practice direction, which can be viewed on the judiciary's website.

### [50.9A.5]   Enforcement of charging order for small amount
The amount of the debt to be recovered by way of sale under a charging order is a relevant consideration in exercising the court's discretion but will not alone be determinative thereof: see *Union Finance Ltd v Leung Wai Ling & Anor* [2000] 2 HKC 821 where Chung J allowed an appeal against a master's decision to refuse an order for sale of a debtor's property on the ground that the amount of the debt was small.

**10.    Funds in court: stop order** (O. 50 r. 10)
    **(1)    The Court, on the application of any person—**
        **(a)    who has a mortgage or charge on the interest of any person in funds in court, or**
        **(b)    to whom that interest has been assigned, or**
        **(c)    who is a judgment creditor of the person entitled to that interest,**
**may make an order prohibiting the transfer, sale, delivery out, payment or other dealing with such funds, or any part thereof, or the income thereon, without notice to the applicant. (See App. A Form 79)**
    **(2)    An application for an order under this rule must be made by summons in the cause or matter relating to the funds in court, or, if there is no such cause or matter, by originating summons.**
    **(3)    The summons must be served on every person whose interest may**

be affected by the order applied for but shall not be served on any other person.

(HK) **(4)**     Without prejudice to the Court's powers and discretion as to costs, the Court may order the applicant for an order under this rule to pay the costs of any party to the cause or matter relating to the funds in question, or of any person interested in those funds occasioned by the application.

**11.     Securities not in court: stop notice** (O. 50 r. 11)

**(1)**     Any person claiming to be beneficially entitled to an interest in any securities of the kinds set out in section 20A(2)(b) of the Ordinance, other than securities in court, who wishes to be notified of any proposed transfer or payment of those securities may avail himself of the provisions of this rule.

**(2)**     A person claiming to be so entitled must file in the Registry—

    **(a)**     an affidavit identifying the securities in question and describing his interest therein by reference to the document under which it arises, and

    **(b)**     a notice in Form No. 80 in Appendix A (a stop notice), signed by the deponent to the affidavit, and annexed to it, addressed to the body or unit trust concerned,

and must serve an office copy of the affidavit, and a copy of the notice sealed with the Seal of the Court on that person or body as provided in rule 2(1)(b).

**(3)**     There must be endorsed on the affidavit filed under this rule a note stating the address to which any such notice as is referred to in rule 12 is to be sent and, subject to paragraph (4), that address shall for the purpose of that rule be the address for service of the person on whose behalf the affidavit is filed.

**(4)**     A person on whose behalf an affidavit under this rule is filed may change his address for service for the purpose of rule 12 by serving on the person or body concerned, a notice to that effect, and as from the date of service of such a notice the address stated therein shall for the purpose of that rule be the address for service of that person.

---

## NOTES

### [50.11.1]     'Stop notices' in respect of dealings in shares, etc

Order 50 rule 11 prescribes the procedure to obtain a 'stop notice' in respect of dealings in securities. The term 'stop notice' is defined in section 55C(1) of the High Court Ordinance. Briefly it is a notice requiring prior notification of dealings in securities. Under rule 11(1) any person claiming a beneficial interest in any securities may issue a stop notice. For example, the beneficial owner of shares registered in the name of a nominee, or a person with an interest in a unit trust, may use this procedure to require advance notice to himself of any transfer or other dealing as mentioned in section 55C(4) of the Ordinance. The purpose is 'to give the company notice of a claim to the shares adverse to the title of the person who may appear as the owner of the shares in the share register. The claim does not have to be a claim which is being pursued in litigation': *Lee v Buckle* [2004] 3 IR 544.

Rule 11 provides that for its purposes 'securities' has the same meaning as in section 20A(2)(b) of the Ordinance. Accordingly a stop notice may be issued in respect of the following:

(i)      government stock,

(ii)     stock of any body incorporated in Hong Kong,

(iii)    stock of bodies or governments outside Hong Kong if registered in a register kept in Hong Kong, and

(iv)    units of any unit trust with a register in Hong Kong.

A stop notice is obtained by filing an affidavit setting out the claimed beneficial interest and attaching the stop notice itself, in accordance with rule 11(2). The prescribed form of affidavit and notice is Form 80 in Appendix A. No hearing is required. The notice will be sealed with the seal of the court upon payment of the requisite fee. The notice must then be served in accordance with Order 50 rule 2(b), that is on the company, unit trust or other body in which the party issuing the notice claims a beneficial interest. Stop notices may be inspected in the court registry by the public.

**12.     Effect of stop notice** (O. 50 r. 12)

**Where a stop notice has been served in accordance with rule 11, then, so long as the stop notice is in force, the person or body on which it is served shall not register a transfer of the securities or take any other steps restrained by the stop notice until 14 days after sending notice thereof, by ordinary pre-paid post, to the person on whose behalf the stop notice was filed, but shall not by reason only of that notice refuse to register a transfer, or to take any other step, after the expiry of that period.**

---

**NOTES**

**[50.12.1]    Stop notice requires 14-days notice of dealings in shares, etc**

The effect of a stop notice is to prohibit the company, unit trust or other body on which it is served from registering any transfer without 14 days advance notice to the person who filed the notice. This gives that person time to apply under Order 50 rule 15 for an order to prohibit such transfer. The primary objective of the procedure 'is to protect a beneficial interest in shares against actions by the person who is registered as the owner of the shares in the share register of the company': *Lee v Buckle* [2004] 3 IR 544, 554 There it was held that a stop notice operates like an injunction. It may there fore be argued that a stop notice, like an injunction, operates *in personam* and the remedy for breach lies in contempt proceedings. *Quaere* whether a transfer of shares in breach of a stop notice would be effective, and whether the fact stop notices may be inspected in the registry ousts the possibility of a *bona fide* purchaser for value without notice.

**[50.12.2]    Registered post not required**

In 1991, the provision in Order 10 with respect to postal service of writs was amended so as to stipulate that service is to be by registered post rather than by ordinary post (Rules of the Supreme Court (Amendment) (No 3) Rules 1991). Somewhat surprisingly, this rule was not at the same time amended.

**13.      Amendment of stop notice** (O. 50 r. 13)

If any securities are incorrectly described in a stop notice which has been filed and of which a sealed copy has been served in accordance with rule 11, an amended stop notice may be filed and served in accordance with the same procedure and shall take effect as a stop notice on the day on which the sealed copy of the amended notice is served.

**14.      Withdrawal, etc. of stop notice** (O. 50 r. 14)

(1)      The person on whose behalf a stop notice was filed may withdraw it by serving a request for its withdrawal on the person or body on whom the notice was served.

(2)      Such request must be signed by the person on whose behalf the notice was filed and his signature must be witnessed by a practising solicitor.

(3)      The Court, on the application of any person claiming to be beneficially entitled to an interest in the securities to which a notice under rule 11 relates, may by order discharge the notice.

(4)      An application for an order under paragraph (3) must be made by originating summons, and the summons must be served on the person on whose behalf a stop notice was filed.

The summons shall be in Form No. 10 in Appendix A.

---

**NOTES**

**[50.14.1]      Discharge of stop notice**

In *Lee v Buckle* [2004] 3 IR 544 it was held that a stop notice will be discharged if it is apparent that the ultimate outcome of the claim (if successful) 'will be a monetary award and not the retention of the shares'. This is because the procedure 'is designed to preserve the shares *in specie* while there is an unresolved claim . . . so that they will be available to satisfy the claim, if successful'.

**15.      Order prohibiting transfer, etc. of securities** (O. 50 r. 15)

(1)      The Court, on the application of any person claiming to be beneficially entitled to an interest in any securities of the kinds set out in section 20A(2)(b) of the Ordinance may by order prohibit the person or body concerned from registering any transfer of the securities or taking any other step to which section 55C(4) of the Ordinance applies. (See App. A, Form 81) (L.N. 356 of 1988)

The order shall specify the securities to which the prohibition relates, the name in which they stand and the steps which may not be taken, and shall state whether the prohibition applies to the securities only or to the dividends or interest as well.

(2)      An application for an order under this rule must be made by summons. (L.N. 152 of 2008)

An originating summons under this rule shall be in Form No. 10 in Appendix A.

(3)      The Court, on the application of any person claiming to be entitled to an interest in any securities to which an order under this rule relates, may vary or

**discharge the order on such terms (if any) as to costs or otherwise as it thinks fit.**
**(Enacted 1988)**

---

**NOTES**

**[50.15.1]** **'Stop orders' in respect of dealings in shares, etc**
Order 50 rule 15 provides for 'stop orders' in respect of dealings in securities of the same type as may be made the subject of a 'stop notice' under rule 11. Essentially the court is empowered to prohibit the transfer of shares, unit trusts or government stock on the application of a person claiming a beneficial interest therein. Insofar as this rule applies to company shares, it makes no distinction between public and private companies: *Ong Yip Chung Henry v Chou Tai Ting & Ors* HCA 9171/1998 (Cheung J; 21.01.1999).

The power to make a stop order is clearly discretionary. This flows from the use of the permissive 'may' in rule 15(1).

A stop order should be in Form 81 in Appendix A. That form contemplates an undertaking in damages. In *Re Mee Di Weaving Factory Ltd* [1998] 1 HKC 592 the court, on making a stop order in respect of shares registered in the name of a deceased person, required an undertaking as to damages in favour of the company whose shares were involved. However no such undertaking was required in favour of the deceased's estate since there was no grant of representation, and pending that no damages could be suffered.

**[50.15.2]** **Injunction to supplement stop order**
The court appears to have jurisdiction to supplement a stop order with an injunction. See *Re International Peaceful Interests Ltd* [1986] HKLR 120 where, after a stop order was made in respect of the shares of a company, the underlying assets of the company were sold, and the party claiming a beneficial interest in the shares sought an injunction to restrain disposition of the proceeds of sale. The jurisdiction to grant such an injunction was conceded and the court expressed the view that *Mareva* injunction principles should apply, though at the end of the day an injunction was refused.

## ORDER 51

### RECEIVERS: EQUITABLE EXECUTION

**1.    Appointment of receiver by way of equitable execution** (O. 51 r. 1)
    **(1)    Where an application is made for the appointment of a receiver by way of equitable execution, the Court in determining whether it is just or convenient that the appointment should be made shall have regard to the amount claimed by the judgment creditor, to the amount likely to be obtained by the receiver and to the probable costs of his appointment and may direct an inquiry on any of these matters or any other matter before making the appointment. (See App. A, Form 84)**

---

## NOTES

### [51.1.1]    Rule 1

The court's jurisdiction to appoint a receiver, by way of equitable execution, is conferred by section 21L subsections 1 and 5 of the High Court Ordinance which provide:

> 21L(1) The Court of First Instance may by order (whether interlocutory or final) grant an injunction or appoint a receiver in all cases in which it appears to the Court of First Instance to be just or convenient to do so.
>
> ...
>
> (5)    The power of the Court of First Instance to appoint a receiver by way of equitable execution shall operate in relation to all legal estates and interests in land; and that power –
>
> (a)    may be exercised in relation to an estate or interest in land whether or not a charge has been imposed on that land under section 20 for the purpose of enforcing the judgment, order, decree or award in question; and
>
> (b)    shall be in addition to, and not in derogation of, any power of any court to appoint a receiver in proceedings for enforcing such a charge.

As to the circumstances in which it is appropriate to appoint a receiver by way of equitable execution see generally Booth, *Enforcing Judgments in Hong Kong* (LexisNexis 2004), ch 9. One advantage of this method of execution is that a receiver may receive periodic payments in the future. This can save the cost of proceeding by way of garnishee order each time a payment becomes due.

Although the court has power to appoint an equitable receiver in respect of an interest in land, the judgment creditor will normally prefer to seek a charging order and sale of the property. However where sale of the property may be difficult (for example, where the judgment debtor is a co-owner), appointment of a receiver may be appropriate, as in *Chan Ching Kit Katherine v Lam Sik Shi & Anor* HCMP 2239/ 2000 (Kwan J; 24.06.2002).

**[51.1.2]** **Form of order**

In *Hong Kong and Shanghai Banking Corp v Star Trans International Ltd* [1988] 2 HKLR 549 (CA), the court noted that there were differences in wording between Form No 82 (summons for appointment of a receiver) and Form No 84 (order appointing receiver by way of equitable execution), in a case where the actual court order followed the wording of Form 82, thus omitting important parts of Form 84, in particular the paragraph to the effect that the appointment shall be without prejudice to the rights of any prior incumbrancers. The court observed that in cases where forms derive from Chancery practice there were often real differences between the form of summons, which describes the relief sought in shorthand form, and the form of order, which spells out the relief in detail. The court went on to doubt that the actual order made could be 'rewritten' under the slip rule, or that the detailed terms of Form 84 could be implied into it. However, the court nevertheless noted that the order made had to be judged against and viewed within the context of the underlying law. The applicable law, in the instant case, included the principle (as it was expressed by Lord Halsbury in *Re Standard Manufacturing Co* [1891] 1 Ch 627, 641) that 'an execution creditor takes subject to all equities'.

**2.** **Masters may appoint receiver etc.** (O. 51 r. 2)

**A master shall have power to make an order for the appointment of a receiver by way of equitable execution and to grant an injunction if, and only so far as, the injunction is ancillary or incidental to such order.**

---

**NOTES**

**[51.2.1]** **Origin and scope of Order 51 rule 2**

Order 51 rule 2 was introduced in 1988. Its purpose is to make clear that a receiver by way of equitable execution may be appointed by a master. It is an adaptation of the similarly numbered rule under the former Rules of the Supreme Court in Eng land and Wales. The equivalent power in England is now CPR 69.2, read together with CPR 2.4.

**3.** **Application of rules as to appointment of receiver, etc.** (O. 51 r. 3)

**An application for the appointment of a receiver by way of equitable execution may be made in accordance with Order 30, rule 1, and rules 2 to 6 of that Order shall apply in relation to a receiver appointed by way of equitable execution as they apply in relation to a receiver appointed for any other purpose. (See App. A, Forms 82, 83)**

**ORDER 52**

**COMMITTAL**

1.　　**Committal for contempt of court** (O. 52 r. 1)
　　　**The power of the Court or of the Court of Appeal to punish for contempt of court may be exercised by an order of committal made by a single Judge or by a single justice of appeal. (See App. A, Form 85)**
　　　　**(Enacted 1988)**

---

**NOTES**

**[52.1.1]　　Cross-reference**
See also Order 45 rules 5–9, and the commentary thereunder, which prescribe and govern, in general terms, the availability of committal proceedings to enforce judgments and orders to abstain from doing an act, or to do an act within a specified time, these being failures and omissions commonly described as 'civil contempt.'

**[52.1.2]　　Terms of Order, or judgment, sought to be enforced must be clear**
It is 'well established that punishment for contempt is only imposed where the order contravened is clear and unambiguous': *Sino Wood Investment Ltd v Wong Kam Yin* [2006] 1 HKC 1, 7D (CFA), referring to *Redwing Ltd v Redwing Forest Products Ltd* (1947) 177 LT 387 and *Iberian Trust Ltd v Founders Trust and Investment Co Ltd* [1932] 2 KB 87. See also *Grand Union Insurance Co Ltd v Clyde & Co* [1988] HKC 464; *Harrow London Borough Council v Johnstone* [1997] 1 All ER 929 (HL) and *AG v Newspaper Publishing plc* [1997] 1 WLR 926, 935. Any ambiguity in an order must be resolved in favour of the alleged contemnor: *Shell Electric Mfg (Holdings) Co Ltd v Liu Chi Kuen Tony & Anor* [2003] 3 HKC 331. Similarly, where it is sought to enforce any undertaking by committal, the terms of such undertaking must be clearly understood (see *Winner Food Products Ltd v Chung Yat Ming* [1988] HKC 473; [1989] I HKLR 371).

**[52.1.3]　　Strict compliance with procedural requirements necessary**
Form No 85 in Appendix A to the rules is the form prescribed for orders of committal. In the case of *Re M* [1989] 2 HKLR 117, the Court of Appeal (Silke VP, Power and Penlington JJA) considered the validity of a committal order which had been approved by the court below, but did not comply with the prescribed Form in that it did not state what the contempt was. The court cited *Chiltern DC v Keane* [1985] 1 WLR 619 with approval and applied the principle that procedural requirements must be strictly complied with in cases involving the liberty of the individual and found the order to be fundamentally defective. In the result the appeal against the order of committal was allowed. For an exposition of the attitude of the English courts as to procedural irregularities, see *Nicholls v Nicholls* [1997] 1 WLR 314, at 326.

**[52.1.4]　　Extraterritorial contempt**
A prohibitory order which does not say anything about geographical limitation is

presumed to be limited to Hong Kong. It follows that unless the order expressly applies outside Hong Kong the court will not punish by way of contempt an infringing act committed outside the SAR. See *Shell Electric Mfg (Holdings) Co Ltd v Liu Chi Kuen Tony & Anor* [2003] 3 HKC 331.

**(HK)2.    Grant of leave to apply for committal** (O. 52 r. 2)
**(HK) (1)    No application for an order of committal against any person may be made unless leave to make such an application has been granted in accordance with this rule.**

**(2)    An application for such leave must be made ex parte to a judge, and must be supported by a statement setting out the name and description of the applicant, the name, description and address of the person sought to be committed and the grounds on which his committal is sought, and by an affidavit, to be filed before the application is made, verifying the facts relied on.**

**(3)    The applicant must give notice of the application for leave not later than the preceding day to the Registrar and must at the same time lodge with the Registrar copies of the statement and affidavit.**

**(HK) (4)    The judge may determine the application for leave without a hearing, unless a hearing is requested in the notice of application, and need not sit in open court; and in any case the Registrar shall serve a copy of the judge's order on the applicant.**

**(HK) (5)    Where an application for leave is refused by a judge or is granted on terms, the applicant may appeal against the judge's order to the Court of Appeal within 10 days after such order.**

**(HK) (6)    Without prejudice to the powers conferred by Order 20, rule 8, the judge hearing an application for leave may allow the applicant's statement to be amended on such terms, if any, as the judge thinks fit.**

**(HK) (7)    If the judge grants leave he may impose such terms as to costs and as to giving of security as he thinks fit.**

---

**NOTES**

**[52.2.1]    The leave requirement**
An application for an order of committal is made by originating summons to a judge (Order 52 rule 3). Prior leave to apply is required by Order 52 rule 2(1). The leave requirement is 'a filter process . . . intended to avoid persons being harassed by applications for committal which are either obviously unfounded or oppressive, or perhaps applications which have some suspicion of oppression about them': *Fabrique Ebel Société Anonyme v MBO Far East (HK) Ltd* [1985] 1 HKC 166, 168F-G. See also *Hotung v Ho Yuen Ki* CACV 178/2006 (Yuen JA & Barma J; 25.09.2009).

**[52.2.2]    The statement and affidavit in support of an application for leave**
An application for leave to seek an order for committal is made by statement identifying the alleged contemnor and stating the grounds on which his committal is sought which statement must in turn be supported by an affidavit verifying the facts relied on.

Failure to file the statement as a separate document, as contemplated by Order 52 rule 2(2) was considered by the Court of Appeal in *Re M* [1989] 2 HKLR 117. That case was decided on another point and the question of the consequences of failure to file a separate statement was left open.

Order 52 rule 2(2) requires that the alleged contemnor be identified by name, description and address. In *SA Development Ltd v Wing Hang Bank Ltd* [1997] 1 HKC 82 (CA), at 87–C it was held that committal proceedings were a nullity from inception where addressed to 'the officers of the Wing Hang Bank, San Po Kong Branch' without naming the individuals concerned.

The statement should set out the allegations against the alleged contemnor with a degree of particularity similar to that required of a criminal charge. In *Nicolas Pappadis & Anor v Chan Shing-sheung Barry & Ors* [1989] 2 HKLR 511 (CA), at 520F–G Hunter JA quoted *Chiltern District Council v Keane* [1985] 1 WLR 619, 622 where Sir John Donaldson MR said:

> what is required is that the person alleged to be in contempt shall know, with sufficient particularity to enable him to defend himself, what exactly he is said to have done or omitted to do which constitutes contempt of court.

See also *Incorporated Owners of United Building v Ng Yuk Ming & Ors* [1994] 3 HKC 637 where leave to apply for an order of committal was set aside where the allegations were insufficiently particularised.

It has been held that as the statement is presented to the court in support of an *ex parte* application, there is a duty of full and frank disclosure. See *Chou Yi Feng v Chou Yi Chen & Ors* HCA 4393/2001 (Chung J; 23.11.2002) where a statement was found to be defective for failing to alert the court at the *ex parte* stage to the lack of personal service or any order dispensing with the same or permitting substituted service.

**[52.2.3]    Grant of leave discretionary**

The court's power to grant leave to apply for committal is discretionary, and like any discretionary power it must be exercised judicially: *Century Equipment Co Ltd v Excellent Electrical Co Ltd* HCA 2542/1998 (Yeung J; 03.06.1999). Leave may be refused where, as in that case, the purpose of the order allegedly disobeyed has already been achieved; or where the alleged contempt is trivial: see the discussion in *Yau Ngai & Ors v Yau Tak & Ors* HCA 1309/2007 (Deputy Judge L Chan; 05.09.2008).

**[52.2.4]    Appeal against decision on leave application**

Order 52 rule 2(5) expressly provides that an applicant may appeal within 10 days against a refusal to grant leave to apply for committal, or where leave is granted on terms. The provision applies only to the applicant, not the respondent: *Incorporated Owners of United Building v Ng Yuk Ming & Ors* [1994] 3 HKC 637, 640D-F. If the respondent wishes to challenge the grant of leave, the remedy is apply for leave to be set aside. See below.

As noted by the court in *Oosterveld v The Ka Wah Bank Ltd & Anor* HCA 2142/1985 (Deputy Judge Barnett; 16.07.1985) (para 19), an appeal against an *ex parte* refusal of leave to apply for committal should likewise proceed *ex parte*. However, in that case the appeal was dealt with *inter partes* without objection.

**[52.2.5]    Application to set aside leave**

A grant of leave to apply for committal may be set aside like any other *ex parte* order. See Order 32 rule 6 and the commentary thereunder. One of the grounds on which leave may be set aside is material non-disclosure. See, for example, *RACP Pharmaceutical Holdings Ltd v Li Xiaobo & Anor* HCA 490/2007 (Deputy Judge Gill; 14.04.2008).

**[52.2.6]    Costs of application for leave**

Since the application for leave to apply for committal may be dealt with *ex parte* in chambers, by way of paper application, appearance before the court is not strictly necessary. In *O'Shaughnessy v Gunson & Anor* HCA 9218/1999 (Chung J; 13.04.2000) the court disallowed counsel's fees for attending at the application for leave.

**3.    Application for order after leave to apply granted** (O. 52 r. 3)

**(1)    When leave has been granted to make an application for an order of committal, the application shall be made by originating summons to a judge and unless the Court granting leave has otherwise directed, there must be at least 8 clear days between the service of the originating summons and the day named therein for the hearing. (L.N. 125 of 1991) (L.N. 152 of 2008)**

**(1A)    The originating summons shall state the grounds in respect of which leave for making an application for an order of committal has been granted. (L.N. 108 of 2002) (L.N. 152 of 2008)**

**(2)    Unless within 14 days after such leave was granted the originating summons is entered for hearing the leave shall lapse. (L.N. 152 of 2008)**

**(3)    The originating summons, accompanied by a copy of the statement and affidavit in support of the application for leave under rule 2, must be served personally on the person sought to be committed. (L.N. 152 of 2008)**

**(4)    Without prejudice to the powers of the Court under Order 65, rule 4, the Court may dispense with service of the originating summons under this rule if it thinks it just to do so. (L.N. 152 of 2008)**

---

**NOTES**

**[52.3.1]    Numbering**

There is no rule 4 in Order 52.

**[52.3.2]    Procedure after grant of leave**

Order 52 rule 3 provides that when leave to apply for committal is granted the applicant must within 14 days enter a notice of motion for hearing the application. The notice of motion must state the grounds in respect of which leave has been granted: rule 3(1A).

Personal service of the notice of motion and other relevant papers is required: rule 3(3). The personal service requirement applies equally to notice of an adjourned hearing: *Secretary for Justice v Choy Bing Wing* [2005] 4 HKC 416, 426E–F. The court has power to dispense with service in exceptional cases: rule 3(4). In *Choy Bing Wing* (above, at 426G–I) it was held that the power to dispense with service may be exercised in advance or *ex post facto*, and that it should be exercised in a manner which 'best reflects the requirements of justice'. See also the commentary under Order 45 rule 7.

**5. Saving for power to commit without application for purpose** (O. 52 r. 5)

Nothing in the foregoing provisions of this Order shall be taken as affecting the power of the Court of First Instance or the Court of Appeal to make an order of committal of its own motion against a person guilty of contempt of court.

**6. Provisions as to hearing** (O. 52 r. 6)

(1) Subject to paragraph (2), the Court hearing an application for an order of committal may sit in private in the following cases, that is to say—

    (a) where the application arises out of proceedings relating to the wardship or adoption of an infant or wholly or mainly to the guardianship, custody, maintenance or upbringing of an infant, or rights of access to an infant;

    (b) where the application arises out of proceedings relating to a person suffering or appearing to be suffering from mental disorder within the meaning of the Mental Health Ordinance (Cap. 136);

    (c) where the application arises out of proceedings in which a secret process, discovery or invention was in issue;

    (d) where it appears to the Court that in the interests of the administration of justice or for reasons affecting the security of Hong Kong the application should be heard in private;

but, except as aforesaid, the application shall be heard in open court.

(2) If the Court hearing an application in private by virtue of paragraph (1) decides to make an order of committal against the person sought to be committed, it shall in open court state—

    (a) the name of that person,

    (b) in general terms the nature of the contempt of court in respect of which the order of committal is being made, and

    (c) the length of the period for which he is being committed.

(3) Except with the leave of the Court hearing an application for an order of committal, no grounds shall be relied upon at the hearing except the grounds as stated in the originating summons under rule 3(1A). (L.N. 108 of 2002) (L.N. 152 of 2008)

The foregoing provision is without prejudice to the powers of the Court under Order 20, rule 8.

(4) If on the hearing of the application the person sought to be committed expresses a wish to give oral evidence on his own behalf, he shall be entitled to do so.

---

**NOTES**

## [52.6.1] Hearing in open court

An application for an order of committal must be heard in open court except in the limited circumstances set out in Order 52 rule 6(1). This is a fundamental requirement and failure to comply cannot be cured by the application of Order 2 rule 1 (which provides that non-compliance with the rules shall be treated as an irregularity and not a nullity). See *C v C & A* [2003] 4 HKC 141 where it was held that a judgment summons in matrimonial proceedings is in the nature of a contempt application and that the same requirement for a hearing in open court applies.

## [52.6.2] Approach of the court

The law of contempt exists 'to maintain the supremacy of the law and the due and unobstructed administration of justice': *Aqua-Leisure Industries Inc v Aqua Splash Ltd (No 3)* [2002] 1 HKC 495, 499E, citing *Moy v Chan Luen Ying* [1964] HKLR 579, 587–88. (Note that the decision of Deputy Judge To in *Aqua-Leisure* was set aside on appeal, on other grounds: see [2003] 1 HKC 1.) In exercising its contempt power the court will bear in mind the 'signal importance' of demonstrating to litigants that court orders are to be obeyed unless bad on their face: *Abu Dhabi National Tanker Co v Lam Ming Chi* [1998] 4 HKC 320, 336E, per Stone J, cited with approval by Chu J in *Re Texgar Ltd* [2001] 2 HKC 426, 432G.

## [52.6.3] The distinction between civil and criminal contempt

Contempts are classified as civil or criminal. The difference was explained in *Secretary for Justice v Choy Bing Wing* [2005] 4 HKC 416, 441A–C in the following terms:

> A civil contempt involves a breach of a court order. If there is such a breach, it is normally for an aggrieved party – invariably the party in whose favour the court order has been made – to raise the matter by way of a complaint to the court. A criminal contempt is broader in compass, involving conduct which interferes with the due administration of justice. A criminal contempt is a matter for the Secretary for Justice to raise, acting as guardian of the public interest in ensuring the protection of the due administration of justice.

See also *A Ltd v Z* [1982] 1 All ER 556 (CA) and *AG v Times Newspapers Ltd* [1991] 2 WLR 994 (HL).

Order 52 applies to both civil and criminal contempt proceedings: *Choy Bing Wing* (above).

Where it occurs in the context of civil proceedings, the distinction between civil and criminal contempt is of little significance, save with regard to the rules of evidence. See *Aqua-Leisure Industries Inc & Anor v Aqua Splash Ltd (No 3)* [2002] 1 HKC 495, 503C–D (reversed on other grounds at [2003] 1 HKC 1), where the distinction was described as 'unhelpful and meaningless'.

Where wilful interference with the administration of justice occurs in the context of criminal proceedings, the categorisation of the contempt as 'criminal' requires that the criminal law should prevail as to the procedures applied. The defendant is not a compellable witness and the plaintiff is not entitled to an order for discovery against him: *Secretary for Justice v Apple Daily Ltd & Anor* [2000] 2 HKC 739 (CFI) (applying dicta of Lord Denning in *Comet Products UK Ltd v Hawkex Plastics Ltd & Anor* [1971] 2 QB 67, 74; *Jennison v Baker* [1972] 2 QB 52 and *Attorney General v Newspaper Publishing plc* [1988] Ch 333). It is not necessary for an allegation of criminal contempt to be tried on indictment. The notice of motion procedure under Order 52 rule 3 may be used. See *Choy Bing Wing* (above).

**[52.6.4]     Standard of proof**
On an application for committal for contempt the criminal standard of proof applies. See *K Yu Sein Trading Co Ltd & Anor v Talakchand* [1982] HKLR 171, 177E (CA) citing *Re Bramblevale Ltd* [1970] 1 Ch 128. In those decisions some of the judges preferred to put the test as one 'consistent with the gravity of the charge', but this seems to amount to the same thing – proof beyond reasonable doubt is required because the alleged contemnor faces the possibility of imprisonment.

The criminal standard applies whether the alleged contempt is civil or criminal: *Cartier International BV & Ors v Kaybee International Ltd* [1985] HKLR 127, 132I–J (CA).

**[52.6.5]     The mental element in civil contempt**
On an application for committal for civil contempt, although the criminal standard of proof applies, there is no requirement to demonstrate *mens rea* in the sense that the alleged contemnor intended to disobey the order. It is sufficient to prove (a) that the alleged contemnor knew the facts, and (b) that the alleged contempt was not accidental: *Citybase Property Management Ltd v Kam Kyun Tak & Ors (No 1)* [2003] 2 HKC 98, 103H-I (per Ma J as he then was). Sir Gerard Brennan NPJ appears to have approved of this aspect of the judgment in *Citybase* in the Court of Final Appeal's judgment in *Kao, Lee & Yip (a firm) v Koo Hoi Yan Donald* [2009] 5 HKC 36 (CFA) (para 45) where he added 'it is clear that liability for civil contempt does not depend on a contumacious intent'.

**[52.6.6]     Evidence**
Affidavit evidence is 'invariably used in committal proceedings unless otherwise directed by the court' and hearsay evidence is permissible: see *Citybase Property Management Ltd v Kam Kyun Tak & Ors ( No 1)* [2003] 2 HKC 98, 103 D-E. In that case, Ma J described the use of affidavit and hearsay evidence as an anomaly given the criminal standard of proof applies.

The use of affidavit evidence, and in particular the use of affidavits containing statements of 'information and belief' was considered in *Aqua-Leisure Industries Inc v Aqua Splash Ltd (No 3)* [2002] 1 HKC 495. Deputy Judge To held that on a motion to commit for civil contempt, affidavit evidence was admissible in terms of the rules applicable in respect of civil proceedings, generally (set out in Order 38 rule 2) under which there was a right to seek and a discretion for the court to order cross-examination of the deponent. However, whether such affidavits could contain statements of 'information or belief' depended upon whether the proceedings were 'final' or 'interlocutory' in nature this, in turn, depending upon the nature of the order, breach of which was alleged. Where, as in the instant case, the main action had been concluded and the purpose of the committal proceedings was solely punitive, the application to commit ought to be regarded as 'final' and not merely as 'interlocutory'. The decision of Deputy Judge To was set aside on appeal: see [2003] 1 HKC 1. On the appeal it was argued that the final or interlocutory issue went to the question whether the old or new rules as to admissibility of hearsay evidence were applicable. However, as a result of the Court of Appeal's ruling on other points, this issue was rendered academic. See the judgment of Le Pichon JA, at 17D–H.

The court will be slow to exercise its discretion to grant leave to cross-examine the alleged contemnor's affidavit. See the commentary under Order 38 rule 2.

### [52.6.7] Summary of procedure on application for committal for breach of court order

The procedures to be followed in bringing an application for committal for contempt are found in various rules under Orders 45 and 52. They were succinctly summarised by Ma J in *Citybase Property Management Ltd v Kam Kyun Tak & Ors (No 1)* [2003] 2 HKC 98 in the context of an application for committal for breach of a court order. The learned judge's summary, at 102A-I brings together the requirements in a manner which is easy to understand. For the benefit of readers we produce extracts below with cross-references to the commentary elsewhere in this work. The learned judge said:

> Before considering whether a contempt has been committed where the breach of a court order is involved, the court must be satisfied of the following:
>
> (1) The relevant order, together with an appropriate penal notice, must generally have been personally served on the alleged contemnor: RHC O 45 r 7(2)(a), (4). This, however, is the general rule. Personal service will not necessarily be required to be shown in relation to an order requiring a person to abstain from doing something, if the person to be served (the alleged contemnor) was present in court when the order was made or that person was notified of the terms of the order . . . [see the commentary under Order 45 rule 7]
>
> (2) The relevant order must also contain . . . a penal notice. Where there has been a failure in this regard, the court nevertheless has the [discretion] to enforce the order . . . [see the commentary under Order 45 rule 7(6)]. However, it is in my view, essential that the alleged contemnor shall be told, whether by being present in court or by being notified by telephone, telegram or otherwise, that the consequences of breaching any order made is to be held in contempt of court and liable to a process or execution . . . It would be an extremely rare exercise of discretion under O 45 r 7(6) for the court to dispense with this requirement . . .
>
> (3) Next, the applicant must obtain leave from the court to make an application for committal: O 52 r 2(1). The application for leave is made *ex parte* and must be accompanied by an affidavit and a statement providing details of the alleged contemnor and the facts of the contempt alleged: see O 52 r 2(2).
>
> (4) Where leave is granted, the applicant must apply by motion [now originating summons] to a judge and serve the motion [now originating summons] together with the affidavit evidence and statement used for the *ex parte* application for leave, on the alleged contemnor at least eight clear days before the hearing: O 52 r 3. Service should be personal (see O 52 r 3(3)) but the court has the discretion to dispense with this if it is just to do so: O 52 r 3(4).
>
> Once the above requirements are complied with to the satisfaction of the court, the court is then in a position first to determine whether a contempt has occurred and secondly, if so, to make an order for committal or impose some other form of punishment. The final stage of the hearing is the determination of costs.

**[52.6.8]    Submission of no case to answer**
There are conflicting authorities as to whether the respondent to a committal application is required to make an election as to calling evidence before embarking on a submission of no case to answer. See the commentary under Order 35 rule 7

**[52.6.9]    Application for committal of officer of body corporate**
As to the circumstances in which an order directed to a body corporate may be enforced by committal of its officer or director, see the commentary under Order 45 rule 5.

**[52.6.10]    Costs**
Costs are commonly awarded on the indemnity basis against contemnors. See the commentary under Order 62 rule 28. The reason for this was explained in *Lau Yee Ching v Wong Tak Kwong & Ors* CACV 385/2005 (Rogers & Woo VPP; Le Pichon JA; 03.03.2006). There it was said that the complainant in committal proceedings stands to gain no benefit other than enforcement of the order which is the subject of the committal application, and yet incurs expense for the benefit of the court. Insofar as an order for indemnity costs is itself a penalty, the court can adjust the other penalties imposed on the contemnor to ensure the overall penalty is not disproportionate. In *Koo Hoi Yan Donald v Kao, Lee & Yip (a firm)* FACV 27/2007 (14.09.2009) (para 12) the Court of Final Appeal considered *Lau Yee Ching* and agreed that the need to bring proceedings to force compliance with the court's order is a relevant factor, but emphasised that indemnity costs was a matter of judicial discretion calling for evaluation of all relevant circumstances.

**7.    Power to suspend execution of committal order** (O. 52 r. 7)
    **(1)    The Court by whom an order of committal is made may by order direct that the execution of the order of committal shall be suspended for such period or on such terms or conditions as it may specify.**
    **(2)    Where execution of an order of committal is suspended by an order under paragraph (1), the applicant for the order of committal must, unless the Court otherwise directs, serve on the person against whom it was made a notice informing him of the making and terms of the order under that paragraph.**

**8.    Discharge of person committed** (O. 52 r. 8)
    **(1)    The Court may, on the application of any person committed to prison for any contempt of court, discharge him.**
    **(2)    Where a person has been committed for failing to comply with a judgment or order requiring him to deliver any thing to some other person or to deposit it in court or elsewhere, and a writ of sequestration has also been issued to enforce that judgment or order, then, if the thing is in the custody or power of the person committed, the commissioners appointed by the writ of sequestration may take possession of it as if it were the property of that person and, without prejudice to the generality of paragraph (1), the Court may discharge the person committed and may give such directions for dealing with the thing taken by the commissioners as it thinks fit.**

**9.      Saving for other powers** (O. 52 r. 9)

**Nothing in the foregoing provisions of this Order shall be taken as affecting the power of the Court to make an order requiring a person guilty of contempt of court, or a person punishable by virtue of any written law in like manner as if he had been guilty of contempt of the Court of First Instance, to pay a fine or to give security for his good behaviour, and those provisions, so far as applicable, and with the necessary modifications, shall apply in relation to an application for such an order as they apply in relation to an application for an order of committal.**

----

**NOTES**

**[52.9.1]      Range of sentences which may be imposed on contemnor**
The term 'committal' refers to committal to prison. However Order 52 rule 9 makes it clear that other sentences such as a fine or good behaviour bond are possible.

**[52.9.2]      Sentencing considerations**
The primary consideration in imposing sentence for contempt is the 'signal importance' of demonstrating to litigants that court orders must be obeyed: *Abu Dhabi National Tanker Co v Lam Ming Chi & Anor* [1998] 4 HKC 320, 336E; *Re Texgar Ltd* [2001] 2 HKC 426, 432G-I.

A contempt may be 'purged' by compliance and tendering a genuine apology. The apology should be made personally by *viva voce* evidence or on affidavit rather than through counsel: *Sino Wood Investment Ltd v Wong Kam Yin* HCA 307/2002 (Deputy Judge Saunders; 30.01.2006).

In *Texgar* (above) 21 days imprisonment was imposed for contempts consisting of failure to comply, within time, with an order for disclosure; failure, ultimately, to make full and frank disclosure; failure to comply with an order for payment into court and misleading the court. In *Citybase Property Management Ltd v Kam Kyun Tak & Ors (No 2)* [2003] 2 HKC 108, 111E-G 6 weeks' imprisonment was imposed for contempt consisting of breach of an injunction granted to enforce a deed of mutual covenant. In *Oriental Daily Publisher Ltd & Anor v Ma Chiu Sing* HCA 606/2008 (Poon J; 12.09.2008) the defendant, who on 7 occasions displayed defamatory banners in breach of court injunctions, was sentenced to 7 terms of 6 weeks imprisonment to be served consecutively, but the Court of Appeal, taking the view that the totality of the sentence was too great, ordered release of defendant after he had served only about 20 weeks of the sentence ([2009] 2 HKLRD 558). In *Banca Popolare di Vincenza Soc Coop & Anor v Alutech (FE) Co Ltd & Ors* HCA 1973/2007 (Saunders J; 11.09.2008) breach of a *Mareva* injunction prohibiting disposal of assets worldwide was punished by 6 months imprisonment. In *Secretary for Justice v Ocean Technology Ltd & Ors* [2010] 1 HKC 456 contempt consisting of breach of an injunction restraining the making of unlicensed radio broadcasts was punished by fines of $10,000 per contemnor, a figure which was fixed taking into account the amount of costs each was ordered to pay ($50,000).

Special considerations arise when the court is called upon to sentence a person for a contempt which has already been dealt with by way of criminal prosecution.

See *Slade v Slade* [2009] EWCA 748 (17.07.2009), a case concerning the sentence for a contempt consisting of a breach of undertaking not to harass or pester, which had already been the subject of a criminal prosecution for malicious damage.

## [52.9.3]    Court may refuse to hear party until contempt is purged

Where a contempt of court 'impedes the course of justice' and there is no other effective means of securing compliance, the court may refuse to hear the contemnor further in the same proceedings until the contempt is purged: *Hadkinson v Hadkinson* [1952] 2 All ER 567 (CA). However the court will hear an appeal against the order giving rise to the contempt: *Hotung v Ho Yuen Ki* [2007] 4 HKLRD 384 (CA) (para 29 *et seq*); *Questnet Ltd v Rinck* HCA 1475/2006 (Saunders J; 18.02.2008).

## ORDER 53

### APPLICATIONS FOR JUDICIAL REVIEW

**1A.    Interpretation** (O. 53 r. 1A)
**In this Order —**
"application for judicial review" includes an application in accordance with
    this Order for a review of the lawfulness of —
    (a)    an enactment; or
    (b)    a decision, action or failure to act in relation to the exercise of
           a public function;
"interested party", in relation to an application for judicial review, means any
    person (other than the applicant and respondent) who is directly affected
    by the application.

(L.N. 152 of 2008)

**1.      Cases appropriate for application for judicial review** (O. 53 r. 1)
        (1)    An application for judicial review must be made if the applicant is
seeking —
        (a)    an order for mandamus, prohibition or certiorari; or
        (b)    an injunction under section 21J of the Ordinance restraining a
               person from acting in any office in which he is not entitled to
               act.
        (2)    An application for judicial review may be made if the applicant is
seeking —
        (a)    a declaration; or
        (b)    an injunction (not being an injunction mentioned in paragraph
               (1)(b)).
        (3)    An application for judicial review may include an application for
an award of damages, restitution or the recovery of a sum due but may not seek
such a remedy alone.

(L.N. 152 of 2008)

---

## NOTES

### [53.1.1]    Scope of judicial review

Order 53 rule 1 sets out the types of relief which it is appropriate to seek by way of
application for judicial review. The rule should be read together with section 21K of
the High Court Ordinance. Although the rule was repealed and replaced as part of
the civil justice reforms taking effect in April 2009, the amendments were largely
cosmetic, and did not affect the legal position.

        Generally speaking, judicial review is not concerned with the merits of the
impugned decision. Judicial review is not equivalent to an appeal, and on review the
court will not substitute its opinion for the opinion of the administrative authority. It is

not for the court to consider the wisdom of government policies: *Clean Air Foundation Ltd & Anor v HKSAR* HCAL 35/2007 (Hartmann J; 26.07.2007). Rather judicial review is concerned with the underpinnings of the decisions of administrative authorities. See *Secretary for Justice v Cheung Chung Chit* [2003] 4 HKC 49. In *Re Right Centre Co Ltd* [1990] 1 HKLR 250, 262C-E Godfrey J summarised the scope of judicial review as follows:

> the function of the Court, on an application for judicial review, is merely to see whether any allegation of illegality, impropriety or irrationality is made against the respondent; and if so, to consider whether that allegation is justified. So that there shall be no doubt about it, I shall explain what these hurdles involve. First, illegality. This involves proving that the decision was wrong as a matter of law. Secondly, impropriety. This involves proving that the process by which the decision was arrived at (not the decision itself) was unfair, or otherwise flawed in some way. Thirdly, irrationality. This involves proving, not that a reasonable man could have come to a different decision, but that no rational person, properly directing himself as to the relevant law and properly appreciating the relevant facts, could possibly have come to the decision under challenge.

The three heads of judicial review as enunciated by Godfrey J in the above passage derive from the House of Lords decision in *Council of Civil Service Unions v Minister for the Civil Service* [1985] AC 374.

Judicial review is a supervisory jurisdiction by which the Court of First Instance reviews decisions of inferior courts and tribunals. It does not lie against a decision of a judge of the High Court: *Sit Kwok Keung v CIR* CACV 23/2005 (Rogers VP & Sakhrani J; 03.06.2005), referring to *Re Racal Communications Ltd* [1981] AC 374. However, judicial review will lie against a High Court judge sitting in another capacity, such chairman of a commission under the Commissions of Inquiry Ordinance (Cap 86): *Secretary for Justice v Commission of Inquiry on Allegations Relating to the HK Institute of Education* [2009] 3 HKC 102 (paras 35-42), referring to *Mahon v Air New Zealand* [1984] 1 AC 808 (PC). See also *Yau Kwong Man v Long-term Prison Sentences Review Board* HCAL 34/2004 (Tang J; 27.10.2004) where the court quashed the decision of a statutory board chaired by a High Court judge. The remedy also lies against the Registrar or a master of the High Court (see, for example *Ng Ai Kheng Jasmine v Master M Yuen & Anor* HCAL 46/2003 (Chu J; 08.03.2004)) and against a District Court judge (*Nattrass v AG* [1996] 1 HKC 480) or magistrate (*Chan Tit Shau v Secretary for Justice* [2003] 2 HKC 225). That said, it must be borne in mind that judicial review is not appropriate where an appeal would lie – see the commentary some paragraphs hence on the duty to exhaust other remedies before applying for judicial review.

**[53.1.2]    Relief that may be granted by way of judicial review**
The common law prerogative writs of mandamus, prohibition, certiorari and quo warranto have been abolished in Hong Kong: see section 46 of the High Court Ordinance and the schedule thereto. In their place is the modern procedure of judicial review under which the court may grant orders of a similar nature. The types of order which may be granted by way of judicial review are set out in sections 21I, 21J and 21K of the High Court Ordinance as well as Order 53 rule 1. They are:

(1)    Order of mandamus, that is an order requiring a public official to perform a function or duty imposed by law;

(2)    Order of prohibition, that is an order prohibiting a public official from taking a particular course of action;

(3)    Order of certiorari, that is an order quashing a decision taken by a public (or in some cases private) decision-making body; and

(4)    Injunction to restrain a person from acting in an office to which he is not entitled. This is the modern equivalent of quo warranto.

Other types of injunction, and declarations, may be sought by way of judicial review rather than ordinary action where the context is one of public law: rule 1(2). A claim to damages may be joined with an application for judicial review and the court may grant relief accordingly. See section 21K(4) of the Ordinance and Order 53 rules 1(3) and 7.

    With regard to interim relief, see Order 53 rule 3(10) and the commentary thereunder.

### [53.1.3]    Relief discretionary

All relief by way of judicial review is in the discretion of the court. In the exercise of its discretion the court may refuse to grant relief even where the applicant's case is made out. See *Re Mitchell & Ors* [1976] HKLR 1005; *Re an application by Lawe William Enterprises Ltd* [1990] 1 HKLR 365 and *Mok Kwong Ching v Secretary for the Civil Service & Anor* HCMP 4100/1996 (Yeung J; 11.09.1997) (citing *R v Secretary of State for the Environment ex p Walters* The Times, 02.09.1997).

    For example even though procedural impropriety has been demonstrated, relief might be denied if the court is of the view the result would have been the same any way. However it is 'rare' for a court to refuse relief in cases where there has been procedural impropriety. See *Leung Fuk Wah Oil v Commissioner of Police* [2002] 3 HKC 1, 10H–11E (CA) *and Chu Ping Tak Tim v Commissioner of Police* HCAL 3672/2001 quoting extensively from an article by Bingham LJ published at [1991] Public Law 64:

> Judges of the highest distinction have held that an applicant who has been unlawfully and unfairly denied a right to be heard may be denied relief if the outcome would have been no different if he had been heard. Sir William Wade has referred to 'the dubious doctrine that a hearing would make no difference,' and in a recent case [*R v Chief Constable of the Thames Valley Police Forces, ex p Cotton* [1990] IRLR 344] I gave six reasons for expecting (by which I really meant hoping) that such cases would be of great rarity …

> (i)    Unless the subject of the decision has had an opportunity to put his case, it may not be easy to know what case he could or would have put if he had had the chance.

> (ii)    As memorably pointed out by Megarry J in *John v Rees* [1970] Ch 345, experience shows that that which is confidently expected is by no means always that which happens.

> (iii)    It is generally desirable that decision-makers should be reasonably receptive to argument, and it would therefore be unfortunate if the complainant's position became weaker as the decision-maker's mind became more closed.

(iv)   In considering whether the complainant's representations would have made any difference to the outcome, the court may unconsciously stray from its proper province of reviewing the propriety of the decision-making process into the forbidden territory of evaluating the substantial merits of the decision.

(v)    This is a field in which appearances are generally thought to matter.

(vi)   Where a decision-maker is under a duty to act fairly the subject of the decision may properly be said to have a right to be heard, and rights are not to be lightly denied.

One of the 'rare' cases where the court has in its discretion refused relief by way of judicial review despite a finding of procedural impropriety is *Lam Ping Cheung Andrew v Law Society of Hong Kong* [2007] 1 HKC 123. There it was held that the Law Society had not given a solicitor sufficient opportunity to be heard on a disciplinary and suspension matter, but dismissed the solicitor's application for judicial review on the ground the Law Society would inevitably have come to the same decision.

See also section 21K(6) of the High Court Ordinance which specifically empowers the court to refuse an application for judicial review where by reason of undue delay it considers relief would cause substantial hardship or substantially prejudice the rights of any person or would be detrimental to good administration.

## [53.1.4]   Advisory or hypothetical applications

An application for judicial review may be dismissed if there is no, or is no longer any, real dispute between the parties.

In *Chit Fai Motors Co Ltd v Commissioner for Transport* [2004] 1 HKC 465, the Court of Appeal set out the circumstances in which it is appropriate for the court to hear an application for judicial review notwithstanding the fact the issue may have been rendered academic or hypothetical by events. In that case, the licence which was the subject of an application for judicial review had expired by the time of the substantive hearing and the judge at first instance dismissed the application for that reason. On appeal, it was held that there were good reasons for the issue to be decided by the court, in particular there was a likelihood the same point would arise in future between the same parties. The law was reviewed again in *Leung TC William Roy v Secretary for Justice* [2006] 4 HKLRD 211 (CA) where (at para 28) it was held that it is a matter of discretion rather than jurisdiction whether an application which is said to be advisory or hypothetical can be heard.

In the case of applications for a declaration or injunction by way of judicial review, section 21K(2) of the High Court provides that the court must be satisfied that it would be 'just and convenient' for the relief to be granted, having regard to all the circumstances of the case and other criteria set out in the subsection. The court will be reluctant to grant a declaration which is of a purely advisory nature. See *Cheung Man Wai v Director of Social Welfare* [2000] 3 HKLRD 255, 259. In *Pang Yiu Hung Rob ert v Commissioner of Police* [2002] 4 HKC 579 it was argued that a declaration should not be granted as to the true construction of a statutory provision since there was no issue between the parties on that point. It was submitted that it would not be 'just and convenient' for the court to do so. Hartmann J ruled against this submission on the ground that the legislation was 'far from clear' (at 607I) and the facts giving rise to the application were not hypothetical (at 609E). The cases of *Gouriet v Union of Post Office Workers* [1978] AC 435 and *R v Secretary of State for the Home*

*Department, ex p Mehari* [1994] QB 474 were cited as to when it is appropriate for a court to grant a declaration in such circumstances.

**[53.1.5]    Judicial review only appropriate in cases involving questions of public law**

Order 53 rule 1(1) provides that applications in the nature of the old prerogative writs of mandamus, prohibition, certiorari and quo warranto must be made by way of judicial review. Under rule 1(2) applications for a declaration or injunction may also be made by way of judicial review if, having regard to the circumstances, judicial review rather than ordinary action is appropriate.

Claims made by ordinary action for relief which should be sought by way of judicial review will be struck out: *O'Reilly v Mackman* [1983] 2 AC 237 (HL); *Chow Wai Hung v HK Gov't* [1983] 2 HKC 537; *Tsui Kin Kwok Johnnie v Commr of Police* HCAL 50/2009 (A Cheung J; 29.01.2010). Conversely judicial review proceedings which raise issues more appropriately determined in an ordinary action will also be dismissed: *Ex p Lavelle* [1983] 1 WLR 23; *Re Tsang Shing-kung Harris* [1986] HKLR 356. However, in certain circumstances the court may, instead of dismissing such a judicial review, direct that the application continue as if it were an action commenced by writ of summons under Order 53 rule 9(5).

Judicial review is the appropriate procedure when applying for a declaration or injunction in relation to a decision made within the realm of 'public' as opposed to 'private' law: *CCSU v Minister for the Civil Service* [1985] AC 374, 409B–C. For example, a decision made by a government official, department or agency exercising a governmental function pursuant to statutory or prerogative power will usually be considered to be within the realm of public law and thus susceptible to judicial review. Likewise decisions of public bodies which may be independent of the government but exercise statutory power or carry out public functions. The distinction between public and private law functions is not always easy to make and is perhaps best explained by examples.

(1)    *Decisions of public bodies not amenable to judicial review*

Decisions of government and public bodies of a commercial character, or acting as landlord, tenant, purchaser or vendor, are considered to be private and not susceptible to judicial review. See the comprehensive discussion in *Ngo Kee Construction Co Ltd v HK Housing Authority* [2001] 1 HKC 492. The following are some examples:

•    Decision as to the grant, extension or modification of a government lease of land: *Kam Lan Koon & Ors v SJ* [1999] 3 HKC 591 (CA); *Rank Profit Industries Ltd v Director of Lands* CACV 94/2007 (07.05.2008).

•    Decision whether to permit development of land made under contractual provisions in a government lease rather than under planning or land use leg islation: *Canadian Overseas Dev't Co Ltd v AG* [1991] 1 HKC 233 (CA), following *Hang Wah Chong Investment Co Ltd v AG* [1981] HKLR 336 (PC).

•    Decision of the Housing Authority to issue an occupation permit: *Re Occupation Permit No 18555* [1991] 2 HKLR 104, 109F–G.

•    Decision of the MTR Corporation (at the time wholly owned by the government and incorporated by statute) relating to distribution of newspapers within its pre cincts: *Hong Kong Standard Newspapers Ltd v MTR Corp* HCMP 2587/1992 (Mayo J; 05.03.1993).

- Decision of the Airport Authority (a government owned body incorporated by statute) choosing one tenderer over another: *Matteograssi SpA v Airport Authority* [1998] 3 HKC 25 (CA).

- Decision of the Environment, Transport and Works Bureau to remove a contractor from the list of those approved to carry out public works: *Lee Chau Mou t/a Chau Mou Eng'g Co v Secretary for the Environment, Transport & Works* HCAL 111/2006 (Chu J; 06.06.2007).

- Decision not to take enforcement action in respect of alleged breaches of a government tenancy: *Cheung Shing Scrap Metals Recycling Ltd v Director of Lands* HCAL 54/2008 (Poon J; 20.05.2009).

(2)     *Decisions of a public body which may or may not be amenable to judicial review*

Decisions in relation to government leases may be subject to judicial review when they are made by government not acting not purely as landlord, but 'determining as a matter of policy what conditions to impose': *The Home Restaurant Ltd v AG* [1987] HKLR 237, 245B-C. Likewise where such a decision is required to be made with regard to competing public interests, or where a legitimate expectation arises from a policy statement as to how the government will exercise its power: *Hong Kong & China Gas Co Ltd v Director of Lands* [1997] 3 HKC 520 (affirmed on appeal – see CACV 10/1998).

(3)     *Challenge to constitutionality of legislation*

Where an issue of constitutionality arises in civil or criminal proceedings it may be ventilated in those proceedings as a point of law. The CALL practice direction (below) provides for such proceedings to be transferred to the Constitutional and Administrative Law list, but this is rarely done.

Where such an issue arises in the absence of ongoing proceedings, it should be raised by way of judicial review rather than ordinary action: *Lee Miu Ling v AG* [1996] 1 HKC 124, 135 (CA). There Litton VP held that a challenge to legislation providing for functional constituencies in the legislature should have been brought by way of judicial review instead of originating summons. In *Lau Wong Fat v AG* (1996) 7 HKPLR 148 the court struck out a writ and statement of claim challenging the validity of legislation permitting women to inherit New Territories land. Cheung J said that the requirement that public law litigation proceed by way of judicial review was not a mere matter of putting form over substance 'because the procedure under Order 53 contains important safeguards against groundless or unmeritorious claims'.

In *Financial Services & Systems Ltd v SJ* HCAL 101/2006 (Fung J; 06.07.2007) (para 24) the Court of Appeal's decision in *Leung TC William Roy* (above) was interpreted as holding that the court has a discretion to grant a declaration by way of judicial review on the constitutionality of legislation even in the absence of a judgment, order, decision or other proceeding to challenge.

(4)    *Public sector employment disputes*

Public sector employment disputes may in some, but not all, circumstances properly be the subject of judicial review proceedings. The key is whether the dispute involves legislative provisions such as restrictions on dismissal: *R v East Berkshire Health Authority, ex p Walsh* [1985] 1 QB 152, 164 (CA). Thus in *Spruce v HKU* [1993] 2 HKLR 65 (PC) a university lecturer proceeded by way of judicial review in a dispute over termination for cause under subsidiary legislation. However in *Sit Ka Yin Priscilla v EOC* [1998] 1 HKC 278 and again in *Chik Po Yee v Vocational Training Council* CACV 78/2006 (Ma CJHC, Stock JA & Reyes J; 25.04.2007) it was held that judicial review was not appropriate where public authority employees were terminated under contractual provisions. Even a termination under statutory power may not be judicially reviewable where the statute excludes application of public law concepts such as natural justice: *Fung Yiu Bun v Commissioner of Police* [2002] 4 HKC 15.

Aspects of employment in the Hong Kong civil service and disciplined services are regulated by legislative instrument such as Ordinance, subsidiary legislation and executive order. Disciplinary proceedings are a notable example. Judicial review is often appropriate in such cases. Examples include *Re Ling Sik-ho* [1990] 2 HKLR 388 (police officer disciplined for making false statement); *Mok Kwong Ching v Scty for Civil Service* HCMP 4100/1996 (Yeung J; 11.09.1997) (legal aid counsel denied housing benefit); *Ratcliffe v Scty for Civil Service* [1999] 4 HKC 412 (CA) (police superintendent disciplined for alleged sexual harassment); *Pang Tak Kwai v Commissioner of Correctional Services* [2001] 4 HKC 412 (CA) (technical instructor disciplined for taking peanuts into high security prison); and *Leung Fuk Wah Oil v Commissioner of Police* [2003] 3 HKC 1 (CA) (police officer dismissed for impairment of operational efficiency arising from bankruptcy). In *Khan v AG* [1986] HKLR 972 (CA) an auxiliary policeman obtained relief by way of ordinary action after having been dismissed under legislative power. However the first instance proceedings in that case were commenced in 1980, before Order 53 was enacted in its current form. Today it is likely that the applicant would be required to proceed by way of judicial review under *O'Reilly v Mackman* (above).

(5)    *Private sector employment disputes*

Contractual disciplinary procedures may expressly or impliedly incorporate public law duties such as natural justice, fairness and absence of bias. Failure to comply is a breach of contract and a remedy may be sought by writ of summons – judicial review is not appropriate: *Chik Po Yee* (above).

(6)    *Educational institutions*

Many educational institutions in Hong Kong are incorporated or regulated by statute, whether or not publicly funded. There are many instances where the result has been judicial review of decisions made by or in respect of such institutions. Some examples relating to employment disputes with such institutions are referred to above. Other examples include the following:

*    *Re Mitchell* [1976] HKLR 1005 – judicial review of censure of a university employee;

*    *Ng Chor Kiu v Director of Education* HCAL 28/1998 (Sears J; 12.11.1998) –

judicial review of appointment of a new principal;

- *Dr Wang Tze Sam v AG* HCMP 936/1996 (Sears J; 12.06.1996) – judicial review concerning public funding of a private school, but limited to non-contractual issues;
- *Liang Ting Sen Thomas v Director of Education* HCAL 2241/2000 (Hartmann J; 22.12.2000) – judicial review of refusal to certify buildings as suitable for use as school premises;
- *'R' v English Schools Foundation* [2004] 3 HKC 343 – judicial review of expulsion of a pupil from a school system incorporated by statute and partly publicly funded.

(7)    *The Jockey Club*

There are some decisions in which disciplinary proceedings by the Hong Kong Jockey Club (a company incorporated by guarantee) have been subject to judicial review. See, for example *Moses v Royal Hong Kong Jockey Club* HCMP 1450/1981 (Mayo J; 19.11.1981); *Hall v ICAC* [1987] HKLR 210; (1987) 17 HKLJ 220. However *Moses* pre-dates the decision of the House of Lords in *O'Reilly v Mackman* [1983] 2 AC 237 and *Hall* centred on a decision of the ICAC. It appears open to argument whether judicial review would lie against Jockey Club disciplinary proceedings in future.

(8)    *Professional and disciplinary bodies*

Professional bodies such as the Law Society, although private (the Law Society is a company limited by guarantee), have statutory licensing and disciplinary powers. They are clearly subject to judicial review when exercising those powers. See the following examples:

- *Brook v Law Society of Hong Kong* [1997]–[1998] 1 HKCFAR 228 – admission of foreign lawyer as solicitor
- *Sze Hei Fa Helena v Chinese Medicine Practitioners Board* CACV 236/2003 (Le Pichon, Cheung & Yuen JJA; 07.09.2004) – registration of Chinese medicine practitioner
- *Chan Po Fun Peter v Hong Kong Society of Accountants* [2002] 2 HKC 250 – disciplinary proceedings against professional accountant
- *Tse Wai Chun Paul v Solicitors Disciplinary Tribunal* [2002] 4 HKC 1 (CA); FAMV 46/2002 – disciplinary proceedings against solicitor
- *Re A Committee of Inquiry ex p A Barrister* [1990] 1 HKLR 216 (CA) – dis ciplinary proceedings against barrister
- *Preliminary Investigation Committee of the Dental Council of Hong Kong v Tomlin* [1996] 1 HKC 714 (CA) – disciplinary proceedings against a dentist
- *Chow Siu Shek David v Medical Council of Hong Kong* [2002] 2 HKC 235 – registration of a medical practitioner

Note that in many instances there is a statutory right of appeal against a disciplinary decision by a professional body. As discussed below, remedies such as an appeal should, where available and suitable, be pursued before seeking judicial review.

**[53.1.6]    Judicial review of decisions reached in stages or later reconsidered**

Where a decision is reached in stages, it is not appropriate to seek judicial review until the complete decision has been made on the merits. This is so even though the grounds of objection arise earlier. See *Cheng Kai Man William v Panel on Take-overs and Mergers & Anor (No 1)* [1994] 1 HKC 390 where leave to apply for judicial review was sought of a decision which had been made in a piecemeal fashion. The grounds of complaint against the decision (bias) had been raised earlier but not been pursued. The respondent objected that the applicant sought leave to apply for judicial review more than three months after the grounds first arose. Kaplan J held, at 395F–H, that the three-month period did not begin to run until the date of the complete decision. Kaplan J stated:

> It would be strange if [the applicant] had been obliged to seek leave to apply for judicial review before any decision adverse to him, on the merits, had been made.

Where a public authority reconsiders an earlier decision the subsequent decision may supersede and replace the earlier decision and become the decision of which review should be sought: see *Hong Kong and China Gas Co Ltd v Director of Lands* [1997] 3 HKC 520, at 524A–D, per Keith J. The learned judge said:

> I have been persuaded that it is appropriate for the company to be challenging the later decision. Although the later decision had the effect of confirming the earlier decision, it can properly be said to have superseded and replaced it. That is because it followed a reconsideration of the issue … If a public officer decides to reconsider an earlier decision made by him or his subordinate, the decision made following that reconsideration is amenable to judicial review even if it amounts to the confirmation of the earlier decision.

In his decision the learned judge cited *McCarthy & Stone (Developments) Ltd v Richmond-upon-Thames LBC* [1992] 2 AC 48. His decision was later affirmed on appeal to the Court of Appeal.

In *Hussain v The Registrar of Births and Deaths* CACV 77/2000 (Rogers Ag CJHC, Leong & Keith JJA; 13.10.2000) (reversed on other grounds: see (2001) 4 HKCFAR 429) the Court of Appeal had before it an application for judicial review of a decision to refuse correction of birth certificates issued some 15 years earlier. The respondent objected that the application was long out of time because the real decisions being challenged were the ones taken 15 years earlier. This argument was rejected by the Court of Appeal. Keith JA, at 45F–M (dissenting in result, but concurring on this point), referred to his decision in *Hong Kong and China Gas Co Ltd v Director of Lands* (above) and said:

> Although the decision made in 1999 had the effect of confirming the earlier decisions made in 1984 and 1985, the decision made in 1999 can properly be said to have superseded and replaced them. That is because the decision made in 1999 followed a reconsideration of the issue by the [respondent].

**[53.1.7]**  **Review of decisions of the executive branch of government**

Judicial review lies against the executive branch of government, including the Chief Executive of the HKSAR, the principal officials and the heads of government departments and bureaux. Article 35(2) of the Basic Law provides that Hong Kong residents have 'the right to institute legal proceedings in the courts against the acts of the executive authorities and their personnel'. That may have the effect of rendering unconstitutional the recognised limitations on judicial review of the executive authorities. Those limitations include the following:

(1)    *Restriction on granting injunction* – section 16 of the Crown Proceedings Ordinance (Cap 300) (which retains its colonial title pending revision in the on-going adaptation of laws exercise) restricts the court's power to grant an injunction against the government and its servants. In *Wong Tsz Jam v Commissioner of Police* [2008] 5 HKLRD 164 (CA) it was held that section 16 is based on the premise that declaratory relief is adequate and that it did not infringe the principle of equality before the law. In Hogg & Monahan, *Liability of the Crown,* (3rd ed, 2000) p 32-33 it is argued that the section does not prohibit injunctions against government servants in respect of unauthorised acts.

(2)    *Restriction on review of CE-in-Council* – section 64(3) of the Interpretation and General Clauses Ordinance (Cap 1) purports to oust judicial review of the Chief Executive-in-Council in respect of any decision on an appeal or objection provided for by statute. However the section is ineffective to oust review on questions going to jurisdiction, including compliance with the rules of natural justice: *Bahadur v Director of Immigration & Anor* [2001] 3 HKLRD 225, expressly applying to section 64(3) the principles laid down in *Anisminic v Foreign Compensation Commission* [1969] 2 AC 147 (HL). (Note that in *Shawnavasudeen Musahuddeen v Director of Immigration* HCAL 1727/2000 (A Cheung J; 15.11.2002) the government indicated it did not accept *Bahadur* as authoritative on this point, given that the decision was on an interlocutory application, and that it would, at a suitable time seek to re-argue the issue. However, as of late 2007 it does not appear that this has happened.)  See also *Ng Chun-kwan v CIR* [1976] HKLR 94, 102; *Re Tse Cho* [1979] HKLR 339, 344; *R v Director of Immigration & Anor ex p Do Giau & Ors* [1992] 1 HKLR 287.

(3)    *Prerogative powers* – under the common law, the executive branch of government has prerogative powers, some of which are not subject to judicial review.

Prerogative powers include governmental functions such as defence and foreign affairs and the prerogative of mercy. Cases from other common law jurisdictions often refer to the prerogative with the prefix 'royal'. However, since such powers derive from the common law, which applies in Hong Kong under the Basic Law, they should continue to have application in this jurisdiction. Note, however that prerogative powers must give way to statute (*AG v DeKeyser's Royal Hotel* [1920] AC 508) including the Basic Law. In *Ch'ng Poh v CE* HCAL 182/2002 (Hartmann J; 03.12.2003) it was said that the Basic Law, 'while giving the Chief Executive certain prerogative powers, does not seek to place him above the law; his powers are defined by and therefore constrained by the Basic Law'. It may be argued that the Chinese sovereign should have the right to exercise common law prerogative powers in regard to defence and foreign affairs in connection with the HKSAR, which are reserved to it under the Basic Law, whereas the local administration should be entitled to exercise those within its sphere of competence. Such a division of the right to exercise prerogative powers was long ago recognised in respect of Canada: see *Liquidators of the Maritime Bank of Canada v Receiver-General of New Brunswick* [1892] AC 437 (PC).

It was once thought that prerogative powers and the exercise thereof were never justiciable in a court of law. The court's power was limited to identifying the existence and extent of a prerogative power. Now it is recognised that justiciability depends not on the source, but the nature of the power; and that if the exercise of power affects the rights of the citizen it will not be non-justiciable solely because the power derives from the prerogative: *CCSU v Minister for the Civil Service* [1985] 1 AC 374. The effect of that decision and subsequent cases concerning judicial review of the prerogative is discussed in a comprehensive fashion in *Black v Chrétien & Anor* (2001) 199 DLR (4th) 228 (Ontario Court of Appeal).

**[53.1.8]     Duty to exhaust other remedies before applying for judicial review**
Where other avenues of redress (such as an appeal) lie against the decision complained of, those should normally be pursued before applying for judicial review: *Stock Exchange of Hong Kong Ltd v Onshine Securities Ltd* [1994] 1 HKC 319 (CA). The reason for this rule is explained in *R v IRC ex p Preston* [1985] AC 835, 852 (quoted with approval in *Chow Shun Chiu v HKSAR* [2002] 1 HKC 30):

> a remedy by way of judicial review is not to be made available where an alternative remedy exists ... Judicial review is a collateral challenge: it is not an appeal. Where Parliament has provided by statute appeal procedures ... it will only be very rarely that the courts will allow the collateral process of judicial review to be used to attack an appealable decision.

In *Stock Exchange of Hong Kong Ltd v New World Development Co Ltd & Ors* [2006] 2 HKC 533 the Court of Final Appeal overturned decisions below which allowed a judicial review to proceed in advance of an internal disciplinary enquiry. The CFA held that the judicial review was premature.

In *Chow Kwong Fai Edward v Inland Revenue Board of Review* [2004] 3 HKC 216 it was held that a challenge to a decision of the Inland Revenue Board of Review should have been brought by way of judicial review rather than by way of case stated under the Inland Revenue Ordinance (Cap 112). The taxpayer's grievance boiled down to irrationality and procedural impropriety which were matters most appropriately investigated on an application for judicial review. Nevertheless the court allowed the application under the case stated procedure to go ahead.

Where an administrative appeal lies to the Chief Executive, section 64(3) of the Interpretation and General Clauses Ordinance (Cap 1) provides that judicial review may instead, or in addition, be sought. See *PCCW Media Ltd v Broadcasting Authority & Anor* HCAL 97/2005 (Reyes J; 01.12.2005), citing *Bahadur v Director of Immigration* [2001] 3 HKLRD 225, 233F–H.

In the Malaysian case of *QRS Brands Bhd v Suruhanjaya Sekuriti & Anor* [2006] 3 MLJ 164 (CA) it was held that the availability of an alternative remedy is only relevant to the merits of the substantive application and should not be dealt with at the leave stage.

**[53.1.9]     Residual jurisdiction to allow judicial review where applicant could
            have appealed**
However, the court retains a jurisdiction to grant relief by way of judicial review, in exceptional circumstances, even though the applicant could have appealed. See *Au Wing Lun, William v The Solicitors Disciplinary Tribunal & The Law Society of*

*Hong Kong* (CACV 4154/2001). There, the majority of the Court of Appeal (Rogers VP and Le Pichon JA), with Yuen JA dissenting on this point, granted relief by way of judicial review although the applicant could have availed himself of an appeal. Le Pichon JA held that there were 'exceptional circumstances' to grant judicial review in the particular case, citing *R v Inland Revenue Commissioners ex p Preston* [1985] AC 835 and *Leech v Deputy Governor of Parkhurst Prison* [1988] 1 AC 533. Rogers VP said that the decision subject to review was 'not only so clearly wrong but so manifestly unjust that it cannot be allowed to stand'.

### [53.1.10]   Judicial review of criminal proceedings

It is not appropriate to apply for judicial review of criminal proceedings where an adequate remedy such as an appeal lies within the criminal process: *Jetex HVAC Equipments Ltd v Commissioner for Labour* [1994] 3 HKC 42, 47; *Secretary for Justice v Lee Wai Man* [1999] 1 HKLRD 572; *Chow Shun Chiu v HKSAR* [2001] 1 HKC 30. Nor is it appropriate to interrupt criminal proceedings by seeking review on points of law which arise in the course of the proceedings: *Mo Yuk Ping v Secretary for Justice* [2005] 3 HKC 476, 483C–E (CA); *Ma Zhujiang v Secretary for Justice* HCAL 129/2005 (Chu J; 31.10.2005). This is so even where the review arises from a jurisdictional point: *Tse So So v Secretary for Jus tice* HCAL 160/2005 (Lam J; 19.12.2005). The exercise of prosecutorial discretion on questions such as whether to proceed with a public prosecution will not normally be reviewable, though there is inherent power to prevent abuse of process: *Keung Siu Wah v AG* [1990] 2 HKLR 238 (CA); *Matalulu v DPP* [2003] 2 HKC 457 (FijiSC); *Kwan Sun Chu Pearl v Department of Justice* [2005] 3 HKC 441 (CFI) (appeal to the Court of Appeal dismissed — [2006] 3 HKC 207); *RV v Director of Immigration & Anor* HCAL 2/2008 (Hartmann J; 10.03.2008).

However there are circumstances in which judicial review is appropriate in the criminal context. For example:

* *Nattrass v AG* [1996] 1 HKC 480 – the defendant in a criminal case successfully applied for judicial review of the trial judge's decision to recuse himself.
* *Re Cheng Kai Nam Gary* [2002] 1 HKC 41 – the court heard a pre-trial application for judicial review of the district court's refusal to list a criminal case before a Chinese-speaking judge. Leave to apply was refused on the merits.
* *Secretary for Justice v Cheung Chung Chit* [2003] 4 HKC 49 – judicial review of a judge's order of a permanent stay of criminal proceedings was considered appropriate because there was no statutory right of appeal. See also *Secretary for Justice v Shum Chiu* HCAL 101/2005 (Hartmann J; 22.12.2005).
* *Dairy Farm Co Ltd v Director of Food & Environmental Hygiene* HCAL 59/2004 (Chu J; 18.08.2004); [2005] 3 HKC 1 (CA) – judicial review of a magistrate's refusal to order a permanent stay was heard on an expedited basis during an adjournment of the trial.
* *Yeung Chun Pong & Ors v Secretary for Justice* [2005] 3 HKC 447 –judicial review of a magistrate's decision that there was no jurisdiction to consider an *autrefois* plea at the committal stage.
* *Inglis v Loh Lai Kuen Eda* [2005] 3 HKC 115 – judicial review of a

magis trate's refusal to allow counsel to enter a plea of guilty on behalf of the defendant.

Such circumstances will be comparatively rare. In *Ng Pak Min v HKSAR* HCAL 70/ 1999 (Stock J; 27.07.1999) it was said that judicial review is an 'avenue of lastresort', and that only in 'the most exceptional circumstances' would a court stop criminal proceedings *in limine.* In *Yeung Chun Pong v SJ (No 2)* [2006] 3 HKC 31, 34F-G the Court of Appeal reminded practitioners of the 'strong presumption against entertaining judicial review applications that interrupt criminal proceedings'. See also *Yeung Chun Pong v SJ (No 4)* [2008] 2 HKC 46 (CA) (para 62 *et seq*).

The burden on the applicant in seeking leave to apply for judicial review may be heavier when the impugned decision arises in the criminal process. In *Re Wong Tung Kin* [1989] 1 HKLR 93 Sears J held that the court should interfere in the criminal process only where the impugned decision is 'outrageous'. However in *Lee Wai Man* (above) the court doubted that Sears J had intended to suggest that a heavier burden applies.

### [53.1.11]   Constitutional and administrative law list

Applications for judicial review must be brought on the court's Constitutional and Administrative Law List, which also applies to applications for habeas corpus, election petitions, appeals from the Obscene Articles Tribunal and other cases involving the Basic Law or Bill of Rights if transferred to the list by a judge. The list was established by practice direction 26.1, the text of which may be viewed free-of-charge on the judiciary website www.judiciary.gov.hk or that of the Hong Kong Legal Information Institute www.hklii.org.

### [53.1.12]   Judicial review practice direction

Practice direction SL3 sets out various matters of procedure to be followed on applications which come within the Constitutional and Administrative Law List. Part 1 of the practice direction deals with applications for judicial review. The practice direction dates from 1998 and has since been amended, most recently when the civil justice reforms came into force in 2009. The up-to-date text of the practice direction may be downloaded from the judiciary website www.judiciary.gov.hk or that of the Hong Kong Legal Information Institute www.hklii.org, both of which are accessible to the general public free-of-charge.

**2.      Joinder of claims for relief** (O. 53 r. 2)

**On an application for judicial review any relief mentioned in rule 1(1) or (2) may be claimed as an alternative or in addition to any other relief so mentioned if it arises out of or relates to or is connected with the same matter.**

**3.      Grant of leave to apply for judicial review** (O. 53 r. 3)

**(1)    No application for judicial review shall be made unless the leave of the Court has been obtained in accordance with this rule.**

**(2)    An application for leave must be made ex parte by filing in the Registry—**

  **(a)    a notice in Form No. 86 in Appendix A containing a statement of —**

  **(i)    the name and description of the applicant;**

　　　　(ii)　　**the name and description of the respondent;**

　　　　(iii)　**the relief sought and the grounds on which it is sought;**

　　　　(iv)　**the name and description of all interested parties (if any) known to the applicant;**

　　　　(v)　　**the name and address of the applicant's solicitors (if any); and**

　　　　(vi)　**if no solicitor acts for the applicant, the applicant's address for service; and**

　　(b)　　**an affidavit verifying the facts relied on. (L.N. 152 of 2008)**

　　**(3)　The judge may determine the application for leave without a hearing, unless a hearing is requested in the notice of application, and need not sit in open court; and in any case the Registrar shall serve a copy of the judge's order on the applicant. (L.N. 152 of 2008)**

**(HK)　(4)　Where an application for leave is refused by a judge or is granted on terms, the applicant may appeal against the judge's order to the Court of Appeal within 14 days after such order. (L.N. 152 of 2008)**

　　**(6)　Without prejudice to its powers conferred by Order 20 rule 8, the Court hearing an application for leave may allow the applicant's statement to be amended, whether by specifying different or additional grounds or relief or otherwise, on such terms, if any, as the Court thinks fit.**

　　**(7)　The Court shall not grant leave unless it considers that the applicant has a sufficient interest in the matter to which the application relates.**

　　**(8)　Where leave is sought to apply for an order of certiorari to remove for the purpose of its being quashed any judgment, order, conviction or other proceeding which is subject to appeal and a time is limited for the bringing of the appeal, the Court may adjourn the application for leave until the appeal is determined or the time for appealing has expired.**

　　**(9)　If the Court grants leave it may impose such terms as to costs and as to giving security as it thinks fit.**

　　**(10)　Where leave to apply for judicial review is granted, then—**

　　(a)　　**if the relief sought is an order of prohibition or certiorari and the Court so directs, the grant shall operate as a stay of the proceedings to which the application relates until the determination of the application or until the Court otherwise orders;**

　　(b)　　**if any other relief is sought, the Court may at any time grant in the proceedings such interim relief as could be granted in an action begun by writ.**

---

## NOTES

### [53.3.1]　The leave requirement

Section 21K(3) of the High Court Ordinance provides that an application for judicial review requires prior leave of the court. Leave is to be obtained in accordance with the rules of court. The leave requirement is repeated in Order 53 rule 3(1), which goes on to set out the procedures to be followed.

　　The leave requirement, coupled with the affidavit to verify the facts relied on (as required by Order 53 rule 3(2)(b)) serves the 'public interest in good administration' by operating as a 'safeguard against groundless or unmeritorious claims': *O'Reilly v Mackman* [1983] 2 AC 238, 280G-281B. In successive editions of the English Supreme Court Practice slightly stronger language was used. It was said that the purpose of the leave requirement was to 'eliminate frivolous, vexatious or hopeless applications for judicial review without the need for a substantive *inter partes* judicial review hearing'. In *Re Keung Siu Wah* HCMP 659/1989 (Mayo J; 03.07.1989) (appeal dismissed – see [1990] 2 HKLR 238) it was noted that no authority was cited for this more strongly worded proposition. In *Chan Po Fun Peter v Cheung CW Winnie & Anor* [2007] 5 HKC 145 (CFA) (para 14) the Chief Justice made no mention of the stronger language, instead describing the leave requirement as 'an important filter' the purpose of which is 'to prevent public authorities from being unduly vexed with unarguable challenges'.

### [53.3.2] Form of application for leave

Order 53 rule 3(2) provides that an application for leave to apply for judicial review should be made by notice in form 86 in appendix A to these rules. If leave is granted it will subsequently be necessary to issue and serve an originating summons in form 86A – see rule 5. These forms date from the civil justice reforms which took effect in April 2009. The previous form 86A was the notice of application for leave, and if leave was granted it was necessary to issue a notice of motion. The differences between the previous forms and those replacing them are largely technical rather than substantive. The notice of application for leave must state, *inter alia*, the relief sought and the grounds upon which it is sought. In *Lau Kong Yung (an infant) v Director of Immigration* [1999] 4 HKC 731 (CFA) Litton PJ described the requirements of Order 53 rule 3(2)(a) as 'mandatory' (at 773C). The learned judge went on to emphasise that the grounds should be stated clearly and succinctly. He said, at 773G–H:

> Grounds for quashing the exercise of administrative power by the court if well-founded should be capable of being stated clearly and succinctly, in a few numbered paragraphs. I would emphasise the word *few*.

The facts relied on in the application must be verified by affidavit: rule 3(2)(b). The affidavit requirement makes the law of perjury applicable at the leave stage and thus discourages groundless claims: *O'Reilly v Mackman* [1983] 2 AC 238, 280G.

### [53.3.3] Test on application for leave

The court now applies the 'arguability test' in considering whether to grant leave to apply for judicial review. The criterion is 'reasonable arguability'. A reasonably arguable case 'is one which enjoys realistic prospects of success'. See *Chan Po Fun Peter v Cheung CW Winnie & Anor* [2007] 5 HKC 145 (CFA) (para 15).

The arguability test derives from *R v Legal Aid Board ex p Hughes* (1992) 24 HLR 698, 702-3. Its adoption in Hong Kong in late 2007 marked a tightening-up of the burden on an applicant for leave to apply for judicial review. As Li CJ said in *Chan Po Fun* (above) (at para 13), the arguability test 'undoubtedly imposes a higher threshold', as compared to the 'potential arguability test' which had previously been applied in Hong Kong. The previous test had been approved by the Court of Appeal in *Ho Ming Sai v Director of Immigration* [1994] 1 HKLR 21. It derived from *IRC v National Federation of Self-Employed and Small Businesses Ltd* [1982] AC 617, 664 and merely required the applicant 'to satisfy the court that on *further* consideration at a *subsequent* hearing an arguable case *might* be demonstrated': *Chan Po Fun* (above, at para 12), and see *Vo Thi Do v Director of Immigration* (1996) 7 HKPLR 136 (CA).

The shift which *Chan Po Fun* (above) represents was not unexpected. In June 2000 it had been suggested that the test be re-examined: *Wong Chung Ki & Anor v Chief Executive & Anor* [2003] 1 HKC 404 (CA), 414B-C. And in *Shem Yin Fun v Director of Legal Aid & Anor* [2003] 1 HKC 568, 573C-574D Chu J had already indicated that it was appropriate to adopt a more flexible approach in certain circumstances.

*Chan Po Fun* (above) clearly overrules *Ho Ming Sai* (above) and the other earlier Hong Kong authorities. The result is that applications for leave to apply for judicial review now require closer scrutiny by the Court of First Instance and may more frequently be the subject of *inter partes* oral hearings rather than being disposed of *ex parte* on the papers. In the words of the Chief Justice in *Chan Po Fun* (at para 17):

> With the discarding of the potential arguability test and the adoption of the arguability test, more time may need to be spent by the judge in dealing with leave applications than previously. 'A quick perusal' of the material may not be sufficient in reaching a decision whether the arguability test is satisfied. In appropriate cases, the judge may require an oral hearing, with notice to the respondent in suitable cases. [Ed note – 'quick perusal' is the term used in the *IRC v National Federation of Self-Employed* case (above)].

The judgment in *Chan Po Fun* was largely based on consideration of the previous authorities. The Chief Justice noted that there had been a similar shift in the United Kingdom, and suggested that relevant authorities may not have been considered in *Ho Ming Sai*. The decision was clearly influenced by policy considerations as well. At para 14 the Chief Justice balanced the right of access to the courts with the public interest in good public administration. Regard might also be had to the Chief Justice's speech at the ceremonial opening of the legal year 2006 referring to the number of judicial review applications having 'grown tremendously', a 'flood' of right of abode applications in 2000 and 2001 and the need for the public to understand the limitations on the court's role. The text of the speech can be viewed on the judiciary's website.

As a result of the CFA's decision in *Chan Po Fun*, it is now clear that at the leave stage the court will no longer confine itself to weeding out hopeless cases, but should consider the merits more closely to determine whether the application has 'realistic prospects of success'. In *Yeung Chung Pong & Ors v SJ (No 4)* [2008] 2 HKC 46 (CA) it was said that the new test will 'serve as a more realistic filter' (para 17).

## [53.3.4]    Hearing of the application for leave

An application for leave will be dealt with on the papers, without a hearing, unless a hearing is requested in the Notice of Application or by the judge (rule 3(3)) or unless the intended respondent intervenes and seeks an inter partes hearing on the question of leave.

By para 1.6 of the Constitutional and Administrative Law List practice direction (see commentary under Order 53 rule 1), the hearing of an application for leave to apply for judicial review will take place in open court unless the judge hearing the application orders otherwise. In *Sit Ka Yin Priscilla v Equal Opportunities Commission* [1998] 1 HKC 278 the applicant sought to have the application for leave to be heard in chambers. The application was refused by Keith J since the applicant's main reason was to avoid embarrassment. The judge held that there was a particular interest in applications for judicial review to be held in public 'because they relate to decisions made in the public field, and the public has a legitimate interest to be informed about them'.

It might be said that a more principled approach would be for the application for leave to proceed *ex parte*, and then if leave be granted for the Secretary for Justice to consider whether to apply to have that leave set aside (as to which, see below).

The Court of Appeal has approved this 'more principled approach' in *Thoong Coc Duong v Director of Immigration* (1996) 7 HKPLR 145, CA. The court said that, where leave has been granted *ex parte*, application to set aside the order should be made to the same judge for review of his decision or to a different High Court judge.

**[53.3.5]    Ex parte application**
An application for leave to apply for judicial review 'must be made *ex parte*' (rule 3(2)). However, intended respondents who anticipate applications for judicial review sometimes request, and are given, an opportunity to be heard at the leave stage. In other cases the court itself may invite an intended respondent to make submissions at the leave stage. In *Re Osman* [1988] 2 HKLR 378, at 387C, the Court of Appeal held that it was 'perfectly proper' for a judge to permit the intended respondent to be heard on an application for leave. The result is often a lengthy hearing on the question of leave which goes well into the merits of the application. This is in principle wrong, as the leave application is only intended to be a low-threshold filtering mechanism to ensure that there are matters which require further investigation. However, in some cases it may save the court time and costs by filtering out applications for judicial review which would otherwise proceed to even lengthier substantive hearings.

**[53.3.6]    Order 53 rule 3(7) – applicant must have 'standing'**
Section 21K(3) of the High Court Ordinance prohibits the court from granting leave to apply for judicial review unless it 'considers that the applicant has a sufficient interest in the matter to which the application relates'. This stipulation is repeated in Order 53 rule 3(7). 'Sufficient interest' in this context is usually referred to as 'standing' or '*locus standi*'. The question of *locus standi* relates to the court's jurisdiction, not discretion: *Anderson Asphalt Ltd v Town Planning Board* [2006] 4 HKC 50 (appeal allowed on other grounds – [2007] 2 HKC 579). Standing does not depend on nationality: *Dayang Kayang Dawila v Mahkamah Anak Negeri* [2005] 5 MLJ 603. Provided the 'sufficient interest' test is met, there is no barrier to a non-citizen or non-resident applying for judicial review, though the constitutional guarantee under article 35(2) of the Basic Law is limited to residents.

The purpose of the standing requirement is to enable the court 'to prevent abuse by busybodies, cranks or other mischief-makers': *Gouriet v Union of Post Office Workers* [1978] AC 435, quoted with approval in *Re Au Shui-yuen Alick* [1991] 2 HKLR 79, 101B.

The court's approach to issues of standing has become more relaxed. 'There is now a clearly discernible trend away from the restrictive and highly technical approach to *locus standi*: *Re a Marine Court Investigation* [1987] HKLR 549, 560A–

B quoting from de Smith, Judicial Review of Administrative Action (4ᵗʰ).

*IRC v National Federation of Self-Employed and Small Businesses Ltd* [1982] AC 617 is regarded as the leading authority on *locus standi*. See *Re Au Shui-yuen Alick* [1991] 2 HKLR 79, 98I. It has been applied in Hong Kong since *Re an appli cation by Hong Kong Orient Shipping Co Ltd SA & Ors* [1981] HKC 245. In *IRC*, Lord Diplock said at 644:

> It would, in my view, be a grave lacuna in our system of public law if a pressure group, like the federation, or even a single public spirited taxpayer, were prevented by outdated technical rules of *locus standi* from bringing the matter to the attention of the court to vindicate the rule of law and get the unlawful conduct stopped.

The same passage was quoted with approval in *Re Medical Defence Union Ltd* HCMP 1950/1989 (Barnett J; 15.02.1990) (appeal to the Court of Appeal allowed in part on other grounds – see [1991] 1 HKLR 429). 'In summary, it can be said that today the court ought not to decline jurisdiction to hear an application for judicial review on the ground of lack of standing to any responsible person or group seeking, on reasonable grounds, to challenge the validity of governmental action': *AECS v Secretary for the Civil Service & Anor* CACV 260/1995 (Bokhary, Mortimer & Ching JJA; 22.11.1996), quoting deSmith (5ᵗʰ) p 122 as an accurate statement of the law.

Examples of cases where the court has considered whether the applicant had sufficient *locus standi* include the following:

- *Anderson Asphalt Ltd v Town Planning Board* [2007] 2 HKC 579 – an asphalt producer had standing to challenge a decision to grant temporary planning permission to enable a competitor to produce asphalt on agricultural land.

- *Leung TC William Roy v Secretary for Justice* [2005] 3 HKC 77, 98C (CFI); [2006] 4 HKLRD 211 (CA) – a homosexual man had sufficient interest to challenge the constitutionality of legislation criminalising certain types of homosexual behaviour, despite the fact he had not been charged with any offence.

- *Re Chan Yu Nam & Anor* [2006] 1 HKC 392 – taxi drivers were refused leave to apply for judicial review of an increase in tolls for passage through a tunnel regulated by Ordinance. The increase had been awarded in arbitration proceedings to which the drivers were not a party.

- *Keane v DLA* CACV 49/2000 (Godfrey VP, Rogers & Keith JJA; 15.06.2000) - a barrister had standing to challenge a decision of the Director of Legal Aid not to assign him as counsel for an aided person.

- *Chu Woan-Chyi Theresa & Ors v Director of Immigration* CACV 331/2003 (Rogers VP & Le Pichon JA; 05.07.2004) – the chairman of an organisation which held a conference had sufficient standing to join as an applicant in judicial review proceedings by non-residents who were denied permission to enter Hong Kong to attend the conference. Leave to appeal to the Court of Final Appeal was refused both by the Court of Appeal (judgment dated 07.09.2004) and by the CFA itself: FAMV 17/2004 (Li CJ; Bokhary PJ & Ribeiro PJ; 17.12.2004).

- *Re a Marine Court Investigation* [1987] HKLR 549, 560A-B – expert wit nesses criticised in a Marine Court investigation had standing to seek judicial review of the findings although they were not parties to the Marine Court proceedings.

- *Cheung Ernest v Christie (Permanent Magistrate)* [1983] 2 HKC 562 – a court prosecutor, as a representative of the Attorney General who had control of prosecutions (now Secretary for Justice), had sufficient interest to apply for judicial review of a decision of a magistrate.
- *Re Medical Defence Union & Bascombe* [1991] 1 HKLR 429, 443E-F (CA) – the court was not prepared to grant a declaration as to the conduct of an inquest on the application of medical insurers and a doctor who had no complaint about the result.
- *Re Au Shui-yuen Alick* [1991] 2 HKLR 79, 96H *et seq* – a person facing prosecution by the ICAC did not have standing to challenge the fact a witness against him was being detained by the ICAC rather than in a prison.
- *Re Anthony Chi Hing Chua* CACV 137 & 150/1991 (Fuad VP, Clough & Penlington JJA; 07.01.1992) – a pharmacist and self-styled 'whistleblower' had no standing to apply for judicial review to compel the re-opening of an inquest which did not concern him.
- *AECS v Chief Executive* [1998] 2 HKC 138 – a civil servants' association had standing to challenge the legality of an executive order governing the public service.

A decision to grant leave to apply for judicial review is not conclusive on the question of standing. The issue may be revisited at the substantive hearing in light of all the evidence. See *AECS & Ors v Secretary for the Civil Service* HCMP 3037/1994 (Keith J; 31.10.1995), para 37.

### [53.3.7]    Conditional leave
The court has express power under Order 53 rule 3(9) to impose conditions as to costs or security when it grants leave to apply for judicial review. It is rare for this power to be exercised.

In *AECS & Ors v Secretary for the Civil Service* HCMP 3037/1994 (Keith J; 31.10.1995) para 19(i), the court granted leave subject to the condition that further affidavit evidence be filed within a fixed time. One of the applicants failed to comply with the condition and the court later found that his leave had lapsed. See the subsequent judgment in those proceedings, dated 31.10.1995.

In *Fung Chi Man & Ors v Director of Immigration* CACV 220/2010 (Stock VP & Hartmann JA; 19.01.2011) the court made an 'observation' on granting leave that no argument inconsistent with a judgment which had earlier been handed down should be run. On appeal it was held that the observation was a case management direction which might be reviewed if there were a change of circumstances such as an amendment. It was not part of the order itself, and was not a term imposed on the grant of leave. It followed that no appeal lay under Order 53 rule 3(4).

### [53.3.8]    Order 53 rule 3(10) – Stay of underlying proceedings; interim relief; bail; interim injunction
If the court so directs, a grant of leave to apply for prohibition or certiorari by way of judicial review will operate as a stay of the proceedings to which it relates: rule 3(10)(a). As an example, see *Egan v ICAC* [1991] HKC 119, 125H (CA) where the

court directed a stay of criminal proceedings pending a judicial review. The power to make such a direction is discretionary and may be exercised whenever it is appropriate to do so: *Anglo Starlite Insurance Co Ltd v The Insurance Authority* [1992] 2 HKLR 31, 36. In *Re University of Hong Kong* HCMP 2332/1990 (Godfrey J; 03.10.1990) the court considered the degree of hardship which would be suffered by each side and decided in favour of directing a stay. In *Super Lion Enterprises Ltd v Commissioner of Rating & Valuation* [2006] 1 HKLRD 239 the court used as a starting point the guidelines for grant of an interlocutory injunction.

The power is to grant a stay of the proceedings to which the application for judicial review relates. In this context 'proceedings' includes 'any procedure by which a decision challengeable on judicial review is reached and implemented': *R v Licensing Authority, ex p Smith Kline (No 2)* [1990] 1 QB 574, 604E. Thus in *Anglo Starlite* (above) the Hong Kong court found it had jurisdiction to stay the implementation or enforcement of decisions which were challenged in a pending judicial review.

Where other relief is sought by way of judicial review the court may grant interim relief at any stage: rule 3(10)(b). An example of such interim relief would be an interim injunction. This was recognised in *Re M* [1994] 1 AC 377 (HL) where an interim mandatory injunction against a minister of the Crown, pending consideration of an application for leave to apply for judicial review, was upheld. The discretion under rule 3(10)(b) is exercised so as to preserve the *status quo* pending a substantive decision so as to ensure that the applicant, if ultimately successful, will not be denied the benefit of success: *Society for Protection of the Harbour Ltd v Chief Executive in Council & Ors* [2003] 4 HKC 1, 5G-7B.

It will usually be appropriate to give the opposing party an early opportunity to be heard on the application for interim relief such as a stay. In *Super Lion Enterprises* (above) the Court granted a stay *ex parte* at the leave stage, coupled with liberty to the opposing party to apply to set it aside. In other cases the Court will grant *ex parte* leave to apply, and fix an early *inter partes* directions hearing on the question of a stay: *Society for Protection of the Harbour* (above) (para 7). In *Anglo Starlite* (above) the Court appears to have adopted the second approach, and granted an interim stay pending the *inter partes* hearing.

In *Thoong Coc Duong v Director of Immigration* (1996) 7 HKPLR 145 (CA) a stay of a removal order was granted pending judicial review of a decision to refuse permission to remain in Hong Kong.

Where damages are claimed in an application for judicial review the court should have power to make an order for interim payment under Part II of Order 29, but not where the claim to damages is doomed to failure: *Jones v MIB* HCAL 139/2005 (A Cheung J; 12.12.2005).

The court has inherent jurisdiction to grant bail in pending judicial review cases. See *R v Secretary of State ex p Turkoglu* [1988] QB 398 and *R (Sezek) v Secretary of State* [2002] 1 WLR 348, 354A. In *Le Tu Phuong & Anor v Director of Immigration* [1994] 2 HKLR 127, 132 Litton JA (sitting as a single judge of the Court of Appeal) doubted the existence of this jurisdiction in Hong Kong. However in *PV v Director of Immigration* [2004] 3 HKC 637 it was held that the judgment of Litton JA was not binding and the English authority was to be preferred.

Applications for interim relief in judicial review proceedings are normally heard in open court: see paragraph 1.6 of the CALL Practice Direction (above).

### [53.3.9]    Costs of leave application

When a leave application is dealt with in the usual way, that is *ex parte* and on the papers, it is not the usual practice to make an order for costs. The costs of the leave application will, nevertheless, form part of the applicant's costs in the cause should there ultimately be an order for costs in its favour, since the substantive application for leave will be based on the papers filed on the leave application.

Where leave to apply for judicial review is refused after a contested hearing, it will not normally be appropriate for the court to order costs in favour of the putative respondent: *Cheung Wai Mei v Coroner* HCAL 24/2007 (Hartmann J; 09.03.2007) (para 25). There the court made no order as to costs, observing that a contested leave application is *ex parte* in the sense that the respondent remains a putative respondent unless and until leave is granted; further that the putative respondent appeared as a matter of public duty to assist the court. The court said:

> Although there may be occasions when the court, in the exercise of its discretion, considers that an application for leave is so frivolous, so vexatious or motivated for a tactical purpose that indicates bad faith that it should award costs, nothing of that kind can be asserted in the present case.

Likewise in *Hall v SJ* HCAL 5/2006 (Hartmann J; 30.06.2006) the court made no order as to the costs of a contested leave hearing. In *Lo Siu Lan & Anor v HK Housing Authority* CACV 378/2004 (Ma CJHC, Stock & Le Pichon JJA; 01.03.2005) 'no order as to costs' of a rolled-up hearing of the leave application and the substantive judicial review on an urgent basis was upheld by the Court of Appeal. However, in *Sky Wide Development Ltd & Ors v Building Authority* [2009] 1 HKC 450 it was held that there is no 'special rule' in Hong Kong whereby no order as to costs will be the norm. The court held that *Cheung Wai Mei* (above) does not lay down any principle of general application (para 12) and went on to order an unsuccessful applicant to pay the costs of respondents for attending a leave hearing at the invitation of the court.

Other Hong Kong cases in which costs have been ordered against an unsuccessful applicant following a contested hearing at the leave stage include *Re Osman* [1988] 2 HKLR 378, 387C and *Ng Pak Min v HKSAR* HCAL 70/1999 (Stock J; 27.07.1999).

### [53.3.10]    Setting aside leave

Where leave to apply for judicial review has been granted *ex parte* the respondent may apply at an *inter partes* hearing for that leave to be set aside. Leave may be set aside where the application is doomed to failure as a matter of law (as in *Re Wong Tung Kin* [1989] 1 HKLR 93) or where at the *ex parte* stage the applicant has not made full and frank disclosure.

The principles applicable on an application to set aside leave were summarised by Cheung JA in *To Kin Wah v Tuen Mun District Officer & Ors (No 2)* [2003] 4 HKC 213, 218 (CA) as follows:

> (1)    Applications to set aside may be made on a number of grounds including want of reviewability, the existence of an alternative remedy, want of arguability and material non-disclosure such as the failure to disclose the existence of an ouster clause (*R v Cornwall County Council ex p Huntington* [1992] 3 All ER 566) or not pursuing an appeal when there were no exceptional circumstances making

that course inappropriate (*R v Law Society ex p Kingsley* [1996] COD 59).

(2)    An application to set aside should only be made in exceptional circumstances such as where the respondent can demonstrate that the proceedings are funda mentally misconceived or doomed to fail (*Re Wong Tung Kin* [1989] 1 HKLR 93) or that there has been material non-disclosure. Orders setting aside the grant of leave will be made only in very plain cases (*R v Bromsgrove District Council, ex p Judge* [1992] COD 129). The application should be made, if possible, to the judge who granted leave if he is available.

(3)    Applications to set aside should be made timeously or not at all. *Ng Enterprises Ltd v Urban Council* [1995] 2 HKC 571; *R v Derbyshire County Council, ex p Noble* [1989] COD 285; *R v Secretary of State for the Environment, ex p Upton Brickworks Ltd* [1992] COD 301. The grounds on which the application to set aside are made must be specified with particularity in the application (*R v Lloyd's of London, ex p Briggs* [1992] COD 456). On an application to set aside the court should not permit the application to set aside to be used as a vehicle for rehearsing arguments that should be canvassed at a substantive hearing for that would defeat the purpose of the O 53 procedure which is to enable applications for judicial review to be heard within a short space of time.

As to the circumstances in which the court will set aside leave to apply for judicial review on the ground of material non-disclosure at the *ex parte* stage, see *Kan Hung Chung v Director of Immigration* [2008] 2 HKC 323, and see generally the commentary under Order 32 rule 6.

The respondent should apply to set aside leave rather than lodge an appeal save in 'the most exceptional of circumstances': *Thoong Coc Duong & Ors v Director of Immigration* (1996) 7 HKPLR 145 (CA), per Litton VP at 147A–B. In that case the Court of Appeal dismissed an appeal against an *ex parte* order granting leave in circumstances where the respondent had failed to first apply to the High Court to set aside leave. Litton VP stated (at 146H–I):

> Where a High Court judge has made an ex parte order – and particularly in the circumstances of a case such as this where he did so without even a hearing – such an ex parte order is by definition provisional and is liable therefore to be reviewed either by the judge himself or, if it be necessary, by another High Court judge: if needs be, upon an ex parte application, on a really urgent matter.

Litton VP went on to state (at 147A–B) that insofar as the appeal was against the *ex parte* order granting leave, it verged upon an abuse of process.

Different considerations apply where leave has been granted at an *inter partes* hearing. In *Chan Mei Yee v Director of Immigration (No 2)* [2000] 1 HKC 238 the respondent applied to strike out the notice of motion on the ground that it disclosed no reasonable claim in public law. Leave had been granted at an *inter partes* hearing. Cheung J held that the respondent's application was not appropriate and dismissed it expressly without going into the merits.

**[53.3.11]  Appeal against refusal of leave**
Order 53 rule 3(4) provides that an applicant who is refused leave to apply for judicial review (or granted leave on condition) may appeal to the Court of Appeal within 14 days. Where leave is granted on some of the grounds, but refused on others, an appeal lies against the refusal of leave on those others: *Chan Clarence v Commissioner of*

*Police* FAMV 15/2010 (Bokhary Chan & Ribeiro PJJ; 14.09.2010) (para 2), rejecting the suggestion to the contrary in *Chiu Kin Ho v Commissioner of Police* CACV 374/ 2004 (Cheung JA & Yam J; 02.03.2005). Prior to the civil justice reforms which took effect in 2009 the appeal period was only 10 days. Such an appeal may be brought as of right: the requirement in section 14AA of the High Court Ordinance that leave to appeal be obtained in the case of interlocutory appeals to the Court of Appeal does not apply: see Order 59 rule 21(1)(g). Note that under Order 59 rule 4 the time for appealing begins to run immediately the order is made, rather than from the later date on which it is likely to be drawn up and entered.

No appeal lies against a case management direction that a particular line of argument shall not be run. However, such a direction may be reviewed if there is a change of circumstances such as an amendment. See *Fung Chi Man & Ors v Director of Immigration* CACV 220/2010 (Stock VP & Hartmann JA; 19.01.2011).

The corresponding English rule provides that an application for leave to apply for judicial review which has been rejected may be 'renewed' by means of a hearing in open court. There is no such renewal procedure in Hong Kong and, accordingly, Form 86B has been omitted from the Hong Kong rules.

In *Philip Nicholls* CACV 124/1995 (Nazareth VP, Liu JA & Leong J; 07.07.1995) the absence of a renewal procedure in Hong Kong was noted. It was held that as a result, in Hong Kong, once leave has been refused, the judge is *functus officio*, and the applicant's remedy is to appeal.

Where leave to apply for judicial review has been refused *ex parte*, the appeal may likewise proceed *ex parte*, as in *Terrado v Director of Immigration* CACV 92/ 2006 (Le Pichon JA & Stone J; 03.08.2006).

As to appeals against an order granting or refusing judicial review after a substantive hearing see Order 53 rule 13.

**[53.3.12]    Extension of time to appeal against refusal of leave**
The court's powers to extend time under Order 3 rule 5 and Order 59 rule 15 apply to an appeal against refusal of leave to apply for judicial review. In *Po Fun Chan Peter v Cheung* HCAL 162/2005 (Chu J; 06.03.2006) it was observed that in exercising its discretion to extend time the court will have regard to the reasons for the delay, prejudice to the opposing party and the merit or prospects of the intended appeal.

**4.      Delay in applying for relief** (O. 53 r. 4)
   **(1)    An application for leave to apply for judicial review shall be made promptly and in any event within three months from the date when grounds for the application first arose unless the Court considers that there is good reason for extending the period within which the application shall be made. (L.N. 356 of 1988)**
   **(2)    Where the relief sought is an order of certiorari in respect of any judgment, order, conviction or other proceeding, the date when grounds for the application first arose shall be taken to be the date of that judgment, order, conviction or proceeding.**
   **(3)    The preceding paragraphs are without prejudice to any statutory provision which has the effect of limiting the time within which an application for judicial review may be made.**

**NOTES**

**[53.4.1]     Time limitation on application for leave**

Section 21K(6) of the High Court Ordinance provides that the court may refuse to grant leave to apply for judicial review, or the relief sought, where there has been 'undue delay'. Order 53 rule 4(1) is more specific, stipulating that applications for leave must be brought promptly and in any event within three months. The primary requirement is promptness, and 'the fact that an application has been made within three months from the date when the grounds for the application first arose does not necessarily mean that it has been made promptly': *R v Stratford-on-Avon DC ex p Jackson* [1985] 1 WLR 1319, 1322–3, quoted with approval in *Re Right Centre Ltd* [1990] 1 HKLR 250, 260B–D. As a result it is possible that 'an applicant who has filed his application for leave within the three months time period will still be judged to be guilty of undue delay': *Law Chun Loy v SJ* HCAL 13/2005 (Hartmann J; 26.10.2006) (para 9).

The three-month period begins to run from the date of the 'complete decision' of which review is sought: *Cheng Kai Man William v Panel on Take-overs and Mergers* [1994] 1 HKC 390, 395G–H. The fact that reasons for a decision are to be given later does not stop time from running: *Commissioner for Television & Entertainment Licensing v Amusement Game Centres Appeal Board* [2004] 2 HKC 476 (CA).

The three-month time limitation was introduced in Hong Kong in 1988 and earlier in England. Older decisions should be considered with care.

**[53.4.2]     Extension of time**

Order 53 rule 4(1) empowers the court to extend the time to apply for leave to seek judicial review if there is 'good reason'. It is recognised that a person who delays application pending the result of a relevant test case may have good reason for an extension of time: *Re Ho Thi Diem* [1994] 2 HKC 708. Likewise, there are cases in which a delay in obtaining legal aid to apply for judicial review is considered good reason to allow an extension of time.

In *Re Chan Yu Nam & Anor* [2006] 1 HKC 392 the applicants sought to excuse delay of one month outside the three month period relying on the time taken to consult lawyers and experts. The court expressed the view that such time 'is an ordinary incident of any litigation and cannot by itself excuse delay'.

**4A.     Service of order granting leave** (O. 53 r. 4A)

(1)     **Where leave to make an application for judicial review is granted, the Court may also give directions as to the management of the case.**

(2)     **The applicant for judicial review shall, within 14 days after the leave was granted, serve the order granting leave and any directions given under paragraph (1) on —**

(a)     **the respondent; and**

(b)     **such interested parties as may be directed by the Court.**

**(L.N. 152 of 2008)**

## NOTES

**[53.4A.1]  Case management directions**
Order 53 rule 4A(1) expressly empowers the court to give case management directions when granting leave to apply for judicial review. It was introduced as part of the civil justice reforms taking effect in April 2009. The power itself is not new, the court having previously given directions of a case management nature by exercise of inherent jurisdiction. It is expected that directions given by the court on granting leave will be noted on form CALL-1 (annexed to the practice direction, above) by which the court makes known its decision on a leave application.

## [53.4A.3]  Service
Order 53 rule 4A(2) provides that the applicant must serve an order granting leave to apply for judicial review, along with any directions given by the court, on the respondent and any other interested parties as directed by the court, within 14 days. See the definition of 'interested party' in rule 1A. See also rule 5(3) which requires that the applicant subsequently serve the originating summons for judicial review on 'all persons directly affected' which may not be the same group as directed by the court under rule 4A(2).

**5.  Mode of applying for judicial review** (O. 53 r. 5)
   **(1) When leave has been granted to make an application for judicial review, the application must be made by originating summons in Form No. 86A in Appendix A to a judge sitting in open court or, if the judge granting leave has so ordered, to a judge in chambers. (L.N. 152 of 2008)**
   **(3)  The originating summons must be served on all persons directly affected and, where it relates to any proceedings in or before a court and the object of the application is either to compel the court or an officer of the court to do any act in relation to the proceedings or to quash them or any order made therein, the originating summons must also be served on the clerk or registrar of the court and, where any objection to the conduct of the judge is to be made, on that judge. (L.N. 152 of 2008)**
   **(4)  Unless the Court granting leave has otherwise directed, there must be at least 10 days between the service of the originating summons and the day named therein for the hearing (L.N. 152 of 2008)**
   **(5)  An originating summons must be issued for hearing within 14 days after the grant of leave. (L.N. 152 of 2008)**
   **(6)  An affidavit giving the names and addresses of, and the places and dates of service on, all persons who have been served with the originating summons must be filed within 7 days of such service and, if any person who ought to be served under this rule has not been served, the affidavit must state that fact and the reason for it; and the affidavit shall be before the Court on the hearing of the originating summons. (L.N. 152 of 2008)**
   **(7)  If on the hearing of the originating summons the Court is of opinion that any person who ought, whether under this rule or otherwise, to have been served has not been served, the Court may adjourn the hearing on**

**such terms (if any) as it may direct in order that the originating summons may be served on that person. (L.N. 152 of 2008)**

---

## NOTES

### [53.5.1]     Mode of applying for judicial review

Order 53 rule 5(1) provides that where leave has been granted to apply for judicial review, the application shall be made by the special form of originating summons prescribed for judicial review proceedings, being form no 86A in appendix A of these rules. This form and form No 86 (the form of application for leave) date from the civil justice reforms which took effect in April 2009. They differ from what they replaced in a largely technical rather than substantive fashion. The main difference is that the substantive application for judicial review is now made by originating summons rather than notice of motion.

In Order 53 rule 5 of the former English Rules of the Supreme Court, separate modes of application were prescribed for judicial review applications in civil and criminal matters. No such distinction is made in Hong Kong, with the result that rule 5(2) is omitted from these rules.

### [53.5.2]     Who is to be served with the originating summons?

Order 53 rule 5(3) provides that the originating summons by which judicial review is sought following a grant of leave to apply must be served 'on all parties directly affected'. That may include the maker of the decision which is the subject of the application for judicial review as well as any other parties who might have an interest in the decision which is challenged. The persons to be served may or may not be the same as those required by rule 4A to be served with the order granting leave. See the commentary under that rule.

*Delegated decisions* – where a decision-maker delegates the task of making a particular decision it is the delegate who should be served and named as a respondent: see *Singh & Ors v Secretary for Security & Anor* (1996) 6 HKPLR 440. In that case judicial review was sought of deportation orders. Although the power to make a deportation order is formally vested in the Chief Executive of the HKSAR, the actual decisions complained of had been made by the Secretary for Security. Keith J held, at 445G–H and 448H–I, that the Secretary had acted pursuant to power deemed to have been delegated to him by virtue of section 63 of the Interpretation and General Clauses Ordinance (Cap 1). In the circumstances it was the Secretary and not the Chief Executive who should have been named as respondent. Leave to amend accordingly was granted under Order 53 rule 6(2).

*Decisions of inferior courts* – Order 53 rule 5(3) provides that where judicial review is sought of a decision of an inferior court the originating summons should be served on the clerk or Registrar of the court. It will not be appropriate to serve the judge or magistrate who made the decision complained of unless, in the words of Order 53 rule 5(3), 'any objection to the conduct of the judge is to be made'. In *Nattrass v Attorney General* [1996] 1 HKC 480 the defendant in a criminal trial in the District Court sought judicial review of the trial judge's decision part way through the trial to stand down from the case. The trial judge's decision was challenged on the basis that it was wrong in law. It was held that because the judicial review challenged only the correctness of the trial judge's decision in law, and did not raise objections to his conduct, the judge was not a person to be served. The originating summons need only have been served on the Registrar of the District Court. In the *Nattrass* case the judge had been served at his own request and he appeared by counsel at the judicial review. The court held that the only avenue by which he might be heard was Order 53 rule 9(1), but leave to appear under that rule was refused on the ground that the judge was not a 'proper person to be heard' on the review.

In *Hospital Authority v A District Judge* [2002] 2 HKC 98 Hartmann J noted at 101E–F that it was 'quite proper' that a district judge had chosen not to be legally represented on an application for judicial review of his decision not to authorise detention under the Mental Health Ordinance (Cap 136). It is not clear whether the patient, or his mother (who had initiated the application to the district judge) were served, but the application proceeded *ex parte*. It is submitted that this is in principle undesirable. It would be more appropriate for the patient's interests to be represented by the Official Solicitor or at least for an *amicus curiae* to be appointed.

**[53.5.3]    Where a party properly served is not a respondent**
In *Tomlin v The Preliminary Investigation Committee of the Dental Council of Hong Kong* [1995] 1 HKC 533, the Court of Appeal held that although a party was properly served under rule 5(3) he should not be named as a respondent in the title of the action where no relief is claimed against him. Mortimer JA (at 537I) disapproved of the commentary at paragraph 53/1–14/39 of the 1995 *Supreme Court Practice* and said (at 538B–C):

> ... there can be no reason, practical or otherwise, for requiring parties to proceedings under review to be made named respondents in the title when no relief of any kind is sought against them. Even if the English cases had said otherwise, for my part, I would not have followed them. There are no rules which regulate the title of applications for judicial review. As a practical guide I would say that parties against whom relief is sought in the proceedings should be named as parties in the title but no other parties should be so named.

**[53.5.4]    Hearing in chambers or open court**
Order 53 rule 5(1) provides that an application for judicial review is normally heard in open court.

Exceptionally, the judge granting leave to apply for judicial review may order that the application proceed in chambers. The circumstances in which such an order would be made must be very rare. The Hong Kong court has been known to do so in cases where the parties reach an agreement as to the form of order which should be made and wish to save costs by avoiding a hearing in open court. The court should then adjourn into open court to make the order.

In *Re the Takeovers and Mergers Panel* [1996] 3 HKC 379, Keith J refused an application for a judicial review to be heard in chambers. The applicants were seeking review of private proceedings which had resulted in a private reprimand. They feared that if the review were to proceed in open court the private nature of the proceedings under review would be lost. The learned judge held that judicial review proceedings in particular should be held in open court unless justice would be denied. Measures could be taken to preserve privacy. For example, directions could be given that the applicants' names not be disclosed.

**5A.    Affidavit evidence (O. 53 r. 5A)**
At the hearing of the application for judicial review, no affidavit may be relied on unless —
          (a)    rule 6(3), (4) or (5), as the case may be, has been complied with as regards the use of affidavits;
          (b)    the affidavit has been served in accordance with any direction of the Court; or
          (c)    the Court grants leave.

                                                            **(L.N. 152 of 2008)**

**NOTES**

**[53.5A.1]   Restrictions on use of affidavit evidence**
Order 53 rule 5A restricts the use of affidavits on an application for judicial review unless certain procedural requirements have been complied with. See generally rule 3(2)(b) which requires an application for leave to apply for judicial review to be supported by an affidavit verifying the facts relied on, rule 6(2) which allows the court to permit further affidavits to be used by the applicant, and rule 6(4) which requires the respondent to file any affidavit evidence within 56 days.

**5B.    Court's powers to hear any person** (O. 53 r. 5B)
          **(1)    Any person may apply for leave to —**
          (a)    file evidence; or
          (b)    make representations at the hearing of the application for judicial review.
          **(2)    An application under paragraph (1) must be made promptly.**
          **(3)    The Court shall not grant leave under paragraph (1) unless the applicant appears to the Court to be a proper person to be heard at the hearing of the application for judicial review.**

                                                            **(L.N. 152 of 2008)**

**NOTES**

**[53.5B.1]   Power to give interveners opportunity to be heard**
Order 53 rule 5B expressly empowers the court to permit anyone to be heard on a judicial review, either by filing evidence or making representations at the hearing, provided the person appears to the court to be a proper person to be heard. This is, in effect, a power to permit interveners to join in judicial review proceedings. Potential interveners may have been alerted to the judicial review application by service of the order granting leave as required by rule 4A. The rule was introduced as part of the civil justice reforms, taking effect in April 2009. Although the rule is new, the power is not, as a similar power previously existed (and continues to exist) in Order 53 rule 9(1).

An intervener is different from an *amicus curiae*. An *amicus* is counsel with a duty to assist the court impartially, whereas an intervener is a party who is free to advocate a particular position. See *Secretary for Justice & Anor v Chan Wah & Ors* (2000) 3 HKCFAR 293.

**6.    Statements and affidavits** (O. 53 r. 6)

(1)    **Copies of the statement in support of an application for leave under rule 3 must be served with the originating summons and, subject to paragraph (2), no grounds shall be relied upon or any relief sought at the hearing except the grounds and relief set out in the statement. (L.N. 152 of 2008)**

(2)    **The Court may on the hearing of the originating summons allow the applicant to amend his statement, whether by specifying different or additional grounds or relief or otherwise, on such terms, if any, as it thinks fit and may allow further affidavits to be used by him. (L.N. 152 of 2008)**

(3)    **Where the applicant intends to ask to be allowed to amend his statement or to use further affidavits, he shall give notice of his intention and of any proposed amendment to every other party.**

(4)    **Any respondent who intends to use an affidavit at the hearing shall file it in the Registry as soon as practicable and in any event, unless the Court otherwise directs, within 56 days after service upon him of the documents required to be served by paragraph (1).**

**(L.N. 404 of 1991)**

(5)    **Each party to the application must supply to every other party copies of every affidavit which he proposes to use at the hearing, including, in the case of the applicant, the affidavit in support of the application for leave under rule 3.**

(6)    **A reference to a party in paragraphs (3) and (5) includes a reference to an interested party on whom the applicant is required under rule 4A(2) to serve the order granting leave for judicial review.  (L.N. 152 of 2008)**

---

NOTES

**[53.6.1]    Rule 6(1) – applicant may not rely on other grounds**

Rule 6(1) prescribes what must be served with the originating summons and goes on to restrict the applicant to the grounds and relief claimed in the statement.  The effect of this restriction is that 'only the grounds included in the application for leave may be argued at the substantive hearing for judicial review': *Ng Ai Kheng Jasmine v Master M Yuen & Anor* HCAL 46/2003 (Chu J; 08.03.2004).  In that case the applicant's attempt to rely on expansions and additions to the original grounds, without obtaining leave, was described as 'improper'.

A party who wishes to expand the scope of his judicial review should apply for leave under rule 6(2).

**[53.6.2]    Rule 6(2) – amendment**

Rule 6(2) gives the court power to permit an applicant to amend its statement in support of an application for judicial review (meaning the statement in form 86 filed pursuant to rule 3(2) in support of the application for leave to apply for judicial review). Prior notice to the other parties is required by rule 6(3). It should be noted that rule 6(2) contemplates the amendment power being exercised at the hearing of the substantive application for judicial review and not at a prior interlocutory hearing. However this does not preclude an interlocutory application where appropriate: see Order 53 rule 8.

See also Order 53 rule 3(6) concerning amendment at the hearing of an application for leave to apply for judicial review.

The court's power to permit amendment under Order 53 rule 6(2) is clearly discretionary. In *Lau Kong Yung (an infant) v Director of Immigration* [1999] 4 HKC 731 Litton PJ used colourful language to express his view that the discretion should be exercised sparingly. His Lordship said, at 773G–H:

> Once leave to apply for judicial review is granted, amendment of the grounds should rarely occur. All too often applications are made for amendment after leave to issue proceedings has been granted, as if O 53 r 3 were simply the portals to a playground of infinite possibilities where the administrators could then be made to leap through more and more hoops of fire. It is up to the judges of the High Court to stop this kind of extravaganza.

Delay, and possible consequences such as prejudice, or detriment to good administration, are relevant on an amendment application: *Chan Mei Yiu Paddy & Ors v SJ* HCAL 16-18/2007 (Saunders J; 03.08.2007) (para 14–15). These are the grounds on which leave to apply for judicial review, or any relief claimed, may be refused in the discretion of the court: High Court Ordinance, s 21K(6).

The amendment power appears to be sufficiently broad to enable the court to allow substitution of parties: see *Singh & Ors v Secretary for Security & Anor* (1996) 6 HKPLR 440, 448I–449A where leave to amend so as to substitute respondents was granted.

In *HK Aircrew Officers Association v Director of Civil Aviation & Anor* HCAL 51/1999 (Stock J; 28.10.1999) the court refused an application to amend, taking the view that it would raise an entirely new point which could have been raised earlier and would result in an adjournment of the hearing.

**[53.6.3]    Evidence by affirmation**

Evidence in judicial review proceedings is by way of affidavit or affirmation. Given the nature of judicial review, it is comparatively rare for issues of fact to arise. When they do, the appropriate step is to apply under Order 38 rule 2(3) for an order that the maker of the affidavit attend to be cross-examined thereon. In this regard see also the commentary under Order 53 rule 8.

See also rule 5A which restricts the use of affidavit evidence on a judicial review application unless certain procedural requirements have been complied with.

**[53.6.4] Applicant's evidence**

The applicant must file an affidavit in support of the application for leave to apply for judicial review: Order 53 rule 3(2)(b). The application for leave is normally made *ex parte* and it follows that there is a duty of full and frank disclosure. Failure to make full and frank disclosure at the *ex parte* stage may result in leave being set aside. See the commentary under Order 53 rule 3.

An applicant who wishes to rely on further evidence after the *ex parte* stage must apply for leave on notice. See Order 53 rule 6(2) and (3). In *Shun Fat Container Service Co Ltd & Ors v Commissioner for Transport* [1989] 2 HKC 301, 310B-D it was said that leave will only be granted in the 'most unusual circumstances'.

**[53.6.5]    Rule 6(4) - respondent's evidence**
Order 53 rule 6(4) requires that a respondent who wishes to rely on evidence at the substantive judicial review hearing should file affidavits as soon as practicable and in any event within 56 days after being served with the papers. Respondents sometimes proceed on the assumption they are entitled to the full 56-day period. However the rule clearly emphasises 'as soon as practicable'. In *Shun Fat Container Service Co Ltd & Ors v Commissioner for Transport* [1989] 2 HKC 301, 310A-B the court urged respondents to put in their evidence as soon as possible. The time for the respondent to file evidence may be extended. In *Cho Man Kit v Broadcasting Authority* HCAL 69/2007 (Hartmann J 25.09.2007) the court was critical of the respondent's delay but granted an extension in view of the 'overriding importance that the court has full evidence before it' (para 13).

In preparing its evidence the respondent has a duty to place its 'cards face upwards on the table', that is to disclose all relevant facts and produce relevant documentary exhibits. See *Chit Fai Motors Co Ltd v Comr for Transport* [2004] 1 HKC 465, 477A (CA), and *Dr Kwong Kwok Hay v Medical Council of HK (No 2)* [2007] 4 HKC 446 (CA) (para 6, 15), both referring to *R v Lancashire County Council ex p Huddleston* [1986] 2 All ER 941, 945. For a thorough discussion of this duty of candour, and the consequences of failure to comply, see *Chu Woan Chyi & Ors v Director of Immigration* [2009] 6 HKC 77 (CA).

**[53.6.6]    Admissibility of evidence**
In *Tran Van Tien v Director of Immigration (No 1)* (1996) 7 HKPLR 173 Keith J stated (at 175H–I) that 'there are three categories of evidence which have conventionally been regarded as admissible on applications for judicial review'. The three categories are those identified in *R v Secretary of State for the Environment, ex p Powis* [1981] 1 WLR 584 as follows:

1)    Since the court is exercising a supervisory jurisdiction, it is necessary for the court to see the material which was before the person or body who made the decision challenged. If there is doubt as to what that material was, the court can receive evidence to resolve that doubt.

2)    If the jurisdiction of the person or body who made the decision challenged depends on a question of fact or if there is an issue as to whether essential procedural requirements were observed, the court can receive evidence to determine the jurisdictional fact or procedural error.

3)    If it is alleged that the proceedings were tainted by misconduct on the part of the person or body who made the decision challenged or of one of the parties to the proceedings, the court can receive evidence to prove the particular misconduct alleged.

In *Tran Van Tien* Keith J went on to consider whether there is a fourth category of admissible evidence 'where a decision in public law is made in ignorance of or contrary to the true facts' in which case the court might receive evidence 'to demonstrate the true facts on which the decision should have been based'. *Ex p Do Giau & Ors* [1992] 1 HKLR 287 was referred to (and see *Nguyen Ho v Director of Immigration* [1991] 1 HKLR 576). Keith J proceeded to examine all of the evidence in order to determine whether the facts on which the impugned decision was based were 'plainly wrong' (at 177H–I). He concluded that they were not, and ruled the evidence inadmissible (at 185B–C).

Admission of evidence in the fourth category operates as an exception to the normal rule in judicial review that evidence which was not before the decision-maker will not be admissible in challenging the decision. See *Singh & Ors v Secretary for Security & Anor* (1996) 6 HKPLR 440, 455C–F.

### [53.6.7]    Fresh evidence
The court may admit fresh evidence, that is evidence which was not before the decision-maker being reviewed, if it comes within the principles laid down in *Ex p Powis* [1981] 1 WLR 584: see *Yu Chee Yin v Commissioner of the ICAC* [2001] 2 HKC 91, 104F–H, citing *Re Lo Wing Tong* [1990] 1 HKLR 325, 337 (CA). The *Powis* principles are set out above in the discussion on admissibility.

### [53.6.8]    Hearsay
Affidavits in applications for judicial review may contain hearsay evidence: *Re Chan Heung Mui* [1993] 1 HKLR 126; *Cheung Francis & Anor v Insider Dealing Tribunal* [1999] 4 HKC 585 (CA). In regard to hearsay in affidavits see generally the commentary under Order 41 rule 5.

**7.    Claim for damages** (O. 53 r. 7)
**(1)    On an application for judicial review the judge may, subject to paragraph (2), award damages to the applicant if—**
> **(a)    he has included in the statement in support of his application for leave under rule 3 a claim for damages arising from any matter to which the application relates, and**
> **(b)    the Court is satisfied that, if the claim had been made in an action begun by the applicant at the time of making his application, it could have been awarded damages.**

**(2)    Order 18, rule 12, shall apply to a statement relating to a claim for damages as it applies to a pleading.**

**8.    Application for discovery, interrogatories, cross-examination, etc.**
(O. 53 r. 8)
**(1)    Unless the judge otherwise directs, any interlocutory application in proceedings on an application for judicial review may be made to any judge in chambers or a master.**

**(2)    In this paragraph "interlocutory application" includes an application for an order under Order 24 or 26 or Order 38, rule 2(3), or for an order dismissing the proceedings by consent of the parties.**

**(3)    This rule is without prejudice to any statutory provision or rule of law restricting the making of an order against the Crown.**

## NOTES

**[53.8.1]    Interlocutory applications in judicial review proceedings**
Order 53 rule 8(2) expressly contemplates applications for discovery, interrogatories and cross-examination being made in judicial review proceedings, as well as applications for dismissal by consent. Other forms of interlocutory relief are not necessarily precluded: *Re Williamson* [2008] NICA 52 (05.12.2008) (para 6).

Under rule 8, interlocutory applications may be made to a judge in chambers or a master. However, the practice is for such applications to be heard by a judge rather than a master. See also paragraph 1.6 of practice direction SL3 which provides that in certain circumstances such applications should be made in open court.

**[53.8.2]    Discovery of documents in judicial review**
There is no automatic discovery in judicial review proceedings. Order 24 rule 2, which provides for exchange of lists of documents in actions commenced by writ, does not apply. However, the court has power under Order 24 rules 3 and 7 to order discovery in any cause or matter. It may exercise those powers to order discovery in judicial review proceedings if justice so requires: *O'Reilly v Mackman* [1983] 2 AC 237, 282C–D (HL). Order 53 rule 8 specifically contemplates such applications.

The court has tended to adopt a restrictive approach on applications for discovery in judicial review, but this appears to be changing. The restrictive approach is evident in *IRC v National Federation of Self-Employed and Small Businesses Ltd* [1982] AC 617, 654 where Lord Scarman said that in judicial review discovery 'should be limited strictly to documents relevant to the issue which emerges from the affidavit'. That passage was quoted with approval in *Law Sze Yan v Chinese Medicine Practitioners Board* [2007] 4 HKC 224 HCAL 41/2005 (Chu J; 28.10.2005), where it was held that the test for ordering discovery is higher in judicial review than in other civil proceedings. In *Au Shui-yuen Alick v Ford* [1991] 1 HKLR 525 it was held that it is not sufficient for the applicant to show that the documents sought are relevant or that production is desirable.

Change was signalled in *Tweed v Parades Commission for Northern Ireland* [2007] 2 WLR 1 (HL) where it was held that the courts should adopt a more flexible, less prescriptive approach and assess the need for disclosure on the facts of the individual case. The 'more liberal' approach in *Tweed* (above) was approved as more appropriate in *Chan Mei Yiu Paddy & Ors v SJ* [2007] 4 HKC 224 (Saunders J; 28.06.2007). *Chu Woan Chyi & Ors v Director of Immigration* [2005] 4 HKC 303 may also be seen as an example of the more liberal approach. In that case discovery of documents relating to the immigration 'watch list' was ordered in a judicial review based on allegations that immigration powers had been used in a manner inconsistent with freedom of religion. It is noteworthy that these cases adopting a 'more liberal' approach all concern human rights.

The more liberal approach will not make discovery generally available in judicial review. Order 24 rule 8 and 13 continue to require that the court refuse an order for discovery where not necessary for fair disposal of the proceedings or for saving costs, though para 10 of  *Chan Mei Yiu Paddy* (above) may be read as suggesting otherwise.

In *Bahadur v Director of Immigration* HCAL 34/1999 (Stock J; 15.06.1999) discovery of government immigration policy was refused although apparently referred to in an affirmation. No mention was made of Order 24 rule 10 under which a party 'shall be entitled' to inspect documents referred to in an affirmation.

### [53.8.3]    Interrogatories in judicial review

The provisions of Order 26 regarding discovery by way of interrogatories apply in judicial review proceedings: *O'Reilly v Mackman* [1983] 2 AC 237, 282 (HL). Rule 1(1) thereof now provides that interrogatories may be served without order in 'any cause or matter' where necessary for the fair disposition of the case or for saving costs. Such interrogatories without order may not be served on the government: Order 26 rule 3(3). Thus where discovery by way of interrogatories is sought against the government it is necessary to apply for leave under Order 26 rule 4.

The circumstances in which interrogatories will be 'necessary', etc in judicial review proceedings (as required by Order 26 rule 1) will be limited for the same rea sons as set out above with respect to discovery of documents.

A party who objects to providing answers to interrogatories served without order may apply under Order 26 rule 3 to have them varied or withdrawn. Order 53 rule 8 clearly contemplates such an application in the context of judicial review proceedings.

Interrogatories which amount to a 'fishing expedition' will not be allowed to stand. It is not permissible to administer interrogatories in order to discover a mistake in the decision-making process: *R v Independent Television Commission ex p TSW Broadcasting Ltd* [1996] JR 185, 192. Thus leave to apply for judicial review will not be granted on the basis that grounds for review might reveal themselves once interrogatories are served and answered: *Re Huang Jing* HCAL 63/1998 (Stock J; 24.08.1998).

### [53.8.4]    Application for cross-examination

The court's power to order the maker of an affidavit to attend to be cross-examined thereon is found in Order 38 rule 2. The power is clearly discretionary. As to the approach of the court in exercising the discretion in judicial review proceedings see *R v Director of Immigration & Anor ex p Do Giau & Ors* [1992] 1 HKLR 287, 343–5 and see Clark & McCoy, *Hong Kong Administrative Law* (2nd edn, 1993) pp 513–514. It is clear that cross-examination is rarely considered necessary and will not normally be allowed in judicial review proceedings. Clark & McCoy (*loc cit*) attribute this to the fact that findings of fact are not normally open to judicial review.

For an example of a case where leave to cross-examine was granted see *Re Pham Van Ngo & Ors* [1991] 1 HKLR 499 where the Secretary for Security and a government refugee co-ordinator were examined. See also *Chan Sau Mui & Ors v Director of Immigration* HCMP 356/1992 (Liu J; 07.04.1992) (overturned on appeal – CACV 60&70/1992 (Sir Derek Cons Ag CJ; Nazareth JA & Bokhary J; 29.05.1992)).

It has been held that there is no 'general power' to order a person who has not submitted affidavit evidence to attend to be cross-examined in judicial review proceedings. See *Re Williamson* [2008] NICA 52 (05.12.2008) (para 18). In that case the Northern Ireland Court of Appeal upheld a judge's refusal to issue *subpoenae* which would require prominent politicians to attend to be cross-examined.

**9.      Hearing of application for judicial review** (O. 53 r. 9)

(1)   On the hearing of any originating summons under rule 5, any person who desires to be heard in opposition to or in support of the originating summons, and appears to the Court to be a proper person to be heard, shall be heard, notwithstanding that he has not been served with the originating summons. (L.N. 152 of 2008)

(2)   Where the relief sought is or includes an order of certiorari to remove any proceedings for the purpose of quashing them, the applicant may not question the validity of any order, warrant, commitment, conviction, inquisition or record unless before the hearing of the originating summons he has lodged with the Registrar a copy thereof verified by affidavit or accounts for his failure to do so to the satisfaction of the Court hearing the originating summons. (L.N. 152 of 2008)

(3)   Where an order of certiorari is made in any such case as is referred to in paragraph (2), the order shall, subject to paragraph (4), direct that the proceedings shall be quashed forthwith on their removal into the Court of First Instance.

(4)   Where the relief sought is an order of certiorari and the Court is satisfied that there are grounds for quashing the decision to which the application relates, the Court may, in addition to quashing it, remit the matter to the court, tribunal or authority concerned with a direction to reconsider it and reach a decision in accordance with the findings of the Court.

(5)   Where the relief sought is a declaration, an injunction or damages and the Court considers that it should not be granted on an application for judicial review but might have been granted if it had been sought in an action begun by writ by the applicant at the time of making his application, the Court may, instead of refusing the application, order the proceedings to continue as if they had been begun by writ; and Order 28, rule 8, shall apply. (L.N. 152 of 2008)

------------------

**NOTES**

**[53.9.1]      Rule 9(1) – intervention of 'proper person to be heard'**
Order 53 rule 9(1) provides that the court shall hear any person who appears to be a proper person to be heard on an application for judicial review, though that person has not been served. In *Nattrass v AG* [1996] 1 HKC 480, 489 it was held that a District Court judge whose decision was impugned on a judicial review application was not a proper party to be heard since it was his decision, not his conduct, which was challenged.

Rule 9(1) was amended as part of the civil justice reforms taking effect in April 2009 so as to extend to parties who wish to be heard in support of an application for judicial review, whereas previously it was expressed to apply only to parties who wished to be heard in opposition. The amendment would appear to overrule *Tong Tim Nui & Ors v HK Housing Authority* [1999] 4 HKC 466, 482A-F (CA) insofar as it was there held that the court could not permit parties who had never applied for a judicial review of their own cases to join. The amendment was relied upon in

*Gurung Ganga Devi v Director of Immigration* HCAL 131/2008 (Saunders J; 23.09.2009) (paras 25–26) to enable the daughter of the applicant for judicial review to be heard on a family reunion issue which was not open to the applicant herself.

See also Order 53 rule 5B which gives the court a power to permit parties to intervene in judicial review proceedings.

**[53.9.2]    Rule 9(5) – order for proceedings to continue as if begun by writ**

Order 53 rule 9(5) empowers the court to order that an application for judicial review continue as if it were an action commenced by writ of summons. The power only applies where the relief sought is a declaration, an injunction or damages; it does not apply where a prerogative order such as mandamus, prohibition or certiorari is sought. The latter types of relief must be sought by way of judicial review: Order 53 rule 1(1)(a).

The power is discretionary and will not be interfered with lightly on appeal: *Leonard v Commissioner of Police* CACV 239/2007 (Cheung JA & Chu J; 19.02.2008). In that case the power was exercised on the ground there were substantial factual disputes between the parties, and although there is power to allow cross-examination on affidavits, this would only rarely be done in a judicial review. In *Wong Kei Kwong v Principal Assistant Sect'y for the Civil Service* HCAL 49/2007 (Saunders J; 15.02.2008) (paras 8-13) the court proceeded with a judicial review, treating it as though commenced by writ, where at the substantive hearing it was objected that the application concerned private law. The court said it would be a 'futile waste of expense' to require the applicant to start over again using a different procedure. In *Matteograssi SpA v Airport Authority* [1998] 3 HKC 25 (CA) it was said that a judicial review application which had boiled down to a claim for damages alone should have been the subject of an order under rule 9(5).

**[53.9.3]    Rule 9(5) – joinder of additional parties**

This rule cannot be construed to allow joinder of parties to a claim for damages where those parties have never applied for leave to apply for judicial review: *Nguyen Tuan Cuong & Ors v Secretary for Justice* [1999] 1 HKC 242.

**[53.9.4]    Costs of judicial review applications**

The general rule (under Order 62 rule 3) that costs shall follow the event applies in judicial review proceedings: *Leung Kwok Hung v President of the Legislative Council* HCAL 87/2006 (Hartmann J; 327.04.2007), referring to *R v Lord Chancellor ex p Child Poverty Action Group* [1999] 1 WLR 347. However, there are numerous cases where the court has departed from the general rule where judicial review has been sought on matters of public importance. In landmark right of abode litigation such as *Ng Ka Ling v Director of Immigration* [1999] 1 HKC 291 the Court of Final Appeal made no order as to costs. In *Leung* (above) the court made no order as to costs against a legislative councillor who unsuccessfully sought judicial review on a point of legislative procedure. See also the commentary under Order 62 rule 3 concerning protective costs orders, and under Order 62 rule 28 concerning indemnity costs, for discussion of cases where the court has protected private litigants in costs where they bring proceedings in the public interest.

As to costs at the leave stage, see the commentary under Order 53 rule 3.

**[53.9.5]    Costs where multiplicity of respondents**

Where a judicial review application involving more than one respondent is unsuccessful, the applicant should normally be liable for only one set of the respondents' costs. See *Shiu Wing Steel Ltd v Director of Environmental Protection & Anor* CACV 350/2003 (Ma CJHC, Stock JA & Stone J; 18.03.2005). Ma CJHC set out the follow factors as guidance for the exercise of discretion as to costs in such cases:

(1)    The mere fact that a person has the necessary *locus standi* to appear does not by itself entitle that person to an order for costs should the outcome be successful: see *R v Registrar of Companies, ex p Central Bank of India* [1986] QB 1114, 1162F.

(2)    Where several parties appear having the same interest in proceedings, the starting point is that the unsuccessful party should not have to pay more than one set of costs: - *R v Industrial Disputes Tribunal, ex p American Express Co Inc* [1954] 1 WLR 1118; *Ex p Central Bank of India* (above) at 1162F-G. The rationale here is simply that an unsuccessful party should not have to pay for costs which are unnecessarily incurred. Either the different parties with the same interest engage the same solicitors and counsel or they adopt the position of one of the other parties.

(3)    Where, however, the party can show that there is a separate issue on which he was entitled to be heard, being an issue not covered by the other party or parties in the proceedings, he would be entitled to his costs: - see *Bolton Metropolitan District Council* [1995] 1 WLR 1176, 1178H.

In *Shiu Wing Steel* the Court of Appeal, considering the above factors, ordered the unsuccessful applicant to pay the costs of the government, but not the costs of an interested statutory body which also appeared and was represented separately. The Court of Appeal's judgment was reversed on other grounds – see [2006] 4 HKC 111 (CFA). In *PCCW-HKT Telephone Ltd v Telecommunications Authority* [2007] 5 HKC 36 (CA) it was held that it is even less likely that the court will order more than one set of costs *on appeal*, by which time the issues should have crystallised and the extent to which there are separate interests clarified.

It is clear that the court retains a discretion to order more than one set of costs where appropriate. See, for example *Incorporated Owners of Wah Kai Industrial Centre & Ors v Secretary for Justice & Ors* HCAL 120/1999 (Cheung J; 03.05.2000) where the court ordered the unsuccessful applicant to pay the costs of the government and of a government-owned corporation which appeared separately, which was considered appropriate because of technical arguments. See also *Kaisilk Development Ltd v Secretary for Planning, Environment and Lands* HCAL 148/ 1999 (Cheung J; 15.06.2000) where the unsuccessful applicant was ordered to pay two sets of respondents' costs on the ground they had independent interests requiring separate representation. And see *Hong Kong Aircrew Officers Ass'n v Director-General of Civil Aviation & Anor* HCAL 96/2008 (A Cheung J; 04.09.2009) where the unsuccessful applicant was ordered to pay the 2nd respondent's solicitors costs, but only part of counsel's fee, on the ground that the same counsel could have been instructed to appear for both respondents.

The court's usual reluctance to order more than one set of costs on a judicial review application was referred to in a security for costs application in *To Kin Wah v Tuen Mun District Officer & Ors* [2003] 1 HKC 366, 371I-372A (CA).

**[53.9.6]    Uncontested applications**
Where the parties reach agreement as to the manner in which a judicial review application should be resolved, the procedure set out in paragraph 1.11 of the directions governing the Constitutional and Administrative Law List should be followed. The procedures under Order 21 for withdrawal and discontinuance of an action commenced by writ are 'inappropriate' for judicial review proceedings: *Po Fun Chan Peter v Cheung* HCAL 162/2005 (Chu J; 06.02.2006). Where an applicant no longer wishes to pursue the matter because the respondent has provided the relief sought, there may be no order for costs or the respondent may be ordered to pay the applicant's costs: *R v Liverpool City Council ex p Newman & Ors* [1992] 2 TLR 510.

**[53.9.7]    Costs against public officers**
The question of whether costs should be ordered against a public officer who unsuccessfully opposes an application for judicial review was considered by the Court of Appeal in *China Light & Power Co Ltd v Warner Banks, Esq, Coroner* [1995] 1 HKC 40. In that case a coroner had appeared by counsel and had vigorously contested the application. Noting the differences between the situations in Hong Kong and England, the Court of Appeal affirmed an order for costs against the coroner, which it was acknowledged would be paid from public funds and not by the coroner personally (per Mortimer JA at 49F–50D).

**10.    Saving for person acting in obedience to mandamus** (O. 53 r. 10)
       **No action or proceeding shall be begun or prosecuted against any person in respect of anything done in obedience to an order of mandamus.**

**12.    Consolidation of applications** (O. 53 r. 12)
       **Where there is more than one application pending under section 21K of the Ordinance against several persons in respect of the same office, and on the same grounds, the Court may order the applications to be consolidated.**

**13.    Order made by judge may be set aside, etc.** (O. 53 r. 13)
**(HK) An appeal shall lie, from an order of a judge granting or refusing an application for judicial review, to the Court of Appeal, which may set aside or confirm any such order or substitute such order as ought to have been made.**

---

**NOTES**

**[53.13.1]    Appeal from order granting or refusing judicial review**
Order 53 rule 13 provides that an appeal lies to the Court of Appeal against an order granting or refusing an application for judicial review. As this rule is subsidiary legislation it does not in itself confer jurisdiction on the Court of Appeal. It is necessary to look to the High Court Ordinance (Cap 4) for the extent of the jurisdiction of the Court of Appeal.
       In *AG v Alick Au Shui-yuen* [1992] 1 HKLR 88 (CA) and *Tan Soon-gin George v H H Judge Cameron & Anor* [1992] 1 HKLR 149 (CA); [1992] 2 AC 205 (PC) it was held that the Court of Appeal's jurisdiction in judicial review matters is confined to

those arising in civil matters. This was because section 13(2)(a) of the High Court Ordinance provides for appeal to the Court of Appeal from any decision of the Court of First Instance in a civil cause or matter, whereas the provisions conferring jurisdiction in criminal matters did not extend to judicial review. The effect of those decisions was reversed by the enactment of section 14A of the High Court Ordinance (Cap 4) in 1993. That section expressly provides for appeals to the Court of Appeal from judicial review proceedings arising in a criminal context. As a result Order 53 rule 13 now correctly reflects the jurisdiction of the Court of Appeal as laid down in the High Court Ordinance.

As to appeals against decisions at the leave stage (and applications to set aside leave) see Order 53 rule 3(4) and the commentary thereunder.

**14.   Meaning of "Court"** (O. 53 r. 14)
**In relation to the hearing by a judge of an application for leave under rule 3 or of an application for judicial review, any reference in this Order to "the Court" shall, unless the context otherwise requires, be construed as a reference to the judge.**
**(Enacted 1988)**

---

**NOTES**

**[53.14.1]   Master has no jurisdiction to hear application for leave**
Order 53 rule 14 restricts the meaning of 'the Court' as used in the Order, to judges. The broader meaning of 'the Court' under Order 1 rule 4(2), which includes the Registrar and masters, is excluded. The effect is that only a judge of the High Court may hear an application for leave to apply for judicial review or, if leave has been granted, the substantive application.

**15.   Transitional provisions relating to Part 24 of the Amendment Rules 2008**
   (O. 53 r. 15)
   **(1)   Where, immediately before the commencement of the Amendment Rules 2008, an application for leave to apply for judicial review is pending, then nothing in Part 24 of the Amendment Rules applies in relation to the application and (if leave is granted) the subsequent application for judicial review, and this Order as in force immediately before the commencement continues to apply as if that Part had not been made.**
   **(2)   Where, immediately before the commencement of the Amendment Rules 2008, an application for judicial review is pending, then nothing in Part 24 of the Amendment Rules 2008 applies in relation to the application, and this Order as in force immediately before the commencement continues to apply as if that Part had not been made. (L.N. 152 of 2008)**

---

**NOTES**

**[53.15.1]    Applications filed before April 2009**

Order 53 rule 15 provides that applications for judicial review which had already been taken out when the order was amended as part of the civil justice reforms taking effect in April 2009, are not affected by those amendments and the previous provisions of the Order will apply. The transitional provision applies even if only an application for leave to apply for judicial review was pending when the amendments came into force. One of the principal differences is that the former requirement for an applicant to issue a notice of motion on being granted leave continues to apply rather than the new form of originating summons.

## ORDER 54

### APPLICATIONS FOR WRIT OF HABEAS CORPUS

---

## NOTES

### [54.0.1]    References
For accounts of the substantive law of habeas corpus see: Sharpe, *The Law of Habeas Corpus* (Oxford: Clarendon Press, 2nd edn, 1989); Clark, 'Liberty and Security of the Person: Habeas Corpus' in Wacks (ed) *Human Rights in Hong Kong* (HK: OUP, 1992); Clark & McCoy, *The Most Fundamental Legal Right: Habeas Corpus in the Commonwealth* (Oxford: Clarendon Press, 2000); Clark & McCoy, *Habeas Corpus: Australia, New Zealand and South Pacific* (Sydney: Federation Press, 2000). See also Gordon, *Crown Office Proceedings* (London: Sweet & Maxwell, looseleaf).

### [54.0.2]    Sources of law of habeas corpus
The law and procedure relating to habeas corpus in Hong Kong derives from the Basic Law, local legislation including this Order, the common law and practice direction.

### (1)    *The Basic Law*
The Basic Law not only applies the common law to the Hong Kong SAR (article 8) but also contains specific provision against arbitrary or unlawful arrest, detention or imprisonment (article 28).

### (2)    *Local statutory provisions*
The principal statutory provision touching on habeas corpus in Hong Kong is section 22A of the High Court Ordinance (Cap 4). Section 22A 'contains detailed habeas corpus provisions faithful to the "freedom of the person" and "no arbitrary or unlawful detention" guarantees extended to all persons in Hong Kong' under the Basic Law: *Thang Thieu Quyen v Director of Immigration* [1998] 3 HKC 247, 274F–G (CFA) (per Bokhary PJ, dissenting partly in result).

See also sections 23 (repeated applications) and 24 (appeals) of the High Court Ordinance. These are discussed below.

In practice habeas corpus applications often arise in extradition cases. See for example *Cheung Ying-lun v Government of Australia* [1990] 1 WLR 1497 (PC); *Chong Bing Keung Peter v USA* [2000] 1 HKC 256 (CA). Section 12 of the Fugitive Offenders Ordinance (Cap 503) expressly requires that the alleged fugitive be informed in ordinary language of the right to apply for habeas corpus.

Section 13D(1C) of the Immigration Ordinance (Cap 115) touches on habeas corpus in that it permits the Director of Immigration to ask persons detained under that Ordinance but released by way of habeas corpus to enter into recognizances.

**(3)   Common law**

Habeas corpus exists at common law (*Re Lo Tsun Man & Ors* (1910) 5 HKLR 166, 172; *Thongchai Sanguandikul v USA* [1993] 2 HKLR 475, 476 (CA)). The common law right to obtain a writ of habeas corpus is expressly preserved by section 22A(14) of the High Court Ordinance (Cap 4), but subject to the relevant statutory provisions.

**(4)   Practice directions**

Applications for habeas corpus are placed on the Constitutional and Administrative Law List and are subject to the practice direction governing that list (No 26.1) as well as the directions made by the judge in the charge of the list pursuant to Order 72 rule 2(3) (SL 3). These are reproduced in the commentary under Order 53 rule 1 (above).

**[54.0.3]   History**

Habeas corpus is a remedy which traces back to at least the 13th century (*AG v Chiu Tat-cheong David* [1992] 2 HKLR 84, 107 (CA)) and attained its modern form in the latter part of the 17th century. During the colonial era the Application of English Law Ordinance (Cap 88) applied the English law of habeas corpus to Hong Kong both through adoption of English common law and by specific application of the Habeas Corpus Acts of 1679 and 1816.

The Application of English Law Ordinance (Cap 88) did not survive the resumption of Chinese sovereignty over Hong Kong. In its place article 8 of the Basic Law of the HKSAR applies the common law, and local Ordinances have been enacted to replace UK statutes which previously applied. For a discussion of this process and its legal consequences see *HKSAR v Ma Wai Kwan David & Ors* [1997] 2 HKC 315, 328H–329D (CA).

So far as habeas corpus is concerned, article 28(2) of the Basic Law now provides that no Hong Kong resident shall be subjected to arbitrary or unlawful arrest, detention or imprisonment. In addition, section 22A of the High Court Ordinance (Cap 4) was enacted to replace the UK Habeas Corpus Acts. One year after the resumption of Chinese sovereignty it was said of these changes that 'the substance of habeas corpus in Hong Kong is the same now as it was then': *Thang Thieu Quyen v Director of Immi gration* [1998] 3 HKC 247, 274E–F (CFA) (per Bokhary PJ, dissenting partly in result). The transition was sufficiently smooth that fugitives arrested before 1 July 1997 could lawfully be detained after that date even though the new arrangements for extradition were not complete. See *Yang Chung Chun Robert v USA & Anor* [1997] 3 HKC 338.

**[54.0.4]   Types of habeas corpus**

Originally there were many types of writ of habeas corpus. According to section 46 and the Schedule to the High Court Ordinance (Cap 4) all are abolished in Hong Kong save the writ of habeas corpus *ad subjiciendum* (to produce the detained person to the court). However, two other types of writ of habeas corpus continue to be mentioned in other legislation.

First, Section 2GC of the Arbitration Ordinance (Cap 341) provides that the court may grant a writ of habeas corpus *ad testificandum* (to bring a prisoner to court to give evidence) in aid of arbitration proceedings. Section 2GC was added by Ordinance 75 of 1996 and thus predates the legislation amending the Schedule to the High Court Ordinance so as to abolish the writ of habeas corpus *ad testificandum* (Ordinance 95 of 1997). Applying the doctrine of implied repeal, the later Ordinance should prevail.

Secondly, Order 54 rule 9 mentions not only the writ of habeas corpus *ad testificandum* but also the writ of habeas corpus *ad respondendum* (to bring up a prisoner to face action by a creditor or other claimant). The latter does not appear to have any continuing existence in Hong Kong. See the commentary under rule 9.

The other types of habeas corpus which originally existed, such as habeas corpus *cum causa*, habeas corpus *ad prosequendum*, habeas corpus *satisfaciendum*, habeas corpus *ad deliberendum* and habeas corpus *recipias* appear to have no existence in current Hong Kong law.

### [54.0.5]  Comparison with English Order
Since the implementation of the Woolf reforms in England, Order 54 in that jurisdiction is found in Schedule 1 to the Civil Procedure Rules.

Hong Kong's Order 54 is largely the same as its English equivalent. However rule 11 is omitted in Hong Kong and there are some differences in wording.

### [54.0.6]  The future of habeas corpus – merger with judicial review?
There is a significant trend of suggestion in the cases to the effect that habeas corpus will ultimately conflate with judicial review. See Simon Brown LJ 'Habeas Corpus – A New Chapter' [2000] Public Law 31, reviewing *Ex p Cheblak* [1991] 1 WLR 890; *Ex p Muboyana* [1991] 4 All ER 72 and *MB v The Managers of Warley Hospital* (English Court of Appeal, 30.07.1998). Habeas corpus and judicial review are historically distinct and are governed by different statutory provisions (*Ex parte Khawaja* [1984] AC 74, 99E) but it has been said, with reference to that authority, that there is 'no substantive distinction' between the 'ancient remedy' of habeas corpus and 'the modern approach of judicial review': *Re Pham Van Ngo & Ors* [1991] 1 HKLR 499, 506.

**1.    Application for writ of habeas corpus ad subjiciendum** (O. 54 r. 1)

(1)    An application for a writ of habeas corpus ad subjiciendum shall be made to a single judge in court, except that—

    (b)    at any time when no judge is sitting in court, it may be made to a judge otherwise than in court; and

    (c)    any application on behalf of a minor must be made in the first instance to a judge otherwise than in court.

(2)    An application for such writ may be made ex parte and, subject to paragraph (3), must be supported by an affidavit by the person restrained showing that it is made at his instance and setting out the nature of the restraint.

(3)    Where the person restrained is unable for any reason to make the affidavit required by paragraph (2), the affidavit may be made by some other person on his behalf and that affidavit must state that the person restrained is unable to make the affidavit himself and for what reason.

## NOTES

**[54.1.1]     Application for habeas corpus – two-stage process**
Applications for habeas corpus are dealt with in a two-stage process. It is said that the writ is a writ of right and not a writ of course, meaning that there is an initial stage at which the court considers whether to proceed further to a full hearing on the merits: *In re Corke* [1954] 1 WLR 899. Order 54 rule 1 deals with the first stage (which may be *ex parte*) at which a judge may order the issue of a writ of habeas corpus. If the writ is issued there will be a second stage where the substantive issue is heard in full as between the parties pursuant to Order 54 rule 8.

**[54.1.2]     Jurisdiction reposes in judges of CFI**
Habeas corpus jurisdiction reposes in the judges of the Court of First Instance and not the Court of Appeal. The jurisdiction of judges of the CFI is express in section 22A(1) of the High Court Ordinance (Cap 4) and is reflected in sections 23(1) and 24 thereof. The Court of Appeal is a creature of statute and has no jurisdiction to hear an original application for a writ of habeas corpus. See *In re Carroll (No1)* [1931] 1 KB 104; *Chung Tse Ching & Anor v Commissioner of Correctional Services* [1988] HKC 251 (CA) and *Re Meng Ching Hai* [1990] 1 HKC 185 (CA). However an appeal lies as of right to the Court of Appeal from any decision on an application for habeas corpus: High Court Ordinance, section 24.

**[54.1.3]     Jurisdiction – territorial considerations**
The writ of habeas corpus runs to any place within the Hong Kong SAR, including its territorial waters, save diplomatically protected premises (*Re Sun Yat Sen* (26.10.1896) in Short & Mellor, *The Practice on the Crown Side of the KBD* (2nd edn), (London: Stevens, 1908) p 318). The writ does not extend outside the Hong Kong SAR: *Re Ning Yi-ching* (1939) 56 TLR 3, 6. It follows that the detainor must be inside Hong Kong when the writ is issued.

**[54.1.4]     Form of application**
An *ex parte* application for issue of a writ of habeas corpus may be made on affidavit without any originating process. For the *inter partes* stage, form 87 in appendix A, a special type of originating summons, should be used. In the event an *ex parte* application is adjourned to enable the respondent to be heard at the initial stage, form 88 is used.

**[54.1.5]     Who may apply?**
Section 22A(2) of the Ordinance provides that the application may be made by the person detained, by another person on that person's behalf or by a person who claims to be legally entitled to the custody of another person. The identity of the applicant must be made clear: *Re W* [2006] 1 HKC 468, 474D-I.
    A number of issues arise in this context, as discussed below.

(1)     *Persons on bail or recognizance*
The prevailing view appears to be that any person in detention, whether the detention

is actual or notional, may apply for habeas corpus. Thus persons who are on bail or recognizance may apply. See *Re Cheung Kam Ping* HCMP 634/1978 (Li J; 19.12.1978) and *Re Lee Ka Ming* [1991] 1 HKLR 307, 313I (reversed on other grounds at [1991] 1 HKC 153 (CA)) and *USA v Jennings* [1983] 1 AC 624, 627. However the question is not free from doubt. In *Li Hong Mi* (1917) 12 HKLR 54, 55 the court proceeded on the basis of a concession that habeas corpus did not lie. In *AG v Chiu Tat-cheong, David & Anor* [1992] 2 HKLR 84, 107 (CA) Fuad JA doubted that a person on bail could apply for habeas corpus, pointing to a lack of examples. In *Re Chung Tu Quan & Ors* [1995] 1 HKC 566, 582D, Keith J said that habeas corpus is an inappropriate remedy for a person released on his own recognizance.

(2)     *Participants in witness protection programme*
In *Re W* [2006] 1 HKC 468 the court rejected a submission that a person cloistered under the Witness Protection Ordinance (Cap 564) is *per se* in a form of custody. It was held that under the Ordinance a witness enters the programme voluntarily and may leave at any time. As a result, participation in the programme 'does not constitute any form of detention'.

(3) *Persons released prior to hearing*
If the person is released before the conclusion of a habeas corpus application the court will proceed no further: *Barnardo v Ford* [1892] AC 326, 333; *Sestan v Director of Area Mental Health Services* [2007] NZSC 5. Habeas corpus does not lie in respect of a prior detention, even if it was illegal: *Re Ogunade* HCAL 155/2005 (Chu J; 09.12.2005). However the released person could still seek damages for false imprisonment by ordinary civil action.

(4)     *Application by third party*
Section 22A(2) of the High Court Ordinance expressly provides that an application for habeas corpus may be made by another person on behalf of the person who is alleged to be unlawfully detained. This reflects a jurisdiction tracing back at least as far as *The Hottentot Venus* (1810) 13 East 195; 104 ER 344.

Order 54 rule 1(3) provides that the affidavit in support may be made by that other person if the detained person cannot do so.

The person making the application must have a degree of 'standing', not be a 'mere stranger or perhaps vexatious volunteer'. For this reason, and to establish responsibility for matters such as costs, the identity of the applicant must be made clear. See *Re W* [2006[ 1 HKC 468, 474, citing *Ex parte Child* (1854) 15 CB 237, 238.

The court must be satisfied that the detained person could not make the application personally because of mental state (including infancy) or because of being held *in communicado* without access to a lawyer: *Li Kui Yu v Superintendent of Labourers* [1906] SALR (TS) 181, 184 (Transvaal SCt). Where the evidence is that the person on whose behalf the application is made chose to remain in custody the case will not be heard: *Re Winara Parata* (1880) 1 Oliver, Bell's & Fitzgerald's Reports 31 (NZFC) (prisoner indicated that he did not want the application made); *Ex parte Mughal* [1973] 1 WLR 1133, 1136F.

(5)     *Nationality and status of applicant*
An application for habeas corpus may be made by any person detained in Hong Kong regardless of nationality and residence status. The remedy is available to illegal immigrants as well as lawful residents: *AG v Kwok-A-Sing* (1873) LR 5 PC 179 (PC from HK); *Re Lo Tsun Man & Ors* (1910) 5 HKLR 166, 172; *Re Lam Yuk-kuen & Anor* [1990] 2 HKLR 38, 42H.

(6)     *Children*
Age is not a barrier to an application for habeas corpus. See *Re Lam Yuk-kuen & Anor* [1990] 2 HKLR 38 (2 year old girl); *Re Lee Ka Ming* [1991] 1 HKLR 307 (7 year old boy); *Re Pham Van Ngo & Ors* [1991] 1 HKLR 499 where 111 people including 4 children were freed). An application on behalf of a child must be made by another person (see for example *Re Liu Chak-lai* HCMP 2586/1993 (Bewley J; 09.07.1993) (SCMP 10 & 22.07.1993)) and the initial hearing will be in chambers: Order 54 rule 1(1)(c).

(7)     *Persons imprisoned for debt*
Habeas corpus may issue in cases where debtors are detained: *Re an Application by the Official Solicitor (No 1)* [1983] 2 HKC 259 (Full Bench). Orders 48 and 49B provide for detention of debtors in certain circumstances.

(8)     *Joinder of multiple applicants*
In *Chieng A Lac v Director of Immigration* [1997] HKLRD 271 the respondent objected to the joinder of a large number of applicants in a single application for habeas corpus, but the court held that it was appropriate.

**[54.1.6]     Against whom may habeas corpus be sought?**
The writ runs in both civil and criminal matters and against public officials as well as private individuals. It is said that the sovereign has an interest in any unlawful detention. See *Re Sung Man Cho* (1931) 25 HKLR 62, 76 and *R v Jackson* [1891] 1 QB 671. Examples may best illustrate the extent to which the writ may lie.

(1)     *Public officials*
Habeas corpus is most frequently sought in cases of detention by public officials such as the Commissioner for Correctional Services and the Director of Immigration. The test is not actual physical custody or control but whether the person to whom the writ is directed has the legal right to control the applicant. Hence the writ will lie against a senior official although it is actually subordinate officers who have physical custody: *Ex p O'Brien* [1923] 2 KB 361, 398.

(2)     *Private individuals*
The writ lies in cases of private detention, such as child custody disputes: *EH v DH* [1962] HKLR 559 (FC).

(3)     *Corporations*
In principle the writ may lie against a body corporate but it is preferable to name the

responsible officer thereof otherwise difficulty arises in enforcement by way of contempt proceedings. See *In re J M Carroll (an infant)* [1931] 1 KB 317 (CA) at 363–64 per Slesser LJ.

(4) *Where uncertainty as to identity of person detaining*
In *Jones v Skelton* [2007] 2 NZLR 178 (NZSC) there was a degree of uncertainty as to which of 6 persons might be detaining a child who had been abducted. The court ordered each of the 6 to bring the child before the court, with the rider that any of them unable to do so should file and serve an affidavit containing information as to their knowledge of the whereabouts of the child, details of any contact they had had with him, what efforts they had made to locate him and the location of the person thought to have physical custody.

## [54.1.7]    Respondent to habeas corpus application
The person against whom habeas corpus is sought will obviously be named as a respondent to the application. In addition, the Secretary for Justice may intervene and appear as a party: *Lam Ngok Yeung v Director of Immigration & Anor* [1985] 2 HKC 725, 727D-F. It is established practice for the requesting country to be joined as a respondent where the application arises from extradition proceedings: *Chan Hok Shek v Superintendent of Lai Chi Kok Reception Centre & Gov't of the USA* [2010] 3 HKC 94.

## [54.1.8]    Scope of habeas corpus
On a habeas corpus application the court may examine not only whether there exists a warrant, order or other legal authority authorising the detention, but may look behind any such authority to make sure it has a sound legal basis.
    No person has inherent power to detain or to authorise detention: either the power is conferred by law or it does not exist. Detention cannot be justified on the basis of state necessity: *Entick v Carrington* (1765) 19 St Tr 1029, 1073. High office of itself does not confer power to order detention: *Re Iu Ki Shing* (1908) 3 HKLR 20, 34.
    Detention under legislation which is no longer in force is without jurisdiction and unlawful: *Eng Sui Hang v USA* HCMP 3484/1990 (Jones J; 22.06.1990) (referred to in the subsequent case of *Re Eng Sui Hang* [1991] 1 HKLR 606, 608B–C).
    Specific issues as to the scope of habeas corpus are discussed below:

(1)    *Procedural or technical error*
The court is careful to ensure that all prescribed procedures are followed in the process leading up to a person's detention. Procedural protections are matters that go to jurisdiction and must be complied with: *Leung Afu v Superintendent of Victoria Gaol* The Daily Press, 15.06.1887; *Re Chan Kum Cheun* (1892) 5 HKLR 182, 183. Failure to follow prescribed procedures may render the detention unlawful. The court will insist that procedures are complied with and that powers are not used for ulterior purposes: *Re Luong Bat Kien* [1973]–[1976] HKC 71, 74. Procedural requirements are not necessarily only those laid down by statute.
    However the court will be slow to release a detained person on the ground of a purely technical procedural error which has nothing to do with the merits. See *Mayuret*

*Tankanchophat v USA* [1992] 1 HKLR 401, 406 (CA) and *Fung Chuen-kan & Anor v USA* [1994] 1 HKLR 163, 168 (CA) (joint warrant in extradition case erroneous but a mere technical defect).

### (2) *Natural justice*
In *Chu Wing Hei v AG* [1946]–[1972] HKC 536, 542H–I, it was held that an order for detention was unlawful on the ground the person had not been told the grounds alleged to justify his detention. In *Re Lam Yuk-kuen & Anor* [1990] 2 HKLR 38, 42 it was held an order for detention of an illegal immigrant under section 32(4)(b) of the Immigration Ordinance was unlawful because it had been obtained in breach of natural justice in that the illegal immigrant had not been given notice.

### (3) *Reasonableness*
In *Fidelis Emem v Superintendent of Victoria Prison* [1998] 2 HKLRD 448, 453D the court proceeded on the basis that reasonableness in the '*Wednesbury*' sense or otherwise is not a matter to be taken into account in habeas corpus proceedings. However the court acknowledged that such an issue would be relevant on judicial review.

### (4) *Detention ordered by superior court of record*
The writ is not available to test the lawfulness of detention ordered by a superior court of record (in Hong Kong the Court of First Instance and the Court of Appeal). The Court of First Instance 'cannot test the validity of its own decisions': *Chung Tse Ching v Commissioner of Correctional Services* [1988] HKC 251, 255B (CA), citing *Re Kray* [1965] Ch 736, 745A and *Re Hastings (No 3)* [1959] Ch 368, 377. See also *Re Seven Witnesses* (1906) 2 HKLR 179, 182 (overruled on another point in *Chang Hang Kiu v Piggott* [1909] AC 312).

### (5) *Detention ordered by judge sitting as commissioner*
Although the writ of habeas corpus does not lie against the High Court itself, it is available to test the legality of detention ordered by a High Court judge sitting in another capacity such as under the Commissions of Inquiry Ordinance (Cap 86). See *Re So Sau-chung* [1966] HKLR 523, 552).

### (6) *Detention ordered by district judge or magistrate*
The writ will lie to test the lawfulness of a sentence imposed by an inferior court such as the district court. See for example *Cheung Yuk-ha v R* [1979] HKLR 95, 96. Further, where a magistrate is required to have evidence of certain matters (as in extradition cases), the absence of evidence goes to jurisdiction and vitiates the order for detention: *Re A-Kam & 12 Ors*, The China Mail 18.11.1881; *Re Wong Cheong Wai* [1989] 2 HKC 226. In extradition proceedings, the existence or adequacy of evidence is tested with reference to the time the magistrate orders committal: *Thongchai Sanguandikul v USA* [1993] 2 HKLR 475, 483, 484.

### (7) *Detention for a limited purpose*
Where detention is for a limited purpose, it may be construed as being subject also to

a reasonable time limitation after which continued detention is unlawful. On application for habeas corpus the lawfulness of detention is judged as at the date of the hearing, not the date of taking the person into custody: *Re Pham Van Ngo & Ors* [1991] 1 HKLR 499, 507G. Hence the writ lies to test the continued lawfulness of detention which, though unimpeachable on the date it began, has, by effluxion of time, become unlawful.

The leading authorities in this context are: *Tan Te Lam v Superintendent of Tai A Chau Detention Centre* [1997] AC 97 (PC); *Director of Immigration & Anor v Long Quoc Tuong & Ors* [1998] 1 HKC 290 (CA); and *Thang Thieu Quyen v Director of Immigration* [1998] 3 HKC 247 (CFA).

Unlimited detention is frowned upon by the courts. See *Re Liew Kar-seng v Governor in Council* [1989] 1 HKLR 607; *R v Director of Immigration ex p Santiago* [1989] 1 HKC 293; *Pham Van Ngo & Ors* [1991] 1 HKLR 499, 507I; *Re Chung Tu Quan* [1995] 1 HKC 566; *Cong Siu Lay v Superintendent of Whitehead Detention Centre* [1995] 2 HKC 822, 823G.

### (8) *Challenge to prison conditions*

Prison conditions *per se* cannot be challenged by habeas corpus: *Chieng A Lac v Director of Immigration* [1997] HKLRD 271, 293B–295H. However the writ is available to challenge the particular part of the institution a prisoner is detained in, if there are legal rules governing such things: *Re Sakchai Suwannapeng* [1990] 2 HKLR 231, 236.

### (9) *Threat of re-arrest*

The threat of re-arrest in the event of release will not deter the court from granting relief. Section 22A(12) restricts re-detention following release to cases where there is a material change in circumstances.

### (10) *Embarrassment to executive*

The court will not be impressed by concerns that release will cause embarrassment or inconvenience to the executive branch of government: *Re Pham Van Ngo & Ors* [1991] 1 HKLR 499, 510B.

### (11) *Extradition cases*

An application for habeas corpus in the context of extradition proceedings is not con fined to the formal validity of the detention order. The court is entitled to examine the merits. See *Gibson v USA* [2007] UKPC 52 (para 18), referring to *Knowles v USA* [2006] UKPC 38.

### [54.1.9] The affidavit in support

An application for issue of a writ of habeas corpus must normally be supported by an affidavit setting out the relevant facts. The purpose of the affidavit is to show 'some ground on which the court can see that the applicant may be unlawfully detained': *In re Corke* [1954] 1 WLR 899.

In exceptional circumstances the court may dispense with the affidavit requirement: *Re Sakchai Suwannapeng* [1990] 2 HKLR 231. This might be allowed where the applicant is held *in communicado* and is not able to make an affidavit: *Re Parker & Ors (Canadian Prisoners' Case)* (1839) 5 M&W 32; 151 ER 15. However the application might not be heard if the applicant fails to file an affidavit without reasonable explanation: *Re Cope land's Application* [1990] NI 301, 304.

A number of issues arise with respect to the content of the affidavit in support, as set out below.

### (1)    *Full and frank disclosure*

Full and frank disclosure is required in an affidavit in support of an application for issue of a writ of habeas corpus. Failure to disclose parallel proceedings or the exact status of the applicant may result in the application being dismissed: *Re Bhagwan Singh* (1914) 17 DLR 63 (BCSC) (failure to disclose that applicant on bail at time of application). In *Re W* [2006] 1 HKC 468 the court expressed disapproval of the failure to disclose the fact the person allegedly detained (under the Witness Protection Ordinance) was con nected with another who was a suspect in ICAC corruption investigations.

### (2)    *Hearsay*

An affidavit in habeas corpus proceedings may contain hearsay if it is not practical for the relevant facts to be demonstrated by direct evidence. See *Chieng A Lac & Ors v Director of Immigration & Ors (No 1)* (1997) 7 HKPLR 233 citing *Ex parte Rahman* [1996] 4 All ER 945 (QB), affirmed at [1998] QB 136 (CA).

### (3)    *Legal matters*

An affidavit is normally confined to matters of fact. See the commentary under Order 41. However in habeas corpus proceedings an affidavit may be used to demonstrate defects in jurisdiction: see *Poon Yuk Sim* (1956) 40 HKLR 12.

### (3)    *Further affidavits*

If the court finds that the affidavit in support is inadequate it may order that a further affidavit be filed: *Kek Peng-teng* [1969] HKLR 564, 568.

### [54.1.10]    Listing priority

Applications for habeas corpus are accorded priority over all other business of the court: *Re Tse Sun-miu* [1994] 2 HKLR 78, 83 (CA), citing *Ex parte Cheblak* [1991] 1 WLR 890, 894. In *Re Liu Chak-lai* HCMP 2586/1993 (Bewley J; 09.07.1993) (SCMP 10 & 22.07.1993) a murder trial was adjourned in order that the judge could hear a habeas corpus application. The emphasis in habeas corpus is on provision of a speedy and efficient remedy since unlawful detention cannot be tolerated. See *Re Poon Yuk Sim* (1956) 40 HKLR 12, 15.

### [54.1.11]    Urgent cases

An urgent application for habeas corpus can be made at any time of day or night. Outside of court hours such applications can be entertained at the residence of a judge. The power to hear such applications outside court is express in Order 54 rule 1(1)(b). See the discussion below concerning hearings in open court or *in camera*.

See for example *Tolentino v Custodian of Victoria Immigration Centre* [1993] 1

HKC 19 where the application was made at the Chief Justice's official residence at 10.00 pm on the eve of Chinese New Year. See also *Yoo Soon-nam v AG* [1976] HKLR 702, 703: application at 12.30 a.m.

In case of a need to make an urgent application outside of court hours, practitioners should telephone the clerk to the duty judge on the mobile telephone number provided in Law Society circulars from time to time.

### [54.1.12]   Ex parte hearing

Section 22A(3) of the High Court Ordinance (Cap 4) and Order 54 rule 1(2) expressly provide that an application for a writ of habeas corpus may be made *ex parte*.

In *Cheng Chui Ping v Superintendent of Tai Lam Centre for Women & Anor* [2000] 3 HKC 777, 780F–G Stock J said that in his experience the application is normally heard *ex parte* at the initial stage. He described the case before him as 'unusual' in that it came on for hearing at the initial stage *inter partes*. Earlier, in *Thongchai Sanguandikul v USA* [1993] 2 HKLR 475, 482 (CA) Litton JA had suggested that to avoid delay in extradition cases the court should be more ready to use its power under Order 54 rule 2 to direct an *inter partes* hearing at the initial stage.

### [54.1.13]   Hearing in open court or in camera

As a general rule an application for a writ of habeas corpus and the return will be heard in open court although section 22A(4) of the High Court Ordinance (Cap 4) makes provision for applications to be heard *in camera* in exceptional circumstances. Two such exceptional circumstances are dealt with in Order 54 rule 1. First, rule 1(1)(b) provides that when no judge is sitting in court an application for habeas corpus may be made 'otherwise than in court'. This would apply outside of court hours: see the dis cussion of urgent cases above. Secondly, rule 1(1)(c) provides that an application on behalf of a minor must in the first instance be made to a judge otherwise than in court. See *EH v DH* [1962] HKLR 559, 562 (child custody case heard in chambers).

Technically a hearing *in camera* may be distinguishable from a hearing in chambers in that although the public is excluded the formalities of open court may apply.

Where an application for habeas corpus is heard *in camera* the court's decision and reasons must nevertheless be announced in open court: High Court Ordinance (Cap 4), section 22A(4).

### [54.1.14]   The test at the initial stage

At the initial stage the applicant 'need not convince the court of the merits of his case but should raise an arguable case which deserves further consideration': *Cheng Chui Ping v Superintendent of Tai Lam Centre for Women & Anor* [2000] 3 HKC 777, 781D–E citing Sharpe (2nd edn) (above). Or as stated in *Chong Bing Keung Peter v USA* [2000] 1 HKC 256, 259G–H (CA) (also citing Sharpe):

> It is probably enough that a doubt is raised in the mind of the judge regarding the validity of the detention and an arguable case be shown which deserves further consideration.

### [54.1.15]   Availability of alternative remedy

Where there is an alternative and equally effective remedy the court may decline to issue the writ. The availability of another remedy does not remove the right to apply for habeas corpus; rather the court in its discretion leaves it to the applicant to pursue the other remedy. See *Re Tse Sun-miu* [1994] 2 HKLR 78 (CA) per Bokhary JA at 82–83, citing *Ex Parte Azam* [1974] AC 18, 31F–H.

Judicial review is frequently an alternative to habeas corpus. See *Re Vonchai Tumtonkitkul* [1982] HKC 181 where the court permitted an applicant to seek judicial review as an alternative to habeas corpus. In *Re Sakchai Suwannapeng* [1990] 2 HKLR 231, 232 the court adjourned an application for habeas corpus on the ground it had sufficient power within the ambit of judicial review to do justice.

Habeas corpus is not appropriate where the prisoner has an avenue of appeal against detention: *Re Corke* [1954] 1 WLR 899; *Re Yu Kin Chun Philip* [1987] HKLR 123; *Re Tse Sun-miu* [1994] 2 HKLR 78 (CA). This will be the case where the prisoner is detained under a sentence of imprisonment following conviction for an offence, as in *Re Pearce* HCAL 20/2007 (Hartmann J; 23.02.2007).

Matters such as delay in inferior courts are best dealt with by mandamus (*Re McAleenan's Application* [1985] NI 496, 506; or by the abuse of process doctrine: *Jago v District Court of NSW* (1989) 168 CLR 23 (HCA).

**[54.1.16]   Order to be made at initial stage**

If at the initial stage the court is satisfied the application has substance it *must*, according to section 22A(5) of the High Court Ordinance (Cap 4), either:

(a)   order the issue of a writ of habeas corpus directing the detainor to bring the applicant before the court and to certify the grounds for the applicant's detention; or

(b)   order the detainor to appear before the court to justify the lawfulness of the detention.

In the usual course of events the result will be a second stage hearing, pursuant to rule 8, at a later date. However in *Cheng Chui Ping v Superintendent of Tai Lam Centre for Women & Anor* [2000] 3 HKC 777, where the application was heard *inter partes* at the initial stage, the court proceeded to the second stage hearing immediately.

At the initial stage the court may also order release of the applicant under Order 54 rule 4. See the commentary thereunder.

Where at the initial stage the court is satisfied that the application has no substance it may dismiss it: section 22A(5) High Court Ordinance (Cap 4). Alternatively the court may direct an *inter partes* hearing under Order 54 rule 2.

**[54.1.17]   Restriction on repeat applications**

It was once considered possible in England for an applicant to go from court to court and judge to judge making repeated applications for habeas corpus. Upon the enactment of the Judicature Act 1873 there were no longer separate courts of law and equity so the first possibility ceased. See *Eshugbayi Eleko v Officer Administering the Government of Nigeria* [1928] AC 459 (PC). And note that in Hong Kong law and equity have all along been administered in the same courts.

In *Eshugbayi* the Privy Council left open the possibility of repeat applications to different judges within the court, but this was doubted in *Re Hastings (No 3)* [1959] Ch 368, 378.

In Hong Kong today section 23(1) of the High Court Ordinance (Cap 4) expressly prohibits fresh applications on the same ground unless fresh evidence is adduced. Fresh evidence does not include evidence which was available at the time of the original application and could have been used by the applicant but was not. See *Re Law Kin Man* (1992) HKPLR 332 (CA) confirming [1993] 1 HKLR 83; and *Thongchai Sanguandikul v USA* [1993] 2 HKLR 475 (CA) confirming HCMP 287/ 1993 (Jones J; 19.05.1993).

However if a ground of application was not relied on due to inadvertence, error of judgment or incompetence, 'it cannot be said that such ground was fairly available' and it may be raised in a fresh application: *Re Yeung Yan Chi* [1996] 2 HKLR 309.

**2.      Power of Court to whom ex parte application made** (O. 54 r. 2)

**(1)      The judge to whom an application under rule 1 is made ex parte may make an order forthwith for the writ to issue, or may— (See App. A, Forms 87, 88)**

> **(a)      where the application is made otherwise than in court, direct that an originating summons for the writ be issued, or that an application therefor be made by originating summons to a judge in court; (L.N. 152 of 2008)**

> **(b)      where the application is made to a judge in court, adjourn the application so that notice thereof may be given, or direct that an application be made by originating summons. (L.N. 152 of 2008)**

**(2)      The summons must be served on the person against whom the issue of the writ is sought and on such other persons as the judge may direct, and, unless the judge otherwise directs, there must be at least 8 clear days between the service of the summons or notice and the date named therein for the hearing of the application. (L.N. 152 of 2008)**

**(3)      An originating summons under this rule must be in Form No. 87 in Appendix A.  (L.N. 152 of 2008)**

---

## NOTES

### [54.2.1]      Comparison with English rule
There are several differences between the wording of Order 54 rule 2 and its English counterpart. These largely reflect the different manner in which the courts are organised in the two jurisdictions. Note that the English rule 2(1)(c) is omitted in Hong Kong.

### [54.2.2]      Purpose and scope of Order 54 rule 2
Order 54 rule 2 provides that the court may, when an application is made *ex parte* at the initial stage, give directions for the application to be heard on notice to the opposing party. In *Thongchai Sanguandikul v USA* [1993] 2 HKLR 475, 482 (CA) Litton JA suggested that to avoid delay in extradition cases the court should be more ready to use its power under this rule.

Where the application is *prima facie* strong, the practice is to issue the writ immediately. See Order 54 rule 4 and the commentary thereunder, and see *Re Liu Chak-lai* HCMP 2586/1993 (Bewley J; 09.07.1993) (SCMP 10 & 22.07.1993).

**3.　　Copies of affidavits to be supplied** (O. 54 r. 3)
**Every party to an application under rule 1 must supply to every other party on demand copies of the affidavits which he proposes to use at the hearing of the application.**

**4.　　Power to order release of person restrained** (O. 54 r. 4)
**Without prejudice to rule 2(1), the judge hearing an application for a writ of habeas corpus ad subjiciendum may in his discretion order that the person restrained be released, and such order shall be a sufficient warrant to any superintendent of a prison, constable or other person for the release of the person under restraint.**

---

**NOTES**

**[54.4.1]　　Immediate release at initial stage**
Order 54 rule 4 provides that on an application for habeas corpus the court may order the immediate release of the applicant. See *Re Lee Ka-ming* [1991] 1 HKLR 307, 309C and *Cong Siu Lay & Ors v Superintendent of Whitehead Detention Centre* [1995] 2 HKC 822 as examples.

**5.　　Directions as to return to writ** (O. 54 r. 5)
**Where a writ of habeas corpus ad subjiciendum is ordered to issue, the judge by whom the order is made shall give directions as to the judge before whom, and the date on which, the writ is returnable.**

---

**NOTES**

**[54.5.1]　　Directions on issue of writ**
Order 54 rule 5 provides that on issuing a writ of habeas corpus the court may make directions as to which judge, and when, the substantive hearing shall take place. Section 22A(7) of the Ordinance provides that the person to whom the writ is directed must no later than the time specified by way of such direction, produce the detained person and make a formal return to the writ. Extension of time is possible for 'good reason'.

Any such direction as to the particular judge before whom the substantive application shall be heard does not go to jurisdiction: *Law Kin Man v Commissioner of Correctional Services* (1992) 2 HKPLR 332 (CA). There a notice which stated that the return was to be made before a particular judge did not deprive the court of jurisdiction when the matter came on for hearing before another judge.

**[54.5.2]　　Discovery**
There is power to order discovery in habeas corpus proceedings. However the circumstances in which discovery is necessary will be rare. In *Vo Thi Do v Director*

*of Immigration & Anor* [1998] 1 HKLRD 729, 749C–J (CA) an order for discovery in habeas corpus proceedings was set aside on appeal on the ground it amounted to a fishing expedition and did not meet the requirements of Order 24 rule 13(1).

### [54.5.3]    Security for costs

Given that habeas corpus concerns the fundamental right of liberty of the person it would be wrong in principle for the court to order security for costs against an applicant.

Different considerations may apply on appeal, depending on whether the habeas corpus application arises in a civil or criminal context. In *Thongchai Sanguandikul v USA* [1992] HKLY 12; CACV 123/1992 (Litton JA; 28.10.1992) it was held that where a habeas corpus appeal arises in a criminal context there is no jurisdiction to order security for costs. However in *In re Carroll* [1931] 1 KB 104 (CA) security for costs was ordered against an appellant who had failed to obtain relief (in a civil context) below. Scrutton LJ said (at 109): 'the fact that the appeal relates to an application for habeas corpus is of itself no ground for preventing the court ordering security'.

**6.    Service of writ and notice** (O. 54 r. 6)

**(1)    Subject to paragraphs (2) and (3), a writ of habeas corpus ad subjiciendum must be served personally on the person to whom it is directed.**

**(2)    If it is not possible to serve such writ personally, or if it is directed to a superintendent of a prison or other public official, it must be served by leaving it with a servant or agent of the person to whom the writ is directed at the place where the person restrained is confined or restrained.**

**(3)    If the writ is directed to more than one person, the writ must be served in manner provided by this rule on the person first named in the writ, and copies must be served on each of the other persons in the same manner as the writ.**

**(4)    There must be served with the writ a notice (in Form No 90 in Appendix A) stating the judge before whom and the date on which the person restrained is to be brought and that in default of obedience proceedings for committal of the party disobeying will be taken.**

---

### NOTES

#### [54.6.1]    Form of writ of habeas corpus

See Order 54 rule 10 and the commentary thereunder.

#### [54.6.2]    Service of writ

Order 54 rule 6 provides that a writ of habeas corpus must be served personally unless personal service is not possible or the writ is directed to a public official. In those cases the writ must be served by leaving it with a servant or agent at the place of detention: rule 6(2).

Failure to serve a writ properly or at all may be fatal to the proceedings since in that event the court has no jurisdiction to proceed: *Re Meng Ching Hai* [1990] 1 HKC 185, 187A. In *R v Rowe* (1894) 11 TLR 29 copies were served rather than the original. It was held that the respondents could not be punished for contempt for non-compliance even though they had initially appeared in court in response to the copies they received.

### [54.6.3]     Notice to be served with writ

Order 54 rule 6(4) provides that a form of penal notice must be served with the writ of habeas corpus, expressly informing the person to whom the writ is directed that disobedience may result in committal for contempt. The notice must be in form No 90 in Appendix A.

The contents of the notice under this rule do not go to jurisdiction: *Law Kin Man v Commissioner of Correctional Services* (1992) 2 HKPLR 332 (CA) confirming [1993] 1 HKLR 83. There a notice which stated that the return was to be made before a particular judge did not deprive the court of jurisdiction when the matter came on for hearing before another judge.

**7.     Return to the writ** (O. 54 r. 7)

**(1)     The return to a writ of habeas corpus ad subjiciendum must be indorsed on or annexed to the writ and must state all the causes of the detainer of the person restrained.**

**(2)     The return may be amended, or another return substituted therefor, by leave of the judge before whom the writ is returnable.**

---

## NOTES

### [54.7.1]     The return

The return is the respondent's answer to the writ of habeas corpus. Its purpose is to state the respondent's justification for detaining the applicant. In *Chan Cho Tei v AG* HCMP 463/1980 (Roberts CJ & Zimmern J; 03.06.1980) it was held that in the return the custodian under a warrant ought to show the following:

1)     that the warrant was issued under a valid power;
2)     that the person who issued the warrant had proper authority to do so;
3)     that the subject was one of a class of persons subject to warrants issued under that power; and
4)     the evidence relied on to reach the factual conclusions.

Where it is not possible to comply with the writ the respondent must nevertheless make a return stating why it is not possible to comply: section 22A(8) High Court Ordinance. For example, if the subject of the application is not detained (any longer or at all) so that it is not possible for the respondent to bring that person before the court in obedience to the writ, these facts should be stated in a 'nil' return. See for example *Re W* [2006] 1 HKC 468.

The return need not be accompanied by affidavit evidence, but if it is ambiguous and the ambiguities are not clarified by affidavit, the return may be held bad: *R v Roberts* (1869) 2 F&F 272; 175 ER 1056.

The return is a jurisdictional document and becomes part of the court record: *Bushell's Case* (1670) Vaughan 135, 137; 124 ER 1006, 1007; *Re Meng Ching Hai* [1990] 1 HKC 185, 187A (CA).

## [54.7.2]    Failure to provide any or any proper return

If the detainor makes no reply or no adequate reply the court may extend the time for compliance (section 22A(7), High Court Ordinance) and adjourn to a new hearing date: *Archer's Case* (1701) Fort 196; 92 ER 816. In *Cheung Ying-lun v Australia* [1990] 2 HKLR 99, 103 the court expressed strong disapproval of failure to comply in a timely fashion.

If ultimately there is still non-compliance the detainor may be fined or imprisoned for contempt: High Court Ordinance, section 22A(13), and see *R v Woodward* (1889) 5 TLR 565.

In the absence of a proper return the court has no discretion to refuse the remedy, but must grant it to the applicant as a matter of right. See the commentary under Order 54 rule 8, below.

## 8.    Procedure at hearing of writ (O. 54 r. 8)

**When a return to a writ of habeas corpus ad subjiciendum is made, the return shall first be read, and motion then made for discharging or remanding the person restrained or amending or quashing the return, and where that person is brought up in accordance with the writ, his counsel shall be heard first, then counsel for the Crown, and then one counsel for the person restrained in reply.**

---

## NOTES

### [54.8.1]    Interpretation of Order 54 rule 8 after 01.07.1997

The term 'the Crown' in Order 54 rule 8 should be construed as meaning the HKSAR government by virtue of the Reunification Ordinance and Schedule 8 to the Interpretation and General Clauses Ordinance (Cap 1).

### [54.8.2]    Procedure at substantive hearing

At the substantive hearing the reading of the return is the first order of business. Even a nil return must be read into the record to show that the writ has been complied with. If the return on its face provides legal justification for deprivation of liberty the court 'must immediately inquire into the circumstances surrounding the detention' (High Court Ordinance, Cap 4, section 22A(9)). The judge examines the truth of the facts alleged in the return: *Re Meng Ching Hai* [1990] 1 HKC 185, 186H–I (CA). The judge does so in accordance with the order of hearing laid down by Order 54 rule 8.

Unless the court is satisfied the detention is lawful the court must order release of the person: High Court Ordinance (Cap 4), section 22A(9) and (10).

### [54.8.3]    Burden of proof

At the substantive hearing the initial burden is on the applicant to produce evidence to put the legality of the detention in issue: *Superintendent of Tai A Chau Detention Centre v Tan Te Lam & Ors* [1995] 3 HKC 339, 353D–F (CA). In *Re W* [2006] 1 HKC 468 Hartmann J described this as a burden to demonstrate a *prima facie* case. If the applicant is able to put the lawfulness of the detention in issue, the burden shifts to the respondent. See *Re Pham Van Ngo & Ors* [1991] 1 HKLR 499, 506I citing *Liversidge v Anderson* [1942] AC 206 ('every imprisonment is *prima facie* unlawful and it is for the person directing imprisonment to justify it'). See also *Chung Tu Quan* [1995] 1 HKC 566, 583B–F and *Chan Cho Tei v AG* HCMP 463/ 1980 (Roberts CJ & Zimmern J; 03.06.1980).

**[54.8.4]    Standard of proof**
Habeas corpus proceedings are civil in nature and the standard of proof is the balance of probabilities: *Lee Yu Ying v Lee Yip Tang & Anor* [1983] 1 HKC 434, 437F; *Re an Application by the Official Solicitor (No 1)* [1983] 2 HKC 259; 274F-G. Once the burden has shifted to the respondent 'clear and cogent' evidence that a detention is lawful or that there is no detention is required: *Re W* [2006] 1 HKC 468, citing *Truong* (1994) 31 ALD 729, 731.

**[54.8.5]    Order to be made on substantive hearing**
Section 22A(9) of the High Court Ordinance provides that after inquiry into the circumstances the court 'must' order release of the applicant 'unless satisfied that the detention is lawful'. However this does not cater to all circumstances. In *Re Vonchai Tumtonkitkul* [1982] HKC 181 the court did not order the release of the applicant, but varied the order of a magistrate committing the applicant to detention pending extradition. This had the effect of reducing the scope of the charges for which the applicant could be extradited and tried abroad. In *Re W* [2006] 1 HKC 468 it was found that the person on whose behalf the application was brought was not detained at all and the application was dismissed. In *Re Tse Sun-miu* [1994] 2 HKLR 78,83 (CA) Bokhary JA said that release is not a 'matter of course':

> If in any instance it is by no means clear that the detention is unlawful, so that the lawfulness or otherwise of the reason given for the detention constitutes a substantial issue; if such issue would most appropriately be dealt with in a criminal appeal; and if the detainee's bid for freedom would, all things considered and looked at realistically in the round, be best served by leaving him to pursue such appeal: then the High Court has the power to leave him to do so.

In *Ex p Santiago* [1989] 1 HKC 293 the court adjourned the proceedings generally with liberty to restore where it was satisfied the detention was currently lawful, but might later become unlawful if it became apparent the purpose of the detention (removal from Hong Kong) had no reasonable prospect of success.

The court also has power to allow applications for habeas corpus to be withdrawn: *Chieng A Lac v Director of Immigration* [1997] HKLRD 271, 284F.

**[54.8.6]    Damages**
The purpose of habeas corpus is remedial, not punitive or compensatory. Thus the court will not award damages for an illegal detention on a habeas corpus application but will leave it to the successful applicant to seek damages for false imprisonment in separate proceedings. See *Yoo Soon-nam v AG* [1976] HKLR 702; *Pham Van Ngo & Ors v AG* HCA 4895/1990 (Patrick Chan J: 30.07.1993).

**[54.8.7]    Costs**
In contested habeas corpus proceedings arising in a civil context, costs will invariably follow the event. See *Chun Lun v Acting Superintendent of Victoria Gaol* (Hong Kong

Daily Press; 20.05.1897); *Leung Kun Yau v F H May* (Hong Kong Daily Press 13.09.1901); *Re Poon Yuk Sim* (1956) 40 HKLR 12, 25; and *Chen Chong Gui v Senior Superintendent of Lai Chi Kok Reception Centre & Anor* [1997] 3 HKC 210, 227H (CFI), [1998] 1 HKC 522, 544H (CA). If the parties compromise and the application is withdrawn they must bear their own costs (*Re Leung Toi Sam* [1959] HKLR 342, 354) in the absence of agreement to the contrary.

Where a habeas corpus application arises in a criminal context the modern practice in Hong Kong appears to be that costs will similarly follow the event. Although the Costs in Criminal Cases Ordinance (Cap 492) has no application this practice is supported by the fact that habeas corpus proceedings (in whatever context they arise) are civil in nature. There is some earlier authority in Hong Kong to the effect that costs will not be awarded against the government in these cases: see *Re Lo Tsun Man* (1910) 5 HKLR 166, 179; *Re Li Sam* (1931) 25 HKLR 58, 61 and *Re Sun Ah Wan* (1910) 5 HKLR 72, 82. And this continues to be the case in other jurisdictions: see *USA v Bowe* [1990] 1 AC 500, 535E–F.

### [54.8.8]    Restriction on re-detention after release

Section 22A(12) of the High Court Ordinance provides that a person released on a habeas corpus application may not be re-detained on the same or similar ground unless there has been a material change in circumstances. This rule traces back to the Habeas Corpus Act 1679 and older cases continue to be of authority. See *AG v Kwok-A-Sing* (1873) LR 5 PC 179, 202 (PC from HK); *Ng Hung-yiu v USA* [1992] 2 HKLR 383 and *Re Sung Man Cho* (1931) 25 HKLR 62, 71.

In *Vincente Sotto v Welch* (1914) 9 HKLR 1, 8, 14, it was held that the prohibition on re-detention applies only after a full hearing on the merits.

**9.     Bringing up prisoner to give evidence, etc.** (O. 54 r. 9)

**(1)    An application for a writ of habeas corpus ad testificandum or of habeas corpus ad respondendum must be made on affidavit to a judge in chambers.**

---

### NOTES

### [54.9.1]    Comparison with English rule

Rule 9(2) in England has no equivalent in Hong Kong. That rule deals with the bringing up of prisoners, otherwise than by a writ of habeas corpus, to give evidence in any cause or matter, civil or criminal, before any court, tribunal or justice.

In Hong Kong see section 12 of the Prisons Ordinance (Cap 234) and section 81 of the Evidence Ordinance (Cap 8).

### [54.9.2]    Order 54 rule 9 – applications for habeas corpus ad testificandum and habeas corpus ad respondendum

Order 54 rule 9 provides that applications for the writs of habeas corpus *ad testificandum* (to bring up a prisoner to testify) and of habeas corpus *ad respondendum* (to bring up a prisoner to face action by a creditor or other claimant) should be made on affidavit to a judge in chambers.

According to section 46 of the High Court Ordinance and the Schedule to that

Ordinance both those types of writ have been abolished in Hong Kong. The Schedule was amended by Ordinance 95/1997 so as to delete those types of writ of habeas corpus from the list of writs which exist in this jurisdiction. See also the definition section of the High Court Ordinance which confines the term 'writ of habeas corpus' to the writ of habeas corpus *ad subjiciendum*.

Nevertheless habeas corpus *ad testificandum* continues to be mentioned in section 2GC of the Arbitration Ordinance (Cap 341) (see the commentary under Order 54 rule 1 above). In other contexts the writ of habeas corpus *ad testificandum* is replaced by section 81 of the Evidence Ordinance (Cap 8) and by the 'body order': see the commentary under Order 38 rule 14.

The writ of habeas corpus *ad respondendum* does not appear to be mentioned in any primary legislation in Hong Kong and a search of the judiciary's database at late 2004 produced no judgments referring to this type of writ. Presumably it has been replaced by the procedure for arrest and examination of debtors under Orders 44A, 48 and 49B of these rules.

**10.    Form of writ** (O. 54 r. 10)
    **A writ of habeas corpus must be in Form No 89, 91 or 92 in Appendix A, whichever is appropriate.**
    **(Enacted 1988)**

------

**NOTES**

**[54.10.1]    Order 54 rule 10 – form of writ of habeas corpus**
The form of writ of habeas corpus *ad subjiciendum* is No 89 in Appendix A to these rules. The other two prescribed forms mentioned in rule 10 (forms 91 and 92) were in fact repealed in 1997. They were forms of writ of habeas corpus of types which were abolished that year – see the commentary under rule 9 above.

Section 22A(7) of the Ordinance suggests that the writ itself must specify the time and date for the person to whom it is directed to produce the person alleged to be detained and to make the formal return. Form No 89 does not cater to this requirement, though the prescribed form of Notice to be served with the writ (Form No 90) does. In *Re W* [2006] 1 HKC 468 it was argued that a writ in Form No 89 was 'invalid' in this regard but no ruling was made on the point.

## ORDER 55

### APPEALS TO THE HIGH COURT
### FROM COURT, TRIBUNAL OR PERSON: GENERAL

1.    **Application** (O. 55 r. 1)

(1)    **Subject to paragraphs (2), (3) and (4), this Order shall apply to every appeal which by or under any enactment lies to the Court of First Instance from any court, tribunal or person.**

(2)    **This Order shall not apply to—**

(a)    **an appeal by case stated,**

(HK)  (b)    **an appeal under the Magistrates Ordinance (Cap. 227), or**

(HK)  (c)    **any appeal to which Order 73 applies.**
**(L.N. 363 of 1990)**

(4)    **The following rules of this Order shall, in relation to an appeal to which this Order applies, have effect subject to any provision made in relation to that appeal by any other provision of these rules or by or under any enactment.**

(5)    **In this Order references to a Tribunal shall be construed as references to any Tribunal constituted by or under any enactment other than any of the ordinary courts of law.**

---

**NOTES**

**[55.1.1]    Scope of order**
This Order governs appeals from various inferior statutory tribunals to a single judge of the Court of First Instance. When dealing with such an appeal, the starting point must be the Ordinance and subsidiary legislation which establish the tribunal to be appealed from. It is usually there that one will discover the circumstances in which an appeal may be lodged.

The provisions of this Order are general for all tribunal appeals within its scope, and must in each case be read together with the specific rules, if any, made to govern proceedings in the particular tribunal.

**[55.1.2]    Examples of the appellate jurisdiction of the Court of First Instance**

(1)    *Appeals from the Small Claims Tribunal*
Appeal lies under section 28 of the Small Claims Tribunal Ordinance (Cap 338) from decisions of the Small Claims Tribunal to the Court of First Instance. Appeal may be made on any ground involving a question of law alone or on the ground that the claim was outside the jurisdiction of the tribunal. Leave to appeal must be sought from the Court of First Instance.

(2)    *Appeals from the Labour Tribunal*
Appeal lies under section 32(1) of the Labour Tribunal Ordinance (Cap 25) from decisions of the Labour Tribunal to the Court of First Instance on the grounds that

the award, order or determination was erroneous in point of law or outside the jurisdiction of the tribunal. Leave of the Court of First Instance is required.

### (3)    *Appeals under the Buildings Ordinance*

Appeal lies under section 7(4) of the Buildings Ordinance (Cap 123) from a decision of the disciplinary board to a judge of the Court of First Instance, from a decision of the board finding that an authorised person or registered structural engineer has been guilty of negligence or misconduct.

### (4)    *Appeals under the Pilotage Ordinance*

Appeal lies under section 20 of the Pilotage Ordinance (Cap 84) from a decision of the Board of Investigation (established under section 19 of the Ordinance) to the Court of First Instance. A further appeal lies to the Court of Appeal (*Chan Chung-fai v The Pilotage Authority* [1979] HKLR 562 (CA)).

### (5)    *Appeals from the Obscene Articles Tribunal*

Appeal lies under section 30 of the Control of Obscene and Indecent Articles Ordinance (Cap 390) to the Court of First Instance from decisions of the Obscene Articles Tribunal on points of law.  Such appeals are assigned to the Constitutional and Administrative Law List but are governed by Order 55.  See practice direction 26.1 and para 2.1 of the directions thereunder (known as PD SL3).

### (6)    *Appeals under the Estate Duty Ordinance*

Section 22 of the Estate Duty Ordinance (Cap 111) provides for appeals to the Court of First Instance from decisions of the Commissioner in respect of property alleged by the Commissioner to be worth more than $200,000.  Where the alleged value is a lower figure, appeal lies to the district court.

### (7)    *Appeals under the Copyright Ordinance*

Section 176 of the Copyright Ordinance (Cap 528) provides for appeals from the Copyright Tribunal to the Court of First Instance on any point of law.

### (8)    *Appeals under the Chinese Medicine Ordinance*

Section 141(1) of the Chinese Medicine Ordinance (Cap 549) provides for appeals to the Court of First Instance from any decision of the Medicines Board under that Ordinance.

### [55.1.3]    Appeals to the Court of First Instance which are not governed by Order 55

Order 55 rule 1(2) lists certain types of appeal to the Court of First Instance which are *not* governed by this Order.  They are:

- *Appeal by case stated* – for example appeals under section 69 of the Inland Revenue Ordinance (Cap 112). See the discussion below.
- *Appeals from magistrates* – appeals from magistrates in criminal matters are generally governed by Part VII of the Magistrates Ordinance (Cap 227) and these rules do not apply.  However this Order does apply to appeals from a magistrate under section 4(2) of the Costs in Criminal Cases Rules (Cap

492): *HKSAR v Wai Sau Cheong* [2003] 1 HKC 640.

- *Order 73 appeals* – Order 73 makes provision for arbitration proceedings and any appeal to which that Order applies is not subject to Order 55.

### [55.1.4] Appeals under the Trade Marks Ordinance

For appeals to the Court of First Instance from the Registrar of Trade Marks, see Order 100.

### [55.1.5] Appeals from the Inland Revenue Board of Review

Under section 69(1) of the Inland Revenue Ordinance (Cap 112) either the appellant or the Commissioner of Inland Revenue may make an application requiring the Board of Review to state a case on a question of law for the opinion of the Court of First Instance

As for the function of the court on such appeals, see *Rico Internationale Ltd v Commissioner of Inland Revenue* [1965] HKLR 493 and *Commissioner of Inland Revenue (No 2) v Hong Kong Whampoa Dock Co Ltd* [1960] HKLR 166, at 199.

Appeal lies on law alone (*Shun Lee Investment Co Ltd v Commissioner of Inland Revenue* [1967] HKLR 712).

As for the proper method of stating a case, see *Commissioner of Inland Revenue v Aspiration Land Investment Ltd* [1991] 1 HKLR 409.

The provisions of Order 55 do *not* apply to such appeals as they proceed by way of case stated (see Order 55 rule 1(2)(a)). The procedure regulating such appeals is to be found in the Inland Revenue Ordinance.

**(HK)2.   Court to hear appeal** (O. 55 r. 2)

**Except where it is otherwise provided by these rules or under any enactment, an appeal to which this Order applies shall be heard and determined by a single judge.**

**(L.N. 363 of 1990)**

---

### NOTES

### [55.2.1]   Appeal to be heard by a single judge

In *Re CHM Finance (HK) Ltd* [1990] 1 HKLR 248, it was held that an appeal under Order 55 should be heard and determined by two or more judges. As a result of amendments to Order 55 rule 2 in 1988 and 1990, that decision should no longer be followed.

**3.   Bringing of appeal** (O. 55 r. 3)

**(1)An appeal to which this Order applies shall be by way of rehearing and must be brought by originating motion.**

**(2)   Every notice of the motion by which such an appeal is brought must state the grounds of the appeal and, if the appeal is against a judgment, order or other decision of a court, must state whether the appeal is against the whole or a part of that decision and, if against a part only, must specify the part.**

**(3)   The bringing of such an appeal shall not operate as a stay of**

proceedings on the judgment, determination or other decision against which the appeal is brought unless the Court by which the appeal is to be heard or the court, tribunal or person by which or by whom the decision was given so orders.

---

## NOTES

**[55.3.1]     Appeal by way of rehearing**
Order 55 rule 3(1) provides that an appeal under this Order is by way of rehearing. This means the court will consider the evidence and submissions afresh without the witnesses being recalled: see the commentary under Order 59 rule 3. However, there is express power to receive fresh evidence whether by affidavit or otherwise – see Order 55 rule 7(2).

It has been suggested that that an appeal under Order 55 is not a rehearing in its full sense. See *Licoman Herbal Research Lab Ltd v Chinese Medicines Board* HCMP 2420/2009 (Chung J; 29.11.2010). In that case, the court was referred to authorities concerning appeals from the Registrar of Trade Marks to the effect that great weight should be attached to the decision below; *ie* the Registrar being an expert, his decision should only be disturbed for mistake of law or having clearly come to a wrong conclusion. Note, however, that appeals from the Registrar of Trade Marks are not governed by this Order, but by Order 100.

**4.     Service of notice of motion and entry of appeal** (O. 55 r. 4)
    **(1)     The persons to be served with notice of the motion by which an appeal to which this Order applies is brought are the following—**
        **(a)     if the appeal is against a judgment, order or other decision of a court, the registrar or clerk of the court and any party to the proceedings in which the decision was given who is directly affected by the appeal;**
        **(b)     if the appeal is against an order, determination, award or other decision of a tribunal, government department or other person, the chairman of the tribunal, government department or person, as the case may be, and every party to the proceedings (other than the appellant) in which the decision appealed against was given.**
    **(2)     The notice must be served, and the appeal entered, within 28 days after the date of the judgment, order, determination or other decision against which the appeal is brought.**
    **(3)     In the case of an appeal against a judgment, order or decision of a court, the period specified in paragraph (2) shall be calculated from the date of the judgment or order or the date on which the decision was given.**
    **(4)     In the case of an appeal against an order, determination, award or other decision of a tribunal, government department or other person, the period specified in paragraph (2) shall be calculated from the date on which notice of the decision was given to the appellant by the person who made the decision or by a person authorized in that behalf to do so.**

## NOTES

### [55.4.1]   Parties to an appeal
By virtue of rule 4(1)(b) the tribunal whose decision is appealed against must be served with the appeal papers. However, it is incorrect to name the tribunal as the respondent to the appeal. The parties to the appeal are the same parties who appeared in the proceedings before the tribunal. In *East Touch Publisher Ltd v TELA* [1996] 3 HKC 195 Keith J had before him an appeal against a decision of the Obscene Articles Tribunal. The learned judge said (at 198C):

> The tribunal is named as the respondent to this appeal. This is not uncommon practice. However, the practice is wrong. The parties to an appeal are the same parties to the proceedings from which the appeal is brought.

The learned judge went on to grant leave under Order 15 rule 6(2)(b)(i) to substitute the complainant in the proceedings below for the tribunal as the respondent on the appeal.

### [55.4.2]   Time for appealing
Order 55 rule 4(2) provides that the appellant has 28 days within which to serve a notice of originating motion appealing against a decision to which Order 55 applies. The 28-day period begins to run on the date of the judgment of the court below (Order 55 rule 4(3)), or, in the case of other decision-making bodies, on the date notice of the decision is 'given to the appellant'. There are conflicting decisions in England as to what is meant by 'given to the appellant'. One view is that a decision is 'given' for this purpose when sent to the appellant, another that it is 'given' when received by him. In *Yue Bob Ken, Bobby v Hon Ying Chu, Leon M Lee* HCMP 6366/ 1998 (Leong JA; 24.12.1998), the court treated a decision as having been given to the intended appellant on the day it was pronounced in the presence of her represen tative. (Note that this appears to have been an appeal to the Court of Appeal rather than the Court of First Instance, so Order 55 should not apply).

### [55.4.3]   Extension of time for appealing
Extension of time to appeal under Order 55 may be granted under Order 3 rule 5. In *Le Thi Bich Thuy Kitty v Sheraton International (HK) Ltd* HCLA 34/2004 (Lam J; 04.06.2004) it was held that the merits of the intended appeal are relevant to an extension application and that the registrar should be 'stringent' in approaching such applications. In *Leung Kam Tong v Italy Leone Int'l Group (Asia) Ltd* HCMP 2415/ 2005 (Deputy Judge Mayo; 06.12.2005) an extension application was dismissed partly for lack of explanation of the delay.

**5.    Date of hearing of appeal** (O. 55 r. 5)
    **Unless the Court having jurisdiction to determine the appeal otherwise directs, an appeal to which this Order applies shall not be heard sooner than 21 days after service of notice of the motion by which the appeal is brought.**

**6.  Amendment of grounds of appeal, etc.** (O. 55 r. 6)
    **(1)   The notice of the motion by which an appeal to which this Order**

applies is brought may be amended by the appellant, without leave, by supplementary notice served not less than 7 days before the day appointed for the hearing of the appeal, on each of the persons on whom the notice to be amended was served.

(2)   Within 2 days after service of a supplementary notice under paragraph (1) the appellant must lodge two copies of the notice in the office in which the appeal is entered.

(3)   Except with the leave of the Court hearing any such appeal, no grounds other than those stated in the notice of the motion by which the appeal is brought or any supplementary notice under paragraph (1) may be relied upon by the appellant at the hearing; but that Court may amend the grounds so stated or make any other order, on such terms as it thinks just, to ensure the determination on the merits of the real question in controversy between the parties.

(4)   The foregoing provisions of this rule are without prejudice to the powers of the Court under Order 20.

**6A.    Interlocutory applications** (O. 55 r. 6A)

(1)   Unless the Court otherwise directs, any interlocutory application in proceedings to which this Order applies may be made to any judge or a master.

In this paragraph "interlocutory application" includes an application for the extension of time for the service of a notice of motion or the entry of the appeal or for the amendment of the notice of motion.

(2)   This rule is without prejudice to any statutory provision or rule of law restricting the making of an order against the Crown.

(L.N. 404 of 1991)

**7.    Powers of court hearing appeal** (O. 55 r. 7)

(1)   In addition to the power conferred by rule 6(3), the Court hearing an appeal to which this Order applies shall have the powers conferred by the following provisions of this rule.

(2)   The Court shall have power to receive further evidence on questions of fact, and the evidence may be given in such manner as the Court may direct either by oral examination in court, by affidavit, by deposition taken before an examiner or in some other manner.

(3)   The Court shall have power to draw any inferences of fact which might have been drawn in the proceedings out of which the appeal arose.

(4)   It shall be the duty of the appellant to apply to the judge or other person presiding at the proceedings in which the decision appealed against was given for a signed copy of any note made by him of the proceedings and to furnish that copy for the use of the Court; and in default of production of such a note, or, if such note is incomplete, in addition to such note, the Court may hear and determine the appeal on any other evidence or statement of what occurred in those proceedings as appears to the Court to be sufficient.

Except where the Court otherwise directs, an affidavit or note by a person present at the proceedings shall not be used in evidence under this paragraph unless it was previously submitted to the person presiding at the

**proceedings for his comments.**

**(5)   The Court may give any judgment or decision or make any order which ought to have been given or made by the court, tribunal or person and make such further or other order as the case may require or may remit the matter with the opinion of the Court for rehearing and determination by it or him.**

**(6)   The Court may, in special circumstances, order that such security shall be given for the costs of the appeal as may be just.**

**(7)   The Court shall not be bound to allow the appeal on the ground merely of misdirection, or of the improper admission or rejection of evidence, unless in the opinion of the Court substantial wrong or miscarriage has been thereby occasioned.**

---

## NOTES

### [55.7.1]     Powers of court on appeal – constitutional considerations
The powers of the court on appeal under this Order are sufficiently broad to cure any defect in the composition of the tribunal below with regard to the right to an independent and impartial tribunal under article 10 of the Hong Kong Bill of Rights. See *R v Lift Contractors' Disciplinary Board, ex p Otis Elevator Co (HK) Ltd* (1995) 5 HKPLR 78. On the other hand see *Leary v National Union of Vehicle Builders* [1971] Ch 34, 49 where it was said that 'failure of natural justice in the trial body cannot be cured by a sufficiency of natural justice in an appellate body'.

### [55.7.2]     Power to admit fresh evidence
On an appeal under Order 55, the court has power to admit fresh evidence whether by affidavit or otherwise: rule 7(2). This is equivalent to the power of the Court of Appeal under Order 59 rule 10(2). See the commentary thereunder.

### [55.7.3]     Power to draw inferences of fact
On an appeal under Order 55, the court has power to draw inferences of fact which might have been drawn below: rule 7(3). This is equivalent to the power of the Court of Appeal under Order 59 rule 10(3). See the commentary thereunder.

### [55.7.4]     Power to remit for rehearing
Under Order 55 rule 7(5), the court has power to remit a matter to the tribunal below or grant other relief. In the unusual case of *Curtis v Chairman of London Rent Assessment Committee* [1999] QB 92, the court remitted the matter to the tribunal for fresh consideration on the appeal of the party which had been successful below. The successful party objected to the reasoning of the tribunal below.

### [55.7.5]     Security for costs of appeal
Order 55 rule 7(6) gives the court power to order security for the costs of an appeal 'in special circumstances'. This power cannot be used to order security for the costs of an appeal from a master to a single judge since those appeals are governed by Order 58, not Order 55: *Mo Chi Man v Young Wai Yi* HCMP 7402/1999 (Cheung J; 01.02.2000) and *Perennial Cable (HK) Ltd v Popbridge Industrial Ltd* [2000] 1 HKC 564.

**[55.7.6]    Appeals on points of misdirection or admissibility of evidence**

Order 55 rule 7(7) provides that where the tribunal below misdirected itself or erred on a point of admissibility of evidence, the court is not bound to allow the appeal unless the result is a 'substantial wrong or miscarriage'. The effect of the rule is 'to provide guidance on the exercise of the judicial discretion' as to what order to make: *Ip Wah v Cheung Chun Chiu* HCMP 251/2007 (Yuen JA & Chu J; 22.06.2007), concerning section 35(1) of the Labour Tribunal Ordinance, which provides that on an appeal to the CFI the court may (a) allow the appeal, (b) dismiss the appeal, or (c) remit the matter to the tribunal. In result the court may dismiss an appeal where it is satisfied that even without the error below, the result would be the same: *Knight v Dorset CC* [1997] EWCA Civ 1496. Thus, it has been observed, appeals to which rule 7(7) applies are 'difficult to sustain': *Re Selleys Pty Ltd* HCMP 82/2006 (Deputy Judge Carlson; 21.07.2006).

In *Ip Wah* (above) the Court of Appeal dismissed an argument that rule 7(7) does not apply to appeals from the Labour Tribunal.

Rule 7(7) applies only in cases of misdirection or wrongful admission or rejection of evidence. See *Winning Co v Director of Fire Services* HCMP 4459/1999 (Deputy Judge To; 29.02.2000) where it was found the rule did not apply to an appeal based on failure to discharge the burden of proof.

**8.      Right of government department to appear and be heard** (O. 55 r. 8)

**Where an appeal to which this Order applies is against any order, determination or other decision of a government department, the department shall be entitled to appear and be heard in the proceedings on the appeal.**

**(Enacted 1988)**

---

**NOTES**

**[56-57.0.1]  Orders 56 and 57 omitted**

Orders 56 and 57 have been omitted from the Hong Kong rules. Under the previous English RSC those Orders dealt with appeals by way of case stated and Divisional Court proceedings.

## ORDER 58

### APPEALS FROM MASTERS

1.    **Appeals from certain decisions of masters to a judge in chambers**
(O. 58 r. 1)
**(1)    Except as provided by rule 2, Order 5, rule 6, and Order 12, rule 1, an appeal shall lie to a judge in chambers from any judgment, order or decision of a master, irrespective of whether the judgment, order or decision was given or made on the basis of written submissions only or after hearing. (L.N. 152 of 2008)**

**(2)    The appeal shall be brought by serving on every other party to the proceedings in which the judgment, order or decision was given or made a notice to attend before the judge on a day specified in the notice or as on such other day as may be directed.**

**(3)    Unless the Court otherwise orders, the notice must be issued within 14 days after the judgment, order or decision appealed against was given or made and must be served within 5 days after issue and an appeal to which this rule applies shall not be heard sooner than 2 clear days after such service. (L.N. 404 of 1991; L.N. 129 of 2000)**

**(4)    Except so far as the Court may otherwise direct, an appeal under this rule shall not operate as a stay of the proceedings in which the appeal is brought.**

**(5)    No further evidence (other than evidence as to matters which have occurred after the date on which the judgment, order or decision was given or made) may be received on the hearing of an appeal under this rule except on special grounds. (L.N. 152 of 2008)**

---

## NOTES

**[58.1.1]    Scope of Order 58 rule 1 – appeal as of right from master to single judge**

Order 58 rule 1 provides that most decisions of a master may be appealed to a single judge of the Court of First Instance sitting in chambers. The exceptions are:

(a)    decisions of a final rather than interlocutory character which by rule 2 must be appealed to the Court of Appeal, and

(b)    decisions under Order 5 rule 6 and Order 12 rule 1 giving or refusing leave for a company to be represented by director, which are deemed to be final.

An appeal to a single judge under this rule lies as of right, unlike interlocutory appeals to the Court of Appeal, which generally require leave to appeal. The Chief Justice's working party on civil justice reform, which recommended the leave requirement for interlocutory appeals to the Court of Appeal (implemented by section 14AA of the High Court Ordinance, in force in 2009), decided that the pre-existing position whereby appeals from a master to a single judge lay as of right should continue (final report, recommendation 109). However, a further appeal to the Court of Appeal will require leave if the decision is of the type which comes within section 14AA of the High Court Ordinance. Likewise the leave requirement in section 14(3)(e) of the High Court Ordinance for appeals relating only to costs applies only to appeals to the Court of Appeal, and not appeals under this Order from a master to a single judge: *Honnin Development Ltd v Ho Ming & Anor* HCA 16376/1999 (Poon J; 14.12.2000).

Masters have power to determine interlocutory applications with or without an oral hearing: see Order 32 rule 11A. That provision came into force as part of the civil justice reforms in 2009, and at the same time Order 58 rule 1(1) was amended to make clear that an appeal lies to a single judge whether the master's decision was made after an oral hearing or on the basis of written submissions.

In *Official Receiver v Chan Hing To* [2007] 2 HKC 43 (CA) it was suggested that the procedure under Order 58 for appeals from a master to a single judge could theoretically be bypassed by an appeal direct to the Court of Appeal. However, in that case such an appeal was struck out on the ground there were good reasons why the Order 58 proce dure should be followed instead. Since that decision was handed down, section 14AA of the High Court Ordinance has come into force, whereby leave to appeal to the Court of Appeal is required in respect of most interlocutory decisions (see Order 59 rules 2A, 2B and 21 and the commentary thereunder). It seems highly unlikely that leave to appeal would be granted where the avenue of an appeal as of right to a single judge is available.

### [58.1.2]      Time
Notice of an appeal from a master to a single judge must be 'issued' within 14 days of the judgment, order or decision to be appealed: Order 58 rule 1(3). Note that time runs from the date the decision 'was given or made', not from the later date on which the order is sealed by the court. It would appear that the notice is 'issued' when presented to the court for filing. The notice must be served on every other party to the proceedings with 14 days of being issued, leaving at least 2 clear days between service and the hearing: rule 1(2)&(3).

### [58.1. 3]      Extension of time to appeal
The court's general power under Order 3 rule 5 to extend time applies to appeals from a master to a single judge under Order 58.

The factors relevant to the exercise of the court's discretion in this context are well established. In *Lai Yuen Wah v Hoi Kwong Printing Co Ltd* [2003] 1 HKC 447, 450F–G Deputy Judge Saunders enumerated them as follows:

(a)      the length of the delay
(b)      the reasons for the delay
(c)      the chances of the appeal being successful, and
(d)      the degree of prejudice to the defendant

See also *Wong Kam Hong v Triangle Motors Ltd* [1998] 2 HKC 219, 224D–E and *Hsiao Hsiu Yang v Chu Wai Ting* HCA 5909/1999 (Chu J; 05.12.2003).

The reasons for delay should be explained on affidavit to the satisfaction of the court: *Postwell Ltd v Cheng Kap Sang* [2004] 2 HKLRD 355. In the absence of such an affidavit there is no basis on which the court can exercise its discretion to grant an extension: *Chan Kong v Chan Li Chai Medical Fty (HK) Ltd & Ors* HCA 4101/2001 (Deputy Judge Saunders; 10.03.2006).

Other factors may be relevant in individual cases. See *Chiu Sin-chung v Yu Yan-yan Angela & Anor* [1993] 1 HKLR 225, 227-8, elaborating on the above list. In *Wong Tsz Yuk v Commissioner of Police & Anor* HCA 1699/2008 (Chung J; 29.04.2010) the court took the view that waiting for the master's reasons for the decision to be appealed is not a valid reason for delay. This was because an appeal under Order 58 rule 1 is by way of fresh hearing, so the master's reasons for decision are of little use on such an appeal.

A development in the law after delivery of the judgment to be appealed is not of itself considered a justifiable reason to extend the time for an appeal. See *Leung Yiu & Ors v Birkenhead Properties and Investments Ltd* [1998] 1 HKC 561; *Lam Yun Wah Dominic & Anor v Chan Kan Hei & Anor* [2000] 4 HKC 500, 504I (CA).

The court's approach in evaluating the relevant factors was considered in *Lai Yuen Wah* (above). Deputy Judge Saunders doubted the strict approach taken in some earlier cases such as *Tong Yi Sang & Anor v Fung Law & Ng & Ors* [1993] 2 HKC 665. He said that the 'modern approach' is not 'mechanistic', but reflects the fact the 'court has the widest measure of discretion in which the merits of a potential appeal and the prejudice to the other side are more relevant factors'. The deputy judge referred to *Finnegan v Parkside Health Authority* [1998] 1 WLR 411 (CA).

### [58.1. 4]    Jurisdiction

The court has jurisdiction to hear an appeal under this order notwithstanding that the proceedings have been stayed by virtue of the order which is the subject of the appeal. See *Lam Fei Hong v Wong Kam Fong & Ors* [1999] 2 HKC 781 per Keith J. Otherwise 'there could never be an appeal from an order for a stay unless the order expressly permitted it' (per Keith J at 783G–H).

A single judge on appeal from a master under this order has power in appropriate circumstances to set aside the master's order on the basis that the appealing party was absent at the hearing below: see *Pak Tim Chun v Tung Yung Metals Factory* [1998] 3 HKC 691 (CA).

It has been suggested that no appeal lies as to the sufficiency of security ordered by a master as a condition of leave to defend under Order 14. See Hong Kong Civil Procedure 2001 citing *Hoare v Morshead* [1903] 2 KB 359 (CA). However, in *Wong Hung Yu Richard v Wu Ming Fat Simon* [2002] 2 HKC 687 Ma J held (at 689H) that *Hoare v Morshead* 'is not authority for this proposition at all'. The learned judge held that if that case remains good law at all, it is confined to the *form* of security rather than the *quantum* of security. Further, since it is now invariable to order that the security be paid into court the rule would not now have much applica tion anyway.

### [58.1.5]    On appeal the application is heard afresh

An appeal under Order 58 from a master to a judge in chambers is an actual rehearing in the sense that the judge hears the application afresh. This differs from appeals to the Court of Appeal, where there is only nominally a rehearing. In *Wai Cheong Co Ltd v Kiu May Construction Co Ltd* [1983] 2 HKC 403, Clough J, citing *Evans v Bartlam* [1937] AC 473, 478, said, at 409 C–E:

> It is settled practice that an appeal from the Master to the Judge in Chambers is by way of an actual re-hearing of the application which led to the order under appeal. It is for

that reason that the judge treats the matter as if it came before him for the first time, although the appellant always has to open the appeal. The judge exercises the same discretion as that previously exercised by the Master with due respect to the Master's decision but the judge is unfettered by it.

See also *Killenny Ltd & Ors v AG* CACV 157/1995 (Litton VP, Godfrey & Liu JJA; 20.10.1995) where it was noted that this practice exists despite the fact that Order 58 is silent in this regard.

It follows that where the appeal is against a discretionary decision, the judge in chambers should be prepared to exercise the discretion afresh and not be bound by the rule in the Court of Appeal that discretionary decisions should be interfered with only when clearly wrong (*Kung Wong Sau-hin v CP Lin & Co* [1988] 2 HKLR 209 (CA)).

It follows that new issues or points not argued before the master may be raised on the appeal to a judge in chambers. See *El Vince Ltd v Wu Wen Sheng* [2001] 4 HKC 107, 112H where Kwan J held that a party was entitled to raise a point on appeal notwithstanding its agreement not to raise the point before the master. The learned judge cited *Magec Aviation Ltd v Fayair (Jersey) Co Ltd* (English QBD, 25 March 1997, unreported).

It follows from the fact that an appeal under Order 58 is by way of an actual rehearing that new evidence not before the master may be adduced. See the commentary below under the heading '*New evidence*'.

**[58.1. 6]     Respondent's Notice and Notice of Cross-Appeal**
In view of the fact that an appeal under Order 58 proceeds by way of fresh hearing it is not strictly necessary for a respondent to give formal notice of any point he would wish to take by way of cross-appeal. However, the court has observed that whatever the technical position, it is sensible and courteous to give such notice where appropriate: *Chinakong Manufactory Ltd v Uniden Hong Kong* [1992] 1 HKC 481, 484A–B.

There is no procedure under Order 58 for the filing of a Respondent's Notice seek ing to affirm a master's decision on other reasons. Further, it is not appropriate to adapt the procedure for such notice found in Order 59 rule 6 for appeals to the Court of Appeal: see *Morigood Development Ltd v Sunny Trading Co (a firm)* [1999] 2 HKC 710, 718A–D. In that case Keith J held that there was no need for a Respondent's Notice procedure under Order 58, as masters are not required to give reasons.

**[58.1.7]     Appeals as to costs**
A judge in chambers should not allow an appeal against a costs order made by a master unless it can be shown that the order made is unreasonable or erroneous in law or the master either failed to take into account proper matters or took into account matters that should not have been taken into account: *China Venturetechno Int'l Co Ltd v New Century Chain Development* [1996] 2 HKC 68 (CFI); CACV 20/ 1996 (Nazareth VP; Bokhary & Liu JJA; 03.07.1996); *Wong Chi Keung v Farspeed Int'l Ltd & Ors* HCPI 262/2003 (Deputy Judge Gill; 21.11.2005), citing *Hoddle v CCF Construction Ltd* [1992] 2 All ER 550. The burden which the appellant carries on such an appeal 'is not an easy one': *Lam Sik Shi v Lam Sik Ying* HCMP 1464/ 2004 (Deputy Judge Carlson; 16.02.2006); but where it is demonstrated that the master has not exercised the discretion correctly, the single judge on appeal may

look at the question afresh: *Paul Y-ITC Construction Ltd v Kin Shing Co Ltd* [1999] 1 HKC 511, 515G-H.

### [58.1. 8]  Appeals as to pre-judgment interest rate

As with an appeal against costs, a single judge should be reluctant to interfere with a master's discretion in fixing the rate of pre-judgment interest payable on a judgment: *Tago Ltd v Process Automation Int'l Ltd* HCA 1133/2006 (Deputy Judge Muttrie; 18.05.2006). Different considerations will apply where interest is awarded not as a matter of discretion but as part of the plaintiff's cause of action: see the commentary under Order 42 rule 1.

### [58.1. 9]  Further evidence on appeal from master to single judge

Order 58 rule 1(5) expressly provides for further evidence which was not before the master to be placed before the single judge on appeal. There is no restriction on such further evidence if it relates to matters which occurred after the date of the master's decision being appealed. However 'special grounds' are required if the evidence could have been, but was not, adduced before the master.

Rule 1(5) was introduced as part of the civil justice reforms which came into force on 2 April 2009. In *Aggressive Construction Co Ltd v Yick Wai Cheong* HCA 1889/2008 (Deputy Judge Au; 29.06.2009) (para 24) the court rejected an argument that it applies only to proceedings issued after that date. It was sufficient that the application to adduce new evidence had been taken out after 2 April 2009. Previously there was no express power by which the court could admit new evidence on appeal to a single judge, though it was accepted that there was a discretion to do so: *Core Resources (FE) Ltd v Sky Finders Ltd* [1992] 1 HKLR 193. At that time, because of the nature of such an appeal as a rehearing 'as though the matter was before the judge for the first time', the court was 'much more ready to admit further evidence . . . than on appeal to the Court of Appeal': *Wong Hung Yu Richard v Wu Ming Fat Simon* [2002] 2 HKC 687, 690H, per Ma J. As a result of the 'special grounds' requirement in rule 1(5), that should no longer be the case. The 'special grounds' requirement is the same as that which has long applied in the Court of Appeal: see Order 59 rule 10(2). Moreover, the Chief Justice's working part on civil justice reform, in recommending this change, specifically referred to *Ladd v Marshall* [1954] 1 WLR 1489 which set out the criteria applied under the 'special grounds' test in the Court of Appeal (final report, para 645, n 534).

Shortly after rule 1(5) came into force the court adopted the *Ladd v Marshall* criteria on an application for leave under the new provision. See *Chan Yau v Chan Calvin & Anor* HCA 666/2007 (Sakhrani J; 15.05.2009) (para 19); and *Fortis Insurance Co (Asia) Ltd v Lam Hau Wah Inneo* HCA 1840/2009 (Fok J; 30.03.2010) (para 15-17). For discussion of those criteria, see the commentary under Order 59 rule 10(2). In addition, certain aspects of the approach taken by the court on Order 58 appeals prior to the introduction of rule 1(5) appear to remain valid. They include:

(a)  Leave may be refused if the new evidence entails a radical change of the party's case or raises matters which should have been dealt with before: *Core Resources* (above) (198).

(b)  Leave may be refused where the party, despite being given the opportunity to do so, failed to adduce further evidence below: *Wong Hung Yu Richard* (above) (690F).

## [58.1. 10]   Procedure on application for leave to adduce further evidence

An application for leave to adduce further evidence on appeal to a single judge should be made by summons. In most cases it will be appropriate for the summons to be returnable at the appeal hearing itself. See *So Kam Wing & Anor v Seapower Resources Int'l Ltd* [2000] 2 HKC 50. An earlier hearing of the leave application could result in disproportionate costs being incurred. However an earlier hearing may be necessary if, should the application be successful, the other party will require time to prepare evidence in response, as in *Wong Hung Yu Richard* (above) (691C–F).

Where the application for leave to adduce further evidence was initially made to the master, but refused, it is not appropriate to make a fresh application by summons before the single judge. Rather the master's refusal should itself be made the subject of an appeal (or cross-appeal) to the single judge from the master: *Jindal Exports Ltd v Waco Trading Co Ltd* [2000] 2 HKC 46, 47I. However the judge should consider the appeal with regard to the fresh evidence on the basis of the facts and circumstances as they exist at the time of the appeal, rather than as they were before the master: *Ip Yin Ping & Ors v Ip Anne* [2003] 2 HKC 595, 599G–H.

## [58.1. 11]   Practice direction

Practice direction 5.4 gives guidance as to preparation of bundles, *dramatis personae*, chronology of events, skeleton arguments and lists of authorities for appeals under Order 58 from a master to a single judge. Revisions to this practice direction took effect in 2009 along with the civil justice reforms coming into force. It is now provided that the written decision of the master, if any, should be included in the hearing bundle. The updated text of the practice direction may be viewed on the judiciary website www.judiciary.gov.hk or that of the Hong Kong Legal Information Institute www.hklii.org, both of which are accessible by the general public free-of-charge.

This practice direction also governs interlocutory summonses set down for hearing before a judge, or for 30 minutes or more before a master, under Order 32 rule 1. See the commentary under that rule for reference to cases in which the court has criticised the failure of parties to comply with the practice direction and warned of possible costs consequences.

## [58.1. 12]   No security for costs

The court has no power to order security for costs of an appeal to a single judge under Order 58. See *Brand Farrar Buxbaum LLP v Samuel-Rozenbaum Diamond Ltd & Ors* [2003] 1 HKLRD 600, 609D *et seq* where it was held that the absence of an express power is deliberate, and cannot be filled by reliance on inherent jurisdiction.

**2.     Appeals from certain decisions of masters to Court of Appeal** (O. 58 r. 2)
**An appeal shall lie to the Court of Appeal from any judgment, order or decision (other than an interlocutory judgment, order or decision) of a master, given or made—**

       **(HK)  (a)     on the hearing or determination of any cause, matter, question or issue tried before him under Order 14, rule 6(2) and Order 36, rule 1;**

| | | |
|---|---|---|
| | **(b)** | **on an assessment of damages under Order 37 or otherwise; or** |
| **(HK)** | **(c)** | **on the hearing or determination of an application under Order 84A, rule 3; or (L.N. 127 of 1995)** |
| **(HK)** | **(d)** | **on the hearing or determination of an application under Order 49B; or** |
| **(HK)** | **(e)** | **on the hearing of a petition for winding-up or bankruptcy.** |
| | | **(L.N. 404 of 1991)** |

---

**NOTES**

**[58.2.1]    Appeal from master to Court of Appeal**

Appeals from a master are normally made to a single judge of the Court of First Instance under Order 58 rule 1. In certain circumstances, laid down in Order 58 rule 2, an appeal from a master's decision must be made direct to the Court of Appeal. Broadly speaking the appeal will be to the Court of Appeal where the master's decision was of a final rather than interlocutory character, or made in exercise of a master's limited jurisdiction in open court. For example, where the parties have consented to an order under Order 36 rule 1 that a trial take place before a master, the resulting judgment would be appealable direct to the Court of Appeal. In *Kwok Ying Lung v Ko Chi Hung & Anor* [2001] 3 HKC 480 it was suggested that such an appeal might be incompetent if the order providing for the trial before a master did not record the consent of the parties thereto.

In *Lam Shing Chin t/a New Cotton Trading Co v Luen Hing Fat Textile Ltd* [1989] 2 HKC 485, 488F–489E Bokhary J held that notwithstanding Order 58 rule 2(d) (which provides that an appeal against a master's order under Order 49B shall be to the Court of Appeal) a single judge had power to hear an appeal against an order for imprisonment under that Order where the order complained of had been made without jurisdiction.

Rule 2(e), in providing for appeals from a master to the Court of Appeal in winding-up and bankruptcy matters, does not apply to ancillary orders such as an order suspending discharge of a bankrupt (*Re Chung Kwok Yiu Ringo* [2001] 2 HKLRD 749) or an order for disqualification of a company director (*Re Forever Wise Investment Ltd* [2006] 3 HKLRD 885 (CA)).

Appeals from a master to the Court of Appeal under rule 2 will usually, if not always, lie as of right. This is because the types of appeal which come within the ambit of rule 2 are either not interlocutory, and thus not subject to the leave requirement in section 14AA of the High Court Ordinance, or they are listed in Order 59 rule 21 which sets out the interlocutory appeals to which the leave requirement in section 14AA does not apply.

**[58.2.2]    Time**

Order 58 rule 2 does not stipulate the time within which an appeal from a master to the Court of Appeal shall be issued. Instead the times specified in Order 59 rule 4 are generally applicable. See Order 59 rule 1 which provides that that Order applies 'so far as applicable' to appeals from a master to the Court of Appeal. Those times should give way to specific provision made elsewhere, such as was formerly the case with section 98(2) of the Bankruptcy Ordinance.

**7.     Appeal from judgment, etc. of judge in interpleader proceedings**
(O. 58 r. 7)

**(1)    Any judgment, order or decision of a judge given or made in summarily determining under Order 17, rule 5(2)(b) or (c), any question at issue between claimants in interpleader proceedings shall be final and conclusive against the claimants and all persons claiming under them unless leave to appeal to the Court of Appeal is given by the judge or the Court of Appeal.**

**(2)    Where an interpleader issue is tried by a judge (with or without a jury), an appeal shall lie to the Court of Appeal, without the leave of the judge or that Court, from any judgment, order or decision given or made by the judge on the trial.**

**(3)    (Repealed, L.N. 152 of 2008)**

**(Enacted 1988)**

---

**NOTES**

**[58.7.1]     Leave to appeal to Court of Appeal required from certain decisions of judge in interpleader proceedings**

Order 58 rule 7 provides that summary determination by a judge of a question arising in interpleader proceedings is final and conclusive unless leave to appeal to the Court of Appeal is granted. The requirement for leave to appeal is found in section 14(3)(f) of the High Court Ordinance, which provides that leave may be granted by the Court of First Instance or the Court of Appeal.

By its own terms the rule applies only to decisions of a 'judge'. The word 'judge' is not defined in these rules or in the High Court Ordinance but clearly it does not include the Registrar or a master, both of which are defined in Order 1 rule 4. Given that this rule does not apply to decisions of masters, its inclusion in Order 58 seems strange.

## ORDER 59

### APPEALS TO THE COURT OF APPEAL

1.    **Application of Order to appeals** (O. 59 r. 1)

**(1)    This Order applies, subject to the provisions of these rules with respect to particular appeals, to every appeal to the Court of Appeal (including so far as it is applicable thereto, any appeal to that Court from a master or other officer of the High Court or from any tribunal from which an appeal lies to that Court under or by virtue of any enactment) not being an appeal for which other provision is made by these rules and references to "the court below" apply to any Court, tribunal or person from which such appeal lies.**

**(2)    For the avoidance of doubt and without prejudice to the generality of paragraph (1), this Order, unless the context otherwise requires, applies in relation to an appeal to the Court of Appeal from the District Court. (L.N. 152 of 2008)**

---

**NOTES**

**[59.1.1]    Scope of Order 59**
Order 59 lays down the procedures to be followed on appeals to the Court of Appeal. Rule 1(1) provides that the Order applies to all appeals to the Court of Appeal save where provision is made elsewhere for a particular type of appeal. In this regard see Orders 60A and 61 which make provision for appeals from certain tribunals, thereby ousting the application of Order 59: *Gallium Development Ltd & Ors v Winning Properties Management Ltd & Anor* CACV 186/2003 (Registrar Levy; 31.10.2003).

Rule 1(2) makes it clear that the provisions of Order 59 are intended to have general application to appeals from the District Court. With regard to such appeals, reference should also be made to section 63 of the District Court Ordinance (Cap 336) by which leave to appeal is required, and to Order 59 rule 2A, which governs the procedure when such an application for leave to appeal is brought before the Court of Appeal.

**[59.1.2]    No appeal against reasons**
An appeal to the Court of Appeal must be against the substantive judgment or order made below, not simply against the reasons for that judgment or order. This follows from the fact that the jurisdiction of the Court of Appeal in civil matters is expressed by section 14(1) of the High Court Ordinance to relate to judgments and orders, which 'are not to be equated with the reasons leading to that result': *Lo Kai Bun v Pong Man Yi & Ors* CACV 127/2006 (Stock & Yuen JJA and Waung J; 13.12.2006), citing (at para 18) *Cie Noga SA v Australia and New Zealand Banking Group Ltd* [2003] 1 WLR 307, 328.

**[59.1. 3]    Appeals as to costs**
Section 14(3)(e) of the High Court Ordinance (Cap 4) provides that leave to appeal is required against a decision 'relating only to costs' where costs are in the discretion of the court below. Leave is not required to include an appeal on costs in an appeal

on substantive issues: *Re Wing Fai Construction Co Ltd* CACV 244/2004 (Yeung JA; 06.10.2005) (para 18).

Where leave is required, it may be granted by the court or tribunal below, or by the Court of Appeal. This situation differs from that in England where leave may only be granted by the court or tribunal below. As a result the '*Scherer* principle' (Court of Appeal may entertain appeal on costs where court or tribunal below did not exercise its discretion or did not exercise it judicially) does not apply in Hong Kong: *Ho Lee Man v Wong Wai Kai* [1993] 1 HKC 183 (CA), not following *Scherer v Counting Instruments Ltd* [1986] 1 WLR 615 and *Prudential Enterprises Ltd v PH Shek Ltd* [1990] 2 HKLR 79.

Failure to obtain leave deprives the Court of Appeal of jurisdiction with the result that the appeal cannot be entertained: *A Solicitor v Law Society of Hong Kong* [1995] 1 HKC 834. It has been held in England that the irregularity of failure to obtain leave to appeal may be waived by the opposing party applying for security for costs of the appeal: *Knighthood Assurance Consultants Ltd v Meacher* (1976) 120 SJ 117 (CA), but this was expressly not followed by the Hong Kong Court of Appeal in *Kwan Chui Kwok Ying & Anor v Tao Wai Chun & Ors* CACV 296/2006 (Cheung & Yeung JJA and Chung J; 17.12.2007).

In an appeal exclusively against a costs order it is not permissible to challenge findings on the substantive issues below: *Baron v Hartford Fire Insurance Co & Ors* [1999] 2 HKC 388 (CA).

For the procedure on applying for leave to appeal against interlocutory and costs orders, see Order 59 rule 2B and the commentary thereunder.

**[59.1. 4]    Appeals as to quantum of damages**
The Court of Appeal will not interfere with a decision as to the quantum of damages 'unless it can be demonstrated … that it is in serious error': *King Light Industrial Ltd v Lo Wai Keung* [1994] 3 HKC 54, 58F per Mayo J. In that case the Court of Appeal quoted with approval from the decision of Greer LJ in *Flint v Lovell* [1935] 1 KB 354 where it was said, at 359:

> … this court will be disinclined to reverse the finding of a trial judge as to the amount of damages merely because they think that if they had tried the case in the first instance they would have given a lesser sum. In order to justify reversing the trial judge on the question of the amount of damages it will generally be necessary that this court should be convinced either that the judge acted upon some wrong principle of law, or that the amount awarded was so extremely high or so very small as to make it, in the judgment of this court, an entirely erroneous estimate of the damage to which the plaintiff is entitled.

**[59.1. 5]    Interlocutory appeals**
See Order 59 rule 2B with regard to interlocutory appeals to the Court of Appeal in respect of which leave to appeal is required by section 14AA of the High Court Ordinance, and Order 59 rule 21 with regard to those interlocutory appeals which may be brought as of right.

**2.    Application of Order to applications for new trial** (O. 59 r. 2)
**This Order (except so much of rule 3(1) as provides that an appeal shall be by way of rehearing and except rule 11 (1)) applies to an application to the**

Court of Appeal for a new trial or to set aside a verdict, finding or judgment after trial with or without a jury, as it applies to an appeal to that Court, and references in this Order to an appeal and to an appellant shall be construed accordingly.

General Provisions as to Appeals

**2A.    Application to Court of Appeal for leave to appeal** (O. 59 r. 2A)

(1)    An application to the Court of Appeal for leave to appeal must be made by a summons supported by a statement setting out –

    (a)    the reasons why leave should be granted; and

    (b)    if the time for appealing has expired, the reasons why the application was not made within that time.

(2)    An application under paragraph (1) must be made inter partes if the proceedings in the court below are inter partes.

(3)    An application under paragraph (1) must include, where necessary, an application to extend the time for appealing.

(4)    A party who intends to resist an application under paragraph (1) made inter partes shall, within 14 days after the application is served on him, file in the Court of Appeal and serve on the applicant a statement as to why the application should not be granted.

(5)    The Court of Appeal may –

    (a)    determine the application without a hearing on the basis of written submissions only; or

    (b)    direct that the application be heard at an oral hearing,

and in both cases, the Court of Appeal may give such directions as it thinks fit in relation to the application.

(6)    Where the Court of Appeal grants the application, it may impose such terms as it thinks fit.

(7)    Subject to paragraph (8), if the application is determined on the basis of written submissions only, a party aggrieved by the determination may, within 7 days after he has been given notice of the determination, request the Court of Appeal to reconsider the determination at an oral hearing inter partes.

(8)    Where the Court of Appeal determines the application on the basis of written submissions only, it may, if it considers that the application is totally without merit, make an order that no party may under paragraph (7) request the determination to be reconsidered at an oral hearing inter partes.

(9)    An oral hearing held pursuant to a request under paragraph (7) may be before the Court of Appeal consisting of –

    (a)    the Justice of Appeal; or

    (b)    one or more of the Justices of Appeal,

who have determined the application on the basis of written submissions only.

(L.N. 152 of 2008)

---

**NOTES**

**[59.2A.1]   Scope of Order 59 rule 2A**
Order 59 rule 2A deals with the procedure on application to the Court of Appeal for leave to appeal. It applies to appeals from the Court of First Instance in matters which originated in the Labour Tribunal or the Small Claims Tribunal in respect of which an appeal lies to the Court of Appeal only with leave of the Court of Appeal itself. See section 35A of the Labour Tribunal Ordinance (Cap 25) and section 29A of the Small Claims Tribunal Ordinance (Cap 338). It also applies where leave to appeal may be granted by the court below or by the Court of Appeal and, having been refused leave by the court below, a fresh application is made to the Court of Appeal. Examples are appeals from the Lands Tribunal (section 11AA(1) of the Lands Tribunal Ordinance (Cap 17)), District Court (see section 63 of the District Court Ordinance (Cap 336)) and interlocutory appeals from the Court of First Instance (see section 14AA of the High Court Ordinance).

**[59.2A. 2]   Where either court below or Court of Appeal may grant leave to appeal**
Where application for leave to appeal may be made to the court below or to the Court of Appeal, the application should be made to the court below in the first instance, and only if that fails is it appropriate to make an application direct to the Court of Appeal. See Order 59 rules 2B(1) and 14(4).

**[59.2A. 3]   Application to be made inter partes**
Order 59 rule 2A(2) provides that an application to the Court of Appeal for leave to appeal must be made *inter partes* if the matter was dealt with *inter partes* below. This provision supersedes, in part, the former rule 14(2A) which required that certain applications to the Court of Appeal be made *ex parte*. *First Int'l Bank of Israel Ltd v DRA Trading Ltd* DCCJ 2216/2003 (Deputy Judge WK Kwok; 13.07.2006) should no longer be followed insofar as it held that application to the Court of Appeal for leave to appeal from the District Court should be made *ex parte*.

**[59.2A. 4]   Form and content of application**
An application to the Court of Appeal for leave to appeal is made by summons: Order 59 rule 2A(1). Although neither the rule nor the relevant provisions of the practice direction on civil appeals says so, it may be that in principle the summons should be an originating summons since there is no pending appeal within which to issue an interlocutory summons. However, since the application is to the Court of Appeal rather than the Court of First Instance, it would appear that the usual provisions with regard to originating summonses in Order 28 are inappropriate.

The application must be supported by a statement of the reasons why leave should be granted: Order 59 rule 2A(1)(a). In part B of the practice direction on civil appeals (see below) it is provided that draft grounds of appeal and skeleton arguments should be submitted and that in most cases this will fulfill the requirement for a statement of reasons. If the application is late, such that an extension of time is required, the reasons for the delay should be stated: rule 2A(1)(b), and formal application for extension of time should be included in the summons: rule 2A(3). The practice direction suggests that affidavit evidence justifying an extension of time is appropriate.

The practice direction provides that two sets of the required documents should be lodged with the court.

### [59.2A. 5] Time for making application for leave to appeal
Order 59 rule 2A does not prescribe a time within which application should be made to the Court of Appeal for leave to appeal. Such time is prescribed by the individual legislative provisions permitting application for leave to be made to the Court of Appeal. See for example RDC Order 58 rule 2(4) which allows 14 days from the date on which the District Court refuses leave to appeal for an application to be made to the Court of Appeal.

### [59.2A. 6] Late applications for leave to appeal
Order 59 rule 2A(b) expressly contemplates extension of time for applying to the Court of Appeal for leave to appeal. That provision was previously found in rule 14(2)(a). The power to grant extensions of time is found in Order 3 rule 5.

An application for extension of time to apply for leave to appeal is a matter of discretion: *George YC Mok & Co v Trade Advisers Co Ltd* [2003] 4 HKC 96 (CA) (para 18).

With regard to extension of time for service of a notice of appeal, see Order 59 rule 15 and the commentary thereunder.

### [59.2A. 7] Opportunity for respondent to make representations
An application to the Court of Appeal for leave to appeal must be made *inter partes* if the proceedings below were *inter partes*: see above. Any party who wishes to oppose the grant of leave to appeal is required by rule 2A(4) to file and serve a statement in writing as to why. According to part B of the practice direction on civil appeals (see below) the opposing party should also set out any grounds on which it contends leave should only be granted on terms. The practice direction also contemplates the opposing party relying on affidavit evidence. It goes on to state that the requirement for a statement will in most cases be fulfilled by filing a skeleton argument and any such affidavit evidence.

### [59.2A. 8] Constitution of bench hearing application for leave
An application under this rule may be dealt with by a single judge of the Court of Appeal, or a bench of two justices of appeal rather than the usual 3. See sections 34B(4)(aa) and 35 of the High Court Ordinance. Any determination by a single judge may be the subject of a fresh application to the Court of Appeal under rule 2C. See also Order 59 rule 14(12) which provides for fresh applications to the Court of Appeal from a determination by a single judge.

### [59.2A.9] Determination of the application for leave to appeal on paper
An application to the Court of Appeal for leave to appeal may be determined on the basis of written submissions or an oral hearing: rule 2A(5). The wording of the provision is such that it is up to the Court of Appeal to decide which to choose. However, according to para 9 of the practice direction on civil appeals, the parties should assist the court by stating in their written submissions whether the application

can be determined on the basis of written submissions, with reasons.

### [59.2A.10] Request for reconsideration of application dealt with on paper

A party aggrieved by a decision determined on the basis of written submissions only may, within 7 days of notification of the determination, request reconsideration at an oral hearing: rule 2A(7). The practice direction on civil appeals (para 11) contemplates additional written submissions, if any, being submitted with such a request.

There is no right to such a reconsideration. The court dealing with the application on paper may, if it is of the view that the application for leave to appeal is 'totally without merit' direct that no party may request a reconsideration: rule 2A(8). However, notwithstanding such a direction, if leave to appeal has been refused by a single judge, an aggrieved party may make a fresh application to a Court of Appeal consisting of two justices of appeal: see rule 2C, and see *Ever Harvest Tobacco & Liquor Bonded Warehouse Ltd v Force 8 Cellars Ltd* HCMP 914/2009 (Tang VP & Chu J; 16.06.2009) (para 3).

In the event of an oral reconsideration of an application which has been dealt with on paper, the bench may consist of or include one or more of the justices of appeal who dealt with the application in writing: rule 2A(9).

Costs may be awarded against a party who requests reconsideration at an oral hearing but fails to change the result of the paper hearing: *Fosh v Cardiff University* [2009] EWCA Civ 38 (03.02.2009).

### [59.2A. 11] Refusal of leave to appeal final

A decision by the Court of Appeal to refuse leave to appeal may not be further appealed. See section 14AB of the High Court Ordinance. The Chief Justice's working party on civil justice reform envisaged that this limitation would be restricted to refusals of leave in relation to 'purely interlocutory questions' (recommendation 113), but such restriction is not expressly found in section 14AB. Thus it appears to apply, for example, to refusals of leave to appeal against substantive judgments of the District Court.

The working party took into account the decision of the Court of Final Appeal in *A Solicitor v Law Society of Hong Kong* [2004] 1 HKLRD 214 on the constitutionality of restrictions on appeals to the CFA, and came to the view that the recommended restric tion would be valid. See paragraphs 648-9 of the final report.

In fact even before section 14AB came into force as part of the civil justice reforms in 2009 it was held that '[subject] to a constitutional challenge, no appeal lies to the Court of Final Appeal from a refusal by the Court of Appeal to grant leave to appeal to that intermediate tribunal': *HLF v MTC* [2004] 3 HKLRD 241; (2004) 7 HKCFAR 167, at 177 HKCFAR.

**2B.   Application for leave to appeal against interlocutory and other judgments or orders of Court** (O. 59 r. 2B)

    **(1)   Subject to paragraph (4) and any other enactment, an application for leave to appeal against —**

        **(a)   an interlocutory judgment or order of the Court;**

        **(b)   a judgment or order of the Court specified in section 14(3)(e) or (f) of the Ordinance; or**

      (c)      **any other judgment or order of the Court against which an appeal may be made with leave of the Court or the Court of Appeal,**

**may only be made to the Court in the first instance within 14 days from the date of the judgment or order.**

      **(2)   So far as is practicable, the application must be made to the judge or master against whose judgment or order leave to appeal is sought.**

      **(3)   Where the Court refuses the application, a further application for leave to appeal may be made to the Court of Appeal within 14 days from the date of the refusal.**

      **(4)   If the Court of Appeal allows, the application may be made direct to the Court of Appeal within 14 days from the date of the judgment or order.**

      **(5)   An application under this rule must be made inter partes if the proceedings to which the judgment or order relates are inter partes.**

**(L.N. 152 of 2008)**

---

## NOTES

### [59.2B.1]   Scope of Order 59 rule 2B – General requirement for leave to appeal interlocutory decisions to Court of Appeal

Order 59 rule 2B concerns applications for leave to appeal interlocutory decisions to the Court of Appeal. It applies to appeals against interlocutory decisions of 'the Court', which means the Court of First Instance: see Order 1 rule 4. Such an appeal may be an appeal from a judge of the CFI, or from a master if it concerns a decision of a type which by Order 58 rule 2 must be appealed from the master to the Court of Appeal rather than to a single judge of the CFI.

Rule 2B applies principally to those interlocutory orders for which leave to appeal to the Court of Appeal is required by High Court Ordinance, s 14AA.

Rule 2B also applies to appeals against costs orders, and those against summary determinations in interpleader proceedings, for which leave to appeal is required by section 14(3)(e) and (f) of the High Court Ordinance respectively, and any other appeal from the CFI which requires leave either of the CFI or the Court of Appeal itself.

### [59.2B.2]   Which interlocutory appeals require leave?

The requirement under section 14AA(1) of the High Court Ordinance that leave be obtained to appeal an interlocutory order is subject to exceptions.

First, section 14AA(5) provides that the leave requirement does not apply to decisions before the section came into force in 2009 as part of the civil justice reforms.

Secondly, section 14AA(2) provides that the rules of court may specify interlocutory judgments and orders to which the leave requirement will not apply, such that an appeal lies of right. That is done by Order 59 rule 21. See that rule and the commentary thereunder.

Thirdly, there is the fundamental question whether any particular judgment or order is interlocutory or final. There is no definition of 'interlocutory' in the Ordinance or rules for this purpose. However, the question has been considered in many cases. Most of those cases concern the time within which notice of appeal must be served under the former Order 59 rule 4, which previously stipulated different times for interlocutory and final orders. The reasoning in them should apply here and provide guidance as to how to determine whether any particular judgment or order is 'interlocutory' and thus possibly subject to the leave to appeal requirement.

The general rule which emerges from the cases is that a judgment or order will only be considered to be 'final' if the application giving rise to it would necessarily have resulted in a final determination on the merits. The Hong Kong courts have preferred this 'application' approach whereby one looks at the nature of the application rather than the result. See *First Pacific Bank Ltd v Fung* [1990] 1 HKLR 527, 529G-I (CA); *B+B Construction Ltd v Sun Alliance & London Insurance plc* (2000) 3 HKCFAR 503; and *Shell HK Ltd v Yeung Wai Man Kiu Yip Co Ltd* (2003) 6 HKCFAR 222. Hence, although an order striking out a statement of claim results in judgment in favour of the defendant, the order is nevertheless interlocutory because, if the application had failed, the matter would have gone on to trial. See *Wai Hung Stationery Co & Ors v HKSAR & Ors* [1998] 2 HKC 229 (CFA). Under this 'application' approach an order may also be regarded as final if, 'although not finally determinative of the entire cause or matter, it is finally determinative of a crucial or substantial issue in the cause or matter': *Hip Hing Timber Co Ltd v Tang Man Kit* (2004) 7 HKCFAR 212 (para 38).

By contrast the 'order' approach has been adopted in Australia, Malaysia and British Columbia. By that approach the court looks at the order actually made to determine whether it is a final disposition of the dispute. See *Carr v Finance Corp of Australia Ltd* (1981) 147 CLR 246; *Ratnam v Cumarasamy* (1962) 28 MLJ 330, 333 (approved by the Privy Council in *Haron bin Mhd Zaid v Central Securities (Holdings) Bhd* [1983] 1 AC 16); and *Forest Glen Wood Products Ltd v Minister of Forests* [2008] BCCA 480 (paras 19-24) (distinguishing *Salaman v Warner* [1891] 1 QB 734 (CA)).

If, applying the application approach, it is determined that a decision is interlocutory rather than final, this does not necessarily mean leave to appeal is required. The next question to ask is whether the decision comes within one of the exceptions referred to above whereby certain interlocutory appeals are not subject to the leave requirement.

**[59.2B.3]   Grant of leave to appeal may be restricted to particular issue**
Leave to appeal an interlocutory decision to the Court of Appeal may be granted 'in respect of a particular issue arising out of the interlocutory judgment or order': High Court Ordinance, section 14AA(3)(a). This appears to mean that the court granting leave may restrict the grounds of appeal which may be argued at the substantive appeal.

**[59.2B.4]   Leave to appeal may be subject to conditions**
The court granting leave to appeal an interlocutory decision to the Court of Appeal may impose conditions 'to secure the just, expeditious and economical disposal of the appeal': High Court Ordinance, section 14AA(3)(b). Such conditions might include the grant of a stay of the order pending the appeal, security for costs and a time-table to be followed by the parties to avoid delay to the main action being brought on for trial.

**[59.2B.5]    Timing, forum and procedure for application for leave to appeal**

An application for leave to appeal under this rule should in the first instance be made (so far as practicable) to the judge or master who made the order it is sought to appeal: rule 2B(2). The Chief Justice's working party envisaged such applications being made, so far as possible, at the original hearing so as to avoid the need for separate oral hearings of applications for leave. See recommendation 112 in the final report. At para 646 of the final report, the working party outlined the following procedure, which it said had the support of the judges of the Court of Appeal:

(a)    The question of leave to appeal, like costs, should routinely be addressed whenever a judge hears an interlocutory application. If the application is disposed of *ex tempore*, the judge ought to decide there and then whether to grant leave to appeal after hearing the parties on that subject.

(b)    If the judge is to hand his decision down later, he should invite the parties to address him in advance on whether leave should be granted whether the application succeeds or fails (without necessarily having decided whether to appeal if the decision goes against them). He should then deal with leave to appeal in the decision handed down without further submissions. If the lateness of the day makes it inconvenient to enter into a discussion of leave to appeal at the end of the argument and the decision is to be handed down, the judge might invite the parties to file written submissions on this question. Having just heard the application, the judge ought to be well placed to make a decision without much further assistance.

(c)    Adopting the foregoing procedure, a fresh hearing to apply for leave to appeal before the CFI judge should hardly ever be needed.

The procedure envisaged by the working party (above) was not adopted in mandatory form. Rule 2B(1) permits the application for leave to be made within 14 days of the decision to be appealed.

The application for leave to appeal 'may only be made to the Court in the first instance' within that 14–day period: rule 2B(1). This means the Court of First Instance has no power to extend the time for making the application: *Wynn Resorts (Macau) SA v Mong Henry* [2009] 5 HKC 515; *Vos v Global Fair Industrial Ltd & Ors* HCA 4200/1995 (To J; 23.04.2010). The applicant may, however, seek an extension of time by making the leave application direct to the Court of Appeal: *Tang Fu Sun v Tang Lik Yuen* HCMP 887/2010 (Tang VP & Yeung JA; 16.07.2010).

The Court of Appeal may permit the judge or master below to be bypassed, and an application for leave to appeal to be made direct to it: rule 2B(4). A prospective appellant who seeks to do so should, according to the practice direction on civil appeals (para 13), submit affidavit evidence and/or written submissions as to why leave is sought from the Court of Appeal directly.

Where an application to the judge or master below is unsuccessful, a fresh application for leave may be made to the Court of Appeal within 14 days of the refusal: rule 2B(3). That application may be dealt with by a single judge (section 35(1) High Court Ordinance), and if unsuccessful may be renewed by way of fresh application to a bench consisting of no less than 2 justices of appeal under rule 2C. The Chief Justice's working party envisaged that applications to the Court of Appeal would normally be dealt with on paper: final report, recommendation 112.

The power to do so is found in rule 14A. Continuing the numbered paragraphs quoted above from paragraph 646 of the final report, the working party outlined the following procedure with regard to such applications:

(d)     Where the CFI refuses leave, the applicant should be entitled to apply in writing to the Court of Appeal which should generally deal with the leave application on the papers and without an oral hearing. The application for leave should be accompanied by the applicant's brief written submissions setting out the grounds for seeking leave and, within a specified time after being served with the papers, the respondent should file any brief submissions he wishes to make resisting leave.

(e)     When dealing with such leave applications on the papers, the Court of Appeal would be duly constituted by two Justices of Appeal, as provided for by section 34B(4)(a) of the HCO.

(f)     The Court of Appeal ought to have powers either (i) to grant leave; (ii) to refuse leave; or exceptionally (iii) to summon the parties for an oral hearing on the question of leave either before the two judges who have considered the papers or before a panel of three judges (for example, where the two judges are unable to agree). It may, of course, be the better course simply to grant leave where there is no agreement between the two judges originally seised of the matter.

(g)     Where the Court of Appeal refuses leave, it should not be required to give reasons beyond stating in the order dismissing the application the ground upon which leave is refused (eg ... that the application has no reasonable prospects of success, or that it has been made out of time, and so forth).

### [59.2B.6]   Application for stay of execution where leave to appeal required
In *Joint & Several Liquidators of United Pacific Trading Ltd (in liq) v Liao Zhe* HCCW 424/2006 (Kwan J; 03.07.2009) the court took the view that it was not appropriate to grant a stay of execution pending appeal against an interlocutory order where, although a notice of appeal had been filed, leave to appeal had not been sought.

### [59.2B.7]   The threshold test for leave to appeal
Section 14AA(4) of the High Court Ordinance provides that leave to appeal shall not be granted unless:

(a)     the appeal has a reasonable prospect of success, or
(b)     there is some other reason in the interests of justice why the appeal should be heard.

The section applies only to interlocutory appeals to the Court of Appeal for which leave is required by section 14AA(1), and not to the other types of order for which leave is required by other provisions (as to which see above). For the criteria applied on applications for leave to appeal from the District Court, see the commentary on section 63 of the District Court Ordinance in volume 2 of the loose-leaf edition of this work, referring to *Ma Bik Yung v Ko Chuen* [2009] 3 HKC 359, and see *Commissioner of Inland Revenue v Nam Tai Trading Co Ltd* [2009] 3 HKC 421.

The criteria set out in section 14AA(4)(a) and (b) are similar, but not identical, to those set out in CPR 52.3(6). In England the first criterion is a 'real' prospect of success, as compared to Hong Kong's 'reasonable' prospect of success. The Chief

Justice's working party noted (final report, para 655) that the English provision:

> had been taken to mean the opposite of 'fanciful', which, if adopted in the leave to appeal context, would import a very low threshold for the grant of leave. An appeal while not 'fanciful' may be little more than just arguable and quite likely to fail.

The working party was of the view that the test in Hong Kong should be 'more stringent' and in recommendation 115 put forward the 'reasonable' prospect of success test which is implemented by section 14AA(4)(a). The working party explained what it had in mind in the following passages from its final report:

> 656. In the Working Party's view, the test should be more stringent than merely having to show that the appeal is arguable and 'not fanciful', but considerably less stringent than having to show a 'probability' of success . . . the Working Party considers it desirable to adopt as the test for granting leave a requirement *'that the appeal has reasonable prospects of success'*. It is hoped that this would convey the notion that the prospects of succeeding in the appeal must be 'reasonable' and therefore more than 'not fanciful', without having to be 'probable' – just 'reasonable'. As pointed out in the Interim Report, this was the sense attributed to the phrase 'reasonable prospects of success' in the Court of Appeal cases discussing the differences, if any, between the test for refusing summary judgment and for setting aside a default judgment (See *Yeu Shing Construction Co Ltd v Pioneer Concrete (HK) Ltd* [1987] 2 HKC 187, 191, per Silke VP; and *Premier Fashion Wears Ltd v Li Hing-chung* [1994] 1 HKLR 377, 383, per Godfrey JA).

> 657. It appears to the Working Party that such a threshold would be fair. If an applicant cannot show that the proposed interlocutory appeal has reasonable prospects of success, a refusal of leave does him no injustice. Most interlocutory decisions are discretionary and it is well-established that an appellate tribunal will not interfere with a discretionary decision of the court below unless it is wrong in principle or is plainly wrong, even if the appellate court might itself have made a different decision. Accordingly, a refusal of leave to appeal where there are no reasonable prospects of success will often be a kindness to the applicant, saving him the costs of arriving at the same result after a full hearing of the appeal.

The above reasoning of the working party was referred to in *Wynn Resorts (Macau) SA v Mong Henry* [2009] 5 HKC 515, leading Chu J to state (*obiter*, at para 19):

> To meet the 'reasonable prospect of success' test, an applicant is required to show more than just an arguable case, but an appeal that has merits and ought to be heard, although he does not have to demonstrate that the appeal will probably succeed.

See also *Re Wing Fai Construction Co Ltd* HCCW 735/2002 (Kwan JA; 08.12.2009) (para 5) where the above passage was quoted with approval. See, however, *Aggressive Construction Co Ltd v Data-form Eng'g Ltd* HCA 2143/2008 (Deputy Judge To; 13.10.2009) (paras 5-8) where 'reasonable' prospect of success in section 14AA is equated with 'realistic' prospect of success and 'arguable case', and it was said that the test is no more onerous than that adopted in *Ma Bik Yung* (above) for appeals from the District Court. In *SMSE v KL* [2009] 4 HKLRD 125 (CA) (para 18) the court rejected an argument that the threshold test could not be met where grounds of appeal had not yet been formulated.

Concerning what the working party said in the passage above about an appellate tribunal's reluctance to interfere with discretionary decisions, reference may be made to *Hymer v MTR Corp & Ors* [2000] 2 HKLRD 589, 600G-601C (CA) citing *Kerry Foodstuffs Co Ltd v Phulsawat Navy Co Ltd* [1999] 3 HKC 523 and *Birkett v James* [1978] AC 297. In *Hymer* it was said (*loc cit*) that the Court of Appeal has only a 'reviewing function' and will only interfere with a discretionary decision if the judge below 'erred in principle'. Such considerations will certainly be relevant on an application for leave to appeal a discretionary decision since the prospects of success are affected. That has been the experience in other jurisdictions where leave to appeal interlocutory decisions is required. The review of authorities in *Gulamani v Chandra* [2009] BCCA 206 (para 12-13) may be of interest in this regard. See also the Canadian case of *Rolls-Royce Corp v Universal Helicopters Newfoundland Ltd & Ors* [2009] NLCA 58 (para 24) where it was said that 'the hurdle to be overcome by an appellant is much higher when the court is being asked to review a discretionary decision'.

With regard to the 'some other reason' criterion in section 14AA(4)(b), the working party said as follows (final report, para 658):

> There should also be a discretion to grant leave to appeal for cases which may not pass the reasonable prospects of success test but where 'there is some other compelling reason why the appeal should be heard'. For instance, the Court of Appeal may wish to take the opportunity to provide much needed clarification in an area of the law or to entertain an argument that the law ought to be changed, even though it is questionable whether the appellant has less than reasonable prospects of success.

The example of a need for clarification reflects the alternative basis for allowing an appeal against an exercise of discretion as set out in *Hymer* (above), that is where the decision 'raises issues in an area where it is desirable to promote consistency'. Other examples of 'some other reason' to grant leave to appeal might include the following:

(a)    Where the matter will be going to the Court of Appeal anyway, such as where there is an appeal (as of right) against a grant of Order 14 summary judgment in respect of part of a claim, and leave is sought to appeal the grant of leave to defend the balance of the claim.

(b)    Where an appeal could ultimately save costs and court time by resulting in a final determination of the dispute, thereby avoiding the need for a lengthy trial.

## [59.2B. 8]    Other factors to be taken into account on application for leave to appeal

The court is not obliged to grant leave to appeal if one or both of the criteria in section 14AA(4) are met. Rather the wording of the section is simply to prohibit the court from granting leave unless one of the criteria is satisfied. As the Chief Justice's working party described it in the above passage, the test is a 'threshold'. Passing the test gets the applicant for leave in the door in the sense that the application will be considered, but the court must still be persuaded to exercise its discretion in favour of granting leave. Thus other factors may be taken into account, and at the end of the day leave may be refused even though the threshold test is met.

It would not be possible to set out an exhaustive list of such other factors. In *Ho Yuen Ki Winnie & Anor v Ho Hung Sun Stanley* HCMP 1009/2009 (Le Pichon & Hartmann JJA; 24.08.2009) (para 16) the court referred to para 643 of the final report on CJR and said it was relevant to bear in mind that the leave requirement 'was introduced largely to address satellite litigation on interlocutory issues (often of only marginal significance to the outcome of the litigation)'. Clearly the underlying objectives in Order 1A rule 1 will be relevant. Reference may be made to cases from other jurisdictions where factors similar to the underlying objectives have been taken into account:

*Proportionality and expense* – In *Piglowska v Piglowska* [1999] 3 All ER 632 (HL) Lord Hoffman said (at 644j), in relation to an appeal on matters of value judgment 'on which reasonable people may differ':

> To allow successive appeals in the hope of producing an answer which accords with perfect justice is to kill the parties with kindness.

Lord Hoffman continued, expressing the view (at 645b–c) that the resources of the parties could be taken into account:

> I would only add that even if a case does raise an important point of practice or principle, the Court of Appeal should consider carefully whether it is fair to have it decided at the expense of parties with very limited resources or whether it should wait for a more suitable vehicle.

The above comments should be relevant in Hong Kong where the court is enjoined to apply the underlying objectives of 'cost-effectiveness' and 'reasonable proportion and procedural economy' (Order 1A, rule 1(1) (a) and (c)), and to consider, in man aging cases, the relative cost and benefit of taking a particular step (Order 1A rule 4(2)(h)).

*Expeditiousness* – In *Ho Yuen Ki Winnie & Anor v Ho Hung Sun Stanley & Anor* HCA 391/2006 (A Cheung J; 25.05.2009) the court took into account the slow progress of an action in refusing leave to appeal against a discovery order. A fresh application for leave came before two judges of the Court of Appeal who held that even if the appeal had reasonable prospects of success, leave would be refused for reasons of cost and delay: see HCMP 1009/2009 (Le Pichon & Hartmann JJA; 24.08.2009) (para 22). Also relevant should be the expeditiousness objective in Order 1A rule 1(1)(b). In British Columbia, where the court takes into account 'whether the appeal will unduly hinder the progress of the action', leave to appeal an interlocutory decision has been refused, even though it could not be said to be 'without merit', on the ground that an appeal would 'unduly interfere with the orderly and timely disposition' of the action in that the trial dates, which had already been fixed, would be lost: *Honour v Canada (AG)* [2008] BCCA 346 (paras 7, 15 & 17). Similarly, in *Oriental Press Group Ltd & Anor v Fevaworks Solutions Ltd* HCA 2140/2008 (Yam J; 23.11.2009) leave to appeal was refused in part because the case was at the verge of going to trial, and the court considered that it was 'not appropriate at this stage to ask the Court of Appeal to decide on an interlocutory matter'. The proposed appeal was against refusal of an interlocutory injunction.

*Overall justice* – In Australia the courts may refuse leave to appeal an interlocutory order on the ground that no substantial injustice is caused. See *Niemann v Electronic Industries Ltd* [1978] VR 431, 441 (lines 0–15) (Vic FCt) where Murphy J referred to authority dating back to 1901 and said:

> If the order is seen to be clearly wrong, this is not alone sufficient. It must be shown, in addition, to effect a substantial injustice by its operation.

See also *BHP Petroleum Pty Ltd v Oil Basins Ltd* [1985] VR 756, 758 (Vic FCt) and *SA Gov't Financing Authority v Bank of NZ* [2002] SASC 56 (SA FCt). In Hong Kong Order 1A rule 2(2) could be construed as permitting the court to take a similar approach: it is there provided that in giving effect to the underlying objectives the court should always recognise that the primary aim is the just resolution of disputes.

**[59.2B. 9]   Criteria on application for leave to appeal case management decision**
The criteria set out in section 14AA(4) of the High Court Ordinance for the grant of leave to appeal interlocutory decisions to the Court of Appeal apply equally to case management decisions as to other interlocutory decisions for which leave to appeal is required. However, because of the nature of case management decisions, it seems less likely that the criteria will be satisfied. As pointed out in the final report of the Chief Justice's working party on civil justice reform (para 659), the Court of Appeal has repeatedly held that it will not interfere with case management decisions taken by first instance judges in exercise of their discretion except in cases of plain error. Reference is made to *Carrian Investments Ltd (in liq) v Price Waterhouse Int'l* [1994] 1 HKLR 150, 153-4 (CA). The final report also refers to *Cheung Yee Mong Edmond (an infant) v So Kwok Yan Bernard* [1996] 1 HKC 604 (CA); [1996] 2 HKLR 48 (CA), where at 608I HKC Bokhary JA said:

> Case management is pre-eminently within the province of the trial judge. And it is only in wholly exceptional circumstances that we will interfere.

The final report goes on to quote from *Bellenden v Satterthwaite* [1948] 1 All ER 343, 345 where Asquith LJ said that an appellate body is only entitled to interfere with discretionary decisions which exceed 'the generous ambit within which reasonable disagreement is possible'. The report continues (at para 661):

> Accordingly, where a CFI judge makes a case management decision which is not wrong in principle and which does not 'exceed the generous ambit within which reasonable disagreement is possible', it would not be regarded as appealable [on the test now set out in section 14AA(4) HCO] and leave would be refused. On the other hand, a case management decision which raises a significant point of principle would necessarily enable the aggrieved party to contend that the judge had erred in principle in the exercise of his discretion so that, assuming the appeal had reasonable prospects of success it would qualify for leave . . . Indeed, even if it is questionable whether the appeal has reasonable prospects of success, the fact that it raises a significant point of principle may suffice to justify the grant of leave on the basis that it provides 'some other compelling reason why the appeal should be heard'.

In result the working party was of the view that it was unnecessary to recommend a more stringent test for leave to appeal case management decisions. The view that leave to appeal case management decisions would normally be refused was confirmed shortly after Order 59 rule 2B came into force: *Chinachem Charitable Foundation Ltd v Chan Chun Chuen & Ors* HCMP 901/2009 (Rogers VP; 18.05.2009). In that case leave to appeal a decision to permit a party to adduce evidence of a replacement expert witness was refused both by the trial judge and again by a single judge of the Court of Appeal. The experience in other jurisdictions is similar. For example, in *Honour v Canada (AG)* [2008] BCCA 346 (para 16) (09.09.2008) leave to appeal against an order for disclosure of computer records was refused, the court citing the reluctance to interfere with discretionary decisions by way of case management; and in *Ovlas*

*Trad ing SA v Strand (London) Ltd & Ors* [2009] EWCA Civ 250 (27.04.2009) leave to appeal orders refusing leave to amend, and requiring disclosure of financial information, was refused on the same ground. Note that in England CPR PD 52 para 4.4 sets out specific guidance on leave to appeal case management decisions, stating that the court may take into account whether:

(1)    the issue is of sufficient significance to justify the costs of an appeal;

(2)    the procedural consequences of an appeal (*eg* loss of trial date) outweigh significance of the case management decision;

(3)    it would be more convenient to determine the issue at or after trial.

See also that part of commentary in the above paragraph on the threshold test concerning discretionary decisions.

**[59.2B. 10]  Criteria on application for leave to appeal decision of CFI judge on appeal from a master**

There is no requirement for leave to appeal under Order 58 from a master to a single judge of the Court of First Instance. However, it seems implicit that a further appeal to the Court of Appeal will require leave if the decision is of the type which comes within section 14AA of the High Court Ordinance. In that event the criteria for granting leave as set out in section 14AA(4) apply in the same way as with other interlocutory appeals. In its final report the Chief Justice's working party decided against adopting the position in England, where a more stringent test is applied on second appeals (final report, para 664 *et seq*).

**[59.2B. 11]  Interlocutory appeals during the course of trial**

Even prior to the introduction of section 14AA and the requirement for leave to appeal interlocutory orders to the Court of Appeal, such appeals were generally considered undesirable once trial was underway. See *Lam Choi King v Yeung Fook Chi t/a Yeung Yat Fat Wood Co & Ors* [1991] 1 HKC 219, 226G-227D (CA). In *To Kan Chi v Pui Man Yau & Ors* [1998] 3 HKC 371, 390G-H (CFA) Litton PJ said that such appeals should be 'strongly discouraged'. See also *CKW Co Ltd v SJ* [2005] 1 HKC 109.

    Similar considerations are likely to influence the court now in considering whether to grant leave to appeal to the Court of Appeal once trial is underway.

**2C.    Refusal by single judge of application for leave to appeal** (O. 59 r. 2C)

    **(1)    Notwithstanding rule 2A(8), where an application for leave to appeal made under rule 2A(1) or 2B(3) is determined (with or without a hearing) by a single Justice of Appeal, a party aggrieved by the determination may, within 7 days from the date of the refusal, make a fresh application to the Court of Appeal.**

    **(2)    The party is entitled to have the fresh application determined by the Court of Appeal consisting of 2 Justices of Appeal.**

    **(3)    The Justice of Appeal who has previously determined the application may sit in the Court of Appeal determining the fresh application.**

                                                                            **(L.N. 152 of 2008)**

## NOTES

**[59.2C.1]    Fresh application after refusal of leave by single judge**

Applications to the Court of Appeal for leave to appeal under Order 59 rules 2A and 2B may be dealt with by a single judge. The power of a single judge to do so is found in section 35(1) of the High Court Ordinance. Rule 2C provides that where such an application has been determined by a single judge, an aggrieved party may make a fresh application to the Court of Appeal within 7 days of the refusal. The fresh application should be made in the original miscellaneous proceedings by which leave was sought from a single judge, rather than by fresh HCMP application: *Ever Harvest Tobacco & Liquor Bonded Warehouse Ltd v Force 8 Cellars Ltd* HCMP 914/2009 (Tang VP & Chu J; 16.06.2009) (para 5). The practice direction on civil appeals (para 14) provides that the aggrieved party may, if it wishes, make additional written submissions.

Such a fresh application may be dealt with by a bench consisting of two justices of appeal instead of the usual three: section 34B(4)(aa) HCO. It is expressly provided in rule 2C(3) that the bench dealing with the fresh application may include the judge or judges who heard the application for leave earlier on. The latter provision infringes the principle that no one shall be a judge in his or her own cause (*nemo judex sua causa*). Insofar as that is a principle of common law, the legislative provision is unobjectionable. However, it is not difficult to contemplate a clever litigator coming up with a constitutional argument against its validity.

The heading to rule 2C suggests that a fresh application for leave is only possible under the rule where a single judge has *refused* leave to appeal. However the body of the rule does not seem to be so confined. In *RK v YS* HCMP 1410/2010 (Le Pichon & Kwan JJA; 07.09.2010) the Court of Appeal entertained an application to set aside leave which had been *granted* by a single justice of appeal. The application was dis missed, but not on jurisdictional grounds. The court applied *The Iran Nabuvat* [1990] 1 WLR 1115 (CA) where it was held that leave granted by a single justice of appeal will not be set aside unless it can be shown by reference to a decisive factor, such as a statute or authority overlooked before the single judge, that the appeal will inevitably fail.

**3.     Notice of appeal** (O. 59 r. 3)

**(1)    An appeal to the Court of Appeal shall be by way of rehearing and must be brought by motion, and the notice of the motion is referred to in this Order as "notice of appeal".**

**(2)    Notice of appeal may be given either in respect of the whole or in respect of any specified part of the judgment or order of the court below; and every such notice must specify the grounds of the appeal and the precise form of the order which the appellant proposes to ask the Court of Appeal to make.**

**(3)    Except with the leave of the Court of Appeal or a single judge, the appellant shall not be entitled on the hearing of an appeal to rely on any grounds of appeal, or to apply for any relief, not specified in the notice of appeal. (L.N. 404 of 1991)**

**(5)    A notice of appeal must be served on all parties to the proceedings**

in the court below who are directly affected by the appeal; and, subject to rule 8, it shall not be necessary to serve the notice on parties not so affected.

(6)    No notice of appeal shall be given by a respondent in a case to which rule 6(1) relates.

---

**NOTES**

**[59.3.1]    Appeal by way of rehearing – comparison with English rules**
Order 59 rule 3(1) provides that an appeal shall be by way of 'rehearing'. This means that the Court of Appeal will consider the evidence and submissions. In this respect the procedure in Hong Kong is the same as that which applied in England before the introduction of CPR 52.11. Under that provision, in England an appeal is now usually a 'review' rather than a rehearing, and the Court of Appeal may only interfere with the decision below in relatively limited circumstances. Hong Kong decided against adopting the current English position (Chief Justice's working party on civil justice reform, final report, recommendation 121).

So far as the evidence is concerned the Court of Appeal does not rehear the witnesses, rather in the case of an appeal on a question of fact it considers the evidence in writing. See *Hongkong and Shanghai Banking Corp v Chan Yiu-wah & Anor* [1988] 1 HKLR 457, at 475B–C (CA) per Fuad JA, citing with approval the following passage from the speech of Viscount Sankey in *Powell v Streatham Manor Nursing Home* [1935] AC 243:

> It is perfectly true that an appeal is by way of rehearing, but it must not be forgotten that the Court of Appeal does not rehear the witnesses. It only reads the evidence and rehears the counsel.

In *Tang Kwok Ming v Daxprofit Scaffolding Ltd* [1999] 1 HKC 657 (CA) Godfrey JA reiterated the law in the following words, at 663D–F:

> The approach of an appellate court to appeals on fact is well-established. An appeal to this court is by way of re-hearing. Accordingly, it is the duty of this court to re-consider all the materials before the judge, to make up its own mind, not disregarding the judgment below but carefully weighing and considering it, not shrinking from overruling it, if on full consideration it comes to the conclusion that the trial judge's finding was wrong. But that does not mean that this court will re-try the case. The re-hearing is a re-hearing on the papers.

As a consequence of the fact that an appeal is a rehearing, the Court of Appeal does not confine itself to the question whether the court below came to the correct decision on the basis of the material it had before it. The Court of Appeal has power to admit further evidence (Order 59 rule 10(2)) even of facts occurring after the decision under appeal. An appellate court will also give effect to intervening changes of the law: *Quilter v Mapleson* (1882) 9 QBD 672; *Lau Kong Yung (an infant) v Director of Immigration* [1999] 4 HKC 731 (CFA). An intervening development of the common law material to the particular case will be applied by the appellate court on the basis of the declaratory theory whereby decisions of the court are said to declare the common law as it has always been. Legislative amendments are not normally retrospective, but if so they will, if material, be applied by the appellate court.

**[59.3. 2]    Rule 3(2) – Contents of a notice of appeal**

In addition to permitting a notice of appeal to be confined to part of the judgment below, this paragraph sets down two requirements for all notices of appeal: (1) that they specify the grounds of the appeal, and (2) that they specify the precise form of the order which the appellant proposes to ask the Court of Appeal to make. The first of those requirements has been the subject of judicial comment in Hong Kong. In *Leung Kin Hung v Cheng Mui* [1982] HKLR 383, the Court of Appeal held that grounds of appeal which state merely that the trial judge 'erred in law' in holding as he did, are lacking in that they fail to give 'any indication as to how it is suggested that the judge did err or what the questions of law would be'.

Separate notices of appeal are required to appeal against separate orders made at separate hearings, even though they may arise from the same proceedings: *Re Wing Fai Construction Co Ltd* CACV 244/2004 (Yeung JA; 06.10.2005).

As to the proper manner of setting out the title to an appeal, see the practice direction on civil appeals (PD 4.1), para 16.

**[59.3. 3]    Failure to obtain leave to appeal where required**

Where leave to appeal is required, 'a valid notice of appeal cannot be served until and unless leave to appeal has been granted': *Kwan Chui Ying & Anor v Tao Wai Chun & Ors* CACV 296/2006 (Cheung & Yeung JJA, Chung J; 09.05.2008 (para 7). See also the Australian case of *Permanent Custodians Ltd v Palmer* [2009] VSCA 80 (24.04.2009) where it was said that a purported appeal was 'incompetent' for failure to obtain leave to appeal, notwithstanding advice from the registry staff which the appellant had allegedly received. If it is not possible to obtain leave within the time prescribed for service of the notice of appeal, the court should be sympathetic to an application for an extension of time, as in *Re Wing Fung Construction (HK) Ltd* [2006] 1 HKC 72.

With regard to when leave to appeal is required, see Order 59 rules 2A, 2B and 21 and the commentary thereunder, and with regard to the time for service of a notice of appeal see rule 4.

**[59.3. 4]    Rule 3(4) – omitted in Hong Kong**
              **The lists of appeals – comparison with English rules**

In England it is provided by Order 59 rule 3(4) that every notice of appeal must specify the list of appeals to which it is to be assigned. That provision has been omitted from the Hong Kong rules. In Hong Kong the procedure governing the listing of appeals is dealt with in part D of the practice direction on civil appeals.

**[59.3. 5]    Power to strike out notice of appeal**

The Court of Appeal has power to strike out a notice of appeal. See the discussion of that topic in the commentary under Order 59 rule 10.

**4.    Time for appealing** (O. 59 r. 4)

    **(1)    Except as otherwise provided by these rules, a notice of appeal must be served under rule 3(5) within —**

                **(a)    in the case where leave to appeal to the Court of Appeal is required under section 14AA (not being a case to which sub-**

paragraph (b) applies) or section 14(3)(e) or (f) of the Ordinance, 7 days after the date on which leave to appeal is granted;

(b)     in the case of an appeal from a judgment, order or decision given or made in the matter of the winding up of a company, or in the matter of any bankruptcy, 28 days from the date of the judgment, order or decision; and

(c)     in any other case, 28 days from the date of the judgment, order or decision concerned.

(L.N. 152 of 2008)

(2)     In the case where an appeal may lie from a judgment of the Court of First Instance under Division 3 of Part II of the Hong Kong Court of Final Appeal Ordinance (Cap 484), the following period of time shall be disregarded in determining the period referred to in paragraph (1) —

(a)     where an application has been made under section 27C of that Ordinance, the period from the date on which the judgment is given to the date on which the application is determined; or

(b)     where an application has been made under section 27D of that Ordinance, the period from the date on which the judgment is given to the date on which the application is determined.

(11 of 2002 s. 7)

(3)     (Repealed, L.N. 152 of 2008)

(4)     In relation to an appeal from the District Court, a notice of appeal must be served under rule 3(5) within —

(a)     in the case where leave to appeal to the Court of Appeal is required under section 63(1) or (1B) of the District Court Ordinance (Cap. 336), 7 days after the date on which leave to appeal is granted; and

(b)     in the case of an appeal from an order specified in section 63(3) of the District Court Ordinance (Cap. 336) or an order for imprisonment given or made under Order 49B of the Rules of the District Court (Cap. 336 sub. leg. H), 28 days after the date on which the order is made.

(L.N. 152 of 2008)

## NOTES

**[59.4.1]     Time within which notice of appeal must be served**

A notice of appeal must be served within the time prescribed by Order 59 rule 4. Rule 4(1) is the general provision. It was replaced as part of the civil justice reforms taking effect in 2009. The new provision is significantly different from its predecessor in the following respects:

(a)     Time now begins to run immediately that leave to appeal is granted or, where leave is not required, from the date of the judgment, order or decision to be appealed. Previously time did not run until the order to be appealed had been drawn up and entered. This topic is discussed further below.

(b)     The time for service of a notice of appeal against an interlocutory order has been adjusted, reflecting the introduction of the general requirement for leave to appeal such orders (as to which see rules 2A, 2B and 21).

A notice of appeal must be served on all parties to the proceedings giving rise to the appeal, who are directly affected by the appeal: rule 3(5). It appears that all must be served within the time prescribed by rule 4. The times may be summarised briefly as follows:

(a)     *Interlocutory appeals* – 7 days from the grant of leave to appeal, if leave is required by section 14AA of the High Court Ordinance (rule 4(1)(a)); 28 days from date of the decision if by virtue of Order 59 rule 21 leave to appeal is not required (rule 4(1)(c)).

(b)     *Winding-up and bankruptcy matters* – 28 days from the date of the decision in all cases, whether interlocutory or final and whether leave is required or not (rule 4(1)(b)).

(c)     *Appeals against final decisions* – 28 days from the date of the decision (rule 4(1)(c)).

(d)     *Appeals from District Court* – 7 days from the grant of leave to appeal (rule 4(4)(a)); 28 days if the decision comes within section 63(3) of the District Court Ordinance, which prescribes certain orders which may be appealed without leave, or if it is an order for imprisonment of a judgment debtor under Order 49B RDC (rule 4(4)(b)).

The time periods prescribed by Order 59 rule 4 do not apply where there is express provision elsewhere applying to a specific type of appeal: *Mita Kobyo Kabushiki Kaisha v Mitac Inc* [1993] 1 HKC 207. Although that case concerned the now-repealed Trade Marks Ordinance (Cap 43) (which has been replaced by Cap 559), the stated principle should still apply.

**[59.4.2]     Comparison with English rules**
In England appeals to the Court of Appeal are governed by part 52 of the CPR. The English provisions regarding appeals are significantly different from their Hong Kong counterparts. For one thing, leave to appeal is required in most cases, whereas Hong Kong does not require leave to appeal from final orders of the Court of First Instance, nor from many interlocutory orders (as set out in Order 59 rule 21). For another, the time for appealing is generally 21 days from the date of the decision, as compared to 7 or 28 days in Hong Kong, depending on the type of decision.

**[59.4. 3]     When time begins to run**
As noted above, the time within which notice of appeal must be served begins to run immediately that leave to appeal is granted or, where leave is not required, from the date of the judgment, order or decision to be appealed. Prior to implementation of the civil justice reforms in 2009, time did not run until the order to be appealed had been 'sealed or otherwise perfected'. This is a significant change. Previously parties could postpone the time for service of notice of appeal simply by delaying the process of drawing up of the order and submitting it for approval and to be sealed. This change does not appear to have been specifically recommended by the Chief Justice's working party on civil justice reform. However the Registrar has previously complained about

delays in drawing up orders: see the Registrar's paper on drawing up orders of the court dated November 2007 (circulated to solicitors under Law Society circular 07-709).

Difficulties could arise in cases where the court's judgment or order is pronounced at the end of the hearing, with reasons to be given later. Rule 4(1)(c) says that time runs 'from the date of the judgment, order or decision' which should mean the date on which it is pronounced, not the later date when reasons are given. See Order 42 rule 3(2) which provides that a judgment or order shall normally be dated as of the day on which it is pronounced, given or made. In most cases it is preferable to consider and reflect on the court's reasons before deciding whether to appeal, and yet that may not be possible given the running of time. As a result, the court should be lenient in granting extensions of time to appeal where the delay is attributable to reasons being given only after a judgment or order is pronounced.

### [59.4. 4]     When running of time for serving notice of appeal is suspended

The time for service of a Notice of Appeal does not run during the summer vacation (which is the month of August – Order 64 rule 1), unless the court otherwise directs. See section 31(1) of the High Court Ordinance, and see *Chung Fai Eng'g Co v Maxwell Eng'g Co Ltd* [2001] 3 HKC 24. Likewise time does not run when a memorandum of application for legal aid to appeal is lodged with the court in the proceedings below. Section 15 of the Legal Aid Ordinance (Cap 91) provides for a 42 day stay of proceedings in that event, and it has been held that this applies to the proposed appeal even though it has not yet been launched: *Brook v Law Society of Hong Kong (No 1)* [1998] 1 HKC 595 (CA).

Order 59 rule 4(2) also provides, in effect, for suspension of the running of time, in cases where it is possible to apply for a certificate or for leave to appeal from the Court of First Instance direct to the Court of Final Appeal (under sections 27A-F of the Court of Final Appeal Ordinance (Cap 484)). The suspension is of the time for appeal to the Court of Appeal, not the CFA. It leaves open the possibility of an appeal to the Court of Appeal in the event that the application for a certificate or for leave to go direct to the CFA is refused.

### [59.4. 5]     Extension of time to appeal

The general power of the High Court under Order 3 rule 5 to extend time even after expiration applies in the Court of Appeal. See that rule and the commentary thereunder. In addition the court below may extend (or abridge) the time for appealing to the Court of Appeal provided that application is made before expiration of the relevant period: see Order 59 rule 15. The court's case management power under Order 1B rule 2(a) to 'extend or shorten the time for compliance with any rule' is also relevant.

The factors which will generally be taken into account on an application for extension of time to appeal (or 'leave to appeal out of time') were set out concisely in *China Light & Power Co Ltd v Ford* [1998] 1 HKLRD 382, 385-6 (CA) in the following terms:

(1)     the length of delay;
(2)     the reasons for the delay;
(3)     the chances of the appeal succeeding . . .; and
(4)     the degree of prejudice to the potential respondent if the application is granted.

See also *Chinko v Director of Immigration* HCMP 1634/2006 (Cheung & Yeung JJA; 14.02.2007) (para 20).

The above list is not exhaustive. Extension of time is discretionary and the court should 'look at the matter in the round . . . to see what the consequences might be': *Mak Hau Shing v Oriental Press Group & Ors* [1996] 3 HKC 12, 22D (CA). In *Chinko v Director of Immigration* HCMP 1634/2006 (Tang JA; 04.12.2006) the court was prepared to take into account the fact the case involved human rights.

A change in the understanding of the law by a subsequent decision does not by itself justify an extension of time. However there may be exceptional circumstances in a particular case which would justify an extension. Those circumstances must be so exceptional as to be very rare. See *HKSAR v Hung Chan Wa & Anor* (2006) 9 HKCFAR 614 (para 23-25); *Lau Luen Hung Thomas v Insider Dealing Tribunal & Anor* FAMV 46/2009 (CFA; 04.12.2009) (para 7). This applies equally to civil and criminal cases: *Tsang Yiu Kai & Ors v Insider Dealing Tribunal* [2008] 1 HKC 376 (CA) (para 33).

We now turn to look at the relevant factors listed in the *China Light & Power* case (above) one by one.

*(1) length of delay* – the court will be most ready to grant an extension of time where the delay is for a trifling period, and least ready to do so where a lengthy period of time has passed. In calculating the length of delay any period of time during which proceedings are stayed by virtue of an application for legal aid (Legal Aid Ordinance (Cap 91), s 15) should be excluded: *Brook v Law Society of HK (No 1)* [1998] 1 HKC 595.

*(2) Reasons for the delay* – delay may be excused where there is a good reason why the normal time limit could not be complied with. Delay in obtaining legal aid beyond the 42-day statutory stay may be excusable: *Chen v Whirlpool (HK) Ltd* HCMP 1877/ 2005 (Cheung JA; 12.10.2005). In *Pak Tim Chun v Tung Yung Metals Factory* [1998] 3 HKC 691 (CA) the court found delay of 2 years excusable where the prospective appellant had never received notice of the proceedings below. Delay on the part of legal advisors will not normally be considered excusable, though the court may be flexible where an action against solicitors would not provide an adequate remedy: *BR (Iran) v Secretary of State* [2007] EWCA Civ 198 (para 18). The decision in *BR (Iran)* is not regarded as authority for the proposition that delay by lawyers may be disregarded in all judicial review proceedings: *Leung Kwok Hung v President of the Legislative Council* HCMP 1227/2007 (Tang VP; 10.08.2007). The reasons for the delay should be explained on affidavit. It is 'inexcusable' for a solicitor merely to depose that the time for giving notice of appeal was thought to be longer – an explanation as to how he or she came to think so is required: *Secretary for Justice v Hong Kong & Yaumati Ferry Co Ltd* [2001] 1 HKC 125, 128F-129A. Similarly it is not acceptable for a solicitor to say only that notice of appeal was not served in time due to 'oversight': *King Fung Construction Work Co Ltd v Yip Kwai Chor & Anor* HCMP 51/2008 (Yuen JA; 16.01.2008) (para 14).

*(3) Chances of success* – the party seeking an extension of time must show that there is 'a reasonable chance of succeeding in the appeal': *Mak Hau Shing* (above, at 16G-H). In *Leung Kwok Hung* (above) the court adopted this 'reasonable prospects' test, rejecting an argument that under *Chen v Whirpool (HK) Ltd* [2006] 1 HKLRD 171 the applicant need only show that the appeal is not 'bound to fail'. An extension

will be refused where, on account of lack of prospects of success, it would be 'pointless' (*Mak Hau Shing* (*loc cit*)), or 'futile' (*Chinko v Director of Immigration* HCMP 1634/2006 (Cheung & Yeung JJA; 14.02.2007 (para 24)). The extent to which the merits are relevant may vary from case to case depending on factors such as the extent to which the delay is excusable: *Tridant Eng'g Co Ltd v Mansion Holdings Ltd* [2001] HKLRD 783.

*(4) Prejudice* – where the opposing party has changed its position, treating the result below as final on the ground the appeal period has expired, an extension of time might cause prejudice. On this ground an extension of time may be refused unless the prejudice can be compensated by an order for costs. In *Wong Yuk Fung v Woo Chor Wah & Anor* CACV 242/2004 (Cheung & Tang JJA; A Cheung J; 09.05.2005) (leave to appeal to the CFA dismissed on 28.10.2005) an application for leave to appeal out of time against an order allowing joinder of an additional defendant was refused partly on the ground that during the period of delay that defendant had taken part in the proceedings. Prejudice may be minimised or avoided if the prospective appellant puts the opposing party on notice of a possible appeal at an early stage.

**[59.4.6]     Abridgement of time to appeal**
The court's power under Order 3 rule 5 to abridge time applies in the Court of Appeal. In the unusual case of *Lo Siu Lan & Anor v Hong Kong Housing Authority* CACV 378/2004 (Ma CJHC; Stock & Le Pichon JJA; 17.12.2004) the Court of Appeal abridged the time for lodging an appeal from the usual 28 days to only two days. The order was made without opposition from the appellant. However Ma CJHC noted that in the absence of consent 'exceptional reasons' need to be shown; 'urgency is not necessarily enough by itself' to justify such an order. Leave to appeal to the CFA on the abridgement of time issue was refused: see FAMV 14/2005 (Bokhary, Chan & Ribeiro PJJ; 26.05.2005.

Note that there is no power to abridge the time for appealing to the Court of Final Appeal: see *Lo Siu Lan & Anor v Hong Kong Housing Authority* FAMP 2/2004, [2005] 2 HKLRD 208.

**5.     Setting down appeal** (O. 59 r. 5)
**(1)    Within 7 days after the date on which service of the notice of appeal was effected, the appellant must lodge with the Registrar —**
      **(a)     a copy of the sealed judgment or order and a copy of the reasoned decision (if any); and**
      **(b)     two copies of the notice of appeal, one of which shall be indorsed with the amount of the fee paid, and the other indorsed with a certificate of the date of service of the notice.**
                                                **(L.N. 152 of 2008)**
**(2)    Upon the said documents being left, the Registrar shall file one copy of the notice of appeal and cause the appeal to be set down in the list of appeals; and the appeal shall come on to be heard according to its order in that list unless the Court of Appeal or a judge of that Court otherwise orders.**
**(3)    Within 4 days after an appeal has been set down, the appellant must give notice to that effect to all parties on whom the notice of appeal was**

**served. (L.N. 152 of 2008)**

---

**NOTES**

**[59.5.1]     Procedure after service of notice of appeal**
After serving the notice of appeal, the appellant is required by Order 59 rule 5(1) to lodge with the Registrar a sealed copy of the judgment or order appealed and a copy of the reasoned judgment, if any, together with two copies of the notice of appeal. The notice of appeal is considered to be an originating document for the purposes of the High Court Fees Rules and a filing fee is payable.

It is important that the sequence of events as set out in rule 5(1) be followed. The notice of appeal should be served *before* it is lodged with the Registrar along with the other documents. In *Wong Hon Sheung v Daikaco Co Ltd & Ors* [1997] 3 HKC 676, 679B-E (CA) it was noted that the registry had sometimes allowed notices of appeal to be filed on an undertaking or understanding that they will be served on the same day, and observed that this was not proper compliance with the rule.

The required documents must be lodged with the Registrar within the 7-day period stipulated in rule 5(1). In the event of failure to comply with the time limit an extension must be obtained or the appeal cannot proceed: *Cheung Man Yu v Lau Yuen Ching & Ors* HCMP 542/2003 (Yeung & Ma JJA; 07.03.2003).

Note that rule 5(1) was amended as part of the civil justice reforms which took effect in 2009 so as to stipulate that it is a *sealed* copy of the judgment or order appealed which must lodged. Given that the time for service of the notice of appeal runs from the date the judgment or order is pronounced (see rule 4 above and the commentary thereunder) and that time is needed for approval of a draft judgment or order before it will be sealed by the court, it is clear that parties who are considering an appeal will delay drawing up a judgment or order and having it sealed at their own risk.

**[59.5.2]     Duty to set down appeal**
Once the appellant has complied with rule 5(1), the Registrar is required by rule 5(2) to 'set down', that is enter, the appeal in the list of appeals. There are in fact 3 lists of appeals – see para 8 of practice direction 4.1. The duty to set down the appeal lies with the Registrar, not the appellant: *Wong Shu-tao v Choi Shuen-lan* CACV 71/ 1979 (Huggins JA; 01.02.1980); *China Weal Ltd v Lam Sau Wah* [2000] 4 HKC 227 (CA). See, however, *A Solicitor v Law Society of Hong Kong* [1998] 2 HKC 88 (CA) in which the court appears to have proceeded on the basis that it was the duty of the appellant to set down an appeal and that failure to do so in a timely fashion could result in the appeal being struck out.  This could be a merely semantic point, since the term 'set down' is at times used rather loosely to describe the various steps by which an appeal is launched – see *Gallium Development Ltd & Ors v Winning Properties Management Ltd & Anor* CACV 186/2003 (Registrar Levy; 31.10.2003) and *Hoong Chiu Kai v Wai Yip Dispensary Ltd & Anor* [2003] 3 HKC 424 (CA) as examples.

**[59.5.3]     Notice of setting down appeal**
After an appeal has been set down, the appellant is required to give notice to that

effect, within 4 days, to the parties who have been served with the notice of appeal: see Order 59 rule 5(3) (which was numbered 5(4) prior to the civil justice reforms which took effect in April 2009). There is no form for giving such notice prescribed by these rules, but there is a commonly used form which can be found on the judi ciary website. In *Tang Sing Yu & Ors v Tang Tat Kwong & Ors* CACV 361/ 2004 (Yuen JA; 26.01.2006) it was doubted that any such notice is required to be filed in the registry and a letter was deemed to be sufficient. It has been held that the notice may be given orally: *China Weal Ltd v Lam Sau Wah* [2000] 4 HKC 227, 230E-F (CA), but see Order 66 rule 2(5) which provides that any notice required under the rules may not be given orally except with leave.

An appellant who fails to comply with the 4-day time limit should seek an extension of time under Order 3 rule 5. Failure to do so may result in the appeal being struck out. An application for such an extension is a matter of the court's discretion: *Honestwin Ltd v Mezely Trading Ltd* CACV 311/1998 (Rogers JA; 19.04.1999). In that case the court reluctantly granted an extension where it appeared there had been a deliberate decision not to comply with the rules of court. In *Mok Pak Keung v Wong Ip Ming* CACV 78/2000 (Rogers ACJHC & Keith JA; 08.09.2000) an extension was refused on the ground that it would be futile since the appeal lacked merit. However in *Cheung Chung Fat v Toyo Advertising Co Ltd* [1997] 3 HKC 459 (CA), 461I-462E the court considered the failure to give notice of setting down within time to be the 'merest technicality' and dismissed an application to set aside the notice of appeal with costs.

**[59.5.4] Application to fix hearing date**
After an appeal has been set down and notice thereof has been given, application should be made to the Registrar of Civil Appeals to fix a hearing date in accordance with paragraphs 18 and 19 of practice direction 4.1. In practice it should be up to the appellant to take the initiative to fix a date, but there does not appear to be any barrier to the respondent doing so. See *Re HY & HT Lee Brothers & Co Ltd* CACV 307 & 328/1999 (Mayo VP, Keith & Stock JJA; 29.05.2001) (para 7).

There is no prescribed time limit to apply to fix a hearing date. However in *Law Siu Hong Albert & Ors v Cheung Kin Ping* CACV 114/1997 (Leong & Woo JJA; 03.08.2000) the court held it could consider whether to allow a date to be fixed where there has been excessive delay, citing inherent power to regulate its own business and to prevent delay. In *Yu Man v PricewaterhouseCoopers* HCMP 71/2006 (Yuen JA; 05.06.2006) the court was of the view *Law Siu Hong* was in conflict with *Chan Cheryl* (below) and held that an application for extension of time to fix a hearing date is unnecessary.

Order 59 rule 5(2) provides that an appeal 'shall come on to be heard according to its order' in the list of appeals unless otherwise ordered. However, as noted in *Chan Cheryl v Ngai Po Lun Paul* [1990] 1 HKC 148, 153B (CA), the practice in Hong Kong is for all appeals to be given fixed dates. This is apparently the reason the practice direction requires an application to be made to fix a date. In *Yu Man* (above) the court considered that since the rule must take precedence over the practice direction, an appeal must come on for hearing even if no application is made to fix a date.

An appeal will normally be fixed for hearing on the earliest available date in accordance with para 18 of the practice direction. Applications to vacate or vary a hearing date on the ground of availability of counsel must be supported by a certificate from instructing solicitors setting out the information stipulated in para 19 of the practice direction. Where other grounds are relied on, very detailed information should be given on affidavit as to why the hearing date is inappropriate. See *Tai Fook Futures Ltd v Cheung Moon Hoi Jeff* CACV 103/2005 (Yuen JA; 10.10.2006) where the application of a litigant in person to vacate a hearing date was dismissed on the ground of lack of sufficient information.

**[59.5.5]     Practice direction**
Practice direction 4.1 concerns civil appeals to the Court of Appeal. It covers various aspects of the procedure to be followed in applying for leave to appeal, and with regard to preparation for the hearing of an appeal, such as submission of hearing bundles and skeleton arguments. The practice direction was substantially revised with effect from the coming into force of the civil justice reforms in 2009. Its updated text can be viewed on the judiciary's website www.judiciary.gov.hk or that of the Hong Kong Legal Information Institute www.hklii.org, both of which are accessible by the general public free-of-charge.

**[59.5.6]     Costs consequences of failure to comply with practice direction**
In *Chan King Wan & Anor v Honest Scaffold General Contractor Co Ltd & Anor* [2001] 1 HKC 415 the Court of Appeal disallowed as between solicitor and client the costs of preparation of the appeal bundles for failure to prepare a core bundle and inclusion of more than 1,600 pages of documents of which only 3 were referred to at the appeal hearing. Likewise the costs of preparation of a transcript of the evidence at trial was disallowed as the transcript was not referred to on the appeal.

**[59.5.7]     Application for the adjournment of an appeal**
A good explanation upon reasonable notice must be given where the parties seek an adjournment of the hearing of the appeal: *Wong Man-hung Patrick v Haruna Co Ltd* [1997] 2 HKC 71. In this case one day before the hearing the parties filed a consent summons stating that appeal was 'to be adjourned sine die with liberty to restore'; no reasons were given in support. The appellant's solicitors then sent a fax asking the court for an adjournment. The parties did not appear at the hearing and the appeal was dismissed for want of prosecution. 'Applications to the court, and particularly arguments in support, should not be pursued by fax. The courts do not engage in hearings and arguments by correspondence even by those means', per Nazareth VP.

**[59.5.8]     Language of hearing of an appeal**
The choice of which official language to use in an appeal is, as in all legal proceedings in Hong Kong, up to the court hearing the matter: Official Languages Ordinance (Cap 5), s 5. Rule 3 of the High Court Civil Procedure (Use of Language) Rules (subsidiary legislation under Cap 5) provides that paramount consideration must be given to the just and expeditious disposal of the proceedings.

Guidance from the court on the choice of language to be used in appeals is set out in Law Society circular 00-341, the full text of which can be viewed in the Law Society's website. The main points are:

•       It is expected that a Notice of Appeal will be in the same official language as the judgment appealed.

- An appeal will normally be heard in the same official language as the proceedings below.
- If a party wishes on appeal to switch to the other official language, directions should be sought from the court.
- The party seeking a change of language on appeal will be responsible to pay for translation of the transcript below, subject to the possibility of recovery on taxation.

6.     **Respondent's notice** (O. 59 r. 6)

       **(1)   A respondent who, having been served with a notice of appeal, desires—**

      (a)     **to contend on the appeal that the decision of the court below should be varied, either in any event or in the event of the appeal being allowed in whole or in part, or**

      (b)     **to contend that the decision of the court below should be affirmed on grounds other than those relied upon by that court, or**

      (c)     **to contend by way of cross-appeal that the decision of the court below was wrong in whole or in part,**

**must give notice to that effect, specifying the grounds of his contention and, in a case to which sub-paragraph (a) or (c) relates, the precise form of the order which he proposes to ask the Court to make.**

       **(2)   Except with the leave of the Court of Appeal or a single judge, a respondent shall not be entitled on the hearing of the appeal to apply for any relief not specified in a notice under paragraph (1) or to rely, in support of any contention, upon any ground which has not been specified in such a notice or relied upon by the court below. (L.N. 404 of 1991)**

**(HK)   (3)   Any notice given by a respondent under this rule (in this Order referred to as a "respondent's notice") must be served on the appellant, and on all parties to the proceedings in the court below who are directly affected by the contentions of the respondent, and must be served—**

      (a)     **where the notice of appeal related to an interlocutory order, within 14 days, and**

      (b)     **in any other case, within 21 days,**

**after the service of the notice of appeal on the respondent.**

       **(4)   A party by whom a respondent's notice is given must, within 2 days after service of the notice, furnish 2 copies of the notice to the Registrar.**

7.     **Amendment of notice of appeal and respondent's notice** (O. 59 r. 7)

       **(1)   A notice of appeal or respondent's notice may be amended—**

      (a)     **by or with the leave of the Court of Appeal or a single judge at any time;(L.N. 404 of 1991)**

      (b)     **without such leave, by supplementary notice served not less than three weeks before the date fixed for the hearing of the appeal.**

       **(2)   A party by whom a supplementary notice is served under this rule must, within 2 days after service of the notice, furnish two copies of the notice to**

the Registrar.

**8.     Directions of the Court as to service** (O. 59 r. 8)

(1)     The Court of Appeal or a single judge may in any case direct that a notice of appeal or respondent's notice be served on any party to the proceedings in the court below on whom it has not been served, or on any person not party to those proceedings. **(L.N. 404 of 1991)**

(2)     Where a direction is given under paragraph (1) the hearing of the appeal may be postponed or adjourned for such period and on such terms as may be just and such judgment may be given and such order made on the appeal as might have been given or made if the persons served in pursuance of the direction had originally been parties.

**9.     Documents to be lodged by appellant** (O. 59 r. 9)

(1)     Not less than 14 days before the date on which the appeal is listed for hearing the appellant must cause to be lodged with the Registrar the number of copies for which paragraph (2) provides of each of the following documents, namely—

    (a)     the notice of appeal;

    (b)     the respondent's notice;

    (c)     any supplementary notice served under rule 7;

    (d)     the judgment or order of the court below;

    (e)     the originating process by which the proceedings in the court below were begun, any interlocutory or other related process which is the subject of the appeal, the pleadings (including particulars), if any, and, in the case of an appeal in an Admiralty cause or matter, the preliminary acts, if any;

    (f)     the transcript of the official shorthand note, if any, of the judgment or order of the court below or, in the absence of such a note, the judge's note of his reasons for giving the judgment or making the order;

    (g)     such parts of the transcript of the official shorthand note, if any, of the evidence given in the court below as are relevant to any question at issue on the appeal or, in the absence of such a note, such parts of the judge's note of the evidence as are relevant to any such question;

    (h)     any list of exhibits made under Order 35, rule 11, or the schedule of evidence, as the case may be;

(HK)(i)     such documents, affidavits, exhibits, or parts of exhibits, as were in evidence in the court below and as are relevant to any question at issue on the appeal. **(L.N. 152 of 2008)**

(2)     Unless otherwise directed the number of copies to be lodged in accordance with paragraph (1) is three copies except—

    (a)     where the appeal is to be heard by two judges in which case it is two copies; or

    (b)     in the case of an appeal in an Admiralty cause or matter, in which case it is four copies or, if the Court of Appeal is to hear

**the appeal with assessors, six copies.**

**(2A) When the transcripts, if any referred to in items (f) and (g) of paragraph (1) have been bespoken by the appellant and paid for, the number of such transcripts required in accordance with paragraph (2) shall be sent by the appellant direct to the Registrar. (L.N. 152 of 2008)**

**(3) At any time after an appeal has been set down in accordance with rule 5 the Registrar may give such directions in relation to the documents to be produced at the appeal, and the manner in which they are to be presented, and as to other matters incidental to the conduct of the appeal, as appear best adapted to secure the just, expeditious and economical disposal of the appeal.**

**(4) The directions referred to in paragraph (3) may be given without a hearing provided always that the Registrar may at any time issue a summons requiring the parties to an appeal to attend before him and any party to an appeal may apply at any time for an appointment before the Registrar.**

## NOTES

### [59.9.1] Comparison with English rules
Order 59 rule 9 is taken from the rule of the same number in the former English Rules of the Supreme Court.

The position in England was amended significantly with the advent of the Civil Procedure Rules. See para 5.6 of English practice direction 52.

### [59.9.2] Documentation to be lodged for the appeal hearing
Order 59 rule 9(1) requires that the appellant lodge with the Registrar copies of relevant documentation not less than 14 days before the date on which the appeal is listed for hearing. Prior to the civil justice reforms which took effect in 2009, the documents did not need to be lodged until 7 days before the hearing, though the parties were requested to comply earlier.

The documentation to be lodged is specified in paragraphs (a) to (i) of rule 9(1). It includes the documents filed in the appeal itself (notice of appeal, respondent's notice, *etc*) as well as the originating process, pleadings and judgment or order below. Evidence adduced in the proceedings below should also be included, limited to such of the evidence as is relevant to any question at issue on the appeal: rule 9(1)(i). The documentation should be organised in bundles in accordance with part IV of practice direction 4.1. It is emphasised in that part of the practice direction that by the time a matter reaches the Court of Appeal much of the documentation below is no longer relevant and should not be included in the appeal bundles.

The appellant is required to lodge the appropriate number of copies of the appeal bundles in accordance with rule 9(2). That will normally be two copies where the appeal will be heard by two judges, and three copies for a 3-judge bench. More copies are required for Admiralty appeals and where the Court of Appeal will sit with assessors.

### [59.9.3] Failure to lodge appeal bundles in time
Failure to lodge appeal bundles with the Registrar within the time stipulated in Order 59 rule 9(1) will usually result in the appeal date being vacated with an order for

costs thrown away against the appellant or its legal representative: *Nagata & Ors v New Japan Securities Int'l (HK) Ltd (No 2)* [1994] 1 HKC 141, 143F-G (CA). In that case it was suggested that the court may even consider whether the appeal should be dismissed.

**[59.9.4]    Lists of authorities**

Practice direction 5.5 provides that every party to an appeal must submit a list of authorities. The practice direction, which is available on the judiciary's website, also applies in part to proceedings in the Court of First Instance (see para 10 of practice direction 5.4). The parties' duty is merely to list the authorities to be relied upon, not to provide copies unless requested to do so. The primary responsibility for making sure copies are made available is placed on the Clerk of Court. In practice, however, the parties' legal advisers often prepare bundles of authorities for use at the hearing.

The up-to-date text of the relevant practice directions can be viewed on the judiciary website www.judiciary.gov.hk or that of the Hong Kong Legal Information Institute www.hklii.org, both of which are accessible by the general public free-of-charge.

**10.    General powers of the Court** (O. 59 r. 10)

**(1)    In relation to an appeal the Court of Appeal shall have all the powers and duties as to amendment and otherwise of the Court of First Instance.**

**(2)    The Court of Appeal shall have power to receive further evidence on questions of fact, either by oral examination in court, by affidavit, or by deposition taken before an examiner, but no such further evidence (other than evidence as to matters which occurred after the date of the trial or hearing) shall be admitted except on special grounds. (L.N. 152 of 2008)**

**(3)    The Court of Appeal shall have power to draw inferences of fact and to give any judgment and make any order which ought to have been given or made, and to make such further or other order as the case may require.**

**(4)    The powers of the Court of Appeal under the foregoing provisions of this rule may be exercised notwithstanding that no notice of appeal or respondent's notice has been given in respect of any particular part of the decision of the court below or by any particular party to the proceedings in that court, or that any ground for allowing the appeal or for affirming or varying the decision of that court is not specified in such a notice; and the Court of Appeal may make any order, on such terms as the Court thinks just, to ensure the determination on the merits of the real question in controversy between the parties.**

**(5)    The Court of Appeal may, in special circumstances, order that such security shall be given for the costs of an appeal as may be just.**

**(6)    The powers of the Court of Appeal in respect of an appeal shall not be restricted by reason of any interlocutory order from which there has been no appeal.**

**(7)    Documents impounded by order of the Court of Appeal shall not be delivered out of the custody of that Court except in compliance with an order of that Court (L.N.362 of 1997):**

**Provided that where a Law Officer or the Director of Public**

Prosecutions makes a written request in that behalf, documents so impounded shall be delivered into his custody.

(8)   Documents impounded by order of the Court of Appeal, while in the custody of that Court, shall not be inspected except by a person authorized to do so by an order of that Court.

(9)   In any proceedings incidental to any cause or matter pending before the Court of Appeal, the powers conferred by this rule on the Court may be exercised by a single judge: (L.N. 404 of 1991)

Provided that the said powers of the Court of Appeal shall be exercisable only by that Court or a single judge in relation to—

(a)   the grant, variation, discharge or enforcement of an injunction, or an undertaking given in lieu of an injunction; and

(b)   the grant or lifting of a stay of execution or proceedings.

---

## NOTES

### [59.10.1]   Rule 10(1) – interlocutory powers of Court of Appeal – case management of appeals

Order 59 rule 10(1) extends to the Court of Appeal the powers and duties 'as to amendment and otherwise' of the Court of First Instance. Thus the Court of Appeal may exercise the amendment power under Order 20, even to the extent of granting leave to amend the pleadings relied on below: *Snellink v Data General HK Ltd* CACV 83/1989 (Yang CJ; Clough & Power JJA; 05.07.1989). Likewise the Court of Appeal may use the 'slip rule' (Order 20 rule 11): *Aqua-Leisure Industries Inc & Anor v Aqua Splash Ltd* [2003] 2 HKLRD 422. It may exercise the power under Order 15 rule 6 to add parties, even so as to permit a new party who did not appear below to join in an appeal: *Ming An Insurance Co (HK) Ltd v Chan Man Dun & Anor* CACV 96/2005 (Yuen JA; 15.03.2006). The power to extend time under Order 3 rule 5 is available to the Court of Appeal, supplementing the express power under Order 59 rule 15 – see the commentary thereunder.

The Chief Justice's working party on civil justice reform (2004) was of the view that rule 10, together with rule 9(3) and the relevant provisions of the practice direction on civil appeals (above) give the Court of Appeal all the case management powers which the Court of First Instance has (final report, para 673–675).

### [59.10.2]   Inherent powers of Court of Appeal

Apart from this rule the Court of Appeal also has a limited inherent jurisdiction to do whatever is necessary in connection with proceedings which come before it. This jurisdiction is unlike the broad inherent jurisdiction of the Court of First Instance because the Court of Appeal is considered in general to have only the jurisdiction given it by the High Court Ordinance. See *So Wing Keung v Sing Tao Ltd & Anor* [2005] 2 HKLRD 11 (CA).

### [59.10.3]   Power to strike out an appeal

The Court of Appeal has inherent power to strike out an appeal. The purpose is to prevent abuse. The power is 'seldom exercised'. See *Swordland Ltd v Wharf Properties Ltd* [1994] 2 HKC 223, 226F–G (CA).

The power extends to striking out an *ex parte* application for leave to appeal out of time. See *FHK v YSY* HCMP 1325/2006 (Tang VP; 23.05.2007) where such an order was made.

Circumstances in which the power may be exercised include the following:

- Out of time: *Kuok Hong Neng v Yuen Sik Wah* [2004] 1 HKC 618.
- Academic: *Kuok* (above); *Gay v Yip Shut Yuen* [2004] 1 HKC 615.
- No jurisdiction: *Chan Cheuk Tong v Director of Lands* [1996] 3 HKC 485 (CA); *Ng Shek Po v Director of Lands* [1996] 4 HKC 616 (CA). Note that both those decisions concerned appeals from a tribunal under Order 60A, but in principle they should apply to appeals under Order 59 as well. See also *Swordland* (above).
- Another venue more appropriate: *Official Receiver v Chan Hing To* [2007] 2 HKC 43 (CA).
- Abuse of process: *Tay Choo Wah v Singapore-Johore Express (Pte) Ltd* [1991] 2 HKC 180, 184B–F (CA) (*obiter*), citing *Aviagents Ltd v Balstravest Investments Ltd* [1966] 1 WLR 150 and *Burgess v Stafford Hotel Ltd* [1990] 1 WLR 1215 (CA).
- Delay in prosecuting appeal: *Incorporated Owners of Tuen Mun Hung Cheung Industrial Centre v United HK Ltd* CACV 652/2000 (Mayo VP, Woo JA & Stone J; 12.07.2001). See also *Interasia Bag Manufacturers Ltd v Commis sioner of Inland Revenue* CACV 400/2004 (Tang VP, Cheung JA & Stone J; 06.11.2009) (para 35) where the court took into account the underlying objective of expeditiousness (O 1A r 1(b)) in striking out a notice of appeal and dismissing the appeal for want of prosecution.

### [59.10.4]  Rule 10(2) – Power of the Court of Appeal to receive further evidence

Order 59 rule 10(2) gives the Court of Appeal power to receive further evidence not adduced below, if 'special grounds' are shown. The provision was amended as part of the civil justice reforms in force in 2009 so as to extend the 'special grounds' requirement to all appeals: previously it applied only appeals 'from a judgment after trial or hearing of any cause or matter on the merits', thus not to interlocutory appeals. The special grounds requirement never applied to evidence as to matters which occur after the date of the trial or hearing, and that continues to be the case.

In *Ladd v Marshall* [1954] 1 WLR 1489; [1954] 3 All ER 745 it was held that there are three criteria to be considered on an application to adduce further evidence on appeal. It was held that all three grounds must be satisfied before the Court of Appeal will allow fresh evidence to be adduced at an appeal:

(1)  it must be shown that the evidence could not have been obtained for use at the trial below with reasonable diligence;

(2)  it must be shown that the evidence, if received, would probably have an important influence on the result of the case, though not necessarily decisive; and

(3)  it must be shown that the evidence would probably be accepted as truthful.

In addition to the *Ladd v Marshall* criteria, since the implementation of the civil justice reforms on 2 April 2009, the underlying objectives in Order 1A should also be taken into account: *Dhami & Anor v Lloyds TSB General Insurance Ltd* [2009] EWCA 1326 (Civ) (09.12.2009) (para 16).

For policy reasons the court's approach is restrictive: the societal interest in the finality of litigation must be balanced against the interests of the individual litigant: *Paper Reclaim Ltd v Aotearoa Int'l Ltd* [2007] NZSC 1. There it was said that it is incumbent on the parties to 'apply their minds diligently', prior to trial, to what documents are available, and that a bare assertion that a document was mislaid or forgotten is not enough. In *Camberra Investment Ltd v Chan Wai Tak* CACV 75/1988 (Silke VP, Hunter & Penlington JJA; 13.12.1988) (an unreported decision delivered the same day as the substantive judgment, which is reported at [1989] 1 HKLR 568) an application for leave to call evidence which had been available at trial but had not been adduced because it was not thought to be relevant, was dismissed.

In *Kwan Chi On v Kwan Tit On Daniel* [1996] 1 HKC 137 the Hong Kong Court of Appeal, applying *Ladd v Marshall*, allowed fresh evidence to be admitted. It was suggested that the second criterion laid down in *Ladd v Marshall* (see above) may be more easily satisfied where there is a *prima facie* case of wilful deception in the court below.

In *Ratcliffe v Secretary for the Civil Service* [1999] 4 HKC 237 the Court of Appeal refused to allow further evidence to be adduced on an appeal on the ground that it failed to meet the second and third criteria in *Ladd v Marshall*. The Court of Appeal was of the view the 'evidence was not such as is presumably to be believed and that, if believed, would be conclusive; or that if given, it would probably have an important influence on the result of the appeal' (per Nazareth VP at 242F–G).

*Public law cases* – In public law cases (such as judicial review) the Court of Appeal has a greater degree of flexibility to permit new evidence to be adduced. Although the *Ladd v Marshall* criteria apply, there is a discretion to depart from them in 'wholly exceptional' circumstances: *Kwong Kwok Hay v Medical Council of HK* (No 2) [2007] 4 HKC 446 (CA) (paras 10–11) (reversing the decision reported at [2007] 3 HKLRD 213), referring to *E v Secty of State for the Home Department* [2004] QB 1044 (CA).

*Appeals against summary judgment or refusal to set aside default judgment'* – It has been suggested that the court may be more ready to permit fresh evidence on an appeal against a summary judgment than on an appeal against judgment after trial. This is because 'the standard of diligence' required of the defendant in preparing opposition to a summary judgment application 'will not be so high as that required in preparing for trial'. See *Langdale v Danby* [1983] 1 WLR 1123, referred to in *Chan Yau v Chan Calvin & Anor* HCA 666/2007 (Sakhrani J; 15.05.2009) (para 20). In *Forward v West Sussex County Council* [1995] 1 WLR 1469 (CA) the court accepted that the same point applied on an application to set aside a default judgment. However, the Hong Kong court declined to follow *Forward* after implementation of the civil justice reforms. See *Bank of China (HK) Ltd v Certain Aim Ltd* [2011] 1 HKC 135. That case was an appeal to a single judge under Order 58 from a master's refusal to set aside a default judgment. The court was construing Order 58 rule 1(5), which empowers the court to permit fresh evidence on such appeals. It was said that the rule was introduced to curb the undesirable pre-CJR practice of seeking to adduce further rounds of evidence, and that the spirit of the rule would be defeated if parties were allowed to revert to the previous practice.

**[59.10.5]   Power to allow new points to be argued on appeal**

The court has a discretion to allow new points, not argued below, to be raised on appeal. See *Cathay Pacific Flight Attendants Union v Director of Civil Aviation* [2007] 2 HKC 393 (CA) where Ma CJHC set out the following guidance as to when and how this discretion will be exercised:

    (1)    Where new points are sought to be raised on appeal (not having been raised in the court below), it is for the Court of Appeal to decide in its discretion whether or not to allow this.

    (2)    Where pure points of law are involved, the Court of Appeal may be more inclined to allow these to be raised than if factual questions or mixed law/fact issues are involved.

    (3)    Where in particular any factual questions are sought to be raised, the Court of Appeal will be anxious to ensure that no prejudice to the other side will be caused. This is equally applicable to pure points of law but is more acute when factual issues are involved.

    (4)    If the court does allow new factual points to be raised, the other side must be given sufficient opportunity to meet them. It does not follow from this that just because the other side may be given an opportunity to deal with new factual issues that leave will be given to raise them. The time for going into the facts is before the trial court. It is not for the appeal courts to try and determine disputed facts.

    (5)    The Court of Appeal will almost invariably expect an explanation to be given as to why new points raised on appeal (whether of fact or law) were not raised in the court below. This is an important facet of the court's discretion.

    (6)    It is also incumbent on the party seeking to raise new points on appeal to alert the court and the other party or parties that this is the case. It will not be good practice merely to 'slip in' new points without there being some prior indication of this.

    (7)    Where appropriate, an application should be made to amend pleadings or in judicial review proceedings, the Form 86A application for leave to apply for judicial review.

Ma CJHC went on to say that underpinning the above procedural requirements 'is not a slavish regard to technicality, but quite simply fairness and being above board in litigation'. The application to raise new points was dismissed.

With regard to the requirement that there be an explanation why the new point was not raised below (point (5) above), it has been held in Australia that the fact new counsel is briefed for the appeal, who identifies a new point, is not a satisfactory explanation: *Sunset Vineyard Management Pty Ltd v Southcorp Wines Pty Ltd* [2008] VSCA 96 (06.06.2008) (para 38).

See also the judgment Bokhary PJ in *Flywin Co Ltd v Strong & Associates Ltd* (2002) 5 HKCFAR 356.

It is up to the party seeking to raise new points to apply for leave to do so. In the absence of such an application, and an order allowing it, the appellate court should refrain from investigating issues not raised, even though they might well have been raised, before the trial judge: *Lawrence v Poorah* [2008] UKPC 21 (PC) (para 19).

**[59.10.6]** **Rule 10(3) – power to draw inferences of fact Circumstances in which the Court of Appeal will interfere with findings of fact below**

As a general rule the Court of Appeal will not interfere with the primary findings of fact of the trial judge: see *Tang Kwok Ming v Daxprofit Scaffolding Ltd* [1999] 1 HKC 657 where Godfrey JA said, at 663E–F:

> This court will not usurp the function of the trial judge, ie to find the facts. It will certainly not disturb his findings of primary fact where these are based on the credibility of the witnesses or the preference of the evidence of one witness for that of another.

In *Rossington Investments Ltd v Lam Ping Kwong & 3rd Party* [2002] 4 HKC 671 Mayo VP held (at 678D) that the Court of Appeal will only interfere with a trial judge's primary findings of fact if the appellant demonstrates:

> (1) that there is no evidence to support it; or (2) that it is contrary to documentary or other incontrovertible evidence which the judge overlooked.

The applicable principles were summarised more fully in *A Solicitor v The Law Society of Hong Kong* CACV 302/2002 (Woo VP, Cheung JA & Burrell J; 18.02.2004) (reported at [2006] 2 HKC 40, but omitting that part of the judgment relevant here) where, at para 19, Woo VP said:

> The principles laid down in the… authorities can be summarised as follows:
>
> (a) If the Court of Appeal is to reverse the trial judge's decision on the facts, it 'must not merely entertain doubt whether the decision below is right, but be convinced it is wrong'.
>
> (b) The Court of Appeal will certainly not disturb the judge's findings of primary fact where they are based on the credibility of the witnesses or the preference of the evidence of one witness for that of another because he enjoyed the advantages of receiving the evidence in its living state at first-hand.
>
> (c) In order to disturb a finding of primary fact, the Court of Appeal has to be satisfied that the judge's conclusion is plainly wrong in the sense that either (1) that there is no evidence to support it; or (2) that it is contrary to documentary or other incontrovertible evidence that the judge overlooked. It is not enough to show there is little evidence to support the judge's finding, or that it was 'contrary to the weight of the evidence'. The weight of the evidence is a matter for the trial judge. It does not matter how many witnesses say one thing, and how few say the contrary. The judge is perfectly entitled to prefer the evidence of the few to that of the many.

However, under Order 59 rule 10(3) the Court of Appeal has an express power to draw its own inferences from the primary findings of fact. In *Hongkong and Shanghai Banking Corp v Chan Yiu-wah & Anor* [1988] 1 HKLR 457 (CA) (citing *Benmax v Austin Motor Co Ltd* [1955] AC 371, per Viscount Simonds at 373–4) Fuad JA said, at 476E–F:

> The cases, I would note here, draw a distinction between the trial judge's view of the conflicting testimony and the inferences which he draws from the facts which are not in dispute. They also draw a distinction between the finding of a specific fact and a finding which is in reality an inference drawn from facts specifically found. Where the

drawing of proper inferences is concerned an appellate court will more readily form an independent opinion, subject to the weight which must always be given to the opinion of the trial judge.

The rationale for the general rule that an appellate court will not normally interfere with the trial judge's primary findings of fact is that the appellate judges do not have the advantage of seeing and hearing the witnesses themselves. See *Clarke v Edinburgh Tramways Co* [1919] SC (HL) 37, cited with approval on this point by Fuad JA in *Hongkong and Shanghai Banking Corp v Chan Yiu-wah & Anor* [1988] 1 HKLR 457, at 475D–H. Putting it another way, Bokhary PJ in *Ting Kwok Keung v Tam Dick Yuen* [2002] 1 HKC 601, 612A–B (CFA) referred to 'the trial judge's advantage of having received the evidence at first-hand'. In *Edinburgh Tramways* Lord Shaw had said that before interfering with findings of fact based on the trial judge's observation of the witnesses, an appellate judge should ask:

> Am I – who sit here without those advantages, sometimes broad and sometimes subtle, which are the privilege of the judge who heard and tried the case – in a position, not having those privileges, to come to a clear conclusion that the judge who had them was plainly wrong? If I cannot be satisfied in my own mind that the judge with those privileges was plainly wrong, then it appears to me to be my duty to defer to his judgment.

This 'plainly wrong' test for interfering with the trial judge's primary findings of fact was applied by the Court of Appeal in *Lau Lap Che Richard v Wong Sut Fan Villette* [1996] 1 HKC 165 at 167H, per Nazareth VP.

By contrast, the Court of Appeal is considered to be in as good a position as the trial judge to draw inferences of fact from the primary findings: see *Tang Kwok Ming v Daxprofit Scaffolding Ltd* [1999] 1 HKC 657 at 663G (CA), per Godfrey JA.

What are the circumstances in which the Court of Appeal may find that a trial judge's findings of fact are 'plainly wrong'? In *Ting Kwok Keung v Tam Dick Yuen & Ors* [2002] 1 HKC 601 (CFA) Bokhary PJ said it is 'impossible to lay down anything in the nature of a code on this subject'. It is therefore necessary to look at the various cases for examples. The Court of Appeal elaborated on this question in *Aktieselskabet Dansk Skibsfinansiering v Wheelock Marden & Co Ltd & Ors* [1998] 3 HKC 153. There Godfrey and Liu JJA described the burden on the party seeking to convince the Court of Appeal that a trial judge's findings of primary fact were unjustified is a 'heavy one'. The court continued, at 162D–H:

> In respect of a judge's finding of primary fact, particularly a finding based on the credibility of a witness, before we disturb such a finding, we must be satisfied that there was no evidence to support it; or that it ran counter to documentary or other incontrovertible evidence which the judge must have overlooked; or that it can only have been based on a misapprehension of the facts of some faulty process of reasoning.

See also *Tsui Cheung Hing v Tsui Hing Lan* [1999] 4 HKC 259 (CA), following the *Wheelock Marden* decision. And see *Tam Yu Hung v Chu Man On* [1996] 2 HKC 337 where the Court of Appeal overturned a decision of the Lands Tribunal on the ground that a crucial finding was vitiated for never having been put in evidence (at 341B–C).

## [59.10.7]    Rule 10(3) – power to make judgment or order which ought to have been made

In *Nagata & Ors v New Japan Securities International (HK) Ltd (No 1)* [1994] 1 HKC 134 the Court of Appeal used its power under Order 59 rule 10(3) to grant leave to amend a pleading, which leave it had held had been wrongly refused below.

## [59.10.8]    Rule 10(5) – security for costs in the Court of Appeal

Order 59 rule 10(5) empowers the Court of Appeal to order security for the costs of an appeal. The power is stated to be exercisable 'in special circumstances'. The overriding consideration is whether 'special (not exceptional) circumstances exist which make it just to order security': *Chung Kau v Hong Kong Housing Authority & Ors* [2004] 2 HKLRD 650. That test differs from the criteria applied in the Court of First Instance under Order 23 rule 1. Nevertheless similar factors are taken into account. For example, in many cases security for costs of an appeal is ordered on the ground of lack of assets within the jurisdiction or impecuniosity. With regard to those grounds see generally the commentary under Order 23 rule 1, and in relation specifically to appeals see *To Kin Wah v Tuen Mun District Office & Ors* [2003] 1 HKC 366 where it is was said that once it is demonstrated that the appellant is impecunious, security will likely be ordered, unless the appellant demonstrates countervailing factors 'that would tilt the balance or discretion in his favour'.

The categories of 'special circumstances' are 'not closed', and security for the costs of an appeal may be ordered on the ground the respondent could have difficulty enforcing a costs order, which 'may be demonstrated by the appellant trying to evade payment of the judgment or costs order that had been made against him in the court below': *Wai Yip Hin v Wong Po Kit* CACV 336/2008 (Cheung JA; 24.02.2009) (para 4).

The merits of the appeal are relevant. In *To Kin Wah* (above) Ma JA (as he then was) said (at para 15):

> If there is a strong likelihood of the appeal succeeding, then it may not be appropriate or right to order security for costs. On the other hand, if the appeal is merely arguable or if it can really go either way, an order for security will generally be made where other factors exist in support of such a course.

Thus the Court of Appeal will be reluctant to order security if the result would be to force the appellant to abandon a meritorious appeal, but ready to do so if the appeal appears hopeless: *Bank of China (HK) Ltd v Fu Ming Kong Michael & Anor* CACV 240/2005 (Rogers VP; 19.10.2005); or if the appeal is an abuse of process: *Tang On Kwai & Ors v Tang Hoi Wo* CACV 181/2008 (Tang VP; 25.09.2008). A detailed examination of the merits is not necessary or desirable: *Chung Kau* (above); *Kwangtung Provincial Bank v Chin Kam Chiu* CACV 121/2005 (Yuen JA; 20.10.2005).

In relation to companies the relevant provision is section 357 of the Companies Ordinance (Cap 32), which by its own terms applies not only to first instance actions, but to other legal proceedings. See the discussion of that power to order security in the commentary under Order 23 rule 1.

Where security for costs has been given in respect of proceedings at first instance, the court has a discretion under Order 59 rule 13 to stay payment out pending an appeal: *Akai Holdings Ltd (in liq) v Kasikorn Bank* CACV 177/2008 (Le Pichon JA; 24.08.2009) following *Stabilad Ltd v Stephens & Carter Ltd* [1999] 1 WLR 1201 (CA).

**[59.10.9]    Quantum of security**
The amount of security to be given is calculated on the party and party basis. References in English authorities to the 'standard' basis should be construed accordingly. See *Herman Iskandar v Bonardy Leo* CACV 117/1987 (Silke VP; 28.09.1987).

The quantum of security should be confined to the costs of the appeal, and not include the costs below: *Oldham, Li & Nie v Wong Lin Chooi* CACV 319/2005 (Tang JA; 08.11.2005).

**[59.10.10]    Rule 10(9) – powers of a single judge**
Order 59 rule 10(9) provides that a single judge may exercise the powers conferred on the Court of Appeal under that rule. The provision is probably not necessary as section 35 of the High Court Ordinance already provides that a single judge may make any order or direction not involving determination of the appeal and any interim order to prevent prejudice, but subject to discharge or variation by the Court of Appeal. See the discussion under Order 59 rule 14(12).

**[59.10.11]    Appeal may be allowed by consent**
Where the parties are agreed that an appeal should be allowed, they may apply for an order by consent summons. The application may be dealt with by a single judge of the Court of Appeal, who must decide whether it is proper to make the order sought: *Hong Kong Kam Lan Koon Ltd v Realray Investments Ltd* CACV 146/2005 (Rogers VP; 27.02.2006).

Where the appeal is against a considered judgment the consent summons should be supported by an affidavit or other information explaining the position in order that the court may be satisfied that the judgment below was wrong: *Johannesen & Anor v Cibean Development Co Ltd* [1998] 2 HKC 616 (CA), 621I-622B, per Nazareth VP. If the parties do not satisfy the court with such an explanation in writing, the court may make enquiries or require a hearing as was the case in *Johannesen*. In *Re A Solicitor* CACV 1218/2001 (Rogers VP, Le Pichon & Yuen JJA; 30.09.2002) the court was not prepared to deal with the application on paper because of the 'serious nature' of allegations concerning proceedings before the Solicitors Disciplinary Tribunal.

In England the procedures to be followed on an application to allow an appeal by consent were laid down in *Hadfield v Knowles & Anor* [1996] 1 WLR 1003. These were quoted with general approval in *Johannesen* (at 621). Though they may not have been formally adopted in Hong Kong they contain useful guidance particularly with regard to cases involving an infant or patient, or a structured settlement.

**[59.10.12]    Absence of appellant**
The absence of the appellant at the appeal hearing does not justify the court in dismissing the appeal without a consideration of the merits. See *Ford v China Light and Power Co Ltd & Anor* [1997] 2 HKC 14 (JCPC) and *Tsui Cheung Hing v Tsui Hing Lan* [1999] 4 HKC 259 (CA).

**[59.10.13]    Power to dismiss appeal without hearing**
Where an appellant no longer wishes to pursue the appeal, it may request that the appeal be dismissed under part H of practice direction 4.1. The request is submitted in writing and no hearing is required. The procedure does not apply to minors or parties

under disability. Where the appellant is content with an order that the appeal be dismissed with costs to the respondent, there is no need to seek the respondent's consent. However if some other order as to costs is sought the respondent must countersign the request. In either event the appeal will (subject to endorsement by a justice of appeal in chambers) be dismissed and struck out from the list without a hearing.

Appellants' solicitors should inform the court as soon as possible if their client no longer wishes to prosecute an appeal. If they fail to do so they may be liable to a wasted costs order under Order 62 rule 8(2). See *Incorporated Owners of Nine Queen's Road Central & Anor v Minkind Development Ltd* [2004] 1 HKC 270, per Nazareth VP at 290C *et seq.*

### [59.10.14]   Costs of appeal
The Court of Appeal has the same power as the Court of First Instance to make orders as to costs, including the costs of the proceedings below.

In *Tung Wing Steel Co Ltd v Brasimet Comercio E Industria SA & Ors* [1993] 2 HKC 249 the Court of Appeal considered whether it could be bound by an order below as to the costs of further proceedings. Wong J stated (at 253C–D):

> It must be very rare indeed for a single judge of the High Court to make provision for future costs occasioned in the Court of Appeal. If such an order is ever made it must be upon very special and unusual circumstances. I am not satisfied that this is such a case.

**11.   Powers of the Court as to new trials** (O. 59 r. 11)

**(1)   On the hearing of any appeal the Court of Appeal may, if it thinks fit, make any such order as could be made in pursuance of an application for a new trial or to set aside a verdict, finding or judgment of the court below.**

**(2)   The Court of Appeal shall not be bound to order a new trial on the ground of misdirection, or of the improper admission or rejection of evidence, or because the verdict of the jury was not taken upon a question which the judge at the trial was not asked to leave to them, unless in the opinion of the Court of Appeal some substantial wrong or miscarriage has been thereby occasioned.**

**(3)   A new trial may be ordered on any question without interfering with the finding or decision on any other question; and if it appears to the Court of Appeal that any such wrong or miscarriage as is mentioned in paragraph (2) affects part only of the matter in controversy, or one or some only of the parties, the Court may order a new trial as to that part only, or as to that party or those parties only, and give final judgment as to the remainder.**

**(4)   In any case where the Court of Appeal has power to order a new trial on the ground that damages awarded by a jury are excessive or inadequate, the Court may, in lieu of ordering a new trial—**

> **(a)   with the consent of all parties concerned, substitute for the sum awarded by the jury such sum as appears to the Court to be proper;**

> **(b)   with the consent of the party entitled to receive or liable to pay the damages, as the case may be, reduce or increase the sum**

awarded by the jury by such amount as appears to the Court to be proper in respect of any distinct head of damages erroneously included in or excluded from the sum so awarded; but except as aforesaid the Court of Appeal shall not have power to reduce or increase the damages awarded by a jury.

(5)   A new trial shall not be ordered by reason of the ruling of any judge that a document is sufficiently stamped or does not require to be stamped.

**12.   Evidence on appeal** (O. 59 r. 12)

Where any question of fact is involved in an appeal, the evidence taken in the court below bearing on the question shall, subject to any direction of the Court of Appeal or a single judge, be brought before that Court as follows— (L.N. 404 of 1991)

      (a)    in the case of evidence taken by affidavit, by the production of a true copy of such affidavit;

      (b)    in the case of evidence given orally, by a copy of so much of the transcript of the official shorthand note as is relevant or by a copy of the judge's note, where he has intimated that in the event of an appeal his note will be sufficient, or by such other means as the Court of Appeal or a single judge, may direct. (L.N. 404 of 1991)

## NOTES

**[59.12.1]   Fresh evidence**

In exceptional circumstances the Court of Appeal may receive further evidence, not adduced below (see Order 59 rule 10(2) and the commentary thereon).

**12A.   Non-disclosure of payment into court** (O. 59 r. 12A)

    (1)   Where—

      (a)    any question on an appeal in an action for a debt, damages or salvage relates to liability for the debt, damages or salvage or to the amount thereof, and

      (b)    money was paid into court under Order 22, in the proceedings in the court below before judgment,

neither the fact of the payment nor the amount thereof nor the terms of any relevant offer made in accordance with Order 22 shall be stated in the notice of appeal or the respondent's notice or in any supplementary notice or be communicated to the Court of Appeal until all such questions have been decided. This rule shall not apply in the case of an appeal as to costs only or an appeal in an action to which a defence of tender before action was pleaded. (L.N. 152 of 2008)

(2)   For the purpose of complying with this rule the appellant must cause to be omitted from the copies of the documents lodged by him under rule 9(d) and (f) every part thereof which states that money was paid into court in

**the proceedings in that court before judgment.**

---

## NOTES

### [59.12A.1]  Duty not to disclose sanctioned payment or sanctioned offer

Order 59 rule 12A prohibits disclosure to the Court of Appeal of the fact or amount of a sanctioned payment or sanctioned offer made under Order 22 in the proceedings below until the Court of Appeal has decided any issues arising on the appeal in relation to liability and quantum. The rule is the equivalent in the Court of Appeal of Order 22 rule 25, which applies in the Court of First Instance. See the commentary under that rule. The purpose is to avoid any appearance that the decision of the Court of Appeal may be influenced by knowledge of any such payment.

In the case of appeals from the District Court, the rule extends to sanctioned payments made under the District Court Rules: see Order 59 rule 19(4B).

In *Shek Kam Tin v Chan Fuk Sang & Anor* [1977–79] HKC 178, 180; [1979] HKLR 532, 534 an appeal had to be adjourned as a result of information concerning a payment in having been included in the appeal bundle. The responsible solicitors were ordered to pay the costs thrown away. *Shek Kam Tin* should be read in light of the fact it was decided before rule12A was enacted in Hong Kong. Insofar as it suggests the fact of a payment into court (as opposed to the amount) may be disclosed to the Court of Appeal, it should no longer be followed.

In *Chan Kam Hoi v Dragages et Travaux Publics* [1997] 2 HKC 567 the court referred with approval to the commentary under Order 22 in this work and held that this is a 'mandatory requirement of law' (per Nazareth VP, at 569) with the result that a statement in a Notice of Appeal referring to a payment in below was ordered to be struck out.

**13.  Stay of execution, etc. (O 59 r. 13)**

**(1)  Except so far as the court below or the Court of Appeal or a single judge may otherwise direct–**

> **(a)  an appeal shall not operate as a stay of execution or of proceedings under the decision of the court below;**
>
> **(b)  no intermediate act or proceeding shall be invalidated by an appeal.**

**(2) On an appeal from the court below, interest for such time as execution has been delayed by an appeal shall be allowed unless the court below otherwise orders. (L.N. 152 of 2008)**

---

## NOTES

### [59.13.1]  Stay of execution pending appeal

By virtue of Order 59 rule 13(1)(a) an appeal does not operate as a stay of execution. If the appellant wishes to avoid execution of the judgment against him pending appeal he must make a specific application to the court for a stay.

*Forum* – An application for a stay of execution may be made to the court below or to the Court of Appeal: Order 59 rule 13(1). However, it should not be made to the Court of Appeal in the first instance unless there is good reason: see Order 59 rule 14(4). In *Caine Tai Investment Co Ltd & Ors v Ayala International Finance Ltd & Anor* [1983] 1 HKC 163, 164B–C the trial judge was on leave and the Court of Appeal accepted that this constituted special circumstances justifying the application being brought before the Court of Appeal in the first instance.

*Discretion* – The court's power to grant a stay of execution is 'an unfettered discretion the exercise of which depends on the circumstances of each individual case': see *Caine Tai Investment Co Ltd & Ors v Ayala International Finance Ltd & Anor* [1983] 1 HKC 163, 166H–I, citing *AG v Emerson* (1890) 24 QBD 56 and *The Ratata* [1897] P 118, 132.

*Principles* – The principles to be applied on an application for a stay of execution pending appeal have been stated differently in different Hong Kong cases. In the *Caine Tai* case at 165C the Court of Appeal referred to *Wilson v Church (No 2)* (1879) 12 Ch D 454 as the 'leading authority' and held that the applicant for a stay had to show two things:

> ... firstly, that the appeal appears to be bona fide; and secondly, that failure to give the stay sought would result in the appeal, if successful, being nugatory.

See also *Yip Alice & Ors v Wong Shun* [2002] 3 HKC 510, 514C–D where the Court of Appeal again approved of *Wilson v Church (No 2)* and went on to quote from *Linotype-Hell Finance Ltd v Baker* [1992] 4 All ER 887 where Staughton LJ said:

> ... if a defendant can say that without a stay of execution he will be ruined and that he has an appeal which has some prospect of success, that is a legitimate ground for granting a stay of execution.

In *Humphreys Estate (Queen's Gardens) Limited v AG & Anor* CACV 92/1985 (Cons, Fuad & Kempster JJA; 07.06.1985) the court started from the proposition that it should be 'reluctant to deprive a successful litigant of the fruits of the litigation' pending appeal. The applicant for a stay faced a 'difficult task'. However, the court was prepared to grant the stay where there was reason to fear that the appellant would not be able to recover his money if successful on appeal. Cons JA stated:

> As a general rule the only ground for a stay is an affidavit showing that if the damages and costs were paid, there is no reasonable probability of getting them back if the appeal succeeds.

In *World Trade Centre Group Ltd & Anor v Resourceful River Ltd & Anor* CACV 70/1993 (Litton JA; 12.05.1993) the court considered the strength of the grounds of appeal and the financial status of the appellant in coming to the conclusion not to grant a stay. Litton JA said:

> ... a party should not be deprived of the fruits of a judgment in his favour except on good grounds being shown. Obviously if an applicant were able to demonstrate that he has very strong grounds of appeal, that something has grievously gone wrong with the process of law in the court below, then this court would be inclined to make such order as to ensure that the appeal would not be rendered nugatory in the meanwhile. In those circumstances perhaps the court may not examine very closely the financial situation of the appellant. On the other hand if the grounds of appeal appear weak then the court would look more closely into the alleged impecuniosity and prospective financial ruin.

The above-quoted passage was cited with approval in *Fung Wai Kwong William v Insider Dealing Tribunal* [2001] 1 HKC 44 where the Court of Appeal refused to grant a stay of execution in circumstances where the appellant was capable of paying the judgment and the opposing party being the government there was no risk of being unable to recover the funds in the event of the appeal being successful.

In *Whale View Investment Ltd v Kensland Realty Ltd & Ors* [2001] 3 HKC 15 (concerning an application for a stay pending appeal to the Court of Final Appeal) Keith JA at 18I–19B adopted a 'good reasons' test and held that the court should compare the injustice which could be caused to either party as a result of the grant or refusal of a stay. Keith JA found some support in the decision of the Court of Appeal in *Super Keen Investments Ltd v Global Time Investments Ltd* CACV 285/1998 (unreported). However, the majority of the court in the *Whale View Investment Ltd* case (Le Pichon JA, with Stock JA agreeing) found against any such balancing exercise. The majority found favour with English cases holding that a stay of execution will only be granted in very exceptional circumstances: see per Le Pichon JA at 21D–22C, citing *Emmerson v Ind Coope & Co* (1886) 55 LJ Ch 903, *Youssoupoff v Metro-Goldwyn-Mayer Pictures* (1934) 50 TLR 581 (CA) and *Smith Hogg & Co v Black Sea and Baltic General Insurance Ltd* (1940) 162 LT 11 (CA). It may be that the somewhat stricter approach in the *Whale View Investment Ltd* case can be confined to final appeals, but see the minority judgment of Keith JA at 18G–H where his Lordship stated he was unable to find thinking of that kind in the relevant authorities.

In *Star Play Dev't Ltd v Bess Fashion Management Co Ltd* [2007] 5 HKC 84 (a 2002 decision not reported until 2007), Ma J, as he then was set out comprehensive guidance on the exercise of the court's discretion to grant a stay of execution pending appeal. To save space, here we set out only a summary of what the court said (at para 9) regarding two factors commonly raised, that is that without a stay the appeal would be rendered nugatory, and the merits of the appeal:

(1)   In determining whether an appeal would be rendered nugatory the court must first have regard to the nature of the order that is the subject matter of the appeal. If the order appealed against is a money judgment, the court will require evidence as to why the levying of execution will result in the appeal being rendered nugatory, such as an appreciable risk that the respondent to the appeal would not be able to repay in the event of a successful appeal. Where the order appealed is, for example, an injunction (particularly a mandatory injunction) or order for possession of premises, it may well be that the nature of the order will by itself almost be determinative of the question as without a stay, more often than not, it is likely an appeal would be rendered nugatory.

(2)   Whatever the nature of the order or judgment appealed from, the court will require evidence as to why an appeal will be rendered nugatory in the event of a stay not being granted. The requisite quality of the evidence will depend on the nature of the order or judgment appealed against.

(3)   Where it is said that the levying of execution would result in financial ruin or serious financial consequences for the appellant, the court will require good evidence to support this contention, such as the production of accounts or other documents to justify the assertion. A bare assertion is unlikely to meet with much sympathy.

(4)   An appeal being rendered nugatory does not mean in all cases that without a stay the appellant faces financial ruin or the loss of all his property. Demonstrating that the failure to grant a stay would have a serious deleterious effect is enough.

(5)     Relevance of merits or strength of the appeal – while it is impractical and even undesirable for the court in dealing with an application for a stay of execution to go deeply into the merits and strengths of an appeal, it must form a preliminary view of those aspects.

(6)     The existence of an arguable appeal (that is, one with reasonable prospects of success) cannot *by itself* amount to sufficient reason to justify a stay, but is the minimum requirement before a court would even consider granting a stay.

(7)     The existence of a strong appeal or a strong likelihood that the appeal would succeed, will usually by itself enable a stay to be granted because this would constitute a good reason for a stay.

(8)     Where it is demonstrated that an appeal would be rendered nugatory if a stay is not granted, the court may require no more than the existence of an arguable appeal. Correspondingly, where it cannot be shown that an appeal would be rendered nugatory if a stay were not granted, the court will require, in the absence of any other factors, the appellant to demonstrate strong grounds of appeal or a strong likelihood of success [As an example see *Harilela Hotels Ltd v Hospitality Marketing Concepts (HK) Ltd* HCA 2523/2004 (Waung J; 05.12.2006)].

(9)     The court must not at any stage forget the position of the successful party. It is always relevant to consider the prejudice that would be caused to the successful party (the respondent in the appeal) in the event a stay is granted and if necessary, to impose conditions so as to minimise the prejudice caused to him. *A fortiori*, the court must consider any contention that the appeal would be rendered nugatory to him (in the event the appeal is dismissed) should a stay of execution be imposed.

The above observations were reiterated by the learned judge in *Wenden Eng'g Service Co Ltd v Lee Shing Yue Construction Co Ltd* HCCT 90/1999 (Ma J; 17.07.2002) and have been applied in many subsequent cases.

The effect of point (6) above is that the court may wish to consider the merits of the appeal first, and only if that threshold is passed, go on to consider whether refusal of a stay would render the appeal nugatory: *Lee Theatre Realty Ltd v Tong Wah Jor & Ors* CACV 279/2009 (Cheung JA; 02.03.2010).

**[59.13.2]     Ex parte application for stay of execution to be avoided**
In *Brand Farrar Buxbaum LLP v Samuel-Rozenbaum Diamond Ltd & Ors* HCA 5191/1998 (Ma J; 08.05.2002) the court deplored the practice of applying *ex parte* for stays of execution save in cases of extreme urgency or where there is a genuine need for secrecy. The court observed that even in cases of urgency it was preferable to apply *inter partes*, seeking an abridgement of time if necessary, or at the very least to apply *ex parte* on notice (as to which see the commentary under Order 29 rule 1). In the *Brand Farrar Buxbaum* case indemnity costs were ordered against the party who was found to have abused the *ex parte* procedure.

**[59.13.3]     Costs of application for stay of execution**
Where an application for a stay of execution pending appeal is successful, the appropriate order as to costs is that they be in the cause of the appeal. However, where the application is refused, the costs of and occasioned by the application

will more likely be ordered against the unsuccessful applicant. See *Cheng Ying Hung v Yuen Chak Construction Co Ltd* [2004] 1 HKC 503, 506F–H.

A party who successfully resists a stay of execution pending appeal is at risk as to the costs of execution in the event the appeal is allowed: *Active Profit Ltd v Nissho Iwai HK Corp Ltd & Ors* [2005] 3 HKC 499 (CA).

**[59.13.4]  Interest to run during stay of execution**
Order 59 rule 13(2) provides that unless otherwise ordered by the court below, interest runs during the time that execution of a judgment or order is delayed pending appeal. It will apply whether there is a formal stay of execution pending appeal, or the court in its discretion declines to grant a writ of execution pending determination of the appeal. This deters unsuccessful defendants from lodging appeals simply to 'buy time', and compensates plaintiffs whose judgments are upheld on appeal for the extra time they are deprived of the fruits of the judgment.

**[59.13.5]  Stay of proceedings pending appeal etc**
Order 59 rule 13(1)(a) also provides that an appeal does not operate as a stay of proceedings unless the court so orders. The court's power to grant such a stay is preserved by section 16(3) of the High Court Ordinance (Cap 4). With regard to bankruptcy proceedings, see also s 104 of the Bankruptcy Ordinance (Cap 6).

A stay of proceedings prevents further action from being taken. Thus a stay pending appeal prevents the judgment creditor from applying for a writ of execution or taking other action to enforce the judgment. However, it does not vitiate the judgment itself, and the judgment debtor remains a judgment debtor unless and until the judgment is set aside on appeal. Thus in *Re Ho Ying Pat Bobby* HCB 1946/2009 (Harris J; 07.01.2010) (para 2) it was held that a temporary stay of bankruptcy proceedings against a solicitor would not affect his status as a bankrupt, and his practising certificate would remain automatically terminated.

There are various circumstances in which a stay of proceedings pending appeal might be appropriate.

First, a stay of proceedings may be appropriate pending an interlocutory appeal which might resolve the whole dispute. In such a case costs and court time might be saved by granting a stay of the underlying proceedings pending the appeal. On the other hand, the court will take into account the fact that if the appeal fails, a stay will cause delay in bringing the action to trial. See for example, *Hoi Sing Construction Co Ltd v ITC Corp Ltd* HCA 11433/1998 (Deputy Judge Carlson; 26.09.2005).

Secondly, it may be appropriate to stay an action pending judgment in another case which could have an effect on the particular case. In *Tan Man Kou & Anor v Chime Corp Ltd* HCMP 4146/2001 (Kwan J; 11.03.2005) the court stayed 8 sets of proceedings pending an appeal to the Court of Final Appeal in a related case which could render them 'pointless and academic', causing 'substantial wasted costs' (para 34).

The court's approach in considering such a temporary stay is 'to consider the balance of convenience and fairness as between the parties': *Clinton Eng'g Ltd v B-Tech (Holdings) Ltd* HCA 3608/1998 (Recorder Liao SC; 28.09.2001); *SWE Ltd v Chong Lai Fun* HCA 1064/2004 (Reyes J; 28.10.2004) (para 27); *Tan Man Kou* (above) (para 14). It is a matter of 'case management': *Tan Man Kou* (*loc cit*). Even before the civil justice reforms came into force in 2009 it was said that the court should exercise its discretion to grant a stay 'to ensure that its procedures are used in a logical, fair and cost-efficient manner": *SWE* (above) (para 27). Those considerations will now be all the more important in light of the underlying objectives in Order 1A rule 1.

For stay of proceedings pending mediation, see the commentary under Order 1A rule 4(2)(e).

**[59.13.6]    Power to stay payment out of security for costs pending appeal**
The court has a discretion under Order 59 rule 13 to stay payment out of security for costs pending an appeal: *Akai Holdings Ltd (in liq) v Kasikorn Bank* CACV 177/ 2008 (Le Pichon JA; 24.08.2009) following *Stabilad Ltd v Stephens & Carter Ltd* [1999] 1 WLR 1201 (CA).

**14.    Applications to the Court of Appeal** (O. 59 r. 14)
**(1)    Unless otherwise directed, every application to the Court of Appeal or a single judge which is not made ex parte must be made by summons and such summons must be served on the party or parties affected at least 2 clear days before the day on which it is heard or, in the case of an application which is made after the expiration of the time for appealing, at least 7 days before the day on which the summons is heard. (L.N. 404 of 1991)**

**(1A) In support of any application (whether made ex parte or inter partes) the applicant shall lodge with the Registrar such documents as the Court of Appeal or a single judge may direct, and rule 9(3) and (4) shall apply, with any necessary modifications, to applications as they apply to appeals. (L.N. 404 of 1991)**

**(2)    (Repealed, L.N. 152 of 2008)**
**(2A)  (Repealed, L.N. 152 of 2008)**
**(2B)  (Repealed, L.N. 152 of 2008)**

**(3)    Where an ex parte application has been refused by the court below, an application for a similar purpose may be made to the Court of Appeal ex parte within 7 days after the date of the refusal.**

**(3A) Where an application made to the Court of Appeal ex parte under paragraph (3) is granted, notice of the order granting the application must be served on the party or parties affected. (L.N. 152 of 2008)**

**(3B) A party on whom a notice has been served is entitled, within 7 days after service of the notice, to apply to the Court of Appeal to have the order granting the application reconsidered inter partes in open court. (L.N. 152 of 2008)**

**(4)    Wherever under these rules an application may be made either to the court below or to the Court of Appeal, it shall not be made in the first instance to the Court of Appeal, except where there are special circumstances which make it impossible or impracticable to apply to the court below.**

**(5)    Where an application is made to the Court of Appeal with regard to arbitration proceedings before a judge-arbitrator or judge-umpire which would, in the case of an ordinary arbitrator or umpire, be made to the Court of First Instance, the provisions of Order 73, rule 5, shall apply as if, for the words "the Court", wherever they appear in that rule, there were substituted the words "the Court of Appeal" and as if, for the words "arbitrator" and**

"umpire", there were substituted the words "judge-arbitrator" and "Judge-umpire" respectively.

(6)     Where an application is made to the Court of Appeal under section 23(5) of the Arbitration Ordinance (Cap. 341) (including any application for leave), notice thereof must be served on the judge-arbitrator or judge-umpire and on any other party to the reference.

(HK)(6A) In this rule "judge-arbitrator" and "Judge-umpire" mean a judge appointed as sole arbitrator or, as the case may be, as umpire by or by virtue of an arbitration agreement.

(7)     An application which may be heard by a single judge, shall, unless otherwise directed, be heard in chambers. (L.N. 152 of 2008)

(8)     (Repealed, L.N. 404 of 1991)

(9)     (Repealed, L.N. 404 of 1991)

(10)   A single judge may refer to the Court of Appeal any matter which he thinks should properly be decided by that Court, and, following such reference, that Court may either dispose of the matter or refer it back to a single judge or the Registrar, with such directions as that Court thinks fit.

(11)   (Repealed, L.N. 404 of 1991)

(12)   An appeal shall lie to the Court of Appeal from any determination by a single judge and shall be brought by way of fresh application made within 10 days of the determination appealed against. (L.N. 152 of 2008)

(13)   This rule does not apply in relation to an application for leave to appeal. (L.N. 152 of 2008)

---

NOTES

**[59.14.1]    Scope of Order 59 rule 14**
Order 59 rule 14 deals with various types of application of an interlocutory nature which may be made in relation to an appeal to the Court of Appeal. Rule 14(2) and (2A) previously dealt with general applications for leave to appeal, but those provisions were repealed and replaced by rules 2A, 2B, 2C and 21 as part of the civil justice reforms which took effect in 2009.

**[59.14.2]    Applications to a single judge**
Applications to the Court of Appeal not involving determination of an appeal may be dealt with by a single judge: see section 35(1) of the High Court Ordinance. That expressly includes applications for leave to appeal. However it does not extend to an application to strike out an appeal since striking out amounts to a determination of the appeal and hence does not come within the subsection: *Koon Wing Yee v Insider Dealing Tribunal* CACV 358/2005 (Ma CJHC, Tang VP & Stock JA; 07.12.2006).

See also section 34A HCO in relation to criminal matters, Order 3 rule 5(4) which contemplates applications for extension of time being heard by a single judge of the Court of Appeal, and Order 59 rule 10(9) concerning exercise of the Court of Appeal's powers under that rule.

**[59.14.3]    Appeal from determination of single judge**
Order 59 rule 14(12) provides that an appeal lies from a decision of a single judge to

the Court of Appeal. See also section 35(3) HCO which provides that every decision of a single judge may be discharged or varied by the Court of Appeal. Such an appeal or application may be made to a bench consisting of two justices of appeal: see section 34B(4) of the High Court Ordinance, and see *Yip Alice & Ors v Wong Shun* [2002] 3 HKC 510, 513F, describing commentary to the contrary in another work as 'misleading'. Note that applications for leave to appeal are outside the scope of this rule: rule 14(13). Specific provision is made in rule 2C for an application for leave to appeal which has been determined by a single judge to be the subject of a fresh application before two justices of appeal.

A party appealing under rule 14(12) against an exercise of discretion by a single judge 'has a high hurdle to surmount'. It must show that the judge 'plainly was in error'. It may do so by pointing to a factor which was not drawn to the judge's attention or to a decisive statutory provision which was overlooked. See *Chau Cheuk Yiu v Poon Kit Sang* HCMP 121/2010 (Le Pichon & Yuen JJA; 13.08.2010) (para 2–4), quoting from *The Iran Nabuvat* [1990] 1 WLR 1115. *Chau Cheuk Yiu* was an appeal against a single judge's decision to grant an extension of time to appeal. Le Pichon JA said (para 4) that the court should 'be very sparing in the exercise of the jurisdiction to set aside an extension of time so granted'.

In *Yip Alice* (above) it was also held that the Court of Appeal may exercise the single judge's discretion afresh where no reasons were given, distinguishing *Wren v Braunston Canal Services* [1990] The Times, Nov 23.

On appeal against a single judge's decision to grant an application, the court applies a high threshold. See *Chau Cheuk Yiu v Poon Kit Sang & Ors* HCMP 121/2010 (Le Pichon & Kwan JJA; 13.08.2010) where an appeal against a single judge's grant of an extension of time to appeal was dismissed. It was held that on such an appeal against an exercise of discretion it was necessary to show that the judge 'plainly was in error'.

**14A.   Determination of interlocutory application** (O. 59 r. 14A)

**(1)   The Court of Appeal (including a single judge thereof) may, in relation to a cause or matter pending before the Court of Appeal, determine an interlocutory application without a hearing on the basis of written submissions only.**

**(2)   Where it considers it necessary or expedient, the Court of Appeal (including a single judge thereof) may direct that the interlocutory application shall be heard before the Court of Appeal consisting of 2 or 3 Justices of Appeal.**

**(3)   For the avoidance of doubt, nothing in this rule precludes a judge of the Court of First Instance from sitting as an additional judge of the Court of Appeal in accordance with section 5(2) of the Ordinance.**

**(L.N. 152 of 2008)**

---

**NOTES**

**[59.14A.1]   Disposal of interlocutory application without a hearing**
Order 59 rule 14A(1) provides that an interlocutory application arising from an appeal to the Court of Appeal may be determined on the basis of written submissions. Such a

procedure would be suitable for routine applications such as for security for the costs of an appeal.

Alternatively such applications may be determined with an oral hearing before a single judge (see section 35 of the High Court Ordinance, and see the commentary under the preceding rule), or, if so directed by the court, before 2 or 3 justices of appeal: rule 14A(2).

**15.    Extension of time** (O. 59 r. 15)

**Without prejudice to the power of the Court of Appeal or a single judge under Order 3, rule 5, to extend or abridge the time prescribed by any provision of this Order, the period for serving notice of appeal under rule 4 or for making application ex parte under rule 14(3) may be extended or abridged by the court below on application made before the expiration of that period. (L.N. 404 of 1991)**

---

**NOTES**

**[59.15.1]    Power to grant extension of time to serve notice of appeal**
Order 59 rule 15 provides *inter alia* that the court below may grant an extension of time for serving notice of appeal. However, by the express terms of the rule, that power can only be exercised prior to expiration of the prescribed time. See *Re Wing Fung Construction (HK) Ltd* [2006] 1 HKC 72. Once the time has expired application must be made to the Court of Appeal under Order 3 rule 5, and may be heard by a single judge thereof but not the registrar or a master: *Chan Cheryl v Ngai Po Lun Paul* [1990] 1 HKC 148, 151D-G (CA). A hearing is required. See *Chung Fai Engineering Co (a firm) v Maxwell Engineering Co Ltd* HCMP 4473/2000 (Keith JA; 21.09.2000).

Special Provisions as to Particular Appeals

**16.    Appeal against decree nisi** (O. 59 r. 16)
**(1)    The following provisions of this rule shall apply to any appeal to the Court of Appeal in a matrimonial cause against a decree nisi of divorce or nullity of marriage.**

**(1A) An appeal lies as of right to the Court of Appeal from a decree nisi granted by the Court. (L.N. 152 of 2008)**

**(2)    The period of 28 days specified in rule 4 shall be calculated from the date on which the decree was pronounced and rule 15 shall not apply in relation to that period.**

**(3)    The appellant must, within the period mentioned in paragraph (2) produce to the Registrar a sealed copy of the decree appealed against and leave with him a copy of that decree and two copies of the notice of appeal (one of which shall be indorsed with the amount of the fee paid and the other indorsed with a certificate of the date of service of the notice); and the appeal shall not be competent unless this paragraph has been complied with. (L.N. 404 of 1991)**

**(4)    For the purposes of rule 5 the leaving of the said copies shall be**

sufficient for the setting down of the appeal and rule 5(1) shall not apply.

(5)    A party who intends to apply ex parte to the Court of Appeal to extend the period referred to in paragraphs (2) and (3) must give notice of his intention to the appropriate Registrar before the application is made; and where any order is made by the Court of Appeal extending the said period, it shall be the duty of the Registrar forthwith to give notice of the making of the order and of the terms thereof to the appropriate Registrar.

(6)    In this rule "the appropriate Registrar" means—

    (a)    in relation to a cause pending in a district court, the registrar of that court.

(Ordinance 10 of 2008, s 30)

_____

## NOTES

**[59.16.1]**    **Appeal against decree nisi of divorce or nullity**

Order 59 rule 16(1) sets out certain special provisions for appeals to the Court of Appeal against decrees *nisi* of divorce or nullity. Rule 16(1A) specifically provides that there is a right to appeal to the Court of Appeal from such a decree granted by 'the Court', which is defined in Order 1 to mean the Court of First Instance. See also Order 59 rule 21(1)(*l*) which exempts such decrees from the requirement for leave to appeal against interlocutory orders.

**19.**    **Appeal from District Court** (O. 59 r. 19)

(1)    The following provisions of this rule shall apply to any appeal to the Court of Appeal from a District Court other than an appeal against a decree nisi of divorce or nullity of marriage.

(2)    The notice of appeal must be served on the registrar of the District Court as well as on the party or parties required to be served under rule 3.

(3)    (Repealed, L.N. 152 of 2008)

(4)    Except where the Court of Appeal or a single judge otherwise directs, an affidavit or note by a person present in the District Court shall not be used in evidence before the Court of Appeal unless it was previously submitted to the judge for his comments. (L.N. 404 of 1991) (L.N. 152 of 2008)

(4A)    Rule 12A shall apply in any case where money was paid into court by the defendant before judgment in district court proceedings in satisfaction of the plaintiff's cause of action or of one or more causes joined in one action or on account of a sum admitted by the defendant to be due to the plaintiff.

(4B)    Rule 12A(1) applies as if a reference to Order 22 were a reference to Order 22 of the Rules of the District Court (Cap. 336 sub. leg. H). (L.N. 152 of 2008)

(5)    Rule 13(1)(a) shall apply subject to the provisions of section 66 of the District Court Ordinance (Cap. 336).

_____

## NOTES

**[59.19.1]    Leave to appeal from District Court**
Leave to appeal to the Court of Appeal is required in respect of all decisions of the District Court in exercise of its civil jurisdiction: District Court Ordinance (Cap 336), s 63. Leave may be granted by the District Court itself or by the Court of Appeal, but it is not appropriate to apply to the Court of Appeal unless the District Court has already refused leave: RDC Order 58 rule 2(4A); RHC Order 59 rule 14(4). The procedure for applying to the District Court for leave to appeal is governed by RDC Order 58, and by RHC Order 59 rule 2A for applications to the Court of Appeal.

Until the repeal in 1993 of what was then section 53 of the District Court Ordinance, there was a procedure whereby a party could apply to the District Court for review of its own decision, rather than appealing.

**20.    Appeals in cases of contempt of court** (O. 59 r. 20)
**(1)    In the case of an appeal to the Court of Appeal against an order of committal or other punishment for contempt of Court made by a judge of the Court of First Instance, the notice of appeal must be served on the Registrar as well as on the party or parties required to be served under rule 3. (See App. A, Form 99)**

**This paragraph shall not apply in relation to an appeal to which rule 19 applies.**

**(2)    Where, in the case of such an appeal as is mentioned in paragraph (1), the appellant is in custody, the Court of Appeal may order his release on his giving security (whether by recognizance, with or without sureties, or otherwise and for such reasonable sum as that Court may fix) for his appearance within 10 days after the judgment of the Court of Appeal on the appeal shall have been given, before the court from whose order or decision the appeal is brought unless the order or decision is reversed by that judgment.**

**(3)    An application for the release of a person under paragraph (2) pending an appeal to the Court of Appeal must be made by motion, and the notice of the motion must, at least 24 hours before the day named therein for the hearing, be served on the Registrar and on all parties to the proceedings who are directly affected by the appeal.**

**(Enacted 1988)**

Cases Where Leave to Appeal is Not Required
for Interlocutory Appeals

**21.    Judgments and orders to which section 14AA(1) of the Ordinance not apply** (O. 59 r. 21)
**(1)    Judgments and orders to which section 14AA(1) of the Ordinance (leave to appeal required for interlocutory appeals) does not apply and accordingly an appeal lies as of right from them are the following —**

    **(a)    a judgment or order determining in a summary way the substantive rights of a party to an action;**

    **(b)    an order made under section 52A(4) of the Ordinance;**

    **(c)    an order prohibiting a debtor from leaving Hong Kong under**

Order 44A, rule 3(1);

(d)    an order for the imprisonment of a judgment debtor under Order 49B;

(e)    an order of committal for contempt of court under Order 52, rule 1;

(f)    an order granting any relief made at the hearing of an application for judicial review;

(g)    an order under Order 53, rule 3 refusing to grant leave to apply for judicial review;

(h)    an order granting an application for a writ of habeas corpus ad subjiciendum;

(i)    an order under Order 73 (other than an order against which leave to appeal is required under the Arbitration Ordinance (Cap. 341);

(j)    a judgment given inter partes under Order 83A, rule 4, or Order 84A, rule 3 or in a mortgage action within the meaning of Order 88, rule 1;

(k)    an order under Order 121; and

(l)    a decree nisi of divorce or nullity of marriage.

(2)  Without affecting the generality of paragraph (1)(a), the following are judgments and orders determining in a summary way the substantive rights of a party –

(a)    a summary judgment under Order 14 or Order 86;

(b)    an order striking out an action or other proceedings or a pleading or any part of a pleading under Order 18, rule 19 or under the inherent jurisdiction of the Court;

(c)    a judgment or order determining any question of law or the construction of any document under Order 14A, rule 1(1);

(d)    a judgment or order made under Order 14A, rule 1(2) dismissing any cause or matter upon determination of a question of law or construction of any document;

(e)    a judgment on any question or issue tried pursuant to an order under Order 33, rule 3;

(f)    an order dismissing or striking out an action or other proceedings for want of prosecution;

(g)    a judgment obtained pursuant to an "unless" order;

(h)    an order refusing to set aside a judgment in default;

(i)    an order refusing to allow an amendment of a pleading to introduce a new claim or defence or any other new issue; and

(j)    a judgment or order on admissions under Order 27, rule 3.

(3)  A direction as to whether a judgment or order is one that is referred to in paragraph (1)(a) may be sought from the judge who made or will make the judgment or order.

(4)  A reference to an order specified in paragraph (1)(b), (c), (d), (e), (f), (h), (i), (k) and (l) includes an order refusing, varying or discharging the order.

(L.N. 152 of 2008)

## NOTES

### [59.21.1] Scope of Order 59 rule 21 – leave not required to appeal certain interlocutory appeals

Order 59 rule 21 lists those interlocutory appeals to the Court of Appeal for which leave to appeal is not required. Under section 14AA(1) of the High Court Ordinance leave is generally required for such appeals, but section 14AA(2) goes on to stipulate that the rules of court may prescribe judgments and orders to which that requirement will not apply. Pursuant to the latter provision, rule 21 exempts many interlocutory judgments and orders from the leave requirement. Generally it is judgments and orders of a final character, or affecting the liberty of the person, which are exempted.

Note also that the leave requirement does not apply to any interlocutory judgment or order of the CFI made before section 14AA came into operation in 2009: see HCO section 14AA(5).

### [59.21.2] Rule 21(1)(a) – summary determination of substantive rights

Order 59 rule 21(1)(a) provides that summary determinations of the substantive rights of a party are not subject to the leave requirement for interlocutory appeals. Rule 21(2) sets out a non-exhaustive list of judgments and orders which are considered to be summary determinations of substantive rights. The list includes summary judgment, striking out of pleadings, refusal to set aside default judgment and judgment on admissions.

It is important to note that the exemption only applies where the result of the interlocutory application is a determination of substantive rights. Thus on an Order 14 summons, for example, the exemption only applies if the court grants summary judgment. It does not apply if the court dismisses the application or grants leave to defend. This is because it is only if summary judgment is granted that there is a determination of substantive rights – the result of dismissal of the summons or a grant of leave to defend is that the matter must proceed to trial for determination of substantive rights. Accordingly, a grant of summary judgment comes within the exemption and may be appealed as of right, whereas dismissal of the summons or grant of leave to defend does not come within the exemption and leave to appeal would be required.

The position with regard to self-executing orders (see Order 32 rule 11B) is complex in this regard. If by such an order a Draconian consequence is imposed for non-compliance, such as dismissal of the action, then the question whether the order determines substantive rights will depend on whether the order is complied with. Consider, for example, an unless order providing that the plaintiff's action be struck out unless further and better particulars of the statement of claim are provided within a specified time, or unless further discovery is provided. If the order is complied with, the action will proceed and there is no summary determination of rights. However, if it is not complied with the parties' substantive rights are determined against the plaintiff, which can no longer proceed with its claims. Is such an order one which requires leave to appeal or not? If it results in judgment then it comes within rule 21(2)(g), and is a determination of substantive rights which may be appealed without leave. Otherwise the appropriate procedure would appear to be an application under Order 2 rule 5 for relief from the sanction.

**[59.21.3]   Direction of the court where uncertain whether order comes within rule 21(1)(a)**

In cases of uncertainty whether a judgment or order constitutes a summary determination of substantive rights, rule 21(3) provides that a direction may be sought from the judge who made or will make the judgment or order.

**[59.21.4]   Rule 21(1)(b) – wasted costs order**

Order 59 rule 21(1)(b) exempts wasted costs orders against legal representatives from the general requirement for leave to appeal an interlocutory order. Such orders are provided for in section 52A(4) of the High Court Ordinance and Order 62 rules 8-8E.

**[59.21.5]   Rule 21(1)(c), (d) & (e) – liberty of the person**

Wrongful deprivation of liberty is obviously intolerable and must be remedied without delay. As a result, the sanctions provided for under these rules whereby a person's liberty may be restricted in connection with civil proceedings are exempted from the requirement that leave be obtained for an appeal to the Court of Appeal. The exempted sanctions are:

(1)   *Rule 21(1)(c)* – order under section 21B of the High Court Ordinance and Order 44A RHC prohibiting a debtor from leaving Hong Kong.

(2)   *Rule 21(1)(d)* – imprisonment of judgment debtor following examination under Order 49B RHC: see the commentary under rule 1B of that Order.

(3)   *Rule 21(1)(e)* – committal (imprisonment) under Order 52 RHC for contempt of court.

The effect of the above provisions is that an appeal to the Court of Appeal lies as of right in the event an order of the type concerned is made by a judge of the Court of First Instance. Orders prohibiting debtors from leaving Hong Kong and those imprisoning judgment debtors following examination may be made by masters. However, the general provision whereby a master's decision may be appealed to a single judge of the High Court under Order 58 rule 1 does not apply: such an appeal must be made to the Court of Appeal: Order 58 rule 2(d). Leave to appeal is not required.

**[59.21.6]   Rule 21(1)(f), (g) & (h) – judicial review and habeas corpus**

Judgments and orders granting relief by way of judicial review, or refusing leave to apply for judicial review may be appealed to the Court of Appeal as of right: Order 59 rule 21(1)(f) & (g). The same applies to an order in accordance with Order 54 granting an application for a writ of habeas corpus *subjiciendum* (to produce a detained person to the court): rule 21(1)(h). Orders refusing such an application are not specifically mentioned; nevertheless such an order would appear to come within the general provision of rule 21(1)(a) being a summary determination of substantive rights, and thus exempt from the leave requirement.

**[59.21.7]   Rule 21(1)(i) – arbitration proceedings**

Under section 23 of the Arbitration Ordinance (Cap 341) an appeal lies from a determination in an arbitration to the court on any question of law provided that the parties consent or with leave of the court. Without disturbing any such leave requirement under the Ordinance, Order 59 rule 21(1)(i) provides that an appeal lies as of right to the Court of Appeal from any order under Order 73, which concerns arbitration matters which come before the court.

### [59.21.8]    Rule 21(1)(j) – default judgment in money lenders', hire-purchase and mortgage actions

Order 83A rule 4 gives the court power to grant leave to enter judgment in default of notice of intention to defend or in default of defence, in money lenders' actions. Order 84A rule 3 makes the same provision for actions arising out of hire-purchase and conditional sales agreements. By virtue of Order 59 rule 21(1)(j), an appeal to the Court of Appeal lies as of right from any such judgment. The provision extends to judgments in mortgage actions under Order 88. All of these types of orders may be made by masters. Default judgment under Order 84A rule 3 (in a hire purchase or conditional sale action) must be appealed direct from the master to the Court of Appeal: Order 58 rule 2(c), and the provision being commented on here makes it clear that such an appeal may proceed as of right. With regard to the judgments in money lenders' and mortgage actions which are covered by this provision, an appeal lies from a master to a single judge of the Court of First Instance under Order 58 rule 1 (for which no leave is required), and this provision would only be relevant in the event of a further appeal from the single judge to the Court of Appeal.

### [59.21.9]    Rule 21(1)(k) – proceedings under Child Abduction and Custody Ordinance

An appeal to the Court of Appeal from a judgment or order under Order 121, which provides for applications under the Child Abduction and Custody Ordinance (Cap 512), lies as of right: Order 59 rule 21(1)(k).

### [59.21.10]   Rule 21(1)(l) – matrimonial proceedings

By virtue of Order 59 rule 21(1)(l) a decree *nisi* of divorce or nullity of marriage is exempted from the requirement for leave to appeal against interlocutory orders. See also Order 59 rule 16(1A) which expressly provides that an appeal lies as of right from a decree *nisi* granted by the CFI.

---

## NOTES

### [60.0.11]    Numbering

There is no Order 60 in the Hong Kong rules. The Order of the same number in the former English RSC concerned appeals to the Court of Appeal from the Restrictive Practices Court, which existed under the Restrictive Practices Court Act 1976. There is no equivalent court in Hong Kong.

## ORDER 60A

## (HK) APPEALS FROM TRIBUNALS TO COURT OF APPEAL
## ON A QUESTION OF LAW OTHER THAN BY WAY OF CASE STATED

---

## NOTES

### [60A.0.1]   Comparison with English rules
Order 60A is unique to Hong Kong in the sense that there was no Order of that number in the former English RSC.

**1.   Application of Order** (O. 60A r. 1)
   **This Order applies to appeals that lie from any tribunal to the Court of Appeal on a question of law other than by way of case stated.**

---

## NOTES

### [60A.1.1]   Scope of Order
This Order provides the procedure for appeals to the Court of Appeal against decisions of tribunals where such appeals may be made on questions of law other than by case stated. The right to appeal is a matter of statute and not common law. Reference should normally be made to the Ordinance governing the particular tribunal.
   In *Ng Chiu Yuen Jacob v Lam Che Cheung* [1999] 1 HKC 468 the Court of Appeal dismissed an appeal on the ground that it related solely to disputes of fact and not to questions of law.

### [60A.1.2]   Appeals from Lands Tribunal
This Order governs appeals under section 11(2) of the Lands Tribunal Ordinance (Cap 17) from decisions of the Lands Tribunal to the Court of Appeal against a determination or order of the tribunal on the ground that such determination or order is erroneous in point of law. Leave to appeal is required by section 11AA(1) of the Lands Tribunal Ordinance (applicable only to judgments orders and decisions delivered after the commencement of that provision in 2009 as part of the civil justice reforms). According to section 11(3), subject to subsection (4), any appeal under subsection (2) shall be brought in such manner and shall be subject to such conditions as are prescribed by the Rules of the High Court. Subsection (4) says that the time within which a notice of appeal must be served shall be calculated from the date of the making of the determination or order appealed from. This differs from the normal provision governing appeals to the Court of Appeal (see Order 59 rule 4(1)) where the time for making an appeal runs from the date the judgment or order is sealed or otherwise perfected.

### [60A.1.3]   Appeals from Labour Tribunal
Order 60A does not apply to appeals from the Labour Tribunal. This is because such appeals are initially to the Court of First Instance (with leave, on a point of law or

jurisdiction only, pursuant to the Labour Tribunal Ordinance (Cap 25), s 32) whereas Order 60A applies only to appeals to the Court of Appeal. A Labour Tribunal appeal to the Court of First Instance may in certain circumstances result in a subsequent appeal to the Court of Appeal (section 35A), but any such appeal is from the Court of First Instance and not the Tribunal itself, hence Order 60A still does not apply.

Appeals to the Court of First Instance, such as those from the Labour Tribunal, are governed by Order 55.

See *Lin Zhen Man t/a Yat Chong Electric Co v Soo Yun Wah* [1999] 1 HKC 630 (CFA) for discussion of appeals from the Labour Tribunal to the Court of First Instance and beyond.

**2.      Notice of appeal from tribunal** (O. 60A r. 2)

**(1)    An appeal to which the Order applies must be brought by motion, notice of which is referred to in this Order as "notice of appeal".**

**(2)    A notice of appeal must specify the grounds of the appeal, together with the question of law to be decided by the Court of Appeal.**

---

**NOTES**

**[60A.2.1]    Notice of appeal must state question of law**

The notice of appeal from the tribunal to the Court of Appeal must state the grounds of appeal and the question of law to be decided: rule 2(2).

Given that appeals under this Order are limited to questions of law, failure to state a point of law is fatal and the appeal may be struck out under inherent jurisdiction: *Chan Cheuk Tong v Director of Lands* [1996] 3 HKC 485 (CA); *Ng Shek Po & Anor v Director of Lands* [1996] 4 HKC 616 (CA).

Non-compliance with rule 2(2) can be cured by amendment: *Parasram v Kuscene Development Ltd* [1991] 2 HKC 13, 15I-16A (CA).

**3.      Time for appealing** (O. 60A r. 3)

**Subject to the provisions of any Ordinance, a notice of appeal must be served on all parties to the proceedings before the tribunal, and on the tribunal, within 28 days of the date on which the judgment or order of the tribunal was given. (L.N. 152 of 2008)**

---

**NOTES**

**[60A.3.1]    Time for service of notice of appeal**

Order 60A rule 3 provides that a notice of appeal from a tribunal to the Court of Appeal in accordance with the Order must be served within 28 days of the judgment or order appealed. The time, which was previously 21 days, was increased to 28 days as part of the civil justice reforms which took effect in April 2009.

Note that the notice of appeal must be served not only on the other parties, but on the tribunal itself.

**4.     Setting down appeal** (O. 60A r. 4)

**(1)     The appellant must, within 7 days after service of the notice of appeal, or within such further time as may be allowed by the Registrar, produce to the Registrar—**

> **(a)     a copy of the sealed judgment or order of the tribunal and a copy of its reasoned decision (if any); (L.N. 152 of 2008)**
>
> **(b)     2 copies of the notice of appeal, one of which shall be endorsed with the amount of the fee paid, and the other endorsed with a certificate of the date of service of the notice.**

**(2)     Upon the said documents being left, the Registrar shall file one copy of the notice of appeal and cause the appeal to be set down in the list of appeals; and the appeal shall come on to be heard according to its order in that list unless the Court of Appeal or a single judge or the Registrar otherwise orders.**

---

**NOTES**

**[60A.4.1]     Procedure on setting down appeal**
Order 60A rule 4, not Order 59 rule 5, prescribes the procedures for setting down an appeal from a tribunal to which this Order applies: *Gallium Development Ltd & Ors v Winning Properties Management Ltd & Anor* CACV 186/2003 (Registrar Levy; 31.10.2003). In that case it was held that a sealed copy of the order of the Lands Tribunal is not required to set down the appeal.

**5.     Application of Order 59** (O. 60A r. 5)

**Order 59, rules 9 and 10 shall, so far as applicable, apply to an appeal to which this Order applies.**

**(L.N. 356 of 1988)**

---

**NOTES**

**[60A.5.1]     Powers of the Court of Appeal**
According to Order 60A rule 5, Order 59 rule 10 shall, so far as is applicable, apply to an appeal to which Order 60A applies. For the effect of this rule, see the notes under Order 59 rule 10.

Also relevant in this context is section 13(4) of the High Court Ordinance which provides that, for the purposes of and incidental to the hearing and determination of an appeal to the Court of Appeal, the Court of Appeal shall have all the authority and jurisdiction of the court or tribunal from which the appeal was brought. The effect is that, for example, when hearing an appeal from the Lands Tribunal, the Court of Appeal will have all the powers of the Lands Tribunal in making appropriate orders.

**6.     Duty of Registrar to notify tribunal of result** (O. 60A r. 6)

**The Registrar shall notify the tribunal of the decision of the Court of Appeal on the appeal and of any direction given by the Court therein.**

**(Enacted 1988)**

## ORDER 61

### APPEALS FROM TRIBUNALS TO COURT OF APPEAL BY WAY OF CASE STATED

2.    **Statement of case by tribunals** (O. 61 r. 2)

(1)    **Where any tribunal is empowered or may be required to state a case on a question of law for determination by the Court of Appeal, any party to the proceedings who is aggrieved by the tribunal's refusal to state a case may apply to the Court of Appeal or a single judge of that Court for an order requiring the tribunal to state a case.**

(2)    **An application under this rule must be made by motion and the notice of the motion, stating in general terms the grounds of the application, together with the question of law on which it is desired that a case shall be stated and any reasons given by the tribunal for its refusal, must within 28 days after the refusal, be served on the clerk or registrar of the tribunal and on every other party to the proceedings before the tribunal. (L.N. 152 of 2008)**

(3)    **Within 2 days after service of the notice of motion, the applicant must lodge two copies of the notice with the Registrar who shall enter the motion in the list of appeals.**

(4)    **Where a tribunal is ordered under this rule to state a case, the tribunal must, within such period as may be specified in the order, state a case stating the facts on which the decision of the tribunal was based and the decision, sign it and cause it to be sent by post to the applicant.**

(4A)    **Where the decision of the tribunal in respect of which a case is stated states all the relevant facts found by the tribunal and indicates the questions of law to be decided by the Court of Appeal, a copy of the decision signed by the person who presided at the hearing shall be annexed to the case, and the facts so found and the question of law to be decided shall be sufficiently stated in the case by referring to the statement thereof in the decision.**

---

## NOTES

### [61.2.1]    Comparison with English rules
Order 61 rule 1 of the former English RSC has been omitted from the Hong Kong rules. It deals specifically with appeals by way of case stated from the English Lands Tribunal. Appeals from the Hong Kong Lands Tribunal are dealt with by the Court of Appeal under Order 60A (above).

Order 61 rule 2(4A) is taken from Order 61 rule 1(4) of the former English RSC. Whereas the former English RSC applies to appeals from the Lands Tribunal, in Hong Kong the rule has general effect.

### [61.2.2]    Scope of Order 61
Order 61 governs some aspects of the procedure for an appeal from a tribunal to the Court of Appeal by case stated on a point of law. Such an appeal may only be brought where provided for in primary legislation, which is rare.

The following are some examples of legislation providing for reference of points of law to the Court of Appeal by way of case stated:

- Air Pollution Control Ordinance (Cap 311) s 36
- Waste Disposal Ordinance (Cap 354) s 29
- Water Pollution Control Ordinance (Cap 358) s 34
- Dumping at Sea Ordinance (Cap 466) s 31
- Hong Kong War Memorial Pensions Ordinance (Cap 386) s 15

**[61.2.3]   Rule 2 – order to compel tribunal to state case**

Order 61 rule 2 provides a remedy to a party aggrieved by the failure or refusal of a tribunal to state a case. The aggrieved party may, under the rule, apply for an order to compel the tribunal to state a case. The rule applies where a tribunal is empowered or may be required to state a case on a question of law for determination by the Court of Appeal. Note that the time for making application was increased from 21 to 28 days under the civil justice reforms taking effect in 2009.

**3.     Proceedings on case stated** (O. 61 r. 3)

**(1)     The party at whose instance a case has been stated by any tribunal to which this Order applies must, within 28 days after receiving the case— (L.N. 152 of 2008)**

> **(a)     serve on every other party to the proceedings before the tribunal a copy of the case, together with a notice setting out his contentions on the question of law, and**

> **(b)     serve a copy of the notice on the clerk or registrar of the tribunal.**

**(2)     Within 2 days after service of the notice, the said party must lodge the case and two copies of the notice with the Registrar who shall enter the case in the list of appeals, and the case shall not be heard until after the expiration of 28 days from the date of entry. (L.N. 152 of 2008)**

**(3)     Where any enactment under which the case is stated provides that a government department shall have a right to be heard in the proceedings on the case, a copy of the case and of the notice served under paragraph (1) must be served on that department and on the Secretary for Justice.**

**(4)     On the hearing of the case, the Court of Appeal may amend the case or order it to be sent back to the tribunal for amendment.**

**(5)     Order 59, rule 10, shall, so far as applicable, apply in relation to a case stated by a tribunal to which this Order applies.**

**(6)     The Registrar shall notify the clerk or registrar of the tribunal of the decision of the Court of Appeal on the case and of any directions given by that Court thereon.**

**(Enacted 1988)**

---

**NOTES**

**[61.3.1]     Comparison with English rule**

Note that in Hong Kong, unlike England, service of the Secretary for Justice is required where a government department has a right to be heard on a reference by case stated. See rule 3(3).

**[61.3.2] Scope of hearing**

In *Commissioner of Inland Revenue v Emerson Radio Corp* [1999] 2 HKC 255, 263G-264E (CA) Rogers JA held that the Court of Appeal is not confined to questions of law raised in the case stated. The other judges on that appeal did not make this point, nor is it dealt with in the subsequent appeal to the CFA ([2000] 1 HKC 155), but it may be supported by Order 61 rule 3(4) which allows the Court of Appeal to amend the case stated.

On the other hand, the decision might be distinguishable on the basis that it did not concern an appeal to the Court of Appeal under Order 61, but an appeal to the Court of First Instance under the Inland Revenue Ordinance, which was subsequently further appealed to the Court of Appeal.

## COSTS

## ORDER 62

### PRELIMINARY

1. **Interpretation** (O. 62 r. 1)

   **(1)   In this Order—**

"certificate" includes allocatur;

(HK) "contentious business" means business done, whether as a barrister, solicitor or advocate, in or for the purpose of proceedings begun before the Court or before an arbitrator appointed under the Arbitration Ordinance (Cap 341) not being common form probate business; (10 of 2005 s 166):

"costs" include fees, charges, disbursements, expenses and remuneration;

"the Court" means the High Court or any one or more judges thereof, whether sitting in Court or in chambers, the Registrar or assistant registrar or master;

(HK) "District Court" means the District Court established under the provisions of the District Court Ordinance (Cap 336), and any judge of that court;

"legal representative", in relation to a party to proceedings, means a counsel or solicitor conducting litigation on behalf of the party; (L.N. 152 of 2008)

(HK) "mentally disordered person" means a person who is so far disabled in mind or who is so mentally ill or subnormal due to arrested or incomplete development of mind as to render it either necessary or expedient that he, either for his own sake or in the public interest, should be placed and kept under control;

(HK) "non-contentious business" means any business done by and as a solicitor which is not contentious business;

"party entitled to be heard on taxation" means –

   (a)   a party entitled to payment of costs;

   (b)   a party who has acknowledged service or taken any part in the proceedings which gave rise to the taxation proceedings, and who is directly liable under a costs order made against him;

   (c)   a person who has given the party entitled to payment of costs and the Registrar written notice that he has a financial interest in the outcome of the taxation; or

   (d)   a person in respect of whom a direction has been given under rule 21(3).

(L.N. 152 of 2008)

"taxed costs" means costs taxed in accordance with this Order;

(HK) "taxing master" means the Registrar as taxing master;

"wasted costs order" means an order made under section 52A(4) of the Ordinance. (L.N. 152 of 2008)

(2)   In this Order, references to a fund, being a fund out of which costs are to be paid or which is held by a trustee or personal representative, include references to any estate or property whether immovable or personal held for the benefit of any person or class of persons; and references to a fund held by a trustee or personal representative include references to any fund to which he is entitled (whether alone or together with any other person) in that capacity, whether the fund is for the time being in his possession or not.

---

## NOTES

**[62.1.1]   General note on interpretation of Order 62 with reference to English cases**

Order 62 of the Hong Kong rules is substantially the same as its equivalent in England as it existed prior to April 1986. In that month (and subsequently) there have been substantial amendments to the English rules on costs which have not been adopted in Hong Kong. As a result, English decisions since April 1986 need to be considered in light of the differing rules in the two jurisdictions.

## 2.   Application (O. 62 r. 2)

**(HK)(1)   This Order shall apply to all proceedings in the Court, except non-contentious or common form probate proceedings and proceedings in matters of prize.**

**(2)   Where by virtue of any Ordinance the costs of or incidental to any proceedings before an arbitrator or umpire or before a tribunal or other body constituted by or under any Ordinance, not being proceedings in the High Court, are taxable in the Court of First Instance, the following provisions of this Order, that is to say, rule 7(4), rule 8D (except paragraph (4)), rule 8E, rule 9D(1) and (4), rules 13 and 13A, rules 14 to 16, rule 17(1), rules 17A and 17B, rule 18, rules 21 (except paragraph (4)), 21A, 21B, 21C and 21D, rules 22 to 26, rule 28A (except paragraphs (4) and (7)), rules 32A and 32B and rules 33 to 35, shall have effect in relation to proceedings for taxation of those costs as they have effect in relation to proceedings for taxation of the costs of or arising out of proceedings in the High Court. (L.N. 152 of 2008)**

**(2A)   Where rule 22 has effect under paragraph (2), a reference to the Court of First Instance in rule 22(9)(a) is to be construed as a reference to the arbitrator, umpire, tribunal or other body, as the case may be. (L.N. 152 of 2008)**

**(3)   This Order shall have effect subject to the provisions of the District Court Ordinance (Cap 336) and to any rules made thereunder and to any other enactment.**

**(4)   The powers and discretion of the Court as to costs under sections 52A and 52B of the Ordinance and under the enactments relating to the costs of criminal proceedings to which this Order applies shall be exercised subject to and in accordance with this Order. (L.N. 152 of 2008)**

## NOTES

### [62.2.1]  Proceedings to which Order 62 applies

Order 62 rule 2 sets out the extent to which the Order applies to legal proceedings. Subject to certain exceptions, the Order applies to all contentious proceedings in the High Court, and to taxation in the Court of First Instance of costs awarded in certain alternative dispute resolution (ADR), and certain tribunals.

### [62.2.2]  Application to probate and administration matters

Order 62 does not apply to non-contentious probate proceedings (meaning unopposed applications under the Non-Contentious Probate Rules (Cap 10) for grants of probate or letters of administration in relation to the estate of a deceased person): rule 2(1). However, the exception does not extend to contentious probate proceedings of the type governed by Order 76, and the Order does apply to those.

### [62.2.3]  Application to proceedings in prize

Order 62 does not apply to 'proceedings in matters of prize': rule 2(1). Such proceedings, which must be very rare, are in relation to ships or property captured at sea as spoils of war. In relation to such proceedings see also item 4 in the table to Order 1 rule 2(2).

### [62.2.4]  Application to alternative dispute resolution

Rule 2(2) applies certain of the provisions of Order 62 to proceedings before an arbitrator or umpire where by statute the costs of such proceedings are taxable in the Court of First Instance. With regard to arbitrations, see section 2GJ(2) of the Arbitration Ordinance (Cap 341), which provides that costs awarded in arbitration proceedings are taxable by the Court of First Instance unless the award otherwise directs.

### [62.2.5]  Application to tribunal proceedings

Rule 2(2) applies some of the provisions of Order 62 to taxation of costs awarded by statutory tribunals where, by Ordinance, such costs are taxable in the Court of First Instance. An example is section 12(2) of the Lands Tribunal Ordinance (Cap 17), which has been interpreted as providing that costs in that tribunal should be taxed in the CFI: *Incorporated Owners of Honour Building v Lou Chui-sim & Anor* LDBM 266/1999 (Judge Li; 17.07.2001); *Leung Yin Ling v IO of No 165 Wong Nai Chung Rd* [2002] 4 HKC 328.

### [62.2.6]  Application to criminal proceedings

Order 62 applies to orders for costs in criminal proceedings: rule 2(4). However, this is subject to the Costs in Criminal Cases Ordinance (Cap 492) and subsidiary legislation thereunder which contain specific provisions with regard to such costs. Under rule 5(2)(b) of the Costs in Criminal Cases Rules (Cap 492A) awards of costs in criminal proceedings in the Court of First Instance or Court of Appeal are taxed by the Registrar of the High Court. Certain of the provisions of Order 62 are expressly applied to such taxations: see rule 8(3) of Cap 492A, applying Order 62 rules 33 and 34.

**[62.2.7]    Rule 2(4) – ambit of the court's discretion as to costs**

Section 52A(1) of the High Court Ordinance gives the court 'full power' to determine 'by whom and to what extent' costs are to be paid. This power extends to the making of costs orders against non-parties by virtue of HCO section 52A(2), which was amended to that effect by the Civil Justice (Miscellaneous Amendments) Ordinance (No 3 of 2008) in force from 2009. See Order 62 rule 6A with respect to costs against non-parties.

Order 62 rule 2(4) provides that the court's discretion as to costs is to be exercised in accordance with this Order. The provision applies to the broad discretion under section 52A, as well as the power under section 52B in relation to costs only proceedings (as to which see rule 11A), and to costs orders in criminal cases. This has the effect of narrowing the ambit of the discretion somewhat, in that Order 62 contains specific guidance as to the incidence and quantum of costs. See in particular rule 3(2), which stipulates that costs shall generally follow the event; rule 5, which stipulates certain matters which should be taken into account, and rule 28 which regulates the amount of costs to be allowed on taxation.

**[62.2.8]    Contribution cases**

The court's discretion with respect to costs is fettered in contribution cases by section 6 of the Civil Liability (Contribution) Ordinance (Cap 377), which provides that a plaintiff who commences more than one action against defendants, who are jointly or otherwise together liable to compensate him, will be entitled to costs only on the first judgment.

**[62.2.9]    Costs of amicus curiae**

There is a discretion to order a party to pay the costs of an *amicus curiae* appointed to assist the court in a particular case. The discretion should be exercised 'sparingly'. See *Lau Wing Hong v Wong Wor Hung (No 2)* [2007] 3 HKC 574. In that case an *amicus* was appointed by the court, with concurrence of the parties, and instructed by the registrar of the High Court, to be paid out of public funds. On discontinuance of the relevant part of the plaintiffs' claim they were ordered to pay 2/3 of the costs of the *amicus*.

## ENTITLEMENT TO COSTS

3.    **Order as to entitlement to costs** (O. 62 r. 3) (L.N. 152 of 2008)

(1)    **Subject to the provisions of this Order, no party shall be entitled to recover any costs of or incidental to any proceedings from any other party to the proceedings except under an order of the Court.**

(2)    **If the Court in the exercise of its discretion sees fit to make any order as to the costs of or incidental to any proceedings (other than interlocutory proceedings), the Court shall, subject to this Order, order the costs to follow the event, except when it appears to the Court that in the circumstances of the case some other order should be made as to the whole or any part of the costs. (L.N. 152 of 2008)**

(2A)    **If the Court in the exercise of its discretion sees fit to make any order as to the costs of or incidental to any interlocutory proceedings, it may, subject** to this Order, order the costs to follow the event or make such other order as it sees fit. (L.N. 152 of 2008)

(3)    The costs of and occasioned by any amendment made without leave in the writ of summons or any pleading shall be borne by the party making the amendment, unless the Court otherwise orders.

(4)    The costs of and occasioned by any application to extend the time fixed by these rules, or any direction or order thereunder, for serving or filing any document or the doing of any other act (including the costs of any order made on the application) shall be borne by the party making the application, unless the Court otherwise orders.

(5)    If a party on whom a notice to admit facts is served under Order 27, rule 2, refuses or neglects to admit the facts within 7 days after the service on him of the notice or such longer time as may be allowed by the Court, the costs of proving the facts shall be paid by him, unless the Court otherwise orders.

(6)    If a party—

(a)    on whom a list of documents is served in pursuance of any provision of Order 24, or

(b)    on whom a notice to admit documents is served under Order 27, rule 5,

gives notice of non-admission of any of the documents in accordance with Order 27, rule 4(2) or 5(2) as the case may be, the costs of proving that document shall be paid by him, unless the Court otherwise orders.

(7)    Where a defendant by notice in writing and without leave discontinues his counterclaim against any party or withdraws any particular claim made by him therein against any party, that party shall, unless the Court otherwise directs, be entitled to his costs of the counterclaim or his costs occasioned by the claim withdrawn, as the case may be, incurred to the time of receipt of the notice of discontinuance or withdrawal.

(8)    (Repealed, L.N. 152 of 2008)

(9)    Where any person claiming to be a creditor—

(a)    seeks to establish his claim to a debt under any judgment or order in accordance with Order 44, or

(b)    comes in to prove his title, debt or claim in relation to a company in pursuance of any such notice as is mentioned in Order 102, rule 13,

he shall, if his claim succeeds, be entitled to his costs incurred in establishing it, unless the Court otherwise directs, and, if his claim or any part of it fails, may be ordered to pay the costs of any person incurred in opposing it.

(10)    Where a claimant is entitled to costs under paragraph (9), the amount of the costs shall be fixed by the Court unless it thinks fit to direct taxation, and the amount fixed or allowed shall be added to the claimant's debt.

(11)    Where a claimant (other than a person claiming to be a creditor) having established a claim to be entitled under a judgment or order in accordance with Order 44 has been served with notice of the judgment or order pursuant to rule 3 or 15 of that Order, he shall, if he acknowledges service of the notice be entitled as part of his costs of action (if allowed) to costs incurred in establishing his claim, unless the Court otherwise directs; and where such a claimant fails

to establish his claim or any part of it he may be ordered to pay the costs of any person incurred in opposing it.

(12)     Where an application is made in accordance with Order 24, rule 7A or Order 29, rule 7A, for an order under section 41, 42 or 44 of the Ordinance, the person against whom the order is sought shall be entitled, unless the Court otherwise directs, to his costs of and incidental to the application and of complying with any order made thereon and he may, after giving the applicant 7 days' notice of his intention to do so, tax such costs and, if they are not paid within 4 days after taxation, sign judgment for them.

---

## NOTES

### [62.3.1]    Rule 3(1) – no recovery of costs except under order

Order 62 rule 3(1) provides that as a general rule, costs may only be recovered under an order of the court. Exceptions are provided for elsewhere in Order 62, notably rules 10 and 11. Those provide, *inter alia*, that a party against whom proceedings have been withdrawn or discontinued without leave may claim taxed costs without the need for an order.

The court may make an order for costs under its general power in section 52A of the High Court Ordinance and this Order whether or not a claim to costs has been pleaded. See Order 18 rule 15(1). It is sometimes said that costs are always in issue. Different considerations apply where a claim to costs, or a particular level of costs, arises from contract – see above.

See Order 42 rule 5B(6) for the court's power to make an order *nisi* as to costs.

### [62.3.2]    Rule 3(2) – when court shall order costs to follow the event

Order 62 rule 3(2) states the general rule that costs shall follow the event. It provides that when making an order for costs other than in interlocutory proceedings, the court 'shall' order that costs follow the event unless in the circumstances of the case some other order should be made. In other words the rule prescribes that in general the court's broad discretion under section 52A of the Ordinance to determine 'by whom' costs should be paid, should be exercised so as to require the unsuccessful party to pay the successful party's costs.

Prior to amendment of rule 3(2) as part of the civil justice reforms, in effect from April 2009, the rule that costs 'shall' follow the event applied equally to interlocutory and other proceedings. Now under rule 3(2A) the court 'may' order that costs of interlocutory proceedings follow the event. The purpose of the amendment was to facilitate the court making use of costs orders to deter unreasonable interlocutory applications. See the commentary on the costs of interlocutory applications some paragraphs below.

The meaning of an order that costs follow the event was described in the following words in *Like Soon Co Ltd v Tsai Kui Kan & Ors* [1986] HKC 142, 144A–B (CA):

> ... we have always understood the expression 'costs to follow the event' to mean that the costs expended in obtaining the particular decision that the court has just made should be recovered by the party in whose favour that decision went. Or if the court were dealing with more than one matter, or more than two parties, then the costs should be recovered by each successful party.

### [62.3.3] Circumstances in which the court will make an order other than that costs follow the event

The rule that costs shall follow the event is not absolute. The court retains a discretion in all cases. This point is expressed emphatically in *Donald Campbell & Co Ltd v Pollak* [1927] AC 732, 811:

> A successful [litigant] … has no doubt, in the absence of special circumstances, a reasonable expectation of obtaining an order for the payment of his costs … but he has no right to costs unless and until the court awards them to him, and the court has an absolute and unfettered discretion to award or not to award them.

Order 62 rule 3(2) expressly qualifies the rule that costs shall follow the event by providing that the court may make some other order as to the whole or any part of the costs in the circumstances of the case. Relevant circumstances as to when a successful party may be denied part of the costs, or even ordered to pay costs to the unsuccessful party, are set out in *Re Elgindata Ltd (No 2)* [1992] 1 WLR 1207, 1214A–C (CA) where the following 4 principles were expressed by Nourse LJ:

(i)   Costs are in the discretion of the court.

(ii)  They should follow the event, except when it appears to the court that in the circumstances of the case some other order should be made.

(iii) The general rule does not cease to apply simply because the successful party raises issues or makes allegations on which he fails, but where that has caused a significant increase in the length or cost of the proceedings he may be deprived of the whole or a part of his costs.

(iv)  Where the successful party raises issues or makes allegations improperly or unreasonably, the court may not only deprive him of his costs but may order him to pay the whole or a part of the unsuccessful party's costs.

The above principles clearly apply in Hong Kong: see *La Chemise Lacoste SA v Crocodile Garments Ltd* [2000] 4 HKC 317, 327B-E (CA); *KWKM v KSW* CACV 432/2006 (Yuen JA & Chu J; 15.06.2007). They are frequently cited by the court in considering whether to depart from 'costs follow the event'. See, for example, *Chow Kee James t/a Tapbo Civil Eng'g Co v Transway Construction & Eng'g Ltd* HCCT 11/2006 (Deputy Judge Gill; 23.05.2007). However, they are not an exhaustive list of the circumstances in which the court may depart from the usual order. This is clear from the cases discussed in the following paragraphs.

In exercising its discretion as to costs the court will take into account all of the relevant circumstances. The fact that a party succeeded on a point raised by the court itself is irrelevant: *Wong Hing Cheong v Wah E Investment Ltd & Anor* [2002] 3 HKC 59, 69F–G (CA).

See also Order 62 rule 7 which gives the court an express power to depart from the principle that costs follow the event in cases of misconduct or neglect.

### [62.3.4] Order for proportion or fraction of costs

The court may, in exercise of its discretion, limit the extent to which costs are recovered by reference to a proportion, such as a fraction or percentage, or by reference to the costs of a particular stage of the proceedings. The power to make such orders is express in Order 62 rule 9(4)(a). See also Order 62 rule 5(1)(f) and 5(2)(a). It is sometimes exercised to reflect shared success. See the commentary concerning those rules.

**[62.3.5]   No order as to costs**

The court may in its discretion expressly make no order as to costs.

In *Wong Hing Cheong & Anor v Wah E Investment Ltd & Anor* [2002] 3 HKC 59 (paras 31–33) the Court of Appeal held that no order as to costs was fair where a party discontinued claims of 'substantial merit' following an erroneous decision by the court below on a point of jurisdiction. At para 30 Rogers VP expressed the view that it was irrelevant whether a case is decided on a point raised by the parties or the court.

In *Secretary for Justice v Lau Kwok Fai Bernard & Anor* (2005) 8 HKCFAR 304 no order as to costs was made against the losing litigants in a constitutional challenge brought in the public interest. See the discussion below on the costs of public interest litigation.

In *Solicitor v Law Society of Hong Kong & Secretary for Justice (No 2)* [2004] 2 HKLRD 754 the Court of Final Appeal held that as a general rule costs will not be ordered against an intervenor in important constitutional cases. In that case the Secretary for Justice had intervened in litigation over the constitutional validity of legislation.

In *Lion Will Investment Ltd v Triple Will Ltd* CACV 200/1992 (Power VP, Nazareth & Bokhary JJA; 23.07.1993) (para 17) it was argued that no order as to costs is 'usual' on a vendor and purchaser summons under section 12 of the Conveyancing and Property Ordinance (Cap 219). The Court of Appeal did not doubt that to be the case. However an examination of the authorities suggests that such an order is often the result of agreement of the parties or consent, rather than exercise of the court's discretion. See, for example *Lo Shea Chung & Anor v Lo Hung Biu* [1997] 2 HKC 723 (CA); *Goldful Way Dev't Ltd v Wellstable Dev't Ltd* [1999] 1 HKLRD 563; *WOC Finance Co Ltd v Wing On Cheong Investment Co Ltd* [2000] 2 HKLRD 713 and *Leonart Ltd v Turn Fine Dev't Ltd* [2001] 3 HKLRD 353. This is perhaps explained by the fact that in certain instances a vendor purchaser summons is taken out to benefit both sides by clarifying title or contractual rights, unlike the more common hostile litigation.

In *Chan Ka Lim v Chow Wai Kin* CACV 405/2007 (Rogers VP, Le Pichon & Cheung JJA; 14.10.2008) the Court of Appeal made no order as to costs of an appeal and a cross-appeal, both of which were successful, where the net result was a variation of the quantum of damages ordered below by less than one-half of one percent. Le Pichon JA said (at para 40) that the variation was '*de minimis*', and that neither party could be said to have been successful.

Where a judgment of the court is silent as to costs the result is that neither party will have any claim to costs. This follows from rule 3(1) which provides that (save as provided elsewhere in Order 62) no party is entitled to recover costs except under an order. However the situation may be different with respect to an interlocutory order which is silent as to costs, and the court subsequently makes an order for the general costs of the action. In such case the order for the general costs of the action has been interpreted to extend to the costs of the interlocutory order: *Friis v Paramount Bagwash Co Ltd* [1940] 2 KB 654.

**[62.3.6]   Reverse order as to costs**

There are cases in which the court has been prepared to depart from the rule that costs follow the event to such an extent that it orders the successful party to pay the unsuccessful party's costs. See *Spruce v University of Hong Kong* CACV 58/1991 (Cons Ag CJ, Kempster & Macdougall JJA; 20.08.1991) (reversed on appeal on other grounds: see [1993] 2 HKLR 65 (PC)). However, such an order is appropriate 'only in the most unusual circumstances': *Union Base Ltd v Tsang Shek Tong* [1998] 2 HKC 349, 351G-H (CA). It appears that there must be some fault attributable to the successful party to justify such a costs order. It is not a proper judicial exercise of discretion to order a completely successful party to pay costs: *Kierson v Joseph L Thompson & Sons, Ltd* [1913] 1 KB 587 (CA).

### [62.3.7] Costs where only nominal or trivial damages awarded

A plaintiff who is awarded only a nominal amount of damages may not be regarded as successful for the purpose of the rule that costs follow the event. In *Elpe Int'l (FE) Ltd v Hewlett Packard (HK) Ltd* CACV 58/1993 (Power VP, Nazareth & Bokhary JJA; 30.07.1993) (para 32) Bokhary JA cited *Anglo-Cyprian Trade Agencies Ltd v Paphos Wine Industries Ltd* [1951] 1 All ER 873 and *Alltrans Express Ltd v CVA Holdings Ltd* [1984] 1 WLR 394 and said:

> So the courts do not proceed on the basis that a party who recovers anything, even if only nominal damages, is *prima facie* entitled to costs provided he is not confronted by a payment into court of as much or more than what he recovered. Rather, the courts, looking at the realities, ask themselves the question, 'who really won?'

See also *Gallium Dev't Ltd & Ors v Winning Ppty Management Ltd* CACV 186/2003 (Woo VP, Le Pichon & Yuen JJA; 06.07.2005) citing *Anglo-Cyprian* (above) and *The Zinnia* [1984] 2 Lloyd's Rep 211. It has been held that the same principle applies where only a 'small or trivial' amount is awarded: *Hong Chi Fat Thomas & Anor v Alexander Sung Wai Yip* DCCJ 3196/2004 (Deputy Judge KW Wong; 12.09.2007) (para 23).

The result may be no order as to costs, as in *Tai Yip Dyeing Fty Ltd v Kong Hoi Sang* HCA 2917/2004 (Saunders J; 04.04.2007). Such an order is 'the usual practice' in defamation cases where the jury awards only nominal damages: *Ki Ping Ki Paul v Oriental Daily Publisher Ltd* [1999] 3 HKC 672, 675D, referring to *Martin v Benson* [1927] 1 KB 771 and *Pamplin v Express Newspapers (No 2)* [1988] 1 WLR 116. Alternatively the court may apportion costs as between plaintiff and defendant, as in *Tsun Fat Finance Co Ltd v Commissioner of Police* HCA 7017/2000 (Deputy Judge Fung; 04.10.2002). Or the court may go so far as to order the plaintiff to pay the defendant's costs, as in *Hong Chi Fat Thomas* (above).

### [62.3.8] Cost of litigation over estate or trust

See also the commentary under Order 62 rule 6 concerning the costs of contentious probate litigation, and the costs of personal representatives and trustees.

The costs of all parties in non-hostile litigation over an estate or trust (for example on a construction point) will normally be paid out of the fund. However where the litigation is hostile (such as where there are factual disputes) costs will normally follow the event. See *Hongkong Bank Trustee Ltd v Lee See Ching John* [1998] 2 HKC 706, 707H-708F. Similar principles were applied in relation to a Chinese *t'ong* or *t'so* in *To Kan Chi & Ors v To Kin Wah & Anor* HCMP 509/2002 (Yam J; 29.09.2005); CACV 68/2006 (Rogers VP & Chu J; 27.02.2007). See also the commentary under Order 85 concerning the *Beddoe* order, by which trustees may protect themselves against personal liability for costs.

### [62.3.9]   Costs of minority shareholder

A minority shareholder who brings proceedings for the benefit of the company may seek a pre-emptive order for indemnification by the company in costs. See *Chung Sau Ling & Anor v Asia Women's League Ltd & Ors* [2001] 3 HKC 410, 415D–F, citing *Wallersteiner v Moir (No 2)* [1975] QB 373. The criteria applicable on an application for such an order are similar to those applicable on an application for a *Beddoe* order: see the commentary under Order 85. Where the shareholder brings such an action with leave of the court under part IVAA of the Companies Ordinance (Cap 32) the power to make an order of indemnification in costs is under section 168BI. In *Re F&S Express Ltd* [2005] 4 HKLRD 743 it was held that such an order should not be made without evidence as to the company's ability to pay.

### [62.3.10]   Costs of public interest litigation

Where proceedings are brought for the benefit of a large class of persons or the public generally, it may be appropriate for the court to depart from the usual rule that costs follow the event: *Scott v HKSAR* [2004] 2 HKLRD 989 (para 15) (judgment ultimately upheld by the CFA, including the costs order – see *Secretary for Justice v Lau Kwok Fai Bernard & Anor* (2005) 8 HKCFAR 304). Such an order may take the form of no order as to costs (as in *Scott* and landmark right of abode cases like *Chong Fung Yuen v Director of Immigration* (2001) 4 HKCFAR 234), or an order that the private litigant bringing the proceedings be indemnified in costs (as in *Society for the Protection of the Harbour Ltd v Town Planning Board* [2003] 4 HKC 463 (CFI); (2004) 7 HKCFAR 114). As to indemnity costs in these circumstances, see the commentary under Order 62 rule 28.

The principles governing the court's discretion to depart, in public interest cases, from the usual rule that costs follow the event are discussed comprehensively in *Chu Hoi Dick & Anor v Secretary for Home Affairs* (No 2) [2007] 4 HKC 428. There (at para 29) the court reformulated the 3 criteria laid down by Kirby J in *Oshlack v Richmond River Council* (1998) 193 CLR 72; 152 ALR 83 (HCA) in the following terms:

(a)   A litigant has properly brought proceedings to seek guidance from the court on a point of general public importance so that the litigation is for the benefit of the community as a whole to warrant the costs of the litigation be borne by the public purse as costs incidental to good public administration;

(b)   The judicial decision has contributed to the proper understanding of the law in question;

(c)   The litigant has no private gain in the outcome.

See also *Chan Noi Heung & Ors v Chief Executive in Council* CACV 197/2007 (Ma CJHC, Tang VP & Lam J; 16.03.2009) approving *Chu Hoi Dick* and *Oshlack* and making it clear costs will be awarded against a litigant who mounts alleged public interest litigation which is in fact unmeritorious.

### [62.3.11]   Protective costs orders in public interest litigation

The court has power to make pre-emptive costs orders to protect applicants who bring public interest cases. This jurisdiction traces back at least to *R v Lord Chancellor (ex p CPAG)* [1999] 1 WLR 347. In England such orders are known as 'protective costs orders' or 'PCO'. In Canada they are referred to as 'advance' costs orders and were recognised at the highest level in *British Columbia (Minister of Forests) v Okanagan Indian Band* [2003] 3 SCR 371 (SCC).

In *R (Corner House Research) v Secretary of State for Trade & Industry* [2005] 4 All ER 1 the English Court of Appeal reviewed developments in various common law jurisdictions and noted that the power to make such orders had been recognised in Ireland as well. The court set out the governing principles for grant of a PCO as follows (at para 74):

1.  A PCO may be made at any stage of the proceedings, on such conditions as the court thinks fit, provided that the court is satisfied that:
    (i)    the issues raised are of general public importance;
    (ii)   the public interest requires that those issues should be resolved;
    (iii)  the applicant has no private interest in the outcome of the case;
    (iv)   having regard to the financial resources of the applicant and the respondent(s) and to the amount of costs that are likely to be involved it is fair and just to make the order;
    (v)    if the order is not made the applicant will probably discontinue the proceedings and will be acting reasonably in doing so.
2.  If those acting for the applicant are doing so *pro bono* this will be likely to enhance the merits of the application for a PCO.
3.  It is for the court, in its discretion, to decide whether it is fair and just to make the order in the light of the considerations set out above.

In both Canada and England the courts have used cautionary language suggesting that protective costs orders should only be granted in exceptional cases. However it has been suggested that the exceptionality test may have been applied so as to set 'too high a threshold', thereby preventing the PCO jurisdiction from making a 'significant contribution to remedying the access to justice deficit it was intended to deal with': see *R (Compton) v Wiltshire Primary Care Trust* [2008] EWCA Civ 749 (01.07.2008), quoting from the Report on Access to Environmental Justice.

A protective costs order may provide that all costs be borne by the public purse, as in the *British Columbia (Minister of Forests)* case (above). Before seeking such an order the applicant should first explore other possible funding options: *Little Sisters Book & Art Emporium v Commissioner of Customs & Revenue* [2007] SCC 2. Alternatively a PCO may limit the extent of the parties' liability to costs in advance, as in *Compton* (above) and *R (Buglife Invertebrate Conservation Trust) v Thurrock Thames Gateway Development Corp* [2008] EWCA Civ 1209 (04.11.2008). In *Corner House* (above) the court limited the extent to which the applicant could recover costs and protected it against any adverse order as to costs.

For the procedure to be followed in applying for a protective costs order at first instance and on appeal, see the *Buglife* case (above) at para 29 *et seq*, summarising what was held in *Corner House* (above).

See also Order 1B rule 1(2)(l) and the commentary thereunder, which arguably could be relevant on an application for a protective costs order.

For discussion of protective costs orders generally, see Zuckerman, Editor's Note, (2009) 28 CJQ 161 and McColgan, 'Limiting the Costs of Litigation – Protective Costs Orders in the Court of Appeal' (2009) 28 CJQ 169.

**[62.3.12]   Costs of environmental litigation**
In England the court may have regard to the Aarhus Convention in exercising its discretion as to the costs of environmental litigation. Article 9(4) of the convention (formally the UNECE Convention on Access to Information, Public Participation in Decision-making and Access to Justice in Environmental Matters) provides that procedures for environmental challenges should not be 'prohibitively expensive'. That requirement 'should be taken as applying to the total potential liability of claimants, including the threat of adverse costs orders': *Morgan & Anor v Hinton Organics (Wessex) Ltd & Anor* [2009] EWCA Civ 107 (02.03.2009). The Aarhus convention does not apply in Hong Kong. However the Hong Kong courts have indicated a willingness to depart from the usual order as to costs in cases of *public interest* environmental litigation, as in *Society for the Protection of the Harbour Ltd v Town Planning Board* [2003] 4 HKC 463 (CFI); (2004) 7 HKCFAR 114 (CFA) (see above).

**[62.3.13]   Effect of the Legal Aid Ordinance on recovery of costs**
The Legal Aid Ordinance (Cap 91) does not fetter the court's power to make costs orders, but it restricts the enforcement of such orders against legally aided persons and the legal aid fund. In the words of Bokhary PJ, discussing the relevant provisions of the Ordinance in *Common Luck Investment Ltd v Director of Legal Aid* (2005) 5 HKCFAR 467:

> Section 19(1) empowers the courts to make orders for costs in favour of or against legally aided persons in the same manner and in the same extent as they may make orders for costs in favour of or against other persons. But it provides that such orders may only be enforced against legally aided persons and the Director to the extent permitted by section 16C.

Bokhary PJ went on to set out the types of proceedings in which a non-aided person may look to the Director to meet an order for costs against an aided person:

(1)   any claim to which he was a defendant (s 16C(1)(b)(i));
(2)   any petition to which he was a respondent (s 16C(1)(b)(i));
(3)   any appeal to which he was a respondent (s 16C(1)(b)(i));
(4)   any counterclaim to which he was a defendant to counterclaim(s 16C(1)(b)(ia));
(5)   any cross-petition to which he was the respondent (s 16C(1)(b)(ia))
(6)   any cross-appeal to which he was the respondent to cross-appeal (s 16C(1)(b)(ia)); and
(7)   an appeal and the proceedings below even where he was the appellant if the legally aided person had been the plaintiff below (s 16C(1)(b)(ib)).

In the court below it was suggested that the circumstances in which the Director is liable for costs ordered against aided persons should be broadened: see [2002] 1 HKC 1, 16I.

Reference should also be made to s 17(3) of the Legal Aid Ordinance which empowers the court to order an aided person to be personally responsible for the costs of aided proceedings brought or defended improperly. It is not the spirit of that provision to expose an aided person to costs as a result of inapt legal advice: *Tang Ka Hung Robert v Tang Tim Chue* HCAP 7/2006 (Chu J; 27.09.2007).

**[62.3.14]   Costs where plaintiff does not succeed against all defendants**

Where a plaintiff succeeds, but not against all defendants, it may be unjust to apply strictly the rule that costs shall follow the event. Strict application would require an order that the plaintiff be entitled to its costs against the unsuccessful defendant(s) only, and that it pay the costs of the others. However the plaintiff may be regarded as having been justified in suing all defendants, despite losing against some. In such cases the court may mitigate injustice to the plaintiff by making a '*Bullock*' or '*Sanderson*' order.

*Bullock order* – an order that the plaintiff pay the successful defendant's costs, and that the unsuccessful defendant reimburse the plaintiff for the same. See *Bullock v London General Omnibus Co* [1907] 1 KB 264 (CA).

*Sanderson order* – an order that the unsuccessful defendant pay the successful defendant's costs directly, in addition to the plaintiff's costs. See *Sanderson v Blyth Theatre Co* [1903] 2 KB 533 (CA).

*Where Bullock or Sanderson order appropriate* – a *Bullock* or *Sanderson* order will be made where it was reasonable for the plaintiff to join all defendants: *Leung Lai-ha v Hon Sau-ling* [1993] 1 HKLR 86 (CA). In that case the court made a *Sanderson* order where joinder of the drivers of both vehicles involved in a collision was reasonable because they blamed each other. See also *General Accident Insurance Asia Ltd v Hampton Winter & Glynn* [1998] 4 HKC 398, 419H-I and see *Yeung Kwok Wo v Hoi Hing Steel Fixing Works Co* HCPI 136/2004 (Deputy Judge Muttrie; 13.11.2006). Such an order is appropriate where the plaintiff is in a dilemma as to which defendant to sue, but not where the doubt is limited to a matter of law, nor where the causes of action are separate and distinct: *Chu Keung Fai v Success Insurance Ltd* HCA 4517/1981 (Deputy Judge Cruden; 13.03.1987) (paras 15 & 22). A *Bullock* or *Sanderson* order may also be appropriate in accident cases where both the owner and the driver of a vehicle are sued, but judgment is given against only the driver, if there were reasonable grounds to believe that the driver was driving as servant or agent of the owner: *Cheng Wai Chuen & Anor v Tsang Kwai Yan & Anor* HCPI 1409/2003 (Sakhrani J; 02.12.2005). In Australia it has been authoritatively held that the plaintiff must go further than showing just that it was reasonable to join more than one defendant. In *Gould v Vaggelas* [1985] HCA 85, 157 CLR 215, 229-230 the High Court of Australia held that 'the mere fact that the joinder of two defendants was reasonable does not mean that the unsuccessful defendant should be ordered to pay, directly or indirectly, the costs of the successful defendant ... if nothing that the unsuccessful defendant has said or done has led the plaintiff to sue the other defendant, who ultimately was held not to be liable, it is difficult to see any reason why the unsuccessful defendant should be required to pay for the plaintiff's error or overcaution'. The High Court approved the statement in *Steppke v National Capital Dev't Commission* (1978) 21 ACTR 23, 30 that there is a condition for the making of such an order 'namely that the conduct of the unsuccessful defendant has been such as to make it fair to impose some liability on it for the costs of the successful defendant'. Thus more recently in *Dominello v Dominello & Anor* [2009] NSWCA 257 (29.08.2009) (paras 19-20) it was held that there 'must be something more than a denial of liability which would be present in every case brought against two or more defendants ... [t]hat something more will typically involve a positive assertion, express or implied, that the relevant defendant is not liable because the other is'.

*Choosing between Bullock and Sanderson order* - In choosing between a *Bullock* or a *Sanderson* order, the court has a discretion, and in cases where one party may be in financial difficulty a 'dominant consideration' is the 'balance of hardship': *China Everbright Finance Ltd v Chan Yung & Anor* HCA 18300/1999 (Deputy Judge Muttrie; 12.12.2006). In that case the court made a *Bullock* order to 'guarantee' that a successful defendant get its costs from the plaintiff, taking into account the fact the other defendant appeared to be in financial difficulty and would probably be unable to pay costs.

**[62.3.15]   Costs of interlocutory proceedings 'may' follow the event**
The general rule in Order 62 rule 3(2) that costs shall follow the event previously applied equally to interlocutory and final judgments and orders. It was amended as part of the civil justice reforms taking effect in 2009 so as to express the general rule, so far as interlocutory proceedings are concerned, in permissive rather than mandatory language. The general rule that costs 'shall' follow the event in rule 3(2) is now restricted to proceedings other than interlocutory proceedings, and rule 3(2A) provides that in the case of interlocutory proceedings the court 'may' order that costs follow the event. The new provision applies not just to interlocutory applications, but to 'costs of or incidental to any interlocutory proceedings'. The intention is that it apply to all manner of steps taken at the interlocutory stage: see below.

For the purpose of an interlocutory application the 'event' to be followed is success or failure on that application, regardless of the final outcome of the litigation: *Like Soon Co Ltd v Tsai Kui Kan & Ors* [1986] HKC 142, 144A-B (CA).

**[62.3.16]   Adverse costs orders to penalise unreasonable interlocutory conduct**
As a result of the amendments to rule 3 in effect from 2009 (referred to above) as read together with rule 5(1)(e) (which requires the court to take into account the conduct of the parties when exercising its discretion as to costs), it is clear that the court will be ready to penalise a party for unreasonable interlocutory conduct, regardless of success on the interlocutory application or at trial. The power to penalise such conduct should be seen as additional to the pre-existing power of the court under Order 62 rule 7 to make adverse costs orders in cases of misconduct or neglect.

These amendments implemented recommendation 122 in the final report of the Chief Justice's working party on civil justice reform. That recommendation was as follows:

> The principle that the costs should normally 'follow the event' should continue to apply to the costs of the action as a whole. However, in relation to interlocutory applications, that principle should be an option (which would often in practice be adopted) but should not be the prescribed 'usual order'. Costs orders aimed at deterring unreasonable interlocutory conduct after commencement of the proceedings should be given at least equal prominence in practice, with the court being directed to have regard to the underlying objectives [in Order 1A] . . .

The working party was of the view that costs orders should be used 'as a primary means of discouraging unreasonable procedural conduct at the interlocutory stage, whichever party ultimately wins the case'. It envisaged the court making 'stringent' costs orders 'in relation to inappropriately verified pleadings, over-elaborate witness statements and expert reports, unnecessary interlocutory applications or appeals, seeking relief from self-executing sanctions, unnecessarily insisting on oral hearings to challenge decisions taken on the papers and so forth' (final report, para 699).

The working party recommended that the power to penalise unreasonable interlocutory conduct not be applied to pre-action conduct, in order to avoid front-loaded costs (final report, para 701). However it left open the possibility that pre-action protocols could provide for pre-action conduct to be penalised.

See also Order 62 rule 5(1)(aa) and rule 7(2)(aa), which require the court to have regard to the underlying objectives when exercising its discretion as to costs.

## [62.3.17]  Other types of costs orders on interlocutory applications

It has long been the case that the court may, instead of making an order for the costs of an interlocutory application to follow the result of that application, make an order linking the costs of the application to the ultimate result of the litigation, or to defer decision on such costs until that ultimate result is known. Some of such orders were described succinctly in the judgment of Lord Denning MR in *JT Stratford & Son Ltd v Lindley (No 2)* [1969] 1 WLR 1547, 1552-1553. He said:

*Costs in the cause* 'means that the costs of those interlocutory proceedings are to be awarded according to the final award of costs in the action. If the plaintiff wins and gets an order for his costs, he gets those interlocutory costs as part of his costs'.

*Plaintiff's costs in the cause* 'means that if the plaintiff wins he gets the costs of the interlocutory proceedings: but, if he loses, he does not have to pay the other side's costs of them.'

*Plaintiff's (or defendant's) costs in any event* 'means that, no matter who wins or loses, when the case is decided, or settled, the plaintiff is to have the costs of those interlocutory proceedings'.

*Plaintiff's (or defendant's) costs* 'means that if the plaintiff is to have the cost of the interlocutory proceedings without waiting for a decision', in other words the plaintiff's costs may be taxed and payment claimed forthwith. For further discussion of 'forthwith' costs orders see the commentary under Order 62 rules 4 and 9A.

Not mentioned in Lord Denning's judgment are the following types of order sometimes made at the interlocutory stage:

*Costs reserved*, meaning that the question of costs is postponed for consideration at a later stage. It is then up to the parties to ask for an order on the reserved costs if they wish. That is usually done at the conclusion of the suit. In the absence of a subsequent order specifically dealing with reserved costs, those costs 'forming no part of the costs of the action are left where they lie': *PBM (HK) Ltd v Tang Kam Lun Allan* HCA 12138/1997 (Master de Souza; 28.08.2006). Note that 'costs reserved' had a different meaning in England where it was defined in the previous RSC O 62 r 3(6) so as to mean that the costs in question would be to the party in whose favour costs are ordered at the conclusion of the proceedings, unless otherwise ordered.

*Costs of and occasioned by* ... is the form of order often made where the court grants a party an indulgence, such as leave to amend, or an adjournment. In *ASM Assembly Automation Ltd v Chan Lo Kwan* HCA 7622/1999 (Master Kwan; 29.04.2006) the court framed the following test as to which costs come within such an order:

Would this item of costs have been incurred by the receiving party irrespective of whether there was an adjournment? If the answer is 'yes', then the paying party should not be liable for that item of costs. But if the answer is 'no', then the paying party should be liable for it.

*Costs thrown away* is a term which was defined in the previous English RSC O 62 r 3(6) as the costs of proceedings which are 'ineffective or subsequently set aside'. The English definition was adopted in *Shoei Co Ltd v LeRoy Orient Co Ltd & Ors* HCCL 30/1997 (Master Jones; 11.05.1997) although not included in the Hong Kong rules. Costs thrown away include the defendant's costs of an application to set aside an irregular default judgment, and should be paid by the plaintiff to the defendant: *Hughes v Justin* [1894] 1 QB 667, 669 (CA); *Bolt & Nut Co (Tipton) Ltd v Rowlands Nicholls & Co Ltd* [1964] 2 QB 10.

'*Costs*' and '*Costs in any event*' were defined in the previous English RSC O 62 r 3(6) to mean that the party in whose favour the order was made would be entitled to costs of the particular proceeding whatever the outcome of the cause or matter in which it arose. Orders for 'costs in any event' are also made in Hong Kong, the 'event' referring to 'the final outcome of the litigation': *Like Soon Co Ltd v Tsai Kui Kan & Ors* [1986] HKC 1452, 144A-B (CA). Costs under an order referring to the event cannot normally be taxed until the conclusion of the proceedings – see the commentary under Order 62 rule 4.

### [62.3.18]    Summary assessment of costs of interlocutory applications

The quantum of costs of an interlocutory application may, instead of being referred to taxation, be summarily assessed by the court. See Order 62 rule 9A and the commentary thereunder.

### [62.3.19]    Costs of counterclaim

When giving judgment in an action where there is a counterclaim the court should consider the costs of the plaintiff's claim and the defendant's counterclaim separately. The usual rule that costs follow the event will apply to the main claim and the counterclaim as if they were independent actions and two separate orders as to costs will normally be made. See *Union Base Ltd v Tsang Shek Tong* [1998] 2 HKC 349, 351I. In that case the plaintiff succeeded on the main claim and the defendant succeeded on the counterclaim. The trial judge directed a set-off of the two amounts due and gave judgment for the plaintiff for the net balance, ordering costs in favour of the defendant. The Court of Appeal held that the costs order was inappropriate and granted costs of the main claim to the plaintiff, and 3/4 of the costs of the counterclaim to the defendant. See also *Great Quality Corp Ltd v Emery Airfreight Corp* HCCL 67/1997 (Stone J; 24.12.2008) where it was held that 'no order as to costs' on dismissal of both claim and counterclaim for want of prosecution was inappropriate, and that costs of dismissal of each should follow the event.

With regard to separate judgments on claim and counterclaim, see Order 15 rule 2 and the commentary thereunder.

### [62.3.20]    Costs consequences of discontinuation of counterclaim or withdrawal of claim therein – rule 3(7)

Order 62 rule 3(7) provides that where a counterclaim is discontinued, or any claim in it is withdrawn, the opposing party will normally be entitled to costs up to that moment. It thus applies to counterclaims the same regime as applies in respect of discontinuation or withdrawal of the plaintiff's claims under rule 10(1) of this Order.

**[62.3.21]  Costs of counterclaim on acceptance of sanctioned payment**
Order 62 rule 3(8) previously provided for the costs of a counterclaim where a payment into court expressly taking into account the counterclaim was accepted. The provision was repealed with effect from 2009 when Order 22 was completely revised, introducing the new sanctioned payment procedure. Now see Order 22 rule 20(3).

**[62.3.22]  Costs of a non-existent party**
A solicitor who issues proceedings warrants that his client exists and may be liable in costs if that is not the case. See the commentary under Order 15 rule 4 and under Order 62 rule 8.

In the reverse situation where it is the defendant which does not exist in law, and an action is dismissed on that basis, the person who has defended on behalf of the 'defendant' may be entitled to costs. See *Fu Lok Man James v Chief Bailiff of the High Court (No 1)* [2003] 2 HKC 672 (CA), citing the definition of 'defendant' in section 2 of the High Court Ordinance (Cap 4) which includes any person served.

**[62.3.23]  Costs of creditor proving claim under O 44 or 102 – rule 3(9)–(11)**
Order 62 rule 3(9)-(11) provides that a creditor who succeeds in proving a debt claim in the somewhat unusual circumstances governed by Order 44 and Order 102 rule 13, the creditor shall normally be entitled to costs. Order 44 rules 4 to 8 concern administration of estates and trusts, under direction of the court, and make provision for creditors to prove their claims against such estates and trusts. Order 102 rules 7 to 13 provide for creditors of companies to prove their claims in cases where the company seeks a reduction of share capital or similar order.

**[62.3.24]  Costs of non-party disclosure, etc order – rule 3(12)**
Order 62 rule 3(12) provides that an order for disclosure before action, or against a non-party, under sections 41 and 42 of the High Court Ordinance (as to which see the commentary under Order 24 rule 7A), should normally award costs of the application and of compliance to the person against whom the order is made. The provision also extends to orders under Order 29 rule 7A in exercise of the court's power under section 44 HCO to order inspection, taking of samples, *etc*, before action.

**[62.3.25]  Interest on costs**
An order for payment of costs is considered to be a judgment debt on which interest will be payable pursuant to section 49 of the High Court Ordinance. See the commentary under Order 42 rule 1 as to determination of the rate of interest on a judgment debt. Interest on costs may be disallowed, or the period or rate may be reduced by a taxing master where there has been 'undue delay' in taxation of costs: see Order 62 rule 22(5)(c).

Although the issue is not free from controversy, the prevailing view is that interest runs from the date of the order for costs even though the costs are not quantified until a later date such as when agreed or taxed. See *Caltex Oil Hong Kong v The Director of Buildings and Lands* [1994] HKDCLR 31 applying the House of Lords' decision in *Hunt v R M Douglas (Roofing) Ltd* [1990] AC 398. There Lord Ackner had explained (at 415) that the balance of justice was in favour of costs running from the moment of the order (the '*incipitur* rule') rather than from the later date of taxation (the '*allocatur* rule'). He gave the following reasons:

1.  It is the unsuccessful party to the litigation who, *ex hypothesi*, has caused the costs unnecessarily to be incurred. Hence the order made against him. Since interest is not awarded on costs incurred and paid by the successful party before judgment, why should he suffer the added loss of interest on costs incurred and paid after judgment but before the taxing master gives his certificate?

2.  Since ... payments of costs are likely nowadays to be made to lawyers prior to taxation, then the application of the *allocatur* rule would generally speaking do greater injustice than the operation of the *incipitur* rule. Moreover, the *incipitur* rule provides a further necessary stimulus for payments to be made on account of costs and disbursements prior to taxation, for costs to be made readily agreed, and for taxation, when necessary, to be expedited, all of which are desirable developments. Barristers, solicitors and expert witnesses should not be expected to finance their clients' litigation until it is completed and the taxing master's certificate obtained. If interest is not payable on costs between judgment and the completion of taxation, then there is an incentive to delay payment, delay disbursements and taxation ...

Whilst the above policy reasons clearly militate in favour of the '*incipitur* rule', the House of Lords decision gives rise to an anomaly in that interest runs at a time when the principal amount has yet to be ascertained. In *Thomas v Bunn* [1991] AC 362, 380 Lord Ackner recognised that his earlier judgment created this anomaly.

In Hong Kong it has been held that there is no debt in respect of costs until they have been quantified. See *Re Golden Always Ltd & Anor* [1996] 3 HKC 252 where Le Pichon J held that there is no obligation to pay until an allocatur has been presented to the paying party. An appeal to the Court of Appeal was allowed to the extent it was held that the obligation to pay arises once the quantum has been certified, whether or not the allocatur is served. But it was not doubted that there is no obligation to pay prior to the amount of costs being certified: see *Australian Telephone Distributors Pty Ltd (in liq) v Golden Always Ltd & Anor* [1996] 2 HKLR 325. It is thus difficult to see how *Hunt* can continue to be followed in Hong Kong. For if there is no debt prior to quantification then clearly there can be no judgment debt within section 49. In *Wong Wai Chun v Lewin* [2000] 2 HKC 271, this line of argument was rejected. Master Poon distinguished the *Golden Always* case on the basis it did not concern interest, and followed *Caltex Oil*. However, this may not be the end of the matter. In *Caltex Oil*, the Presiding Officer in the Lands Tribunal considered *Hunt* to be binding in Hong Kong. After the resumption of Chinese sovereignty, that should no longer be the case.

In England under the former Order 22 payment into court procedure it was held that interest did not run on costs payable by reason of acceptance of such a payment: *Legal Aid Board v Russell* [1990] 2 QB 607 (CA); [1991] 2 AC 317 (HL). This was because the entitlement to costs arose under the rules of court as they then were, and not under a judgment. This should not be the case in Hong Kong as a result of Order 62 rule 10(5), which expressly provides that for the purposes of section 49 of the High Court Ordinance (interest on judgments) an order for costs is deemed to have been made when the event giving rise to the entitlement to costs occurred. The rule expressly applies to costs payable under the sanctioned payment and sanctioned offer procedures in Order 22 as amended with effect from April 2009. Note also the provisions of Order 22 rules 23 and 24 with regard to enhanced interest on costs where a sanctioned payment or sanctioned offer is not accepted, and the offeree fails to do better at trial.

**4. Stage of proceedings at which costs to be dealt with** (O. 62 r. 4)

**(1) Costs may be dealt with by the Court at any stage of the proceedings or after the conclusion of the proceedings; and any order of the Court for the payment of any costs may, if the Court thinks fit, and the person against whom the order is made is not an assisted person, require the costs to be paid forthwith notwithstanding that the proceedings have not been concluded.**

**(2) In the case of an appeal the costs of the proceedings giving rise to the appeal, as well as the costs of the appeal and of the proceedings connected with it, may be dealt with by the Court hearing the appeal; and in the case of any proceedings transferred or removed to the Court of First Instance from any other court or tribunal, the costs of the whole proceedings, both before and after the transfer or removal, may (subject to any order of the court or tribunal ordering the transfer or removal) be dealt with by the Court to which the proceedings are transferred or removed. (L.N. 152 of 2008)**

**(3) Where under paragraph (2) the Court makes an order as to the costs of any proceedings before another court or tribunal, rules 28, 31 and 32 shall not apply in relation to those costs, but, except in relation to costs of proceedings transferred or removed from the District Court or the Lands Tribunal, the order—**

    **(a) shall specify the amount of the costs to be allowed, or**

    **(b) shall direct that the costs shall be assessed by the court or tribunal before which the proceedings took place or taxed by an officer of that court or tribunal, or**

    **(c) if the order is made on appeal from the District Court or the Lands Tribunal in relation to proceedings in that court or tribunal, may direct that the costs shall be taxed by the taxing master.**

**(L.N. 152 of 2008)**

---

**NOTES**

**[62.4.1] Time at which order as to costs may be made**

Under this rule an order for costs may be made at any stage of the proceedings. This enables the court to make costs orders concerning interlocutory applications. See the commentary under Order 62 rule 3.

However, an order as to the costs of an action as a whole will not be made without the final disposition of the action: see *Ta Tung China & Arts Ltd v Fontana Restaurant Ltd & Ors* [1999] 1 HKC 404 (CA). In that case one of three defendants admitted liability and the action was thereby effectively compromised. Some years later the issue of the costs relating to the other defendants arose. The Court of Appeal held that the question of those costs could not be resolved unless the action was brought to a conclusion. That could be done by the plaintiff discontinuing the action or by proceeding to what would be an extremely limited trial. See the judgment of Mortimer VP at 407B–F.

**[62.4.2] Appeals as to costs**
See the commentary under Order 58 rule 1 (appeals from masters) and Order 59 rule 1 (appeals to the Court of Appeal).

**[62.4.3] Costs of appeal**
The general rule that costs follow the event (see rule 3) applies on appeal, with the result that the Court of Appeal will normally allow a successful appellant the costs of the appeal as well as the costs below. Where, however, an appeal succeeds on a ground which was not argued below, the Court of Appeal may depart from the usual rule. In *Glynn v Commissioner of Inland Revenue* CACV 51/1998 (Cons VP, Clough and Hunter JJA; 16.02.1989), the Court of Appeal was asked to follow *The Mersey Railway Co* (1888) 17 Ch 610 and refuse costs to the appellant who had succeeded on the basis of authority which had not been cited in the court below. The Court of Appeal was unwilling to go that far, but did order that the appellant have only three-quarters of its costs of the appeal, with no costs to be awarded in respect of the proceedings below.

5.  **Special matters to be taken into account in exercising discretion** (O. 62 r. 5)
    **(1)  The Court in exercising its discretion as to costs shall, to such extent, if any, as may be appropriate in the circumstances, take into account — (L.N. 152 of 2008)**
    > **(aa)  the underlying objectives set out in Order 1A, rule 1; (L.N. 152 of 2008)**
    > **(a)  any such offer of contribution as is mentioned in Order 16, rule 10, which is brought to its attention in pursuance of a reserved right to do so;**
    > **(b)  any payment of money into court and the amount of such payment;**
    > **(c)  any written offer made under Order 33, rule 4A(2);**
    > **(d)  any written offer which is expressed to be "without prejudice save as to costs" and which relates to any issue in the proceedings, but the Court may not take the offer into account if, at the time it is made, the party making it could have protected his position as to costs by means of a sanctioned payment or a sanctioned offer under Order 22; (L.N. 152 of 2008)**
    > **(e)  the conduct of all the parties; (L.N. 152 of 2008)**
    > **(f)  whether a party has succeeded on part of his case, even if he has not been wholly successful; and (L.N. 152 of 2008)**
    > **(g)  any admissible offer to settle made by a party, which is drawn to the Court's attention. (L.N. 152 of 2008)**
    **(2)  For the purpose of paragraph (1)(e), the conduct of the parties includes —**
    > **(a)  whether it was reasonable for a party to raise, pursue or contest a particular allegation or issue;**
    > **(b)  the manner in which a party has pursued or defended his case or a particular allegation or issue;**

**(c)** **whether a claimant who has succeeded in his claim, in whole or in part, exaggerated his claim; and**

**(d)** **conduct before, as well as during, the proceedings.**

**(L.N. 152 of 2008)**

## NOTES

### [62.5.1]   Origin and scope of Order 62 rule 5
Order 62 rule 5 stipulates particular matters which 'shall' be taken into account by the court, as appropriate in the circumstances, in exercising its discretion as to costs. The rule was substantially amended with effect from 2 April 2009, as part of the civil justice reforms. In *Chan Lai Ying & Ors v Lee Lim & Anor* HCA 1413/2005 (Deputy Judge Au; 25.06.2009) (para 38) it was doubted that the amendments apply to costs incurred prior that date. The matters to be taken into account are considered one by one below.

### [62.5.2]   Rule 5(1)(aa) – underlying objectives to be taken into account
Order 62 rule 5(1)(aa) provides that the 'underlying objectives' of these rules as set out in Order 1A should be taken into account by the court in exercising its discretionary powers as to costs. This provision is strictly speaking unnecessary, because Order 1A rule 2 already provides that the court 'shall seek to give effect to the underlying objectives' when exercising any of its powers. However the inclusion of this specific provision in Order 62 rule 5 serves to emphasise that the court's powers in relation to costs are a key tool in controlling the civil litigation process.

See also Order 62 rule 7(2)(aa) which similarly directs the court to have regard to the underlying objectives when considering whether a party should be penalised in costs for misconduct or neglect in legal proceedings.

### [62.5.3]   Rule 5(1)(a) – offer of contribution to be taken into account
Order 16 rule 10 provides that where a party may be found liable to contribute to a debt or damages which may be recovered against another party to the action, a without prejudice offer in writing as to the extent of contribution may be made. Order 62 rule 5(1)(a) provides that such an offer shall be taken into account by the court in exercising its discretion as to costs.

### [62.5.4]   Rule 5(1)(b) – Payment of money into court to be taken into account
Order 62 rule 5(1)(b) provides that in exercising its discretion as to costs, the court shall take into account any payment of money into court and the amount thereof. The provision does not appear to affect payments into court of money by way of sanctioned payment under Order 22 or Order 62A, since the costs consequences of such payments are set out in those Orders themselves. Rather the provision appears to apply to payment into court pursuant to the court's case management power in Order 1B rule 1(3) and (4) to require such a payment as a condition of an order, and payments into court by a party in procedural default ordered by the court pursuant to Order 2 rule 3. Such payments are security for any sum payable by that party in the proceedings. Thus, in taking them into account the court may direct payment out. It is unlikely that such payments will, in themselves affect the incidence or quantum of costs.

**[62.5.5]   Rule 5(1)(c) – offer to accept proportion of liability to be taken into account**

Order 62 rule 5(1)(c) directs the court to take into account written offers under Order 33 rule 4A(2) when exercising its discretion as to costs. That provision enables a party to make a written without prejudice offer to accept a proportion of liability where the court has ordered a split trial. Although the rule does not expressly say so, it is clear that where such an offer is not bettered at the trial on liability, the party who failed to accept it may be responsible for the offeror's costs thereof. Such an offer is similar to a *Calderbank* offer, as to which see below.

**[62.5.6]   Rule 5(1)(d) – 'Calderbank' offers**

Order 62 rule 5(1)(d) mandates the court to take into account written offers 'without prejudice save as to costs' when exercising its discretion as to costs. Such offers are commonly known as '*Calderbank*' offers after the case of *Calderbank v Calderbank* [1975] 3 All ER 333 in which the English Court of Appeal recognised that a party who fails to accept such an offer, and eventually does no better, may face an adverse costs order. See also *Cutts v Head* [1984] Ch 290. Such offers were later given a legislative basis in the former Order 22 rule 14, which was repealed with effect from 2009 as part of the civil justice reforms, when the sanctioned offer and sanctioned payment procedures under the new Order 22 were introduced. Despite the repeal of that rule, the right of parties to make settlement proposals in any manner they choose is expressly preserved by Order 22 rule 2(4). See also the commentary under that rule as to the continued recognition of *Calderbank* offers.

Rule 5(1)(d) expressly provides that a *Calderbank* offer should not be taken into account where the party could, instead of making such an offer, have protected its position by sanctioned payment or sanctioned offer under Order 22. The sanctioned payment and sanctioned offer procedures are available in most circumstances. As a result *Calderbank* offers will only continue to be relevant to the exercise of the court's discretion as to costs in relatively limited circumstances. One of those circumstances will be in relation to taxation of costs. Although there is specific provision under Order 62A for sanctioned offers and sanctioned payments in relation to taxation of costs, there is no prohibition on the court taking into account a *Calderbank* offer where those procedures could have been used. Order 62A rule 2(3) expressly preserves the right of a party to make a costs offer otherwise than by way of sanctioned offer or sanctioned payment. Furthermore, Order 62A does not apply where either party is or has been legally aided: O 62A, r1(2), so the *Calderbank* offer will remain the primary tool for making offers in respect of liability to pay costs in such proceedings.

The court may also be entitled to take into account a *Calderbank* offer, despite the availability of the sanctioned payment procedure, where the offeror faces insurmountable difficulty in quantifying the amount to be paid: *Limbu Netra Kumar v Yau Lee Construction Co Ltd & Anor* HCPI 234/2002 (Suffiad J; 21.09.2007) (para 8).

Where a *Calderbank* offer has been made, and may be taken into account by the court, the following points are relevant:

*What constitutes a Calderbank offer? –* A *Calderbank* offer may be made 'by a simple statement that the correspondence or negotiations are without prejudice save as to costs or an express reservation … that the contents of any offer may be brought to the attention of the court on the question of costs': *National Commercial Bank Ltd v Kanashi (FE) Ltd & Anor* [2005] 2 HKC 81, 86E-F, per Ma J (as he then was). In that case an offer made 'entirely without prejudice to our client's rights herein' was held not to be a *Calderbank* offer, the court emphasising the use of the word 'entirely'.

*Calderbank offer must be clear* – A *Calderbank* offer must be sufficiently clear that the offeree knows what is being offered: *C&H Eng'g v F Klucznic & Sons Ltd* [1992] FSR 667, 671. In *Luk Kwan Hung Nelson v Victory Mark Investment Ltd* [2004] 2 HKC 305 (para 10) a proposal which was uncertain to the extent that its acceptance without further query or negotiation would not have resulted in a binding agreement, was held not to have the effect of a *Calderbank* offer.

*Interest and costs* – It is not necessary for a *Calderbank* offer on the principal sum claimed as debt or damages to include matters such as interest, or incidence and quantum of costs and disbursements, since it is always open to a party to make an offer in whole or in part: *Wong Wai Chun & Anor v Lewin* [2000] 2 HKC 271, 275D–F. However, the offer must be clear as to exactly what it covers – see above.

*Costs consequences of Calderbank offer* – A *Calderbank* offer 'should influence but not govern' the exercise of the court's discretion as to costs: *Luk Kwan Hung Nelson* (above) (para 14). The question to be asked is whether the recipient of the offer 'ought reasonably to have accepted [it]': *Butcher v Wolfe* [1999] 1 FLR 334, 340 (quoted with approval in *Luk Kwan Hung Nelson*, above). If so, the recipient may be deprived of costs incurred thereafter, or ordered to pay the subsequent costs of the offeror.

*Time for Calderbank offer to remain open* – The court may refuse to take into account a *Calderbank* offer which does not remain open for acceptance long enough for the offeree to consider it: *Wong Yik Po & Ors v Director of Lands* [1996] 1 HKC 586.

*Calderbank offer before commencement of proceedings* – In *Oriental Press Group Ltd & Anor v Apple Daily Ltd (No 2)* [1997] 3 HKC 615, 620F-I it was held that a *Calderbank* offer made before issue of the writ should not be taken into account as to the costs of the proceedings because 'its effect was spent when the plaintiffs rejected it and commenced proceedings'. It was said the defendant should have admitted liability and renewed its offer after issue of the writ. However the case may be seen as turning on its own facts rather than laying down a general principle.

*Court should not be informed* – The fact that a *Calderbank* offer has been made may not be brought to the attention of the court until the question of costs comes to be determined. This follows from the fact that the offer comes within the without prejudice rule, meaning it may not be disclosed without the consent of all relevant parties. But such an offer is without prejudice *save as to costs*, meaning that consent is not required to bring it to the attention of the court on the question of costs, once such question arises.

**[62.5.7]   Rule 5(1)(e) – conduct of the parties to be taken into account**
Order 62 rule 5(1)(e) requires the court to take into account the conduct of all the parties when exercising its discretion as to costs. Rule 5(2) gives guidance as to what the 'conduct of the parties' includes. The two provisions are substantially similar to England's CPR 44.3(4)(a) and (5). Factors such as whether it was reasonable for a

party to argue a particular issue, and whether a successful party exaggerated its claim, are listed in both the Hong Kong and English provisions. These are factors which the court has long taken into account in considering how to exercise its discretion as to costs. See the commentary concerning the court's powers under Order 62 rule 9(4) (a) to limit recovery of costs by proportion or by issue. See also Order 62 rule 7 as to costs arising from misconduct and neglect. The significance of the inclusion of 'conduct of the parties' in rule 5 (with effect from April 2009) is that the court is now expressly mandated to consider the same when exercising its discretion as to costs.

Rule 5(2) also expressly extends the rule to pre-action conduct. In order for pre-action conduct to be reflected in a costs order it is not necessary to show that it caused the bringing of an unsuccessful claim, or of some increased expenditure in the course of a claim, though those factors are plainly relevant: *Bank of Tokyo-Mitsubishi UFJ Ltd & Anor v Baskan Gida Sanayi Ve Pazarlama AS & Ors* [2009] EWHC 1696 (Ch) (14.07.2009) (paras 20-24).

As to the appropriate time to raise questions of conduct, see the next paragraph of commentary.

The following extracts from the commentary in our sister publication in the UK, The Civil Court Practice, on the equivalent CPR provisions, will be instructive in Hong Kong as to how the court may, in exercising its discretion as to costs, reflect the conduct of the parties. The Civil Court Practice says, at para CPR 44[3]:

> **Conduct of parties** Direction for the court as to the nature of the conduct to be taken into account is given in CPR 44.3(5) [Order 62 rule 5(2) in Hong Kong]. In particular the court may take into account conduct before and during the proceedings and whether the parties have followed a pre-action Protocol [the CPR provision with regard to taking into account pre-action protocols is omitted in Hong Kong]. The conduct must, however be related to the proceedings: *Hall v Rover Financial Services Ltd (GB)* [2002] EWCA Civ 1514 and *Groupama Insurance Co Ltd v Overseas Partners Re Ltd & Aon Ltd* [2003] EWCA Civ 1846, [2004] 1 All ER (Comm) 893.
>
> For examples of conduct that may be taken into account, see *Oksuzoglu v Kay* [1998] 2 All ER 361 (CA) where the defendant could have, but did not, make admissions which would have reduced the length and cost of the trial and *Butcher v Wolfe* [1999] 2 FCR 165, [1999] 1 FLR 334 (CA), where the claimant was ordered to pay all of the costs of the action for unreasonably refusing to negotiate. For decisions under the CPR see for example *Re Burfoot & Anor (bankrupts)* [2000] TLR 634 (17.08.2000) and *Adam Phones Ltd v Goldschmidt & Ors* [1999] 4 All ER 486 and *Painting v University of Oxford* [2005] EWCA Civ 161 (03.02.2005), [2005] TLR 86 (15.02.2005) in which the court imposed a cost penalty against the successful applicant for the disproportionate nature of the application and *Liverpool City Council v Rosemary Chavasse Ltd and Walton Group plc* [1999] 36 LS Gaz R 29 (CA) where the successful claimant only recovered 50% of costs because of a failure to negotiate or deal with matters expeditiously. Such conduct may be a breach of the obligation of the parties to help the court to achieve the overriding objective (CPR 1.3) [in Hong Kong see Order 1A rule 3 which lays down the duty of the parties and their legal representatives to assist the court to further the underlying objectives]. As to conduct during the proceedings that the court may take into account see *King v Telegraph Group Ltd* [2004] EWCA Civ 613, [2004] NLJR 823 . . .

The Civil Court Practice continues at para CPR 44.3[6]:

> **"conduct"** An overriding dynamic of the CPR is the use by the court of the costs provisions as a management tool to achieve the overriding objective [in Hong Kong 'underlying objectives' – see Order 1A], eg to penalise, through the award of costs orders, conduct of a party which is considered by the court to interfere for instance with the expeditious disposal of the claim or the identification of issues at an early stage. The court has always

been able to take into account a party's conduct when considering costs and has done so. Thus under the pre-CPR regime, in *Butcher v Wolfe* [1999] 2 FCR 165, [1999] 1 FLR 334 (CA) the court took into account attempts to settle the claim before the action commenced to decide that the successful party, the claimant [plaintiff], should pay both parties' costs. It is suggested that the courts will follow pre-CPR examples where conduct has been taken into account in the award of costs, for example late amendment of a statement of case [statement of claim in Hong Kong], with success in the claim only arising from the amendment (*Beoco Ltd v Alfa Laval Co Ltd & Anor* [1995] QB 137, [1994] 4 All ER 464 (CA)), but the emphasis on conduct in this rule is to ensure the court has that factor prominent in its mind at all times when considering the award of costs for or against a party …

In *Technicom Interiors Design Eng'g Ltd v Tse Yuet Yi & Anor* DCCJ 5965/2008 (Deputy Judge R Yu; 02.11.2010) (para 154-9) the court ordered indemnity costs against a party in respect of a document (a Scott table) which it considered to be of no use. In doing so the court referred to Order 62 rule 5(1)(e), the purpose of which was said to be to give greater flexibility to award indemnity costs to reflect conduct.

### [62.5.8]   Adverse costs consequences of refusal to mediate or negotiate

It has been held in both England and Hong Kong that an unreasonable refusal to try to resolve a dispute through mediation may result in an adverse costs order. See *Halsey v Milton Keynes General NHS Trust* [2004] EWCA Civ 576 (11.05.2004) (quoted at length in the commentary under Order 1A rule 4(2)(e) concerning the court's duty to encourage use of ADR), and see *Supply Chain & Logistics Technology Ltd v NEC Hong Kong Ltd* HCA 1939/2006 (Lam J; 29.01.2009). The possibility of such an order now finds expression in para 4 of the mediation practice direction (PD 31), which came into force at the beginning of 2010. It is there provided that unreasonable failure of a party to engage in mediation where this can be established by admissible materials is one of the relevant circumstances to be taken into account by the court in exercising its discretion on costs. PD 31 goes on to provide in para 5:

> The Court will not make any adverse costs order against a party on the ground of unreasonable failure to engage in mediation where:
>
> (1)   The party has engaged in mediation to the minimum level of participation agreed to by the parties or as directed by the Court prior to the mediation in accordance with paragraph 13 of this PD.
> (2)   A party has a reasonable explanation for not engaging in mediation. The fact that active without prejudice settlement negotiations between the parties are progressing is likely to provide such a reasonable explanation. However, where such negotiations have broken down, the basis for such explanation will have gone and the parties should then consider the appropriateness of mediation. The fact that the parties are actively engaged in some other form of ADR to settle the dispute may also provide a reasonable explanation for not engaging in mediation in the meantime.

In *Golden Eagle Int'l (Group) Ltd v GR Investment Holdings Ltd* [2010] 5 HKC 317 it was held that in Hong Kong the burden is on the refusing party to provide a reasonable explanation for not agreeing to mediate, rather than on the willing party to show that mediation had a reasonable prospect of success. In this respect the Hong Kong court departed from *Halsey*. In *Incorporated Owners of Shatin New Town v Yeung Kui* CACV 45/2009 (Cheung JA, Stone & Lunn JJ; 05.02.2010) (para 8) the court refused to make an adverse costs order for refusal to mediate, taking into account the fact the case involved a point of law on interpretation of a DMC which affected many co-owners.

As mentioned in the above passage from The Civil Court Practice, a refusal to negotiate with a view to settlement resulted in a successful plaintiff recovering only 50% of its costs in *Liverpool City Council v Rosemary Chavasse Ltd and Walton Group plc* [1999] 36 LS Gaz R 29 (CA). See also *Painting v University of Oxford* [2005] EWCA Civ 161 where a successful plaintiff who failed or refused to negotiate with the defendant was allowed costs only up to the date the defendant was granted leave to withdraw a sanctioned payment on the ground of new evidence, and was ordered to pay the defendant's costs thereafter. Longmore LJ said (at para 27):

> Mrs Painting herself made no attempt to negotiate, made no offer of her own and made no response to the offers of the University. That would not have mattered in pre-CPR days but, to my mind, that now matters very much. Negotiation is supposed to be a two-way street, and a claimant who makes no attempt to negotiate can expect, and should expect, the courts to take that into account when making the appropriate order as to costs.

In *Golden Eagle* (above) (para 46) the court ordered costs on the common fund basis against a party which had unreasonably refused to mediate.

**[62.5.9]    Other examples of conduct being reflected in costs**
Exaggeration of a claim is another aspect of conduct to be taken into account. It is expressly mentioned in rule 5(2)(c). In *Widlake v BAA Ltd* [2009] EWCA Civ 1256 (23.11.2009) the English Court of Appeal held that the 'dishonesty' of a successful plaintiff who had exaggerated a personal injuries claim 'must be penalised' (para 44). Taking into account the plaintiff's failure to negotiate as well, the court concluded that the right order was no order for costs. The court below had gone so far as to order the successful plaintiff to pay the defendant's costs, saying that there had been an attempt to manipulate the civil justice system. On appeal Ward LJ said: (para 41):

> I sound a word of caution: lies are told in litigation every day up and down the country and quite rightly do not lead to a penalty being imposed in respect of them. There is a considerable difference between a concocted claim and an exaggerated claim and judges must be astute to measure how reprehensible the conduct is.

In *Malmesbury & Ors v Strutt & Parker* [2008] EWHC 424 (QB) (18.03.2008) (para 85) the English court distinguished between 3 levels of exaggeration which may have an effect on costs. In descending order they are (i) the worst case, of exaggeration which is deliberate and involves dishonesty as in *Painting* (above), (ii) unreasonable conduct, in the middle and (iii) exaggeration meaning no more than that the claimant recovered only a fraction of the claim advanced. Jack J went on to say that exaggeration may occur without fault, but even then it may be appropriate for it to be reflected in the order as to costs.

In *Noorani v Calver (No 2/Costs)* [2009] EWHC 592 (QB) a plaintiff who flatly refused to consider a suggestion that he should withdraw a defamation action despite being shown evidence which demonstrated the claim was unmeritorious, but later sought to discontinue during trial, was ordered to pay indemnity costs to the defendant. The defendant's pre-trial conduct was described as 'eminently fair and reasonable' (para 17). Coulson J (at para 9) gave the following examples of indemnity costs orders being made on grounds of conduct:

- *Amoco (UK) Exploration Co v British American Offshore Ltd* [2002] BLR 135 – use of litigation for ulterior commercial purposes;
- *Clark v Associated Newspapers* [1998] EWHC Patents 345 – the making of an unjustified personal attack by one party on the other;
- *Wates Construction Ltd v HGP Greentree Alchurch Evans Ltd* [2006] BLR 45 – the pursuit of a hopeless claim (or a claim which the party pursuing it should have realised was hopeless).

The above decisions on indemnity costs should be read in light of the fact that in England there are only two bases for taxation of costs – the standard basis and the indemnity basis. In Hong Kong where we retain intermediate steps between party and party and indemnity costs (such as common fund and solicitor client), the court must consider not only whether to order costs on a higher basis, but which basis.

It has been suggested that the costs of pursuing an alternative claim may be disallowed as unreasonable under this rule if a party fails to decide which is primary and which secondary and expend effort and costs in preparation accordingly. See *Lam So Chai v Cheung Sai Lui t/a Hoi Fung Stevedore & Transportation Co* HCPI 360/2007 (Fung J; 03.07.2009) (para 18) (*obiter*). With regard to pleading in the alternative generally, see Order 18 rule 12A and the commentary thereunder.

In *Wong Shui Lam v Hospital Authority* HCPI 151/2009 (Master Roy Yu; 31.12.2009) the defendant was ordered to pay indemnity costs of the statement of claim. It was said (para 37) that the defendant's conduct was 'unreasonable' and 'oppressive' in failing to respond to the plaintiff's pre-action letters in accordance with the personal injuries list practice direction (PD 18.1). The costs of the statement of claim could have been avoided if the defendant had complied.

It has also been suggested that failure or refusal to apply promptly to transfer an action from the High Court to the District Court where it becomes clear that the quantum is within the jurisdiction of the latter, is conduct which the court will not hesitate to take into account under this provision: *Hung Chor Hung John v Li Kwok Kin & Anor* HCPI 251/2009 (Master Marlene Ng; 10.11.2009) (para 72).

In the Canadian case of *Jayetileke v Blake* [2010] BCSC 1478 (CanLII) the court penalised a party in costs for having relied on expert evidence from a psychiatrist who 'was nothing more than an advocate thinly disguised in the cloak of an expert'.

### [62.5.10]   Appropriate time to raise issues of conduct

In England there are two separate provisions as to when the court should, in exercising its powers as to costs, consider the conduct of the parties:

(a) CPR 44.3 (4), which mandates the court to have regard to conduct in 'deciding what order (if any) to make about costs'; and

(b) CPR 44.5(3), by which the court must have regard to conduct 'in deciding the amount of costs'.

Thus it is crystal clear in England that conduct is relevant both when determining the incidence of costs, and when it comes to assessment or taxation of those costs. By contrast, in Hong Kong there is only Order 62 rule 5(1)(e), requiring the court to take into account conduct 'in exercising its discretion as to costs'. Despite the difference in wording between the rules in the two jurisdictions, the position is probably the same. The court exercises discretion both in deciding the incidence of costs and in determining the amount, so Hong Kong's rule 5(1)(e) is capable of applying at both stages.

Our sister publication in the UK, The Civil Court Practice says (at para CPR 44[3]) that as a 'general rule' the appropriate time to raise issues of conduct is at the assessment (or taxation) of costs. The cases of *Nugent & Killick v Michael Goss Aviation* [2002] EWHC 1281 (QB) and *Shirley v Caswell* [2001] 1 Costs LR 1 (CA) are cited. However The Civil Court Practice goes on to refer to *Aaron v Shelton* [2004] EWHC 1162 (QB); [2004] 3 All ER 561 where it was held that in many instances the issue of conduct should be raised at the time the costs order is made, and failure to do so may result in the point being lost to the party who wishes to make it. In *Aaron v Shelton* Jack J said (at paras 20-21):

> ... where a party wishes to raise in relation to costs a matter concerning the conduct of his opposing party (either before the litigation or during it), it is his duty to raise it before the judge making the costs order where appropriate to do so. One situation where it will be appropriate is where the judge making the costs order is in a position to deal with the matter by reason of his involvement in the case ... where a party faces the making of an order that he pay the costs of an action ... but he considers that he should not be liable to pay the whole of those costs ... he should make an application to that effect to the judge who is considering what orders as to costs should be made, that is, the trial judge in the case of a trial. If he does not do so it is not open to him when the costs come to be assessed [taxed] to raise the same matter ... as a ground for the reduction of the costs which he would otherwise have to pay. If he is uncertain whether a matter he wishes to raise falls within that category, he should raise the matter before the judge. The judge can then consider whether he should deal with it or specifically direct that it should be considered by the costs judge [taxing master].
>
> ... it is an abuse of the court's process to raise an issue before the costs judge [taxing master] which was not but should have been raised before the judge making the order for payment of costs.

Reflecting on the authorities referred to in The Civil Court Practice, we would suggest that conduct in relation to specific items of work should be raised on assessment or taxation, whereas conduct in relation to the overall approach to a case should be raised before the judge or judicial officer deciding on the incidence of costs. The taxing master is in the best position to decide whether a particular letter was necessary, whether it was appropriate to instruct counsel to undertake a specific aspect of the case, whether an item of work could have been delegated to a less expensive fee-earner, etc. On the other hand the judge or other judicial officer who has heard the application or trial will be in the better position to decide whether a party exaggerated the claim, raised hopeless issues or caused the hearing to be prolonged.

### [62.5.11] Manner in which court to reflect conduct at taxation or assessment stage

When the court takes into account conduct at the assessment or taxation stage, it cannot in so doing undermine the earlier order as to incidence of costs. In *Business Environment Bow Lane Ltd v Deanwater Estates Ltd* [2009] EWHC 2014 (Ch) (31.07.2009) the taxing master assessed a receiving party's costs of a preliminary issue at nil because that party ultimately failed badly at trial due to exaggeration. The taxing master's assessment was set aside on the ground it would undermine the costs order in respect of the preliminary issue. It was held (para 41) that the taxing master should have determined the costs of the preliminary issue taking into account conduct in relation to that issue, and not by reference to what happened at the end of the day.

In assessing the quantum of costs the court may reduce the amount recoverable by a percentage to reflect conduct of which it disapproves. However, this should be done only after considering the items of costs one by one, and then looking at the result in the round and considering at that stage whether to apply a percentage reduction. See *Booth v Britannia Hotels Ltd* [2002] EWCA Civ 579 (26.03.2002) (para 25).

**[62.5.12]     Rule 5(1)(f) – partial success to be taken into account**
Order 62 rule 5(1)(f) provides that the court shall take into account, in exercising its discretion as to costs, success on part of a litigant's case, even where not wholly successful. This provision states expressly that which has long been adopted in some cases where the court will tailor its order as to costs to reflect shared success on different issues. See the commentary on that topic under Order 62 rule 3.

Rule 5(1)(f) is in the same terms as England's CPR 44.3(4)(b), in relation to which our sister publication in the UK, The Civil Court Practice, says (at para CPR 44[4]):

> **Success on all or some of the issues** Whilst the general rule [Order 62 rule 3 in Hong Kong] is that costs follow the event, repeating to a certain extent earlier authority (*Re Elgindata (No 2)* [1993] 1 All ER 232, [1992] 1 WLR 1207 (CA)), the court will now examine individual issues to determine the just order; see *BCCI SA (in liq) v Ali & Ors (No 4)* [2000] TLR 156 (02.03.2000) ... For a review of the current position see *Phonographic Performance Ltd v AEI Rediffusion Music Ltd* [1999] 2 All ER 299 (CA).
>
> In a case where it was claimed that a child's learning difficulties should have been diagnosed by various head teachers and educational psychologists and the claim succeeded against one defendant but failed and was withdrawn against the others, the court allowed the claimant [plaintiff] only 70% of his costs: *Clark v Devon County Council* [2005] TLR 223 (22.04.2005), [2005] EWCA Civ 266, [2005] 1 FCR 752. The claimant had failed on certain clearly defined issues and the 30% reduction was made in order to reflect his success rate.
>
> Where neither party is completely successful this does not by itself, justify making no order as to costs. The question who is the successful party, for the purposes of applying the general rule, may be determined by reference to who ultimately has to write the cheque: *Day v Day* [2006] EWCA Civ 415 (14.03.2006) [para 17].

The Civil Court Practice continues at para [44.3[10]:

> **Costs of separate issues** If a party succeeds in an action the benefit of an order for costs carries with it the general costs of the action, which without an order to the contrary, includes the costs of part of the claim or defence on which he has failed. If however the successful party has failed on an issue of substance the court may take that failure into account under both [Order 62 rule 5(1)(f) and rule 5(2)(a)]. Whether a party should have pursued or contested an issue is part of the conduct to be considered by the court. The successful party may be ordered to pay the costs of the unsuccessful party in relation to a particular issue without evidence of impropriety or unreasonableness: *Summit Property Ltd v Pitmans (a firm) (Costs)* [2001] EWCA Civ 2020 (19.11.2001), [2002] CPLR 97 [para 16]. Unless the costs of an issue are very clearly definable rather than making an order relating to the costs of the particular issue, the courts will make an order that the paying party pay a proportion of the receiving party's costs in accordance with CPR 44.3(6)(a) and 44.3(7) [no express equivalents in Hong Kong]; an approach adopted in *Budgen v Andrew Gardner Partnership* [2002] EWCA Civ 1125, [2002] All ER (D) 528 (Jul), [2002] TLR 379 (09.09.2002).

Although *Butcher v Wolfe* [1999] 2 FCR 165, [1999] 1 FLR 334 (CA) was decided under the old rules it reflected the principles subsequently established by the CPR that the court has the discretion not only to disallow costs for the successful party but also to award costs to the unsuccessful party.

See also the commentary concerning the court's power under Order 62 rule 9(4)(a) to apportion costs by issue.

**[62.5.13]    Rule 5(1)(g) – open offers**
Order 62 rule 5(1)(g) provides that in exercising its discretion as to costs the court shall take into account any admissible offer to settle which is drawn to its attention. The use of the adjective 'admissible' confines the provision to offers which are not subject to the 'without prejudice' rule (as to which see the commentary under Order 24 rule 2). Thus the provision applies to open offers and, provided all relevant parties consent, to offers which were originally made on a without prejudice basis.

The purpose of this provision is to emphasise that notwithstanding the introduction of the sanctioned settlement proposals under Order 22, the court's residual discretion as to costs under section 52A of the High Court Ordinance still enables it 'to make an adverse costs order reflecting an unreasonable rejection of an "unsanctioned" offer': Chief Justice's working party on civil justice reform, final report (para 319). The provision implements recommendation 42 of the final report which reads:

> The rules should make it clear that the court will continue to exercise its discretion as to costs in relation to any offers of settlement which do not meet the requirements to qualify as sanctioned offers.

The court's power to take into account an open offer differs from that in relation to *Calderbank* offers in that it is not subject to the 'exclusionary' rule in Order 62 rule 5(1)(d) whereby the court may not take into account a *Calderbank* offer where the offeror could have protected itself by making a sanctioned payment or sanctioned offer under Order 22. See *Ming An Insurance Co (HK) Ltd v Ritz-Carlton Ltd (No 3)* [2009] 3 HKC 255 (CFA).

**6.    Restriction of discretion to order costs** (O. 62 r. 6)
**(1)    Notwithstanding anything in this Order or in section 52A of the Ordinance—**
> **(a)    unless the Court is of opinion that there was no reasonable ground for opposing the will, no order shall be made for the costs of the other side to be paid by the party opposing a will in a probate action who has given notice with his defence to the party setting up the will that he merely insists upon the will being proved in solemn form of law and only intends to cross-examine the witnesses produced in support of the will.**

**(2)    Where a person is or has been a party to any proceedings in the capacity of trustee, personal representative or mortgagee, he shall, unless the Court otherwise orders, be entitled to the costs of those proceedings, in so far as they are not recovered from or paid by any other person, out of the fund held by the trustee or personal representative or the mortgaged property, as the case may be; and the Court may otherwise order only on the ground that the trustee, personal representative or mortgagee has acted unreasonably or, in the case of**

**a trustee or personal representative, has in substance acted for his own benefit rather than for the benefit of the fund.**

---

## NOTES

### [62.6.1]  Costs of probate action

Order 62 rule 6(1) protects a party to a probate action from an adverse costs order where he gives notice that he merely seeks that the will be proved in solemn form and only intends to cross-examine the witnesses. Where a party challenging a will does not have the costs protection of rule 6(1), the court will normally order that costs follow the event, but subject to important exceptions. See *Kung Nina v Wang Din Shin (No 2)* (2006) 9 HKCFAR 800 (CFA) where Ribeiro PJ quoted with approval from *Spiers v English* [1907] P 122, 123 and said (at paras 12, 15 & 17):

> Accordingly the general rule where opposition to a will is unsuccessful is that costs follow the event. However, if the case can be shown to fall into one or other of the two exceptions, the order is, in the first category (where litigation is caused by the conduct of the testator or the residual beneficiary) for the costs to come out of the estate; and in the second category (where circumstances lead reasonably to an investigation of the will's validity) for there to be no order as to costs . . .
>
> A case may fall *prima facie* within one of the two exceptions, but if opposition to the will goes beyond putting the proponent to strict proof of its validity and takes the form of hostile litigation, the general rule whereby costs follow the event is likely to be applicable. This is implicitly recognised by O 62 r 6(1)(c) . . .
>
> It follows that in exercising its discretion, the court draws a distinction between litigation reasonably undertaken by a person in order to require the validity of a will to be investigated by the court, and litigation which is fundamentally hostile, where the opposing party takes it upon himself to establish a positive case such as of forgery, fraud or undue influence, with a view to defeating the will and advancing his own claim to the estate over that of the will's proponent.

### [62.6.2]  Costs of trustee, personal representative or mortgagee

Order 62 rule 6(2) protects a trustee, personal representative or mortgagee as to costs incurred in such capacity. Any costs not recovered from the opposing party will normally be recoverable out of the fund or property concerned. In *Man Ping Nam v Man Tim Lup & Ors* HCMP 2417/2007 (Recorder A Ho SC; 31.03.2010) (para 5) the court applied the same principle to the costs of the manager of a Chinese *wui*. It appears that the sub-rule does not affect the rights of third parties in whose favour costs are ordered – the third party may look to the trustee, personal representative or mortgagee to pay those costs, leaving it to that person to seek indemnity from the fund or property: *Lee Shuk Yee v Kwok Wing Yun Edwin (No 2)* [2006] 3 HKC 396 (CA) (note that this rule is not referred to in that decision).

The court retains a discretion to make an order depriving a trustee (*etc*) of indemnity where the trustee has acted 'unreasonably' or 'for his own benefit': rule 6(2). Those terms refer to the trustee's actions in respect of the proceedings, not to its actions through the life of the trust: *Hillhead Ltd v Hotung* HCMP 2757/2005 (Deputy Judge Muttrie; 30.03.2007).

In *Hotung v Ho Yuen Ki & Ors* HCA 571/2003 (Tang JA; 17.06.2005) it was held that a trustee had acted unreasonably within the meaning of this rule. The trustee had taken an active part in proceedings between the settlor and beneficiaries of the trust whereas she ought, in the court's view, to have taken a neutral stance. The court declined to allow the trustee to recover costs from the trust property.

In *Cheung Man Kwong Thomas v Mok Chun Bor* DCCJ 2133/2007 (Judge Mimmie Chan; 02.10.2009) an administrator whose defence of a claim went beyond merely putting the plaintiff to proof, thereby prolonging the trial, was permitting to recover only half of his costs from the estate.

See the commentary under Order 85 rule 2 as to the circumstances in which the court may grant a *Beddoe* order protecting a trustee as to costs in advance.

**6A. Costs orders in favour of or against non-parties** (O. 62, r 6A)

**(1)   Where the Court is considering whether to exercise its power under section 52A or 52B of the Ordinance to make a costs order in favour of or against a person who is not a party to the relevant proceedings —**

> **(a)   that person must be joined as a party to the proceedings for the purposes of costs only; and**
>
> **(b)   that person must be given a reasonable opportunity to attend a hearing at which the Court shall consider the matter further.**

**(2)   This rule does not apply where the Court is considering whether to make —**

> **(a)   a wasted costs order; or**
>
> **(b)   an order under section 41 or 42 of the Ordinance.**

**(L.N. 152 of 2008)**

---

**NOTES**

**[62.6A.1]   Power to order costs against non-parties**

Section 52A(2) of the High Court Ordinance empowers the court to order costs against a person who is not a party to the relevant proceedings, if it is in the interests of justice to do so. The subsection was enacted by the Civil Justice (Miscellaneous Amendments) Ordinance (No 3 of 2008), in effect from April 2009. It replaced a subsection which prevented the court from ordering costs against non-parties in the absence of an express provision in an Ordinance authorising such an order. As a result of the amendment, the position in Hong Kong is the same as that in England, where it was recognised in *Aiden Shipping Co Ltd v Interbulk Ltd* [1986] 1 AC 965 (HL) that the power to make such orders existed. Hong Kong decisions holding that orders for costs could not be made against non-parties should no longer be followed. They include *The CR Pointe Noire* [2006] 1 HKC 614 and *Best Consultants Ltd v Aurasound Speakers Ltd* [2005] 4 HKC 357 (CFI) and CACV 41/2006 (Yuen JA & Sakhrani J; 17.10.2006).

Order 62 rule 6A applies equally to applications under section 52A(2) for costs orders against non-parties and to costs only proceedings under section 52B (as to which see Order 62 rule 11A and the commentary thereunder). By its own terms the rule does not apply to the following:

> ☐   Applications for wasted costs orders against legal representatives, as to which see Order 62 rule 8-8E; and
>
> ☐   Applications for disclosure before action or against non-parties under sections 41 and 42 of the High Court Ordinance. As to such orders see Order 24 rule 7A.

**[62.6A.2]   Procedure on application for costs order against non-party**

Order 62 rule 6A provides that where an order for costs is sought against a non-party, that person must be joined as a party and given an opportunity to attend a hearing at which the court will consider the matter, which must mean an opportunity to be heard at an oral hearing, with the result that the court's power under Order 32 rule 11A to deal with interlocutory matters on paper is excluded.

**[62.6A.3]   Circumstances in which costs order againstnon-party may be appropriate**

There are some cases pre-dating the current section 52A(2) in which there were good reasons to seek costs against non-parties, though in some the court considered it could not do so because of the wording of that sub-section as it was prior to April 2009. These cases provide some guidance as to when a costs order against a non-party may be appropriate. They include:

☐   *The CR Pointe Noire* (above) where a costs order was sought against an insurer because the insured, which was the party to the proceedings, had gone into liquidation.

☐   *HK Housing Authority v Hsin Yieh Architects & Associates Ltd & Ors* [2005] 2 HKC 201 (paras 4-6) where a costs order was sought against an insurer which was funding the insured's defence, although liability under the insurance policy was denied.

☐   *Re Datacom Wire & Cable Co Ltd* [2000] 2 HKC 241, 244F where costs of winding-up proceedings were ordered against an unsuccessful opposing contributory.

☐   *Best Consultants Ltd v Aurasound Speakers Ltd* (above) where a costs order was refused against a director who filed affirmations in opposition to a winding-up petition.

☐   *The MV Liberty Container (No 2)* [2007] 3 HKC 332 (CFA) where costs were ordered against the funder of a party's defence.

After the current power to order costs in favour of or against a non-party came into force as part of the civil justice reforms in April 2009, there was no rush of cases seeking such orders. One noteworthy case is *Tse Ping Shun David & Anor v Lai Ho Man Shan Grace & Anor* CACV 97/2009 (Rogers VP, Le Pichon & Kwan JJA; 30.04.2010). There (para 48) the Court of Appeal expressed the view that there was a case for saying that an estate agent should be responsible for legal costs of litigation resulting from the 'mess' created by her 'inept' drafting of an agreement for sale and purchase of company shares as a means of acquiring a property registered in the company's name.

Examples of cases in which costs orders have actually been made against non–parties since CJR include the following:

•   *Chiu Tak Kwong v Tan Yufang* HCAP 9/2006 (Deputy Judge L Chan; 11.06.2010); [2010] 5 HKLRD 718 where costs were ordered against non–parties who had been served with notice of the action pursuant to Order 15 rule 13A, and thereby stood to benefit from it. The non–parties gave assistance to the plaintiff in the hope of personal gain, but declined to join as parties in an attempt to shield themselves from an adverse costs order.

- *Incorporated Owners of Hoi Hei Wa Ting v Cheung Chi Wai & Ors* LDBM 21/2010 (Deputy Judge Kot; 29.07.2010); [2010] HKCU 2848 where costs were ordered against the former chairman of the management committee of an owners' incorporation who had improperly used the name of the Incorporated Owners to bring proceedings against rival committee members.

**[62.6A.4]   Considerations to be taken into account on application for costs order against non-party**

Guidance as to the exercise of the court's discretion to order costs against a non-party was laid down in *Symphony Group plc v Hodgson* [1994] QB 179 (CA), which continues to be followed in England – see *Oriakhel v Groupama Insurance Co Ltd & Ors* [2008] EWCA Civ 748 (04.07.2008). The guidance should be highly persuasive in Hong Kong.

In *Symphony Group* Balcombe LJ said, at 192H–194D:

> In my judgment the following are material considerations to be taken into account, although I do not suggest that there may not be others which are relevant.
>
> (1)   An order for the payment of costs by a non-party will always be exceptional: see per Lord Goff in *Aiden Shipping* [above] at 980F. The judge should treat any application for such an order with considerable caution.
>
> (2)   It will be even more exceptional for an order for the payment of costs to be made against a non-party, where the applicant has a cause of action against the non-party and could have joined him as a party to the original proceedings. Joinder as a party to the proceedings gives the person concerned all the protection conferred by the rules, as to *eg* the framing of the issues by pleadings; discovery of documents and the opportunity to pay into court or to make a *Calderbank* offer … and the knowledge of what the issues are before giving evidence.
>
> (3)   Even if the applicant can provide a good reason for not joining the non-party against whom he has a valid cause of action, he should warn the non-party at the earliest opportunity of the possibility that he may seek to apply for costs against him. At the very least this will give the non-party an opportunity to apply to be joined as a party to the action under O 15, r 6(2)(b)(i) or (ii).
>
> (4)   An application for payment of costs by a non-party should normally be determined by the trial judge: see *Bahai v Rashidian* [1985] 1 WLR 1337.
>
> (5)   The fact that the trial judge may in the course of his judgment in the action have expressed views on the conduct of the non-party constitutes neither bias nor the appearance of bias. Bias is the antithesis of the proper exercise of a judicial function: see *Bahai v Rashidian* [above] 1342H, 1346F.
>
> (6)   The procedure for the determination of costs is a summary procedure, not necessarily subject to all the rules that would apply in an action. Thus, subject to any relevant statutory exceptions, judicial findings are inadmissible as evidence of the facts upon which they were based in proceedings between one of the parties to the original proceedings and a stranger: see *Hollington v F Hewthorn & Co Ltd* [1943] KB 587; Cross on Evidence, 7th ed (1990) pp 100-101. Yet in the summary procedure for the determination of the liability of a solicitor to pay the costs of an action to which he was not a party, the judge's findings of fact may be admissible: see *Brendon v Spiro* [1938] 1 KB 176, 192, cited with approval by this court in *Bahai v Rashidian* [above] 1343D, 1345H. This departure from basic principles can only be justified if the connection of the non-party with the original proceedings was so close that he will not suffer any injustice by allowing this exception to the general rule. [In Hong Kong see Order 62 rule 8 as to wasted costs orders against legal representatives].

(7)  Again, the normal rule is that witnesses in either civil or criminal proceedings enjoy immunity from any form of civil action in respect of evidence given during those proceedings. One reason for this immunity is so that witnesses may give their evidence fearlessly: see *Palmer v Durnford Ford* [1992] QB 483, 487. In so far as the evidence of a witness in proceedings may lead to an application for the costs of those proceedings against him or his company, it introduces yet another exception to a valuable general principle. [See also the commentary below on costs orders against witnesses.]

(8)  The fact that an employee, or even a director or the managing director, of a company gives evidence in an action does not normally mean that the company is taking part in that action, in so far as that is an allegation relied upon by the party who applies for an order for costs against a non-party company: see *Gleeson v J Wippell & Co Ltd* [1977] 1 WLR 510, 513.

(9)  The judge should be alert to the possibility that an application against a non-party is motivated by resentment of an inability to obtain an effective order for costs against a legally aided litigant. The courts are well aware of the financial difficulties faced by parties who are facing legally aided litigants at first instance, where the opportunity of a claim against the Legal Aid Board under section 18 of the Legal Aid Act 1988 [in Hong Kong see section 16C of the Legal Aid Ordinance (Cap 91)] is very limited. Nevertheless the Civil Legal Aid (General) Regulations 1989 ... lay down conditions designed to ensure that there is no abuse of legal aid by the legally assisted person [in Hong Kong see *inter alia* s 17(3) of the Legal Aid Ordinance (Cap 91)] and these are designed to protect the other party to the litigation as well as the Legal Aid Fund. The court will be very reluctant to infer that solicitors to a legally aided party have failed to discharge their duties under the regulations – see *Orchard v South Eastern Electricity Board* [1987] QB 565 – and in my judgment this principle extends to a reluctance to infer that any maintenance by a non-party has occurred.

In *Oriakhel* (above) Jacob LJ described principles (2) and (3) above as 'an obvious application of the basic principles of natural justice'.

**[62.6A.5]  Costs order against witness**

See generally principle (6) in the judgment of Balcombe LJ in the *Symphony Group* case, quoted above.

In *Oriakhel* (above) the English Court of Appeal held (para 31) that it was not appropriate to order costs against the non-party in the particular case. The non-party against whom costs were sought (a witness in the primary litigation) could have been, but was not, joined as a party thereto. It remained possible to sue him for dishonest conspiracy and to claim the costs of the primary litigation as damages. The findings in the primary litigation were not admissible against him because he did not have such a close connection with the primary claim that he must be bound by the result. See the discussion below on the issue of when the findings of fact in the primary litigation will be binding on a non-party.

**[62.6A.6]  Costs order against expert**

In *Phillips v Symes* [2004] EWHC 2330 (Ch), [2004] 4 All ER 519 it was held that a psychiatric expert witness had a case to answer in respect of costs allegedly wasted as a result of his conclusion, said to be in breach of duty, that a party was incapable of managing his affairs. Peter Smith J expressed the view (at para 71) that although a non-party should normally be warned of a possible costs application against him, this was not the case with an expert witness who had signed the declaration of duty to the court as required by Order 38 rule 37C.

**[62.6A.7]    Order for costs against the funder of litigation**
In *Oriakhel* (above) the English Court of Appeal held that the making of an order
for costs against a non-party does not depend upon it being shown that the non-party
was a 'funder or controller' of the primary litigation. However, the fact of funding
or controlling litigation will clearly be relevant on such an application. In *The MV
Liberty Container (No 2)* [2007] 3 HKC 332 (para 31) the Court of Final Appeal
held that costs should not normally be ordered against a 'pure' funder, meaning one
who has no personal interest in the litigation and does not seek to control its course,
but merely facilitates access to justice; 'but justice will normally require that a self-
interested funder ... be ordered to pay the costs of the funded litigant's successful
opponent'. An example of a case where costs were ordered against a non–party which
was had not just funded the litigation, but had supervised and controlled it is *Kuwait
Airways Corp v Iraqi Airways Co* [2008] EWHC 2039 (TCC).

**[62.6A.8]    Restrictions on evidence admissible against non-party where costs
              sought**
In *Oriakhel* (above), Jacob LJ considered whether the findings in the primary
litigation were admissible as against the non-party against whom a costs order was
sought. Referring to *Globe Equities v Globe Legal Services* [1999] BLR 232 and
*Dymocks Franchise Systems v Todd* [2004] UKPC 39, [2004] 1 WLR 2807 (PC), he
had the following to say (at para 31(d)):

> The findings in the primary claim are not admissible against Mr Khan pursuant to
> Balcombe LJ's sixth point [see the quotation from *Symphony Group v Hodgson* (above),
> and see the above commentary on costs orders against witnesses]. Where a non-party
> effectively has controlled the primary litigation (as for instance in *Globe* or *Dymocks*) it
> is, in the language of estoppel, a 'privy' and will be bound by the result. But that is not the
> case here. One cannot say that Mr Khan had such a close connection or 'proximity' (to use
> Morritt LJ's word in *Globe*) with the primary claim that he must be bound by the result.
> He neither funded it nor controlled it – it was not his claim even though, if the findings
> are correct, he stood to benefit from it. True it is that in the primary judgment Mr Khan
> was found to be a co-conspirator and a liar but neither of these matters taken separately
> or together are enough to bind him. Mr Khan must be free to contend that he was not a
> conspirator and adduce evidence to support his own defence.

See also the commentary under Order 62 rule 8B (concerning costs orders against
legal representatives) and *Secretary of State for Trade & Industry v Bairstow* [2003]
EWCA Civ 321; [2004] 4 All ER 325 (CA) cited therein.

**[62.6A.9]    Costs-only proceedings**
Order 62 rule 6A applies also to applications under section 52B of the High Court
Ordinance for costs where the parties have reached settlement without proceedings
being commenced. Such applications are known as 'costs only proceedings'. With
regard to such proceedings, see also Order 62 rule 11A.

**7.    Costs arising from misconduct or neglect** (O. 62 r. 7)
    **(1)    Where in any cause or matter any thing is done or omission is made
improperly or unnecessarily by or on behalf of a party, the Court may direct
that any costs to that party in respect of it shall not be allowed to him and that
any costs occasioned by it to other parties shall be paid by him to them.**

(2)    Without prejudice to the generality of paragraph (1), the Court shall for the purpose of that paragraph have regard in particular to the following matters, that is to say—

(aa) the underlying objectives set out in Order 1A, rule 1; (L.N. 152 of 2008)

(a)    the omission to do any thing the doing of which would have been calculated to save costs;

(b)    the doing of any thing calculated to occasion, or in a manner or at a time calculated to occasion, unnecessary costs;

(c)    any unnecessary delay in the proceedings.

(3)    The Court may, instead of giving a direction under paragraph (1) in relation to any thing done or omission made, direct the taxing master to inquire into it and, if it appears to him that such a direction as aforesaid should have been given in relation to it, to act as if the appropriate direction had been given.

(4)    The taxing master shall, in relation to any thing done or omission made in the course of taxation, have the same power to disallow or to award costs as the Court has under paragraph (1) to direct that costs shall be disallowed to or paid by any party. (L.N. 152 of 2008)

(5)    (Repealed L.N. 152 of 2008)

---

**NOTES**

**[62.7.1]    Costs penalty for improper or unnecessary act or omission**
Order 62 rule 7 gives the court a discretion to deprive a successful party of costs, and even to order costs in favour of the unsuccessful party. Such an order penalises a party responsible for anything done or omitted 'improperly or unnecessarily'. In *Wang Din Shin v Nina Kung* CACV 460/2002 (Yeung & Yuen JJA, Waung J; 19.04.2005) Yuen JA held (at para 40) that the discretion only comes into play where the 'improperly or unnecessarily' test is met. See also *Chinney Construction Co Ltd v Po Kwong Marble Factory Ltd* HCCT 7/2005 (A Cheung J; 07.10.2005). It has been held that in this context the word 'unnecessarily' should not be construed as applying to anything done which was not, with the wisdom of hindsight, strictly necessary: *Akai Holdings Ltd (in liq) v Kasikornbank PCL* FACV 16/2009 (CFA; 21.01.2011) (per Lord Neuberger NPJ, giving the CFA's unanimous judgment) (para 6). There a party put its case in two alternative ways and succeeded on both. The opposing party argued that the costs of the appeal were inflated by the unnecessary additional argument. It was held that where a party has two alternative ways of putting its case, it is normally not unreasonable to run them both, especially in a big money case.

The words 'misconduct or neglect' which appear in the heading to Order 62 rule 7 are not repeated in the body of the rule itself. In England, the court considered such an omission in relation to the provisions of CPR 44 (which are similar, but by no means identical to the Hong Kong rule) in *Haji-Ioannou v Frangos & Ors* [2006] EWCA Civ 1663 (06.12.2006); [2007] 3 All ER 938. It was said (para 10) that the words did not limit the court's jurisdiction, but pointed 'to the nature of the court's discretion'. In Hong Kong reference should be made to section 18(3) of the Interpretation and General Clauses Ordinance (Cap 1) which provides that headings do not have legislative effect.

Rule 7(2)(aa), which was added as part of the civil justice reforms which took effect in 2009, requires the court to have regard to the underlying objectives in Order 1A when considering whether to make an order under the rule.

The rule would justify a refusal to grant costs to a successful plaintiff who omitted to send a letter before action in circumstances where such a letter would have provoked an immediate settlement. In *Wealthy Plus Ltd v Lai Man Ho* [2001] 4 HKC 691 a District Court judge concluded that the plaintiff 'could have obtained everything' he could legitimately have asked for from the defendants 'without resort to litigation' and ordered the plaintiff to pay a large measure of the defendant's costs. The district judge adopted the approach used by Simon Brown LJ in *Butcher v Wolfe* [1999] 1 FLR 334, where *Roache v News Group Newspaper Ltd* (unreported) was quoted.

In *Lee Tso Fong v Kwok Wai Sun & Anor (No 2)* [2008] 5 HKC 97 the court deprived a successful defendant of costs where she had severely contested the claim on concocted evidence, causing the trial to take 11 days instead of 4.

**8. Personal liability of legal representative for costs – wasted costs order (O. 62 r. 8)**

   **(1)**   The Court may make a wasted costs order against a legal representative, only if —

      **(a)**   the legal representative, whether personally or through his employee or agent, has caused a party to incur wasted costs as defined in section 52A(6) of the Ordinance; and

      **(b)**   it is just in all the circumstances to order the legal representative to compensate the party for the whole or part of those costs.

   **(2)**   A wasted costs order may —

      **(a)**   disallow the costs as between the legal representative and his client; and

      **(b)**   direct the legal representative to —

         **(i)**   repay to his client costs which the client has been ordered to pay to other parties to the proceedings; or

         **(ii)**   indemnify other parties against costs incurred by them.

   **(3)**   The Court shall give the legal representative a reasonable opportunity to attend a hearing to give reasons why it should not make the order.

   **(4)**   When the Court makes a wasted costs order, it shall —

      **(a)**   specify the amount to be disallowed or paid; or

      **(b)**   direct a master to decide the amount of costs to be disallowed or paid.

   **(5)**   The Court may give directions about the procedure that should be followed in each case in order to ensure that the issues are dealt with in a way that is fair and is as simple and summary as the circumstances permit.

   **(6)**   The Court may direct that notice must be given to the legal representative's client, in such manner as the Court may direct —

      **(a)**   of any proceedings under this rule; or

      **(b)**   of any order made under this rule against his legal representative.

   **(7)**   Before making a wasted costs order, the Court may direct a master to inquire into the matter and report to the Court.

**(8)** The Court may refer the question of wasted costs to a master, instead of making a wasted costs order.

**(9)** The Court may, if it thinks fit, direct or authorize the Official Solicitor to attend and take part in any proceedings or inquiry under this rule, and may make such order as it thinks fit as to the payment of his costs.

(L.N. 152 of 2008)

## NOTES

### [62.8.1]   Origin and scope of Order 62 rules 8-8E

Order 62 rules 8-8E came into force as part of the civil justice reforms in 2009. They regulate the exercise of the court's power under section 52A(4)–(7) of the High Court Ordinance to make 'wasted costs' orders against legal representatives. Those paragraphs were inserted into section 52A by the Civil Justice (Miscellaneous Amendments) Ordinance (No 3 of 2008) which came into force in 2009 along with the civil justice reforms. The most significant aspect of the new paragraphs is that they extend the power to make costs orders which was previously recognised to exist in relation to solicitors, so that it may now be exercised against barristers as well.

Rule 8(2) provides for three types of costs orders against legal representatives. They are orders:

    (a)      disallowing costs as between legal representative and client: rule 8(2)(a); and

    (b)(i)   directing the legal representative to repay costs which the client has been ordered to pay other parties: rule 8(2)(b)(i); or

    (b)(ii) directing the legal representative to indemnify other parties against costs incurred by them: rule 8(2)(b)(ii).

It will be noted that the rule is worded in such a way that the choice is not between 3 self-contained types of order, but between (a) above coupled, perhaps, with either with (b)(i) or (b)(ii) above, but not both.

The position was the same under the former rule 8(1) (which is still relevant to costs incurred prior to April 2009 – see the commentary under Order 62 rule 36) save that it applied only in relation to solicitors.

### [62.8.2]   Scenarios where question of costs against legal representative may arise

There are three factual scenarios in which the question of costs against a legal representative may arise.

First, where the legal representative is a party to litigation. In such a case the court has power under section 52A(1) of the High Court Ordinance to order the lawyer-litigant to pay costs just like any other litigant. The general provisions of Order 62 will apply.

Secondly, where the legal representative represents a party to litigation. In this scenario section 52A(4) of the Ordinance empowers the court to make a 'wasted costs' order against the legal representative. It is likely only in this scenario that Order 62 rules 8-8E are relevant.

Thirdly, where a barrister or solicitor acts or advises in a non-contentious matter. Prior to the amendments in effect in 2009 as part of civil justice reform it was held that in this scenario the court has no power to order costs against a solicitor: *AIE Co Ltd v Kay Kam Yu* [1997] 1 HKLRD 161. This remains the case if the power under section 52A(4) to make wasted costs orders in respect of costs incurred by a 'party' is restricted to parties to legal proceedings in the court. The precise ambit of 'party' is not clear in this regard from the definition of that word in section 2 of the Ordinance. The definition includes but is not restricted to parties to court proceedings. The situation of barristers and solicitors should be the same in regard to this scenario. Note, however that it is always open to a client to challenge a solicitor's bill (whether in relation to contentious or non-contentious matters) by solicitor and own client taxation under section 67 of the Legal Practitioners Ordinance (Cap 159) – see the commentary under Order 106.

**[62.8.3] The meaning of 'wasted costs'**
The term 'wasted costs' is defined by section 52A(6) of the High Court Ordinance to mean costs incurred as a result of 'an improper or unreasonable act or omission', or 'undue delay or other misconduct or default'. More or less the same definition previously appeared in Order 62 rule 8 itself – see the commentary under Order 62 rule 36. In *Mok Lai Chun v Everwise Investment Ltd & Ors* CACV 323/2006 (Tang VP, Sakhrani & Reyes JJ; 19.11.2007) it was said that those words set out a 'stringent' test.

The meaning of 'improper' and 'unreasonable' in the definition of wasted costs was considered in detail in *Ridehalgh v Horsefield* [1994] Ch 205 (quoted with approval in the final report of the Chief Justice's working party on civil justice reform, para 547). 'Improper' includes violation of the rules of professional conduct but is not limited to that: conduct 'which would be regarded as improper according to the consensus of professional (including judicial) opinion can be fairly stigmatised as such whether or not it violates the letter of a professional code'. 'Unreasonable' means 'conduct which is vexatious, designed to harass the other side rather than advance the resolution of the case'.

'Misconduct' means breach of duty to the court: *Ridehalgh* (above, at 227C-D), cited with approval in *KB Chau & Co (a firm) v China Finance Trust and Investment Corp* [1996] 1 HKC 420, 427 (CA).

There are some cases where a wasted costs order is based on breach of duty to the opposing party. See for example *KB Chau & Co* (above), citing *Myers v Elman* [1940] AC 282 and *Tang Man Kit & Anor v Hip Hing Timber Co Ltd & Anor (No 2)* [2002] 1 HKC 630. This may come within 'default'.

Mistake or error of judgment may not necessarily be enough to justify making a wasted costs order: *Yau Chiu Wah v Gold Chief Investment Ltd & Anor (No 2)* [2003] 3 HKC 91, 103B; *The Tian Xiang 2 Hao* HCAJ 322/2001 (Reyes J; 18.10.2003) (upheld on appeal – CACV 327/2003).

In Hong Kong, unlike England, the definition of wasted costs does not extend to costs resulting from negligence or incompetence. See *Dolphin Advertising Ltd v Tronken Enterprises Ltd* [2010] 1 HKC 137 (paras 9-10) in which it is noted that the Chief Justice's working party on civil justice reform rejected a proposal to include negligence in the definition. However it has been suggested that negligence which is 'serious' or 'gross' may amount to misconduct, and hence be within the definition: *Yau Chiu Wah* (above, at 103B).

**[62.8.4]   Wasted costs incurred before April 2009**
Order 62 rules 8 to 8E do not apply to costs incurred prior to April 2009 when they came into force as part of the civil justice reforms. In relation to such prior costs, the previous Order 62 rule 8 continues to apply by virtue of the transitional provisions in Order 62 rule 36. See the commentary under that rule which includes, for the sake of convenience, the text of the former rule 8.

**[62.8.5]   Meaning of 'legal representative' – extension of the wasted costs jurisdiction to barristers**
As mentioned above, section 52A of the High Court Ordinance was amended as part of the civil justice reforms taking effect in 2009 so as to extend the court's power to make wasted costs orders so that it now applies as against barristers in addition to solicitors. Such an order may be made against a 'legal representative', which is defined in section 52A(7) HCO and Order 62 rule 1(1) to mean counsel or solicitor conducting litigation on behalf of a party.

**[62.8.6]   Trainee solicitors, law costs draftsmen, legal executives, etc**
Trainee solicitors, law costs draftsmen and legal executives are not included in the definition of 'legal representative' in section 52A(7) HCO and Order 62 rule 1 for the purpose of wasted costs orders, although they have the right of audience before the court in certain proceedings. However in any case where such a person is at fault there will be a solicitor with responsibility for the conduct of the proceedings against whom a wasted costs order could be made: see rule 8(1)(a) whereby a legal representative may be responsible for wasted costs caused by an 'employee or agent'. See also the definition of 'wasted costs' in section 52A(6) of the Ordinance which extends to acts and misconduct on the part of any legal representative 'whether personally or through an employee or agent'.

**[62.8.7]   Comparison with English rules**
In England the power to make wasted costs orders against legal representatives is found in section 51(6) of the Supreme Court Act 1981. Its exercise is regulated by section II of CPR part 48. Prior to the extension of the power in Hong Kong taking effect in 2009, the Chief Justice said that although the reach of the English provisions was 'much wider' than their Hong Kong equivalent, English authorities were of assistance as the nature of the jurisdiction was essentially similar. See *Ma So So Josephine v Chin Yuk Lun Francis & Anor* [2004] 3 HKLRD 294 (CFA). As a result of the amendments taking effect in Hong Kong in 2009 the gap between the two jurisdictions has been closed, and English authorities will be all the more useful in Hong Kong.

**[62.8.8]   Wasted costs order may be made against party's own legal representative or that of opposing party**
The court may make a wasted costs order not only against a party's own legal representative but also against the legal representatives of the opposing party: See Order 62 rule 8(2)(b)(ii) and *Medcalf v Mardell & Ors* [2002] UKHL 27; [2003] 1 AC (HL). Application may be made by the party itself rather than waiting for the court to act of its own motion: *Que Jocelyn Co (t/a Scented Delights) v Broadair Express Ltd* [1999] 3 HKC 393, 396I.

One reason a party might wish to seek a wasted costs order against the opposing party's legal representatives is where the opposing party itself is impecunious and unable to pay a costs order against it. This may have been a factor in *KB Chau & Co (a firm) v China Finance Trust & Investment Corp* [1996] 1 HKC 420 (CA). However, it has been observed that the wasted costs jurisdiction should not be used as a 'back-door' means of recovering costs not recoverable against impoverished litigants: *Dolphin Advertising Ltd v Tronken Enterprises Ltd* [2010] 1 HKC 137 (para 7), quoting from *Ridehalgh v Horsefield* [1994] Ch 323/2006.

### [62.8.9] Jurisdiction of master

The Registrar and masters have jurisdiction to deal with applications for wasted costs orders. This is because Order 62 rule 8 provides for such orders to be made by 'the Court', which is defined in Order 1 rule 4(2) to include any judge, registrar or master. See also *Que Jocelyn Co (t/a Scented Delights v Broadair Express Ltd* [1999] 3 HKC 393.

### [62.8.10] Extent of costs which may be ordered against legal representative

Order 62 rule 8(4) requires that the court, when making a wasted costs order against a legal representative, either fix the amount, or direct that the amount be determined by a master.

The amount of wasted costs to be disallowed or paid may be all or part of what has been incurred: section 52A(4), High Court Ordinance. However, it should not exceed the amount incurred: although there is a punitive element to such an order, it is also compensatory and its amount should not exceed the quantum of costs incurred or wasted. See *Ma So So* (above) (para 7).

In *KB Chau & Co (a firm) v China Finance Trust and Investment Corp* [1996] 1 HKC 420, 433D-E (CA) a solicitor was ordered to pay wasted costs on the solicitor and own client basis, and the costs of the wasted costs application on the indemnity basis. In *Ma So So* (above) the Court of Final Appeal expressed the view (at para 94 *et seq*) that it is not appropriate to order costs of the application on the indemnity basis as a demonstration of disapproval of the solicitor's conduct in the proceedings from which the application arises. Ribeiro PJ said:

> The wasted costs order itself is the response (both punitive and compensatory) to the misconduct which attracted the disapproval. That disapproval cannot be allowed to spill over into the costs order made in the O 62 r 8 proceedings where there has been no procedural or other impropriety justifying a special costs order in the latter proceedings.

**8A. Court may make wasted costs order on its own motion or on application**
(O. 62 r. 8A)

**(1) The Court may make a wasted costs order against a legal representative on its own motion.**

**(2) A party may apply for a wasted costs order —**

**(a) orally in the course of a hearing; or**

**(b) by making an interlocutory application by summons.**

**(3) Where a party applies for a wasted costs order by making an interlocutory application by summons, the party shall serve the summons on —**

**(a) the legal representative concerned;**

    **(b)**   **any party represented by that legal representative; and**

    **(c)**   **any other person as may be directed by the Court,**

**not less that 2 clear days before the day specified in the summons for its hearing.**

    **(4)**   **An application for a wasted costs order shall not be made or dealt with until the conclusion of the proceedings to which the order relates, unless the Court is satisfied that there is reasonable cause for the application to be made or dealt with before the conclusion of the proceedings.**

    **(5)**   **Unless there are exceptional circumstances making it inappropriate to do so, an application for a wasted costs order shall be heard by the judge or master who conducted the proceedings to which the order relates.**

**(L.N. 152 of 2008)**

## NOTES

### [62.8A.1]   Who may initiate application for wasted costs order?

Order 62 rule 8A provides that an application for a wasted costs order may be initiated by a party making an application, or by the court of its own motion. In this regard the rule codifies the situation which prevailed before it came into force. See *Que Jocelyn Co (t/a Scented Delights v Broadair Express Ltd* [1999] 3 HKC 393. *Castle City Ltd v Choi Yue Dev't Ltd* [1995] 2 HKC 593 appears to be an example of a case where the court raised a wasted costs issue of its own motion.

### [62.8A.2]   In what circumstances is it appropriate to apply for a wasted costs order?

Prior to the amendments to the wasted costs jurisdiction which took effect in 2009, it was said that it 'is a summary jurisdiction and should be strictly confined to questions which are apt for summary determination': *Ma So So Josephine v Chin Yuk Lun Francis & Anor* [2004] 3 HKLRD 294 (CFA) (para 8). This now finds expression in rule 8(5). See also rule 8B(1)(a)(ii) whereby the court must be satisfied that wasted costs proceedings are justified notwithstanding the likely costs. Thus the earlier cases concerning the circumstances in which the wasted costs procedure is appropriate will continue to be of guidance.

In *Bermuda Trust (HK) Ltd v Cai Guo Xiang & Ors* CACV 143/2006 (Tang VP, Yuen JA & A Cheung J; 04.01.2008) (para 60) the court quoted with approval from *Harley v McDonald* [2001] 2 AC 678 (PC from NZ) where it was said that insofar as the jurisdiction may be invoked for breach of duty in conduct of a case, it should be confined to matters such as:

> [f]ailures to appear, conduct which leads to an otherwise avoidable step or prolongation of a hearing by gross repetition or extreme slowness in the presentation of evidence or argument.

In *Harley* Lord Hope went on to say (at 704C-D) that issues about duties owed to the client and the conduct of the case outside the courtroom are 'unlikely' to be appropriate to be determined under the summary jurisdiction. Instead, in such cases, a complaint to a professional body, or a separate action, should be considered.

## [62.8A.3]    Procedure in making application for wasted costs order

Observations as to the procedure which should be followed on an application for a wasted costs order were made by the Chief Justice in *Ma So So Josephine v Chin Yuk Lun Francis & Anor* [2004] 3 HKLRD 294 (CFA). That predates the amendments allowing the court to make a costs order against counsel. Nevertheless, it is likely to be relevant to the new power which came into effect in 2009. See para 3 of practice direction 14.5, which was amended with effect from the same date so to state.

The following procedural points made in *Ma So So* are noteworthy:

-    The application should usually be dealt with at the conclusion of the proceedings. This is to avoid any risk of disruption of the proceedings and intimidation (para 19) [now see rule 8A(4) and, as to avoiding intimidation, see rule 8C].
-    The application should usually be heard by the judge who dealt with the proceedings (para 19) [now see rule 8A(5)].
-    The solicitor [or counsel] should be informed of the conduct complained of, how such conduct caused costs to be incurred or wasted and all other circumstances relied on (para 21) [now see rule 8B(3)].
-    Elaborate pleadings should be avoided; likewise the formal process of discovery (para 21) [now see rule 8(5)].

Practice direction 14.5, which took effect on 2 April 2009 along with the new rules 8-8E, contains additional guidance as to the procedure to be followed in making a wasted costs application. The following points are of note:

-    Para 14 – although the application may be made orally at a hearing, it should normally be made by *inter partes* summons in the proceedings in which wasted costs are alleged to have been incurred.
-    Para 15 – by rule 8A(3) the summons must be served on the legal representative against whom the order is sought and any person represented by that legal representative, as well as any other person as may be directed by the court.
-    Paras 16, 17, 18 – particulars specifying the conduct complained of, and what wasted costs were caused must be given in the application.
-    Para 19 – the application should be supported by an affidavit verifying the particulars of the complaint and identifying the evidence or other material relied upon.

The full text of the practice direction can be viewed on the judiciary's website www. judiciary.gov.hk, or that of the Hong Kong Legal Information Institute www.hklii. org, both of which are accessible by the general public free-of-charge.

## [62.8A.4]    Timing of application for wasted costs order

According to paras 4 and 5 of practice direction 14.5 (as amended with effect from 2009, along with the coming into force of the new legislation and rules on wasted costs orders), the court may make a wasted costs order against a legal representative 'at any time'; however an application by a party, under rule 8A(2), should usually not be made or dealt with until after the relevant proceedings have concluded: rule 8A(4). The reason is to avoid disruption of proceedings and the risk of intimidation. This reflects what was said in para 19 of the CFA's judgment in *Ma So So Josephine* (above).

#### [62.8A.5] Delay in applying for wasted costs order

Delay in applying for a wasted costs order is a factor relevant to the exercise of the court's discretion at the first stage whether to allow the application to proceed. See *Kwok Chin Wing v Kao, Lee & Yip* HCCW 743/2002 (Kwan J; 18.07.2007), in particular at paras 20-21. In that case the court dismissed an application for a wasted costs order partly on the ground of delay of about 19 months after the conclusion of the proceedings from which it arose. It was said that a late application could place the opposite party in difficulty, as evidence might no longer be available.

As to the stages in which the court will consider making a wasted costs order, see rule 8B.

#### 8B. Stages of considering whether to make a wasted costs order (O. 62 r. 8B)

**(1)** **The Court shall consider whether to make a wasted costs order in 2 stages —**

    **(a)** **in the first stage, the Court must be satisfied that —**

        **(i)** **it has before it evidence or other material which, if unanswered, would be likely to lead to a wasted costs order being made; and**

        **(ii)** **the wasted costs proceedings are justified notwithstanding the likely costs involved; and**

    **(b)** **in the second stage (even if the Court is satisfied under sub-paragraph (a)), the Court shall consider, after giving the legal representative an opportunity to give reasons why the Court should not make a wasted costs order, whether it is appropriate to make the order in accordance with rule 8.**

**(2)** **On an application for a wasted costs order, the Court may proceed to the second stage described in paragraph (1)(b) without first adjourning the hearing if it is satisfied that the legal representative has already had a reasonable opportunity to give reasons why the Court should not make a wasted costs order. In other cases the Court shall adjourn the hearing before proceeding to the second stage.**

**(3)** **On an application for a wasted costs order, any evidence in support must identify —**

    **(a)** **what the legal representative is alleged to have done or failed to do; and**

    **(b)** **the costs that he may be ordered to pay or which are sought against him.**

(L.N. 152 of 2008)

---

#### NOTES

#### [62.8B.1] Two-stage process

Order 62 rule 8B(1) provides that an application for a wasted costs order should proceed in two stages. See also *Ma So So Josephine v Chin Yuk Lun Francis & Anor* [2004] 3 HKLRD 294 (CFA) concerning the similar two-stage process under the previous rule 8.

At the first stage the court will consider whether it should proceed with the application. The court will only proceed beyond this stage if it is satisfied that, in effect, there is a case for the legal representative to answer on the evidence, and that it is justifiable to proceed notwithstanding the extra costs which will be incurred. As stated in *Ma So So Josephine* (above, para 16), at the initial stage the court will consider factors such as the strength of the case shown by the applicant and the proportionality of the exercise. Thus the court may decline to proceed beyond the first stage if it appears that the costs of doing so would be out of proportion to the amount of wasted costs claimed. An example is *Party for the Civil Rights and Livelihood of the People of HK Ltd v Public Bank (HK) Ltd* DCCJ 1302/2009 (Deputy Judge E Shum; 22.12.2009) (para 36).

### [62.8B.2] Legal representative's opportunity to be heard

Order 62 rule 8(3) requires the court to give a reasonable opportunity to a legal representative to attend a hearing to oppose an application for a wasted costs order. This is reinforced by rule 8B(2) which provides that if at the first stage the court decides to proceed, it must adjourn the hearing unless the legal representative has already had a reasonable opportunity to oppose the application, in which event the court may proceed to the second stage immediately.

Failure to give the legal representative a proper opportunity to be heard on the wasted costs order will result in the order being set aside: *Johnson, Stokes & Master (a firm) v Hoshing Holdings Ltd & Ors* [1994] 1 HKC 237 (CA).

The court has no power to compel the legal representative to appear. It should merely provide the opportunity and leave it to the legal representative to decide whether take advantage of it, or 'to let the matter go by default': *KB Chau & Co (a firm) v China Finance Trust and Investment Corp* [1996] 1 HKC 420, 425D-E (CA).

The legal representative's opportunity to be heard applies at both stages of the application. This is clear from the wording of rule 8B(2). See also *Ma So So Josephine v Chin Yuk Lun Francis* [2004] 3 HKLRD 294 (CFA) (para 18).

### [62.8B.3] Evidence on application for wasted costs order

Order 62 rule 8B(3) stipulates certain matters which must be covered by the evidence in support of an application for a wasted costs order.

It has been held that on application for a wasted costs order against a solicitor the court's findings of facts between the parties to the proceedings may be admissible. This is an exception to the general rule of evidence that judicial findings are not admissible as against a non-party to the proceedings in which they were made. See principle (6) enunciated by Balcombe LJ in *Symphony Group plc v Hodgson* [1994] QB 179 (CA), quoted in the commentary under rule 6A above concerning costs against non-parties and see the commentary under rule 6A on evidence against non-parties. According to the judgment of Balcombe LJ, the exception applies to any non-party whose connection with the original proceedings was sufficiently close that he will not suffer any injustice. Thus it should extend to counsel against whom wasted costs orders are sought. In *Re Prudential Enterprises Ltd (No 2)* [2004] 2 HKC 205 (para 9) the rationale for the exception as set out in the judgment of Balcombe LJ was not doubted though it was found inapplicable in the particular case. An interesting survey of the cases on the general rule and its exceptions can be found in *Secretary of State for Trade & Industry v Bairstow* [2003] EWCA Civ 321; [2004] 4 All ER 325 (CA).

**[62.8B.4]   The court's approach**

In *Ma So So* (above) the Chief Justice set out the manner in which the court should approach the exercise of its discretion to make a wasted costs order. It appears that the Chief Justice was referring to the exercise at the second, substantive stage, where the court considers the merits of the application. He said that the court should deal with the following questions:

    (1)    Whether the solicitor was responsible for (i) acting improperly or without reasonable cause or (ii) for undue delay or any other misconduct or default in any proceedings.

    (2)    Whether such conduct of the solicitor caused costs to be incurred or wasted. This is a question of causation. The causal link between the solicitor's conduct and the extent of costs incurred or wasted must be established.

    (3)    Whether the court should exercise its discretion to make an order.

In light of the amendments to the relevant legislation taking effect in 2009, the above passage should now apply equally to wasted costs applications against barristers. As noted above, practice direction 14.5, which was amended with effect from the same date, provides in para 3 that the general principles of *Ma So So* are now likely to be relevant to wasted costs applications whether against a solicitor or counsel.

**[62.8B.5]   Burden of proof**

The burden of proof is on the applicant at both stages of a wasted costs application. However there may be an evidential burden on the legal representative if the matter proceeds to the second stage. See *Ma So So* (above) (para 21).

**[62.8B.6]   Examples of wasted costs orders against solicitors**

The circumstances in which wasted costs orders will be made against solicitors are perhaps best described by examples:

*(1)   Costs unnecessarily incurred*

In *Sin Hua Bank Ltd v Sung Foo Kee Ltd* [1993] 1 HKC 65, 68F–H (CA) solicitors were ordered to show cause why the costs of including unnecessary documents in an appeal bundle should not be disallowed as between them and their own client as costs incurred improperly or without reasonable cause.

*(2)   Dereliction of duty*

In *Kwok Ka v Mak Siu Hing & Anor* [1999] 2 HKC 410, 422 the court disallowed costs as between two parties and their solicitors and ordered the solicitors to repay to their clients any costs which the clients had been ordered to pay. This was done on the ground that 'on each side there was such a dereliction of duty on the part of solicitors'. In *Ho Lee Man v Wong Wai Kai (No 2)* [1993] 1 HKC 193, 202 (CA) it was held that solicitors were guilty of 'gross dereliction of duty' in lodging an appeal against an order for costs without first obtaining leave as required under the High Court Ordinance. They were held liable for all the costs of the appeal, meaning they could not charge their own client and had to pay the opposing party's costs.

*(3)   Wrongly ceasing to act*

In *Que Jocelyn Co (t/a Scented Delights) v Broadair Express Ltd (No 2)* [1999] 4 HKC 381 the court ordered a solicitor to repay costs to a client on the ground the solicitor had wrongly ceased to act. It was held that there was an 'entire' contract between solicitor and client which the solicitor had breached, resulting in a total failure of consideration. Although Order 62 rule 8 is referred to in the judgment, on closer analysis the basis of the order as to costs may more properly be regarded as founded in the law of contract.

### (4) Abuse of process
In *Ma So So Josephine v Chin Yuk Lun Francis & Anor* [2004] 3 HKLRD 294 (CFA) it was held that a solicitor had abused the process of the court by starting an action knowing it to be false. The solicitor was ordered to indemnify the opposing parties for the entire costs of the action on a solicitor-and-own-client basis.

### (5) Mareva injunction cases
In *KB Chau & Co (a firm) v China Finance Trust and Investment Corp* [1995] 2 HKLR 567; [1996] 1 HKC 420 a solicitor was ordered to pay the wasted costs of a *Mareva* injunction for breach of duty. In particular the solicitor had obtained an *ex parte Mareva* injunction on the basis of an affirmation by the client giving the false impression that the plaintiff was a financially sound merchant bank when it fact it had virtually no assets.

### (6) Failed vendor and purchaser summons
In *Castle City Ltd v Choi Yue Development Ltd* [1995] 2 HKC 593, 597–8 the court considered it arguable that a solicitor should pay the costs of a failed vendor purchaser summons if the proceedings had in fact been brought for protection of the solicitor rather than the client.

### (7) Acting for non-existent party
A solicitor who commences proceedings on behalf of a non-existent party, or a party which does not have the legal capacity to sue, may be liable for the costs of the opposing party. See *Tang Man Kit & Anor v Hip Hing Timber Co Ltd (No 2)* [2002] 1 HKC 630, and see the commentary under Order 15 rule 4. In *Chan Chi Ming v Brilliant Rise Container Depot Ltd & Anor* [2008] 1 HKC 487 the court considered that solicitors who defended on behalf of a deregistered company had acted without proper authority and were liable to pay wasted costs for that reason. An appeal to the Court of Appeal was allowed (CACV 202/2008) after the company was reinstated and its acts validated by order of the court on application of the solicitors who had been ordered to pay wasted costs.

### (8) Acting for impecunious client
A solicitor who knowingly conducts litigation on behalf of a client who is unable to pay costs may be ordered to satisfy a costs order unmet by the client. See *Mainwaring v Goldtech Investments Ltd* The Times 19.02.1991; *Charles Sin Cho Chiu v Tin Tin Publication Development Ltd* HCA 6662/1997 (Deputy Judge Li; 11.01.2002). However, the fact that a solicitor acts without fee is not of itself a basis for a personal costs order since it is in the public interest and recognised as proper for legal professionals to do so where necessary to provide access to justice. See *Count Tolstoy-Miloslavsky v Lord Aldington* [1996] 2 All ER 556, 565h-j (CA).

### (9) Acting without proper authority
A solicitor who acts in legal proceedings without proper authority may be personally liable in costs. See *Re Raja Enterprises* [1978] HKLR 249 where a solicitor acted for a

company on the basis of instructions from a person who had no authority to give them, and see *Ma Hing Yin Caroline v Crowncity Engineering Ltd* HCPI 83/2005 (Deputy Judge Muttrie; 16.05.2006) where solicitors were ordered to pay costs incurred in proceedings brought without proper authority on behalf of the estate of a deceased person. In *Chan Chi Ming* (above), solicitors who acted for a deregistered company could not escape a wasted costs order on the ground they had reasonably relied on a board resolution and did not know of the deregistration (however the wasted costs order was set aside on appeal after the solicitors procured the reinstatement of the company and an order of the court validating its acts). Liability in these cases is said to arise from breach of the solicitor's warranty of authority: *The Tian Xiang 2 Hao* CACV 327/2003 (Rogers VP & Chu J; 02.03.2004) (para 14). See the discussion of the solicitor's warranty of authority under Order 15 rule 4. Where proceedings are commenced with proper authority, but that authority comes to an end, whether by mental incapacity of the client (as in *Yonge v Toynbee* [1910] 1 KB 215) or revocation (as in *Chun Fai Garment Factory v Seaguide Import & Export Ltd* [1992] HKDCLR 31), the opposing party may look to the solicitor to pay costs subsequently incurred if the solicitor continues to act.

*(10)   Fault attributable to registry*
In *Chung Fai Engineering Co v Maxwell Engineering Co Ltd* [2001] 3 HKC 24 the court declined to make a costs order against solicitors where it transpired that their application for an extension of time to appeal had been necessitated not by their own fault, but by the registry's mistaken calculation of the time allowed for giving notice of appeal.

*(11)   Acting without client's instructions*
Failure to obtain client's instructions at various stages of a contentious matter resulted in a wasted costs order in *Lam Rogerio Sou Fung v Ku Ling Yu John t/a John Ku & Co* HCMP 1916/2007 (Master de Souza; 23.12.2009). The handling solicitor disclosed privileged documents without instructions to do so, leading to further enquiries and extra costs. The solicitor had also unsuccessfully sought costs on the common fund basis against the opposing party where there were no special features, and he did so without explaining the consequences of not succeeding to the client.

*(12) Acting in hopeless case*

In *Dolphin Advertising Ltd v Tronken Enterprises Ltd* [2010] 1 HKC 137 (para 7) it was held that continuing to prosecute an action once it should have been obvious that it was bound to fail was not, of itself, a ground for making a wasted costs order against solicitors. However in *Re Labour Buildings Ltd* CACV 37/2010 (Rogers VP, Le Pichon JA & Stone J; 26.04.2010) a substantial wasted costs order was made against solicitors who pursued a hopeless appeal even after they knew it was not going to proceed. In the subsequent case of *Chan Wai Tung v Tang Kwok Kwong & Ors* [2010] 6 HKC 446 (DCt) the court took was of the view that failure of a solicitor to inform the client if a continuing action has no prospects of success as a matter of law, constitutes improper conduct which, if unanswered, is likely to lead to a wasted costs order.

**[62.8B.7] Circumstances in which counsel may be ordered to pay wasted costs**
Wasted costs orders may be made against counsel both in relation to conduct in court, and preparatory matters such as settling pleadings and preparing skeleton arguments: *Medcalf v Mardell & Ors* [2003] 1 AC 120 (HL).

In *Medcalf* the House of Lords allowed counsel's appeal against a wasted costs order for making allegations of fraud in a draft amended notice of appeal, a supplementary skeleton argument and at a hearing. The wasted costs order was based on breach of the equivalent of para 113(b) of the Hong Kong Bar Association's Code of Conduct, by which counsel may not allege fraud without reasonably credible material establishing a *prima facie* case of fraud. The House of Lords did not doubt that a wasted costs order could be based on a breach of the Code of Conduct, but allowed the appeal because counsel were hampered in defending themselves by lay client's refusal to waive privilege (a subject dealt with below).

Our sister publication in the UK, The Civil Court Practice 2008 (at CPR 48.7[7]) gives the following guidance as to wasted costs orders against counsel under the equivalent provisions in the CPR:

> A barrister in sole practice should not rely on his solicitor to notify him of the date of the case: *Re a Barrister (Wasted Costs Order) (No 4 of 1992)* [1994] The Times, 15 March (CA). However where an adjournment has to be granted to allow a barrister to conclude a case which overruns, a judge should take account of difficulties over time estimates: *Re a Barrister (Wasted Costs Order) (No 4 of 1993)* [1995] The Times, 21 April (CA). A wasted costs order could be made against counsel who makes unsustainable complaints about the judge's interventions to prevent a waste of time: *R v Naylor* [1995] The Times, 8 Feb (CA). Nor should an order be made where a point taken is fairly arguable: *Sampson v John Boddy Timber Ltd* [1995] NLJR 851 (CA).

In *Whyte v Brosch & Ors* (1998) 45 NSWLR 354 the New South Wales Court of Appeal accepted an apology from counsel for the late filing of written submissions and chronologies, which was partly a result of difficulty in obtaining instructions from the lay client, and decided not to make a costs order against the legal representatives. However the court went on to give the following warning:

> In a case where the opposing party seeks an adjournment of proceedings by reason of the late filing of submissions, if the Court grants the adjournment in accordance with its usual approach, the profession ought to be aware that the Court can order that costs thrown away by any adjournment should be paid by the legal practitioner responsible for the failure.

Subsequently, in *Kendirjian v Ayoub (No 2)* [2008] NSWCA 255 the same court ordered an appellant's solicitor and counsel to indemnify lay client (on a 50:50 basis) for costs payable to the opposing party as a result of failure to file proper written submissions in advance of an appeal hearing, which had necessitated further written submissions from each side.

Cases from Canada and New Zealand must be considered bearing in mind the fact that their legal professions are formally fused and barristers are officers of the court. Nevertheless guidance can be obtained from those jurisdictions concerning conduct of legal practitioners performing the functions of counsel. Both jurisdictions adopt a cautious approach. In *Young v Young* (1994) 108 DLR (4th) 193 the Supreme Court of Canada, holding that a costs order was wrongly made against an advocate at first instance, set up a bad faith test. In the words of McLachlin J at 284, with whom the majority concurred:

Any member of the legal profession might be subject to a compensatory order for costs if it is shown that repetitive and irrelevant material, and excessive motions and applications, characterised the proceedings in which they were involved, and that the lawyer acted in bad faith in encouraging this abuse and delay.

In *Harley v McDonald* [2001] 2 AC 678 (PC from NZ) a costs order had been made against a barrister who pursued a hopeless case even after a clear warning by the court at the interlocutory stage. The Privy Council was of the view that the lawyer had done nothing worse than pursue the client's instructions, and set aside the costs order. Likewise in *HKSAR v Tang Ka Hung & Anor* [2011] 1 HKC 1 (para 52) a wasted costs order (in a criminal case) was set aside on the ground that counsel had been acting in accordance with instructions. However, in *Baryluk v Campbell* [2009] CanLII 34042 (Ont SC) where, in pursuing a hopeless case, counsel apparently went beyond client's instructions and made allegations against the judiciary amounting to a 'baseless and scurrilous attack on judges', in her own capacity, counsel was ordered to be jointly and severally liable for 50% of the party and party costs payable to the opposing party.

In *Rao v Goundar* [1998] FJHC 72 (22.05.1998) the Fiji High Court considered there were grounds to make a wasted costs order against counsel who failed to appear in court on time.

**[62.8B.8]    Legal representative may be hampered by privilege**

A legal representative against whom a wasted costs order is sought may be constrained by legal professional privilege in mounting a defence. Unless such privilege is waived by the client (expressly or impliedly) the legal representative may be 'unable to disclose what advice and warnings he had given to his client and what instructions were received'. If so, the court must 'make full allowance for his inability to tell the whole story': *Ma So So* (above). Thus in *Medcalf v Mardell* [2003] 1 AC 120 (HL) (para 23) Lord Bingham said that the court should not make a wasted costs order against a practitioner who is precluded by legal professional privilege from advancing a full answer to the complaint, unless satisfied that nothing could be said to influence the exercise of discretion, and that in all the circumstances it is fair to make the order; further that 'only exceptionally could these exacting conditions be satisfied'. The Chief Justice's working party on civil justice reform, referring to this aspect of Lord Bingham's speech, said that the same approach would almost certainly be adopted in Hong Kong (final report, para 572).

Where a lay client brings a wasted costs application against his or her own legal representative, privilege is impliedly waived: *Yau Chiu Wah v Gold Chief Investment Ltd & Anor (No 2)* [2003] 3 HKC 91, 104A. However, where the application is made by someone else, such as the opposing party, privilege restrains the legal representative unless expressly waived by the lay client.

In *Yau Chiu Wah* Ma JA summarised the relevant points in regard to privilege as follows (at 104D-I):

(1) Where a solicitor facing an application for a wasted costs order is unable to give a full account of events by reason of privileged material (and the client does not waive privilege) the court must proceed very carefully. As [Lord Bingham said in *Ridehalgh v Horsefield* [1994] Ch 205, 184], '[s]peculation is one thing,

the drawing of inferences sufficiently strong to support orders potentially very damaging to the practitioner concerned is another'.

(2) It is perhaps only on rare occasions that a court will, even after making full allowance for the handicap the solicitor finds himself in, conclude there is no room for doubt in holding that the solicitor has been at fault. The reason for this is that a court must necessarily proceed with the utmost caution where it does not have the full facts before it.

(3) Where a solicitor's professional reputation is at risk of being tarnished (an inevitable consequence of an order under Order 62 rule 8), the court must be fair to him in the light of the handicap on privileged material . . .

(4) Lord Bingham ... summarises the position in this way at 185, '[w]here a wasted costs order is sought against a practitioner precluded by legal professional privilege from giving his full answer to the application, the court should not make an order unless, proceeding with extreme care, it is (a) satisfied that there is nothing that the practitioner could say, if unconstrained, to resist the order and (b) that it is in all the circumstances fair to make the order'.

**8C. Application for wasted costs order not to be used as means of intimidation**
(O. 62 r. 8C)

**(1)   A party shall not by himself or by another person on his behalf threaten another party or any of that party's legal representatives with an application for a wasted costs order with a view to coercing or intimidating either of them to do or refrain from doing anything.**

**(2)   A party shall not indicate to another party or any of that party's legal representatives that he intends to apply for a wasted costs order unless he is satisfied that he is able to —**

> **(a)   particularize the behaviour of the legal representative from which the wasted costs concerned are alleged to result; and**
>
> **(b)   identify the evidence or other materials on which he relies in support of the allegation.**

**(L.N. 152 of 2008)**

---

**NOTES**

**[62.8C.1]   Discretion to make wasted costs order to be exercised with care**
The court's power to make wasted costs orders against legal representatives is discretionary. The discretion is 'seldom exercised' and should be used 'with care and discretion, and only in clear cases': *Ho Lee Man v Wong Wai Kai (No 2)* [1993] 1 HKC 193, 195I-196H (CA). In that case Litton JA, citing with approval *Orchard v South Eastern Electricity Board* [1987] QB 565, explained:

> If a solicitor should run the risk of being personally liable for the costs every time his client takes a wrong step, this would have a profoundly harmful effect on the normal conduct of civil litigation. A solicitor, instead of doing his best in the circumstances for his client, would tremulously be looking to his own pocket, fearful of the consequences if he loses.

The point made by the learned judge in the above passage is now express in the legislation:

- □   section 52A(5) of the High Court Ordinance requires the court, in considering whether to make a wasted costs order, to 'take into account the interest that there be fearless advocacy under the adversarial system of justice'.
- □   Order 62 rule 8C provides an application for a wasted costs order must not be used as a means of coercing or intimidating another party's legal representative.

**8D. Personal liability of legal representative for costs – supplementary provisions** (O. 62 r. 8D)

**(1)   Where in any proceedings before a taxing master, the legal representative representing any party is guilty of neglect or delay or puts any other party to any unnecessary expense in relation to those proceedings, the taxing master may direct the legal representative personally to pay costs to any of the parties to those proceedings.**

**(2)   Where any legal representative fails to file a bill of costs (with the documents required by this Order) for taxation within the time fixed by or under this Order or otherwise delays or impedes the taxation, then, unless the taxing master otherwise directs, the legal representative shall not be allowed the fees to which he would otherwise be entitled for drawing the bill of costs and for attending the taxation.**

**(3)   If, on the taxation of costs to be paid out of a fund other than funds provided by the Legislative Council pursuant to section 27 of the Legal Aid Ordinance (Cap 91), one-sixth or more of the amount of the bill for those costs is taxed off, the legal representative whose bill it is shall not be allowed the fees to which he would otherwise be entitled for drawing the bill and for attending the taxation.**

**(4)   In any proceedings in which the party by whom the fees prescribed by any enactment relating to court fees are payable is represented by a legal representative, if the fees or any part of the fees payable under that enactment are not paid as prescribed, the Court may, on the application of the Official Solicitor by summons, order the legal representative personally to —**

- **(a)   pay that amount in the manner so prescribed; and**
- **(b)   pay the costs of the Official Solicitor of the application.**

**(5)   A legal representative shall not be directed or ordered under this rule to pay any costs or fees, nor shall he be disallowed under this rule any fees, unless he has been given a reasonable opportunity to give reasons why —**

- **(a)   the direction or order should not be made; or**
- **(b)   he should not be disallowed the fees.**

**(6)   When a taxing master makes a direction under paragraph (1), he —**

- **(a)   shall specify the amount to be paid; and**
- **(b)   may give directions about the procedure that should be followed in each case in order to ensure that the issues are dealt with in a way that is fair and is as simple and summary as the circumstances permit.**

**(7)   The Court or a taxing master may direct that notice must be given to the legal representative's client, in such manner as the Court or the taxing**

**master may direct, of any direction or order made under this rule against his legal representative.**

---

NOTES

**[62.8D.1]**    **Costs against legal representative in relation to taxation proceedings and court fees**

Order 62 rule 8D(1), (2), (3) and (4), which respectively concern neglect and delay (*etc*) in proceedings before a taxing master; delay (*etc*) in filing a bill of costs; taxation of costs to be paid out of a fund other than the legal aid fund; and non-payment of court fees, were found in rule 8(6), (7) and (8) before the amendments taking effect in 2009 pursuant to civil justice reform. For the previous rule, see the commentary under Order 62 rule 36.

**8E. Stages of considering whether to make direction under rule 8D(1)**
     (O. 62 r. 8E)

     **(1)**    **The taxing master shall consider whether to make a direction under rule 8D(1) in 2 stages —**

         **(a)**    **in the first stage, the taxing master must be satisfied that —**

             **(i)**    **he has before him evidence or other material which, if unanswered, would be likely to lead to a direction under rule 8D(1) being made; and**

             **(ii)**    **the direction is justified notwithstanding the likely costs involved; and**

         **(b)**    **in the second stage (even if the taxing master is satisfied under sub-paragraph (a)), the taxing master shall consider, after giving the legal representative an opportunity to give reasons why the taxing master should not make the direction, whether it is appropriate to make the direction.**

     **(2)**    **On an application for a direction under rule 8D(1), the taxing master may proceed to the second stage described in paragraph (1)(b) without first adjourning the hearing if he is satisfied that the legal representative has already had a reasonable opportunity to give reasons why the taxing master should not make the direction. In other cases the taxing master shall adjourn the hearing before proceeding to the second stage.**

     **(3)**    **On an application for a direction under rule 8D(1), any evidence in support must identify —**

         **(a)**    **what the legal representative is alleged to have done or failed to do; and**

         **(b)**    **the costs that he may be directed to pay or which are sought against him.**

                                              **(L.N. 152 of 2008)**

**[62.8E.1]**    **Two-stage process**

Order 62 rule 8E provides that an application for a wasted costs order in relation to taxation proceedings or court fees should, like an application in relation to other proceedings, proceed in two stages. It follows closely the provisions of rule 8B as to the two-stage procedure in relation to applications for costs wasted in other proceedings. See the commentary under rule 8B which should be applicable, *mutatis mutandis*, here.

**9. Taxed costs, fractional costs or costs summarily assessed for non-interlocutory applications** (O. 62 r. 9)

**(1)    Subject to this order, where by or under these rules or any order or direction of the Court costs are to be paid to any person, that person shall be entitled to his taxed costs.**

**(2)    Paragraph (1) shall not apply to costs which by or under any order or direction of the Court —**

**(a)    are to be paid to a receiver appointed by the Court of First Instance under section 21L of the Ordinance in respect of his remuneration, disbursements or expenses; or**

**(b)    are to be assessed or settled by a taxing master,**

**but rules 28, 28A, 31 and 32 shall apply in relation to the assessment or settlement by a taxing master of costs which are to be assessed or settled as aforesaid as they apply in relation to the taxation of costs by a taxing master.**

**(3)    Where a writ in an action is endorsed in accordance with Order 6, rule 2(1)(b), and judgment is entered on failure to give notice of intention to defend or in default of defence for the amount claimed for costs (whether alone or together with any other amount claimed), paragraph (1) of this rule shall not apply to those costs, but if the amount claimed for costs as aforesaid is paid in accordance with the indorsement (or is accepted by the plaintiff as if so paid) the defendant shall nevertheless be entitled to have those costs taxed.**

**(4)    The Court in awarding costs to any person may direct that, instead of taxed costs, that person shall be entitled —**

**(a)    to a proportion specified in the direction of the taxed costs or to the taxed costs from or up to a stage of the proceedings so specified; or**

**(b)    to a sum of money summarily assessed in lieu of taxed costs. (L.N. 152 of 2008)**

**(5)    This rule does not apply to costs of an interlocutory application. (L.N. 152 of 2008)**

### [62.9.1]    Scope of Order 62 rule 9

Order 62 rule 9 sets out the circumstances in which a receiving party is entitled to taxed costs, empowers the court to limit entitlement to costs to a proportion of the taxed amount, and provides for summary assessment of costs of non-interlocutory applications in lieu of taxation. These topics are discussed individually below.

### [62.9.2]    When party entitled to taxed costs

Order 62 rule 9(1) provides that a receiving party is normally entitled to proceed to taxation of the amount of costs payable. However, this is subject to exceptions. By rule 9(2) it does not apply where the costs are to be paid in respect of receiver's remuneration, or where the costs are to be assessed or settled by a taxing master. By rule 9(3) a party who obtains default judgment on a writ indorsed with the '14-

day costs indorsement' (as to which see Order 6 rule 2(1)(b) and the commentary thereunder) is entitled only to the amount claimed in the indorsement, and not to taxed costs.

See also the schedules to Order 62 under which costs recoverable are fixed in other circumstances, such as where judgment is obtained short of trial.

### [62.9.3]   Rule 9(4)(a) – Court's power to limit recovery of costs by proportion or stage

Order 62 rule 9(4)(a) empowers the court to limit a receiving party's recovery of costs to a proportion of the taxed costs, or to the costs of a particular stage of the proceedings. See also Order 62 rule 5(1)(f) and 5(2)(a) and the commentary thereunder.

*Proportional costs* – There are many examples of cases where the court has limited recovery of costs to a percentage or fraction of the taxed costs. They include:

- □  *Glynn v Commr of Inland Revenue* CACV 51/1988 (Cons VP, Clough & Hunter JJA; 16.02.1989) where a party was awarded only three-quarters of its costs of the appeal on which it succeeded, with no order as to the costs below, partly because the appeal succeeded on a point only raised by the court itself on appeal.

- □  *Choy Bing Wing v HK & Shanghai Hotels Ltd* [1995] 2 HKC 435 (CA) where an appellant who succeeded on an argument first put forward on appeal was given its costs of the appeal, but only 75% of the costs below.

- □  *Chung Man Yau & Anor v Sihon Co Ltd* [1997] 3 HKC 197, 209C-D (CA) where a successful plaintiff whose misconceived claims had protracted a trial was allowed only three-quarters of his costs in a personal injuries action. However, the Court of Appeal overturned an order that he pay two-thirds of the defendant's costs, noting that the defendant had taken none of the 'well recognised' steps to protect itself in costs.

- □  *To Kan Chi v Pui Man Yau* [1998] 3 HKC 361 (CA) where a costs order in favour of the government in respect of its successful appeal was limited to 75% because it had adopted a 'somewhat confusing stance' which had increased costs.

- □  *Woonsing Ltd v Wong Yi Ming* HCA 6744/1998 (Chu J; 26.02.2001) where a plaintiff which succeeded only because of a late amendment to the statement of claim, was entitled to recover only 50% of its costs from the defendant.

- □  *Ho Lai Chuen Cadia v Xerox (HK) Ltd* [2003] 2 HKC 603 (CA), where the Court of Appeal overturned the trial judge's order limiting the successful plaintiff to 85% of its costs. Rogers VP said, at 606A-B: 'if a plaintiff makes a claim which is disputed on liability as well as quantum and recovers, it is, generally, entitled to costs, save insofar as it may be found at fault for having increased those costs unnecessarily'.

*Costs of particular stage of proceedings* – Examples of cases where the court has limited a party's recovery of costs to the costs of a particular stage of the proceedings include cases where the court has concluded a party ought to have accepted a settlement proposal, and the failure to do so is reflected in the order as to costs thereafter. See the discussion of *Calderbank* offers in the commentary concerning Order 62 rule 5(1)(d).

Other examples are cases where the result of the case is affected by a late amendment. See the commentary on that topic under Order 20 rule 5.

**[62.9.4]  Rule 9(4)(a) – Apportionment of costs in cases of shared success on different issues**

The court's power under Order 62 rule 9(4)(a) to limit recovery of costs to a proportion or stage of costs clearly enables it to apportion costs to reflect success on some issues and failure on others. An example is *Vincent v SCMP Publishers Ltd (No 2)* [2004] 2 HKC 570 (CA) where each of the parties had succeeded on some issues. The plaintiff was ordered to pay two-thirds of the costs of the appeal, and the defendant one-third, with liability under the two orders to be set off. The costs order was left undisturbed on appeal to the Court of Final Appeal reported at (2005) 8 HKCFAR 605.

The traditional view has been that such an order reflecting shared success on different issues is by no means automatic or usual. See principle (iii) set out in the *Elgindata* case, quoted in the commentary under Order 62 rule 3 as to when the court will make an order other than that costs follow the event. It is there stated that a successful party should only be deprived of the whole or part of the costs of the action 'where that has caused a significant increase in the length or cost of the proceedings'. In England the courts may now be more ready to fashion the costs order so as to reflect the outcome on different issues. See *AEI Rediffusion Music Ltd v Phonographic Performance Ltd* [1999] 1 WLR 1507. In *Akai Holdings Ltd (in liq) v Kasikorn Bank* [2008] 6 HKC 82 it was argued that this was part of 'the modern approach to discourage the parties from increasing the costs of the action and of narrowing the issues to those at the heart of the case'. However the Hong Kong court declined to adopt that approach. Stone J said (at para 26-27):

> For my own part I am able to identify no predisposition in the Hong Kong courts similar to that to which Lord Woolf made reference in *AEI Rediffusion Music Ltd* [above], that is, to a movement away from the *Elgindata* approach towards a situation wherein, as Lord Woolf expressed it, even prior to the fundamental changes in English civil procedure there had been a change of emphasis abroad requiring the courts to be more ready to make separate orders reflective of the outcome of different issues, and that the new Civil Procedure Rules simply had accentuated this pre-existing tendency. I do not consider this to be the case in Hong Kong.

Stone J confirmed (at para 29) the court's adherence to the approach he had set out in *Cooperatieve Centrale (Rabobank, HK Branch) v Bank of China* HCCL 56/2001 (Stone J; 23.07.2004) (para 13), where he had said:

> … as a matter of general approach to the issue of trial costs the occasions which justify the 'filleting' of costs according to the success or failure of any specific issue arising for decision within the composite whole are likely to be relatively few and far between …

Since then Order 62 rule 5(1)(f) and rule 5(2)(a) have come into force (in effect from April 2009). The first of those provisions requires the court to take into account, when exercising its discretion as to costs, the fact that a party's case may have been partially, though not wholly, successful. The second of those provisions specifically directs the court, when exercising its discretion as to costs, to consider whether it was reasonable for a party to raise, pursue or contest a particular allegation or issue in proceedings. Those provisions could be interpreted as a basis for the court to take the approach which Stone J declined to adopt in the *Akai Holdings* case (above). That is certainly the view which has been taken in England of similar provisions in CPR Part 44. In *AEI* (above) (at 1523) Lord Woolf said:

> The most significant change of emphasis of the new Rules is to require courts to be more ready to make separate orders which reflect the outcome of different issues. In doing this the new Rules are reflecting a change of practice which has already started. It is now clear that a too robust application of the 'follow the event principle' encourages litigants to increase the costs of litigation, since it discourages litigants from being selective as to the points they take. If you recover all your costs as long as you win, you are encouraged to leave no stone unturned in your effort to do so.

However, in *Kam Hing Trading (HK) Ltd v People's Insurance Co of China (HK) Ltd* HCCL 27/2009 (Stone J; 15.12.2010) (para 21) the reluctance to engage in 'filleting' of costs by issue, at least in the context of the commercial court, was re–emphasised in post–CJR Hong Kong.

### [62.9.5]   Single taxation of costs apportioned on grounds of shared success
The form of order made in *Vincent v SCMP* (above) requires taxation of two sets of costs, and a set off. In *Golden Bright Manufacturer Ltd v Sunlight Electronic Toys Manufacturing Co Ltd & Anor* HCA 927/2001 (Deputy Judge Gill; 08.11.2007) the court preferred to simplify matters by ordering taxation of one set of costs, to be discounted by 40%. The court referred to *Bayer Corp & Bayer plc v Octapharma Ltd* [1999] FSR 926 where it was said that it is undesirable to double the complex process of taxation by requiring examination of the bills of costs of both sides. The approach taken in *Golden Bright* is to be recommended insofar as it can save costs on taxation.

### [62.9.6]   Summary assessment of costs
Order 62 rule 9(4)(b) provides for the summary assessment of the quantum of costs in lieu of taxation. The provision was amended as part of the civil justice reforms taking effect in 2009, replacing the previous 'gross sum' of costs in lieu of taxation. The new provision is similar to its predecessor, but it does not apply to interlocutory applications: rule 9(5). Summary assessment of costs of interlocutory applications is now dealt with by rule 9A.

In *Kennedy v Kelly Cheng & Anor* FACV 30/2008 (CFA; 12.01.2010) (para 3) Bokhary PJ said that it would be 'wholly impracticable' to order gross sum assessment after a final appeal, as that would have to be done by the judges concerned at each level.

### [62.9.7]   When summary assessment of costs appropriate
The power under rule 9(4)(b) to order payment of a summarily assessed quantum of costs is clearly discretionary. However, exercise of the discretion is subject to rule 9C(1)(a), which provides that such an order shall not be made where there are 'substantial grounds' for disputing the sum claimed such that the matter cannot be dealt with summarily. Additionally (in the case of interlocutory applications), by rule 9C(1)(b) and (c), such an order shall not be made where the receiving party is a legally aided person or party under disability, and that party's legal representative (or guardian *ad litem, etc*) does not waive the right to claim a further sum. This reflects the fact that in such cases the legal representative may be entitled to claim common fund costs, recoverable out of the client's winnings, over and above what is recovered on the party and party basis. If such claim is not waived, there may have to be a

taxation anyway, at which it may be necessary to consider which items are properly party and party, and which common fund.

See also the commentary under rule 9A as to when summary assessment of the costs of interlocutory applications is appropriate.

### [62.9.8]   Matters to be considered by court on summary assessment of costs
See the commentary under rule 9A, concerning summary assessment of the costs of interlocutory applications. The same considerations should apply here.

### [62.9.9]   Time for payment of summarily assessed costs
Where the court has summarily assessed costs under rule 9(4)(b), those costs must be paid within 14 days or such other period as the court may specify. See rule 9B.

### [62.9.10]   Appeal against summary assessment of costs
Some guidance as to the court's approach on an appeal against a summary assessment of costs might be obtained from the cases concerning appeals from gross sum assessments under the former gross sum assessment procedure.

In *Fairview Park Property Management Ltd v Sun Wai Chun* [1999] 4 HKC 42 (CA) a gross sum assessment of costs was considered on appeal. It was noted that the judge had before him relevant costs schedules, and the Court of Appeal declined to interfere with what it regarded as an exercise of discretion.

Leave to appeal a gross sum assessment of costs was refused in *The Columbus Caravelle* HCAJ 282/2000 (Waung J; 06.11.2003), the judge noting that such assessments save costs and avoid delay.

**9A. Summary assessment of costs of interlocutory application** (O. 62 r. 9A)
    **(1)   Where the Court has determined an interlocutory application at any stage of proceedings and orders a party to pay costs in respect of the interlocutory application to any other party, it may, if it considers it appropriate to do so but subject to rule 9C —**
        **(a)   make a summary assessment of the costs by ordering payment of a sum of money to that other party in lieu of taxed costs;**
        **(b)   make a summary assessment of the costs by ordering payment of a sum of money to that other party in lieu of taxed costs but subject to the right of either party to have the costs taxed pursuant to paragraph (2); or**
        **(c)   order that the costs be taxed in accordance with this Order.**
    **(2)   Where the Court has made an order under paragraph (1)(b), either party to the interlocutory application is entitled to have the costs in respect of the interlocutory application taxed in accordance with this Order.**
    **(3)   Upon taxation pursuant to paragraph (2) —**
        **(a)   if the amount of taxed costs in respect of the interlocutory application equals the amount paid pursuant to an order made under paragraph (1)(b), the taxing master shall direct that no further amount is payable in respect of the taxed costs;**

     (b)  if the amount of the taxed costs in respect of the interlocutory application exceeds the amount paid pursuant to an order made under paragraph (1)(b), the taxing master may —

        (i)  direct the party against whom the order was made to pay the shortfall; or

        (ii)  set off the shortfall against any other costs to which the party against whom the order was made is entitled and direct payment of any balance; and

     (c)  if the amount paid pursuant to an order made under paragraph (1)(b) exceeds the amount of the taxed costs in respect of the interlocutory application, the taxing master may —

        (i)  direct the party in whose favour the order was made to pay the difference; or

        (ii)  set off the difference against any other costs to which the party in whose favour the order was made is entitled and direct payment of any balance.

  (4)  Where —

     (a)  the amount paid pursuant to an order made under paragraph (1) (b) equals or exceeds the amount of the taxed costs in respect of the interlocutory application; or

     (b)  the taxed costs in respect of the interlocutory application do not materially exceed the amount paid pursuant to an order made under paragraph (1)(b),

the taxing master may make such order as to the costs of the taxation or such other order as he considers appropriate.

  (5)  In determining whether the taxed costs materially exceed the amount paid pursuant to an order made under paragraph (1)(b), the taxing master shall, in addition to any other matter that he may consider relevant, have regard to —

     (a)  the amount by which the taxed costs exceed the amount paid pursuant to the order made under paragraph (1)(b); and

     (b)  whether the exceeded amount is disproportionate to the costs of the taxation.

                                    **(L.N. 152 of 2008)**

## NOTES

**[62.9A.1]** **Origin of Order 62 rule 9A, and comparison with previous rule**

Order 62 rule 9A was completely replaced as part of the civil justice reforms, taking effect in 2009. It provides for the summary assessment of the costs of interlocutory applications. For summary assessment of non-interlocutory proceedings, see rule 9(4) (b) and the commentary thereunder. The current rule 9A replaced a rule giving the court power to order interim payment of an approximation of the amount of costs which would be allowed on taxation in respect of an interlocutory costs order (as to which see *Wellcherry Ltd v Wellcherry Ltd* CACV 36/2000 (Godfrey VP & Rogers JA; 23.05.2000)). The purpose of that rule was to provide the receiving party with early recompense for its expenditure of costs without having to wait for formal taxation: *Dallah Albaraka (Ireland) Ltd v Symphony Gems NV & Ors* HCA 2555/2003 (Stone

J; 21.01.2005). Now rule 9B requires payment of summarily assessed costs within 14 days, but there is no express provision for part payment pending taxation. In *Re Hawkins Dev't Ltd* [2010] 1 HKC 131 it was held that there is thus a procedural lacuna, and inherent jurisdiction was relied upon to fill the gap. The court ordered payment out of court of money deposited as security for costs, in part satisfaction of a costs order, pending taxation.

Under the previous rule 9A it was held that once the receiving party's costs had been taxed, the rule no longer applied (*Green Park Properties Ltd v Dorku Ltd* [2001] 4 HKC 496, where an interim payment order made on adjournment of a review of taxation was set aside). There would appear to be no reason why the same should not apply under the current rule 9A.

**[62.9A.2]    Summary assessment or taxation of costs of interlocutory application**
Order 62 rule 9A(1) provides that when making an order for costs of an interlocutory application, the court may, instead of ordering costs of the application to be taxed, make a summary assessment of those costs, with or without the right of either party to proceed to taxation if not satisfied with the summary assessment. The power extends to the Registrar and masters: this follows from the grant of the power to 'the Court', which is defined in Order 1 rule 4(2) to include any judge of the Court of First Instance sitting in court or chambers and the Registrar or any master.

This power is not new in the sense that prior to the civil justice reforms rule 9(4)(b) provided for gross sum assessments of costs, and at the time extended to interlocutory applications. However, the Chief Justice's working party considered that the application of that provision was 'uneven', referring to the interim report where it was reported that its use was 'highly exceptional' except in relation to small items such as time summonses heard by masters. The working party envisioned 'a more systematic and better-informed process of summary assessment' (final report, para 536) and that it be used more widely. Under the Costs practice direction (PD 14.3), para 6, the court will give preference to summary assessment, or provisional taxation without a hearing (as to which see O 62 rule 21B), rather than full taxation, when it comes to the costs of interlocutory applications.

The Chief Justice's working party saw summary assessment as having two main features, which it clearly saw as advantages. There are (final report, para 529):

(a)    Immediacy of payment. Rule 9B requires payment of summarily assessed costs within 14 days whereas an order for costs 'in any event' does not result in an ascertained sum which must be paid until after the conclusion of the proceedings. This feature serves as a sanction against making unwarranted interlocutory applications or resisting meritorious ones; and

(b)    Saving the costs of taxation by assessing the costs of interlocutory applications in a 'broad-brush' way.

Another advantage of the summary assessment procedure is that no taxation fee is payable: see para 39(3) of the Costs practice direction, PD 14.3.

Rule 9A should be read together with rules 9B-9D.

**[62.9A.3]    Summary assessment may be made subject to right to seek taxation**
Under Order 62 rule 9A(1) the court's choice as to the manner of assessment of costs of an interlocutory application is not limited to summary assessment and taxation.

Instead the court may choose the middle ground of rule 9A(1)(b) and make a summary assessment of the costs subject to the right of either party to proceed to taxation. It appears that in the event of such an order the paying party cannot delay making payment by electing to proceed to taxation. The wording of rule 9A(3) suggests that the summarily assessed amount of costs must be paid in accordance with rule 9B and then, if either party proceeds to taxation, there will, after such taxation, be a direction of the taxing master as to payment of any outstanding balance or repayment of excess.

A party unhappy with the amount allowed on a summary assessment should consider carefully before proceeding to taxation. This is because rule 9A(4)(b) clearly contemplates that an adverse order as to the costs of taxation may be made if the amount allowed on taxation does not 'materially exceed' the amount which was determined on the summary assessment. In considering whether the taxed costs materially exceed the summarily assessed amount, the court will consider not only the two amounts, but will consider any gain in proportion to the costs of the taxation: see rule 9A(5).

**[62.9A.4] Circumstances in which summary assessment of costs appropriate**
The power under rule 9A to assess summarily the costs of an interlocutory application is clearly discretionary. The discretion is subject to rule 9C, which provides that such an order shall not be made where there are 'substantial grounds' for disputing the sum claimed which cannot be dealt with summarily, or, in the case of a legally aided person or party under disability, where the representative does not waive the right to claim a further sum.

In recommending adoption of the summary assessment of costs procedure, the Chief Justice's working party on civil justice reform intended that such orders be made in circumstances much more broad than those in which the previous interim payment procedure under the former rule 9A had been used. That power, the working party noted (at para 545), was 'only exercisable where the application or resistance to the application is frivolous or vexatious' or for some other reason the order was just. By contrast, the provisional summary assessment power was envisaged by the working party 'to cover all such cases, but should be wider and more general, enabling the court to make a provisional summary assessment where appropriate, for instance where this is likely to save costs', meaning the costs of taxation.

Insofar as the summary assessment procedure is available in cases of frivolous or vexatious conduct, the decisions concerning use of its predecessor in such cases may be relevant. They include *Roger SK Wong t/a Roger SK Wong & Co v Thomas & Anor* HCA 27/2004 (Deputy Judge To; 30.03.2004) and *Re Kennedy (No 3)* [2005] 2 HKC 73.

Under the previous procedure it was held that where the quantum of costs cannot readily be estimated the court should make an order under Order 62 rule 4(1) that costs be taxed and paid forthwith: *True Rank Holdings Ltd v Lam & Ors* HCMP 4078/2003 (Deputy Judge Muttrie; 11.02.2004). The same should apply where under the new procedure there is difficulty in summarily assessing the quantum of costs. Likewise, the fact that the paying party claims lack of money should not be a ground to refuse the order, just as was the case under the previous procedure: *BS Moorjani v Ka Wah Bank Ltd* HCA 16440/1998 (Yam J; 03.09.2002).

**[62.9A.5] Materials to be considered by court on summary assessment – the 'statement of costs'**

Under the interim payment procedure under the former rule 9A, it was recognised that it was incumbent on the receiving party to put forward 'some materials, albeit not in great details, as to the level of costs incurred … and the components thereof so as to justify the amount': *Re Prudential Enterprise Ltd* HCCW 594/1999 (Chu J; 03.11.2003). A form of 'statement of costs' was devised by the Registrar. See the Registrar's note on assessment of costs attached to Law Society circular 08-214, which may be viewed on the members' zone of the Law Society's website. By Order 32 rule 11A(3)(c) masters are now empowered to direct the filing of statements of costs when dealing with interlocutory applications. The court has warned that parties who fail to comply with such a direction may be penalised in costs: see *Grand Victory Dev't Ltd v Ke Junxiang* HCA 2120/2008 (Master Levy; 22.05.2009) where it was said that a non-compliant receiving party may be disallowed costs for attending a summary assessment hearing, or face a global reduction of recoverable costs. The Chief Justice's working party on civil justice reform envisaged (at para 537) an automatic direction for the filing of a statement of costs where an interlocutory application is to be dealt with on paper, and that where heard orally, the parties be required to have available at the hearing statements of costs which would be claimed if awarded, showing:

(i)   the number of hours claimed
(ii)  the hourly rate claimed
(iii) the grade of fee earner
(iv)  the amount and nature of any disbursement to be claimed other than counsel's fee for appearing at the hearing
(v)   the amount of solicitors' costs to be claimed for attending or appearing at the hearing; and
(vi)  the fees of counsel to be claimed in respect of the hearing.

In the case of summary assessment of the costs of an interlocutory application, the required information should be set out in the form of 'Statement of Costs for Summary Assessment under Order 62 rule 9A' in Appendix A to the Costs practice direction, PD 14.3. In *World Chinese Business Investment Foundation Ltd & Ors v Shine Rainbow Marketing Ltd & Ors* [2010] 2 HKC 294 (Registrar Au-Yeung; 12.02.2010) practitioners were reminded to comply with para 8 of PD 14.3, which provides that the statement should be lodged and served together with the skeleton argument for the substantive interlocutory hearing.

**[62.9A.6] The court's approach on summary assessment**

According to para 13 of the practice direction on Costs (PD 14.3) the court will take a 'broad-brush' approach on summary assessment of costs, and it will not embark on a 'mini-taxation'. To facilitate this being done, it is provided in para 11 of the practice direction that a summary assessment will be conducted by the judge or master who dealt with the substantive application, who will obviously be familiar with the case. Because of the approach taken by the court, the practice direction advises (in para 13) that prolixity in the Statement of Costs is unacceptable, and costs for its preparation will not generally be allowed.

In *Ip Tsz Lam Ada v Pearl Wisdom Ltd* HCA 2482/2007 (Sakhrani J; 30.04.2009) the court confirmed the broadbrush approach. Referring to the underlying objectives in Order 1A rule 1, in particular (a) cost-effectiveness and (c) reasonable proportion and procedural economy, the court found a claim of more than $600,000 as the costs of an amendment application to be 'unreasonable and disproportionate' and reduced it to less than $100,000.

**9B. Time for complying with direction or order for summary assessment** (O. 62 r. 9B)

**(1)   A party shall comply with a direction or order under rule 9(4)(b) or 9A(1)(a) or (b) for payment of a sum of money —**

   **(a)   within 14 days of the date of the direction or order; or**

   **(b)   by such date as the Court may specify.**

**(2)   Paragraph (1) does not apply if the party is an aided person.**

**(L.N. 152 of 2008)**

---

**NOTES**

**[62.9B.1]   Time for payment of summarily assessed costs**

Order 62 rule 9B provides that when costs have been summarily assessed, whether under rule 9(4)(b) (which applies to costs orders not relating to interlocutory matters) or under rule 9A(1) (which applies to interlocutory orders), the amount assessed must be paid within 14 days, unless the court has specified another time for payment. With regard to interlocutory orders under rule 9A(1)(b) where there is an option to proceed to taxation, payment cannot be delayed by electing to challenge the summary assessment by taking up that option.

**9C. When summary assessment not allowed** (O. 62 r. 9C)

**(1)   No direction or order may be made under rule 9(4)(b) or 9A(1)(a) or (b) for the payment of a sum of money if —**

   **(a)   the paying party shows substantial grounds for disputing the sum claimed for costs that cannot be dealt with summarily;**

   **(b)   the receiving party is an aided person, and the legal representative acting for the receiving party has not waived the right to any further sum of money in respect of the costs of the interlocutory application; or**

   **(c)   the receiving party is a person under disability as defined in Order 80, rule 1, and the legal representative (or the next friend or guardian ad litem) acting for the person under disability has not waived the right to any further sum of money in respect of the costs of the interlocutory application.**

**(2)   In this rule —**

**"paying party" means the party against whom a direction or order under rule 9(4)(b) or 9A(1)(a) or (b) is made;**

**"receiving party" means the party in whose favour a direction or order under rule 9(4)(b) or 9A(1)(a) or (b) is made.**

**(L.N. 152 of 2008)**

**NOTES**

**[62.9C.1]   Restriction on use of summary assessment procedure**
Order 62 rule 9C restricts the court's discretion to use the summary assessment of
costs procedure. The rule provides that the procedure shall not be used where there
are 'substantial grounds' for disputing the sum claimed which cannot be dealt with
summarily. Further the procedure shall not be used where the receiving party is a
legally aided person or a party under disability unless the legal representative waives
any right to further costs. The latter two restrictions protect the rights of possibly
vulnerable parties, who may later be responsible for the balance of legal costs
incurred on their behalf out of money recovered. They are expressed to be in respect
of interlocutory applications. However, in *Ma Hoi Ki v Li Chi Chuen & Anor* [2009]
2 HKC 488 (para 27) it was suggested that they should in fact extend to any costs of
the application, cause or matter.

   In *Sun Hung Kai Investment Services Ltd v Quality Prince Ltd & Ors* HCA
1995/2008 (Master C Chan; 12.08.2009) the court refused an application by both
parties for taxation of costs instead of summary assessment. Referring to the cost-
effectiveness and fair distribution of resources objectives of civil justice reform, the
court noted that taxation takes up a lot of court time and that the costs of taxation are
often not in proportion to the claim. Summary assessment had the advantage of the
hearing master doing the assessment 'while the case is still fresh in his mind and he
can easily decide what is necessary and proper'.

**9D. When to tax costs** (O. 62 r. 9D)
   **(1)   Subject to paragraphs (2) and (4), the costs of any proceedings shall not
be taxed until the conclusion of the action.**
   **(2)   If it appears to the Court when making a costs order that all or any
part of the costs ought to be taxed at an earlier stage it may order accordingly.**
   **(3)   No order may be made under paragraph (2) in a case where the person
against whom the costs order is made is an aided person.**
   **(4)   Where it appears to a taxing master that there is no likelihood of any
further order being made in a cause or matter, he may order the person entitled
to payment of the costs of any interlocutory proceedings which have taken place
to commence taxation proceedings in accordance with rule 21.**
                                                        **(L.N. 152 of 2008)**

**[62.9D.1]   The timing of taxation proceedings**
Order 62 rule 9D provides that costs orders should be taxed at the conclusion of the
action, unless the court makes an order for an earlier taxation or it appears to the court
that the case will go no further. This is a salutary provision since by the conclusion
of the action there may be several different costs orders which can be considered by
the parties in their totality with a view to overall settlement or, if no settlement, can
be taxed together.

   Rule 9D was added as part of the civil justice reforms which took effect on 2
April 2009. Previously a party was entitled to proceed to taxation of an interlocutory
costs order immediately unless the order was expressed to be for costs 'in any event',
meaning they were not taxable or recoverable until the conclusion of the case:

*Aktieselskabet Dansk Skibsfinansiering v Wheelock Marden & Co Ltd* [1994] 1 HKC 607. Under the new rule 8D, the 'default position' is that a party in whose favour a costs order is made may proceed to taxation only after conclusion of an action 'unless the costs order specifies taxation to be "forthwith" or at some designated time': *Big Boss Investment Ltd v So Lai Kei & Anor* [2010] 1 HKLRD 793.

If an action is struck out, stayed or settled, it may be considered to have come to a conclusion so that taxation might ensue: *Sang Hing Mechanical & Electrical Eng'g Ltd v Arnhold & Co Ltd* [2005] 1 HKLRD 540.

**[62.9D.2] Order for costs to be taxed and paid forthwith**
In appropriate cases the court orders costs to be taxed and paid forthwith. Such an order is a departure from general rule expressed in Order 62 rule 9D that costs are to be taxed (and therefore paid) at the conclusion of an action.

An order for costs to be taxed and paid forthwith is sometimes intended to reflect disapproval of the conduct of the paying party. For example, since the implementation of the civil justice reforms in 2009 such orders are considered appropriate to discourage parties from unnecessarily and unreasonably maintaining or resisting interlocutory applications. See *Wong Yau Kwan & Ors v Zhang Hongjie & Ors* HCCW 574/2009 (Poon J; 19.05.2010) (para 4) referring to *Hui Yin Sang v Tsoi Ping Kwan* HCA 392/2008 (Sakhrani J; 14.07.2009) (para 17).

In the case of costs which are summarily assessed rather than taxed, there is no real need for an express order for payment forthwith because Order 62 rule 9B stipulates that such costs must be paid within 14 days unless otherwise ordered.

**10. When a party may sign judgment for costs without an order (O. 62 r. 10)**
**(1) Where a plaintiff by notice in writing and without leave either wholly discontinues his action against any defendant or withdraws any particular claim made or question raised by him therein as against any defendant, the defendant may tax his costs of the action or his costs occasioned by the matter withdrawn, as the case may be, and, if the taxed costs are not paid within 4 days after taxation, may sign judgment for them. (See App. A, Form 50)**
**(2) (Repealed, L.N. 152 of 2008)**
**(3) (Repealed, L.N. 152 of 2008)**
**(4) (Repealed, L.N. 152 of 2008)**
**(5) In the circumstances mentioned in this rule, Order 22, rules 20 and 21 and Order 25, rule 1C(6) an order for costs shall be deemed to have been made to the effect described and, for the purposes of section 49 of the Ordinance, the order shall be deemed to have been entered up on the date on which the event which gave rise to the entitlement to cost occurred. (L.N. 403 of 1992) (L.N. 152 of 2008)**

---

**NOTES**

**[62.10.1] Rule 10(1) – costs on discontinuance or withdrawal without leave**
Order 62 rule 10(1) provides that where an action has been discontinued or withdrawn without leave, the defendant may proceed to tax its costs. The purpose is to enable the defendant to recover its costs without the need for a court order, which would

normally be required by Order 62 rule 3(1). With regard to counterclaims, the equivalent provision is Order 62 rule 3(7).

The situation is different where leave is granted to discontinue or withdraw. When granting leave the court has a discretion as to what costs order to make. See the commentary under Order 21 rule 2, and see *Robbins & Anor v Peaktop Technologies (USA) HK Ltd* HCMP 2456/2006 (Barma J; 16.05.2007) where the court rejected an argument that Order 62 rule 10 applies where a party applies for leave to withdraw.

### [62.10.2]   Costs on acceptance of payment into court
Order 62 rule 10(2), (3) and (4) were repealed as part of the civil justice reforms which took effect on 02.04.2009. They provided that a plaintiff who accepted money paid into court under the former Order 22 was entitled to tax his costs. The payment into court procedure was repealed by the civil justice reforms and replaced with the sanctioned offer and sanctioned payment procedures in a wholly new Order 22. However, the transitional provision in Order 22 rule 28 preserves the prior Order 22 procedures, including the repealed provisions of Order 62 rule 10, in cases where a payment into court had been made and disposal of it was pending when the civil justice reforms came into force.

### [62.10.3]   Rule 10(5) – deemed order for costs
Order 62 rule 10(5) deems an order for costs to have been made in each of the circumstances provided for in the rule whereby a party may tax costs (under rule 11) without an order. For the purposes of section 49 of the High Court Ordinance (interest on judgments), the order is deemed to have been entered when the event giving rise to the entitlement to costs occurred. The effect, so far as costs payable on acceptance of a sanctioned payment or sanctioned offer under Order 22 is concerned, is that interest runs on those costs from the acceptance, and *Legal Aid Board v Russell* [1990] 2 QB 607 (CA); [1991] 2 AC 317 (HL) (where it was held that interest does not run in such cases) is ousted.

As to interest on costs generally, see the commentary under Order 62 rule 3.

The District Court equivalent of this rule (which is in the same terms and has the same number) was held to be of no effect in *Ho Kin Chung v Tsang Hiu Sang* [2001] 1 HKC 110, 120H-I. It was held that the rule is inconsistent with the court's discretion under the District Court Ordinance to determine by whom and to what extent costs shall be paid. The provision in the Ordinance must prevail over the rule, which is subsidiary legislation. The equivalent provision in the High Court Ordinance (section 52A) is expressly subject to the rules of court, and it follows that so far as the High Court is concerned, there is no inconsistency between the two provisions. In other words the validity of Order 62 rule 10(5) RHC is not in question. In any event *Ho Kin Chung* was doubted in some respects by *Cho Ho Kuen v Yu Kwok Wah & Ors* [2001] 3 HKC 566 (CA), and in *Ngai Chu Sing v Chan Wai Ho* DCPI 547/2003 (para 5) the court considered it to have been 'disapproved' thereby.

### 11.  When order for taxation of costs not required (O. 62 r. 11)
**(1)   Where an action, petition or summons is dismissed with costs, or a motion is refused with costs, or an order of the Court directs the payment of any costs, or any party is entitled under rule 10 to tax his costs, no order directing the taxation of those costs need be made.**

**(2)   Where a summons is taken out to set aside with costs any proceeding on the ground of irregularity and the summons is dismissed but no direction is given as to costs, the summons is to be taken as having been dismissed with costs.**

**11A.  Commencement of costs-only proceedings** (O. 62 r. 11A)
**(1)   Proceedings under section 52B(2) of the Ordinance may be commenced by originating summons in Form No. 10 in Appendix A.**
**(2)   The originating summons must be accompanied by —**
**(a)   an affidavit exhibiting the agreement referred to in section 52B(1) of the Ordinance; and**
**(b)   the plaintiff's bill of costs or statement of costs.**
**(3)   An acknowledgement of service of the originating summons must be in Form No. 15A in Appendix A.**
**(4)   A master may make a summary assessment of or an order for taxation of the costs that are the subject matter of the proceedings commenced in accordance with paragraph (1).**
**(5)   Orders 13A, 22 and 27 and Order 28, rules 1A, 4(3) to (5) and 7 to 9 do not apply in relation to the proceedings commenced in accordance with paragraph (1) unless otherwise directed by the Court.**

(L.N. 152 of 2008)

**NOTES**

**[62.11A.1]   Costs only proceedings**
Order 62 rule 11A governs the commencement of 'costs only proceedings' under section 52B of the High Court Ordinance. Such proceedings may be commenced where a civil dispute has been settled without issue of a writ and, although the parties have agreed who is to pay the costs of and incidental to the dispute, there is no agreement as to the amount of those costs. The agreement between the parties must be in writing: s 52B(1)(b). Proceedings may be commenced in relation to costs, and the court may by section 52B(3) make various types of order in relation to such costs, including an order that they be taxed or assessed.

Costs only proceedings derive from CPR 44.12A in England and Wales, which is in terms similar to s 52B, save that the CPR provide that costs only proceedings must be dismissed if opposed. Our sister publication in the UK, The Civil Court Practice, notes (at CPR 44.12A[3]) that this aspect of the English provision has caused concern. It has not been adopted in Hong Kong. In any event it is difficult to contemplate why costs only proceedings would be opposed, given that the jurisdiction to bring such an application is predicated on there being an agreement as to liability for costs. In all likelihood, any opposition would be to *quantum*, rather than the bringing of the application itself.

The Chief Justice's working party on civil justice reform recommended the adoption of costs only proceedings in Hong Kong partly because of concerns that pre-action protocols (which are contemplated by the civil justice reforms, though adopted only to a limited extent, such as in cases within the personal injuries list) could result in the front-loading of costs which would be an extra hurdle to achieving amicable settlement of civil disputes. The working party said (at para 134):

Where the substance of a dispute is settled, the parties are often able to reach a global settlement covering the costs incurred. However, this is not always the case and costs can be a fatal sticking point. Such costs may be in more significant amounts where pre-action protocols have been observed and so may become a more important factor in determining whether settlement can be achieved. A defendant who is prepared to accept liability and to pay the damages claimed may nevertheless regard the claimant's costs incurred in meeting protocol obligations to be unreasonably high and unacceptable. It is therefore important that the front-loaded costs generated by pre-action protocols should not be allowed to undermine settlements achievable on the substantive dispute.

Costs only proceedings allow the parties to settle the substantive dispute, including liability for costs, and apply to the court for adjudication of the quantum of such costs.

### [62.11A.2]  Procedure in costs only proceedings

Aspects of the procedure in costs only proceedings under section 52B HCO are governed by Order 62 rule 6A. It is there provided that the party against which it is proposed to seek costs by means of costs only proceedings is entitled to an opportunity to be heard.

Rule 11A provides that the application should be commenced by originating summons in Form No 10 in appendix A, which is the expedited form, and must be supported by affidavit evidence exhibiting the agreement of the parties settling the dispute. According to para 41 of the Costs practice direction, the affidavit should additionally show compliance with statutory requirements and 'briefly describe the claim or dispute which the agreement to pay costs relates and the terms of settlement'.

The originating summons must be accompanied by the bill of costs or statement of costs of the party claiming costs: rule 11A(2)(b). The bill or statement of costs should be in form A or B annexed to the Costs practice direction (see para 40 of the practice direction).

A special form of acknowledgement of service for costs only proceedings is prescribed in form No 15A in appendix A. This form gives the defendant the opportunity to indicate an intention to contest liability for costs (which seems a rather unlikely event given that the costs only jurisdiction is based on an agreement to pay costs) or the amount of those costs.

According to practice direction 14.2, an originating summons commencing costs only proceedings will in the first instance be returnable before a master in chambers (open to the public).

Once an order is made for taxation in costs only proceedings, the Costs practice direction should be followed. See generally part C of that practice direction.

### [62.11A.3]  Summary assessment or taxation

Order 62 rule 11A(4) provides that costs claimed by way of costs only proceedings may be summarily assessed by a master, or referred to taxation. According to paragraph 39 of the Costs practice direction, the plaintiff may elect in the originating summons by which costs only proceedings are commenced to proceed by way of summary assessment or taxation.

With regard to summary assessment generally, see Order 62 rules 9(4)(b) and 9A, and the commentary thereunder.

**12. Powers of taxing masters to tax costs** (O. 62 r. 12)

    (1)   A taxing master shall have power to tax —

        (a)   the costs of or incidental to any proceedings in the High Court;

        (aa) the costs that are the subject matter of the proceedings commenced in accordance with rule 11A(1);

        (b)   the costs directed by an award made on a reference to arbitration under any enactment or pursuant to an arbitration agreement to be paid; and

        (c)   any other costs the taxation of which is directed by an order of the Court.

(L.N. 152 of 2008)

**NOTES**

**[62.12.1]  Enlargement of powers of taxing master**

Order 62 rule 12 sets out the circumstances in which a taxing master has power to tax costs. The rule was amended as part of the civil justice reform with effect from 2009, in particular by adding rule 12(1)(aa) to provide expressly that the taxing master has power to tax costs to which costs-only proceedings relate (as to which, see rule 11A and the commentary thereunder).

**13. Powers of certain judicial clerks to tax costs** (O. 62 r. 13)

    (HK)(1)  A Chief Judicial Clerk shall have power to transact all such business and exercise all such authority as under rule 21B of this Order may be transacted and exercised by the taxing master and to issue a certificate for any costs taxed by him. (L.N. 152 of 2008)

    (1A)  Paragraph (1) only applies if the amount of the bill of costs does not exceed the sum of $200,000. (L.N. 152 of 2008)

    (2)  Paragraph (1) shall not be taken as empowering a Chief Judicial Clerk to tax any costs the taxation of which is set down for hearing under rule 21B(4) or 21C(1). (L.N. 152 of 2008)

    (3)  In exercising the powers conferred on him by this Order, a Chief Judicial Clerk shall comply with any directions given to him by a taxing master.

(L.N. 343 of 1989)

**NOTES**

**[62.13.1]  Chief judicial clerk may deal with taxation up to $200,000**

Order 62 rule 13 provides that a chief judicial clerk may exercise the powers of a taxing master under rule 21B with regard to taxing a bill of costs without a hearing or setting it down for hearing, where the bills of costs claims no more than $200,000. The rule was amended as part of the civil justice reforms which took effect in April 2009 so as to add that power. It replaces the previous system of provisional taxation whereby a taxing master or chief judicial clerk could, without a hearing, assess a bill of costs claiming up to $100,000 and notify the parties the amount proposed to be allowed (the former Order 62 rule 13 and 21(4)).

**13A. Taxing master may give directions** (O. 62 r. 13A)

   **(1)**   **A taxing master may give directions —**

      **(a)**   **for the just and expeditious disposal of the taxation of a bill of costs; and**

      **(b)**   **for saving the costs of taxation.**

   **(2)**   **Without limiting the generality of paragraph (1), a taxing master may give directions as to —**

      **(a)**   **the form and contents of a bill of costs;**

      **(b)**   **the filing of papers and vouchers;**

      **(c)**   **the manner in which —**

         **(i)**   **any objections to a bill of costs may be raised; and**

         **(ii)**   **any reply to those objections may be made; and**

      **(d)**   **the steps to be taken or things to be done at any stage of the taxation proceedings.**

**(L.N. 152 of 2008)**

---

**NOTES**

**[62.13A.1]**   **Power of taxing master to give directions**

Order 62 rule 13A gives the taxing master express powers to give directions relating to the taxation of a bill of costs. The rule was introduced as part of the civil justice reforms which took effect in April 2009. It gives a legislative basis to the previous practice whereby directions as to the conduct of taxations were given at a call-over hearing under practice direction 14.3.

A taxing master may refuse to proceed with a taxation if directions given under this rule have not been complied with: rule 21A(3). Alternatively the taxing master may proceed provided that the party in default was duly served with the taxation notice and bill of costs: rule 24(1). If it is necessary for taxation proceedings to be adjourned because of failure to comply with directions, the taxing master may make an order in respect of the costs thrown away: rule 26(2).

**[62.13A.2]**   **Standard directions**

The practice direction on Costs prescribes standard directions which take effect on service of the notice of commencement of taxation ('NOCT') under rule 21, unless otherwise directed. Those directions (PD 14.3, para 21) are:

(1) Within 28 days of service of the NOCT, the paying party shall file and serve a list of objections, failing which the receiving party may apply to the taxing Master for the bill to be taxed as drawn as provided for in paragraph 23 below.

(2) In the event that no settlement on the whole bill can be reached within 28 days after service of the list of objections, the receiving party shall file and serve an application in the form of Appendix E ('Application to Set Down a Bill for Taxation').

See rule 21A with regard to setting down a bill for taxation.

**[62.13A.3]   Failure to comply with direction to file list of objections**

As mentioned above, a paying party who fails to file and serve a list of objections to the receiving party's bill of costs in accordance with the standard directions, may find that the bill will be taxed as drawn. In *Citi Creation Investment Ltd v IO Kwai Wan Industrial Bldg & Ors* LDBM 180/2009 (Judge HC Wong; 22.03.2010) it was held that thereafter it remains open to the paying party to apply under rule 21B for a taxation hearing.

**[62.13A.4]   Direction as to preparation of taxation bundle**

Order 62 rule 13A(2)(b) empowers the taxing master to give directions as to the filing of papers and vouchers for the purpose of a taxation. See part 2(f) (para 28 *et seq*) of the Costs practice direction as to the preparation and filing of documents in a bundle for the purposes of provisional taxation or taxation with a hearing.

**[62.13A.5]   Transfer of issue to a judge for decision**

A taxing master may refer a preliminary point arising on a taxation of costs for decision by a judge. The power to do so is under Order 32 rule 12. See *Chun Wo Construction & Eng'g Co Ltd v China Win Eng'g Ltd* HCCT 37/2006 (Lam J; 12.06.2008) (para 108); *To Kan Chi & Ors v Miller Peart* HCMP 2111/2005 (Master Ho; 12.05.2010) (para 21).

**14.  Supplementary powers of taxing masters** (O. 62 r. 14)

**A taxing master may, in the discharge of his functions with respect to the taxation of costs—**

    **(a)   take an account of any dealing in money made in connection with the payment of the costs being taxed, if the Court so directs;**

    **(b)   require any party represented jointly with any other party in any proceedings before him to be separately represented;**

    **(c)   examine any witness in those proceedings;**

    **(d)   direct the production of any document which may be relevant in connection with those proceedings;**

    **(e)   correct any clerical mistake in any certificate or order, or any error arising therein from any accidental slip or omission.**

**NOTES**

**[62.14.1]   Resolution of factual issues in taxation proceedings**

Order 62 rule 14(c) and (d) empower the taxing master to examine any witness and direct the production of relevant documents. As to the exercise of this power, the following points emerge from *Hotung v Hillhead Ltd & Ors* HCA 1738/2006 (Master Marlene Ng; 31.12.2009) (para 136 *et seq*):

•   These powers should only be exercised if there is a genuine and relevant factual issue which cannot be resolved in any other way.

•   The power to order production of documents is limited to documents relevant to the taxation, and is subject to any claim to privilege.

**15. Disposal of business by one taxing master for another** (O. 62 r. 15)

(1)   If, apart from this paragraph, a taxing master has power to tax any costs, the taxation of which has been assigned to some other taxing master, he may tax those costs and if, apart from this paragraph, he has power to issue a certificate for the taxed costs he shall issue a certificate for them.

(2)   Any taxing master may assist any other taxing master in the taxation of any costs the taxation of which has been assigned to that other officer.

(3)   On an application in that behalf made by a party to any cause or matter, a taxing master may, and if the circumstances require it shall, hear and dispose of any application in the cause or matter on behalf of the taxing master by whom the application would otherwise be heard.

**16. Extension etc., of time** (O. 62 r. 16)

(1)   A taxing master may—

(a)   extend the period within which a party is required by or under this Order to begin proceedings for taxation or to do anything in or in connection with proceedings before that master;

(b)   extend the period provided by rule 33(2) beyond the signing of the taxing officer's certificate by setting the certificate aside;

(c)   where no period is specified by or under this Order or by the Court for the doing of anything in or in connection with such proceedings, specify the period within which the thing is to be done.

(2)   Where an order of the Court specifies a period within which anything is to be done by or before a taxing master, then unless the Court otherwise directs, the taxing master may from time to time extend the period so specified on such terms (if any) as he thinks just.

(3)   A taxing master may extend any such period as is referred to in the foregoing provisions of this rule although the application for extension is not made until after the expiration of that period.

**17. Interim certificates** (O. 62 r. 17)

(1)   A taxing master may from time to time in the course of the taxation of any costs by him issue an interim certificate for any part of those costs which has been taxed.

(2)   If, in the course of the taxation of a solicitor's bill to his own client, it appears to the taxing master that in any event the solicitor will be liable in connection with that bill to pay money to the client, he may from time to time issue an interim certificate specifying an amount which in his opinion is payable by the solicitor to his client.

(3)   On the filing of a certificate issued under paragraph (2), the Court may order the amount specified therein to be paid forthwith to the client or into court.

_____

**NOTES**

**[62.17.1]   Interim certificate for costs and immediate payment**

Order 62 rule 17 'clearly caters for the situation whereby the taxing master before the completion of the taxation considers appropriate to order part payment of the costs claimed': see *SY Engineering Co Ltd v Hong Kong Housing Authority* [2001] 2 HKC 226, 229E–F. An interim certificate may only be granted in respect of part of the costs which have been taxed: rule 17(1). This may be in respect of items of costs already taxed when a taxation is adjourned part heard (as in *SY Engineering*), or in respect of items to which no objection is made in the paying party's list of objections: *Tsang Sau Hing Beatrice & Anor v Yeung Man Loong Maxly & Ors* [2009] 5 HKC 154.

**17A.  Final certificate** (O. 62 r. 17A)
    **(1)   A taxing master shall, after the conclusion of taxation proceedings before him, issue a final certificate specifying the amount of taxed costs and the amount of money payable under rule 32B.**
    **(2)   A taxing master shall not issue a final certificate unless the period within which an application for review of his decision may be made under rule 33(2) has expired.**
    **(3)   A taxing master may set aside a final certificate for good reasons and on such terms as he thinks fit.**
                                                        **(L.N. 152 of 2008)**

**17B.  Taxing master may set aside his own decision** (O. 62 r. 17B)
    **If a party entitled to be heard on taxation fails to raise any objection to a bill of costs or to appear at a hearing set down under rule 21B(4) or 21C(1), a decision of a taxing master made against that party may be set aside or varied by the taxing master for good reasons and on such terms as he thinks fit.**
                                                        **(L.N. 152 of 2008)**

**18.  Power of taxing master where party liable to be paid and to pay costs** (O. 62 r. 18)
    **Where a party entitled to be paid costs is also liable to pay costs, the taxing master may—**
            **(a)   tax the costs which that party is liable to pay and set off the amount allowed against the amount he is entitled to be paid and direct payment of any balance, or**
            **(b)   delay the issue of a certificate for the costs he is entitled to be paid until he has paid or tendered the amount he is liable to pay.**

---

**NOTES**

**[62.18.1]   Set off where defendant legally aided**
This rule sensibly provides for set off of costs payable by one party against costs payable to him by the opposing party.
    Special considerations arise where the defendant is legally aided or is a defendant by way of counterclaim. Under section 16C of the Legal Aid Ordinance (Cap 91) neither the Director of Legal Aid nor the aided person is liable for a plaintiff's costs against an aided defendant beyond the level of the aided person's contribution. In *Tam Kwok Kit v Addchance Ltd* (2000) HCA 12519 of 1997 (1 June 2000; Master Poon), it was held that the Director and the aided person are equally protected with respect to the costs of a counterclaim against a legally aided

plaintiff. There the trial judge had ordered the legally aided plaintiff to pay two-thirds of the defendant's costs of the counterclaim, and had also ordered that the defendant pay one-half of the aided plaintiff's costs of the main claim. The defendant sought an order enabling it to set off the one against the other under this rule. Master Poon held that the legally aided plaintiff, being a defendant under the counterclaim, was not susceptible to such a set off, nor was the Director liable.

**19. Taxation of bill of costs comprised in account** (O. 62 r. 19)

**(1) Where the Court directs an account to be taken and the account consists in part of a bill of costs, the Court may direct a taxing master to tax those costs and the taxing master shall tax the costs in accordance with the direction and shall return the bill of costs, after taxation thereof, together with his report thereon to the Court.**

**(2) A taxing master taxing a bill of costs in accordance with a direction under this rule shall have the same powers, and the same fees shall be payable in connection with the taxation, as if an order for taxation of the costs had been made by the Court.**

---

**NOTES**

**[62.19.1] Numbering**
There is no rule 20 in Order 62. The rule of equivalent number in the former English Rules of the Supreme Court gave taxing officers supplementary powers to take account of dealings in money in connection with payment of the costs being taxed, require separate representation of parties, examine witnesses and order production of documents.

**PROCEDURE ON TAXATION**

**21. Mode of commencing proceedings for taxation** (O. 62 r. 21)

**(1) A party entitled to payment of the costs of any action to be taxed may commence proceedings for the taxation of those costs by filing in the Court —**

    **(a) a notice of commencement of taxation; and**

    **(b) his bill of costs.**

**(2) The party shall serve a copy of the notice of commencement of taxation and of the bill of costs on every other party entitled to be heard on taxation within 7 days after the notice and the bill of costs were filed in the Court.**

**(3) The Court may give directions as to the service of a copy of the notice of commencement of taxation and of the bill of costs on any other person who may have a financial interest in the outcome of the taxation.**

**(4) It is not necessary for a copy of the notice of commencement of taxation or of the bill of costs to be served on any party who has not acknowledged service in the proceedings which gave rise to the taxation, except where —**

    **(a) an order for the taxation of the bill of costs of a solicitor is made under section 67 of the Legal Practitioners Ordinance (Cap 159) at the instance of the solicitor; or**

    **(b) the Court otherwise orders.**

**(5)** **A party shall, when he files a notice of commencement of taxation, pay to the Court a prescribed taxing fee.**

**(6)** **A person who has been served with a copy of the notice of commencement of taxation and of the bill of costs pursuant to paragraph (3) shall, within 7 days of the service, give notice in writing to the taxing master and all other parties entitled to be heard on taxation, stating —**

      **(a)** **his financial interest in the outcome of the taxation; and**

      **(b)** **whether he intends to take part in the taxation proceedings.**

**(7)** **A person who fails to comply with paragraph (6) is not entitled to —**

      **(a)** **receive from the Registrar or from any other party entitled to be heard on taxation any notice, application or other document relating to the taxation; and**

      **(b)** **to take part in the taxation proceedings.**

**(L.N. 152 of 2008)**

---

## NOTES

### [62.21.1]   Taxation of costs – commencement and procedure

If an award of costs is not summarily assessed under rule 9(4)(b) or 9A of Order 62, it will be necessary to proceed to taxation. Order 62 rule 21 provides that proceedings for the taxation of costs are to be commenced by filing a Notice of Commencement of Taxation together with the bill of costs to be taxed. The form of notice is set out in Annex D to practice direction on costs, and is referred to therein as the 'NOCT'. The form of bill of costs to be followed is chronological, and not by type of work. It is set out in Annex B to the practice direction.

Rule 21 goes on to make provision for service of the notice and bill and with regard to who may be heard on the taxation. See also the definition of 'party entitled to be heard on taxation' in Order 62 rule 1. Rule 21 was replaced as part of the civil justice reforms, taking effect in 2009. See also rules 21A-21D which were introduced at the same time.

*Service* – It will be noted that service is not limited to the parties to the proceedings: under rule 2(3) the court may direct service of anyone else who has a financial interest in the taxation. This could include an insurer or funder. Where such a direction has been made, the person concerned is a 'party entitled to be heard on taxation' within the definition of that term in Order 62 rule 1.

*Payment of taxation fee* – With regard to the taxation fee required to be paid in accordance with rule 2(5), see the High Court Fees Rules, subsidiary legislation under the High Court Ordinance (Cap 4). For refund of taxation fee where settlement is reached before the actual taxation, see Order 62 rule 21D.

*Response required from party who wishes to be heard* – Anyone served with the notice of commencement and bill by direction of the court under rule 21(3) must give written notice to the taxing master or will not be entitled to take part in the taxation: rule 21(6) and (7).

Taxation procedure is governed by part 2 of the Costs practice direction. In paragraph 21 it provides for standard directions to take effect. By those directions the paying party is required to file and serve a list of objections to the bill of costs within 28 days after the service of the notice of commencement of taxation. The form of list of objections is set out in Annex C to the practice direction. It is provided in the standard directions that if the paying party fails to file a list of objections, the receiving party may apply to the master for the bill to be taxed as drawn. That may be done by completing Part A of the Application to Set a Bill Down for Taxation (Annex E to the Costs practice direction) accordingly. On the other hand if a list of objections is filed, then, under the standard directions, if no settlement is reached on the whole bill within 28 days, the receiving party shall apply under rule 21A to set down the bill for taxation.

See also rule 13A which gives the taxing master wide power to give directions for the just and expeditious disposal of a taxation and for saving costs.

### [62.21.2]   Practice direction on costs

A practice direction on matters relating to the taxation of costs (PD 14.3) was issued contemporaneously with the amendments to Order 62 which came into force in 2009 as part of the civil justice reforms. The text of the Costs practice direction can be viewed on the judiciary website www.judiciary.gov.hk or that of the Hong Kong Legal Information Institute www.hklii.org, both of which are accessible by the general public free-of-charge.

### [62.21.3]   Prescribed form of bill of costs and list of objections

Annexes B and C to the practice direction on Costs set out respectively the forms of bill of costs and list of objections which should be followed in taxation proceedings and costs only proceedings. They came into effect along with the civil justice reforms in 2009. The form of bill of costs is chronological in format, whereas previously the commonly used format was by type of work. The previous format was criticised by the High Court masters as 'fragmented', 'repetitious and tedious' (para 780, final report, Chief Justice's working party on civil justice reform).

The chronological format was first published before the civil justice reforms came into force in 2009, with encouragement from the Registrar for it to be used (see Law Society circular 08-213). Now, under para 17 of the Costs practice direction, its use is more or less mandatory: para 17 of the practice direction says that it 'shall' be used as far as practicable. The paragraph goes on to provide that if there are special reasons why the prescribed format cannot be used, directions should be sought from the taxing master before the bill of costs is drafted. By para 18 the same applies to the prescribed form of list of objections.

### [62.21.4]   Hourly basis for recovery of solicitors' charges on party and party taxation

The prescribed form of bill of costs (see above) contemplates use of an hourly rate system with regard to recovery of party and party costs in relation to services provided by fee earners. This formalises a practice which has long been followed.

Under part I of the 1st schedule to Order 62, fixed amounts are recoverable for certain services provided by solicitors' firms which are suitable for junior unqualified staff. However, for other services, including those of qualified and unqualified fee earners, item 5 thereof merely provides that the Registrar may 'allow such fee as he thinks proper'. Since that provision was introduced in 1988 it has been accepted practice for the taxing master to exercise that discretion by reference to the length of time spent in each item of work, and an hourly rate which varies according to the status and experience of the fee earner concerned. Indicative hourly rates are published and used as guidance by the taxing masters in deciding what to allow on taxation for services provided by a particular fee earner. The full list of indicative hourly rates for services going back to 1985 can be viewed in Law Society circulars issued from time to time, for example circular 08-213. The indicative hourly rates which have applied for work done from July 1997 are as follows:

| No of Years of Practice | High Court | District Court |
|---|---|---|
| Newly admitted | From 1,600 to 2,000 | From 1,066 to 1,280 |
| 2 – 4 years | From 2,000 to 2,500 | From 1,350 to 1,650 |
| 5 – 6 years | From 2,400 to 3,000 | From 1,600 to 2,000 |
| 7 – 8 years | From 2,900 to 3,500 | From 1,900 to 2,300 |
| Over 10 years | From 3,200 to 4,000 | From 2,100 to 2,600 |
| Trainee Solicitor | From 1,066 to 1,300 | From 700 to 860 |
| Litigation Clerk | From 800 to 1,000 | From 533 to 660 |
| Law Costs Draftsman | 1,600 | 1,600 |

The above rates are set by the Law Society, not the court: *Re Maintain Profits Ltd* HCCW 345/2004 (Registrar Chan; 28.04.2006). They are not binding on the court but serve as a 'guideline' (*Wharf Properties Ltd v Eric Cumine Associates* [1992] 2 HKLR 273, 283), or 'reference point' (*Re Maintain Profits Ltd*, above). A note form the court appended to the above table of hourly rates as published by the Law Society states as follows:

> Members should note that the Masters will be paying more attention to the level at which work has been done *eg* if the work could have been done by a trainee solicitor or even a clerk, the costs will be allowed only on that basis. Conversely, if the work is that which would normally be done by counsel or the solicitor is exercising particular expertise and taking unusual responsibility then he may be allowed more than the norm.

Thus in *Re Maintain Profits Ltd* (above), the Registrar allowed a rate in excess of the published maximum of $4,000 in a specialist field. However in *The Delta Pia* HCAJ 31/2002 (Waung J; 25.06.2003) the court considered that $3,500 rather than $4,000 was the 'top end of the scale' at a time of economic downturn.

**[62.21.5]   Parties encouraged to agree quantum of costs**
As is the case with any civil dispute, parties are encouraged to try to settle a claim for costs by agreement. Solicitors 'have a paramount duty towards the court and such duty, in a taxation matter expressly includes the duty to discuss and negotiate the bill, in order to reduce the items in dispute as far as possible, whatever instruction they may have from their lay clients': *SY Eng'g Co Ltd v HK Housing Authority* [2001] 2 HKC 226, 231G. That decision was based, in part, on the wording of the former practice direction 14.3 which required the parties to negotiate to try to reduce the number of items in issue before the substantive taxation hearing. The practice direction which came into force with the civil justice reforms in 2009 goes further, requiring the receiving party in the form of application to set a bill down for taxation (appendix E to PD 14.3) to state that it has used its best endeavours 'to reach an agreement on the whole of the bill or on as many items as possible'.

In the *SY Eng'g* case, a costs order *nisi* was made against solicitors who failed to comply with the duty.

**21A.  Application for taxation to be set down** (O. 62 r. 21A)

**(1)   Upon compliance with the directions given by a taxing master under rule 13A relating to the steps to be taken or things to be done before the taxation is set down, the party who has commenced taxation proceedings under rule 21 may apply to the taxing master for setting down the taxation.**

**(2)   The party shall, within 7 days after making an application under paragraph (1), serve a copy of the application on every other party entitled to be heard on taxation.**

**(3)   A taxing master may refuse to proceed with taxation if he is of the opinion that any direction referred to in paragraph (1) has not been complied with.**

(L.N. 152 of 2008)

---

**NOTES**

**[62.21A.1]   Taxation must be set down if no settlement**
If the parties are unable to reach agreement on the quantum of costs after considering the bill of costs and the list of objections, the taxation must be set down under Order 62 rule 21A. The rule says that this is to be done 'upon' compliance with the directions given by the taxing master. The standard directions seem to contemplate a period of 28 days after service of the list of objections for the parties to attempt to reach settlement before application is made to set down the taxation: see para 21(b) of the Costs practice direction. The date within which the application to set down must be filed is important because the Costs practice direction provides in para 24 that the date cannot be postponed without permission of the taxing master, and that such permission will only be granted if 'good reasons' are shown. It is stated that a wish to discuss settlement will not generally be regarded as a good reason as the parties 'should have made use of the prior period' for that purpose.

Application to set down a taxation should be made in the prescribed form, which is Annex E to the Costs practice direction.

Upon receipt of an application to set down a bill for taxation, the taxing master will decide which procedure will be followed in accordance with para 26 of the costs practice direction. The options for the taxing master to choose from, as set out in that paragraph, are the following:

(a)  tax the bill as drawn, if the taxing master is satisfied that the Notice of Commencement of Taxation and the bill have been duly served in accordance with rule 21, but the paying party has failed to file a list of objections;

(b)  set down the bill for taxation by a Chief Judicial Clerk under rule 13 if the amount claimed does not exceed $200,000 (the maximum of a Chief Judicial Clerk's jurisdiction under that rule);

(c)  set down the bill for provisional taxation by a taxing master under rule 21B if the amount claimed exceeds $200,000;

(d) set down the bill (wholly or partly) for taxation with a hearing under rule 21C (whether the amount claimed exceeds $200,000 or not), if there is good reason to do so;

(e) give other directions as are seen to be fit.

The form of application to set down a bill for taxation contemplates parties requesting an oral hearing if they so wish, in which event reasons should be stated. The taxing master's decision with regard to the above options will be communicated to the parties by means of a Notice of Setting Down a Bill for Taxation, in the form set out in Annex F to the Costs practice directions.

**[62.21A.2] Order for part payment pending taxation**
Order 62 rule 9A previously empowered the court to order interim payment, pending taxation, of an approximation of the amount likely to be recovered. The rule was repealed and replaced as part of the civil justice reforms which took effect in 2009. Now rule 9B requires payment of summarily assessed costs within 14 days, but there is no express provision for part payment pending taxation. In *Re Hawkins Dev't Ltd* [2010] 1 HKC 131 it was held that there is thus a procedural lacuna, and inherent jurisdiction was relied upon to fill the gap. The court ordered payment out of court of money deposited as security for costs, in part satisfaction of a costs order, pending taxation.

**21B. Provisional taxation** (O. 62 r. 21B)
   **(1)   Unless the taxation is set down for hearing under rule 21C(1), the taxing master may —**
         **(a)   tax the bill of costs without a hearing; and**
         **(b)   make an order nisi as to —**
               **(i)   the amount which he allows in respect of the whole or part of the bill of costs; and**
               **(ii)   the costs of the taxation.**
   **(2)   Where the taxing master has taxed the bill of costs without a hearing and made an order nisi under paragraph (1), the party who has applied for setting down the taxation under rule 21A(1) shall serve a copy of the order nisi on every other party entitled to be heard on taxation.**
   **(3)   The order nisi becomes absolute 14 days after it is made unless a party entitled to be heard on taxation applies to the taxing master within the 14-day period for a hearing.**
   **(4)   The taxing master shall set down the taxation for hearing upon application made by a party under paragraph (3) and that party shall serve a notice of the hearing on every other party entitled to be heard on taxation.**
   **(5)   The taxing master may order that party to pay any costs of the hearing if the taxed costs do not materially exceed the amount allowed under paragraph (1)(b)(i).**
   **(6)   In determining whether the taxed costs materially exceed the amount allowed under paragraph (1)(b)(i), the taxing master shall, in addition to any other matter that he may consider relevant, have regard to —**
         **(a)   the amount by which the costs taxed at the hearing exceed the amount allowed under paragraph (1)(b)(i); and**

   **(b)   whether the exceeded amount is disproportionate to the costs of the hearing.**

                                                    **(L.N. 152 of 2008)**

---

## NOTES

### [62.21B.1]   Provisional taxation without a hearing

Order 62 rule 21B provides for provisional taxation of a bill of costs whereby the taxing master may make an order *nisi* as to the amount to be allowed on a bill of costs and in relation to the costs of taxation, without a hearing. The rule was introduced as part of the civil justice reforms taking effect in 2009. Under the former rule 21(4) there was also a power of provisional taxation of a bill of costs, but it was limited to bills claiming no more than $100,000.

The Costs practice direction which came into force along with the civil justice reforms in 2009 clearly contemplates that provisional taxation without a hearing will be the norm. In para 26(4) it is provided that the taxing master shall only set down a bill for hearing if satisfied that there is good reason to do so. See also para 6 of the same practice direction (PD 14.3) where it is stated that with regard to the costs of interlocutory applications, summary assessment (under O 62 r 9A), or provisional taxation without a hearing under this rule, are to be given preference by the court over the full traditional taxation procedure.

A party dissatisfied with the amount of costs allowed by an order *nisi* under this rule may apply under rule 21B(3) within 14 days for a hearing. The taxing master is then required by rule 21B(4) to set the bill down for a hearing, even if the paying party failed to comply with the standard direction under rule 13A to file and serve a list of objections: *Citi Creation Investment Ltd v IO Kwai Wan Industrial Bldg & Ors* LDBM 180/2009 (Judge HC Wong; 22.03.2010). If at the hearing the taxing master does not order an amount which materially exceeds the order *nisi*, the party who requested the hearing may be ordered to pay the costs thereof. This serves as a disincentive for receiving parties to challenge an order *nisi* unless there are solid grounds. Strangely there is no express equivalent discouraging paying parties from seeking a hearing in the hope of reducing the amount of the order *nisi*. However, on general principles it would appear open for the taxing master to order a paying party to pay the costs of such a hearing unless the result was a significant reduction.

Rule 21B implements recommendation 134 in the final report of the Chief Justice's working party on civil justice reform. That was an adoption of proposal 60 in the interim report. At para 617 of the interim report it was suggested that the court will have studied the papers before deciding whether to proceed by way of provisional taxation, or to set the matter down for an oral taxation. In para 777 of the final report, it was noted that some groups took the view the discretion to proceed by way of provisional taxation without a hearing 'should obviously not be exercised in relation to complex taxations after long cases'.

### 21C. Taxation with a hearing (O. 62 r. 21C)

**(1)   Where the taxing master is satisfied that there is a good reason to do so, he may, either of his own motion or on application by a party entitled to be heard on taxation, set down for hearing the taxation of the whole or part of the bill of costs.**

**(2)** Upon notification by the taxing master of the date of hearing, the party who applied for setting down shall serve a notice of the hearing on every other party entitled to be heard on taxation within 7 days after the notification.

(L.N. 152 of 2008)

**NOTES**

**[62.21C.1]** **When taxation with a hearing appropriate**
It is clear from the practice direction on costs that taxation with a hearing is intended to be exceptional; that wherever possible the provisional taxation procedures will be followed instead. It is provided that taxation with a hearing will only be ordered if there is 'good reason' to do so. See in particular para 26 of the Costs practice direction as to choice of procedure by the taxing master. A party may request a taxation hearing in the application to set down, the form for which requires that reasons be given.

**21D. Withdrawal of bill of costs** (O. 62 r. 21D)
**(1)** A party who has filed a bill of costs shall pay the prescribed fee to the Court if he withdraws the bill of costs within 7 days after his application to the taxing master for setting down the taxation under rule 21A(1) is made.
**(2)** The Court shall deduct the fee payable under paragraph (1) from the amount paid under rule 21(5) and refund the balance to the party.
**(3)** The party is not entitled to any refund of the balance of the amount paid under rule 21(5) except –
    **(a)** under paragraph (2); or
    **(b)** where the Court otherwise directs.

(L.N. 152 of 2008)

**NOTES**

**[62.21D.1]**
*Refund of taxation fee on withdrawal of bill of costs*
Order 62 rule 21D provides that a party who withdraws a bill of costs before it is taxed will still be responsible for all or part of the court fee. Refund of the court fee is generally in the discretion of the court under rule 21D(3)(b). That discretion will generally be exercised in accordance with para 27 of the Costs practice direction. It is there provided that to encourage settlement, the court fee payable will be reduced by a higher percentage the sooner the bill of costs is withdrawn, resulting in refund of a greater proportion of the fee. The paragraph provides for reduction of the court fee by 90% if the bill is withdrawn within the 2nd week after the application to set down, which reduces in steps to 10% reduction if withdrawn during the 6th week.

**[62.21D.2]** **Rules 21 – 21D apply prospectively only**
Rules 21 to 21D, all of which were added to the rules in their present form by the civil justice reforms taking effect in 2009, do not apply in relation to taxation of a bill of costs filed prior to the amendments coming into force. See Order 62 rule 37 and the commentary thereunder.

**22. Delay in service of notice of commencement of taxation or in proceeding with taxation** (O. 62 r. 22)

(1)  If, within 3 months after the completion date, the person entitled to payment of costs has neither –

> (a)  agreed the amount of those costs with the person liable to pay them; nor
>
> (b)  served upon such person a copy of a notice of commencement of taxation in accordance with rule 21(2),

the taxing master, on the application of the person liable to pay such costs and on not less than 7 days' notice to the person entitled to payment of those costs, may make an order under paragraph (3).

(2)  If, after the proceedings for the taxation of a bill of costs have commenced in accordance with rule 21(1), the person entitled to payment of costs has neither —

> (a)  agreed the amount of those costs with the person liable to pay them; nor
>
> (b)  proceeded with the taxation,

the taxing master, on the application of the person liable to pay such costs and on not less than 7 days' notice to the person entitled to payment of those costs, may make an order under paragraph (3).

(3)  The taxing master —

> (a)  may order that the person entitled to payment of the costs must commence taxation proceedings in accordance with rule 21 or proceed with the taxation, within such period as may be specified in the order; and
>
> (b)  may further order that that person shall not be entitled to commence those taxation proceedings or proceed with the taxation unless the person does commence those taxation proceedings or proceed with the taxation within the specified period or such extended period as may be allowed by the taxing master.

(4)  The taxing master may make an order under paragraph (3) subject to such conditions as he thinks fit, including a condition that the person liable to pay the costs to be taxed shall pay a sum of money into court.

(5)  On the taxation of a bill of costs, whether or not an order has been made under paragraph (3), the taxing master, if he is satisfied that there has been undue delay in commencing taxation proceedings or in proceeding with the taxation –

> (a)  may make such order as he thinks fit as to the costs of any application or as to the costs of the taxation;
>
> (b)  may disallow any part of the costs to be taxed pursuant to the costs order; and
>
> (c)  may, in relation to the taxed costs or any part of those costs, disallow interest or reduce the period for which interest is payable or the rate at which interest is payable.

(6)  Where a party entitled to payment of costs fails to proceed with taxation after filing the notice of commencement of taxation under rule 21(1), the taxing

master in order to prevent any other parties being prejudiced by that failure, may —

    (a)  allow the party so entitled a nominal or other sum for costs; or

    (b)  certify the failure and the costs of the other parties.

    (7)  A party is not entitled to commence taxation proceedings under rule 21 —

    (a)  after the expiry of 2 years from the completion date; or

    (b)  where the Court has extended the period specified in sub-paragraph (a), after the expiry of the period as extended,

whichever is the later.

    (8)  Where the completion date is before the commencement of this rule, paragraph (7)(a) has effect as if for the words "completion date", there were substituted the words "commencement of this rule".

    (9)  In this rule, "completion date" means —

    (a)  in relation to a costs order made by the Court of First Instance —

        (i)  the date of the judgment or order of the Court of First Instance which disposes of the action;

       (ii)  the date on which the Court of First Instance makes the costs order, or if the order is an order nisi, the date on which the order is made absolute or varied (as the case may be);

      (iii)  the date on which the taxing master orders under rule 9D(4) the person entitled to payment of the costs of any interlocutory proceedings in the Court of First Instance to commence taxation proceedings; or

      (iv)  where the person entitled to payment of costs is entitled to tax those costs without an order of the Court of First Instance directing the taxation of them, the date on which he becomes entitled to tax those costs,

    whichever is the later; and

    (b)  in relation to a costs order made by the Court of Appeal —

        (i)  the date of the judgment or order of the Court of Appeal which disposes of the appeal;

       (ii)  the date on which the Court of Appeal makes the costs order, or if the order is an order nisi, the date on which the order is made absolute or varied (as the case may be);

      (iii)  the date on which the taxing master orders under rule 9D(4) the person entitled to payment of the costs of any interlocutory proceedings in the Court of Appeal to commence taxation proceedings; or

      (iv)  where the person entitled to payment of costs is entitled to tax those costs without an order of the Court of Appeal directing the taxation of them, the date on which he becomes entitled to tax those costs,

    whichever is the later.

**(L.N. 152 of 2008)**

## NOTES

### [62.22.1]  Provisions to discourage delay in taxation of costs
Order 62 rule 22 contains various provisions to discourage delay in the taxation of costs. The rule was repealed and replaced as part of the civil justice reforms in effect in 2009. Avoidance of delay is desirable not least because interest runs on costs from the date of the order: see the commentary on this topic under Order 62 rule 3. Interest runs at the judgment rate which is higher than commercial rates of interest.

See also Order 62 rule 8D which provides for wasted costs orders against legal representatives responsible for delay in taxation of costs.

### [62.22.3]  Power to order receiving party to proceed
Rule 22(3)(a) empowers the taxing master to order a receiving party to commence or proceed with taxation within a specified period, and rule 22(3)(b) provides that the taxing master may additionally order that the receiving party shall be barred from commencing or proceeding with taxation if the order under (a) is not complied with. Such orders may be made in respect of delay whether before or after taxation proceedings are commenced:

*Delay before commencing taxation* – Rule 22(1) provides that such orders may be made where a receiving party has neither agreed the quantum of costs nor commenced taxation within 3 months. Time runs from the 'completion date', which is defined in rule 22(9). Read together with rule 9D, the definition more or less boils down to the date on which the receiving party was entitled to instigate taxation proceedings.

*Delay after commencing taxation* – Rule 22(2) provides for such orders to be made if there is delay after the commencement of taxation.

An order under rule 22(3) may be subject to conditions: rule 22(4). Specifically mentioned is the condition that the paying party be required to pay a sum of money into court. It is difficult to imagine circumstances in which such an order would be made, since an order under rule 22(3) presupposes default on the part of the receiving party, not the paying party.

### [62.22.4]  Power to penalise delay in taxation of costs
Rule 22(5) provides that a taxing master may impose financial sanctions on a party who is responsible for delay in taxation proceedings. Three types of financial sanction are specified: (a) an order for costs of any application or of the taxation; (b) disallowance of part of the taxed costs; and (c) disallowance of interest or reduction of the period for which interest runs or the rate of interest on costs. It appears that the court's power is to make any one or more of those three types of order. Before rule 22 came into force in its present form as part of the civil justice reforms in April 2009, the taxing master had no power to reduce interest on costs. This was held in *Hotung v Ho Yuen Ki & Ors (No 3)* [2009] 2 HKC 378, which may be taken to have been overruled by rule 22(5) to that extent.

A similar power previously existed under rule 22(3) and the cases thereon will continue to be of guidance. In *AG v Commodore Electronics Ltd* [1994] 1 HKC 660 the taxing master ordered a global reduction of 20% of the taxed costs to reflect undue delay in proceeding to taxation. There had been delay of 21/2 years between the order for costs and the taxation hearing. The purpose of such an order is to 'encourage timely taxation': *PBM (HK) Ltd v Tang Kam Lun Allan* HCA 12138/1997 (Master de Souza; 28.08.2006). Proof of prejudice is not necessary because delay necessarily causes prejudice on account of the paying party's liability to pay interest from the date of the costs order: *Re Madam Tan* HCA 6086/1994 (Master Kwan; 20.07.1999). In that case the master ordered a global reduction of 8% on the taxed costs for unexplained delay of 11 months in filing the taxation bill. See also *Dollarwell Investments Ltd v Donald Koo Hoi Yan* HCA 12307/1995 (Master de Souza; 06.10.2005) where a 30% global reduction was ordered on account of 28 months delay, and *PBM (HK) Ltd* (above) where a 15% reduction was ordered for 'inordinate, unjustified and inexcusable' delay of 16 months.

Where delay in any proceedings before a taxing master is attributable to a party's legal representative, the court may make a wasted costs requiring the legal representative to pay costs to any party. See Order 62 rule 8D.

See also reg 8(1) of the Legal Aid (Scale of Fees) Regulations (Cap 91) which similarly provides for disallowance or reduction of solicitors' profit costs on the ground of delay in legal aid taxations.

### [62.22.5]   Power to prevent prejudice to other parties

Rule 22(6) empowers the court to allow only a nominal (or other) sum of money in respect of costs where the receiving party has commenced taxation proceedings, but delayed thereafter. This power is expressly intended to prevent prejudice to the other parties and seems to contemplate application being made by such parties. Provision is also made for the other parties' costs: rule 22(6)(b).

### [62.22.6]   2-year limitation period for commencing taxation

Rule 22(7) provides for what is, in effect, a 2-year limitation period for the commencement of taxation proceedings, but subject to the possibility of extension of time.

### 23. (Repealed L.N. 152 of 2008)

### [62.23.1]   Deposit of vouchers and papers

Order 62 rule 23 was repealed as part of the civil justice reforms implemented in 2009. It required the receiving party who has filed a bill of costs to deposit the relevant papers and vouchers in respect of the costs claimed with the taxing master no later than 2 days before the day appointed for the taxation hearing. The matter is now dealt with by way of directions of the taxing master given pursuant to Order 62 rule 13A(2)(b). See the commentary under that rule.

### 24. **Taxation** (O. 62 r. 24)

**(1)   The taxing master may proceed to taxation of a bill of costs under rule 21B(1) notwithstanding that a party entitled to be heard on taxation has failed to comply with any direction given by him relating to the steps to be taken or things to be done before the taxation proceeds under rule 21B, if the taxing master is satisfied that a copy of the notice of commencement of taxation and of the bill of costs were duly served in accordance with rule 21(2) on the party.**

**(2)** If, at the date and time of a hearing under rule 21B(4) or 21C(2), a party entitled to be heard on taxation does not appear before the taxing master in person or by his representative, the taxing master may proceed to taxation of the bill of costs in the absence of the party or of his representative, if the taxing master is satisfied that the party has been served with a notice of the hearing in accordance with rule 21B(4) or 21C(2), or has been otherwise informed of the hearing.

**(3)** If the taxing master is not so satisfied, he –

    **(a)** must adjourn the hearing for such period as he may consider necessary to enable service of the notice of the adjourned hearing or of the bill of costs or both to be effected on the party; and

    **(b)** may make such order as he may consider appropriate in relation to costs thrown away by the adjournment.

**(L.N. 152 of 2008)**

## NOTES

**[62.24.1]** **Taxation may proceed despite failure to comply with directions or to appear**

Order 62 rule 24(1) provides that the taxing master may proceed to tax a bill of costs notwithstanding failure of a party to comply with directions, if satisfied that the party was duly served. Rule 24(2) make similar provision in cases where a party entitled to be heard fails to appear at a taxation hearing. In either case, the taxing master must adjourn the hearing if not satisfied as to service: rule 24(3).

If it is the paying party who fails to comply with directions, or fails to attend, in all likelihood the taxing master will tax the bill as drawn. See the standard directions in para 21 of the Costs practice direction, para 26 thereof and the form of application to set down a taxation in Annex E thereto.

## 25. (Repealed L.N. 152 of 2008)

**[62.25.1]** **Replacement of '3-column' format of bill of costs**

Order 62 rule 25 previously provided for the 3-column form of bill of costs whereby professional charges and disbursements were set out in separate columns in the bill. It has been replaced by a new format, as to which see the commentary under Order 62 rule 21.

## 26. Power to adjourn (O. 62 r. 26)

**(1)** The taxing master by whom any taxation proceedings are being conducted may, if he thinks it necessary to do so, adjourn those proceedings from time to time. **(L.N. 152 of 2008)**

**(2)** If the taxation proceedings are adjourned because a party has failed to comply with any directions given under rule 13A, the taxing master may make such order as he may consider appropriate in relation to costs thrown away by the adjournment. **(L.N. 152 of 2008)**

**[62.26.1] Limited power of taxing master to adjourn taxation**

A taxing master has power under Order 62 rule 26(1) (formerly numbered as 26(2)) to adjourn taxation proceedings from time to time. In addition the court has an inherent jurisdiction to adjourn a taxation hearing quite independent of Order 62 rule 26: see *Plus Lucky Ltd v Chin Yuk Lun Francis & Ors* [2003] 3 HKC 80, 86A-B.

In the *Plus Lucky* case it was held that the power to adjourn under Order 62 rule 26 may not be exercised so as in effect to stay execution of an order for payment of costs pending appeal. To do so would amount to a usurpation of the power reserved to the trial judge and the Court of Appeal to grant a stay of execution under Order 59 rule 13. Rather, the power to adjourn under Order 62 rule 26 may only be exercised where 'necessary ... for the expedient and efficient disposal of the taxation'. See the judgment of Deputy Judge To in *Plus Lucky* at 85F-I.

The court's inherent power to adjourn a taxation hearing should be exercised only when good cause is shown. Two principles need to be borne in mind. First, a successful litigant should not be deprived of the fruits of his success unless the trial judge or the Court of Appeal grants a stay of execution. Secondly, the expenditure of unnecessary court time and expense should be avoided. The second principle is subject to the first and it is impracticable for the taxing master to consider the merits of the pending appeal. See the judgment of Deputy Judge To in *Plus Lucky* at 86B – 87G, citing *Star Play Development Ltd v Bess Fashion Management Co Ltd* [2007] 5 HKC 84; *Roselodge Ltd v Castle* [1966] 2 Lloyd's Rep 113, 114; *Re Schindler Lifts (HK) Ltd and Dickson Construction Ltd* [1993] 1 HKLR 45, and preferring the judgment of Keith JA in *Re HY & HT Lee Brothers and Co Ltd* CACV 307 & 328/1999 (29.11.2000, unreported) over that of Woolf LJ in *Malliez v Redland Plasterboard Overseas Ltd* (22.09.1992, unreported).

Rule 26(2) expressly empowers the court to order payment of costs thrown away in the event a taxation is adjourned because of failure to comply with directions.

**27. Powers of taxing master taxing costs payable out of fund** (O. 62 r. 27)

**(1)    Where any costs are to be paid out of a fund the taxing master may give directions as to the parties who are entitled to attend on the taxation of those costs and may disallow the costs of attendance of any party not entitled to attend by virtue of the directions and whose attendance he considers unnecessary.**

**(2)    Where the Court has directed that a bill of costs be taxed for the purpose of being paid out of a fund the taxing master by whom the bill is being taxed may, if he thinks fit, adjourn the taxation for a reasonable period and direct the party whose bill it is to send to any person having an interest in the fund a copy of the bill, or of any part thereof, free of charge together with a letter containing the following information, that is to say—**

**(a)    that the bill of costs, a copy of which or of part of which is sent with the letter, has been referred to a taxing master for taxation;**

**(b)    the name of the taxing master and the address of the office at which the taxation is proceeding;**

**(c)    the time appointed by the taxing master at which the taxation will be continued; and**

**(d)    such other information, if any, as the taxing master may direct.**

**NOTES**

### BASES AND SCALES FOR TAXATION AND ASSESSMENT OF COSTS
### (L.N. 152 OF 2008)

**28. Costs payable to one party by another or out of a fund** (O. 62 r. 28)

(1)    This rule applies to costs which by or under these rules or any order or direction of the Court are to be paid to a party to any proceedings either by another party to those proceedings or out of any fund (other than a fund which the party to whom the costs are to be paid holds as trustee or personal representative).

(2)    Subject to the following provisions of this rule, costs to which this rule applies shall be taxed on the party and party basis, and on a taxation on that basis there shall be allowed all such costs as were necessary or proper for the attainment of justice or for enforcing or defending the rights of the party whose costs are being taxed.

(3)    The Court in awarding costs to which this rule applies may in any case in which it thinks fit to do so order or direct that the costs shall be taxed on the common fund basis or on the indemnity basis. (L.N. 125 of 1991)

(4)    On a taxation on the common fund basis, being a more generous basis than that provided for by paragraph (2), there shall be allowed a reasonable amount in respect of all costs reasonably incurred, and paragraph (2) shall not apply; and accordingly in all cases where costs are to be taxed on the common fund basis the ordinary rules applicable on a taxation as between solicitor and client where the costs are to be paid out of a common fund in which the client and others are interested shall be applied, whether or not the costs are in fact to be so paid.

(4A)    On a taxation on the indemnity basis all costs shall be allowed except insofar as they are of an unreasonable amount or have been unreasonably incurred and any doubts which the taxing master may have as to whether the costs were reasonably incurred or were reasonable in amount shall be resolved in favour of the receiving party; and in these rules the term "the indemnity basis" in relation to the taxation of costs shall be construed accordingly. (L.N. 125 of 1991)

(5)    The Court in awarding costs to which this rule applies to any person may if it thinks fit and if—

(a)    the costs are to be paid out of a fund, or

(b)    the person to whom the costs are to be paid is or was a party to the proceedings in the capacity of trustee or personal representative,

order or direct that the costs shall be taxed as if that person were a trustee of the fund or as if the costs were to be paid out of a fund held by that person, as the case may be, and where the Court so orders or directs rule 31(2) shall have effect in relation to the taxation in substitution for paragraph (2) of this rule.

(6)    The foregoing provisions of this rule shall be without prejudice to the powers of the Court under section 44A of the District Court Ordinance (Cap 336). (L.N. 152 of 2008)

**NOTES**

**[62.28.1]   The indemnity principle**
The purpose of an order for costs is to compensate a litigant for the legal expenses he has incurred. The degree to which he will be compensated depends on a number of factors, not least the basis on which it is ordered his costs be taxed (as to which see below). There is an over-riding principle that a litigant cannot recover on taxation anything more than he has paid or is liable to pay his solicitors on account of costs and disbursements. The indemnity principle was stated in the following terms in a practice note at [1998] 1 WLR 1674D, cited with approval in *Building Authority v Business Rights Ltd* [1999] 3 HKC 247, 251G-H:

> The indemnity principle is as follows: an order for costs between parties allows the receiving party to claim from the paying party only an indemnity in respect of the costs covered by the order. Receiving parties cannot therefore recover a sum in excess of their liability to their own solicitors. On the taxation of a bill, the indemnity principle is to be applied on an item by item basis rather than on a global basis . . .

See also the proviso to section 59(1)(b) of the Legal Practitioners Ordinance (Cap 159) which provides that where there is an agreement between solicitor and client as to remuneration for contentious business, the client shall not be entitled to recover more than the amount payable by him to the solicitor from any other person under any order for the payment of costs.

The indemnity principle 'does not require that costs have been paid, but it does require that there be a legal liability to pay': *Wentworth v Rogers* [2006] NSWCA 145 (per Basten JA at para 126). In Hong Kong the situation is different with regard to counsel's fees, which must have been paid to be recoverable: see the commentary on counsel's fees under Order 62 rule 32. A contingency fee agreement is unenforceable, so there is no legal liability to pay, and nothing for the opposing party to indemnify: *Bank of China (HK) Ltd v Well Lok Printing Ltd* HCMP 3925/2002 (Master J Wong; 07.11.2007).

In *Holiday Resorts (Management) Co Ltd v Chan Yuk Yan & Ors* HCA 7665/1998 (Registrar Chan; 02.05.2001) a solicitor had agreed to charge the client only the amount recovered from the opposing party. The registrar took the view that such an arrangement infringed the indemnity principle saying (at para 6):

> In this case unless I am satisfied that the amount that I have allowed does not exceed the sum the receiving party is liable to pay their solicitors I will not issue the certificate (commonly known as the allocatur) certifying the amount that is due and payable by the paying party.

The English Court of Appeal appears to have taken a different view in *Thai Trading Co v Taylor* [1998] QB 781 where Millett LJ said (at para 33):

> there is nothing unlawful in a solicitor acting for a party to litigation to agree to forgo all or part of his fee if he loses, provided that he does not seek to recover more than his ordinary profit costs and disbursements if he wins.

However, that decision was doubted in the subsequent case of *Hughes v Kingston Upon Hull CC* [1999] QB 1193 (DC) and again in *Awwad v Geraghty & Co (a firm)* [2001] QB 570 (CA). In *Unruh v Seeberger & Anor* [2007] 2 HKC 609 (para 109) the Court of Final Appeal left open the question which approach should be adopted in Hong Kong.

The indemnity principle does not prevent recovery of costs where a third party such as an insurer, trade union, spouse or friend has provided financial assistance to the successful litigant. See *Lam Lai Wah Susanna v Pacific Century Insurance Co Ltd* [2003] 2 HKC 520 (CA). The applicable principles were summarised concisely by Yuen JA at 523E-H in the following terms:

(1) The first question to be asked is: did the winning party employ the solicitors in the action? In answering this question, it matters not that the solicitors were chosen or appointed for the winning party by a third party on his behalf, so long as they acted for him with his knowledge and assent.

(2) If the answer is 'Yes', it is presumed that the winning party had a *prima facie* obligation to remunerate the solicitors, because that would be the ordinary basis on which a professional person is employed to represent a party.

(3) It is for the losing party to rebut that presumption. The presumption is *not* rebutted simply by evidence that a third party had also undertaken to pay the solicitors' costs. However, the presumption would be rebutted if there is evidence of an agreement made by the solicitors with the winning party, or with the third party, that under no circumstances would the winning party be liable to them for the costs of the litigation incurred on his behalf.

In *Lam Lai Wah Susanna* the successful litigant's costs had been paid by her boyfriend. In the absence of evidence that the successful litigant would not reimburse the boyfriend even in the event the proceedings were unsuccessful, the Court of Appeal allowed her appeal against an order that there be no order as to costs.

In *Lam Lai Wah Susanna* the Court of Appeal cited the following English cases where costs were allowed notwithstanding financial assistance from a third party:

☐ *Adams v London Improved Motor Coach Builders Ltd* [1921] 1 KB 495, [1920] All ER 340 (CA) where a trade union financed litigation on behalf of one of its members;

☐ *Davies v Taylor (No 2)* [1974] AC 225, [1973] 1 All ER 959, [1973] 2 WLR 610 (HL) where an insurance company had undertaken to indemnify a litigant for costs;

☐ *Lewis v Averay (No 2)* [1973] 2 All ER 229; [1973] 1 WLR 510, where an automobile association had instructed and paid the winning party's solicitors; and

☐ *R v Miller* [1983] 1 WLR 1056, where the defendant's employers had undertaken to pay his costs in a criminal case.

A subsequent example is *Hotung v Hotung* [2007] 1 HKLRD 548 (Master de Souza; 09.01.2007) where a party was permitted to recover party and party costs in respect of which her father had given her an indemnity. It was held that despite the arrangement between father and daughter, the daughter remained personally liable to her solicitors for their costs and disbursements so there was no infringement of the indemnity principle.

In *Fairbairn v Roberts & Ors* HCMP 4200/2003 (Chu J; 02.04.2004) the court dismissed an application by a paying party for discovery to assist it in rebutting the presumption set out at point (2) above. There was uncontradicted affidavit evidence to the effect the indemnity principle had not been infringed. In *Cheung Kong (Holdings) Ltd v Chan Wai Yip Albert* HCA 16790/1998 (Waung J; 30.07.2002) an appeal was allowed against a master's order requiring the receiving party's solicitors to file an affidavit stating whether there was any agreement relating to solicitors' costs. The receiving party's legal representatives had provided the court with confirmation there was no such agreement.

It is asserted in another work that the indemnity principle applies only to the amount allowed on taxation, so the amount claimed in the bill of costs may be greater. If that was ever true, it can no longer be. This is because para 17(7) of the Costs practice direction (PD 14.3), which came into effect with the civil justice reforms in April 2009, requires that a solicitor putting forward a bill of costs shall certify that the amount claimed does not exceed the party's liability to the solicitor's firm. See *Yeung Yeuk Sut v Tse Chun Yip & Ors* HCA 682/2006 (Registrar Au-Yeung; 02.02.2010) (para 14-15). The certificate appears on the prescribed forms of statement of costs (for summary assessment under rule 9A) and of bill of costs (appendices A and B respectively to PD 14.3).

### [62.28.2]   'Costs' includes disbursements
The word 'costs' is defined in Order 62 rule 1 to include disbursements and expenses. Thus the recoverability of disbursements is governed by the same criteria as laid down for costs in Order 62 rule 28.

With regard to recoverability of counsel's fees, see also the commentary under Order 62 rule 32.

### [62.28.3]   Costs of government counsel
Government counsel within the Department of Justice have the status of both barrister and solicitor by virtue of the Legal Officers Ordinance (Cap 87). The recovery of costs incurred by a government department represented by government counsel is governed by the Legal Officers (Fees and Costs) Rules, subsidiary legislation under the same Ordinance. It has been held that where the government has been represented in court proceedings by a single government counsel performing both the functions of barrister and solicitor, no brief fee will be recoverable on taxation of the government's costs: see *Building Authority v Tam Chung Ching Denis* [1997] 3 HKC 260. See also *Building Authority v Business Rights Ltd* [1999] 3 HKC 247. There Burrell J held that it would offend the indemnity principle to allow government counsel who handles a case alone a brief fee of the type payable to a member of the private bar. Assessment of government counsel's costs on an hourly rate is more appropriate. Nevertheless (*obiter*) a reduced brief fee might be appropriate so long as it does not result in excessive recovery by the government. Note that this is a judgment of a single judge of the Court of First Instance on appeal from a master under Order 58, and not a judgment of the Court of Appeal as stated in the report.

It is understood that government departments (at least those which do not run on a 'trading fund' basis) are not required to pay for the services of government counsel when the Department of Justice is instructed to act for them in contentious proceedings. In practice, costs are nevertheless ordered in favour of the government and when recovered, such costs are paid into the general revenue pursuant to the Legal Officers Ordinance (Cap 87) section 10(2). Although this practice appears to infringe the indemnity principle it is authorised by the Crown Proceedings Ordinance (Cap 300) s 17. See the cases of *AG v Shillibeer* (1854) 154 ER 1356, *Lord Advocate v Stewart* (No 2) (1899) 63 JP 473 and *Re Southbourne Sheet Metal Co Ltd* [1993] 1 WLR 244 dealing with similar legislation in the UK. See also *Ling Yuk Sing v Secretary for the Civil Service & Anor* [2010] 5 HKC 169 where it was held that the indemnity principle must be applied flexibly and reasonably and that the starting point is that the costs of government lawyers are to be taxed on the same basis as private lawyers.

**[62.28.4]   Costs of 'in house' counsel**
Where legal work is undertaken by a party's own employee, such as 'in house' counsel, costs in respect thereof are recoverable notwithstanding the fact the employee is paid no extra salary for the work done. See for example *Lloyds Bank Ltd v Eastwood* [1975] Ch 112, cited with approval in *Building Authority v Business Rights Ltd* [1999] 3 HKC 247, 252 D–F.

**[62.28.5]   Costs incidental to, or prior to proceedings, including costs of mediation**
The court's general discretion as to costs in section 52A(1) of the High Court Ordinance is expressed to be in relation to costs 'of and incidental to' proceedings. Negotiations with a view to settlement are included in para 5(a)(x) of the 1st Schedule, Part I of Order 62 as costs which may be recoverable. As a result, certain costs not part of the legal proceedings themselves may be recoverable. This may include costs incurred prior to proceedings being commenced, or of an alternative dispute resolution procedure ('ADR') used in attempt to settle.

In *The Golden Georgia* HCAJ 45/2004 (Master de Souza; 21.06.2006), (quoting from *SA Pescheries Ostendaises v Merchant Marine Insurance Co* [1928] 2 KB 751, 757) it was said that pre-action costs 'ultimately proving of use and service in the action' may be recoverable.

In *Chun Wo Construction & Eng'g Co Ltd v China Win Eng'g Ltd* HCCT 37/2006 (Lam J; 12.06.2008) the court considered whether the costs of mediation, which had been of some assistance in resolving the dispute, were recoverable in legal proceedings. In the particular case it was held that they were not, because the parties had not agreed to depart from the governing mediation rules (Clause 13(i) of the Hong Kong International Arbitration Centre's Mediation Rules, which provides that each party shall bear its own costs unless otherwise agreed) (those rules may be viewed on www.hkiac.org). However, the court (at para 90 *et seq*) made some important *obiter* observations on the recovery of the costs of mediation, which may be summarised as follows:

☐   As a matter of principle the costs of mediation may be recoverable like costs incurred in negotiations.
☐   Costs of a failed post-action mediation may be recovered as costs incidental to the court proceedings (citing *Vellacott v Convergence Group plc* [2007] EWHC 1774 (Ch) and *Eagleson v Liddell* [2001] EWCA Civ 155).
☐   'It is a question of fact whether a mediation is so closely connected with a piece of litigation such that the costs of mediation can properly be described as costs incidental to a set of legal proceedings. If a mediation takes place a long time ago before parties commence legal proceedings, the court may be slow to conclude that the costs of such a mediation should be taxable as costs incidental to the legal proceedings' (citing *Lobster Group Ltd v Heidelberg Graphic Equipment Ltd* [2008] EWHC 413 (TCC) (06.03.2008) [2008] 2 All ER 1173).

In *Lobster Group Ltd v Heidelberg Graphic Equipment Ltd* [2008] EWHC (TCC); [2008] 2 All ER 1173 the English court distinguished between pre-action and post-action mediation and observed (para 17) that the costs of the latter were more likely to be recoverable as being incidental to the proceedings. With regard to the former it was said (para 12) that 'the greater the distance in time between the incurring of the costs and the commencement of proceedings, the greater will be the likelihood that the losing party will have good grounds to dispute its liability to reimburse such costs'.

The specimen forms of mediation notice and response in the appendices to PD 31 contemplate the parties agreeing in advance whether the cost of mediation could be recoverable as costs of the proceedings if the mediation fails.

### [62.28.6]  Apportionment between jointly liable defendants
Where costs are ordered against more than one defendant, who are jointly and severally liable for the same, the court may nevertheless assess costs wholly attributable to steps taken in respect of one defendant against that defendant only. See *Stumm v Dixon* (1889) 22 QBD 529 (CA) where it was held that where a defendant had served a separate defence, it alone was liable for the plaintiff's costs incurred in relation thereto.

### [62.28.7]  Time when costs order becomes a debt
An order that a litigant pay costs does not give rise to a debt until the amount payable has been ascertained by taxation or agreement: *Australian Telephone Distributors Pty Ltd (in liq) v Golden Always Ltd & Anor* [1996] 2 HKLR 325. In that case, it had been held at first instance that there is no obligation to pay until an allocatur has been served (see *Re Golden Always Ltd & Anor* [1996] 3 HKC 252) but the Court of Appeal held that once the amount of costs has been certified it immediately becomes due and payable.

### [62.28.8]  The bases of taxation
This rule sets out the bases on which costs may be taxed as between the parties to proceedings or where costs are to be paid out of a fund. The basis on which costs are to be taxed determines which items of work performed by a party's solicitor and which disbursements incurred must be paid for by the party against whom the costs award is made, and, subject to the schedules to this rule, influence the amount recoverable in respect of any such item.

Note that there is now a considerable divergence between the English and Hong Kong rules on the question of the bases of taxation. In England all of the old bases were replaced in April 1986 with just two new bases, being the 'standard basis' and the 'indemnity basis'. The Hong Kong Court of Appeal expressed support, *obiter*, for a similar amendment of Hong Kong's rules in *Lakhan v Wu Wing Tat & Anor* [1987] 3 HKC 54, but no such amendment was incorporated into the 1988 Hong Kong rules. The result is that English decisions on the bases of taxation since April 1986 must be read with caution in Hong Kong, and the leading decision in *EMI Records Ltd v Ian Cameron Wallace Ltd* [1983] 1 Ch 59 remains highly persuasive in Hong Kong though it is now largely irrelevant in England.

**[62.28.9]    The party and party basis**

Rule 28(2) stipulates that costs to which this rule applies shall normally be taxed on the party and party basis. In *EMI Records Ltd v Ian Cameron Wallace Ltd* [1983] 1 Ch 59, at 63G, Megarry V-C described the 'necessary or proper' test set down in this sub-rule as the 'essence' of party and party costs and went on to describe this as the strictest of the normal bases of taxation. In *C Art Ltd v Ability Manufacturing Ltd* [1990] 1 HKC 407, 409G-H it was held that recovery on the party and party scale includes:

> action taken by a prudent solicitor, protecting the rights of his client, and instructing a specialist counsel to settle the statement of claim in proceedings where it is intended that he will be briefed to appear at trial, and stand by those pleadings, except in the most simple and straightforward proceedings . . .'

The court went on to hold that party and party costs will not necessarily extend to a conference with counsel.

In *Tai Hing Cotton Mill Ltd v Liu Chong Hing Bank Ltd* [1982] HKLR 387, it was held that the cost of travelling time, air fares and hotel accommodation of a London silk were not 'necessary or proper' in the circumstances of the case and thus could not be recovered on a party and party taxation because capable local counsel would have done the job for the brief fee only, thus saving the other expenses.

The party and party basis is a minimal basis, and will normally leave the successful party substantially out of pocket. In *Commissioner of Inland Revenue v Aspiration Land Investment Ltd* HCIA 10/1989 (Kaplan J; 14.12.1990) it was observed that the party and party basis would leave a party 'between 40% and 30% out of pocket'. The level of recovery under the party and party scale has been criticised as inadequate (see Hunsworth, in *Law Lectures for Practitioners 1991* (Hong Kong: Hong Kong Law Journal Ltd, 1991)).

**[62.28.10]    The common fund basis**

Rule 28(3) empowers the court to award costs as between opposing litigants on the 'common fund basis', and sub-rule (4) lays down what costs shall be allowed on this 'more generous basis'. In *EMI Records Ltd v Ian Cameron Wallace Ltd* [1983] 1 Ch 59, at 63G–64B, Megarry V-C referred to *Giles v Randall* [1915] 1 KB 290, at 295, and said that a common fund taxation is, in practice,

> little more than a party and party taxation conducted 'on a more generous scale' ... It is sometimes said that on average a common fund taxation produces a figure 5 to 10 per cent higher than a party and party taxation; and that may be so.

It has been held that the 'more generous' basis applicable on a common fund taxation relates to 'approach' and not quantum of individual items claimed: see *Ngan Wun Yeung v Lok Sin Tong Benevolent Society, Kowloon & Ors* [2000] 2 HKC 404, per Master Poon. The result in the case before Master Poon was that no enhancement of the quantum of counsel's fees was allowed. The master did not follow *Gibbs v Gibbs* [1952] P 332, preferring *Lyon v Lyon* [1952] 2 All ER 831, and cited with approval the commentary on the latter decision in the Lord Chancellor's *Notes for Guidance on the Taxation of Civil Costs* (July 1984).

*When common fund costs appropriate* – for the court to order taxation on the more generous common fund scale, instead of the usual party and party scale, 'there should be some special or unusual feature in the case to justify the court in exercising its discretion in that way': *Kung Kwok Wai David v Citibank NA* [1989] 2 HKC 48, 52C–G (CA), quoting *Preston v Preston* [1982] Fam 17, 38. One example is where a party has unreasonably prosecuted or defended an action. See *Chiu Chi Lai v Well Speed Ltd* [1997] 4 HKC 144, 148H–I where such an order was made against an unsuccessful party who had resisted the application 'to the very end' in spite of clear authorities. And see *Chau Yee Chai Henry v Chan Yuk Kwan* HCAP 10/2004 (A Cheung J; 07.11.2005) where common fund costs were ordered against the defendant in a probate action who really had no defence and had defended for a collateral purpose. In *Cheung Wei Man Vivien & Anor v Centaline Property Agency Ltd & Ors* HCA 286/2000 (Lam J; 15.12.2006) (para 32) the court ordered costs on the common fund basis against a party who had unreasonably conducted the litigation in a manner which disproportionately escalated costs.

*Legal aid cases* – section 20A of the Legal Aid Ordinance (Cap 91) provides for common fund taxation where an aided person is a party to proceedings. It is common practice to differentiate between the party and party element, being costs which may be recoverable from the opposing party depending on the order of the court, and the aided person's 'own costs' comprising additional costs over and above those allowable on the party and party scale, but permissible on the common fund scale and payable by the legal aid fund to an aided person's assigned solicitors and counsel. An example is the costs of assigned solicitors reporting periodically to the Director of Legal Aid, as they are required to do.

*Parties under disability* – Where an order for costs is made in favour of a party under disability (as to which see Order 80) on settlement of an action it is usual for the court to order that the opposing party pay those costs on the common fund basis. See *Tai Chau Yung & Anor v Ng Jim & Anor* [1999] 2 HKLRD 549. There Suffiad J quoted from the *1985 Supreme Court Practice* where it was stated:

> The reason for this practice is that it is difficult for the court to judge on the adequacy of the settlement without knowing how much the plaintiff will receive net of costs.

Suffiad J also noted that an order for common fund costs would protect the amount of the settlement for the benefit of the party under disability and went on to order common fund costs in the case before him 'primarily on the basis to ensure that the plaintiff, particularly the two infants, are adequately compensated'.

In relation to personal injuries list actions, see also para 189 of PD 18.1, which provides that save as otherwise ordered by the judge, the proper order for costs in respect of compromised proceedings on behalf of a party under disability is on the common fund basis.

In *Wai Yin Wa v Laminate Enterprises Ltd* HCPI 514/1997 (Master Barnes; 23.12.1999) it was held that the costs of a party under disability should be ordered on the common fund basis whether the case was compromised by settlement or concluded after a full assessment. However in *Fung Wing Yee v Chen Jung Chien* HCPI 657/2007 (Suffiad J; 30.04.2010) (para 12-14) the court read *Wai Yin Wa* as based on the special features of the particular case, and not as of general application. The fact that the plaintiff was a minor was not, *per se*, such a matter as would warrant the exercise of discretion to order costs on the common fund basis after a full assessment of damages.

In *Ma Ka Lai (by the mother and next friend Ho Mei Chun) v Katafygiotis Lampros* HCPI 982/2001 (Seagroatt J; 21.01.2003) the court departed from the usual practice and ordered costs on the party and party scale only. It was a 'relatively simple claim' and the infant's solicitors had waived any claim to further costs meaning that the infant client would not be prejudiced. Similarly in *Lam Wing Sam (a minor) v Landfit Enterprises Ltd* DCEC 370/99 (HH Judge Carlson; 21.02.2002) the usual practice was not adopted. The ground was that there was no difficulty in approving the settlement.

### [62.28.11]   The trustee basis
Rule 28(5) permits the court to award costs on the higher 'trustee' basis laid down by rule 31(2) in cases where the costs are to be paid out of a fund or to a trustee. As to the level of recovery under this basis of taxation, see the annotation to rule 31.

### [62.28.12]   The indemnity basis
*Power to order costs on indemnity basis* – An amendment to rule 28 in 1991 ended a period of uncertainty as to whether the Hong Kong court has power to order that costs be taxed on an indemnity basis. Rule 28(3), as amended, now makes it clear that there is such power, and rule 28(4A) now sets out the extent to which costs are to be allowed on an indemnity basis taxation.

It had long been thought that the court had an inherent power to order costs to be taxed on an indemnity basis. In *EMI Records Ltd v Ian Cameron Wallace Ltd* [1983] 1 Ch 59, at 70C–E, Megarry V-C stated:

> the court has power in contentious proceedings to order the unsuccessful party to pay the successful party's costs on bases other than those contained in rule 28; and these include orders for costs on the solicitor and own client basis, on the solicitor and client basis, or on an indemnity basis.

Although the situation changed in England with the amendments of April 1986 (see the commentary on the bases of taxation, above), many assumed that the *EMI* case continued to represent the law in Hong Kong on this point. However, the decision in *Hanwa Co (HK) Ltd v Everbright Shipping Co Ltd & Ors* HCAJ 153/1988 (Barnett J; 09.12.1988), cast doubt on this. Barnett J there held that rule 28 constitutes a complete scheme for the award of costs between parties when read together with section 52A of the Ordinance and rule 2(4) of this Order, and that, therefore, 'on a true construction of our legislation, a court has no power to award costs between parties other than on a party and party or common fund basis'. The court specifically held that it had no power to award costs on an indemnity basis. In a subsequent first instance decision, the court doubted the correctness of the *Hanwa* decision: this was in *Overseas Trust Bank Ltd v Coopers & Lybrand* [1991] 1 HKLR 177, where the court, *obiter*, held that in the light of the breadth of the discretion conferred on it by section 52A of the Ordinance in matters relating to costs, the decision in *Hanwa* could not stand. It was pointed out that in at least one Privy Council decision, on appeal from Hong Kong, the power to order indemnity costs in this jurisdiction was recognised and exercised (*Pacific Insurance Co Ltd v Wong* [1989] 1 WLR 602). In *Commissioner of Inland Revenue v Aspiration Land Investment Ltd* HCIA 10/1989 (Kaplan J; 14.12.1990) the court was faced with the conflicting judgments in *Hanwa* and the *Overseas Trust Bank* case, and expressly preferred the latter, holding that it did have jurisdiction to order indemnity costs.

*Quantum to be allowed on indemnity taxation* – The 1991 amendments not only clarified the existence of the court's power to make indemnity basis costs orders, they also set down in legislation for the first time in Hong Kong the criteria to be applied on such a taxation. This is done in rule 28(4A), inserted as part of the 1991 amendments. This provision is the same as Order 62 rule 12(2) of the former English RSC, so the English cases thereunder will have persuasive value.

*When indemnity costs are appropriate* – Indemnity costs have long been ordered against contemnors: *EMI* (above, at 64H). Approval of this practice was expressed in the *Aspiration Land* case (above). In *Re Kennedy (No 3)* [2005] 2 HKC 73 indemnity costs were ordered *in favour* of an alleged contemnor who successfully resisted the application for committal. Indemnity costs may be appropriate in cases of proceedings which are an abuse of process (*Aspiration Land*, above), scandalous or vexatious, or initiated or prosecuted maliciously, or for an ulterior motive, or in an oppressive manner (*Choy Yee Chun v Bondstar Development Ltd* [1997] HKLRD 1327), commenced for an illegitimate purpose (*Yip Peter v Asian Electronics Ltd* [1998] 2 HKC 96) or otherwise an 'affront to the court' (*Wu Ka v Wu Kuo Cheng* [2003] 3 HKLRD 658). In *UBC Construction Ltd v Sung Foo Kee Ltd* HCCT 11/1991 (Kaplan J; 19.07.1993) indemnity costs were ordered in respect of certain items where witnesses had made an 'absurd' contention of fact based on an 'outrageous' attempt by late amendment to induce a settlement, adding 'considerably to the costs'. In *Yu Tim Sheung v SJ* HCPI 1395/2006 (Deputy Judge Carlson; 03.06.2008) indemnity costs were ordered against an unsuccessful plaintiff who had lied at trial on issues of liability and quantum, though it was recognised that such an order would not be made in every such case. Indemnity costs are no longer limited to cases of deception, underhand conduct, ulterior motive or improper purpose: *Sung Foo Kee Ltd v Pak Lik Co* [1996] 3 HKC 570, 575-6 (CA); *Re Hyundai Engineering & Construction Co Ltd* HCCW 1299/2001 (Kwan J; 08.03.2002). In those cases the court quoted with approval from English authority to the effect that indemnity costs are appropriate in cases of bad faith, personal vendetta, improper or oppressive conduct and costs incurred irrationally or out of proportion. In *Technicon Eng'g Ltd v Chan Lee Kwok & Anor* DCCJ 607/2007 (Judge Mimmie Chan; 28.09.2007) the court ordered indemnity costs against a plaintiff who named the wrong defendant on the writ, having failed to conduct a business registration search. In addition, indemnity costs may be ordered in any other circumstances where the court considers such an order appropriate: see *Town Planning Board v Society for Protection of the Harbour Ltd (No 2)* (2004) 7 HKCFAR 114 where Li CJ noted (at para 17) that 'the courts have emphasised the undesirability of attempting to define the circumstances in which orders for indemnity costs are to be made' and that the discretion is not fettered beyond the requirement that taxation on an indemnity basis must be appropriate. In *Technicom Interiors Design Eng'g Ltd v Tse Yuet Yi & Anor* DCCJ 5965/2008 (Deputy Judge R Yu; 02.11.2010) (para 159) the court took the view that Order 62 rule 5(1)(e) now allows the court greater flexibility to award indemnity costs. That provision, which was introduced as part of the Civil Justice Reforms in 2009, mandates the court to take into account the conduct of parties when exercising its discretion as to costs.

*Indemnity costs on non-disclosure* – An order for indemnity costs may be appropriate against a party who has failed in its duty to make full and frank disclosure on an *ex parte* application. However, this will not be 'automatically' so. See the judgment of Keith JA in *New Asia Energy Ltd v Concord Oil (HK) Ltd* [2000] 2 HKC

681, 690H–I. In that case the Court of Appeal set aside an order for indemnity costs made below.

*Contractual provision as to indemnity costs* – It is common for mortgage, credit card and other loan agreements to provide that a lender shall be entitled to indemnity costs in recovery proceedings. The court will normally exercise its discretion as to costs so as to enforce such an agreement: see below.

*Indemnity costs on extension of time after lengthy delay* – An order for indemnity costs may be appropriate against a party who is granted an extension of time after lengthy delay: see *Leung Yee & Anor v Ng Yiu Ming & Anor* [2001] 1 HKC 342 (CA) at 361I–362A.

*Indemnity costs in cases of misconduct* – In *Lam Lai Wah Susanna v Pacific Century Insurance Co Ltd* [2003] 2 HKC 520 (CA) costs were ordered on an indemnity basis where a solicitor made an affirmation which was 'obviously wrong' (at 525I) and the manner in which the proceedings had been initiated and carried on constituted an 'affront to the court' (at 526I-527A).

*Indemnity costs in proceedings brought for public benefit* – Indemnity costs may be ordered in favour of a private litigant who brings proceedings in the public interest and for public benefit rather than for personal gain. See *Society for Protection of the Harbour Ltd v Town Planning Board* [2003] 4 HKC 463, 467E. In that case Chu J cited the following overseas cases where it had been held that indemnity costs may be awarded to a party who pursues an important point of law with wide socio-cultural, environmental or constitutional implications:

- *New Zealand Maori Council v AG of New Zealand* [1994] 1 AC 466, 485G–H;
- *Oshlack v Richmond River Council* (1998) 193 CLR 72, 80-81, 91;
- *Reilly PCJ v Wachowich CJPC* (1999) Lexis 1380 (upheld by the Alberta Court of Appeal at [2000] AJ No 1029; and
- *Re Reference s 6(2) of the Territorial Court Act (NWT)* (1997) 152 DLR (4th) 132.

The judgment of Chu J was upheld on appeal to the Court of Final Appeal, and there the costs of the appeal were also ordered to be paid on the indemnity basis. See *Town Planning Board v Society for the Protection of the Harbour Ltd* (2004) 7 HKCFAR 114.

*Indemnity costs for improper conduct* – See the commentary under Order 62 rule 5(1)(e).

**[62.28.13]   Other bases**

Costs are sometimes awarded on the 'solicitor and client' scale: this is equivalent to the common fund basis (see *EMI Records Ltd v Ian Cameron Wallace Ltd* [1983] 1 Ch 59, at 63A). There is also the 'solicitor and own client' basis of taxation, governed by Order 62 rule 29. Although primarily intended for taxations as between solicitors and their own clients pursuant to the provisions of the Legal Practitioners Ordinance (Cap 159), if *EMI* is correct then the court may order taxation on this basis as between opposing litigants as well. However, if the *Hanwa* case (see commentary on the indemnity basis, above) is to be followed this would not be possible, as it was held there that rule 28 is a complete code for awarding costs as between opposing litigants, and although the effect of that decision has now been reversed by amendment to the rules clarifying the situation with respect to indemnity costs, there is no equivalent legislation for solicitor and own client costs, and the reasoning in *Hanwa* has not been overruled by a higher court. See *Hirst v Agrava-Kerr* [1992] 1 HKLR 414 as an example of a case where a losing party was ordered to pay costs on the solicitor and own client basis to the winning party, for reasons of improper conduct. However, such orders will be very rare as between opposing parties to litigation. See *Cathay Pacific Airways Flight Attendants Union v Cheung & Choy (a firm)* HCMP 1863/2007 (Bharwaney J; 04.05.2010) where it was noted that the quantum allowed on a solicitor and own client taxation may exceed indemnity costs, since anything authorised by the client will be allowed, even if unreasonable.

### [62.28.14]    Contract as to level of costs

The court's discretion as to costs under section 52A of the Ordinance cannot be fettered by contract: *Chekiang First Bank v Fong Siu Kin & Anor* [1997] 2 HKC 302, 309E-F (CA). However 'where parties have contractually provided for the basis upon which costs are to be quantified, the court would in the normal course of events give effect to that': (per Litton VP at 309F, citing *Gomba Holdings v Minories Finance* [1993] Ch 171, 191B). See also *Goodwell Property Management Ltd v Basesmart Development Ltd & Anor* [1990] 1 HKLR 1.

In *Hang Seng Credit Card Ltd & Ors v Tsang Nga Lee & Ors* [2000] 3 HKC 269 the court cited the Unconscionable Contracts Ordinance (Cap 458) in refusing to award indemnity costs as provided in a credit card agreement. However in *Yeung Kwok Fan & Anor v Standard Chartered Bank* [2001] 4 HKC 486, 490C-D (where Cap 458 was not engaged) the court held that 'commercial behaviour' and 'financial arrogance' were not relevant to its exercise of discretion. To the extent that *Yeung Kwok Fan* suggested there was a contractual right to indemnity costs notwithstanding the court's discretion under s 52A, it was not followed in *Standard Chartered Bank (HK) Ltd v Sweetmart Garment Works Ltd & Ors* [2010] 5 HKC 143. In *Standard Chartered* the court emphasised that in *Chekiang First Bank* the Court of Appeal had held that the court's discretion could not be fettered by contract. It held (para 36) that there was no basis to depart from the usual party and party basis despite an indemnity costs provision. Leave to appeal the *Standard Chartered* decision was granted on 11.08.2010.

In *Wing Hang Bank Ltd v Crystal Jet International Ltd & Ors* [2002] 3 HKC 279 a mortgage provided that the bank would be entitled to costs on the solicitor and own client basis. There was no equivalent provision in a parallel guarantee. However, it was held that since the guarantee was for all sums due under the mortgage, the guarantor should be equally liable in costs (appeal on other grounds dismissed at [2005] 2 HKC 638).

A contractual term providing for costs to be paid on a basis other than the usual party and party basis may not be given effect by the court unless it is pleaded: *Credit Agricole v Crossland Industries Corp & Anor* [1988] HKC 676. However where the receiving party is the defendant in proceedings arising from an agreement it is 'legal nonsense' for him to counterclaim solely for costs in accordance with the agreement: *Yeung Kwok Fan & Anor v Standard Chartered Bank* [2001] 4 HKC 486, 495B–E.

**[62.28.15]    High Court cases within the jurisdiction of District Court**
A plaintiff who chooses to issue proceedings in the Court of First Instance which could also have been commenced in the District Court will generally recover only such amount of costs as would be awarded in the District Court: *Yuen Yiu Kwong v Chan Kwok Chuen & Ors* [2003] 2 HKC 617. However the court retains a discretion to award costs on the High Court scale where there was a 'reasonable prospect' of obtaining judgment in a higher amount: *Lai Ki v B+B Construction Co Ltd & Ors* [2003] 3 HKC 322, 329E-F. The matter should be considered from the point of view of the time when the writ was issued and the circumstances which prevailed at that time: *Wong Wai Man v Yi Wo Yuen Aged Sanatorium Centre Ltd* HCPI 77/2007 (Suffiad J; 09.09.2008) (para 14), referring to *Hopkins v Rees & Kirby Ltd* [1959] 1 WLR 740, 742. In *Express Engineering Ltd v Cheng Chun Ying & Anor* [1993] 1 HKC 410 such an order was made in respect of a counterclaim to a High Court action. The same 'reasonable prospect' test applies where proceedings are taken in the District Court but damages awarded below the upward limit of the exclusive jurisdiction of the Small Claims Tribunal. See *Cheng Yu Tin Alvin v Ho Hon Ka* [2006] 3 HKC 473 (CA) where it was held that a plaintiff in the District Court, awarded damages in the middle range of the jurisdiction of the tribunal, was entitled only to the costs on the tribunal's scale.

In considering which scale of costs to apply in such cases, the court should take into account the underlying objectives in Order 1A rule 1. These include cost-effectiveness and procedural economy. In *May Fung Co Ltd v Wing Lung Industrial Ltd & Ors* [2009] 5 HKLRD 590 (Lam J; 09.10.2009) (paras 8-9) the court said that 'these underlying objectives point to the importance of conducting litigation in the appropriate forum', and that *prima facie* 'it is not cost-effective to pursue a claim in a more expensive manner by litigating in the Court of First Instance as opposed to the District Court'.

Where the court's order does not specify which scale should apply, it should be the lower scale. See *OWT Asia Ltd v CPCNet HK Ltd* [2007] 2 HKLRD 224 where it was said (at para 11):

> Thus, in the absence of a specific statement that the High Court scale should apply, an order for costs made in favour of a plaintiff where the amount recovered (not including interest, which the District Court is equally able to award) falls within the jurisdiction of the District Court, should be understood as requiring taxation of such costs on the District Court scale.

In personal injuries cases the proper forum is to be decided after giving credit for employees' compensation which has been received: *Lai Ki* at 329F-G, and see *Yuen Yiu Kwong* at 622E expressly doubting *Lam Sui Wo v Leung Kam Tin* [1990] 1 HKC 456 in this regard. However no account is to be taken of contributory negligence unless it was admitted: *Lai Ki* (above, at para 7); *Leung Po Chun v Yat Lee Booth-Construction Co Ltd & Anor* HCPI 1099/2006 (Deputy Judge Carlson; 22.11.2007).

In considering whether the District Court or the Court of First Instance was appropriate for a particular claim, it is the principal amount of the judgment which is relevant. Interest should not be taken into account. See *Cheung Kai Chi v Chun Wo Contractors Ltd & Anor* HCPI 572/2004 (Deputy Judge L Chan; 19.06.2008).

Where proceedings are settled any agreement between the parties as to the scale of costs should appear in the consent order, but if there is no such agreement an application should be made by way of summons to a master to determine the appropriate scale: *Lai Ki* at 329H. In *Lai Ki* Seagroatt J indicated that the same should apply where money within the District Court jurisdiction is paid into the High Court and accepted, but this aspect of the decision may be *per incuriam* as it appears to contradict the decision of the Court of Appeal in *Cho Ho Kuen v Yu Kwok Wah & Ors* [2001] 3 HKC 566. See the commentary under Order 62 rule 10.

In cases where there has been a transfer between the Court of First Instance and the District Court see section 44A of the District Court Ordinance (Cap 336), and see the commentary under Order 78 rule 1.

Costs incurred in the Court of First Instance may be ordered to be paid on the District Court scale from a reasonable time after it became clear that it was appropriate for the proceedings to be transferred to that court: *Chak Wing Keung & Ors v BSC Home Improvement Centres Ltd* HCPI 880/2002 (Suffiad J; 19.10.2005).

The principles discussed here, as laid down in *Lai Ki v B&B Construction Co Ltd & Ors* (above) are not confined to personal injury cases, and are of 'general application': *Windix Industries Ltd v Telesonic Enterprises Ltd & Anor* HCA 1274/2007 (Suffiad J; 28.11.2008). In that case those principles were applied in a copyright infringement claim. In *OWT* (above) they were applied in a breach of contract case.

See also the discussion of the related topic of the costs consequences of acceptance of a sanctioned payment in an amount within the District Court's jurisdiction, in the commentary under Order 22 rule 20.

### [62.28.16] Appeals
The Court of Appeal is reluctant to interfere on appeal with an order by the trial judge as to the basis of taxation of costs to be paid to the receiving party. This is a matter for the judge's discretion. See *Lakhan v Wu Wing Tat & Anor* [1987] 3 HKC 54. As to appeals against orders as to costs generally, see the commentary under Order 59 rule 1.

### [62.28.17] Costs of taxation
The paying party will usually be ordered to pay the receiving party's costs of taxation. However, the result may be different where the paying party has protected itself by making a *Calderbank* offer (as to which see the commentary under Order 62 rule 5(1) (d)), or where there has been a sanctioned offer or sanctioned payment on account of costs under Order 62A.

In *SY Eng'g Co Ltd v HK Housing Authority* [2001] 2 HKC 226 solicitors for a paying party were ordered (*nisi*) to pay personally 2/3 of the costs of a taxation where they had not complied with the practice direction by negotiating the bill with the other side and attempting to reduce the number of items in dispute.

All the costs of taxation, including costs of preparation of the bill and considering the list of objections were disallowed on the ground of exaggeration in *Manova Int'l Ltd v Giga Technology Co Ltd & Anor* HCA 733/2009 (Registrar Au-Yeung; 26.02.2010). The receiving party had claimed $270,000 as compared to $110,000 allowed on taxation. See the commentary under Order 62 rule 5(1)(e) concerning the relevance of the conduct of the parties in exercising the discretion as to costs.

In *Manova* (para 22) the court warned that in future costs of taxation might be disallowed where summary assessment was clearly appropriate. See the commentary under Order 62 rules 9(4)(b) and 9A concerning summary assessment.

**28A. Costs of a litigant in person** (O. 62 r. 28A)

**(1)   On a taxation of the costs of a litigant in person there may, subject to the provisions of this rule, be allowed such costs as would have been allowed if the work and disbursements to which the costs relate had been done or made by a solicitor on the litigant's behalf.**

**(2)   The amount allowed in respect of any item shall be such sum as the taxing master thinks fit not exceeding, except in the case of a disbursement, two-thirds of the sum which in the opinion of the taxing master would have been allowed in respect of that item if the litigant had been represented by a solicitor.**

**(3)   Where in the opinion of the taxing master the litigant has not suffered any pecuniary loss in doing any work to which the costs relate, he shall not be allowed in respect of the time reasonably spent by him on the work more than $200 an hour.**

**(4)   A litigant who is allowed costs in respect of attending court to conduct his own case shall not be entitled to a witness allowance in addition.**

**(5)   Nothing in Order 6, rule 2(1)(b), or rule 32(4) of this Order or the Second Schedule to this Order shall, unless otherwise specified therein, apply to the costs of a litigant in person. (L.N. 152 of 2008)**

**(6)   For the purposes of this rule a litigant in person does not include a litigant who is a practising solicitor but includes a company or other corporation which is acting without a legal representative. (L.N. 152 of 2008)**

**(7)   This rule applies, with the necessary modifications, to a summary assessment under rules 9(4)(b), 9A(1)(a) and (b) and 11A(4), as it applies to the taxation of the costs of a litigant in person, if the party entitled to the sum is a litigant in person. (L.N. 152 of 2008)**

---

**NOTES**

**[62.28A.1]   Costs of a litigant in person**
At one time a litigant in person was entitled to recover by way of costs only out-of-pocket expenses: *Buckland v Watts* [1970] 1 QB 27; [1969] 2 All ER 985. This position was remedied in England by the Litigants in Person (Costs and Expenses) Act 1975. The failure of Hong Kong to follow the English reform was criticised at (1980) 10 HKLJ 257. Order 62 rule 28A ameliorates the position of the litigant in person in Hong Kong. It entitles the litigant in person to recover, in addition to out-of-pocket expenses, up to $200 per hour for time reasonably spent, or, where pecuniary loss is shown, as much as 2/3 of what would have been allowed if a solicitor had been instructed. Pecuniary loss must be demonstrated by admissible evidence: *Lam Chit Man v Lam Chi To* [2004] 2 HKLRD 104 (CA). The absence, in Hong Kong, of primary legislation equivalent to the English Act was considered by the Court of Appeal in *Tse Ming Cheung v Wilkinson & Grist* [1991] 1 HKLR 30. The burden of proof is on the litigant in person to establish pecuniary loss by affidavit: *Audrey Chow Securities Ltd v Yung Lung Biu Albert & Ors* HCA 147/1998 (Master Levy; 15.07.2009) (para 13).

The out-of-pocket expenses which a litigant in person may recover include travelling expenses. In the case of a litigant from overseas these may include the cost of coming to Hong Kong for the purpose of the proceedings. This is so even though no such expense would have been incurred had the litigant instructed a solicitor in Hong Kong to appear for him. However, the overall quantum of expenses may not exceed the amount which would have been allowed by way of costs if a solicitor had been instructed. See *Tse Ming Cheung v Wilkinson & Grist* [1991] 1 HKLR 30 (CA).

The indemnity principle 'has no application to cases where litigants are acting in person': *Leung Yin Ling v IO of 165 Wong Nai Chung Rd* LDBM 63/2000 (Ag Reg Kwang; 08.08.2002), distinguishing *Gundry v Sanibury* [1910] 1 KB 645. Hence a litigant in person may recover amounts under this rule which it is not actually obliged to pay to another party. The costs awarded under this rule are paid to the litigant in person itself. (Note that the decision in *Leung Yin Ling* was set aside on other grounds at [2002] 4 HKC 328). The indemnity principle has no application because the litigant in person has a statutory right, without reference to costs actually paid to a fee earner: *Au Wing Lun v Tam Mei Kam & Ors* HCA 811/2007 (Master Yuen; 31.10.2008) (para 53).

An order for costs in favour of a litigant in person on the indemnity basis does not oust application of this rule: *Au Wing Lun* (above) (at para 45).

**[62.28A.2]  Costs of a company 'in person'**
Where a company acts 'in person', through a director, with leave under Order 5 rule 6(2), it may recover costs in accordance with this rule: see *Typhoon 8 Research Ltd v Seapower Resources International Ltd & Anor* [2002] 2 HKLRD 660. In that case the Court of Appeal expressly did not follow *Australian Telephone Distributors Pty Ltd v Golden Always Ltd* [1996] 3 HKC 401 where a differently constituted Court of Appeal had held that a company represented by a director is not a 'litigant in person' for the purposes of Order 62 rule 28A. In the *Typhoon 8* case the Court of Appeal distinguished *Jonathan Alexander Ltd v Proctor* [1996] 1 WLR 518 which had been relied upon in the *Australian Telephone* case. See also *Leung Yin Ling* (above).

With effect from April 2009, rule 28A(6) was amended as part of the civil justice reform so as to expressly extend the rule to companies and other corporations acting without a legal representative.

**29. Costs payable to a solicitor by his own client** (O. 62 r. 29)
**(1)  On the taxation of a solicitor's bill to his own client (except a bill to be paid out of funds provided by the Legislative Council pursuant to section 27 of the Legal Aid Ordinance (Cap 91), or a bill with respect to non-contentious business) all costs shall be allowed except in so far as they are of an unreasonable amount or have been unreasonably incurred.**

**(2)  For the purposes of paragraph (1), all costs incurred with the express or implied approval of the client shall, subject to paragraph (3), be conclusively presumed to have been reasonably incurred and, where the amount thereof has been expressly or impliedly approved by the client, to have been reasonable in amount.**

**(3)  For the purposes of paragraph (1), any costs which in the circumstances of the case are of an unusual nature and such that they would not be allowed on a taxation of costs in a case to which rule 28(2) applies, shall, unless the**

solicitor expressly informed his client before they were incurred that they might not be so allowed, be presumed, until the contrary is shown, to have been unreasonably incurred.

(4)    In paragraphs (2) and (3), the references to the client shall be construed—

(a)    if the client was at the material time a mentally disordered person within the meaning of the Mental Health Ordinance (Cap 136) and represented by a person acting as guardian ad litem or next friend, as references to that person acting, where necessary, with the authority of the Court;

(b)    if the client was at the material time a minor and represented by a person acting as guardian ad litem or next friend, as references to that person.

## NOTES

### [62.29.1]    Solicitor and own client taxation

Order 62 rule 29 sets out the criteria applicable on taxation as between solicitor and own client, that is assessment of the amount the client is liable to pay where that is in dispute with the solicitor. As to the circumstances in which the court may order such a taxation, see sections 67 and 68 of the Legal Practitioners Ordinance (Cap 159) and the commentary under Order 106 rule 2. The rule will also apply where the court orders taxation of *inter partes* costs on the solicitor and own client basis rather than the usual party and party basis.

By its own terms rule 29 does not apply to taxation of solicitors' charges payable out of the legal aid fund. The relevant provisions for such taxations are found in the Legal Aid Ordinance and regulations which apply the common fund basis. Likewise the rule does not apply to taxation of solicitors' bills rendered in respect of non-contentious business. The criteria applicable on such a taxation are found in rule 5 of the Solicitors (General) Costs Rules, subsidiary legislation under the Legal Practitioners Ordinance (see the commentary under Order 106 rule 2).

On taxation to which rule 29 applies 'all costs shall be allowed except in so far as they are of an unreasonable amount or have been unreasonably incurred'. This resembles the trustee basis 'in that it allows everything except any items which fall within the words of disallowance': *EMI Records Ltd v Ian Cameron Wallace Ltd* [1983] 1 Ch 59, 64E-G. In deciding what costs were reasonably incurred or of a reasonable amount, the taxing master is assisted by subrule (2) which deems costs incurred with the client's approval to be reasonable, and subrule (3) which creates a rebuttable presumption that costs of an 'unusual nature' have been unreasonably incurred unless the solicitor informed the client in advance.

30. **Costs payable to solicitor where money recovered by or on behalf of infant, etc.** (O. 62 r. 30)

(1)    **This rule applies to—**

(a)    **any proceedings in which money is claimed or recovered by or on behalf of, or adjudged or ordered or agreed to be paid to, or for the benefit of, a person who is a minor or a mentally disordered person within the meaning of the Mental Health Ordinance**

(Cap 136) or in which money paid into court is accepted by or on behalf of such a person; and

(b)   any proceedings under the Fatal Accidents Ordinance (Cap 22), in which money is recovered by or on behalf of, or adjudged or ordered or agreed to be paid to, or for the benefit of, the widow of the person whose death gave rise to the proceedings in satisfaction of a claim under the said Ordinance or in which money paid into court is accepted by her or on her behalf in satisfaction of such a claim, if the proceedings were for the benefit also of a person who, when the money is recovered, or adjudged or ordered or agreed to be paid, or accepted, is a minor; and

(c)   any proceedings in the Court of Appeal on an application or appeal made in connection with any such proceedings to which this rule applies by virtue of the foregoing provisions of this paragraph.

(2)   Unless the Court otherwise directs the costs payable to his solicitor by any plaintiff in any proceedings to which this rule applies by virtue of paragraph (1)(a) or (b), being the costs of those proceedings or incident to the claim therein or consequent thereon, shall be taxed under rule 29; and no costs shall be payable to the solicitor of any plaintiff in respect of those proceedings, except such amount of costs as may be certified in accordance with this rule on the taxation under rule 29 of the solicitor's bill to that plaintiff.

(3)   On the taxation under rule 29 of a solicitor's bill to any plaintiff in any proceedings to which this rule applies by virtue of paragraph (1)(a) or (b) who is his own client, the taxing master shall also tax any costs payable to that plaintiff in those proceedings and shall certify—

(a)   the amount allowed on the taxation under rule 29, the amount allowed on that taxation of any costs payable to the plaintiff in those proceedings and the amount (if any), by which the first-mentioned amount exceeds the other, and

(b)   where necessary, the proportion of the amount of the excess payable respectively by, or out of money belonging to, any party to the proceedings who is a minor or a mentally disordered person within the meaning of the Mental Health Ordinance (Cap 136) or the widow of the man whose death gave rise to the proceedings and any other party.

(4)   Paragraphs (2) and (3) shall apply in relation to any proceedings to which this rule applies by virtue of paragraph (1)(c) as if for references to a plaintiff there were substituted references to the party, whether appellant or respondent, who was the plaintiff in the proceedings which gave rise to the first-mentioned proceedings.

(5)   Nothing in the foregoing provisions of this rule shall prejudice a solicitor's lien for costs.

(6)   Where in any proceedings to which this rule applies directions given by the Court under Order 80, rule 12 provide for the transfer or payment of money to or into a District Court and for the payment to the solicitor of any plaintiff in the proceedings of an amount in respect of costs out of the money so transferred or paid, the taxing master by whom those costs are taxed shall send a copy of his certificate to the registrar of the District Court.

(7)    **The foregoing provisions of this rule shall apply in relation to—**

    (a)    **a counterclaim by or on behalf of a person who is a minor or a mentally disordered person within the meaning of the Mental Health Ordinance (Cap 136) and a counterclaim consisting of or including a claim under the Fatal Accidents Ordinance (Cap 22) by or on behalf of the widow of the man whose death gave rise to the claim; and**

    (b)    **a claim made by or on behalf of a person who is a minor or a mentally disordered person as aforesaid in an action by any other person for relief under section 504 of the Merchant Shipping Act, 1894 (1894 c. 60 U.K.), and a claim consisting of or including a claim under the Fatal Accidents Ordinance (Cap 22) made by or on behalf of that widow in such an action,**

**as if for references to a plaintiff there were substituted references to a defendant.**

---

## NOTES

### [62.30.1]    Costs payable by party under disability to be taxed

Order 62 rule 30 provides that costs payable by or on behalf of an infant or mentally disordered person to a solicitor must be taxed as between solicitor and own client under rule 29. The rule also applies to proceedings brought by a person of full capacity under the Fatal Accidents Ordinance (Cap 22) for the benefit of an infant or mentally disordered person.

Infants and mentally disordered persons are parties under disability to whom Order 80 applies in relation to the conduct of civil litigation, settlement and handling of money recovered. Mentally handicapped persons also come within the definition of party under disability in Order 80 rule 1, but strangely Order 62 rule 30 does not expressly extend to them.

Order 62 rule 30 is necessary because an infant or mentally disordered person does not have conduct of civil claims on his or her own behalf, and may not be competent to enter into an agreement with a solicitor as to costs. The purpose of the rule is to put the court in the position of protecting the disabled party's interests.

## 31. Costs payable to a trustee out of the trust funds, etc. (O. 62 r. 31)

    **(1)    This rule applies to every taxation of the costs which a person who is or has been a party to any proceedings in the capacity of trustee or personal representative is entitled to be paid out of any fund which he holds in that capacity.**

    **(2)    On any taxation to which this rule applies, no costs shall be disallowed except in so far as those costs or any part of their amount should not, in accordance with the duty of the trustee or personal representative as such, have been incurred or paid, and should for that reason be borne by him personally.**

---

## NOTES

### [62.31.1]    Taxation on the trustee basis

Order 62 rule 31 lays down the trustee basis for taxation of costs. It is expressed to apply to every case in which a trustee is entitled to be paid costs out of the trust fund. By virtue of Order 62 rule 28(5) it may also be awarded in other cases in which costs are to be paid out of a fund and in other cases involving trustees and personal representatives.

In *EMI Records Ltd v Ian Cameron Wallace Ltd* [1983] 1 Ch 59, at 64D, Megarry V-C, differentiating this basis of taxation from the party and party and common fund bases, said:

> it will be observed that here the thrust of the taxation has been shifted from what is to be included to what is to be excluded; it is no longer a question of allowing only those items which are necessary or proper, whether on a more generous scale or not, but instead has become a matter of prohibiting the disallowance of any item unless it falls within the words of exception.

**32. Scales of costs** (O. 62 r. 32)

**(1)  Subject to the foregoing rules and the following provisions of this rule, the scale of costs contained in the First Schedule of this Order, together with the notes and general provisions contained in that Schedule, shall apply to the taxation of all costs incurred in relation to contentious business done after the commencement of these rules.**

**(2)  On a taxation in relation to which rule 29 or rule 31(2) has effect and in other special cases costs may at the discretion of the taxing master be allowed—**

**(a)  in relation to items not mentioned in the said scale; or**

**(b)  of an amount higher than that prescribed by the said scale.**

**(3)  Where the amount of a solicitor's remuneration in respect of non-contentious business connected with sales, purchases, leases, mortgages and other matters of conveyancing or in respect of any other non-contentious business is regulated (in the absence of agreement to the contrary) by any rules for the time being in force under the Legal Practitioners Ordinance (Cap 159), the amount of the costs to be allowed on taxation in respect of the like contentious business shall be the same, notwithstanding anything in the scale contained in the First Schedule. (L.N. 152 of 2008)**

**(4)  Notwithstanding paragraph (1), costs shall, unless the Court otherwise orders, be allowed in the cases to which the Second Schedule to this Order applies in accordance with the provisions of that Schedule.**

---

**NOTES**

**[62.32.1]  The scales of costs**

By virtue of Order 62 rule 32 the provisions of the two Schedules to Order 62 govern the level of recovery on most party and party taxations.

Schedule 2 lays down fixed costs which will normally be recoverable as between parties where judgment is entered by default, or under Order 14 or in respect of other matters such as garnishee proceedings. The amounts were substantially increased as part of the civil justice reforms which came into force on 2 April 2009. Note that the final costs in Schedule 2 apply only in the absence of an order to the contrary: Order 62 rule 32(4). It is thus open to a party to apply for costs to be assessed in the usual way, by taxation or agreement, which will usually result in a higher level of recovery. See the commentary under Order 49 rule 10 (garnishee proceedings) for examples of cases where the court has ordered that a party's costs be taxed rather than be fixed under Schedule 2.

Schedule 2 does not apply to litigants in person: see Order 62 rule 28A(5).

Schedule 1 applies to party and party taxations arising from disputes which are not resolved by default or on summary judgment. The main provision is paragraph 5 which grants the Registrar a general discretion to allow such amount as he thinks proper in respect of a solicitor's work. This discretion has for many years been exercised in accordance with guidelines. These provide that a solicitors' work will be recoverable on a party and party taxation on an hourly rate basis (rates suggested by the Law Society). The hourly rate depends on when the work was done and the seniority of the solicitor attending. See the guidance issued by the Law Society reproduced under Order 62 rule 21. It is important to note that the guidelines are not binding and that the court retains an unfettered discretion.

**[62.32.2]    Quantum of costs on party and party taxation**
See the commentary under Order 62 rule 21 and 28.

**[62.32.3]    Counsel's fees**
In order to be recoverable on taxation counsel's fee must have been paid. If it has not been paid there is no disbursement to recover. See *Mong Man Wai v H H Lau & Co* [2003] 4 HKC 587, 602D – 603C citing *Re Taxation of Costs, Re a Solicitor* [1936] 1 KB 523. In *Mong Man Wai* Deputy Judge A Cheung noted that the situation had been changed by legislation in England, but not Hong Kong, where para 2(1)(b) of Part II of the 1st Schedule to Order 62 specifically provides that counsel's fees shall not be allowed on taxation unless a receipt signed by counsel is produced before the taxing master's certificate is issued (except legal aid taxations and counsel instructed by the government).

*Counsel's fees generally – Two stage process for assessing counsel's fees –* In *Re Greater Beijing Expressways Ltd (No 4)* [2005] 2 HKC 185 it was held that the assessment of counsel's fees is a two-stage process. First the court considers whether it was 'necessary or proper' in terms of Order 62 rule 28(2) to instruct counsel to do the work in question. (The 'necessary or proper' criterion applies to taxations on the party and party basis; different criteria apply to taxations on other bases). Secondly, if it was 'necessary or proper' to instruct counsel, the court goes on to consider how much should be allowed in accordance with para 2(5) of Part II of the 1st Schedule to Order 62. Para 2(5) was amended (with prospective effect only) as part of the civil justice reforms taking effect in 2009: see the discussion below.

*Counsel's fee for work done before 2009 amendment –* Prior to the amendment of para 2(5) of Part II of the 1st Schedule to Order 62, it was there provided that every fee paid to counsel 'shall be allowed in full on taxation, unless the taxing master is satisfied that the same is excessive and unreasonable', in which event the taxing master's discretion as to costs was to be exercised having regard to all relevant circumstances and the matters set out in 1st Sched, Part II, para 1(2). By virtue of the transitional provisions in Order 62 rule 37(2) that test continues to apply to work done before the amendment came into force, even where the taxation takes place afterward. The Chief Justice's working party on civil justice reform said (final report, para 768) that this test 'appears to be at least as generous as the common fund and solicitor and own client bases of taxation'. The 'hypothetical counsel' test (which derives from *Simpson Motor Sales (London) Ltd v Hendon Corp (No 2)* [1965] 1 WLR 112 and has been used in Hong Kong since at least 1968: see *Re Tai Shun Investment Co Ltd v CIR* HCIA 2/1967 (Registrar Oliver; 14.12.1968)) may be applied at the second of the two stages referred to above: *Re Greater Beijing Expressways Ltd* (above, at 193D-E) 'so long as it is remembered that one is doing so on a more generous basis than that applicable to the other items in a party and party taxation'. Under the hypothetical counsel test, the measure of counsel's fee is what a hypothetical counsel, who does not insist on the high fees sometimes demanded by fashionable counsel, but is capable of conducting the case effectively, would be content to take: *Tai Hing Cotton Mill Ltd v Liu Chong Hing Bank Ltd* [1982] HKLR 387 389H-I.

*Counsel's fee for work done after 2009 amendment* - The new test, applicable to work done after commencement, gives greater scope to the taxing master to reduce the amount allowed in respect of counsel's fee on taxation. Para 2(5) now provides that the amount of counsel's fees 'is in the discretion of the taxing master' and in all cases the discretion is to be exercised having regard to all relevant circumstances and the matters set out in 1st Sched, Part II, para 1(2). Thus the presumption in favour of allowing counsel's fee in full unless the paying party shows that it is 'excessive and unreasonable' no longer applies and in its place the taxing master has a broad discretion. The new test implements recommendation 131 of the Chief Justice's working party on civil justice reform. In the interim report it had been said (at para 607.2) that it was 'difficult to see any justification' for the previous, more generous, test, which was described as 'exceptional', and might even 'encourage solicitors to pay counsel's fees without questioning them, on the footing that their clients are likely to recover such fees from the other side without their being taxed down'.

*Certificate for counsel* – Counsel's fees are in certain circumstances not recoverable unless the court has granted a certificate. Such certificates are given only in respect of counsel's attendances before the court and do not relate to other work: *Gao Hai Yin & Anor v Keeneye Holdings Ltd & Ors* HCA 1315/2009 (Chung J; 27.08.2009) (para 16, 17). The circumstances in which a certificate for counsel is required were broadened by the civil justice reforms which took effect in 2009. Previously, a certificate for counsel was only required for an appearance before a master in chambers, or more than one counsel appearing before a judge in chambers. Para 2(3) of Part II of the First Schedule to Order 62 now provides that a certificate for counsel is also required for appearances by more than one counsel before a master in open court or any hearing before a judge or the Court of Appeal. In earlier cases it was held that a certificate for two counsel was not required in the Court of Appeal. Those cases will continue to apply to counsel's fees for work done before the 2009 amendments, by virtue of the transitional provision in Order 62 rule 37. Those cases include *S v L* CACV 205/2007 (Rogers VP & Le Pichon JA; 12.10.2007) (para 24) and *Cheung Sun Lam v Lai Kam Man* [2008] 5 HKLRD 1. In cases where a certificate is not required, the taxing master retains a discretion whether to allow counsel's fees: *Bank of China v Xinyuan Trading Co Ltd* CACV 276/1998 (Godfrey VP, Rogers & Ribeiro JJA; 21.06.2000) (para 3). The purpose of amending the First Schedule so as to require a certificate for counsel in broader circumstances was to reduce the amount of time spent in argument before the taxing master as to the exercise of this discretion. So far as appearance in the Court of Appeal is concerned, the amendment was not intended to effect a change of substance. See *Chan Hei Ling Helen v Medical Council of Hong Kong* CACV 403/2006 (Le Pichon & Cheung JJA; Stone J; 21.07.2009). In that case a certificate for two counsel was granted, the court saying that the previous practice whereby parties were considered to be entitled to instruct leading counsel in the Court of Appeal if they choose remained unchanged. Subsequently, in *UDL Holdings Ltd & Anor v Leung Yuet Keung & Anor* CACV 356/2008 (Rogers VP, Le Pichon JA & Sakhrani J; 14.09.2009) (para 17) it was said that since parties would frequently forget to request a certificate, and nearly every case in the Court of Appeal merits the attendance of two counsel, the practice in respect of substantive appeals would be to grant a certificate unless the matter is raised specifically. In *Cheung Cho Kam Sindy v Cheung Yuet Ying Rose* CACV 178/2008 (Rogers VP, Le Pichon JA & Stone J; 08.12.2009) (para 12) it was clarified that 'even if people do not ask for it, they will be entitled to a certificate for two counsel into the Order'.

*Taxing master's discretion to allow fees of more than one counsel* – The manner in which the taxing master's discretion to allow fees of the level appropriate to leading counsel, or of two counsel, was considered in detail in *Xinyuan Trading Co Ltd v NPH Petrochemical Ltd* HCA 18159/1998 (Master Poon; 25.09.2000). The master referred to the abrogation of the two counsel rule (leading counsel may now appear in Hong Kong without a junior) and held that the first step is to ask 'whether it was necessary or proper to instruct a leader'. The master held that the 'necessary or proper' test is the appropriate one in Hong Kong, distinguishing *Juby v London Fire & Civil Defence Authority* (unreported, QBD; 24.04.1990) where a reasonableness test was applied. The master set out the following (non-exhaustive) list of relevant factors:

(1)  the nature of the case
(2)  difficult questions of fact or law
(3)  the complexity, difficulty or novelty of the issues involved
(4)  the skill, specialised knowledge or expertise required for the case
(5)  where money or property is involved, its amount or value
(6)  the importance of the matter to client
(7)  the general importance of the case, for example as affecting other cases
(8)  if a junior counsel has already been instructed, the experience, competency and seniority of that junior
(9)  whether the other side has instructed a leader: see *British Metals Corporation Ltd v Ludlow Brothers* (1913) Ltd [1938] Ch 787 [where it was held that the mere fact one side has instructed two counsel is not of itself to sufficient to justify allowing the other side to recover for two counsel, though it is a factor which may be taken into account: see *Wing Hong Construction Ltd v Tin Wo Eng'g Co Ltd* HCCT 13/2010 (Saunders J; 03.06.2010)].

The next question is whether it was 'necessary or proper' in the circumstances to instruct a junior in addition to a leader. Factors include:

(1)  assisting with the proper preparation of the case, for example, when the case was complex or heavy documentation is involved
(2)  assisting with the court proceedings by, for example, examining or cross-examining some witnesses, or dealing with a certain part of the case, for example, expert evidence or damages, etc
(3)  carrying out legal research on difficult or novel questions of law.

Where a case is considered suitable for two counsel, the taxing master should ignore the fact a third counsel was instructed on a complimentary basis and allow the fees of the two paid counsel: *Cheung Sun Lam v Lai Kam Man* [2007] 2 HKLRD 688 (appeal dismissed – CACV 281/2007).

*Counsel's brief fee* – Counsel's brief fee 'covers all the work done by way of preparation for representation at the trial and attendance on the first day of trial': *Loveday v Renton & Anor (No 2)* [1992] 3 All ER 184, 190, cited with approval in *Yeung Shu & Anor v Alfred Lau & Co (a firm) & Anor (third party)* [2000] 1 HKC 505 (CA) and *Ngan Wun Yeung v Lok Sin Tong Benevolent Society, Kowloon & Ors* [2000] 2 HKC 404. Thus no separate fee will be allowed for written submissions, skeleton arguments, *dramatis personae*, chronologies, etc, where those are required. It is counsel's responsibility to negotiate a brief fee which is adequate to cover such preparatory matters. Thus, in assessing the quantum of the brief fee, the need for such preparatory work should be taken into account: *Loveday* (above, 191b-e). There (at 190-191) it was held that in heavy litigation, additional preparatory work such as meetings of the team of lawyers and experts may be required, and this should be taken into account in assessing quantum of the brief fee. No separate fee for refreshing memory and re-reading papers is recoverable when there is a time gap in the trial: *Onway Eng'g Ltd v Chinney Construction Co Ltd* HCCT 10/2002 (Sakhrani J; 17.01.2008). Both the Law Society's guidance notes (reproduced below) and the Bar Code provide that once the formal brief has been delivered to counsel the brief fee will normally be payable even if the hearing does not go ahead. However this does not mean that the brief fee will be recoverable on taxation: see *Leung Kang Wai v Ng Yat Wing & Anor* HCPI 1224/1995 (Master Poon; 25.08.2000) where counsel's brief fee was mostly taxed off in circumstances where counsel had not actually begun preparation. In *Interlego AG v Tyco Industries Inc & Ors* HCA 4231/1984 (Master Perrior; 22.12.1989), it was held that counsel's brief fee includes one pre-trial conference.

*Counsel's fees for advisory work* – Advisory work by counsel during the course of preparation for the trial is considered to be covered by the brief fee and will not be recoverable as a separate item on party and party taxation. However advisory work done long before the trial may be considered 'separate and discrete from the brief fee' and hence recoverable as a separate item on taxation provided it meets the 'necessary or proper' test in Order 62 rule 28(2): *Yeung Shu & Anor v Alfred Lau & Co (a firm) & Anor (third party)* [2000] 1 HKC 505 (CA), per Ribeiro JA at 509D. In *Chan Shiu Wah v Wu Kwok On* [2000] 3 HKC 200, 205G-H counsel's fee for pre-action advice on liability, quantum and evidence was not allowed on taxation on the ground it was not necessary in a simple personal injury action.

*Refreshers* – In *Ngan Wun Yeung v Lok Sin Tong Benevolent Society, Kowloon & Ors* [2000] 2 HKC 404, 417H-I it was submitted that there is a 'usual practice' whereby counsel's refreshers are charged at 50% of the brief. Master Poon held that any such practice had not been approved by the court and that on taxation the amount of a refresher fee remained in the discretion of the court. Counsel are not entitled to charge refreshers for days not sitting in court, but may charge for work done on such days which is not covered by the brief fee, such as perusal of a new and unanticipated expert report: *Onway* (above).

*Unused refreshers* - Under an agreement between the Law Society and the Bar known as the 'Vine Formula' a solicitor would in certain circumstances be expected to pay counsel half refreshers for unused days where a case settles or finishes early.

See Law Society circulars 58/66, 6/81 and 200/89. However the Vine Formula has no application on taxation and counsel's fees for unused refreshers are not normally allowed. See *The Magway* HCAJ 14/1999 (Waung J; 08.05.2000). In any event the Vine Formula appears to have fallen into desuetude and is no longer mentioned in the Law Society's guidance notes on counsel's fees (reproduced below).

*Counsel's fee for settling statement of claim* – the settling of a statement of claim is part of the essential 'stock-in-trade' of the bar and counsel's fee for this task should be allowed on taxation: see *Chan Shiu Wah v Wu Kwok On* [2000] 3 HKC 200 at 204B–C, per Seagroatt J on appeal from a master.

*Counsel's fee for settling witness statements and (in personal injuries cases) the Revised Statement of Damages* – in *Chan Shiu Wah v Wu Kwok On* [2000] 3 HKC 200 at 204E–H Seagroatt J held, on appeal from a master, that it is not counsel's work to settle witness statements nor the Revised Statement of Damages in a personal injuries case. It was held that counsel's fee therefor had rightly been taxed off by the master. However in *Woo Hing Keung Lawrence v CEF Brokerage Ltd* HCCL 39/2004 (Master Ng; 03.03.2010) (paras 69-74) counsel's fees for preparing a witness statement were allowed in a complicated case.

*Counsel's fee for drafting correspondence* – in *Ngan Wun Yeung v Lok Sin Tong Benevolent Society, Kowloon & Ors* [2000] 2 HKC 404, 415B-F counsel's fee for drafting correspondence was not allowed on taxation for the reason that letters can be written by any reasonably competent solicitor. However such fees were allowed in *Re Greater Beijing Expressways Ltd (No 4)* [2005] 2 HKC 185 (paras 33-35) where the letter required 7 hours work and was a prelude to an application to the court.

*Counsel's fee for preparing affidavit* – counsel's fees for settling an affidavit were allowed in *Re Greater Beijing Expressways* (above) (para 17-27), having regard to the fact that the affidavit was the principal one to be relied upon in resisting an important application.

*Counsel's fee for perusal of documents* - perusal of documents will normally be considered to be part of counsel's conference or brief fee, and not a separate item recoverable on party and party taxation. However in a complicated or difficult case, a separate fee for perusal may be recoverable. See *Woo Hing Keung Lawrence* (above) (paras 54-68).

*Counsel's fee for pre-trial review* – it is proper for a solicitor to instruct counsel to appear at a pre-trial review and counsel's fee for that should be recoverable: see *Chan Shiu Wah v Wu Kwok On* [2000] 3 HKC 200 at 204I.

*Agreement as to counsel's fees* – In paragraph 2(a) of Part II of the First Schedule to Order 62 it is provided that counsel's fee shall not be allowed unless its amount has been agreed between solicitor and counsel. As a matter of professional conduct, counsel's brief (or 'backsheet') should state the agreed fee (except in legally aided cases where instead the legal aid certificate number should be stated) However, this requirement is not a matter of law and does not prevent counsel's fee from being allowed on taxation. See *Portric Co Ltd v Golden Dragon Engineering Co Ltd* [1984] HKC 343.

*Fees of overseas counsel* – in applying the 'hypothetical counsel' test (see above) to overseas counsel admitted for a particular case in Hong Kong, the comparator is a hypothetical *local* counsel. See *Mariner Int'l Hotels Ltd & Anor v Sino Land Co Ltd* FACV 3/2006 (Ag Registrar Au-Yeung; 09.08.2008) where it was said (at para 6(f)) to be best 'to approach the question of quantum of the London silk's brief by asking what a local eminent silk, with special expertise in an area of law, able to conduct an appeal effectively, would be content to receive . . .'. The fees of overseas counsel may be recovered on the basis of a refresher for each day away from his or her own jurisdiction: *Interlego AG v Tyco Industries Inc & Ors* HCA 4231/1984 (Master Perrior; 22.12.1989). Travelling expenses and hotel bills are not recoverable where this would impose a greater liability for costs than would have arisen if local counsel had been instructed: *Tai Hing Cotton Mill Ltd v Liu Chong Hing Bank Ltd & Ors (No 2)* [1986] HKC 20 (PC). Overseas counsel who have not, or have not yet, been admitted for a particular case in Hong Kong are sometimes briefed to advise or draft pleadings. It is arguable that such fees should not be recoverable as a disbursement since they cannot be the fees of 'counsel'.

*Procedure for taxation of counsel's fees* – the taxing master may prefer to group together all of counsel's fees in respect of different stages of the proceedings rather than deal with them on the usual 'fragmented' basis which makes it difficult 'to see the whole picture': *Incorporated Owners of Kiu Sun Factory Bldg & Anor v Greenswood Pty Ltd* HCMP 5020/2000 (Registrar Chan; 12.12.2003).

In this connection it is relevant to note the guidance provided by the Law Society under Circular 00-334(PA), which reads as follows:

### NOTES FOR GUIDANCE IN AGREEING FEES WITH COUNSEL

Experience has shown that many of the disputes between solicitors and counsel over fees arise from a failure by either or both to address potential problems at the time that instructions are delivered. With a view to reducing these problems, the Society has prepared the following notes for guidance which solicitors should take into account.

A.  HEARINGS

Matters to be considered when instructing counsel:

1.  Have specific instructions preferably in writing been obtained from the client to brief counsel?
2.  Counsel may be asked to provide an estimate of the fees. This may be done by sending the full set of papers to counsel in accordance with a prior arrangement with him or his clerk to provide such an estimate.
3.  Marking of Counsel's diary
    (a)  The marking of counsel's diary does not commit either counsel or solicitor, and no fees are payable.
    (b)  If after the marking of counsel's diary, the counsel is approached by another solicitor offering a brief during the same period in question or part thereof, counsel (who by that time should have agreed the brief as well as refreshers) would be obliged to approach the 1st solicitor and specify terms as to the manner in which the agreed brief fee and refreshers should become payable. If the 1st solicitor does not agree to the terms, then counsel will be free to accept the brief from the 2nd solicitor. In such event, the 1st solicitor need not pay counsel anything in relation to the reserved dates.
4.  Brief Fees

When a brief fee is quoted make sure that the following points are clarified:
    (a)  Conferences

        Ascertain:-

(i)    If pre-hearing conferences are included and if so whether there is a limit to the number of conferences.

(ii)   If the agreed fee includes conferences with the lay client and/or expert witnesses.

(iii)  If the brief or refresher fees includes conferences which may take place at the end of the day's hearing or otherwise during the course of the hearing.

(iv)   If conferences are not included in the brief or refresher fees – this should be made clear as should the charging rate to be applied for such conferences. If they are to take place other than in counsel's chambers or the precinct of the court, has agreement been reached on whether counsel is to be paid for the time spent travelling to and from the conference in addition to the time advising in conference and if so at what rate?

(v)    Where leading counsel is engaged are consultations between leading and junior counsel during the course of litigation included in their respective agreed fees?

(b)    Refreshers

       Agree:-

(i)    What constitutes a refresher? Is it payable only for a whole day in court or in full for part of a day?

(ii)   Arrangements regarding lost days (e.g. when, during the course of the hearing, the case is adjourned due to the illness of one of the parties or their advisers). Is a refresher payable in such circumstances?

(iii)  Clarify whether refresher fees are payable and at what rate in the event that the case is concluded in a shorter period than that originally reserved in counsel's diary.

(iv)   The arrangements for taking judgment. Will counsel be paid a refresher at the agreed rate or will special arrangements apply?

(v)    Clarify whether any additional preparation fees will be charged if the hearing is adjourned part-heard for a substantial period of time.

(c)    Lump sum

       If counsel is to be paid an inclusive fee for conducting the case it is essential not only that solicitor and counsel are agreed as to precisely what work is covered by the lump sum fee but also that both lawyers and lay client are in no doubt what their respective positions will be if the case is not concluded within a specified time.

(d)    Trial

       When fees become payable:-

(i)    Unless *otherwise agreed*, the brief fee is payable once the brief has been delivered to counsel.

(ii)   Solicitors and barristers may also consider whether they wish to agree that the brief can be deemed to have been delivered under the "10-day rule" i.e. if the fee has been agreed and counsel has not been released 10 days before the hearing.

(iii)  An express agreement should be made about when counsel fees become payable even if, for whatever reason, the hearing or trial is cancelled or postponed. The parties should remind themselves of the need for counsel to be properly prepared for the hearing.

(iv)   Briefs are as a rule delivered and accepted on the understanding that counsel may be justifiably prevented from attending at Court. Counsel is entitled to return a brief if there is a subsequent commitment in the Court of Appeal even if those dates were fixed after acceptance of the existing brief in which counsel appeared in the Court below.

### B.    OPINIONS AND SETTLING PLEADINGS

1.    Agreement should always be reached on the fees payable. Instructions may be delivered to counsel with a request for particulars of the charge rate and an estimate of his fees. Once that estimate has been given and the lay client has agreed counsel will be expected to abide by it but may revert back to the instructing solicitor in exceptional circumstances if he realises that the estimated figure is likely to be exceeded.

2.    There should be agreement at the outset whether the fees quoted for an opinion include conferences with the lay client.

3.    Similarly, there should be agreement as to whether fees are payable for telephone conferences and what the charge rate will be.

4.    If the counsel is unable to prepare the documents the instructing solicitor should be advised and a request made for the return of the papers.

### C.    FORMULAE FOR COSTS

1.    Before agreeing any formula for costs with counsel the solicitor should make sure that the lay client fully understands the terms of the proposed formula. Lay client should be asked to give his consent in writing.

2.    Solicitor and counsel should consider and advise the client on all the contingencies that can be reasonably foreseen having regard to the particular set of circumstances, for example when it is that he will become bound by the arrangement; whether there is any likelihood of settlement and, if so, when it may occur and the possibility of illness of the judge, counsel or litigants which may increase the costs to be incurred.

3.    Any formula which is to be adopted should be comprehensively set out in a memorandum of understanding.

### D.    TAXING OF FEES IN LEGALLY-AIDED CASES

Fees payable to counsel in Legally-Aided cases

These are governed by the *Legal Aid (Scale of Fees) Regulations*.

Regulation 4 states:

"*The fees payable by the Director to counsel acting for an aided person shall be such as may be allowed on taxation or, in default of taxation, as may be fixed by the Director, not exceeding such amount as in the opinion of the Director would have been allowed if there had been taxation*".

Members' attention is drawn to the *obiter* comments of Seagroatt J. in the case *Chan Shiu Wah v Wu Kwok On* (PI Action No. 1123 of 1997). The Judge indicated that where counsel's fees have been taxed off or reduced on the basis that such work was "solicitors' work", counsel should look for payment of those fees from the taxed profit costs of the instructing solicitor.

The Law Society is of the opinion that in relation to the division of work between solicitors and counsel the onus is on counsel to return the papers to the solicitor forthwith if he is of the view that there is a risk that any work done by him will be taxed off or reduced. Where counsel fails to do so then he would be bound by the provisions in Regulation 4.

### E.    PAYMENT OF COUNSEL'S FEES

1.    Time for payment

Counsel's fees must be paid or challenged promptly, *and in any event within 2 months* from the submission of counsel's fee note.

2.    Failure to pay counsel's fees

Principle 12.04 of the *Hong Kong Solicitors' Guide to Professional Conduct* states:

*"In the absence of reasonable excuse a solicitor is personally liable as a matter of professional conduct for the payment of a barrister's proper fees. Failure to obtain funds on account of a barrister's fees shall not of itself constitute reasonable excuse."*

### [62.32.4]    Solicitors' responsibility to pay counsel's fee taxed off

It has been held that a solicitor is responsible to pay counsel's fee to the extent agreed even though the fee is reduced or disallowed on taxation: see *Chan Shiu Wah v Wu Kwok On* [2000] 3 HKC 200 at 206H–I, per Seagroatt J. See also *Cheng Ma Choi v Tai Fong Textile Finishing Work Ltd* HCPI 563/1995 (Seagroatt J; 01.03.1999). However the situation is different where counsel is assigned by the Director of Legal Aid. Under the Legal Aid Regulations counsel's fee shall be such as may be allowed on taxation. See *Ngan Wun Yeung v Lok Sin Tong Benevolent Society, Kowloon & Ors* [2000] 2 HKC 404, 409F–H where Master Poon said:

> if counsel's fees are taxed at the inter partes taxation of the aided client's bill of costs, the Director if only liable to pay to counsel the taxed fees and nothing more.
>
> Contrast this with a non-legal aid case. Fees payable to counsel acting for a party is a matter of agreement between them. Counsel is normally entitled to his fees in full irrespective of the outcome of taxation. The paying party has to pay the fees as allowed to the receiving party. Any difference between the fees claimed and allowed is to be borne by the receiving party himself.

In *Chan Shiu Wah* (above) it was observed that counsel would be bound by an agreement with instructing solicitors to accept whatever fee is allowed on taxation. It appears that this is necessarily the case where the lay client is legally aided (Legal Aid (Scale of Fees) Regulations (Cap 91) regs 4 & 5). Note, however, that para 124 of the Hong Kong Bar Association's Code of Conduct prohibits barristers from agreeing fees dependent upon or related to a contingency.

### [62.32.5]    Inter-jurisdictional litigation

Where litigation has an inter-jurisdictional aspect, the travelling expenses of a solicitor to confer with legal advisers who are co-ordinating the litigation overseas may be allowed as a disbursement. See *Interlego AG v Tyco Industries Inc & Ors* HCA 4231/1984 (Master Perrior; 22.12.1989).

### [62.32.6]    District court hourly rates

In the District Court, hourly rates on party and party taxation will normally be allowed at two-thirds of the High Court rate. See the guidance reproduced under Order 62 rule 21 above and see RDC Order 62 rule 32 (1A).

### 32A.    Liability for costs of taxation (O. 62 r. 32A)

(1)    **A party entitled to payment of any costs to be taxed is also entitled to his costs of the taxation except where —**

(a)    **any Ordinance, any of these rules or any relevant practice direction provides otherwise; or**

(b)    **the Court makes some other order in relation to all or part of the costs of the taxation.**

**(2)   In deciding whether to make some other order, the Court shall have regard to the underlying objectives set out in Order 1A, rule 1 and all the circumstances, including —**

    **(a)   the conduct of all the parties in relation to the taxation;**

    **(b)   the amount, if any, by which the bill of costs has been reduced; and**

    **(c)   whether it was reasonable for a party to claim the costs of a particular item or to dispute that item.**

**(L.N. 152 of 2008)**

_____

## NOTES

**[62.32A.1]   Receiving party's general entitlement to costs of taxation**
Order 62 rule 32A provides that a receiving party is generally entitled to the costs of taxation, except where otherwise provided by Ordinance, rules or practice direction. It derives from England's CPR 47.18(1). The rule provides for a general entitlement only, because it expressly preserves the right of the court to make some other order as to the costs of taxation. The court is directed, in considering whether to make some other order, to have regard to the matters set out in rule 32A(2). There is no express mention of *Calderbank* offers 'without prejudice save as to costs', but these should also be taken into account as the court is required to have regard to 'all the circumstances'. With regard to *Calderbank* offers, see Order 62 rule 5(1)(d) and the commentary on that provision.

See also Order 62 rule 8D(3) whereby a receiving party's legal representative may be deprived of the costs of taxation if more than one-sixth is taxed off a bill of costs payable by a fund (other than the legal aid fund).

**32B. Reimbursement for taxing fees** (O. 62 r. 32B)
**Upon the issue of a final certificate under rule 17A, the party liable to pay costs shall pay to the party entitled to payment of the costs an amount of money equivalent to the prescribed taxing fee calculated on the basis of the amount of costs allowed.**

**(L.N. 152 of 2008)**

_____

## NOTES

**[62.32B.1]   Paying party must reimburse receiving party for taxation fee**
Order 62 rule 32B provides that a paying party must reimburse the receiving party for the taxing fee which is paid to the court under the High Court Fees Rules (subsidiary legislation under the High Court Ordinance (Cap 4)). The taxing fee paid on filing a bill of costs for taxation is an *ad valorem* amount based on the total claimed. If the bill is reduced on taxation, the taxing fee will also reduce, and the paying party is liable only for the reduced amount.

No taxing fee is payable on filing a bill of costs on behalf of a legally aided person. However a notional taxing fee is added to the amount payable by the party ordered to pay an aided person's costs, and that money is later paid over by the Director of Legal Aid to the court. See section 16B(c) of the Legal Aid Ordinance (Cap 91).

**32C. Court's powers in relation to misconduct** (O. 62 r. 32C)
    (1)    **The Court may make an order under this rule where –**
        (a)  **a party or his legal representative, in connection with a summary assessment or taxation of costs, fails to comply with a rule, practice direction or an order of the Court; or**
        (b)  **it appears to the Court that the conduct of a party or his legal representative, before or during the proceedings which gave rise to the summary assessment or taxation, was unreasonable or improper.**
    (2)    **For the purpose of paragraph (1), the conduct of a party or his legal representative does not include any conduct before the commencement of the action.**
    (3)    **Where paragraph (1) applies, the Court may –**
        (a)  **by order disallow all or part of the costs being summarily assessed or taxed; or**
        (b)  **order the party at fault or his legal representative, to pay costs that he has caused any other party to incur.**
    (4)    **Where –**
        (a)  **the Court makes an order under paragraph (3) against a legally represented party; and**
        (b)  **the party is not present when the order is made,**

**the party's solicitor shall notify his client in writing of the order not later than 7 days after the solicitor receives notice of the order and shall inform the Court in writing that he has done so.**
    (5)    **In this rule, "client" includes a person on whose behalf the solicitor acts and any other person who has instructed the solicitor to act or who is liable to pay the solicitor's costs.**

**(L.N. 152 of 2008)**

**[62.32C.1]   Sanctions for misconduct in relation to taxation**
Order 62 rule 32C expressly empowers the court to impose sanctions for misconduct of a party or legal representative in relation to a summary assessment or taxation of costs, or in proceedings giving rise to the same. The type of misconduct which triggers operation of the rule is:
    ☐    failure to comply with a rule, practice direction or order in connection with summary assessment or taxation; and
    ☐    unreasonable or improper conduct in the proceedings giving rise to the summary assessment or taxation.

By rule 32C(3) the court may disallow all or part of the costs being assessed or taxed, or impose a costs penalty.
    Rule 32C derives from England's CPR 44.14. The Chief Justice's working party on civil justice reform recommended that Hong Kong adopt a similar provision (final report, recommendation 136). Of the English provision, our sister publication in the UK, The Civil Court Practice says (at CPR 44.14[1]):

> **Misconduct** See the notes to CPR 48.7 [in Hong Kong Order 62 rule 8] dealing with 'wasted costs orders' for a discussion of the principles under which the court will act when dealing with misconduct.

The reference in CPR 44.14(1)(b) [Order 62 rule 32C(1)(b) in Hong Kong] to 'conduct of a party' does not entitle the applicant to raise a range of issues concerning the very subject-matter of the claim and the court should deal with the application in a way which is proportionate to the amounts involved: *Kaminski v Somerville College* [2000] CLY 467.

As to the meaning of 'misconduct' and the relationship of CPR 44.14 and CPR 47.8 [Order 62 rule 22 in Hong Kong, dealing with delay in taxation proceedings] see *Haji-Ioannou v Frangos* [2006] EWCA Civ 1663, [2006] NLJR 1918.

The court may exercise its management powers under CPR 3.1 [Order 1B rule 1 in Hong Kong] to debar the paying party from taking part in the detailed assessment [taxation] unless that party complies with an order for an interim payment: *Days Healthcare UK Ltd v Pihsiang Machinery Manufacturing Co Ltd* [2006] EWHC 1444 (QB) [2006] 4 All ER 233.

For example, where at the trial, the successful party is proved to have forged a material document the trial judge should consider making an order under paragraph (2) [rule 32C(1)(b) in Hong Kong] for the disallowance of costs claimed or for the payment of costs incurred by the other side: *Ultraframe (UK) Ltd v Fielding (No 2)* [2007] The Times, 8 Jan (CA).

Save insofar as rule 32C expressly applies in relation to and at the stage of assessment or taxation of costs, it does not seem to add much to Order 62 rule 5(1)(e) (by which the court takes into account the conduct of parties in exercising its discretion as to costs), rule 7(1) (which empowers the court to impose sanctions for improper or unnecessary conduct and rule 8 (which provides for wasted costs orders).

**REVIEW**

**33. Application to taxing master for review** (O. 62 r. 33)

**(1)  Any party to any taxation proceedings who is dissatisfied with the allowance or disallowance in whole or in part of any item by a taxing master, or with the amount allowed by a taxing master in respect of any item —**

 **(a)  may apply to the taxing master to review his decision in respect of that item; and**

 **(b)  may not apply to a judge for an order to review the decision until after its review by the taxing master.**

**(L.N. 152 of 2008)**

**(2)  An application under this rule for review of a taxing master's decision may be made at any time within 14 days after the conclusion of the taxation in which that decision was made or such shorter period as may be fixed by the taxing master:**

 **Provided that no application under this rule for review of a decision in respect of any item may be made after the signing of the taxing master's final certificate dealing with that item. (L.N. 152 of 2008)**

**(3)  Every applicant for review under this rule must at the time of making his application deliver to the taxing master objections in writing specifying by a list the items or parts of items the allowance or disallowance of which or the amount allowed in respect of which, is objected to and stating concisely the nature and grounds of the objection in each case, and must deliver a copy of the objections to each other party (if any) who attended on the taxation of those items or to whom the taxing master directs that a copy of the objections shall be delivered.**

**(3A)** If an applicant fails to comply with paragraph (3), the taxing master may dismiss the application. (L.N. 152 of 2008)

**(4)** Any party to whom a copy of the objections is delivered under this rule may, within 14 days after delivery of the copy to him or such shorter period as may be fixed by the taxing master, deliver to the taxing master answers in writing to the objections stating concisely the grounds on which he will oppose the objections, and shall at the same time deliver a copy of the answers to the party applying for review and to each other party (if any) to whom a copy of the objections has been delivered or to whom the taxing master directs that a copy of the answers shall be delivered.

**(5)** An application under this rule for review of the taxing master's decision in respect of any item shall not prejudice the power of the taxing master under rule 17 to issue an interim certificate in respect of items his decision as to which is not objected to.

---

## NOTES

### [62.33.1] Cross-reference
See also the Legal Aid Regulations (Cap 91), regs 10, 11 & 12, for review of costs allowed the lawyers assigned for a legally aided person.

### [62.33.2] Review of taxation of costs
Order 62 rules 33, 34 and 35 provide a procedure for review of taxation of costs. Any party dissatisfied with a taxing master's decision on any item in a bill of costs may apply to the master for a review of taxation under rule 33. The review will be conducted before the same taxing master in accordance with rule 34. Thereafter, there may be a further review before a judge under rule 35.

The review procedures should be exhausted before bringing an appeal against the decision of the taxing master: *CFK v LLL* [2003] 3 HKC 190 (CA).

Where a party is dissatisfied with some aspect of a taxation other than a decision to allow or disallow any item in the bill being taxed, for example where a party is dissatisfied with a decision by the taxing master on procedure, an appeal would be appropriate since such a challenge does not come within the review procedure. See *Re Macro (Ipswich) Ltd* [1996] 1 WLR 145 and *R v Taxing Officer ex p Bee-Line Roadways Int'l Ltd* The Times 11.02.1982, both cited in *CFK v LLL* [2003] 3 HKC 190, 194D-E (CA).

### [62.33.3] Time for applying for review of taxation
An application to a taxing master for review of a decision on taxation of costs should be made within 14 days after conclusion of the taxation: Order 62 rule 33(2). Extension of time is possible under Order 62 rule 16. Order 62 rule 33(2) provides that in any event an application for review must be made before the signing of the taxing master's certificate dealing finally with any objected item but the certificate may be set aside under rule 16(1)(b) so as to extend time. See *A Solicitor v Law Society of HK* [2007] 4 HKC 165.

**[62.33.4] Form of application for review of taxation**
Order 62 rule 33 does not specify the form of application for review of taxation. Practitioners commonly use a form headed 'Notice of Application for Review of Taxation'. In *AG v Commodore Electronics Ltd* [1994] 1 HKC 660, Master Gould suggested (at 661E-G) that application should be made by summons or at least the procedures which apply to a summons should be followed.

**[62.33.5] Contents of application for review of taxation**
Order 62 rule 33(3) provides that a party applying for review of taxation must prepare a written list of the items in respect of which objection is raised and state concisely the nature and grounds of the objection. A review of taxation is not just another opportunity for the taxing master to consider the items in more detail and the party applying for review must present fresh evidence or argument: *Glendon Rowell v Pacific International Insurance Co Ltd* HCCT 2/2000 (Master HC Wong; 29.08.2001). In that decision, Master Wong referred to *Smart International Industrial Ltd v Twinkle Step Investment Ltd* HCA 9883/1997 and CACV 201/1998 (Master B Kwan; 15.08.2000) where an application for review which merely repeated the objections filed on the original taxation was struck out.

**[62.33.6] Procedure**
Order 62 rule 33(3) provides that the party applying for review of taxation must deliver its written objections with the application and serve other relevant parties. In the past failure to deliver objections in a timely fashion was sometimes treated leniently. In *Lam Fong & Anor v Mak Ming* HCPI 395/1997 (Master Kwan; 30.09.1999) such failure was said to be a procedural irregularity which could be remedied by an adjournment with costs in case of any prejudice being caused. And in *A Solicitor v Law Society of HK* [2007] 4 HKC 165 it was held that failure to deliver objections with the application was not fatal. Since then, the new rule 33(3A) has come into force as part of the civil justice reforms. It expressly provides that failure to comply with the procedural requirements of rule 33(3) may result in the application for review being dismissed.

The party served with objections to the taxation has 14 days from delivery thereof to provide written answers thereto: rule 33(4).

**[62.33.7] Who may apply for review of taxation?**
Obviously the party to the proceedings who has been ordered to pay costs may apply for review of taxation of those costs. In addition, a legal representative who is not a party to the proceedings, but the subject of a 'wasted costs' order under Order 62 rule 8 has standing to apply for a review: *Yeung Shu Lam Wilson v Chan Sui Tung & Anor* [2005] 1 HKC 309, 317I (CA).

**[62.33.8] Review of taxation in criminal cases**
In *HKSAR v Cheung Siu Ki* [1997] 3 HKC 344, it was held that where a deputy registrar of the High Court had taxed costs under an order of the district court in a criminal case there was no power in the deputy registrar or a judge to review the taxation. This situation is now ameliorated by section 21 of the Costs in Criminal Cases Ordinance (Cap 492) which expressly provides for review of taxation and by

rule 8 of the Costs in Criminal Cases Rules which provides that Order 62 rules 33 and 34 will apply on such a review.

**34. Review by taxing master** (O. 62 r. 34)
**(HK)(1)    A review under rule 33 shall be carried out by the taxing master to whom the taxation was originally assigned.**

**(2)    On reviewing any decision in respect of any item, a taxing master may receive further evidence and may exercise all the powers which he might exercise on an original taxation in respect of that item, including the power to award costs of and incidental to the proceedings before him; and any costs awarded by him to any party may be taxed by him and may be added to or deducted from any other sum payable to or by that party in respect of costs.**

**(3)    On a hearing of a review under rule 33 a party to whom a copy of objections was delivered under paragraph (4) of that rule shall be entitled to be heard in respect of any item to which the objections relate notwithstanding that he did not deliver written answers to the objections under that paragraph.**

**(4)    A taxing master who has reviewed a decision in respect of any item shall issue his certificate accordingly and, if requested to do so by any party to the proceedings before him, shall state in his certificate or otherwise in writing by reference to the objections to that decision the reasons for his decision on the review, and any special facts or circumstances relevant to it. A request under this paragraph must be made within 14 days after the review or such shorter period as may be fixed by the taxing master.**

---

**NOTES**

**[62.34.1]    Review before same taxing master**
Order 62 rule 34(1) provides that a review of taxation shall be carried out by the taxing master who dealt with the taxation of costs giving rise to the review. In *Fenn Kar Bak Lily v Goh Kim Lay & Anor* HCA 9177/1992 (Keith J; 08.12.1998), it was held that the rationale for this rule 'is that the taxing master who carried out the original taxation will know why a particular item had or had not been allowed'.

In the *Fenn Kar Bak Lilly* case, the taxing master had retired and was not available to conduct the review. Noting that the original taxation had proceeded by default and that the master had allowed the whole of the receiving party's bill as drawn without considering the items one by one, Keith J held that under the inherent jurisdiction of the court he could order that the review be conducted by another master.

**[62.34.2]    Fresh evidence on application for review**
Order 62 rule 34(2) expressly provides that a taxing master may receive fresh evidence on an application for review. It has been held that the taxing master's discretion to admit fresh evidence on review 'is in no way fettered' by considerations such as those which apply in the Court of Appeal: *Kung Wong Sau-hin v C P Lin & Co* [1988] 2 HKLR 209, 212B-C. In that case, the Court of Appeal held that parts of an affidavit should have been admitted on an application for review of taxation notwithstanding the fact the evidence was available at the time of the original taxation but had not been used.

**[62.34.3]  Reasons for decision on review**

Order 62 rule 34(4) provides that if requested by a party within 14 days of a review the taxing master shall give written reasons for the decision on review. Such a request is necessary if there is to be a further review before a judge: rule 35(1). The taxing master's reasons need not be lengthy or detailed, but should 'fairly reveal ... the process of reasoning whereby the objection in question was allowed or disallowed ... with a statement of the matters ... taken into account or disregarded in the process': *Re Gibson's Settlement Trusts* [1981] Ch 179, 192, quoted with approval in *Union (V-Tex) Shirt Factory Ltd v Union V-Tex Realty Ltd* HCA 219/1976 (Clough J; 14.11.1984).

**[62.34.4]  Costs of review of taxation**

The costs of a review of taxation will normally follow the event.

Where the review concerns the fees of counsel assigned for a legally aided party, costs of the review may be awarded against the assigned solicitor. Regulation 12 of the Legal Aid Regulations (Cap 159) provides that such a review is to be conducted as if the assigned solicitor is the dissatisfied party. In *Ngan Wun Yeung v Lok Win Tong Benevolent Society & Ors* [2000] 2 HKC 404, such a review was unsuccessful and the court, noting it had no jurisdiction to order counsel to pay the costs of the review, ordered that the assigned solicitors do so. Under the civil justice reforms which came into force in April 2009 the court was given power to order counsel to pay costs, but only in the rare circumstances in which a wasted costs order would be appropriate. See generally the commentary under Order 62 rule 8.

**35.  Review of taxing master's certificate by a judge** (O. 62 r. 35)

**(1)  Any party who is dissatisfied with the decision of a taxing master to allow or to disallow any item in whole or in part on review under rule 34, or with the amount allowed in respect of any item by a taxing master on any such review, may apply to a judge for an order to review the taxation as to that item or part of an item if, but only if, one of the parties to the proceedings before the taxing master requested that officer in accordance with rule 34(4) to state the reasons for his decision in respect of that item or part on the review. (L.N. 152 of 2008)**

**(2)  An application under this rule for review of a taxing master's decision in respect of any item may be made at any time within 14 days after the taxing master's certificate in respect of that item is signed, or such longer time as the taxing master at the time when he signs the certificate, or the Court at any time, may allow.**

**(3)  An application under this rule shall be made by summons and shall, except where the judge thinks fit to adjourn into court, be heard in chambers.**

**(4)  Unless the judge otherwise directs, no further evidence shall be received on the hearing of an application under this rule, and no ground of objection shall be raised which was not raised on the review by the taxing master but, save as aforesaid, on the hearing of any such application the judge may exercise all such powers and discretion as are vested in the taxing master in relation to the subject-matter of the application.**

(5)   If the judge thinks fit to exercise in relation to an application under this rule the power of the Court to appoint assessors under section 53 of the Ordinance, the judge shall appoint not less than 2 assessors, of whom one shall be a taxing master.

(6)   On an application under this rule the judge may make such order as the circumstances require, and in particular may order the taxing master's certificate to be amended or, except where the dispute as to the item under review is as to amount only, order the item to be remitted to the same or another taxing master for taxation.

(7)   In this rule "Judge" means a judge in person.

---

## NOTES

### [62.35.1]   Application to judge for review of taxation

Order 62 rule 35 provides that following a taxation review before the taxing master, a dissatisfied party may apply for review by a judge. There must have been a prior request to the taxing master under rule 34(4) for written reasons – see the final clause of rule 35(1). In the absence of the required written reasons, an application to a judge for review is 'incompetent': *Bank of China (HK) Ltd v Villa King Enterprises Ltd* HCMP 5727/1999 (Waung J; 26.10.2004) (para 11). This is because the judge's function on a review is to examine the reasons, rather than conduct a fresh taxation. See the discussion of the scope of review below.

Application for such a review is made by summons, which will normally be heard in chambers: rule 35(3). The summons must be issued within 14 days after issue of the taxing master's certificate: rule 35(2).

### [62.35.2]   No application to judge until after review by master

Application to a judge for an order that a taxation be reviewed may only be made after there has been a review by the taxing master: see rule 33(1)(b). That provision was added as part of the civil justice reforms which took effect in April 2009. Insofar as *CFK v LLL* [2003] 3 HKC 190, 193H-I (CA) suggested that review by a judge is possible in the High Court without there having been a prior review by the taxing master, it is overruled.

Indemnity costs were ordered against a party who wrongly applied to a judge for a review of taxation without fist seeking a review by the taxing master in *Tang Woung Shiu v Tang Kun Yeung & Anor* HCA 5527/1998 (Sakhrani J; 15.09.2006).

### [62.35.3]   Time for making application – taxing master's certificate should be signed first

Order 62 rule 35(2) provides that an application to a judge for review of taxation may be made within 14 days after the taxing master's certificate has been signed. It follows that an application made before the certificate has been signed is 'premature': *Fenn Kar Bak Lily v Goh Kim Lay & Anor* HCA 9177/1992 (Yuen J; 04.10.1999). However such a premature application is not a nullity and the court may hear the review *de bene esse* conditional upon the issue of the required certificate: *Cheung Sun Lam v Lai Kam Man & 11 Ors* [2007] 2 HKLRD 688.

## [62.35.4]  Scope of review by a judge

A review of taxation by a judge is confined to the evidence and objections which were raised on review before the taxing master, unless the judge otherwise directs. The judge's function is to look at the taxing master's reasons to see whether they are valid, not to conduct a fresh taxation: *Bank of China (HK) Ltd v Villa King Enterprises Ltd* HCMP 5727/1999 (Waung J; 26.10.2004) (para 11). To allow or disallow any item on a bill of costs, or to fix the amount recoverable, is a matter of discretion on the part of the taxing master, and the judge will only interfere if the taxing master made an error of law, took into account irrelevant matters or failed to take into account relevant matters: *Lin Zhen Man v Topfine Machinery Co Ltd* [2010] 1 HKLRD 135. In *China Property Development (Holdings) Ltd v Mandecly Ltd & Ors* (Chung J; 07.07.2008) (para 35) and again in *Hui Kee Chun v Privacy Commissioner* HCA 1980/2006 (Chung J; 11.05.2010) (para 15) it was said that the starting point is that the court will not generally interfere with the decision of a taxing master on a question relating to fact or the amount of costs, and set out the following list of exceptions, deriving from Halsbury's Laws of Hong Kong:

(a)  some question of principle is involved;
(b)  the taxing master has not had reasonably sufficient material before him;
(c)  he has taken into account irrelevant matters;
(d)  he has not taken into account relevant matters; or
(e)  he has acted upon a wrong principle or adopted the wrong approach.

## [62.35.5]  Judge may be assisted by assessors on review of taxation

Rule 35(5) provides that the court may appoint assessors to assist a judge on a review of taxation. This was done in *Lam Put v Tai Yieh Construction & Engineering Co Ltd* [1992] 1 HKC 291 where the only issue was the charges of a medical witness for attendance at court. One of the assessors must be a taxing master and in the *Lam Put* case the other was a practising solicitor.

## [62.35.6]  Criminal cases

In *HKSAR v Cheung Siu Ki* [1997] 3 HKC 344, it was held that a judge of the Court of First Instance has no jurisdiction under this rule to review taxation of costs in a criminal case. It appears that this continues to be the case although rule 8 of the Costs in Criminal Cases Rules (Cap 492) now provides for review before the registrar and that Order 62 rules 33 and 34 shall apply on such a review.

### TRANSITIONAL

**36. Transitional provision relating to Part 16 of Amendment Rules 2008**
   (O. 62 r. 36)
   **Rules 8, 8A, 8B, 8C, 8D and 8E do not apply in relation to any costs incurred before the commencement of the Amendment Rules 2008, and rule 8 as in force immediately before the commencement continues to apply in relation to those costs as if Part 16 had not been made.**

**(L.N. 152 of 2008)**

**[62.36.1]    Repealed rule 8 continues to apply to costs incurred before April 2009**
Order 62 rule 36 provides that the provisions of rules 8-8E, which regulate the court's power to make wasted costs orders against legal representatives, do not apply to costs incurred before those rules came into force as part of the civil justice reforms in 2009. Instead, the former rule 8 continues to apply in relation to such costs. Unlike the new rules 8-8E, the former rule 8 does not apply to barristers. See the discussion of the amendments which took effect in 2009 under Order 62 rule 8 above.

For the convenience of readers the text of the former rule 8 is set out below:

8.    *Personal liability of solicitor for costs (the former O. 62 r.8)*
(1) Subject to the following provisions of this rule, where in any proceedings costs are incurred improperly or without reasonable cause or are wasted by undue delay or by any other misconduct or default, the Court may make against any solicitor whom it considers to be responsible whether personally or through a servant or agent an order –

    (a)    disallowing the costs as between the solicitor and his client; and

    (b)    directing the solicitor to repay to his client costs which the client has been ordered to pay to other parties to the proceedings; or

    (c)    directing the solicitor personally to indemnify such other parties against costs payable by them.

(2) No order under this rule shall be made against a solicitor unless he has been given a reasonable opportunity to appear before the Court and show cause why the order should not be made except where any proceeding in Court or in chambers cannot conveniently proceed, and fails or is adjourned without useful progress being made, -

    (a)    because of the failure of the solicitor to attend in person or by a proper representative; or

    (b)    because of the failure of the solicitor to deliver any document for the use of the Court which ought to have been delivered or to be prepared with any proper evidence or account or otherwise to proceed.

(3) Before making an order under this rule the Court may, if it thinks fit refer the matter (except in the case of undue delay in the drawing up of, or in any proceedings under, an order or judgment as to which the Registrar has reported to the Court) to a taxing master for inquiry and report and direct the solicitor in the first place to show cause before the taxing master.

(4) The Court may, if it thinks fit, direct or authorize the Official Solicitor to attend and take part in any proceedings or inquiry under this rule, and may make such order as it thinks fit as to the payment of his costs. (L.N. 375 of 1991)

(5) The Court may direct that notice of any proceedings or order against a solicitor under this rule shall be given to his client in such manner as may be specified in the direction.

(6) Where in any proceedings before a taxing master the solicitor representing any party is guilty of neglect or delay or puts any other party to any unnecessary expense in relation to those proceedings, the taxing master may direct the solicitor to pay costs personally to any of the parties in those proceedings, and where any solicitor fails to leave his bill of costs [with the documents required by this Order] for taxation within the time fixed by or under this Order or otherwise delays or impedes the taxation, then, unless the taxing master otherwise directs, the solicitor shall not be allowed the fees to which he would otherwise be entitled for drawing his bill of costs and for attending the taxation.

(7) If, on the taxation of costs to be paid out of a fund other than funds provided by the Legislative Council pursuant to section 27 of the Legal Aid Ordinance (Cap 91), one sixth or more of the amount of the bill for those costs is taxed off, the solicitor whose bill it is shall not be allowed the fees to which he would otherwise be entitled for drawing the bill and for attending the taxation.

(8) In any proceeding in which the party by whom the fees prescribed by any enactment relating to court fees are payable is represented by a solicitor, if the fees or any part of the fees payable under the said enactment are not paid as therein prescribed,

the Court may, on the application of the Official Solicitor by summons, order the solicitor personally to pay that amount in the manner so prescribed and to pay the costs of the Official Solicitor of the application. (L.N. 375 of 1991)

It can be seen that in many respects the former rule 8, above, is the same as the current rules 8 to 8E, save that it applies only to solicitors whereas the new provisions extend to barristers as well. Bearing that in mind, the commentary under the new provisions will largely be relevant here.

**[62.36.2]   Juridical basis for wasted costs orders under previous rule 8**
The juridical basis for making wasted costs orders in respect of costs incurred before the new provisions came into force is somewhat uncertain. In *Ho Lee Man v Wong Wai Kai (No 2)* [1993] 1 HKC 193, 195G (CA) it was said that the power derived from the court's inherent jurisdiction to exercise control over its own officers, including solicitors. That may have been historically correct, but it does not sit comfortably with section 52A(2) of the High Court Ordinance as it was worded before the civil justice reforms came into force. It was there provided that the court could not make a costs order against a non-party in the absence of specific primary legislation. See *AIE Co Ltd v Kay Kam Yu* [1997] 1 HKLRD 161, 163 (CA). Rather than inherent jurisdiction, it might be argued that the pre-CJR power to make wasted costs orders against solicitors is section 3(2) of the Legal Practitioners Ordinance (Cap 159) which provides that a solicitor is an officer of the court *and subject to the jurisdiction thereof in accordance with the HCO*. In *Yau Chiu Wah v Gold Chief Investment Ltd & Anor (No 2)* [2003] 3 HKC 91, 101I, Ma JA also referred to rule 2(f) of the Solicitors Practice Rules (which provides that a solicitor should not do or permit to be done anything which would compromise or impair his duty to the court). However, this is probably of academic interest only: there is no saving provision for the previous section 52A(2), and its replacement, expressly empowering the court to make costs orders against non-parties, arguably applies to costs incurred before the amendment came into force.

**[62.36.3]   Circumstances where wasted costs order appropriate in respect of pre-2009 cost**
The circumstances in which a wasted cost order will be made in respect of costs incurred before the new provisions came into force are more or less the same as under the current provisions (Order 62 rules 8-8E), save that there is no provision for orders against barristers. The commentary under those rules will be useful in relation to the making of such orders in respect of costs whether incurred before or after the current provisions came into force. However, it must be remembered that the power to make wasted costs orders against barristers arises only under the new provisions and does not have retrospective effect.

**37. Transitional provisions relating to Part 23 of Amendment Rules 2008**
    (O. 62 r. 37)
    **(1)   Where a party entitled to require any costs to be taxed has filed his bill of costs before the commencement of the Amendment Rules 2008, nothing in Part 23 of the Amendment Rules 2008 applies in relation to the taxation, and**

Order 62 as in force immediately before the commencement applies in relation to the taxation as if it had not been amended by that Part.

    (2)   Where —

        (a)   a party entitled to require any costs to be taxed files his bill of costs after the commencement of the Amendment Rules 2008; but

        (b)   any item of work to which the costs or charges specified in the First Schedule or Part III of the Second Schedule of this Order relate was undertaken before the commencement,

then the First Schedule or Part III of the Second Schedule of this Order as in force immediately before the commencement applies in relation to that item of work as if it had not been amended by Part 23 of the Amendment Rules 2008.

    (3)   Where —

        (a)   a party entitled to require any costs to be taxed files his bill of costs after the commencement of the Amendment Rules 2008; but

        (b)   the writ of summons was issued before the commencement, then Part I and Part II of the Second Schedule of this Order as in force immediately before the commencement applies in relation to the writ of summons issued before the commencement as if they had not been amended by Part 23 of the Amendment Rules 2008.

    (4)   No costs for work undertaken before the commencement of the Amendment Rules 2008 are to be disallowed if those costs would have been allowed under this Order as in force immediately before the commencement.

(L.N. 152 of 2008)

**[62.37.1]   2009 amendments not applicable in respect of certain prior matters**
Order 62 rule 37 provides that the amendments to the Order effected by Part 23 of the Amendment Rules 2008 (in force from April 2009) will not apply in relation to a bill of costs which has already been filed at the time of commencement. Similarly, where a bill of costs is filed after commencement, the amendments do not fully apply if the writ was issued previously. Significantly, rule 37(4) provides that no costs for work done before commencement shall be disallowed if they would have been recoverable under the previous provisions. As a result, the following important new provisions (as well as others which may be regarded of lesser importance) will not apply to the relevant costs:

    ☐   The amendment of the basis on which counsel's fee is assessed by the taxing master under Order 62, first schedule, part II (as to which, see the commentary on counsel's fees under Order 62 rule 32).

    ☐   Enlarged powers of judicial clerks in relation to taxations, under O 62 rule 13.

    ☐   The express power of the taxing master to give directions as to the conduct of a taxation under the new rule 13A.

    ☐   The new rule 17A in relation to the taxing master's final certificate of costs.

    ☐   Power of the taxing master to set aside his or her own decision under the new rule 17B.

    ☐   The new rules 21, 21A, 21B, 21C, 21D and the replaced rule 24, as to taxation procedure.

    ☐   The replaced rule 22 in relation to delay in proceeding to taxation.

- □   The repeal of the former rules 23 and 25.
- □   The new rule 32A as to liability for the costs of taxation.
- □   The new rule 32C as to the court's powers in relation costs in cases of to misconduct.

## [62.37.2]   Schedules to Order 62

The schedules to Order 62 are set out below. They are the scales of costs which, under rule 32 of the Order, apply in calculating the amount of costs recoverable in various situations.

    The scales were substantially revised as part of the civil justice reforms which came into effect in 2009. However, under the transitional provisions in Order 62 rule 37, the previous scales will continue to apply in some circumstances where an action was commenced and costs incurred prior to the new scales taking effect. The previous scales will therefore continue to be relevant for some time. As a result, we reproduce the schedules below in the form of previous schedules marked up with the deletions and additions made as part of the 2009 amendments, so that readers can see both the previous and current versions.

## [62.37.3]

### FIRST SCHEDULE        [rule 32]

### PART I

#### SCALE OF COSTS

| Item | Particulars | Charges |
|---|---|---|
| ~~1.~~ | ~~Mechanical preparation of documents~~ | |
| | ~~(a) for the top copy, per page~~ | |
| | ~~(i) quarto size or above.........................................~~ | ~~$50~~ |
| | ~~(ii) less than quarto size...................................~~ | ~~$30~~ |
| ~~(b)~~ | ~~for additional copies, either by photographic means, printing, carbon or any other method, per page of whatever size... ... ... ... ... ... ... ... ... ... ... ... ... ...~~ | ~~$3~~ |
| <u>1</u> | <u>Preparation of a bundle of copies of documents, including the costs of copying and collating the documents and compiling (including indexing and pagination) the bundle, per page of in respect whatever size............................................</u> | <u>$4 per page in of the first bundle, and $1 per page in respect of each subsequent bundle</u> |
| <u>1A.</u> | <u>Copying of documents, per page of whatever size</u> | <u>$1</u> |
| 2. | **Attendance suitable for unqualified staff, such as for filing of documents, delivery or collection of papers and to make appointments, whether such attendance are made by qualified or** | |
| | **unqualified persons, for each attendance** | **$100** |
| | | **$110** |

3.   Attendance for necessary search and inquires—such fee as the Registrar thinks proper but not less than $100 $50 for each attendance.

4.   Service of any documents—such fee as the Registrar thinks proper but not less than $50 in each case.

5.   The Registrar may allow such fee as he thinks proper in respect of every other matter or thing not hereinbefore specially mentioned.

Note to item 5: This item is intended to cover—

(a)   the doing of any work not otherwise provided for and which was properly done in preparing for a trial, hearing or appeal, or before a settlement of the matters in dispute, including—

     (i)   The client: taking instructions to sue, defend, counter-claim,appeal or opose etc.: attending upon and corresponding with client;

     (ii)   Witnesses: interviewing and corresponding with witnesses and potential witnesses, taking and preparing proofs of evidence and, where appropriate, arranging attendance at Court, including issue of subpoena;

     (iii)   Expert evidence: obtaining and considering reports or advice from experts and plans, photographs and models; where appropriate arranging their attendance at Court, including issue of subpoena;

     (iv)   Inspections: inspecting any property or place material to the proceedings;

     (v)   Searches and Inquiries: making searches in Government Registries and elsewhere for relevant documents;

     (vi)   Special damages: obtaining details of special damages and making or obtaining any relevant calculations;

     (vii)   Other parties: attending upon and corresponding with other parties or their solicitors;

     (viii)   Discovery: perusing, considering or collating documents for affidavit or list of documents; attending to inspect or produce for inspection any documents required to be produced or inspected by order of the Court or by virtue of Order 24;

     (ix)   Documents: drafting, perusing, considering and collating any relevant documents (including pleadings, affidavits, cases and instructions to and advice from counsel, orders and judgments) and any law involved;

     (x)   Negotiations: work done in connection with negotiations with a view to settlement;

     (xi)   Attendances: attendances at Court (whether in Court or chambers) for the hearing of any summons or other application, on examination of any witness, on the trial or hearing of a cause or matter, on any appeal and on delivery of any judgment; attendances on counsel in conference, and any other necessary attendances;

     (xii)   Interest: where relevant the calculation of interest on damages; and

     (xiii)   Notices: preparation and service of miscellaneous notices, including notices to witnesses to attend court; and

(b)   the general care and conduct of the proceedings.

## PART II

### GENERAL

**Discretionary costs**

~~1.(1) Where in the foregoing provisions of this Schedule there is entered in the third column against any item specified in the second column an upper and a lower sum of money, the amount of costs to be allowed in respect of that item shall (subject to any order of the Court fixing the costs to be allowed) be in the discretion of the taxing master, within the limits of the sums so entered.~~

(2)   In exercising his discretion under this paragraph or under rule 32(2) in relation to any item, the taxing master shall have regard to all relevant circumstances, and in particular to—

    (a)   the complexity of the item or of the cause or matter in which it arises and the difficulty or novelty of the questions involved;

    (b)   the skill, specialized knowledge and responsibility required of, and the time and labour expended by, the solicitor or counsel;

    (c)   the number and importance of the documents (however brief) prepared or perused;

    (d)   the place and circumstances in which the business involved is transacted;

    (e)   the importance of the cause or matter to the client;

    (f)   where money or property is involved, its amount or value;

    (g)   any other fees and allowances payable to the solicitor or counsel in respect of other items in the same cause or matter, but only where work done in relation to those items has reduced the work which would otherwise have been necessary in relation to the item in question.

**Fees to counsel**

2.   (1)   Except in the case of taxation under the Legal Aid Ordinance (Cap 91) and taxations of fees payable by the Crown, no fee to counsel shall be allowed unless—

    (a)   before taxation its amount has been agreed by the solicitor instructing counsel; and

    (b)   before the taxing master issues his certificate a receipt for the fees signed by counsel is produced to him.

(2)   No retaining fee to counsel shall be allowed on any taxation of costs in relation to which rule 28(2) has effect.

(3)   No costs shall be allowed in respect of counsel appearing before a master in chambers, or of more counsel than one appearing before a ~~judge in chambers, unless the master or judge~~ master in open court or a judge or the Court of Appeal, unless the master or judge or the Court of Appeal, as the case may be, has certified the attendance as being proper in the circumstances of the case.

(4)   A refresher fee, the amount of which shall be in the discretion of the taxing master, shall be allowed to counsel, either for each period of five hours or part thereof, after the first, during which a trial or hearing is proceeding or, at the discretion of the taxing master, in respect of any day, after the first day, on which the attendance of counsel at the place of trial is necessary.

~~(HK)(5)   Every fee paid to counsel shall be allowed in full on taxation, unless the taxing master is satisfied that the same is excessive and unreasonable, in which event the taxing master shall exercise his discretion having regard to all the relevant circumstances and in particular to the matters set out in paragraph 1(2).~~

(5)   The amount of fees to be allowed to counsel is in the discretion of the taxing master who shall, in exercising his discretion, have regard to all relevant circumstances and in particular to the matters set out in paragraph 1(2).

**Items to be authorized, certified etc.**

4. (1) In an action arising out of an accident on land due to a collision or apprehended collision, the costs of preparing a plan (other than a sketch plan) of the place where the accident happened shall not be allowed unless—

    (a)    before the trial the Court authorized the preparation of the plan, or

    (b)    notwithstanding the absence of an authorization under sub-paragraph (a) the taxing officer is satisfied that it was reasonable to prepare the plan for use at the trial.

(2) The costs of calling an expert witness with regard to any question as to which a court expert is appointed under Order 40 (or a scientific adviser is appointed under Order 103 rule 27) shall not be allowed on a taxation of costs in relation to which rule 28(2) or (3) has effect unless the Court at the trial has certified that the calling of the witness was reasonable.

(3) If any action or claim for a declaration under section 8(1) of the Registration of Patents Ordinance (Cap 42) proceeds to trial, no costs shall be allowed to the parties delivering any particulars of breaches or particulars of objection in respect of any issues raised in those particulars and relating to that patent except in so far as those issues or particulars have been certified by the Court to have been proven or to have been reasonable and proper.

**Attendances in Chambers—equity jurisdiction**

5. (1) The following provisions of this paragraph apply in relation to every hearing in chambers in the equity jurisdiction of the Court.

(3) Where on any such hearing as aforesaid the Court certifies that the speedy and satisfactory disposal of the proceedings required and received from the solicitor engaged in them exceptional skill and labour in the preparation for the hearing, the taxing master in taxing the costs to be allowed for instructions in relation to the summons or application shall take the certificate into account.

**Copies of documents**

7. (1) There shall be allowed for printing copies of any document the amount properly paid to the printer; and where any part of a document is properly printed in a foreign language or as a facsimile or in any unusual or special manner, or where any alteration becomes necessary after the first proof of the document, there shall be allowed such an amount as the taxing master thinks reasonable, such amount to include any attendances on the printer.

(2) The solicitor for a party entitled to take printed copies of any documents shall be allowed the amount he pays for such number of copies as he necessarily or properly takes.

(3) The allowance for printed copies of documents under item 1 of Part I of this Schedule shall be made in addition to the allowances under the foregoing provisions of this paragraph and shall, subject to sub-paragraph (4), be made for such printed copies as may be necessary or proper—

    (a)    of any pleading, for service on the opposite party;

    (b)    of any special case, for filing;

    (c)    of any pleading or special case, for the use of the Court;

    (d)    of any affidavit, for attestation in print;

    (e)    of any pleading, special case or evidence for the use of counsel in court; or

    (f)    of any other document necessarily and properly copied and not otherwise provided for.

(4) The allowance under item 1 of Part I shall not be made in relation to printed copies of documents for the use of the Court or of counsel where written copies have been made before printing, and shall not be made more than once in the same cause or matter. (Enacted 1988)

**[62.37.4]**

**SECOND SCHEDULE**          [rule 32]

~~Fixed Costs~~

~~For the purposes of this Schedule there shall be five Scales, namely—~~

| ~~Scale Applicable~~ | ~~Sum of Money~~ |
|---|---|
| ~~Scale I~~ | ~~Exceeding $ 50 but not exceeding $ 200~~ |
| ~~Scale II~~ | ~~Exceeding $ 200 but not exceeding $ 500~~ |
| ~~Scale III~~ | ~~Exceeding $ 500 but not exceeding $ 2000~~ |
| ~~Scale IV~~ | ~~Exceeding $ 2000 but not exceeding $ 5000~~ |
| ~~Scale V~~ | ~~Exceeding $ 5000~~ |

~~The Scale of Costs in garnishee proceedings shall be determined—~~

~~(a)   as regards the costs of the judgment creditor, by the amount recovered against the garnishee; and~~

~~(b)   as regards the costs of the garnishee or the judgment debtor, by the amount claimed by the judgment creditor in the garnishee proceedings.~~

**PART I**

COSTS ON JUDGMENT WITHOUT TRIAL FOR A LIQUIDATED SUM
OR UNDER ORDER 13A

1.    The scale of costs set out in Part II of this Schedule (which includes the scale prescribed pursuant to section 72 of the District Court Ordinance (Cap 336) shall apply in relation to the following cases if the writ of summons therein was issued after ~~1 January 1966~~ the commencement of the Amendment Rules 2008, and was indorsed with a claim for a debt or liquidated demand only, that is to say—

> (a)    cases in which the defendant pays the amount claimed within the time and in the manner required by the indorsement of the writ;
>
> (b)    cases in which the plaintiff obtains judgment on failure to give notice of intention to defend under Order 13, rule 1, or judgment in default of defence under Order 19, rule 2.
>
> ~~(c)   cases in which the plaintiff obtains judgment under Order 14, rule 3, either unconditionally or unless that sum is paid into court or to the plaintiff's solicitors.~~

1A.    The scale of costs set out in Part II of this Schedule applies in relation to cases in which the plaintiff obtains judgment under Order 13A without a hearing.

2.    Notwithstanding anything in paragraph 1 or 1A of this Schedule or in the said scale, no costs shall be allowed in any case to which the said paragraph 1 or 1A applies unless—

> (a)    the Court orders costs to be allowed; or
>
> (b)    in a case to which sub-paragraph (b) of paragraph 1 applies, judgment or an order for judgment, as the case may be, is obtained within 28 days after the service of the writ or within such further time as the Court may allow.

3.    In every case to which the said scale applies there shall be added to the basic costs set out in the said scale the fee which would have been payable on the issue of a writ for the amount recovered.

# PART II

## SCALE OF COSTS

| Item | Scale |
|------|-------|
| | $ |

**Basic Costs**

**To be allowed in cases under—**

| Item | Scale |
|------|-------|
| ~~sub-paragraph (a) of paragraph 1~~ | ~~400.00~~ |
| ~~sub-paragraph (b) of paragraph 1~~ | ~~505.00~~ |
| ~~sub-paragraph (c) of paragraph 1~~ | ~~650.00~~ |
| sub-paragraph (a) of paragraph 1 | 9000 if the plaintiff is legally represented and 500 if the plaintiff is not legally represented |
| sub-paragraph (b) of paragraph 1 | 10,000 if the plaintiff is legally represented and 600 if the plaintiff is not legally represented |
| paragraph 1A | 10,000 if the plaintiff is legally represented and 600 if the plaintiff is not legally represented |

**Additional Costs**

| | Item | Scale |
|--|------|-------|
| 1. | For each additional defendant after the first | ~~65.00~~ 500.00 |
| 2. | Where substituted service is ordered and effected, for each defendant served | ~~500.00~~ 1000.00 |
| ~~3.~~ | ~~Where service out of the jurisdiction is ordered and effected~~ | ~~225.00~~ |
| ~~4.~~ | ~~In the case of judgment in default of defence or judgment under Order 14, rule 3, where notice of intention to defend is given after the time limited therefor and the plaintiff makes an affidavit of service for the purpose of a judgment on failure to give notice of intention to defend (the allowance to include the search fee)~~ | ~~120.00~~ |
| ~~5.~~ | ~~In the case of judgment under Order 14, rule 3, where an affidavit of service of summons is required~~ | ~~120.00~~ |
| ~~6.~~ | ~~In the case of judgment under Order 14, rule 3, for each adjournment of the summons~~ | ~~50.00~~ |
| ~~7.~~ | ~~In the case of judgment on failure to give notice of intention to defend on an application by notice under Order 83A, rule 4, (which applies to moneylenders' actions)—~~ | |
| | ~~(a) where judgment is given for interest at a rate exceeding 48 per cent per annum on production of an affidavit justifying the rate~~ | ~~120.00~~ |
| | ~~(b) in any other case~~ | ~~60.00~~ |
| | ~~(c) for each additional defendant after the first~~ | ~~30.00~~ |

## PART III

### MISCELLANEOUS

| Item | Scale |
|------|-------|
| | $ |

1.　Where a plaintiff or defendant signs judgment for costs under ~~rule 11~~ rule 10, there shall be allowed—
　　cost of the judgment　　　　　　　　　　　　　　~~120.00~~ 1000.00

2.　Where upon the application of any person who has obtained a judgment or order against a debtor for the recovery or payment of money a garnishee order is made under Order 49 against a garnishee attaching debts owing or accruing from him to the debtor, the following costs shall be allowed—

　　(a)　to the garnishee, to be deducted by him from any debt owing by him as aforesaid before payments to the applicant—
　　　　(i)　if no affidavit used　　　　　　　　　　~~50.00~~ 100.00
　　　　(ii)　if affidavit used　　　　　　　　　　~~100.00~~ 300.00

　　~~(b)　to the applicant, to be retained unless the Court otherwise orders, out of the money recovered by him under the garnishee order and in priority to the amount of the debt owing to him under the judgment or order—~~
　　　　　　~~basic costs　　　　　　　　　　　　　150.00~~
　　　　　　~~additional costs where the garnishee fails to attend the hearing of the application and an affidavit of service is required　　　　　50.00~~

~~3.　Where a charging order is made—~~
　　~~(a)　in respect of any stock, funds, annuities or shares, or any dividends or interest thereon or produce thereof, under Order 50; or~~
　　~~(b)　in respect of any partnership property or profits, under section 25 of the Partnership Ordinance (Cap 38);~~
　　~~there shall be allowed—~~
　　　　~~basic costs　　　　　　　　　　　　　　575.00~~
　　　　~~additional costs where an affidavit of service is required　50.00~~

4.　Where a writ of execution within the meaning of Order 46, rule 1 is issued against any party, there shall be allowed—

　　cost of issuing execution　　　　　　　　　　~~170.00~~ 600.00

**(Enacted 1988)**
**(L.N. 152 of 2008)**

## ORDER 62A

### COSTS OFFER AND PAYMENTS INTO COURT

### I. PRELIMINARY

1.  **Interpretation and application** (O. 62A r. 1)
    **(1)** In this Order –
"costs offer" means an offer to settle –
> **(a)** a party's entitlement to costs that are the subject of a taxation; and
> **(b)** the costs of the taxation;

"offeree" means the party to whom a costs offer is made;

"offeror" means the party who makes a costs offer;

"paying party" means the party liable to pay costs;

"receiving party", in relation to a paying party, means the party who is entitled to payment of costs from that paying party;

"relevant date", in relation to a taxation, means –
> **(a)** the date on which the bill of costs is taxed under Order 62, rule 21B(1); or
> **(b)** the date set down under Order 62, rule 21C(1) for hearing the taxation;

"sanctioned offer" means a costs offer made (otherwise than by way of a payment into court) in accordance with this Order;

"sanctioned payment" means a costs offer made by way of a payment into court in accordance with this Order;

"sanctioned payment notice" means the notice relating to a sanctioned payment required to be filed under rule 8(2).

**(2)** This Order does not apply to or in relation to a party who is or has been an aided person in the relevant proceedings.

(L.N. 152 of 2008)

---

## NOTES

### [62A.1.1] Origin and scope of Order 62A

Order 62A is based on Order 22. Both provide for sanctioned payments and sanctioned offers to settle claims made in court proceedings. The difference is that whereas Order 22 applies to settlement in relation to the debt, damages or other cause of action claimed by the plaintiff in the action, Order 62A applies to the costs of the action which are subject to taxation.

Order 62A was added to the rules with effect from April 2009 as part of the civil justice reforms. The Chief Justice's working party on civil justice reform was of the view that the cost of taxations is often disproportionate and that as a result, 'a mechanism which enables either party to make a sanctioned payment or offer which forces the other party to give serious thought to settling a dispute as to costs and to avoiding an expensive hearing ought to be promoted' (final report, para 771). In the interim report it had been noted that 'court officers report that the *Calderbank* procedure is insufficiently used' (para 611). The result was recommendation 132 in the final report, that 'sanctioned offers and payments should be extended to pending costs taxations', which has been implemented by Order 62A.

Section 55B of the High Court Ordinance, added by the Civil Justice (Miscellaneous Amendments) Ordinance 2008, expressly empowers the rules committee to make provision as they have done in Order 62A to disallow costs or interest on costs, and to increase the rate of interest payable on costs, by way of sanction against a party who does not accept a proposal on costs which is ultimately not bettered.

In England the CPR do not have an express equivalent to Order 62A making specific provision for sanctioned payments and sanctioned offers in relation to costs. The idea appears to have been adopted from the New South Wales SCR, which were referred to in the interim report on civil justice reform (para 612).

#### [62A.1.2] Order not applicable to legally aided cases

Order 62A rule 1(2) provides that the Order does not apply in cases where either party is or has been legally aided in the relevant proceedings. This exception was made at the suggestion of the Legal Aid Department: see para 773 of the final report of the Chief Justice's working party on civil justice reform. The stated reason is simply that legally aided parties are subject to 'a different regime for the control of costs'. Possibly the Legal Aid Department had in mind the difficulty sometimes encountered in seeking consent of unsophisticated aided persons to terms of settlement as to costs when the result may be that some of the costs incurred on their behalf may have to be recovered out of their damages as common fund costs rather than being paid by the opposing party as party and party costs.

Nevertheless it will still be open to either party in such proceedings to make a settlement proposal in the form of a *Calderbank* offer 'without prejudice save as to costs', as to which see the commentary under Order 62 rule 5(1)(d).

#### [62A.1.3] Calderbank offer as to costs of legally aided person

A *Calderbank* offer as to the costs of a legally aided person should differentiate between the amounts offered in respect of profit costs, counsel's fees and other disbursements: *Tso Wing Yu Anita v Lau Siu Fan & Anor* [1998] 2 HKC 286, 291. This is because in legally aided cases the fees of counsel and experts cannot be agreed in advance. Thus an aided person's advisers need this extra information to facilitate discussion with counsel and experts whether they are prepared to accept the proposal.

**2. Offer to settle with specified consequences** (O. 62A r. 2)

**(1) Any party to a taxation may make a costs offer in accordance with this Order.**

**(2) An offer made under paragraph (1) has the consequences specified in rules 18, 19 and 20 (as may be applicable).**

**(3) Nothing in this Order prevents a party from making a costs offer in whatever way he chooses, but if that costs offer is not made in accordance with this Order, it does not have the consequences specified in this Order, unless the Court so orders.**

**(L.N. 152 of 2008)**

**NOTES**

**[62A.2.1]   Types of offer to settle costs under Order 62A**
Order 62A rule 2 provides that any party to a taxation may make a 'costs offer' in accordance with the Order. The term 'costs offer' is defined in rule 1 to mean an offer to settle costs which are subject to taxation and the costs of the taxation. The wording of the definition suggests that the offer must cover both of those elements.

The order provides for the sanctioned payment which may be made by the paying party under rule 3 as a costs offer, and the sanctioned offer which may be made by the receiving party under rule 4.

**[62A.2.2]   Other types of offer to settle**
Order 62A rule 2(3) expressly preserves the right of a party to make a costs offer of any type. The sanctioned payment and sanctioned offer procedures provided by Order 62A are therefore clearly intended to be additional to other settlement procedures which have long been used in practice. However a costs offer which is not a sanctioned payment or sanctioned offer within Order 62A will only have Order 62A consequences if the court so orders.

Order 62 rule 5(1)(g) provides that when exercising its discretion as to costs, the court shall take into account any admissible offer to settle made by a party. In the context of taxation of costs, this means the court shall take into account any open offer. With regard to '*Calderbank*' offers (offers 'without prejudice save as to costs') special provision is made in Order 62 rule 5(1)(d) for these to be taken into account. That provision does not apply where a sanctioned payment or sanctioned offer under Order 22 could have been made, but there is no similar exception for Order 62A sanctioned payments and offers. Thus there is no impediment to making a '*Calderbank*' offer in relation to taxation of costs despite the repeal of the former Order 22 rule 14 which gave such offers recognition within these rules. Further, such an offer in relation to taxation shall be taken into account by the court. However, if not accepted, the consequences will not necessarily be the same as if a sanctioned offer or sanctioned payment under Order 62A had been made. The Steering Committee on Civil Justice Reform expressed the view that Order 62A rule 2(3) is wide enough to enable the court to consider a *Calderbank* offer, but added that the party making such an offer would have to justify why it is not made in accordance Order 62A. See the Steering Committee's responses to comments received at the consultation stage (LegCo paper CJRS 3/2008).

With regard to *Calderbank* offers generally, see the commentary under Order 62 rule 5.

**II. MANNER OF MAKING SANCTIONED OFFER
OR SANCTIONED PAYMENT**

**3.   Paying party's costs offer requires sanctioned payment** (O. 62A r. 3)

**(1)   A costs offer by a paying party does not have the consequences specified in this Order unless it is made by way of a sanctioned payment.**

**(2)   A sanctioned payment may be made at any time before the relevant date.**

**(L.N. 152 of 2008)**

## NOTES

### [62A.3.1]   Payment required for paying party's offer

Order 62A rule 3 provides that the consequences specified in this order, such as enhanced costs and interest as set out in part IV of the Order, only apply to a paying party's offer in respect of costs where made by way of sanctioned payment. That necessitates paying the money into court. The rule is substantially similar to Order 22 rule 3, which applies to settlement of the substantive claims in an action rather than costs. See the commentary under that rule, which will largely be relevant here.

### [62A.3.2]   When sanctioned payment may be made

Order 62A rule 3(2) provides that a sanctioned payment in respect of costs may be made at any time before the 'relevant date', which is defined in rule 1.

**4.   Receiving party's costs offer requires sanctioned offer** (O. 62A r. 4)

**A costs offer by a receiving party does not have the consequences specified in this Order unless it is made by way of a sanctioned offer.**

(L.N. 152 of 2008)

### [62A.4.1]   Receiving party's sanctioned offer

Order 62A rule 4 provides that the enhanced costs and interest consequences of a sanctioned offer in respect of costs, as set out in part IV of the Order, only apply to a receiving party's settlement proposal if made by way of sanctioned offer. It is in largely the same terms as Order 22 rule 4. The commentary concerning that rule will be relevant here, bearing in mind the fact that it concerns offers in relation to the substantive relief sought in the proceedings, whereas this rule is concerned with the quantum of costs.

**5.   Form and content of sanctioned offer** (O. 62A r. 5)

    **(1)   A sanctioned offer must be in writing.**

    **(2)   A sanctioned offer may relate to the whole or part of the costs.**

    **(3)   A sanctioned offer must state whether it relates to the whole or part of the costs, and if it relates to part of the costs, to which part does it relate.**

    **(4)   A sanctioned offer may be made at any time before the relevant date.**

    **(5)   A sanctioned offer must provide that after the expiry of 14 days from the date the sanctioned offer is made, the offeree may only accept it if –**

        **(a)   the parties agree on the liability for and quantum of costs of taxation incurred after the period; or**

        **(b)   the Court grants leave to accept it.**

(L.N. 152 of 2008)

## NOTES

### [62A.5.1]   How to make a sanctioned offer in relation to costs

Order 62A rule 5 provides that a sanctioned offer in respect of costs must be made in writing. No form is prescribed. Thus it should be sufficient to set out the terms of the offer in a letter. Nor is there any requirement for the offer to be filed in court. Care should be taken to include the information stipulated by rule 5(3) and (5). It is also necessary for the terms of the offer to be clear. See the commentary under Order 22 rule 5 regarding the need for precision in formulating the terms of a sanctioned offer and the consequences of non-compliance which should be relevant here, bearing in mind that it concerns offers in relation to the substantive relief claimed in an action, whereas this rule concerns costs only.

**6.  Service of sanctioned offer** (O. 62A r. 6)
**A receiving party who makes a sanctioned offer shall serve the sanctioned offer on the paying party.**

(L.N. 152 of 2008)

**7.  Withdrawal or diminution of sanctioned offer** (O. 62A r. 7)
**(1)  A sanctioned offer may not be withdrawn or diminished before the expiry of 14 days from the date the sanctioned offer is made unless the Court grants leave to withdraw or diminish it.**

**(2)  If there is subsisting an application to withdraw or diminish a sanctioned offer, the sanctioned offer may not be accepted unless the Court grants leave to accept it.**

**(3)  If the Court dismisses an application to withdraw or diminish a sanctioned offer or grants leave to diminish the sanctioned offer, it may by order specify the period within which the sanctioned offer or diminished sanctioned offer may be accepted.**

**(4)  If a sanctioned offer is withdrawn, it does not have the consequences specified in this Order.**

(L.N. 152 of 2008)

**[62A.7.1]    When sanctioned offer may be withdrawn or reduced**
A receiving party's sanctioned offer in respect of costs is generally open for acceptance for 14 days. See Order 62A rule 14. Order 62A rule 7 provides that during that 14 day period the offer may be withdrawn or diminished only with leave of the court. The circumstances in which the court will grant such leave will be similar to those in which it will grant leave to withdraw or diminish an offer under Order 22 in respect of the substantive claim. See the commentary under Order 22 rule 10 which will largely be relevant here.

**8.  Notice of sanctioned payment** (O. 62A r. 8)
**(1)  A sanctioned payment may relate to the whole or part of the costs.**
**(2)  A paying party who makes a sanctioned payment shall file with the Court a notice in Form No. 93 in Appendix A, that –**
- **(a)  states the amount of the payment;**
- **(b)  states whether the payment relates to the whole or part of the costs, and if it relates to part of the costs, to which part it relates;**
- **(c)  if an interim payment of costs has been made, states that the paying party has taken into account the interim payment;**
- **(d)  if it is expressed not to be inclusive of interest, states –**
  - **(i)   whether interest is offered; and**

(ii) if so, the amount offered, the rate or rates offered and the period or periods for which it is offered; and

(e) if a sum of money has been paid into court as security for the costs of the action, cause or matter, states whether the sanctioned payment has taken into account that sum of money.

**(L.N. 152 of 2008)**

---

NOTES

**[62A.8.1]** **The sanctioned payment notice in respect of costs**
A paying party making a sanctioned payment in respect of costs must pay the money into court and file and serve a notice in form 93 in appendix A of these rules. The requirements of Order 62A rules 8 and 9 in that regard are substantially the same as those in Order 22 rules 8 and 9 in relation to sanctioned payments on account of the substantive claims in legal proceedings. See the commentary under those rules.

**9. Service of sanctioned payment** (O. 62A r. 9)
A paying party who makes a sanctioned payment shall –
(a) serve the sanctioned payment notice on the receiving party; and
(b) file with the Court a certificate of service of the notice.

**(L.N. 152 of 2008)**

---

NOTES

**[62A.9.1]** **Service of notice of sanctioned payment in respect of costs**
See the commentary under rule 8 above. Note that a certificate of service must be filed in court.

**10. Withdrawal or diminution of sanctioned payment** (O. 62A r. 10)
(1) A sanctioned payment may not be withdrawn or diminished before the expiry of 14 days from the date the sanctioned payment is made unless the Court grants leave to withdraw or diminish it.
(2) If there is subsisting an application to withdraw or diminish a sanctioned payment, the sanctioned payment may not be accepted unless the Court grants leave to accept it.
(3) If the Court dismisses an application to withdraw or diminish a sanctioned payment or grants leave to diminish the sanctioned payment, it may by order specify the period within which the sanctioned payment or diminished sanctioned payment may be accepted.
(4) If a sanctioned payment is withdrawn, it does not have the consequences specified in this Order.

**(L.N. 152 of 2008)**

---

NOTES

**[62A.10.1]** **Withdrawal or reduction of sanctioned payment in respect of costs**
A paying party's sanctioned payment in respect of costs is generally open for acceptance for 14 days. See Order 62A rule 13(1). Order 62A rule 10 provides that

during that 14 day period the offer may be withdrawn or diminished only with leave of the court. The circumstances in which the court will grant such leave will be similar to those in which it will grant leave to withdraw or diminish a sanctioned payment under Order 22 in respect of the substantive claim. See the commentary under Order 22 rule 10 which will largely be relevant here.

**11. Time when sanctioned offer or sanctioned payment is made and accepted** (O. 62A r. 11)

**(1)    A sanctioned offer is made when it is served on the offeree.**

**(2)    A sanctioned payment is made when a sanctioned payment notice is served on the offeree.**

**(3)    An amendment to a sanctioned offer is effective when its details are served on the offeree.**

**(4)    An amendment to a sanctioned payment is effective when notice of the amendment is served on the offeree.**

**(5)    A sanctioned offer or a sanctioned payment is accepted when notice of its acceptance is served on the offeror.**

(L.N. 152 of 2008)

**NOTES**

**[62A.11.1]    Time when sanctioned offer or payment is made and accepted**
Order 62A rule 11 is the same as Order 22 rule 12. It makes for claims to costs the same provisions as its Order 22 equivalent does for the principal amount claimed by way of cause of action. The commentary under Order 22 rule 12 should largely be relevant here.

**12. Clarification of sanctioned offer or sanctioned payment notice** (O. 62A r. 12)

**(1)    The offeree may, within 7 days of a sanctioned offer or sanctioned payment being made, request the offeror to clarify the offer or payment notice.**

**(2)    If the offeror does not give the clarification requested under paragraph (1) within 7 days of service of the request, the offeree may, before the relevant date, apply for an order that he does so.**

**(3)    If the Court makes an order pursuant to an application made under paragraph (2), it shall specify the date when the sanctioned offer or sanctioned payment is to be treated as having been made.**

(L.N. 152 of 2008)

**NOTES**

**[62A.12.1]    Right to seek clarification of sanctioned offer or payment in respect of costs**
Order 62A rule 12 is in substantially the same terms as Order 22 rule 14(1), (2) and (3). The commentary concerning the latter should be relevant here, bearing in mind the fact that the provisions of this Order concern sanctioned proposals in relation to costs, whereas Order 22 concerns such proposals in relation to the cause of action claimed.

### III. ACCEPTANCE OF SANCTIONED OFFER
### OR SANCTIONED PAYMENT

**13. Time for acceptance of paying party's sanctioned payment** (O. 62A r. 13)

**(1)** Subject to rule 10(2) and paragraph (2), a receiving party may accept a sanctioned payment at any time before the relevant date without requiring the leave of the Court if he files with the Court and serves on the paying party a written notice of acceptance not later than 14 days after the payment was made.

**(2)** If the receiving party does not accept a paying party's sanctioned payment within the 14-day period specified in paragraph (1), then the receiving party may –

    **(a)** if the parties agree on the liability for and quantum of costs of taxation incurred after the expiry of the period, accept the payment without the leave of the Court; and

    **(b)** if the parties do not agree on the liability for and quantum of costs of taxation incurred after the expiry of the period, only accept the payment with the leave of the Court.

**(3)** Where the leave of the Court is required under paragraph (2), the Court shall, if it grants leave, make an order as to costs.

**(4)** A notice of acceptance of a sanctioned payment must be in Form No. 93A in Appendix A.

**(L.N. 152 of 2008)**

---

**NOTES**

**[62A.13.1]  Time and manner of acceptance of sanctioned payment**

Order 62A rule 13 stipulates the time and manner in which a receiving party may accept a paying party's sanctioned payment in relation to costs. Generally speaking the sanctioned payment may be accepted within 14 days simply by serving a written notice of acceptance in form 93A in appendix A to the rules. Leave of the court is required to accept the sanctioned payment after the 'relevant date' (defined in Order 62 rule 1 to mean the date of provisional taxation under Order 62 rule 21B or the date on which the court sets down the bill for hearing under Order 62 rule 21C). Late acceptance (*ie* after 14 days) is permissible under rule 13(2) provided the parties agree as to the liability and quantum of the costs of taxation after expiry of the usual time for acceptance, or with leave of the court, in which event the court will decide on costs: rule 13(3).

**[62A.13.2]  Solicitor's duty in advising on sanctioned payment**

See the commentary under Order 22 rule 15, which will be relevant here, bearing in mind the fact that Order 22 concerns sanctioned offers and payments in respect of the substantive cause of action in legal proceedings, whereas this Order is concerned with costs.

**[62A.13.3]  Late acceptance of sanctioned payment**

See the commentary under Order 22 rule 15, which will be relevant here, bearing in mind the fact that Order 22 concerns sanctioned offers and payments in respect of the substantive cause of action in legal proceedings, whereas this Order is concerned with costs.

**14. Time for acceptance of receiving party's sanctioned offer** (O. 62A r. 14)

**(1)  Subject to rule 7(2) and paragraph (2), a paying party may accept a sanctioned offer at any time before the relevant date without requiring the leave of the Court if he files with the Court and serves on the receiving party a written notice of acceptance not later than 14 days after the offer was made.**

**(2)  If the paying party does not accept a receiving party's sanctioned offer within the 14-day period specified in paragraph (1), then the paying party may —**

> **(a)  if the parties agree on the liability for and quantum of costs of taxation incurred after the expiry of the period, accept the offer without the leave of the Court; and**
>
> **(b)  if the parties do not agree on the liability for and quantum of costs of taxation incurred after the expiry of the period, only accept the offer with the leave of the Court.**

**(3)  Where the leave of the Court is require under paragraph (2), the Court shall, if it grants leave, make an order as to costs.**

**(L.N. 152 of 2008)**

**[62A.14.1]  Time considerations and solicitor's duty**
See the commentary under Order 62A rule 13, in relation to sanctioned payments in respect of costs, which is relevant here as well, on a *mutatis mutandis* basis.

**15. Payment out of a sum in court on acceptance of sanctioned payment** (O. 62A r. 15)

**Subject to rule 16(4), where a sanctioned payment is accepted, the receiving party may obtain payment out of the sum in court by making a request for payment in Form No. 93B in Appendix A.**

**(L.N. 152 of 2008)**

**[62A.15.1]  Order not required for payment out**
The effect of Order 62A rule 15 is that an order is not normally required for payment out of court of money accepted under a sanctioned payment in regard to costs. This is subject to the exception laid down by rule 16(4), whereby an order for payment out is required in certain cases where a sanctioned payment is made by one or more, but not all of the paying parties. It is also subject to rule 17 concerning parties under disability.

**16. Acceptance of sanctioned payment made by one or more, but not all, paying parties** (O. 62A r. 16)

**(1)  This rule applies where the receiving party wishes to accept a sanctioned payment made by one or more, but not all, of a number of paying parties.**

**(2)  If the paying parties are jointly or severally liable to pay costs, the receiving party may accept the payment in accordance with rule 13 if —**

> **(a)  he discontinues the proceedings for taxation against those paying parties who have not made the payment; and**

   (b)  those paying parties give written consent to the acceptance of the
        payment.

   (3)   If the paying parties are not jointly, but severally liable to pay costs, the
receiving party may —

   (a)  accept the payment in accordance with rule 13; and

   (b)  continue with his proceedings for taxation against the other
        paying parties.

   (4)   In all other cases the receiving party shall apply to the Court for —

   (a)  an order permitting a payment out to him of any sum in court;
        and

   (b)  such order as to costs relating to the taxation as the Court
        considers appropriate.

                                                            (L.N. 152 of 2008)


**[62A.16.1]    Origin and scope of Order 62A rule 16**
Order 62A rule 16 is in substantially the same terms as Order 22 rule 18, and the
commentary concerning the latter should be applicable here, on a *mutatis mutandis*
basis, bearing in mind that it concerns the substantive claim whereas this rule
concerns costs.


**17. Cases where court order is required to enable acceptance of sanctioned offer
     or sanctioned payment** (O. 62A r. 17)

   Where a sanctioned offer or a sanctioned payment is made in proceedings
to which Order 80, rule 10 (Compromise, etc., by person under disability)
applies —

   (a)  the offer or payment may be accepted only with the leave of the
        Court; and

   (b)  no payment out of any sum in court may be made without a court
        order.

                                                            (L.N. 152 of 2008)

_____

**NOTES**

**[62A.17.1]    Parties under disability**
Order 62A rule 17 extends to sanctioned offers and sanctioned payment in relation
to costs the requirement under Order 80 rule 10 that settlement on behalf of a party
under disability must be approved by the court. It provides that no such offer or
payment may be accepted without leave of the court, and no money in court may be
paid out without an order.

## IV. CONSEQUENCES OF SANCTIONED OFFER
## OR SANCTIONED PAYMENT

**18. Consequences of acceptance of sanctioned offer or sanctioned payment** (O. 62A r. 18)

(1)   If a sanctioned offer or sanctioned payment relates to the whole costs and is accepted, the taxation is stayed.

(2)   In the case of acceptance of a sanctioned offer which relates to the whole costs —

      (a)   the stay is upon the terms of the offer; and

      (b)   either party may apply to enforce those terms without the need to commence new proceedings.

(3)   If a sanctioned offer or a sanctioned payment which relates to part only of the costs is accepted, the taxation is stayed as to that part.

(4)   If the approval of the Court is required before a settlement as to costs can be binding, any stay which would otherwise arise on the acceptance of a sanctioned offer or a sanctioned payment takes effect only when that approval has been given.

(5)   Any stay arising under this rule does not affect the power of the Court —

      (a)   to enforce the terms of a sanctioned offer;

      (b)   to deal with any question of costs (including interest on costs) relating to the taxation; or

      (c)   to order payment out of court of any sum paid into court.

(6)   Where —

      (a)   a sanctioned offer has been accepted; and

      (b)   a party alleges that —

          (i)   the other party has not honoured the terms of the offer; and

          (ii)   he is therefore entitled to a remedy for breach of contract,

the party may claim the remedy by applying to the Court without the need to commence new proceedings unless the Court orders otherwise.

**(L.N. 152 of 2008)**

## NOTES

**[62A.18.1]   Consequences of acceptance of sanctioned proposal on costs**
Order 62A rule 18 provides for a stay of the taxation where a sanctioned offer or sanctioned payment in respect of costs is accepted (subject to court approval where required under rule 17). The rule goes on to provide that a sanctioned offer which has been accepted may be enforced by application to the court without the need to commence new proceedings. (There is no equivalent provision in regard to sanctioned payments since such a settlement proposal must be made by payment of money into court, so enforcement will not be necessary). Save that it applies to costs rather than the cause of action claimed in the proceedings, rule 18 closely resembles Order 22 rule 22. The commentary under the latter should be relevant here.

**19. Costs consequences where receiving party fails to better sanctioned payment**
(O. 62A r. 19)

**(1)** This rule applies where upon taxation a receiving party fails to better a sanctioned payment.

**(2)** The taxing master may by order disallow all or part of any interest otherwise payable under section 49 of the Ordinance on the whole or part of the amount of the costs awarded to the receiving party for some or all of the period after the latest date on which the payment could have been accepted without requiring the leave of the Court.

**(3)** The taxing master may also —

    (a) order the receiving party to pay the costs of the taxation on the indemnity basis after the date on which the payment was made; and

    (b) order that the paying party is entitled to interest on those costs at a rate not exceeding 10% above judgment rate.

**(4)** Where this rule applies, the taxing master shall make the orders referred to in paragraphs (2) and (3) unless he considers it unjust to do so.

**(5)** In considering whether it would be unjust to make the orders referred to in paragraphs (2) and (3), the taxing master shall take into account all the circumstances of the case including —

    (a) the terms of the sanctioned payment;

    (b) the stage in the proceedings at which the sanctioned payment was made;

    (c) the information available to the parties at the time when the sanctioned payment was made; and

    (d) the conduct of the parties with regard to the giving or refusing to give information for the purposes of enabling the payment to be made or evaluated.

**(6)** The power of the taxing master under this rule is in addition to any other power it may have to award or disallow interest.

**(L.N. 152 of 2008)**

---

**NOTES**

**[62A.19.1]** **Power to impose costs and interest sanctions on receiving party for failure to accept sanctioned offer or payment**

Order 62A rule 19 provides for costs and interest sanctions against a receiving party who fails to accept a sanctioned payment in respect of costs, and ultimately achieves no better result in regard to the costs claimed. It is in most material respects the same as Order 22 rule 23, which applies to the similar situation where a plaintiff fails to accept a sanctioned offer or sanctioned payment in respect of the cause of action, but ultimately achieves no better result. See the commentary under Order 22 rule 23.

*Manova Int'l Ltd v Giga Technology Co Ltd & Anor* HCA 733/2009 (Registrar Au-Yeung; 26.02.2010) is an example of a case where costs and interest sanctions under rule 19 were imposed on a receiving party which failed to beat the paying party's sanctioned payment. The court rejected the receiving party's argument that sanctions should not be imposed because the amount allowed on taxation was only slightly below the sanctioned payment.

**20. Costs and other consequences where receiving party does better than he proposed in his sanctioned offer** (O. 62A r. 20)

**(1)   This rule applies where upon taxation a paying party is held liable for more than the proposals contained in a receiving party's sanctioned offer.**

**(2)   The taxing master may order interest on the whole or part of the amount of the costs allowed to the receiving party at a rate not exceeding 10% above judgment rate for some or all of the period after the date on which the sanctioned offer was served on the paying party.**

**(3)   The taxing master may also order that the receiving party is entitled to—**

> **(a)   his costs on the indemnity basis after the date on which the sanctioned offer was served on the paying party; and**
>
> **(b)   interest on those costs at a rate not exceeding 10% above judgment rate.**

**(4)   Where this rule applies, the taxing master shall make the orders referred to in paragraphs (2) and (3) unless he considers it unjust to do so.**

**(5)   In considering whether it would be unjust to make the orders referred to in paragraphs (2) and (3), the taxing master shall take into account all the circumstances of the case including –**

> **(a)   the terms of the sanctioned offer;**
>
> **(b)   the stage in the proceedings at which the sanctioned offer was made;**
>
> **(c)   the information available to the parties at the time when the sanctioned offer was made; and**
>
> **(d)   the conduct of the parties with regard to the giving or refusing to give information for the purposes of enabling the offer to be made or evaluated.**

**(6)   The power of the taxing master under this rule is in addition to any other power he may have to award interest.**

**(L.N. 152 of 2008)**

---

**NOTES**

**[62A.20.1]   Power to impose costs and interest sanctions on paying party for failure to accept sanctioned offer**

Order 62A rule 20 provides for costs and interest sanctions against a paying party who fails to accept a sanctioned offer, but ultimately achieves no better result in regard to the costs claimed against it. The rule is in most material respects the same as Order 22 rule 24, which applies to the similar situation where a defendant is held liable for more than the proposals contained in the plaintiff's sanctioned offer. See the commentary under Order 22 rule 24.

**V. MISCELLANEOUS**

**21. Restriction on disclosure of sanctioned offer or sanctioned payment** (O.62A r. 21)

(1) **A sanctioned offer is treated as "without prejudice save as to costs".**

(2) **The fact that a sanctioned payment has been made must not be communicated to the taxing master until the amount of the costs to be allowed have been decided.**

(3) **Paragraph (2) does not apply –**

    (a) **where the taxation has been stayed under rule 18 following acceptance of a sanctioned payment; and**

    (b) **where the fact that there has or has not been a sanctioned payment may be relevant to the question of the costs of the issue of liability.**

**(L.N. 152 of 2008)**

**NOTES**

**[62A.21.1]   Origin and scope of Order 62A rule 21**
Order 62 rule 21 provides that a sanctioned offer or sanctioned payment in regard to costs should not be disclosed to the court until the amount of costs to be allowed has been decided. It is in most respects the same as Order 22 rule 25, which applies in regard to such payments and offers in regard to the claims in an action. See the commentary under Order 22 rule 25.

**22. Interest** (O. 62A r. 22)

(1) **Unless —**

    (a) **a receiving party's sanctioned offer; or**

    (b) **a sanctioned payment notice,**

**indicates to the contrary, any such offer or payment is to be treated as inclusive of all interest until the last date on which it could be accepted without requiring the leave of the Court.**

(2) **Where a receiving party's sanctioned offer or a sanctioned payment notice is expressed not to be inclusive of interest, the offer or notice must state —**

    (a) **whether interest is offered; and**

    (b) **if so, the amount offered, the rate or rates offered and the period or periods for which it is offered.**

**(L.N. 152 of 2008)**

**NOTESA**

**[62A.22.1]   Interest on sanctioned payment or offer**
Order 62A rule 22 provides that unless otherwise indicated, a sanctioned offer or payment in respect of costs is to be treated as inclusive of interest. The rule is in all material respects the same as Order 22 rule 26. The commentary under Order 22 rule 26 will be relevant here, bearing in mind the fact that here we are concerned with costs, whereas Order 22 is concerned with the substantive claims in an action.

# GENERAL AND ADMINISTRATIVE PROVISIONS

## ORDER 63

### THE REGISTRY

---

## NOTES

### [63.0.1]   Comparison with English rules

Order 63 derives from the Order of the same number in the former English RSC. Some of the former English rules were omitted, and there are many differences in wording, largely because the High Court in Hong Kong has no formal divisions and only one registry.

### [63.0.2]   Functions of the High Court registry

The High Court registry issues originating process by which actions are commenced, and acts as a repository for the filing of subsequent documents in such actions and on appeal. In addition the registry issues summonses and fixes hearing dates. The Registrar has significant powers (also exercised by masters) over the conduct of proceedings in the Court of First Instance at the interlocutory stage.

### [63.0.3]   Registry practice

From time to time the High Court registry issues guidance on registry practice. See Law Society circular 06–79 for a consolidated statement which remains valid as at late 2007. The circular can be viewed in the members' zone of the Law Society's website.

### [63.0.4]   Numbering

There is no rule 1 in Order 63. The equivalent in the former English Rules of the Supreme Court dealt with distribution of business within various departments of the court.

## 2.   Practice master (O. 63 r. 2)

**Subject to the direction of the Registrar one of the masters shall be present at the Registry on every day on which the Registry is open for the purpose of superintending the business performed there and giving any directions which may be required on questions of practice and procedure.**

---

## NOTES

### [63.2.1]   Role of practice master

Order 63 rule 2 was introduced in 1988 to provide a formal basis for the office of practice master. Each day the registry is open, one master is designated to act as practice master. The practice master will normally be available each afternoon to deal with *ex parte* applications which require a hearing, such as applications for prohibition orders. The practice master may also be available to deal with urgent matters, though contested matters which may require lengthy argument may be more appropriate for the duty judge.

**3. Date of filing to be marked, etc.** (O. 63 r. 3)

**(1) Any document filed in the Registry in any proceedings must be marked showing the date on which the document was filed.**

**(2) Particulars of the time of delivery at the Registry of any document for filing, the date of the document and the title of the cause or matter of which the document forms part of the record shall be entered in books kept in the Registry for the purpose.**

**(L.N. 127 of 1995)**

---

**NOTES**

**[63.3.1] Comparison with English rules**
Order 63 rule 3(1) differs from its counterpart of the same number in the former English RSC in that the latter provides for every document filed to be 'sealed with a seal showing the date on which the document was filed'.

**[63.3.2] Inherent power to backdate court document**
The court has an inherent jurisdiction to order the backdating of a writ of summons: *Cinerent Ltd v GAN Assurances* HCA 593/2009 (Recorder P Fung SC; 14.12.2009). In that case the plaintiff presented its writ and paid the court fee on 2 March, but the writ was not actually issued until the next day. This gave rise to a potential contractual limitation point. The court ordered that the writ should be deemed for all purposes to have been issued on 2 March.

**3A. Filing of documents in the Registry** (O. 63 r. 3A)

**(1) Subject to paragraph (2) and to Order 12 rule 1(3), any document to be filed in Court in accordance with these rules or by order of the Court shall be filed by delivering such document to the Registry by hand.**

**(2) When any document is to be filed by a litigant in person, not being a director representing a body corporate by leave of the Court given pursuant to Order 5 rule 6(3) or Order 12 rule 1(2A), such document may by filed by sending it by post to the Registry, and the date of filing thereof shall be the date the document is received by the Registry. (L.N.127/95)**

---

**NOTES**

**[63.3A.1] Comparison with English rules**
Order 63 rule 3A is unique to Hong Kong in the sense that there was no rule of the equivalent number in the former English RSC. The rule was possibly thought necessary in Hong Kong because of the requirement of Order 18 rule 5A (which did not exist under the English RSC) that pleadings be filed.

**[63.3A.2]    Method of filing documents in court**

The normal method of filing documents in court is delivering them by hand to the registry: Order 63 rule 3A(1). By sub-rule 2, litigants in person are permitted to file documents by post. This does not apply to companies which have been granted leave to be represented by a director, nor to any party represented by a solicitor. Note however that Order 12 rule 1(3) provides that an acknowledgement of service may be filed by any party by handing it in or by post to the registry.

There is no provision in Hong Kong for filing by fax or by electronic means. Filing by fax is specifically prohibited by part III of practice direction 24.1, the text of which can be viewed on the judiciary website www.judiciary.gov.hk or that of the Hong Kong Legal Information Institute www.hklii.org, both of which are accessible by the general public free-of-charge.

**4.    Right to inspect, etc. certain documents filed in the Registry** (O. 63 r. 4)

**(1)    Any person shall, on payment of the prescribed fee, be entitled during such hours as the Registrar may direct to search for, inspect and obtain a copy of any of the following documents filed in the Registry, namely—**

> **(a)    the copy of any writ of summons or other originating process,**
>
> **(b)    any judgment or order given or made in court or the copy of any such judgment or order, and**
>
> **(c)    with the leave of the Court, which may be granted on an application made ex parte, any other document.**

**(2)    Nothing in the foregoing provisions shall be taken as preventing any party to a cause or matter searching for, inspecting and obtaining a copy of any affidavit or other document filed in the Registry in that cause or matter or filed therein before the commencement of that cause or matter but made with a view to its commencement.**

---

**NOTES**

**[63.4.1]    Comparison with English rules**

There are some differences between the wording of Order 63 rule 4 and its counterpart of the same number in the former English RSC, but they are not of any substance and do not affect the general position as to access to documents in the court file.

**[63.4.2]    Limited right of public to inspect and copy documents in court file**

Order 63 rule 4 gives the public a right to inspect and take copies of documents filed in civil proceedings. The right is limited in two ways. First it applies only to the writ or originating process, and any judgment or order given in court – rule 4(1)(c) stipulates that inspection of other documents in the court file requires leave. Secondly the court has inherent jurisdiction to restrict access even to those documents inspection of which does not require leave. See *Re Kong Wah Holdings Ltd (in liq) (No 3)* [2007] 3 HKC 631, doubting *obiter dicta* in *Hunsworth v AG* [1996] 3 HKC 519, 523D (CA) to the effect that the right is 'unqualified'. Leave is also required to inspect any document filed in relation to an application by a person subject to a vexatious litigant order, for leave under section 27A of the High Court Ordinance to commence or continue proceedings: see Order 32A rule 6.

The rule does not apply to proceedings of a criminal nature such as an application for a letter of request for evidence to be taken in another jurisdiction in support of a possible criminal prosecution in Hong Kong: *Hunsworth v Registrar* [1997] 4 HKC 405.

### [63.4.3]  Inspection and copying of court file by parties
Order 63 rule 4(2) makes it clear that the limitations set out in the rule for access to the court file by members of the public do not apply to the parties to the proceedings. See also the Registrar's administrative direction on search and inspection of court files (ref SC 101/16/28 VI) (annexed to Law Society circular 06-79 which can be viewed on the members' zone of the Law Society's website).

The definition of 'party' in section 2 of the High Court Ordinance (which applies to these rules) is broad. However, it is not so broad as to permit 'interested parties' to inspect the court file without leave: see *Re Peregrine Investments Holdings Ltd* [1999] 2 HKLRD 722 where former directors of a company were refused leave to inspect the court file relating to an application by the Financial Secretary for appointment of an inspector.

### [63.4.4]  Copy only of originating process to be inspected
Rule 4(1)(a) provides that the right to inspect originating process is the right to inspect a copy thereof. By Part I of Practice Direction 24.1 when a writ of summons or other originating process is tendered for sealing at the registry, the party tendering the same is required to lodge an additional copy, which is the copy for inspection.

### [63.4.5]  Public interest immunity
The rights under Order 63 rule 4 are subject to public interest immunity and may be refused on that ground: *Apple Daily Ltd v Commissioner of the ICAC* [2000] 1 HKC 295, 311B–D (CA).

### [63.4.6]  Restrictions on right to inspect
The extent to which parties and members of the public may inspect a court file under Order 63 rule 4 is subject to additional restrictions set out elsewhere in the rules. Order 32A rule 6 provides no one may inspect documents filed on an application under section 27A of the High Court Ordinance without leave. That section enables persons who are subject to vexatious litigant orders to apply for leave to commence or continue proceedings. Order 67 rule 6A provides that leave is required to inspect or copy an affidavit in support of a solicitor's application for a declaration of having ceased to act.

### [63.4.7]  Inspection of court file by solicitors
Solicitors are required to seek leave to search and inspect a court file: Order 63 rule 4(1)(c). Leave should be sought by praecipe, and a small fee is payable (except in legally aided cases). See the Registrar's administrative direction on search and inspection of court files, which can be obtained from the court (Ref: SC 101/16/28 VI) or downloaded from Law Society circular 06–79 which can be viewed on the members zone of the Law Society's website.

**5. Deposit of documents** (O. 63 r. 5)

Where the Court orders any documents to be lodged in court, they must, unless otherwise directed, be deposited in the Registry.

**8. Inspection, etc. of powers of attorney** (O. 63 r. 8)

(1) An index shall be kept in the Registry of all powers of attorney which have been deposited in the Registry prior to 1 October 1972.

(2) Any person shall, on payment of the prescribed fee, be entitled to—

    (a) search the index;

    (b) inspect any power of attorney and any document which has been deposited together with the power of attorney; and

    (c) office copies of the power of attorney and any document relating thereto,

and a copy of such power of attorney and document may be presented at the Registry to be marked as office copies.

(3) Any person shall, on payment of the prescribed fee, be entitled to—

    (a) search the register of enduring powers of attorney kept under section 9(4) of the Enduring Powers of Attorney Ordinance (Cap 501);

    (b) inspect any enduring power of attorney lodged under section 9(3) of that Ordinance; and

    (c) office copies of the enduring power of attorney,

and a copy of such enduring power of attorney may be presented at the Registry to be marked as an office copy. (L.N. 284 of 1997)

---

**NOTES**

**[63.8.1] Registration and inspection of powers of attorney**

There is no requirement in the Powers of Attorney Ordinance (Cap 31) for powers of attorney to be filed at the High Court.

Under the Enduring Powers of Attorney Ordinance (Cap 501) a register of enduring powers of attorney is created and paragraph (3) of this rule governs inspection of powers of attorney lodged under that Ordinance.

**9. Restriction on removal of documents** (O. 63 r. 9)

No document filed in or in the custody of the Registry of the High Court shall be taken out of that Registry without the leave of the Court.

---

**NOTES**

**[63.9.1] Power to permit withdrawal of filed document**

In *Axona International Credit and Commerce Ltd (in liq) v PT Susukan Agung & Ors* [1985] 1 HKC 452, 460I–461F the court refused an application by a party for liberty to remove its own solicitor's affidavit from the court file. Without doubting the jurisdiction to make such an order it was held that if there was anything 'unethical or improper' about the affidavit it should remain on file 'to provide a basis for any necessary action'.

**10. Enrolment of instruments** (O. 63 r. 10)

Any deed which by virtue of any written law is required or authorized to be enrolled in the High Court may be enrolled in the Registry.

In this rule "deed" includes assurances and other instruments.

**(Enacted 1988)**

## ORDER 64

### SITTINGS, VACATIONS AND OFFICE HOURS

**1.   Sittings of the High Court** (O. 64 r. 1)

**(1)   The sittings of the Court of Appeal and of the Court of First Instance shall be three in every year, that is to say—**

    **(a)   the Winter sittings which shall begin on 4 January and end on the Thursday before Easter Sunday;**

    **(b)   the Spring sittings which shall begin on the second Monday after Easter Sunday and end on 31 July;**

    **(c)   the Autumn sittings which shall begin on 1 September and end on 23 December.**

**(L.N. 404 of 1991)**

## NOTES

### [64.1.1]   Court sitting hours

Court sitting hours are governed by practice direction 8.1, which can be viewed on the judiciary's website www.judiciary.gov.hk or that of the Hong Kong Legal Information Institute www.hklii.org, both of which are accessible by the general public free-of-charge. The usual sitting hours, subject to variation at the discretion of the presiding judge or master, are 10 am to 1 pm and 2.30 pm to 4.30 pm in the High Court. Sitting hours in the District Court begin 30 minutes earlier at 9.30 a.m., but otherwise are the same.

### [64.1.2]   Adjournment of court proceedings in case of inclement weather

By virtue of section 3(1) of the Judicial Proceedings (Adjournment During Gale Warnings) Ordinance (Cap 62), all judicial proceedings set down for hearing, or being conducted, stand adjourned when a gale warning (number 8 typhoon signal or higher) or black rainstorm warning is in force. However such proceedings may be continued during the period such a warning is in force under section 3(2) of the Ordinance.

Section 4 of the Ordinance provides that judicial proceedings which have been adjourned by virtue of section 3 shall resume on the next day (not being a public holiday) after the day on which the warning ceases.

The provisions of sections 3 and 4 are subject to section 6 of the Ordinance, which empowers the Chief Justice to order the adjournment or resumption of any judicial proceedings. According to information provided by the judiciary administrator and circulated to solicitors by Law Society circular 10-273, the Chief Justice has decided that the power will be exercised as follows:

    **(a)   Resumption on the same day**

        (i)   if the gale or rainstorm warning is lowered or cancelled at or before 6:00 am, all adjourned judicial proceedings for the previous day(s) will be resumed at 9:30 am on the same day which is a working day (including Saturday).

        (ii)   If the gale or rainstorm warning is lowered or cancelled between 6:00 am and 11:00 am or at 11:00 am on a working day other than a Saturday, all adjourned proceedings for the morning and the previous day(s), if any, will be resumed at 2:30 pm on the same day.

**(b)   Resumption on the next day**

(i)    If the gale or rainstorm warning is lowered or cancelled after 11:00 am, all adjourned proceedings for that day and the previous day(s), if any, will be resumed at 9:30 am the next day (including Saturday), which is not a public holiday.

(ii)   If the gale or rainstorm warning is lowered or cancelled after 6:00 am on a Saturday, all adjourned proceedings for the morning and the previous day(s), if any, will be resumed at 9:30 am the next day, which is not a public holiday.

The above provisions apply with regard to judicial proceedings. Different arrangements are in place for court registries and offices, as set out in the said Law Society circular:

(a)    If the gale or rainstorm warning signal is lowered at or before 6.00 a.m. on Monday to Friday and on Saturday, all Registries/offices will be opened at their usual times in the morning;

(b)    If the gale or rainstorm warning signal is lowered between 6.00 a.m. and 11.00 a.m. or at 11.00 a.m. on Monday to Friday, all Registries/offices will be re-opened at their usual time in the afternoon;

(c)    If the gale or rainstorm warning is lowered after 11.00 a.m. Monday to Friday, subject to the circumstances prevailing at the time, all Registries/offices will re-open in the afternoon as soon as staff return to work. However, all Registries/offices will remain closed if the gale or rainstorm warning signal is lowered after 3.00 p.m. [i.e. 2 hours or less before the normal registries/offices' closing hour (5.00 p.m.)] on a whole working day; and

(d)    The Registries/offices will remain closed on a Saturday if the gale or rainstorm warning signal is lowered after 6.00 a.m.

## [64.1.3]   Court vacations

The intervals between sittings of the High Court as set down in Order 64 rule 1 are known as the court 'vacation': Order 1 rule 4. See Order 64 rules 2, 3 and 3A as to the circumstances in which the court will sit in vacation and the types of business which may be done. See also the commentary under Order 3 rule 3 as to the suspension of time for taking steps in civil proceedings during the summer vacation, that is the month of August.

**2.   Court of Appeal** (O. 64 r. 2)

**(1)   The Court of Appeal shall sit in vacation on such days as the Chief Justice may, from time to time direct to hear such appeals or applications as require to be immediately or promptly heard and to hear other appeals and applications if the Chief Justice determines that sittings are necessary for that purpose.**

**(2)   Any party to an appeal may at any time apply to the Court of Appeal for an order that the appeal be heard in vacation and, if that Court is satisfied that the appeal requires to be immediately or promptly heard, it may make an order accordingly and fix a date for the hearing.**

**(3)   The Court of Appeal may hear such other appeals in vacation as that Court may direct.**

**(4)   The provisions of O. 59, r. 10(9) shall apply to the powers conferred on the Court of Appeal by this rule.**

**3.   Court of First Instance** (O. 64 r. 3)

**(1)   One or more judges of the Court of First Instance shall sit in vacation on such days as the Chief Justice may, from time to time direct, to hear such causes, matters or applications as require to be immediately or promptly heard and to hear other causes, matters or applications if the Chief Justice determines that sittings are necessary for that purpose.**

**(2)   Any party to a cause or matter may at any time apply to the Court for an order that such cause or matter be heard in vacation and, if the Court is satisfied that the cause or matter requires to be immediately or promptly heard, it may make an order accordingly and fix a date for the hearing.**

**(3)   Any judge of the Court of First Instance may hear such other causes or matters in vacation as the Court may direct.**

**NOTES**

**[64.3.1]   Order for hearing during vacation**
Order 64 rule 2(2) provides that any party may apply for an order that a hearing take place in vacation in the Court of Appeal. Rule 3(2) makes the same provision for the Court of First Instance. On such an application a 'high or stringent' standard is required: *Re Lawe William Enterprises Ltd* HCMP 1638/1989 (Jones J; 27.07.1989). In that case the application was rejected on the ground its underlying purpose was to suit the convenience of counsel. It was also suggested that an application under rule 3(2) should be made on notice to the opposing party.

**3A. Business in vacation** (O. 64 r. 3A)
**(HK)(1)   Upon application by any party to an action or matter, the Court may, if it thinks fit—**

**(a)   complete such action or matter in vacation if it is part-heard; and**

**(b)   deliver judgment in such action or matter in vacation.**

**NOTES**

**[64.3A.1]   Vacation business**
The type of business which may be conducted during a vacation is governed by Practice Direction 8.2. With effect from 24 April 2006, the practice direction reads as follows:

VACATION BUSINESS IN THE HIGH COURT

1.   The following classes of applications can be issued and made returnable in vacations:-
   (1)   Before a judge:
      (a)   for injunction;
      (b)   for committal;
      (c)   for appraisal and sale of a vessel in the admiralty jurisdiction;
      (d)   interlocutory application that can be issued and made returnable before a master in vacation;
      (e)   application referred by a master to a judge; and
      (f)   appeal from a master in relation to an application that comes within sub-paragraph (3) below.

(2) Before a judge in companies and bankruptcy matters:

 (a) the hearing of a contested winding-up or bankruptcy petition on the first working day of each week at 9:30 a.m.;

 (b) the hearing of an application to set aside a statutory demand before a Judge;

 (c) for a validation order under s 182 of the Companies Ordinance (Cap 32) or s 42 of the Bankruptcy Ordinance (Cap 6);

 (d) for injunction;

 (e) for appointment of an interim receiver or provisional liquidator or for the protection or preservation of assets or status;

 (f) concerning schemes of arrangement and reductions of capital redemption reserve funds and share premium accounts; and

 (g) for leave to institute or defend proceedings or effect a compromise.

(3) Before a master:

 (a) to set aside writ or judgment;

 (b) to set aside writ or service for irregularity of jurisdiction;

 (c) to renew writ;

 (d) for leave to issue and serve writ out of jurisdiction;

 (e) for substituted service;

 (f) for interim payment;

 (g) for particulars, if summons under O 14 issued;

 (h) for time, in interpleader and cases where pleadings are to be served in vacation;

 (i) for the extension of time under s 86 of the Companies Ordinance (Cap 32);

 (j) for stay of proceedings by consent;

 (k) for judgment under O 14;

 (l) for leave to enter judgment;

 (m) for an order by consent;

 (n) for approval of infant settlement;

 (o) for assessment of damages, where both parties consent to the matter being dealt with in vacation;

 (p) interpleaders

 (q) for payment out after judgment;

 (r) for enforcement of any judgment or order;

 (s) for stay of execution;

 (t) for relief against forfeiture;

 (u) to vacate *lis pendens*;

 (v) to tax bills of costs;

 (w) appeals against the refusal by the Director of Legal Aid to grant legal aid;

 (x) in an admiralty action, for the arrest or release of a vessel or cargo and any matter relating to the crew;

 (y) in companies winding-up proceedings:

  (i) uncontested applications for winding-up orders;

  (ii) for the appointment of a liquidator and/or committee of inspection; and

  (iii) for warrant of arrest;

   (z)   in bankruptcy proceedings:
      (i)    uncontested applications for receiving orders;
      (ii)   for an interim order under s 20A of the Bankruptcy Ordinance (Cap 6);
      (iii)  for the appointment of a creditors' committee or trustee;
      (iv)   order for redirection of mail;
      (v)    for warrant of arrest;
      (vi)   for statutory dispensation or release;
      (vii)  application to object the automatic discharge of a bankrupt;
      (viii) for annulment of a bankruptcy order; and
      (ix)   for a validation order under s 42 of the Bankruptcy Ordinance (Cap 6).

2.   In addition to the types of business set out in paragraph 1, the following matters may be set down for hearing in vacation:
   (a)   An action assigned to the Fixture List or Running List in accordance with para 3 of Practice Direction 5.1, and
   (b)   Proceedings in the Court of First Instance,

if all parties thereto signify agreement to this effect to either the Listing Master or Listing Judge at the time leave to set down is granted or to the listing officer at the time of fixing a date for hearing.

3.   Where a party considers any other summons or application should be immediately or promptly heard, application for leave to proceed in vacation may be made to a master. The application may be made orally or by submission of a certificate signed by counsel or, if counsel has not been instructed in the matter, by solicitor.

## [64.3A.2]   Application for leave to proceed in vacation

Under practice direction 8.2, the types of applications and summonses listed in paragraph 1 may automatically be issued and heard during a court vacation.

Other applications and summonses may also be heard during vacation if leave to proceed is obtained from a master under paragraph 3 of the practice direction. Such an application is within the discretion of the master. It was once complained that there was a degree of 'laxity' in dealing with such applications: *Li Ip Man Lui v Thomas Li Wang Chung* HCMC 109/1966 (Rigby J; 08.06.1968). However it is now clear that the master should adopt a high standard in scrutinising such applications: *Midland Realty Int'l Ltd v Lee Ngok Wah* HCA 9581/1983 (Jones J; 09.08.1983). The application in the *Midland Realty* case was refused on the ground the party making it had been taking a 'leisurely approach', and no evidence was produced to substantiate the ground on which it was made.

## 7.   High Court Offices: days on which open and office hours (O. 64 r. 7)

**(1)   The offices of the High Court shall be open on every day of the year except—**
   **(a)   Saturdays from 1 p.m.,**
   **(b)   Sundays,**
   **(c)   Christmas Eve or, if that day is a Sunday, then 23 December from 1 p.m.,**

    **(ca) Lunar New Year's Eve from 1 p.m.,**

    **(e)  general holidays under the General Holidays Ordinance (Cap 149), (35 of 1998 s 5)**

    **(f)  such other days as the Chief Justice may direct. (L.N. 403 of 1992)**

    **(2)  The hours during which any office of the High Court shall be open to the public shall be such as the Chief Justice may from time to time direct.**

## ORDER 65

### SERVICE OF DOCUMENTS

**1.   When personal service required** (O. 65 r. 1)
**(1)   Any document which by virtue of these rules is required to be served on any person need not be served personally unless the document is one which by an express provision of these rules or by order of the Court is required to be so served.**
**(2)   Paragraph (1) shall not affect the power of the Court under any provision of these rules to dispense with the requirement for personal service.**

**2.   Personal service: how effected** (O. 65 r. 2)
**Personal service of a document is effected by leaving a copy of the document with the person to be served.**

## NOTES

**[65.2.1]   Personal service – who may be served?**
Personal service is of diminished importance since the introduction of postal service (see Order 10 rule 1(2)) in 1979.

Personal service is only effective on a defendant if he is at the time of service present in Hong Kong. If the defendant is outside Hong Kong the plaintiff must proceed in accordance with Order 11.

Even a fleeting presence in Hong Kong is sufficient to found valid service on a defendant: *Colt Industries v Sarlie* [1966] 1 All ER 673. See also *Maharanee of Baroda v Wildenstein* [1972] 2 QB 283. However, service may be set aside if a defendant is induced to enter Hong Kong by fraud or trickery in order to serve him: *Watkins v North American Land and Timber Co Ltd* (1904) 20 TLR 534. Moreover the court may decline to exercise its jurisdiction over a person served in Hong Kong where the dispute would best be resolved somewhere else – see the commentary under Order 12 rule 8.

**[65.2.2]   Manner of effecting personal service**
Order 65 rule 2 provides that personal service is effected by 'leaving a copy of the document with the person to be served'. What do those words mean? In *Goggs v Lord Huntingtower* (1844) 152 ER 1297 it was held that delivery of the document to a servant is not valid, even where the servant subsequently gives the document to his master. If the person to be served refuses to accept the same it will be sufficient to touch him with it, or to throw it down in his presence: *Rose v Kempthorne* (1910) 103 LT 730. See also *Buxbaum v Samuel-Rozenbaum HK Ltd* CACV 141/2005 (Rogers VP, Le Pichon & Yuen JJA; 10.05.2006). The person being served should be informed in brief terms the nature of the document: *Ko Sin Yun v Chan Chuen* DCCJ 6693/2004 (Judge H C Wong; 24.02.2006). Provided the person being served knows the nature of the document, and 'has been given a sufficient degree of possession of the document to enable him to exercise dominion over it for any period of time however brief, the document has been left with him in the sense intended by the rule':

*Dynasty Line Ltd (provisional liquidators appointed) v Sukamto Sia & Anor* [2009] 4 HKC 184 (CA) (para 21). In that case it was held that it was sufficient for the process server to tell the defendant that the package consisted of 'court documents', and it was not necessary to say that it was a writ.

A defendant's conduct may constitute waiver of strict compliance with the rules governing personal service: *Yuen On Investment Co Ltd v Chiu Tak Kan* [1961] HKLR 463. In addition, a defendant who files an acknowledgment of service in accordance with Order 12 is deemed (unless the contrary is shown) to have been duly served: see Order 10 rule 1(5).

**[65.2.3]   Restriction on personal service in court precinct**
Older cases suggest that it is an act of contempt of court to serve court documents within the precinct of the court. The more modern view is that such service would constitute contempt only in extremely rare circumstances. The service will be considered valid unless it has interfered with the judicial process. See *Fung Tak Chi v Billion Eagle Ltd* [2010] 4 HKLRD 571 referring to *Re O'Sullivan* (1995) 129 ALR 295. In *Fung* it was held that service in a conference room after a court hearing was not invalid.

**3.   Personal service on body corporate** (O. 65 r. 3)
**(1)   Personal service of a document on a body corporate may, in cases for which provision is not otherwise made by any written law, be effected by serving it in accordance with rule 2 on the chairman or president of the body, or the clerk, secretary, treasurer or other similar officer thereof.**
**(2)   Where a writ is served on a body corporate in accordance with Order 10, rule 1(2), that rule shall have effect as if for the reference to the usual or last known address of the defendant there were substituted a reference to the registered or principal office of the body corporate and as if for the reference to the knowledge of the defendant there were substituted a reference to the knowledge of a person mentioned in paragraph (1).**

---

**NOTES**

**[65.3.1]   Scope of this rule**
Although the heading above this rule suggests that it is concerned only with *personal* service of bodies corporate it actually goes further and deals with the alternative to personal service permitted under Order 10 rule 1(2), service by post or delivery, in respect of bodies corporate. The rule does not, however, deal with 'ordinary' service of bodies corporate, that is, service of documents other than the originating process and similar documents required to be served personally or in accordance with Order 10 rule 1(2). 'Ordinary' service is dealt with in rule 5 of this order.

This rule must be read together with Part XI of the Companies Ordinance (Cap 32) and other enactments which make provision for service of process on bodies corporate.

**[65.3.2]   Cross-reference**
See also the commentary under Order 10 rule 1.

**[65.3.3]  Failure to comply**

Where there is failure to comply with the procedures laid down for service of a body corporate the court has a discretion under Order 2 rule 1 to overlook the same where this best serves the interests of justice. See, for example, *LG Electronics Hong Kong Ltd v Bank of Taiwan* [2001] 4 HKC 421 where Kwan J made an order that service of an overseas company which did not comply with the applicable provisions was nevertheless good. In that case such an order was justified by the fact it was clear the proceedings had actually come to the notice of the defendant; further the defendant had not raised the service point in a timely fashion.

**[65.3.4]  Service on solicitor**

Bodies corporate such as companies are usually represented by solicitors from the outset of a civil dispute. Thus it is common to rely on Order 10 rule 1(4) whereby a party's solicitor may accept service on its behalf. However there is no legal requirement that a plaintiff investigate whether a corporate defendant is represented or whether its solicitors have instructions to accept service: *Winly Proper Ltd v In-time Int'l Development Ltd* DCCJ 6000/2004 (Judge Chow; 20.09.2005). The plaintiff is free to use the other procedures for service of a body corporate discussed in this commentary.

**[65.3.5]  Service of companies incorporated in Hong Kong under the Companies Ordinance**

Service of companies incorporated in Hong Kong under the Companies Ordinance (Cap 32) may be effected either under Order 65 rule 3(2) or under section 356 of that Ordinance. The legal provisions related to those two types of service are not identical, so it may be a good idea to include a covering letter expressly stating which provision is being relied upon.

**[65.3.6]  Service of company by post**

Order 65 rule 3(2) contemplates service of a company by post under Order 10 rule 1. Section 356 of the Ordinance makes express provision for such service. The former provides for service by registered post, whilst the latter stipulates 'post', without specifying ordinary or registered.

It has been held that Order 10 rule 1 is not intended to apply to service of companies, that rule 1(7) thereof has the effect of removing companies from its scope since specific provision is made elsewhere (section 356) for service of companies by post. See *Treasure Land Property Consultants (a firm) v United Smart Development Ltd* [1995] 3 HKC 30, 34H-I (CA). However in *Guangdong Int'l Trust & Investment Corp HK (Holdings) Ltd v Yuet Wah (HK) Wah Fat Ltd* [1997] 2 HKC 696, 700B-D the contrary conclusion was reached by referring to Order 65 rule 3(2) which, it was said, had not been drawn to the Court of Appeal's attention in the earlier case. It is submitted that the later decision is the correct one, and that the true position is that postal service may be effected on a company under either of the two legislative provisions.

**[65.3.7]  Service of company by 'leaving'**

Section 356 of the Companies Ordinance provides for service by 'leaving', i.e. by messenger, at a company's registered office. In *Po Kwong Marble Factory Ltd v Wah*

*Yee Decoration Co Ltd* [1996] 4 HKC 157, 160A-D (CA) it was held that service by leaving at an office marked with a sign bearing the company's name was irregular since that place was not in fact the company's registered address. No objection was taken in that case to the fact that service by leaving was attempted outside office hours.

Service by 'leaving' under section 356 does not require that the document be left with a person: *UCCA Formwork (HK) Ltd v Wui Fai Eng'g Co Ltd* DCCJ 5220/2007 (Deputy Judge Ko; 29.05.2008) (para 16). However, as acknowledged in that case, failure to leave the document with a person or to obtain a chop evidencing receipt, may cause difficulty in proving that the service actually took place.

It appears that where a company's registered address does not include a room number, service by leaving the writ anywhere in the registered address will be effective. See *UDL Contracting Ltd v Apple Daily Printing Ltd & Anor* [2008] 2 HKC 534 where it was said:

> A company which chooses to give a number on a street instead of say, a specific room number in a building, cannot be heard to complain if the document is left at the entrance to the place designated by the given address.

In that case service by throwing the papers over the security barrier at the entrance to the registered address was held to be valid.

Order 65 rule 3(2), referring back to Order 10 rule 1, provides for service by insertion into a letter box at the registered or principal office of a company, but contains no general provision for service by 'leaving'.

### [65.3.8]   Service of company at 'principal' office
Order 65 rule 3(2) provides for service at the 'principal' office of a company. In this context 'principal' office means one actually used by it. Service at an office which has been vacated by the company will not be valid. See *Guangdong Int'l Trust & Investment Corp HK (Holdings) Ltd v Yuet Wah (HK) Wah Fat Ltd* [1997] 2 HKC 696, 700I–701C.

### [65.3.9]   Service of company at 'registered' office
Both Order 65 rule 3(2) and section 356 of the Companies Ordinance provide for service at the registered office of a Hong Kong incorporated company. The registered office is, of course, the address recorded as such in the Companies Registry for legal purposes. Very often it is not the company's actual address, but the office of a solicitor, accountant or company secretarial service.

In *Stevenson, Wong & Co (a firm) v Goldsense Technology Ltd* [2007] 1 HKLRD 217, where a company which had given a non-existent address in its notice of registered office, but actually received the writ, it was held that service was valid as the company should not be permitted to rely upon its own default in incorrectly describing the address.

### [65.3.10]   Consequences of non receipt
It is clear that service by post addressed to a company's registered office will be valid under section 356 whether or not it is actually received. This results from section 8 of Cap 1 whereby service is deemed to be effected upon posting the document properly addressed with pre-paid postage. See *A/S Catherineholm v Norequipment Trading*

*Ltd* [1972] 2 QB 314, 322A where it was held that service under the equivalent English legislation was valid notwithstanding the demolition of the building in which the registered office was located. See also *Chung Shun Land Investment Co Ltd v Steadman* HCA 4215/1985 (Deputy Judge Barnett; 01.07.1986); *Kwok Chong Kow v Johnson Engineering Transportation Co Ltd* DCEC 126/1984 (Judge E Li; 20.12.1984); *Ho Kwok Wah v Group Jewellery Arts Ltd* [2000] 3 HKC 595 (CA); and *Winly Proper Ltd v In-time Int'l Development Ltd* DCCJ 6000/2004 (Judge Chow; 20.09.2005).

**[65.3.11]**   **Change of registered office**
If a company changes its registered office it is required by section 92(2) of the Companies Ordinance to notify the Registrar of Companies within 14 days. However the Ordinance does not state when such a change takes effect. It has been held that service at the registered address as recorded by the companies registry will not be valid if the company has in fact already submitted notification of change of registered address: *Guangdong Int'l Trust & Investment Corp HK (Holdings) Ltd v Yuet Wah (HK) Ltd* [1997] 2 HKC 696.

**[65.3.12]**   **Deemed date of service**
When a company is served under Order 65 rule 3(2), service is deemed by Order 10 rule 1(3)(a) to be effected 7 days after posting. Where section 356 is relied upon, service is deemed by section 8 of Cap 1 to be effected on the date when the document would be delivered in the 'ordinary course of post'. Just when a document will be delivered in the 'ordinary course of post' is a question of fact to be determined not by judicial notice, but by evidence: *Treasure Land Property Consultants (a firm) v United Smart Development Ltd* [1995] 3 HKC 30, 35B-I (CA). Thus it is advisable to use the post office's double-registered service by which a certificate of delivery will be returned to the sender.

**[65.3.13]**   **Bodies corporate incorporated by statute or prerogative instrument**
Where a body corporate is incorporated by statute or prerogative instrument, section 356 of the Companies Ordinance does not apply and some other mode of service must be relied on. In some instances the incorporating statute or prerogative instrument may contain a provision authorising service in a particular way, often in terms similar to section 356, but this is not common in Hong Kong.

In the absence of any guidance in the incorporating statute or charter, service will normally be effected on such a body corporate by post to, or by leaving the document to be served at, the registered or principal office of the corporation, pursuant to Order 65 rule 3(2), read together with Order 10 rule 1(2).

**[65.3.14]**   **Service of body corporate by personal service of officer thereof**
Order 65 rule 3(1) authorises service of bodies corporate by personal service on an officer of the corporation.

This method of service is available only, in the words of rule 3(1), 'in cases for which provision is not otherwise made by any written law'. Such provision has been made for companies and oversea companies under the Companies Ordinance. Moreover, it is expressly contemplated in Order 65 rule 3(2) that service by post or delivery under Order 10 rule 1(2) be possible on all bodies corporate. Thus, it may be that sufficient provision for service of bodies corporate has otherwise been made to render the procedure under rule 3(1) redundant.

**[65.3.15]    Foreign companies with places of business in Hong Kong**
As is the case with Hong Kong companies, foreign companies which have places of business in Hong Kong may be served either under the provisions of this rule read together with Order 10 rule 1(2), or under special provisions found in the Companies Ordinance.

Section 333(1)(c) of the Companies Ordinance requires an 'oversea' company (defined in section 332) which establishes a place of business in Hong Kong to register with the Registrar of Companies the name and address of at least one person in Hong Kong authorised to accept service on its behalf. Under section 338(1) of the Ordinance process is deemed sufficiently served on such a company if addressed to such person 'and left at or sent by post to his address ...'.

In the event that an oversea company which has established a place of business in Hong Kong fails to register the name of a person who may be served on its behalf, or for some reason it is not possible to serve the person whose name has been registered, service under section 338(1) will not be valid and section 338(2) applies instead: *LG Electronics HK Ltd v Bank of Taiwan* [2001] 4 HKC 421, 427B-H. Section 338(2) provides that the document may be served by leaving or by post at 'any place of business' which the oversea company may have in Hong Kong. It is not necessary for the place at which service is effected to be a principal place of business: *Ho Tai Kwan v Global Innovative Systems Inc* HCA 12/2007 (Sakhrani J; 14.08.2007). Alternatively, if the oversea company no longer has a place of business in Hong Kong, service may be effected under section 338(2)(b) by registered post to its registered office in the place of incorporation, with a copy by registered post to its principal place of business (if any) or, in default of any such addresses, at any place in Hong Kong where the company has had a place of business in Hong Kong within the previous 3 years. Service out of Hong Kong under section 338(2)(b) is not expressed to be subject to the usual requirement (see Order 11 rule 1) that leave is required for service *ex juris*. In principle the provisions of the section, being in primary legislation, should take precedence over Order 11 (see s 28(1)(b) of Cap 1).

**[65.3.16]    Foreign companies – what is a 'place of business' in Hong Kong**
Sections 333 and 338 of the Companies Ordinance apply only to oversea companies which establish places of business in Hong Kong. Similarly, foreign companies may not be served under Order 65 rule 3 unless they have an office in Hong Kong.

'Place of business' is defined in section 341 of the Companies Ordinance in restrictive terms and it is a question of fact whether the defendant has established a place of business entitling the plaintiff to serve it in Hong Kong: *English Sewing (HK) Ltd & Ors v Eastern Shipping Lines Inc* [1984] HKLR 5 (CA). In deciding whether a foreign company has a 'place of business' in Hong Kong for the purposes of service, the Hong Kong courts apply English decisions. See, for example, *The Artemis* [1983] HKLR 364 citing *Okura & Co, Ltd v Forsbacka Jernverks Aktiebolag* [1914] 1 KB 715 and see *Yuasa Trading Co (HK) Ltd & Anor v Selina Shipping SA* HCCL 8/1989 (Mayo J; 16.06.1989); [1989] HKLY 1078 citing those authorities and *South India Shipping v Export Import Bank* [1985] 2 All ER 219. In the *Yuasa Trading Co (HK)*

*Ltd* case Mayo J refused to pierce the corporate veil in deciding whether a company registered in Panama had been properly served at a 'place of business' in Hong Kong. The evidence showed that the Panamanian company was under control of residents of Hong Kong and that an address in Hong Kong was recorded with the authorities in Panama. However, the learned judge held that *The Evpo Agnic* [1988] 1 WLR 1090 was good authority and declared that valid service had not been effected at the Hong Kong address.

*Burden of proof* – the burden of establishing whether an oversea company has established a place of business in Hong Kong is on the plaintiff: *English Sewing (HK) Ltd & Ors v Eastern Shipping Lines Inc* [1984] HKLR 5 (CA); *Ahola Josephine Ann v LA Gear Inc & Anor* [1994] 2 HKC 640, 641G. The standard is the civil standard of proof: *Elsinct (Asia-Pacific) Ltd v Commercial Bank of Korea Ltd* [1994] 3 HKC 365.

*Agents* – it is possible but unlikely that by conducting business in Hong Kong through an agent an oversea company has itself established a place of business in the SAR. In *MCY Finance Ltd SA Ors v Hong Kong Shanghai (Shipping) Ltd* [1986] HKC 323; (1987)17 HKLJ 372 it was held that by such an arrangement the principal had not established a place of business in Hong Kong and service under section 338(2) of the Companies Ordinance was set aside. In such cases the plaintiff may apply for leave under Order 10 rule 2 to serve the local agent on behalf of the overseas principal.

*Business conducted by visitors* – it has been held that a foreign company which sends representatives to Hong Kong to conduct business in a hotel room has not established a place of business in the SAR and may not be served under section 338(2): see *Peter Pang v Windsor Industries Inc* [1977] HKLR 271, 272.

*Representative offices* – a 'representative' office which undertakes promotional activities and may seek to create business for an oversea company, but does not enter into any legal obligations locally, is not a place of business for the purpose of service: *Elsinct (Asia-Pacific) Ltd v Commercial Bank of Korea Ltd* [1994] 3 HKC 365. In this context 'legal obligations' (as used in section 341 of the Companies Ordinance) does not necessarily include the renting of premises and employing staff. It is 'necessary to consider the office's main activities [in Hong Kong] in the light of the company's paramount and subsidiary objects and see whether such activities create legal obligations': see the *Elsinct* case at 373. Further, the fact that the oversea company may have been registered under the Business Registration Ordinance (Cap 310) and may have filed profits tax returns does not necessarily mean that it has established a business within the meaning of section 341: *Murdock v Dresser-Rand Services SARL* [2002] 2 HKC 85, 95G–I. However, in *Zhong You (China) Design Co v Fuyuan Landmark (Shenzhen) Ltd* [1996] 2 HKC 342, 346I–347I there was evidence that all correspondence addressed to the Hong Kong office was brought to the attention of one of the officers of an oversea company and that contracts were entered into in Hong Kong. It was there held that a place of business had been established in Hong Kong.

*Order 11* – where service is not possible in Hong Kong, the appropriate procedure is, of course, to apply under Order 11 to serve out of the jurisdiction.

## 4. Substituted service (O. 65 r. 4)

**(1)   If, in the case of any document which by virtue of any provision of these rules is required to be served personally or in the case of a document to which**

Order 10, rule 1, applies, it appears to the Court that it is impracticable for any reason to serve that document in the manner prescribed on that person, the Court may make an order for substituted service of that document.

(2)   An application for an order for substituted service may be made by an affidavit stating the facts on which the application is founded.

(3)   Substituted service of a document, in relation to which an order is made under this rule, is effected by taking such steps as the Court may direct to bring the document to the notice of the person to be served.

## NOTES

### [65.4.1]   Order for substituted service
Order 65 rule 4 empowers the court to permit substituted service, that is service in a manner other than personal service, where personal service is impracticable. The rule applies only where personal service is required under the RHC. It does not apply to non-judicial documents such as a statutory demand: see PD 3.1, para 2.2, and see *Re Fung Kwok On William* HCB 9590/2008 (Recorder Patrick Fung SC; 06.08.2010) (para 36).

### [65.4.2]   Application by affidavit
An application for substituted service may be (and usually is) made by affidavit submitted to the court registry: Order 65 rule 4(2). The application will be considered by a master without a hearing, unless the master requires one. Proceeding *ex parte* by paper application without a hearing does not infringe human rights guarantees since any *ex parte* order may be set aside at an *inter partes* hearing under Order 32 rule 6. See *Poon Ting Chau v Wong Kwok Chi* HCMP 5314/2002 (Chu J; 20.10.2006).

### [65.4.3]   Jurisdiction
The court will not normally assert jurisdiction over a defendant by ordering substituted service of him if he was not within Hong Kong at the time of the issue of the writ: *Wilding v Bean* [1891] 1 QB 100. The reason for this rule is that personal service could not have been effected on the defendant if he was not present in the jurisdiction when the writ was issued.

Where, however, the defendant was within the jurisdiction when the writ was issued, but subsequently left and has stayed out of the jurisdiction, substituted service may be ordered: *Jay v Budd* [1898] 1 QB 12; *Laurie v Carroll* (1958) 98 CLR 310. In the reverse situation, where the defendant was outside the jurisdiction when the writ was issued but subsequently returns, substituted service may not be allowed: *Myerson v Martin* [1979] 3 All ER 667.

An exception to the rule in *Wilding v Bean* is where it is shown that the defendant left the jurisdiction in order to evade service: see *Re Urquhart* (1890) 24 QBD 723.

### [65.4.4]   The test for a substituted service order
In order to obtain an order for substituted service it is necessary to demonstrate to the court that it is 'impracticable for any reason' to effect service by the usual methods: Order 65 rule 4(1). This is a threshold requirement which, when satisfied, gives the court a discretion whether to make the order: *Chan Yeuk Mui v Ng Shu Chi* [1999]

2 HKC 702 (CA). In order to satisfy the threshold requirement the applicant should provide affidavit evidence showing the steps it has taken to try to effect service in the usual way. It is normally expected that the applicant will have made inquiries at any address previously associated with the person to be served, and with the telephone directory inquiries service.

There is a paucity of readily accessible Hong Kong and English authority as to what constitutes 'impracticable' in this context. In *Chan Yeuk Mui* (above) the court upheld a substituted service order where the plaintiff had demonstrated that it was 'impossible' to locate the defendant at any of his known addresses, or through local enquiries. However the court did not discuss the ambit of the impracticability requirement. Impracticability is clearly something less than impossibility. This point has been made in authorities from Canadian jurisdictions where a similar 'impractical' requirement applies. In *Marlowe v Capital Health Authority* [2009] ABQB 105 (Alta QB) it was said (at para 32):

> The test for impracticality of service does not require that a plaintiff exhaust every possibility for personal service before seeking an order for substitutional service. He only needs to show that it is unduly difficult or expensive to serve the [document] personally.

The impracticability may be 'for any reason'. A ground frequently relied on is evasion of service. See, for example, *Poon Ting Chau v Wong Kwok Chi* HCMP 5314/2002 (Chu J; 20.10.2006) where the court refused to set aside a substituted service order where it was 'obvious that [the party] was resisting personal service'. And, as the above quotation from *Marlowe* suggests, cost may be a relevant reason.

### [65.4.5]  Method of substituted service

An order permitting substituted service will stipulate the method by which service is to be effected. It is up to the party applying for the order to suggest an appropriate method. In *Porter v Freudenberg* [1915] 1 KB 857 (CA) it was held that the method of substituted service should be such that there is a high probability of the writ coming to the attention of the person to be served. This was described as a 'requirement' in *Chan Yeuk Mui v Ng Shu Chi* [1999] 2 HKC 702, 706H-I (CA). However, it is now recognised that this requirement, if it exists, is not absolute. See *Abbey National plc v Frost* [1999] 1 WLR 1080 (CA) where it was noted that the wording of the relevant rule had been amended in the 1960s, and a substituted service order was restored despite the fact there was no likelihood the writ would reach the defendant or come to his knowledge. The defendant was a solicitor who had chosen to disappear and the order was for service of the writ on the solicitors indemnity fund. The English court was satisfied that at least in the circumstances of the particular case, any practice whereby there should be a likelihood of the writ coming to the attention of the defendant did not fetter the court's broad discretion under the rule. See also *Chen Ar Mee & Anor v Lee* DCCJ 1068/2004 (Judge Yuen; 21.04.2006) where *Abbey National* was referred to and there was no dispute that there is a discretion to order service on the solicitors indemnity fund.

The choice of a method of substituted service likely to bring notice to the party to be served will depend on the facts of the individual case. In some cases it may be appropriate to serve the document on another person who is closely connected with the person to be served and likely to inform him of it. In others service might be effective by posting the document at premises the party to be served is likely to enter. However, not just any premises will be appropriate. In *Marlowe v Capital Health Authority* [2009] ABQB 105 the Alberta Queen's Bench was highly critical of a substituted order permitting service of two doctors by posting at the main entrance to a hospital. Ross JCQBA said (at para 36):

> To even suggest that defendants can be personally served by posting to the door of an institution the size of the University of Alberta Hospital is ludicrous and has the effect of making the court look foolish.

It is common for an order for substituted service to specify that the method of service be by way of advertisement in a newspaper. As observed by Rogers JA in *Chan Yeuk Mui v Ng Shu Chi* [1999] 2 HKC 704, 707A, often 'advertisements will be the only practical way'. Service by way of advertisement should be in a publication known to be read by the party to be served, or in the absence of any information as to what the party to be served reads, then in a widely circulating newspaper published in a language which the person to be served reads. In *Re Vong Wun Man* HCB 11934/2004 (Kwan J; 23.06.2006) a bankruptcy order was set aside where substituted service had been effected by publication in a Hong Kong newspaper whereas the alleged bankrupt was a resident of Macau. Note that Part II of Practice Direction 24.1 provides that any such advertisement must be in the language of the newspaper in which it is published.

Electronic means of communication such as e–mail are not yet regarded as a safe and secure means of service, though substituted service by e–mail may be allowed together with more traditional means: *Deacons v Wu Chen Kuo Stanley* [2010] 6 HKC 153.

### [65.4.6] Setting aside order as to substituted service

In *Chan Yeuk Mui v Ng Shu Chi* [1999] 2 HKC 702 the Court of Appeal considered the circumstances in which an order for substituted service will be set aside. Rogers JA held, at 707D–E:

> As with any ex parte order, the court would have power to review the order inter partes. If the application had been defective or had been made on the basis of evidence which was shown to be wrong, then no doubt it would be set aside.

Rogers JA held that an order for substituted service 'should not be set aside lightly' particularly where 'the order had been made following established practice' (at 707G–H).

In that case the Court of Appeal went on to affirm an order for substituted service where there was no evidence that the Registrar had exercised the discretion wrongly.

Substituted service is not considered irregular merely because it fails to bring the proceedings to the attention of the party to be served. However, where the defendant seeks to set aside a resulting default judgment, 'the absence of the writ coming to the attention of the defendant should be taken as a valid reason why the defendant should be permitted to argue that he has a defence to the plaintiff's claim which should be permitted to stand': *Chan Yeuk Mui* (above, at 707H).

In *Chan Kam Kee v Chan Kam Man* [1998] 3 HKC 416, 420A-G a substituted service order was set aside where there was no information as to the whereabouts of the party to be served, and thus no way the court could be satisfied that the party to be served would receive notice of the document. However, that judgment should no longer be followed without consideration of the fact that it relied on the lower court judgment in *Abbey National plc v Frost*, which was reversed on appeal: (see [1999] 1 WLR 1080, discussed above). Only if the Hong Kong court, in a considered decision, decides not to follow the updated English position, would it be regarded as authoritative. The same may be said of *Alpha Star Enterprises Ltd v Personal Representative of Tang Mei Shin (deceased)* [2002] 4 HKC 218.

**[65.4.7]  Substituted service of foreign corporation**
Where a foreign company cannot be served in its place of registration because it has no domicile there, the court may order substituted service in Hong Kong, provided that the provisions of Order 11 rule 1 are also met: see *Tillemont Shipping Corp SA & Anor v Taitexma Enterprise Corp & Ors* [1993] 2 HKC 129 (CA).

**5.  Ordinary service: how effected** (O. 65 r. 5)
    **(1)**  **Service of any document, not being a document which by virtue of any provision of these rules is required to be served personally or a document to which Order 10, rule 1, applies, may be effected—**
        **(a)**  **by leaving the document at the proper address of the person to be served, or**
        **(b)**  **by post, or**
        **(c)**  **where the proper address for service includes a numbered box at a document exchange, by leaving the document at that document exchange or at a document exchange which transmits documents every business day to that document exchange, or**
        **(d)**  **in such other manner as the court may direct.**
**In these rules "document exchange" means any document exchange, or exchanges under the control of the same operator, for the time being approved by the Chief Justice.**

                                                 **(L.N. 223 of 1995)**
    **(2)**  **For the purposes of this rule, and of section 8 of the Interpretation and General Clauses Ordinance (Cap 1), in its application to this rule, the proper address of any person on whom a document is to be served in accordance with this rule shall be the address for service of that person, but if at the time when service is effected that person has no address for service his proper address for the purposes aforesaid shall be—**
        **(a)**  **in any case, the business address of the solicitor (if any) who is acting for him in the proceedings in connection with which service of the document in question is to be effected, or**
        **(b)**  **in the case of an individual, his usual or last known address, or**
        **(c)**  **in the case of individuals who are suing or being sued in the name of a firm, the principal or last known place of business of the firm within the jurisdiction, or**
        **(d)**  **in the case of a body corporate, the registered or principal office of the body.**

(2A)    **Any such document which is left at a document exchange in accordance with paragraph (1)(c) shall, unless the contrary is proved, be deemed to have been served on the business day following the day on which it is left.**

(3)    **Nothing in this rule shall be taken as prohibiting the personal service of any document or as affecting any enactment which provides for the manner in which documents may be served on bodies corporate.**

(4)    **In this rule "business day" means a day other than a general holiday.**

## NOTES

### [65.5.1]   'Ordinary' service

After service of originating process has been acknowledged pursuant to Order 12, subsequent documents in High Court proceedings are served by 'ordinary' service pursuant to Order 65 rule 5. Such documents include summonses and other documents related to pre-trial applications, whether served by a plaintiff or a defendant.

Where a solicitor is acting for a party the usual practice in Hong Kong is to effect 'ordinary' service by hand to the solicitor's office stated in the originating process or acknowledgement of service, pursuant to Order 65 rule 5(1)(a). Service by post and the document exchange ("DX" service) are also expressly authorised by rule 5(1)(b) and (c) respectively.

### [65.5.2]   Rule 5(1)(b) – Ordinary service *by post* of documents not required to be served personally

Service of a document by post is effected by 'properly addressing, pre-paying the postage thereon and dispatching it': Interpretation and General Clauses Ordinance (Cap 1), section 8.

In *Chung Shun Land Investment Co Ltd v Steadman* HCA 4215/1985 (Deputy Judge Barnett; 01.07.1986); [1986] HKLY 732, it was held that a summons could be served either by ordinary post or by registered post under this provision.

Section 8 of Cap 1 provides that service by post is deemed to be effected on the day it would be delivered 'in the ordinary course of post' unless the contrary is shown. That provision has given rise to uncertainty and litigation, since it cannot always be certain when the post office will deliver a letter. See the commentary under Order 10 rule 1. How long does it take a posted letter to reach the addressee? How much longer when the letter is registered? Practice direction 19.2 seeks to remove the uncertainty by deeming the time within which ordinary service by post is effected. The practice direction, effective 2 October 2003, reads as follows:

Service of Documents by post:

Ordinary course of post

1.   Under section 8 of the Interpretation and General Clauses Ordinance, Cap 1, service by post is deemed to have been effected, unless the contrary is proved, at the time at which the document or notice would be delivered in the ordinary course of post.

2.   To avoid uncertainty as to the date of service, delivery in the ordinary course of post under the relevant rules governing proceedings in the High Court, District Court, Lands Tribunal and Family Court, shall be deemed, subject to proof to the contrary, to have been effected:

     (a)   in the case of registered post, on the fourth working day after posting; and

     (b)   in the case of ordinary post, on the second working day after posting.

'Working day' shall mean any day of the week excluding Sundays, public holidays, and gale warning days or black rainstorm warning days as defined in section 71(2) of the Interpretation and General Clauses Ordinance, Cap 1 and published in the Gazette.

3. Affidavits of service shall state whether the document was dispatched by registered or ordinary post. If this information is omitted, it shall be assumed that ordinary post was used.

4. The President of the Lands Tribunal has determined, pursuant to section 10(4)(b) of the Lands Tribunal Ordinance, that these Practice Directions shall apply to proceedings in the Lands Tribunal.

5. Nothing in this Practice Direction shall be taken to affect the provisions relating to service or originating process under the relevant rules of court.

### [65.5.3] Service by fax

Service by fax is not authorised by these rules, though it is under the equivalent rules in England. This difference was noted by Keith J with surprise in *Aqua-Leisure Industries Inc v Aqua Splash Ltd (No 1)* [1999] 3 HKC 338 (at 342D).

### [65.5.4] Rule 5(2) – Address for service

The address for service of a party represented by a solicitor will normally be that solicitor's office address.

A document posted to or left at a party's address for service is validly served even though the party might not actually receive notice. In *The Chung Shun Land Investment Co Ltd v Steadman* HCA 4215/1985 (Deputy Judge Barnett; 01.07.1986), [1986] HKLY 732, an *inter partes* summons and, subsequently, an appointment to tax a bill of costs were served by posting them to the defendant's address for service. It was held that the service and the resulting orders of the court were valid notwithstanding the fact that in each case the documents were eventually returned to the plaintiff's solicitors undelivered. The court referred to *A/S Catherineholm v Norequipment Trading Ltd* [1972] 2 All ER 538 and held that should a party wish to have the service set aside in such circumstances, it was incumbent on such a party to show some merits, 'a triable issue' in the words of the court in *Catherineholm.*

Solicitors have been advised by the Law Society that it is good practice when effecting ordinary service at another solicitor's office to state the recipient's reference so as to enable the responsible fee earner to be identified. See Law Society circular 89–42, which can be viewed on the members' zone of the Law Society website.

### [65.5.5] Rule 5(2)(c) – address for service of a firm

Service at the address of a firm's principal or last known place of business under rule 5(2)(c) is not valid where notice has been given of another address: see *Morigood Development Ltd v Sunny Trading Co (a firm)* [1999] 2 HKC 710, 714I–715A.

**6. Service on Secretary for Justice in proceedings which are not by or against the Crown** (O. 65 r. 6)

**Where for the purpose of or in connection with any proceedings in the High Court, not being civil proceedings by or against the Crown within the meaning of Part III of the Crown Proceedings Ordinance (Cap 300), any document is required by any written law or these rules to be served on the Secretary for Justice, section 14 of the said Ordinance and Order 77, rule 4, shall apply in**

relation to the service of the document as they apply in relation to the service of documents required to be served on the Crown for the purpose of or in connection with any civil proceedings by or against the Crown.

7. **Effect of service after certain hours** (O. 65 r. 7)

Any document (other than a writ of summons or other originating process) service of which is effected under rule 2 or under rule 5(1)(a) between 1 pm on a Saturday and midnight on the following day or after four in the afternoon on any other weekday shall, for the purpose of computing any period of time after service of that document, be deemed to have been served on the Monday following that Saturday or on the day following that other weekday, as the case may be.

8. **Affidavit of service** (O. 65 r. 8)

Except as provided in Order 10, rule 1(3)(b) and Order 81, rule 3(2)(b), an affidavit of service of any document must state by whom the document was served, the day of the week and date on which it was served, where it was served and how.

---

**NOTES**

**[65.8.1] Affidavits of service**
Order 65 rule 8 sets out certain formal requirements for an affidavit of service. For affidavits of service generally, see the commentary under Order 10 rule 1(3)(b). See also practice direction 24.1, para 8, which stipulates that an affidavit of service in support of an application for judgment in default of notice of intention to defend a monetary claim should depose to the fact that the relevant form for admission under Order 13A was served along with the originating process, as required by Order 13A rule 13.

9. **No service required in certain cases** (O. 65 r. 9)

Where by virtue of these rules any document is required to be served on any person but it is not required to be served personally or in accordance with Order 10, rule 1(2), and at the time when service is to be effected that person is in default as to acknowledgment of service or has no address for service, the document need not be served on that person unless the Court otherwise directs or any of these rules otherwise provides.

---

**NOTES**

**[65.9.1] Where service not required**
Order 65 rule 9 provides that in the absence of an express requirement for service personally or under Order 10 rule 1, or a direction from the court, there is no need to serve a document on a person who has not acknowledged service or has no address for service. An example is a notice of assessment of damages, which is not required to be served personally (see Order 37 rule 1(1)). See *Chiu Po Ling v Wong Yuet* DCPI 115/2006 (Deputy Judge Wahab; 22.02.2007) where the court was satisfied it could proceed with an assessment of damages where the defendant could not be served

because her only known address was a building which had been demolished. Other examples include an application by summons, and an appeal from a master to a single judge under Order 58: see *Lok Wai Yuk (administratrix) v Cheung Che Hung* DCCJ 4275/2007 (Deputy Judge H Au-Yeung; 24.09.2010) (para 38 *et seq*).

Order 65 rule 9 does not apply on an application for a writ of specific delivery to enforce a judgment for delivery of goods (Order 45 rule 4(2)), nor to an application for leave to enter default judgment on a claim under a hire-purchase or conditional sale agreement (Order 84A rule 3(2)(b)), mortgage (Order 88 rule 6(2)), or in a claim in tort between husband and wife (Order 89 rule 1(4)).

**10. Service of process on Sunday** (O. 65 r. 10)

**(1)   No process shall be served or executed within the jurisdiction on a Sunday, except, in case of urgency, with the leave of the Court.**

**(2)   For the purposes of this rule "process" includes a writ, judgment, notice, order, petition, originating or other summons or warrant.**

**(Enacted 1988)**

---

**NOTES**

**[65.10.1]   Admiralty actions**
Order 65 rule 10 does not apply in the Admiralty jurisdiction (see Order 75 rule 11(3)).

**[65.10.2]   Constitutional considerations**
Order 65 rule 10 does not have the effect of favouring Christians or discriminating against Jewish persons by making the latter but not the former susceptible to service on their Sabbath: *Buxbaum v Samuel-Rozenbaum HK Ltd* CACV 141/2005 (Rogers VP, Le Pichon & Yuen JJA; 10.05.2006).

## ORDER 66

### PAPER, PRINTING, NOTICES AND COPIES

**1. Quality of paper** (O. 66 r. 1)

**Unless the nature of the document renders it impracticable, every document prepared by a party for use in the Court must be on paper of durable quality, having a margin not less than 35 mm wide, to be left blank on the left side of the face of the paper and on the right side of the reverse.**

---

**NOTES**

**[66.1.1]   Type of paper to be used**

Order 66 rule 1 sets out the requirements as to the type of paper to be used in preparing documents for use in court. Although A4 size paper is now usually used in Hong Kong, this is not mandated by the rules, unlike England where the former Order 66 rule 1 and the subsequent CPR PD 5 stipulate that A4 size paper must be used.

This rule contemplates both sides of the paper being used, though this is not usually done. See also Order 41 rule 1(5).

**2. Regulations as to printing, etc.** (O. 66 r. 2)

**(1) Except where these rules otherwise provide, every document prepared by a party for use in the High Court must be produced by one of the following means, that is to say, printing, writing (which must be clear and legible) and typewriting otherwise than by means of a carbon, and may be produced partly by one of those means and partly by another or others of them.**

**(2) For the purposes of these rules a document shall be deemed to be printed if it is produced by type lithography or stencil duplicating.**

**(3) Any type used in producing a document for use as aforesaid must be such as to give a clear and legible impression and must be not smaller than 11 point type for printing or elite type for type lithography, stencil duplicating or typewriting.**

**(4) Any document produced by a photographic or similar process giving a positive and permanent representation free from blemishes shall, to the extent that it contains a facsimile of any printed, written or typewritten matter, be treated for the purposes of these rules as if it were printed, written or typewritten, as the case may be.**

**(5) Any notice required by these rules may not be given orally except with the leave of the Court.**

**3. Copies of documents for other party** (O. 66 r. 3)

**(1) Where a document prepared by a party for use in the High Court is printed the party by whom it was prepared must, on receiving a written request from any other party entitled to a copy of that document and on payment of the proper charges, supply him with such number of copies thereof, not exceeding ten, as may be specified in the request.**

(2) Where a document prepared by a party for use in the High Court is written or typewritten, the party by whom it was prepared must supply any other party entitled to a copy of it, not being a party on whom it has been served, with one copy of it and, where the document in question is an affidavit, of any document exhibited to it.

The copy must be ready for delivery within 48 hours after a written request for it, together with an undertaking to pay the proper charges, is received and must be supplied thereafter on payment of those charges.

**4.**    **Requirements as to copies** (O. 66 r. 4)

(2) Before a copy of a document is supplied to a party under these rules, it must be indorsed with the name and address of the party or solicitor by whom it was supplied.

(3) The party by whom a copy is supplied under rule 3, or, if he sues or appears by a solicitor, his solicitor, shall be answerable for the copy being a true copy of the original or of an office copy, as the case may be.

(Enacted 1988)

## ORDER 67

### CHANGE OF SOLICITOR

**1.   Notice of change of solicitor** (O. 67 r. 1)

(1)   **A party to any cause or matter who sues or defends by a solicitor may change his solicitor without an order for that purpose but, unless and until notice of the change is filed and copies of the notice are lodged and served in accordance with this rule, the former solicitor shall, subject to rules 5 and 6, be considered the solicitor of the party until the final conclusion of the cause or matter, whether in the Court of First Instance or the Court of Appeal.**

(2)   **Notice of a change of solicitor must be filed, and a copy thereof lodged in the Registry.**

(3)   **The party giving the notice must serve on every other party to the cause or matter (not being a party in default as to acknowledgment of service) and on the former solicitor a copy of the notice indorsed with a memorandum stating that the notice has been duly filed in the Registry.**

(4)   **The party giving the notice may perform the duties prescribed by this rule in person or by his new solicitor.**

---

## NOTES

### [67.1.1]   Comparison with English rules

Order 67 is based on the Order of the same number in the former English RSC. It was modified for Hong Kong to reflect the fact there is only one High Court registry in this jurisdiction. The equivalent provision in England is now CPR part 42.

### [67.1.2]   Purpose and scope of Order 67

The main purpose of Order 67 is to make provision to ensure that opposing parties are informed of any change of legal representation, and may know at what address 'ordinary service' (see Order 65 rule 5) may be effected after such a change in a subsisting action. It requires that notice be given where a party changes solicitors (rule 1), appoints a solicitor where it has previously acted in person (rule 3) or, having been represented by a solicitor decides to discharge the solicitor and act in person (rule 4). It also caters for the situation where a party who ceases to have legal representation fails to give notice, leaving the other side in uncertainty (rule 5) and where a solicitor who has ceased to act wishes to be absolved of the responsibility of remaining on the record (rule 6).

### [67.1.3]   Solicitor's lien on client's papers

A solicitor who has ceased to act is in most circumstances entitled to a lien on the client's papers. The solicitor may refuse to release those papers to the client or the client's new solicitor until all outstanding costs are paid: *Leo, Abse & Cohen v Evan G Jones (Builders) Ltd* The Times 21.04.1984 (CA). There are some exceptions, for example where a third party's rights are affected: *Re Hawkes* [1898] 2 Ch 1.

A lien may arise even though no bill of costs has been issued by the solicitor, and may be asserted against a client even though that client is party to an agreement whereby its costs will be paid by another: *Li Fu Yat Tso v George Y C Mok & Co* [2007] 1 HKC 150. The lien may be exercised over any of the client's property which has come into the hands of the solicitor in that capacity: *George Y C Mok & Co v Tang Kwong Ming* [2000] 3 HKC 445, 449G.

According to para 1 of the commentary to principle 5.23 in the Hong Kong Solicitors' Guide to Professional Conduct, a solicitor's lien 'is passive in nature and does not entitle a solicitor to sell or dispose of a client's property'.

The existence and extent of a solicitor's lien depend on whether the retainer is terminated by the solicitor or the client, and the grounds. See the discussion below.

**[67.1.4]    Retainer terminated by the solicitor**
A solicitor who terminates the solicitor-client relationship may be ordered to deliver the client's papers to the replacement solicitor on the latter's undertaking to preserve the outgoing solicitor's lien and to return the papers at the end of the new solicitor's representation: *Gamlen Chemical Ltd v Rochem Ltd* [1980] 1 WLR 614 (CA). The power to make such an order is a matter of discretion, to be exercised in the interests of justice, bearing in mind the competing interests of solicitor and client: *A v B* [1984] 1 All ER 265, 274h-j. The court's general power to order a solicitor to deliver a client's papers is recognised in section 65(1) of the Legal Practitioners Ordinance (Cap 159) and Order 106 rule 3.

A solicitor is only entitled to terminate the retainer for 'good reason': see the commentary under principle 5.22 in the Hong Kong Solicitors' Guide to Professional Conduct.

Where the 'entire contract' rule applies (as to which see Law Society circular 01-302, referred to in the commentary under rule 6 below), a solicitor terminating the retainer before completion of the matter without good reason may not be entitled to any costs; hence no lien would arise. See *Underwood, Son & Piper v Lewis* [1894] 2 QB 306 (CA); *Chin Yuk Lun Francis & Anor v Lo & Lo* HCMP 1142/2005 (Deputy Judge To; 07.07.2006) (para 10); *Morrison Voss v Smith* [2007] BCCA 296 (paras 32, 56).

See also Order 1A rule 3 and the commentary thereunder concerning the solicitor's duty to the court not to put forward unarguable points. That duty may entitle a solicitor to terminate a client's retainer if the client persists in instructions which would result in it being infringed: *Richard Buxton (Solicitors) v Mills-Owens* [2010] EWCA Civ 122 (23.02.2010) (para 43).

**[67.1.5]    Retainer terminated by the client**
Where, for its own reasons, the client discharges the solicitor, the latter is entitled to retain the former's papers until outstanding costs are paid and the court has no power to compel the solicitor to release the same: *Gamlen Chemical Ltd v Rochem Ltd* [1980] 1 WLR 614 (CA). Nevertheless as a matter of conduct, rather than duty, the solicitor should normally voluntarily release the papers to the new solicitor on a satisfactory undertaking as to outstanding costs: see para 4 of the commentary under principle 5.23 of the Hong Kong Solicitors' Guide to Professional Conduct.

Where the client discharges the solicitor on grounds of misconduct, it is probable that the solicitor is not entitled to a lien: *Hughes v Hughes* [1958] 3 All ER 175 (CA) (*obiter*). This should be the case if the solicitor is not entitled to payment.

3. **Notice of appointment of solicitor** (O. 67 r. 3)

   **Where a party, after having sued or defended in person, appoints a solicitor to act in the cause or matter on his behalf, the change may be made without an order for that purpose and rule 1(2), (3) and (4) shall, with the necessary modifications, apply in relation to a notice of appointment of a solicitor as they apply in relation to a notice of change of solicitor.**

---

NOTES

**[67.3.1] Numbering**
There is no rule 2 in Order 67. The rule of the equivalent number in the former English RSC dealt with change of agent in cases where one solicitor acts as agent for another.

4. **Notice of intention to act in person** (O. 67 r. 4)

   **Where a party, after having sued or defended by a solicitor, intends and is entitled to act in person, the change may be made without an order for that purpose and rule 1 shall, with the necessary modifications, apply in relation to a notice of intention to act in person as it applies in relation to a notice of change of solicitor except that the notice of intention to act in person must contain an address for service of the party giving it.**

---

NOTES

**[67.4.1] Address for service of party giving notice of intention to act in person**
Order 67 rule 4 provides that when a party who has been represented by a solicitor gives notice of intention to act in person, he must give an address for service. Although the rule does not expressly say so, that address must be in Hong Kong: *Dianoor International Ltd v Subramaniam* HCA 806/2008 (Deputy Judge L Chan; 19.11.2010). In that case the court referred to Order 12 rule 3 which requires a defendant acknowledging service in person to give an address for service in Hong Kong. The court set aside a notice of intention to act in person which gave an address in Dubai. The result was that the solicitors who had represented the party concerned remained on record.

5. **Removal of solicitor from record at instance of another party** (O. 67 r. 5)
   (1) **Where—**
       (a) **a solicitor who has acted for a party in a cause or matter has died or become bankrupt or cannot be found or has failed to take out a practising certificate or has been struck off the roll of solicitors or has been suspended from practising or has for any other reason ceased to practise, and**
       (b) **the party has not given notice of change of solicitor or notice of intention to act in person in accordance with the foregoing provisions of this Order,**

any other party to the cause or matter may apply to the Court, or if an appeal to the Court of Appeal is pending in the cause or matter, to the Court of Appeal, for an order declaring that the solicitor has ceased to be the solicitor acting for the first-mentioned party in the cause or matter, and the Court or Court of Appeal, as the case may be, may make an order accordingly.

(2)   An application for an order under this rule must be made by summons and the summons must, unless the Court or Court of Appeal, as the case may be, otherwise directs, be served on the party to whose solicitor the application relates. (L.N. 152 of 2008)

The application must be supported by an affidavit stating the grounds of the application.

(3)   Where an order is made under this rule the party on whose application it was made must—

(a)   serve on every other party to the cause or matter (not being a party in default as to acknowledgment of service) a copy of the order, and

(b)   procure the order to be entered in the Registry, and

(c)   leave at the Registry a copy of the order and a certificate signed by him or his solicitor that the order has been duly served as aforesaid.

(4)   An order made under this rule shall not affect the rights of the solicitor and the party for whom he acted as between themselves.

## NOTES

### [67.5.1]   Application to remove another party's solicitor

Order 67 rule 5 provides for application by one party to remove another party's solicitor from the record where that solicitor has ceased to act. The rule applies where despite the fact a solicitor has ceased to act for a party, that party has not given notice of change of solicitor or to act in person, thus leaving it uncertain at what address that party is to be served. The rule covers cases where the other party's solicitor of record has died, become bankrupt, disappeared or lost the right to practise by failing to take out a practising certificate or by disciplinary action. The address for service of a party whose solicitor is removed under this rule is thereafter determined in accordance with rule 7.

In addition to this rule the court has inherent power to restrain another party's solicitor from acting in cases of bias (*Re L* [2001] 1 WLR 100), risk of breach of confidentiality (*Bolkiah v KPMG* [1999] 2 AC 222; *Time Success Profits Ltd v Andrew Lam & Co* [2004] 1 HKC 214) or conflict of interest (*Nishimatsu-Costain-China Harbour JV v Ip Kwan & Co* [2000] 2 HKC 445 (CA)).

### 6.   Withdrawal of solicitor who has ceased to act for party (O. 67 r. 6)

(1)   Where a solicitor who has acted for a party in a cause or matter has ceased so to act and the party has not given notice of change in accordance with rule 1, or notice of intention to act in person in accordance with rule 4, the solicitor may apply to the Court for an order declaring that the solicitor has ceased to be the solicitor acting for the party in the cause or matter, and the

Court or Court of Appeal, as the case may be, may make an order accordingly, but, unless and until the solicitor—

    (a)  serves on every party to the cause or matter (not being a party in default as to acknowledgment of service) a copy of the order, and

    (b)  procures the order to be entered in the Registry, and

    (c)  leaves at the Registry a copy of the order and a certificate signed by him that the order has been duly served as aforesaid,

he shall, subject to the foregoing provisions of this Order, be considered the solicitor of the party till the final conclusion of the cause or matter whether in the Court of First Instance or Court of Appeal.

    (2)  An application for an order under this rule must be made by summons which must, unless the Court or the Court of Appeal, as the case may be, otherwise directs, be served on the party for whom the solicitor acted. The application must be supported by an affidavit stating the grounds of the application. (L.N. 363 of 1990)

    (3)  An order made under this rule shall not affect the rights of the solicitor and the party for whom he acted as between themselves.

    (4)  Notwithstanding anything in paragraph (1), where the certificate of an assisted person within the meaning of the Legal Aid Ordinance (Cap 91) is revoked or discharged, the solicitor who acted for the assisted person shall cease to be the solicitor acting in the cause or matter as soon as his retainer is determined under that Ordinance; and if the assisted person whose certificate has been revoked or discharged desires to proceed with the cause or matter without legal aid and appoints that solicitor or another solicitor to act on his behalf, the provisions of rule 3 shall apply as if that party had previously sued or defended in person.

---

## NOTES

### [67.6.1]  Application for order declaring solicitor has ceased to act

Order 67 rule 6 allows solicitors to apply for an order declaring that they have ceased to act for their client. The solicitors will be relieved of the responsibilities of solicitors on the record once the order has been made, drawn up and entered and served on every party.

In order to obtain a declaration under this rule the solicitors must demonstrate that they have ceased to act and yet the client has not appointed other solicitors in their place nor given notice of intention to act in person. It is not appropriate for solicitors who wish to cease to act to apply under this rule – the court cannot relieve them of the responsibility of solicitors on record unless they have already ceased to act for the client. See *Tang Hing-kwong & Anor v Ip & Willis* HCA 7988/2000 (Deputy Judge Carlson; 01.11.2002).

Solicitors cease to act when the retainer is terminated. It may be terminated by the client or by the solicitor. It may also be terminated by operation of law where, for example, the client ceases to have requisite mental capacity: *Yonge v Toynbee* [1910] 1 KB 215 (CA). Chapter 4(5) of the Hong Kong Solicitors' Guide to Professional Conduct, vol 1, (2nd ed) sets out the circumstances in which a solicitor is entitled to terminate the retainer. A frequent ground on which solicitors cease to act is where they are unable to obtain instructions from the client. Another frequent ground is failure of the client to pay invoices or provide costs on account. Such money disputes must be considered in light of the 'entire contract' rule whereby in the absence of agreement to the contrary it is implied that a solicitor agrees to act through to completion of a matter. The Law Society has brought this rule to the attention of the profession and pointed out that interim invoices may not be issued without prior agreement with the client. See Law Society Circular 01–302 (PA), which reads as follows:

CIRCULAR 01-302 (PA)                                    29 October 2001

### LAW SOCIETY GUIDANCE NOTE

#### Retainer Letters

1. **The Entire Contract Rule and the Interim Bills ("the Rule")**

   Members should be aware that this Rule applies generally to the retainer between a solicitor and client **in the absence of any agreement to the contrary**. The law is quite clear in that an *"entire contract is a contract to complete the work for which the retainer was given and cannot generally be terminated before completion of the work"*.

   e.g. If a client has retained a solicitor to sue a third party for damages for breach of contract, the client cannot obtain any benefit from the contract until judgment has been obtained against the third party, thus the contract between the solicitor and his client is "entire". (See generally *Cordery on Solicitors* Section 4)

2. **Principle 4.08 of the Hong Kong Solicitors' Guide to Professional Conduct ("the Guide") states:**

   "If a solicitor wishes to render interim bills he *must* have the agreement of his client.

   *Commentary*

   1. It is advisable that an agreement for interim payments be evidenced in writing.

   2. Without such an agreement, a solicitor cannot sue for his profit costs until the work the subject of the retainer is completed and a bill rendered, nor can he justifiably terminate his retainer if a client refuses to make such a payment."

   3. Members should therefore review their practice in relation to interim bills and ensure that an agreement has been reached with the client that such bills can be issued.

   4. Members should review the following information (which is not exhaustive) to determine the contents of an appropriate retainer letter:-

      • Scope of the retainer and services to be provided by the firm

      • Agreement on circumstances permitting termination of the retainer (See Principle 5 of the Guide)

      • Best estimate of the costs of the matter in hand (See Principle 4 of the Guide)

      • Money on account of costs and the right to ask for additional funds for work in progress

      • Hourly rates of Principal in charge of the matter

      • Hourly rates of Assistants

      • Hourly rates of Support staff where appropriate

      • Method of billing: whether in units of 6 mins etc, charges for phone calls etc

      • Client's agreement to pay interim bills e.g. monthly

- Appropriate receipts for payments of fees and/or disbursements
- Interest charges on outstanding bills
- Charges for travelling and waiting time attending court hearings
- Information on barristers fees where appropriate

5.  In the current economic climate it would be prudent for solicitors to review their Work in Progress and maintain the firm's cash flow by issuing regular interim bills.

There is authority to the effect that it is an implied term of a solicitor's retainer that the client will provide funds on account to meet disbursements: see *Robins v Goldingham* (1872) LR 13 Eq 440. Solicitors may terminate the contract of retainer if the client fails to do so: *The Hong Kong Solicitors' Guide to Professional Conduct* (vol 1) principle 5.22(2). However, failure to pay profit costs during the course of the retainer is not good reason to terminate in the absence of agreement to the contrary: principles 4.07 and 5.22.

### [67.6.2] Time for making application

Solicitors have been advised that they should not wait until shortly before a substantial hearing before applying under this rule to cease to act. See Law Society circular 98–128 (PA), which so far as material reads as follows:

**O. 67 r. 6: Withdrawal of Solicitor who has ceased
to act for party in Civil or Commercial Matters**

The Registrar has advised the Law Society that a substantial number of applications pursuant to O. 67 r. 6 are made "very shortly before the date fixed for a substantive hearing".

The Registrar has stated that, in future, solicitors may encounter difficulties in obtaining orders to withdraw **"… if the application is made less than 2 working weeks before the date fixed for a substantial argument".**

### [67.6.3] Service on client

Under rule 6(2) of this Order an application by solicitors for a declaration that they have ceased to act must be served on the party for whom they acted unless otherwise ordered. In *Aqua-Leisure Industries Inc v Aqua Splash Ltd (No 1)* [1999] 3 HKC 338 Keith J held (at 342C–D) that such an application had not been properly served. Nevertheless the court was prepared to make the order sought on the ground that the documents before the court demonstrated that the party had indeed terminated its instructions to the solicitors. In *Au Yeung On v Che Shing Cheong Wilfred* HCMP 4745/1999 (Deputy Judge To; 20.06.2006) a master's order declaring that solicitors had ceased to act was held to be a 'nullity' where the client could not have been given notice as he was dead and there was no grant of representation.

### [67.6.4] Opposing party not to be served

An application by solicitors for a declaration that they have ceased to act for a party is a matter between those solicitors and the party. It is not appropriate that the opposing party be served. See *Aqua-Leisure Industries Inc v Aqua Splash Ltd (No 1)* [1999] 3 HKC 338. There Keith J said (at 341H) that the opposing party is 'not entitled to be given notice of the application, or to make representations on it'. The learned judge referred to the English case of *Re Creehouse Ltd* [1983] 1 WLR 77.

**[67.6.5] Date from which cease to act order takes effect**
It should be noted that an order under paragraph (1) of this rule declaring that a solicitor has ceased to act is not effective until that solicitor complies with sub-paragraphs (a), (b) and (c) thereof. Pending such compliance, service on the solicitor of record will be valid. See *Bank of China (HK) Ltd v Sze Wang & Anor* HCMP 2825/2001 (Chu J; 16.02.2005).

**[67.6.6] Preservation of confidentiality**
Documents filed in support of a solicitor's application for a declaration of ceasing to act are confidential and should be sealed by the court. The filed document may not be inspected save with leave of the court under rule 6A. Although confidential, the documents are not privileged: *Fairview Park Management Ltd v Sun Wai Chun* [1999] 4 HKC 42 (CA). See also *Man Fong Hang v Man Ping Nam & Ors (No 2)* [2003] 4 HKC 245 where *Fairview Park Management* was followed in this regard on the basis that it was binding, though its correctness in law was questioned by counsel. In the *Fairview Park* case it was also held that a judge who had seen the confidential documents was not thereby deemed to have been biased.

Administrative arrangements have been adopted by the court for preservation of confidentiality. These are circulated to the profession from time to time for example under para 16 of Law Society circular 06-79 which reads:

**Steps to follow in application to cease to act**

1. The solicitor who initiates an application for ceasing to act should mark on the top of an affidavit in support with a request:

   **"REQUEST the affidavit/affirmation to be put in an envelope and not to be inspected without leave of the Court."**

2. The Registrar has given a standing direction that the request be accepted except in special circumstances.

3. On the rare occasion that the request is rejected, the party initiating the application will be notified and will have the right to make representation thereon.

4. If the request is granted, the affidavit/affirmation will be given a folio number and put in an envelope marked with a folio number and also with the following note in both Chinese and English:

   **"Affidavit/Affirmation in support of the application for ceasing to act. Pursuant to O. 67 r. 6A, this envelope cannot be opened and inspected without leave of the Court."**

5. The envelope with the document will be sealed with chop and staple. The envelope will be placed separate from the main proceeding papers. It will be kept either in the correspondence file to which outsiders do not have access or on the left side of the main file where the correspondences are kept, as the case may be.

6. Among the main proceeding papers a different colour sheet will be inserted in place of the affidavit in accordance with the folio number and will be written thereon the following note:

   **"The affidavit/affirmation in support of the application for ceasing to act has been put in a sealed envelope to be kept in the correspondence file/left side of the file."**

7. In case of search, the counter clerk of the Registry shall detach the correspondence file from the main file or remove from the main file the envelope together with the

other materials not to be disclosed, as the case may be, before giving the main file to the searcher. This may reduce the chance of the searcher having access to the envelope and the document therein.

8.   At the time of hearing of the application, the Master's clerk will retrieve the affidavit from the envelope and place it before the Master. After hearing the affidavit shall be put back to the envelope and sealed again as before. The envelope with the document will be kept in the former place i.e. the correspondence file or the left side of the main file, as the case may be.

## (HK)6A.   Leave required to inspect affidavits (O. 67, r. 6A)

**(HK) Notwithstanding the provisions of Order 63, rule 4(2), the leave of the Court or the Court of Appeal, as the case may be, is required before inspection can be made, or any copy obtained, of any affidavit made or filed pursuant to rule 6(2).**

**(Added L.N. 167 of 1994)**

_____

## NOTES

### [67.6A.1]   Leave to inspect
An affidavit filed in support of an application declaring a solicitor has ceased to act may not be inspected by anyone without leave of the court. In the unusual case of *Man Fong Hang v Man Ping Nam & Ors (No 2)* [2003] 4 HKC 245 the court granted leave to the opposing party in the substantive litigation where the solicitor's application to cease to act was brought shortly before trial and at the same time the former client was seeking an adjournment.

7.   **Address for service of party whose solicitor is removed, etc.** (O. 67 r. 7)
     **Where—**
     **(a)   an order is made under rule 5, or**
     **(b)   an order is made under rule 6, and the applicant for that order has complied with rule 6(1), or**
     **(c)   the certificate of an assisted person within the meaning of the Legal Aid Ordinance (Cap 91) is revoked or discharged,**

**then, unless and until the party to whose solicitor or to whom, as the case may be, the order or certificate relates either appoints another solicitor and complies with rule 3 or, being entitled to act in person, gives notice of his intention so to do and complies with rule 4, his last known address or, where the party is a body corporate, its registered or principal office shall, for the purpose of the service on him of any document not required to be served personally, be deemed to be his address for service.**

_____

## NOTES

### [67.7.1]   Provision to be strictly construed
It has been held that the provision in this rule that a litigant's address for service shall be deemed to be his last known address must be strictly complied with. Thus service at the address given for a plaintiff on the writ commencing the proceedings was liable to be set aside *ex debito justitiae* where it was known by the defendant that the

plaintiff no longer lived there. See *Al-Tobaishi v Aung* [1994] TLR 138 (10 March) (CA), referring to *White v Weston* [1968] 2 QB 647.

**9.   Order to apply to matrimonial causes and matters** (O. 67 r. 9)
   **This Order shall have effect in relation to matrimonial causes and matters and, in its application to such a cause or matter, any reference in rules 4 and 7 to an address for service shall be construed as a reference to the address for service required by the rules in force by virtue of the provisions of section 10 or made under section 54 of the Matrimonial Causes Ordinance (Cap 179).**

                                                                    **(Enacted 1988)**

_____

**NOTES**

**[67.9.1]   Comparison with English rules**
There is no rule 8 in Hong Kong's Order 67. The rule of the equivalent number in the former English RSC dealt with matters arising from the fact that in England there are formal divisions in the Supreme Court, and there are district registries in addition to the central office.
   Order 67 rule 9 was repealed in England in 1968.

## ORDER 68

### OFFICIAL SHORTHAND NOTE

**1. Official shorthand note of all evidence, etc.** (O. 68 r. 1)

**(1)** In every action or other proceeding in the Court of First Instance which is tried or heard with witnesses, an official shorthand note shall, unless the judge otherwise directs, be taken of any evidence given orally in court and of any summing up by the judge and of any judgment delivered by him, and, if any party so requires the note so taken shall be transcribed and such number of transcripts as any party may demand shall be supplied to him at the charges authorized by any scheme in force providing for the taking of official shorthand notes of proceedings in the Court of First Instance.

**(2)** Nothing in this rule shall be construed as prohibiting the supply of transcripts to persons not parties to the proceedings.

**(3)** The powers of the Court of Appeal under this Order may be exercised by a single judge of that Court or by the registrar of civil appeals.

---

**NOTES**

**[68.1.1] Audio recording of proceedings**
Most legal proceedings in Hong Kong are now recorded. The requirement in Order 68 rule 1 for an official shorthand note is satisfied by such audio recordings. See rule 8 which deems any reference to a shorthand note to include a record made by mechanical means.

This rule does not apply to interlocutory hearings which do not involve oral evidence: *Lam Chit Man t/a Yat Cheong Electric Co v The Pacific Insurance Co Ltd & Anor* CACV 2795/2001; [2001–2003] HKCLRT 156 (CA) (para 10). As a result a note or recording of such hearings is not strictly required. In practice, however, such hearings are recorded.

A party who requires a transcript of proceedings may obtain one on payment of prescribed charges: rule 1(1). Further provisions with regard to payment are found in subsequent rules of this Order.

**2. Evidence when not to be transcribed** (O. 68 r. 2)

**(1)** If the judge intimates that in the event of an appeal his note will be sufficient, the shorthand note of the evidence need not be transcribed for the purposes of an appeal.

**(2)** If the parties agree or the judge is of opinion that the evidence or some part of the evidence of any witness would, in the event of an appeal, be of no assistance to the Court of Appeal, the shorthand note of such evidence need not be transcribed for the purposes of an appeal.

**(3)** If any party requires a transcript of any such evidence as aforesaid the charge therefor shall be borne by that party in any event.

**NOTES**

### [68.2.1]   Transcription of shorthand note for use at appeal

Order 68 rule 2 makes provisions with regard to the transcription of a judge's shorthand note for the purposes of appeal. By virtue of rule 8 it applies also to mechanical recording, which is now the norm in Hong Kong. The effect of the rule is to obviate the need for a transcription where the trial judge is of the view that it is not necessary, and of parts of evidence at trial which the parties or the judge take the view would be of no assistance to the Court of Appeal. The rule does not displace or undermine the right of a party under rule 1 to require that a transcript be produced: *Lam Chit Man t/a Yat Cheong Electric Co v The Pacific Insurance Co Ltd & Anor* CACV 2795/2001; [2001–2003] HKCLRT 156 (CA) (para 9).

### [68.2.2]   Cost of transcription

Order 68 rule 2(3) provides that a party who requires a transcript which the judge or other party does not consider necessary, must bear the cost in any event. In other words the cost is not recoverable on party and party taxation. In *Wing Hing Provision, Wine & Spirits Trading Co Ltd v Hanjin Shipping Co Ltd* HCA 9510/1995 (Waung J; 05.07.1999) (para 13) a party was allowed to recover such cost despite its opponent's objection on the ground that the transcript had been obtained to assist the court, and with the permission of the court.

See also rule 4 in relation to payment for transcripts.

**3.   Payment for transcripts out of public funds: excepted proceedings**
(O. 68 r. 3)

**Rules 4 and 5 shall not apply in relation to a transcript of a note taken in proceedings in connection with which legal aid might have been given under the Legal Aid Ordinance (Cap 91) whether or not such aid was given thereunder to any party to the proceedings.**

**4.   Payment for transcripts for the Court of Appeal** (O. 68 r. 4)

**(1)   An appellant shall not be required to pay for the transcript to which a certificate given under this rule relates but, except as aforesaid, any transcript required for the Court of Appeal shall be paid for by the appellant in the first instance.**

**(2)   Where the judge by whom any such proceeding as is referred to in rule 1 was tried or heard or the Court of Appeal is satisfied that an appellant in that proceeding is in such poor financial circumstances that the cost of a transcript would be an excessive burden on him, and, in the case of a transcript of evidence, that there is reasonable ground for the appeal, the judge or the Court of Appeal, as the case may be, may certify that the case is one in which it is proper that the said cost should be borne by public funds.**

**(3)   An application for a certificate under this rule must be made in the first instance to the judge; if the application is refused, the application (if any) to the Court of Appeal must be made within 7 days after the refusal.**

**(4)   Where an application is made to the Court of Appeal for a certificate under this rule, then, if the Court of Appeal is of opinion that for the purpose of**

determining the application it is necessary for that Court to see a transcript of the summing up and judgment, with or without a transcript of the evidence, the Court of Appeal may certify that both transcripts or, as the case may be, only a transcript of the summing up and judgment may properly be supplied for the use of that Court at the expense of public funds.

(5)  No transcript supplied for the use of the Court of Appeal under a certificate given under paragraph (4) shall be handed to the appellant except by direction of the Court of Appeal.

(6)  Where the judge or the Court of Appeal certifies under paragraph (2) that there is reasonable ground for the appeal, the appellant may be supplied with as many free copies of the transcript referred to in the certificate as will, together with any free copies already supplied under a certificate given under paragraph (4), make up a total of one for his own use and three for the use of the Court of Appeal.

(7)  References in this rule to an appellant include references to an intending appellant.

**5. Payment for transcript for poor respondent** (O. 68 r. 5)

(1)  Where the judge by whom any such proceeding as is referred to in rule 1 was tried or heard or the Court of Appeal is satisfied that the respondent to an appeal in that proceeding is in such poor financial circumstances that the cost of obtaining a transcript, or a specified part thereof, for the purpose of resisting the appeal would be an excessive burden on him, the judge or the Court of Appeal, as the case may be, may certify that the case is one in which it is proper that the cost of the transcript or that part thereof, as the case may be, should be borne by public funds, and where such a certificate is given the respondent shall not be required to pay the said cost.

(2)  Rule 4(3) shall apply in relation to an application for a certificate under this rule as it applies in relation to an application for a certificate under that rule.

---

**NOTES**

**[68.5.1]  Poor respondent may obtain transcript with public funds**
Order 68 rule 5 provides that the court may certify that an impecunious respondent to an appeal is entitled to obtain a transcript of the proceedings below out of public funds. The rule applies only to respondents, not appellants: *Lam Chit Man t/a Yat Cheong Electric Co v The Pacific Insurance Co Ltd & Anor* CACV 2795/2001; [2001–2003] HKCLRT 156.

**[68.5.2]  Numbering**
Rules 6 and 7 are omitted from Order 68. The rules of the same number in the former English RSC dealt with transcripts for use in appeals from county courts, and an official referee's power to direct that a shorthand note be taken of proceedings before him or her.

**8.   Mechanical recording** (O. 68 r. 8)

In this Order any reference to a shorthand note of any proceedings shall be construed as including a reference to a record of the proceedings made by mechanical means.

**8A. Definition** (O. 68 r. 8A)

In this Order "transcript" includes the transcript of the official shorthand note and any official typescript of the Judge's manuscript note.

**(Enacted 1988)**

# PROVISIONS AS TO PROCEEDINGS OF A COUNTRY OR PLACE OUTSIDE HONG KONG

**(L.N. 39 of 1999)**

## ORDER 69

### SERVICE OF PROCESS FROM A COUNTRY OR PLACE OUTSIDE HONG KONG

**(L.N. 39 of 1999)**

1.  **Definitions** (O. 69 r. 1)
    In this Order—
"**a convention country**" means a foreign country in relation to which there subsists a civil procedure convention providing for service in that country of process of the Court of First Instance, and includes a country which is a party to the Convention on the Service Abroad of Judicial and Extra-Judicial Documents in Civil or Commercial Matters signed at The Hague on 15 November 1965;
"**process**" includes a citation;
"**process server**" means the process server appointed under rule 4 or his authorized agent;
"**taxing master**" means a taxing master of the High Court.

2.  **Applications** (O. 69 r. 2)
    This Order applies to the service on a person in Hong Kong of any process in connection with civil or commercial proceedings in a court or tribunal of a country or place outside Hong Kong where the Registrar receives a written request for service—
    (a) from the Chief Secretary for Administration with a recommendation by him that service should be effected; (L.N. 362 of 1997)
    (b) where the court or tribunal is in a convention country, from a consular or other authority of that country; or
    (c) where the court or tribunal is in the Mainland of China, from the judicial authorities of the Mainland of China. (L.N. 39 of 1999)

3.  **Service of process** (O. 69 r. 3)
    (1) If the request is in a language other than either or both of Hong Kong's official languages, it shall be accompanied by a translation of the request in either of Hong Kong's official languages, 2 copies of the process and, unless the court or tribunal of a country or place outside Hong Kong certifies that the person to be served understands the language of the process, 2 copies of the translation of the process. (L.N. 39 of 1999)
    (2) Subject to paragraphs (3) and (5) and to any enactment providing for the manner of service of documents on corporate bodies, the process shall be served by the process server's leaving a copy of the process and a copy of the translation or certificate, as the case may be, with the person to be served.

(3)   The provisions of Order 10, rule 1(2)(b) regarding service by insertion through a letter-box shall apply to the service of process from a country or place outside Hong Kong as they apply to the service of writs, except that service may be proved by an affidavit or by a certificate or report in such form as the Registrar may direct. (L.N. 39 of 1999)

(4)   The process server shall send to the Registrar a copy of the process and an affidavit, certificate or report proving due service of process or stating the reason why service could not be effected, as the case may be, and shall, if the Court so directs, specify the costs incurred in effecting or attempting to effect service.

(5)   Order 65, rule 4 (substituted service) shall apply to the service of process from a country or place outside Hong Kong as it applies to the service of writs, except that the Registrar may make an order for substituted service of process from a country or place outside Hong Kong on the basis of the process server's affidavit, certificate or report, without an application being made to him in that behalf. (L.N. 39 of 1999)

(6)   The Registrar shall send a certificate, together with a copy of the process, to the consular or other authority, the judicial authorities of the Mainland of China or the Chief Secretary for Administration, as the case may be, stating— (L.N. 362 of 1997; L.N. 39 of 1999)

   (a)   when and how service was effected or the reason why service could not be effected, as the case may be;
   (b)   where appropriate, the amount certified by the taxing master to be the costs of effecting or attempting to effect service.

(7)   The certificate under paragraph (6) shall be sealed with the seal of the High Court for use out of the jurisdiction.

---

## NOTES

### [69.3.1]   Service of process of courts and tribunals of Mainland China
Order 69 was amended with effect from 30 March 1999 to implement an agreement between the Hong Kong and Mainland authorities for service of process. This agreement replaced arrangements in place prior to the transfer of sovereignty. See the commentary under Order 11 rule 5A.

**4.   Appointment of process server** (O. 69 r. 4)
   **The process server for the purposes of this Order shall be the Chief Bailiff.**
                                                            **(Enacted 1988)**

## ORDER 70

### OBTAINING EVIDENCE FOR FOREIGN COURTS, ETC.

**1. Interpretation and exercise of jurisdiction** (O. 70 r. 1)

**(1)** **In this Order "the Ordinance" means the Evidence Ordinance (Cap 8) and expressions used in this Order which are used in the Ordinance shall have the same meaning as in the Ordinance.**

**(2)** **The power of the Court of First Instance to make an order under section 76 or section 76 as extended by section 77B of the Ordinance may be exercised by the Registrar.**

**(L.N. 403 of 1992)**

---

**NOTES**

**[70.1.1]    Order 70 – evidence for foreign courts**

Order 70 lays down the procedures to be followed in invoking the court's powers under Part VIII of the Evidence Ordinance (Cap 8) to gather evidence to assist courts of other jurisdictions. That legislation implements aspects of the 1970 Hague Convention on the Taking of Evidence Abroad by which Hong Kong may receive requests from other jurisdictions for assistance in obtaining evidence from persons here. For a discussion of the Convention and its legal status in Hong Kong see the commentary under Order 39 rule 2.

Requests from foreign jurisdictions for assistance in taking evidence in Hong Kong are made by 'letters of request', sometimes also referred to as 'letters rogatory'.

**[70.1.2]    Proceedings must have been instituted or be contemplated in the foreign court**

Section 75 of the Evidence Ordinance provides that an application under Order 70 must be in respect of proceedings which 'have been instituted' or are 'contemplated' in the foreign court making the request for assistance. In *Re Binoy & Court of the Special Judge Delhi, India* [1995] 1 HKC 305 it was held that the question whether proceedings had been instituted abroad is to be determined in accordance with the law of the place abroad. In *Camaro Trading Co Ltd v Nissei Sangyo America Ltd* [1994] 3 HKC 94 the Court of Appeal considered whether proceedings were 'contemplated' before the American court making the request. The majority held that proceedings were not contemplated in America because the administrative action (by the United States tax authorities) which they would challenge had not yet been taken.

**[70.1.3]    Criminal proceedings abroad**

Part VIII of the Evidence Ordinance extends to requests to obtain evidence in respect of criminal matters abroad (see section 77B of the Ordinance).

Criminal proceedings of a 'political character' are not within the scope of the section (see section 77B(3) of Cap 8). In *Crown Solicitor v Kitingan* [1994] 1 HKC 516, a request for assistance from a court in Malaysia was refused on the ground that the criminal proceedings were of a political character. It was held that the onus is on the party asserting that the proceedings abroad are of a political character to demonstrate the same. In *Kitingan*, it was also held that the application was an abuse of process since the evidence gathered would not have been admissible in the requesting country.

It has been held that a request from an investigating magistrate in a civil law jurisdiction where magistrates conduct criminal investigations is not a request from a 'court or tribunal' within the meaning of section 75(a) of Cap 8 and hence not one which may be the subject of an order under the relevant legislation. See *Re Troielli* [1995] 2 HKC 785.

With regard to criminal matters, reference should also be made to the Mutual Legal Assistance in Criminal Matters Ordinance (Cap 525) and Order 115A of these rules. Applications to the court for assistance under that legislation are subject to different criteria.

### [70.1.4]   Scope of statutory scheme

It has been held that the provisions of Order 70 and Part VIII of the Evidence Ordinance (Cap 8) are a 'comprehensive self-contained code governing the court's power to order discovery in aid of foreign proceedings' (see *Manufacturer's Life Insurance Co of Canada v Harvest Hero International Ltd & Ors* [2001] 1 HKC 435 at 442B). As a result in that case the court dismissed an application based on the principles laid down by the House of Lords in *Norwich Pharmacal Co v Customs and Excise Commissioners* [1974] AC 133 for discovery in aid of foreign proceedings. Stone J held that the court had no jurisdiction save under the statutory scheme.

The judgment of Stone J was set aside on appeal on the ground that the court's jurisdiction to make a *Norwich Pharmacal* order is separate and distinct from the jurisdiction under the statutory scheme to assist foreign courts. See CACV 631/2001 (Rogers VP and Le Pichon JA; 12.03.2002). The Court of Appeal did not disturb the holding of Stone J that the statutory scheme is a self-contained code where it applies.

### [70.1.5]   Order for production of documents

A person ordered to be examined may be required to produce documents: section 76(2) (b). However, this is subject to the restrictions set out in section 76(4). In particular, a person cannot be required to produce documents other than 'particular documents' specified in the order: section 76(4)(b). To put it another way, an order to produce documents in this context is not to be used to enable the requesting party to have discovery of documents: *Re Moreno* [1987] 3 HKC 279.

In *Re Q Ltd* [1997] 4 HKC 439, 443H-444C, the court set out the 'key principles' to be applied on an application for production of documents under this Order, deriving from the English cases of *Rio Tinto Zinc Corp v Westinghouse Electric Corp* [1978] AC 547, *In re Asbestos Insurance Coverage Cases* [1985] 1 WLR 331, *In re State of Norway's Application* [1987] 1 QB 433 and *Panayiotou v Sony Music Ltd* [1994] Ch 143, 153F):

(a)   s 76(4)(b) has to be strictly construed so that the documents ordered to be produced to assist a foreign court must be 'particular documents' ... although a compendious description is allowed insofar as the documents are particularised ...

(b)   the particular documents must be directly material to prove issues raised bona fide and with adequate particularisation ...

(c)   it must appear to the court that the documents are in existence and they are or are likely to be in the possession, custody or power of the person ordered to produce them, as opposed to conjectural documents ...

(d)   no general documents can be ordered and a fishing exercise is not allowed ... and

(e)   unless a case of bad faith is made out, the court should give effect to a letter of request as far as possible by applying a blue pencil to severely reduce the documents to be produced ... although the court cannot substitute a different category of documents from that requested or redraft the request in different terms.

See also *Mid Pacific Services Inc & Ors v Crown Solicitor* [1992] 1 HKLR 367.

### [70.1.6]   Intrusion on bank's duty of confidentiality

In considering an application under Order 70 for evidence to be taken from a bank, the duty of confidentiality between the bank and its customers is a matter to be taken into account. See *Re Q Ltd* (above, at 447F-I where Woo J said:

> Where the evidence requested from a bank concerns a person against whom the foreign proceedings is brought and the evidence is material to prove certain allegations of fact raised bona fide in those proceedings, the public interest to assist the foreign court will properly outweigh any duty of confidence owed by the bank to such person. On the other hand, if the information concerns a customer of the bank not shown to be material to the proof of any issue in the foreign proceedings, ordering the disclosure of the information would be an unjustified breach of confidence which the court should not require.

In *Prediwave Corp & Anor v New World TMT Ltd* [2007] 4 HKC 207 (CA) (para 54) it was held that the same considerations should apply even where the evidence sought from the bank concerns a non-party to the foreign proceedings (albeit, in that case, a closely connected party), and that ultimately it is a question of balancing the public interest to assist the foreign court and the duty of confidence owed by the bank to its customer. In *Prediwave* the Court of Appeal varied the order below so as to restrict it to a specific bank account rather than all accounts maintained by the bank's customer.

**2.   Application for order** (O. 70 r. 2)

**(1)   Subject to rule 3 an application for an order under the Ordinance must be made ex parte and must be supported by affidavit.**

**(2)   There shall be exhibited to the affidavit the request in pursuance of which the application is made, and if the request is not in the English language, a translation thereof in that language.**

---

### NOTES

### [70.2.1]   Ex parte application

Order 70 rule 2 provides that an application for an order for the taking of evidence in Hong Kong for a foreign court is made *ex parte* by affidavit. In practice the applicant need only submit an affidavit (containing the information required by rule 2). Such an application may (and normally will) be dealt with by a master: Order 70 rule 1(2). A hearing is not normally required.

In *Lehman Brothers Commercial Corp v China International United Petroleum & Chemicals Co Ltd* HCMP 2550/1996 (Keith J; 07.08.1996), it was suggested that although the practice of dispensing with a hearing is 'sensible' it may not be lawful in the absence of express provision in the rules. It was also suggested that the rules may not support the making of such an application without originating process.

### [70.2.2]   Application to set aside order

Like all *ex parte* orders, an order for taking evidence in aid of a foreign court may be set aside at a subsequent *inter partes* hearing. See Order 32 rule 6 and the commentary thereunder.

In *Re Troielli* [1995] 2 HKC 785, an application was made to set aside a master's order under Order 70 rule 1 on various grounds including non-disclosure at the *ex parte* stage. Barnett J said:

> Provided any non-disclosure was not deliberate and the matter undisclosed was not seriously prejudicial, the usual approach should be to exercise discretion in favour of the requesting court.

In *Prediwave* (above) (para 62) the Court of Appeal found that a failure at the *ex parte* stage to provide particulars of the defence of the opposing party did not amount to a material non-disclosure.

### [70.2.3]   Security for costs of application to set aside

The court has power to order security for costs of an application to set aside an *ex parte* order that witnesses attend to be examined in aid of a foreign court. See *Credit Lyonnais Bank Nederland NV v Century Insurance Ltd* [1993] 1 HKLR 210.

3.  **Application by Law Officer (International Law) in certain cases** (O. 70 r. 3)
    **Where a request—**
    - **(a)  is received by the Chief Secretary for Administration and sent by him to the Registrar with an intimation that effect should be given to the request without requiring an application for that purpose to be made by the agent in Hong Kong of any party to the matter pending or contemplated before the foreign court or tribunal; or**
    - **(b)  is received by the Registrar in pursuance of a Civil Procedure Convention providing for the taking of the evidence of any person in Hong Kong for the assistance of a court or tribunal in the foreign country, and no person is named in the document as the person who will make the necessary application on behalf of such party,**

**the Registrar shall send the document to the Law Officer (International Law) and the Law Officer (International Law) may make an application for an order under the Ordinance, and take such other steps as may be necessary, to give effect to the request.**

**(L.N. 362 of 1997; L.N. 322 of 1998)**

4.  **Person to take and manner of taking examination** (O. 70 r. 4)
    **(1)   Any order made in pursuance of this Order for the examination of a witness may order the examination to be taken before any fit and proper person nominated by the person applying for the order or before such other qualified person as to the Court seems fit.**

(2) Subject to rule 6 and to any special directions contained in any order made in pursuance of this Order for the examination of any witness, the examination shall be taken in manner provided by Order 39, rules 5 to 10 and 11(1) to (3), and an order may be made under Order 39, rule 14, for payment of the fees and expenses due to the examiner, and those rules shall apply accordingly with any necessary modifications.

(3) Any order made in pursuance of this Order for the examination of a witness shall permit the cross-examination of the witness by a person who—

    (a) has the examiner's approval to do so; and

    (b) is affected by the examination or his legal representative. (87 of 1997 ss 1(2) & 36)

---

## NOTES

**[70.4.1]   Before whom the examination should take place**

Order 70 rule 4 provides that the Hong Kong court will appoint the person before whom an examination under Order 70 will take place. High Court practice form PF152 envisages the examination taking place before a barrister. A barrister or other person who is not a judicial officer within the meaning of section 3 of the Oaths and Declarations Ordinance (Cap 11) has power to take oaths and affirmations when directed to take an examination under this Order. See Order 114 rule 2.

**5.   Dealing with deposition** (O. 70 r. 5)

Unless any order made in pursuance of this Order for the examination of any witness otherwise directs, the examiner before whom the examination was taken must send the deposition of that witness to the Registrar, and the Registrar shall—

    (a) give a certificate sealed with the Seal of the Court for use out of the jurisdiction identifying the documents annexed thereto, that is to say, the request, the order of the Court for examination and the deposition taken in pursuance of the order; and

    (b) send the certificate with the documents annexed thereto to the Chief Secretary for Administration, or, where the request was sent to the Registrar by some other person in accordance with a Civil Procedure Convention, to that other person, for transmission to the court or tribunal out of the jurisdiction requesting the examination.

**6.   Claim to privilege** (O. 70 r. 6)

(1) The provisions of this rule shall have effect where a claim by a witness to be exempt from giving any evidence on the ground specified in section 77(1) (b) of the Ordinance is not supported or conceded as mentioned in subsection (2) of that section.

(2) The examiner may, if he thinks fit, require the witness to give the evidence to which the claim relates and, if the examiner does not do so, the Court

may do so, on the ex parte application of the person who obtained the order under section 76.

   (3)   If such evidence is taken—

      (a)  it must be contained in a document separate from the remainder of the deposition of the witness;

      (b)  the examiner shall send to the Registrar with the deposition a statement signed by the examiner setting out the claim and the ground on which it was made;

      (c)  on receipt of the statement the Registrar shall, notwithstanding anything in rule 5, retain the document containing the part of the witness's evidence to which the claim relates and shall send the statement and a request to determine the claim to the foreign court or tribunal with the documents mentioned in rule 5;

      (d)  if the claim is rejected by the foreign court or tribunal, the Registrar shall send to that court or tribunal the document containing that part of the witness's evidence to which the claim relates, but if the claim is upheld he shall send the document to the witness, and shall in either case notify the witness and the person who obtained the order under section 76 of the court or tribunal's determination.

**(Enacted 1988)**

---

**NOTES**

**[70.6.1]**   **Rules of evidence on examination under Order 70**

Section 77 of the Evidence Ordinance (Cap 8) provides that a person being examined pursuant to an order under Order 70 rule 1 cannot be compelled to give evidence which he could not be compelled to give in Hong Kong or in the requesting jurisdiction. In other words, compellability of a witness, and privilege, as understood in Hong Kong and in the jurisdiction abroad apply on the examination.

Privilege is not in itself a ground to refuse or set aside an order for examination under Order 70. Rather, privilege should be claimed at the actual examination in answer to specific questions. See *Jim Beam Brands Co v Kentucky Importers Pty Ltd & Anor* [1992] 2 HKC 581; [1994] 1 HKLR 1.

Order 70 rule 6 sets out the procedure to be followed where a claim is made that under the law of the requesting jurisdiction the evidence is not compellable. In such cases, the evidence may be taken, but it must then be retained by the Hong Kong court pending determination by the foreign court on the issue as to compellability.

## ORDER 71

### RECIPROCAL ENFORCEMENT OF FOREIGN JUDGMENTS

**2. Application for registration** (O. 71 r. 2)

**(1) An application under section 4 of the Foreign Judgments (Reciprocal Enforcement) Ordinance (Cap 319), (in this Order referred to as "the Ordinance") in respect of a judgment to which the Ordinance applies to have the judgment registered in the Court may be made ex parte, but the Court may direct a summons to be issued. (See App. A, Form 63)**

**(2) If the Court directs a summons to be issued, the summons shall be an originating summons.**

**(3) An originating summons under this rule shall be in Form No. 10 in Appendix A.**

---

**NOTES**

**[71.2.1] Enforcement of foreign judgments**
Order 71 lays down the procedure for registration of foreign judgments under the Foreign Judgments (Reciprocal Enforcement) Ordinance (Cap 319) ('FJREO'). Once registered such judgments may be enforced in Hong Kong. The requirements for registration under the Ordinance were summarised as follows in *Morgan Stanley & Co Int'l Ltd v Pilot Lead Investments Ltd* [2006] 4 HKC 93:

> In order to be capable of being registered under FJREO, a foreign judgment must satisfy the following prerequisites:
>
> (1) It must come from a superior court of a designated country: s 3(2).
> (2) It must be final and conclusive as between the parties thereto: s 3(2)(a).
> (3) There is payable thereunder a sum of money, not being a sum payable in respect of taxes or other charges of a like nature or in respect of a fine or other penalty: s 3(2)(b).
> (4) It is given after the coming into operation of the order directing that the provisions of FJREO shall extend to that foreign country: s 3(2)(c).

It follows from (3) above that an order for specific performance, not being a judgment for the payment of a sum of money, is not registrable under the Ordinance: *Cova Enterprises Ltd v Ruddy Tjanaka* [2004] 1 HKC 94. A *Mareva* injunction granted by a court in another jurisdiction is not registrable in Hong Kong under the Ordinance for the same reason, and additionally because it is interlocutory rather than final: *Westpac New Zealand Ltd v Gao Hui & Ors* HCZZ 27/2009 (Deputy Judge Carlson; 25.05.2009). A party who wishes to enforce an overseas *Mareva* injunction in Hong Kong should apply for a local injunction in aid of the foreign proceedings under Order 29 rule 8A. See the commentary under that rule.

In principle, the judgment to be registered and enforced in Hong Kong should not differ from that given by the foreign court. However, in *Lai Ling Ling v Chun Foo Keung* [2005] 3 HKC 589 it was held there is jurisdiction to make a supplemental order. That case concerned an order for ancillary relief in matrimonial proceedings in Singapore, and may be confined to its own facts.

**[71.2.2]   Jurisdictions designated under Cap 319 – effect of reunification**

The lists of jurisdictions in the schedules to the FJREO, being the jurisdictions whose judgments may be registered thereunder, must now be read in conjunction with section 2A of the Interpretation and General Clauses Ordinance (Cap 1). It is there provided that legislative provisions previously conferring privileges on the United Kingdom and Commonwealth countries shall cease to have legal effect save where reciprocity is in place. The jurisdictions scheduled under the Ordinance include some within and some without the Commonwealth. So what is the legal status of the Ordinance and this Order post 1997? Philip Smart of the University of Hong Kong has doubted a judgment of the Court of First Instance to the effect that the Ordinance (Cap 319) was not affected by the transfer of sovereignty – see *Hong Kong Lawyer*, April 2002, 50, commenting on *Koninljike Philips Electronics NV v Utran Technology Development Ltd* HCMP 4509/2000 (Deputy Judge Woolley; 26.10.2001). Mr Smart described the judgment as *per incuriam* for failure to take into account s 2A of Cap 1 and went on to suggest that the situation is no different as between Commonwealth and non-Commonwealth jurisdictions. In Mr Smart's view a party now seeking to enforce a judgment under the Ordinance (Cap 319) 'must be in a position to satisfy the Hong Kong court (by appropriate evidence as to the content of the foreign law) that the foreign jurisdiction in question gives reciprocal treatment to judgments of the HKSAR courts'. In the particular case a judgment of a Netherlands court was held registrable under the Ordinance notwithstanding an express finding by the judge that the Netherlands would no longer enforce HKSAR judgments (the treaty which applied during the colonial era having ceased to have effect).

Mr Smart's line of argument appears to have been rejected in *Prime Credit Leasing Sdn Bhd v Tan Cho Lung Raymond* [2006] 4 HKC 547. There it was held (at paras 43–45) that the focus of inquiry is 'whether the Chief Executive in Council is satisfied that substantial reciprocity of treatment by [the foreign jurisdiction] will be assured at the time of and after the handover', and that it is not necessary to undertake a fact finding exercise as to whether the foreign jurisdiction continues to give reciprocal enforcement after 01.07.1997. The court found that Malaysian judgments were still enforceable under the FJREO.

In order to assist practitioners on the question of reciprocity after 1997 the Department of Justice has made inquiries and reported its findings in correspondence with the Law Society.

See in particular circular 06–724, reproducing correspondence received from that department. The correspondence reads as follows:

3 November 1997

Ms Joyce Wong
Director of Practitioners Affairs
The Law Society of Hong Kong
1403 Swire House,                                                   By Fax & By Post
11 Chater Road,
Central, Hong Kong

Dear Ms Wong

**Foreign Judgments (Reciprocal Enforcement) Ordinance (Cap 319)**

Thank you for your letter of 23 October enquiring about foreign jurisdictions which continue to recognise and enforce HKSAR judgments under their own domestic legislation.

We have indeed written to all the jurisdictions designated under the Foreign Judgments (Reciprocal Enforcement) Ordinance (Cap 319) to enquire about their treatment of HKSAR judgments. I would like to set out below the background to these enquiries. This letter includes our understanding of the current legislative provisions in Hong Kong for registration of foreign judgments in civil and commercial matters, though you will appreciate that the courts are the authority for interpreting the law and that in any event legislation can be amended by the legislature.

General Background

The enforcement in the HKSAR of civil and commercial judgments from elsewhere is dealt with mainly by registration under the Foreign Judgments (Reciprocal Enforcement) Ordinance (Cap 319). An Order made under that Ordinance designates those jurisdictions whose judgments the HKSAR courts will enforce. The Order includes both Commonwealth and non-Commonwealth jurisdictions (but not the UK). Jurisdictions are designated on the basis of reciprocity.

Reciprocity with the Commonwealth jurisdictions designated under Cap 319 was previously established by a Commonwealth Scheme. Reciprocity with non-Commonwealth jurisdictions was established by bilateral agreements concluded with them by the UK; such agreements have ceased to apply to Hong Kong since 1 July 1997. Arrangements for the enforcement in Hong Kong of judgments from the UK itself were formerly implemented by the Judgments (Facilities for Enforcement) Ordinance (Cap 9), which did not require reciprocity.

The Legislative Consequences of Reunification

The operation of both Ordinances has been affected by the enactment of section 2A(2)(b) of the Interpretation and General Clauses Ordinance (Cap 1) (inserted by section 5 of the Hong Kong Reunification Ordinance) which implements a decision of the National People's Congress dated 23 February 1997. Under section 2A(2)(b) provisions in any Ordinance in Hong Kong that confer privileges on the UK or other Commonwealth countries, *other than provisions giving effect to reciprocal arrangements*, have no further effect.

The Foreign Judgments (Reciprocal Enforcement) Ordinance (Cap 319)

Cap 319 should, in the light of section 2A(2)(b) of Cap 1, still apply to Commonwealth jurisdictions which demonstrate reciprocity by continuing to recognise and enforce HKSAR judgments. And there is also no reason why Cap 319 should cease to apply to non-Commonwealth jurisdictions designated under it, as long as they too continue to recognise and enforce HKSAR judgments (although such reciprocity would necessarily be other than as a result of the bilateral agreements with the UK).

With a view to clarifying the legal position, we have written to all the jurisdictions designated under Cap 319 to find out whether HKSAR judgments can be recognised and enforced there. So far, Australia and Bermuda have replied. Australia has confirmed that the same recognition and enforcement facilities as existed prior to 1 July 1997 for judgments from Hong Kong are still available in Australia. Bermuda has informed us that it could no longer recognise and enforce judgments from the HKSAR because Bermuda's relevant legislation only applies to 'any part of Her Majesty's dominion outside the UK'.

The position between the UK and the HKSAR

The reciprocity requirements of section 2A(2)(b) are, however, not fulfilled in the case of judgments from the UK. That is because in the UK the enforcement of Hong Kong judgments was provided for in Part II of the Administration of Justice Act 1920, which only operated on the basis that Hong Kong was a part of the Commonwealth and therefore ceased to apply to Hong Kong from 1 July. In view of the resultant lack of enforcement facilities in the UK for judgments from the HKSAR, it appears to be the case that the relevant legislation in Hong Kong, namely the Judgments (Facilities for Enforcement) Ordinance (Cap 9), has in turn ceased to apply to UK judgments, by virtue of the failure to satisfy the reciprocity requirement of section 2(A)(2)(b) of Cap 1.

The Common Law

Notwithstanding the absence of reciprocal statutory arrangements, whether with jurisdictions designated under Cap 319 or other jurisdictions, judgments may still be enforced in Hong Kong under the common law.

I hope this letter helps to clarify the position. As you have requested, we shall keep the Law Society informed of the results of our enquiries with foreign jurisdictions designated under Cap 319.

Yours sincerely,


(David Little)
Law Officer (International Law)

---

8 December 1997

Ms Joyce Wong
Director of Practitioners Affairs
The Law Society of Hong Kong
1403 Swire House,                                                     By Fax & By Post
11 Chater Road,
Central, Hong Kong

Dear Ms Wong

### Foreign Judgments (Reciprocal Enforcement) Ordinance (Cap 319)

When I wrote to you on 3 November on the subject of reciprocal enforcement of judgments, I promised to keep the Law Society informed of the results of our enquiries with foreign jurisdictions designated under the Foreign Judgments (Reciprocal Enforcement) Ordinance (Cap 319).

Since 3 November, we have received further substantive replies, from New Zealand, Israel and Germany.

The Consulate General of New Zealand has confirmed that judgments of the Hong Kong Special Administrative Region ("HKSAR") can be recognised and enforced in New Zealand in the same manner as applied to Hong Kong judgments prior to 1 July 1997.

The Consulate General of Israel has confirmed that judgments from the courts of the HKSAR will be recognised and enforced in Israel after 1 July 1997 provided that reciprocity is maintained by the HKSAR courts.

The Consulate General of Germany has indicated that in  view of the continued designation of Germany under the HKSAR's legislation (Cap 319), the German Government presumes that German courts will continue to recognise and enforce judgments of the HKSAR courts.

In summary the replies received from the above countries appear to confirm that reciprocity of treatment is maintained between HKSAR and the respective countries on reciprocal enforcement of judgments. You will appreciate, however, that the application and interpretation of Cap 319 in relation to judgments from these countries is a matter for the HKSAR courts.

Yours sincerely,


(David Little)
Law Officer (International Law)

---

23 January 1998

Ms Joyce Wong
Director of Practitioners Affairs
The Law Society of Hong Kong
1403 Swire House,                                    By Fax & By Post
11 Chater Road,
Central, Hong Kong

Dear Ms Wong

**Foreign Judgments (Reciprocal Enforcement)
Ordinance (Cap 319)**

I last wrote to you on 8 December 1997 on the results of our enquiries with foreign jurisdictions designated under the Foreign Judgments (Reciprocal Enforcement) Ordinance (Cap 319). Since the date of that letter, we have received some further information, from Belgium and Brunei. The purpose of this letter is to provide you with a synopsis of our latest information. I should reiterate that the application and interpretation of Cap 319 in relation to judgments from the above-mentioned countries is a matter for the HKSAR courts.

**Belgium**
The Consulate General of Belgium has confirmed that under the Judicial Code of Belgium (Article 570) judgments of the Hong Kong Special Administrative Region ("HKSAR") can be recognised and enforced in Belgium. Applications must comply with the requirements of the Judicial Code.

**Brunei**
The Attorney General's Chambers of Brunei have informed us that the relevant legislation in Brunei is the Emergency (Reciprocal Enforcement of Foreign Judgments) Order 1996. It appears that the HKSAR is not at present designated in it.

**Israel**
You will recall that I mentioned in my letter of 8 December that the Israeli Consulate General had earlier confirmed that judgments of the HKSAR would still be enforced by the courts in Israel subject to reciprocity being maintained by the HKSAR courts. The Israeli Consulate General has subsequently supplemented that information by pointing out that according to its Foreign Judgments Enforcement Law of 1958 (as amended), recognition (as opposed to enforcement) of foreign judgments is, as a general rule, based on Agreements with the States of origin of the foreign judgments. However, Article 11 of the 1958 Law provides that the Israeli courts, in dealing with and for the purposes of a matter within their jurisdiction, may recognise foreign judgments if they consider it lawful and just to do so, even if the conditions set out in the Law have not been fulfilled.

Yours sincerely,


(David Little)
Law Officer (International Law)

12 March 1998

Ms Joyce Wong
Director of Practitioners Affairs
The Law Society of Hong Kong
1403 Swire House,                           By Fax & By Post
11 Chater Road,
Central, Hong Kong

Dear Ms Wong

**Foreign Judgments (Reciprocal Enforcement)
Ordinance (Cap 319)**

I am writing to inform the Law Society of the latest results of our enquiries with foreign jurisdictions designated under the Foreign Judgments (Reciprocal Enforcement) Ordinance (Cap 319). Since my last letter dated 23 January 1998 on this subject, we have received information from France and the Netherlands, judgments from both of which are enforceable under the Ordinance.

**France**
France appears to reciprocate for judgments from the Hong Kong SAR because the French authorities have confirmed that civil and commercial judgments of the Hong Kong SAR courts can continue to be recognised and executed in France, insofar as decisions rendered by the courts of France in civil and commercial matters continue to be recognized and executed in the Hong Kong SAR.

**The Netherlands**
The authorities in the Netherlands have indicated that in the absence of an international agreement between the Hong Kong SAR and the Netherlands on reciprocal enforcement of civil and commercial judgments, judgments of the Hong Kong SAR courts can still be recognised in the Netherlands but not enforced and/or executed.

I would like to remind you that the purpose of my letters on this subject is merely to provide a synopsis of our latest information; the application and interpretation of the law on foreign judgments is a matter for the courts.

Yours sincerely,


(David Little)
Law Officer (International Law)

---

18 January 1999

Dear Sirs,

**Re: Reciprocal Enforcement of Judgments: Malaysia**

I refer to your letter of 15 January to Mr David Little which has been passed to me for reply.

Malaysia remains designated in Part 2 of the First Schedule to the Foreign Judgments (Reciprocal Enforcement) Order (Cap 319, sub-leg.) (the "Order"). Section 3(1) of The Foreign Judgments (Reciprocal Enforcement) Ordinance (Cap 319) (the "Ordinance"), in gist, provides that the Chief Executive in Council may extend the effect of the Ordinance to a foreign country if he is satisfied that there is substantial reciprocity of treatment regarding enforcement of judgments between Hong Kong and that foreign country.

You may be aware that we have been trying to ascertain from jurisdictions designated in the Order whether judgments of the HKSAR court would continue to be recognised and enforced in these jurisdictions in the same way as Hong Kong judgments were enforced and recognised prior to 1 July 1997. So far we have not yet received a substantive reply from the Government of Malaysia.

In any event, the interpretation of the Ordinance, including the Order, is a matter for the court. As Malaysia is still a jurisdiction designated in the Order, I do not see any reason why an application to register a Malaysian judgment cannot be made under the Ordinance in accordance with the procedure stipulated in Order 71 of the High Court Rules, Cap 4 (sub-leg.).

Yours sincerely,

(Frank Poon)
Deputy Principal Government Counsel
(International Law)

---

19 May, 1999

Ms Joyce Wong
The Law Society of Hong Kong
3/F Wing On House
71 Des Voeux Road
Central
Hong Kong

Dear Ms Wong,

    (1)    Reciprocal Enforcement of Judgments

    (2)    Resealing of Grants of Probate and
            Letters of Administration

I am writing to provide the latest results of our enquiries on the above topics. I am pleased to be able to convey the following information to you for the benefit of your members but must reiterate our earlier caveat that the interpretation and application of the law on these subjects are, of course, matters upon which they must take their own advice.

**Singapore**

We have been informed by the Attorney General's Chambers of Singapore that Part I of their Reciprocal Enforcement of Foreign Judgments Act has been extended to judgments of the HKSAR, by the Reciprocal Enforcement of Foreign Judgments (Hong Kong Special Administrative Region of the People's Republic of China) Order 1999.

The Attorney General's Chambers of Singapore has informed us that the Probate and Administration (Hong Kong Special Administrative Region of the People's Republic of China) Notification 1999 has been made, applying the effect of section 46(1)(b) of Singapore's Probate and Administration Act to the Hong Kong SAR.

**Italy**

Arrangements for the reciprocal recognition and enforcement of judgments between Hong Kong and Italy were formerly provided for in a treaty between Italy and the UK. The treaty has ceased to apply to the HKSAR since 1 July 1997. Nevertheless, we have been informed that civil and commercial judgments of the HKSAR may still be recognized and enforced in Italy on the basis of reciprocity, in the same way as before.

Yours faithfully,

(David Little)
Law Officer (International Law)

---

6 January 2003

Ms Joyce Wong
The Law Society of Hong Kong
3/F, Wing On House
71 Des Voeux Road Central
Hong Kong

Dear Ms Wong,

## Reciprocal Enforcement of Judgments and
## Reciprocal Enforcement of Maintenance Orders

I am writing to provide some further information about our enquiries overseas on the above topics.

The Consulate General of India has confirmed the continued enforceability in India of judgments from Hong Kong under Section 44-A of the Civil Procedure Code of India.

The Attorney General's Chambers of Brunei has informed us that the Hong Kong Special Administration Region of the People's Republic of China has been designated as a reciprocating territory under the Maintenance Orders Reciprocal Enforcement Notification 2002 for the purpose of their Maintenance Orders Reciprocal Enforcement Act (Chapter 175).

In summary, the replies received from the above jurisdictions appear to confirm that reciprocity of treatment is maintained between the HKSAR and the respective jurisdictions on the above matters. Although we cannot undertake to provide advice on the interpretation and application of the law on these matters, we hope this information is helpful to your members.

Yours sincerely,


(Ian Wingfield)
Law Officer (International Law)

---

29 November 2006

Dear Ms Wong,

## Reciprocal Enforcement of Maintenance Orders and
## Reciprocal Enforcement of Judgments

I am writing to provide some further information about our enquiries on the above topics.

The Consulate General of Malaysia has recently informed us that the Maintenance Orders (Facilities for Enforcement) Order 2003 among others, has amended the Schedule of the Maintenance Orders (Facilities for Enforcement) Act 1949 by substituting the word "Hong Kong, Colony of" with "Hong Kong Special Administrative Region of the People's Republic of China"; and the Reciprocal Enforcement of Judgments (Extension of Part II) Order 2003 among others, has amended the First Schedule of the Reciprocal Enforcement of Judgments Act 1958 by substituting the word "Hong Kong" with "Hong Kong Special Administrative Region of the People's Republic of China". Both Orders were passed on 11 December 2003, gazetted on 22 January 2004 and came into force on 23 January 2004.

Although we cannot undertake to provide advice on the interpretation and application of the law on these matters, we hope this information is helpful to your members.

Yours sincerely,


(Ian Wingfield)
Law Officer (International Law)

### [71.2.3] 'Laundering' of foreign judgments under Cap 319

In *Morgan Stanley & Co Int'l Ltd v Pilot Lead Investments Ltd* [2006] 4 HKC 93 the court suggested (*obiter*) that the practice of 'laundering' foreign judgments is permissible under Cap 319. By this practice a judgment from a jurisdiction which is not designated for the purposes of Cap 319 is first registered in a jurisdiction which is designated, and then the registered judgment of the designated jurisdiction is in turn registered in Hong Kong. However there are powerful arguments against recognition of judgments which have been laundered this way. See, for example, *Owen v Rocketinfo Inc* [2008] BCCA 502 where the practice was held to be inconsistent with the purpose of the equivalent statute in British Columbia, which, like Hong Kong's Cap 319, is intended to facilitate enforcement only of judgments of reciprocating jurisdictions.

### [71.2.4] Enforcement of other foreign judgments

Order 71 rules 1 to 13 are concerned only with enforcement of judgments from jurisdictions to which the Foreign Judgments (Reciprocal Enforcement) Ordinance (Cap 319) continues to apply. Judgments from other jurisdictions may be enforced by other procedural routes. See generally Clarke 'Reciprocal Enforcement of Judgments' *Law Lectures for Practitioners 1989* (HKLJ), 99. Broadly speaking there are two such routes.

### [71.2.5] Judgments (Facilities for Enforcement) Ordinance (Cap 9)

First, there is the Judgments (Facilities for Enforcement) Ordinance (Cap 9) which implemented in Hong Kong a Commonwealth scheme for reciprocal enforcement of judgments. For the reasons set out in the letter dated 3 November 1997 reproduced above, that Ordinance ceased to apply to UK judgments with effect from 1 July 1997. The question of its continuing application to judgments of other Commonwealth jurisdictions listed in its Schedule will depend on the existence of reciprocity.

### [71.2.6] Common law

Secondly, at common law there is a cause of action on a judgment from a jurisdiction outside Hong Kong. The cause of action is the judgment itself and the underlying issues need not be pleaded or re-litigated. A fresh action in Hong Kong pleading the judgment to be enforced is required.

By statute, the common law cause of action applies only to judgments which are not enforceable under either of the two Ordinances providing for registration of foreign judgments in Hong Kong. See section 8 of the Foreign Judgments (Reciprocal Enforcement) Ordinance (Cap 319) and see section 5 of the Foreign Judgments (Restriction on Recognition and Enforcement) Ordinance (Cap 46). Furthermore, section 3 of Cap 46 provides that foreign judgments obtained in breach of an agreement under which the dispute was to be settled in another manner will not be enforceable in Hong Kong.

### [71.2.7] What must be shown in common law action on overseas judgment

The requirements for enforcement of a non-Hong Kong judgment at common law were summarised concisely by Deputy Judge Jeremy Poon in *Korea Data Systems Co Ltd v Chiang Jay Tien & Anor* [2001] 3 HKC 239, 245D–E as follows:

It is well-established that a foreign judgment for a monetary sum may be enforced at common law in Hong Kong if:

(a)  The foreign court granting the judgment has the requisite jurisdiction to adjudicate upon the cause or matter that gave rise to the judgment.

(b)  The judgment is final and conclusive.

(c)  The judgment is not impeachable according to the rules on conflict of laws in Hong Kong.

The learned Deputy Judge cited with approval the judgments of Lord Herschell and Lord Watson in *Nouvion v Freeman* (1889) 15 App Cas 1.

The three criteria set out in the judgment of Deputy Judge Poon are examined in detail in major works on the conflict of laws, for example Cheshire & North, *Private International Law* and Dicey & Morris, *The Conflict of Laws*. The three criteria may be briefly elaborated as follows:

(a)  *Jurisdiction* – The foreign court must have had jurisdiction in accordance with the common law principles of private international law (*Gurdyal Singh v The Rajah of Faridkote* [1894] AC 670). These require that the party against whom it is sought to enforce the foreign judgment have a connection with the foreign jurisdiction. The connection can be physical presence (*Emmanuel v Symon* [1908] 1 KB 302) or in the case of a body corporate, the carrying on of business (*Littauer Glove Corporation v FW Millington Ltd* (1928) 44 TLR 746). Taking a step to invoke the jurisdiction of the foreign court such as initiating the proceedings or counterclaiming or submitting to the jurisdiction of the foreign court by agreement or taking part in the proceedings is also a sufficient connection: (*Schibsby v Westenholz* (1870) LR 6 QB 161; *Feyerick v Hubbard* (1902) 71 LJKB 509). However taking steps solely to contest the foreign court's jurisdiction or to oppose the seizure of property do not constitute submission to the foreign court's jurisdiction: see the Foreign Judgments (Restriction on Recognition and Enforcement) Ordinance (Cap 46), section 4.

(b)  *Final and conclusive* – The foreign judgment must be final and conclusive in accordance with the law applicable in the court granting the judgment: see *Chiyu Banking Corp Ltd v Chan Tin Kwan* [1996] 2 HKLR 395 as explained in *Korea Data Systems Co Ltd v Chiang Jay Tien & Anor* [2001] 3 HKC 239, 246B–247E. A judgment may be final and conclusive for this purpose even though it is not a judgment on the merits: see *Nintendo of America Inc v Bung Enterprises Ltd* [2000] 2 HKC 629. Thus default and summary judgments may be considered final and conclusive. The fact a judgment may be appealed does not mean it is not final and conclusive. However judgments which are liable to variation by the same court are not final and thus are not enforceable by means of the common law cause of action. Maintenance orders are an example (*Harrop v Harrop* [1920] 3 KB 386) as are certain types of judgment of the courts of mainland China which are subject to reconsideration on protest (*Chiyu Banking Corp Ltd v Chan Tin Kwan* [1996] 3 HKC 239). In *Haining Han Lin Sofa Co Ltd v AGX Lines Ltd* HCA 1298/2008 (Sakhrani J; 18.08.2009) it was held that a civil mediation statement issued by the Shanghai Maritime Court on settlement of civil proceedings was a final judgment enforceable in Hong Kong. The court accepted the plaintiff's expert evidence on this point, there being no such evidence from the defendant.

(c)   *Not impeachable* – Certain types of foreign judgment are considered 'impeachable' under the common law rules of private international law. Such a judgment will not be enforced by means of the common law cause of action. Foreign judgments obtained by fraud (*Vadala v Lawes* (1890) 25 QBD 310) or in proceedings conducted in a manner contrary to common law notions of natural justice (*Crawley v Isaacs* (1867) 16 LT 529) are impeachable. Foreign judgments of a penal or revenue nature are not enforceable at common law (*Huntington v Attrill* [1893] AC 150) nor any other judgment the enforcement of which would be contrary to public policy (*Re Macartney* [1921] 1 Ch 522). The ground of impeachment constitutes a defence to the action brought on the foreign judgment. Similarly an action on a foreign judgment which is inconsistent with one already rendered in Hong Kong would on general principles be impeachable on the ground of *res judicata* or issue estoppel.

The above criteria apply only to judgments *in personam* for a fixed sum of money (*Grant v Easton* (1883) 13 QBD 302). Other types of judgment such as those for specific performance are not enforceable at common law. However in certain circumstances judgments *in rem* are enforceable at common law (*Minna Craig Steamship Co v Chartered Bank of India* [1897] 1 QB 55).

**[71.2.8]   Enforcement of judgments and orders of courts of Taiwan and other unrecognised jurisdictions**
The government of Taiwan and its instrumentalities, including its courts, are not recognised by Hong Kong's sovereign power, the People's Republic of China, as legally valid. Nevertheless, judgments and orders of Taiwan courts may be given effect in Hong Kong, subject to certain conditions. In *Chen Li Hung & Anor v Ting Lei Miao & Ors* [2000] 1 HKC 461 the Court of Final Appeal held that Taiwan court orders will be recognised and enforceable in Hong Kong where:-

(a)   they concern private, and opposed to public, rights;
(b)   it is in the interests of justice to give effect to the order; and
(c)   there are no adverse consequences to the sovereign's interests of public policy.

The same principles would apply to judgments and orders of the courts of any other jurisdiction not recognised by the sovereign power in international law.

**[71.2.9]   Relitigation of dispute decided abroad**
A cause of action on which judgment has been given abroad may be relitigated in Hong Kong. The rule by which a cause of action is said to merge with the judgment does not apply to foreign judgments (*Re Flynn (No 2)* [1969] 2 Ch 403). Hence a foreign judgment which is not enforceable by statute, nor recognised as giving rise itself to a cause of action in Hong Kong may be given effect by fresh suit on the underlying cause of action.

**[71.2.10]   Enforcement of judgments as between Hong Kong and the Mainland**
Civil and commercial judgments and orders of designated Mainland courts may be enforced by registration in Hong Kong under the Mainland Judgments (Reciprocal Enforcement) Ordinance (No 9 of 2008), which came into force on 1st August 2008. The procedure for such registration is governed by Order 71A. Section 21 of the

Ordinance provides for the issue of certified copies of Hong Kong judgments to facilitate enforcement in the Mainland under the relevant legal provisions there. The procedure for making application for a certified copy for that purpose is governed by Order 71B.

See the commentary under Orders 71A and 71B.

3.  **Evidence in support of application** (O. 71 r. 3)
    (1)  **An application for registration must be supported by an affidavit—**
        (a)  **exhibiting the judgment or a verified or certified or otherwise duly authenticated copy thereof and, where the judgment is not in the English language, a translation thereof in that language certified by a notary public or authenticated by affidavit;**
        (b)  **stating the name, trade or business and the usual or last known place of abode or business of the judgment creditor and the judgment debtor respectively, so far as known to the deponent;**
        (c)  **stating to the best of the information or belief of the deponent—**
            (i)   **that the judgment creditor is entitled to enforce the judgment;**
            (ii)  **as the case may require, either that at the date of the application the judgment has not been satisfied, or the amount in respect of which it remains unsatisfied;**
            (iv)  **that at the date of the application the judgment can be enforced by execution in the country of the original court and that, if it were registered, the registration would not be, or be liable to be, set aside under section 6 of the Ordinance;**
        (d)  **specifying the amount of the interest, if any, which under the law of the country of the original court has become due under the judgment up to the time of registration.**
    (2)  **Where a judgment sought to be registered is in respect of different matters, and some, but not all, of the provisions of the judgment are such that if those provisions had been contained in separate judgments, those judgments could properly have been registered, the affidavit must state the provisions in respect of which it is sought to register the judgment.**
    (3)  **The affidavit must be accompanied by such other evidence with respect to the enforceability of the judgment by execution in the country of the original court, and of the law of that country under which any interest has become due under the judgment, as may be required having regard to the provisions of the Order in Council extending the Ordinance to that country.**

4.  **Security for costs** (O. 71 r. 4)
    **Save as otherwise provided by any relevant Order in Council, the Court may order the judgment creditor to give security for the costs of the application for registration and of any proceedings which may be brought to set aside the registration.**

5.  **Order for registration** (O. 71 r. 5)
    (1)  **An order giving leave to register a judgment must be drawn up by, or on behalf of, the judgment creditor.**

(2) Except where the order is made on summons, no such order need be served on the judgment debtor.

(3) Every such order shall state the period within which an application may be made to set aside the registration and shall contain a notification that execution on the judgment will not issue until after the expiration of that period.

(4) The Court may, on an application made at any time while it remains competent for any party to apply to have the registration set aside, extend the period (either as originally fixed or as subsequently extended) within which an application to have the registration set aside may be made.

6. **Register of judgments** (O. 71 r. 6)

(1) There shall be kept in the Registry under the direction of the Registrar a register of the judgments ordered to be registered under the Ordinance.

(2) There shall be included in each such register particulars of any execution issued on a judgment ordered to be so registered.

7. **Notice of registration** (O. 71 r. 7)

(1) Notice of the registration of a judgment must be served on the judgment debtor by delivering it to him personally or by sending it to him at his usual or last known place of abode or business or in such other manner as the Court may direct.

(2) Service of such a notice out of the jurisdiction is permissible without leave, and Order 11, rules 5, 6 and 8, shall apply in relation to such a notice as they apply in relation to notice of a writ.

(3) The notice of registration must state—

    (a) full particulars of the judgment registered and the order for registration,

    (b) the name and address of the judgment creditor or of his solicitor or agent on whom, and at which, any summons issued by the judgment debtor may be served,

    (c) the right of the judgment debtor to apply to have the registration set aside, and

    (d) the period within which an application to set aside the registration may be made.

9. **Application to set aside registration** (O. 71 r. 9)

(1) An application to set aside the registration of a judgment must be made by summons supported by affidavit.

(2) The Court hearing such application may order any issue between the judgment creditor and the judgment debtor to be tried in any manner in which an issue in an action may be ordered to be tried.

(HK)(3) The Court may, either of its own motion or on an application made by the judgment creditor, and if, having regard to all the circumstances of the case it thinks it just to do so, impose such terms, as to giving security or otherwise, as a condition of the further conduct of an application under this rule, as it thinks fit. (L.N. 127 of 1995)

## NOTES

### [71.9.1]   Fraud

In *Maydwell v WFM Motor (Pty) Ltd* [1997] 2 HKC 244 the Privy Council had before it an appeal from Hong Kong in a case where a judgment debtor had applied to set aside registration in Hong Kong of a New South Wales judgment on the basis that the judgment had been obtained by fraud. Lord Browne-Wilkinson stated at 246C–D:

> There is no dispute as to the applicable law. The registration of a foreign judgment will be set aside if it has been obtained by fraud. In cases of doubt, the court will direct a preliminary issue to be heard to determine whether or not the judgment was obtained by fraud: but no such preliminary issue will be directed unless there is evidence disclosing at least a prima facie case of fraud.

In that case the court found that there was no basis on which it could be held that the judgment had been obtained by fraud and its registration in Hong Kong was upheld.

See the commentary under Order 42 rule 3 as to the setting aside of domestic judgments obtained by fraud.

### 10.  Issue of execution (O. 71 r. 10)

(1)   Execution shall not issue on a judgment registered under the Ordinance until after the expiration of the period which, in accordance with rule 5(3), is specified in the order for registration as the period within which an application may be made to set aside the registration or, if that period has been extended by the Court, until after the expiration of that period as so extended.

(2)   If an application is made to set aside the registration of a judgment, execution on the judgment shall not issue until after such application is finally determined.

(3)   Any party wishing to issue execution on a judgment registered under the Ordinance must produce to the Registrar an affidavit of service of the notice of registration of the judgment and any order made by the Court in relation to the judgment.

### 11.  Determination of certain questions (O. 71 r. 11)

If, in any case under the Ordinance, any question arises whether a foreign judgment can be enforced by execution in the country of the original court, or what interest is payable under a foreign judgment under the law of the original court, that question shall be determined in accordance with the provisions in that behalf contained in the Order in Council extending the Ordinance to that country.

### 12.  Rules to have effect subject to Orders in Council (O. 71 r. 12)

The foregoing rules shall, in relation to any judgment registered or sought to be registered under the Ordinance, have effect subject to any such provisions contained in the Order in Council extending the Ordinance to the country of the original court as are declared by the Order to be necessary for giving effect to the agreement made between Hong Kong and that country in relation to matters with respect to which there is power to make those rules.

**13. Certified copy of judgment** (O. 71 r. 13)

(1)   An application under section 12 of the Ordinance for a certified copy of a judgment entered in the Court of First Instance must be made ex parte to the Registrar on affidavit.

(2)   An affidavit by which an application under section 12 of the Ordinance is made must—

    (a)   give particulars of the proceedings in which the judgment was obtained;

    (b)   (repealed L.N. 103 of 1994)

    (c)   state whether the defendant did or did not object to the jurisdiction, and, if so, on what grounds;

    (d)   show that the judgment is not subject to any stay of execution;

    (e)   state that the time for appealing has expired or, as the case may be, the date on which it will expire and in either case whether notice of appeal against the judgment has been entered; and

    (f)   state the rate at which the judgment carries interest.

(4)   The certified copy of the judgment shall be an office copy sealed with the Seal of the High Court and indorsed with a certificate signed by the Registrar certifying that the copy is a true copy of a judgment obtained in the Court of First Instance of Hong Kong and that it is issued in accordance with section 12 of the Ordinance.

(5)   There shall also be issued a certificate (signed by the Registrar and sealed with the Seal of the High Court) having annexed to it a copy of the writ, originating summons or other process by which the proceedings were begun, and stating—

    (a)   the manner in which the writ or such summons or other process was served on the defendant or that the defendant acknowledged service thereof,

    (b)   what objections, if any, were made to the jurisdiction,

    (c)   what pleadings, if any, were served,

    (d)   the grounds on which the judgment was based,

    (e)   that the time for appealing has expired or, as the case may be, the date on which it will expire,

    (f)   whether notice of appeal against the judgment has been entered, and

    (g)   such other particulars as it may be necessary to give to the court in the foreign country in which it is sought to obtain execution of the judgment,

and a certificate (signed and sealed as aforesaid) stating the rate at which the judgment carries interest.

---

**NOTES**

**[71.13.1]   Numbering sequence – comparison with English rules**

Note that rules 14 to 40 are omitted in Hong Kong. The equivalents in the English Rules of the Supreme Court concerned enforcement of judgments of other parts of the United Kingdom and the European Union. The relevant English rules are now found in Part 74 of the English CPR.

## ENFORCEMENT OF RECOMMENDATIONS ETC UNDER THE MERCHANT SHIPPING (LINER CONFERENCES) ORDINANCE (CAP 482)

**41. Application for registration** (O. 71 r. 41)

An application under section 10 of the Merchant Shipping (Liner Conferences) Ordinance (Cap 482) (in this Order referred to as "the Liner Conferences Ordinance") for the registration of a recommendation, determination or award shall be made by originating summons, which shall be in Form No. 10 in Appendix A. **(L.N. 152 of 2008)**

**42. Evidence in support of application** (O. 71 r. 42)

(1)  An application under section 10 of the Liner Conferences Ordinance for the registration of a recommendation must be supported by an affidavit—

    (a)  exhibiting a verified or certified or otherwise duly authenticated copy of the recommendation and the reasons therefor and of the record of settlement;

    (b)  where the recommendation and reasons or the record of settlement or the acceptance of the recommendation is not in the English language, a translation thereof into English certified by a notary public or authenticated by affidavit;

    (c)  exhibiting copies of the acceptance of the recommendation by the parties upon whom it is binding, where the acceptance was in writing, or otherwise verifying the acceptance;

    (d)  giving particulars of the failure to implement the recommendations; and

    (e)  verifying that none of the grounds which would render the recommendation unenforceable under section 10(2) of the Liner Conferences Ordinance is applicable. **(L.N. 152 of 2008)**

(2)  An application under section 10 of the Liner Conferences Ordinance for the registration of a determination or award as to costs must be supported by an affidavit—

    (a)  exhibiting a verified or certified or otherwise duly authenticated copy of the recommendation or other document containing the pronouncement on costs; and

    (b)  stating that such costs have not been paid.

**(L.N. 152 of 2008)**

**43. Order for registration** (O. 71 r. 43)

(1)  An order giving leave to register a recommendation, determination or award under section 10 of the Liner Conferences Ordinance must be drawn up by or on behalf of the party making the application for registration. **(L.N. 152 of 2008)**

(2)  Such an order shall contain a provision that the reasonable costs of registration be taxed.

**44. Register of recommendations etc.** (O. 71 r. 44)

(1)    There shall be kept in the Registry under the direction of the Registrar a register of the recommendations, determinations and awards ordered to be registered under section 10 of the Liner Conferences Ordinance. (L.N. 152 of 2008)

(2)    There shall be included in such register particulars of the enforcement of a recommendation, determination or award so registered.

**(Enacted 1988)**

---

NOTES

**[71.44.1]   Registration and enforcement of decisions under the Liner Conferences Convention 1974**

Order 71 rules 41–44 provide for the registration in Hong Kong of recommendations, determinations and awards of conciliators under the Geneva Convention on the Code of Conduct for Liner Conferences 1974.

Liner conferences are competition reduction agreements between shipping lines whereby they agree to operate under common freight rates or conditions on certain routes. The Geneva Convention of 1974 provides for settlement of disputes. The Merchant Shipping (Liner Conferences) Ordinance (Cap 482) provides for enforcement in Hong Kong. That Ordinance, which was enacted in 1995, replaced United Kingdom legislation which had extended to Hong Kong during the colonial era. Order 71 was amended to reflect the localisation of the relevant primary legislation as part of the civil justice reforms which took effect in 2009.

## ORDER 71A

### RECIPROCAL ENFORCEMENT OF MAINLAND JUDGMENTS

**1. Interpretation** (O. 71A r. 1)

**In this Order —**

**"choice of Mainland court agreement", "judgment creditor", "judgment debtor", "Mainland", "Mainland judgment", "original court" and "registered judgment" have the meanings assigned to them by section 2 of the Ordinance; "the Ordinance" means the Mainland Judgments (Reciprocal Enforcement) Ordinance (Cap 597).**

**(Ordinance 9 of 2008)**

---

**NOTES**

**[71A.1.1]    Origin and scope of Order 71A**

Order 71A governs the procedure to be followed when applying for registration of a Mainland judgment in Hong Kong's Court of First Instance. Such registration is provided for by the Mainland Judgments (Reciprocal Enforcement) Ordinance (Cap 597), ('MJ(RE)O') which came into force on 1st August 2008 (see LN 195 of 2008) That Ordinance implements, in Hong Kong, the 'Arrangement on Reciprocal Recognition and Enforcement of Judgments in Civil and Commercial Matters by the Courts of the Mainland and of the Hong Kong SAR Pursuant to Choice of Court Agreements between Parties Concerned'. The text of the 'Arrangement' can be viewed on the website of the HKSAR Department of Justice, in Chinese with 'courtesy' English translation.

The Arrangement and the Ordinance also deal with the enforcement of Hong Kong judgments in the Mainland, the procedure for which is governed by Order 71B.

**[71A.1.2]    Which Mainland judgments may be registered in HK?**

Section 2 of MJ(RE)O defines 'Mainland judgment' broadly so as to apply to 'a judgment, ruling, conciliatory statement or order of payment'. However the provisions for registration of Mainland judgments by no means apply to all decisions of a judicial character from other parts of China. As succinctly stated by Michelle Tsang of the Department of Justice in HK Lawyer, July 2008, p 60:

> In a nutshell, the Arrangement only covers money judgments on contractual disputes relating to civil or commercial matters whereby the parties concerned have made a prior express agreement to submit to the exclusive jurisdiction of the courts of either the Mainland or Hong Kong.

The following are some of the limitations on the scope of MJ(RE)O as to which Mainland judgments and orders may be registered and enforced in Hong Kong under the Ordinance:

- *No application to Macau and Taiwan* – Section 2 of the Ordinance defines 'Mainland' to mean 'any part of China other than Hong Kong, Macau and Taiwan', thus excluding judgments of the court systems of the latter two places from its scope. See the commentary under Order 71 rule 2 as to enforcement of those judgments by common law action.

- *'Choice of court' agreement required* – As succinctly expressed in the article by Tsang (above), 'the jurisdiction of the court giving the judgment must derive from an exclusive choice of court agreement between the parties'. This requirement is found in section 5(2)(a)(i) of the MJ(RE)O, by which the judgment must be one of a 'chosen court', which term is defined in section 2 to mean a court specified in a 'choice of Mainland court agreement', which in turn is defined in section 3(2) of the Ordinance. It is important to note that the relevant choice of court agreement must have been made on or after the date the Ordinance came into force (01.08.2008): section 5(2)(b).

- *Must be judgment of a 'designated court'* – The judgment must be one of a 'designated court': MJ(RE)O, s 5(2)(a)(i). Schedule 1 of the Ordinance lists 'designated courts' as the Supreme People's Court, a Higher People's Court, an Intermediate People's Court and a 'recognized' Basic People's Court ('BPC'). A separate list of recognised BPCs will be published by the Secretary for Justice in the Gazette pursuant to section 25 of the Ordinance. According to the article by Tsang (above) the purpose is to address concerns that some BPCs may lack experience in handling foreign related disputes. Judgments of BPCs only qualify for registration under the Ordinance if the particular BPC was on the recognised list at the date of the choice of court agreement and at the date of judgment: section 26. A list of BPCs with jurisdiction over non-Mainland parties (as at 31.05.2006) is annexed to the Arrangement. It appears that the Secretary for Justice may choose any or all of these as recognised BPCs for the purpose of the Ordinance.

- *Money judgments only* – Section 5(2)(e) of the Ordinance restricts registration to judgments 'for the payment of a sum of money (not being a sum payable in respect of taxes or other charges of a like nature or in respect of a fine or other penalty)'. The qualification in brackets reflects the position at common law – see the commentary under Order 71 rule 2.

- *Enforcement limited to 'civil and commercial' judgments* – The MJ(RE)O applies only to judgments in 'civil or commercial matters'. This is stipulated in the definition of 'Mainland judgment' in section 2.

- *Judgments under employment and consumer contracts excluded* – The choice of court agreement, which is required for the Ordinance to apply (see above), must be one concluded by parties to a 'specified contract': MJ(RE)O, s 3. The term 'specified contract' is defined in section 2 to exclude contracts of employment and contracts with a natural person 'for personal consumption, family or other non-commercial purposes'. According to the article by Tsang (above), this definition is based on article 2(1) of the Hague Convention on Choice of Courts Agreements 2005.

- *Must be a final judgment* – The Hong Kong court's power to register Mainland judgments is restricted to judgments which are 'final and conclusive as between the parties': MJ(RE)O, s 5(2)(c). Section 6(1) of the Ordinance lists certain types of Mainland judgments which are to be treated as final and conclusive for this purpose.

- *Judgment must be enforceable in the Mainland* – Only judgments which are 'enforceable in the Mainland' may be registered in Hong Kong: MJ(RE)O, s 5(2)(d). For this purpose section 6(2) deems a Mainland judgment to comply, in the absence of proof to the contrary, if certified by the court giving it to be final and enforceable in the Mainland.
- *Only judgments given after 01.08.2008* – Section 5(2)(a) of MJ(RE)O restricts the court's power to register Mainland judgments to those 'given on or after the date of the commencement of this Ordinance', which was 1st August 2008 (see LN 195 of 2008). In addition the choice of court agreement between the parties must also have been entered into after commencement – see above.

### [71A.1.3]    Legal effect of registration of Mainland judgment

A Mainland judgment registered under Order 71A has the same legal effect in Hong Kong as a judgment of the Court of First Instance. Section 14(2)(a) of MJ(RE)O provides that 'proceedings may be taken on the judgment'. This presumably means that the procedures for enforcement of Hong Kong judgments (see generally Order 45 rule 1) will be available on application in the usual way once a Mainland judgment has been registered in Hong Kong; likewise the procedures for examination of judgment debtors under Orders 44A, 48 and 49B. However section 15 of the Ordinance provides for what is in effect an automatic stay of execution of a registered Mainland judgment during the time the judgment debtor may apply to set aside the registration, and pending disposal of any such application, as to which see Order 71A rule 8.

### [71A.1.4]    Interest on registered Mainland judgment

Section 12 of MJ(RE)O provides that a Mainland judgment registered under the Ordinance shall be registered for an amount including interest payable under Mainland law up to the date of registration.

Post-registration interest is dealt with by section 14(2), which provides that a registered Mainland judgment carries interest from the day of registration as if it were a judgment of the Court of First Instance. This presumably means that the Hong Kong legal provisions for post-judgment interest, whether under the terms of the judgment itself or by statute, will apply. With regard to those provisions see the commentary under Order 42 rule 1.

### [71A.1.5]    Setting aside registration of Mainland judgment

See Order 71A rule 8 and the commentary thereunder.

### [71A.1.6]    Restriction on bringing common law action

Section 22 of MJ(RE)O provides that no proceedings shall be brought on a cause of action which is already the subject of a Mainland judgment if that judgment has been registered under the Ordinance or an application for such registration is pending. It appears that in other circumstances a plaintiff is free to bring fresh proceedings in Hong Kong. See the commentary under Order 71 rule 2 as to the common law action on a judgment of another jurisdiction.

### [71A.1.7]    Mainland judgments which have been partly satisfied

A party applying for registration of a Mainland judgment in Hong Kong is required to disclose whether enforcement action has been taken in the Mainland and whether the judgment is wholly or only partly unsatisfied: see rule 3(1)(c)(iii) and (iv). If the judgment has been partly satisfied, it will be registered only in respect of the outstanding balance: MJ(RE)O, s 10.

### [71A.1.8]  Defence or counterclaim based on Mainland judgment

Section 16 of MJ(RE)O provides that certain Mainland judgments may be relied upon in Hong Kong proceedings by way of defence or counterclaim. The provision applies to registered Mainland judgments provided they have not been set aside on any ground other than payment in full. It also applies to unregistered Mainland judgments provided that the criteria for registration are met, and, if registered, registration of the judgment would not be liable to be set aside.

The section goes on to preserve the criteria for recognition of Mainland judgments as they exist at common law.

## 2.  Application for registration (O. 71A, r. 2)

(1)  **An application under section 5(1) of the Ordinance to have a Mainland judgment registered in the Court may be made ex parte, but the Court may direct a summons to be issued.**

(2)  **If the Court directs a summons to be issued, the summons shall be an originating summons.**

(3)  **An originating summons under this rule shall be in Form No. 10 in Appendix A.**

**(Ordinance 9 of 2008)**

---

## NOTES

### [71A.2.1]  Application for registration of Mainland judgment may be made ex parte or inter partes

Order 71A rule 2(1) contemplates application for registration of a Mainland judgment being made either *ex parte* or *inter partes*. No guidance is given as to which route should be followed in which circumstances. In principle *inter partes* application should be the norm, and *ex parte* application will only be justified in unusual circumstances such as where there is a need to avoid giving the judgment debtor advance warning because of grounds to believe assets will be disposed of to defeat the judgment creditor.

When application is made *ex parte* the court has power to direct that a summons be issued. Such a direction is in effect a direction that the application be heard *inter partes*. Where an application for registration is granted *ex parte* the judgment creditor will be entitled to apply to set the registration aside not just under Order 71A rule 8, but under Order 32 rule 6 which provides that any *ex parte* order may be set aside. See the commentary under that rule.

### [71A.2.2]  Form of application for application to register Mainland judgment

Order 71A rule 2(2) & (3) stipulate that an *inter partes* application for registration of a Mainland judgment should be made by originating summons in form No 10, which is the expedited form. The rule is silent as to the form of *ex parte* application. In the absence of an express requirement an *ex parte* originating summons is not appropriate – see Order 7 rule 2 and the commentary thereunder. It would therefore appear that application should be made by affidavit.

**[71A.2.3]    Time limit for registration of Mainland judgment**
Application for registration of a Mainland judgment must be made within two years of the date on which the judgment takes effect, or from the last day for performance if specified in the judgment. See section 7 of the MJ(RE)O.

3.  **Evidence in support of application for registration of Mainland judgments**
    (O. 71A, r. 3)
    **(1)    An application for registration of a Mainland judgment shall be supported by an affidavit —**
        **(a)    exhibiting —**
            **(i)    a copy of the Mainland judgment duly sealed by the original court;**
            **(ii)    the original or a verified or certified or otherwise duly authenticated copy of the relevant choice of Mainland court agreement;**
            **(iii)    a certificate issued by the original court certifying that the judgment is final and enforceable in the Mainland; and**
            **(iv)    where the judgment creditor is a body of persons, the documents specified for the purposes of this sub-subparagraph in paragraph (2);**
        **(b)    stating the name, trade or business and the usual or last known place of abode or business of the judgment creditor and the judgment debtor respectively, so far as known to the deponent;**
        **(c)    stating to the best of the information or belief of the deponent —**
            **(i)    that at the date of the application, the judgment is enforceable in the Mainland;**
            **(ii)    that the judgment creditor is entitled to enforce the judgment;**
            **(iii)    whether any action has been taken to enforce the judgment in the Mainland and, if so, the details of such enforcement;**
            **(iv)    as the case may require, either that at the date of the application the judgment has not been satisfied or the amount in respect of which it remains unsatisfied at that date; and**
            **(v)    if the judgment were registered, the registration would not be, or be liable to be, set aside under section 18 or 19 of the Ordinance;**
        **(d)    specifying the amount of the interest, if any, which by the law of the Mainland has become due under the judgment up to the time of registration together with the costs duly certified by the original court for the judgment.**
    **(2)    The documents specified for the purposes of paragraph (1)(a)(iv) are -**
        **(a)    if the judgment creditor is a body of persons incorporated, formed or established under the law of Hong Kong, a verified or certified or otherwise duly authenticated copy of its certificate of incorporation or similar documents;**

    (b)  if the judgment creditor is a body of persons incorporated, formed or established under the law of any place other than Hong Kong, a verified or certified or otherwise duly authenticated copy of documents stating that its incorporation, formation or establishment was in accordance with the law of the place where it was so incorporated, formed or established.

    (3)  Where a Mainland judgment sought to be registered is in respect of different matters, and that some, but not all, of the provisions of the judgment would, if contained in separate Mainland judgments that are the subjects of applications for registration under section 5(1) of the Ordinance, satisfy the requirements specified in section 5(2)(a) to (e) of the Ordinance, the affidavit shall state the provisions in respect of which it is sought to register the judgment.

    (4)  The affidavit shall be accompanied by any evidence relevant to the enforceability of the Mainland judgment, and of the law of the Mainland under which any interest has become due under the judgment.

(Ordinance 9 of 2008)

## NOTES

**[71A.3.1]  Origin and scope of Order 71A rule 3**
Order 71A rule 3 stipulates the information which must be set out in the affidavit in support of an application for registration of a Mainland judgment. The requirements of the rule are clearly based on Order 71 rule 3 (which applies to applications for registration of foreign judgments) with some additional provisions reflecting the terms of the Mainland-HKSAR Arrangement on reciprocal enforcement of judgments.

**4.  Security for costs** (O. 71A, r. 4)
    The Court may order the judgment creditor to give security for the costs of the application for registration of a Mainland judgment and of any proceedings which may be brought to set aside the registration.

(Ordinance 9 of 2008)

## NOTES

**[71A.4.1]  Security for costs of application for registration of Mainland judgment**
Order 71A rule 4 empowers the court to order a judgment creditor to give security for the costs of an application for registration of a Mainland judgment. No criteria for making such an order are stated. Presumably, therefore, the established criteria for ordering security for costs under Order 23 and section 357 of the Companies Ordinance (Cap 32) will apply. See the commentary under Order 23.

**5.  Order for registration** (O. 71A, r. 5)
    (1)  An order for registration of a Mainland judgment shall be drawn up by or on behalf of the judgment creditor, and the order so drawn up shall —
        (a)  state the period within which an application may be made to set aside the registration; and

(b)  **contain a notification that execution on the judgment will not be issued until after the expiration of that period.**

(2)  **Except where the order is made on summons, the order so drawn up is not required to be served on the judgment debtor.**

(Ordinance 9 of 2008)

---

## NOTES

**[71A.5.1]    Contents of order for registration**
An order for registration of a Mainland judgment must contain the information stipulated in Order 71A rule 5. This includes notification that execution of the judgment will not be issued until after expiration of the time within which application to set aside may be made. That time is fixed by the court making the order: see the commentary under Order 71A rule 8.

**[71A.5.2]    Service of order for registration**
The order for registration of a Mainland judgment need only be served if it was made on summons: Order 71A rule 5(2). That means it need not be served if the application was heard *ex parte*. By whichever means the application was heard, notice of the order must be given in accordance with rule 7 – see below.

**6.  Register of Mainland judgments** (O. 71A, r. 6)
(1)  **The Registrar shall keep in the Registry a register of the Mainland judgments ordered to be registered under the Ordinance.**
(2)  **There shall be included in such register particulars of any execution issued on a Mainland judgment.**

(Ordinance 9 of 2008)

**[71A.6.1]    Origin and scope of Order 71A rule 6**
Order 71A rule 6 requires the court registry to keep a register of Mainland judgments which are registered in Hong Kong, and of execution issued on such judgments. The wording of the rule is virtually identical to that of Order 71 rule 6 (which applies to foreign judgments registered under Cap 319).

**7.  Notice of registration** (O. 71A, r. 7)
(1)  **The judgment creditor shall serve a notice of registration of a Mainland judgment on the judgment debtor by delivering it to him personally or by sending it to him at his usual or last known place of abode or business or in such other manner as the Court may direct.**
(2)  **Service of such a notice out of the jurisdiction is permissible without leave, and Order 11, rules 5A and 8A, shall apply in relation to such a notice as they apply in relation to a writ.**
(3)  **The notice of registration shall set out —**
  (a)  **full particulars of the registered judgment and the order for registration;**
  (b)  **the name and address of the judgment creditor or of his solicitor or agent on whom, and at which, any summons issued by the judgment debtor may be served;**

    **(c)** **the right of the judgment debtor to apply to have the registration set aside; and**

    **(d)** **the period within which an application to set aside the registration may be made.**

**(Ordinance 9 of 2008)**

## NOTES

### [71A.7.1] Form of notice of registration of Mainland judgment

Order 71A rule 7 requires that notice of registration of a Mainland judgment be served on the judgment debtor, and sets out the information which must be included in such notice. However, it does not specify any particular form. The information which must be given in the notice goes beyond what would normally be included in the order for registration as drawn up and entered, so service of a sealed copy of the order may not be sufficient. It appears that a letter setting out the required particulars, and enclosing a sealed copy of the order for registration would comply. However, service of the order itself is not expressly required unless it was made on *inter partes* application. See rule 5(2).

### [71A.7.2] Manner of service of notice of registration

Notice of registration of a Mainland judgment must normally, according to Order 71A rule 7, be served on the judgment debtor personally or at the usual or last known place of abode or business, that is in a manner similar to service of a writ or originating summons. This is a salutary provision in cases where the application for registration was heard *ex parte* without prior notice to the judgment debtor. However it may result in a waste of costs and time where the application was heard *ex parte* or on notice and the judgment debtor is represented by solicitors. In that event a direction from the court for another manner of service, such as 'ordinary' service as normally takes place between solicitors on record (see Order 65 rule 5 and the commentary thereunder) might be sought.

### [71A.7.3] Leave not required to serve notification ex juris

Where notification of registration of a Mainland judgment is required to be served outside Hong Kong, leave to serve out is not required: see Order 71A rule 7(2).

### [71A.7.4] Affidavit of service of notice of registration

An affidavit of service of the notification of registration of a Mainland judgment must be produced in support of any application for execution of the judgment. See rule 9.

**8. Application to set aside registration** (O. 71A, r. 8)

    **(1)** **An application to set aside the registration of a registered judgment shall be made by summons supported by affidavit.**

    **(2)** **The Court hearing such application may order any issue between the judgment creditor and the judgment debtor to be tried in any manner in which an issue in an action may be ordered to be tried.**

**(3)   The Court may, either of its own motion or on an application made by the judgment creditor, and if having regard to all the circumstances of the case it thinks it just to do so, impose such terms (whether as to giving security or otherwise) as it thinks fit as a condition of the further conduct of an application under this rule.**

(Ordinance 9 of 2008)

------------------------

**NOTES**

**[71A.8.1]   Time for making application to set aside registration of Mainland judgment**

An order for registration of a Mainland judgment must specify the time within which an application to set aside registration may be made: MJ(RE)O, s 17(1). The order when drawn up must state the period specified by the court: Order 71A rule 5(1)(a). No guidance is given as to how long a period should be allowed, rather the matter appears to be left in the discretion of the court.

Section 17(2) of MJ(RE)O permits the court to extend the time which has been specified for application to set aside registration, and to grant further extensions.

**[71A.8.2]   Grounds for setting aside registration of Mainland judgment**

Section 18 of MJ(RE)O provides that registration of a Mainland judgment may be set aside. Eleven grounds for setting aside are listed.

Application to set aside may be made 'by any party against whom a registered judgment may be enforced'. This wording suggests that someone other than the judgment debtor, such as an insurer or possibly a guarantor, may apply.

According to the article by Tsang (above), the grounds on which registration of a Mainland judgment may be set aside are similar to those for setting aside foreign judgments registered under Cap 319. Reference should be made to MJ(RE)O for the precise grounds on which registration may be set aside. In brief, they are as follows (adopting the lettering in section 18(1) of the Ordinance), with our commentary:

(a)   *Judgment does not satisfy the registration criteria* – a judgment which should not have been registered in the first place, because it does not meet the criteria set out in section 5(2) of the Ordinance, may be set aside under this provision.

(b)   *Registration in contravention of the Ordinance* – where registration of a judgment contravenes the Ordinance, it may be set aside. Thus where the application for registration was made after expiration of the 2 year limitation specified in section 7, or where the registration failed to take into account a part payment as required by section 10, it may be set aside.

(c)   *Choice of court agreement invalid* – If the choice of Mainland court agreement between the parties is invalid under Mainland law, registration may be set aside unless the court giving the judgment determined that the agreement was valid.

(d)   *Judgment satisfied* – Registration of a Mainland judgment may be set aside if it has been paid.

(e) *Exclusive Hong Kong jurisdiction* – Registration may be set aside if, according to Hong Kong law, the Hong Kong courts have exclusive jurisdiction over the dispute.

(f) *Failure of judgment debtor to appear* – If the judgment debtor did not appear before the Mainland court, because of failure to comply with the summonsing procedure under Mainland law, or because of insufficient time in accordance with Mainland law, registration may be set aside.

(g) *Fraud* – A Mainland judgment obtained by fraud may be set aside. According to the article by Tsang (above), setting aside on this ground should follow 'the common law principles applicable when fraud is alleged in resisting the enforcement of a foreign judgment'.

(h) *Existing judgment or award in HK* – Where the cause of action giving rise to the Mainland judgment is the subject of a Hong Kong judgment or a Hong Kong arbitral award between the parties, registration may be set aside.

(i) *Prior recognition of the judgment in Hong Kong* – In the event of the same cause of action between the parties having already given rise to recognition or enforcement in Hong Kong of a judgment or arbitral award outside Hong Kong, registration may be set aside.

(j) *Public policy* – Registration may be set aside if enforcement of the judgment would be contrary to public policy. The decision of the Court of Final Appeal in *Hebei Import & Export Corp v Polytek Engineering Co Ltd* [1999] 2 HKC 205 with regard to refusal to enforce arbitral awards on public policy grounds is likely to be instructive. See the discussion of that case and others in the commentary under Order 73 rule 10.

(k) *Judgment reversed or set aside in Mainland* – Under this ground, registration in Hong Kong may be set aside if the Mainland judgment has been reversed on appeal or set aside on retrial.

**[71A.8.3] Setting aside registration of Mainland judgment for breach of natural justice**

According to the article by Tsang (above), it is implicit in the grounds for setting aside under section 18 of the Ordinance that a Mainland judgment obtained in breach of natural justice may be set aside. She explains why it was not considered necessary to include this ground specifically in the legislation:

There have been suggestions that the defence of 'natural justice' should also be included in s 18. The suggestion has not been adopted as the Arrangement does not specify 'natural justice' as a ground for refusing to enforce a judgment. This is necessarily the case, as the term 'natural justice' is not known to the legal system of the Mainland. In any case, the grounds now listed in section 18 are sufficient to embrace the common law concept of natural justice.

At common law, natural justice is generally concerned with procedural safeguards upholding the fundamental principles of justice and fairness. The notion of natural justice traditionally consists of two fundamental rules: (a) no one may be a judge in his or her own cause; and (b) one's defence must always be fairly heard.

In the *Explanatory Report on the 2005 Hague Choice of Court Agreements Convention* [Hartley & Dogauchi, 2007], it is suggested that the three grounds for refusal of recognition or enforcement – namely failure to properly notify the defendant, fraud and public policy – have considerable overlap [and] these grounds 'all relate, wholly or partly, to procedural fairness' which is 'also known as . . . natural justice' . . . Given these comments, it may be fairly argued that, in the context of the Ordinance, the principle of natural justice is now subsumed by s 18(1).

### [71A.8.4]   Setting aside where appeal or retrial pending

The court may set aside registration of a Mainland judgment where it is satisfied that an appeal against the judgment is pending or that there has been an order for a retrial of the case: MJ(RE)O s 19. The section expressly provides that the court may adjourn the application to set aside until the appeal or retrial is likely to be disposed of.

### [71A.8.5]   Re-registration after setting aside

In certain circumstances, a fresh application for registration of a Mainland judgment may be brought after registration has been set aside. Those circumstances are set out in section 20(2) and (3) of MJ(RE)O. Briefly they are:

*   Where registration was set aside under section 18(1)(a) on the ground the Mainland judgment was not enforceable under Mainland law and the judgment subsequently becomes enforceable;
*   Where registration was set aside under section 19 of the Ordinance on the ground of a pending appeal or retrial, and that appeal or retrial has been disposed of.
*   Where a Mainland judgment is set aside under section 18(1)(b) on the ground the amount registered should have reflected a part payment, the court may order registration for the balance owing.

## 9.   Issue of execution (O. 71A, r. 9)

**Any party wishing to issue execution on a registered judgment shall produce to the Registrar an affidavit of service of the notice of registration of the judgment and any order made by the Court in relation to the judgment.**

**(Ordinance 9 of 2008)**

### [71A.9.1]   Execution of registered Mainland judgment

A Mainland judgment which has been registered under MJ(RE)O may be the subject of execution in accordance with Hong Kong law and procedures. See the commentary under Order 71A rule 1.

### [71A.9.2]   Affidavit of service required for execution of Mainland judgment

A party applying for a writ of execution in Hong Kong on a registered Mainland judgment is required by rule 9 to produce an affidavit of service of the notice of registration. As to the manner of service see rule 7.

## 10.   Application for registration of part of Mainland judgments (O. 71A, r. 10)

**In the case of an application for registration of any part of a Mainland judgment under section 5(1) of the Ordinance —**

**(a)   rule 2 applies to such an application;**

    (b)   unless the context otherwise requires, a reference to a Mainland judgment (however described) in this Order shall be construed as a reference to that part of the Mainland judgment; and

    (c)   the other provisions of this Order shall, subject to all necessary modifications, be construed and have application accordingly.

                                     **(Ordinance 9 of 2008)**

---

## NOTES

**[71A.10.1]   Registration of part of Mainland judgment**
Where a Mainland judgment contains provisions which, if in a separate judgment, would be registrable in Hong Kong, as well as provisions which are not registrable, the court may order registration of the eligible part under section 9 of MJ(RE)O.

**11. Evidence in support of application for registration of part of Mainland judgments** (O. 71A, r. 11)

    **(1)**   Subject to paragraph (2), in the case of an application for registration of any part of a Mainland judgment under section 5(1) of the Ordinance, in addition to the information specified in rule 3(1), the affidavit submitted in support of the application shall also state to the best of the information or belief of the deponent that the sum of money ordered to be paid under that part of the judgment is due.

    **(2)**   Where —

        **(a)**   the Court has under section 5(2) of the Ordinance ordered a part of a Mainland judgment to be registered; and

        **(b)**   the registration has not been set aside under section 18 or 19 of the Ordinance,

then notwithstanding rule 3, any application subsequently made for registration of any other part of the judgment under section 5(1) of the Ordinance shall be supported by an affidavit specified for the purposes of this paragraph in paragraph (3).

    **(3)**   An affidavit specified for the purposes of paragraph (2) shall —

        **(a)**   cite the Mainland judgment;

        **(b)**   state to the best of the information or belief of the deponent —

            **(i)**   that the sum of money ordered to be paid under the part of the judgment sought to be registered under the application is due; and

            **(ii)**   any other information relevant to the application; and

        **(c)**   exhibit a copy of the last order made by the Court under section 5(2) of the Ordinance for registration of any other part of the judgment.

                                       **(9 of 2008 s 27)**

**NOTES**

**[71A.11.1]    Affidavit in support of application for registration of part of Mainland judgment**

Order 71A rule 11 stipulates the information which must be set out in the affidavit in support of registration of part of such a judgment. As to registration of part of a Mainland judgment, see the commentary under rule 10.

## ORDER 71B

### CERTIFIED COPIES OF JUDGMENTS GIVEN BY COURT OF FINAL APPEAL AND HIGH COURT

1. **Interpretation** (O. 71B, r. 1)

   **In this Order -**

   **"choice of Hong Kong court agreement" has the meaning assigned to it by section 2 of the Ordinance;**

   **"judgment" includes any judgment, order and allocatur in civil or commercial matters;**

   **"Mainland" has the meaning assigned to it by section 2 of the Ordinance;**

   **"the Ordinance" means the Mainland Judgments (Reciprocal Enforcement) Ordinance (Cap 597).**

   **(Ordinance 9 of 2008)**

---

## NOTES

### [71B.1.1]   Origin and scope of Order 71B

Order 71B governs the procedure to be followed when applying for a certified copy of a Hong Kong judgment for the purpose of enforcing it in the Mainland. Section 21 of the Mainland Judgments (Reciprocal Enforcement) Ordinance (Cap 597), ('MJ(RE)O') which came into force on 1st August 2008 (see LN 195 of 2008) gives the High Court jurisdiction to issue certified copies of judgments for that purpose.

The actual procedures for registration and enforcement of a Hong Kong judgment in the Mainland once the certified copy has been obtained are a matter for Mainland law. That law is expressed in the 'Arrangement on Reciprocal Recognition and Enforcement of Judgments in Civil and Commercial Matters by the Courts of the Mainland and of the Hong Kong SAR Pursuant to Choice of Court Agreements between Parties Concerned'. The Arrangement can be viewed in its Chinese original and 'courtesy' English translation on the website of the HKSAR Department of Justice. It appears that the Arrangement takes direct effect in the Mainland without the need for implementing legislation.

### [71B.1.2]   Which Hong Kong judgments may be registered in the Mainland?

Article 2 of the Arrangement provides that any judgment, order or allocatur of the Court of Final Appeal, Court of Appeal, Court of First Instance or of the District Court may be enforced in the Mainland under its terms. This is subject to various other provisions of the Arrangement. In particular, it is clear from the preamble that the Arrangement is limited to 'judgments in civil and commercial matters', where the parties have entered into a choice of court agreement, meaning an agreement expressly designating a court of the HKSAR as 'having sole jurisdiction' for resolving disputes in a 'particular legal relationship' (art 3).

Although the Arrangement is worded very differently from a statute in the common law system, it is clear that the intention is that Hong Kong judgments shall be enforceable in the Mainland in the same circumstances that Mainland judgments may be registered and enforced in Hong Kong under MJ(RE)O. In that regard see the commentary under Order 71A.

## 2. Certified copies of judgments (O. 71B, r. 2)

(1)    An application under section 21 of the Ordinance for a certified copy of a judgment given by the Court of Final Appeal or the High Court shall be made ex parte to the Registrar on affidavit.

(2)    The affidavit shall —

(a)   exhibit the original or a verified or certified or otherwise duly authenticated copy of the relevant choice of Hong Kong court agreement;

(b)   give particulars of the proceedings in which the judgment was obtained;

(c)   state the amount in respect of which the judgment remains unsatisfied at the date of the application;

(d)   state whether the defendant did or did not object to the jurisdiction and, if he objected, on what grounds;

(e)   state whether any action has been taken to enforce the judgment in Hong Kong and, if so, the details of such enforcement;

(f)   show that the judgment is not subject to any stay of execution;

(g)   state that the time for appealing has expired or, as the case may be, the date on which it will expire and in either case whether any notice of appeal against the judgment has been entered; and

(h)   state the rate at which the judgment carries interest.

(3)    The certified copy of the judgment shall be an office copy sealed with the seal of the High Court and indorsed with a certificate signed by the Registrar certifying that the copy is a true copy of a judgment obtained in the Court of Final Appeal or the High Court, as the case may be, and that it is issued in accordance with section 21 of the Ordinance.

(4)    The certificate issued by the High Court under section 21(3) of the Ordinance shall have annexed to it a copy of the writ, originating summons or other process by which the proceedings were begun and a copy of the reasoned judgment (if any), and state —

(a)   what pleadings, if any, were served;

(b)   the manner in which the writ or such summons or other process was served on the defendant or that the defendant acknowledged service of the writ or summons or process;

(c)   the amount in respect of which the judgment remains unsatisfied at the date of the application as stated by the deponent in the affidavit by which the application is made;

(d)   what objections, if any, were made to the jurisdiction;

(e)   the date from which the judgment takes effect;

(f)   whether any action has been taken to enforce the judgment in Hong Kong and, if so, the details of such enforcement;

(g) that the time for appealing has expired or, as the case may be, the date on which it will expire;

(h) whether any notice of appeal against the judgment has been entered;

(i) the rate at which the judgment carries interest; and

(j) such other particulars as it may be necessary to give to the court in the Mainland in which it is sought to obtain execution of the judgment.

(5) the certificate shall be signed by the Registrar and sealed with the seal of the High Court.

(Ordinance 9 of 2008)

---

**NOTES**

**[71B.2.1] Origin and scope of Order 71B rule 2**

Order 71B rule 2 stipulates the information which must be set out in the affidavit in support of an application for a certified copy of a Hong Kong judgment which the applicant intends to use for the purpose of seeking registration in the Mainland. The requirements of the rule are clearly based on Order 71 rule 13 (which applies to applications for registration in foreign jurisdictions of Hong Kong judgments).

**[71B.2.3] Procedure on application for certified copy of Hong Kong judgment sought to be enforced in Mainland**

In order to apply for enforcement of a Hong Kong judgment in the Mainland of China, the judgment creditor must first obtain a certified copy of the judgment in accordance with section 21 of MJ(RE)O and Order 71B rule 2. The rule provides that application for the certified copy is to be made *ex parte* by affidavit. The affidavit should set out the information as required by rule 2(2).

The affidavit should be submitted to the court together with a draft certificate to be issued by the Registrar. The following form of certificate has been made available by the court as a practice form (see Law Society circular 08-592):

IN THE HIGH COURT OF THE

HONG KONG SPECIAL ADMINISTRATIVE REGION

COURT OF FIRST INSTANCE

ACTION NO. _____ OF 20

---

BETWEEN

Plaintiff

AND

Defendant

---

CERTIFICATE ISSUED UNDER SECTION 21(3) OF THE
MAINLAND JUDGMENTS (RECIPROCAL ENFORCEMENT)
ORDINANCE, CAP 597
AND
ORDER 71B, RULE 2 OF THE RULES OF THE HIGH COURT

I,   , Registrar of the High Court of the Hong Kong Special Administrative region hereby certify that the Plaintiff obtained judgment in respect of [a claim for debt] against the Defendant on [date] in the Court of First Instance. A certified true copy of the judgment ("the Judgment") is enclosed as Annexure 1.

[A copy of the reasoned judgment is enclosed as Annexure 2.]

The Judgment can be enforced by execution in Hong Kong.

I also certify that:

1.    The pleadings in this action consisted of:
      (a)    [The Writ of summons issued on [date] with the Statement of Claim endorsed], a copy of which is enclosed as Annexure 3.
      (b)    [set out others]

2.    The Defendant duly acknowledged service of the writ on [date]. [Or state the manner in which the writ of summons or other process was served on the defendant.]

3.    The Judgment was for the sum of HK$[      ] together with interest thereon from        to the date of judgment at the rate of [      % per annum] and thereafter at judgment rate until payment, together with costs to be taxed if not agreed.

4.    The costs have been taxed and interest is allowed in the sum of [HK$      ] on [date]. A copy of the certificate of costs is enclosed as Annexure 4.

5.    The amount in respect of which the judgment remains unsatisfied at the date of application as stated by the Plaintiff [or name of deponent] in the affidavit by which the application was made is HK$[      ]. A breakdown of the calculation is enclosed as Annexure 5.

6.    No objection has been made to the jurisdiction of the court. [Or state the objection to jurisdiction taken.]

7.    The judgment takes effect from [date].

8.    The judgment [is/is not] subject to any stay of execution. The steps taken to enforce the judgment in Hong Kong are [give details].

9.    [The time for appealing has expired and no notice of appeal against the judgment has been entered in the High Court.]

10.   [Give other particulars necessary to the court in the Mainland.]

Dated the                    day of 20 .

                    Registrar of the High Court
                    of the Hong Kong
                    Special Administrative Region
                    [seal of the High Court]

Note: The contents of this Practice Form can be adapted as the circumstances require.

# SPECIAL PROVISIONS AS TO PARTICULAR PROCEEDINGS

## ORDER 72

### (HK) PARTICULAR PROCEEDINGS

**1.  Application and interpretation** (O. 72 r. 1)

(1)   This Order applies to particular proceedings, and the other provisions of these rules apply to those actions subject to the provisions of this Order.

(2)   In this Order "particular proceedings" means a type of proceedings for which provision has been made by the Chief Justice for separate listing.

**2.  The Various Lists** (O. 72 r. 2)

(1)   There may be lists, in which actions and other proceedings may be entered in accordance with the provisions of this Order, and a judge shall be in charge of each list. **(L.N. 307 of 1998)**

(2)   In this Order references to the judge shall be construed as references to the judge for the time being in charge of a particular list.

(3)   The judge shall have control of the proceedings in his particular list and, subject to the provisions of this Order and to any directions of the judge, the powers of a judge in chambers (including those exercisable by the Registrar) shall, in relation to any proceedings in such an action (including any appeal from any judgment, order or decision of the Registrar, given or made prior to the transfer of the action or proceedings to the relevant list) be exercisable by the judge.

(4)   Paragraph (3) shall not be construed as preventing the powers of the judge being exercised by some other judge.

---

## NOTES

### [72.2.1]   Origin and scope of Order 72

Order 72 makes provision for the establishment of lists of particular types of proceedings, often referred to as specialist lists. The consequence of an action being listed on one of the specialist lists is that it will usually be tried before a particular judge, or one of a group of judges, who are assigned to deal with the particular type of case. The Hong Kong system of specialist lists is rather different from what prevails in England and Wales. There, unlike Hong Kong, there are formal divisions within the court, such as the Chancery Division and the Queen's Bench Division.

A number of specialist lists have been established in Hong Kong pursuant to Order 72. This is normally done by practice directions which govern the procedures to be followed. The various lists are discussed one by one below.

### [72.2.2]   The commercial list

There has long been a commercial list in Hong Kong. It is now the subject of practice direction SL1.1, which took effect on 1 November 2009. The practice direction says (para 2) that the function of the list 'is to facilitate the disposal of actions involving commercial matters'.

The commercial list practice direction contains specific provisions in relation to case management summonses. The intention appears to be to displace the provisions of Order 25 and the case management practice direction (PD 5.2) which would otherwise apply. A special form of information sheet, set out in appendix A to the practice direction, is required to be lodged with the clerk to the judge no later than 7 days before the hearing of the 1ˢᵗ case management summons. Standard directions to be made at the 1ˢᵗ case management conference in most commercial list cases are set out in paragraph 11 of the practice direction. Appendix B is the commercial list checklist for pre-trial review, to be lodged no later than 28 days in advance.

Also relevant are practice direction SL1, which specifies commercial list applications which are to be dealt with by a master, and part (3A) of practice direction 11.1, which deals with urgent applications to the commercial list judge. The updated text of these practice directions can be downloaded from the judiciary's website or that of the Hong Kong legal information institute.

The choice of whether to place an action on the commercial list appears to be left to the plaintiff at the time the writ is issued. In *Idmiston Ltd v Asian Master Enterprises Ltd & Anor* CACV 1/1989 (Cons VP, Clough JA & O'Connor J; 17.03.1989) Cons VP said (at para 6), referring to Order 72 rule 4, that 'a plaintiff may enter his action in the Commercial List by simply noting the writ or the originating summons in the top left hand corner'. The current practice is to insert an action number beginning with 'HCCL' rather than the 'HCA' used for ordinary High Court actions. An action which is not commenced on the commercial list may at a later stage be transferred to it under Order 72 rule 5.

Guidance as to the type of cases which are appropriate for the commercial list is set out in *Idmiston* (above) (para 5), where Cons VP said:

> The Commercial List was introduced in Hong Kong, I think, in the late 1960s, although it did not become active until 1976. It followed the precedent set in England at the end of the last century when a special list was set up to deal with 'causes arising out of the ordinary transactions of merchants and traders; amongst others, those relating to the construction of mercantile documents, export or import of merchandise, affreightment, insurance, banking and mercantile agency and mercantile usages'. Those words I have taken from the original notice issued by the Queen's Bench Division of the High Court of England in 1895. And they are words which, with only one change, have since been incorporated into the English Rules of the Supreme Court. Although we have nothing of a similar nature in our own rules, it seems to me that they still provide very useful guidance as to what is a commercial cause.

*Idmiston* was an appeal against an order transferring 3 actions which 'raised questions of commercial fraud' to the commercial list. It was held (at para 11) that actions of that nature 'would not necessarily be excluded from transfer to the Commercial List', though it was considered there were sufficient High Court judges with knowledge of the commercial world that transfer was not necessary in the particular case. See also:

•   *Advance Finance Ltd v Pang Sze-mui Loretta & Ors* [1986] HKLR 523, 537F-H where the majority of the Court of Appeal were of the view that an action concerning alleged breach of fiduciary duties by company directors should not have been entered in the commercial list.

- *K Master & Co Ltd v Eagle Star Insurance Co Ltd* [1968] HKLR 215 where a claim under a marine insurance policy for damage to cargo during shipment was held to be suitable for the commercial list.

**[72.2.3]**

### *The construction and arbitration list*

The construction and arbitration list was established in 1986. It is now governed by practice direction 6.1 which came into force along with the civil justice reforms in 2009 and consolidated 3 previous practice directions. Construction and arbitration list actions are designated with action numbers beginning with 'HCCT'.

The practice direction gives the following non-exhaustive list of classes of action which are 'within' the HCCT list:

(1)     civil or mechanical engineering;

(2)     building or other construction work;

(3)     claims by or against engineers, architects, surveyors and other professional persons or bodies engaged in matters relating to the construction industry; and,

(4)     applications relating to arbitration whether arising under the Arbitration Ordinance (Cap 341), RHC Order 73 or otherwise.

The practice direction provides that a plaintiff or applicant may enter an action in the HCCT list, but goes on to give the judge in charge of the list control over which actions shall be included. It is provided that the judge in charge of the list may, of his own motion or on application, remove an action from the list or transfer an action pending elsewhere in the High Court (other than in another specialist list) to the HCCT list.

The practice direction gives detailed guidance on matters of procedure, including mediation and case management. It can be viewed on the judiciary website www.judiciary.gov.hk and that of the Hong Kong Legal Information Institute www.hklii.org, both of which are accessible by the general public free-of-charge.

**[72.2.4]**    **The personal injuries list**

All actions claiming damages arising out of death or personal injury, including medical negligence claims, should be commenced in the personal injuries list. However actions within the jurisdiction of the Admiralty Court (as to which see Order 75) are excluded from the list, and employees' compensation cases (which are dealt with in the District Court) have their own list and practice direction.

The personal injuries list became compulsory for the cases to which it applies in 1996. It is governed by practice direction 18.1 which was substantially revised in 2009 along with the coming into force of the civil justice reforms. The practice direction is very detailed and sets out mandatory procedures to be followed at every stage of a personal injury claim, including pre-action protocols. It can be viewed in its updated form on the judiciary website www.judiciary.gov.hk and that of the Hong Kong Legal Information Institute www.hklii.org, both of which are accessible by the general public free-of-charge.

Actions on the personal injuries list are designated with action numbers beginning with 'HCPI' (or 'DCPI' in the District Court).

In *I v L* [2005] 4 HKLRD 301 it was argued that some provisions of the personal injury practice direction depart from the requirements of the Rules of the High Court, and to that extent are ultra vires. The court acknowledged that the rules take precedence over a practice direction, but found no conflict in the particular case.

In *Wong Shui Lam v Hospital Authority* HCPI 151/2009 (Master Roy Yu; 31.12.2009) (para 37) indemnity costs were ordered against a defendant for 'unreasonable' and 'oppressive' conduct in failing to comply with the personal injuries list practice direction (PD 18.1).

### [72.2.5]   Interim payments in personal injury cases

Guidance on interim payments in personal injury cases is provided in a note dated 5 May 2003 from the judge in charge of the personal injuries list. This note was made known to solicitors by Law Society circular 03-286 (PA) which is available to members on the society's website. Its main points are as follows:

- An interim payment is on account of damages and is intended for the plaintiff, not for the lawyers. It is not a payment in respect of costs and is not subject to the Legal Aid Department's first charge.
- An interim payment should be remitted to the plaintiff without deduction or, where the plaintiff is under disability, paid into court.
- Solicitors acting for a plaintiff must notify the court of any interim payment received.
- An interim payment should not be held in a non-interest bearing account.

For interim payments generally see Order 29 part II. Note that the guidance in the above note as to informing the court of an interim payment appears to be contrary to Order 29 rule 15.

### [72.2.6]   Interest on general damages in personal injury cases

Guidance on when interest runs on general damages claimed in a personal injury action was issued by the judge in charge of the personal injuries list in a note dated 15 August 2003. The text of the note is included in Law Society circular 03-286 (PA) which is available to members on the society's website. Its main points are as follows:

- Strict entitlement to such interest in the absence of agreement runs only from the date of service of the writ.
- Plaintiffs' solicitors should take steps to protect the client's position in regard to interest, particularly where the quantification of a claim is a drawn out affair, and the amount of interest would be significant.
- Where there is delay in issue and service of a writ, such as where discussions are underway, the plaintiff can be protected by agreement as to the date from which interest will run.
- If such agreement cannot be reached, a writ should be issued and served on a protective basis.
- Where such a protective writ has been issued the parties may write to the court asking for the check-list review not to be 'triggered' for 2 or 3 months in order to enable the negotiations to continue. This should preferably be done by a joint letter to the court at the same time as the writ is issued. The plaintiff's solicitors

will be expected to notify the court if such negotiations break down so that the progress provided for by the practice direction can be restored.

• The court is unlikely to be concerned with an examination of a dispute over interest, in considering whether the parties have observed the spirit of the practice direction, save in the most exceptional of circumstances.

### [72.2.7]    The constitutional and administrative law list

The constitutional and administrative law list came into being in 1998, replacing the previous administrative law list. Practice direction 26.1 provides that the following types of cases 'shall' be assigned to the list:

(a)    applications for judicial review;

(b)    applications for habeas corpus;

(c)    election petitions;

(d)    appeals from decisions of the Obscene Articles Tribunal; and

(e)    such other civil cases which raise an issue under the Basic Law of the HKSAR or the Hong Kong Bill of Rights Ordinance (Cap 383) for determination and which a judge of the Court of Fist Instance or a judge of the District Court certifies as suitable for transfer to the list.

Proceedings on the list are designated with action numbers beginning with the letters 'HCAL'. It is the responsibility of solicitors, not registry staff, to ensure that papers filed in court commencing proceedings which come within the list are marked with the HCAL designation so that they will be placed on the list: *Chiang Lai Wan v Tang Siu Tong & Anor* [1998] 3 HKC 613, 632.

Detailed guidance on matters of procedure to be followed in relation to proceedings on the list is given in the form of directions from the judge in charge of the list, which are set out in a separate practice direction, numbered SL3. Revisions to that practice direction took effect in 2009 when the civil justice reforms came into force. Its updated text, and that of practice direction 26.1 which establishes the list, can be viewed on the judiciary website www.judiciary.gov.hk and that of the Hong Kong Legal Information Institute www.hklii.org, both of which are accessible by the general public free-of-charge.

### [72.2.8]    The Admiralty list

An Admiralty list exists and is governed by practice direction 1, a revision of which came into force in 2009 along with the civil justice reforms. According to the practice direction, the function of the Admiralty list is 'to facilitate the disposal of Admiralty actions (whether *in rem* or *in personam*)'. Proceedings within the list are designated with action numbers beginning 'HCAJ'. The practice direction can be viewed on the judiciary website www.judiciary.gov.hk and that of the Hong Kong Legal Information Institute www.hklii.org, both of which are accessible by the general public free-of-charge.

With regard to admiralty actions generally, see Order 75 and the commentary thereunder.

### [72.2.9]    Probate actions

No formal list has been established for probate actions, but they are given their own distinction actions numbers beginning with the letters 'HCAP', and they are subject to particular procedures. See generally Order 76, which deals with contentious probate proceedings, and see also the Non-contentious Probate Rules (subsidiary legislation under Cap 10) which, despite their name, govern some aspects of procedure in relation to contentious probate matters. Practice direction 20.2 is also relevant – it provides that leave is required to issue a writ commencing a probate action.

### [72.2.10] Insolvency and companies matters
No formal list has been established by practice direction for insolvency and companies matters. However they are normally dealt with by the 'companies court'. Insolvency matters of various types are given distinctive action numbers, for example 'HCB' for bankruptcy proceedings and 'HCCW' for winding-up. See the list of case types in the commentary under Order 1 rule 9. There is no special designation for other types of company proceedings.

In 2009 a practice direction was issued to deal with case management of bankruptcy and winding-up petitions, as well as petitions presented under section 168A of the Companies Ordinance (Cap 32). Also relevant is part (4) of practice direction 11.1, as amended with effect from 1 November 2009, which deals with urgent applications to the companies judge. Both practice directions can be viewed on the judiciary website, or that of the Hong Kong Legal Information Institute.

### [72.2.11] Numbering
There is no rule 3 in Order 72. The rule of the same number in the former English RSC dealt with district registries, which do not exist in Hong Kong.

**4.   Entry of action in particular list when action begun** (O. 72 r. 4)

**(1)   Before a writ or originating summons by which particular proceedings are to be begun is issued out of the Registry, it may be marked in the top left hand corner with words identifying the relevant list, and on the issue of a writ or summons so marked the action begun thereby shall be entered in that list.**

**(2)   If the plaintiff intends to issue the writ or originating summons by which particular proceedings are to be begun out of the Registry and to mark it in accordance with paragraph (1), and the writ or the originating summons, as the case may be, is to be served out of the jurisdiction, an application for leave to issue the writ or summons and to serve the writ or the summons out of the jurisdiction may be made to the judge.**

**(3)   The affidavit in support of an application made to the judge by virtue of paragraph (2) must, in addition to the matters required by Order 11, rule 4(1), to be stated, state that the plaintiff intends to mark the writ or originating summons in accordance with paragraph (1) of this rule.**

**(4)   If the judge hearing an application made to him by virtue of paragraph (2) is of opinion that the action in question should not be entered in the list in question, he may adjourn the application to be heard by the Registrar.**

**5.   Transfer of action to particular list after action begun** (O. 72 r. 5)

**(1)   At any stage of the proceedings in any action any party thereto may apply by summons to the judge to transfer the action to a particular list.**

**(3)**   **If, at any stage of the proceedings in any action, it appears to the Court that the action may be one suitable for trial in a particular list and any party wishes the action to be transferred to that list, then the Court may adjourn any hearing so that it can proceed before the judge and be treated by him as a summons to transfer the action to that list.**

## NOTES

**[72.5.1]**   **Order for transfer of proceedings to a specialist list**

Order 72 rule 5 provides that any party may apply for an order that an action be transferred to one of the specialist lists established under rule 2. The application must be made by summons to 'the judge', which by rule 2(2) means the judge in charge of the particular list. In *Terkildsen & Anor v Barber Asia Ltd & Ors* HCA 1963/2003 (Saunders J; 30.10.2009) (para 29, 30) it was held that other judges do not have jurisdiction. The Commercial List practice direction (PD SL1.1) provides (para 6) that the powers of the judge in charge of the list shall, when necessary, be exercised by another judge. Sensible as that provision is, it cannot take precedence over these rules, which have legislative effect. In *K Master & Co Ltd v Eagle Star Insurance Co Ltd* [1968] HKLR 215 it was held that the power under rule 5 may be exercised in spite of the fact that a party objects to the proposed transfer. Note that the practice directions governing some of the specialist lists contain their own provisions with regard to transfer. This rule takes precedence over any such practice direction: *K Master & Co Ltd* (above). Note also that in some cases those practice directions contemplate an order for transfer being made without any party having applied for such an order: see for example the construction and arbitration list practice direction which now provides that the court may make such an order of its own motion.

**6.**   **Removal of action from particular list** (O. 72 r. 6)

    **(1)**   **The judge may, of his own motion or on the application of any party, order an action in a particular list to be removed from that list.**

    **(2)**   **Where an action is in a particular list by virtue of rule 4, an application by a defendant or third party for an order under this rule must be made within 7 days after giving notice of intention to defend.**

**7.**   **Pleadings in particular proceedings** (O. 72 r. 7)

    **(1)**   **The pleadings in an action in a particular list may be in the form of points of claim, or of defence, counterclaim, defence to counterclaim or reply, as the case may be, and must be as brief as possible.**

    **(2)**   **Without prejudice to Order 18, rule 12(1), no particulars shall be applied for or ordered in an action in the particular list designated the commercial list except such particulars as are necessary to enable the party applying to be informed of the case he has to meet or as are for some other reason necessary to secure the just, expeditious and economical disposal of any question at issue in the proceedings.**

    **(3)**   **The foregoing provisions are without prejudice to the power of the judge to order that an action in a particular list shall be tried without pleadings or further pleadings, as the case may be.**

**NOTES**

**[72.7.1]    Scope of Rule 7**
According to Order 72 rule 7(1), the pleadings in an action in a particular list may be in the form of points of claim, or of defence, counterclaim, defence to counterclaim or reply, as the case may be, and must be as brief as possible. Strong criticism was made of the drafting of the points of claim in *Advance Finance Ltd (in liquidation) v Pang Sze Mui, Loretta & Ors* [1986] HKLR 523,537 G-H Huggins VP said:

> I agree with Fuad JA that this was not an appropriate case to be entered in the Commercial List. If it had been, it is impossible to understand how anyone could believe that the Points of Claim were as brief as possible.

**8.    Directions in particular proceedings** (O. 72 r. 8)
   **(1)    Notwithstanding anything in Order 25, rule 1(1B)(b), any party to particular proceedings may take out a case management summons before the pleadings are deemed to be closed. (L.N. 152 of 2008)**
   **(2)    Where an application is made to transfer an action to a particular list, Order 25, rules 2 to 7, shall, with the omission of so much of rule 7(1) as requires the parties to serve a notice specifying the orders and directions which they desire and with any other necessary modifications, apply as if the application were a case management summons. (L.N. 152 of 2008)**

**9.    (Repealed 13 of 1995 s 20)**

**NOTES**

**[72.9.1]    Repeal of Order 72 rule 9 – abolition of special juries**
Order 72 rule 9 was repealed by the Administration of Justice (Miscellaneous Provisions) Ordinance (13 of 1995). It previously made provision for trial by special jury. Special juries were abolished by the same amending Ordinance, which repealed provisions of the Jury Ordinance (Cap 3). Special juries were not in practice used anyway. The equivalent rule in England was repealed in 1971.
   For trial by common jury in civil cases, see the commentary under Order 33 rule 5.

**10. Production of certain documents in marine insurance actions** (O. 72 r. 10)
   **(1)    Where in an action in a particular list relating to a marine insurance policy an application for an order under Order 24, rule 3, is made by the insurer, then, without prejudice to its powers under that rule, the Court, if satisfied that the circumstances of the case are such that it is necessary or expedient to do so, may make an order, either in Form No. 94 in Appendix A or in such other form as it thinks fit, for the production of such documents as are therein specified or described.**
   **(2)    An order under this rule may be made on such terms, if any, as to staying proceedings in the action or otherwise, as the Court thinks fit.**
   **(3)    In this rule "the Court" means the judge.**

                                                                    **(Enacted 1988)**

**NOTES**

**[72.10.1]   Discovery in marine insurance actions**
In *K Master & Co Ltd v Eagle Star Insurance Ltd* [1968] HKLR 215, discovery of documents was granted under Order 72 rule 10. The court stated that it has additional inherent jurisdiction to order the fullest discovery of documents in marine insurance actions.

## ORDER 73

### ARBITRATION PROCEEDINGS

**2.   Matters for a judge in court** (O. 73 r. 2)

(1)   Subject to section 2D of the Arbitration Ordinance (Cap 341), every application or request to the Court—

> (a)   to remit an award under section 24 of that Ordinance (Cap 341), or
>
> (b)   to remove an arbitrator or umpire under section 25(1) of that Ordinance, or
>
> (c)   to set aside an award under section 25(2) of that Ordinance, or
>
> (HK)(d)   for leave to appeal under section 23(2) of that Ordinance, or
>
> (e)   to determine, under section 23A(l) of that Ordinance, any question of law arising in the course of a reference, or
>
> (HK)(f)   to make an order under section 2GE of that Ordinance, or (L.N. 152 of 2008)
>
> (HK)(g)   to decide, under article 13(3) of the Fifth Schedule to that Ordinance, on a challenge to an arbitrator, or (L.N. 363 of 1990)
>
> (HK)(h)   to decide, under article 14(1) of the Fifth Schedule to that Ordinance, on the termination of an arbitrator's mandate, or (L.N. 363 of 1990)
>
> (HK)(i)   to set aside an arbitral award under article 34 of the Fifth Schedule to that Ordinance, (L.N. 363 of 1990)

may be made by originating summons in Form No. 10 in Appendix A to a single judge in court. (L.N. 373 of 1990) (L.N. 152 of 2008)

(2)   Any appeal to the Court of First Instance under section 23(2) of the Arbitration Ordinance (Cap 341) may be made by originating summons in Form No. 10 in Appendix A to a single judge in court which may be included in the originating summons for leave to appeal, where leave is required. (L.N. 152 of 2008)

(3)   An application for a declaration that an award made by an arbitrator or umpire is not binding on a party to the award on the ground that it was made without jurisdiction may be made by originating summons in Form No. 10 in Appendix A to a single judge in court. (L.N. 152 of 2008)

## NOTES

### [73.2.1]   Numbering

There is no rule 1 in Order 73.

### [73.2.2]   Order 73 – comparison with English rules

Order 73 is based on the Order of the same number in the English Rules of the Supreme Court as they existed prior to amendments which took effect in January 1997. However it is not an exact copy. For example, a number of the paragraphs under rule 2(1) as well as rules 11 to 18 are unique to Hong Kong.

The Arbitration Act 1996 (in force 31.01.1997) introduced extensive reforms in England. The amendments applied with prospective effect only leaving the prior law intact for arbitrations already underway. At the same time the English Order 73 was replaced by a wholly new Order in three parts.

The English Order 73 was replaced with CPR Part 62 in 2002 which retains the 3-part layout, with Part II dealing with arbitrations governed by the law as it existed prior to the Arbitration Act 1996 coming into force.

The effect of the amendments in England is such that care must be taken when seeking guidance from authorities and secondary sources from that jurisdiction when considering points of procedure when arbitration matters come before the Hong Kong court.

### [73.2.3]   Order 73 updated

The Arbitration Ordinance (Cap 341) was extensively amended in 1996 and again in 2000 (Ordinances 75 of 1996 and 2 of 2000). Both amending Ordinances contained transitional provisions to preserve the prior law for arbitrations already underway. Notwithstanding those amendments, Order 73 was left largely unchanged. As a result there were some anomalies including a reference to a section of the Ordinance which had been repealed (Order 73 rule 2(1)(f) continued to refer to section 29A of the Ordinance for more than a decade after that section was repealed in 1996). In *Ng Fung Hong Ltd v ABC* [1998] 1 HKC 213, 216 C–D it was said that Order 73 was 'out of date'. The Order was amended as part of the civil justice reforms taking effect in 2009, including correction of the anomalies which had been pointed out. The Order should no longer be out of date.

### [73.2.4]   Distinction between different types of arbitrations

In construing the provisions of Order 73 it should be borne in mind that there are different types of arbitrations, and that the Arbitration Ordinance deals with them separately.

'International' arbitrations are those to which the UNCITRAL Model Law on Commercial Arbitration applies. See the definition of 'international arbitration agreement' in section 2(1) of the Ordinance and see article 1(3) of the Model Law. The text of the Model Law is set out in Schedule 5 to the Ordinance. It is defined in section 2(1) of the Ordinance to mean 'the Model Law on International Commercial Arbitration adopted by the United Nations Commission on International Trade Law on 21 June 1985'. So far as Hong Kong law is concerned, the UNCITRAL Model Law applies to international arbitration agreements by virtue of section 34C of the Arbitration Ordinance.

An arbitration agreement which does not come within the definition of 'international arbitration agreement' is 'domestic'. See the definition of 'domestic arbitration agreement' in section 2(1).

'Convention awards', are awards made in a place (other than China or any part thereof) which is a party to the Convention on the Recognition and Enforcement of Foreign Arbitral Awards adopted by the United Nations Conference on International Commercial Arbitration on 10 June 1958 ('the New York Convention'). See the definitions of 'Convention award' and 'the New York Convention' in section 2(1) of the Ordinance. The text of the New York Convention is set out in Schedule 3 to the Ordinance.

'Mainland awards', as defined by section 2(1) are those made pursuant to the Arbitration Law of the PRC.

The distinction between the different types of arbitration is important because Order 73 deals with matters arising from the court's jurisdiction over arbitrations as set out in the Ordinance, and that jurisdiction does not apply uniformly to all arbitration agreements. For example, part IA of the Ordinance applies to both domestic and international arbitration agreements (section 2AD), whereas part II will only extend to an international arbitration agreement if the agreement so provides or with consent (section 2M), and part IIA may or may not apply to either type of agreement depending on the circumstances (sections 34A and 34B). Part IIIA of the Ordinance applies to Mainland awards and part IV to Convention awards.

### [73.2.5]　Order 73 rule 2 – applications under the Arbitration Ordinance which must be made to a single judge in court

Order 73 rule 2 deals with the manner in which certain types of applications to the court under the provisions of the Arbitration Ordinance (Cap 341) and the UNCITRAL Model Law on Commercial Arbitration (which is Schedule 5 to the Ordinance) are to be made. It provides that the applications listed in the rule may be made by originating summons (in form No 10 which is the 'expedited' or 'short' form). The consequence is that the application would normally be heard by a judge in open court, pursuant to Order 28. The rule is expressly subject to section 2D of the Ordinance which provides that any party may apply for proceedings to be heard 'otherwise than in open court'. The types of application which come within the rule are:

*Rule 2(1)(a) –*　　applications under section 24 to remit an award – the court has power under section 24 of the Ordinance to remit any matter to an arbitrator for reconsideration.

*Rule 2(1)(b) –*　　applications under section 25(1) to remove an arbitrator or umpire – section 25(1) of the Ordinance empowers the court to remove an arbitrator or umpire for misconduct.

*Rule 2(1)(c) –*　　applications to set aside an award under section 25(2) - section 25(2) empowers the court to set aside an arbitration award on the ground of misconduct of the arbitrator or umpire, or where the arbitration or award was improperly procured.

*Rule 2(1)(d) –*　　applications under section 23(2) for leave to appeal – section 23(2) of the Ordinance provides that an appeal lies to the court on any question of law arising out of an arbitration award. Under subsection (3), such an appeal requires consent of all parties or leave of the court. Note that the English equivalent of rule 2(1)(d) was revoked in 1983. Note also that rule 2(1)(d) was previously in conflict with rule 3(2)(a), but that was repealed along with the civil justice reforms which took effect in 2009. See the commentary under Order 73 rule 3.

*Rule 2(1)(e) –*　　applications under section 23A(1) for the determination of any question of law arising in an arbitration – section 23A(1) of the Ordinance gives the court jurisdiction to determine any question of law arising in the course of a reference. Consent of the arbitrator or of all of the parties is required. The court is enjoined not to exercise this jurisdiction unless it is satisfied the determination might produce substantial costs savings and that the question of law is one which would likely result in a grant of leave to appeal: s 23A(2). As to what constitutes a question of law for the purpose of this provision, see *Unistress Building Construction Ltd v Humphrey's Estate (Forrestdale) Ltd* [1991] 1 HKC 519. There it was held that an issue whether or not particulars should be given was not a point of law.

*Rule 2(1)(f) –*   *applications under section 2GE of the Ordinance* – section 2GE of the Ordinance empowers the court (in the absence of an arbitral tribunal in existence) to dismiss a party's claim and prohibit it from commencing fresh proceedings where it has delayed unreasonably in prosecuting a claim subject to an arbitration agreement. Prior to 1996 a similar provision was contained in section 29A(2) of the Ordinance.

*Rule 2(1)(g) –*   *challenge to arbitrator* - article 13(3) of the UNCITRAL model law provides that a party who has unsuccessfully challenged the choice of an arbitrator may request that the court decide the challenge.

*Rule 2(1)(h) –*   *termination of arbitrator's mandate* – article 14(1) of the UNCITRAL model law provides for application to the court to determine any controversy as to whether an arbitrator's mandate has been terminated.

*Rule 2(1)(i) –*   *application to set aside arbitral award* – article 34 of the UNCITRAL model law provides for application to set aside an arbitral award within 3 months on the grounds set out in that article.

## [73.2.6]   Construction and arbitration list

All applications under the Arbitration Ordinance or this Order should be brought on the Construction and Arbitration list. See Order 73 rule 6 and the commentary thereunder.

## [73.2.7]   Appeal against arbitral award

As noted above, an appeal under section 23(2) of the Arbitration Ordinance requires consent of all parties or leave of the court. The court's appellate jurisdiction is limited to questions of law.

Guidance as to applications for leave is laid down in practice direction 6.1 which may be viewed on the judiciary's website. Briefly, as amended in 2009, it provides as follows:

(1)   The application shall contain a succinct statement of each alleged error of law, with reference to the relevant part of the award and reasons. A copy of the award and reasons and any documents expressly incorporated therein, shall accompany the application.

(2)   A respondent who wishes to uphold the award on grounds other than those expressed in it should provide a succinct statement of such grounds in numbered paragraphs no later than 7 days before the application for leave is to be heard, with reference to the appropriate parts of the award and reasons.

(3)    Affidavit evidence is required in support of, and in response to, any contention of a question of law concerning a term of contract or an event which is not a one-off clause or event.

Once consent or leave to appeal is obtained, Order 73 rule 2(2) provides that the appeal may be made by originating summons to a single judge. It is there provided that the originating summons may be included in the application for leave to appeal. In *Carl Int'l (HK) Ltd v Ernest Komrowski & Co* [1996] 2 HKC 490, 494B-C the court recommended that this single document procedure be used to avoid trouble and expense.

### [73.2.8]    Criteria for grant of leave to appeal

In considering an application for leave to appeal under section 23 of the Arbitration Ordinance the Hong Kong courts apply the principles laid down in *The Nema* [1982] AC 724. See *Lee Chang Yung Chemical Industry Corp v PT Dover Chemical Co* [1990] 1 HKC 132; [1990] 2 HKLR 257 and *Ha Hau Kwan Fong Mary v IO of Golden Plaza* HCCT 9/2002 (Ma J; 28.05.2002). In the latter case it was said the test is 'stringent'. Where parties have chosen arbitration the court should interfere as little as possible: *Downer & Co Ltd v Airport Authority* [2000] 1 HKLRD 556, 560 (CA). The presumption of finality of an arbitral award is stronger where a one-off event or clause is involved. In the *Ha Hau Kwan Fong Mary* case it was said (at para 22):

> Where a one-off event or clause is involved, the applicant for leave must demonstrate quickly and easily that the arbitrator was plainly or obviously wrong. Where, on the other hand, the event or clause is not one off or that the case has important repercussions, all that needs to be demonstrated is that the arbitrator was arguably wrong or that the point on appeal is capable of serious argument.

See also *Swire Properties Ltd v SJ* [2003] 3 HKC 347 (CFA); *Mak's Construction Co Ltd v Sun Fook Kong (Civil) Ltd* HCCT 20/2002 (Ma J; 27.06.2002), (para 17–18) and *Incorporated Owners of Casio Mansion v Leung Yau Building Ltd* HCCT 55/2006 (Deputy Judge Poon; 12.10.2006).

The court's appellate jurisdiction over arbitration awards is limited to questions of law, not including errors of law on the face of the award: sections 23(1) & (2). As to when findings of fact might be so perverse as to give rise to a question of law, see *Hong Kong Institute of Education v Aoki Corp (No 2)* [2004] 2 HKC 397, 426B *et seq*; [2004] 2 HKLRD 760. In *Penta-Ocean Construction Co Ltd v CWF Piling & Civil Eng'g Co Ltd* HCCT 10/2007 (A Cheung J; 15.06.2007) the court found that an arbitrator had made a mistake of law by adopting the wrong standard of proof.

For a detailed discussion of this topic, see McInnis, *Hong Kong Construction Law*, (LexisNexis), division XVIII.

### [73.2.9]    Amendment of grounds of application for leave to appeal

An application for leave to appeal an arbitral award must be brought within 30 days. See Order 73 rule 5 and the commentary thereunder. It has been held that an application to vary or add to the grounds on which leave is sought must, if the 30-day period has expired, include an application for leave to appeal out of time. The application must be supported by an affidavit giving the reasons for the inability to comply with the stipulated time limit. See *Woon Lee Construction Co Ltd v Holyrood Ltd* HCCT 43/2010 (Saunders J; 26.10.2010) (para 10).

**[73.2.10]   Application for declaration**

Order 73 rule 2(3) provides that an application for a declaration that an arbitral award is not binding on a party for want of jurisdiction may be made by originating summons to a single judge.

Applications for such declarations are not mentioned in the Arbitration Ordinance. It appears that the source of jurisdiction is the court's general power to grant declaratory relief, as to which see Order 15 rule 16 and the commentary thereunder.

On such an application the court may consider the question of jurisdiction *de novo* - it may reconsider the arguments and receive new evidence: *Carrier HK Ltd v Dickson Construction Co Ltd* [2005] 4 HKC 142 (para 3). Note that the judgment in *Carrier* refers to rule 3(2) whereas rule 2(3) appears to be the correct rule.

**3.   Matters for judge in chambers or master** (O. 73 r. 3)

**(1)   Subject to the foregoing provisions of this Order and the provisions of this rule, the jurisdiction of the Court of First Instance or a judge thereof under the Arbitration Ordinance (Cap 341), may be exercised by a judge in chambers or a master.**

**(2)   Any application under section 23(5) or (7) of the Arbitration Ordinance (Cap 341) (including any application for leave) must be made to a judge in chambers. (L.N. 152 of 2008)**

**(3)   Any application to which this rule applies may, where an action is pending, be made by summons in the action, and in any other case may be made by an originating summons in Form No. 10 in Appendix A. (L.N. 152 of 2008)**

**(4)   Where an application is made under section 23(5) of the Arbitration Ordinance (Cap 341) (including any application for leave) the summons must be served on the arbitrator or umpire and on any other party to the reference.**

---

**NOTES**

**[73.3.1]   Scope of Order 73 rule 3**

Order 73 rule 3(1) provides that applications to the court under the Arbitration Ordinance may generally be dealt with by a judge in chambers or a master. However this must be read subject to rule 3(2) which specifies that certain applications under section 23 of the Ordinance must be made to a judge in chambers.

Rule 3(3) prescribes that applications to the court should be made by summons in the action, or, if no action is pending, by originating summons.

**[73.3.2]   Applications for leave to appeal**

Order 73 rule 3(2) provides that applications under section 23(5) and (7) of the Arbitration Ordinance (which provide for application to the court for an order that an arbitrator give sufficient reasons, and for leave to appeal from the Court of First Instance to the Court of Appeal) shall be made to a judge in chambers. Rule 3(2) expressly extends to applications for leave to appeal in relation to such relief, meaning such applications for leave should also be made to a judge in chambers. See also rule 6A.

Previously rule 3(2) also expressly extended to applications for leave to appeal under section 23(2) of the Ordinance (appeal on a question of law arising out of an arbitral agreement), purporting to require that such applications be made to a judge in chambers. To that extent it was in conflict with rule 2(1)(d) which provides that such applications for leave shall be made to a judge in open court. The conflict was the subject of judicial comment in *Carl Int'l (HK) Ltd v Ernst Kamrowski & Co* [1996] 2 HKC 490, 492-4; *China Link Construction Co Ltd v China Insurance Co Ltd* [2002] 1 HKLRD 844 and *Ha Hau Kwan Fong Mary v IO of Golden Plaza* HCCT 9/2002 (Ma J; 28.05.2002) (paras 34-39). The position was clarified with the amendment to rule 3 as part of the civil justice reforms taking effect in 2009: such applications should be made to a judge in open court pursuant to rule 2(1)(d).

### [73.3.3]  Costs of unsuccessful application for leave to appeal

In *A v R* [2010] 3 HKC 67 the court warned that henceforth, in the absence of special circumstances, when an order for enforcement of an arbitral award has been unsuccessfully challenged, the court would consider awarding costs against the losing party on an indemnity basis. Reyes J said that it should be expected that arbitration awards would be enforced as a matter of course, and that applications to appeal against or set aside an award, or for an order refusing enforcement, should be 'exceptional events'. In *Wing Hong Construction Ltd v Tin Wo Eng'g Co Ltd* HCCT 13/2010 (Saunders J; 03.06.2010) (para 26) *A v R* was followed. The court distinguished a decision of the Court of Appeal and concluded that ' as a matter of principle in the special circumstances of arbitration proceedings, where an applicant fails to successfully establish a basis to challenge an award, the proper award of costs will usually be an award of indemnity costs'. See also *Hung Wan Construction Co Ltd v HK Housing Authority* HCCT 21/2010 (Saunders J; 29.07.2010).

### [73.3.4]  Application for stay of proceedings in favour of arbitration

Where a party makes a claim by ordinary action in breach of an agreement to refer disputes to arbitration, the court has power to stay the action. See section 6 of the Arbitration Ordinance and art 8 of the UNCITRAL Model Law. An application for such a stay is not governed by Order 73, but should be brought by summons in the action pursuant to Order 12 rule 8. See the commentary under that rule.

### [73.3.5]  Dismissal for want of prosecution

A power similar to that of the court to dismiss for want of prosecution is given to arbitrators by section 2GE of the Arbitration Ordinance.

Where an arbitration award comes before the court, such as on appeal on a point of law, there is also jurisdiction to dismiss for want of prosecution. See *China Link Construction Co Ltd v China Insurance Co Ltd* [2002] 1 HKLRD 844. There it was held that it is not necessary to show prejudice as would be required in such an application in relation to an action commenced by writ (see *Birkett v James* [1978] AC 297 and the other authorities referred to in the commentary under Order 34 rule 2). In *China Link* (at 854) it was said:

> while inexcusable delay is still obviously to be shown, there is no need for the applicant seeking to strike out for want of prosecution to demonstrate that prejudice has been caused to him consequent upon the delay. This arises from the nature of arbitrations and the importance of speed...

I do not wish to lay down guidelines on how the discretion is to be exercised, but obviously the reasons for the delay and the period of delay itself are relevant. While the existence of prejudice is not a requisite factor to be shown in such applications, nevertheless the existence of prejudice resulting from delay may of course be relevant.

### [73.3.6] Other relief of an interlocutory nature which may be granted by the court in respect of an arbitration

Section 2GC(1) of the Arbitration Ordinance empowers the court to make a wide range of orders of an interlocutory nature in relation to an arbitration. These include orders for inspection or preservation of property and interim injunctions.

### [73.3.7] Restriction on reporting proceedings in chambers

Section 2E of the Arbitration Ordinance imposes restrictions on the publication of information relating to arbitration proceedings heard otherwise than in open court. The procedure laid down by practice direction 25.1 whereby most chambers hearings are open to the public does not apply.

### [73.3.8] Applications which may be made to a master

Order 73 rule 3(1) specifically authorises applications under the Arbitration Ordinance to be made to a master. The jurisdiction of the master goes no further than as specifically conferred in legislation such as these rules: *American Express Int'l Inc v Ng Pak Sang* [1987] 1 HKC 522, 524-5, referring to *Firman v Ellis* [1978] QB 886, 909.

The broad jurisdiction conferred on masters by the rule is cut down by rule 3(2) which provides that specified types of application must be made to a judge.

The provisions of this rule as to a master's jurisdiction should be read together with practice direction SL2 which provides that applications in proceedings in the Construction and Arbitration List should be made to a judge, save that applications of the following type should be made to a master unless otherwise ordered by a judge:

(a) applications for entry of default judgment;
(b) applications concerning enforcement of judgments; and
(c) assessments of damages.

Practice direction 6.1 provides (in para 10) that any application relating to an arbitration should normally be listed to be heard by the judge in charge of the Construction and Arbitration List, or another designated judge. It is expressly stated that this extends to actions which are not on the List. In *Rondabosh Int'l Ltd v China Ping An Insurance (HK) Co Ltd* HCA 581/2009 (Reyes J; 29.12.2009) (para 23) practitioners were reminded to follow PD 6.1 in this regard, and it was said that only in exceptional cases would applications relating to arbitration be entertained by a master.

Where a case in the Construction and Arbitration List reaches the Court of Appeal, interlocutory applications should be made to a judge of that Court pursuant to Order 59 rule 14.

### [73.3.9] Hearing of application under Arbitration Ordinance

An originating summons for leave to appeal an arbitral award, or to set aside an *ex parte* order for enforcement of an award, will normally be listed for an initial

30-minute hearing. This initial hearing 'should not be treated by parties as a simple call-over for directions'. The court may scrutinise the application and if no viable case is disclosed, 'then in the interests of saving time and cost the court can dispose of the relevant summons even in an initial 30 minute hearing': *G v M* HCCT 36/2009 (Reyes J; 14.09.2009) (para 6).

**4. Application for interim injunction under section 2GC(1) of Arbitration Ordinance** (O. 73 r. 4)

**(1)    An application for an interim injunction or any other interim measure under section 2GC(1) of the Arbitration Ordinance (Cap 341) in relation to an arbitration proceeding (whether in Hong Kong or in a place outside Hong Kong) must be made by originating summons in Form No. 10 in Appendix A.**

**(2)    Where the application is in relation to an arbitration proceeding outside Hong Kong, rules 1, 2, 3, 4, 7(1), 7A and 8 of Order 29 apply with any necessary modifications to the application as they apply to an application for interlocutory relief in an action or proceeding in the High Court.**

**(3)    Upon hearing of the originating summons, the Court may direct that all or part of the hearing be conducted in open court.**

**(L.N. 152 of 2008)**

---

**NOTES**

**[73.4.1]    Origin and scope of Order 73 rule 4**

Order 73 rule 4 was added to the rules as part of the civil justice reform, taking effect in 2009. It regulates the procedure for applications under section 2GC of the Arbitration Ordinance (Cap 341) for interim relief in relation to arbitral proceedings. The rule provides that such an application is to be commenced by originating summons in form No 10, which is the expedited form. Any affidavit evidence relied upon must be filed and served in accordance with Order 28 rule 1A.

**[73.4.2]    Order 29 applies to Order 73 rule 4 applications**

Order 73 rule 4 expressly provides that on an application to the court for interim relief in relation to arbitration proceedings outside Hong Kong, most of the provisions of Order 29 with regard to interim relief apply. They include rule 1 (interim injunctions), rule 2 (detention and preservation of property), rule 3 (taking of samples), rule 4 (sale of perishable property) and rule 7A (inspection of property). See the commentary under Order 29 as to the circumstances in which such relief will be granted. So far as arbitration proceedings inside Hong Kong are concerned, see section 2GC of the Arbitration Ordinance which gives similar powers to the court.

**[73.4.3]    Application for *Mareva* injunction in aid of arbitration proceedings outside Hong Kong**

As mentioned above, Order 73 rule 4 regulates the procedure for applications under section 2GC of the Arbitration Ordinance. That section was amended by the Civil Justice (Miscellaneous Amendments) Ordinance (No 3 of 2008), in force from 2009, so as to extend the court's power to grant interim relief in relation to arbitration proceedings to such proceedings which have been or will be commenced in a place outside Hong Kong. In this regard it implements recommendations 45, 46 and 47 in the final report of the Chief Justice's working party on civil justice reform, which concern the grant of interim relief in aid of court proceedings and arbitrations outside Hong Kong.

The working party had particularly in mind the desirability of the Hong Kong court's power to grant *Mareva* injunctions being exercised in aid of court proceedings and arbitrations in other jurisdictions. The intention was to reverse the effect of *Mercedes Benz AG v Leiduck* [1996] 1 AC 284 where the Privy Council, on appeal from Hong Kong, held that there was no jurisdiction to grant a *Mareva* injunction in Hong Kong in support of litigation in another jurisdiction. See the discussion of the working party's report in the commentary under Order 29 rule 8A concerning the court's power to grant interim relief in relation to overseas court proceedings. As stated there, the position in Hong Kong would now appear to be as the House of Lords expressed it to be in England in *Channel Tunnel Group Ltd v Balfour Beatty Construction Ltd* [1993] AC 334, that although an interim injunction is incidental to an attempt to enforce substantive rights, and cannot exist in isolation, it is no longer necessary that it be ancillary to a claim for relief to be granted within the jurisdiction. The circumstances in which the court will exercise this power in relation to arbitrations outside Hong Kong will be substantially similar to those in relation to court proceedings elsewhere. For guidance on the exercise of the court's discretion, see the extensive commentary under Order 29 rule 8A.

The court's power to grant a *Mareva* injunction or other interim relief in aid of arbitration proceedings in another jurisdiction may only be exercised if the arbitration proceedings are capable of giving rise to an arbitral award which is enforceable in Hong Kong under the Arbitration Ordinance or any other Ordinance: Arbitration Ordinance, s 2GC(1A). Thus in *Prema Birkdale Horticulture (Macau) Ltd v Venetian Orient Ltd* [2009] 5 HKC 485, [2009] 5 HKLRD 89 the court was able to entertain an application for a *Mareva* injunction in aid of an arbitration in Macau, both Hong Kong and Macau being parties to the New York Convention. In that case it was said (para 8) that a court exercising this new jurisdiction must still abide by the general principles governing the grant of interim injunctions and other interim relief. The application was refused.

In *Hornor Resources (Int'l) Co Ltd v Savvy Resources Ltd* [2010] 4 HKC 50 a *Mareva* injunction which had been granted in Hong Kong proceedings was continued after those proceedings were stayed because of an arbitration clause and an exclusive jurisdiction clause. In considering continuation of the injunction the court considered the usual factors on which a *Mareva* injunction will be granted.

**[73.4.4] Service out of the jurisdiction**
On an application under Order 73 rule 4 for interim relief in relation to arbitration proceedings outside Hong Kong, it will often be necessary to seek leave to serve a party out of the jurisdiction. Specific power for the court to permit such service is granted by Order 73 rule 7(1B).

5. **Time limits and other special provisions as to appeals and applications under the Arbitration Ordinance** (O. 73 r. 5)
   (1) **An application to the Court—**
       (a) **to remit an award under section 24 of the Arbitration Ordinance (Cap 341), or**

    **(b)**  **to set aside an award under section 25(2) of that Ordinance or otherwise, or**

    **(c)**  **to direct an arbitrator or umpire to state the reasons for an award under section 23(5) of that Ordinance,**

**must be made, and the summons must be served, within 30 days after the award has been made and published to the parties. (L.N. 152 of 2008)**

    **(2)**  **In the case of an appeal to the Court under section 23(2) of the Arbitration Ordinance (Cap 341), the summons must be served, and the appeal entered, within 30 days after the award has been made and published to the parties:**

    **Provided that, where reasons material to the appeal are given on a date subsequent to the publication of the award, the period of 30 days shall run from the date on which the reasons are given. (L.N. 152 of 2008)**

    **(3)**  **An application, under section 23A(1) of the Arbitration Ordinance (Cap 341), to determine any question of law arising in the course of a reference, must be made within 30 days after the arbitrator or umpire has consented to the application being made, or the other parties have so consented. (L.N. 152 of 2008)**

    **(4)**  **For the purpose of paragraph (3) the consent must be given in writing.**

    **(5)**  **In the case of every appeal or application to which this rule applies, the summons must state the grounds of appeal or application and, where the appeal or application is founded on evidence by affidavit, or is made with the consent of the arbitrator or umpire or of the other parties, a copy of every affidavit intended to be used, or as the case may be, of every consent given in writing, must be served with that summons. (L.N. 152 of 2008)**

---

**NOTES**

**[73.5.1]    Scope of Order 73 rule 5**
Order 73 rule 5 sets down the time limits for making various types of application to the court under the Arbitration Ordinance and goes on, in rule 5(5), to require that the grounds relied upon must be stated in the document by which the originating application to the court is made.

**[73.5.2]    Time limit for appeals and applications under Arbitration Ordinance**
Order 73 rule 5 prescribes a time limit of 30 days for various applications to the court in relation to arbitration awards. They are applications to remit an award under section 24 of the Arbitration Ordinance, applications under s 25(2) to set aside an award, applications under s 23(5) to direct the statement of reasons for an award and appeals under section 23(2). The rule was amended with effect from 2009 so as to enlarge the time from 21 days to 30 days. The application must be made, and the summons served, within the 30 day period.

    Time runs from the date on which the award is 'made and published to the parties'. In the case of an appeal against an arbitral award, time runs from the date reasons for the award are given, if that be subsequent to the publication of the award: see the proviso to rule 5(2).

An award may be 'made and published to the parties' even though the arbitrator insists on payment before releasing it. See *Kwan Lee Construction Co Ltd v Elevator Parts Eng'g Co Ltd* [1997] 1 HKC 97, 108F-109G (CA) where it was held that an award was 'made and published' on the day the arbitrator informed the parties it could be obtained in writing upon payment of outstanding fees of $137,550. The court followed *The Archipelagos* [1979] 2 Lloyd's Rep 289, 292 where it was held that time runs whether the payment demanded is reasonable or not. If a party considers the amount demanded unreasonable, the procedure under section 21 of the Ordinance may be followed. It is there provided that the court may order release of the award on payment into court of the amount demanded, and that the arbitrator's charges be taxed. Note that under section 2GK of the Ordinance the parties are jointly and severally liable to pay the tribunal's fees and expenses and any agreement between the parties to the contrary is only effective as between themselves.

In the case of an appeal against an arbitral award, the time prescribed by rule 5(2) is for the appeal to be 'entered'. That suggests the notice of appeal must be served and the appeal set down within the 30-day period. Such appeals require leave, but no time limit is specified for applying for leave. Thus, as a matter of practice, the court treats the 30-day period as applying to the leave application, and encourages parties to use the procedure in rule 2(2) whereby the notice of appeal and the application for leave to appeal may be included in a single document. See *Carl Int'l (HK) Ltd v Ernest Komrowski & Co* [1996] 2 HKC 490, 494-5, referring to *Mebro Oil SA v Gatoil Int'l Inc* [1985] 2 Lloyd's Rep 234. In the *Carl Int'l* case the court suggested that rule 5(2) be amended to reflect this practice. In *China Link Construction Co Ltd v China Insurance Co Ltd* [2002] 1 HKLRD 844, 877 the courted noted with regret that the suggested amendment had not yet been made.

### [73.5.3]   Extension of time

The court's general powers under Order 1B rule 1(2)(a) and Order 3 rule 5 to grant extensions of time apply to the time limits laid down in Order 73 rule 5.

Previously the court took the view that the time was 'extremely short', and that it would be inclined to be lenient on an application for extension of time where a party has taken reasonable steps to protect its right: *Kwan Lee Construction Co Ltd v Elevator Parts Eng'g Co Ltd* [1997] 1 HKC 97, 109B (CA). However, a party who simply allowed time to slip, even though legally represented, might be refused an extension of time, as in *Wong Bik Ling Kitty v Crowe Insurance Group (HK) Ltd* [2000] 1 HKC 23 (CA). When those cases were decided, the time limit was 21 days. It was increased to 30 days as part of the civil justice reforms implemented on 2 April 2009. After that amendment it was held, without referring to the earlier authority, that there has to be 'compelling and cogent reason' for the court to grant an extension: *G v M* HCCT 36/2009 (Reyes J; 14.09.2009). In that case the court dismissed a late summons when the applicant put forward no material on which the court could exercise its discretion to extend time.

On an application to extend the time for appealing an arbitral award under section 23(2) of the Ordinance, the merits of the proposed appeal may be considered. See *Kwan Lee Construction* (above), but note the dissenting judgment of Mayo JA on this point.

**[73.5.4]   Rule 5(5) – service of affidavit evidence**
Order 73 rule 5(5) requires that any affidavit evidence in support of an application under the rule must be served together with the summons by which the application is made. The is because the respondent is entitled to know the facts and matters relied on in support of the application at the earliest opportunity: *Free Form Construction Co Ltd v Shinryo (HK) Ltd* [2008] 3 HKC 415. In that case the court refused leave for an applicant to rely on a late affirmation, citing prejudice to the respondent.

**6.   Applications and appeals to be heard in a particular list** (O. 73 r. 6)
   **(1)   Any matter which is required, by rule 2 or 3, to be heard by a judge, shall be entered in a particular list unless the Judge in charge of such list otherwise directs.**
   **(2)   Nothing in the foregoing paragraph shall be construed as preventing the powers of the Judge in charge of a particular list from being exercised by any judge of the Court of First Instance.**

**NOTES**

**[73.6.1]   Construction and arbitration list**
Order 73 rule 6 requires that matters to be heard by a judge under the preceding provisions of the Order be entered in a particular list unless otherwise ordered. The relevant list is the Construction and Arbitration List which is governed by practice direction 6.1. See also the commentary on the particular lists under Order 72 rule 2.

**6A. Originating summons to be heard in chambers** (O. 73, r. 6A)
   **An originating summons referred to in rules 2, 3 and 5 may be heard in chambers if the judge, whether of his own motion or at the request of one or more of the parties, so decides. (L.N. 152 of 2008)**

**NOTES**

**[73.6A.1]   Power to hear originating summons in chambers**
Rule 6A, which was added to Order 73 with effect from 2009, provides that the court may direct that an originating summons under the preceding rules of the Order be heard in chambers. Thus the requirement in rule 2(1) for originating summonses to be heard before a judge in open court may be overridden by direction of the court. See also rule 3(2).

**7.   Service out of the jurisdiction of summons and order** (O. 73, r. 7)
**(HK)(1)   Subject to paragraphs (1A) and (1B), service out of the jurisdiction of —**
   **(a)   any originating summons under the Arbitration Ordinance (Cap 341), or**
   **(b)   any order made on such a summons,**
**is permissible with leave of the Court provided that the arbitration to which the summons or order relates is granted by Hong Kong law or has been, is being, or is to be held within the jurisdiction. (L.N. 152 of 2008)**

**(1A)** **Service out of the jurisdiction of an originating summons for leave to enforce an award is permissible with the leave of the Court whether or not the arbitration is governed by Hong Kong law.**

**(1B)** **Service out of the jurisdiction of an originating summons by which an application for an interim injunction or any other interim measure under section 2GC(1) of the Arbitration Ordinance (Cap 341) is made is permissible with the leave of the Court. (L.N. 152 of 2008)**

**(2)** **An application for the grant of leave under this rule must be supported by an affidavit stating the grounds on which the application is made and showing in what place or country the person to be served is, or probably may be found; and no such leave shall be granted unless it shall be made sufficiently to appear to the Court that the case is a proper one for service out of the jurisdiction under this rule.**

**(3)** **Order 11, rules 5, 6 and 8, shall apply in relation to any such summons or order as is referred to in paragraph (1) or (1B) as they apply in relation to a writ. (L.N. 152 of 2008)**

## NOTES

**[73.7.1] Scope of Order 73 rule 7**
Order 73 rule 7 provides for service of court process out of the jurisdiction in proceedings under the Arbitration Ordinance. The rule displaces, for such proceedings, the provisions of Order 11 which might otherwise apply. Order 11 rule 9 expressly excludes certain of the rules in that Order from application. The displacement is not complete – Order 73 rule 7(3) expressly applies rules 5, 6 and 8 of Order 11. The rule was amended with effect from 2009 so as to extend to applications for interim injunctions or other interim relief under section 2GC(1) of the Arbitration Ordinance (Cap 341). Such applications are brought by originating summons under Order 73 rule 4. See the commentary under that rule.

**[73.7.2] Leave to serve out of the jurisdiction**
Leave is generally required for service out of the jurisdiction of court documents relating to proceedings governed by Order 73. Rule 7 sets out 3 different factual scenarios in which leave may be granted:
(1) *Arbitrations 'granted' by Hong Kong law* – Rule 7(1) empowers the court to grant leave to serve out of the jurisdiction originating summonses and orders made thereon in relation to arbitrations 'granted' by Hong Kong law. The word 'granted' is probably an error, as the context (rule 7(1A) in particular) suggests that the intended criterion may be 'governed' by Hong Kong law.
(2) *Enforcement of arbitral award* – Rule 7(1A) provides for the grant of leave to serve outside Hong Kong an originating summons seeking leave to enforce an arbitral award. By its express terms the provision applies whether or not the award sought to be enforced arose from an arbitration governed by Hong Kong law. Although this rule expressly extends to any order made on such a summons (rule 7(1)(b)), rule 10(5) provides that leave to serve such an order out of the jurisdiction is not required.

(3)    *Application for interim relief* – Applications for an interlocutory injunction or other interim relief in aid of an arbitration outside Hong Kong (as to which see Order 73 rule 4 and the commentary thereunder) are the subject of rule 7(1B). Leave to serve an originating summons seeking such relief may be granted.

Each of the above scenarios is subject to rule 7(2), by which leave will not be granted unless it is 'made sufficiently to appear' to the court that 'the case is a proper one for service out of the jurisdiction'. This gives the court a discretion to refuse leave, or if leave has already been granted, to set it aside on grounds such as *forum non conveniens*. See Order 11 rule 4(2) (where the same wording appears) and the commentary thereunder.

It has been held in England that the jurisdiction to grant leave to serve out of the jurisdiction is limited to parties to the arbitration giving rise to the court proceedings: *The Cienvik* [1996] 2 Lloyd's Rep 395; *Tate & Lyle Industries Ltd v Cia Usina Bulhoes & Anor* [1997] 1 Lloyd's Rep 355, 357 (CA).

### [73.7.3]   The affidavit in support
An application under rule 7 for leave to serve out of the jurisdiction must be supported by an affidavit (or affirmation) setting out the matters stipulated by rule 7(2). As the application will be *ex parte*, the other party not having been served, there is a duty of full and frank disclosure. See generally the commentary under Order 32 rule 6.

### [73.7.4]   Procedure on application for leave
An application for leave to serve out of the jurisdiction under rule 7 may be made *ex parte* by submitting the affidavit (or affirmation) in support to the registry. Such applications are not of the type which, under practice direction SL 2, may in the ordinary course of events be dealt with by a master.

**8.   Registration in High Court of foreign awards** (O. 73 r. 8)
   **Where an award is made in proceedings on an arbitration in any territory to which sections 3 to 9 of the Foreign Judgments (Reciprocal Enforcement) Ordinance (Cap 319) extend, being a part to which the said Ordinance has been applied, then, if the award has, in pursuance of the law in force in the place where it was made, become enforceable in the same manner as a judgment given by a court in that place, Order 71 shall apply in relation to the award as it applies in relation to a judgment given by that court, subject, however, to the following modifications—**

   **(a)   for references to the country of the original court there shall be substituted references to the place where the award was made; and**

   **(b)   the affidavit required by rule 3 of the said Order must state (in addition to the other matters required by that rule) that to the best of the information or belief of the deponent the award has, in pursuance of the law in force in the place where it was made, become enforceable in the same manner as a judgment given by a court in that place.**

## NOTES

### [73.8.1] Scope of Order 73 rule 8

Order 73 rule 8 provides that arbitral awards from some jurisdictions outside Hong Kong, namely those jurisdictions to which the Foreign Judgments (Reciprocal Enforcement) Ordinance (Cap 319) extends and has been applied, may be registered in Hong Kong pursuant to Order 71. The effect is that the award becomes enforceable in the same way as a Hong Kong judgment. The award from the place outside Hong Kong must have become enforceable in the same manner as a judgment in the place where made. Order 71 applies subject to the modifications set out in rule 8(a) and (b).

Arbitral awards, orders and directions from Hong Kong or places outside Hong Kong which are not within the scope of Cap 319 may be enforced in Hong Kong in the same way as a judgment, with leave of the court: Arbitration Ordinance, s 2GG. With regard to awards from the Mainland of China, see s 40B, and see s 42 for Convention awards. Order 73 rule 8 does not apply in such cases unless the arbitration concerned is from a place to which Cap 319 applies. See instead rules 10 and 10A. In addition an arbitration award may be enforced by ordinary common law action based on the implied promise to pay the award: *National Ability SA v Tinna Oils & Chemicals Ltd* [2009] EWCA Civ 1330 (11.12.2009) (para 5).

An application to the court to enforce an arbitration award, like a common law action based on the implied promise, is subject to the 6 year limitation period in section 4(1)(c) of the Limitation Ordinance (Cap 347): *National Ability* (above), construing the equivalent legislation in England.

**9. Registration of awards under Arbitration (International Investment Disputes) Act 1966** (O. 73 r. 9)

**(1) In this rule and in any provision of these rules as applied by this rule—**
**"the Act of 1966" means the Arbitration (International Investment Disputes) Act 1966 (1966 c. 41 U.K.);**
**"award" means an award rendered pursuant to the Convention;**
**"judgment creditor" and "judgment debtor" mean respectively the person seeking recognition or enforcement of an award and the other party to the award.**

**(2) Subject to the provisions of this rule, the following provisions of Order 71, namely rules 3(1) (except subparagraphs (c)(iv) and (d) thereof), 7 (except paragraph (3)(c) and (d) thereof) and 10(3) shall apply with the necessary modifications in relation to an award as they apply in relation to a judgment to which the Foreign Judgments (Reciprocal Enforcement) Ordinance (Cap 319) applies.**

**(3) An application to have an award registered in the Court of First Instance under section 1 of the Act of 1966 may be made by originating summons which shall be in Form 10 in Appendix A. (L.N. 152 of 2008)**

**(4) The affidavit required by Order 71, rule 3, in support of an application for registration shall–**
      **(a) in lieu of exhibiting the judgment or a copy thereof, exhibit a copy of the award certified pursuant to the Convention; and**

    **(b)**  in addition to stating the matters mentioned in paragraph (1)(c)(i) and (ii) of the said rule 3, state whether at the date of the application the enforcement of the award has been stayed (provisionally or otherwise) pursuant to the Convention and whether any, and if so what, application has been made pursuant to the Convention, which, if granted, might result in a stay of the award.

  **(5)**  There shall be kept in the Registry under the direction of the Registrar a register of the awards ordered to be registered under the Act of 1966 and particulars shall be entered in the register of any execution issued on such an award.

  **(6)**  Where it appears to the Court on granting leave to register an award or on an application made by the judgment debtor after an award has been registered—

    **(a)**  that the enforcement of the award has been stayed (whether provisionally or otherwise) pursuant to the Convention; or

    **(b)**  that an application has been made pursuant to the Convention, which, if granted, might result in a stay of the enforcement of the award,

the Court shall, or, in the case referred to in subparagraph (b) may, stay execution of the award for such time as it considers appropriate in the circumstances.

  **(7)**  An application by the judgment debtor under paragraph (6) shall be made by summons and supported by affidavit.

                                                                 **(L.N. 363 of 1990)**

---

## NOTES

**[73.9.1]**  **Arbitration awards of International Centre for Settlement of Investment Disputes**

Order 73 rule 9 provides for the registration in Hong Kong of arbitral awards of the International Centre for Settlement of Investment Disputes (ICSID). ICSID was created under the auspices of the World Bank in 1966 and is based in Washington DC. See generally the background information on ICSID set out in *ETI Euro Telecom Int'l NV v Republic of Bolivia & Anor* [2008] EWCA Civ 880.

This rule refers to the 1966 UK Act which included ICSID in its schedule. It appears that the UK Act no longer has any direct application in Hong Kong since the resumption of Chinese sovereignty. To that extent at least the rule is outdated. However it is possible that an ICSID award would be considered an award pursuant to an international arbitration agreement within the meaning of the Arbitration Ordinance (Cap 341) and subject to recognition in Hong Kong by that means.

**10. Enforcement of settlement agreement under section 2C of the Arbitration Ordinance or of award under section 2GG of that Ordinance** (O. 73 r. 10)

  **(1)**  An application for leave—

**(HK)(a)**  under section 2C of the Arbitration Ordinance (Cap 341) to enforce a settlement agreement, or (L.N. 363 of 1990)

    **(b)**  under section 2GG of that Ordinance to enforce an award on an arbitration agreement, (L.N. 363 of 1990; 2 of 2000 s 15) in the same manner as a judgment or order may be made ex parte but the Court hearing the application may direct a summons to be issued.

(2)   If the Court directs a summons to be issued, the summons may be an originating summons which shall be in Form No. 10 in Appendix A. (L.N. 152 of 2008)

(3)   An application for leave must be supported by affidavit-

(a)   exhibiting—

(HK)(i)   where the application is under section 2C of the Arbitration Ordinance (Cap 341), the arbitration agreement and the original settlement agreement or, in either case, a copy thereof;

(L.N. 363 of 1990)

(ii)   where the application is under section 2GG of the Arbitration Ordinance (Cap 341), the arbitration agreement and the original award or, in either case, a copy thereof; (L.N. 363 of 1990; 2 of 2000 s 15)

(iii)   where the application is under section 40B(1) or 42(1) of the Arbitration Ordinance (Cap 341), the documents required to be produced by section 40D or 43, as the case may be, of that Ordinance, (2 of 2000 s 15)

(b)   stating the name and the usual or last known place of abode or business of the applicant (hereinafter referred to as "the creditor") and the person against whom it is sought to enforce the settlement agreement or award (hereinafter referred to as "the debtor") respectively,

(c)   as the case may require, either that the settlement agreement or award has not been complied with or the extent to which it has not been complied with at the date of the application.

(4)   An order giving leave must be drawn up by or on behalf of the creditor and must be served on the debtor by delivering a copy to him personally or by sending a copy to him at his usual or last known place of abode or business or in such other manner as the Court may direct.

(5)   Service of the order out of the jurisdiction is permissible without leave, and Order 11, rules 5, 6 and 8, shall apply in relation to such an order as they apply in relation to a writ.

(6)   Within 14 days after service of the order or, if the order is to be served out of the jurisdiction, within such other period as the Court may fix, the debtor may apply to set aside the order and the settlement agreement or award shall not be enforced until after the expiration of that period or, if the debtor applies within that period to set aside the order, until after the application is finally disposed of.

(HK)(6A)   An application under paragraph (6) to set aside the order must be made by summons supported by affidavit, and such affidavit must be filed at the same time as the summons. (L.N. 127 of 1995)

(7)   The copy of the order served on the debtor shall state the effect of paragraph (6).

**(8)   In relation to a body corporate this rule shall have effect as if for any reference to the place of abode or business of the creditor or the debtor there were substituted a reference to the registered or principal address of the body corporate; so, however, that nothing in this rule shall affect any enactment which provides for the manner in which a document may be served on a body corporate.**

---

## NOTES

### [73.10.1]   Scope of Order 73 rule 10

Order 73 rule 10 prescribes the procedures to be followed on an application to enforce a settlement agreement or arbitral award under the Arbitration Ordinance. The rule refers to applications to enforce a settlement agreement under section 2C and to enforce an award under section 2GG. Reading those two sections together it is clear that with leave of the court any such settlement or award may be enforced in Hong Kong regardless of place of origin. However where it is sought to enforce an award from a jurisdiction to which the Foreign Judgments (Reciprocal Enforcement) Ordinance (Cap 319) extends and has been applied, the procedure under rule 8 should be followed.

An application to the court to enforce an arbitration award, like a common law action based on the implied promise to pay an award, is subject to the 6 year limitation period in section 4(1)(c) of the Limitation Ordinance (Cap 347). See *National Ability SA v Tinna Oils & Chemicals Ltd* [2009] EWCA Civ 1330 (11.12.2009) (para 5), construing the equivalent legislation in England.

### [73.10.2]   Ex parte procedure

Rule 10(1) provides that an application under the rule may be made *ex parte* but the court may direct a summons to be issued. It has been held that in order to save costs and court time the *ex parte* procedure should normally be followed, leaving it to the court to decide whether to call for an *inter partes* hearing. See *Zhejiang Province Import & Export Co v Siemssen & Co (HK) Trading Ltd* HCMP 144/1992 (Kaplan J; 02.06.1992; [1993] ADRLJ 183, 184) where it was said:

> In my judgment the *ex parte* procedure should be used and only if the court directs should a summons be issued. I mention this because I have had two cases recently where the originating summons was served upon the defendant and the first hearing before me was an *inter partes* hearing. Unless there is no contest, the matter is bound to be adjourned to enable the defendants to file evidence as to why the award should not be enforced. That hearing serves no useful purpose and is a waste of costs and court time.
>
> It is far preferable to leave the initiative with the defendant. If he does not contest the matter, costs are kept to a bare minimum. If he does contest the matter he can apply to set aside the *ex parte* order and file evidence in support. There may or may not have to be a hearing for directions depending on the issues raised.
>
> If the *ex parte* procedure is not used, the court will require an explanation, and if not satisfied, will consider disallowing the costs of the first return day.

### [73.10.3]   The affidavit in support

An application under rule 10 must be supported by an affidavit complying with subrule (3). In relation to applications to enforce Mainland awards, see in addition the requirements as to evidence laid down in section 40D of the Ordinance; and in relation to New York Convention awards, see section 43.

It is not permissible to rely on information and belief evidence (hearsay) in the affidavit in support of an application under rule 10. Order 41 rule 5(2), which provides that affidavits for use in interlocutory proceedings may contain information and belief evidence, does not apply: *Medison Co Ltd v Victor (FE) Ltd* [2000] 2 HKC 502, 506F-I. In that case the court was not prepared to strike out an affidavit containing such evidence. The offending material could be edited or excised and in any event it supported the party who objected to it: see at 507C-E.

Where the application is made *ex parte*, there should, in principle, be a duty of full and frank disclosure. However, *Shenzhen Kai Long Investment & Dev't Co Ltd v CEC Electrical Manufacturing (Int'l) Co Ltd* HCMP 1885/2000 (A Cheung J; 30.10.2003) suggests (para 84) that the court may take a more relaxed attitude toward that duty, given the detailed provisions in the Ordinance and rules as to evidence that an applicant must provide.

### [73.10.4] Interim stay of enforcement on grant of leave

Where an order is made granting leave to enforce an arbitral award, the right to enforce is held in abeyance for an interim period to allow the defendant time to apply to set it aside. Rule 10(6) provides that the award shall not be enforced for 14 days from service of the order, or such longer period as the court allows the defendant to apply to set it aside. In the event of such an application, the prohibition on enforcement continues until final disposition of the application.

The interim prohibition on enforcement comes into effect automatically by operation of rule 10(6), but in practice the court may expressly grant a stay to the same effect. In *China Nanhai Oil Joint Service Corp Shenzhen Branch v Gee Tai Holdings Co Ltd* [1994] 3 HKC 375, 388-9 it was said:

> Order 73 ... provides a very simple method for dealing with applications under the New York Convention. The plaintiff takes out an originating summons for leave to enforce the award as a judgment of the court. If the papers are in order and comply with the Arbitration Ordinance and rules, the judge grants the order but stays enforcement for 14 days to enable the defendant, if so advised, to apply to set aside the *ex parte* order. If an application is made to set aside the order, then the stay continues until the matter has been disposed of.

### [73.10.5] Application to set aside ex parte order for enforcement

Order 73 rule 10(6) provides that the party against whom an order is made for enforcement of a settlement agreement or arbitral award (referred to as the 'debtor'), may apply to set aside the order within 14 days of service (or such other period as the court may fix where service is out of the jurisdiction). The grounds on which leave to enforce a Convention award will be refused, or set aside, are set out in section 44 of the Arbitration Ordinance. For a discussion of many of these grounds see *Karaha Bodas Co LLC v Perusahaan Perambangan Minydak dan Gas Bumi Negara* [2007] 5 HKC 91 (CA) (appeal to the CFA dismissed – see [2009] 2 HKC 303.

Rule 10(6A) provides that the application to set aside must be made by summons and must be supported by affidavit. In *Shanghai City Foundation Works Corp v Sunlink Ltd* [2001] 3 HKC 521, 524C-F it was held that such applications should normally be determined on the affidavit evidence rather than oral evidence. The court referred to *JJ Agro Industries (P) Ltd v Texuna Int'l Ltd* [1994] 1 HKLR 89 where the court heard oral evidence on an allegation of fraud, but regarded this as exceptional.

**[73.10.6]   Costs of unsuccessful application to set aside order for enforcement**
In *A v R* [2010] 3 HKC 67 the court warned that henceforth, in the absence of special circumstances, when an order for enforcement of an arbitral award has been unsuccessfully challenged, the court would consider awarding costs against the losing party on an indemnity basis. Reyes J said that it should be expected that arbitration awards would be enforced as a matter of course, and that applications to appeal against or set aside an award or for an order refusing enforcement should be 'exceptional events'. In *Wing Hong Construction Ltd v Tin Wo Eng'g Co Ltd* HCCT 13/2010 (Saunders J; 03.06.2010) (para 26) *A v R* was followed. The court distinguished a decision of the Court of Appeal and concluded that 'as a matter of principle in the special circumstances of arbitration proceedings, where an applicant fails to successfully establish a basis to challenge an award, the proper award of costs will usually be an award of indemnity costs'. See also *Hung Wan Construction Co Ltd v HK Housing Authority* HCCT 21/2010 (Saunders J; 29.07.2010).

**[73.10.7]   Enforcement of arbitral awards as between Hong Kong and the Mainland – effect of the transfer of sovereignty and the enactment of part IIIA of the Ordinance**
Following an agreement concluded in 1999, Mainland arbitral awards are enforceable in Hong Kong, and Hong Kong awards are likewise enforceable in the Mainland, restoring the pre-1997 position. The agreement was implemented in Hong Kong by the enactment of part IIIA of the Arbitration Ordinance (sections 40A-40G), which came into force on 01.02.2000. Effective the same day, the agreement took effect in the Mainland by Supreme People's Court Notice. See *Fa Shi* [2000] No 3 and see Morgan, 'Enforcement of Chinese Arbitral Awards Complete Once More – But with a Difference' (2000) 30 HKLJ 375.

The implementation of the agreement filled a lacuna created upon the resumption of Chinese sovereignty over Hong Kong. Prior to 1997, Hong Kong and Mainland awards were enforceable in each other's jurisdiction under the New York Convention on International Arbitration. However that convention applies only between foreign states and thus ceased to apply as between Hong Kong and the Mainland upon reunification. During the period from 01.07.1997 to 31.01.2000 there was no mechanism for enforcement of awards between the two jurisdictions. The Hong Kong court did not have jurisdiction to enforce a Mainland award under the Ordinance. See *Ng Fung Hong Ltd v ABC* [1998] 1 HKC 213, 214F-H and *Shandong Textiles Import & Export Corp v Da Hua Non-ferrous Metals Co Ltd* [2002] 2 HKC 122, 137D-F. This undesirable consequence was avoided in *Hebei Import & Export Corp v Polytek Engineering Co Ltd* [1999] 2 HKC 205 (CFA) where both the Mainland arbitral award and the proceedings to enforce it in Hong Kong pre-dated the transfer of sovereignty and it was held the New York Convention continued to apply. In other cases Mainland awards could only be enforced by common law action.

The biting provision of the Ordinance for enforcement in Hong Kong of Mainland awards is section 40B which provides that now they may, subject to the provisions of part IIIA, be enforced under section 2GG.

The agreement and part IIIA of the Ordinance have a retrospective aspect in that they permit the enforcement not only of arbitral awards given after implementation, but also earlier awards which could not be enforced during the period 1997–2000. See *Shandong Textiles* (above). Para 10 of the agreement and section 40G of the Ordinance even permit enforcement of awards where leave to enforce had been refused during the lacuna period. Thus no question of *res judicata* will arise on a fresh application to enforce such an award.

The agreement itself does not have the force of law in Hong Kong. Where it is sought to enforce a Mainland award in Hong Kong, reference should be made to the provisions of part IIIA of the Ordinance by which it is implemented. However the agreement may be instructive in understanding part IIIA, or when considering enforcement in the Mainland of a Hong Kong award. Its text can be downloaded in its Chinese original and English translation from the 'intracountry' section of the Department of Justice 'BLIS' website, concerning 'Arrangements with the Mainland and the Macao SAR', and can also be viewed in Law Society circular 07-669, available to members on the Law Society's website. The English translation of the agreement, which, perhaps significantly, is called an 'arrangement', reads as follows:

Arrangement Concerning Mutual Enforcement of Arbitral Awards Between
the Mainland and the Hong Kong Special Administrative Region

In accordance with the provision of Article 95 of the Basic Law of the Hong Kong Special Administrative Region of the People's Republic of China and through mutual consultations between the Supreme People's Court and the Government of the Hong Kong Special Administrative Region (HKSAR) the Courts of the HKSAR agree to enforce the awards made pursuant to the Arbitration Law of the People's Republic of China by the arbitral authorities in the Mainland (the list to be supplied by the Legislative Affairs Office of the State Council through the Hong Kong and Macao Affairs Office of the State Council) and the People's Courts of the Mainland agree to enforce the awards made in the HKSAR pursuant to the Arbitration Ordinance of the HKSAR. The following arrangement is made in respect of mutual enforcement of arbitral awards by the Mainland and the HKSAR:

1. Where a party fails to comply with an arbitral award, whether made in the Mainland or in the HKSAR, the other party may apply to the relevant court in the place where the party against whom the application is filed is domiciled or in the place where the property of the said party is situated to enforce the award.

2. For the purpose of Article 1 above, 'relevant court', in the case of the Mainland, means the Intermediate People's Court of the place where the party against whom the application is filed is domiciled or the place in which the property of the said party is situated and, in the case of the HKSAR, means the High Court of the HKSAR.

   If the place where the party against whom the application is filed is domiciled or the place where the property of the said party is situated falls within the jurisdiction of different Intermediate People's Courts of the Mainland, the applicant may apply to any one of the People's Courts to enforce the award. The applicant shall not file his application with two or more People's Courts.

   If the place where the party against whom the application is filed is domiciled or the place where the property of the said party is situated is in the Mainland as well as in the HKSAR, the applicant shall not file applications with relevant courts of the two places at the same time. Only when the result of the enforcement of the award by the court of one place is insufficient to satisfy the liabilities may the applicant apply to the court of another place for enforcement of the outstanding liabilities. The total amount recovered from enforcing the award in the courts of the two places one after the other shall in no case exceed the amount awarded.

3. The applicant shall submit the following documents in applying to the relevant court for enforcement of an award, made either in the Mainland or the HKSAR:

    i)    An application for enforcement;

    ii)   The arbitral award;

    iii)  The arbitration agreement.

4.    An application for enforcement shall contain the following:

    (1)    Where the applicant is a natural person, his name and address; where the applicant is a legal entity or any other organisation, its name and address and the name of its legally authorised representative;

    (2)    Where the party against whom the application is filed is a natural person, his name and address; where the party against whom the application is filed is a legal entity or any other organisation, its name and address and the name of its legally authorised representative;

    (3)    Where the applicant is a legal entity or any other organisation, a copy of the enterprise registration record shall be submitted. Where the applicant is a foreign legal entity or any other foreign organisation, the corresponding notarisation and authentication material shall be submitted;

    (4)    The grounds for and the particulars of the application for enforcement; the place where the property of the party against whom the application is filed is situated and the status of the property.

Application for enforcement made in the Mainland shall be in the Chinese language. If the arbitral award or arbitration agreement is not in the Chinese language, the applicant shall submit a duly certified Chinese translation of it.

5.    The time limit for an applicant to apply to the relevant court for enforcement of the arbitral award, whether made in the Mainland or in the HKSAR, shall be governed by the law on limitation period of the place of enforcement.

6.    Upon receipt of an application for enforcement from an applicant, the relevant court shall handle the application and enforce the award according to the legal procedure of the place of enforcement.

7.    The party against whom an application is filed may, after receiving notice of an arbitral award, whether made in the Mainland or in the HKSAR, adduce evidence to show any of the situations set out below. Upon such evidence being examined and any of the said situations being found proved, the relevant court may refuse to enforce the arbitral award:

    (1)    A party to the arbitration agreement was, under the law applicable to him, under some incapacity, or the arbitration agreement was not valid under the law to which the parties subjected it, or, failing any indication thereon, under the law of the place in which the arbitral award was made;

    (2)    The party against whom the application is filed was not given proper notice of the appointment of the arbitrator or was otherwise unable to present his case;

    (3)    The award deals with a difference not contemplated by or not falling within the terms of the submission to arbitration, or the award contains decisions on matters beyond the scope of the submission to arbitration. However, if the award contains decisions on matters submitted to arbitration that can be separated from those not so submitted, that part of the award which contains decisions on matters submitted to arbitration shall be enforced;

    (4)    The composition of the arbitral authority or the arbitral procedure was not in accordance with agreement of the parties or, failing such agreement, with the law of the place where the arbitration took place;

    (5)    The award has not yet become binding on the parties, or has been set aside or suspended by the court or in accordance with the law of the place where the arbitration took place;

           If the relevant court finds that under the law of the place of enforcement, the dispute is incapable of being settled by arbitration, then the court may refuse to enforce the award.

The enforcement of the award may be refused if the court of the Mainland holds that the enforcement of the arbitral award in the Mainland would be contrary to the public interests of the Mainland, or if the court of the HKSAR decides that the enforcement of the arbitral award in Hong Kong would be contrary to the public policy of the HKSAR.

8.   The applicant, in applying to the relevant court to enforce an arbitral award, whether made in the Mainland or in the HKSAR, shall pay the enforcement fees prescribed by the court of enforcement.

9.   Applications made after 1st July, 1997 for enforcement of arbitral awards, whether made in the Mainland or in the HKSAR, shall be enforced according to this Arrangement.

10.  In respect of applications for enforcement made between 1st July, 1997 and the coming into force of this Arrangement, both parties agree that:

Where the applications for enforcement cannot, for some reasons, be made to the court of the Mainland or the court of the HKSAR between 1st July, 1997 and the coming into force of this Arrangement, then, in the case of the applicant being a legal entity or any other organisation, the application for enforcement may be made within six months after this Arrangement comes into force and, in the case of the applicant being a natural person, the application for enforcement may be made within one year after this Arrangement comes into force.

Parties to cases which the court of the Mainland or the HKSAR had, between 1st July, 1997 and the coming into force of this Arrangement, refused to handle or to enforce the award, shall be allowed to make fresh application for enforcement.

11.  Any problem arising in the course of implementing this Arrangement and any amendment to this Arrangement shall be resolved through consultations between the Supreme People's Court and the Government of the HKSAR.

Although the agreement and part IIIA of the Ordinance do not apply to Macau and Taiwan, arbitral agreements from those jurisdictions should nevertheless be enforceable in Hong Kong as a result of section 2GG(2) of the Ordinance (which applies to all jurisdictions outside Hong Kong).

The mainland judicial authorities have clarified that *ad hoc* arbitral awards made in the HKSAR are enforceable in the Mainland, subject to article 7 of the arrangement (above). See Law Society circular 07-699. *Ad hoc* arbitral awards are those made where although the parties have no prior arbitration agreement, they agree to refer a dispute to arbitration, or where the parties administer an arbitration themselves rather than using the arbitration centre. It has also been clarified that arbitral awards made in Hong Kong by international and foreign arbitration institutions are enforceable in the Mainland under the arrangement: see the notification to this effect from the Supreme People's Court dated 30.12.2009, reproduced in Law Society circular 10-41.

### [73.10.8]   Restrictions on enforcement of Mainland awards in Hong Kong

A Mainland award will not be enforced in Hong Kong where application has been made for enforcement there, unless the award has not been fully satisfied by means of that enforcement. See section 40C of the Ordinance implementing para 2(3) of the agreement.

### [73.10.9]   Grounds for refusal of enforcement of Mainland awards in Hong Kong

Paragraph 7 of the agreement between the Hong Kong and Mainland authorities sets out the grounds on which each jurisdiction may refuse to enforce an arbitral award from the other. So far as enforcement in Hong Kong is concerned, these are implemented in section 40E of the Arbitration Ordinance. Briefly, the grounds are, following the subsection numbers in section 40E:

(2) (a) a party to the arbitration agreement was (under the law applicable to him) under some incapacity – see Order 80 of these rules as to 'disability'
  (b) invalid arbitration agreement
  (c) lack of notice or inability to present case
  (d) the award goes beyond the scope of the submission to arbitration (but see subsection (4) below)
  (e) improper composition of the tribunal or improper procedure
  (f) the award is not yet binding or has been set aside or suspended

(3) matter not susceptible to arbitration in Hong Kong, or enforcement contrary to public policy
(4) where the award goes beyond the scope of the submission to arbitration, those aspects which are within the scope of the submission may nevertheless be enforced.

### [73.10.10] Refusal to enforce arbitral award on public policy grounds

As set out above, section 40E(3) of the Arbitration Ordinance provides that the Hong Kong court may refuse to enforce a Mainland arbitral award on public policy grounds. The precise wording of the subsection is 'it would be contrary to public policy to enforce the award'. Paragraph 7 of the agreement refers to the public policy 'of the HKSAR'. There is a similar provision in section 44(3) of the Ordinance in relation to enforcement of New York Convention awards.

The circumstances in which the court may refuse to enforce an arbitral award on the ground of public policy were considered in *Hebei Import & Export Corp v Polytek Engineering Co Ltd* [1999] 2 HKC 205 (CFA) with regard to New York Convention awards. In *Hebei* Litton PJ said (at 211A-D):

> As can be seen, refusal of enforcement on public policy grounds in subsection (3) is a residual remedy. It would be an unusual case where the 'competent authority' in subsection 2(f) has ruled in favour of the validity of the award, yet the court in the enforcement jurisdiction nevertheless concludes that enforcement should be denied for public policy reasons. The practical result, as counsel for the appellant Ms Audrey Eu SC points out, can be extremely unjust: The claimant cannot *enforce* the award because the award has, in effect, been nullified in the eyes of the enforcement court, yet it cannot ask for the arbitration to be instituted afresh in the supervisory jurisdiction because the court in that jurisdiction has *upheld* its validity.
>
> The expression *public policy* as it appears in s 44(3) is a multi-faceted concept. Woven into this concept is the principle that courts should recognise the validity of decisions of foreign arbitral tribunals as a matter of comity, and give effect to them, unless to do so would violate the most basic notions of morality and justice. It would take a very strong case before such a conclusion can be properly reached, when the facts giving rise to the allegation have been made the subject of challenge in proceedings in the supervisory jurisdiction, and such challenge has failed.

Bokhary PJ stated (at 215G-H and 216H-I):

> In my view there must be compelling reasons before enforcement of a Convention award can be refused on public policy grounds. This is not to say that the reasons must be so extreme that the award falls to be cursed by bell, book and candle. But the reasons must go beyond the minimum which would justify setting aside a domestic judgment or award ...
>
> Before a Convention jurisdiction can, in keeping with its being a party to the Convention, refuse enforcement of a Convention award on public policy grounds, the award must be so fundamentally offensive to that jurisdiction's notions of justice that,

despite its being a party to the Convention, it cannot reasonably be expected to overlook the objection.

In *Shanghai City Foundation Works Corp v Sunlink Ltd* [2001] 3 HKC 521 the court followed *Hebei* with regard to a Mainland award.

### [73.10.11]  Enforcement of Mainland award by defence, set-off etc
Section 40B(2) of the Arbitration Ordinance provides that a Mainland award which is enforceable under part IIIA may be relied upon 'by way of defence, set off or otherwise in any legal proceedings in Hong Kong'. However it has been held that this is not permissible without first following the procedures of part IIIA. In *Yu Long Trading Int'l Co Ltd v Sino-Jinlink Petrochemical Co Ltd* HCMP 2768/2000 (Burrell J; 24.10.2000) it was held that a Mainland award could not be set up as a counterclaim to an application for leave to enforce another Mainland award since Part IIIA and Order 73 had not been followed.

### [73.10.12]  Mainland award may be enforced by third party
A Mainland award may be enforced in Hong Kong by a third party. See *Sam Ming City Forestry Economic Co v Lam Pun Hung* [2001] 3 HKC 573 (CA) where it was said (at 579E):

> ... a person who was not a party to a Mainland arbitration proceedings but was the sole beneficiary of the Mainland award may enforce it in Hong Kong ... As the beneficiary of the award which was made between the plaintiffs and the defendants, the second plaintiff is in the analogous position of a third person not being a party to a cause who may invoke Order 45 rule 9(1) to enforce an order to his benefit.

### [73.10.13]  Questions of law on application to enforce arbitral award from outside Hong Kong
Where on an application in relation to an arbitration outside Hong Kong there arises a question of the law of another jurisdiction, the court will proceed on the basis that the law of the other jurisdiction is the same as Hong Kong's unless there is expert evidence to the contrary. See *Cheng Hang Chu & Ors v China Treasure Enterprise Ltd* [2000] 2 HKC 814, concerning enforcement of a Mainland award under Orders 14 and 14A of these rules, and see generally the commentary under Order 38 rule 7.

### [73.10.14]  Leave to enforce arbitral award which is under appeal
Leave to enforce an arbitral award may be granted despite the fact it is under appeal. This may be less likely where the appeal is on the merits. In *Société nationale d'operations pétrolières de la Côte d'Ivoire v Keen Lloyd Resources Ltd* [2004] 3 HKC 452 the court refused to set aside leave to enforce an arbitral award which was under appeal, and thereby automatically stayed, in France. In the same case the court later refused a stay of enforcement (see HCCT 55/2001 (Burrell J; 11.03.2002)), relying on the fact that the appeal was not on the merits. In the latter decision it was said (at para 13-14):

> I find that an appeal to set aside an award and an appeal on the merits are different animals. The French law plainly provides for the former but not the latter. The distinction is important because the general principles set out above and the ICC rules are such that a mere application (or appeal) to set aside (on maybe technical grounds) should have no

effect on the binding nature of the award. The type of appeal which does affect the binding nature of the award is confined to an appeal on the merits …

Mr Harris' strongest point is that, in France, once the 'appeal' procedure to set aside the award is commenced it has the automatic effect of staying any enforcement procedures, in France. It would be odd, he submits, for an award to be enforceable in Hong Kong but not in the country whence the award originated. I do not consider it to be so. Individual countries are bound to have different rules, laws and regulations governing arbitral laws and procedure. This court's concern is to apply the law applicable in Hong Kong to foreign awards. That law contains a strong pro-enforcement bias consistent with the general principle of finality and comity. If an inconsistency emerges between this and a foreign country's domestic regime then so be it. This court should be cautious before allowing the foreign regime to influence decisions in this jurisdiction.

The court held that the award under appeal was not to be regarded as one which 'has not yet become binding on the parties' pursuant to section 44(2)(f) of the Arbitration Ordinance.

(HK)**10A.    Other provisions as to applications to set aside an order made under rule 10** (O. 73 r. 10A)

**(HK)    Where a debtor has applied to set aside an order made under rule 10, the Court may, either of its own motion or on an application made by the creditor, and if, having regard to all the circumstances of the case it thinks it just to do so, impose such terms, as to giving security or otherwise, as a condition of the further conduct of the application, as it thinks fit. (L.N. 167 of 1994)**

**NOTES**

**[73.10A.1]    Security for costs of application to set aside leave**
Order 73 rule 10A empowers the court to impose terms, as to security or otherwise, on an application to set aside leave to enforce a settlement agreement or arbitral award under rule 10. The power exists where application has been made by the 'debtor', meaning the person against whom it is sought to enforce the settlement agreement or arbitral award (see rule 10(3)(b)).

Under rule 10A the court may order security for the amount of the creditor's claim, or security for costs. See, for example, *Karaha Bodas Co LLC v Persusahaan Pertambangan Minydak dan Gas Bumi Negara* [2003] 2 HKC 200. There it was held (at para 9) that the criteria on application for either type of security are:

(i)    the merits of the challenge to the award; and
(ii)    the ease or difficulty of enforcement and whether it will be rendered more difficult as enforcement is delayed.

It has been held that the debtor may not seek security for costs against the creditor on such an application. The debtor is in a position analogous to that of a plaintiff in an action, and like Order 23, this rule does not permit an order for security for costs in those circumstances. See *TK Bulkhandling Gmbh v Meridian Success Int'l Ltd* HCMP 4765/1998 (Findlay J; 30.11.1998). There it was also held that Order 23 does not apply on an application to set aside leave to enforce, because such an application is not an 'action'. In *FG Hemisphere Associates LLC v Democratic Republic of the Congo & Ors* HCMP 928/2008 (Deputy Judge Mayo; 22.10.2008) it was held that there is no jurisdiction to order security for costs against a creditor seeking to enforce an award under rule 10.

**11. Payments into court** (O. 73 r. 11)

**(HK)(1)   In any arbitration proceedings any party to the reference may at any time pay into court a sum of money in satisfaction of any claim against him under the reference.**

**(2)   On making payment into court under this rule, and on increasing any such payment already made the party making payment must give notice thereof in Form No. 100 in Appendix A to all other parties to the reference; and within 3 days after receiving the notice the recipient parties must send the party making payment a written acknowledgment of its receipt.**

**(3)   A party who has made payment into court under this rule may, without leave, give notice of an increase in such a payment but, subject to that and without prejudice to paragraph (5), a notice of payment may not be withdrawn or amended without leave of the Court which may be granted on such terms as may be just.**

**(4)   Where there are two or more matters in dispute in the arbitration proceedings and money is paid into court under this rule in respect of all, or some only of, those matters, the notice of payment–**

    **(a)   must state that the money is paid in respect of all those matters in dispute or, as the case may be, must specify the matters in respect of which payment is made, and**

    **(b)   where the party makes separate payments in respect of each, or any two of those matters in dispute, must specify the sum paid in respect of that matter or, as the case may be, those matters.**

**(5)   Where a single sum of money is paid into court under this rule in respect of two or more matters in dispute, then, if it appears to the Court that any party to the arbitration proceedings is embarrassed by the payment, the Court may order the party making payment to amend the notice of payment so as to specify the sum paid in respect of each matter in dispute.**

**(6)   For the purposes of this rule, a claim under a reference to arbitration shall be construed as a claim in respect, also, of such interest as might be included in the award if the award were made at the date of the payment into court.**

---

## NOTES

### [73.11.1]   Payment into court in an arbitration

Order 73 rule 11 provides a procedure similar to that under Order 22, as the latter was prior to the implementation of the civil justice reforms in April 2009, whereby a party to an arbitration may make a payment into court by way of offer of settlement. See also rules 12 and 16 with regard to payment into court in respect of a counterclaim.

Although the procedure laid down by the rule is for payment into court, it relates not to court proceedings arising out of an arbitration, but to the substantive dispute in the arbitration itself. This is clear from rule 11(1) which provides for payment into court in 'any arbitration proceedings'. Although that term is not defined, it is used in the Ordinance (for example in section 2GB) to mean proceedings before an arbitrator, in distinction to proceedings before the court arising from an arbitration.

So far as court proceedings arising out of an arbitration are concerned, the view has been expressed by the judiciary administration that the sanctioned payment and sanctioned offer procedures under the current Order 22 are applicable: see the commentary under Order 22 rule 1.

### [73.11.2]  Origin of rule 11
Order 73 rule 11 traces back to the Commercial Arbitration report of the Hong Kong Law Reform Commission, 1981 (paras 8.27 – 8.28), which can be viewed on the LRCHK website. It followed a recommendation of the Commercial Court Committee Report on Arbitration in England (July 1978, Cmnd 7284).

The procedure is similar to, but does not expressly replace, the practice whereby the party against whom arbitration proceedings are brought could make a sealed offer of settlement not be opened by the arbitrator until the question of liability had been established.

### [73.11.3]  Comparison with Order 22
The procedures under Order 73 for payment into court in arbitration proceedings largely follow those set out in the former Order 22 for actions. However different forms are used (forms 100 and 101, rather than 23 and 24) to reflect the different nature of an arbitration. Likewise there are some differences in terminology – the relevant rules under Order 73 refer to 'claims' and 'matters in dispute' rather than cause (or causes) of action. In *Hanson Jay & Associates Ltd v AG* [1989] 1 HKC 74, 77D (CA) the court proceeded on the basis that the term 'matters in dispute' used in Order 73 has the same meaning as 'causes of action' used in the former Order 22.

### [73.11.4]  Calderbank offers in arbitration proceedings
Order 73 does not contain an equivalent of the former Order 22 rule 14 which formalised the procedure whereby a written offer of settlement may be made (commonly referred to as a *'Calderbank'* letter), with possible costs consequences for the offeree if not accepted or exceeded by the final award. Nor does it contain an equivalent of Order 62 rule 5(1)(d) which now provides for the court to take into account *Calderbank* offers in exercising its discretion as to costs. Nevertheless, since the procedure originally came into existence by judicial recognition (*Calderbank v Calderbank* [1975] 3 All ER 333) rather than by legislation, there is no reason of principle whereby such an offer cannot be made and taken into account by an arbitrator.

In *Chinney Construction Co Ltd v Po Kwong Marble Factory Ltd* [2005] 3 HKC 262, 280 it was held the prohibition on taking into account a *Calderbank* offer where a payment into court could instead have been made does not apply in arbitration proceedings.

### [73.11.5]  Notice of payment in and acknowledgement thereof
Rule 11(2) provides that a party making payment in must give notice thereof in the requisite form, and further, that the parties receiving such notice must, within 3 days thereafter, give written acknowledgement of receipt of the notice.

**[73.11.6]   Payment into court in respect of more than one 'matter in dispute'**
Where payment into court is made under rule 11 in respect of more than one matter in dispute in the arbitration, the notice of payment in should apportion the sum between the various matters. If the party fails to do so, the court may make an order requiring the notice to be amended (rule 11(5)).

In *Hanson Jay & Associates Ltd* (above) it was held there is no jurisdiction to make an order under rule 11(5) in respect of money paid into court prior to the commencement of the arbitration. This seems strange because, according to rule 13(3), rule 11(5) only applies to payment in made before the hearing of an arbitration begins (which means the hearing of the substantive issues: *Vianini Lavori SPA v HK Housing Authority* [1992] 2 HKLR 131, 138).

**[73.11.7]   Payment in to take account of interest**
Payment into court in respect of an arbitration should take into account interest to which the claiming party may be entitled: rule 11(6). It follows that if the payment in is not accepted, and at the conclusion of the arbitration the paying party is found liable for an amount which, when interest is added, exceeds what was paid in, the paying party will be liable in costs as if the payment in had never been made. There was an equivalent provision in the former Order 22 rule 1(8). Its purpose was to reverse the effect of *Jefford v Gee* [1970] 2 QB 130, 149-50 (CA). There it had been held that since a claim for interest under statute is not itself a cause of action and forms no part of the debt or damages claimed, a defendant making a payment into court need not include an additional sum to cover interest that might be awarded. See *Vianini Lavori SPA v AG* HCMP 3333/1991 (Kaplan J; 10.01.1991). In that case it was held that a party may get round rule 11(6) by expressly stipulating that its payment in does not include interest. The opposing party would then be free to accept it and apply for an award of interest on top.

**[73.11.8]   Increase of payment into court**
When a payment into court has not been accepted, the paying party made wish to increase the amount so as to make it more attractive. Order 73 rule 11(2) expressly contemplates this being done by making a top-up payment and giving fresh notice in form 100. The form of notice should be adapted to make it clear that the payment is intended to be in addition to that made earlier, and in respect of the same matter, if that be the case.

Such a top-up payment may be made at any time (rule 11(1)), and no leave is required (rule 11(3)).

**[73.11.9]   Decrease or withdrawal of payment into court**
The court's leave is required if it is wished to withdraw or amend a payment into court: Order 73 rule 11(3). This means that that if a party wishes to reduce the amount of the offer made by means of payment in, whether in part or by withdrawing it entirely; or to amend the terms of the notice as to which aspects of the arbitration it is intended to settle, application must be made to the court. Leave is not required to increase an existing offer: see above.

An application to withdraw or amend a payment into court under this rule is discretionary: *Unistress Bldg Construction Ltd v Humphreys Estate (Forrestdale) Ltd*

HCMP 3268 & 3311/1991 (Kaplan J; 16.03.1992) (para 24). In that case the court took into account the factors under which the court would grant leave to withdraw or reduce a payment into court under the former Order 22 procedure. Similar factors continue to be relevant where it is sought to withdraw or reduce a sanctioned offer or sanctioned payment under the current Order 22. For discussion of these factors, see the commentary under Order 22 rule 10.

#### [73.11.10]   Costs consequences of payment into court under rule 11

Under the previous Order 22 payment into court procedure (for court proceedings), the court was enjoined by the then Order 62 rule 5(b) to take such a payment into account in exercising its discretion as to costs. There is no express equivalent in rule 11 for payments into court in regard to arbitrations. However in *Vianini Lavori v AG* (above) the court had no doubt that the arbitrator could and would take such a payment into account in exercising his discretion on costs. It is therefore to be expected that where a party does not accept such a payment in, but does no better in the arbitration, it may be deprived of costs by the arbitrator, or even ordered to pay the opposing party's costs after the payment in. The following passage from *Findlay v Railway Executive* [1950] 2 All ER 969, 971 (CA) is relevant:

> The main purpose of the rules for payment into court is the hope that further litigation will be avoided, the plaintiff being encouraged to take out the sum paid in, if it be a reasonable sum, whereas, if he goes on and gets a smaller sum, he will be penalised wholly or to some extent in costs. Once, therefore, the money has been paid in, the *lis* between the parties simply is: Is that sum sufficient to cover the damage which has been suffered.

On the question of when a payment into court may be considered to have been better than the ultimate result, the pre-CJR cases discussed in the commentary under Order 22 rule 23 should be relevant.

#### 12.  Payment in by party who has counterclaimed (O. 73 r. 12)

**(HK)   Where a party, who makes by counterclaim in the arbitration proceedings a claim against any other party to the arbitration proceedings, pays a sum or sums of money into court under rule 11, the notice of payment must state if it be the case, that in making the payment he has taken into account and intends to satisfy the matter in dispute, or matters in dispute, as the case may be, under his counterclaim.**

#### 13.  Acceptance of money paid into court (O. 73 r. 13)

**(HK)(1)   Where money is paid into court under rule 11, then, subject to paragraph (2), within 14 days after the receipt of the notice of payment or, where more than one payment has been made or the notice has been amended, within 14 days after receipt of the notice of the last payment or the amended notice but, in any case, before the hearing of the arbitration proceedings begins, a party to the arbitration proceedings may–**

> **(a)   where the money was paid in respect of the matter in dispute or all the matters in dispute in respect of which he claims, accept the money in satisfaction of that matter in dispute or those matters in dispute, as the case may be, or**

    **(b)** **where the money was paid in respect of some only of the matters in dispute in respect of which he claims, accept in satisfaction of any such matter in dispute the sum specified in respect of that matter in dispute in the notice of payment,**

**by giving notice in Form No. 101 in Appendix A to all other parties to the arbitration proceedings.**

    **(2)** **Where after the hearing of the arbitration proceedings has begun–**
        **(a)** **money is paid into court under rule 11, or**
        **(b)** **money in court is increased by a further payment into court under that rule,**

**any party may accept the money in accordance with paragraph (1) within 2 days after receipt of the notice of payment or notice of the further payment, as the case may be, but, in any case, before the arbitrator publishes his award.**

    **(3)** **Rule 11(5) shall not apply in relation to money paid into court after the hearing of the arbitration proceedings has begun.**

    **(4)** **On a party accepting any money paid into court all further proceedings in the arbitration proceedings or in respect of the specified matter in dispute or matters in dispute, as the case may be, to which the acceptance relates shall be stayed.**

    **(5)** **Where money is paid into court by a party who made a counterclaim in the arbitration proceedings and the notice of payment stated, in relation to any sum so paid, that in making the payment the party had taken into account and satisfied the matter in dispute, or matters in dispute, as the case may be, in respect of which he claimed, then, on the claimant party accepting that sum, all further proceedings on the counterclaim or in respect of the specified matter or matters in dispute, as the case may be, shall be stayed.**

    **(6)** **A party to arbitration proceedings who has accepted any sum paid into court shall, subject to rule 14, be entitled to receive payment of that sum in satisfaction of the matter or matters in dispute to which the arbitration proceedings relate.**

---

## NOTES

### [73.13.1]   Time for acceptance of payment into court

The time within which payment into court in respect of proceedings before an arbitrator may be accepted is normally 14 days. The 14 days runs from the date of the payment in or any subsequent increase or amendment thereof: Order 73 rule 13(1).

    The time for acceptance is reduced to 2 days if the payment in, increase or amendment is made after the arbitration proceedings have begun: rule 13(2). However the court has jurisdiction to entertain an application for leave for late acceptance of such a payment in: *Unistress Bldg Construction Ltd v Humphreys Estate (Forrestdale) Ltd* HCMP 3268 & 3311/1991 (Kaplan J; 16.03.1992) (para 23).

### [73.13.2]   Effect of acceptance of payment into court

On acceptance of a payment into court, the arbitration proceedings are automatically stayed by Order 73 rule 13(4). Where the payment was in relation to only a specified part of the dispute, only that part will be stayed. The party who has accepted the payment in may then apply for the money to be paid out. In certain circumstances an order of the court is necessary for payment out: see rule 14.

## 14. Order for payment out of money accepted required (O. 73 r. 14)

**(HK)(1)** **Where a party to arbitration proceedings accepts any sum paid into court and that sum was paid into court by some but not all of the other parties to the arbitration proceedings the money in court shall not be paid out except under paragraph (2) or in pursuance of an order of the Court, and the order shall deal with the whole costs of the arbitration proceedings or the matter in dispute to which the payment relates, as the case may be.**

**(2)** **Where an order of the Court is required under paragraph (1), then if, either before or after accepting the money paid into court by some only of the other parties the party discontinues the arbitration proceedings against all the other parties and those parties consent in writing to the payment out of that sum, it may be paid out without an order of the Court.**

**(3)** **Where after the hearing of the arbitration proceedings has begun a claimant party accepts any money paid into court and all further proceedings in the arbitration proceedings or in respect of the matter in dispute or matters in dispute, as the case may be, to which the acceptance relates are stayed by virtue of rule 13(4), then, notwithstanding anything in paragraph (2), the money shall not be paid out except in pursuance of an order of the Court, and the order shall deal with the whole costs of the arbitration proceedings or with the costs relating to the matter in dispute or matters in dispute as the case may be, to which the arbitration proceedings relate.**

## NOTES

**[73.14.1]** **Where court order required for payment out on acceptance**
Order 73 rule 14 sets out various circumstances in which an order of the court is necessary for payment out of money which has been paid in by way of offer to settle proceedings before an arbitrator, and has been accepted. They are:

(1) *Where there are multiple parties and the acceptance does not relate to all –* Leave is required unless the accepting party discontinues the arbitration against the nonpaying parties, and they consent. See also Order 22 rule 18, which makes similar provision in respect of sanctioned offers and sanctioned payments.

(2) *Where payment accepted only after arbitration has begun –* an order of the court is required for payment out of court of money accepted only after the arbitration has begun. This is because substantial additional costs may have been incurred from commencement of the arbitration. The rule requires the court, when granting leave for payment out, to deal with all issues as to costs. See rule 13 (2) for payment into court made only after the arbitration has begun.

## 15. Money remaining in court (O. 73 r. 15)

**(HK)** **If any money paid into court in connection with arbitration proceedings is not accepted in accordance with rule 13, the money remaining in court shall not be paid out except in pursuance of an order of the Court which may be made**

**at any time before during or after the hearing of the arbitration proceedings; and where such an order is made before the hearing the money shall not be paid out except in satisfaction of the matter or matters in dispute in respect of which it was paid in.**

---

## NOTES

### [73.15.1]    Court order required for payment out of money not accepted

Order 73 rule 15 provides that an order of the court is required for payment out of money which was paid in as an offer of settlement of arbitral proceedings, but not accepted. It is to the same effect as Order 22A rule 1, which applies to unaccepted payments into court in relation to High Court actions. The commentary under that provision will largely be relevant here, and reference should be made to it.

### 16. Counterclaim (O. 73 r. 16)

**(HK)    A party to arbitration proceedings against whom a counterclaim is made may pay money into court in accordance with rule 11, and that rule and rules 13 (except paragraph (5)), 14 and 15 shall apply accordingly with the necessary modifications.**

### 17. Non-disclosure of payment into court; amendment of arbitrators award (O. 73 r. 17)

**(HK)    Except in arbitration proceedings in which all further proceedings are stayed after the hearing has begun by virtue of rule 13(4), the fact that money has been paid into court under the foregoing provisions of this Order shall not be communicated to the arbitrator until he has published his award, whereupon the arbitrator may amend his award by adding thereto such directions as he may think proper with respect to the payment of the costs of the reference.**

---

## NOTES

### [73.17.1]    Restriction on disclosure of payment into court

Order 73 rule 17 provides that a payment into court in arbitration proceedings should not be disclosed to the arbitrator until the proceedings have come to a conclusion. It is to the same effect as Order 22 rule 25(2), which applies to sanctioned offers and sanctioned payments. The commentary in relation to that provision will largely be relevant to Order 73 rule 17 as well.

### 18. Investment of money in court (O. 73 r. 18)

**(HK)    Cash under the control of or subject to the order of the Court may be invested in any manner specified in the High Court Suitors' Funds Rules (Cap 4 sub. leg.) and the Trustee Ordinance (Cap 29).**

**(Enacted 1988)**

## NOTES

### [73.18.1]   Provisions as to investment of money in court

Order 73 rule 18 provides for the manner in which money paid into court by way of offer of settlement of arbitration proceedings should be invested. It is identical to Order 22A rule 4, which applies to money paid into court to settle High Court actions. See the commentary under that rule, which should be equally applicable here.

## ORDER 74

### (Repealed L.N. 343 of 1989)

## ORDER 75

### (HK) ADMIRALTY PROCEEDINGS

---

## NOTES

**[75.0.1]**

The present Order 75 (see LN 117 of 1988) came into operation on 24 February 1989 upon the commencement of the Supreme Court (Amendment) Ordinance 1989 (see Ordinance No 3 of 1989, section 5).

The Hong Kong High Court in its Admiralty jurisdiction generally follows the practice of the English Admiralty Court (per Hogan CJ in *Taiyo Gyogyo Kabushiki Kaisha v The United Trawler No 5* (1956) 40 HKLR 131, at 141–142 (F Ct)). This continues to be the case since reunification.

For a brief history of the Admiralty Court and its jurisdiction, see Wiswall, *The Development of Admiralty Jurisdiction and Practice since 1800* (1970); *Lovio v Boit* (1815) 7 Fed Cas 418, at 421, per Story J; and the dissenting judgment of Sir John Donaldson MR (as he then was) in *The Goring* [1987] 2 Lloyd's Rep 15 (CA).

For details of Admiralty practice, see Meeson, *Admiralty Jurisdiction and Practice* (3rd ed, 2003); Meeson, *Practice and Procedure of the Admiralty Court: forms and precedents* (1986); and *Roscoe's Admiralty Practice*, 5th ed by Hutchinson (1987 reprint, Professional Books Ltd) referred to by Liu J in *Armco Pacific Ltd v Lim Juliano* [1989] 2 HKC 237.

For useful court forms and precedents, see *Atkin's Encyclopaedia of Court Forms* (above); and Colinvaux et al, *Forms and Precedents* (1973), being Volume 6 of the British Shipping Laws series.

**[75.0.2]    Jurisdiction of the Admiralty court - history**

The forerunner of those sections of the High Court Ordinance which authorise the present Admiralty jurisdiction of the High Court is the Administration of Justice Act 1956, applicable in Hong Kong until 1985 by virtue of SI No 1547 of 1962 (see *The Union Darwin* [1983] HKLR 248. The 1956 Act implemented in the United Kingdom the 1952 International Convention on the Unification of Certain Rules Relating to the Arrest of Sea-going Ships, and in interpreting the 1956 Act (and its successors, including sections 12A–E of Hong Kong's High Court Ordinance), it is permissible to look to the 1952 Convention (per Lord Diplock in *The Eschersheim (The Jade)* [1976] 2 Lloyd's Rep 1, at 6 (HL); per Kempster JA in *The Rolita* [1989] 1 HKLR 394, at 397 (CA)).

Prior to the Supreme Court (Amendment) Ordinance 1989, the source of the High Court's Admiralty jurisdiction was the Colonial Courts of Admiralty Act 1890, in particular, section 2(2).

The Admiralty jurisdiction conferred by the 1890 Act was fixed to be that existing in England in 1890 and not that of the English Admiralty Court as it might be from time to time (*The Yuri Maru* [1927] AC 906 (PC, from Ex Ct, Canada); *The Hai Jye* [1961] HKLR 567, especially at 590–606).

Under the 1890 Act, the Admiralty jurisdiction of the High Court of Hong Kong could only be extended by (UK) Orders in Council. The most recent of these, the Admiralty Jurisdiction (Hong Kong) Order 1985, provided that the local Admiralty jurisdiction would be, with some minor amendments, identical to that of the English Admiralty Court under the Supreme Court Act 1981, sections 20–24.

### [75.0.3]   Jurisdiction of the Admiralty court - present

The Admiralty jurisdiction of the High Court in Hong Kong is now provided for in the High Court Ordinance by virtue of the Supreme Court (Amendment) Ordinance 1989 (in force from 24 February 1989). The amending Ordinance did not alter the Admiralty jurisdiction of the High Court, which remains identical in most respects to that of the English courts, but merely conferred upon that court its Admiralty jurisdiction by a local statute. This was done under the enlarged powers of the Hong Kong legislature conferred by legislation enacted with a view to the localisation, before 1997, of United Kingdom legislation applicable in Hong Kong (see the Hong Kong (Legislative Power) Orders-in-Council 1986 and 1989, pursuant to the Hong Kong Act 1985).

By the Supreme Court (Amendment) Ordinance 1989, section 4, the Admiralty Jurisdiction (Hong Kong) Order 1985 and the Colonial Courts of Admiralty Act 1890, in so far as they were part of the law of Hong Kong, were repealed.

With effect from 1 July 1997 the High Court's Admiralty jurisdiction derives solely from local statute under authority of the Basic Law of the HKSAR. In some instances the local legislation incorporates UK enactments by reference. See the commentary under Order 75 rule 1.

### [75.0.4]   The mode of exercise of Admiralty jurisdiction

Subject to certain restrictions on entertainment of actions *in* personam in collision and similar cases (see section 12C of the High Court Ordinance), an action *in* personam may be brought in the High Court in all cases within the Admiralty jurisdiction of the High Court (section 12B(1) of the High Court Ordinance).

The most significant consequence of being within the Admiralty jurisdiction is that in most cases where the Admiralty Court has jurisdiction, the plaintiff can (a) bring an action *in rem* by serving a writ on the 'particular' vessel (the vessel in connection with which the claim arises), and in some cases a sister ship of the particular vessel, thereby giving the court jurisdiction when the owner himself has not been served, and (b) obtain pre-judgment security by the associated arrest of the vessel.

### [75.0.5]   Particular restrictions on Admiralty jurisdiction

The Admiralty Court has no jurisdiction if the claim is not within the Admiralty jurisdiction specified in the High Court Ordinance (sections 12A–12E of the High Court Ordinance). Whether there is Admiralty jurisdiction is important because certain actions (in particular, *in rem* proceedings) may be brought, and certain causes of action (for example, for salvage) may be heard, only in the Admiralty Court.

## [75.0.6]    Limitation by subject matter and locality

The jurisdiction of the Admiralty Court is limited by subject matter (see section 12A(2)–(3) of the High Court Ordinance) and by locality, the Admiralty Court often having jurisdiction only when the events relating to the claim have taken place in tidal waters (*The Goring* [1987] 2 Lloyd's Rep 15, 35 (CA), per Bingham LJ, affd [1988] 1 Lloyd's Rep 397 (HL)). Limitation by locality is probably less important in Hong Kong than in countries with large internal waterways.

## [75.0.7]    Stay of proceedings in favour of another forum

As with other High Court actions, the court may order a stay of admiralty proceedings in order to enforce an agreement that the dispute be resolved in another jurisdiction or by arbitration or where in the circumstances another jurisdiction is considered more appropriate. See generally the commentary under Order 12 rule 8.

## [75.0.8]    Stay of proceedings commenced in breach of choice of jurisdiction clause

The court's power to order a stay of proceedings commenced in Hong Kong in breach of an agreement to litigate elsewhere is discretionary. The discretion should be exercised by granting a stay unless strong cause for not doing so is shown: *The K H Enterprise* [1994] 2 HKLR 134, 150 (PC, from Hong Kong). See also *The Mahkutai* [1994] 1 HKLR 212 (CA). However, the court should not consider itself obliged to stay proceedings brought in breach of such an agreement: *The Fehmarn* [1957] 2 Lloyd's Rep 551 (CA); *Konsumex Foreign Trade Co & Ors v Sun Luen Transportation Co & Ors* [1990] 1 HKC 247. There are well-established circumstances in which the court might refuse a stay. Some of these are discussed below.

## [75.0.9]    Mixed claims

Where there is a joinder of claims under various bills of lading, some of which contain choice of forum clauses and others not, the court may decline to order a stay of *in rem* proceedings. In such cases the court may apply a hybrid of the tests laid down in *The Eleftheria* [1969] 1 Lloyd's Rep 237 and *Spiliada Maritime Corp v Cansulex Ltd* [1987] AC 460 (HL). The court will consider 'the interests of all the parties and the ends of justice'. See *The Frinton* [1990] 2 HKLR 700 per Fuad VP at 713I-J.

## [75.0.10]    Unfairness – loss of juridical advantage

In *The Andhika Samyra* [1989] 1 HKLR 198 (following *The Hollandia* (*sub nom The Morviken*) [1983] AC 565; 1 Lloyd's Rep 1 (HL)) the court refused to give effect to a choice of forum clause the effect of which would have been to restrict a shipowner's liability to an amount less than that provided for by the Hague-Visby Rules as applied in Hong Kong. This decision was criticised by Murphy at (1990) 20 HKLJ 86.

## [75.0.11]    Waiver

A party may waive its right to rely on an exclusive jurisdiction clause where it has itself commenced proceedings in another jurisdiction: see *The Thorscan* [1998] 4 HKC 536 (CA). In that case a bill of lading provided that any dispute should be decided in the jurisdiction where the carrier had its principal place of business, which was the Netherlands Antilles. The carrier had commenced proceedings in the metropolitan Netherlands, unsuccessfully. The Hong Kong Court of Appeal refused to stay Hong Kong proceedings against the carrier on the ground it had thereby made a final election waiving its right to insist on dispute resolution in its principal place of business.

**[75.0.12)   Stay of proceedings commenced in breach of arbitration clause**
The existence of an arbitration clause may similarly persuade the court to stay proceedings. See generally Order 73 and the commentary thereunder. Arbitration agreements are common in maritime transactions.

**[75.0.13]   Distinction between 'international' and 'domestic' arbitration agreements**
There is a distinction between 'international' and 'domestic' arbitration agreements. If the agreement is 'domestic', as defined in section 2(1) of the Arbitration Ordinance (Cap 341), the court has a discretion under section 6 of that Ordinance whether to order a stay. If the agreement is 'international' the court is obliged to order a stay: see UNCITRAL Model Law, article 8, and sections 34A & 34C of the Arbitration Ordinance (Cap 341). However, it has been said that 'there is a convergence between the international and domestic regimes' with respect to stays of proceedings. See Kaplan *et al*, Hong Kong and China Arbitration – Cases and Materials (1994, Butterworths, pp 1-3, citing, *inter alia*, *Hayter v Nelson & Home Insurance Co* [1990] 2 Lloyd's Rep 265, *Icos Vibro Ltd v SFK Construction Management Ltd* [1992] 1 HKC 296 and *Guangdong Agriculture Co v Conagra International (Far East) Ltd* [1993] 1 HKLR 113.

**[75.0.14]   Requirement for written arbitration agreement**
Clauses contained in bills of lading and purporting to incorporate by reference arbitration clauses from charterparties may not comply with the requirement in article 7(2) of the Model Law that an arbitration agreement must be in writing. See *Hissan Trading Co Ltd v Orkin Shipping Corp* [1993] 2 HKLR 360. There it was held that a bill of lading which incorporated the arbitration clause of a charterparty to which neither the plaintiff nor the defendant was a party did not satisfy the requirement for writing. This was because the bill of lading was not signed by both parties. Also the court held that correspondence between the parties could not be relied upon since the wording of article 7(2) precludes the adoption of memoranda in writing postdating the agreement to arbitrate. See however *William Co v Chu Kong Agency Co Ltd & Anor* [1993] 2 HKC 377 in which Kaplan J held that writing which postdated the agreement to arbitrate could provide a record of the agreement. To decide otherwise, the learned judge said, would place an unnecessarily narrow construction on article 7(2) which did not do justice to the language used and would produce a result in conflict with commercial reality. (See further, Kaplan *et al*, Hong Kong and China Arbitration – Cases and Materials (1994, Butterworths), pp 170-171, and Kaplan 'Just how successful is the Model Law?' (1994) The New Gazette (December) pp 40–43.

**[75.0.15]   Security on stay in favour of arbitration**
It has been suggested that if the Admiralty court orders a stay of proceedings *in rem* in favour of a clause providing for foreign arbitration, the court has no authority to

retain the ship in Hong Kong pending the foreign arbitration award. See *The Ledesco Uno* [1977] HKLR 490; [1978] Lloyd's Rep 99 and see *The Vasso* [1984] 1 Lloyd's Rep 235 (CA) where Goff LJ said (at 242) 'the court's jurisdiction to arrest a ship in an action *in rem* should not be exercised for the purpose of providing security for an award which may be made in arbitration proceedings'.

However if a stay is granted in exercise of the court's discretion under section 6 of the Arbitration Ordinance, it may be ordered that security be posted to secure the award which may be made in the arbitration proceedings. Such security will replace arrest of a vessel. Where a mandatory stay is granted under article 8 of the Model Law no such term may be imposed *(The Vasso)*. Nonetheless it has been held that where it is shown that an arbitration award is unlikely to be satisfied by the defendant, the security available in the action *in rem* may be ordered to stand: *The Vasso* (at 242); *The Rena K* [1978] 1 Lloyd's Rep 545; *The Tuyuti* [1984] 2 Lloyd's Rep 51 (CA); *The Alacrity* [1994] 2 HKC 659; *The Britannia* [1998] 1 HKC 221.

**[75.0.16] Stay of proceedings on other grounds**
See the commentary under Order 12 rule 8 as to other circumstances in which the Hong Kong court will decline to exercise its jurisdiction, notably where there are ongoing proceedings elsewhere, or another jurisdiction is considered more appropriate on the facts of the case.

**[75.0.17] Government immunity**
Ships and cargo belonging to the governments of the Mainland of China and the HKSAR are immune from admiralty action *in rem*. They may not be arrested. See section 12E(2)(c) and (4) of the High Court Ordinance and section 25 of the Crown Proceedings Ordinance (Cap 300). This reflects the common law: see *The Broadmayne* [1916] P 64 (CA). See also Jackson, Enforcement of Maritime Claims (3rd ed, 2000), para 12.137.

Furthermore the government is not liable in tort in respect of any ship, dock or harbour owned by it: see section 4(6) of the Crown Proceedings Ordinance (Cap 300) and see *Cheung Moon Chee v Commissioner of Police* [1992] 1 HKC 271.

**[75.0.18] Foreign sovereign immunity**
A foreign sovereign is, *prima facie*, immune from suits *in rem*. See *The Parlement Belge* (1880) 5 PD 197; *Young v The Scotia* [1903] AC 501 (PC, from Newfoundland) and *Chiu Chik Seng & Ors v The French Government* HCAJ 11/1946 (Williams J; 30.05.1947). However, a vessel owned by a foreign sovereign which is operated as an ordinary merchant ship is no longer entitled to sovereign immunity (*The Philippine Admiral* [1976] 1 Lloyd's Rep 234; [1976] HKLR 512 (PC, from Hong Kong). See also *The Rung Ra Do* [1994] 3 HKC 621, a case involving a sister ship arrest of a vessel alleged to be owned by the government of North Korea. And see *Trendtex Trading v Central Bank of Nigeria* [1977] 1 All ER 881.

Under the normal principles of public international law a foreign sovereign may waive immunity allowing the court to hear an action against it. See for example *Kahan v Pakistan Federation* [1951] 2 KB 1003.

See also Order 75 rule 5(5) which requires that prior notice be given to the local consul of a foreign state before arrest of a ship belonging to the foreign state in connection with a claim for possession or wages.

**[75.0.19] Admiralty list practice direction**
Proceedings listed on the Admiralty list are governed by a practice direction which was substantially revised in 2009 when the civil justice reforms came into force. The updated text of the practice direction may be downloaded from the judiciary's website www.judiciary.gov.hk and that of the Hong Kong Legal Information Institute www.hklii.org, both of which are accessible by the general public free-of-charge.

The practice direction provides that the function of the Admiralty list is to facilitate the disposal of Admiralty actions, whether *in rem* or *in personam*. It goes on to set out procedures to be followed on interlocutory applications, the standard directions the court will normally make at the case management stage. Annexed to the practice direction are the forms of case management questionnaire and pre-trial review checklist to be followed in Admiralty actions.

**[75.0.20] Costs**
In a judgment in November 2003 it was noted that the gross sum assessment procedure for costs had been followed in the Admiralty jurisdiction in Hong Kong for 'many years': *The Columbus Caravelle* HCAJ 282/2000 (Waung J; 06.11.2003). See Order 62 rule 9 and the commentary thereunder as to the gross sum procedure generally.

**1. Application and interpretation** (O. 75 r. 1)
**(1)   This Order applies to Admiralty causes and matters, and the other provisions of these rules apply to those causes and matters subject to the provisions of this Order. (See App B Form 14)**
**(2)   In this Order—**
**"action in rem" means an Admiralty action in rem;**
**"caveat against arrest" means a caveat entered in the caveat book under rule 6;**
**"caveat against release and payment" means a caveat entered in the caveat book under rule 14;**
**"caveat book" means the book kept in the Registry in which caveats issued under this Order are entered;**
**"collision regulations" means the regulations made or deemed to be made under section 93 of the Merchant Shipping (Safety) Ordinance (Cap 369);**
**"limitation action" means an action by shipowners or other persons under the Merchant Shipping Acts 1894 to 1984, the Merchant Shipping (Liability and Compensation for Oil Pollution) Ordinance (Cap 414), the Merchant Shipping (Limitation of Shipowners Liability) Ordinance (Cap 434) or the Bunker Oil Pollution (Liability and Compensation) Ordinance (Cap 605) for the limitation of the amount of their liability in connection with a ship or other property; (L.N. 363 of 1990; 14 of 2009, s 35)**
**"ship" includes any description of vessel used in navigation.**

**NOTES**

**[75.1.1]   References to United Kingdom legislation**
In Order 75 rule 1 and elsewhere in this Order there are references to United Kingdom legislation such as the Merchant Shipping Acts. United Kingdom legislation no longer has any direct application in Hong Kong. However, as a transitional arrangement such legislation may continue to apply if expressly adopted in a local statute. See section 2A(2)(e) of the Interpretation and General Clauses Ordinance (Cap 1). With regard to shipping matters, section 12A(1)(c) of the High Court Ordinance expressly preserves 'any other Admiralty jurisdiction' which the court had prior to amendment of the Ordinance in 1989. However, for the most part, UK shipping legislation which once applied in Hong Kong has been replaced by local legislation.

**2A. Proceedings against, or concerning, the International Oil Pollution Compensation Fund** (O. 75 r. 2A)
  **(2)   For the purposes of section 27(1) of the Merchant Shipping (Liability and Compensation for Oil Pollution) Ordinance (Cap 414) any party to proceedings brought against an owner or guarantor in respect of liability under section 6 of that Ordinance may give notice to the Fund of such proceedings by serving notice in writing on the Fund together with a copy of the writ and copies of the pleadings (if any) served in the action.**
                                                                **(L.N. 363 of 1990)**
  **(3)   The Court shall, on the application made ex parte by the Fund grant leave to the Fund to intervene in any proceedings to which the preceding paragraph applies, whether notice of such proceedings has been served on the Fund or not, and paragraphs (3) and (4) of rule 17 shall apply to such an application.**
  **(4)   Where judgment is given against the Fund in any proceedings under section 25 of the Merchant Shipping (Liability and Compensation for Oil Pollution) Ordinance (Cap 414), the Registrar shall cause a stamped copy of the judgment to be sent by post to the Fund.**
                                                                **(L.N. 363 of 1990)**
  **(5)   The Fund shall notify the Registrar of the matters set out in section 25(11)(b) of the Merchant Shipping (Liability and Compensation for Oil Pollution) Ordinance (Cap 414) by a notice in writing sent by post to, or delivered at, the Registry.**
                                                                **(L.N. 363 of 1990)**

**3.   Issue of writ and acknowledgment of service** (O. 75 r. 3)
  **(1)   An action in rem may be begun by writ; and the writ must be in Form No 1 in Appendix B. (L.N. 152 of 2008)**
  **(2)   The writ by which an Admiralty action in personam is begun must be in Form No 1 in Appendix A.**
  **(3)   The writ by which a limitation action is begun must be in Form No 2 in Appendix B.**
  **(4)   Subject to the following paragraphs Order 6, rule 7, shall apply in relation to a writ by which an Admiralty action is begun.**

(5)    An acknowledgment of service in an action in rem or a limitation action shall be in Form No 2B in Appendix B.

(6)    A defendant to an action in rem in which the writ has not been served, or a defendant to a limitation action who has not been served with the writ, may, if he desires to take part in the proceedings, acknowledge the issue of the writ by handing in at, or sending to, the Registry an acknowledgment of issue in the same form as an acknowledgment of service but with the substitution for the references therein to service of references to issue of the writ.

(7)    These rules shall apply, with the necessary modifications, in relation to an acknowledgment of issue or service in Form 2B in Appendix B as they apply in relation to an acknowledgment of service in Form No. 14 in Appendix A which contains a statement to the effect that the defendant intends to contest the proceedings to which the acknowledgment relates.

## NOTES

### [75.3.1]    Writ in rem against more than one ship

In *The Halla Liberty* [2000] 1 HKC 659 it was argued that it was not permissible to plead claims with regard to seven ships within one writ. This, it was said, followed from the wording of sections 12A and 12B of the High Court Ordinance, which distinguish between the singular and the plural of the word 'ship' (see at 667A-B). The argument was made in the context of an application under Order 12 rule 8 to set aside the writ on jurisdictional grounds. Stone J dismissed the argument (at 668F-669B). The learned judge appeared to recognise the distinction in the statute contended for, but went on to hold 'I do not consider that jurisdiction per se is negated by reason solely of the fact that but one writ has been issued and not seven'.

### [75.3.2]    Service of writ in rem

With regard to the validity and extension of writs in rem, see the commentary under Order 75 rule 8. As to the manner of service of a writ *in rem*, see Order 75 rule 11 and the commentary thereunder.

### [75.3.3]    Order 75 rule 3(1) – Action in rem may be commenced by writ or originating summons

Order 75 rule 3(1) previously provided that an action in rem 'must' be commenced by writ. With effect from 2009 it was amended to provide that such an action 'may' be commenced by writ. That was done as a consequence of amendments to Order 5, which now provides that most civil proceedings may be commenced by writ or originating summons.

*Indorsement as to head of jurisdiction* – There is no specific requirement that a particular head of jurisdiction (*ie* statutory provision under which the action is brought) be indorsed on a writ *in rem*. If such an indorsement is included, it may be stated in the alternative. See *The Pacific Bear* [1979] HKLR 125, 130.

### [75.3.4]    Advantages of action in rem

An action *in rem* is brought against a vessel, freight or cargo ('the *res*'), rather than against a legal or natural person. The principal advantage of an action *in rem* is that it permits the plaintiff to arrest the property concerned (or, in certain circumstances, a sister ship) thereby securing the claim.

In addition there can be a procedural advantage – where the *res* is present in and served in Hong Kong, the court has jurisdiction even though the personal defendant (usually the owner of the *res*) is outside Hong Kong and has not been served. See *The New Hailong* HCAJ 56/1994 (Barnett J; 23.12.1994) where it was held that jurisdiction is founded 'as of right' where a vessel is arrested in Hong Kong (but subject to the court's discretion to decline to exercise its jurisdiction, as to which see the commentary prior to Order 75 rule 1 on stay of proceedings).

**[75.3.5]  Where an action in rem lies**
An action *in rem* lies only for claims with the Admiralty jurisdiction. See *The Rolita* [1989] 1 HKLR 394 (CA). The extent of the Admiralty jurisdiction is set out in section 12A of the High Court Ordinance.

**[75.3.6]  Action in rem by members of crew**
Section 12A(2)(n) of the High Court Ordinance provides that an Admiralty action may be brought by a master or crew for wages. In this context 'crew' may include persons who do not sail with the vessel every day: see *The Tai Shan* HCAJ 344/2001 (Waung J; 09.10.2002). As to the crew's priority on sale of a ship see Order 75 rule 22 and the commentary thereunder.

**[75.3.7]  Action in rem against sister ship**
Section 12A(2)(e)-(q) of the High Court Ordinance lists the type of case which admits of an action *in rem* against a sister ship. Certain preconditions need to be met. See the commentary under Order 75 rule 5. The types of claim listed are not mutually exclusive: *The Eschersheim* [1976] 2 Lloyd's Rep 1, 7 (HL).

**[75.3.8]  Action in rem in respect of maritime lien**
Section 12B(3) of the High Court Ordinance provides the court with jurisdiction *in rem* where there is a claim in respect of a maritime lien or other charge on any ship, aircraft or other property for the amount claimed.

The term 'maritime lien' is not defined in the relevant legislation. It should be distinguished from a statutory right *in rem*, that is a claim which gives rise to an action *in rem* only by virtue of the High Court Ordinance, section 12A.

Maritime liens attach only to claims for salvage, damage done by a ship, wages and disbursements, bottomry and respondentia. Foreign maritime liens will only be recognised if they correspond to local law: *The Halcyon Isle* [1981] AC 221 (PC, from Singapore).

The terms 'maritime lien' and 'other charge' in section 12B(3) of the High Court Ordinance have been interpreted narrowly. 'Maritime lien' is taken to mean a local maritime lien. 'Other charge' is restricted to a foreign claim having the characteristics of a claim which would attract a local maritime lien or to 'charges' which by statute are equated to maritime liens. See *The Accrux* [1965] 1 Lloyd's Rep 565; *The Pacific Bear* [1979] HKLR 125, 131.

**[75.3.9]  Residual jurisdiction in rem**
Section 12A(1)(c) of the High Court Ordinance preserves any residual admiralty jurisdiction which existed in Hong Kong prior to the commencement of the 1989

amendments to the Ordinance. This includes some aspects of jurisdiction *in rem*. One example may be the jurisdiction exercised by the English court in *The Despina GK* [1982] 2 Lloyd's Rep 555. It was there held that an action *in rem* will lie by way of enforcement of a foreign judgment *in rem*.

### [75.3.10]    Order 75 rule 3(2) – An Admiralty action may be in personam

Section 12B(1) of the High Court Ordinance provides that an action *in personam* may be brought in the Admiralty jurisdiction of the Court of First Instance. Section 12C limits this Admiralty jurisdiction *in personam*, in certain factual scenarios, to cases where there is a specified connection with Hong Kong. Order 75 rule 3(2) provides that an Admiralty action *in personam* shall be commenced by writ in the same form as that used for general civil actions (form No 1 in Appendix A).

### [75.3.11]    Acknowledgement of service of writ in rem

Order 75 rule 3(5) prescribes a special form of acknowledgement of service for an action *in rem* or limitation action (form No 2B in Appendix B).

### [75.3.12]    Only registered owner may acknowledge service of writ in rem

For the purposes of a writ *in rem* against the owner of a ship, 'owner' is taken to mean the registered owner save in the most unusual circumstances. It follows that only the registered owner may properly acknowledge service. See *The Tian Xiang 2 Hao* HCAJ 322/2001 (Reyes J; 08.10.2003) where an acknowledgement of service filed on behalf of a party claiming to be beneficial owner was set aside. Citing *The Able Lieutenant* [2002] 6 MLJ 433 it was held that the proper course for the party claiming beneficial ownership was to apply under Order 75 rule 17 for leave to intervene in the action.

### [75.3.13]    Acknowledgement of unserved writ in rem

Order 75 rule 3(6) permits a defendant to acknowledge issue of a writ which has not yet been served. This enables the defendant to make a 'pre-emptive strike': *The Tuyuti* [1984] 2 Lloyd's Rep 51, 53 (CA). In that case the defendant shipowners acknowledged issue of the writ so as to enable them to make an application for a stay of proceedings. Although the stay was granted the associated warrant of arrest was allowed to stand.

In *The Pacific Bear* [1979] HKLR 125 the court considered whether a defendant could abuse this rule to avoid arrest in a case where a writ is issued in respect of more than one ship. Cons J said, at 129:

> Furthermore by judicious choice of ships a defendant might be able to emasculate the new found remedy of the plaintiffs [ie arrest of sister ships]. Only one ship may be arrested. The defendant would enter appearance for that one of his ships least likely to call within the jurisdiction, and the others could then continue to call with impunity. To my mind that cannot be right. The Act gives the choice to the plaintiff. It must be the fact of arrest, or similar action, and not the fact of service, which demonstrates the exercise of that choice.

### [75.3.14]    Duration and renewal of writ in rem

See the commentary under Order 75 rule 8.

**[75.3.15]   Amendment of Admiralty writ**

An Admiralty writ may be amended like a writ commencing an ordinary action. As noted in the commentary under Order 20 rule 5, special considerations arise where it is sought to amend so as to introduce a new cause of action which has become statute barred. In *The Almerinda* [2002] 1 HKC 75 the Court of Final Appeal refused leave to appeal against a decision allowing amendment of an Admiralty writ after expiration of the 12-month period prescribed by art III r 6 of the Hague-Visby Rules. The CFA, at 79H-I agreed with the view of the Court of Appeal that the rule 'did not operate so as to impose a time-bar against subsequent amendments to add further grounds of liability, whether in the shape of new causes of action' or otherwise.

**4.   Service of writ out of jurisdiction** (O. 75 r. 4)

**(1)   Subject to the following provisions of this rule, service out of the jurisdiction of a writ containing any claim for damage, loss of life or personal injury arising out of a collision between ships or the carrying out of or omission to carry out a manoeuvre in the case of one or more of two or more ships or non-compliance on the part of one or more of two or more ships with the collision regulations, every limitation action and every action to enforce a claim under section 6 or 25 of the Merchant Shipping (Liability and Compensation for Oil Pollution) Ordinance (Cap 414) or section 5 of the Bunker Oil Pollution (Liability and Compensation) Ordinance (Cap 605) is permissible with the leave of the Court if, but only if— (L.N. 363 of 1990, 14 of 2009 s 36 )**

> **(a)   the defendant has his habitual residence or a place of business in Hong Kong; or**
>
> **(b)   the cause of action arose within the territorial waters of Hong Kong; or**
>
> **(c)   an action arising out of the same incident or series of incidents is proceeding in the Court or has been heard and determined in the Court; or**
>
> **(d)   the defendant has submitted or agreed to submit to the jurisdiction of the Court.**

**(2)   Order 11, rule 4(1), (2) and (4), shall apply in relation to an application for the grant of leave under this rule as it applies in relation to an application for the grant of leave under rule 1 of that Order. (L.N. 152 of 2008)**

**(3)   Paragraph (1) shall not apply to an action in rem.**

**(4)   The proviso to rule 7(1) of Order 6 and Order 11, rule 1(2), shall not apply to a writ by which any Admiralty action is begun.**

---

**NOTES**

**[75.4.1]   Service outside Hong Kong of Admiralty writ in personam**

Order 75 rule 4 empowers the court to grant leave to serve an Admiralty writ *in personam* out of Hong Kong in certain factual scenarios. This fills the gap created by Order 11 rule 1(4) (by which the general power under Order 11 rule 1 to grant leave to serve *ex juris* does not apply in more or less the same factual scenarios).

Broadly speaking the factual scenarios catered for by rule 4 are:

- Claims arising out of a collision between ships, failure to carry out a manoeuvre or non-compliance with collision regulations
- Limitation actions (defined in rule 1)
- Claims under the Merchant Shipping (Liability and Compensation for Oil Pollution) Ordinance (Cap 414).

In order to obtain leave it must be demonstrated that the claim has one of the qualifying connections with Hong Kong listed in paragraphs (a) to (d) of rule 4(1). These are discussed below.

The criteria laid down by rule 4 are broadly the same as those in section 12C of the High Court Ordinance which defines the ambit of the court's Admiralty jurisdiction *in personam*.

Unlike ordinary actions, leave is always required for service *ex juris* in the Admiralty jurisdiction: Order 75 rule 4(4) excludes application of Order 11 rule 1(2) (which provides that in certain circumstances an ordinary writ may be served out of Hong Kong without the need to obtain leave) in Admiralty actions.

Save as excluded by this rule and Order 11 rule 1(4), the general rules governing service outside Hong Kong apply in the Admiralty context. Likewise considerations such as *forum non conveniens* under which the court may stay Hong Kong proceedings in favour of another forum. See *The Adhiguna Meranti* [1987] HKLR 904 (CA), *The Oceania Queen* HCAJ 276/1985 (Mayo J; 29.01.1988) and see the commentary under Order 12 rule 8.

The power under this rule to grant leave to serve a writ out of the jurisdiction does not extend to writs in rem: see rule 4(3) and the commentary below.

Echoing section 12C of the Ordinance, rule 4 provides that leave will only be granted if there is a sufficient connection with Hong Kong. The types of connection which qualify are set out in rule 4(1)(a) to (d) and are discussed below.

**[75.4.2]  Rule 4(1)(a) – 'place of business in Hong Kong'**

Rule 4(1)(a) provides that if a defendant is habitually resident in Hong Kong or has a place of business here, that is a sufficient connection with the SAR for leave to be granted to serve an Admiralty writ out of the jurisdiction.

Habitual residence probably equates with ordinary residence, a term used elsewhere in these rules.

The test for determining whether a defendant has a place of business in Hong Kong in this context is likely to be the same as that applied where a plaintiff seeks to serve a body corporate at its 'place of business' in Hong Kong under the Companies Ordinance (see the commentary under Order 65 rule 3). In *The Artemis* [1983] HKLR 364 the Court of Appeal laid down guidelines for determining the question in such cases. The Court of Appeal held that the question is one of fact (following *The World Harmony* [1965] 1 Lloyd's Rep 244) with the onus of proof falling on the plaintiff (following *The Theodohos* [1977] 2 Lloyd's Rep 428). See also *Yuasa Trading Co (HK) Ltd v Selina Shipping* [1989] HKLY 1078; HCCL 8/1989 (Mayo J; 16.06.1989); and *MCY Finance Ltd SA & Ors v Hong Kong Shanghai (Shipping) Ltd* [1986] HKC 323, (1987) 17 HKLJ 372.

**[75.4.3]**   **Rule 4(1)(b) – cause of action arising within territorial waters of Hong Kong**

Under Order 74 rule 4(1)(b) there is sufficient connection with Hong Kong to obtain leave to serve an Admiralty writ out of the jurisdiction if the cause of action arose within the territorial waters of Hong Kong.

As to the precise boundaries of the Hong Kong SAR and its territorial waters see Order of the State Council of the PRC, No 221, (01.07.1997) (reproduced in vol 1 of the looseleaf edition of the Laws of Hong Kong).

**[75.4.4]**   **Writ in rem may not be served out of the jurisdiction**

Order 75 rule 4(3) excludes writs *in rem* from the ambit of the court's power to grant leave to serve an Admiralty writ outside Hong Kong. It is considered not possible for service of a writ *in rem* to be effected out of the jurisdiction. Likewise substituted service of a writ *in rem* is not normally appropriate. See *The Good Herald* [1987] 1 Lloyd's Rep 236, 238 and see the commentary under Order 75 rule 11.

**5.   Warrant of arrest** (O. 75 r. 5)

    **(1)**   **After a writ has been issued in an action in rem a warrant in Form No 3 in Appendix B for the arrest of the property against which the action or any counterclaim in the action is brought may, subject to the provisions of this rule, be issued at the instance of the plaintiff or of the defendant, as the case may be.**

    **(3)**   **A party applying for the issue out of the Registry of a warrant to arrest any property shall procure a search to be made in the caveat book for the purpose of ascertaining whether there is a caveat against arrest in force with respect to that property.**

    **(4)**   **A warrant of arrest shall not be issued until the party applying for it has filed an affidavit requesting issue of the warrant together with an affidavit made by him or his agent containing the particulars required by paragraph (8) so, however, that the Court may, if it thinks fit, allow the warrant to issue notwithstanding that the affidavit does not contain all those particulars.**

    **(5)**   **Except with the leave of the Court, a warrant of arrest shall not be issued in an action in rem against a foreign ship belonging to a port of a State having a consulate in Hong Kong, being an action for possession of the ship or for wages, until notice that the action has been begun has been sent to the consul.**

    **(6)**   **Except with the leave of the Court, a warrant of arrest shall not be issued in an action in rem in which there is a claim arising out of bottomry until the bottomry bond and, if the bond is in a foreign language, a notarial translation thereof is produced to the Registrar.**

    **(7)**   **Where, by, or under, any convention or treaty, Hong Kong has undertaken to minimise the possibility of arrest of ships of another state, no application shall be made for the issue of a warrant of arrest in an action in rem against a ship owned by that state until a notice in Form No 15 in Appendix B has been served on a consular officer at the consular office of, or acting on behalf of, that state in Hong Kong.**

(8)   An affidavit required by paragraph (4) must state—

   (a)   in every case—

      (i)   the nature of the claim or counterclaim and that it has not been satisfied and, if it arises in connection with a ship, the name of that ship; and

      (ii)   the nature of the property to be arrested and, if the property is a ship, the name of the ship and her port of registry; and

   (b)   in the case of a claim against a ship in rem by virtue of paragraph (10)—

      (i)   the name of the person who would be liable on the claim in an action in personam ("the relevant person"); and

      (ii)   that the relevant person was when the cause of action arose the owner or charterer of, or in possession or in control of, the ship in connection with which the claim arose; and

      (iii)   that at the time of the issue of the writ the relevant person was either the beneficial owner of all the shares in the ship in respect of which the warrant is required or (where appropriate) the charterer of it under a charter by demise; and

   (c)   in the case of a claim for possession of a ship or for wages, the nationality of the ship in respect of which the warrant is required and that the notice (if any) required by paragraph (5) has been sent;

   (e)   in the case of a claim in respect of a liability incurred under Section 6 of the Merchant Shipping (Liability and Compensation for Oil Pollution) Ordinance (Cap 414), the facts relied on as establishing that the Court is not prevented from entertaining the action by reason of section 18(1) of that Ordinance; and (L.N. 363 of 1990)

   (f)   in the case of a claim in respect of a liability incurred under section 5 of the Bunker Oil Pollution (Liability and Compensation) Ordinance (Cap 605), the facts relied on as establishing that the Court is not prevented from entertaining the action by reason of section 18(2) of that Ordinance. (14 of 2009 s 37)

(9)   The following documents shall, where appropriate, be exhibited to an affidavit required by paragraph (4)—

   (a)   a copy of any notice sent to a consul under paragraph (5);

   (b)   a certified copy of any bottomry bond, or of the translation thereof, produced under paragraph (6).

   (c)   a copy of any notice served on a consular officer under paragraph (7).

(10)   The claims against a ship in rem coming within the provisions of sub-paragraph (b) (whether or not the claim gives rise to a maritime lien on that ship) are—

   (a)   for damage done by a ship;

   (b)   for loss of life or personal injury sustained in consequence of any defect in a ship or in her apparel or equipment or in consequence of the wrongful act, neglect or default of the owners, charterers or persons in possession or control of a ship or the master or crew of a ship or any other person for whose wrongful acts, neglects or defaults the owners, charterers or persons in possession or control of a ship are responsible, being an act, neglect or default in the navigation or management of a ship in the loading, carriage or discharge of goods on, in or from the ship or in the embarkation, carriage or disembarkation of persons on, in or from the ship;

(c)   for loss of or damage to goods carried in a ship;

(d)   those arising out of any agreement relating to the carriage of goods in a ship or to the use or hire of a ship;

(e)   those in the nature of salvage (including any claim arising by virtue of the application by or under section 9 of the Civil Aviation Ordinance (Cap 448), of the law relating to salvage to aircraft and their apparel and cargo); (L.N. 152 of 2008)

(f)   those in the nature of towage or pilotage in respect of a ship or an aircraft when an action in rem may be brought against that aircraft if, at the time when the action is brought, it is beneficially owned by the person who would be liable on the claim in an action in personam;

(g)   those in respect of goods or materials supplied to a ship for her operation or maintenance;

(h)   those in respect of the construction, repair or equipment of a ship or dock charges or dues;

(i)   those by a master or member of a crew of a ship for wages (including any sum allotted out of wages or adjudged by a superintendent to be due by way of wages);

(j)   those by a master, shipper, charterer or agent in respect of disbursements made on account of a ship;

(k)   those arising out of an act which is or is claimed to be a general average act;

(l)   those arising out of bottomry.

And where the person who would be liable on the claim in an action in personam ("the relevant person") was, when the cause of action arose, the owner or charterer of, or in possession or in control of, the ship and at the time when the action is brought is either the beneficial owner of that ship as respects all the shares in it or the charterer of it under a charter by demise or, in the case of any other ship, where the relevant person is the beneficial owner as respects all the shares in it at the time when the action is brought.

## NOTES

### [75.5.1]   Numbering

Note that there is no paragraph (d) in Order 75 rule 5(8): rule 5(8)(e) comes immediately after rule 5(8)(c). In the former English RSC, rule 5(8)(d) required that the affidavit required by rule 5(4) must state, where appropriate, that the notice as required by rule 5(7) had been served on a consular officer. It is not known why this requirement was omitted from the Hong Kong rules; however a possible reason is that it is redundant in view of rule 5(9)(a) which in any event requires that a copy of the notice be exhibited to the affidavit.

## [75.5.2]  Arrest of property
Order 75 rule 5(1) empowers the court to issue a warrant of arrest of property against which an action *in rem* has been commenced. A warrant will not be issued as a matter of course; the court has a discretion to refuse to issue it (*The Vasso (formerly Andria)* [1984] 1 Lloyd's Rep 235, at 241 (CA); *The Amigo* [1991] 2 HKC 491; *cf Taiyo Gyogyo Kabushiki Kaisha v The United Trawler No 5* (1956) 40 HKLR131, at 145 (F Ct), per Reece J). It seems that the discretion to refuse an arrest warrant is seldom exercised (*The Vanessa Ann* [1985] 1 Lloyd's Rep 549, 551 (QB, Ad Ct) per Staughton J). In The *Yuan Tong* No 6 [2003] 3 HKC 428 a warrant for arrest of a ship was refused where there was no information as to the ship's whereabouts. Waung J held that an application for an arrest warrant should not be made until the solicitors are in a position to inform the court that the ship has arrived in or is on its way to Hong Kong. It was held that it is up to the solicitors, not the Marine Department or the court bailiff to keep track of the whereabouts of the ship.

Note that *The Varna* [1993] 2 Lloyd's Rep 253 (CA), which held that the issuance of a warrant of arrest is not discretionary, does not apply in Hong Kong since that decision was decided on 1986 amendments to Order 75 rule 5 of the English Rules of the Supreme Court, which amendments have not been incorporated into the Hong Kong Rules.

Where an arrest is wrongful, damages for wrongful arrest may only be brought where there is *mala fides* or *crassa negligentia*. The wrongfulness of the arrest alone does not entitle the shipowner to damages (*The Amigo* HCAJ 115/1991 (Barnett J; 22.02.1994)), relying on *The Evangelismos* (1858) Swa 378 (PC) and *The Walter D Wallet* [1893] P 202).

## [75.5.3]  Prior arrest in another jurisdiction not a bar
The fact that a vessel was previously arrested in another jurisdiction in respect of the same claim, and has been released, is not a bar to a second arrest in Hong Kong. As an example see *The Silver Ocean* HCAJ 208/2000 (Waung J; 03.12.2001).

## [75.5.4]  Power to order arrest before issue of writ
There are conflicting authorities on the question whether the court has power to issue a warrant of arrest before proceedings have been commenced. The question is important in cases where a warrant is sought urgently on account of imminent departure of a vessel outside of court hours.

In *The Dragon Supreme* [1997] 3 HKC 405 Keith J held that there was no pre-writ jurisdiction to issue an arrest warrant. This decision was based on the opening words of rule 5(1) ('After a writ has been issued ...') and on rule 5(4) (which provides that a warrant shall not be issued until the affidavit in support has been filed). The judge recognised that his decision left a gap, and recommended that Hong Kong adopt Order 6 rule 7A of the former English RSC whereby certain types of writ may be issued even when the registry is closed. As at early 2008, despite the passage of more than a decade, that has not been done.

In *The Dragon No 1* [1998] 3 HKC 684 Waung J expressly doubted the judgment of Keith J saying (at 688E-G) that 'the issue of the writ before the issue of the warrant might not be such a strict statutory requirement which absolutely prohibits the court from exercising its discretion to grant the warrant'. This view was stated by Waung J to be 'somewhat tentative' (at 689D), and may not be regarded as part of the ratio of the decision which was to issue a second warrant rather than to release the vessel.

### [75.5.5] Power to order arrest in absence of debt

A vessel may be arrested as security for a claim based on an 'event of default' as defined in a mortgage document even in advance of any payment becoming overdue: *The Maule* [1997] 1 HKC 231 (PC).

### [75.5.6] Application for warrant of arrest to be made by affidavit

Order 75 rule 5(4) provides that a party seeking a warrant of arrest of property in an admiralty action shall do so by filing an affidavit. The affidavit must request the issue of a warrant of arrest and contain the particulars required by rule 5(8). The application is made *ex parte* and will normally be considered by the Registrar.

### [75.5.7] Factors considered by court on application for warrant of arrest

The court's first concern in dealing with an application for a warrant of arrest is whether the action is *prima facie* one which comes within the Admiralty jurisdiction: *The Amigo* [1991] 2 HKC 491. Otherwise the court is not at this stage concerned with the merits, but only with what is 'material to the granting or refusal of an arrest warrant': *The Cynthia G* HCAJ 367/1984 (Clough J; 06.02.1985).

Where the affidavit is made by a solicitor on instructions of the plaintiff it is the registrar's duty 'to enquire into any matter…that gives rise to doubts as to whether the grounds of belief expressed are genuinely those of both the plaintiff and the solicitor': *The Cynthia G* HCAJ 367/1984 (Clough J; 06.02.1985). In *The Kum Susan Ho* HCAJ 156/1982 (Mayo J; 02.06.1982) proceedings were set aside and a vessel released from arrest where a solicitor's affidavit in support of the arrest warrant was based on hearsay evidence and did not satisfy the burden of proof.

### [75.5.8] Duty of full and frank disclosure on application for arrest warrant

As with all *ex parte* applications there is a duty of full and frank disclosure when applying for a warrant of arrest in the Admiralty jurisdiction. Breach of the duty may result in the warrant being set aside. See generally the commentary under Order 32 rule 6 concerning setting aside *ex parte* orders for material non-disclosure.

An arrest warrant will not be set aside for immaterial non-disclosure: *The Tat Yau 8* [1998] 4 HKC 108, 114I-115F. The test to be applied was stated as follows by the Singapore Court of Appeal in *The Damavand* [1993] 2 SLR 717, 731:

> [W]hether the fact is relevant to the making of the decision whether or not to issue the warrant of arrest, that is, a fact which should properly be taken into consideration when weighing all the circumstances of the case, though it need not have the effect of leading to a different decision being made.

Thus a warrant will be set aside where the undisclosed material 'would have been taken into account': *The Cynthia G* HCAJ 367/1984 (Clough J; 06.02.1985). In *The J*

*Faster* [2000] 1 HKC 652, 657G-658A Waung J set aside an arrest warrant obtained without disclosure of evidence which went 'to the heart of the plaintiff's case against the defendant'.

Since the merits are not relevant at the arrest stage, non-disclosure thereof will not necessarily be fatal: *The Harima* [1987] HKLR 770 (CA); *The Trust* CACV 164/1991 (Penlington & Nazareth JJA, Liu J; 30.04.1991).

The person making the affidavit in support of the application for an arrest warrant can only be expected to disclose facts which are, or ought to be, within his knowledge. In *The Silver Ocean* HCAJ 208/2000 (Waung J; 03.12.2001) the court refused to set aside a warrant where it was 'inherently highly improbable' that the party knew or ought to have known the facts which were not disclosed.

Disclosure means bringing the material to the attention of the court. It may not be sufficient if it is buried in a stack of papers. See *The Vasiliy Golovnin* [2007] SGHC 116 (31.07.2007) where Tan Lee Meng J said in the Singapore High Court:

> clearly it is of no use putting it in if the judge either cannot or does not read it. It is just as much not disclosed as if it had not been put in at all. Unless the document is presented to the eyes and/or the ears of the judge, it is not disclosed.

The court may also set aside an arrest warrant 'as a matter of public policy to discourage the abuse of its procedure': *The Cynthia G* (above).

### [75.5.9] Arrest of foreign ship - prior notice to consulate
Where it is sought to arrest a foreign ship from a country which has consular representation in Hong Kong prior notice to the consul is required if the action is for possession of the ship or for wages. See Order 75 rule 5(5). The fact that such notice has been given must be stated in the affidavit in support of the application for the arrest warrant: Order 75 rule 5(8)(c).

### [75.5.10] Power to arrest in support of arbitration
The court has power to maintain the arrest of a vessel notwithstanding the mandatory stay of proceedings by virtue of an arbitration agreement. See *The Britannia* [1998] 1 HKC 221, citing *The Tuyuti* [1984] 1 QB 838, [1984] 2 Lloyd's Rep 51 and *The Bazias* [1993] QB 673. This jurisdiction is exceptional, limited to allowing security in the *res* to be retained for the purpose of execution of an anticipated arbitration award and does not extend to allowing other aspects of the Admiralty jurisdiction *in rem* to continue: *The Halla Liberty* HCAJ 400/1997 (Stone J; 24.07.1998) (para 13).

### [75.5.11] Affidavit should identify property to be arrested
The affidavit in support of an application for a warrant of arrest should make clear whether arrest is sought of the vessel alone or also the cargo laden thereon: see *The Asia Star* HCAJ 1/1999 (Waung J; 23.06.2000).

### [75.5.12] Special requirements for affidavit in particular cases
In certain types of Admiralty claims, such as those for loss of life or personal injury (see the list in Order 75 rule 5(10)) the affidavit in support of an application for a warrant of arrest must include information such as the name of the person who would be liable *in personam*. The information which must be set out is stipulated by Order 75 rule 5(8)(b).

The list of claims in rule 5(10) is similar to that set out in section 12A(2)(e)-(q) of the High Court Ordinance. It is only in respect of these claims that sister ship arrest is possible.

**[75.5.13]  Order 75 rule 5(8)(b)(i) – meaning of person 'who would be liable in personam'**

The meaning of 'the person who would be liable' on the claim if the action were brought *in personam* (which must be stated in the affidavit in support of an arrest warrant in cases to which rule 5(8)(b)(i) applies) is well established. It means the person who would be liable if the claim is successful, not the person who is in fact liable. Actual liability is not an issue to be determined at this preliminary stage. See *The Harima* [1987] HKLR 770 (CA), citing *The St Elefterio* [1957] P 179, 186. In *The Harima* a defendant argued that the bill of lading on which the action *in rem* was founded was void for illegality and, therefore, the defendant shipowner was not a 'person who would be liable...' The court held it was unnecessary at this stage to go into the merits and so long as the defendant would be liable if the bill of lading were not void, a warrant of arrest could issue.

**[75.5.14]  Order 75 rule 5(8)(b)(ii) – connection with ship giving rise to cause of action**

In those cases to which it applies, Order 75 rule 5(8)(b)(ii) requires that the affidavit state the connection between the person who would be liable if the action were *in personam* and the ship in connection with which the cause of action arose. Four types of connection are specified. The person must be (i) owner, (ii) charterer, (iii) in possession or (iv) in control, of the ship. These reflect the requirements of section 12B(4)(b) of the High Court Ordinance as to when an action *in rem* may be brought. As to the meaning of 'owner' in this context, see *The Convenience Container* [2006] 4 HKC 435 (appeal dismissed: [2007] 4 HKC 489).

The relevant time is when the cause of action arose.

**[75.5.15]  Sister ship arrest – ownership issues**

Regarding ownership and sister ship arrest, vessels owned by a series of one-ship companies will not usually be treated as sister ships notwithstanding that the one-ship companies are owned by a single holding company or the same individual shareholders, unless there is some real indication that the registration of the one-ship companies as owners is a sham (*The Evpo Agnic* [1988] 2 Lloyd's Rep 411 (CA), reversing Sheen J; *The Neptune* [1986] HKLR 345, 348–351; *cf The Maritime Trader* [1981] 2 Lloyd's Rep 153 (QB, Ad Ct) and *The Saudi Prince* [1982] 2 Lloyd's Rep 255 (QB, Ad Ct), both being decisions of Sheen J). But see *The Rung Ra Do* [1994] 3 HKC 621, a case involving the sister ship arrest of a vessel alleged to have been owned by the government of North Korea.

Regarding charterers and sister ship arrest, where the 'relevant person' contemplated in rule 5(10) (and section 12B(4)(a) of the High Court Ordinance), ie the person who would be liable on the claim in an action *in personam*, is a charterer (whether time, voyage or by demise), a ship of which he is the sole beneficial owner at the time when the action is brought is liable to arrest as a 'sister ship', although properly it is not one in that the two ships are not owned by the same person (*The Span Terza* [1982] 1 Lloyd's Rep 225 (CA); *The Sextum (ex Ercole Lauro)* [1982] 2

Lloyd's Rep 532; [1982] HKLR 356; *The Riau v The Djatianom* [1982] HKLR 427; cf *The Evpo Agnic* [1988] 2 Lloyd's Rep 411, at 414 (CA)).

A wrongdoing vessel under demise charter can be arrested (section 12B(4)(i)), but a vessel under demise to the relevant person cannot be arrested as a sister ship (section 12B(4)(ii)); *The Union Darwin* [1983] HKLR 248 is now obsolete on this point.

#### [75.5.16]   Order 75 rule 5(8)(b)(iii) - connection with ship to be arrested

In addition to stating the connection between the person who would be liable *in personam* and the ship in connection with which the cause of action arose (see above), the affidavit must state that person's connection with the ship to be arrested (which may be a sister ship). That person must be the beneficial owner of the ship or demise charterer thereof. The relevant time is the issue of the writ. This additional information will be relevant on an application to arrest a sister ship.

#### [75.5.17]   Restriction on arrest of more than one sister ship

A plaintiff may issue writs against more than one sister ship but may only serve and arrest one of them in respect of a single cause of action: section 12B(8) of the High Court Ordinance. As to interpretation of that section see *The Banco* [1971] 1 Lloyd's Rep 49 (CA); *The Berny* [1977] 2 Lloyd's Rep 533 and *The Stephan J* [1985] 2 Lloyd's Rep 344, 346.

In *The Neptune* [1986] HKLR 345 a plaintiff who had already arrested a ship in Sri Lanka arrested a second one in Hong Kong. It sought to justify the second arrest with a suggestion the two vessels might not be sister ships. Nazareth J set aside the second arrest warrant on the ground the claims against both ships were identical and the principle laid down in *The Banco* would be infringed if more than one arrest were allowed.

In *The K H Enterprise* [1989] 1 HKLR 465 Mayo J, citing *The Stephan J* [1985] 2 Lloyd's Rep 344, held that a second arrest was permissible since the first arrested vessel was not in fact a sister ship and had been arrested by mistake. A prior arrest will only preclude a subsequent one where the prior arrest was of a ship against which an action *in rem* could be brought.

#### [75.5.18]   Establishing beneficial ownership of sister ship to be arrested

In order to obtain an arrest warrant against a sister ship, it must be established that the sister ship is beneficially owned by the person who would be liable if an action were brought *in personam*. The court will look behind the registered ownership in order to determine the question of beneficial ownership. See *The Rung Ra Do* [1994] 3 HKC 621, citing *I Congreso Del Partido* [1978] QB 500 and The *Aventicum* [1978] 1 Lloyd's Rep 184 (QB). In *The Rung Ra Do*, a case of sister ship arrest, the court found that the registered owner of the sister ship was a state enterprise through which the government of North Korea was exercising beneficial ownership.

#### [75.5.19]   Change of ownership of ship to be arrested

Changes to ownership of a ship after a writ has been issued will not enable arrest to be evaded: see *The Monica S* [1967] 2 Lloyd's Rep 113 (CA). In *The Silver Ocean* HCAJ 208/2000 (Waung J; 03.12.2001) it was said that the principle arising from the *Monica S*:

... gives to a maritime claimant the right to arrest a ship even in the possession of a new owner provided that the writ is issued before the change of ownership. The new owner in such circumstances has to live with the consequences so to speak of the sins of the former owner and his remedy is not to have the ship released from arrest but to seek indemnity against the previous owner who very often is not worth suing. The principle of *Monica S* is well known to all maritime lawyers and the fact that the new owner will suffer by the arrest does not in any way influence the admiralty court's decision and duty to have a vessel arrested so long as the writ in question was issued before the change of ownership.

Likewise the fact the ship has gone off demise charter will not affect the power to arrest: *The Deichland* [1988] 2 Lloyd's Rep 454, 456 (reversed on appeal on other grounds – see [1989] 2 Lloyd's Rep 113 (CA)).

**[75.5.20]   Order 75 rule 5(10) – list of claims where special requirements for affidavit apply**

Order 75 rule 5(10) is a list of the types of claim to which rule 5(8)(b) applies. In other words it lists the claims where an affidavit in support of an application for an arrest warrant is subject to special requirements as to the information to be provided.

Rule 5(10) is unhappily worded. First, in the opening sentence the reference to 'sub-paragraph (b)' should be to 'subparagraph (8)(b)'. Secondly, the final sentence appears to be incomplete - though it has 105 words it does not seem to have a predicate. The sentence may be intended to be a proviso to the whole of rule 5(10), or perhaps the last item in the list therein set down. It is not clear.

Rule 5(10)(e) continues to refer to the Civil Aviation Act 1949 (UK) although that Act was repealed so far as it applied to Hong Kong by section 15 of the Civil Aviation Ordinance (Cap 448), enacted in 1994.

**6.   Caveat against arrest** (O. 75 r. 6)

**(1)   A person who desires to prevent the arrest of any property must file in the Registry a praecipe, in Form No 5 in Appendix B, signed by him or his solicitor undertaking–**

   **(a)   to acknowledge issue or service (as may be appropriate) of the writ in any action that may be begun against the property described in the praecipe, and**

   **(b)   within 3 days after receiving notice that such an action has been begun, to give bail in the action in a sum not exceeding an amount specified in the praecipe or to pay the amount so specified into court,**

**and on the filing of the praecipe a caveat against the issue of a warrant to arrest the property described in the praecipe shall be entered in the caveat book.**

**(2)   The fact that there is a caveat against arrest in force shall not prevent the issue of a warrant to arrest the property to which the caveat relates.**

**NOTES**

**[75.6.1]   Caveat against arrest**

A person who wishes to prevent arrest of any property subject to the Admiralty jurisdiction may file a caveat under Order 75 rule 6. The person must undertake in the caveat (*inter alia*) to post bail up to a specified amount if an action is commenced.

Whilst such a caveat does not preclude the issue of a warrant for arrest it will clearly be taken into account.

The purpose of the caveat procedure is 'to avoid the necessity of the usual procedure in admiralty of causing the warrant to be issued … and for security to be furnished [for] release from arrest': *The Jian She* 33 [2001] 2 HKC 493, 496G.

In the event of an arrest warrant being sought a party is obliged to search the caveat book (Order 75 rule 5(3)) and will be required to give full and frank disclosure in accordance with the usual practice.

### [75.6.2]   Caveat by owner – effect on demise charterer
A bail bond posted by an owner pursuant to a caveat is limited to itself and does not extend to liability of a demise charterer. See *The Jian She* 33 [2001] 2 HKC 493.

### 7.   Remedy where property protected by caveat is arrested (O. 75 r.7)
**Where any property with respect to which a caveat against arrest is in force is arrested in pursuance of a warrant of arrest, the party at whose instance the caveat was entered may apply to the Court by motion for an order under this rule and, on the hearing of the application, the Court, unless it is satisfied that the party procuring the arrest of the property had a good and sufficient reason for so doing, may by order discharge the warrant and may also order the last-mentioned party to pay to the applicant damages in respect of the loss suffered by the applicant as a result of the arrest.**

### 8.   Service of writ in action in rem (O. 75 r. 8)
**(1)   Subject to paragraph (2), a writ by which an action in rem is begun must be served on the property against which the action is brought save that–**

> **(a)   where that property is freight it must be served on the cargo in respect of which the freight is payable or on the ship in which that cargo was carried, or**

> **(b)   where the property has been sold by the bailiff, the writ may not be served on that property, but a sealed copy of it must be filed in the Registry and the writ shall be deemed to have been duly served on the day on which it was filed.**

**(2)   A writ need not be served or filed as mentioned in paragraph (1) if the writ is deemed to have been duly served on the defendant by virtue of Order 10, rule 1 (4) or (5).**

**(3)   Where by virtue of this rule a writ is required to be served on any property, then, if the plaintiff wishes service of the writ to be effected by the bailiff, he must file in the Registry a praecipe in Form No 6 in Appendix B and lodge–**

> **(a)   the writ and a copy thereof, and**

> **(b)   an undertaking to pay on demand all expenses incurred by the bailiff or his substitute in respect of the service of the writ,**

**and thereupon the bailiff or his substitute shall serve the writ on the property described in the praecipe.**

**(3A)   Where a writ is served on any property by the bailiff or his substitute the person effecting service must indorse on the writ the following particulars, that is to say, where it was served, the property on which it was served, the day**

of the week and the date on which it was served, the manner in which it was served and the name and the address of the person effecting service, and the indorsement shall be evidence of the facts stated therein.

(4)　Where the plaintiff in an action in rem, or his solicitor, becomes aware that there is in force a caveat against arrest with respect to the property against which the action is brought, he must serve the writ forthwith on the person at whose instance the caveat was entered.

(5)　Where a writ by which an action in rem is begun is amended under Order 20, rule 1, after service thereof, Order 20, rule 1 (2), shall not apply and, unless the Court otherwise directs on an application made ex parte, the amended writ must be served on any intervener and any defendant who has acknowledged issue or service of the writ in the action or, if no defendant has acknowledged issue or service of the writ, it must be served in accordance with paragraph (1) of this rule.

---

## NOTES

### [75.8.1]　Manner of service of writ in rem
Order 75 rule 8 provides that a writ *in rem* must be served on the ship or cargo. As to the manner of effecting service on the ship or cargo see Order 75 rule 11 and the commentary thereunder. The plaintiff may have the writ served by the bailiff under rule 8(3), on giving an undertaking to meet all expenses incurred.

Where the ship or cargo has been sold by the bailiff, service is deemed upon filing a sealed copy of the writ in court: rule 8(1)(b). In *The Convenience Container* [2006] 4 HKC 435 (para 59) (CFI) the court observed that there is no difference in nature between an action *in rem* against an unsold ship and such an action against the proceeds of sale (appeal dismissed:[2007] 4 HKC 489.

### [75.8.2]　When a writ in rem need not be served
The provisions of Order 10 rule 1(4) and (5) whereby service is deemed to have been effected if a solicitor accepts service or a defendant acknowledges service despite not having actually been served, apply in Admiralty proceedings: Order 75 rule 8(2).

### [75.8.3]　Duration and renewal of writ
The provisions of Order 6 rule 8 as to duration and renewal of a writ apply to Admiralty proceedings. Thus a writ *in rem* is valid for 12 months in the first instance and may thereafter be renewed in the discretion of the court.

The criteria to be applied on an application to renew a writ *in rem* are different from those which apply to an ordinary writ *in personam*: *The Chong Bong* [1997] 3 HKC 579, 589F–G. In that case (at 590B-E) the court cited with approval *The Berny* [1979] 1 QB 80 where three circumstances were set out as to when the court will allow renewal of a writ *in rem*. Those circumstances may be summarised as follows:
(1)　None of the ships proceeded against have been or will be present within the jurisdiction during the currency of the writ, or
(2)　If any of the ships have or will come within the jurisdiction during the currency of the writ, the circumstances are such that the visit will not afford reasonable opportunity to serve the writ and arrest the vessel; or

(3)    If any of the ships have or will come within the jurisdiction during the currency of the writ their value is not great enough to provide adequate security for the claim, whereas the value of other ships proceeded against would be sufficient.

The above list should not be considered exhaustive, as there may be other circumstances in which the court may extend the validity of a writ *in rem*. There is a duty to serve such a writ promptly: *The Vita* [1990] 1 Lloyd's Rep 528. It is incumbent on the plaintiff to take all reasonable steps to effect service of the writ during its initial currency: *The Oriental Lily* [2005] 2 HKC 343; *The Zhu Sheng 2* HCAJ 68/2007 (Reyes J; 24.04.2009). Thus extensions are not to be expected as a matter of course and plaintiffs cannot expect sympathy from the court for unexplained delay. However, where the defendant is party to the delay, or where the plaintiff delays in the hope of saving costs, the court may be amenable to an extension: *The Mouna* [1990] 2 Lloyd's Rep 7. In *The Fen He* [1996] 4 HKC 380, an *ex parte* order renewing a writ was set aside at a subsequent *inter partes* hearing because the plaintiff had not acted expeditiously in serving the writ during its initial validity, and on the ground of material non disclosure at the *ex parte* stage.

**9.   Committal of solicitor failing to comply with undertaking** (O. 75 r. 9)
     **Where the solicitor of a party to an action in rem fails to comply with a written undertaking given by him to any other party or his solicitor to acknowledge issue or service of the writ in the action, give bail or pay money into court in lieu of bail, he shall be liable to committal.**

---

**NOTES**

**[75.9.1]   Cross-reference**
As to committal, see Order 52 and the commentary thereunder.

**10. Execution, etc., of warrant of arrest** (O. 75 r. 10)
     **(1)   A warrant of arrest is valid for 12 months beginning with the date of its issue.**
     **(2)   A warrant of arrest may be executed only by the bailiff or his substitute.**
     **(3)   A warrant of arrest shall not be executed until an undertaking to pay on demand the fees of the bailiff and all expenses incurred by him or on his behalf in respect of the arrest of the property and the care and custody of it while under arrest has been lodged in the bailiff's office.**
     **(4)   A warrant of arrest shall not be executed if the party at whose instance it was issued lodges a written request to that effect with the bailiff.**
     **(5)   A warrant of arrest issued against freight may be executed by serving the warrant on the cargo in respect of which the freight is payable or on the ship in which that cargo was carried or on both of them.**
     **(6)   Subject to paragraph (5), a warrant of arrest must be served on the property against which it is issued.**
     **(7)   Within 7 days after the service of a warrant of arrest, the warrant must be filed, in the Registry by the bailiff.**

## NOTES

### [75.10.1]  Service of warrant of arrest
Order 75 rule 10(2) provides that a warrant of arrest may only be executed by the bailiff or his substitute.

An arrest warrant is executed by affixing it to the property to be arrested. See Order 75 rule 11(1) and the commentary thereunder.

### [75.10.2]  Undertaking to pay bailiff's fees and expenses
Before the bailiff will execute a warrant of arrest an undertaking to pay his fees and expenses must be lodged.

### [75.10.3]  Liability for damage arising from arrest
The liability of the HKSAR government and of the bailiff for damage resulting from arrest of property is limited. See the commentary under Order 47 rule 6. Moreover, since 1 April 1983 the bailiff has not effected insurance for loss or damage to property under arrest. Parties seeking the arrest of property should take out 'port risks' or other appropriate insurance.

**11.  Service on ships, etc.: how effected** (O. 75 r. 11)
**(1)  Subject to paragraph (2), service of a warrant of arrest or writ in an action in rem against a ship, freight or cargo shall be effected by–**
> **(a)  affixing the warrant or writ for a short time on any mast of the ship or on the outside of any suitable part of the ship's superstructure, and**
> **(b)  on removing the warrant or writ, leaving a copy of it affixed (in the case of the warrant) in its place or (in the case of the writ) on a sheltered, conspicuous part of the ship.**

**(2)  Service of a warrant of arrest or writ in an action in rem against freight or cargo or both shall, if the cargo has been landed or transhipped, be effected–**
> **(a)  by placing the warrant or writ for a short time on the cargo and, on removing the warrant or writ, leaving a copy of it on the cargo, or**
> **(b)  if the cargo is in the custody of a person who will not permit access to it, by leaving a copy of the warrant or writ with that person.**

**(3)  Order 65, rule 10, shall not apply to a warrant of arrest or a writ in rem.**

## NOTES

### [75.11.1]  Service of writ in rem
Unless a solicitor acting on behalf of the owner of a ship endorses on the writ a statement that he accepts service of the writ in accordance with Order 10, rule 1(4), or a defendant acknowledges service of a writ in accordance with Order 10, rule 1(5), despite the fact that the writ has not been duly served, a writ *in rem* must be served on the property against which the action is brought in accordance with Order 75, rule 11. An order for substituted service is normally inappropriate to a writ *in rem* (*The Good*

*Herald* [1987] 1 Lloyd's Rep 236, at 238 (QB, Ad Ct)). See, however, *The S S Illinois v The Ocean Tramp* HCAJ 4/1965 (Rigby SPJ; 19.04.1969) where it was impossible to serve the writ *in rem* in the usual manner since the vessel had sunk and an order was made permitting service to be effected on the purported owners (appealed on another point at [1970] HKLR 52).

Service on the property means, by virtue of Order 75 rule 11, affixing the document on the mast or the exterior of any suitable part of the ship's superstructure. It is not sufficient to serve the ship's master: *The Prins Bernhard* [1964] P 117. Such affixation is generally notional and need only be for a short time. Order 75 rule 11(1)(b) provides that thereafter a copy may be left in an appropriate place, depending on the type of document.

In *The Deichland* [1989] 2 Lloyd's Rep 113, at 115 (CA), Neill LJ described the way in which the writ was served in that case. A trainee legal executive in the employment of the plaintiff's solicitors served the writ upon the vessel by affixing the original writ on the window near the ship's bridge for a short time and then, upon removing the original writ, leaving the sealed service copy in its place, accompanied by an appropriate form of acknowledgement of service. The procedure is different in Hong Kong where the original writ is filed in the registry and the plaintiff given sealed copies. The original writ cannot be removed from the court file (Order 63 rule 9) and the correct procedure in Hong Kong is to serve a sealed copy: *The Chen Da 513* [1998] 2 HKC 500.

### [75.11.2]   Irregular service

Irregular service, for example, where the master is shown a copy of the writ in his cabin and nothing more, may result in service being set aside (*The Prins Bernhard* [1964] P 117; cf *The Sullivar* [1965] 2 Lloyd's Rep 350 (Ad Div)). The court will be particularly concerned with the sufficiency of service of the writ *in rem* when default judgment is sought under Orders 13 and 19. In the Canadian case of *Key Marine Industries Ltd v The Ship 'Glen Coe', Jada Fishing Co Ltd et al*, T-238-95 (20 March 1995) (FCTD), an application for default judgment was refused because the Statement of Claim (the originating process in the Federal Court) was attached not to the main mast or other conspicuous part of the ship, as required by the Rules, but to the outside of the hull in drydock, and it was conceivable that the ship could have been floated out of the drydock with the Statement of Claim unnoticed.

### [75.11.3]   Service on a Sunday

Order 75 rule 11(3) excludes application of Order 65 rule 10 to writs *in rem* and warrants of arrest. The effect is that they may be served on a Sunday unlike other court process.

**12. Applications with respect to property under arrest** (O. 75 r. 12)

**(1)   The bailiff may at any time apply to the Court for directions with respect to property under arrest in an action and may, or, if the Court so directs, shall, give notice of the application to any or all of the persons referred to in paragraph 2.**

(2)   The bailiff shall send by hand or by post a copy of any order made on an application under paragraph (1) to all those persons who, in relation to that property, have–

     (a)   entered a caveat which is still in force; or

     (b)   caused a warrant for the arrest of the property to be executed by the bailiff; or

     (c)   acknowledged issue or service of the writ in any action in which the property is under arrest; or

     (d)   intervened in any action in which the property is under arrest.

(3)   A person other than the bailiff may make an application under this rule by summons or motion in the action in which the property is under arrest and the summons or notice of motion together with copies of any affidavits in support must be served upon the bailiff and all persons referred to in paragraph (2) unless the court otherwise orders on an application made ex parte.

(4)   Unless otherwise directed by the Registrar, the bailiff shall serve a copy of any notice of motion or summons on the property under arrest.

**13. Release of property under arrest** (O. 75 r. 13)

(1)   Except where property arrested in pursuance of a warrant of arrest is sold under an order of the Court, property which has been so arrested shall only be released under the authority of an instrument of release (in this rule referred to as a "release"), in Form No 7 in Appendix B, issued out of the Registry.

(3)   A release shall not be issued with respect to property as to which a caveat against release is in force, unless, either–

     (a)   at the time of the issue of the release the property is under arrest in one or more other actions, or

     (b)   the Court so orders.

(4)   A release may be issued at the instance of any party to the action in which the warrant of arrest was issued if the Court so orders, or, subject to paragraph (3), if all the other parties, except any defendant who has not acknowledged issue or service of the writ, consent.

(6)   Before a release is issued, the party applying for its issue must, unless paragraph (3)(a) applies, give notice to any person at whose instance a subsisting caveat against release has been entered, or to his solicitor, requiring the caveat to be withdrawn.

(7)   Before property under arrest is released in compliance with a release issued under this rule, the party at whose instance it was issued must, in accordance with the directions of the bailiff, either–

     (a)   pay the fees of the bailiff already incurred and lodge in the bailiff's office an undertaking to pay on demand the other fees and expenses in connection with the arrest of the property and the care and custody of it while under arrest and of its release, or

     (b)   lodge in the bailiff's office an undertaking to pay on demand all such fees and expenses, whether incurred or to be incurred.

(8)   The Court, on the application of any party who objects to directions given to him by the bailiff under paragraph (7), may vary or revoke the directions.

**NOTES**

**[75.13.1]    Release of arrested property**
Order 75 rule 13(4) provides that arrested property may be released by consent of all the parties (save any defendant which has not acknowledged service) or by order of the court.

**[75.13.2]    Release by order of the court**
The court's power to order release of arrested property is discretionary. In exercising the discretion the court may take into account the manner in which, or the purpose for which the plaintiff has proceeded (*The Vasso* [1984] 1 Lloyd's Rep 235, 241 (CA). Release from arrest will not normally be ordered by the court unless the arrest was wrongful or adequate security has been provided (*The Alacrity* [1994] 2 HKC 659, citing *The Myrto* [1977] 2 Lloyd's Rep 243 and *The APJ Shalin* [1991] 2 Lloyd's Rep 62.

See *The Hero II* HCAJ 131/2000 (Waung J; 31.05.2000) as an example of a case where plaintiffs applied to the court for release of a vessel from arrest where a caveator was withholding consent.

**[75.13.3]    Challenge to jurisdiction**
It has been held that Order 75 rule 13 does not confer upon the court a jurisdiction additional to that found in Order 12 rule 8 to consider jurisdictional issues: *The Tian Sheng No 8* [2000] 3 HKC 285 (CFA).

**14.  Caveat against release etc.** (O. 75 r. 14)
**(1)    Where a person claiming to have a right of action in rem against any property which is under arrest or the proceeds of sale thereof wishes to be served with notice of any application to the Court in respect of that property or those proceeds, he must file in the Registry a praecipe in Form No 9 in Appendix B and, on the filing of the praecipe, a caveat shall be entered in the caveat book.**
**(2)    Where the release of any property under arrest is delayed by the entry of a caveat under this rule, any person having an interest in that property may apply to the Court by motion for an order requiring the person who procured the entry of the caveat to pay to the applicant damages in respect of the loss suffered by the applicant by reason of the delay, and the Court, unless it is satisfied that the person procuring the entry of the caveat had a good and sufficient reason for so doing, may make an order accordingly.**

**NOTES**

**[75.14.1]    Remedy of third party who wishes to resist release from arrest**
A third party may arrest a ship already arrested, and in such a case he will not be required to pay the costs of arrest (as provided for in Order 75 rule 10(3)). But if the first arrester procures a release from arrest (pursuant to rule 13) the second arrester becomes liable for the costs of maintaining the arrest. In *The Falcon* [1981] 1 Lloyd's Rep 13 (QB, Ad Ct), Sheen J set out the practice and the reasons for it regarding the liability of arresting parties for the expenses and fees of the bailiff.

**[75.14.2]   Caveat against release from arrest**

Rather than effect a second arrest of the ship a plaintiff might instead file a caveat against release under this rule. If he does so he will be served with notice of any application to the court in respect of that property. The availability of the caveat procedure means that in relation to a ship already under arrest a claimant may ensure that the security does not disappear without his knowledge; at the same time he will not be (potentially) burdened with the costs of arrest nor even with the costs of issuing a writ, as a caveator need not issue one.

In *The New Asia* HCAJ 41/1967 (Briggs J; 29.03.1969) the court described as 'the grossest negligence' an arrangement whereby instead of entering a caveat there was a gentleman's agreement between the parties' solicitors not to seek release of the proceeds of sale of an arrested vessel.

On the other hand, the issue of a writ is advisable, because a shipowner may sell his vessel notwithstanding that it is under arrest (although not if a commission for appraisement and sale of the vessel has been issued pursuant to rule 23); and if he does so the caveator will not, except in claims giving rise to a maritime lien and certain limited cases enumerated in section 12B(2), be entitled to issue a writ *in rem* against the arrested vessel as it will now not be beneficially owned by the 'relevant person' at the time when the action is brought (see section 12B(4) of the High Court Ordinance and rule 5 and the notes thereto).

**15. Duration of caveats** (O. 75 r. 15)

(1)   **Every caveat entered in the caveat book is valid for 12 months beginning with the date of its entry but the person at whose instance a caveat was entered may withdraw it by filing a praecipe in Form No 10 in Appendix B.**

(2)   **The period of validity of a caveat may not be extended, but this provision shall not be taken as preventing the entry of successive caveats.**

**16. Bail** (O. 75 r. 16)

(1)   **Bail on behalf of a party to an action in rem must be given by bond in Form No 11 in Appendix B; and the sureties to the bond must enter into the bond before a commissioner for oaths or a solicitor exercising the powers of a commissioner for oaths under section 7A of the Legal Practitioners Ordinance (Cap 159) not being a solicitor who, or whose partner, is acting as solicitor or agent for the party on whose behalf the bail is to be given.**

(2)   **Subject to paragraph (3), a surety to a bail bond must make an affidavit stating that he is able to pay the sum for which the bond is given.**

(3)   **Where a corporation is a surety to a bail bond given on behalf of a party, no affidavit shall be made under paragraph (2) on behalf of the corporation unless the opposite party requires it, but where such an affidavit is required it must be made by a director, manager, secretary or other similar officer of the corporation.**

(4)   **The party on whose behalf bail is given must serve on the opposite party a notice of bail containing the names and addresses of the persons who have given bail on his behalf and of the commissioner before whom the bail bond was entered into; and after the expiration of 24 hours from the service of the notice (or sooner with the consent of the opposite party) he may file the bond**

**and must at the same time file the affidavits (if any) made under paragraph (2) and an affidavit proving due service of the notice of bail to which a copy of that notice must be exhibited.**

---

## NOTES

### [75.16.1]  Bail bond to release arrested property

Defendants are encouraged by arrest to settle the claim or put up bail or other security to procure release of the property from arrest. Order 75 rule 16 lays down the requirements for posting a bail bond.

If bail or other adequate security is provided the plaintiff can seek release from arrest under rule 13(4). If the plaintiff does not do so the defendant may apply under the same rule, the question of release being a matter for the court upon application by 'any party to the action', and it is likely that if the defendant puts up sufficient security the court will order release (*The Gay Tucan* [1968] 2 Lloyd's Rep 245).

### [75.16.2]  Quantum of bail

A party is entitled to 'sufficient security to cover the amount of his claim with interest and costs on the basis of his reasonably best argued case' (*The Moschanthy* [1971] 1 Lloyd's Rep 37, 44; cf *Taiyo Gyogyo Kabushiki Kaisha v The United Trawler No 5* (1956) 40 HKLR 131, 141 and 145-6 (F Ct)).

The identity of bail with the ship means that the bail bond is limited to the value of the ship if the ship is worth less than the amount of the bond *(The Staffordshire* (1872) LR 4 PC 194 (PC on appeal from Ireland).

In practice the provision of a bail bond is almost unheard of and security by way of payment into court is unusual (*The Alacrity* [1994] 2 HKC 659). Instead private security arrangements are more usually used.

As to the manner in which the court will assess the quantum of bail in the absence of private arrangements such as those provided by a protection and indemnity (P & I) club, see the *The Hua Tian Long* HCAJ 59/2008 (Stone J; 14.05.2008).

### [75.16.3]  Guarantee or undertaking in place of bail bond

Private security in the form of a guarantee or letter of undertaking is often used in place of a bail bond. It is a matter of agreement of the parties as to what form of security is acceptable. A plaintiff is entitled to reject any offer of private security and require a bail bond: *The Saudi Star* (unreported (1982), discussed by Mathews in [1983] LCMLQ 99).

Under such a guarantee an independent and creditworthy body (*eg* a bank, insurance company or protection and indemnity (P & I) club) agrees to pay on demand any sum in respect of the particular claim agreed by the parties or ordered by the court. Such arrangements are entirely contractual between the guarantor and the plaintiff, and no interest or right in the ship is created thereby.

An example of a guarantee is given in Jackson, Enforcement of Maritime Claims (3rd ed, 2000) para 15.140. A guarantee given by a defendant's P & I club is reproduced in *The Deichland* [1989] 2 Lloyd's Rep 113, 115 (CA).

**[75.16.4]  Form and adequacy of private security**
The court will not normally enter the arena and adjudicate upon competing proposals for security put forward by the parties to the action. It is a matter for agreement between the parties.

However, in *The Silver Ocean* HCAJ 208/2000 (Waung J; 03.12.2001) the court had to consider the form and adequacy of security which had been given in mainland China to secure release from arrest. The context was a second arrest in Hong Kong which was objected to on the ground of the security given in the mainland. Waung J said:

> It is universally recognised by all mature maritime jurisdictions that to avoid the arrest of a ship or to secure the release of an arrested ship, a proper security in the full amount of the claim plus interest and costs is required. A proper security for most maritime courts would generally be either a bank guarantee or a guarantee from a reputable insurance company or P & I Club … Cash of course would be acceptable to the maritime courts. What is important is that the security accepted can be easily enforceable without too much dispute and that it is not capable of fluctuating in value. For that reason, it is extremely rare to see a maritime court accepting stocks and shares or real estate properties. Real estate properties are particularly inappropriate as security for maritime claims because its enforceable values are often very uncertain and in shipping time to investigate real estate as security is a luxury few can afford. I do not know of a single instance where real estate had been accepted by the Admiralty court of Hong Kong or of Singapore or of England for the release of an arrested ship.

Waung J went on to dismiss the application for discharge of the Hong Kong warrant of arrest on the ground the security given in the mainland was effectively worthless.

**[75.16.5]  Legal effect of bail bond or other security**
The filing of a bail bond will operate to extinguish the maritime lien (see Jackson, Enforcement of Maritime Claims (3rd ed, 2000) para 15.134. However the same is not true with respect to a guarantee or undertaking. A court is unlikely to find that for all purposes (in particular, the sale of the vessel to which the lien attaches) an undertaking or guarantee given by, for example, insurers, and accepted by the plaintiff, extinguishes the maritime lien (see *The Birchglen* (1990) 36 FTR 92; cf Thomas, Maritime Liens (1980) 291, n 4).

**[75.16.6]  Jurisdiction of court over private security arrangements**
Notwithstanding some authority to the effect that the court has no power to order security for the release of a vessel in any form other than bail or payment into court, Barnett J in *The Alacrity* [1994] 2 HKC 659 held that the court does have 'a measure of jurisdiction over private security arrangements' (*eg* undertakings, indemnities, guarantees).

This proposition was stated more forcefully in *The Mahkutai* [1994] 1 HKLR 212 (CA) where Litton JA said, at 227:

> The security [a bank guarantee] put up by the defendants was inextricably linked with the plaintiffs' action in rem. The arrangements between the parties, which led to the defendants causing the Standard Chartered Bank to give the bank guarantee, must contain by implication an agreement that the Admiralty Court should have jurisdiction to order its cancellation, release or surrender in circumstances in which the court would release a bail bond or order the payment out of money paid into court by way of security. A similar power was exercised by the court in *The Vasso* [1984] QB 477 where the P & I Club had

given a contractual undertaking to secure the release of The "Vasso" from arrest; the court ordered the release of the P & I Club from its undertaking upon holding that the arrest was an abuse of the process of the court.

## 17. Interveners (O. 75 r. 17)

**(1)    Where property against which an action in rem is brought is under arrest or money representing the proceeds of sale of that property is in court, a person who has an interest in that property or money but who is not a defendant to the action may, with the leave of the Court, intervene in the action.**

**(2)    An application for the grant of leave under this rule must be made ex parte by affidavit showing the interest of the applicant in the property against which the action is brought or in the money in court.**

**(3)    A person to whom leave is granted under this rule shall thereupon become a party to the action.**

**(4)    The Court may order that a person to whom it grants leave to intervene in an action shall, within such period or periods as may be specified in the order, serve on any other party to the action such notice of his intervention and such pleadings as may be so specified.**

## NOTES

### [75.17.1]    Application by non-party to intervene

A third party who claims an interest in arrested property (or proceeds of sale paid into court) may apply under Order 75 rule 17 for leave to intervene in the proceedings. The application is made *ex parte* by affidavit showing the applicant's interest. Such an application is clearly a matter of the court's discretion.

A third party who claims a beneficial interest in property should apply under this rule rather than acknowledge issue of the writ as if it were a defendant (*The Tian Xiang 2 Hao* HCAJ 322/2001 (Reyes J; 08.10.2003), citing *The Able Lieutenant* [2002] 6 MLJ 433).

## 18. Preliminary acts (O. 75 r. 18)

**(1)    In an action to enforce a claim for damage, loss of life or personal injury arising out of a collision between ships, the following provisions of this rule shall apply unless the Court otherwise orders.**

**(2)    The plaintiff must within 2 months after service of the writ on any defendant and the defendant must within 2 months of acknowledging issue or service of the writ file in the Registry a document in two parts (in these rules referred to as a preliminary act) containing a statement of the following–**

      **Part One**
- **(i)     the names of the ships which came into collision and their ports of registry;**
- **(ii)    the length, breadth, gross tonnage, horsepower and draught at the material time of the ship and the nature and tonnage of any cargo carried by the ship;**
- **(iii)   the date and time (including the time zone) of the collision;**
- **(iv)    the place of the collision;**
- **(v)     the direction and force of the wind;**

    (vi)  the state of the weather;

   (vii)  the state, direction and force of the tidal or other current;

  (viii)  the position, the course steered and speed through the water of the ship when the other ship was first seen or immediately before any measures were taken with reference to her presence, whichever was the earlier;

   (ix)  the lights or shapes (if any) carried by the ship;

    (x)  (a)  the distance and bearing of the other ship if and when her echo was first observed by radar;

          (b)  the distance, bearing and approximate heading of the other ship when first seen;

   (xi)  what light or shape or combination of lights or shapes (if any) of the other ship was first seen;

  (xii)  what other lights or shapes or combinations of lights or shapes (if any) of the other ship were subsequently seen before the collision, and when;

 (xiii)  what alterations (if any) were made to the course and speed of the ship after the earlier of the two times referred to in article (viii) up to the time of the collision, and when, and what measures (if any), other than alterations of course or speed, were taken to avoid the collision, and when;

 (xiv)  the heading of the ship, the parts of each ship which first came into contact and the approximate angle between the two ships at the moment of contact;

  (xv)  what sound signals (if any) were given, and when;

 (xvi)  what sound signals (if any) were heard from the other ship, and when.

Part Two

    (i)  a statement that the particulars in Part One are incorporated in Part Two;

   (ii)  any other facts and matters upon which the party filing the preliminary act relies;

  (iii)  all allegations of negligence or other fault which the party filing the preliminary act makes;

  (iv)  the remedy or relief which the party filing the preliminary act claims.

(3)   Part Two of the preliminary act shall be deemed to be the pleading of the person filing the preliminary act (in the case of the plaintiff his statement of claim and in the case of the defendant his defence and, where appropriate, his counterclaim) and the provisions of these rules relating to pleadings shall apply to it save insofar as this rule and rule 20 provide otherwise.

(4)   The Court may order that Part Two of the preliminary act need not be filed by the plaintiff or defendant and give directions for the further conduct of the action.

(5)   Every preliminary act shall before filing be sealed by the proper officer and be filed in a sealed envelope which shall not be opened except as provided in paragraph (7) or by order of the Court.

(6)   A plaintiff must serve notice of filing his preliminary act on every defendant who acknowledges issue or service of the writ within 3 days of receiving notice of that acknowledgment or upon filing his preliminary act, whichever is the later. A defendant must, upon filing his preliminary act, serve notice that he has done so on the plaintiff and on every other defendant who has acknowledged issue or service of the writ.

(7)   Any party may inspect and bespeak a copy of the preliminary act of any other party upon filing in the Registry a consent signed by that other party or his solicitor.

(8)   Order 18, rule 20 (close of pleadings) shall not apply; and for the purposes of Order 18, rule 14 (denial by joinder of issue), Order 20, rule 3 (amendment of pleadings without leave) and Order 24, rules 1 and 2 (discovery of documents) the pleadings shall be deemed to be closed–

> (a)   at the expiration of 7 days after service of the reply or, if there is no reply but only a defence to counterclaim, after service of the defence to counterclaim, pursuant to leave given under rule 20; or

> (b)   if neither a reply nor a defence to counterclaim is served, at the expiration of 7 days after the last preliminary act in the action was served pursuant to paragraph (9).

(9)   Within 14 days after the last preliminary act in the action is filed each party must serve on every other party a copy of his preliminary act.

(10)   At any time after all preliminary acts have been filed any party may apply to the Court for an order that–

> (a)   one or more parties file in the Registry particulars of the damages claimed by them and serve a copy thereof on every other party; and

> (b)   that the damages be assessed prior to or at the trial on liability.

The application must be made by summons to the Registrar even if it is made after the issue of a case management summons. (L.N. 152 of 2008)

(11)   When an order is made under paragraph (10) the claim or claims concerned shall be treated as referred to the Registrar for assessment and rules 41 and 42 shall apply unless the Registrar otherwise directs.

(L.N. 404 of 1991)

---

NOTES

### [75.18.1]   'Preliminary act' in collision cases

Order 75 rule 18(2) requires that in cases claiming for damage, loss of life or personal injury resulting from a collision between ships a document known as a 'preliminary act' must be filed by each party at an early stage of the proceedings. This document must provide the particulars set out under rule 18(2) concerning the vessels involved and the circumstances of their position, movement and precautionary measures at the relevant time.

The requirement to file a 'preliminary act' applies only to claims for damage, loss of life or personal injury arising from a collision between ships. As to when a ship is a ship or otherwise, see the definitions of that word in Order 75 rule 1 and section 12E(1) of the High Court Ordinance. See also *The Craighill* [1910] P 207 (a floating landing stage is not a ship) and *The Lian Shun* HCAJ 44/2004 (Waung J; 24.09.2004) (a barge is a ship).

**[75.18.2]  Purpose and function of the 'preliminary act'**
The purpose and function of the 'preliminary act' are well described in Roscoe, Admiralty Jurisdiction and Practice (5th ed by Hutchinson) (1987 Reprint, Professional Books Ltd) commenting on the former Order 19, rule 28 of the English RSC. It is there stated that the purpose of the preliminary act is to place the material circumstances of a collision in a formal document whilst the facts are fresh in the minds of the parties (citing *The Vortigern* (1858) Swa 518). The facts stated in the preliminary act function as formal admissions (citing *The Seacombe; The Devonshire* [1912] P 21, 59).

Part Two of a preliminary act stands as a pleading (Order 75 rule 18(3)). Unlike normal pleadings the preliminary act is filed 'blind', that is without knowledge of the other party's document. Preliminary acts are sealed upon filing and may not be inspected save by consent or order (rule 18(5) & (7)) though notice must be given by each party on the other of having filed the document (rule 18(6)). Only later are the preliminary acts served (rule 18(9)). The purpose of blind filing is 'to prevent the plaintiff from adjusting his case to meet facts advanced by the defendant': *Wong Wai Fong (administratrix) v Leung Cho Sze* [1982] HKC 263, 265H quoting with approval from *The Vortigern* (1859) Swa 518.

**[75.18.3]  Power to dispense with 'preliminary act'**
The court has power to order that the preliminary act be dispensed with in a particular case (rule 18(1)). In *Wong Wai Fong* (above, at 266A-C) a plaintiff who had failed to lodge a preliminary act argued that the document would add little to the statement of claim and sought a direction dispensing with the preliminary act. Fuad J dismissed this suggestion emphatically:

> I am bound to say at once that I do not think it would be right to dispense with the need to file a preliminary act by the plaintiff, by treating the Statement of Claim as a preliminary act even if the plaintiff agrees to be bound by the facts in the Statement of Claim. I think that this would be to drive a coach and horses through the rules and might lead to confusion and difficulty at the trial.'

**[75.18.4]  Amendment of 'preliminary act'**
In Roscoe's Admiralty Jurisdiction and Practice (above) it is observed that the court will not generally allow amendments to a preliminary act either before or at the hearing (citing *The Miranda* (1882) 7 PD 185, *The Frankland* (1872) LR 3 Ad & Ecc 511 and *The Seacombe; The Devonshire* [1912] P 21, 59). However, where the required particulars are not fully set out the court will order necessary additions if the information is or should be in the possession of the party (citing *The Godiva* (1886) 11 PD 20).

**19. Failure to lodge preliminary act: proceedings against party in default**
(O. 75 r. 19)
**(1)   Where in such an action as is referred to in rule 18(1) the plaintiff fails to lodge a preliminary act within the prescribed period, any defendant who has lodged such an act may apply to the Court by summons for an order to dismiss**

the action, and the Court may by order dismiss the action or make such other order on such terms as it thinks just.

(2)　Where in such an action, being an action in personam, a defendant fails to lodge a preliminary act within the prescribed period, Order 19, rules 2 and 3, shall apply as if the defendant's failure to lodge the preliminary act within that period were a failure by him to serve a defence on the plaintiff within the period fixed by or under these rules for service thereof, and the plaintiff, if he has lodged a preliminary act may, subject to Order 77, rule 9, accordingly enter judgment against that defendant in accordance with the said rule 2 or the said rule 3, as the circumstances of the case require.

(3)　Where in such an action, being an action in rem, a defendant fails to lodge a preliminary act within the prescribed period, the plaintiff, if he has lodged such an act, may apply to the Court by motion for judgment against that defendant, and it shall not be necessary for the plaintiff to file or serve a statement of claim or an affidavit before the hearing of the motion.

(4)　On the hearing of a motion under paragraph (3) the Court may make such order as it thinks just, and where the defendant does not appear on the hearing and the Court is of opinion that judgment should be given for the plaintiff provided he proves his case, it shall order the plaintiff's preliminary act to be opened and require the plaintiff to satisfy the Court that his claim is well founded.

The plaintiff's evidence may, unless the Court otherwise orders, be given by affidavit without any order or direction in that behalf.

(5)　Where the plaintiff in accordance with a requirement under paragraph (4) satisfies the Court that his claim is well founded, the Court may give judgment for the claim with or without a reference to the Registrar and may at the same time order the property against which the action is brought to be appraised and sold and the proceeds to be paid into court or make such order as it thinks just.

(6)　The Court may, on such terms as it thinks just, set aside any judgment entered in pursuance of this rule.

(7)　In this rule references to the prescribed period shall be construed as references to the period within which by virtue of rule 18(2) or of any order of the Court the plaintiff or defendant, as the context of the reference requires, is required to lodge a preliminary act. (L.N. 404 of 1991)

---

**NOTES**

**[75.19.1]　Collision cases – default of filing preliminary act**
Order 75 rule 19(1) provides for dismissal of an action if the plaintiff fails to lodge a preliminary act in a collision case of the type to which rule 18 applies. Application is made by summons. In *Wong Wai Fong (administratrix) v Leung Cho Sze* [1982] HKC 263, 265E-F the court observed that although the rules should be obeyed, the penalty for default (dismissal) is 'a Draconian one and the court will be reluctant to impose it unless the justice of the matter so dictates'. In that case the court went on to allow the plaintiff a further 7 days to file a preliminary act, bearing in mind the case concerned two small fishing vessels and the facts were not complicated.

Where it is the defendant who fails to lodge a preliminary act default judgment may be entered. If the action is *in personam*, Order 19 of these rules applies and the plaintiff may enter default judgment in accordance with that order (see Order 75 rule 19(2)). On the other hand where the action is *in rem* the plaintiff must apply to the court by motion (see rule 19(3)) and is required to satisfy the court the claim is well founded. Evidence to prove the claim may be given by affidavit. See rule 19(4).

**20. Special provisions as to pleadings in collision, etc. actions** (O. 75 r. 20)

(1) Notwithstanding anything in Order 18, rule 3, the plaintiff in any such action as is referred to in rule 4(1) may not serve a reply or a defence to counterclaim on the defendant except with the leave of the Court. (L.N. 356 of 1988)

(2) Subject to paragraph (3), in any such action Order 18, rule 13(3) shall not apply to any allegation of fact in–

    (a) a statement of claim contained in Part Two of a preliminary act; or

    (b) a counterclaim (whether contained in Part Two of a preliminary act or not),

and notwithstanding Order 18, rule 14(3) but without prejudice to the other provisions of that rule, there is an implied joinder of issue on the statement of claim or counterclaim. (L.N. 404 of 1991)

(3) Paragraph (2) does not apply to a counterclaim if the plaintiff has served a defence to counterclaim pursuant to leave given under paragraph (1). (L.N. 404 of 1991)

---

**NOTES**

**[75.20.1] Collision cases – leave required to serve reply or defence to counterclaim**

Order 75 rule 20 provides that no reply or defence to counterclaim shall be served without leave of the court in collision and similar cases of the type described in rule 4(1).

**21. Judgment by default** (O. 75 r. 21)

(1) Where a writ is served under rule 8(4) on a party at whose instance a caveat against arrest was issued, then if–

    (a) the sum claimed in the action begun by the writ does not exceed the amount specified in the undertaking given by that party or his solicitor to procure the entry of that caveat, and

    (b) that party or his solicitor does not within 14 days after service of the writ fulfil the undertaking given by him as aforesaid,

the plaintiff may, after filing an affidavit verifying the facts on which the action is based, apply to the Court for judgment by default.

(2) Judgment given under paragraph (1) may be enforced by the arrest of the property against which the action was brought and by committal of the party at whose instance the caveat with respect to that property was entered.

(3)   Where a defendant to an action in rem fails to acknowledge service of the writ within the time limited for doing so, then, on the expiration of 14 days after service of the writ and upon filing an affidavit proving due service of the writ, an affidavit verifying the facts on which the action is based and, if a statement of claim was not indorsed on the writ, a copy of the statement of claim, the plaintiff may apply to the Court for judgment by default.

Where the writ is deemed to have been duly served on the defendant by virtue of Order 10, rule 1(4), or was served by the bailiff or his substitute under rule 8 of this Order, an affidavit proving due service of the writ need not be filed under this paragraph, but the writ indorsed as mentioned in the said rule 1(4) or indorsed as mentioned in rule 8(3A) must be lodged with the affidavit verifying the facts on which the action is based.

(4)   Where a defendant to an action in rem fails to serve a defence on the plaintiff, then, after the expiration of the period fixed by or under these rules for service of the defence and upon filing an affidavit stating that no defence was served on him by that defendant during that period, an affidavit verifying the facts on which the action is based and, if a statement of claim was not indorsed on the writ, a copy of the statement of claim, the plaintiff may apply to the Court for judgment by default.

(5)   Where a defendant to a counterclaim in an action in rem fails to serve a defence to counterclaim on the defendant making the counterclaim, then, subject to paragraph (6), after the expiration of the period fixed by or under these rules for service of the defence to counterclaim and upon filing an affidavit stating that no defence to counterclaim was served on him by the first-mentioned defendant during that period, an affidavit verifying the facts on which the counterclaim is based and a copy of the counterclaim, the defendant making the counterclaim may apply to the Court for judgment by default.

(6)   No application may be made under paragraph (5) against the plaintiff in any action to enforce a claim for damage, loss of life or personal injury arising out of a collision between ships or the carrying out of or omission to carry out a manoeuvre in the case of one or more of two or more ships or non-compliance on the part of one or more of two or more ships with the collision regulations.

(7)   An application to the Court under this rule must be made by motion and if, on the hearing of the motion, the Court is satisfied that the applicant's claim is well founded it may give judgment for the claim with or without a reference to the Registrar and may at the same time order the property against which the action or, as the case may be, counterclaim is brought to be appraised and sold and the proceeds to be paid into court or may make such other order as it thinks just.

(8)   In default actions in rem evidence may, unless the Court otherwise orders, be given by affidavit without any order or direction in that behalf.

(9)   The Court may, on such terms as it thinks just, set aside or vary any judgment entered in pursuance of this rule.

(10)   Order 13 and Order 19 (except rule 1) shall not apply to actions in rem.

## NOTES

### [75.21.1]   Default judgment

Order 75 rule 21 provides for default judgment in various types of Admiralty cases. Note the rule does not apply to failure to lodge a preliminary act in collision and similar cases for which special provision is made in rule 19.

The types of case to which rule 21 applies are:

Rule 21(1) – default in complying with an undertaking in a caveat against arrest;
Rule 21(3) – default in acknowledging service of a writ *in rem*;
Rule 21(4) – default of defence in an action *in rem*;
Rule 21(5) – default of defence to counterclaim in an action *in rem*.

In order to obtain default judgment under this rule it is necessary to apply by motion and satisfy the court the claim is well founded. Evidence by affidavit is permissible. See rule 21(7). Order 8 rule 2 applies and the motion for default judgment should be heard *inter partes* on two clear days notice: *The Tai Wah 18* [1996] 4 HKC 725.

### 22. Order for sale of ship: determination of priority of claims (O. 75 r. 22)

(1)   **Where in an action in rem against a ship the Court has ordered the ship to be sold, any party who has obtained or obtains judgment against the ship or proceeds of sale of the ship may–**

    (a)   **in a case where the order for sale contains the further order referred to in paragraph (2), after the expiration of the period specified in the order under paragraph (2)(a), or**

    (b)   **in any other case, after obtaining judgment,**

**apply to the Court by motion for an order determining the order of priority of the claims against the proceeds of sale of the ship.**

(2)   **Where in an action in rem against a ship the Court orders the ship to be sold, it may further order–**

    (a)   **that the order of priority of the claims against the proceeds of sale of the ship shall not be determined until after the expiration of 90 days, or of such other period as the Court may specify, beginning with the day on which the proceeds of sale are paid into court;**

    (b)   **that any party to the action or to any other action in rem against the ship or the proceeds of sale thereof may apply to the Court in the action to which he is a party to extend the period specified in the Order;**

    (c)   **that within 7 days after the date of payment into court of the proceeds of sale the bailiff shall send for publication in the Gazette and such other newspaper, if any, as the Court may direct, a notice complying with paragraph (3).**

(3)   **The notice referred to in paragraph (2)(c) must state–**

    (a)   **that the ship (naming her) has been sold by order of the Court in an action in rem, identifying the action;**

    (b)   **that the gross proceeds of the sale, specifying the amount thereof, have been paid into court;**

    (c)　**that the order of priority of the claims against the said proceeds will not be determined until after the expiration of the period (specifying it) specified in the order for sale; and**

    (d)　**that any person with a claim against the ship or the proceeds of sale thereof, on which he intends to proceed to judgment should do so before the expiration of that period.**

    **(4)　The bailiff must lodge in the Registry a copy of each newspaper in which the notice referred to in paragraph (2)(c) appeared.**

    **(5)　The expenses incurred by the bailiff in complying with an order of the Court under this rule shall be included in his expenses relating to the sale of the ship.**

    **(6)　An application to the Court to extend the period referred to in paragraph (2)(a) must be made by motion, and a copy of the notice of motion must, at least 3 days before the day fixed for the hearing thereof, be served on each party who has begun an action in rem against the ship or the proceeds of sale thereof.**

    **(7)　In this rule "the Court" means the judge in person.**

## NOTES

### [75.22.1]　Order for sale of ship

The court has power to order sale of a vessel which is under arrest whether at the interlocutory stage or following entry of judgment. An order for sale at the interlocutory stage is described by the Latin term '*pendente lite*'.

    Sale *pendente lite* may be ordered where no security is deposited with a view to release of the vessel from arrest. Other considerations such as hardship to the vessel's owners are largely irrelevant. See *The Fook Hing* HCAJ 116/2000 (Waung J; 03.07.2000).

    Sale after entry of judgment will be ordered as a means of enforcing a judgment for payment of money.

### [75.22.2]　Priority as to proceeds of sale

The vessel is sold free of prior incumbrances such as mortgages and liens: *The Accrux* [1962] 1 Lloyd's Rep 405. However prior incumbrancers are entitled to a degree of priority on payment out of the proceeds of sale.

    The proceeds of sale are paid into court pursuant to rule 24 and the money is paid out of court to claimants according to the following general priorities:

(1)　the bailiff's fees and expenses of arrest and sale (*The Falcon* [1981] 1 Lloyd's Rep 13, at 17 (QB, Ad Ct)), including any shipbroker's commission payable (*Den Norske Bank AS v Asset Century Ltd t/a Dairy On Co & Anor* [1990] 2 HKC (CA));

(2)　the plaintiff's costs of the action (*The Falcon*, at 17);

(3)　creditors, according to the local priority rules: *The Halcyon Isle* [1981] AC 221 (PC from Singapore); *The Pacific Bear* [1979] HKLR 125. Priority goes to crew and salvors. Crew are entitled to a maritime lien which gives them priority over mortgagees, but the lien is personal and cannot be asserted by an assignee: *The Sparti* [2000] 3 HKC 323. With regard to the priority enjoyed by crew see *The Pointer Apitong* HCAJ 353/1990 (Barnett J; 14.10.1991), and with regard priority for emoluments due to a vessel's master see *The SS Sumbawa ex Grandhing* HCAJ 10/1968 (Briggs J; 03.07.1968). Mortgagees enjoy priority over claims for towage, but rank behind claims for salvage: *The Dragon Sunrise* [1998] 3 HKC 633, 636A-B.

(4)    the residue is paid to the owners.

The court has jurisdiction to reopen orders relating to priorities (presumably before payment out of the funds in court) in order to avoid 'the infliction of an injustice upon parties who have a prior legal claim over those funds' (per Sir Robert Phillimore in *The Markland* (1871) LR 3 A & E 340 (H Ct of Ad), quoted by Hunter J in *The Fortune Founder* [1987] HKLR 156, at 159).

In *The Fortune Founder*, while acknowledging the jurisdiction to do so, Hunter J declined to set aside an order stating priorities, notwithstanding that the plaintiff mortgagee was possessed in law of a priority over the claim of a manning agent, because the mortgagee had failed to bring its claim before the court at a sufficiently early date.

### [75.22.3]   Other enforcement action

If the proceeds are insufficient and the action has been defended, the plaintiff may proceed, as any judgment creditor, against any other property of the defendant in the jurisdiction (or have the judgment recognised and enforced outside the jurisdiction) but the plaintiff may not bring another action *in rem*, the claims having merged with the judgment (see *The Alletta* [1974] 1 Lloyd's Rep 40 (QB, Ad Ct); cf *The Daien Maru No 18* [1986] 1 Lloyd's Rep 387 (Singapore H Ct), explained in a note of the case by Chong in (1986) 28 Mal LR 102).

On the other hand, 'A judgment creditor who has obtained a final judgment against a shipowner by proceeding *in rem* in a foreign Admiralty Court can bring an action *in rem* in this Court [the English Admiralty Court] against that ship to enforce the decree of the foreign Court if that is necessary to complete the execution of that judgment, provided that the ship is the property of the judgment debtor at the time when she is arrested' (*The Despina GK* [1982] 2 Lloyd's Rep 555, at 559 (QB, Ad Ct)).

Similarly, an action *in rem* would seem to lie for enforcement of an arbitration award if the claim in respect of which the arbitration award was given is one for which an *in rem* action would lie independent of the arbitration agreement (*The Saint Anna* [1983] 1 Lloyd's Rep 637 (QB, Ad Ct)).

### 23. Appraisement and sale of property (O. 75 r. 23)

**(1)   A commission for the appraisement and sale of any property under an order of the Court shall not be issued until the party applying for it has filed a praecipe in Form No 12 in Appendix B.**

**(2)   Such a commission must, unless the Court otherwise orders, be executed by the bailiff and must be in Form No 13 in Appendix B.**

**(3)   A commission for appraisement and sale shall not be executed until an undertaking in writing satisfactory to the bailiff to pay the fees and expenses of the bailiff on demand has been lodged in the bailiff's office.**

**(4)    The bailiff shall pay into court the gross proceeds of the sale of any property sold by him under a commission for sale and shall bring into court the account relating to the sale (with vouchers in support) for taxation.**

**(5)    On the taxation of the bailiff's account relating to a sale any person interested in the proceeds of the sale shall be entitled to be heard, and any decision of the Registrar made on the taxation to which objection is taken may be reviewed in the same manner and by the same persons as any decision of the Registrar made in taxation proceedings under Order 62, and rules 33 to 35 of that Order shall apply accordingly with the necessary modifications.**

## NOTES

### [75.23.1]    Execution of order for sale
An order for 'appraisement' and sale of property must be executed by the bailiff unless the court otherwise orders: rule 23(2).

However this does not mean the bailiff must do the work himself. In practice the bailiff will instruct valuers and shipbrokers to do the work. The form of Commission for Appraisement and Sale (No 13 in Appendix B) expressly contemplates appointment of expert valuers. The use of international shipbrokers is thought to result in attracting greater interest and possibly higher prices than simply advertising in a local newspaper.

The court may order that sums paid to professionals and brokers be included in the bailiff's costs and expenses. See *Den Norske Bank AS v Asset Century Ltd t/a Dairy On Co & Anor* [1990] 2 HKC (CA).

### [75.23.2]    Sale at less than appraised value
Approval of the court is required for sale of the property at an amount less than the appraised value. See *Armco Pacific Ltd v Lim Juliano* [1989] 2 HKC 237, 239D-I.

### [75.23.3]    Duty of mortgagee as to price
Sale of a vessel by the bailiff is not a mortgagee sale. Indeed any attempt by a mortgagee to try to sell the property would be an interference with the bailiff's commission and punishable by contempt: *Armco Pacific Ltd v Lim Juliano* [1989] 2 HKC 237, 243G, citing *The Jarvis Brake* [1976] 2 Lloyd's Rep 320, 321. It follows that authorities as to the duty of a mortgagee as to the price to be obtained on sale are not applicable. However, the shipowner, and by parity of reasoning a mortgagee, has a duty to keep the bailiff briefed of information which might lead to a higher price being obtained. If it is alleged this duty is breached the onus is on the party who so asserts to prove it. See *Armco Pacific Ltd v Lim Juliano* [1989] 2 HKC 237 holding inapplicable authorities on a mortgagee's duty such as *Cuckmere Brick Co Ltd v Mutual Finance Co Ltd* [1971] Ch 949 (CA) and *Tse Kwong Lam v Wong Chit Sen* [1983] 2 HKC 1; [1983] 1 WLR 1349 (PC from Hong Kong).

### [75.23.4]    Undertaking as to bailiff's expenses
Order 75 rule 23(3) provides that an undertaking must be given to cover the bailiff's fees and expenses of executing a commission for appraisement and sale of property. The requirements for the undertaking are set out in rule 23A.

The expenses of discharging cargo from a ship arrested and sold by order of the court are to be borne by the cargo owners and do not form part of the bailiff's expenses; they are, therefore, not a first charge on the proceeds of sale even where the arrest is not at the instance of the cargo owner (*The Mingren Development* [1979] HKLR 159 (H Ct); cf *The Myrto* [1977] 2 Lloyd's Rep 243 (QB, Ad Ct); [1978] 1 Lloyd's Rep 11, the Court of Appeal expressing no opinion on this point).

**[75.23.5]   Sale by public tender or private sale**
Although the court may have jurisdiction to permit private sale of a ship by a judgment creditor, this is in general undesirable and sale by public tender should be the norm. This is in part because sale by public tender brings the matter to the attention of potential claimants around the world who may then seek a share of the sale proceeds. See *The Margo L* [1998] 1 HKC 217 where the court refused an application by a judgment creditor to sell a vessel by private sale to a named buyer at a particular price.

**23A.  Undertaking as to expenses, etc.** (O. 75 r. 23A)
    **(1)   Every undertaking under rule 8(3), 10(3), 13(7) or 23(3) shall be given in writing to the satisfaction of the bailiff.**
    **(2)   Where a party is required by rule 8(3), 10(3), 13(7) or 23(3) to give to the bailiff an undertaking to pay any fees or expenses, the bailiff may require from time to time the deposit with him of such sum as he considers reasonable to meet those fees and expenses.**
    **(3)   The Court may, on the application of any party who is dissatisfied with a direction or determination of the bailiff under rule 13(7) or this rule, vary or revoke the direction or determination.**

**24.  Payment into and out of court** (O. 75 r. 24)
    **(1)   Subject to this rule, Order 22 shall apply in relation to an Admiralty action (other than a limitation action) as it applies to an action for a debt or damages. (L.N. 152 of 2008)**
    **(2)   Subject to paragraphs (3) and (4), money paid into court shall not be paid out except in pursuance of an order of the judge in person.**
    **(3)   The Registrar may, with the consent of the parties interested in money paid into court, order the money to be paid out to the person entitled thereto in the following cases, that is to say–**
        **(a)   where a claim has been referred to the Registrar for decision and all the parties to the reference have agreed to accept the Registrar's decision and to the payment out of any money in court in accordance with that decision;**
        **(b)   where property has been sold and the proceeds of sale thereof paid into court and the parties are agreed as to the persons to whom the proceeds shall be paid and the amount to be paid to each of those persons;**
        **(c)   where in any other case there is no dispute between the parties.**

**(4)   Where in an Admiralty action money has been paid into court pursuant to an order made under Order 29, rule 12, the Registrar may make an order under rule 13(1) of that Order for the money to be paid out to the person entitled thereto.**

---

## NOTES

### [75.24.1]   Application of Order 22 to Admiralty proceedings

Order 75 rule 24(1) applies the sanctioned offer and sanctioned payment procedures under Order 22 to Admiralty actions generally. However Order 22 rule 17, by which a party which has accepted a sanctioned payment may apply for payment out by filing the prescribed form, does not apply to Admiralty proceedings. Its application is ousted by rule 24(2), (3) and (4), by which money in court may not be paid out in an Admiralty action save by order of a judge or the Registrar.

Previously rule 24 excluded the time limits in Order 22 from applying in Admiralty proceedings. Instead a reasonable time was allowed. See *The Vasili Shelgunov* [1989] 1 Lloyd's Rep 542 (CA). As a result of amendment of rule 24 with effect from 2009, the time limits for accepting a sanctioned offer or sanctioned payment as set out in Order 22 should now apply in Admiralty actions.

## 25.  Case management summons (O. 75 r. 25)

**(1)   Order 25 shall apply to Admiralty actions (other than limitation actions) as it applies to other actions, except that–**

> **(a)   the case management summons shall be returnable in not less than 7 weeks; (L.N. 152 of 2008)**
>
> **(b)   any notice under Order 25, rule 7(1), must be served within 21 days after service of the case management summons on the party giving the notice; and (L.N. 152 of 2008)**
>
> **(c)   unless a judge in person otherwise directs, the case management summons shall be heard by a judge in person. (L.N. 152 of 2008)**

**On or before the day on which any party serves on any other party a notice under Order 75, rule 7, he must lodge 2 copies of the notice in the Registry.**

**(2)   An order made on the case management summons shall determine whether the trial is to be without assessors or with one or more assessors. (L.N. 152 of 2008)**

**(3)   The trial shall be before a judge without a jury unless, on the ground that there are special reasons to the contrary, an order made on the case management summons otherwise provides. (L.N. 152 of 2008)**

**(5)   Any such order or direction as is referred to in paragraph (2) or (3) (including an order made on appeal) may be varied or revoked by a subsequent order or direction made or given at or before the trial by the judge in person or, with the judge's consent by the Registrar.**

**NOTES**

**[75.25.1]   Application of Order 25 case management procedure**
Order 75 rule 25 provides that the case management procedures under Order 25 apply to Admiralty actions. An exception is limitation actions (as to which see Order 75 rule 37), which are expressly excluded. See, however, Order 75 rule 38(7) which provides that in certain circumstances the Registrar may direct that a case management summons be taken out in such an action.

Rule 25(1)(a) and (b) prescribe different time limits for case management procedures in Admiralty actions. Note also rule 25(1)(c) which provides that an Admiralty case management summons shall normally be heard by a judge in person, whereas for other actions such summonses may be dealt with by a master and on paper under Order 25 rule 1A(4).

See also practice direction No 1, governing the Admiralty list, which was substantially revised in 2009 and deals with various aspect of case management of actions within the list.

**26. Fixing date for trial, etc.** (O. 75 r. 26)
   **(1)   Subject to paragraph (2), the date for trial of an Admiralty action shall be fixed by the judge at the hearing of the case management summons unless a judge in person otherwise directs. (L.N. 152 of 2008)**

   **(2)   Where an action is ordered to be tried without pleadings or a case management summons is directed to be heard by the Registrar the date for trial shall be fixed by the Registrar. (L.N. 152 of 2008)**

   **(3)   Order 34 shall apply to Admiralty actions subject to the following and any other necessary modifications—**
   
   **(a)   the bundles referred to in rule 3(1) shall include any preliminary acts and any particulars filed pursuant to an order under rule 18(10)(a) of this Order, and where trial with one or more assessors has been ordered an additional bundle shall be lodged for the use of each assessor;**
   **(L.N. 404 of 1991)**
   
   **(b)   "the proper officer" shall mean the chief judicial clerk of the Registry; and**
   
   **(c)   in an action which has been ordered to be tried with an assessor or assessors the solicitor to the party setting it down must file in the Registry an undertaking to pay the proper fee and expenses of such assessor or assessors.**

   **(4)   If all the parties to an action consent, the action may be withdrawn without the leave of the Court at any time before trial by filing in the Registry a written consent to the action being withdrawn signed by all the parties.**

**27. Stay of proceedings in collision, etc. actions until security given** (O. 75 r. 27)
   **Where an action in rem, being an action to enforce any such claim as is referred to in rule 2(l)(a), is begun and a cross action *in rem* arising out of the same collision or other occurrence as the first mentioned action is subsequently**

begun, or a counterclaim arising out of that occurrence is made in the first mentioned action, then–

   (a)   **if the ship in respect of or against which the first mentioned action is brought has been arrested or security given to prevent her arrest, but**

   (b)   **the ship in respect of or against which the cross action is brought or the counterclaim made cannot be arrested and security has not been given to satisfy any judgment given in favour of the party bringing the cross action or making the counterclaim,**

the Court may stay proceedings in the first mentioned action until security is given to satisfy any judgment given in favour of that party.

**28.  Inspection of ship, etc.** (O. 75 r. 28)

Without prejudice to its powers under Order 29, rules 2 and 3, and Order 35, rule 8, the Court may, on the application of any party, make an order for the inspection by the assessors (if the action is tried with assessors), or by any party or witness, of any ship or other property, whether real or personal, the inspection of which may be necessary or desirable for the purpose of obtaining full information or evidence in connection with any issue in the action.

___

## NOTES

### [75.28.1]   Order for inspection

Order 75 rule 28 empowers the court to order inspection of a ship or other property in connection with an issue arising in Admiralty proceedings. The rule stipulates that the power may be exercised where 'necessary or desirable for the purpose of obtaining full information or evidence'. The 'key words' are 'full information and evidence': *The Goodeast* [1997] 3 HKC 250, 252D. In that case, the court initially refused to order inspection on the ground that the plaintiffs were on a fishing expedition but reversed its decision on reconsideration with the benefit of new material.

The rule provides that the full information or evidence sought must be 'in connection with any issue in the action'. Those words are to be construed 'broadly so as to cover matters which, on the materials presently available, may reasonably be regarded as of relevance to probable issues': *Owners of the Ship Da Qing 236 v Owners of the Ships or Vessels Gunung Klabat etc* HCAJ 333/1983 (Kempster J; 31.10.1983) (para 7). In that case an early general inspection of a damaged ship was ordered despite objection that it was beyond the scope of the issues as defined in the generally indorsed writ. The court was of the view that delay until after the preliminary act was filed under rule 18, or the close of pleadings, by which time the issues would be more clearly defined, would prejudice the shipowner, who had every reason to want to repair the ship before then.

The court may order a shipowner to permit the opposing party's surveyor to have access to the vessel for the purpose of inspection and taking photographs: *The Mare Del Nord* [1990] 1 Lloyd's Rep 40, 43.

Rule 28 is expressly without prejudice to the powers of the court to order preservation of property and the taking of samples under Order 29 rules 2 and 3, and under Order 35 rule 8 for inspection by the court. In *The Inchon Glory* HCAJ

117/1992 (Barnett J; 17.06.1992) a preservation order extending to documents was made *ex parte,* but later set aside on the ground there had been no urgency and the matter should have been heard *inter partes.* See the commentary under Order 29 rule 3 as to the matters the court took into account in that case.

**[75.28.2]    Factors to be considered on application for inspection order**
The court's power under Order 75 rule 28 to order inspection is clearly discretionary. Some of the matters which the Admiralty court should take into account in exercising the discretion (under this rule or under Order 29) were set out in *The Inchon Glory* HCAJ 117/1992 (Barnett J; 17.06.1992). The following non-exhaustive list deriving from *The Mare Del Nord* [1990] 1 Lloyd's Rep 40 was approved:

1.  The plaintiffs' evidence on affidavit must show a good arguable case on the merits. Particularly, the evidence must show that there was damage which should not be treated as *de minimis.*
2.  The taking of a sample (or such other relief as may be granted) must be shown to be such that it may assist the judge at trial. The longer the lapse of time between the moment when damage occurred and the moment when a sample is to be taken, the more difficult it will be to show that the order is likely to be of assistance at trial. If there is any doubt, it is in the interest of justice to preserve evidence rather than let pass an opportunity of obtaining such evidence.
3.  Shipowners must be protected from unnecessary interference with the running of their ships. Provided, however, a shipowner is fully protected against any damage which he may suffer, the type of relief being afforded to a plaintiff may be no more burdensome than discovery which can put a shipowner to a great deal of trouble and inconvenience. Both processes help a court to ascertain the true facts …
4.  A plaintiff should be required to give an undertaking in damages.
5.  If satisfied that the plaintiff has a good arguable case and that the evidence obtained may assist at trial, the court should take account of undertakings given by the plaintiff and balance the inconvenience which might be caused to the shipowner and others against the possible benefit to the plaintiff.

See also the commentary by *M Dockray* at [1990] LMCLQ 319. And see *The tug De Ping* HCAJ 3/2000 (Waung J; 10.01.2000) where an application for an inspection order was refused on the ground the applicant was fishing for material which might improve its forensic position in a very ordinary case of a something having gone wrong as sea.

**[75.28.3]    Order for inspection in aid of arbitration**
In *The Lady Muriel* [1995] 2 HKC 320, 325I (CA) it was held that where the parties have entered into a binding foreign arbitration agreement the Hong Kong court should not normally make an inspection order unless prior approval of the arbitrators has been obtained. However the court would not rule out the possibility of making an order in a case of great urgency. Godfrey JA said (at 324G-I) that if there was a risk of serious and irreparable damage being caused to the party seeking to inspect the court might make an order for inspection as an 'interim measure of protection' even without prior approval of the arbitrators.

**[75.28.4]    Numbering**
There is no rule 29 in Order 75. The rule of that number in the former English RSC dealt with the taking of a shorthand note of oral evidence, and was repealed in 1971.

Court hearings in Hong Kong are now routinely tape-recorded, so no such note is necessary.

**30. Examination of witnesses and other persons** (O. 75 r. 30)

(1)   The power conferred by Order 39, rule 1, shall extend to the making of an order authorizing the examination of a witness or person on oath before a judge sitting in court as if for the trial of the cause or matter, without that cause or matter having been set down for trial or called on for trial.

(2)   The power conferred by the said rule 1 shall also extend to the making of an order, with the consent of the parties, providing for the evidence of a witness being taken as if before an examiner, but without an examiner actually being appointed or being present.

(3)   Where an order is made under paragraph (2), it may make provision for any consequential matters and, subject to any provision so made, the following provisions shall have effect–

> (a)   the party whose witness is to be examined shall provide a shorthand writer to take down the evidence of the witness;
>
> (b)   any representative, being counsel or solicitor, of either of the parties shall have authority to administer the oath to the witness;
>
> (c)   the shorthand writer need not himself be sworn but shall certify in writing as correct a transcript of his notes of the evidence and deliver it to the solicitor for the party whose witness was examined, and that solicitor must file it in the Registry;
>
> (d)   unless the parties otherwise agree or the Court otherwise orders, the transcript or a copy thereof shall, before the transcript is filed, be made available to the counsel or other persons who acted as advocates at the examination, and if any of those persons is of opinion that the transcript does not accurately represent the evidence he shall make a certificate specifying the corrections which in his opinion should be made therein, and that certificate must be filed with the transcript.

(4)   In actions in which preliminary acts fall to be filed under rule 18, an order shall not be made under Order 39, rule 1, authorizing any examination of a witness before the preliminary acts have been filed, unless for special reasons the Court thinks fit so to direct.

**31. Trial without pleadings** (O. 75 r. 31)

Order 18, rule 21 shall apply to Admiralty as it applies to other actions except that the summons must be served on every other party not less than 7 days before the day specified in the summons for the hearing thereof.

**32. Further provisions with respect to evidence** (O. 75 r. 32)

(3)   (Repealed 2 of 1999 s 6)

(7)   Unless the Court otherwise directs, an affidavit for the purposes of rule 19(4), 21 or 38(2) may, except in so far as it relates to the service of a writ, contain statements of information or belief with the sources and grounds thereof.

## NOTES

**[75.32.1]   Repeal of rule 32(3)**
By virtue of the Evidence (Amendment) Ordinance 1999 (No 2 of 1999), rule 32(3) of this Order was repealed for civil proceedings commenced on or after 1 June 1999. The sub-rule continues to apply to proceedings commenced prior to that date. See the commentary under Order 38 rule 22.

**33. Proceedings for apportionment of salvage** (O. 75 r. 33)
   **(1)   Proceedings for the apportionment of salvage the aggregate amount of which has already been ascertained shall be begun by originating motion.**
   **(3)   On the hearing of the motion the judge may exercise any of the jurisdiction conferred by section 556 of the Merchant Shipping Act 1894 (1984 c. 60 U.K.).**

## NOTES

**[75.33.1]   Apportionment of salvage**
Order 75 rule 33 provides that proceedings for apportionment of salvage shall be commenced by originating motion. For a discussion of the principles applied by the Admiralty court in apportioning amongst different salvors see Kennedy & Rose, The Law of Salvage (6th ed, 2002) ch 17.
   See the commentary under Order 75 rule 1 as to interpretation of the reference in this rule to the UK Merchant Shipping Act 1894 after the resumption of Chinese sovereignty over Hong Kong.

**34. Notice of motion in actions in rem** (O. 75 r. 34)
   **(1)   The affidavits, if any, in support of a motion in an action in rem must be filed in the Registry before the notice of motion is issued, unless the Court gives leave to the contrary.**
   **(2)   A notice of motion, except a motion for judgment in default, must be served on all caveators together with copies of the affidavits, if any, in support of the motion 2 clear days at least before the hearing, unless the Court gives leave to the contrary.**

**35. Agreement between solicitors may be made order of court** (O. 75 r. 35)
   **(1)   Any agreement in writing between the solicitors of the parties to a cause or matter, dated and signed by those solicitors, may, if the Registrar thinks it reasonable and such as the judge would under the circumstances allow, be filed in the Registry, and the agreement shall thereupon become an order of court and have the same effect as if such order had been made by the judge in person.**

## NOTES

**[75.35.1]   Order 75 rule 35 – order by agreement**
Order 75 rule 35 provides for consent orders in the Admiralty jurisdiction. The parties need only file their agreement in the registry and, if approved by the registrar (as

reasonable, and such as the judge would under the circumstances allow) it is deemed to be an order of the court. The consent summons and consent order procedures (see the commentary under Order 42 rule 5A) need not be followed.

### [75.35.2] Omission of Order 75 rule 36

There is no rule 36 in Order 75 of the Hong Kong rules. The rule of the equivalent number in the former English RSC dealt with Admiralty proceedings commenced by originating summons.

### 37. Limitation action: parties (O. 75 r. 37)

**(1) In a limitation action the person seeking relief shall be the plaintiff and shall be named in the writ by his name and not described merely as the owner of, or as bearing some other relation to, a particular ship or other property.**

**(2) The plaintiff must make one of the persons with claims against him in respect of the casualty to which the action relates defendant to the action and may make any or all of the others defendants also.**

**(3) At least one of the defendants to the action must be named in the writ by his name but the other defendants may be described generally and not named by their names.**

**(4) The writ must be served on one or more of the defendants who are named by their names therein and need not be served on any other defendant.**

**(5) In this rule and rules 38, 39 and 40 "name" includes a firm name or the name under which a person carries on his business, and where any person with a claim against the plaintiff in respect of the casualty to which the action relates has described himself for the purposes of his claim merely as the owner of, or as bearing some other relation to, a ship or other property, he may be so described as defendant in the writ and, if so described, shall be deemed for the purposes of the rules aforesaid to have been named in the writ by his name.**

---

### NOTES

### [75.37.1] Limitation actions

A 'limitation action', as defined in rule 1, means an action by shipowners or other persons under the Merchant Shipping Acts 1894 to 1984 for the limitation of the amount of their liability in connection with a ship or other property. The reference to United Kingdom legislation should now be read in light of the Hong Kong Reunification Ordinance (Cap 1026). See the commentary under Order 75 rule 1.

Limitation actions are within the Admiralty jurisdiction of the High Court (section 12A(1)(b) and (3)(c) of the High Court Ordinance). Order 75 rule 37 sets out the requirements for joining and naming the parties to a limitation action.

A limitation fund must be constituted in accordance with the provisions of the Merchant Shipping (Limitation of Shipowners Liability) Ordinance (Cap 434) (brought into operation on 1 October 1993 (LN 381 of 1993)). Section 12 of that Ordinance brings into force in Hong Kong the Convention on Limitation of Liability for Maritime Claims 1976. The text of the convention is set out in the Second Schedule of the Ordinance.

For the rate of interest to be applied for the purposes of paragraph 1 of Article 11 of the Convention on Limitation of Liability for Maritime Claims 1976, see section 19 of the Ordinance.

**[75.37.2] Omission of Order 75 rule 37A**
Order 75 of the former English RSC contained rule 37A. That rule, which is omitted in Hong Kong, provided for a limitation fund to be constituted by payment into court.

**38. Limitation action: summons for decree or directions** (O. 75 r. 38)

(1) Within 7 days after the acknowledgment of issue or service of the writ by one of the defendants named therein by their names or, if none of them acknowledges issue or service, within 7 days after the time limited for acknowledging service, the plaintiff, without serving a statement of claim, must take out a summons returnable in chambers before the Registrar asking for a decree limiting his liability or, in default of such a decree, for directions as to the further proceedings in the action.

(2) The summons must be supported by an affidavit or affidavits proving—
   (a) the plaintiff's case in the action, and
   (b) if none of the defendants named in the writ by their names has acknowledged service, service of the writ on at least one of the defendants so named.

(3) The affidavit in support of the summons must state—
   (a) the names of all the persons who, to the knowledge of the plaintiff, have claims against him in respect of the casualty to which the action relates, not being defendants to the action who are named in the writ by their names, and
   (b) the address of each of those persons, if known to the plaintiff.

(4) The summons and every affidavit in support thereof must, at least 7 clear days before the hearing of the summons, be served on any defendant who has acknowledged issue or service of the writ.

(5) On the hearing of the summons the Registrar, if it appears to him that it is not disputed that the plaintiff has a right to limit his liability, shall make a decree limiting the plaintiff's liability and fix the amount to which the liability is to be limited.

(6) On the hearing of the summons the Registrar, if it appears to him that any defendant has not sufficient information to enable him to decide whether or not to dispute that the plaintiff has a right to limit his liability, shall give such directions as appear to him to be appropriate for enabling the defendant to obtain such information and shall adjourn the hearing.

(7) If on the hearing or resumed hearing of the summons the Registrar does not make a decree limiting the plaintiff's liability, he shall give such directions as to the further proceedings in the action as appear to him to be appropriate including, in particular, a direction requiring the taking out of a case management summons under Order 25 and, if he gives no such direction, a direction fixing the period within which any notice under Order 38, rule 21, must be served. (L.N. 152 of 2008)

**(8)** Any defendant who, after the Registrar has given directions under paragraph (7), ceases to dispute the plaintiff's right to limit his liability must forthwith file a notice to that effect in the Registry, and serve a copy on the plaintiff and on any other defendant who has acknowledged issue or service of the writ.

**(9)** If every defendant who disputes the plaintiff's right to limit his liability serves a notice on the plaintiff under paragraph (8), the plaintiff may take out a summons returnable in chambers before the Registrar, asking for a decree limiting his liability; and paragraphs (4) and (5) shall apply to a summons under this paragraph as they apply to a summons under paragraph (1).

## NOTES

**[75.38.1]   Application for decree limiting liability**

Order 75 rule 38 provides that a plaintiff must apply for a decree limiting liability, or for directions, before serving a statement of claim. The rule applies to plaintiffs seeking to limit their liability in limitation actions. See the definition of 'limitation action' in Order 75 rule 1(2), which was amended by Ordinance 14 of 2009, s 35, to extend to actions for the limitation of liability under two additional statutes.

It has been held that an application by summons for a limitation decree 'is to be brought before the Registrar and to be heard by the Registrar and not by the Admiralty Judge': *The Equator Crystal* [1998] 4 HKC 568, 570D. This was said to be because rule 38 repeatedly refers to the Registrar. This situation was to be contrasted with 'the trial of a limitation action by the Admiralty Judge and not by the Registrar'. The equivalent rule in the former English RSC was different, expressly providing for applications to be made to 'the Admiralty registrar or district judge'.

Note that the Admiralty List practice direction (PD 1.1), which was repealed and replaced with effect from 2 April 2009, provides in para 4 that the Admiralty judge is to have 'control' of the matters in the list and interlocutory applications, and may make directions and orders regulating the conduct or trial of such matters.

## 39. Limitation action: proceedings under decree (O. 75 r. 39)

**(1)** Where the only defendants in a limitation action are those named in the writ by their names and all the persons so named have either been served with the writ or acknowledged the issue thereof, any decree in the action limiting the plaintiff's liability (whether made by the Registrar or on the trial of the action)—

    (a)   need not be advertised, but

    (b)   shall only operate to protect the plaintiff in respect of claims by the persons so named or persons claiming through or under them.

**(2)** In any case not falling within paragraph (1), any decree in the action limiting the plaintiff's liability—

    (a)   shall be advertised by the plaintiff in such manner and within such time as may be provided by the decree;

    (b)   shall fix a time within which persons with claims against the plaintiff in respect of the casualty to which the action relates may file their claims, and, in cases to which rule 40 applies, take out a summons, if they think fit, to set the order aside.

(3)   The advertisement to be required under paragraph (2)(a) shall, unless for special reasons the Registrar thinks fit otherwise to provide, be a single advertisement in each of 3 newspapers specified in the decree, identifying the action, the casualty and the relation of the plaintiff thereto (whether as owner of a ship involved in the casualty or otherwise as the case may be), stating that the decree has been made and specifying the amounts fixed thereby as the limits of the plaintiff's liability and the time allowed thereby for the filing of claims and the taking out of summonses to set the decree aside.

The plaintiff must within the time fixed under paragraph (2)(b) file in the Registry a copy of each newspaper in which the advertisement required under paragraph (2)(a) appears.

(4)   The time to be allowed under paragraph (2)(b) shall, unless for special reasons the Registrar thinks fit otherwise to provide, be not less than 2 months from the latest date allowed for the appearance of the advertisements; and after the expiration of the time so allowed no claim may be filed or summons taken out to set aside the decree except with the leave of the Registrar.

(5)   Save as aforesaid, any decree limiting the plaintiff's liability (whether made by the Registrar or on trial of the action) may make any such provisions as is authorized by section 504 of the Merchant Shipping Act, 1894 (1894 c. 60 U.K.).

**40. Limitation action: proceedings to set aside decree** (O. 75 r. 40)

(1)   Where a decree limiting the plaintiff's liability (whether made by Registrar or on trial of the action) fixes a time in accordance with rule 39(2), any person with a claim against the plaintiff in respect of the casualty to which the action relates, who–

    (a)  was not named by his name in the writ as a defendant to the action, or

    (b)  if so named, neither was served with the writ nor has acknowledged the issue thereof,

may, within that time, after acknowledging issue of the writ, take out a summons returnable in chambers before the Registrar, asking that the decree be set aside.

(2)   The summons must be supported by an affidavit or affidavits showing that the defendant in question has a bona fide claim against the plaintiff in respect of the casualty in question and that he has sufficient prima facie grounds for the contention that the plaintiff is not entitled to the relief given him by the decree.

(3)   The summons and every affidavit in support thereof must, at least 7 clear days before the hearing of the summons, be served on the plaintiff and any defendant who has acknowledged issue or service of the writ.

(4)   On the hearing of the summons the Registrar, if he is satisfied that the defendant in question has a bona fide claim against the plaintiff and sufficient prima facie grounds for the contention that the plaintiff is not entitled to the relief given him by the decree, shall set the decree aside and give such directions as to the further proceedings in the action as appear to him to be

appropriate including, in particular, a direction requiring the taking out of a case management summons under Order 25. (L.N. 152 of 2008)

**41. References to Registrar** (O. 75 r. 41)

(1)   Any party (hereafter in this rule referred to as the "claimant") making a claim which is referred to the Registrar for decision must within 2 months after the order is made, or, in a limitation action, within such other period as the Court may direct, file his claim and, unless the reference is in such an action, serve a copy of the claim on every other party.

(2)   At any time after the claimant's claim has been filed or, where the reference is in a limitation action, after the expiration of the time limited by the Court for the filing of claims but, in any case, not less than 28 days before the day appointed for the hearing of the reference, any party to the cause or matter may apply to the Registrar by case management summons as to the proceedings on the reference, and the Registrar shall give such directions, if any, as he thinks fit including, without prejudice to the generality of the foregoing words, a direction requiring any party to serve on any claimant, within such period as the Registrar may specify, a defence to that claimant's claim. (L.N. 152 of 2008)

(3)   The reference shall be heard on a day appointed by the Registrar and, unless the reference is in a limitation action or the parties to the reference consent to the appointment of a particular day, the appointment must be made by order on an application by summons made by any party to the cause or matter.

(4)   An appointment for the hearing of a reference shall not be made until after the claimant has filed his claim or, where the reference is in a limitation action, until after the expiration of the time limited by the Court for the filing of claims.

(5)   Not later than 7 days after an appointment for the hearing of a reference has been made the claimant or, where the reference is in a limitation action, the plaintiff must enter the reference for hearing by lodging in the Registry a praecipe requesting the entry of the reference in the list for hearing on the day appointed.

(6)   Not less than 14 days before the day appointed for the hearing of the reference the claimant must file—

  (a)   a list, signed by him and every other party, of the items (if any) of his claim which are not disputed, stating the amount (if any) which he and the other parties agree should be allowed in respect of each such item, and

  (b)   such affidavits or other documentary evidence as is required to support the items of his claim which are disputed;

and, unless the reference is in a limitation action, he must at the same time serve on every other party a copy of every document filed under this paragraph.

(7)   If the claimant fails to comply with paragraph (1) or (6)(b), the Court may, on the application of any other party to the cause or matter, dismiss the claim.

**NOTES**

**[75.41.1]   Reference to registrar after judgment**
Just as with ordinary civil cases there may be a split trial of an Admiralty action. See the commentary under Order 33 rules 3 and 4. Once judgment on liability has been given by a judge, there may be a reference to the registrar for assessment of the quantum of damages.

Order 75 rule 41 sets down the procedure to be followed on such a reference.

The sequence of events prescribed by Order 75 rule 41 is as follows. First the claimant must within 2 months file and serve its claim and then an appointment for hearing the reference may be fixed. Before the hearing the claimant must ensure that a list is prepared and signed by all parties setting out which items are not in dispute and the agreed amount to be allowed. This list, together with affidavits and documentary evidence must be filed no less than 14 days prior to the hearing.

**[75.41.2]   Directions on reference to Registrar**
Order 75 rule 41(2) provides that a party who wishes to seek directions in respect of a reference to the Registrar should apply to the Registrar by summons. In February 2004 the profession was notified by the Registrar that the previous practice of an initial call-over hearing was discontinued and that rule 41(2) should be followed where directions are sought: see Law Society circular 04-54 (PA).

**42.  Hearing of reference** (O. 75 r. 42)
      **(1)   Unless a judge in person otherwise orders, a reference shall be heard in public.**
      **(2)   The Registrar may adjourn the hearing of a reference from time to time as he thinks fit.**
      **(3)   Subject to paragraph (2), evidence may be given orally or by affidavit or in such other manner as may be agreed upon.**
      **(4)   When the hearing of the reference has been concluded, the Registrar shall—**
            **(a)   reduce to writing his decision on the question arising in the reference (including any order as to costs) and cause it to be filed;**
            **(b)   cause to be filed either with his decision or subsequently such statement (if any) of the grounds of the decision as he thinks fit; and**
            **(c)   send to the parties to the reference notice that he has done so.**
      **(5)   Where no statement of the grounds of the Registrar's decision is filed with his decision and no intimation has been given by the Registrar that he intends to file such a statement later, any party to the reference may, within 14 days after the filing of the decision, make a written request to the Registrar to file such a statement.**

**43.  Objection to decision on reference** (O. 75 r. 43)
      **(1)   Any party to a reference to the Registrar may, by motion in objection, apply to set aside or vary the decision of the Registrar on the reference, but notice of the motion, specifying the points of objection to the decision, must be**

filed within 28 days after the date on which notice of the filing of the decision was sent to that party under rule 42(4) or, if a notice of the filing of a statement of the grounds of the decision was subsequently sent to him thereunder, within 28 days after the date on which the notice was sent.

(2)   The decision of the Registrar shall be deemed to be given on the date on which it is filed, but, unless he or the judge otherwise directs, the decision shall not be acted upon until the time has elapsed for filing notice of a motion in objection thereto.

(3)   A direction shall not be given under paragraph (2) without the parties being given an opportunity of being heard but may, if the Registrar announces his intended decision at the conclusion of the hearing of the reference, be incorporated in his decision as reduced to writing under rule 42(4).

---

## NOTES

**[75.43.1]   Objection to decision of registrar under Order 75 rules 41 & 42**
Order 75 rule 43 sets up a procedure which may be invoked by a party who objects to a decision of the registrar on a reference under rules 41 and 42. The aggrieved party must within 28 days file a 'motion in objection' specifying the points of objection to the registrar's order.

An objection under rule 43 will be heard by a single judge. However, in several respects the procedure is unlike that of a rehearing before a single judge on appeal from a master under Order 58. First, an objection under rule 43 will be heard in open court, as in *Hong Kong Macau Hydrofoil Co Ltd v Ng Chun Wai & Anor* [1990] 2 HKC 536. Secondly, there are older English cases which suggest that as on an appeal to the Court of Appeal there are restrictions on the raising of new points and adducing new evidence: see for example *The Princess Helena* (1861) 167 ER 91.

The objection review procedure under rule 43 is the only avenue of redress in cases to which it applies. The Court of Appeal has no jurisdiction to hear an appeal direct from a decision of the registrar on a reference under rules 41 & 42. See *The 'Flying Flamingo' and the 'Flying Goldfinch'* CACV 196/1989 (Fuad VP, Hunter & Penlington JJA; 08.03.1990) where the Court of Appeal 'very reluctantly' felt constrained to hold that the objecting party had to proceed under rule 43 first, and only after having done so could there be an appeal to the Court of Appeal.

## 45. Drawing up and entry of judgments and orders (O. 75 r. 45)
Every judgment given or order made in an Admiralty cause or matter, except an order which by virtue of Order 42, rule 4, is not required to be drawn up, shall be drawn up in the Registry and shall be entered by an officer of the Registry in the book kept for the purpose.

## 46. Inspection of documents filed in Registry (O. 75, r. 46)
(1)   Order 63, rule 4, shall apply in relation to documents filed in the Registry.

(2)   For the purpose of Order 63, rule 4, a decree made by the Registrar in a limitation action and a decision and any statement of the grounds of that decision filed under rule 42 shall be deemed to have been made or given in court.

**(Enacted 1988)**

---

## NOTES

### [75.46.1]   Leave to inspect court file

Order 75 rule 46 makes it clear that Admiralty proceedings are subject to the provisions of Order 63 rule 4 as to when leave is required to inspect documents in the court file. See the commentary under that rule.

Non-parties require leave to inspect the caveat book kept pursuant to Order 75 rules 6 and 14: see the information from the Registrar circulated in Law Society circular 09-234 (which may be viewed on the members' zone of the Law Society's website).

## ORDER 76

### CONTENTIOUS PROBATE PROCEEDINGS

**1.  Application and interpretation** (O. 76 r. 1)

**(1)  This Order applies to probate causes and matters, and the other provisions of these rules apply to those causes and matters including applications for the rectification of a will subject to the provisions of this Order.**

**(2)  In these rules "probate action" means an action for the grant of probate of the will, or letters of administration of the estate, of a deceased person or for the revocation of such a grant or for a decree pronouncing for or against the validity of an alleged will, not being an action which is non-contentious or common form probate business.**

**(3)  In this Order, "will" includes a codicil.**

---

### NOTES

**[76.1.1]  Cross-reference**
In contemplation of proceedings under this Order, regard should also be had to the Non-Contentious Probate Rules, subsidiary legislation under the Probate and Administration Ordinance (Cap 10) which, in spite of their names, prescribe some of the procedures relevant to contentious probate proceedings such as the issue of caveats against a grant of representation being made and the procedure whereby a warning may be issued to such a caveator requiring him to commence proceedings under this Order.

**[76.1.2]  Proof of death**
A probate action may only be brought to prove the will of a person who has died. It is not appropriate in such an action to seek a declaration that the person has died. In *Wang Din Shin v Wang Nina* [1999] 4 HKC 263 (CA) the Court of Appeal struck out a probate action where the fact of death was in dispute. Godfrey JA held that in the circumstances of the case the probate action was 'a nonsense' and 'misconceived' (at 267E–F). The correct procedure where a person had gone missing but there was no proof of death was to seek leave (under rule 52 of the Non-Contentious Probate Rules, Cap 10) to swear to the death of the missing person. The common law assists with a presumption of death after seven years. In the meantime, the court has power to appoint a receiver of the missing person's property.

**[76.1.3]  No application for revocation of grant in ordinary action**
The specific procedures laid down in this Order must be followed in any application to the court for revocation of a grant of representation. The court may not make such an order in an ordinary action. See *Ng Dok Sing v Yao Jack & Anor* HCA 4039/1980 (Liu J; 09.07.1982).

**[76.1.4]  Type of action to which Order 76 applies – comparison with Order 85**
Order 76 rule 1 provides that the Order applies to probate actions, which are defined as actions for the grant or revocation of a grant of representation (probate or letters of administration). An application for rectification of a will is not a probate action and

should proceed by ordinary writ or originating summons depending on whether there are substantial disputes of fact: *Leung Po Chu v Ho Hung Ying Donna & Ors* [2010] 3 HKLRD 403; [2010] 5 HKC 33. It is not appropriate in the context of a probate action to raise issues as to who is entitled to distribution of the estate of the deceased: that is a matter of administration of the estate, and should be dealt with by proceedings under Order 85: *Liu Yu Wei v Lee Wai Hing* HCAP 1/2006 (Chu J; 14.08.2007).

**2.  Requirements in connection with issue of writ** (O. 76 r. 2)
    **(1)  A probate action may be begun by writ. (L.N. 152 of 2008)**
    **(2)  Before a writ beginning a probate action is issued it must be indorsed with a statement of the nature of the interest of the plaintiff and of the defendant in the estate of the deceased to which the action relates.**

**NOTES**

**[76.2.1]  Leave to issue writ required**
Practice Direction 20.2 provides that leave of the Probate Registrar is required to issue a writ commencing a probate action. The leave application is made by lodging the original and one copy of the writ with the Probate Registry. If leave is granted, this will be endorsed on the duplicate.

**[76.2.2]  Summary judgment on probate action**
Previously a probate action was required by rule 2(1) to be commenced by writ, and on that basis it was held that Order 14 applies and the court could grant summary judgment: *Re Lau Siu Wah* [2005] 1 HKC 364; *Poncet v Kho* HCAP 19/2003 (A Cheung J; 13.03.2007). The rule was amended with effect from 2009 to provide that a probate action 'may' be commenced by writ. The previous cases should still apply, and summary judgment be available, where the writ procedure is adopted.

**[76.2.3]  Discovery in probate action**
Communications between a solicitor and an attesting witness of a will are not privileged to the extent that they concern evidence on attestation and execution: *Chinachem Charitable Foundation Ltd v Chan Chun Chuen & Ors* [2009] 2 HKC 365 (para 15).

**[76.2.4]  Costs**
The costs of a probate action will not normally be ordered against a defendant who gives notice that he only requires proof of a will in solemn form and only intends to cross-examine the witnesses who support the will. See Order 62 rule 6(1)(c).

**3.  Parties to action for revocation of grant** (O. 76 r. 3)
    **Every person who is entitled or claims to be entitled to administer the estate of a deceased person under or by virtue of an unrevoked grant of probate of his will or letters of administration of his estate shall be made a party to any action for revocation of the grant.**

**NOTES**

**[76.3.1]   Application for revocation of a grant – who should be joined?**
Order 76 rule 3 provides that all parties who may be entitled to probate or administration of an estate shall be joined in an application for revocation of a grant. In the case of an application to revoke letters of administration granted in respect of the estate of an intestate, the persons who must be joined will be all those who under the relevant legislation may apply for a grant of representation.

In *Cheng Sau Kam v Eng Audrey* [2000] 3 HKLRD 484 it was held the defendant had no *locus standi* to challenge a grant of probate as she had no interest under either of 2 competing wills. Only the person named as executor and beneficiary under the subsequent will could do so, but he was not a party to the proceedings.

In the interesting case of *Yeung Chi Ding & Ors v Yeung Tse Chun* HCAP 1/1979 (Liu J; 23.07.1985) the court had first to decide that a son of the deceased had been adopted out of the family under Chinese law before coming to the conclusion that the son was not a necessary party under this rule.

Order 76 does not apply to an application for a declaration of relationship which would entitle a person to apply for a grant or to benefit from an estate. See *Re the Estate of Fong Iong* HCMP 6014/2001 (Chu J; 07.12.2001).

Nor does it apply to an application for revocation of a grant where it is the grantee who makes the application. In such a case the application is non-contentious and may be made by *ex parte* originating summons. See *Re Estate of Cheng Ki Sang* [2009] 2 HKLRD 533 where an administrator applied for revocation of the grant on the ground that a will was subsequently found.

**4.   Lodgment of grant in action for revocation (O. 76 r. 4)**
   **(1)   Where, at the commencement of an action for the revocation of a grant of probate of the will or letters of administration of the estate of a deceased person, the probate or letters of administration, as the case may be, have not been lodged in court, then–**
   (a)   **if the action is commenced by a person to whom the grant was made, he shall lodge the probate or letters of administration in the Registry within 7 days after the issue of the writ;**
   (b)   **if any defendant to the action has the probate or letters of administration in his possession or under his control, he shall lodge it or them in the Registry within 14 days after the service of the writ upon him.**
   **(2)   Any person who fails to comply with paragraph (1) may, on the application of any party to the action, be ordered by the Court to lodge the probate or letters of administration in the Registry within a specified time; and any person against whom such an order is made shall not be entitled to take any step in the action without the leave of the Court until he has complied with the order.**

## NOTES

### [76.4.1]  Purpose of Order 76 rule 4

Order 76 rule 4 requires that a grant of probate or letters of administration must be lodged with the court when there is an application for revocation thereof. The purpose is 'to ensure that nothing could be done on the strength of the grant in the meantime': *Ho Wai Yin v Cheng Suet Yee* HCAP 18/2003 (Lam J; 13.02.2004).

Where assets have already been distributed, the lodgment of the grant may not be sufficient protection to ensure against disposition of the assets. In such a case, the court may grant injunctive relief pending determination of the revocation application. On an application for such an injunction, the normal principles as to injunctive relief will apply: *Ho Wai Yin* (above).

**5.  Affidavit of testamentary scripts** (O. 76 r. 5)

**(1)  Unless the Court otherwise directs, the plaintiff and every defendant who has acknowledged service of the writ in a probate action must swear an affidavit—**

> **(a)  describing any testamentary script of the deceased person, whose estate is the subject of the action, of which he has any knowledge or, if such be the case, stating that he knows of no such script; and**

> **(b)  if any such script of which he has knowledge is not in his possession or under his control, giving the name and address of the person in whose possession or under whose control it is or, if such be the case, stating that he does not know the name or address of that person.**

**(2)  Any affidavit required by this rule must be filed, and an office copy thereof and any testamentary script referred to therein which is in the possession or under the control of the deponent, must be lodged in the Registry within 14 days after the acknowledgment of service by a defendant to the action or, if no defendant acknowledges service and the Court does not otherwise direct, before an order is made for the trial of the action.**

**(3)  Where any testamentary script required by this rule to be lodged in the Registry or any part thereof is written in pencil, then, unless the Court otherwise directs, a facsimile copy of that script, or of the page or pages thereof containing the part written in pencil, must also be lodged in the Registry and the words which appear in pencil in the original must be underlined in red ink in the copy.**

**(4)  Except with the leave of the Court, a party to a probate action shall not be allowed to inspect an affidavit filed, or any testamentary script lodged, by any other party to the action under this rule, unless and until an affidavit sworn by him containing the information referred to in paragraph (1) has been filed.**

**(5)  In this rule "testamentary script" means a will or draft thereof, written instructions for a will made by or at the request or under the instructions of the testator and any document purporting to be evidence of the contents, or to be a copy, of a will which is alleged to have been lost or destroyed.**

**6. Failure to acknowledge service** (O. 76 r. 6)

(1) **Order 13 shall not apply in relation to a probate action.**

(2) **Where any of several defendants to a probate action fails to acknowledge service of the writ, the plaintiff may, after the time for acknowledging service has expired and upon filing an affidavit proving due service of the writ, or notice of the writ, on that defendant proceed with the action as if that defendant had acknowledged service.**

(3) **Where the defendant, or all the defendants, to a probate action, fails or fail to acknowledge service of the writ, then, unless on the application of the plaintiff the Court orders the action to be discontinued, the plaintiff may after the time limited for acknowledging service by the defendant apply to the Court for an order for trial of the action.**

(4) **Before applying for an order under paragraph (3) the plaintiff must file an affidavit proving due service of the writ, or notice of the writ, on the defendant and, if no statement of claim is indorsed on the writ, he must lodge a statement of claim in the judge's chambers.**

(5) **Where the Court grants an order under paragraph (3), it may direct the action to be tried on affidavit evidence.**

---

**NOTES**

**[76.6.1]   Procedure on failure to acknowledge service or default of pleadings**
Order 76 rule 6 provides that the usual procedures for entry of judgment in default of acknowledgment of service (under Order 13) do not apply to a probate action. Similarly Order 76 rule 10 provides that judgment in default of pleading (under Order 19) does not apply.

In *Re Lau Siu Wah* [2005] 1 HKC 364 it was held that the combined effect of Order 76 rules 6 and 10 is as follows:

> If a defendant defaults in acknowledging service of the writ or if there is default in service of a defence, the plaintiff has two alternatives: (1) to apply for an order for trial (normally on affidavit evidence); or (2) to apply for an order that the action be discontinued or dismissed, and for a grant of probate or letters of administration to be made to the person entitled thereto under Order 76 rule 11...

**7. Service of statement of claim** (O. 76 r. 7)

**The plaintiff in a probate action must, unless the Court gives leave to the contrary or unless a statement of claim is indorsed on the writ, serve a statement of claim on every defendant who acknowledges service of the writ in the action and must do so before the expiration of 6 weeks after acknowledgment of service by that defendant or of 8 days after the filing by that defendant of an affidavit under rule 5, whichever is the later.**

**8. Counterclaim** (O. 76 r. 8)

(1) **Notwithstanding anything in Order 15, rule 2(1), a defendant to a probate action who alleges that he has any claim or is entitled to any relief or remedy in respect of any matter relating to the grant of probate of the will, or letters of administration of the estate, of the deceased person which is the subject of the action must add to his defence a counterclaim in respect of that matter.**

**(2)** If the plaintiff fails to serve a statement of claim, any such defendant may, with the leave of the Court, serve a counterclaim and the action shall then proceed as if the counterclaim were the statement of claim.

**9. Contents of pleadings** (O. 76 r. 9)

**(1)** Where the plaintiff in a probate action disputes the interest of a defendant he must allege in his statement of claim that he denies the interest of that defendant.

**(2)** In a probate action in which the interest by virtue of which a party claims to be entitled to a grant of letters of administration is disputed, the party disputing that interest must show in his pleading that if the allegations made therein are proved he would be entitled to an interest in the estate.

**(3)** Without prejudice to Order 18, rule 7, any party who pleads that at the time when a will, the subject of the action, was alleged to have been executed the testator did not know and approve of its contents must specify the nature of the case on which he intends to rely, and no allegation in support of that plea which would be relevant in support of any of the following other pleas, that is to say—

    (a)  that the will was not duly executed;

    (b)  that at the time of the execution of the will the testator was not of sound mind, memory and understanding; and

    (c)  that the execution of the will was obtained by undue influence or fraud,

shall be made by that party unless that other plea is also pleaded.

---

NOTES

**[76.9.1]   Defence putting plaintiff to proof**
A defendant who merely wishes to put a plaintiff to proof of a will in solemn form and to cross-examine the witnesses supporting a will should, in the defence, give notice accordingly. See Order 62 rule 6(1)(c) whereby a defendant who does so may be protected against the costs of the action.

**10. Default of pleadings** (O. 76 r. 10)

**(1)** Order 19 shall not apply in relation to a probate action.

**(2)** Where any party to a probate action fails to serve on any other party a pleading which he is required by these rules to serve on that other party, then, unless the Court orders the action to be discontinued or dismissed, that other party may, after the expiration of the period fixed by or under these rules for service of the pleading in question, apply to the Court for an order for trial of the action; and if an order is made the Court may direct the action to be tried on affidavit evidence.

---

NOTES

**[76.10.1]   Procedure on failure to acknowledge service or default of pleadings**
See the commentary under Order 76 rule 6.

**11.  Discontinuance and dismissal** (O. 76 r. 11)

**(1)   Order 21 shall not apply in relation to a probate action.**

**(2)   At any stage of the proceedings in a probate action the Court may, on the application of the plaintiff or of any party to the action who has acknowledged service of the writ therein, order the action to be discontinued or dismissed on such terms as to costs or otherwise as it thinks just, and may further order that a grant of probate of the will, or letters of administration of the estate, of the deceased person, as the case may be, which is the subject of the action, be made to the person entitled thereto.**

**(3)   An application for an order under this rule may be made by summons or by notice under Order 25, rule 7. (L.N. 152 of 2008)**

---

**NOTES**

**[76.11.1]   Order for discontinuance or dismissal of action**

Order 76 rule 11 empowers the court to order that an action be discontinued or dismissed and to make an order for a grant of representation to the person entitled thereto. In *Leung May Chow, Karen & Anor v Leung May Chun, Alison Aliance* HCAP 7/1993 (Yam J; 04.11.1997) the court exercised this power in a case where a defendant's defence and counterclaim had already been struck out.

**12.  Compromise of action: trial on affidavit evidence** (O. 76 r. 12)

**Where, whether before or after the service of the defence in a probate action, the parties to the action agree to a compromise, the Court may order the trial of the action on affidavit evidence.**

---

**NOTES**

**[76.12.1]   Trial after terms of settlement agreed**

Where the parties to a probate action agree on terms of settlement, it is not possible to follow the procedures applicable to ordinary actions whereby judgment may be entered by consent. Instead a trial is required, though the trial may, under Order 76 rule 12, be on affidavit evidence. A trial is necessary because the court has a duty to give effect to the wishes of the testator regardless of what the parties may have agreed: *Kan Mui v Lai Chung Hei & Ors* HCAP 7/2001 (Poon J; 25.02.2008).

Where the parties wish to save costs, it may be appropriate to apply under Order 36 rule 1 for an order that the trial take place before a master. Solicitors have the right of audience at a trial before a master. Such an order was made in *Mak Xiu Chang v Chan Ying Lun Allan* HCAP 1/1994 (no written judgment).

**13.  Application for order to bring in will, etc.** (O. 76 r. 13)

**(1)   Any application in a probate action for an order under section 7(1) of the Probate and Administration Ordinance (Cap 10) shall be for an order requiring a person to bring a will or other testamentary paper into the Registry or to attend in court for examination.**

**(2)   An application under paragraph (1) shall be made by summons in the action, which must be served on the person against whom the order is sought.**

(3)    Any application in a probate action for the issue of a subpoena under section 7(3) of the Probate and Administration Ordinance (Cap 10) shall be for the issue of a subpoena requiring a person to bring into the Registry a will or other testamentary paper.

(4)    An application under paragraph (3) may be made ex parte and must be supported by an affidavit setting out the grounds of the application.

(5)    An application under paragraph (3) shall be made to a master who may, if the application is granted, authorize the issue of a subpoena accordingly.

(6)    Any person against whom a subpoena is issued under section 7(3) of the Probate and Administration Ordinance (Cap 10) and who denies that the will or other testamentary paper referred to in the subpoena is in his possession or under his control may file an affidavit to that effect.

## NOTES

### [76.13.1]    Primary legislation

Section 7(1) of the Probate and Administration Ordinance (Cap 10), to which paragraph (1) of this rule refers, provides as follows:

> The court may, on motion or petition or otherwise, in a summary way, whether any proceedings are or are not pending in the court with respect to any probate or administration, order any person to produce and bring into the Registry, or otherwise as the court may direct, any paper or writing being or purporting to be testamentary which may be shown to be in the possession or under the control of such person.

Section 7(3) of the Probate and Administration Ordinance, to which paragraph (3) of this rule refers, provides:

> The Registrar may, whether or not any proceedings are pending in the court, issue a subpoena requiring any person to produce and bring into the Registry any paper or writing being or purporting to be testamentary, which may be shown to be in the possession, within the power, or under the control of such person; and such person, upon being duly served with the said subpoena, shall be bound to produce and bring in such paper or writing, and shall be subject to the like process of contempt in case of default as if he had been a party to proceedings in the court, and had been ordered by a judge to produce and bring in such paper and writing.

### 14. Administration pendente lite (O. 76 r. 14)

(1)    An application under section 40 of the Probate and Administration Ordinance (Cap 10) for an order for the grant of administration may be made by summons.

(2)    Where an order for a grant of administration is made under the said section 40, Order 30, rules 2, 4 and 6 and (subject to section 60 of the Probate and Administration Ordinance (Cap 10)) rule 3 shall apply as if the administrator were a receiver appointed by the Court.

## NOTES

### [76.14.1]    Appointment of administrator pendente lite

Order 76 rule 14 concerns applications for appointment of an administrator *pendente lite*. The power to make such appointments is found in section 40 of the Probate and

Administration Ordinance (Cap 10). It is there provided that when a probate action is under way the court may appoint an administrator to take charge of the estate of a deceased (subject to the court's direction and control).

As to the factors the court will take into account in deciding whether to appoint an administrator *pendente lite*, see *Hung Jin Mui v Tang Chui Yuk Angela & Anor* HCAP 4/1997 (Le Pichon J; 11.02.1998), citing *Re Bevan* [1948] 1 All ER 271 and *Bellew v Bellew* (1865) 13 LT 247. See also *Lai Wai Pang v Kwok Li Shuk Han* HCAP 13/2000 (A Cheung J; 16.05.2003).

The appointment of an administrator *pendente lite* is interlocutory in that the appointment is intended only for the interim period while proceedings are under way. Application for the appointment is made by summons in the pending probate action (rule 14(1)). There is no power to make the appointment in the absence of a pending probate action; however in those circumstances a receiver may be appointed to protect the assets in the estate: see *Wang Din Shin v Wang Nina* [1999] 4 HKC 263 (CA).

**[76.14.2]  Documents to be filed in support of application**
An application for appointment of an administrator *pendente lite* should be supported by an affidavit setting out the name and qualifications of the proposed administrator, and the value of the estate to be administered. In addition the following documents should be furnished to the court:
(i)   affidavit of fitness of the proposed administrator by a disinterested party; and
(ii)  consent to act.

See *Choy Po Chun & Anor v Au Wing Lun* HCAP 7/2010 (Master Levy; 06.05.2010) (para 23).

**[76.14.3]  Costs of administrator pendente lite**
The costs of an administrator *pendente lite* will, insofar as not necessary in any event, normally be costs in the cause of the pending probate action. See *Hung Jin Mui v Tang Chui Yuk Angela & Anor* HCAP 4/1997 (Le Pichon J; 11.02.1998), citing *Fisher & Joy v Fisher* (1879) 4 PD 231 and *Re Howlett* [1950] P 177. The administrator *pendente lite* is entitled to be paid from the moment of appointment until the conclusion of the suit, or any appeal: *Taylor v Taylor* (1881) 6 PD 29.

Where an administrator *pendente lite* conducts litigation on behalf of the estate, the question of the administrator's right to recover the costs thereof from the estate is not a matter to be decided in the context of those proceedings. It is a matter between the administrator and the beneficiary of the estate. See *Nina Kung v Tan Man Kou & Anor* FACV 6/2004 (Bokhary, Chan & Ribeiro PJJ; Mortimer & Lord Scott NPJJ; 18.02.2005).

**15.  Probate counterclaim in other proceedings** (O. 76 r. 15)
**(1)   In this rule "probate counterclaim" means a counterclaim in any action other than a probate action by which the defendant claims any such relief as is mentioned in rule 1(2).**

**(2)   Subject to the following paragraphs, this Order shall apply with the necessary modifications to a probate counterclaim as it applies to a probate action.**

**(3)  A probate counterclaim must contain a statement of the nature of the interest of the defendant and of the plaintiff in the estate of the deceased to which the counterclaim relates.**

**(4)  Before it is served a probate counterclaim must be indorsed with a memorandum signed by a master showing that the counterclaim has been produced to him for examination and that three copies of it have been lodged with him.**

## NOTES

**[76.15.1]  Probate counterclaims**
Order 76 rule 15 deals with 'probate counterclaims'. Such a counterclaim is one which, in an action which has not been commenced as a probate action, claims relief of a type which comes within the definition of 'probate action' in rule 1(2).

The rule applies the provisions of this Order to probate counterclaims and goes on to add some special requirements as to pleading (the nature of the interests of the opposing parties in the deceased's estate must be stated) and as to indorsement by a master before service. Note that the requirement that a probate counterclaim be indorsed by a master before service had no equivalent in the former English Rules of the Supreme Court.

## 16. Rectification of wills (O. 76 r. 16)
**(1)  Where an application is made for rectification of a will, and the grant has not been lodged in court, rule 4 shall apply, with the necessary modifications, as if the proceedings were a probate action.**

**(2)  A copy of every order made for the rectification of a will shall be sent to the principal Registry for filing, and a memorandum of the order shall be endorsed on, or permanently annexed to, the grant under which the estate is administered.**

**(Enacted 1988)**

## NOTES

**[76.16.1]  Application for rectification of will**
Order 76 rule 16 applies to applications for rectification of wills under section 23A of the Wills Ordinance (Cap 30). It is there provided that the court may order that a will be rectified so as to carry out the testator's intentions in cases of clerical error or failure to understand the testator's instructions.

In *Wu Man Shan v Registrar of Probate* [2006] 2 HKC 106 it was held that rule 55 of the English Non-Contentious Probate Rules 1987 should be followed on an application for rectification of a will in Hong Kong. That rule, the full text of which is quoted in the judgment, provides in summary:

(1)  Application may be made to a judge or registrar, unless a probate action has been commenced.
(2)  The application shall be supported by an affidavit setting out the grounds of the application together with such evidence as can be adduced as to the testator's intentions and as to whichever of the following matters are in issue:-
    (a)  in what respects the testator's intentions were not understood; or

(b)    the nature of any alleged clerical error.

(3)    Unless otherwise directed, notice of the application shall be given to every person having an interest under the will whose interest might be prejudiced by the rectification and any comments in writing by any such person shall be exhibited to the affidavit in support.

As to the mode of commencing such proceedings, in *Wu Man Shan* (above at para 9) the court expressed the following view:

(c)    If an application for a grant has been filed with the probate registry, an application for rectification may be made to the registrar within that application.

(d)    On the other hand, if application for a grant has not yet been filed, *ex parte* miscellaneous proceedings should be issued, with or without notice to the interested parties, depending on the circumstances. The registrar or master does not have jurisdiction.

(e)    The registrar or master may refer the matter to a judge pursuant to s 6(2) of the Probate and Administration Ordinance and Order 32 rule 12 of these rules.

(f)    When a probate action has been commenced, any application for rectification of a will shall be brought by separate miscellaneous proceedings before a judge in chambers with notice to all interested or affected parties.

The court went on to hold that in the particular case, where it was sought to rectify a trivial clerical error (wrong name stated in the interpretation clause) the application could be made *ex parte*.

## ORDER 77

### PROCEEDINGS BY AND AGAINST THE CROWN

---

## NOTES

### [77.0.1]    Order 77 – preliminary note on colonial language

Order 77, which deals with civil proceedings by and against the government, has not been amended to reflect the resumption of Chinese sovereignty in 1997. Pending appropriate amendment under the ongoing adaptation of laws exercise, references to 'the Crown' should be interpreted as provided in Schedule 8 to the Interpretation and General Clauses Ordinance (Cap 1), introduced by the Reunification Ordinance on 1 July 1997. It is there provided that in certain circumstances references to 'the Crown' are to be taken as references to the Central People's Government, and in others to the government of the HKSAR. See the blue pages distributed to subscribers with Issue 8 of this work in August 1997.

### [77.0.2]    Comparison with English rules

Hong Kong's Order 77 differs from the equivalent in the former English Rules of the Supreme Court in that rules 2, 5, 8 and 13 are omitted.

### [77.0.3]    Primary legislation

The provisions of Order 77 should be read together with the Crown Proceedings Ordinance (Cap 300) which is the statutory basis for many civil claims against the government. Pending amendment under the on-going Adaptation of Laws exercise, that Ordinance must, like this Order, be construed in accordance with the interpretative devices enacted by the Reunification Ordinance in 1997 (see above).

At common law it was not possible to bring civil claims in contract or tort against the government. The government and the courts both exercised power in the name of the Crown and it was thought not possible for the monarch to summon herself to appear in her own court. The private citizen's remedy was at best the reasonable expectation of *ex gratia* compensation. This unsatisfactory situation was remedied in the 20th century by statute, in Hong Kong, by the Crown Proceedings Ordinance. See in particular section 3 of that Ordinance which enables the private citizen to make claims for compensation against the government.

### [77.0.4]    Appropriate defendant in proceedings against government

Section 13(1) of the Crown Proceedings Ordinance (Cap 300) provides that the Secretary for Justice should be named as defendant in proceedings against the government under that Ordinance. The same is true when the government is said to be vicariously liable for the acts of a government servant: it is the government itself which may be vicariously liable, not the head of the department or unit in which the tortfeasor is employed. See *Lai Hing v Cater & AG* [1976] HKLR 1022 where the court struck out proceedings as against the Commissioner of the ICAC personally for alleged torts committed by ICAC officers, leaving the action to proceed against the Attorney General (as the Secretary for Justice was then known) as the government's representative under the Ordinance.

The situation is sometimes different in proceedings concerning government property. Under the Financial Secretary Incorporation Ordinance (Cap 1015) the FS is constituted as a corporation sole known as The Financial Secretary Incorporated for the purpose of holding government property which may be transferred to it. There are many examples of proceedings in which the FSI is named as the party to proceedings concerning tenancy agreements entered into in respect of government-owned buildings which have been transferred to that corporation.

In the case of judicial review proceedings under Order 53, where allegations of illegality, procedural impropriety or irrationality are made against the holder of a government office or instrumentalities of the state, claiming public law relief, it is appropriate to name the particular government office or body as a party. There are many examples where the Chief Executive of the HKSAR, the Secretary for the Civil Service, the Director of Immigration and many other government offices have been named as parties in such proceedings.

**1.  Application and interpretation** (O. 77 r. 1)

**(1)   These rules apply to civil proceedings to which the Crown is a party subject to the following rules of this Order.**

**(2)   In this Order–**

**"civil proceedings by the Crown" and "civil proceedings against the Crown" have the same respective meanings as in Part III of the Crown Proceedings Ordinance (Cap 300), and do not include any of the proceedings specified in section 19(3) of that Ordinance;**

**"civil proceedings to which the Crown is a party" has the same meaning as it has for the purposes of Part V of the Crown Proceedings Ordinance (Cap 300), by virtue of section 2(4) of that Ordinance;**

**"order against the Crown" means any order (including an order for costs) made in any civil proceedings by or against the Crown, or in connection with any arbitration to which the Crown is a party, in favour of any person against the Crown or against a government department or against an officer of the Crown as such;**

**"order" includes a judgment, decree, rule, award or declaration.**

**3.  Particulars to be included in indorsement of claim** (O. 77 r. 3)

**(1)   In the case of a writ which begins proceedings against the Crown the indorsement of claim required by Order 6, rule 2, shall include a statement of the circumstances in which the Crown's liability is alleged to have arisen and as to the government department and officers of the Crown concerned.**

**(2)   If in civil proceedings against the Crown a defendant considers that the writ does not contain a sufficient statement as required by this rule, he may, before the expiration of the time limited for acknowledging service of the writ, apply to the plaintiff by notice for a further and better statement containing such information as may be specified in the notice.**

**(3)   Where a defendant gives a notice under this rule, the time limited for acknowledging service of the writ shall not expire until 4 days after the defendant has notified the plaintiff in writing that the defendant is satisfied with the statement supplied in compliance with the notice, or 4 days after the Court**

has, on the application of the plaintiff by summons served on the defendant not less than 7 days before the return day, decided that no further information as to the matters referred to in paragraph (1) is reasonably required.

4.  **Service on the Crown** (O. 77 r. 4)

(1)  Order 10, Order 11 and any other provision of these rules relating to service out of the jurisdiction shall not apply in relation to the service of any process by which civil proceedings against the Crown are begun.

(HK)(2)  Personal service of any document required to be served on the Crown for the purpose of or in connection with any civil proceedings is not requisite; but where the proceedings are by or against the Crown service on the Crown must be effected by service on the Secretary for Justice.

(3)  In relation to the service of any document required to be served on the Crown for the purpose of or in connection with any civil proceedings by or against the Crown, Order 65, rules 5 and 9, shall not apply, and Order 65, rule 7, shall apply as if the reference therein to rules 2 and 5(1)(a) of that Order were a reference to paragraph (2) of this rule.

6.  **Counterclaim and set-off** (O. 77 r. 6)

(1)  Notwithstanding Order 15, rule 2, and Order 18, rules 17 and 18, a person may not in any proceedings by the Crown make any counterclaim or plead a set-off if the proceedings are for the recovery of, or the counterclaim or set-off arises out of a right or claim to repayment in respect of, any taxes, duties or penalties.

(2)  Notwithstanding Order 15, rule 2, and Order 18, rules 17 and 18, no counterclaim may be made, or set-off pleaded, without the leave of the Court, by the Crown in proceedings against the Crown, or by any person in proceedings by the Crown—

      (a)  if the Crown is sued or sues in the name of a government department and the subject-matter of the counterclaim or set-off does not relate to that department; or

      (b)  if the Crown is sued or sues in the name of the Secretary for Justice.

(3)  Any application for leave under this rule must be made by summons.

---

## NOTES

[**77.6.1**]  **Restriction on counterclaim and set-off in proceedings involving the government**

Order 77 rule 6 imposes, for the purpose of proceedings involving the government, restrictions on the usual right to counterclaim or rely on the defence of set-off. No counterclaim or set-off is permitted against or in respect of taxes, duties or penalties owing to or repayable by the government. In other circumstances a cross claim is possible, but leave is required. The court's discretion to grant such leave has been described as 'seemingly unfettered': *Paul Y Construction Co Ltd v AG* [1992] 2 HKLR 120. There (at 122) Kaplan J described the rationale of the rule in the following terms:

The rationale behind this rule would seem to be based upon the fact that the [Secretary for Justice] can be sued in one capacity, but may seek to set-off or counterclaim in another. For instance, A could sue the [SJ] in respect of medical negligence. This would, effectively, be an action against the Department of Medical and Health. The [SJ] could seek to set-off against any sums found to be due to A in the medical negligence action a sum said to be owed by A to another government department, for instance the Building Ordinance Office, in respect of the cost of work carried out by that office for which A is liable under that Ordinance. It is to keep an eye on situations such as this, that the leave of the court is required.

The court went on to hold that in exercising its discretion, it was necessary to look at all the circumstances.

**7.   Summary judgment** (O. 77 r. 7)

(1)   **No application shall be made against the Crown–**

(a)   **under Order 14, rule 1, or Order 86, rule 1, in any proceedings against the Crown;**

(b)   **under Order 14, rule 5, in any proceedings by the Crown; or**

(c)   **under Order 14A, rule 1, in any proceedings by or against the Crown. (L.N. 165 of 1992)**

(2)   **Where an application is made by the Crown under Order 14, rule 1, Order 14, rule 5, or Order 86, rule 1, the affidavit required in support of the application must be made by—**

(a)   **the solicitor acting for the Crown, or**

(b)   **an officer duly authorized by the solicitor so acting or by the department concerned;**

**and the affidavit shall be sufficient if it states that in the deponent's belief the applicant is entitled to the relief claimed and there is no defence to the claim or part of a claim to which the application relates or no defence except as to the amount of any damages claimed.**

**9.   Judgment in default** (O. 77 r. 9)

(1)   **Except with the leave of the Court, no judgment in default of notice of intention to defend or of pleading shall be entered against the Crown in civil proceedings against the Crown or in third party proceedings against the Crown.**

(2)   **Except with the leave of the Court, Order 16, rule 5(1)(a), shall not apply in the case of third party proceedings against the Crown.**

(3)   **An application for leave under this rule may be made by summons and the summons must be served not less than 7 days before the return day. (L.N. 152 of 2008)**

**10.  Third party notices** (O. 77 r. 10)

(1)   **Notwithstanding anything in Order 16, a third party notice (including a notice issuable by virtue of Order 16, rule 9) for service on the Crown shall not be issued without the leave of the Court, and the application for the grant of such leave must be made by summons, and the summons must be served on the plaintiff and the Crown.**

(2)   **Leave to issue such a notice for service on the Crown shall not be granted unless the Court is satisfied that the Crown is in possession of all such**

information as it reasonably requires as to the circumstances in which it is alleged that the liability of the Crown has arisen and as to the departments and officers of the Crown concerned.

## 11. Interpleader: application for order against Crown (O. 77 r. 11)

No order shall be made against the Crown under Order 17, rule 5(3), except upon an application by summons served not less than 7 days before the return day.

## 12. Discovery and interrogatories (O. 77 r. 12)

(1) Order 24, rules 1 and 2, shall not apply in civil proceedings to which the Crown is a party.

(2) In any civil proceedings to which the Crown is a party any order of the Court made under the power conferred by section 24(1) of the Crown Proceedings Ordinance (Cap 300), shall be construed as not requiring the disclosure of the existence of any document the existence of which it would, in the opinion of the Chief Secretary for Administration, be injurious to the public interest to disclose. (L.N. 362 of 1997)

(3) Where in any such proceedings an order of the Court directs that a list of documents made in answer to an order for discovery against the Crown shall be verified by affidavit, the affidavit shall be made by such officer of the Crown as the Court may direct.

(4) Where in any such proceedings an order is made under the said section 24 for interrogatories to be answered by the Crown, the Court shall direct by what officer of the Crown the interrogatories are to be answered.

(5) (Repealed L.N. 404 of 1991)

---

## NOTES

### [77.12.1] Discovery and interrogatories against the government

At common law no order for discovery or interrogatories could be made against the government: *Cowie v AG* [1948] HKLR 42. Now there is statutory power under section 24 of the Crown Proceedings Ordinance (Cap 300) to make such orders. An order is always required – Order 77 rule 12(1) provides that the automatic discovery procedure laid down in Order 24 rules 1 and 2 does not apply to proceedings to which the government is a party, and Order 26 rule 3(3) provides that interrogatories without order shall not be served on the government.

Order 77 rule 12(2) preserves the government's immunity from discovery where disclosure would, in the opinion of the Chief Secretary, be injurious to the public interest. See also Order 24 rule 15. Rules 12(3) and (4) require that the court direct which government officer shall make any affidavit verifying a list of documents, or answering any interrogatories.

## 14. Evidence (O. 77 r. 14)

(1) Civil proceedings against the Crown may be instituted under Order 39, rule 15, in any case in which the Crown is alleged to have an interest or estate in the honour, title, dignity or office or property in question.

(2) For the avoidance of doubt it is hereby declared that any powers exercisable by the Court in regard to the taking of evidence are exercisable in proceedings between subjects.

**15. Execution and satisfaction of orders** (O. 77 r. 15)

(1) Nothing in Orders 45 to 52 shall apply in respect of any order against the Crown. (See App A Form 96.)

(2) An application under the proviso to subsection (1) of section 21 of the Crown Proceedings Ordinance (Cap 300), for a direction that a separate certificate shall be issued under that subsection with respect to the costs (if any) ordered to be paid to the applicant, may be made to the Court ex parte without summons.

(3) Any such certificate must be in Form No 95 or 96 in Appendix A, whichever is appropriate.

**16. Attachment of debts, etc.** (O. 77 r. 16)

(1) No order–
    (a) for the attachment of debts under Order 49, or
    (b) for the appointment of a sequestrator under Order 45, or
    (c) for the appointment of a receiver under Order 30 or 51,

shall be made or have effect in respect of any money due or accruing due, or alleged to be due or accruing due, from the Crown.

(1A) No application shall be made under paragraph (2) unless the order of the Court to be enforced is for a sum of money amounting in value to at least $5,000.

(2) Every application to the Court for an order under section 23(1) of the Crown Proceedings Ordinance (Cap 300), restraining any person from receiving money payable to him by the Crown and directing payment of the money to the applicant or some other person must be made by summons and, unless the Court otherwise directs, served–
    (a) on the Crown at least 15 days before the return day, and
    (b) on the person to be restrained or his solicitor at least 7 days after the summons has been served on the Crown and at least 7 days before the return day.

(2A) An application under paragraph (2) must be supported by an affidavit–
    (a) setting out the facts giving rise to the application;
    (b) stating the name and last known address of the person to be restrained;
    (c) identifying the order to be enforced and stating the amount of such order and the amount remaining unpaid under it at the time of the application, and
    (d) identifying the particular debt from the Crown in respect of which the application is made.

(3) Order 49, rules 5 and 6, shall apply in relation to such an application as is mentioned in paragraph (2) for an order restraining a person from receiving money payable to him by the Crown as those rules apply to an application under

Order 49, rule 1, for an order for the attachment of a debt owing to any person from a garnishee, except that the Court shall not have power to order execution to issue against the Crown.

---

NOTES

**[77.16.1]    'Attachment' of debts owing by government**
Under Order 77 rule 16 money owing by the government is not susceptible to execution in the usual way by garnishee order (*etc*). However, this is really more a matter of form than substance. The rule prohibits the making of such orders against the government in the spirit of the common law's respect for the sovereign. However, the same effect can be achieved under section 23(1) of the Crown Proceedings Ordinance (Cap 300) which empowers the court to make an order restraining a person from receiving money from the government and directing its payment to another. See *AG v Ng Shiu-fai* [1977] DCLR 51. Where the application seeks to divert to a third party money owing by the government, they are 'in effect garnishee proceedings': *Goodpoint Holdings Ltd v Seabrook* [1997] 2 HKC 541.

The procedure for such applications is regulated by Order 77 rule 16(2).

**[77.16.2]    Bail money**
In *Goodpoint Holdings* (above, at 546H-I) it was held that cash bail advanced by an outsider on behalf of the defendant in a criminal case is not susceptible to attachment under rule 16. This, it was said, is because, in the event the defendant does not abscond, the money is subject to a trust in favour of the person who advanced it. However, *dicta* in a later case suggests that this rationale may not be correct. See *Registrar, District Court v Li Kai & Anor* [2006] 3 HKC 379, 389H-I (CA) where, without referring to the earlier case, Ma CJHC said that as far as the court is concerned bail money is considered to be a payment made by the accused himself regardless of who actually provides the money and under what conditions.

**17. Proceedings relating to postal packets** (O. 77 r. 17)
   **(1)    An application by any person under section 7(3) of the Crown Proceedings Ordinance (Cap 300), for leave to bring proceedings in the name of the sender or addressee of a postal packet or his personal representatives must be made by originating summons.**
   **(2)    The Crown and the person in whose name the applicant seeks to bring proceedings must be made defendants to a summons under this rule.**
   **(3)    A summons under this rule shall be in Form No 10 in Appendix A.**

**18. Applications under section 25 of Crown Proceedings Ordinance** (O. 77 r. 18)
   **(2)    An application such as is referred to in section 25(2) of the Crown Proceedings Ordinance (Cap 300) may be made to the Court at any time before trial by summons, or may be made at the trial of the proceedings. (L.N. 152 of 2008)**

**(Enacted 1988)**

## ORDER 78

### DISTRICT COURT PROCEEDINGS TRANSFERRED OR REMOVED TO THE COURT OF FIRST INSTANCE

**1. Application and interpretation** (O. 78 r. 1)

(1) **This Order applies where an order has been made under section 41 or 42 of the District Court Ordinance (Cap 336), for the transfer, or under section 15 of the Crown Proceedings Ordinance (Cap 300), for the removal, of proceedings from the District Court to the Court of First Instance. (28 of 2000) (L.N. 152 of 2008)**

(2) **Where only the proceedings on a counterclaim are transferred, this Order shall apply as if the party setting up the counterclaim were the plaintiff and the party resisting it the defendant, and references in this Order to the plaintiff and the defendant shall be construed accordingly.**

(3) **References in the following provisions of this Order to the plaintiff and the defendant shall, in relation to proceedings begun in the District Court otherwise than by writ, be construed as references to the applicant and the respondent respectively. (L.N. 152 of 2008)**

---

**NOTES**

**[78.1.1]  Scope of Order 78**
Order 78 governs the procedure to be followed when an action is transferred from the District Court to the Court of First Instance.

Power to order transfer from the District Court to the Court of First Instance is found in the District Court Ordinance (Cap 336) and in the Crown Proceedings Ordinance (Cap 300) (which retains its colonial title pending revision in the on-going adaptation of laws exercise) .

**[78.1.2]  Transfer to the Court of First Instance under the District Court Ordinance**
The District Court Ordinance, as amended with effect from 1 September 2000, provides in sections 41 and 42 that the District Court may order that an action or proceeding be transferred to the Court of First Instance either of its own motion or on the application of any party.

Section 41 deals with claims which are beyond the jurisdiction of the District Court. It provides that the District Court may either transfer the claim to the Court of First Instance or, if it thinks fit, strike out the action or proceeding if it appears that the plaintiff knew or ought to have known that the District Court had no jurisdiction. Section 41 goes on, in subsection (3) to deal with the situation where a claim brought within the limits of the District Court's jurisdiction is met with a counterclaim beyond that court's jurisdiction. It is provided that the District Court may (either on its own motion or on application) transfer the whole proceedings or the counterclaim alone (save any defence of set-off) to the Court of First Instance.

Section 41(3)(c) of the District Court Ordinance, read together with section 41(4), allows the District Court to refer the question of transfer to a judge of the Court of

First Instance for decision. For an illustration of such a case under the law as it was prior to 1 September 2000, see *Estraymo Co Ltd v Gracious Industries Ltd* DCCJ 10312/1983 (Judge E Li; 09.02.1984).

Section 42 provides the District Court with an additional power to transfer proceedings to the Court of First Instance without regard to the District Court's jurisdictional limits.

*Hearing required* – In *Inchcape (HK) Ltd v Performa* (Asia) Ltd [1992] 2 HKC 364 it was held that natural justice requires that the parties be heard before an order for transfer is made from the Court of First Instance to the District Court. The same reasoning should apply on transfer from the District Court to the CFI. In *Hang Seng Credit Card Ltd v Tsang Nga Lee* [2000] 3 HKC 269, 281G it was held that *Inchcape* should no longer be followed, but this appears to relate to other aspects of the *Inchcape* decision.

### [78.1.3]   Transfer under the Crown Proceedings Ordinance

Section 15(1) of the Crown Proceedings Ordinance (Cap 300) provides that proceedings shall be transferred from the district court to the Court of First Instance where proceedings have been instituted against the government in the District Court and the government applies to the Court of First Instance with a certificate from the Secretary for Justice to the effect that the proceedings may involve an important point of law or be decisive of other cases arising out of the same matter or are, for other reasons, more fit to be tried in the Court of First Instance. Order 78 now provides the procedure to be followed in effecting such transfer. This has remedied the former position (see *Crown Trading Co v Ming Hop Hing Garment Factory* [1965] HKLR 190).

### [78.1.4]   Costs consequences of transfer between District Court and Court of First Instance

As a general rule the costs allowed on taxation in respect of proceedings in the District Court are 2/3 of those which would be allowed in the Court of First Instance: see the commentary under Order 62. Where fixed costs are applicable, the District Court has its own scale, which is lower than that applicable in the High Court.

Section 44A of the District Court Ordinance (as amended with effect from 1 September 2000) makes provision as to costs where there has been a transfer to or from the Court of First Instance. In brief, it is there provided that the court making an order for costs on transfer, or where there has been a transfer, may exercise its discretion taking into account the circumstances of the particular case and the differing scales. See also Order 62 rule 4(2).

In *Lai Hing-tong v AG* [1990] 1 HKLR 56 (before the 2000 amendments), where proceedings were transferred from the District Court to the Court of First Instance, the plaintiff was awarded costs on the High Court scale for the period after transfer, with no order as to the costs incurred in the District Court. In *Sunbeam Investments Ltd v Mannitop Investment Co Ltd* [2008] 5 HKC 250 proceedings were transferred to the Court of First Instance because the District Court had no jurisdiction to grant the injunction claimed. After transfer, the claim for an injunction was not pursued and the plaintiff accepted payment into court of an amount that was within the District Court's jurisdiction. The plaintiff was awarded pre-transfer costs on the District Court scale and post-transfer costs on the High Court scale.

**[78.1.5]    Transfer of case from the High Court to the District Court**
Order 78 deals with transfer from the District Court to the Court of First Instance. For transfer in the opposite direction, that is from the CFI to the District Court, see section 43 of the District Court Ordinance (Cap 336) and see Order 25 rule 3(c) of these rules.

**2.   Duties of officer** (O. 78, r. 2)
**On receipt by the Registrar of the documents relating to the transfer or removal, the Registrar must forthwith —**

      **(a)   file the said documents and make an entry of the filing thereof in the cause book,**

      **(c)   give notice to all parties to the proceedings in the District Court that the action is proceeding in the Court of First Instance and that the defendant is required to acknowledge service of the notice in writing.**

                                     **(L.N. 356 of 1988) (L.N. 152 of 2008)**

**NOTES**

**[78.2.1]   Numbering**
Note that there is no paragraph (b) in Order 78 rule 2.

**3.   Acknowledgement of service** (O. 78, rule 3)
**(1)   The defendant must, within 7 days after receipt of the notice referred to in rule 2, acknowledge service in writing of the notice of transfer or removal. (L.N. 152 of 2008)**

**(2)   Where the defendant has not, before the proceedings are transferred or removed to the Court, acknowledged service of the writ or the originating summons by which the proceedings were begun in the District Court, he shall file an acknowledgement of service in accordance with Order 12, rules 1, 3, 5 and 9 within 14 days after receipt of the notice referred to in rule 2. (L.N. 152 of 2008)**

**4.   Judgment on failure to give notice of intention to defend** (O. 78, r. 4)
**(1)   If the defendant fails, or all the defendants (if more than one) fail, to give notice of intention to defend within the period prescribed by rule 3(2), the plaintiff, after having caused an address for service to be entered in the cause book, may, with the leave of the Court, enter judgment against the defendant or defendants, as the case may be, with costs. (L.N. 152 of 2008)**

**(2)   An application for leave under this rule must be made by summons which must, notwithstanding anything in Order 65, rule 9, be served on the defendant, and the address for service of the defendant shall be his address for service in the proceedings in the District Court. (L.N. 152 of 2008)**

**NOTES**

**[78.4.1]   Example**
For an example of a case where the court entered judgment in default under Order 78 rule 4 see *Wong Kum Chi v Lee Tit Ying* HCMP 363/2002 (Á Cheung J; 08.10.2002).

**5.   Case management summons or summary judgment** (O. 78, r. 5)

(1)   Unless the plaintiff has entered judgment against a defendant under rule 4(1) or has entered judgment (final or interlocutory) or applied for judgment against a defendant under Order 19, the plaintiff must, within 7 days after a notice under rule 2 is given, cause an address for service to be entered in the cause book and either — (L.N. 152 of 2008)

    (a)   take out and serve on the defendant a case management summons returnable in not less than 21 days, or (L.N. 152 of 2008)

    (b)   except where the defendant is the Crown, make an application under Order 14, rule 1, for judgment against the defendant;

and where a summons is served on the defendant under sub-paragraph (a), Order 25, rules 2 to 7, shall, with any necessary modifications, apply as if that summons were a case management summons under that Order. (L.N. 152 of 2008)

(2)   If the plaintiff fails either to take out such a summons, or make such an application, as is referred to in paragraph (1) within the period prescribed thereby the defendant or any defendant may take out such a summons or may apply for an order dismissing the action.

(3)   On the hearing of an application to dismiss the action the Court may either dismiss the action on such terms as may be just or may deal with the application as if it were a case management summons. (L.N. 152 of 2008)

(Enacted 1988)

---

## NOTES

### [78.5.1]   Procedure after transfer

Order 78 rule 5 provides that after an action has been transferred under the Order, the plaintiff must either take out a case management summons or apply for summary judgment. If the plaintiff fails to do so, the defendant may take out a case management summons or apply for dismissal of the action. Such an application for dismissal is similar to the application contemplated by Order 25 rule 1(4)(b).

## ORDER 79

### TRIBUNAL PROCEEDINGS TRANSFER OR REMOVAL TO THE COURT OF FIRST INSTANCE

**1. Tribunal proceedings; transfer or removal to the Court of First Instance** (O. 79 r. 1)

**(HK) Save as is otherwise provided by Ordinance or rules of court when a matter is transferred or removed from a tribunal to the Court of First Instance it shall be set down before a master who shall make such directions as he sees fit for the further conduct of the proceedings.**

**(Enacted 1988)**

## NOTES

### [79.1.1]  Comparison with English rules
Order 79, dealing with transfer of proceedings from a tribunal to the Court of First Instance, deals with a different subject than the Order of the same number in the former English Rules of the Supreme Court (which dealt with criminal proceedings).

### [79.1.2]  Power to transfer proceedings from tribunal to CFI
The Lands Tribunal, Small Claims Tribunal and Labour Tribunal all have power to order the transfer of proceedings to the Court of First Instance. The criteria laid down in their governing statutes differ. However, generally speaking the tribunal's power will be exercised in respect of proceedings which are complex or raise difficult points of law or where there are other proceedings between the same parties on-going in the Court of First Instance. In the case of the Labour Tribunal, a stale claim (more than one year old) may not be dealt with there, but may be dealt with in court on transfer.

A tribunal's power to order transfer is discretionary but it should not be exercised without some 'good and sufficient reason': *Chapman v Thai Airways Int'l Ltd* HCSA 1/1995 (Power VP, Bokhary and Mortimer JJA; 01.03.1995). One judge has said that an order for transfer will only be justified where 'necessary in the interests of justice': *Ho Siu Mei v Solution House Ltd* HCSA 5/1997 (Litton VP, Godfrey and Liu, JJA, 16.04.1997). It should be borne in mind that transfer to a court will result in loss of advantages such as 'speedy, simple and informal procedures, and the exclusion of legal representation': *Leung Muk Lan v Country Club Publishing Co Ltd* HCMP 48512/1998 (Chan CJHC, Nazareth VP & Liu JA; 13.10.1998). If the tribunals are too ready to transfer cases to the higher courts, 'the purpose of the legislation will be frustrated': *Lo Suk Ling Villy v The Methodist Church Hong Kong* HCA 8395/1997 (Chung J; 12.01.2001).

### [79.1.3]  Procedure after order of transfer
Upon transfer to the Court of First Instance a claim commenced in a tribunal will be assigned an action number and the parties will be called before a master for a directions hearing in accordance with Order 79 rule 1. It is not necessary to issue a writ of summons. The practice and procedure of the Court of First Instance, including these rules, applies after transfer: see *Murdock v Dresser-Rand Service SARL* [2002]

2 HKC 85, 88C. The master will accordingly give directions relating to pleadings, discovery and witness statements. Though not specifically required by Order 79 rule 1 the master should also direct that the reasons the adjudicating officer in the tribunal made the transfer order be provided: *Leung Muk Lan v Country Club Publishing Co Ltd* HCMP 4851/1998 (Chan CJHC, Nazareth VP and Liu JA; 13.10.1998).

## ORDER 80

### DISABILITY

**1. Interpretation** (O. 80 r. 1)
**In this Order—**
**"mentally incapacitated person"** means a mentally disordered person or a
mentally handicapped person (within the meaning of the Mental Health
Ordinance (Cap 136)) who by reason of mental disorder or mental handicap,
as the case may be, is incapable of managing and administering his property
and affairs; (81 of 1997 s 59)
**"the Ordinance"** means the Mental Health Ordinance (Cap 136);
**"person under disability"** means a person who is a minor or a mentally
incapacitated person. (81 of 1997 s 59)

## NOTES

#### [80.1.1] Comparison with English rules
Order 80 is taken from the Order of the same number in the former English Rules of
the Supreme Court. The equivalent provision now is Part 21 of the Civil Procedure
Rules. In the English CPR the terms 'children' and 'patient' are now used instead of
'party under disability', 'infant' and 'mentally incapacitated person'.

#### [80.1.2] Definition of 'minor'
In Hong Kong law a minor is a person who has not attained the age of 18 years: see
the definitions of 'adult', 'infant' and 'minor' in section 3 of the Interpretation and
General Clauses Ordinance (Cap 1) as amended by the Age of Majority (Related
Provisions) Ordinance 1990.

#### [80.1.3] Mental health legislation
Prior to the reversion of Hong Kong to Chinese sovereignty, the primary legislation
relevant to those provisions of this Order which relate to mental disability was the
Mental Health Act 1983 c 20 (UK). The law has since been localised and reference
should now be made to the Mental Health Ordinance (Cap 136) as amended by
Ordinance No 81 of 1997.

#### [80.1.4] Inquiry as to mental fitness – practice direction
Where a question arises as to whether a person is mentally incapacitated, the court
may, under section 7 of Cap 136, order an inquiry. The procedures to be followed
on such an inquiry are set out in detail in practice direction 30.1, in force from 31
October 2005. The full text of the practice direction, together with annexed forms, is
available on the judiciary's website.

Where such a question arises in the context of on-going legal proceedings, it may
be appropriate to seek a direction of the court that the Official Solicitor investigate:
*Harbin v Masterman* [1896] 1 Ch 351, 365 & 367 (CA).

Pending investigation into possible mental incapacity, the court may appoint an interim representative and direct the commencement of proceedings to preserve property: *Re Madam L* [2004] 4 HKC 114, 124C-F.

**[80.1.5]   Management of property and affairs of mentally incapacitated persons**
With regard to proceedings concerning the management of property and affairs of mentally incapacitated persons, see Law Society circular 10–615 and the various sources referred to therein. The circular can be viewed on the Law Society's website.

**2.   Person under disability must sue, etc. by next friend or guardian ad litem**
(O. 80 r. 2)
**(1)   A person under disability may not bring, or make a claim in, any proceedings except by his next friend and may not acknowledge service, defend, make a counterclaim or intervene in any proceedings, or appear in any proceedings under a judgment or order notice of which has been served on him, except by his guardian ad litem.**

**(2)   Subject to the provision of these rules, anything which in the ordinary conduct of any proceedings is required or authorized by a provision of these rules to be done by a party to the proceedings shall or may, if the party is a person under disability, be done by his next friend or guardian ad litem.**

**(3)   Except where the Official Solicitor is acting as next friend or guardian ad litem, a next friend or guardian ad litem of a person under disability must act by a solicitor.**

**(L.N. 375 of 1991)**

**NOTES**

**[80.2.1]   Procedure where a party is 'under disability'**
Order 80 rule 2 provides that legal proceedings may not be commenced or continued by or against a person under disability save by a 'next friend' or 'guardian *ad litem*'. A 'next friend' represents a plaintiff or applicant, and a 'guardian *ad litem*' represents a person under disability who is a defendant or respondent. Such a representative may not act in person, save that the Official Solicitor, when appointed representative, need not seek outside representation. Although this order applies in the Court of Final Appeal (see rule 76 of the Court of Final Appeal Rules), that court appears to have allowed a next friend to appear in person in *Wu Yee Pak v Un Fong Leung & Ors* [2005] 2 HKLRD 169.

**[80.2.2]   'Debarring' order**
The court has power to make a 'debarring' order to prevent a party under disability from continuing proceedings without a next friend or guardian *ad litem*. In *Chan Sai Lun Henry v Chan Wai Wah Lily-Ann* [2000] 1 HKC 453 (CA) it was held that where the disability is mental incapacity, such an order cannot be made unless the existence of such incapacity has previously been determined under the Mental Health Ordinance (Cap 136). However in *Ho Po Chu v Tung Chee Hwa & Ors* [2006] 1 HKC 527 (CA), *Chan* was said to be *per incuriam* in this regard. It was held that such an order may be made without a formal determination under Cap 136 provided there is 'clear medical evidence to prove the incapacity': *Ho*, 542C-D.

A debarring order should only be made 'in exceptional cases': *Ho* (above, at 539I). Instead, the court may stay the proceedings pending appointment of a next friend or guardian *ad litem* or, when faced with bizarre proceedings brought by a mentally incapacitated person the court may use its power to strike out: *Ho* (above, at 540C-D).

### [80.2.3]  Costs of party under disability
Where costs are awarded in favour of a party under disability, it is usual for the court to order that they be taxed on the common fund basis. See the commentary under Order 62 rule 28. Order 62 rule 30 requires that costs payable by or on behalf of a party under disability are required to be taxed as between solicitor and own client under Order 62 rule 29. For some reason this requirement does not expressly extend to mentally handicapped persons. See the commentary under Order 62 rule 30.

### [80.2.4]  No power to order costs against next friend
Historically in England costs have been ordered against next friends. See, for example, *Golds v Kerr* [1884] WN 46. At present CPR 21.9 contemplates costs orders against next friends in England. However the situation has been different in Hong Kong. In *Wu Yee Pak v Un Fong Leung & Ors* [2005] 2 HKLRD 169, 175 the Court of Final Appeal declined to make an order for costs against a next friend, saying there was no power to do so, and that in any event it would not be appropriate in the particular case. The CFA did not refer to any authorities to support its finding of lack of jurisdiction. The explanation may lie in the fact that a next friend is not a party to the proceedings: see *In re Corsellis, Lawton v Elwes* (1884) 52 LJ 399. When *Wu Yee Pak* (above) was decided the power to order costs against non-parties was very limited. However, as part of the civil justice reforms which took effect on 2 April 2009 those restrictions have been abolished and the court now has a broad discretion to order costs against non-parties when it is just to do so. See Order 62 rule 6A and the commentary thereunder.

**3.   Appointment of next friend or guardian ad litem** (O. 80 r. 3)

**(2)   Except as provided by paragraph (4) or (5) or by rule 6, an order appointing a person next friend or guardian ad litem of a person under disability is not necessary.**

**(3)   Where a person is authorized under Part II of the Ordinance to conduct legal proceedings in the name of a person or on his behalf, that person shall be entitled to be next friend or guardian ad litem, as the case may be, of the mentally incapacitated person in any proceedings to which his authority extends unless, in a case to which paragraph (4) or (5) or rule 6 applies, some other person is appointed by the Court under that paragraph or rule to be next friend or guardian ad litem, as the case may be, of the mentally incapacitated person in those proceedings. (81 of 1997 s 59)**

**(4)   Where a person has been or is next friend or guardian ad litem of a person under disability in any proceedings, no other person shall be entitled to act as such friend or guardian, as the case may be, of the person under disability in those proceedings unless the Court makes an order appointing him such friend or guardian in substitution for the person previously acting in that capacity.**

(5) Where, after any proceedings have been begun, a party to the proceedings becomes a mentally incapacitated person, an application must be made to the Court for the appointment of a person to be next friend or guardian ad litem, as the case may be, of that party. (81 of 1997 s 59)

(6) Except where the next friend or guardian ad litem, as the case may be, of a person under disability has been appointed by the Court–

(a) the name of any person shall not be used in a cause or matter as next friend of a person under disability,

(b) service shall not be acknowledged in a cause or matter for a person under disability, and

(c) a person under disability shall not be entitled to appear by his guardian ad litem on the hearing of a petition, summons or motion which, or notice of which, has been served on him,

unless and until the documents listed in paragraph (8) have been filed in the Registry.

(8) The documents referred to in paragraph (6) are the following–

(a) a written consent to be next friend or guardian ad litem, as the case may be, of the person under disability in the cause or matter in question given by the person proposing to be such friend or guardian; and

(b) where the person proposing to be such friend or guardian of the person under disability, being a mentally incapacitated person, is authorized under Part II of the Ordinance to conduct the proceedings in the cause or matter in question in the name of the mentally incapacitated person or on his behalf, an office copy, sealed with the seal of the High Court, of the order or other authorization made or given under the said Part II by virtue of which he is so authorized; and (25 of 1998 s 2)

(c) except where the person proposing to be such friend or guardian of the person under disability, being a mentally incapacitated person, is authorized as mentioned in sub-paragraph (b) a certificate made by the solicitor for the person under disability certifying–

(i) that he knows or believes, as the case may be, that the person to whom the certificate relates is a minor or a mentally incapacitated person, giving (in the case of a mentally incapacitated person) the grounds of his knowledge or belief; and

(ii) where the person under disability is a mentally incapacitated person, that there is no person authorized as aforesaid; and

(iii) except where the person named in the certificate as next friend or guardian ad litem, as the case may be, is the Official Solicitor, that the person so named has no interest in the cause or matter in question adverse to that of the person under disability.

(L.N. 375 of 1991; 81 of 1997 s 59)

**NOTES**

**[80.3.1]    Comparison with English rules**
Order 80 rule 3 differs from the rule of the same number in the former English Rules of the Supreme Court in some minor details, reflecting the jurisdiction of the Court of Protection which has no formal equivalent in Hong Kong.

**[80.3.2]    Appointment of next friend or guardian ad litem**
By virtue of Order 80 rule 3 it is not always necessary to seek a court order for appointment of a next friend or guardian *ad litem*. Exceptions where an order is required are laid down there and in Order 80 rule 6. In addition, the committee of a mentally incapacitated person, being subject to the supervision of the court, should obtain the sanction of the court to commence proceedings as next friend: *Re YPC* [2008] 2 HKC 359. Such a committee is discharged on the death of the mentally incapacitated person, and should seek directions of the court as to the continuation of the litigation: *Re IWY* [2008] 2 HKC 366.
      A next friend or guardian *ad litem* will normally be a family member or close acquaintance. It is essential that the representative has no conflict of interest in the subject matter of the proceedings.

**[80.3.3]    Role of the Official Solicitor**
In the absence of a person willing and able to act as representative, the Official Solicitor may be appointed. In Hong Kong the Official Solicitor is the Director of Legal Aid, who maintains a separate office in this capacity. In this context see practice direction 17.1 which deals with appointment of the Official Solicitor to represent infants where no other person is available.
      The duties of the Official Solicitor are laid down in section 4 of the Official Solicitor Ordinance (Cap 416). It has been held that as an officer of the court the Official Solicitor is duty bound to act if so requested by the court: see *Chow Hui shui-yee v Chow Sung-ming* (1986) 16 HKLJ 280. See also *Mok Shum Pik Ying v Mok Kam Bor* [1986] HKDCLR 25, 26F where the Official Solicitor conceded that if appointed by the court he would act. However, in the absence of an order or direction of the court, it is a matter of the Official Solicitor's own discretion whether to act: see section 4(1)(b) of the Ordinance.
      The Official Solicitor cannot act without instructions and it is reasonable for him to refuse, for example, to defend an action where he is unable to obtain instructions. In such cases the Official Solicitor may agree to be appointed solely for the purpose of accepting service of a writ. Where the Official Solicitor is appointed to represent a deceased's estate, Order 15 rule 6A(5A) expressly provides that the appointment is limited to accepting service unless otherwise ordered. Further information on the role of the Official Solicitor can be found in Law Society circular 05-647.

**[80.3.4]    Failure to comply**
Failure to comply with the requirement that a next friend or guardian *ad litem* be appointed for a person under disability will render any subsequent order of the court voidable: see *John v John & Goff* [1965] P 289. In that case the court

granted a decree absolute of divorce notwithstanding the failure to appoint a representative.

## [80.3.5] Nomenclature

A party to proceedings who is represented by a next friend or guardian *ad litem* will be so described in pleadings. For example, an infant plaintiff should be described in the heading to a writ or pleading as 'AB, an infant, by his father and next friend, CD'.

## [80.3.6] Documents to be filed

By virtue of rule 3(6) an action involving a person under disability cannot proceed until the documents listed in rule 3(8) have been filed in court. Those documents are normally the written consent of the next friend or guardian *ad litem* to act as such, and a solicitor's certificate to the effect that that person has no interest adverse to that of the person under disability. Exceptions are where the person appointed is the official solicitor or where the person has been authorised under Part II of the Mental Health Ordinance (Cap 136) (which deals with 'Management of Property and Affairs of Mentally Incapacitated Persons').

The usual form of consent and solicitor's certificate are as follows:

(heading as in action)

### CONSENT TO ACT AS NEXT FRIEND OF MINOR

I, (name) of (address), (state relationship to the party under disability) CONSENT to be the next friend / guardian *ad litem* of (the party under disability) in these proceedings, AND I authorise (name of solicitors) of (address of solicitors) to use my name as the next friend / guardian *ad litem* of the said (party under disability) and to act on my behalf.

Dated this        day of        , XXXX

                                     signature of next
                                     friend / guardian
                                     ad litem

(heading as in action)

### CERTIFICATE BY MINOR'S SOLICITOR AS TO NEXT FRIEND

I, (name of solicitor) of (address of solicitor) HEREBY CERTIFY THAT:

1. I know that (name of party under disability) of (address of party under disability) is a minor, the grounds of my knowledge being ...

2. (name of next friend / guardian *ad litem*) of (address of next friend / guardian *ad litem*) has no interest in the case or matter in question adverse to that of the minor.
Dated this        day of        , XXXX

                                     signature of solicitor

The reason for the first part of the solicitor's certificate is to show that the solicitor has 'a basis for knowing or believing that the claimant is a [party under disability] otherwise any appointment of a next friend is not only redundant but improper': *Chan Kin Shing v K Wah Asphalt Ltd* DCEC 639/2009 (Judge Marlene Ng; 04.08.2009 (para 16). In that case the court directed that a party take out an *ex parte* summons for leave to amend a certificate which did not comply with the requirements of Order 80 rule 3(8).

### [80.3.7] Different procedure in matrimonial proceedings

The procedure to be followed for the appointment of a guardian *ad litem* in matrimonial proceedings was set out clearly by Judge Hansen in *Mok Shum Pik Ying v Mok Kam Bor* [1986] HKDCLR 25. He laid down the following principles:

1. Wherever the petitioner's solicitor has reason to believe that the respondent is, or may be, a person under a disability within the meaning of the Mental Health Ordinance (Cap 136), at that stage, under rule 105(3) of the Matrimonial Causes Rules (Cap 179) (ie before service) the petitioner's solicitor should refer the matter to the Crown Solicitor to see whether or not he consents to act as guardian ad litem.

2. The petitioner's solicitor is duty bound to provide the Crown Solicitor with all such information he has in his possession that is relevant to the Crown Solicitor's considerations.

3. It is unethical and a breach of professional practice for the petitioner's solicitor to seek privileged medical information in relation to the respondent's condition. He should not do so or be requested to do so.

4. If the Crown Solicitor then consents to act, the papers are served on him and the matter proceeds in the normal way, subject to his right to apply to take himself off the record if the respondent is no longer in need of a guardian ad litem.

5. If the Crown Solicitor does not consent to act, the papers are served in the normal way. It may be, at the stage when the petitioner applies for directions in the usual way, that the Judge may refuse them because he is concerned that the respondent is a person under a disability, notwithstanding that the Crown Solicitor has refused his consent. Indeed the position may be reached even though the Crown Solicitor has never been approached.

6. It is then incumbent on, and the duty of, the petitioner's solicitor to apply to the Court under rule 105(5) of the Matrimonial Causes Rules for directions as to whether or not the Crown Solicitor should be appointed to act as guardian ad litem. Counsel for the Crown Solicitor stated that the Crown Solicitor would argue that the Crown Solicitor could only be appointed where he consents, but he accepted that if the Court appointed the Crown Solicitor as guardian ad litem the Crown Solicitor would accept the appointment.

### [80.3.8] Change of next friend or guardian ad litem

Order 80 rule 3(4) provides, in effect that an order of the court is necessary for appointment of a new, or replacement, next friend or guardian *ad litem*. In *Re Corsellis* (1884) 50 LT (NS) 703 (CA) it was held that the court has jurisdiction to remove a next friend who is not properly conducting the litigation, provided that the next friend is given an opportunity to be heard.

### [80.3.9] Appointment of next friend or guardian ad litem after commencement of proceedings

Order 80 rule 3(5) provides that where a party becomes mentally incapacitated after proceedings are commenced, an application to the court is required for appointment of a next friend or guardian *ad litem*. Such an application may be opposed. In *Chan Ka Yi v DBS Bank (HK) Ltd* [2010] 5 HKC 1 the court considered the procedure to be followed on such a contested application. It was held that it was not necessary to have a preliminary trial of the issue. Instead, the court may appoint a next friend on an interlocutory basis, leaving the issue of mental incapacity to be decided along with all the other issues at a single trial.

**[80.3.10] Numbering**

There is no rule 4 or 5 in Hong Kong's Order 80.

6. **Appointment of guardian where person under disability does not acknowledge service** (O. 80 r. 6)

   (1) Where–

   (a) in an action against a person under disability begun by writ, or by originating summons, no acknowledgment of service is given in the action for that person, or

   (b) the defendant to an action serves a defence and counterclaim on a person under disability who is not already a party to the action, and no acknowledgment of service is given for that person,

an application for the appointment by the Court of a guardian ad litem of that person must be made by the plaintiff or defendant, as the case may be, after the time limited (as respects that person) for acknowledging service and before proceeding further with the action or counterclaim.

   (2) Where a party to an action has served on a person under disability who is not already a party to the action a third party notice within the meaning of Order 16 and no acknowledgment of service is given for that person to the notice, an application for the appointment by the Court of a guardian ad litem of that person must be made by that party after the time limited (as respects that person) for acknowledging service and before proceeding further with the third party proceedings.

   (3) Where in any proceedings against a person under disability begun by petition or motion, that person does not appear by a guardian ad litem at the hearing of the petition or motion, as the case may be, the Court hearing it may appoint a guardian ad litem of that person in the proceedings or direct that an application be made by the petitioner or applicant, as the case may be, for the appointment of such a guardian.

   (5) An application under paragraph (1) or (2) must be supported by evidence proving–

   (a) that the person to whom the application relates is a person under disability,

   (b) that the person proposed as guardian ad litem is willing and a proper person to act as such and has no interest in the proceedings adverse to that of the person under disability,

   (c) that the writ, originating summons, defence and counterclaim or third party notice, as the case may be, was duly served on the person under disability, and

   (d) subject to paragraph (6), that notice of the application was, after the expiration of the time limited for acknowledging service and at least 7 days before the day named in the notice for hearing of the application, so served on him.

   (6) If the Court so directs, notice of an application under paragraph (1) or (2) need not be served on a person under disability.

(7) An application for the appointment of a guardian ad litem made in compliance with a direction of the Court given under paragraph (3) must be supported by evidence proving the matters referred to in paragraph (5)(b).

## NOTES

### [80.6.1] Comparison with English rules

Order 80 rule 6(4) is omitted in Hong Kong. The equivalent in the former English Rules of the Supreme Court dealt with actions in the Chancery Division. There are no formal divisions within the Court of First Instance in Hong Kong.

### 7. Application to discharge or vary certain orders (O. 80 r. 7)

An application to the Court on behalf of a person under disability served with an order made ex parte under Order 15, rule 7, for the discharge or variation of the order must be made—

    (a) if a next friend or guardian ad litem is acting for that person in the cause or matter in which the order is made, within 14 days after the service of the order on that person;

    (b) if there is no next friend or guardian ad litem acting for that person in that cause or matter, within 14 days after the appointment of such a friend or guardian to act for him.

### 8. Admission not to be implied from pleading of person under disability (O. 80 r. 8)

Notwithstanding anything in Order 18, rule 13(1), a person under disability shall not be taken to admit the truth of any allegation of fact made in the pleading of the opposite party by reason only that he has not traversed it in his pleadings.

### 9. Discovery and interrogatories (O. 80 r. 9)

Orders 24 and 26 shall apply to a person under disability and to his next friend or guardian ad litem.

### 10. Compromise, etc., by person under disability (O. 80 r. 10)

Where in any proceedings money is claimed by or on behalf of a person under disability, no settlement, compromise or payment and no acceptance of money paid into court, whenever entered into or made, shall so far as it relates to that person's claim be valid without the approval of the Court.

## NOTES

### [80.10.1] Court approval of compromise or settlement on behalf of party under disability

Order 80 rule 10 requires that court approval be obtained for any settlement or compromise of legal proceedings on behalf of a party under disability. Order 80 rule 11 extends the requirement to settlements achieved prior to the commencement of legal proceedings. For the sake of convenience commentary under both rules is placed after the test of Order 80 rule 11.

**11. Approval of settlement** (O. 80 r. 11)

(1) Where, before proceedings in which a claim for money is made by or on behalf of a person under disability (whether alone or in conjunction with any other person) are begun, an agreement is reached for the settlement of the claim, and it is desired to obtain the Court's approval to the settlement, then the claim may be made in proceedings begun by originating summons, and in the summons an application may also be made for—

(a) the approval of the Court to the settlement and such orders or directions as may be necessary to give effect to it or as may be necessary or expedient under rule 12, or

(b) alternatively, directions as to the further prosecution of the claim. (L.N. 152 of 2008)

(2) Where in proceedings under this rule a claim is made under the Fatal Accidents Ordinance (Cap 22), the originating summons must include the particulars mentioned in section 5(4) of the Fatal Accidents Ordinance (Cap 22).

(4) An originating summons under this rule shall be in Form No 10 in Appendix A.

(5) In this rule "settlement" includes a compromise.

---

**NOTES**

**[80.11.1] Comparison with English rules**
Order 80 rule 11 is taken from the rule of the same number in the former English Rules of the Supreme Court. Rule 11(3) of the English RSC, which dealt with district registries, was omitted in Hong Kong where there are no such registries. The equivalent rule in England under the Civil Procedure Rules, which came into force in 1999, is CPR 21.10.

**[80.11.2] Cross-reference**
Order 80 rule 11 should be read together with Order 62 rule 30 which provides that, unless the court otherwise directs, the costs payable to his solicitor by any plaintiff under a disability shall be taxed. This rule is clearly made for the protection of plaintiffs under disability.

**[80.11.3] Claim under Fatal Accidents Ordinance**
Rule 11(2) provides that where an application is made for approval under this rule of a settlement of proceedings under the Fatal Accidents Ordinance (Cap 22), the particulars mentioned in section 5(4) of that Ordinance must be set out. The required particulars are of the persons for whom and on whose behalf the action is brought and the nature of the claim.

**[80.11.4] Approval of settlement involving party under disability**
Court approval is required for settlement of any legal proceedings (Order 80 rule 10) or, before proceedings have been issued, any claim (Order 80 rule 11) on behalf of an infant or other party under disability. An application for approval should be made by interlocutory summons in the action or, where proceedings have not yet been commenced, by originating summons under Order 80 rule 11.

Unless and until approval of the court has been obtained no agreement between the parties as to settlement on behalf of a party under disability will be binding: see *Dietz v Lennig Chemicals Ltd* [1969] 1 AC 170 (HL). In that case the House of Lords set aside court approval of a settlement on the basis that it had been obtained on the basis of a misapprehension as to the true state of the facts, thus refusing to enforce the underlying 'agreement'.

The personal injuries list practice direction (PD 18.1), para 187, provides that an application for approval of a settlement under rule 10 and 11 should be made following practice forms PF 170 and PF 171 as set out in volume 2 of the English Supreme Court Practice 1999. Those are Queen's Bench Masters' practice forms. For ease of reference, Hong Kong adaptations of those forms are set out below. Although PD 18.1 applies only to actions on the personal injuries list, the forms it prescribes are suitable for use in other cases as well.

It is inappropriate for the consent order procedure to be used: PD 18.1 para 183. A hearing will be required and it should not be assumed that the court will 'rubber stamp' the settlement; the parties should be prepared to explain why the court should approve it: *Ablan (intending administratrix) v Skanska-Shui On-Balfour Beatty-Joint Venture & Anor* [2000] 1 HKLRD 491. The application should be supported by relevant information. In *So Long Him v Ho Kai Lun Ricky & Anor* [2009] 2 HKC 506 (para 14) Judge Marlene Ng said:

> In discharging its duty for Order 80 approval of disability settlement, the key or perhaps even sole question for the court is whether the proposed compromise is fair and for the benefit of the person under disability. It is therefore necessary for the legal representatives acting for the minor or mentally incapacitated person to explain how the proposed settlement is arrived at and why the court should approve it.

Information going to the court's jurisdiction, such as evidence of the party's disability (birth certificate for an infant, or evidence of mental incapacitation) and in personal injuries cases the latest medical reports, should be provided and may be given by affidavit: *So Long Him* (above) (para 20). It will also usually be necessary to make available to the court confidential information of a contentious nature going into the merits of the plaintiff's claim, the chances of success and so forth. This may include counsel's advice on the merits, and medical reports which have not been disclosed. According to para 186 of PD 18.1 such information should be in the form of a memorandum prepared by the solicitor having prime responsibility for the matter, containing 'full details of all relevant matters'. That includes information concerning related litigation (such as employees' compensation proceedings) and payments which have been made or are being held in court. More important, the memorandum should, in every case, show that the solicitor having prime responsibility for the matter has 'considered the correct question, namely, whether the proposed settlement is of benefit to the minor or the mentally incapacitated person upon a comprehensive assessment of the primary information and material': *So Long Him* (above) (para 23). The learned judge continued:

> It is not enough (as sometimes occurs in the Order 80 applications that have come before this court) for the legal representatives to tender an opinion that the proposed settlement is reasonable or that the proposed settlement is agreed to by the next friend.

It is the usual practice for counsel's advice on the proposed settlement to be annexed to the memorandum. However, counsel's advice may not be necessary and in simple, low quantum cases in the District Court it should be remembered that counsel's fees might not be recoverable on taxation: *Ma Hoi Ki v Li Chi Chuen & Anor* [2009] 2 HKC 488 (para 18).

The memorandum delving into contentious matters should be kept confidential. In particular counsel's advice in support of approval of the settlement should not be made known to the opposing party because it may delve into perceived weaknesses of the plaintiff's case, which should not be disclosed in case the settlement is not approved and the action proceeds to trial: *Ablan* (above). The same is true of medical reports which have not been disclosed. The point was reinforced by Judge Ng in *So Long Him* (above) (para 16):

> Such a memorandum must be lodged and not filed, and the hearing of the application for approval of disability settlement is not open to the public (see Practice Direction 25.1). The reason for this is straightforward. The court requires a frank and realistic assessment as to the prospects of success of the claim in order [to] decide whether the settlement is fair and of benefit to the person under disability. The next friend and the legal representatives acting for the person under disability must not be inhibited about giving a candid assessment, and confidential information concerning the minor or the mentally incapacitated person should not be unnecessarily disclosed, especially when there is always the possibility that the settlement may not be approved and the case proceeds to trial.

An application for approval of a settlement on behalf of a party under disability may be dealt with by a master. This follows from the use of the term 'the Court' in rule 10, which is defined in Order 1 rule 4(2) to include the Registrar and masters. See also Order 32 rule 11 and the commentary thereunder.

**[80.11.5]   Special considerations in cases of mental incapacity**
The court may withhold approval of a settlement in favour of a mentally incapacitated person until consideration is given to making application under Part II of the Mental Health Ordinance (Cap 136). That part provides, *inter alia*, for appointment of a committee to manage the property and affairs of the person. See *Re LWO* [2005] 3 HKC 174. In *Re CK* HCMP 1150/2006 (Lam J; 04.08.2006) the court noted that although a mentally incapacitated person is sufficiently protected in personal injury litigation by the fact the next friend must be represented by a solicitor, who has a duty to protect the mentally incapacitated person's interest, the situation changes once an award is made. The next friend's authority is thereafter limited and legal representation is not required. The court set out (at para 21) the following non-exhaustive list of factors which could be relevant in deciding whether Part II proceedings should be pursued before seeking approval of a settlement on behalf of a mentally incapacitated person ('MIP'):

(a)   The condition of the MIP including his or her age and prognosis;
(b)   The future needs and requirements of the MIP;
(c)   The quantum of the award;
(d)   The background and experience of the next friend including the relationship of the next friend with the MIP and the ability of the next fiend to keep proper account and to appreciate his duty;
(e)   The adequacy of advice regarding the duty of a next friend as canvassed above;
(f)   The needs and resources of the MIP's family;
(g)   The likelihood of applications to use the funds in court for acquisitions of a capital nature;

(h)    The attitude of the primary carer of the MIP and to a lesser extent, the attitude of the immediate family members of the MIP;

(i)    The possible alternatives in terms of investment of the funds as opposed to leaving the monies in court.

Where a mentally incapacitated person's claim is settled before action, and the committee is authorised by the court, under part II of the Mental Health Ordinance, to enter into the settlement agreement, it is not necessary to seek additional approval of the settlement under Order 80 rule 11: *Re MK* HCMP 851/2005 (Lam J; 27.02.2009).

**[80.11.6]    Costs considerations under O 80 rr 10 & 11**

Costs of compromised proceedings on behalf of a party under disability will normally be on the common fund basis. The solicitors for the party under disability will be expected to waive any additional costs not recoverable from the defendant or produce a statement of the maximum amount of costs which would be charged against the plaintiff's damages for approval of the court. Any uncertainty as to whether the settlement figure may be reduced by costs may result in the compromise not being approved by the court. See *Ma Hoi Ki v Li Chi Chuen & Anor* [2009] 2 HKC 488 (Judge Marlene Ng; 25.03.2009) (paras 20 - 23), referring to Halsbury's Laws of Hong Kong and various authorities cited therein; and in relation to personal injuries actions see PD 18.1, para 189-190. The parties should consider use of the summary assessment procedure for costs under Order 62 rule 9(4)(b) and 9A, particularly where the compromise is reached before proceedings are commenced: *Ma Hoi Ki* (above) (para 28-30).

In *Ma Hoi Ki* (above) (para 18) the court stated (*obiter*) that the underlying objectives in Order 1A rule 1 apply with 'equal vigour' to an application for approval of a compromise on behalf of a party under disability, referring in particular to objectives (c) 'reasonable proportion and procedural economy', and (d) 'fairness between the parties'. The court's comment was in the context of the recoverability of counsel's fees for advising on low quantum cases in the District Court. As mentioned above, in that case the court suggested that counsel's advice on settlement on behalf of a party under disability may not be necessary, and in simple, low quantum cases in the District Court counsel's fees might not be recoverable even on the common fund basis: *Ma Hoi Ki v Li Chi Chuen & Anor* (above) (para 18).

**[80.11.7]    Forms for use under O 80 rr 10 & 11**

As mentioned above, Hong Kong's PD 18.1 provides (in para 187) that an application for approval of a settlement on behalf of a party under disability should be made using PF 170 and PF 171 as set out in volume 2 of the English Supreme Court Practice 1999. Those are Queen's Bench Masters' practice forms. The following are adaptations of the English PF 170 and 171, taking into account Hong Kong law and procedure. Although PD 18.1 applies only to actions on the personal injuries list, the forms it prescribes are suitable for use in other cases as well. Obviously further adaptations will be necessary to suit the circumstances of any particular case. In particular, these forms assume that the compromise is reached after proceedings are commenced, such that approval is sought by *inter partes* summons. Where compromise is reached before proceedings have been commenced, it would be necessary to seek approval by originating summons.

### Summons for approval of personal injury settlement where action in being

(Title as in action)

(O 80 r 10 RHC)

### SUMMONS

Let all parties attend before the Master in Chambers (closed to the public) at the High Court, 38 Queensway, Hong Kong on ___ day the _____ day of ____, 20XX at _____ o'clock in the _____ noon on the hearing of an application by the Plaintiff for an Order that the terms of compromise in the form of the draft Order attached hereto be approved and made an Order of the Court.

Dated the _____ day of _____, 20XX

### Draft Order

Upon hearing Counsel [*the Solicitors*] for the Plaintiff and Counsel [*the Solicitors*] for the Defendant the following terms of compromise are approved and made an Order of the Court: -

### Terms of compromise

1. That the Plaintiff may accept the sum of $_____ [*do not state the sum in the draft Order*] in satisfaction of this claim.

2. That the said sum be satisfied as follows:-

[*set out the means by which this sum is to be satisfied and the time within which such satisfaction is to be completed. If there is money in Court this should be stated (leaving the sum in blank) and stating how such money in Court is to be allocated.*]

3. That the said sum be invested [*set out investment directions ordered by the Master, if any*]

4. That the Plaintiff's solicitor shall apply for such further Order not later than _____ days after the date of this Order.

5. That the Defendant do pay the Plaintiff's costs to be taxed on the common fund basis [*the Plaintiff's solicitor waiving any claim to further costs, if that is the case, failing which attach a statement of maximum costs which would be deducted from damages for approval of the court*]

6. That there be liberty to apply for an Order that taxation of the Plaintiff's costs be dispensed with on the Court being informed of the sums to be received by way of costs, disbursements and expenses by the Plaintiff's solicitor.

7. [*If applicable*] That the Plaintiff's own costs be taxed in accordance with the Legal Aid Regulations.

8. That upon payment by the Defendant of the sum referred to at paragraph 2 of this draft Order and costs [*he/she/it*] be discharged from liability in respect of each and every claim made by the Plaintiff against [*him/her/it*] in this action.

9. [*If applicable*] That any interest accumulated to the date of this Order on any money in Court paid by or on behalf of the Defendant be paid out to the Defendant's solicitors without further Order and that any interest accruing after the date of this Order be applied in the same way as if it were part of the sum referred to at paragraph 2 of this draft Order.

10. That either party be at liberty to make application to the Court for the purpose of carrying this Order into effect.

11.    That save for the liberty granted at paragraph 10 of this Order all further proceedings be stayed.

Dated the _____ day of _____, 20XX.

It is not clear why the English forms stipulate that the settlement amount should be omitted from the draft order. If that is done, the information as to quantum must be communicated to the court in some other fashion, as the whole purpose of the exercise is to obtain the court's approval as to the terms of settlement.

Form PF 171 is the form for use in fatal accident cases. It is substantially the same as PF 170, but additionally includes a clause apportioning the settlement sum in accordance with Order 80 rule 15. A Hong Kong adaptation of that clause might be along these lines:

The said sum of $_____ is apportioned as follows: –
(a)    to the claim of the Plaintiff under the Law Amendment and Reform (Consolidation) Ordinance (Cap 23) $_____;
(b)    to the personal claim of the Plaintiff under the Fatal Accidents Ordinance (Cap 22) $_____; and
(c)    to the personal claim of the minor _____ under the Fatal Accidents Ordinance (Cap 22) $_____.

## 12.  Control of money recovered by person under disability (O. 80 r. 12)

(1)    Wherein any proceedings—

    (a)    money is recovered by or on behalf of, or adjudged or ordered or agreed to be paid to, or for the benefit of, a person under disability, or

    (b)    money paid into court is accepted by or on behalf of a plaintiff who is a person under disability,

the money shall be dealt with in accordance with directions given by the Court, under this rule and not otherwise.

(2)    Directions given under this rule may provide that the money shall, as to the whole or any part thereof, be paid into the Court and invested or otherwise dealt with there.

(3)    Without prejudice to the foregoing provisions of this rule, directions given under this rule may include any general or special directions that the Court thinks fit to give and, in particular, directions as to how the money is to be applied or dealt with and as to any payment to be made, either directly or out of the amount paid into court and whether before or after the money is transferred to or paid into a District Court, to the plaintiff, or to the next friend in respect of moneys paid or expenses incurred for or on behalf or for the benefit of the person under disability or for his maintenance or otherwise for his benefit or to the plaintiff's solicitor in respect of costs.

(4)    Where in pursuance of directions given under this rule money is paid into the Court of First Instance to be invested or otherwise dealt with there, the money (including any interest thereon) shall not be paid out, nor shall any securities in which the money is invested, or the dividends thereon, be sold, transferred or paid out of court, except in accordance with an order of the Court.

(5)    The foregoing provisions of this rule shall apply in relation to a counterclaim by or on behalf of a person under disability, as if for references to

**a plaintiff and a next friend there were substituted references to a defendant and to a guardian ad litem respectively. (81 of 1997 s 59)**

## NOTES

### [80.12.1] Comparison with English rules

Order 80 rule 12(3) differs from its counterpart in the former English rules of the Supreme Court by the addition of the following italicised words:

> ... directions as to how the money is to be applied or dealt with and as to any payment to be made either directly or out of the amount paid into court _and whether before or after the money is transferred to or paid into a District Court_, to the plaintiff ...'.

These words are added in view of the fact that the High Court has power to control money recovered by a person under a disability and may order that it be transferred or paid into the district court.

### [80.12.2] Application of rule 12

Although Order 80 rules 10 and 11 apply only to claims for money, rule 12 applies to claims for declaratory relief which will result in money being recovered: _Kwai Fun Luk Vanessa v Kwai Kun Choi_ HCA 4261/2003 (Deputy Judge Muttrie; 05.01.2006).

### [80.12.3] Power to direct how money is to be applied or dealt with

Order 80 rule 12(3) gives the court power to direct how money in court held for the benefit of a person under disability is to be applied or dealt with. In _Re C_ HCMP 15/2002 (Lam J; 14.03.2007) (para 12–13) it was observed that the rule suggests that the power is confined to payments for the benefit or maintenance of the person under disability, and legal costs. The court observed that by contrast, section 10A of the Mental Health Ordinance (Cap 136) gives the court a wider power which includes payments for the benefit of family members and other persons or purposes for which the party under disability might be expected to provide.

### [80.12.4] Interim payments

Interim payments to a party under disability under Order 29 part II should be made known to the court (despite Order 29 rule 15) and should not be held in an account which bears no interest. See the guidance note dated 5 May 2003 from the judge then in charge of the personal injury list, included with practice direction 18.1 on the judiciary's website. See also the commentary under Order 72 rule 2. In such cases it is appropriate to apply under Order 80 rule 12 for directions as to how the money should be dealt with.

### [80.12.5] Transfer to District Court

Note Order 62 rule 30(6) which provides for a copy of a taxing master's certificate of costs to be sent to the Registrar of the District Court where there has been a transfer under this rule. See also rule 13, below.

**13. Provisions supplementary to rule 12** (O. 80 r. 13)

**(HK)(3)  Where money is ordered to be transferred to or paid into a District Court, the Registrar shall send a sealed copy of the judgment or order to the Registrar of the District Court.**

**NOTES**

**[80.13.1]   Numbering sequence**
Note that there is no rule 14 in Order 80.

**15. Proceedings under Fatal Accidents Ordinance: apportionment by Court**
   (O. 80 r. 15)
   **(1) Where a single sum of money is paid into court under Order 22, in satisfaction of a cause of action under the Fatal Accidents Ordinance (Cap 22) and a cause of action under Part IV or IVA of the Law Amendment and Reform (Consolidation) Ordinance (Cap 23), and that sum is accepted, the money shall be apportioned between the different causes of action by the Court either when giving directions for dealing with it under rule 12 (if that rule applies) or when authorizing its payment out of court. (L.N. 152 of 2008)**
   **(2)   Where, in an action in which a claim under the Fatal Accidents Ordinance (Cap 22) is made by or on behalf of more than one person, a sum in respect of damages is adjudged or ordered or agreed to be paid in satisfaction of the claim, or a sum of money paid into court under Order 22, is accepted in satisfaction of the cause of action under the said Ordinance, then, unless the sum has been apportioned between the persons entitled thereto by a jury, it shall be apportioned between those persons by the Court. (L.N. 152 of 2008)**
   **The reference in this paragraph to a sum of money paid into court shall be construed as including a reference to part of a sum so paid, being the part apportioned by the Court under paragraph (1) to the cause of action under the said Ordinances.**

**NOTES**

**[80.15.1]   Comparison with English rule**
Order 80 rule 15 is adapted from the rule of the same number in the previous English RSC. That was replaced by rule 37.4 of the Civil Procedure Rules which came into force in England in 1999.

**[80.15.2]   Apportionment of money accepted in settlement of claims on death**
Order 80 rule 15 provides for the division between surviving dependants and beneficiaries of money accepted in settlement of their claims arising from the death of a deceased.
   Such apportionment will be necessary in fatal accident claims where proceedings are brought on behalf of more than one surviving dependant and are settled by acceptance of a sanctioned payment of a single sum of money. This is because the Fatal Accidents Ordinance (Cap 22) provides, in section 5(3), that only one action may be brought for the benefit of all surviving dependants, and in section 6(6) that money paid into court in satisfaction of a cause of action under the Ordinance may be in one sum without specifying any person's share. Furthermore, under LARCO (Cap 23) causes of action belonging to the deceased may survive for the benefit of his or her estate, which may devolve to a person or group of persons not exactly the same as the dependants entitled to the FAO (Cap 22) relief. Order 22 rule 14(4) expressly

provides that a plaintiff is not entitled to require a defendant to clarify a sanctioned payment by apportioning it between the causes of action.

Solicitors should consider carefully whether it is appropriate to act or continue to act for more than one dependant or beneficiary in relation to a question of apportionment, as conflicts of interest can easily arise.

**16. Service of certain documents on person under disability** (O. 80 r. 16)

**(1)  Where in any proceedings a document is required to be served personally or in accordance with Order 10, rule 1 (2) on any person and that person is a person under disability this rule shall apply.**

**(2)  Subject to the following provisions of this rule and to Order 24, rule 16(3) and Order 26, rule 6(3) the document must be served–**

> **(a)  in the case of a minor who is not also a mentally incapacitated person, on his father or guardian or, if he has no father or guardian, on the person with whom he resides or in whose care he is;**

> **(b)  in the case of a mentally incapacitated person, on the person (if any) who is authorized under Part II of the Ordinance to conduct in the name of the mentally incapacitated person or on his behalf the proceedings in connection with which the document is to be served or, if there is no person so authorized, on the person with whom he resides or in whose care he is;**

**and must be served in the manner required by these rules with respect to the document in question. (81 of 1997 s 59)**

**(3)  Notwithstanding anything in paragraph (2), the Court may order that a document which has been, or is to be, served on the person under disability or on a person other than a person mentioned in that paragraph shall be deemed to be duly served on the person under disability.**

**(4)  A judgment or order requiring a person to do, or refrain from doing, any act, a notice of motion or summons for the committal of any person, and a writ of subpoena against any person, must, if that person is a person under disability, be served personally on him unless the Court otherwise orders.**

**This paragraph shall not apply to an order for interrogatories or for discovery or inspection of documents.**

**(Enacted 1988)**

---

**NOTES**

**[80.16.1]  Manner of service of party under disability**

Order 80 rule 16 lays down the requirements for service of a party under disability. Generally speaking, documents such as originating process, which are normally required to be served personally or by post under Order 10, should be served in a like manner, but not on the disabled person directly, but, in the case of a child, on the father or guardian, and in the absence of such, on a person with whom the child lives or in whose care he or she is; and in the case of a mentally incapacitated person on the person authorised under the Mental Health Ordinance to conduct legal proceedings on that person's behalf, or in the absence of such authorisation, on the person with whom the incapacitated person lives or in whose care he or she is.

This rule does not apply to 'ordinary' service (such as service of interlocutory documents after service of the originating process has been acknowledged) and it follows that the general provisions of Order 65 apply with regard thereto.

**[80.16.2]   Deemed service of party under disability**

Order 80 rule 16(3) empowers the court to order that good service on a party under disability be deemed to have been effected. This power does not appear to extend so as to permit the court to dispense with the appointment of a next friend or guardian *ad litem*: *Easy Fortune Ppty Ltd v Lai Moon Wing & Anor* DCCJ 5098/2006 (Judge Leung; 14.01.2008) (para 16).

## ORDER 81

### PARTNERS

**1.  Actions by and against firms within jurisdiction** (O. 81 r. 1)

**Subject to the provisions of any written law, any 2 or more persons claiming to be entitled, or alleged to be liable, as partners in respect of a cause of action and carrying on business within the jurisdiction may sue, or be sued, in the name of the firm (if any) of which they were partners at the time when the cause of action accrued.**

## NOTES

### [81.1.1]  Comparison with English rules

Order 81 rule 1 is expressed to be 'Subject to the provisions of any written law', whereas the equivalent in the former English Rules of the Supreme Court was 'Subject to the provisions of any enactment'.

Under the Civil Procedure Rules in England, provisions concerning actions by and against partners are no longer consolidated in a single part equivalent to Hong Kong's Order 81.

### [81.1.2]  Use of the firm name

Order 81 rule 1 permits a partnership to sue or be sued in the name of the firm. This is a matter of convenience. There may be so many partners that it would be unwieldy to have to name and serve them all individually; alternatively, the identity of the partners may be unascertained or subject to change. By its own terms, the rule applies only to partners 'carrying on business within the jurisdiction'. A writ wrongly using the firm name in respect of a partnership which does not carry on business in Hong Kong is irregular, but not a nullity: *Dinardo & Ors t/a One Sylvan Road North Associates v Lark Int'l Ltd* HCA 14565/1998 (Yuen J; 02.06.1999); *NIFSMBC-V2006S1 Investment Limited Partnership & Anor v Gainday Investments Ltd* HCA 2738/2008 (Reyes J; 17.09.2009). In both those cases the court was prepared to allow the proceedings to be amended so as to cure the irregularity, no prejudice having been caused to the other parties.

It must be remembered that the rule does not in any way confer legal personality on the partnership. A partnership is not a body corporate and the partners are personally liable for any claims against it. In *Kao, Lee & Yip (a firm) v Koo Hoi-yan Donald & Ors* [1994] 2 HKC 228 (CA) Godfrey JA, delivering the judgment of the Court of Appeal, made this point (at 231E–G) in the following words:

> We recall that in English (and Hong Kong) law a 'firm' as such has no existence; partners carry on business, both as principals and its agents for each other, within the scope of the partnership business; the firm name is a mere expression, not a legal entity, although for convenience Order 81 permits partners to sue or be sued in that name: see, to this effect, *Sadler v Whitman* [1910] 1 KB 868, per Farwell LJ at p 889. Because English law does not recognise the existence of a 'firm', as distinct from the members of it, a partner cannot sue or be sued by his 'firm', either before or after he ceases to be a partner: see *Meyer & Co v Faber* [1923] 2 Ch 421, per Warrington LJ at p 439. Order 81, although it enables the firm name to be used in actions between partners, does not in any way 'alter the substantive law': see per Lord Sterndale MR, in the same case, at p 435.

We draw attention to all this because, at times during the argument, it appeared that he plaintiffs in the action, having used the style or firm name of 'Kao, Lee & Yip' in which to sue the defendants, were under the mistaken impression that the 'firm' did indeed have some separate existence independent of its partners from time to time, and in particular on 1 October 1993, the date when the cause of action (if any) accrued; for example, on the first page of their skeleton argument, the plaintiffs inaccurately describe 'the plaintiff' as 'the firm itself'.

It is important to note that under the law of partnership only the partners at the time of accrual of the cause of action are entitled to the benefit of any cause of action the firm might have, alternatively be liable for any cause of action against it. Accordingly rule 2 of this Order provides for disclosure of partners' names when an action is brought in the name of a firm, and rule 4 that a firm must acknowledge service not in its trading name, but in the names of the partners allegedly liable. See generally *Chan, Leung & Cheung (a firm) v Tse Mei Lin & Anor* [2004] 2 HKC 283.

### [81.1.3]    Indemnity as to costs of unwilling partner

A partner who is unwilling to be involved in litigation commenced by the firm may be compelled to be a co-plaintiff (notwithstanding Order 15 rule 4(2)), but is entitled to an indemnity from his partners as to costs. See *Kao, Lee & Yip (a firm) v Koo Hoi Yan Donald & Ors* [2002] 3 HKC 323, 332D, per Ma J, citing *Whitehead v Hughes* (1834) 2 C&M 318, 319. The court may order that the indemnity be backed by security. In the *Kao, Lee & Yip* case the court held that a retired partner who was no longer willing to participate in an action commenced by the firm (and had nothing to gain therefrom) was entitled to an indemnity as to costs to be backed by security in the amount of $4.5 million. The high figure resulted from the court's finding that the retired partner could potentially be liable for the full amount of any costs which might be ordered against the partnership.

### [81.1.4]    Actions commenced against firm and a partner jointly

In *Tak Wo v Lai Ming Tak Kee Dyeing and Bleaching Factory* [1962] DCLR 87, action was commenced against a firm and one of the partners in his own name. The court held, following *West of England Steamship Owners Protection & Indemnity Association Ltd v John Holman & Sons* [1957] 3 All ER 421, that this was illogical because the partner is already sued when the firm is sued. The court observed that it might, however, be convenient to add the name of a partner who is outside the jurisdiction if it is thought desirable to serve him personally. The same was held by Huggins J in *Sun Hing Co v Brilliant Investment Co Ltd* [1966] HKLR 310 (F Ct) where he said, at 318:

> The action was brought against a firm and against the partners of that firm in their own names. In my view, for reasons which I have given elsewhere [*Tak Wo v Lai Ming Tak Kee* (above)], as a general rule this is entirely wrong and is strongly to be discouraged in cases where, as here, there is no good reason for adopting such procedure.

### [81.1.5]    Actions wrongly commenced by sole trader in firm name

These rules do not permit a sole trader to commence proceedings using his or her business name, though the reverse is true (see Order 81 rule 9, under which the plaintiff may use the defendant's trading name in commencing proceedings). For convenience, plaintiffs may, however, add their trading name by way of further description in order to show the sole trader's connection to the matters at issue, eg 'Chan Hon Fat t/a [trading as] Hop Hing Garment Factory' is a familiar and useful formula.

In the case of an action wrongly commenced by a sole trader in a firm name, the courts have consistently held that this is a mere irregularity that can be cured by amendment (*The Holland Pacific Trading Co v Fung Tang* (1920) 15 HKLR 72; *Nam Hoi Shoes Factory v Empire Trading Co (HK) Ltd* [1960] HKLR 99; *Wong Ming-chun t/a Tai Tak School v Hong Kong Times Ltd* [1968] HKLR 99).

In *Kin Wah Garment Manufacturing Co v Ping Man Store Grocery Department* [1957] DCLR 73 the court declined to make such an amendment of its own motion where, despite suggestion, the plaintiff had failed to apply. As a result the court felt it had no alternative but to refuse to give judgment to the plaintiff.

**[81.1.6]  Action wrongly commenced against company as if it were a firm**

In *WA Somerville & Co Ltd v Golden Carriage Restaurant (a firm)* [1966] HKLR 273 the plaintiff used the procedure now found in Order 81 rule 9 to sue a firm, and obtained default judgment. It transpired that the firm was in fact a limited company. It was held that the judgment must be set aside, though leave to amend the writ was given. In granting leave to amend the court distinguished *Davies v Elsby Bros, Ltd* [1960] 3 All ER where it was held that such an amendment was not possible because in that case the limitation period had expired. With regard to amendment after expiration of the limitation period, now see Order 20 rule 5 and the commentary thereunder.

**2.  Disclosure of partners names** (O. 81 r. 2)

**(1)  Any defendant to an action brought by partners in the name of a firm may serve on the plaintiffs or their solicitor a notice requiring them or him forthwith to furnish the defendant with a written statement of the names and places of residence of all the persons who were partners in the firm at the time when the cause of action accrued; and if the notice is not complied with the Court may order the plaintiffs or their solicitor to furnish the defendant with such a statement and to verify it on oath or otherwise as may be specified in the order, or may order that further proceedings in the action be stayed on such terms as the Court may direct.**

**(2)  When the names of the partners have been declared in compliance with a notice or order given or made under paragraph (1), the proceedings shall continue in the name of the firm but with the same consequences as would have ensued if the persons whose names have been so declared had been named as plaintiffs in the writ.**

**(3)  Paragraph (1) shall have effect in relation to an action brought against partners in the name of a firm as it has effect in relation to an action brought by partners in the name of a firm but with the substitution, for references to the defendant and the plaintiffs, of references to the plaintiff and the defendants respectively, and with the omission of the words "or may order" to the end.**

**3. Service of writ** (O. 81 r. 3)

(1)  Where by virtue of rule 1 partners are sued in the name of a firm, the writ may, except in the case mentioned in paragraph (3), be served–

    (a)  on any one or more of the partners, or

    (b)  at the principal place of business of the partnership within the jurisdiction, on any person having at the time of service the control or management of the partnership business there, or

    (c)  by sending a copy of the writ by registered post (in accordance with Order 10, rule 1(2)) to the firm at the principal place of business of the partnership within the jurisdiction;

and, subject to paragraph (2), where service of the writ is effected in accordance with this paragraph, the writ shall be deemed to have been duly served on the firm, whether or not any member of the firm is out of the jurisdiction.

(L.N. 165 of 1992)

(2)  Where a writ is served on a firm in accordance with paragraph (1)(c)–

    (a)  the date of service shall, unless the contrary is shown, be deemed to be the seventh day (ignoring Order 3, rule 2(5)) after the date on which the copy was sent to the firm, and

    (b)  any affidavit proving due service of the writ must contain a statement to the effect that–

        (i)  in the opinion of the deponent (or, if the deponent is the plaintiff's solicitor or an employee of that solicitor, in the opinion of the plaintiff) the copy of the writ, if sent to the firm at the address in question, will have come to the knowledge of one of the persons mentioned in paragraph (1)(a) or (b) within 7 days thereafter, and

        (ii)  the copy of the writ has not been returned to the plaintiff through the post undelivered to the addressee.

(3)  Where a partnership has, to the knowledge of the plaintiff, been dissolved before an action against the firm is begun, the writ by which the action is begun must be served on every person within the jurisdiction sought to be made liable in the action.

(4)  Every person on whom a writ is served under paragraph (1)(a) or (b) must at the time of service be given a written notice stating whether he is served as a partner or as a person having the control or management of the partnership business or both as a partner and as such a person; and any person on whom a writ is so served but to whom no such notice is given shall be deemed to be served as a partner.

---

**NOTES**

**[81.3.1]  Comparison with English rule**

Order 81 rule 3(1)(c) of the Hong Kong rules speaks of service 'by registered post in accordance with Order 10, rule 1(2)'. The provision of the same number in the former English RSC spoke of service 'by ordinary 1ˢᵗ class post …'. See the commentary under Order 10 rule 1 as to the differences between the Hong Kong and English rules on service by post.

**[81.3.2]    Manner of service of a partnership**

Where the members of a partnership are sued in the firm name they should be served in accordance with the provisions of Order 81 rule 3(1). Three methods of service are set down there:

1.    Personal service on one or more of the partners (rule 3(1)(a)).

2.    Personal service of the person 'having control or management of the partnership business' at the principal place of business (rule 3(1)(b)). Such service may be effected on an employee of the partners, but not on an outside agent, as it cannot be said that the partners' business is carried on at the agent's premises: *Baillie v Goodwin & Co* (1886) 33 ChD 604.

3.    Service by registered post to the firm's principal place of business (rule 3(1)(c)). Service may be valid in spite of sending the writ to the wrong address, if it is actually received: *Austin Rover Group Ltd v Crouch Butler Savage Associates* [1986] 1 WLR 1102 (CA); but is irregular if sent to a former principal place of business and not actually received by the partners: *Tse Fui v Hung Cheung Kwong* [2007] 2 HKC 348 (CA).

**[81.3.3]    Contents of affidavit of service**

In *Tak Wo v Lai Ming Tak Kee Dyeing and Bleaching Factory* [1962] DCLR 87, the plaintiffs were criticised for failing to utilise the customary form of affidavit, viz 'I ... did personally serve A.B., a partner in the above-named defendant firm of X.Y. & Co ...'.

In *Davie, Boag & Co Ltd v Tak Hing Construction Co (a firm)* [1965] HKLR 1 an affidavit of service on a partnership stating that the writ had been served on a person having 'charge' of the defendant firm was rejected as improper. For service on a firm to be effective, if not made on one or more of the partners, it had to be effected at the principal place of business of the firm within the jurisdiction on a person having, at the time of service, control or management of the partnership business.

**4.    Acknowledgment of service in an action against firm** (O. 81 r. 4)

(1)    **Where persons are sued as partners in the name of their firm, service may not be acknowledged in the name of the firm but only by the partners thereof in their own names, but the action shall nevertheless continue in the name of the firm.**

(2)    **Where in an action against a firm the writ by which the action is begun is served on a person as a partner, that person, if he denies that he was a partner or liable as such at any material time, may acknowledge service of the writ and state in his acknowledgment that he does so as a person served as a partner in the defendant firm but who denies that he was a partner at any material time.**

**An acknowledgment of service given in accordance with this paragraph shall, unless and until it is set aside, be treated as an acknowledgment by the defendant firm.**

(3)    **Where an acknowledgment of service has been given by a defendant in accordance with paragraph (2), then–**

(a)    **the plaintiff may either apply to the Court to set it aside on the ground that the defendant was a partner or liable as such at a** material time or may leave that question to be determined at a later stage of the proceedings;

    (b)  the defendant may either apply to the Court to set aside the service of the writ on him on the ground that he was not a partner or liable as such at a material time or may at the proper time serve a defence on the plaintiff denying in respect of the plaintiff's claim either his liability as a partner or the liability of the defendant firm or both.

    (4)  The Court may at any stage of the proceedings in an action in which a defendant has acknowledged service in accordance with paragraph (2), on the application of the plaintiff or of that defendant, order that any question as to the liability of that defendant or as to the liability of the defendant firm be tried in such manner and at such time as the Court directs.

    (5)  Where in an action against a firm the writ by which the action is begun is served on a person as a person having the control or management of the partnership business, that person may not acknowledge service of the writ unless he is a member of the firm sued.

5.    **Enforcing judgment or order against firm** (O. 81 r. 5)

    (1)  Where a judgment is given or order made against a firm, execution to enforce the judgment or order may, subject to rule 6, issue against any property of the firm within the jurisdiction.

    (2)  Where a judgment is given or order made against a firm, execution to enforce the judgment or order may, subject to rule 6 and to the next following paragraph, issue against any person who–

    (a)  acknowledged service of the writ in the action as a partner, or

    (b)  having been served as a partner with the writ of summons, failed to acknowledge service of it in the action, or

    (c)  admitted in his pleading that he is a partner, or

    (d)  was adjudged to be a partner.

    (3)  Execution to enforce a judgment or order given or made against a firm may not issue against a member of the firm who was out of the jurisdiction when the writ of summons was issued unless he–

    (a)  acknowledged service of the writ in the action as a partner, or

    (b)  was served within the jurisdiction with the writ as a partner, or

    (c)  was, with the leave of the Court given under Order 11, served out of the jurisdiction with the writ as a partner;

and, except as provided by paragraph (1) and by the foregoing provisions of this paragraph, a judgment or order given or made against a firm shall not render liable, release or otherwise affect a member of the firm who was out of the jurisdiction when the writ was issued.

    (4)  Where a party who has obtained a judgment or order against a firm claims that a person is liable to satisfy the judgment or order as being a member of the firm, and the foregoing provisions of this rule do not apply in relation to that person, that party may apply to the Court for leave to issue execution against that person, the application to be made by summons which must be served personally on that person.

**(5)** **Where the person against whom an application under paragraph (4) is made does not dispute his liability, the Court hearing the application may, subject to paragraph (3), give leave to issue execution against that person, and, where that person disputes his liability, the Court may order that the liability of that person be tried and determined in any manner in which any issue or question in an action may be tried and determined.**

---

**NOTES**

**[81.5.1] Execution against partnership**

Order 81 rule 5 makes provision for enforcement of judgments and orders which have been entered against partnerships.

Execution may be levied against any property of the partnership within the jurisdiction, pursuant to rule 5(1).

Further, enforcement proceedings may be taken against the assets of individual partners, because partnerships do not generally have limited liability. Rule 5(2)-(5) regulates such enforcement proceedings. A judgment creditor is not required to exhaust the remedy of enforcement against property of the partnership before proceeding to enforce against the assets of individual partners: *Lily Fenn & Partners (a firm) v Ng Wai Hin Jacky t/a Jacky Ng & Co* DCCJ 4077/2009 (Deputy Judge Alfred Chan; 05.03.2010).

Rule 5(2) provides for enforcement against any person who (a) acknowledged service as a partner, or (b) failed to acknowledge service after being served as a partner, or (c) admitted in a pleading to being a partner, or (d) was held by the court to be a partner.

Other cases, where there may be an issue as to whether the person against whom it is sought to enforce the judgment is in fact liable as a partner of the firm, are catered for by rule 5(4). There may be an issue as to whether the person is a partner at all, or as to whether the timing of the liability being incurred and membership in the partnership coincide, it being a 'fundamental principle' that a partner is not liable for debts incurred before he joins the partnership: *Hong Kong & Overseas Dev't Co Ltd v Yeung Fat Construction Co* HCMP 2520/1985 (Penlington J; 09.01.1986). In such cases the judgment creditor or party seeking to enforce the judgment or order must apply by summons for leave to enforce against that person. The summons must be served personally on the person against whom enforcement is sought, and if the application is contested the court may try the issue of whether that person is liable as a partner.

Rule 5(3) restricts the enforcement of judgments or orders against a partner who was not in Hong Kong when the writ was issued.

Rule 5 applies whether the firm is a foreign or Hong Kong partnership carrying on business in the jurisdiction: *Brand Farrar Buxbaum LLP v Samuel-Rozembaum Diamond Ltd & Ors* CACV 272/2004 (Cheung JA & A Cheung J; 24.03.2005) (para 13). In that case the court permitted enforcement against a partner who contended that the partnership was entitled to limited liability under California law on the ground that the firm was not registered under the Limited Partnerships Ordinance (Cap 37), with the result that every partner was deemed to be a general partner by s 4 thereof.

**[81.5.2]   Sole proprietors**

It has been held in *Lynn v Consolidated Sales Ltd* [1970] HKLR 373 (F Ct) that the mere fact of Order 81 rule 9 applying to the case of a defendant trading in a name other than his own cannot result in that individual being treated as a firm, which *ex hypothesi* he is not, for the purpose of execution under Order 81 rule 5(4) against alleged partners. In principle, however, there is no barrier to execution being levied against the personal assets of a sole proprietor who has been sued in his business name pursuant to Order 81 rule 9, and against whom judgment has been entered accordingly. A sole proprietor does not have limited liability and is personally responsible for his or her business debts.

**6.   Enforcing judgment or order in actions between partners, etc.** (O. 81 r. 6)

> **(1)   Execution to enforce a judgment or order given or made in–**
>
> > **(a)   an action by or against a firm in the name of the firm against or by a member of the firm, or**
> >
> > **(b)   an action by a firm in the name of the firm against a firm in the name of the firm where those firms have one or more members in common,**

**shall not issue except with the leave of the Court.**

**(2)   The Court hearing an application under this rule may give such directions, including directions as to the taking of accounts and the making of inquiries, as may be just.**

---

**NOTES**

**[81.6.1]   Execution against dissolved partnership**

In *Tam Tat-ting v Chan Chiu-wan* [1957] DCLR 126, the plaintiff claimed a sum of money being the plaintiff's share of the partnership business. It appeared, however, that the partnership had been dissolved prior to the action. The court held that the correct cause of action was on an account stated. Mills-Owen DJ said, at 127:

> … it was common ground between the parties that the partnership had already been dissolved prior to the commencement of these proceedings. Certainly if the partnership had still been subsisting it would not have been open to the plaintiff to sue the defendant as his partner for his share in the partnership business in a common law action; the appropriate proceedings would have been an action for dissolution and accounts as it is only upon a dissolution and the taking or settlement of accounts that the share due to any partner may properly be ascertained (*Green v Hertzog* [1954] 1 WLR 1309 applied). With regard to the partnership dealings the partners are not debtors and creditors, the one with the other, until the partnership is dissolved and a final settlement of accounts arrived at. But immediately such a settlement is arrived at the law implies a promise by the indebted partner to pay the amount or amounts due to the other partner or partners in consideration of the dissolution and mutual settlement of accounts; alternatively the settled amount or amounts may be claimed as an account stated (*Foster v Allanson* (1788) 2 Term Rep 479, 483). Accordingly the question in this action is whether there has in fact been a binding settlement of accounts as between the plaintiff and defendant following the admitted dissolution of their former partnership.

**7.   Attachment of debts owed by firm** (O. 81 r. 7)

**(1)   An order may be made under Order 49, rule 1, in relation to debts due or accruing due from a firm carrying on business within the jurisdiction notwithstanding that one or more members of the firm is resident out of the jurisdiction.**

**(2)   An order to show cause under the said rule 1 relating to such debts as aforesaid must be served on a member of the firm within the jurisdiction or on some other person having the control or management of the partnership business.**

**(3)   Where an order made under the said rule 1 requires a firm to appear before the Court, an appearance by a member of the firm constitutes a sufficient compliance with the order.**

**8.   Actions begun by originating summons** (O. 81 r. 8)

**Rules 2 to 7 shall, with the necessary modifications, apply in relation to an action by or against partners in the name of their firm begun by originating summons as they apply in relation to such an action begun by writ.**

**9.   Application to person carrying on business in another name** (O. 81 r. 9)

**An individual carrying on business within the jurisdiction in a name or style other than his own name, may, whether or not he is within the jurisdiction, be sued in that name or style as if it were the name of a firm, and rules 2 to 8 shall, so far as applicable, apply as if he were a partner and the name in which he carries on business were the name of his firm.**

---

**NOTES**

**[81.9.1]   Sole proprietor may be sued in business name**

Order 81 rule 9 provides that an individual carrying on business within the jurisdiction in a name or style other than his own name, may, whether or not he is within the jurisdiction, be sued in that name or style as if it were the name of a firm. It should be noted that this provision only applies to individuals who are sued, not individuals who are suing (see Order 81 rule 1 above).

Referring to the rationale of the rule, Pickering J said in *Lynn v Consolidated Sales Ltd* [1970] HKLR 373 (F Ct):

> In our view Order 81 rule 9 applies to cases where an individual trades under a name other than his own and is a procedural rule designed to prevent such a person from escaping liability by reason of his creditor's unawareness of the true name of the person operating the business with which the creditor has been dealing.

This rule does not apply to companies which carry on business under trading names which differ from their registered corporate names. This is because the word 'individual' in Order 81 rule 9 does not include a body corporate. See *Survival Technology v Loh & Co* [1986] HKC 64 (CA). However it is common (and unobjectionable) to name the company and add by way of description its trading name, *eg* ABC Ltd t/a XYZ Restaurant.

**10. Applications for orders charging partners interest in partnership property, etc.** (O. 81 r. 10)

**(1)** Every application to the Court by a judgment creditor of a partner for an order under section 25 of the Partnership Ordinance (Cap 38) (which authorizes the Court of First Instance or a judge thereof to make certain orders on the application of a judgment creditor of a partner, including an order charging the partner's interest in the partnership property), and every application to the Court by a partner of the judgment debtor made in consequence of the first-mentioned application, must be made by summons.

**(2)** A master may exercise the powers conferred on a judge by the said section 25.

**(3)** Every summons issued by a judgment creditor under this rule, and every order made on such a summons, must be served on the judgment debtor and on such of his partners as are within the jurisdiction.

**(4)** Every summons issued by a partner of a judgment debtor under this rule, and every order made on such a summons, must be served–

    **(a)** on the judgment creditor, and

    **(b)** on the judgment debtor, and

    **(c)** on such of the other partners of the judgment debtor as do not join in the application and are within the jurisdiction.

**(5)** A summons or order served in accordance with this rule on some only of the partners shall be deemed to have been served on all the partners of the partnership.

**(Enacted 1988)**

---

**NOTES**

**[81.10.1]   Rule 10(1)**
Section 25 of the Partnership Ordinance (Cap 38) to which this rule refers, provides:

(1)   A writ of execution shall not issue against any partnership property except on a judgment against the firm.

(2)   The court or a judge may, on the application by summons of any judgment creditor of a partner, make an order charging that partner's interest in the partnership property and profits with payment of the amount of the judgment debt and interest thereon, and may, by the same or a subsequent order, appoint a receiver of that partner's share of profits (whether already declared or accruing), and of any other money which may be coming to him in respect of the partnership, and direct all accounts and inquiries, and give all other orders and directions, which might have been directed or given if the charge had been made in favour of the judgment creditor by the partner, or which the circumstances of the case may require.

(3)   The other partner or partners shall be at liberty at any time to redeem the interest charged, or, in case of a sale being directed, to purchase the same.

(4)   This section shall apply in the case of a cost-book company as if the company were a partnership within the meaning of this Ordinance.

**[81.10.2] Rule 10(4) and (5)**

In the former English RSC, rules 10(4) and (5) of Order 81 contained references to 'cost book companies'. These are omitted from the Hong Kong rule, though section 25(4) of the Partnership Ordinance (see above) applies that section to such companies.

## ORDER 82

### DEFAMATION ACTIONS

1.  **Application** (O. 82 r. 1)
    **These rules apply to actions for libel or slander subject to the following rules of this Order.**

**NOTES**

**[82.1.1]	Scope of Order 82**
Order 82 rule 1 provides that the Order applies to actions for libel or slander, that is, defamation actions. It also applies in certain circumstances to actions for malicious prosecution or false imprisonment: see Order 82 rule 5.

**[82.1.2]	Parties to a defamation action**
Defamation actions are normally brought by individuals. They may also be brought by bodies corporate. *Oriental Daily Publisher Ltd v Easy Finder Ltd* [1998] 1 HKC 546 (CA) is a Hong Kong example. The situation may be different with public bodies. In *Derbyshire County Council v Times Newspapers Ltd* [1993] AC 534 it was held that for public policy reasons a local authority could not maintain an action for defamation. However, in *Hong Kong Polytechnic University v Next Magazine Ltd (No 2)* [1997] 1 HKLRD 514 (CA) it was held, distinguishing *Derbyshire*, that a university (incorporated by statute) could proceed with a defamation action.

   An unincorporated association may not bring a defamation action, nor may the members of such an association bring such an action in the form of representative proceedings under Order 15 rule 12. It is necessary for the members to be individual plaintiffs. See *Hong Kong Children's Ass'n v Chan Mei Kee & Anor* HCA 9588/2000 (Suffiad J; 01.02.2001).

**[82.1.3]	Defamation actions involving communications between solicitors**
Communications between solicitors in relation to litigious matters are considered to be made in the course of the proceedings before the court and are absolutely privileged. However, where the maker of a statement steps outside the confines of the judicial proceedings and embarks on an independent course of conduct, the privilege does not apply. See *Wong Shui Kee Roger v Victor LL Chu & Ors* [2001] 3 HKC 589 (affirmed on appeal: see [2003] 1 HKC 125) citing *Royal Aquarium and Summer and Winter Garden Society Ltd v Parkinson* [1892] 1 QB 431 and *Seaman v Nethercliff* (1876) 2 CPD 53.

2.  **Indorsement of claim in libel action** (O. 82 r. 2)
    **Before a writ in an action for libel is issued it must be indorsed with a statement giving sufficient particulars of the publications in respect of which the action is brought to enable them to be identified.**

3.  **Obligation to give particulars** (O. 82 r. 3)
    **(1)   Where in an action for libel or slander the plaintiff alleges that the words or matters complained of were used in a defamatory sense other than**

their ordinary meaning, he must give particulars of the facts and matters on which he relies in support of such sense.

(2)   Where in an action for libel or slander the defendant alleges that, in so far as the words complained of consist of statements of fact, they are true in substance and in fact, and in so far as they consist of expressions of opinion, they are fair comment on a matter of public interest, or pleads to the like effect, he must give particulars stating which of the words complained of he alleges are statements of fact and of the facts and matters he relies on in support of the allegation that the words are true.

(3)   Where in an action for libel or slander the plaintiff alleges that the defendant maliciously published the words or matters complained of, he need not in his statement of claim give particulars of the facts on which he relies in support of the allegation of malice, but if the defendant pleads that any of those words or matters are fair comment on a matter of public interest or were published on a privileged occasion and the plaintiff intends to allege that the defendant was actuated by express malice, he must serve a reply giving particulars of the facts and matters from which the malice is to be inferred.

(4)   This rule shall apply in relation to a counterclaim for libel or slander as if the party making the counterclaim were the plaintiff and the party against whom it is made the defendant.

---

## NOTES

### [82.3.1]   Defamatory words must be pleaded
In a defamation action the actual language used must be pleaded. See *Yung Chi Kin Larry v Leung Tin Wai & Ors* [1993] 1 HKC 143, 155 (CA), citing *Harris v Warre* (1879) 4 CPD 125; and see *Tai Yip Dyeing Fty Ltd v Kong Hoi Sang* [2007] 1 HKLRD 608 (para 23), an action for slander of title. However, in the case of slander, given the 'transitory nature' of speech, it is acceptable to add, after the offending words, 'or substantially similar defamatory words', as in *Ho Yuen Ki Winnie & Anor v Ho Hung Han Stanley* HCA 391/2006 (Poon J; 20.07.2007).

### [82.3.2]   Reference to the plaintiff must be pleaded
Where allegedly defamatory words which do not expressly refer to the plaintiff are relied upon, it is necessary to plead the facts which it is said link those words to the plaintiff. In *Lee York Fai v Yue Sin Man Anna* CACV 184/2007 (Cheung & Yeung JJA, Lam J; 19.12.2007), the court found that the words actually spoken did not contain an express reference to the plaintiff, and since the plaintiff had not pleaded an alternative case as to how the words referred to him, the action failed.

### [82.3.3]   Rule 3(1) – particulars of innuendo
Order 82 rule 3(1) requires that particulars be given where it is contended that the words or matters complained of were used in a defamatory sense other than their ordinary meaning. This means that particulars of an allegation of defamation by innuendo must be given. The purpose is to enable the defendant to know the extended meaning relied on in order to know the case to be met: *Yam Chi Ming Stephen v Sing Pao Newspaper Co Ltd* [2006] 3 HKC 10 (para 32).

Where the defamatory sense in which the words were allegedly used is special to some particular persons, the innuendo is said to be 'legal' as opposed to 'popular', and the particular persons and circumstances known to them must be pleaded: *Beijing Television v Brightec Ltd & Ors* [1999] 2 HKC 665 (CA).

**[82.3.4]   Rule 3(2) – pleading justification or fair comment**
Order 82 rule 3(2) provides that where a party wishes to rely on the defence of justification (truth), or fair comment on a matter of public interest, particulars must be given.

It has been held that 'comment may only be defended as fair comment if it is comment on facts (meaning true facts) stated or sufficiently indicated': *Brent Walker Group plc v Time Out Ltd* [1991] 2 QB 33, 44H (CA). Thus, particulars of this defence should clearly indicate what is contended to be fact and what is intended to be comment thereon. See *Channel Seven Adelaide (Pty) Ltd v Manock* [2007] HCA 60 where the High Court of Australia found that a pleading merely setting out facts did not raise a defence of fair comment.

**[82.3.5]   Rule 3(3) – malice**
Order 82 rule 3(3) provides that a plaintiff who wishes to rely on malice to defeat a defence based on fair comment or qualified privilege is required to give particulars thereof. 'Particulars of malice must be expressly and specifically pleaded': *Omar Zarina v Chow Yee Ping & Anor* HCA 3699/2002 (A Cheung J; 24.09.2004). Under the rule, if such particulars are not included in the Statement of Claim, the plaintiff is obliged to serve a Reply containing the same.

Particulars alleging a threat to take legal action are not sufficient to comply with this rule since such a threat is not capable of constituting malice. See *Lo Ki Chung v Hong Kong Nam Hoi (Sha Tau District) Ass'n Ltd* HCA 39/2003 (Deputy Judge Poon; 22.07.2004).

**[82.3.6]   Discovery and the 'newspaper rule'**
In defamation actions there are certain limitations on discovery. A defendant is not entitled to rely on discovery to obtain particulars of a plea of justification, or truth: *Loh v Salamon* [1980] HKC 383; [1980] HKLR 806. Further, the 'newspaper rule' applies in Hong Kong and the court will not order interlocutory discovery as to the source of an alleged libel published in news media: *Sham v Eastweek Publisher Ltd* [1995] 1 HKC 264 (CA). In that case an order for *Norwich Pharmacal* discovery was set aside on the ground the 'newspaper rule' applied. For an interesting discussion of cases on the 'newspaper rule' from around the common law world, see *KLW Holdings Ltd v Singapore Press Holdings Ltd* [2002] 4 SLR 417 where it was held that the rule does not apply in Singapore and the court expressly disagreed with the Hong Kong Court of Appeal's judgment in *Sham* (above). See also *Ashworth Hospital Authority v MGN Ltd* [2002] 1 WLR 2033 where the House of Lords upheld a *Norwich Pharmacal* order requiring a newspaper to disclose its source of information it had published on the grounds the order was necessary and proportionate in the particular case.

**[82.3.7]    Particulars in relation to damages for libel**

The defendant in a libel action 'is entitled to plead, and to seek to establish, facts directly relevant to the contextual background of the publication' for the purpose of assessment of damages: *Warren v Random House Group Ltd* [2008] EWCA Civ 834 (16.07.2008) (para 70). Thus the defendant can plead facts which suggest the publication was at least partially true. The court described these as '*Burnstein*' particulars, referring to *Burnstein v Times Newspapers Ltd* [2001] 1 WLR 579 (CA).

**[82.3.8]    Issue as to meaning of allegedly defamatory words**

Order 82 rule 3A of the former English Rules of the Supreme Court provided for determination by the court as a separate issue whether allegedly defamatory words are capable of bearing a particular meaning. The rule was not adopted in Hong Kong. However, it has been suggested (*obiter*) that this might be done in Hong Kong under Order 14A. See *Ho Yuen Ki Winnie* (above).

**4.    Provisions as to payment into court** (O. 82 r. 4)

**(1)    Where in an action for libel or slander against several defendants sued jointly the plaintiff, in accordance with Order 22, accepts money paid into court by any of those defendants in satisfaction of his cause of action against that defendant, then, notwithstanding anything in that Order, the action shall be stayed as against that defendant only, but— (L.N. 152 of 2008)**

> **(a)    the sum recoverable under any judgment given in the plaintiff's favour against any other defendant in the action by way of damages shall not exceed the amount (if any) by which the amount of the damages exceeds the amount paid into court by the defendant as against whom the action has been stayed, and**

> **(b)    the plaintiff shall not be entitled to his costs of the action against the other defendant after the date of the payment into court unless either the amount of the damages awarded to him is greater than the amount paid into court and accepted by him or the judge is of opinion that there was reasonable ground for him to proceed with the action against the other defendant.**

**(2)    Where in an action for libel a party pleads the defence for which section 4 of the Defamation Ordinance (Cap 21) provides, Order 22, rule 25, shall not apply in relation to that pleading. (L.N. 152 of 2008)**

**5.    Statement in open court** (O. 82 r. 5)

**(1)    Where a party wishes to accept money paid into court in satisfaction of a cause of action for libel or slander, malicious prosecution or false imprisonment, that party may before or after accepting the money apply to a judge in chambers by summons for leave to make in open court a statement in terms approved by the judge.**

**(2)    Where a party to an action for libel or slander, malicious prosecution or false imprisonment which is settled before trial desires to make a statement in open court, an application must be made to the Court for an order that an action be set down for trial, and before the date fixed for the trial a statement must be submitted for the approval of the judge before whom it is to be made.**

**(L.N. 404 of 1991)**

## NOTES

### [82.5.1]   Leave to make statement in open court

Where a defamation action is settled prior to trial by acceptance of money paid into court or otherwise, the parties may seek to make a statement in open court concerning the alleged defamation. Order 82 rule 5 caters for this practice. The rule extends to actions for malicious prosecution and false imprisonment which may equally impugn the reputation of a defendant.

The court's leave is required for the making of such a statement in open court. In *Spiegel v Bennett* HCA 9012/1994 (Findlay J; 20.10.1994) there were disputes of fact which impeded the court's grant of leave in a case of libel which was 'not of the most serious'. The court amended the draft statement to reflect those concerns rather than resolve them at a further hearing.

**6.   Interrogatories not allowed in certain cases** (O. 82 r. 6)

**In an action for libel or slander where the defendant pleads that the words or matters complained of are fair comment on a matter of public interest or were published on a privileged occasion, no interrogatories as to the defendant's sources of information or grounds of belief shall be allowed.**

**7.   Evidence in mitigation of damages** (O. 82 r. 7)

**In an action for libel or slander in which the defendant does not by his defence assert the truth of the statement complained of, the defendant shall not be entitled on the trial to give evidence in chief, with a view to mitigation of damages, as to the circumstances under which the libel or slander was published, or as to the character of the plaintiff, without the leave of the judge, unless 7 days at least before the trial he furnishes particulars to the plaintiff of the matters as to which he intends to give evidence.**

**8.   Fulfilment of offer of amends under section 25 of the Defamation Ordinance** (O. 82 r. 8)

**(1)   An application to the Court under section 25 of the Defamation Ordinance (Cap 21) to determine any question as to the steps to be taken in fulfilment of an offer of amends made under that section must, unless the application is made in the course of proceedings for libel or slander in respect of the publication to which the offer relates, be made before a judge in chambers.**

**(2)   An originating summons by which such an application is made shall be in Form No 10 in Appendix A.**

**(Enacted 1988)**

## (HK) ORDER 83A

### MONEY LENDERS' ACTIONS

**1. Application and interpretation** (O. 83A r. 1)

**(1) These rules apply to a money lender's action subject to the following rules of this Order.**

**(2) In these rules—**

**"money lender" has the meaning assigned to it by section 2 of the Money Lenders Ordinance (Cap 163);**

**"money lender's action" means an action for the recovery of money lent by a money lender or for the enforcement of any agreement or security relating to money so lent, being an action brought by the lender or an assignee.**

---

## NOTES

### [83A.1.1] Application of Order 83A

Order 83A applies to money lenders' actions as defined in rule 1(2). It is necessary to look to section 2 of the Money Lenders Ordinance (Cap 163) for a definition of the term 'money lender'. Essentially, a money lender is someone who carries on a business of making loans. The making of a single loan or several isolated loans does not constitute carrying on business. See Allcock 'The Money Lenders Ordinance' (1981) 11 HKLJ 293, 301–302 and the authorities cited there, and see *Harvester Stock Investment Co v Kwan Siu May* [1987] 1 HKC 271.

Banks and certain other financial institutions which are subject to separate regulatory regimes are not subject to the Money Lenders Ordinance. Similarly, certain types of loan such as those made by pawnbrokers, or by employer to employee, are not covered. See Allcock at 303–313. It follows that Order 83A does not apply to actions brought by such lenders to recover money lent by them.

In *The Cavalry* [1987] HKLR 287, it was held that the 1911 Money Lenders Ordinance (now repealed) applied only to lenders carrying on business in Hong Kong or holding themselves out to be doing so. Hunter J said (at 294H-I) that the Ordinance was 'plainly directed primarily to domestic transactions'. The same is undoubtedly true with respect to the current Ordinance, enacted during the colonial era when the Hong Kong legislature was subject to a presumption against the extraterritorial effect of legislation. On the extraterritoriality point, see *Ka Wah Bank Ltd v Low Chung Song & Ors* HCA 4191/1987 (Deputy Judge Cruden; 23.06.1988) (appeal allowed on other grounds – see [1989] 1 HKLR 451) citing Craies on Statute Law.

### [83A.1.2] Historical cross-reference

Prior to 1988, the equivalent of the current Order 83A was numbered 83.

**2. Commencement of money lenders action** (O. 83A r. 2)

**(1) Every money lender's action may be begun by writ. (L.N. 152 of 2008)**

**(2) Before a writ beginning a money lender's action is issued it must be indorsed with a statement that at the time of the making of the loan or contract or the giving of the security in question the lender was licensed as a money lender.**

**NOTES**

**[83A.2.1]   Indorsement as to status of plaintiff as licensed money lender**
Order 83A rule 2 requires that a writ commencing a money lender's action 'must' be indorsed with a statement that the plaintiff was a licensed money lender at the time of the loan (or other dealing) sued upon. This reflects section 23 of the Money Lenders Ordinance whereby a loan made by a money lender is not recoverable in court proceedings unless the court is satisfied that the money lender was licensed at the relevant time. In *New China Hong Kong Finance Ltd (in liq) v To Sau Ching* [2001] 4 HKC 304 the consequences of failure to comply with this requirement were considered. Judge Carlson (construing the district court equivalent of this rule, which is in the same terms) held that although the wording of the rule is mandatory, failure to comply is a mere irregularity capable of being cured by amendment. Failure to comply did not render the action a nullity. In that case, the defect having been cured by amendment, the court entered summary judgment under Order 14. Judge Carlson expressly declined to follow the decision in *Welfare Co v Hickok Plastic Manufactory* [1965] HKDCLR 190.

**3.   Particulars to be included in statement of claim** (O. 83A r. 3)
**Every statement of claim in a money lender's action (whether indorsed on the writ or not) must state–**
    **(a)   the date on which the loan was made;**
    **(b)   the amount actually lent to the borrower;**
    **(c)   the rate per cent per annum of interest charged;**
    **(d)   the date when the contract for repayment was made;**
    **(g)   the amount repaid;**
    **(h)   the amount due but unpaid;**
    **(i)   the date upon which such unpaid sum or sums became due; and**
    **(j)   the amount of interest accrued due and unpaid on every such sum.**

**NOTES**

**[83A.3.1]   Particulars in money lender's claim**
Order 83A rule 3 specifies particulars which must be pleaded in the statement of claim in a 'money lender's action', a term which is defined in rule 1(2).
The particulars which are required to be pleaded reflect section 18 of the Money Lenders Ordinance (Cap 163) which requires that the terms of a money lender's transaction be recorded in a memorandum signed personally by the borrower. Failure to comply with the section renders the loan and any security for it unenforceable, save by exercise of the court's discretion under section 18(3). In *Konew Finance Ltd v Wong Kai Ming & Ors (No 2)* [2001] 4 HKC 218, the court exercised that discretion in favour of a money lender where the breaches were considered 'technical'. In *Treasure Spot Finance Co Ltd v Li Chik Ming* HCA 5387/2001 (Recorder P Fung SC; 10.07.2007) where a late allegation of failure to comply with section 18 of the Ordinance arose, the court was of the view that Order 18 rule 8 (an allegation of illegality must be specifically pleaded) applied.

In *Emperor Futures Ltd & Anor v La Belle Fashions Ltd & Anor* CACV 1476/2001 (Rogers VP, Le Pichon and Yuen JJA; 10.12.2002), the Court of Appeal, faced with a late application to amend a money lender's pleading so as to cure non-compliance with this rule, remitted the case to the Court of First Instance. On further appeal, the Court of Final Appeal was of the view that the amendments were, by that stage, 'matters of formality' and the court, 'having all the materials necessary to deal with the matter, should do so at once': *Emperor Finance Ltd v La Belle Fashions Ltd & Anor* [2003] 3 HKLRD 995 (CFA).

*Rule 3(b) – the 'borrower'* – In *Emperor Finance Ltd* [2003] 3 HKLRD 995, the Court of Final Appeal declined to follow a line of Australian and New Zealand authority to the effect that the requirement in section 18(1) of the Ordinance for a memorandum setting out the terms of a money lender's transaction only applies where the borrower is a natural person. However, since money lenders might have been relying on that line of authority the courts would, for a reasonable transitional period, exercise the discretion under section 18(3) in favour of enforcing non-complying loans to bodies corporate.

*Rule 3(c) – interest rate* – Section 18(2)(i) of the Ordinance provides that the memorandum recording the terms of a money lender's transaction shall state the rate of interest 'expressed as a rate per cent per annum'. The purpose is to allow the borrower to know 'exactly what rate of interest will be charged over the life of the loan'; floating rates such as the commonly used formula 'X % above the HSBC best lending rate from time to time' do not comply: *Emperor Finance Ltd* [2003] 3 HKLRD 995 (CFA). However, the court has a discretion under section 18(3) to permit enforcement of non-complying loan agreements. In *Emperor Finance Ltd* [2003] 3 HKLRD 995 the Court of Final Appeal exercised this discretion in favour of the money lender where, notwithstanding a non-complying memorandum, the borrower had in fact been sent daily statements showing the amount of interest charged in dollars and cents.

4. **Judgment on failure to give notice of intention to defend or in default of defence** (O. 83A r. 4)

   **(1) In a money lender's action judgment on failure to give notice of intention to defend or in default of defence shall not be entered except with the leave of the Court.**

   **(2)  (a)  An application for the grant of leave under this rule must be made by summons supported by an affidavit which must–**

   **(i)  prove that the money is due and payable;**

   **(ii)  give the particulars required by rules 2 and 3; and**

   **(iii)  exhibit a true copy of any agreement or security relating to the money lent,**

   **and the original agreement or security must be produced at the hearing of the summons.**

   **(b)  The summons and a copy of the affidavit in support and of any exhibits referred to therein must, notwithstanding anything in Order 65, rule 9 be served on the defendant not less than 4 clear days before the day fixed for the hearing of the summons.**

**(3)** If the application is for leave to enter judgment on failure to give notice of intention to defend, the summons shall not be issued until after the time limited for acknowledgment of service of the writ.

**(4)** On the hearing of such application, whether the defendant appears or not, the Court–

    **(a)** may exercise the powers of the court under section 25 of the Money Lenders Ordinance (Cap 163);

    **(b)** where it refuses leave under this rule to enter judgment on a claim or any part of a claim, may make or give any such order or directions as it might have made or given had the application been an application under Order 14, rule 1, for judgment on the claim.

**5.**    **(Repealed L.N. 129 of 2000)**

                                                                **(Enacted 1988)**

## NOTES

### [83A.4.1]   Leave required to enter default judgment

Order 83A rule 4(1) provides that in a money lender's action, unlike most civil claims, leave of the court is required before judgment may be entered on failure to give notice of intention to defend or default of defence. The subsequent paragraphs of rule 4 set out the procedural requirements for obtaining such leave.

In *National Resources Capital Ltd v Tsang Kin Man* DCCJ 3175/2002 (Deputy Judge CP Pang; 11.12.2002), leave to enter judgment in default of defence was refused under the equivalent district court rule (which is in the same terms). The court held that the security which the money lender sought to enforce was void as contrary to public policy, being a sham attempt to circumvent the requirements of the Housing Ordinance in regard to subsidised home ownership scheme flats.

### [83A.4.2]   Other powers exercisable on application for leave to enter default judgment

On an application under rule 4, the court is not necessarily confined to a choice between granting or refusing leave to enter judgment. Rule 4(4) expressly provides that on such an application the court may exercise its power under section 25 of the Ordinance. It is there provided that the court may reopen an 'extortionate' transaction (defined as one which requires grossly exorbitant payments or is grossly contrary to ordinary principles of fair dealing). This power 'gives the court a very wide and unfettered discretion to do justice between the parties': *Lee Leo v Cheong Oi Sum Ader* [1993] 2 HKC 736, 738I.

In *Wong Kwai Fun v Li Fung* [1994] 1 HKC 549, the court declared that security given by a borrower was unenforceable and void, and in exercise of its power under section 25 made an order to the effect that the borrower need only repay the principal amount of the loan. However, in *Cheung Bing Sum Juana v Lee Leo* [1996] 4 HKC 130 (PC), it was held that section 25 could not be used to set aside the transfer of a flat since that transaction had insufficient connection with the loan to constitute security.

Rule 4(4) goes on to provide that where the court refuses leave to enter judgment it may give such directions as it could have done if the application had been under Order 14 rule 1. Order 14 rule 6 provides for directions for the future conduct of an action which wholly or partly survives a summary judgment application.

## ORDER 84A

### (HK) ACTIONS ARISING OUT OF HIRE-PURCHASE OR CONDITIONAL SALE AGREEMENTS

**1. Application and interpretation** (O. 84A r. 1)

(1) These rules apply to actions to which this Order applies subject to the following Order.

(2) This Order applies to any action arising out of a hire-purchase agreement or a conditional sale agreement brought against the hirer or buyer of the goods to which the agreement relates or a guarantor, if the writ beginning the action is indorsed with a claim for money, not being–

    (a) a claim for unliquidated damages, or

    (b) a claim for no more than the amount of any instalment or instalments of the hire-purchase price or total purchase price, as the case may be, which is due and unpaid.

(3)   (a)   In this Order–

"hire-purchase agreement" means an agreement for the bailment of goods under which the bailee may buy the goods, or under which the property in the goods will or may pass to the bailee;

"conditional sale agreement" means an agreement for the sale of goods under which the purchase price or part of it is payable by instalments, and the property in the goods is to remain in the seller (notwithstanding that the buyer is to be in possession of the goods) until such conditions as to the payment of instalments or otherwise as may be specified in the agreement are fulfilled;

"contract of guarantee", in relation to a hire-purchase agreement, credit-sale agreement or conditional sale agreement, means a contract, made at the request (express or implied) of the hirer or buyer, either to guarantee the performance of the hirer's or buyer's obligations under the hire-purchase agreement, credit-sale agreement or conditional sale agreement, or to indemnify the owner or seller against any loss which he may incur in respect of that agreement, and "guarantee" shall be considered accordingly;

"buyer" in relation to a conditional sale agreement, means the person who agrees to purchase goods under the agreement and includes a person to whom the rights or liabilities of that person under the agreement have passed by assignment or by operation of law;

"hire-purchase price" (subject to sub-paragraph (b)) means the total sum payable by the hirer under a hire-purchase agreement in order to complete the purchase of goods to which the agreement relates, exclusive of any sum payable as a penalty or as compensation or damages for a breach of the agreement;

"**total purchase price**" (subject to sub-paragraph (b)) means the total sum payable by the buyer under a credit-sale agreement or a conditional sale agreement, exclusive of any sum payable as a penalty or as compensation or damages for a breach of the agreement;

"**hirer**" means the person who takes or has taken goods from an owner under a hire-purchase agreement and includes a person to whom the hirer's rights or liabilities under the agreement have passed by assignment or by operation of law; and

"**goods**", "**buyer**" (except in relation to a conditional sale agreement) have the meanings assigned to them respectively by the Sale of Goods Ordinance (Cap 26).

(b)   For the purposes of this Order, any sum payable by the hirer under a hire-purchase agreement, or by the buyer under a conditional sale agreement, by way of a deposit or other initial payment, or credited or to be credited to him under the agreement on account of any such deposit or payment, whether that sum is to be or has been paid to the owner or seller or to any other person or is to be or has been discharged by a payment of money or by the transfer or delivery of goods or by any other means, shall form part of the hire-purchase price or total purchase price, as the case may be.

## NOTES

### [84A.1.1]   Scope of Order 84A

Order 84A applies to actions for money owing under hire-purchase and conditional sale agreements. It is confined to claims for liquidated sums not exceeding the amount owing under the agreement. Claims for unliquidated amounts or amounts exceeding the amount owing by way of instalment or total purchase price under the agreement are expressly excluded by rule 1(2)(a) and (b). Hence, the order will apply where, for example, the plaintiff claims:

(a)   a liquidated sum in respect of an unpaid instalment or instalments; or

(b)   where the seller has elected to terminate the agreement for non-payment, the whole amount remaining unpaid (after allowing set-off for any amount recovered by the seller on resale of the goods).

This Order also applies to actions against a guarantor. It does not apply to actions by the hirer or buyer under the agreement.

For a discussion of the law on deficiency claims under hire purchase contracts see Allcock, 'Hire Purchase Deficiency Claims' (1986) 16 HKLJ 227. The forthcoming hire-purchase legislation mentioned in that article appears never to have been enacted.

### 2.   Particulars to be included in statement of claim (O. 84A r. 2)

Every statement of claim in an action to which this Order applies (whether indorsed on the writ or not) must state the circumstances in which the claim mentioned in rule 1(2) arises.

**NOTES**

**[84A.2.1]   Particulars which must be pleaded**

Order 84A rule 2 provides that a statement of claim to which this Order applies must state the 'circumstances' in which the claim arises. This means that the plaintiff should give particulars, not only of the agreement, the parties and the alleged breach, but, so far as applicable, of the other matters which are defined in rule 1(3). Since the claim must be liquidated, the statement of claim should set out a calculation of the amount owing after any set-off for money received on resale of the goods.

3.   **Judgment on failure to give notice of intention to defend or in default of defence** (O. 84A r. 3)

    **(1)   In an action to which this Order applies judgment on failure to give notice of intention to defend or in default of defence shall not be entered except with the leave of the Court.**

    **(2)   (a)   An application for the grant of leave under this rule must be made by summons supported by an affidavit which must–**

        **(i)   give the particulars required by rule 2; and**

        **(ii)   exhibit a true copy of the hire-purchase or conditional sale agreement, the original of which must be produced at the hearing of the summons.**

      **(b)   The summons and a copy of the affidavit in support and of any exhibits referred to therein must, notwithstanding anything in Order 65, rule 9, be served on the defendant not less than 4 clear days before the day fixed for the hearing of the summons.**

    **(3)   If the application is for leave to enter judgment on failure to give notice of intention to defend, the summons shall not be issued until after the time limited for acknowledgment of service of the writ.**

    **(4)   The plaintiff must produce to the Court hearing an application for the grant of leave under this rule the hire-purchase or conditional sale agreement to which the action relates.**

    **(5)   Unless the Court hearing such application grants leave to enter judgment for the amount claimed or, having power to do so, transfers the action to a District Court, it shall (whether or not the defendant appears on the hearing) try the action.**

                                                          **(Enacted 1988)**

**NOTES**

**[84A.3.1]   Default judgment**

Order 84A rule 3 provides that leave of the court is required to enter default judgment. Leave may not be granted where a defence has been filed: *Capita Corp HK Ltd v Lam Kam Yin & Anor* HCA 9626/1998 (V Bokhary J; 12.01.1999).

**[84A.3.2]   Procedure on application for leave to enter default judgment**

An application for leave to enter default judgment under Order 84A rule 3 is made by summons and affidavit. The particulars required by rule 2 must be verified in the affidavit. This can be done by reference to the statement of claim if one has already have been filed. Otherwise the particulars should be set out in the affidavit. A true copy of the agreement must be exhibited to the affidavit: rule 3(2)(a)(ii).

### [84A.3.3]   Service of summons for leave to enter default judgment
The usual two-clear day rule for service of a summons does not apply on an application under this Order for leave to enter default judgment. Rule 3(2)(b) expressly stipulates that there must be no less than four clear days between service and the hearing date.

### [84A.3.4]   Original agreement must be produced at hearing
In addition to exhibiting a true copy of the agreement to the affidavit in support of an application for leave to enter default judgment, it is necessary to produce the original agreement to the court at the hearing for leave to enter default judgment. See rule 3(4).

### [84A.3.5]   Court will consider whether plaintiff mitigated loss
In some cases to which this Order applies the creditor will already have seized the goods and resold them, recovering part of the money owing. (Unlike some other jurisdictions, there is no requirement in Hong Kong that the creditor elect either to 'seize and sell' or to sue – the creditor may seize and sell, and then pursue the debtor for the balance owing.) In such cases, the question may arise whether the creditor mitigated its loss by obtaining an appropriate price on resale of the goods seized. In *Wayfoong Credit Ltd v Cheung Wai Wah Samuel* [1990] 1 HKC 367, it was held that the court may look into the question of mitigation of loss even on an application for default judgment. In that case, Master Perrior found that the creditor had not taken reasonable steps to mitigate its loss and allowed the creditor only an amount based on the depreciation value of the chattel (a motor car) for tax purposes, less allowance for a forced sale. See also *Kone Elevator (HK) Ltd v Senfield Ltd* DCCJ 4544/2001 (Deputy Judge Yu; 06.02.2002).

### [84A.3.6]   Appeal
Order 58 rule 2(c) provides that an appeal against a hearing or determination by a master under Order 84A rule 3 lies to the Court of Appeal. However, this applies only in the event of a trial, as contemplated by Order 84A rule 3(5). It does not apply where default judgment is entered. See *Capita Corp HK Ltd v Lam Kam Yin & Anor* HCA 9626/1998 (V Bokhary J; 12.01.1999).

**ORDER 85**

**ADMINISTRATION AND SIMILAR ACTIONS**

1.   **Interpretation** (O. 85 r. 1)
    In this Order "administration action" means an action for the administration under the direction of the Court of the estate of a deceased person or for the execution under the direction of the Court of a trust.

---

**NOTES**

**[85.1.1]   Comparison with English rules**
Order 85 is based on the English Order of the same number, as it existed before the Woolf reforms came into effect. The relevant English rules are now found in CPR part 64.

2.   **Determination of questions, etc., without administration** (O. 85 r. 2)
    (1)   An action may be brought for the determination of any question or for any relief which could be determined or granted, as the case may be, in an administration action and a claim need not be made in the action for the administration or execution under the direction of the Court of the estate or trust in connection with which the question arises or the relief is sought.
    (2)   Without prejudice to the generality of paragraph (1), an action may be brought for the determination of any of the following questions–
        (a)   any question arising in the administration of the estate of a deceased person or in the execution of a trust;
        (b)   any question as to the composition of any class of persons having a claim against the estate of a deceased person or a beneficial interest in the estate of such a person or in any property subject to a trust;
        (c)   any question as to the rights or interests of a person claiming to be a creditor of the estate of a deceased person or to be entitled under a will or on the intestacy of a deceased person or to be beneficially entitled under a trust.
    (3)   Without prejudice to the generality of paragraph (1), an action may be brought for any of the following reliefs–
        (a)   an order requiring an executor, administrator or trustee to furnish and, if necessary, verify accounts;
        (b)   an order requiring the payment into court of money held by a person in his capacity as executor, administrator or trustee;
        (c)   an order directing a person to do or abstain from doing a particular act in his capacity as executor, administrator or trustee;
        (d)   an order approving any sale, purchase, compromise or other transaction by a person in his capacity as executor, administrator or trustee;
        (e)   an order directing any act to be done in the administration of the estate of a deceased person or in the execution of a trust which

> **the Court could order to be done if the estate or trust were being administered or executed, as the case may be, under the direction of the Court.**

## NOTES

### [85.2.1]  Order 85 applies to 'domestic' litigation involving trust or estate

Order 85 provides for what has been described as 'domestic' litigation involving a trust or estate. The term 'friendly' litigation is also sometimes used. It does not apply to 'hostile' litigation. Domestic litigation in this context is litigation concerning the trustee's obligations in administering the trust. See *Standard Chartered Bank Hong Kong Trustee Ltd & Anor v Brogan* [1990] 2 HKC 560, 563G where domestic litigation was described as follows:

> In domestic litigation, a trustee seeking directions from the court as to what he should do in or about the execution of the trust may institute proceedings in a summary way, in which somebody representing the beneficial interest in the trust estate is constituted a party. The order made in such proceedings protects the trustee from any adverse criticism if he follows the course of action directed by the court.

By contrast hostile litigation involves a substantive dispute with an outsider, or between beneficiaries *inter se* or between beneficiary and trustee.

### [85.2.2]  *Beddoe* orders

Where hostile litigation is contemplated a trustee may seek advance protection as to the costs of those proceedings by applying under Order 85 for a *Beddoe* order. The *Beddoe* order takes its name from *Re Beddoe* [1893] 1 Ch 547. Such an order authorises the trustee to commence or defend hostile proceedings, and provides that the trustee shall be entitled to be indemnified by the trust fund for unrecovered costs. See *Sin Hua Bank Trustee Ltd v Ip Cheung-kwok & Ors* [1992] 1 HKLR 212 (CA). There Clough JA (at 215-216) referred to Order 62 rule 6(2) which provides that a trustee is entitled to costs out of the trust fund unless it has acted unreasonably or for its own benefit, and said:

> In practice the court will in its discretion give advance protection to a trustee who contemplates bringing or defending proceedings. It may make a *Beddoe* order giving him leave … to bring or defend an action and indemnify himself in respect of his costs if he is unsuccessful …

A *Beddoe* order protects the trustee against the possibility its costs would not be paid out of the fund under Order 62 rule 6(2): *Re Estate of Lee Mentor* HCAG 5212/1991 (Yam J; 30.06.2000). Such an order may be sought by a trustee or a person standing in the position of a trustee, such as the liquidators of a company: *Re Peregrine Investments Holdings Ltd & Ors* [1999] 3 HKC 291, 308G-H (CA). There Mortimer VP said that a *Beddoe* order enables such a person to 'bring proceedings with confidence that the proceedings are justified and that he will not be called upon to pay costs personally'.

*Beddoe* orders are usually sought where the trust becomes embroiled in a dispute with a third party. However such an order may also be made in the event of hostile litigation between the trustee and a beneficiary. In *Chui Pak Ming Norman & Anor v Leung Sai Lun Robert & Ors* [2001] 2 HKC 286 the Court of Appeal upheld a

*Beddoe* order granted to administrators of an estate in respect of an action against beneficiaries to recover misappropriated property. However in *Leung May Chow Karen & Anor (administrices) v Leung May Chun Alison Aliance* HCMP 148/2005 (Master J Wong; 21.02.2006) the court declined to grant the administrices of an estate the protection of a *Beddoe* order to defend proceedings against them brought by a beneficiary alleging wilful default in the administration of the estate. See that case and *Re Kennedy (No 3)* [2005] 2 HKC 73, 75H-76H for a discussion of the different types of litigation in which trustees may become involved, and when a *Beddoe* order might be granted.

A *Beddoe* order may be limited. See for example *Chui Pak Ming Norman* (above) where such an order was limited to the completion of discovery.

### [85.2.3]    May beneficiary be granted a Beddoe order?

There is some authority suggesting that just as a trustee may seek advance protection as to costs by means of a *Beddoe* order, so may a beneficiary. See *McDonald & Ors v Horn & Ors* [1995] 1 All ER 961 where such an order was made in favour of the members of an occupational pension scheme in respect of proceedings against the pension fund trustee.

### [85.2.4]    Procedure on application for Beddoe order

An application for a *Beddoe* order should be made promptly: *Sin Hua Bank Trustee Ltd* (above, 218).

The application should be made by originating application under Order 85 rule 2, not by summons in the hostile proceedings the trustee proposes to commence or defend. This is because the issues on a *Beddoe* application do not concern the hostile party unless he is a beneficiary of the trust. However a mistake in this regard may not affect the validity of a *Beddoe* order: *Wang Din Shin v Nina Kung* CACV 1643/2001 (Rogers VP & Suffiad J; 04.09.2001) (para 22).

It is necessary for the court to form a view about the trustee's prospects of success: *Re Dallaway (deceased)* [1982] 1 WLR 756; [1982] 3 All ER 118. This may involve placing counsel's advice before the court. As a result the application should not be heard by the judge who will eventually deal with the substantive litigation since it would be inappropriate for that judge to be informed of the trustee's views on the strengths and weaknesses of the case and what legal advice has been received: *Hillhead Ltd v Hotung & Ors* [2003] 3 HKC 558, 559G. Likewise care should be taken not to serve counsel's advice on any hostile party: *Chui Pak Ming Norman* (above, 290E-F) citing *Re Moritz* [1960] Ch 251.

### [85.2.5]    Factors to be considered on application for Beddoe order

On an application for a *Beddoe* order the burden is on the trustee to show that the proposed course of action in the hostile litigation is *'prima facie* proper and in the interest of the trust': *Sin Hua Bank Trustee Ltd* (above, 216). The trustee has a duty to protect the trust property against adverse proceedings and a *Beddoe* order will be appropriate in such cases. However where the dispute is between the persons entitled, the trustee should remain neutral, with the result that a *Beddoe* order will not be granted in respect of the costs of substantive participation in the litigation: *HSBC International Trustee Ltd v Tam Mei Kam* HCMP 716/2004 (Lam J; 11.10.2004).

In the *HSBC International Trustee Ltd* case (above) the court listed four relevant considerations on an application for a *Beddoe* order:

(a)    the strength of the party's case;

(b)    the likely order as to costs at the trial: it must appear that the judge at the trial could properly exercise his discretion only by ordering the applicants' costs be paid out of the trust estate, see *McDonald v Horn* [1995] 1 All ER 961;

(c)    the justice of the application; and

(d)    any special circumstances.

The above list traces back to *National Anti-Vivisection Society Ltd v Duddington & Ors* The Times 23.11.1989, summarising the earlier cases, and was refined in *Re Biddencare Ltd* [1994] 2 BCLC 160, *McDonald v Horn* (above) and *Alsop Wilkinson v Neary* [1996] 1 WLR 1220, 1226. It appears to apply generally to applications for pre-emptive costs orders, of which the *Beddoe* order is a type. See the commentary under Order 62 rules 3 and 6(2) for discussion of other types of pre-emptive costs orders.

#### [85.2.6]    Action by beneficiary for administration of estate

Order 85 rule 2 is the appropriate provision for a beneficiary to bring proceedings against the trustee for administration of the trust property: see *Chan Chun Wah v Chan Chun Wai Patrick & Anor* [1987] 2 HKC 397. There Godfrey J held that an action by a beneficiary for a vesting order under section 70(2) of the Probate and Administration Ordinance (Cap 10) was misconceived. The beneficiary could not claim a beneficial interest in trust property under that law pending administration of the estate. The remedy was an administration action under Order 85 rule 2. Godfrey J stated, at 398G–H:

> Not until there has been an assent can it be said with certainty whether or not a particular asset will be needed for the payment of debts or other liabilities; and until these have been discharged, it cannot be said what assets there will be in the residuary estate. Accordingly, the general rule is that no beneficiary can assert that he has any legal or equitable interest in any of the assets which are still unadministered; for the whole right of property in them is vested in the personal representatives. The beneficiary has merely a right to require the deceased's estate to be duly administered. Apart from specific gifts, the rights of the beneficiaries are accordingly protected, not by conferring equitable interests upon them, but by the control exercised by the court, whether under a will or an intestacy, to secure the due administration of the assets in the interests of the beneficiaries and of other persons concerned.

See also *Cheung Lily & Anor v Standard Chartered Bank Hong Kong Trustee Ltd & Ors* [1988] 1 HKLR 613 (CA) where it was held (per Kempster JA at 617G–H) that beneficiaries of an estate had 'good grounds' to bring an administration action under Order 85 rule 2 against the executor for the determination of a question whether certain assets formed part of the estate of a deceased. And see *Liu Yu Wei v Lee Wai Hing* HCAP 1/2006 (Chu J; 14.08.2007) where it was held that an action by a person claiming an interest in an estate should be brought under Order 85, and that Order 76 is inappropriate.

**[85.2.7]  Order against trustee for disclosure**

Order 85 rule 2(3) empowers the court to order an executor, administrator or trustee to do or refrain from doing a range of different things. In *Hotung v Ho Yuen Ki* [2007] 4 HKLRD 384 (CA) a beneficiary obtained under this provision an order that the trustee supply a wide range of documents and information. Yuen JA observed (at para 35-6) that although rule 2(3)(a) may apply only to accounts and not other documents, the more 'general terms' of rule 2(3)(c) permitted the court to make an order of the type sought by the beneficiary.

**3.  Parties** (O. 85 r. 3)

**(1)  All the executors or administrators of the estate or trustees of the trust, as the case may be, to which an administration action or such an action as is referred to in rule 2 relates must be parties to the action, and where the action is brought by executors, administrators or trustees, any of them who does not consent to being joined as a plaintiff must be made a defendant.**

**(2)  Notwithstanding anything in Order 15, rule 4(2), and without prejudice to the powers of the Court under that Order, all the persons having a beneficial interest in or claim against the estate or having a beneficial interest under the trust, as the case may be, to which such an action as is mentioned in paragraph (1) relates need not be parties to the action; but the plaintiff may make such of those persons, whether all or any one or more of them, parties as, having regard to the nature of the relief or remedy claimed in the action, he thinks fit.**

**(3)  Where, in proceedings under a judgment or order given or made in an action for the administration under the direction of the Court of the estate of a deceased person, a claim in respect of a debt or other liability is made against the estate by a person not a party to the action, no party other than the executors or administrators of the estate shall be entitled to appear in any proceedings relating to that claim without the leave of the Court, and the Court may direct or allow any other party to appear either in addition to, or in substitution for, the executors or administrators on such terms as to costs or otherwise as it thinks fit.**

**NOTES**

**[85.3.1]  Parties to proceedings under Order 85**

Order 85 rule 3(1) provides that all of the executors or trustees must be parties to proceedings of the type dealt with by this Order. However, it is not necessary to join all persons with a beneficial interest: rule 3(2). Thus in *Hotung v Ho Yuen Ki* [2007] 4 HKLRD 384 (CA) (para 51) it was held that proceedings by one of three beneficial owners of company shares in respect of which there was a single share certificate were 'competent'. In *Standard Chartered Bank HK Trustee Ltd v Brogan* [1990] 2 HKC 560, 563F Godfrey J doubted whether proceedings were properly constituted where no beneficiary had been joined.

**4.  Grant of relief in action begun by originating summons** (O. 85 r. 4)

**In an administration action or such an action as is referred to in rule 2, the Court may make any certificate or order and grant any relief to which the plaintiff may be entitled by reason of any breach of trust, wilful default or other**

misconduct of the defendant notwithstanding that the action was begun by originating summons, but the foregoing provision is without prejudice to the power of the Court to make an order under Order 28, rule 8, in relation to the action.

## NOTES

### [85.4.1]   Administration action by way of originating summons

In *Ho Chi Mei v Ho Che Ying & Anor* HCA 1002/2008 (Lam J; 04.02.2010) the court took the view that an administration action ought to have been begun by originating summons rather than writ. No reason was given. Perhaps the court had in mind Order 5 rule 4, by which an action in which the sole or principal question is the construction of a written document is considered appropriate for the originating summons procedure. That would certainly apply to an administration action involving construction of a will. However, there is clearly no absolute bar on an administration action being commenced by writ. Order 5 rule 3, which previously required certain actions to be commenced by originating summons, was abolished as part of the civil justice reforms which came into force on 2 April 2009. Moreover Order 85 rule 4 expressly preserves the court's power to make an order under Order 28 rule 8 that an administration action continue as if begun by writ.

The main thrust of Order 85 rule 4 is to enable the court to grant relief for breach of trust, wilful default or misconduct in an administration action notwithstanding it was commenced by originating summons. It may have been intended to facilitate administration actions proceeding by originating summons notwithstanding the requirement in the former Order 5 rule 2 that actions including a claim based on an allegation of fraud be commenced by writ. Order 5 rule 2 was repealed with effect from 2 April 2009.

**5.   Judgments and orders in administration actions** (O. 85 r. 5)

   **(1)   A judgment or order for the administration or execution under the direction of the Court of an estate or trust need not be given or made unless in the opinion of the Court the questions at issue between the parties cannot properly be determined otherwise than under such a judgment or order.**

   **(2)   Where an administration action is brought by a creditor of the estate of a deceased person or by a person claiming to be entitled under a will or on the intestacy of a deceased person or to be beneficially entitled under a trust, and the plaintiff alleges that no or insufficient accounts have been furnished by the executors, administrators or trustees, as the case may be, then, without prejudice to its other powers, the Court may–**

   **(a)   order that proceedings in the action be stayed for a period specified in the order and that the executors, administrators or trustees, as the case may be, shall within that period furnish the plaintiff with proper accounts;**

   **(b)   if necessary to prevent proceedings by other creditors or by other persons claiming to be entitled as aforesaid, give judgment or make an order for the administration of the estate to which the**

**action relates and include therein an order that no proceedings are to be taken under the judgment or order, or under any particular account or inquiry directed, without the leave of the judge in person.**

**6. Conduct of sale of trust property** (O. 85 r. 6)

**Where in an administration action an order is made for the sale of any property vested in executors, administrators or trustees, those executors, administrators or trustees, as the case may be, shall have the conduct of the sale unless the Court otherwise directs.**

**(Enacted 1988)**

**NOTES**

**[85.6.1] History of rule**
The power of the court to direct a sale was considered in *Ip Cheung Kwok v Sin Hua Bank Trustee Ltd* [1990] 1 HKLR 497, 525-256. The Court of Appeal held that the power to direct a sale had historically been conferred on the English Court of Chancery by section 55 of the Chancery Procedure Act 1852. That power had been retained in England by section 21 of the Judicature Act 1873, section 18 of the Judicature Act 1925 and section 19 of the Supreme Court Act 1981. It is preserved in Hong Kong by section 12(2) of the High Court Ordinance. In this case the propriety of the court's order of sale had been challenged on the ground that the time was inappropriate for sale. The court ruled that arrangements for sale should proceed without further inhibition.

## ORDER 86

### ACTIONS FOR SPECIFIC PERFORMANCE ETC: SUMMARY JUDGMENT

1. **Application by plaintiff for summary judgment** (O. 86 r. 1)
   **(1)   In any action begun by writ indorsed with a claim–**
       **(a)   for specific performance of an agreement (whether in writing or not) for the sale, purchase, exchange, mortgage or charge of any property, or for the grant or assignment of a lease of any property, with or without an alternative claim for damages, or**
       **(b)   for rescission of such an agreement, or**
       **(c)   for the forfeiture or return of any deposit made under such an agreement,**
   **the plaintiff may, on the ground that the defendant has no defence to the action, apply to the Court for judgment.**
   **(2)   An application may be made against a defendant under this rule whether or not he has acknowledged service of the writ.**

---

**NOTES**

**[86.1.1]   Summary judgment under Order 86**
Under Order 86 rule 1 the court has power to grant summary judgment in certain types of non-money claims which are excluded from the scope of Order 14. An application under Order 86 is only appropriate where it is demonstrable on affidavit evidence that the defendant has no real defence to the action: see *Man Earn Ltd v Wing Ting Fong* [1996] 1 HKC 225 (CA). See also the commentary under Order 14.

Some of the major differences between the summary judgment procedures under Order 14 and Order 86 were set out in *Yau Fook Hong Co Ltd v Pang Cheung So* [1986] HKC 313, 318H–I (CA):

(a)   in the UK, O 86 applies only to the Chancery Division; despite the fact that we have no such division in Hong Kong, the scope of the two orders is still an important matter ... because both jurisdictions have the same O 14 r 1(3): 'This Order shall not apply to an action to which O 86 applies';

(b)   unlike the position under O 14, an application under O 86 can be made whether or not the defendant has acknowledged service ...

(c)   under O 86, it is not essential that a statement of claim has been served.

Despite the differences between Order 14 and Order 86 the legal principles as to whether summary judgment ought to be granted are the same: *Super Town Investments Ltd v Ives Developments Ltd & Ors* HCA 86/2006 (Deputy Judge To; 22.05.2007) (para 5).

**[86.1.2]   Claim for specific performance**
Order 86 rule 1(1)(a) provides for summary judgment in an action for specific performance. It has been held that such an action is not premature, and summary judgment may be granted under this Order, even though the writ is issued before the due date for performance. See *Kou Lau Ru Ling & Ors v Tse Sui Luen* [2000] 2

HKC 644. There the Court of Appeal (at 655H–1, per Ribeiro JA) applied *Khatijabai Jiwa Hasham v Zenab* [1960] AC 316 (PC) where Lord Tucker had observed (at 329) that specific performance being an equitable remedy, it was only necessary to show circumstances which would justify intervention by the court, and that could be done by way of declaratory relief.

### [86.1.3]  Claim for rescission

Order 86 rule 1(1)(b) provides for summary judgment in an action for rescission of an agreement. It has been held that the word 'rescission' in this rule is not used in the narrow sense of rescission *ab initio* but in the broad sense of being released from an agreement including release by termination or discharge on breach. See *Yau Fook Hong Co Ltd v Pang Cheung So* [1986] HKC 313 (CA).

**2.  Manner in which application under rule 1 must be made** (O. 86 r. 2)

**(1)   An application under rule 1 shall be made by summons supported by an affidavit verifying the facts on which the cause of action is based and stating that in the deponent's belief there is no defence to the action. Unless the Court otherwise directs, an affidavit for the purposes of this paragraph may contain statements of information or belief with the sources and grounds thereof.**

**(2)   The summons must set out or have attached thereto minutes of the judgment sought by the plaintiff.**

**(3)   The summons, a copy of the affidavit in support and of any exhibit referred to therein must be served on the defendant not less than 4 clear days before the return day.**

**NOTES**

### [86.2.1]  Application by summons and affidavit

Order 86 rule 2(1) provides that an application under rule 1 must be made by summons with supporting affidavit.

The summons must set out or have attached 'minutes of the judgment sought'. It has been held that 'this means no more than that the defendant must set out, by individual paragraphs, the complete terms of the order it seeks in the summons': *Fantasy Gift Int'l Co Ltd v Gold Luck Int'l Ltd* HCA 2548/2007 (Burrell J; 09.09.2008) (para 12).

With regard to the affidavit in support, the cases concerning the requirements for an affidavit in support of an Order 14 summons should be applicable here. See the commentary under Order 14 rule 2.

**3.  Judgment for plaintiff** (O. 86 r. 3)

**(1)   Unless on the hearing of an application under rule 1 either the Court dismisses the application or the defendant satisfies the Court that there is an issue or question in dispute which ought to be tried or that there ought for some other reason to be a trial of the action, the Court may give judgment for the plaintiff in the action.**

**(2)   The Court may by order, and subject to such conditions, if any, as may be just, stay execution of any judgment given against the defendant under this**

rule until after the trial of any counterclaim made or raised by the defendant in the action. (L.N. 356 of 1988)

**4.   Leave to defend** (O. 86 r. 4)

(1)   A defendant may show cause against an application under rule 1 by affidavit or otherwise to the satisfaction of the Court.

(2)   The Court may give a defendant against whom such an application is made leave to defend the action either unconditionally or on such terms as to giving security or time or mode of trial or otherwise as it thinks fit.

(3)   On the hearing of such an application the Court may order a defendant showing cause or, where that defendant is a body corporate, any director, manager, secretary or other similar officer thereof, or any person purporting to act in any such capacity–

    **(a)**   to produce any document;

    **(b)**   if it appears to the Court that there are special circumstances which make it desirable that he should do so, to attend and be examined on oath.

## NOTES

**[86.4.1]   Manner in which cause may be shown**

Order 86 rule 4(1) provides that a defendant may, in an application for summary judgment under this Order, show cause by affidavit. The defendant may do so even where the particular defence is not pleaded. See *Country Rich Development Ltd v Yau* HCA 1670/2005 (Deputy Judge Poon; 24.05.2006) para 13. The wording of rule 4(1) is such that an affidavit is not required – the defendant may show cause 'otherwise'. Where the defendant seeks to raise a fact-sensitive defence, an affidavit will be indispensable. The court's task in relation to such an affidavit is 'to determine two questions, namely whether what the defendant says is believable and, secondly, if it is, whether what the defendant says amounts to an arguable defence in law': *Fine Elite Group Ltd v Cheng Wai Tao* HCA 1269/2008 (Fok J; 27.04.2010) (para 52). This is the same task the court performs on an application under Order 14.

**[86.4.2]   Leave to defend**

Order 86 rule 4(2) provides that leave to defend may be granted either unconditionally or on terms. In this regard it is substantially identical to Order 14 rule 4(3). See the commentary under that rule.

**[86.4.3]   Appeal against grant of unconditional leave to defend**

The Court of Appeal will rarely interfere with a decision below to grant unconditional leave to defend. See the commentary under Order 14 rule 4. An example of a case making this point in the context of Order 86 is *Ng Lung Sang Anita v Lam Yuk Lan* [1999] 4 HKC 106, 109I–110I (CA).

**5.   Directions** (O. 86 r. 5)

Where the Court orders that a defendant have leave to defend the action, the Court shall give directions as to the further conduct of the action, and Order 25, rules 2 to 7, shall, with the omission of so much of rule 7(1) as requires parties to serve a notice specifying the orders and directions which they require and with any other necessary modifications, apply as if the application under rule 1 were a case management summons. (L.N. 152 of 2008)

6.  **Costs** (O. 86 r. 6)

If the plaintiff makes an application under rule 1 where the case is not within this Order, or if it appears to the Court that the plaintiff knew that the defendant relied on a contention which would entitle him to unconditional leave to defend, then, without prejudice to Order 62, and, in particular, to rule 4(1) thereof, the Court may dismiss the application with costs and may, if the plaintiff is not an aided person, require the costs to be paid by him forthwith.

7.  **Setting aside judgment** (O. 86 r. 7)

Any judgement given against a defendant who does not appear at the hearing of an application under rule 1 may be set aside or varied by the Court on such terms as it thinks just.

8.  **(HK) Application for summary judgment on counterclaim** (O. 86 r. 8)

(1)   Where a defendant to an action begun by writ has served a counterclaim claiming against the plaintiff such relief as appears in rule 1(1) the defendant may, on the ground that the plaintiff has no defence to a claim made in the counterclaim or to a particular part of such a claim, apply to the court for judgment against the plaintiff on that claim or that part.

(2)   Rules 2, 3, 4, 5, 6 and 7 shall apply in relation to an application under this rule as they apply in relation to an application under rule 1 but with the following modifications—

> (a)   references to the plaintiff and defendant shall be construed as references to the defendant and plaintiff respectively;
>
> (b)   the words in rule 3(2) "any counterclaim made or raised by the defendant in" shall be omitted;
>
> (c)   the reference in rule 4(2) to the action shall be construed as a reference to the counterclaim to which the application under this rule relates.

(L.N. 356 of 1988)

9.  **(HK) Right to proceed with residue of action or counterclaim** (O. 86 r. 9)

(1)   Where on an application under rule 1 the plaintiff obtains judgment on a claim or a part of a claim against any defendant, he may proceed with the action as respects any other claim or as respects the remainder of the claim or against any other defendant.

(2)   Where on an application under rule 8 a defendant obtains judgment on a claim or part of a claim made in a counterclaim against the plaintiff, he may proceed with the counterclaim as respects any other claim or against any other defendant to the counterclaim.

(L.N. 356 of 1988)

## ORDER 87

### DEBENTURE HOLDERS' ACTIONS: RECEIVER'S REGISTER

**1. Receivers register** (O. 87 r. 1)

**Every receiver appointed by the Court in an action to enforce registered debentures or registered debenture stock shall, if so directed by the Court, keep a register of transfers of, and other transmissions of title to, such debentures or stock (in this Order referred to as "the receiver's register").**

---

## NOTES

### [87.1.1]   Where receiver's register required

Order 87 rule 1 gives the court a discretion to direct, on appointing a receiver in an action to enforce registered debentures or registered debenture stock, that a register of transfers (*etc*) be kept. Such a direction is appropriate where there are numerous debentures involved: see Kerr & Hunter on Receivers and Administrators, 2005, para 7-51.

**2. Registration of transfers, etc.** (O. 87 r. 2)

**(1)   Where a receiver is required by rule 1 to keep a receiver's register, then, on the application of any person entitled to any debentures or debenture stock by virtue of any transfer or other transmission of title, and on production of such evidence of identity and title as the receiver may reasonably require, the receiver shall, subject to the following provisions of this rule, register the transfer or other transmissions of title in that register.**

**(2)   Before registering a transfer the receiver must, unless the due execution of the transfer is proved by affidavit, send by post to the registered holder of the debentures or debenture stock transferred at his registered address a notice stating–**

    **(a)   that an application for the registration of the transfer has been made, and**

    **(b)   that the transfer will be registered unless within the period specified in the notice the holder informs the receiver that he objects to the registration,**

**and no transfer shall be registered until the period so specified has elapsed. The period to be specified in the notice shall in no case be less than 7 days after a reply from the registered holder would in the ordinary course of post reach the receiver if the holder had replied to the notice on the day following the day when in the ordinary course of post the notice would have been delivered at the place to which it was addressed.**

**(3)   On registering a transfer or other transmission of title under this rule the receiver must indorse a memorandum thereof on the debenture or certificate of debenture stock, as the case may be, transferred or transmitted, containing a reference to the action and to the order appointing him receiver.**

**3. Application for rectification of receivers register** (O. 87 r. 3)

(1) Any person aggrieved by any thing done or omission made by a receiver under rule 2 may apply to the Court for rectification of the receiver's register, the application to be made by summons in the action in which the receiver was appointed.

(2) The summons shall in the first instance be served only on the plaintiff or other party having the conduct of the action but the Court may direct the summons or notice of the application to be served on any other person appearing to be interested.

(3) The Court hearing an application under this rule may decide any question relating to the title of any person who is party to the application to have his name entered in or omitted from the receiver's register and generally may decide any question necessary or expedient to be decided for the rectification of that register.

**4. Receivers register evidence of transfers, etc.** (O. 87 r. 4)

Any entry made in the receiver's register, if verified by an affidavit made by the receiver or by such other person as the Court may direct, shall in all proceedings in the action in which the receiver was appointed be evidence of the transfer or transmission of title to which the entry relates and, in particular, shall be accepted as evidence thereof for the purpose of any distribution of assets, notwithstanding that the transfer or transmission has taken place after the making of a certificate in the action certifying the holders of the debentures or debenture stock certificates.

**5. Proof of title of holder of bearer debenture, etc.** (O. 87 r. 5)

(1) This rule applies in relation to an action to enforce bearer debentures or to enforce debenture stock in respect of which the company has issued debenture stock bearer certificates.

(2) Notwithstanding that judgment has been given in the action and that a certificate has been made therein certifying the holders of such debentures or certificates as are referred to in paragraph (1), the title of any person claiming to be such a holder shall (in the absence of notice of any defect in the title) be sufficiently proved by the production of the debenture or debenture stock certificate, as the case may be, together with a certificate of identification signed by the person producing the debenture or certificate identifying the debenture or certificate produced and certifying the person (giving his name and address) who is the holder thereof.

(3) Where such a debenture or certificate as is referred to in paragraph (1) is produced in the Registry, the solicitor of the plaintiff in the action must cause to be indorsed thereon a notice stating–

    (a) that the person whose name and address is specified in the notice (being the person named as the holder of the debenture or certificate in the certificate of identification produced under paragraph (2)) has been recorded in the Registry as the holder of the debenture or debenture stock certificate, as the case may be, and

    (b)   that that person will, on producing the debenture or debenture stock certificate, as the case may be, be entitled to receive payment of any dividend in respect of that debenture or stock unless before payment a new holder proves his title in accordance with paragraph (2), and

    (c)   that if a new holder neglects to prove his title as aforesaid he may incur additional delay, trouble and expense in obtaining payment.

    **(4)**   The solicitor of the plaintiff in the action must preserve any certificates of identification produced under paragraph (2) and must keep a record of the debentures and debenture stock certificates so produced and of the names and addresses of the persons producing them and of the holders thereof, and, if the Court requires it, must verify the record by affidavit.

**6.   Requirements in connection with payments** (O. 87 r. 6)

    **(1)**   Where in an action to enforce any debentures or debenture stock an order is made for payment in respect of the debentures or stock, the Registrar shall not make a payment in respect of any such debenture or stock unless either there is produced to him the certificate for which paragraph (2) provides or the Court has in the case in question for special reason dispensed with the need for the certificate and directed payment to be made without it.

    **(2)**   For the purpose of obtaining any such payment the debenture or debenture stock certificate must be produced to the solicitor of the plaintiff in the action or to such other person as the Court may direct, and that solicitor or other person must indorse thereon a memorandum of payment and must make and sign a certificate certifying that the statement set out in the certificate has been indorsed on the debenture or debenture stock certificate, as the case may be, and send the certificate to the Registrar.

**(Enacted 1988)**

## ORDER 88

### MORGAGE ACTIONS

1. **Application and interpretation** (O. 88 r. 1)

(1) **This Order applies to any action (whether begun by writ or originating summons) by a mortgagee or mortgagor or by any person having the right to foreclose or redeem any mortgage, being an action (other than an action to which rule 5A applies) in which there is a claim for any of the following reliefs, namely–**

(a) **payment of moneys secured by the mortgage,**

(b) **sale of the mortgaged property,**

(c) **foreclosure,**

(d) **delivery of possession (whether before or after foreclosure or without foreclosure) to the mortgagee by the mortgagor or by any other person who is or is alleged to be in possession of the property,**

(e) **redemption,**

(f) **reconveyance of the property or its release from the security,**

(g) **delivery of possession by the mortgagee.**

(2) **In this Order "mortgage" includes a legal and an equitable mortgage and a legal and an equitable charge, and references to a mortgagor, a mortgagee and mortgaged property shall be construed accordingly.**

(3) **An action to which this Order applies is referred to in this Order as a mortgage action.**

(4) **These rules apply to mortgage actions subject to the following provisions of this Order.**

---

## NOTES

### [88.1.1] Scope of Order 88

Although rule 1 applies to 'mortgage actions', defined in that rule by reference to seven specific forms of relief, the most usual claims are for (1) payment of moneys secured by the mortgage (rule 1(1)(a)), and (2) delivery of possession (rule 1(1)(d): *Hua Chiao Commercial Bank Ltd v Yang Hsiang Yang & Anor* HCMP 3816/1992 (Le Pichon J; 24.11.1995). In some cases an additional claim is made for the sale of the mortgaged property (rule 1(1)(b)) to perfect the mortgagee's remedies: *Startford Ltd v Lam Mui Fong* HCMP 91/1995 (Yam J; 08.12.1995). Most actions will also include a claim for costs. The basis on which costs are claimed should be disclosed: for example, whether costs are claimed under the usual statutory and common law rules (as to which see Order 62) or under a specific term in the mortgage agreement.

The type of remedies provided by several of the forms of relief, listed in this Order, is usually available without the need for court proceedings. These remedies are usually available to the mortgagee by virtue of express or implied powers under the mortgage, or as implied into the mortgage by the terms of section 51 of the Conveyancing and Property Ordinance (Cap 219) ('CPO'): see, however, section 51(3) and (5). In general, the remedies provided by the CPO are enforceable by a mortgagee in respect of a mortgage executed after November 1984. The two more important and effective mortgagee's powers are those of the taking of possession and the sale of the land: see sections 44 to 56A and Fourth Schedule, CPO. Section 51 also empowers the mortgagee to appoint a receiver to exercise these remedies on its behalf, but as agent of the mortgagor. Neither remedy requires the leave of the court if these powers can be exercised lawfully and effectively by the mortgagee: *Guang Xin Enterprises Ltd v Leung Kwai Mui* [1996] 4 HKC 572. In exercising these remedies, due observance must be paid to the terms of the mortgage and the common law: *Parker-Tweedale v Dunbar Bank plc* [1991] 1 Ch 23; *China and South Sea Bank Ltd v Tan Soon Gin* [1989] 1 HKC 155; [1990] 2 WLR 56. But if the mortgagee sells to himself, his agent or trustee, then the sale is not valid. Only the court, under this Order, can grant leave for the mortgagee to bid at an auction of the mortgaged land: *Tang Ying Ki & Ors v Maxtime Transportation Ltd* [1996] 3 HKC 257.

The consequence of the availability of remedies given to the mortgagee by the mortgage or the CPO is that most sales of mortgaged property, and the taking of physical possession, are exercised outside the operation of Order 88.

Where the mortgagee does enforce the remedies against the security then it must observe the procedure set out in this Order. Application can be way of originating summons supported by an affidavit or affirmation, or by writ. The mortgagor is entitled to appear and be heard, and to oppose the application on admissible ground. Alternatively the mortgagor may apply to redeem the security, with a right of appeal as a substantive right. The rights, title and interest of the mortgagor in the land cannot be extinguished except in accordance with the procedure set out in this Order, and only after the mortgagor has exhausted his substantive rights of appeal. This reflects a fundamental rule of natural justice: *audi alteram partem*. One consequence is that when payment is being sought from the mortgagor, he must be given details of the exact amount said to be owing.

In considering the operation of this Order, it should be noted that there are specific differences between the terms of the Hong Kong Order, and the equivalent in England, in particular rules 2 and 3 of the English rules are not found in the Hong Kong rules.

**[88.1.2]  Comparison with the English rules**
There are numerous differences between Order 88 of the Hong Kong rules and its counterpart in the former English RSC.

(a)   the insertion, in Hong Kong, of the words '(other than an action to which rule 5A applies)' in rule 1(1);

(b)   the absence of rule 2 and rule 3 from the Hong Kong rules. In England rule 2 provides that mortgage actions shall be assigned to the Chancery Division, and rule 3 deals with district registries;

(c)   rule 4(3) has been repealed in the English rules, and a consequent removal of the latter part of rule 4(4) has also been removed from those rules. The repeal was effected in 1990.

(d)   the words '(other than an action to which rule 5A applies)' are included in the English rule 5(1);

(e)   the English rule 5(2) includes specific reference to a charge;

(f)   the English rule 5(2A) is not included in the Hong Kong rules;

(g)   the English rules 5(4) and (6) are more extensive than the Hong Kong rules; and

(h)   rule 5A contains some inconsequential differences from the English rule.

### [88.1.3]   Rule 1 – jurisdiction

By virtue of rule 1, Order 88 applies to any action for any of the types of relief listed in rule 1(1) paras (a) to (g), other than an action for the enforcement of a charging order by sale. Actions for the enforcement of charging orders by sale are governed by Order 88 rule 5A, which appears to be self-contained. Proceedings under this Order are normally brought in the Court of First Instance but the District Court also has a limited jurisdiction: see, for example section 37(1)(c) of the District Court Ordinance (Cap 336) which confers on that court jurisdiction in foreclosure and redemption of mortgages where the amount owing does not exceed HK$1,000,000.

The Order 88 procedure is not limited to enforcement of deeds, but extends to actions to enforce claims for personal debt secured by mortgage: see *Wing Hang Bank Ltd v Kit Choy Development Ltd & Anor* [2005] 3 HKC 312, 315I-316H (CA).

A mortgage action properly brought under Order 88 may extend to claiming other types of relief, such as relief against the guarantor of the mortgage: *Hang Seng Bank Ltd v Perfecta Dyeing Works Ltd & Ors* HCMP 1375/2008 (Deputy Judge L Chan; 13.02.2009) (para 39).

Pursuant to the terms of section 15 of the Legal Aid Ordinance (Cap 91) there will be an automatic stay of proceedings where an application for legal aid has been filed or legal aid is discharged; that stay may be lifted by the court: *Lee Shiu Ming v Yeo Hiap Seng (Hong Kong) Ltd* [1994] 1 HKC 18.

### [88.1.4]   Hearing before master in chambers

Mortgage actions commenced by originating summons under Order 88 are normally listed for initial hearing before a master in chambers. In 'Jurisdiction and Authority of Masters in Mortgage Proceedings under Order 88' (Hong Kong Lawyer, April 2002, 77) Mark Bradley expressed the view that on hearing such a summons the master has three choices:

(1)   to determine the matter summarily on the affidavit evidence if there is no appearance by the defendant;

(2)   to determine the matter summarily on the affidavit evidence in a manner similar to the Order 14 summary judgment procedure; or

(3)   if serious issues of fact emerge from the affidavit evidence, incapable of being resolved without oral testimony, to refer the matter to a judge to be heard in open court.

Mr Bradley's view as to summary determination of an Order 88 originating summons in chambers is supported by the judgment of Ma J in *Wing Hang Bank Ltd v Liu Kam Ying & Ors* [2002] 2 HKC 57, 60A–C, citing with approval *International Bank of Asia Ltd v Kewpaisal Warranuch* HCMP 1421/1998 (Yuen J; 04.03.1999).

### [88.1.5]   Burden of proof in summary proceedings

On an application under Order 88 for summary determination of a mortgage action the burden is on the plaintiff rather than on the defendant. In this respect the procedure under Order 88 differs from that under Order 14: *Wing Hang Bank Ltd v Liu Kam Ying & Ors* [2002] 2 HKC 57, 60A–C, citing *International Bank of Asia Ltd v Kewpaisal Warranuch* HCMP 1421/1998(Yuen J; 04.03.1999). In the *Wing Hang Bank* case Ma J said, at 60 H–I:

> Unlike O 14 applications where the defendant is obliged to provide sufficient grounds to justify the action continuing to trial, the burden in summary judgment applications under the originating summons procedure is on the plaintiff to justify its entitlement to summary judgment. However, once this is *prima facie* demonstrated on the evidence, it is then up to the defendant to show that he does have a defence or defences to the claim.

**[88.1.6]   Mortgage action after repayment of the debt**
In *China State Bank Ltd v Goboway Investment Ltd* [2002] 1 HKC 566 it was held that where after a mortgage action had been commenced the debt ceased to be secured, it was no longer a mortgage action and the master had no jurisdiction to enter final judgment under this Order. The matter had to be referred to a judge for trial in open court under Order 28 rule 9. The court found support in the English case of *Newnham v Brown* [1966] 1 WLR 875.

In the *China State Bank* case Deputy Judge Longley went on to refer to Order 28 rule 9 and said that save in exceptional cases an originating summons should be set down for substantive hearing in open court before a judge. Mr Bradley, in the article referred to above, expressed the view that this aspect of the judgment in the *China State Bank* case was *obiter* and that in the absence of issues of fact the master continues to have jurisdiction to give final judgment in mortgagee actions under Order 88.

**[88.1.7]   Bankruptcy proceedings not appropriate while contested mortgagee action pending**
A bankruptcy order should not be made in favour of a mortgagee when a contested mortgagee action is pending. See *Re Lam Lam* [2003] 2 HKC 293 (CA). In that case, the Court of Appeal set aside a bankruptcy order made in favour of a mortgagee where there was also a contested mortgagee action which was nearing readiness for trial. Rogers VP said, at 296B, that bankruptcy petitions 'are not proceedings in which complicated questions of fact or law should be decided'.

**[88.1.8]   Originating process – writ or originating summons**
A mortgage action can be commenced either by originating summons or by writ: Order 5 rule 4(1); Order 88 rule 1(1). The choice of originating process is up to the plaintiff. The factors set out in Order 5 rule 4(2) are relevant in deciding which originating process to use: *Chase Manhattan Bank v Sybella Ltd* HCMP 2159/1999 (Chung J; 26.10.1999). Where there is unlikely to be any substantial dispute of fact, an originating summons is appropriate. If later issues of fact emerge, the court may order that the action continue as if begun by writ and that any affidavits shall stand as pleadings: Order 28 rules 4(5) and 8(1).

Mortgage actions which are not disposed of summarily by a master in chambers (see above) will normally be heard by a judge in chambers whether commenced by originating summons or writ. See the commentary under Order 28 rule 9.

## [88.1.9]   Rule 1(2) – meaning of 'mortgage' and similar terms

Rule 1(2) defines the term 'mortgage' for the purpose of Order 88 broadly, so as to include legal and equitable mortgages and charges. It goes on to extend the same broad definition to consequent terms such as 'mortgagor' and 'mortgagee'. It should be noted that since 1 November 1984 a legal mortgage over land takes the form of a charge by way of deed, although the incidents of this charge correspond to those of the traditional mortgage: section 44, CPO. The terminology used in the CPO is somewhat confusing in that it intermingles the words 'charge' and 'mortgage'. For the purpose of Order 88, the definition contained under rule 1(2) should be noted.

'Mortgage', as defined in this rule, would also include those mortgages not entered into by the parties as consensual transactions. As a result this Order would apply for appropriate relief in respect of a charge over land imposed by the court as the appropriate form of relief in respect of a constructive trust: *Hui Mei v Cheng Yau Shing* [1996] 4 HKC 145. Further, the charge over land created by the manager of a multi-storey building pursuant to powers given by the Deed of Mutual Covenant where the chargor has not executed the charge document would also come within this Order: *Incorporated Owners of Kingsford Industrial Centre v Austria Property Management* [1997] 3 HKC 753; *Beacon Heights (Management) Ltd v Leung Ping Hung, Antonio* [1995] 1 HKLR 181. However, this Order does not apply to a quasi-security, such as that found in *Cheung Bing Sum Juana v Lee Leo* [1996] 4 HKC 130 where there were two transactions, one a contract of loan and one a sale and purchase agreement by the borrower as vendor in favour of the lender as purchaser. This is because the sale and purchase agreement provided the remedy against the land for default under the loan. As such the transaction did not function as a mortgage over the land.

If the plaintiff is seeking recovery of money lent, by way of action on the debt, this Order does not apply because the action is personal against the defendant. However, if the plaintiff brings action under the mortgage as collateral security for the loan, then this Order applies because the proceedings are against the land: *National Westminster Bank v Kitch* [1996] 1 WLR 1316 (CA); *Ryan v O'Sullivan* [1956] VLR 99; *The National Bank of Tasmania Ltd (in liq) v McKenzie* [1920] VLR 411; *Common Luck Investment Ltd v Cheung Kam Chuen* [1999] 2 HKC 719.

In *Daiwa Bank v Shum Shek Chiu & Anor* [2005] 1 HKC 243, 250A-F it was held that proceedings under Order 88 were competent against a party who alleged to be only a guarantor, but had executed a legal charge as principal debtor. In the circumstances the *National Westminster Bank* case (above) was distinguishable.

*Order 14 inapplicable* – One consequence of the fact that the action is a 'mortgage' action under this Order, is that Order 14 does not apply: *Overseas Trust Bank v Aik San Realty Ltd* [1985] 2 HKC 551. It was there held that Order 88 applies to those actions undertaken by a mortgagee, *qua* mortgagee, with a right to foreclose or redeem, suing as a mortgagee and relying on the mortgage to enforce his rights.

*Subsequent mortgagees* – An action under Order 88 can be undertaken by a first or subsequent mortgagee subject to the rights of the first mortgagee to whom notice of the proceedings under this Order must be given: *Startford Ltd v Lam Mui Fong* HCMP 91/1995 (Yam J; 08.12.1995).

*Invalid or unenforceable mortgages* – The validity and enforceability of the mortgage will be relevant. For example, in *Startford*, the mortgagor raised defences of *non est factum*, misrepresentation and illegality; although in the opinion of the court, none of these had been made out: see also *Hua Chiao Commercial Bank Ltd v Yang Hsiang Yang & Anor* HCMP 3816/1992 (Le Pichon J; 24.11.1995). When such defences are raised it may be appropriate for the action to be proceeded with as if it had been commenced by writ. The mortgagor may claim that the mortgage is unenforceable because he is a third party to the loan transaction, although he has mortgaged his land to secure the repayment for the loan made to the debtor. It is in this type of transaction that questions of vitiating factors, such as undue influence, may be relied upon to render the mortgage unenforceable: *Barclays Bank plc v O'Brien* [1993] 4 All ER 417 (HL): cf *Dunbar Bank v Nadeem* [1997] 1 All ER 253.

### [88.1.10]    What debts may be claimed by way of mortgage action?

There is a distinction between a debt and the money secured by a mortgage.

'Debt' connotes a contractual liability incurred by the debtor in favour of the creditor for the repayment of a sum of money, and in certain cases the payment also of interest: *Castling v Aubect* (1802) 2 East 325; *Esso v Marden* [1975] 3 All ER 558. The creditor may recover the money due by way of a simple action in debt where a liquidated sum is being sought.

Where the debtor is also bound by a collateral contract of security, then the creditor can take action on the debt, or under the contract as damages for breach of the contract, or as a personal action on the personal covenant to pay contained in the mortgage contract. No such action is a mortgage action for the purpose of this Order. To enforce its claim the creditor must obtain a judgment and proceed to enforce it in the usual way (see Order 45). If the judgment debtor owns or has an interest in land, then that land can be attached in execution by a charging order under Order 50, and Order 88 rule 5A provides for the enforcement of such an order against land owned by the debtor.

Action to recover money secured by a mortgage relates to that which enables the taking of an action, such as for possession or foreclosure, where there has been default in observance of the terms of the mortgage. The mortgage contract is a collateral contract under which the debt obligation is subsumed into the contract of security by which the land of the debtor is secured for repayment of the loan: *Goss v Chilcott* [1997] 2 All ER 110. As a collateral contract, the mortgage acts to enable the mortgagor's land to be burdened with due performance of the mortgagor's obligations, and on default of these obligations for action such as that referred to in this rule to be taken against the land.

### [88.1.11]    Limitation considerations

Under the Limitation Ordinance (Cap 347) there are different limitation periods for actions in debt and mortgage actions: see *Barnes & Anor v Glenton & Ors* [1899] 1 QB 885. An action in simple debt will normally be governed by the six-year limitation period for actions in contract and tort as stipulated by section 4 of the Ordinance, whereas the period is 20 years for actions to recover money secured by a mortgage (see section 19 of the Limitation Ordinance and note that the 20-year period has been reduced to 12 years for causes of action arising after the commencement of the

Limitation (Amendment) Ordinance 1991 on 1 July 1991). In each case, when the limitation period has expired, the defendant has an accrued right to plead a time bar, though the underlying cause of action does not necessarily extinguish.

In recent years, the question of the barring of time in respect of several mortgages in the New Territories has been considered in the context of title defects. In these cases the mortgages were entered into and, generally, the last payments were made decades previously. As no further demands for payment had been made within the intervening 20 or more so years, the courts declared that the mortgagee's rights to relief for non-payment had been barred. The typical judgment then decided that the mortgagee would no longer

> be able to maintain an action to recover the principal sum secured by the mortgage, nor maintain any foreclosure action nor any claim to interest by reason of s 19(1), (2) and (5) of the Limitation Ordinance (Cap 347) – see (*Broada Ltd v Chow Cheuk Yin* [1997] 3 HKC 168, per Le Pichon J at 169).

This would mean that action under Order 88 would not be available to the mortgagee to seek any of the forms of relief therein detailed: *Fung Kam Cheung & Ors v Kwok Yiu Wing & Ors* [1991] 1 HKC 321; *Cheng Tin Loi & Anor v Li Yung Hing & Anor* [1999] 3 HKC 699.

**[88.1.12]  Rule 1(1)(c) – foreclosure**
An order for foreclosure results in the mortgagee becoming the owner of the mortgaged land absolutely (as against the mortgagor): for a discussion on foreclosure see *Yarrangah Pty Ltd v National Australia Bank Ltd* [1999] NSWSC 97. It involves the destruction of the mortgagor's 'equity of redemption', and the discharge of the personal covenant to pay. As a consequence the mortgagor cannot thereafter recover the land unless, in rare cases, the foreclosure is reopened.

*Reopening of foreclosure order* – In appropriate circumstances a foreclosure order absolute can be set aside to permit the mortgagor to redeem. One factor permitting the mortgagor to apply to reopen the foreclosure is where the mortgagee seeks recovery of any outstanding liability under the personal covenant to pay. By pursuing the covenant to pay, the mortgagee can be said to be treating the mortgage as still subsisting, hence giving the mortgagor the opportunity to reopen, redeem the mortgage and thereby recover possession. Even if the mortgagor is not in a position to redeem, it may still be possible to reopen the foreclosure order and seek an appropriate remedy on the basis of fraud on the part of the mortgagee. Factors to be considered in this application include the promptness in which the application is made, the nature of the property as regards its commercial value or any particular value associated with the identity of the mortgagor: *Campbell v Holyland* (1877) 7 Ch D 166; *Hang Seng Bank Ltd v Mee Cheong Investment Co Ltd* [1970] HKLR 94: note in particular *Frencher Ltd (in liq) & Anor v The Bank of East Asia Ltd* [1995] 2 HKC 263 where the application to reopen the foreclosure order absolute was refused. Apart from the mortgagor, the right to reopen the order absolute for foreclosure is also given to those with an interest in the equity of redemption: *Gee v Liddell* [1913] 2 Ch 62; *Francis v Harrison* (1880) 43 Ch D 183. The court may be moved to reopen the foreclosure by the presence of the matters referred to in *Hang Seng Bank Ltd v Mee Cheong Investment Co Ltd* [1970] HKLR 94. One such matter may be the sale of the land by the mortgagee between the time of the foreclosure *nisi* and absolute: *Hang Seng Bank Ltd v Yeung Sau-min* [1986] HKLR 273.

*Cross-reference to CPO* – Under the CPO a legal mortgage over land takes effect as a legal charge, that is a hypothecation under which the land is designated as that which can be seized on default. The charge is only an encumbrance against title. Hence, in any successful action for foreclosure of land subject to a legal charge, it is necessary that regard be had to section 53(2) of the CPO which provides that the order absolute for foreclosure will operate to assign the mortgagor's estate to the mortgagee, unless the order otherwise provides.

### [88.1.13]    Rule 1(1)(d) – delivery of possession to the mortgagee
Subject to contrary intention, section 50 of the CPO empowers the mortgagee, on default of payment, to appoint a receiver to exercise the powers set out in the Fourth Schedule including that in paragraph 2 which enable the receiver to 'take possession of the mortgaged land and, for that purpose, to take any legal proceedings'. The exercise of these powers is subject to paragraph 11 of that schedule. Where the mortgagee or the receiver is able to take physical possession personally, or to take possession by receipt of rent and profits from a lawful tenant, there will be no need to bring a mortgage action under this order: *Standard Chartered Bank v Grow Up Trading Ltd & Ors* [1999] 3 HKC 530.

The action for relief under this order is an action for possession of mortgaged land: cf Order 113 used, for example, where the owner wishes to recover possession against a squatter, *Wu Koon Tai & Anor v Wu Yau Lio* [1996] 3 HKC 559.

Unless the mortgage provides otherwise, and this would need to be a clear, express provision to the contrary, the mortgagee has a right to take possession on default of payment of the principal sum; in addition, the mortgage may extend this right to other cases of default under the mortgage. As the right arises on default of payment, the mortgagor would find it difficult to establish a defence against the mortgagee taking possession, either personally or through a receiver. But where for some reason, and in particular where the mortgagee wishes to sell the land, there are problems in physically taking possession or obtaining the rents and profits, the mortgagee can apply under this order for possession. Similarly, there would be no practical defence to the court ordering possession if the mortgagee is able to make out its case.

In England, section 36 of the Administration of Justice Act 1970 empowers the court to stay or suspend the order for possession where it is likely that the mortgagor will be able to pay off the mortgage debt within a reasonable time: *Birmingham Citizens Permanent Building Society v Caunt & Anor* [1962] 1 All ER 163; *Halifax Building Society v Clark & Anor* [1973] 2 All ER 33. The English courts consider that this statutory power only operates where the mortgagee is seeking an order for possession under the equivalent of this order; so in *Ropaigealach v Barclays Bank plc* [1998] 3 WLR 17 the English Court of Appeal declined to order a stay, or to suspend the mortgagee's right to possession, where the mortgagee had taken possession under the mortgage contract without the assistance of the court under this order.

Section 36 does not apply in Hong Kong: see *Chekiang First Bank Ltd v Ko Hoi Luen & Anor* [1999] 3 HKLRD 360 where Keith J held that the master had been in error in adjourning the hearing to give time to pay. It was not clear whether this had been time to pay the whole of the outstanding amount and interest within a short time, or merely the arrears of principal and interest. However, his Lordship added:

> [the master] was only entitled to adjourn the hearing to enable the defendants to pay off the whole of the outstanding amount due under the charge plus interest, and even then only if the Defendants had demonstrated that they could do that in a short time (at 362).

The order made by the court was indicative that because there was no evidence that the mortgagors could have paid the outstanding principal and interest, it was proper to make an order for possession. But an order was made also that:

> An order for the redelivery-up by the Bank to the Defendants of vacant possession of the premises in the event of the Defendants paying to the Bank all the sums secured by the legal charge, though that order for redelivery-up is subject and without prejudice to the due exercise by the Bank of the power of sale for the time being vested in it (at 363).

Thus the mortgagee was entitled to the order for delivery-up of possession, and if the mortgagors were able to pay between the time of possession and sale, they could recover the land.

The operation of section 36 of the UK Act, within the court's discretion, would prevent the carrying out of the order, pending payment within a time set by the court. The effect in England would be different in that not only would possession not have to be delivered to the mortgagee during the time of suspension or stay, but the mortgagee would not be in a position to sell with vacant possession. The position in Hong Kong would be that part of the order in the *Ko Hoi Luen* case set out above.

*Claim for possession by subsequent mortgagee* – A second mortgagee is able to obtain possession under this Order subject to the rights of the first mortgagee. Prior notice to the first mortgagee is required : *Startford Ltd v Lam Mui Fong* HCMP 91/1995 (Yam J; 08.12.1995).

*Possession as against tenants* – Where the mortgagor has entered into a tenancy agreement contrary to the terms of the mortgage contract without the leave of the mortgagee, then the mortgagee is not bound by that tenancy and will not be disentitled from seeking possession merely because of the existence of the tenancy. In *Po Sang Bank Ltd v Luxton Development Ltd & Ors* [2000] 3 HKLRD 231, this general principle was adopted where there was no estoppel against, or waiver on the part of, the mortgagee, with the result that the mortgagee was entitled to possession as against the tenants holding from the mortgagor. See also *Taylor v Ellis & Anor* [1960] Ch 368. However, where the land is subject to a tenancy to which the mortgagee has consented, or which is in existence at the time the mortgage is effected, then the mortgagee will only be entitled to physical possession if that tenancy has been properly terminated; until then the mortgagee will be entitled to the rents and profits. Note that unlike other claims for possession, it is not required in a mortgage action to give notice to occupants and obtain leave to issue a writ of possession: see Order 45 rule 3.

*Possession as against lien holders* – In *The Commercial Bank of Hong Kong Ltd v Wellstandard Textiles Co Ltd & Anor* HCMP 3785/1991 (Jones J; 31.05.1993), the party in possession claimed to hold under a lien, as the unpaid vendor of the property in a sale to the mortgagor; he also claimed that the mortgagee had had notice of the lien at the time of entry into the mortgage. However, the mortgagee was held to be a bona fide mortgagee without knowledge of the occupier's lien, and that 'mere speculation' that the mortgagee had had knowledge was insufficient to deny the bona fide without notice status to the mortgagee. Hence, the mortgagee was successful in the action for possession.

### [88.1.14]   Comparison with English rules

Rules 2 and 3 have been omitted in Hong Kong. Their English counterparts (pre-CPR) deal with administrative matters which are not applicable in Hong Kong: in England rule 2 provides that mortgage actions shall be assigned to the Chancery division, and rule 3 deals with district registries.

**4.   Claim for possession: failure by a defendant to acknowledge service (O. 88 r. 4)**

**(1)   Where in a mortgage action begun by originating summons, being an action in which the plaintiff is the mortgagee and claims delivery of possession or payment of moneys secured by the mortgage or both, any defendant fails to acknowledge service of the originating summons, the following provisions of this rule shall apply, and references in those provisions to the defendant shall be construed as references to any such defendant.**

**This rule shall not be taken as affecting Order 28, rule 3, or rule 5(2), in so far as it requires any document to be served on, or notice given to, a defendant who has acknowledged service of the originating summons in the action.**

**(2)   Not less than 4 clear days before the day fixed for the first hearing of the originating summons the plaintiff must serve on the defendant a notice of appointment for the hearing and a copy of the affidavit in support of the summons.**

**(3)   Where the plaintiff claims delivery of possession there must be indorsed on the outside fold of the copy of the affidavit served on the defendant a notice informing the defendant that the plaintiff intends at the hearing to apply for an order to the defendant to deliver up to the plaintiff possession of the mortgaged property and for such other relief (if any) claimed by the originating summons as the plaintiff intends to apply for at the hearing.**

**(4)   Where the hearing is adjourned, then, subject to any directions given by the Court, the plaintiff must serve notice of the appointment for the adjourned hearing, together with a copy of any further affidavit intended to be used at that hearing, on the defendant not less than 2 clear days before the day fixed for the hearing.**

**A copy of any affidavit served under this paragraph must be indorsed in accordance with paragraph (3).**

**(5)   Service under paragraph (2) or (4), and the manner in which it was effected, may be proved by a certificate signed by the plaintiff, if he sues in person, and otherwise by his solicitor.**

**The certificate may be indorsed on the affidavit in support of the summons or, as the case may be, on any further affidavit intended to be used at an adjourned hearing.**

**(6)   A copy of any exhibit to an affidavit need not accompany the copy of the affidavit served under paragraph (2) or (4).**

(7)  Where the plaintiff gives notice to the defendant under Order 3, rule 6, of his intention to proceed, service of the notice, and the manner in which it was effected, may be proved by a certificate signed as mentioned in paragraph (5).

---

NOTES

**[88.4.1]   Rule 4 – failure to acknowledge service of originating summons**
The provisions of rule 4 apply to actions for possession, or for the payment of money secured by the mortgage, or both.

The rule applies where the defendant has failed to acknowledge service of the originating summons or writ. Despite this failure on the defendant's part, the plaintiff is required to serve, on the defendant, any subsequent document, such as notice of appointment for hearing (Order 28 rule 3(3)), and copies of all affidavits in support of the sum being claimed (Order 88 rule 4(2)). If there has been no acknowledgment of service filed within 14 days, the plaintiff can make an appointment for hearing of the action, and must then 'not less than 4 clear days before the day fixed for the first hearing' serve notice of the hearing.

See Order 10 and the commentary thereunder for the law governing service of process and see also Order 65 as to service on companies. Of particular note is Order 10 rule 4 which provides specifically for service in actions for the possession of land: by virtue of Order 10 rule 4(2) a copy of the originating summons or writ must be posted in a 'conspicuous place on or at the entrance to the premises or land'. Note Order 10 rule 5 also. Unless there has been due service, no order or judgment will be made.

Observance of rule 4(2) and rule 5 of this order should be referred to in an affidavit of service.

Despite the defendant's failure to acknowledge service, rule 4 requires that notice of the appointment for hearing must be served on the defendant. This provides an example of where the general rule does not apply; Order 65 rule 9 provides that there is no need for service in such a case unless the court so directs or the rules so provide.

Service should be effected at the same address as that where the originating summons or the writ was served.

In interpreting the requirement of service of the notice 'not less than 4 clear days' there is a conflict between Order 3 rule 2 and section 71 of the Interpretation and General Clauses Ordinance (Cap 1), with the result that the latter prevails over rule 2 in cases of conflict: *Mohan v McElney* [1983] HKLR 308 (see I [461]). Section 71 provides that the calculation of the four clear days does not include:

(a)   the day of the hearing; the section and rule 2(3) are similar; or

(b)   any public holiday, gale warning day, or black rainstorm warning day, 'Black rainstorm warning day' and 'gale warning day' are defined in section 71(2) of Cap 1. There is no definition of 'public holiday' in this section. However, Order 3 rule 2(5) which provides similarly to section 71 does define a 'general holiday'. These days are excluded where the time is less than six days, however, Order 3 rule 2 applies a similar principle where the timing is less than seven days.

Rather than an affidavit or affirmation, a certificate of service and the manner it was effected by the plaintiff or where legally represented by his solicitor will be sufficient for the purposes of rule 4(2) and (4).

**[88.4.2]   Application to set aside default judgment under Order 88**
Where judgment is entered under Order 88 rule 4 in default of notice of intention to defend, and the respondent alleges service of process was irregular, the court will apply the principles applicable under Order 13: see *Liu Chong Hing Bank Ltd v Union World (HK) Ltd & Ors* [2005] 1 HKC 20 (CA).

**[88.4.3]   Rule 4(3) – indorsement as to application for possession**
Rule 4(3) requires that the copy of the affidavit or affirmation to be served on the defendant must be indorsed, on the outside fold, with the fact that the plaintiff intends to apply for an order for delivery-up of possession, and for any other claimed relief. When the hearing is adjourned and notice of this is served on the defendant, that notice too must contain the appropriate indorsement.

Where the defendant does not attend the hearing, and the court considers the indorsement to be defective, for example it does not contain sufficient information of the relief being sought, then the court may decide not to enter judgment.

**[88.4.4]   Rule 4(4) – adjournment of the hearing**
Rule 4(4) provides that where the hearing is adjourned, subject to directions of the court, the plaintiff must service notice of the appointment for the adjourned hearing, and any further affidavit or affirmation on the defendant not less than two clear days before the new date fixed for the hearing.

The adjournment of the hearing contrasts to the situation where the hearing has been completed and a stay or suspension of the order or judgment is sought by the defendant. There are only limited circumstances when this would be approved. One situation would be where the mortgagor has contracted to sell to a third party, and there is a binding sale and purchase agreement: *Barrett v Halifax Building Society* (1995) 28 HLR 634; *Cheltenham and Gloucester plc v Krausz* [1997] 1 All ER 21. Another would be where there is a possibility of the mortgagor paying the full amount due, then there is a restricted right to stay the execution of the order: *Chekiang First Bank Ltd v Ko Hoi Luen* [1999] 3 HKLRD 360.

**[88.4.5]   Comparison with English rule**
Paragraph (3) of this rule has no counterpart in England. The paragraph of that number was repealed in England in 1990.

**5.   Action for possession or payment: evidence** (O. 88 r. 5)
   **(1)   The affidavit in support of the originating summons by which an action to which this rule applies is begun must comply with the following provisions of this rule.**

   **This rule applies to a mortgage action begun by originating summons in which the plaintiff is the mortgagee and claims delivery of possession or payment of moneys secured by the mortgage or both.**

(2) **The affidavit must exhibit a true copy of the mortgage and the original mortgage must be produced at the hearing of the summons.**

(3) **Where the plaintiff claims delivery of possession the affidavit must show the circumstances under which the right to possession arises and except where the Court in any case or class of case otherwise directs, the state of the account between the mortgagor and mortgagee with particulars of–**

    (a) **the amount of the advance,**

    (b) **the amount of the periodic payments required to be made,**

    (c) **the amount of any interest or instalments in arrear at the date of the originating summons and at the date of the affidavit, and**

    (d) **the amount remaining due under the mortgage.**

(4) **Where the plaintiff claims delivery of possession, the affidavit must give particulars of every person who to the best of the plaintiff's knowledge is in possession of the mortgaged property.**

(5) **If the mortgage creates a tenancy other than a tenancy at will between the mortgagor and mortgagee, the affidavit must show how and when the tenancy was determined and if by service of notice when the notice was duly served.**

(6) **Where the plaintiff claims payment of moneys secured by the mortgage, the affidavit must prove that the money is due and payable and give the particulars mentioned in paragraph (3).**

(7) **Where the plaintiff's claim includes a claim for interest to judgment, the affidavit must state the amount of a day's interest.**

---

## NOTES

### [88.5.1]    Rule 5 – evidence

Rule 5 stipulates the evidence which must be filed in support of an action by way of originating summons where the plaintiff mortgagee seeks delivery-up of possession, or payment of the money secured by the mortgage, or both. Rule 5(1) to (5) apply where the plaintiff seeks delivery of possession. Rule 5(6) also applies where the claim relates to the recovery of money secured by the mortgage. Rule 5(7) applies where the plaintiff also claims interest to the date of judgment. Rule 5 refers to the evidence necessarily produced to enable the court to consider giving judgment or making any order.

The affidavit or affirmation, which must be filed in support of the originating summons, must comply with the requirements of this rule and Order 41 as appropriate.

The first requirement is that a true copy of the mortgage must be exhibited to the affidavit or affirmation, and that the original mortgage must be produced at the hearing. Further, a copy of any material documents containing terms of the mortgage, which are not included in the actual mortgage, must also be exhibited to the affidavit or affirmation, and the originals must be produced at the hearing. In *Cheang Kwok Sam v Chui Kin Wing & Anor* [1995] 1 HKC 637, the security transaction was found to comprise an oral contract of loan together with a formal sale and purchase agreement under which the vendor (the borrower) agreed to sell the land to the purchaser (the lender) on default of repayment by the borrower. This transaction was treated as an equitable mortgage because:

the equity of redemption could be separately agreed and [did not have] to be contained in some [written] instrument as the transfer of a property to a mortgagee (per Nazareth VP at 642).

The sale and purchase agreement would have been such a document or instrument a copy of which is required to be exhibited, and the original required to be produced under this order.

Documents coming under this rule may also include those where the mortgagor whose land is made security for the loan is not the party who has received the loan money: *Goss v Chilcott* [1997] 2 All ER 110. This would be a case in which, although the action is commenced by originating summons, yet because of the presence of arguable law or facts, the action should be conducted as if it had been begun by writ.

The affidavit or affirmation must comply with Order 41, especially rule 5(1), which provides that it must contain 'only such facts as the deponent is able of his own knowledge to prove'. The affidavit or affirmation must not contain legal arguments or submissions. The plaintiff's solicitor should not be a deponent of facts which are not within his or her personal knowledge. Hence, the deponent must be the person with first-hand knowledge, such as a bank officer where the plaintiff is the lending bank.

The affidavit or affirmation must contain information on the circumstances in which the right to possession arises. The mortgage can authorise, expressly or impliedly, the mortgagee to take physical possession, or enter into the receipt of the rents and profits on default by the mortgagor: sections 44(2) and 51 of the CPO. This right is exercisable not only on default of repayment or of payment of interest but also where there has been breach of any other covenant in the mortgage. An express provision in the mortgage relating to 'events of default' will extend the power of the mortgagee in this regard.

The defendant is entitled to know, at least as of the date the originating summons is filed, the exact amount for which he is said to be liable, so that he is able to decide whether to pay or to contest the action. If the information is deficient, then the defendant is in a prejudicial position. Fairness requires that he know how much he owes. The affidavit or affirmation must also indicate the state of the account between the parties; it must contain details of matters such as:

(a)   The amount of the advance – If the advance is not a fixed sum but is linked to banking facilities, then all details of the amounts lent must be set out in the affidavit or affirmation. There may well be dispute between the parties resulting from clauses in the mortgage which provide for 'all monies', or 'all obligations': *Re Modular Design Group Pty Ltd* (1994) 35 NSWLR 96; *Re Rudd & Son* [1986] 2 BCC 989. These clauses can refer to sums, not advanced to the mortgagor as loan money. Yet the mortgage treats these sums as recoverable as 'money secured by a mortgage'. This will be so in respect of sums expended by the mortgagee, without the consent knowledge of the mortgagor, for expenses such as costs of litigation undertaken by the mortgagee to protect the secured property: *Bank of Scotland v Wright* [1991] BCLC 244; *Fountain v Bank of America National Trust & Savings Association* (1992) 5 PBR 97, at 401.

However, where the loan money has been paid to a third party, the mortgagee may give the mortgagor some allowance against the more severe terms of the mortgage on the basis that the mortgagor was unaware of these terms: *ANZ v Petrick* [1996] 2 VR 638. In any case the court may read down the clause so that the plaintiff will need to go to full trial, even if the action was begun by originating summons: *Re Bankrupt Estate of Murphy* (1996) 149 ALR 46.

(b) The amount of periodic payments required to be made – If the mortgage does not contain these details, that fact should be incorporated in the affidavit or affirmation. A mortgage to secure an overdraft facility usually will not be subject to pre-arranged periodic payments.

(c) The amount of instalments and/or interest in arrears – The amount due at the time of issue of the summons or writ may have been reduced by the time of the hearing. A supplemental affidavit or affirmation must then be filed to ensure that any order made by the court, at the hearing, will reflect the amount then due. Alternatively, after the hearing, application can be made to amend the sealed order; on default of such amendment the order can be set aside as irregular.

(d) The rate of interest charged – The rate of interest that can be charged may be uncertain, for example, where the mortgagee claims capitalised or compound interest. If the mortgage does not expressly or impliedly provide for compound interest, and the mortgage is not to secure a bank loan in a traditional form, then compound interest is probably not chargeable: *Westdeutsche Landesbank Girozentral v Islington LBC* [1996] 2 All ER 959. See also *BNP Paribas v Pang Kwai Ling* [2003] 1 HKC 20. In that case the mortgagee claimed compound interest by implication from banking practice, citing *National Bank of Greece SA v Pinios Shipping Co (No 1)* [1990] 1 AC 637. However there was no evidence of such a banking practice in Hong Kong and the court refused to order compound interest. Note that the contractual rate of interest does not apply in the post-judgment period unless the contract so provides, and the court so orders. Otherwise post judgment interest accrues at the judgment rate pursuant to statute.

The affidavit or affirmation should also contain:

(a) particulars of every person who, to the best of the plaintiff's knowledge, is in possession of the mortgaged property. Even if the interest of the person in possession does not bind the mortgagee, the affidavit or affirmation must contain details known to the plaintiff;

(b) proof that the money is due and payable. Where rule 5(6) applies so that the plaintiff is seeking possession as well as the payment of money due, then further information is required: rule 5(3);

(c) the amount due as daily interest where the plaintiff is claiming interest under rule 5(7). The principles on which this is calculated must be set out accurately otherwise a supplemental affidavit or affirmation must be filed;

(d) the amount remaining due under the mortgage; and

(e) particulars of any claim to costs – many mortgages give the mortgagor a contractual right to costs which may exceed the amount recoverable under the party and party basis (see commentary under Order 62). In such cases the court will usually make an order for costs in accordance with the contractual provision. In this connection see *Gomba Holdings Ltd v Minories Finance (No 2)* [1992] 4 All ER 588. In the absence of an express provision in the mortgage, costs on enforcement will be ordered to be taxed on the standard party to party basis: *Re Adelphi Hotel (Brighton) Ltd* [1953] 2 All ER 498.

Where the defendant disputes claimed costs and expenses, the best way is to proceed to taxation under Order 62: *Barclays Bank plc v Jeffrey* [1997] EWCA 4096.

**5A. Action for the enforcement of charging order by sale** (O. 88 r. 5A)
    **(1)   This rule applies to a mortgage action to enforce a charging order by sale of the property charged.**
    **(2)   The affidavit in support of the originating summons must–**
        **(a)  identify the charging sought to be enforced and the subject-matter of the charge;**
        **(b)  specify the amount in respect of which the charge was imposed and the balance outstanding at the date of the affidavit;**
        **(c)  verify, so far as is known, the debtor's title to the property charged;**
        **(d)  identify any other incumbrances on the property charged stating, so far as is known, the names and addresses of the incumbrancers and the amounts owing to them;**
        **(e)  set out the plaintiff's proposals as to the manner of sale of the property charged together with estimates of the gross price which would be obtained on a sale in that manner and of the costs of such sale;**
        **(f)  where the property charged consists of land in respect of which the plaintiff claims delivery of possession, give particulars of every person who to the best of the plaintiff's knowledge is in possession of the property charged or any part of it.**

## NOTES

**[88.5A.1]   Comparison with English rule**
Rule 5A in the Hong Kong rules differs from its English counterpart in the following ways:

(a)   the word 'charging' in paragraph (2)(a) of the Hong Kong rule reads 'charging order' in England; (this would appear to be the result of a mistake in the Hong Kong rules)

(b)   the word 'incumbrances' in paragraph (2)(d) of the Hong Kong rule reads 'incumbrancer' in England; and

(c)   paragraph (2)(f) of the Hong Kong rules omits an additional subparagraph which in England makes special provision for dwelling houses.

**[88.5A.2]   Rule 5A – enforcement of charging orders**
A charging order is an order made under Order 50, as provided for in sections 20, 20A and 20B of the High Court Ordinance. It is used to enforce a judgment debt against land owned by the debtor (see VI [2411]). The charging order functions as an equitable charge. It enables the sale of the land in satisfaction of the debt. An application for an order for sale to enforce a charging order should be brought by originating summons pursuant to this Order, and not in the original proceedings in which the charging order was made. See *Urban Property Management Ltd & Anor v*

*Tsang Wing Lam* DCMP 3128/2009 (Judge Poon; 20.10.2010). Rule 5A sets out the requirements for the affidavit in support of the originating summons.

See the commentary under Order 50 rule 9A for discussion of the court's power to appoint a person to convey title to a purchaser when it grants an order for sale pursuant to a charging order.

It should be noted that the charging order will be ineffective against the land if, at the time the order is made, the judgment debtor had already contracted to sell the land to a third party who was *bona fide* and who paid good consideration for the land. The purchaser will take priority over the creditor even if the purchaser has failed to register the contract; one reason against the creditor taking priority is that the creditor is not regarded as a *bona fide* purchaser for sale: section 3(2) of the Land Registration Ordinance (Cap 218); *Ng Kam-ha v Vincent Sina Traders (HK) Ltd* [1987] 2 HKC 517.

### [88.5A.3] Enforcement of charging order against co-owner

The court's power to order sale of property to enforce a charging order extends to partial interests: the court may order sale of the interest of a joint tenant or tenant-in-common. However as a matter of discretion the court will rarely make such an order: *Chan Ching Kit Katherine v Lam Sik Shi & Anor* HCMP 2239/2000 (Kwan J; 24.06.2002). It was there said that such a sale is 'often not practicable', apparently referring to the obvious difficulty in finding a buyer for a partial interest and the low price achievable.

In *Chan Ching Kit* the holder of a charging order against the half share of a tenant-in-common sought to use the Partition Ordinance in order to obtain an order for sale of the whole property. It was held that this could not be done. However, the court granted the alternative application for appointment of a receiver by way of equitable execution under Order 51 to receive the judgment debtor's share in the rent and profits of the property.

### 6. Action by writ: judgment in default (O. 88 r. 6)

**(1) Notwithstanding anything in Order 13 or Order 19, in a mortgage action begun by writ judgment on failure to give notice of intention to defend or in default of defence shall not be entered except with the leave of the Court.**

**(2) An application for the grant of leave under this rule must be made by summons and the summons must, notwithstanding anything in Order 65, rule 9, be served on the defendant.**

**(3) Where a summons for leave under this rule is issued, rule 4(2) to (7) shall apply in relation to the action subject to the modification that for references therein to the originating summons, and for the reference in paragraph (2) to the notice of appointment, there shall be substituted references to the summons.**

**(4) Where a summons for leave under this rule is issued in an action to which rule 5 would apply had the action been begun by originating summons, the affidavit in support of the summons must contain the information required by that rule.**

**NOTES**

**[88.6.1]    Rule 6 – default judgment on mortgage action by writ**
Rule 6 provides that where a mortgage action has been commenced by writ, it is not possible to obtain a judgment in default of notice of intention to defend or of a defence under the usual provisions of Order 13 and Order 19. As the White Book notes, this factor removes the advantages of commencing action by writ. This provision applies only to mortgage actions.

**7.    Foreclosure in redemption action** (O. 88 r. 7)
**Where foreclosure has taken place by reason of the failure of the plaintiff in a mortgage action for redemption to redeem, the defendant in whose favour the foreclosure has taken place may apply by summons for an order for delivery to him of possession of the mortgaged property, and the Court may make such order thereon as it thinks fit. (L.N. 152 of 2008)**

**(Enacted 1988)**

**NOTES**

**[88.7.1]    Rule 7 – possession on failure to redeem**
Where an order for foreclosure has been made, after the defendant has unsuccessfully sought redemption, rule 7 empowers the plaintiff to then apply by summons for an order for delivery-up of possession: *Frencher Ltd v Bank of East Asia Ltd* [1995] 2 HKC 263.

## ORDER 89

### PROCEEDINGS BETWEEN HUSBAND AND WIFE

**1. Determination of questions as to property** (O. 89 r. 1)

**(HK)(1)** Proceedings under section 6 of the Married Persons Status Ordinance (Cap 182) may be begun by originating summons. (L.N. 152 of 2008)

**2. Provisions as to actions in tort** (O. 89 r. 2)

(1) This rule applies to any action in tort brought by one of the parties to a marriage against the other during the subsistence of the marriage.

(2) On the first application by summons in an action to which this rule applies, the Court shall consider, if necessary of its own motion, whether the power to stay the action under section 5(2) of the Married Persons Status Ordinance (Cap 182) should or should not be exercised. (L.N. 152 of 2008)

(3) Notwithstanding anything in Order 13 or Order 19, judgment on failure to give notice of intention to defend or in default of defence shall not be entered in an action to which this rule applies except with the leave of the Court.

(4) An application for grant of leave under paragraph (3) must be made by summons and the summons must, notwithstanding anything in Order 65, rule 9, be served on the defendant.

(5) If the summons is for leave to enter judgment on failure to give notice of intention to defend, the summons shall not be issued before the time limited for acknowledging service of the writ.

**(Enacted 1988)**

## ORDER 90

### PROCEEDINGS CONCERNING MINORS

**3.  Application to make a minor a ward of court** (O. 90 r. 3)

(1)   Where an action to which a minor is a party is proceeding, an application to make that minor a ward of court may be made by summons in the action; in any other case an application to make a minor a ward of court may be made by originating summons.(L.N. 152 of 2008)

(2)   Where there is no person other than the minor who is a suitable defendant, an application may be made ex parte to the Registrar for leave to issue either an ex parte originating summons or an originating summons with the infant as defendant thereto; and, except where such leave is granted, the minor shall not be made a defendant to an originating summons under this rule in the first instance.

(3)   Particulars of any summons under this rule shall be recorded in the register of wards.

(3A)   The date of the minor's birth shall, unless otherwise directed, be stated in the summons and the plaintiff shall—

(a)   on issuing the summons or before or at the first hearing thereof lodge in the Registry a certified copy of the entry in the birth register book kept under the Births and Deaths Registration Ordinance (Cap 174) or, as the case may be, in the Adopted Children Register maintained under the Adoption Ordinance (Cap 290), relating to the minor, or

(b)   at the first hearing of the summons apply for directions as to proof of birth of the minor in some other manner.

(3B)   The name of each party to the proceedings shall be qualified by a brief description in the body of the summons, of his interest in, or relationship to, the minor.

(4)   Unless the Court otherwise directs, the summons shall state the whereabouts of the minor or, as the case may be, that the plaintiff is unaware of his whereabouts.

(5)   Every defendant other than the minor shall, forthwith after being served with the summons—

(a)   lodge in the Registry a notice stating the address of the defendant and the whereabouts of the minor or, as the case may be, that the defendant is unaware of his whereabouts, and

(b)   unless the Court otherwise directs, serve a copy of the notice on the plaintiff.

(6)   Where any party other than the minor changes his address or becomes aware of any change in the whereabouts of the minor after the issue of, as the case may be, service of the summons, he shall, unless the Court otherwise directs, forthwith lodge notice of the change in the Registry and serve a copy of the notice on every other party.

(7)   The summons shall contain a notice to the defendant informing him of the requirements of paragraphs (5) and (6).

**(8)    In this rule any reference to the whereabouts of a minor is a reference to the address at which and the person with whom he is living and any other information relevant to the question where he may be found.**

---

## NOTES

### [90.3.1]    Numbering
There is no rule 1 or rule 2 in Order 90.

### [90.3.2]    Wardship takes effect on issue of application – indorsement as to contempt
Section 26(2) of the High Court Ordinance provides that a child becomes a ward of court upon the making of a wardship application. The purpose is to preserve the *status quo* pending decision of the court. As a consequence it is a contempt to remove the child from Hong Kong without leave and it is provided in Practice Direction 23.1 that the application must be endorsed with notice to that effect. The practice direction goes on to provide for notice to the Director of Immigration in cases where there are grounds for fearing an unauthorised removal of a ward from the jurisdiction. The text of the practice direction can be viewed on the judiciary's website.

See Order 90 rule 4 as to when a child ceases to be a ward of court.

### [90.3.3]    Nature and extent of wardship
In the case of *In re Y (minors)* [1984] HKLR 204, 205 I-J Jackson-Lipkin J described the court's wardship jurisdiction as 'ancient', deriving from the role of the sovereign as *parens patriae*. He said the jurisdiction gives the wardship judge 'complete and absolute control' over matters such as care and control of the child, financial support, schooling and so forth. The paramount consideration in exercising the warship jurisdiction is the welfare of the child: *K v K* HCMP 700 /1995 (Seagroatt J:04.06.1996). However, the court's wardship jurisdiction cannot be used so as to over-ride the powers of the Director of Immigration to remove a non-resident from Hong Kong. See *In the matter of C ( a minor)* [1989] 2 HKLR 652 and *Mok Chi Hung & Anor v Director of Immigration* [2001] 1 HKC 281, 295F both citing *In re Mohamed Arif (an infant)* [1968] 1 Ch 643. It is an abuse of process to use the court's wardship jurisdiction to try to thwart the powers of the Director of Immigration: *Zuniga v Zuniga* HCMP 788/1994 (Kaplan J; 20.05.1994). The court will only exercise its wardship jurisdiction where there is an imminent or immediate need to afford protection for a child. It will not do so simply on the basis that there may be a need in the future: *M v Y & Anor* [2009] 6 HKC 360.

The jurisdiction can be exercised in order to obtain medical treatment for a child against the wishes of the parents, as in *Re C (a minor)* [1994] 1 HKLR 60.

### [90.3.4]    Parties
The parties to wardship proceedings are often the parents, having adverse interests after breakdown of their relationship. Order 90 rule 3(2) provides that wardship proceedings may be commenced *ex parte* where no defendant with adverse interests is readily identifiable. In some cases it may be considered necessary for the child to have separate representation and in such cases the Official Solicitor may be appointed:

see *Re M and P* (1982) 12 HKLJ 227, citing *Re S (infants)* [1967] 1 WLR 396. In *In the matter of C (a minor)* [1989] 2 HKLR 652 the court allowed the Attorney General to intervene in wardship proceedings to represent the Director of Immigration who opposed the application.

Unlike certain other types of applications in the family jurisdiction, leave is required to serve wardship proceedings out of the jurisdiction. See *Re S (a minor)* [1992] 2 HKLR 39.

**[90.3.5]   Procedure where there are concurrent divorce proceedings**
Where there are on-going proceedings under the Matrimonial Causes Ordinance as well as for wardship, the two should be dealt with together by the same judge so as to avoid any conflict. If the matrimonial proceedings are before the District Court they should be transferred to the High Court for the purpose. See *In re Y (minors)* [1984] HKLR 204, 206 E-I.

**[90.3.6]   Procedure at hearing**
It has been held that 'in wardship matters the court is essentially inquisitorial in its approach and not adversarial': *K v K* HCMP 700/1995 (Seagroatt J; 04.06.1996). However, in *D v G* [2002] 1 HKLRD 52 (CA), a child abduction case, the Court of Appeal was highly critical of a judge who undertook some inquiries on his own in the absence of the parties.

**[90.3.7]   Evidence on wardship application**
Hearsay evidence has historically been admissible in wardship proceedings in the High Court. The reason is that the welfare of the child is the paramount consideration rather than the rights of the parties. See *Re W (Children)* [2010] UKSC 12 (03.03.2010) (para 5). In that case the UK Supreme Court went on to consider the circumstances in which a child may be summoned to give evidence in any family proceedings.

**3A. Enforcement of order by bailiff** (O. 90 r. 3A)
**The power of the Court of First Instance to secure, through an officer attending upon the Court, compliance with any direction relating to a ward of court may be exercised by an order addressed to the bailiff.**

**4.   When minor ceases to be ward of court** (O. 90 r. 4)
**(1)   A minor who, by virtue of section 26(2) of the High Court Ordinance, becomes a ward of court on the issue of a summons under rule 3 shall cease to be a ward of court–**
      **(a)   if an application for an appointment for the hearing of the summons is not made within the period of 21 days after the issue of the summons, at the expiration of that period;**
      **(b)   if an application for such an appointment is made within that period, on the determination of the application made by the summons unless the judge hearing it orders that the minor be made a ward of court.**

**(2)** Nothing in paragraph (1) shall be taken as affecting the power of the Court under section 26(3) of the said Ordinance to order that any minor who is for the time being a ward of court shall cease to be a ward of court.

**(3)** If no application for an appointment for the hearing of a summons under rule 3 is made within the period of 21 days after the issue of the summons, a notice stating whether the applicant intends to proceed with the application made by the summons must be left at the Registry immediately after the expiration of that period.

## NOTES

**[90.4.1]  Numbering**
Order 90 rule 4B follows immediately after Order 90 rule 4, there being no rule 4A.

**4B. Hearing of an application to make a minor a ward of Court**
    (O. 90 r. 4B)
**(HK)**  An application to make a minor a ward of court may be disposed of in chambers and shall be heard by a judge.

**5.  Applications under the Guardianship of Minors Ordinance** (O. 90 r. 5)
Where there is pending any action or other proceeding by reason of which a minor is a ward of court, any application under the Guardianship of Minors Ordinance (Cap 13) with respect to that minor may be made by summons in the proceedings; and in any other case any such application may be made by originating summons. **(L.N. 152 of 2008)**

**6.  Defendants to summons** (O. 90 r. 6)
**(1)**  Where the minor with respect to whom an application under the Guardianship of Minors Ordinance (Cap 13) is made is not the plaintiff he shall not, unless the Court otherwise directs, be made a defendant to the summons or, if the application is made by ordinary summons, be served with the summons, but, subject to paragraph (2), any other person appearing to be interested in, or affected by, the application shall be made a defendant or be served with the summons, as the case may be.
**(2)**  The Court may dispense with service of the summons (whether originating or ordinary) on any person and may order it to be served on any person not originally served.

**7.  Hearing of applications as to guardianship, maintenance, etc.** (O. 90 r. 7)
**(1)**  Applications as to the guardianship of minors may be disposed of in chambers and shall be heard by a judge.
**(2)**  Applications as to the maintenance and advancement of any minor may be disposed of in chambers.

**8.  Verification and passing of guardians accounts** (O. 90 r. 8)
**(HK)**  A guardian's account must be verified and passed in the same manner as that provided by Order 30 in relation to a receiver's account or in such other manner as the Court may direct.

**10. Removal of guardianship proceedings from the District Court** (O. 90 r. 10)

(1)   An application for an order under section 24 of the Guardianship of Minors Ordinance (Cap 13) for the removal of an application from a District Court into the Court may be made by an originating summons and, unless the Court otherwise directs, the summons need not be served on any person. (L.N. 152 of 2008)

(2)   The application may be heard by a master, but, if an order is made for the removal to the Court of the application to the District Court, that application shall be heard by a judge.

(HK)(3A)   Section 44, subsections (1), (2) (except the proviso) and (4), of the District Court Ordinance (Cap 336) shall apply to an application ordered to be transferred to the Court under this rule.

(5)   The application so removed shall proceed in the Court as if it had been made by originating summons.

**11. Application of Matrimonial Causes Rules** (O. 90 r. 11)

(1)   The provisions of the Matrimonial Causes Rules (Cap 179 sub. leg.) relating to proceedings under section 48 of the Matrimonial Causes Ordinance (Cap 179) shall apply, with the necessary modifications, to proceedings under sections 13(1), 14 and 15 of the Guardianship of Minors Ordinance (Cap 13).

(2)   The provisions of the Matrimonial Causes Rules (Cap 179 sub. leg.) relating to the drawing up and service of orders shall apply to proceedings under this Order as if they were proceedings under those rules.

**(Enacted 1988)**

**NOTES**

**[90.11.1]   Numbering**
There is no Order 91 in Hong Kong. The equivalent in the former English Rules of the Supreme Court dealt with revenue proceedings. In Hong Kong provisions of the Inland Revenue Ordinance govern such proceedings. See the commentary under Order 55 rule 1.

**ORDER 92**

**LODGMENT, INVESTMENT, ETC. OF FUNDS IN COURT**

---

**NOTES**

**[92.1.1] Comparison with English rule**
Order 92 rule 1 is omitted from the Hong Kong rules as the equivalent English rule deals with payment into court under the Life Assurance Companies (Payment into Court) Act 1896.

**2. Payment into court under the Trustee Ordinance** (O. 92 r. 2)
    **(1)   Subject to paragraph (2), any trustee wishing to make a payment into court under section 62 of the Trustee Ordinance (Cap 29) must make and file an affidavit setting out–**
        **(a)   a short description of the trust and of the instrument creating it or, as the case may be, of the circumstances in which the trust arose,**
        **(b)   the names of the persons interested in or entitled to the money or securities to be paid into court with their addresses so far as known to him,**
        **(c)   his submission to answer all such inquiries relating to the application of such money or securities as the Court may make or direct, and**
        **(d)   an address where he may be served with any summons or order, or notice of any proceedings, relating to the money or securities paid into court.**
    **(2)   Where the money or securities represents a legacy, or residue or any share thereof, to which a minor or a person resident outside Hong Kong is absolutely entitled, no affidavit need be filed under paragraph (1) and the money or securities may be paid into court in the manner prescribed by the High Court Suitors' Funds Rules (Cap 4 sub. leg.) for the time being in force.**

---

**NOTES**

**[92.2.1] Application by trustee to pay funds into court**
Order 92 rule 2 deals with applications under section 62 of the Trustee Ordinance (Cap 29). That section enables a trustee to apply to pay trust funds into court. Trustees may wish to apply where trust funds are unclaimed. A common example is where solicitors hold unclaimed funds, the beneficial owner of which cannot be ascertained or traced. This includes funds which had been paid to solicitors on account. Such a application may be made by affidavit (subject to rule 2)).
    The applicant trustee is entitled to its costs of the application. In practice, the trustee may submit a summary of the costs claimed with its affidavit, for consideration by the court, so as to avoid the need for taxation.

In *Re Celestial Finance Ltd HCMP 657/2005* (Deputy Judge L Chan; 21.06.2005) the court ordered that advertisements be published in local newspapers where a securities trader was granted leave to pay unclaimed funds into court.

**4.   Notice of lodgment** (O. 92 r. 4)
**Any person who has lodged money or securities in court in accordance with rule 2 must forthwith send notice of the lodgment to every person appearing from the affidavit on which the lodgment was made to be entitled to, or to have an interest in, the money or securities lodged.**

**5.   Applications with respect to funds in court** (O. 92 r. 5)
    **(1)   Where an application to the Court—**
        **(a)   for the payment or transfer to any person of any funds in court standing to the credit of any cause or matter or for the transfer of any such funds to a separate account or for the payment to any person of any dividend of or interest on any securities or money comprised in such funds;**
        **(b)   for the investment, or change of investment, of any funds in court;**
        **(c)   for payment of the dividends of or interest on any funds in court representing or comprising money or securities lodged in court under any enactment; or**
        **(d)   for the payment or transfer out of court of any such funds as are mentioned in sub-paragraph (c),**
**is made the application may be disposed of in chambers.**

    **(2)   Subject to paragraph (3), any such application must be made by summons and, unless the application is made in a pending cause or matter or an application for the same purpose has previously been made by petition or originating summons, the summons must be an originating summons.**

    **(3)   Where an application under paragraph (1)(d) is required to be made by originating summons, then, if the funds to which the application relates do not exceed $50,000 in value, the application may be made ex parte to a master and the master may dispose of the application or may direct it to be made by originating summons. Unless otherwise directed, an ex parte application under this paragraph shall be made by affidavit.**

    **(5)   This rule does not apply to any application for an order under Order 22A. (L.N. 152 of 2008)**

                                                  **(Enacted 1988)**

---

**NOTES**

**[92.5.1]   Numbering of Order 92 rule 5**
Note that paragraph (4) is omitted from Order 92 rule 5. This results from differences between the English and Hong Kong judicial administration at the time rule 5 was enacted in 1988.

**[92.5.2]   Scope of order 92 rule 5**
Order 92 rule 5 provides for applications in relation to payment out and management of funds in court. See also Order 22A.

**[92.5.3]  Mode of application**

An application under Order 92 rule 5 may be made by interlocutory summons if there are on-going proceedings between the parties. However, if there are no such proceedings, or any such proceedings have come to a conclusion, the application must be made by originating summons. See *Killenny Ltd & Ors v AG* CACV 157/1995 (Litton VP, Godfrey & Liu JJA; 20.10.1995) and *Re Hongkew Holdings Ltd* HCMP 2523/1993 (Rogers J; 17.07.1996).

**[92.5.4]  Parties**

Where an application is made under Order 92 rule 5 by interlocutory summons in pending proceedings, the parties will, of course, be the parties to those proceedings. Otherwise (that is where the application is required to be commenced by originating summons) the parties should be those with adverse claims to the funds in court.

Exceptionally, where the amount is less than $50,000, and the application relates to payment out of a dividend or interest on funds in court, the application may be made *ex parte* on affidavit (rule 5(3)) and dealt with by a master.

It is not appropriate to join the Secretary for Justice or the Financial Secretary as respondent to an originating application under this rule, even where they have appeared in underlying proceedings, unless the government has a claim to beneficial interest in the funds: *Killenny Ltd & Ors v AG* CACV 157/1995 (Litton VP, Godfrey & Liu JJA; 20.10.1995).

## ORDER 93

### THE VARIATION OF TRUSTS ORDINANCE

**6.　Application under Variation of Trusts Ordinance** (O. 93 r. 6)
**(2)　In addition to any other persons who are necessary and proper defendants to the originating summons by which an application under section 3 of the Variation of Trusts Ordinance (Cap 253), is made, the settlor and any other person who provided property for the purposes of the trusts to which the application relates must, if still alive and not the plaintiff, be made a defendant unless the Court for some special reason otherwise directs.**

**14.　(Repealed, 23 of 2002 s 126)**

## NOTES

**[93.14.1]　Numbering**
There is no Order 94 in Hong Kong. The equivalent in the former English Rules of the Supreme Court dealt with appeals to the Queen's Bench Division under various statutes. In Hong Kong reference may be made to Orders 55, 60A and 61.

## ORDER 95

### THE BILLS OF SALE ORDINANCE AND BANKRUPTCY ORDINANCE

**1. Rectification of register** (O. 95 r. 1)

(1) Every application to the Court under section 20 of the Bills of Sale Ordinance (Cap 20) for an order–

(a) that any omission to register a bill of sale or an affidavit of renewal thereof within the time prescribed by that Ordinance be rectified by extending the time for such registration, or

(b) that any omission or mis-statement of the name, residence or occupation of any person be rectified by the insertion in the register of his true name, residence or occupation,

must be made by affidavit ex parte to a master.

(2) Every application for such an order as is described in paragraph (1) shall be supported by an affidavit setting out particulars of the bill of sale and of the omission or mis-statement in question and stating the grounds on which the application is made.

---

## NOTES

### [95.1.1] Bills of Sale Ordinance (Cap 20)

The Bills of Sale Ordinance (Cap 20), which is modelled after the UK Bills of Sale Act 1878 and the Bills of Sale Act (1878) Amendment Act 1882, requires all bills of sale to comply with certain requirements and to be properly registered in order to be valid. The Ordinance governs all bills of sale whether they are made or given to secure the payment of money or otherwise (*ie* bills to secure the performance of obligations other than the payment of money). A bill of sale may be described as a document of title to chattels, entitling the grantee of the bill to seize or take possession of the chattels (which remain in the possession of the grantor) which are comprised in or made subject to such bill of sale under certain circumstances. Bills of sale pose a danger to lenders who are unaware that the parties to whom they are extending credit on the strength of apparent ownership of goods, have in fact conveyed or charged the goods to another. Registration of bills of sale prevents such frauds upon creditors by secret bills of sale of personal chattels (see long title of the Ordinance).

### [95.1.2] Registration

By virtue of section 7 of the Ordinance, every bill of sale to which the Ordinance applies must be duly attested and registered within seven clear days after the execution thereof, or, if it is executed in any place out of Hong Kong, then within seven clear days after the time at which it would, in the course of post, arrive in Hong Kong if posted immediately after the execution thereof. See Order 3 rule 2(4) for the meaning of 'clear days' – where the act is required to be done a specified number of clear days before or after a specified date, at least that number of days must intervene between the day on which the act is done and that date. In addition, section 25 of the Ordinance stipulates that when the time for registering a bill of sale expires on a Sunday or other day on which the offices of the High Court are closed, such registration shall be valid if made on the next following day on which the offices are opened. A security bill (*ie* a bill of sale made or given by way of security for the payment of money) shall be void in respect of the chattels comprised therein unless attested and registered as required by the section. Any other bill of sale would be deemed fraudulent and void as against any of the persons stipulated in the section and to the extent stated therein (see subsection (b) of section 7 of the Ordinance). Section 9 of the Ordinance sets out the mode of registering the bills of sale.

### [95.1.3]    Renewal of registration

Section 10 of the Ordinance states that the registration of a bill of sale must be renewed once at least every five years, and in the event that a period of five years elapses from the registration or the renewed registration of a bill of sale without a renewal or further renewal, as the case may be, the registration shall become void. The renewal of a registration is effected by filing with the Registrar an affidavit stating the details specified in the section. The form of such affidavit is set out in Form 1 of the Schedule to the Ordinance.

### [95.1.4]    Correction of errors in registration

A judge, on being satisfied that an omission or misstatement of the name, residence or occupation of any person was accidental or due to inadvertence, may order such omission or misstatement to be rectified by the insertion in the register of the true name, residence, or occupation – see section 20 of the Ordinance and this rule. In *Crew v Cummings* (1888) 21 QBD 420, the party registering the bill of sale omitted to include a description of the residence and occupation of one of the attesting witnesses to the bill in the affidavit accompanying the bill, as required under section 10 of the UK Bills of Sale Act 1878 (equivalent to section 9 of the Ordinance). An application under section 14 of the 1878 Act (equivalent to section 20 of the Ordinance) to rectify this omission was not permitted on the basis that the said section only permitted a rectification of the register, and the description of the residence and occupation of the attesting witness did not form part of the register (see section 19 of the Ordinance for the details which do form part of the register).

### [95.1.5]    Extension of time for registration

Under section 20 of the Ordinance and this rule, a judge, on being satisfied that the omission to register a bill of sale or an affidavit of renewal thereof within the time prescribed by the Ordinance was accidental or due to inadvertence, may extend the time for such registration, on such terms and conditions, if any, as to security, notice by advertisement or otherwise, or to any other matter, as he thinks fit to direct. However, *Crew v Cummings* (1888) 21 QBD 420, held that an extension of time to register a bill of sale could not be granted so as to defeat a title already *bona fide* vested in an execution creditor. Similarly, in *Re Parsons, Ex parte Furber* [1893] 2 QB 122, the Court of Appeal held that the time for registration of a bill of sale could not be extended to defeat vested rights of a trustee in bankruptcy. In *Re Spiral Globe Ltd* [1902] 1 Ch 396, Swinfen Eady J was prepared to extend time for registration of a charge under section 15 of the UK Companies Act 1900 (which was in *pari materia* with section 14 of the UK Bills of Sale Act 1878) provided that the order for extension included the words: 'This order to be without prejudice to the rights of parties acquired prior to the time when such [debentures] shall be actually registered.' It would therefore appear that the discretion of a judge in extending time for registration cannot be exercised to defeat rights of persons which have actually accrued in the meantime and which would be prejudicially affected if registration were allowed without saving and protecting those rights. However, it would appear from the case of *Re Kris Cruises Ltd* [1949] Ch 138 that this protection is only for the benefit of secured creditors whose rights have accrued in respect of the assets of the debtor and does not extend to protect unsecured creditors of the grantor where no bankruptcy has intervened.

### [95.1.6] Comparision with English rule
Prior to 26 April 1999, Order 95, rules 1, 2, 3, 4 and 6 of the English Rules of the Supreme Court were in *pari materia* with the corresponding rules of Order 95 of the Hong Kong Rules of the High Court. However, the English Civil Procedure Rules 1998 ('CPR') which came into force on 26 April 1999 have resulted in Order 95 of the English Rules being re-enacted in Schedule 1 of the CPR. In the process, all of the rules in the said Order 95 have undergone amendment. Save and except for rule 2, all the amendments are minor.

**2.  Entry of satisfaction** (O. 95 r. 2)

   **(1)   Every application under section 21 of the Bills of Sale Ordinance (Cap 20) to a master for an order that a memorandum of satisfaction be written on a registered copy of a bill of sale must–**

   **(a)   if a consent to the satisfaction signed by the person entitled to the benefit of the bill of sale can be obtained, be made ex parte;**

   **(b)   in all other cases, be made by originating summons.**

   **(2)   An ex parte application under paragraph (1)(a) must be supported by–**

   **(a)   particulars of the consent referred to in that paragraph; and**

   **(b)   an affidavit by a witness who attested the consent verifying the signature on it.**

   **(3)   An originating summons under paragraph (1)(b) must be served on the person entitled to the benefit of the bill of sale and must be supported by evidence that the debt (if any) for which the bill of sale was made has been satisfied or discharged.**

   **(4)   An originating summons under paragraph (1)(b) shall be in Form No 10 in Appendix A.**

---

### NOTES

### [95.2.1] Application under section 2
Section 21 of the Ordinance provides that the Registrar may order a memorandum of satisfaction to be written upon any registered copy of a bill of sale, on the prescribed evidence being given that the debt, if any, for which such bill of sale was made or given has been satisfied or discharged. This rule provides that where consent to the satisfaction of the bill is signed by the person entitled to the benefit thereof is obtained, the application may be made *ex parte*. In other cases, it must be an *inter partes* application made by originating summons. See also rules 1, 2 and 3 of the Bill of Sales Rules (Cap 20B).

**[95.2.2]    Effect of satisfaction**

The entry of satisfaction brings the operation of the bill of sale to an end. A bill of sale which has been paid off cannot be set up against an execution creditor even though satisfaction has not been entered – *Waterton v Baker* (1868) 17 LT 494.

**3.   Restraining removal on sale of goods seized** (O. 95 r. 3)

**An originating summons by which an application to the Court under the proviso to section 14 of the Bills of Sale Ordinance (Cap 20) must be made shall be in Form No 10 in Appendix A.**

**4.   Search of register** (O. 95 r. 4)

**The Registrar shall, on a request in writing giving sufficient particulars, and on payment of the prescribed fee, cause a search to be made in the register of bills of sale and issue a certificate of the result of the search.**

---

**NOTES**

**[95.4.1]    Prescribed fee**

See regulation 2 of the Bills of Sale (Fees) Regulations) (Cap 20A).

**6.   Assignment of book debts** (O. 95 r. 6)

**(1)   There shall continue to be kept in the Registry a register of assignment of book debts.**

**(2)   Every application for registration of an assignment of a book debt under section 48 of the Bankruptcy Ordinance (Cap 6) shall be made by producing at the Registry—**

> **(a)   a true copy of the assignment, and of every schedule thereto, and**
>
> **(b)   an affidavit verifying the date and the time, and the due execution of the assignment in the presence of the deponent, and setting out the particulars of the assignment, and of the parties thereto.**

**(3)   On an application being made in accordance with the preceding paragraph, the documents there referred to shall be filed and the particulars of the assignment and the parties to it, shall be entered in the register.**

**(Enacted 1988)**

---

**NOTES**

**[95.6.1]    Registration of book debts**

Under section 48 of the Bankruptcy Ordinance (Cap 6), where a person engaged in any trade or business makes an assignment to any other person of his existing or future book debts or any class thereof and is subsequently adjudicated bankrupt, the assignment shall be void against any trustee as regards any book debts which have not been paid before the date of the bankruptcy order, unless the assignment has been registered with the Registrar in a register to be kept by him for that purpose.

**[95.6.2]    Numbering**

There is no Order 96, 97, 98 or 99 in Hong Kong.

## ORDER 100

### THE TRADE MARKS ORDINANCE

**2.   Appeals and applications under the Trade Marks Ordinance** (O. 100 r. 2)

(1)   Every appeal to the Court under the Trade Marks Ordinance (Cap 559), shall be heard and determined by a single judge.

(2)   Subject to rule 3, every application to the Court under the said Ordinance may be begun by originating summons in Form No. 10 in Appendix A. (L.N. 152 of 2008)

(3)   The summons by which any such application is made must be served on the Registrar of Trade Marks.

(4)   Where the Registrar of Trade Marks refers to the Court an application under the said Ordinance made to him, then, unless within one month after receiving notification of the decision to refer, the applicant makes to the Court the application referred, he shall be deemed to have abandoned it.

(5)   The period prescribed in relation to an appeal to which paragraph (1) applies or the period prescribed by paragraph (4) in relation to an application or appeal to which that paragraph applies may be extended by the Registrar of Trade Marks on the application of any party interested and may be so extended although the application is not made until after the expiration of that period, but the foregoing provision shall not be taken to affect the power of the Court under Order 3, rule 5, to extend that period.

(6)   (Repealed, 35 of 2000 s 98.)

## NOTES

### [100.2.1]   Numbering
There is no rule 1 in Hong Kong's Order 100.

### [100.2.2]   Appeals under Trade Marks Ordinance
Section 84 of the Trade Marks Ordinance (Cap 559) provides that an appeal lies from any decision of the Registrar of Trade Marks under that Ordinance to the Court of First Instance. The Registrar is entitled to appear and be heard in support of the decision or order, and indeed may be directed by the court to appear. Order 100 rule 2(1) and (5) makes some provision for such appeals. See also Order 55 which also appears to apply to such appeals.

### [100.2.3]   Further evidence on trade mark appeal
The intention behind the rules is that parties to a disputed application for registration of a trade mark should put in all their evidence in one go, and the court will be slow to grant leave to adduce further evidence on appeal. See *Chi Wing & Anor t/a Singapore Headway Medicine Co v Eng Kwan Lan t/a Kam Ying Trading Co* HCMP 730/2007 (A Cheung J; 06.09.2007).

**[100.2.4]	Applications under Trade Marks Ordinance**

Applications to the Court of First Instance under the Trade Marks Ordinance (Cap 559) are governed by Order 100. Applications for revocation (s 52) or rectification (s 57) of a trade mark are examples.

Such applications are made by notice of originating motion (rule 2(2)). The notice must be served on the Registrar of Trade Marks (rule 2(3)). In *Re Yoshida & Co Ltd* [2004] 2 HKC 577, 581D-E (CA), an application for rectification of the trade marks register, it was noted that there is nothing in these rules or in the Trade Marks Ordinance which requires that the proprietor of the trade mark be made a respondent to such an application, but proceeded on the assumption that this was the case and that the proprietor should be served. The court held that such service could be effected at the address for service recorded in the register of trade marks, and that it is not necessary to obtain leave to serve out of the jurisdiction. Further, the court may proceed if it is satisfied that adequate notice was received even though the prescribed procedures for service were not followed.

**[100.2.5]	Call-over hearing**

Practice Direction 22.1 provides that the first hearing of an originating motion under Order 100 will be for directions, rather like a call-over hearing. The text of the practice direction can be viewed on the judiciary's website.

**[100.2.6]	Court's approach on appeal under Trade Marks Ordinance**

On an appeal under Order 100 rule 2(1) to a single judge against a decision of the registrar of trade marks, the court will only interfere where it is satisfied that the registrar 'acted on some wrong principle, for example, has not approached the problem in the right way, or has taken into consideration matter which he ought not to have taken into consideration, or has omitted to take into consideration matters which were proper for consideration': *Re 'Hicaliq' the Trade Mark* HCMP 638/1994 (Rogers J; 15.07.1994) (para 4), ; *Prince Sovereign and Device Trade Mark* [1989] 2 HKC 247, 251G. This is particularly so with regard to findings of fact: *Chi Wing & Anor t/a Singapore Headway Medicine Co v Eng Kwan Lan t/a Kam Ying Trading Co* HCMP 730/2007 (Recorder A Chan SC; 28.03.2008) (para 5).

**3.	Proceedings for infringement of registered trade mark: validity of registration disputed** (O. 100 r. 3)

**(1)	Where in any proceedings a claim is made for relief for infringement of the right to the use of a registered trade mark, the party against whom the claim is made may in his defence put in issue the validity of the registration of that trade mark or may counterclaim for an order that the register of trade marks be rectified by cancelling or varying the relevant entry or may do both those things.**

**(2)	A party to any such proceedings who in his pleading (whether a defence or counterclaim) disputes the validity of the registration of a registered trade mark must serve with the pleading particulars of the objections to the validity of the registration on which he relies in support of the allegation of invalidity.**

**(3)	A party to any such proceedings who counterclaims for an order that the register of trade marks be rectified must serve on the Registrar of Trade Marks a copy of the counterclaim together with a copy of the particulars mentioned in**

paragraph (2); and the Registrar of Trade Marks shall be entitled to take such part in the proceedings as he may think fit but need not serve a defence or other pleading unless ordered to do so by the Court.

**(Enacted 1988)**

## ORDER 102

### THE COMPANIES ORDINANCE

1.  **Definitions** (O. 102 r. 1)
    **In this Order—**
    **"the Ordinance" means the Companies Ordinance (Cap 32).**

**NOTES**

**[102.1.1]    Scope of Order 102**
Order 102 regulates the procedure to be followed on various types of application for relief under the Companies Ordinance. However, it does not apply to winding-up which is governed by the Companies (Winding-up) Rules. Order 1 rule 2 provides that the Rules of the High Court do not apply to winding-up proceedings.

In *Hill & Anor v O'Driscoll & Anor* [1998] 2 HKLRD 994, indemnity costs were awarded against plaintiffs who wrongly proceeded under Order 102 instead of making an application under winding-up proceedings.

Order 102, together with the Companies Ordinance and subsidiary legislation, can be regarded as a 'code' which must be followed where applicable, leaving no room for inherent jurisdiction. See *YJK Co Ltd & Anor v Kazuo Aizawa & Ors* HCA 8177/1998 (Deputy Judge To; 24.11.1999).

2.  **Applications to be made by originating summons** (O. 102 r. 2)
    **(1)    Except in the case of applications made in proceedings relating to the winding up of companies, applications made pursuant to section 168A of the Ordinance and the applications mentioned in rule 5, every application under the Ordinance may be made by originating summons. (L.N. 152 of 2008)**
    **(2)    An originating summons under this rule shall be in Form No 10 in Appendix A unless the application made by the summons is–**
    
      **(a)    an application under section 167 of the Ordinance for an order to make provision for all or any of the matters mentioned in subsection (1) of that section where an order sanctioning the compromise or arrangement to which the application relates has previously been made, or**

      **(b)    an application under section 302 of the Ordinance for an order directing a receiver or manager of a company to make good any such default as is mentioned in subsection (1) of that section, or**

      **(c)    an application under section 306 of the Ordinance for an order directing a company and any officer thereof to make good any such default as is mentioned in that section.**

    **(3)    (Repealed, 28 of 2003 s 120)**
    **(4)    An application under section 168BD of the Ordinance for leave to dispense with the service of a written notice required by that section may be made by ex parte originating summons. (L.N. 80/2005)**

## NOTES

### [102.2.1]  Parties

Order 102 rule 2 provides that various types of application relating to the affairs of a company are to be commenced by originating summons. An example is application under section 114B of Cap 32 where it is impracticable to hold a meeting of the company in accordance with the prescribed procedures.

It is inappropriate for the company itself to be a party to proceedings relating to its internal affairs, such as an application under section 114B. See *Jiang Shaoliang v Zhang Xinneng* HCMP 877/2001 (Yuen J; 29.05.2001). The proper parties in that case were the one director who wished to hold a meeting and the other director who could not be located.

It is no longer necessary to name the Secretary for Justice as a party to proceedings to reinstate a company which has been deregistered and whose property is deemed *bona vacantia* under the Companies Ordinance (Cap 32). In this regard the decision in *Wong Shuk-ying & Anor v AG* [1987] HKLR 985 should no longer be followed. It had there been held that the Secretary for Justice was a proper party to protect the government's interest because if an order were made reinstating the company, its property would cease to be *bona vacantia.* However, the Registrar of Companies now acts as agent for the government in such cases and it is no longer necessary to name the Secretary for Justice as a separate party. The new procedure was announced to the profession with Law Society circular 01-355 (PA) which reads as follows:

CIRCULAR 01-355 (PA)                                             10 December 2001

#### COMPANIES

##### Applications under S 291AB of the Companies Ordinance, Cap 32 for Reinstatement of Deregistered Companies

Under Section 291AB of the Companies Ordinance, Cap 32, an aggrieved party may apply to the Court for an order that the Registrar of Companies reinstate the registration of a company that was deregistered under S 291AA.

While the Originating Summons in such applications will normally only name the Registrar of Companies as the respondent to the proceedings, there have been a few occasions where the Secretary of Justice ("SJ") has also been named as a party to the proceedings, either upon request by the Judge or at the initiation of the solicitors. In such circumstances, the SJ will write to seek instructions from the Companies Registry ("CR"). As requested by the Hon. Yuen J., the CR has advised the Society that the CR, having the authority to act as agent on behalf of the government on bona vacantia cases, will settle the terms of the Consent Summonses for the applications directly with the applicants and the SJ's services will not normally be required.

**Members should thus take note that with immediate effect, all applications made under S 291AB need only name the Registrar of Companies as the respondent.**

### [102.2.2]  Application for leave to bring derivative action

An application under Part IVAA of the Companies Ordinance for leave to bring a derivative action should be made by originating summons under Order 102 rule 2. Prior notice to the company is required unless the court grants leave to dispense therewith. See Section 168BD of the Ordinance. Order 102 rule 2(4) specifically provides that an application for leave to dispense with prior notice may be made *ex parte*.

See also the commentary under Order 15 rule 12, and as to costs see the commentary under Order 62 rule 3.

## 3.   (Repealed, L.N. 152 of 2008)

NOTES

**[102.3.1]   Application for rectification of register of members**
Order 102 rule 3 previously provided that application to the court under section 100 of the Companies Ordinance (Cap 32) for rectification of the register of members of a company should be made by originating summons or originating motion. It was repealed as part of the civil justice reforms, taking effect in 2009, by which originating motions were generally abolished. See Order 5 and the commentary thereunder.

Now the general provision for making applications under the Ordinance, rule 2, will apply and applications previously governed by this rule should be made by originating summons.

## 4.   (Repealed, L.N. 152 of 2008)

NOTES

**[102.4.1]   Repeal of Order 102 rule 4**
Order 102 rule 4 previously provided that certain types of applications under the Companies Ordinance (Cap 32) were to be made by originating motion. It was repealed as part of the civil justice reforms, taking effect in 2009, by which originating motions were generally abolished. See Order 5 and the commentary thereunder.

Now the general provision for making applications under the Ordinance, rule 2, will apply and applications previously governed by this rule should be made by originating summons.

Set out below is a brief discussion of some of the types of application which came within the previous rule 4.

**[102.4.2]   Applications under section 143 of Cap 32**
Order 102 rule 4(1)(c) previously provided that applications under section 143 of the Companies Ordinance (Cap 32) for an order for investigation of the affairs of a company be made by originating motion. Such applications should now be made by originating summons in accordance with Order 102 rule 2.

The principles applicable on an application under section 143 of the Companies Ordinance are set out concisely in numbered paragraphs in *Re San Imperial Corp Ltd* HCMP 127 & 179/1978 (Yang J; 01.05.1978).

**[102.4.3]   Applications under section 290 of Cap 32**
Section 290 of the Companies Ordinance (Cap 32) empowers the court to declare void the dissolution of a company. It was previously provided in Order 102 rule 4(1) (f) that where such a company had not been wound up, the application should be

made by originating motion. With regard to companies which have been wound up, see *Re Max Win Eng'g Ltd* HCMP 1913/2002 (Kwan J; 24.05.2002), referring to rules 5(1)(c) and 7(1) of the Companies (Winding-up) Rules.

*Parties to application under section 290* – The Registrar of Companies should be named as a respondent where the company has not been wound up. However, where the company was wound up prior to dissolution it is not necessary, but common practice, for the Registrar to be joined. See *Classic Rolls Ltd & Anor v Kennic Lai Hang Lui* HCMP 4914/2002 (Kwan J; 24.10.2003).

In the *Max Win* case (above), the court was of the view that in addition to the Registrar of Companies, the former liquidator and insurers should have been named as respondents. The insurers were interested because the application was brought by a former employee of the company who wished to bring an action for damages for personal injury suffered at work. Despite the non-joinder, the court exercised its discretion to proceed with the application on the ground that all interested parties had been given notice.

The company itself cannot be made a party to an application under section 290 since it ceased to exist upon dissolution: see *Classic Rolls* (above).

*Costs of application under section 290* – In *Max Win* (above), although the application was unsuccessfully opposed, the court did not make any order as to costs, leaving it to the applicant to claim those costs in the intended personal injury action.

**5. Applications to be made by petition** (O. 102 r. 5)

**(1) The following applications under the Ordinance must be made by petition, namely applications—**

**(a) under section 8 to cancel the alteration of a private company's objects, (28 of 2003 s 120)**

**(b) under section 25A to cancel the alteration of a condition contained in a private company's memorandum, (28 of 2003 s 120)**

**(c) under section 48B to confirm a reduction of the share premium account of a company,**

**(d) under section 50 to sanction the issue by a company of shares at a discount,**

**(e) under section 49 to confirm a reduction of the capital redemption reserve fund of a company,**

**(f) under section 59 to confirm a reduction of the share capital of a company,**

**(g) under section 64 to cancel any variation or abrogation of the rights attached to any class of shares in a company,**

**(h) under section 166 to sanction a compromise or arrangement between a company and its creditors or any class of them or between a company and its members or any class of them,**

**(i) under section 291(7) for an order restoring the name of a company to the register, where the application is made in conjunction with an application for the winding up of the company,**

**(j) under section 323 to cancel the alteration of the form of a company's constitution, and**

(k)  under section 358(2) for relief from liability of an officer of a
company or a person employed by a company as auditor.

## NOTES

**[102.5.1]   Application to wind up under s 168A should be commenced by
petition**
Order 102 rule 5 prescribes that certain types of application under the Companies
Ordinance must be commenced by petition. There is no mention in the rule of
applications to wind up a company on the just and equitable ground in section 168A
of the Ordinance. Nevertheless it has been held that such an application must be
commenced by petition. See *Leung Chi Kai Mintis v China-Tech Engineering Co Ltd
& Ors* [2002] 3 HKC 605. There Chung J found that section 168A, which itself states
that an application thereunder shall be made by petition, takes precedence over Order
102 rule 5. That decision appears to have been preserved by the amendment of Order
102 rule 2 taking effect in 2009, which excluded applications under section 168A of
the Ordinance from the general requirement that applications under the Companies
Ordinance be commenced by originating summons.

6.   **Entitlement of proceedings** (O. 102 r. 6)
  (2)   Every originating summons and petition by which any such proceedings
are begun and all affidavits, notices and other documents in those proceedings
must be entitled in the matter of the company in question and in the matter of
the Ordinance. (L.N. 152 of 2008)
  (3)   (Repealed 28 of 2003 s 120)

7.   **Case management summons** (O. 102 r. 7)
  (1)   After presentation of a petition by which any such application as is
mentioned in rule 5 is made, the petitioner, except where his application is one of
those mentioned in paragraph (2), must take out a case management summons
under this rule. (L.N. 152 of 2008)
  (2)   The applications referred to in paragraph (1) are—
    (a)   an application under section 50 of the Ordinance to sanction the
issue by a company of shares at a discount,
    (b)   an application under section 166 of the Ordinance to sanction a
compromise or arrangement unless there is included in the petition
for such sanction an application for an order under section 167 of
the Ordinance, and
    (c)   an application under section 291(7) of the Ordinance for an order
restoring the name of a company to the register.
  (3)   On the hearing of the summons the Court may by order give such
directions as to the proceedings to be taken before the hearing of the petition as
it thinks fit including, in particular, directions for the publication of notices and
the making of any inquiry.
  (4)   Where the application made by the petition is to confirm a reduction of
the share capital, the share premium account or the capital redemption reserve
fund, of a company, then, without prejudice to the generality of paragraph (3),
the Court may give directions—

(a) **for an inquiry to be made as to the debts of, and claims against, the company or as to any class or classes of such debts or claims;**

(b) **as to the proceedings to be taken for settling the list of creditors entitled to object to the reduction and fixing the date by reference to which the list is to be made;**

and the power of the Court under section 59(3) of the Ordinance to direct that section 59(2) thereof shall not apply as regards any class or classes of creditors may be exercised on any hearing of the summons.

(5) **Rules 8 to 13 shall have effect subject to any directions given by the Court under this rule.**

## NOTES

### [102.7.1]   Case management of rule 5 proceedings
Order 102 rule 7 provides that in most of the proceedings commenced by petition under rule 5 the petitioner must take out a case management summons. With regard to case management summonses generally, see Order 25.

### [102.7.2]   Case management of bankruptcy, winding-up and s 168A petitions
Provisions as to the case management of bankruptcy and winding-up petitions, and petitions for relief under s 168A of the Companies Ordinance are set out in practice direction 3.4, which came into force in 2009 along with the civil justice reforms. The practice direction may be viewed on the judiciary website www.judiciary.gov.hk and that of the Hong Kong Legal Information Institute www.hklii.org, both of which are available to the public free of charge.

### [102.7.3]   Interlocutory application by letter
In appropriate circumstances the Companies court will entertain applications of an interlocutory nature by letter. Practice direction 3.5, which took effect on 19 May 2010 requires that such an application by letter must be supported by submissions identifying:

(a)   the relevant legal principles: statutory provisions and legal authorities;

(b)   the evidence and facts relied on; and

(c)   how it is contended that the relevant legal principles are satisfied.

The practice direction makes it clear that the court may insist that an application be made by summons rather than letter.

**8.   Inquiry as to debts: company to make list of creditors** (O. 102 r. 8)
(1)   **Where under rule 7 the Court orders such an inquiry as is mentioned in paragraph (4) thereof, the company in question must, within 7 days after the making of the order, file in the Registry an affidavit made by an officer of the company competent to make it verifying a list containing—**

(a) **the name and address of every creditor entitled to any debt or claim to which the inquiry extends,**

(b) **the amount due to each creditor in respect of such debt or claim or, in the case of a debt or claim which is subject to any contingency** or sounds only in damages or for some other reason does not bear a certain value, a just estimate of the value thereof, and

(c)  the total of those amounts and values.

(2)  The deponent must state in the affidavit his belief that at the date fixed by the Court as the date by reference to which the list is to be made there is no debt or claim which, if that date were the commencement of the winding up of the company, would be admissible in proof against the company, other than the debts or claims set out in the list and any debts or claims to which the inquiry does not extend, and must also state his means of knowledge of the matters deposed to.

(3)  The list must be left at the office mentioned in paragraph (1) not later than one day after the affidavit is filed.

### 9.  Inspection of list of creditors (O. 102 r. 9)

(1)  Copies of the list made under rule 8 with the omission, unless the Court otherwise directs, of the amount due to each creditor and the estimated value of any debt or claim to which any creditor is entitled, shall be kept at the registered office of the company and at the office of that company's solicitor.

(2)  Any person shall be entitled during ordinary business hours, on payment of a fee of one dollar, to inspect the said list at any such office and to take extracts therefrom.

### 10.  Notice to creditors (O. 102 r. 10)

Within 7 days after filing the affidavit required by rule 8 the company must send by post to each creditor named in the list exhibited to the affidavit, at his last known address, a notice stating–

(a)  the amount of the reduction sought to be confirmed,

(b)  the effect of the order directing an inquiry as to debts and claims,

(c)  the amount or value specified in the list as due or estimated to be due to that creditor, and

(d)  the time fixed by the Court within which, if he claims to be entitled to a larger amount, he must send particulars of his debt or claim and the name and address of his solicitor, if any, to the company's solicitor.

### 11.  Advertisement of petition and list of creditors (O. 102 r. 11)

After filing the affidavit required by rule 8 the company must insert, in such newspapers and at such times as the Court directs, a notice stating—

(a)  the date of presentation of the petition and the amount of the reduction thereby sought to be confirmed,

(b)  the inquiry ordered by the Court under rule 7,

(c)  the places where the list of creditors may be inspected in accordance with rule 9, and

(d)  the time within which any creditor not named in the list who claims to be entitled to any debt or claim to which the inquiry extends must send his name and address, the name and address of his solicitor, if any, and particulars of his debt or claim to the company's solicitor.

**12. Affidavit as to claims made by creditors** (O. 102 r. 12)

Within such time as the Court directs the company must file in the Registry an affidavit made by the company's solicitor and an officer of the company competent to make it–

    (a)  proving service of the notices mentioned in rule 10 and advertisement of the notice mentioned in rule 11,

    (b)  verifying a list containing the names and addresses of the persons (if any) who in pursuance of such notices sent in particulars of debts or claims, specifying the amount of each debt or claim,

    (c)  distinguishing in such list those debts or claims which are wholly, or as to any and what part thereof, admitted by the company, disputed by the company or alleged by the company to be outside the scope of the inquiry, and

    (d)  stating which of the persons named in the list made under rule 8, and which of the persons named in the list made under this rule, have been paid or consent to the reduction sought to be confirmed.

**13. Adjudication of disputed claims** (O. 102 r. 13)

If the company contends that a person is not entitled to be entered in the list of creditors in respect of any debt or claim or in respect of the full amount claimed by him in respect of any debt or claim, then, unless the company is willing to secure payment of that debt or claim by appropriating the full amount of the debt or claim, the company must, if the Court so directs, send to that person by post at his last known address a notice requiring him—

    (a)  within such time as may be specified in the notice, being not less than 4 clear days after service thereof, to file an affidavit proving his debt or claim or, as the case may be, so much thereof as is not admitted by the company, and

    (b)  to attend the adjudication of his debt or claim at the place and time specified in the notice, being the time appointed by the Court for the adjudication of debts and claims.

**NOTES**

**[102.13.1]  Creditor's costs**

A creditor who proves its claim in an inquiry under Order 102 rule 13 will normally be entitled to costs. See Order 62 rule 3(9).

**14. Certifying lists of creditors entitled to object to reduction** (O. 102 r. 14)

The list of creditors entitled to object to such reduction as is mentioned in rule 7(4), as settled by the Court under section 59(2) of the Ordinance shall be certified and filed by the Registrar and his certificate shall—

    (a)  specify the debts or claims (if any) disallowed by the Court;

    (b)  distinguish the debts or claims (if any) the full amount of which is admitted by the company, the debts or claims (if any) the full amount of which, though not admitted by the company, the company is willing to appropriate, the debts or claims (if any) the amount of which has been fixed by adjudication of the Court under section 59(2) of the Ordinance and other debts or claims;

(c)    specify the total amount of the debts or claims payment of which has been secured by appropriation under the said section 59(2);

(d)    show which creditors consent to the reduction and the total amount of their debts or claims;

(e)    specify the creditors who sought to prove their debts or claims under rule 13 and state which of such debts or claims were allowed.

## 15. Evidence of consent of creditor (O. 102 r. 15)

The consent of a creditor to such reduction as is mentioned in rule 7(4) may be proved in such manner as the Court thinks sufficient.

## 16. Time, etc. of hearing of petition for confirmation of reduction (O. 102 r. 16)

(1)    A petition for the confirmation of any such reduction as is mentioned in rule 7(4) shall not, where the Court has directed an inquiry pursuant to that rule, be heard before the expiration of at least 8 clear days after the filing of the certificate mentioned in rule 14.

(2)    Before the hearing of such a petition, a notice specifying the day appointed for the hearing must be published at such times and in such newspapers as the Court may direct.

## 17. Restriction on taking effect of order under section 50 (O. 102 r. 17)

Unless the Court otherwise directs, an order under section 50 of the Ordinance sanctioning the issue of shares at a discount shall direct that an office copy of the order be delivered to the Registrar of Companies within 10 days after the making of the order or such extended time as the Court may allow and that the order shall not take effect until such copy has been so delivered.

(Enacted 1988)

## ORDER 103

### THE REGISTRATION OF PATENTS ORDINANCE: THE PATENTS ACTS 1949 TO 1961 AND 1977

1.  **Definitions** (O. 103 r. 1)
    **In this Order—**
    **"existing patent" means a patent mentioned in section 127(2)(a) or (c) of the Act;**
    **"the Act" means the Patents Act 1977 (1977 c. 37 U.K.);**
    **"the Ordinance" means the Registration of Patents Ordinance (Cap 42).**

## NOTES

**[103.1.1]   Order 103 obsolete**

Order 103 is now obsolete. It was enacted to provide for proceedings in the court under the UK Patents Act 1977 and the Registration of Patents Ordinance (Cap 42) which implemented the UK patent system in Hong Kong during the colonial era (see *Re Wing Yick Bamboo Scaffolders Ltd* [2002] 1 HKC 395, 397E–F). The UK Act ceased to have force in Hong Kong with the resumption of Chinese sovereignty and the Ordinance has been repealed (Patents Ordinance (Cap 514) section 154). A new system for Hong Kong was enacted locally on 27 June 1997 and the relevant primary legislation is now the Patents Ordinance (Cap 514).

Rather strangely Order 103 has been neither repealed nor replaced. In *Re Wing Yick Bamboo Scaffolders Ltd* [2002] 1 HKC 395 Chu J said (at 397H–I) 'Despite the repeal of the old Ordinance and the enactment of the new Patents Ordinance, O 103 has not been updated nor amended'. The English equivalent of Order 103 was revoked in 1984 and replaced by the new Order 104, but that has not been adopted in Hong Kong: see *Re Low Ban Chai* [1999] 1 HKC 413 where Yuen J nevertheless followed 'roughly' the procedure under the English Order 104 in the absence of any relevant Hong Kong rule.

Although the new legislation includes transitional arrangements (see section 155 and the Patent (Transitional Arrangement) Rules enacted under section 158) deeming the continuation of prior patent rights it does not appear that Order 103 has any continuing relevance to them.

**19. Actions for infringement: particulars of pleading** (O. 103 r. 19)
    **(1)   The plaintiff in an action for infringement of a patent must serve with his statement of claim particulars of the infringements relied on.**
    **(2)   If a defendant in such an action disputes the validity of the patent, he must serve with his defence particulars of the objections to the validity of the patent on which he relies in support of the allegation of invalidity.**
    **(3)   If a defendant in such an action alleges, as a defence to the action, that at the time of the infringement there was in force a contract or licence relating to the patent made by or with the consent of the plaintiff and containing a condition or term void by virtue of section 44 of the Act, he must serve on the plaintiff particulars of the date of, and parties to, each such contract or licence and particulars of each such condition or term.**

**(4)**   A defendant to such an action who applies by counterclaim in the action for a declaration under section 8(1) of the Ordinance must, with his counterclaim, serve particulars of the grounds on which he relies in support of his counterclaim.

## 20. Particulars of infringements (O. 103 r. 20)

Particulars of infringements of a patent must specify which of the claims in the specification of the patent are alleged to be infringed and must give at least one instance of each type of infringement alleged.

## 21. Particulars of objections (O. 103 r. 21)

**(1)**   Particulars of objections to the validity of a patent must state every ground on which the validity of the patent is disputed and must include such particulars as will clearly define every issue which it is intended to raise.

**(2)**   If the grounds stated in the particulars of objections include want of novelty or want of any inventive step, the particulars must state the manner, time and place of every prior publication or user relied upon and, if prior user is alleged, must—

    (a)   specify the name of every person alleged to have made such user,

    (b)   state whether such user is alleged to have continued until the priority date of the claim in question or of the invention, as may be appropriate, and, if not, the earliest and latest date on which such user is alleged to have taken place,

    (c)   contain a description, accompanied by drawings, if necessary, sufficient to identify such user, and

    (d)   if such user relates to machinery or apparatus, state whether the machinery or apparatus is in existence and where it can be inspected.

    **(3)**   If in the case of an existing patent—

    (a)   one of the grounds stated in the particulars of objection is that the invention, so far as claimed in any claim of the complete specification, is not useful, and

    (b)   it is intended, in connection with that ground, to rely on the fact that an example of the invention which is the subject of any such claim cannot be made to work, either at all or as described in the specification,

the particulars must state the fact and identify each such claim and must include particulars of each such example, specifying the respects in which it is alleged that it does not work or does not work as described.

---

## NOTES

### [103.21.1]   Settlement of dispute over validity of patent

Where settlement is reached in on-going proceedings concerning the validity of a patent, the court cannot give judgment in favour of validity by judgment in default of opposition. This is because a patent confers proprietary rights *in rem*. See *Conor Medsystems Inc v Angiotech Pharmaceuticals Inc* [2008] UKHL 49. In that case the respondent to an appeal against a judgment finding that a patent was not valid withdrew its opposition to the appeal, and the House of Lords therefore invited the Comptroller General of Patents to assist with arguments against validity of the patent.

## 22. Amendment of particulars (O. 103 r. 22)

Without prejudice to Order 20, rule 5, the Court may at any stage of the proceedings allow a party to amend any particulars served by him under the foregoing provisions of this Order on such terms as to costs or otherwise as may be just.

## 23. Further particulars (O. 103 r. 23)

The Court may at any stage of the proceedings order a party to serve on any other party further or better particulars of infringements or of objections.

## 24. Restrictions on admission of evidence (O. 103 r. 24)

(1) Except with the leave of the judge hearing any action or other proceeding relating to a patent, no evidence shall be admissible in proof of any alleged infringement, or of any objection to the validity, of the patent, if the infringement or objection was not raised in the particulars of infringements or objections, as the case may be.

(2) In any action or other proceeding relating to a patent, evidence which is not in accordance with a statement contained in particulars of objections to the validity of the patent shall not be admissible in support of such an objection unless the judge hearing the proceeding allows the evidence to be admitted.

(3) If any machinery or apparatus alleged to have been used before the priority date mentioned in rule 21(2)(b) is in existence at the date of service of the particulars of objections, no evidence of its user before that date shall be admissible unless it is proved that the party relying on such user offered, where the machinery or apparatus is in his possession, inspection of it to the other parties to the proceedings, or, where it is not, did his best to obtain inspection of it for those parties.

## 25. Proceedings for infringement: admissions must be requested (O. 103 r. 25)

(1) In an action for infringement of a patent (whether or not any other relief is claimed) each party must, within 14 days after service of a reply or answer or after the expiration of the period fixed for service thereof, write to each other party from whom he requires an admission for the purpose of the action or proceedings requesting him to make the admission, and the party receiving the request must within 14 days after the receipt thereof reply in writing making the admission or stating that he refuses to make it.

(2) No order shall be made authorizing a party to any such action or proceedings to serve any interrogatory on any other party unless the first-mentioned party requested that other party in accordance with paragraph (1) to admit the facts sought to be proved by the answer to the interrogatory and the other party refused or failed to comply with the request.

**26. Proceedings for infringement: case management summons** (O. 103 r. 26)

(1)   In such an action, and in such proceedings, as are referred to in rule 25(1), the plaintiff or petitioner must—

(a)   within one month after the date on which the last reply to a request made under rule 25(1) is received or after the date on which the period fixed for making such a reply expires, whichever first occurs, or

(b)   if no request for an admission is made by any party to the action or proceedings, within one month after service of a reply or answer or after the expiration of the period fixed for service thereof,

take out a case management summons as to the place and mode of trial returnable in not less than 21 days, and if the plaintiff or petitioner does not take out such a summons in accordance with this paragraph, the defendant or respondent, as the case may be, may do so. (L.N. 152 of 2008)

The summons may be heard in chambers or in court as the Court thinks fit.

(2)   The Court hearing a summons under this rule may give such directions—

(a)   for the service of further pleadings or particulars,

(b)   the discovery of documents,

(c)   (subject to rule 25(2)) for the service of interrogatories and of answers thereto,

(d)   for the taking by affidavit of evidence relating to matters requiring expert knowledge, and for the filing of such affidavits and the service of copies thereof on the other parties,

(e)   for the service on the other parties, by any party desiring to submit experimental proof, of full and precise particulars of the experiments proposed and of the facts which he claims to be able to establish thereby,

(f)   for the making of experiments, tests, inspections or reports,

(g)   for the hearing, as a preliminary issue, of any question that may arise (including any question as to the construction of the specification or other documents),

and otherwise as the Court thinks necessary or expedient for the purpose of defining and limiting the issues to be tried, restricting the number of witnesses to be called at the trial of any particular issue and otherwise securing that the case shall be disposed of, consistently with adequate hearing, in the most expeditious manner.

Where evidence is directed to be given by affidavit, the deponents must attend at the trial for cross-examination unless, with the concurrence of the Court, the parties otherwise agree.

(3)   Order 24, rules 1 and 2, shall not apply in an action for infringement of a patent.

(4)   No action for a declaration under section 8(1) of the Ordinance shall be set down for trial unless and until a summons under this rule in the action or proceedings has been taken out and the directions given on the summons have been carried out or the time fixed by the Court for carrying them out has expired.

(5)   An action for a declaration under section 8(1) of the Ordinance shall not be tried sooner than 21 days after the action has been set down for trial.

**27. Appointment of scientific adviser** (O. 103 r. 27)

(1)   In an action for infringement of a patent and in any proceedings under the Ordinance, the Court may at any time, and on or without the application of any party, appoint an independent scientific adviser to assist the Court or to inquire and report on any question of fact or of opinion not involving questions of law or construction.

(2)   The Court may nominate the scientific adviser and shall settle the question or instructions to be submitted or given to him.

(3)   The remuneration of any adviser appointed under this rule shall be fixed by the Court and shall include the costs of making any report and a proper daily fee for any day on which he is required to attend before the Court.

(4)   Order 40, rules 2, 3, 4 and 6, shall apply in relation to an adviser appointed under this rule and any report made by him as they apply in relation to a Court expert and a report made by him.

**NOTES**

**[103.27.1]   Numbering**
There is no rule 28 in Order 103.

**29. Application for rectification of register of patents in Hong Kong** (O. 103 r. 29)

An application to the Court for an order that the register of patents be rectified must be made by originating summons, except where it is made by way of counterclaim in proceedings for infringement or by originating summons in proceedings for an order under section 52 of the Trustee Ordinance (Cap 29).

**(Enacted 1988) (L.N. 152 of 2008)**

**NOTES**

**[103.29.1]   Application for rectification of register of patents**
Order 103 rule 29 was amended taking effect in 2009 to make it clear that applications for rectification of the register of patents should normally be made by originating summons. There had previously been some doubt arising from the replacement of the primary legislation, the Patents Ordinance (Cap 514), as noted in *Re Wing Yick Bamboo Scaffolders Ltd* [2002] 1 HKC 395.

**[103.29.2]   Numbering**
Order 104 has been omitted from the Hong Kong rules. The Order of the same number in the former English RSC provided for proceedings relating to patents and registered designs. In *Re Low Ban Chai* [1999] 1 HKC 413 Yuen J had before her what appeared to be the first such application since the enactment of the Patents Ordinance 1997. The learned judge noted the absence of rules of court in Hong Kong and gave directions to bring notice of the application to interested parties, by advertisement

in the gazette, following roughly Order 104 rule 3 of the former English rules. The equivalent provisions in England are now found in CPR Part 63.

Order 105 is also omitted in Hong Kong.

## ORDER 106

### PROCEEDINGS RELATING TO SOLICITORS:
### THE LEGAL PRACTITIONERS ORDINANCE

1.  **Definitions** (O. 106 r. 1)
    **In this Order–**
    **"the Ordinance" means the Legal Practitioners Ordinance (Cap 159);**
    **"appeal" means an appeal against any order made by the disciplinary tribunal on an application or complaint under the Ordinance; (L.N. 275 of 1998)**
    **"disciplinary tribunal" means the Solicitors Disciplinary Tribunal constituted in accordance with section 9B of the Ordinance; (L.N. 275 of 1998)**
    **"Society" means The Law Society of Hong Kong.**

    **(L.N. 275 of 1998)**

---

**NOTES**

**[106.1.1]    Comparison with English rules**
Order 106 is based upon the English Order of the same number. When the Woolf reforms were implemented with the enactment of the Civil Procedure Rules, the English Order 106 was retained. The Hong Kong rules have equivalents in the surviving English Order 106, but there are additional rules in the English Order which have not been adopted in Hong Kong.

**[106.1.2]    Scope of Order 106**
Order 106 deals with proceedings relating to solicitors under the Legal Practitioners Ordinance (Cap 159). These include appeals to the Court of Appeal against decisions of the Solicitors' Disciplinary Tribunal and applications to the Court of First Instance relating to remuneration of solicitors.

**[106.1.3]    Disciplinary proceedings against solicitors**
The court has inherent jurisdiction to enforce honourable conduct on the part of solicitors by virtue of their being officers of the court: *Re H A Grey* [1892] 2 QB 440, 443. The jurisdiction is both penal and compensatory: *Myers v Elman* [1940] AC 282, 319. The penal jurisdiction is in practice no longer exercised and is left to the Solicitors Disciplinary Tribunal: *R & T Thew Ltd v Reeves (No 2)* [1982] 1 QB 1283, 1286A. Proceedings in the tribunal are governed by the Solicitors Disciplinary Tribunal Proceedings Rules, subsidiary legislation under the Legal Practitioners Ordinance (Cap 159). The power to make a compensatory costs order against a solicitor remains with the court and in Hong Kong is governed by Order 62 rule 8.

**[106.1.4]    Solicitors' Disciplinary Tribunal**
According to section 9A(1) of the Legal Practitioners Ordinance, whenever the Council of the Law Society considers that the conduct of a solicitor, trainee solicitor, foreign lawyer or employee of a solicitor or foreign lawyer should be inquired into and investigated as a result of a complaint made to it or otherwise, the matter will be submitted to the Tribunal Convenor of the Solicitors' Disciplinary Tribunal Panel who will appoint a Tribunal to inquire into and investigate the

matter. If the Tribunal concludes that a *prima facie* case has been shown, it will conduct a hearing and have the same powers as a court in respect of such matters as enforcing the attendance of witnesses and adjourning the hearing (section 11(1) of the Legal Practitioners Ordinance). Upon finding that a solicitor has been guilty of misconduct, the Tribunal is empowered to strike the solicitor off the roll or suspend him, permit the solicitor to continue to practice subject to conditions, order him to repay fees to his client, order him to pay a financial penalty, or censure him. It may also order the solicitor to pay the costs of the proceedings. It may cancel or suspend a trainee solicitor contract. In respect of a foreign lawyer, the Tribunal may cancel or suspend his registration or impose conditions on his registration.

**[106.1.5]   Status of the Solicitors Disciplinary Tribunal – application of the Hong Kong Bill of Rights and the ICCPR**

In *Tse Wai Chun Paul v Solicitors Disciplinary Tribunal & The Law Society of Hong Kong* [2002] 4 HKC 1 Le Pichon JA, giving the judgment of the Court of Appeal, held as follows:

(i)    The Solicitors Disciplinary Tribunal is not a court 'of the classic kind' and under the '*Tehrani*' principle (*Tehrani v United Kingdom Council for Nursing, Midwifery and Health Visiting* [2001] 1 IRLR 208) its proceedings are not required to be held in public. Section 9B(4) of the Legal Practitioners Ordinance, which provides that the Tribunal shall sit *in camera*, does not contravene the requirements of the ICCPR or the Hong Kong Bill of Rights as to hearings in public and is not unconstitutional.

(ii)   (*Obiter*) the Tribunal is not a 'public authority' for the purposes of section 7 of the Hong Kong Bill of Rights Ordinance (BORO) and thus is not bound by that Ordinance.

(iii)  The requirement of Order 106 rule 12(1) that the appellant shall not be named in the originating motion does not prevent a solicitor-appellant from publicising appeal proceedings which he/she has brought. Such an appeal is heard in public, with the effect that there could in any event be no breach of BORO since the rights prescribed by ICCPR and BORO can be satisfied by a public appeal even though the decision subject to the appeal was delivered in private.

Leave to appeal to the Court of Final Appeal was refused (FAMV 46/2002 (Li CJ; Bokhary & Chan PJJ; 13.02.2003)) on the ground there was no reasonable prospect of the CFA coming to a different result. However, in the subsequent case of *Solicitor (301/02) v Law Society of Hong Kong* [2006] 2 HKC 40 (CA) a substantially different result was reached on two of the above points. First, it was held that the tribunal is a court, at least for the purposes of article 35 of the Basic Law (which guarantees the right of access to the courts); secondly, it was held by a majority that the tribunal is a public authority and bound by the Hong Kong Bill of Rights Ordinance. The first of those issues reached the Court of Final Appeal in another context in *Stock Exchange of HK Ltd v New World Development Co Ltd & Ors* [2006] 2 HKC 533. The CFA held that BL 35 applies only to judicial organs, and not to tribunals such as the Disciplinary Committee of the stock exchange. It specifically disapproved of the finding in CACV 302/2002 that the Solicitors' Disciplinary Tribunal is a court within BL 35.

**[106.1.6] Role of the clerk to the Solicitors Disciplinary Tribunal**

The members of the Solicitors Disciplinary Tribunal are assisted by a clerk, who is a practising solicitor chosen from a panel.

The clerk should not have any role in the decision-making process: *Au Wing Lun, William v The Solicitors Disciplinary Tribunal & Anor* CACV 4154/2001 (Rogers VP; Le Pichon & Yuen JJA; 09.09.2002). In that case the clerk had drafted the tribunal's findings, thereby giving rise to what the majority described as a 'grave suspicion that at the very least justice does not appear to have been done'. The majority referred to *Re Sawyer and Ontario Racing Commission* (1979) 24 DLR (2d) 673, (1980) 99 DLR (3d) 561 (CA); *Khan v College of Physicians and Surgeons of Ontario* (1992) 9 OR (3d) 641; *The King v Sussex Justices* [1924] 1 KB 256; and *R v Salford Assessment Committee* [1937] 2 All ER 98, 103.

This issue arose again in *Solicitors A & B v Law Society of Hong Kong* [2005] 2 HKC 573 (CA) (leave to appeal to CFA refused – see CACV 269/2004 (Rogers VP, Le Pichon JA & Burrell J; 23.11.2005)) where the tribunal sought to justify reliance on the clerk to draft findings on the basis that the clerk did not take part in the decision-making process and, unlike the tribunal members, is remunerated. In *Law Society of Hong Kong v Solicitor* [2006] 1 HKLRD 49 (CA) it was held that the clerk should take no part at all in drafting the decision of the tribunal, nor conduct research for its use.

The above decisions on the role of the clerk to the Solicitors Disciplinary Tribunal should be read in the light of the subsequent decision in *Medical Council of Hong Kong v Helen Chan* [2010] 4 HKC 539 (CFA) which would seem to permit the legal adviser to a professional disciplinary tribunal to have some role in drafting the decision.

**[106.1.7] Costs of proceedings before the Solicitors Disciplinary Tribunal**

The rule that costs will normally follow the event applies in solicitors' disciplinary matters: *A Solicitor (274/06) v Law Society of Hong Kong* [2007] 5 HKC 58 (CA). There it was held that in Hong Kong, unlike England, there is no general rule that costs of unsuccessful disciplinary proceedings should not be ordered against the Law Society. It is clear from *Au Wing Lun* (above) that the tribunal should only depart from the rule that costs follow the event in circumstances where a court would be likely to do so. There it was held that it was wrong in principle for the tribunal to order a solicitor to pay costs in relation to a charge of which he was acquitted, unless he had raised issues or made allegations improperly or unreasonably. Further it was wrong to order a solicitor to pay costs in relation to a disciplinary complaint which was made not against him, but his clerk.

For a concise summary of the factors which should be taken into account by the tribunal in determining the question of costs, see *A Solicitor v Law Society of Hong Kong* [2005] 4 HKC 290 (CA) (para 24). See also *A Solicitor v Law Society of Hong Kong* CACV 149/2008 (Rogers VP, Le Pichon JA & Poon J; 16.06.2009) (para 20) where the court criticised the costs incurred in engaging a solicitor with 10 years experience as clerk to the tribunal. It was said that justification should be required for employment of anyone other than an unqualified clerical or secretarial person.

It was once common for solicitors found guilty of misconduct to be ordered to pay costs on the indemnity basis. The power to make such an order is found in section 10(2)(e) of the Legal Practitioners Ordinance (Cap 159). However in *Solicitor*

*(301/02) v Law Society of Hong Kong* [2006] 2 HKC 40 (CA) it was held that such orders should only be made in exceptional circumstances. Insofar as the reasoning in that judgment is based on art 35 of the Basic Law (right of access to the courts) it may now be open to reconsideration in view of the CFA's judgment in the *Stock Exchange of HK* case where it was held that art 35 does not apply to the tribunal (see above).

### [106.1.8]   Standard of proof before the Tribunal

It has long been held in Hong Kong that disciplinary proceedings against solicitors are not criminal in nature and the criminal standard of proof does not apply. See, for example, *Re a Solicitor* [1988] 2 HKLR 137, 145C (CA). In many cases in Hong Kong and elsewhere the courts have held that the standard of proof is flexible, depending on the gravity of the charge. After a full review of these authorities, the Court of Final Appeal confirmed in *A Solicitor (24/07) v Law Society of Hong Kong* [2008] 2 HKC 1 that the civil standard applies in the solicitors' disciplinary tribunal, but the less probable the prosecution case, the stronger the evidence needs to be to prove it. In so deciding the CFA declined to follow *Campbell v Hamlet* [2005] 3 All ER 1116 where the Privy Council held that the criminal standard should apply in disciplinary proceedings against lawyers. The CFA's judgment expressly applies to other disciplinary tribunals as well.

### [106.1.9]   Appeal from the Solicitors Disciplinary Tribunal to the Court of Appeal

Section 13 of the Legal Practitioners Ordinance (Cap 159) provides for appeals from the Solicitors Disciplinary Tribunal to the Court of Appeal. See the commentary under Order 106 rule 11.

**2.   Jurisdiction under Part VI of the Ordinance exercisable by judge in chambers, etc.** (O. 106 r. 2)

**(1)   Any application to the Court under Part VI of the Ordinance may be disposed of in chambers.**

**(2)   The jurisdiction of the Court under Part VI of the Ordinance may be exercised by a judge in chambers.**

---

## NOTES

### [106.2.1]   Proceedings under Part VI of the Legal Practitioners Ordinance: Taxation as between solicitor and own client

Order 106 rule 2 concerns applications under Part VI of the Legal Practitioners Ordinance (Cap 159). That part of the Ordinance deals with remuneration of solicitors. Of particular note is section 67 which empowers the court to order taxation of a solicitor's bill of costs as between the solicitor and own client. This enables the court to resolve disputes with clients as to the quantum of solicitors' bills. The section also provides for taxation of the bills of foreign lawyers.

Order 106 rule 2 provides that proceedings under part VI of the Ordinance may be dealt with in chambers, and may be exercised by a judge. In practice such proceedings are usually dealt with by masters.

**[106.2.2]    Jurisdiction to conduct solicitor and own client taxation**

The power to tax a bill of costs as between solicitor and client is vested exclusively in the Court of First Instance. The District Court has no jurisdiction: *Kao, Lee & Yip v High View Properties Ltd & Anor* [1988] 1 HKLR 555 (CA). Where a solicitor claims unpaid costs in the District Court and the amount is disputed, that court should transfer the matter to the CFI for taxation: *Oldham, Li & Nie v Wong Lin Chooi* [2006] 2 HKC 397 (CA). The Small Claims Tribunal has no power to refer a solicitor and own client bill for taxation: *Chan & Kong v Sky Blue Investment Ltd* [1999] 2 HKC 703.

The jurisdiction to tax a solicitor's bill extends to charges for any work done by a solicitor who is retained as a solicitor, even if the work is not strictly solicitor's work. See *Super Strategy Investments Ltd & Anor v Kao, Lee & Yip (a firm)* HCMP 1752/2007 (Fung J; 19.02.2008); [2008] 5 HKC 71 (Saunders J; 19.06.2008). where it was held that the court's powers under part VI of the Ordinance applied to a solicitor's consultancy fee in relation to a property redevelopment because the solicitor had been retained as such. The court distinguished the position in the United Kingdom where the relevant legislation is worded differently, and explained *Re Baker, Lees & Co* [1903] 1 KB 189 (charges for acting as 'parliamentary agent' not liable to be taxed) and *Allen v Aldridge* (1884) 49 ER 633 (charges of a solicitor as 'steward of a manor' likewise not subject to taxation). The decision of Saunders J in *Super Strategy* was appealed. While the Court of Appeal dismissed the appeal ([2009] 3 HKC 92), it preferred (at para 16) to leave open the question whether a solicitor can make a contract with a client to undertake solicitor's work and also provide services distinct from the services of a solicitor.

**[106.2.3]    Right to solicitor and own client taxation within one month of delivery of the bill**

Section 67(1) of the Legal Practitioners Ordinance provides that the court 'shall' order taxation where application is made within one month of delivery of the bill. The party seeking taxation (whether solicitor, foreign lawyer or client) is entitled to an order for taxation 'as of right': *South Horizon Int'l Petroleum Ltd v Crump & Co* [2001] 3 HKC 304, 309E (reversed by the Court of Appeal on other grounds at [2002] 1 HKC 620).

**[106.2.4]    Discretion to order taxation of solicitor and own client bill after one month from delivery**

After the expiration of one month from the delivery of a solicitor's bill the court 'may' order taxation: section 67(2). The discretion should generally be exercised in favour of taxation 'unless the application is an abuse of proceedings or not *bona fide* made': see *Simmons & Simmons v Dillon* HCA 2784/2003 (Deputy Judge To; 14.02.2006) where the court refused an application for taxation which it considered to be a 'delaying tactic'. Terms, other than terms as to the costs of the taxation, may be imposed. Such terms may include an order for interim payment on account of the solicitor's bill: *Tin Tin Publication Development Co Ltd v John Ho & Tsui* HCMP 6586/2000 (Waung J; 26.04.2001); *To Kan Chi & Ors v Miller Peart* [2007] 3 HKC 585 (para 107). In the latter case it was also argued that the court may order payment into court of security for the solicitor's bill, but no such order was made in the circumstances of the case (para 116).

**[106.2.5]   Limitation on power to order taxation after 12 months from delivery or if bill has been paid – 'special circumstances' requirement**

The power to order taxation of a solicitor's bill is subject to the proviso to section 67(2) whereby if more than 12 months has expired since delivery, or the bill has been paid, special circumstances must be shown. The 12 month period runs from the date of delivery of the solicitor's bill (or, where there are interim bills, from the date of the final bill – see below). If the application is made within 12 months the 'special circumstances' requirement does not apply even if the court does not give its decision until later: *ETC Environmental Technology Ltd v Alvan Liu & Partners* [2004] 4 HKC 433 (CA).

The purpose of the limitation on the court's power to order taxation after 12 months is to 'protect solicitors who are entitled to payment for services rendered within a reasonable time': *Cheung Chi Keung v Ince & Co* HCMP 304/2005 (Burrell J; 05.12.2005).

In this context 'special circumstances' is to be given a 'wide, comprehensive and flexible' interpretation: *Re Norman* (1886) 16 QBD 673, 677. The test is 'stringent': *South Horizons Int'l Petroleum Ltd v Crump & Co* [2002] 1 HKC 620, 626B (CA). There must be something 'out of the ordinary', something which is 'serious' and 'justifies not only an ordinary taxation but a special one': *Clayton Wong & Co v Springbok Shipping (HK) Ltd* [1997] 3 HKC 710, 713H-I (CA). Apparent overcharging may be taken into account: *Re A Solicitor* [1961] 1 Ch 491, 504; *Mong Man Wai v H H Lau & Co* [2003] 4 HKC 587, 605H-606C. The court may take into account the fact that on payment of the bill the client reserved its rights: *Clayton Wong & Co*, above, at 714H-I). However the client may not by reserving rights override the time limits prescribed by the legislation: *South Horizons* (above, at 626C-D).

In *Greaterchinaherbs.com Ltd v Deacons* HCMP 1079/2002 (Master Woolley; 06.08.2002) it was argued that failure by a solicitor to comply with the duty to inform a client of the right to apply for taxation may constitute 'special circumstances'. That duty is expressed in the commentary to principle 4.11 of the Hong Kong Solicitors' Guide to Professional Conduct as arising when there is a 'dispute' or 'query' about a bill. In *Greaterchinaherbs.com* the court observed (*obiter*) that something more than a simple enquiry is required, that the query should be in the nature of a complaint before the duty arises.

**[106.2.6]   No taxation more than 12 months after payment**

Once 12 months have expired after payment of a solicitor's bill no order for taxation may be made: see paragraph (ii) of the proviso to section 67(2). The court 'has no jurisdiction to order taxation': *Chin Yuk Lun Francis & Anor v Lo & Lo* HCMP 1142/2005 (Deputy Judge To; 07.07.2006) (para 8).

**[106.2.7]   Calculation of time where bills issued in series**

Where a solicitor issues a series of bills in respect of the same matter, the time within which application for solicitor and own client taxation must be made may run from the final bill: *Wang Yoeh Yu Ruth v Chan Victoria* [1988] HKC 687, citing *Chamberlain v Boodle & King* [1982] 1 WLR 1443, 1446. For a lengthy and learned discussion of when a series of solicitor's bills may be considered to be a single bill for this purpose, see *Chin Yuk Lun Francis* (above), citing *Romer v Haslam* [1893] 2 QB 286. The following important points are elucidated in *Chin Yuk Lun*:

- A 'final' bill is not necessarily the last in the series (citing with approval *De Cotiis v Owen Bird* (1998) 51 BCLR (3d) 272 (BCCA).
- A solicitor may issue 'final' bills at natural breaks in handling a matter with the result that more than one of a series of bills may be considered final.
- Time will run from delivery of the final in a series of bills even if it is withdrawn – a solicitor may not, by withdrawing the final bill, prejudice the client's right to seek taxation.

See also *Lee Chi Enterprises Co Ltd v KC Ho & Fong* HCMP 61/2007 (Recorder A Ho, SC; 13.09.2007) where it was held that a group of bills issued over about 13 months, all relating to conduct of a High Court action to which the client was a party, constituted a series.

## [106.2.8]    Effect of agreement between solicitor and client as to costs

Agreements between solicitor and client as to charges for non-contentious work are permitted. Such agreements are enforceable, but may be cancelled by the court or the amount payable reduced on taxation. See section 56 of the Legal Practitioners Ordinance and see *Lau Leung Wa & Anor v Lau Yue Kui & Anor* HCAP 10/2001 (Chung J; 10.03.2006).

In *Chin Yuk Lun Francis* (above) it was stated (at para 34), in a case involving contentious work, that the statutory power to order taxation 'overrides the agreement between the client and the solicitor'.

## [106.2.9]    Taxation application of third parties

A third party who, although not the solicitor's client, has paid or is liable to pay the solicitor's bill, may apply for taxation of the bill in the same way as the client may: Legal Practitioners Ordinance, s 68. In *Oriental Properties LLC v JSM* HCMP 1281/2005 (Deputy Judge Gill; 15.05.2006) the court refused to order such a taxation where the solicitors' costs which the third party sought to tax were in reality part of an overall debt which the third party had assumed.

## [106.2.10]    Procedure for taxation as between solicitor and own client

An application for an order for taxation of a solicitor's bill as between solicitor and own client should be made by originating summons in Form 10 in Appendix A to these rules: see Order 106 rule 5. Such an application will normally be brought before a master in chambers, though it is also possible, under Order 106 rule 2(2), to bring the application before a judge in chambers.

The Registrar usefully summarised the procedure for solicitor and own client taxations under section 67 of the Ordinance in *Good Harvest Investment Co Ltd v Jewkes Chan & Partners* HCMP 4770/2000 (Mr Registrar Chan; 15.08.2001). The learned registrar stated:

> For the sake of clarity I set out the procedure which this type of case should follow:
>
> (a) An application for taxation of the bill under section 67 should be made by way of originating summons in form No 10 (Order 106 rule 2 and rule 5).
> (b) Acknowledgment of service with notice of intention to defend within the period specified in Order 12 rules 5 and 9.
> (c) The plaintiff should file with the court and serve on the defendant the affidavit evidence he intends to rely on, at least, setting out the issues and exhibiting the bill pursuant to Order 28 rules 1A(1) and (3).

(d)   Whether the defendant needs to file any affidavit evidence and whether the plaintiff has to file further affidavit evidence thereafter pursuant to Order 28 rule 1A(4) and (5) depends very much on the circumstances and the issues raised.

(e)   At the appointed time as set out in the originating summons before the master the parties should bear in mind and consider at least the following issues:

   (i)    whether the application is made under subsection (1) or subsection (2) of section 67 of the Legal Practitioners Ordinance;

   (ii)   whether an itemised bill should be ordered (section 63);

   (iii)  whether certain issues should be heard and disposed of before the substantive taxation hearing; and

   (iv)   what are the appropriate directions sought.

*Right of audience* – At the initial stage, when at the hearing of the originating summons the court considers whether to order that the solicitor's bill be taxed, law costs draftsmen do not have the right of audience. However, they do have the right of audience at the subsequent taxation. See *Tang Lik Yuen v Joseph Leung & Associates* HCMP 2046/2009 (Registrar Au–Yeung; 30.10.2009).

*Order for itemised bill* – A solicitor's bill in relation to 'contentious business' may 'either contain detailed items or be for a gross sum': Legal Practitioners Ordinance (Cap 159), s 63. (The term 'contentious business' is defined in the Ordinance to include any business done in any court, whether as solicitor or as advocate.) A gross sum bill should contain 'sufficient particulars to enable the client to judge the fairness of the charges': *Kao Lee & Yip v Carey & Lui* [1999] 1 HKC 88, 91G, quoting Cook on *Costs*. The client has a right under s 63(a) to demand a detailed bill within a limited time and, on taxation, the court has power to require that details be given (s 63(c)). That power need not be exercised in every case as a properly cast gross sum bill should 'largely be capable of taxation without additional information' (*Kao Lee & Yip* at 93F-G). Where the court orders that a gross sum bill be itemised for the purposes of taxation, with the result that additional items not included in the original bill are claimed, the court may have regard to those additional items – the original bill is 'in the nature of an interim bill' and adjustments are permissible. See *Hampton Winter & Glynn (a firm) v Campbell* HCA 2176/1996 (Master Chu; 18.09.1997). As to itemisation of solicitors' bills in non-contentious matters, see Law Society practice direction B1.

*Discovery* – When ordering a solicitor and own client taxation the court may direct that the client be at liberty to inspect the solicitor's file before the taxation hearing. In *Good Harvest Investment Co Ltd v Jewkes Chan & Partners* HCMP 4770/2000 (Mr Registrar Chan; 15.08.2001) it was held that it was inappropriate to make such an order prior to the filing of evidence by the parties.

### [106.2.11]   Criteria applicable on solicitor and own client taxation

The criteria applicable on a taxation as between solicitor and own client are different in contentious and non-contentious cases. Where the solicitor was retained by the client to handle contentious business Order 62 rule 29 applies. In respect of non-contentious business the criteria are those laid down in rule 5 of the Solicitors (General) Costs Rules (Cap 159). The terms 'contentious business' and 'non-contentious business' are defined in section 2 of the Legal Practitioners Ordinance with the former including business conducted in any court, whether as solicitor or advocate, and the latter including commercial and conveyancing matters. In this context 'court' includes courts both within and outside Hong Kong: see *South Horizon International Petroleum Ltd v Crump & Co* [2001] 3 HKC 304, 311E–H (reversed by the Court of Appeal on other grounds at [2002] 1 HKC 620).

Rule 5 of the Solicitors (General) Costs Rules provides that costs for non-contentious business shall be a 'fair and reasonable' amount, having regard to all the circumstances of the case and in particular to seven enumerated factors. Those factors include the degree of complexity and responsibility involved, the number of documents and the time spent by the solicitor as well as the weightiness of the matter measured by value and importance to the client. In *China Creator Estate Ltd v K C Ho & Fong* HCMP 2689/1987 (Ribeiro J; 03.01.2000, unreported) the court emphasised that under rule 5 the number of hours spent by the solicitor 'may be an insignificant indicator of what would constitute a fair and reasonable fee'.

**[106.2.12]   Taxation of counsel's fees and other disbursements**
The court's power to tax a solicitor's bill as between the solicitor and his own client applies to all items on the bill, whether profit costs or disbursements such as counsel's fees.

The following principles in relation to taxation of disbursements emerge from the decision in *Mong Man Wai v H H Lau & Co* [2003] 4 HKC 587:

(i)   The court has no power to tax a disbursement which does not appear on a solicitor's bill, even though it has been paid. In the words of Deputy Judge A Cheung (at 595 C–D) section 67 'is simply not engaged'.

(ii)   The court has an inherent jurisdiction over its own officers to order a solicitor to deliver a bill (at 595G–H citing *Storer v Johnson* (1890) 15 App Cas 203; *Re Thomas* [1894] 1 QB 747; *Re Foster, Barnato v Foster* [1920] 3 KB 306) and other authorities.

(iii)   There 'can be no objection in principle' to the court making an order in exercise of its inherent jurisdiction requiring a solicitor to deliver a bill of costs in respect of counsel's fees as disbursements, and once that has been done, to order taxation of the bill pursuant to section 67 (see at 596 B–C).

(iv)   It is 'a basic right of a client that he should be supplied with a complete bill containing the whole of the fees, charges and disbursements, so as to enable him to check the bill and form a fair opinion' (at 604 E–F).

(v)   The fact that a disbursement has been paid directly by the lay client and not by the solicitor is no obstacle to inclusion on the solicitor's bill, nor to taxation, since the client makes payment as agent of the solicitor (see at 603 G-604B, citing *Re Osborn & Osborn* [1913] 3 KB 862).

In *Mong Man Wai* the court made orders in accordance with the above principles in the unusual factual scenario of counsel's fees having been paid directly by the lay client, and the lay client subsequently wishing to seek taxation thereof.

**[106.2.13]   Costs of solicitor and own client taxation**
Section 67(5) of the Legal Practitioners Ordinance provides that if on a solicitor and own client taxation one-sixth or more is taxed off, the solicitor shall pay the costs, but otherwise the client shall pay. If the bill relates to non-contentious work at least half of which is not the subject of a scale charge then only one-fifth needs to be taxed off for the solicitor to be ordered to pay the costs.

The above general rule applies unless the order for taxation otherwise provides. In *Stevenson, Wong & Lai v Yue Feng Knitting Factory Ltd* HCMP 2470/2000 (Master Kwan; 17.03.2001), a master ordered that two solicitors' bills be taxed, and that costs be reserved. Later, the two bills were taxed before a different master. Following that taxation, the second master held that she was not bound by the one-sixth rule since the first master, in reserving costs, had meant that the taxing master would have discretion over costs.

Under the Ordinance the one-sixth rule does not apply if it is the solicitor who applies for taxation and the client does not attend.

A solicitor in whose favour costs are ordered may charge for providing details of a gross sum bill. The client who applies for taxation of a gross sum bill runs the risk of being responsible for all the costs of the taxation. See *Kao Lee & Yip v Carey & Lui* [1999] 1 HKC 88, 93H-I.

**3. Power to order solicitor to deliver cash account, etc.** (O. 106 r. 3)

**(1)** **Where the relationship of solicitor and client exists or has existed, the Court may, on the application of the client or his personal representative, make an order for—**

> **(a) the delivery by the solicitor of a cash account;**
>
> **(b) the payment or delivery up by the solicitor of money or securities;**
>
> **(c) the delivery to the plaintiff of a list of the moneys or securities which the solicitor has in his possession or control on behalf of the plaintiff;**
>
> **(d) the payment into or lodging in court of any such moneys or securities.**

**(2)** **An application for an order under this rule must be made by originating summons.**

**(3)** **If the defendant alleges that he has a claim for costs, the Court may make such order for the taxation and payment, or securing the payment, thereof and the protection of the defendant's lien, if any, as the Court thinks fit.**

---

**NOTES**

**[106.3.1] Comparison with English rule**

Order 106 rule 4 of the English rules deals with petitions in the Chancery Division and has been omitted from the Hong Kong rules.

**5. Form of originating summons** (O. 106 r. 5)

**An originating summons by which an application under the Ordinance, or any application for an order under rule 3, is made shall be in Form No 10 in Appendix A.**

---

**NOTES**

**[106.5.1] Sequence of rules**

Note that rules 5A to 9 are omitted from Hong Kong's Order 106.

**10. Service of documents** (O. 106 r. 10)

(1) **Any document required to be served on the Society in proceedings under this Order shall be served by sending it by prepaid post to the secretary of the Society.**

(2) **Subject to paragraph (1), any document not required to be served personally which is to be served on a defendant to proceedings under this Order shall, unless the Court otherwise directs, be deemed to be properly served by sending it by prepaid post to the defendant at his last known address.**

**11. Constitution of the Court of Appeal to hear appeals** (O. 106 r. 11)

**Every appeal shall be heard by the Court of Appeal consisting, unless the Chief Justice otherwise directs, of not less than 3 judges.**

---

NOTES

**[106.11.1] Composition of Court of Appeal on appeal from Solicitors Disciplinary Tribunal**

Order 106 rule 11, in providing that an appeal to the Court of Appeal from the Solicitors Disciplinary Tribunal shall normally be heard by not less than 3 judges, does not reflect section 34B(4) of the High Court Ordinance (which provides that the Court of Appeal may sit with only 2 judges where the parties consent). In principle the Ordinance should prevail: see section 28(1)(b) of Cap 1.

**[106.11.2] Appeal by solicitor to the Court of Appeal**

Section 13(1) of the Legal Practitioners Ordinance (Cap 159) provides that a solicitor aggrieved by any order made by the Solicitors Disciplinary Tribunal may appeal to the Court of Appeal. Unlike appeals by the Law Society, there is no general leave requirement. However, where the appeal relates solely to costs, section 14(3)(e) of the High Court Ordinance (Cap 4) applies and the solicitor appellant must obtain leave from the tribunal or from the Court of Appeal: see *A Solicitor v Law Society of Hong Kong* [1995] 1 HKC 834 (CA).

Section 13(1) goes on to provide that the provisions of Order 59 shall apply on the hearing of such an appeal. However, to the extent that Order 106 differs from Order 59 the former shall prevail: *Re a Solicitor* [1988] 2 HKLR 137 (CA), per Barker JA at 144H. Notwithstanding Order 59 rule 4 the time for giving notice of appeal is 21 days (as compared to 28 days for other appeals). The Law Society should be named as respondent to an appeal by a solicitor under section 13(1). It is not appropriate to name the tribunal as respondent – *Solicitor (301/02) v Law Society of HK* [2006] 2 HKC 40, 47I (CA) where the Court of Appeal ordered that the tribunal be struck out as a respondent.

In *Au Wing Lun, William v The Solicitors Disciplinary Tribunal & The Law Society of Hong Kong* (CACV 4154/2001) the solicitor had sought judicial review of the Tribunal rather than availing himself of the statutory appeal process. Yuen JA found against the solicitor on this ground. However, the majority of the Court of Appeal was prepared to allow the appeal on exceptional grounds. Rogers VP said that the decision of the Tribunal on costs was 'not only so clearly wrong but so manifestly unjust that it cannot be allowed to stand'. Le Pichon JA said that there were 'exceptional circumstances'.

**[106.11.3]   Further appeal to Court of Final Appeal**
It is now clear that a solicitor who is not satisfied by a decision of the Court of Appeal on appeal from the Solicitors Disciplinary Tribunal may seek leave to appeal to the Court of Final Appeal.

Section 13(1) of the Legal Practitioners previously stated that an appeal by a solicitor to the Court of Appeal 'shall be final', purportedly ousting the possibility of a further appeal. In *Solicitor v The Law Society of Hong Kong & Secretary for Justice* (2003) 6 HKCFAR 570 (FACV 7/2003) it was held that this finality provision was void on the ground of repugnancy to UK legislation during the colonial era and hence did not become part of the law of Hong Kong on 1 July 1997. The finality provision was repealed by Ordinance No 10 of 2005.

**[106.11.4]   Appeal by Law Society to Court of Appeal**
Previously there was no express right on the part of the Law Society to appeal an order of the Solicitors Disciplinary Tribunal. In 2000 section 13(2A) was added to the Legal Practitioners Ordinance (Cap 159), providing that the Council of the Law Society may, with leave of the Court of Appeal, appeal an order of the Solicitors Disciplinary Tribunal. In *Law Society of Hong Kong v A Solicitor* [2002] 1 HKC 585 (CA) it was argued that this provision does not extend so as to permit an appeal against an *ex parte* order of the tribunal summarily dismissing a complaint against a solicitor. The Court of Appeal set aside leave on the ground that the single judge who had granted it had been misled, leaving open the jurisdictional question.

In the subsequent case of *Law Society of Hong Kong v A Solicitor* [2002] 2 HKC 115 the jurisdiction issue was revisited and it was held that the Court of Appeal does have the power to entertain an appeal against summary dismissal by the Solicitors Disciplinary Tribunal. The court distinguished *Re Stromberg and the Law Society of Saskatchewan* (1996) 132 DLR (4th) 470 (QB) (Sask) and allowed the appeal.

**12. Title, service, etc. of notice of motion** (O. 106 r. 12)
   **(1)   The notice of the originating motion by which an appeal is brought must be entitled in the matter of a solicitor, or, as the case may be, a solicitor's clerk, without naming him, and in the matter of the Ordinance.**
   **(2)   Unless the Court otherwise orders, the persons to be served with such notice are every party to the proceedings before the disciplinary tribunal and the Society. (L.N. 275 of 1998)**
   **(3)   The notice must be served within 21 days from the day on which the order appealed against is pronounced. (L.N. 275 of 1998)**
   **(4)   (Repealed L.N. 275 of 1998)**

**13. Society to produce certain documents** (O. 106 r. 13)
   **(1)   Within 7 days after being served with notice of the originating motion by which an appeal is brought the Society must lodge in the Registry 3 copies of each of the following documents—**
          **(a)   the order appealed against, prefaced by the statement of the disciplinary tribunal's findings required by section 12 of the Ordinance,**

(b) **any document lodged by a party with the disciplinary tribunal which is relevant to a matter in issue on the appeal, and**

(c) **the transcript of the shorthand note, or, as the case may be, the note taken by the chairman of the disciplinary tribunal, of the evidence in the proceedings before the committee. (L.N. 275 of 1998)**

(2) **At the hearing of the appeal the Court shall direct by whom the costs incurred in complying with paragraph (1) are to be borne and may order them to be paid to the Society by one of the parties notwithstanding that the Society does not appear at the hearing.**

## NOTES

### [106.13.1]  Comparison with other appeals
In placing the burden on the Law Society to lodge the appeal documents in every case, this rule differs from the general rule for appeals to the Court of Appeal, Order 59 rule 9, which places the burden on the appellant in each case. In *Re a Solicitor* [1988] 2 HKLR 137, Barker JA held that this rule ousts application of Order 59 rule 9 for the purpose of appeals to the Court of Appeal from the Disciplinary Committee of the Law Society of Hong Kong.

### 14. Restriction on requiring security for costs (O. 106 r. 14)
**No person other than an appellant who was the applicant in the proceedings before the disciplinary tribunal or, in the case of an application to that tribunal by a solicitor to procure his name to be removed from the roll, was an objector, shall be ordered to give security for the costs of an appeal. (L.N. 275 of 1998)**

## NOTES

### [106.14.1]  Comparison with English rule
Under the Hong Kong rule, unlike the equivalent English rule, an objector, in the case of an application to the Disciplinary Tribunal by a solicitor to have his name removed from the roll, may be ordered to give security for costs.

### 15. Disciplinary tribunals opinion may be required (O. 106 r. 15)
**The Court may direct the disciplinary tribunal to furnish the Court with a written statement of their opinion on the case which is the subject-matter of an appeal or on any question arising therein, and where such a direction is given, the clerk to the disciplinary tribunal must as soon as may be lodge 3 copies of such statement in the Registry and at the same time send a copy to each of the parties to the appeal. (L.N. 275 of 1998)**

### 16. Persons entitled to be heard on appeal (O. 106 r. 16)
**A person who has not been served with notice of the originating motion by which an appeal is brought but who desires to be heard in opposition to the appeal shall, if he appears to the Court to be a proper person to be so heard, be entitled to be so heard.**

**17. Discontinuance of appeal** (O. 106 r. 17)

(1)   An appellant may at any time discontinue his appeal by serving notice of discontinuance on the clerk to the disciplinary tribunal and every other party to the appeal and, if the appeal has been entered, by lodging a copy of the notice in the Registry. (L.N. 275 of 1998)

(2)   Where an appeal has been discontinued in accordance with paragraph (1), it shall be treated as having been dismissed with an order for payment by the appellant of the costs of and incidental to the appeal, including any costs incurred by the Society in complying with rule 13(1).

(Enacted 1988)

---

**NOTES**

**[106.17.1]   Numbering**
There is no Order 107, 108, 109, 110, 111 or 112 in Hong Kong.

**ORDER 113**

**SUMMARY PROCEEDINGS FOR POSSESSION OF LAND**

1.      **Where a person claims possession of land which he alleges is occupied solely by a person or persons (not being a tenant or tenants holding over after the termination of the tenancy) who entered into or remained in occupation without his licence or consent or that of any predecessor in title of his, the proceedings may be brought by originating summons in accordance with the provisions of this Order.**

---

**NOTES**

**[113.1.1]**    **Scope of order**
Where, in addition to possession of the land concerned, the plaintiff seeks damages for trespass, it is submitted that proceedings should be commenced by way of writ of summons under Order 6 rather than this Order.

**[113.1.2]**    **Where summary procedure not appropriate**
In some cases the summary procedure provided by this Order will not be appropriate. An example is where there are triable issues of fact. In such cases the appropriate order to be made is that the proceedings be continued under Order 28 rule 8(1) as if the proceedings had been begun by writ, and for consequential directions. See *Mutual Luck Investment Ltd v Chiu Yim Man & Ors* [1999] 3 HKC 399; *Star Ferry Co Ltd v Chuen Wah Trading Co* [1992] 1 HKC 415; *Goldmen Electronic Co Ltd v Shum Wai Man* [2002] 2 HKC 324; *Ricas Properties Ltd v Armed Forces Trading Co Ltd & Ors* [2008] 5 HKC 210. However, the authorities do not support the contention that the Order 113 procedure is only intended for uncontested cases. See *Vipac Engineers & Scientists Ltd v Karpovich & Anor* [1989] 2 HKC 358, 359I where Godfrey J said that the right test is:

> The right test, in my view, is whether the issue between parties is one which the defendant is entitled to have sent to a trial – whether it be an issue of fact or law. If the issue is seen on analysis to be capable of determination in only one way, in favour of the plaintiff, then, as it seems to me, it is proper for the court to exercise the power conferred on it by O 113 and determine the matter, however vigorous the contest may have been.

The above passage continues to be applied: see *Aegis Capital Ltd v Wai Sik Yin Felicia* HCMP 851/2009 (Fung J; 23.06.2010).

**[113.1.3]**    **Occupant an undisclosed principal tenant**
In proceedings for summary possession against a named tenant, a third party, claiming that the named tenant was agent for it as undisclosed principal, may not resist the application on the basis of 'holding over' within the meaning of Order 113 rule 1 where the contract shows that the agent is the true and only principal. See *Shui On Centre Co Ltd v Persons Unknown & Anor* [2002] 2 HKC 263.

**1A. Jurisdiction of masters** (O. 113 r. 1A)
     **Proceedings under this Order may be heard and determined by a master, who may refer them to a judge if he thinks they should properly be decided by the judge. (L.N. 404 of 1991)**

**2.   Form of originating summons** (O. 113 r. 2)

The originating summons shall be in Form No 11A in Appendix A and no acknowledgment of service of it shall be required.

**3.   Affidavit in support** (O. 113 r. 3)

The plaintiff shall file in support of the originating summons an affidavit stating—

    (a)   his interest in the land;

    (b)   the circumstances in which the land has been occupied without licence or consent and in which his claim to possession arises; and

    (c)   that he does not know the name of any person occupying the land who is not named in the summons.

**NOTES**

**[113.3.1]   The affidavit in support - hearsay not permitted**

An application under Order 113 must be supported by an affidavit which sets out the matters stipulated in rule 3. Hearsay evidence on 'information or belief' is not admissible, though it was under the English rule of the same number from which the Hong Kong rule is derived. See *Mutual Luck Investment Ltd v Chiu Yim Man & Ors* [1999] 3 HKC 399, 404 where it was held that evidence by the plaintiff's solicitor was inadmissible hearsay. In England Order 113 was replaced by Part 55 of the CPR.

**4.   Service of originating summons** (O. 113 r. 4)

    **(1)**   Where any person in occupation of the land is named in the originating summons, the summons together with a copy of the affidavit in support shall be served on him—

    (a)   personally, or

**(HK)(aa)**   by sending a copy of the summons and of the affidavit by ordinary post to him at the premises, or

    (b)   by leaving a copy of the summons and of the affidavit, or sending them to him, at the premises, or

    (c)   in such other manner as the Court may direct.

    **(2)**   The summons shall, in addition to being served on the named defendants (if any) in accordance with paragraph (1), be served, unless the Court otherwise directs, by—

    (a)   affixing a copy of the summons and a copy of the affidavit to the main door or other conspicuous part of the premises, and

    (b)   if practicable, inserting through the letter-box at the premises a copy of the summons and a copy of the affidavit enclosed in a sealed envelope addressed to "the occupiers".

    **(2A)**   Every copy of an originating summons for service under paragraph (1) or (2) shall be sealed with the seal of the High Court.

    **(3)**   Order 28, rule 3, shall not apply to proceedings under this Order.

## NOTES

**[113.4.1]    Service of originating summons claiming possession of land**
By its own terms this rule applies only to service of originating summonses claiming possession of land. With respect to writs of summons seeking similar relief there is specific provision in Order 10 rule 4.

**5.    Application by occupier to be made a party** (O. 113 r. 5)
    **Without prejudice to Order 15, rules 6 and 10, any person not named as a defendant who is in occupation of the land and wishes to be heard on the question whether an order for possession should be made may apply at any stage of the proceedings to be joined as a defendant.**

## NOTES

**[113.5.1]    Joinder of party no longer in occupation of land**
Order 113 rule 5 provides that any person in occupation of the land may apply to be joined as a defendant. In *Hilder Co Ltd v Persons Unknown* HCMP 1868/2000 (Reyes J; 29.01.2007) the court allowed joinder of a person who was no longer in occupation of the land. This was justified by the criteria laid down in Order 15 rule 6, to which this rule is expressly subject.

**6.    Order for possession** (O. 113 r. 6)
    **(1)    A final order shall, except in case of urgency and by leave of the Court, not be made less than 5 clear days after the date of service. (L.N. 165 of 1992)**
    **(2)    An order for possession in proceedings under this Order shall be in Form No 42A in Appendix A.**
    **(3)    Nothing in this Order shall prevent the Court from ordering possession to be given on a specified date, in exercise of any power which could have been exercised if possession had been claimed in an action begun by writ.**

**7.    Writ of possession** (O. 113 r. 7)
    **(1)    Order 45, rule 3(2), shall not apply in relation to an order for possession under this Order but no writ of possession to enforce such an order shall be issued after the expiry of 3 months from the date of the order without the leave of the Court.**
    **An application for leave may be made ex parte unless the Court otherwise directs.**
    **(2)    The writ of possession shall be in Form No 66A in Appendix A.**

**8.    Setting aside order** (O. 113 r. 8)
    **The judge may, on such terms as he thinks just, set aside or vary any order made in proceedings under this Order.**

**(Enacted 1988)**

**NOTES**

**[113.8.1]    Jurisdiction of master to set aside order**
Although rule 8 provides only for a judge to set aside or vary an order made under Order 113, the jurisdiction may be exercised by a master. This flows from Order 32 rule 11, the application of which is not precluded by rule 8: *Hilder Co Ltd v Persons Unknown* HCMP 1868/2000 (Reyes J; 29.01.2007).

## ORDER 114

### (HK) COMMISSIONERS FOR OATHS

**1.   Appointment of commissioners for oaths** (O. 114 r. 1)

**(HK)(1)   The Chief Justice may, by a commission signed by him, appoint fit and proper persons to be commissioners to administer oaths and take declarations, affirmations, and attestations of honour, and may revoke any such appointment.**

**(1A)   The power of appointment under paragraph (1) may, by a notice in writing signed by the Chief Justice, be delegated to the Registrar. (L.N. 167 of 1994)**

**(2)   Every person so appointed shall be styled a commissioner for oaths and shall have all the powers and discharge all the duties which now belong to the office of a commissioner to administer oaths.**

---

**NOTES**

**[114.1.1]   Barristers, solicitors, notaries and justices of the peace**
Solicitors holding current practising certificates, notaries and justices of the peace all enjoy the powers of commissioners for oaths. See Legal Practitioners Ordinance (Cap 159), section s 7A and 40B(2)(c), and the Justices of the Peace Ordinance (Cap 510, section 5.

Barristers are not commissioners for oaths in Hong Kong, unlike the situation in England under the Commissioner for Oaths Acts. However a barrister who is 'acting judicially' may take oaths and affirmations by virtue of section 3 of the Oaths and Declarations Ordinance (Cap 11). Further, where a barrister is directed to take an examination (such as under Order 70), there is authority to administer oaths and affirmations under Order 114 rule 2.

**[114.1.2]   Powers of Commissioners for Oaths**
Commissioners for oaths have power to administer oaths and to take affidavits, affirmations and statutory declarations (Oaths and Declarations Ordinance, section 12). The power is exercisable only in Hong Kong. See *Ka Wah Bank Ltd v Low Chung Song & Ors* HCA 4191/1987 (Deputy Judge Cruden; 23.06.1988) (appeal allowed on other grounds – see [1989] 1 HKLR 451) where it was held that an affirmation taken by a Hong Kong solicitor in Taiwan for use in Hong Kong was inadmissible. See also *Yiu Ping Fong & Anor v Lam Lai Hing Lana* [1998] 4 HKC 476 where it was held that statutory declarations made outside Hong Kong are not admissible even if made before a notary of the jurisdiction in which they are made. See Order 41 rule 12 and the commentary thereunder as to the manner in which oaths and affirmations may be made outside of Hong Kong before a Chinese consular official and otherwise.

**2.   Officers of the court to administer oaths** (O. 114 r. 2)

**(HK)   Every person who, being an officer of or performing duties in relation to the Court, is for the time being so authorized by the Court or by or in pursuance of any rules or orders regulating the procedure of the Court,**

**and every person directed to take an examination in any cause or matter in the Court, shall have authority to administer any oath or take any affidavit required for any purpose connected with his duties.**

**(Enacted 1988)**

## ORDER 115

### DRUG TRAFFICKING (RECOVERY OF PROCEEDS) ORDINANCE (CAP 405)

**1. Interpretation** (O. 115 r. 1)

**(1) In this Order "the Ordinance" means the Drug Trafficking (Recovery of Proceeds) Ordinance (Cap 405), and a section referred to by number means the section so numbered in the Ordinance.**

**(2) Expressions used in this Order which are used in the Ordinance have the same meanings in this Order as in the Ordinance.**

---

**NOTES**

**[115.1.1] History and origin of Order 115**
Order 115 was enacted pursuant to the Drug Trafficking (Recovery of Proceeds) Ordinance (Cap 405) in relation to restraint, charging and confiscation orders in respect of the alleged proceeds of drug trafficking. It is similar but not identical to the Order of the same number in the former English Rules of the Supreme Court. The English Order 115 was retained when the Civil Procedure Rules generally replaced the RSC in the late 1990s. Hence subsequent English decisions will have considerable persuasive force in Hong Kong.

**[115.1.2] Human rights considerations**
Our sister publication in the UK (The Civil Court Practice 2007) says of human rights considerations arising in respect of the equivalent legislation there:

> Confiscation proceedings as part of the sentencing process following conviction are not within art 6.2 of the Human Rights Convention [European Convention for the Protection of Human Rights and Fundamental Freedoms] and the procedures provide a fair hearing, as required by art 6.1: *R v Benjafield* [2002] UKHL 2, [2003] 1 AC 1099, [2002] 1 All ER 815; *R v Rezvi* [2002] UKHL 1 [2002] 1 All ER 801.

**2. Assignment of proceedings** (O. 115 r. 2)

**Subject to Order 32, rule 18, and to rule 12, the jurisdiction of the Court under the Ordinance shall be exercised by a judge of the Court in chambers notwithstanding that the originating process is an originating summons. (L.N. 296 of 1996) (L.N. 152 of 2008)**

**2A. Application for confiscation order where person has died or absconded** (O. 115 r. 2A)

**(1) An application for a confiscation order under section 3 where the defendant has died or absconded shall be made by the Secretary for Justice. (89 of 1995, s 30) (L.N. 296 of 1996) (L.N. 362 of 1997) (L.N. 152 of 2008)**

**(2) An application under paragraph (1) may be made by originating summons in Form No. 10 in Appendix A. (L.N. 152 of 2008)**

**NOTES**

**[115.2A.1]   Comparison with English rules**
Order 115 rule 2A is entirely different from the rule of the same number in the English RSC (which rule was retained when the CPR came into force). Rule 2A in England deals with the title to proceedings under Order 115.

**[115.2A.2]   Numbering**
The equivalent Order in England contains rule 2B, which is omitted in Hong Kong.

**3.   Application for restraint order or charging order** (O. 115 r. 3)
    **(1)   An application for a restraint order under section 10 or for a charging order under section 11 (to either of which may be joined an application for the appointment of a receiver) shall be made by the Secretary for Justice ex parte. (L.N. 296 of 1996) (L.N. 362 of 1997) (L.N. 152 of 2008)**
    **(1A)   An application under paragraph (1) may be made by originating summons in Form No. 10 in Appendix A. (L.N. 152 of 2008)**
    **(2)   An application under paragraph (1) shall be supported by an affidavit, which shall—**
        **(a)   state, as the case may be, the grounds for believing that—**
            **(i)   the defendant has benefited from drug trafficking; or**
            **(ii)   the Court of First Instance will be satisfied as specified in section 15(1A); (89 of 1995 s 30; 25 of 1998 s 2)**
        **(b)   state, as the case may be—**
            **(i)   that proceedings have been instituted against the defendant for a drug trafficking offence (giving particulars of the offence) and that they have not been concluded;**
            **(ii)   that, whether by the laying of an information or otherwise, a person is to be charged with a drug trafficking offence;**
            **(iii)   that an application for a confiscation order has been made in respect of the defendant where section 3(1)(a)(ii) or (7) is applicable; or**
            **(iv)   that an application has been made under section 15(1A) in respect of a confiscation order made against the defendant; (89 of 1995 s 30)**
        **(c)   to the best of the deponent's ability, give full particulars of the realisable property in respect of which the order is sought and specify the person or persons holding such property;**
        **(d)   where proceedings have not been instituted, verify that the Secretary for Justice is to have the conduct of the proposed proceedings;**
        **(e)   where proceedings have not been instituted, indicate when it is intended that they should be instituted.**
    **(3)   An originating summons under paragraph (1A) shall be entitled in the matter of the defendant, naming him, and in the matter of the Ordinance, and all subsequent documents in the matter shall be so entitled. (L.N. 152 of 2008)**

**(4)** **Unless the Court otherwise directs, an affidavit under paragraph (2) may contain statements of information or belief with the sources and grounds thereof.**

---

**NOTES**

**[115.3.1]    Procedure – ex parte application by originating motion**

Order 115 rule 3 provides that an application for a restraint order or a charging order under the primary legislation (Cap 405) shall be made by the Secretary for Justice *ex parte* by originating motion. As to the contents of the originating motion, in *Re C* [1990] 1 HKLR 127, 128I-J it was said that the terms of the order sought should be:

> … set out in the body of the originating motion (for example, by saying 'the following terms' or 'the terms set out in the schedule hereto', and then setting them out as indicated) or incorporated by reference (for example, by saying 'the terms set out in the draft order annexed hereto', or something similar).

The *ex parte* summons will be heard in chambers notwithstanding that the originating process is a motion: rule 2.

**4.    Restraint order and charging order** (O. 115 r. 4)

**(1)    A restraint order may be made subject to conditions and exceptions, including but not limited to conditions relating to the indemnifying of third parties against expenses incurred in complying with the order, and exceptions relating to reasonable living expenses and reasonable legal expenses of the defendant, but the Secretary for Justice shall not be required to give an undertaking to abide by any order as to damages sustained by the defendant as a result of the restraint order. (89 of 1995 s 30)**

**(2)    Unless the Court otherwise directs, a restraint order made ex parte shall have effect until a day which shall be fixed for the hearing inter partes of the application and a charging order shall be an order to show cause, imposing the charge until such day.**

**(3)    Where a restraint order is made the Secretary for Justice shall serve copies of the order and of the affidavit in support on the defendant and on all other named persons restrained by the order and shall notify all other persons or bodies affected by the order of its terms.**

**(4)    Where a charging order is made the Secretary for Justice shall, unless the Court otherwise directs, serve copies of the order and of the affidavit in support on the defendant and, where the property to which the order relates is held by another person, on that person and shall serve a copy of the order on such of the persons or bodies specified in Order 50, rule 2(1)(b) to (d) as shall be appropriate.**

---

**NOTES**

**[115.4.1]    Duration of ex parte restraint order**

Rule 4(2) provides that unless the court otherwise orders, an *ex parte* restraint order will normally only have effect until the return day for an *inter partes* hearing. In *Re C* (above) the court was invited to make an *ex parte* restraining order effective 'until further order'. The court declined to do so and instead the judge ascertained that the court would be available for an *inter partes* hearing on the following day and expressly made the order effective only to that date and time.

**[115.4.2]   Third parties have no right to be heard**
Third parties who may claim an interest in the property which is the subject of a confiscation order application have no right to be heard on the application. Their interests are catered for at a later stage when application is made for an order appointing a receiver to realise the property when they have, by section 12(8) of Cap 405, a right to be heard. See *Secretary for Justice v Lee Chau Ping & Anor* [1999] 2 HKC 103, 116G-I, and see the commentary under Order 115 rule 7.

**5.   Discharge or variation of order** (O. 115 r. 5)
**(1)   Any person or body on whom a restraint order or a charging order is served or who is notified of such an order may apply by summons to discharge or vary the order.**
**(2)   The summons and any affidavit in support shall be served on the Secretary for Justice and, where he is not the applicant, on the defendant, not less than 2 clear days before the date fixed for the hearing of the summons. (L.N. 296 of 1996)**
**(3)   Upon the Court being notified that proceedings for the offences have been concluded or that the amount payment of which is secured by a charging order has been paid into court, any restraint order or charging order, as the case may be, shall be discharged.**

**NOTES**

**[115.5.1]   Right to apply for discharge or variation of order**
Order 115 rule 5 provides that any person served with a restraining or charging order may apply for discharge or variation thereof. In *Re C* (above) the court insisted that an *ex parte* restraining order contain an express provision giving the person against whom it was made liberty to apply to discharge the order.

**6.   Further application by Secretary for Justice** (O. 115 r. 6)
**(1)   Where a restraint order or a charging order has been made the Secretary for Justice may apply (and, if so, by summons) or, where the case is one of urgency, ex parte— (L.N. 296 of 1996)**
    **(a)   to discharge or vary such order; or**
    **(b)   for a restraint order or a charging order in respect of other realisable property; or**
    **(c)   for the appointment of a receiver.**
**(2)   An application under paragraph (1) shall be supported by an affidavit which, where the application is for a restraint order or a charging order, shall to the best of the deponent's ability give full particulars of the realisable property in respect of which the order is sought and specify the person or persons holding such property.**

(3)   The summons and affidavit in support shall be served on the defendant and, where one has been appointed in the matter, on the receiver, not less than 2 clear days before the date fixed for the hearing of the summons. (L.N. 296 of 1996)

(4)   Rule 4(3) and (4) shall apply to the service of restraint orders and charging orders respectively made under this rule on persons other than the defendant.

7.   **Realisation of property** (O. 115 r. 7)

(1)   An application under section 12 must be made by the Secretary for Justice. (L.N. 152 of 2008)

(1A)   The application may, where there have been proceedings against the defendant in the Court of First Instance, be made by summons and may otherwise be made by originating summons in Form No. 10 in Appendix A. (L.N. 152 of 2008)

(2)   The summons or originating summons, as the case may be, shall be served with the evidence in support not less than 7 days before the date fixed for the hearing of the summons on— (L.N. 152 of 2008)

   (a)   the defendant;
   (b)   any person holding any interest in the realisable property to which the application relates; and
   (c)   the receiver, where one has been appointed in the matter.

(3)   The application shall be supported by an affidavit, which shall, to the best of the deponent's ability, give full particulars of the realisable property to which it relates and specify the person or persons holding such property, and a copy of the confiscation order, of any certificate issued by the Court under section 6(2) and of any charging order made in the matter shall be exhibited to such affidavit.

(4)   The Court may, on an application under section 12, exercise the power conferred by section 13(1) to direct the making of payments by the receiver.

---

**NOTES**

**[115.7.1]   Application for realisation of property**

Order 115 rule 7 deals with applications under section 12 of Cap 405 which empowers the court *inter alia* to appoint a receiver in respect of realisable property which is the subject of a confiscation order in proceedings for a drug trafficking offence which have not concluded and order delivery of possession of such property and payments to such receiver.

Rule 7(2)(b) provides that any person with an interest in the property to which such an application relates shall be served. Our sister publication in the UK, The Civil Court Practice (the 'green book') 2008 says of the provision of the same number in the English RSC (which was retained when the CPR came into force):

**Any person holding any interest in the reliasable property.** Where an application is made to the High Court to realise property to satisfy a confiscation order made by the Crown Court, a person with an interest in the property has a right to be heard [in Hong Kong see section 12(8) of Cap 405]. It is not an abuse of process for such a person to re-open questions of title to the property which have already been addressed and decided by the Crown Court: *Re Norris* [2001] UKHL 34, [2001] 3 All ER 961, [2001] 1 WLR 1388, [2001] 3 FCR 97.

**Conflicting claims.** The conflicting claims of a co-owner and the prosecutor must be determined in accordance with s 15, the principles referred to in *Bank of Ireland Home Mortgages Ltd v Bell* [2001] 3 FCR 134, [2001] 2 FLR 809 and the rights recognised by articles 5 and 8 of the Convention on Human Rights. In a case where the convicted person's wife was a co-owner of the home and had applied, on divorce, for a transfer of the husband's interest it was held that the wife's claim to continue to live in the property and her claim to a transfer were both rights in relation to the property for the purposes of s 31(4) of the Act: *Re A, A v A* [2002] EWHC 611 (Admin/Fam), [2002] 2 FCR 481, [2002] 2 FLR 274. The Court of Appeal agreed that the court's power to order a transfer of property under s 24 of the Matrimonial Causes Act 1973 was exercisable, although it would defeat the claims to the husband's property made under s 29 of the Drug Trafficking Act 1994: *Customs & Excise Comrs v A* [2002] EWCA Civ 1039, [2002] All ER (D) 312 (Jul), [2003] 1 FLR 164. In cases where the matrimonial assets are tainted to the knowledge of the other spouse, they should not ordinarily, as a matter of justice and public policy, be distributed: *Crown Prosecution Service v Richards* (2006) Times, 10 July (CA). When applying ss 4(4)(a) and 7 of the 1994 Act, the value of the house which was included in the confiscation order is to be taken as the net value after deducting the building society loan: *R v Walls (Andrew)* (2002) Times, 6 Nov (CA).

**8.  Receivers** (O. 115 r. 8)

**(1)    Subject to this rule, the provisions of Order 30, rules 2 to 8 shall apply where a receiver is appointed in pursuance of a charging order or under section 10 or 12.**

**(2)    Where the receiver proposed to be appointed has been appointed receiver in other proceedings under the Ordinance, it shall not be necessary for an affidavit of fitness to be sworn or for the receiver to give security, unless the Court otherwise orders.**

**(3)    Where a receiver has fully paid the amount payable under the confiscation order and any sums remain in his hands, he shall apply by case management summons as to the distribution of such sums. (L.N. 152 of 2008)**

**(4)    A summons under paragraph (3) shall be served with any evidence in support not less than 7 days before the date fixed for the hearing of the summons on—**

> **(a)    the defendant; and**
>
> **(b)    any other person who held property realised by the receiver.**

**NOTES**

**[115.8.1]    Receivers appointed to realise confiscated property**
Order 115 rule 8 lays down procedures governing receivers appointed to realise confiscated property. The rule applies the general provisions relating to court-appointed receivers in Order 30 rule 2–8. The rule is substantially the same as its counterpart of the same number in the English RSC, which was retained when the CPR came into force. However, the English provision has an additional paragraph, providing for application by a receiver to be discharged from office. Our sister publication in the UK, The Civil Court Practice 2008 says of the English provision:

> **Remuneration of receiver.** A receiver's remuneration and expenses should come in the first place from the estate under his, or her, control and then, if a confiscation order

is made, from any sums realised and remitted to the justice's clerk under s 81 of the Drug Trafficking Act 1994 [in Hong Kong see section 13 of Cap 405]. The receiver's right to remuneration from the estate is not affected by the defendant being acquitted: *Hughes v Customs & Excise Comrs* [2002] EWCA Civ 670, [2002] 4 All ER 633, [2003] 1 WLR 177.

See also the discussion of receiver's remuneration in money laundering cases in *Heath Sinclair v Glatt & Ors* [2009] EWCA Civ 176.

**9. Variation of confiscation order** (O. 115 r. 9)

**(1)   The Secretary for Justice or the defendant may apply by summons for an order under section 15(1). (89 of 1995 s 30)**

**(2)   A summons under paragraph (1) shall be served, with any supporting evidence, not less than 7 days before the date fixed for the hearing of the summons on—**

(a)   **where the Secretary for Justice is making the application, the defendant;**

(b)   **where the defendant is making the application, the Secretary for Justice,**

**and, in either case, on the receiver, where one has been appointed in the matter. (89 of 1995 s 30)**

**(3)   The Secretary for Justice may apply by summons for an order under section 15(1A). (89 of 1995 s 30)**

**10. Compensation** (O. 115 r. 10)

**An application for an order under section 27 shall be made by summons, which shall be served, with any supporting evidence, on the person alleged to be in default and on the Secretary for Justice not less than 7 days before the date fixed for the hearing of the summons.**

**11. Disclosure of information** (O. 115 r. 11)

**(1)   An application under section 23 shall be made by the Secretary for Justice by summons, which shall state the nature of the order sought and whether material sought to be disclosed is to be disclosed to a receiver appointed under section 10 or 12 or in pursuance of a charging order or to an authorized officer.**

**(2)   The summons and affidavit in support shall be served on the public body—**

(a)   **not less than 7 days before the date fixed for the hearing of the summons; and**

(b)   **where the public body is a Government Department, in accordance with Order 77, rule 4.**

**(3)   The affidavit in support of an application under paragraph (1) shall state the grounds for believing that the conditions in section 23(4) and, if appropriate, section 23(7) are fulfilled.**

**12. Exercise of powers under section 29** (O. 115 r. 12)

**The powers conferred on the Court by section 29 may be exercised by a judge in chambers and a Master.**

**13. Application for registration** (O. 115 r. 13)

An application for registration of an external confiscation order under section 29(1) may be ex parte.

_____

**NOTES**

**[115.13.1]   Numbering**

There is no rule 14 in Order 115. The rule of the equivalent number in the former English Rules of the Supreme Court dealt with applications for registration of confiscation orders under section 37 of the Drug Trafficking Act 1994 which provided for enforcement of such orders as between different parts of the United Kingdom.

**15. Evidence in support of application under section 29(1)** (O. 115 r. 15)

An application for registration of an external confiscation order must be supported by an affidavit –

- (a)  exhibiting the order or a verified or certified or otherwise duly authenticated copy thereof and, where the order is not in the English language, a translation thereof into English certified by a notary public or authenticated by affidavit; and
- (b)  stating –
    - (i)  that the order is in force and is not subject to appeal;
    - (ii)  where the person against whom, or in relation to whose property, the order was made did not appear in the proceedings, that he received notice of the proceedings, in accordance with the law of the designated country concerned, in sufficient time to enable him to defend them; (89 of 1995 s 30)
    - (iii)  in the case of money, either that at the date of the application the sum payable under the order has not been paid or the amount which remains unpaid, as may be appropriate, or, in the case of other property, the property which has not been recovered; and
    - (iv)  to the best of the deponent's knowledge, particulars of what property the person against whom, or in relation to whose property, the order was made holds in Hong Kong, giving the source of the deponent's knowledge. (89 of 1995 s 30)

**16. Register of orders** (O. 115 r. 16)

(1) The Registrar shall keep a register of the orders registered nder the Ordinance.

(2) There shall be included in such register particulars of any variation or setting aside of a registration, of any variation, satisfaction or discharge of a registered order, and of any execution issued on such an order.

**17. Notice of registration** (O. 115 r. 17)

(1)   Notice of the registration of an order must be served on the person against whom, or in relation to whose property, it was obtained by delivering it

to him personally or by sending it to him at his usual or last known address or place of business or in such other manner as the Court may direct. **(89 of 1995 s 30)**

(2)   Service of such a notice out of the jurisdiction is permissible without leave, and Order 11, rules 5, 6 and 8 shall apply in relation to such a notice as they apply in relation to a writ.

(3)   The notice shall state the period within which an application may be made to vary or set aside the registration and that the order will not be enforced until after the expiration of that period.

**18. Application to vary or set aside registration** (O. 115 r. 18)

An application by the person against whom, or in relation to whose property, an order was made to vary or set aside the registration of an order must be made to a judge by summons supported by affidavit. **(89 of 1995 s 30)**

**19. Enforcement of order** (O. 115 r. 19)

(1)   An order registered under the Ordinance shall not be enforced until after the expiration of the period specified in accordance with rule 17(3) or, if that period has been extended by the Court, until after the expiration of the period so extended.

(2)   If an application is made under rule 18, an order shall not be enforced until after such application is determined.

**20. Variation, satisfaction and discharge of registered order** (O. 115 r. 20)

Upon the Court being notified by the applicant for registration that an order which has been registered has been varied, satisfied or discharged, particulars of the variation, satisfaction or discharge, as the case may be, shall be entered in the register.

**21. Rules to have effect subject to orders** (O. 115 r. 21)

Rules 12 to 20 shall have effect subject to the provisions of any order made under section 28.

---

**NOTES**

**[115.21.1]   Order 115 rules 12–21**

Rules 12 to 21 of Order 115 are due to be repealed by the Mutual Legal Assistance in Criminal Matters Ordinance (87 of 1997, now Cap 525). Although most of that Ordinance was brought into force in 1997 and 1998, the provision repealing rules 12 to 21 was still not in force as at late 2007.

**22. Statement relating to drug trafficking** (O. 115 r. 22)

**(HK)(1)   Where the Secretary for Justice or the defendant proposes to tender to the Court any statement or other document under section 5 he shall give a copy thereof as soon as practicable to the defendant or the Secretary for Justice, as the case may be, and to the appropriate officer of the court. (89 of 1995 s 30)**

(2)   Any statement tendered to the Court by the Secretary for Justice under section 5(1) shall include the following particulars, namely—

    (a)   the name of the defendant;

    (b)   the name of the person who made the statement;

    (c)   such information known to the person who made the statement as is relevant to—

        (i)   where section 3(1)(a)(ii) is applicable, the determination whether the defendant could have been convicted in respect of the drug trafficking offence or offences concerned;

        (ii)   the determination whether the defendant has benefited from drug trafficking;

        (iii)   the assessment of the value of the defendant's proceeds of drug trafficking.

                                        **(89 of 1995 s 30)**

---

## NOTES

**[115.22.1]**   **Statement in support of application for confiscation order**

Section 5 of Cap 405 provides that on an application for a confiscation order the prosecution may tender a statement of relevant matters. Order 115 rule 22(2) stipulates certain particulars which must be included in such a statement. The significance of such a statement is that it may take the place of evidence in circumstances where the subject of the application has died or absconded so there is no criminal conviction to rely on and the court is required to decide whether the defendant 'could have been convicted': *Secretary for Justice v Lee Chau Ping & Anor* [1999] 2 HKC 103.

**23. Investigation into drug trafficking - discharge and variation of orders**

    (O. 115 r. 23)

(1A)   An authorized officer shall make an application for an order under section 20 or a warrant under section 21 ex parte to a judge by laying an information on oath. (L.N. 142 of 1990)

(HK)(1)   Where an order under section 20 has been made, the person required to comply with it may apply in writing to the appropriate officer of the Court for the order to be discharged or varied, and on hearing such an application the Court may discharge the order or make such variations to it as it thinks fit.

(2)   Subject to paragraph (3), where a person proposes to make an application under paragraph (1) for the discharge or variation of an order, he shall give a copy of the application, not later than 48 hours before the making of the application, to the authorized officer by whom the application for an order was made, or if such officer is not known or cannot be found, to another authorized officer, together with a notice indicating the time and place at which the application for discharge or variation is to be made.

(3)   The Court may direct that paragraph (2) need not be complied with if it is satisfied that the person making the application has good reason to seek a discharge or variation of the order as soon as possible and it is not practicable to comply with that paragraph.

**24. Application for continued detention of seized property** (O. 115 r. 24)

(1)   An application under section 24C(2) for an order to authorize the continued detention of seized property may be made by originating summons in Form No. 10 in Appendix A. (L.N. 152 of 2008)

(2)   An application under paragraph (1) shall be supported by an affidavit, which shall—

    (a)   state what the seized property consists of (including, in the case of money, the amount and currency thereof) and the date on which and the place at which it was seized;

    (b)   state the grounds for suspecting that the seized property is specified property; and

    (c)   give particulars, in terms of the matters referred to in section 24C(2)(b), as to why the continued detention of the seized property is justified. (L.N. 296 of 1996)

**25. Order for continued detention of seized property** (O. 115 r. 25)

(1)   Where an order is made under section 24C(2), the applicant shall, as soon as practicable, serve a copy of the order on each person affected by the order.

(2)   An order under section 24C(2) shall be in Form No. 108 in Appendix A.

(3)   In rules 26(3) and (4), 27, 28(2) and 29(3) and (4), "affected person", in relation to any summons or order referred to in those rules, means a person—

    (a)   on whom a copy of an order made under section 24C(2) has been served pursuant to paragraph (1) where the seized property (or any part thereof ) the subject of the summons or first-mentioned order is or was the subject of the second-mentioned order; or

    (b)   in respect of whom the Court has made an order under rule 31 in connection with the summons or first-mentioned order. (L.N. 296 of 1996)

**26. Application for further detention of seized property** (O. 115 r. 26)

(1)   An application under section 24C(3) for an order to authorize the further detention of seized property shall be made by summons in the proceedings commenced under rule 24.

(2)   An application under paragraph (1) shall be supported by an affidavit, which shall—

    (a)   state the grounds for suspecting that the seized property is specified property; and

    (b)   give particulars, in terms of the matters referred to in section 24C(2)(b), as to why the continued detention of the seized property is justified.

(3)   The summons and the affidavit in support shall be served on each affected person not less than 5 clear days before the date fixed for the hearing of the summons.

(4)   Affidavit evidence in response to the summons shall be served by an affected person on—

    (a)   the Secretary for Justice on behalf of the applicant; and

    (b)   each other affected person,

not less than 2 clear days before the date fixed for the hearing of the summons. (L.N. 296 of 1996)

**27. Order for further detention of seized property** (O. 115 r. 27)

Where an order is made under section 24C(3), the applicant shall, as soon as is practicable, serve a copy of the order on each affected person. (L.N. 296 of 1996)

**28. Application for release of seized property** (O. 115 r. 28)

(1)  An application under section 24C(4)(a) for the release of seized property detained by an order under section 24C(2) or (3) shall be made by summons which shall state the grounds on which the application is made.

(2)  The summons and any affidavit in support shall be served on—

    (a)  the Secretary for Justice on behalf of the authorized officer who obtained the order by virtue of which the seized property is detained; and

    (b)  each other affected person,

not less than 5 clear days before the date fixed for the hearing of the summons.

(3)  Any affidavit in opposition to the summons shall be served on—

    (a)  the person who made the application under paragraph (1); and

    (b)  each of the other persons referred to in paragraph (2)(a) and (b),

not less than 2 clear days before the date fixed for the hearing of the summons.
(L.N. 296 of 1996)

**29. Application for forfeiture of seized property** (O. 115 r. 29)

(1)  An application under section 24D(1) for the forfeiture of seized property shall be made by summons in the proceedings under which any order under rule 24 has been obtained.

(2)  An application under paragraph (1) shall be supported by an affidavit, which shall state the grounds for believing that the seized property—

    (a)  in whole or in part directly or indirectly represents any person's proceeds of drug trafficking;

    (b)  has been used in drug trafficking; or

    (c)  is intended for use in drug trafficking.

(3)  The summons and the affidavit in support referred to in paragraphs (1) and (2) shall be served on each affected person not less than 14 clear days before the date fixed for the hearing of the summons.

(4)  Any affidavit in opposition to the summons shall be served by an affected person on—

    (a)  the Secretary for Justice on behalf of the applicant; and

    (b)  each other affected person,

not less than 5 clear days before the date fixed for the hearing of the summons. (L.N. 296 of 1996)

**30. Release of seized property** (O. 115 r. 30)

Where in relation to any seized property—

(a)  an order under section 24C(2) expires without an order being made under section 24C(3);

(b)  an order under section 24C(3) expires without a further order being made thereunder; or

(c)  a direction is obtained under section 24C(4),

then, unless the Court has directed that an issue be stated and tried as between affected persons, the property shall be forthwith released on such terms, if any, as the Court thinks fit to the person from whom the property was seized or to such other person as appears to be entitled to it. (L.N. 296 of 1996)

**31. Joinder and payment into Court** (O. 115 r. 31)

(1)  Without prejudice to its powers under Order 15, rule 6, the Court may either of its own motion or on application order that any person who may be affected by any order made by it be joined as a party to the proceedings.

(2)  The Court may order that the property which is the subject of an application or order shall be paid into or lodged in Court on such terms as it thinks fit. (L.N. 296 of 1996)

**32. Service of documents** (O. 115 r. 32)

(1)  Without prejudice to Order 65, any documents required to be served on a party under rules 25 to 29 may be served in accordance with the provisions of this rule.

(2)  Where documents are required to be served on a party from whom property has been seized and that party has provided an authorized officer with an address or facsimile number at which any such document may be served, the documents may be served by leaving them at or sending them by registered mail to that address or by sending it by facsimile to the number provided.

(3)  If that party has refused to provide an authorized officer with any such address or facsimile number and there is no other method of serving him or if it is otherwise not possible to serve a party, the documents may be served on that party by exhibiting them on a notice board at a place to which the public have access on the ground floor of the High Court Building but where any application made under rule 25, 26, 27, 28 or 29 is so served, the applicant shall state in his affidavit of service why this method of service has been adopted and the Court shall consider whether to give directions for some other form of service (including substituted service) by the applicant.

(4)  A body corporate which is not incorporated in Hong Kong and which is not registered under Part XI of the Companies Ordinance (Cap 32) may be served by leaving the document to be served at or by sending it by registered mail to the registered office or principal place of business of that body corporate. (L.N. 296 of 1996)

**33. Power to extend or abridge time** (O. 115 r. 33)

Rules 26(3) and (4), 28(2) and (3), and 29(3) and (4) shall not operate to prejudice the power of the Court under Order 3, rule 5, to extend or abridge the period within which a person is required or authorized by any of those rules to do any act in any proceedings. (L.N. 296 of 1996)

## ORDER 115A

### (HK) MUTUAL LEGAL ASSISTANCE IN CRIMINAL MATTERS ORDINANCE (CAP 525)

1.  **Interpretation** (O. 115A r. 1)
    **(1)   In this Order "the Ordinance" means the Mutual Legal Assistance in Criminal Matters Ordinance (Cap 525), and a section referred to by number in rules 3 to 12 means the section so numbered in the Ordinance and in rules 13 to 18 means the section so numbered in Schedule 2 to the Ordinance.**
    **(2)   Expressions used in this Order which are used in the Ordinance (including Schedule 2 to the Ordinance) have the same meanings in this Order as in the Ordinance.**

___

**NOTES**

**[115A.1.1]   History and scope of Order 115A**
Order 115A was enacted along with the Mutual Legal Assistance in Criminal Matters Ordinance (No 87 of 1997) (now Cap 525). The Ordinance makes provision for mutual legal assistance in criminal matters as between Hong Kong and other jurisdictions, but it does not apply in respect of other parts of China (s 3(1)). The provisions of Order 115A are largely concerned with applications under part VI of Cap 525 for registration in Hong Kong of external orders for confiscation of the proceeds of crime.

2.  **Assignment of proceedings** (O. 115A r. 2)
    **Subject to rule 3, the jurisdiction of the Court under the Ordinance shall be exercised by a judge of the Court in chambers.**

3.  **Exercise of powers under section 28** (O. 115A r. 3)
    **The powers conferred on the Court by section 28 may be exercised by a judge in chambers and a Master.**

4.  **Application for registration** (O. 115A r. 4)
    **An application for registration of an external confiscation order under section 28(1) may be ex parte.**

5.  **Evidence in support of application under section 28(1)** (O. 115A r. 5)
    **An application for registration of an external confiscation order must be supported by an affidavit—**
    (a)   **exhibiting the order or a verified or certified or otherwise duly authenticated copy thereof and, where the order is not in the English language, a translation thereof into English certified by a notary public or authenticated by affidavit; and**
    (b)   **stating—**
        (i)   **that the order is in force and is not subject to appeal;**
        (ii)  **where the person against whom, or in relation to whose property, the order was made did not appear in the**

proceedings, that he received notice of the proceedings, in accordance with the law of the place outside Hong Kong concerned, in sufficient time to enable him to defend them;

(iii)  in the case of money, either that at the date of the application the sum payable under the order has not been paid or the amount which remains unpaid, as may be appropriate, or, in the case of other property, the property which has not been recovered; and

(iv)  to the best of the deponent's knowledge, particulars of what property the person against whom, or in relation to whose property, the order was made holds in, or controls from, Hong Kong, giving the source of the deponent's knowledge.

**6.  Register of orders** (O. 115A r. 6)

(1)  The Registrar shall keep a register of the orders registered under the Ordinance.

(2)  There shall be included in such register particulars of any variation or setting aside of a registration, of any variation, satisfaction or discharge of a registered order, and of any execution issued on such an order.

**7.  Notice of registration** (O. 115A r. 7)

(1)  Notice of the registration of an order must be served on the person against whom, or in relation to whose property, it was obtained by delivering it to him personally or by sending it to him at his usual or last known address or place of business or in such other manner as the Court may direct.

(2)  Service of such a notice out of the jurisdiction is permissible without leave, and Order 11, rules 5, 6 and 8 shall apply in relation to such a notice as they apply in relation to a writ.

(3)  The notice shall state the period within which an application may be made to vary or set aside the registration and that the order will not be enforced until after the expiration of that period.

**8.  Application to vary or set aside registration** (O. 115A r. 8)

An application by the person against whom an order was made to vary or set aside the registration of an order must be made to a judge by summons supported by affidavit.

---

**NOTES**

**[115A.8.1]  No security for costs**

*In Anwide Co Ltd v AG* [1994] 2 HKC 114 (CA) it was held that security for costs was not available against an applicant under the former Order 115 rule 18 (repealed by Ordinance 87 of 1997). The same should apply under rule 8 of this Order.

In *Anwide* the Court of Appeal held that the applicant did not stand as plaintiff and that the court had no jurisdiction to make an order for security for costs.

**9. Enforcement of order** (O. 115A r 9)

(1)   An order registered under the Ordinance shall not be enforced until after the expiration of the period specified in accordance with rule 7(3) or, if that period has been extended by the Court, until after the expiration of the period so extended.

(2)   If an application is made under rule 8, an order shall not be enforced until after such application is determined.

**10. Variation, satisfaction and discharge of registered order** (O. 115A r. 10)

Upon the Court being notified by the applicant for registration that an order which has been registered has been varied, satisfied or discharged, particulars of the variation, satisfaction or discharge, as the case may be, shall be entered in the register.

**11. Rules to have effect subject to orders** (O. 115A r. 11)

Rules 3 to 10 shall have effect subject to the provisions of any order made under section 27.

**12. Investigation or proceeding relating to criminal matter discharge and variation of orders** (O. 115A r. 12)

(1)   An authorized officer shall make an application for an order under section 15 ex parte to a judge by laying an information on oath.

(2)   Where an order under section 15 has been made, the person required to comply with it may apply in writing to the appropriate officer of the Court for the order to be discharged or varied, and on hearing such an application the Court may discharge the order or make such variations to it as it thinks fit.

(3)   Subject to paragraph (4), where a person proposes to make an application under paragraph (2) for the discharge or variation of an order, he shall give a copy of the application, not later than **48 hours** before the making of the application, to the authorized officer by whom the application for an order was made, or if such officer is not known or cannot be found, to another authorized officer, together with a notice indicating the time and place at which the application for discharge or variation is to be made.

(4)   The Court may direct that paragraph (3) need not be complied with if it is satisfied that the person making the application has good reason to seek a discharge or variation of the order as soon as possible and it is not practicable to comply with that paragraph.

---

**NOTES**

**[115A.12.1]   Owner has no right to be heard**

Order 115A rule 12(2) permits a person required to comply with an order under section 15 of Cap 525 to apply to the court for discharge or variation. This does not give the owner of the documents or things, as opposed to the person required to comply, a right to be heard on the question whether they should be transmitted overseas: *Re Anson Garment Ltd* [2006] 2 HKC 246, para 100.

**13. Application for restraint order or charging order** (O. 115A r. 13)

(1)   An application for a restraint order under section 7 or for a charging order under section 8 (to either of which may be joined an application for the appointment of a receiver) may be made by the Secretary for Justice ex parte by originating summons. (L.N. 362 of 1997) (L.N. 152 of 2008)

(2)   An application under section 7(4) or 8(3) shall be supported by an affidavit which shall—

(a)   state, where applicable, the grounds for believing that an external confiscation order may be made in the proceedings instituted or to be instituted in the place outside Hong Kong concerned.

(b)   to the best of the deponent's ability, give particulars of the realisable property in respect of which the order is sought and specify the person or persons holding such property;

(c)   in a case to which section 6(2) applies, indicate when it is intended that proceedings should be instituted in the place outside Hong Kong concerned.

(3)   An originating summons under paragraph (1) shall be entitled in the matter of the defendant, naming him, and in the matter of the Ordinance, and all subsequent documents in the matter shall be so entitled. (L.N. 152 of 2008)

(4)   Unless the Court otherwise directs, an affidavit under paragraph (2) may contain statements of information or belief with the sources and grounds thereof.

**14. Restraint order and charging order** (O. 115A r. 14)

(1)   A restraint order may be made subject to conditions and exceptions, including but not limited to conditions relating to the indemnifying of third parties against expenses incurred in complying with the order, and exceptions relating to reasonable living expenses and reasonable legal expenses of the defendant, but the Secretary for Justice shall not be required to give an undertaking to abide by any order as to damages sustained by the defendant as a result of the restraint order.

(2)   Unless the Court otherwise directs, a restraint order made ex parte shall have effect until a day which shall be fixed for the hearing inter partes of the application and a charging order shall be an order to show cause, imposing the charge until such day.

(3)   Where a restraint order is made the Secretary for Justice shall serve copies of the order and of the affidavit in support on the defendant and on all other named persons restrained by the order and shall notify all other persons or bodies affected by the order of its terms.

(4)   Where a charging order is made the Secretary for Justice shall, unless the Court otherwise directs, serve copies of the order and of the affidavit in support on the defendant and, where the property to which the order relates is held by another person, on that person and shall serve a copy of the order on such of the persons or bodies specified in Order 50, rule 2(1)(b) to (d) as shall be appropriate.

**15. Discharge or variation of order** (O. 115A r. 15)

(1)   Any person or body on whom a restraint order or a charging order is served or who is notified of such an order may apply by summons to discharge or vary the order.

(2)   The summons and any affidavit in support shall be lodged with the Court and served on the Secretary for Justice and, where he is not the applicant, on the defendant, not less than 2 clear days before the date fixed for the hearing of the summons.

(3)   Upon the Court being notified that proceedings have been concluded any restraint or charging order shall be discharged.

**16. Further application by Secretary for Justice** (O. 115A r. 16)

(1)   Where a restraint order or a charging order has been made the Secretary for Justice may apply by summons or, where the case is one of urgency, ex parte—

(a)   to discharge or vary such order;

(b)   for a restraint order or a charging order in respect of other realisable property;

or

(c)   for the appointment of a receiver.

(2)   An application under paragraph (1) shall be supported by an affidavit which, where the application is for a restraint order or a charging order, shall to the best of the deponent's ability give full particulars of the realisable property in respect of which the order is sought and specify the person or persons holding such property.

(3)   The summons and affidavit in support shall be lodged with the Court and served on the defendant and, where one has been appointed in the matter, on the receiver, not less than 2 clear days before the date fixed for the hearing of the summons.

(4)   Rule 14(3) and (4) shall apply to the service of restraint orders and charging orders respectively made under this rule on persons other than the defendant.

**17. Realisation of property** (O. 115A r. 17)

(1)   An application under section 9 shall, where there have been proceedings against the defendant in the Court of First Instance, be made by the Secretary for Justice by summons and shall otherwise be made by originating summons. (L.N. 362 of 1997) (L.N. 152 of 2008)

(2)   The summons or originating summons, as the case may be, shall be served with the evidence in support not less than 7 days before the date fixed for the hearing of the summons on— (L.N. 152 of 2008)

(a)   the defendant;

(b)   any person holding any interest in the realisable property to which the application relates; and;

(c)   the receiver, where one has been appointed in the matter.

(3) The application shall be supported by an affidavit, which shall, to the best of the deponent's ability, give full particulars of the realisable property to which it relates and specify the person or persons holding such property.

(4) The Court may, on an application under section 9, exercise the power conferred by section 10(1) to direct the making of payments by the receiver.

## 18. Receivers (O. 115A r. 18)

(1) Subject to this rule, the provisions of Order 30, rules 2 to 8 shall apply where a receiver is appointed in pursuance of a charging order or under section 7 or 9.

(2) Where the receiver proposed to be appointed has been appointed receiver in other proceedings under the Ordinance, it shall not be necessary for an affidavit of fitness to be sworn or for the receiver to give security, unless the Court otherwise orders.

(3) Where a receiver has fully paid the amount payable under the external confiscation order and any sums remain in his hands, he shall apply by case management summons as to the distribution of such sums. (L.N. 152 of 2008)

(4) A summons under paragraph (3) shall be served with any evidence in support not less than 7 days before the date fixed for the hearing of the summons on—

 (a) the defendant; and

 (b) any other person who held property realised by the receiver.

**(87 of 1997 ss 1(2) & 36)**

---

## NOTES

**[115A.18.1]**   **Receivers appointed in respect of confiscated property**

See the commentary under Order 115 rule 8 which should be applicable *mutatis mutandis* here.

## ORDER 116

### (HK) ORGANIZED AND SERIOUS CRIMES ORDINANCE (CAP 455)

PART II—POWERS OF INVESTIGATION

**1. Interpretation** (O. 116 r. 1)

**(1) In this Order "the Ordinance" means the Organized and Serious Crimes Ordinance (Cap 455), and a section referred to by number means the section so numbered in the Ordinance.**

**(2) Expressions used in this Order which are used in the Ordinance have the same meanings in this Order as in the Ordinance.**

**NOTES**

**[116.1.1] History of order**
This Order came into operation on 22 April 1995 when sections 3 to 24 of the Organized and Serious Crimes Ordinance (No 82 of 1994) (now Cap 455) came into force (LN 157 and LN 156 of 1995).

**2. Application of this Order** (O. 116 r. 2)
**This Order applies to applications—**
    **(a) by the Secretary for Justice under section 3 for an order authorizing the Secretary for Justice to require a person to furnish information or produce material;**
    **(b) by the Secretary for Justice or an authorized officer under section 4 for an order that a person make material available; and**
    **(c) by an authorized officer under section 5 for the issue of a search warrant.**

**3. Assignment of proceedings** (O. 116 r. 3)
**For the purposes of this Order, the jurisdiction of the Court under the Ordinance shall be exercised by a judge of the Court in chambers.**

**NOTES**

**[116.3.1] Jurisdiction of magistrate**
Sections 4 and 5 of the Organized and Serious Crimes Ordinance provide for application to be made to the Court of First Instance for certain orders and warrants related to investigations under that Ordinance. Order 116 rules 3 and 5 provide that such applications shall be heard in chambers closed to the public.

Under the Ordinance, the district court also has jurisdiction to issue warrants in some circumstances. Furthermore, it has been held that the power of magistrates to issue warrants is not ousted: *Philip KH Wong & Kennedy YH Wong & Co (a firm) & Anor v ICAC* [2008] 2 HKC 479 (CA).

**4.    Applications under section 3, 4 or 5** (O. 116 r. 4)

(1)    An application to which this Order applies—

(a)    shall be made by laying an information on oath;

(b)    may, where a judge so directs, be heard at a place other than within the court premises.

(2)    At the hearing of an application to which this Order applies the Court may receive evidence from the applicant.

**5.    Application to be heard in camera** (O. 116 r. 5)

(1)    An application to which this Order applies, and any other application provided for in this Order, shall be heard in camera.

(2)    The information and all other documents relating to such application shall be treated as confidential and shall, immediately on the determination of the application, be placed in a packet and sealed by order of the judge by whom the application was heard.

(3)    The packet shall be kept in the custody of the Court in a place to which the public has no access or in such other place as the judge may authorize and—

(a)    shall not be opened or its contents removed except by order of a judge;

(b)    shall not be destroyed except pursuant to an order of the Court.

**6.    Discharge or variation of order under section 3 or 4** (O. 116 r. 6)

(1)    An application under section 3(17) for the discharge or variation of an order made under section 3 or under section 4(7) for the discharge or variation of an order made under section 4(2) or (6) shall be made to a judge by summons supported by affidavit.

(2)    The summons and affidavit in support—

(a)    shall set out the grounds on which the applicant relies in seeking the discharge or variation of the order; and

(b)    shall be lodged with the Court and served on the Secretary for Justice not less than 3 clear days before the date fixed for the hearing of the summons.

(3)    On the hearing of the application the Court may discharge the order or make such variation as it thinks fit.

**7.    Claim of legal privilege in relation to order under section 3 or 4** (O. 116 r. 7)

(1)    If in the course of the exercise by an authorized officer of powers conferred by an order made under section 3 a claim of legal privilege is made in respect of any information, the person making the claim shall—

(a)    within 3 days of making the claim, apply to the Court by summons supported by affidavit for a declaration that the information is subject to legal privilege; and

(b)    not less than 3 clear days before the hearing of the application, serve a copy of the summons and affidavit on the Secretary for Justice.

(2)    If in the course of the exercise by an authorized officer of powers conferred by an order made under section 3 or 4 a claim of legal privilege is made in respect of any material, the person making the claim shall—

     (a)    in the presence of the authorized officer, secure the material in a sealed container;

     (b)    immediately deposit the sealed container with the Court;

     (c)    within 3 days of depositing the material with the Court, apply to the Court by summons supported by affidavit for a declaration that the material is subject to legal privilege; and

     (d)    not less than 3 clear days before the hearing of the application, serve a copy of the summons and affidavit on the Secretary for Justice.

8.    Claim of legal privilege in relation to search warrant issued under section 5 (O. 116 r. 8)

If in the course of execution by an authorized officer of a warrant issued under section 5 a claim of legal privilege is made in respect of any material, the person making the claim shall—

     (a)    secure the material in a sealed container in the presence of the authorized officer and hand the sealed container to the authorized officer for safe keeping pending an application by the person under this rule;

     (b)    within 3 days of making the claim of legal privilege, apply to the Court by summons supported by affidavit for a declaration that the material is subject to legal privilege; and

     (c)    not less than 3 clear days before the hearing of the application, serve a copy of the summons and affidavit on the authorized officer and the Secretary for Justice. (L.N. 156 of 1995)

## ORDER 117

### (HK) ORGANIZED AND SERIOUS CRIMES ORDINANCE (CAP 455)

PART IV—ENFORCEMENT, ETC. OF CONFISCATION ORDERS

**1. Interpretation** (O. 117 r. 1)

**(1) In this Order "the Ordinance" means the Organized and Serious Crimes Ordinance (Cap 455), and a Part or section referred to by number means the Part or section so numbered in the Ordinance.**

**(2) Expressions used in this Order which are used in the Ordinance have the same meanings in this Order as in the Ordinance.**

___

**NOTES**

**[117.1.1]   History of order**

Order 117 came into operation on 22 April 1995 when sections 3 to 24 of the Organized and Serious Crimes Ordinance (Cap 455) came into force (LN 157 and LN 156 of 1995).

**2. Application of this Order** (O. 117 r. 2)

**This Order applies to applications under Part IV.**

___

**NOTES**

**[117.2.1]   Scope of Order 117**

The Organized and Serious Crimes Ordinance (Cap 455) empowers the court to order the confiscation of the proceeds of crime. Order 117 applies to proceedings under Part IV of that Ordinance, where provision is made for the enforcement of confiscation orders (or anticipated orders) by means of restraint order and charging order.

It has been held that confiscation proceedings under Cap 455 are partly criminal and partly civil in nature, and that the court's power to strike out for want of prosecution is available. See *Secretary for Justice v Yiu Chik Chuen* [2006] 1 HKC 507.

**3. Assignment of proceedings** (O. 117 r. 3)

**The jurisdiction of the Court under the Ordinance shall, for the purposes of this Order, be exercised by a judge of the Court in chambers.**

**3A. Application for confiscation order where person has died or absconded** (O. 117 r. 3A)

**An application for a confiscation order under section 8 where the defendant has died or absconded may be made by the Secretary for Justice by originating summons. (90 of 1995 s 27)**

**4. Application for restraint order or charging order** (O. 117 r. 4)

**(1)   An application for a restraint order under section 15 or for a charging order under section 16 (to either of which may be joined an application for the**

appointment of a receiver) may be made by the Secretary for Justice ex parte by summons.

(2)   An application under paragraph (1) shall be supported by an affidavit, which shall—

- (a)   state, as the case may be, the grounds for believing that—
  - (i)   the defendant has benefited from a specified offence; or
  - (ii)   the Court of First Instance will be satisfied as specified in section 20(1A); (90 of 1995 s 27; 25 of 1998 s 2)
- (b)   state, as the case may be—
  - (i)   that proceedings have been instituted against the defendant for a specified offence (giving particulars of the offence) and that they have not been concluded;
  - (ii)   that, whether by the laying of an information or otherwise, a person is to be charged with a specified offence;
  - (iii)   that an application for an confiscation order has been made in respect of the defendant where section 8(1)(a)(ii) or (7A) is applicable; or
  - (iv)   that an application has been made under section 20(1A) in respect of a confiscation order made against the defendant; (90 of 1995 s 27)
- (c)   to the best of the deponent's ability, give full particulars of the realisable property in respect of which the order is sought and specify the person or persons holding such property;
- (d)   where proceedings have not been instituted, verify that the Secretary for Justice is to have the conduct of the proposed proceedings;
- (e)   where proceedings have not been instituted, indicate when it is intended that they should be instituted.

(3)   A summons under paragraph (1) shall be entitled in the matter of the defendant, naming him, and in the matter of the Ordinance, and all subsequent documents in the matter shall be so entitled.

(4)   Unless the Court otherwise directs, an affidavit under paragraph (2) may contain statements of information or belief with the sources and grounds of the information or belief.

## NOTES

### [117.4.1]   Effect of non-compliance as to contents of affidavit

Order 117 rule 4(2) stipulates that an application for a restraint order or a charging order under Cap 455 'shall' be supported by an affidavit which 'shall' state certain matters adumbrated under that sub-rule. Despite the mandatory wording, it has been held that failure to comply may not be fatal to the application: see *Secretary for Justice v Tan Lam Chuan & 4 Ors* HCMP 6503/2000 (Jackson J; 12.01.2001). In that case the affidavit in support failed to comply in two respects. First, it did not state that the Secretary for Justice would have conduct of the case, as required by rule 4(2)(d), and secondly, it did not state when it was intended to issue proceedings as required by rule 4(2)(e). The court held that these defects were not fatal to the application, distinguishing in this respect dicta of Viscount Simonds in *East Riding CC v Park Estate (Bridlington) Ltd* [1957] AC 223.

**5.    Restraint order and charging order** (O. 117 r. 5)

**(1)    A restraint order may be made subject to conditions and exceptions, including but not limited to conditions relating to the indemnifying of third parties against expenses incurred in complying with the order, and exceptions relating to reasonable living and legal expenses of the defendant, but the Secretary for Justice shall not be required to give an undertaking to abide by any order as to damages sustained by the defendant as a result of the restraint order.**

**(2)    Unless the Court otherwise directs, a restraint order made ex parte shall have effect until a day which shall be fixed for the hearing inter partes of the application and a charging order shall be an order to show cause, imposing the charge until such day.**

**(3)    Where a restraint order is made the Secretary for Justice shall serve copies of the order and of the affidavit in support on the defendant and on all other named persons restrained by the order and shall notify all other persons or bodies affected by the order of its terms.**

**(4)    Where a charging order is made the Secretary for Justice shall—**

> **(a)    unless the Court otherwise directs, serve copies of the order and of the affidavit in support on the defendant and, where the property to which the order relates is held by another person, on that person; and**

> **(b)    serve a copy of the order on such of the persons or bodies specified in Order 50, rule 2(1)(b) to (d) as shall be appropriate.**

## NOTES

### [117.5.1]    Conditions and exceptions to restraint order

Order 117 rule 5 expressly provides that a restraint order may be made subject to conditions and exceptions including 'reasonable living and legal expenses of the defendant'. In *Secretary for Justice v Tan Lam Chuan* (2001) HCMP 6503/2000 (Chung J; 02.01.2001) it was held that:

> a balance ought to be struck between preserving the assets to satisfy any confiscation order which may be made after conviction (if any) and meeting the reasonable requirements of the suspect (or defendant) in the meantime.

Chung J referred to *In re Petes* [1988] 1 QB 871, 879E–F and 880G–H and found that an analogy could be drawn with the court's approach on Mareva injunctions.

### [117.5.2]    Ancillary order for disclosure

It has been held that when the court makes a restraint or charging order under Cap 455 it has an inherent power to order disclosure of the assets of the person whose property is being frozen: see *Secretary for Justice v CKS & Anor* [2000] 2 HKC 592 applying *Re O* [1991] 2 QB 520; [1991] 1 All ER 330 and see *Secretary for Justice v Tan Lam Chuan & 4 Ors* (2001) HCMP 6503/2000 (Jackson J; 12.01.2001).

An order for disclosure should contain a proviso to protect the right against self-incrimination: an undertaking as to use of the information disclosed is insufficient. See *Secretary for Justice v CKS & Anor* [2000] 2 HKC 592, 604F–605A).

**6.   Discharge or variation of order** (O. 117 r. 6)

**(1)   Any person or body on whom a restraint order or a charging order is served or who is notified of such an order may apply by summons to discharge or vary the order.**

**(2)   The summons and any affidavit in support shall be lodged with the Court and served on the Secretary for Justice and, where he is not the applicant, on the defendant, not less than 2 clear days before the date fixed for the hearing of the summons.**

**(3)   Upon the Court being notified that proceedings for the offences have been concluded or that the amount payment of which is secured by a charging order has been paid into court, any restraint order or charging order, as the case may be, shall be discharged.**

---

**NOTES**

**[117.6.1]   Application for variation of order**
Order 117 rule 6 prescribes the procedure to be followed on application under section 15(6) of Cap 455 for discharge or variation of a restraint order.

Anyone affected by a restraint order may apply for discharge or variation, including a bank in which restrained funds are deposited: *Secretary for Justice v Hui Yat Fai & Ors* CACV 187/2004 (Yeung JA & A Cheung J; 08.02.2005).

Variation of a restraint order may be ordered to provide funds for living or legal expenses. The principles governing the exercise of the court's discretion to vary a restraint order for such purposes were laid down in *Secretary for Justice v Tan Lam Chuan & Ors* [2005] 3 HKC 545, 552H *et seq* (CA) and may be summarised as follows:

(1)   The person applying must demonstrate an interest (which may or may not be beneficial) in the property in question, and must show that the variation is justified by reference to that interest.
(2)   Where the person seeking variation wishes to use the restrained property for personal benefit, it is essential to demonstrate a beneficial entitlement to that property.
(3)   In exercising its discretion the court may take into account many factors such as whether full disclosure of assets has been made.

**7.   Further application by Secretary for Justice** (O. 117 r. 7)

**(1)   Where a restraint order or a charging order has been made the Secretary for Justice may apply by summons or, where the case is one of urgency, ex parte—**
**(a)   to discharge or vary such order; or**
**(b)   for a restraint order or a charging order in respect of other realisable property; or**
**(c)   for the appointment of a receiver.**

(2)   An application under paragraph (1) shall be supported by an affidavit which, where the application is for a restraint order or a charging order, shall to the best of the deponent's ability give full particulars of the realisable property in respect of which the order is sought and specify the person or persons holding such property.

(3)   The summons and affidavit in support shall be lodged with the Court and served on the defendant and, where one has been appointed in the matter, on the receiver, not less than 2 clear days before the date fixed for the hearing of the summons.

(4)   Rule 5(3) and (4) shall apply to the service of restraint orders and charging orders respectively made under this rule on persons other than the defendant.

**8.   Consent order for variation of restraint order or charging order** (O. 117 r. 8)

Order 42, rule 5A shall apply to an order for the variation of a restraint order or a charging order pursuant to rule 6 or 7 as it applies to an order for the dismissal, discontinuance or withdrawal of such an order.

**9.   Realisation of property** (O. 117 r. 9)

(1)   An application under section 17 shall, where there have been proceedings against the defendant in the Court of First Instance, be made by the Secretary for Justice by summons and shall otherwise be made by originating summons. (L.N. 362 of 1997) (L.N. 152 of 2008)

(2)   The summons or originating summons, as the case may be, shall be served with the evidence in support not less than 7 days before the date fixed for the hearing of the summons on– (L.N. 152 of 2008)

     (a)   the defendant;

     (b)   any person holding any interest in the realisable property to which the application relates; and

     (c)   the receiver, where one has been appointed in the matter.

(3)   The application shall be supported by an affidavit, which shall, to the best of the deponent's ability, give full particulars of the realisable property to which it relates and specify the person or persons holding such property, and a copy of the confiscation order, of any certificate issued by the Court under section 11(2) and of any charging order made in the matter shall be exhibited to such affidavit.

(4)   The Court may, on an application under section 17, exercise the power conferred by section 18(1) to direct the making of payments by the receiver.

**10. Receivers** (O. 117 r. 10)

(1)   Subject to this rule, the provisions of Order 30, rules 2 to 8 shall apply where a receiver is appointed in pursuance of a charging order or under section 15 or 17.

(2)   Where the receiver proposed to be appointed has been appointed receiver in other proceedings under the Ordinance, it shall not be necessary for an affidavit of fitness to be sworn or for the receiver to give security, unless the Court otherwise orders.

(3) Where a receiver has fully paid the amount payable under the confiscation order and any sums remain in his hands, he shall apply by case management summons as to the distribution of such sums. (L.N. 152 of 2008)

(4) A summons under paragraph (3) shall be served with any evidence in support not less than 7 days before the date fixed for the hearing of the summons on—

   (a) the defendant; and

   (b) any other person who held property realised by the receiver.

**11. Variation of confiscation order** (O. 117 r. 11)

(1) The Secretary for Justice or defendant may apply by summons for an order under section 20(1).

(2) The summons shall be served, with any supporting evidence, not less than 7 days before the date fixed for the hearing of the summons on—

   (a) where the Secretary for Justice is making the application, the defendant;

   (b) where the defendant is making the application, the Secretary for Justice,

and, in either case, on the receiver, where one has been appointed in the matter. (90 of 1995 s 27)

(3) The Secretary for Justice may apply by summons for an order under section 20(1A). (90 of 1995 s 27)

**12. Compensation** (O. 117 r. 12)

An application for an order under section 29 shall be made by summons, which shall be served, with any supporting evidence, on the person alleged to be in default and on the Secretary for Justice not less than 7 days before the date fixed for the hearing of the summons.

**13. Disclosure of information** (O. 117 r. 13)

(1) An application under section 28 shall be made by the Secretary for Justice by summons, which shall state the nature of the order sought and whether material sought to be disclosed is to be disclosed to a receiver appointed under section 15 or 17 or in pursuance of a charging order or to an authorized officer.

(2) The summons and affidavit in support shall be served on the public body–

   (a) not less than 7 days before the date fixed for the hearing of the summons; and

   (b) where the public body is a Government department, in accordance with Order 77, rule 4.

(3) The affidavit in support shall state the grounds for believing that the conditions in section 28(4) and, if appropriate, section 28(7) are fulfilled.

**14. Statement relating to specified offence or organized crime** (O. 117 r. 14)

(1) Where in any proceedings the Secretary for Justice or the defendant proposes to tender to the Court any statement or other document under section 10 he shall give a copy of the statement or other document as soon as practicable

to the defendant or the Attorney General, as the case may be, and to the appropriate officer of the Court.

(2)    A statement tendered to the Court by the Secretary for Justice under section 10(1) shall include the following particulars, namely— **(90 of 1995 s 27)**

  (a)   the name of the defendant;

  (b)   the name of the person by whom the statement is tendered;

  (c)   if the statement is tendered after the defendant has been convicted, the date on which and the place where the relevant conviction occurred;

  (d)   such information known to the person who made the statement as is relevant to—

    (i)   where section 8(1)(a)(ii) is applicable, the determination—

      (A)   whether the defendant could have been convicted in respect of the specified offence or offences concerned;

      (B)   whether the specified offence or any of the specified offences concerned could have been an organized crime;

    (ii)   the determination whether the defendant has benefited from a specified offence or an organized crime;

    (iii)   the assessment of the value of the defendant's proceeds of a specified offence or an organized crime.

**(90 of 1995 s 27)**
**(L.N. 156 of 1995)**

## ORDER 118

### (HK) INTERPRETATION AND GENERAL CLAUSES ORDINANCE (CAP 1)

PART XII – SEARCH AND SEIZURE OF JOURNALISTIC MATERIAL

**1.  Interpretation** (O. 118 r. 1)

**In this Order "the Ordinance" means the Interpretation and General Clauses Ordinance (Cap 1), and a section referred to by number means the section so numbered in the Ordinance.**

**(L.N. 242 of 1996)**

**2.  Application** (O. 118 r. 2)

**This Order applies to proceedings under sections 84, 85 and 87. (L.N. 242 of 1996)**

---

**NOTES**

**[118.2.1]  Scope of order**

Order 118, which is unique to Hong Kong, governs proceedings for the search for and seizure of journalistic material under Part XII of the Interpretation and General Clauses Ordinance, Cap 1. This Order came into force along with the relevant provisions of the Ordinance on 1 August 1996.

**3.  Proceedings under section 84** (O. 118 r. 3)

**(1)   An application for an order under section 84 may be made by originating summons in the expedited form supported by affidavit. (L.N. 152 of 2008)**

**(2)   The affidavit shall contain the evidence relied on to show that the conditions set out in section 84(3) have been fulfilled.**

**(3)   Unless the court otherwise directs, the affidavit may contain statements of information or belief with the sources and grounds of such information or belief.**

**(4)   Notwithstanding Order 28, rule 1A, a copy of the originating summons and affidavit shall be served on the respondent not less than 3 clear days before the date fixed for the hearing of the application.**

**(L.N. 242 of 1996)**

**4.  Proceedings under section 85** (O. 118 r. 4)

**(1)   An application for a warrant under section 85 shall be made ex parte by originating summons in Form No. 11 in Appendix A supported by affidavit. (L.N. 152 of 2008)**

**(2)   The affidavit shall –**

    **(a)   state which of the grounds set out in section 85 is relied on;**

    **(b)   contain the evidence relied on in support of those grounds; and**

    **(c)   specify the name, rank, title and address of the officer who has approved the making of the application.**

**(3)   Unless the court otherwise directs, the affidavit may contain statements of information or belief with the sources and grounds of such information or belief.**

**(4)   All applications under section 85 shall be heard in chambers.**

(L.N. 242 of 1996)

---

## NOTES

### [118.4.1]   Application for production of journalistic material

Order 118 rules 3 and 4 govern applications for orders requiring the production of journalistic material under sections 84 and 85 respectively of the Interpretation and General Clauses Ordinance (Cap 1).

The rule 3 procedure is the least 'intrusive' in that it requires an *inter partes* hearing on no less than three clear days' notice to the respondent, whereas rule 4 allows for *ex parte* applications in chambers. See *So Wing Keung v Sing Tao Ltd & Anor* HCMP 1833/2004 (Hartmann J; 10.08.2004) (doubted on appeal on other grounds – see [2005] 2 HKLRD 11).

### [118.4.2]   Affidavit evidence protected by public interest immunity

Affidavit evidence filed in support of an application under rules 3 or 4 is protected by public interest immunity and disclosure may be refused on that ground. See *Apple Daily Ltd v Commissioner of the ICAC* [2000] 1 HKC 295 (CA). In *So Wing Keung* (above) it was argued that the *Apple Daily* decision was wrong in law in this regard, though it was effectively binding at first instance. The point was not resolved when *So Wing Keung* came before the Court of Appeal.

### [118.4.3]   Application for return of seized material

A party aggrieved by seizure of material under a warrant issued *ex parte* under rule 4 may apply under rule 5 and section 87 of Cap 1 for its return. Order 32 rule 6 (which empowers the court to set aside orders made *ex parte* does not apply in this context. The relevant provisions of Cap 1 and of this Order are 'a complete, self contained code'. See *So Wing Keung v Sing Tao Ltd & Anor* [2005] 2 HKLRD 11 (CA). That decision appears to survive although the Court of Final Appeal said in a subsequent case that it should be confined to applications under the relevant provisions of Cap 1: see *P v Commissioner of the ICAC* [2007] 3 HKC 346 (CFA) (para 42).

**5.   Proceedings under section 87** (O. 118 r. 5)

**(1)   An application for an order under section 87 shall be made by summons which may be supported by affidavit.**

**(2)   The summons shall set out the grounds on which the applicant relies.**

**(3)   A copy of the summons and affidavit (if any) shall be served on the person named in the warrant pursuant to section 86(1)(a) by delivering it to him not less than 3 clear days before the date fixed for the hearing of the summons.**

**(4)   Unless the court otherwise directs, a party wishing to adduce evidence shall do so by affidavit, and such affidavit may contain statements of information or belief with the sources and grounds of such information or belief.**

(L.N. 242 of 1996)

## ORDER 119

### (HK) PREVENTION OF BRIBERY ORDINANCE (CAP 201)

PART III— POWERS OF INVESTIGATION

1.  **Interpretation** (O. 119 r. 1)

    **(1)** In this Order "the Ordinance" means the Prevention of Bribery Ordinance (Cap 201), and a section referred to by number means the section so numbered in the Ordinance.

    **(2)** Expressions used in this Order which are used in the Ordinance have the same meanings in this Order as in the Ordinance.

2.  **Application of this Order** (O. 119 r. 2)

    This Order applies to an application made to the Court under Part III of the Ordinance.

3.  **Assignment of proceedings** (O. 119 r. 3)

    As application to which this Order applies shall be heard by a judge in chambers.

4.  **Form of application** (O. 119 r. 4)

    Subject to rule 6, an application to which this Order applies shall be made ex parte by originating summons in Form No. 11 in Appendix A and, except for an application made under section 14D of the Ordinance, be supported by affidavit. **(L.N. 152 of 2008)**

5.  **Restrictions on access to documents, etc.** (O. 119 r. 5)

    **(1)** The originating summons, affidavit, if any, information and all other documents relating to the application shall be treated as confidential and shall, immediately on the determination of the application, be placed in a packet and sealed by order of the judge by whom the application was heard. **(L.N. 152 of 2008)**

    **(2)** The packet shall be kept in the custody of the Court in a place to which the public has no access or in such other place as the judge may authorize and shall not—

    (a)  be opened;
    (b)  have its contents removed;
    (c)  be copied; or
    (d)  be destroyed,

    except by order of a judge.

6.  **Variation or revocation of orders** (O. 119 r. 6)

    **(1)** An application made under section 14D of the Ordinance shall be made by summons issued in the proceedings in which the order which is sought to vary or revoke was made and shall state, so far as the applicant is able, the grounds on which the application is made.

**(2)   The summons and any affidavit in support shall be served on the Commissioner not less than 3 clear days before the hearing of the application.**

**(L.N. 222 of 1997)**

## NOTES

**[119.6.1]   Scope of Order 119**

Order 119 prescribes the procedures to be followed on applications under Part III of the Prevention of Bribery Ordinance (Cap 201). There the court is empowered to authorise compulsory disclosure of information and to issue restraining orders to freeze the assets of persons subject to ICAC investigations.

**[119.6.2]   Procedure**

Order 119 rule 4 provides that an application under this Order shall generally be made *ex parte*. The application may be dealt with on paper without a hearing: *P v Commissioner of the ICAC* [2007] 3 HKC 346 (CFA). There it was also held that the court has power under Order 32 rule 6 to set aside such an *ex parte* order (approving *X v Commissioner of the ICAC* HCCM 49/2003 (Lugar-Mawson J; 20.10.2003) in this regard), but that material non-disclosure is not a ground.

## ORDER 120

### (HK) CHARITABLE TRUSTS

1. **Appointment or removal of trustee** (O. 120 r. 1)

**(HK)** Where the appointment or removal of any trustee or any other relief, order or direction relating to any charity is deemed desirable, any person mentioned in rule 3 of this Order may make application by summons (without any information, action or petition) to the Court in chambers for such relief, order or direction as the nature of the case may require.

---

**NOTES**

**[120.1.1] History of Order 120**

This Order was previously numbered 115, and some decisions of the court prior to 1989 may refer to that number.

This Order previously governed procedure under the Charities Procedure Act 1812, as applied to Hong Kong. That Act was replaced in Hong Kong by section 57A of the Trustee Ordinance (Cap 29), enacted by Ordinance No 79 of 1997.

2. **Powers of Court** (O. 120 r. 2)

**(HK)** The Court may proceed upon and dispose of such application in chambers, unless it thinks fit otherwise to direct, and shall and may have and exercise thereupon all jurisdiction, power and authority, and may make such orders and give such directions relating to the matter of such application, as might now be exercised, made or given by the Court in an action regularly instituted, or upon petition as the case may require:

Provided that the Court may, where in the circumstances of any such application it sees fit, direct that, for obtaining the relief, order or direction sought for by such application, an information, action or petition, as the case may require, shall be brought or presented and prosecuted, and abstain from further proceeding on such application.

---

**NOTES**

**[120.2.1] Hearing in chambers or open court**

Order 120 rule 2 gives the court a discretion to hear an application to which the Order applies in chambers rather than open court. See the commentary under Order 28 rule 9 as to when, as a general rule, the court will hear an originating summons in chambers.

Given that Order 120 relates only to charitable trusts, which will inevitably have a public purpose, an application should normally be heard in open court.

3. **Applications** (O. 120 r. 3)

**(HK)** An application under rule 1 of this Order may be made by —

      (a) the Secretary for Justice;

> (b) **all or any one or more of the trustees or persons administering the trust, or persons claiming to administer the trust, or persons otherwise interested in the trust; or**
>
> (c) **in the case of any relief, order or direction sought under section 57A of the Trustee Ordinance (Cap 29), 2 or more persons who have the consent in writing of the Secretary for Justice to make the application.**
>
> (79 of 1997 s 4)

## NOTES

### [120.3.1]   Form of application

An application under Order 120 should be made by way of originating summons: Order 5 rule 3. It follows that affidavit evidence should be filed. Where the consent of the Secretary for Justice is required (see rule 3(c)) and has been obtained, this should be exhibited in order to demonstrate procedural compliance.

The court's power to direct that proceedings commenced by originating summons be continued as if commenced by writ (Order 28 rule 8) may be exercised in cases where it is desirable to hear oral evidence to resolve issues of fact. Such an order was made in proceedings under Order 120 known as *Cheung Man Yu v Lau Yuen Ching* CACV 70/2003 (Yuen JA & Stone J; 16.07.2003) but overturned on appeal for procedural reasons.

**4.   Secretary for Justice to be made party to certain applications** (O. 120 r. 4)

**(HK)   Where an application under rule 1 of this Order is made by any trustee or person referred to in rule 3(b) of this Order, the Secretary for Justice shall be made a party to the application unless the Court otherwise orders. (79 of 1997 s 4)**

(L.N. 282 of 1989; L.N. 383 of 1996)

## NOTES

### [120.4.1]   Parties in proceedings relating to charitable trusts

The general rule is that the sovereign as *parens patriae* is the constitutional protector of property subject to charitable trusts. Hence the Secretary for Justice, being the equivalent of Attorney General in Hong Kong, is the proper person to bring proceedings to protect charities. See *Ip Cheung-kwok v Sin Hua Bank Trustee Ltd & Ors* [1990] 2 HKLR 499, 515E–H (CA), citing 5 Hals (4th) 870.

Order 120 rules 3 and 4 provide that in certain circumstances, other persons may also bring such proceedings, provided that the Secretary consents, or is made a party.

In *Ip Cheung-kwok* it was a defendant rather than the plaintiff who contended that certain property was held on charitable trust. The Attorney General was joined as a party but declined to support the contention. As a result, it was argued that the issue could not be advanced and the court had no jurisdiction. The Court of Appeal held (at 523C) that a defendant may contend for the existence of a charitable trust notwithstanding the lack of support from the Secretary for Justice where it does so to protect itself as well as the trust.

**[120.4.2]   Costs**

Where the Secretary for Justice acted in the public interest in proceedings where property was found to be held on charitable trust, it was ordered that the Secretary's costs be paid out of the charity's funds insofar as not recoverable from the opposing party: *Re Tsing Shan Monastery* [2003] 1 HKLRD 237. The Secretary's costs were to be taxed on the common fund basis.

## ORDER 121

### CHILD ABDUCTION AND CUSTODY ORDINANCE (CAP 512)

PROCEEDINGS AND APPLICATIONS

**1.  Interpretation** (O. 121 r. 1)

(1)  In this Order "the Ordinance" means the Child Abduction and Custody Ordinance (Cap 512) and a section referred to by number means the section so numbered in the Ordinance.

(2)  Expressions used in this Order which are used in the Ordinance have the same meanings in this Order as in the Ordinance.

(3)  In this Order, unless the context otherwise requires—

"application" means an application under the Convention or the Ordinance;

"decision" includes a judgment or an order of any judicial authority as well as an order of an administrative authority;

"relevant authority" includes the Court, a District Court and a juvenile court.

**2.  Mode of application** (O. 121 r. 2)

(1)  Subject to paragraph (2), every originating application may be made by originating summons in Form No. 10 in Appendix A. (L.N. 152 of 2008)

(2)  Where an applicant seeks a direction under rule 9 without having filed an originating summons, the Court may, on sufficient cause being shown, allow such an application to be made on the applicant's undertaking to the Court to issue an originating summons as soon as possible and on such other terms, if any, as the Court thinks fit.

**3.  Application for return of a child** (O. 121 r. 3)

(1)  An application for the return of a child shall be supported by an affidavit sworn by the applicant or, if the circumstances of the case justify it, a person duly authorized to swear it on behalf of the applicant, and the affidavit shall, so far as it is possible to do so—

    (a)  state the following—

        (i)   the matters specified in Article 8(a) to (d) of the Convention;

        (ii)  if applicable, the matters stated in Article 8(e) and (f) of the Convention;

        (iii) particulars of any pending or concluded proceedings, including proceedings out of Hong Kong, relating to the child;

        (iv)  any other information which may assist in securing the return of the child;

    (b)  exhibit all relevant documents.

(2)  The affidavit shall be filed at the same time as the application except that, in a case of urgency, the affidavit may be filed as soon as possible after the application.

**4. Application for a declaration under section 10** (O. 121 r. 4)

(1) An application for a declaration that the removal or retention of the child was wrongful shall be supported by an affidavit sworn by the applicant or, if the circumstances of the case justify it, by a person duly authorized to swear it on behalf of the applicant, and the affidavit shall, so far as is possible—

    (a) state—

        (i) full particulars of the request made by the requesting state;

        (ii) the matters specified in Article 8(a) to (c) of the Convention and all other facts on which the applicant relies;

    (b) exhibit all relevant documents.

(2) The affidavit shall be filed at the same time as the application except that, where the case is one of urgency, the affidavit may be filed as soon as possible after the application.

**5. Defendants** (O. 121 r. 5)

(1) The following persons shall be made defendants to an application for the return of a child—

    (a) the person alleged in the affidavit to have brought into Hong Kong the child in respect of whom the application under the Convention is made;

    (b) the person with whom the child is alleged in the affidavit to be;

    (c) any parent or guardian of the child who is not otherwise a party;

    (d) the person in whose favour a decision, including a decision of a relevant authority in a Contracting State other than Hong Kong, relating to custody has been made, if he is not otherwise a party; and

    (e) any other person who has a sufficient interest in the welfare of the child.

(2) The persons referred to in paragraph (1)(b) to (e) shall be made defendants to an application under section 10.

**6. Time for acknowledging service** (O. 121 r. 6)

The time limited for acknowledging service of an originating summons issued pursuant to rule 2 is 7 days after the service of the originating summons, including the day of service, or 14 days after the service of the originating summons, including the day of service, where the service has taken place outside the jurisdiction.

**7. Further evidence** (O. 121 r. 7)

(1) Any defendant may within 5 days after acknowledging service of the originating summons file and serve on the other parties any affidavit on which he intends to rely.

(2) The plaintiff may within 5 days thereafter file and serve on the defendant an affidavit in reply.

**8.   Assignment of proceedings** (O. 121 r. 8)

Every application shall be heard and determined by a judge, except that applications to extend time and to join a defendant may be heard by a Master, and shall be dealt with in chambers unless the Court otherwise directs.

**9.   Interim directions** (O. 121 r. 9)

An application for interim directions under section 7 may, where the case is one of urgency, be made ex parte.

**10.  Stay of proceedings** (O. 121 r. 10)

(1)   A person wishing to give notice under Article 16 of the Convention that there has been a wrongful removal or retention of a child who is the subject of proceedings relating to the merits of rights of custody shall file in the Registry a notice to that effect, which shall contain a concise statement of the nature of those proceedings and shall identify the relevant authority before which they are pending.

(2)   A notice given under paragraph (1) shall be verified on affidavit by the person giving it and the affidavit shall be filed at the same time as the notice.

(3)   The Registrar, upon receipt of such notice and affidavit, shall as soon as practicable, provide the relevant authority with copies thereof.

**11.  Authenticated copy of Courts order** (O. 121 r. 11)

(1)   A person who wishes to make an application under the Convention in a Contracting State other than Hong Kong and who wishes to obtain from the Court an authenticated copy of an order of the Court relating to the child in respect of whom the application is to be made shall apply in writing in that behalf to the Registrar.

(2)   An application under paragraph (1) shall specify, so far as it is possible to do so—

  (a)   the name and date of birth of the child;

  (b)   the date of the order and the short title of the proceedings in which the order was made;

  (c)   the nature of the application which is intended to be made, identifying the Contracting State in which the application is intended to be made;

  (d)   the relationship of the applicant to the child;

  (e)   the address of the applicant.

(3)   On receipt of an application under this rule, the Registrar shall send by post to the applicant at the address indicated in the application an authenticated copy of the order or, if he is unable to locate the order, shall notify the applicant accordingly.

(4)   The authenticated copy of the order shall be an office copy sealed with the Seal of the Court and endorsed with a certificate signed by the Registrar certifying that the copy is a true copy of an order obtained in the Court and that it is issued for the purposes of the Convention.

**(L.N. 119 of 1998)**

**NOTES**

**[121.11.1]  History of Order 121**
Order 121 came into force on 11 February 1998 (LN 119 of 1998), providing procedures for proceedings under the Child Abduction and Custody Ordinance (Cap 512). The Ordinance and this Order implement in Hong Kong the international Convention on Civil Aspects of International Child Abduction.

**[121.11.2]  Principles applicable on application under Child Abduction and Custody Ordinance**
For a discussion of the principles applicable on applications under Order 121 pursuant to the Child Abduction and Custody Ordinance (Cap 512) see, for example, *N v O (Child Retention)* [1998] 4 HKC 574 and *LM v HTS* HCMP 1329/2001 (Hartmann J; 19.04.2001.)

See also *AC v PC* [2005] 2 HKC 90, 103C-D where it was held that it is an 'unspoken' objective of the contention to ensure the best interests of abducted children. In that case it was held that abducted children should remain with the abducting parent since they had, by passage of time, become settled in their environment.

**[121.11.3]  Costs**
In *N v O (Child Retention)* [1998] 4 HKC 574 the court made an order nisi that there be no order as to costs. The successful defendant (mother) applied for a variation of that order seeking that her costs be paid by the father. Hartmann J gave a written judgment on the costs issue (HCMP 4204/1998 (Hartmann J; 06.01.1999)) holding that in proceedings under Order 121 the court should 'be wary of awarding costs against an unsuccessful party except in exceptional circumstances'. Support for this view was found in article 26 of the Hague Convention implemented by the primary legislation (Cap 512).

FORMS

No. 1

Writ of Summons

(O. 6 r. 1)

## IN THE HIGH COURT OF THE
## HONG KONG SPECIAL ADMINISTRATIVE REGION
### COURT OF FIRST INSTANCE

20........ ,No.................

| Between | A.B. | Plaintiff |
| --- | --- | --- |
| | AND | |
| | CD. | Defendant |

TO THE DEFENDANT (name) ............................................................ of (address)
.......................................................................................................................................

THIS WRIT OF SUMMONS has been issued against you by the above- named Plaintiff in respect of the claim set out on the back.

Within (14 days) after the service of this Writ on you, counting the day of service, you must either satisfy the claim or return to the Registry of the High Court the accompanying ACKNOWLEDGMENT OF SERVICE stating therein whether you intend to contest these proceedings or to make an admission.

If you fail to satisfy the claim or to return the Acknowledgment within the time stated, or if you return the Acknowledgment without stating therein an intention to contest the proceedings, the Plaintiff may proceed with the action and judgment may be entered against you forthwith without further notice.

*[If you intend to make an admission, you may complete an appropriate form enclosed in accordance with the accompanying Directions for Acknowledgment of Service.]

Issued from the Registry of the High Court this .......... day of ................... 20 .......

Note: This Writ may not be served later than 12 calendar months beginning with that date unless renewed by order of the Court.

## IMPORTANT

Directions for Acknowledgment of Service are given with the accompanying form.

(Back of No. 1)

*[Statement of Claim]

The Plaintiffs claim is for......................................................................................................

*Where words appear between square brackets delete if inapplicable.

*(Signed if statement of claim indorsed.)

A statement of claim must be verified by a statement of truth in accordance with Order 41A of the Rules of the High Court (Cap. 4 sub. leg. A).

(Where the Plaintiffs claim is for a debt or liquidated demand only: If, within the time for returning the Acknowledgment of Service, the Defendant pays the amount claimed and $..................for costs, further proceedings will be stayed. The money must be paid to the Plaintiff or his Solicitor.)

THIS WRIT was issued by................................................,of.....................................

Solicitors for the said Plaintiff whose address is..............................................................
.......................................................................................................................................
.......................................................................................................................................

*(or where the Plaintiff sues in person.)

THIS WRIT was issued by the said Plaintiff who resides at .........................................
.......................................................................................................................................
and (if the Plaintiff does not reside within the jurisdiction) whose address for service is......................................................................................................................................).

(L.N. 251 of 1997; 25 of 1998 s 2)
(L.N. 152 of 2008)

## No. 8

### Originating summons—general form

### (O. 7 r. 2)

IN THE HIGH COURT OF THE HONG KONG SPECIAL ADMINISTRATIVE REGION
COURT OF FIRST INSTANCE

19........,No...........

(IN THE MATTER OF.....................)

| Between | | |
|---|---|---|
| | *A.B.* | Plaintiff |
| | *AND* | |
| | *C.D.* | Defendant |

To *C.D.* of

Let the defendant, within (14 days) after service of this summons on him, counting the day of service, return the accompanying Acknowledgment of Service to the Registry of the High Court.

By this summons, which is issued on the application of the plaintiff *A.B.* of .........................................., the plaintiff claims against the defendant ............... .....................................(or seeks the determination of the Court on the following questions, namely,................................or as may be).

If the defendant does not acknowledge service, such judgment may be given or order made against or in relation to him as the Court may think just and expedient.

Dated the ...................... day of ...................... 19........

*Note*:—This summons may not be served later than 12 calendar months beginning with the above date unless renewed by order of the Court.

This summons was taken out by ................................................................ of ........................................... solicitors for the said plaintiff..................... whose address is as stated above (or where the plaintiff sues in person. This summons was taken out by the said plaintiff who resides at the above-named address or as may be and (if the plaintiff does not reside within the jurisdiction) whose address for service is.................................................................................................................................).

### IMPORTANT

Directions for Acknowledgment of Service are given with the accompanying form.

(Enacted 1988)

## No. 10

Originating summons-expedited form

(O.7 r. 2; O.29 r. 8A; O.30 r. 9; O.62 r. 11A;
O.73 rr. 2, 3 & 4; O 100 r. 2; O.115 rr. 2A, 3, 7 & 24)

IN THE HIGH COURT OF THE
HONG KONG SPECIAL ADMINISTRATIVE REGION
COURT OF FIRST INSTANCE

20.............,No.............

(IN THE MATTER OF...........................)

Between                     A.B.                       Plaintiff

AND

C.D.                      Defendant

Let C.D. of.................... attend before the Registrar (or Judge) in Chambers, at the High Court, Hong Kong, on................ day, the.............. day of............ 20.., at.....o'clock (or, if no application has yet been made for a day to be fixed, on a day to be fixed) on the hearing of an application by the plaintiff A.B. of................................ ....................that.........................................

And let the defendant within (14 days) after service of this summons on him counting the day of service, return the accompanying Acknowledgment of Service to the Registry of the High Court.

Dated the...............day of...............of 20...............

Note: This summons may not be served later than 12 calendar months beginning with the above date unless renewed by order of the Court.

This summons was taken out by ...................................... of ...................................... solicitors for the said plaintiff whose address is as stated above (or where the plaintiff sues in person:

This summons was taken out by the said plaintiff who resides at............................ and (if the plaintiff does not reside within the jurisdiction) whose address for service is................................................................................................................................).

Note: If a defendant does not attend personally or by his counsel or solicitor at the time and place above-mentioned such order will be made as the Court may think just and expedient.

### IMPORTANT

Directions for Acknowledgment of Service are given with the accompanying form.

(L.N. 251 of 1997; 25 of 1998 s. 2)
(L.N. 152 of 2008)

## No. 11

### Ex parte originating summons

### (O. 7 r. 2, O. 118 r 4(1); O. 119 r. 4)

### IN THE HIGH COURT OF THE HONG KONG SPECIAL ADMINISTRATIVE REGION

20.............., No................

In the matter of.................................................................................................................

Let all parties concerned attend before the Judge in Chambers (or the Master) at the High Court in Hong Kong, on...............day, the...............day of............. 20................,at......o'clock,on the hearing of an application by A.B. that................. ........................

Dated the.........day of...............20

This summons was taken out by....................................of............................... solicitor for the applicant whose address is.............................................................................

(L.N. 313 of 1997; 25 of 1998 s 2)

(L.N. 152 of 2008)

No. 11A

**Originating summons for possession**
(Order 113 rule 2)

19......, No..............

IN THE COURT OF FIRST INSTANCE OF THE HONG KONG
SPECIAL ADMINISTRATIVE REGION

(IN THE MATTER OF.......................)

Between                              *A.B.*                    Plaintiff

                                     *AND*

                                     *C.D.*                    Defendant (if any)
                                                               whose name is
                                                               known

To [*C.D.* and] every [other] person in occupation of................................
Let all persons concerned attend before..................................... Court of First
Instance...............................of Hong Kong in Hong Kong on................................
........................... day, the..............day of...........................19......at.......o'clock, on
the hearing of an application by *A.B.* for an order that he do recover possession
of..........................on the ground that he is entitled to possession and that the person(s)
in occupation is (are) in occupation without licence or consent.
Dated the...............day of.................19......
This summons was taken out by.....................of.................solicitor for the said
plaintiff whose address is..........................[or when the plaintiff acts in person]
This summons was taken out by the said plaintiff who resides at.....................
.....................................and is (State occupation) and (if the plaintiff does not reside
within the jurisdiction) whose address for service is.....................................................
.........................................................................................................................................

*Note*:—Any person occupying the premises may apply to the Court personally
or by counsel or solicitor to be joined as a defendant. If a person occupying the
premises does not attend personally or by counsel or solicitor at the time and place
above-mentioned, such order will be made as the Court may think just and expedient.

(Enacted 1988)

## No. 12

### Notice of appointment to hear originating summons
(Order 28 rule 2)

*(Heading as in summons)*

To (name of defendant) of..........................................................

Take notice that the originating summons issued herein on the..........................
day of..........................19......, will be heard by the Judge in Chambers (or the master)
at the High Court in Hong Kong, on..........................day, the..........................day
of.................. 19......, at..........................o'clock.

You may attend in person, or by your solicitor or counsel. If you fail to attend,
such order will be made as the Court may think just and expedient.

Dated the..........................day of..........................19......

(Signed)..............................................
*Solicitor for the plaintiff.*

(Enacted 1988)

## No. 13

**Notice of originating summons**
(Order 8 rule 3)

19......, No..............

IN THE HIGH COURT OF THE HONG KONG SPECIAL ADMINISTRATIVE REGION

In the matter of...............................................................................

and

In the matter of...............................................................................

Take notice that the High Court of Hong Kong in Hong Kong will be moved (before his Lordship, Mr. Justice...............................................) at the expiration of............ days from the service upon you of this notice (or on............................................... .................. day, the.. day of............. 19......, at the sitting of the Court) or so soon thereafter as counsel can be heard, by counsel on behalf of *A.B.* for an order that.............. (or for the following relief, namely........................................)

And that the costs of and incidental to this (application) (appeal) may be paid by................................................................................................................................

(And further take notice that the grounds of this (application) (appeal) are:...............................................................................................................................

Dated the..........................day of.......................... 19.....

(Signed).....................................................

*C.D.* of................................solicitor for the above named (applicant) (appellant) *A.B.* whose address is................................................. or *A.B.* whose address for service is.............................(applicant) (appellant) in person................................................................................................

To..................of...................

(L.N. 313 of 1997)

(Enacted 1988)

No. 14

Acknowledgment of Service of Writ of Summons

(Order 12 rule 3)

Directions for Acknowledgment of Service

1. The accompanying form of ACKNOWLEDGMENT OF SERVICE should be detached and completed by a Solicitor acting on behalf of the Defendant or by the Defendant if acting in person. After completion it must be delivered or sent by post to the Registry of the High Court at the following address:—

*[insert here the address of the Registry of the High Court]*

2. A Defendant who states in his Acknowledgment of Service that he intends to contest the proceedings MUST ALSO file a DEFENCE which must be written in either the Chinese or the English language with the Registry and serve a copy thereof on the Solicitor for the Plaintiff (or on the Plaintiff if acting in person).

If a Statement of Claim is indorsed on the Writ (i.e. the words "Statement of Claim" appear at the top of the back), the Defence must be filed and served within 28 days after the time for acknowledging service of the Writ, unless in the meantime a summons for judgment is served on the Defendant.

If a Statement of Claim is not indorsed on the Writ, the Defence must be filed and served within 28 days after a Statement of Claim has been served on the Defendant.

If the Defendant fails to file and serve his Defence within the appropriate time, the Plaintiff may enter judgment against him without further notice.

The Defendant's defence must be verified by a statement of truth in accordance with Order 41A of the Rules of the High Court (Cap. 4 sub. leg. A)

3. If the only remedy that the Plaintiff is seeking is the payment of a liquidated amount of money or the payment of an unliquidated amount of money, you may admit the Plaintiffs claim in whole or in part by completing Form No. 16 or 16C (as the case may require) accompanying the Writ of Summons.

A completed Form No. 16 or 16C must be filed with the Registry of the High Court and served on the Plaintiff [or the Plaintiffs Solicitors] within the period for service of the Defence.

4. A Defendant who wishes to dispute the jurisdiction of the Court of First Instance in the proceedings or to argue that the Court of First Instance should not exercise its jurisdiction in the proceedings, and wishes to apply to the Court of First Instance for an order staying the proceedings, must give notice of intention to defend the proceedings and make the application within the time limited for service of a defence.

See attached Notes for Guidance

Notes for Guidance

1. Each Defendant (if there are more than one) is required to complete an Acknowledgment of Service and return it to the Registry of the High Court.

2. For the purpose of calculating the period of 14 days for acknowledging service, a writ served on the Defendant personally is treated as having been served on the day it was delivered to him and a writ served by post or by insertion through the Defendant's letter box is treated as having been served on the seventh day after the date of posting or insertion.] (Note: Not applicable if the defendant is a company served at its registered office.)

3. Where the Defendant is sued in a name different from his own, the form must be completed by him with the addition in paragraph 1 of the words "sued as (the name stated on the Writ of Summons)".

4. Where the Defendant is a FIRM and a Solicitor is not instructed, the form must be completed by a PARTNER by name, with the addition in paragraph 1 of the description "partner in the firm of (.......................)" after his name.

5. Where the Defendant is sued as an individual TRADING IN A NAME OTHER THAN HIS OWN, the form must be completed by him with the addition in paragraph 1 of the description "trading as (.......................)" after his name.

6. Where the Defendant is a LIMITED COMPANY the form must be completed by a Solicitor or by someone authorized to act on behalf of the Company, but the Company can take no further step in the proceedings without a Solicitor acting on its behalf.

7. Where the Defendant is a MINOR or a MENTAL Patient, the form must be completed by a Solicitor acting for a guardian ad litem.

8. A Defendant acting in person may obtain help in completing the form at the Registry of the High Court.

9. These notes deal only with the more usual cases. In case of difficulty a Defendant in person should refer to paragraph 8 above.

(Heading as in No. 1 to be completed by plaintiff)

## ACKNOWLEDGMENT OF SERVICE OF WRIT
## OF SUMMONS

If you intend to instruct a Solicitor to act for you, give him this form IMMEDIATELY. Important: Read the accompanying directions and notes for guidance carefully before completing this form. If any information required is omitted or given wrongly, THIS FORM MAY HAVE TO BE RETURNED.

Delay may result in judgment being entered against a Defendant whereby he or his Solicitor may have to pay the costs of applying to set it aside.

| | | |
|---|---|---|
| See Notes 1, 3, 4 and 5. | 1. | State the full name of the defendant by whom or on whose behalf the service of the originating summons is being acknowledged. |

2. State whether the defendant intends to contest the liability for costs (tick appropriate box)

□ yes   □ no

See Direction 3

3. If the only remedy that the Plaintiff is seeking is the payment of a liquidated amount of money or the payment of an unliquidated amount of money, state whether the Defendant intends to make an admission (tick appropriate box).

□ yes   □ no

If yes, the Defendant may make the admission by completing Form No. 16 or 16C (as the case may require) accompanying the Writ of Summons.

Where words appear between square brackets, delete if inapplicable.

Service of the Writ is acknowledged accordingly

(Signed)[Solicitor]( )
[Defendant in person]

Notes as to Address for Service

Solicitor. Where the Defendant is represented by a Solicitor, stale the Solicitor's place of business in Hong Kong.

Defendant in person. Where the Defendant is acting in person, he must give his residence OR, if he does not reside in Hong Kong, he must give an address in Hong Kong where communications for him should be sent. In the case of a limited company, "residence" means its registered or principal office.

(Back of page (1))

Indorsement by plaintiff's solicitor (or by plaintiff if suing in person) of his name, address and reference, if any.

(L N. 251 of 1997, L.N. 313 of 1997; 25 of 1998 s. 2; L.N. 129 of 2000)
(L.N. 152 of 2008)

---

No. 15

Acknowledgment of Service of Originating Summons – for all cases other than costs-only proceedings under section 52B of the High Court Ordinance

(Order 10 rule 5; Order 12 rule 3(1))

Directions for Acknowledgment of Service

1.   The accompanying form of ACKNOWLEDGMENT OF SERVICE should be detached and completed by a Solicitor acting on behalf of the Defendant or by the Defendant if acting in person. After completion it must be delivered or sent by post to the Registry of the High Court of the following address: -

[insert here the address of the Registry of the High Court]

2.   If the only remedy that the Plaintiff is seeking is the payment of a liquidated amount of money or the payment of an unliquidated amount of money, you may admit the Plaintiff's claim in whole or in part by completing Form No. 16 or 16C (as the case may require) accompanying the Originating Summons.

A completed Form No. 16 or 16C must be filed with the Registry of the High Court and served on the Plaintiff [or the Plaintiff's Solicitors] within the period for filing of the Defendant's affidavit evidence.

3.   A Defendant who wishes to dispute the jurisdiction of the Court of First Instance in the proceedings or to argue that the Court of First Instance should not exercise its jurisdiction in the proceedings, and wishes to apply to the Court of First Instance for an order staying the proceedings, must give notice of intention to defend the proceedings and make the application within the time limited for service of a defence.

See over for Notes for Guidance

[Back of page (1)]

Notes for Guidance

[As in No. 14 substituting "originating summons" for "writ of summons".]

(Heading as in No. 8 or 10 to be completed by plaintiff)

ACKNOWLEDGMENT OF SERVICE
OF ORIGINATING SUMMONS

If you intend to instruct a Solicitor to act for you, give him this form IMMEDIATELY.

Important. Read the accompanying directions and notes for guidance carefully before completing this form. If any information required is omitted or given wrongly, THIS FORM MAY HAVE TO BE RETURNED.

| | | |
|---|---|---|
| See Notes 1, 3, 4 and 5. | 1. | State the full name of the Defendant by whom or on whose behalf the service of the Originating Summons is being acknowledged. |
| | 2. | State whether the defendant intends to contest the proceeding (tick appropriate box)<br><br>□ yes □ no |
| See Direction 3 | 3. | If the only remedy that the Plaintiff is seeking is the payment of a liquidated amount of money or the payment of an unliquidated amount of money, state whether the Defendant intends to make an admission (tick appropriate box).<br><br>□ yes □ no<br><br>If yes, the Defendant may make the admission by completing Form No. 16 or 16C (as the case may require) accompanying the Originating Summons. |

| | | |
|---|---|---|
| Where words appear between square brackets, delete if inapplicable. | Service of the Originating Summons is acknowledged accordingly | (Signed)[Solicitor]( )<br>[Defendant in person] |

**Notes as to Address for Service**

Solicitor. Where the Defendant is represented by a Solicitor, state the Solicitor's place of business in Hong Kong.

Defendant in person. Where the Defendant is acting in person, he must give his residence OR, if he does not reside in Hong Kong, he must give an address in Hong Kong where communications for him should be sent. In the case of a limited company, "residence" Chinese text omitted means its registered or principal office.

(Back of page (1))

Indorsement by plaintiff's Solicitors (or by plaintiff if suing in person) of his name, address and reference, if any.

(Enacted 1988) (L.N. 251 of 1997) (25 of 1998 s.2)
(L.N. 152 of 2008)

Appendices

No. 15A

Acknowledgment of Service of Originating Summons –
for all cases other than costs-only proceedings under section 52B
of the High Court Ordinance

(Order 10 rule 5; Order 12 rule 3(1); Order 62 rule 11A)

*Directions for Acknowledgment of Service*

The accompanying form of ACKNOWLEDGMENT OF SERVICE should be detached and completed by a solicitor acting on behalf of the defendant or by the defendant if acting in person. After completion it must be delivered or sent by post to the Registry of the High Court of the following address: —

[*insert here the address of the Registry of the High Court*]

See over for Notes for Guidance

[Back of page (1)]

Notes for Guidance

[As in No 14 substituting "originating summons" for "writ of summons".]

(Heading as in No. 8 or 10 to be completed by plaintiff)

ACKNOWLEDGEMENT OF SERVICE OF ORIGINATING SUMMONS

If you intend to instruct a solicitor to act for you, give him this form IMMEDIATELY.

*Important*. Read the accompanying directions and notes for guidance *carefully* before completing this form. If any information required is omitted or given wrongly, THIS FORM MAY HAVE TO BE RETURNED.

| | | |
|---|---|---|
| See Notes 1, 3, 4 and 5. | 1. | State the full name of the defendant whose behalf the service of the originating being acknowledged. |
| | 2. | State whether the defendant intends for costs (tick appropriate box). |
| | | □ yes □ no |
| See Direction 3 | 3. | State whether the defendant intends of those costs (tick appropriate box). |
| | | □ yes □ no |
| Where words appear between square brackets, delete if inapplicable. | | Service of the Writ is acknowledged accordingly |

(Signed)[Solicitor]( )
[Defendant in person]
Address for service

*Notes as to Address for Service*

Solicitor. Where the defendant is represented by a Solicitor, state the solicitor's place of business in Hong Kong.

Defendant in person. Where the Defendant is acting in person, he must state his residence OR, if he does not reside in Hong Kong, he must state an address in Hong Kong to which communications for him should be sent. In the case of a limited company, "residence" means its registered or principal office.

(Back of page (1))

Indorsement by plaintiffs solicitors (or by plaintiff if suing in person) of his name, address and reference, if any.

(L.N. 152 of 2008)

———————————

## No. 16

### (Admission (liquidated amount))

O. 13A rules 4(2) & 13(2)

---

*(Heading as in action)*

Explanatory Note

1.  The only claim the plaintiff has made against you is for a liquidated amount of money. You may admit the plaintiffs claim in whole or part by completing this form—

(a) within the period for service of your defence if you have been served with a writ; or

(b) the period for filing of your affidavit evidence if you have been served with an originating summons; *or*

(c) within 14 days after service of the originating process in any other case.

2.  If you have made an admission, you may only be allowed to amend or withdraw your admission if the Court considers it just to do so.

3.  If you do not ask for time to pay, the plaintiff will decide how much and when you should pay.

4.  If you ask for time to pay, the plaintiff will decide whether or not to accept your proposal for payment.

5.  If the plaintiff accepts your proposal for payment, the plaintiff may, within 14 days after the copy of your admission is served on him, request the Court to enter judgment against you.

6.  If the plaintiff does not accept your proposal for payment, the Court will decide how the payment should be made after considering-

    (a) the information set out in this form;

    (b) the reasons why the plaintiff does not accept your proposal for payment; and

    (c) all other relevant matters

7.  The completed form should be filed in the Registry of the High Court.

How to fill in this form

•   Tick the correct boxes and give as much information as you can. Then sign and date the form. If necessary provide details on a separate sheet, add the action number and attach it to this form.

•   If you do not ask for time to pay, you need not complete items 2 to 9 and 11 to 14.

---

| |
|---|
| • If you ask for time to pay, make your offer of payment in item 14. |
| • If you are not an individual, you need not complete items 1 to 9 but you should complete items 10 to 12 and ensure that you comply with the requirement specified in item 13 and provide sufficient details about the assets and liabilities of your firm, company or corporation to support any offer of payment made in item 14. |
| • If you are an individual you need not complete items 10 to 12 and need not comply with the requirement specified in item 13. |
| • You can get help to complete this form at the Registry of the High Court. |

| How much of the claim do you admit? | | |
|---|---|---|
| ☐ | I admit the full amount claimed as shown on the statement of claim or | |
| ☐ | I admit the amount of | $ |

1. Personal Details

Surname

Forename

☐ Mr  ☐ Mrs  ☐ Miss  ☐ Ms

Address

2. Dependants (*people you look after financially*)

| *give details* | |
|---|---|

3. Employment
   - ☐ I am employed as a
   - ☐ My employer is
   - ☐ Jobs other than main job (*give details*)
   - ☐ I am self employed as a
   - ☐ Annual turnover is
   - ☐ I am not in arrears with my mandatory provident fund contributions and income tax.
   - ☐ I am in arrears and I owe

Give details of:

(a) contracts and other work in hand

(b) any sums due for work done

☐ I have been unemployed for _____years_____months

☐ I am a pensioner

4. Bank account and savings *(please list all)*

| Bank account | In credit by $ | Overdrawn by $ |
|---|---|---|
| | | |

5. Residence

I live in

    ☐    my own flat

    ☐    my jointly owned flat

    ☐    public housing estate

    ☐    rented private flat

    ☐    others (please specify)

6. Income

| | | |
|---|---|---|
| My usual take-home pay (including overtime, commission, bonuses etc) | $ | per month |
| My pension(s) | $ | per month |
| Others living in my home give me | $ | per month |
| Other income *(give details below)* | | |
| | $ | per month |
| | $ | per month |
| | $ | per month |
| Total income | $ | per month |

7. Other assets *(please list and indicate their location)*

| |
|---|
| |

8. Expenses

*(Do not include any payments made by other members of the household out of their own income)*

I have regular expenses as follows:

| | | |
|---|---|---|
| Mortgage *(including second mortgage)* | $ | per month |
| Rent | $ | per month |
| Rates and government rent | $ | per month |
| Management fees | $ | per month |
| Domestic helper's salary | $ | per month |
| Gas | $ | per month |
| Electricity | $ | per month |
| Water charges | $ | per month |
| Telephone charges | $ | per month |
| Housekeeping, food, school meals | $ | per month |
| Travelling expenses | $ | per month |
| Children's clothing | $ | per month |
| Tuition fee | $ | per month |
| Maintenance payment | $ | per month |
| Court orders | $ | per month |
| Others | | |
| | $ | per month |
| | $ | per month |
| | $ | per month |
| Total expenses | $ | per month |

9. Liabilities

*(This section is for arrears only. <u>Do not</u> include regular expenses listed in item 8)*

| | |
|---|---|
| Rent arrears | $ |
| Mortgage arrears | $ |
| Rates and government arrears | $ |
| Water charges arrears | $ |
| Fuel debts: Gas | $ |
| Electricity | $ |
| Others | $ |
| Maintenance arrears | $ |
| Loan and credit cards and debts (please list) | $ |
| Others *(give details below)* | |
| | $ |
| | $ |
| Total liabilities | $ |

10. Firm, company or corporation

Name

Address

Tel. no.

11. Assets of firm, company or corporation (*please list*)

| Property, plant and equipment | $ |
|---|---|
| Inventories | $ |
| Goodwill and other intangible assets | $ |
| Loans and receivables | $ |
| Bank balances and cash | $ |
| Others | $ |
| Total | $ |

12. Liabilities of firm, company or corporation *(please list)*

| Trade payables | $ |
|---|---|
| Tax payable | $ |
| Other payables | $ |
| Bank loans | $ |
| Other borrowings | $ |
| Others | $ |
| Total | $ |

13. Attach to this form a copy of the latest audited profit and loss account and balance sheet of the firm, company or corporation.

14. Offer of payment

| ☐ | I can pay the amount admitted on | $ |
|---|---|---|
| | or | |
| ☐ | I can pay by [weekly/ monthly etc] instalments of | $ |

Starting (date)
If you cannot pay immediately, please give brief reasons below:

15. Declaration    I ......................... declare that the details I have given above and in the attached sheet(s) (if any) are true to the best of my knowledge.

And I make this solemn declaration conscientiously believing the same to be true and by virtue of the Oaths and Declaration Ordinance
(Cap.1 1)

| Signed | | Position or office held (If signing on behalf of a firm, company or corporation) With company chop (if applicable) | |

Declared at...................................... in Hong Kong on......................... of 20.................

Before me,
[Signature and designation i.e. Justice of the Peace/Notary Public/Commissioner for Oaths.]

Note    –    Under section 36 of the Crimes Ordinance (Cap 200) a person who knowingly and wilfully makes a statement false in a material particular in a declaration or other document which he is authorized or required to make by an enactment is guilty of an offence.

–    A defendant who is an individual must sign personally. A director of a company must obtain leave to represent the company from a Practice Master before he may sign on behalf of the company.

–    If a plaintiff does not file a request for judgment within 14 days after this form served on him, his claim is stayed until he files the request.

(L.N. 152 of 2008)

## No. 16A

Request for judgment (admission of liquidated amount)

(Order 13A rules 4(3), 9(4) & 10(2))

*(Heading as in action)*

- Remember to sign and date the form. Your signature certifies that the information you have given is correct.

- Return the completed form to the Court.

- The completed form should be filed in the Registry of the High Court.

A    The defendant has admitted the whole of my claim

Tick only one box below and follow the instructions given

    ☐    I accept the defendant's proposal for payment

        Enclose a draft judgment for approval. The Court will enter judgment in accordance with the defendant's proposal.

    ☐    The defendant has not made any proposal for payment.

        Enclose a draft judgment for approval. You can ask for the judgment to be paid by instalments or in one payment.

    ☐    I DO NOT accept the defendant's proposal for payment.

        Enclose a draft judgment for approval. You can say how you want the defendant to pay. Give your reasons for objecting to the defendant's offer of payment. (Continue on the back of this form if necessary.)

        Note:— The Court will notify you and the defendant of its judgment.

I certify that the information given is correct.

Signed           [        ]    Position or office held (If signing on behalf

          (Plaintiff) Plaintiff's   of a firm, company or
          solicitor)(next friend)  corporation)

                                 With company chop (if applicable)

Date

## No. 16B

Reply to part admission of liquidated amount and Request for judgment

(Order 13A rules 5(3) & (5). 9(4) & 10(2))

*(Heading as in action)*

- Please tell the Court what you wish to do by completing the lower half of this form and filing it in the Registry of the High Court within 14 days after the copy of the defendant's admission is served on you. At the same time you must serve a copy on the defendant. If you do not file this form in the Registry of the High Court within the prescribed priod, your claim will be stayed. No further action will be taken by the Court until the form is received.

- You must tick box A or B.

- Remember to sign and date the notice

A ☐ I DO NOT accept the defendant's part admission

   If you tick box A the claim will proceed as a defended claim

B ☐ I ACCEPT the amount admitted by the defendant in satisfaction of my whole claim

   Tick only one box and follow the instructions given

   ☐ I accept the defendant's proposal for payment

    Enclose a draft judgment for approval. The Court will enter judgment in accordance with the offer.

   ☐ The defendant has not made any proposal for payment

    Enclose a draft judgment for approval. You can ask for the judgment to be paid by instalments or in one payment.

   ☐ I DO NOT accept the defendant's proposal for payment.

    Enclose a draft judgment for approval. You can say how you want the defendant to pay. Give your reasons for objecting to the defendant's offer of payment. (Continue on the back of this form if necessary)

Note:— The Court will notify you and the defendant of its judgment.

I certify that the information given is correct.

Signed _____

(Plaintiff) Plaintiff's
solicitor)(next friend)

Position or office held
(If signing on behalf
of a firm, company or
corporation)

With company chop
(if applicable)

Date _____

(L.N. 152 of 2008)

## No. 16C

Admission (unliquidated amount)

O. 13A rules 6(2), 7(2) & 13(2))

*(Heading as in action)*

---

Explanatory Note

1.  The only claim the plaintiff has made against you is for an unliquidated amount of money. You may admit the plaintiffs claim in whole or in part by completing this form—

    (a)   within the period for service of your defence if you have been served with a writ; *or*

    (b)   the period for filing of your affidavit evidence if you have been served with an originating summons; *or*

    (c)   within 14 days after service of the originating process in any other case.

2.  If you have made an admission, you may only be allowed to amend or withdraw your admission if the Court considers it just to do so.

3.  You may offer a specified amount to satisfy the claim. If the amount you offer is accepted by the plaintiff, the plaintiff may request the Court to enter judgment against you for that amount. Alternatively, the plaintiff may request the Court to enter judgment against you for an amount to be decided by the Court and costs.

4.  You may also ask for time to pay. If the plaintiff does not accept your proposal for payment, the Court will decide how the payment should be made after considering-

    (a)   the information set out in this form;

    (b)   the reasons why the plaintiff does not accept your proposal for payment; and

    (c)   all other relevant matters.

5.  The completed form should be filed in the Registry of the District Court.

How to fill in this form

- Tick the correct boxes and give as much information as you can. Then sign and date the form. If necessary provide details on a separate sheet, add the action number and attach it to this form.

- If you do not ask for time to pay, you need not complete items 2 to 9 and 11 and 12.

- If you are not an individual you need not complete items 1 to 9 but you should complete items 10 to 12 and ensure that you comply with the requirement specified in item 13 and provide sufficient details about the assets and liabilities of your firm, company or corporation to support any offer of payment made.

- If you are an individual, you need not complete items 10 to 12 and need not comply with the requirement specified in item 13.

- You can get help to complete this form at the Registry of the District Court.

Part A.    Response to claim (*tick only one box only*)

☐    I admit liability for the whole claim but want the Court to decide the amount I should pay (if you tick this box, you need not complete Part B and items 2 to 9, 11 and 12 and need not comply with the requirement specified in item 13.

OR

☐    I admit liability for the claim and offer to [＿＿＿＿＿＿] in satisfaction
pay                    of the claim

Part B    How are you going to pay the amount you have admitted? (*tick one box only*)

☐    I offer to pay on (date) [＿＿＿＿＿＿＿＿＿＿＿＿＿]

OR

☐    I cannot pay the amount immediately because (state reason)

[＿＿＿＿＿＿＿＿＿＿＿＿＿＿＿＿＿＿＿＿＿＿＿＿]

AND

I offer to pay by instalments [$＿＿＿＿＿] per (week)(month) [＿＿＿＿＿]
starting (date)

## 1. Personal Details

Surname    [＿＿＿＿＿＿＿＿＿＿＿＿＿＿＿＿＿＿＿＿＿＿＿＿]

Forename    [＿＿＿＿＿＿＿＿＿＿＿＿＿＿＿＿＿＿＿＿＿＿＿＿]

☐   Mr   ☐   Mrs   ☐   Miss   ☐   Ms

[＿＿＿＿＿＿＿＿＿＿＿＿＿＿＿＿＿＿＿＿＿＿＿＿]

Address

## 2. Dependants (*people you look after financially*)

| *give details* | |
|---|---|
| | |

3.  Employment

| | | |
|---|---|---|
| ☐ | I am employed as a | |
| ☐ | My employer is | |
| ☐ | Jobs other than main job *(give details)* | |
| ☐ | I am self employed as a | |
| ☐ | Annual turnover is | $ |

☐    I am not in arrears with my mandatory provident fund contributions and income tax.

| | | |
|---|---|---|
| ☐ | I am in arrears and I owe | $ |
| Give details of: <br><br> (a)   contracts and other work in hand | | |
| (b)   any sums due for work done | | |
| ☐   I have been unemployed for | _____years_____months | |
| ☐   I am a pensioner | | |

4.  Bank account and savings *(please list all)*

| Bank account | In credit by $ | Overdrawn by $ |
|---|---|---|
| | | |

5.  Residence

I live in

    ☐    my own flat

    ☐    my jointly owned flat

    ☐    public housing estate

    ☐    rented private flat

    ☐    others (please specify)

6. Income

| | | |
|---|---|---|
| My usual take-home pay (including overtime, commission, bonuses etc) | $ | per month |
| My pension(s) | $ | per month |
| Others living in my home give me | $ | per month |
| Other income *(give details below)* | | |
| | $ | per month |
| | $ | per month |
| | $ | per month |
| Total income | $ | per month |

7. Other assets *(please list and indicate their location)*

| |
|---|
| |

8. Expenses
   *(Do not include any payments made by other members of the household out of their own income)*

   I have regular expenses as follows:

| | | |
|---|---|---|
| Mortgage *(including second mortgage)* | $ | per month |
| Rent | $ | per month |
| Rates and government rent | $ | per month |
| Management fees | $ | per month |
| Domestic helper's salary | $ | per month |
| Gas | $ | per month |
| Electricity | $ | per month |
| Water charges | $ | per month |
| Telephone charges | $ | per month |
| Housekeeping, food, school meals | $ | per month |
| Travelling expenses | $ | per month |
| Children's clothing | $ | per month |
| Tuition fees | $ | per month |
| Maintenance payment | $ | per month |

| | | |
|---|---|---|
| Court orders | $ | per month |
| Others | | |
| | $ | per month |
| | $ | per month |
| | $ | per month |
| Total expenses | $ | per month |

9.  Liabilities

    *(This section is for arrears only. Do not include regular expenses listed in item 8)*

| | |
|---|---|
| Rent arrears | $ |
| Mortgage arrears | $ |
| Rates and government arrears | $ |
| Water charges arrears | $ |
| Fuel debts:          Gas | $ |
| Electricity | $ |
| Others | $ |
| Maintenance arrears | $ |
| Loan and credit cards and debts (please list) | $ |
| Others *(give details below)* | |
| | $ |
| | $ |
| Total liabilities | $ |

10.  Firm, company or corporation

| | |
|---|---|
| Name | |

| | |
|---|---|
| Address | |

| | |
|---|---|
| Tel. no. | |

11. Assets of firm, company or corporation (*please list*)

| Property, plant and equipment | $ |
| Inventories | $ |
| Goodwill and other intangible assets | $ |
| Loans and receivables | $ |
| Bank balances and cash | $ |
| Others | $ |
| Total | $ |

12. Liabilities of firm, company or corporation *(please list)*

| Trade payables | $ |
| Tax payable | $ |
| Other payables | $ |
| Bank loans | $ |
| Other borrowings | $ |
| Others | $ |
| Total | $ |

13. Attach to this form a copy of the latest audited profit and loss account and balance sheet of the firm, company or corporation.

14. Declaration      I .......................... declare that the details I have given above and in the attached sheet(s) (if any) are true to the best of my knowledge.

And I make this solemn declaration conscientiously believing the same to be true and by virtue of the Oaths and Declaration Ordinance (Cap. 11)

Signed          Position or office held (If signing on behalf of a firm, company or corporation)

With company chop (if applicable)

Declared at...................................... in Hong Kong on.......................... of 20................

Before me,
[Signature and designation i.e. Justice of the Peace/Notary Public/Commissioner for Oaths.]

Note  –  Under section 36 of the Crimes Ordinance (Cap 200) a person who knowingly and wilfully makes a statement false in a material particular in a declaration or other document which he is authorized or required to make by an enactment is guilty of an offence.

–  A defendant who is an individual must sign personally. A director of a company must obtain leave to represent the company from a Practice Master before he may sign on behalf of the company.

–  If a plaintiff does not file a request for judgment within 14 days after this form served on him, his claim is stayed until he files the request.

(L.N. 152 of 2008)

**[29.6]**

No. 16D

Request for judgment (admission of unliquidated amount)

(O. 13Ar. 6(3))

*(Heading as in action)*

The defendant has admitted liability to pay the whole of my claim but has not made any proposal for payment.

I request judgment to be entered against the defendant for an amount to be decided by the Court and costs. [Enclose a draft judgment for approval]

| Signed | | Position or office held (If signing on behalf of a firm, company or corporation) | |
| --- | --- | --- | --- |
| | (Plaintiff) Plaintiff's solicitor)(next friend) | | |
| Date | | With company chop (if applicable) | |

The completed form should be filed in the Registry of the High Court.

(L.N. 152 of 2008)

No. 16E

Reply to admission of unliquidated amount and Request for judgment

[rule 7(3)]

(O. 13A rr. 7(3), (5) & (9), 9(4) & 10(2)

*(Heading as in action)*

---

### Important Notes for plaintiff

- You must tick either item A or complete item B and file the form in the Registry of the High Court within 14 days after the copy of the defendant's admission is sent to you.

  At the same time you must send a copy to the defendant. If you do not return the form within the prescribed period, your claim will be stayed. No further action will be taken by the Court until the form is received.

- Remember to sign and date the notice

---

A ☐ I DO NOT accept the amount offered by the defendant in satisfaction of any claim. I wish judgment to be entered for an amount to be decided by the Court.

The Court will give directions for management of the case.

B ☐ I ACCEPT the amount admitted by the defendant in satisfaction of my claim

Tick only one box and follow the instructions given.

☐ I accept the defendant's proposal for payment

Enclose a draft judgment for approval. The Court will enter judgment in accordance with the offer.

☐ I DO NOT accept the defendant's proposal for payment

Enclose a draft judgment for approval. You can say how you want the defendant to pay. Give your reasons for objecting to the defendant's offer of payment. (Continue on the back of this form if necessary)

Note:— The Court will notify you and the defendant of its judgment.

I certify that the information given is correction

| Signed | | Position or office held (If signing on behalf of a firm, | |
|---|---|---|---|
| | (Plaintiff's solicitor)(next friend) | company or corporation) | |
| Date | | With company chop (if applicable) | |

(L.N. 152 of 2008)

---

No. 17

Notice to be indorsed on copy of counterclaim

(Order 15 rule 3(6))

To X.Y.

(1)   Take notice that within [14 days] after service of this defence and counterclaim on you, counting the day of service, you must acknowledge service and state in your acknowledgment whether you intend to contest the proceedings. If you fail to do so or if your acknowledgment does not state your intention to contest the proceedings, judgment may be given against you without further notice.

(2)   If the only remedy that the counterclaiming plaintiff is seeking is the payment of a liquidated amount of money or the payment of an unliquidated amount of money, you may admit the counterclaiming plaintiff's claim in whole or in part by completing Form No. 16 or 16C (as the case may require) accompanying the counterclaim.

   A completed Form No. 16 or 16C must be filed with the Registry of the High Court and served on the counterclaiming plaintiff [or counterclaiming plaintiff's solicitors] within the period for service of the defence to counterclaim.


IMPORTANT

Directions for Acknowledgment of Service are given with the accompanying form.

(L.N. 251 of 1997)
(L.N. 152 of 2008)

## No. 20

### Third party notice claiming contribution or indemnity or other relief or remedy
(Order 16)

19......, No.............

IN THE HIGH COURT OF THE HONG KONG SPECIAL ADMINISTRATIVE REGION

COURT OF FIRST INSTANCE

| | | |
|---|---|---|
| Between | *A.B.* | Plaintiff |
| | AND | |
| | *C.D.* | Defendant |
| | AND | |
| | *T.P.* | Third Party |

### Third Party Notice

[Issued pursuant to the order of.............. dated the........................... day of........
................................................................................................................................ ].

To *T.P.* of............................. in the....................................................... of.........
................................................................................................................................

Take notice that this action has been brought by the plaintiff against the defendant. In it the plaintiff claims against the defendant [*here state the nature of the plaintiff's claim*] as appears from the writ of summons [or originating summons] a copy whereof is served herewith [together with a copy of the statement of claim].

The defendant claims against you [*here state the nature of the claim against the third party as for instance*] to be indemnified against the plaintiff's claim and the costs of this action or contribution to the extent of [one half] of the plaintiff's claim or the following relief or remedy namely...................... on the grounds that (*state the grounds of the claim*).

And take notice that within [14 days] after service of this notice on you, counting the day of service, you must acknowledge service and state in your acknowledgment whether you intend to contest the proceedings. If you fail to do so, or if your acknowledgment does not state your intention to contest the proceedings, you will be deemed to admit the plaintiff's claim against the defendant and the defendant's claim against you and your liability to [indemnify the defendant or to contribute to the extent claimed or to................................. *stating the relief or remedy sought*] and will be bound by any judgment or decision given in the action, and the judgment may be enforced against you in accordance with Order 16 of the Rules of the High Court Chapter 4.

Dated the............. day of............... 19......

(Signed)....................................................
*Solicitor for the defendant*

### IMPORTANT

Directions for Acknowledgment of Service are given with the accompanying form.

(Enacted 1988)

No. 21

**Third party notice where question or issue to be determined**
(Order 16)

*[Title etc. as in No. 20 down to end of first paragraph]*

The defendant requires that the following question or issue, viz. *[here state the question or issue required to be determined]* should be determined not only as between the plaintiff and the defendant but also as between either or both of them and yourself.

And take notice that *[as in No. 20 down to the words "intention to contest the proceedings"]* you will be bound by any judgment or decision in the action so far as it is relevant to the said question or issue, and the judgment may be enforced against you in accordance with Order 16 of the Rules of the High Court Chapter 4.

Dated the..........day of...........19

(Signed)..............................................
*Solicitor for the defendant.*

IMPORTANT

Directions for Acknowledgment of Service are given with the accompanying form.

(Enacted 1988)

No. 23

Notice of sanctioned payment

(Order 22 rule 8(2))

*(Heading as in action)*

To the plaintiff('s solicitor) and to the Director of Legal Aid (if applicable)

Take notice that the defendant(s)......................................... has/have paid
$.......................... (in further amount of $.........................) into court in settlement of
(tick as appropriate)

- ☐    the whole of your claim

- ☐    part of your claim *(give details below)*

- ☐    a certain issue or certain issues arising from your claim *(give details below)*

The (part) (issue or issues) to which it relates is(are): *(give details)*

- ☐    It is in addition to the amount of $..................................... already paid into court on...........................and the total amount in court now offered in settlement is $.......................... *(give total of all payments in court to date)*

- ☐    It is not inclusive of interest and an additional amount of $.......................... is offered for interest *(give details of the rate(s) and period(s) for which the amount of interest if offfered)*

- ☐    It takes into account all (part) of the following counterclaim or set off: *(give details of the party and the part of the counterclaim to which the payment relates)*

- ☐    It takes into account the interim payment(s) made in the following amount(s) on the following date(s): *(give details)*

- ☐    It takes into account the following sum(s) of money that has (have) been paid into court: *(give details)*

- ☐    It is part of the terms of a sanctioned offer set out in (identify the document). If you give notice of acceptance of this sanctioned payment; you will be treated as also accepting the sanctioned offer.

Note: — This notice will need to be modified where an offer or provisional damages is made (Order 22, rule 11)

Signed

Defendent ('s solicitor)

Position or office held
(If signing on
behalf of a firm,
company or
corpoartion)

Date

With company chop
(if applicable)

Note: To the plaintiff

If you wish to accept the payment made into court and the Court's leave for acceptance is not required, you should complete Form No. 24, send it to the defendant and file a copy in the Registry of the High Court.

(L.N. 152 of 2008)

## No. 24

Notice of acceptance of sanctioned payment

(Order 22 rule 15(4))

*(Heading as in action)*

To the defendant('s solicitor) and to the Director of Legal Aid (if applicable)

Take notice that the plaintiff accepts the payment(s) into court totalling $........................... in settlement of (the whole of) (part of) (certain issue(s) arising from) *the plaintiff's claim as set out in the notice of sanctioned payment received on........................... (and abandons the other part(s) of or issue(s) arising from the plaintiff's claim).

| | | |
|---|---|---|
| Signed | | |
| | Plaintiff ('s solicitor) | Position or office held (If signing on behalf of a firm, company or corporation) |
| Date | | With company chop (if applicable) |

* Delete as appropriate

(L.N. 152 of 2008)

No. 25

Notice of request for payment

(Order 22 rule 17)

*(Heading as in action)*

On............................................I accepted the payments) into court totalling $.............
......................... in settlement of (the whole of) (part of) (certain issue(s) arising from)
*my claim as set out in the notice of sanctioned payment received on..........................
.................... (and abandoned the other part(s) of or issue(s) arising from my claim).*

I declare that:

- ☐ the sanctioned payment has been accepted [within 28 days] [after 28 days but costs have been agreed] [less than 28 days before trial but costs have been agreed]*

- ☐ the payment into court was not made with a defence of tender

- ☐ the offeree is not a person under disability

- ☐ [at no time has the offeree been on legal aid in these proceedings] [the offeree has been on legal aid]*

- ☐ there is no pending applications to withdraw or diminish the sanctioned payment

- ☐ [there is only 1 defendant] [the sanctioned payment is made by all defendants] [I have discontinued my claim against those defendants who have not made the sanctioned payment and they have given written consent to the acceptance of the sanctioned payment]*

- ☐ [my claim does not include a claim for provisional damages] [my claim for provisional damages has been disposed of under Order 37, rule 8]*

  *(If any of the above declarations has not been made, the money in court can only be paid out by order of the Court)*

- ☐ a copy of this notice has been serviced on the defendant's solicitor) named below and I request payment of this money held in court to be made to:

| Plaintiff or solicitor's full name/Director of Legal Aid* |
|---|
| Address and telephone number |

| | | | |
|---|---|---|---|
| Signature | | | |
| Note: | Before signing this form please read the notes for guidance overleaf. | | |
| | Incorrectly signed forms may be returned unactioned. | | |
| Signed | | Date | |

### DETAILS OF PLAINTIFF'S SOLICITOR

| |
|---|
| Name of firm |
| Solicitor for |

| |
|---|
| Defendant or solicitor's full name/Director of Legal Aid* |

| |
|---|
| Address and telephone number |

| | | | |
|---|---|---|---|
| Signature | | | |
| Note: | The plaintiff('s solicitor) should obtain the signature of the defendant('s solicitor) on the box below before serving a copy of this notice on him | | |
| Signed | | Date | |

### DETAILS OF PLAINTIFF'S SOLICITOR

| |
|---|
| Name of firm |
| Solicitor for |

\* Delete as appropriate

Notes for guidance on completion of Form No. 25

In order to request payment out of funds in court, file this form, signed and completed in accordance with these notes for guidance in the Registry of the High Court. A copy of this form should also be sent to the defendant('s solicitors).

• When completing this form, please ensure that you tick all of the boxes under the heading: 'I declare that'. If you do not tick all the boxes, the Registry of the High Court will not be able to process your request for payment and will have to return the form to you.

• The form should be signed either by the plaintiff or his solicitor.

• The Accounts Office of the High Court will only issue payment upon receipt of a properly completed Form No. 25 with an original signature. Faxed copies of the form and photocopies of signatures will not be accepted and will be returned to sender.

(L.N. 152 of 2008)

## No. 25A

### Notice of payment into court under order or certificate

(Order 22 rule 27(1))

*(Heading as in action)*

Take notice that the plaintiff/defendant...................................has  paid $..................
...............into court in compliance with the order/certificate
of................................dated..........................

Signed

Plaintiff/Defendent
('s solicitor)

Date

Position or office
held (If signing on
behalf of a firm,
company or
corportion)

With company chop
(if applicable)

### Solicitor's certificate

We certify that—

(a)    the payment is made within time.

*(b)    there is no direction in the order for investment of the money.

*(c)    the Court has directed that the money be invested in the following manner—

Signed                                        Date

### SOLICITOR'S DETAILS

Name of firm

Solicitor for

*    Delete as appropriate

(L.N. 152 of 2008)

No. 26

## List of Documents

(Order 24 rule 5)

*(Heading as in cause or matter)*

## List of Documents

The following is a list of the documents relating to the matters in question in this action which are or have been in the possession, custody or power of the above-named plaintiff (or defendant) *A.B.* and which is served in compliance with Order 24, rule 2 (or the order herein dated the ........ day of ............ 19.....).

1.   The plaintiff (or defendant) has in his possession, custody or power the documents relating to the matters in question in this action enumerated in schedule 1 hereto.

2.   The plaintiff (or defendant) objects to produce the documents enumerated in part 2 of the said schedule 1 on the ground that (stating the ground of objection).

3.   The plaintiff (or defendant) has had, but has not now, in his possession, custody or power the documents relating to the matters in question in this action enumerated in schedule 2 hereto.

4.   Of the documents in the said schedule 2, those numbered .......... in that schedule were last in the plaintiffs (or defendant's) possession, custody or power on (*stating when*) and the remainder on (*stating when*).

*(Here state what has become of the said documents and in whose possession they now are.)*

5.   Neither the plaintiff (or defendant), nor his solicitor nor any other person on his behalf, has now, or ever had, in his possession, custody or power any document of any description whatever relating to any matter in question this action, other than the documents enumerated in schedules 1 and 2 hereto.

SCHEDULE 1

Part 1

*(Here enumerate in a convenient order the documents (or bundles of documents, if of the same nature, such as invoices) in the possession, custody or power of the party in question which he does not object to produce, with a short description of each document or bundle sufficient to identify it.)*

Part 2

*(Here enumerate as aforesaid the documents in the possession, custody or power of the party in question which he objects to produce.)*

## SCHEDULE 2

*(Here enumerate as aforesaid the documents which have been, but at the date of service of the list are not, in the possession, custody or power of the party in question.)*

Dated the............. day of...................... 19........

### *Notice to inspect*

Take notice that the documents in the above list, other than those listed in part 2 of schedule 1 (and schedule 2), may be inspected at (the office of the solicitor of the above-named (plaintiff) (defendant) (*insert address*) *or as may be*) on the................... day of..................................19....., between the hours of............... and...................

To the defendant (or plaintiff) *C.D.* and his solicitor.

Served on the............... day of................ 19........ by........................... of............
.................................solicitor for the (plaintiff)
(defendant).

(Enacted 1988)

No. 27

**Affidavit verifying list of documents**
(Order 24 rule 5)
*(Heading as in cause or matter)*

I, the above-named plaintiff (or defendant) *A.B.*, make oath and say as follows:—

1.   The statements made by me in paragraphs 1,3 and 4 of the list of documents now produced and shown to me marked............................ are true.

2.   The statements of fact made by me in paragraph 2 of the said list are true.

3.   The statements made by me in paragraph 5 of the said list are true to the best of my knowledge, information and belief.

Sworn, etc.
This affidavit is filed on behalf of the plaintiff (or defendant).
(Enacted 1988)

No. 27A
Notice of application for leave to institute
or continue proceedings in court
(O. 32A r. 2)

No..........

IN THE HIGH COURT OF THE HONG KONG SPECIAL
ADMINISTRATIVE REGION COURT OF FIRST INSTANCE

Applicant

Notice of application for leave to
institute or continue proceedings
in court (O. 32A r. 2)

To the Registrar, High Court, Hong Kong

| | |
|---|---|
| Name and address of applicant | |
| Title and reference number of the proceedings in which the order under section 27(1) of the High Court Ordinance (Cap. 4) was made | |
| Order sought | |
| Previous applications for leave which the applicant has made under section 27 of the High Court Ordinance (Cap. 4), and the results of those applications | |
| Signed | Dated |

Grounds on which leave is sought

Note: Grounds must be supported by the affidavit evidence on which the applicant
relies in support of his application

(L.N. 152 of 2008)

No. 28

**Writ of subpoena**
(Order 38 rule 14)

*(Heading as in cause or matter)*

To (names of witnesses)

You are required to attend (at the High Court in Hong Kong at the sittings of the Court of First Instance) on the day fixed for the trial of the above-named cause, notice of which will be given to you, and from day to day thereafter until the end of the trial, to give evidence on behalf of the (plaintiff) or (defendant)*.

Witness.......................... Chief Justice of Hong Kong the.......................... day of ..............................19..... Issued on the..................... day of......................................... 19...... by ............................... solicitor for the ...........................

(*If *duces tecum add*: And it is also required to bring with you and produce at the place aforesaid on the day notified to you (*here describe the documents or things to be produced*).)
(Enacted 1988)

**[78]**

No. 29

**Writ of subpoena: proceedings in chambers**
(Order 38 rule 14)

*(Heading as in cause or matter)*

To (names of witnesses).

You are required to attend before (Mr. Justice..........................) in chambers, at the High Court in Hong Kong on........................................ day the...................day of..................................... 19........... at................................... and so from day to day until your evidence shall have been taken, to give evidence on behalf of the (plaintiff) or (defendant) in the above-named cause (and it is also required to bring with you and produce at the time and place aforesaid *describe the documents or things to be produced.*)

Witness (*as in No. 28*).

Issued (*as in No. 28*).
(Enacted 1988)

## No. 31

## Summons for examination within jurisdiction of
## witness before trial
### (Order 39 rule 1)
*(Heading as in cause or matter)*

Let all parties concerned attend the Judge (or Registrar) in chambers at the High Court in Hong Kong on............... the............................ day of 19........... at...................... o'clock on the hearing of an application on the part of............................. that *A.B.* a witness on behalf of the.......................................... be examined forthwith before a Judge, [the Registrar] or one of the examiners of the Court (or an examiner to be agreed upon) upon the usual terms, and that the costs of this application be (costs in the cause).

Dated the...................... day of.................. 19...........

This summons was taken out by................................................. of ..................... solicitor for the.................................

To the above-named....................... (and.................... his solicitor).
(Enacted 1988)

## No. 32

**Order for examination within jurisdiction of witness before trial**
(Order 39 rule 1)

*(Heading as in cause or matter)*

On hearing (the solicitors on both sides) and on reading the affidavit of...............
.................... filed herein the...................... day of...................... 19................

It is ordered that................................................................................ a witness
on behalf of the............................................................ be examined viva voce on
oath or affirmation before a Judge, the Registrar or one of the examiners of the Court
(or.................................................Esq., the examiner agreed upon or an examiner to
be agreed upon), the plaintiffs (or defendant's) solicitor giving to the defendant's (or
plaintiffs) solicitor...........................................days' notice in writing of the time and
place where the examination is to take place (or state the time and place if fixed by
the order). And it is ordered that the depositions taken at the examination be filed in
the Registry of the High Court, and that office copies thereof may be read and given
in evidence on the trial of this cause, saving all just exceptions, without any further
proof of the absence of the said witness than the affidavit of the solicitor of the party
using the same, as to his belief, and that the costs of this application (and of the
examination) be (costs in the cause).

Dated the............................. day of...............................19...........
(Enacted 1988)

No. 33

**Summons for issue of the letter of request of judicial authority
out of jurisdiction**
(Order 39 rule 2)

*(Heading as in cause or matter)*

Let all parties (*as in No. 31*) on the hearing of an application on the part
of........................ for an order that a letter of request shall issue to the proper judicial
authority of................ for the examination of *E.F.* and *G.H.* and other witnesses on
the plaintiff's (or the defendant's) behalf at........................ in (name of country), and
that the action be stayed until the return of the said letter of request and examination,
and that the costs of and incidental to this application and the said letter of request
and examination be costs in the cause.

Dated, etc. (*conclude as in No. 31*).
(Enacted 1988)

No. 34

**Order for issue of letter of request to judicial authority**
**out of jurisdiction**
(Order 39 rule 2)

*(Heading as in cause or matter)*

On hearing (*as in No. 32*).

It is ordered that a letter of request do issue directed to the proper judicial authority for the examination of the following witnesses, namely:

*E.F.* of..........................................

*G.H.*..............................................

And it is ordered that the depositions taken pursuant thereto when received be filed in the Registry of the High Court and that office copies thereof may be read and given in evidence on the trial of this action, saving all just exceptions, without any further proof of the absence of the said witnesses than the affidavit of the solicitor of the party using the same as to his belief.

And it is ordered that (the trial of this action be stayed until the said depositions have been filed and that) the costs of and incidental to the application for this order and the said letter of request and examination be (costs in the cause).

Dated the..................... day of................. 19...........

(Enacted 1988)

No. 35

**Letter of request for examination of witness out of jurisdiction**
(Order 39 rule 3)

To the Competent Judicial Authority of............................................. in the.............. of.......................................................................

WHEREAS an action is now pending in the High Court of Hong Kong in which
................................................................... is plaintiff and...................................
............................................... is defendant and in which the plaintiff claims ............
.....................................................................................................

AND WHEREAS it has been represented to the said Court that it is necessary for the purposes of justice and for the due determination of the matters in dispute between the parties that the following persons should be examined as witnesses upon oath touching such matters, namely..................... of..................... and..................... of.....................
and it appears that such witnesses are resident within your jurisdiction.

Now I................ the Registrar of the High Court in Hong Kong hereby request that for the reasons aforesaid and for the assistance of the said Court you will be pleased to summon the said witnesses (and such other witnesses as the agents of the said plaintiff and defendant shall humbly request you in writing so to summon) to attend at such time and place as you shall appoint before you, or such other person as according to your procedure is competent to take the examination of witnesses, and that you will cause such witnesses to be examined viva voce (or upon the interrogatories which accompany this letter of request) touching the said matters in question in the presence of the agents of the plaintiff and defendant or such of them as shall, on due notice given, attend the examination.

And I further request that you will permit the agents of both the plaintiff and defendant or such of them as shall be present to examine (upon interrogatories and viva voce upon the subject-matter thereof or arising out of the answers thereto) such witnesses as may, after due notice in writing, be produced on their behalf, and the other party to cross-examine the said witnesses (upon cross-interrogatories and viva voce) and the party producing the witness for examination to re-examine him viva voce.

And I further request that you will be pleased to cause the evidence of the said witnesses (or the answers of the said witness and all additional viva voce questions, whether on examination, cross-examination or re-examination) to be reduced into writing and all books, letters, papers and documents produced on such examination to be duly marked for identification, and that you will be further pleased to authenticate such examination by the seal of your tribunal or in such other way as is in accordance with your procedure and to return it together with (the interrogatories and cross-interrogatories and) a note of the charges and expenses payable in respect of the execution of this request through the British Consul from whom the same was received (or........ one of Her Majesty's Secretaries of State) for transmission to the High Court, Hong Kong.

And I further request that you will cause me, or the agents of the parties if appointed, to be informed of the date and place where the examination is to take place

Dated the.............. day of................. 19.......
(Enacted 1988)

No. 36

## Summons for appointment of examiner to take evidence of witness out of jurisdiction
(Order 39 rule 2)

*(Heading as in cause or matter)*

Let all parties (*as in No. 31*) on the hearing of an application on the part of........ .................................... for an order that (the British Consul at.................................. .......... in (*name of country*) or his deputy) (............................. Esq.) be appointed as special examiner for the purpose of taking the examination, cross-examination, and re-examination, viva voce, on oath or affirmation, of................................................... ....................... and.............................., witnesses on behalf of the.............., at........... ................................ in (*name of country*) on the usual terms and that the costs of and incidental to this application and the said examination be costs in the cause.

Dated, etc. (*conclude as in No. 31*).
(Enacted 1988)

## No. 37

**Order for appointment of examiner to take evidence
of witness out of jurisdiction**
(Order 39 rule 2)

*(Heading as in cause or matter)*

On hearing the solicitors on both sides and on reading the affidavit of................ ........................... filed the............... day of.............. 19.....

It is ordered that the British Consul or his deputy at ................................... (or ............... Esq.) be appointed as special examiner for the purpose of taking the examination, cross-examination and re-examination viva voce, on oath or affirmation, of ............................................ witnesses on the part of ............... at ............... in (*name of country*). The examiner shall be at liberty to invite the attendance of the witnesses and the production of documents, but shall not exercise any compulsory powers. Otherwise such examination shall be conducted in accordance with the procedure followed in the Court of First Instance of Hong Kong. The............... solicitors to give to the ............... solicitors ............... days' notice in writing of the date on which they propose to send out this order to ............... for execution, and that ............... days after the service of such notice the solicitors for the plaintiff and defendant respectively do exchange the names of their agents at .................... ............... to whom notice relating to the examination of the said witnesses may be sent. And that............... days (exclusive of Sunday) before the examination of any witness hereunder notice of such examination shall be given by the agent of the party on whose behalf such witness is to be examined to the agent of the other party, unless such notice be dispensed with. And that the depositions when taken, together with any documents referred to therein, or certified copies of such documents, or of extracts therefrom, be sent by the examiner, under seal, to the Registrar of the High Court in Hong Kong, on or before the............... day of............... next, or such further or other day as may be ordered, there to be filed in the proper office. And that either party be at liberty to read and give such depositions in evidence on the trial of this action, saving all just exceptions. And that the trial of this action be stayed until the filing of such depositions. And that the costs of and incidental to the application for this order and such examination be costs in the cause.

Dated the............... day of............... 19.....
(Enacted 1988)

No. 38

**Notice of Motion**
(Order 8 rule 3)

*(Heading as in cause or matter)*

Take notice that (pursuant to the leave of........................ given on the..............
day of.............. 19.......) the Court (or Mr. Justice..................) will be moved ..........
........................ the.............. day of.............. 19......., at ............ o'clock, or so soon
thereafter as counsel can be heard, by (Mr.................... of....................) counsel for
the above-named plaintiff (or defendant) that.................... and that the costs of the
application be....................

Dated the.............. day of.............. 19.......

(Signed)...........................................
of...........................................
Solicitor for...........................................

*To*

Solicitor for................................................
(Enacted 1988)

No. 39

**Default judgment in action for liquidated demand**
(Order 13 rule 1; Order 19 rule 2; Order 42 rule 1)

*(Heading as in action)*

The.............. day of.................. 19.....

No notice of intention to defend having been given (or no defence having been served) by the defendant herein, it is this day adjudged that the defendant do pay the plaintiff $.................. and.............. costs (or costs to be taxed).

(The above costs have been taxed and allowed at $.............. as appears by a taxing officer's certificate dated the.............. day of.............. 19.....).

(Enacted 1988)

## No. 40

**Default judgment in action for liquidated damages**
(Order 13 rule 2; Order 19 rule 3; Order 42 rule 1)

*(Heading as in action)*

The.............. day of.................. 19.....

No notice of intention to defend having been given (or no defence having been served) by the defendant herein, it is this day adjudged that the defendant to pay the plaintiff damages to be assessed.

---

The amount found due to the plaintiff under this judgment having been certified at $............... as appears by the (Judge's or Registrar's certificate or as may be) filed the............. day of.............. 19....

It is adjudged that the defendant do pay the plaintiff $............. costs to be taxed.

The above costs, etc. (*as in No. 39*).

(*Note:—This form is a combined form of interlocutory and final judgment. The plaintiff may at his option enter interlocutory judgment by omitting the words below the line in the form and enter a separate final judgment in Form No. 43.*)

(Enacted 1988)

## No. 41

### Default judgment in action relating to detention of goods
(Order 13 rule 3; Order 19 rule 4; Order 42 rule 1)

*(Heading as in action)*

The............. day of............. 19....

No notice of intention to defend having been given (or no defence having been served) by the defendant herein.

It is this day adjudged that the defendant do deliver to the plaintiff the goods described in the writ of summons (or statement of claim) as (description of goods) or pay the plaintiff the value of the said goods to be assessed (and also damages for their detention to be assessed).

or

It is this day adjudged that the defendant do pay the plaintiff the value of the goods described in the writ of summons (or statement of claim) to be assessed (and also damages for their detention to be assessed).

---

The value of the said goods having been assessed at $............. (and damages at $.............) as appears by the (Judge's or Registrar's certificate or as may be) filed the.......... day of.................... 19.....

It is adjudged that the defendant do pay the plaintiff $............. and costs to be taxed.

The above costs, etc. (*as in No. 39*).

(*Note:—See the note to No. 40.*)

(Enacted 1988)

No. 42

**Default judgment in action for possession of land**
(Order 13 rule 4; Order 19 rule 5; Order 42 rule 1)

*(Heading as in action)*

The.............. day of.............. 19.....

No notice of intention to defend having been given (or no defence having been served) by the defendant herein, it is this day adjudged that the defendant do give the plaintiff possession of the land described in the writ of summons (or statement of claim) as.................... and pay the plaintiff $.......... costs (or costs to be taxed).

The above costs, etc, *(as in No. 39)*.

(Enacted 1988)

## No. 42A

### **Order for posssession**
(Order 113 rule 6)

*[Heading as in summons]*

Upon hearing............................. and upon reading the affidavit of.....................
........ filed the............... day of.................... 19....., it is ordered that the plaintiff *A.B.*
do recover possession of the land described in the originating summons as...............
............... [and that the defendant ........................................................................ do
pay the plaintiff $................... costs [*or* costs to be taxed]].

The above costs have been taxed and allowed at $............... as appears by a taxing
master's certificate dated the................... day of............................. 19.....

Dated the............. day of............... 19.....

(Enacted 1988)

## No. 43

**Final judgment after assessment of damages, etc.**
(Order 42 rule 1)

*(Heading as in action)*

The..........................day of............19.......

The plaintiff having on the................day of..................... 19....... obtained interlocutory judgment herein against the defendant for damages (or as may be) to be assessed, and the amount found due to the plaintiff having been certified at $.....................as appears by the (Judge's or Registrar's certificate or as may be) filed the day of.....................19.....

It is this day adjudged that the defendant do pay the plaintiff $................. and costs to be taxed.

The above costs, etc. (*as in No. 39*).

(Enacted 1988)

No. 44

## Judgment under Order 14
(Order 14 rule 3; Order 42 rule 1)

*(Heading as in action)*

The.....................day of..................... 19......

The defendant having given notice of intention to defend herein and the Court having under Order 14, rule 3 ordered that judgment as hereinafter provided be entered for the plaintiff against the defendant.

It is this day adjudged that the defendant do pay the plaintiff $................. and $..................... costs (or costs to be taxed)

or

pay the plaintiff damages to be assessed and costs to be taxed

or

deliver to the plaintiff the goods described in the writ of summons (or statement of claim) as..................... (or pay the plaintiff the value of the said goods to be assessed) (and also damages for their detention to be assessed) and costs to be taxed

or

give the plaintiff possession of the land described in the writ of summons (or statement of claim) as..................... and costs to be taxed.

The above costs, etc. (*as in No. 39*).

(Enacted 1988)

No. 45

**Judgment after trial before judge without jury**
(Order 42 rule 1)

*(Heading as in action)*

Dated and entered the....................day of..................... 19.....

This action having been tried before the Honourable Mr. Justice.................... without a jury, at the High Court, Hong Kong, and the said Mr. Justice.................... having on the..................... day of..................... 19..... ordered that judgment as hereinafter provided be entered for the plaintiff (or defendant) (and directed that execution be stayed for the period and on the terms hereinafter provided).

It is adjudged that the defendant do pay the plaintiff $..................... and his costs of action to be taxed (or that the plaintiff do pay the defendant his costs of defence to be taxed or *as may be according to the judge's order*).

(It is further adjudged that execution be stayed for..................... days and if within that time the................................. gives notice of appeal and sets down the appeal, execution be further stayed until the determination of the appeal *or as may be according to the judge's direction*).

The above costs, etc. (*as in No. 39*).

(Enacted 1988)

## No. 46

### Judgment after trial before judge with jury
(Order 42 rule 1)

*(Heading as in action)*

Dated and entered the..................... day of..................... 19......
This action having been tried before the Honourable Mr. Justice...........................
with a jury and the jury having found (*state findings*) and the said Mr.
Justice............................ having on the..................... day of..................... 19......
ordered that judgment as hereinafter provided be entered for (*etc. as in No. 45*).
(Enacted 1988)

## No. 48

**Judgment after decision of preliminary issue**
(Order 33 rule 7; Order 42 rule 1)

*(Heading as in cause or matter)*

Dated and entered the.................... day of.................... 19......

The issue (or question) arising in this cause (or matter) by the order dated the............................... day of.......................... 19...... ordered to be tried before............................... having on the............................... day of...................... ......19...... been tried before the said .................... and the said ........... having found ............................... and having ordered that judgment as hereinafter provided be entered for the.......................... (or having dismissed the cause or matter).

It is adjudged that (the defendant do pay the plaintiff $.................... and his costs of action to be taxed) (the plaintiff do pay the defendant his costs of defence to be taxed) *or as may be according to the order made.*

(Enacted 1988)

## No. 49

**Judgment for liquidated sum against personal representative**
(Order 42 rule 1)

*(Heading as in action)*

Dated and entered the............................... day of............................... 19......
*(Recital as in No. 39, 43–48 according to the circumstances in which judgment was obtained).*

It is adjudged that the defendant as executor (or administrator) of the above named............................. deceased do pay the plaintiff $................... and costs to be taxed, the said sum and costs to be levied of the real and personal estate of the deceased at the time of his death come to the hands of the defendant as such executor (or administrator) to be administered, if he has or shall hereafter have so much thereof in his hands to be administered, and if he has not so much thereof in his hands to be administered, then, as to the costs aforesaid, to be levied of the goods, chattels and other property of the defendant authorized by law to be seized in execution (*or as may be according to the order made*).

The above costs, etc. (*as in No. 39*).
(Enacted 1988)

No. 50

**Judgment for defendant's costs on discontinuance**
(Order 62 rule 10(1))

*(Heading as in action)*

The..................... day of..................... 19......

The plaintiff having by a notice in writing dated the..................... day of..................... 19......, discontinued this action (or withdrawn his claim in this action for.....................) and the defendant's costs of the action (or of the claim withdrawn) having been taxed and allowed at $..................... as appears by a taxing officer's certificate dated the..................... day of..................... 19......, and the plaintiff not having paid the sum within 4 days after taxation.

It is this day adjudged that the plaintiff do pay the defendant $..................... the said taxed costs.

(Enacted 1988)

# No. 51

## (Repealed L.N. 152 of 2008)

No. 52

**Notice of judgment or order**
(Order 44 rule 3)

*(Heading as in cause or matter)*

Take notice that a judgment (or order) of this Court was given (or made) on the..................... day of..................... 19...... by which it was *(state substance of judgment or order)*.

And also take notice that from the time of the service of this notice you (or the infant..................... *or* the patient..................... as may be) will be bound by the said judgment (or order) to the same extent as you (or he) would have been if you (or he) had originally been made a party.

And also take notice that you (or the said infant or patient) may within one month after the service of this notice apply to the Court to discharge, vary or add to the said judgment (or order) and that after acknowledging service of this notice at the Registry of the High Court in Hong Kong, you (or the said infant or patient) may attend the proceedings under the said judgment (or order).

Dated the..................... day of..................... 19......

To......................................................

(Signed).....................................

(Enacted 1988)

(L.N. 126 of 1995; L.N. 251 of 1997; L.N. 313 of 1997; 25 of 1998 s.2)

No. 53

**Writ of fieri facias**
(Order 45 rule 12)

*(Heading as in action)*

To the bailiff.....................................:

Whereas in the above named action it was on the..................... day of.....................
19...... adjudged (or ordered) that the defendant *C.D.* do pay the plaintiff *A.B.*
$..................... (and $..................... costs or costs to be taxed, which costs have been
taxed and allowed at $..................... as appears by the certificate of the taxing officer
dated the..................... day of..................... 19......):

It is required that of the goods, chattels and other property of *C.D.* authorized by
law to be seized in execution you cause to be made the sums of $..................... and
$..................... for costs of execution and also interest on $................. at the rate of 4
per cent per annum from the..................... day of..................... 19...... until payment
(together with bailiffs fees, costs of levying and all other legal, incidental expenses)
and that immediately after execution of this writ you pay *A.B.* in pursuance of the
said judgment (or order) the amount levied in respect of the said sums and interest.

And it is also required that you indorse on this writ immediately after execution
thereof a statement of the manner in which you have executed it and send a copy of
the statement to *A.B.*

And the court has fixed support and maintenance allowance at the rate
of..................... a day.

Witness................................ Chief Justice of Hong Kong, the..................... day
of..................... 19......

This writ was issued by..................... of..................... solicitor for.....................
the..................... (or this writ was issued by *A.B.* (the plaintiff) in person who resides
at.....................).

(Enacted 1988)

## No. 54

### Writ of fieri facias on order for costs
(Order 45 rule 12)

*(Heading as in cause or matter)*

To the bailiff.......................................:

Whereas in the above named cause (or matter) it was on the..................... day of..................... 19...... ordered that the .......................... *C.D.* do pay the.................... *A.B.* costs to be taxed, which costs have been taxed and allowed at $.................... as appears by the taxing officer's certificate dated the ............. day of ................. 19...:

It is required that of the goods, chattels and other property of *C.D.* authorized by law to be seized in execution you cause to be made the sum of $..................... and $..................... for cause of execution, and also interest on $..................... at the rate of 4 per cent per annum from the..................... day of..................... 19...... until payment together with bailiff's fees, cost of levying and all other legal incidental expenses and that immediately after execution of this writ you pay *A.B.* in pursuance of the said order the amount levied in respect of the said sum and interest.

And it is also required (*as in No. 53*).

And the court (*as in No. 53*).

Witness (*as in No. 53*).

This writ (*as in No. 53*).
(Enacted 1988)

No. 56

**Writ of fieri facias after levy of part**
(Order 45 rule 12)

*(Heading as in action)*

To the bailiff..........................................:

Whereas (*as in No. 53*).

And whereas by our writ issued the..................... day of..................... 19...... it is required that of the goods, chattels and other property of *C.D.* you should cause to be made the sums of $..................... and $..................... for costs of execution and also interest on $..................... at 4 per cent per annum from the..................... day of..................... 19.... until payment and should pay *A.B.* in pursuance of the said judgment (or order) the amount levied in respect of the said sums and interest and should indorse on the writ a statement of the manner in which you had executed it and send a copy of the statement to *A.B.*

And whereas the indorsement on the said writ states that by virtue thereof you (or he) caused to be made of the property aforesaid the sum of $.....................

It is required that of the goods, chattels and other property of *C.D.* authorized by law to be seized in execution you cause to be made the sum of $....................., the residue of the said $....................., and $..................... for costs of execution and also interest on $..................... at the rate of 4 per cent per annum from the..................... day of..................... 19...... until payment (*continue as in No. 53*).

And it is also required (*as in No. 53*).

And the court (*as in No. 53*).

Witness (*as in No. 53*).

This writ (*as in No. 53*).
(Enacted 1988)

## No. 57

### Writ of fieri facias against personal representative
(Order 45 rule 12)

*(Heading as in action)*

To the bailiff................................:

Whereas in the above named action it was on the.............. day of..............
19...... adjudged (or ordered) that the defendant *C.D.* as executor (or administrator)
of E.F. deceased do pay the plaintiff A.B. $.............. and $.............. costs (or costs
to be taxed which costs have been taxed and allowed at $.............. as appears by the
certificate of the taxing officer dated the.............. day of.............. 19......), the said
sums and interest to be levied of the real and personal estate of the said *E.F.* at the
time of his death in the hands of the defendant *C.D.* as his executor (or administrator)
to be administered, if he had or should thereafter have so much thereof in his hands
to be administered, (and if he had not, then the said costs to be levied of the goods,
chattels and other property of the defendant *C.D.* authorized by law to be seized in
execution):

It is required that of the real and personal estate of *E.F.* deceased, at the time
of his death, which is in the hands of *C.D.* as his executor (or administrator) to be
administered you cause to be made the sums of $.............. and $..............for costs
of execution and also interest on $.............. at the rate of $4 per cent per annum
from the.......... day of.......... 19...... until payment (together with bailiffs fees, cost
of levying and all other legal incidental expenses) (and if the said *C.D.* has not so
much thereof in his hands to be administered that you cause to be made of the goods,
chattels and other property of *C.D.* authorized by law to be seized in execution the
sum of $.......... for costs) and that immediately after execution of this writ you pay
*A.B.* in pursuance of the said judgment (or order) the amount levied in respect of the
said sums and interest.

And it is also required (*remainder as in No. 53*).

Witness (*as in No. 53*).

This writ (*as in No. 53*).
(Enacted 1988)

No. 63

**Writ of fieri facias to enforce registered judgment**
(Order 45 rule 12; Order 71)

IN THE HIGH COURT OF THE HONG KONG SPECIAL ADMINISTRATIVE REGION

In the matter of the Foreign Judgments (Reciprocal Enforcement) Ordinance (Cap. 319).

and

In the matter of a judgment of (*describe the court*) obtained in (*describe the cause or matter*) and dated the................ day of....................19......

To the bailiff..............................:

Whereas by a judgment dated the............... day of............... 19....... of (*describe the court*) registered in the High Court, Hong Kong pursuant to the Foreign Judgments (Reciprocal Enforcement) Ordinance it was adjudged that *C.D.* do pay *A.B.*................ dollars (or as may be) and the amount now due and owing under the said judgment is equivalent to the sum of $...............

It is required that of the goods, chattels and other property of *C.D.* authorized by law to be seized in execution you cause to be made the sums, of $............... and $............... for costs of execution together with bailiff, officers' fees (*remainder as in No. 53*).

And it is also required (*as in No. 53*).

Witness (*as in No. 53*).

This writ (*as in No. 53*).
(Enacted 1988)

## No. 64

### Writ of delivery of goods, damages and costs
(Order 45 rule 12)

*(Heading as in action)*

To the bailiff..............................:

Whereas in the above named action it was on the............... day of ............... 19.....
adjudged (or ordered) that the defendant *C.D.* do deliver to the plaintiff *A.B.* the
following goods, namely (*describe the goods delivery of which has been adjudged or
ordered*) (and $............... damages) and $............... costs (or costs to be taxed, which
costs have been taxed and allowed at $............... as appears by the certificate of the
taxing officer dated the............... day of............. 19.......):

It is required that you cause the said goods to be delivered to *A.B.* and that of the
goods, chattels and other property of *C.D.* authorized by law to be seized in execution
you cause to be made the sums of $............... and $............... for costs of execution
and also interest on $............... at the rate of $4 per cent per annum from the...............
day of.................. 19...... until payment together with bailiff's fees, costs of levying
and all other legal incidental expenses and that immediately after execution of this
writ you pay *A.B.* in pursuance of the said judgment (or order) the amount levied in
respect of the said sums and interest.

And it is also required that you indorse (*remainder as in No. 53*).

Witness (*as in No. 53*).

This writ (*as in No. 53*).
(Enacted 1988)

No. 65

**Writ of delivery: delivery of goods or value, damages and costs**
(Order 45 rule 12)

*(Heading as in action)*

To the bailiff.............:

Whereas in the above named action it was on the.............. day of..................
19...... adjudged (or ordered) that the defendant *C.D.* do deliver to the plaintiff *A.B.*
the following goods, namely (*describe the goods delivery of which has been adjudged
or ordered*) or do pay him $............... being the assessed value of the said goods, (and
$............... damages) and $............... costs (or costs to be taxed, which costs have
been taxed and allowed at $.......... as appears by the certificate of the taxing officer
dated the.............. day of.................... 19......)

It is required that you cause the said goods to be delivered to *A.B.* and that if
possession of the said goods cannot be obtained by you you cause to be made of the
goods, chattels and other property of *C.D.* authorized by law to be seized in execution
$............... the assessed value of the said goods and pay it to *A.B.*

And it is also required that of the said property of *C.D.* you cause to be made
the sums of $............... for (damages and) costs and $............... for costs of execution
and also interest on $............... at the rate of $4 per cent per annum from the...............
day of.................. 19...... until payment together with bailiff's fees, costs of levying
and all other legal incidental expenses and that immediately after execution of this
writ you pay *A.B.* in pursuance of the said judgment (or order) the amount levied in
respect of the said sums and interest.

And it is also required that you indorse (*remainder as in No. 53*).

Witness (*as in No. 53*).

This writ (*as in No. 53*).
(Enacted 1988)

No. 66

**Writ of possession**
(Order 45 rule 12)

*(Heading as in action)*

To the bailiff...............:

Whereas in the above named action it was on the............... day of...................
19...... adjudged (or ordered) that the defendant *C.D.* do give the plaintiff *A.B.*
possession of (*describe the land delivery of which has been adjudged or ordered*) and
do pay him ($............... and) $............... costs (or costs to be taxed, which costs have
been taxed and allowed at $............... as appears by the taxing officer's certificate
dated the............... day of................... 19......):

It is required that you enter the said land and cause *A.B.* to have possession of it.

And it is also required that of the goods, chattels and other property (*remainder
as in No. 53*).

And we also command you that you indorse (as in No. 53).

Witness (as in No. 53).

This writ (as in No. 53).

(Enacted 1988)

No. 66A

**Writ of Possession**
(Order 113 rule 7)

*(Heading as in summons)*

To the bailiff....................................................:

Whereas it was on the.............day of................................. 19...... ordered that the plaintiff *A.B.* do recover possession of [*describe the land recovery of which has been ordered*] [and that the defendant *C.D.* do pay him $............... costs [or costs to be taxed, which costs have been taxed and allowed at $................. as appears by the taxing master's certificate dated the..............day of.......... 19........]]

It is required that you enter the said land and cause *A.B.* to have possession of it. [And it is also required thai of the goods, chattels and other property [*remainder as in No. 53*].]

Witness (*as in No. 53*).

This writ (*as in No. 53*).

Dated this................day of.................................... 19......

(Enacted 1988)

No. 67

**Writ of sequestration**
(Order 45 rule 12)

*(Heading as in cause or matter)*

To (*names of not less than four commissioners*):

Whereas in the above named action (or matter) in the High Court, Hong Kong it was on the................day of................................. 19...... adjudged (or ordered) that *C.D.* should (pay into Court the sum of $....................or as may be):

You are hereby authorized and directed by this writ that you, or any two or three of you, may enter upon and take possession of all the real and personal estate of the said *C.D.* and may collect, receive and get into your hands the rents and profits of his real estate and all his personal estate and keep the same under sequestration in your hands until the said *C.D.* shall (pay into Court to the credit of the said action or matter the sum of $..................or as may be) and clear his contempt and the said Court make other order to the contrary.

Witness (*as in No. 53*).

This writ was issued (*as in No. 53*).

(Enacted 1988)

## No. 68

### Writ of restitution
(Order 46 rule 1)

*(Heading as in action)*

To the bailiff...................................................:

Whereas in the above named action it was on the......................day of.................
..........19......adjudged (or ordered) that the defendant *C.D.* do give the plaintiff *A.B.*
possession of (*describe the land delivery of which was adjudged or ordered*):

And whereas on the.............day of.................. 19......a writ of possession was
issued pursuant to the said judgment (or order) directing you to give possession of the
said land to the said *A.B.*, but it appearing to the High Court. Hong Kong that certain
other persons have wrongfully taken possession of the said land and the said Court
having on the.............. day of.................... 19...... ordered that a writ of restitution
should issue in respect of the said land:

It is required that you enter the said land and cause *A.B.* to have restitution thereof.

And it is also required that you indorse (*remainder as in No. 53*).

Witness (*as in No. 53*).

This writ (*as in No. 53*).

(Enacted 1988)

No. 69

**Writ of assistance**
(Order 46 rule 1)

*(Heading as in action)*

To the present and any future bailiff..............................................:

Whereas by an order dated the..............day of................... 19...... made in an action in the High Court, Hong Kong between *A.B.*, plaintiff, and *C.D.*, defendant, the said *C.D.* was ordered to give to the said *A.B.* possession of the goods therein described, namely (*describe the goods*), but he the said *C.D.* and other persons have refused to obey the order and keep the possession of the goods in contempt of the said Court:

And whereas by an order made in the said action dated the............. day of......... ..................... 19...... it was ordered that a writ of assistance should issue to give the said *A.B.* possession of the said goods: It is required that you put the said *A.B.* and his assigns into full peaceable and quiet possession of the said goods and defend and keep him and his assigns in such peaceable and quiet possession, when and as often as any interruption thereof is at any time effected, according to the intent of the said orders. And herein you are not in any wise to fail.

Witness (*as in No. 53*).

This writ (*as in No. 53*).
(L.N. 165 of 1992)

No. 71

**Notice of renewal of writ of execution**
(Order 46 rule 8)

*(Heading as in cause or matter)*

Take notice that the writ of............................. issued in this cause (or matter) directed to the bailiff and bearing date the................. day of.................................. .19.......has by order dated the..................day of................................ 19......been renewed for one year beginning with the date of the said order.
To the bailiff.

(Signed)

Solicitor for..................................

(Enacted 1988)

No. 72

**Garnishee order to show cause**
(Order 49 rule 1)

IN THE HIGH COURT OF THE HONG KONG SPECIAL ADMINISTRATIVE REGION

19.......No..........

(Mr. Justice..........................Judge in chambers)

Between                            *A.B.*                     Judgment creditor

                                           AND

                                        *C.D.*                     Judgment debtor

                                        *F.G.*                     Garnishee

Upon reading the affidavit of .......................... filed the .......... day of ................ 19......:

It is ordered by (Mr. Justice....................) that all debts due or accruing due from the above-mentioned garnishee to the above-mentioned judgment debtor (in the sum of $....................) be attached to answer a judgment recovered against the said judgment debtor by the above-named judgment creditor in the High Court on the.............day of...................19.....for the sum (or to answer an order made in the High Court on the............day of...................19.....; ordering payment by the said judgment debtor to the above-named judgment creditor of the sum) of $.............. (debt and $..............costs) and interest at the judgment rate calculated from the date on which maintenance payment is due to the date of payment and surcharge at a rate to be decided by the High Court, as referred to in Order 49, rule 2(ba)(i) and (ii) (together with the costs of the garnishee proceedings) on which judgment (or order) the sum of $..............remains due and unpaid.

And it is ordered that the said garnishee attend Mr. Justice............ in Chambers, at the High Court, in Hong Kong on the..............................day of................ 19..... at........ o'clock, on an application by the said judgment creditor that the garnishee do pay to the said judgment creditor the debt due from the said garnishee to the said judgment debtor, or so much thereof as may be sufficient to satisfy the said judgment (or order) and interest at the judgment rate calculated from the date on which maintenance payment is due to the date of payment and surcharge at a rate to be decided by the High Court, as referred to in Order 49, rule 2(ba)(i) and (ii), together with the costs of the garnishee proceedings.

Dated the...............day of................ 19......

To the above-named garnishee and judgment debtor.
    (Enacted 1988)
    (Ordinance No 18 of 2003)

## No. 73

### Garnishee order absolute where garnishee owes more than judgment debt
(Order 49 rules 1,4)

*(Heading as in No. 72)*

Upon hearing the solicitors for the judgment creditor and the garnishee, and upon reading the affidavit of..................................................... filed herein, and the order to show cause made herein dated the.............day of............................... 19....., whereby it was ordered that all debts due or accruing due from the above-named garnishee to the above-named judgment debtor should be attached to answer a judgment recovered against the said judgment debtor by the above-named judgment creditor in the High Court on the..............day of............................................................. 19..... for the sum (or to answer an order made in the High Court dated the............. day of.................................................. 19...... ordering payment by the said judgment debtor to the above-named judgment creditor of the sum) of $....................(debt and $.....................costs) and interest at the judgment rate calculated from the date on which maintenance payment is due to the date of payment and surcharge at a rate to be decided by the High Court, as referred to in Order 49, rule 2(ba)(i) and (ii) (together with the costs of the garnishee proceedings) on which judgment (or order) the sum of $....................remained due and unpaid:

It is ordered that the said garnishee do forthwith pay to the said judgment creditor $....................being so much of the debt from the said garnishee to the said judgment debtor as is sufficient to satisfy the said judgment debt, $...........interest and $.................... surcharge, as referred to in Order 49, rule 2(ba)(i) and (ii) and costs, together with $.................... the costs of the garnishee proceedings, and that the said garnishee be at liberty to retain $....................for his costs of this application out of the balance of the debt due from him to the judgment debtor.

Dated the.............day of............................... 19......

(Enacted 1988)
(Ordinance No 18 of 2003)

No. 74

## Garnishee order absolute where garnishee owes less than judgment debt

(Order 49 rules 1, 4)
*(Heading as in No. 72)*

Upon hearing (*as in No. 73*).

It is ordered that the said garnishee (after deducting therefrom $..................for his costs of this application) do forthwith pay to the said judgment creditor $.................. the debt due from the said garnishee to the said judgment debtor and $.................. interest and $.................. surcharge, as referred to in Order 49, rule 2(ba)(i) and Order 49, rule 2(ba)(ii). And that the sum of $.................. the costs or the judgment creditor of this application be added to the judgment debt and be retained out of the money recovered by the said judgment creditor under this order and in priority to the

amount of the judgment debt.

Dated the..............day of...................19.....
(Enacted 1988)
(Ordinance No 18 of 2003)

No. 75

**Charging order: notice to show cause**
(Order 50 rule 1)

*(Heading as in cause or matter)*

Upon hearing the................. and upon reading the affidavit of.................filed herein the..........day of.................... 19..... whereby it appears that by a judgment (or order) made in the Court of First Instance on the.........day of....................19......the defendant was ordered to pay to the plaintiff the sum of $.............and $.................. costs on which judgment (or order) the sum of $...............remains due and unpaid and that the defendant has a beneficial interest in the asset specified in the schedule hereto:

It is ordered by (Mr. Justice / Master...................) that unless sufficient cause to the contrary be shown before (Mr. Justice / Master...............at the High Court of Hong Kong, 38 Queensway, Hong Kong) on the......... day of............. 19....., at..........o'clock, the defendant's interest in the said asset shall, and it is ordered that in the meantime it do, stand charged with the payment of $........... due on the said judgment (or order) and (interest thereon at the statutory rate) (interest at the judgment rate calculated from the date on which maintenance payment is due to the date of payment and surcharge at a rate to be decided by the Court, as referred to in Order 50, rule 1 (3)(ba)(i) and Order 50, rule 1 (3)(ba)(ii)) together with the costs of this application.

Dated the............day of...................... 19......

### SCHEDULE

(Describe with full particulars the relevant land, securities, funds or trust, stating, in relation to securities, their full title, the amount of them and the name in which they stand and whether the beneficial interest charged is in the securities only or in dividends or interest as well, and stating, in relation to funds in court, the number of the account).

(L.N. 356 of 1988)

(Ordinance No 18 of 2003)

## No. 76

### Charging order absolute
(Order 50 rule 3)

*(Heading as in cause or matter)*

Upon hearing the.......................and upon reading the affidavits of................
................................and.................................................filed herein the.............day
of........................... 19...... and the order to show cause made herein on the..........day
of................... 19.....:

It is ordered that the interest of the defendant *C.D.* in the asset specified in the schedule hereto stand charged with the payment of $..............., the amount due from the defendant to the plaintiff *A.B.* on a judgment (or order) of the Court of First Instance dated the.........day of.................. 19......, and (interest thereon at the statutory rate) ($.......... interest and $...........surcharge, as referred to in Order 50, rule 1(3)(ba) (i) and Order 50, rule 1(3)(ba)(ii)) together with $........... the costs of this application, the said costs to be added to the judgment debt.

Dated the...........day of................19......

### SCHEDULE

(Describe with full particulars the relevant land, securities, funds or trust, stating, in relation to securities, their full title, the amount of them and the name in which they stand and whether the beneficial interest charged is in the securities only or in dividends or interest as well, and stating, in relation to funds in court, the number of the account).

### STOP NOTICE

To the (describe the person having custody of the security)

Take notice that, in relation to the securities specified in the schedule to this order, you may not, without notice to (name of the plaintiff) at (his address for service) register any transfer, or make any redemption payment, or, in the case of a unit trust, deal with the units, or, where dividends or interest are included in the order, pay any dividend or interest.

### SCHEDULE

(L.N. 356 of 1988)

No. 77

*(Repealed L.N. 356 of 1988)*

No. 78

*(Repealed L.N. 356 of 1988)*

No. 79

**Stop order on capital and income of funds in court
(Order 50 rule 10)**

*(Heading as in cause or matter)*

Upon hearing............................................ for the plaintiff *A.B.* and......................
.................... for the defendant *C.D.* and upon reading the affidavit of...................filed
herein the..........day of................ 19.....:

It is ordered that no part of the capital of (*describe funds*) in court to the credit
of this action (or matter) (*state title of action or matter*), the account of *C.D.*, and of
the sum of $...................cash (being income) in court to the same credit, and of any
interest or dividends to accrue due on the said funds in court, to which the said *C.D.*
is (or may become) entitled, be transferred, sold, paid or otherwise dealt with without
notice to the said *A.B.*

Dated the.............day of.................19.....
(Enacted 1988)

No. 80

**Affidavit and notice under O. 50 r. 11**
(Order 50 rule 11)

IN THE HIGH COURT OF THE HONG KONG SPECIAL ADMINISTRATIVE REGION

In the matter of *(state the settlement or other document under which the deponent's interest arises giving the date and other particulars sufficient to identify the document).*

and

In the matter of Order 50, rule 11, of the Rules of the High Court.

I, *A.B.* (or *C.D.* the solicitor of *A.B.* of............................................ made oath and say that according to the best of my knowledge, information and belief I am (or the said *A.B.* is) beneficially entitled under the above-mentioned settlement (*or as may be*) to an interest in the securities specified in the notice hereto annexed.

Sworn, etc...........

This affidavit is filed on behalf of *A.B.* whose address is................

**Notice to be annexed to affidavit**

To..................Co. Ltd.

Take notice that the securities comprised in and subject to the trusts of the settlement (*or as may be*) referred to in the affidavit to which this notice is annexed consist of the following, namely (*specify the stock, shares, etc. stating the names in which it stands*).

This notice is intended to stop the transfer of the said securities and not the payment of any dividend thereof or interest thereon (or and also the payment of any dividend thereof or interest thereon).

(Signed) *A.B.* (or *C.D. if affidavit sworn by him*).
(Enacted 1988)

## No. 81

### Order on originating summons restraining transfer of stock, etc.
#### (Order 50 rule 15)

IN THE HIGH COURT OF THE HONG KONG SPECIAL ADMINISTRATIVE REGION

20....., No...........

In the matter of the trusts of

..................................................................................................

and

In the matter of Order 50, rule 15, of the Rules of the High Court.

Upon the hearing of the originating summons for an injunction this day made unto this Court by counsel for the applicant *A.B.*:

And the applicant by his counsel undertaking to abide by any order the Court may hereafter make should it decide that the respondents (the.......................... Co. Ltd.) have sustained damage by reason of this order and are entitled to damages which the applicant ought to pay:

It is ordered that (the........................... Co. Ltd.) be restrained until the..........day of.....................20......or further order from permitting the transfer of (*describe stock*) standing in the name of (*state name of holder of stock*) in their books, or any part thereof, and from paying any dividend or interest due or to become due thereon.

Dated the............day of.....................20......

(L.N. 251 of 1997; 25 of 1998 s 2; L.N. 152 of 2008)

## No. 82

### Summons for appointment of receiver
(Order 51 rule 3)

*(Heading as in action)*

Let the defendant *C.D.* attend the (Judge in chambers, at the High Court in Hong Kong) on.....................the........day of................19.... at.........o'clock on the hearing of an application on the part of the plaintiff for an order that a receiver be appointed (or that *P.R.* be appointed receiver) in this action to receive the rents, profits and moneys receivable in respect of the interest of the defendant *C.D.* in the following property, namely (*describe the property*) in or towards satisfaction of the moneys and interest due to the plaintiff under the judgment (or order) in this action dated the........ day of.................19.... and for an order as to the costs of this application.

Dated the............day of...................19.....

This summons was taken out by.................of....................

To the above-named.........................(and his solicitor).

(Enacted 1988)

## No. 83

### Order directing summons for appointment of receiver and granting injunction meanwhile
(Order 51 rule 3)

*(Heading as in action)*

Upon reading the affidavit of...............filed the...............day of................. 19....:

Let the defendant *C.D.* attend the (Judge in chambers, at the High Court in Hong Kong) on the...............day of.................19.....at........... o'clock on the hearing of an application on the part of the plaintiff for the appointment of *P.R.* as receiver in this action, on the usual terms, to receive the rents, profits and moneys receivable in respect of the said defendant's interest in the following property, namely *(describe the property)* in or towards satisfaction of the sum of $...................debt and $........... costs, and interest on the said sums at the rate of $4 per cent per annum from the.......... day of.....................19......due under the judgment (or order) in this action dated the...........day of................19.....

And the plaintiff (by his solicitor) hereby undertaking to abide by any order the Court may hereafter make should it decide that the said defendant has sustained damage by reason of this order and is entitled to damages which the plaintiff ought to pay, it is ordered that the said defendant by himself, his agents or servants, or otherwise, be restrained, and an injunction is hereby granted restraining him, until after the hearing of the above application, from assigning, charging or otherwise dealing with the said property.

Dated the...........day of................. 19......

(Enacted 1988)

## No. 84

**Order appointing receiver by way of equitable execution**
(Order 51 rule 1)

*(Heading as in action)*

Upon hearing................................................... and upon reading the affidavit of............................... filed the........day of............. 19.....:

(*If security ordered*) It is ordered that *P.R.* of...................on first giving security to the satisfaction of the Court, be and is hereby appointed to receive the rents, profits and moneys receivable in respect of the above-named defendant's interest in the following property, namely (*describe the property*). (*If no security ordered and receiver is not the plaintiff*) The plaintiff being answerable for the acts and defaults of the receiver, it is ordered that *P.R.* of...................be and is hereby appointed to receive (*continue as above*) but he shall not receive more than the amount of the judgment debt and allowed costs of obtaining this order without leave of the Court or first giving (at the plaintiffs cost unless otherwise ordered) the usual security to the satisfaction of the Court.

(*If no security ordered and receiver is the plaintiff: as above omitting "The plaintiff being answerable for the acts and defaults of the receiver" and the words after "the Court"*).

(In all cases continue as follows:—)

That this appointment shall be without prejudice to the rights of any prior incumbrances upon the said property who may think proper to take possession of or receive the same by virtue of their respective securities or, if any prior incumbrances is in possession, then without prejudice to such possession.

And that the tenants of premises comprised in the said property do attorn and pay their rents in arrear and growing rents to the receiver.

And that the receiver have liberty, if he shall think proper (but not otherwise), out of the rents, profits and moneys to be received by him to keep down the interest upon the prior incumbrances, according to their priorities, and be allowed such payments, if any, in passing his accounts.

And that the receiver shall on the.......................... day of....................... (*3 months after the date of orde*r), and at such further and other times as may be ordered by the Court leave and pass his accounts, and shall on the......................... day of............. (*4 months after the date of order*) and at such further and other times as may be hereafter ordered by the Court pay the balance or balances appearing due on the accounts so left, or such part thereof as shall be certified as proper to be so paid, such sums to be paid in or towards satisfaction of what shall for the time being be due in respect of the judgment signed on the...........day of.........................for the sum of $...................debt and $...................costs, making together the sum of $...................

And that the costs of the receiver (including his remuneration), the costs of obtaining his appointment, of completing his security (if any), of passing his accounts and of obtaining his discharge shall not exceed ten per cent of the amount due under the said judgment or the amount recovered by the receiver, whichever is the less, provided that not less than.....................be allowed unless otherwise ordered. Such costs shall be taxed unless assessed by the Court and shall be primarily payable out of the sums received by the receiver, but if there shall be no sums received or the amount shall be insufficient, then upon the certificate of the Court being given stating the amount of the deficiency, such certificate to be given after passing the final account, the amount of the deficiency so certified shall be paid by the defendant to the plaintiff.

It is also ordered that the balance (if any) remaining in the hands of the receiver, after making the several payments aforesaid, shall unless otherwise directed by the Court forthwith be paid by the receiver into Court to the credit of this action, subject to further order.

And that any of the parties be at liberty to apply to the Judge in chambers as there may be occasion.

Dated the.............day of.................19.....
(Enacted 1988)

No. 85

**Order of committal**
(Order 52 rule 1)

*(Heading as in action)*

Upon hearing the originating summons dated the..............day of..........
20........ taken out by the solicitor for the plaintiff/plaintiff and upon reading (an
affidavit of...........................................................................................................
........................................................ filed the.................day of...............20.........of
service on the defendant C.D. of a copy of the order of the Court dated the................
day of.............. 20......... and of notice of hearing of this originating summons):

And it appearing to the satisfaction of the Court that the defendant *C.D.* has been
guilty of contempt of court in (*state the contempt*):

It is ordered that for his said contempt the defendant do stand committed
to......................Prison to be there imprisoned (until further order).

(It is further ordered that this order shall not be executed if the defendant *C.D.*
complies with the following terms, namely,.................................................................
...............................................................................................................................).

Dated the...........day of...................20.........

(L.N. 251 of 1997, L.N. 152 of 2008)

No. 85A

**Warrant for committal**
(Order 52 rule 1)

IN THE HIGH COURT OF THE HONG KONG SPECIAL ADMINISTRATIVE REGION
COURT OF FIRST INSTANCE

Between                                    *A.B.*                        Plaintiff

                                           *AND*

                                           *C.D.*                        Defendant

To: The Chief Bailiff and his assistants and the Commissioner of Correctional Services.

WHEREAS by an order of this Court pronounced this day it was ordered that the above-named [here insert name of defendant], do stand committed to Prison for his / her contempt in the said order mentioned.

You are required to apprehend the said [here insert name of defendant], and him / her safely convey to Prison there to be detained and kept in safe custody until such time as the said Order granted by the Honourable Mr. Justice.......................on the.........day of.................. 19.... shall have been complied with and obeyed or until such time as the said [here insert name of defendant] may be discharged by the Court on his / her application.

Dated the...........day of..................... 19......


.................................................................
*A Judge of the Court of First Instance*

(Enacted 1988)

No. 86

Notice of application for leave to apply for judicial review
O. 53 r. 3(2)

No.........................

IN THE HIGH COURT OF THE HONG KONG SPECIAL
ADMINISTRATIVE REGION

COURT OF FIRST INSTANCE

Applicant

Notice of application for leave to apply
for judicial review (O. 53 r. 3(2))

This form must be read together with notes for guidance obtainable from the Registry.

To the Registrar, High Court, Hong Kong

| | |
|---|---|
| Name, description and address of applicant | |
| Name and description of proposed respondent | |
| Judgment, order, decision or other proceeding in respect of which relief is sought | |

### Relief Sought

| | |
|---|---|
| Name, description and address of all interested parties, (if any) known to the applicant | |
| Name and address of applicant's solicitors, or, if no solicitors acting, the address for service of the applicant | |
| Signed | Dated |

*Grounds on which leave is sought*
(If there has been any delay, include reasons here).

Note:- Grounds must be supported by an affidavit which verifies the facts relied on.

## No. 86A
## **Originating summons – judicial review**
### (O. 53 r. 5)

IN THE HIGH COURT OF THE HONG KONG SPECIAL ADMINISTRATIVE REGION
COURT OF FIRST INSTANCE
CONSTITUTIONAL AND ADMINISTRATIVE LAW LIST
NO._____ OF_____

Between                                                    *A.B.*                                          Applicant

                                                    AND

                                                    *C.D.*                                          Respondent

Pursuant to the leave granted by the Honourable_____ on
_____, let all parties concerned appear before the
Honourable_____ on the_____ day of_____ 20_____
at_____ o'clock, on the hearing of an application by *A.B.* for an order that
(or for the following relief, namely):

_____

_____

_____

TAKE NOTICE that an order will also be sought that the costs of and incidental
to this application be paid by_____.

THE GROUNDS FOR THE APPLICATION are those set out in Form No. 86
used on the application for leave to apply for such order (or the grounds for the
application, for which leave had been granted, are as follows:

_____

_____

FURTHER TAKE NOTICE that on the hearing of this application, theapplicant
will use the following affidavit(s) and the exhibits therein referred to:

_____

_____

Dated the_____ day of_____ 20_____.


_____
Solicitor for the applicant
(or where the applicant acts
in person, name of
the applicant)

This summons was taken out by_____, solicitor for the applicant whose address is at_____

(or where the plaintiff acts in person:

This summons was taken out by the applicant whose address for service is at_____
_____ )

To:_____
_____

(Name and address of the respondent or the solicitor for the respondent, and if applicable, name and address of the interested party or other party as directed by the Court).

(L.N. 152 of 2008)

## No. 87

### Originating summons – for writ of habeas corpus ad subjiciendum
(Order 54 rule 2)

IN THE HIGH COURT OF THE HONG KONG SPECIAL ADMINISTRATIVE REGION
COURT OF FIRST INSTANCE
CONSTITUTIONAL AND ADMINISTRATIVE LAW LIST

NO._____ OF _____

Between                                 *A.B.*                    Applicant

AND

*C.D.*                  Respondent

Pursuant to the direction given by the Honourable _____
on_____, let all parties concerned appear before the
Honourable_____on the_____day of 20_____
at_____o'clock, on the hearing of an application by *A.B.* for an
order that a writ of habeas corpus be issued directed to_____
to have *A.B.* brought before the Honourable _____at such time as the
judge_____may direct.

TAKE NOTICE that an order will also be sought that the costs of and incidental
to this application be paid by_____.

THE GROUNDS FOR THE APPLICATION are those set out in the affidavits of
*A.B.* and_____and the exhibits therein respectively referred to used on the
application to the_____ for such order, copies of which
affidavits and exhibits are served herewith.

FURTHER TAKE NOTICE that on the hearing of this application, the applicant
will use the following affidavit(s) and the exhibits therein referred to:

_____

_____

Dated the_____day of_____20_____.


_____
Solicitor for the applicant
(or where the applicant acts
in person, name of the applicant)

This summons was taken out by_____, solicitor for the applicant whose address is at_____

(or where the plaintiff acts in person -:

This summons was taken out by the applicant whose address for service is at _____
_____)

To:_____
_____

(Name and address of the respondent or the solicitor for the respondent, and if applicable, name and address of the other party as directed by the Court)

No. 88

**Notice directed by Court of adjourned application for
writ of habeas corpus**
(Order 54 rule 2)

*(Heading as in No. 87)*

Take notice that an application for the above writ was made to the......................
...................... in the above matter on the.................day of.......................... 19.... when
the said application was adjourned so that notice could be given to you.

Notice is hereby given to you that the said application will be made to the..........
........................................on.........................................the...................day of..........
........................ 19..... at..............o'clock.

(Signed).....................................................

of.....................................................

Solicitor for...................................................

*To*...................................................................
(Enacted 1988)

## No. 89

## Writ of habeas corpus ad subjiciendum
(Order 54 rule 10)

To...................:

It is required that you have in our High Court at the High Court in Hong Kong, on the day at the time specified in the notice served with this writ, *A.B.* being taken and detained under your custody as is said, together with the day and cause of his being taken and detained, by whatsoever name he may be called therein, that our Court may then and there examine and determine whether such cause is legal, and have you there then this writ.

Witness..............................Chief Justice of Hong Kong the.............. day of......................19.....

### *Indorsement*

By order of (Mr. Justice.....................................................................................)
This writ was issued by..............................of....................................... solicitor for...................................................................................................................
(L.N. 313 of 1997; 25 of 1998 s 2)

## No. 90

**Notice to be served with writ of habeas corpus ad subjiciendum**
(Order 54 rule 6)

IN THE HIGH COURT OF THE HONG KONG SPECIAL ADMINISTRATIVE REGION
COURT OF FIRST INSTANCE

*(If in a cause already begun, here insert the title, not otherwise)*

The Honourable Mr. Justice..................................................... has granted a writ of habeas corpus directed to............................................. (or other person having the custody of.......................................... if so) requiring him to have *A.B.* before a judge at the High Court in Hong Kong on the day and at the time specified in the notice together with the day and cause of his being taken and detained.

Take notice that you are required by the said writ to have the said *A.B.* before the Honourable Mr. Justice..................................................... on............................ ..the..........day of............................... 19.... at..............o'clock and to make a return to the said writ. In default thereof the said Court will then, or so soon thereafter as counsel can be heard, be moved to commit you to prison for your contempt in not obeying the said writ.

Dated the............day of............................... 19....

(Signed).....................................................

of.....................................................

Solicitor for.....................................................

*To*.........................................................................
(Enacted 1988)

No. 91

**Writ of habeas corpus ad testificandum**
(Order 54 rule 10)

*[Repealed by Ordinance No. 95 of 1997.]*

No. 92

**Writ of habeas corpus ad respondendum**
(Order 54 rule 10)

*[Repealed by Ordinance No. 95 of 1997.]*

No. 93

**Notice of sanctioned payment (Order 62A)**

(Order 62A rule 8(2))

*(Heading as in action)*

To the receiving party('s solicitor)

Take notice that the paying party....................................has paid $...............................
.............................(a further amount of  $.........................) into court in settlement of

(tick as appropriate)

      □     The whole of your costs including the costs of taxation (for the bill dated..........................................)

      □     part of your costs *(give details below)*

      □     It is in addition to the amount of $.............................. already paid into court on..............................and the total amount in court now offered in settlement of your costs is $............................................*(give total of all payments in court to date)*

      □     It is not inclusive of interest and an additional amount of $.............. .......................... is offered for interest *(give details of the rate(s) and period(s) for which the amount of interest is offered)*

      □     It takes into account the interim payment(s) of costs made in the following amount(s) on the following date(s) *(give details)*

      □     It takes into account the following sum(s) of money that has (have) been paid into court as security for the costs of the action, cause or matter: *(give details)*

| Signed | | Position or office held (If signing on behalf of a firm, company or corporation) | |
|---|---|---|---|
| | Paying party('s solicitor) | | |
| Date | | With company chop (if applicable) | |

Note: To the receiving party

If you wish to accept the payment made into Court and the Court's leave for acceptance is not required, you should complete form No. 93B and file it in the Registry of the High Court, and send a copy to the paying party.

(L.N. 152 of 2008)

No. 93A

**Notice of acceptance sanctioned payment (Order 62A)**

(Order 62A) (Order 62A rule 13(4))

*(Heading as in action)*

To the paying party('s solicitor)

Take notice that the receiving party accepts the payments) into court totalling $.........
........................ in settlement of (whole of) (part of) the receiving party's costs as set
out in the notice of sanctioned payment received on...........................(and abandons
the other part(s) of the costs).

| | | | |
|---|---|---|---|
| Signed | | Position or office held (If signing on behalf of a firm, company or corporation) | |
| | Receiving party('s solicitor) | | |
| Date | | With company chop (if applicable) | |

(L.N. 152 of 2008)

No. 93B

**Notice of request for payment (Order 62A)**

(Order 62A rule 15)

*(Heading as in action)*

On..................................I accepted the payments) into court totalling $...................
...............in settlement of (the whole of) (part of) my costs as set out in the notice of
sanctioned payment received on....................................

I declare that:

      □    the sanctioned payment has been accepted [within 14 days] [after 14 days but liability for and quantum of costs incurred after the 14-day period have been agreed]*

      □    the offeree is not a person under disability

      □    [at no time has the offeree been on legal aid in these proceedings] [the offeree has been on legal aid]*

      □    there is no pending application to withdraw or diminish the sanctioned payment

      □    [there is only one paying party] [the sanctioned payment is made by all paying parties] [I have discontinued the proceedings for taxation against those paying parties who have not made the payment and they have given written consent to the acceptance of the sanctioned payment]*

           *(If any of the above declarations has not been made, the money in court can only be paid out by order of the Court)*

      □    a copy of this notice has been served on the paying party('s solicitor) named below and I request payment of this money held in court to be made to:

| Receiving party or solicitor's full name |
|---|
| |

| Address and telephone number |
|---|
| |

| Signature |
|---|
| Note:      Before signing this form please read the notes for guidance overleaf. Incorrectly signed forms may be returned unactioned. |

| Signed | Date |
|---|---|
| | |

DETAILS OF PLAINTIFF'S SOLICITOR

| Name of firm |
|---|
| |

| Solicitor for |
|---|
| |

| Paying party or solicitor's full name/Director of Legal Aid* |
|---|

| Address and telephone number |
|---|

Signature

Note:　　　　The plaintiff('s solicitor) should obtain the signature of the defendant('s solicitor) on the box below before serving a copy of this notice on him

| Signed | Date |
|---|---|

### DETAILS OF PLAINTIFF'S SOLICITOR

| Name of firm |
|---|

| Solicitor for |
|---|

\* Delete as appropriate

### Notes for guidance on completion of Form No. 93B

In order to request payment out of funds in court, file this form, signed and completed in accordance with these notes for guidance in the Registry of the High Court. A copy of this form should also be sent to the paying party's solicitors.

* When completing this form, please ensure that you tick all of the boxes under the heading: 'I declare that'. If you do not tick all of the boxes, the Registry of the High Court will not be able to process your request for payment and will have to return the form to you.

* The form should be signed either by the receiving party or his solicitor.

* The Accounts Office of the High Court will only issue payment upon receipt of a properly completed Form No. 93B with an original signature. Faxed copies of the form and photocopies of signatures will not be accepted.

* A director of a company must obtain leave to represent the company from a Practice Master before he may sign on behalf of the company.

(L.N. 152 of 2008)

---

No. 94

**Order for production of documents in marine insurance action**
(Order 72 rule 10)

(*Heading as in action*)

Upon hearing..................................................... (and upon reading the affidavit of...................................................filed the..........................day of.................19.....):

It is ordered that the plaintiff and all other persons interested in this action, and in the insurance the subject of this action, do produce and show to the defendant, his solicitors or agents on oath (or by oath of their proper officer) all insurance slips, policies, letters of instruction or other orders for effecting such slips or policies, or relating to the insurance or the subject-matter of the insurance on the ship................ ................................................., or the cargo on board thereof, or the freight thereby, and also all documents relating to the sailing or alleged loss of the said ship, cargo or freight, and all correspondence with any person relating in any manner to the effecting of the insurance on the said ship, cargo or freight, or any other insurance whatsoever effected on the said ship, cargo or freight, on the voyage insured by the policy sued on in this action, or any other policy whatsoever effected on the said ship, or the cargo on board thereof, or the freight thereby on the same voyage. Also all correspondence between the captain or agent of the ship and any other person with the owner or any person before the commencement of or during the voyage on which the alleged loss happened. Also all books and documents, whatever their nature and whether originals, duplicates or copies, which in any way relate or refer to any matter in question in this action and which are now in the custody, possession or power of the plaintiff or any other person on his behalf, his or their, or any of their brokers, solicitors or agents, with liberty for the defendant, his solicitors or agents to inspect and take copies of, or extracts from, any of those books or documents. And that in the like manner the plaintiff and every other person interested as aforesaid do account for all other books and documents relating or referring to any matter in question in this action which were once but are not now in his custody, possession and power.

And that (in the meantime all further proceedings be stayed and that) the costs of and occasioned by this application be costs in the action.

Dated the...............day of..................... 19.....
(Enacted 1988)

No. 95

**Certificate of order against the Government**
(Order 77 rule 15(3))

*(Heading as in cause or matter)*

By a judgment (or order) of this Court dated the................. day of.....................
19.....it was adjudged (or ordered) that (*give particulars of the judgment or ordered*)

I hereby certify that the amount payable to................................. by.....................
.................. in pursuance of the said judgment (or order) is $...............(together with
interest thereon at the rate of ............ per cent per annum until payment and together
with costs which have been taxed and certified by the taxing officer at $.................
Interest is payable on the said costs at the rate of ................. per cent per annum from
the.......... day of.................... 19..... until payment).

(This certificate does not include the amount payable under the said judgment or
order in respect of costs).

Dated the.............day of.....................19....

(Signed).....................................................

(*Note:—The final paragraph is to be included where a separate certificate with
respect to costs has been directed to be issued*).
(Enacted 1988)

No. 96

**Certificate of order for costs against the Government**
(Order 77 rule 15)

*(Heading as in cause or matter)*

By a judgment (or order of this Court dated the.................. day of.......................
19.... it was adjudged (or ordered) that (*give particulars of the judgment or order*).

I hereby certify that the costs payable to......................................by.....................
............. in pursuance of the said judgment (or order) have been taxed and certified
by the taxing officer at $.................(and interest is payable thereon at the rate of
$.................per cent per annum from the..................day of............................ 19.....
until payment).

Dated the...............day of..................... 19.....

(Signed).....................................................

(Enacted 1988)

No. 99

## Order of Court of Appeal to admit prisoner to bail
(Order 59 rule 20)

IN THE COURT OF APPEAL

On appeal from the...................... court

Dated the................day of....................................19.......

Whereas on the.............day of................................19.....*A.B.* was ordered by (*description of court*) to be imprisoned for........................... for contempt of court and the said *A.B.* has appealed to this Honourable Court against the said order:—

And whereas the said *A.B.* has applied to this Honourable Court to be admitted to bail:

Upon reading the notice of motion on behalf of the said *A.B.* and upon hearing Mr......................................... of counsel for the said *A.B.*

It is ordered that upon the said *A.B.* giving security (by his own recognizance) in the sum of $...................with (two) sufficient sureties in the sum of $.............. each before the Registrar for the personal appearance of the said *A.B.* before the.......................court within ten days after the judgment of this Honourable Court on his said appeal shall have been given unless the order of the said court is reversed by that judgment, he, the said *A.B.* be discharged out of the custody of the Commissioner for Correctional Services....................in respect of his commitment as aforesaid.

By the Court

(Enacted 1988)
(Ord. No. 47 of 1997)
(L.N. 39 of 1999)

## No. 100

### Notice of payment into court in connection with arbitration proceedings
(Order 73 rule 11)

In the matter of arbitration proceedings
commenced between    *A.B.*...................................................................... 1st party

                                   *C.D.*.................................................................. 2nd party

                                     *E.F.*.................................................................. 3rd party

etc

Take notice that—

The...........................party.......................................... has paid $..............................
into court. The said $...........................is in satisfaction of (the matter in dispute)
(All the matters in dispute) in respect of which the.............................. party
claims (and after taking into account and satisfying the above-named party's claim
for.......................... in respect of which he counterclaims).

or

The said $...................is in satisfaction of the following matters in dispute in respect
of which the..........................party claims (and after taking into account as above).

or

Of the said $........................, $........................ is in satisfaction of the following
matter in dispute in respect of which the.............................. party claims (and after
taking into account as above) and $........................ is in satisfaction of the following
matter in dispute in respect of which the......................party claim (and after taking
into account as above).

Dated the.............day of....................... 19.....
(Enacted 1988)

No. 101

**Notice of acceptance of money paid into court in connection
with arbitration proceedings**
(Order 73 rule 11)

In the matter of arbitration proceedings
commenced between   *A.B*.......................................................................1st party
                    *C.D*.................................................................. 2nd party
                    *E.F*.................................................................. 3rd party

Take notice that the................party.................accepts the sum of $......................
paid in by the...................... parry in satisfaction of the matter(s) in dispute in respect
of which it was paid in and in respect of which the..........................party claims
(against that party) (and abandons his claim(s) against that party in respect of the
other matter(s) in dispute in the arbitration proceedings).

Dated the..............day of.....................19.....
(Enacted 1988)

No. 102

**Order of issue of warrant of arrest for examination**
(Order 49B rule 1)

IN THE HIGH COURT OF THE HONG KONG SPECIAL ADMINISTRATIVE REGION
COURT OF FIRST INSTANCE

| | | |
|---|---|---|
| Between | *A.B.* | Judgment Creditor |
| | AND | |
| | *C.D.* | Judgment Debtor |

Upon the application of the Judgment Creditor *A.B.* and upon hearing the solicitor for the said Judgment Creditor, and upon reading the affidavit of...............................
......... filed the............day of.................... 19....:

It is ordered that a warrant do issue to the bailiff enjoining him to arrest the Judgment Debtor *C.D.* and to bring him before the Court before the expiry of the day after the day of arrest for examination; and it is further ordered that the bailiff be authorized to release the Judgment Debtor—

1. upon payment to him of the sum of $........................., being the amount of the judgment debt, together with the sum of $.........................for costs of this action and such costs as may be due for the obtaining and execution of this warrant;

2. upon payment to him of the sum of $.........................as security or the provision of bail in that sum by a surety or sureties;

3. upon the surrender to him of the judgment debtor's travel documents.

[*Delete, amend or substitute conditions in accordance with the order of the Court.*]

Dated the.................day of......................... 19.....

*NOTE:* The Judgment Debtor may apply to the Court to discharge this order.
(Enacted 1988)

No. 103

**Order of imprisonment pending further examination**
(Order 49B rule 1A)

IN THE HIGH COURT OF THE HONG KONG SPECIAL ADMINISTRATIVE REGION
COURT OF FIRST INSTANCE

Between                                    *A.B.*                        Judgment Creditor

AND

*C.D.*                        Judgment Debtor

Whereas the examination being conducted under Order 49B rule 1A has been adjourned until............day of...................................... 19....:

It is ordered that a warrant do issue to the bailiff enjoining him to deliver the Judgment Debtor into the custody of the Commissioner of Correctional Services to be kept in a prison as a prisoner for debt until the............day of.............................. .............. 19......and then to bring the Judgment Debtor before the Court for further examination. The Court has fixed the support and maintenance allowance at the rate of $...................... a day.

It is further ordered that the bailiff be authorized to release the Judgment Debtor—

1.    upon payment to him of the sum of $........................., being the amount of the judgment debt, together with the sum of $.........................for costs of this action and such costs as may be due for the obtaining and execution of this warrant

2.    upon payment to him of the sum of $......................... as security or the provision of bail in that sum by a surety or sureties.

[*Delete, amend or substitute conditions in accordance with the order of the Court.*]

Dated the.................day of.........................19......

*NOTE:* The Judgment Debtor may apply to the Court to discharge this order.
(Enacted 1988)

No. 104

### Order for imprisonment for debt
(Order 49B rule 1B)

IN THE HIGH COURT OF THE HONG KONG SPECIAL ADMINISTRATIVE REGION
COURT OF FIRST INSTANCE

Between                                    *A.B.*                      Judgment Creditor

                                               AND

                                               *C.D.*                      Judgment Debtor

[Following examination of the Judgment Debtor under Order 49B rule 1A and upon the Court being satisfied as required by Order 49B rule 1B:] or [Upon the Court being satisfied that the Judgment Debtor has failed to comply with an order made under Order 49B rule 1B(3):]

It is ordered that the bailiff do take the Judgment Debtor and deliver him into the custody of the Commissioner of Correctional Services to be kept in prison as a prisoner for debt for a period of............................... unless he shall be sooner discharged in due course of law.

The Court has fixed the support and maintenance allowance at the rate of $..................a day.

Dated the...............day of.......................... 19.....
(Enacted 1988)

No. 105

**Application for order for imprisonment in default of payment**
(Order 49B rule IB)

IN THE HIGH COURT OF THE HONG KONG SPECIAL ADMINISTRATIVE REGION
COURT OF FIRST INSTANCE

Between                                    *A.B.*                          Judgment Creditor

                                                    AND

                                                    *C.D.*                          Judgment Debtor

TAKE NOTICE that the Judgment. Creditor will apply to the Court on................ day of......................... 19..... for an order for the imprisonment of the Judgment Debtor on the ground that the Judgment Debtor has failed to make payment of the sum of $................as ordered by the Court on............day of.........................19.....

Dated the...............day of.........................19.....
(Enacted 1988)

No. 106

**Order prohibiting departure from Hong Kong**
(Order 44A rule 3)

IN THE HIGH COURT OF THE HONG KONG SPECIAL ADMINISTRATIVE REGION
COURT OF FIRST INSTANCE

Between                               *A.B.*                     Judgment Creditor/
                                                                Plaintiff/Claimant

                                      AND

                                      *C.D.*                     Judgment Debtor/
                                                                Defendant/Person
                                                                against whom
                                                                claim is made

Upon the application of *A.B.* and upon hearing the solicitor for *A.B* and upon reading the affidavit of..........................................filed the....................day of............ ...................... 19....:
It is ordered that *C.D.* is prohibited from leaving Hong Kong. This order shall lapse after the expiry of one month (unless extended or renewed) and shall have no effect if —

1.   C. D. makes payment of the sum of $.........................., being the amount claimed by *A.B.*, [together with the sum of $..........................for costs of this action] and such costs as may be due for the obtaining and execution of this order;

2.   *C.D.* makes payment of the sum of $..........................as security or provides bail in that sum by a surety or sureties;

*[Delete, amend or substitute conditions in accordance with the order of the Court.]*

Dated the.................day of..........................19.....

*NOTE: C.D.* may apply to the Court to discharge this order.
(Enacted 1988)

# No. 107

*(Repealed L.N. 152 of 2008)*

No. 108

**Order for continued detention of
sized property**
(O. 115 r. 25)

IN THE HIGH COURT OF THE HONG KONG SPECIAL ADMINISTRATIVE REGION
COURT OF FIRST INSTANCE

---

IN THE MATTER OF THE DRUG TRAFFICKING (RECOVERY OF
PROCEEDS ORDINANCE (CAP.] 405)

---

Between          [          ]          Applicant

and

[          ]          Respondent

BEFORE THE HONOURABLE MR. JUSTICE..................................................
IN CHAMBERS

## ORDER

UPON the application of [*A.B.*]

AND UPON HEARING [*the said A.B..*]

AND UPON READING the affidavit of [*A.B.*] made on...........................

IT IS ORDERED THAT the sum of $....................seized from [*C.D.*] of.......
...........................(or. from person or persons unknown) at........................................
....................Hong Kong on...................-day, the...................day of...........................
at...............o'clock Hong Kong time by [*E.F.*] of the...................be further detained
for a period of............. days from the date hereof or until further order of this Court.
Dated this................day of...................... 19.........

Registrar.

**Important Notice:**

(1)    A party affected by this order may apply to the Court for its discharge.
(2)    The applicant may apply for an order for the further detention of this money.
(3)    Persons affected by this order will be notified in accordance with the Rules of the Court, or as directed by the Court, of any application made for the release of this money.

(L.N. 296 of 1996)

No. 109

*(Repealed L.N. 152 of 2008)*

APPENDIX B

SPECIAL ADMIRALTY FORMS

No. 1

**Writ of summons in action in rem**
(Order 75 rule 3)

19......, Folio No...........

IN THE HIGH COURT OF THE HONG KONG SPECIAL ADMINISTRATIVE REGION
COURT OF FIRST INSTANCE

Admiralty action in rem against:

[The ship "X" or as may be describing the property against which the action is brought]

| | | |
|---|---|---|
| Between | [The owners of the ship "A" or as may be describing the plaintiffs] | Plaintiffs |
| | [or name] | |
| | and | |
| | [The owners of the ship "X" or as may be describing the property against which the action is brought] | Defendants |

TO THE DEFENDANTS and other persons interested in the ship "X"................
...................................................... registered at the port of
.................................................................................... [or as may be]

THE WRIT OF SUMMONS has been issued by the Plaintiffs against the property described above in respect of the claim set out on the back. Within [14 days] after the service of this Writ, counting the day of service, you must either satisfy the claim or lodge in the Registry of the High Court mentioned below an ACKNOWLEDGMENT OF SERVICE.

If you fail to satisfy the claim or to lodge an Acknowledgment within the time stated, the Plaintiffs may proceed with the action and judgment may be given without further notice to you and if the property described in this Writ is under the arrest of the Court it may be sold by order of the Court.

Issued from the Registry of the High Court this................................day of........
.......................... 19.....

*Note:*—This Writ may not be served later than 12 calendar months beginning with that date unless renewed by order of the Court.

## IMPORTANT

Directions for Acknowledgement of Service are given with the accompanying form.

*[Back of No. 1]*

### *[STATEMENT OF CLAIM]

The Plaintiffs' claim is for

*[Signed if statement of claim indorsed]

---

THIS WRIT was issued by.............................................................. of..............
.................................................................................... Solicitor for the said
Plaintiff whose address is.......................................

*[or where the Plaintiff sues in person

THIS WRIT was issued by the said Plaintiff who resides at...........................
..........................and (if the Plaintiff does not reside within the jurisdiction) whose
address for service is..........................................................................]

### *[Indorsement as to service

(To be completed only when the Writ has been served by the bailiff)

THIS WRIT was served by me at...................................................... on.........,
on.........day, the............day of................................. 19....., by *(state the manner service)*

Signed

Name of bailiff                                                                                    ]

(* Where words appear between square brackets, delete if inapplicable) ]
(Enacted 1988)

## No. 2

### Writ of summons in limitation action
(Order 75 rule 3(3))

19......., Folio No...........

THE HIGH COURT OF THE HONG KONG SPECIAL ADMINISTRATIVE REGION
COURT OF FIRST INSTANCE

Admiralty Jurisdiction

Between                                                                                     Plaintiff

and

Defendant

TO THE DEFENDANT [name]................................................................ of [address]...................................................................................

THIS WRIT OF SUMMONS has been issued against you by the abovenamed Plaintiff in respect of the claim set out on the back.

Unless you admit the claim you must within [14 days] after service of this writ on you, counting the day of service, return to the Registry of the High Court mentioned below the accompanying ACKNOWLEDGMENT OF SERVICE.

If you fail to return the Acknowledgment within the time stated, the Plaintiff may proceed with the action without further notice to you.

Issued from the Registry of the High Court this.................... day of...................... 19.....

*Note:*—This Writ may not be served later than 12 calendar months beginning with that date unless renewed by order of the Court.

### IMPORTANT

Directions for Acknowledgment of Service are given with the accompanying form.

[*Back of No. 2*]

The Plaintiff claims

___

THIS WRIT was issued by............................................................................. .................. of.............................................................................................. .......... Solicitor for the said Plaintiff whose address is............................................. *[or where the Plaintiff sues in person

THIS WRIT was issued by the said Plaintiff who resides at................................... ...............................and (if the Plaintiff does not reside within the jurisdiction) whose address for service is.............................................................................]

(*Where words appear between square brackets, delete if inapplicable)
(Enacted 1988)

## No. 2A

### Notice of writ of summons in limitation action
### to be served out of jurisdiction
(Order 75 rule 3(3))

*[Heading as in action]*

To *C.D.* of

Take notice that *A.B.* of.................................................... has begun an action against you, *C.D.*, in the Court of First Instance in Hong Kong by writ of summons dated the...........day of............................... 19....., which writ is indorsed as follows [copy the indorsement of claim] and unless you admit the Plaintiffs claim you are required within................ days after receipt of this notice, counting the day of receipt, to return to the Registry of the High Court the accompanying Acknowledgment of Service.

And take notice that if you do not return the Acknowledgment within the time stated, the Plaintiff may proceed with the action without further notice to you.

(Signed) *A.B.*...........................................
or X. Y. of
*Solicitors for A.B.*

### IMPORTANT

Directions for Acknowledgment of Service are given with the accompanying form.

(Enacted 1988)

No. 2B

**Acknowledgment of Service of Writ of Summons in
Action in rem or Limitation Action**
(Order 75 rule 3(5))

*Directions for Acknowledgment of Service*

1.    The accompanying form of ACKNOWLEDGMENT OF SERVICE should be detached and completed by a Solicitor acting on behalf of the Defendant or by the Defendant if acting in person. After completion it must be delivered or sent by post to the Registry of the High Court at the following address:—

2.    If in an action in rem a Statement of Claim is indorsed on the Writ (i.e. the words "Statement of Claim" appear at the top of the back), a Defence must be served within 14 days after the time for acknowledging service of the Writ.

If a Statement of Claim is not indorsed on the Writ, a Defence need not be served until 14 days after a Statement of Claim has been served on the Defendant.

If a Defendant fails to serve a defence within the appropriate time, the Plaintiff may apply to the Court for judgment against him and, if the property described in the Writ is under the arrest of the Court, for an order for the sale of that property.

(1)

*[Back of page (1)]*

**Notes for Guidance**

1.    Each Defendant (if there is more than one) is required to complete an Acknowledgment of Service and return it to the Registry of the High Court.

2.    For the purpose of calculating the period of 14 days for acknowledging service, a writ served on the Defendant personally is treated as having been served on the day it was delivered to him and a writ served by post or by insertion through the Defendant's letter box is treated as having been served on the seventh day after the date of posting or insertion.

3.    Where the Defendant is a FIRM and a Solicitor is not instructed, the form must be completed by a PARTNER by name, with the addition of the description "partner in the firm of (..............................) after his name.

4.    Where the Defendant is sued as an individual TRADING IN A NAME OTHER THAN HIS OWN, the form must be completed by him with the addition of the description"trading as (..............................)" after his name.

5.    Where the Defendant is a LIMITED COMPANY the form must be completed by a Solicitor or by someone authorised to act on behalf of the Company, but the Company can take no further step in the proceedings without a Solicitor acting on its behalf.

6.    Where the Defendant is a MINOR or a MENTAL PATIENT, the form must be completed by a Solicitor acting for a guardian ad litem.

7.    A Defendant acting in person may obtain help in completing the form at the Registry of the High Court.

8.    These notes deal only with the more usual cases. In case of difficulty a Defendant in person should refer to paragraph 7 above.

(2)

*[Heading as in No. 1 or 2 to be completed by plaintiff]*

ACKNOWLEDGMENT OF SERVICE
OR WRIT OF SUMMONS IN
ACTION IN REM OR LIMITATION ACTION

If you intend to instruct a Solicitor to act for you, give him this form

IMMEDIATELY

*Important.* Read the accompanying directions and notes for guidance carefully before completing this form. If any information required is omitted or given wrongly, THIS FORM MAY HAVE TO BE RETURNED.

Delay may result in judgment being given against a defendant whereby he or his Solicitor may have to pay the costs of applying to set it aside. Furthermore, the property described in the Writ of Summons, if under arrest of the Court, may be sold by order of the Court.

| | | |
|---|---|---|
| * Where words appear between square brackets, delete if inapplicable | 1. | *[In an action in rem<br>State the description of the Defendant, as stated in the Writ of Summons, by whom or on whose behalf the service of the Writ is being acknowledged.]<br>*[In a limitation action<br>    (a)  If the Defendant by whom or on whose behalf service of the Writ is being acknowledged is named in the Writ, state his full name. If he is sued in a name different from his own, add "sued as (the name stated on the Writ of Summons)".<br>    (b)  If the Defendant by whom or on whose behalf service of the Writ is being acknowledged is one of a class of persons described in the Writ, state his full name.<br>The Defendant should completed (a) or (b), whichever is appropriate and delete the other]. |

Service of the Writ is acknowledged accordingly
*(Signed) [Solicitor]
[Defendant in person]
Address for Service

(*Where words appear between square brackets, delete if inapplicable)

(3)

**Notes as to Address for Service**

Solicitor. Where the Defendant is represented by a Solicitor, state the Solicitor's place of business in Hong Kong.

Defendant in person. Where the Defendant is acting in person, he must give his residence OR, if he does not reside in Hong Kong, he must give an address in Hong Kong where communications for him should be sent. In the case of a limited company "residence" means its registered or principal office.

*[Back of Page (3)]*

Indorsement by plaintiffs solicitor (or by plaintiff if suing in person) of his name, address and reference, if any.

(Enacted 1988)

No. 3

**Warrant of arrest**

(Order 75 rule 5(1))

*(Heading as in action)*

To the Bailiff:

You are hereby required to arrest the ship.............................of the port of..........
............................(and the cargo now or lately laden therein, together with the freight
due for the transportation thereof,) or (and the freight due for the transportation of the
cargo now or lately laden therein,) and to keep the same under safe arrest until you
shall receive further orders from the High Court.

The plaintiff's claim is for *(copy from the writ)*

Taken out by........................................................... (solicitors for) the................
.....................................................

*Bailiff's indorsement as to service*

(Enacted 1988)

## No. 4

**Praecipe for warrant of arrest**
(Order 75 rule 5(4))

*(Heading as in action)*

We................................. of........................................... (solicitors for) the plaintiffs request a warrant to arrest (description of property giving name, if a ship).

Dated the.................day of.................19......

(Signed)....................................................

(Enacted 1988)

## No. 5

### Praecipe for caveat against arrest
(Order 75 rule 6)

*(Description of property giving name, if a ship)*

We...............................of............................................................... (solicitors for..
...........................of.......................................................) request a caveat against the
arrest of (*description of property giving name, if a ship*) and hereby undertake to enter
an acknowledgment of issue or service (as may be appropriate) in any action that may
be begun in the High Court against the said...............................................................
and, within 3 days after receiving notice that such an action has been begun, to give
bail in the action in a sum not exceeding...................dollars or to pay that sum into
court. We consent that the writ of summons and any other document in the action may
be left for us at.............................................

Dated the.................day of.......................... 19.....

(Signed)......................................................
(L.N. 99 of 1993)

No. 6

**Praecipe for service of writ in rem by Bailiff**
(Order 75 rule 8(3))

*(Heading as in action)*

We..........................of.............................................. (solicitors for) the plaintiffs request that the writ of summons left herewith be duly served on..............................
......................

Dated the................day of..........................19.....

(Signed).........................................

(Enacted 1988)

No. 7

**Release**
(Order 75 rule 13(1))

*(Heading as in action)*

To the Bailiff:

Whereas in this action you were required to arrest the...............and to keep the same under safe arrest until you should receive further orders from the High Court. You are hereby required to release the said.............. from the arrest effected by virtue of the warrant in this action.

Taken out by...............................................(solicitors for)...............................
.........................

*Bailiff's indorsement*

On.......................the....................................day of...............................................
19..... the........................ was released from arrest pursuant to this Instrument.

(Signed)....................................................

Bailiff
(Enacted 1988)

## No. 8

**Praecipe for issue of release**
(Order 75 rule 13(6))

*(Heading as in action)*

We.....................................of.......................................................(solicitors for) the plaintiffs (or defendants) in this action against (*description of property giving name, if a ship*), now under arrest, request the issue of a release with respect to the said.......
.........................................................................................................................................

Dated the.................day of........................19......

(Signed).............................................

(Enacted 1988)

## No. 9

### Praecipe for caveat against release and payment
(Order 75 rule 14(1))

*(Description of property giving name, if a ship)*

We........................of................................................ (solicitors for).........................
of........................................... request a caveat against the issue of a release with respect to (*description of property giving name, if a ship*) now under arrest and, should the said property be sold by order of the Court, a caveat against payment out of court of the proceeds of sale.

The intending caveator claims to have an interest [to the extent of approximately $...............*if known*] in the above-mentioned property in respect of [*state nature of claim, e.g. salvage, collision damage, etc.*].

Dated the..................day of.................. 19.....

(Signed).............................................
(Enacted 1988)

## No. 10

### **Praecipe for withdrawal of caveat**
(Order 75 rule 15(1))

*(Description of properly giving name, if a ship)*

We.......................of.............................................. (solicitors for).......................
of...................................... request that the caveat (*state nature of caveat*) entered on
the...........day of............................. 19.... on behalf of.............................................
...be withdrawn.

Dated the..................day of.................... 19.....

(Signed).............................................

(Enacted 1988)

No. 11

**Bail bond**

(Order 75 rule 16(1))

*(Heading as in action)*

WHEREAS this Admiralty action in rem against the above-mentioned property is pending in the High Court and the parties to the said action are the above-mentioned plaintiffs and defendants:

NOW, THEREFORE, WE, *A.B.* of............................................................ and *C.D.* of................................................., hereby jointly and severally submit ourselves to the jurisdiction of the said Court and consent that if they, the above-mentioned defendants, (or plaintiffs, *in the case of a counterclaim*) do not pay what may be adjudged against them in this action, with costs, or do not pay any sum due to be paid by them in consequence of any admission of liability therein or under any agreement by which this action is settled before judgment and which is filed in the said Court, execution may issue against us, our executors or administrators, goods and chattels, for the amount unpaid or an amount of..................... dollars whichever is the less.

*A.B.*

(Signed).....................................................

*C.D.*

(Signed).....................................................

This bail bond was signed by the said *A.B.* and *C.D.*, the sureties, the.............. day of.................... 19......

Before me

a Commissioner for Oaths.

(Enacted 1988)

## No. 12

**Praecipe for commission for appraisement and sale**
(Order 75 rule 23(1))

*(Heading as in action)*

We.......................of............................................... (solicitors for) the plaintiffs (or defendants) request a commission for the appraisement and sale of (*description of property giving name, if a ship*) which was ordered by the Court on the..............day of............................... 19......

Dated the..............day of.....................19.....

(Signed)............................................

(Enacted 1988)

## No. 13

### Commission for Appraisement and Sale
(Order 75 rule 23(2))

(*Heading as in action*)

To the Bailiff:

WHEREAS in this action the Court has ordered (*description of property giving name, if a ship*) to be appraised and sold.

You are hereby authorized and required to choose one or more experienced persons and to swear him or them to appraise the said............................... according to the true value thereof, and such value having been certified in writing by him or them to cause the said........................................ to be sold by (private treaty) (public auction) for the highest price that can be obtained for it, but not for less than the appraised value unless the Court on your application allows it to be sold for less.

AND you are further required, immediately upon the sale being completed, to pay the proceeds thereof into court and to file the certificate of appraisement signed by you and the appraiser or appraisers, and an account of the sale signed by you, together with this commission.

Taken out by................(solicitors for) the.................................
(Enacted 1988)

## No. 14

### Release and Warrant of Possession
(Order 75)

(*Heading as in action*)

To the Bailiff:

WHEREAS in this action the Court has ordered possession of the ship (*name to be stated*), her tackle, apparel and furniture to be delivered up to....................or to his solicitor for his use,........................ You are hereby required to release the said ship, her tackle, apparel and furniture from the arrest made by virtue of the warrant in that behalf and to deliver possession thereof to the said................. or to his solicitor for his use.

Taken out by................. (solicitors for) the.................

### *Bailiff's Indorsement*

On the............day of.........................19...., the ship................ was released from arrest pursuant to this warrant.

(Signed).............................................
Bailiff.

### *Receipt*

Received from the Bailiff on the..........day of............................. 19 the ship........................and everything on board belonging to her.

(Signed).............................................

(Enacted 1988)

No. 15

## Notice to Consular Officer of Intention to
## Apply for Warrant of Arrest
(Order 75 rule 5(7))

(*Heading as in action*)

To the Consular Officer of (*name of State*)

The (*state nationality*) ship (*name*)

TAKE NOTICE that as solicitors for (*name or description of plaintiff as in writ*) we did on the.........day of.......................... 19..........(*or* we intend to) institute proceedings in the High Court of Hong Kong against the.................... above-mentioned ship in respect of a claim by (*name or description of plaintiff*) for (*state nature of claim as indorsed on writ*) and that we intend to apply to the Court to arrest the said ship.

Dated this................day of...................19....

(Signed)...................................................
*Solicitors for the Plaintiff.*
(Enacted 1988)

No. 15

**Notice to Consular Officer of Intention to
Apply for Warrant of Arrest**
(Order 75 rule 5(2))

(Heading as in a Note)

To the Consular Officer of (name of State)

The (name of ship) (ship (name))

TAKE NOTICE that as solicitors for lessors or Assignors of plaintiff or a (?) we did on the ......... day of ............ 19 ....... (or we intend to) institute proceedings in the High Court of Hong Kong against the ............ above-mentioned ship in respect of a claim by (name) for a (description) for (nature of claim as indorsed on writ) and that we intend to apply to the Court to arrest the said ship.

Dated this ............ day of .............19....

(Signed) ...............................
Solicitors for the Plaintiff.
(Practice 1988?)

APPENDIX C

No. 5

**Warrant for bailiff to call upon defendant to give**
**security to produce property**
(Order 44A rule 8)

Action No..............of 19....

IN THE HIGH COURT OF THE HONG KONG SPECIAL ADMINISTRATIVE REGION
COURT OF FIRST INSTANCE

Between               *A.B.*              Plaintiff

AND

*C.D.*            Defendant

To the Bailiff of the said Court:

You are required forthwith to call upon the defendant *C.D.* either by..............
day, the..............day of..............................., 19...., to furnish security in the sum of
S...............................to produce and place at the disposal of the said Court, when
required, his property or the value of the same, or such portion thereof as may be
sufficient to answer any judgment that may be given against him in this action, or
by the said day to appear before the said Court and show cause why he should not
furnish such security; and you are further required, in default of such security being
given, to attach all the movable and immovable property of the said defendant within
Hong Kong until the further order of the said Court.

Witness The Honourable......................................., Chief Justice of the said
Court, the............day of...............................19.....

(Signed).....................................................
*Registrar.*

*Note:—This warrant is to be returned into the Registry immediately after the
execution thereof, with a memorandum indorsed thereon of the date and mode of
execution.*

No. 6 and 7
(*Repealed L.N. 343 of 1989*)

## Appendix C

**Warrant for bailiff to call upon defendant to give
security to produce property**

(Cap. 336, rule 8)

Action No. ............ of 19......

In the Hong Kong ...... the Hong Kong Special Administrative Region

Between The Plaintiff

and

Defendant

To the bailiff of the said Court

You are ordered forthwith to call upon the defendant C. D. either to .........
(a) ..................... any ......... ............... 19...... to furnish security to the sum of
$........... ............... to produce and answer at the disposal of the said Court, when
required, the property or the value of the same, or to in complying thereof, as may be
sufficient to meet of any judgment that may be given against him in this action; or
(b) fail and pay to appear before the said Court and answer cause why he should not
furnish six security; and you are further required, in default of such security being
given, to attach all the moveable and immoveable property of the said defendant within
Hong Kong until the further order of the said Court.

Witness The Honourable ..................................... Chief Justice of the said
Court, the ............ day of ................., 19.......

.....................................
(Signed)

.....................................     Registrar

*Note:—This warrant is to be returned into the Registry immediately after the
execution thereof with a memorandum indorsed thereon of the day and manner of
execution.*

Nos. 6 and 7

[Magistrates' Courts (A. 315 of 1964)]

APPENDIX D

Code of Conduct for Expert Witness
(O. 38 rr. 35, 37B and 37C)

**Application of code**

1.    This code of conduct applies to an expert who has been instructed to give or prepare evidence for the purpose of proceedings in the Court.

**General duty to the Court**

2.    An expert witness has an overriding duty to help the Court impartially and independently on matters relevant to the expert's area of expertise.

3.    An expert witness's paramount duty is to the Court and not to the person from whom the expert has received instructions or by whom he is paid.

4.    An expert witness is not an advocate for a party.

**Declaration of Duty to Court**

5.    A report by an expert witness is not admissible in evidence unless the report contains a declaration by the expert witness that
      (a)   he has read this code of conduct and agrees to be bound by it.
      (b)   he understands his duty to the Court; and
      (c)   he has complied with and will continue to comply with that duty.

6.    Oral expert evidence is not admissible unless an expert witness has declared in writing, whether in a report or otherwise in relation to the proceedings, that-
      (a)   he has read this code of conduct and agrees to be bound by it;
      (b)   he understands his duty to the Court; and
      (c)   he has complied with and will continue to comply with that duty.

**Expert report to be verified**

7.    A report by an expert witness must be verified by a statement of truth in accordance with Order 41A of the Rules of the High Court (Cap. 4 sub. leg. A).

**Form of expert reports**

8.    A report by an expert witness must (in the body of the report or in an annexure) specify —
      (a)   the person's qualifications as an expert;
      (b)   the facts, matters and assumptions on which the opinions in the report are based (a letter of instructions may be annexed).
      (c)   the reasons for each opinion expressed.
      (d)   if applicable, that a particular question or issue falls outside his field of expertise;
      (e)   any literature or other materials utilized in support of the opinions; an.
      (f)   any examinations, tests or other investigations on which he has relied, and the identity and details of the qualifications of the person who carried them out.

9.  If an expert witness who prepares a report believes that it may be incomplete or inaccurate without some qualification, that qualification must be stated in the report.

10. If an expert witness considers that his opinion is not a concluded opinion because of insufficient research or insufficient data or for any other reason, this must be stated when the opinion is expressed.

11. An expert witness who, after communicating an opinion to the party instructing him (or that party's legal representative), changes his opinion on a material matter shall forthwith provide the party (or that party's legal representative) with a supplementary report to that effect which must contain such of the information referred to in section 8(b), (c), (d), (e) and (f) as is appropriate.

**Experts' conference**

12. An expert witness shall abide by any direction of the Court to'
    (a)  confer with any other expert witness;
    (b)  endeavour to reach agreement on material matters for expert opinion; and
    (c)  provide the Court with a joint report specifying matters agreed and matters not agreed and the reasons for any non-agreement.

13. An expert witness shall exercise his independent, professional judgment in relation to such a conference and joint report, and shall not act on any instruction or request to withhold or avoid agreement.

Note: — Proceedings for contempt of court may be brought against a person if he makes, or causes to be made, a false declaration or a false statement in a document verified by a statement of truth without an honest belief in its truth.

(L.N. 152 of 2008)

# Index

*References are to paragraph numbers*

**Account**

    appeal against order made on taking, [43.5.3]

    hearing, [43.5.2]

    interlocutory order for taking, [43.1.1]

    liberty to apply, [43.3.1]

    orders ancillary to an order for taking, [43.1.3]

    outstanding factual issues, [43.1.2]

    procedure for taking, [43.5.1]

**Action**

    defamation, [18.12.13]

    property of bankrupt, concerning, [15.14.4]

    trust property, concerning, [15.14.2]

    untraceable trustee, proceed against, [15.14.3]

**Adjourned hearings**

    claim for possession, for, [88.4.4]

    listing of, [34.2.13]

**Administration**

    determination of questions

        action by beneficiary, [85.2.6]

        *Beddoe* order, [85.2.2]

            beneficiary, [85.2.3]

            factors, [85.2.5]

            procedure on application for, [85.2.4]

        domestic litigation, [85.2.1]

        order against trustee for disclosure, [85.2.7]

    interpretation, comparison with English rules, [85.1.1]

    judgments and orders, [85.6.1]

    originating summons, action by way of, [85.4.1]

    parties to proceedings, [85.3.1]

**Administrative law list.** *See*

**Admiralty list**

    case management procedure, [75.25.1]

    practice direction, [72.2.8], [75.0.19]

**Admiralty proceedings**

    Admiralty court, jurisdiction of

        history, [75.0.2]

        mode of exercise of, [75.0.4]

        particular restrictions on, [75.0.5]

        present, [75.0.3]

    Admiralty list practice direction, [72.2.8], [75.0.19]

    agreement between solicitors, [75.35.1]

    application and interpretation, United Kingdom legislation, [75.1.1]

    application by non-party to intervene, [75.15.1]

    apportionment of salvage, [75.33.1]

    appraisement and sale of property

        duty of mortgagee, [75.23.3]

        less than appraised value, at, [75.23.2]

        order for sale, execution of, [75.23.1]

        public tender/private sale, [75.23.5]

        undertaking, as to bailiff's expenses, [75.23.4]

    arbitration agreements, international and domestic, [75.0.13]

    case management summons, application of, [75.25.1]

    caveat against arrest, [75.6.1]

        owner, effect on demise charterer, [75.6.2]